RAND McNALLY
WORLD ATLAS

RAND McNALLY

Chicago   New York   San Francisco

CONTENTS

USING THE ATLAS.................. I·3 – I·4

WORLD PATTERNS.............. I·5 – I·16
World Terrain............................ I·6 – I·7
World Climate........................... I·8 – I·9
World Vegetation..................... I·10 – I·11
World Population..................... I·12 – I·13
World Environments............... I·14 – I·15
World Time Zones.................... I·16

REFERENCE MAPS.................. 1 – 128
Map Symbols and Index Map................ 1
World...................................... 2 – 3
Europe.................................. 4 – 5
Scandinavia................................. 6
British Isles.................................. 7
Central Europe........................ 8 – 9
France and the Alps.............. 10 – 11
Spain and Portugal................12 – 13
Italy...................................... 14 – 15
Southeastern Europe.............. 16 – 17
Baltic and Moscow Regions......... 18 – 19
Asia...................................... 20 – 21
Northwest
    Asia................................. 22 – 23
Northeast
    Asia................................. 24 – 25
China, Japan, and Korea.......... 26 – 27
Eastern and Southeastern China.. 28 – 29
Japan.................................... 30 – 31
Southeastern Asia................... 32 – 33
Burma, Thailand, and Indochina.. 34 – 35
India and Pakistan....................... 36
Southern India and Sri Lanka........... 37
Northern India and Pakistan........ 38 – 39
Eastern Mediterranean Lands...............40
Africa.................................... 41
Northern Africa........................ 42 – 43
Southern Africa....................... 44 – 45
Eastern Africa and Middle East........... 46
Antarctica............................. 47
Pacific Ocean....................... 48 – 49
Australia.............................. 50 – 51
New Zealand.............................. 52
South America....................... 53
Northern South America.............. 54 – 55
Southern South America................... 56
Southeastern Brazil........................ 57
Colombia, Ecuador, Venezuela,
    and Guyana....................... 58 – 59
Atlantic Ocean..................... 60

North America...................... 61
Mexico.................................. 62 – 63
Central America
    and the Caribbean.................... 64 – 65
Canada................................ 66 – 67
Alberta...................................... 68
British Columbia............................ 69
Manitoba.................................... 70
New Brunswick, Nova Scotia,
    and Prince Edward Island................ 71
Newfoundland............................... 72
Ontario...................................... 73
Quebec...................................... 74
Saskatchewan............................... 75
United States of America............ 76 – 77
Alabama.................................... 78
Alaska...................................... 79
Arizona..................................... 80
Arkansas.................................... 81
California................................... 82
Colorado.................................... 83
Connecticut................................. 84
Delaware.................................... 85
Florida...................................... 86
Georgia..................................... 87
Hawaii...................................... 88
Idaho....................................... 89
Illinois...................................... 90
Indiana..................................... 91
Iowa.. 92
Kansas...................................... 93
Kentucky.................................... 94
Louisiana................................... 95
Maine....................................... 96
Maryland.................................... 97
Massachusetts.............................. 98
Michigan.................................... 99
Minnesota.................................. 100
Mississippi................................. 101
Missouri.................................... 102
Montana.................................... 103
Nebraska................................... 104
Nevada..................................... 105
New Hampshire............................. 106
New Jersey................................. 107
New Mexico................................ 108
New York................................... 109
North Carolina............................. 110
North Dakota.............................. 111
Ohio....................................... 112
Oklahoma.................................. 113
Oregon..................................... 114
Pennsylvania.............................. 115

Rhode Island.............................. 116
South Carolina............................ 117
South Dakota.............................. 118
Tennessee.................................. 119
Texas....................................... 120
Utah.. 121
Vermont.................................... 122
Virginia.................................... 123
Washington................................ 124
West Virginia.............................. 125
Wisconsin.................................. 126
Wyoming................................... 127
North Polar Regions............... 128

INDEX TO
    REFERENCE MAPS........... 129 – 192

WORLD GEOGRAPHICAL
    TABLES...................... 193 – 215
World Political Information...... 193 – 196
General Information...................... 197
Principal Mountains...................... 198
World Oceans, Seas, Gulfs, Lakes,
    Rivers, and Islands........................ 199
World Populations................... 200 – 215

UNITED STATES
GEOGRAPHICAL
    TABLES...................... 216 – 240
United States General Information... 216

**United States Populations
and Zip Codes................. 217 – 240**
Latest 1990 Census Information

Copyright © 1992 by Rand McNally & Company.

Revised Edition.

Library of Congress Cataloging-in-Publication Data

Rand McNally and Company.
    World Atlas.
        p. cm.
    Includes index.
    1. Atlases. I. Title.
G1021.R21 1991 <G&M>   91-16938
912—dc20   CIP
                                          MAP

USING THE ATLAS

Maps and Atlases

Satellite images of the world (figure 1) constantly give us views of the shape and size of the earth. It is hard, therefore, to imagine how difficult it once was to ascertain the look of our planet. Yet from early history we have evidence of humans trying to work out what the world actually looked like.

Twenty-five hundred years ago, on a tiny clay tablet the size of a hand, the Babylonians inscribed the earth as a flat disk (figure 2) with Babylon at the center. The section of the Cantino map of 1502 (figure 3) is an example of a *portolan* chart used by mariners to chart the newly discovered Americas. The maps in this atlas, show the detail and accuracy that cartographers are now able to achieve.

In 1589 Gerardus Mercator used the word *atlas* to describe a collection of maps. Atlases now bring together not only a variety of maps, but an assortment of tables and other reference material as well. They have become a unique and indispensable reference for graphically defining the world and answering the question *where*. With them routes between places can be traced, trips planned, distances measured, places imagined, and our earth visualized.

FIGURE 1

FIGURE 2

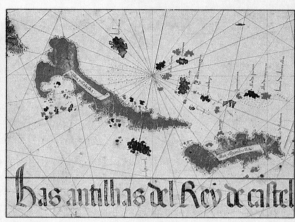

FIGURE 3

Sequence of the Maps

The world is made up of seven major landmasses: the continents of Europe, Asia, Africa, Antarctica, Australia, South America, and North America. The maps in this atlas follow this continental sequence. To allow for the inclusion of detail, each continent is broken down into a series of maps, and this grouping is arranged so that as consecutive pages are turned, a continuous successive part of the continent is shown. Larger-scale maps are used for regions of greater detail or for areas of global significance.

Getting the Information

To realize the potential of an atlas the user must be able to:
1. Find places on the maps
2. Measure distances
3. Determine directions
4. Understand map symbols

Finding Places

One of the most common and important tasks facilitated by an atlas is finding the location of a place in the world. A river's name in a book, a city mentioned in the news, or a vacation spot may prompt your need to know where the place is located. The illustrations and text below explain how to find Yangon (Rangoon), Burma.

Yancheng, China	B9	28
Yandoon, Burma	F3	34
Yangjiang, China	G9	26
Yangon (Rangoon), Burma	B2	32
Yangquan, China	D9	26
Yangtze see Chang, stm., China	E10	26
Yangzhou, China	C8	28

FIGURE 4

1. Look up the place-name in the index at the back of the atlas. Yangon, Burma can be found on the map on page 32, and it can be located on the map by the letter-number key *B2* (figure 4). If you know the general area in which a place is found, you may turn directly to the appropriate map and use the special marginal index.

2. Turn to the map of Southeastern Asia found on page 32. Note that the letters *A* through *H* and the numbers *1* through *11* appear in the margins of the map.

3. To find Yangon, on the map, place your left index finger on *B* and your right index finger on *2*. Move your left finger across the map and your right finger down the map. Your fingers will meet in the area in which Yangon is located (figure 5).

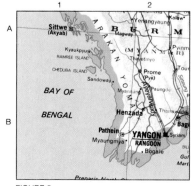

FIGURE 5

FIGURE 10

Measuring Distances

In planning trips, determining the distance between two places is essential, and an atlas can help in travel preparation. For instance, to determine the approximate distance between Paris and Rouen, France, follow these three steps:

1. Lay a slip of paper on the map on page 10 so that its edge touches the two cities. Adjust the paper so one corner touches Rouen. Mark the paper directly at the spot where Paris is located (figure 6).

FIGURE 6

2. Place the paper along the scale of miles beneath the map. Position the corner at 0 and line up the edge of the paper along the scale. The pencil mark on the paper indicates Rouen is between 50 and 100 miles from Paris (figure 7).

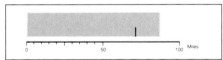

FIGURE 7

3. To find the exact distance, move the paper to the left so that the pencil mark is at 100 on the scale. The corner of the paper stands on the fourth 5-mile unit on the scale. This means that the two towns are 50 plus 20, or 70 miles apart (figure 8).

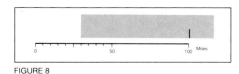

FIGURE 8

Determining Directions

Most of the maps in the atlas are drawn so that when oriented for normal reading, north is at the top of the map, south is at the bottom, west is at the left, and east is at the right. Most maps have a series of lines drawn across them–the lines of *latitude* and *longitude*. Lines of latitude, or *parallels* of latitude, are drawn east and west. Lines of longitude, or *meridians* of longitude, are drawn north and south (figure 9).

Parallels and meridians appear as either curved or straight lines. For example, in the section of the map of Europe (figure 10) the parallels of latitude appear as curved lines. The meridians of longitude are straight lines that come together toward the top of the map. Latitude and longitude lines help locate places on maps. Parallels of latitude are numbered in degrees north and south of the *Equator*. Meridians of longitude are numbered in degrees east and west of a line called the *Prime Meridian*, running through Greenwich, England, near London. Any place on earth can be located by the latitude and longitude lines running through it.

To determine directions or locations on the map, you must use the parallels and meridians. For example, suppose you want to know which is farther north, Bergen, Norway, or Stockholm, Sweden. The map (figure 10) shows that Stockholm is south of the 60° parallel of latitude and Bergen is north of it. Bergen is farther north than Stockholm. By looking at the meridians of longitude, you can determine which city is farther east. Bergen is approximately 5° east of the 0° meridian (Prime Meridian), and Stockholm is almost 20° east of it. Stockholm is farther east than Bergen.

Understanding Map Symbols

In a very real sense, the whole map is a symbol, representing the world or a part of it. It is a reduced representation of the earth; each of the world's features–cities, rivers, etc.–is represented on the map by a symbol. Map symbols may take the form of points, such as dots or squares (often used for cities, capital cities, or points of interest), or lines (roads, railroads, rivers). Symbols may also occupy an area, showing extent of coverage (terrain, forests, deserts). They seldom look like the feature they represent and therefore must be identified and interpreted. For instance, the maps in this atlas define political units by a colored line depicting their boundaries. Neither the colors nor the boundary lines are actually found on the surface of the earth, but because countries and states are such important political components of the world, strong symbols are used to represent them. The Map Symbols page in this atlas identifies the symbols used on the maps.

FIGURE 9

WORLD PATTERNS

The five world maps in this section portray the distribution of major natural and human elements that describe the world's fundamental geographic character. The lines and colors show basic patterns caused by the movement and interaction of land, air, water, and human activity.

The world terrain map on pages I·6 and I·7 portrays the surface of the uppermost layer of the earth's crust. The crust, broken into six gigantic and several smaller plates, floats on denser rock. Constant movement of the plates in the geologic past helped create the terrain features we see today. Motion of the plates along with the erosive force of water, wind, and human development continues to reshape the earth's terrain.

The earth's oceans are in constant motion. Water near the surface and in the deeps flows in well established currents that are like rivers within the ocean. The earth's atmosphere is an ocean of gases with currents that span the globe. The sun drives these moving currents of water and air. The average of the widely varying weather phenomena caused by these movements establishes the patterns of global climate shown on pages I·8 and I·9.

Climate is the single most important factor determining where plants can grow. And vegetation is the major factor determining where animals–including humans– can live. The map on pages I·10 and I·11 shows the distribution of vegetation types that might exist if humans did not intervene. Notice how similar the patterns of vegetation and climate are. Tundra vegetation is associated with polar climates. The rain forests of South America, Africa, and Asia grow in hot, wet climates near the Equator. The steppes of Central Asia and the short-grass prairies of North America grow in cool climates with dry summers. The evergreen forests of northern Eurasia and North America coincide with moist climates with cold winters and cool summers.

The population density map on pages I·12 and I·13 indicates that almost all areas of the earth are inhabited by humankind, from the Poles to the Equator. Humanity's densest settlement has been in the most fertile regions of the earth. These areas combine adequate rainfall and growing season with terrain that is neither too rough nor mountainous. A comparison of the terrain and climate maps with the population map shows this relationship. Abundant mineral deposits as well as people's ability to develop natural resources also explain settlement preferences. Densely settled areas in Southwest Asia, Southeast Asia, and China are rural-agricultural populations. In western Europe,

the northeastern United States, and parts of Japan, high-density regions are urban-industrial in character.

The environment map on pages I·14 and I·15 indicates how human habitation has impacted our planet. Compare this map with the vegetation map that shows what the world might be like if humankind had played a less dominant role. Millions of square miles of land that were once forests or grasslands are now plowed fields and pastures. Much of North America, Europe, and Southeast Asia has been almost completely remade by farmers. Though the urban areas occupy a small percentage of the land area in the world, their impact on the environment is extensive.

Terrain

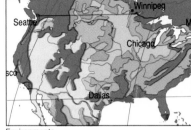

Population

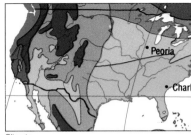

Climate

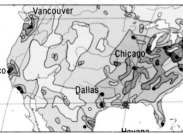

Environments

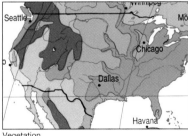

Vegetation

The distribution, relationship, and interaction of the major elements shown on the maps establish fundamental world patterns that distinguish one area from another. Upon the differences and similarities indicated by these patterns the world builds its intriguing variety of cultures and histories.

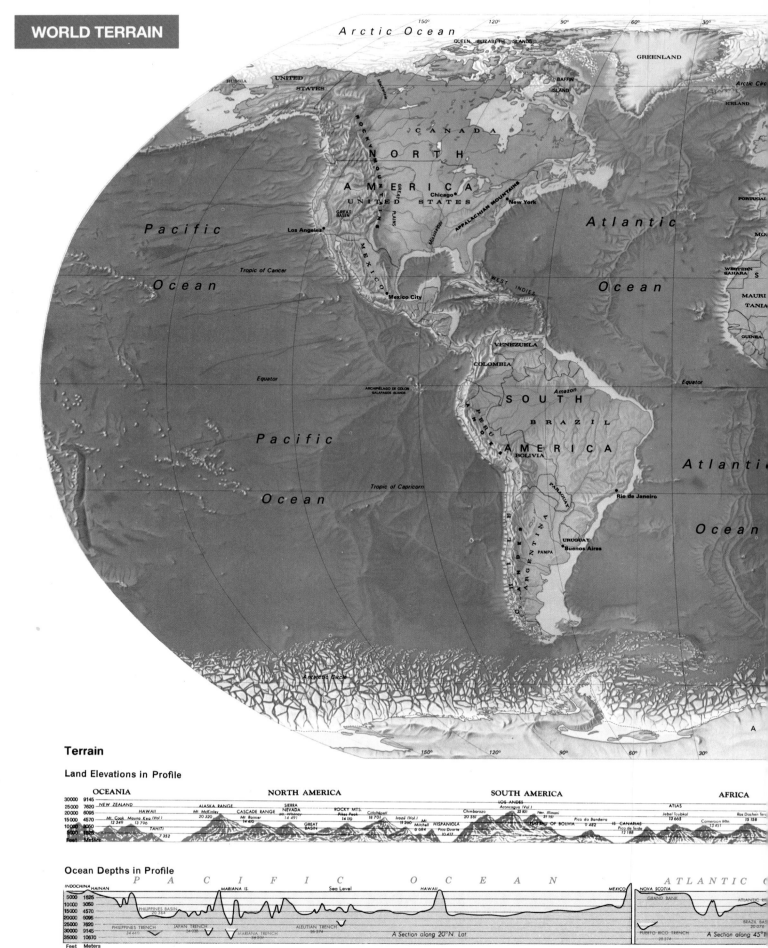

Terrain

Land Elevations in Profile

Ocean Depths in Profile

Elevations and depress

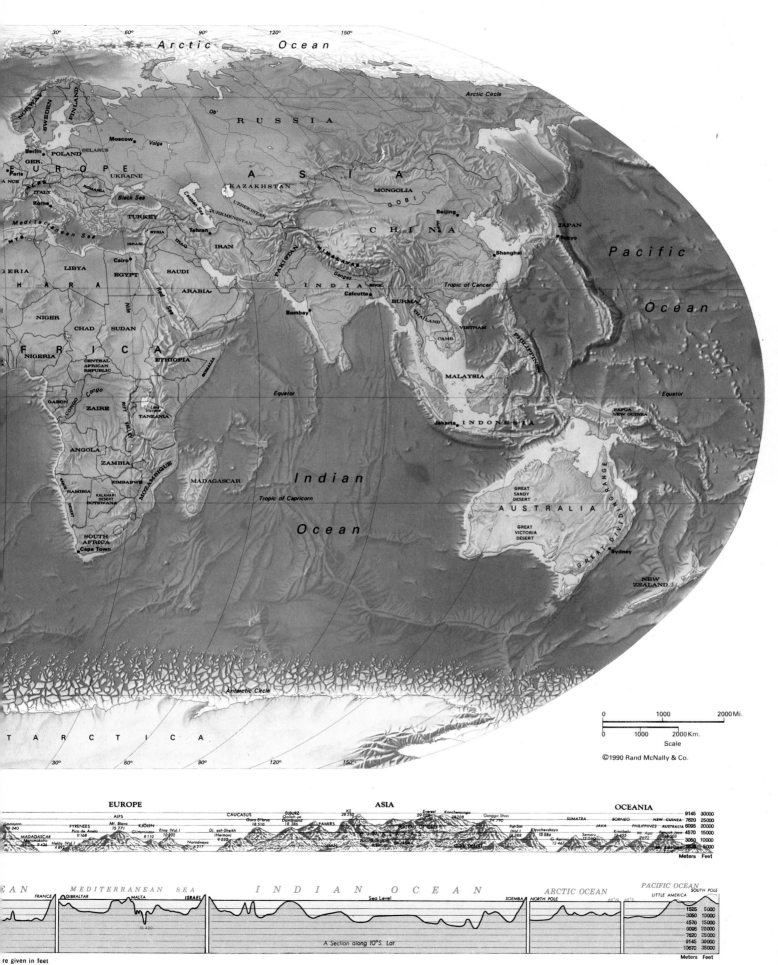

Arctic Ocean

30° 60° 90° 120° 150°

NORWAY SWEDEN FINLAND
EUROPE
Berlin POLAND BELARUS
GER.
Paris UKRAINE
FRANCE
ALPS ITALY ROMANIA
Rome Black Sea
Mediterranean Sea TURKEY
MTS. SYRIA
ISRAEL
IRAQ IRAN
NIGERIA LIBYA EGYPT
Cairo SAUDI
SAHARA ARABIA
NIGER CHAD SUDAN
AFRICA
NIGERIA CENTRAL ETHIOPIA
AFRICAN
REPUBLIC SOMALIA
GABON CONGO
Congo
ZAIRE RIFT Lake
Victoria TANZANIA
VALLEY
ANGOLA
ZAMBIA
NAMIBIA ZIMBABWE MOZAMBIQUE MADAGASCAR
KALAHARI
DESERT BOTSWANA
SOUTH
AFRICA
Cape Town

RUSSIA
Moscow
Volga Ob'
ASIA
KAZAKHSTAN MONGOLIA
Caspian Sea GOBI
UZBEKISTAN
TURKMENISTAN
Tehran CHINA Beijing
Huang JAPAN
HIMALAYAS Tokyo
PAKISTAN Shanghai
Ganges
INDIA Tropic of Cancer
Calcutta
Bombay BURMA
THAILAND VIETNAM
CAMB.
MALAYSIA PHILIPPINES

Pacific
Ocean

Equator Jakarta INDONESIA PAPUA Equator
NEW GUINEA

Indian
Ocean
GREAT
SANDY
DESERT
Tropic of Capricorn AUSTRALIA GREAT
GREAT DIVIDING RANGE
VICTORIA
DESERT
Sydney

NEW
ZEALAND

Antarctic Circle

ANTARCTICA

30° 60° 90° 120° 150°

| 0 | 1000 | 2000 Mi. |
| 0 | 1000 | 2000 Km. |

Scale

©1990 Rand McNally & Co.

EUROPE ASIA OCEANIA

ALPS CAUCASUS ELBURZ K2 Everest Kanchenjunga 9145 30000
Qollen-ye 28,250 29,028 28,208 Gongga Shan
Gora El'brus Damavand 24,790 SUMATRA BORNEO NEW GUINEA 7620 25000
PYRENEES Mt. Blanc 18,510 18,386 Fuji-San
Kilimanjaro Pico de Aneto 15,771 KJÖLEN Etna (Vol.) Dj. esh-Sheikh PAMIRS PHILIPPINES AUSTRALIA 6095 20000
19,340 11,168 Glittertinden 10,902 (Hermon) 12,388 Klyuchevskaya Kinabalu Mt. Apo JAVA 4570 15000
MADAGASCAR 8,110 9,232 15,584 12,000 13,455 9,692 Puncak Jaya 16,503 3050 10000
Maromokotro Hekla (Vol.) Narodnaya Semeru 12,467 1525 5000
9,436 4,892 6,217 Meters Feet

MEDITERRANEAN SEA INDIAN OCEAN ARCTIC OCEAN PACIFIC OCEAN SOUTH POLE
OCEAN FRANCE GIBRALTAR MALTA ISRAEL Sea Level SOEMBA NORTH POLE LITTLE AMERICA
45°N 45°S 1525 5000
3050 10000
16,420 4570 15000
6095 20000
A Section along 10°S. Lat 7620 25000
9145 30000
re given in feet 10670 35000
Meters Feet

I·7

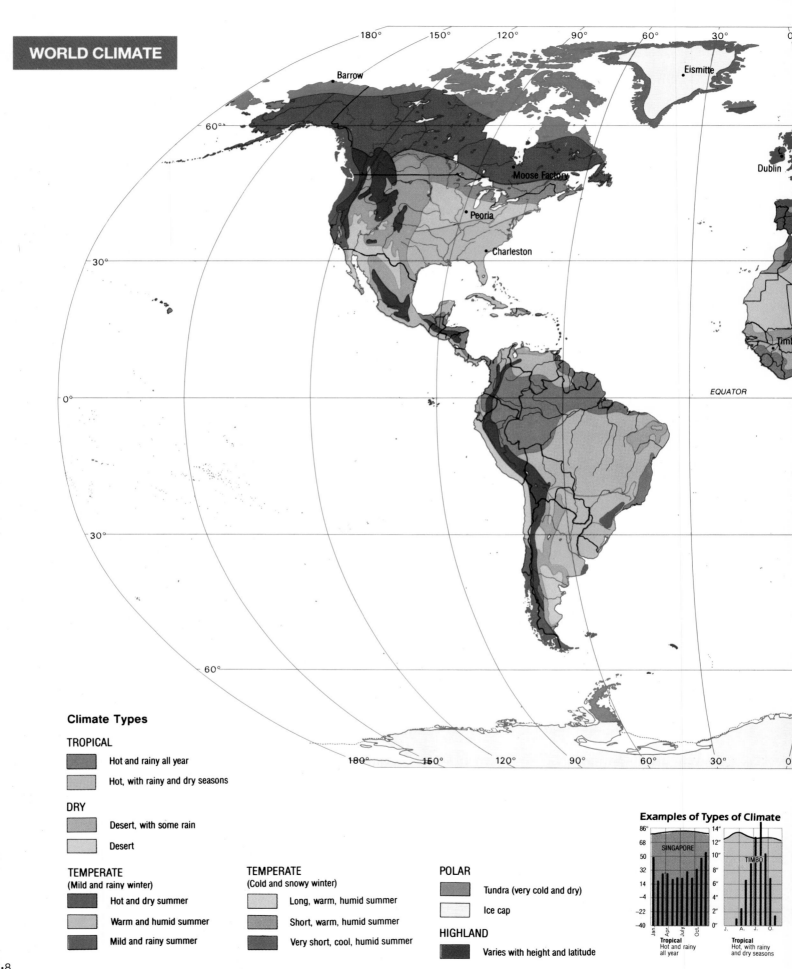

Barrow

Eismitte

Dublin

Moose Factory

Peoria

Charleston

Timb

EQUATOR

Climate Types

TROPICAL

Hot and rainy all year

Hot, with rainy and dry seasons

DRY

Desert, with some rain

Desert

TEMPERATE
(Mild and rainy winter)

Hot and dry summer

Warm and humid summer

Mild and rainy summer

TEMPERATE
(Cold and snowy winter)

Long, warm, humid summer

Short, warm, humid summer

Very short, cool, humid summer

POLAR

Tundra (very cold and dry)

Ice cap

HIGHLAND

Varies with height and latitude

Examples of Types of Climate

SINGAPORE

86°
68°
50°
32°
14°
-4°
-22°
-40°

14"
12"
10"
8"
6"
4"
2"
0"

Jan. Apr. July Oct.

Tropical
Hot and rainy
all year

TIMBO

Tropical
Hot, with rainy
and dry seasons

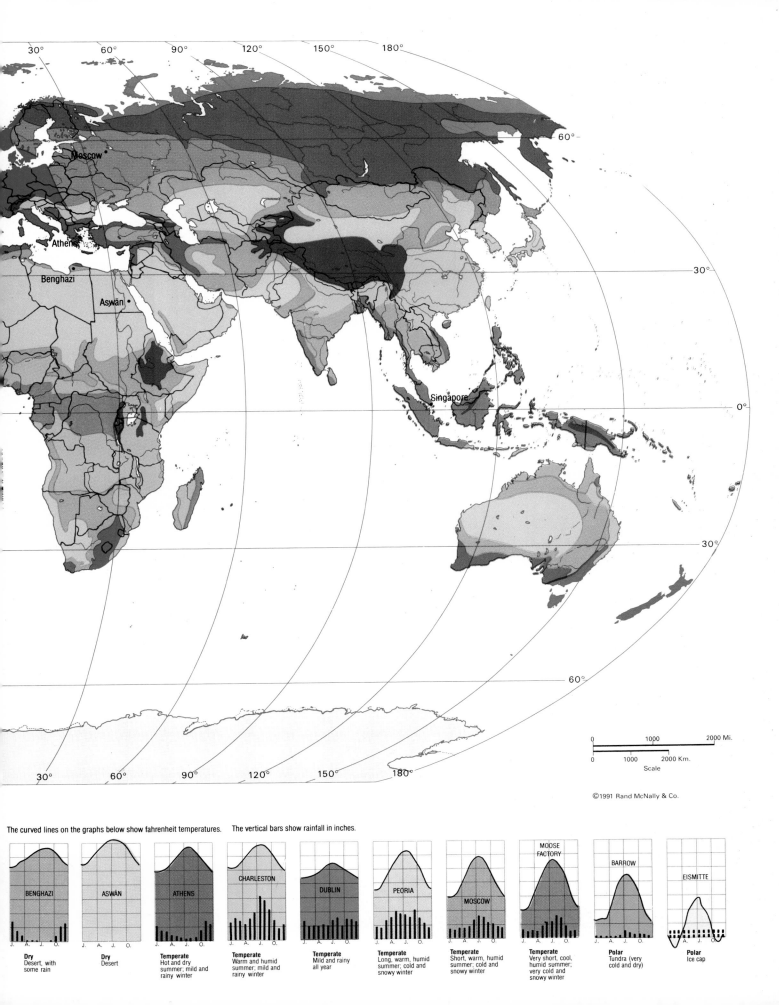

The curved lines on the graphs below show fahrenheit temperatures.   The vertical bars show rainfall in inches.

Dry
Desert, with some rain

Dry
Desert

Temperate
Hot and dry summer; mild and rainy winter

Temperate
Warm and humid summer; mild and rainy winter

Temperate
Mild and rainy all year

Temperate
Long, warm, humid summer; cold and snowy winter

Temperate
Short, warm, humid summer; cold and snowy winter

Temperate
Very short, cool, humid summer; very cold and snowy winter

Polar
Tundra (very cold and dry)

Polar
Ice cap

BENGHAZI

ASWĀN

ATHENS

CHARLESTON

DUBLIN

PEORIA

MOSCOW

MOOSE FACTORY

BARROW

EISMITTE

©1991 Rand McNally & Co.

Scale

0   1000   2000 Mi.

0   1000   2000 Km.

I·9

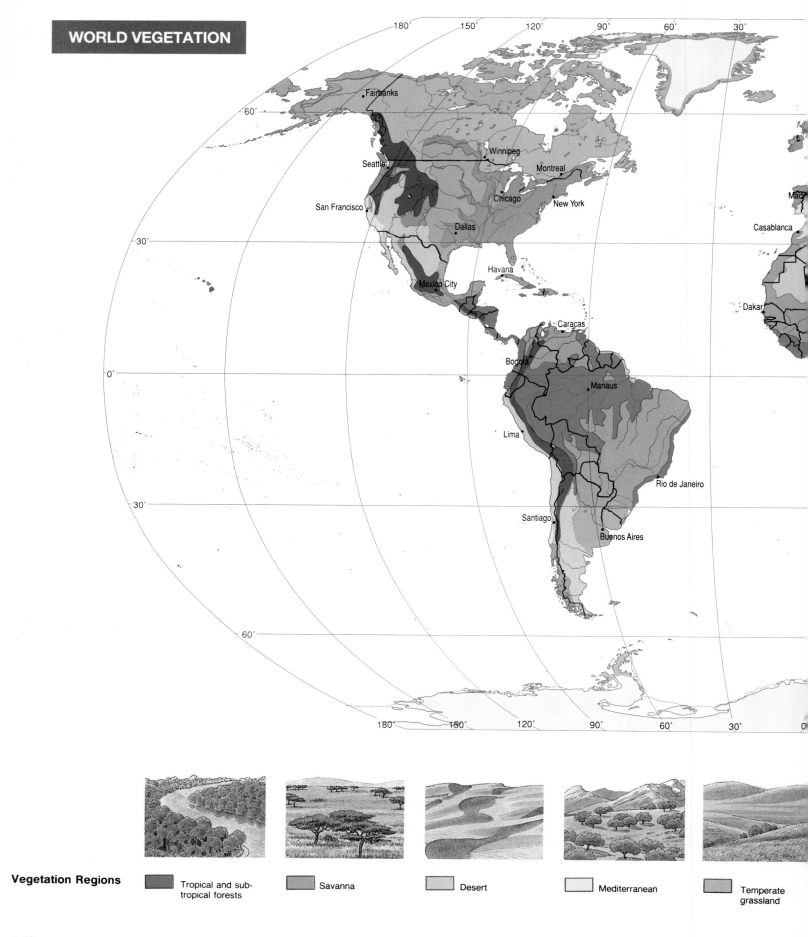

Vegetation Regions

Tropical and sub-tropical forests

Savanna

Desert

Mediterranean

Temperate grassland

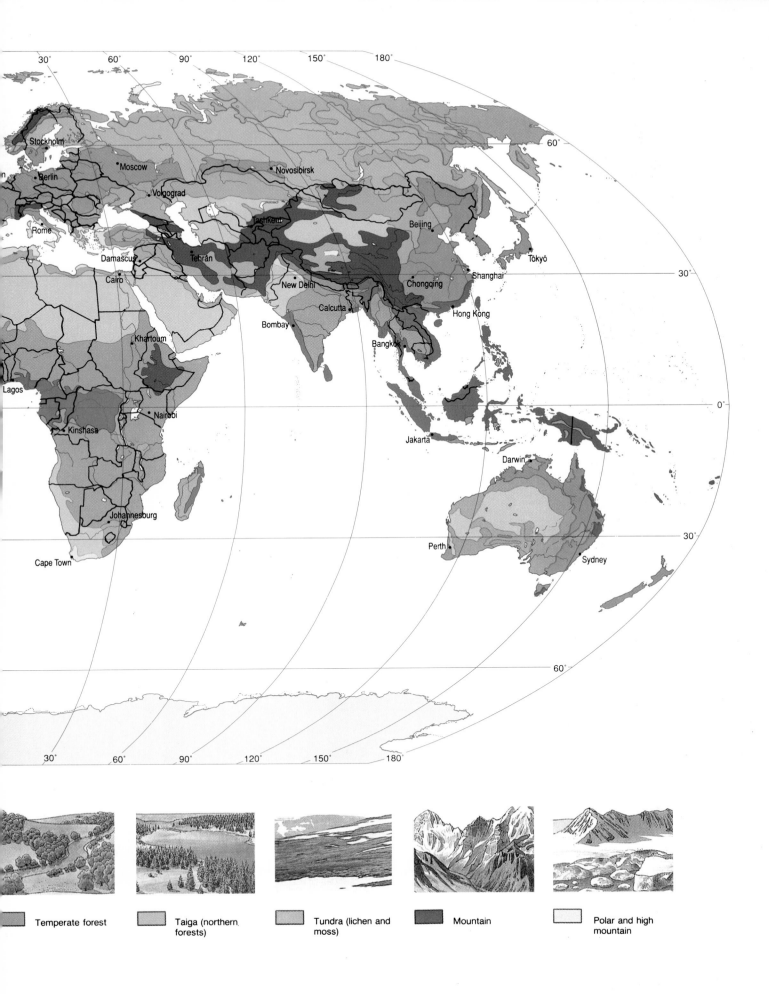

Temperate forest

Taiga (northern forests)

Tundra (lichen and moss)

Mountain

Polar and high mountain

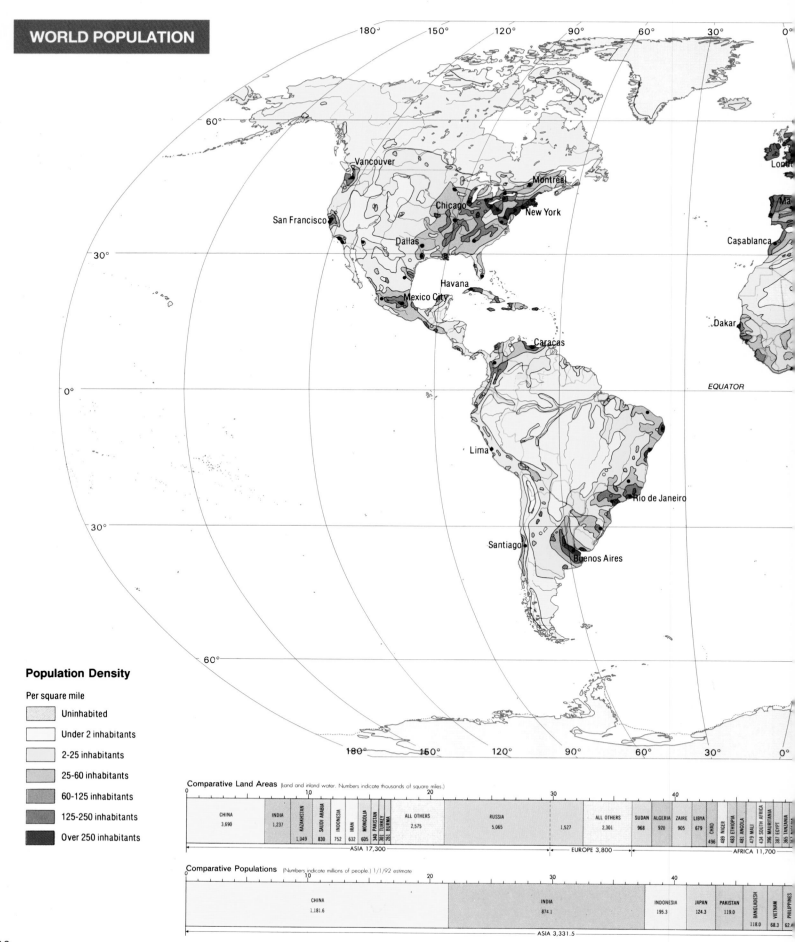

WORLD POPULATION

180° 150° 120° 90° 60° 30° 0°

60°

Vancouver
Montreal
Chicago
New York
San Francisco
Dallas
Havana
Mexico City
Caracas
Lima
Rio de Janeiro
Santiago
Buenos Aires

London
Madrid
Casablanca
Dakar

EQUATOR

30°

0°

30°

60°

180° 150° 120° 90° 60° 30° 0°

Population Density

Per square mile

- Uninhabited
- Under 2 inhabitants
- 2-25 inhabitants
- 25-60 inhabitants
- 60-125 inhabitants
- 125-250 inhabitants
- Over 250 inhabitants

Comparative Land Areas (land and inland water. Numbers indicate thousands of square miles.)

CHINA 3,690	INDIA 1,237	KAZAKHSTAN 1,049	SAUDI ARABIA 830	INDONESIA 752	IRAN 632	MONGOLIA 605	PAKISTAN 340	TURKEY 301	BURMA 261	ALL OTHERS 2,575	RUSSIA 5,065		1,527	ALL OTHERS 2,301	SUDAN 968	ALGERIA 920	ZAIRE 905	LIBYA 679	CHAD 496	NIGER 489	ETHIOPIA 483	ANGOLA 481	MALI 479	SOUTH AFRICA 434	MAURITANIA 396	EGYPT 387	TANZANIA 365

◄—————— ASIA 17,300 ——————► ◄—— EUROPE 3,800 ——► ◄—— AFRICA 11,700

Comparative Populations (Numbers indicate millions of people.) 1/1/92 estimate

CHINA 1,181.6	INDIA 874.1	INDONESIA 195.3	JAPAN 124.3	PAKISTAN 119.0	BANGLADESH 118.0	VIETNAM 68.3	PHILIPPINES 62.4

◄—————————————— ASIA 3,331.5

I·12

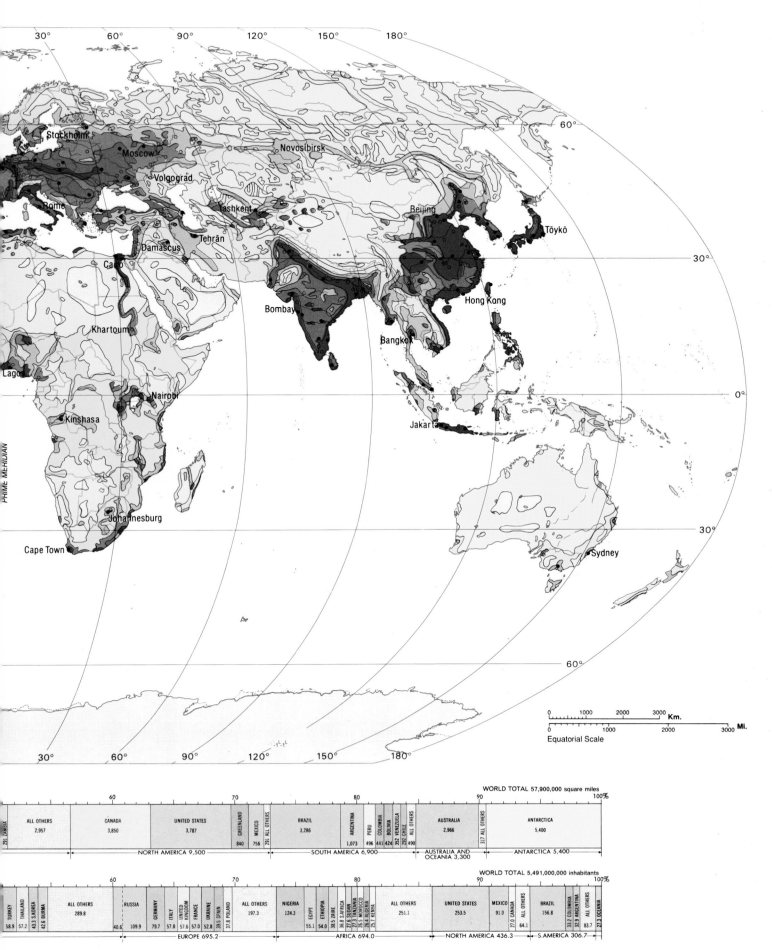

30° 60° 90° 120° 150° 180°

60°

Stockholm
Moscow
Novosibirsk
Volgograd
60°
Rome
Tashkent
Beijing
Tōkyō
Damascus Tehrān
30°
Cairo
Bombay
Hong Kong
Khartoum
Bangkok
Lagos
Nairobi
0°
Kinshasa
Jakarta
Johannesburg
30°
Cape Town
Sydney

PRIME MERIDIAN

60°

0   1000   2000   3000 Km.
0   1000   2000   3000 Mi.
Equatorial Scale

30° 60° 90° 120° 150° 180°

WORLD TOTAL 57,900,000 square miles

	60		70			80						90		100%

| 29.1 ZAMBIA | ALL OTHERS 2,957 | CANADA 3,850 | UNITED STATES 3,787 | GREENLAND 840 | MEXICO 756 | 291 ALL OTHERS | BRAZIL 3,286 | ARGENTINA 1,073 | PERU 496 | COLOMBIA 441 | BOLIVIA 424 | VENEZUELA 352 | 292 CHILE | ALL OTHERS 490 | AUSTRALIA 2,966 | 317 ALL OTHERS | ANTARCTICA 5,400 |

NORTH AMERICA 9,500   SOUTH AMERICA 6,900   AUSTRALIA AND OCEANIA 3,300   ANTARCTICA 5,400

WORLD TOTAL 5,491,000,000 inhabitants

	60		70			80						90		100%

| TURKEY 58.9 | THAILAND 57.2 | S.KOREA 43.3 | BURMA 42.6 | ALL OTHERS 289.8 | RUSSIA 109.9 | GERMANY 79.7 | ITALY 57.8 | UNITED KINGDOM 57.6 | FRANCE 57.0 | UKRAINE 52.8 | SPAIN 39.5 | POLAND 37.8 | ALL OTHERS 197.3 | NIGERIA 124.3 | EGYPT 55.1 | ETHIOPIA 54.0 | S.AFRICA 38.5 | SUDAN 27.6 | TANZANIA 27.3 | MOROCCO 26.5 | ALGERIA 26.4 | KENYA 25.7 | ALL OTHERS 251.1 | UNITED STATES 253.5 | MEXICO 91.0 | CANADA 27.0 | ALL OTHERS 64.1 | BRAZIL 156.8 | COLOMBIA 33.2 | ARGENTINA 32.9 | ALL OTHERS 83.7 | 27.3 OCEANIA |

EUROPE 695.2   AFRICA 694.0   NORTH AMERICA 436.3   S.AMERICA 306.7

I·13

WORLD ENVIRONMENTS

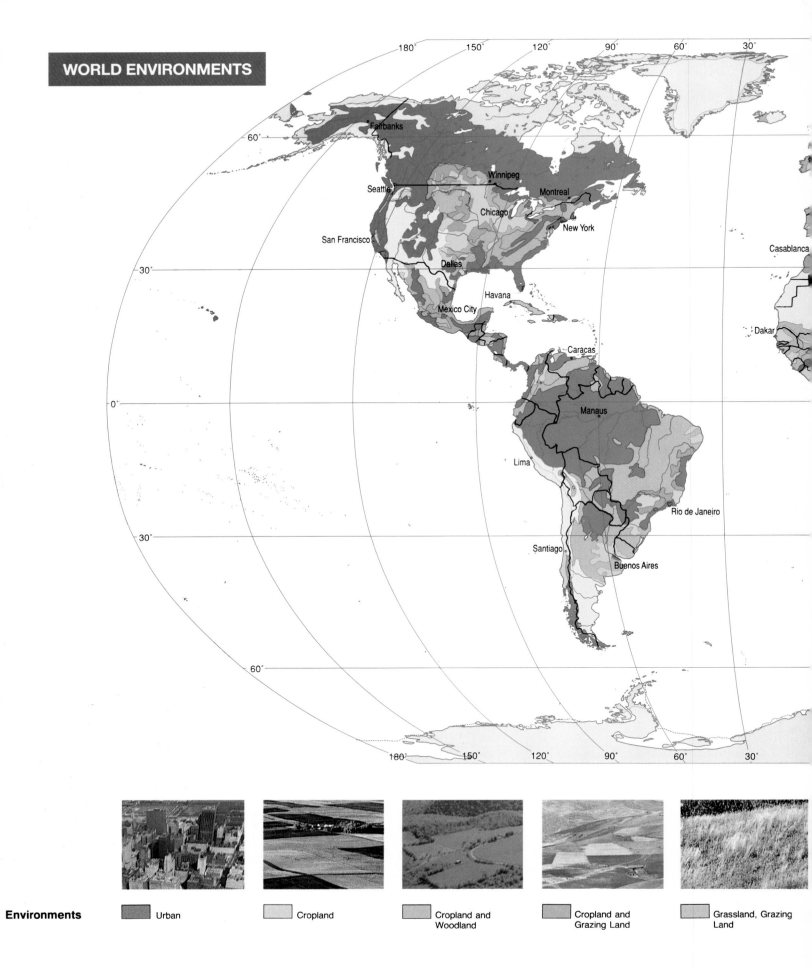

Environments

Urban

Cropland

Cropland and Woodland

Cropland and Grazing Land

Grassland, Grazing Land

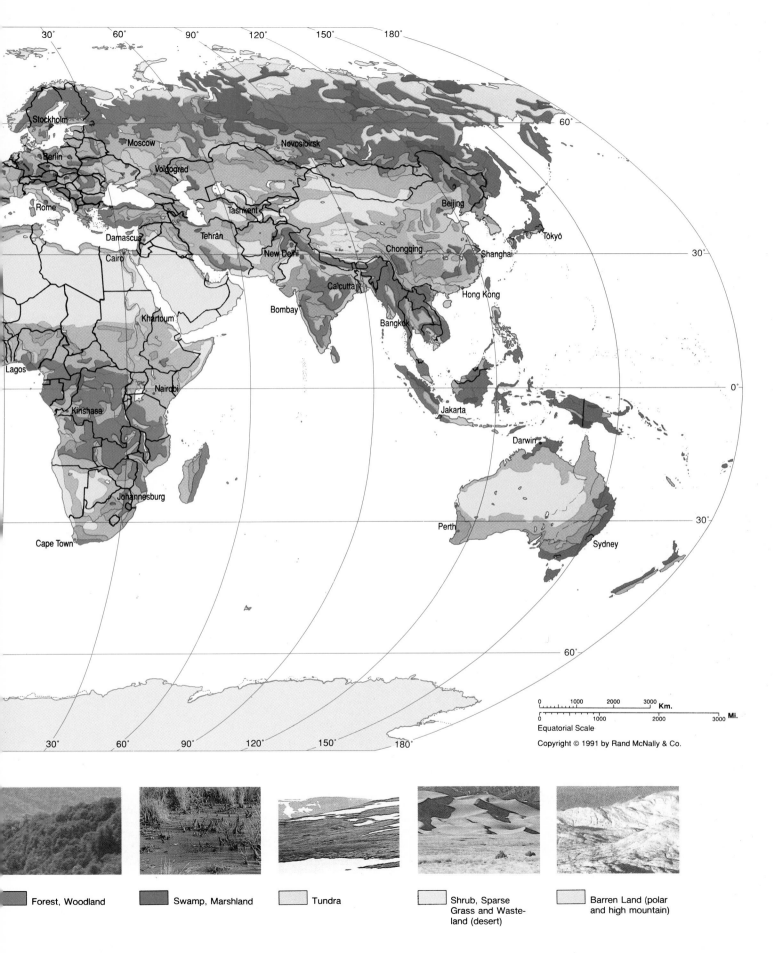

Stockholm
Berlin
Rome
Moscow
Voldograd
Novosibirsk
Damascus
Cairo
Tashkent
Tehrân
New Delhi
Chongqing
Beijing
Shanghai
Tōkyō
Khartoum
Bombay
Calcutta
Hong Kong
Bangkok
Lagos
Nairobi
Kinshasa
Jakarta
Johannesburg
Darwin
Cape Town
Perth
Sydney

30° 60° 90° 120° 150° 180°
60°
30°
0°
30°
60°

30° 60° 90° 120° 150° 180°

0   1000   2000   3000 **Km.**
0   1000   2000   3000 **Mi.**
Equatorial Scale

Copyright © 1991 by Rand McNally & Co.

Forest, Woodland   Swamp, Marshland   Tundra   Shrub, Sparse Grass and Waste- land (desert)   Barren Land (polar and high mountain)

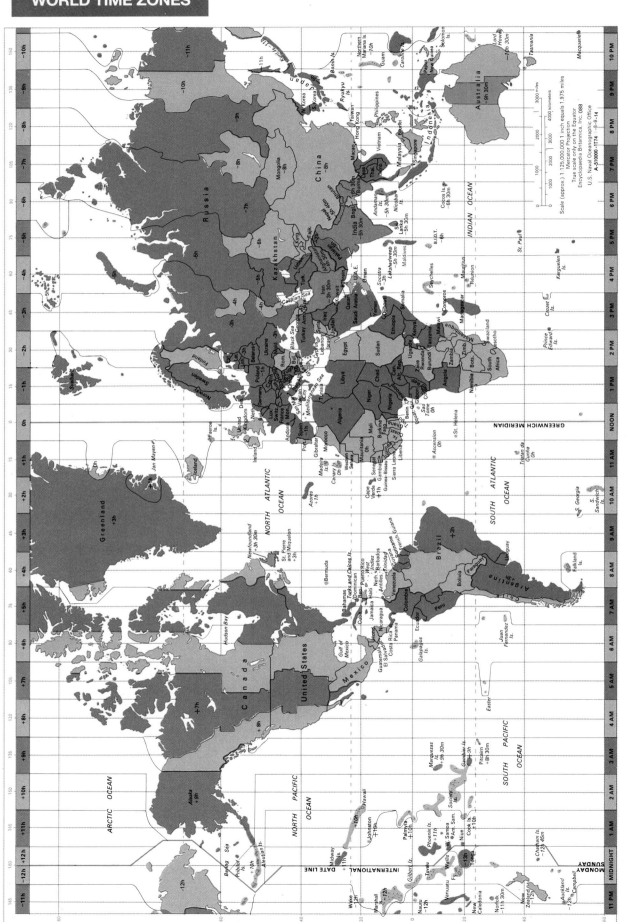

The standard time zone system, fixed by international agreement and by law in each country, is based on a theoretical division of the globe into 24 zones of 15° longitude each. The mid-meridian of each zone fixes the hour for the entire zone. The zero time zone extends 7½° east and 7½° west of the Greenwich meridian, 0° longitude. Since the earth rotates toward the east, time zones to the west of Greenwich are earlier, to the east, later. Plus and minus hours at the top of the map are added to or subtracted from local time to find Greenwich time. Local standard time can be determined for any area in the world by adding one hour for each time zone counted in an easterly direction from

one's own, or by subtracting one hour for each zone counted in a westerly direction. To separate one day from the next, the 180th meridian has been designated as the international date line. On both sides of the line the time of day is the same, but west of the line it is one day later than it is to the east. Countries that adhere to the international zone system adopt the zone applicable to their location. Some countries, however, establish time zones based on political boundaries, or adopt the time zone of a neighboring unit. For all or part of the year some countries also advance their time by one hour, thereby utilizing more daylight hours each day.

Time Zones

Standard time zone of even-numbered hours from Greenwich time

Standard time zone of odd-numbered hours from Greenwich time

Time varies from the standard time zone by half an hour

Time varies from the standard time zone by other than half an hour

h m   hours, minutes

I·16

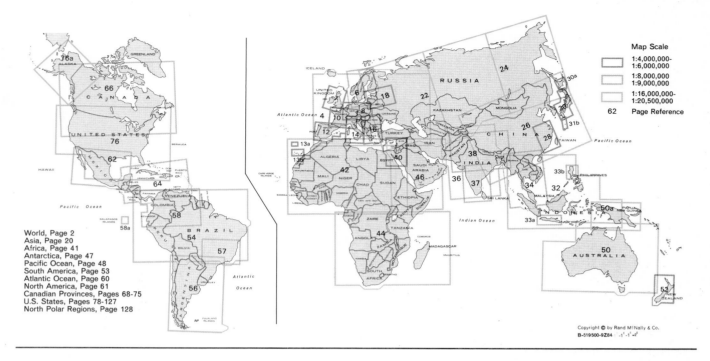

World, Page 2
Asia, Page 20
Africa, Page 41
Antarctica, Page 47
Pacific Ocean, Page 48
South America, Page 53
Atlantic Ocean, Page 60
North America, Page 61
Canadian Provinces, Pages 68-75
U.S. States, Pages 78-127
North Polar Regions, Page 128

World Maps Symbols

Inhabited Localities

The size of type indicates the relative economic and political importance of the locality

Écommoy   Lisieux   **Rouen**

Trouville   **Orléans**   **PARIS**

Bi'r Safājah °   Oasis

Alternate Names

MOSKVA
MOSCOW — English or second official language names are shown in reduced size lettering

Basel
Bâle

Volgograd
(Stalingrad) — Historical or other alternates in the local language are shown in parentheses

Urban Area (Area of continuous industrial, commercial, and residential development)

Capitals of Political Units

BUDAPEST Independent Nation

Cayenne Dependency (Colony, protectorate, etc.)

Recife State, Province, County, Oblast, etc.

Political Boundaries

International (First-order political unit)

Demarcated and Undemarcated
Disputed de jure
Indefinite or Undefined
Demarcation Line

Internal

State, Province, etc. (Second-order political unit)

MURCIA Historical Region (No boundaries indicated)

GALAPAGOS (Ecuador) Administering Country

Transportation

Primary Road
Secondary Road
Minor Road, Trail
Railway
Canal du Midi Navigable Canal
Bridge
Tunnel
TO MALMÖ Ferry

Hydrographic Features

Shoreline
Undefined or Fluctuating Shoreline
Amur River, Stream
Intermittent Stream
Rapids, Falls
Irrigation or Drainage Canal
Reef
The Everglades Swamp
RIMO GLACIER Glacier
L. Victoria Lake, Reservoir
Tuz Gölü Salt Lake
Intermittent Lake, Reservoir
Dry Lake Bed
(395) Lake Surface Elevation

Topographic Features

Matterhorn △ 4478 Elevation Above Sea Level
76 ▽ Elevation Below Sea Level
Mount Cook ▲ 3764 Highest Elevation in Country
133 ▼ Lowest Elevation in Country
Khyber Pass ‿ 1067 Mountain Pass

Elevations are given in meters.
The highest and lowest elevations in a continent are underlined

Sand Area
Lava
Salt Flat

State, Province Maps Symbols

✪ Capital
◦ County Seat
▲ Military Installation
△ Point of Interest
+ Mountain Peak

International Boundary
State, Province Boundary
County Boundary
Railroad
Road
Urban Area

1

World

Europe

ALBANIA...............G11
Amsterdam, 6,965,000 ('89) (1,860,000★) ...E 8
ANDORRA...............G 8
Antwerpen, 497,748 ('87) (1,100,000★) ....E 8
Athínai (Athens), 885,737 ('81) (3,027,331★) ...H12
AUSTRIA...............F10
Barcelona, 1,714,355 ('88) (4,040,000★) ....G 8
BELARUS...............E13
Belfast, 303,800 ('87) (685,000★) ....E 6
BELGIUM...............E 8
Beograd (Belgrade), 1,130,000 ('87) (1,400,000★) G12
Berlin, 3,352,848 ('89) (3,825,000★) E10
Bern, 134,393 ('90) (298,800★) ...F 9
Birmingham, 1,013,995 ('81) (2,675,000★) ...E 7
Bonn, 282,190 ('89) (570,000★) ....E 9
BOSNIA AND HERCEGOVINA.......G11
Bremen, 535,058 ('89) (800,000★) ....E 9
Bruxelles, 136,920 ('87) (2,385,000★) ....E 8
Bucureşti, 1,989,823 ('86) (2,275,000★) G13
Budapest, 2,016,132 ('90) (2,565,000★) F11
BULGARIA...............G12
Cardiff, 262,313 ('81) (625,000★) ....E 7
Char'kov (Kharkov), 1,611,000 ('89) (1,940,000★) F15
CROATIA...............F11
CZECHOSLOVAKIA...............F11
DENMARK...............D 9
Dnepropetrovsk, 1,179,000 ('89) (1,600,000★) F14
Doneck, 1,110,000 ('89) (2,200,000★) F15
Dresden, 518,057 ('89) (670,000★) E10
Dublin, 502,749 ('86) (1,140,000★) ....E 6
Düsseldorf, 569,641 ('89) (1,190,000★) ....E 9
Edinburgh, 433,200 ('89) (630,000★) ....D 7
Essen, 620,594 ('89) (4,950,000★) ....E 9
ESTONIA...............D12
FAEROE ISLANDS......C 6
FINLAND...............C13
Firenze, 425,835 ('87) (640,000★) G10
FRANCE...............F 8
Frankfurt, 625,258 ('89) (1,855,000★) ....E 9
Gdańsk, 461,500 ('89) (909,000★) E11
Genève (Geneva), 165,404 ('90) (460,000★) ....F 9
Genova, 727,427 ('87) (805,000★) ....G 9
GERMANY...............E10
Gibraltar, 30,077 ('88). H 6
Glasgow, 695,630 ('89) (1,800,000★) ....D 7
Göteborg, 431,840 ('90) (710,894★) D10
GREECE...............H12
GUERNSEY...............F 7
Hamburg, 1,603,070 ('89) (2,225,000★) ....E 9
Helsinki, 490,034 ('88) (1,040,000★) C12
HUNGARY...............F11
ICELAND...............B 4
IRELAND...............E 6
ISLE OF MAN...............E 7
İstanbul, 6,748,435 ('90) (7,000,000★) G13
ITALY...............G10
JERSEY...............F 7
Katowice, 365,800 ('89) (2,778,000★) E11
Kazan', 1,094,000 ('89) (1,140,000★) D17
Kijev (Kiev), 2,587,000 ('89) (2,900,000★) E14
København, 466,723 ('90) (1,685,000★) D10
Köln, 937,482 ('89) (1,760,000★) ....E 9
Kraków, 743,700 ('89) (828,000★) E11
LATVIA...............D12
Leipzig, 545,307 ('89) (700,000★) E10
Leningrad see Sankt-Peterburg D14
LIECHTENSTEIN...............F 9
Ljubljana, 233,200 ('87) (316,607▲) F10

★ Population of metropolitan area, including suburbs.

4

Lisboa, 807,167 ('81)
(2,250,000★) ....H 6
LITHUANIA.............D12
Liverpool, 538,809 ('81)
(1,525,000★) ....E 7
Łódź, 851,500 ('89)
(1,061,000★) E11
London, 6,574,009 ('81)
(11,100,000★) ....E 7
LUXEMBOURG...........F 9
Lyon, 413,095 ('82)
(1,275,000★) ....F 8
MACEDONIA...........G12
Madrid, 3,102,846 ('88)
(4,650,000★) .... G 7
MALTA....................H10
Manchester, 437,612 ('81)
(2,775,000★) ....E 7
Marseille, 874,436 ('82)
(1,225,000★) ....G 9
Milano, 1,495,260 ('87)
(3,750,000★) ....F 9
Minsk, 1,589,000 ('89)
(1,650,000★) E13
MOLDOVA...............F13
MONACO.................G 9
Moskva (Moscow),
8,769,000 ('89)
(13,100,000★) D15
München, 1,211,617 ('89)
(1,955,000★) F10
Napoli, 1,204,211 ('87)
(2,875,000★) G10
NETHERLANDS.........E 9
Nižnij Novgorod (Gor'kij),
1,438,000 ('89)
(2,025,000★) D16
NORWAY..................C 9
Nürnberg, 480,078 ('89)
(1,030,000★) F10
Odessa, 1,115,000 ('89)
(1,185,000★) F14
Oslo, 452,415 ('87)
(720,000★) D10
Paris, 2,078,900 ('87)
(9,775,000★) ....F 8
POLAND..................E11
Porto, 327,368 ('81)
(1,225,000★) .... G 6
PORTUGAL............... G 6
Praha, 1,215,656 ('90)
(1,325,000★) E10
Reykjavík, 93,425 ('87)
(137,941★) ....C 3
Rīga, 915,000 ('89)
(1,005,000★) D12
Roma, 2,815,457 ('87)
(3,175,000★) G10
ROMANIA................F12
Rostov-na-Donu,
1,020,000 ('89)
(1,165,000★) F15
Rotterdam, 576,300 ('89)
(1,110,000★) ....E 8
RUSSIA..................D16
Samara (Kuybyshev),
1,257,000 ('89)
(1,505,000★) E18
Sankt-Peterburg,
4,456,000 ('89)
(5,825,000★) D14
SAN MARINO...........G10
Sarajevo, 341,200 ('87)
(479,688★) G11
Saratov, 905,000 ('89)
(1,155,000★) E17
Sevilla, 663,132 ('88)
(945,000★) ....H 6
's-Gravenhage (The
Hague), 443,900 ('89)
(770,000★) ....E 8
Skopje, 444,900 ('87)
(547,214▲) G12
SLOVENIA................F10
Sofija, 1,119,152 ('86)
(1,205,000★) G12
SPAIN......................H 7
Stockholm, 672,187 ('90)
(1,449,972★) D11
SWEDEN..................C11
SWITZERLAND..........F 9
Tallinn, 482,000..........D12
Thessaloniki, 406,413 ('81)
(706,180★) G12
Tiranë, 255,700 ('87)...G11
Torino, 1,035,565 ('87)
(1,550,000★) ....F 9
UKRAINE.................F14
UNITED KINGDOM......E 7
Valencia, 743,933 ('88)
(1,270,000★) ....H 7
Valletta, 9,210 ('89)
(215,000★) H10
Vilnius, 582,000..........E12
Warszawa, 1,651,200
('89) (2,323,000★) E12
Wien (Vienna), 1,482,800
('88) (1,875,000★) E10
YUGOSLAVIA...........G11
Zagreb, 697,925 ('87)..F11
Zürich, 342,861 ('90)
(860,000★) ....F 9

Miller Oblated Stereographic Projection

5

Scandinavia

Denmark

1990 ESTIMATE

Ålborg, 114,000
  (155,019▲) . . . . H 7
Århus, 202,300
  (261,437▲) . . . . H 8
Copenhagen see
  København . . . . I 9
København (Copenhagen),
  466,723
  (1,685,000★) . . . . . I 9
Odense, 140,100
  (176,133▲) . . . . I 8

Finland

1988 ESTIMATE

Helsinki (Helsingfors),
  490,034
  (1,040,000★) F15
Lahti, 74,300
  (108,000★) F15
Oulu, 98,582
  (121,000★) D15
Tampere, 170,533
  (241,000★) F14
Turku (Åbo), 160,456
  (228,000★) F14

Norway

1987 ESTIMATE

Bergen, 209,320
  (239,000★) . . . . F 5
Hammerfest,
  7,208 ('83) A14
Oslo, 452,415
  (720,000★) . . . . G 8
Stavanger, 94,200
  (132,000★) ('85) . . . G 5
Trondheim, 135,010 . . E 8

Sweden

1990 ESTIMATE

Göteborg (Gothenburg),
  431,840 (710,894★) H 8
Helsingborg, 108,359 H 9
Jönköping, 110,860 . H10
Linköping, 120,562 . . G10

Malmö, 232,908
  (445,000★) . . . . I 9
Norrköping, 119,921 G11
Örebro, 120,353 . . . . G10
Stockholm, 672,187
  (1,449,972★) G12
Uppsala, 164,754 . . . . G11
Västerås, 118,386 . . G11

★ Population of metropolitan area, including suburbs.
▲ Population of entire district, including rural area.

6

Lambert Conformal Conic Projection

Kilometers 0 100 200 300 Km.
Miles 0 100 200 300 Mi.

1 : 8 000 000

British Isles

Ireland
1986 CENSUS

Cork, 133,271
(173,694★) . . . . . J 4
Dublin (Baile Átha Cliath),
502,749
(1,140,000★) . . . . H 6
Galway, 47,104 . . . . H 3
Limerick, 56,279
(76,557★) . . . . I 4
Waterford, 39,529
(41,054★) . . . . I 5

Isle of Man
1986 CENSUS

Douglas, 20,368
(28,500★) . . . . . . G 8

United Kingdom
England
1981 CENSUS

Birmingham, 1,013,995
(2,675,000★) . . . . I 11
Blackpool, 146,297
(280,000★) . . . . . H 9
Bournemouth, 142,829
(315,000★) . . . . . K 11
Bradford, 293,336 . H 11
Brighton, 134,581
(420,000★) . . . . . K 12
Bristol, 413,861
(630,000★) . . . . . J 10
Coventry, 318,718
(645,000★) . . . . . I 11
Derby, 218,026
(275,000★) . . . . . I 11
Kingston upon Hull,
322,144 (350,000★) H 12
Leeds, 445,242
(1,540,000★) . . . . H 11
Leicester, 324,394
(495,000★) . . . . . I 11
Liverpool, 538,809
(1,525,000★) . . . . H 10
London, 6,574,009
(11,100,000★) . . . J 12
Manchester, 437,612
(2,775,000★) . . . . H 10
Newcastle upon Tyne,
199,064
(1,300,000★) . . . . G 11
Nottingham, 273,300
(655,000★) . . . . . I 11
Oxford, 113,847
(230,000★) . . . . . J 11
Plymouth, 238,583
(290,000★) . . . . . K 8
Portsmouth, 174,218
(485,000★) . . . . . K 11
Preston, 166,675
(250,000★) . . . . . H 10
Reading, 194,727
(200,000★) . . . . . J 12
Sheffield, 470,685
(710,000★) . . . . . H 11
Southampton, 211,321
(415,000★) . . . . . K 11
Southend-on-Sea,
155,720 . . . . J 13
Stoke-on-Trent, 272,446
(440,000★) . . . . . H 10
Sunderland, 195,064 G 11
Teesside, 158,516 . G 11
Wolverhampton,
263,501 . . . . I 10

Northern Ireland
1987 ESTIMATE

Bangor, 70,700 . . . G 7
Belfast, 303,800
(685,000★) . . . . . G 7
Londonderry, 97,500
(97,200★) . . . . . . G 5
Newtownabbey,
72,300 . . . . G 7

Scotland
1989 ESTIMATE

Aberdeen, 210,700 . D 10
Dundee, 172,540 . . . E 9
Edinburgh, 433,200
(630,000★) . . . . . F 9
Glasgow, 695,630
(1,800,000★) . . . . F 8
Greenock, 58,436
(101,000★)('81) . . F 8
Inverness, 38,204('81) D 8
Paisley, 84,330('81) . . F 8

Wales
1981 CENSUS

Cardiff, 262,313
(625,000★) . . . . . J 9
Newport, 115,896
(310,000★) . . . . . J 9
Swansea, 172,433
(275,000★) . . . . . J 9

★ Population of metropolitan
area, including suburbs.

7

Copyright © by Rand McNally & Co.
B-553600-264

Conic Projection, Two Standard Parallels

Kilometers
Km.
Miles
Mi.
1 : 5 000 000

Central Europe

Austria

1981 CENSUS

Graz, 243,166
 (325,000★)........H15
Innsbruck, 117,287
 (185,000★)........H11
Linz, 199,910
 (335,000★)...... G14
Salzburg, 139,426
 (220,000★)......H13
Vienna see Wien G16
Villach, 52,692
 (65,000★) I13
Wien (Vienna), 1,482,800
 (1,875,000★)('88) .. G16

Belgium

1987 ESTIMATE

Antwerpen (Antwerp),
 479,748
 (1,100,000★)......D 4
Brugge, 117,755
 (223,000★)......D 3
Bruxelles (Brussel),
 136,920
 (2,385,000★)......E 4
Charleroi, 209,395
 (480,000★)...... E 4
Gent (Gand), 233,856
 (465,000★)......D 3
Hasselt, 65,563
 (290,000★)......E 5
Liège, 200,891
 (750,000★)...... E 5
Mons, 89,697
 (242,000★)...... E 3

Czechoslovakia

1990 ESTIMATE

Bratislava, 442,999 .. G17
Brno, 392,285
 (450,000★)......F16
Hradec Králové, 101,302
 (113,000★).......E15
Košice, 237,099 .... G21
Liberec, 104,256
 (175,000★).......E15
Olomouc, 107,044
 (126,000★)......F17
Ostrava, 331,557
 (760,000★)......F18
Plzeň, 175,038
 (210,000★).......F13
Praha (Prague), 1,215,656
 (1,325,000★)......E14
Ústí nad Labem, 106,499
 (115,000★)........E14

Germany

1989 ESTIMATE

Aachen, 233,255
 (535,000★)...... E 6
Augsburg, 247,731
 (405,000★)...... G10
Berlin, 3,352,848
 (3,825,000★)......C13
Bielefeld, 311,946
 (515,000★)...... C 8
Bochum, 389,087....D 7
Bonn, 282,190
 (570,000★)...... E 7
Braunschweig, 253,794
 (330,000★)......C10
Bremen, 535,058
 (800,000★)...... B 8
Bremerhaven, 126,934
 (190,000★)...... B 8
Chemnitz, 311,765
 (450,000★)......E12
Cologne see Köln .. E 6
Dortmund, 587,328 .. D 7
Dresden, 518,057
 (670,000★)......D13
Duisburg, 527,447 .. D 6
Düsseldorf, 569,641
 (1,190,000★)...... D 6
Erfurt, 220,016 ......E11
Essen, 620,594
 (4,950,000★)......D 7
Frankfurt am Main,
 625,258
 (1,855,000★)......E 8
Gelsenkirchen,
 287,255 ....D 7
Hagen, 210,640 ..... D 7
Halle, 236,044
 (475,000★)......D11
Hamburg, 1,603,070
 (2,225,000★)...... B 9
Hannover, 498,495
 (1,000,000★)...... C 9
Karlsruhe, 265,100
 (485,000★)...... F 8
Kiel, 240,675
 (335,000★).......A10
Köln (Cologne), 937,482
 (1,760,000★)...... E 6
Leipzig, 545,307
 (700,000★)......D12
Lübeck, 210,681
 (260,000★)......B10

8

1 : 4 000 000

Magdeburg, 290,579
(400,000★) C11
Mannheim, 300,468
(1,400,000★) . . . . . . F 8
Mönchengladbach,
252,910 (410,000★) D 6
München (Munich),
1,211,617
(1,955,000★) G11
Münster, 248,919 . . . . D 7
Nürnberg, 480,078
(1,030,000★) F11
Potsdam, 142,862 . . . C13
Rostock, 253,990 . . . . A12
Saarbrücken, 188,467
(385,000★) . . . . . . F 6
Stuttgart, 562,658
(1,925,000★) . . . . . . G 9
Wiesbaden, 254,209
(795,000★) . . . . . . E 8
Wuppertal, 371,283
(830,000★) . . . . D 7

Hungary
1990 ESTIMATE

Budapest, 2,016,132
(2,565,000★) H19
Debrecen, 212,247 . . H21
Győr, 129,356 . . . . . . H 7
Miskolc, 196,449 . . . . G20
Pécs, 170,119 . . . . . . I18
Szeged, 175,338 . . . . I20
Szombathely, 85,418 H16

Liechtenstein
1990 ESTIMATE

Vaduz, 4,874 . . . . H 9

Luxembourg
1985 ESTIMATE

Luxembourg, 76,130
(136,000★) . . . . F 6

Netherlands
1989 ESTIMATE

Amsterdam, 6,965,000
(1,860,000★) . . . . . . C 4
Eindhoven, 190,700
(379,377★) . . . . D 5
Groningen, 167,800
(206,781★) . . . . B 6
Nijmegen, 145,400
(240,085★) . . . . D 5
Rotterdam, 576,300
(1,110,000★) . . . . . . D 4
's-Gravenhage (The
Hague), 443,900
(770,000★) . . . . . . C 4
Tilburg, 155,100
(224,934★) . . . . D 5
Utrecht, 230,700
(518,779★) . . . . C 5

Poland
1989 ESTIMATE

Białystok, 263,900 . . B23
Bydgoszcz, 377,900 B18
Częstochowa,
254,600 . . . . E19
Gdańsk (Danzig), 461,500
(909,000★) A18
Gdynia, 250,200 . . . . A18
Katowice, 365,800
(2,778,000★) E19
Kielce, 211,100 . . . . . E20
Kraków, 743,700
(828,000★) E19
Łódź, 851,500
(1,061,000★) D19
Lublin, 339,500
(389,000★) D22
Poznań, 586,500
(672,000★) E17
Radom, 223,600 . . . . D21
Szczecin (Stettin), 409,500
(449,000★) B14
Toruń, 199,600 . . . . . B18
Wałbrzych (Waldenburg),
141,400 (207,000★) E16
Warszawa (Warsaw),
1,651,200
(2,323,000★) C21
Wrocław (Breslau),
637,400 . . . . D17

France and the Alps

France

1982 CENSUS

Aix-en-Provence, 121,327
(126,552★) I12
Alès, 43,268
(70,180★) H11
Amiens, 131,332
(154,498★) . . . . C 9
Angers, 136,038
(195,859★) . . . . E 6
Angoulême, 46,197
(103,552★) . . . . . . G 7
Bayonne, 41,381
(127,477★) . . . . I 5
Belfort, 51,206
(76,221★) E13
Besançon, 113,283
(120,772★) E13
Béziers, 76,647
(81,347★) I10
Bordeaux, 208,159
(640,012★) . . . . . . H 6
Boulogne-Billancourt,
102,582 . . . . D 9
Boulogne-sur-Mer, 47,653
(98,566★) . . . . B 8
Brest, 156,060
(201,145★) . . . . . . D 2
Brive-la-Gaillarde, 51,511
(64,301★) . . . . G 8
Caen, 114,068
(183,526★) . . . . . . C 6
Calais, 76,527
(100,823★) . . . . . . B 8
Cannes, 72,259
(295,525★) I14
Chalon-sur-Saône, 56,194
(78,064★) F11
Chambéry, 53,427
(96,163★) G12
Cherbourg, 28,442
(85,485★) . . . . C 5
Cholet, 55,524 . . . . . . E 6
Clermont-Ferrand,
147,361 (256,189★) G10
Compiègne, 40,384
(62,778★) . . . . C 9
Creil, 34,709
(82,505★) . . . . C 9
Dieppe, 35,957
(41,812★) . . . . C 8
Dijon, 140,942
(215,865★) E12
Douai, 42,576
(202,366★) B10
Dunkerque, 73,120
(195,705★) . . . . . . A 9
Fontainebleau, 15,679
(35,629★) . . . . D 9
Grenoble, 156,637
(392,021★) G12
La Rochelle, 75,840
(102,143★) . . . . . . F 5
Laval, 50,360
(55,984★) . . . . D 6
Le Havre, 199,388
(254,595★) . . . . . . C 7
Le Mans, 147,697
(191,080★) . . . . . . D 7
Lens, 38,244
(327,383★) . . . . . . B 9
Lille, 168,424
(1,020,000★) B10
Limoges, 140,400
(171,689★) . . . . . . G 8
Lorient, 62,554
(104,025★) . . . . . . E 3
Lourdes, 17,425 . . . . . I 6
Lyon, 413,095
(1,275,000★) G11
Mâcon, 38,404
(47,274★) F11
Marseille, 874,436
(1,225,000★) J12
Maubeuge, 36,061
(105,714★) B10
Meaux, 45,005
(55,797★) . . . . D 9
Melun, 35,005
(82,479★) . . . . D 9
Metz, 114,232
(186,437★) C13
Montbéliard, 31,836
(128,194★) E13
Montluçon, 49,912
(67,963★) . . . . F 9
Montpellier, 197,231
(221,307★) I10
Mulhouse, 112,157
(220,613★) E14
Nancy, 96,317
(306,982★) D13
Nantes, 240,539
(464,857★) . . . . . . E 5
Nevers, 43,013
(59,274★) E10
Nice, 337,085
(449,496★) I14
Nîmes, 124,220
(132,343★) I11
Niort, 58,203
(61,959★) . . . . F 6

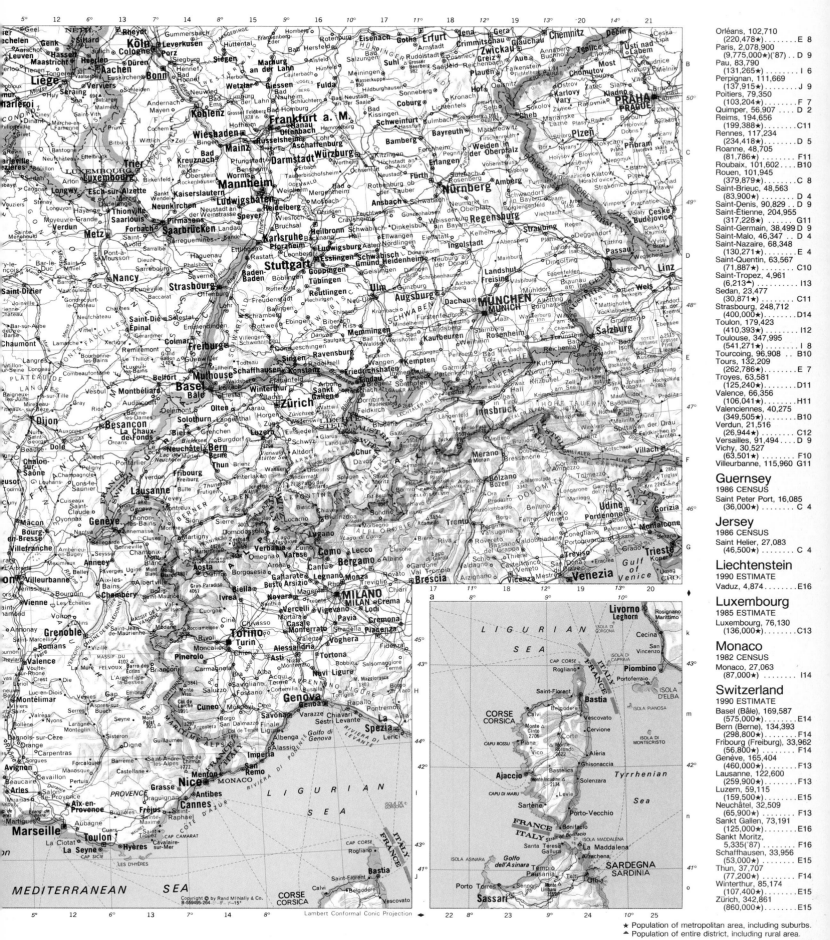

Orléans, 102,710
(220,478★) . . . . E 8
Paris, 2,078,900
(9,775,000★)('87) . . D 9
Pau, 83,790
(131,265★) . . . . I 6
Perpignan, 111,669
(137,915★) . . . . J 9
Poitiers, 79,350
(103,204★) . . . . F 7
Quimper, 56,907 . . . . D 2
Reims, 194,656
(199,388★) C11
Rennes, 117,234
(234,418★) . . . . . . .D 5
Roanne, 48,705
(81,786★) F11
Roubaix, 101,602 . . .B10
Rouen, 101,945
(379,879★) . . . . . . .C 8
Saint-Brieuc, 48,563
(83,900★) . . . . . . .D 4
Saint-Denis, 90,829 . .D 9
Saint-Étienne, 204,955
(317,228★) G11
Saint-Germain, 38,499 D 9
Saint-Malo, 46,347 . .D 4
Saint-Nazaire, 68,348
(130,271★) . . . . . . .E 4
Saint-Quentin, 63,567
(71,887★) C10
Saint-Tropez, 4,961
(6,213★) I13
Sedan, 23,477
(30,871★) C11
Strasbourg, 248,712
(400,000★) D14
Toulon, 179,423
(410,393★) I12
Toulouse, 347,995
(541,271★) . . . . . . I 8
Tourcoing, 96,908 . .B10
Tours, 132,209
(262,786★) . . . . . . .E 7
Troyes, 63,581
(125,240★) D11
Valence, 66,356
(106,041★) H11
Valenciennes, 40,275
(349,505★) B10
Verdun, 21,516
(26,944★) C12
Versailles, 91,494 . . .D 9
Vichy, 30,527
(63,501★) F10
Villeurbanne, 115,960 G11

Guernsey
1986 CENSUS
Saint Peter Port, 16,085
(36,000★) . . . . C 4

Jersey
1986 CENSUS
Saint Helier, 27,083
(46,500★) . . . . C 4

Liechtenstein
1990 ESTIMATE
Vaduz, 4,874 . . . . .E16

Luxembourg
1985 ESTIMATE
Luxembourg, 76,130
(136,000★) C13

Monaco
1982 CENSUS
Monaco, 27,063
(87,000★) I14

Switzerland
1990 ESTIMATE
Basel (Bâle), 169,587
(575,000★) E14
Bern (Berne), 134,393
(298,800★) F14
Fribourg (Freiburg), 33,962
(56,800★) F14
Genève, 165,404
(460,000★) F13
Lausanne, 122,600
(259,900★) F13
Luzern, 59,115
(159,500★) E15
Neuchâtel, 32,509
(65,900★) F13
Sankt Gallen, 73,191
(125,000★) E16
Sankt Moritz,
5,335('87) F16
Schaffhausen, 33,956
(53,000★) E15
Thun, 37,707
(77,200★) F14
Winterthur, 85,174
(107,400★) E15
Zürich, 342,861
(860,000★) E15

★ Population of metropolitan area, including suburbs.
▲ Population of entire district, including rural area.

11

Spain and Portugal

Andorra

1986 CENSUS

Andorra, 18,463 .... C13

Gibraltar

1988 ESTIMATE

Gibraltar, 30,077 .... I 6

Portugal

1981 CENSUS

Almada, 42,607 .... G 2
Barreiro, 50,863 .... G 2
Beja, 19,643 .... G 4
Braga, 63,033 .... D 3
Coimbra, 74,616 .... E 3
Covilhã, 21,807 .... E 4
Évora, 34,851 .... G 4
Faro, 27,974 .... H 4
Funchal, 44,111 .. m21
Guimarães, 21,947 .. D 3
Lisboa (Lisbon), 807,167
  (2,250,000★) ..... G 2
Montijo, 23,017 ..... G 3
Porto, 327,368
  (1,225,000★) ..... D 3
Póvoa de Varzim,
  23,729 .... D 3
Santarém, 19,761 ... F 3
Setúbal, 77,885 .... G 3
Vila do Conde, 20,613 D 3
Vila Nova de Gaia,
  62,469 .... D 3

Spain

1988 ESTIMATE

Albacete, 125,997 .. G10
Alcalá de Guadaira,
  50,935 .... H 6
Alcalá de Henares,
  150,021 .... E 8
Alcantarilla, 28,279 . H10
Alcázar de San Juan,
  26,258 .... F 8
Alcira, 40,575 ..... F11
Alcoy, 66,074 ..... G11
Algeciras, 99,528 ... I 6
Alicante, 261,051 ... G11
Almendralejo, 25,352 G 5
Almería, 157,644 ... I 9
Andújar, 32,300
  (37,020▲) ...... G 7
Antequera, 32,200
  (41,284▲) ...... H 7
Aranjuez, 37,694 ... E 8
Arcos de la Frontera,
  19,600 (27,311▲) . I 6
Arrecife, 36,297 .... p27
Ávila, 45,092 ..... E 7
Avilés, 87,811
  (131,000★) ..... B 6
Badajoz, 106,400
  (122,407▲) ..... G 5
Badalona, 225,229 .. D14
Barcelona, 1,714,355
  (4,040,000★) D14
Baza, 20,910 ...... H 9
Bilbao, 384,733
  (985,000★) ...... B 9
Burgos, 160,561 ... C 8
Burjasot, 35,011 ... F11
Cáceres, 71,598 ... F 5
Cádiz, 156,591
  (240,000★) ...... I 5
Cartagena, 70,000
  (172,710▲) H11
Castellón de la Plana,
  131,809 ....F11
Chiclana de la Frontera,
  43,157 .... I 5
Ciudad Real, 56,300 G 8
Córdoba, 302,301 .. H 7
Coria del Río, 21,844 H 5
Cuenca, 42,222 .... E 9
Don Benito, 24,500
  (29,324▲) ...... G 6
Durango, 27,425 ... B 9
Écija, 30,900
  (35,836▲) ...... H 6
Éibar, 34,355 ..... B 9
Elche, 158,300
  (180,256▲) G11
Elda, 56,756 ...... G11
El Ferrol del Caudillo,
  86,503 (129,000★) . B 3
El Puerto de Santa María,
  49,900 (62,285▲) . I 5
Gandía, 46,100
  (52,646▲) G11
Gavá, 34,613 ..... D14
Gerona, 30,900
  (68,902▲) D14
Getafe, 135,367 ... E 8
Gijón, 262,156 .... B 6
Granada, 263,334 ... H 8
Granollers, 49,045 . D14
Guadalajara, 61,309 . E 8
Hospitalet, 278,449 . D14
Huelva, 137,826 ... H 5
Huesca, 41,841 ... C11
Irún, 54,886 ...... B10
Jaén, 106,435 ..... H 8

★ Population of metropolitan area, including suburbs.
▲ Population of entire district, including rural area.

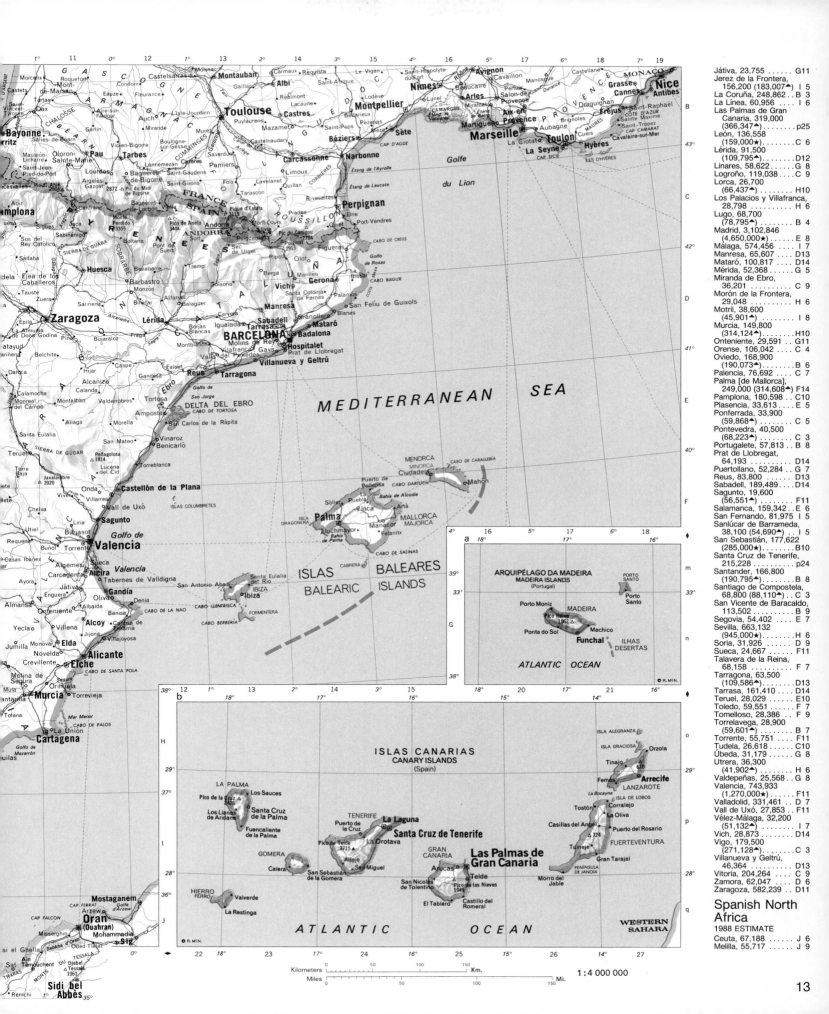

Játiva, 23,755 ...... G11
Jerez de la Frontera,
  156,200 (183,007▲) I 5
La Coruña, 248,862 .. B 3
La Línea, 60,956 ..... I 6
Las Palmas de Gran
  Canaria, 319,000
  (366,347▲) p25
León, 136,558
  (159,000★) ....C 6
Lérida, 91,500
  (109,795▲) D12
Linares, 58,622 .... G 8
Logroño, 119,038 ...C 9
Lorca, 26,700
  (66,437▲) H10
Los Palacios y Villafranca,
  28,798 .... H 6
Lugo, 68,700
  (78,795▲) ....B 4
Madrid, 3,102,846
  (4,650,000★) .... E 8
Málaga, 574,456 ....I 7
Manresa, 65,607 ...D13
Mataró, 100,817 ...D14
Mérida, 52,368 .... G 5
Miranda de Ebro,
  36,201 .... C 9
Morón de la Frontera,
  29,048 .... H 6
Motril, 38,600
  (45,901▲) .... I 8
Murcia, 149,800
  (314,124▲) H10
Onteniente, 29,591 . G11
Orense, 106,042 .... C 4
Oviedo, 168,900
  (190,073▲) ......B 6
Palencia, 76,692 .... C 7
Palma [de Mallorca],
  249,000 (314,608▲) F14
Pamplona, 180,598 .C10
Plasencia, 33,613 ... E 5
Ponferrada, 33,900
  (59,868▲) .... C 5
Pontevedra, 40,500
  (68,223▲) .... C 3
Portugalete, 57,813 .. B 8
Prat de Llobregat,
  64,193 .... D14
Puertollano, 52,284 . G 7
Reus, 83,800 ...... D13
Sabadell, 189,489 ...D14
Sagunto, 19,600
  (56,551▲) F11
Salamanca, 159,342 .. E 6
San Fernando, 81,975 I 6
Sanlúcar de Barrameda,
  38,100 (54,690▲) .. I 5
San Sebastián, 177,622
  (285,000★) B10
Santa Cruz de Tenerife,
  215,228 .... p24
Santander, 166,800
  (190,795▲) ......B 8
Santiago de Compostela,
  68,800 (88,110▲) .. C 3
San Vicente de Baracaldo,
  113,502 .... B 9
Segovia, 54,402 .... E 7
Sevilla, 663,132
  (945,000★) ......H 6
Soria, 31,926 ..... D 9
Sueca, 24,667 ..... F11
Talavera de la Reina,
  68,158 .... F 7
Tarragona, 63,500
  (109,586▲) D13
Tarrasa, 161,410 ...D14
Teruel, 28,029 .... E10
Toledo, 59,551 .... F 7
Tomelloso, 28,386 .. F 9
Torrelavega, 28,900
  (59,601▲) .... B 7
Torrente, 55,751 ... F11
Tudela, 26,618 .... C10
Úbeda, 31,179 .... G 8
Utrera, 36,300
  (41,902▲) .... H 6
Valdepeñas, 25,568 . G 8
Valencia, 743,933
  (1,270,000★) F11
Valladolid, 331,461 . D 7
Vall de Uxó, 27,853 . F11
Vélez-Málaga, 32,200
  (51,132▲) .... I 7
Vích, 28,873 ...... D14
Vigo, 179,500
  (271,128▲) ......C 3
Villanueva y Geltrú,
  46,364 .... D13
Vitoria, 204,264 ... C 9
Zamora, 62,047 ... D 6
Zaragoza, 582,239 .. D11

Spanish North Africa

1988 ESTIMATE

Ceuta, 67,188 ...... J 6
Melilla, 55,717 ..... J 9

1 : 4 000 000

13

Italy

Bosnia and Hercegovina

1987 ESTIMATE

Banja Luka, 130,900	
(193,890▲)	E12
Mostar, 47,606('71)	F12
(162,490▲)('87)	
Sarajevo, 341,200	
(479,688▲)	D 9
Tuzla, 67,300	D11
(129,967▲)	E13

Croatia

1987 ESTIMATE

Osijek, 106,800	
(54,600▲)	L 8
Rijeka, 166,400	
(199,282▲)('87)	L 7
Sisak, 38,421('71)	D 9
(96,014▲)	F11

Zadar, 43,187('71)	E12
Zagreb, 697,925('87)	D13

Italy

1987 ESTIMATE

Acireale, 46,997	L10
Agrigento, 41,200	L 9
Alcamo, 43,072	L 9
Alessandria, 76,100	E 3
Altamura, 54,784	I11
Ancona, 104,409	F 8
Andria, 88,348	H11
Anzio, 30,806	H 7
Arezzo, 74,200	F 6
Asti, 63,600 (75,459▲)	E 3
Avellino, 56,407	I 9
Bagheria, 43,725	K 8
Bari, 362,524	H11
Barletta, 86,954	H11
Benevento, 54,400	H 9
(65,661▲)	
Bergamo, 118,959	D 4
(345,000★)	
Bisceglie, 47,771	H11
Bologna, 432,406	E 6
(525,000★)	
Bolzano (Bozen),	
101,515	C 6
Brescia, 199,286	D 5
Brindisi, 92,280	I12
Busto Arsizio, 78,056	D 3
Cagliari, 220,574	J 4
(305,000★)	
Caltanissetta, 62,352	L 9
Carrara, 65,974	E 5
Caserta, 65,974	H 9
Castellammare [di Stabia],	
68,491	I 9
Catania, 372,486	L10
(550,000★)	
Catanzaro, 102,558	K11
Cerignola, 53,463	F 6
Cesena, 72,600	E 7
Civitavecchia, 50,806	G 6
Como, 91,738	D 4
(165,000★)	
Cosenza, 106,026	J11
(150,000★)	
Cremona, 76,979	D 5
Ferrara, 113,300	E 6
(143,950▲)	F 3
Firenze (Florence), 425,835	
(640,000★)	F 6
Foggia, 155,051	H10
(90,012▲)	E 7
Forlì, 91,200 (110,482▲)	L 9
Gela, 79,378	E 3
Genova (Genoa), 727,427	
(805,000★)	
Grosseto, 56,400	G 6
(70,592▲)	E 6
Iesi, 40,855	E 8
Imola, 48,200 (61,587▲)	F 3
Imperia, 41,481	E 4
(185,000★)	

★ Population of metropolitan area, including suburbs. ▲ Population of entire district, including rural area.

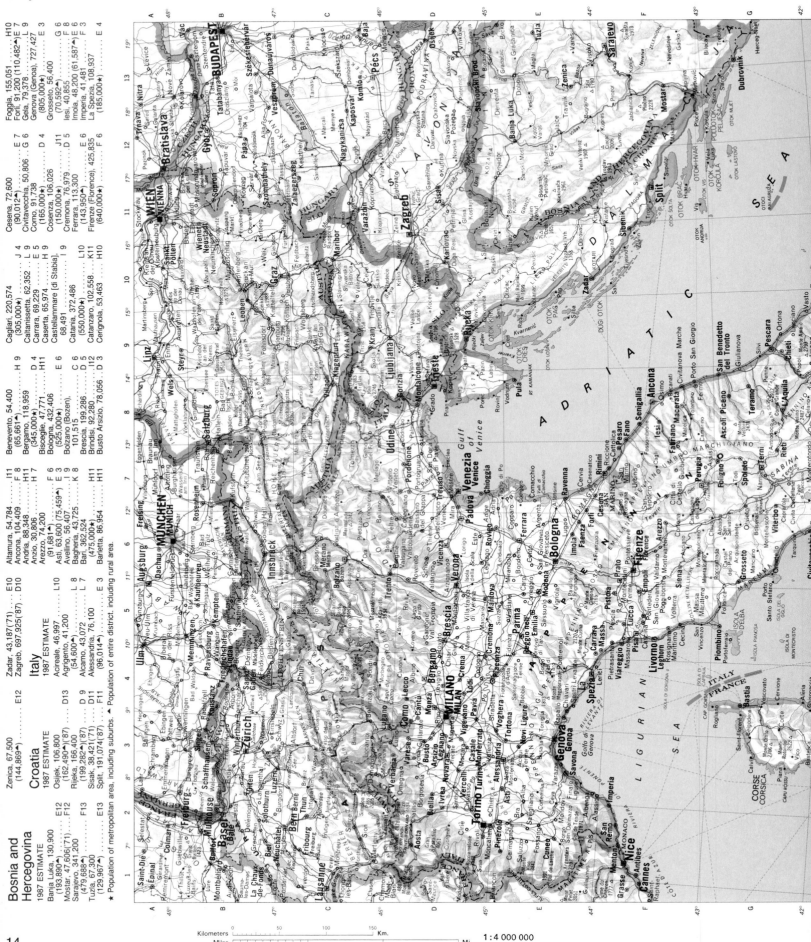

Kilometers 0 50 100 150 Km.

Miles 0 50 100 150 Mi.

1 : 4 000 000

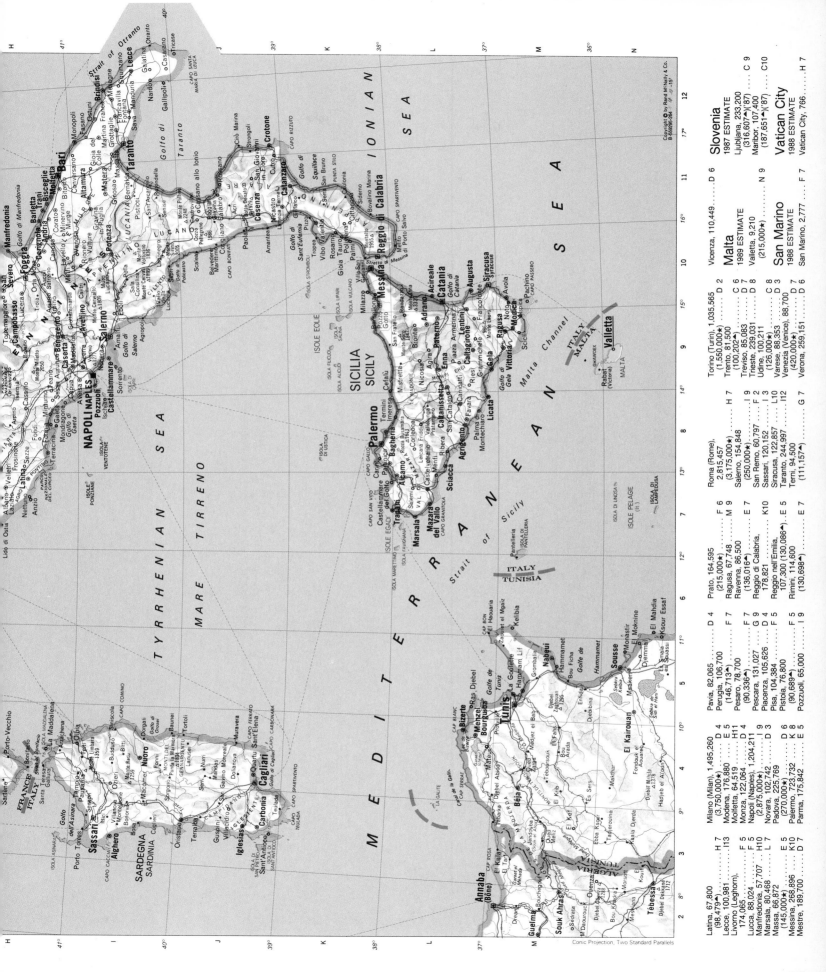

Copyright by Rand McNally & Co.
8-559295-264

Latina, 67,800 .... H 7
(98,479▲)
Lecce, 100,981 .... I13
Livorno (Leghorn),
174,065 .... F 5
Lucca, 88,024 .... F 5
Manfredonia, 57,707 ...... H10
Marsala, 80,468 .... L 7
Massa, 66,872 .... D 3
(145,000★)
Messina, 268,896 .... K10
Mestre, 189,700 .... D 7

Milano (Milan), 1,495,260 .. D 4
(3,750,000★)
Modena, 176,880 .... E 5
Molfetta, 64,519 .... H11
Monza, 122,064 .... D 4
Napoli (Naples), 1,204,211 . I 9
(2,875,000★)
Novara, 102,742 .... D 3
Padova, 225,769 .... D 6
Palermo, 723,732 .... K 8
Parma, 175,842 .... E 5

Pavia, 82,065 .... D 4
Perugia, 106,700 .... F 7
(146,713▲)
Pesaro, 78,700 .... E 7
(90,336▲)
Pescara, 131,027 .... G 9
Piacenza, 105,626 .... D 4
Pisa, 104,384 .... F 5
Pistoia, 76,800 .... E 5
(90,689▲)
Pozzuoli, 65,000 .... I 9
(130,698▲)

Prato, 164,595 .... F 6
(215,000★)
Ragusa, 67,748 .... M 9
Ravenna, 86,500 .... E 7
(136,016▲)
Reggio di Calabria,
178,821 .... K10
Reggio nell'Emilia,
107,300 (130,086▲) ..... E 5
Rimini, 114,600 .... F 5

Roma (Rome),
2,815,457 .... H 7
(3,175,000★)
Salerno, 154,848 .... I 9
(250,000★)
San Remo, 60,797 .... F 2
Sassari, 120,152 .... I 3
Siracusa, 122,857 .... L10
Taranto, 244,997 .... I12
Termi, 94,500 .... G 7
(111,157▲)

Torino (Turin), 1,035,565 .. D 2
(1,550,000★)
Trento, 81,500 .... C 6
Treviso, 85,083 .... D 7
Trieste, 239,031 .... D 8
(250,000★)
Udine, 100,211 .... C 6
Varese, 88,353 .... D 3
Venezia (Venice), 88,700 . D 7
(420,000★)
Verona, 259,151 .... D 6
Vicenza, 110,449 .... D 6

Slovenia
1987 ESTIMATE
Ljubljana, 233,200 .... C 9
(316,607▲)('87)
Maribor, 107,400 .... C10
(187,651▲)('87)

Malta
1989 ESTIMATE
Valletta, 9,210 .... N 9
(215,000★)

San Marino
1988 ESTIMATE
San Marino, 2,777 .... F 7

Vatican City
1988 ESTIMATE
Vatican City, 766 .... F 7

Conic Projection, Two Standard Parallels

Southeastern Europe

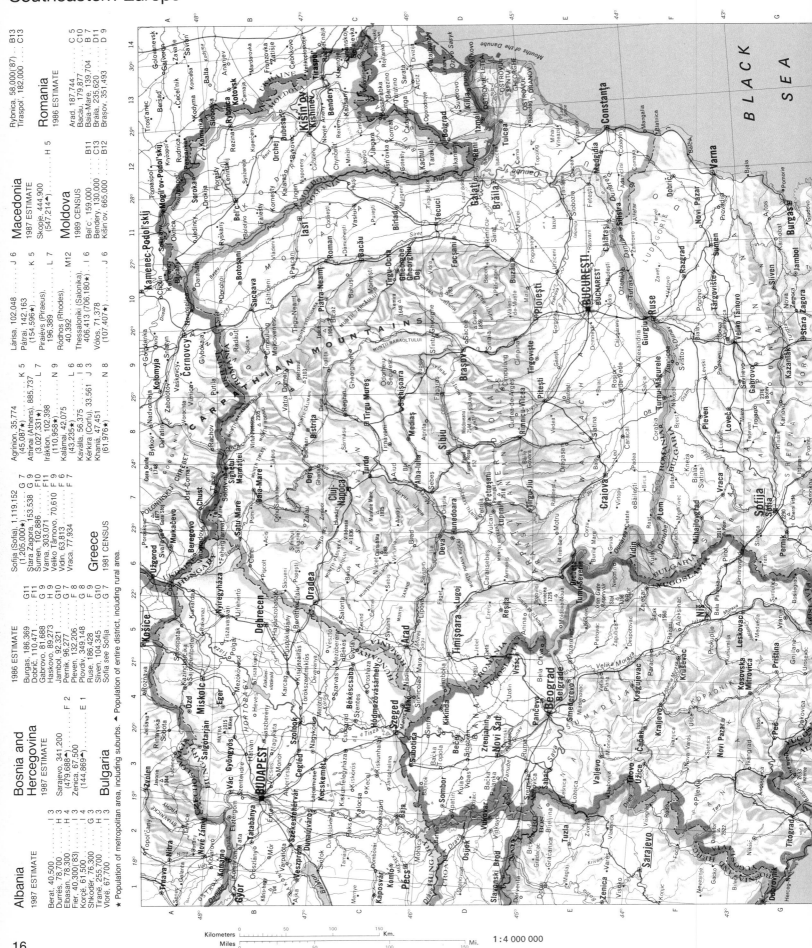

Albania
1987 ESTIMATE

Berat, 40,500 . . . . I 3
Durrës, 78,700 . . . . H 3
Elbasan, 78,300 . . . . I 3
Fier, 40,300(83) . . . . I 4
Korçë, 61,500 . . . . I 4
Shkodër, 76,300 . . . . . . G 3
Tiranë, 255,700 ▲ . . . . . H 3
Vlorë, 67,700 . . . . I 3

Bosnia and Hercegovina
1987 ESTIMATE

Sarajevo, 341,200
   (479,688▲) . . . . F 2
Zenica, 67,500
   (144,869▲) . . . . E 1

Bulgaria
1986 ESTIMATE

Burgas, 186,369 . . . . . . G11
Dobrič, 110,471 . . . . F11
Gabrovo, 81,688 . . . . . . G 9
Haskovo, 89,273 . . . . . . H 9
Jambol, 92,321 . . . . G10
Pernik, 96,277 . . . . G 7
Pleven, 132,206 . . . . . . F 8
Plovdiv, 349,148 . . . . . . F 9
Ruse, 186,428 . . . . F 9
Sliven, 104,345 . . . . G10
Sofija see Sofia

Sofija (Sofia), 1,119,152
   (1,205,000★) . . . . . . G 7
Stara Zagora, 153,538 . . G 9
Šumen, 102,886 . . . . . . F10
Varna, 303,071 . . . . F11
Veliko Tărnovo, 70,610 . . F 9
Vidin, 63,813 . . . . F 8
Vraca, 77,934 . . . . F 7

Greece
1981 CENSUS

Agrínion, 35,774 . . . . . . K 5
Athínai (Athens), 885,737
   (45,087★) . . . . L 7
Iráklion, 102,398
   (110,958★) . . . . L 6
Kalámai, 42,075
   (43,235★) . . . . L 6
Kavála, 56,375 . . . . J 3
Kérkira (Corfu), 33,561 . . J 3
Khaniá, 47,451
   (61,976★) . . . . N 8

Lárisa, 102,048 . . . . J 6
Pátrai, 142,163
   (154,596★) . . . . K 5
Piraiévs (Piraeus),
   196,389
   (3,027,331★) . . . . L 7
Ródhos (Rhodes),
   40,392 . . . . M12
Thessaloníki (Salonika),
   406,413 (706,180★) . . . I 6
Vólos, 71,378
   (107,407★) . . . . J 6

Macedonia
1987 ESTIMATE

Skopje, 444,900
   (547,214▲) . . . . H 5

Moldova
1989 CENSUS

Bel'c', 159,000 . . . . B11
Bendery, 130,000 . . . . . C13
Kišin'ov, 665,000 . . . . . . B12

Romania
1986 ESTIMATE

Arad, 187,744 . . . . C 5
Bacău, 179,877 . . . . C10
Baia-Mare, 139,704 . . . . B 7
Brăila, 235,620 . . . . D11
Brașov, 351,493 . . . . . . D 9

Rybnica, 58,000(87) B13
Tiraspol, 182,000 . . . . . . C13

★ Population of metropolitan area, including suburbs. ▲ Population of entire district, including rural area.

BLACK SEA

Kilometers

Km.

Miles

Mi.

1 : 4 000 000

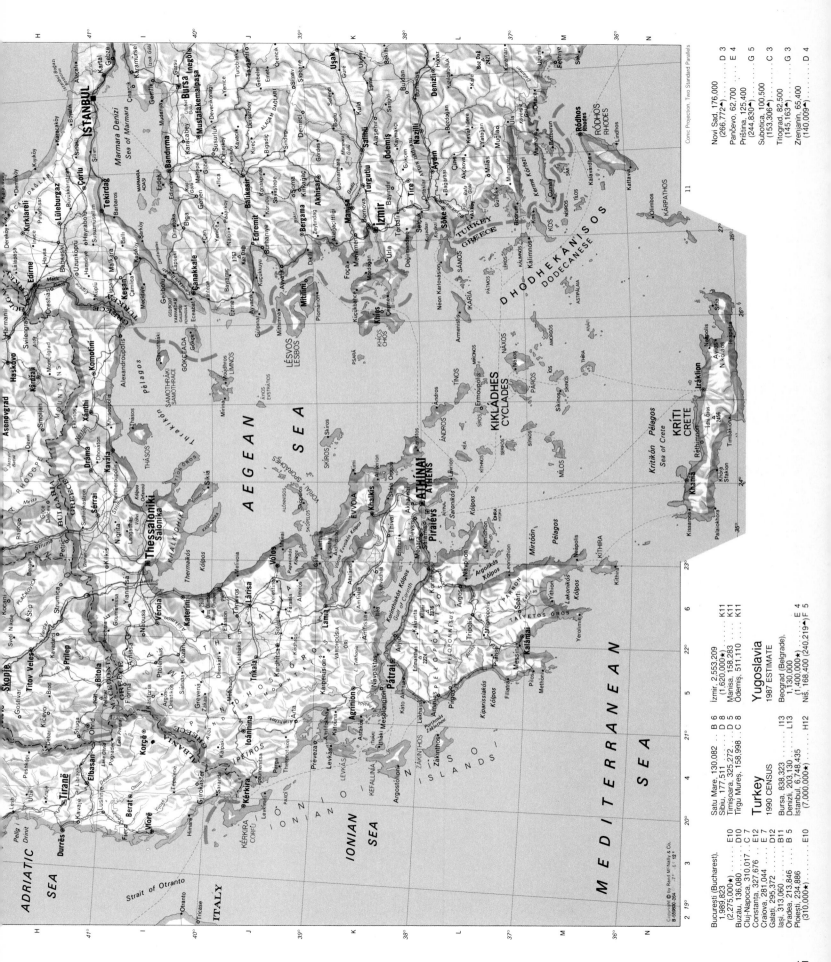

Conic Projection, Two Standard Parallels

Baltic and Moscow Regions

Belarus
1989 CENSUS

Baranoviči, 159,000 .. H 9
Bobrujsk, 223,000 .. H12
Borisov, 144,000 ... G11
Brest, 258,000 ..... I 6
Gomel', 500,000 ... I14
Grodno, 270,000 ... H 6
Lida, 81,000('87) .. H 8
Minsk, 1,589,000
  (1,650,000★) H10
Mogil'ov, 356,000 .. H13
Molodečno,
  87,000('87) ...... G 9
Novopolock,
  90,000('87) F11
Orša, 123,000 ..... G13
Pinsk, 119,000 .... I 9
Polock, 80,000('87) . F11
Rečica, 71,000('87) . I13
Sluck, 55,000('87) .. H10
Svetlogorsk,
  68,000('87) ...... G 3
Vitebsk, 350,000 ... F13
Žlobin, 52,000('87) . I13

Estonia
1989 CENSUS

Kohtla-Järve,
  78,000('87) ... B10
Narva, 81,000('87) .. B11
Pärnu, 53,000('87) .. C 7
Tallinn, 482,000 ... B 7
Tartu, 114,000 .... C 9

Latvia
1989 CENSUS

Daugavpils, 127,000 . F 9
Jelgava, 72,000('87) . E 6
Jūrmala, 65,000('87) . E 6
Liepāja, 114,000 ... E 4
Rēzekne, 35,620('79) E10
Rīga, 915,000
  (1,005,000★) ..... E 7
Ventspils, 52,000('87) D 4

Lithuania
1989 CENSUS

Kaunas, 423,000 .... G 6
Klaipėda (Memel),
  204,000 .... F 4
Panevėžys, 126,000 . F 7
Šiauliai, 145,000 ... F 6
Vilnius, 582,000 .... G 8

Russia
1989 CENSUS

Aleksandrov,
  66,000('87) E21
Aleksin, 72,000('87) . G20
Balachna, 35,359('79) E26

Balašicha, 136,000 . F20
Bežeck, 30,711('79) . D19
Bor, 65,000('87) ... E27
Boroviči, 64,000('87) C16
Br'ansk, 452,000 ... H17
Čechov, 57,000('87) . F20
Čerepovec, 310,000 . B20
Čern'achovsk,
  36,361('79) ..... G 4
Chimki, 133,000 ... F20
Dmitrov, 64,000('87) . E20
Domodedovo,
  51,000('87) F20
Dubna, 64,000('87) . E20
Dzeržinsk, 285,000 . E26
Elektrostal', 153,000 . F21
Furmanov, 44,430('79) D24
Gatčina, 81,000('87) . B13
Gorki see Nižnij
  Novgorod E27
Gr'azi, 41,082('79) .. I22
Gus'-Chrustal'nyj,
  75,000('87) F23
Ivanovo, 481,000 ... D23
Jarcevo, 40,908('79) . F15
Jaroslavl', 633,000 . D22
Jefremov, 58,000('87) H21
Jegorjevsk,
  73,000('87) F22

★ Population of metropolitan
  area, including suburbs.

Copyright © by Rand McNally & Co.
B-579495-264

Kilometers

Miles

1:4 000 000

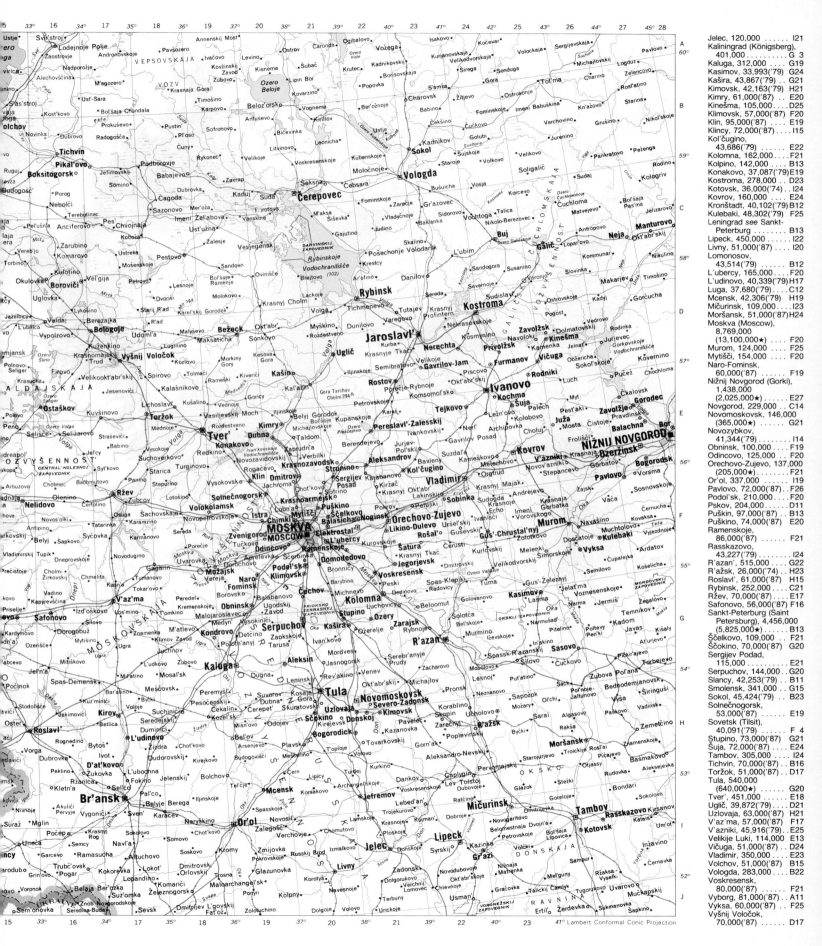

Jelec, 120,000 . . . . . . I21
Kaliningrad (Königsberg),
  401,000 . . . . G 3
Kaluga, 312,000 . . . . G19
Kasimov, 33,993('79) G24
Kašira, 43,867('79) . . G21
Kimovsk, 42,163('79) H21
Kimry, 61,000('87) . . E20
Kinešma, 105,000 . . . D25
Klimovsk, 57,000('87) F20
Klin, 95,000('87) E19
Klincy, 72,000('87) I15
Kol'čugino,
  43,686('79) E22
Kolomna, 162,000 . . . . F21
Kolpino, 142,000 . . . . B13
Konakovo, 37,087('79) E19
Kostroma, 278,000 . . . D23
Kotovsk, 36,000('74) . . I24
Kovrov, 160,000 . . . . . E24
Kronštadt, 40,102('79) B12
Kulebaki, 48,302('79) . F25
Leningrad see Sankt-
  Peterburg B13
Lipeck, 450,000 . . . . . I22
Livny, 51,000('87) I20
Lomonosov,
  43,514('79) B12
L'ubercy, 165,000 . . . . F20
L'udinovo, 40,339('79) H17
Luga, 37,680('79) C12
Mcensk, 42,306('79) . H19
Mičurinsk, 109,000 . . . I23
Moršansk, 51,000('87) H24
Moskva (Moscow),
  8,769,000
  (13,100,000★) F20
Murom, 124,000 . . . . F25
Mytišči, 154,000 . . . . F20
Naro-Fominsk,
  60,000('87) F19
Nižnij Novgorod (Gorki),
  1,438,000
  (2,025,000★) E27
Novgorod, 229,000 . . . C14
Novomoskovsk, 146,000
  (365,000★) G21
Novozybkov,
  41,344('79) I14
Obninsk, 100,000 . . . . F19
Odincovo, 125,000 . . . F20
Orechovo-Zujevo, 137,000
  (205,000★) F21
Or'ol, 337,000 . . . . . . I19
Pavlovo, 72,000('87). . F26
Podol'sk, 210,000 . . . . F20
Pskov, 204,000 . . . . . D11
Puškin, 97,000('87) . . B13
Puškino, 74,000('87) . E20
Ramenskoje,
  86,000('87) F21
Rasskazovo,
  43,227('79) I24
R'azan', 515,000 . . . . G22
R'ažsk, 26,000('74) . . I23
Roslavl', 61,000('87) . H15
Rybinsk, 252,000 . . . . C21
Ržev, 70,000('87) E17
Safonovo, 56,000('87) F16
Sankt-Peterburg (Saint
  Petersburg), 4,456,000
  (5,825,000★) B13
Ščelkovo, 109,000 . . . F21
Ščokino, 70,000('87) . G20
Sergijev Podad,
  115,000 . . . . E21
Serpuchov, 144,000 . . G20
Slancy, 42,253('79) . . B11
Smolensk, 341,000 . . . G15
Sokol, 45,424('79) . . . B23
Solnečnogorsk,
  53,000('87) E19
Sovetsk (Tilsit),
  40,091('79) . . . . . . F 4
Stupino, 73,000('87) . G21
Šuja, 72,000('87) E24
Tambov, 305,000 . . . . I24
Tichvin, 70,000('87) . . B16
Toržok, 51,000('87) . . D17
Tula, 540,000
  (640,000★) G20
Tver', 451,000 . . . . . . E18
Uglič, 39,872('79) . . . D21
Uzlovaja, 63,000('87) H21
V'az'ma, 57,000('87) . F17
V'azniki, 45,916('79) . .E25
Velikije Luki, 114,000 . E13
Vičuga, 51,000('87) . . D24
Vladimir, 350,000 . . . . E23
Volchov, 51,000('87) . B15
Vologda, 283,000 . . . . B22
Voskresensk,
  80,000('87) F21
Vyborg, 81,000('87) . . A11
Vyksa, 60,000('87) . . . F25
Vyšnij Voločok,
  70,000('87) D17

Asia

'Adan, 176,100 ('84)
(318,000★) ....H 7
AFGHANISTAN............F 9
Ahmadābād, 2,059,725
('81) (2,400,000★) ..G10
Al Baṣrah, 616,700
('85)......................F 7
Al-Kuwayt, 44,335 ('85)
(1,375,000★) ....G 7
Alma-Ata,
1,128,000 ('89)
(1,190,000★) E10
Al-Madīnah, 290,000
('80)......................G 6
'Ammān, 936,300 ('89)
(1,450,000★) ....F 6
Ankara, 2,553,209 ('90)
(2,670,000★) ....F 6
ARMENIA..................F 7
Ar-Riyāḍ, 1,250,000
('80)......................G 7
Ašchabad, 398,000
('89)......................F 8
AZERBAIJAN............E 7
Baghdād, 3,841,268
('87)......................F 7
Baku, 1,150,000 ('89)
(2,020,000★) ....E 7
Bangalore,
2,476,355 ('81)
(2,950,000★) H10
Bangkok see Krung
Thep H13
BANGLADESH............G12
Batumi, 136,000 ('89)..E 7
Bayrūt, 509,000 ('82)
(1,675,000★) ....F 6
Beijing (Peking),
6,710,000 ('88)
(6,450,000★) F14
BHUTAN....................G12
Biškek, 616,000 ('89)..E10
Bombay, 8,243,405 ('81)
(9,950,000★) H10
BRUNEI......................I14
BURMA......................G12
Calcutta, 3,305,006 ('81)
(11,100,000★) H11
CAMBODIA................H13
Canton see
Guangzhou G14
Celinograd, 277,000
('89)......................D10
Chabarovsk, 601,000
('89)......................E16
Changchun, 1,822,000
('88) (2,000,000▲)...E15
Changsha, 1,230,000
('88)......................G14
Chengdu, 1,884,000 ('88)
(2,960,000▲) F13
CHINA......................F12
Chongqing (Chungking),
2,502,000 ('88)
(2,890,000▲) G13
Čita, 366,000 ('89)......D14
Colombo, 683,000 ('86)
(2,050,000★) I10
CYPRUS....................F 6
CYPRUS, NORTH..........F 6
Dacca see Dhaka G12
Dalian, 2,280,000 ('88)F15
Damascus see
Dimashq ....F 6
Da Nang, 318,653
('79)......................H13
Delhi, 4,884,234 ('81)
(7,200,000★) G10
Dhaka (Dacca), 2,365,695
('81) (3,430,312★) ..G12

Dimashq (Damascus),
1,326,000 ('88)
(1,950,000★) ....F 6
Dušanbe, 595,000
('89)......................F 9
Esfahān, 986,753 ('86)
(1,175,000★) ....F 8
Frunze see Biškek E10
Fukuoka, 1,160,440 ('85)
(1,750,000★) F16
Fuzhou, 910,000 ('88)
(1,240,000★) G14
George Town, 248,241
('80) (495,000★)......I13
GEORGIA..................E 7
Guangzhou (Canton),
3,100,000 ('88)
(3,420,000▲) G14
Hakodate, 319,194
('85)......................E17
Ha Noi, 1,089,000 ('89)
(1,500,000★) G13
Harbin, 2,710,000
('88)......................E15
Herāt, 177,300 ('88)....F 9
Hiroshima,
1,044,118 ('85)
(1,575,000★) F16
HONG KONG..............G14
Hyderābād, 2,187,262
('81) (2,750,000★) ..H10
INDIA......................G10
INDONESIA................I13
IRAN........................F 8
IRAQ........................F 7
Irkutsk, 626,000 ('89)..D13
Islāmābād, 204,364
('81)......................F10
ISRAEL....................F 6
izmir, 2,553,209 ('90)
(1,620,000★) ....F 5
Jakutsk,
187,000 ('89)..........C15
JAPAN......................F16
Jekaterinbug,
1,367,000 ('89)
(1,620,000★) ....D 9
Jerevan, 1,199,000 ('89)
(1,315,000★) ....E 7
Jerusalem see
Yerushalayim ....F 6
Jiddah, 1,300,000
('80)......................G 6
Jinan, 1,546,000 ('88)
(2,140,000▲) F14
JORDAN....................F 6
Kābol (Kabul), 1,424,400
('88)......................F 9
Kānpur, 1,481,789 ('81)
(1,875,000★) G11
Karāchi, 4,901,627 ('81)
(5,300,000★) ....G 9
Kashi, 146,300 ('86)
(194,500★) F10
Kathmāndū, 235,160
('81) (320,000★) G11
KAZAKHSTAN............E 9
Kermān,
257,284 ('86)...........F 8
Konsomol'sk-na-Amure,
315,000 ('89)..........D16
KOREA, NORTH..........E15
KOREA, SOUTH..........F15
Krasnojarsk, 912,000
('89)......................D12
Krung Thep (Bangkok),
5,716,779 ('88)
(6,450,000★) H13
Kuala Lumpur, 919,610
('80) (1,475,000★)....I13
Kuching, 72,555 ('80)...I14

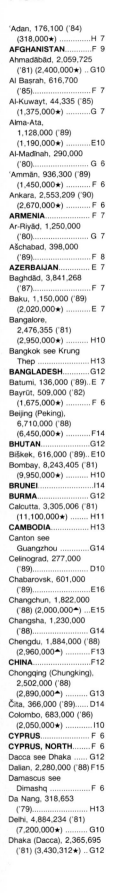
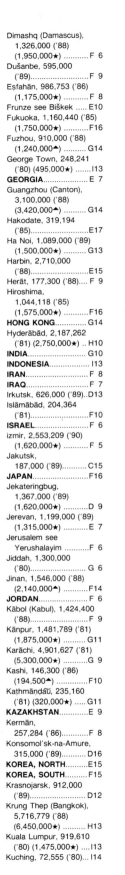

Copyright © by Rand McNally & Co.

A-519695-286

Miles 0 200 400 600 800 1000 Mi.

Kilometers 0 400 800 1200 1600 Km.

1:40 000 000

Kunming, 1,310,000 ('88)
(1,550,000▲) G13
KUWAIT .... G 7
Kyōto,
1,479,218 ('85)........F16
KYRGYZSTAN E10
Kyzyl, 80,000 ('87)......D12
Lahore, 2,707,215 ('81)
(3,025,000★) F10
Lanzhou, 1,297,000 ('88)
(1,420,000▲) F13
LAOS H13
LEBANON .... F 6
Lhasa, 84,400 ('86)
(107,700▲) G12
MACAU G14
Madras, 3,276,622 ('81)
(4,475,000★) H11
Makkah,
550,000 ('80)......... G 6
MALAYSIA I13
MALDIVES I10
Mandalay, 532,949
('83) G12
Manila, 1,587,000 ('90)
(6,800,000★) H15
Mashhad, 1,463,508
('86) .... F 8
Masqaṭ, 50,000 ('81)...G 8
Mawlamyine, 219,961
('83) H12
MONGOLIA E13
Nāgpur, 1,219,461 ('81)
(1,302,066★) G10
Nanjing, 2,390,000
('88) F14
NEPAL G11
New Delhi, 273,036
('81) G10
Novosibirsk, 1,436,000
('89) (1,600,000★) .. D11
Ochotsk, 9,000 .... D17
OMAN .... G 8
Omsk, 1,148,000 ('89)
(1,175,000★) D10
Ōsaka, 2,636,249 ('85)
(1,645,000★) F16
PAKISTAN .... G 9
Patna, 776,371 ('81)
(1,025,000★) G11
Peking see Beijing F14
Peshāwar, 506,896 ('81)
(566,248★) F10
Petropavlovsk-Kamčatskij,
269,000 ('89) D18
PHILIPPINES H15
Phnum Penh, 700,000
('86) H13
Pyŏngyang, 1,283,000
('81) (1,600,000★) ...F15
QATAR .... G 8
Qingdao (Tsingtao),
1,300,000 ('88)........F15
Quetta, 244,842 ('81)
(285,719★) .... F 9
Quezon City, 1,632,000
('90) H15
Rangoon see
Yangon H12
Rāwalpindi, 457,091 ('81)
(1,040,000★) F10
RUSSIA D10
Saigon see Thanh Pho Ho
Chi Minh H13
Samarkand, 366,000
('89) .... F 9
San'ā', 427,150 ('86)...H 7
SAUDI ARABIA .... G 7
Semipalatinsk, 334,000
('89) D11

Sendai, 700,254 ('85)
(1,175,000★) F17
Shanghai,
7,220,000 ('88)
(9,300,000★) F15
Shenyang (Mukden),
3,910,000 ('88)
(4,370,000▲) E15
Shīrāz, 848,289 ('86)...G 8
SINGAPORE I13
Sŏul, 10,522,000 ('89)
(15,850,000★) F15
SRI LANKA I11
Srīnagar, 594,775 ('81)
(606,002★) F10
SYRIA .... F 6
Tabrīz, 971,482 ('86)... F 7
T'aipei, 2,637,100 ('88)
(6,130,000★) G15
TAIWAN G15
Taiyuan, 1,700,000 ('88)
(1,980,000★) F14
TAJIKISTAN F10
Taškent, 2,073,000 ('89)
(2,325,000★) .... E 9
Tbilisi, 1,260,000 ('89)
(1,460,000★) .... E 7
Tehrān, 6,042,584 ('86)
(7,500,000★) .... F 8
THAILAND H13
Thanh Pho Ho Chi Minh
(Saigon), 3,169,000 ('89)
(3,100,000★) H13
Tianjin (Tientsin),
4,950,000 ('88)
(5,540,000▲) F14
Tobol'sk,
82,000 ('87)............ D 9
Tōkyō, 8,354,615 ('85)
(27,700,000★) F16
Tomsk, 502,000 ('89)..D11
TURKEY .... F 6
TURKMENISTAN .... F 9
Ulaanbaatar, 548,400
('89)........................E13
**UNITED ARAB
EMIRATES** .... G 8
Ürümqi, 1,060,000
('88)........................E11
UZBEKISTAN .... E 9
Vārānasi, 708,647 ('81)
(925,000★) G11
Verchojansk, 1,400.....C16
Viangchan, 377,409
('85)........................H13
VIETNAM H13
Vladivostok, 648,000
('89)........................E16
Wuhan, 3,570,000
('88)........................F14
Xiamen, 343,700 ('86)
(546,400▲) G14
Xi'an, 2,210,000 ('88)
(2,580,000▲) F13
Yangon (Rangoon),
2,705,039 ('83)
(2,800,000★) H12
YEMEN .... H 7
Yerevan see Jerevan ..E 7
Yerushalayim (Jerusalem),
493,500 ('89)
(530,000★) .... F 6
Yokohama, 2,992,926
('85)........................F16
Zhangjiakou,
500,000 ('88)
(640,000▲) E14

★ Population of metropolitan area, including suburbs.
▲ Population of entire district, including rural area.

21

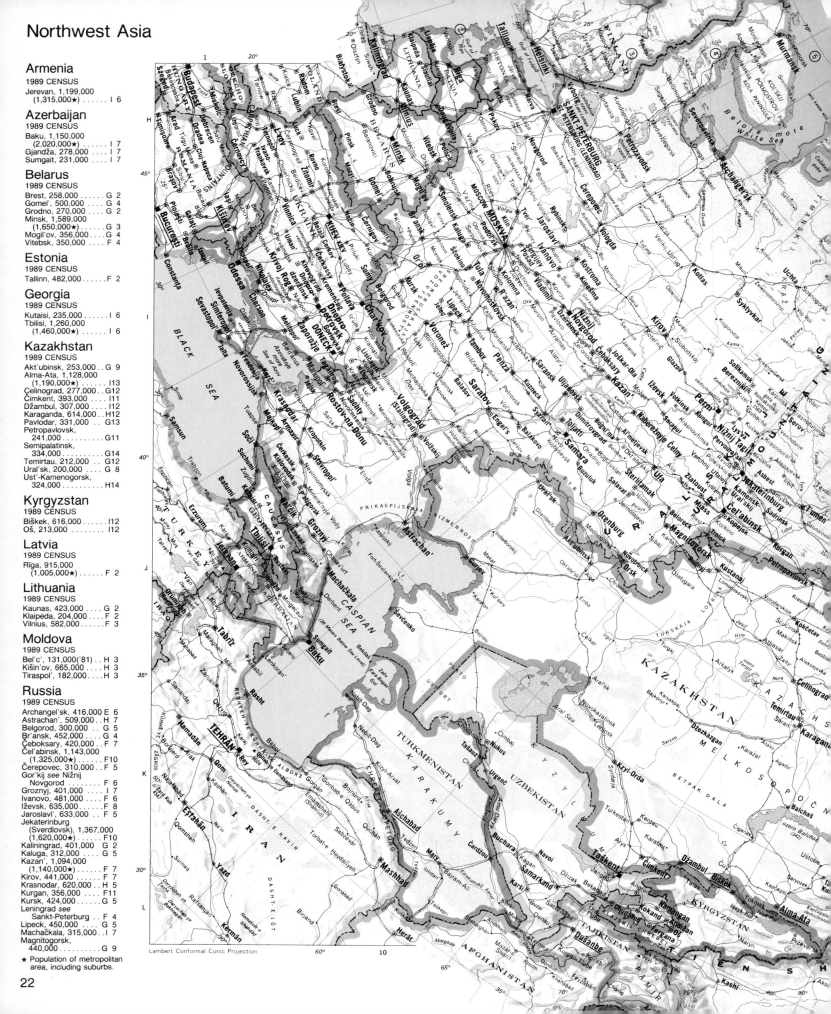

Northwest Asia

Armenia
1989 CENSUS
Jerevan, 1,199,000
(1,315,000★) ...... I 6

Azerbaijan
1989 CENSUS
Baku, 1,150,000
(2,020,000★) .... I 7
Gjandža, 278,000 .... I 7
Sumgait, 231,000 .... I 7

Belarus
1989 CENSUS
Brest, 258,000 ...... G 2
Gomel', 500,000 .... G 4
Grodno, 270,000 .... G 2
Minsk, 1,589,000
(1,650,000★) .... G 3
Mogil'ov, 356,000 .... G 4
Vitebsk, 350,000 .... F 4

Estonia
1989 CENSUS
Tallinn, 482,000 ..... F 2

Georgia
1989 CENSUS
Kutaisi, 235,000 ..... I 6
Tbilisi, 1,260,000
(1,460,000★) ...... I 6

Kazakhstan
1989 CENSUS
Akt'ubinsk, 253,000 .. G 9
Alma-Ata, 1,128,000
(1,190,000★) I13
Čelinograd, 277,000 . G12
Čimkent, 393,000 .. I11
Džambul, 307,000 ... I11
Karaganda, 614,000 . H12
Pavlodar, 331,000 .. G13
Petropavlovsk,
241,000 .... G11
Semipalatinsk,
334,000 .... G14
Temirtau, 212,000 .. G12
Ural'sk, 200,000 .... G 8
Ust'-Kamenogorsk,
324,000 .... H14

Kyrgyzstan
1989 CENSUS
Biškek, 616,000 ...... I12
Oš, 213,000 .... I12

Latvia
1989 CENSUS
Rīga, 915,000
(1,005,000★) ..... F 2

Lithuania
1989 CENSUS
Kaunas, 423,000 .... G 2
Klaipeda, 204,000 ... F 2
Vilnius, 582,000 ..... F 3

Moldova
1989 CENSUS
Bel'c', 131,000('81) .. H 3
Kišin'ov, 665,000 .... H 3
Tiraspol', 182,000 .... H 3

Russia
1989 CENSUS
Archangel'sk, 416,000 E 6
Astrachan', 509,000 .. H 7
Belgorod, 300,000 ... G 5
Br'ansk, 452,000 .... G 4
Čeboksary, 420,000 .. F 7
Čel'abinsk, 1,143,000
(1,325,000★) F10
Čerepovec, 310,000 .. F 5
Gor'kij see Nižnij
Novgorod .... F 6
Groznyj, 401,000 .... I 7
Ivanovo, 481,000 .... F 6
Iževsk, 635,000 ..... F 8
Jaroslavl', 633,000 .. F 5
Jekaterinburg
(Sverdlovsk), 1,367,000
(1,620,000★) F10
Kaliningrad, 401,000 . G 2
Kaluga, 312,000 .... G 5
Kazan', 1,094,000
(1,140,000★) ..... F 7
Kirov, 441,000 ...... F 7
Krasnodar, 620,000 .. H 5
Kurgan, 356,000 .... F11
Kursk, 424,000 ..... G 5
Leningrad see
Sankt-Peterburg . F 4
Lipeck, 450,000 ..... G 6
Machačkala, 315,000 . I 7
Magnitogorsk,
440,000 .... G 9

★ Population of metropolitan
area, including suburbs.

22

Lambert Conformal Conic Projection

Map

BARENTS SEA

NOVAJA ZEMLA

KARSKOJE MORE
KARA SEA
KARA

OSTROV KOMSOMOLEC
SEVERNAJA ZEMLA
OSTROV OKT'ABR'SKOJ REVOL'UCII
OSTROV BOL'ŠEVIK

MORE LAPTEVYCH
LAPTEV SEA

POLUOSTROV TAJMYR
GORY BYRRANGA

SEVERO - SIBIRSKAJA NIZMENNOST'

Vorkuta

Arctic Circle

Noril'sk

SREDNE-SIBIRSKOJE PLOSKOGORJE

RUSSIA

ZAPADNO SIBIRSKAJA RAVNINA

Surgut

Omsk

Novosibirsk
Tomsk
Anžero-Sudžensk
Ačinsk
Krasnojarsk
Kemerovo
Kansk
Belovo
Leninsk-Kuzneckij
Prokopjevsk
Kisel'ovsk
Novokuzneck
Barnaul
Bijsk
Abakan

Bratsk

Semipalatinsk
Ust'-Kamenogorsk

Rubcovsk

ZAPADNYJ SAJAN
VOSTOČNYJ SAJAN
SAJAN MOUNTAINS
SAJANY

Čeremchovo
Usolje-Sibirskoje
Angarsk
Irkutsk

ozero Bajkal
Lake Baikal

Ulan-Ude

STANOVOJE NAGORJE
STANOVOY MOUNTAINS

JABLONOVYJ CHREBET

Čita

CHINA
XINJIANG UYGUR ZIZHIQU
SINKIANG

Yining

MONGOLIA

Ulaanbaatar

Copyright © by Rand McNally & Co.
B-579594-264-10 -9'-13 -20"

Kilometers 0 200 400 600 Km.
Miles 0 200 400 600 Mi.
1:16 000 000

Index

Moskva (Moscow),
8,769,000
(13,100,000★) .... F 5
Murmansk, 468,000 .. D 4
Naberežnyje Čelny,
501,000 .... F 8
Nižnij Novgorod (Gor'kij),
1,438,000
(2,025,000★) ...... F 7
Nižnij Tagil, 440,000 .. F 9
Orenburg, 547,000 .. G 9
Or'ol, 337,000 ...... G 5
Orsk, 271,000 ...... G 9
Penza, 543,000 .... G 7
Perm', 1,091,000
(1,160,000★) ...... F 9
Petrozavodsk,
270,000 .... E 4
R'azan', 515,000 .. G 5
Rostov-na-Donu,
1,020,000
(1,165,000★) ...... H 5
Samara, 1,257,000
(1,505,000★) ...... G 8
Sankt-Peterburg (St.
Petersburg), 4,456,000
(5,825,000★) ...... F 4
Saransk, 312,000 .. G 7
Saratov, 905,000
(1,155,000★) ...... G 7
Smolensk, 341,000 .. G 4
Soči, 337,000 .... I 5
Stalingrad see
Volgograd .... H 6
Stavropol', 318,000 .. H 6
Sverdlovsk see
Jekaterinburg F10
Syktyvkar, 233,000 .. E 8
Taganrog, 291,000 .. H 5
Tambov, 305,000 .. G 6
Toljatti, 630,000 ... G 7
Tula, 540,000
(640,000★) ...... G 5
Tver' (Kalinin),
451,000 .... F 5
Ufa, 1,083,000
(1,100,000★) ..... G 9
Uljanovsk, 625,000 .. G 7
Vladikavkaz, 300,000 .. I 6
Vladimir, 350,000 ... F 6
Volgograd (Stalingrad),
999,000
(1,360,000★) ..... H 6
Vologda, 283,000 .... F 5
Volžskij, 269,000 .. H 6
Voronež, 887,000 .. G 5

Tajikistan
1989 CENSUS
Dušanbe, 595,000 ....J11

Turkmenistan
1989 CENSUS
Aschabad, 398,000 .. J 9

Ukraine
1989 CENSUS
Čerkassy, 290,000 .. H 4
Černigov, 296,000 .. G 4
Char'kov, 1,611,000
(1,940,000★) ...... G 5
Cherson, 355,000 .. H 4
Dneprodzeržinsk,
282,000 .... H 4
Dnepropetrovsk,
1,179,000
(1,600,000★) ...... H 4
Doneck, 1,110,000
(2,200,000★) ...... H 5
Gorlovka, 337,000
(710,000★) ...... H 5
Jalta, 89,000('87) .. I 4
Kijev (Kiev), 2,587,000
(2,900,000★) ...... G 4
Krivoj Rog, 713,000 .. H 4
Lugansk, 497,000 .. H 5
L'vov, 790,000 ..... H 2
Mariupol' (Ždanov),
517,000 .... H 5
Nikolajev, 503,000 .. H 4
Odessa, 1,115,000
(1,185,000★) ...... H 4
Poltava, 315,000 .. H 4
Sevastopol', 356,000 .. I 4
Simferopol', 344,000 .. I 4
Sumy, 291,000 ...... H 4
Vinnica, 374,000 .. H 3
Yalta see Jalta ...... I 4
Zaporožje, 884,000 .. H 5
Žitomir, 292,000 ... G 3

Uzbekistan
1989 CENSUS
Andižan, 293,000 .... I12
Buchara, 224,000 .... J10
Fergana, 200,000 .... I12
Namangan, 308,000 .. I12
Samarkand, 366,000 ..J11
Taškent, 2,073,000
(2,325,000★) I11

Northeast Asia

Russia

1989 CENSUS

Abakan, 154,000 .... G12
Ačinsk, 122,000 .... F12
Alapajevsk,
 51,000('87) .... F 6
Aldan, 20,000('74) .. F19
Alejsk, 31,390('79) . G10
Aleksandrovsk-
 Sachalinskij,
 20,000('74) G22
Angarsk, 266,000 .... G14
Anžero-Sudžensk,
 108,000 .... F11
Arsenjev, 67,000('87) .. I20
Art'om, 73,000('87) .. I20
Art'omovsk,
 17,000('79) G12
Asbest, 83,000('87) .. F 6
Asino, 31,329('79) .. F11
Balej, 25,000('79) ... G17
Barabinsk, 35,035('79) F 9
Barnaul, 602,000
 (665,000★) G10
Belogorsk,
 71,000('87) G19
Belovo, 118,000('87) . G11
Berdsk, 77,000('87) .. G10
Berezniki, 201,000 ... F 5
Bijsk, 233,000 ...... G11
Bikin, 18,000('79) ... H20
Birobidžan,
 82,000('87) G19
Blagoveščensk,
 206,000 .... G19
Bogotol, 29,000('79) . F11
Bolotnoje, 20,000('79) F10
Bratsk, 255,000 ..... F14
Čel'abinsk, 1,143,000
 (1,325,000★) ..... F 6

Čeremchovo,
 73,000('87) G14
Černogorsk,
 80,000('87) G12
Chabarovsk, 601,000 . H21
Chanty-Mansijsk,
 27,961('79) ...... E 7
Cholmsk, 50,000('87) . H22
Čita, 366,000 ...... G16
Čusovoj, 59,000('87) . F 5
Dudinka, 23,000('74) . D11
Gorno-Altajsk,
 39,917('79) G11
Gubacha, 32,461('79) . F 5
Gusinoozersk,
 18,000('79) G15
Igarka, 16,918('74) .. D11
Inta, 58,000('87) .... D 6
Irbit, 53,000('87) .... F 6
Irkutsk, 626,000 .... G14
Iskitim, 69,000('87) .. G10
Issyk-Kul', 64,000('87) I 9
Jakutsk, 187,000 .... E19
Jekaterinburg, 1,367,000
 (1,620,000★) ..... F 6
Jenisejsk, 22,000('79) F12
Jurga, 92,000('87) ... F10
Južno-Sachalinsk,
 157,000 .... H22
Kamen'-na-Obi,
 40,684('79) G10
Kamensk-Ural'skij,
 209,000 .... F 6
Kansk, 110,000 ..... F13
Karpinsk, 36,569('79) F 6
Kemerovo, 520,000 .. F11
Kirensk, 16,000('74) . F15
Kisel'ovsk, 128,000 .. G11
Kizel, 40,157('79) ... F 5
Kolpaševo,
 27,000('79) F10
Komsomol'sk-na-Amure,
 315,000 .... G21
Kopejsk, 99,000('87) . F 6
Korkino, 63,000('81) . G 6
Korsakov, 43,348('79) H22
Krasnojarsk, 912,000 . F12

★ Population of metropolitan
 area, including suburbs.

24

Kilometers
Miles
1:16 000 000

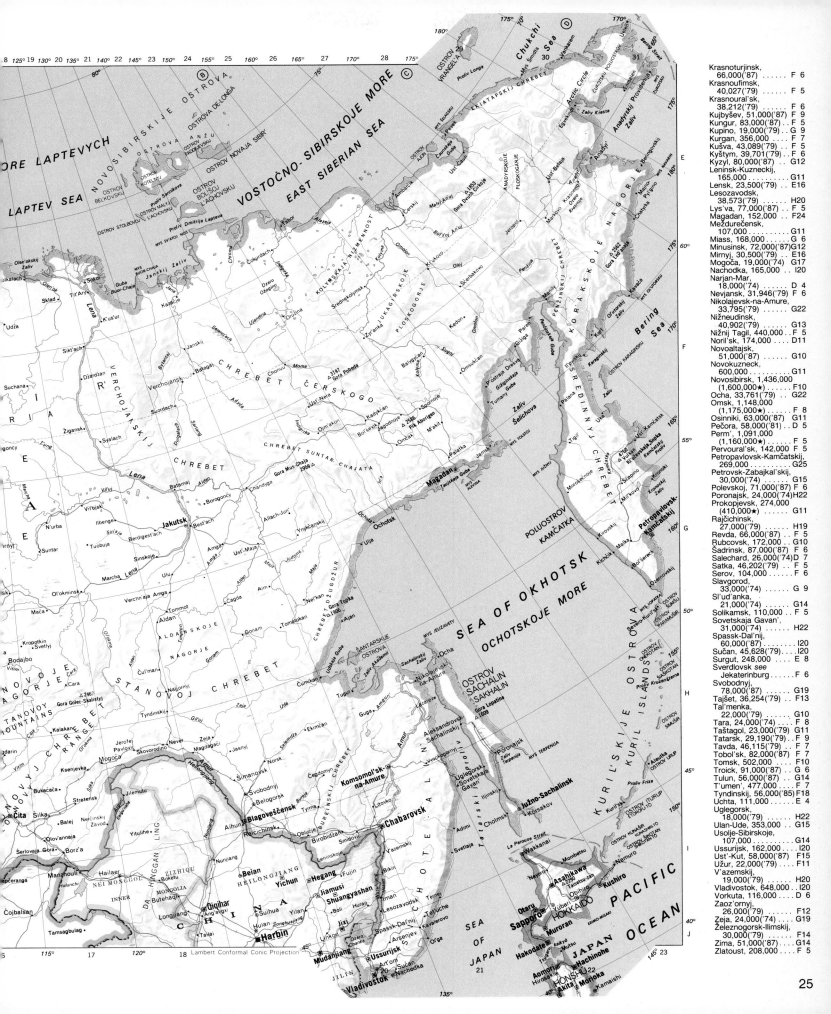

Krasnoturjinsk,
66,000('87) . . . . . F 6
Krasnoufimsk,
40,027('79) . . . . . F 5
Krasnoural'sk,
38,212('79) . . . . . F 6
Kujbyšev, 51,000('87) F 9
Kungur, 83,000('87) . . F 5
Kupino, 19,000('79) . G 9
Kurgan, 356,000 . . . . F 7
Kuša, 43,089('79) . . . F 5
Kyštym, 39,701('79) . . F 6
Kyzyl, 80,000('87) . . G12
Leninsk-Kuzneckij,
165,000 . . . . G11
Lensk, 23,500('79) . . E16
Lesozavodsk,
38,573('79) H20
Lys'va, 77,000('87) . . F 5
Magadan, 152,000 . . F24
Meždurečensk,
107,000 . . . . G11
Miass, 168,000 . . . . . G 6
Minusinsk, 72,000('87) G12
Mirnyj, 30,500('79) . . E16
Mogoča, 19,000('74) . G17
Nachodka, 165,000 . . I20
Narjan-Mar,
18,000('74) . . . . . D 4
Nevjansk, 31,946('79) F 6
Nikolajevsk-na-Amure,
33,795('79) G22
Nižneudinsk,
40,902('79) G13
Nižnij Tagil, 440,000 . F 5
Noril'sk, 174,000 . . . D11
Novoaltajsk,
51,000('87) G10
Novokuzneck,
600,000 . . . . G11
Novosibirsk, 1,436,000
(1,600,000★) F10
Ocha, 33,761('79) . . G22
Omsk, 1,148,000
(1,175,000★) . . . . F 8
Osinniki, 63,000('87) . G11
Pečora, 58,000('81) . . D 5
Perm', 1,091,000
(1,160,000★) . . . . F 5
Pervoural'sk, 142,000 F 5
Petropavlovsk-Kamčatskij,
269,000 . . . . G25
Petrovsk-Zabajkal'skij,
30,000('74) G15
Polevskoj, 71,000('87) F 6
Poronajsk, 24,000('74) H22
Prokopjevsk, 274,000
(410,000★) G11
Rajčichinsk,
27,000('79) H19
Revda, 66,000('87) . . F 5
Rubcovsk, 172,000 . . G10
Šadrinsk, 87,000('87) F 6
Salechard, 26,000('74) D 7
Satka, 46,202('79) . . F 5
Serov, 104,000 . . . . . F 6
Slavgorod,
33,000('74) . . . . . G 9
Sl'ud'anka,
21,000('74) G14
Solikamsk, 110,000 . . F 5
Sovetskaja Gavan',
31,000('74) H22
Spassk-Dal'nij,
60,000('87) I20
Sučan, 45,628('79) . . . I20
Surgut, 248,000 . . . . E 8
Sverdlovsk see
Jekaterinburg . . . . . F 6
Svobodnyj,
78,000('87) G19
Tajšet, 36,254('79) . . F13
Tal'menka,
22,000('79) G10
Tara, 24,000('74) . . . F 8
Taštagol, 23,000('79) G11
Tatarsk, 29,190('79) . F 9
Tavda, 46,115('79) . . F 7
Tobol'sk, 82,000('87) . F 7
Tomsk, 502,000 . . . . F10
Troick, 91,000('87) . . G 6
Tulun, 56,000('87) . . G14
T'umen', 477,000 . . . F 7
Tyndinskij, 56,000('85) F18
Uchta, 111,000 . . . . . E 4
Uglegorsk,
18,000('79) H22
Ulan-Ude, 353,000 . . G15
Usolje-Sibirskoje,
107,000 . . . . G14
Ussurijsk, 162,000 . . I20
Ust'-Kut, 58,000('87) F14
Užur, 22,000('79) . . . F11
V'azemskij,
19,000('79) H20
Vladivostok, 648,000 . I20
Vorkuta, 116,000 . . . D 6
Zaoz'ornyj,
26,000('79) F12
Zeja, 24,000('74) . . . G19
Železnogorsk-Ilimskij,
30,000('79) F14
Zima, 51,000('87) . . . G14
Zlatoust, 208,000 . . . F 5

China, Japan, and Korea

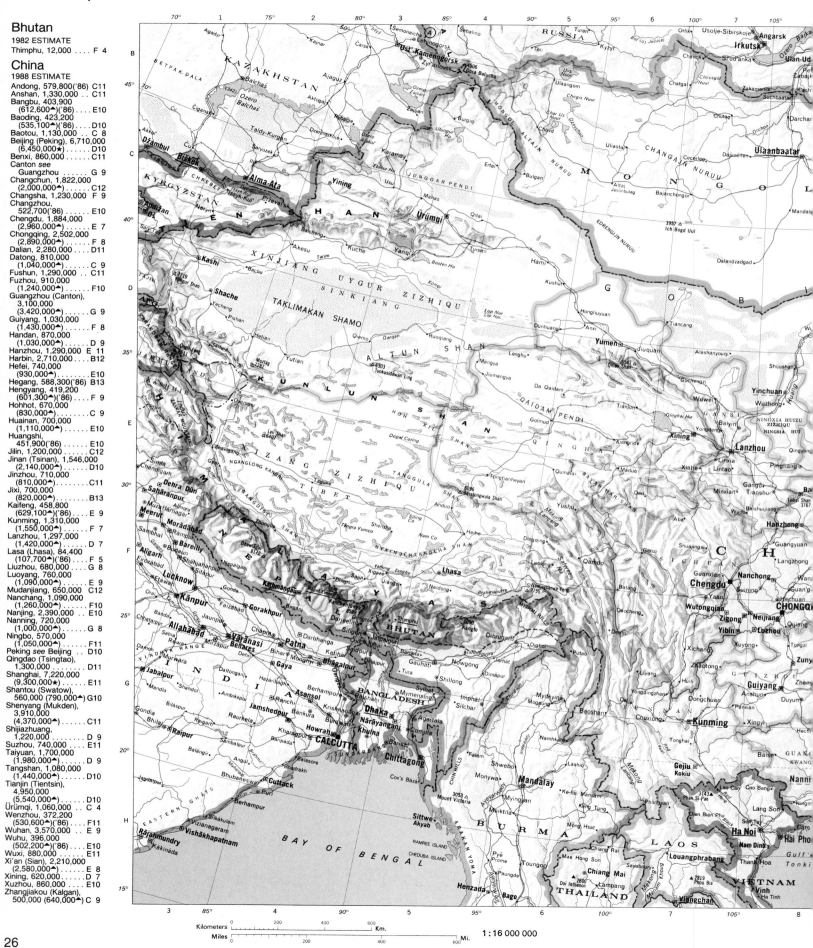

Bhutan
1982 ESTIMATE
Thimphu, 12,000 .... F 4

China
1988 ESTIMATE
Andong, 579,800('86) C11
Anshan, 1,330,000 .. C11
Bangbu, 403,900
(612,600)('86) E10
Baoding, 423,200
(535,100)('86) D10
Baotou, 1,130,000.. C 8
Beijing (Peking), 6,710,000
(6,450,000★).... D10
Benxi, 860,000 .... C11
Canton see
Guangzhou ...... G 9
Changchun, 1,822,000
(2,000,000▲).... C12
Changsha, 1,230,000 F 9
Changzhou,
522,700('86) E10
Chengdu, 1,884,000
(2,960,000▲).... E 7
Chongqing, 2,502,000
(2,890,000▲).... F 8
Dalian, 2,280,000.. D11
Datong, 810,000
(1,040,000▲)...... C 9
Fushun, 1,290,000 .. C11
Fuzhou, 910,000
(1,240,000▲).... F10
Guangzhou (Canton),
3,100,000
(3,420,000▲).... G 9
Guiyang, 1,030,000
(1,430,000▲)...... F 8
Handan, 870,000
(1,030,000▲)...... D 9
Hanzhou, 1,290,000 E 11
Harbin, 2,710,000 .. B12
Hefei, 740,000
(930,000▲)...... E10
Hegang, 588,300('86) B13
Hengyang, 419,200
(601,300▲)('86) .... F 9
Hohhot, 670,000
(830,000▲)...... C 9
Huainan, 700,000
(1,110,000▲).... E10
Huangshi,
451,900('86) E10
Jilin, 1,200,000 .... C12
Jinan (Tsinan), 1,546,000
(2,140,000▲).... D10
Jinzhou, 710,000
(810,000▲)........ C11
Jixi, 700,000
(820,000▲)........ B13
Kaifeng, 458,800
(629,100▲)('86) .. E 9
Kunming, 1,310,000
(1,550,000▲)...... F 7
Lanzhou, 1,297,000
(1,420,000▲)...... D 7
Lasa (Lhasa), 84,400
(107,700▲)('86) .. F 5
Liuzhou, 680,000 .. G 8
Luoyang, 760,000
(1,090,000▲)...... E 9
Mudanjiang, 650,000 C12
Nanchang, 1,090,000
(1,260,000▲).... F10
Nanjing, 2,390,000 .. E10
Nanning, 720,000
(1,000,000▲)...... G 8
Ningbo, 570,000
(1,050,000▲)...... F11
Peking see Beijing .. D10
Qingdao (Tsingtao),
1,300,000 .... D11
Shanghai, 7,220,000
(9,300,000★).... E11
Shantou (Swatow),
560,000 (790,000▲) G10
Shenyang (Mukden),
3,910,000
(4,370,000▲).... C11
Shijiazhuang,
1,220,000 ...... D 9
Suzhou, 740,000 .... E11
Taiyuan, 1,700,000
(1,980,000▲).... D 9
Tangshan, 1,080,000
(1,440,000▲).... D10
Tianjin (Tientsin),
4,950,000
(5,540,000▲).... D10
Ürümqi, 1,060,000 .. C 4
Wenzhou, 372,200
(530,600▲)('86) .. F11
Wuhan, 3,570,000 .. E 9
Wuhu, 396,000
(502,200▲)('86) .. E10
Wuxi, 880,000 ...... E11
Xi'an (Sian), 2,210,000
(2,580,000▲)...... E 8
Xining, 620,000 .... D 7
Xuzhou, 860,000 .... E10
Zhangjiakou (Kalgan),
500,000 (640,000▲) C 9

Kilometers 1:16 000 000
Miles

Zhengzhou, 1,150,000
(1,580,000★) . . . . . E 9
Zibo, 840,000
(2,370,000▲) D10

Hong Kong
1986 CENSUS
Kowloon (Jiulong),
774,781 . . . . G 9
Victoria (Xianggang),
1,175,860
(4,770,000★) . . . . . . G 9

Japan
1985 CENSUS
Asahikawa, 363,631 . . C15
Chiba, 788,930 . . . . . D15
Fukuoka, 1,160,440
(1,750,000★) E13
Hakodate, 319,194 . . C15
Hamamatsu, 514,118 E14
Himeji, 452,917
(660,000★) E13
Hiroshima, 1,044,118
(1,575,000★) E13
Kagoshima, 530,502 . E13
Kanazawa, 430,481 . . D14
Kitakyūshū, 1,056,402
(1,525,000★) E13
Kōbe, 1,410,834 . . . . E14
Kumamoto, 555,719 . . E13
Kurashiki, 413,632 . . E13
Kyōto, 1,479,218 . . . D14
Matsuyama, 426,658 . E13
Nagasaki, 449,382 . . E12
Nagoya, 2,116,381
(4,800,000★) D14
Niigata, 475,630 . . . . D14
Okayama, 572,479 . . E13
Ōsaka, 2,636,249
(16,450,000★) E14
Sapporo, 1,542,979
(1,900,000★) C15
Sendai, 700,254
(1,175,000★) D15
Shizuoka, 468,362
(975,000★) E14
Tōkyō, 8,354,615
(27,700,000★) D14
Utsunomiya, 405,375 D14
Yokohama, 2,992,926 D14

Korea, North
1981 ESTIMATE
Ch'ŏngjin, 490,000 . . C12
Kaesŏng, 259,000 . . D12
Namp'o, 241,000 . . . . D12
P'yŏngyang, 1,283,000
(1,600,000★) D12
Sinŭiju, 305,000 . . . . C11
Wŏnsan, 398,000 . . . D12

Korea, South
1989 ESTIMATE
Chŏnju, 426,473('85) D12
Inch'ŏn, 1,628,000 . . D12
Kwangju, 1,165,000 . . D12
Masan, 448,746
(625,000★)('85) D12
Pusan, 3,773,000
(3,800,000★) D12
Sŏul (Seoul), 10,522,000
(15,850,000★) D12
Taegu, 2,207,000 . . . . D12
Taejŏn, 1,041,000 . . . D12

Macau
1987 ESTIMATE
Macau (Aomen),
429,000 . . . . G 9

Mongolia
1989 ESTIMATE
Ulaanbaatar (Ulan Bator),
548,400 . . . . B 8

Nepal
1981 CENSUS
Kāthmāṇḍau
(Kathmandu), 235,160
(320,000★) . . . . F 4

Taiwan
1988 ESTIMATE
Kaohsiung, 1,342,797
(1,845,000★) G11
T'aichung, 715,107 . . G11
T'ainan, 656,927 . . . . G11
T'aipei, 2,637,100
(6,130,000★) F11

★ Population of metropolitan area, including suburbs.
▲ Population of entire district, including rural area.

27

Eastern and Southeastern China

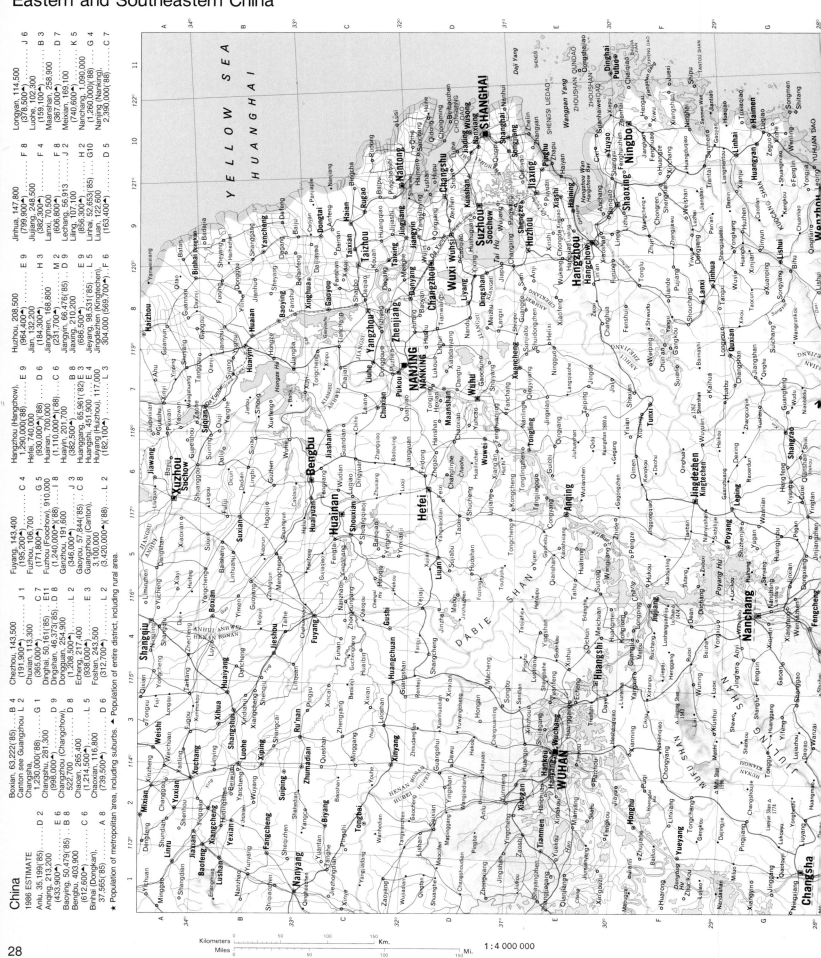

28

Kilometers 0 _____ 50 _____ 100 _____ 150 Km.
Miles 0 _____ 50 _____ 100 _____ 150 Mi.
1 : 4 000 000

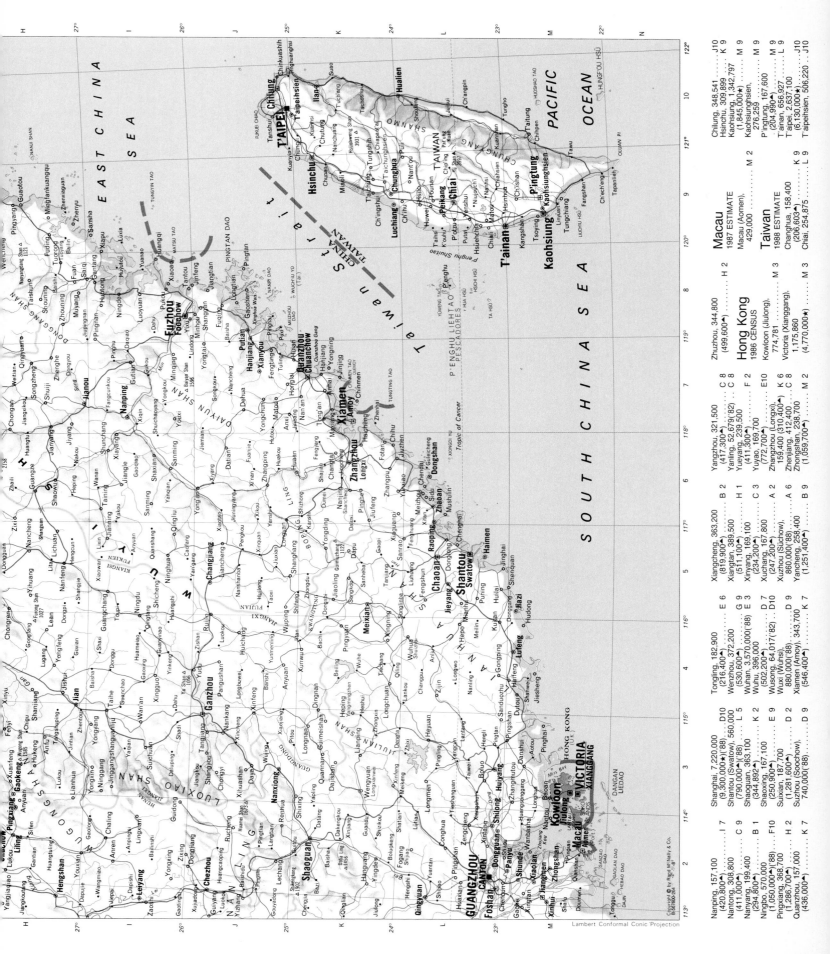

Japan

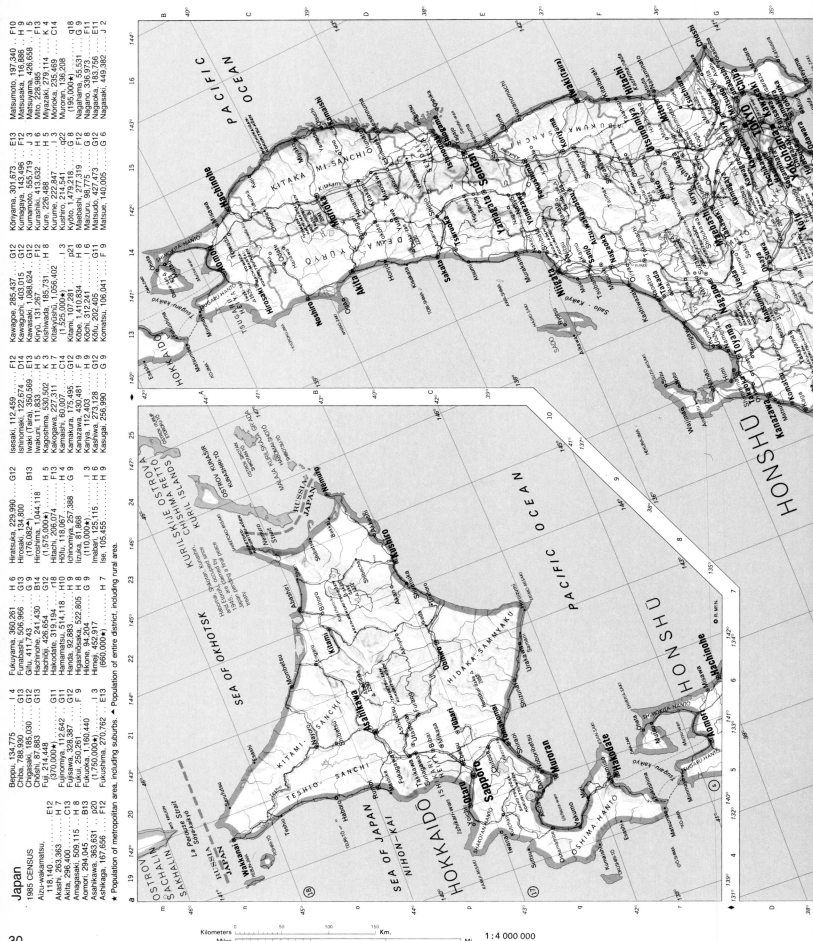

★ Population of metropolitan area, including suburbs. ▲ Population of entire district, including rural area.

PACIFIC OCEAN

SEA OF OKHOTSK

OSTROVA OSTROVA SACHALIN SAKHALIN

RUSSIA
JAPAN

HOKKAIDŌ

HONSHU

Kilometers 0 50 100 150 Km.
Miles 0 50 100 150 Mi.

1:4 000 000

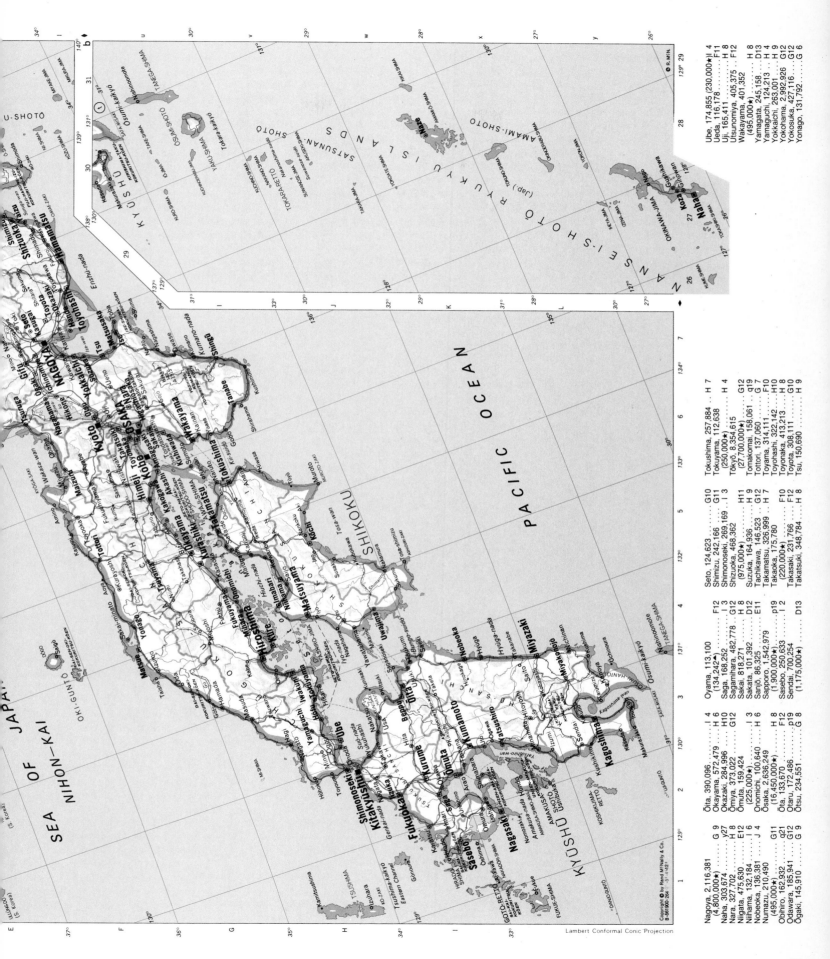

SEA OF JAPAN

NIHON-KAI

PACIFIC OCEAN

KYŪSHŪ

SHIKOKU

NANSEI-SHOTŌ RYUKYU ISLANDS

SATSUNAN-SHOTŌ

AMAMI-SHOTŌ

Lambert Conformal Conic Projection

Nagoya, 2,116,381 . . . . G 9
  (4,800,000★) y27
Naha, 303,674 . . . . H 8
Nara, 327,702 . . . . E12
Niigata, 475,630 . . . . I 6
Niihama, 132,184 . . . . J 4
Nobeoka, 136,381 . . . . G11
Numazu, 210,490 . . . . q21
  (495,000★) . . . .
Obihiro, 162,932 . . . . .q21
Ōdawara, 185,941 . . . . G 9

Ōita, 390,096 . . . . I 4
Okayama, 572,479 . . . . H 6
Okazaki, 284,996 . . . . H10
Ōmiya, 373,022 . . . . G12
Ōmuta, 159,424 . . . . I 3
  (225,000★) . . . .
Onomichi, 100,640 . . . . H 6
Ōsaka, 2,636,249 . . . . H 8
  (16,450,000★) . . . .
Ōta, 133,670 . . . . F12
Otaru, 172,486 . . . . p19
Ōtsu, 234,551 . . . . G 8

Oyama, 113,100 . . . . F12
  (134,242★) . . . .
Saga, 168,252 . . . . I 3
Sagamihara, 482,778 . . . . G12
Sakai, 818,271 . . . . H 8
Sakata, 101,392 . . . . D12
Sanjō, 86,325 . . . . E11
Sapporo, 1,542,979 . . . . p19
  (1,900,000★) . . . .
Sasebo, 250,633 . . . . I 2
Sendai, 700,254 . . . . G 8
  (1,175,000★) . . . .

Seto, 124,623 . . . . G10
Shimizu, 242,166 . . . . G11
Shimonoseki, 269,169 . . . . H 4
Shizuoka, 468,362 . . . . H 7
Suzuka, 164,936 . . . . H11
Tachikawa, 146,523 . . . . G12
Takamatsu, 326,999 . . . . H 7
Takaoka, 175,780 . . . . F10
Takasaki, 231,766 . . . . F12
Takatsuki, 348,784 . . . . H 8

Tokushima, 257,884 . . . . H 7
Toyama, 112,638 . . . . H 4
  (250,000★) . . . .
Tōkyō, 8,354,615 . . . . G12
  (27,700,000★) . . . .
Tomakomai, 158,061 . . . . q19
Tottori, 137,060 . . . . G 7
Toyama, 314,111 . . . . F10
Toyohashi, 322,142 . . . . H10
Toyonaka, 413,213 . . . . H 8
Toyota, 308,111 . . . . G10

Ube, 174,855 (230,000★)I 4
Ueda, 116,178 . . . . F11
Uji, 165,411 . . . . H 8
Utsunomiya, 405,375 . . . . F12
Wakayama, 401,352 . . . .
  (495,000★) . . . . H 8
Yamagata, 245,158 . . . . D13
Yamaguchi, 124,213 . . . . H 4
Yokkaichi, 263,001 . . . . H 9
Yokohama, 2,992,926 . . . . G12
Yokosuka, 427,116 . . . . G12
Yonago, 131,792 . . . . G 6

31

Southeastern Asia

Brunei
1981 CENSUS
Bandar Seri Begawan,
22,777 (64,000★) . . E 5

Burma
1983 CENSUS
Bago,' 150,528 . . . . . B 2
Henzada, 82,005 . . . . . B 2
Mandalay, 532,949 . . A 2
Mawlamyine, 219,961 B 2
Monywa, 106,843 . . . . A 2
Pathein, 144,096 . . . . B 1
Pyè (Prome), 83,332 . . B 2
Sittwe (Akyab),
107,621 . . . . A 1
Yangon (Rangoon),
2,705,039
(2,800,000★) . . . . . . B 2

Cambodia
1986 ESTIMATE
Phnum Pénh, 700,000 C 3

Indonesia
1980 CENSUS
Ambon, 111,914
(207,702▲) . . . . F 8
Balikpapan, 208,040
(279,852▲) . . . . F 6
Bandung, 1,633,000
(1,800,000★)('85) . . m13
Banjarmasin,
424,000('83) . . . . . F 5
Banjuwangi, 90,378 . . n17
Blitar, 78,503
(100,000★) n16
Bogor, 246,946
(560,000★) m13
Cilacap, 127,017 . . . . m14
Cirebon, 223,504
(275,000★) m14
Denpasar, 159,233 . . G 6
Dili, 6,890 (67,039▲) . G 8
Garut, 145,624 . . . . . m13
Jakarta, 9,200,000
(10,000,000★)('89) m13
Jambi, 155,761
(230,046▲) . . . . F 3
Jember, 171,284 . . . . n16
Kediri, 176,261
(221,830▲) m16
Kudus, 154,478 . . . . m15
Kupang, 84,587 . . . . H 7
Madiun, 150,562
(180,000★) m15
Magelang, 123,358
(160,000★) m15
Malang, 547,000('83) m16
Manado, 217,091 . . E 7
Medan, 2,110,000('85)E 2
Padang, 405,600
(657,000★)('83) . . . F 3
Pakanbaru, 186,199 . . E 3
Palembang,
874,000('83) . . . . . F 3
Pangkalpinang, 90,078 F 4
Pasuruan, 95,864
(125,000★) m16
Pekalongan, 132,413
(260,000★) m14
Pemalang, 72,663 . . m14
Pematangsiantar, 150,296
(175,000★) . . . . . . E 2
Pontianak,
343,000('83) . . . . . F 4
Probolinggo, 100,296 m16
Purwokerto, 143,787 m14
Salatiga, 85,740 . . . m15
Samarinda, 182,473
(264,012▲) . . . . . . F 6
Semarang,
1,206,000('83) . . . m15
Sukabumi, 109,898
(225,000★) m13
Surabaya,
2,345,000('85) . . . m16
Surakarta, 491,000
(575,000★)('83) m15
Tanjungkarang-
Telukbetung, 284,167
(375,000★) k12
Tasikmalaya, 192,267 m14
Tegal, 131,440
(340,000★) m14
Tual, 7,833 . . . . G 9
Tulungagung, 91,585 n15
Ujungpandang,
841,000('83) . . . . . G 6
Yogyakarta, 421,000
(510,000★)('83) . . . m15

Laos
1975 ESTIMATE
Louangphrabang,
46,000 . . . . B 3
Paksé, 47,000 . . . . . . B 4
Savannakhet, 53,000 B 3
Viangchan,
377,409('85) . . . . . . B 3

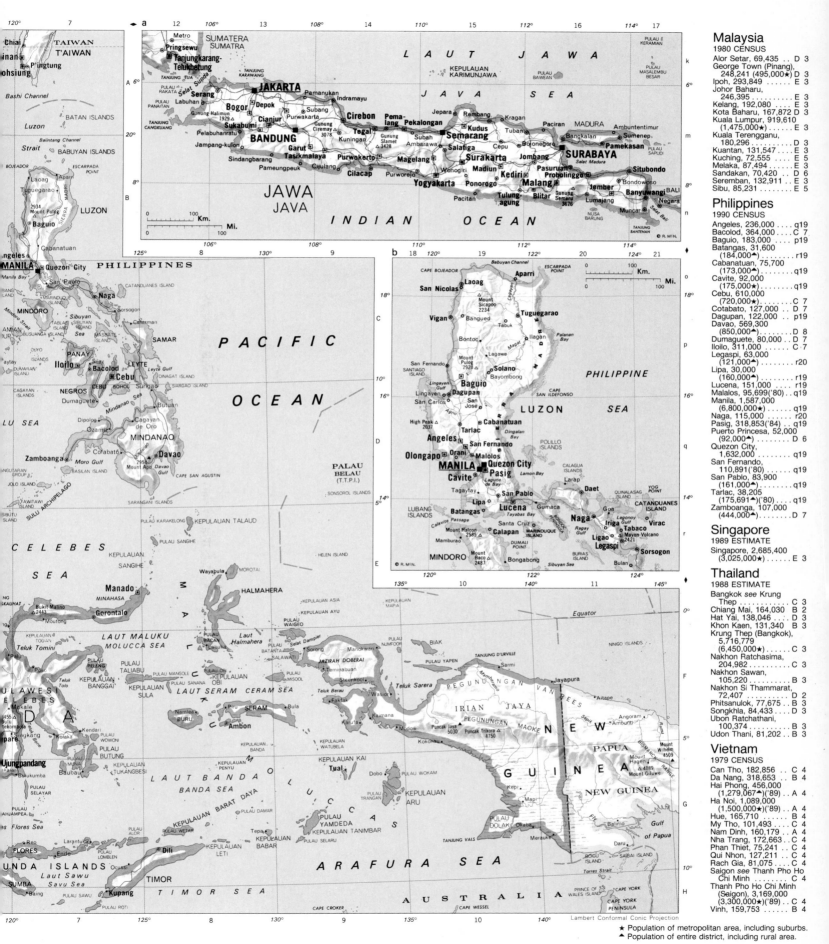

Malaysia
1980 CENSUS
Alor Setar, 69,435 .. D 3
George Town (Pinang),
  248,241 (495,000★) D 3
Ipoh, 293,849 ...... E 3
Johor Baharu,
  246,351 .... E 3
Kelang, 192,080 .... E 3
Kota Baharu, 167,872 D 3
Kuala Lumpur, 919,610
  (1,475,000★) ..... E 3
Kuala Terengganu,
  180,296 .... D 3
Kuantan, 131,547 ... E 3
Kuching, 72,555 .... E 5
Melaka, 87,494 ..... E 3
Sandakan, 70,420 ... D 6
Seremban, 132,911 .. E 3
Sibu, 85,231 ...... E 5

Philippines
1990 CENSUS
Angeles, 236,000 .... q19
Bacolod, 364,000 ... C 7
Baguio, 183,000 .... p19
Batangas, 31,600
  (184,000▲) r19
Cabanatuan, 75,700
  (173,000▲) q19
Cavite, 92,000
  (175,000▲) q19
Cebu, 610,000
  (720,000★) .... C 7
Cotabato, 127,000 .. D 7
Dagupan, 122,000 .. p19
Davao, 569,300
  (850,000▲) ...... D 8
Dumaguete, 80,000 .. D 7
Iloilo, 311,000 ... C 7
Legaspi, 63,000
  (121,000▲) r20
Lipa, 30,000
  (160,000▲) r19
Lucena, 151,000 .... r19
Malolos, 95,699('80) . r19
Manila, 1,587,000
  (6,800,000★) q19
Naga, 115,000 ..... r20
Pasig, 318,853('84) . q19
Puerto Princesa, 52,000
  (92,000▲) .... D 6
Quezon City,
  1,632,000 .... q19
San Fernando,
  110,891('80) q19
San Pablo, 83,900
  (161,000▲) q19
Tarlac, 38,205
  (175,691▲)('80) . q19
Zamboanga, 107,000
  (444,000▲) ...... D 7

Singapore
1989 ESTIMATE
Singapore, 2,685,400
  (3,025,000★) ..... E 3

Thailand
1988 ESTIMATE
Bangkok see Krung
  Thep .... C 3
Chiang Mai, 164,030 . B 2
Hat Yai, 138,046 ... D 3
Khon Kaen, 131,340 . B 3
Krung Thep (Bangkok),
  5,716,779
  (6,450,000★) ..... C 3
Nakhon Ratchasima,
  204,982 .... C 3
Nakhon Sawan,
  105,220 .... B 3
Nakhon Si Thammarat,
  72,407 .... D 2
Phitsanulok, 77,675 .. B 3
Songkhla, 84,433 ... D 3
Ubon Ratchathani,
  100,374 .... B 3
Udon Thani, 81,202 .. B 3

Vietnam
1979 CENSUS
Can Tho, 182,856 .. C 4
Da Nang, 318,653 .. B 4
Hai Phong, 456,000
  (1,279,067▲)('89) . A 4
Ha Noi, 1,089,000
  (1,500,000★)('89) . A 4
Hue, 165,710 ..... B 4
My Tho, 101,493 ... C 4
Nam Dinh, 160,179 . A 4
Nha Trang, 172,663 . C 4
Phan Thiet, 75,241 . C 4
Qui Nhon, 127,211 . C 4
Rach Gia, 81,075 ... C 4
Saigon see Thanh Pho Ho
  Chi Minh .... C 4
Thanh Pho Ho Chi Minh
  (Saigon), 3,169,000
  (3,300,000★)('89) . C 4
Vinh, 159,753 ..... B 4

★ Population of metropolitan area, including suburbs.
▲ Population of entire district, including rural area.

33

Burma, Thailand, and Indochina

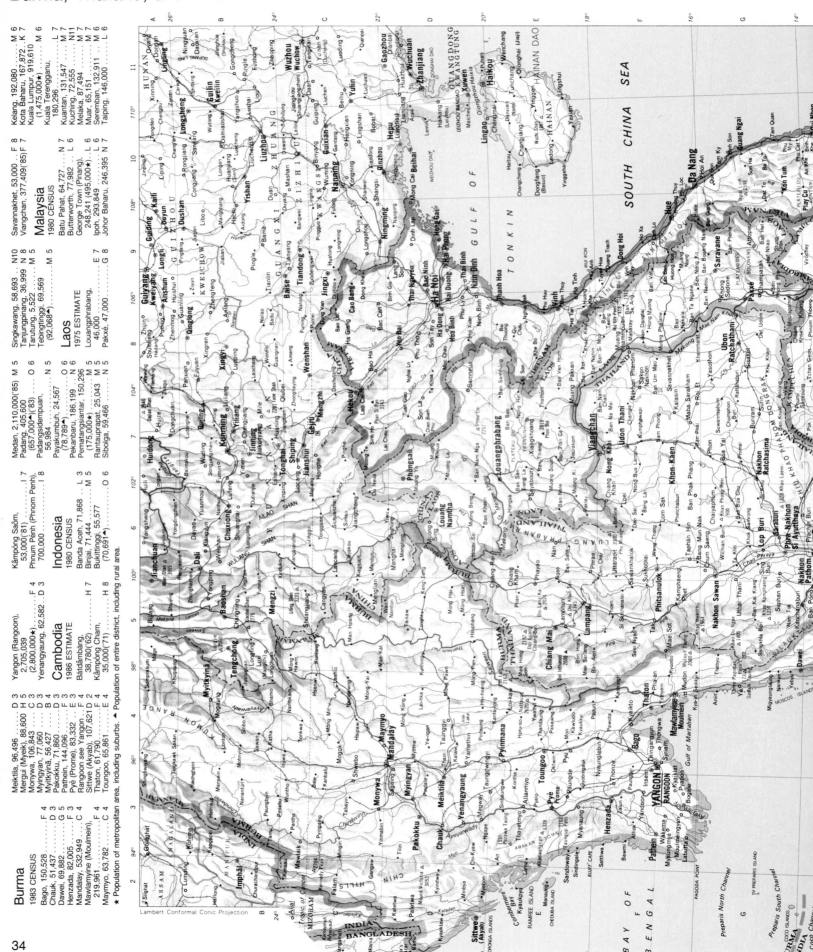

★ Population of metropolitan area, including suburbs. ▲ Population of entire district, including rural area.

Lambert Conformal Conic Projection

34

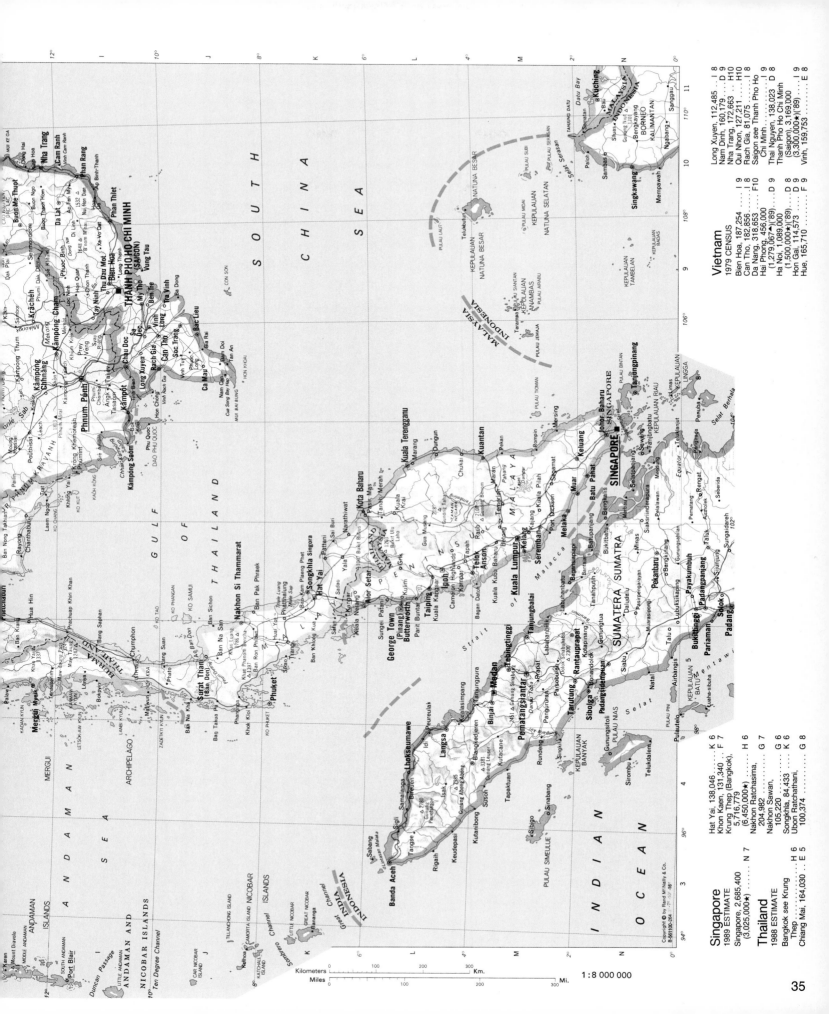

India and Pakistan

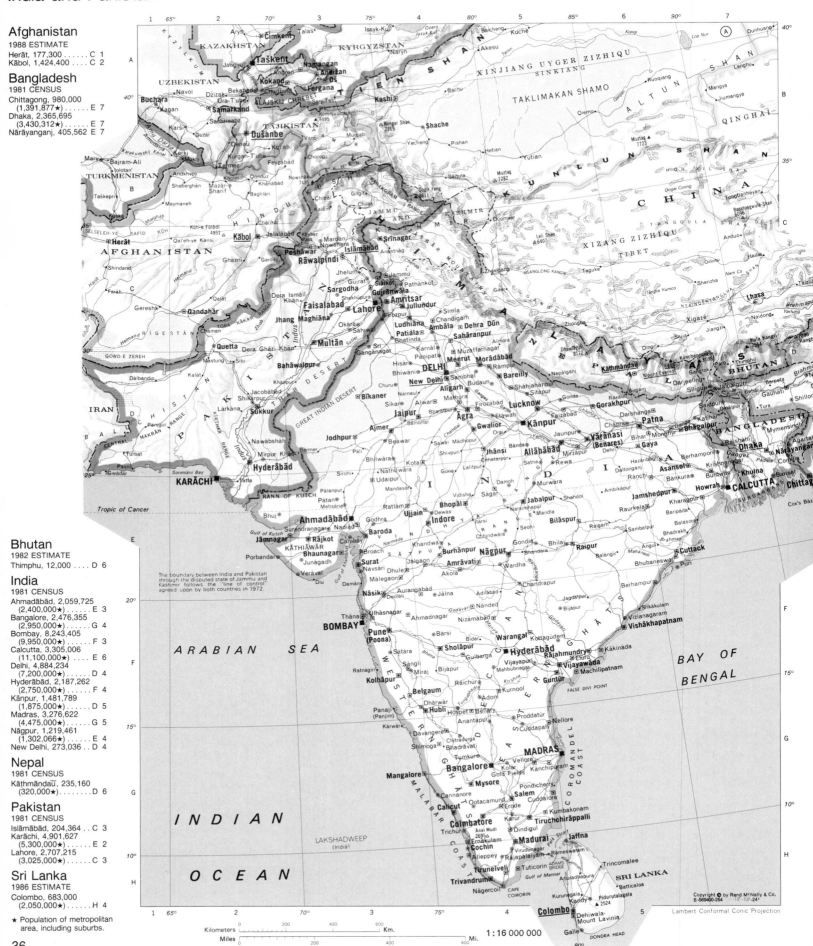

Afghanistan
1988 ESTIMATE
Herāt, 177,300 . . . . . . C 1
Kābol, 1,424,400 . . . . C 2

Bangladesh
1981 CENSUS
Chittagong, 980,000
(1,391,877★) . . . . . . E 7
Dhaka, 2,365,695
(3,430,312★) . . . . . . E 7
Nārāyanganj, 405,562 E 7

Bhutan
1982 ESTIMATE
Thimphu, 12,000 . . . . D 6

India
1981 CENSUS
Ahmadābād, 2,059,725
(2,400,000★) . . . . . . E 3
Bangalore, 2,476,355
(2,950,000★) . . . . . . G 4
Bombay, 8,243,405
(9,950,000★) . . . . . . F 3
Calcutta, 3,305,006
(11,100,000★) . . . . . . E 6
Delhi, 4,884,234
(7,200,000★) . . . . . . D 4
Hyderābād, 2,187,262
(2,750,000★) . . . . . . F 4
Kānpur, 1,481,789
(1,875,000★) . . . . . . D 5
Madras, 3,276,622
(4,475,000★) . . . . . . G 5
Nāgpur, 1,219,461
(1,302,066★) . . . . . . E 4
New Delhi, 273,036 . . D 4

Nepal
1981 CENSUS
Kāthmāndaū, 235,160
(320,000★) . . . . D 6

Pakistan
1981 CENSUS
Islāmābād, 204,364 . . C 3
Karāchi, 4,901,627
(5,300,000★) . . . . . . E 2
Lahore, 2,707,215
(3,025,000★) . . . . . . C 3

Sri Lanka
1986 ESTIMATE
Colombo, 683,000
(2,050,000★) . . . . . . H 4

★ Population of metropolitan
area, including suburbs.

36

The boundary between India and Pakistan
through the disputed state of Jammu and
Kashmir follows the "line of control"
agreed upon by both countries in 1972.

Lambert Conformal Conic Projection

Kilometers   0   200   400   600
                                              Km.
Miles   0   200   400   600
                                              Mi.

1 : 16 000 000

India

1981 CENSUS

Akola, 225,412 . . . . . . B 4
Amrāvati, 261,404 . . B 4
Aurangābād, 284,607
    (316,421★) . . . . . . C 3
Bangalore, 2,476,355
    (2,950,000★) . . . . F 4
Baroda, 734,473
    (744,881★) . . . . . . A 2
Belgaum, 274,430
    (300,372★) . . . . . . E 3
Bhāvnagar, 307,121
    (308,642★) . . . . . . B 2
Bhilai, 290,090
    (490,214★) . . . . . . B 6
Bhubaneswar,
    219,211 . . . . B 8
Bombay, 8,243,405
    (9,950,000★) . . . . . C 2
Calicut, 394,447
    (546,058★) . . . . . . G 3
Cochin, 513,249
    (685,836★) . . . . . . H 4
Coimbatore, 704,514
    (965,000★) . . . . . . G 4
Cuttack, 269,950
    (327,412★) . . . . . . B 8
Dhule, 210,759 . . . . B 3
Gulbarga, 221,325 . . D 4
Guntūr, 367,699 . . . D 6
Hubli, 527,108 . . . . E 3
Hyderābād, 2,187,262
    (2,750,000★) . . . . D 5
Indore, 829,327
    (850,000★) . . . . . . A 3
Kolhāpur, 340,625
    (351,392★) . . . . . . D 3
Madras, 3,276,622
    (4,475,000★) . . . . F 6
Madurai, 820,891
    (960,000★) . . . . . . H 5
Mālegaon, 245,883 . . B 3
Mysore, 441,754
    (479,081★) . . . . . . F 4
Nāgpur, 1,219,461
    (1,302,066★) . . . . . B 5
Nāsik, 262,428
    (429,034★) . . . . . . C 2
Nellore, 237,065 . . . . E 5
Pondicherry, 162,636
    (251,420★) . . . . . . G 5
Pune (Poona), 1,203,351
    (1,775,000★) . . . . C 2
Raipur, 338,245 . . . . B 6
Salem, 361,394
    (518,615★) . . . . . . G 5
Sholāpur, 511,103
    (514,860★) . . . . . . D 3
Surat, 776,583
    (913,806★) . . . . . . B 2
Thāna, 309,897 . . . . C 2
Tiruchchirāppalli, 362,045
    (609,548★) . . . . . . G 5
Trivandrum, 483,086
    (520,125★) . . . . . . H 4
Ulhāsnagar, 273,668 . C 2
Vijayawāda, 454,577
    (543,008★) . . . . . . D 6
Vishākhapatnam, 565,321
    (603,630★) . . . . . . D 7
Warangal, 335,150 . . C 5

Sri Lanka

1986 ESTIMATE

Colombo, 683,000
    (2,050,000★) . . . . . I 5
Dehiwala-Mount Lavinia,
    191,000 . . . . I 5
Kandy, 130,000 . . . . I 6
Kotte, 104,000 . . . . . I 5

★ Population of metropolitan
    area, including suburbs.

37

Northern India and Pakistan

Afghanistan
1981 ESTIMATE
Baghlān, 41,000('82) . . B 3
Ghaznī, 31,196 . . . . . D 3
Jalālābād, 58,000('82) C 4
Kābol, 1,424,400('88) C 3
Khānābād, 27,482 . . B 3
Kholm, 28,788 . . . . . B 2
Mazār-e Sharīf,
130,600('88) . . . . . B 2
Meymaneh, 39,218 . . C 1
Qandahār,
225,500('88) . . . . . E 1
Sheberghān, 19,475 . . B 1

Bangladesh
1981 CENSUS
Barisāl, 172,905 . . . . . I14
Brāhmanbāria, 87,570 I14
Chittagong, 980,000
(1,391,877★) I14
Comilla, 184,132 . . . . I14
Dhaka, 2,365,695
(3,430,312★) I14
Jessore, 148,927 . . . . I13
Khulna, 648,359 . . . . I13
Mymensingh, 190,991 H14
Nārāyanganj, 405,562 I14
Pābna, 109,065 . . . . H13
Rājshāhi, 253,740 . . . H13
Rangpur, 153,174 . . . H13
Saidpur, 126,608 . . . H13
Sirājganj, 106,774 . . H13
Sylhet, 168,371 . . . . H14

Bhutan
1982 ESTIMATE
Thimphu, 12,000 . . . . G13

India
1981 CENSUS
Āgra, 694,191
(747,318★) . . . . G 8
Ahmadābād, 2,059,725
(2,400,000★) . . . . . I 5
Ajmer, 375,593 . . . . . G 6
Alīgarh, 320,861 . . . . G 8
Allāhābād, 616,051
(650,070★) . . . . . . H 9
Alwar, 145,795 . . . . . G 7
Amritsar, 594,844 . . . . E 6
Asansol, 183,375
(1,050,000★) I12
Bareilly, 386,734
(449,425★) . . . . F 8
Baroda, 734,473
(744,881★) . . . . I 5
Bhāgalpur, 225,062 . . H12
Bhātpāra, 260,761 . . . I13
Bhāvnagar, 307,121
(308,642★) . . . . . . J 5
Bhilai, 290,090
(490,214★) . . . . . . J 9
Bhopāl, 671,018 . . . . I 7
Bhubaneswar, 219,211 J11
Bīkaner, 253,174
(287,712★) . . . . . . F 5
Calcutta, 3,305,006
(11,100,000★) I13
Chandīgarh, 373,789
(422,841★) . . . . . . E 7
Cuttack, 269,950
(327,412★) J11
Dehra Dūn, 211,416
(293,010★) . . . . . . E 8
Delhi, 4,884,234
(7,200,000★) . . . . . F 7
Durgāpur, 311,798 . . I12
Gaya, 247,075 . . . . . H11
Ghāziābād, 271,730
(287,170★) . . . . . . F 7
Gorakhpur, 290,814
(307,501★) G10
Gwalior, 539,015
(555,862★) . . . . . . G 8
Howrah, 744,429 . . . . I13
Indore, 829,327
(850,000★) . . . . . . I 6
Jabalpur, 614,162
(757,303★) . . . . . . I 8
Jaipur, 977,165
(1,025,000★) . . . . . G 6
Jammu, 206,135
(223,361★) . . . . . . D 6
Jāmnagar, 277,615
(317,362★) . . . . . . I 4
Jamshedpur, 438,385
(669,580★) I12
Jhānsi, 246,172
(284,141★) . . . . . . H 8
Jodhpur, 506,345
(555,862★) . . . . . . G 5
Jullundur, 408,186
(441,552★) . . . . . . E 6
Kānpur, 1,481,789
(1,875,000★) . . . . . G 9
Kota, 358,241 . . . . . H 6
Lucknow, 895,721
(1,060,000★) . . . . . G 9
Ludhiāna, 607,052 . . E 6
Mathura, 147,493
(160,995★) . . . . . . G 7

★ Population of metropolitan
   area, including suburbs.

38

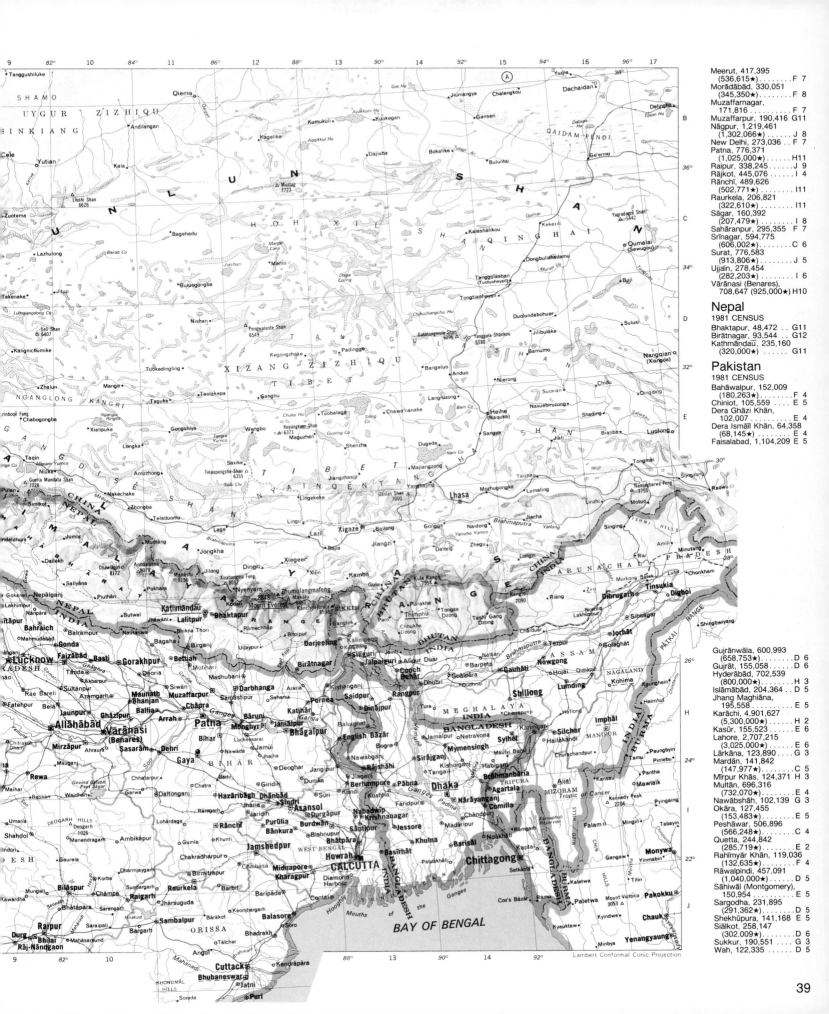

Meerut, 417,395
(536,615★) . . . . F 7
Morādābād, 330,051
(345,350★) . . . . F 8
Muzaffarnagar,
171,816 . . . . F 7
Muzaffarpur, 190,416 G11
Nāgpur, 1,219,461
(1,302,066★) . . . . . J 8
New Delhi, 273,036 . . F 7
Patna, 776,371
(1,025,000★) H11
Raipur, 338,245 . . . . . J 9
Rājkot, 445,076 . . . . . I 4
Rānchī, 489,626
(502,771★) I11
Raurkela, 206,821
(322,610★) I11
Sāgar, 160,392
(207,479★) . . . . I 8
Sahāranpur, 295,355 . F 7
Srīnagar, 594,775
(606,002★) . . . . C 6
Surat, 776,583
(913,806★) . . . . J 5
Ujjain, 278,454
(282,203★) . . . . I 6
Vārānasi (Benares),
708,647 (925,000★) H10

Nepal
1981 CENSUS
Bhaktapur, 48,472 . . G11
Birātnagar, 93,544 . . G12
Kathmāndau, 235,160
(320,000★) G11

Pakistan
1981 CENSUS
Bahāwalpur, 152,009
(180,263★) . . . . F 4
Chiniot, 105,559 . . . . E 5
Dera Ghāzi Khān,
102,007 . . . . E 4
Dera Ismāīl Khān, 64,358
(68,145★) . . . . E 4
Faisalabad, 1,104,209 E 5

Gujrānwāla, 600,993
(658,753★) . . . . D 6
Gujrāt, 155,058 . . . . . D 6
Hyderābād, 702,539
(800,000★) . . . . H 3
Islāmābād, 204,364 . . D 5
Jhang Maghiāna,
195,558 . . . . E 5
Karāchi, 4,901,627
(5,300,000★) . . . . . H 2
Kasūr, 155,523 . . . . . E 6
Lahore, 2,707,215
(3,025,000★) . . . . . E 6
Lārkāna, 123,890 . . . . G 3
Mardān, 141,842
(147,977★) . . . . C 5
Mīrpur Khās, 124,371 H 3
Multān, 696,316
(732,070★) . . . . E 4
Nawābshāh, 102,139 G 3
Okāra, 127,455
(153,483★) . . . . E 5
Peshāwar, 506,896
(566,248★) . . . . C 4
Quetta, 244,842
(285,719★) . . . . E 2
Rahīmyār Khān, 119,036
(132,635★) . . . . F 4
Rāwalpindi, 457,091
(1,040,000★) . . . . . D 5
Sāhiwāl (Montgomery),
150,954 . . . . E 5
Sargodha, 231,895
(291,362★) . . . . D 5
Shekhūpura, 141,168 E 5
Siālkot, 258,147
(302,009★) . . . . D 6
Sukkur, 190,551 . . . . G 3
Wah, 122,335 . . . . . . D 5

Lambert Conformal Conic Projection

39

Eastern Mediterranean Lands

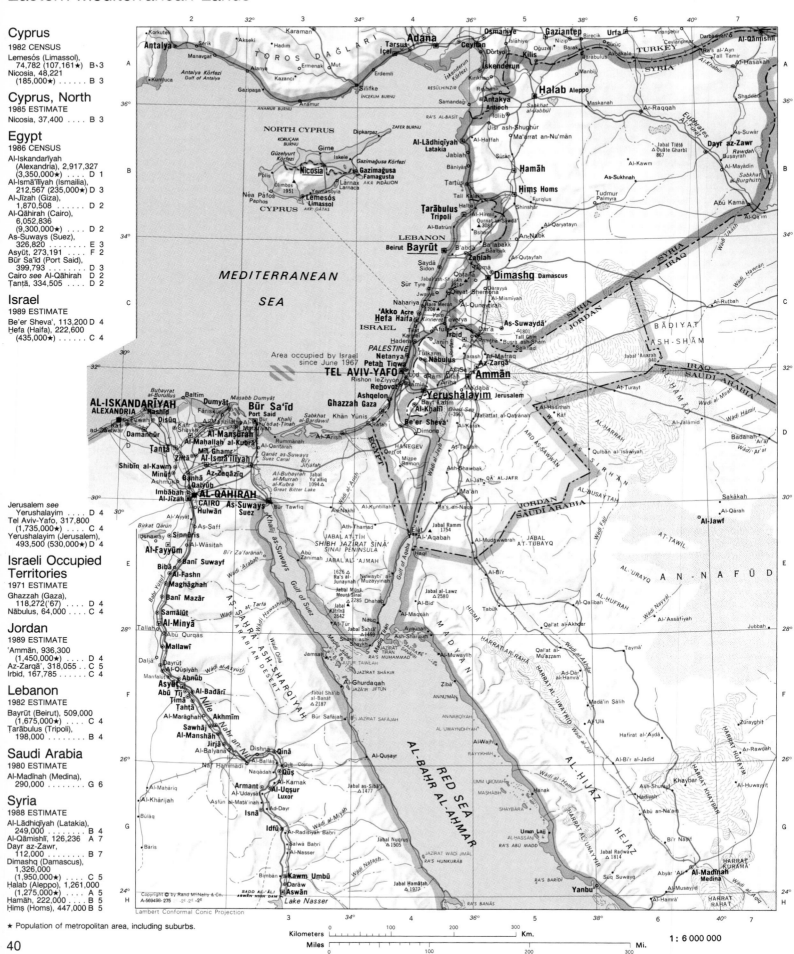

Cyprus
1982 CENSUS

Lemesós (Limassol),
74,782 (107,161★) B 3
Nicosia, 48,221
(185,000★) ...... B 3

Cyprus, North
1985 ESTIMATE

Nicosia, 37,400 .... B 3

Egypt
1986 CENSUS

Al-Iskandarīyah
(Alexandria), 2,917,327
(3,350,000★) .... D 1
Al-Ismā'īlīyah (Ismailia),
212,567 (235,000★) D 3
Al-Jīzah (Giza),
1,870,508 ...... D 2
Al-Qāhirah (Cairo),
6,052,836
(9,300,000★) .... D 2
As-Suways (Suez),
326,820 ...... E 3
Asyūt, 273,191 .... F 2
Būr Sa'īd (Port Said),
399,793 ...... D 3
Cairo see Al-Qāhirah D 2
Tantā, 334,505 .... D 2

Israel
1989 ESTIMATE

Be'er Sheva', 113,200 D 4
Hefa (Haifa), 222,600
(435,000★) ...... C 4
Jerusalem see
Yerushalayim .... D 4
Tel Aviv-Yafo, 317,800
(1,735,000★) .... C 4
Yerushalayim (Jerusalem),
493,500 (530,000★) D 4

Israeli Occupied Territories
1971 ESTIMATE

Ghazzah (Gaza),
118,272('67) .... D 4
Nābulus, 64,000 .... C 4

Jordan
1989 ESTIMATE

'Ammān, 936,300
(1,450,000★) .... D 4
Az-Zarqā', 318,055 .. C 5
Irbid, 167,785 .... C 4

Lebanon
1982 ESTIMATE

Bayrūt (Beirut), 509,000
(1,675,000★) .... C 4
Tarābulus (Tripoli),
198,000 ...... B 4

Saudi Arabia
1980 ESTIMATE

Al-Madīnah (Medina),
290,000 ...... G 6

Syria
1988 ESTIMATE

Al-Lādhiqīyah (Latakia),
249,000 ...... B 4
Al-Qāmishlī, 126,236 .. A 7
Dayr az-Zawr,
112,000 ...... B 7
Dimashq (Damascus),
1,326,000
(1,950,000★) .... C 5
Halab (Aleppo), 1,261,000
(1,275,000★) .... A 5
Hamāh, 222,000 .. B 5
Hims (Homs), 447,000 B 5

★ Population of metropolitan area, including suburbs.

40

Kilometers

Miles

1 : 6 000 000

Africa

Abidjan, 1,950,000 ('83) ....E 3
Accra, 859,640 ('84) (1,250,000★) ('88) ....E 3
Adis Abeba (Addis Ababa), 1,686,300 ('88) (1,500,000★) ....E 7
Alger (Algiers), 1,507,241 ('87) (2,547,983★) ...B 4
ALGERIA ....C 4
Al-Iskandarīyah (Alexandria), 2,917,327 ('86) (3,350,000★) ....B 6
Al-Khartūm (Khartoum), 476,218 ('83) (1,450,000★) ....D 7
Al-Qāhirah (Cairo), 6,052,836 ('86) (9,300,000★) ....B 7
ANGOLA ....G 5
BENIN ....E 4
BOTSWANA ....H 6
Brazzaville, 585,812 ('84) ....F 5
BURKINA FASO ....D 3
BURUNDI ....F 6
Cairo see Al-Qāhirah ..B 7
CAMEROON ....E 4
Cape Town, 776,617 ('85) (1,790,000★) ....I 5
Casablanca, 2,139,204 ('82) (2,475,000★) ..B 3
CENTRAL AFRICAN
REPUBLIC ....E 5
CHAD ....D 5
COMOROS ....G 8
CONGO ....F 5
Dakar, 1,447,642 ('88) D 2
Dar es Salaam, 1,300,000 ('84) ....F 7
DJIBOUTI ....D 8
EGYPT ....C 6
EQUATORIAL
GUINEA ....E 4

ETHIOPIA ....E 7
GABON ....F 5
GAMBIA ....D 2
GHANA ....E 3
GUINEA ....D 2
GUINEA-BISSAU ....D 2
IVORY COAST ....E 3
Johannesburg, 632,369 ('85) (3,650,000★) ....H 6
Kampala, 1,008,707 ('90) ....E 7
KENYA ....E 7
Kinshasa (Léopoldville), 3,000,000 ('86) ....F 5
Lagos, 1,213,000 ('87) (3,800,000★) ....E 4
LESOTHO ....H 6
LIBERIA ....E 3
LIBYA ....C 5
MADAGASCAR ....G 8
MALAWI ....G 7
MALI ....D 3
Maputo (Lourenço Marques), 1,069,727 ('89) ....H 7
MAURITANIA ....D 2
MOROCCO ....B 3
MOZAMBIQUE ....G 7
Nairobi, 1,505,000 ('90) ....F 7
NAMIBIA ....H 5
NIGER ....D 4
NIGERIA ....E 4
RWANDA ....F 6
SAO TOME AND
PRINCIPE ....E 4
SENEGAL ....D 2
SIERRA LEONE ....E 2
SOMALIA ....E 8
SOUTH AFRICA ....I 6
SUDAN ....D 6
SWAZILAND ....H 7
TANZANIA ....F 7
Tarābulus (Tripoli), 990,697 ('84) ....B 5
TOGO ....E 4
Tunis, 596,654 ('84) (1,225,000★) ....B 5
TUNISIA ....B 4
UGANDA ....E 7
WESTERN SAHARA ...C 2
ZAIRE ....F 6
ZAMBIA ....G 6
ZIMBABWE ....G 6

★ Population of metropolitan area, including suburbs.

Copyright © by Rand McNally & Co.
A-580000-286   -1 -1 -1ᴱ
Lambert Azimuthal Equal Area Projection

Miles 0 200 400 600 800 1000 Mi.
Kilometers 0 400 800 1200 1600 Km.
1:40 000 000

41

Northern Africa

Algeria
1987 CENSUS
Alger (Algiers), 1,507,241
(2,547,983★) . . . . . A 6
Annaba (Bône),
305,526 . . . . . . A 7
Batna, 181,601 . . . . . . A 7
Blida, 170,935 . . . . . . A 6
Constantine (Qacentina),
440,842 . . . . A 7
Oran (Wahran),
628,558 . . . . A 5
Sidi bel Abbès,
152,778 . . . . A 5
Skikda, 128,747 . . . . A 7

Benin
1984 ESTIMATE
Cotonou, 478,000 . . G 6
Porto-Novo, 164,000 G 6

Burkina Faso
1985 ESTIMATE
Bobo Dioulasso,
228,668 . . . . F 5
Ouagadougou,
441,514 . . . . F 5

Cameroon
1986 ESTIMATE
Douala, 1,029,731 . . H 7
Yaoundé, 653,670 . . H 8

Central African Republic
1984 ESTIMATE
Bangui, 473,817 . . . . H 9

Chad
1979 ESTIMATE
N'Djamena (Fort-Lamy),
303,000 . . . . F 9

Egypt
1986 CENSUS
Al-Fayyūm, 212,523 . . C12
Al-Iskandarīyah
(Alexandria), 2,917,327
(3,350,000★) B11
Al-Manṣūrah, 316,870
(375,000★) B12
Al-Qāhirah (Cairo),
6,052,836
(9,300,000★) B12
Al-Uqṣur (Luxor),
125,404 . . . . C12
As-Suways (Suez),
326,820 . . . . C12
Aswān, 191,461 . . . . D12
Asyūṭ, 273,191 . . . . C12
Banī Suwayf, 151,813 C12
399,793 . . . . B12
Būr Saʿīd (Port Said),
399,793 . . . . B12
Cairo see Al-Qāhirah . B12
Qinā, 119,794 . . . . . C12
Ṭanṭā, 334,505 . . . . . B12

Equatorial Guinea
1983 CENSUS
Malabo, 31,630 . . . . . . H 7

Gambia
1983 CENSUS
Banjul, 44,536
(95,000★) . . . . F 2

Ghana
1984 CENSUS
Accra, 859,640
(1,250,000★) . . . . . . G 5
Cape Coast, 86,620 . . G 5
Kumasi, 348,880
(600,000★) . . . . G 5
Sekondi-Takoradi,
93,882 . . . . H 5
Tamale, 136,828
(168,091★) . . . . . . G 5

Guinea
1986 ESTIMATE
Conakry, 800,000 . . . . G 3
Kankan, 100,000 . . . . F 4

Guinea-Bissau
1988 ESTIMATE
Bissau, 125,000 . . . . F 2

Ivory Coast
1983 ESTIMATE
Abidjan, 1,950,000 . . G 5
Bouaké, 275,000 . . . G 4
Yamoussoukro,
80,000 . . . . G 4

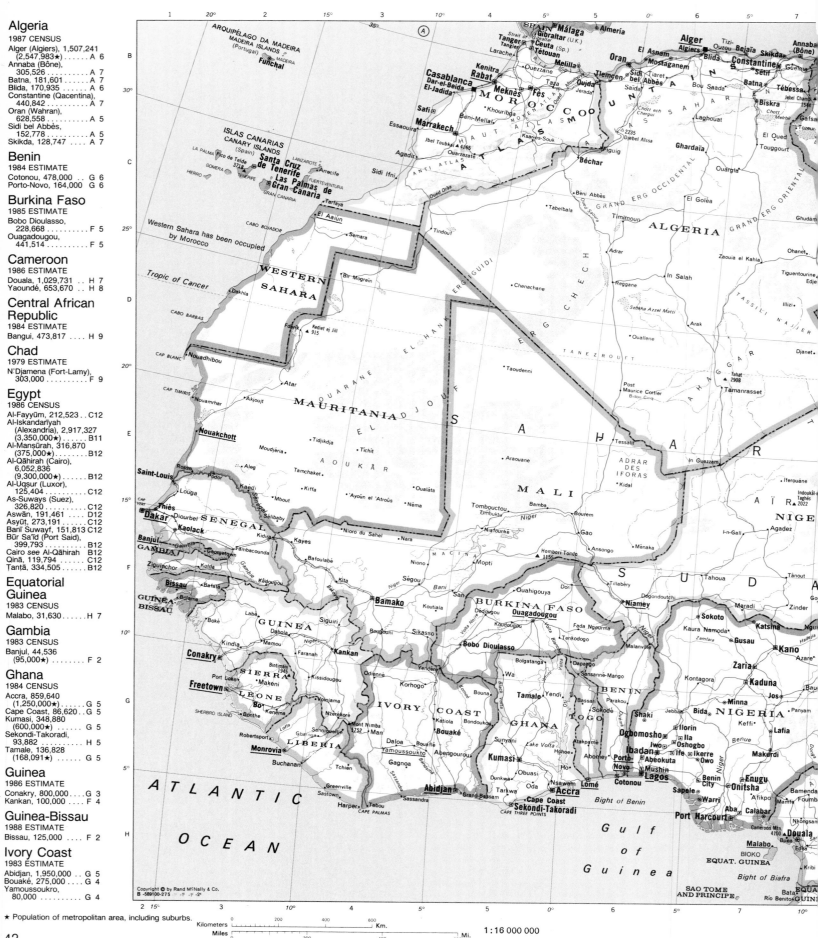

★ Population of metropolitan area, including suburbs.

42

Kilometers 0   200   400   600
                                    Km.
Miles 0   200   400   600
                                    Mi.
1:16 000 000

Liberia
1986 ESTIMATE
Monrovia, 465,000 . . G 3

Libya
1984 CENSUS
Banghāzī, 435,886 . . B10
Ṭarābulus (Tripoli),
 990,697 . . . . B 8
Tripoli *see* Ṭarābulus B 8

Mali
1987 CENSUS
Bamako, 646,163 . . . . F 4
Tombouctou (Timbuktu),
 31,925 . . . . E 5

Mauritania
1987 ESTIMATE
Nouakchott, 285,000 E 2

Morocco
1982 CENSUS
Casablanca (Dar-el-Beida),
 2,139,204
 (2,475,000★) . . . . . B 4
Fès, 448,823
 (535,000★) . . . . . . B 5
Marrakech, 439,728
 (535,000★) . . . . . . B 4
Meknès, 319,783
 (375,000★) . . . . . . B 4
Oujda, 260,082 . . . . B 5
Rabat, 518,616
 (980,000★) . . . . . . B 4
Safi, 197,309 . . . . . B 4
Tanger (Tangier), 266,346
 (370,000★) . . . . . . A 4

Niger
1988 ESTIMATE
Niamey, 398,265 . . . . F 6

Nigeria
1987 ESTIMATE
Aba, 239,800 . . . . . . G 7
Abeokuta, 341,300 . . G 6
Benin City, 183,200 . . G 7
Enugu, 252,500 . . . . G 7
Ibadan, 1,144,000 . . G 6
Ilorin, 380,000 . . . . . G 6
Iwo, 289,100 . . . . . . G 6
Kaduna, 273,200 . . . . F 7
Kano, 538,300 . . . . . F 7
Lagos, 1,213,000
 (3,800,000★) . . . . . G 6
Maiduguri, 255,100 . . F 8
Ogbomosho, 582,900 G 6
Onitsha, 298,200 . . . G 7
Oshogbo, 380,800 . . G 6
Port Harcourt,
 327,300 . . . . H 7
Zaria, 302,800 . . . . . F 7

Senegal
1988 CENSUS
Dakar, 1,447,642 . . . . F 2
Saint-Louis, 160,689 . E 2

Sierra Leone
1985 CENSUS
Freetown, 469,776
 (525,000★) . . . . . . G 3

Sudan
1983 CENSUS
Al-Khartūm (Khartoum),
 476,218
 (1,450,000★) E12
Al-Ubayyid, 140,000 . F12
Būr Sūdān (Port Sudan),
 206,727 . . . . E13
Khartoum *see* Al-
 Khartūm E12
Umm Durmān
 (Omdurman),
 526,287 . . . . E12

Togo
1984 ESTIMATE
Lomé, 400,000 . . . . . . G 6

Tunisia
1984 CENSUS
Bizerte, 94,509 . . . . . A 7
Sfax, 231,911
 (310,000★) . . . . B 8
Tunis, 596,654
 (1,225,000★) . . . . . A 8

Western Sahara
1982 CENSUS
El Aaiún, 93,875 . . . . C 3

Miller Oblated Stereographic Projection

Southern Africa

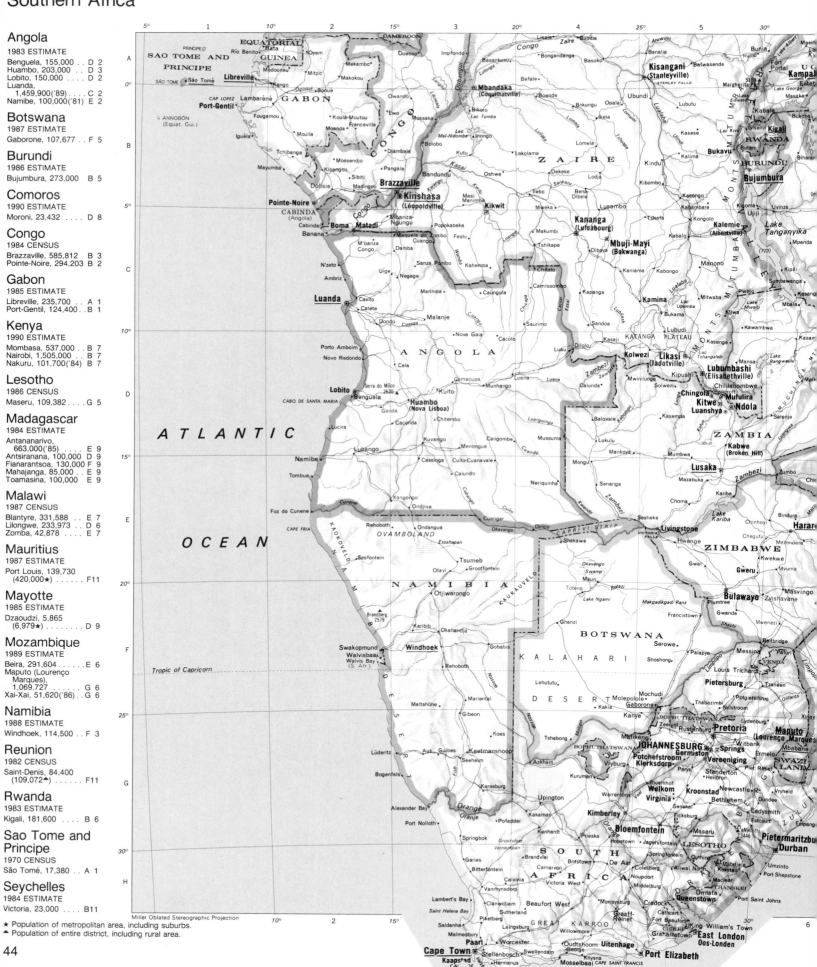

Angola
1983 ESTIMATE
Benguela, 155,000 . . D 2
Huambo, 203,000 . . . D 3
Lobito, 150,000 . . . . D 2
Luanda,
1,459,900('89) . . . . C 2
Namibe, 100,000('81) E 2

Botswana
1987 ESTIMATE
Gaborone, 107,677 . . F 5

Burundi
1986 ESTIMATE
Bujumbura, 273,000   B 5

Comoros
1990 ESTIMATE
Moroni, 23,432 . . . . . D 8

Congo
1984 CENSUS
Brazzaville, 585,812   B 3
Pointe-Noire, 294,203   B 2

Gabon
1985 ESTIMATE
Libreville, 235,700 . . A 1
Port-Gentil, 124,400 . . B 1

Kenya
1990 ESTIMATE
Mombasa, 537,000 . . B 7
Nairobi, 1,505,000 . . B 7
Nakuru, 101,700('84) B 7

Lesotho
1986 CENSUS
Maseru, 109,382 . . . . G 5

Madagascar
1984 ESTIMATE
Antananarivo,
663,000('85) . . . . E 9
Antsiranana, 100,000 D 9
Fianarantsoa, 130,000 F 9
Mahajanga, 85,000 . E 9
Toamasina, 100,000 E 9

Malawi
1987 CENSUS
Blantyre, 331,588 . . E 7
Lilongwe, 233,973 . . D 6
Zomba, 42,878 . . . . E 7

Mauritius
1987 ESTIMATE
Port Louis, 139,730
(420,000★) F11

Mayotte
1985 ESTIMATE
Dzaoudzi, 5,865
(6,979★) . . . . D 9

Mozambique
1989 ESTIMATE
Beira, 291,604 . . . . . E 6
Maputo (Lourenço
Marques),
1,069,727 . . . . . G 6
Xai-Xai, 51,620('86) . . G 6

Namibia
1988 ESTIMATE
Windhoek, 114,500 . . F 3

Reunion
1982 CENSUS
Saint-Denis, 84,400
(109,072▲) F11

Rwanda
1983 ESTIMATE
Kigali, 181,600 . . . . B 6

**Sao Tome and
Principe**
1970 CENSUS
São Tomé, 17,380 . . A 1

Seychelles
1984 ESTIMATE
Victoria, 23,000 . . . . B11

★ Population of metropolitan area, including suburbs.
▲ Population of entire district, including rural area.

Miller Oblated Stereographic Projection

44

Somalia
1984 ESTIMATE
Kismayu, 70,000 . . . . B 8

South Africa
1985 CENSUS
Bloemfontein, 104,381
(235,000★) . . . . . . G 5
Cape Town (Kaapstad),
776,617
(1,790,000★) . . . . H 3
Durban, 634,301
(1,550,000★) . . . . G 6
East London (Oos-
Londen), 85,699
(320,000★) . . . . . H 5
Germiston, 116,718 . . G 5
Johannesburg, 632,369
(3,650,000★) . . . . G 5
Kimberley, 74,061
(145,000★) . . . . . . G 4
King William's Town,
16,123 (48,300★) . . H 5
Klerksdorp, 48,947
(205,000★) . . . . . . G 5
Ladysmith, 25,102
(31,670★) . . . . G 5
Pietermaritzburg, 133,809
(230,000★) . . . . . . G 6
Port Elizabeth, 272,844
(690,000★) . . . . . . H 5
Potchefstroom, 43,766
(78,865★) . . . . G 5
Pretoria, 443,059
(960,000★) . . . . . . G 5
Springs, 68,235 . . . . . G 5
Uitenhage, 54,987 . . . H 5
Vereeniging, 60,584
(525,000★) . . . . . . G 5
Walvisbaai (Walvis Bay),
9,687 (16,607★) . . F 2
Welkom, 54,488
(215,000★) . . . . . . G 5

Swaziland
1986 CENSUS
Mbabane, 38,290 . . G 6

Tanzania
1984 ESTIMATE
Arusha, 69,000 . . . . B 7
Dar es Salaam,
1,300,000 . . . . . . C 7
Mwanza, 110,611('78) B 6
Tanga, 121,000 . . . . C 7
Zanzibar, 133,000('85)C 7

Uganda
1990 ESTIMATE
Kampala, 1,008,707 . . A 6

Zaire
1984 CENSUS
Boma, 88,556 . . . . . . C 2
Bukavu, 171,064 . . . . B 5
Kalemie (Albertville),
70,694 . . . . C 5
Kananga (Luluabourg),
290,898 . . . . C 4
Kikwit, 146,784 . . . . C 3
Kinshasa (Léopoldville),
3,000,000('86) . . . B 3
Kisangani (Stanleyville),
282,650 . . . . A 5
Kolwezi, 201,382 . . . . D 5
Likasi (Jadotville),
194,465 . . . . D 5
Lubumbashi
(Élisabethville),
543,268 . . . . D 5
Matadi, 144,742 . . . . C 2
Mbandaka (Coquilhatville),
125,263 . . . . A 3
Mbuji-Mayi (Bakwanga),
423,363 . . . . C 4

Zambia
1980 CENSUS
Chingola, 130,872 . . D 5
Kabwe (Broken Hill),
127,420 . . . . D 5
Kitwe, 207,500
(283,962★) . . . . . . D 5
Livingstone, 61,296 . . E 5
Luanshya, 61,600
(113,422★) . . . . . . D 5
Lusaka, 535,830 . . . . E 5
Mufulira, 77,100
(138,824★) . . . . . . D 5
Ndola, 250,490 . . . . D 5

Zimbabwe
1983 ESTIMATE
Bulawayo, 429,000 . . F 5
Harare, 681,000
(890,000★) . . . . . . E 6

Kilometers 0 200 400 600 Km.
Miles 0 200 400 600 Mi.
1 : 16 000 000

Eastern Africa and Middle East

Bahrain
1981 CENSUS
Al-Manāmah, 115,054
(224,643★) . . . . . . C 5

Djibouti
1976 ESTIMATE
Djibouti, 120,000 . . . . F 3

Ethiopia
1988 ESTIMATE
Adis Abeba, 1,686,300
(1,500,000★) . . . . G 2
Asmera, 319,353 . . . . E 2

Iran
1986 CENSUS
Ābādān, 296,081('76) . B 4
Bākhtarān, 560,514 . . B 4
Esfahān, 986,753
(1,175,000★) . . . . B 5
Kermān, 257,284 . . . B 6
Shīrāz, 848,289 . . . . C 5

Iraq
1985 ESTIMATE
Al-Basrah, 616,700 . . B 4
Al-Mawsil, 570,926 . . A 3
Baghdād,
3,841,268('87) . . . . B 3

Kuwait
1985 CENSUS
Al-Kuwayt, 44,335
(1,375,000★) . . . . C 4

Oman
1981 ESTIMATE
Masqat (Muscat),
50,000 . . . . D 6

Qatar
1986 CENSUS
Ad-Dawhah (Doha),
217,294 (310,000★) C 5

Saudi Arabia
1980 CENSUS
Al-Madīnah (Medina),
290,000 . . . . D 2
Ar-Riyād (Riyadh),
1,250,000 . . . . . . D 4
Jiddah, 1,300,000 . . D 2
Makkah (Mecca),
550,000 . . . . D 2

Somalia
1984 ESTIMATE
Muqdisho, 600,000 . . H 4

United Arab Emirates
1980 CENSUS
Abū Zaby, 242,975 . . D 5
Dubayy (Dubai),
265,702 . . . . C 6

Yemen
1984 ESTIMATE
'Adan (Aden), 176,100
(318,000★) . . . . . . F 4
San'ā', 427,150('86) . E 3

★ Population of metropolitan
area, including suburbs.

46

Kilometers
200   400   600
Km.
Miles
200   400   600
Mi.
1 : 16 000 000

Copyright ⓒ by Rand McNally & Co.
B-589391-264
Miller Oblated Stereographic Projection

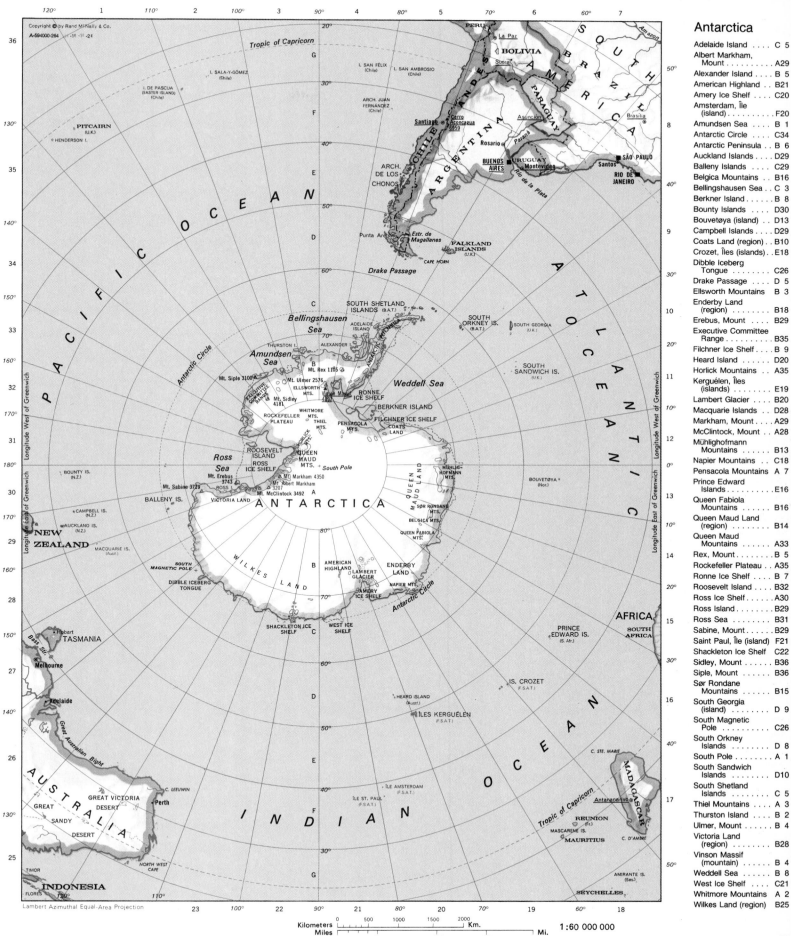

Antarctica

Adelaide Island . . . . C 5
Albert Markham,
  Mount A29
Alexander Island . . . . B 5
American Highland . . B21
Amery Ice Shelf C20
Amsterdam, Île
  (island) F20
Amundsen Sea . . . . B 1
Antarctic Circle C34
Antarctic Peninsula . . B 6
Auckland Islands D29
Balleny Islands C29
Belgica Mountains . . B16
Bellingshausen Sea . . C 3
Berkner Island . . . . . B 8
Bounty Islands D30
Bouvetøya (island) . . D13
Campbell Islands D29
Coats Land (region) . . B10
Crozet, Îles (islands) . . E18
Dibble Iceberg
  Tongue C26
Drake Passage . . . D 5
Ellsworth Mountains . B 3
Enderby Land
  (region) B18
Erebus, Mount B29
Executive Committee
  Range B35
Filchner Ice Shelf . . . . B 9
Heard Island D20
Horlick Mountains . . A35
Kerguélen, Îles
  (islands) E19
Lambert Glacier B20
Macquarie Islands . . D28
Markham, Mount . . A29
McClintock, Mount . . A28
Mühlighofmann
  Mountains B13
Napier Mountains . . C18
Pensacola Mountains A 7
Prince Edward
  Islands E16
Queen Fabiola
  Mountains B16
Queen Maud Land
  (region) B14
Queen Maud
  Mountains A33
Rex, Mount . . . . B 5
Rockefeller Plateau . . A35
Ronne Ice Shelf . . . . B 7
Roosevelt Island B32
Ross Ice Shelf A30
Ross Island B29
Ross Sea B31
Sabine, Mount B29
Saint Paul, Île (island) F21
Shackleton Ice Shelf C22
Sidley, Mount B36
Siple, Mount B36
Sør Rondane
  Mountains B15
South Georgia
  (island) . . . . D 9
South Magnetic
  Pole C26
South Orkney
  Islands . . . . D 8
South Pole . . . . A 1
South Sandwich
  Islands D10
South Shetland
  Islands . . . . C 5
Thiel Mountains . . . . A 3
Thurston Island . . . . B 2
Ulmer, Mount . . . . . B 4
Victoria Land
  (region) B28
Vinson Massif
  (mountain) . . . . . . B 4
Weddell Sea . . . . . . B 8
West Ice Shelf C21
Whitmore Mountains . A 2
Wilkes Land (region) B25

Pacific Ocean

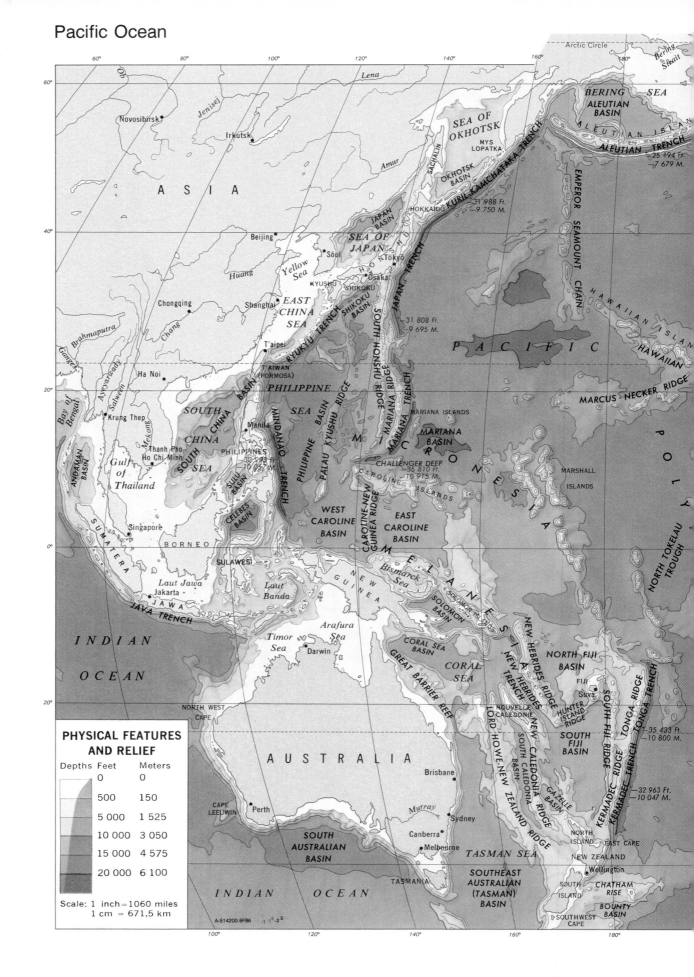

**PHYSICAL FEATURES
AND RELIEF**

Depths	Feet	Meters
	0	0
	500	150
	5 000	1 525
	10 000	3 050
	15 000	4 575
	20 000	6 100

Scale: 1 inch = 1060 miles
1 cm = 671.5 km

A-514200-9F86

140°   120°   100°   80°   60°   40°   20°

Anchorage
Yukon
Mackenzie
GULF OF
ALASKA
GREENLAND
KAP
FARVEL
REYKJANES
RIDGE
LABRADOR
BASIN
HUDSON
BAY
VANCOUVER
Seattle
St. Lawrence
NEWFOUNDLAND
Columbia
NORTH
Montréal
GRAND
BANK NEWFOUNDLAND
RIDGE
MENDOCINO ESCARPMENT
CAPE
MENDOCINO
San Francisco
AMERICA
Missouri
Chicago
New York
Washington
ATLANTIC
OCEAN
MURRAY FRACTURE ZONE
Los Angeles
Colorado
Mississippi
Ohio
CAPE
HATTERAS
Rio Grande
NORTH
AMERICAN
BASIN
O C E A N
Golfo de California
Tropic of Cancer
Honolulu
GULF OF
MEXICAN
BASIN
MEXICO
New
Orleans
Miami
BAHAMAS
MILWAUKEE DEPTH
28,232 Ft.
8,605 M.
La Habana
CLARION   FRACTURE   ZONE
Ciudad de
México
CUBA WEST INDIES
CAYMAN TRENCH
PUERTO RICO TRENCH
MEXICAN TRENCH
(MIDDLE AMERICA TRENCH)
CARIBBEAN
SEA
AVES RIDGE
CLIPPERTON   FRACTURE   ZONE
COLOMBIAN VENEZUELAN
ABYSSAL
PLAIN
BASIN
Caracas
NORTHWEST CHRISTMAS ISLAND
RIDGE
ISTMO
DE
PANAMA
Orinoco
COCOS RIDGE
Santa Fe de Bogotá
Equator
ARCHIPIÉLAGO DE COLÓN
(GALÁPAGOS IS.)
CARNEGIE
RIDGE
Amazon
SOUTH
TUAMOTU
SOCIETY
TUAMOTU
RIDGE
ARCHIPIÉLAGO
RIDGE
Lima
P
E
R
U
AMERICA
AUSTRAL
SEAMOUNT
CHAIN
Tropic of Capricorn
–26,457 Ft.
–8,064 M.
C
H
I
L
E
T
R
E
N
C
H
Paraná
P A C I F I C
O C E A N
PACIFIC
ANTARCTIC
RIDGE
CHILE RISE
Santiago
Montevideo
Buenos
Aires
SOUTHWESTERN
PACIFIC
BASIN
ATLANTIC
OCEAN
ARGENTINE
BASIN

140°   120°   100°   80°   60°   40°

49

...9
...G 9
...........G 8
('86)...F 9
05('86)..C 9
e, 744,828
273,511★)........E10
ken Hill, 22,550 ..F 8
Broome, 5,778('86)..C 4
Bunbury, 26,398...F 3
Bundaberg, 33,024
  (45,161★)........D10
Burketown,
  232('86)..........C 7
Burnie, 20,665('86)..H 9
Busselton,
  7,784('86)........F 3
Cairns, 42,839
  (80,875★)........C 9
Camooweal,
  315('86)..........C 7
Canberra, 247,194
  (271,362★)('86)..G 9
Carnarvon,
  6,847('86)........D 2
Ceduna, 2,877('86)..F 6
Cessnock, 43,870....F10
Charleville,
  3,588('86)........E 9
Charters Towers,
  7,208('86)........D 9
Cloncurry,
  2,297('86)........D 8
Coffs Harbour,
  47,890...........F10
Cooktown, 964('86)..C 9
Coolgardie, 989('86)..F 4
Cooma, 7,406('86)...G 9
Croydon, 229('86)...C 8
Cunnamulla,
  1,697('86)........E 9
Dampier, 2,201('86)..D 3
Darwin, 63,900
  (72,937★)........B 6
Derby, 3,258('86)....C 4
Devonport, 25,370...H 9
Dongara, 1,496('86)..E 2
Dubbo, 32,230......F 9
Elizabeth, 29,998...F 7
Emerald, 5,982('86)..D 9
Esperance,
  6,440('86)........F 4
Geelong, 13,190
  (148,980★).......G 8
Geraldton, 20,968....E 2
Gladstone,
  22,033('86)......D10
Glen Innes,
  5,971('86)........E10
Goondiwindi,
  4,103('86)........E10
Goulburn, 21,580...F 9
Grafton, 15,890.....E10
Griffith, 13,630('86)..F 9
Gympie, 10,772('86)..E10
Halls Creek,
  1,182('86)........C 5
Hay, 2,961('86)......F 8
Hobart, 47,280
  (181,210★)........H 9
Home Hill,
  3,286('86)........C 9
Horsham, 12,850....G 8
Hughenden,
  1,791('86)........D 8
Ingham, 5,202('86)...C 9
Inverell, 9,693('86)..E10
Ipswich, 75,283.....E10
Kalgoorlie, 26,813...F 4
Kingaroy, 6,362('86)..E10
Launceston, 32,150
  (92,350★)........H 9
Leonora, 1,004('86)..E 4
Lismore, 39,450....E10
Longreach,
  3,159('86)........D 8
Mackay, 22,583
  (50,885★)........D 9
Maitland, 47,280....F10
Marble Bar, 332('86)..D 3
Mareeba, 6,614('86)..C 9
Marree, 300('76)....E 7
Meekatharra,
  1,018('86)........E 3

★ Population of metropolitan
  area, including suburbs.

50

Map of Australia, Papua New Guinea, and surrounding region with latitude/longitude grid.

Top margin longitude labels: 135° 7 140° 8 145° 9 150° 10 155° 11

Bottom margin: 7 140° 8 145° 10 11 155° 160° 12 Lambert Conformal Conic Projection

Latitude row labels along right edge: A, B, C, D, E, F, G, H at 10°, 15°, 20°, 25°, 30°, 35°, 40°

Seas and Oceans:
- ura Sea (Arafura Sea)
- Gulf of Carpentaria
- Coral Sea
- Solomon Sea
- PACIFIC OCEAN
- Tasman Sea
- Bass Strait
- Torres Strait

Papua New Guinea / New Guinea region:
BOIGU, SAIBAI, Daru, Popondetta, Gulf of Papua, Port Moresby, OWEN STANLEY RANGE, Esa-Ala, Samarai, TROBRIAND ISLANDS, D'ENTRECASTEAUX ISLANDS, Kulumadau, WOODLARK ISLAND, Losuia, LOUISIADE ARCHIPELAGO, MISIMA I., TAGULA ISLAND, ROSSEL ISLAND, PAPUA NEW GUINEA, NEW GUINEA

Solomon Islands:
VELLA LAVELLA, CHOISEUL, NEW GEORGIA, RENDOVA, VANGUNU, SANTA ISABEL, Gizo, SOLOMON ISLANDS, GUADALCANAL, Honiara, Mt. Popomanaseu 2331

Coral Sea features: OSPREY REEF, BOUGAINVILLE REEF, HOLMES REEFS, WILLIS ISLETS (Austl.), CORINGA ISLETS (Austl.), LIHOU REEFS, TREGOSSE ISLETS (Austl.), MELLISH REEF, ÎLES CHESTERFIELD (N. Cal.), ÎLES DE SABLE (N. Cal.), KENN REEFS, SAUMAREZ REEF, WRECK REEFS, CAYE DE L'OBSERVATOIRE (N. Cal.), BELLONA REEFS, CATO ISLAND, MIDDLETON REEF, ELIZABETH REEF, LORD HOWE ISLAND (N.S.W.), RENNELL ISLAND, INDISPENSABLE REEFS

Australia — northern:
WESSEL ISLANDS, THE ENGLISH COMPANY'S ISLANDS, CAPE ARNHEM, GROOTE EYLANDT, SIR EDWARD PELLEW GROUP, Limmen Bight, MORNINGTON ISLAND, WELLESLEY ISLANDS, BARKLY TABLELAND, Burketown, Normanton, Camooweal, Mount Isa, Duchess, PRINCE OF WALES ISLAND, CAPE YORK, DUIFKEN POINT, Weipa, Albatross Bay, CAPE YORK PENINSULA, Coen, CAPE GRENVILLE, Cooktown, Mareeba, Ravenshoe, Cairns, CAPE GRAFTON, Croydon, Forsayth, Ingham, HINCHINBROOK ISLAND, Halifax Bay, Townsville, Home Hill, Bowen, CUMBERLAND ISLANDS, Charters Towers, Cloncurry, Richmond, Hughenden, Mackay, CAPE PALMERSTON, SWAIN REEFS

GREAT BARRIER REEF, GREAT DIVIDING RANGE

Queensland interior:
SIMPSON DESERT, GREAT ARTESIAN BASIN, Winton, Longreach, Barcaldine, Blackall, Blair Athol, Emerald, Rockhampton, CURTIS, CAPE CAPRICORN, Gladstone, Bundaberg, Hervey Bay, FRASER ISLAND, Maryborough, Gympie, Nambour, Windorah, Yaraka, GREY RANGE, Quilpie, Charleville, Mitchell, Roma, Dalby, Mount Kiangarow 1143, Toowoomba, Ipswich, Brisbane, NORTH STRADBROKE ISLAND, Thargomindah, Cunnamulla, Saint George, Goondiwindi, Warwick, Innamincka, Coopers Creek, Birdsville

South Australia / interior:
Oodnadatta, Warrina, Lake Eyre (North) (Dry Salt Lake), Lake Eyre (South), Marree, The Warburton, Cooper Creek, STURT DESERT, Diamantina, Barcoo, Warrego, Paroo, Milparinka, Tibooburra(?)

Lake Torrens (Dry Salt Lake), Lake Frome (Dry Salt Lake), FLINDERS RANGES, NORTH FLINDERS RANGES, Saint Mary Peak 1165, Woomera, Port Augusta, Whyalla, Port Pirie, Peterborough, Broken Hill, GAWLER RANGES, EYRE PENINSULA, Mount Hope, Lincoln, CAPE CATASTROPHE, Port Lincoln, Spencer Gulf, Gulf Saint Vincent, Elizabeth, Adelaide, KANGAROO ISLAND, Encounter Bay, Investigator Strait, Lake Gairdner (Dry Salt Lake), AUSTRALIA

New South Wales:
NEW SOUTH WALES, Wilcannia, Bourke, Walgett, Moree, Tenterfield, Inverell, Glen Innes, The Round Mountain 1615, Armidale, Grafton, Lismore, Murwillumbah, Coffs Harbour, Tamworth, Narrabri(?), Nyngan, Dubbo, Darling, Macquarie, Lachlan, Cobar(?), Orange, Bathurst, Port Macquarie, Taree, Maitland, Cessnock, Newcastle, SYDNEY, Wollongong, Hay, Griffith, Wagga Wagga, Goulburn, Canberra, A.C.T., Cooma, Bombala, Murrumbidgee, Murray

Victoria:
VICTORIA, Mildura, Swan Hill, Bordertown, Naracoorte, Horsham, Ararat, Bendigo, Shepparton, Wangaratta, Albury, Mount Kosciusko 2230, Mount Buffalo(?), GREAT DIVIDING RANGE, Ballarat, Geelong, MELBOURNE, Morwell, Sale, NINETY MILE BEACH, Orbost, CAPE HOWE, Mount Gambier, Portland, Warrnambool, CAPE OTWAY, WILSONS PROMONTORY, SOUTH EAST POINT, Goulburn River, Loddon River, Avoca River, Glenelg River

Tasmania:
KING ISLAND, FLINDERS ISLAND, FURNEAUX GROUP, Banks Strait, HUNTER ISLAND, Smithton, Burnie, Devonport, Scottsdale, Saint Marys, Zeehan, Mount Ossa 1617, Strahan, Launceston, TASMANIA, New Norfolk, Hobart, BRUNY ISLAND, SOUTH WEST CAPE, SOUTH EAST CAPE

Index column (right side):

M...
Mul...
Murv...
  7,67...
Nambo...
Naracoo...
  4,636('...
Newcastle,
  (425,610★...
New Norfolk,
  6,152('86) ...
Normanton,
  1,109('86) ...
Norseman,
  1,775('86) .....
Northam, 6,377('86)
Nyngan, 2,502('86) .
Onslow, 750('86) ....
Oodnadatta, 200('76)
Orange, 32,980 .....F
Pemberton, 802('86) .F
Perth, 82,413
  (1,158,387★) ......F 3
Peterborough,
  2,239('86) ....F 7
Port Augusta,
  15,752 ....F 7
Port Hedland,
  13,069('86) ......D 3
Port Lincoln, 12,941 ..F 7
Port Macquarie,
  22,884('86) F10
Port Pirie, 15,210 ...F 7
Quilpie, 780('86) ...E 8
Ravensthorpe,
  299('86) ....F 3
Richmond, 704('86) ..D 8
Rockhampton, 58,890
  (61,694★) D10
Roebourne,
  1,269('86) ....D 3
Roma, 6,069('86) ...E 9
Saint George,
  2,323('86) ....G 9
Sale, 13,800 ....G 9
Shepparton, 26,420
  (39,700★) ....G 9
Smithton, 3,414('86) ..H 9
Southern Cross,
  898('86) ....F 3
Swan Hill,
  8,831('86) ....G 8
Sydney, 9,800
  (3,623,550★) F10
Tamworth, 34,430 ...F10
Taree, 38,760 .....F10
Tennant Creek,
  3,503('86) ....C 6
Tenterfield,
  3,370('86) E10
Theodore, 576('86) ..D10
Toowoomba,
  81,071 ....E10
Townsville, 83,339
  (111,972★) ....C 9
Wagga Wagga,
  52,180 ....G 9
Walgett, 2,151('86) ..E 9
Wangaratta, 16,320 ..G 9
Warrnambool,
  24,480 ....G 8
Weipa, 2,406('86) ...B 8
Whyalla, 26,706 ....F 7
Wilcannia, 1,048('86) .F 8
Wiluna, 279('86) ....E 4
Winton, 1,281('86) ..D 8
Wollongong, 174,770
  (236,690★) F10
Woomera,
  1,805('86) ....F 7
Wyndham,
  1,329('86) ....C 5

Indonesia
1980 CENSUS

Jayapura, 60,641 ....k15
Kupang, 84,587 ....B 4
Sorong, 52,041 .....k13

Papua New Guinea
1987 ESTIMATE

Lae, 79,600 ....m16
Madang, 24,700 ....m16
Port Moresby,
  152,100 ....m16
Rabaul, 14,954('80) .k17
Wewak, 23,200 .....k15

51

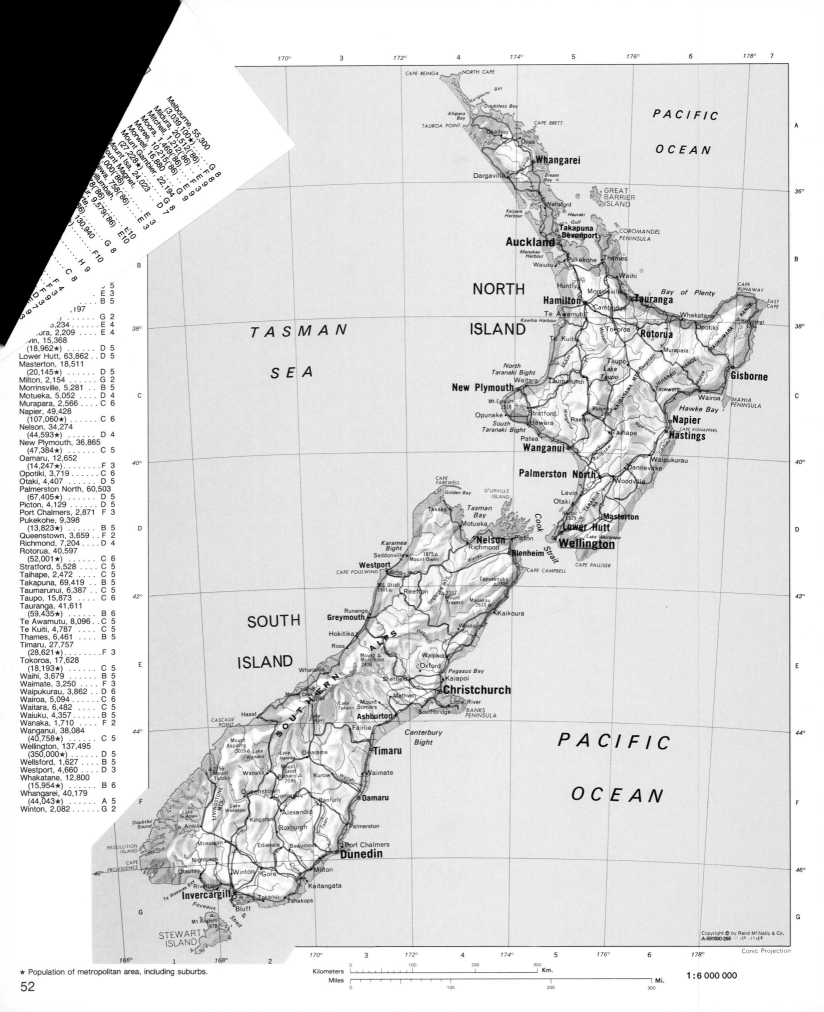

★ Population of metropolitan area, including suburbs.

52

Kilometers
Miles

1 : 6 000 000

Conic Projection

Antofagasta, 185,486
('82)....................F 3
Arequipa, 108,023 ('81)
(446,942) ....E 3
ARGENTINA.............G 4
Asunción, 477,100 ('85)
(700,000★) ....F 5
Barranquilla, 899,781 ('85)
(1,140,000★) ....B 3
Belém, 1,116,578 ('85)
(1,200,000★) ....D 6
Belo Horizonte, 2,114,429
('85) (2,950,000★) ...E 6
Bogotá see Santa Fe de
Bogotá...................C 3
BOLIVIA.................E 4
Brasília, 1,567,709
('85)......................E 6
BRAZIL..................E 5
Buenos Aires, 2,922,829
('80) (10,750,000★) ..G 5
Caracas, 1,816,901 ('81)
(3,600,000★) ....B 4
Cartagena, 531,426
('85)......................B 3
Cayenne, 38,091 ('82).C 5
Chiclayo, 213,095 ('81)
(279,527★) ....D 3
CHILE...................G 3
Ciudad Bolívar, 182,941
('81)......................C 4
COLOMBIA..............C 3
Concepción, 267,891 ('82)
(675,000★) ....G 3
Cuzco, 89,563 ('81)
(184,550★) ....E 3
ECUADOR...............D 3
FALKLAND ISLANDS...I 5
Fortaleza, 1,582,414 ('85)
(1,825,000★) ....D 7
FRENCH GUIANA........C 5
Georgetown, 78,500 ('83)
(188,000★) ....C 5
Guayaquil, 1,572,615 ('87)
(1,580,000★) ....D 3
GUYANA.................C 5
Iquitos, 178,738 ('81)..D 3
João Pessoa, 348,500
('85) (550,000★) .....D 7
La Paz, 992,592 ('85)..E 4
La Plata, 477,175
('80)......................G 5
Lima, 371,122 ('81)
(4,608,010★) ....E 3
Maceió, 482,195 ('85).D 7
Manaus, 809,914 ('85).D 5
Maracaibo, 890,643
('81)......................B 3
Medellín, 1,468,089 ('85)
(2,095,000★) ....C 3
Mendoza, 119,088 ('80)
(650,000★) ....G 4
Montevideo, 1,251,647
('85) (1,550,000★) .. G 5
Natal, 510,106 ('85)....D 7
PARAGUAY...............F 5
Paramaribo, 241,000 ('88)
(296,000★) ....C 5
PERU....................E 3
Porto Alegre, 1,272,121
('85) (2,600,000★) .. G 5
Quito, 1,137,705 ('87)
(1,300,000★) ....D 3
Recife, 1,287,623 ('85)
(2,625,000★) ....D 7
Rio Branco, 109,800 ('85)
(145,486▲) ....D 4
Rio de Janeiro, 5,603,388
('85) (10,150,000★) . F 6
Rosario, 938,120 ('80)
(1,045,000★) ....G 4
Salta, 260,744 ('80).....F 4
Salvador, 1,804,438 ('85)
(2,050,000★) ....E 7
San Miguel de Tucumán,
392,888 ('80)
(525,000★) ....F 4
Santa Fe, 292,165
('80)......................G 4
Santa Fe de Bogotá,
3,982,941 ('85)
(4,260,000★) ....C 3
Santiago, 232,667 ('82)
(4,100,000★) ....G 3
Santos, 460,100 ('85)
(1,065,000★) ....F 6
São Luís, 227,900 ('85)
(600,000★) ....D 6
São Paulo, 10,063,110
('85) (15,175,000★) . F 6
Stanley, 1,200 ('86)......I 5
Sucre, 86,609 ('85)......E 4
SURINAME...............C 5
Teresina, 425,300 ('85)
(525,000★) ....D 6
Trujillo, 202,469 ('81)
(354,301★) ....D 3
URUGUAY................G 5
Valparaíso, 265,355 ('82)
(675,000★) ....G 3
VENEZUELA..............C 4
Vitória, 201,500 ('85)
(735,000★) ....F 6

★ Population of metropolitan area, including suburbs.
▲ Population of entire district, including rural area.

1:40 000 000

53

Miles 0   200   400   600   800   1000 Mi.

Kilometers 0   400   800   1200   1600 Km.

Lambert Azimuthal Equal Area Projection

Copyright © by Rand McNally & Co.

A-540000-286

Northern South America

Bolivia
1985 ESTIMATE

Cochabamba, 317,251G 5
La Paz, 992,592 ..... G 5
Oruro, 178,393 ...... G 5
Potosí, 113,380 ..... G 5
Santa Cruz, 441,717 G 6
Sucre, 86,609 ...... G 5

Brazil
1985 ESTIMATE

Anápolis, 225,840 ... G 9
Aracaju, 360,013 .... F11
Araçatuba, 129,304 . H 8
Bauru, 220,105 ...... H 9
Belém, 1,116,578
  (1,200,000) ...... D 9
Belo Horizonte, 2,114,429
  (2,950,000) G10
Brasília, 1,567,709 . G 9
Campina Grande,
  279,929 .... E11
Campinas, 841,016
  (1,125,000) ..... H 9
Campo Grande,
  384,398 .... H 8
Campos, 187,900
  (366,716★) H10
Caruaru, 152,100
  (190,794) E11
Cuiabá, 220,400
  (279,651▲) .... G 7
Feira de Santana, 278,600
  (355,201) F11
Fortaleza, 1,582,414
  (1,825,000★) ... D11
Goiânia, 923,333
  (990,000★) ..... G 9
Governador Valadares,
  192,300 (216,957▲) G10
João Pessoa, 348,500
  (550,000★) E12
Juàzeiro do Norte,
  159,806 .... E11
Juiz de Fora, 349,720 H10
Jundiaí, 268,900
  (313,652) ...... H 9
Maceió, 482,195 .... E11
Manaus, 809,914 ... D 6
Montes Claros, 183,500
  (214,472★) G10
Natal, 510,106 ..... E11
Niterói, 441,684 .... H10
Petrolina, 92,100
  (225,000) E10
Petrópolis, 170,300 . H10
Piracicaba, 211,000
  (252,079▲) ..... H 9
Porto Velho, 152,700
  (202,011▲) ..... E 6
Presidente Prudente,
  155,883 .... H 8
Recife, 1,287,623
  (2,625,000★) ... E12
Ribeirão Prêto,
  383,125 .... H 9
Rio de Janeiro, 5,603,388
  (10,150,000★) ... H10
Salvador, 1,804,438
  (2,050,000★) ... F11
Santarém, 120,800
  (226,618▲) ..... D 8
Santos, 460,100
  (1,065,000★) ... H 9
São Carlos, 140,383 H 9
São José do Rio Prêto,
  229,221 .... H 9
São Luís, 227,900
  (600,000★) D10
São Paulo, 10,063,110
  (15,175,000★) ... H 9
Sorocaba, 327,468 .. H 9
Teresina, 425,300
  (525,000★) E10
Uberaba, 244,875 ... G 9
Uberlândia, 312,024 . G 9
Vitória, 201,500
  (735,000★) H10
Vitória da Conquista,
  145,800 (198,150▲) F10
Volta Redonda, 219,267
  (375,000★) H10

Colombia
1985 CENSUS

Armenia, 187,130 .... C 3
Barrancabermeja,
  137,406 .... B 4
Barranquilla, 899,781
  (1,140,000★) ..... A 4
Bogotá see Santa Fe de
  Bogotá .... C 4
Bucaramanga, 352,326
  (550,000★) ...... B 4
Buenaventura,
  160,342 .... C 3
Buga, 82,992 ...... C 3
Cali, 1,350,565
  (1,400,000★) .... C 3
Cartagena, 531,426 . A 3
Cúcuta, 379,478
  (445,000★) .... B 4

1 : 16 000 000

Ibagué, 292,965 .... C 3
Manizales, 299,352
 (330,000★) ...... B 3
Medellín, 1,468,089
 (2,095,000★) .... B 3
Montería, 157,466 .. B 3
Neiva, 194,556 .... C 3
Palmira, 175,186 ... C 3
Pasto, 197,407 .... C 3
Pereira, 233,271
 (390,000★) ...... C 3
Popayán, 141,964 ... C 3
Santa Fe de Bogotá,
 3,982,941
 (4,260,000★) ..... C 4
Santa Marta, 177,922 A 4
Tuluá, 99,721 ..... C 3
Valledupar, 142,771 . A 4
Villavicencio, 178,685 C 4

Ecuador
1987 ESTIMATE
Ambato, 126,067 ... D 3
Cuenca, 201,490 .... D 3
Guayaquil, 1,572,615
 (1,580,000★) ..... D 3
Machala, 144,396 ... D 3
Manta, 135,990 .... D 2
Portoviejo, 141,568 .. D 2
Quito, 1,137,705
 (1,300,000★) ..... D 3

French Guiana
1982 CENSUS
Cayenne, 38,091 .... C 8

Guyana
1983 ESTIMATE
Georgetown, 78,500
 (188,000★) ...... B 7

Peru
1981 CENSUS
Arequipa, 108,023
 (446,942★) ...... G 4
Ayacucho, 57,432
 (69,533★) .... F 4
Cajamarca, 62,259 .. E 3
Callao, 264,133 ..... F 3
Cerro de Pasco, 55,597
 (66,373★) .... F 3

Chiclayo, 213,095
 (279,527★) ...... E 3
Chimbote, 223,341 .. E 3
Cuzco, 89,563
 (184,550★) ...... F 4
Huancayo, 84,845
 (164,954★) ...... F 3
Huánuco, 61,812 ... E 3
Ica, 114,786 ...... F 3
Iquitos, 178,738 .... D 4
Lima, 371,122
 (4,608,010★) ..... F 3
Piura, 144,609
 (207,934★) ...... E 2
Sullana, 89,037 ..... D 2
Tacna, 97,173 ..... G 4
Trujillo, 202,469
 (354,301★) ...... E 3
Tumbes, 47,936 ... D 2
Vitarte, 145,504 .... F 3

Suriname
1988 ESTIMATE
Paramaribo, 241,000
 (296,000★) ...... B 7

Venezuela
1981 CENSUS
Acarigua, 91,662 .... B 5
Barinas, 110,462 ... B 4
Barquisimeto, 497,635 A 5
Cabimas, 140,435 ... A 4
Calabozo, 61,995 ... B 5
Caracas, 1,816,901
 (3,600,000★) ..... A 5
Ciudad Bolívar,
 182,941 .... B 6
Ciudad Guayana,
 314,497 .... B 6
Ciudad Ojeda, 83,565 A 4
Cumaná, 179,814 ... A 6
El Tigre, 73,595 ... B 4
Maracaibo, 890,643 .. A 4
Maracay, 322,560 ... A 5
Maturín, 154,976 ... B 4
Mérida, 143,209 ... B 4
Puerto Cabello,
 71,759 .... A 5
Punto Fijo, 71,114 .. A 4
San Cristóbal,
 198,793 .... B 4
Valencia, 616,224 ... A 5
Valera, 102,068 .... B 4

Oblique Conic Conformal Projection

★ Population of metropolitan area, including suburbs.
▲ Population of entire district, including rural area.

55

Southern South America

Argentina
1980 CENSUS
Avellaneda, 334,145 . . C 5
Bahía Blanca, 223,818 D 4
Buenos Aires, 2,922,829
(10,750,000★) . . . . . C 5
Catamarca, 78,799
(90,000★) . . . . B 3
Comodoro Rivadavia,
96,817 . . . . F 3
Concordia, 94,222 . . C 5
Córdoba, 993,055
(1,070,000★) . . . . . C 4
Corrientes, 180,612 . . B 5
La Plata, 477,175 . . . . C 5
Mar del Plata,
414,696 . . . . D 5
Mendoza, 119,088
(650,000★) . . . . C 3
Paraná, 161,638 . . . . C 5
Posadas, 143,889 . . . . B 5
Río Cuarto, 110,254 . . C 4
Rosario, 938,120
(1,045,000★) . . . . . C 4
Salta, 260,744 . . . . . A 3
San Isidro, 289,170 . . C 5
San Juan, 118,046
(300,000★) . . . . C 3
San Miguel de Tucumán,
392,888 (525,000★) B 3
Santa Fe, 292,165 . . C 4
Santiago del Estero,
148,758 (200,000★) B 4

Brazil
1985 ESTIMATE
Bauru, 220,105 . . . . . . A 7
Blumenau, 192,074 . . B 7
Campinas, 841,016
(1,125,000★) . . . . . . A 7
Caxias do Sul,
266,809 . . . . B 6
Curitiba, 1,279,205
(1,700,000★) . . . . . B 7
Florianópolis, 178,400
(365,000★) . . . . B 7
Joinvile, 302,877 . . . . B 7
Jundiaí, 268,900
(313,652▲) . . . . A 7
Londrina, 296,400
(346,676▲) . . . . A 6
Maringá, 196,871 . . . . A 6
Pelotas, 210,300
(277,730▲) . . . . C 6
Piracicaba, 211,000
(252,079▲) . . . . A 7
Ponta Grossa,
223,154 . . . . B 6
Porto Alegre, 1,272,121
(2,600,000★) . . . . . . C 6
Presidente Prudente,
155,883 . . . . A 6
Ribeirão Prêto,
383,125 . . . . A 7
Rio Grande, 164,221 C 6
Santa Maria, 163,900
(196,827▲) . . . . B 6
Santos, 460,100
(1,065,000★) . . . . . . A 7
São Carlos, 140,383 A 7
São Paulo, 10,063,110
(15,175,000★) . . . . A 7
Sorocaba, 327,468 . . A 7

Chile
1982 CENSUS
Antofagasta, 185,486 A 2
Chillán, 118,163 . . . . D 2
Concepción, 267,891
(675,000★) . . . . D 2
Osorno, 95,286 . . . . E 2
Punta Arenas, 95,332 G 2
Rancagua, 139,925 . . C 2
Santiago, 232,667
(4,100,000★) . . . . . . C 2
Talca, 128,544 . . . . . D 2
Talcahuano, 202,368 D 2
Temuco, 157,297 . . . D 2
Valdivia, 100,046 . . . . D 2
Valparaíso, 265,355
(675,000★) . . . . C 2
Viña del Mar, 244,899 C 2

Falkland Islands
1986 ESTIMATE
Stanley, 1,200 . . . . . . G 5

Paraguay
1985 ESTIMATE
Asunción, 477,100
(700,000★) . . . . B 5

Uruguay
1985 CENSUS
Montevideo, 1,251,647
(1,550,000★) . . . . . C 5
Paysandú, 76,191 . . . . C 5
Salto, 80,823 . . . . C 5

★ Population of metropolitan area, including suburbs.
▲ Population of entire district, including rural area.

Copyright © Rand McNally & Co.
B-549200-264

Oblique Conic Conformal Projection

Kilometers 0 200 400 600
0 Km.
Miles 0 200 400 600
0 Mi.

1:16 000 000

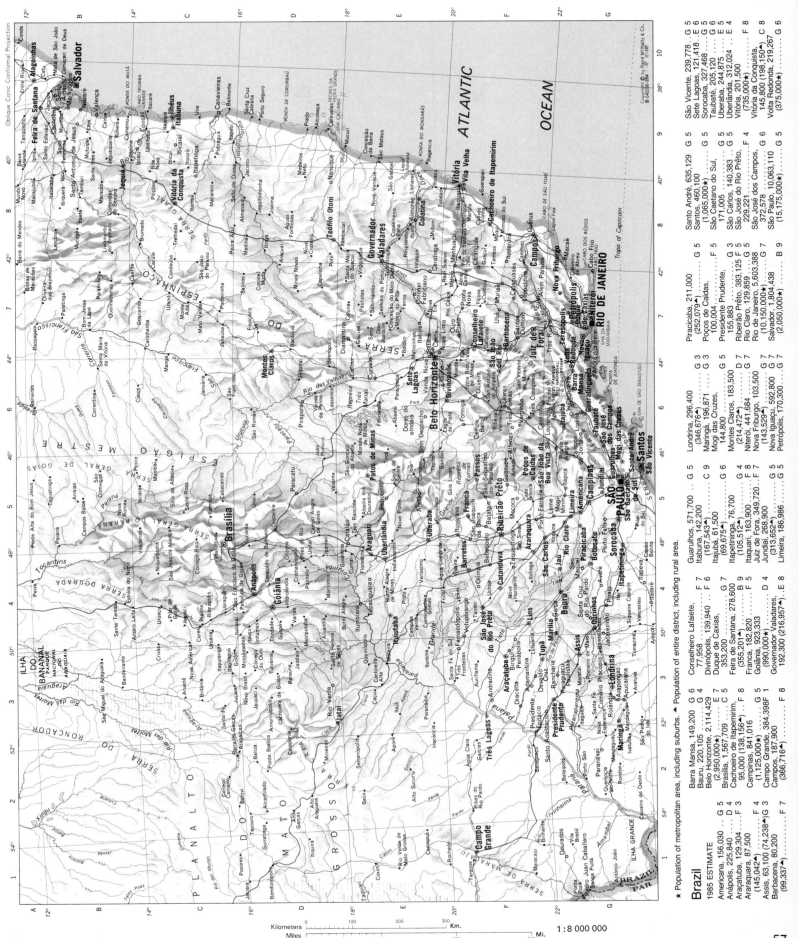

Copyright by Rand McNally & Co.
B-562196264

Oblique Conic Conformal Projection

ATLANTIC

OCEAN

★ Population of metropolitan area, including suburbs. ◆ Population of entire district, including rural area.

Brazil

1985 ESTIMATE

Americana, 156,030	G 5	
Anápolis, 225,840	D 4	
Araçatuba, 129,304	F 3	
Araraquara, 87,500		
(145,042◆)	F 4	
Assis, 63,100 (74,238◆)	G 3	
Barbacena, 80,200		
(99,337◆)	F 7	
Barra Mansa, 149,200	G 6	
Bauru, 220,105	G 4	
Belo Horizonte, 2,114,429		
(2,950,000★)	F 7	
Brasília, 1,567,709	C 5	
Cachoeiro de Itapemirim,		
95,000 (138,156◆)	F 8	
Campinas, 841,016		
(1,125,000★)	G 5	
Campo Grande, 384,398	F 1	
Campos, 187,900		
(366,716◆)	F 8	
Conselheiro Lafaiete,		
77,958	F 7	
Divinópolis, 139,940	F 6	
Duque de Caxias,		
353,200	G 7	
Feira de Santana, 278,600		
(355,201◆)	B 9	
Franca, 182,820		
(214,472◆)	F 5	
Goiânia, 923,333	D 4	
Governador Valadares,		
192,300 (216,957◆)	E 8	
Guarulhos, 571,700	G 5	
(346,676◆)		
Itabuna, 142,200		
(167,543◆)	C 9	
Itajubá, 61,500		
(69,675◆)	G 6	
Mogi das Cruzes,		
144,800	G 7	
Itapetininga, 76,700		
(105,512◆)	G 4	
Itaquari, 163,900	F 8	
Juiz de Fora, 349,720	F 7	
Jundiaí, 268,900		
(143,529◆)	G 5	
Limeira, 186,986	G 5	
Londrina, 296,400	G 3	
Maringá, 196,871	G 3	
Montes Claros, 183,500	D 7	
Niterói, 441,684	G 7	
Nova Friburgo, 103,500	F 7	
Petrópolis, 170,300	G 7	
Piracicaba, 211,000		
(252,079◆)	G 5	
Poços de Caldas,		
100,004	F 5	
Presidente Prudente,		
155,883	G 3	
Ribeirão Prêto, 383,125	F 5	
Rio Claro, 129,859	G 5	
Rio de Janeiro, 5,603,388		
(10,150,000★)	G 7	
Salvador, 1,804,438		
(2,050,000★)	B 9	
Santo André, 635,129	G 5	
Santos, 460,100		
(1,065,000★)	G 5	
São Caetano do Sul,		
171,005	G 5	
São Carlos, 140,383	G 5	
São José do Rio Prêto,		
229,221	F 4	
São José dos Campos,		
372,578	G 6	
São Paulo, 10,063,110		
(15,175,000★)	G 5	
São Vicente, 239,778	G 5	
Sete Lagoas, 121,418	E 6	
Sorocaba, 327,468	G 5	
Taubaté, 205,120	E 5	
Uberaba, 244,875	E 4	
Uberlândia, 312,024	E 4	
Vitória, 201,500		
(735,000★)	F 8	
Vitória da Conquista,		
145,800 (198,150◆)	C 8	
Volta Redonda, 219,267		
(375,000★)	G 6	

Colombia, Ecuador, Venezuela, and Guyana

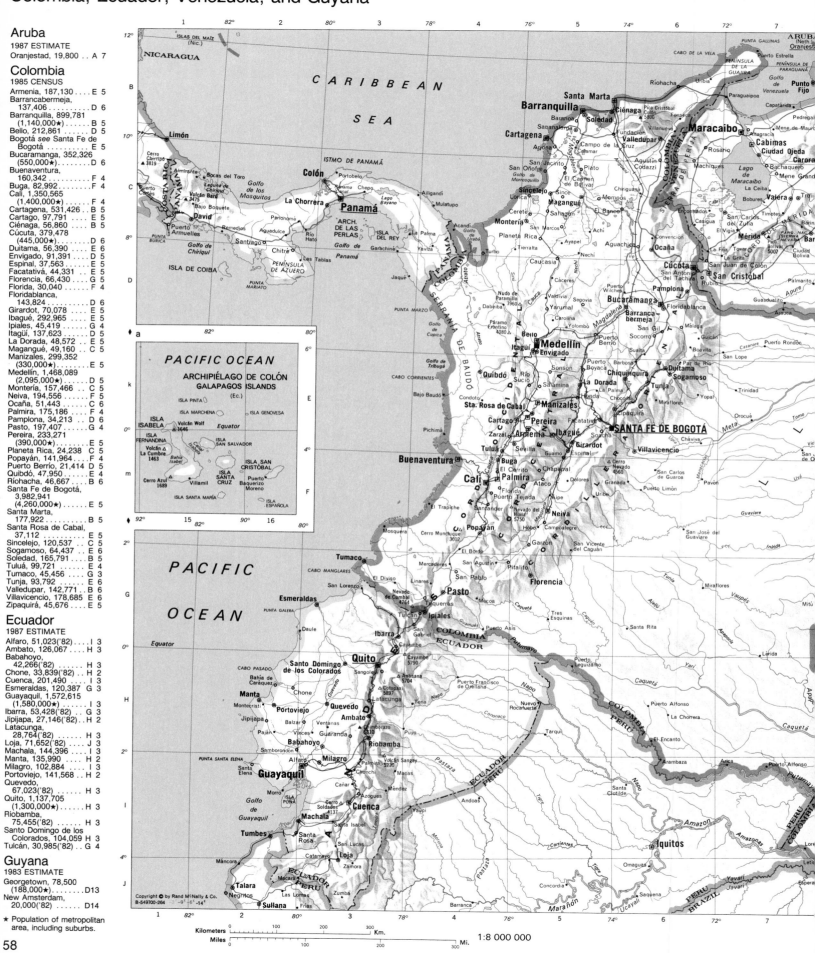

Aruba
1987 ESTIMATE
Oranjestad, 19,800 . . A 7

Colombia
1985 CENSUS
Armenia, 187,130 . . . . E 5
Barrancabermeja, 137,406 . . . . D 6
Barranquilla, 899,781 (1,140,000★) . . . . . B 5
Bello, 212,861 . . . . . . D 5
Bogotá see Santa Fe de Bogotá . . . . E 5
Bucaramanga, 352,326 (550,000★) . . . . . . D 6
Buenaventura, 160,342 . . . . F 4
Buga, 82,992 . . . . F 4
Cali, 1,350,565 (1,400,000★) . . . . . F 4
Cartagena, 531,426 . . B 5
Cartago, 97,791 . . . . E 5
Ciénaga, 56,860 . . . . B 5
Cúcuta, 379,478 (445,000★) . . . . D 6
Duitama, 56,390 . . . . E 5
Envigado, 91,391 . . . D 5
Espinal, 37,563 . . . . . E 5
Facatativá, 44,331 . . . E 5
Florencia, 66,430 . . . E 5
Florida, 30,040 . . . . . F 4
Floridablanca, 143,824 . . . . D 6
Girardot, 70,078 . . . . E 5
Ibagué, 292,965 . . . . E 5
Ipiales, 45,419 . . . . . G 4
Itagüí, 137,623 . . . . . D 5
La Dorada, 48,572 . . E 5
Magangué, 49,160 . . C 5
Manizales, 299,352 (330,000★) . . . . . . E 5
Medellín, 1,468,089 (2,095,000★) . . . . . D 5
Montería, 157,466 . . . C 5
Neiva, 194,556 . . . . . F 5
Ocaña, 51,443 . . . . . C 6
Palmira, 175,186 . . . . F 4
Pamplona, 34,213 . . . D 6
Pasto, 197,407 . . . . . G 4
Pereira, 233,271 (390,000★) . . . . . . E 5
Planeta Rica, 24,238 . C 5
Popayán, 141,964 . . . F 4
Puerto Berrío, 21,414 . D 5
Quibdó, 47,950 . . . . . E 4
Ríohacha, 46,667 . . . B 6
Santa Fe de Bogotá, 3,982,941 (4,260,000★) . . . . . . E 5
Santa Marta, 177,922 . . . . B 5
Santa Rosa de Cabal, 37,112 . . . . E 5
Sincelejo, 120,537 . . C 5
Sogamoso, 64,437 . . . E 6
Soledad, 165,791 . . . B 5
Tuluá, 99,721 . . . . . . E 4
Tumaco, 45,456 . . . . G 3
Tunja, 93,792 . . . . . . E 5
Valledupar, 142,771 . . B 6
Villavicencio, 178,685 E 5
Zipaquirá, 45,676 . . . . E 5

Ecuador
1987 ESTIMATE
Alfaro, 51,023('82) . . . . I 3
Ambato, 126,067 . . . . H 3
Babahoyo, 42,266('82) . . . . . . H 3
Chone, 33,839('82) . . H 2
Cuenca, 201,490 . . . . I 3
Esmeraldas, 120,387 G 3
Guayaquil, 1,572,615 (1,580,000★) . . . . . I 3
Ibarra, 53,428('82) . . G 3
Jipijapa, 27,146('82) . . H 2
Latacunga, 28,764('82) . . . . . . H 3
Loja, 71,652('82) . . . J 3
Machala, 144,396 . . . I 3
Manta, 135,990 . . . . H 2
Milagro, 102,884 . . . I 3
Portoviejo, 141,568 . . H 2
Quevedo, 67,023('82) . . . . . . H 3
Quito, 1,137,705 (1,300,000★) . . . . . . H 3
Riobamba, 75,455('82) . . . . . . H 3
Santo Domingo de los Colorados, 104,059 H 3
Tulcán, 30,985('82) . . G 4

Guyana
1983 ESTIMATE
Georgetown, 78,500 (188,000★) D13
New Amsterdam, 20,000('82) D14

★ Population of metropolitan area, including suburbs.

58

Kilometers
Miles
1:8 000 000
Copyright © by Rand McNally & Co.
B-549700-264

Netherlands Antilles
1981 CENSUS

Willemstad, 31,883
(130,000★) . . . . A 8

Panama
1990 CENSUS

Colón, 54,469
(96,000★) . . . . C 3
David, 65,635 . . . . . . C 1
La Chorrera, 44,110 . . C 3
Panamá, 411,549
(770,000★) . . . . C 3
Puerto Armuelles,
12,562('80) . . . . . . C 1
Santiago, 43,678 . . . . C 2

Trinidad and Tobago
1990 CENSUS

Arima, 29,695 . . . . . . B12
Point Fortin,
6,538('80) B12
Port of Spain, 50,878
(370,000★) B12
San Fernando, 30,092
(75,000★) B12
Scarborough,
6,089('80) B12

Venezuela
1981 CENSUS

Acarigua, 91,662 . . . . C 8
Altagracia de Orituco,
31,582 . . . . C 9
Anaco, 43,607 . . . . C10
Araure, 41,747 . . . . . C 8
Barcelona, 156,461 . . B10
Barinas, 110,462 . . . . C 7
Barquisimeto,
497,635 . . . . B 8
Cabimas, 140,435 . . B 7
Calabozo, 61,995 . . . C 9
Cantaura, 21,236 . . . C10
Caracas, 1,816,901
(3,600,000★) . . . . . B 9
Caripito, 18,172 . . . . B11
Carora, 58,694 . . . . . B 7
Carúpano, 64,579 . . . B11
Ciudad Bolívar,
182,941 . . . . C11
Ciudad Guayana,
314,497 . . . . C11
Ciudad Ojeda (Lagunillas),
83,565 . . . . B 7
Coro, 96,339 . . . . . . B 8
Cumaná, 179,814 . . . B10
El Tigre, 73,595 . . . . C10
El Tocuyo, 22,854 . . C 8
Guanare, 64,025 . . . . C 8
La Guaira, 21,815 . . . B 9
Los Teques, 112,857 . B 9
Machiques, 27,242 . . B 6
Maiquetía, 66,056 . . . B 9
Maracaibo, 890,643 . . B 7
Maracay, 322,560 . . . B 9
Maturín, 154,976 . . . C11
Mérida, 143,209 . . . . C 7
Ocumare del Tuy,
40,666 . . . . B 9
Porlamar, 51,079 . . . . B11
Puerto Ayacucho,
28,248 . . . . E 9
Puerto Cabello,
71,759 . . . . B 8
Puerto la Cruz,
53,881 . . . . B10
Punto Fijo, 71,114 . . B 7
Rosario, 23,914 . . . . B 6
San Carlos, 37,892 . . C 8
San Carlos del Zulia,
31,437 . . . . C 7
San Cristóbal,
198,793 . . . . D 6
San Felipe, 57,526 . . B 8
San Fernando de Apure,
57,308 . . . . D 9
San José de Guanipa,
35,689 . . . . C10
San Juan de Colón,
23,447 . . . . C 6
San Juan de los Morros,
57,219 . . . . C 9
Tinaquillo, 28,168 . . . C 8
Trujillo, 31,774 . . . . . C 7
Tucupita, 27,299 . . . . C11
Upata, 33,238 . . . . . C11
Valencia, 616,224 . . . . C 8
Valera, 102,068 . . . . C 7
Valle de la Pascua,
55,761 . . . . C 9
Yaritagua, 31,936 . . . . B 8
Zaraza, 24,562 . . . . . . C10

Atlantic Ocean

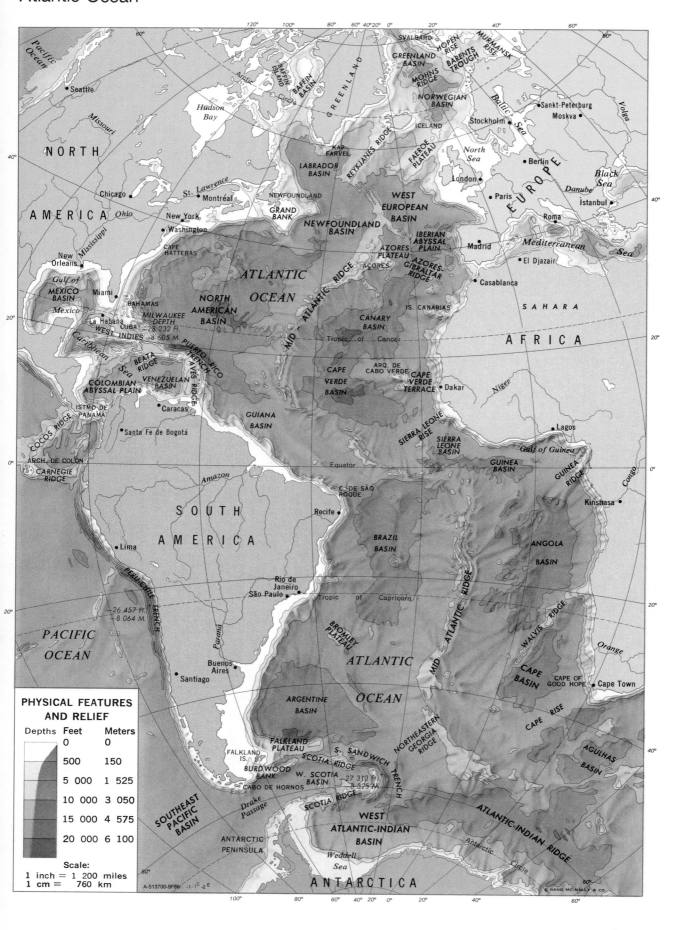

PHYSICAL FEATURES AND RELIEF

Depths	Feet	Meters
	0	0
	500	150
	5 000	1 525
	10 000	3 050
	15 000	4 575
	20 000	6 100

Scale:
1 inch = 1 200 miles
1 cm = 760 km

A-513700-9F86   -1-1E-2 E

© RAND MCNALLY & CO.

Atlanta, 394,017 ('90)..F12
BAHAMAS.............G13
Baltimore, 736,014
('90)................F13
BARBADOS............H14
BELIZE..............H12
Boston, 574,283 ('90). E13
Calgary, 636,104 ('86)
(671,326★) ....D 9
CANADA...............D11
Chicago, 2,783,726
('90)................E12
Ciudad de México (Mexico
City), 8,831,079 ('80)
(14,100,000★) .. H11
COSTA RICA...........H12
CUBA.................G13
Dallas, 1,006,877 ('90) F11
Denver, 467,610 ('90).. F10
Detroit, 1,027,974
('90)................E12
**DOMINICAN
REPUBLIC**...........H13
EL SALVADOR..........H12
GREENLAND............B16
Guadalajara, 1,626,152
('80) (2,325,000★) .. H10
GUATEMALA............H11
HAITI................H13
HONDURAS.............H12
Houston, 1,630,553
('90)................G11
JAMAICA..............H13
Kansas City, 435,146
('90)................F11
La Habana (Havana),
2,036,800 ('87)
(2,125,000★) G12
Los Angeles, 3,485,398
('90)................F 9
Memphis, 610,337
('90)................F11
MÉXICO...............G10
Miami, 358,548 ('90)...G12
Milwaukee, 628,088
('90)................E12
Minneapolis, 368,383
('90)................E11
Montréal, 1,015,420 ('86)
(2,921,357★) E13
New Orleans, 496,938
('90)................G11
New York, 7,322,564
('90)................E13
NICARAGUA............H12
Ottawa, 300,763 ('86)
(819,263★) E13
PANAMA...............I13
Philadelphia, 1,585,577
('90)................F13
Phoenix, 900,013 ('90) F 9
PUERTO RICO..........H14
San Antonio, 935,933
('90)................G11
San Francisco, 723,959
('90)................F 8
Santo Domingo, 1,313,172
('81)................H13
Seattle, 516,259 ('90). E 8
Toronto, 612,289 ('86)
(3,427,168★) E13
**TRINIDAD AND
TOBAGO**.............H14
UNITED STATES........F11
Washington, 606,900
('90)................F13

★ Population of metropolitan
area, including suburbs.

Miles 0   200   400   600   800   1000 Mi.
Kilometers 0   400   800   1200   1600 Km.
1:40 000 000

Mexico

Mexico

1980 CENSUS

Acámbaro, 38,224 .. G 9
Acapulco [de Juárez],
 301,902 .... I10
Aguascalientes,
 293,152 .... G 8
Ameca, 25,946 .... G 7
Apatzingán [de la
 Constitución],
 55,522 .... H 8
Apizaco, 30,498 .... H10
Caborca, 33,696 ... B 3
Campeche, 128,434 H14
Celaya, 141,675 ... G 9
Chihuahua, 385,603 C 6
Chilpancingo [de los
 Bravos], 67,498 ... I10
Ciudad Acuña, 38,898 C 9
Ciudad Chetumal,
 56,709 .... H15
Ciudad del Carmen,
 72,489 .... H14
Ciudad de México (Mexico
 City), 8,831,079
 (14,100,000★) H10
Ciudad de Valles,
 65,609 .... G10
Ciudad Guzmán,
 60,938 .... H 8
Ciudad Hidalgo,
 32,311 .... H 9
Ciudad Juárez,
 544,496 .... B 6
Ciudad Madero,
 132,444 .... F11
Ciudad Mante, 70,647 F10
Ciudad Obregón,
 165,572 .... D 5
Ciudad Victoria,
 140,161 .... F10
Coatzacoalcos,
 127,170 .... H12
Colima, 86,044 .... H 8
Córdoba, 99,972 ... H11
Cuernavaca, 192,770 H10
Culiacán, 304,826 .. E 6
Delicias, 65,504 ... C 7
Durango, 257,915 .. E 7
Empalme, 31,555 .. D 4
Ensenada, 120,483 . B 1
Fresnillo, 56,066 .... F 8
Gómez Palacio,
 116,967 .... E 8
Guadalajara, 1,626,152
 (2,325,000★) ..... G 8
Guadalupe, 370,524 . E 9
Guanajuato, 48,981 . G 9
Guaymas, 54,826 .. D 4
Hermosillo, 297,175 .. D 4
Hidalgo del Parral,
 75,590 .... D 7
Iguala, 66,005 ...... H10
Irapuato, 170,138 .. G 9
Jalapa Enríquez,
 204,594 .... H11
Juchitán [de Zaragoza],
 38,801 .... I12
La Barca, 20,889 .. G 8
Lagos de Moreno,
 44,223 .... G 9
La Paz, 91,453 .... E 4
La Piedad [Cavadas],
 47,441 .... G 8
León [de los Aldamas],
 593,002 .... G 9
Los Mochis, 122,531 . E 5
Manzanillo, 39,088 .. H 7
Matamoros, 188,745 E11
Matehuala, 41,550 .. F 9
Mazatlán, 199,830 .. F 6
Mérida, 400,142 .... G15
Mexicali, 341,559
 (365,000★) ...... A 2
Mexico City see Ciudad
 de México H10
Minatitlán, 106,765 . I12
Monclova, 115,786 .. D 9
Montemorelos, 28,342 E10
Monterrey, 1,090,009
 (2,015,000★) ..... E 9
Morelia, 297,544 .... H 9
Navojoa, 62,901 ... D 5
Nogales, 65,603 .... B 4
Nueva Casas Grandes,
 28,514 .... B 6
Nueva Rosita, 33,121 D 9
Nuevo Laredo,
 201,731 .... D10
Oaxaca [de Juárez],
 154,223 .... I11
Ocotlán, 48,931 ... G 8
Orizaba, 114,848
 (215,000★) H11
Pachuca [de Soto],
 110,351 .... G10
Papantla [de Olarte],
 43,935 .... G11
Pátzcuaro, 32,902 . H 9
Piedras Negras,
 67,455 .... C 9
Poza Rica de Hidalgo,
 166,799 .... G11

★ Population of metropolitan
 area, including suburbs.

Central America and the Caribbean

Antigua and Barbuda
1977 ESTIMATE
Saint Johns, 24,359 . . F17

Bahamas
1982 ESTIMATE
Nassau, 135,000 . . . . B 9

Barbados
1980 CENSUS
Bridgetown, 7,466
(115,000★) H18

Belize
1985 ESTIMATE
Belize City, 47,000 . . F 3
Belmopan, 4,500 . . . . F 3

Cayman Islands
1988 ESTIMATE
Georgetown, 13,700 E 7

Costa Rica
1988 ESTIMATE
Limón, 40,400
(62,600▲) . . . . I 6
San José, 278,600
(670,000★) . . . . . . J 5

Cuba
1987 ESTIMATE
Camagüey, 265,588 D 9
Guantánamo, 179,091 D10
Havana see La
Habana . . . . C 6
Holguín, 199,861 . . D 9
La Habana (Havana),
2,036,800
(2,125,000★) . . . . C 6
Santa Clara, 182,349 C 8
Santiago de Cuba,
364,554 . . . . D10

Dominican Republic
1981 CENSUS
Santiago, 278,638 . . E 12
Santo Domingo,
1,313,172 . . . . . . E 13

El Salvador
1985 ESTIMATE
San Salvador, 462,652
(920,000★) . . . . . H 3
Santa Ana, 137,879 . H 3

Guadeloupe
1982 CENSUS
Basse-Terre, 13,656
(26,600★) F17

Guatemala
1989 ESTIMATE
Guatemala, 1,057,210
(1,400,000★) . . . . G 2

★ Population of metropolitan
area, including suburbs.

64

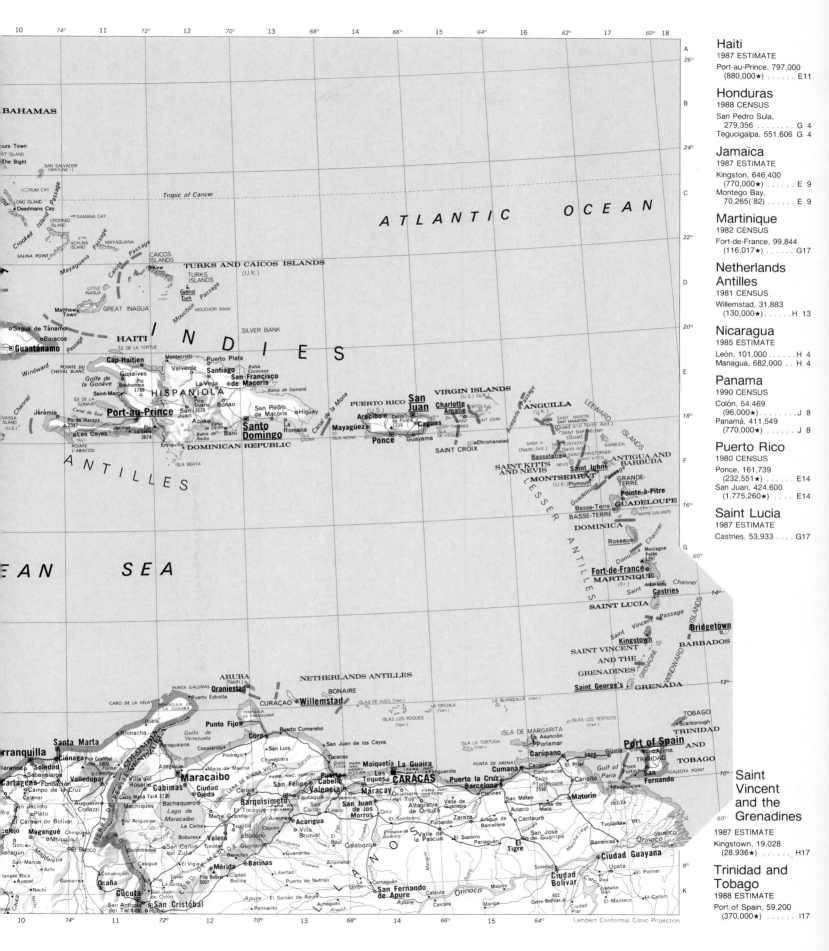

BAHAMAS

ATLANTIC OCEAN

Tropic of Cancer

RUM CAY
LONG ISLAND
Deadmans Cay
CROOKED ISLAND
ACKLINS ISLAND
SALINA POINT
MAYAGUANA

CAICOS ISLANDS

TURKS AND CAICOS ISLANDS
(U.K.)
Kew
TURKS ISLANDS
Grand Turk

MOUCHOIR BANK

SILVER BANK

Sagua de Tánamo
Baracoa
Guantánamo

HAITI
ÎLE DE LA TORTUE
POINTE DU CHEVAL BLANC

Cap-Haïtien
Montecristi
Puerto Plata
Valverde
Gonaïves
Pic Boishomme
Santiago
La Vega
San Francisco de Macoris
Bahía Escocesa
Golfe de la Gonâve
HISPANIOLA
Pico Duarte 3175
Bonao
Bahía de Samaná
Saint-Marc
ÎLE DE LA GONÂVE
San Juan
San Pedro de Macoris
Higuey
Jérémie
Pic de Macaya 2347
Port-au-Prince
Azua
Bahía de Ocoa
La Romana
Les Cayes
Jacmel
La Selle 2674
Santo Domingo
Baní
Enriquillo
DOMINICAN REPUBLIC
ISLA SAONA
ISLA BEATA

Windward Passage

INDIES

ANTILLES

VASSA ISLAND (U.S.)

PUERTO RICO (U.S.)
Arecibo
Mayagüez
San Juan
Cerro de Punta 1338
Caguas
Ponce
Guayama
Canal de la Mona
ISLA MONA
ISLA DE VIEQUES

VIRGIN ISLANDS
(U.S.) (U.K.)
Charlotte Amalie
SAINT JOHN
SAINT THOMAS
SAINT CROIX
Christiansted

Anegada Passage

ANGUILLA
(U.K.)
SAINT MARTIN
SINT MAARTEN
(Guad and Neth. Ant.)
SAINT BARTHÉLEMY
(Guad.)
SABA
(Neth. Ant.)
SINT EUSTATIUS
(Neth. Ant.)
Basseterre
NEVIS
SAINT KITTS AND NEVIS
SAINT KITTS
MONTSERRAT
(U.K.) Plymouth
Saint Johns
ANTIGUA AND BARBUDA
BARBUDA
GRANDE-TERRE
Pointe-à-Pitre
Basse-Terre
GUADELOUPE
BASSE-TERRE
(Fr.)
MARIE-GALANTE
DOMINICA
Roseau
Montagne Pelée 1397
Fort-de-France
MARTINIQUE
(Fr.)
Saint Lucia Channel
Castries
SAINT LUCIA
Saint Vincent Passage
Kingstown
SAINT VINCENT AND THE GRENADINES
GRENADINE IS.
Bridgetown
BARBADOS
WINDWARD ISLANDS
Saint George's
GRENADA

LEEWARD ISLANDS

LESSER ANTILLES

CARIBBEAN SEA

ARUBA
(Neth.)
Oranjestad
PUNTA GALLINAS
CABO DE LA VELA
PENÍNSULA DE LA GUAJIRA
PENÍNSULA DE PARAGUANÁ
Punto Fijo
Uribia
Puerto Estrella
CURAÇAO
Willemstad
BONAIRE
NETHERLANDS ANTILLES
ISLAS DE AVES (Ven.)
LA ORCHILA (Ven.)
LA BLANQUILLA (Ven.)
ISLAS LOS ROQUES (Ven.)
LA TORTUGA (Ven.)
ISLA LA TORTUGA
ISLA DE MARGARITA
La Asunción
Porlamar
ISLAS LOS TESTIGOS (Ven.)
TOBAGO
Scarborough
TRINIDAD AND TOBAGO

Santa Marta
Barranquilla
Ciénaga
Soledad
Pico Cristóbal Colón 5800
Sabanalarga
Rioacha
Maicao
Golfo de Venezuela
COLOMBIA
VENEZUELA
SIERRA DE PERIJÁ
Maracaibo
Cabimas
Ciudad Ojeda
Coro
Puerto Cumarebo
San Juan de los Cayos
Capatárida
Tucacas
Puerto Cabello
San Felipe
Barquisimeto
Valencia
Maracay
Maiquetía
La Guaira
Los Teques
CARACAS
Guatire
Barcelona
Puerto la Cruz
Cumaná
Cariaco
Carúpano
El Pilar
Güiria
Irapa
Port of Spain
Arima
TRINIDAD
GALEOTA POINT
Gulf of Paria
Pedernales
San Fernando
Caripito
Maturín
Lago de Maracaibo
La Ceiba
Trujillo
Boconó
Valera
Mérida
Pico Bolívar 5007
Barinas
Guanare
Ciudad Bolivia
Barcelona
El Tigre
Ciudad Bolívar
Ciudad Guayana
Upata
Ciudad Guayana
ORINOCO
San Cristóbal
San Antonio del Táchira
San Juan de los Morros
Calabozo
Valle de la Pascua
Zaraza
El Socorro
Valle de Guanape
San José de Guanipa
Tucupita
DELTA
Barrancas
Maripa
Caicara
Soledad
Cúcuta

Lambert Conformal Conic Projection

Haiti
1987 ESTIMATE
Port-au-Prince, 797,000
(880,000★) E11

Honduras
1988 CENSUS
San Pedro Sula,
279,356 . . . . G 4
Tegucigalpa, 551,606 G 4

Jamaica
1987 ESTIMATE
Kingston, 646,400
(770,000★) . . . . . E 9
Montego Bay,
70,265('82) . . . . . E 9

Martinique
1982 CENSUS
Fort-de-France, 99,844
(116,017★) G17

Netherlands Antilles
1981 CENSUS
Willemstad, 31,883
(130,000★) . . . . . H 13

Nicaragua
1985 ESTIMATE
León, 101,000 . . . . . H 4
Managua, 682,000 . . H 4

Panama
1990 CENSUS
Colón, 54,469
(96,000★) . . . . J 8
Panamá, 411,549
(770,000★) . . . . . J 8

Puerto Rico
1980 CENSUS
Ponce, 161,739
(232,551★) E14
San Juan, 424,600
(1,775,260★) E14

Saint Lucia
1987 ESTIMATE
Castries, 53,933 . . . G17

Saint Vincent and the Grenadines
1987 ESTIMATE
Kingstown, 19,028
(28,936★) H17

Trinidad and Tobago
1988 ESTIMATE
Port of Spain, 59,200
(370,000★) I17

Canada

ALBERTA..................F10
Alma, 25,923 ('86)
 (29,977★)..............G18
Baie-Comeau, 26,244 ('86)
 (33,047★)..............G19
Banff, 4,208 ('81)......F 9
Barrie, 48,287 ('86)
 (67,703★)..............H17
Bathurst, 14,683 ('86)
 (34,895★)..............G19
Belleville, 36,041 ('86)
 (87,530★)..............H17
Brandon, 38,708 ('86).G13
BRITISH COLUMBIA... F 8
Brockville, 20,880 ('86)
 (37,115★)..............H17
Calgary, 636,104 ('86)
 (671,326★)..............F10
Cambridge, 79,920
 ('86)..................H16
Campbell River, 15,370
 ('81)..................F 7
Campbellton, 9,077 ('86)
 (17,418★)..............G19
CANADA..................D13
Charlottetown, 15,776
 ('86) (53,868★)........G20
Chatham, 42,211 ('86) H16
Chicoutimi, 61,083 ('86)
 (158,468★)..............G18
Chilliwack, 41,337 ('86)
 (50,288★)..............G 8
Churchill, 1,186 ('81)...E14
Corner Brook, 22,719
 ('86) (33,730★)........G21
Cornwall, 46,425 ('86)
 (51,719★)..............G18
Dartmouth, 65,243
 ('86)..................H20
Dawson Creek, 10,544
 ('86)..................E 8
Dolbeau, 8,554 ('86)
 (15,288★)..............G18
Drummondville, 36,020
 ('86) (56,283★)........G18
Edmonton, 573,982 ('86)
 (785,465★)..............F10
Edmundston, 11,497 ('86)
 (22,614★)..............G19
Eskimo Point, 1,189
 ('86)..................D14
Flin Flon, 7,591 ('86)
 (9,211★)..............F12
Fort McMurray, 34,949
 ('86) (48,497★)........E10
Fort Saint John, 13,355
 ('86)..................E 8
Fredericton, 44,352 ('86)
 (65,768★)..............G19
Gander, 10,207 ('86)
 (10,899★)..............G22
Gaspé, 17,350 ('86)....G20
Granby, 38,508 ('86)
 (51,176★)..............G18
Grande-Prairie, 26,471
 ('86)..................E 9
Grand Falls, 9,121 ('86)
 (25,612★)..............G21
Guelph, 78,235 ('86)
 (85,962★)..............H16
Halifax, 113,577 ('86)
 (295,990★)..............H20
Hamilton, 306,728 ('86)
 (557,029★)..............H17
Happy Valley-Goose Bay,
 7,248 ('86)............F20
Hull, 58,722 ('86).....G17
Inuvik, 3,389 ('86).......C 6
Jasper, 3,269 ('81)....F 9
Joliette, 16,845 ('86)
 (34,897★)..............G18
Jonquière, 58,467
 ('86)..................G18
Kamloops, 61,773
 ('86)..................F 8
Kelowna, 61,213 ('86)
 (89,730★)..............G 9
Kenora, 9,621 ('86)
 (15,456★)..............G14
Kirkland Lake, 11,604
 ('86)..................G16
Kitchener, 150,604 ('86)
 (311,195★)..............H16
Kitimat, 11,196 ('86)..F 7
Labrador City, 8,664 ('86)
 (11,301★)..............F19
La Tuque, 10,723 ('86)
 (13,468★)..............G18
Laval, 284,164 ('86)....G18
Lethbridge, 58,841
 ('86)..................G10
Lloydminster, 17,356
 ('86)..................F11
London, 269,140 ('86)
 (342,302★)..............H16
MANITOBA..................F13
Matane, 13,243 ('86)
 (15,361★)..............G19
Medicine Hat, 41,804 ('86)
 (50,734★)..............F10
Midland, 12,092 ('86)
 (35,003★)..............H17
Moncton, 55,468 ('86)
 (102,084★)..............G20

★ Population of metropolitan
 area, including suburbs.

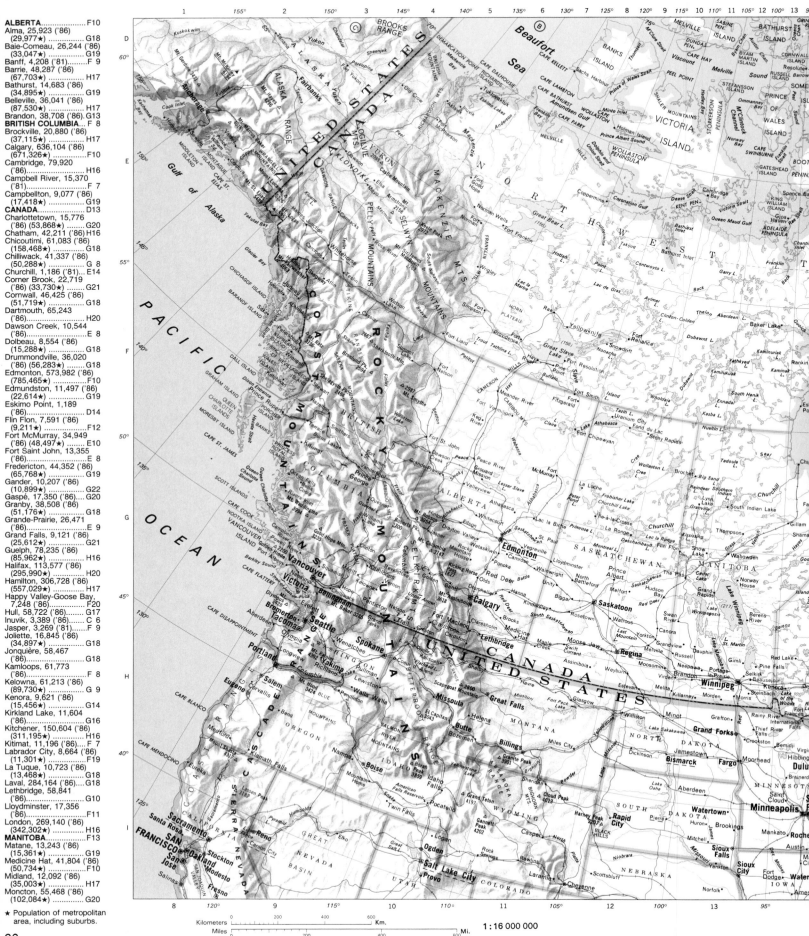

1 : 16 000 000

Montréal, 1,015,420 ('86)
(2,921,357★) G18
Moose Jaw, 35,073 ('86)
(37,219★) F11
Nanaimo, 49,029 ('86)
(60,420★) .... G 8
NEW BRUNSWICK..... G19
NEWFOUNDLAND......F21
New Glasgow, 10,022
('86) (38,737★) G20
Niagara Falls, 72,107
('86)..................... H17
North Bay, 50,623 ('86)
(57,422★) G17
NORTHWEST
TERRITORIES.........C13
NOVA SCOTIA.......... G20
ONTARIO.................. G16
Orillia, 24,077 ('86)
(31,252★) H17
Oshawa, 123,651 ('86)
(203,543★) H17
Ottawa, 300,763 ('86)
(819,263★) G17
Owen Sound, 19,804 ('86)
(27,364★) H16
Pembroke, 14,131 ('86)
(22,560★) G17
Penticton, 23,588 ('86)
(38,966★) .... G 9
Peterborough, 61,049
('86) (87,083★) H17
Portage-la-Prairie, 13,198
('86)..................... G13
Port Alberni, 18,241
('86)..................... G 8
Prince Albert, 33,686 ('86)
(40,841★) F11
PRINCE EDWARD
ISLAND.................. G20
Prince George, 67,621
('86)..................... F 8
Prince Rupert, 15,755
('86) (17,581★) ......F 6
QUÉBEC.................. F18
Québec, 164,580 ('86)
(603,267★) G18
Rankin Inlet, 1,374
('86)..................... D14
Red Deer, 54,425 ('86)F10
Regina, 175,064 ('86)
(186,521★) F12
Saint-Hyacinthe, 38,603
('86) (48,303★) G18
Saint-Jérôme, 23,316 ('86)
(44,048★) G18
Saint John, 76,831 ('86)
(121,265★) G19
Saint John's, 96,216 ('86)
(161,901★) G22
Sarnia, 49,033 ('86)
(85,700★) H16
SASKATCHEWAN......F11
Saskatoon, 177,641 ('86)
(200,665★) F11
Sault Sainte Marie, 80,905
('86) (84,617★) G16
Selkirk, 10,013 ('86).... F13
Sept-Îles (Seven Islands),
25,637 ('86)
(28,050★) F19
Shawinigan, 21,470 ('86)
(61,965★) G18
Sherbrooke, 74,438 ('86)
(129,960★) G18
Sorel, 19,522 ('86)
(46,096★) G18
Sudbury, 88,717 ('86)
(148,877★) G16
Summerside, 8,020 ('86)
(15,614★) G20
Swift Current, 15,666
('86)..................... F11
Sydney Mines, 8,063
('86)..................... G20
Thetford Mines, 18,561
('86) (31,940★) G18
Thunder Bay, 112,272
('86) (122,217★) G15
Timmins, 46,657 ('86). G16
Toronto, 612,289 ('86)
(3,427,168★) H17
Trail, 7,948 ('86)
(20,257★) .... G 9
Trois-Rivières, 50,122
('86) (128,888★) G18
Truro, 12,124 ('86)
(41,516★) G20
Val-d'Or, 22,252 ('86)
(27,178★) G17
Vancouver, 431,147 ('86)
(1,380,729★) .... G 8
Victoria, 66,303 ('86)
(255,547★) .... G 8
Whitehorse, 15,199
('86)..................... D 5
Windsor, 193,111 ('86)
(253,988★) H16
Winnipeg, 594,551 ('86)
(625,304★) G13
Yellowknife, 11,753
('86)..................... D10
YUKON...................... D 5

Alberta

Alberta
1986 CENSUS

Airdrie, 10,390 . . . . . . D 3
Athabasca, 1,970 . . . . B 4
Banff . . . . D 3
Barrhead, 3,991 . . . . . B 3
Beaumont, 3,944 . . . . C 4
Beaverlodge, 1,808 . . B 1
Blackfalds, 1,688 . . . . C 4
Bonnyville, 5,470 . . . . B 5
Bow Island, 1,650 . . . E 5
Brooks, 9,464 . . . . . . D 5
Calgary, 636,104
   (671,326★) . . . . . . D 3
Camrose, 12,968 . . . . C 4
Canmore, 4,182 . . . . . D 3
Cardston, 3,497 . . . . E 4
Carstairs, 1,629 . . . . D 3
Claresholm, 3,382 . . . D 4
Coaldale, 4,796 . . . . E 4
Cochrane, 4,190 . . . . D 3
Cold Lake, 3,195 . . . . B 5
Coronation, 1,310 . . . C 5
Crowsnest Pass,
   6,912 . . . . E 3
Devon, 3,691 . . . . . . C 4
Didsbury, 3,184 . . . . D 3
Drayton Valley, 5,290 C 3
Drumheller, 6,366 . . . D 4
Edmonton, 573,982
   (785,465★) . . . . . . C 4
Edson, 7,323 . . . . . . C 2
Fairview, 2,998 . . . . . A 1
Fort Chipewyan, 922 . f 8
Fort Macleod, 3,123 . E 4
Fort McMurray, 34,949
   (48,497★) . . . . A 5
Fort Saskatchewan,
   11,983 . . . . C 4
Fox Creek, 2,068 . . . B 2
Gibbons, 2,335 . . . . . C 4
Grand Centre, 3,655 . B 5
Grande Cache, 3,646 . C 1
Grande Prairie,
   26,471 . . . . B 1
Grimshaw, 2,579 . . . . A 2
Hanna, 3,017 . . . . . . D 5
High Level, 3,004 . . . F 7
High Prairie, 2,817 . . B 2
High River, 5,096 . . . D 4
Hinton, 8,629 . . . . . . C 2
Innisfail, 5,535 . . . . . C 4
Jasper . . . . C 1
Lac La Biche, 2,553 . . B 4
Lacombe, 6,080 . . . . C 4
La Crete, 689 . . . . . . f 7
Lake Louise, 688 . . . . D 2
Lamont, 1,576 . . . . . C 4
Leduc, 13,126 . . . . . . C 4
Lethbridge, 58,841 . . E 4
Lloydminster, 17,354 . C 5
Magrath, 1,637 . . . . . E 4
Medicine Hat, 41,804
   (50,734★) . . . . D 5
Morinville, 5,364 . . . . C 4
Nordegg, 53 . . . . C 2
Okotoks, 5,214 . . . . . D 4
Olds, 4,871 . . . . C 3
Peace River, 6,288 . . A 2
Penhold, 1,580 . . . . . C 4
Picture Butte, 1,576 . . E 4
Pincher Creek, 3,800 . E 4
Ponoka, 5,473 . . . . . C 4
Provost, 1,725 . . . . . C 5
Raymond, 2,957 . . . . E 4
Redcliff, 3,834 . . . . . D 5
Red Deer, 54,425 . . . C 4
Redwater, 1,982 . . . . C 4
Rimbey, 1,786 . . . . . . C 3
Rocky Mountain House,
   5,182 . . . . C 3
Saint Albert, 36,710 . . C 4
Saint Paul, 5,030 . . . . B 5
Sherwood Park . . . . . C 4
Slave Lake, 5,429 . . . B 3
Smith, 251 . . . . B 3
Spruce Grove, 11,918 C 4
Stettler, 5,147 . . . . . C 4
Stony Plain, 5,802 . . . C 3
Strathmore, 3,544 . . . D 4
Sundre, 1,712 . . . . . . C 3
Swan Hills, 2,403 . . . B 3
Sylvan Lake, 3,937 . . C 4
Taber, 6,382 . . . . E 4
Three Hills, 2,528 . . . D 4
Valleyview, 1,987 . . . B 2
Vegreville, 5,276 . . . . C 4
Vermilion, 3,879 . . . . C 4
Vulcan, 1,420 . . . . . . D 4
Wainwright, 4,665 . . . C 5
Westlock, 4,532 . . . . C 4
Wetaskiwin, 10,071 . . C 4
Whitecourt, 5,737 . . . B 3

★ Population of metropolitan
   area, including suburbs.

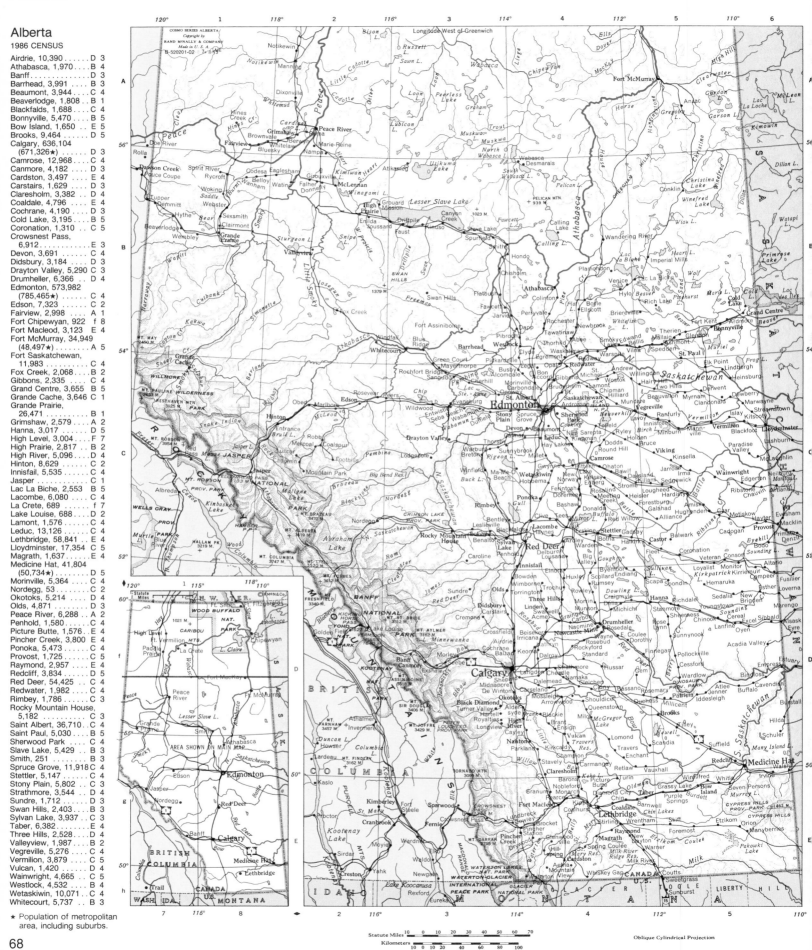

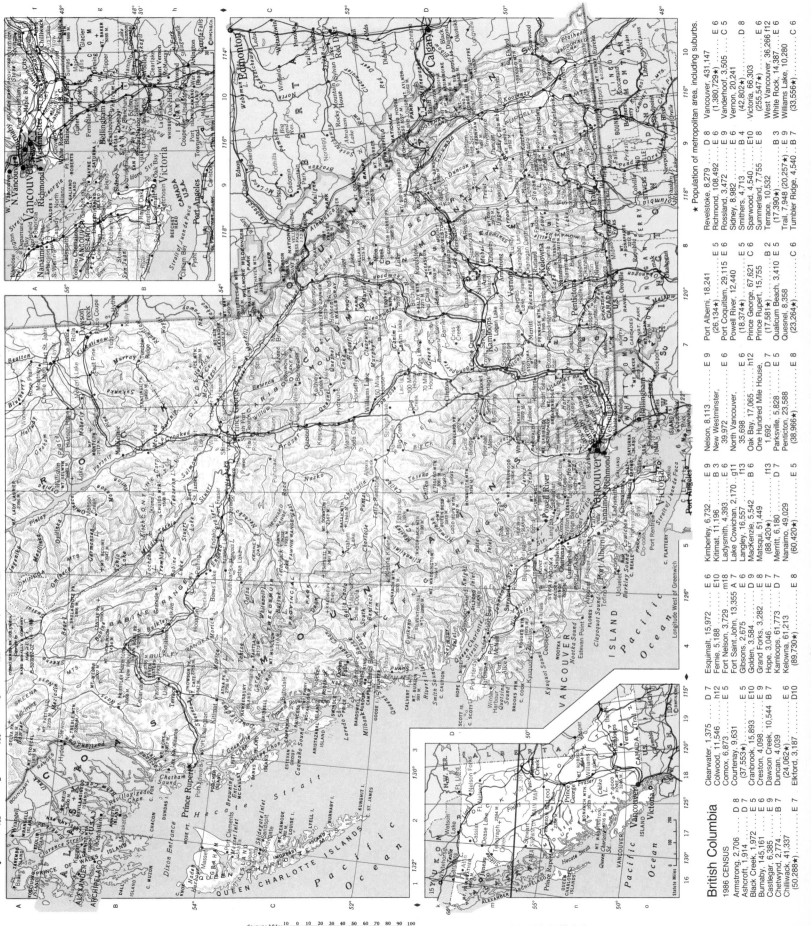

British Columbia

1986 CENSUS

Armstrong, 2,706	D 8	Clearwater, 1,375	D 7	Esquimalt, 15,972	E 6
Ashcroft, 1,914	D 7	Colwood, 11,546	h12	Fernie, 5,188	B 3
Black Creek, 1,972	E 6	Comox, 6,873	E 5	Fort Nelson, 3,729	m18
Burnaby, 145,161	E 6	Courtenay, 9,631	E 5	Fort Saint John, 13,355	A 7
Castlegar, 6,385	E 9	(37,553★)		Gibsons, 2,675	E 6
Chetwynd, 2,774	B 7	Cranbrook, 15,893	E10	Golden, 3,584	D 9
Chilliwack, 41,337	E 7	Creston, 4,098	E 9	Grand Forks, 4,098	E 8
(50,288★)		Dawson Creek, 10,544	B 7	Hope, 3,046	E 7
		Duncan, 4,039	E 6	Kamloops, 61,773	D 7
		Elkford, 3,187	B 7	Kelowna, 61,213	E 8
				(89,730★)	

Kimberley, 6,732	E 9	Nelson, 8,113	E 9	Port Alberni, 18,241	E 5
Kitimat, 11,196	B 3	New Westminster,		(26,134★)	
Ladysmith, 4,393	E 6	39,972	E 6	Port Coquitlam, 29,115	E 6
Lake Cowichan, 2,170,	g11	North Vancouver,		Powell River, 12,440	E 5
Langley, 16,557	f13	35,698	E 6	(18,374★)	
MacKenzie, 5,542	B 6	Oak Bay, 17,065	E 6	Prince George, 67,621	C 6
Matsqui, 51,449		One Hundred Mile House,		(59,683★)	
		1,692	D 7	Prince Rupert, 145,551	
Merritt, 6,180	D 7	Parksville, 5,828	E 5	(17,581★)	B 2
Nanaimo, 49,029	E 5	Penticton, 23,588	E 8	Qualicum Beach, 3,410	E 5
		(38,966★)		Quesnel, 8,358	C 6
				(23,264★)	

Revelstoke, 8,279	D 8	Vancouver, 431,147	D 8
Richmond, 108,492	E 6	(1,380,729★)	
Rossland, 3,472	E 9	Vanderhoof, 3,505	C 5
Sidney, 8,982	E 6	Vernon, 20,241	D 8
Smithers, 4,713	B 4	(42,802★)	
Sparwood, 4,540	E10	Victoria, 66,303	E 6
Summerland, 7,755	E 8	(255,547★)	
Terrace, 10,532		West Vancouver, 36,266	l12
		White Rock, 14,387	E 6
Trail, 7,948 (20,257★)	E 9	Williams Lake, 10,280	
Tumbler Ridge, 4,540	B 7	(33,556★)	C 6

★ Population of metropolitan area, including suburbs.

Statute Miles 10 0 10 20 30 40 50 60 70 80 90 100

Kilometers 10 0 10 20   40   60   80 100 120 140

Oblique Cylindrical Projection

Manitoba

Manitoba
1986 CENSUS

Altona, 2,958 ...... E 3
Arborg, 1,018 ...... D 3
Ashern, 620 .... D 3
Beausejour, 2,535 .. D 3
Birch River, 509 .... C 1
Birtle, 850 .... D 1
Boissevain, 1,572 ... E 1
Brandon, 38,708 .... E 2
Camperville, 588 ... D 1
Carberry, 1,544 .... E 2
Carman, 2,500 ..... E 2
Churchill, 1,109 ...... f 9
Cranberry Portage,
    849 .... B 1
Cross Lake, 580 .... B 3
Crystal City, 487 ... E 2
Dauphin, 8,875 .... D 1
Deloraine, 1,134 .... E 1
Duck Bay, 559 ..... C 1
Easterville, 675 .... C 2
East Selkirk, 572 ... D 3
Elkhorn, 534 ...... E 1
Emerson, 725 ...... E 3
Erickson, 565 ...... D 2
Flin Flon, 7,591
    (9,211★) ...... B 1
Gilbert Plains, 816 .. D 1
Gillam, 1,909 ...... A 4
Gimli, 1,681 ...... D 3
Gladstone, 951 .... D 2
Glenboro, 719 ..... E 2
Grandview, 941 .... D 1
Gretna, 503 .... E 3
Grunthal, 639 ..... E 3
Hamiota, 815 ...... D 1
Hartney, 523 ...... E 1
Killarney, 2,318 .... E 1
Lac du Bonnet, 1,021 D 3
Leaf Rapids, 1,950 .. A 1
Lorette, 1,169 ..... E 3
Lundar, 562 .... D 2
MacGregor, 854 .... E 2
Manitou, 856 ...... E 2
McCreary, 578 ..... D 2
Melita, 1,239 ...... E 1
Minitonas, 559 ..... C 1
Minnedosa, 2,520 .. D 2
Moose Lake, 541 .... C 1
Morden, 5,004 ..... E 2
Morris, 1,613 ...... E 3
Neepawa, 3,314 .... D 2
Niverville, 1,452 ... E 3
Norway House, 633 . C 3
Notre Dame de Lourdes,
    628 .... E 2
Pilot Mound, 819 ... E 2
Pine Falls, 831 ..... D 3
Plum Coulee, 677 .. E 3
Portage la Prairie,
    13,198 .... E 2
Powerview, 724 .... D 3
Reston, 616 .... E 1
Rivers, 1,157 ...... D 1
Riverton, 635 ...... D 3
Roblin, 1,913 ...... D 1
Rossburn, 664 ..... D 1
Russell, 1,669 ..... D 1
Saint Adolphe, 1,059 E 3
Sainte Anne-des-Chênes,
    1,402 .... E 3
Saint Claude, 610 .. E 2
Saint Jean Baptiste,
    571 .... E 3
Saint Malo, 742 .... E 3
Saint Pierre-Jolys,
    912 .... E 3
Sainte Rose du Lac,
    1,030 .... D 2
Selkirk, 10,013 .... D 3
Shoal Lake, 832 .... D 1
Snow Lake, 1,837 .. B 1
Somerset, 534 ..... E 2
Souris, 1,751 ...... E 1
South Indian Lake,
    743 .... A 2
Steinbach, 7,473 ... E 3
Stonewall, 2,349 ... D 3
Swan River, 3,946 .. C 1
Teulon, 953 .... D 3
The Pas, 6,283 .... C 1
Thompson, 14,701 .. B 2
Treherne, 762 ..... E 2
Virden, 3,054 ...... E 1
Wabowden, 571 .... B 2
Wawanesa, 502 .... E 2
Winkler, 5,926 ..... E 3
Winnipeg, 594,551
    (625,304★) .... E 3
Winnipeg Beach, 548 D 3
Winnipegosis, 832 .. D 2

★ Population of metropolitan
area, including suburbs.

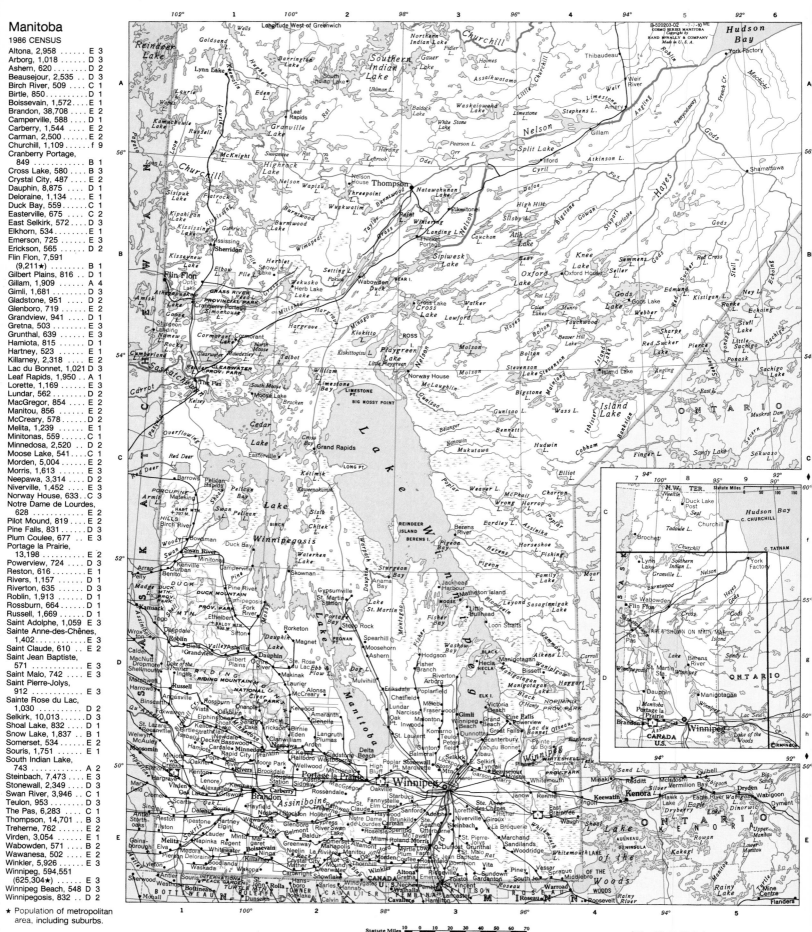

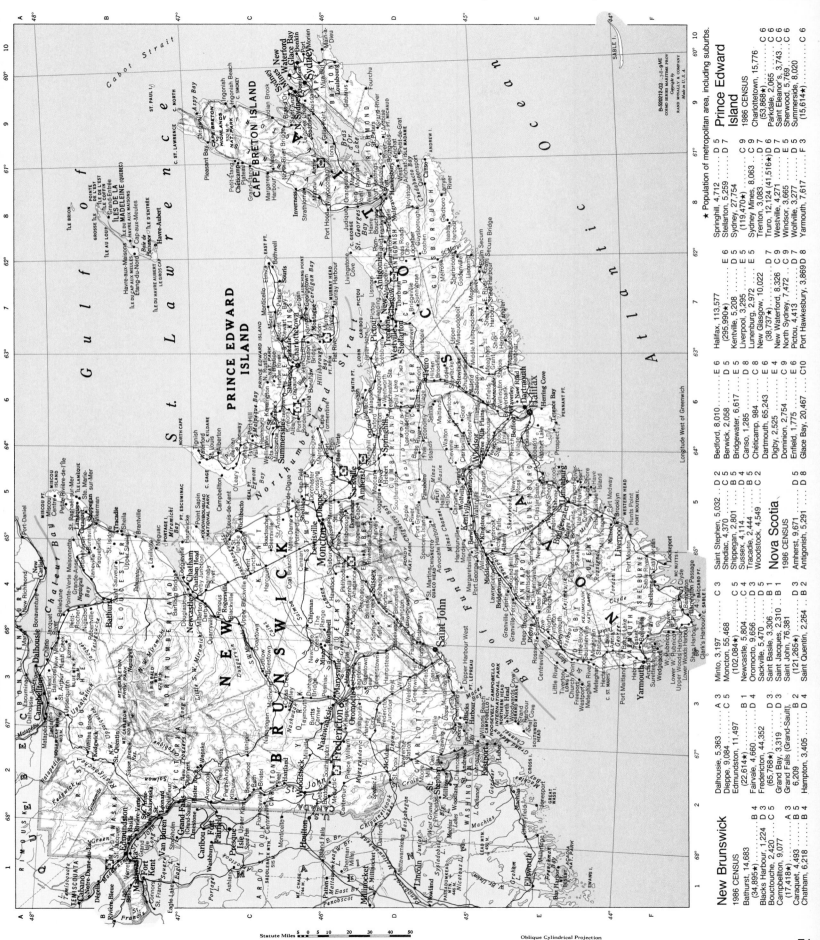

★ Population of metropolitan area, including suburbs.

Prince Edward Island

1986 CENSUS

Charlottetown, 15,776		
(53,868★)	C 6	
Parkdale, 2,065	C 6	
Saint Eleanor's, 3,743	C 6	
Sherwood, 5,769	C 6	
Summerside, 8,020		
(15,614★)	C 6	

New Brunswick

1986 CENSUS

Bathurst, 14,683		
(34,895★)	B 4	
Blacks Harbour, 1,224	C 3	
Bouctouche, 2,420	C 5	
Campbellton, 9,077		
(17,418★)	A 3	
Caraquet, 4,493	B 5	
Chatham, 6,218	B 4	
Dalhousie, 5,363	A 3	
Dieppe, 9,084	C 5	
Edmundston, 11,497		
(22,614★)	B 1	
Fairvale, 4,660	D 4	
Fredericton, 44,352		
(65,768★)	C 3	
Grand Bay, 3,319	D 3	
Grand Falls (Grand-Sault),		
(17,418★)	A 3	
Hampton, 3,405	D 4	
Minto, 3,197	C 3	
Moncton, 55,468		
(102,084★)	C 5	
Newcastle, 5,804	B 4	
Oromocto, 9,656	C 3	
Sackville, 5,470	C 5	
Saint Basile, 3,306	B 1	
Saint Jacques, 2,310	B 1	
Saint John, 76,381		
(121,265★)	D 3	
Saint Quentin, 2,264	B 2	
Saint Stephen, 5,032	C 3	
Shediac, 4,370	C 5	
Shippegan, 2,801	B 5	
Sussex, 4,114	D 4	
Tracadie, 2,444	B 5	
Woodstock, 4,549	C 2	

Nova Scotia

1986 CENSUS

Amherst, 9,671	D 5	
Antigonish, 5,291	D 8	
Bedford, 8,010	E 6	
Berwick, 2,058	D 5	
Bridgewater, 6,617	E 5	
Canso, 1,285	D 8	
Chéticamp, 984	C 8	
Dartmouth, 65,243	E 6	
Digby, 2,525	D 4	
Enfield, 1,775	E 6	
Glace Bay, 20,467	C10	
Halifax, 113,577		
(295,990★)	E 6	
Kentville, 5,208	D 5	
Liverpool, 5,208	E 5	
Lunenburg, 2,972	E 5	
New Glasgow, 10,022	D 7	
New Waterford, 8,326	C 9	
North Sydney, 7,472	C 9	
Pictou, 4,413	D 7	
Port Hawkesbury, 3,869	D 8	
Springhill, 4,712	D 5	
Stellarton, 5,259	D 7	
Sydney, 27,754		
(119,470★)	C 9	
Sydney Mines, 8,063	C 9	
Trenton, 3,083	D 7	
Truro, 12,124 (41,516★)	D 6	
(38,737★)	D 7	
Westville, 4,271	D 7	
Windsor, 3,665	E 5	
Wolfville, 3,277	D 5	
Yarmouth, 7,617	F 3	

Statute Miles 5 0 5 10 20 30 40 50
Kilometers 5 0 5 15 25 35 45 55 65 75

Oblique Cylindrical Projection

Newfoundland

Newfoundland and Labrador

1986 CENSUS

Arnold's Cove, 1,117 . . . E 4
Badger, 1,151 . . . . . D 3
Baie Verte, 2,049 . . . . D 3
Bay Bulls, 1,114 . . . . E 5
Bay Roberts, 4,446 . . . E 5
Bishop's Falls, 4,213 . . D 4
Bonavista, 4,605 . . . . D 5
Botwood, 3,916 . . . . D 4
Buchans, 1,281 . . . . D 3
Burgeo, 2,582 . . . . . E 3
Burin, 2,892 . . . . . E 4
Burnt Islands, 1,042 . . E 2
Carbonear, 5,337
   (13,082★) . . . . . E 5
Carmanville, 987 . . . . D 4
Cartwright, 674 . . . . B 3
Catalina, 1,211 . . . . D 5
Channel-Port-aux-
   Basques, 5,901 . . . E 2
Clarenville, 2,967 . . . D 4
Conception Bay South,
   15,531 . . . . . . E 5
Corner Brook, 22,719
   (33,730★) . . . . . D 3
Cox's Cove, 999 . . . . D 3
Deer Lake, 4,233 . . . . D 3
Dunville, 1,833 . . . . E 5
Durrell, 1,060 . . . . D 4
Englee, 1,012 . . . . C 3
Fogo, 1,153 . . . . . D 4
Fortune, 2,370 . . . . E 4
Gambo, 2,723 . . . . D 4
Gander, 10,207 . . . . D 4
Glenwood, 1,038 . . . . D 4
Glovertown, 2,184 . . . D 4
Grand Bank, 3,732 . . . E 4
Grand Falls, 9,121
   (25,612★) . . . . . D 4
Hampden, 875 . . . . . D 3
Happy Valley-Goose Bay,
   7,248 . . . . B 1
Harbour Breton,
   2,432 . . . . . . E 4
Harbour Grace, 3,053 E 5
Hare Bay, 1,436 . . . . D 4
Hermitage, 831 . . . . E 4
Isle-aux-Morts, 1,203 . E 2
Joe Batt's Arm [-Barr'd
   Islands-Shoal Bay],
   1,232 . . . . . . D 4
King's Point, 923 . . . D 3
Labrador City, 8,664
   (11,301★) . . . . . h 8
Lark Harbour, 829 . . . D 3
La Scie, 1,429 . . . . D 4
Lawn, 1,015 . . . . . E 4
Lewisporte, 3,978 . . . D 4
Lourdes, 937 . . . . . D 2
Marystown, 6,660 . . E 4
Milltown [-Head of Bay
   d'Espoir], 1,276 . . E 4
Mount Pearl, 20,293 . E 5
Musgrave Harbour,
   1,527 . . . . . . D 5
Nain, 1,018 . . . . . g 9
New Harbour, 957 . . . E 5
Norris Arm, 1,127 . . . D 4
Norris Point, 1,010 . . D 3
Pasadena, 3,268 . . . D 3
Placentia, 2,016 . . . E 5
Point Leamington,
   850 . . . . D 4
Port au Port [West-
   Aguathuna-Felix Cove],
   842 . . . . D 2
Pouch Cove, 1,576 . . E 5
Ramea, 1,380 . . . . E 2
Robert's Arm, 1,111 . . D 4
Rocky Harbour, 1,268 D 3
Roddickton, 923 . . . D 3
Rose-Blanche [-Harbour le
   Cou], 967 . . . . . E 2
Saint Alban's, 1,780 . . E 4
Saint Anthony, 3,182 C 4
Saint George's, 1,852 D 2
Saint John's, 96,216
   (161,901★) . . . . E 5
Saint Lawrence,
   1,841 . . . . . . E 4
Shoal Harbour, 1,049 D 4
Spaniard's Bay, 2,190 E 5
Springdale, 3,555 . . . D 4
Stephenville, 7,994 . . D 2
Stephenville Crossing,
   2,252 . . . . . . D 2
Summerford, 1,169 . . D 4
Torbay, 3,730 . . . . E 5
Trepassey, 1,460 . . . E 5
Twillingate, 1,506 . . . D 4
Upper Island Cove,
   2,055 . . . . . . E 5
Victoria, 1,895 . . . . E 5
Wabana (Bell Island),
   4,057 . . . . . . E 5
Wabush, 2,637 . . . . h 8
Wesleyville, 1,208 . . D 5
Whitbourne, 1,151 . . E 5
Windsor, 5,545 . . . . D 4
Witless Bay, 1,022 . . E 5

★ Population of metropolitan
   area, including suburbs.

72

COSMO SERIES NEWFOUNDLAND
Copyright by
RAND McNALLY & COMPANY
Made in U.S.A.
B-520204-02 -6-9-1 ME

Lambert Conformal Conic Projection

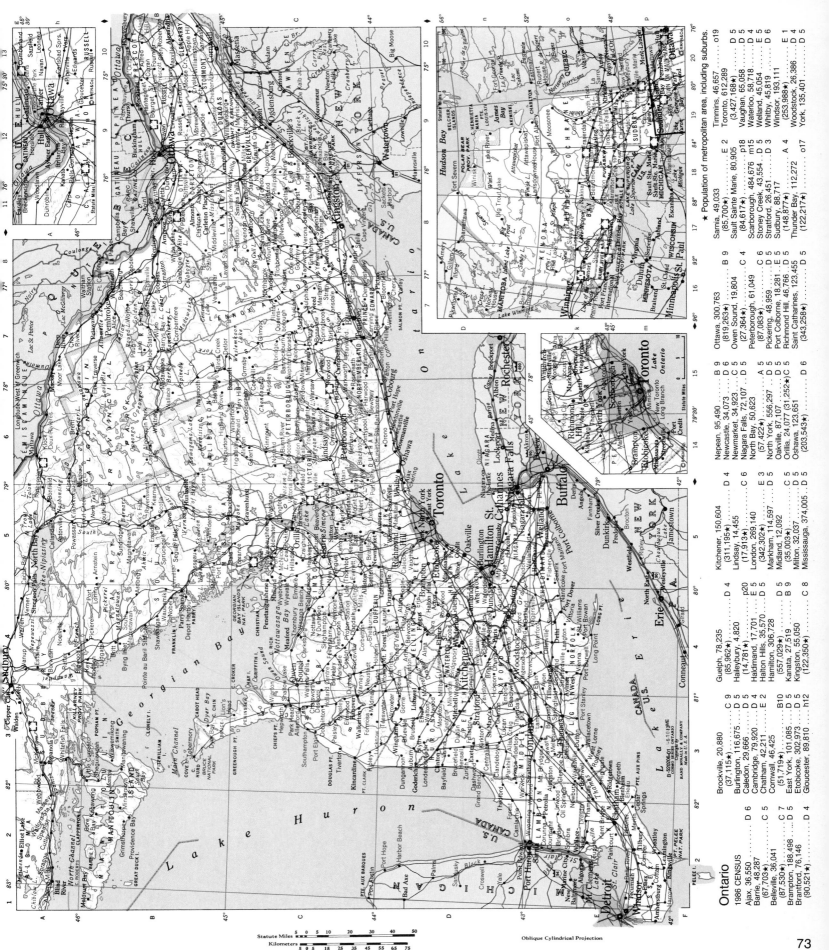

Oblique Cylindrical Projection

* Population of metropolitan area, including suburbs.

Ontario

1986 CENSUS

Ajax, 36,550	D 6	
Barrie, 48,287	C 5	
(67,703★)		
Belleville, 36,041	C 7	
(87,530★)		
Brampton, 188,498	D 5	
Brantford, 76,146	D 4	
(90,521★)		
Brockville, 20,880	C 9	
(37,115★)		
Burlington, 116,675	D 5	
(85,962★)		
Caledon, 29,666	D 4	
Cambridge, 79,920	D 4	
Chatham, 42,211	E 2	
Cornwall, 46,425	B10	
(51,719★)		
East York, 101,085	D 5	
Etobicoke, 302,973	D 5	
Gloucester, 89,810	D 4	
Guelph, 78,235	D 4	
(85,962★)		
Haileybury, 4,820	p20	
(14,781★)		
Haldimand, 17,701	E 5	
Halton Hills, 35,570	D 5	
Hamilton, 306,728	D 5	
(557,029★)		
Kanata, 27,519	B 9	
Kingston, 55,050	C 8	
Kitchener, 150,604	D 4	
(311,195★)		
Lindsay, 14,455	C 6	
(17,913★)		
London, 269,140	D 3	
(342,302★)		
Markham, 114,597	D 5	
Midland, 12,092	C 5	
Mississauga, 374,005	D 5	
Nepean, 95,490	B 9	
Newcastle, 34,073	D 6	
Newmarket, 34,923	C 5	
Niagara Falls, 72,107	D 5	
North Bay, 50,623	A 5	
(57,422★)		
North York, 556,297	D 5	
Oakville, 87,107	D 5	
Orillia, 24,077 (31,252★)	C 5	
Oshawa, 123,651	D 5	
(203,543★)		
Ottawa, 300,763	B 9	
(819,263★)		
Owen Sound, 19,804	C 4	
(27,364★)		
Peterborough, 61,049	C 6	
(87,083★)		
Pickering, 48,959	D 5	
Port Colborne, 18,281	E 5	
Richmond Hill, 46,766	D 5	
(148,877★)		
Saint Catharines, 123,455	D 5	
(343,258★)		
Sarnia, 49,033	E 2	
(85,700★)		
Sault Sainte Marie, 80,905	p18	
(84,617★)		
Scarborough, 484,676	m15	
Stoney Creek, 43,554	D 5	
Stratford, 26,451	D 3	
Sudbury, 88,717	E 5	
(253,988★)		
Thunder Bay, 112,272	E 4	
(122,217★)		
Timmins, 46,657	o19	
Toronto, 612,289	D 5	
(3,427,168★)		
Vaughan, 65,058	D 4	
Waterloo, 58,718	D 4	
Welland, 45,054	E 5	
Whitby, 45,819	D 6	
Windsor, 193,111		
Woodstock, 26,386	D 4	
York, 135,401	D 5	

Statute Miles 5 0 5 10 20 30 40 50

Kilometers 5 0 5 15 25 35 45 55 65 75

Quebec

1986 CENSUS

Alma, 25,923 (29,977★) .... A 6
Ancienne-Lorette,
 13,747 .... C 6
Anjou, 36,916 .... p19
Aylmer East, 28,976 .... D 2
Baie-Comeau, 26,244
 (33,047★) k13
Beaconsfield, 19,301 ... q19

Beauport, 62,869 .... n17
Boucherville, 31,116 ... D 4
Brossard, 57,441 .... q20
Cap-de-la-Madeleine,
 32,800 .... C 5
Charlesbourg, 68,996 ... n17
Châteauguay, 37,865 .... D 4
Chicoutimi, 61,083
 (158,468★) .... A 6
Drummondville, 36,020 .. D 5

Gaspé, 17,350 .... D 4
Gatineau, 81,244
 (51,176★) .... D 2
Granby, 38,508 .... D 5
Grand-Mère, 14,582 ..... C 5
Hull, 58,722 .... D 2
Joliette, 16,845
 (34,897★) .... C 4
Jonquière, 58,467 ...... A 6
Lachine, 34,906 .... D 4
Lachute, 11,586 .... D 5

LaSalle, 75,621 .... q19
La Tuque, 10,723
 (13,468★) .... B 5
Laval, 284,164 .... D 4
Lévis, 18,310 .... C 6
Longueuil, 125,441 ..... D 4
Magog, 13,530 .... D 5
Mascouche, 21,285 ...... D 4
Matane, 13,243
 (15,361★) k13

Montréal, 1,015,420
 (2,921,357★) .... D 4
Montréal-Nord, 90,303 .. p19
Outremont, 23,080 ...... p19
Pierrefonds, 39,605 .... q19
Pointe-Claire, 26,026 .. q19
Québec, 164,580
 (603,267★) .... C 6
Repentigny, 40,778 ..... D 4
Rimouski, 29,672
 (46,210★) .... D 6

Rivière-du-Loup, 13,321
 (22,471★) .... C 6
Rouyn, 17,319
 (36,495★) .... D 1
Saint-Eustache, 32,226 . D 4
Sainte-Foy, 69,615 ..... n17
Saint-Hubert, 66,218 ... q20
Saint-Hyacinthe, 38,603
 (48,303★) .... D 5
Saint-Jean-sur-Richelieu,
 34,745 (59,958★) ..... D 4

Saint-Jérôme, 23,316
 (44,048★) .... C 4
Saint-Laurent, 67,002 .. p19
Salaberry-de-Valleyfield,
 27,942 (38,797★) ..... D 3
Sept-Îles (Seven Islands),
 25,637 (28,050★) h13
Shawinigan, 21,412 ..... C 5

Sorel, 19,522 (46,096★) . C 4
Terrebonne, 31,310 ..... D 4
Thetford Mines, 18,561
 (31,940★) .... C 6
Trois-Rivières, 50,122
 (128,888★) .... C 5
Verdun, 60,246 .... q19
Victoriaville, 21,587
 (21,965★) .... C 5
Ville Saint-Georges, 11,723
 (21,022★) .... C 7

★ Population of metropolitan area, including suburbs.

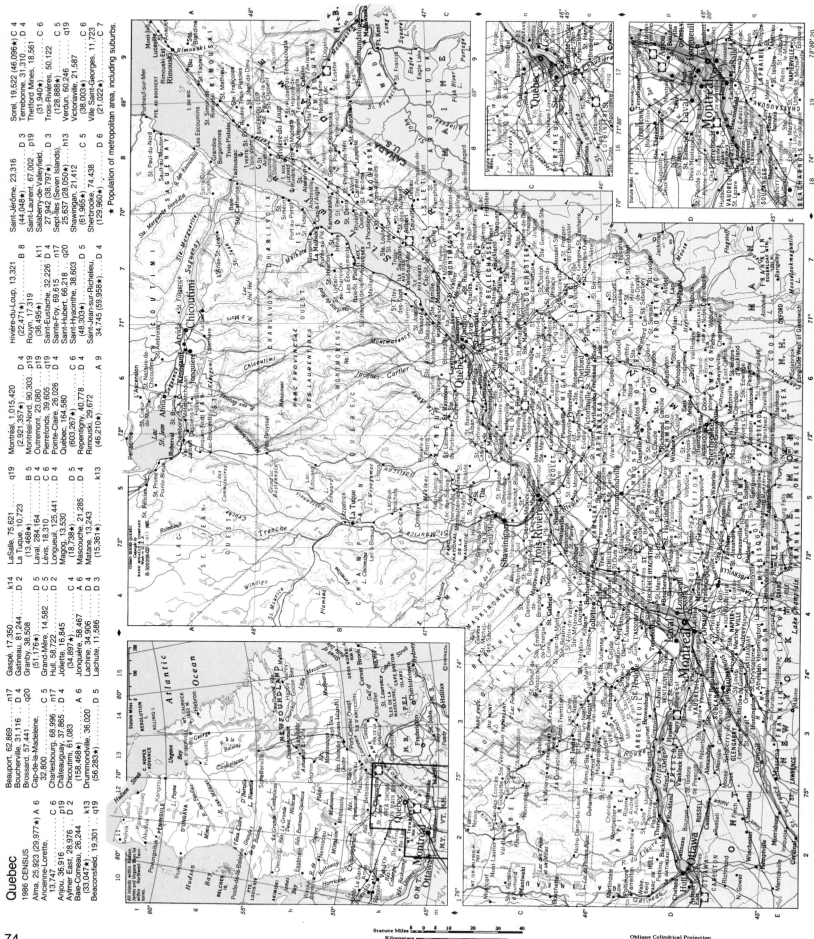

Statute Miles
Kilometers

Oblique Cylindrical Projection

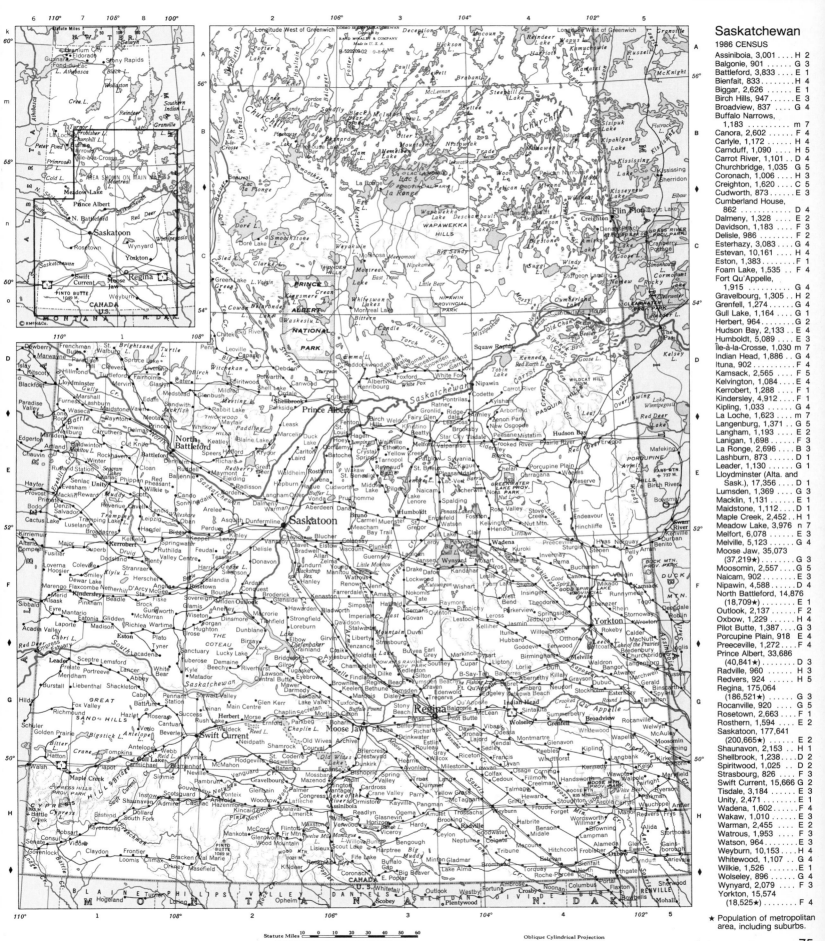

Saskatchewan

1986 CENSUS

Assiniboia, 3,001 . . . . H 2
Balgonie, 901 . . . . . . G 3
Battleford, 3,833 . . . . E 1
Bienfait, 833 . . . . . . H 4
Biggar, 2,626 . . . . . . E 1
Birch Hills, 947 . . . . E 3
Broadview, 837 . . . . . G 4
Buffalo Narrows,
1,183 . . . . m 7
Canora, 2,602 . . . . . F 4
Carlyle, 1,172 . . . . . H 4
Carnduff, 1,090 . . . . H 4
Carrot River, 1,101 . . D 4
Churchbridge, 1,035 . G 5
Coronach, 1,006 . . . H 3
Creighton, 1,620 . . . C 5
Cudworth, 873 . . . . . E 3
Cumberland House,
862 . . . . D 4
Dalmeny, 1,328 . . . . E 2
Davidson, 1,183 . . . . F 3
Delisle, 986 . . . . . . F 2
Esterhazy, 3,083 . . . G 4
Estevan, 10,161 . . . . H 4
Eston, 1,383 . . . . . . F 1
Foam Lake, 1,535 . . . F 4
Fort Qu'Appelle,
1,915 . . . . G 4
Gravelbourg, 1,305 . . H 2
Grenfell, 1,274 . . . . G 4
Gull Lake, 1,164 . . . G 1
Herbert, 964 . . . . . . G 2
Hudson Bay, 2,133 . . F 4
Humboldt, 5,089 . . . E 3
Île-à-la-Crosse, 1,030 m 7
Indian Head, 1,886 . . G 4
Ituna, 902 . . . . F 4
Kamsack, 2,565 . . . . F 5
Kelvington, 1,084 . . . E 4
Kerrobert, 1,288 . . . F 1
Kindersley, 4,912 . . . F 1
Kipling, 1,033 . . . . . G 4
La Loche, 1,623 . . . . m 7
Langenburg, 1,371 . . G 5
Langham, 1,193 . . . . G 2
Lanigan, 1,698 . . . . F 3
La Ronge, 2,696 . . . B 3
Lashburn, 873 . . . . . D 1
Leader, 1,130 . . . . . G 1
Lloydminster (Alta. and
Sask.), 17,356 . . . . D 1
Lumsden, 1,369 . . . . G 3
Macklin, 1,131 . . . . . E 1
Maidstone, 1,112 . . . D 1
Maple Creek, 2,452 . . H 1
Meadow Lake, 3,976 . n 7
Melfort, 6,078 . . . . . E 3
Melville, 5,123 . . . . . G 4
Moose Jaw, 35,073
(37,219★) . . . . G 3
Moosomin, 2,557 . . . G 5
Naicam, 902 . . . . . . E 3
Nipawin, 4,588 . . . . D 4
North Battleford, 14,876
(18,709★) . . . . E 1
Outlook, 2,137 . . . . F 2
Oxbow, 1,229 . . . . . H 4
Pilot Butte, 1,387 . . . G 3
Porcupine Plain, 918 . E 4
Preeceville, 1,272 . . . F 4
Prince Albert, 33,686
(40,841★) . . . . D 3
Radville, 960 . . . . . H 3
Redvers, 924 . . . . . H 5
Regina, 175,064
(186,521★) . . . . . . G 3
Rocanville, 920 . . . . G 5
Rosetown, 2,663 . . . F 1
Rosthern, 1,594 . . . . E 2
Saskatoon, 177,641
(200,665★) . . . . . . E 2
Shaunavon, 2,153 . . . H 1
Shellbrook, 1,238 . . . D 2
Spiritwood, 1,025 . . . D 2
Strasbourg, 826 . . . . F 3
Swift Current, 15,666 G 2
Tisdale, 3,184 . . . . . E 3
Unity, 2,471 . . . . . . E 1
Wadena, 1,602 . . . . F 4
Wakaw, 1,010 . . . . . E 3
Warman, 2,455 . . . . E 2
Watrous, 1,953 . . . . F 3
Watson, 964 . . . . . . E 3
Weyburn, 10,153 . . . H 4
Whitewood, 1,107 . . A 4
Wilkie, 1,526 . . . . . E 1
Wolseley, 896 . . . . . G 4
Wynyard, 2,079 . . . . F 3
Yorkton, 15,574
(18,525★) . . . . F 4

★ Population of metropolitan
area, including suburbs.

United States of America

Akron, 223,019 ('90)...C10
ALABAMA..............E 9
ALASKA................M19
Albany, 101,082 ('90)..C12
Albuquerque, 384,736
  ('90)..................D 5
Amarillo, 157,615 ('90)D 6
Anchorage, 226,338
  ('90)..................M20
Annapolis, 33,187
  ('90)..................D11
ARIZONA...............E 4
ARKANSAS..............E 8.
Atlanta, 394,017 ('90)..E 9
Augusta, 21,325 ('90)..C13
Austin, 465,622 ('90)...E 7
Baltimore, 736,014
  ('90)..................D11
Baton Rouge, 219,531
  ('90)..................E 8
Billings, 81,151 ('90)...B 5
Birmingham, 265,968
  ('90)..................E 9
Bismarck, 49,256 ('90)B 6
Boise, 125,738 ('90)....C 3
Boston, 574,283 ('90)..C12
Buffalo, 328,123 ('90)..C11
CALIFORNIA............D 2
Carson City, 40,443
  ('90)..................D 3
Charleston, 57,287
  ('90)..................D10
Charleston, 80,414
  ('90)..................E11
Charlotte, 395,934
  ('90)..................D10
Chattanooga, 152,466
  ('90)..................D 9
Cheyenne, 50,008
  ('90)..................C 6
Chicago, 2,783,726
  ('90)..................C 9
Cincinnati, 364,040
  ('90)..................D10
Cleveland, 505,616
  ('90)..................C10
COLORADO.............D 5
Colorado Springs, 281,140
  ('90)..................D 6
Columbia, 98,052 ('90)E10
Columbus, 178,681
  ('90)..................E10
Columbus, 632,910
  ('90)..................D10
Concord, 36,006 ('90).C12
CONNECTICUT..........C12
Dallas, 1,006,877 ('90).E 7
DELAWARE.............D11
Denver, 467,610 ('90).D 6
Des Moines, 193,187
  ('90)..................C 8
Detroit, 1,027,974
  ('90)..................C10
Dover, 27,630 ('90).....D11
El Paso, 515,342 ('90).E 5
FLORIDA...............F10
Fort Wayne, 173,072
  ('90)..................C 9
Fort Worth, 447,619
  ('90)..................E 7
Frankfort, 25,968 ('90)D10
Fresno, 354,202 ('90)..D 3
GEORGIA...............E10
Grand Rapids, 189,126
  ('90)..................C 9
Harrisburg, 52,376
  ('90)..................C11
Hartford, 139,739
  ('90)..................C12
Helena, 24,569 ('90)....B 4
Houston, 1,630,553
  ('90)..................F 7
IDAHO.................C 4
ILLINOIS..............C 9
INDIANA...............C 9
Indianapolis, 731,327
  ('90)..................D 9
IOWA..................C 8
Jackson, 196,637 ('90)E 8
Jacksonville, 635,230
  ('90)..................E10
Jefferson City, 35,481
  ('90)..................D 8
Juneau, 26,751 ('90)...N21
KANSAS................D 7
Kansas City, 435,146
  ('90)..................D 8
KENTUCKY.............D 9
Knoxville, 165,121
  ('90)..................D10
Las Vegas, 258,295
  ('90)..................D 3
Lincoln, 191,972 ('90)..C 7
Little Rock, 175,795
  ('90)..................E 8
Los Angeles, 3,485,398
  ('90)..................E 3
LOUISIANA............E 8
Louisville, 269,063
  ('90)..................D 9
Madison, 191,262
  ('90)..................C 9
MAINE.................B13
MARYLAND.............D11

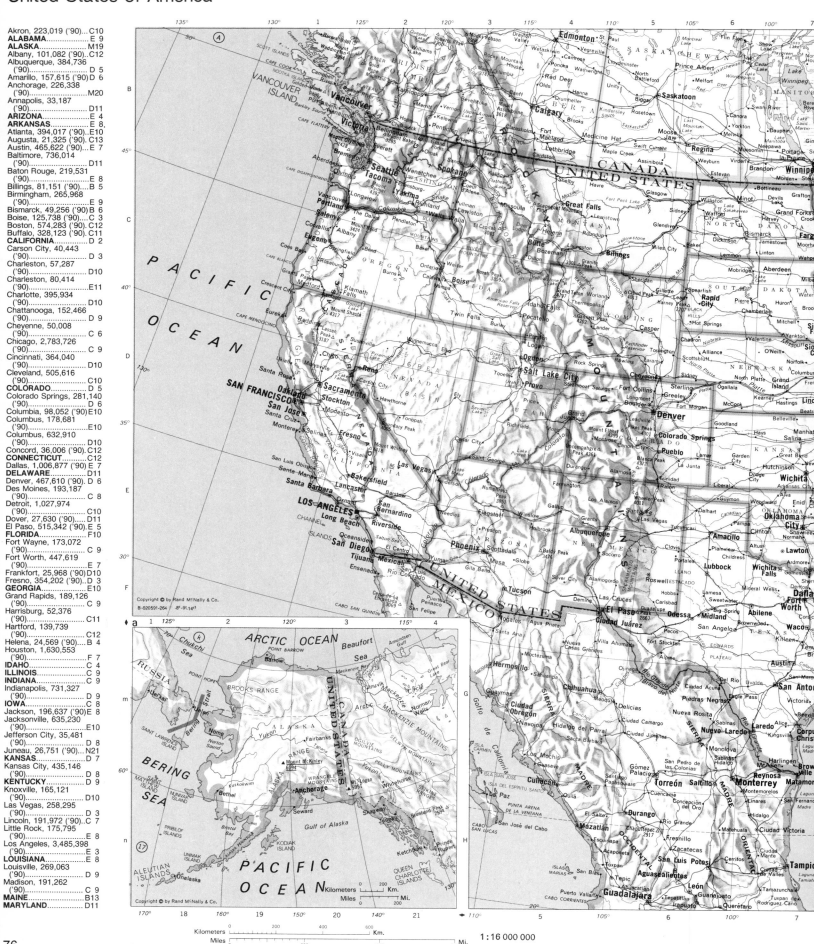

MASSACHUSETTS.....C12
Memphis, 610,337
  ('90)................D 8
Miami, 358,548 ('90)...F10
MICHIGAN...........C10
Milwaukee, 628,088
  ('90)................C 9
Minneapolis, 368,383
  ('90)................C 8
MINNESOTA........B 8
MISSISSIPPI.......E 9
MISSOURI...........D 8
Mobile, 196,278 ('90)..E 9
MONTANA..........B 5
Montgomery, 187,106
  ('90)................C12
Montpelier, 8,247 ('90)C12
Nashville, 487,969
  ('90)................D 9
NEBRASKA.........C 7
NEVADA............D 3
Newark, 275,221 ('90) C12
NEW HAMPSHIRE...C12
NEW JERSEY........C12
NEW MEXICO......E 5
New Orleans, 496,938
  ('90)................F 8
NEW YORK........C11
New York, 7,322,564
  ('90)................C12
Norfolk, 261,229 ('90).D11
NORTH CAROLINA...D11
NORTH DAKOTA....B 6
Oakland, 372,242 ('90) D 2
OHIO................C10
OKLAHOMA.......D 7
Oklahoma City, 444,719
  ('90)................D 7
Olympia, 33,840 ('90)..B 2
Omaha, 335,795 ('90). C 7
OREGON...........C 2
PENNSYLVANIA....C11
Philadelphia, 1,585,577
  ('90)................D11
Phoenix, 900,013 ('90) E 4
Pierre, 12,906 ('90)....C 6
Pittsburgh, 369,879
  ('90)................C11
Portland, 64,358 ('90). C12
Providence, 160,728
  ('90)................C12
Raleigh, 207,951 ('90).D11
Rapid City, 54,523
  ('90)................C 6
Reno, 133,850 ('90)....D 3
RHODE ISLAND.........C12
Richmond, 203,056
  ('90)................D11
Rochester, 231,636
  ('90)................C11
Sacramento, 369,365
  ('90)................D 2
Saint Louis, 396,685
  ('90)................D 8
Saint Paul, 272,235
  ('90)................C 8
Saint Petersburg, 238,629
  ('90)................F10
Salem, 107,786 ('90)...C 2
Salt Lake City, 159,936
  ('90)................C 4
San Antonio, 935,933
  ('90)................F 7
San Diego, 1,110,549
  ('90)................E 3
San Francisco, 723,959
  ('90)................D 2
San Jose, 782,248
  ('90)................D 2
Santa Fe, 55,859 ('90) D 5
Savannah, 137,560
  ('90)................E10
Seattle, 516,259 ('90)..B 2
Shreveport, 198,525
  ('90)................E 8
SOUTH CAROLINA....E10
SOUTH DAKOTA.....C 7
Spokane, 177,196
  ('90)................B 3
Springfield, 105,227
  ('90)................D 9
Syracuse, 163,860
  ('90)................C11
Tacoma, 176,664 ('90) B 2
Tallahassee, 124,773
  ('90)................E10
Tampa, 280,015 ('90)..F10
TENNESSEE.........D 9
TEXAS...............E 7
Toledo, 332,943 ('90)..C10
Topeka, 119,883 ('90). D 7
Trenton, 88,675 ('90)..C12
Tulsa, 367,302 ('90)....D 7
UNITED STATES.....D 7
UTAH................D 4
VERMONT............C12
VIRGINIA...........D11
WASHINGTON.......B 2
Washington, 606,900
  ('90)................D11
WEST VIRGINIA....D10
Wichita, 304,011 ('90). D 7
WISCONSIN.........C 9
WYOMING...........C 5

Alabama

Alabama

1990 CENSUS

Alabaster, 14,732	. .	B	3
Albertville, 14,507	. .	A	3
Alexander City, 14,917	. .	C	4
Andalusia, 9,269	. .	D	3
Anniston, 26,623	. . .	B	4
Arab, 6,321	. . .	A	3
Athens, 16,901	. . . .	A	3
Atmore, 8,046	. . . .	D	2
Attalla, 6,859	. . . .	A	3
Auburn, 33,830	. . . .	C	4
Bay Minette, 7,168	. .	E	2
Bessemer, 33,497	. . .	B	3
Birmingham, 265,968	B	3
Bluff Park, 8,000('85)	g	7
Boaz, 6,928	. . . .	A	3
Brewton, 5,885	. . .	D	2
Center Point, 22,000('85)	. . .	f	7
Chickasaw, 6,649	. .	E	1
Childersburg, 4,579	. .	B	3
Clanton, 7,669	. . .	C	3
Cullman, 13,367	. . .	A	3
Decatur, 48,761	. . . .	A	3
Demopolis, 7,512	. . .	C	2
Dothan, 53,589	. . . .	D	4
Enterprise, 20,123	. .	D	4
Eufaula, 13,220	. . .	C	5
Fairfield, 12,200	. . . .	B	3
Fairhope, 8,485	. . .	E	2
Fayette, 4,909	. . . .	B	2
Florence, 36,426	. . . .	A	2
Fort Payne, 11,838	. .	A	4
Frisco City, 1,581	. . .	D	2
Fultondale, 6,400	. . .	f	7
Gadsden, 42,523	. . .	A	3
Gardendale, 9,251	. .	B	3
Geneva, 4,681	. . . .	D	4
Greenville, 7,492	. . .	D	3
Guntersville, 7,038	. .	A	3
Haleyville, 4,452	. . .	A	2
Hamilton, 5,787	. . . .	A	2
Hartselle, 10,795	. . .	A	3
Homewood, 22,922	. .	g	7
Hueytown, 15,280	. .	g	6
Huntsville, 159,789	. .	A	3
Irondale, 9,454	. . . .	f	7
Jackson, 5,819	. . . .	D	2
Jacksonville, 10,283	. .	B	4
Jasper, 13,553	. . . .	B	2
Lanett, 8,985	. . . . .	C	4
Leeds, 9,946	. . . . .	B	3
Millbrook, 6,050	. . . .	C	3
Mobile, 196,278	. . . .	E	1
Monroeville, 6,993	. .	D	2
Montgomery, 187,106	C	3
Moundville, 1,348	. . . .	C	2
Mountain Brook, 19,810	. . . .	g	7
Muscle Shoals, 9,611	A	2
Northport, 17,366	. . .	B	2
Oneonta, 4,844	. . . .	B	3
Opelika, 22,122	. . . .	C	4
Opp, 6,985	. . . . .	D	3
Oxford, 9,362	. . . .	B	4
Ozark, 12,922	. . . .	D	4
Pelham, 9,765	. . . .	B	3
Pell City, 8,118	. . . .	B	3
Phenix City, 25,312	. .	C	4
Piedmont, 5,288	. . . .	B	4
Pleasant Grove, 8,458	g	7
Prattville, 19,587	. . .	C	3
Prichard, 34,311	. . .	E	1
Rainbow City, 7,673	. .	A	3
Roanoke, 6,362	. . . .	B	4
Russellville, 7,812	. .	A	2
Saraland, 11,751	. . .	E	1
Scottsboro, 13,786	. .	A	3
Selma, 23,755	. . . .	C	2
Sheffield, 10,380	. . .	A	2
Spanish Fort, 3,415('80)	. . . . . .	E	2
Sylacauga, 12,520	. .	B	3
Talladega, 18,175	. .	B	3
Tallassee, 5,112	. . .	C	4
Tarrant, 8,046	. . . .	B	3
Theodore, 6,392('80)	. .	E	1
Tillmans Corner, 5,000('85)	. . . . .	E	1
Troy, 13,051	. . . . .	D	4
Tuscaloosa, 77,759	. .	B	2
Tuscumbia, 8,413	. . .	A	2
Tuskegee, 12,257	. . .	C	4
Vestavia Hills, 19,749	g	7
Warrior, 3,280	. . . .	B	3
Wetumpka, 4,670	. .	C	3

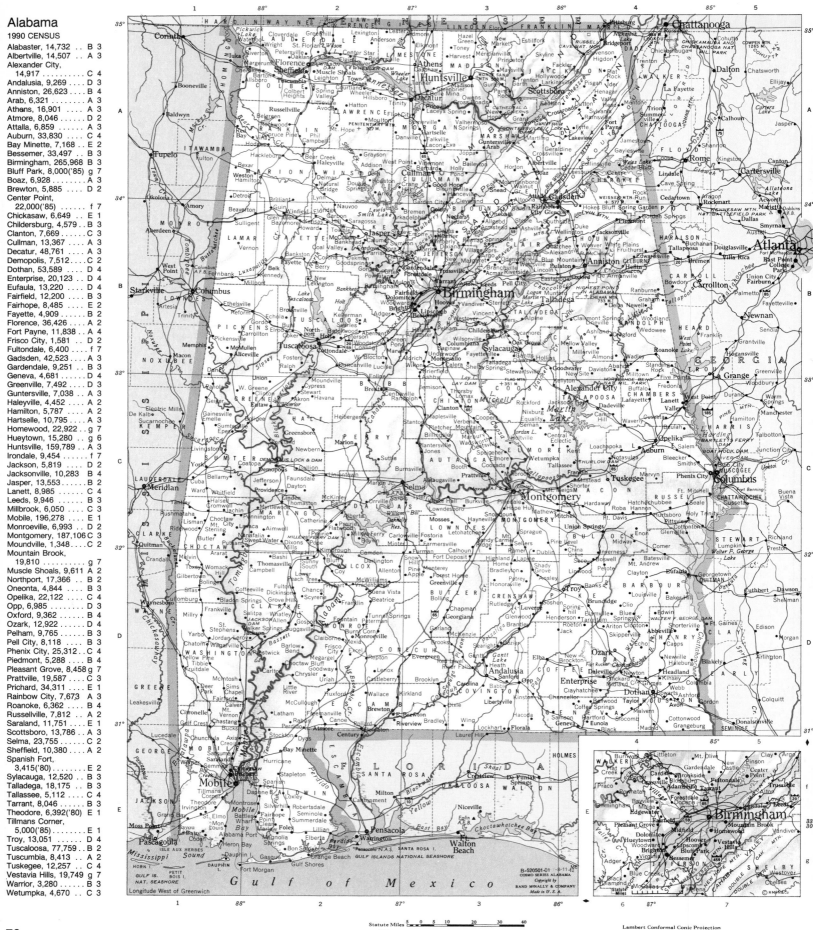

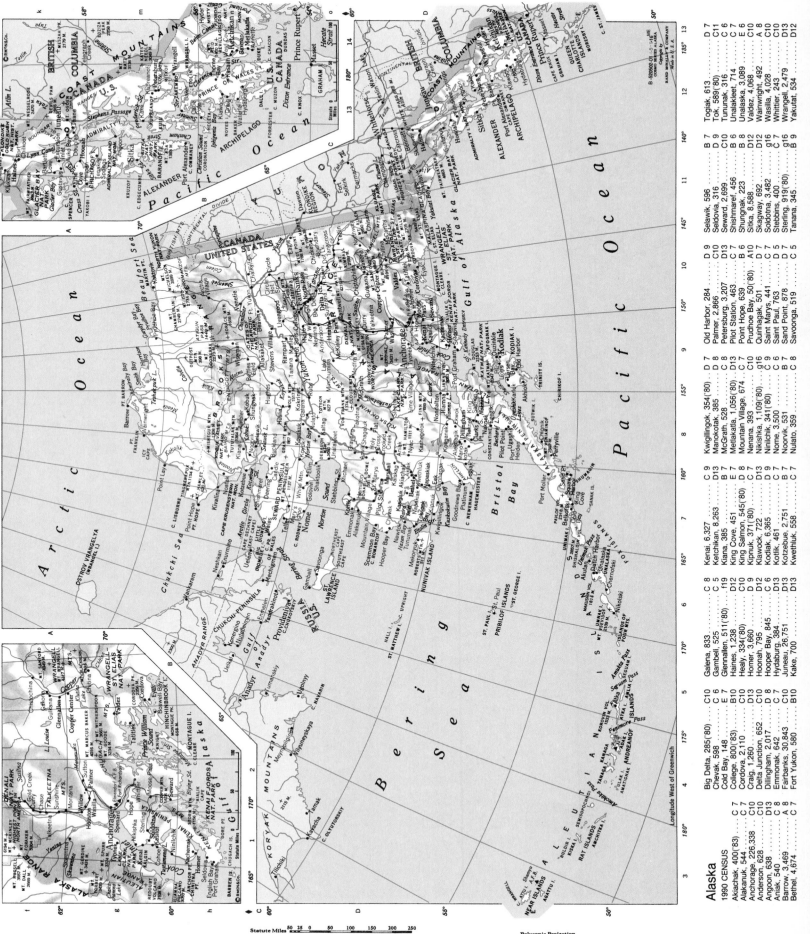

Alaska
1990 CENSUS

Akiachak, 400('83) ..... C 7
Alakanuk, 544 ..... C 7
Anchorage, 226,338 ..... C10
Anderson, 628 ..... C10
Angoon, 638 ..... D13
Aniak, 540 ..... C 8
Barrow, 3,469 ..... A 8
Bethel, 4,674 ..... C 7

Big Delta, 285('80) C10
Chevak, 598 ..... C 6
Cold Bay, 148 ..... E 7
College, 800('83) B10
Cordova, 2,110 ..... C10
Craig, 1,260 ..... D13
Delta Junction, 652 ..... C10
Dillingham, 2,017 ..... D 8
Emmonak, 642 ..... C 7
Fairbanks, 30,843 ..... C10
Fort Yukon, 580 ..... B10

Galena, 833 ..... C 8
Gambell, 525 ..... C 5
Glennallen, 511('80) C10
Haines, 385 ..... D12
Healy, 334('80) C10
Homer, 3,660 ..... D 9
Hoonah, 795 ..... D12
Hooper Bay, 845 ..... C 6
Hydaburg, 384 ..... D13
Juneau, 26,751 ..... D13
Kake, 700 ..... D13

Kenai, 6,327 ..... C 9
Ketchikan, 8,263 ..... D13
Kiana, 385 ..... B 7
King Cove, 451 ..... E 7
King Salmon, 545('80) ..... D 8
Kipnuk, 371('80) ..... C 7
Klawock, 722 ..... D13
Kodiak, 6,365 ..... D 9
Kotlik, 461 ..... C 6
Kotzebue, 2,751 ..... B 7
Kwethluk, 558 ..... C 7

Kwigillingok, 354('80) ..... C 9
Manokotak, 385 ..... D 8
McGrath, 528 ..... C 8
Metlakatla, 1,056('80) D13
Mountain Village, 674 ..... C 7
Nenana, 393 ..... C10
Nikishka, 1,109('80) g16
Ninilchik, 341('80) ..... D 9
Nome, 3,500 ..... C 6
Noorvik, 531 ..... B 7
Nulato, 359 ..... C 8

Old Harbor, 284 ..... D 7
Palmer, 2,866 ..... C10
Petersburg, 3,207 ..... D13
Pilot Station, 463 ..... C 7
Point Hope, 639 ..... B 6
Prudhoe Bay, 50('80) A10
Quinhagak, 501 ..... D 7
Saint Marys, 441 ..... C 7
Saint Paul, 763 ..... D 6
Sand Point, 878 ..... B 7
Savoonga, 519 ..... C 5

Selawik, 596 ..... B 7
Seldovia, 316 ..... D 9
Seward, 2,699 ..... C10
Shishmaref, 456 ..... B 6
Shungnak, 223 ..... B 8
Sitka, 8,588 ..... D12
Skagway, 692 ..... C11
Soldotna, 3,482 ..... g16
Stebbins, 400 ..... C 6
Sterling, 919('80) g16
Tanana, 345 ..... B 9

Togiak, 613 ..... D 7
Tok, 589('80) C11
Tununak, 316 ..... C 6
Unalakleet, 714 ..... C 7
Unalaska, 3,089 ..... E 6
Valdez, 4,068 ..... C10
Wainwright, 492 ..... A 8
Wasilla, 4,028 ..... C10
Whittier, 243 ..... C10
Wrangell, 2,479 ..... D13
Yakutat, 534 ..... D12

B-520502-01 :-5-1-16
COSMO SERIES ALASKA
Compiled by
RAND McNALLY
AND COMPANY
Made in U.S.A.

Longitude West of Greenwich

Statute Miles 50 25 0 50 100 150 200 250
Kilometers 50 0 100 200 300

Polyconic Projection

Arizona

Arizona
1990 CENSUS

Ajo, 5,189('80) . . . . . E 3
Apache Junction,
　18,100 . . . . m 9
Avondale, 16,169 . . . D 3
Bagdad, 2,331('80) . . C 2
Benson, 3,824 . . . . . F 5
Bisbee, 6,288 . . . . . F 6
Black Canyon City,
　850('86) . . . . C 3
Buckeye, 5,038 . . . . D 3
Bullhead City, 21,951 B 1
Camp Verde, 6,243 . . C 4
Casa Grande, 19,082 E 4
Casas Adobes,
　12,155('86) . . . . . D 5
Cashion, 3,014('80) . m 8
Cave Creek, 2,925 . . D 4
Chandler, 90,533 . . . D 4
Chinle, 2,815('80) . . A 6
Chino Valley, 4,837 . C 3
Claypool, 2,362('80) D 5
Clifton, 2,840 . . . . . D 6
Coolidge, 6,927 . . . . E 4
Cottonwood, 5,918 . . C 3
Crane, 2,650('86) . . . E 1
Douglas, 12,822 . . . . F 6
Eagar, 4,025 . . . . . . C 6
El Mirage, 5,001 . . . . k 8
Eloy, 7,211 . . . . E 4
Flagstaff, 45,857 . . . B 4
Florence, 7,510 . . . . D 4
Fort Defiance,
　3,431('80) . . . . . . B 6
Ganado, 3,400('86) . . B 6
Gila Bend, 1,747 . . . C 4
Gilbert, 29,188 . . . . D 4
Glendale, 148,134 . . D 3
Globe, 6,062 . . . . . . D 5
Goodyear, 6,258 . . . . D 3
Grand Canyon,
　1,348('80) . . . . . . A 3
Green Valley,
　7,999('80) . . . . . . F 5
Guadalupe, 5,458 . . . m 9
Holbrook, 4,686 . . . . C 5
Huachuca City, 1,782 F 5
Kayenta, 3,343('80) . A 5
Kearny, 2,262 . . . . . D 5
Kingman, 12,722 . . . B 1
Lake Havasu City,
　24,363 . . . . C 1
Lakeside-Pinetop,
　2,422 . . . . C 6
Litchfield Park, 3,303 m 8
Mammoth, 1,845 . . . E 5
Mesa, 288,091 . . . . . D 4
Miami, 2,018 . . . . . . D 5
Nogales, 19,489 . . . . F 5
Oracle, 2,484('80) . . E 5
Page, 6,598 . . . . A 4
Paradise Valley,
　11,671 . . . . k 9
Parker, 2,897 . . . . . . C 1
Payson, 8,377 . . . . . C 4
Peoria, 50,618 . . . . . D 3
Phoenix, 900,013 . . . D 3
Prescott, 26,455 . . . C 3
Sacaton, 1,951('80) . D 4
Safford, 7,359 . . . . . E 6
Saint Johns, 3,294 . . C 6
San Carlos,
　2,668('80) . . . . . . D 5
San Luis, 70('86) . . . E 3
San Manuel,
　5,443('80) . . . . . . E 5
Scottsdale, 130,069 . D 4
Sedona, 7,720 . . . . . C 4
Sells, 1,864('80) . . . F 4
Show Low, 5,019 . . . C 5
Sierra Vista, 32,983 . F 5
Snowflake, 3,679 . . . C 5
Somerton, 5,282 . . . . E 1
South Tucson, 5,093 . E 5
Sun City, 57,000 . . . k 8
Superior, 3,468 . . . . D 5
Surprise, 7,122 . . . . k 8
Taylor, 2,418 . . . . . . C 5
Tempe, 141,865 . . . . D 4
Thatcher, 3,763 . . . . E 6
Tolleson, 4,434 . . . . m 8
Tombstone, 1,220 . . . F 5
Tuba City, 5,045('80) A 4
Tucson, 405,390 . . . . E 5
Twin Knolls,
　5,210('86) . . . . . . m 9
Wickenburg, 4,515 . . D 3
Willcox, 3,122 . . . . . E 6
Williams, 2,532 . . . . B 3
Window Rock,
　2,230('80) . . . . . . B 6
Winslow, 8,190 . . . . . k 5
Youngtown, 2,542 . . . k 8
Yuma, 54,923 . . . . . E 1

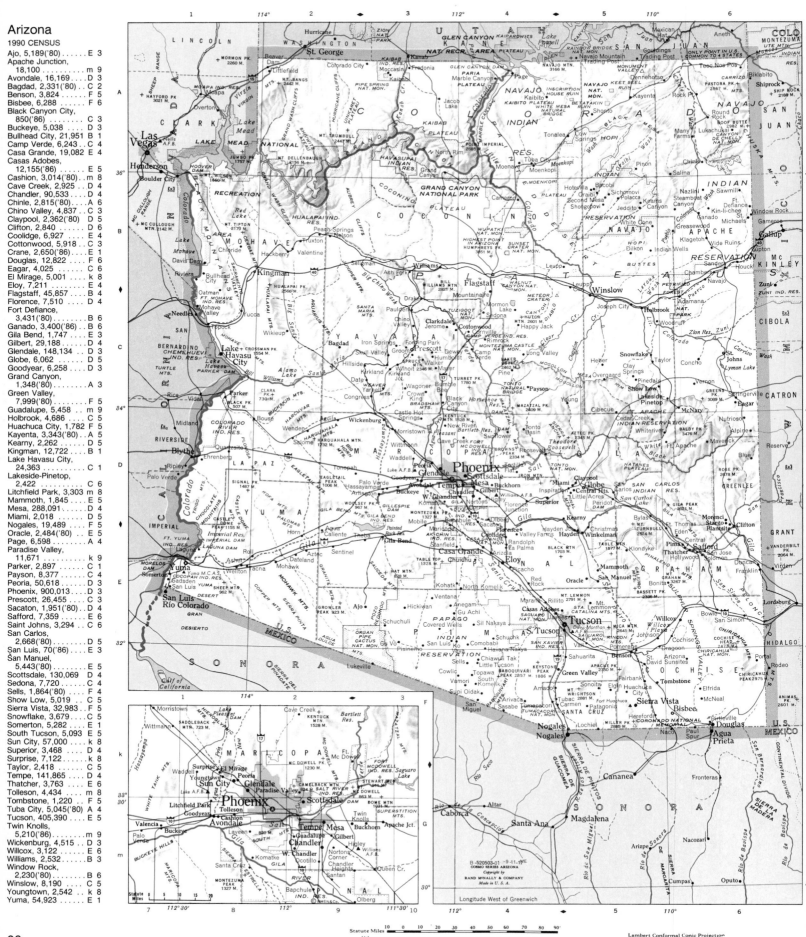

Lambert Conformal Conic Projection

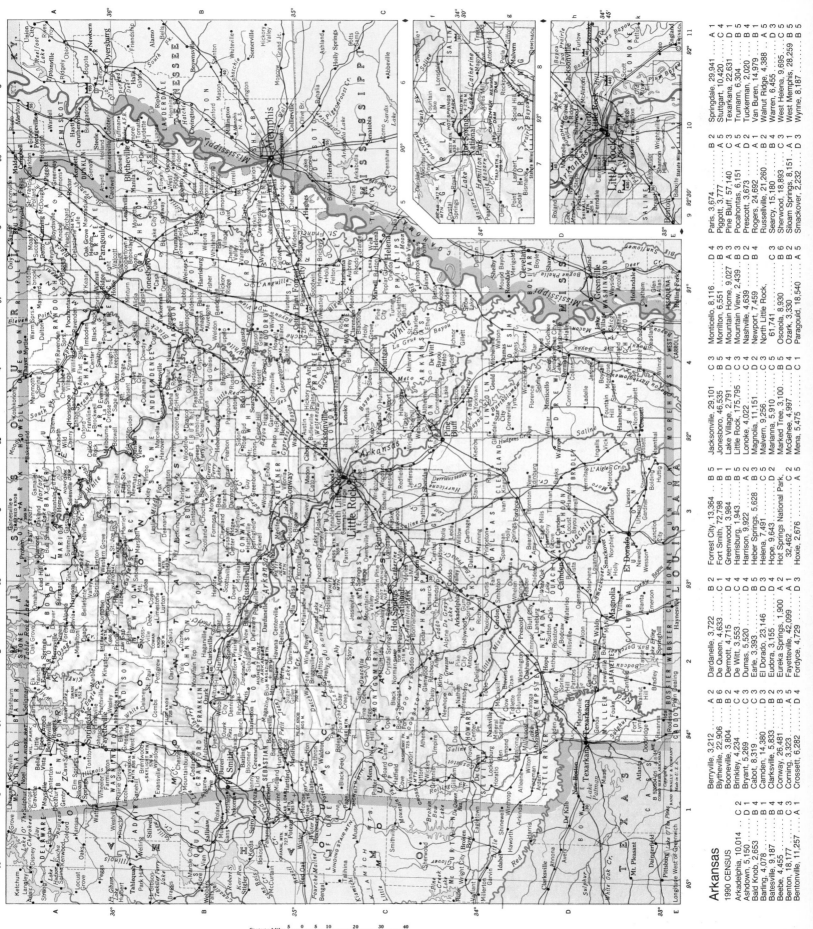

Arkansas
1990 CENSUS

Arkadelphia, 10,014	C 2
Ashdown, 5,150	D 1
Bald Knob, 2,653	B 4
Barling, 4,078	B 1
Batesville, 9,187	B 4
Beebe, 4,455	B 4
Benton, 18,177	C 3
Bentonville, 11,257	A 1
Berryville, 3,212	A 2
Blytheville, 22,906	B 6
Booneville, 3,804	B 2
Brinkley, 4,234	C 4
Bryant, 5,269	C 3
Cabot, 8,319	B 4
Camden, 14,380	D 2
Clarksville, 5,833	B 2
Conway, 26,481	B 3
Corning, 3,323	A 5
Crossett, 6,282	D 3
Dardanelle, 3,722	B 2
De Queen, 4,633	C 1
Dermott, 4,715	D 4
De Witt, 3,553	C 4
Dumas, 5,520	D 4
Earle, 3,393	B 5
El Dorado, 23,146	D 3
Eudora, 3,155	D 4
Eureka Springs, 1,900	A 1
Fayetteville, 42,099	A 1
Fordyce, 4,729	D 3
Forrest City, 13,364	B 5
Fort Smith, 72,798	B 1
Greenwood, 3,984	B 1
Harrisburg, 1,943	B 5
Harrison, 9,922	A 2
Heber Springs, 5,628	B 3
Helena, 7,491	C 5
Hope, 9,643	D 2
Hot Springs National Park, 32,462	C 2
Hoxie, 2,676	B 5
Jacksonville, 29,101	C 3
Jonesboro, 46,535	B 5
Lake Village, 2,791	D 4
Little Rock, 175,795	C 3
Lonoke, 4,022	C 4
Magnolia, 11,151	D 2
Malvern, 9,256	C 3
Marianna, 5,910	C 5
Marked Tree, 3,100	B 6
McGehee, 4,997	D 4
Mena, 5,475	C 1
Monticello, 8,116	D 4
Morrilton, 6,551	B 3
Mountain Home, 9,027	A 3
Mountain View, 2,439	B 3
Nashville, 4,639	D 2
Newport, 7,459	B 4
North Little Rock, 61,741	C 3
Osceola, 8,930	B 6
Ozark, 3,330	B 2
Paragould, 18,540	A 5
Paris, 3,674	B 2
Piggott, 3,777	A 5
Pine Bluff, 57,140	C 3
Pocahontas, 6,151	A 5
Prescott, 3,673	D 2
Rogers, 24,692	A 1
Russellville, 21,260	B 2
Searcy, 15,180	B 4
Sherwood, 18,893	C 3
Siloam Springs, 8,151	A 1
Smackover, 2,232	D 3
Springdale, 29,941	A 1
Stuttgart, 10,420	C 4
Texarkana, 22,631	D 1
Trumann, 6,304	B 5
Tuckerman, 2,020	B 5
Van Buren, 14,979	B 1
Walnut Ridge, 4,388	A 5
Warren, 6,455	D 3
West Helena, 9,695	C 5
West Memphis, 28,259	B 5
Wynne, 8,187	B 5

Statute Miles 0 5 10 20 30 40
Kilometers 5 0 5 15 25 35 45 55

Lambert Conformal Conic Projection

RAND M?NALLY & COMPANY
Made in U.S.A.
© England

California

California

1990 CENSUS

Alameda, 76,459 . . . . h 8
Alhambra, 82,106 . . . m12
Anaheim, 266,406 . . . F 5
Antioch, 62,195 . . . . h 9
Bakersfield, 174,820 . E 4
Berkeley, 102,724 . . . D 2
Beverly Hills, 31,971 . m12
Burbank, 93,643 . . . . E 4
Calexico, 18,633 . . . . F 6
Chico, 40,079 . . . . . C 3
Chula Vista, 135,163 . . F 6
Compton, 90,454 . . . . n12
Concord, 111,348 . . . h 8
Costa Mesa, 96,357 . .n13
Daly City, 92,311 . . . h 8
Davis, 46,209 . . . . . C 3
Downey, 91,444 . . . . n12
East Los Angeles,
  126,379 . . . . . . m12
El Cajon, 88,693 . . . . F 5
El Centro, 31,384 . . . F 6
Escondido, 108,635 . . F 5
Eureka, 27,025 . . . . B 1
Fairfield, 77,211 . . . . C 2
Fremont, 173,339 . . . D 2
Fresno, 354,202 . . . . D 4
Fullerton, 114,144 . . . n13
Garden Grove,
  143,050 . . . . . . n13
Glendale, 180,038 . . . m12
Hayward, 111,498 . . h 8
Huntington Beach,
  181,519 . . . . . . F 4
Indio, 36,793 . . . . . F 5
Inglewood, 109,602 . . n12
Irvine, 110,330 . . . . n13
Lancaster, 97,291 . . . E 4
Lompoc, 37,649 . . . . E 3
Long Beach, 429,433 F 4
Los Angeles,
  3,485,398 . . . . . E 4
Marysville, 12,324 . . . C 3
Menlo Park, 28,040 . . k 8
Merced, 56,216 . . . . D 3
Modesto, 164,730 . . . D 3
Monterey, 31,954 . . . D 3
Napa, 61,842 . . . . . C 2
Newport Beach,
  66,643 . . . . . . n13
Norwalk, 94,279 . . . . n12
Oakland, 372,242 . . . D 2
Oceanside, 128,398 . . F 5
Ontario, 133,179 . . . E 5
Orange, 110,658 . . . . n13
Oxnard, 142,216 . . . . F 4
Palm Springs, 40,181 F 5
Palo Alto, 55,900 . . . D 2
Pasadena, 131,591 . . E 4
Pomona, 131,723 . . . E 5
Redding, 66,462 . . . . B 2
Redwood City,
  66,072 . . . . . . D 2
Richmond, 87,425 . . . D 2
Riverside, 226,505 . . F 5
Sacramento, 369,365 C 3
Salinas, 108,777 . . . D 3
San Bernardino,
  164,164 . . . . . . E 5
San Clemente, 41,100 F 5
San Diego, 1,110,549 F 5
San Francisco,
  723,959 . . . . . . D 2
San Jose, 782,248 . . D 3
San Juan Capistrano,
  26,183 . . . . . . F 5
San Luis Obispo,
  41,958 . . . . . . E 3
San Mateo, 85,486 . . D 2
Santa Ana, 293,742 . F 5
Santa Barbara,
  85,571 . . . . . . E 4
Santa Clara, 93,613 . D 2
Santa Cruz, 49,040 . . D 2
Santa Maria, 61,284 . E 3
Santa Monica, 86,905 m12
Santa Rosa, 113,313 C 2
Simi Valley, 100,217 . E 4
South Gate, 86,284 . . n12
South Lake Tahoe,
  21,586 . . . . . . C 4
Stockton, 210,943 . . . D 3
Sunnyvale, 117,229 . . k 8
Torrance, 133,107 . . . F 4
Tulare, 33,249 . . . . . D 4
Turlock, 42,198 . . . . D 3
Vallejo, 109,199 . . . . C 2
Ventura (San
  Buenaventura),
  92,575 . . . . . . E 4
Visalia, 75,636 . . . . D 4
West Covina, 96,086 m13
Westminster, 78,118 . n12
Whittier, 77,671 . . . . F 4
Yuba City, 27,437 . . . C 3

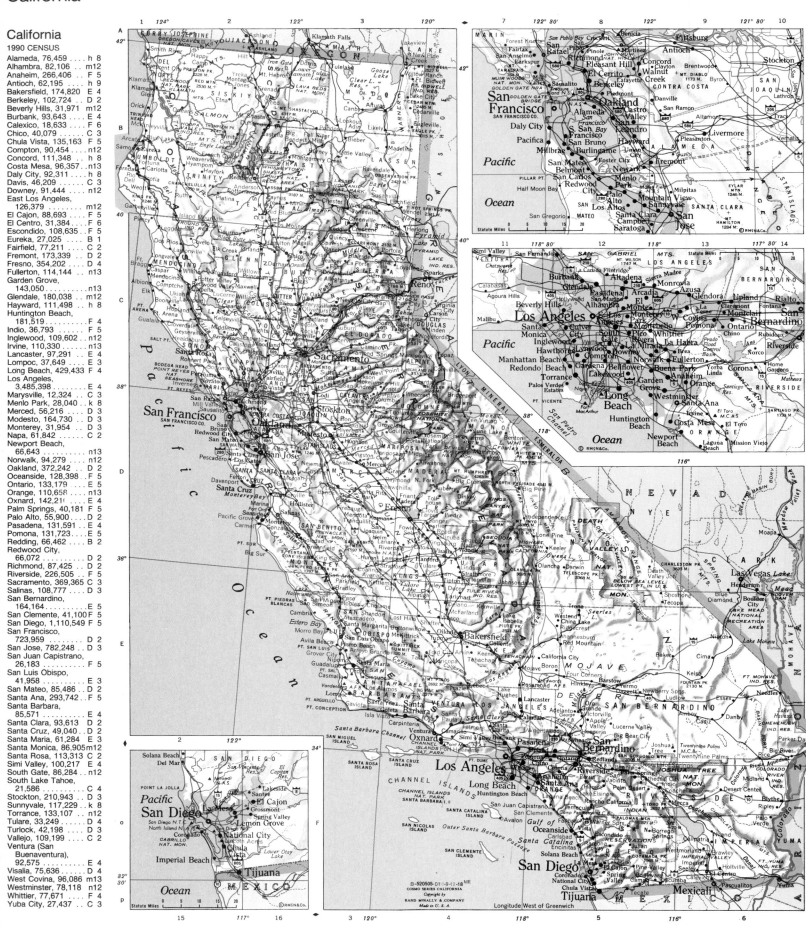

Statute Miles
Kilometers

Lambert Conformal Conic Projection

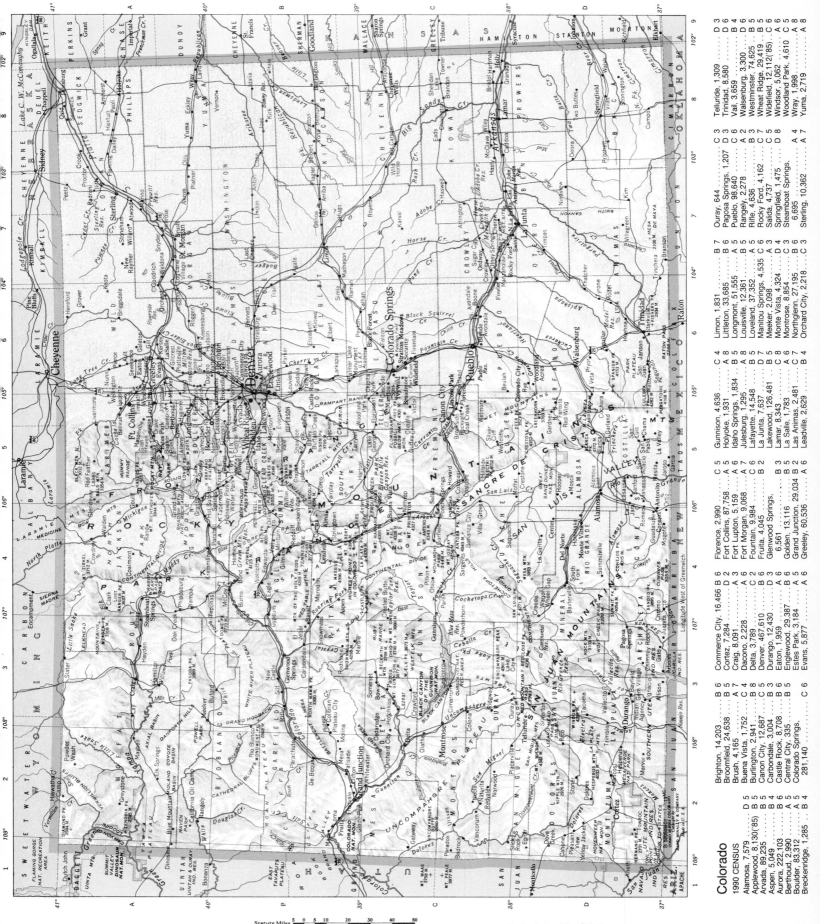

Statute Miles 5 0 5 10 20 30 40 50
Kilometers 5 0 5 15 25 35 45 55 65 75

Lambert Conformal Conic Projection

Colorado

1990 CENSUS

Alamosa, 7,579	D 5	
Applewood, 8,130(’85)	B 5	
Arvada, 89,235	B 5	
Aspen, 5,049	B 4	
Aurora, 222,103	A 5	
Berthoud, 2,990	A 5	
Boulder, 83,312	A 5	
Breckenridge, 1,285	B 4	
Brighton, 14,203	B 6	
Broomfield, 24,638	B 5	
Brush, 4,165	A 7	
Buena Vista, 1,752	C 4	
Burlington, 2,941	B 8	
Canon City, 12,687	C 5	
Carbondale, 3,004	B 4	
Castle Rock, 8,708	B 6	
Central City, 335	B 5	
Colorado Springs,		
281,140	C 6	
Commerce City, 16,466	B 6	
Cortez, 7,284	D 2	
Craig, 8,091	A 3	
Dacono, 2,228	A 6	
Delta, 3,789	C 2	
Denver, 467,610	B 6	
Durango, 12,430	D 3	
Eaton, 1,959	A 6	
Englewood, 29,387	B 6	
Estes Park, 3,184	A 5	
Evans, 5,877	A 6	
Florence, 2,990	C 5	
Fort Collins, 87,758	A 5	
Fort Lupton, 5,159	A 6	
Fort Morgan, 9,068	A 7	
Fountain, 9,984	C 6	
Fruita, 4,045	B 2	
Glenwood Springs,		
6,561	B 3	
Golden, 13,116	B 5	
Grand Junction, 29,034	B 2	
Greeley, 60,536	A 6	
Gunnison, 4,636	C 4	
Holyoke, 1,931	A 8	
Idaho Springs, 1,834	B 5	
Julesburg, 1,295	A 8	
Lafayette, 14,548	B 5	
La Junta, 7,637	D 7	
Lakewood, 126,481	B 5	
Lamar, 8,343	C 8	
La Salle, 1,783	A 6	
Las Animas, 2,481	C 7	
Leadville, 2,629	B 4	
Limon, 1,831	B 7	
Littleton, 87,758	B 6	
Longmont, 51,555	A 5	
Louisville, 12,361	B 5	
Loveland, 37,352	A 5	
Manitou Springs, 4,535	C 6	
Meeker, 2,098	B 2	
Monte Vista, 4,324	D 4	
Montrose, 8,854	C 3	
Northglenn, 27,195	B 6	
Orchard City, 2,218	C 3	
Ouray, 644	C 3	
Pagosa Springs, 1,207	D 3	
Pueblo, 98,640	C 6	
Rangely, 2,278	A 2	
Rifle, 4,636	B 3	
Rocky Ford, 4,162	C 7	
Salida, 4,737	C 5	
Springfield, 1,475	D 8	
Steamboat Springs,		
6,695	A 4	
Sterling, 10,362	A 7	
Telluride, 1,309	D 3	
Trinidad, 8,580	D 6	
Vail, 3,659	B 4	
Walsenburg, 3,300	D 6	
Westminster, 74,625	B 5	
Wheat Ridge, 29,419	B 5	
Widefield, 12,112(’85)	C 6	
Windsor, 5,062	A 5	
Woodland Park, 4,610	C 5	
Wray, 1,998	A 8	
Yuma, 2,719	A 8	

Connecticut

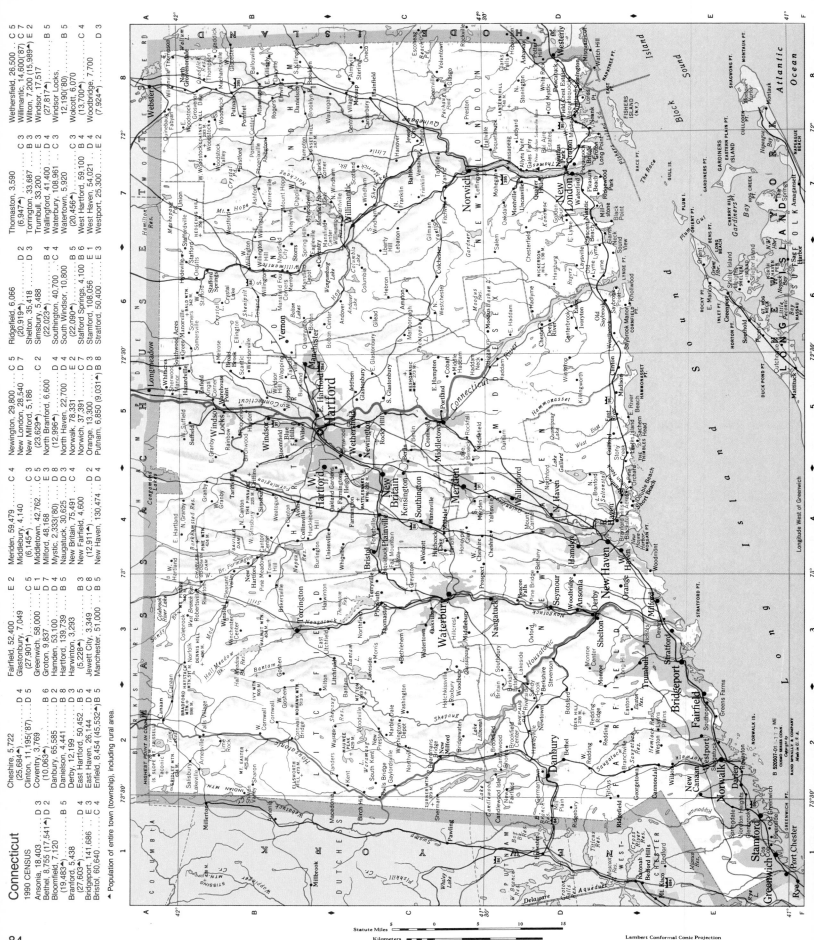

Connecticut

1990 CENSUS

Ansonia, 18,403	D 3	
Bethel, 8,755 (17,541▲)	D 2	
Bloomfield, 7,120		
(19,483▲)	B 5	
Branford, 5,438		
(27,603▲)	D 4	
Bridgeport, 141,686 . .	E 3	
Bristol, 60,640	C 4	

Cheshire, 5,722		
(25,684▲)	D 4	
Clinton, 11,195('87) . .	D 5	
Coventry, 3,769		
(10,063▲)	B 6	
Danbury, 65,585	D 2	
Danielson, 4,441	B 8	
Derby, 12,199	D 3	
East Hartford, 50,452 .	B 5	
East Lyme, 26,144 . . .	D 6	
Enfield, 8,454 (45,532▲)	B 5	

Fairfield, 52,400	E 2	
Glastonbury, 7,049		
(27,901▲)	C 5	
Greenwich, 58,000 . .	E 1	
Groton, 9,837	D 7	
Hamden, 53,100	D 4	
Hartford, 139,739 . . .	B 5	
Harwinton, 3,293		
(5,228▲)	B 3	
Jewett City, 3,349 . . .	C 8	
Manchester, 51,000 . .	B 5	

Meriden, 59,479		
(6,066▲)	D 4	
Middletown, 42,762 . .	D 5	
Milford, 48,168	D 4	
Mystic, 2,333('80) . . .	D 7	
Naugatuck, 30,625 . .	D 3	
New Britain, 75,491 . .	C 4	
(12,911▲)	D 2	
New Haven, 130,474 .	D 4	

Newington, 29,800 . .	C 4	
New London, 28,540 .	D 7	
New Milford, 5,186		
(23,629▲)	C 2	
North Branford, 6,600		
(12,996▲)	D 4	
Southington, 40,700 .	C 4	
South Windsor, 10,800	B 5	
Norwalk, 78,331	E 2	
Norwich, 37,391	C 7	
Orange, 13,300	D 3	
Putnam, 6,850 (9,031▲)	B 8	

Ridgefield, 6,066		
(20,919▲)	D 2	
Shelton, 35,418	D 3	
Simsbury, 5,488		
(22,023▲)	B 4	
Wallingford, 40,700 . .	C 4	
Waterbury, 108,961 . .	C 3	
Watertown, 5,920		
(20,456▲)	C 3	
Stafford Springs, 4,100	B 6	
Stamford, 108,056 . .	E 1	
Stratford, 50,400 . . .	E 3	

Thomaston, 3,590		
(6,947▲)	C 3	
Torrington, 33,687 . .	B 3	
Trumbull, 33,200 . . .	E 3	
Wallingford, 41,400 . .	D 4	
Waterbury, 108,961 . .	C 3	

Wethersfield, 26,500 .	C 5	
Willimantic, 14,600('87)	C 7	
Wilton, 7,200 (15,989▲)	E 2	
Windsor, 17,517		
(27,817▲)	B 5	
Windsor Locks,		
12,190('80)	B 5	
Wolcott, 6,070		
(13,700▲)	C 4	
Woodbridge, 7,700		
(7,924▲)	D 3	

▲ Population of entire town (township), including rural area.

Statute Miles

Kilometers

Lambert Conformal Conic Projection

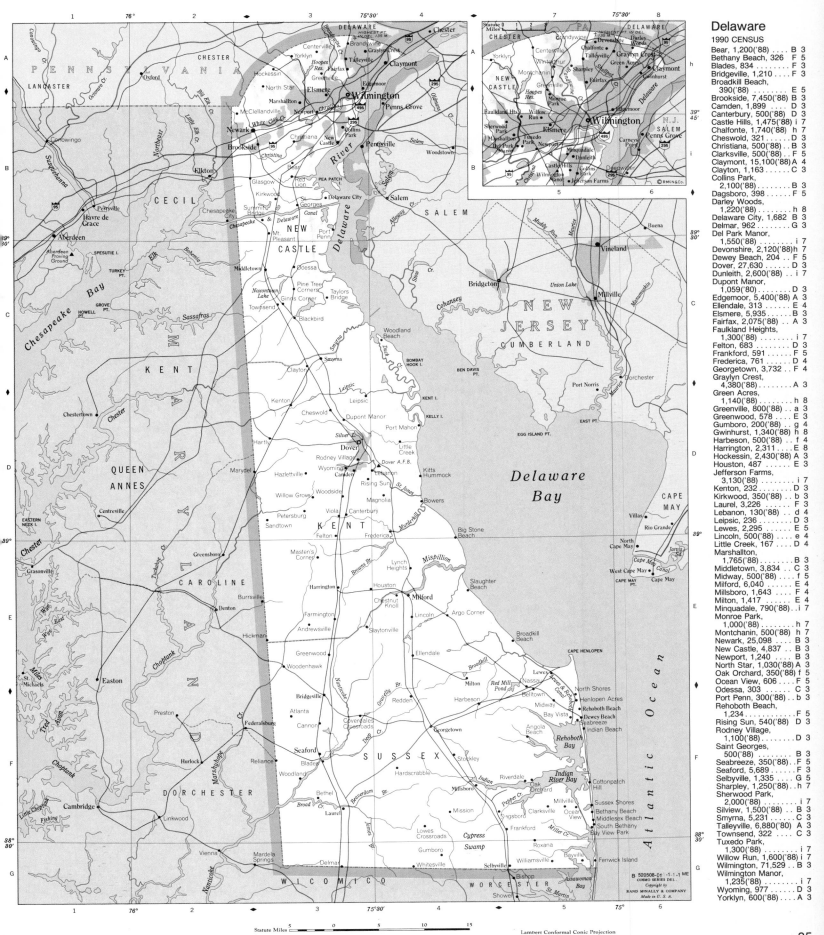

Delaware

1990 CENSUS

Bear, 1,200('88) .... B 3
Bethany Beach, 326 . F 5
Blades, 834 .... F 3
Bridgeville, 1,210 .. F 3
Broadkill Beach,
  390('88) .... E 5
Brookside, 7,450('88) B 3
Camden, 1,899 ..... D 3
Canterbury, 500('88) D 3
Castle Hills, 1,475('88) i 7
Chalfonte, 1,740('88) h 7
Cheswold, 321 ..... D 3
Christiana, 500('88) . B 3
Clarksville, 500('88) . F 5
Claymont, 15,100('88) A 4
Clayton, 1,163 ...... C 3
Collins Park,
  2,100('88) .... B 3
Dagsboro, 398 ..... F 5
Darley Woods,
  1,220('88) .... h 8
Delaware City, 1,682 B 3
Delmar, 962 .... G 3
Del Park Manor,
  1,550('88) .... i 7
Devonshire, 2,120('88)h 7
Dewey Beach, 204 .. F 5
Dover, 27,630 ..... D 3
Dunleith, 2,600('88) . i 7
Dupont Manor,
  1,059('80) .... D 3
Edgemoor, 5,400('88) A 3
Ellendale, 313 ..... E 4
Elsmere, 5,935 .... B 3
Fairfax, 2,075('88) . A 3
Faulkland Heights,
  1,300('88) .... i 7
Felton, 683 .... D 3
Frankford, 591 .... F 5
Frederica, 761 ..... D 4
Georgetown, 3,732 . F 4
Graylyn Crest,
  4,380('88) .... A 3
Green Acres,
  1,140('88) .... h 8
Greenville, 800('88) . a 3
Greenwood, 578 ... E 3
Gumboro, 200('88) .. g 4
Gwinhurst, 1,340('88) h 8
Harbeson, 500('88) .. f 4
Harrington, 2,311 .. E 8
Hockessin, 2,430('88) A 3
Houston, 487 ...... E 3
Jefferson Farms,
  3,130('88) .... i 7
Kenton, 232 .... D 3
Kirkwood, 350('88) .. b 3
Laurel, 3,226 ...... F 3
Lebanon, 130('88) .. d 4
Leipsic, 236 .... D 3
Lewes, 2,295 ...... E 5
Lincoln, 500('88) .... e 4
Little Creek, 167 ... D 4
Marshallton,
  1,765('88) .... B 3
Middletown, 3,834 .. C 3
Midway, 500('88) ... f 5
Milford, 6,040 ..... E 4
Millsboro, 1,643 ... F 4
Milton, 1,417 ...... E 4
Minquadale, 790('88) . i 7
Monroe Park,
  1,000('88) .... h 7
Montchanin, 500('88) h 7
Newark, 25,098 .... B 3
New Castle, 4,837 .. B 3
Newport, 1,240 .... B 3
North Star, 1,030('88) A 3
Oak Orchard, 350('88) f 5
Ocean View, 606 .... F 5
Odessa, 303 .... C 3
Port Penn, 300('88) .. b 3
Rehoboth Beach,
  1,234 .... F 5
Rising Sun, 540('88) . D 3
Rodney Village,
  1,100('88) .... D 3
Saint Georges,
  500('88) .... B 3
Seabreeze, 500('88) . F 5
Seaford, 5,689 ..... F 3
Selbyville, 1,335 ... G 5
Sharpley, 1,250('88) . h 7
Sherwood Park,
  2,000('88) .... i 7
Silview, 1,500('88) .. B 3
Smyrna, 5,231 ..... C 3
Talleyville, 6,880('80) A 3
Townsend, 322 .... C 3
Tuxedo Park,
  1,300('88) .... i 7
Willow Run, 1,600('88) i 7
Wilmington, 71,529 . B 3
Wilmington Manor,
  1,235('88) .... i 7
Wyoming, 977 ..... D 3
Yorklyn, 600('88) ... A 3

Florida

Florida

1990 CENSUS

Altamonte Springs, 34,879	D 5	
Bartow, 14,716	E 5	
Belle Glade, 16,177	F 6	
Boca Raton, 61,492	F 6	
Boynton Beach, 46,194	F 6	
Bradenton, 43,779	E 4	
Brandon, 36,300	E 4	
Brownsville, 18,058('80)	s13	
Cape Canaveral, 8,014	D 6	
Cape Coral, 74,991	F 5	
Carol City, 52,800	s13	
Clearwater, 98,784	E 4	
Cocoa, 17,722	D 6	
Coral Gables, 40,091	G 6	
Cutler Ridge, 20,886('80)	s13	
Davie, 47,217	F 6	
Daytona Beach, 61,921	C 5	
Deerfield Beach, 46,325	F 6	
De Land, 16,491	C 5	
Delray Beach, 47,181	F 6	
Dunedin, 34,012	D 4	
Fort Lauderdale, 149,377	F 6	
Fort Myers, 45,206	F 5	
Fort Pierce, 36,830	E 6	
Fort Walton Beach, 21,471	u15	
Gainesville, 84,770	C 4	
Hallandale, 30,996	G 6	
Hialeah, 188,004	G 6	
Hollywood, 121,697	F 6	
Homestead, 26,866	G 6	
Jacksonville, 635,230	B 5	
Kendall, 53,100	s13	
Key Largo, 7,447('80)	G 6	
Key West, 24,832	H 5	
Kissimmee, 30,050	D 5	
Lake City, 10,005	B 4	
Lakeland, 70,576	D 5	
Lake Worth, 28,564	F 6	
Largo, 65,674	E 4	
Lauderdale Lakes, 27,341	r13	
Lealman, 19,873('80)	p10	
Leesburg, 14,903	D 5	
Leisure City, 17,905('80)	s13	
Margate, 42,985	F 6	
Melbourne, 59,646	D 6	
Merritt Island, 44,300	D 6	
Miami, 358,548	G 6	
Miami Beach, 92,639	G 6	
Miramar, 40,663	s13	
Naples, 19,505	F 5	
New Smyrna Beach, 16,543	C 6	
North Fort Myers, 17,200('83)	F 5	
North Miami, 49,998	G 6	
North Miami Beach, 35,359	s13	
Oakland Park, 26,326	r13	
Ocala, 42,045	C 4	
Orlando, 164,693	D 5	
Ormond Beach, 29,721	C 5	
Palm Bay, 62,632	D 6	
Panama City, 34,378	u16	
Pembroke Pines, 65,452	r13	
Pensacola, 58,165	u14	
Pine Hills, 35,600	D 5	
Pinellas Park, 43,426	E 4	
Plantation, 66,692	r13	
Plant City, 22,754	D 4	
Pompano Beach, 72,411	F 6	
Port Charlotte, 43,300	F 5	
Port Orange, 35,317	C 6	
Riviera Beach, 27,639	F 6	
Saint Augustine, 11,692	C 5	
Saint Petersburg, 238,629	E 4	
Sanford, 32,387	D 5	
Sarasota, 50,961	E 4	
Sebring, 8,900	E 5	
South Miami Heights, 18,000('83)	s13	
Sweetwater Creek, 18,000('83)	p10	
Tallahassee, 124,773	B 2	
Tampa, 280,015	E 4	
Tarpon Springs, 17,906	D 4	
Titusville, 39,394	D 6	
Venice, 16,922	E 4	
Vero Beach, 17,350	E 6	
West Palm Beach, 67,643	F 6	
West Pensacola, 30,200	u14	
Winter Haven, 24,725	D 5	
Winter Park, 22,242	D 5	

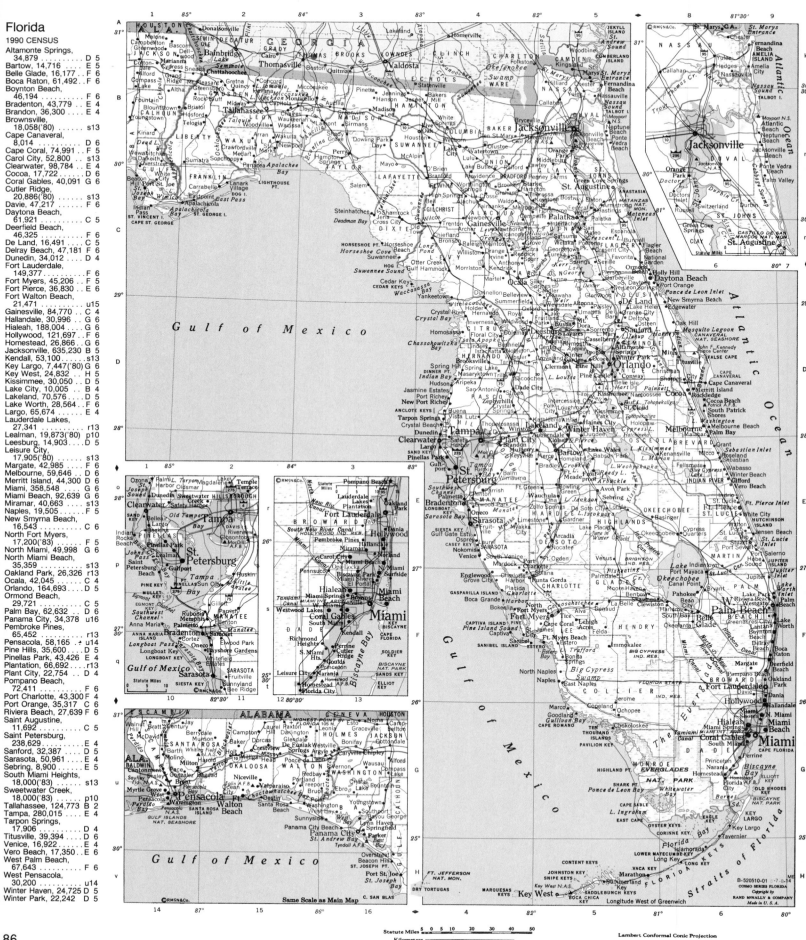

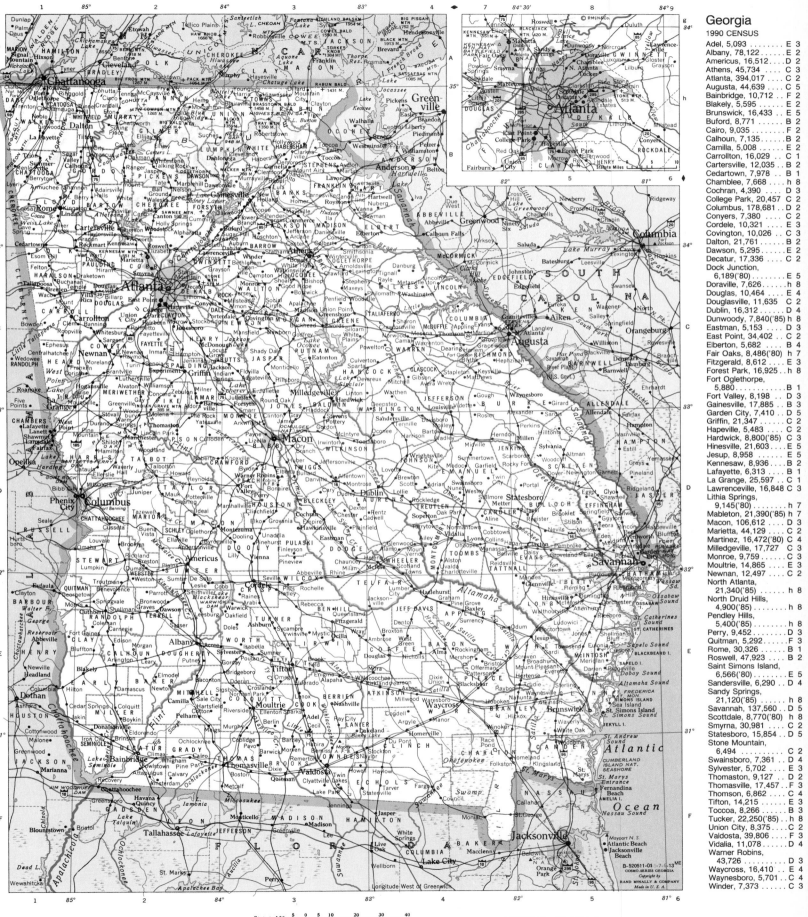

1990 CENSUS

Adel, 5,093 . . . . E 3
Albany, 78,122 . . . . . D 2
Americus, 16,512 . . . D 2
Athens, 45,734 . . . . . C 3
Atlanta, 394,017 . . . . C 2
Augusta, 44,639 . . . . C 5
Bainbridge, 10,712 . . F 2
Blakely, 5,595 . . . . . E 2
Brunswick, 16,433 . . . E 5
Buford, 8,771 . . . . . . B 2
Cairo, 9,035 . . . . F 2
Calhoun, 7,135 . . . . . B 2
Camilla, 5,008 . . . . . E 2
Carrollton, 16,029 . . . C 1
Cartersville, 12,035 . . B 2
Cedartown, 7,978 . . . B 1
Chamblee, 7,668 . . . . h 8
Cochran, 4,390 . . . . . D 3
College Park, 20,457 . C 2
Columbus, 178,681 . . D 2
Conyers, 7,380 . . . . . C 2
Cordele, 10,321 . . . . E 3
Covington, 10,026 . . . C 3
Dalton, 21,761 . . . . . B 2
Dawson, 5,295 . . . . . E 2
Decatur, 17,336 . . . . C 2
Dock Junction,
6,189('80) . . . . . . E 5
Doraville, 7,626 . . . . h 8
Douglas, 10,464 . . . . E 4
Douglasville, 11,635 . C 2
Dublin, 16,312 . . . . . D 4
Dunwoody, 7,840('85) h 8
Eastman, 5,153 . . . . . D 3
East Point, 34,402 . . . C 2
Elberton, 5,682 . . . . . C 4
Fair Oaks, 8,486('80) h 7
Fitzgerald, 8,612 . . . . E 3
Forest Park, 16,925 . . h 8
Fort Oglethorpe,
5,880 . . . . B 1
Fort Valley, 8,198 . . . D 2
Gainesville, 17,885 . . B 3
Garden City, 7,410 . . D 5
Griffin, 21,347 . . . . . C 2
Hapeville, 5,483 . . . . C 2
Hardwick, 8,800('85) . C 3
Hinesville, 21,603 . . . E 5
Jesup, 8,958 . . . . E 5
Kennesaw, 8,936 . . . . B 2
Lafayette, 6,313 . . . . B 1
La Grange, 25,597 . . . C 1
Lawrenceville, 16,848 C 3
Lithia Springs,
9,145('80) . . . . h 7
Mableton, 21,390('85) h 7
Macon, 106,612 . . . . D 3
Marietta, 44,129 . . . . C 2
Martinez, 16,472('80) C 4
Milledgeville, 17,727 . C 3
Monroe, 9,759 . . . . . C 3
Moultrie, 14,865 . . . . E 3
Newnan, 12,497 . . . . C 2
North Atlanta,
21,340('85) . . . . . . h 8
North Druid Hills,
4,900('85) . . . . h 8
Pendley Hills,
5,400('85) . . . . h 8
Perry, 9,452 . . . . D 3
Quitman, 5,292 . . . . . F 3
Rome, 30,326 . . . . . . B 1
Roswell, 47,923 . . . . B 2
Saint Simons Island,
6,566('80) . . . . E 5
Sandersville, 6,290 . . D 4
Sandy Springs,
21,120('85) . . . . . . h 8
Savannah, 137,560 . . D 5
Scottdale, 8,770('80) h 8
Smyrna, 30,981 . . . . C 2
Statesboro, 15,854 . . D 5
Stone Mountain,
6,494 . . . . C 2
Swainsboro, 7,361 . . . D 4
Sylvester, 5,702 . . . . E 3
Thomaston, 9,127 . . . D 2
Thomasville, 17,457 . . F 3
Thomson, 6,862 . . . . C 4
Tifton, 14,215 . . . . . E 3
Toccoa, 8,266 . . . . . . B 3
Tucker, 22,250('85) . . h 8
Union City, 8,375 . . . C 2
Valdosta, 39,806 . . . . F 3
Vidalia, 11,078 . . . . . D 4
Warner Robins,
43,726 . . . . D 3
Waycross, 16,410 . . . E 4
Waynesboro, 5,701 . . C 4
Winder, 7,373 . . . . . . C 3

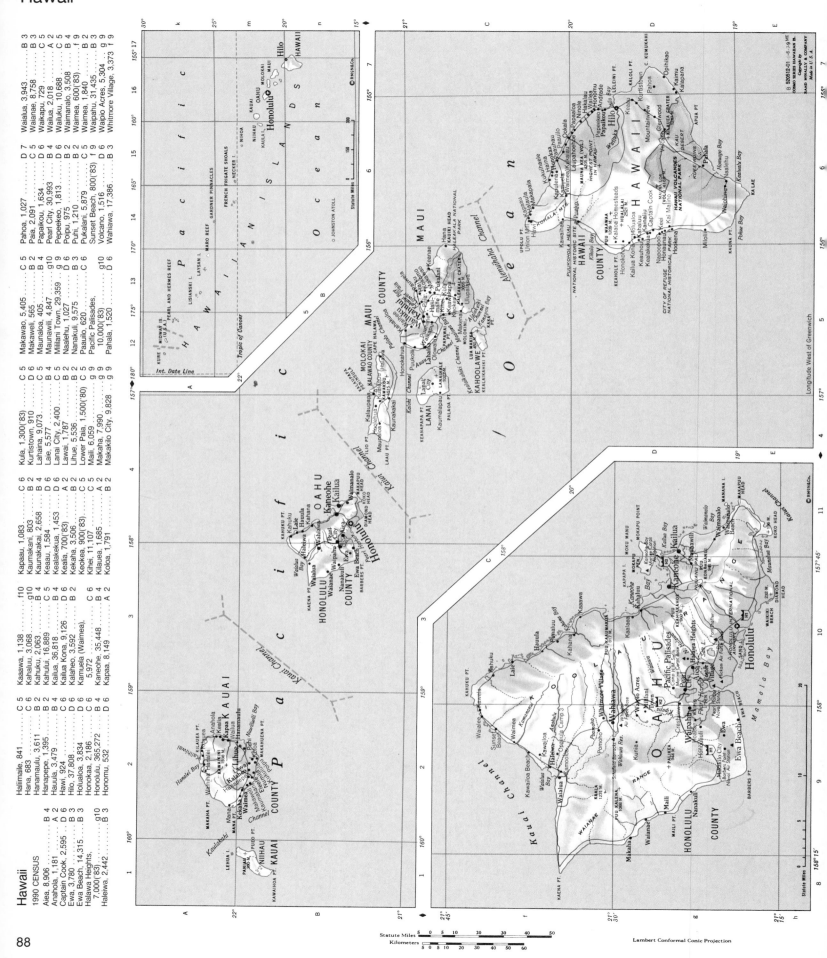

Hawaii

1990 CENSUS

Lambert Conformal Conic Projection

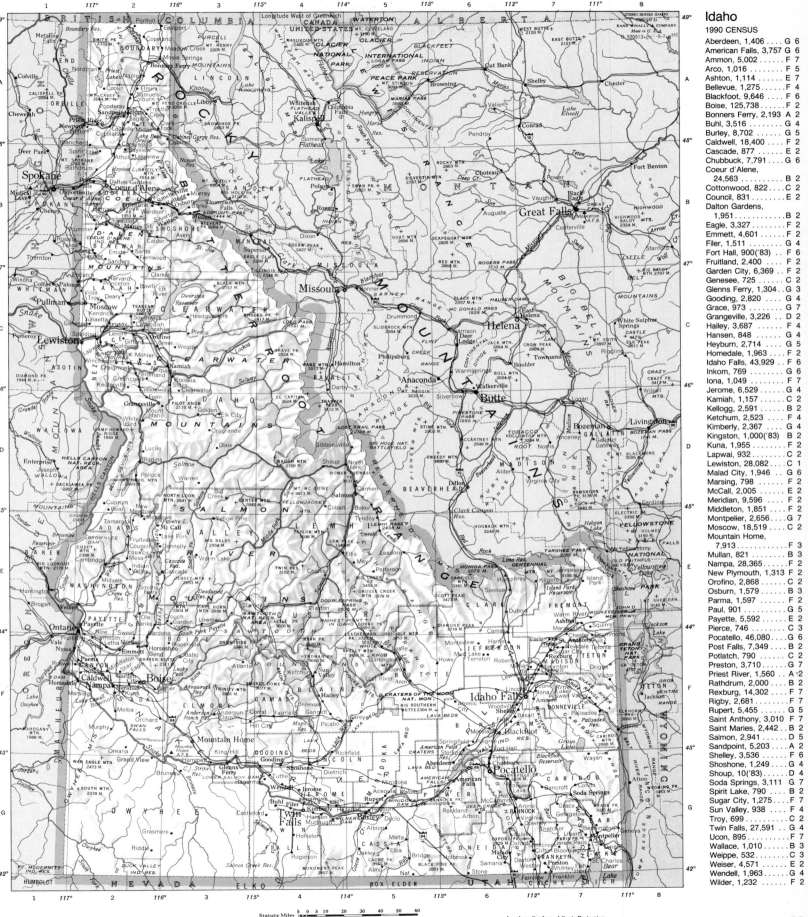

Idaho

Idaho

1990 CENSUS

Aberdeen, 1,406 . . . . G 6
American Falls, 3,757 G 6
Ammon, 5,002 . . . . . F 7
Arco, 1,016 . . . . F 5
Ashton, 1,114 . . . . . E 7
Bellevue, 1,275 . . . . F 4
Blackfoot, 9,646 . . . . F 6
Boise, 125,738 . . . . . F 2
Bonners Ferry, 2,193 A 2
Buhl, 3,516 . . . . . . G 4
Burley, 8,702 . . . . . G 5
Caldwell, 18,400 . . . F 2
Cascade, 877 . . . . . . E 2
Chubbuck, 7,791 . . . G 6
Coeur d'Alene,
  24,563 . . . . B 2
Cottonwood, 822 . . . . C 2
Council, 831 . . . . E 2
Dalton Gardens,
  1,951 . . . . B 2
Eagle, 3,327 . . . . F 2
Emmett, 4,601 . . . . . F 2
Filer, 1,511 . . . . G 4
Fort Hall, 900('83) . . F 6
Fruitland, 2,400 . . . . F 2
Garden City, 6,369 . . F 2
Genesee, 725 . . . . . C 2
Glenns Ferry, 1,304 . . G 3
Gooding, 2,820 . . . . G 4
Grace, 973 . . . . G 7
Grangeville, 3,226 . . . D 2
Hailey, 3,687 . . . . . . F 4
Hansen, 848 . . . . . . G 4
Heyburn, 2,714 . . . . G 5
Homedale, 1,963 . . . F 2
Idaho Falls, 43,929 . . F 6
Inkom, 769 . . . . F 7
Iona, 1,049 . . . . F 7
Jerome, 6,529 . . . . . G 4
Kamiah, 1,157 . . . . . C 2
Kellogg, 2,591 . . . . . B 2
Ketchum, 2,523 . . . . F 4
Kimberly, 2,367 . . . . G 4
Kingston, 1,000('83) . B 2
Kuna, 1,955 . . . . . . F 2
Lapwai, 932 . . . . . . C 2
Lewiston, 28,082 . . . C 1
Malad City, 1,946 . . . G 6
Marsing, 798 . . . . . . F 2
McCall, 2,005 . . . . . E 2
Meridian, 9,596 . . . . F 2
Middleton, 1,851 . . . F 2
Montpelier, 2,656 . . . G 7
Moscow, 18,519 . . . . C 2
Mountain Home,
  7,913 . . . . F 3
Mullan, 821 . . . . . . B 3
Nampa, 28,365 . . . . F 2
New Plymouth, 1,313 F 2
Orofino, 2,868 . . . . . C 2
Osburn, 1,579 . . . . . B 3
Parma, 1,597 . . . . . F 2
Paul, 901 . . . . G 5
Payette, 5,592 . . . . . F 2
Pierce, 746 . . . . C 3
Pocatello, 46,080 . . . G 6
Post Falls, 7,349 . . . . B 2
Potlatch, 790 . . . . . . C 2
Preston, 3,710 . . . . . G 7
Priest River, 1,560 . . A ·2
Rathdrum, 2,000 . . . . B 2
Rexburg, 14,302 . . . . F 7
Rigby, 2,681 . . . . . . F 7
Rupert, 5,455 . . . . . G 5
Saint Anthony, 3,010 . F 7
Saint Maries, 2,442 . . B 2
Salmon, 2,941 . . . . . D 5
Sandpoint, 5,203 . . . A 2
Shelley, 3,536 . . . . . F 6
Shoshone, 1,249 . . . . G 4
Shoup, 10('83) . . . . . D 4
Soda Springs, 3,111 . G 7
Spirit Lake, 790 . . . . B 2
Sugar City, 1,275 . . . F 7
Sun Valley, 938 . . . . F 4
Troy, 699 . . . . C 2
Twin Falls, 27,591 . . G 4
Ucon, 895 . . . . F 7
Wallace, 1,010 . . . . . B 3
Weippe, 532 . . . . . . C 3
Weiser, 4,571 . . . . . E 2
Wendell, 1,963 . . . . G 4
Wilder, 1,232 . . . . . F 2

Statute Miles
Kilometers

Lambert Conformal Conic Projection

89

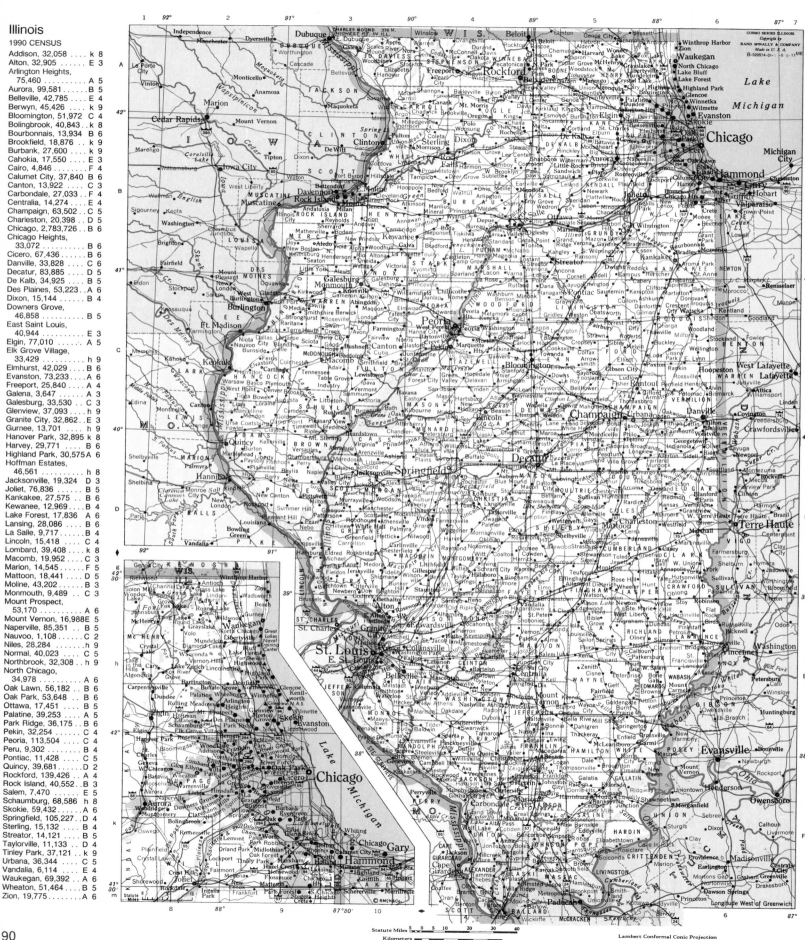

Illinois

Illinois
1990 CENSUS

Addison, 32,058 .... k 8
Alton, 32,905 .... E 3
Arlington Heights, 75,460 .... A 5
Aurora, 99,581 .... B 5
Belleville, 42,785 .... E 4
Berwyn, 45,426 .... k 9
Bloomington, 51,972 C 4
Bolingbrook, 40,843 .. k 8
Bourbonnais, 13,934 B 6
Brookfield, 18,876 .. k 9
Burbank, 27,600 .... k 9
Cahokia, 17,550 .... E 3
Cairo, 4,846 ...... F 4
Calumet City, 37,840 B 6
Canton, 13,922 .... C 3
Carbondale, 27,033 .. F 4
Centralia, 14,274 ... E 4
Champaign, 63,502 .. C 5
Charleston, 20,398 .. D 5
Chicago, 2,783,726 .. B 6
Chicago Heights, 33,072 .... B 6
Cicero, 67,436 .... B 6
Danville, 33,828 .... C 6
Decatur, 83,885 .... C 5
De Kalb, 34,925 .... B 5
Des Plaines, 53,223 .. A 6
Dixon, 15,144 .... B 4
Downers Grove, 46,858 .... B 5
East Saint Louis, 40,944 .... E 3
Elgin, 77,010 .... A 5
Elk Grove Village, 33,429 .... h 9
Elmhurst, 42,029 .... B 5
Evanston, 73,233 .... A 6
Freeport, 25,840 .... A 4
Galena, 3,647 .... A 3
Galesburg, 33,530 .. C 3
Glenview, 37,093 .. h 9
Granite City, 32,862 .. E 3
Gurnee, 13,701 .... A 6
Hanover Park, 32,895 k 8
Harvey, 29,771 .... B 6
Highland Park, 30,575 A 6
Hoffman Estates, 46,561 .... k 8
Jacksonville, 19,324 D 3
Joliet, 76,836 ...... B 5
Kankakee, 27,575 .... C 6
Kewanee, 12,969 .... B 4
Lake Forest, 17,836 A 6
Lansing, 28,086 .... B 6
La Salle, 9,717 ..... B 4
Lincoln, 15,418 .... C 4
Lombard, 39,408 .. k 8
Macomb, 19,952 .... C 3
Marion, 14,545 .... F 5
Mattoon, 18,441 .... D 5
Moline, 43,202 .... B 3
Monmouth, 9,489 .... C 3
Mount Prospect, 53,170 .... A 6
Mount Vernon, 16,988 E 5
Naperville, 85,351 .. B 5
Nauvoo, 1,108 .... C 2
Niles, 28,284 ..... h 9
Normal, 40,023 .... C 5
Northbrook, 32,308 .. h 9
North Chicago, 34,978 .... A 6
Oak Lawn, 56,182 .. B 6
Oak Park, 53,648 .. B 6
Ottawa, 17,451 .... B 5
Palatine, 39,253 .... A 5
Park Ridge, 36,175 .. B 6
Pekin, 32,254 .... C 4
Peoria, 113,504 .... C 4
Peru, 9,302 ...... B 4
Pontiac, 11,428 .... C 5
Quincy, 39,681 .... D 2
Rockford, 139,426 .. A 4
Rock Island, 40,552 .. B 3
Salem, 7,470 ...... E 4
Schaumburg, 68,586 .. h 8
Skokie, 59,432 ..... A 6
Springfield, 105,227 .. D 4
Sterling, 15,132 .... B 4
Streator, 14,121 .... B 5
Taylorville, 11,133 .. D 4
Tinley Park, 37,121 .. k 9
Urbana, 36,344 .... C 5
Vandalia, 6,114 .... E 4
Waukegan, 69,392 .. A 6
Wheaton, 51,464 .. B 5
Zion, 19,775 .... A 6

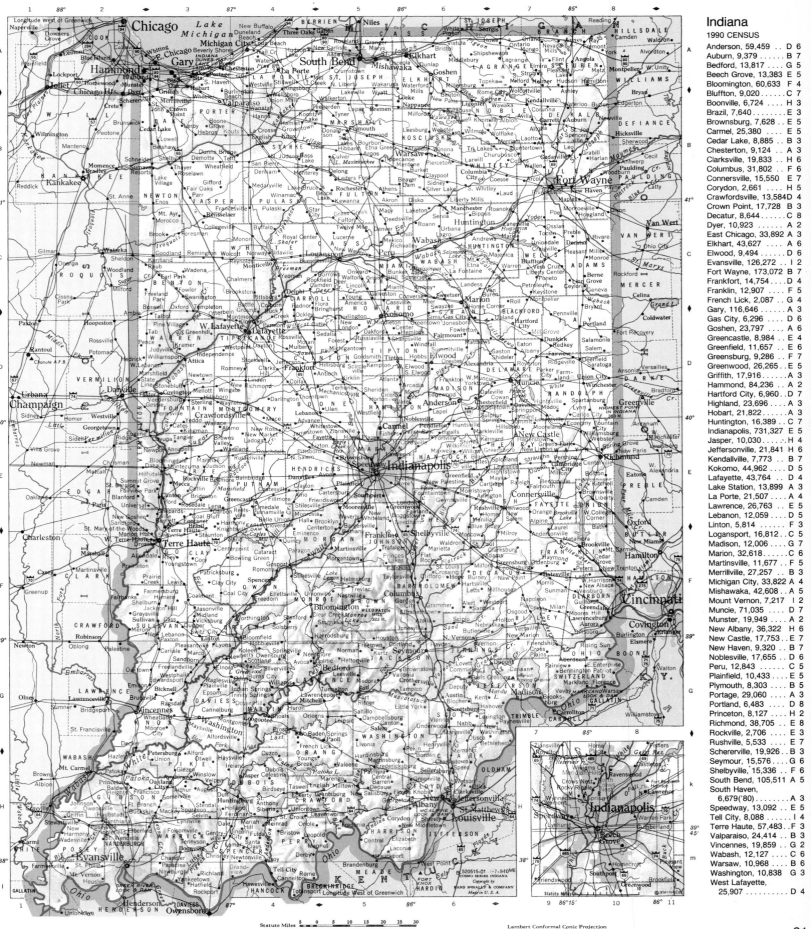

Indiana
1990 CENSUS

Anderson, 59,459 .. D 6
Auburn, 9,379 ..... B 7
Bedford, 13,817 ... G 5
Beech Grove, 13,383 E 5
Bloomington, 60,633 F 4
Bluffton, 9,020 .... C 7
Boonville, 6,724 ... H 3
Brazil, 7,640 ...... E 3
Brownsburg, 7,628 . E 5
Carmel, 25,380 .... E 5
Cedar Lake, 8,885 . B 3
Chesterton, 9,124 . A 3
Clarksville, 19,833 . H 6
Columbus, 31,802 . F 6
Connersville, 15,550 E 7
Corydon, 2,661 .... H 5
Crawfordsville, 13,584 D 4
Crown Point, 17,728 B 3
Decatur, 8,644 ...... C 8
Dyer, 10,923 ...... A 2
East Chicago, 33,892 A 3
Elkhart, 43,627 .... A 6
Elwood, 9,494 ..... D 6
Evansville, 126,272 . I 2
Fort Wayne, 173,072 B 7
Frankfort, 14,754 .. D 4
Franklin, 12,907 ... F 5
French Lick, 2,087 . G 4
Gary, 116,646 ... A 3
Gas City, 6,296 ... D 6
Goshen, 23,797 ... A 6
Greencastle, 8,984 . E 4
Greenfield, 11,657 . E 6
Greensburg, 9,286 . F 7
Greenwood, 26,265 . E 5
Griffith, 17,916 .... A 3
Hammond, 84,236 .. A 2
Hartford City, 6,960 . D 7
Highland, 23,696 .. A 3
Hobart, 21,822 .... A 3
Huntington, 16,389 . C 7
Indianapolis, 731,327 E 5
Jasper, 10,030 .... H 4
Jeffersonville, 21,841 H 6
Kendallville, 7,773 . B 7
Kokomo, 44,962 .. D 5
Lafayette, 43,764 .. D 4
Lake Station, 13,899 A 3
La Porte, 21,507 ... A 4
Lawrence, 26,763 .. E 5
Lebanon, 12,059 .. D 5
Linton, 5,814 ..... F 3
Logansport, 16,812 . C 5
Madison, 12,006 .. G 7
Marion, 32,618 .... C 6
Martinsville, 11,677 . F 5
Merrillville, 27,257 . A 3
Michigan City, 33,822 A 4
Mishawaka, 42,608 . A 5
Mount Vernon, 7,217 I 2
Muncie, 71,035 ... D 7
Munster, 19,949 ... A 2
New Albany, 36,322 H 6
New Castle, 17,753 . E 7
New Haven, 9,320 .. B 7
Noblesville, 17,655 . D 6
Peru, 12,843 ..... C 5
Plainfield, 10,433 .. E 5
Plymouth, 8,303 ... B 5
Portage, 29,060 ... A 3
Portland, 6,483 ... D 8
Princeton, 8,127 .. H 2
Richmond, 38,705 . E 8
Rockville, 2,706 ... E 3
Rushville, 5,533 ... E 7
Schererville, 19,926 . B 3
Seymour, 15,576 ... G 6
Shelbyville, 15,336 . F 6
South Bend, 105,511 A 5
South Haven,
   6,679('80) ...... A 3
Speedway, 13,092 . E 5
Tell City, 8,088 ...... I 4
Terre Haute, 57,483 . F 3
Valparaiso, 24,414 .. A 3
Vincennes, 19,859 .. G 2
Wabash, 12,127 ... C 6
Warsaw, 10,968 ... B 6
Washington, 10,838 . G 3
West Lafayette,
   25,907 .... D 4

Iowa

1990 CENSUS

Algona, 6,015	.... A 3	
Altoona, 7,191	.... C 6	
Amana, 540(87)	.... C 6	
Ames, 47,198	.... B 4	
Anamosa, 5,100	.... B 6	
Ankeny, 18,482	.... C 4	
Atlantic, 7,432	.... C 2	
Bettendorf, 28,132	.... C 7	

Boone, 12,392	.... B 4	
Burlington, 27,208	.... D 6	
Camanche, 4,436	.... C 7	
Carroll, 9,579	.... B 3	
Cedar Falls, 34,298	.... B 5	
Cedar Rapids, 108,751	.... C 6	
Centerville, 5,936	.... D 5	
Chariton, 4,616	.... C 4	
Charles City, 7,878	.... A 5	
Cherokee, 6,026	.... B 2	
Clarinda, 5,104	.... D 2	

Clear Lake, 8,183	.... A 4	
Clinton, 29,201	.... C 7	
Clive, 7,462	.... e 8	
Coralville, 10,347	.... C 6	
Council Bluffs, 54,315	.... C 2	
Creston, 7,911	.... C 3	
Davenport, 95,333	.... C 7	
Decorah, 8,063	.... A 6	
Denison, 6,604	.... B 2	
Des Moines, 193,187	.... C 4	
Dubuque, 57,546	.... B 7	

Estherville, 6,720	.... A 3	
Evansdale, 4,638	.... B 5	
Fairfield, 9,768	.... C 6	
Forest City, 4,430	.... A 4	
Fort Dodge, 25,894	.... B 3	
Fort Madison, 11,618	.... D 6	
Glenwood, 4,571	.... C 2	
Grinnell, 8,902	.... C 5	
Hampton, 4,133	.... B 4	
Harlan, 5,148	.... C 2	
Hiawatha, 4,986	.... B 6	

Humboldt, 4,438	.... B 3	
Independence, 5,972	.... B 6	
Indianola, 11,340	.... C 4	
Iowa City, 59,738	.... C 6	
Iowa Falls, 5,424	.... B 4	
Jefferson, 4,292	.... B 3	
Keokuk, 12,451	.... D 6	
Knoxville, 8,232	.... C 4	
Le Mars, 8,454	.... B 1	
Manchester, 5,137	.... B 6	
Maquoketa, 6,111	.... B 7	

Marion, 20,403	.... B 6	
Marshalltown, 25,178	.... B 5	
Mason City, 29,040	.... A 4	
Mount Pleasant, 8,027	.... D 6	
Muscatine, 22,881	.... C 6	
Nevada, 6,009	.... B 4	
New Hampton, 3,660	.... A 5	
Newton, 14,789	.... C 4	
Oelwein, 6,493	.... B 6	
Orange City, 4,940	.... B 1	
Oskaloosa, 10,632	.... C 5	

Ottumwa, 24,488	.... C 5	
Pella, 9,270	.... C 5	
Perry, 6,652	.... C 3	
Red Oak, 6,264	.... D 2	
Sheldon, 4,937	.... A 2	
Shenandoah, 5,572	.... D 2	
Sioux Center, 5,074	.... A 1	
Sioux City, 80,505	.... B 1	
Spencer, 11,066	.... A 2	
Spirit Lake, 3,871	.... A 2	
Storm Lake, 8,769	.... B 2	

Urbandale, 23,500	.... C 4	
Vinton, 5,103	.... B 5	
Washington, 7,074	.... C 5	
Waterloo, 66,467	.... B 5	
Waukon, 4,019	.... A 6	
Waverly, 8,539	.... B 5	
Webster City, 7,894	.... B 4	
West Branch, 1,908	.... C 6	
West Des Moines, 31,702	.... C 4	
Windsor Heights, 5,190	.... e 8	

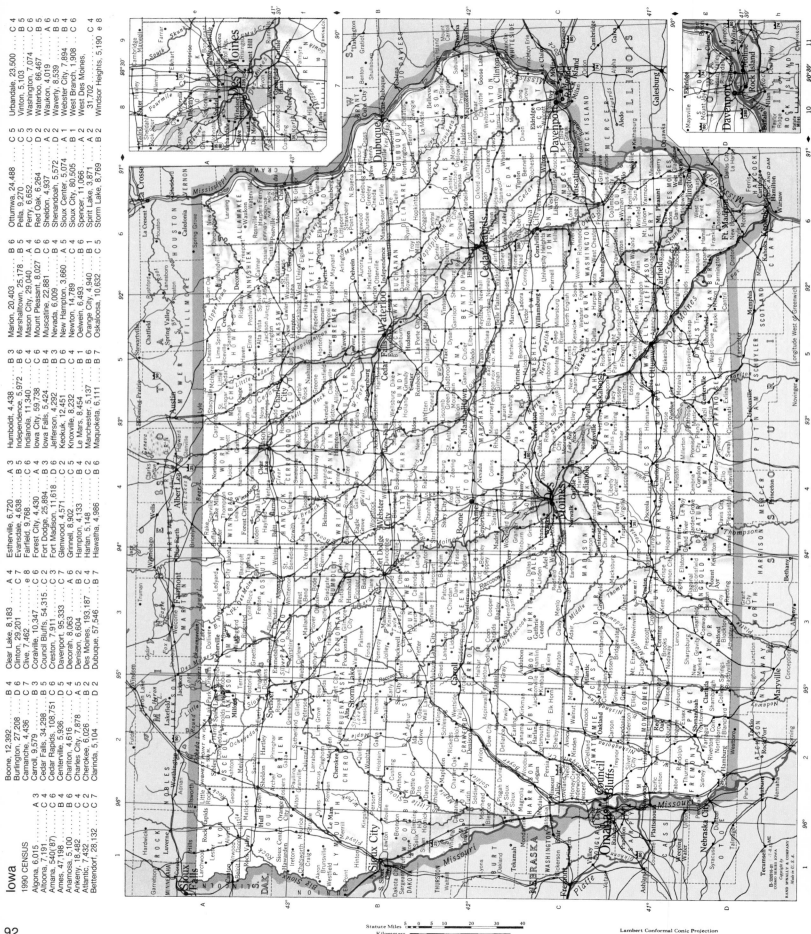

Statute Miles

Kilometers

Lambert Conformal Conic Projection

B-509056-01
OSMO SERIES IOWA
RAND McNALLY & COMPANY

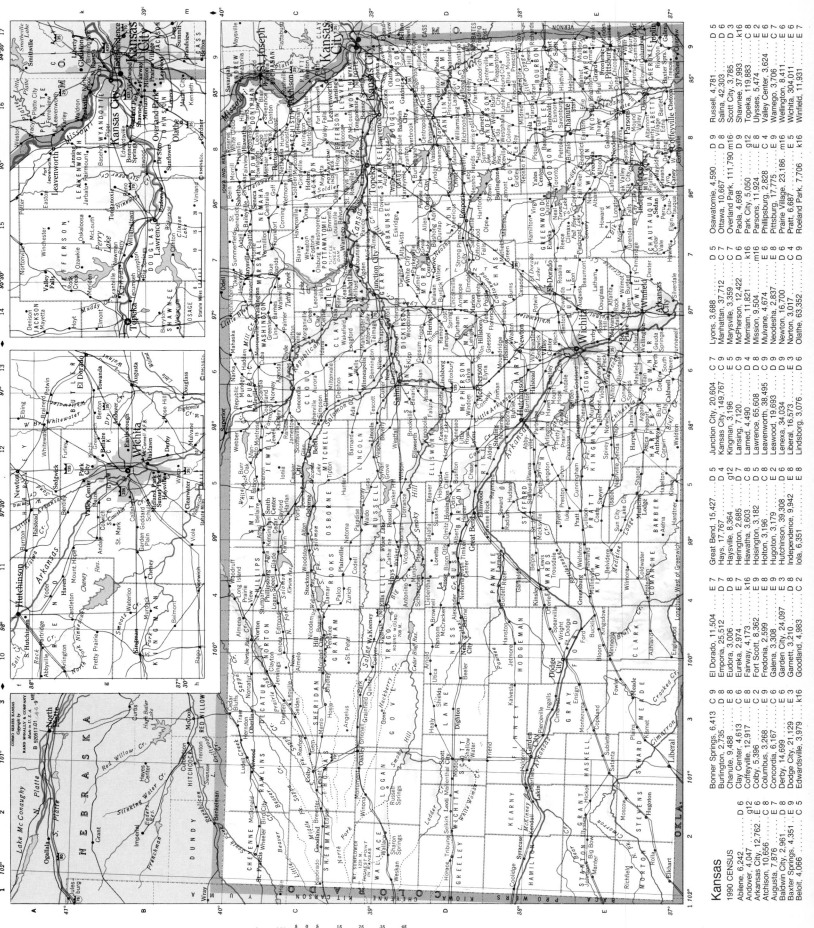

Statute Miles 5 0 5 15   25   35   45
Kilometers 5 0 5 15 25 35 45 55 65

Lambert Conformal Conic Projection

Kansas
1990 CENSUS

Abilene, 6,242	D 6	
Andover, 4,047	g12	
Arkansas City, 12,762	E 6	
Atchison, 10,656	C 8	
Augusta, 7,876	E 7	
Baldwin City, 2,961	D 8	
Baxter Springs, 4,351	E 9	
Beloit, 4,066	C 5	
Bonner Springs, 6,413	C 9	
Burlington, 2,735	D 8	
Chanute, 9,488	E 8	
Clay Center, 4,613	C 6	
Coffeyville, 12,917	E 8	
Colby, 5,396	C 2	
Columbus, 3,268	E 9	
Concordia, 6,167	C 6	
Derby, 14,699	E 7	
Dodge City, 21,129	D 4	
Edwardsville, 3,979	k16	
El Dorado, 11,504	D 7	
Emporia, 25,512	D 8	
Eudora, 3,006	C 8	
Eureka, 2,974	D 7	
Fairway, 4,173	k16	
Fort Scott, 8,362	D 8	
Fredonia, 2,599	E 8	
Galena, 3,308	E 9	
Garden City, 24,097	D 3	
Garnett, 3,210	D 8	
Goodland, 4,983	C 2	
Great Bend, 15,427	D 5	
Hays, 17,767	D 4	
Haysville, 8,364	g12	
Herington, 2,685	D 7	
Hiawatha, 3,603	C 8	
Hoisington, 3,182	D 5	
Holton, 3,196	C 8	
Hugoton, 3,179	E 2	
Hutchinson, 39,308	D 6	
Independence, 9,942	E 8	
Iola, 6,351	D 8	
Junction City, 20,604	C 7	
Kansas City, 149,767	C 9	
Kingman, 3,196	E 5	
Lansing, 7,120	C 8	
Larned, 4,490	D 4	
Lawrence, 65,608	C 8	
Leavenworth, 38,495	C 8	
Leawood, 19,693	m16	
Lenexa, 34,034	m16	
Liberal, 16,573	E 3	
Lindsborg, 3,076	D 6	
Lyons, 3,688	D 5	
Manhattan, 37,712	C 7	
Marysville, 3,359	C 7	
McPherson, 12,422	D 6	
Merriam, 11,821	k16	
Mission, 9,504	m16	
Mulvane, 4,674	E 7	
Neodesha, 2,837	E 8	
Newton, 16,700	D 6	
Norton, 3,017	C 4	
Olathe, 63,352	D 9	
Osawatomie, 4,590	D 9	
Ottawa, 10,667	C 7	
Overland Park, 111,790	m16	
Paola, 4,698	D 9	
Park City, 5,050	g12	
Parsons, 11,924	E 8	
Phillipsburg, 2,828	C 4	
Pittsburg, 17,775	E 9	
Prairie Village, 23,186	m16	
Pratt, 6,687	D 5	
Roeland Park, 7,706	k16	
Russell, 4,781	D 5	
Salina, 42,303	D 6	
Scott City, 3,785	D 3	
Shawnee, 37,993	k16	
Topeka, 119,883	C 7	
Ulysses, 5,474	E 2	
Valley Center, 3,624	E 7	
Wamego, 3,706	C 7	
Wellington, 8,411	E 6	
Wichita, 304,011	E 6	
Winfield, 11,931	E 7	

Kentucky

Kentucky
1990 CENSUS

Alexandria, 5,592 . . . . . B 5
Ashland, 23,622 . . . . . . B 7
Barbourville, 3,658 . . . . D 6
Bardstown, 6,801 . . . . . C 4
Bellevue, 6,997 . . . . . . h13
Benton, 3,899 . . . . f 9
Berea, 9,126 . . . . C 5
Bowling Green, 40,641 . . D 3

Campbellsville, 9,577 . . . C 4
Carrollton, 3,715 . . . . . B 4
Cave City, 1,953 . . . . . . C 2
Central City, 4,979 . . . . C 2
Columbia, 3,845 . . . . . . D 4
Corbin, 7,419 . . . . D 6
Covington, 43,264 . . . . . A 5
Cumberland, 3,112 . . . . . C 7
Cynthiana, 6,497 . . . . . . B 5
Danville, 12,420 . . . . . . C 5
Dayton, 6,576 . . . . D 3

Edgewood, 8,143 . . . . . . h13
Elizabethtown, 18,167 . . . C 4
Elsmere, 6,847 . . . . A 5
Erlanger, 15,979 . . . . . . A 5
Flatwoods, 7,335 . . . . . . B 7
Florence, 18,624 . . . . . . A 5
Fort Mitchell, 7,438 . . . . h13
Fort Thomas, 16,032 . . . . h14
Fort Wright, 6,570 . . . . . h13
Frankfort, 25,968 . . . . . B 5
Franklin, 7,607 . . . . D 3

Georgetown, 11,414 . . . . B 5
Glasgow, 12,351 . . . . . . C 4
Greenville, 4,689 . . . . . . C 2
Harrodsburg, 7,335 . . . . B 4
Hazard, 5,416 . . . . C 6
Henderson, 25,945 . . . . . C 2
Hopkinsville, 29,809 . . . . C 2
Independence, 10,444 . . . h13
Jeffersontown, 23,221 . . . B 4
Lawrenceburg, 5,911 . . . . B 5
Lebanon, 5,695 . . . . C 4

Leitchfield, 4,965 . . . . . . C 3
Lexington, 225,366 . . . . . B 5
London, 5,757 . . . . C 5
Louisville, 269,063 . . . . . B 4
Ludlow, 4,736 . . . . h13
Madisonville, 16,200 . . . . C 2
Mayfield, 9,935 . . . . f 9
Maysville, 7,169 . . . . . . B 6
Middlesboro, 11,328 . . . . D 6
Monticello, 5,357 . . . . . . D 5
Morehead, 8,357 . . . . . . B 6

Morganfield, 3,776 . . . . . C 2
Mount Sterling, 5,362 . . . B 6
Mount Washington,
  5,226 . . . . B 4
Murray, 14,439 . . . . f 9
Newport, 21,155 . . . . . . A 5
Nicholasville, 13,603 . . . . C 5
Owensboro, 53,549 . . . . . C 2
Paducah, 27,256 . . . . . . e 9
Paintsville, 4,354 . . . . . . C 7
Paris, 8,730 . . . . B 5

Pikeville, 6,324 . . . . C 7
Prestonsburg, 3,558 . . . . C 7
Princeton, 6,940 . . . . . . C 2
Providence, 4,123 . . . . . C 2
Radcliff, 19,772 . . . . C 4
Richmond, 21,155 . . . . . C 5
Russell, 4,014 . . . . B 7
Russellville, 7,454 . . . . . D 3
Saint Matthews, 15,800 . . B 4
Scottsville, 4,278 . . . . . . D 3
Shelbyville, 6,238 . . . . . . B 4

Shepherdsville, 4,805 . . . C 4
Shively, 15,535 . . . . B 4
Somerset, 10,733 . . . . . . k14
Taylor Mill, 5,530 . . . . . . D 4
Tompkinsville, 2,861 . . . . D 4
Valley Station,
  20,000('84) g11
Versailles, 7,269 . . . . . . B 5
Williamsburg, 5,493 . . . . D 6
Wilmore, 4,215 . . . . C 5
Winchester, 15,799 . . . . . C 5

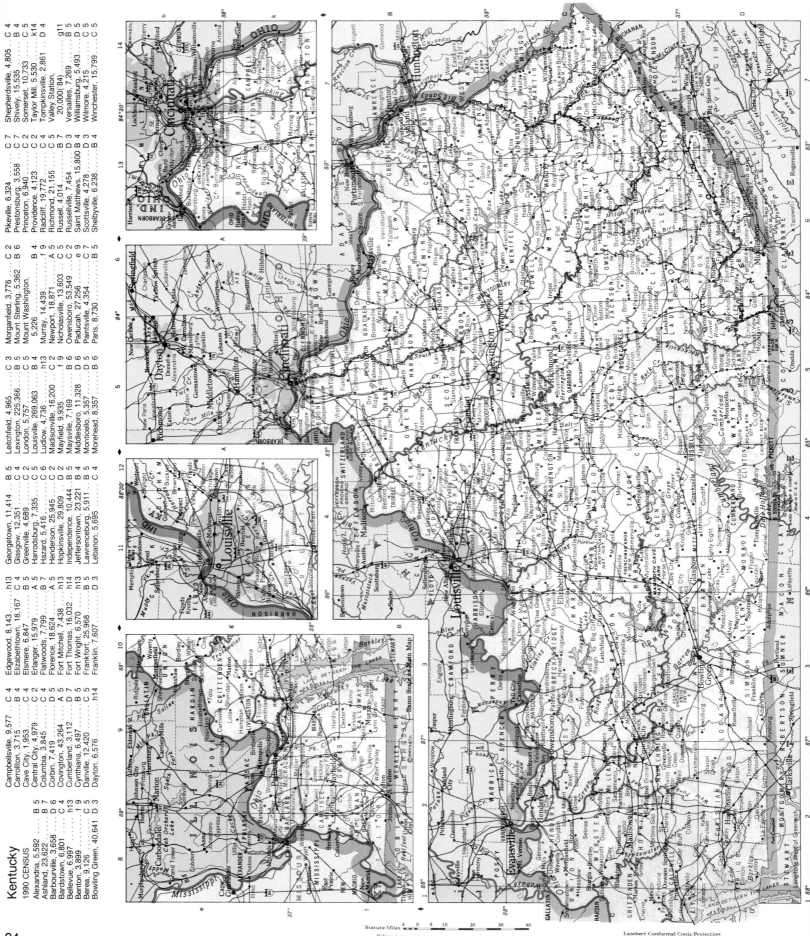

Statute Miles

Kilometers

Lambert Conformal Conic Projection

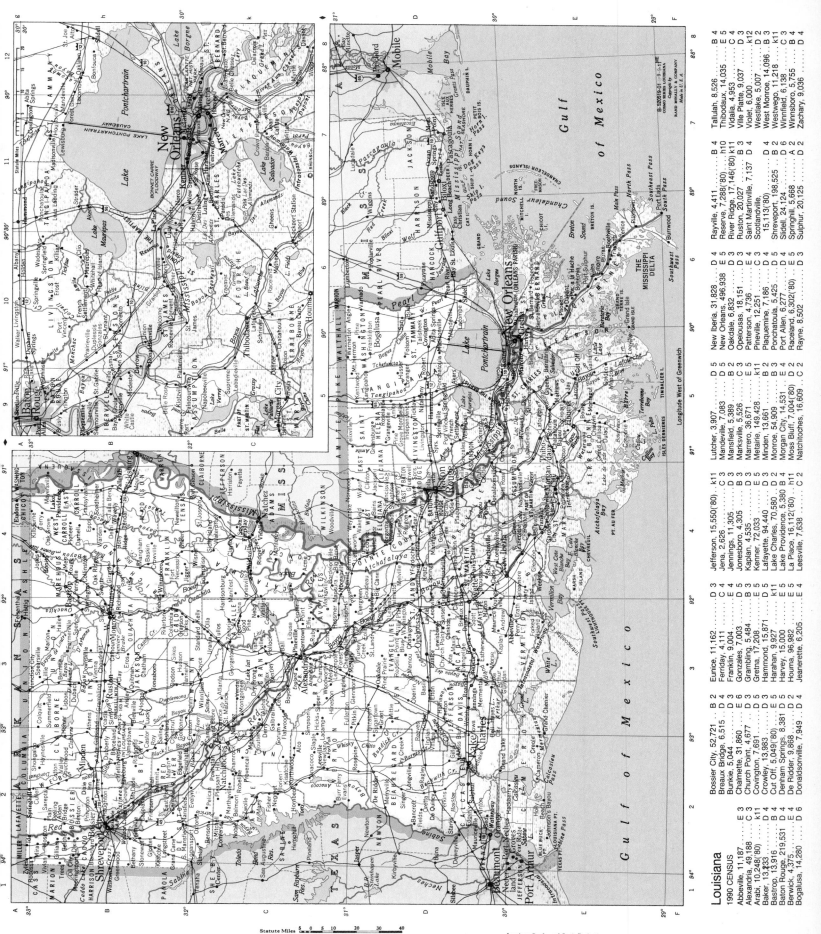

Louisiana
1990 CENSUS

Abbeville, 11,187	E 3	
Alexandria, 49,188	C 3	
Arabi, 10,248('80)	k11	
Baker, 13,233	D 4	
Bastrop, 13,916	B 4	
Baton Rouge, 219,531	D 4	
Berwick, 4,375	E 4	
Bogalusa, 14,280	D 6	

Bossier City, 52,721	B 2	
Breaux Bridge, 6,515	D 4	
Bunkie, 5,044	D 3	
Chalmette, 31,860	E 6	
Church Point, 4,677	D 3	
Covington, 7,691	D 5	
Crowley, 13,983	D 3	
Cut Off, 5,049('80)	E 5	
Denham Springs, 8,381	D 5	
De Ridder, 9,868	C 2	
Donaldsonville, 7,949	D 4	

Eunice, 11,162	D 3	
Ferriday, 4,111	C 4	
Franklin, 9,004	E 4	
Gonzales, 7,003	D 4	
Grambling, 5,484	B 3	
Gretna, 17,208	E 5	
Hammond, 15,871	D 5	
Harahan, 9,927	k11	
Harvey, 15,000	k11	
Houma, 96,982	E 5	
Jeanerette, 6,205	E 4	

Jefferson, 15,550('80)	k11	
Jena, 2,626	C 3	
Jennings, 11,305	D 3	
Jonesboro, 4,305	B 3	
Kaplan, 4,535	E 3	
Kenner, 72,033	E 5	
Lafayette, 94,440	D 4	
Lake Charles, 70,580	D 2	
Lake Providence, 5,380	B 4	
La Place, 16,112('80)	h11	
Leesville, 7,638	C 2	

Lutcher, 3,907	D 5	
Mandeville, 7,083	D 5	
Mansfield, 5,389	B 2	
Marksville, 5,526	D 3	
Marrero, 36,671	E 5	
Metairie, 149,428	E 5	
Minden, 13,661	B 2	
Monroe, 54,909	B 3	
Morgan City, 14,531	E 4	
Moss Bluff, 7,004('80)	D 2	
Natchitoches, 16,609	C 2	

New Iberia, 31,828	D 4	
New Orleans, 496,938	E 5	
Oakdale, 6,832	D 3	
Opelousas, 18,151	D 3	
Patterson, 4,736	E 4	
Pineville, 12,251	C 3	
Plaquemine, 7,186	D 4	
Ponchatoula, 5,425	D 5	
Port Allen, 5,277	D 4	
Raceland, 6,302('80)	E 5	
Rayne, 8,502	D 3	

Rayville, 4,411	B 4	
Reserve, 7,288('80)	h10	
River Ridge, 17,146('80)	k11	
Ruston, 20,027	B 3	
Saint Martinville, 7,137	D 4	
Scotlandville, 15,113('80)	D 4	
Shreveport, 198,525	B 2	
Slidell, 24,124	D 6	
Springhill, 5,668	A 2	
Sulphur, 20,125	D 2	

Tallulah, 8,526	B 4	
Thibodaux, 14,035	E 5	
Vidalia, 4,953	C 4	
Ville Platte, 9,037	D 3	
Violet, 6,000	k12	
Westlake, 5,007	D 2	
West Monroe, 14,096	B 3	
Westwego, 11,218	k11	
Winnfield, 6,138	C 3	
Winnsboro, 5,755	B 4	
Zachary, 9,036	D 4	

B-520519-01
COSMO PRESS LOUISIANA
RAND M?NALLY & COMPANY
Copyright by
Made in U.S.A.

Maine

Maine
1990 CENSUS

Auburn, 24,309 .... D 2
Augusta, 21,325 .... D 3
Bangor, 33,181 .... D 4
Bar Harbor, 2,685
  (4,443▲) .... D 4
Bath, 9,799 .... E 3
Belfast, 6,355 .... D 3
Berwick, 2,378
  (5,995▲) .... E 2
Biddeford, 20,710 .... E 2
Brewer, 9,021 .... D 4
Bridgton, 1,639
  (4,307▲) .... D 2
Brunswick, 10,990
  (20,906▲) .... E 3
Bucksport, 2,853
  (4,825▲) .... D 4
Calais, 3,963 .... C 5
Camden, 3,743
  (5,060▲) .... D 3
Caribou, 9,415 .... B 5
Dexter, 3,118
  (4,419▲) .... C 3
Dixfield, 1,725
  (2,574▲) .... D 2
Dover-Foxcroft, 2,974
  (4,657▲) .... C 3
Eastport, 1,965 .... D 6
Ellsworth, 5,975 .... D 4
Fairfield, 3,169
  (6,718▲) .... D 3
Farmingdale, 2,014
  (2,918▲) .... D 3
Farmington, 3,583
  (7,436▲) .... D 2
Fort Fairfield, 2,282
  (3,998▲) .... B 5
Fort Kent, 2,375
  (4,268▲) .... A 4
Fryeburg, 1,644
  (2,968▲) .... D 2
Gardiner, 6,746 .... D 3
Gorham, 4,052
  (11,856▲) .... E 2
Hallowell, 2,534 .... D 3
Hampden, 2,300
  (5,974▲) .... D 4
Houlton, 5,730
  (6,613▲) .... B 5
Kennebunk, 3,294
  (8,004▲) .... E 2
Kennebunkport, 1,685
  (3,356▲) .... E 2
Kittery, 5,465
  (9,372▲) .... E 2
Lewiston, 39,757 .... D 2
Lincoln, 3,524
  (5,587▲) .... C 4
Livermore Falls, 2,441
  (3,455▲) .... D 2
Madawaska, 4,165
  (4,803▲) .... A 4
Madison, 2,788
  (4,725▲) .... D 3
Mexico, 3,207
  (3,344▲) .... D 2
Milford, 1,688
  (2,884▲) .... D 4
Milo, 2,255 (2,600▲) .... C 4
Newport, 1,748
  (3,036▲) .... D 3
Norway, 2,653
  (4,754▲) .... D 2
Oakland, 3,387
  (5,595▲) .... D 3
Old Town, 8,317 .... D 4
Pittsfield, 3,117
  (4,190▲) .... D 3
Portland, 64,358 .... E 2
Presque Isle, 10,550 .... B 5
Richmond, 1,578
  (3,072▲) .... D 3
Rockland, 7,972 .... D 3
Rumford, 6,256
  (7,078▲) .... D 2
Saco, 15,181 .... E 2
Sanford, 10,268
  (20,463▲) .... E 2
Scarborough, 2,280
  (12,518▲) .... E 2
Skowhegan, 6,517
  (8,725▲) .... D 3
South Berwick, 2,120
  (5,877▲) .... E 2
South Portland,
  23,163 .... E 2
Thomaston, 2,348
  (3,306▲) .... D 3
Topsham, 4,657
  (8,746▲) .... E 3
Waterville, 17,173 .... D 3
Westbrook, 16,121 .... E 2
Wilton, 2,262
  (4,242▲) .... D 2
Winslow, 5,903
  (7,997▲) .... D 3
Winthrop, 3,264
  (5,968▲) .... D 3
Yarmouth, 2,981
  (7,862▲) .... E 2
York, 3,130 (9,818▲) .... E 2

▲ Population of entire town (township), including rural area.

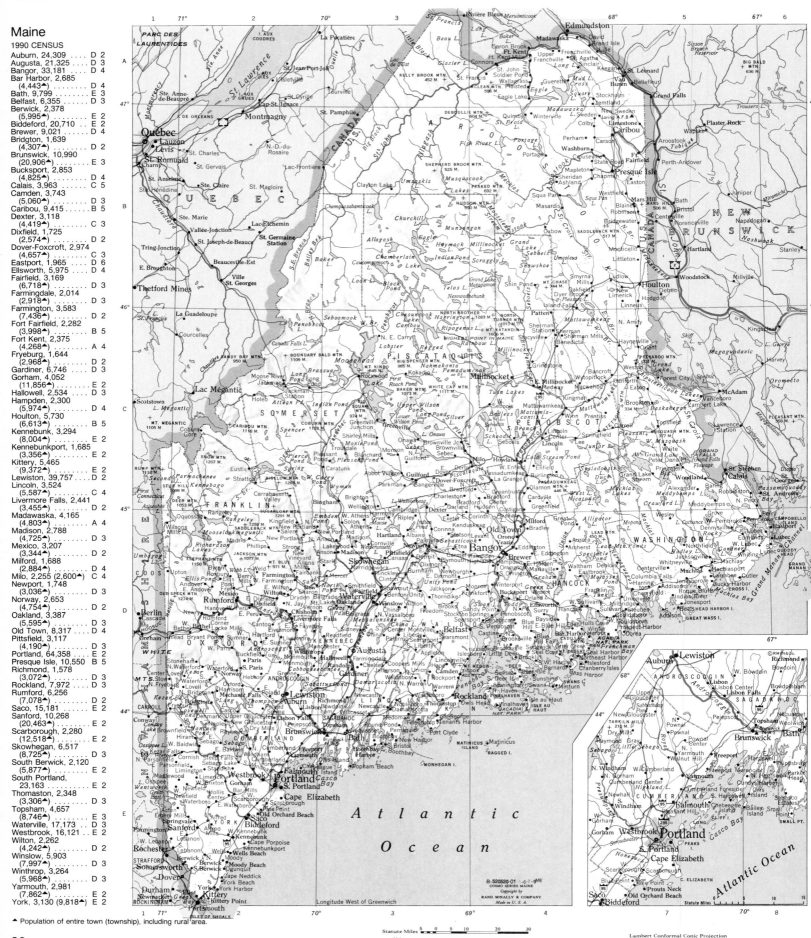

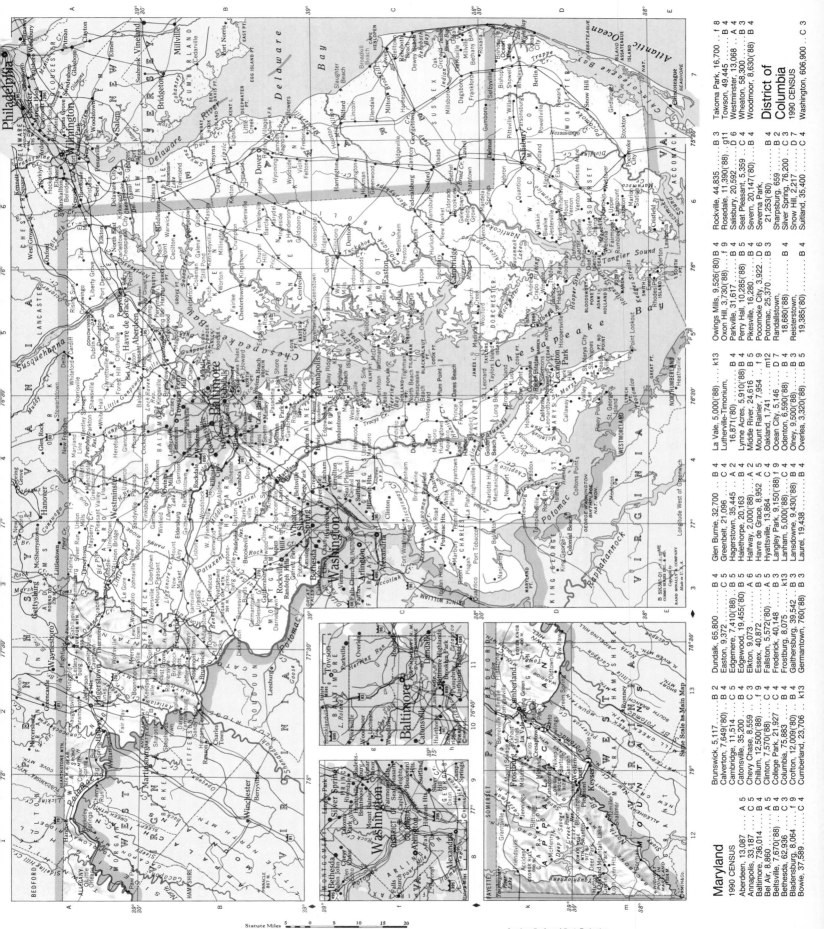

Maryland
1990 CENSUS

Aberdeen, 13,087	A 5		
Annapolis, 33,187	B 4		
Baltimore, 736,014	A 5		
Bel Air, 8,860	A 5		
Beltsville, 7,670('88)	B 4		
Bethesda, 62,936	f 9		
Bladensburg, 8,064	C 4		
Bowie, 37,589			

Brunswick, 5,117	B 2		
Calverton, 7,649('80)	B 4		
Cambridge, 11,514	C 5		
Catonsville, 35,200	B 4		
Chevy Chase, 8,559	C 3		
Chillum, 12,500('88)	f 9		
Clinton, 7,570('88)	C 4		
College Park, 21,927	C 4		
Columbia, 75,883	B 4		
Crofton, 12,009('80)	B 4		
Cumberland, 23,706	k13		

Dundalk, 65,800	B 5		
Easton, 9,372	C 5		
Edgemere, 7,410('88)	B 5		
Edgewood, 19,455('80)	A 6		
Elkton, 9,073	A 6		
Essex, 40,872	B 5		
Fallston, 5,572('80)	A 5		
Frederick, 40,148	B 3		
Frostburg, 8,075	k13		
Gaithersburg, 39,542	B 3		
Germantown, 760('88)	B 3		

Glen Burnie, 32,700	B 4		
Greenbelt, 21,096	C 4		
Hagerstown, 35,445	A 2		
Halfway, 2,000('88)	A 2		
Havre de Grace, 8,952	A 5		
Hyattsville, 13,864	C 4		
Langley Park, 9,150('88)	f 9		
Lanham, 5,000('88)	C 4		
Lansdowne, 9,430('88)	B 4		
Laurel, 19,438	B 4		

La Vale, 5,000('88)	k13		
Lutherville-Timonium, 16,871('80)	B 4		
Lynne Acres, 5,910('88)	B 5		
Middle River, 24,616	B 5		
Mount Rainier, 7,954	f 9		
Oakland, 1,741	m12		
Ocean City, 5,146	D 7		
Odenton, 6,590('88)	B 4		
Olney, 9,500('88)	B 3		
Overlea, 3,320('88)	B 5		

Owings Mills, 9,526('80)	B 4		
Oxon Hill, 3,730('88)	g11		
Parkville, 31,617	B 4		
Perry Hall, 10,285('88)	B 5		
Pikesville, 16,280	B 4		
Pocomoke City, 3,922	D 6		
Potomac, 25,370	B 3		
Randallstown, 21,253('80)	B 4		
Reisterstown, 19,385('80)	B 4		

Rockville, 44,835	B 3		
Rosedale, 11,390('88)	B 4		
Salisbury, 20,592	D 6		
Seat Pleasant, 5,359	C 4		
Severn, 20,147('80)	B 4		
Severna Park, 21,253('80)	B 4		
Sharpsburg, 659	B 2		
Silver Spring, 76,200	C 3		
Snow Hill, 2,217	D 7		
Suitland, 35,400	C 4		

Takoma Park, 16,700	f 8		
Towson, 49,445	A 4		
Westminster, 13,068	A 3		
Wheaton, 58,300	B 3		
Woodmoor, 8,630('88)	B 4		

District of Columbia
1990 CENSUS

Washington, 606,900	C 3

Massachusetts

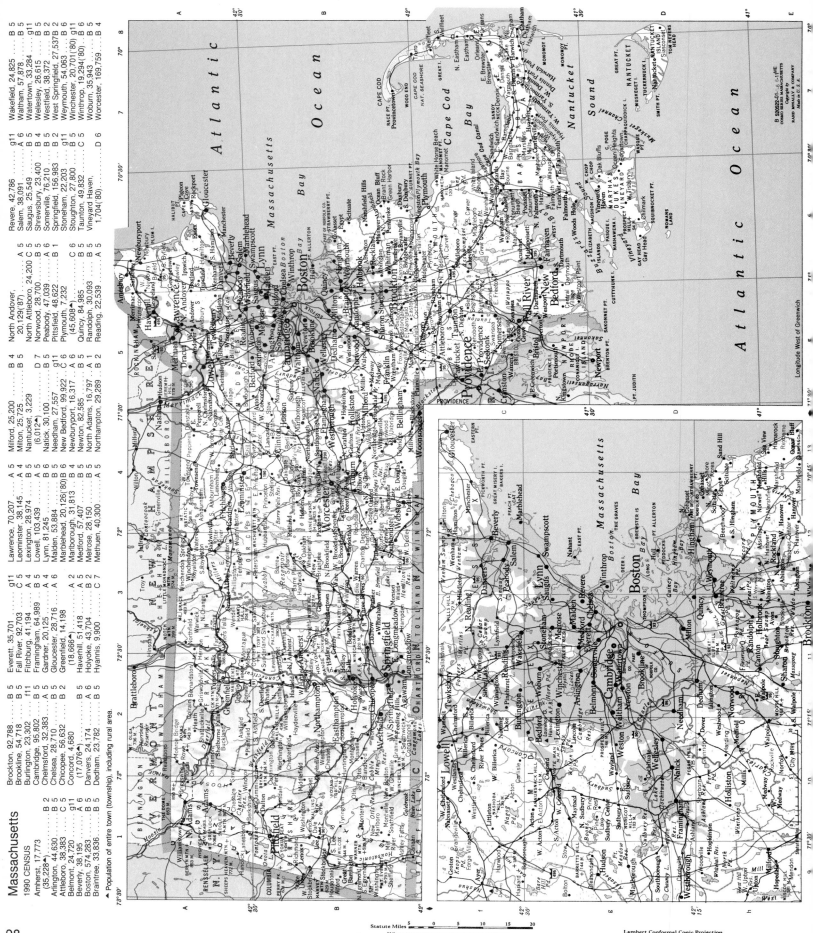

1990 CENSUS

Amherst, 17,773 .... B 2
    (35,228▲)
Arlington, 44,630 .... C 5
Attleboro, 38,383 .... B 5
Belmont, 24,720 .... g11
    (17,076▲)
Beverly, 38,195 .... B 5
Boston, 574,283 .... B 5
Braintree, 33,836 .... B 5

Brockton, 92,788 .... B 5
Brookline, 54,718 .... B 5
Burlington, 23,302 .... f11
Cambridge, 95,802 .... B 5
Chelmsford, 32,383 .... A 5
Chicopee, 56,632 .... B 2
Concord, 4,680 .... A 4
    (18,666▲)
Danvers, 24,174 .... A 6
Dedham, 23,782 .... B 5

Everett, 35,701 .... B 5
Fall River, 92,703 .... B 5
Fitchburg, 41,194 .... f11
Framingham, 64,989 .... B 5
Gardner, 20,125 .... A 4
Gloucester, 28,716 .... B 2
Greenfield, 14,198 .... A 2

Haverhill, 51,418 .... A 5
Holyoke, 43,704 .... B 2
Hyannis, 9,900 .... C 7

Lawrence, 70,207 .... A 5
Leominster, 38,145 .... A 4
Lexington, 28,974 .... B 5
Lowell, 103,439 .... A 5
Lynn, 81,245 .... B 6
Malden, 53,884 .... B 5
Marblehead, 20,126('80) B 6
Marlborough, 31,813 .... B 4
Medford, 57,407 .... B 5
Melrose, 28,150 .... A 5
Methuen, 40,300 .... A 5

Milford, 25,200 .... B 4
Milton, 25,725 .... B 5
Nantucket, 3,229 .... D 7
    (6,012▲)
Natick, 30,100 .... B 5
Needham, 27,557 .... g11
New Bedford, 99,922 ...... C 6
Newburyport, 16,317 ...... A 6
Newton, 82,585 .... B 5
North Adams, 16,797 ...... A 1
Northampton, 29,289 ...... B 2

North Andover,
  20,129('87) .... A 5
North Attleboro, 24,200 .. B 5
Norwood, 28,700 .... B 5
Peabody, 47,039 .... B 6
Pittsfield, 48,622 .... B 1
Plymouth, 7,232 .... C 6
    (45,608▲) .... C 6
Quincy, 84,985 .... B 5
Randolph, 30,093 .... B 5
Reading, 22,539 .... A 5

Revere, 42,786 .... B 5
Salem, 38,091 .... B 6
Saugus, 25,549 .... g11
Shrewsbury, 23,400 .... B 4
Somerville, 76,210 .... B 5
Springfield, 156,983 ...... B 2
Stoneham, 22,203 .... B 6
Stoughton, 27,800 .... g11
Taunton, 49,832 .... C 5
Vineyard Haven,
  1,704('80) .... D 6

Wakefield, 24,825 .... B 5
Waltham, 57,878 .... B 5
Watertown, 33,284 .... g11
Wellesley, 26,615 .... B 5
Westfield, 38,372 .... B 2
West Springfield, 27,537 B 2
Weymouth, 54,063 .... B 6
Winchester, 20,701('80) g11
Winthrop, 19,294('80) .... B 5
Woburn, 35,943 .... B 5
Worcester, 169,759 .... D 4

▲ Population of entire town (township), including rural area.

Statute Miles
Kilometers

Lambert Conformal Conic Projection

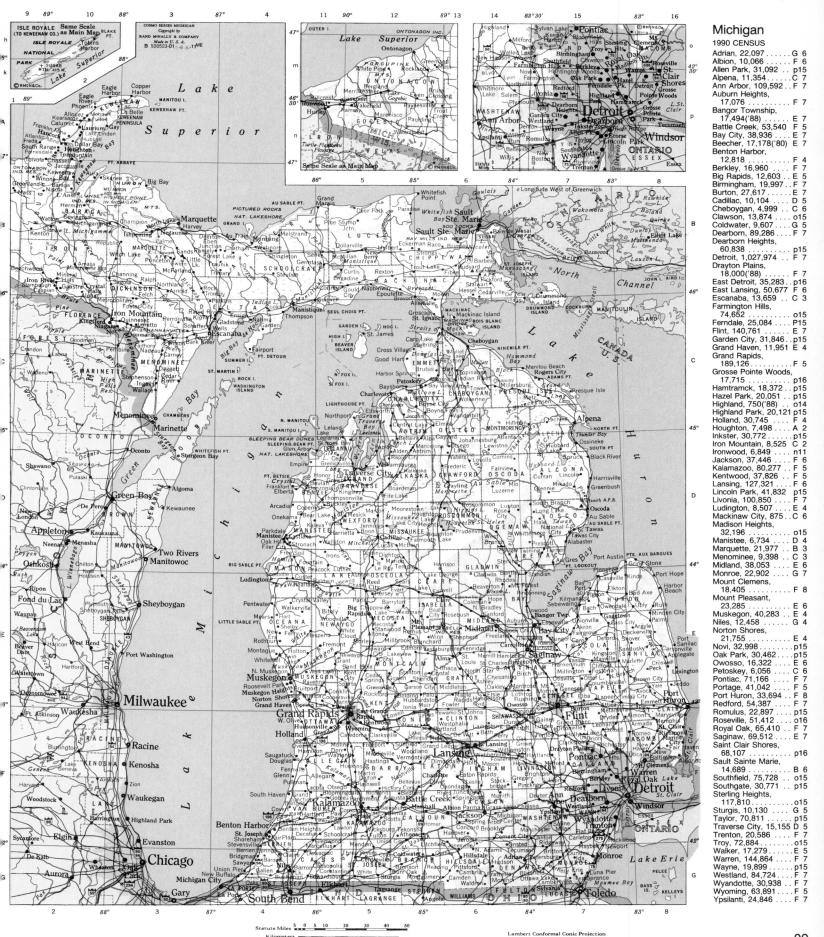

Michigan

1990 CENSUS

Adrian, 22,097 . . . . . . G 6
Albion, 10,066 . . . . . . F 6
Allen Park, 31,092 . . p15
Alpena, 11,354 . . . . C 7
Ann Arbor, 109,592 . . F 7
Auburn Heights,
17,076 . . . . F 7
Bangor Township,
17,494('88) . . . . . . E 7
Battle Creek, 53,540 . F 5
Bay City, 38,936 . . . E 7
Beecher, 17,178('80) . E 7
Benton Harbor,
12,818 . . . . F 4
Berkley, 16,960 . . . . F 7
Big Rapids, 12,603 . . E 5
Birmingham, 19,997 . . F 7
Burton, 27,617 . . . . . E 7
Cadillac, 10,104 . . . D 5
Cheboygan, 4,999 . . C 6
Clawson, 13,874 . . . o15
Coldwater, 9,607 . . . G 5
Dearborn, 89,286 . . . F 7
Dearborn Heights,
60,838 . . . . p15
Detroit, 1,027,974 . . F 7
Drayton Plains,
18,000('88) . . . . . . F 7
East Detroit, 35,283 . p16
East Lansing, 50,677 . F 6
Escanaba, 13,659 . . C 3
Farmington Hills,
74,652 . . . . p15
Ferndale, 25,084 . . . P15
Flint, 140,761 . . . . . . E 7
Garden City, 31,846 . p15
Grand Haven, 11,951 E 4
Grand Rapids,
189,126 . . . . F 5
Grosse Pointe Woods,
17,715 . . . . p16
Hamtramck, 18,372 . . p15
Hazel Park, 20,051 . . p15
Highland, 750('88) . . o14
Highland Park, 20,121 p15
Holland, 30,745 . . . . F 4
Houghton, 7,498 . . . A 2
Inkster, 30,772 . . . . . p15
Iron Mountain, 8,525 C 2
Ironwood, 6,849 . . . n11
Jackson, 37,446 . . . . F 6
Kalamazoo, 80,277 . . F 5
Kentwood, 37,826 . . F 5
Lansing, 127,321 . . . F 6
Lincoln Park, 41,832 p15
Livonia, 100,850 . . . F 7
Ludington, 8,507 . . . E 4
Mackinaw City, 875 . C 6
Madison Heights,
32,196 . . . . o15
Manistee, 6,734 . . . . D 4
Marquette, 21,977 . . B 3
Menominee, 9,398 . . C 3
Midland, 38,053 . . . . E 6
Monroe, 22,902 . . . . G 7
Mount Clemens,
18,405 . . . . F 8
Mount Pleasant,
23,285 . . . . E 6
Muskegon, 40,283 . . E 4
Niles, 12,458 . . . . . . F 5
Norton Shores,
21,755 . . . . E 4
Novi, 32,998 . . . . . . p15
Oak Park, 30,462 . . . p15
Owosso, 16,322 . . . . E 6
Petoskey, 6,056 . . . . C 6
Pontiac, 71,166 . . . . F 7
Portage, 41,042 . . . . F 5
Port Huron, 33,694 . . F 8
Redford, 54,387 . . . . F 7
Romulus, 22,897 . . . p15
Roseville, 51,412 . . . o16
Royal Oak, 65,410 . . F 7
Saginaw, 69,512 . . . E 7
Saint Clair Shores,
68,107 . . . . p16
Sault Sainte Marie,
14,689 . . . . B 6
Southfield, 75,728 . . o15
Southgate, 30,771 . . p15
Sterling Heights,
117,810 . . . . o15
Sturgis, 10,130 . . . . G 5
Taylor, 70,811 . . . . . p15
Traverse City, 15,155 D 5
Trenton, 20,586 . . . . F 7
Troy, 72,884 . . . . . . o15
Walker, 17,279 . . . . E 5
Warren, 144,864 . . . F 7
Wayne, 19,899 . . . . p15
Westland, 84,724 . . . F 7
Wyandotte, 30,938 . . F 7
Wyoming, 63,891 . . . F 5
Ypsilanti, 24,846 . . . F 7

Minnesota

Minnesota
1990 CENSUS

Albert Lea, 18,310 . . G 5
Alexandria, 7,838 . . . E 3
Andover, 15,216 . . . m12
Anoka, 17,192 . . . . E 5
Apple Valley, 34,598 . n12
Austin, 21,907 . . . . . G 6
Bemidji, 11,245 . . . . C 4
Blaine, 38,975 . . . . m12
Bloomington, 86,335 F 5
Brainerd, 12,353 . . . D 4
Brooklyn Center,
  28,887 . . . . E 5
Brooklyn Park,
  56,381 . . . . F 5
Burnsville, 51,288 . . . F 5
Champlin, 16,849 . . m12
Chisholm, 5,290 . . . C 6
Cloquet, 10,885 . . . . D 6
Columbia Heights,
  18,910 . . . . . . m12
Coon Rapids, 52,978 E 5
Cottage Grove,
  22,935 . . . . n13
Crookston, 8,119 . . . C 2
Crystal, 23,788 . . . . E 5
Detroit Lakes, 6,635 . D 3
Duluth, 85,493 . . . . D 6
Eagan, 47,409 . . . . n12
East Bethel, 8,050 . . E 5
East Grand Forks,
  8,658 . . . . C 2
Eden Prairie, 39,311 . n12
Edina, 46,070 . . . . . F 5
Ely, 3,968 . . . . C 7
Fairmont, 11,265 . . . G 4
Faribault, 17,085 . . . F 5
Fergus Falls, 12,362 . D 2
Fridley, 28,335 . . . m12
Golden Valley, 20,971 n12
Grand Marais, 1,171 . k 9
Grand Rapids, 7,976 C 5
Hastings, 15,445 . . . F 6
Hibbing, 18,046 . . . C 6
Hopkins, 16,534 . . m12
Hutchinson, 11,523 . F 4
International Falls,
  8,325 . . . . B 5
Inver Grove Heights,
  22,477 . . . . n12
Lakeville, 24,854 . . . F 5
Litchfield, 6,041 . . . E 4
Little Falls, 7,232 . . . E 4
Mankato, 31,477 . . . F 4
Maple Grove, 38,736 m12
Maplewood, 30,954 . . n12
Marshall, 12,023 . . . F 3
Minneapolis, 368,383 F 5
Minnetonka, 48,370 . . F 5
Montevideo, 5,499 . . F 3
Moorhead, 32,295 . . D 2
Morris, 5,613 . . . . . E 3
Mound, 9,634 . . . . . n11
Mounds View, 12,541 m12
New Brighton, 22,207 m12
New Hope, 21,853 . . n12
New Ulm, 13,132 . . . F 4
Northfield, 14,684 . . F 5
North Mankato,
  10,164 . . . . F 4
North St. Paul,
  12,376 . . . . m13
Owatonna, 19,386 . . F 5
Pipestone, 4,554 . . . G 2
Plymouth, 50,889 . . m12
Prior Lake, 11,482 . . F 5
Ramsey, 12,408 . . . E 5
Red Wing, 15,134 . . F 6
Redwood Falls, 4,859 F 3
Richfield, 35,710 . . . F 5
Robbinsdale, 14,396 . F 5
Rochester, 70,745 . . F 6
Roseville, 33,485 . . m12
Saint Cloud, 48,812 . E 4
Saint Louis Park,
  43,787 . . . . n12
Saint Paul, 272,235 . F 5
Saint Peter, 9,421 . . F 4
Shakopee, 11,739 . . F 5
Shoreview, 24,587 . m12
South St. Paul,
  20,197 . . . . n12
Stillwater, 13,882 . . E 6
Thief River Falls,
  8,010 . . . . B 2
Virginia, 9,410 . . . . C 6
Waseca, 8,385 . . . . F 5
West Saint Paul,
  19,248 . . . . n12
White Bear Lake,
  24,704 . . . . E 5
Willmar, 17,531 . . . E 3
Winona, 25,399 . . . F 7
Woodbury, 20,075 . . F 6
Worthington, 9,977 . . G 3

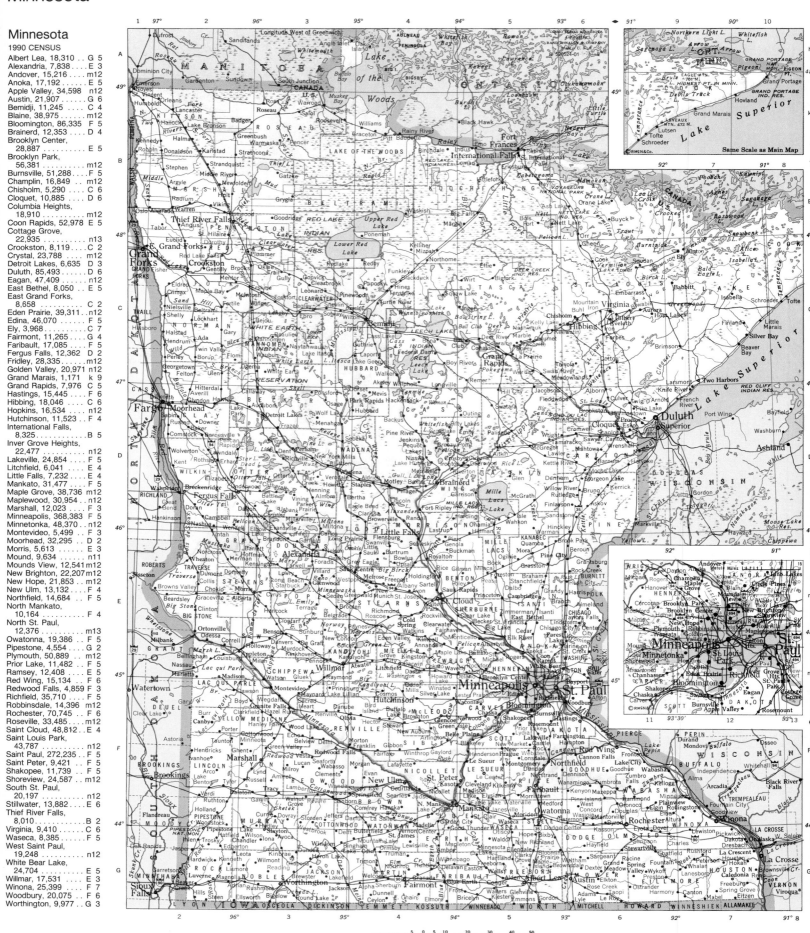

Statute Miles
Kilometers

Lambert Conformal Conic Projection

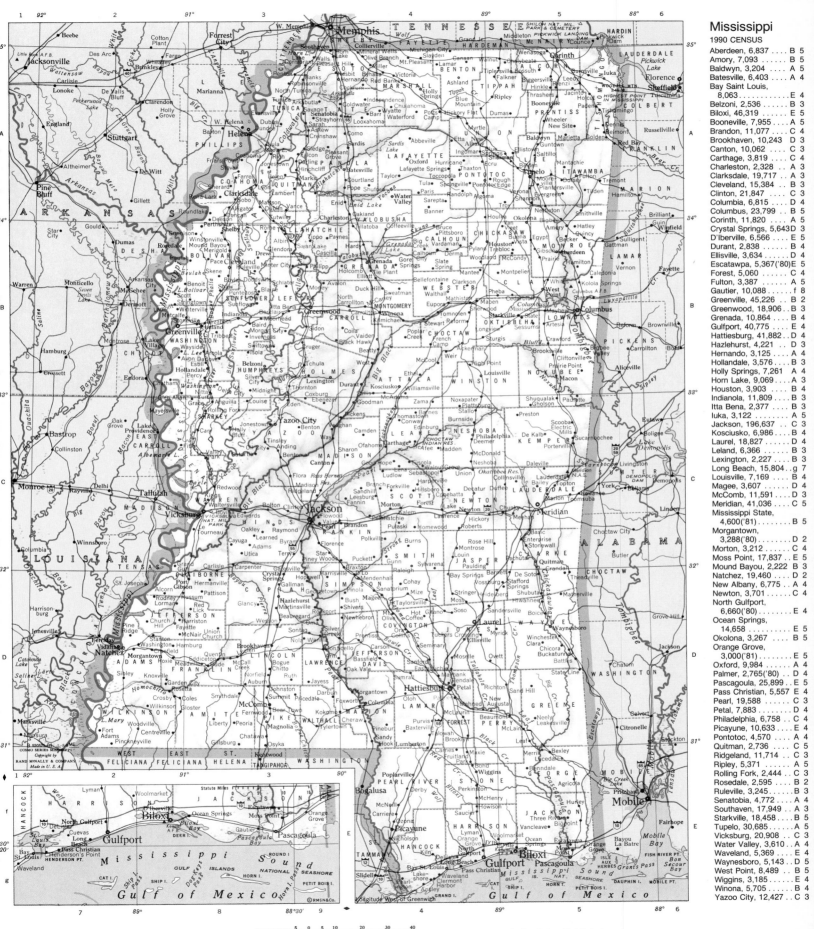

Mississippi
1990 CENSUS

Aberdeen, 6,837 . . . . . . B 5
Amory, 7,093 . . . . . . B 5
Baldwyn, 3,204 . . . . . A 5
Batesville, 6,403 . . . . A 4
Bay Saint Louis,
  8,063 . . . . E 4
Belzoni, 2,536 . . . . . . B 3
Biloxi, 46,319 . . . . . . E 5
Booneville, 7,955 . . . . A 5
Brandon, 11,077 . . . . . C 4
Brookhaven, 10,243 . . D 3
Canton, 10,062 . . . . . C 3
Carthage, 3,819 . . . . . C 4
Charleston, 2,328 . . . . A 3
Clarksdale, 19,717 . . . A 3
Cleveland, 15,384 . . . B 3
Clinton, 21,847 . . . . . C 3
Columbia, 6,815 . . . . . D 4
Columbus, 23,799 . . . . B 5
Corinth, 11,820 . . . . . A 5
Crystal Springs, 5,643 D 3
D'Iberville, 6,566 . . . . E 5
Durant, 2,838 . . . . . . B 4
Ellisville, 3,634 . . . . . D 4
Escatawpa, 5,367('80) E 5
Forest, 5,060 . . . . . . C 4
Fulton, 3,387 . . . . . . A 5
Gautier, 10,088 . . . . . f 8
Greenville, 45,226 . . B 2
Greenwood, 18,906 . . B 3
Grenada, 10,864 . . . . B 4
Gulfport, 40,775 . . . . E 4
Hattiesburg, 41,882 . . D 4
Hazlehurst, 4,221 . . . D 3
Hernando, 3,125 . . . . A 4
Hollandale, 3,576 . . . B 3
Holly Springs, 7,261 . . A 4
Horn Lake, 9,069 . . . . A 3
Houston, 3,903 . . . . . B 4
Indianola, 11,809 . . . . B 3
Itta Bena, 2,377 . . . . B 3
Iuka, 3,122 . . . . A 5
Jackson, 196,637 . . . . C 3
Kosciusko, 6,986 . . . . B 4
Laurel, 18,827 . . . . . D 4
Leland, 6,366 . . . . . . B 3
Lexington, 2,227 . . . . B 3
Long Beach, 15,804 . . g 7
Louisville, 7,169 . . . . B 4
Magee, 3,607 . . . . . . D 4
McComb, 11,591 . . . . D 3
Meridian, 41,036 . . . . C 5
Mississippi State,
  4,600('81) . . . . B 5
Morgantown,
  3,288('80) . . . . D 2
Morton, 3,212 . . . . . . C 4
Moss Point, 17,837 . . E 5
Mound Bayou, 2,222 . . B 3
Natchez, 19,460 . . . . D 2
New Albany, 6,775 . . A 4
Newton, 3,701 . . . . . C 4
North Gulfport,
  6,660('80) . . . . E 4
Ocean Springs,
  14,658 . . . . E 5
Okolona, 3,267 . . . . B 5
Orange Grove,
  3,000('81) . . . . E 5
Oxford, 9,984 . . . . . . A 4
Palmer, 2,765('80) . . D 4
Pascagoula, 25,899 . . E 5
Pass Christian, 5,557 E 4
Pearl, 19,588 . . . . . . C 3
Petal, 7,883 . . . . D 4
Philadelphia, 6,758 . . C 4
Picayune, 10,633 . . . . E 4
Pontotoc, 4,570 . . . . A 4
Quitman, 2,736 . . . . . C 5
Ridgeland, 11,714 . . . C 3
Ripley, 5,371 . . . . . . A 5
Rolling Fork, 2,444 . . C 2
Rosedale, 2,595 . . . . B 2
Ruleville, 3,245 . . . . B 3
Senatobia, 4,772 . . . . A 4
Southaven, 17,949 . . A 3
Starkville, 18,458 . . . B 5
Tupelo, 30,685 . . . . . A 5
Vicksburg, 20,908 . . C 3
Water Valley, 3,610 . . A 4
Waveland, 5,369 . . . . E 4
Waynesboro, 5,143 . . D 5
West Point, 8,489 . . . B 5
Wiggins, 3,185 . . . . . E 4
Winona, 5,705 . . . . . B 4
Yazoo City, 12,427 . . C 3

Missouri

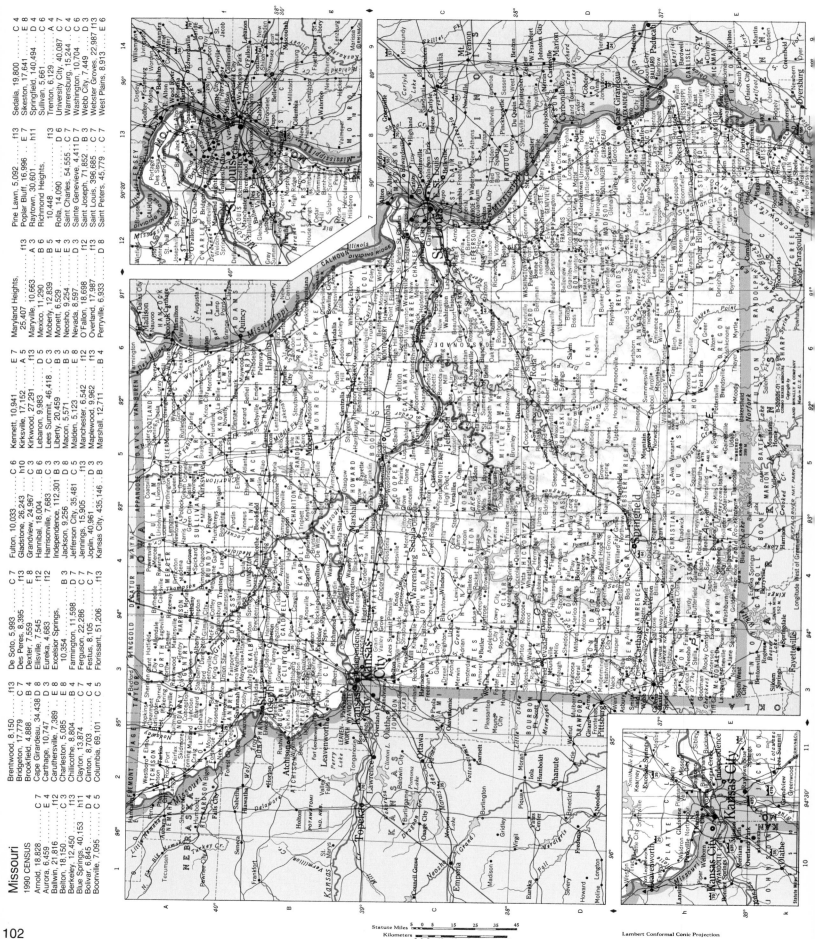

Missouri

1990 CENSUS

Arnold, 18,828	C 7	
Aurora, 6,459	E 4	
Ballwin, 21,816	f12	
Belton, 18,150	C 3	
Berkeley, 12,450	f13	
Blue Springs, 40,153	h11	
Bolivar, 6,845	D 4	
Boonville, 7,095	C 5	

Brentwood, 8,150	f13	
Bridgeton, 17,779	C 7	
Brookfield, 4,888	B 4	
Cape Girardeau, 34,438	D 8	
Carthage, 10,747	D 3	
Caruthersville, 7,389	E 8	
Charleston, 5,085	E 8	
Chillicothe, 8,804	B 4	
Clayton, 13,874	C 7	
Clinton, 8,703	C 4	
Columbia, 69,101	C 5	

De Soto, 5,993	C 7	
Des Peres, 8,395	f13	
Dexter, 7,559	E 8	
Ellisville, 7,545	f12	
Eureka, 4,683	f12	
Excelsior Springs, 10,354	B 3	
Farmington, 11,598	D 7	
Ferguson, 22,286	C 7	
Festus, 8,105	C 7	
Florissant, 51,206	f13	

Fulton, 10,033	C 6	
Gladstone, 26,243	h10	
Grandview, 24,967	E 8	
Harrisonville, 7,683	C 3	
Independence, 112,301	B 3	
Jackson, 9,256	D 8	
Jefferson City, 35,481	C 5	
Joplin, 40,961	D 3	
Kansas City, 435,146	B 3	

Kennett, 10,941	E 7	
Kirksville, 17,152	A 5	
Kirkwood, 27,291	f13	
Lebanon, 9,983	D 5	
Lees Summit, 46,418	C 3	
Liberty, 20,459	B 3	
Macon, 5,571	B 5	
Malden, 5,123	E 8	
Manchester, 6,542	f13	
Maplewood, 9,962	D 3	
Marshall, 12,711	B 4	

Maryland Heights, 25,407	f13	
Maryville, 10,663	A 3	
Mexico, 11,290	B 6	
Moberly, 12,839	B 5	
Monett, 6,529	E 4	
Neosho, 9,254	D 6	
Nevada, 8,597	D 3	
O'Fallon, 18,698	D 3	
Overland, 17,987	f13	
Perryville, 6,933	B 4	

Pine Lawn, 5,092	f13	
Poplar Bluff, 16,996	E 7	
Raytown, 30,601	h11	
Richmond Heights, 10,448		
Rolla, 14,090	D 6	
Saint Charles, 54,555	C 7	
Sainte Genevieve, 4,411	D 7	
Saint Joseph, 71,852	B 3	
Saint Louis, 396,685	C 7	
Saint Peters, 45,779	f13	

Sedalia, 19,800	C 4	
Sikeston, 17,641	E 8	
Springfield, 140,494	D 4	
Sullivan, 5,661	C 7	
Trenton, 6,129	A 4	
University City, 40,087	C 7	
Warrensburg, 15,244	C 4	
Washington, 10,704	C 6	
Webb City, 7,449	D 3	
Webster Groves, 22,987	f13	
West Plains, 8,913	E 6	

Statute Miles
Kilometers

Lambert Conformal Conic Projection

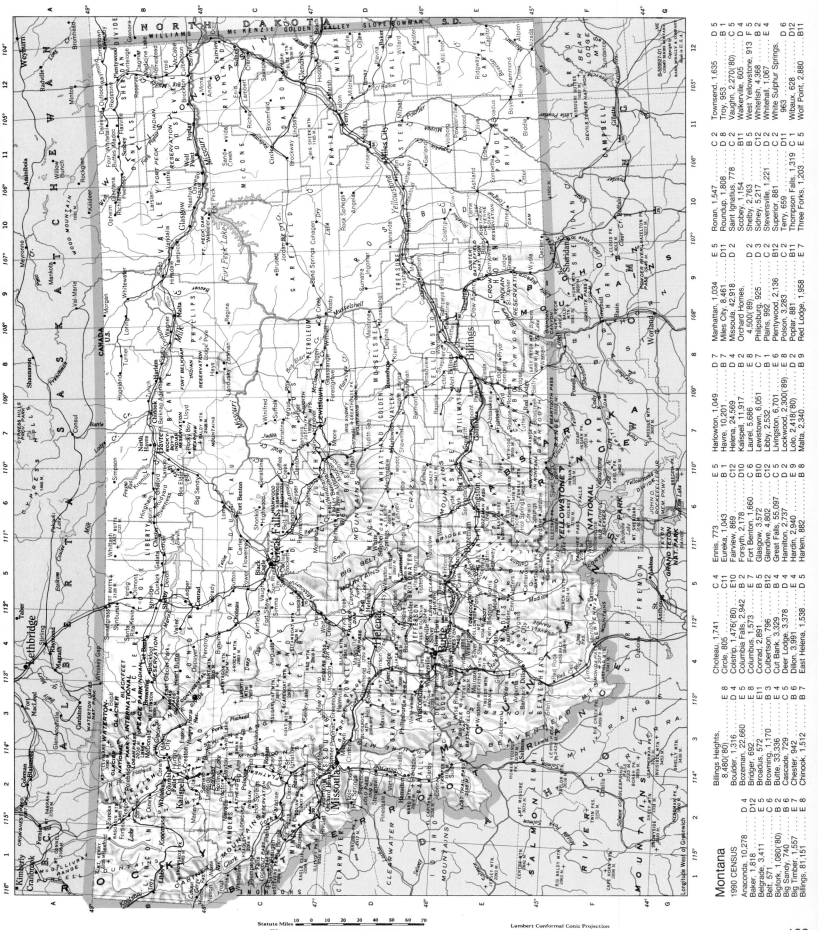

Montana

1990 CENSUS

Anaconda, 10,278	D 12	
Baker, 1,818	E 5	
Belgrade, 3,411	C 6	
Belt, 571	B 2	
Bigfork, 1,080(/80)	B 2	
Big Sandy, 740	B 6	
Big Timber, 1,557	E 7	
Billings, 81,151	E 8	

Billings Heights, 8,480(/80)	E 8	
Boulder, 1,316	D 4	
Bozeman, 22,660	E 5	
Bridger, 692	E 8	
Broadus, 572	E 11	
Browning, 1,170	B 3	
Butte, 33,336	D 4	
Cascade, 729	C 5	
Chester, 942	B 6	
Chinook, 1,512	B 7	

Choteau, 1,741	C 4	
Circle, 805	C 11	
Colstrip, 1,476(/80)	E 10	
Columbia Falls, 2,942	B 2	
Columbus, 1,573	E 7	
Conrad, 2,891	B 5	
Culbertson, 796	B 12	
Cut Bank, 3,329	B 4	
Deer Lodge, 3,378	D 4	
Dillon, 3,991	E 4	
East Helena, 1,538	D 5	

Ennis, 773	E 5	
Eureka, 1,043	B 1	
Fairview, 869	C 12	
Forsyth, 2,178	D 10	
Fort Benton, 1,660	C 6	
Glasgow, 3,572	B 10	
Glendive, 4,802	C 12	
Great Falls, 55,097	C 5	
Hamilton, 2,737	D 2	
Hardin, 2,940	E 9	
Harlem, 882	B 8	

Harlowton, 1,049	D 7	
Havre, 10,201	B 7	
Helena, 24,569	D 4	
Kalispell, 11,917	C 6	
Laurel, 5,686	C 7	
Lewistown, 6,051	C 7	
Libby, 2,532	B 12	
Livingston, 6,701	C 5	
Lockwood, 2,300(/89)	E 8	
Lolo, 2,418(/80)	D 2	
Malta, 2,340	B 8	

Manhattan, 1,034	E 5	
Miles City, 8,461	D 11	
Missoula, 42,918	D 2	
Orchard Homes, 4,500(/89)		
Philipsburg, 925	D 3	
Plains, 992	D 2	
Plentywood, 2,136	B 12	
Polson, 3,283	C 2	
Poplar, 881	B 11	
Red Lodge, 1,958	E 7	

Ronan, 1,547	C 2	
Roundup, 1,808	D 8	
Saint Ignatius, 778	C 2	
Scobey, 1,154	B 11	
Shelby, 2,763	B 5	
Sidney, 5,217	C 12	
Stevensville, 1,221	D 2	
Superior, 881	C 2	
Terry, 659	D 11	
Thompson Falls, 1,319	C 1	
Three Forks, 1,203	E 5	

Townsend, 1,635	D 5	
Troy, 953	B 1	
Vaughn, 2,270(/80)	C 5	
Walkerville, 605	D 4	
West Yellowstone, 913	F 5	
Whitefish, 4,368	B 2	
Whitehall, 1,067	E 4	
White Sulphur Springs, 963	D 6	
Wibaux, 628	C 12	
Wolf Point, 2,880	B 11	

Statute Miles
10 0 10 20 30 40 50 60 70

Kilometers
10 0 10 30 50 70 90

Lambert Conformal Conic Projection

Nebraska

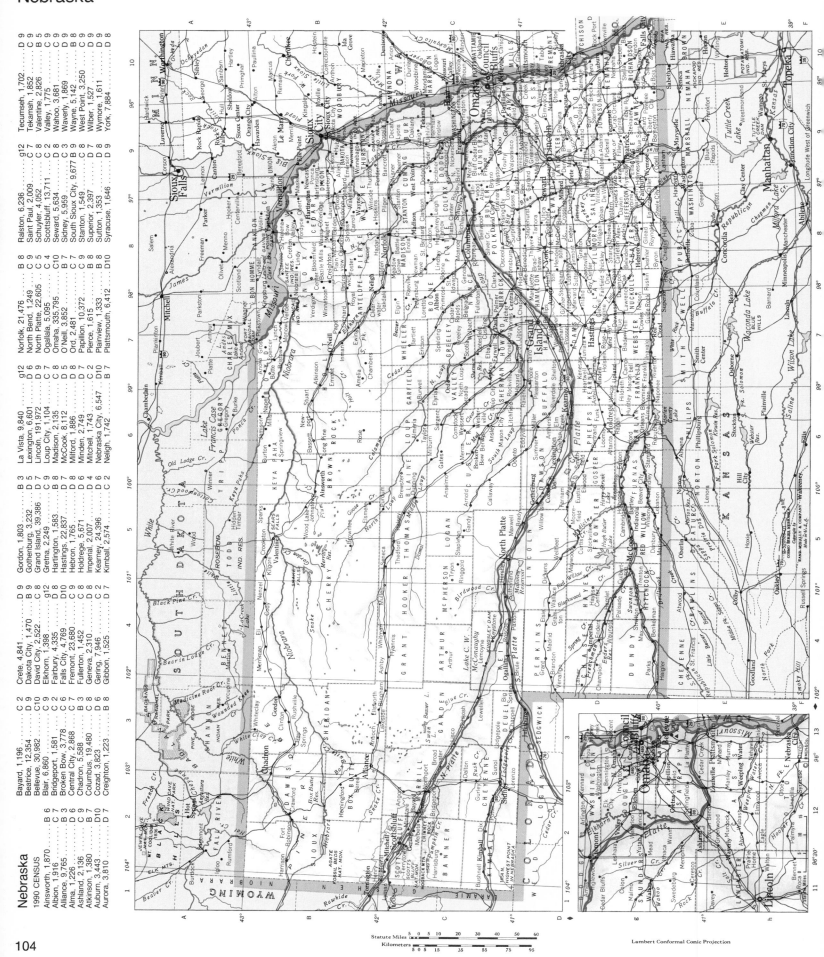

Statute Miles
Kilometers

Lambert Conformal Conic Projection

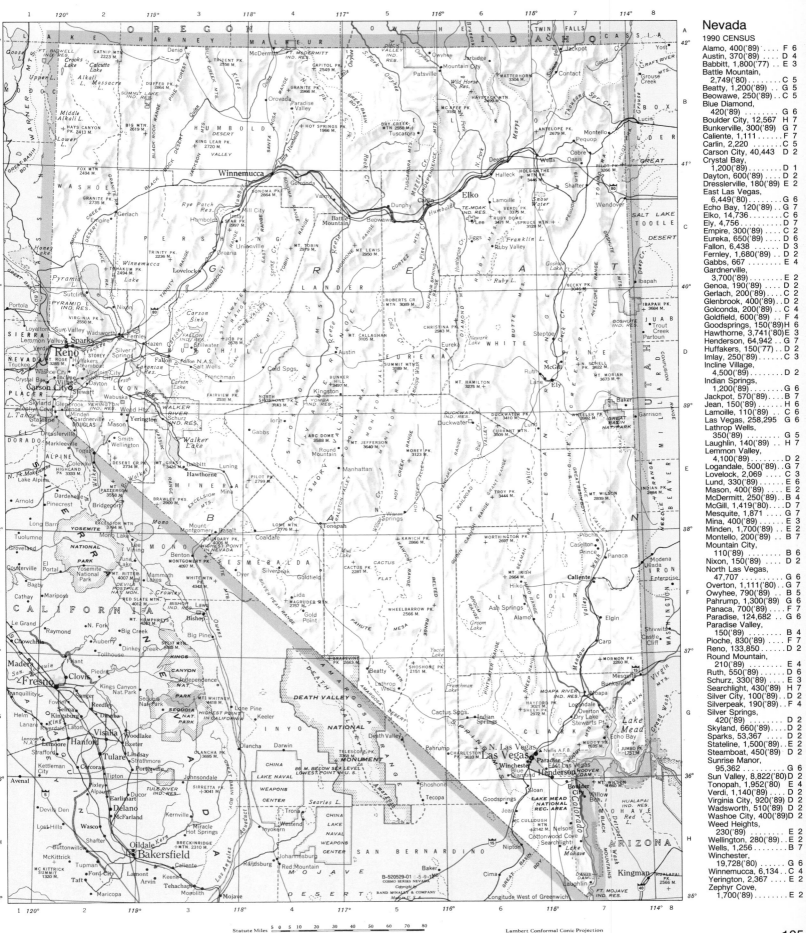

Nevada
1990 CENSUS

Alamo, 400('89) .... F 6
Austin, 370('89) .... D 4
Babbitt, 1,800('77) .. E 3
Battle Mountain,
2,749('80)....... C 5
Beatty, 1,200('89) .... G 5
Beowawe, 250('89) .. C 5
Blue Diamond,
420('89) .... G 6
Boulder City, 12,567 . H 7
Bunkerville, 300('89) . G 7
Caliente, 1,111 ...... F 7
Carlin, 2,220 .... C 5
Carson City, 40,443 .. D 2
Crystal Bay,
1,200('89) .... D 1
Dayton, 600('89) .... D 2
Dresslerville, 180('89) E 2
East Las Vegas,
6,449('80) .... G 6
Echo Bay, 120('89) .. G 7
Elko, 14,736........ C 6
Ely, 4,756.......... D 7
Empire, 300('89) .... C 2
Eureka, 650('89) .... D 6
Fallon, 6,438 .... D 3
Fernley, 1,680('89) .. D 2
Gabbs, 667 .... E 4
Gardnerville,
3,700('89) .... E 2
Genoa, 190('89) .... D 2
Gerlach, 200('89) .... C 2
Glenbrook, 400('89) . D 2
Golconda, 200('89) .. C 4
Goldfield, 600('89) .. F 4
Goodsprings, 150('89) H 6
Hawthorne, 3,741('80)E 3
Henderson, 64,942 .. G 7
Huffakers, 150('77) .. D 2
Imlay, 250('89) ..... C 3
Incline Village,
4,500('89) .... D 2
Indian Springs,
1,200('89) .... G 6
Jackpot, 570('89) .... B 7
Jean, 150('89) ...... H 6
Lamoille, 110('89) ... C 6
Las Vegas, 258,295 . G 6
Lathrop Wells,
350('89) .... G 5
Laughlin, 140('89) ... H 7
Lemmon Valley,
4,100('89) .... D 2
Logandale, 500('89) .G 7
Lovelock, 2,069 ..... C 3
Lund, 330('89) ...... E 6
Mason, 400('89) .... E 2
McDermitt, 250('89) .. B 4
McGill, 1,419('80) ... D 7
Mesquite, 1,871 .... G 7
Mina, 400('89) ...... E 3
Minden, 1,700('89) .. E 2
Montello, 200('89) .. B 7
Mountain City,
110('89) .... B 6
Nixon, 150('89) ..... D 2
North Las Vegas,
47,707 .... G 6
Overton, 1,111('80) .. G 7
Owyhee, 790('89) ... B 5
Pahrump, 1,300('89) . G 6
Panaca, 700('89) .... F 7
Paradise, 124,682 ... G 6
Paradise Valley,
150('89) .... B 4
Pioche, 830('89) .... F 7
Reno, 133,850...... D 2
Round Mountain,
210('89) .... E 4
Ruth, 550('89) ...... D 6
Schurz, 330('89) .... E 3
Searchlight, 430('89) . H 7
Silver City, 100('89) . D 2
Silverpeak, 190('89) .. F 4
Silver Springs,
420('89) .... D 2
Skyland, 660('89).... D 2
Sparks, 53,367 ..... D 2
Stateline, 1,500('89) . D 2
Steamboat, 450('89) . D 2
Sunrise Manor,
95,362 .... G 6
Sun Valley, 8,822('80)D 2
Tonopah, 1,952('80) . E 4
Verdi, 1,140('89) .... D 2
Virginia City, 920('89) D 2
Wadsworth, 510('89) . D 2
Washoe City, 400('89)D 2
Weed Heights,
230('89) .... E 2
Wellington, 280('89) .. E 2
Wells, 1,256 .... B 7
Winchester,
19,728('80) ...... G 6
Winnemucca, 6,134 .. C 4
Yerington, 2,367 .... E 2
Zephyr Cove,
1,700('89)........ E 2

Statute Miles
Kilometers

Lambert Conformal Conic Projection

New Hampshire

New Hampshire

1990 CENSUS

Alton, 975 (3,286▲) . . D 4
Amherst, 850
 (9,068▲) . . . . . . E 3
Antrim, 1,142
 (2,360▲) . . . . . . D 3
Ashland, 1,479
 (1,915▲) . . . . . . C 3
Bedford, 1,400
 (12,563▲) . . . . . E 3
Berlin, 11,824 . . . . B 4
Bristol, 1,258
 (2,537▲) . . . . . . C 3
Charlestown, 1,294
 (4,630▲) . . . . . . D 2
Claremont, 13,902 . D 2
Colebrook, 1,131
 (2,444▲) . . . . . . g 7
Concord, 36,006 . . D 3
Conway, 1,781
 (7,940▲) . . . . . . C 4
Derry, 12,248
 (29,603▲) . . . . . E 4
Dover, 25,042 . . . . D 5
Durham, 8,448
 (11,818▲) . . . . . D 5
Enfield, 1,581
 (3,979▲) . . . . . . C 2
Epping, 1,384
 (5,162▲) . . . . . . D 4
Exeter, 8,947
 (12,481▲) . . . . . E 5
Farmington, 3,284
 (5,739▲) . . . . . . D 4
Franklin, 8,304 . . . D 3
Goffstown, 2,700
 (14,621▲) . . . . . E 3
Gorham, 2,180
 (3,173▲) . . . . . . B 4
Greenville, 1,447
 (2,231▲) . . . . . . E 3
Hampton, 6,779
 (12,278▲) . . . . . E 5
Hanover, 6,861
 (9,212▲) . . . . . . C 2
Henniker, 1,538
 (4,151▲) . . . . . . D 3
Hinsdale, 1,546
 (3,936▲) . . . . . . E 2
Hooksett, 1,868
 (8,767▲) . . . . . . D 4
Hudson, 6,248
 (19,530▲) . . . . . E 4
Jaffrey, 2,684
 (5,361▲) . . . . . . E 2
Keene, 22,430 . . . . E 2
Laconia, 15,743 . . . C 4
Lancaster, 2,134
 (3,522▲) . . . . . . B 3
Lebanon, 12,183 . . C 2
Lisbon, 1,151
 (1,664▲) . . . . . . B 3
Littleton, 4,480
 (5,827▲) . . . . . . B 3
Manchester, 99,567 . E 4
Marlborough, 1,184
 (1,927▲) . . . . . . E 2
Meredith, 1,202
 (4,837▲) . . . . . . C 3
Merrimack, 1,300
 (22,156▲) . . . . . E 4
Milford, 6,269
 (11,795▲) . . . . . E 3
Milton, 1,000 (3,691▲)D 5
Nashua, 79,662 . . . E 4
New London, 1,335
 (3,180▲) . . . . . . D 3
Newmarket, 3,749
 (7,157▲) . . . . . . D 5
Newport, 4,388
 (6,110▲) . . . . . . D 2
Northfield, 1,375
 (4,263▲) . . . . . . D 3
North Hampton, 1,000
 (3,637▲) . . . . . . E 5
Peterborough, 2,100
 (5,239▲) . . . . . . E 3
Pittsfield, 1,584
 (3,701▲) . . . . . . D 4
Plaistow, 1,850
 (7,316▲) . . . . . . E 4
Plymouth, 3,628
 (5,811▲) . . . . . . C 3
Portsmouth, 25,925 . D 5
Raymond, 1,192
 (8,713▲) . . . . . . D 4
Rochester, 26,630 . . D 5
Rollinsford, 1,173
 (2,645▲) . . . . . . D 5
Rye, 835 (4,612▲) . . D 5
Salem, 12,000
 (25,746▲) . . . . . E 4
Somersworth, 11,249 D 5
Tilton, 1,380 (3,240▲)D 3
Troy, 1,318 (2,097▲) . E 2
Whitefield, 1,005
 (1,909▲) . . . . . . B 3
Winchester, 1,732
 (4,038▲) . . . . . . E 2
Wolfeboro, 2,000
 (4,807▲) . . . . . . C 4

◄ Population of entire town (township), including rural area.

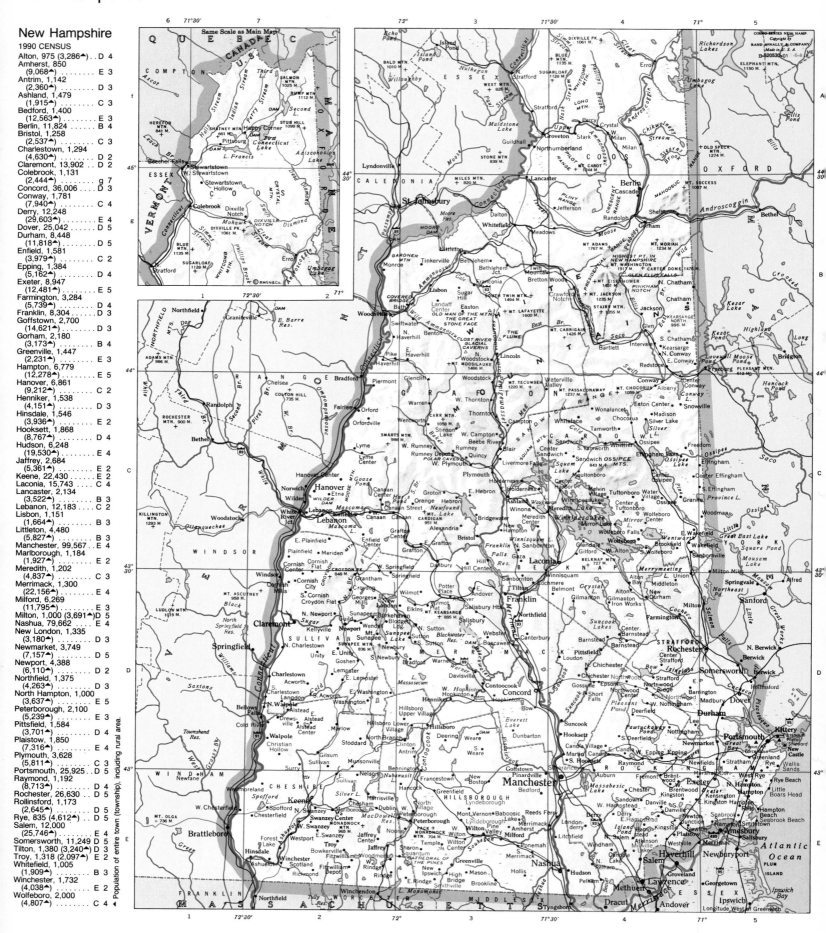

Statute Miles

Kilometers

Lambert Conformal Conic Projection

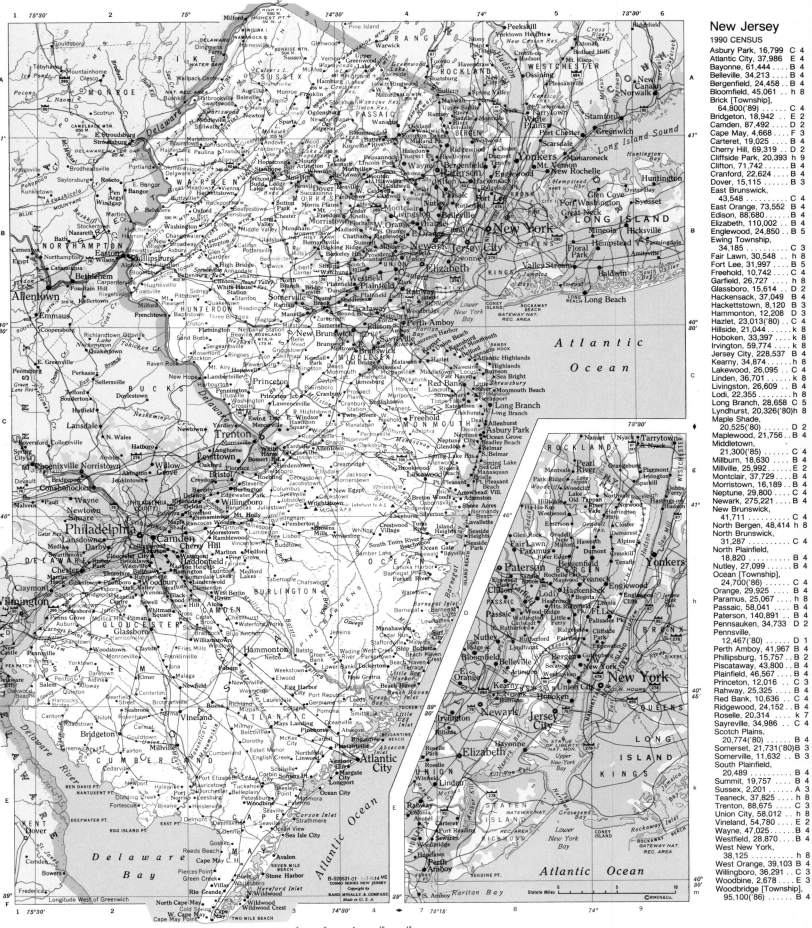

New Jersey

1990 CENSUS

Asbury Park, 16,799 . . C 4
Atlantic City, 37,986 . . E 4
Bayonne, 61,444 . . . . B 4
Belleville, 34,213 . . . . B 4
Bergenfield, 24,458 . . B 4
Bloomfield, 45,061 . . h 8
Brick [Township],
64,800('89) . . . . . . C 4
Bridgeton, 18,942 . . . E 2
Camden, 87,492 . . . . D 2
Cape May, 4,668 . . . F 3
Carteret, 19,025 . . . . B 4
Cherry Hill, 69,319 . . . D 2
Cliffside Park, 20,393 h 9
Clifton, 71,742 . . . . . B 4
Cranford, 22,624 . . . . B 4
Dover, 15,115 . . . . . B 3
East Brunswick,
43,548 . . . . C 4
East Orange, 73,552 . . B 4
Edison, 88,680 . . . . . B 4
Elizabeth, 110,002 . . B 4
Englewood, 24,850 . . B 5
Ewing Township,
34,185 . . . . C 3
Fair Lawn, 30,548 . . . h 8
Fort Lee, 31,997 . . . . B 5
Freehold, 10,742 . . . . C 4
Garfield, 26,727 . . . . h 8
Glassboro, 15,614 . . . D 2
Hackensack, 37,049 . B 4
Hackettstown, 8,120 . B 3
Hammonton, 12,208 . D 3
Hazlet, 23,013('80) . . C 4
Hillside, 21,044 . . . . k 8
Hoboken, 33,397 . . . k 8
Irvington, 59,774 . . . k 8
Jersey City, 228,537 . B 4
Kearny, 34,874 . . . . h 8
Lakewood, 26,095 . . C 4
Linden, 36,701 . . . . k 8
Livingston, 26,609 . . B 4
Lodi, 22,355 . . . . . . h 8
Long Branch, 28,658 C 5
Lyndhurst, 20,326('80)h 8
Maple Shade,
20,525('80) . . . . . D 2
Maplewood, 21,756 . . B 4
Middletown,
21,300('85) . . . . . C 4
Millburn, 18,630 . . . . B 4
Millville, 25,992 . . . . E 2
Montclair, 37,729 . . . B 4
Morristown, 16,189 . . B 4
Neptune, 29,800 . . . . C 4
Newark, 275,221 . . . . B 4
New Brunswick,
41,711 . . . . C 4
North Bergen, 48,414 h 8
North Brunswick,
31,287 . . . . C 4
North Plainfield,
18,820 . . . . B 4
Nutley, 27,099 . . . . . B 4
Ocean [Township],
24,700('86) . . . . . C 4
Orange, 29,925 . . . . B 4
Paramus, 25,067 . . . h 8
Passaic, 58,041 . . . . B 4
Paterson, 140,891 . . B 4
Pennsauken, 34,733 . D 2
Pennsville,
12,467('80) . . . . . D 1
Perth Amboy, 41,967 B 4
Phillipsburg, 15,757 . . B 2
Piscataway, 43,800 . . B 4
Plainfield, 46,567 . . . B 4
Princeton, 12,016 . . . C 3
Rahway, 25,325 . . . . B 4
Red Bank, 10,636 . . . C 4
Ridgewood, 24,152 . . B 4
Roselle, 20,314 . . . . k 7
Sayreville, 34,986 . . . C 4
Scotch Plains,
20,774('80) . . . . . B 4
Somerset, 21,731('80)B 3
Somerville, 11,632 . . C 4
South Plainfield,
20,489 . . . . B 4
Summit, 19,757 . . . . B 4
Sussex, 2,201 . . . . . A 3
Teaneck, 37,825 . . . h 8
Trenton, 88,675 . . . . C 3
Union City, 58,012 . . h 8
Vineland, 54,780 . . . E 2
Wayne, 47,025 . . . . . B 4
Westfield, 28,870 . . . B 4
West New York,
38,125 . . . . h 8
West Orange, 39,103 B 4
Willingboro, 36,291 . . C 3
Woodbine, 2,678 . . . E 3
Woodbridge [Township],
95,100('86) . . . . . B 4

New Mexico

New Mexico
1990 CENSUS

Alameda, 5,900('87) . . . . B 3
Alamogordo, 27,596 . . . E 4
Albuquerque, 384,736 B 3
Anthony, 3,285('80) . . . F 3
Armijo, 14,600('87) . . . k 7
Artesia, 10,610 . . . . . . E 5
Aztec, 5,479 . . . . A 2
Bayard, 2,598 . . . . E 1
Belen, 6,547 . . . . C 3
Bernalillo, 5,960 . . . . . B 3
Bloomfield, 5,214 . . . . A 2
Carlsbad, 24,952 . . . . E 5
Carrizozo, 1,075 . . . . . D 4
Cedar Crest,
  1,200('87) . . . . k 8
Central, 1,835 . . . . E 1
Chama, 1,048 . . . . A 3
Chimayo, 1,993('80) . . A 4
Clayton, 2,484 . . . . . . A 6
Clovis, 30,954 . . . . . . C 6
Crownpoint,
  1,134('87) . . . . B 1
Deming, 10,970 . . . . . E 2
Dona Ana, 950('87) . . . E 3
Dulce, 1,648('80) . . . . A 2
Espanola, 8,389 . . . . . B 3
Eunice, 2,676 . . . . E 6
Farmington, 33,997 . . A 1
Five Points,
  4,200('87) . . . . B 3
Fort Sumner, 1,269 . . . C 5
Fort Wingate,
  950('87) . . . . B 1
Gallup, 19,154 . . . . . . B 1
Grants, 8,626 . . . . B 2
Hagerman, 961 . . . . . D 5
Hatch, 1,136 . . . . E 2
Hobbs, 29,115 . . . . . . E 6
Hurley, 1,534 . . . . E 1
Isleta, 1,246('80) . . . . C 3
Jal, 2,156 . . . . E 6
Jemez Pueblo,
  1,503('80) . . . . B 3
Kirtland, 2,358('87) . . . A 1
La Luz, 1,194('80) . . . . D 4
La Mesa, 900('87) . . . . E 3
Las Cruces, 62,126 . . . E 3
Las Vegas, 14,753 . . . B 4
Lordsburg, 2,951 . . . . E 1
Los Alamos,
  11,039('80) . . . . B 3
Los Lunas, 6,013 . . . . C 3
Los Ranchos de
  Albuquerque, 3,955 B 3
Loving, 1,243 . . . . E 5
Lovington, 9,322 . . . . . E 6
Magdalena, 861 . . . . . C 2
Mescalero, 1,259('80) D 4
Mesilla, 1,975 . . . . E 3
Milan, 1,911 . . . . B 2
Moriarty, 1,399 . . . . . . C 3
Mountainair, 926 . . . . C 3
Mountain View,
  2,300('87) . . . . C 3
Paradise Hills,
  5,096('80) . . . . B 3
Portales, 10,690 . . . . . C 6
Questa, 1,707 . . . . A 4
Ranchos de Taos,
  1,411('80) . . . . A 4
Raton, 7,372 . . . . A 5
Rio Rancho, 32,505 . . B 3
Roswell, 44,654 . . . . . D 5
Ruidoso, 4,600 . . . . . . D 4
Ruidoso Downs, 920 . D 4
San Felipe Pueblo,
  1,465('80) . . . . B 3
Santa Cruz, 975('87) . . B 3
Santa Fe, 55,859 . . . . B 4
Santa Rosa, 2,263 . . . C 5
Santo Domingo Pueblo,
  2,082('80) . . . . B 3
Shiprock, 7,237('80) . . A 1
Silver City, 10,683 . . . E 1
Socorro, 8,159 . . . . . . C 3
Springer, 1,262 . . . . . A 5
Sunland Park, 8,179 . . F 3
Taos, 4,065 . . . . A 4
Taos Pueblo,
  1,030('87) . . . . A 4
Tesuque, 1,014('80) . . B 4
Texico, 966 . . . . C 6
Thoreau, 1,099('80) . . B 1
Tierra Amarilla,
  900('87) . . . . A 3
Tohatchi, 1,011('80) . . B 1
Truth or Consequences
  (Hot Springs), 6,221 D 2
Tucumcari, 6,831 . . . . B 6
Tularosa, 2,615 . . . . . D 3
Tyrone, 950('87) . . . . . E 1
University Park,
  4,353('80) . . . . E 3
Zuni, 5,551('80) . . . . . B 1

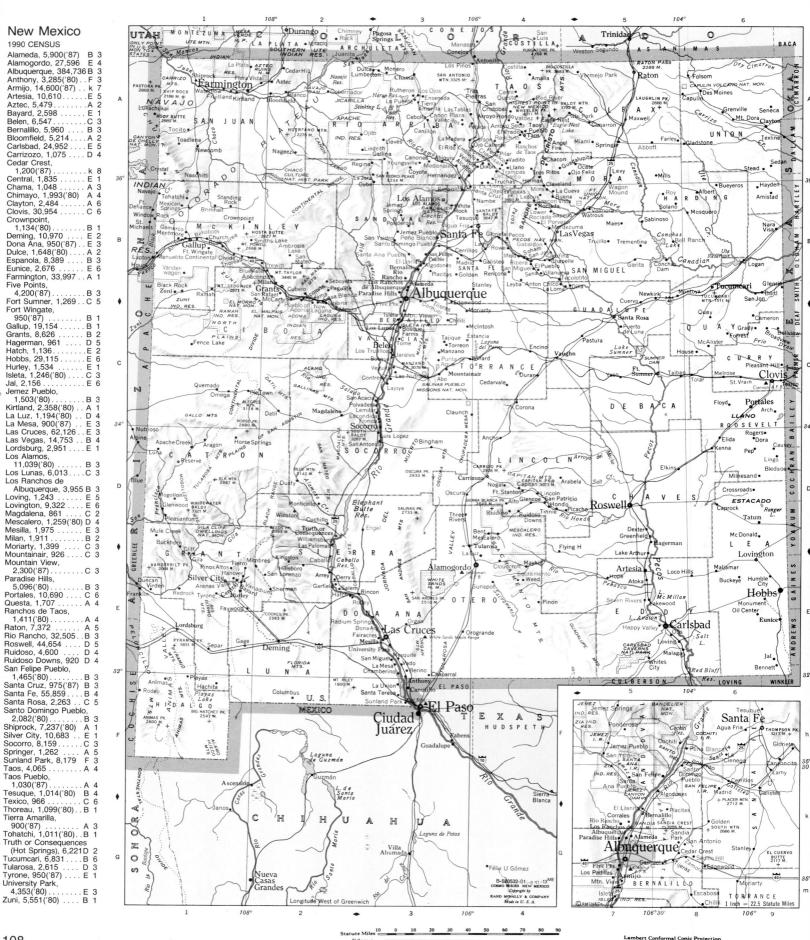

B-520532-01 · 8-81-13·ME
COSMO SERIES NEW MEXICO
Prepared by
RAND McNALLY & COMPANY
Made in U.S.A.

Longitude West of Greenwich

Statute Miles
Kilometers

Lambert Conformal Conic Projection

1 Inch = 22.5 Statute Miles

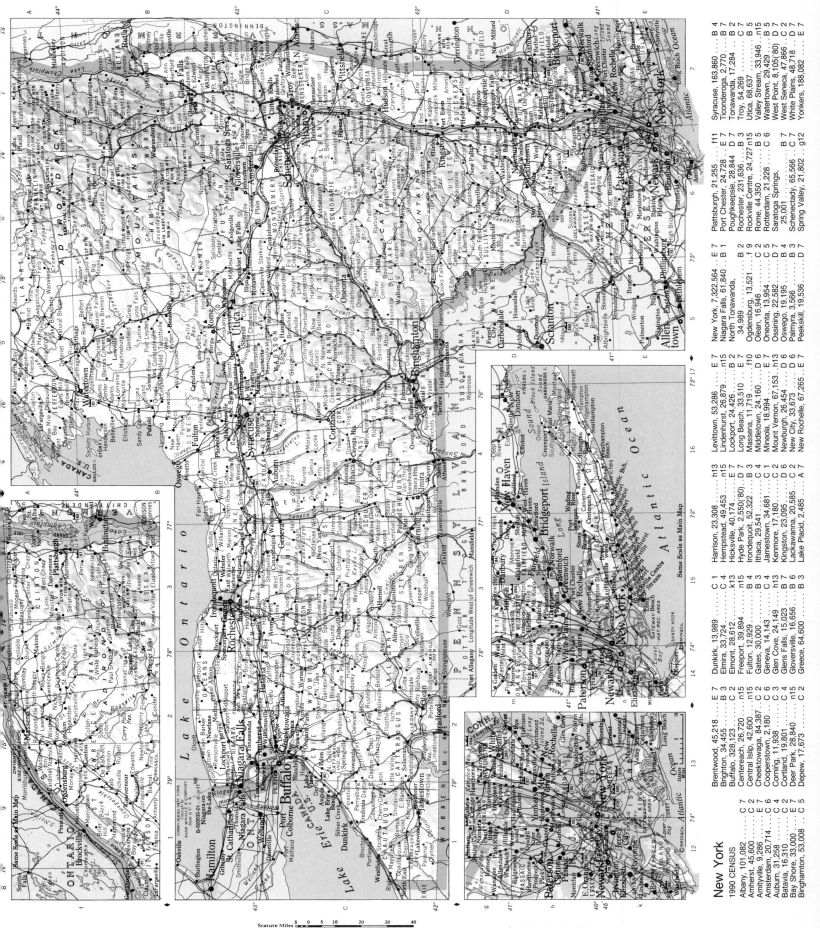

New York

1990 CENSUS

Albany, 101,082	C 7		
Amherst, 45,600	C 2		
Amityville, 9,286	E 7		
Amsterdam, 20,714	C 6		
Auburn, 31,258	C 4		
Batavia, 16,310	C 3		
Bay Shore, 33,000	E 7		
Binghamton, 53,008	D 5		
Brentwood, 45,218	E 7		
Brighton, 34,455	B 3		
Buffalo, 328,123	C 2		
Centereach, 26,720	n15		
Central Islip, 42,600	n15		
Cheektowaga, 84,387	C 2		
Cooperstown, 2,180	C 6		
Corning, 11,938	C 4		
Cortland, 19,801	C 4		
Deer Park, 28,840	E 7		
Depew, 17,673	C 2		
Dunkirk, 13,989	C 1	Levittown, 53,308	h13
Elmira, 33,724	C 4	Lindenhurst, 49,453	n15
Elmont, 28,612	k13	Lockport, 24,426	B 3
Freeport, 39,894	B 4	Long Beach, 33,510	E 7
Fulton, 12,929	B 4	Massena, 11,719	A 6
Gates, 30,000	C 4	Middletown, 24,160	D 6
Geneva, 14,143	C 4	Mineola, 18,994	E 7
Glen Cove, 24,149	h13	Mount Vernon, 67,153	h13
Glens Falls, 15,023	B 7	Newburgh, 26,454	D 6
Gloversville, 16,656	B 6	New City, 33,673	D 6
Greece, 64,600	C 2	New Rochelle, 67,265	E 7
Harrison, 23,308	C 4		
Hempstead, 49,453	C 4	New York, 7,322,564	E 7
Hicksville, 40,174	E 7	Niagara Falls, 61,840	B 1
Hyde Park, 2,550(′80)	D 7	North Tonawanda,	
Irondequoit, 52,322	B 3	34,989	B 2
Ithaca, 29,541	C 4	Ogdensburg, 13,521	f 9
Jamestown, 34,681	D 6	Olean, 16,946	D 6
Kenmore, 17,180	E 7	Oneonta, 21,228	C 5
Kingston, 23,095	C 2	Rotterdam, 21,228	C 5
Lackawanna, 20,585	C 2	Saratoga Springs,	D 7
Lake Placid, 2,485	A 7	25,001	B 7
		Schenectady, 65,566	C 7
		Spring Valley, 21,802	g12

Syracuse, 163,860	B 4	
Ticonderoga, 2,770	B 7	
Tonawanda, 17,284	B 2	
Troy, 54,269	B 5	
Utica, 68,637	n15	
Valley Stream, 33,946	n15	
Watertown, 29,429	B 5	
West Point, 8,105(′80)	D 7	
West Seneca, 47,866	C 2	
White Plains, 48,718	E 7	
Yonkers, 188,082	g12	

Plattsburgh, 21,255 f11
Port Chester, 24,728 E 7
Poughkeepsie, 28,844 D 7
Rockville Centre, 24,727 n15
Rome, 44,350 B 5
Oneonta, 21,228 C 6

Statute Miles
Kilometers

Lambert Conformal Conic Projection

North Carolina

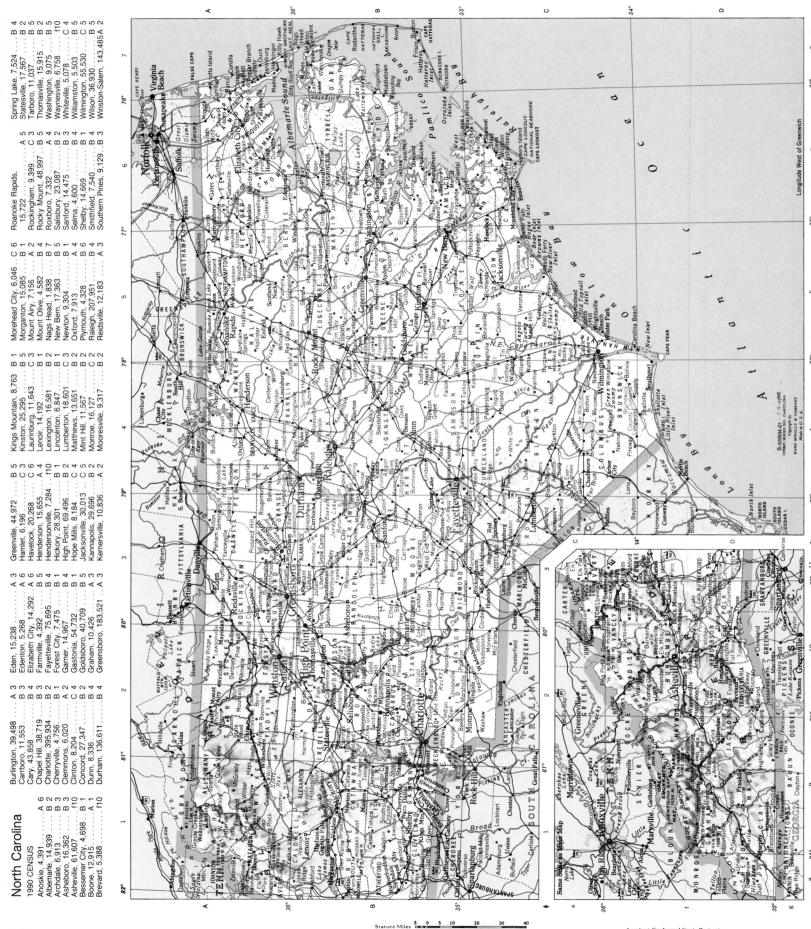

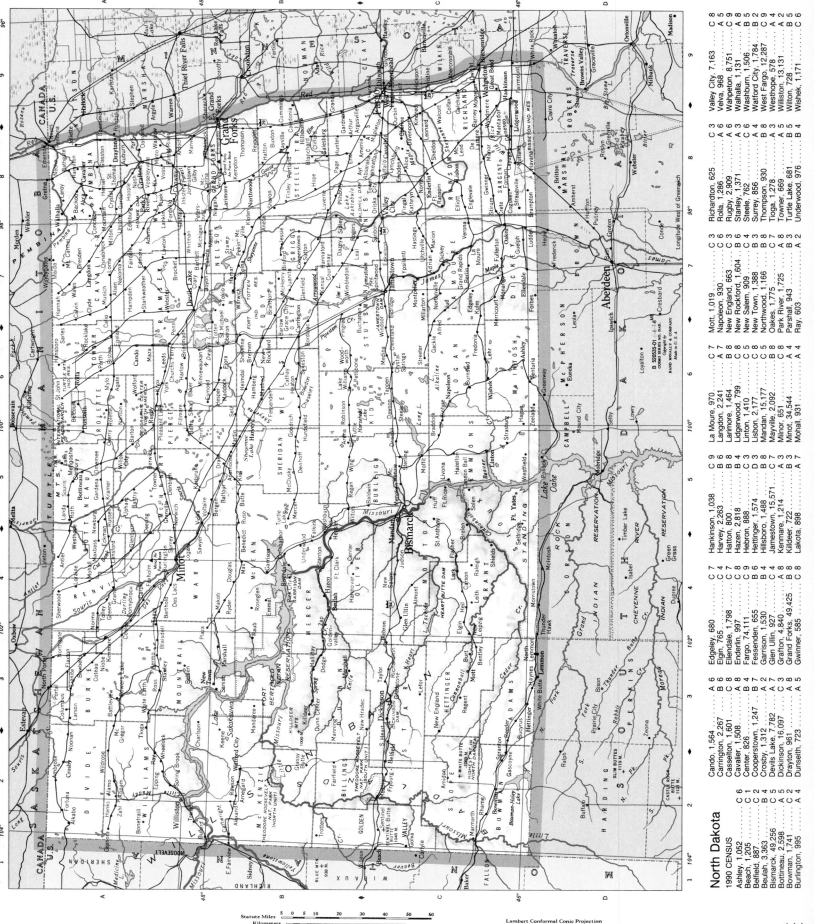

North Dakota

North Dakota

1990 CENSUS

Ashley, 1,052	C 6		
Carrington, 2,267	C 1		
Beach, 1,205	B 2		
Belfield, 887	B 2		
Beulah, 3,363	C 5		
Bismarck, 49,256	A 5		
Bottineau, 2,598	C 2		
Bowman, 1,741	C 2		
Burlington, 995	A 4		

Cando, 1,564	C 7		
Carrington, 2,267	B 6		
Casselton, 1,601	C 8		
Cavalier, 1,508	B 4		
Center, 826	B 7		
Cooperstown, 1,247	A 7		
Crosby, 1,312	A 2		
Devils Lake, 7,782	A 7		
Dickinson, 16,097	A 8		
Drayton, 961	A 8		
Dunseith, 723	A 5		

Edgeley, 680	C 7		
Elgin, 765	B 6		
Ellendale, 1,798	B 4		
Enderlin, 997	C 3		
Fargo, 74,111	D 3		
Fessenden, 655	B 6		
Garrison, 1,530	B 4		
Glen Ullin, 927	A 7		
Gratton, 4,840	A 3		
Grand Forks, 49,425	A 8		
Gwinner, 585	A 5		

Hankinson, 1,038	C 7		
Harvey, 2,263	C 4		
Hatton, 800	C 7		
Hazen, 2,818	B 4		
Hebron, 888	C 9		
Hettinger, 1,574	B 6		
Hillsboro, 1,488	B 4		
Jamestown, 15,571	C 7		
Kenmare, 1,214	A 3		
Killdeer, 722	B 8		
Lakota, 898	C 8		

La Moure, 970	C 7		
Langdon, 2,241	A 7		
Larimore, 1,464	B 8		
Lidgerwood, 799	C 8		
Linton, 1,410	C 5		
Lisbon, 2,177	C 8		
Mandan, 15,177	B 8		
Mayville, 2,092	C 7		
Minot, 651	A 3		
Minot, 34,544	B 3		
Mohall, 931	A 7		

Mott, 1,019	C 7		
Napoleon, 930	A 7		
New England, 663	B 6		
New Rockford, 1,604	C 8		
New Salem, 909	C 5		
New Town, 1,388	B 3		
Northwood, 1,166	C 5		
Oakes, 1,775	C 7		
Park River, 1,725	A 8		
Parshall, 943	B 3		
Ray, 603	A 2		

Richardton, 625	C 3		
Rolla, 1,286	A 6		
Rugby, 2,909	C 3		
Stanley, 1,371	A 3		
Steele, 762	C 6		
Surrey, 856	A 4		
Thompson, 930	B 8		
Tioga, 1,278	A 3		
Towner, 669	C 5		
Turtle Lake, 681	B 5		
Underwood, 976	B 4		

Valley City, 7,163	C 8		
Velva, 968	A 5		
Wahpeton, 8,751	C 9		
Walhalla, 1,131	A 8		
Washburn, 1,506	B 5		
Watford City, 1,784	B 2		
West Fargo, 12,287	C 9		
Westhope, 578	A 4		
Williston, 13,131	A 2		
Wilton, 728	B 5		
Wishek, 1,171	C 6		

Statute Miles

Kilometers

Lambert Conformal Conic Projection

111

Ohio

1990 CENSUS

Akron, 223,019 ... A 4
Alliance, 23,376 ... A 4
Ashland, 20,079 ... B 3
Ashtabula, 21,633 ... C 3
Athens, 21,265 ... C 3
Austintown, 23,300 ... A-5
Barberton, 27,623 ... C 1
Beavercreek, 33,626 ... C 1

Bellefontaine, 12,142 ... B 2
Boardman, 38,596 ... A 5
Bowling Green, 28,176 ... h 9
Brook Park, 22,865 ... h 9
Brunswick, 28,230 ... A 4
Canton, 84,161 ... B 4
Chillicothe, 21,923 ... C 3
Cincinnati, 364,040 ... C 3
Cleveland, 505,616 ... A 5
Cleveland Heights,
54,052 ... C 1

Columbus, 632,910 ... C 2
Cuyahoga Falls, 48,950 ... A 4
Dayton, 182,044 ... C 1
Defiance, 16,768 ... A 1
Delaware, 20,030 ... B 2
East Cleveland, 33,096 ... g 9
Eastlake, 21,161 ... A 4
Elyria, 56,746 ... A 4
Euclid, 54,875 ... A 4
Fairborn, 31,300 ... C 1

Fairfield, 39,729 ... n12
Findlay, 35,703 ... A 2
Fostoria, 14,983 ... A 2
Fremont, 17,648 ... A 2
Garfield Heights, 31,739 ... h 9
Greenville, 12,863 ... C 1
Hamilton, 61,368 ... C 1
Ironton, 12,751 ... D 3
Kent, 28,835 ... A 4
Kettering, 60,569 ... C 1
Lakewood, 59,718 ... A 4

Lancaster, 34,507 ... C 3
Lima, 45,549 ... B 1
Lorain, 71,245 ... A 3
Mansfield, 50,627 ... B 3
Maple Heights, 27,089 ... h 9
Marietta, 15,026 ... C 4
Marion, 34,075 ... B 2
Massillon, 31,007 ... B 4
Medina, 19,231 ... A 4
Mentor, 47,358 ... A 4
Middletown, 46,022 ... C 1

Mount Vernon, 14,550 ... B 3
Newark, 44,389 ... B 3
New Philadelphia,
15,698 ... B 4
Niles, 21,128 ... A 5
North Olmsted, 34,204 ... h 9
Norwalk, 14,731 ... A 3
Norwood, 23,674 ... o13
Oxford, 18,937 ... C 1
Parma, 87,876 ... A 4
Parma Heights, 21,448 ... h 9

Piqua, 20,612 ... B 1
Portsmouth, 22,676 ... D 3
Reynoldsburg, 25,748 ... C 3
Salem, 12,233 ... B 5
Sandusky, 29,764 ... A 3
Shaker Heights, 30,831 ... B 3
South Euclid, 23,866 ... g 9
Springfield, 70,487 ... C 2
Steubenville, 22,125 ... B 5
Stow, 27,702 ... A 4
Strongsville, 35,308 ... A 4

Tiffin, 18,604 ... A 2
Toledo, 332,943 ... D 3
Upper Arlington, 34,128 ... B 2
Urbana, 11,353 ... C 3
Warren, 50,793 ... A 5
Westerville, 30,269 ... B 3
Whitehall, 20,572 ... m11
Wooster, 22,191 ... B 4
Xenia, 24,664 ... A 5
Youngstown, 95,732 ... A 5
Zanesville, 26,778 ... C 4

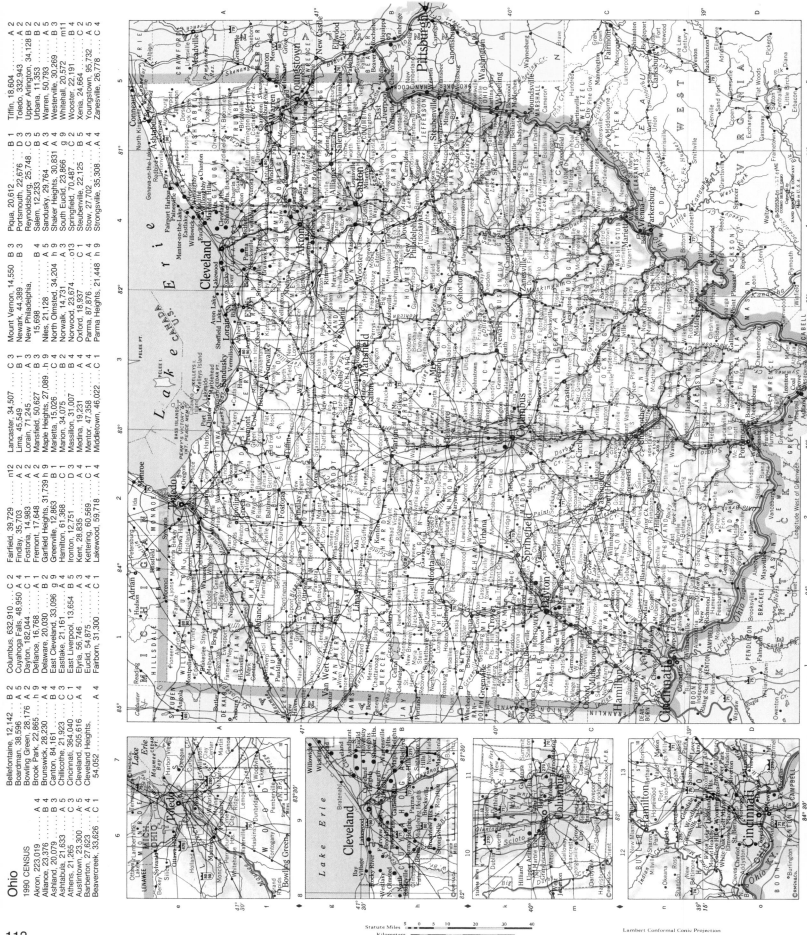

Statute Miles 5 0 5 10 20 30 40

Kilometers 5 0 5 15 25 35 45 55

Lambert Conformal Conic Projection

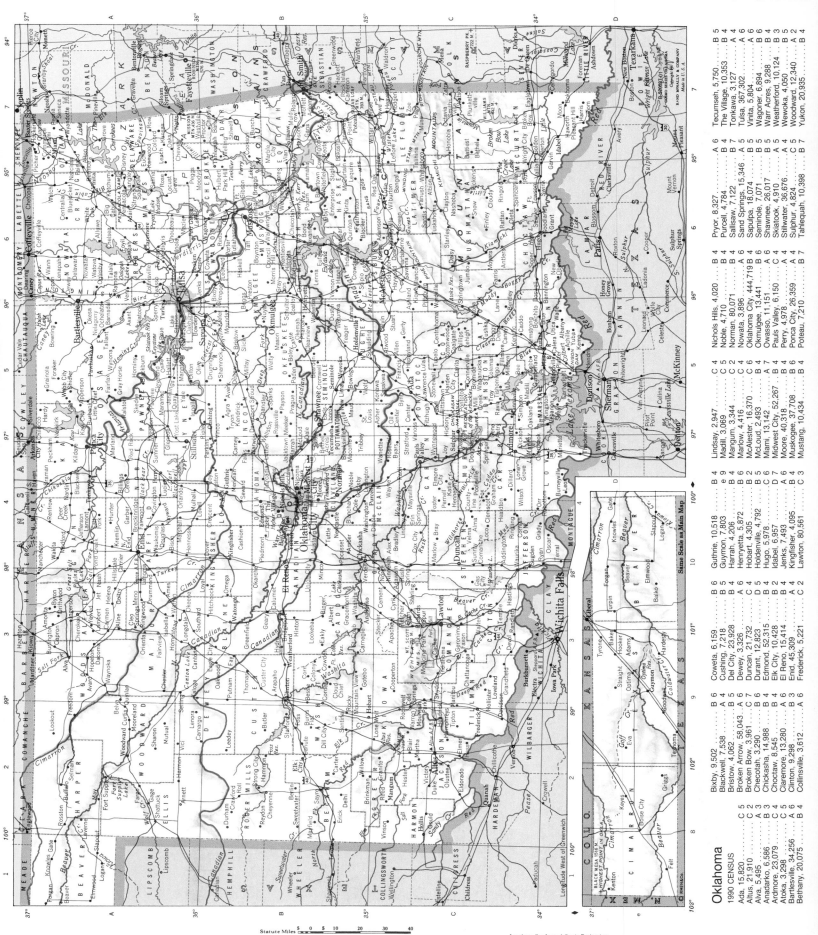

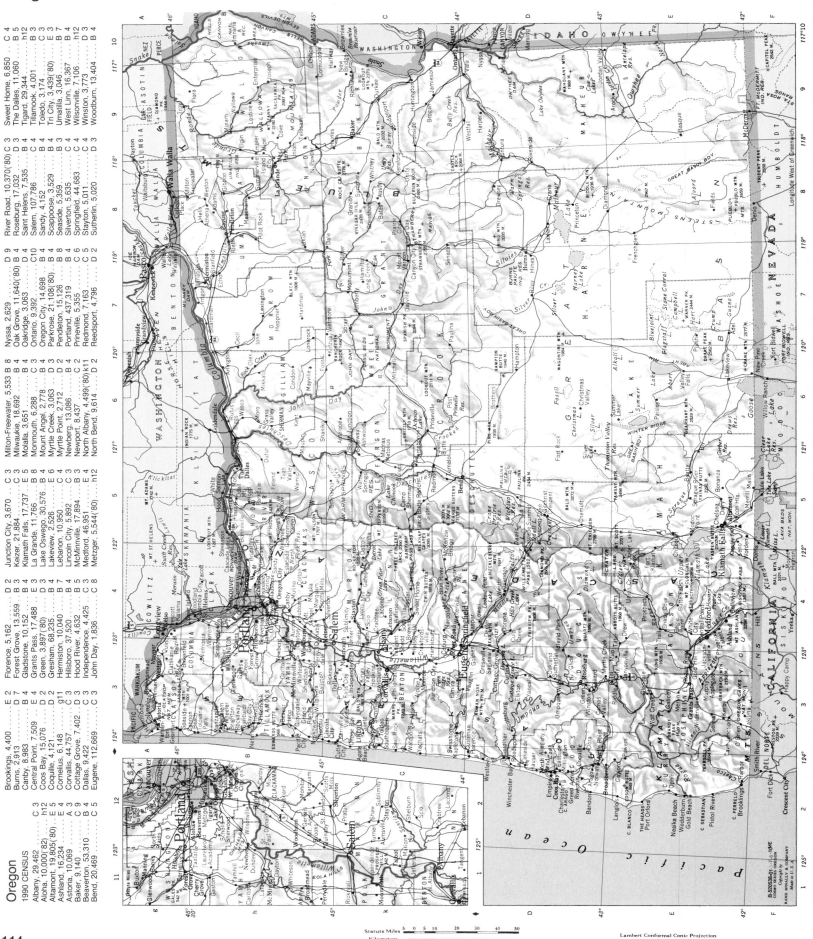

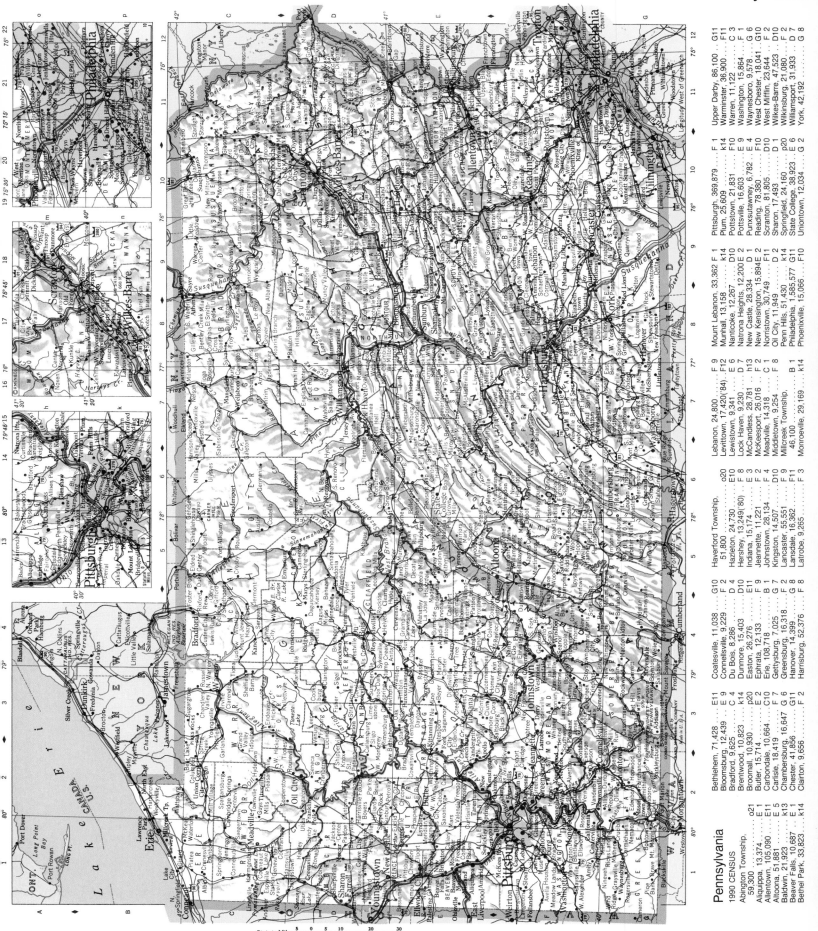

Pennsylvania

1990 CENSUS

Abington Township, 59,300	...	o21
Aliquippa, 13,374	...	E 1
Allentown, 105,090	...	E11
Altoona, 51,881	...	F 5
Baldwin, 21,923	...	k13
Beaver Falls, 10,687	...	E 1
Bethel Park, 33,823	...	k14

Bethlehem, 71,428	...	E11
Bloomsburg, 12,439	...	E 9
Bradford, 9,625	...	C 4
Brentwood, 10,823	...	k14
Broomall, 10,930	...	p20
Butler, 15,714	...	E 2
Carbondale, 10,664	...	C10
Carlisle, 18,419	...	F 7
Chambersburg, 16,647	...	G 6
Chester, 41,856	...	G11
Clairton, 9,656	...	F 2

Coatesville, 11,038	...	G10
Connellsville, 9,229	...	F 2
Du Bois, 8,286	...	D 4
Dunmore, 15,403	...	D10
Easton, 26,276	...	E11
Ephrata, 12,133	...	F 9
Erie, 108,718	...	B 1
Gettysburg, 7,025	...	G 7
Greensburg, 16,318	...	F 2
Hanover, 14,399	...	G 8
Harrisburg, 52,376	...	F 8

Haverford Township, 51,800	...	o20
Hazleton, 24,730	...	E10
Hershey, 13,249(80)	...	F 8
Indiana, 15,174	...	E 3
Jeannette, 11,221	...	F 2
Johnstown, 28,134	...	F 4
Kingston, 14,507	...	D10
Lancaster, 55,551	...	F 9
Lansdale, 16,362	...	F11
Latrobe, 9,265	...	F 3

Lebanon, 24,800	...	F 9
Levittown, 17,420(84)	...	F12
Lewistown, 9,341	...	E 6
Lock Haven, 9,230	...	D 7
McCandless, 28,781	...	h13
McKeesport, 26,016	...	F 2
Meadville, 14,318	...	C 1
Middletown, 9,254	...	F 8
Millcreek Township, 46,100	...	B 1
Monroeville, 29,169	...	F10

Mount Lebanon, 33,362	...	k14
Munhall, 13,158	...	k14
Nanticoke, 9,341	...	D10
Natrona Heights, 12,200	...	E 2
New Castle, 28,334	...	E 1
New Kensington, 15,894	...	E 2
Norristown, 30,749	...	F11
Oil City, 11,949	...	D 2
Penn Hills, 51,430	...	k14
Phoenixville, 15,066	...	F10

Pittsburgh, 369,879	...	G11
Plum, 25,609	...	F11
Pottstown, 21,831	...	C 3
Pottsville, 16,603	...	F 1
Punxsutawney, 6,782	...	G 6
Reading, 78,380	...	G10
Scranton, 81,805	...	D10
Sharon, 17,493	...	D 1
Springfield, 24,160	...	p20
State College, 38,923	...	E 6
Uniontown, 12,034	...	G 2

Upper Darby, 86,100	...	G11
Warminster, 36,900	...	F11
Warren, 11,122	...	C 3
Washington, 15,864	...	F 1
Waynesboro, 9,578	...	G 6
West Chester, 18,041	...	G10
West Mifflin, 23,644	...	F 2
Wilkes-Barre, 47,523	...	D10
Wilkinsburg, 21,080	...	F 2
Williamsport, 31,933	...	D 7
York, 42,192	...	G 8

Statute Miles

Kilometers

Lambert Conformal Conic Projection

Rhode Island

Rhode Island
1990 CENSUS

Abbott Run Valley,
1,050('87) . . . . B 4
Adamsville, 600('87) . . E 6
Albion, 1,600('87) . . B 4
Allenton, 600('87) . . . E 4
Anthony, 2,980('87) . .D 3
Arnold Mills, 600('87) . B 4
Ashton, 820('87) . . . . B 4
Barrington,
16,174('80) . . . . . . D 5
Berkeley, 830('87) . . B 4
Block Island, 620('87) . h 7
Branch Village,
400('87) . . . . B 3
Bristol, 20,128('80) . . D 5
Burdickville, 500('87) F 2
Carolina, 650('87) . . . F 2
Central Falls, 17,637 B 4
Charlestown, 1,500
(6,478▲) . . . . F 2
Chepachet, 900('87) . B 2
Common Fence Point,
860('87) . . . . D 6
Coventry, 6,980
(31,083▲) . . . . . . D 3
Cranston, 76,060 . . . . C 4
Davisville, 500('87) . . E 4
Diamond Hill, 810('87) B 4
East Greenwich,
10,211('87) . . . . . D 4
East Matunuck,
500('87) . . . . F 3
East Providence,
50,380 . . . . C 4
Esmond, 4,320('87) . . B 4
Forestdale, 530('87) . B 3
Glendale, 700('87) . . B 2
Greenville, 7,576('80) C 3
Harmony, 820('87) . . . D 3
Harris, 1,050('87) . . . .D 3
Hope, 270('87) . . . . . D 3
Hopkinton, 550
(6,873▲) . . . . F 1
Island Park,
1,240('87) . . . . . . E 6
Jamestown,
4,040('87) . . . . . . F 5
Johnston, 26,800 . . . . C 4
Kenyon, 400('87) . . . . F 2
Kingston, 5,479('80) . F 3
La Fayette, 640('87) . E 4
Little Compton, 500
(3,339▲) . . . . E 6
Lonsdale, 3,850('87) . B 4
Manville, 3,030('87) . . B 4
Mapleville, 1,300('87) B 4
Matunuck, 550('87) . . G 3
Middletown, 3,350
(19,460▲) . . . . . . E 5
Mount View, 610('87) . D 4
Narragansett, 3,342
(14,985▲) . . . . . . F 4
Newport, 28,227 . . . . F 5
North Kingstown, 2,750
(23,786▲) . . . . . . E 4
North Providence,
32,090 . . . . C 4
Oakland, 600('87) . . . B 2
Pascoag, 3,807('80) . B 2
Pawtucket, 72,644 . . . C 4
Peace Dale,
3,100('87) . . . . . . F 3
Plum Beach, 400('87) E 4
Portsmouth, 3,540
(16,857▲) . . . . . . E 6
Primrose, 500('87) . . B 3
Providence, 160,728 . C 4
Quidnessett,
3,300('87) . . . . . . E 4
Quidnick, 2,300('87) . D 3
Quonochontaug,
1,500('87) . . . . . . G 2
Saunderstown,
400('87) . . . . E 4
Saylesville, 3,510('87) B 4
Shannock, 950('87) . . F 2
Shores Acres,
410('87) . . . . E 4
Slatersville, 2,330('87) A 3
South Hopkinton,
900('87) . . . . F 1
Tiverton, 7,653
(14,312▲) . . . . . . D 6
Union Village,
2,150('87) . . . . . . B 3
Usquepaug, 400('87) F 3
Valley Falls,
10,892('80) . . . . . B 4
Wakefield, 3,450('87) F 3
Warren, 10,640('87) . D 5
Warwick, 85,427 . . . . D 4
Westerly, 16,477
(21,605▲) . . . . . . F 1
West Kingston,
1,150('87) . . . . . . F 3
West Warwick,
29,268 . . . . D 3
Woonsocket, 43,877 . A 3
Yorktown Manor,
2,520('87) . . . . . . C 3

▲ Population of entire town (township), including rural area.

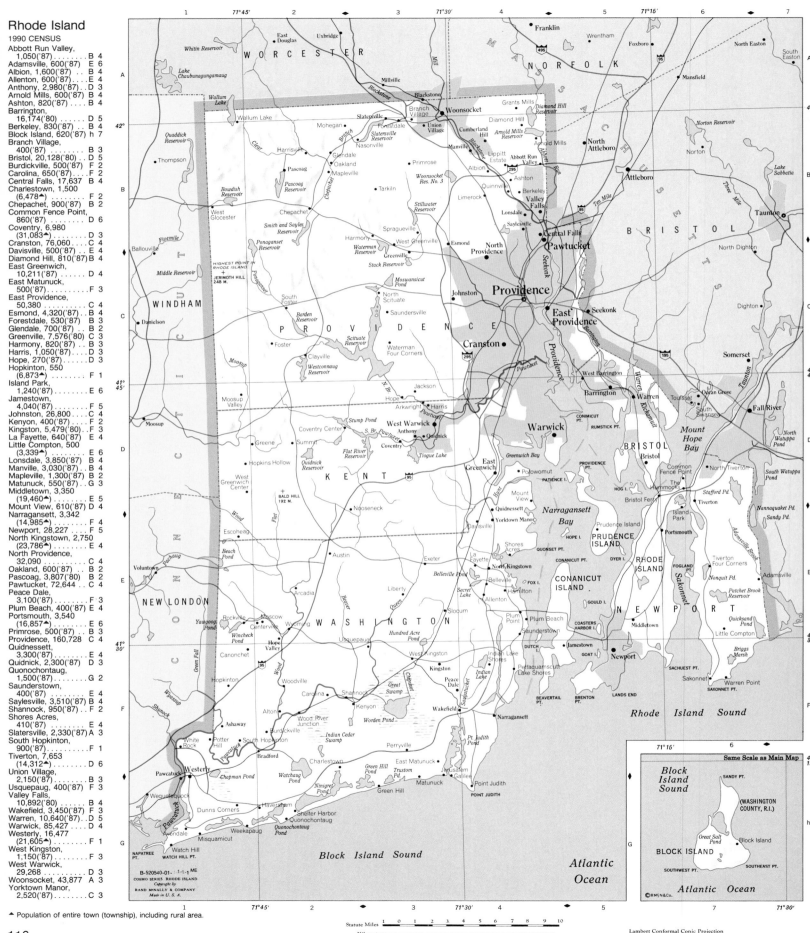

116

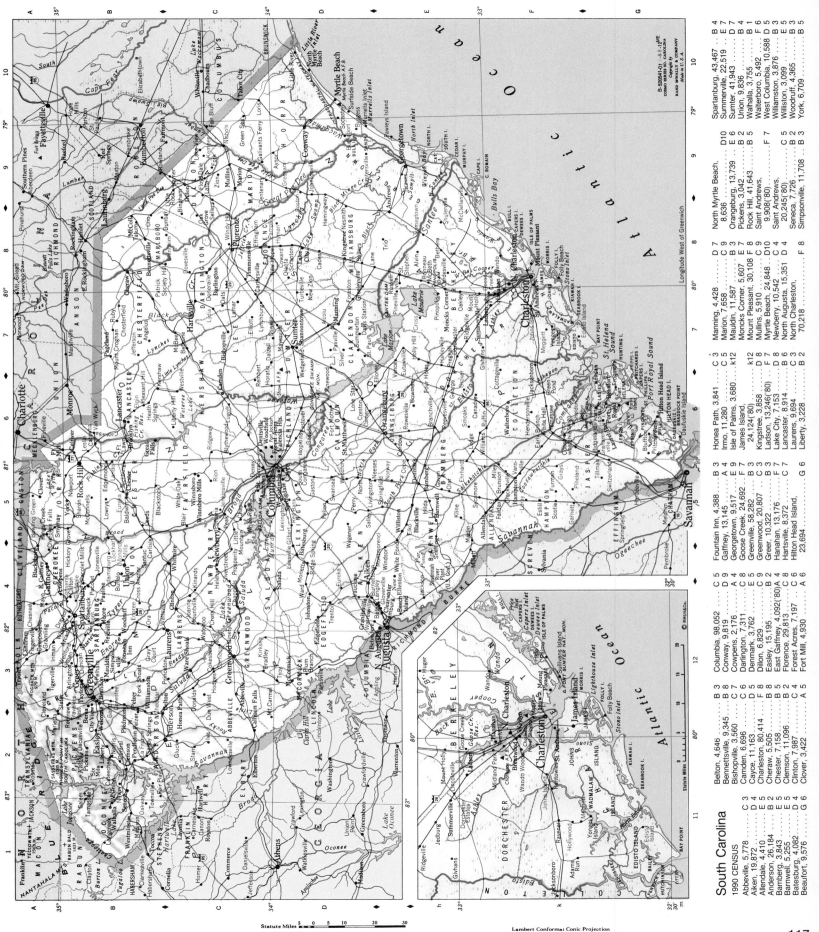

South Carolina

South Carolina
1990 CENSUS

Abbeville, 5,778	C 3
Aiken, 19,872	D 4
Allendale, 4,410	E 5
Anderson, 26,184	B 2
Bamberg, 3,843	E 5
Barnwell, 5,255	E 5
Batesburg, 4,082	D 4
Beaufort, 9,576	G 6

Belton, 4,646	B 3
Bennettsville, 9,345	C 7
Bishopville, 3,560	C 6
Camden, 6,696	C 6
Cayce, 11,163	D 5
Charleston, 80,414	F 8
Cheraw, 5,505	C 7
Chester, 7,158	B 5
Clemson, 11,096	B 2
Clinton, 7,987	C 4
Clover, 3,422	A 5

Columbia, 98,052	D 5
Conway, 9,819	C 9
Cowpens, 2,176	A 4
Darlington, 7,311	C 7
Denmark, 3,762	E 5
Dillon, 6,829	C 8
Easley, 15,195	B 3
East Gaffney, 4,092('80)A 4	
Florence, 29,813	C 7
Forest Acres, 7,197	D 5
Fort Mill, 4,930	A 6

Fountain Inn, 4,388	C 3
Gaffney, 13,145	A 4
Georgetown, 9,517	E 9
Goose Creek, 24,692	F 7
Greenville, 58,282	B 3
Greenwood, 20,807	C 3
Greer, 10,322	B 3
Hanahan, 13,176	F 7
Hartsville, 8,372	C 7
Hilton Head Island,	
23,694	G 6

Honea Path, 3,841	C 3
Irmo, 11,280	C 5
Isle of Palms, 3,680	k12
James Island,	
24,124('80)	k12
Kingstree, 3,858	D 8
Ladson, 13,246('80)	F 7
Lake City, 7,153	D 8
Lancaster, 8,914	B 6
Laurens, 9,694	C 3
Liberty, 3,228	B 2

Manning, 4,428	D 7
Marion, 7,658	C 9
Mauldin, 11,587	B 3
Moncks Corner, 5,607	E 7
Mount Pleasant, 30,108	F 8
Mullins, 5,910	C 9
Myrtle Beach, 24,848	D10
Newberry, 10,542	C 4
North Augusta, 15,351	D 4
North Charleston,	
70,218	F 8

North Myrtle Beach,	
8,636	D10
Orangeburg, 13,739	E 6
Pickens, 3,042	B 2
Rock Hill, 41,643	B 5
Saint Andrews,	
9,908('80)	C 9
Saint Andrews,	
20,245('80)	D10
Seneca, 7,726	C 5
Simpsonville, 11,708	B 3

Spartanburg, 43,467	B 4
Summerville, 22,519	E 7
Sumter, 41,943	D 7
Union, 9,836	B 4
Walhalla, 3,755	B 1
Walterboro, 5,492	F 6
West Columbia, 10,588	D 5
Williamston, 3,876	B 3
Williston, 3,099	E 5
Woodruff, 4,365	B 3
York, 6,709	B 5

Copyright by
COSMO SERIES SO. CAROLINA
RAND McNALLY AND COMPANY
Made in U.S.A.
B-520541-01 -6 9 -12 ME

Lambert Conformal Conic Projection

Statute Miles
Kilometers

South Dakota

1990 CENSUS

Aberdeen, 24,927	C 8
Alcester, 843	B 7
Arlington, 908	C 8
Armour, 854	D 7
Belle Fourche, 4,335	C 2
Beresford, 1,849	D 9
Box Elder, 2,680	D 2
Brandon, 3,543	D 9

Britton, 1,394	B 8
Brookings, 16,270	C 9
Burke, 756	D 7
Canton, 2,787	D 9
Centerville, 887	D 9
Chamberlain, 2,347	D 6
Clark, 1,292	C 8
Clear Lake, 1,247	C 9
Custer, 1,741	D 2
Deadwood, 1,830	D 2
Dell Rapids, 2,484	D 9

De Smet, 1,172	C 8
Edgemont, 906	D 2
Elk Point, 1,423	E 9
Eureka, 1,197	B 6
Faulkton, 809	C 6
Flandreau, 2,311	C 9
Fort Pierre, 1,854	C 5
Freeman, 1,293	D 8
Garretson, 924	C 9
Gettysburg, 1,510	C 6
Gregory, 1,384	D 6

Groton, 1,196	C 8
Hartford, 1,262	D 9
Highmore, 835	C 6
Hot Springs, 4,325	D 2
Howard, 1,156	C 8
Huron, 12,448	C 7
Ipswich, 965	C 6
Kadoka, 736	D 4
Lake Andes, 846	D 7
Lake Preston, 663	C 8
Lead, 3,632	D 2

Lemmon, 1,614	B 3
Lennox, 1,767	D 9
Madison, 6,257	C 8
Marion, 831	D 8
Martin, 1,151	D 4
McLaughlin, 780	B 5
Menno, 768	D 8
Milbank, 3,879	B 9
Miller, 1,678	C 7
Mitchell, 13,798	D 7
Mobridge, 3,768	B 5

North Sioux City, 2,019	E 9
Onida, 761	C 5
Parker, 984	D 8
Parkston, 1,572	D 8
Philip, 1,077	C 4
Pierre, 12,906	C 5
Platte, 1,311	D 7
Presho, 654	D 5
Rapid City, 54,523	D 2
Redfield, 2,770	C 7
Saint Francis, 815	D 5

Salem, 1,289	D 8
Scotland, 968	D 8
Selby, 707	B 5
Sioux Falls, 100,814	D 9
Sisseton, 2,181	B 8
Spearfish, 6,966	C 2
Springfield, 834	E 8
Sturgis, 5,330	C 2
Tyndall, 1,201	E 8
Valley Springs, 739	D 9
Vermillion, 10,034	E 9

Volga, 1,263	C 9
Wagner, 1,462	D 7
Wall, 834	D 3
Watertown, 17,592	B 8
Webster, 2,017	B 8
Wessington Springs, 1,083	C 7
Whitewood, 891	C 2
Winner, 3,354	D 6
Woonsocket, 766	C 7
Yankton, 12,703	E 8

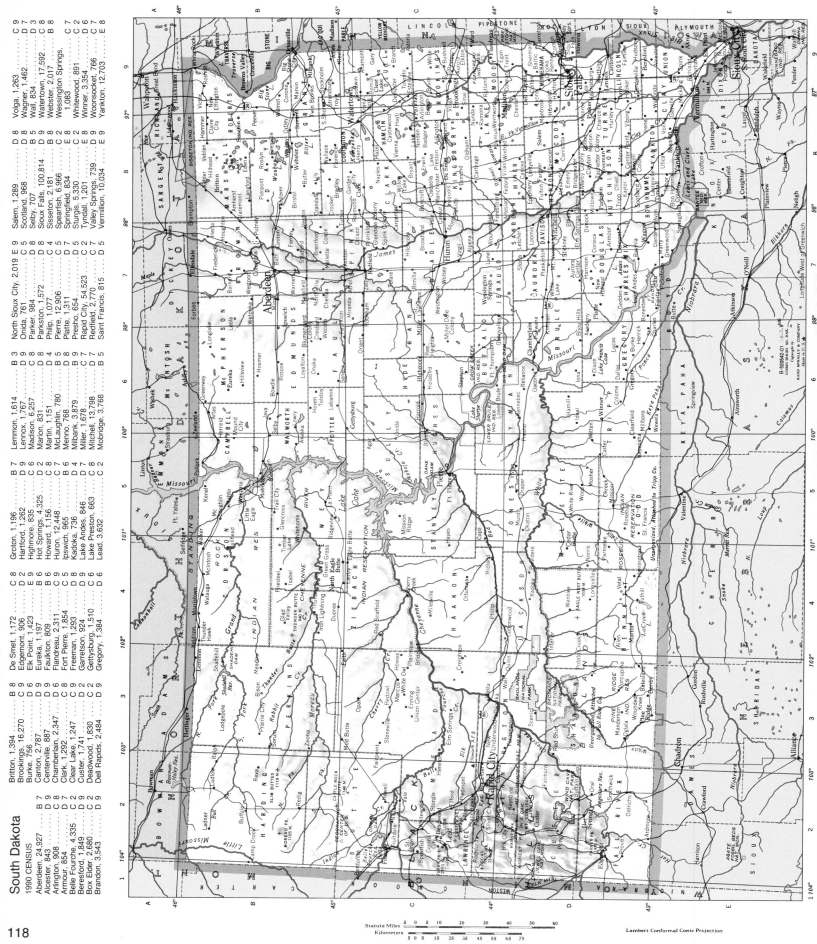

Statute Miles

Kilometers

Lambert Conformal Conic Projection

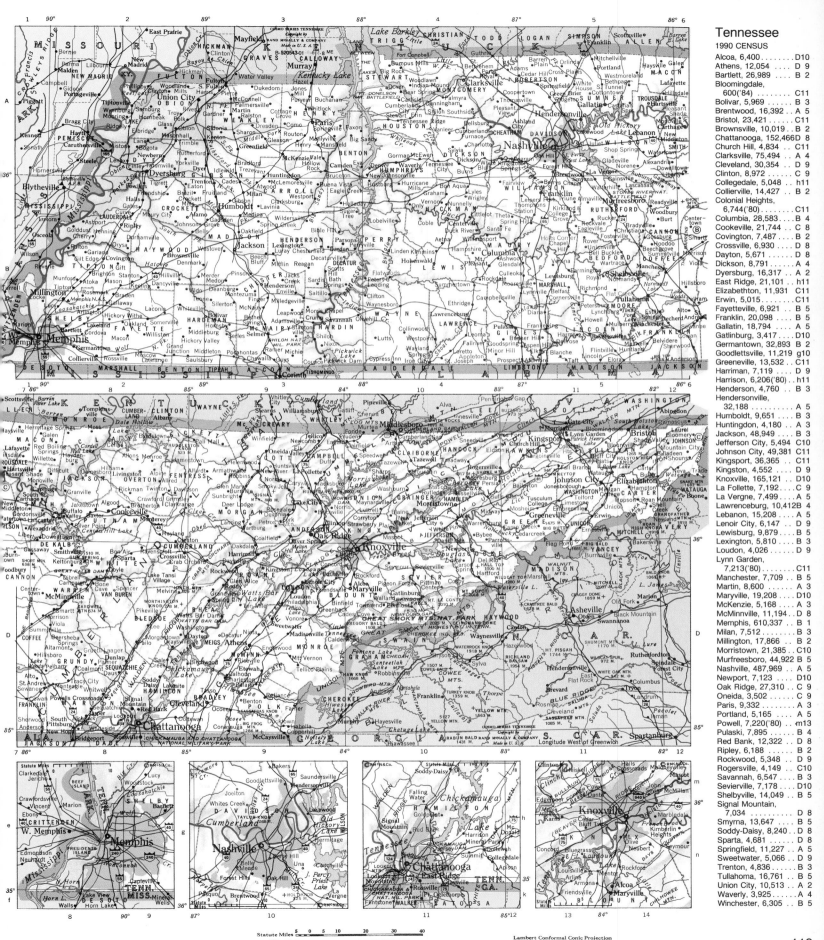

Tennessee

1990 CENSUS

Alcoa, 6,400 . . . . D10
Athens, 12,054 . . . D 9
Bartlett, 26,989 . . . . B 2
Bloomingdale,
  600('84) C11
Bolivar, 5,969 . . . . . . B 3
Brentwood, 16,392 . . A 5
Bristol, 23,421 . . . . C11
Brownsville, 10,019 . . B 2
Chattanooga, 152,466 D 8
Church Hill, 4,834 . . C11
Clarksville, 75,494 . . . A 4
Cleveland, 30,354 . . D 9
Clinton, 8,972 . . . . . C 9
Collegedale, 5,048 . . h11
Collierville, 14,427 . . B 2
Colonial Heights,
  6,744('80) C11
Columbia, 28,583 . . B 4
Cookeville, 21,744 . . C 8
Covington, 7,487 . . . B 2
Crossville, 6,930 . . D 8
Dayton, 5,671 . . . . D 8
Dickson, 8,791 . . . . A 4
Dyersburg, 16,317 . . A 2
East Ridge, 21,101 . . h11
Elizabethton, 11,931 C11
Erwin, 5,015 . . . . . . C11
Fayetteville, 6,921 . . B 5
Franklin, 20,098 . . . B 5
Gallatin, 18,794 . . . A 5
Gatlinburg, 3,417 . . D10
Germantown, 32,893 B 2
Goodlettsville, 11,219 g10
Greeneville, 13,532 . . C11
Harriman, 7,119 . . . D 9
Harrison, 6,206('80) . . h11
Henderson, 4,760 . . B 3
Hendersonville,
  32,188 . . . . A 5
Humboldt, 9,651 . . . B 3
Huntingdon, 4,180 . . A 3
Jackson, 48,949 . . . . B 3
Jefferson City, 5,494 C10
Johnson City, 49,381 C11
Kingsport, 36,365 . . C11
Kingston, 4,552 . . . D 9
Knoxville, 165,121 . . D10
La Follette, 7,192 . . . C 9
La Vergne, 7,499 . . . A 5
Lawrenceburg, 10,412 B 4
Lebanon, 15,208 . . . A 5
Lenoir City, 6,147 . . D 9
Lewisburg, 9,879 . . . B 5
Lexington, 5,810 . . . B 3
Loudon, 4,026 . . . . D 9
Lynn Garden,
  7,213('80) C11
Manchester, 7,709 . . B 5
Martin, 8,600 . . . . . . A 3
Maryville, 19,208 . . D10
McKenzie, 5,168 . . . A 3
McMinnville, 11,194 . . D 8
Memphis, 610,337 . . B 1
Milan, 7,512 . . . . . . B 3
Millington, 17,866 . . B 2
Morristown, 21,385 . . C10
Murfreesboro, 44,922 B 5
Nashville, 487,969 . . A 5
Newport, 7,123 . . . . D10
Oak Ridge, 27,310 . . C 9
Oneida, 3,502 . . . . C 9
Paris, 9,332 . . . . . . A 3
Portland, 5,165 . . . . A 5
Powell, 7,220('80) . . m13
Pulaski, 7,895 . . . . B 4
Red Bank, 12,322 . . D 8
Ripley, 6,188 . . . . B 2
Rockwood, 5,348 . . D 9
Rogersville, 4,149 . . C10
Savannah, 6,547 . . . B 3
Sevierville, 7,178 . . D10
Shelbyville, 14,049 . . B 5
Signal Mountain,
  7,034 . . . . D 8
Smyrna, 13,647 . . . B 5
Soddy-Daisy, 8,240 . . D 8
Sparta, 4,681 . . . . D 8
Springfield, 11,227 . . A 5
Sweetwater, 5,066 . . D 9
Trenton, 4,836 . . . . . B 3
Tullahoma, 16,761 . . B 5
Union City, 10,513 . . A 2
Waverly, 3,925 . . . . A 4
Winchester, 6,305 . . B 5

Texas

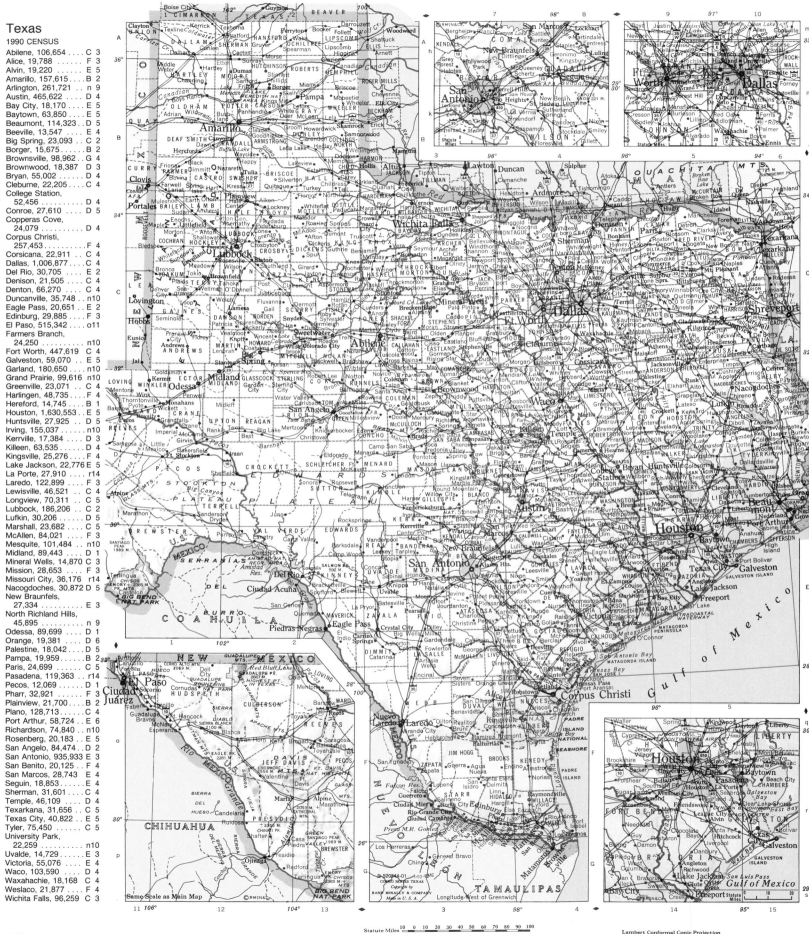

Texas

1990 CENSUS

Abilene, 106,654 .... C 3
Alice, 19,788 ...... F 3
Alvin, 19,220 ...... E 5
Amarillo, 157,615 .... B 2
Arlington, 261,721 .. n 9
Austin, 465,622 .... D 4
Bay City, 18,170 .... E 5
Baytown, 63,850 .... D 5
Beaumont, 114,323 .. D 5
Beeville, 13,547 .... E 4
Big Spring, 23,093 .. C 2
Borger, 15,675 ...... B 2
Brownsville, 98,962 .. G 4
Brownwood, 18,387 .. D 3
Bryan, 55,002 ...... D 4
Cleburne, 22,205 .... C 4
College Station,
  52,456 .... D 4
Conroe, 27,610 .... D 5
Copperas Cove,
  24,079 .... D 4
Corpus Christi,
  257,453 .... F 4
Corsicana, 22,911 .. C 4
Dallas, 1,006,877 .. C 4
Del Rio, 30,705 .... E 2
Denison, 21,505 .... C 4
Denton, 66,270 .... C 4
Duncanville, 35,748 .. n10
Eagle Pass, 20,651 .. E 2
Edinburg, 29,885 .. F 3
El Paso, 515,342 .. o11
Farmers Branch,
  24,250 .... n10
Fort Worth, 447,619 .. C 4
Galveston, 59,070 .. E 5
Garland, 180,650 .. n10
Grand Prairie, 99,616 n10
Greenville, 23,071 .. C 4
Harlingen, 48,735 .. F 4
Hereford, 14,745 .. B 1
Houston, 1,630,553 .. E 5
Huntsville, 27,925 .. D 5
Irving, 155,037 ...... n10
Kerrville, 17,384 .. D 3
Killeen, 63,535 .... D 4
Kingsville, 25,276 .. F 4
Lake Jackson, 22,776 E 5
La Porte, 27,910 .. r14
Laredo, 122,899 .. F 3
Lewisville, 46,521 .. C 4
Longview, 70,311 .. C 5
Lubbock, 186,206 .. C 2
Lufkin, 30,206 .... D 5
Marshall, 23,682 .. C 5
McAllen, 84,021 .. F 3
Mesquite, 101,484 .. n10
Midland, 89,443 .. D 1
Mineral Wells, 14,870 C 3
Mission, 28,653 .... F 3
Missouri City, 36,109 r14
Nacogdoches, 30,872 D 5
New Braunfels,
  27,334 .... E 3
North Richland Hills,
  45,895 .... n 9
Odessa, 89,699 .... D 1
Orange, 19,381 .... D 6
Palestine, 18,042 .. D 5
Pampa, 19,959 .... B 2
Paris, 24,699 ...... C 5
Pasadena, 119,363 .. r14
Pecos, 12,069 .... D 1
Pharr, 32,921 .... F 3
Plainview, 21,700 .. B 2
Plano, 128,713 .... C 4
Port Arthur, 58,724 .. E 6
Richardson, 74,840 .. n10
Rosenberg, 20,183 .. E 5
San Angelo, 84,474 .. D 2
San Antonio, 935,933 E 3
San Benito, 20,125 .. F 4
San Marcos, 28,743 .. E 4
Seguin, 18,853 .... E 4
Sherman, 31,601 .... C 4
Temple, 46,109 .... D 4
Texarkana, 31,656 .. C 5
Texas City, 40,822 .. E 5
Tyler, 75,450 ...... C 5
University Park,
  22,259 .... n10
Uvalde, 14,729 .... E 3
Victoria, 55,076 .... E 4
Waco, 103,590 .... D 4
Waxahachie, 18,168 .. C 4
Weslaco, 21,877 .. F 4
Wichita Falls, 96,259 C 3

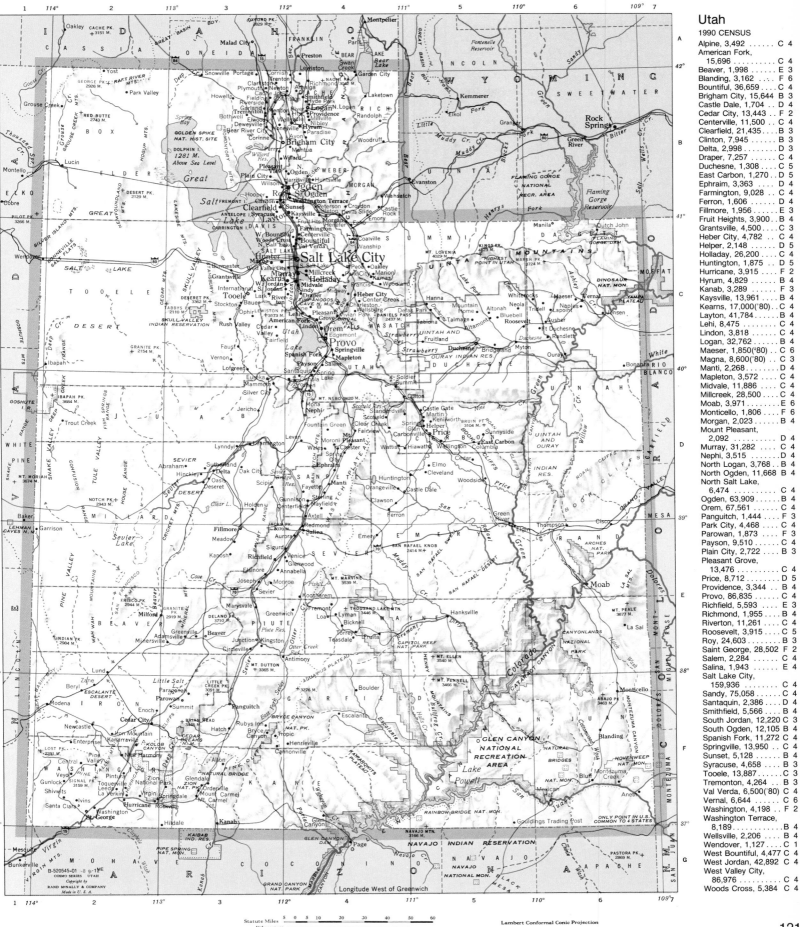

Utah

Utah

1990 CENSUS

Alpine, 3,492 . . . . . . C 4
American Fork,
  15,696 . . . . C 4
Beaver, 1,998 . . . . . . E 3
Blanding, 3,162 . . . . F 6
Bountiful, 36,659 . . . . C 4
Brigham City, 15,644 B 3
Castle Dale, 1,704 . . . D 4
Cedar City, 13,443 . . F 2
Centerville, 11,500 . . C 4
Clearfield, 21,435 . . . B 3
Clinton, 7,945 . . . . . . C 4
Delta, 2,998 . . . . D 3
Draper, 7,257 . . . . . . C 4
Duchesne, 1,308 . . . . C 5
East Carbon, 1,270 . . D 5
Ephraim, 3,363 . . . . . D 4
Farmington, 9,028 . . . C 4
Ferron, 1,606 . . . . . . D 4
Fillmore, 1,956 . . . . . E 3
Fruit Heights, 3,900 . . B 4
Grantsville, 4,500 . . . C 3
Heber City, 4,782 . . . C 4
Helper, 2,148 . . . . . . D 5
Holladay, 26,200 . . . . C 4
Huntington, 1,875 . . . D 5
Hurricane, 3,915 . . . . F 2
Hyrum, 4,829 . . . . . . B 4
Kanab, 3,289 . . . . . . F 3
Kaysville, 13,961 . . . B 4
Kearns, 17,000('80) . . C 4
Layton, 41,784 . . . . . B 4
Lehi, 8,475 . . . . C 4
Lindon, 3,818 . . . . . . C 4
Logan, 32,762 . . . . . . B 4
Maeser, 1,850('80) . . C 6
Magna, 8,600('80) . . C 3
Manti, 2,268 . . . . D 4
Mapleton, 3,572 . . . . C 4
Midvale, 11,886 . . . . C 4
Millcreek, 28,500 . . . C 4
Moab, 3,971 . . . . E 6
Monticello, 1,806 . . . F 6
Morgan, 2,023 . . . . . B 4
Mount Pleasant,
  2,092 . . . . D 4
Murray, 31,282 . . . . . C 4
Nephi, 3,515 . . . . D 4
North Logan, 3,768 . . B 4
North Ogden, 11,668 B 4
North Salt Lake,
  6,474 . . . . C 4
Ogden, 63,909 . . . . . B 4
Orem, 67,561 . . . . . . C 4
Panguitch, 1,444 . . . F 3
Park City, 4,468 . . . . C 4
Parowan, 1,873 . . . . F 3
Payson, 9,510 . . . . . . C 4
Plain City, 2,722 . . . B 3
Pleasant Grove,
  13,476 . . . . C 4
Price, 8,712 . . . . D 5
Providence, 3,344 . . . B 4
Provo, 86,835 . . . . . . C 4
Richfield, 5,593 . . . . E 3
Richmond, 1,955 . . . . B 4
Riverton, 11,261 . . . . C 4
Roosevelt, 3,915 . . . . C 5
Roy, 24,603 . . . . B 3
Saint George, 28,502 F 2
Salem, 2,284 . . . . . . C 4
Salina, 1,943 . . . . . . E 4
Salt Lake City,
  159,936 . . . . C 4
Sandy, 75,058 . . . . . . C 4
Santaquin, 2,386 . . . D 4
Smithfield, 5,566 . . . B 4
South Jordan, 12,220 C 3
South Ogden, 12,105 B 4
Spanish Fork, 11,272 C 4
Springville, 13,950 . . C 4
Sunset, 5,128 . . . . . . B 4
Syracuse, 4,658 . . . . B 3
Tooele, 13,887 . . . . . C 3
Tremonton, 4,264 . . . B 4
Val Verda, 6,500('80) C 4
Vernal, 6,644 . . . . . . C 6
Washington, 4,198 . . F 2
Washington Terrace,
  8,189 . . . . B 4
Wellsville, 2,206 . . . B 4
Wendover, 1,127 . . . C 1
West Bountiful, 4,477 C 4
West Jordan, 42,892 C 4
West Valley City,
  86,976 . . . . C 4
Woods Cross, 5,384 . C 4

Statute Miles   5 0 5 10   20   30   40   50   60
Kilometers   5 0 5   20   40   60   80

Lambert Conformal Conic Projection

Vermont

Vermont
1990 CENSUS

Arlington, 700
  (2,299▲) . . . . E 2
Barre, 9,482 . . . . C 4
Barton, 908 . . . . B 4
Bellows Falls, 3,313 . . . . E 4
Bennington, 9,349
  (16,451▲) . . . . F 2
Bethel, 1,016
  (1,866▲) . . . . . . D 3
Bradford, 672 . . . . . . D 4
Brandon, 1,925
  (4,223▲) . . . . . . D 2
Brattleboro, 8,596
  (12,241▲) . . . . . . F 3
Bristol, 1,801 . . . . . . C 2
Burlington, 39,127 . . . C 2
Castleton, 600
  (4,278▲) . . . . D 2
Chester, 550 (2,832▲) E 3
Chester Depot, 500 . . E 3
Derby Line, 855 . . . . A 4
Dorset, 550 (1,918▲) . E 2
East Arlington, 600 . . E 2
East Barre, 700 . . . . C 4
East Middlebury, 500 D 2
East Montpelier, 600
  (2,239▲) . . . . C 4
Enosburg Falls, 1,350 B 3
Essex, 800 (16,498▲) B 2
Essex Junction, 8,396 C 2
Fair Haven, 2,887 . . . D 2
Forest Dale, 350 . . . . D 2
Gilman, 500 . . . . C 5
Graniteville, 500 . . . . C 4
Hardwick, 1,400
  (2,964▲) . . . . B 4
Hartford, 500 . . . . . . D 4
Hartford, 500
  (9,404▲) . . . . . . D 4
Hyde Park, 450 . . . . . D 2
Jericho, 1,300
  (4,302▲) . . . . . . B 3
Johnson, 1,470 . . . . . B 3
Ludlow, 1,123 . . . . . . E 3
Lyndonville, 1,255 . . . B 4
Manchester, 561 . . . . E 2
Middlebury, 5,591
  (8,034▲) . . . . . . C 2
Milton, 1,578 . . . . . . B 2
Montpelier, 8,247 . . . C 3
Morrisville, 1,984 . . . . B 3
Newport, 4,434 . . . . . B 4
North Bennington,
  1,520 . . . . F 2
North Clarendon, 500 D 3
Northfield, 1,889 . . . . C 3
Northfield Falls, 600 . C 3
North Springfield, 750 E 3
North Troy, 723 . . . . . B 4
Norwich, 1,000
  (3,093▲) . . . . . . D 4
Orleans, 806 . . . . . . B 4
Pittsford, 650
  (2,919▲) . . . . . . D 2
Plainfield, 600
  (1,302▲) . . . . . . C 4
Poultney, 1,731 . . . . . D 2
Proctor, 1,979 . . . . . A 2
Proctorsville, 480 . . . E 3
Putney, 1,100
  (2,352▲) . . . . . . F 3
Quechee, 550 . . . . . . D 4
Randolph, 2,200
  (4,764▲) . . . . . . D 3
Richford, 1,425 . . . . . B 3
Richmond, 650
  (3,729▲) . . . . . . C 3
Riverton, 150 . . . . . . C 3
Rochester, 500
  (1,181▲) . . . . . . D 3
Rutland, 18,230 . . . . . D 3
Saint Albans, 7,339 . . B 2
Saint Johnsbury, 7,150
  (7,608▲) . . . . . . C 4
Saxtons River, 541 . . E 3
Shaftsbury, 700
  (3,368▲) . . . . . . E 2
South Burlington,
  12,809 . . . . C 2
South Royalton, 700 . D 3
Springfield, 5,603
  (9,579▲) . . . . . . E 4
Stamford, 400 (773▲) F 2
Stowe, 450 . . . . B 3
Swanton, 2,360 . . . . . B 2
Vergennes, 2,578 . . . C 2
Wallingford, 1,141
  (2,184▲) . . . . . . E 3
Warren, 350 (1,172▲) C 3
Waterbury, 1,702 . . . . C 3
Waterbury Center,
  500 . . . . C 3
Websterville, 600 . . . C 4
West Pawlet, 350 . . . E 2
West Rutland, 2,448 . D 2
Williamstown, 650
  (2,839▲) . . . . . . C 3
Wilmington, 550
  (1,968▲) . . . . . . F 3
Windsor, 3,714 . . . . . E 4
Winooski, 6,649 . . . . C 2
Woodstock, 1,037 . . . D 3

▲ Population of entire town (township), including rural area.

122

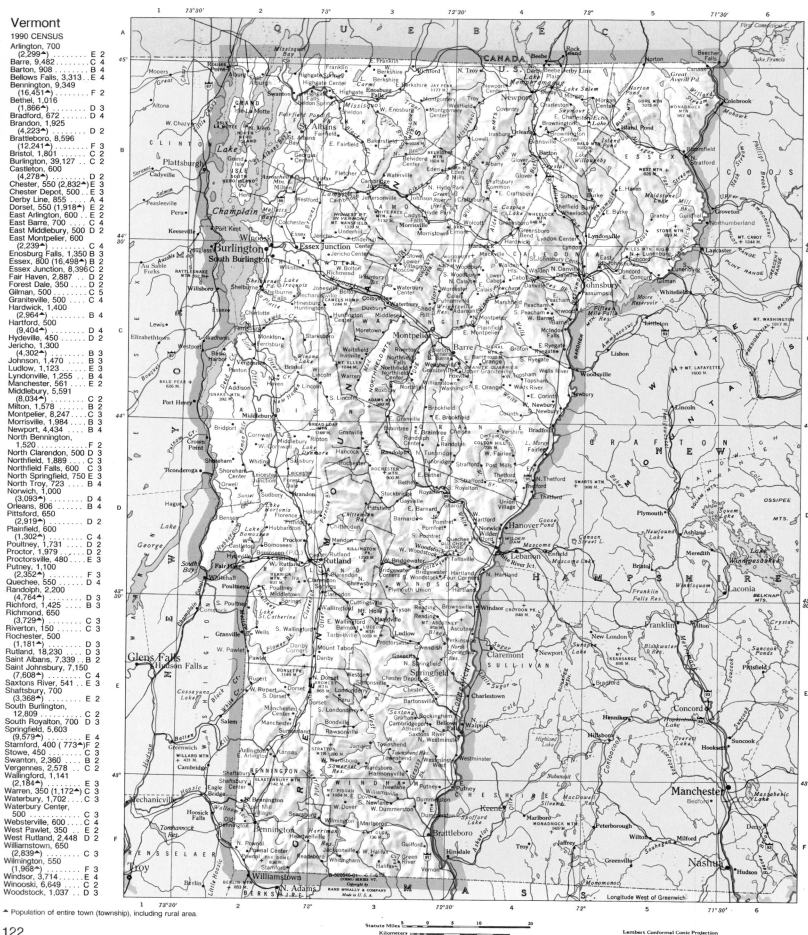

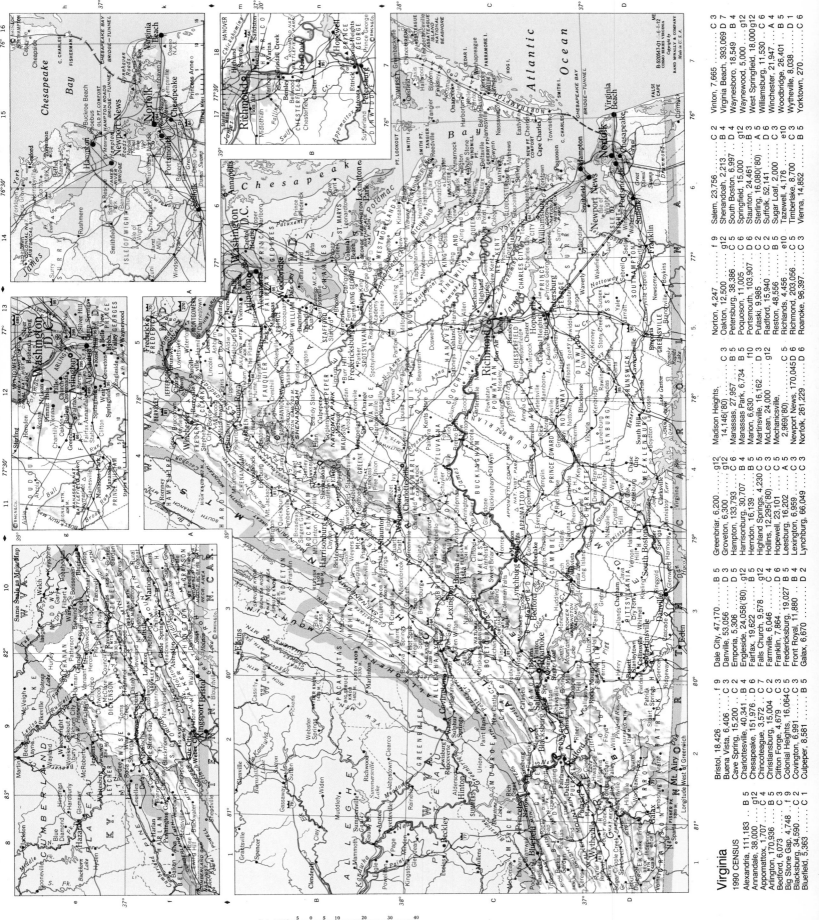

Statute Miles 5 0 5 10 20 30 40
Kilometers 5 0 5 15 25 35 45 55

Lambert Conformal Conic Projection

Virginia

1990 CENSUS

Alexandria, 111,183	B 5	
Annandale, 50,975	g12	
Appomattox, 1,707	C 5	
Arlington, 170,936	B 5	
Bedford, 6,073	C 3	
Big Stone Gap, 4,748	f 9	
Blacksburg, 34,590	C 2	
Bluefield, 5,363	C 1	
Bristol, 18,426	f 9	
Buena Vista, 6,406	C 3	
Cave Spring, 15,200	C 2	
Charlottesville, 40,341	B 4	
Chincoteague, 3,572	C 7	
Christiansburg, 15,004	C 2	
Clifton Forge, 4,679	C 3	
Colonial Heights, 16,064	C 5	
Covington, 6,991	C 2	
Culpeper, 8,581	B 5	
Dale City, 47,170	B 5	
Danville, 53,056	D 3	
Emporia, 5,306	D 5	
Englesid, 24,058(80)	g12	
Fairfax, 19,622	B 5	
Falls Church, 9,578	g12	
Farmville, 6,046	C 4	
Franklin, 7,864	D 6	
Fredericksburg, 19,027	B 5	
Front Royal, 11,880	B 4	
Galax, 6,670	D 2	
Greenbriar, 6,200	C 3	
Groveton, 6,300	D 3	
Hampton, 133,793	C 6	
Harrisonburg, 30,707	B 4	
Herndon, 16,139	B 5	
Highland Springs, 4,230	C 5	
Hollins, 12,295(80)	C 2	
Hopewell, 23,101	C 5	
Leesburg, 16,202	A 5	
Lexington, 6,959	C 3	
Lynchburg, 66,049	C 3	
Madison Heights, 14,146(80)	C 3	
Manassas, 27,957	B 5	
Manassas Park, 6,734	g12	
Marion, 6,630	D 6	
Martinsville, 16,162	C 3	
McLean, 24,000	g12	
Mechanicsville, 2,969(80)	C 5	
Newport News, 170,045	C 6	
Norfolk, 261,229	D 6	
Norton, 4,247	f 9	
Oakton, 12,500	g12	
Petersburg, 38,386	C 5	
Poquoson, 11,005	C 6	
Portsmouth, 103,907	D 6	
Pulaski, 9,985	C 2	
Radford, 15,940	C 2	
Reston, 48,556	B 5	
Richlands, 4,456	e10	
Richmond, 203,056	C 5	
Roanoke, 96,397	C 3	
Salem, 23,756	C 2	
Shenandoah, 2,213	B 4	
South Boston, 6,997	D 4	
Springfield, 15,000	g12	
Staunton, 24,461	B 3	
Sterling, 16,080(80)	A 5	
Suffolk, 52,141	D 6	
Sugar Loaf, 2,000	B 5	
Tazewell, 4,176	e10	
Timberlake, 8,700	C 3	
Vienna, 14,852	B 5	
Vinton, 7,665	C 3	
Virginia Beach, 393,069	D 7	
Waynesboro, 18,549	B 4	
Waynewood, 5,000	g12	
West Springfield, 18,000	g12	
Williamsburg, 11,530	C 6	
Winchester, 21,947	A 4	
Woodbridge, 26,401	B 5	
Wytheville, 8,038	D 1	
Yorktown, 270	C 6	

Washington

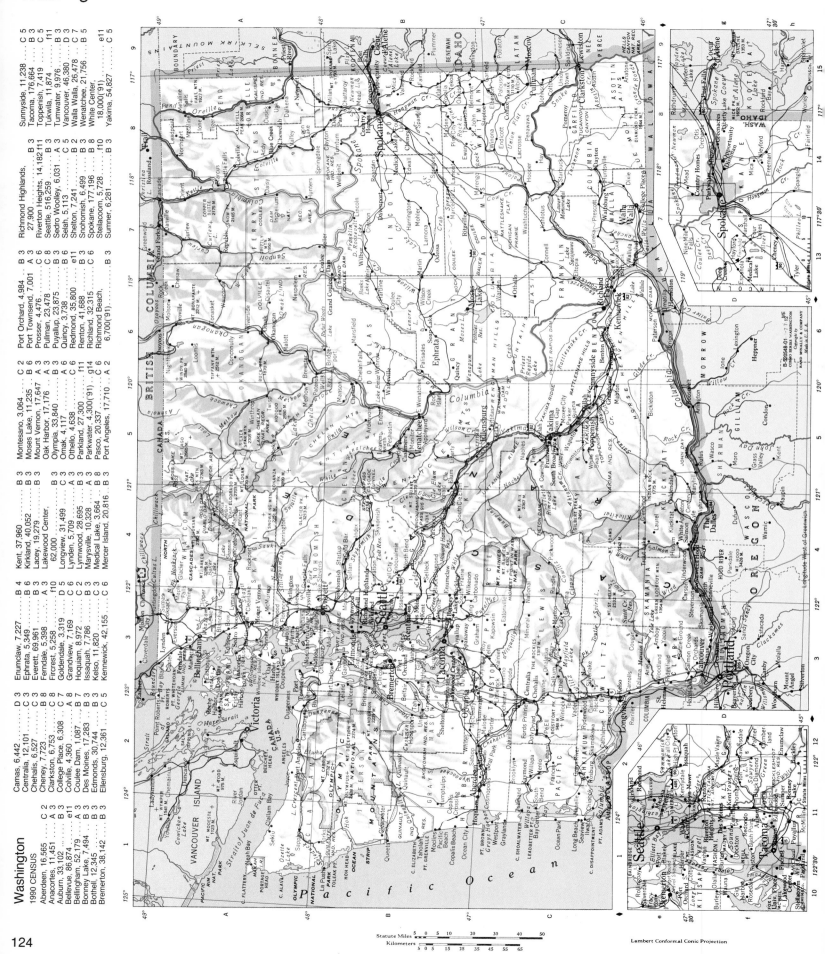

Washington

1990 CENSUS

Aberdeen, 16,565	C 2
Anacortes, 11,451	B 3
Auburn, 33,102	B 3
Bellevue, 86,874	e11
Bellingham, 52,179	A 3
Bonney Lake, 7,494	B 3
Bothell, 12,345	B 3
Bremerton, 38,142	B 3

Camas, 6,442	D 3
Centralia, 12,101	C 3
Chehalis, 6,527	C 3
Cheney, 7,723	B 8
Clarkston, 6,753	C 8
College Place, 6,308	C 7
Colville, 4,360	A 8
Coulee Dam, 1,087	B 7
Des Moines, 17,283	f11
Edmonds, 30,744	B 3
Ellensburg, 12,361	B 3

Enumclaw, 7,227	B 4
Ephrata, 5,349	B 6
Everett, 69,961	A 3
Ferndale, 5,398	A 3
Fircrest, 5,258	f10
Goldendale, 3,319	D 5
Grandview, 7,169	C 6
Hoquiam, 8,972	C 2
Issaquah, 7,786	B 3
Kelso, 11,820	C 3
Kennewick, 42,155	C 5

Kent, 37,960	B 3
Kirkland, 40,052	B 3
Lacey, 19,279	A 3
Lakewood Center, 62,000	
Longview, 31,499	C 3
Lynden, 5,709	A 3
Lynnwood, 28,695	C 2
Marysville, 10,328	B 3
Medical Lake, 3,664	B 8
Mercer Island, 20,816	C 6

Montesano, 3,064	C 2
Moses Lake, 11,235	B 6
Mount Vernon, 17,647	A 3
Oak Harbor, 17,176	A 3
Olympia, 33,840	C 3
Omak, 4,117	A 6
Othello, 4,638	C 6
Parkland, 27,300	f11
Parkwater, 4,300('91)	g14
Pasco, 20,337	C 6
Port Angeles, 17,710	A 2

Port Orchard, 4,984	B 3
Port Townsend, 7,001	A 3
Prosser, 4,476	C 6
Pullman, 23,478	C 8
Puyallup, 23,875	B 3
Quincy, 3,738	B 6
Redmond, 35,800	e11
Renton, 41,688	B 3
Richland, 32,315	C 6
Richmond Beach, 6,700('91)	B 3

Richmond Highlands, 27,900	
Riverton Heights, 14,182	f11
Seattle, 516,259	B 3
Sedro Woolley, 6,031	A 3
Selah, 5,113	C 5
Shelton, 7,241	B 2
Snohomish, 6,499	B 8
Spokane, 177,196	B 8
Steilacoom, 5,728	f10
Sumner, 6,281	B 3

Sunnyside, 11,238	C 5
Tacoma, 176,664	B 3
Toppenish, 7,419	f11
Tukwila, 11,874	f11
Tumwater, 9,976	B 3
Vancouver, 46,380	D 3
Walla Walla, 26,478	C 7
Wenatchee, 21,756	B 5
White Center, 18,000('91)	e11
Yakima, 54,827	C 5

Statute Miles 5 0 5 10 20 30 40 50
Kilometers 5 0 5 15 25 35 45 55 65

Lambert Conformal Conic Projection

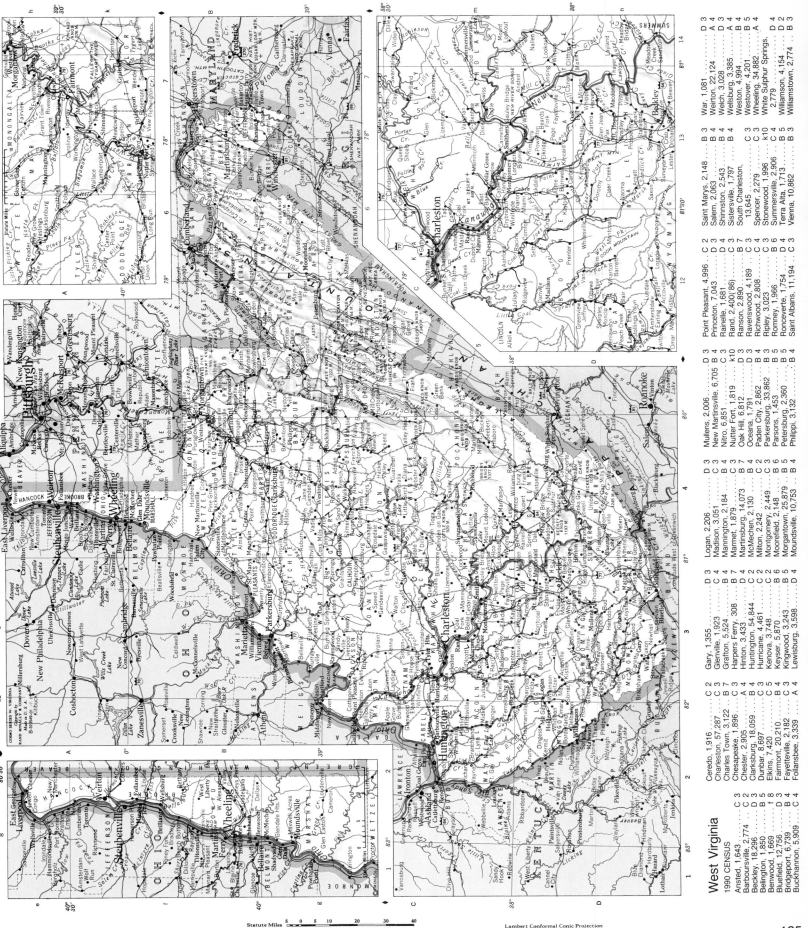

West Virginia

1990 CENSUS

Place		
Ansted, 1,643	C	3
Barboursville, 2,774	C	2
Beckley, 18,296	C	3
Belington, 1,850	B	5
Benwood, 1,669	f	8
Bluefield, 12,756	D	3
Bridgeport, 6,739	B	4
Buckhannon, 5,909	C	4
Ceredo, 1,916	C	2
Charleston, 57,287	C	3
Charles Town, 3,122	B	7
Chesapeake, 1,896	C	3
Chester, 2,905	A	4
Clarksburg, 18,059	B	4
Dunbar, 8,697	C	3
Elkins, 7,420	C	5
Fairmont, 20,210	B	4
Fayetteville, 2,182	C	3
Follansbee, 3,339	C	4
Gary, 1,355	D	3
Glenville, 1,923	C	3
Grafton, 5,524	B	4
Harpers Ferry, 308	B	7
Hinton, 3,433	D	4
Huntington, 54,844	C	2
Hurricane, 4,461	C	2
Kenova, 3,748	C	2
Keyser, 5,870	B	6
Kingwood, 3,243	B	5
Lewisburg, 3,598	D	4
Logan, 2,206	D	3
Madison, 3,051	C	3
Mannington, 2,184	B	4
Marmet, 1,879	C	3
Martinsburg, 14,073	B	7
McMechen, 2,130	A	4
Milton, 2,242	C	2
Montgomery, 2,449	C	3
Moorefield, 2,148	B	6
Morgantown, 25,879	B	5
Moundsville, 10,753	B	4
Mullens, 2,006	D	3
New Martinsville, 6,705	B	4
Nutter Fort, 1,819		
Oak Hill, 6,812	B	4
Oceana, 1,791		
Paden City, 2,862	B	4
Parkersburg, 33,862	B	3
Parsons, 1,453	B	5
Petersburg, 2,360	B	5
Philippi, 3,132	B	4
Point Pleasant, 4,996	C	2
Princeton, 7,043	D	3
Rainelle, 1,681	C	3
Rand, 2,400 (86)		
Ranson, 2,890	B	7
Ravenswood, 4,189	C	3
Richwood, 2,808	C	4
Ripley, 3,023	C	2
Romney, 1,966	B	6
Ronceverte, 1,754	D	4
Saint Albans, 11,194	C	3
Saint Marys, 2,148	D	3
Salem, 2,063	D	4
Shinnston, 3,028	A	4
Sistersville, 1,797	B	4
South Charleston, 13,645	C	3
Spencer, 2,279	C	3
Stonewood, 1,996	k	10
Summersville, 2,906	B	6
Terra Alta, 1,713	B	5
Vienna, 10,862	C	3
War, 1,081	D	3
Weirton, 22,124	A	4
Welch, 3,028	D	3
Wellsburg, 3,385	B	4
Weston, 4,994	B	5
Westover, 4,201	A	4
Wheeling, 34,882	A	4
White Sulphur Springs, 2,779	D	4
Williamson, 4,154	D	2
Williamstown, 2,774	B	3

Statute Miles 5 0 5 10 20 30 40

Kilometers 5 0 5 15 25 35 45 55

Lambert Conformal Conic Projection

Wisconsin

Wisconsin

1990 CENSUS

Allouez, 14,431 . . . . h 9
Antigo, 8,276 . . . . . C 4
Appleton, 65,695 . . . . D 5
Ashland, 8,695 . . . . . B 3
Ashwaubenon, 16,376 D 5
Baraboo, 9,203 . . . . . E 4
Beaver Dam, 14,196 . . E 5
Beloit, 35,573 . . . . . F 4
Brookfield, 35,184 . . . m11
Brown Deer, 12,236 . m12
Burlington, 8,855 . . . . F 5
Cedarburg, 9,895 . . . . E 6
Chippewa Falls,
  12,727 . . . . D 2
Cudahy, 18,659 . . . . F 6
De Pere, 16,569 . . . . D 5
Eau Claire, 56,856 . . . D 2
Fond du Lac, 37,757 . . E 5
Fort Atkinson, 10,227 F 5
Franklin, 21,855 . . . . n11
Germantown, 13,658 . E 5
Glendale, 14,088 . . . . m12
Grafton, 9,340 . . . . . E 6
Green Bay, 96,466 . . . D 6
Greendale, 15,128 . . . F 6
Greenfield, 33,403 . . . n11
Hayward, 1,897 . . . . . B 2
Howard, 9,809 . . . . . D 5
Hudson, 6,378 . . . . . . D 1
Janesville, 52,133 . . . F 4
Kaukauna, 11,982 . . . D 5
Kenosha, 80,352 . . . . F 6
La Crosse, 51,003 . . . E 2
Lake Geneva, 5,979 . . F 5
Little Chute, 9,207 . . . D 5
Madison, 191,262 . . . E 4
Manitowoc, 32,520 . . . D 6
Marinette, 11,843 . . . . C 6
Marshfield, 19,291 . . . D 3
Menasha, 14,711 . . . . D 5
Menomonee Falls,
  26,840 . . . . E 5
Menomonie, 13,547 . . D 2
Mequon, 18,885 . . . . E 6
Merrill, 9,860 . . . . . . C 4
Middleton, 13,289 . . . E 4
Milwaukee, 628,088 . . E 6
Monona, 8,637 . . . . . E 4
Monroe, 10,241 . . . . F 4
Muskego, 16,813 . . . . F 5
Neenah, 23,219 . . . . D 5
New Berlin, 33,592 . . n11
New London, 6,658 . . D 5
Oak Creek, 19,513 . . n12
Oconomowoc, 10,993 E 5
Oconto, 4,474 . . . . . . D 6
Onalaska, 11,284 . . . . E 2
Oshkosh, 55,006 . . . . D 5
Park Falls, 3,104 . . . . C 3
Platteville, 9,708 . . . . F 3
Portage, 8,640 . . . . . . E 4
Port Washington,
  9,338 . . . . E 6
Prairie du Chien,
  5,659 . . . . E 2
Racine, 84,298 . . . . . F 6
Reedsburg, 5,834 . . . E 4
Rhinelander, 7,427 . . . C 4
Rice Lake, 7,998 . . . . C 2
River Falls, 10,610 . . . D 1
Saint Francis, 9,245 . . n12
Shawano, 7,598 . . . . . D 5
Sheboygan, 49,676 . . . E 6
Shorewood, 14,116 . . . E 6
South Milwaukee,
  20,958 . . . . F 6
Stevens Point, 23,006 D 4
Stoughton, 8,786 . . . . F 4
Sturgeon Bay, 9,176 . D 6
Sun Prairie, 15,333 . . E 4
Superior, 27,134 . . . . B 1
Tomah, 7,570 . . . . . . E 3
Two Rivers, 13,030 . . D 6
Watertown, 19,142 . . . E 5
Waukesha, 56,958 . . . F 5
Waupun, 8,207 . . . . . E 5
Wausau, 37,060 . . . . D 4
Wauwatosa, 49,366 . m12
West Allis, 63,221 . . . m11
West Bend, 23,916 . . . E 5
Weston, 8,775('80) . . D 4
Whitefish Bay, 14,272 m12
Whitewater, 12,636 . . F 5
Wisconsin Dells,
  2,393 . . . . E 4
Wisconsin Rapids,
  18,245 . . . . D 4

Statute Miles 5 0 5 10 20 30 40

Kilometers 5 0 5 15 25 35 45 55

Lambert Conformal Conic Projection

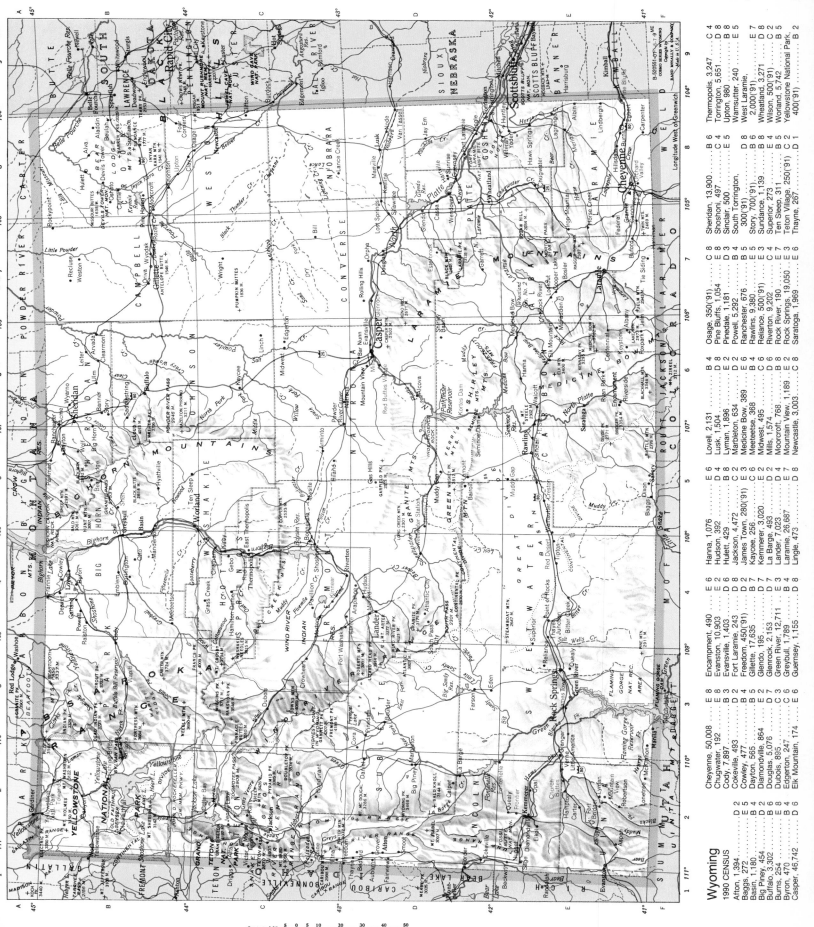

Wyoming
1990 CENSUS

Afton, 1,394	D 2	Hanna, 1,076	E 6
Baggs, 272	E 5	Hudson, 392	D 4
Basin, 1,180	B 4	Hulett, 429	B 8
Dayton, 565	B 5	Jackson, 4,472	C 2
Diamondville, 864	E 2	James Town, 280('91)	E 3
Big Piney, 454	D 2	Kaycee, 256	C 6
Buffalo, 3,302	B 6	Kemmerer, 3,020	D 2
Burns, 254	E 8	La Barge, 493	D 2
Byron, 470	B 4	Lander, 7,023	C 4
		Laramie, 26,687	E 7
Cheyenne, 50,008	E 8	Lingle, 1,155	D 8
Chugwater, 192	E 8	Lovell, 2,131	B 4
Cody, 7,897	B 3	Lusk, 1,504	D 8
Cokeville, 493	D 2	Lyman, 1,896	E 2
Cowley, 477	B 4	Marbleton, 634	D 2
		Medicine Bow, 389	E 6
Douglas, 5,076	D 7	Meeteetse, 368	C 4
Dubois, 895	C 3	Midwest, 495	C 6
Edgerton, 247	C 6	Mills, 1,574	D 6
Elk Mountain, 174	E 6	Moorcroft, 768	B 8
Encampment, 490	E 6	Mountain View, 1,189	E 2
Evanston, 10,903	E 2	Newcastle, 3,003	C 8
Evansville, 1,403	D 6	Osage, 350('91)	C 8
Fort Laramie, 243	D 8	Pine Bluffs, 1,054	E 8
Freedom, 450('91)	D 2	Pinedale, 1,181	D 3
Gillette, 17,635	B 7	Powell, 5,292	B 4
Glendo, 195	D 7	Ranchester, 676	B 5
Glenrock, 2,153	D 7	Rawlins, 9,380	E 5
Green River, 12,711	E 3	Reliance, 500('91)	E 3
Greybull, 1,789	B 4	Riverton, 9,202	C 4
Guernsey, 1,155	D 8	Rock River, 190	E 7
		Rock Springs, 19,050	E 3
		Saratoga, 1,969	E 6
		Sheridan, 13,900	B 5
		Shoshoni, 1,054	C 4
		Sinclair, 500	E 5
		South Torrington, 300('91)	D 8
		Story, 700('91)	B 6
		Sundance, 1,139	B 8
		Superior, 273	E 3
		Ten Sleep, 311	C 4
		Teton Village, 250('91)	C 2
		Thayne, 267	D 1
		Thermopolis, 3,247	C 4
		Torrington, 5,651	D 8
		Upton, 980	C 8
		Wamsutter, 240	E 5
		West Laramie, 2,000('91)	E 7
		Wheatland, 3,271	D 8
		Wilson, 500('91)	C 2
		Worland, 5,742	B 4
		Yellowstone National Park, 400('91)	B 2

Longitude West of Greenwich

Statute Miles 5 0 5 10 20 30 40 50
Kilometers 5 0 5 15 25 35 45 55 65 75

Lambert Conformal Conic Projection

North Polar Regions

Anchorage, 226,338
('90).....................C27
Archangel'sk, 416,000
('89)........................C 8
BELGIUM..................D12
Berlin, 3,352,848 ('89)
(3,825,000★)..........D11
CANADA.....................D22
Chicago, 2,783,726
('90)........................E21
CHINA.........................F 2
Churchill, 1,186 ('81)...D22
CZECHOSLOVAKIA....E11
DENMARK..................D11
Dublin, 502,749 ('86)
(1,140,000★)..........D13
Dutch Harbor, 20 ('81) D29
Edmonton, 573,982 ('86)
(785,465★)..............D24
ESTONIA....................C10
FAEROE ISLANDS.....C13
Fairbanks, 30,843
('90).....................C27
FINLAND....................C10
FRANCE.....................E12
Gander, 10,207 ('86)
(10,899★)................E18
GERMANY..................D11
Godthåb, 12,217 ('90)..C18
GREENLAND...............B17
Hammerfest, 7,208
('83)........................B10
Happy Valley-Goose Bay,
7,248 ('86)................D19
Helsinki, 490,034 ('88)
(1,040,000★)..........C10
ICELAND....................C14
Igarka, 16,918 ('79)......C 4
IRELAND....................D13
JAPAN.......................F35
Jekaterinburg, 1,367,000
('89) (1,620,000★).. D 6
Juneau, 26,751 ('90)....D26
Kijev (Kiev), 2,587,000
('89) (2,900,000★)... D 9
KOREA, NORTH..........E36
KOREA, SOUTH..........F36
LATVIA.......................C10
LITHUANIA.................C10
Leningrad, 4,456,000 ('89)
(5,825,000★)............D 9
LUXEMBOURG............E12
Magadan, 152,000
('89).......................D33
MONGOLIA.................E 2
Moskva (Moscow),
8,769,000 ('89)
(13,100,000★)..........D 9
Murmansk, 468,000
('89).........................C 9
NETHERLANDS...........D12
New York, 7,322,564
('90)........................E20
Nižnij Novgorod (Gorky),
1,438,000 ('89)
(2,025,000★)............D 8
Nome, 3,500 ('90)........C29
Noril'sk, 174,000 ('89)..C 4
NORWAY....................C12
Novosibirsk, 1,436,000
('89) (1,600,000★).. D 4
Ōsaka, 2,636,249 ('85)
(16,450,000★).........F35
Oslo, 452,415 ('87)
(720,000★)..............D11
Ottawa, 300,763 ('86)
(819,263★)..............E20
Paris, 2,078,900 ('87)
(9,775,000★)............E12
POLAND.....................D11
Québec, 164,580 ('86)
(603,267★)..............E20
Reykjavík, 93,425 ('87)
(137,941★)..............C15
RUSSIA......................C 4
Saint John's, 96,216 ('86)
(161,901★)..............E18
Sankt-Peterburg,
4,456,000 ('89)
(5,825,000★)............D 9
Seattle, 516,259 ('90)..E25
Shenyang (Mukden),
3,910,000 ('88)
(4,370,000▲)...........E36
Sŏul (Seoul), 10,522,000
('89) (15,850,000★).F36
Stockholm, 672,187 ('90)
(1,449,972★)...........D11
SWEDEN....................C11
Thule, 551 ('90)...........B19
Tōkyō, 8,354,615 ('85)
(27,700,000★).........F35
Ulaanbaatar (Ulan Bator),
548,400 ('89)...........E 2
UNITED KINGDOM.....D13
UNITED STATES........F22
Vancouver, 431,147 ('86)
(1,380,729★)...........E25
Vladivostok, 648,000
('89).......................E35
Vorkuta, 116,000 ('89) C 6
Warszawa, 1,651,200
('89) (2,323,000★) ..D10
Winnipeg, 594,551 ('86)
(625,304★)..............E22

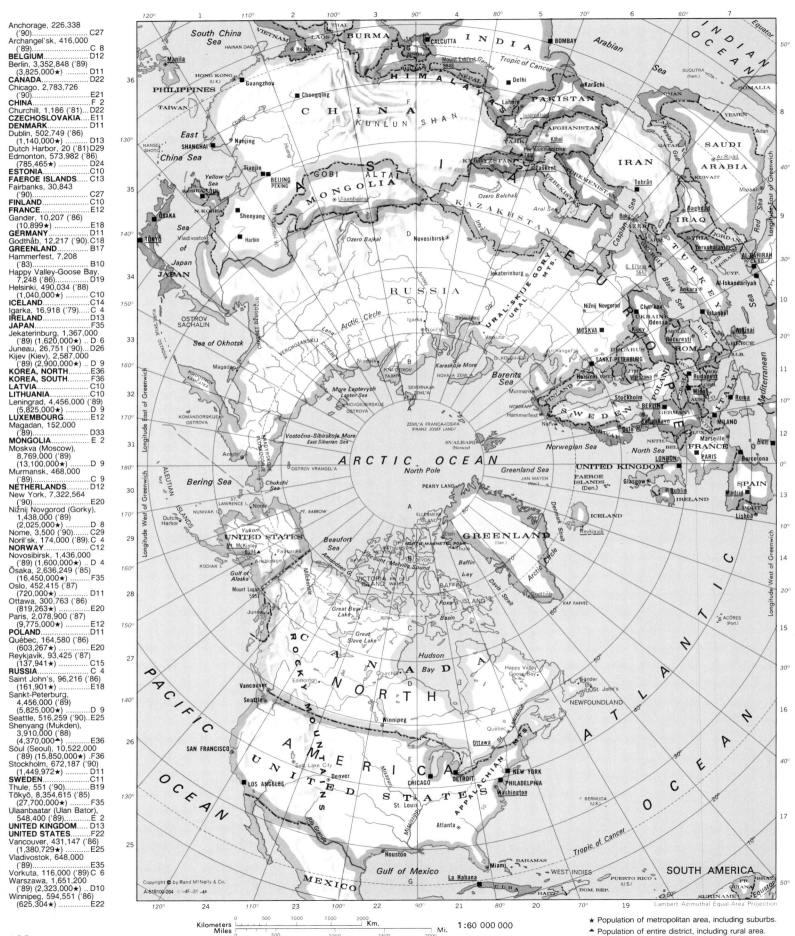

★ Population of metropolitan area, including suburbs.

▲ Population of entire district, including rural area.

Copyright © by Rand McNally & Co.

A-519100-264

Kilometers · Miles · Km. · Mi. · 1:60 000 000

Lambert Azimuthal Equal-Area Projection

Index to World Reference Maps

Introduction to the Index

This universal index includes in a single alphabetical list approximately 38,000 names of features that appear on the reference maps. Each name is followed by the name of the country or continent in which it is located, a map-reference key and a page reference.

Names The names of cities appear in the index in regular type. The names of all other features appear in *italics*, followed by descriptive terms (hill, mtn., state) to indicate their nature.

Names that appear in shortened versions on the maps due to space limitations are spelled out in full in the index. The portions of these names omitted from the maps are enclosed in brackets — for example, Acapulco [de Juárez].

Abbreviations of names on the maps have been standardized as much as possible. Names that are abbreviated on the maps are generally spelled out in full in the index.

Country names and names of features that extend beyond the boundaries of one country are followed by the name of the continent in which each is located. Country designations follow the names of all other places in the index. The locations of places in the United States, Canada, and the United Kingdom are further defined by abbreviations that indicate the state, province, or political division in which each is located.

All abbreviations used in the index are defined in the List of Abbreviations below.

Alphabetization Names are alphabetized in the order of the letters of the English alphabet. Spanish *ll* and *ch*, for example, are not treated as distinct letters. Furthermore, diacritical marks are disregarded in alphabetization — German or Scandinavian *ä* or *ö* are treated as *a* or *o*.

The names of physical features may appear inverted, since they are always alphabetized under the proper, not the generic, part of the name, thus: 'Gibraltar, Strait of'. Otherwise every entry,

whether consisting of one word or more, is alphabetized as a single continuous entity. 'Lakeland', for example, appears after 'La Crosse' and before 'La Salle'. Names beginning with articles (Le Havre, Den Helder, Al Manşūrah) are not inverted. Names beginning 'St.', 'Ste.' and 'Sainte' are alphabetized as though spelled 'Saint'.

In the case of identical names, towns are listed first, then political divisions, then physical features. Entries that are completely identical are listed alphabetically by country name.

Map-Reference Keys and Page References The map-reference keys and page references are found in the last two columns of each entry.

Each map-reference key consists of a letter and number. The letters appear along the sides of the maps. Lowercase letters indicate reference to inset maps. Numbers appear across the tops and bottoms of the maps.

Map reference keys for point features, such as cities and mountain peaks, indicate the locations of the symbols. For extensive areal features, such as countries or mountain ranges, locations are given for the approximate centers of the features. Those for linear features, such as canals and rivers, are given for the locations of the names.

Names of some important places or features that are omitted from the maps due to space limitations are included in the index. Each of these places is identified by an asterisk (*) preceding the map-reference key.

The page number generally refers to the main map for the country in which the feature is located. Page references to two-page maps always refer to the left-hand page.

List of Abbreviations

Afg.	Afghanistan	*ctry.*	country	Isr.	Israel	N.H., U.S.	New Hampshire, U.S.	Som.	Somalia
Afr.	Africa	C.V.	Cape Verde	Isr. Occ.	Israeli Occupied	Nic.	Nicaragua	Sp. N. Afr.	Spanish North Africa
Ak., U.S.	Alaska, U.S.	Cyp.	Cyprus		Territories	Nig.	Nigeria	Sri L.	Sri Lanka
Al., U.S.	Alabama, U.S.	Czech.	Czechoslovakia	Jam.	Jamaica	N. Ire., U.K.	Northern Ireland, U.K.	*state*	state, republic, canton
Alb.	Albania	D.C., U.S.	District of Columbia,	Jord.	Jordan	N.J., U.S.	New Jersey, U.S.	St. Hel.	St. Helena
Alg.	Algeria		U.S.	Kaz.	Kazakhstan	N. Kor.	North Korea	St. K./N	St. Kitts and Nevis
Alta., Can.	Alberta, Can.	De., U.S.	Delaware, U.S.	Kir.	Kiribati	N.M., U.S.	New Mexico, U.S.	St. Luc.	St. Lucia
Am. Sam.	American Samoa	Den.	Denmark	Ks., U.S.	Kansas, U.S.	N. Mar. Is.	Northern Mariana	*stm.*	stream (river, creek)
anch.	anchorage	*dep.*	dependency, colony	Kuw.	Kuwait		Islands	S. Tom./P.	Sao Tome and
And.	Andorra	*depr.*	depression	Ky., U.S.	Kentucky, U.S.	Nmb.	Namibia		Principe
Ang.	Angola	*dept.*	department, district	Kyrg.	Kyrgyzstan	Nor.	Norway	St. P./M.	St. Pierre and
Ant.	Antarctica	*des.*	desert	*l.*	lake, pond	Norf. I.	Norfolk Island		Miquelon
Antig.	Antigua and Barbuda	Dji.	Djibouti	La., U.S.	Louisiana, U.S.	N.S., Can.	Nova Scotia, Can.	*strt.*	strait, channel, sound
Ar., U.S.	Arkansas, U.S.	Dom.	Dominica	Lat.	Latvia	Nv., U.S.	Nevada, U.S.	St. Vin.	St. Vincent and the
Arg.	Argentina	Dom. Rep.	Dominican Republic	Leb.	Lebanon	N.W. Ter.,	Northwest Territories,		Grenadines
Arm.	Armenia	Ec.	Ecuador	Leso.	Lesotho	Can.	Can.	Sud.	Sudan
Aus.	Austria	El Sal.	El Salvador	Lib.	Liberia	N.Y., U.S.	New York, U.S.	Sur.	Suriname
Austl.	Australia	Eng., U.K.	England, U.K.	Liech.	Liechtenstein	N.Z.	New Zealand	*sw.*	swamp, marsh
Az., U.S.	Arizona, U.S.	Eq. Gui.	Equatorial Guinea	Lith.	Lithuania	Oc.	Oceania	Swaz.	Swaziland
Azer.	Azerbaijan	*est.*	estuary	Lux.	Luxembourg	Oh., U.S.	Ohio, U.S.	Swe.	Sweden
b.	bay, gulf, inlet, lagoon	Est.	Estonia	Ma., U.S.	Massachusetts, U.S.	Ok., U.S.	Oklahoma, U.S.	Switz.	Switzerland
Bah.	Bahamas	Eth.	Ethiopia	Mac.	Macedonia	Ont., Can.	Ontario, Can.	Tai.	Taiwan
Bahr.	Bahrain	Eur.	Europe	Madag.	Madagascar	Or., U.S.	Oregon, U.S.	Taj.	Tajikistan
Barb.	Barbados	Faer. Is.	Faeroe Islands	Malay.	Malaysia	Pa., U.S.	Pennsylvania, U.S.	Tan.	Tanzania
B.A.T.	British Antarctic	Falk. Is.	Falkland Islands	Mald.	Maldives	Pak.	Pakistan	T./C. Is.	Turks and Caicos
	Territory	Fin.	Finland	Man., Can.	Manitoba, Can.	Pan.	Panama		Islands
B.C., Can.	British Columbia, Can.	Fl., U.S.	Florida, U.S.	Marsh. Is.	Marshall Islands	Pap. N. Gui.	Papua New Guinea	*ter.*	territory
Bdi.	Burundi	*for.*	forest, moor	Mart.	Martinique	Para.	Paraguay	Thai.	Thailand
Bel.	Belgium	Fr.	France	Maur.	Mauritania	P.E.I., Can.	Prince Edward Island,	Tn., U.S.	Tennessee, U.S.
Bela.	Belarus	Fr. Gu.	French Guiana	May.	Mayotte		Can.	Tok.	Tokelau
Ber.	Bermuda	Fr. Poly.	French Polynesia	Md., U.S.	Maryland, U.S.	*pen.*	peninsula	Trin.	Trinidad and Tobago
Bhu.	Bhutan	F.S.A.T.	French Southern and	Me., U.S.	Maine, U.S.	Phil.	Philippines	Tun.	Tunisia
B.I.O.T.	British Indian Ocean		Antarctic Territory	Mex.	Mexico	Pit.	Pitcairn	Tur.	Turkey
	Territory	Ga., U.S.	Georgia, U.S.	Mi., U.S.	Michigan, U.S.	*pl.*	plain, flat	Turk.	Turkmenistan
Bngl.	Bangladesh	Gam.	Gambia	Micron.	Federated States of	*plat.*	plateau, highland	Tx., U.S.	Texas, U.S.
Bol.	Bolivia	Geor.	Georgia		Micronesia	Pol.	Poland	U.A.E.	United Arab Emirates
Boph.	Bophuthatswana	Ger.	Germany	Mid. Is.	Midway Islands	Port.	Portugal	Ug.	Uganda
Bos.	Bosnia and	Gib.	Gibraltar	*mil.*	military installation	P.R.	Puerto Rico	U.K.	United Kingdom
	Hercegovina	Grc.	Greece	Mn., U.S.	Minnesota, U.S.	*prov.*	province, region	Ukr.	Ukraine
Bots.	Botswana	Gren.	Grenada	Mo., U.S.	Missouri, U.S.	Que., Can.	Quebec, Can.	Ur.	Uruguay
Braz.	Brazil	Grnld.	Greenland	Mol.	Moldova	*reg.*	physical region	U.S.	United States
Bru.	Brunei	Guad.	Guadeloupe	Mon.	Monaco	*res.*	reservoir	Ut., U.S.	Utah, U.S.
Br. Vir. Is.	British Virgin Islands	Guat.	Guatemala	Mong.	Mongolia	*rf.*	reef, shoal	Uzb.	Uzbekistan
Bul.	Bulgaria	Gui.	Guinea	Monts.	Montserrat	Reu.	Reunion	Va., U.S.	Virginia, U.S.
Burkina	Burkina Faso	Gui.-B.	Guinea-Bissau	Mor.	Morocco	R.I., U.S.	Rhode Island, U.S.	*val.*	valley, watercourse
c.	cape, point	Guy.	Guyana	Moz.	Mozambique	Rom.	Romania	Vat.	Vatican City
Ca., U.S.	California, U.S.	Hi., U.S.	Hawaii, U.S.	Mrts.	Mauritius	Rw.	Rwanda	Ven.	Venezuela
Cam.	Cameroon	*hist.*	historic site, ruins	Ms., U.S.	Mississippi, U.S.	S.A.	South America	Viet.	Vietnam
Camb.	Cambodia	*hist. reg.*	historic region	Mt., U.S.	Montana, U.S.	S. Afr.	South Africa	V.I.U.S.	Virgin Islands (U.S.)
Can.	Canada	H.K.	Hong Kong	*mth.*	river mouth or channel	Sask., Can.	Saskatchewan, Can.	*vol.*	volcano
Cay. Is.	Cayman Islands	Hond.	Honduras	*mtn.*	mountain	Sau. Ar.	Saudi Arabia	Vt., U.S.	Vermont, U.S.
Cen. Afr.	Central African	Hung.	Hungary	*mts.*	mountains	S.C., U.S.	South Carolina, U.S.	Wa., U.S.	Washington, U.S.
Rep.	Republic	*i.*	island	Mwi.	Malawi	*sci.*	scientific station	Wal./F.	Wallis and Futuna
Christ. I.	Christmas Island	Ia., U.S.	Iowa, U.S.	N.A.	North America	Scot., U.K.	Scotland, U.K.	Wi., U.S.	Wisconsin, U.S.
clf.	cliff, escarpment	I.C.	Ivory Coast	N.B., Can.	New Brunswick, Can.	S.D., U.S.	South Dakota, U.S.	W. Sah.	Western Sahara
co.	county, parish	Ice.	Iceland	N.C., U.S.	North Carolina, U.S.	Sen.	Senegal	W. Sam.	Western Samoa
Co., U.S.	Colorado, U.S.	*ice*	ice feature, glacier	N. Cal.	New Caledonia	Sey.	Seychelles	*wtfl.*	waterfall
Col.	Colombia	Id., U.S.	Idaho, U.S.	N. Cyp.	North Cyprus	Sing.	Singapore	W.V., U.S.	West Virginia, U.S.
Com.	Comoros	Il., U.S.	Illinois, U.S.	N.D., U.S.	North Dakota, U.S.	S. Kor.	South Korea	Wy., U.S.	Wyoming, U.S.
cont.	continent	In., U.S.	Indiana, U.S.	Ne., U.S.	Nebraska, U.S.	S.L.	Sierra Leone	Yugo.	Yugoslavia
C.R.	Costa Rica	Indon.	Indonesia	Neth.	Netherlands	Slo.	Slovenia	Yukon, Can.	Yukon Territory, Can.
crat.	crater	I. of Man	Isle of Man	Neth. Ant.	Netherlands Antilles	S. Mar.	San Marino	Zam.	Zambia
Cro.	Croatia	Ire.	Ireland	Newf., Can.	Newfoundland, Can.	Sol. Is.	Solomon Islands	Zimb.	Zimbabwe
Ct., U.S.	Connecticut, U.S.	*is.*	islands						

Index

A

Name	Map Ref	Page
Aachen, Ger.	E6	8
Aalen, Ger.	G10	8
Aalst, Bel.	E4	8
Äänekoski, Fin.	E15	6
Aarau, Switz.	E15	10
Aarschot, Bel.	E4	8
Aba, China	E7	26
Aba, Nig.	G7	42
Ābādān, Iran	B4	46
Abaeté, Braz.	E6	57
Abajo Peak, mtn., Ut., U.S.	F6	121
Abakan, Russia	G12	24
Abancay, Peru	F4	54
Abashiri, Japan	o22	30a
Abasolo, Mex.	E7	62
Abaya, Lake, l., Eth.	G2	46
Abaza, Russia	G12	24
Abbadia San Salvatore, Italy	G6	14
Abbaye, Point, c., Mi., U.S.	B2	99
Abbeville, Fr.	B8	10
Abbeville, Al., U.S.	D4	78
Abbeville, Ga., U.S.	E3	87
Abbeville, La., U.S.	E3	95
Abbeville, S.C., U.S.	C3	117
Abbeville, co., S.C., U.S.	C2	117
Abbotsford, Wi., U.S.	D3	126
Abbottābād, Pak.	C5	38
Abbott Butte, mtn., Or., U.S.	E4	114
Abbott Run, stm., U.S.	B4	116
Abbott Run Valley, R.I., U.S.	B4	116
'Abd al-Kūrī, i., Yemen	F5	46
Abe, Lake, l., Afr.	F3	46
Abéché, Chad	F10	42
Abejar, Spain	D9	12
Abengourou, I.C.	G5	42
Abeokuta, Nig.	G6	42
Aberayron, Wales, U.K.	I8	7
Aberdeen, Scot., U.K.	D10	7
Aberdeen, Id., U.S.	G6	89
Aberdeen, Md., U.S.	A5	97
Aberdeen, Ms., U.S.	B5	101
Aberdeen, N.C., U.S.	B3	110
Aberdeen, Oh., U.S.	D2	112
Aberdeen, S.D., U.S.	B7	118
Aberdeen, Wa., U.S.	C2	124
Aberdeen Lake, l., N.W. Ter., Can.	D13	66
Aberdeen Proving Ground, mil., Md., U.S.	A5	97
Abernathy, Tx., U.S.	C2	120
Abert, Lake, l., Or., U.S.	E6	114
Abert Rim, clf., Or., U.S.	E6	114
Aberystwyth, Wales, U.K.	I8	7
Abhā, Sau. Ar.	E3	46
Abidjan, I.C.	G5	42
Abilene, Ks., U.S.	D6	93
Abilene, Tx., U.S.	C3	120
Abingdon, Il., U.S.	C3	90
Abingdon, Md., U.S.	B5	97
Abingdon, Va., U.S.	f10	123
Abington, Ma., U.S.	B6	98
Abington [Township], Pa., U.S.	o21	115
Abisko, Swe.	B12	6
Abita Springs, La., U.S.	D5	95
Abitibi, stm., Ont., Can.	o19	73
Abitibi, Lake, l., Can.	G17	66
Abohar, India	E6	38
Abomey, Benin	G6	42
Aborigen, Pik, mtn., Russia	E23	24
Abraham Lake, res., Alta., Can.	C2	68
Abraham Lincoln Birthplace National Historic Site, hist., Ky., U.S.	C4	94
Abrantes, Port.	F3	12
Absaroka Range, mts., U.S.	F7	127
Absarokee, Mt., U.S.	E7	103
Absecon, N.J., U.S.	E4	107
Absecon Inlet, b., N.J., U.S.	E4	107
Abū 'Alī, i., Sau. Ar.	C4	46
Abu Dhabi see Abū Ẓaby, U.A.E.	D5	46
Abū Hamad, Sudan	E12	42
Abū Kamāl, Syria	B7	40
Abukuma-sanchi, mts., Japan	E13	30
Abū Madd, Ra's, c., Sau. Ar.	D2	46
Abunã, Braz.	E5	54
Abū Shajarah, Ra's, c., Sudan	D13	42
Abū Ẓaby, U.A.E.	D5	46
Academia, Oh., U.S.	B3	112
Acadia, co., La., U.S.	D3	95
Acadia National Park, Me., U.S.	D4	96
Acajutla, El Sal.	H3	64
Acámbaro, Mex.	G9	62
Acaponeta, Mex.	F7	62
Acapulco [de Juárez], Mex.	I10	62
Acarai Mountains, mts., S.A.	C7	54
Acaraú, Braz.	D10	54
Acarigua, Ven.	C8	58
Acatlán [de Osorio], Mex.	H10	62
Acayucan, Mex.	I12	62
Accomack, co., Va., U.S.	C7	123
Accoville, W.V., U.S.	D3	125
Accra, Ghana	G5	42
Acerra, Italy	I9	14
Achaguas, Ven.	D8	58
Achalpur, India	B4	37
Acheng, China	B12	26
Achí, Col.	C5	58
Achill Island, i., Ire.	H2	7
Achtubinsk, Russia	H7	22
Ačinsk, Russia	F12	24
Acireale, Italy	L10	14
Ackerman, Ms., U.S.	B4	101
Ackley, Ia., U.S.	B4	92
Acklins Island, i., Bah.	C10	64
Acoma Indian Reservation, N.M., U.S.	C2	108
Aconcagua, Cerro, mtn., Arg.	C2	56
Açores (Azores), is., Port.	D11	2
Acquapendente, Italy	G6	14
Acqui Terme, Italy	E3	14
Acre, stm., S.A.	E5	54
Acri, Italy	J11	14
Acton, Ma., U.S.	B5	98
Acton Vale, Que., Can.	D5	74
Acushnet, Ma., U.S.	C6	98
Acworth, Ga., U.S.	B2	87
Ada, Mn., U.S.	C2	100
Ada, Oh., U.S.	B2	112
Ada, Ok., U.S.	C5	113
Ada, co., Id., U.S.	F2	89
Ada, Mount, mtn., Ak., U.S.	m22	79
Adair, Ia., U.S.	C3	92
Adair, Ok., U.S.	A6	113
Adair, co., Ia., U.S.	C3	92
Adair, co., Ky., U.S.	C4	94
Adair, co., Mo., U.S.	A5	102
Adair, co., Ok., U.S.	B7	113
Adair, Cape, c., N.W. Ter., Can.	B18	66
Adairsville, Ga., U.S.	B2	87
Adairville, Ky., U.S.	D3	94
Adak Island, i., Ak., U.S.	E4	79
Adak Naval Station, mil., Ak., U.S.	E4	79
Ādam, Oman	D6	46
Adamantina, Braz.	F3	57
Adamawa, mts., Afr.	G8	42
Adam Island, i., Md., U.S.	D5	97
Adams, Ma., U.S.	A1	98
Adams, Mn., U.S.	G6	100
Adams, N.Y., U.S.	B4	109
Adams, Wi., U.S.	E4	126
Adams, co., Co., U.S.	B6	83
Adams, co., Id., U.S.	E2	89
Adams, co., Il., U.S.	D2	90
Adams, co., In., U.S.	C8	91
Adams, co., Ia., U.S.	C3	92
Adams, co., Ms., U.S.	D2	101
Adams, co., Ne., U.S.	D7	104
Adams, co., N.D., U.S.	C3	111
Adams, co., Oh., U.S.	D2	112
Adams, co., Pa., U.S.	G7	115
Adams, co., Wa., U.S.	B7	124
Adams, co., Wi., U.S.	D4	126
Adams, Mount, mtn., N.H., U.S.	B4	106
Adams, Mount, mtn., Wa., U.S.	C4	124
Adams Bridge, rf., Asia	H5	37
Adams Point, c., Mi., U.S.	C7	99
Adamstown, Pa., U.S.	F9	115
Adamsville, Al., U.S.	f7	78
Adamsville, R.I., U.S.	E6	116
Adamsville, Tn., U.S.	B3	119
Adamsville Brook, stm., R.I., U.S.	E6	116
'Adan (Aden), Yemen	F4	46
Adana, Tur.	H15	4
Adapazan, Tur.	G14	4
Adarama, Sudan	E12	42
Ad-Dabbah, Sudan	E12	42
Ad-Dammām, Sau. Ar.	C5	46
Ad-Dawādimī, Sau. Ar.	D3	46
Ad-Dawhah (Doha), Qatar	D4	46
Addis, La., U.S.	D4	95
Addis Ababa see Adis Abeba, Eth.	G2	46
Addison, Ct., U.S.	C5	84
Addison, Il., U.S.	k8	90
Addison, N.Y., U.S.	C3	109
Addison, co., Vt., U.S.	C2	122
Ad-Dīwānīyah, Iraq	B3	46
Ad-Duwaym, Sudan	F12	42
Addyston, Oh., U.S.	o12	112
Adel, Ga., U.S.	E3	87
Adel, Ia., U.S.	C3	92
Adelaide, Austl.	F7	50
Adelaide Peninsula, pen., N.W. Ter., Can.	C13	66
Adelanto, Ca., U.S.	E5	82
Aden, Gulf of, b.	F4	46
Aden see 'Adan, Yemen	F4	46
Adieu, Cape, c., Austl.	F6	50
Adige, stm., Italy	D7	14
Adigrat, Eth.	F2	46
Ādilābād, India	C5	37
Adimi, Russia	H21	24
Adirondack Mountains, mts., N.Y., U.S.	A6	109
Adis Abeba, Eth.	G2	46
Admiralty Bay, b., Ak., U.S.	A9	79
Admiralty Inlet, b., N.W. Ter., Can.	B15	66
Admiralty Island, i., Ak., U.S.	m22	79
Admiralty Islands, is., Pap. N. Gui.	k16	50a
Adobe Creek, N.M., U.S.	*B3	108
Adobe Creek Reservoir, res., Co., U.S.	C7	83
Adolfo López Mateos, Presa, res., Mex.	E6	62
Ādoni, India	E4	37
Adour, stm., Fr.	I7	10
Adra, Spain	I8	12
Adrano, Italy	L9	14
Adrar, Alg.	C5	42
Adria, Italy	D7	14
Adrian, Ga., U.S.	D4	87
Adrian, Mi., U.S.	G6	99
Adrian, Mn., U.S.	G3	100
Adrian, Mo., U.S.	C3	102
Adriatic Sea, Eur.	G11	4
Advance, Mo., U.S.	D8	102
Adyča, stm., Russia	D21	24
Aegean Sea, Eur.	J8	16
Afars and Issas see Djibouti, ctry., Afr.	F3	46
Afghanistan, ctry., Asia	C1	36
Afikpo, Nig.	G7	42
Afjord, Nor.	E8	6
Afmadu, Som.	A8	44
Afognak Island, i., Ak., U.S.	D9	79
Africa	D6	41
Afton, Ia., U.S.	C3	92
Afton, Mn., U.S.	F6	100
Afton, Ok., U.S.	A7	113
Afton, Wy., U.S.	D2	127
'Afula, Isr.	C4	40
Afyon, Tur.	H14	4
Agadez, Niger	E7	42
Agadir, Mor.	B4	42
Agalega Islands, is., Mrts.	D11	44
Agalta, Cordillera de, mts., Hond.	G5	64
Agapa, Russia	C11	24
Agartala, India	I14	38
Agate Fossil Beds National Monument, Ne., U.S.	B2	104
Agattu Island, i., Ak., U.S.	E2	79
Agawam, Ma., U.S.	B2	98
Agen, Fr.	H7	10
Agency, Ia., U.S.	D5	92
Agency, Mo., U.S.	B3	102
Āghā Jārī, Iran	B4	46
Agira, Italy	L9	14
Agnone, Italy	H9	14
Āgra, India	G8	38
Āgreda, Spain	D10	12
Agrigento, Italy	L8	14
Agrínion, Grc.	K5	16
Agropoli, Italy	I9	14
Agua Caliente, Mex.	F7	62
Agua Caliente Grande, Mex.	D5	62
Aguachica, Col.	C6	58
Agua Clara, Braz.	F2	57
Agua Fria, N.M., U.S.	B3	108
Agua Fria, stm., Az., U.S.	D3	80
Agua Prieta, Mex.	B5	62
Aguascalientes, Mex.	G8	62
Águas Formosas, Braz.	D8	57
Águeda, Port.	E3	12
Águeda, Spain	E6	12
Aguilar, Spain	H7	12
Aguilar, Co., U.S.	D6	83
Águilas, Spain	H10	12
Agulhas, Cape, c., S. Afr.	H3	44
Agustín Codazzi, Col.	B6	58
Agustín Codazzi, Col.	I11	64
Ahaggar, mts., Alg.	D7	42
Ahipara Bay, b., N.Z.	A4	52
Ahklun Mountains, mts., Ak., U.S.	D7	79
Ahlen, Ger.	D7	8
Ahmadābād, India	I5	38
Ahmadnagar, India	C3	37
Ahmadpur East, Pak.	F4	38
Ahmar Mountains, mts., Eth.	G3	46
Ahoskie, N.C., U.S.	A6	110
Ahtanum Creek, stm., Wa., U.S.	C5	124
Ahu, China	A7	28
Ahuacatlán, Mex.	G7	62
Ahvāz, Iran	B4	46
Ahvenanmaa (Åland), is., Fin.	F12	6
Aialik, Cape, c., Ak., U.S.	D10	79
Aichach, Ger.	G11	8
Aiea, Hi., U.S.	B4	88
Aihun, China	A12	26
Aijal, India	I15	38
Aiken, S.C., U.S.	D4	117
Aiken, co., S.C., U.S.	D4	117
Ailsa Craig, Ont., Can.	D3	73
Aim, Russia	F20	24
Aimorés, Braz.	E8	57
Ainslie Lake, l., N.S., Can.	C8	71
Ainsworth, Ne., U.S.	B6	104
Aipe, Col.	F5	58
Air, mts., Niger	E7	42
Airdrie, Alta., Can.	D3	68
Aire-sur-l'Adour, Fr.	I6	10
Air Force Island, i., N.W. Ter., Can.	C18	66
Air Park West, Ne., U.S.	*D9	104
Aisne, stm., Fr.	C10	10
Aïssa, Djebel, mtn., Alg.	B5	42
Aitape, Pap. N. Gui.	k15	50a
Aitkin, Mn., U.S.	D5	100
Aitkin, co., Mn., U.S.	D5	100
Aix, Mount, mtn., Wa., U.S.	C4	124
Aix-en-Provence, Fr.	I12	10
Aix-la-Chapelle see Aachen, Ger.	E6	8
Aix-les-Bains, Fr.	G12	10
Aizu-wakamatsu, Japan	E12	30
Ajaguz, Kaz.	H10	24
Ajan, Russia	F21	24
Ajan, stm., Russia	C13	24
Ajax, Ont., Can.	D6	73
Ajdābiyah, Libya	B10	42
Ajjer, Tassili n', plat., Alg.	C7	42
'Ajlūn, Jord.	C4	40
Ajmer, India	G6	38
Ajo, Az., U.S.	E3	80
Ajo, Cabo de, c., Spain	B8	12
Ajon, Ostrov, i., Russia	D27	24
Ajtos, Bul.	G11	16
Akademii, Zaliv, b., Russia	G21	24
Akaltara, India	A7	37
Akan, Japan	p22	30a
'Akasha East, Sudan	D12	42
Akashi, Japan	H7	30
Akçakale, Tur.	A6	40
Ak-Chin Indian Reservation, Az., U.S.	E3	80
Akesu, China	C3	26
Akharnaí, Grc.	K7	16
Akhisar, Tur.	H13	4
Akiachak, Ak., U.S.	C7	79
Akimiski Island, i., N.W. Ter., Can.	F16	66
Akita, Japan	C13	30
Akjoujt, Maur.	E3	42
'Akko (Acre), Isr.	C4	40
Aklavik, N.W. Ter., Can.	C6	66
Akō, Japan	H7	30
Akobo, stm., Afr.	G12	42
Akola, India	B4	37
Akordat, Eth.	E2	46
Akot, India	B4	37
Akpatok Island, i., N.W. Ter., Can.	D19	66
Akron, Co., U.S.	A7	83
Akron, Ia., U.S.	B1	92
Akron, In., U.S.	B5	91
Akron, N.Y., U.S.	B2	109
Akron, Oh., U.S.	A4	112
Akron, Pa., U.S.	F9	115
Aksaray, Tur.	H14	4
Akşehir, Tur.	H14	4
Aksum, Eth.	F2	46
Akt'ubinsk, Kaz.	G9	22
Akureyri, Ice.	B4	6a
Āl, Nor.	F7	6
Alabama, state, U.S.	C3	78
Alabama, stm., Al., U.S.	D2	78
Alabaster, Al., U.S.	B3	78
Alachua, Fl., U.S.	C4	86
Alachua, co., Fl., U.S.	C4	86
Alagoinhas, Braz.	B9	57
Alagón, Spain	D10	12
Alagón, stm., Spain	E5	12
Alajuela, C.R.	I5	64
Alakanuk, Ak., U.S.	C7	79
Alalakeiki Channel, strt., Hi., U.S.	C5	88
Al-'Alamayn, Egypt	B11	42
Alamance, co., N.C., U.S.	B3	110
Al-'Amārah, Iraq	B4	46
Alameda, Ca., U.S.	h8	82
Alameda, N.M., U.S.	B3	108
Alameda, co., Ca., U.S.	D3	82
Alameda Naval Air Station, mil., Ca., U.S.	h8	82
Alamito Creek, stm., Tx., U.S.	p12	120
Alamo, Ga., U.S.	D4	87
Alamo, Nv., U.S.	F6	105
Alamo, Tn., U.S.	B2	119
Alamo, Tx., U.S.	F3	120
Alamogordo, N.M., U.S.	E4	108
Alamo Heights, Tx., U.S.	E3	120
Alamo Hueco Mountains, mts., N.M., U.S.	F1	108
Alamo Indian Reservation, N.M., U.S.	C2	108
Alamo Lake, res., Az., U.S.	C2	80
Alamosa, Co., U.S.	D5	83
Alamosa, co., Co., U.S.	D4	83
Alamosa, stm., Co., U.S.	D4	83
Alamosa Creek, stm., N.M., U.S.	D2	108
Alamosa East, Co., U.S.	D5	83
Alanäs, Swe.	D10	6
Alanya, Tur.	A3	40
Alapaha, Ga., U.S.	E3	87
Alapaha, stm., U.S.	E3	87
Alaşehir, Tur.	K12	16
Alashanyouqi, China	C7	26
Alaska, state, U.S.	C9	79
Alaska, Gulf of, b., Ak., U.S.	D10	79
Alaska Peninsula, pen., Ak., U.S.	D8	79
Alaska Range, mts., Ak., U.S.	C9	79
Alassio, Italy	E3	14
Alatna, stm., Ak., U.S.	B9	79
Alava, Cape, c., Wa., U.S.	A1	124
Alazeja, stm., Russia	C24	24
Alba, Italy	E3	14
Albacete, Spain	G10	12
Alba de Tormes, Spain	E6	12
Albaida, Spain	G11	12
Albanel, Lac, l., Que., Can.	F18	66
Albania, ctry., Eur.	G11	4
Albano Laziale, Italy	H7	14
Albany, Austl.	G3	50
Albany, Ca., U.S.	h8	82
Albany, Ga., U.S.	E2	87
Albany, Il., U.S.	B3	90
Albany, In., U.S.	D7	91
Albany, Ky., U.S.	D4	94
Albany, La., U.S.	g10	95
Albany, Mn., U.S.	E4	100
Albany, Mo., U.S.	A3	102
Albany, N.Y., U.S.	C7	109
Albany, Or., U.S.	C3	114
Albany, Tx., U.S.	C3	120
Albany, Wi., U.S.	F4	126
Albany, co., N.Y., U.S.	C6	109
Albany, co., Wy., U.S.	E7	127
Albany, stm., Ont., Can.	o18	73
Albatross Bay, b., Austl.	B8	50
Al-Batrūn, Leb.	B4	40
Al-Bawītī, Egypt	C11	42
Albemarle, N.C., U.S.	B2	110
Albemarle, co., Va., U.S.	C4	123
Albemarle Lake, l., Ms., U.S.	C2	101
Albemarle Sound, strt., N.C., U.S.	A6	110
Albenga, Italy	E3	14
Albergaria-a-Velha, Port.	E3	12
Albert, Fr.	B9	10
Albert, Lake, l., Afr.	A6	44
Albert City, Ia., U.S.	B3	92
Albert Lea, Mn., U.S.	G5	100
Albert Nile, stm., Ug.	H12	42
Alberta, prov., Can.	C4	68
Alberta, Mount, mtn., Alta., Can.	C2	68
Alberton, P.E.I., Can.	C5	71
Albertson, N.Y., U.S.	k13	109
Albertville, Fr.	G13	10
Albertville, Al., U.S.	A3	78
Albertville see Kalemie, Zaire	C5	44
Albi, Fr.	I9	10
Albia, Ia., U.S.	C5	92
Albino, Italy	D4	14
Albion, Il., U.S.	E5	90
Albion, In., U.S.	B7	91
Albion, Mi., U.S.	F6	99
Albion, Ne., U.S.	C7	104
Albion, N.Y., U.S.	B2	109
Albion, Pa., U.S.	C1	115
Albion, R.I., U.S.	B4	116
Albion, Wa., U.S.	C8	124
Alborán, Isla de, i., Spain	J8	12
Ålborg, Den.	H7	6
Alborz, Reshteh-ye Kūhhā-ye, mts., Iran	J8	22
Albufeira, Port.	H3	12
Albuñol, Spain	I8	12
Albuquerque, N.M., U.S.	B3	108
Alburquerque, Spain	F4	12
Alburtis, Pa., U.S.	F10	115
Albury, Austl.	G9	50
Alcácer do Sal, Port.	G3	12
Alcalá de Guadaira, Spain	H6	12
Alcalá de Henares, Spain	E8	12
Alcalá la Real, Spain	H8	12
Alcamo, Italy	L7	14
Alcanar, Spain	E12	12
Alcañices, Spain	D5	12
Alcântara, Braz.	D10	54
Alcântara, Spain	F5	12
Alcantarilla, Spain	H10	12
Alcázar de San Juan, Spain	F8	12
Alcira, Spain	F11	12
Alcoa, Tn., U.S.	D10	119
Alcobaça, Braz.	D9	57
Alcobaça, Port.	F3	12
Alcolu, S.C., U.S.	D7	117
Alcona, co., Mi., U.S.	D7	99
Alconchel, Spain	G4	12
Alcorn, co., Ms., U.S.	A5	101
Alcoy, Spain	G11	12
Aldabra Islands, atoll, Sey.	C9	44
Aldan, Russia	F19	24
Aldan, stm., Russia	E20	24
Aldanskoje Nagorje, plat., Russia	F19	24
Alden, Ia., U.S.	B4	92
Alden, Mn., U.S.	G5	100
Alden, N.Y., U.S.	C2	109
Alder Brook, stm., Vt., U.S.	B4	122
Aldershot, Eng., U.K.	J12	7
Aldrich, Al., U.S.	B3	78
Aledo, Il., U.S.	B3	90
Aleg, Maur.	E3	42
Alegres Mountain, mtn., N.M., U.S.	C2	108
Alegrete, Braz.	B5	56
Alejsk, Russia	G10	24
Aleksandrov, Russia	E21	18
Aleksandrovsk-Sachalinskij, Russia	G22	24
Aleksejevsk, Russia	F15	24
Aleksin, Russia	G20	18
Além Paraíba, Braz.	F7	57
Alençon, Fr.	D7	10
Alenuihaha Channel, strt., Hi., U.S.	C5	88
Aleppo see Halab, Syria	A5	40
Alert Bay, B.C., Can.	D4	69
Alès, Fr.	H11	10
Alessandria, Italy	E3	14
Alessano, Italy	J13	14
Ålesund, Nor.	E6	6
Aleutian Islands, is., Ak., U.S.	E3	79
Aleutian Range, mts., Ak., U.S.	D9	79
Aleutka, Russia	H24	24
Alevina, Mys, c., Russia	F24	24
Alex, Ok., U.S.	C4	113
Alexander, co., Il., U.S.	F4	90
Alexander, co., N.C., U.S.	B1	110
Alexander, Lake, l., Mn., U.S.	D4	100
Alexander Archipelago, is., Ak., U.S.	D12	79
Alexander Bay, S. Afr.	G3	44
Alexander City, Al., U.S.	C4	78
Alexander Island, i., Ant.	B6	47
Alexandra, N.Z.	F2	52
Alexandretta, Gulf of see iskenderun Körfezi, b., Tur.	A4	40
Alexandria, Ont., Can.	B10	73
Alexandria, In., U.S.	D6	91
Alexandria, Ky., U.S.	B5	94
Alexandria, La., U.S.	C3	95
Alexandria, Mn., U.S.	E3	100
Alexandria, Tn., U.S.	A5	119
Alexandria, Va., U.S.	B5	123
Alexandria see Al-Iskandarīyah, Egypt	B11	42
Alexandroúpolis, Grc.	I9	16
Alexis, Il., U.S.	B3	90
Alfalfa, co., Ok., U.S.	A3	113
Alfaro, Ec.	I3	58
Alfaro, Spain	C10	12
Alfarràs, Spain	D12	12
Al-Fāshir, Sudan	F11	42
Al-Fayyūm, Egypt	C12	42
Alfeld, Ger.	D9	8
Alfenas, Braz.	F6	57
Alfred, Ont., Can.	B10	73
Alfred, N.Y., U.S.	C3	109
Algarve, hist. reg., Port.	H3	12
Algeciras, Spain	I6	12
Algemesí, Spain	F11	12
Alger, Alg.	A6	42
Alger, Oh., U.S.	B2	112
Alger, co., Mi., U.S.	B4	99
Algeria, ctry., Afr.	C5	42
Al-Ghaydah, Yemen	E5	46
Alghero, Italy	I3	14
Al-Ghurdaqah, Egypt	C12	42
Algiers see Alger, Alg.	A6	42
Algoma, Wi., U.S.	D6	126
Algona, Ia., U.S.	A3	92
Algona, Wa., U.S.	B3	124
Algonac, Mi., U.S.	F8	99
Algonquin, Il., U.S.	A5	90
Algonquin Provincial Park, Ont., Can.	B6	73
Algood, Tn., U.S.	C8	119
Algorta, Ur.	C5	56
Al-Hadīthah, Iraq	B3	46
Al-Haffah, Syria	B5	40
Al-Hamād, pl., Sau. Ar.	B2	46
Alhama de Granada, Spain	H8	12
Al-Hārīq, Sau. Ar.	D4	46
Alhambra, Ca., U.S.	m12	82
Al-Harūj al-Aswad, hills, Libya	C9	42
Al-Hasakah, Syria	A7	40
Alhaurín el Grande, Spain	I7	12
Al-Hawrah, Yemen	F4	46
Al-Hijāz (Hejaz), reg., Sau. Ar.	C2	46
Al-Hillah, Iraq	B3	46
Al-Hirmil, Leb.	B5	40
Al-Hudaydah, Yemen	F3	46
Al-Hufūf, Sau. Ar.	C4	46
Aliaga, Spain	E11	12
Alicante, Spain	G11	12
Alice, Tx., U.S.	F3	120
Alice Lake, l., Mn., U.S.	C7	100
Alice Springs, Austl.	D6	50
Aliceville, Al., U.S.	B1	78
Alīgarh, India	G8	38
Alijos, Escollos, Mex.	E2	62
Alingsås, Swe.	H9	6
Alīpur Duār, India	G13	38
Aliquippa, Pa., U.S.	E1	115
Al-Iskandarīyah (Alexandria), Egypt	B11	42
Al-Ismā'īlīyah, Egypt	B12	42
Aliwal North, S. Afr.	H5	44
Alix, Alta., Can.	C4	68
Al-Jabal al-Akhḍar, mts., Oman	D6	46
Al-Jafr, Jord.	D5	40
Al-Jaghbūb, Libya	C10	42
Al-Jawf, Libya	D10	42
Al-Jawf, Sau. Ar.	C2	46
Al-Jazīrah, reg., Sudan	F12	42

Name	Map Ref	Page
Aljezur, Port.	H3	12
Al-Jīzah, Egypt	B12	42
Al-Junaynah, Sudan	F10	42
Aljustrel, Port.	H3	12
Alkali Lake, l., Nv., U.S.	B2	105
Alkali Lake, l., Or., U.S.	E6	114
Alkaline Lake, l., N.D., U.S.	C6	111
Al-Karak, Jord.	D4	40
Al-Kawm, Syria	B6	40
Al-Khābūr, stm., Syria	A7	40
Al-Khalīl, Isr. Occ.	D4	40
Al-Khandaq, Sudan	E12	42
Al-Khārijah, Egypt	C12	42
Al-Khartūm (Khartoum), Sudan	E12	42
Al-Khasab, Oman	C6	46
Al-Khubar, Sau. Ar.	C5	46
Al-Khums, Libya	B8	42
Alkmaar, Neth.	C4	8
Al-Kuwayt, Kuw.	C4	46
Allach-Jun', Russia	E21	24
Al-Lādhiqīyah (Latakia), Syria	B4	40
Allagash, stm., Me., U.S.	B3	96
Allagash Lake, l., Me., U.S.	B3	96
Allahābād, India	H9	38
Allamakee, co., Ia., U.S.	A6	92
Allan, Sask., Can.	F2	75
Allanche, Fr.	G9	10
Allanmyo, Burma	E3	34
Allardt, Tn., U.S.	C9	119
Allatoona Lake, res., Ga., U.S.	B2	87
Allegan, Mi., U.S.	F5	99
Allegan, co., Mi., U.S.	F5	99
Allegany, N.Y., U.S.	C2	109
Allegany, co., Md., U.S.	k13	97
Allegany, co., N.Y., U.S.	C2	109
Allegany Indian Reservation, N.Y., U.S.	C2	109
Allegheny, co., N.C., U.S.	A1	110
Allegheny, co., Va., U.S.	C2	123
Allegheny, co., Pa., U.S.	E2	115
Allegheny, stm., U.S.	E2	115
Allegheny Reservoir, res., U.S.	B4	115
Allemands, Lac Des, l., La., U.S.	E5	95
Allen, Ok., U.S.	C5	113
Allen, co., In., U.S.	B7	91
Allen, co., Ks., U.S.	E8	93
Allen, co., Ky., U.S.	D3	94
Allen, co., La., U.S.	D3	95
Allen, co., Oh., U.S.	B1	112
Allen, Mount, mtn., Ak., U.S.	C11	79
Allendale, N.J., U.S.	A4	107
Allendale, S.C., U.S.	E5	117
Allendale, co., S.C., U.S.	F5	117
Allen Park, Mi., U.S.	p15	99
Allenton, R.I., U.S.	E4	116
Allenton, Wi., U.S.	E5	126
Allentown, Pa., U.S.	E11	115
Allentsteig, Aus.	G15	8
Alleppey, India	H4	37
Aller, stm., Ger.	C9	8
Allerton, Point, c., Ma., U.S.	B6	98
Allgäuer Alpen, mts., Eur.	H10	8
Alliance, Ne., U.S.	B3	104
Alliance, Oh., U.S.	B4	112
Alligator, stm., N.C., U.S.	B6	110
Alligator Lake, l., Me., U.S.	D4	96
Allison, Ia., U.S.	B5	92
Allison, co., Ia., U.S.	G2	115
Allison Park, Pa., U.S.	h14	115
Alliston, Ont., Can.	C5	73
Al-Līth, Sau. Ar.	D3	46
Allouez, Wi., U.S.	h9	126
Alloway Creek, stm., N.J., U.S.	D2	107
Allumette Lake, l., Can.	B7	73
Allyn, Wa., U.S.	A3	124
Alma, Que., Can.	A6	74
Alma, Ar., U.S.	B1	81
Alma, Ga., U.S.	E4	87
Alma, Ks., U.S.	C7	93
Alma, Mi., U.S.	E6	99
Alma, Ne., U.S.	D6	104
Alma, Wi., U.S.	D2	126
Alma-Ata, Kaz.	I9	24
Almada, Port.	G2	12
Al-Madīnah (Medina), Sau. Ar.	D2	46
Al-Mafraq, Jord.	C5	40
Almagro, Spain	G8	12
Al-Manāmah, Bahr.	C5	46
Almanor, Lake, l., Ca., U.S.	B3	82
Almansa, Spain	G10	12
Al-Mansūrah, Egypt	B12	42
Al-Marj, Libya	B10	42
Almas, Pico das, mtn., Braz.	F10	54
Al-Masīrah, i., Oman	D6	46
Almazán, Spain	D9	12
Almelo, Neth.	C6	8
Almenara, Braz.	D8	57
Almendralejo, Spain	G5	12
Almería, Spain	I9	12
Al'metjevsk, Russia	G8	22
Al-Minyā, Egypt	C12	42
Almirante, Pan.	J6	64
Al-Mismīyah, Syria	C5	40
Almodôvar, Port.	H3	12
Almodóvar del Campo, Spain	G7	12
Almont, Mi., U.S.	F7	99
Almonte, Ont., Can.	B8	73
Almonte, Spain	H5	12
Almora, India	F8	38
Al-Mubarraz, Sau. Ar.	C4	46
Al-Mubarraz, Sau. Ar.	D4	46
Al-Muglad, Sudan	F11	42
Al-Muharraq, Bahr.	C5	46
Al-Mukallā, Yemen	F4	46
Al-Mukhā, Yemen	F3	46
Al-Muwaylih, Sau. Ar.	C2	46
Alnwick, Eng., U.K.	F11	7
Aloândia, Braz.	D4	57
Aloha, Or., U.S.	h12	114
Alor, Pulau, i., Indon.	G7	32
Alora, Spain	I7	12
Alor Setar, Malay.	K6	34
Aloysius, Mount, mtn., Austl.	E5	50
Alpena, Mi., U.S.	C7	99
Alpena, co., Mi., U.S.	D7	99
Alpharetta, Ga., U.S.	B2	87
Alphonse Island, i., Sey.	C10	44
Alpiarça, Port.	F3	12
Alpine, Az., U.S.	D6	80
Alpine, Tx., U.S.	D1	120
Alpine, Ut., U.S.	C4	121
Alpine, co., Ca., U.S.	C4	82
Alps, mts., Eur.	F9	4
Al-Qadārif, Egypt	F13	42
Al-Qāhirah (Cairo), Egypt	B12	42
Al-Qāmishlī, Syria	A7	40
Al-Qaryah ash-Sharqīyah, Libya	B8	42
Al-Qaryatayn, Syria	B5	40
Al-Qasr, Egypt	C11	42
Al-Qatīf, Sau. Ar.	C4	46
Al-Qatrūn, Libya	D8	42
Al-Qaysūmah, Sau. Ar.	C4	46
Al-Qunaytirah, Syria	C4	40
Al-Qunfudhah, Sau. Ar.	E3	46
Al-Qusayr, Egypt	C12	42
Al-Qutayfah, Syria	C5	40
Alsace, hist. reg., Fr.	E14	10
Alsasua, Spain	C9	12
Alsfeld, Ger.	E9	8
Alta, Nor.	B14	6
Alta, Ia., U.S.	B2	92
Altadena, Ca., U.S.	m12	82
Altagracia, Ven.	B7	58
Altagracia de Orituco, Ven.	C9	58
Altaj, mts., Asia	B4	26
Altamaha, stm., Ga., U.S.	E5	87
Altamira, Braz.	D8	54
Altamont, Il., U.S.	D5	90
Altamont, Ks., U.S.	E8	93
Altamont, Or., U.S.	E5	114
Altamont, Tn., U.S.	D8	119
Altamonte Springs, Fl., U.S.	D5	86
Altamura, Italy	I11	14
Altar, Mex.	B4	62
Altar, Desierto de, des., Mex.	B3	62
Altata, Mex.	E6	62
Altavista, Va., U.S.	C3	123
Altdorf, Switz.	F15	10
Altenburg, Ger.	E12	8
Altheimer, Ar., U.S.	C4	81
Altiplano, plat., S.A.	G5	54
Alto, Ga., U.S.	B3	87
Alto, N.M., U.S.	D4	108
Alto Araguaia, Braz.	D2	57
Alton, Il., U.S.	E3	90
Alton, Ia., U.S.	B2	92
Alton, Mo., U.S.	E6	102
Alton, N.H., U.S.	D4	106
Altona, Man., Can.	E3	70
Alton Bay, N.H., U.S.	D4	106
Altoona, Al., U.S.	A3	78
Altoona, Fl., U.S.	D5	86
Altoona, Ia., U.S.	C4	92
Altoona, Pa., U.S.	E5	115
Altoona, Wi., U.S.	D2	126
Alto Parnaíba, Braz.	E9	54
Altötting, Ger.	G12	8
Altun Shan, mts., China	D4	26
Alturas, Ca., U.S.	B3	82
Altus, Ok., U.S.	C2	113
Altus Air Force Base, mil., Ok., U.S.	C2	113
Altus Reservoir, res., Ok., U.S.	C2	113
Al-'Ubaylah, Sau. Ar.	D5	46
Al-Ubayyid, Sudan	F12	42
'Alula, Som.	F5	46
Alum Bank, Pa., U.S.	F4	115
Alum Creek, stm., Oh., U.S.	k11	112
Alva, Fl., U.S.	F5	86
Alva, Ok., U.S.	A3	113
Alvarado, Mex.	H12	62
Alvarado, Tx., U.S.	C4	120
Álvaro Obregón, Presa, res., Mex.	D5	62
Älvdalen, Swe.	F10	6
Alvin, Tx., U.S.	E5	120
Alvinston, Ont., Can.	E3	73
Älvkarleby, Swe.	F11	6
Alvord Lake, l., Or., U.S.	E8	114
Älvsbyn, Swe.	D13	6
Al-Wajh, Sau. Ar.	C2	46
Alwar, India	G7	38
Alzamaj, Russia	F13	24
Ama, La., U.S.	k11	95
Amadeus, Lake, l., Austl.	D6	50
Amadjuak Lake, l., N.W. Ter., Can.	C18	66
Amador, co., Ca., U.S.	C3	82
Amagansett, N.Y., U.S.	n16	109
Amagasaki, Japan	H8	30
Amakusa-nada, Japan	J2	30
Amakusa-shotō, is., Japan	J3	30
Amāl, Swe.	G9	6
Amalapuram, India	D7	37
Amalfi, Italy	I9	14
Amalner, India	J6	38
Amambaí, stm., Braz.	G1	57
Amambaí, Serra de, mts., S.A.	H7	54
Amami-Ō-shima, i., Japan	w29	31b
Amami-shotō, is., Japan	x29	31b
Amana, l., U.S.	C6	92
Amantea, Italy	J11	14
Amares, Port.	D3	12
Amargosa, stm., U.S.	D5	82
Amargosa Desert, des., U.S.	G5	105
Amargosa Range, mts., U.S.	G5	105
Amarillo, Tx., U.S.	B2	120
Amatignak Island, i., Ak., U.S.	E4	79
Amazon (Solimões) (Amazonas), stm., S.A.	D7	54
Ambāla, India	E7	38
Ambarčik, Russia	D26	24
Ambāsamudram, India	H4	37
Ambato, Ec.	H3	58
Ambatolampy, Madag.	E9	44
Ambatondrazaka, Madag.	E9	44
Amberg, Ger.	F11	8
Ambérieu-en-Bugey, Fr.	G1	10
Ambert, Fr.	G10	10
Ambikāpur, India	I10	38
Ambilobe, Madag.	D9	44
Amble, Eng., U.K.	F11	7
Ambler, Pa., U.S.	F11	115
Amboise, Fr.	E7	10
Ambon, Indon.	F8	32
Ambositra, Madag.	F9	44
Ambovombe, Madag.	G9	44
Amboy, Il., U.S.	B4	90
Ambridge, Pa., U.S.	E1	115
Ambrières, Fr.	D6	10
Ambriz, Ang.	C2	44
Âmbūr, India	F5	37
Amchitka Island, i., Ak., U.S.	E3	79
Amchitka Pass, strt., Ak., U.S.	E4	79
Ameca, Mex.	G7	62
Amecameca [de Juárez], Mex.	H10	62
Amelia, La., U.S.	E4	95
Amelia, Oh., U.S.	C1	112
Amelia, co., Va., U.S.	C5	123
Amelia Court House, Va., U.S.	C5	123
Amelia Island, i., Fl., U.S.	k9	86
American, stm., Ca., U.S.	C3	82
American Falls, Id., U.S.	G6	89
American Falls Dam, Id., U.S.	G6	89
American Falls Reservoir, res., Id., U.S.	F5	89
American Fork, Ut., U.S.	C4	121
American Highland, plat., Ant.	B20	47
American Samoa, dep., Oc.	G1	2
Americus, Ga., U.S.	D2	87
Americus, Ks., U.S.	D7	93
Amersfoort, Neth.	C5	8
Amery, Wi., U.S.	C1	126
Ames, Ia., U.S.	B4	92
Amesbury, Ma., U.S.	A6	98
Amfilokhía, Grc.	K5	16
Ámfissa, Grc.	K6	16
Amga, Russia	E20	24
Amga, stm., Russia	E20	24
Amgun', stm., Russia	G21	24
Amherst, Ma., U.S.	B2	98
Amherst, N.H., U.S.	E3	106
Amherst, N.Y., U.S.	C2	109
Amherst, Oh., U.S.	A3	112
Amherst, Tx., U.S.	C1	120
Amherst, Va., U.S.	C3	123
Amherst, Wi., U.S.	D4	126
Amherst, co., Va., U.S.	C3	123
Amherstburg, Ont., Can.	E1	73
Amherstdale, W.V., U.S.	n12	125
Amiens, Fr.	C9	10
Amīndīvi Islands, is., India	G2	37
Amirante Islands, is., Sey.	C10	44
Amisk Lake, l., Sask., Can.	C4	75
Amistad National Recreation Area, Tx., U.S.	E2	120
Amistad Reservoir, res., N.A.	C9	62
Amite, La., U.S.	D5	95
Amite, co., Ms., U.S.	D3	101
Amite, stm., La., U.S.	D5	95
Amity, Or., U.S.	B3	114
Amityville, N.Y., U.S.	E7	109
Amlia Island, i., Ak., U.S.	E5	79
'Ammān, Jord.	D4	40
Ammon, Id., U.S.	F7	89
Ammonoosuc, stm., N.H., U.S.	B3	106
Amo, stm., Asia	G13	38
Amory, Ms., U.S.	B5	101
Åmot, Nor.	G6	6
Amoy see Xiamen, China	K7	28
Amposta, Spain	E12	12
Amrāvati, India	B4	37
Amreli, India	J4	38
Amritsar, India	E6	38
Amroha, India	F8	38
Amsterdam, Neth.	C4	8
Amsterdam, N.Y., U.S.	C6	109
Amstetten, Aus.	G14	8
Am Timan, Chad	F10	42
Amu Darya (Amudarja), stm., Asia	I10	22
Amukta Pass, strt., Ak., U.S.	E5	79
Amundsen Gulf, b., N.W. Ter., Can.	B8	66
Amundsen Sea, Ant.	B1	47
Amuntai, Indon.	F6	32
Amur (Heilongjiang), stm., Asia	G21	24
An, Burma	E3	34
Anabar, stm., Russia	C16	24
Anaco, Ven.	C10	58
Anacoco, La., U.S.	C2	95
Anaconda, Mt., U.S.	D4	103
Anaconda Range, mts., Mt., U.S.	E3	103
Anacortes, Wa., U.S.	A3	124
Anacostia, stm., U.S.	C4	97
Anacostia, Northwest Branch, stm., Md., U.S.	B3	97
Anadarko, Ok., U.S.	B3	113
Anadyr', Russia	E29	24
Anadyr, stm., Russia	E29	24
Anadyrskij Zaliv, b., Russia	E30	24
Anagni, Italy	H8	14
Anaheim, Ca., U.S.	F5	82
Anahola, Hi., U.S.	A2	88
Anahuac, Tx., U.S.	E5	120
Ana María, Golfo de, b., Cuba	D7	64
Anambas, Kepulauan, is., Indon.	M9	34
Anamosa, Ia., U.S.	B6	92
Anamur, Tur.	H14	4
Anamur Burnu, c., Tur.	A3	40
Anan, Japan	I7	30
Anand, India	I5	38
Anantapur, India	E4	37
Anantnāg (Islāmābād), India	D6	38
Anápolis, Braz.	D4	57
Ana Sierra, mts., Az., U.S.	E9	80
Anbang, China	E9	28
Ancienne-Lorette, Que., Can.	C6	74
Anclote Keys, is., Fl., U.S.	D4	86
Ancona, Italy	F8	14
Ancud, Chile	E2	56
Ancud, Golfo de, b., Chile	E2	56
Andalucía, hist. reg., Spain	H7	12
Andalusia, Al., U.S.	D3	78
Andalusia, Il., U.S.	B3	90
Andaman Islands, is., India	H2	34
Andaman Sea, Asia	I3	34
Andermatt, Switz.	F15	10
Andernach, Ger.	E7	8
Anderson, Ak., U.S.	C10	79
Anderson, Ca., U.S.	B2	82
Anderson, In., U.S.	D6	91
Anderson, Mo., U.S.	E3	102
Anderson, S.C., U.S.	B2	117
Anderson, co., Ks., U.S.	D8	93
Anderson, co., Ky., U.S.	C4	94
Anderson, co., S.C., U.S.	B2	117
Anderson, co., Tn., U.S.	C9	119
Anderson, co., Tx., U.S.	D5	120
Anderson, stm., N.W. Ter., Can.	C7	66
Anderson, stm., In., U.S.	H4	91
Anderson, Mount, mtn., Wa., U.S.	B2	124
Anderson Ranch Reservoir, res., Id., U.S.	F3	89
Andes, mts., S.A.	F4	53
Andes, Lake, l., S.D., U.S.	D7	118
Andhra Pradesh, state, India	D5	37
Andižan, Uzb.	I12	22
Andkhvoy, Afg.	B1	38
Andong, China	C11	26
Andong, S. Kor.	D12	26
Andorra, And.	C13	12
Andorra, ctry., Eur.	G8	4
Andover, Ks., U.S.	g12	93
Andover, Ma., U.S.	A5	98
Andover, Mn., U.S.	m12	100
Andover, N.Y., U.S.	C2	109
Andover, Oh., U.S.	A5	112
Andover Lake, res., Ct., U.S.	C6	84
Andradina, Braz.	F3	57
Andreanof Islands, is., Ak., U.S.	E4	79
Andrew, co., Mo., U.S.	B3	102
Andrew Island, i., N.S., Can.	D9	71
Andrews, In., U.S.	C6	91
Andrews, N.C., U.S.	f9	110
Andrews, S.C., U.S.	E8	117
Andrews, Tx., U.S.	C1	120
Andrews, co., Tx., U.S.	C1	120
Andrews Air Force Base, mil., Md., U.S.	C4	97
Andria, Italy	H11	14
Androka, Madag.	G8	44
Ándros, i., Grc.	L8	16
Androscoggin, co., Me., U.S.	D2	96
Androscoggin, stm., Me., U.S.	D2	96
Androscoggin Lake, l., Me., U.S.	D2	96
Andros Island, i., Bah.	B8	64
Andros Town, Bah.	B9	64
Andújar, Spain	G7	12
Anduo, China	D14	38
Anegada Passage, strt., N.A.	E16	64
Anfeng, China	B11	26
Anfu, China	H3	28
Ang'angxi, China	B11	26
Angara, stm., Russia	F13	24
Angarsk, Russia	G14	24
Ånge, Swe.	E10	6
Ángel, Salto (Angel Falls), wtfl, Ven.	E11	58
Ángel de la Guarda, Isla, i., Mex.	C3	62
Angeles, Phil.	q19	32
Angeles Point, c., Wa., U.S.	A2	124
Angel Falls see Ángel, Salto, wtfl, Ven.	E11	58
Ångelholm, Swe.	H9	6
Angelina, co., Tx., U.S.	D5	120
Angels Camp, Ca., U.S.	C3	82
Angermünde, Ger.	B13	8
Angers, Fr.	E6	10
Angerville, Fr.	D8	10
Angicos, Braz.	E11	54
Angier, N.C., U.S.	B4	110
Ångk Tasaŏm, Camb.	I8	34
Angleton, Tx., U.S.	E5	120
Angmagssalik, Grnld.	C25	66
Angol, Chile	D2	56
Angola, In., U.S.	A8	91
Angola, N.Y., U.S.	C1	109
Angola, ctry., Afr.	D3	44
Angola Swamp, sw., N.C., U.S.	C5	110
Angoon, Ak., U.S.	D13	79
Angostura Reservoir, res., S.D., U.S.	D2	118
Angoulême, Fr.	G7	10
Angra dos Reis, Braz.	G6	57
Anguilla, Ms., U.S.	C3	101
Anguilla, dep., N.A.	E16	64
Anguille, Cape, c., Newf., Can.	E2	72
Angul, India	J11	38
Anhai, China	K7	28
Anhui, prov., China	E10	26
Aniak, Ak., U.S.	C8	79
Animas, stm., U.S.	D3	83
Animas Mountains, mts., N.M., U.S.	F1	108
Animas Peak, mtn., N.M., U.S.	F2	108
Animas Valley, val., N.M., U.S.	F1	108
Anita, Ia., U.S.	C3	92
Anjār, India	I4	38
Anji, China	E8	28
Anjiang, China	F9	26
Anjou, Que., Can.	p19	74
Anjouan, i., Com.	D8	44
Ankang, China	E9	26
Ankara, Tur.	H14	4
Ankavandra, Madag.	E9	44
Ankazoabo, Madag.	F8	44
Ankazobe, Madag.	E9	44
Ankeny, Ia., U.S.	C4	92
Anklesvar, India	B2	37
Anlong, China	B8	34
Anlu, China	D2	28
Ann, Cape, c., Ma., U.S.	A6	98
Anna, Il., U.S.	F4	90
Anna, Oh., U.S.	B1	112
Anna, Lake, res., Va., U.S.	B5	123
Annaberg-Buchholz, Ger.	E12	8
An-Nabk, Syria	B5	40
An-Nafūd, des., Sau. Ar.	C3	46
An-Najaf, Iraq	B3	46
Anna Maria, Fl., U.S.	p10	86
Anna Maria Island, i., Fl., U.S.	q10	86
Annandale, Mn., U.S.	E4	100
Annandale, Va., U.S.	g12	123
Annapolis, Md., U.S.	C5	97
Annapolis, stm., N.S., Can.	E4	71
Annapolis Junction, Md., U.S.	B4	97
Annapolis Royal, N.S., Can.	E4	71
Annapurna, mtn., Nepal	F10	38
Ann Arbor, Mi., U.S.	F7	99
Anna Regina, Guy.	D13	58
An-Nāsirīyah, Iraq	B4	46
Annawan, Il., U.S.	B4	90
Anne Arundel, co., Md., U.S.	B4	97
Annecy, Fr.	G13	10
Annemasse, Fr.	F13	10
Annette, Ak., U.S.	n24	79
Anniston, Al., U.S.	B4	78
Annobón, i., Eq. Gui.	B1	44
Annonay, Fr.	G11	10
An-Nuhūd, Sudan	F11	42
Annville, Pa., U.S.	F8	115
Anoka, Mn., U.S.	E5	100
Anoka, co., Mn., U.S.	E5	100
Anqing, China	E6	28
Anren, China	I2	28
Ansbach, Ger.	F10	8
Anshan, China	C11	26
Anshun, China	A8	34
Anson, Me., U.S.	D3	96
Anson, Tx., U.S.	C3	120
Anson, co., N.C., U.S.	B2	110
Ansonia, Ct., U.S.	D3	84
Ansonia, Oh., U.S.	B1	112
Ansted, W.V., U.S.	C3	125
Antakya (Antioch), Tur.	H15	4
Antalaha, Madag.	D10	44
Antalya, Tur.	H14	4
Antalya, Gulf of see Antalya Körfezi, b., Tur.	A2	40
Antalya Körfezi, b., Tur.	A2	40
Antananarivo, Madag.	E9	44
Antarctica	A18	47
Antarctic Peninsula, pen., Ant.	C6	47
Antelope, co., Ne., U.S.	B7	104
Antelope Creek, stm., Wy., U.S.	C7	127
Antelope Island, i., Ut., U.S.	B3	121
Antelope Peak, mtn., Nv., U.S.	B7	105
Antelope Range, mts., Nv., U.S.	D7	105
Antelope Reservoir, res., Or., U.S.	E9	114
Antelope Wash, val., Nv., U.S.	D5	105
Antequera, Spain	H7	12
Antero, Mount, mtn., Co., U.S.	C4	83
Antero Reservoir, res., Co., U.S.	C5	83
Anthon, Ia., U.S.	B2	92
Anthony, Fl., U.S.	C4	86
Anthony, Ks., U.S.	E5	93
Anthony, N.M., U.S.	F3	108
Anthony, R.I., U.S.	D3	116
Anthony, Tx., U.S.	o11	120
Anthony Creek, stm., W.V., U.S.	D4	125
Anti Atlas, mts., Mor.	B4	42
Antibes, Fr.	I14	10
Anticosti, Île d', i., Que., Can.	k14	74
Antietam National Battlefield, hist., Md., U.S.	B2	97
Antigo, Wi., U.S.	C4	126
Antigua and Barbuda, ctry., N.A.	F17	64
Antioch, Ca., U.S.	h9	82
Antioch, Il., U.S.	A5	90
Antioch see Antakya, Tur.	H15	4
Antisana, vol., Ec.	H3	58
Antlers, Ok., U.S.	C6	113
Antofagasta, Chile	A2	56
Antofalla, Salar de, pl., Arg.	B3	56
Anton, Tx., U.S.	C1	120
Antongila, Helodrano, b., Madag.	E9	44
António Enes, Moz.	E7	44
Antônio João, Braz.	G1	57
Antonito, Co., U.S.	D5	83
Antora Peak, mtn., Co., U.S.	C4	83
Antrim, N.H., U.S.	D3	106
Antrim, co., Mi., U.S.	C5	99
Antrodoco, Italy	G8	14
Antsirabe, Madag.	E9	44
Antsiranana, Madag.	D9	44
Antwerp, Oh., U.S.	A1	112
Antwerp see Antwerpen, Bel.	D4	8
Antwerpen (Antwerp), Bel.	D4	8
Anuradhapura, Sri L.	H6	37
Anxi, China	C6	26
Anxi, China	J7	28
Anyang, China	D9	26
Anyi, China	G4	28
Anyuan, China	H2	28
Anyuan, China	J4	28
Anžero-Sudžensk, Russia	F11	24
Anzio, Italy	H7	14
Anžu, Ostrova, is., Russia	B23	24
Aoiz, Spain	C10	12
Aomori, Japan	B13	30
Aóós (Vijosë), stm., Eur.	J4	16
Aôral, Phnum, mtn., Camb.	H8	34
Aosta, Italy	D2	14
Aoukâr, reg., Maur.	E4	42
Aozou, Chad	D9	42
Apache, Ok., U.S.	C3	113
Apache, co., Az., U.S.	B6	80
Apache Junction, Az., U.S.	m9	80
Apache Peak, mtn., Az., U.S.	F5	80
Apalachee Bay, b., Fl., U.S.	B2	86
Apalachicola, Fl., U.S.	C1	86
Apalachicola, stm., Fl., U.S.	B1	86
Apalachicola Bay, b., Fl., U.S.	C1	86
Apaporis, stm., S.A.	H7	58
Aparri, Phil.	B7	32
Apatzingán [de la Constitución], Mex.	H8	62
Apeldoorn, Neth.	C5	8
Apennines see Appennino, mts., Italy	F7	14
Apex, N.C., U.S.	B4	110
Apishapa, stm., Co., U.S.	D6	83
Apizaco, Mex.	H10	62
Aplington, Ia., U.S.	B5	92

Index

Name	Map Ref	Page
Apo, Mount, mtn., Phil.	D8	32
Apolda, Ger.	D11	8
Apollo, Pa., U.S.	E2	115
Apopka, Fl., U.S.	D5	86
Apopka, Lake, l., Fl., U.S.	D5	86
Aporé, Braz.	E2	57
Apostle Islands, is., Wi., U.S.	A3	126
Apostle Islands National Lakeshore, Wi., U.S.	A3	126
Appalachia, Va., U.S.	f9	123
Appalachian Mountains, mts., N.A.	D10	76
Appanoose, co., Ia., U.S.	D5	92
Appennino (Apennines), mts., Italy	F7	14
Appiano, Italy	C6	14
Apple, stm., Wi., U.S.	C1	126
Apple Creek, Oh., U.S.	B4	112
Applegate, Or., U.S.	E3	114
Applegate, stm., Or., U.S.	E3	114
Appleton, Mn., U.S.	E2	100
Appleton, Wi., U.S.	D5	126
Appleton City, Mo., U.S.	C3	102
Apple Valley, Ca., U.S.	E5	82
Apple Valley, Mn., U.S.	n12	100
Applewood, Co., U.S.	*B5	83
Appleyard, Wa., U.S.	B5	124
Appling, co., Ga., U.S.	E4	87
Appomattox, Va., U.S.	C4	123
Appomattox, co., Va., U.S.	C4	123
Appomattox, stm., Va., U.S.	C4	123
Appomattox Court House National Historical Park, Va., U.S.	C4	123
Apua Point, c., Hi., U.S.	D6	88
Apucarana, Braz.	G3	57
Apure, stm., Ven.	D9	58
Apurímac, stm., Peru	F4	54
Aqaba, Gulf of, b.	E4	40
Āqcheh, Afg.	B2	38
Āq Koprūk, Afg.	B2	38
Aquarius Mountains, mts., Az., U.S.	C2	80
Aquidauana, Braz.	H7	54
Arab, Al., U.S.	A3	78
'Arab, Bahr al-, stm., Sudan	G11	42
Arabelo, Ven.	E10	58
Arabi, La., U.S.	k11	95
Arabian Desert see Sharqiyah, Aş-Şahrā' al-, des., Egypt	C12	42
Arabian Sea	E17	2
Aracaju, Braz.	F11	54
Aracati, Braz.	D11	54
Araçatuba, Braz.	F3	57
Aracena, Spain	H5	12
Araçuaí, Braz.	D7	57
Arad, Rom.	C5	16
Arafura Sea	G9	32
Arago, Cape, c., Or., U.S.	D2	114
Aragon, Ga., U.S.	B1	87
Aragón, hist. reg., Spain	D11	12
Araguacema, Braz.	E9	54
Aragua de Barcelona, Ven.	C10	58
Araguari, Braz.	E4	57
Arak, Alg.	C6	42
Arāk, Iran	B4	46
Arakan Yoma, mts., Burma	E3	34
Aral Sea, Asia	H10	22
Arambaza, Braz.	I6	58
Aranda de Duero, Spain	D8	12
Arandas, Mex.	G8	62
Ārani, India	F5	37
Aran Island, i., Ire.	G4	7
Aran Islands, is., Ire.	H3	7
Aranjuez, Spain	E8	12
Aransas, co., Tx., U.S.	E4	120
Aransas Bay, b., Tx., U.S.	E4	120
Aransas Pass, Tx., U.S.	F4	120
Aranyaprathet, Thai.	H7	34
Arao, Japan	I3	30
Arapaho, Ok., U.S.	B3	113
Arapahoe, Ne., U.S.	D6	104
Arapahoe, co., Co., U.S.	B6	83
Arapiraca, Braz.	E11	54
Arapongas, Braz.	G3	57
Araraquara, Braz.	F4	57
Ararat, Austl.	G8	50
Ararat, Mount see Ağrı Dağı, mtn., Tur.	H16	4
Arauca, Col.	D7	58
Araure, Ven.	C8	58
Arāvalli Range, mts., India	H5	38
Araxá, Braz.	E5	57
Araya, Punta de, c., Ven.	B10	58
Arba Minch, Eth.	G2	46
Arbois, Fr.	F12	10
Arbon, Switz.	E16	10
Arborg, Man., Can.	D3	70
Arbroath, Scot., U.K.	E10	7
Arbuckle, Ca., Fl., U.S.	E5	86
Arbuckle Mountains, mts., Ok., U.S.	C4	113
Arbuckles, Lake of the, res., Ok., U.S.	C5	113
Arcachon, Fr.	H5	10
Arcade, Ca., U.S.	*C3	82
Arcade, Ga., U.S.	B3	87
Arcade, N.Y., U.S.	C2	109
Arcadia, Ca., U.S.	m12	82
Arcadia, Fl., U.S.	E5	86
Arcadia, In., U.S.	D5	91
Arcadia, La., U.S.	B3	95
Arcadia, Mo., U.S.	D7	102
Arcadia, S.C., U.S.	B4	117
Arcadia, Wi., U.S.	D2	126
Arcanum, Oh., U.S.	C1	112
Arcata, Ca., U.S.	B1	82
Arc Dome, mtn., Nv., U.S.	E4	105
Archangel'sk, Russia	E6	22
Archbald, Pa., U.S.	m18	115
Archbold, Oh., U.S.	A1	112
Archdale, N.C., U.S.	B3	110
Archer, Fl., U.S.	C4	86
Archer, co., Tx., U.S.	C3	120
Archer City, Tx., U.S.	C3	120
Arches National Park, Ut., U.S.	E6	121
Archidona, Spain	H7	12
Archie, Mo., U.S.	C3	102
Archuleta, co., Co., U.S.	D3	83
Arcis-sur-Aube, Fr.	D11	10
Arco, Id., U.S.	F5	89
Arcola, Il., U.S.	D5	90
Arcos de la Frontera, Spain	I6	12
Arctic Bay, N.W. Ter., Can.	B15	66
Arctic Ocean	A32	128
Arda, stm., Eur.	H9	16
Ardabil, Iran	J7	22
Ardalstangen, Nor.	F6	6
Ardennes, reg., Eur.	E5	8
Ardlussa, Scot., U.K.	E7	7
Ardmore, Al., U.S.	A3	78
Ardmore, In., U.S.	A5	91
Ardmore, Ok., U.S.	C4	113
Ardmore, Tn., U.S.	B5	119
Ardsley, N.Y., U.S.	g13	109
Åre, Swe.	E9	6
Arecibo, P.R.	E14	64
Arena, Point, c., Ca., U.S.	C2	82
Arena, Punta, c., Mex.	F5	62
Arenac, co., Mi., U.S.	D7	99
Arenas de San Pedro, Spain	E6	12
Arendal, Nor.	G7	6
Arequipa, Peru	G4	54
Arès, Fr.	H5	10
Arévalo, Spain	D7	12
Arezzo, Italy	F6	14
Arganda, Spain	E8	12
Arga-Sala, stm., Russia	D15	24
Argelès-Gazost, Fr.	I7	10
Argenta, Italy	E6	14
Argenta, Il., U.S.	D5	90
Argentan, Fr.	D6	10
Argentat, Fr.	G8	10
Argentera, mtn., Italy	E2	14
Argentina, ctry., S.A.	C4	56
Argentino, Lago, l., Arg.	G2	56
Argenton-sur-Creuse, Fr.	F8	10
Argonne, reg., Fr.	C12	10
Argos, Grc.	L6	16
Argos, In., U.S.	B5	91
Argostólion, Grc.	K4	16
Argun' (Ergun), stm., Asia	A11	26
Argyle, Mn., U.S.	B2	100
Argyle, Wi., U.S.	F4	126
Århus, Den.	H8	6
Ariano Irpino, Italy	H10	14
Arica, Chile	G4	54
Arica, Col.	I7	58
Arichat, N.S., Can.	D8	71
Arid, Cape, c., Austl.	F4	50
Arīhā (Jericho), Jord.	D4	40
Arikaree, stm., U.S.	B8	83
Arima, Trin.	I17	64
Arinos, stm., Braz.	F7	54
Aripuanã, stm., Braz.	E7	54
Ariquemes, Braz.	E6	54
Arismendi, Ven.	C8	58
Ariton, Al., U.S.	D4	78
Arizona, state, U.S.	C4	80
Arizona Sunsites, Az., U.S.	F6	80
Arizpe, Mex.	B4	62
Arjay, Ky., U.S.	D6	94
Arjeplog, Swe.	C11	6
Arjona, Col.	B5	58
Arkabutla Lake, res., Ms., U.S.	A4	101
Arkadelphia, Ar., U.S.	C2	81
Arkansas, co., Ar., U.S.	C4	81
Arkansas, state, U.S.	C3	81
Arkansas, stm., U.S.	D8	76
Arkansas City, Ks., U.S.	E6	93
Arklow, Ire.	I6	7
Arkoma, Ok., U.S.	B7	113
Arkonam, India	F5	37
Arktičeskogo Instituta, Ostrova, is., Russia	B10	24
Arles, Fr.	I11	10
Arlington, Ga., U.S.	E2	87
Arlington, Ma., U.S.	B5	98
Arlington, Mn., U.S.	F4	100
Arlington, Ne., U.S.	C9	104
Arlington, N.Y., U.S.	D7	109
Arlington, N.C., U.S.	A2	110
Arlington, Oh., U.S.	B2	112
Arlington, S.C., U.S.	B3	117
Arlington, S.D., U.S.	C8	118
Arlington, Tn., U.S.	B2	119
Arlington, Tx., U.S.	n9	120
Arlington, Vt., U.S.	E2	122
Arlington, Va., U.S.	B5	123
Arlington, Wa., U.S.	A3	124
Arlington, co., Va., U.S.	g12	123
Arlington, Lake, res., Tx., U.S.	n9	120
Arlington Heights, Il., U.S.	A5	90
Arma, Ks., U.S.	E9	93
Armada, Mi., U.S.	F8	99
Armagh, Que., Can.	C7	74
Armavir, Russia	H6	22
Armenia, Col.	E5	58
Armenia, ctry., Asia	I6	22
Armentières, Fr.	B9	10
Armidale, Austl.	F10	50
Armijo, N.M., U.S.	k7	108
Armour, S.D., U.S.	D7	118
Armstrong, B.C., Can.	D8	69
Armstrong, Ia., U.S.	A3	92
Armstrong, co., Pa., U.S.	E2	115
Armstrong, co., Tx., U.S.	B2	120
Armstrong, Mount, mtn., Yukon, Can.	D6	66
Armstrong Creek, stm., W.V., U.S.	m13	125
Arnaudville, La., U.S.	D4	95
Arnedo, Spain	C9	12
Arnett, W.V., U.S.	D3	125
Arnhem, Neth.	C6	8
Arnhem, Cape, c., Austl.	B7	50
Arnhem Land, reg., Austl.	B6	50
Árnissa, Grc.	I5	16
Arno, stm., Italy	F5	14
Arnold, Mn., U.S.	D6	100
Arnold, Mo., U.S.	C7	102
Arnold, Ne., U.S.	C5	104
Arnold, Pa., U.S.	h14	115
Arnold Mills Reservoir, res., R.I., U.S.	B4	116
Arnold's Cove, Newf., Can.	E4	72
Arnolds Park, Ia., U.S.	A2	92
Arnprior, Ont., Can.	B8	73
Arnsberg, Ger.	D8	8
Arnstadt, Ger.	E10	8
Arona, Italy	D3	14
Aroostook, co., Me., U.S.	B4	96
Arpajon, Fr.	D9	10
Ar-Rab' al-Khālī, des., Asia	D5	46
Ar-Rahad, Sudan	F12	42
Ar-Ramādī, Iraq	B3	46
Ar-Ramthā, Jord.	C4	40
Arran, Island of, i., Scot., U.K.	F7	7
Ar-Raqqah, Syria	B6	40
Arras, Fr.	B9	10
Arrecife, Spain	C3	42
Arriaga, Mex.	I13	62
Ar-Riyāḍ (Riyadh), Sau. Ar.	D4	46
Arronches, Port.	F4	12
Arrowhead Mountain Lake, res., Vt., U.S.	B2	122
Arrowrock Reservoir, res., Id., U.S.	F3	89
Arrowwood Lake, res., N.D., U.S.	B7	111
Arroyo de la Luz, Spain	F5	12
Arroyo Grande, Ca., U.S.	E3	82
Ar-Ruṣayriṣ, Sudan	F12	42
Ar-Rutbah, Iraq	C7	40
Arsenjev, Russia	I20	24
Ārta, Grc.	J4	16
Artá, Spain	F15	12
Artemisa, Cuba	C6	64
Artemus, Ky., U.S.	D6	94
Artenay, Fr.	D8	10
Arter, Mount, mtn., Wy., U.S.	D4	127
Artesia, N.M., U.S.	E5	108
Arthabaska, Que., Can.	C6	74
Arthur, Ont., Can.	D4	73
Arthur, Il., U.S.	D5	90
Arthur, co., Ne., U.S.	C4	104
Arthur, Lake, l., La., U.S.	D3	95
Arthur, Lake, res., Pa., U.S.	E1	115
Arthur Kill, stm., N.J., U.S.	k8	107
Arthurs Town, Bah.	B10	64
Artigas, Ur.	C5	56
Art'om, Russia	I20	24
Art'omovsk, Russia	G12	24
Artvin, Tur.	G16	4
Aru, Kepulauan, is., Indon.	G9	32
Arua, Ug.	H12	42
Aruanã, Braz.	C3	57
Aruba, dep., N.A.	H13	64
Arunachal Pradesh, ter., India	F16	38
Aruppukkottai, India	H5	37
Arusha, Tan.	B7	44
Aruwimi, stm., Zaire	A5	44
Arvada, Co., U.S.	B5	83
Arvi, India	B5	37
Arvidsjaur, Swe.	D12	6
Arvika, Swe.	G9	6
Arvin, Ca., U.S.	E4	82
Arvon, Mount, mtn., Mi., U.S.	B2	99
Arvonia, Va., U.S.	C4	123
Arzachena, Italy	H4	14
Arzignano, Italy	D6	14
Arzúa, Spain	C3	12
Asadābād, Afg.	C4	38
Asahi-dake, mtn., Japan	p20	30a
Asahikawa, Japan	p20	30a
Asansol, India	I12	38
Asbestos, Que., Can.	D6	74
Asbury, N.J., U.S.	C4	107
Ascensión, Mex.	E10	62
Ascension, co., La., U.S.	D5	95
Ascensión, Bahía de la, b., Mex.	H16	62
Aschabad, Turk.	J9	22
Aschaffenburg, Ger.	F9	8
Aschersleben, Ger.	D11	8
Asciano, Italy	F6	14
Ascoli Piceno, Italy	G8	14
Ascoli Satriano, Italy	H10	14
Aseb, Eth.	F3	46
Åsele, Swe.	D11	6
Åsen, Nor.	E8	6
Asenovgrad, Bul.	G8	16
Ashaway, R.I., U.S.	F1	116
Ashburn, Ga., U.S.	E3	87
Ashburton, N.Z.	E3	52
Ashcroft, B.C., Can.	D7	69
Ashdown, Ar., U.S.	D1	81
Ashe, co., N.C., U.S.	A1	110
Asheboro, N.C., U.S.	B3	110
Ashepoo, stm., S.C., U.S.	F6	117
Ashern, Man., Can.	D2	70
Asherton, Tx., U.S.	E3	120
Asheville, N.C., U.S.	f10	110
Ash Flat, Ar., U.S.	A4	81
Ashford, Eng., U.K.	J13	7
Ashford, Al., U.S.	D4	78
Ashford, W.V., U.S.	m12	125
Ash Grove, Mo., U.S.	D4	102
Ashibetsu, Japan	p20	30a
Ashikaga, Japan	F12	30
Ashizuri-zaki, c., Japan	J6	30
Ashkhabad see Aschabad, Turk.	J9	22
Ashland, Al., U.S.	B4	78
Ashland, Il., U.S.	D3	90
Ashland, Ks., U.S.	E4	93
Ashland, Ky., U.S.	B7	94
Ashland, Me., U.S.	B4	96
Ashland, Ma., U.S.	g10	98
Ashland, Mo., U.S.	C5	102
Ashland, Ne., U.S.	C9	104
Ashland, N.H., U.S.	C3	106
Ashland, Oh., U.S.	B3	112
Ashland, Or., U.S.	E4	114
Ashland, Pa., U.S.	E9	115
Ashland, Va., U.S.	C5	123
Ashland, Wi., U.S.	B3	126
Ashland, co., Oh., U.S.	B3	112
Ashland, co., Wi., U.S.	B3	126
Ashland City, Tn., U.S.	A4	119
Ashland Reservoir, res., Ma., U.S.	h10	98
Ashley, N.D., U.S.	C6	111
Ashley, Oh., U.S.	B3	112
Ashley, Pa., U.S.	n17	115
Ashley, co., Ar., U.S.	D4	81
Ashley, stm., S.C., U.S.	F7	117
Ashley Creek, stm., Ut., U.S.	C6	121
Ashmore, Il., U.S.	D5	90
Ashokan Reservoir, res., N.Y., U.S.	D6	109
Ashqelon, Isr.	D4	40
Ash-Shaqrā', Sau. Ar.	C4	46
Ash-Shāriqah, U.A.E.	C6	46
Ash-Shawbak, Jord.	D4	40
Ashtabula, Oh., U.S.	A5	112
Ashtabula, co., Oh., U.S.	A5	112
Ashtabula, Lake, res., N.D., U.S.	B8	111
Ashton, Id., U.S.	E7	89
Ashton, Il., U.S.	B4	90
Ashton, Md., U.S.	B3	97
Ashton, R.I., U.S.	B4	116
Ashuanipi Lake, l., Newf., Can.	h8	72
Ashuelot, stm., N.H., U.S.	E2	106
Ashville, Al., U.S.	B3	78
Ashville, Oh., U.S.	C3	112
Ashwaubenon, Wi., U.S.	D5	126
Asia	D12	84
Asia, Kepulauan, is., Indon.	E9	32
Asia Minor, reg., Tur.	H14	4
Asino, Russia	F11	24
'Asīr, reg., Sau. Ar.	E3	46
'Asīr, Ras, c., Som.	F5	46
Askham, S. Afr.	G4	44
Askvoll, Nor.	F5	6
Asmara see Asmera, Eth.	E2	46
Asmera, Eth.	E2	46
Asotin, Wa., U.S.	C8	124
Asotin, co., Wa., U.S.	C8	124
Asotin Creek, stm., Wa., U.S.	C8	124
Aspang Markt, Aus.	H16	8
Aspen, Co., U.S.	B4	83
Aspen Butte, mtn., Or., U.S.	E4	114
Aspermont, Tx., U.S.	C2	120
Aspinwall, Pa., U.S.	k14	115
Aspiring, Mount, mtn., N.Z.	F2	52
Aspres-sur-Buëch, Fr.	H12	10
Aspy Bay, b., N.S., Can.	C9	71
Assabet, stm., Ma., U.S.	g9	98
Aş-Şabyā, Sau. Ar.	E3	46
As-Sallūm, Egypt	B11	42
Assam, state, India	G15	38
As-Samāwah, Iraq	B4	46
Assateague Island, i., U.S.	D7	97
Assateague Island National Seashore, U.S.	D7	97
Assawoman Bay, b., Md., U.S.	D7	97
Assen, Neth.	C6	8
Assiniboine, stm., Can.	E2	70
Assiniboine, Mount, mtn., Can.	D3	69
Assis, Braz.	G3	57
Assisi, Italy	F7	14
As-Sulaymānīyah, Iraq	A4	46
As-Sulaymānīyah, Sau. Ar.	D4	46
As-Sulayyil, Sau. Ar.	D4	46
Assumption, Il., U.S.	D4	90
Assumption, co., La., U.S.	E4	95
Assumption Island, i., Sey.	C9	44
Aş-Şuwār, Syria	B7	40
Aş-Şuwayda', Syria	C5	40
As-Suways (Suez), Egypt	C12	42
Asti, Italy	E3	14
Astorga, Spain	C5	12
Astoria, Il., U.S.	C3	90
Astoria, Or., U.S.	A3	114
Astove Island, i., Sey.	D9	44
Astrachan', Russia	H7	22
Astrakhan see Astrachan', Russia	H7	22
Astudillo, Spain	C7	12
Asunción, Para.	B5	56
Aswān, Egypt	D12	42
Aswān High Dam, Egypt	D12	42
Asyūṭ, Egypt	C12	42
Atacama, Desierto de, des., Chile	A3	56
Atacama, Puna de, plat., S.A.	A3	56
Atacama, Salar de, pl., Chile	A3	56
Ataco, Col.	F5	58
Atakpamé, Togo	G6	42
Atami, Japan	G12	30
Atar, Maur.	D3	42
Atascadero, Ca., U.S.	E3	82
Atascosa, co., Tx., U.S.	E3	120
'Aṭbarah, Sudan	E12	42
'Atbarah (Atbara), stm., Afr.	E12	42
Atchafalaya, stm., La., U.S.	D4	95
Atchafalaya Bay, b., La., U.S.	E4	95
Atchison, Ks., U.S.	C8	93
Atchison, co., Ks., U.S.	C8	93
Atchison, co., Mo., U.S.	A2	102
Ateca, Spain	D10	12
Athabasca, Alta., Can.	B4	68
Athabasca, stm., Alta., Can.	f8	68
Athabasca, Lake, l., Can.	m7	75
Athena, Or., U.S.	B8	114
Athenry, Ire.	H4	7
Athens, Ont., Can.	C9	73
Athens, Al., U.S.	A3	78
Athens, Ga., U.S.	C3	87
Athens, Il., U.S.	D4	90
Athens, Mi., U.S.	F5	99
Athens, N.Y., U.S.	C7	109
Athens, Oh., U.S.	C3	112
Athens, Pa., U.S.	C8	115
Athens, Tn., U.S.	D9	119
Athens, Tx., U.S.	C5	120
Athens, W.V., U.S.	D3	125
Athens, co., Oh., U.S.	C3	112
Athens see Athínai, Grc.	L7	16
Athínai (Athens), Grc.	L7	16
Athlone, Ire.	H5	7
Athol, Ma., U.S.	A3	98
Ati, Chad	F9	42
Atienza, Spain	D9	12
Atik Lake, l., Man., Can.	B4	70
Atikonak Lake, l., Newf., Can.	h8	72
Atka Island, i., Ak., U.S.	E5	79
Atkins, Ar., U.S.	B3	81
Atkins, Va., U.S.	D1	123
Atkinson, Il., U.S.	B3	90
Atkinson, Ne., U.S.	B7	104
Atkinson, N.H., U.S.	E4	106
Atkinson, co., Ga., U.S.	E4	87
Atlanta, Ga., U.S.	C2	87
Atlanta, In., U.S.	D5	91
Atlanta, Mi., U.S.	C6	99
Atlanta, Tx., U.S.	C5	120
Atlantic, Ia., U.S.	C2	92
Atlantic, N.C., U.S.	C6	110
Atlantic, co., N.J., U.S.	E3	107
Atlantic Beach, Fl., U.S.	m9	86
Atlantic City, N.J., U.S.	E4	107
Atlantic Highlands, N.J., U.S.	C4	107
Atlantic Ocean	F10	2
Atlantic Peak, mtn., Wy., U.S.	D3	127
Atlas Mountains, mts., Afr.	B5	42
Atlas Saharien, mts., Alg.	B6	42
Atmore, Al., U.S.	D2	78
Atna Peak, mtn., B.C., Can.	C3	69
Atoka, Ok., U.S.	C5	113
Atoka, Tn., U.S.	B2	119
Atoka, co., Ok., U.S.	C5	113
Atoka Reservoir, res., Ok., U.S.	C5	113
Atotonilco el Alto, Mex.	G8	62
Atrato, stm., Col.	D4	58
Aṭ-Ṭafīlah, Jord.	D4	40
Aṭ-Ṭā'if, Sau. Ar.	D3	46
Attala, co., Ms., U.S.	B4	101
Attalla, Al., U.S.	A3	78
Attawapiskat, stm., Ont., Can.	n18	73
Attica, In., U.S.	D3	91
Attica, Ks., U.S.	E5	93
Attica, N.Y., U.S.	C2	109
Attica, Oh., U.S.	A3	112
Attleboro, Ma., U.S.	C5	98
Attopeu, Laos	G9	34
Attow, Ben, mtn., Scot., U.K.	D7	7
Attu Island, i., Ak., U.S.	E2	79
Attūr, India	G5	37
Atwater, Ca., U.S.	D3	82
Atwater, Mn., U.S.	E4	100
Atwood, Ont., Can.	D3	73
Atwood, Il., U.S.	D5	90
Atwood, Ks., U.S.	C2	93
Atwood, Tn., U.S.	B3	119
Atwood Lake, res., Oh., U.S.	B4	112
Auau Channel, strt., Hi., U.S.	C5	88
Aubagne, Fr.	I12	10
Aube, stm., Fr.	D11	10
Auberry, Ca., U.S.	D4	82
Aubigny-sur-Nère, Fr.	E9	10
Aubin, Fr.	H9	10
Auburn, Al., U.S.	C4	78
Auburn, Ca., U.S.	C3	82
Auburn, Il., U.S.	D4	90
Auburn, In., U.S.	B7	91
Auburn, Ky., U.S.	D3	94
Auburn, Me., U.S.	D2	96
Auburn, Ma., U.S.	B4	98
Auburn, Mi., U.S.	E6	99
Auburn, Ne., U.S.	D10	104
Auburn, N.Y., U.S.	C4	109
Auburn, Wa., U.S.	B3	124
Auburndale, Fl., U.S.	D5	86
Auburn Heights, Mi., U.S.	F7	99
Aubusson, Fr.	G9	10
Auch, Fr.	I7	10
Aucilla, stm., Fl., U.S.	B3	86
Auckland, N.Z.	B5	52
Audincourt, Fr.	E13	10
Audrain, co., Mo., U.S.	B6	102
Audubon, Ia., U.S.	C3	92
Audubon, N.J., U.S.	D2	107
Audubon, co., Ia., U.S.	C2	92
Aue, Ger.	E12	8
Auglaize, co., Oh., U.S.	B1	112
Auglaize, stm., Oh., U.S.	A1	112
Au Gres, Mi., U.S.	D7	99
Augsburg, Ger.	G10	8
Augusta, Italy	L10	14
Augusta, Ar., U.S.	B4	81
Augusta, Ga., U.S.	C5	87
Augusta, Ks., U.S.	E7	93
Augusta, Ky., U.S.	B6	94
Augusta, Me., U.S.	D3	96
Augusta, Wi., U.S.	D2	126
Augusta, co., Va., U.S.	B3	123
Augustus, Mount, mtn., Austl.	D3	50
Aulander, N.C., U.S.	A5	110
Auld, Lake, l., Austl.	D4	50
Aulneau Peninsula, pen., Ont., Can.	E4	70
Ault, Co., U.S.	A6	83
Aumont-Aubrac, Fr.	H10	10
Aumsville, Or., U.S.	k12	114
Aurangābād, India	C3	37
Auray, Fr.	E4	10
Aurelia, Ia., U.S.	B2	92
Aurich, Ger.	B7	8
Auriflama, Braz.	F3	57
Aurillac, Fr.	H9	10
Aurora, Ont., Can.	C5	73
Aurora, Co., U.S.	B6	83
Aurora, Il., U.S.	B5	90
Aurora, In., U.S.	F8	91
Aurora, Mn., U.S.	C6	100
Aurora, Mo., U.S.	E4	102
Aurora, Ne., U.S.	D7	104
Aurora, Oh., U.S.	A4	112
Aurora, S.D., U.S.	C9	118
Aurora, Ut., U.S.	E4	121
Aurora, co., S.D., U.S.	D7	118
Aus, Nmb.	G3	44
Au Sable, Mi., U.S.	D7	99
Au Sable, stm., Mi., U.S.	D6	99
Ausable, stm., N.Y., U.S.	f11	109
Au Sable Forks, N.Y., U.S.	f11	109
Au Sable Point, c., Mi., U.S.	B4	99
Au Sable Point, c., Mi., U.S.	D7	99
Auschwitz see Oświęcim, Pol.	h7	8
Austell, Ga., U.S.	h7	87
Austin, In., U.S.	G6	91
Austin, Mn., U.S.	G6	100
Austin, Nv., U.S.	D4	105
Austin, Tx., U.S.	D4	120
Austin, co., Tx., U.S.	E4	120
Austin, Lake, l., Austl.	E3	50

Name	Map Ref	Page
Austin Channel, strt., N.W. Ter., Can.	A12	66
Austintown, Oh., U.S.	A5	112
Austinville, Va., U.S.	D2	123
Australia, ctry., Oc.	D6	50
Australian Capital Territory, ter., Austl.	G9	50
Austria, ctry., Eur.	F10	4
Autauga, co., Al., U.S.	C3	78
Autaugaville, Al., U.S.	C3	78
Autlán de Navarro, Mex.	H7	62
Autun, Fr.	E10	10
Auxier, Ky., U.S.	C7	94
Auxi-le-Château, Fr.	B9	10
Auxonne, Fr.	E12	10
Auxvasse, Mo., U.S.	B6	102
Auyán Tepuy, mtn., Ven.	E11	58
Auzances, Fr.	F9	10
Ava, Mo., U.S.	E5	102
Avallon, Fr.	E10	10
Avalon, Ca., U.S.	F4	82
Avalon, Pa., U.S.	h13	115
Avalon, Lake, res., N.M., U.S.	E5	108
Avalon Peninsula, pen., Newf., Can.	E5	72
Avaré, Braz.	G4	57
Aveiro, Port.	E3	12
Avella, Pa., U.S.	F1	115
Avellaneda, Arg.	C5	56
Avellino, Italy	I9	14
Avenal, Ca., U.S.	E3	82
Avery, co., N.C., U.S.	e11	110
Avesnes, Fr.	B10	10
Avesta, Swe.	F11	6
Avezzano, Italy	G8	14
Aviemore, Scot., U.K.	D9	7
Avignon, Fr.	I11	10
Ávila, Spain	E7	12
Avilés, Spain	B6	12
Avilla, In., U.S.	B7	91
Avis, Pa., U.S.	D7	115
Avispa, Cerro, mtn., Ven.	G10	58
Aviston, Il., U.S.	E4	90
Aviz, Port.	F4	12
Avoca, Ia., U.S.	C2	92
Avoca, Pa., U.S.	m18	115
Avola, Italy	M10	14
Avon, Ct., U.S.	B4	84
Avon, Il., U.S.	C3	90
Avon, Ma., U.S.	B5	98
Avon, Mn., U.S.	E4	100
Avon, N.Y., U.S.	C3	109
Avon, Oh., U.S.	A3	112
Avondale, Az., U.S.	D3	80
Avondale, Co., U.S.	C6	83
Avondale, Ga., U.S.	G10	115
Avondale Estates, Ga., U.S.	h8	87
Avondale, La., U.S.	e8	92
Avon Lake, Oh., U.S.	A3	112
Avonmore, Pa., U.S.	E3	115
Avon Park, Fl., U.S.	E5	86
Avoyelles, co., La., U.S.	C3	95
Avranches, Fr.	D5	10
Awbārī, Libya	C8	42
Awe, Loch, l., Scot., U.K.	E7	7
Awjilah, Libya	C10	42
Axiós (Vardar), stm., Eur.	I6	16
Axis, Al., U.S.	E1	78
Axtell, Ne., U.S.	D6	104
Ayabe, Japan	G8	30
Ayacucho, Peru	F4	54
Ayamonte, Spain	H4	12
Ayapel, Col.	C5	58
Ayaviri, Peru	F4	54
Aybak, Afg.	B3	38
Ayden, N.C., U.S.	B5	110
Ayer, Ma., U.S.	A4	98
Ayers Cliff, Que., Can.	D5	74
Ayeyarwady (Irrawaddy), stm., Burma	G3	34
Áyion Óros, pen., Grc.	I8	16
Aylesbury, Eng., U.K.	J12	7
Áyios Nikólaos, Grc.	N9	16
Aylesford, N.S., Can.	D5	71
Aylmer, Mount, mtn., Alta., Can.	D3	68
Aylmer East, Que., Can.	D2	74
Aylmer Lake, l., N.W. Ter., Can.	D11	66
Aylmer West, Ont., Can.	E4	73
Ayora, Spain	F10	12
'Ayoûn el 'Atroûs, Maur.	E4	42
Ayr, Scot., U.K.	F8	7
Ayre, Point of, c., I. of Man	G8	7
Ayu, Kepulauan, is., Indon.	E9	32
Ayvalik, Tur.	J10	16
Azambuja, Port.	F3	12
Azamgarh, India	G10	38
Azare, Nig.	F8	42
Azerbaijan, ctry., Asia	I7	22
Aziscohos Lake, l., Me., U.S.	C1	96
Azle, Tx., U.S.	n9	120
Azogues, Ec.	I3	58
Azores see Açores, is., Port.	D11	2
Azov, Sea of see Azovskoje more, Eur.	H5	22
Azovskoje more (Sea of Azov), Eur.	H5	22
Aztec, N.M., U.S.	A2	108
Aztec Peak, mtn., Az., U.S.	D5	80
Aztec Ruins National Monument, N.M., U.S.	A1	108
Azua, Dom. Rep.	E12	64
Azuaga, Spain	G6	12
Azuero, Península de, pen., Pan.	K7	64
Azul, Arg.	C5	56
Azul, Côte d', Fr.	I14	10
Azusa, Ca., U.S.	m13	82
Az-Zaqāzīq, Egypt	D2	40
Az-Zarqā', Jord.	C5	40
Az-Zāwiyah, Libya	B8	42
Azzel Matti, Sebkha, pl., Alg.	C6	42

B

Name	Map Ref	Page
Ba, stm., Viet.	H10	34
Babaeski, Tur.	H11	16
Babahoyo, Ec.	H3	58
Babar, Kepulauan, is., Indon.	G8	32
Babb Creek, stm., Pa., U.S.	C7	115
Babbitt, Mn., U.S.	C7	100
Babbitt, Nv., U.S.	E3	105
B'abdā, Leb.	C4	40
Bāb el-Mandeb see Mandeb, Bāb el-, strt.	F3	46
Babine, stm., B.C., Can.	B4	69
Babine Lake, l., B.C., Can.	B5	69
Babine Range, mts., B.C., Can.	B5	69
Bābol, Iran	J8	22
Baboquivari Mountains, mts., Az., U.S.	F4	80
Baboquivari Peak, mtn., Az., U.S.	F4	80
Babuyan Islands, is., Phil.	B7	32
Babylon, N.Y., U.S.	n15	109
Baca, co., Co., U.S.	D8	83
Bacabal, Braz.	D10	54
Bacan, Pulau, i., Indon.	F8	32
Bacău, Rom.	C10	16
Bac Can, Viet.	C8	34
Bacerac, Mex.	B5	62
Bachaquero, Ven.	C7	58
Bachta, Russia	E11	24
Bachu, China	D2	26
Back, stm., N.W. Ter., Can.	C13	66
Back, stm., ..., U.S.	h12	117
Backbone Mountain, mtn., U.S.	m12	97
Backnang, Ger.	G9	8
Bac Lieu, Viet.	J8	34
Bac Ninh, Viet.	D9	34
Bacolod, Phil.	C7	32
Bacon, co., Ga., U.S.	E4	87
Baconton, Ga., U.S.	E2	87
Bacoor, Phil.	q19	33b
Bad, stm., S.D., U.S.	C5	118
Bad, stm., Wi., U.S.	B3	126
Badagara, India	G3	37
Badajia, China	B9	28
Badajoz, Spain	G5	12
Badalona, Spain	D14	12
Badanah, Sau. Ar.	H13	8
Bad Aussee, Aus.	E8	99
Bad Axe, Mi., U.S.	C9	71
Baddeck, N.S., Can.	A11	8
Bad Doberan, Ger.	E7	8
Bad Ems, Ger.	G16	8
Baden, Aus.	D4	73
Baden, Ont., Can.	E15	10
Baden, Switz.	E1	115
Baden, Pa., U.S.	G8	8
Baden-Baden, Ger.	H13	8
Badgastein, Aus.	D3	72
Badger, Newf., Can.	E9	8
Bad Hersfeld, Ger.	E8	8
Bad Homburg [vor der Höhe], Ger.	E7	8
Bad Honnef, Ger.	B2	110
Badin, N.C., U.S.	B2	110
Badin Lake, res., N.C., U.S.	H13	8
Bad Ischl, Aus.	E10	8
Bad Kissingen, Ger.	F7	8
Bad Kreuznach, Ger.	D3	118
Badlands, hills, S.D., U.S.	C2	111
Badlands, reg., U.S.	D3	118
Badlands National Park, S.D., U.S.	D10	8
Bad Lauterberg, Ger.	E8	8
Bad Nauheim, Ger.	E10	8
Bad Neustadt an der Saale, Ger.	B10	8
Bad Oldesloe, Ger.	H12	8
Bad Reichenhall, Ger.	B3	126
Bad River Indian Reservation, Wi., U.S.	E10	8
Bad Salzungen, Ger.	B10	8
Bad Schwartau, Ger.	B10	8
Bad Segeberg, Ger.	H11	8
Bad Tölz, Ger.	I6	37
Badulla, Sri L.	C5	127
Badwater Creek, stm., Wy., U.S.	D9	8
Bad Wildungen, Ger.	G10	8
Bad Wörishofen, Ger.	H7	12
Baena, Spain	H8	12
Baeza, Spain	F3	42
Bafatá, Gui.-B.	B14	61
Baffin Bay, b., N.A.	E4	120
Baffin Bay, b., Tx., U.S.	C18	66
Baffin Island, i., N.W. Ter., Can.	A5	44
Bafwasende, Zaire	G11	38
Bagaha, India	D3	37
Bāgalkot, India	M6	34
Bagansiapiapi, Indon.	L11	16
Bagarası, Tur.	C2	80
Bagdad, Az., U.S.	u14	86
Bagdad, Fl., U.S.	B3	46
Bagdad see Baghdād, Iraq	G16	24
Bagdarin, Russia	C6	56
Bagé, Braz.	E5	127
Baggs, Wy., U.S.	B3	46
Baghdād, Iraq	K8	14
Bagheria, Italy	B3	38
Baghlān, Afg.	D1	38
Baghrān Khowleh, Afg.	C3	100
Bagley, Mn., U.S.	I7	10
Bagnères-de-Bigorre, Fr.	J7	10
Bagnères-de-Luchon, Fr.	H11	10
Bagnols-sur-Cèze, Fr.	p19	32
Bago, Burma	B9	64
Baguio, Phil.	B9	64
Bahamas, ctry., N.A.	F5	38
Bahāwalnagar, Pak.	F4	38
Bahāwalpur, Pak.	F4	64
Bahía, Islas de la, is., Hond.	D4	56
Bahía Blanca, Arg.	H2	58
Bahía de Caráquez, Ec.	C4	62
Bahía Kino, Mex.	F2	46
Bahir Dar, Eth.	C5	46
Bahrain, ctry., Asia	B7	16
Baia-Mare, Rom.	B7	16
Bai Bung, Muy, c., Viet.	J8	34
Baicheng, China	B11	26
Baicheng, China	C3	26
Baidoa, Som.	H3	46
Baie-Comeau, Que., Can.	k13	74
Baie-d'Urfé, Que., Can.	q19	74
Baie-Saint-Paul, Que., Can.	B7	74
Baie Verte, Newf., Can.	D3	72
Baignes-les-Juifs, Fr.	E11	10
Baiju, China	B9	28
Bailén, Spain	G8	12
Bailey, co., Tx., U.S.	B1	120
Bailey Island, Me., U.S.	g8	96
Bailey Island, i., S.C., U.S.	k11	117
Baileys Crossroads, Va., U.S.	g12	123
Bainbridge, Ga., U.S.	F2	87
Bainbridge, In., U.S.	E4	91
Bainbridge, N.Y., U.S.	C5	109
Bainbridge Island, i., Wa., U.S.	e10	124
Bain-de-Bretagne, Fr.	E5	10
Baing, Indon.	H7	32
Baird, Tx., U.S.	C3	120
Bairdford, Pa., U.S.	h14	115
Baird Inlet, b., Ak., U.S.	C7	79
Baird Mountains, mts., Ak., U.S.	B7	79
Bais, Fr.	D6	10
Baise, China	C9	34
Baishuijiang, China	E8	26
Baiyin, China	D7	26
Baiyunebo, China	C9	26
Baja, Hung.	I18	8
Baja, Punta, c., Mex.	C4	62
Baja California, pen., Mex.	D3	62
Bajanchongor, Mong.	B7	26
Bajkal, Ozero (Lake Baykal), l., Russia	G15	24
Bajkal'skoje, Russia	F15	24
Bajkit, Russia	E13	24
Bajkonyr, Kaz.	H11	22
Bajo Baudó, Col.	E4	58
Baker, La., U.S.	D4	95
Baker, Mt., U.S.	D12	103
Baker, Or., U.S.	C9	114
Baker, co., Fl., U.S.	B4	86
Baker, co., Ga., U.S.	E2	87
Baker, co., Or., U.S.	C9	114
Baker, Mount, mtn., Wa., U.S.	A4	124
Baker Air Force Base, mil., Ar., U.S.	B6	81
Baker Butte, mtn., Az., U.S.	C4	80
Baker Island, i., Ak., U.S.	n22	79
Baker Lake, N.W. Ter., Can.	D13	66
Baker Lake, l., Me., U.S.	B3	96
Baker Lake, res., Wa., U.S.	A4	124
Bakersfield, Ca., U.S.	E4	82
Bakers Island, i., Ma., U.S.	f12	98
Bakerstown, Pa., U.S.	h14	115
Bakhtarān, Iran	B4	46
Bakhtegān, Daryācheh-ye, l., Iran	C5	46
Bakır, stm., Tur.	J11	16
Bakoye, stm., Afr.	F4	42
Baku, Azer.	I7	22
Balabac Island, i., Phil.	D6	32
Balabac Strait, strt., Asia	D6	32
Ba'labakk (Baalbek), Leb.	C7	46
Balachna, Russia	E26	18
Bālāghāt, India	J9	38
Bālāghāt Range, mts., India	C4	37
Balaguer, Spain	D12	12
Balakovo, Russia	G7	22
Balallan, Scot., U.K.	C6	7
Balāngīr, India	B7	37
Balašicha, Russia	F20	18
Balasore, India	J12	38
Balašov, Russia	G6	22
Balaton, Mn., U.S.	F3	100
Balaton, l., Hung.	I17	8
Balbriggan, Ire.	H6	7
Balcarres, Sask., Can.	G4	75
Balchaš, Ozero, l., Kaz.	H9	24
Bald Eagle Lake, l., Mn., U.S.	m12	100
Bald Eagle Lake, l., Mn., U.S.	C7	100
Baldhill Dam, N.D., U.S.	B7	111
Bald Knob, mtn., Wy., U.S.	D2	127
Bald Knob, Ar., U.S.	B4	81
Bald Mountain, mtn., Or., U.S.	D5	114
Bald Mountain, mtn., Or., U.S.	C9	114
Bald Mountain, mtn., Wy., U.S.	B5	127
Bald Mountains, mts., N.C., U.S.	f10	110
Baldwin, Fl., U.S.	B5	86
Baldwin, Ga., U.S.	B3	87
Baldwin, La., U.S.	E4	95
Baldwin, Mi., U.S.	E5	99
Baldwin, Pa., U.S.	k14	115
Baldwin, S.C., U.S.	B5	117
Baldwin, Wi., U.S.	D1	126
Baldwin, co., Al., U.S.	E2	78
Baldwin, co., Ga., U.S.	C3	87
Baldwin City, Ks., U.S.	D8	93
Baldwinsville, N.Y., U.S.	B4	109
Baldwinville, Ma., U.S.	A3	98
Baldwyn, Ms., U.S.	A5	101
Baldy Mountain, mtn., B.C., Can.	D7	69
Baldy Mountain, mtn., Man., Can.	D1	70
Baldy Mountain, mtn., Mt., U.S.	B7	103
Baldy Mountain, mtn., N.M., U.S.	A4	108
Baldy Peak, mtn., Az., U.S.	D6	80
Baleares, Islas (Balearic Islands), is., Spain	F14	12
Balearic Islands see Baleares, Islas, is., Spain	E15	12
Baleine, Rivière à la, stm., Que., Can.	g13	74
Balej, Russia	G17	24
Balfate, Hond.	G4	64
Balfour, N.C., U.S.	f10	110
Bali, i., Indon.	G5	32
Bali, Laut (Bali Sea), Indon.	G5	32
Balikesir, Tur.	H13	4
Balikpapan, Indon.	F6	32
Balimo, Pap. N. Gui.	G11	32
Balingen, Ger.	G8	8
Balintang Channel, strt., Phil.	B7	32
Baliza, Braz.	D2	57
Balkan Mountains see Stara Planina, mts., Eur.	G8	16
Balkh, Afg.	B2	38
Balkhash, Lake see Balchaš, Ozero, l., Kaz.	H9	24
Ball, La., U.S.	C3	95
Ballachulish, Scot., U.K.	E7	7
Ballālpur, India	C5	37
Ballarat, Austl.	G8	50
Ballard, co., Ky., U.S.	e8	94
Ball Club Lake, l., Mn., U.S.	C5	100
Ballenas, Canal de, strt., Mex.	C3	62
Ball Ground, Ga., U.S.	B2	87
Ballia, India	H11	38
Ballina, Ire.	G3	7
Ballinger, Tx., U.S.	D3	120
Ballinrobe, Ire.	H3	7
Ball Mountain Lake, res., Vt., U.S.	E3	122
Ballston Spa, N.Y., U.S.	B7	109
Ballwin, Mo., U.S.	f12	102
Bally, Pa., U.S.	F10	115
Ballycastle, N. Ire., U.K.	F6	7
Ballymena, N. Ire., U.K.	G6	7
Ballyshannon, Ire.	G4	7
Balmoral, N.B., Can.	B3	71
Balmoral, Scot., U.K.	D9	7
Balmville, N.Y., U.S.	D6	109
Balovale, Zam.	D4	44
Balrāmpur, India	G10	38
Balsam Lake, Wi., U.S.	C1	126
Balsam Lake, l., Wi., U.S.	C1	126
Balsas, Braz.	E9	54
Baltasar Brum, Ur.	C5	56
Baltic, Ct., U.S.	C7	84
Baltic, S.D., U.S.	D9	118
Baltic Sea, Eur.	H12	6
Baltijsk, Russia	G2	18
Baltijskaja Kosa, spit, Eur.	A19	8
Baltimore, Ire.	J3	7
Baltimore, Md., U.S.	B4	97
Baltimore, Oh., U.S.	C3	112
Baltimore, co., Md., U.S.	B4	97
Baltimore Highlands, Md., U.S.	h11	97
Baluchistan, hist. reg., Asia	D1	36
Bālurghāt, India	H13	38
Balygyčan, Russia	E24	24
Balzar, Ec.	H3	58
Bamako, Mali	F4	42
Bambama, stm., Nic.	H6	64
Bambari, Cen. Afr. Rep.	G10	42
Bamberg, Ger.	F10	8
Bamberg, S.C., U.S.	E5	117
Bamberg, co., S.C., U.S.	E5	117
Bamenda, Cam.	G8	42
Bāmīān, Afg.	C2	38
Banalia, Zaire	A5	44
Banana, Zaire	C2	44
Bananal, Ilha do, i., Braz.	F8	54
Banana River, b., Fl., U.S.	D6	86
Banās, Ra's, c., Egypt	D13	42
Banbridge, N. Ire., U.K.	G6	7
Banbury, Eng., U.K.	I11	7
Bancroft, Ont., Can.	B7	73
Bancroft, Ia., U.S.	A3	92
Bānda, India	H9	38
Banda, Kepulauan, is., Indon.	F8	32
Banda, Laut (Banda Sea), Indon.	G8	32
Banda Aceh, Indon.	D2	32
Bandama, stm., I.C.	G4	42
Bandar Beheshtī, Iran	C7	46
Bandar-e 'Abbās, Iran	C6	46
Bandar-e Būshehr, Iran	C5	46
Bandar-e Lengeh, Iran	C5	46
Bandar Seri Begawan, Bru.	E5	32
Banded Peak, mtn., Co., U.S.	D4	83
Bandeira, Pico da, mtn., Braz.	F8	57
Bandelier National Monument, N.M., U.S.	B3	108
Bandera, co., Tx., U.S.	E3	120
Banderas, Bahía de, b., Mex.	G7	62
Bandırma, Tur.	G13	4
Bandon, Ire.	J4	7
Bandon, Or., U.S.	D2	114
Bandundu, Zaire	B3	44
Bandung, Indon.	m13	32
Banes, Cuba	D10	64
Banff, Scot., U.K.	D10	7
Banff National Park, Alta., Can.	D2	68
Bangalore, India	F4	37
Bangassou, Cen. Afr. Rep.	H10	42
Banggai, Kepulauan, is., Indon.	F7	32
Banggi, Pulau, i., Malay.	D6	32
Banghāzī, Libya	B10	42
Bangil, Indon.	m16	33a
Bangka, i., Indon.	F4	32
Bangkalan, Indon.	m16	33a
Bangkinang, Indon.	N6	34
Bangkok see Krung Thep, Thai.	H6	34
Bangladesh, ctry., Asia	E6	36
Bangor, N. Ire., U.K.	G7	7
Bangor, Wales, U.K.	H8	7
Bangor, Me., U.S.	D4	96
Bangor, Mi., U.S.	F4	99
Bangor, Pa., U.S.	E11	115
Bangor, Wis., U.S.	E3	126
Bangor Township, Mi., U.S.	E7	99
Bangs, Tx., U.S.	D3	120
Bangs, Mount, mtn., Az., U.S.	A2	80
Bangui, Cen. Afr. Rep.	H9	42
Bangweulu, Lake, l., Zam.	D5	44
Bani, Dom. Rep.	E12	64
Banī Mazār, Egypt	C12	42
Banister, stm., Va., U.S.	D4	123
Banī Suwayf, Egypt	C12	42
Bāniyās, Syria	B4	40
Banja Luka, Bos.	E12	14
Banjarmasin, Indon.	F5	32
Banjul, Gam.	F2	42
Bankhead Lake, res., Al., U.S.	B2	78
Banks, co., Ga., U.S.	B3	87
Banks Island, i., B.C., Can.	C2	69
Banks Island, i., N.W. Ter., Can.	B8	66
Banks Lake, res., Wa., U.S.	B6	124
Banks Strait, strt., Austl.	H9	50
Banner, co., Ne., U.S.	C2	104
Banner Elk, N.C., U.S.	A1	110
Banning, Ca., U.S.	F5	82
Bannock, co., Id., U.S.	G6	89
Bannock Peak, mtn., Id., U.S.	F6	89
Bannock Range, mts., Id., U.S.	G6	89
Bannu, Pak.	D4	38
Baños de Cerrato, Spain	D7	12
Ban Phak Phraek, Thai.	J6	34
Ban Pong, Thai.	H5	34
Banská Bystrica, Czech.	G19	8
Bānswāra, India	I6	38
Bantam, stm., Ct., U.S.	B3	84
Bantam Lake, l., Ct., U.S.	C3	84
Bantry, Ire.	J3	7
Banyak, Kepulauan, is., Indon.	M4	34
Banyuwangi, Indon.	n17	33a
Baoding, China	D10	26
Baofeng, China	B2	28
Bao Ha, Viet.	C8	34
Baoji, China	E8	26
Baoshan, China	B5	34
Baotou, China	C8	26
Baoying, China	B8	28
Ba'qūbah, Iraq	B3	46
Baquedano, Chile	A3	56
Baraboo, Wi., U.S.	E4	126
Baraboo, stm., Wi., U.S.	E3	126
Baracoa, Cuba	D10	64
Baraga, Mi., U.S.	B2	99
Baraga, co., Mi., U.S.	B2	99
Baram, stm., Malay.	E5	32
Bārāmati, India	C3	37
Bāramūla, India	C6	38
Baranagar, India	I13	38
Baranoa, Col.	B5	58
Baranof Island, i., Ak., U.S.	m22	79
Baranoviči, Bela.	H9	18
Barataria, La., U.S.	E5	95
Barataria Bay, b., La., U.S.	E6	95
Barat Daya, Kepulauan, is., Indon.	G8	32
Barbacena, Braz.	F7	57
Barbados, ctry., N.A.	H18	64
Barbar, Sudan	E12	42
Barbas, Cabo, c., W. Sah.	D2	42
Barbastro, Spain	C12	12
Barbate de Franco, Spain	I6	12
Barber, co., Ks., U.S.	E5	93
Barbers Point, c., Hi., U.S.	B3	88
Barbers Point Naval Air Station, mil., Hi., U.S.	g9	88
Barberton, Oh., U.S.	A4	112
Barbezieux, Fr.	G6	10
Barbosa, Col.	E6	58
Barbour, co., Al., U.S.	D4	78
Barbour, co., W.V., U.S.	B4	125
Barboursville, W.V., U.S.	C2	125
Barbourville, Ky., U.S.	D6	94
Barbuda, i., Antig.	F17	64
Barcaldine, Austl.	D9	50
Barcelona Pozzo di Gotto, Italy	K10	14
Barcelona, Spain	D14	12
Barcelona, Ven.	B10	58
Barcelos, Braz.	D6	54
Barcelos, Port.	D3	12
Barcroft, Lake, res., Va., U.S.	g12	123
Barden Reservoir, res., R.I., U.S.	C2	116
Bardera, Som.	H3	46
Bardīyah, Libya	B11	42
Bardstown, Ky., U.S.	C4	94
Bardufoss, Nor.	B12	6
Bardwell, Ky., U.S.	f9	94
Bardwell Lake, res., Tx., U.S.	C4	120
Bareilly, India	F8	38
Barents Sea, Eur.	B8	128
Barfleur, Fr.	C5	10
Bargersville, In., U.S.	E5	91
Bari, Italy	H11	14
Barīkowt, Afg.	C4	38
Barillas, Guat.	G2	64
Barinas, Ven.	C7	58
Barinitas, Ven.	C7	58
Barīpāda, India	J12	38
Barīsāl, Bngl.	I14	38
Barisan, Pegunungan, mts., Indon.	F3	32
Barito, stm., Indon.	F5	32
Barker Heights, N.C., U.S.	f10	110
Barkhamsted Reservoir, res., Ct., U.S.	B3	84
Barkley, Lake, res., U.S.	f10	94
Barkley Sound, strt., B.C., Can.	E5	69
Barkly Tableland, plat., Austl.	C7	50
Bark Point, c., Wi., U.S.	B2	126
Barksdale Air Force Base, mil., La., U.S.	B2	95
Bar-le-Duc, Fr.	D12	10
Barlee, Lake, l., Austl.	E3	50
Barletta, Italy	H11	14
Barling, Ar., U.S.	B1	81
Barlow, Ky., U.S.	e8	94
Barmer, India	H4	38
Barmouth, Wales, U.K.	I8	7
Barnaul, Russia	G10	24
Barnegat Bay, b., N.J., U.S.	D4	107
Barnegat Inlet, b., N.J., U.S.	D4	107
Barnes, co., N.D., U.S.	B7	111
Barnesboro, Pa., U.S.	E4	115
Barnes Sound, strt., Fl., U.S.	G6	86
Barnesville, Ga., U.S.	C2	87
Barnesville, Mn., U.S.	D2	100
Barnesville, Oh., U.S.	C4	112
Barneville-Carteret, Fr.	C5	10
Barnhart, Mo., U.S.	C7	102
Barnsdall, Ok., U.S.	A5	113
Barnsley, Eng., U.K.	H11	7
Barnstable, Ma., U.S.	C7	98
Barnstable, co., Ma., U.S.	C7	98
Barnstaple, Eng., U.K.	J8	7
Barnwell, S.C., U.S.	E5	117
Barnwell, co., S.C., U.S.	E5	117
Baroda, India	I5	38
Barpeta, India	G14	38
Barqah (Cyrenaica), reg., Libya	B10	42
Barques, Pointe aux, c., Mi., U.S.	D8	99
Barquisimeto, Ven.	B8	58
Barra, Braz.	F10	54
Barra, Ponta da, c., Moz.	F7	44
Barrackville, W.V., U.S.	B4	125
Barra do Corda, Braz.	E9	54
Barra Falsa, Ponta da, c., Moz.	F7	44
Barra Mansa, Braz.	G6	57

Name	Map Ref	Page
Barrancabermeja, Col.	D6	58
Barranca del Cobre, Parque Nacional, Mex.	D6	62
Barrancas, Ven.	C11	58
Barrancos, Port.	G5	12
Barranquilla, Col.	B5	58
Barras, Braz.	D10	54
Barrax, Spain	F9	12
Barre, Vt., U.S.	C4	122
Barre, Lake, l., La., U.S.	E5	95
Barre Falls Reservoir, res., Ma., U.S.	B4	98
Barreiras, Braz.	B6	57
Barreiro, Port.	G2	12
Barreiros, Braz.	E11	54
Barrême, Fr.	I13	10
Barren, co., Ky., U.S.	D4	94
Barren, stm., Ky., U.S.	C3	94
Barren Island, b., Md., U.S.	D5	97
Barren Islands, is., Ak., U.S.	h15	79
Barren River Lake, res., Ky., U.S.	D3	94
Barretos, Braz.	F4	57
Barrett, W.V., U.S.	D3	125
Barrhead, Alta., Can.	B3	68
Barrie, Ont., Can.	C5	73
Barrie Island, i., Ont., Can.	B2	73
Barrière, B.C., Can.	D7	69
Barrington, Il., U.S.	A5	90
Barrington, N.J., U.S.	D2	107
Barrington, R.I., U.S.	D5	116
Barrington, stm., R.I., U.S.	C5	116
Barron, Wi., U.S.	C2	126
Barron, co., Wi., U.S.	C2	126
Barron Lake, Mi., U.S.	G4	99
Barrow, Ak., U.S.	A8	79
Barrow, co., Ga., U.S.	B3	87
Barrow, Point, c., Ak., U.S.	A8	79
Barrow Creek, Austl.	D6	50
Barrow-in-Furness, Eng., U.K.	G9	7
Barrow Island, i., Austl.	D3	50
Barrow Strait, strt., N.W. Ter., Can.	B14	66
Barry, Il., U.S.	D2	90
Barry, co., Mi., U.S.	F5	99
Barry, co., Mo., U.S.	E4	102
Barrys Bay, Ont., Can.	B7	73
Bārsi, India	C3	37
Barstow, Ca., U.S.	E5	82
Bar-sur-Aube, Fr.	D11	10
Barth, Ger.	A12	8
Bartholomew, co., In., U.S.	F6	91
Bartholomew, Bayou, stm., U.S.	D4	81
Bartica, Guy.	D13	58
Bartlesville, Ok., U.S.	A6	113
Bartlett, N.H., U.S.	B4	106
Bartlett, Tn., U.S.	B2	119
Bartlett, Tx., U.S.	D4	120
Bartlett Reservoir, res., Az., U.S.	D4	80
Bartletts Ferry Dam, U.S.	C4	78
Barton, Oh., U.S.	B5	112
Barton, Vt., U.S.	B4	122
Barton, co., Ks., U.S.	D5	93
Barton, co., Mo., U.S.	D3	102
Barton, stm., Vt., U.S.	B4	122
Bartonville, Il., U.S.	C4	90
Bartow, Fl., U.S.	E5	86
Bartow, co., Ga., U.S.	B2	87
Barú, Volcán, vol., Pan.	J6	64
Bāruni, India	H11	38
Baruun Urt, Mong.	B9	26
Barvas, Scot., U.K.	C6	7
Basalt, Co., U.S.	B4	83
Basankusu, Zaire	A3	44
Basatongwula Shan, mtn., China	D14	38
Bascuñán, Cabo, c., Chile	B2	56
Basehor, Ks., U.S.	k16	93
Basel (Bâle), Switz.	E14	10
Bashan Lake, l., Ct., U.S.	D6	84
Bashaw, Alta., Can.	C4	68
Bashi Channel, strt., Asia	G11	26
Basilan Island, i., Phil.	D7	32
Basildon, Eng., U.K.	J13	7
Basile, La., U.S.	D3	95
Basin, Wy., U.S.	B4	127
Basingstoke, Eng., U.K.	J11	7
Basīrhāt, India	I13	38
Basīt, Ra's al-, c., Syria	B4	40
Baskahegan Lake, l., Me., U.S.	C5	96
Baskatong, Réservoir, res., Que., Can.	G17	66
Basking Ridge, N.J., U.S.	B3	107
Basoko, Zaire	A4	44
Basra see Al-Baṣrah, Iraq	B4	40
Bassano, Alta., Can.	D4	68
Bassano del Grappa, Italy	D6	14
Bassari, Togo	G6	42
Bassas da India, rf., Reu.	F7	44
Basse-Terre, Guad.	F17	64
Basseterre, St. K./N.	F16	64
Basse-Terre, i., Guad.	F17	64
Bassett, Ne., U.S.	B6	104
Bassett, Va., U.S.	D3	123
Bassett Peak, mtn., Az., U.S.	E5	80
Bass Islands, is., Oh., U.S.	A3	112
Bass Lake, In., U.S.	B4	91
Bass Strait, strt., Austl.	G9	50
Basswood Lake, l., Mn., U.S.	B7	100
Basti, India	G10	38
Bastogne, Bel.	E8	8
Bastrop, La., U.S.	B4	95
Bastrop, Tx., U.S.	D4	120
Bastrop, co., Tx., U.S.	D4	120
Bastuträsk, Swe.	D13	6
Bata, Eq. Gui.	H7	42
Bataan Peninsula, pen., Phil.	q19	33b
Batabanó, Golfo de, b., Cuba	C6	64
Batagaj, Russia	D20	24
Bataiporã, Braz.	F2	57
Bataipora, Braz.	G2	57
Batāla, India	E6	38
Batalha, Port.	F3	12
Batamaj, Russia	E19	24
Batang, China	E6	26
Batangas, Phil.	r19	33b
Batan Islands, is., Phil.	A7	32
Batanta, Pulau, i., Indon.	F9	32
Batatais, Braz.	F5	57
Batavia, Il., U.S.	B5	90
Batavia, N.Y., U.S.	C2	109
Batavia, Oh., U.S.	C1	112
Batchelor Bay, b., N.C., U.S.	B6	110
Bātdâmbâng, Camb.	H7	34
Batepito, Mex.	B5	62
Bates, co., Mo., U.S.	C3	102
Batesburg, S.C., U.S.	D4	117
Batesville, Ar., U.S.	B4	81
Batesville, In., U.S.	F7	91
Batesville, Ms., U.S.	A4	101
Bath, N.B., Can.	C2	71
Bath, Ont., Can.	C8	73
Bath, Eng., U.K.	J10	7
Bath, Me., U.S.	E3	96
Bath, N.Y., U.S.	C3	109
Bath, Pa., U.S.	E11	115
Bath, S.C., U.S.	D4	117
Bathurst, N.B., Can.	B4	71
Bath, co., Ky., U.S.	B6	94
Bath, co., Va., U.S.	B3	123
Bathurst, Cape, c., N.W. Ter., Can.	B7	66
Bathurst Inlet, N.W. Ter., Can.	C11	66
Bathurst Inlet, b., N.W. Ter., Can.	C11	66
Bathurst Island, i., Austl.	B6	50
Bathurst Island, i., N.W. Ter., Can.	A12	66
Batiscan, stm., Que., Can.	B5	74
Batna, Alg.	A7	42
Baton Rouge, La., U.S.	D4	95
Batouri, Cam.	H8	42
Batsto, stm., N.J., U.S.	D3	107
Batten Kill, stm., U.S.	E2	122
Batticaloa, Sri L.	I6	37
Battle, stm., Can.	F10	66
Battle Creek, Ia., U.S.	B2	92
Battle Creek, Mi., U.S.	F5	99
Battle Creek, Ne., U.S.	C8	104
Battle Ground, In., U.S.	C4	91
Battle Ground, Wa., U.S.	D3	124
Battle Lake, Mn., U.S.	D3	100
Battle Mountain, Nv., U.S.	C5	105
Battle Mountain, mtn., Wy., U.S.	E5	127
Batu, mtn., Eth.	G2	46
Batu, Kepulauan, is., Indon.	O5	34
Batu Pahat, Malay.	N7	32
Baturité, Braz.	D11	54
Baubau, Indon.	G7	32
Bauchi, Nig.	F7	42
Baud, Fr.	E3	10
Baudette, Mn., U.S.	B4	100
Bauld, Cape, c., Newf., Can.	C4	72
Baume-les-Dames, Fr.	E13	10
Baunei, Italy	I4	14
Bauru, Braz.	G4	57
Baús, Braz.	E2	57
Bautzen, Ger.	D14	8
Bawean, Pulau, i., Indon.	G5	32
Baxley, Ga., U.S.	E4	87
Baxter, Ia., U.S.	C4	92
Baxter, Mn., U.S.	D4	100
Baxter, Tn., U.S.	C8	119
Baxter, co., Ar., U.S.	A3	81
Baxter Springs, Ks., U.S.	E9	93
Bay, Ar., U.S.	B5	81
Bay, co., Fl., U.S.	u16	86
Bay, co., Mi., U.S.	E6	99
Bay, Laguna de, l., Phil.	q19	33b
Bayamo, Cuba	D9	64
Bayan Har Shan, mts., China	E6	26
Bayard, Ne., U.S.	C2	104
Bayard, N.M., U.S.	E1	108
Bayberry, N.Y., U.S.	*B4	109
Bayboro, N.C., U.S.	B6	110
Bay Bulls, Newf., Can.	E5	72
Bay City, Mi., U.S.	E7	99
Bay City, Or., U.S.	B3	114
Bay City, Tx., U.S.	E5	120
Bay de Verde, Newf., Can.	D5	72
Bayerische Alpen, mts., Eur.	H11	8
Bayeux, Fr.	C6	10
Bayfield, Ont., Can.	D3	73
Bayfield, Co., U.S.	D3	83
Bayfield, Wi., U.S.	B3	126
Bayfield, co., Wi., U.S.	B2	126
Bayındır, Tur.	K11	16
Baykonur see Bajkonyr, Kaz.	H11	22
Baylor, co., Tx., U.S.	C3	120
Bay Mills Indian Reservation, Mi., U.S.	B6	99
Bay Minette, Al., U.S.	E2	78
Bayo, Spain	B3	12
Bayona, Spain	C3	12
Bayonne, Fr.	I5	10
Bayonne, N.J., U.S.	B4	107
Bayou Bodcau Reservoir, res., La., U.S.	B2	95
Bayou D'Arbonne Lake, res., La., U.S.	B3	95
Bayou George, Fl., U.S.	u16	86
Bayou Goula, La., U.S.	D4	95
Bayou La Batre, Al., U.S.	E1	78
Bay Point, c., S.C., U.S.	G7	117
Bayport, Mn., U.S.	E6	100
Bayport, N.Y., U.S.	n15	109
Bayramiç, Tur.	J10	16
Bayreuth, Ger.	F11	8
Bay Ridge, Md., U.S.	C5	97
Bay Roberts, Newf., Can.	E5	72
Bayrūt (Beirut), Leb.	C4	40
Bays, Lake of, l., Ont., Can.	B5	73
Bay Saint Louis, Ms., U.S.	E4	101
Bay Shore, N.Y., U.S.	E7	109
Bayshore Gardens, Fl., U.S.	q10	86
Bay Springs, Ms., U.S.	D4	101
Bayt Lahm, Isr. Occ.	D4	40
Baytown, Tx., U.S.	E5	120
Bayview, Al., U.S.	f7	78
Bay Village, Oh., U.S.	h9	112
Baza, Spain	H9	12
Bazaruto, Ilha do, i., Moz.	F7	44
Bazas, Fr.	H6	10
Be, Nosy, i., Madag.	D9	44
Beach, Il., U.S.	h9	90
Beach, N.D., U.S.	C1	111
Beachburg, Ont., Can.	B8	73
Beach City, Oh., U.S.	B4	112
Beach Haven Inlet, b., N.J., U.S.	D4	107
Beach Pond, res., U.S.	C8	84
Beachville, Ont., Can.	D4	73
Beachwood, N.J., U.S.	D4	107
Beachy Head, c., Eng., U.K.	K13	7
Beacon, N.Y., U.S.	D7	109
Beacon Falls, Ct., U.S.	D3	84
Beaconsfield, Que., Can.	q19	74
Beadle, co., S.D., U.S.	C7	118
Beagle Gulf, b., Austl.	B6	50
Beale, Cape, c., B.C., Can.	E5	69
Bealanana, Madag.	D9	44
Bear, De., U.S.	B3	85
Bear, stm., U.S.	B3	121
Bear Creek, Al., U.S.	A2	78
Bear Creek, stm., U.S.	E2	93
Bear Creek, stm., Or., U.S.	E4	114
Bear Creek, stm., Wy., U.S.	E8	127
Bearden, Ar., U.S.	D3	81
Beardstown, Il., U.S.	C3	90
Bear Inlet, b., N.C., U.S.	C5	110
Bear Lake, co., Id., U.S.	G7	89
Bear Lake, l., U.S.	A4	121
Bear Lake, l., Wi., U.S.	C2	126
Bear Lodge Mountains, mts., Wy., U.S.	B8	127
Bear Mountain, mtn., Or., U.S.	D4	114
Bearpaw Mountains, mts., Mt., U.S.	B7	103
Bear River, N.S., Can.	E4	71
Bear River City, Ut., U.S.	B3	121
Beartooth Pass, Wy., U.S.	B3	127
Beartooth Range, mts., U.S.	E7	103
Bear Town, Ms., U.S.	D3	101
Beasain, Spain	B9	12
Beas de Segura, Spain	G9	12
Beata, Isla, i., Dom. Rep.	F12	64
Beatrice, Ne., U.S.	D9	104
Beatton, stm., B.C., Can.	E8	66
Beatty, Nv., U.S.	G5	105
Beattyville, Ky., U.S.	C6	94
Beaucaire, Fr.	I11	10
Beaufort, N.C., U.S.	C6	110
Beaufort, S.C., U.S.	G6	117
Beaufort, co., N.C., U.S.	B5	110
Beaufort, co., S.C., U.S.	G6	117
Beaufort Marine Corps Air Station, mil., S.C., U.S.	F6	117
Beaufort Sea, N.A.	B7	61
Beaufort West, S. Afr.	H4	44
Beaugency, Fr.	E8	10
Beauharnois, Que., Can.	D4	74
Beau Lake, l., Me., U.S.	A3	96
Beauly, Scot., U.K.	D8	7
Beaumont, Alta., Can.	C4	68
Beaumont, Ms., U.S.	D5	101
Beaumont, Tx., U.S.	D5	120
Beaumont-sur-Sarthe, Fr.	D7	10
Beaune, Fr.	E11	10
Beauport, Que., Can.	n17	74
Beaupré, Que., Can.	B7	74
Beaupréau, Fr.	E5	10
Beauregard, co., La., U.S.	D2	95
Beausejour, Man., Can.	D3	70
Beauvais, Fr.	C9	10
Beauval, Sask., Can.	B2	75
Beauvoir-sur-Niort, Fr.	F6	10
Beaver, Pa., U.S.	E1	115
Beaver, Ut., U.S.	E3	121
Beaver, W.V., U.S.	D3	125
Beaver, co., Ok., U.S.	e10	113
Beaver, co., Pa., U.S.	E1	115
Beaver, co., Ut., U.S.	E2	121
Beaver, stm., Can.	D7	66
Beaver, stm., Can.	B2	75
Beaver, stm., U.S.	A2	113
Beaver, stm., N.Y., U.S.	B6	109
Beaver, stm., R.I., U.S.	E2	116
Beaver, stm., Ut., U.S.	E2	121
Beaverbank, N.S., Can.	E6	71
Beaver Brook, stm., U.S.	E4	106
Beaver City, Ne., U.S.	D6	104
Beavercreek, Oh., U.S.	C1	112
Beaver Creek, stm., U.S.	E4	104
Beaver Creek, stm., U.S.	C8	127
Beaver Creek, stm., N.D., U.S.	C1	111
Beaver Creek, stm., N.D., U.S.	C5	111
Beaver Creek, stm., Ok., U.S.	C3	113
Beaver Creek, stm., Tn., U.S.	m13	119
Beaver Creek, stm., Wy., U.S.	D4	127
Beaverdale, Pa., U.S.	F4	115
Beaverdam Branch, stm., De., U.S.	F3	85
Beaver Dam, Ky., U.S.	C3	94
Beaver Dam, Wi., U.S.	E5	126
Beaver Falls, Pa., U.S.	E1	115
Beaverhead, co., Mt., U.S.	E3	103
Beaverhead, stm., Mt., U.S.	E4	103
Beaverhead Mountains, mts., U.S.	D5	89
Beaverhill Lake, l., Alta., Can.	C4	68
Beaver Island, i., Mi., U.S.	C5	99
Beaver Lake, l., Ar., U.S.	A2	81
Beaverlodge, Alta., Can.	B1	68
Beaver Meadows, Pa., U.S.	E10	115
Beaver Run Reservoir, res., Pa., U.S.	F2	115
Beavertail Point, c., R.I., U.S.	F4	116
Beaverton, Mi., U.S.	E6	99
Beaverton, Or., U.S.	B4	114
Beāwar, India	G6	38
Bebedouro, Braz.	F4	57
Bécancour, Que., Can.	C5	74
Becerreá, Spain	C4	12
Béchar, Alg.	B5	42
Becharof Lake, l., Ak., U.S.	D8	79
Beckemeyer, Il., U.S.	E4	90
Becker, Mn., U.S.	E5	100
Becker, co., Mn., U.S.	D3	100
Beckham, co., Ok., U.S.	B2	113
Beckley, W.V., U.S.	D3	125
Beckum, Ger.	D8	8
Becky Peak, mtn., Nv., U.S.	D7	105
Bédarieux, Fr.	I10	10
Bedford, Que., Can.	D5	74
Bedford, Eng., U.K.	I12	7
Bedford, In., U.S.	G5	91
Bedford, Ia., U.S.	D3	92
Bedford, Ky., U.S.	B4	94
Bedford, Ma., U.S.	B5	98
Bedford, N.H., U.S.	E3	106
Bedford, Oh., U.S.	A4	112
Bedford, Pa., U.S.	F4	115
Bedford, Va., U.S.	C3	123
Bedford, co., Pa., U.S.	G4	115
Bedford, co., Tn., U.S.	B5	119
Bedford, co., Va., U.S.	C3	123
Bedford Hills, N.Y., U.S.	D7	109
Bee, co., Tx., U.S.	E4	120
Beebe, Que., Can.	D5	74
Beebe, Ar., U.S.	B4	81
Beecher, Il., U.S.	B6	90
Beecher, Mi., U.S.	*E7	99
Beech Fork, stm., Ky., U.S.	C4	94
Beech Grove, In., U.S.	E5	91
Beech Island, S.C., U.S.	E4	117
Beemer, Ne., U.S.	C9	104
Bee Ridge, Fl., U.S.	q11	86
Beersheba see Be'er Sheva', Isr.	D4	40
Be'er Sheva', Isr.	D4	40
Beeton, Ont., Can.	C5	73
Beeville, Tx., U.S.	E4	120
Befale, Zaire	A4	44
Befandriana, Madag.	E9	44
Beggs, Ok., U.S.	B5	113
Begi, Eth.	G1	46
Behbehān, Iran	C5	40
Behm Canal, strt., Ak., U.S.	n24	79
Bei'an, China	B12	26
Beihai, China	D10	26
Beijing (Peking), China	D10	26
Beijing Shih, China	C10	26
Beipiao, China	C11	26
Beira, Moz.	E6	44
Beirut see Bayrūt, Leb.	C4	40
Beja, Port.	G4	12
Béja, Tun.	M4	14
Bejaïa, Alg.	A7	42
Béjar, Spain	E6	12
Békéscsaba, Hung.	I21	8
Bekily, Madag.	F9	44
Bela, India	H9	38
Bel Air, Md., U.S.	A5	97
Belaja Cerkov', Ukr.	H4	22
Belalcázar, Spain	G6	12
Bel Alton, Md., U.S.	D4	97
Belampalli, India	C5	37
Belarus, ctry., Eur.	H10	18
Belaya Tserkov' see Belaja Cerkov', Ukr.	H4	22
Belcamp, Md., U.S.	B5	97
Belcherāgh, Afg.	C1	38
Belcher Islands, is., N.W. Ter., Can.	E17	66
Belchertown, Ma., U.S.	B3	98
Belchite, Spain	D11	12
Belcourt, N.D., U.S.	A6	111
Belden, Ms., U.S.	A5	101
Belding, Mi., U.S.	E5	99
Beled Weyne, Som.	H4	46
Beled, Braz.	D9	54
Belen, N.M., U.S.	C3	108
Belén, Para.	A5	56
Belfair, Wa., U.S.	B3	124
Belfast, N. Ire., U.K.	G7	7
Belfast, Me., U.S.	D3	96
Belfield, N.D., U.S.	C2	111
Belford, N.J., U.S.	C4	107
Belfort, Fr.	E13	10
Belfry, Ky., U.S.	C7	94
Belgaum, India	E3	37
Belgium, Wi., U.S.	E6	126
Belgium, ctry., Eur.	E8	4
Belgorod, Russia	G5	22
Belgrade, Mn., U.S.	E4	100
Belgrade, Me., U.S.	D3	96
Belgrade see Beograd, Yugo.	E4	16
Belhaven, N.C., U.S.	B6	110
Belin, Fr.	H6	10
Belington, W.V., U.S.	B5	125
Belitung, i., Indon.	F4	32
Belize, ctry., N.A.	F3	64
Belize City, Belize	F3	64
Belknap, co., N.H., U.S.	C3	106
Belknap Crater, crat., Or., U.S.	C5	114
Bell, co., Ky., U.S.	D6	94
Bell, co., Tx., U.S.	D4	120
Bellac, Fr.	F8	10
Bella Coola, stm., B.C., Can.	C4	69
Bellaire, Ks., U.S.	g12	93
Bellaire, Mi., U.S.	D5	99
Bellaire, Oh., U.S.	C5	112
Bellaire, Tx., U.S.	r14	120
Bellamy, Al., U.S.	C1	78
Bellary, India	E4	37
Bellavista, Peru	E3	54
Bella Vista, Ar., U.S.	A1	81
Bellbrook, Oh., U.S.	C1	112
Belle, Mo., U.S.	C6	102
Belle, W.V., U.S.	C3	125
Belle, stm., La., U.S.	k9	95
Belleair, Fl., U.S.	p10	86
Belle Bay, b., Newf., Can.	E4	72
Belle Chasse, La., U.S.	E5	95
Bellefontaine, Oh., U.S.	B2	112
Bellefonte, Pa., U.S.	E6	115
Belle Fourche, S.D., U.S.	C2	118
Belle Fourche, stm., U.S.	C3	118
Belle Fourche Reservoir, res., S.D., U.S.	C2	118
Bellegarde, Fr.	F12	10
Belle Glade, Fl., U.S.	F6	86
Belle Isle, Fl., U.S.	D5	86
Belle Isle, i., Newf., Can.	C4	72
Belle Isle, Strait of, strt., Newf., Can.	C3	72
Belle Meade, Tn., U.S.	g10	119
Belle Plaine, Ia., U.S.	C5	92
Belle Plaine, Ks., U.S.	E6	93
Belle Plaine, Mn., U.S.	F5	100
Bédarieux, Fr.	I10	10
Belle River, Ont., Can.	E2	73
Belle Rose, La., U.S.	D4	95
Belle Vernon, Pa., U.S.	F2	115
Belleview, Fl., U.S.	C4	86
Belle View, Va., U.S.	g12	123
Belleville, Ont., Can.	C7	73
Belleville, Il., U.S.	E4	90
Belleville, Ks., U.S.	C6	93
Belleville, Mi., U.S.	p15	99
Belleville, N.J., U.S.	B4	107
Belleville, Pa., U.S.	E6	115
Belleville, Wi., U.S.	F4	126
Belleville Pond, l., R.I., U.S.	E4	116
Bellevue, Id., U.S.	F4	89
Bellevue, Ia., U.S.	B7	92
Bellevue, Ky., U.S.	h13	94
Bellevue, Mi., U.S.	F5	99
Bellevue, Ne., U.S.	C10	104
Bellevue, Oh., U.S.	A3	112
Bellevue, Pa., U.S.	F1	115
Bellevue, Wa., U.S.	e11	124
Belley, Fr.	G12	10
Bellflower, Ca., U.S.	n12	82
Bellingham, Wa., U.S.	A3	124
Bellingham, Ma., U.S.	B5	98
Bellingshausen Sea, Ant.	B4	47
Bellinzona, Switz.	F16	10
Bell Island, i., Newf., Can.	C4	72
Bellmawr, N.J., U.S.	D2	107
Bello, Col.	D5	58
Bellows Falls, Vt., U.S.	E4	122
Bell Peninsula, pen., N.W. Ter., Can.	D16	66
Bellport, N.Y., U.S.	n16	109
Bells, Tn., U.S.	B2	119
Bells Creek, stm., W.V., U.S.	m13	125
Belluno, Italy	C7	14
Bell Ville, Arg.	C4	56
Bellville, Oh., U.S.	B3	112
Bellville, Tx., U.S.	E4	120
Bellwood, Il., U.S.	k9	90
Bellwood, Pa., U.S.	E5	115
Bellwood, Va., U.S.	n18	123
Belmar, N.J., U.S.	C4	107
Belmond, Ia., U.S.	B4	92
Belmont, Ont., Can.	E3	73
Belmont, Ca., U.S.	h8	82
Belmont, Ma., U.S.	g11	98
Belmont, Ms., U.S.	A5	101
Belmont, N.H., U.S.	D4	106
Belmont, N.C., U.S.	B1	110
Belmont, W.V., U.S.	B3	125
Belmont, Wi., U.S.	F3	126
Belmont, co., Oh., U.S.	C4	112
Belmonte, Braz.	C9	57
Belmonte, Port.	E4	12
Belmonte, Spain	B5	12
Belmopan, Belize	F3	64
Belmullet, Ire.	G2	7
Belo, Madag.	E8	44
Beloeil, Que., Can.	D4	74
Belogorsk, Russia	G19	24
Belo Horizonte, Braz.	E7	57
Beloit, Ks., U.S.	C5	93
Beloit, Oh., U.S.	B5	112
Beloit, Wi., U.S.	F4	126
Beloit North, Wi., U.S.	*F4	126
Beloje, Ozero, l., Russia	A20	22
Beloje more (White Sea), Russia	D5	22
Belorado, Spain	C8	12
Belorechensk, Russia	G9	22
Belorussia see Belarus, ctry., Eur.	H10	18
Belovo, Russia	G11	24
Belpre, Oh., U.S.	C4	112
Belt, Mt., U.S.	C6	103
Belted Range, mts., Nv., U.S.	F5	105
Belton, Mo., U.S.	C3	102
Belton, S.C., U.S.	B3	117
Belton, Tx., U.S.	D4	120
Belton Lake, res., Tx., U.S.	D4	120
Beltrami, co., Mn., U.S.	B4	100
Beltsville, Md., U.S.	B4	97
Belucha, Gora, mtn., Asia	H11	24
Belvedere, S.C., U.S.	D4	117
Belvedere Marittimo, Italy	J10	14
Belvidere, Il., U.S.	A5	90
Belvidere, N.J., U.S.	B2	107
Belyj, Ostrov, i., Russia	C8	24
Belyj Jar, Russia	F11	24
Belzoni, Ms., U.S.	B3	101
Bement, Il., U.S.	D5	90
Bemidji, Mn., U.S.	C4	100
Bemidji, Lake, l., Mn., U.S.	C4	100
Benabarre, Spain	C12	12
Bena-Dibele, Zaire	B4	44
Benavente, Port.	G3	12
Benavente, Spain	C6	12
Benavides, Tx., U.S.	F3	120
Benbrook Lake, res., Tx., U.S.	n9	120
Bend, Or., U.S.	C5	114
Ben Davis Point, c., N.J., U.S.	E2	107
Bendeleben, Mount, mtn., Ak., U.S.	B7	79
Bendigo, Austl.	G8	50
Benedict, Md., U.S.	C4	97
Benedito Leite, Braz.	E10	54
Benevento, Italy	H9	14
Benewah, co., Id., U.S.	B2	89
Bengal, Bay of, b., Asia	C6	28
Bengbu, China	C6	28
Benghazi see Banghāzī, Libya	B10	42
Bengkalis, Indon.	N7	32
Bengkulu, Indon.	F3	32
Benguela, Ang.	D2	44
Benham, Ky., U.S.	D7	94
Ben Hill, co., Ga., U.S.	E3	87
Beni, stm., Bol.	F5	54
Béni Abbès, Alg.	B5	42
Benicarló, Spain	E12	12
Benicia, Ca., U.S.	C2	82
Beni-Mellal, Mor.	B4	42
Benin, ctry., Afr.	G6	42
Benin, Bight of, b., Afr.	G6	42
Benin City, Nig.	G7	42
Benisa, Spain	G12	12
Benito Juárez, Presa, res., Mex.	I12	62
Benjamin Constant, Braz.	D4	54

Name	Map Ref	Page
Benjamín Hill, Mex.	B4	62
Benkelman, Ne., U.S.	D4	104
Benld, Il., U.S.	D4	90
Bennett, Co., U.S.	B6	83
Bennett, co., S.D., U.S.	D4	118
Bennettsville, S.C., U.S.	B8	117
Bennington, Ne., U.S.	g12	104
Bennington, N.H., U.S.	D3	106
Bennington, Vt., U.S.	F2	122
Bennington, co., Vt., U.S.	F2	122
Benoit, Ms., U.S.	B2	101
Bénoué (Benue), stm., Afr.	G8	42
Bensenville, Il., U.S.	B6	90
Bensheim, Ger.	F8	8
Bensley, Va., U.S.	C5	123
Benson, Az., U.S.	F5	80
Benson, Mn., U.S.	E3	100
Benson, N.C., U.S.	B4	110
Benson, co., N.D., U.S.	A6	111
Benson, co., Co., U.S.	D7	83
Bentley, Alta., Can.	C3	68
Bentleyville, Pa., U.S.	F1	115
Benton, Ar., U.S.	C3	81
Benton, Il., U.S.	E5	90
Benton, Ks., U.S.	E6	93
Benton, Ky., U.S.	f9	94
Benton, La., U.S.	B2	95
Benton, Pa., U.S.	D9	115
Benton, Tn., U.S.	B7	119
Benton, Wi., U.S.	F3	126
Benton, co., Ar., U.S.	A1	81
Benton, co., Co., U.S.	C3	91
Benton, co., Ia., U.S.	B5	92
Benton, co., Mn., U.S.	E4	100
Benton, co., Ms., U.S.	A4	101
Benton, co., Mo., U.S.	C4	102
Benton, co., Or., U.S.	C3	114
Benton, co., Tn., U.S.	A3	119
Benton, co., Wa., U.S.	C6	124
Benton City, Wa., U.S.	C6	124
Benton Harbor, Mi., U.S.	F4	99
Benton Heights, Mi., U.S.	F4	99
Bentonville, Ar., U.S.	A1	81
Ben Treang, Viet.	I9	34
Bent's Old Fort National Historic Site, hist., Co., U.S.	C7	83
Benue (Bénoué), stm., Afr.	G7	42
Benwood, W.V., U.S.	f8	125
Benzie, co., Mi., U.S.	D4	99
Beograd (Belgrade), Yugo.	E4	16
Beowawe, Nv., U.S.	C5	105
Beppu, Japan	I4	30
Berau, Teluk, b., Indon.	F9	32
Berbera, Som.	F4	46
Berbérati, Cen. Afr. Rep.	H9	42
Berchtesgaden, Ger.	H13	8
Berck, Fr.	B8	10
Berdigest'ach, Russia	E19	24
Berdsk, Russia	G10	24
Berea, Ky., U.S.	C5	94
Berea, Oh., U.S.	A4	112
Berea, S.C., U.S.	B3	117
Berens, stm., Can.	C3	70
Beresford, S.D., U.S.	D9	118
Berg, Nor.	B11	6
Berga, Spain	C13	12
Bergama, Tur.	J11	16
Bergamo, Italy	D4	14
Bergen, Nor.	F5	6
Bergen, co., N.J., U.S.	A4	107
Bergen [auf Rügen], Ger.	A13	8
Bergenfield, N.J., U.S.	B4	107
Bergen op Zoom, Neth.	D4	8
Bergerac, Fr.	H7	10
Bergland, Mi., U.S.	m12	99
Bergstrom Air Force Base, mil., Tx., U.S.	D4	120
Berhala, India	H13	38
Berhampore, India	C8	37
Berhampur, India	E29	24
Beringovskij, Russia	D30	128
Bering Sea	D30	128
Bering Strait, strt.	m18	76a
Berja, Spain	I9	12
Berkåk, Nor.	E7	6
Berkeley, Ca., U.S.	D2	82
Berkeley, Mo., U.S.	f13	102
Berkeley, R.I., U.S.	B4	116
Berkeley, co., S.C., U.S.	E8	117
Berkeley, co., W.V., U.S.	B6	125
Berkeley Heights, N.J., U.S.	B4	107
Berkeley Springs, W.V., U.S.	B6	125
Berkley, Mi., U.S.	F7	99
Berkner Island, i., Ant.	B8	47
Berks, co., Pa., U.S.	F9	115
Berkshire, co., Ma., U.S.	B1	98
Berkshire Hills, hills, Ma., U.S.	B1	98
Berlin, Ger.	C13	8
Berlin, Ct., U.S.	C5	84
Berlin, Md., U.S.	D7	97
Berlin, N.H., U.S.	B4	106
Berlin, N.J., U.S.	D3	107
Berlin, Pa., U.S.	G4	115
Berlin, Wi., U.S.	E5	126
Berlin Lake, res., Oh., U.S.	A4	112
Bermeo, Spain	B9	12
Bermuda, dep., N.A.	F14	10
Bern (Berne), Switz.	B3	108
Bernalillo, N.M., U.S.	B3	108
Bernalillo, co., N.M., U.S.	C3	108
Bernardsville, N.J., U.S.	B3	107
Bernasconi, Arg.	D4	56
Bernau bei Berlin, Ger.	C13	8
Bernay, Fr.	C7	10
Bernburg, Ger.	D11	8
Berne, In., U.S.	C8	91
Bernice, La., U.S.	B3	95
Bernie, Mo., U.S.	E8	102
Bernier Island, i., Austl.	D2	50
Bernina, Piz, mtn., Eur.	F16	10
Beroroha, Madag.	F9	44
Berre, Étang de, b., Fr.	I12	10
Berrien, co., Ga., U.S.	E3	87
Berrien, co., Mi., U.S.	F4	99
Berrien Springs, Mi., U.S.	G4	99
Berry, Al., U.S.	B2	78
Berryessa, Lake, res., Ca., U.S.	C2	82
Berry Hill, Tn., U.S.	g10	119
Berry Islands, is., Bah.	B9	64
Berryville, Ar., U.S.	A2	81
Berryville, Va., U.S.	A5	123
Berthierville, Que., Can.	C4	74
Berthoud, Co., U.S.	A5	83
Berthoud Pass, Co., U.S.	B5	83
Bertie, co., N.C., U.S.	A5	110
Bertoua, Cam.	H8	42
Bertrand, Mo., U.S.	E8	102
Bertrand, Ne., U.S.	D6	104
Berwick, Ia., U.S.	e8	92
Berwick, La., U.S.	E4	95
Berwick, Me., U.S.	E2	96
Berwick, Pa., U.S.	D9	115
Berwick-upon-Tweed, Eng., U.K.	F10	7
Berwyn, Alta., Can.	A2	68
Berwyn, Il., U.S.	k9	90
Berwyn, Pa., U.S.	o20	115
Besalampy, Madag.	E8	44
Besançon, Fr.	E13	10
Beskid Mountains, mts., Eur.	F19	8
Bessemer, Al., U.S.	B3	78
Bessemer, Mi., U.S.	n11	99
Bessemer, Pa., U.S.	E1	115
Bessemer City, N.C., U.S.	B1	110
Best'ach, Russia	E19	24
Betanzos, Spain	B3	12
Bétaré Oya, Cam.	G8	42
Betatakin Ruin, hist., Az., U.S.	A5	80
Bethalto, Il., U.S.	E3	90
Bethany, Ct., U.S.	D4	84
Bethany, Il., U.S.	D5	90
Bethany, Mo., U.S.	A3	102
Bethany, Ok., U.S.	B4	113
Bethany, W.V., U.S.	A4	125
Bethany Beach, De., U.S.	F5	85
Bethel, Ak., U.S.	C7	79
Bethel, Ct., U.S.	D2	84
Bethel, Me., U.S.	D2	96
Bethel, N.C., U.S.	B5	110
Bethel, Oh., U.S.	D1	112
Bethel, Vt., U.S.	D3	122
Bethel Park, Pa., U.S.	k14	115
Bethel Springs, Tn., U.S.	C3	119
Bethesda, Md., U.S.	B4	112
Bethesda, Oh., U.S.	B4	112
Bethlehem, S. Afr.	G5	44
Bethlehem, Ct., U.S.	C3	84
Bethlehem, N.H., U.S.	B3	106
Bethlehem, Pa., U.S.	E11	115
Bethlehem see Bayt Laḥm, Jord.	D4	40
Béthune, Fr.	B9	10
Beticos, Sistemas, mts., Spain	H9	12
Betioky, Madag.	F8	44
Betong, Malay.	M6	34
Betroka, Madag.	F9	44
Betsiboka, stm., Madag.	E9	44
Betsie, Point, c., Mi., U.S.	D4	99
Betsy Layne, Ky., U.S.	C7	94
Bette, mtn., Libya	D9	42
Bettendorf, Ia., U.S.	C7	92
Bettiah, India	G11	38
Betül, India	B4	37
Betzdorf, Ger.	E7	8
Beulah, Co., U.S.	C6	83
Beulah, N.D., U.S.	B4	111
Beulah, Lake, l., Ms., U.S.	B3	101
Beulaville, N.C., U.S.	C5	110
B. Everett Jordan Lake, res., N.C., U.S.	B3	110
Beverley, Austl.	F3	50
Beverley, Eng., U.K.	H12	7
Beverley Head, c., Newf., Can.	D2	72
Beverly, Ma., U.S.	A6	98
Beverly, N.J., U.S.	C3	107
Beverly, Oh., U.S.	C4	112
Beverly, W.V., U.S.	C5	125
Beverly Hills, Ca., U.S.	m12	82
Beverly Shores, In., U.S.	A4	91
Bexar, co., Tx., U.S.	E3	120
Bexley, Oh., U.S.	m11	112
Beypore, India	G3	37
Bežeck, Russia	D19	18
Béziers, Fr.	J12	38
Bhadrakh, India	F3	38
Bhadravati, India	F3	37
Bhagalpur, India	H12	38
Bhakkar, Pak.	E4	38
Bhaktapur, Nepal	G11	38
Bhandara, India	B5	37
Bharatpur, India	G7	38
Bhatinda, India	E6	38
Bhatpara, India	I13	38
Bhavnagar, India	J5	38
Bhilai, India	B6	37
Bhilwara, India	H6	38
Bhima, stm., India	D4	37
Bhimavaram, India	D6	37
Bhind, India	G8	38
Bhiwandi, India	C2	37
Bhiwani, India	F7	38
Bhopal, India	I7	38
Bhubaneswar, India	J11	38
Bhuj, India	I3	38
Bhusawal, India	B3	37
Bhutan, ctry., Asia	D7	36
Bia, Phou, mtn., Laos	E7	34
Biafra, Bight of, Afr.	H7	42
Biak, i., Indon.	F10	32
Biała Podlaska, Pol.	C23	8
Białystok, Pol.	B23	8
Biarritz, Fr.	I5	10
Biasca, Switz.	F15	10
Bibai, Japan	p19	30a
Bibb, co., Al., U.S.	C2	78
Bibb, co., Ga., U.S.	D3	87
Biberach an der Riss, Ger.	G9	8
Bic, Que., Can.	A9	74
Bic, Île du, i., Que., Can.	A9	74
Biche, Lac la, l., Alta., Can.	B4	68
Bicknell, In., U.S.	G3	91
Bida, Nig.	G7	42
Bidar, India	D4	37
Biddeford, Me., U.S.	E2	96
Bideford, Eng., U.K.	J8	7
Bidwell, Mount, mtn., Ca., U.S.	B3	82
Biel [Bienne], Switz.	E14	10
Bielefeld, Ger.	C8	8
Bieler Lake, l., N.W. Ter., Can.	B18	66
Bielersee, l., Switz.	E14	10
Biella, Italy	D3	14
Bielsko-Biała, Pol.	F19	8
Bien Hoa, Viet.	I9	34
Bienville, co., La., U.S.	B2	95
Bienville, Lac, l., Que., Can.	g12	74
Big, stm., Mo., U.S.	c7	102
Biga, Tur.	I11	16
Bigadiç, Tur.	J12	16
Big Bald, mtn., Ga., U.S.	B2	87
Big Bald Mountain, mtn., N.B., Can.	B3	71
Big Baldy, mtn., Id., U.S.	E3	89
Big Baldy Mountain, mtn., Mt., U.S.	D6	103
Big Bay De Noc, b., Mi., U.S.	C4	99
Big Bear City, Ca., U.S.	E5	82
Big Belt Mountains, mts., Mt., U.S.	D5	103
Big Bend, Wi., U.S.	n11	126
Big Bend Dam, S.D., U.S.	C6	118
Big Bend National Park, Tx., U.S.	E1	120
Big Birch Lake, l., Mn., U.S.	E4	100
Big Black, stm., Me., U.S.	B3	96
Big Black, stm., Ms., U.S.	C3	101
Big Blue, stm., In., U.S.	E6	91
Big Burro Mountains, mts., N.M., U.S.	E1	108
Big Cabin Creek, stm., Ok., U.S.	A6	113
Big Coal, stm., W.V., U.S.	C3	125
Big Costilla Peak, mtn., N.M., U.S.	A4	108
Big Creek, stm., Tn., U.S.	e8	119
Big Creek Lake, res., Al., U.S.	E1	78
Big Cypress Indian Reservation, Fl., U.S.	F5	86
Big Cypress Swamp, sw., Fl., U.S.	F5	86
Big Darby Creek, stm., Oh., U.S.	C2	112
Big Delta, Ak., U.S.	C10	79
Big Duke Dam, N.C., U.S.	B2	110
Big Eau Pleine, stm., Wi., U.S.	D3	126
Big Eau Pleine Reservoir, res., Wi., U.S.	D4	126
Big Escambia Creek, stm., U.S.	D2	78
Big Flats, N.Y., U.S.	C4	109
Bigfork, Mt., U.S.	B2	103
Bigfork, stm., Mn., U.S.	B5	100
Biggs, Ca., U.S.	C3	82
Big Hatchet Peak, mtn., N.M., U.S.	F1	108
Big Hole, stm., Mt., U.S.	E4	103
Big Hole National Battlefield, hist., Mt., U.S.	E3	103
Big Horn, co., Mt., U.S.	E9	103
Big Horn, co., Wy., U.S.	B4	127
Bighorn Canyon National Recreation Area, U.S.	F8	103
Bighorn Lake, res., U.S.	E8	103
Bighorn Mountains, mts., U.S.	B5	127
Big Horn Mountains, mts., Az., U.S.	D2	80
Big Kandiyohi Lake, l., Mn., U.S.	F4	100
Big Lake, Mn., U.S.	E5	100
Big Lake, Tx., U.S.	D2	120
Big Lake, l., Me., U.S.	C5	96
Biglerville, Pa., U.S.	G7	115
Big Lookout Mountain, mtn., Or., U.S.	C9	114
Big Lost, stm., Id., U.S.	F5	89
Big Mossy Point, c., Man., Can.	C2	70
Big Mountain, mtn., Nv., U.S.	B2	105
Big Muddy, stm., Il., U.S.	F4	90
Big Nemaha, stm., Ne., U.S.	D10	104
Big Otter, stm., Va., U.S.	C3	123
Big Pine Lake, l., Mn., U.S.	D3	100
Big Pine Mountain, mtn., Ca., U.S.	E4	82
Big Piney, Wy., U.S.	D2	127
Big Piney, stm., Mo., U.S.	D5	102
Bigpoint, Ms., U.S.	E5	101
Big Rapids, Mi., U.S.	E5	99
Big Rib, stm., Wi., U.S.	C3	126
Big River, Sask., Can.	D2	75
Big Sable Point, c., Mi., U.S.	D4	99
Big Sandy, Mt., U.S.	B6	103
Big Sandy, Tx., U.S.	C5	120
Big Sandy, stm., U.S.	C2	125
Big Sandy, stm., Az., U.S.	C2	80
Big Sandy, stm., Tn., U.S.	B3	119
Big Sandy, stm., Wy., U.S.	D3	127
Big Sandy Creek, stm., W.V., U.S.	C3	125
Big Sandy Lake, l., Mn., U.S.	D5	100
Big Sandy Reservoir, res., Wy., U.S.	D3	127
Big Sheep Mountain, mtn., Mt., U.S.	C11	103
Big Sioux, stm., U.S.	E9	118
Big Smoky Valley, val., Nv., U.S.	E4	105
Big Snowy Mountains, mts., Mt., U.S.	D7	103
Big Southern Butte, mtn., Id., U.S.	F5	89
Big South Fork, stm., Ky., U.S.	k13	94
Big Spring, Tx., U.S.	C2	120
Big Stone, co., Mn., U.S.	E2	100
Big Stone City, S.D., U.S.	B9	118
Big Stone Gap, Va., U.S.	f9	123
Big Stone Lake, l., U.S.	E2	100
Big Sunflower, stm., Ms., U.S.	B3	101
Big Thompson, stm., Co., U.S.	A5	83
Big Timber, Mt., U.S.	E7	103
Big Trout Lake, l., Ont., Can.	n17	73
Big Walnut Creek, stm., Oh., U.S.	m11	112
Big Wood, stm., Id., U.S.	F4	89
Bikoro, Zaire	B3	44
Bilaspur, India	I10	38
Bilauktaung Range, mts., Asia	G5	34
Bilbao, Spain	B9	12
Bilimora, India	B2	37
Bilk Creek Mountains, mts., Nv., U.S.	B3	105
Billerica, Ma., U.S.	A5	98
Billings, Mo., U.S.	D4	102
Billings, Mt., U.S.	E8	103
Billings, co., N.D., U.S.	B2	111
Billings Heights, Mt., U.S.	E8	103
Bill Williams, stm., Az., U.S.	C1	80
Bill Williams Mountain, mtn., Az., U.S.	B3	80
Bilma, Niger	E8	42
Biloxi, Ms., U.S.	E5	101
Biloxi, stm., Ms., U.S.	E4	101
Biloxi Bay, b., Ms., U.S.	f8	101
Biltmore Forest, N.C., U.S.	f10	110
Bimini Islands, is., Bah.	B8	64
Bina-Etawa, India	H8	38
Bindura, Zimb.	E6	44
Binéfar, Spain	D12	12
Binga, Monte, mtn., Afr.	E6	44
Bingamon Creek, stm., W.V., U.S.	k10	125
Bingen, Ger.	F7	8
Bingen, Wa., U.S.	D4	124
Binger, Ok., U.S.	B3	113
Bingham, Me., U.S.	C3	96
Bingham, co., Id., U.S.	F6	89
Binghamton, N.Y., U.S.	C5	109
Binhai (Dongkan), China	A8	28
Binjai, Indon.	M5	34
Bintimani, mtn., S.L.	G3	42
Biograd, Cro.	F10	14
Bioko, i., Eq. Gui.	H7	42
Bir, India	C3	37
Birao, Cen. Afr. Rep.	F10	42
Biratnagar, Nepal	G12	38
Birch, stm., W.V., U.S.	C4	125
Birch Island, i., Man., Can.	C2	70
Birch Lake, l., Mn., U.S.	C7	100
Birch River, Man., Can.	C1	70
Birch Run, Mi., U.S.	E7	99
Birchwood City, Md., U.S.	*f9	97
Birchy Bay, Newf., Can.	D4	72
Bird Creek, stm., Ok., U.S.	A6	113
Bird Island, Mn., U.S.	F4	100
Bird Island, i., N.C., U.S.	D4	110
Birdsboro, Pa., U.S.	F10	115
Birdum, Austl.	C6	50
Birecik, Tur.	A5	40
Birganj, Nepal	G11	38
Birigui, Braz.	F3	57
Biril'ussy, Russia	F12	24
Birjand, Iran	K9	22
Birkenfeld, Ger.	F7	8
Birkenhead, Eng., U.K.	H9	7
Bîrlad, Rom.	C11	16
Birmingham, Eng., U.K.	I11	7
Birmingham, Al., U.S.	B3	78
Birmingham, Mi., U.S.	F7	99
Birmitrapur, India	I11	38
Bir Mogrein, Maur.	C3	42
Birobidžan, Russia	H20	24
Biron, Wi., U.S.	D4	126
Birr, Ire.	H5	7
Bi'r Safājah, Egypt	C12	42
Birtle, Man., Can.	D1	70
Bisbee, Az., U.S.	F6	80
Biscarrosse, Fr.	H5	10
Biscay, Bay of, b., Eur.	G7	4
Biscayne, Key, i., Fl., U.S.	s13	86
Biscayne Bay, b., Fl., U.S.	G6	86
Biscayne National Monument, Fl., U.S.	G6	86
Biscayne Park, Fl., U.S.	s13	86
Bisceglie, Italy	H11	14
Bischofshofen, Aus.	H13	8
Biscoe, N.C., U.S.	B3	110
Bishnupur, India	I12	38
Bishop, Ca., U.S.	D4	82
Bishop, Tx., U.S.	F4	120
Bishop Auckland, Eng., U.K.	G11	7
Bishop's Falls, Newf., Can.	D4	72
Bishopville, S.C., U.S.	C7	117
Biškek, Kyrg.	I12	22
Biskra, Alg.	B7	42
Bismarck, Il., U.S.	C6	90
Bismarck, Mo., U.S.	D7	102
Bismarck, N.D., U.S.	C5	111
Bismarck Archipelago, is., Pap. N. Gui.	m16	50a
Bismarck Range, mts., Pap. N. Gui.	m15	50a
Bison Peak, mtn., Co., U.S.	B5	83
Bissau, Gui.-B.	F2	42
Bistineau, Lake, res., La., U.S.	B2	95
Bistrița, Rom.	B8	16
Bitola, Mac.	H5	16
Bitonto, Italy	H11	14
Bitter Creek, stm., Wy., U.S.	E4	127
Bitterfeld, Ger.	D12	8
Bitterfontein, S. Afr.	H3	44
Bitter Lake, l., S.D., U.S.	B8	118
Bitterroot, stm., Mt., U.S.	D2	103
Bitterroot Range, mts., U.S.	B3	89
Bitti, Italy	I4	14
Biwabik, Mn., U.S.	C6	100
Biwa-ko, l., Japan	G9	30
Bixby, Ok., U.S.	B6	113
Biyang, China	C2	28
Bizen, Japan	H7	30
Bizerte, Tun.	L4	14
Black (Lixian) (Da), stm., Asia	D8	34
Black, stm., Az., U.S.	D5	80
Black, stm., Ar., U.S.	B4	81
Black, stm., Ca., U.S.	C4	82
Black, stm., La., U.S.	C4	95
Black, stm., Mi., U.S.	E8	99
Black, stm., N.Y., U.S.	B4	109
Black, stm., N.C., U.S.	C4	110
Black, stm., S.C., U.S.	*D8	117
Black, stm., Vt., U.S.	*E3	122
Black, stm., Vt., U.S.	B4	122
Black, stm., Wi., U.S.	D3	126
Blackall, Austl.	D9	50
Black Bear Creek, stm., Ok., U.S.	A4	113
Blackbeard Island, i., Ga., U.S.	E5	87
Blackburn, Eng., U.K.	H10	7
Blackburn, Mount, mtn., Ak., U.S.	C11	79
Black Butte, mtn., Mt., U.S.	F5	103
Black Butte Lake, res., Ca., U.S.	C2	82
Black Canyon, val., Co., U.S.	C3	83
Black Canyon City, Az., U.S.	C3	80
Black Canyon of the Gunnison National Monument, Co., U.S.	C3	83
Black Creek, B.C., Can.	E5	69
Black Creek, Wi., U.S.	D5	126
Black Creek, stm., U.S.	B1	108
Black Creek, stm., S.C., U.S.	B7	117
Black Diamond, Alta., Can.	D3	68
Black Diamond, Wa., U.S.	B4	124
Blackduck, Mn., U.S.	C4	100
Black Eagle, Mt., U.S.	C5	103
Black Earth, Wi., U.S.	E4	126
Blackfalds, Alta., Can.	C4	68
Blackfeet Indian Reservation, Mt., U.S.	B4	103
Blackfoot, Id., U.S.	F6	89
Blackfoot, stm., Mt., U.S.	C3	103
Blackfoot Mountains, mts., Id., U.S.	F7	89
Blackfoot Reservoir, res., Id., U.S.	G7	89
Blackford, co., In., U.S.	D7	91
Black Forest, Co., U.S.	C6	83
Black Forest see Schwarzwald, mts., Ger.	G8	8
Blackhall Mountain, mtn., Wy., U.S.	E6	127
Black Hawk, S.D., U.S.	C2	118
Black Hawk, co., Ia., U.S.	B5	92
Black Hills, mts., U.S.	C2	118
Blackjack Mountain, mtn., Ga., U.S.	h8	87
Black Lake, Que., Can.	C6	74
Black Lake, l., Mi., U.S.	C6	99
Black Lake, l., N.Y., U.S.	f9	109
Black Lick, Pa., U.S.	F3	115
Blacklick Estates, Oh., U.S.	*m11	112
Black Mesa, mtn., Ok., U.S.	e8	113
Blackmore, Mount, mtn., Mt., U.S.	E6	103
Black Mountain, N.C., U.S.	f10	110
Black Mountain, mtn., U.S.	D7	94
Black Mountain, mtn., Az., U.S.	E4	80
Black Mountain, mtn., Co., U.S.	A5	83
Black Mountain, mtn., Id., U.S.	C3	89
Black Mountain, mtn., Or., U.S.	B7	114
Black Mountain, mtn., Wy., U.S.	B5	127
Black Mountain, mtn., Wy., U.S.	D7	127
Black Mountains, mts., Az., U.S.	B1	80
Black Peak, mtn., Az., U.S.	C1	80
Black Pine Peak, mtn., Id., U.S.	G5	89
Blackpool, Eng., U.K.	H9	7
Black Range, mts., N.M., U.S.	D2	108
Black River Falls, Wi., U.S.	D3	126
Black Rock, Ar., U.S.	A4	81
Black Rock, N.M., U.S.	B1	108
Black Rock Desert, des., Nv., U.S.	B3	105
Black Rock Range, mts., Nv., U.S.	B3	105
Blacksburg, S.C., U.S.	A4	117
Blacksburg, Va., U.S.	C2	123
Black Sea	G14	4
Blacks Fork, stm., U.S.	E3	127
Blacks Harbour, N.B., Can.	D3	71
Blackshear, Ga., U.S.	E4	87
Blackstone, Ma., U.S.	B4	98
Blackstone, Va., U.S.	C5	123
Blackstone, stm., R.I., U.S.	B4	116
Black Thunder Creek, stm., Wy., U.S.	C8	127
Blackville, N.B., Can.	C4	71
Blackville, S.C., U.S.	E5	117
Black Volta (Volta Noire), stm., Afr.	G5	42
Blackwalnut Point, c., Md., U.S.	C5	97
Black Warrior, stm., Al., U.S.	C2	78
Blackwater, stm., Fl., U.S.	u15	86
Blackwater, stm., Md., U.S.	D5	97
Blackwater, stm., N.H., U.S.	D3	106
Blackwater, stm., Va., U.S.	D6	123
Blackwater Reservoir, res., N.H., U.S.	D3	106
Blackwell, Ok., U.S.	A4	113
Blackwood, N.J., U.S.	D2	107
Bladenboro, N.C., U.S.	C4	110
Bladensburg, Md., U.S.	f9	97
Blades, De., U.S.	F3	85
Blagoevgrad, Bul.	G7	16
Blagoveščensk, Russia	G19	24
Blaine, Me., U.S.	B5	96
Blaine, Mn., U.S.	m12	100
Blaine, Tn., U.S.	C10	119
Blaine, Wa., U.S.	A3	124
Blaine, co., Id., U.S.	F4	89
Blaine, co., Mt., U.S.	B7	103
Blaine, co., Ne., U.S.	C6	104
Blaine, co., Ok., U.S.	B3	113
Blaine Lake, Sask., Can.	E2	75
Blair, Ne., U.S.	C9	104
Blair, Ok., U.S.	C2	113
Blair, W.V., U.S.	n12	125
Blair, Wi., U.S.	D2	126
Blair, co., Pa., U.S.	E5	115
Blair Athol, Austl.	D9	50
Blairstown, Ia., U.S.	C5	92
Blairsville, Ga., U.S.	B2	87
Blairsville, Pa., U.S.	F3	115
Blake Island, i., Wa., U.S.	e11	124
Blakely, Ga., U.S.	E2	87
Blakely, Pa., U.S.	m18	115
Blake Point, c., Mi., U.S.	h10	99
Blanc, Cap, c., Afr.	D2	42
Blanc, Mont (Monte Bianco), mtn., Eur.	G13	10
Blanca Peak, mtn., Co., U.S.	D5	83
Blanchard, La., U.S.	B2	95
Blanchard, Ok., U.S.	B4	113
Blanchard, stm., Oh., U.S.	A1	112
Blanchardville, Wi., U.S.	F4	126
Blanchester, Oh., U.S.	C2	112
Blanco, Tx., U.S.	D3	120

Name	Map Ref	Page
Blanco, co., Tx., U.S.	D3	120
Blanco, Cape, c., Or., U.S.	E2	114
Bland, Mo., U.S.	C6	102
Bland, co., Va., U.S.	C1	123
Blanding, Ut., U.S.	F6	121
Blandinsville, Il., U.S.	C3	90
Blanes, Spain	D14	12
Blangkejeren, Indon.	M4	34
Blangy-sur-Bresle, Fr.	C8	10
Blanquilla, Isla, i., Ven.	B10	58
Blantyre, Mwi.	E7	44
Blasdell, N.Y., U.S.	C2	109
Blawnox, Pa., U.S.	k14	115
Blaye-et-Sainte-Luce, Fr.	G6	10
Bleckley, co., Ga., U.S.	D3	87
Bled, Slo.	C9	14
Bledsoe, co., Tn., U.S.	D8	119
Blende, Co., U.S.	C6	83
Blenheim, Ont., Can.	E3	73
Blenheim, N.Z.	D4	52
Blennerhassett, W.V., U.S.	B3	125
Biéré, Fr.	E7	10
Blida, Alg.	A6	42
Blind, stm., La., U.S.	h10	95
Blind River, Ont., Can.	A2	73
Blissfield, Mi., U.S.	G7	99
Blitar, Indon.	n16	32
Block Island, R.I., U.S.	h7	116
Block Island, i., R.I., U.S.	h7	116
Block Island Sound, strt., U.S.	G2	116
Bloemfontein, S. Afr.	G5	44
Bloemhof, S. Afr.	G5	44
Blois, Fr.	E8	10
Blood Mountain, mtn., Ga., U.S.	B3	87
Bloodsworth Island, i., Md., U.S.	D5	97
Bloodvein, stm., Can.	D3	70
Bloody Foreland, c., Ire.	F4	7
Bloomer, Wi., U.S.	C2	126
Bloomfield, Ont., Can.	D7	73
Bloomfield, Ct., U.S.	B5	84
Bloomfield, In., U.S.	F4	91
Bloomfield, Ia., U.S.	D5	92
Bloomfield, Ky., U.S.	C4	94
Bloomfield, Mo., U.S.	E8	102
Bloomfield, Ne., U.S.	B8	104
Bloomfield, N.J., U.S.	h8	107
Bloomfield, N.M., U.S.	A2	108
Bloomfield Hills, Mi., U.S.	o15	99
Bloomingdale, Ga., U.S.	D5	87
Bloomingdale, Il., U.S.	k8	90
Bloomingdale, N.J., U.S.	A4	107
Bloomingdale, Tn., U.S.	C11	119
Blooming Prairie, Mn., U.S.	G5	100
Bloomington, Ca., U.S.	C4	90
Bloomington, In., U.S.	F4	91
Bloomington, Mn., U.S.	F5	100
Bloomington, Tx., U.S.	E4	120
Bloomington, Wi., U.S.	F3	126
Bloomington, Lake, res., Il., U.S.	C5	90
Bloomsburg, Pa., U.S.	E9	115
Bloomville, Oh., U.S.	A2	112
Blora, Indon.	m15	33a
Blossburg, Pa., U.S.	C7	115
Blossom, Tx., U.S.	C5	120
Blount, co., Al., U.S.	B3	78
Blount, co., Tn., U.S.	D10	119
Blountstown, Fl., U.S.	B1	86
Blountville, Al., U.S.	A3	78
Blountville, Tn., U.S.	C11	119
Blowing Rock, N.C., U.S.	A1	110
Bludenz, Aus.	H9	8
Blue, stm., Co., U.S.	B4	83
Blue, stm., In., U.S.	H5	91
Blue, stm., Mo., U.S.	k10	102
Blue, stm., Ok., U.S.	C5	113
Blue Ash, Oh., U.S.	o13	114
Blue Buck Point, c., La., U.S.	E2	95
Blue Creek, W.V., U.S.	m13	125
Blue Creek, stm., W.V., U.S.	m13	125
Blue Cypress Lake, l., Fl., U.S.	E6	86
Blue Diamond, Nv., U.S.	G6	105
Blue Earth, Mn., U.S.	G4	100
Blue Earth, co., Mn., U.S.	G4	100
Blue Earth, stm., Mn., U.S.	G4	100
Bluefield, Va., U.S.	C1	123
Bluefield, W.V., U.S.	D3	125
Bluefields, Nic.	H6	64
Blue Grass, Ia., U.S.	C7	92
Blue Hill, Me., U.S.	D4	96
Blue Hill, Ne., U.S.	D7	104
Blue Hill Range, hills, Ma., U.S.	h11	98
Blue Hills, Ct., U.S.	B5	84
Blue Island, Il., U.S.	B6	90
Bluejoint Lake, l., Or., U.S.	E7	114
Blue Lake, Ca., U.S.	B2	82
Blue Mesa Reservoir, res., Co., U.S.	C3	83
Blue Mound, Il., U.S.	D4	90
Blue Mountain, Ms., U.S.	A4	101
Blue Mountain, mtn., Mt., U.S.	C12	103
Blue Mountain, mtn., N.M., U.S.	D2	108
Blue Mountain, mtn., Pa., U.S.	F6	115
Blue Mountain Lake, res., Ar., U.S.	B2	81
Blue Mountain Peak, mtn., Jam.	E9	64
Blue Nile (Al-Bahr al-Azraq), stm., Afr.	F12	42
Blue Point, Me., U.S.	g7	96
Blue Rapids, Ks., U.S.	C7	93
Blue Ridge, Ga., U.S.	B2	87
Blue Ridge, Va., U.S.	C3	123
Blue Ridge, mtn., U.S.	E10	76
Blue Ridge Summit, Pa., U.S.	G7	115
Blue Springs, Mo., U.S.	h11	102
Bluestone, stm., W.V., U.S.	D3	125
Bluestone Lake, l., W.V., U.S.	D4	125
Bluewell, W.V., U.S.	D3	125
Bluff City, Tn., U.S.	C11	119
Bluff Creek, stm., Ok., U.S.	A4	113
Bluff Lake, res., Ms., U.S.	B5	101
Bluffs, Il., U.S.	D3	90
Bluffton, In., U.S.	C7	91
Bluffton, Oh., U.S.	B2	112
Bluffton, S.C., U.S.	G6	117
Blumenau, Braz.	B7	56
Bly, Or., U.S.	E5	114
Blying Sound, strt., Ak., U.S.	h17	79
Blyth, Ont., Can.	D3	73
Blyth, Eng., U.K.	F11	7
Blythe, Ca., U.S.	F6	82
Blytheville, Ar., U.S.	B6	81
Bø, Nor.	B10	6
Bø, Nor.	G7	6
Bo, S.L.	G3	42
Boaco, Nic.	H5	64
Boalsburg, Pa., U.S.	E6	115
Boardman, Oh., U.S.	A5	112
Boardman, Or., U.S.	B7	114
Boa Vista, Braz.	C6	54
Boavita, Col.	D6	58
Boaz, Al., U.S.	A3	78
Bobbili, India	C7	37
Bobbio, Italy	E4	14
Bobcaygeon, Ont., Can.	C6	73
Böblingen, Ger.	G9	8
Bobo Dioulasso, Burkina	F5	42
Bobrujsk, Bela.	H12	18
Bobtown, Pa., U.S.	G2	115
Bobures, Ven.	C7	58
Boby, Pic, mtn., Madag.	F9	44
Boca Chica Key, i., Fl., U.S.	H5	86
Boca Ciega Bay, b., Fl., U.S.	p10	86
Bôca do Acre, Braz.	E5	54
Boca Grande, Fl., U.S.	F4	86
Boca Raton, Fl., U.S.	F6	86
Bocas del Toro, Pan.	J6	64
Bocholt, Ger.	D6	8
Bochum, Ger.	D7	8
Bodajbo, Russia	F16	24
Bodega Head, c., Ca., U.S.	C2	82
Bodele, reg., Chad	E9	42
Boden, Swe.	D13	6
Bodensee, l., Eur.	H9	8
Bodhan, India	C4	37
Bodie Island, i., N.C., U.S.	B7	110
Bodināyakkanūr, India	G4	37
Bodø, Nor.	C10	6
Boende, Zaire	B4	44
Boën-sur-Lignon, Fr.	G10	10
Boerne, Tx., U.S.	E3	120
Boeuf, stm., La., U.S.	C4	95
Boeuf, Lake, l., La., U.S.	k10	95
Bogale, Burma	F3	34
Bogalusa, La., U.S.	D6	95
Bogart, Ga., U.S.	C3	87
Bogata, Tx., U.S.	C5	120
Bogenfels, Nmb.	G3	44
Boger City, N.C., U.S.	B1	110
Bognes, Nor.	B10	6
Bogor, Indon.	m13	32
Bogorodick, Russia	H21	18
Bogorodsk, Russia	E26	18
Bogota, N.J., U.S.	h8	107
Bogotá see Santa Fe de Bogotá, Col.	E5	58
Bogotol, Russia	F11	24
Bogra, Bngl.	H13	38
Bogučany, Russia	F13	24
Bogue Chitto, Ms., U.S.	D3	101
Bogue Chitto, stm., U.S.	D5	95
Bogue Inlet, b., N.C., U.S.	C5	110
Bogue Phalia, stm., Ms., U.S.	B3	101
Bo Hai, b., China	D10	26
Bohain-en-Vermandois, Fr.	C10	10
Bohemia see Čechy, hist. reg., Czech.	F14	8
Bohemian Forest, mts., Eur.	F12	8
Bohol, i., Phil.	D7	32
Boiano, Italy	H9	14
Boigu, i., Austl.	A8	50
Boiling Springs, N.C., U.S.	B1	110
Boiling Springs, Pa., U.S.	F7	115
Bois Blanc Island, i., Mi., U.S.	C6	99
Bois Brule, stm., Wi., U.S.	B2	126
Boischâtel, Que., Can.	C6	74
Bois-des-Filion, Que., Can.	p19	74
Bois de Sioux, stm., Mn., U.S.	E2	100
Boise, Id., U.S.	F2	89
Boise, co., Id., U.S.	F3	89
Boise City, Ok., U.S.	e8	113
Boissevain, Man., Can.	E1	70
Boissevain, Va., U.S.	e10	123
Boistfort Peak, mtn., Wa., U.S.	C2	124
Boizenburg, Ger.	B10	8
Bojador, Cabo, c., W. Sah.	C3	42
Bojeador, Cape, c., Phil.	B7	32
Bojnūrd, Iran	J9	22
Bojonegoro, Indon.	m15	33a
Boké, Gui.	F3	42
Boketu, China	B11	26
Boknafjorden, Nor.	G5	6
Boksitogorsk, Russia	B16	18
Bokungu, Zaire	B4	44
Bolama, Gui.-B.	F2	42
Bolbec, Fr.	C7	10
Bolesławiec, Pol.	D15	8
Boley, Ok., U.S.	B5	113
Bolgatanga, Ghana	F5	42
Boli, China	B13	26
Bolingbrook, Il., U.S.	k8	90
Bolívar, Arg.	D4	56
Bolivar, Mo., U.S.	D4	102
Bolivar, Oh., U.S.	B4	112
Bolivar, Tn., U.S.	B3	119
Bolivar, W.V., U.S.	B7	125
Bolivar, co., Ms., U.S.	B3	101
Bolívar, Cerro, mtn., Ven.	D11	58
Bolívar, Lake, l., Ms., U.S.	B3	101
Bolívar, Pico, mtn., Ven.	C7	58
Bolivia, ctry., S.A.	G5	54
Bollène, Fr.	H11	10
Bollinger, co., Mo., U.S.	D7	102
Bollnäs, Swe.	F11	6
Bollullos par del Condado, Spain	H5	12
Bolobo, Zaire	B3	44
Bologna, Italy	E6	14
Bologoje, Russia	D17	18
Bolotnoje, Russia	F10	24
Bolsena, Italy	G6	14
Bol'šereck, Russia	G25	24
Bol'ševik, Russia	E23	24
Bol'ševik, Ostrov, i., Russia	B14	24
Bol'šoj An'uj, stm., Russia	D26	24
Bol'šoj Begičev, Ostrov, i., Russia	C16	24
Bol'šoj L'achovskij, Ostrov, i., Russia	C22	24
Bolton, Eng., U.K.	H10	7
Bolton, Ms., U.S.	C3	101
Bolton Lakes, l., Ct., U.S.	B6	84
Bolton Landing, N.Y., U.S.	B7	109
Bolzano (Bozen), Italy	C6	14
Boma, Zaire	C2	44
Bombala, Austl.	G9	50
Bombay, India	C2	37
Bombay Hook Island, i., De., U.S.	C4	85
Bom Despacho, Braz.	E6	57
Bom Jesus da Lapa, Braz.	B7	57
Bomoseen, Lake, l., Vt., U.S.	D2	122
Bomu (Mbomou), stm., Afr.	H10	42
Bon, Cap, c., Tun.	A8	42
Bon Accord, Alta., Can.	C4	68
Bon Air, Va., U.S.	C5	123
Bonaire, Ga., U.S.	D3	87
Bonaire, i., Neth. Ant.	H13	64
Bonanza Peak, mtn., Wa., U.S.	A5	124
Bonao, Dom. Rep.	E12	64
Bonaparte, Mount, mtn., Wa., U.S.	A6	124
Bonaparte Archipelago, is., Austl.	B5	50
Bonarbridge, Scot., U.K.	D8	7
Bonasila Dome, mtn., Ak., U.S.	C7	79
Bonaventure, Que., Can.	A4	71
Bonavista, Newf., Can.	D5	72
Bonavista, Cape, c., Newf., Can.	D5	72
Bonavista Bay, b., Newf., Can.	G22	66
Bonavista Bay, b., Newf., Can.	D5	72
Bond, co., Il., U.S.	E4	90
Bondeno, Italy	E6	14
Bondo, Zaire	H10	42
Bondoukou, I.C.	G5	42
Bondowoso, Indon.	m16	33a
Bondsville, Ma., U.S.	B3	98
Bonduel, Wi., U.S.	D5	126
Bondurant, Ia., U.S.	C4	92
Bone, Teluk, b., Indon.	F7	32
Bone Lake, l., Wi., U.S.	C1	126
Bongandanga, Zaire	A4	44
Bongor, Chad	F9	42
Bonham, Tx., U.S.	C4	120
Bon Homme, co., S.D., U.S.	D8	118
Bonifacio, Capo, c., Italy	J10	14
Bonifay, Fl., U.S.	u16	86
Bonita Springs, Fl., U.S.	F5	86
Bonn, Ger.	E7	8
Bonneauville, Pa., U.S.	G7	115
Bonne Bay, b., Newf., Can.	D3	72
Bonner, co., Id., U.S.	A2	89
Bonners Ferry, Id., U.S.	A2	89
Bonner Springs, Ks., U.S.	C9	93
Bonnet Carre Floodway, La., U.S.	h11	95
Bonne Terre, Mo., U.S.	D7	102
Bonneval, Fr.	D8	10
Bonneville, Fr.	F13	10
Bonneville, co., Id., U.S.	F7	89
Bonneville Dam, U.S.	B4	114
Bonneville Peak, mtn., Id., U.S.	F6	89
Bonneville Salt Flats, pl., Ut., U.S.	C2	121
Bonney Lake, Wa., U.S.	B3	124
Bonnie Doone, N.C., U.S.	B4	110
Bonny Reservoir, res., Co., U.S.	B8	83
Bonnyville, Alta., Can.	B5	68
Bono, Ar., U.S.	B5	81
Bonorva, Italy	I3	14
Bon Secour, Al., U.S.	E2	78
Bonthe, S.L.	G3	42
Bonteaux, Tx., U.S.	B8	120
Booker T. Washington National Monument, Va., U.S.	C3	123
Boomer, W.V., U.S.	C3	125
Boone, Ia., U.S.	B4	92
Boone, N.C., U.S.	A1	110
Boone, co., Ar., U.S.	A2	81
Boone, co., Il., U.S.	A5	90
Boone, co., In., U.S.	D4	91
Boone, co., Ia., U.S.	B3	92
Boone, co., Ky., U.S.	B5	94
Boone, co., Mo., U.S.	B5	102
Boone, co., Ne., U.S.	C7	104
Boone, co., W.V., U.S.	C3	125
Boone, stm., Ia., U.S.	B4	92
Boone Lake, res., Tn., U.S.	C11	119
Booneville, Ar., U.S.	B2	81
Booneville, Ms., U.S.	A5	101
Boonsboro, Md., U.S.	A2	97
Boonton, N.J., U.S.	B4	107
Boonville, In., U.S.	H3	91
Boonville, Mo., U.S.	C5	102
Boonville, N.Y., U.S.	B5	109
Boonville, N.C., U.S.	A2	110
Boothbay Harbor, Me., U.S.	E3	96
Boothia, Gulf of, b., N.W. Ter., Can.	B14	66
Boothia Peninsula, pen., N.W. Ter., Can.	B14	66
Booths Creek, stm., W.V., U.S.	h11	125
Boothville, La., U.S.	E6	95
Booué, Gabon	B2	44
Boquete, Pan.	J6	64
Boquillas del Carmen, Mex.	C8	62
Bor, Russia	E27	18
Bor, Sudan	G12	42
Boraha, Nosy, i., Madag.	E9	44
Borah Peak, mtn., Id., U.S.	E5	89
Borås, Swe.	H9	6
Bordeaux, Fr.	H6	10
Borden, co., Tx., U.S.	C2	120
Borden Peninsula, pen., N.W. Ter., Can.	B16	66
Bordentown, N.J., U.S.	C3	107
Bordertown, Austl.	G8	50
Borgå (Porvoo), Fin.	F15	6
Borgarnes, Ice.	C3	4
Borger, Tx., U.S.	B2	120
Borgne, Lake, b., La., U.S.	D6	95
Borgo, Italy	C6	14
Borgo San Dalmazzo, Italy	E2	14
Borgosesia, Italy	D3	14
Borgo Val di Taro, Italy	E4	14
Borisov, Bela.	G11	18
Borja, Spain	D10	12
Borjas Blancas, Spain	D12	12
Borken, Ger.	D6	8
Borlänge, Swe.	F10	6
Borlu, Tur.	K12	16
Borneo (Kalimantan), i., Asia	E5	32
Bornholm, i., Den.	I10	6
Bornova, Tur.	K11	16
Borogoncy, Russia	E20	24
Boron, Ca., U.S.	E5	82
Boronga Islands, is., Burma	E2	34
Borovici, Russia	C16	18
Borrego Springs, Ca., U.S.	F5	82
Bort-les-Orgues, Fr.	G9	10
Borūjerd, Iran	B4	46
Borz'a, Russia	G17	24
Bosa, Italy	I3	14
Bosanska Gradiška, Bos.	D12	14
Bosanska Krupa, Bos.	E11	14
Bosanski Novi, Bos.	D11	14
Bosanski Petrovac, Bos.	E11	14
Bosaso, Som.	F4	46
Boscobel, Wi., U.S.	E3	126
Boshan, China	D10	26
Bosnia and Hercegovina, ctry., Eur.	E12	14
Bosporus see İstanbul Boğazı, strt., Tur.	H13	16
Bosque, co., Tx., U.S.	D4	120
Bossangoa, Cen. Afr. Rep.	G9	42
Bossembélé, Cen. Afr. Rep.	G9	42
Bossier, co., La., U.S.	B2	95
Bossier City, La., U.S.	B2	95
Bosten Hu, l., China	C4	26
Boston, Eng., U.K.	I12	7
Boston, Ga., U.S.	F3	87
Boston, Ma., U.S.	B5	98
Boston Bay, b., Ma., U.S.	B6	98
Boston Mountains, mts., Ar., U.S.	B2	81
Boswell, In., U.S.	C3	91
Boswell, Ok., U.S.	C6	113
Boswell, Pa., U.S.	F3	115
Botād, India	I4	38
Boteti, stm., Bots.	F4	44
Botetourt, co., Va., U.S.	C3	123
Bothell, Wa., U.S.	B3	124
Bothnia, Gulf of, b., Eur.	E12	6
Bothwell, Ont., Can.	E3	73
Botkins, Oh., U.S.	B1	112
Botoşani, Rom.	B10	16
Botswana, ctry., Afr.	F4	44
Bottenhavet (Selkämeri), b., Eur.	F12	6
Bottenviken (Perämeri), b., Eur.	D14	6
Bottineau, N.D., U.S.	A5	111
Bottineau, co., N.D., U.S.	A4	111
Botucatu, Braz.	G4	57
Botwood, Newf., Can.	D4	72
Bouaflé, I.C.	G4	42
Bouaké, I.C.	G4	42
Bouar, Cen. Afr. Rep.	G9	42
Bou Arada, Tun.	M4	14
Boucherville, Que., Can.	D4	74
Bouctouche, N.B., Can.	C5	71
Boudreaux, Lake, l., La., U.S.	E5	95
Bou Ficha, Tun.	M5	14
Bougainville Reef, rf., Austl.	C9	50
Bougouni, Mali	F4	42
Bouillon, Bel.	F5	8
Boulder, Co., U.S.	A5	83
Boulder, Mt., U.S.	D4	103
Boulder, co., Co., U.S.	A5	83
Boulder City, Nv., U.S.	H7	105
Boulevard Heights, Md., U.S.	f9	97
Boulogne-Billancourt, Fr.	D9	10
Boulogne-sur-Gesse, Fr.	I7	10
Boulogne-sur-Mer, Fr.	B8	10
Bouna, I.C.	G5	42
Boundary, co., Id., U.S.	A2	89
Boundary Bay, b., Wa., U.S.	A3	124
Boundary Peak, mtn., Nv., U.S.	F3	105
Bound Brook, N.J., U.S.	B3	107
Bountiful, Ut., U.S.	C4	121
Bourbeuse, stm., Mo., U.S.	C6	102
Bourbon, In., U.S.	B5	91
Bourbon, Mo., U.S.	C6	102
Bourbon, co., Ks., U.S.	E9	93
Bourbon, co., Ky., U.S.	B5	94
Bourbonnais, Il., U.S.	B6	90
Bourbonnais, hist. reg., Fr.	F9	10
Bourbonne-les-Bains, Fr.	E12	10
Bourem, Mali	E5	42
Bourg, La., U.S.	E5	95
Bourganeuf, Fr.	G8	10
Bourg-en-Bresse, Fr.	F12	10
Bourges, Fr.	E9	10
Bourg-Lastic, Fr.	G9	10
Bourgogne, hist. reg., Fr.	E11	10
Bourgoin, Fr.	G12	10
Bourg-Saint-Andéol, Fr.	H11	10
Bourg-Saint-Maurice, Fr.	G13	10
Bourke, Austl.	F9	50
Bournemouth, Eng., U.K.	K11	7
Bou Saâda, Alg.	A6	42
Bouse, Az., U.S.	D2	80
Boussac, Fr.	F9	10
Bousso, Chad	F9	42
Boutte, La., U.S.	k11	95
Bøvågen, Nor.	F5	6
Bovalino Marina, Italy	K11	14
Bovec, Slo.	C8	14
Bøverdal, Nor.	F7	6
Bovey, Mn., U.S.	C5	100
Bovina, Tx., U.S.	B1	120
Bow, N.H., U.S.	D3	106
Bow, stm., Alta., Can.	D4	68
Bowden, Alta., Can.	D4	68
Bowdish Reservoir, res., R.I., U.S.	B1	116
Bowdon, Ga., U.S.	C1	87
Bowen, Austl.	C9	50
Bowie, Az., U.S.	E6	80
Bowie, Md., U.S.	C4	97
Bowie, Tx., U.S.	C4	120
Bowie, co., Tx., U.S.	C5	120
Bow Island, Alta., Can.	E5	68
Bow Lake, l., N.H., U.S.	D4	106
Bowling Green, Fl., U.S.	E5	86
Bowling Green, Ky., U.S.	D3	94
Bowling Green, Mo., U.S.	B6	102
Bowling Green, Oh., U.S.	A2	112
Bowling Green, S.C., U.S.	A5	117
Bowling Green, Va., U.S.	B5	123
Bowman, Ga., U.S.	B3	87
Bowman, N.D., U.S.	C2	111
Bowman, S.C., U.S.	E6	117
Bowman, co., N.D., U.S.	C2	111
Bowman Creek, stm., Pa., U.S.	m16	115
Bowman-Haley Lake, res., N.D., U.S.	C2	111
Bowron, stm., B.C., Can.	C7	69
Bowstring Lake, l., Mn., U.S.	C5	100
Box Butte, co., Ne., U.S.	B2	104
Box Butte Reservoir, res., Ne., U.S.	B2	104
Box Elder, S.D., U.S.	C2	118
Box Elder, co., Ut., U.S.	B2	121
Boxford, Ma., U.S.	A6	98
Boxian, China	B4	28
Boyce, La., U.S.	C3	95
Boyceville, Wi., U.S.	C1	126
Boyd, Tx., U.S.	C4	120
Boyd, co., Ky., U.S.	B7	94
Boyd, co., Ne., U.S.	B7	104
Boyd Lake, l., Me., U.S.	C4	96
Boyer, stm., Ia., U.S.	C2	92
Boyertown, Pa., U.S.	F10	115
Boykins, Va., U.S.	D5	123
Boyle, Alta., Can.	B4	68
Boyle, Ire.	H4	7
Boyle, Ms., U.S.	B3	101
Boyle, co., Ky., U.S.	C5	94
Boyne City, Mi., U.S.	C6	99
Boynton Beach, Fl., U.S.	F6	86
Boysen Reservoir, res., Wy., U.S.	C4	127
Boys Town, Ne., U.S.	g12	104
Bozburun, Tur.	M12	16
Bozeman, Mt., U.S.	E5	103
Bozeman Pass, Mt., U.S.	E6	103
Bozoum, Cen. Afr. Rep.	G9	42
Bra, Italy	E2	14
Bracciano, Italy	G7	14
Bracebridge, Ont., Can.	B5	73
Bräcke, Swe.	E10	6
Bracken, co., Ky., U.S.	B5	94
Brackenridge, Pa., U.S.	h15	115
Brackettville, Tx., U.S.	E2	120
Braddock, Pa., U.S.	k14	115
Braddock Heights, Md., U.S.	B2	97
Braddock Point, c., S.C., U.S.	G6	117
Bradenton, Fl., U.S.	E4	86
Bradenville, Pa., U.S.	F3	115
Bradford, Ont., Can.	C5	73
Bradford, Eng., U.K.	H11	7
Bradford, Ar., U.S.	B4	81
Bradford, Oh., U.S.	B1	112
Bradford, R.I., U.S.	F2	116
Bradford, Tn., U.S.	A3	119
Bradford, Vt., U.S.	D4	122
Bradford, co., Fl., U.S.	C4	86
Bradford, co., Pa., U.S.	C8	115
Bradfordwoods, Pa., U.S.	h13	115
Bradley, Il., U.S.	B6	90
Bradley, Me., U.S.	D4	96
Bradley, W.V., U.S.	D3	125
Bradley, co., Ar., U.S.	D3	81
Bradley, co., Tn., U.S.	D9	119
Bradley Beach, N.J., U.S.	C4	107
Bradner, Oh., U.S.	A2	112
Bradshaw, Mt., U.S.	B5	97
Bradshaw Mountains, mts., Az., U.S.	C3	80
Brady, Tx., U.S.	D3	120
Braga, Port.	D3	12
Bragado, Arg.	D4	56
Bragança, Port.	D5	12
Braham, Mn., U.S.	E5	100
Brāhmanbāria, Bngl.	I14	38
Brāhmani, stm., India	J11	38
Brahmaputra (Yarlung), stm., Asia	G15	38
Braich y Pwll, c., Wales, U.K.	I8	7
Braidwood, Il., U.S.	B5	90
Brăila, Rom.	D11	16
Brainerd, Mn., U.S.	D4	100
Braintree, Ma., U.S.	B5	98
Brake, Ger.	B8	8
Brampton, Ont., Can.	D5	73
Bramsche, Ger.	C7	8
Bramwell, W.V., U.S.	D3	125
Branch, co., Mi., U.S.	G5	99
Branch, stm., R.I., U.S.	B3	116
Branch, stm., Wi., U.S.	h10	126
Branch Lake, l., Me., U.S.	D4	96
Branch Village, R.I., U.S.	B3	116
Branchville, S.C., U.S.	E6	117
Branco, stm., Braz.	C6	54
Brandberg, mtn., Nmb.	F2	44
Brandbu, Nor.	F8	6
Brandenburg, Ger.	C12	8
Brandenburg, Ky., U.S.	C3	94
Brandon, Man., Can.	E2	70
Brandon, Fl., U.S.	E4	86
Brandon, Ms., U.S.	C4	101
Brandon, S.C., U.S.	B3	117
Brandon, S.D., U.S.	D9	118
Brandon, Vt., U.S.	D2	122
Brandon, Wi., U.S.	E5	126
Brandvlei, S. Afr.	H4	44
Brandy Peak, mtn., Or., U.S.	E3	114
Brandywine, Md., U.S.	C4	97
Brandywine Creek, stm., U.S.	A3	85
Branford, Ct., U.S.	D4	84
Branford Hills, Ct., U.S.	D4	84
Br'ansk, Russia	H17	18
Branson, Mo., U.S.	E4	102
Brantford, Ont., Can.	D4	73
Brantley, Al., U.S.	D3	78
Brantley, co., Ga., U.S.	E4	87
Brantôme, Fr.	G7	10
Brant Rock, Ma., U.S.	B6	98
Brantville, N.B., Can.	B5	71
Bras d'Or Lake, l., N.S., Can.	D9	71
Brasília, Braz.	C5	57
Braşov, Rom.	D9	16
Brasstown Bald, mtn., Ga., U.S.	B3	87
Brassua Lake, res., Me., U.S.	C3	96
Bratenahl, Oh., U.S.	g9	112
Bratislava, Czech.	G17	8

Name	Map Ref	Page
Bratsk, Russia	F14	24
Bratskoje Vodochranilišče, res., Russia	F14	24
Brattleboro, Vt., U.S.	F3	122
Braunau [am Inn], Aus.	G13	8
Braunschweig, Ger.	C10	8
Brava, Som.	H3	46
Brava, Costa, Spain	D15	12
Bravo del Norte (Rio Grande), stm., N.A.	F6	76
Brawley, Ca., U.S.	F6	82
Brawley Peaks, mts., Nv., U.S.	E3	105
Braxton, co., W.V., U.S.	C4	125
Bray, Ire.	H6	7
Bray, Ok., U.S.	C4	113
Bray Island, i., N.W. Ter., Can.	C17	66
Braymer, Mo., U.S.	B4	102
Brazeau, stm., Alta., Can.	C2	68
Brazil, In., U.S.	E3	91
Brazil, ctry., S.A.	E7	54
Brazoria, In., U.S.	r14	120
Brazoria, co., Tx., U.S.	E5	120
Brazos, co., Tx., U.S.	D4	120
Brazos, stm., Tx., U.S.	D4	120
Brazzaville, Congo	B3	44
Brčko, Bos.	E2	16
Brea, Ca., U.S.	n13	82
Breakenridge, Mount, mtn., B.C., Can.	E7	69
Breathitt, co., Ky., U.S.	C6	94
Breaux Bridge, La., U.S.	D4	95
Brebes, Indon.	m14	33a
Breckenridge, Co., U.S.	B4	83
Breckenridge, Mi., U.S.	E6	99
Breckenridge, Mn., U.S.	D2	100
Breckenridge, Tx., U.S.	C3	120
Breckinridge, co., Ky., U.S.	C3	94
Brecksville, Oh., U.S.	A4	112
Brecon Beacons National Park, Wales, U.K.	J9	7
Breda, Neth.	D4	8
Bredstedt, Ger.	A8	8
Breese, Il., U.S.	E4	90
Bréhal, Fr.	D5	10
Brekstad, Nor.	E7	6
Bremen, Ger.	B8	8
Bremen, Ga., U.S.	C1	87
Bremen, In., U.S.	A5	91
Bremen, Oh., U.S.	C3	112
Bremer, co., Ia., U.S.	B5	92
Bremerhaven, Ger.	B8	8
Bremerton, Wa., U.S.	B3	124
Bremond, Tx., U.S.	D4	120
Brenham, Tx., U.S.	D4	120
Brenner Pass, Eur.	B6	14
Breno, Italy	D5	14
Brent, Al., U.S.	C2	78
Brent, Fl., U.S.	u14	86
Brenton Point, c., R.I., U.S.	F5	116
Brentwood, Ca., U.S.	h9	82
Brentwood, Md., U.S.	f9	97
Brentwood, Mo., U.S.	f13	102
Brentwood, N.Y., U.S.	E7	109
Brentwood, Pa., U.S.	k14	115
Brentwood, S.C., U.S.	k11	117
Brentwood, Tn., U.S.	A5	119
Brescia, Italy	D5	14
Breslau see Wrocław, Pol.	D17	8
Bressanone, Italy	C6	14
Bressuire, Fr.	F6	10
Brest, Bela.	I6	18
Brest, Fr.	D2	10
Bretagne, hist. reg., Fr.	D3	10
Breton Islands, is., La., U.S.	E6	95
Breton Sound, strt., La., U.S.	E6	95
Brevard, N.C., U.S.	f10	110
Brevard, co., Fl., U.S.	E6	86
Brevoort Lake, l., Mi., U.S.	B6	99
Brewer, Me., U.S.	D4	96
Brewster, Ma., U.S.	C7	98
Brewster, N.Y., U.S.	D7	109
Brewster, Oh., U.S.	B4	112
Brewster, Wa., U.S.	A6	124
Brewster, co., Tx., U.S.	E1	120
Brewster Islands, is., Ma., U.S.	g12	98
Brewton, Al., U.S.	D2	78
Brežice, Slo.	D10	14
Bria, Cen. Afr. Rep.	G10	42
Brian Boru Peak, mtn., B.C., Can.	B4	69
Briançon, Fr.	H13	10
Brian Head, mtn., Ut., U.S.	F3	121
Briare, Fr.	E9	10
Briceville, Tn., U.S.	C9	119
Brick [Township], N.J., U.S.	C4	107
Bricquebec, Fr.	C5	10
Bridal Veil Falls, wtfl, Ut., U.S.	C4	121
Bridgehampton, N.Y., U.S.	n16	109
Bridgeport, Al., U.S.	A4	78
Bridgeport, Ct., U.S.	E3	84
Bridgeport, Il., U.S.	E6	90
Bridgeport, Mi., U.S.	E7	99
Bridgeport, Ne., U.S.	C2	104
Bridgeport, Oh., U.S.	B5	112
Bridgeport, Pa., U.S.	o20	115
Bridgeport, Tx., U.S.	C4	120
Bridgeport, Wa., U.S.	B6	124
Bridgeport, W.V., U.S.	B4	125
Bridger, Mt., U.S.	E8	103
Bridger Peak, mtn., Wy., U.S.	E5	127
Bridger Range, mts., Mt., U.S.	E6	103
Bridgeton, Mo., U.S.	C7	102
Bridgeton, N.J., U.S.	E2	107
Bridgetown, Barb.	H18	64
Bridgetown, N.S., Can.	E4	71
Bridgeville, De., U.S.	F3	85
Bridgeville, Pa., U.S.	k13	115
Bridgewater, Ma., U.S.	C6	98
Bridgewater, N.J., U.S.	B3	107
Bridgewater, Va., U.S.	B4	123
Bridgman, Mi., U.S.	G4	99
Bridgton, Me., U.S.	D2	96
Bridgwater, Eng., U.K.	J9	7
Bridlington, Eng., U.K.	G12	7
Briec, Fr.	D2	10
Brielle, N.J., U.S.	C4	107
Brienne-le-Château, Fr.	D11	10
Brienz, Switz.	F15	10
Brig, Switz.	F14	10
Brigantine, N.J., U.S.	E4	107
Brigantine Beach, N.J., U.S.	E4	107
Brigden, Ont., Can.	E2	73
Briggs Marsh, sw., R.I., U.S.	F6	116
Brigham City, Ut., U.S.	B3	121
Brighton, Ont., Can.	C7	73
Brighton, Eng., U.K.	K12	7
Brighton, Al., U.S.	B3	78
Brighton, Co., U.S.	B6	83
Brighton, Il., U.S.	D3	90
Brighton, Ia., U.S.	C6	92
Brighton, Mi., U.S.	F7	99
Brighton, N.Y., U.S.	B3	109
Brighton, Tn., U.S.	B2	119
Brighton Indian Reservation, Fl., U.S.	E5	86
Brihuega, Spain	E9	12
Brilliant, Al., U.S.	A2	78
Brilliant, Oh., U.S.	B5	112
Brillion, Wi., U.S.	D5	126
Brilon, Ger.	D8	8
Brimfield, Il., U.S.	C4	90
Brindisi, Italy	I12	14
Brinkley, Ar., U.S.	C4	81
Brinnon, Wa., U.S.	B3	124
Brioude, Fr.	G10	10
Brisbane, Austl.	E10	50
Briscoe, co., Tx., U.S.	B2	120
Bristol, N.B., Can.	C2	71
Bristol, Eng., U.K.	J10	7
Bristol, Ct., U.S.	C4	84
Bristol, In., U.S.	A6	91
Bristol, N.H., U.S.	C3	106
Bristol, R.I., U.S.	D5	116
Bristol, Tn., U.S.	C11	119
Bristol, Vt., U.S.	C2	122
Bristol, Va., U.S.	f9	123
Bristol, co., Ma., U.S.	C5	98
Bristol, co., R.I., U.S.	D5	116
Bristol Bay, b., Ak., U.S.	D7	79
Bristol Channel, strt., U.K.	J8	7
Bristol [Township], Pa., U.S.	F12	115
Bristow, Ok., U.S.	B5	113
British Columbia, prov., Can.	C6	69
British Honduras see Belize, ctry., N.A.	F3	64
British Indian Ocean Territory, dep., A.	G17	2
British Mountains, mts., N.A.	C5	66
British Solomon Islands see Solomon Islands, ctry., Oc.	G23	2
Britstown, S. Afr.	H4	44
Britt, Ia., U.S.	A4	92
Brittany see Bretagne, hist. reg., Fr.	D3	10
Britton, S.D., U.S.	B8	118
Brive-la-Gaillarde, Fr.	G8	10
Briviesca, Spain	C8	12
Brno, Czech.	F16	8
Broach, India	B2	37
Broad, stm., S.C., U.S.	C5	117
Broad Brook, Ct., U.S.	B5	84
Broadford, Scot., U.K.	D7	7
Broadkill, stm., De., U.S.	E4	85
Broadkill Beach, De., U.S.	E5	85
Broad Law, mtn., Scot., U.K.	F9	7
Broad Run, stm., Va., U.S.	g11	123
Broadus, Mt., U.S.	E11	103
Broadview Heights, Oh., U.S.	h9	112
Broadwater, co., Mt., U.S.	D5	103
Broadway, N.C., U.S.	B3	110
Broadway, Va., U.S.	B4	123
Brockport, N.Y., U.S.	B3	109
Brockton, Ma., U.S.	B5	98
Brockton Reservoir, res., Ma., U.S.	h11	98
Brockville, Ont., Can.	C9	73
Brockway, Pa., U.S.	D4	115
Brodeur Peninsula, pen., N.W. Ter., Can.	B15	66
Brodhead, Ky., U.S.	C5	94
Brodhead, Wi., U.S.	F4	126
Brodheadsville, Pa., U.S.	E11	115
Broken Arrow, Ok., U.S.	A6	113
Broken Bow, Ne., U.S.	C6	104
Broken Bow, Ok., U.S.	C7	113
Broken Bow Lake, res., Ok., U.S.	C7	113
Brokopondo, Sur.	B8	54
Brome, Lac, l., Que., Can.	D5	74
Bromptonville, Que., Can.	D6	74
Bromsgrove, Eng., U.K.	I10	7
Bronlund Peak, mtn., B.C., Can.	E7	66
Brønnøysund, Nor.	D9	6
Bronson, Mi., U.S.	G5	99
Bronte, Italy	L9	14
Bronx, co., N.Y., U.S.	E7	109
Bronxville, N.Y., U.S.	h13	109
Brook, In., U.S.	C3	91
Brooke, co., W.V., U.S.	A4	125
Brookfield, N.S., Can.	D6	71
Brookfield, Ct., U.S.	D2	84
Brookfield, Il., U.S.	k9	90
Brookfield, Mo., U.S.	B4	102
Brookfield, Va., U.S.	*B5	123
Brookfield, Wi., U.S.	m11	126
Brookfield Center, Ct., U.S.	D2	84
Brookhaven, Ms., U.S.	D3	101
Brookhaven, W.V., U.S.	h11	125
Brookings, Or., U.S.	E2	114
Brookings, S.D., U.S.	C9	118
Brookings, co., S.D., U.S.	C9	118
Brookland, Ar., U.S.	B5	81
Brooklandville, Md., U.S.	B4	97
Brooklet, Ga., U.S.	D5	87
Brookline, Ma., U.S.	B5	98
Brooklyn, N.S., Can.	E5	71
Brooklyn, Ct., U.S.	B8	84
Brooklyn, Ia., U.S.	C5	92
Brooklyn, Mi., U.S.	F6	99
Brooklyn, Ms., U.S.	D4	101
Brooklyn, Oh., U.S.	h9	112
Brooklyn, S.C., U.S.	B6	117
Brooklyn, Wi., U.S.	F4	126
Brooklyn Center, Mn., U.S.	m12	100
Brooklyn Park, Md., U.S.	h11	97
Brooklyn Park, Mn., U.S.	m12	100
Brookneal, Va., U.S.	C4	123
Brook Park, Oh., U.S.	h9	112
Brookport, Il., U.S.	F5	90
Brooks, Alta., Can.	D5	68
Brooks, Ky., U.S.	g11	94
Brooks, co., Ga., U.S.	F3	87
Brooks, co., Tx., U.S.	F3	120
Brooks Air Force Base, mil., Tx., U.S.	k7	120
Brookshire, Tx., U.S.	E5	120
Brookside, Al., U.S.	f7	78
Brookside, De., U.S.	B3	85
Brooks Range, mts., Ak., U.S.	B9	79
Brookston, In., U.S.	C4	91
Brooksville, Fl., U.S.	D4	86
Brooksville, Ky., U.S.	B5	94
Brooksville, Ms., U.S.	B5	101
Brookville, In., U.S.	F8	91
Brookville, Oh., U.S.	C1	112
Brookville, Pa., U.S.	D3	115
Brookville Lake, res., In., U.S.	E7	91
Brookwood, Al., U.S.	B2	78
Brookwood, N.J., U.S.	C4	107
Broomall, Pa., U.S.	p20	115
Broome, Austl.	C4	50
Broome, co., N.Y., U.S.	C5	109
Broomfield, Co., U.S.	B5	83
Broons, Fr.	D4	10
Brossard, Que., Can.	q20	74
Brou, Fr.	D8	10
Broussard, La., U.S.	D4	95
Broward, co., Fl., U.S.	F6	86
Browerville, Mn., U.S.	D4	100
Brown, co., Il., U.S.	D3	90
Brown, co., In., U.S.	F5	91
Brown, co., Ks., U.S.	C8	93
Brown, co., Mn., U.S.	F4	100
Brown, co., Oh., U.S.	D2	112
Brown, co., S.D., U.S.	B7	118
Brown, co., Tx., U.S.	D3	120
Brown, co., Wi., U.S.	D6	126
Brown, Point, c., Wa., U.S.	C1	124
Brown City, Mi., U.S.	E8	99
Brown Deer, Wi., U.S.	m12	126
Brownfield, Tx., U.S.	C1	120
Browning, Mt., U.S.	B3	103
Brownlee Dam, U.S.	E2	89
Brownlee Reservoir, res., U.S.	C10	114
Browns, stm., Vt., U.S.	B2	122
Browns Branch, stm., De., U.S.	E3	85
Brownsburg, In., U.S.	E5	91
Brownsburg, Que., Can.	D3	74
Brownsdale, Mn., U.S.	G6	100
Browns Inlet, b., N.C., U.S.	C5	110
Browns Mills, N.J., U.S.	D3	107
Browns Peak, mtn., Az., U.S.	D4	80
Brownstown, In., U.S.	G5	91
Browns Valley, Mn., U.S.	E2	100
Brownsville, Fl., U.S.	s13	86
Brownsville, Ky., U.S.	C3	94
Brownsville, Or., U.S.	C4	114
Brownsville, Pa., U.S.	F2	115
Brownsville, Tn., U.S.	B2	119
Brownsville, Tx., U.S.	G4	120
Brownton, Mn., U.S.	F4	100
Brownville, Me., U.S.	C3	96
Brownville Junction, Me., U.S.	C3	96
Brownwood, Tx., U.S.	D3	120
Brownwood, Lake, res., Tx., U.S.	D3	120
Broxton, Ga., U.S.	E4	87
Bruay-en-Artois, Fr.	B9	10
Bruce, Ms., U.S.	B4	101
Bruce, Wi., U.S.	C2	126
Bruce, Mount, mtn., Austl.	D3	50
Bruce National Park, Ont., Can.	B3	73
Bruce Peninsula, pen., Ont., Can.	B3	73
Bruceton, Tn., U.S.	A3	119
Bruchsal, Ger.	F8	8
Bruck an der Leitha, Aus.	H16	8
Bruck an der Mur, Aus.	H15	8
Bruderheim, Alta., Can.	C4	68
Brugge, Bel.	D3	8
Bruin Point, mtn., Ut., U.S.	D5	121
Brule, co., S.D., U.S.	D6	118
Brule, stm., U.S.	C5	126
Brule Lake, l., Mn., U.S.	k9	100
Brundidge, Al., U.S.	D4	78
Bruneau, stm., Id., U.S.	G3	89
Brunei, ctry., Asia	E5	32
Brunico, Italy	C6	14
Brunkeberg, Nor.	G7	6
Bruno, Sask., Can.	E3	75
Brunsbüttel, Ger.	B9	8
Brunswick, Ga., U.S.	E5	87
Brunswick, Me., U.S.	E3	96
Brunswick, Md., U.S.	B2	97
Brunswick, Mo., U.S.	B4	102
Brunswick, Oh., U.S.	A4	112
Brunswick, co., N.C., U.S.	C4	110
Brunswick, co., Va., U.S.	D5	123
Brunswick Naval Air Station, mil., Me., U.S.	E3	96
Brush, Co., U.S.	A7	83
Brushy Mountains, mts., N.C., U.S.	B1	110
Brus Laguna, Hond.	G5	64
Brusly, La., U.S.	D4	95
Brussels see Bruxelles, Bel.	E4	8
Brussels, Ont., Can.	D3	73
Bruxelles (Brussel), Bel.	E4	8
Bryan, Oh., U.S.	A1	112
Bryan, Tx., U.S.	D4	120
Bryan, co., Ga., U.S.	D5	87
Bryan, co., Ok., U.S.	D5	113
Bryans Road, Md., U.S.	C3	97
Bryant, Ar., U.S.	C3	81
Bryantville, Ma., U.S.	B6	98
Bryce Canyon National Park, Ut., U.S.	F3	121
Bryn Mawr, Wa., U.S.	e11	124
Bryson City, N.C., U.S.	f9	110
Brzeg, Pol.	E17	8
Bsharrī, Leb.	B5	40
Bucaramanga, Col.	D6	58
Buccaneer Archipelago, is., Austl.	C4	50
Buchanan, Lib.	G3	42
Buchanan, Ga., U.S.	C1	87
Buchanan, Mi., U.S.	G4	99
Buchanan, Va., U.S.	C3	123
Buchanan, co., Ia., U.S.	B6	92
Buchanan, co., Mo., U.S.	B3	102
Buchanan, co., Va., U.S.	e9	123
Buchan Gulf, b., N.W. Ter., Can.	B18	66
Buchans, Newf., Can.	D3	72
Buchara, Uzb.	J10	22
Bucharest see Bucureşti, Rom.	E10	16
Buchholz, Ger.	B9	8
Buckatunna, Ms., U.S.	D5	101
Bückeburg, Ger.	C9	8
Buckeye, Az., U.S.	D3	80
Buckeye Lake, Oh., U.S.	C3	112
Buckhannon, W.V., U.S.	C4	125
Buck Hill Falls, Pa., U.S.	D11	115
Buckhorn Lake, res., Ky., U.S.	C6	94
Buckingham, Que., Can.	D2	74
Buckingham, co., Va., U.S.	C4	123
Buckley, Wa., U.S.	B3	124
Bucklin, Ks., U.S.	E4	93
Bucklin, Mo., U.S.	B5	102
Buckner, Mo., U.S.	h11	102
Bucks, co., Pa., U.S.	F11	115
Buckskin Mountains, mts., Az., U.S.	C2	80
Bucksport, Me., U.S.	D4	96
Bucksport, S.C., U.S.	D9	117
Bucureşti (Bucharest), Rom.	E10	16
Bucyrus, Oh., U.S.	B3	112
Buda, Tx., U.S.	D4	120
Budapest, Hung.	H19	8
Budaun, India	F8	38
Budd Lake, l., N.J., U.S.	B3	107
Buddusò, Italy	I4	14
Bude, Eng., U.K.	K8	7
Bude, Ms., U.S.	D3	101
Buea, Cam.	H7	42
Buechel, Ky., U.S.	B4	94
Buena, N.J., U.S.	D3	107
Buena Park, Ca., U.S.	n12	82
Buena Vista, Bol.	G6	54
Buena Vista, Co., U.S.	C4	83
Buena Vista, Fl., U.S.	D4	86
Buena Vista, Va., U.S.	C3	123
Buena Vista, co., Ia., U.S.	B2	92
Buenópolis, Braz.	D6	57
Buenos Aires, Arg.	C5	56
Buffalo, Ia., U.S.	C7	92
Buffalo, Ks., U.S.	E8	93
Buffalo, Mn., U.S.	E5	100
Buffalo, Mo., U.S.	D4	102
Buffalo, N.Y., U.S.	C2	109
Buffalo, Ok., U.S.	A2	113
Buffalo, S.C., U.S.	B4	117
Buffalo, Tx., U.S.	D5	120
Buffalo, W.V., U.S.	C3	125
Buffalo, Wi., U.S.	D2	126
Buffalo, Wy., U.S.	B6	127
Buffalo, co., Ne., U.S.	D6	104
Buffalo, co., S.D., U.S.	C6	118
Buffalo, co., Wi., U.S.	D2	126
Buffalo, stm., Ar., U.S.	B3	81
Buffalo, stm., Mn., U.S.	D2	100
Buffalo, stm., Tn., U.S.	B4	119
Buffalo, stm., Wi., U.S.	D2	126
Buffalo Bill Reservoir, res., Wy., U.S.	B3	127
Buffalo Center, Ia., U.S.	A4	92
Buffalo Creek, stm., W.V., U.S.	f8	125
Buffalo Creek, stm., W.V., U.S.	h10	125
Buffalo Creek, stm., W.V., U.S.	n12	125
Buffalo Grove, Il., U.S.	h9	90
Buffalo Lake, Mn., U.S.	F4	100
Buffalo Lake, l., Alta., Can.	C4	68
Buffalo Lake, l., N.W. Ter., Can.	D9	66
Buffalo Lake, res., Tx., U.S.	B1	120
Buffalo Lake, res., Wi., U.S.	E4	126
Buffumville Lake, res., Ma., U.S.	B4	98
Buford, Ga., U.S.	B2	87
Bug, stm., Eur.	E12	4
Buga, Col.	F4	58
Bugøynes, Nor.	B17	6
Bugsuk Island, i., Phil.	D6	32
Bugul'ma, Russia	G8	22
Buhl, Id., U.S.	G4	89
Buhl, Mn., U.S.	C6	100
Buhler, Ks., U.S.	D6	93
Buies Creek, N.C., U.S.	B4	110
Buj, Russia	C24	18
Bujalance, Spain	H7	12
Bujaraloz, Spain	D11	12
Bujumbura, Bdi.	B5	44
Bukačača, Russia	G17	24
Bukama, Zaire	C5	44
Bukavu, Zaire	B5	44
Bukittinggi, Indon.	F3	32
Bukoba, Tan.	B6	44
Bukovina, hist. reg., Eur.	B9	16
Bula, Indon.	F9	32
Bulan, Ky., U.S.	C6	94
Bulandshahr, India	F7	38
Bulawayo, Zimb.	F5	44
Buldan, Tur.	K12	16
Buldāna, India	B4	37
Bulgan, Mong.	B6	26
Bulgaria, ctry., Eur.	G12	4
Bulkley, stm., B.C., Can.	B4	69
Bull Creek, stm., S.D., U.S.	B2	118
Bulle, Switz.	F14	10
Bullfinch, Austl.	F3	50
Bullfrog Creek, stm., Fl., U.S.	p11	86
Bullhead City, Az., U.S.	B1	80
Bull Island, i., S.C., U.S.	F8	117
Bull Island, i., S.C., U.S.	D9	117
Bullitt, co., Ky., U.S.	C4	94
Bulloch, co., Ga., U.S.	D5	87
Bullock, Al., U.S.	C4	78
Bullock, co., Al., U.S.	C4	78
Bullock Creek, Mi., U.S.	E6	99
Bull Run, stm., Va., U.S.	g11	123
Bull Run Rock, mtn., Or., U.S.	C8	114
Bulls Bay, b., S.C., U.S.	F8	117
Bulls Gap, Tn., U.S.	C10	119
Bull Shoals, Ar., U.S.	A3	81
Bull Shoals Lake, res., U.S.	A3	81
Bully Creek Reservoir, res., Or., U.S.	C9	114
Bulsār, India	B2	37
Bulukumba, Indon.	G7	32
Bumba, Zaire	A4	44
Bumping, stm., Wa., U.S.	C4	124
Buna, Tx., U.S.	D6	120
Bunbury, Austl.	F3	50
Buncombe, co., N.C., U.S.	f10	110
Buncrana, Ire.	F5	7
Bundaberg, Austl.	D10	50
Bündi, India	H6	38
Bundoran, Ire.	G4	7
Bungo-suidō, strt., Japan	I5	30
Bunia, Zaire	A6	44
Bunker Hill, Il., U.S.	D4	90
Bunker Hill, In., U.S.	C5	91
Bunker Hill, W.V., U.S.	B6	125
Bunker Hill, W.V., U.S.	m12	125
Bunker Hill, mtn., Nv., U.S.	D4	105
Bunkerville, Nv., U.S.	G7	105
Bunkie, La., U.S.	D3	95
Bunnell, Fl., U.S.	C5	86
Buñol, Spain	F11	12
Buntok, Indon.	F5	32
Buolkalach, Russia	C17	24
Buon Me Thuot, Viet.	H10	34
Buor-Chaja, Guba, b., Russia	C20	24
Buor-Chaja, Mys, c., Russia	C20	24
Bura, Kenya	B7	44
Burao, Som.	G4	46
Buras, La., U.S.	E6	95
Buraydah, Sau. Ar.	C3	46
Burbank, Ca., U.S.	E4	82
Burbank, Il., U.S.	k9	90
Burbank, Wa., U.S.	C7	124
Burdickville, R.I., U.S.	F2	116
Burdur, Tur.	H14	4
Burdwān, India	I12	38
Bureau, co., Il., U.S.	B4	90
Bureinskij Chrebet, mts., Russia	G20	24
Bureja, stm., Russia	G20	24
Burfjord, Nor.	B13	6
Burgas, Bul.	G11	16
Bur Gavo, Som.	B8	44
Burgaw, N.C., U.S.	C5	110
Burg [bei Magdeburg], Ger.	C11	8
Burgdorf, Switz.	E14	10
Burgeo, Newf., Can.	E3	72
Burgettstown, Pa., U.S.	F1	115
Burghausen, Ger.	G12	8
Burghūth, Sabkhat al-, l., Syria	B7	40
Burgin, China	B4	26
Burgin, Ky., U.S.	C5	94
Burglengenfeld, Ger.	F12	8
Burgos, Spain	C8	12
Burgsteinfurt, Ger.	C7	8
Burgundy see Bourgogne, hist. reg., Fr.	E11	10
Burhaniye, Tur.	J10	16
Burhānpur, India	B4	37
Burica, Punta, c., N.A.	J6	64
Burin, Newf., Can.	E4	72
Burin Peninsula, pen., Newf., Can.	E4	72
Buriram, Thai.	G7	34
Burjasot, Spain	F11	12
Burkburnett, Tx., U.S.	B3	120
Burke, S.D., U.S.	D6	118
Burke, co., Ga., U.S.	C4	87
Burke, co., N.C., U.S.	B1	110
Burke, co., N.D., U.S.	A3	111
Burke Channel, strt., B.C., Can.	C4	69
Burkesville, Ky., U.S.	D4	94
Burketown, Austl.	C7	50
Burkina Faso, ctry., Afr.	F5	42
Burk's Falls, Ont., Can.	B5	73
Burleigh, co., N.D., U.S.	C5	111
Burleson, Tx., U.S.	n9	120
Burleson, co., Tx., U.S.	D4	120
Burley, Id., U.S.	G5	89
Burlingame, Ca., U.S.	h8	82
Burlingame, Ks., U.S.	D8	93
Burlington, Ont., Can.	D5	73
Burlington, Co., U.S.	B8	83
Burlington, Ia., U.S.	D6	92
Burlington, Ks., U.S.	D8	93
Burlington, Ky., U.S.	A5	94
Burlington, Ma., U.S.	f11	98
Burlington, N.J., U.S.	C3	107
Burlington, N.C., U.S.	A3	110
Burlington, N.D., U.S.	A4	111
Burlington, Vt., U.S.	C2	122
Burlington, Wa., U.S.	A3	124
Burlington, Wi., U.S.	F5	126
Burlington, co., N.J., U.S.	D3	107
Burlington Beach, In., U.S.	B3	91
Burlington Junction, Mo., U.S.	A2	102
Burma, ctry., Asia	A2	32
Burnaby, B.C., Can.	E6	69
Burnet, Tx., U.S.	D3	120
Burnet, co., Tx., U.S.	D3	120
Burnett, co., Wi., U.S.	C1	126
Burney, Ca., U.S.	B3	82
Burnham, Pa., U.S.	E6	115
Burnie, Austl.	H9	50
Burns, Or., U.S.	D7	114
Burns, Tn., U.S.	A4	119
Burns, Wy., U.S.	E8	127
Burns Flat, Ok., U.S.	B2	113
Burnside, Ky., U.S.	D5	94
Burns Lake, B.C., Can.	B5	69
Burns Paiute Indian Reservation, Or., U.S.	D7	114
Burnsville, Mn., U.S.	n12	100
Burnsville, Ms., U.S.	A5	101
Burnsville, N.C., U.S.	f10	110
Burnsville Lake, res., W.V., U.S.	C4	125
Burnt Islands, Newf., Can.	E2	72
Burnt Mills, Lake, l., Va., U.S.	k14	123
Burntside Lake, l., Mn., U.S.	C6	100
Burntwood, stm., Man., Can.	B2	70
Burravoe, Scot., U.K.	A11	7
Burr Oak, Mi., U.S.	G5	99
Burr Oak Reservoir, res., Oh., U.S.	C3	112
Burrton, Ks., U.S.	D6	93
Bursa, Tur.	G13	4
Būr Sa'īd (Port Said), Egypt	B12	42
Būr Sūdān (Port Sudan), Sudan	E13	42

Name	Map Ref	Page
Burt, co., Ne., U.S.	C9	104
Burt Lake, l., Mi., U.S.	C6	99
Burton, Mi., U.S.	F7	99
Burton, Oh., U.S.	A4	112
Burton upon Trent, Eng., U.K.	I11	7
Burtts Corner, N.B., Can.	C3	71
Buru, i., Indon.	F8	32
Burundi, ctry., Afr.	B5	44
Burwell, Ne., U.S.	C6	104
Burwick, Scot., U.K.	C10	7
Bury Saint Edmunds, Eng., U.K.	I13	7
Busalla, Italy	E3	14
Buşayrah, Syria	B7	40
Bushnell, Fl., U.S.	D4	86
Bushnell, Il., U.S.	C3	90
Bush River, b., Md., U.S.	B5	97
Buşrá ash-Shām, Syria	C5	40
Busselton, Austl.	F3	50
Busto Arsizio, Italy	D3	14
Busuanga Island, i., Phil.	C7	32
Buta, Zaire	H10	42
Butare, Rw.	B5	44
Butehaqi, China	B11	26
Bute Inlet, b., B.C., Can.	D5	69
Butler, Al., U.S.	C1	78
Butler, Ga., U.S.	D2	87
Butler, In., U.S.	B8	91
Butler, Ky., U.S.	B5	94
Butler, Mo., U.S.	C3	102
Butler, N.J., U.S.	B4	107
Butler, Oh., U.S.	B3	112
Butler, Pa., U.S.	E2	115
Butler, Wi., U.S.	m11	126
Butler, co., Al., U.S.	D3	78
Butler, co., Ia., U.S.	B5	92
Butler, co., Ks., U.S.	E7	93
Butler, co., Ky., U.S.	C3	94
Butler, co., Mo., U.S.	E7	102
Butler, co., Ne., U.S.	C8	104
Butler, co., Oh., U.S.	C1	112
Butler, co., Pa., U.S.	E2	115
Butner, N.C., U.S.	A4	110
Buttahatchee, stm., U.S.	B5	101
Butte, Mt., U.S.	E4	103
Butte, co., Ca., U.S.	C3	82
Butte, co., Id., U.S.	F5	89
Butte, co., S.D., U.S.	C2	118
Butte des Morts, Lake, l., Wi., U.S.	D5	126
Butte Mountains, mts., Nv., U.S.	D6	105
Butternut Lake, l., Wi., U.S.	C5	126
Butterworth, Malay.	L6	34
Butt of Lewis, c., Scot., U.K.	C6	7
Buttonwillow, Ca., U.S.	E4	82
Butts, co., Ga., U.S.	C3	87
Butuan, Phil.	D8	32
Butung, Pulau, i., Indon.	F7	32
Bützow, Ger.	B11	8
Buxtehude, Ger.	B9	8
Buxton, N.C., U.S.	B7	110
Büyükmenderes, stm., Tur.	L11	16
Buzançais, Fr.	F8	10
Buzău, Rom.	D10	16
Búzi, stm., Moz.	F6	44
Buzuluk, Russia	G8	22
Buzzards Bay, Ma., U.S.	C6	98
Buzzards Bay, b., Ma., U.S.	C6	98
Byam Channel, strt., N.W. Ter., Can.	A11	66
Byam Martin Island, i., N.W. Ter., Can.	A12	66
Bydgoszcz, Pol.	B18	8
Byers, Co., U.S.	B6	83
Byesville, Oh., U.S.	C4	112
Byhalia, Ms., U.S.	A4	101
Bylas, Az., U.S.	D5	80
Bylot Island, i., N.W. Ter., Can.	B17	66
Byng, Ok., U.S.	C5	113
Byrdstown, Tn., U.S.	C8	119
Byron, Ga., U.S.	D3	87
Byron, Il., U.S.	A4	90
Byron, Mn., U.S.	F6	100
Byron, Wy., U.S.	B4	127
Byrranga, Gory, mts., Russia	B14	24
Bytantaj, stm., Russia	D20	24
Bytom (Beuthen), Pol.	E18	8
Byxelkrok, Swe.	H11	6

C

Caacupé, Para.	B5	56
Cabaiguán, Cuba	C8	64
Caballo Mountains, mts., N.M., U.S.	E2	108
Caballo Reservoir, res., N.M., U.S.	E2	108
Cabanatuan, Phil.	q19	32
Cabano, Que., Can.	B9	74
Cabarrus, co., N.C., U.S.	B2	110
Cabbage Swamp, sw., Fl., U.S.	m9	86
Cabell, co., W.V., U.S.	C2	125
Cabeza del Buey, Spain	G6	12
Cabimas, Ven.	B7	58
Cabin Creek, W.V., U.S.	m13	125
Cabin Creek, stm., W.V., U.S.	m13	125
Cabinda, Ang.	C2	44
Cabinda, dept., Ang.	C2	44
Cabinet Gorge Reservoir, res., U.S.	B1	103
Cabinet Mountains, mts., Mt., U.S.	B1	103
Cabin John, Md., U.S.	C3	97
Cabo Frio, Braz.	G7	57
Cabonga, Réservoir, res., Que., Can.	k11	74
Cabool, Mo., U.S.	D5	102
Caborca, Mex.	B3	62
Cabot, Ar., U.S.	C3	81
Cabot, Mount, mtn., N.H., U.S.	A4	106
Cabot Head, c., Ont., Can.	B3	73
Cabot Strait, strt., Can.	G21	66
Cabri, Sask., Can.	G1	75
Cabrillo National Monument, Ca., U.S.	o15	82
Cabrobó, Braz.	E11	54
Cabruta, Ven.	D9	58
Çaçador, Braz.	B6	56
Čačak, Yugo.	F4	16
Cacapon, stm., W.V., U.S.	B6	125
Cáceres, Braz.	G7	54
Cáceres, Col.	D5	58
Cáceres, Spain	F5	12
Cache, Ok., U.S.	C3	113
Cache, co., Ut., U.S.	B4	121
Cache, stm., Ar., U.S.	C4	81
Cache, stm., Il., U.S.	F4	90
Cache Bay, Ont., Can.	A5	73
Cache Creek, B.C., Can.	D7	69
Cache la Poudre, stm., Co., U.S.	A5	83
Cache Mountain, mtn., Ak., U.S.	B10	79
Cache Peak, mtn., Id., U.S.	G5	89
Cachoeira, Braz.	B9	54
Cachoeira do Sul, Braz.	C6	56
Cachoeiro de Itapemirim, Braz.	F8	57
Cacólo, Ang.	D3	44
Caconda, Ang.	D3	44
Cactus Flat, pl., Nv., U.S.	F5	105
Cactus Peak, mtn., Nv., U.S.	F5	105
Caddo, Ok., U.S.	C5	113
Caddo, co., La., U.S.	B2	95
Caddo, co., Ok., U.S.	B3	113
Caddo, stm., Ar., U.S.	C2	81
Caddo Creek, stm., Ok., U.S.	C4	113
Caddo Lake, res., U.S.	B2	95
Cader Idris, mtn., Wales, U.K.	I9	7
Cadillac, Fr.	H6	10
Cadillac, Mi., U.S.	D5	99
Cadillac Mountain, mtn., Me., U.S.	D4	96
Cádiz, Spain	I5	12
Cadiz, Ky., U.S.	D2	94
Cadiz, Oh., U.S.	B4	112
Cádiz, Golfo de, b., Eur.	I4	12
Cadott, Wi., U.S.	D2	126
Caen, Fr.	C6	10
Caernarvon, Wales, U.K.	H8	7
Caesar Creek Lake, res., Oh., U.S.	C2	112
Caeté, Braz.	E7	57
Cagayan de Oro, Phil.	D7	32
Cagayan Islands, is., Phil.	D7	32
Cagda, Russia	F20	24
Cagles Mill Lake, res., In., U.S.	F4	91
Cagli, Italy	F7	14
Cagliari, Italy	J4	14
Caguas, P.R.	E14	64
Cahaba, stm., Al., U.S.	C2	78
Caha Mountains, mts., Ire.	J3	7
Cahirciveen, Ire.	J2	7
Cahokia, Il., U.S.	E3	90
Cahore Point, c., Ire.	I6	7
Cahors, Fr.	H8	10
Caiapó, Serra, mts., Braz.	D2	57
Caibarién, Cuba	C8	64
Caicara, Ven.	D9	58
Caicos Islands, is., T./C. Is.	D12	64
Caicos Passage, strt., N.A.	C11	64
Caillou Bay, b., La., U.S.	E5	95
Caillou Lake, l., La., U.S.	E5	95
Cairnbrook, Pa., U.S.	F4	115
Cairngorm Mountains, mts., Scot., U.K.	D9	7
Cairns, Austl.	C9	50
Cairo, Ga., U.S.	F2	87
Cairo, Il., U.S.	F4	90
Cairo, Ne., U.S.	D7	104
Cairo see Al-Qāhirah, Egypt	B12	42
Caiundo, Ang.	E3	44
Cajamarca, Peru	E3	54
Cajàzeiras, Braz.	E11	54
Cakovec, Cro.	C11	14
Calabar, Nig.	H7	42
Calabozo, Ven.	C9	58
Calahorra, Spain	C10	12
Calais, Fr.	B8	10
Calais, Me., U.S.	C5	96
Calais, Pas de (Strait of Dover), strt., Eur.	K14	7
Calamar, Col.	B5	58
Calamian Group, is., Phil.	C6	32
Calamocha, Spain	E10	12
Calamus, stm., Ne., U.S.	B6	104
Calanda, Spain	E11	12
Călăraşi, Rom.	E11	16
Calatayud, Spain	D10	12
Calaveras, co., Ca., U.S.	C3	82
Calcasieu, co., La., U.S.	D2	95
Calcasieu, stm., La., U.S.	D2	95
Calcasieu Lake, l., La., U.S.	E2	95
Calcasieu Pass, strt., La., U.S.	E2	95
Calçoene, Braz.	C8	54
Calcutta, India	I13	38
Calcutta, Oh., U.S.	B5	112
Calcutta Lake, l., Nv., U.S.	B2	105
Caldas da Rainha, Port.	F2	12
Calderwood, Tn., U.S.	D10	119
Caldron Falls Reservoir, res., Wi., U.S.	C5	126
Caldwell, Ks., U.S.	E6	93
Caldwell, N.J., U.S.	B4	107
Caldwell, Oh., U.S.	C4	112
Caldwell, Tx., U.S.	D4	120
Caldwell, co., Ky., U.S.	C2	94
Caldwell, co., La., U.S.	B3	95
Caldwell, co., Mo., U.S.	B3	102
Caldwell, co., N.C., U.S.	B1	110
Caldwell, co., Tx., U.S.	E4	120
Caledon, Ont., Can.	D5	73
Caledonia, Mi., U.S.	F5	99
Caledonia, Mn., U.S.	G7	100
Caledonia, Ms., U.S.	B5	101
Caledonia, N.Y., U.S.	C3	109
Caledonia, co., Vt., U.S.	C4	122
Calera, Al., U.S.	B3	78
Calera, Ok., U.S.	D5	113
Calexico, Ca., U.S.	F6	82
Calhoun, Ga., U.S.	B2	87
Calhoun, Ky., U.S.	C2	94
Calhoun, co., Al., U.S.	B4	78
Calhoun, co., Ar., U.S.	D3	81
Calhoun, co., Fl., U.S.	B1	86
Calhoun, co., Ga., U.S.	E2	87
Calhoun, co., Il., U.S.	D3	90
Calhoun, co., Ia., U.S.	B3	92
Calhoun, co., Mi., U.S.	F5	99
Calhoun, co., Ms., U.S.	B4	101
Calhoun, co., S.C., U.S.	D6	117
Calhoun, co., Tx., U.S.	E4	120
Calhoun, co., W.V., U.S.	C3	125
Calhoun City, Ms., U.S.	B4	101
Calhoun Falls, S.C., U.S.	C2	117
Cali, Col.	F4	58
Calico Rock, Ar., U.S.	A3	81
Caliente, Nv., U.S.	F7	105
Calicut, India	G3	37
California, Mo., U.S.	C5	102
California, Pa., U.S.	F2	115
California, state, U.S.	D4	82
California, Golfo de, b., Mex.	D4	62
California Aqueduct, Ca., U.S.	E4	82
Calimere, Point, c., India	G5	37
Calipatria, Ca., U.S.	F6	82
Calispell Peak, mtn., Wa., U.S.	A8	124
Calistoga, Ca., U.S.	C2	82
Calitri, Italy	I10	14
Callac, Fr.	D3	10
Callaghan, Mount, mtn., Nv., U.S.	D5	105
Callahan, co., Tx., U.S.	C3	120
Callao, Peru	F3	54
Callaway, co., Mo., U.S.	C6	102
Calling Lake, l., Alta., Can.	B4	68
Callosa de Ensarriá, Spain	G11	12
Calloway, co., Ky., U.S.	f9	94
Calmar, Alta., Can.	C4	68
Calmar, Ia., U.S.	A6	92
Caloosahatchee, stm., Fl., U.S.	F5	86
Caltagirone, Italy	L9	14
Caltanissetta, Italy	L9	14
Calumet, Que., Can.	D3	74
Calumet, Mi., U.S.	A2	99
Calumet, co., Wi., U.S.	D5	126
Calumet, Lake, l., Il., U.S.	k9	90
Calumet City, Il., U.S.	B6	90
Calunda, Ang.	D4	44
Calvert, Tx., U.S.	D4	120
Calvert, co., Md., U.S.	C4	97
Calvert City, Ky., U.S.	e9	94
Calverton, Md., U.S.	*B4	97
Calverton Park, Mo., U.S.	f13	102
Calvinia, S. Afr.	H3	44
Camacho, Mex.	E8	62
Camacupa, Ang.	D3	44
Camaguán, Ven.	C9	58
Camagüey, Cuba	D9	64
Camaná, Peru	G4	54
Camanche, Ia., U.S.	C7	92
Camano Island, i., Wa., U.S.	A3	124
Camapuã, Braz.	E1	57
Camaquã, Braz.	C6	56
Camas, Spain	H5	12
Camas, Wa., U.S.	D3	124
Camas, co., Id., U.S.	F4	89
Ca Mau, Viet.	J8	34
Cambados, Spain	C3	12
Cambay, India	I5	38
Cambodia (Kampuchea), ctry., Asia	C3	32
Cambrai, Fr.	B10	10
Cambria, Ca., U.S.	E3	82
Cambria, Wi., U.S.	E4	126
Cambria, co., Pa., U.S.	E4	115
Cambrian Mountains, mts., Wales, U.K.	I9	7
Cambridge, Ont., Can.	D4	73
Cambridge, Eng., U.K.	I13	7
Cambridge, Il., U.S.	B3	90
Cambridge, Ia., U.S.	C4	92
Cambridge, Md., U.S.	C5	97
Cambridge, Ma., U.S.	B5	98
Cambridge, Mn., U.S.	E5	100
Cambridge, Ne., U.S.	D5	104
Cambridge, N.Y., U.S.	B7	109
Cambridge, Oh., U.S.	B4	112
Cambridge, Wi., U.S.	F4	126
Cambridge Bay, N.W. Ter., Can.	C11	66
Cambridge City, In., U.S.	E7	91
Cambridge Reservoir, res., Ma., U.S.	g10	98
Cambridge Springs, Pa., U.S.	C1	115
Cambuci, Braz.	F8	57
Camden, Al., U.S.	D2	78
Camden, Ar., U.S.	D3	81
Camden, De., U.S.	D3	85
Camden, In., U.S.	C4	91
Camden, Me., U.S.	D3	96
Camden, N.J., U.S.	D2	107
Camden, N.Y., U.S.	B5	109
Camden, Oh., U.S.	C1	112
Camden, S.C., U.S.	C6	117
Camden, Tn., U.S.	A3	119
Camden, co., Ga., U.S.	F5	87
Camden, co., Mo., U.S.	C5	102
Camden, co., N.J., U.S.	D3	107
Camden, co., N.C., U.S.	A6	110
Camdenton, Mo., U.S.	D5	102
Camelback Mountain, mtn., Az., U.S.	k9	80
Cameron, Az., U.S.	B4	80
Cameron, La., U.S.	E2	95
Cameron, Mo., U.S.	B3	102
Cameron, Tx., U.S.	D4	120
Cameron, W.V., U.S.	B4	125
Cameron, Wi., U.S.	C2	126
Cameron, co., Pa., U.S.	D5	115
Cameron, co., Tx., U.S.	F4	120
Cameron Highlands, Malay.	L6	34
Cameron Hills, hills, Can.	E9	66
Cameroon, ctry., Afr.	G8	42
Cameroon Mountain, mtn., Cam.	H7	42
Cametá, Braz.	D9	54
Camilla, Ga., U.S.	E2	87
Camino, Ca., U.S.	C3	82
Camiranga, Braz.	D9	54
Camissombo, Ang.	C4	44
Cam Lo, Viet.	F9	34
Cammack Village, Ar., U.S.	C3	81
Camocim, Braz.	D10	54
Camooweal, Austl.	C7	50
Camorta Island, i., India	J2	34
Camp, co., Tx., U.S.	C5	120
Campana, Isla, i., Chile	F1	56
Campanero, Cerro, mtn., Ven.	D9	58
Campbell, Ca., U.S.	k8	82
Campbell, Fl., U.S.	D5	86
Campbell, Mo., U.S.	E7	102
Campbell, Oh., U.S.	A5	112
Campbell, co., Ky., U.S.	B5	94
Campbell, co., S.D., U.S.	B5	118
Campbell, co., Tn., U.S.	C9	119
Campbell, co., Va., U.S.	C3	123
Campbell, co., Wy., U.S.	B7	127
Campbellford, Ont., Can.	C7	73
Campbell Hill, hill, Oh., U.S.	B2	112
Campbell Lake, l., Or., U.S.	E7	114
Campbellsburg, In., U.S.	G5	91
Campbellsburg, Ky., U.S.	B4	94
Campbells Creek, stm., W.V., U.S.	m13	125
Campbellsport, Wi., U.S.	E5	126
Campbellsville, Ky., U.S.	C4	94
Campbellton, N.B., Can.	A3	71
Campbellton, Newf., Can.	D4	72
Campbelltown, Scot., U.K.	F7	7
Campeche, Mex.	H14	62
Campeche, Bahía de, b., Mex.	H13	62
Camperville, Man., Can.	D1	70
Camp Hill, Al., U.S.	C4	78
Camp Hill, Pa., U.S.	F8	115
Campina Grande, Braz.	E11	54
Campinas, Braz.	G5	57
Camp H. M. Smith Marine Corps Base, mil., Hi., U.S.	g10	88
Camp Howard Ridge, mtn., Id., U.S.	D2	89
Camp Lejeune Marine Corps Base, mil., N.C., U.S.	C5	110
Campoalegre, Col.	F5	58
Campo Alegre de Goiás, Braz.	D5	57
Campobasso, Italy	H9	14
Campobello Island, i., N.B., Can.	E3	71
Campo Belo, Braz.	F6	57
Campo de Criptana, Spain	F8	12
Campo de la Cruz, Col.	B5	58
Campo Grande, Braz.	F1	57
Campo Maior, Braz.	D10	54
Campos, Braz.	F8	57
Campos do Jordão, Braz.	G6	57
Camp Pendleton Marine Corps Base, mil., Ca., U.S.	A6	82
Camp Point, Il., U.S.	C2	90
Camp Springs, Md., U.S.	f9	97
Campti, La., U.S.	C2	95
Campton, N.H., U.S.	C3	106
Camp Verde, Az., U.S.	C4	80
Camp Verde Indian Reservation, Az., U.S.	C4	80
Camrose, Alta., Can.	C4	68
Cam Ranh, Viet.	I10	34
Canaan, Ct., U.S.	A2	84
Canaan, N.H., U.S.	C2	106
Canaan, stm., N.B., Can.	C4	71
Canada, ctry., N.A.	D14	66
Canada Bay, b., Newf., Can.	C3	72
Canada Falls Lake, res., Me., U.S.	C2	96
Canadensis, Pa., U.S.	D11	115
Canadian, Tx., U.S.	B2	120
Canadian, co., Ok., U.S.	B3	113
Canadian, stm., U.S.	D6	76
Canajoharie, N.Y., U.S.	C6	109
Canakkale, Tur.	G13	4
Çanakkale Boğazı (Dardanelles), strt., Tur.	I10	16
Canal Flats, B.C., Can.	D10	69
Canal Fulton, Oh., U.S.	B4	112
Canal Winchester, Oh., U.S.	C3	112
Canandaigua, N.Y., U.S.	C3	109
Canandaigua Lake, l., N.Y., U.S.	C3	109
Cananea, Mex.	B4	62
Cañar, Ec.	I3	58
Canaries, Islas (Canary Islands), is., Spain	C2	42
Canary Islands see Canarias, Islas, is., Spain	C2	42
Cañas, C.R.	I5	64
Canastota, N.Y., U.S.	B5	109
Canaveral, Cape, c., Fl., U.S.	D6	86
Canaveral National Seashore, Fl., U.S.	D6	86
Canavieiras, Braz.	C9	57
Canberra, Austl.	G9	50
Canby, Mn., U.S.	F2	100
Canby, Or., U.S.	B4	114
Cancale, Fr.	D5	10
Cancon, Fr.	H7	10
Cancún, Mex.	G16	62
Candeleda, Spain	E6	12
Candiac, Que., Can.	q19	74
Candle Lake, l., Sask., Can.	D3	75
Candler, co., Ga., U.S.	D4	87
Candlewood, Lake, l., Ct., U.S.	D1	84
Candlewood Isle, Ct., U.S.	D2	84
Candlewood Shores, Ct., U.S.	D2	84
Cando, N.D., U.S.	A6	111
Candor, N.C., U.S.	B3	110
Cane, La., U.S.	C2	95
Cañete, Spain	E10	12
Caney, Ks., U.S.	E8	93
Caney, stm., Ok., U.S.	A5	113
Caney Creek, stm., Tx., U.S.	r14	120
Caney Fork, stm., Tn., U.S.	C8	119
Canfield, Oh., U.S.	A5	112
Canfranc, Spain	C11	12
Cangas de Onís, Spain	B6	12
Cangombe, Ang.	D3	44
Canguçu, Braz.	C6	56
Cangzhou, China	D10	26
Caniapiscau, stm., Que., Can.	g13	74
Caniapiscau, Lac, l., Que., Can.	F19	66
Canicattì, Italy	L8	14
Canisteo, N.Y., U.S.	C3	109
Canisteo, stm., N.Y., U.S.	C3	109
Canistota, S.D., U.S.	D8	118
Cañitas, Mex.	F8	62
Çankin, Tur.	G14	4
Canmore, Alta., Can.	D3	68
Cannanore, India	G3	37
Cannelton, In., U.S.	I4	91
Cannes, Fr.	I14	10
Canning, N.S., Can.	D5	71
Cannon, co., Tn., U.S.	B5	119
Cannon, stm., Mn., U.S.	F5	100
Cannon Air Force Base, mil., N.M., U.S.	C6	108
Cannonball, stm., N.D., U.S.	C5	111
Cannon Beach, Or., U.S.	B3	114
Cannondale, Ct., U.S.	E2	84
Cannon Falls, Mn., U.S.	F6	100
Cannonsburg, Ky., U.S.	B7	94
Cannonsville Reservoir, res., N.Y., U.S.	C5	109
Canon, Ga., U.S.	B3	87
Canon City, Co., U.S.	C5	83
Canonsburg, Pa., U.S.	F1	115
Canosa [di Puglia], Italy	H11	14
Cantábrica, Cordillera, mts., Spain	B7	12
Cantalejo, Spain	D8	12
Cantanhede, Port.	E3	12
Cantaura, Ven.	C10	58
Canterbury, Eng., U.K.	J14	7
Canterbury, De., U.S.	D3	85
Canterbury Bight, N.Z.	F3	52
Can Tho, Viet.	I8	34
Canton, Ct., U.S.	B4	84
Canton, Ga., U.S.	B2	87
Canton, Il., U.S.	C3	90
Canton, Ks., U.S.	D6	93
Canton, Ma., U.S.	B5	98
Canton, Ms., U.S.	C3	101
Canton, Mo., U.S.	A6	102
Canton, N.Y., U.S.	f9	109
Canton, N.C., U.S.	f10	110
Canton, Oh., U.S.	B4	112
Canton, Ok., U.S.	A3	113
Canton, Pa., U.S.	C8	115
Canton, S.D., U.S.	D9	118
Canton, Tx., U.S.	C5	120
Canton see Guangzhou, China	L2	30
Canton Lake, res., Ok., U.S.	A3	113
Cantonment, Fl., U.S.	u14	86
Cantù, Italy	D4	14
Canutillo, Tx., U.S.	o11	120
Canyon, Tx., U.S.	B2	120
Canyon, co., Id., U.S.	F2	89
Canyon de Chelly National Monument, Az., U.S.	A6	80
Canyon Ferry Lake, res., Mt., U.S.	D5	103
Canyon Lake, Tx., U.S.	E3	120
Canyon Lake, res., Tx., U.S.	E3	120
Canyonlands National Park, Ut., U.S.	E6	121
Canyonville, Or., U.S.	E3	114
Cao Bang, Viet.	C9	34
Capac, Mi., U.S.	F8	99
Cap-à-l'Aigle, Que., Can.	B7	74
Cap-aux-Meules, Que., Can.	B8	71
Cap-de-la-Madeleine, Que., Can.	C5	74
Cape Breton Highlands National Park, N.S., Can.	C9	71
Cape Breton Island, i., N.S., Can.	C9	71
Cape Broyle, Newf., Can.	E5	72
Cape Canaveral, Fl., U.S.	D6	86
Cape Charles, Va., U.S.	C6	123
Cape Coast, Ghana	G5	42
Cape Cod Bay, b., Ma., U.S.	C7	98
Cape Cod Canal, Ma., U.S.	C6	98
Cape Cod National Seashore, Ma., U.S.	C7	98
Cape Coral, Fl., U.S.	F5	86
Cape Dorset, N.W. Ter., Can.	D17	66
Cape Elizabeth, Me., U.S.	E2	96
Cape Fear, stm., N.C., U.S.	C4	110
Cape Girardeau, Mo., U.S.	D8	102
Cape Girardeau, co., Mo., U.S.	D8	102
Cape Hatteras National Seashore, N.C., U.S.	B7	110
Cape Horn Mountain, mtn., Id., U.S.	E3	89
Cape Island, i., S.C., U.S.	E9	117
Cape Lookout National Seashore, N.C., U.S.	C6	110
Cape May, N.J., U.S.	F3	107
Cape May, co., N.J., U.S.	E3	107
Cape May Court House, N.J., U.S.	E3	107
Capers Inlet, b., S.C., U.S.	k12	117
Capers Island, i., S.C., U.S.	G6	117
Capers Island, i., S.C., U.S.	F8	117
Cape Sable Island, i., N.S., Can.	F4	71
Cape Town (Kaapstad), S. Afr.	H3	44
Cape Verde, ctry., Afr.	E11	2
Cape York Peninsula, pen., Austl.	B8	50
Cap-Haïtien, Haiti	E11	64
Capim, stm., Braz.	D9	54
Capitan, N.M., U.S.	D4	108
Capitan Mountains, mts., N.M., U.S.	D4	108
Capitan Peak, mtn., N.M., U.S.	D4	108
Capitol Heights, Ia., U.S.	e8	92
Capitol Heights, Md., U.S.	C4	97
Capitol Peak, mtn., Nv., U.S.	B4	105
Capitol Reef National Park, Ut., U.S.	E4	121
Čapljina, Bos.	F12	14
Cap-Pelé, N.B., Can.	C5	71
Capreol, Ont., Can.	p19	73
Capri, Italy	I9	14
Caprivi Strip, hist. reg., Nmb.	E4	44
Cap-Rouge, Que., Can.	n17	74
Cap-Saint-Ignace, Que., Can.	B7	74
Captain Cook, Hi., U.S.	D6	88
Captieux, Fr.	H6	10
Captiva, Fl., U.S.	F4	86
Captiva Island, i., Fl., U.S.	F4	86
Capua, Italy	H9	14
Capulin Volcano National Monument, N.M., U.S.	A6	108
Caquetá (Japurá), stm., S.A.	D5	54
Çara, Russia	F17	24
Cara, stm., Russia	F17	24
Caracaraí, Braz.	C6	54
Caracas, Ven.	B9	58
Carajás, Serra dos, mts., Braz.	E8	54
Carangola, Braz.	F7	57
Caraquet, N.B., Can.	B5	71

Name	Map Ref	Page
Caratasca, Laguna de, b., Hond.	G6	64
Caratinga, Braz.	E7	57
Carauari, Braz.	D5	54
Caravaca, Spain	G10	12
Caravelas, Braz.	D9	57
Caraway, Ar., U.S.	B5	81
Carballo, Spain	B3	12
Carberry, Man., Can.	E2	70
Carbon, co., Mt., U.S.	E7	103
Carbon, co., Pa., U.S.	E10	115
Carbon, co., Ut., U.S.	D5	121
Carbon, co., Wy., U.S.	E5	127
Carbondale, Co., U.S.	B3	83
Carbondale, Il., U.S.	F4	90
Carbondale, Ks., U.S.	D8	93
Carbondale, Pa., U.S.	C10	115
Carbonear, Newf., Can.	E5	72
Carboneras de Guadazaon, Spain	F10	12
Carbon Hill, Al., U.S.	B2	78
Carbonia, Italy	J3	14
Carcagente, Spain	F11	12
Carcassonne, Fr.	I9	10
Carcross, Yukon, Can.	D6	66
Cárdenas, Cuba	C7	64
Cárdenas, Mex.	F10	62
Cardiff, Wales, U.K.	J9	7
Cardigan, Wales, U.K.	I8	7
Cardinal, Ont., Can.	C9	73
Cardigan Bay, b., P.E.I., Can.	C7	71
Cardigan Bay, b., Wales, U.K.	I8	7
Cardington, Oh., U.S.	B3	112
Cardston, Alta., Can.	E4	68
Cardwell, Mo., U.S.	E7	102
Cardžou, Turk.	J10	22
Carencro, La., U.S.	D3	95
Carentan, Fr.	C5	10
Caretta, W.V., U.S.	D3	125
Carey, Id., U.S.	F5	89
Carey, Oh., U.S.	B2	112
Carey, Lake, l., Austl.	E4	50
Caribbean Sea	G10	64
Cariboo Mountains, mts., B.C., Can.	C7	69
Caribou, Me., U.S.	B5	96
Caribou, co., Id., U.S.	G7	89
Caribou, i., N.S., Can.	D7	71
Caribou Lake, l., Me., U.S.	C3	96
Caribou Mountains, mtn., Id., U.S.	F7	89
Caribou Mountains, mts., Alta., Can.	f7	68
Caribou Range, mts., Id., U.S.	F7	89
Carignan, Fr.	C12	10
Cariñena, Spain	D10	12
Carinhanha, Braz.	C7	57
Caripito, Ven.	B11	58
Carl Blackwell, Lake, res., Ok., U.S.	A4	113
Carleton, Mi., U.S.	F7	99
Carleton, Mount, mtn., N.B., Can.	B3	71
Carleton Place, Ont., Can.	B8	73
Carlin, Nv., U.S.	C5	105
Carlinville, Il., U.S.	D4	90
Carlisle, Eng., U.K.	G10	7
Carlisle, Ar., U.S.	C4	81
Carlisle, In., U.S.	G3	91
Carlisle, Ia., U.S.	C4	92
Carlisle, Ky., U.S.	B5	94
Carlisle, Oh., U.S.	C1	112
Carlisle, Pa., U.S.	F7	115
Carlisle, co., Ky., U.S.	f8	94
Carl Junction, Mo., U.S.	D3	102
Carlow, Ire.	I6	7
Carlsbad, Ca., U.S.	F5	82
Carlsbad, N.M., U.S.	E5	108
Carlsbad Caverns National Park, N.M., U.S.	E5	108
Carlstadt, N.J., U.S.	h8	107
Carlton, Mn., U.S.	D6	100
Carlton, Or., U.S.	B3	114
Carlton, co., Mn., U.S.	D6	100
Carlyle, Il., U.S.	E4	90
Carlyle Lake, res., Il., U.S.	E4	90
Carmacks, Yukon, Can.	D5	66
Carmagnola, Italy	E2	14
Carman, Man., Can.	E2	70
Carmanville, Newf., Can.	D4	72
Carmarthen, Wales, U.K.	J8	7
Carmaux, Fr.	H9	10
Carmel, Ca., U.S.	D3	82
Carmel, In., U.S.	E5	91
Carmel, N.Y., U.S.	D7	109
Carmel Head, c., Wales, U.K.	H8	7
Carmen, Isla, i., Mex.	E4	62
Carmen, Isla del, i., Mex.	H14	62
Carmen de Patagones, Arg.	E4	56
Carmi, Il., U.S.	E5	90
Carmi, Lake, l., Vt., U.S.	B3	122
Carmona, Spain	H6	12
Carnarvon, Austl.	D2	50
Carnarvon, S. Afr.	H4	44
Carnation, Wa., U.S.	B4	124
Carndonagh, Ire.	F5	7
Carnegie, Ok., U.S.	B3	113
Carnegie, Pa., U.S.	F1	115
Carnegie, Lake, l., Austl.	E4	50
Carneys Point, N.J., U.S.	D2	107
Carniche, Alpi, mts., Eur.	C8	14
Car Nicobar Island, i., India	J2	36
Carnsore Point, c., Ire.	I6	7
Caro, Mi., U.S.	E7	99
Carol City, Fl., U.S.	s13	86
Caroleen, N.C., U.S.	B1	110
Carolina, Braz.	E9	54
Carolina, Col.	D5	58
Carolina, R.I., U.S.	F2	116
Carolina, W.V., U.S.	k10	125
Carolina Beach, N.C., U.S.	C5	110
Caroline, co., Md., U.S.	C6	97
Caroline, co., Va., U.S.	C5	123
Caroní, stm., Ven.	D11	58
Carora, Ven.	B7	58
Carpathian Mountains, mts., Eur.	F12	4
Carpații Meridionali, mts., Rom.	D8	16
Carpentaria, Gulf of, b., Austl.	B7	50
Carpenter Dam, Ar., U.S.	g7	81
Carpentersville, Il., U.S.	A5	90
Carpentras, Fr.	H12	10
Carpi, Italy	E5	14
Carpinteria, Ca., U.S.	E4	82
Carquefou, Fr.	E5	10
Carrabelle, Fl., U.S.	C2	86
Carrauntoohill, mtn., Ire.	I3	7
Carrara, Italy	E5	14
Carrboro, N.C., U.S.	B3	110
Carreta, Punta, c., Peru	F3	54
Carrickfergus, N. Ire., U.K.	G7	7
Carrickmacross, Ire.	H6	7
Carrie, Mount, mtn., Wa., U.S.	B2	124
Carrier, Ms., U.S.	E4	101
Carrier Mills, Il., U.S.	F5	90
Carrillo, Mex.	D8	62
Carrington, N.D., U.S.	B6	111
Carrington Island, i., Ut., U.S.	C3	121
Carrión de los Condes, Spain	A7	12
Carrizo Creek, stm., U.S.	A4	120
Carrizo Mountain, mtn., N.M., U.S.	D4	108
Carrizo Mountains, mts., U.S.	A6	80
Carrizo Springs, Tx., U.S.	*E3	120
Carrizozo, N.M., U.S.	D4	108
Carroll, Ia., U.S.	B3	92
Carroll, co., Ar., U.S.	A2	81
Carroll, co., Ga., U.S.	C1	87
Carroll, co., Il., U.S.	A4	90
Carroll, co., In., U.S.	C4	91
Carroll, co., Ia., U.S.	B3	92
Carroll, co., Ky., U.S.	B4	94
Carroll, co., Md., U.S.	A3	97
Carroll, co., Ms., U.S.	B4	101
Carroll, co., Mo., U.S.	B4	102
Carroll, co., N.H., U.S.	C4	106
Carroll, co., Oh., U.S.	B4	112
Carroll, co., Tn., U.S.	B3	119
Carroll, co., Va., U.S.	D2	123
Carrollton, Al., U.S.	B1	78
Carrollton, Ga., U.S.	C1	87
Carrollton, Il., U.S.	D3	90
Carrollton, Ky., U.S.	B4	94
Carrollton, Mi., U.S.	E7	99
Carrollton, Mo., U.S.	B4	102
Carrollton, Oh., U.S.	B4	112
Carrolltown, Pa., U.S.	E4	115
Carrot, stm., Can.	D4	75
Carry Falls Reservoir, res., N.Y., U.S.	f10	109
Čarsk, Kaz.	H10	24
Carson, Ia., U.S.	C2	92
Carson, Wa., U.S.	D4	124
Carson, co., Tx., U.S.	B2	120
Carson, stm., Nv., U.S.	D2	105
Carson City, Mi., U.S.	E6	99
Carson City, Nv., U.S.	D2	105
Carson Lake, l., Nv., U.S.	D3	105
Carson Sink, l., Nv., U.S.	D3	105
Carson Spring, Tn., U.S.	D10	119
Carstairs, Alta., Can.	D3	68
Carswell Air Force Base, mil., Tx., U.S.	n9	120
Cartagena, Col.	B5	58
Cartagena, Spain	H11	12
Cartago, Col.	E5	58
Cartago, C.R.	J6	64
Carter, co., Ky., U.S.	B6	94
Carter, co., Mo., U.S.	E7	102
Carter, co., Mt., U.S.	E12	103
Carter, co., Ok., U.S.	C4	113
Carter, co., Tn., U.S.	C11	119
Carteret, N.J., U.S.	B4	107
Carteret, co., N.C., U.S.	C6	110
Carter Mountain, mtn., Wy., U.S.	B3	127
Carters Lake, res., Ga., U.S.	B2	87
Cartersville, Ga., U.S.	B2	87
Carterville, Il., U.S.	F4	90
Carterville, Mo., U.S.	D3	102
Carthage, Il., U.S.	C2	90
Carthage, In., U.S.	E6	91
Carthage, Ms., U.S.	C4	101
Carthage, Mo., U.S.	D3	102
Carthage, N.Y., U.S.	B5	109
Carthage, N.C., U.S.	B3	110
Carthage, Tn., U.S.	C8	119
Carthage, Tx., U.S.	C5	120
Cartier Island, i., Austl.	B4	50
Cartwright, Newf., Can.	B3	72
Cartwright, Ok., U.S.	D5	113
Caruaru, Braz.	E11	54
Carúpano, Ven.	B11	58
Caruthersville, Mo., U.S.	E8	102
Carver, Ma., U.S.	C6	98
Carver, Mn., U.S.	F5	100
Carver, co., Mn., U.S.	F5	100
Carville, La., U.S.	h9	95
Cary, Il., U.S.	A5	90
Cary, N.C., U.S.	B4	110
Caryville, Tn., U.S.	C9	119
Casablanca (Dar-el-Beida), Mor.	B4	42
Casacalenda, Italy	H9	14
Casa Grande, Az., U.S.	E4	80
Casa Grande National Monument, Az., U.S.	E4	80
Casale Monferrato, Italy	D3	14
Casarano, Italy	I13	14
Casas Adobes, Az., U.S.	E5	80
Casas Ibáñez, Spain	F10	12
Cascade, Co., U.S.	C6	83
Cascade, Id., U.S.	E2	89
Cascade, Ia., U.S.	B6	92
Cascade, Mt., U.S.	C5	103
Cascade, co., Mt., U.S.	C5	103
Cascade Locks, Or., U.S.	B5	114
Cascade Range, mts., N.A.	C2	76
Cascade Reservoir, res., Id., U.S.	E3	89
Cascade Tunnel, Wa., U.S.	B4	124
Cascais, Port.	G2	12
Cascina, Italy	F5	14
Casco Bay, b., Me., U.S.	E3	96
Caserta, Italy	H9	14
Caseville, Mi., U.S.	E7	99
Casey, Il., U.S.	D6	90
Casey, co., Ky., U.S.	C5	94
Casey Key, i., Fl., U.S.	E4	86
Cashion, Az., U.S.	m8	80
Cashmere, Wa., U.S.	B5	124
Cashton, Wi., U.S.	E3	126
Casigua, Ven.	C6	58
Caspe, Spain	D11	12
Casper, Wy., U.S.	D6	127
Casper Mountain, mtn., Wy., U.S.	D6	127
Caspian, Mi., U.S.	B2	99
Caspian Lake, l., Vt., U.S.	B4	122
Caspian Sea	G17	4
Cass, co., Il., U.S.	D3	90
Cass, co., In., U.S.	C5	91
Cass, co., Ia., U.S.	C3	92
Cass, co., Mi., U.S.	G4	99
Cass, co., Mn., U.S.	D4	100
Cass, co., Mo., U.S.	C3	102
Cass, co., Ne., U.S.	D9	104
Cass, co., N.D., U.S.	C8	111
Cass, co., Tx., U.S.	C5	120
Cass, stm., Mi., U.S.	E7	99
Cassai (Kasai), stm., Afr.	C4	44
Cassano allo Ionio, Italy	J11	14
Cass City, Mi., U.S.	E7	99
Casselberry, Fl., U.S.	D5	86
Casselman, Ont., Can.	B9	73
Casselman, stm., U.S.	k12	97
Casselton, N.D., U.S.	C8	111
Cassia, co., Id., U.S.	G5	89
Cassiar, B.C., Can.	m17	69
Cassinga, Ang.	E3	44
Cassino, Italy	H8	14
Cass Lake, Mn., U.S.	C4	100
Cass Lake, l., Mn., U.S.	C4	100
Cassopolis, Mi., U.S.	G4	99
Cassville, Ga., U.S.	B2	87
Cassville, Mo., U.S.	E4	102
Cassville, Wi., U.S.	F3	126
Castalia, Oh., U.S.	A3	112
Castanea, Pa., U.S.	D7	115
Castanheira de Pêra, Port.	E3	12
Castel del Piano, Italy	G6	14
Castelfranco Veneto, Italy	D6	14
Castellammare del Golfo, Italy	K7	14
Castellammare [di Stabia], Italy	I9	14
Castellane, Fr.	I13	10
Castellón de la Plana, Spain	F11	12
Castelnaudary, Fr.	I8	10
Castelo Branco, Port.	F4	12
Castelsarrasin, Fr.	H8	10
Castelvetrano, Italy	L7	14
Castets, Fr.	I5	10
Castiglione del Lago, Italy	F7	14
Castilla, Peru	E2	54
Castilla la Nueva, hist. reg., Spain	F8	12
Castillo de San Marcos National Monument, Fl., U.S.	n9	86
Castine, Me., U.S.	D4	96
Castleberry, Al., U.S.	D2	78
Castle Dale, Ut., U.S.	D4	121
Castle Dome Mountains, mts., Az., U.S.	D1	80
Castle Dome Peak, mtn., Az., U.S.	D1	80
Castlegar, B.C., Can.	E9	69
Castle Hayne, N.C., U.S.	C5	110
Castle Hills, De., U.S.	i7	85
Castle Mountain, mtn., Yukon, Can.	D5	66
Castle Mountains, mts., Mt., U.S.	D6	103
Castle Peak, mtn., Co., U.S.	B4	83
Castle Peak, mtn., Id., U.S.	E4	89
Castle Point, Mo., U.S.	f13	102
Castle Rock, Co., U.S.	B6	83
Castle Rock, Wa., U.S.	C3	124
Castle Rock, mtn., Or., U.S.	C8	114
Castle Rock Lake, res., Wi., U.S.	E4	126
Castleton, Vt., U.S.	D2	122
Castletown, I. of Man	G8	7
Castletown Berehaven, Ire.	J3	7
Castlewood, Va., U.S.	f9	123
Castor, Alta., Can.	C5	68
Castor, stm., Mo., U.S.	D7	102
Castres, Fr.	I9	10
Castries, St. Luc.	G17	64
Castro, co., Tx., U.S.	B1	120
Castro Daire, Port.	E4	12
Castro del Río, Spain	H7	12
Castropol, Spain	B4	12
Castro Valley, Ca., U.S.	h8	82
Castrovillari, Italy	J11	14
Castroville, Tx., U.S.	E3	120
Castuera, Spain	G6	12
Caswell, co., N.C., U.S.	A3	110
Catacamas, Hond.	G5	64
Cataguases, Braz.	F7	57
Catahoula, co., La., U.S.	C4	95
Catahoula Lake, l., La., U.S.	C3	95
Catalão, Braz.	E5	57
Catalina, Newf., Can.	D5	72
Catalina, Chile	B3	56
Catamarca, Arg.	B3	56
Catamayo, Ec.	I3	58
Catanduanes Island, i., Phil.	C7	32
Catanduva, Braz.	F4	57
Catania, Italy	L10	14
Catanzaro, Italy	K11	14
Cataouatche, Lake, l., La., U.S.	k11	95
Catarman, Phil.	C7	32
Catasauqua, Pa., U.S.	E11	115
Catastrophe, Cape, c., Austl.	F7	50
Cataumet, Ma., U.S.	C6	98
Catawba, co., N.C., U.S.	B1	110
Catawba, stm., S.C., U.S.	B6	117
Catawba, South Fork, stm., N.C., U.S.	B1	110
Catawissa, Pa., U.S.	E9	115
Catete, Ang.	C2	44
Cathance, Lake, l., Me., U.S.	D5	96
Cathcart, S. Afr.	H5	44
Cathedral City, Ca., U.S.	F5	82
Cathedral of the Pines, N.H., U.S.	E3	106
Catherine, Lake, res., Ar., U.S.	C3	81
Cat Island, i., Bah.	B10	64
Cat Island, i., Ms., U.S.	f12	98
Cat Island, i., S.C., U.S.	E9	117
Catlettsburg, Ky., U.S.	B7	94
Catlin, Il., U.S.	C6	90
Catnip Mountain, mtn., Nv., U.S.	B2	105
Catoche, Cabo, c., Mex.	G16	62
Cato Island, i., Austl.	D11	50
Catoosa, Ok., U.S.	A6	113
Catoosa, co., Ga., U.S.	B1	87
Catorce, Mex.	F9	62
Catron, co., N.M., U.S.	D1	108
Catskill, N.Y., U.S.	C7	109
Catskill Mountains, mts., N.Y., U.S.	C6	109
Catt, Mount, mtn., B.C., Can.	B3	69
Cattaraugus, co., N.Y., U.S.	C2	109
Cattaraugus Creek, stm., N.Y., U.S.	C2	109
Cattaraugus Indian Reservation, N.Y., U.S.	C2	109
Cattolica, Italy	F7	14
Catus, Fr.	H8	10
Caubvick, Mount (Mont d'Iberville), mtn., Can.	f9	72
Cauca, stm., Col.	D5	58
Caucasia, Col.	C5	58
Caucasus, mts., Eur.	I6	22
Caucomgomoc Lake, l., Me., U.S.	B3	96
Caudry, Fr.	B10	10
Caulonia, Italy	K11	14
Caunskaja Guba, b., Russia	D27	24
Cauquenes, Chile	D2	56
Caura, stm., Ven.	D10	58
Caussade, Fr.	H8	10
Cauvery, stm., India	G5	37
Cavalaire-sur-Mer, Fr.	I13	10
Cavalier, N.D., U.S.	A8	111
Cavalier, co., N.D., U.S.	A7	111
Cavan, Ire.	G5	7
Cave City, Ar., U.S.	B4	81
Cave City, Ky., U.S.	C4	94
Cave Creek, Az., U.S.	D4	80
Cave Junction, Or., U.S.	E3	114
Cave Point, c., Wi., U.S.	D6	126
Cave Run Lake, res., Ky., U.S.	B6	94
Cave Spring, Ga., U.S.	B1	87
Cave Spring, Va., U.S.	C2	123
Cavetown, Md., U.S.	A2	97
Caviana, Ilha, i., Braz.	C8	54
Cavite, Phil.	q19	33b
Cawood, Ky., U.S.	D6	94
Cawston, B.C., Can.	E8	69
Caxambu, Braz.	F6	57
Caxias, Braz.	D10	54
Caxias do Sul, Braz.	B6	56
Caxito, Ang.	C2	44
Cayambe, Ec.	H4	58
Cayambe, vol., Ec.	H4	58
Cayce, S.C., U.S.	D5	117
Cayenne, Fr. Gu.	C8	54
Cayman Brac, i., Cay. Is.	E8	64
Cayman Islands, dep., N.A.	E7	64
Cayuga, Ont., Can.	E5	73
Cayuga, co., N.Y., U.S.	C4	109
Cayuga Heights, N.Y., U.S.	C4	109
Cayuga Lake, l., N.Y., U.S.	C4	109
Cazenovia, N.Y., U.S.	C5	109
Cazères, Fr.	I8	10
Cazin, Bos.	E10	14
Cazorla, Spain	H8	12
Čeboksary, Russia	F7	22
Cebollar, Arg.	B3	56
Cebreros, Spain	E7	12
Cebu, Phil.	C7	32
Cebu, i., Phil.	C7	32
Cecerleg, Mong.	B7	26
Cechov, Russia	F20	18
Čechy, hist. reg., Czech.	F14	8
Cecil, co., Md., U.S.	A6	97
Cecil Field Naval Air Station, mil., Fl., U.S.	B5	86
Cecilia, Ky., U.S.	C4	94
Cecina, Italy	F5	14
Cedar, co., Ia., U.S.	C6	92
Cedar, co., Mo., U.S.	D4	102
Cedar, co., Ne., U.S.	B8	104
Cedar, stm., U.S.	C6	92
Cedar, stm., Ne., U.S.	C7	104
Cedar, stm., Wa., U.S.	B4	124
Cedar Bluff, Al., U.S.	A4	78
Cedar Bluff Reservoir, res., Ks., U.S.	D4	93
Cedar Bluff Two, Tn., U.S.	D9	119
Cedar Breaks National Monument, Ut., U.S.	F3	121
Cedarburg, Wi., U.S.	E6	126
Cedar City, Ut., U.S.	F2	121
Cedar Creek, stm., N.J., U.S.	D4	107
Cedar Creek, stm., N.D., U.S.	C3	111
Cedar Creek, stm., Oh., U.S.	e7	112
Cedar Creek Lake, res., Tx., U.S.	C4	120
Cedaredge, Co., U.S.	C3	83
Cedar Falls, Ia., U.S.	B5	92
Cedar Grove, N.J., U.S.	B4	107
Cedar Grove, W.V., U.S.	C3	125
Cedar Grove, Wi., U.S.	E6	126
Cedar Hill, Mo., U.S.	g12	102
Cedar Hill, Tx., U.S.	n10	120
Cedarhurst, N.Y., U.S.	k13	109
Cedar Island, i., N.C., U.S.	C6	110
Cedar Island, i., S.C., U.S.	E9	117
Cedar Island, i., Va., U.S.	C7	123
Cedar Key, Fl., U.S.	C3	86
Cedar Keys, is., Fl., U.S.	C3	86
Cedar Lake, In., U.S.	B3	91
Cedar Lake, l., Man., Can.	C1	70
Cedar Lake, res., Il., U.S.	F4	90
Cedar Mountain, mtn., Ca., U.S.	B3	82
Cedar Point, c., Md., U.S.	D5	97
Cedar Point, c., Oh., U.S.	e7	112
Cedar Rapids, Ia., U.S.	C6	92
Cedar Springs, Mi., U.S.	E5	99
Cedartown, Ga., U.S.	B1	87
Cedar Vale, Ks., U.S.	E7	93
Cedarville, Oh., U.S.	C2	112
Cedarville, Ca., U.S.	B3	82
Cedros, Isla, i., Mex.	C2	62
Ceduna, Austl.	F6	50
Cefalù, Italy	K9	14
Čegdomyn, Russia	G20	24
Cegléd, Hung.	H19	8
Cehegín, Spain	G10	12
Cela, Ang.	D3	44
Čel'abinsk, Russia	F10	22
Celano, Italy	G8	14
Celanova, Spain	C4	12
Celaya, Mex.	G9	62
Cele, China	B9	38
Celebes Sea, Asia	E7	32
Celebes see Sulawesi, i., Indon.	F7	32
Celina, Oh., U.S.	B1	112
Celina, Tn., U.S.	C8	119
Celina, Tx., U.S.	C4	120
Celinograd, Kaz.	G8	24
Celje, Slo.	C10	14
Celle, Ger.	C10	8
Cement, Ok., U.S.	C3	113
Cementon, Pa., U.S.	E10	115
Centennial Mountains, mts., Id., U.S.	E7	89
Center, Co., U.S.	D4	83
Center, N.D., U.S.	B4	111
Center, Tx., U.S.	D5	120
Centerbrook, Ct., U.S.	D6	84
Centerburg, Oh., U.S.	B3	112
Centereach, N.Y., U.S.	n15	109
Centerfield, Ut., U.S.	D4	121
Center Hill Lake, res., Tn., U.S.	C8	119
Center Moriches, N.Y., U.S.	n16	109
Center Mountain, mtn., Id., U.S.	D3	89
Center Point, Al., U.S.	f7	78
Center Point, Ia., U.S.	B6	92
Centerville, In., U.S.	E8	91
Centerville, Ia., U.S.	D5	92
Centerville, La., U.S.	E4	95
Centerville, Ma., U.S.	C7	98
Centerville, Oh., U.S.	C1	112
Centerville, Pa., U.S.	F2	115
Centerville, S.D., U.S.	D9	118
Centerville, Tn., U.S.	B4	119
Centerville, Ut., U.S.	C4	121
Central, N.M., U.S.	E1	108
Central, S.C., U.S.	B2	117
Central, Cordillera, mts., Bol.	G6	54
Central, Cordillera, mts., Col.	E5	54
Central, Cordillera, mts., Peru	E3	54
Central, Massif, mts., Fr.	G10	10
Central, Planalto, plat., Braz.	G9	54
Central, Sistema, mts., Spain	E6	12
Central African Republic, ctry., Afr.	G10	42
Central City, Co., U.S.	B5	83
Central City, Il., U.S.	E4	90
Central City, Ia., U.S.	B6	92
Central City, Ky., U.S.	C2	94
Central City, Ne., U.S.	C7	104
Central City, Pa., U.S.	F4	115
Central Falls, R.I., U.S.	B4	116
Central Heights, Az., U.S.	D5	80
Central Islip, N.Y., U.S.	n15	109
Centralia, Il., U.S.	E4	90
Centralia, Mo., U.S.	B5	102
Centralia, Wa., U.S.	C3	124
Central Lake, Mi., U.S.	C5	99
Central Makrān Range, mts., Pak.	D1	36
Central Park, Wa., U.S.	C2	124
Central Point, Or., U.S.	E4	114
Central Square, N.Y., U.S.	B4	109
Central Valley, Ca., U.S.	B2	82
Central Valley, N.Y., U.S.	D6	109
Central Village, Ct., U.S.	C8	84
Centre, Al., U.S.	A4	78
Centre, co., Pa., U.S.	E6	115
Centre Hall, Pa., U.S.	E6	115
Centreville, Al., U.S.	C2	78
Centreville, Il., U.S.	E3	90
Centreville, Md., U.S.	B5	97
Centreville, Ms., U.S.	D2	101
Centuria, Wi., U.S.	C1	126
Century, Fl., U.S.	u14	86
Cepu, Indon.	m15	33a
Ceram Sea see Seram, Laut, Indon.	F8	32
Cerbat Mountains, mts., Az., U.S.	B1	80
Ceredo, W.V., U.S.	C2	125
Čeremchovo, Russia	G14	24
Čerepovec, Russia	B20	18
Ceres, Ca., U.S.	D3	82
Ceresco, Ne., U.S.	C9	104
Céret, Fr.	J9	10
Cereté, Col.	C5	58
Cerf Island, i., Sey.	C10	44
Cerignola, Italy	H10	14
Cérilly, Fr.	F9	10
Čerkassy, Ukr.	H4	22
Čerkessk, Russia	I6	22
Čern'achovsk, Russia	G4	18
Černigov, Ukr.	G4	22
Černobyl' (Chernobyl), Ukr.	G4	22
Černogorsk, Russia	G12	24
Černovcy, Ukr.	H3	22
Černyševskij, Russia	E16	24
Cerralvo, Isla, i., Mex.	E5	62
Cerritos, Mex.	F9	62
Cerro de Pasco, Peru	F3	54
Cerro Gordo, Il., U.S.	D5	90
Cerro Gordo, co., Ia., U.S.	A4	92
Čerskij, Russia	D26	24
Čerskogo, Chrebet, mts., Russia	E23	24
Cervera del Río Alhama, Spain	C10	12
Cervera de Pisuerga, Spain	C7	12
Cervia, Italy	E7	14
Cesena, Italy	E7	14
Cesenatico, Italy	E7	14
České Budějovice, Czech.	G14	8
Cessnock, Austl.	F10	50
Ceuta, Sp. N. Afr.	A4	42
Ceyhan, Tur.	A4	40
Ceylânpınar, Tur.	A5	40
Ceylon see Sri Lanka, ctry., Asia	H5	35
Chabanais, Fr.	G7	10
Chabarovsk, Russia	H21	24
Chachoengsao, Thai.	H6	34
Chaco, stm., N.M., U.S.	A1	108
Chaco Culture National Historic Park, N.M., U.S.	A2	108

Name	Map Ref	Page
Chacon, Cape, c., Ak., U.S.	n24	79
Chad, ctry., Afr.	E9	42
Chad, Lake (Lac Tchad), l., Afr.	F8	42
Chadbourn, N.C., U.S.	C4	110
Chadds Ford, Pa., U.S.	G10	115
Chadron, Ne., U.S.	B3	104
Chadwicks, N.Y., U.S.	B5	109
Chaffee, Mo., U.S.	D8	102
Chaffee, co., Co., U.S.	C4	83
Chaffin, Ma., U.S.	B4	98
Chaghcharān, Afg.	C1	38
Chagny, Fr.	F11	10
Chagos Archipelago, is., B.I.O.T.	G17	2
Chagrin Falls, Oh., U.S.	A4	112
Chaîne Annamitique, mts., Asia	F9	34
Chakachamna Lake, l., Ak., U.S.	g15	79
Chake Chake, Tan.	C7	44
Chalais, Fr.	G7	10
Chalbi Desert, des., Kenya	H2	44
Chalcuapa, El Sal.	H3	64
Chaleur Bay, b., Can.	A7	71
Chalfonte, De., U.S.	h7	85
Chāligaon, India	B3	37
Chalk River, Ont., Can.	A7	73
Challans, Fr.	F5	10
Challis, Id., U.S.	E4	89
Chalmette, La., U.S.	E6	95
Chalonnes-sur-Loire, Fr.	E6	10
Châlons-sur-Marne, Fr.	D11	10
Chalon-sur-Saône, Fr.	F11	10
Châlus, Fr.	G7	10
Cham, Ger.	F12	8
Chama, N.M., U.S.	A3	108
Chama, Rio, stm., N.M., U.S.	A3	108
Chaman, Pak.	E2	38
Chambal, stm., India	G7	38
Chamberlain, S.D., U.S.	D6	118
Chamberlain Lake, l., Me., U.S.	B3	96
Chamberlin, Mount, mtn., Ak., U.S.	B10	79
Chambers, co., Al., U.S.	C4	78
Chambers, co., Tx., U.S.	E5	120
Chambersburg, Pa., U.S.	G6	115
Chambers Island, i., Wi., U.S.	C6	126
Chambéry, Fr.	G12	10
Chambi, Jebel, mtn., Tun.	A7	42
Chamblee, Ga., U.S.	h8	87
Chambly, Que., Can.	D4	74
Chambon-sur-Voueize, Fr.	F9	10
Chamisal, N.M., U.S.	A4	108
Chamonix-Mont-Blanc, Fr.	G13	10
Champagne, hist. reg., Fr.	D11	10
Champagnole, Fr.	F12	10
Champaign, Il., U.S.	C5	90
Champaign, co., Il., U.S.	C5	90
Champaign, co., Oh., U.S.	B2	112
Champassak, Laos	G8	34
Champion, Oh., U.S.	A5	112
Champlain, Lake, l., N.A.	C12	76
Champlin, Mn., U.S.	m12	100
Chāmrājnagar Rāmasamudram, India	G4	37
Chañaral, Chile	B2	56
Chance, Md., U.S.	D6	97
Chanch, Mong.	A7	26
Chanchelulla Peak, mtn., Ca., U.S.	B2	82
Chandalar, stm., Ak., U.S.	B10	79
Chandausi, India	F8	38
Chandeleur Islands, is., La., U.S.	E7	95
Chandeleur Sound, strt., La., U.S.	E6	95
Chandīgarh, India	E7	38
Chandler, Que., Can.	k14	74
Chandler, Az., U.S.	D4	80
Chandler, In., U.S.	H3	91
Chandler, Ok., U.S.	B5	113
Chandler, Tx., U.S.	C5	120
Chandler Heights, Az., U.S.	m9	80
Chāndpur, Bngl.	I14	38
Chāndpur, India	F8	38
Chandrapur, India	C5	37
Chandyga, Russia	E21	24
Chang (Yangtze), stm., China	E10	26
Changain Nuruu, mts., Mong.	B6	26
Changchun, China	C12	26
Changde, China	F9	26
Changhua, Tai.	K9	28
Changjiang, China	J5	28
Changli, China	D10	26
Changsha, China	G1	28
Changshu, China	D9	28
Changzhi, China	D9	26
Changzhou (Changchow), China	D8	28
Chanhassen, Mn., U.S.	n11	100
Chanka, Ozero (Xingkathu), l., Asia	I20	24
Channahon, Il., U.S.	B5	90
Channapatna, India	F4	37
Channel Islands, is., Eur.	C4	10
Channel Islands National Park, Ca., U.S.	F4	82
Channel Lake, l., Il., U.S.	H8	90
Channel-Port-aux-Basques, Newf., Can.	E2	72
Channelview, Tx., U.S.	r14	120
Chantada, Spain	C4	12
Chantajskoje, Ozero, l., Russia	D12	24
Chanthaburi, Thai.	H7	34
Chantilly, Va., U.S.	g12	123
Chantrey Inlet, b., N.W. Ter., Can.	C13	66
Chanute, Ks., U.S.	E8	93
Chanute Air Force Base, mil., Il., U.S.	C5	90
Chaoan, China	L5	28
Chao Phraya, stm., Thai.	G6	34
Chapala, Lago de, l., Mex.	G8	62
Chaparral, Col.	F5	58
Chapčeranga, Russia	H16	24
Chapel Hill, N.C., U.S.	B3	110
Chapel Hill, Tn., U.S.	B5	119
Chaplin Lake, l., Sask., Can.	G2	75
Chapman, Ks., U.S.	D6	93
Chapman Pond, l., R.I., U.S.	F1	116
Chapmanville, W.V., U.S.	D2	125
Chappaquiddick Island, i., Ma., U.S.	D7	98
Chappell, Ne., U.S.	C3	104
Chāpra, India	H11	38
Chapultepec, mtn., Mex.	F8	62
Charadai, Arg.	B5	56
Charcas, Mex.	F9	62
Chardon, Oh., U.S.	A4	112
Charenton, La., U.S.	E4	95
Chari, stm., Afr.	F9	42
Chārīkār, Afg.	C3	38
Chariton, Ia., U.S.	C4	92
Chariton, co., Mo., U.S.	B4	102
Chariton, stm., U.S.	A5	102
Charity, Guy.	D13	58
Char'kov, Ukr.	G5	22
Charleroi, Bel.	E4	8
Charleroi, Pa., U.S.	F2	115
Charles, co., Md., U.S.	C3	97
Charles, stm., Ma., U.S.	B5	98
Charles, Cape, c., Va., U.S.	C6	123
Charles A. Goodwin Dam, Ct., U.S.	B3	84
Charlesbourg, Que., Can.	n17	74
Charles City, Ia., U.S.	A5	92
Charles City, co., Va., U.S.	C5	123
Charles Island, i., N.W. Ter., Can.	D18	66
Charles Mill Lake, res., Oh., U.S.	B3	112
Charles Mix, co., S.D., U.S.	D7	118
Charles Mound, hill, Il., U.S.	A3	90
Charleston, Ar., U.S.	B1	81
Charleston, Il., U.S.	D5	90
Charleston, Ms., U.S.	A3	101
Charleston, Mo., U.S.	E8	102
Charleston, Or., U.S.	D2	114
Charleston, S.C., U.S.	F8	117
Charleston, Tn., U.S.	D9	119
Charleston, W.V., U.S.	C3	125
Charleston, co., S.C., U.S.	F8	117
Charleston Air Force Base, mil., S.C., U.S.	k11	117
Charleston Naval Shipyard, mil., S.C., U.S.	k12	117
Charleston Peak, mtn., Nv., U.S.	G6	105
Charlestown, In., U.S.	H6	91
Charlestown, N.H., U.S.	D2	106
Charlestown, R.I., U.S.	F2	116
Charles Town, W.V., U.S.	B7	125
Charleville, Austl.	E9	50
Charleville-Mézières, Fr.	C11	10
Charlevoix, Mi., U.S.	C5	99
Charlevoix, co., Mi., U.S.	C5	99
Charlevoix, Lake, l., Mi., U.S.	C5	99
Charlo, N.B., Can.	B3	71
Charlotte, Mi., U.S.	F6	99
Charlotte, N.C., U.S.	B2	110
Charlotte, Tn., U.S.	A4	119
Charlotte, Tx., U.S.	E3	120
Charlotte, co., Fl., U.S.	F5	86
Charlotte, co., Va., U.S.	C4	123
Charlotte Amalie, V.I.U.S.	E15	64
Charlotte Hall, Md., U.S.	D4	97
Charlotte Harbor, Fl., U.S.	F4	86
Charlotte Harbor, b., Fl., U.S.	F4	86
Charlottenberg, Swe.	G9	6
Charlottesville, Va., U.S.	B4	123
Charlottetown, P.E.I., Can.	C6	71
Charlton, co., Ga., U.S.	F4	87
Charmco, W.V., U.S.	C4	125
Charmes, Fr.	D13	10
Charny, Que., Can.	C6	74
Charolles, Fr.	F11	10
Chārsadda, Pak.	C4	38
Charters Towers, Austl.	D9	50
Chartres, Fr.	D8	10
Char Us Nuur, l., Mong.	B5	26
Chascomús, Arg.	D5	56
Chase, B.C., Can.	D8	69
Chase, Md., U.S.	B5	97
Chase, co., Ks., U.S.	D7	93
Chase, co., Ne., U.S.	D4	104
Chase City, Va., U.S.	D4	123
Chase Field Naval Air Station, mil., Tx., U.S.	E4	120
Chaska, Mn., U.S.	F5	100
Chassahowitzka Bay, b., Fl., U.S.	D4	86
Chassell, Mi., U.S.	B2	99
Chatanbulag, Mong.	C8	26
Chatanga, Russia	C14	24
Chatanga, stm., Russia	C14	24
Chatangskij Zaliv, b., Russia	C15	24
Châteaubriant, Fr.	E5	10
Château-du-Loir, Fr.	E7	10
Châteaudun, Fr.	D8	10
Château-Gontier, Fr.	E6	10
Châteauguay, Que., Can.	D4	74
Château-Landon, Fr.	D9	10
Châteaulin, Fr.	D2	10
Châteaumeillant, Fr.	F9	10
Châteauneuf-de-Charente, Fr.	G6	10
Châteauneuf-sur-Loire, Fr.	E9	10
Château-Renault, Fr.	E7	10
Châteauroux, Fr.	F8	10
Château-Richer, Que., Can.	C6	74
Château-Thierry, Fr.	C10	10
Châtellerault, Fr.	F7	10
Chatfield, Mn., U.S.	G6	100
Chatgal, Mong.	A7	26
Chatham, N.B., Can.	B4	71
Chatham, Ont., Can.	E2	73
Chatham, Eng., U.K.	J13	7
Chatham, Il., U.S.	D4	90
Chatham, La., U.S.	B3	95
Chatham, Ma., U.S.	C8	98
Chatham, N.J., U.S.	B4	107
Chatham, N.Y., U.S.	C7	109
Chatham, Va., U.S.	D3	123
Chatham, co., Ga., U.S.	E5	87
Chatham, co., N.C., U.S.	B3	110
Chatham, co., N.C., U.S.	C6	123
Chatham Strait, strt., Ak., U.S.	m22	79
Châtillon, Italy	D2	14
Châtillon-Coligny, Fr.	E9	10
Châtillon-sur-Indre, Fr.	F8	10
Châtillon-sur-Seine, Fr.	E11	10
Chatom, Al., U.S.	D1	78
Chatsworth, Ga., U.S.	B2	87
Chatsworth, Il., U.S.	C5	90
Chatsworth Reservoir, res., Ca., U.S.	m11	82
Chattahoochee, Fl., U.S.	B2	86
Chattahoochee, co., Ga., U.S.	D2	87
Chattahoochee, stm., U.S.	E1	87
Chattanooga, Tn., U.S.	D8	119
Chattaroy, W.V., U.S.	D2	125
Chattooga, co., Ga., U.S.	B1	87
Chattooga, stm., U.S.	B1	117
Chatuge Lake, res., U.S.	g9	110
Chau Doc, Viet.	I8	34
Chauk, Burma	D3	34
Chaumont, Fr.	D12	10
Chauncey, Oh., U.S.	C3	112
Chauny, Fr.	C10	10
Chautauqua, co., Ks., U.S.	E7	93
Chautauqua, co., N.Y., U.S.	C1	109
Chautauqua Lake, l., N.Y., U.S.	C1	109
Chauvigny, Fr.	F7	10
Chauvin, La., U.S.	E5	95
Chavakkad, India	G4	37
Chaves, Port.	D4	12
Chaves, co., N.M., U.S.	D5	108
Cháviva, Col.	E6	58
Chbukha Dzong, Bhu.	G13	38
Cheaha Mountain, mtn., Al., U.S.	B4	78
Cheat, Shavers Fork, stm., W.V., U.S.	B5	125
Cheatham, co., Tn., U.S.	A4	119
Chebanse, Il., U.S.	C6	90
Cheboygan, Mi., U.S.	C6	99
Cheboygan, co., Mi., U.S.	C6	99
Chech, Erg, des., Afr.	C5	42
Checotah, Ok., U.S.	B6	113
Chedabucto Bay, b., N.S., Can.	D8	71
Cheduba Island, i., Burma	E2	34
Cheektowaga, N.Y., U.S.	C2	109
Cheeseman Lake, res., Co., U.S.	B5	83
Chehalem Mountains, mts., Or., U.S.	h12	114
Chehalis, Wa., U.S.	C3	124
Chehalis, stm., Wa., U.S.	C2	124
Cheju-do, i., S. Kor.	E12	26
Chelan, Wa., U.S.	B5	124
Chelan, co., Wa., U.S.	B4	124
Chelan, Lake, l., Wa., U.S.	A5	124
Chelan Mountains, mts., Wa., U.S.	A5	124
Chełm, Pol.	D23	8
Chełmno, Pol.	B18	8
Chelmsford, Eng., U.K.	J13	7
Chelmsford, Ma., U.S.	A5	98
Chelsea, Que., Can.	D2	74
Chelsea, Al., U.S.	g7	78
Chelsea, Ma., U.S.	B5	98
Chelsea, Mi., U.S.	F6	99
Chelsea, Ok., U.S.	A6	113
Cheltenham, Eng., U.K.	J10	7
Cheltenham, Md., U.S.	C4	97
Chelva, Spain	F11	12
Chelyabinsk see Čel'abinsk, Russia	F10	22
Chelyan, W.V., U.S.	C3	125
Chemehuevi Indian Reservation, Ca., U.S.	E6	82
Chemnitz, Ger.	E12	8
Chemquasabamticook Lake (Ross Lake), l., Me., U.S.	B3	96
Chemung, co., N.Y., U.S.	C4	109
Chemung, stm., Pa., U.S.	C8	115
Chemung Lake, l., Ont., Can.	C6	73
Chenāb, stm., Asia	E5	38
Chenachane, Alg.	C6	42
Chenango, co., N.Y., U.S.	C5	109
Chenango, stm., N.Y., U.S.	C5	109
Chenango Bridge, N.Y., U.S.	C5	109
Chenes, River Aux, b., La., U.S.	k12	95
Chénéville, Que., Can.	D2	74
Cheney, Ks., U.S.	E6	93
Cheney, Wa., U.S.	B8	124
Cheney Reservoir, res., Ks., U.S.	E6	93
Cheneyville, La., U.S.	C3	95
Chengde, China	C10	26
Chengdu, China	E7	26
Chengutu, Zimb.	E6	44
Chenoa, Il., U.S.	C5	90
Chenoweth, Or., U.S.	B5	114
Chepachet, R.I., U.S.	B2	116
Chepachet, stm., R.I., U.S.	B2	116
Chepo, Pan.	J8	64
Chequamegon Bay, b., Wi., U.S.	B3	126
Cheraw, S.C., U.S.	B8	117
Cherbourg, Fr.	C5	10
Chergui, Chott ech l., Alg.	B6	42
Cherkassy see Čerkassy, Ukr.	H4	22
Chernigov see Černigov, Ukr.	G4	22
Chernobyl see Černobyl', Ukr.	G4	22
Cherokee, Al., U.S.	A2	78
Cherokee, Ia., U.S.	B2	92
Cherokee, Ks., U.S.	E9	93
Cherokee, Ok., U.S.	A3	113
Cherokee, co., Al., U.S.	A4	78
Cherokee, co., Ga., U.S.	B2	87
Cherokee, co., Ia., U.S.	B2	92
Cherokee, co., Ks., U.S.	E9	93
Cherokee, co., N.C., U.S.	f8	110
Cherokee, co., Ok., U.S.	B6	113
Cherokee, co., S.C., U.S.	A4	117
Cherokee, co., Tx., U.S.	D5	120
Cherokee Indian Reservation, N.C., U.S.	f9	110
Cherokee Lake, res., Tn., U.S.	C10	119
Cherokees, Lake O' The, res., Ok., U.S.	A7	113
Cherokee Village, Ar., U.S.	A4	81
Cherry, co., Ne., U.S.	B4	104
Cherry Creek, stm., S.D., U.S.	C3	118
Cherry Hill, N.J., U.S.	D2	107
Cherry Point Marine Corps Air Station, mil., N.C., U.S.	C6	110
Cherryvale, Ks., U.S.	E8	93
Cherry Valley, Il., U.S.	A5	90
Cherryville, N.C., U.S.	B1	110
Cherson, Ukr.	H4	22
Chesaning, Mi., U.S.	E6	99
Chesapeake, Oh., U.S.	D3	112
Chesapeake, Va., U.S.	D6	123
Chesapeake, W.V., U.S.	C3	125
Chesapeake and Delaware Canal, U.S.	B3	85
Chesapeake Bay, b., U.S.	D11	76
Chesapeake Bay Bridge-Tunnel, Va., U.S.	D7	123
Chesapeake Beach, Md., U.S.	C4	97
Chesapeake City, Md., U.S.	A6	97
Chesdin, Lake, res., Va., U.S.	C5	123
Cheshire, Ct., U.S.	D4	84
Cheshire, co., N.H., U.S.	E2	106
Cheshire Reservoir, res., Ma., U.S.	A1	98
Chesley, Ont., Can.	C3	73
Chesnee, S.C., U.S.	A4	117
Chester, Eng., U.K.	H10	7
Chester, Ca., U.S.	B3	82
Chester, Ct., U.S.	D6	84
Chester, Il., U.S.	F4	90
Chester, Md., U.S.	C5	97
Chester, Mt., U.S.	B6	103
Chester, N.H., U.S.	E4	106
Chester, N.Y., U.S.	D6	109
Chester, Pa., U.S.	G11	115
Chester, S.C., U.S.	B5	117
Chester, Vt., U.S.	E3	122
Chester, W.V., U.S.	A4	125
Chester, co., Pa., U.S.	G10	115
Chester, co., S.C., U.S.	B5	117
Chester, co., Tn., U.S.	B3	119
Chester, stm., Md., U.S.	B5	97
Chester Basin, N.S., Can.	E5	71
Chester Depot, Vt., U.S.	E3	122
Chesterfield, In., U.S.	D6	91
Chesterfield, S.C., U.S.	B7	117
Chesterfield, co., S.C., U.S.	B7	117
Chesterfield, co., Va., U.S.	C5	123
Chesterfield, Îles, is., N. Cal.	C11	50
Chesterfield Inlet, N.W. Ter., Can.	D14	66
Chesterfield Inlet, b., N.W. Ter., Can.	D14	66
Chesterton, In., U.S.	A3	91
Chestertown, Md., U.S.	B5	97
Chesterville, Ont., Can.	B9	73
Chesuncook Lake, l., Me., U.S.	C3	96
Cheswick, Pa., U.S.	h14	115
Cheswold, De., U.S.	D3	85
Cheta, stm., Russia	C13	24
Chetac, Lake, l., Wi., U.S.	C2	126
Chetco, stm., Or., U.S.	E2	114
Chetek, Wi., U.S.	C2	126
Chetek, Lake, l., Wi., U.S.	C2	126
Chetopa, Ks., U.S.	E8	93
Chetumal Bay, b., N.A.	H15	62
Chetwynd, B.C., Can.	B7	69
Chevak, Ak., U.S.	C6	79
Cheval Blanc, Pointe du, c., Haiti	E11	64
Cheviot, Oh., U.S.	C1	112
Chevreuil, Point, c., La., U.S.	E4	95
Chevy Chase, Md., U.S.	C3	97
Chewack, stm., Wa., U.S.	A5	124
Chewelah, Wa., U.S.	A8	124
Cheyenne, Ok., U.S.	B2	113
Cheyenne, Wy., U.S.	E8	127
Cheyenne, co., Co., U.S.	C8	83
Cheyenne, co., Ks., U.S.	C2	93
Cheyenne, co., Ne., U.S.	C2	104
Cheyenne, stm., U.S.	C4	118
Cheyenne, Dry Fork, stm., Wy., U.S.	C7	127
Cheyenne River Indian Reservation, S.D., U.S.	B4	118
Cheyenne Wells, Co., U.S.	C8	83
Chezhou, China	J1	28
Chhatarpur, India	H8	38
Chhindwāra, India	I8	38
Chi, stm., Thai.	G8	34
Chiai, Tai.	L9	28
Chiali, Tai.	L9	28
Chiang Khan, Thai.	F6	34
Chiang Mai, Thai.	E5	34
Chiang Rai, Thai.	E5	34
Chiari, Italy	D4	14
Chiavari, Italy	E4	14
Chiavenna, Italy	C4	14
Chiba, Japan	G13	30
Chiblow Lake, l., Ont., Can.	A1	73
Chibougamau, Que., Can.	k12	74
Chibuto, Moz.	F6	44
Chicago, Il., U.S.	B6	90
Chicago Heights, Il., U.S.	B6	90
Chicago Sanitary and Ship Canal, Il., U.S.	k8	90
Chicamacomico, stm., Md., U.S.	C6	97
Chicapa, stm., Afr.	C4	44
Chichagof Island, i., Ak., U.S.	m22	79
Chichén Itzá, Mex.	G15	62
Chichibu, Japan	G12	30
Chickahominy, stm., Va., U.S.	C5	123
Chickamauga, Ga., U.S.	B1	87
Chickamauga and Chattanooga National Military Park	k11	119
Chickamauga Dam, Tn., U.S.	h11	119
Chickamauga Lake, res., Tn., U.S.	D8	119
Chickasaw, Al., U.S.	E1	78
Chickasaw, co., Ia., U.S.	A5	92
Chickasaw, co., Ms., U.S.	B5	101
Chickasawhay, stm., Ms., U.S.	D5	101
Chickasaw National Recreation Area, Ok., U.S.	C5	113
Chickasha, Ok., U.S.	B4	113
Chickasha, Lake, res., Ok., U.S.	B3	113
Chickwolnepy Stream, stm., N.H., U.S.	A4	106
Chiclana de la Frontera, Spain	I5	12
Chiclayo, Peru	E3	54
Chico, Ca., U.S.	C3	82
Chicoa, Moz.	E6	44
Chicopee, Ga., U.S.	B3	87
Chicopee, Ma., U.S.	B2	98
Chicora, Pa., U.S.	E2	115
Chicot, Lake, l., Ar., U.S.	D4	81
Chicot Island, i., La., U.S.	E6	95
Chicoutimi, Que., Can.	A6	74
Chicoutimi, stm., Que., Can.	A6	74
Chidambaram, India	G5	37
Chidley, Cape, c., Can.	D20	66
Chiefland, Fl., U.S.	C4	86
Chieri, Italy	D2	14
Chieti, Italy	G9	14
Chifeng, China	C10	26
Chigasaki, Japan	G12	30
Chignecto, Cape, c., N.S., Can.	D5	71
Chignecto Bay, b., Can.	D5	71
Ch'ihu, Tai.	L9	28
Chihuahua, Mex.	C6	62
Chikaskia, stm., U.S.	A4	113
Chik Ballāpur, India	F4	37
Chikmagalūr, India	F3	37
Chilakalūrupet, India	D6	37
Chilapa de Alvarez, Mex.	I10	62
Chilās, Pak.	C6	38
Childersburg, Al., U.S.	B3	78
Childress, Tx., U.S.	B2	120
Childress, co., Tx., U.S.	B2	120
Chile, ctry., S.A.	C2	56
Chilete, Peru	E3	54
Chilhowie, Va., U.S.	f10	123
Chililabombwe (Bancroft), Zam.	D5	44
Chilka Lake, l., India	C8	37
Chilko, stm., B.C., Can.	D6	69
Chilko Lake, l., B.C., Can.	D5	69
Chillán, Chile	D2	56
Chillicothe, Il., U.S.	C4	90
Chillicothe, Mo., U.S.	B4	102
Chillicothe, Oh., U.S.	C3	112
Chilliwack, B.C., Can.	E7	69
Chillum, Md., U.S.	f9	97
Chiloé, Isla de, i., Chile	E2	56
Chilok, Russia	G16	24
Chiloquin, Or., U.S.	E5	114
Chilpancingo [de los Bravos], Mex.	I10	62
Chilton, Wi., U.S.	D5	126
Chilton, co., Al., U.S.	C3	78
Chilung, Tai.	J10	28
Chilwa, Lake, l., Afr.	E7	44
Chimacum, Wa., U.S.	A3	124
Chimayo, N.M., U.S.	A4	108
Chimborazo, vol., Ec.	H3	54
Chimbote, Peru	E3	54
Chimkent see Čimkent, Kaz.	I11	22
Chimki, Russia	F20	18
Chimney Rock, mtn., Ne., U.S.	C2	104
China, ctry., Asia	D7	26
China Grove, N.C., U.S.	B2	110
China Lake, l., Me., U.S.	D3	96
Chinandega, Nic.	H4	64
Chincha Alta, Peru	F3	54
Chincilla de Monte Aragón, Spain	G10	12
Chincoteague, Va., U.S.	C7	123
Chincoteague Bay, b., U.S.	D7	97
Chinde, Moz.	E7	44
Chindwin, stm., Burma	C3	34
Chingleput, India	F5	37
Chingola, Zam.	D5	44
Ch'ingshui, Tai.	K9	28
Chin Hills, hills, Burma	D2	34
Chinhoyi, Zimb.	E6	44
Chiniot, Pak.	E5	38
Chinitna Point, c., Ak., U.S.	h15	79
Chinju, S. Kor.	D12	26
Chinko, stm., Cen. Afr. Rep.	G10	42
Chinkuashih, Tai.	J10	28
Chinle, Az., U.S.	A6	80
Chinmen Tao, i., Tai.	K7	28
Chino, Ca., U.S.	F5	82
Chinon, Fr.	E7	10
Chinook, Mt., U.S.	B7	103
Chinook, Wa., U.S.	C2	124
Chinook, Lake, res., Or., U.S.	C5	114
Chino Valley, Az., U.S.	C3	80
Chinshan, Tai.	J10	28
Chioggia, Italy	D7	14
Chipata, Zam.	D6	44
Chipita Park, Co., U.S.	C6	83
Chipley, Fl., U.S.	u16	86
Chipman, N.B., Can.	C4	71
Chipola, stm., Fl., U.S.	B1	86
Chippewa, co., Mi., U.S.	B6	99
Chippewa, co., Mn., U.S.	E3	100
Chippewa, co., Wi., U.S.	C2	126
Chippewa, stm., Mn., U.S.	E3	100
Chippewa, stm., Wi., U.S.	D2	126
Chippewa, Lake, l., Wi., U.S.	C2	126
Chippewa Falls, Wi., U.S.	D2	126
Chipuxet, stm., R.I., U.S.	F3	116
Chiquimula, Guat.	G3	64
Chiquinquirá, Col.	E6	58
Chīrāla, India	E6	37
Chirfa, Niger	D8	42
Chirgis Nuur, l., Mong.	B5	26
Chiricahua Mountains, mts., Az., U.S.	F6	80
Chiricahua National Monument, Az., U.S.	F6	80
Chiricahua Peak, mtn., Az., U.S.	F6	80
Chiriguaná, Col.	C6	58
Chirikof Island, i., Ak., U.S.	D8	79
Chiriquí, Golfo de, b., Pan.	K6	64
Chiriquí, Laguna de, b., Pan.	J7	64
Chirripó, Cerro, mtn., C.R.	J6	64
Chisago, co., Mn., U.S.	E6	100
Chisago City, Mn., U.S.	E6	100
Chisholm, Mn., U.S.	C6	100
Chisholm, Ok., U.S.	C6	100
Chishtiān Mandi, Pak.	F5	38
Chisos Mountains, mts., Tx., U.S.	E1	120
Chitato, Ang.	C4	44
Chitembo, Ang.	D3	44
Chitina, Ak., U.S.	g19	79
Chitipa, Mwi.	C6	44
Chitorgarh, India	H6	38
Chitose, Japan	q19	30a
Chitradurga, India	F4	37
Chitrāl, Pak.	B5	38
Chitré, Pan.	K7	64
Chittagong, Bngl.	I14	38
Chittenango, N.Y., U.S.	B5	109
Chittenden, co., Vt., U.S.	C2	122

Name	Map Ref	Page
Chittenden Reservoir, res., Vt., U.S.	D3	122
Chittoor, India	F5	37
Chiusi, Italy	F6	14
Chivasso, Italy	D2	14
Choapan, Mex.	I12	62
Chocolate Mountains, mts., U.S.	F6	82
Chocontá, Col.	E6	58
Choctaw, Ok., U.S.	B4	113
Choctaw, co., Al., U.S.	C1	78
Choctaw, co., Ms., U.S.	B4	101
Choctaw, co., Ok., U.S.	C6	113
Choctawhatchee Bay, b., Fl., U.S.	u15	86
Choctaw Indian Reservation, Ms., U.S.	C4	101
Choele-Choel, Arg.	D3	56
Cholet, Fr.	E6	10
Cholmsk, Russia	H22	24
Choluteca, Hond.	H4	64
Choma, Zam.	E5	44
Chomutov, Czech.	E13	8
Chon Buri, Thai.	H6	34
Chone, Ec.	H2	58
Ch'ŏngjin, N. Kor.	C12	26
Ch'ŏngju, S. Kor.	D12	26
Chongmingdao, i., China	D10	28
Chongqing, China	F8	26
Chŏnju, S. Kor.	D12	26
Chonos, Archipiélago de los, is., Chile	F2	56
Chonui, Russia	D22	24
Choptank, stm., Md., U.S.	C6	97
Chōshi, Japan	G13	30
Chos Malal, Arg.	D2	56
Choteau, Mt., U.S.	C4	103
Chouteau, Ok., U.S.	A6	113
Chouteau, co., Mt., U.S.	C6	103
Chovd, Mong.	B5	26
Chövsgöl Nuur, l., Mong.	A7	26
Chowan, co., N.C., U.S.	A6	110
Chowan, stm., N.C., U.S.	A6	110
Chowchilla, Ca., U.S.	D3	82
Chrisman, Il., U.S.	D6	90
Christanshåb, Grnld.	C22	66
Christchurch, N.Z.	E4	52
Christian, co., Il., U.S.	D4	90
Christian, co., Ky., U.S.	D2	94
Christian, co., Mo., U.S.	E4	102
Christian, Cape, c., N.W. Ter., Can.	B19	66
Christiana, De., U.S.	B3	85
Christiana, Pa., U.S.	G9	115
Christiansburg, Va., U.S.	C2	123
Christian Sound, strt., Ak., U.S.	n22	79
Christiansted, V.I.U.S.	F15	64
Christina, stm., Alta., Can.	A5	68
Christina, stm., De., U.S.	B3	85
Christina, Lake, l., Mn., U.S.	D3	100
Christina Peak, mtn., Nv., U.S.	D6	105
Christmas, Fl., U.S.	D5	86
Christmas Island, dep., Oc.	H4	32
Christmas Lake, l., Or., U.S.	D6	114
Christopher, Il., U.S.	F4	90
Chroma, stm., Russia	C22	24
Chrzanów, Pol.	E19	8
Chubbuck, Id., U.S.	G6	89
Chugach Islands, is., Ak., U.S.	h16	79
Chugach Mountains, mts., Ak., U.S.	g18	79
Chūgoku-sanchi, mts., Japan	H5	30
Chugwater, Wy., U.S.	E8	127
Chugwater Creek, stm., Wy., U.S.	E8	127
Chukai, Malay.	L7	34
Chukchi Sea	C30	128
Chula Vista, Ca., U.S.	F5	82
Chulucanas, Peru	E2	54
Chumphon, Thai.	G6	34
Chum Saeng, Thai.	G6	34
Chunchi, Ec.	I3	58
Ch'unch'ŏn, S. Kor.	D12	26
Chunchula, Al., U.S.	E1	78
Ch'ungju, S. Kor.	D12	26
Chungking see Chongqing, China	F8	26
Chungli, Tai.	K10	28
Chungyang Shanmo, mts., Tai.	L10	28
Chuŏr Phnum Krâvanh, mts., Asia	H7	34
Chupadera Mesa, mtn., N.M., U.S.	D3	108
Chupaderos, Mex.	F8	62
Chuquicamata, Chile	A3	56
Chur, Switz.	F16	10
Church Hill, Tn., U.S.	C11	119
Churchill, Man., Can.	f9	70
Churchill, co., Nv., U.S.	D3	105
Churchill, stm., Can.	E13	66
Churchill, stm., Newf., Can.	h9	72
Churchill, Cape, c., Man., Can.	f9	70
Churchill, Mount, mtn., B.C., Can.	E6	69
Churchill Falls, wtfl, Newf., Can.	h9	72
Churchill Lake, l., Sask., Can.	m7	75
Churchill Lake, l., Me., U.S.	B3	96
Church Point, La., U.S.	D3	95
Church Rock, N.M., U.S.	B1	108
Churchton, Md., U.S.	C4	97
Churchville, N.Y., U.S.	B3	109
Churu, India	F6	38
Churubusco, In., U.S.	B7	91
Churuguara, Ven.	B8	58
Chuska Mountains, mts., Az., U.S.	A6	80
Chutag, Mong.	B7	26
Chuxian, China	C7	28
Chuxiong, China	B6	34
Chuzhir, Russia	G15	24
Cianjur, Indon.	G4	32
Cibecue, Az., U.S.	C5	80
Cibinong, Indon.	m13	33a
Cibola, co., N.M., U.S.	C1	108
Cibolo Creek, stm., Tx., U.S.	h7	120
Cicero, Il., U.S.	B6	90
Cicero, In., U.S.	D5	91
Ciechanów, Pol.	C20	8
Ciego de Avila, Cuba	D8	64
Ciempozuelos, Spain	E8	12
Ciénaga, Col.	B5	58
Cienfuegos, Cuba	C7	64
Cieszyn, Pol.	F18	8
Cieza, Spain	G10	12
Cifuentes, Spain	E9	12
Cikampek, Indon.	m13	33a
Cilacap, Indon.	m14	33a
Cilleruelo de Bezana, Spain	C8	12
Cimarron, Ks., U.S.	E3	93
Cimarron, N.M., U.S.	A5	108
Cimarron, co., Ok., U.S.	e8	113
Cimkent, Kaz.	I11	22
Çınarcık, Tur.	I13	16
Cincinnati, Oh., U.S.	C1	112
Çine, Tur.	L12	16
Çiney, Bel.	E5	8
Cinnaminson, N.J., U.S.	D3	107
Cipa, stm., Russia	F17	24
Cipolletti, Arg.	D3	56
Circle, Ak., U.S.	B11	79
Circle, Mt., U.S.	C11	103
Circle Pines, Mn., U.S.	m12	100
Circleville, Oh., U.S.	C3	112
Cirebon, Indon.	m14	32
Cirencester, Eng., U.K.	J11	7
Ciriè, Italy	D2	14
Cirò Marina, Italy	J12	14
Cisco, Tx., U.S.	C3	120
Cispus, stm., Wa., U.S.	C4	124
Cissna Park, Il., U.S.	C6	90
Cistierna, Spain	C6	12
Cita, Russia	G16	24
Citra, Fl., U.S.	C4	86
Citronelle, Al., U.S.	D1	78
Citrus, co., Fl., U.S.	D4	86
Città di Castello, Italy	F7	14
City View, S.C., U.S.	B3	117
Ciudad, Mex.	F7	62
Ciudad Acuña, Mex.	C9	62
Ciudad Altamirano, Mex.	H9	62
Ciudad Bolívar, Ven.	C11	58
Ciudad Bolivia, Ven.	C7	58
Ciudad Camargo, Mex.	D7	62
Ciudad Chetumal, Mex.	H15	62
Ciudad del Carmen, Mex.	H14	62
Ciudad del Maíz, Mex.	F10	62
Ciudad de México (Mexico City), Mex.	H10	62
Ciudad de Nutrias, Ven.	C8	58
Ciudad de Valles, Mex.	G10	62
Ciudadela, Spain	E15	12
Ciudad Guayana, Ven.	C11	58
Ciudad Guzmán, Mex.	H8	62
Ciudad Hidalgo, Mex.	H9	62
Ciudad Ixtepec, Mex.	I12	62
Ciudad Jiménez, Mex.	D7	62
Ciudad Juárez, Mex.	B6	62
Ciudad Madero, Mex.	F11	62
Ciudad Mante, Mex.	F10	62
Ciudad Melchor Múzquiz, Mex.	D9	62
Ciudad Obregón, Mex.	D5	62
Ciudad Ojeda (Lagunillas), Ven.	B7	58
Ciudad Piar, Ven.	D11	58
Ciudad Real, Spain	G8	12
Ciudad Rodrigo, Spain	E5	12
Ciudad Victoria, Mex.	F10	62
Civita Castellana, Italy	G7	14
Civitanova Marche, Italy	F8	14
Civitavecchia, Italy	G6	14
Civray, Fr.	F7	10
C.J. Strike Reservoir, res., Id., U.S.	G3	89
Clackamas, Or., U.S.	h12	114
Clackamas, co., Or., U.S.	B4	114
Clacton-on-Sea, Eng., U.K.	J14	7
Claflin, Ks., U.S.	D5	93
Claiborne, co., La., U.S.	B2	95
Claiborne, co., Ms., U.S.	D3	101
Claiborne, co., Tn., U.S.	C10	119
Claiborne, Lake, res., La., U.S.	B3	95
Clair, N.B., Can.	B1	71
Claire, Lake, l., Alta., Can.	f8	68
Clair Engle Lake, res., Ca., U.S.	B2	82
Clairton, Pa., U.S.	F2	115
Clallam, co., Wa., U.S.	B1	124
Clallam Bay, Wa., U.S.	A1	124
Clamecy, Fr.	E10	10
Clam Lake, l., Wi., U.S.	C1	126
Clan Alpine Mountains, mts., Nv., U.S.	D4	105
Clanton, Al., U.S.	C3	78
Clanwilliam, S. Afr.	H3	44
Clara City, Mn., U.S.	F3	100
Clara Peak, mtn., Az., U.S.	C2	80
Clare, Mi., U.S.	E6	99
Clare, co., Mi., U.S.	E6	99
Claremont, Ca., U.S.	m13	82
Claremont, N.H., U.S.	D2	106
Claremont, N.C., U.S.	B1	110
Claremont, mtn., Ca., U.S.	C3	82
Claremore, Ok., U.S.	A6	113
Claremorris, Ire.	H3	7
Clarence, Ia., U.S.	C6	92
Clarence, Mo., U.S.	B5	102
Clarence Strait, strt., Ak., U.S.	n23	79
Clarendon, Ar., U.S.	C4	81
Clarendon, Tx., U.S.	B2	120
Clarendon, co., S.C., U.S.	D7	117
Clarendon, stm., Vt., U.S.	E2	122
Clarendon Hills, Il., U.S.	k9	90
Clarenville, Newf., Can.	D4	72
Claresholm, Alta., Can.	D4	68
Claridge, Pa., U.S.	F2	115
Clarinda, Ia., U.S.	D2	92
Clarines, Ven.	C10	58
Clarion, Ia., U.S.	B4	92
Clarion, Pa., U.S.	D3	115
Clarion, co., Pa., U.S.	D3	115
Clarion, stm., Pa., U.S.	D3	115
Clarión, Isla, i., Mex.	H2	62
Clarissa, Mn., U.S.	D4	100
Clark, N.J., U.S.	B4	107
Clark, S.D., U.S.	C8	118
Clark, co., Ar., U.S.	C2	81
Clark, co., Id., U.S.	E6	89
Clark, co., Il., U.S.	D6	90
Clark, co., In., U.S.	H6	91
Clark, co., Ks., U.S.	E4	93
Clark, co., Ky., U.S.	C5	94
Clark, co., Mo., U.S.	A6	102
Clark, co., Nv., U.S.	G6	105
Clark, co., Oh., U.S.	C2	112
Clark, co., S.D., U.S.	C8	118
Clark, co., Wa., U.S.	D3	124
Clark, co., Wi., U.S.	D3	126
Clark, Lake, l., Ak., U.S.	C9	79
Clark, Point, c., Ont., Can.	C3	73
Clarkdale, Az., U.S.	C3	80
Clarkdale, Ga., U.S.	h7	87
Clarke, co., Al., U.S.	D2	78
Clarke, co., Ga., U.S.	C3	87
Clarke, co., Ia., U.S.	D4	92
Clarke, co., Ms., U.S.	C5	101
Clarke, co., Va., U.S.	A4	123
Clarkfield, Mn., U.S.	F3	100
Clarks, La., U.S.	B3	95
Clarks, stm., Ky., U.S.	f9	94
Clarksburg, Md., U.S.	B3	97
Clarksburg, W.V., U.S.	B4	125
Clarksdale, Ms., U.S.	A3	101
Clarks Grove, Mn., U.S.	G5	100
Clark's Harbour, N.S., Can.	F4	71
Clarks Hill, In., U.S.	D4	91
Clarkson, Ky., U.S.	C3	94
Clarkson, Ne., U.S.	C8	104
Clarks Summit, Pa., U.S.	m18	115
Clarkston, Ga., U.S.	h8	87
Clarkston, Mi., U.S.	F7	99
Clarkston, Ut., U.S.	B3	121
Clarkston, Wa., U.S.	C8	124
Clarksville, Ar., U.S.	B2	81
Clarksville, De., U.S.	F5	85
Clarksville, In., U.S.	H6	91
Clarksville, Ia., U.S.	B5	92
Clarksville, Tn., U.S.	A4	119
Clarksville, Tx., U.S.	C5	120
Clarksville, Va., U.S.	D4	123
Clarkton, Mo., U.S.	E8	102
Clarkton, N.C., U.S.	C4	110
Clatskanie, Or., U.S.	A3	114
Clatsop, co., Or., U.S.	A3	114
Claude, Tx., U.S.	B2	120
Clausthal-Zellerfeld, Ger.	D10	8
Clawson, Mi., U.S.	o15	99
Claxton, Ga., U.S.	D5	87
Clay, Ky., U.S.	C2	94
Clay, co., Al., U.S.	B4	78
Clay, co., Ar., U.S.	A5	81
Clay, co., Fl., U.S.	B5	86
Clay, co., Ga., U.S.	E2	87
Clay, co., Il., U.S.	E5	90
Clay, co., In., U.S.	F3	91
Clay, co., Ia., U.S.	A2	92
Clay, co., Ks., U.S.	C6	93
Clay, co., Ky., U.S.	C6	94
Clay, co., Mn., U.S.	D2	100
Clay, co., Ms., U.S.	B5	101
Clay, co., Mo., U.S.	B3	102
Clay, co., Ne., U.S.	D7	104
Clay, co., N.C., U.S.	f9	110
Clay, co., S.D., U.S.	E8	118
Clay, co., Tn., U.S.	C8	119
Clay, co., Tx., U.S.	C3	120
Clay, co., W.V., U.S.	C3	125
Clay Center, Ks., U.S.	C6	93
Clay Center, Ne., U.S.	D7	104
Clay City, Il., U.S.	E5	90
Clay City, In., U.S.	F3	91
Clay City, Ky., U.S.	C6	94
Clay Creek, stm., S.D., U.S.	D8	118
Claymont, De., U.S.	A4	85
Claypool, Az., U.S.	D5	80
Claysburg, Pa., U.S.	F5	115
Claysville, Pa., U.S.	F1	115
Clayton, Al., U.S.	D4	78
Clayton, De., U.S.	C3	85
Clayton, Ga., U.S.	B3	87
Clayton, In., U.S.	E4	91
Clayton, Mo., U.S.	f13	102
Clayton, N.J., U.S.	D2	107
Clayton, N.M., U.S.	A6	108
Clayton, N.Y., U.S.	A4	109
Clayton, N.C., U.S.	B4	110
Clayton, Ok., U.S.	C6	113
Clayton, co., Ga., U.S.	C2	87
Clayton, co., Ia., U.S.	B6	92
Claytor Lake, res., Va., U.S.	C2	123
Clear, stm., R.I., U.S.	B2	116
Clear Boggy Creek, stm., Ok., U.S.	C5	113
Clear Creek, co., Co., U.S.	B5	83
Clear Creek, stm., Tn., U.S.	C9	119
Clear Creek, stm., W.V., U.S.	n13	125
Cleare, Cape, c., Ak., U.S.	D10	79
Clearfield, Ky., U.S.	B6	94
Clearfield, Pa., U.S.	D5	115
Clearfield, Ut., U.S.	B3	121
Clearfield, co., Pa., U.S.	D5	115
Clear Fork, stm., W.V., U.S.	D3	125
Clear Fork, stm., W.V., U.S.	n13	125
Clearlake, Ca., U.S.	C2	82
Clear Lake, Ia., U.S.	A4	92
Clear Lake, S.D., U.S.	C9	118
Clearlake, Wa., U.S.	A3	124
Clear Lake, Wi., U.S.	C1	126
Clear Lake, l., Ia., U.S.	A4	92
Clear Lake, l., Ut., U.S.	D3	121
Clear Lake, res., Ca., U.S.	C2	82
Clear Lake Reservoir, res., Ca., U.S.	B3	82
Clear Lake Shores, Tx., U.S.	r15	120
Clear Stream, stm., N.H., U.S.	g7	106
Clearwater, B.C., Can.	D7	69
Clearwater, Fl., U.S.	E4	86
Clearwater, Ks., U.S.	E6	93
Clearwater, S.C., U.S.	E4	117
Clearwater, co., Id., U.S.	C3	89
Clearwater, co., Mn., U.S.	C3	100
Clearwater, stm., Can.	A5	68
Clearwater, stm., Id., U.S.	C2	89
Clearwater, stm., Mn., U.S.	C3	100
Clearwater, Lake, res., Mo., U.S.	D7	102
Clearwater Mountains, mts., Id., U.S.	C2	89
Cleburne, Tx., U.S.	C4	120
Cleburne, co., Al., U.S.	B4	78
Cleburne, co., Ar., U.S.	B3	81
Cle Elum, Wa., U.S.	B5	124
Cle Elum, stm., Wa., U.S.	B4	124
Cle Elum Lake, res., Wa., U.S.	B4	124
Clementon, N.J., U.S.	D3	107
Clemmons, N.C., U.S.	A2	110
Clemson, S.C., U.S.	B2	117
Clendenin, W.V., U.S.	C3	125
Clendening Lake, res., Oh., U.S.	B4	112
Cleona, Pa., U.S.	F9	115
Clermont, Que., Can.	B7	74
Clermont, Fr.	C9	10
Clermont, Fl., U.S.	D5	86
Clermont, co., Oh., U.S.	C1	112
Clermont-Ferrand, Fr.	G10	10
Cles, Italy	C6	14
Cleveland, Al., U.S.	A3	78
Cleveland, Ga., U.S.	B3	87
Cleveland, Mn., U.S.	F5	100
Cleveland, Ms., U.S.	B3	101
Cleveland, N.C., U.S.	B2	110
Cleveland, Oh., U.S.	A4	112
Cleveland, Ok., U.S.	A5	113
Cleveland, Tn., U.S.	D9	119
Cleveland, Tx., U.S.	D5	120
Cleveland, Wi., U.S.	k10	126
Cleveland, co., Ar., U.S.	D3	81
Cleveland, co., N.C., U.S.	B1	110
Cleveland, co., Ok., U.S.	B4	113
Cleveland, Mount, mtn., Mt., U.S.	B3	103
Cleveland Heights, Oh., U.S.	A4	112
Cleves, Oh., U.S.	o12	112
Clewiston, Fl., U.S.	F6	86
Clifden, Ire.	H2	7
Cliff Island, i., Me., U.S.	g7	96
Clifford, Ont., Can.	D4	73
Cliffside, N.C., U.S.	B1	110
Cliffside Park, N.J., U.S.	h9	107
Clifton, Az., U.S.	D6	80
Clifton, Co., U.S.	B2	83
Clifton, Il., U.S.	C6	90
Clifton, N.J., U.S.	B4	107
Clifton, S.C., U.S.	B4	117
Clifton, Tn., U.S.	B4	119
Clifton, Tx., U.S.	D4	120
Clifton Forge, Va., U.S.	C3	123
Clifton Knolls, N.Y., U.S.	C7	109
Clifton Springs, N.Y., U.S.	C3	109
Clinch, co., Ga., U.S.	F4	87
Clinch, stm., U.S.	D9	119
Clinch Mountain, mtn., U.S.	C10	119
Clingmans Dome, mtn., U.S.	D10	119
Clinton, B.C., Can.	D7	69
Clinton, Ont., Can.	D3	73
Clinton, Ar., U.S.	B3	81
Clinton, Ct., U.S.	D5	84
Clinton, Il., U.S.	C5	90
Clinton, In., U.S.	E3	91
Clinton, Ia., U.S.	C7	92
Clinton, Ky., U.S.	f9	94
Clinton, La., U.S.	D4	95
Clinton, Me., U.S.	D3	96
Clinton, Md., U.S.	C4	97
Clinton, Ma., U.S.	B4	98
Clinton, Mi., U.S.	F7	99
Clinton, Mn., U.S.	E2	100
Clinton, Mo., U.S.	C4	102
Clinton, N.Y., U.S.	B5	109
Clinton, N.C., U.S.	C4	110
Clinton, Ok., U.S.	B3	113
Clinton, S.C., U.S.	C4	117
Clinton, Tn., U.S.	C9	119
Clinton, Ut., U.S.	B3	121
Clinton, Wa., U.S.	B3	124
Clinton, Wi., U.S.	F5	126
Clinton, co., Il., U.S.	E4	90
Clinton, co., In., U.S.	D4	91
Clinton, co., Ia., U.S.	C7	92
Clinton, co., Ky., U.S.	D4	94
Clinton, co., Mi., U.S.	F6	99
Clinton, co., Mo., U.S.	B3	102
Clinton, co., N.Y., U.S.	f11	109
Clinton, co., Oh., U.S.	C2	112
Clinton, co., Pa., U.S.	D6	115
Clinton-Colden Lake, l., N.W. Ter., Can.	D11	66
Clinton Lake, res., Ks., U.S.	m15	93
Clinton Reservoir, res., N.J., U.S.	A4	107
Clintonville, Wi., U.S.	D5	126
Clintwood, Va., U.S.	e9	123
Clio, Al., U.S.	D4	78
Clio, Mi., U.S.	E7	99
Clio, S.C., U.S.	B8	117
Clive, Ia., U.S.	e8	92
Clogher Head, c., Ire.	H6	7
Cloncurry, Austl.	D8	50
Clonmel, Ire.	I5	7
Cloppenburg, Ger.	C8	8
Cloquet, Mn., U.S.	D6	100
Cloquet, stm., Mn., U.S.	C6	100
Closter, N.J., U.S.	B5	107
Clothier, W.V., U.S.	n12	125
Cloud, co., Ks., U.S.	C6	93
Cloudcroft, N.M., U.S.	E4	108
Cloud Peak, mtn., Wy., U.S.	B5	127
Clover, S.C., U.S.	A5	117
Cloverdale, Al., U.S.	A2	78
Cloverdale, Ca., U.S.	C2	82
Cloverdale, In., U.S.	E4	91
Cloverport, Ky., U.S.	C3	94
Clovis, Ca., U.S.	D4	82
Clovis, N.M., U.S.	C6	108
Clute, Tx., U.S.	r14	120
Clutha, stm., N.Z.	G2	52
Clyde, N.W. Ter., Can.	B19	66
Clyde, Ks., U.S.	C6	93
Clyde, N.Y., U.S.	B4	109
Clyde, N.C., U.S.	f10	110
Clyde, Oh., U.S.	A3	112
Clyde, Tx., U.S.	C3	120
Clyde, stm., Scot., U.K.	F9	7
Clyde, Firth of, est., Scot., U.K.	F7	7
Clymer, Pa., U.S.	E3	115
Coachella, Ca., U.S.	F5	82
Coachella Canal, Ca., U.S.	F6	82
Coacoyole, Mex.	E6	62
Coahoma, Tx., U.S.	C2	120
Coahoma, co., Ms., U.S.	A3	101
Coal, co., Ok., U.S.	C5	113
Coal, stm., W.V., U.S.	C3	125
Coal Branch, N.B., Can.	C4	71
Coal City, Il., U.S.	B5	90
Coalcomán de Matamoros, Mex.	H8	62
Coal Creek, stm., Ok., U.S.	B6	113
Coaldale, Alta., Can.	E4	68
Coal Fork, W.V., U.S.	C3	125
Coal Fork, stm., W.V., U.S.	m13	125
Coalgate, Ok., U.S.	C5	113
Coal Grove, Oh., U.S.	D3	112
Coalhurst, Alta., Can.	E4	68
Coalinga, Ca., U.S.	D3	82
Coalmont, Tn., U.S.	D8	119
Coalville, Ut., U.S.	C4	121
Coalwood, W.V., U.S.	D3	125
Coari, Braz.	D6	54
Coasters Harbor Island, i., R.I., U.S.	E5	116
Coast Mountains, mts., N.A.	E6	66
Coast Ranges, mts., U.S.	C2	76
Coatepeque, Guat.	G2	64
Coatesville, Pa., U.S.	G10	115
Coaticook, Que., Can.	D6	74
Coats, N.C., U.S.	B4	110
Coats Island, i., N.W. Ter., Can.	D16	66
Coats Land, reg., Ant.	B10	47
Coatzacoalcos, Mex.	H12	62
Cobalt, Ont., Can.	p19	73
Cobb, co., Ga., U.S.	C2	87
Cobb, stm., Mn., U.S.	G5	100
Cobble Mountain Reservoir, res., Ma., U.S.	B2	98
Cobbosseecontee Lake, l., Me., U.S.	D3	96
Cobden, Ont., Can.	B8	73
Cobden, Il., U.S.	F4	90
Cobequid Mountains, mts., N.S., Can.	D5	71
Cobham, stm., Can.	C4	70
Cobija, Bol.	F5	54
Cobleskill, N.Y., U.S.	C6	109
Cobourg, Ont., Can.	D6	73
Côbuè, Moz.	D6	44
Cobun Creek, stm., W.V., U.S.	h11	125
Coburg, Ger.	E10	8
Coburg, Or., U.S.	C3	114
Coburg Island, i., N.W. Ter., Can.	A17	66
Cochabamba, Bol.	G5	54
Cocheco, stm., N.H., U.S.	D5	106
Cochin, India	H4	37
Cochise, co., Az., U.S.	F5	80
Cochise Head, mtn., Az., U.S.	E6	80
Cochiti Indian Reservation, N.M., U.S.	h8	108
Cochiti Reservoir, res., N.M., U.S.	B3	108
Cochituate, Ma., U.S.	g10	98
Cochituate, Lake, l., Ma., U.S.	g10	98
Cochran, Ga., U.S.	D3	87
Cochran, co., Tx., U.S.	C1	120
Cochrane, Alta., Can.	D3	68
Cochrane, Ont., Can.	o19	73
Cochranton, Pa., U.S.	C1	115
Cocke, co., Tn., U.S.	D10	119
Cockeysville, Md., U.S.	B4	97
Cockrell Hill, Tx., U.S.	n10	120
Coco, stm., N.A.	G6	64
Coco, Isla del, i., C.R.	B1	64
Cocoa, Fl., U.S.	D6	86
Cocoa Beach, Fl., U.S.	D6	86
Coco Channel, strt., Asia	H2	34
Coco Islands, is., Burma	G2	34
Coconino, co., Az., U.S.	B3	80
Cocopah Indian Reservation, Az., U.S.	E1	80
Côcos, Braz.	C6	57
Cocula, Mex.	G8	62
Cod, Cape, c., Ma., U.S.	C7	98
Codajás, Braz.	D6	54
Coden, Al., U.S.	E1	78
Codigoro, Italy	E7	14
Codington, co., S.D., U.S.	C8	118
Codogno, Italy	D4	14
Codroipo, Italy	D7	14
Cody, Wy., U.S.	B3	127
Coeburn, Va., U.S.	f9	123
Coen, Austl.	B8	50
Coetivy Island, i., Sey.	C11	44
Coeur d'Alene, Id., U.S.	B2	89
Coeur d'Alene, stm., Id., U.S.	B2	89
Coeur d'Alene Indian Reservation, Id., U.S.	B2	89
Coeur d'Alene Lake, res., Id., U.S.	B2	89
Coeur d'Alene Mountains, mts., Id., U.S.	B2	89
Coffee, co., Al., U.S.	D3	78
Coffee, co., Ga., U.S.	E4	87
Coffee, co., Tn., U.S.	B5	119
Coffeeville, Ms., U.S.	B4	101
Coffey, co., Ks., U.S.	D8	93
Coffeyville, Ks., U.S.	E8	93
Coffs Harbour, Austl.	F10	50
Coggon, Ia., U.S.	B6	92
Cognac, Fr.	G6	10
Cohansey, stm., N.J., U.S.	E2	107
Cohasset, Ma., U.S.	B6	98
Cohasset, Mn., U.S.	C5	100
Cohocton, stm., N.Y., U.S.	C3	109
Cohoes, N.Y., U.S.	C7	109
Cohoon, Lake, res., Va., U.S.	k14	123
Cohutta Mountain, mtn., Ga., U.S.	B2	87
Coiba, Isla de, i., Pan.	K7	64
Coimbatore, India	G4	37
Coimbra, Braz.	F7	57
Coimbra, Port.	E3	12
Coin, Spain	I7	12
Cojbalsan, Mong.	B9	26
Cokato, Mn., U.S.	E4	100
Coke, co., Tx., U.S.	D2	120
Cokeville, Wy., U.S.	D2	127
Çokurdach, Russia	C23	24

Name	Map Ref	Page
Colatina, Braz.	E8	57
Colbert, Ok., U.S.	D5	113
Colbert, co., Al., U.S.	A2	78
Colborne, Ont., Can.	C7	73
Colby, Ks., U.S.	C2	93
Colby, Wi., U.S.	D3	126
Colchester, Eng., U.K.	J13	7
Colchester, Ct., U.S.	C6	84
Colchester, Vt., U.S.	C3	90
Colcord, Ok., U.S.	A7	113
Cold, stm., N.H., U.S.	C4	106
Cold, stm., N.H., U.S.	D2	106
Cold Bay, Ak., U.S.	E7	79
Cold Lake, Alta., Can.	B5	68
Cold Spring, Ky., U.S.	A5	94
Cold Spring, Mn., U.S.	E4	100
Coldwater, Ont., Can.	C5	73
Coldwater, Ks., U.S.	E4	93
Coldwater, Mi., U.S.	G5	99
Coldwater, Ms., U.S.	A4	101
Coldwater, stm., Ms., U.S.	B1	112
Coldwater, stm., Ms., U.S.	A3	101
Coldwater Creek, stm., U.S.	e9	113
Cole, co., Mo., U.S.	C5	102
Colebrook, N.H., U.S.	g7	106
Colebrook River Lake, res., Ct., U.S.	A3	84
Cole Camp, Mo., U.S.	C4	102
Coleen, stm., Ak., U.S.	B11	79
Coleman, Mi., U.S.	E6	99
Coleman, Tx., U.S.	D3	120
Coleman, Wi., U.S.	C5	126
Coleman, co., Tx., U.S.	D3	120
Coleraine, N. Ire., U.K.	F6	7
Coleraine, Mn., U.S.	C5	100
Coles, co., Il., U.S.	D5	90
Colesberg, S. Afr.	H5	44
Colfax, Ca., U.S.	C3	82
Colfax, Il., U.S.	C5	90
Colfax, Ia., U.S.	C4	92
Colfax, La., U.S.	C3	95
Colfax, Wa., U.S.	C8	124
Colfax, Wi., U.S.	D2	126
Colfax, co., Ne., U.S.	C8	104
Colfax, co., N.M., U.S.	A5	108
Colhué Huapi, Lago, l., Arg.	F3	56
Colima, Mex.	H8	62
Colima, Nevado de, mtn., Mex.	H8	62
Colinas, Braz.	E10	54
Coll, i., Scot., U.K.	E6	7
College, Ak., U.S.	B10	79
Collegedale, Tn., U.S.	h11	119
College Park, Ga., U.S.	C2	87
College Park, Md., U.S.	C4	97
College Place, Wa., U.S.	C7	124
College Station, Ar., U.S.	C3	81
College Station, Tx., U.S.	D4	120
Collegeville, In., U.S.	C3	91
Collegeville, Pa., U.S.	F11	115
Colleton, co., S.C., U.S.	F6	117
Collier, co., Fl., U.S.	F5	86
Collier Bay, b., Austl.	C4	50
Colliers, W.V., U.S.	f8	125
Collierville, Tn., U.S.	B2	119
Collin, co., Tx., U.S.	C4	120
Collingdale, Pa., U.S.	p20	115
Collingswood, N.J., U.S.	D2	107
Collingsworth, co., Tx., U.S.	B2	120
Collingwood, Ont., Can.	C4	73
Collins, Ms., U.S.	D4	101
Collins Park, De., U.S.	i8	85
Collinsville, Al., U.S.	A4	78
Collinsville, Ct., U.S.	B4	84
Collinsville, Il., U.S.	E4	90
Collinsville, Ms., U.S.	C5	101
Collinsville, Ok., U.S.	A6	113
Collinsville, Va., U.S.	D3	123
Collinwood, Tn., U.S.	B4	119
Collooney, Ire.		
Colmar, Fr.	D14	10
Colmar Manor, Md., U.S.	f9	97
Colmenar, Spain	I7	12
Colmenar de Oreja, Spain	E8	12
Colmenar Viejo, Spain	E8	12
Colo, Ia., U.S.	B4	92
Cologne see Köln, Ger.	E6	8
Coloma, Mi., U.S.	F4	99
Colomb-Béchar see Béchar, Alg.	B5	42
Colombia, ctry., S.A.	C4	54
Colombo, Sri L.	I5	37
Colón, Cuba	C7	64
Colón, Pan.	J8	64
Colon, Mi., U.S.	G5	99
Colon, Archipiélago de (Galapagos Islands), is., Ec.	m15	58a
Colonia Dora, Arg.	B4	56
Colonial Beach, Va., U.S.	B6	123
Colonial Heights, Tn., U.S.	C11	119
Colonial Heights, Va., U.S.	C5	123
Colonial National Historical Park, Va., U.S.	C6	123
Colonia Vicente Guerrero, Mex.	B1	62
Colonie, N.Y., U.S.	C7	109
Coloradas, Lomas, hills, Arg.	E3	56
Colorado, co., Tx., U.S.	E4	120
Colorado, state, U.S.	B5	83
Colorado, stm., Arg.	D4	56
Colorado, stm., N.A.	E4	76
Colorado, stm., Tx., U.S.	D3	120
Colorado City, Az., U.S.	A3	80
Colorado City, Co., U.S.	D6	83
Colorado City, Tx., U.S.	C2	120
Colorado City, Lake, res., Tx., U.S.	C2	120
Colorado National Monument, Co., U.S.	B2	83
Colorado River Aqueduct, Ca., U.S.	F6	82
Colorado River Indian Reservation, Ca., U.S.	D1	80
Colorado Springs, Co., U.S.	C6	83
Colotlán, Mex.	G8	62
Colquitt, Ga., U.S.	E2	87
Colquitt, co., Ga., U.S.	E3	87
Colstrip, Mt., U.S.	E10	103
Colton, S.D., U.S.	D9	118
Coltons Point, Md., U.S.	D4	97
Columbia, Al., U.S.	D4	78
Columbia, Il., U.S.	E3	90
Columbia, Ky., U.S.	C4	94
Columbia, Md., U.S.	B4	97
Columbia, Ms., U.S.	D4	101
Columbia, Mo., U.S.	C5	102
Columbia, N.C., U.S.	B6	110
Columbia, Pa., U.S.	F9	115
Columbia, S.C., U.S.	C5	117
Columbia, Tn., U.S.	B4	119
Columbia, co., Ar., U.S.	D2	81
Columbia, co., Fl., U.S.	B4	86
Columbia, co., Ga., U.S.	C4	87
Columbia, co., N.Y., U.S.	C7	109
Columbia, co., Or., U.S.	B3	114
Columbia, co., Pa., U.S.	D9	115
Columbia, co., Wa., U.S.	C7	124
Columbia, co., Wi., U.S.	E4	126
Columbia, stm., N.A.	G8	60
Columbia, Mount, mtn., Can.	C2	68
Columbia City, In., U.S.	B7	91
Columbia City, Or., U.S.	B4	114
Columbia Falls, Mt., U.S.	B2	103
Columbia Heights, Mn., U.S.	m12	100
Columbia Mountains, mts., B.C., Can.	C7	69
Columbiana, Al., U.S.	B3	78
Columbiana, Oh., U.S.	B5	112
Columbiana, co., Oh., U.S.	B5	112
Columbiaville, Mi., U.S.	E7	99
Columbus, Ga., U.S.	D2	87
Columbus, In., U.S.	F6	91
Columbus, Ks., U.S.	E9	93
Columbus, Ms., U.S.	B5	101
Columbus, Mt., U.S.	E7	103
Columbus, Ne., U.S.	C8	104
Columbus, N.M., U.S.	F2	108
Columbus, N.C., U.S.	f10	110
Columbus, Oh., U.S.	C2	112
Columbus, Tx., U.S.	E4	120
Columbus, Wi., U.S.	E4	126
Columbus, co., N.C., U.S.	C4	110
Columbus Air Force Base, mil., Ms., U.S.	B5	101
Columbus Grove, Oh., U.S.	B1	112
Columbus Junction, Ia., U.S.	C6	92
Columbus Lake, res., Ms., U.S.	B5	101
Colusa, Ca., U.S.	C2	82
Colusa, co., Ca., U.S.	C2	82
Colver, Pa., U.S.	E4	115
Colville, Wa., U.S.	A8	124
Colville, stm., Ak., U.S.	B9	79
Colville, stm., Wa., U.S.	A8	124
Colville Indian Reservation, Wa., U.S.	A6	124
Colvos Passage, strt., Wa., U.S.	f10	124
Colwich, Ks., U.S.	E6	93
Colwood, B.C., Can.	h12	69
Comacchio, Italy	E7	14
Comal, co., Tx., U.S.	E3	120
Comanche, Ok., U.S.	C4	113
Comanche, Tx., U.S.	D3	120
Comanche, co., Ks., U.S.	E4	93
Comanche, co., Ok., U.S.	C3	113
Comanche, co., Tx., U.S.	D3	120
Comandante Fontana, Arg.	B5	56
Comayagua, Hond.	G4	64
Combahee, stm., S.C., U.S.	F6	117
Combarbalá, Chile	C2	56
Combeaufontaine, Fr.	E12	10
Comber, Ont., Can.	E2	73
Combermere Bay, b., Burma	E2	34
Combined Locks, Wi., U.S.	h9	126
Combourg, Fr.	D5	10
Combs, Ky., U.S.	C6	94
Comer, Ga., U.S.	B3	87
Comfort, Tx., U.S.	E3	120
Comilla, Bngl.	I14	38
Comitán [de Domínguez], Mex.	I13	62
Comite, stm., La., U.S.	D4	95
Commentry, Fr.	F9	10
Commerce, Ga., U.S.	B3	87
Commerce, Ok., U.S.	A7	113
Commerce, Tx., U.S.	C5	120
Commerce City, Co., U.S.	B6	83
Committee Bay, b., N.W. Ter., Can.	C15	66
Common Fence Point, R.I., U.S.	D6	116
Como, Italy	D4	14
Como, Ms., U.S.	A4	101
Como, Lago di, l., Italy	C4	14
Comodoro Rivadavia, Arg.	F3	56
Comorin, Cape, c., India	H4	37
Comox, B.C., Can.	E5	69
Compiègne, Fr.	C9	10
Compton, Que., Can.	D6	74
Compton, Ca., U.S.	n12	82
Comstock, Mi., U.S.	F5	99
Con, stm., Viet.	E8	34
Cona, stm., Russia	E16	24
Conakry, Gui.	G3	42
Conanicut Island, i., R.I., U.S.	E5	116
Conanicut Point, c., R.I., U.S.	E5	116
Concarneau, Fr.	E3	10
Conceição do Araguaia, Braz.	E9	54
Concepción, Arg.	B3	56
Concepción, Bol.	G6	54
Concepción, Chile	D2	56
Concepción, Para.	A5	56
Concepción, Laguna, l., Bol.	G6	54
Concepción, Volcán, vol., Nic.	I5	64
Concepción del Oro, Mex.	E9	62
Concepción del Uruguay, Arg.	C5	56
Conception, Point, c., Ca., U.S.	E3	82
Conception Bay, b., Newf., Can.	E5	72
Conception Bay South, Newf., Can.	E5	72
Conchas Lake, res., N.M., U.S.	B5	108
Conches, Fr.	D7	10
Concho, co., Tx., U.S.	D3	120
Concho, stm., Tx., U.S.	D2	120
Conchos, stm., Mex.	C7	62
Concord, Ca., U.S.	h8	82
Concord, Ma., U.S.	B5	98
Concord, Mi., U.S.	F6	99
Concord, Mo., U.S.	g13	102
Concord, N.H., U.S.	D3	106
Concord, N.C., U.S.	B2	110
Concord, stm., Ma., U.S.	A5	98
Concordia, Arg.	C5	56
Concordia, Mex.	F6	62
Concordia, Ks., U.S.	C6	93
Concordia, Mo., U.S.	C4	102
Concordia, co., La., U.S.	C4	95
Concrete, Wa., U.S.	A4	124
Condé, Fr.	I7	10
Condom, Fr.		
Condon, Or., U.S.	B6	114
Condoto, Col.	E4	58
Conecuh, co., Al., U.S.	D2	78
Conecuh, stm., Al., U.S.	D3	78
Conegliano, Italy	D7	14
Conejos, co., Co., U.S.	D4	83
Conejos, stm., Co., U.S.	D4	83
Conejos Peak, mtn., Co., U.S.	D4	83
Conemaugh, Pa., U.S.	F4	115
Conemaugh River Lake, res., Pa., U.S.	F3	115
Confolens, Fr.	F7	10
Congamond Lakes, U.S.	A4	84
Congaree, stm., S.C., U.S.	D6	117
Congaree Swamp National Monument, S.C., U.S.	D6	117
Congo, ctry., Afr.	B2	44
Congo (Zaire), stm., Afr.	C2	44
Congress, Az., U.S.	C3	80
Conimicut Point, c., R.I., U.S.	D5	116
Conitaca, Mex.	E6	62
Conklin, N.Y., U.S.	C5	109
Conn, Lough, l., Ire.	G3	7
Connaught, hist. reg., Ire.	H3	7
Conneaut, Oh., U.S.	A5	112
Conneaut Creek, stm., Oh., U.S.	A5	112
Conneaut Lake, l., Pa., U.S.	C1	115
Connecticut, stm., U.S.	C12	76
Connecticut, state, U.S.	C5	84
Connell, Wa., U.S.	C7	124
Connellsville, Pa., U.S.	F2	115
Connemara, reg., Ire.	H3	7
Connersville, In., U.S.	E7	91
Conover, N.C., U.S.	B1	110
Conowingo, Md., U.S.	A5	97
Conrad, Ia., U.S.	B5	92
Conrad, Mt., U.S.	B5	103
Conroe, Tx., U.S.	D5	120
Conselheiro Lafaiete, Braz.	F7	57
Conshohocken, Pa., U.S.	F11	115
Con Son, is., Viet.	J9	34
Consort, Alta., Can.	C5	68
Constance, Lake see Bodensee, l., Eur.	H9	8
Constanța, Rom.	E12	16
Constantina, Spain	H6	12
Constantine (Qacentina), Alg.	A7	42
Constantine, Mi., U.S.	G5	99
Constantine, Cape, c., Ak., U.S.	D8	79
Consuegra, Spain	F8	12
Contai, India	J12	38
Contas, Rio de, stm., Braz.	C9	57
Content Keys, is., Fl., U.S.	H5	86
Continental, Oh., U.S.	A1	112
Continental Peak, mtn., Wy., U.S.	D4	127
Continental Reservoir, res., Co., U.S.	D3	83
Contoocook, N.H., U.S.	D3	106
Contoocook, stm., N.H., U.S.	D3	106
Contra Costa, co., Ca., U.S.	D3	82
Contrecoeur, Que., Can.	D4	74
Contres, Fr.	E8	10
Contwoyto Lake, l., N.W. Ter., Can.	C10	66
Convención, Col.	C6	58
Conversano, Italy	I12	14
Converse, In., U.S.	C6	91
Converse, co., Wy., U.S.	C7	127
Convoy, Oh., U.S.	B1	112
Conway, Ar., U.S.	B3	81
Conway, Fl., U.S.	D5	86
Conway, Mo., U.S.	D5	102
Conway, N.H., U.S.	C4	106
Conway, N.C., U.S.	A5	110
Conway, Pa., U.S.	E1	115
Conway, S.C., U.S.	D9	117
Conway, co., Ar., U.S.	B3	81
Conway, Lake, res., Ar., U.S.	B3	81
Conway Lake, l., N.H., U.S.	C4	106
Conway Springs, Ks., U.S.	E6	93
Conyers, Ga., U.S.	C2	87
Cooch Behār, India	G13	38
Cook, Mn., U.S.	C6	100
Cook, co., Ga., U.S.	E3	87
Cook, co., Il., U.S.	B6	90
Cook, co., Mn., U.S.	k9	100
Cook, Cape, c., B.C., Can.	D4	69
Cook, Mount, mtn., N.Z.	E3	52
Cooke, co., Tx., U.S.	C4	120
Cookes Peak, mtn., N.M., U.S.	E2	108
Cookeville, Tn., U.S.	C8	119
Cook Inlet, b., Ak., U.S.	D9	79
Cook Islands, dep., Oc.	H2	2
Cook Point, c., Md., U.S.	C5	97
Cookshire, Que., Can.	D6	74
Cookson, Ok., U.S.	B7	113
Cookstown, N. Ire., U.K.	G6	7
Cook Strait, strt., N.Z.	D5	52
Cooktown, Austl.	C9	50
Cooleemee, N.C., U.S.	B2	110
Coolgardie, Austl.	F4	50
Coolidge, Az., U.S.	E4	80
Coolidge, Ga., U.S.	E3	87
Cooma, Austl.	G9	50
Coon Rapids, Ia., U.S.	C3	92
Coon Rapids, Mn., U.S.	E5	100
Coon Valley, Wi., U.S.	E2	126
Cooper, Tx., U.S.	C5	120
Cooper, co., Mo., U.S.	C5	102
Cooper, stm., S.C., U.S.	F8	117
Cooper Mountain, mtn., Ak., U.S.	g17	79
Coopersburg, Pa., U.S.	F11	115
Cooperstown, N.Y., U.S.	C6	109
Cooperstown, N.D., U.S.	B7	111
Coopersville, Mi., U.S.	E5	99
Coos, co., N.H., U.S.	A4	106
Coos, co., Or., U.S.	D2	114
Coos, stm., Or., U.S.	D2	114
Coos Bay, Or., U.S.	D2	114
Coosa, co., Al., U.S.	C3	78
Coosa, stm., U.S.	C3	78
Coosada, Al., U.S.	C3	78
Coosawhatchie, stm., S.C., U.S.	F5	117
Copan, Ok., U.S.	A6	113
Copan Reservoir, res., Ok., U.S.	A6	113
Copenhagen see København, Den.	I9	6
Copiah, co., Ms., U.S.	D3	101
Copiapó, Chile	B2	56
Coplay, Pa., U.S.	E10	115
Copparo, Italy	E6	14
Copper, stm., Ak., U.S.	C11	79
Copper Butte, mtn., Wa., U.S.	A7	124
Coppermine, N.W. Ter., Can.	C9	66
Coppermine, stm., N.W. Ter., Can.	C10	66
Copper Mountain, mtn., Wy., U.S.	C5	127
Copper Mountains, mts., Az., U.S.	E2	80
Coquille, Or., U.S.	D2	114
Coquimbo, Chile	B2	56
Coral Gables, Fl., U.S.	G6	86
Coral Harbour, N.W. Ter., Can.	D16	66
Coral Sea, Oc.	B10	50
Coralville, Ia., U.S.	C6	92
Coralville Lake, res., Ia., U.S.	C5	92
Corantijn (Corentyne), stm., S.A.	E14	58
Coraopolis, Pa., U.S.	E1	115
Corato, Italy	H11	14
Corbeil-Essonnes, Fr.	D9	10
Corbigny, Fr.	E10	10
Corbin, Ky., U.S.	D5	94
Corcoran, Ca., U.S.	D4	82
Corcoran, Mn., U.S.	m11	100
Corcovado, Golfo de, b., Chile	E2	56
Corcovado, Volcán, vol., Chile	E2	56
Corcubión, Spain	C2	12
Cordele, Ga., U.S.	E3	87
Cordell, Ok., U.S.	B3	113
Cordell Hull Lake, res., Tn., U.S.	C8	119
Cordes, Fr.	H8	10
Córdoba, Arg.	C4	56
Córdoba, Mex.	H11	62
Córdoba, Spain	H7	12
Cordova, Al., U.S.	B2	78
Cordova, Ak., U.S.	C10	79
Cordova, N.M., U.S.	A4	108
Cordova Peak, mtn., Ak., U.S.	C10	79
Corentyne (Corantijn), stm., S.A.	E14	58
Corfu see Kérkira, Grc.	J3	16
Coria, Spain	F5	12
Coria del Río, Spain	H5	12
Corigliano Calabro, Italy	J11	14
Corinna, Me., U.S.	D3	96
Corinne, Ut., U.S.	B3	121
Corinne Key, i., Fl., U.S.	G6	86
Corinth, Ms., U.S.	A5	101
Corinth, N.Y., U.S.	B7	109
Corinth see Kórinthos, Grc.	L6	16
Corinto, Braz.	E7	57
Cork, Ire.	J4	7
Corlay, Fr.	D3	10
Corleone, Italy	L8	14
Corleto Perticara, Italy	I11	14
Corlu, Tur.	H11	16
Cormorant Lake, l., Man., Can.	B1	70
Cornelia, Ga., U.S.	B3	87
Cornélio Procópio, Braz.	G3	57
Cornelius, N.C., U.S.	B2	110
Cornelius, Or., U.S.	g11	114
Cornell, Wi., U.S.	C2	126
Corner Brook, Newf., Can.	D3	72
Cornersville, Tn., U.S.	B5	119
Cornfield Point, c., Ct., U.S.	D6	84
Cornie Bayou, stm., U.S.	D3	81
Corning, Ar., U.S.	A5	81
Corning, Ca., U.S.	C2	82
Corning, Ia., U.S.	D3	92
Corning, N.Y., U.S.	C3	109
Cornish, Me., U.S.	E2	96
Corno Grande, mtn., Italy	G8	14
Cornville, Az., U.S.	C4	80
Cornwall, Ont., Can.	B10	73
Cornwall, Pa., U.S.	F9	115
Cornwallis Island, i., N.W. Ter., Can.	A14	66
Cornwall on Hudson, N.Y., U.S.	D6	109
Coro, Ven.	B8	58
Corocoro, Bol.	G5	54
Coroico, Bol.	G5	54
Coromandel Coast, India	F6	37
Coromandel Peninsula, pen., N.Z.	B5	52
Corona, Ca., U.S.	F5	82
Coronado, Ca., U.S.	F5	82
Coronado National Memorial, Az., U.S.	F5	80
Coronation, Alta., Can.	C5	68
Coronation Gulf, b., N.W. Ter., Can.	C10	66
Coronation Island, i., Ak., U.S.	n22	79
Coronel Dorrego, Arg.	D4	56
Coronel Fabriciano, Braz.	E7	57
Coronel Pringles, Arg.	D4	56
Coronel Suárez, Arg.	D4	56
Coropuna, Nevado, mtn., Peru	G4	54
Corpus Christi, Tx., U.S.	F4	120
Corpus Christi Naval Air Station, mil., Tx., U.S.	F4	120
Corral de Almaguer, Spain	F8	12
Correctionville, Ia., U.S.	B2	92
Correggio, Italy	E5	14
Corrente, stm., Braz.	B7	57
Corrib, Lough, l., Ire.	H3	7
Corrientes, Arg.	B5	56
Corrientes, Cabo, c., Col.	E4	58
Corrientes, Cabo, c., Cuba	D5	64
Corrientes, Cabo, c., Mex.	G7	62
Corrigan, Tx., U.S.	D5	120
Corriganville, Md., U.S.	k13	97
Corry, Pa., U.S.	C2	115
Corse (Corsica), i., Fr.	m19	14
Corsica, S.D., U.S.	D7	118
Corsica see Corse, i., Fr.	m19	14
Corsicana, Tx., U.S.	C4	120
Corson, co., S.D., U.S.	B4	118
Corson Inlet, b., N.J., U.S.	E3	107
Cortemilia, Italy	E3	14
Cortez, Co., U.S.	D2	83
Cortez, Fl., U.S.	q10	86
Cortez Mountains, mts., Nv., U.S.	C5	105
Cortina d'Ampezzo, Italy	C7	14
Cortland, Il., U.S.	B5	90
Cortland, N.Y., U.S.	C4	109
Cortland, Oh., U.S.	A5	112
Cortland, co., N.Y., U.S.	C4	109
Corum, Tur.	G14	4
Corumbá, Braz.	G7	54
Corumbá, stm., Braz.	D5	57
Corunna, Mi., U.S.	F6	99
Corvallis, Or., U.S.	C3	114
Corydon, In., U.S.	H5	91
Corydon, Ia., U.S.	D4	92
Corydon, Ky., U.S.	C2	94
Coryell, co., Tx., U.S.	D4	120
Cosamaloapan [de Carpio], Mex.	H12	62
Cosenza, Italy	J11	14
Coshocton, Oh., U.S.	B4	112
Coshocton, co., Oh., U.S.	B4	112
Cosmoledo Group, is., Sey.	C9	44
Cosmopolis, Wa., U.S.	C2	124
Cosmos, Mn., U.S.	F4	100
Cosne-sur-Loire, Fr.	E9	10
Cossatot, stm., Ar., U.S.	C1	81
Costa Mesa, Ca., U.S.	n13	82
Costa Rica, Mex.	C4	62
Costa Rica, ctry., N.A.	I5	60
Costilla, co., Co., U.S.	D5	83
Cotabato, Phil.	D7	32
Coteau-Landing, Que., Can.	D3	74
Cotentin, pen., Fr.	C5	10
Cotonou, Benin	G6	42
Cotopaxi, vol., Ec.	H3	58
Cottage Grove, Mn., U.S.	n13	100
Cottage Grove, Or., U.S.	D3	114
Cottage Grove Reservoir, res., Or., U.S.	D3	114
Cottam, Ont., Can.	E2	73
Cottbus, Ger.	D14	8
Cotter, Ar., U.S.	A3	81
Cottiennes, Alpes (Alpi Cozie), mts., Eur.	H13	14
Cottle, co., Tx., U.S.	B2	120
Cottleville, Mo., U.S.	f12	102
Cotton, co., Ok., U.S.	C3	113
Cotton Plant, Ar., U.S.	B4	81
Cottonport, La., U.S.	C3	95
Cotton Valley, La., U.S.	B2	95
Cottonwood, Al., U.S.	D4	78
Cottonwood, Az., U.S.	C3	80
Cottonwood, Ca., U.S.	B2	82
Cottonwood, Id., U.S.	C2	89
Cottonwood, Mn., U.S.	F3	100
Cottonwood, co., Mn., U.S.	F3	100
Cottonwood, stm., Ks., U.S.	D7	93
Cottonwood, stm., Mn., U.S.	F3	100
Cottonwood Creek, stm., Wy., U.S.	C4	127
Cottonwood Falls, Ks., U.S.	D7	93
Cotui, Dom. Rep.	E12	64
Cotulla, Tx., U.S.	E3	120
Coudersport, Pa., U.S.	C5	115
Cougar Reservoir, res., Or., U.S.	C4	114
Couhé, Fr.	F7	10
Coulee Creek, stm., Wa., U.S.	g13	124
Coulee Dam, Wa., U.S.	B7	124
Coulee Dam National Recreation Area, Wa., U.S.	A7	124
Coulommiers, Fr.	D10	10
Coulterville, Il., U.S.	E4	90
Counce, Tn., U.S.	B3	119
Council, Id., U.S.	E2	89
Council Bluffs, Ia., U.S.	C2	92
Council Grove, Ks., U.S.	D7	93
Council Grove Lake, res., Ks., U.S.	D7	93
Council Mountain, mtn., Id., U.S.	E3	89
Country Homes, Wa., U.S.	B8	124
Coupeville, Wa., U.S.	A3	124
Courtenay, B.C., Can.	E5	69
Courte Oreilles, Lac, l., Wi., U.S.	C2	126
Courtland, Ont., Can.	E4	73
Courtland, Al., U.S.	A2	78
Courtland, Va., U.S.	D5	123
Coushatta, La., U.S.	B2	95
Coutances, Fr.	C5	10
Coutras, Fr.	G6	10
Cove Creek, stm., Ut., U.S.	E3	121
Covedale, Oh., U.S.	o12	112
Coventry, Eng., U.K.	I11	7
Coventry, Ct., U.S.	B6	84
Coventry, R.I., U.S.	D3	116
Cove Point, c., Md., U.S.	D5	97
Covilhã, Port.	E4	12
Covina, Ca., U.S.	m13	82
Covington, Ga., U.S.	C3	87
Covington, In., U.S.	D3	91
Covington, Ky., U.S.	A5	94
Covington, La., U.S.	D5	95
Covington, Oh., U.S.	B1	112
Covington, Tn., U.S.	B2	119
Covington, Va., U.S.	C3	123
Covington, co., Al., U.S.	D3	78
Covington, co., Ms., U.S.	D4	101
Cowan, Tn., U.S.	B5	119
Cowan, Lake, l., Austl.	F4	50
Cowansville, Que., Can.	D5	74
Cowarts, Al., U.S.	D4	78
Cow Creek, stm., Wa., U.S.	C7	124
Coweta, Ok., U.S.	B6	113
Coweta, co., Ga., U.S.	C2	87
Cowee Mountains, mts., N.C., U.S.	f9	110
Cowen, Mount, mtn., Mt., U.S.	E6	103
Cow Head, Newf., Can.	D3	72
Cowichan Bay, B.C., Can.	g12	69
Cowley, Wy., U.S.	B4	127

Name	Map Ref	Page
Cowley, co., Ks., U.S.	E7	93
Cowlington, Ok., U.S.	B7	113
Cowlitz, co., Wa., U.S.	C2	124
Cowlitz, stm., Wa., U.S.	C3	124
Cowpasture, stm., Va., U.S.	B3	123
Cowpen Mountain, mtn., Ga., U.S.	B2	87
Cowpens, S.C., U.S.	A4	117
Coxim, Braz.	E1	57
Coxsackie, N.Y., U.S.	C7	109
Cox's Bāzār, Bngl.	J14	38
Cox's Cove, Newf., Can.	D2	72
Coyhaique, Chile	F2	56
Cozad, Ne., U.S.	D6	104
Cozumel, Isla de, i., Mex.	G16	62
Crab Creek, stm., Wa., U.S.	C6	124
Crab Orchard, Ky., U.S.	C5	94
Crab Orchard, Tn., U.S.	D9	119
Crab Orchard, W.V., U.S.	n13	125
Crab Orchard Lake, res., Il., U.S.	F4	90
Crabtree, Pa., U.S.	F3	115
Crabtree Mills, Que., Can.	D4	74
Cradock, S. Afr.	H5	44
Crafton, Pa., U.S.	k13	115
Craig, Ak., U.S.	D13	79
Craig, Co., U.S.	A3	83
Craig, co., Ok., U.S.	A6	113
Craig, co., Va., U.S.	C2	123
Craig Air Force Base, mil., Al., U.S.	C3	78
Craig Creek, stm., Va., U.S.	C2	123
Craighead, co., Ar., U.S.	B5	81
Craigsville, Va., U.S.	B3	123
Craigsville, W.V., U.S.	C4	125
Crailsheim, Ger.	F10	8
Craiova, Rom.	E7	16
Cramerton, N.C., U.S.	B1	110
Cranberry Lake, l., N.Y., U.S.	A6	109
Cranberry Portage, Man., Can.	B1	70
Cranbrook, B.C., Can.	E10	69
Crandall, Tx., U.S.	n10	120
Crandon, Wi., U.S.	C5	126
Crane, Az., U.S.	*E1	80
Crane, Mo., U.S.	E4	102
Crane, Tx., U.S.	D1	120
Crane, co., Tx., U.S.	D1	120
Crane Creek, stm., Oh., U.S.	e7	112
Crane Creek Reservoir, res., Id., U.S.	E2	89
Crane Lake, l., Il., U.S.	C3	90
Crane Lake, l., Mn., U.S.	B6	100
Crane Mountain, mtn., Or., U.S.	E6	114
Crane Prairie Reservoir, res., Or., U.S.	D5	114
Cranford, N.J., U.S.	B4	107
Cranston, R.I., U.S.	C4	116
Craon, Fr.	E6	10
Craponne, Fr.	G10	10
Crater Lake, l., Or., U.S.	E4	114
Crater Lake National Park, Or., U.S.	E4	114
Craters of the Moon National Monument, Id., U.S.	F5	89
Cratéus, Braz.	E10	54
Crato, Braz.	E11	54
Crauford, Cape, c., N.W. Ter., Can.	B16	66
Craven, co., N.C., U.S.	B5	110
Crawford, Ga., U.S.	C3	87
Crawford, Ms., U.S.	B5	101
Crawford, Ne., U.S.	B2	104
Crawford, co., Ar., U.S.	B1	81
Crawford, co., Ga., U.S.	D3	87
Crawford, co., Il., U.S.	D6	90
Crawford, co., In., U.S.	H4	91
Crawford, co., Ia., U.S.	B2	92
Crawford, co., Ks., U.S.	E9	93
Crawford, co., Mi., U.S.	D6	99
Crawford, co., Mo., U.S.	D6	102
Crawford, co., Oh., U.S.	B3	112
Crawford, co., Pa., U.S.	C1	115
Crawford, co., Wi., U.S.	E3	126
Crawford Lake, l., Me., U.S.	C5	96
Crawford Notch State Park, N.H., U.S.	B4	106
Crawfordsville, Ar., U.S.	B5	81
Crawfordsville, In., U.S.	D4	91
Crawfordville, Fl., U.S.	B2	86
Crazy Mountains, mts., Mt., U.S.	D6	103
Crazy Peak, mtn., Mt., U.S.	D6	103
Crazy Woman Creek, stm., Wy., U.S.	B6	127
Creal Springs, Il., U.S.	F5	90
Cree, stm., Sask., Can.	E11	66
Creedmoor, N.C., U.S.	A4	110
Creek, co., Ok., U.S.	B5	113
Cree Lake, l., Sask., Can.	m7	75
Creemore, Ont., Can.	C4	73
Creighton, Ne., U.S.	B8	104
Creighton, Pa., U.S.	h14	115
Creil, Fr.	C9	10
Crema, Italy	D4	14
Cremona, Italy	D5	14
Crenshaw, Ms., U.S.	A3	101
Crenshaw, co., Al., U.S.	D3	78
Creola, Al., U.S.	E1	78
Cres, Cro.	E9	14
Cresaptown, Md., U.S.	k13	97
Crescent, Ok., U.S.	B4	113
Crescent, Or., U.S.	D5	114
Crescent Lake, l., Wa., U.S.	A2	124
Crescent City, Ca., U.S.	B1	82
Crescent City, Fl., U.S.	C5	86
Crescent Lake, l., Fl., U.S.	C5	86
Crescent Lake, l., Or., U.S.	D5	114
Crescent Springs, Ky., U.S.	h13	94
Cresco, Ia., U.S.	A5	92
Creskill, N.J., U.S.	h9	107
Cresson, Pa., U.S.	F4	115
Cressona, Pa., U.S.	E9	115
Crest, Fr.	H12	10
Crested Butte, Co., U.S.	C4	83
Crest Hill, Il., U.S.	k8	90
Crestline, Oh., U.S.	B3	112
Creston, B.C., Can.	E9	69
Creston, Ia., U.S.	C3	92
Creston, Oh., U.S.	B4	112
Crestone Peak, mtn., Co., U.S.	D5	83
Crestview, Fl., U.S.	u15	86
Crestview, Hi., U.S.	g10	88
Crestwood, Ky., U.S.	B4	94
Crestwood Village, N.J., U.S.	D4	107
Creswell, Or., U.S.	D3	114
Crete, Il., U.S.	B6	90
Crete, Ne., U.S.	D9	104
Crete see Kríti, i., Grc.	N8	16
Creve Coeur, Il., U.S.	C4	90
Crevillente, Spain	G11	12
Crewe, Eng., U.K.	H10	7
Crewe, Va., U.S.	C4	123
Criciúma, Braz.	B7	56
Cricket, N.C., U.S.	A1	110
Cridersville, Oh., U.S.	B1	112
Crikvenica, Cro.	D9	14
Crimea see Krymskij poluostrov, pen., Ukr.	H4	22
Crimmitschau, Ger.	E12	8
Crisfield, Md., U.S.	E6	97
Crisp, co., Ga., U.S.	E3	87
Cristalândia, Braz.	F9	54
Cristalina, Braz.	D5	57
Cristianópolis, Braz.	D4	57
Cristóbal Colón, Pico, mtn., Col.	B6	58
Crittenden, Ky., U.S.	B5	94
Crittenden, co., Ar., U.S.	B5	81
Crittenden, co., Ky., U.S.	e9	94
Crivitz, Wi., U.S.	C6	126
Crnomelj, Slo.	D10	14
Croatia, ctry., Eur.	D10	14
Crocker, Mo., U.S.	D5	102
Crockett, Ca., U.S.	g8	82
Crockett, Tx., U.S.	D5	120
Crockett, co., Tn., U.S.	B2	119
Crockett, co., Tx., U.S.	D2	120
Crofton, Ky., U.S.	C2	94
Crofton, Md., U.S.	B4	97
Crofton, Ne., U.S.	B8	104
Croix, Lac la, l., Mn., U.S.	B6	100
Croker, Cape, c., Ont., Can.	C4	73
Croker Island, i., Austl.	B6	50
Cromarty, Scot., U.K.	D8	7
Cromona, Ky., U.S.	C7	94
Cromwell, Ct., U.S.	C5	84
Crook, co., Or., U.S.	C6	114
Crook, co., Wy., U.S.	B8	127
Crooked, stm., Or., U.S.	C6	114
Crooked Creek, stm., Pa., U.S.	C7	115
Crooked Creek Lake, res., Pa., U.S.	E3	115
Crooked Island, i., Bah.	C10	64
Crooked Island Passage, strt., Bah.	C10	64
Crooked Lake, l., Fl., U.S.	E5	86
Crooked Lake, l., Mn., U.S.	B7	100
Crooks, S.D., U.S.	D9	118
Crooks Lake, l., Nv., U.S.	B2	105
Crookston, Mn., U.S.	C2	100
Crooksville, Oh., U.S.	C3	112
Crosby, Mn., U.S.	D5	100
Crosby, N.D., U.S.	A2	111
Crosby, Tx., U.S.	r14	120
Crosby, co., Tx., U.S.	C2	120
Crosby, Mount, mtn., Wy., U.S.	C3	127
Crosbyton, Tx., U.S.	C2	120
Cross, co., Ar., U.S.	B5	81
Cross Bay, b., Man., Can.	C2	70
Cross City, Fl., U.S.	C3	86
Cross Creek, stm., W.V., U.S.	f8	125
Crossett, Ar., U.S.	D4	81
Crossfield, Alta., Can.	D3	68
Cross Island, i., Me., U.S.	D5	96
Crosslake, Mn., U.S.	D4	100
Cross Lake, Man., Can.	B3	70
Cross Lake, l., Me., U.S.	A4	96
Cross Lake, res., La., U.S.	B2	95
Cross Lanes, W.V., U.S.	C3	125
Crossman Peak, mtn., Az., U.S.	C1	80
Cross Plains, Tn., U.S.	A5	119
Cross Plains, Tx., U.S.	C3	120
Cross Plains, Wi., U.S.	E4	126
Cross Sound, strt., Ak., U.S.	k21	79
Crossville, Al., U.S.	A4	78
Crossville, Il., U.S.	E5	90
Crossville, Tn., U.S.	D8	119
Croswell, Mi., U.S.	E8	99
Crothersville, In., U.S.	G6	91
Crotone, Italy	J12	14
Croton-on-Hudson, N.Y., U.S.	D7	109
Crouse, Ky., U.S.	B11	110
Crow, stm., Mn., U.S.	F4	100
Crow Agency, Mt., U.S.	E9	103
Crow Creek, stm., U.S.	A6	83
Crow Creek Indian Reservation, S.D., U.S.	C6	118
Crowder, Ms., U.S.	A3	101
Crowell, Tx., U.S.	C3	120
Crowley, La., U.S.	D3	95
Crowley, Tx., U.S.	n9	120
Crowley, co., Co., U.S.	C7	83
Crowley, Lake, res., Ca., U.S.	D4	82
Crowleys Ridge, mtn., U.S.	B5	81
Crown Point, In., U.S.	B3	91
Crown Point, La., U.S.	k11	95
Crownpoint, N.M., U.S.	B1	108
Crown Prince Frederick Island, i., N.W. Ter., Can.	B15	66
Crow Peak, mtn., Mt., U.S.	D5	103
Crowsnest Pass, Alta., Can.	E3	68
Crowsnest Pass, Can.	E3	68
Crow Wing, co., Mn., U.S.	D4	100
Crow Wing, stm., Mn., U.S.	D4	100
Croydon, Austl.	C8	50
Crozet, Va., U.S.	B4	123
Crozon, Fr.	D2	10
Cruces, Cuba	C7	64
Crump Lake, l., Or., U.S.	E7	114
Cruz Alta, Braz.	B6	56
Cruz del Eje, Arg.	C4	56
Cruzeiro do Sul, Braz.	E4	54
Crystal, Mn., U.S.	m12	100
Crystal, stm., Co., U.S.	B3	83
Crystal Bay, Nv., U.S.	D1	105
Crystal Bay, b., Fl., U.S.	D4	86
Crystal Beach, Fl., U.S.	D4	86
Crystal City, Man., Can.	E2	70
Crystal City, Mo., U.S.	C7	102
Crystal City, Tx., U.S.	E3	120
Crystal Falls, Mi., U.S.	B2	99
Crystal Lake, Ct., U.S.	B6	84
Crystal Lake, Fl., U.S.	u16	86
Crystal Lake, Il., U.S.	A5	90
Crystal Lake, l., Ct., U.S.	B6	84
Crystal Lake, l., Mi., U.S.	D4	99
Crystal Lake, l., N.H., U.S.	D4	106
Crystal Lake, l., Vt., U.S.	B4	122
Crystal Lawns, Il., U.S.	k8	90
Crystal Pond, res., Ct., U.S.	B7	84
Crystal River, Fl., U.S.	D4	86
Crystal Springs, Ms., U.S.	D3	101
Cuando (Kwando), stm., Afr.	E4	44
Cuangar, Ang.	E3	44
Cuango, Ang.	C3	44
Cuango (Kwango), stm., Afr.	C3	44
Cuanza, stm., Ang.	C3	44
Cuauhtémoc, Mex.	C6	62
Cuautla, Mex.	H10	62
Cuba, Port.	G4	12
Cuba, Il., U.S.	C3	90
Cuba, Mo., U.S.	C6	102
Cuba, N.M., U.S.	A3	108
Cuba, N.Y., U.S.	C2	109
Cuba, ctry., N.A.	D8	64
Cuba City, Wi., U.S.	F3	126
Cubango (Okavango), stm., Afr.	E3	44
Cubero, N.M., U.S.	B2	108
Cucharas, Mex.	F7	62
Cucharas, stm., Co., U.S.	D6	83
Cudahy, Wi., U.S.	F6	126
Cuddalore, India	G5	37
Cuddapah, India	E5	37
Cuddy Mountain, mtn., Id., U.S.	E2	89
Čudskoje Ozero (Peipsi Järv), l., Eur.	C10	18
Cuéllar, Spain	D7	12
Cuenca, Ec.	I3	58
Cuenca, Spain	E9	12
Cuencamé [de Ceniceros], Mex.	E8	62
Cuernavaca, Mex.	H10	62
Cuero, Tx., U.S.	E4	120
Cuers, Fr.	I13	10
Cuervos, Mex.	A2	62
Cuevas del Almanzora, Spain	H10	12
Cuglieri, Italy	I3	14
Cuiabá, Braz.	G7	54
Cuiseaux, Fr.	F12	10
Cuito, stm., Ang.	E3	44
Cuíto-Cuanavale, Ang.	E3	44
Cuivre, West Fork, stm., Mo., U.S.	B6	102
Čukotskij, Mys, c., Russia	E31	24
Čukotskij Poluostrov, pen., Russia	D30	24
Culberson, co., Tx., U.S.	o12	120
Culbertson, Mt., U.S.	B12	103
Culbertson, Ne., U.S.	D5	104
Culebra Peak, mtn., Co., U.S.	D5	83
Culiacán, Mex.	E6	62
Cullen, La., U.S.	B2	95
Cullman, Al., U.S.	A3	78
Cullman, co., Al., U.S.	A3	78
Culloden, W.V., U.S.	C2	125
Cullowhee, N.C., U.S.	f9	110
Cul'man, Russia	F18	24
Culpeper, Va., U.S.	B4	123
Culpeper, co., Va., U.S.	B5	123
Culver, In., U.S.	B5	91
Culver City, Ca., U.S.	m12	82
Culvers Lake, l., N.J., U.S.	A3	107
Culym, Russia	F10	24
Cumalı, Tur.	M11	16
Cumaná, Ven.	B10	58
Cumanacoa, Ven.	B11	58
Cumbal, Nevado de, mtn., Col.	G4	58
Cumberland, B.C., Can.	E5	69
Cumberland, Ky., U.S.	D7	94
Cumberland, Md., U.S.	k13	97
Cumberland, Wi., U.S.	C2	126
Cumberland, co., Il., U.S.	D5	90
Cumberland, co., Ky., U.S.	D4	94
Cumberland, co., Me., U.S.	E2	96
Cumberland, co., N.J., U.S.	E2	107
Cumberland, co., N.C., U.S.	C4	110
Cumberland, co., Pa., U.S.	F7	115
Cumberland, co., Tn., U.S.	D8	119
Cumberland, co., Va., U.S.	C4	123
Cumberland, stm., U.S.	D4	94
Cumberland, Lake, res., Ky., U.S.	D5	94
Cumberland Center, Me., U.S.	g7	96
Cumberland Foreside, Me., U.S.	E2	96
Cumberland Gap, Tn., U.S.	D6	94
Cumberland Gap National Historical Park, U.S.	D6	94
Cumberland Hill, R.I., U.S.	B4	116
Cumberland Island National Seashore, Ga., U.S.	F5	87
Cumberland Islands, is., Austl.	D9	50
Cumberland Lake, l., Sask., Can.	C4	75
Cumberland Peninsula, pen., N.W. Ter., Can.	C19	66
Cumberland Sound, strt., N.W. Ter., Can.	C19	66
Cumbres Pass, Co., U.S.	D4	83
Cumikan, Russia	G21	24
Cuming, co., Ne., U.S.	C9	104
Cumming, Ga., U.S.	B2	87
Cumnock, Scot., U.K.	F8	7
Čuna, stm., Russia	F13	24
Cun'a, stm., Russia	E13	24
Cunani, Braz.	C8	54
Cunene, stm., Afr.	E2	44
Cuneo, Italy	E2	14
Cunnamulla, Austl.	E9	50
Cunningham, Ky., U.S.	f9	94
Cupar, Scot., U.K.	E9	7
Cupar, Sask., Can.	G3	75
Curaçao, i., Neth. Ant.	H13	64
Curecanti National Recreation Area, Co., U.S.	C3	83
Curepipe, Mrts.	F11	44
Curiapo, Ven.	C12	58
Curicó, Chile	C2	56
Curitiba, Braz.	B7	56
Curlew Creek, stm., Wa., U.S.	A7	124
Curlew Lake, l., Wa., U.S.	A7	124
Curralinho, Braz.	D9	54
Currant Mountain, mtn., Nv., U.S.	E6	105
Current, stm., U.S.	A5	81
Currituck, co., N.C., U.S.	A6	110
Curry, co., N.M., U.S.	C6	108
Curry, co., Or., U.S.	E2	114
Curtis, Ne., U.S.	D5	104
Curtisville, Pa., U.S.	E2	115
Curvelo, Braz.	E6	57
Curwensville, Pa., U.S.	E4	115
Curwensville Lake, res., Pa., U.S.	E4	115
Curwood, Mount, mtn., Mi., U.S.	B2	99
Cushing, Ok., U.S.	B5	113
Cushman, Lake, res., Wa., U.S.	B2	124
Cusseta, Ga., U.S.	D2	87
Custer, S.D., U.S.	D2	118
Custer, co., Co., U.S.	C5	83
Custer, co., Id., U.S.	E4	89
Custer, co., Mt., U.S.	D11	103
Custer, co., Ne., U.S.	C6	104
Custer, co., Ok., U.S.	B2	113
Custer, co., S.D., U.S.	D2	118
Custer Battlefield National Monument, Mt., U.S.	E9	103
Cut Bank, Mt., U.S.	B4	103
Cut Bank Creek, stm., N.D., U.S.	A4	111
Cutchogue, N.Y., U.S.	m16	109
Cuthbert, Ga., U.S.	E2	87
Cutler Ridge, Fl., U.S.	s13	86
Cut Off, La., U.S.	E5	95
Cutro, Italy	J11	14
Cuttack, India	J11	38
Cuttyhunk Island, i., Ma., U.S.	D6	98
Cuxhaven, Ger.	B8	8
Cuyahoga, co., Oh., U.S.	A4	112
Cuyahoga, stm., Oh., U.S.	A4	112
Cuyahoga Falls, Oh., U.S.	A4	112
Cuyama, stm., Ca., U.S.	E4	82
Cuyamaca Peak, mtn., Ca., U.S.	F5	82
Cuyo Islands, is., Phil.	C7	32
Cuyuni, stm., S.A.	D13	58
Cuzco, Peru	F4	54
C.W. McConaughy, Lake, res., Ne., U.S.	C4	104
Cyclades see Kikládhes, is., Grc.	L8	16
Cynthiana, In., U.S.	H2	91
Cynthiana, Ky., U.S.	B5	94
Cypress Creek, stm., Tx., U.S.	r14	120
Cypress Hills Provincial Park, Sask., Can.	H1	75
Cypress Lake, l., Fl., U.S.	D5	86
Cypress Quarters, Fl., U.S.	E6	86
Cypress Swamp, sw., U.S.	F4	85
Cyprus, ctry., Asia	B3	40
Cyril, Ok., U.S.	C3	113
Czechoslovakia, ctry., Eur.	F11	4
Częstochowa, Pol.	E19	8
D		
Dabeiba, Col.	D4	58
Dabhoi, India	I5	38
Dabie Shan, mts., China	D4	28
Dabola, Gui.	F3	42
Dacca see Dhaka, Bngl.	I14	38
Dachaidan, China	B16	38
Dachau, Ger.	G11	8
Dacono, Co., U.S.	A6	83
Dacula, Ga., U.S.	C3	87
Dadanawa, Guy.	F13	58
Dade, co., Fl., U.S.	G6	86
Dade, co., Ga., U.S.	B1	87
Dade, co., Mo., U.S.	D4	102
Dade City, Fl., U.S.	D4	86
Dadeville, Al., U.S.	C4	78
Dādra and Nagar Haveli, ter., India	B2	37
Dādu, Pak.	G2	38
Daet, Phil.	q20	33b
Daggett, co., Ut., U.S.	C6	121
Dagsboro, De., U.S.	F5	85
Dagupan, Phil.	p19	33b
Dahan-e Qowmghī, Afg.	C2	38
Da Hinggan Ling, mts., China	C11	26
Dahlak Archipelago, is., Eth.	E3	46
Dahlak Kebir Island, i., Eth.	E3	46
Dahlonega, Ga., U.S.	B3	87
Dahomey see Benin, ctry., Afr.	G6	42
Dahra, Libya	C9	42
Dahy, Nafūd ad-, des., Sau. Ar.	D4	46
Daimiel, Spain	F8	12
Daingerfield, Tx., U.S.	C5	120
Dairen see Dalian, China	D11	26
Dakar, Sen.	F2	42
Dakhla, W. Sah.	D2	42
Dakota, co., Mn., U.S.	F5	100
Dakota, co., Ne., U.S.	B9	104
Dakota City, Ne., U.S.	B9	104
Dalandzadgad, Mong.	C7	26
Da Lat, Viet.	I10	34
Dālbandin, Pak.	D1	36
Dalby, Austl.	E10	50
Dale, In., U.S.	H4	91
Dale, co., Al., U.S.	D4	78
Dale City, Va., U.S.	B5	123
Dale Hollow Lake, res., Tn., U.S.	C8	119
Daleville, Al., U.S.	D4	78
Daleville, In., U.S.	D6	91
Dalhart, Tx., U.S.	A1	120
Dalhousie, N.B., Can.	A3	71
Dalhousie, Cape, c., N.W. Ter., Can.	B7	66
Dali, China	B6	34
Dalian, China	D11	26
Dall, Mount, mtn., Ak., U.S.	f15	79
Dallam, co., Tx., U.S.	A1	120
Dallas, Ga., U.S.	C2	87
Dallas, N.C., U.S.	B1	110
Dallas, Or., U.S.	C3	114
Dallas, Pa., U.S.	D10	115
Dallas, Tx., U.S.	C4	120
Dallas, co., Al., U.S.	C3	78
Dallas, co., Ar., U.S.	D3	81
Dallas, co., Ia., U.S.	C3	92
Dallas, co., Mo., U.S.	D4	102
Dallas, co., Tx., U.S.	C4	120
Dallas Center, Ia., U.S.	C4	92
Dallas City, Il., U.S.	C2	90
Dallas Naval Air Station, mil., Tx., U.S.	n9	120
Dallastown, Pa., U.S.	G8	115
Dall Island, i., Ak., U.S.	n23	79
Dalmacija, hist. reg., Eur.	F11	14
Dalmatia see Dalmacija, hist. reg., Eur.	F11	14
Daloa, I.C.	G4	42
Dalqū, Sudan	D12	42
Dalton, Ga., U.S.	B2	87
Dalton, Ma., U.S.	B1	98
Dalton, Oh., U.S.	B4	112
Dalton, Pa., U.S.	C10	115
Daltonganj, India	H11	38
Dalton Gardens, Id., U.S.	B2	89
Dalwallinu, Austl.	F3	50
Daly City, Ca., U.S.	h8	82
Damān, India	B2	37
Damān, ter., India	B2	37
Damar, Pulau, i., Indon.	G8	32
Damariscotta, Me., U.S.	D3	96
Damariscotta Lake, l., Me., U.S.	D3	96
Damascus, Md., U.S.	B3	97
Damascus, Va., U.S.	f10	123
Damascus see Dimashq, Syria	C5	40
Damāvand, Qolleh-ye, mtn., Iran	J8	22
Damba, Ang.	C3	44
Damoh, India	I8	38
Dampar, Tasek, l., Malay.	M7	34
Dampier, Austl.	D3	50
Dampier, Selat, strt., Indon.	F9	32
Dampier Archipelago, is., Austl.	D3	50
Dan, stm., U.S.	D3	123
Dana, In., U.S.	E3	91
Da Nang, Viet.	F10	34
Danakil Plain, pl., Eth.	F3	46
Danbury, Ct., U.S.	D2	84
Danbury, Tx., U.S.	r14	120
Dand, Afg.	E1	38
Dandridge, Tn., U.S.	C10	119
Dandong, China	C11	26
Dangla, Eth.	F2	46
Dania, Fl., U.S.	F6	86
Daniels, co., Mt., U.S.	B11	103
Danielson, Ct., U.S.	B8	84
Daniels Pass, Ut., U.S.	C4	121
Danilov, Russia	C23	18
Danlí, Hond.	G4	64
Dannemora, N.Y., U.S.	f11	109
Dansville, N.Y., U.S.	C3	109
Dante, Va., U.S.	f9	123
Danube, stm., Eur.	G13	4
Danube, Mouths of the, mth., Eur.	D13	16
Danvers, Il., U.S.	C4	90
Danvers, Ma., U.S.	A6	98
Danville, Que., Can.	D5	74
Danville, Ar., U.S.	B2	81
Danville, Ca., U.S.	h9	82
Danville, Il., U.S.	C6	90
Danville, In., U.S.	E4	91
Danville, Ia., U.S.	D6	92
Danville, Ky., U.S.	C5	94
Danville, Oh., U.S.	B3	112
Danville, Pa., U.S.	E8	115
Danville, Va., U.S.	D3	123
Danyang, China	C8	28
Danzig, Gulf of, b., Eur.	A19	8
Danzig see Gdańsk, Pol.	A18	8
Daocheng, China	F7	26
Dapango, Togo	F6	42
Daphne, Al., U.S.	E2	78
Dar'ā, Syria	C5	40
Darakht-e Yahyá, Afg.	E3	38
Dārayyā, Syria	C5	40
Darbāsīyah, Syria	A7	40
Darbhanga, India	G11	38
Darby, Mt., U.S.	D2	103
Darby, Pa., U.S.	G11	115
Darchan, Mong.	B8	26
Dardanelle, Ar., U.S.	B2	81
Dardanelle, Lake, res., Ar., U.S.	B2	81
Dardanelles see Çanakkale Boğazı, strt., Tur.	I10	16
Dare, co., N.C., U.S.	B7	110
Dar es Salaam, Tan.	C7	44
Dargaville, N.Z.	A4	52
Dari, China	E6	26
Darien, Ct., U.S.	E2	84
Darien, Ga., U.S.	E5	87
Darien, Wi., U.S.	F5	126
Dariganga, Mong.	B9	26
Darjeeling, India	G13	38
Darke, co., Oh., U.S.	B1	112
Darley Woods, De., U.S.	h8	85
Darling, stm., Austl.	F9	50
Darling, Lake, res., N.D., U.S.	A4	111
Darling Range, mts., Austl.	F3	50
Darlington, Eng., U.K.	G11	7
Darlington, In., U.S.	D4	91
Darlington, Md., U.S.	A5	97
Darlington, S.C., U.S.	C8	117
Darlington, Wi., U.S.	F3	126
Darlington, co., S.C., U.S.	C8	117
Darmstadt, Ger.	F8	8
Darnah, Libya	B10	42
Daroca, Spain	D10	12
Darrah, Mount, mtn., Can.	E3	68
Darrington, Wa., U.S.	A4	124
Dartmoor National Park, Eng., U.K.	K9	7
Dartmouth, Eng., U.K.	K9	7
Daru, Pap. N. Gui.	G11	32
Darwin, Austl.	B6	50
Dašinčilen, Mong.	B7	26
Dassel, Mn., U.S.	E4	100
Datia, India	H8	38
Datil Mountains, mts., N.M., U.S.	C2	108
D'at'kovo, Russia	H17	18
Datong, China	C9	26
Datu, Tanjung, c., Asia	M10	34
Dāūd Khel, Pak.	D4	38
Daufuskie Island, i., S.C., U.S.	G6	117
Daugavpils, Lat.	F9	18
Daulatābād (Shirin Tagāo), Afg.	B1	38
Daule, Ec.	G2	58

Name	Map Ref	Page
Dauphin, Man., Can.	D1	70
Dauphin, co., Pa., U.S.	F8	115
Dauphin, stm., Man., Can.	D2	70
Dauphin Island, Al., U.S.	E1	78
Dauphin Island, i., Al., U.S.	E1	78
Dauphin Lake, l., Man., Can.	D2	70
Dävanagere, India	E3	37
Davao, Phil.	D8	32
Davao, b., Phil.	D8	32
Davao Gulf, b., Phil.	D8	32
Daveluyville, Que., Can.	C5	74
Davenport, Fl., U.S.	D5	86
Davenport, Ia., U.S.	C7	92
Davenport, Ok., U.S.	B5	113
Davenport, Wa., U.S.	B7	124
David, Pan.	J6	64
David City, Ne., U.S.	C8	104
Davidson, N.C., U.S.	B2	110
Davidson, co., N.C., U.S.	B2	110
Davidson, co., Tn., U.S.	A5	119
Davidsville, Pa., U.S.	F4	115
Davie, Fl., U.S.	F6	86
Davie, co., N.C., U.S.	B2	110
Daviess, co., In., U.S.	G3	91
Daviess, co., Ky., U.S.	C2	94
Daviess, co., Mo., U.S.	B3	102
Davis, Ca., U.S.	C3	82
Davis, Ok., U.S.	C4	113
Davis, W.V., U.S.	B5	125
Davis, co., Ia., U.S.	D5	92
Davis, co., Ut., U.S.	C3	121
Davis, Mount, mtn., Pa., U.S.	G3	115
Davis Creek, stm., W.V., U.S.	m12	125
Davis Dam, U.S.	H7	105
Davis Islands, is., Fl., U.S.	p11	86
Davis Lake, l., Or., U.S.	E5	114
Davis-Monthan Air Force Base, mil., Az., U.S.	E5	80
Davison, Mi., U.S.	E7	99
Davison, co., S.D., U.S.	D7	118
Davis Strait, strt., N.A.	C21	66
Davisville, R.I., U.S.	E4	116
Davos, Switz.	F16	10
Dawa (Daua), stm., Afr.	H3	46
Dawei, Burma	G5	34
Dawes, co., Ne., U.S.	B2	104
Daws Island, i., S.C., U.S.	G6	117
Dawson, Ga., U.S.	E2	87
Dawson, Mn., U.S.	F2	100
Dawson, co., Ga., U.S.	B2	87
Dawson, co., Mt., U.S.	C11	103
Dawson, co., Ne., U.S.	D6	104
Dawson, co., Tx., U.S.	C1	120
Dawson, Mount, mtn., B.C., Can.	D9	69
Dawson Creek, B.C., Can.	B7	69
Dawson Springs, Ky., U.S.	C2	94
Dax, Fr.	I5	10
Day, co., S.D., U.S.	B8	118
Dayr az-Zawr, Syria	B7	40
Daysland, Alta., Can.	C4	68
Dayton, In., U.S.	D4	91
Dayton, Ia., U.S.	B3	92
Dayton, Ky., U.S.	h14	94
Dayton, Md., U.S.	B4	97
Dayton, Mn., U.S.	m12	100
Dayton, Nv., U.S.	D2	105
Dayton, Oh., U.S.	C1	112
Dayton, Or., U.S.	B3	114
Dayton, Tn., U.S.	D8	119
Dayton, Tx., U.S.	D5	120
Dayton, Va., U.S.	B4	123
Dayton, Wa., U.S.	C8	124
Dayton, Wy., U.S.	B5	127
Daytona Beach, Fl., U.S.	C5	86
Da Yunhe, China	E10	26
Dayville, Ct., U.S.	B8	84
De Aar, S. Afr.	H4	44
Dead, North Branch, stm., Me., U.S.	C2	96
Dead, South Branch, stm., Me., U.S.	C2	96
Dead Creek, stm., Vt., U.S.	C2	122
Dead Diamond, stm., N.H., U.S.	g7	106
Dead Indian Peak, mtn., Wy., U.S.	B3	127
Dead Lake, l., Mn., U.S.	D3	100
Dead Lakes, l., Fl., U.S.	B1	86
Deadman Bay, b., Fl., U.S.	C3	86
Deadman Creek, stm., Wa., U.S.	g14	124
Deadmans Cay, Bah.	C10	64
Dead Sea, l., Asia	D4	40
Deadwood, S.D., U.S.	C2	118
Deadwood Reservoir, res., Id., U.S.	E3	89
Deaf Smith, co., Tx., U.S.	B1	120
Deale, Md., U.S.	C4	97
Deal Island, Md., U.S.	D6	97
Deal Island, i., Md., U.S.	D6	97
Dean, co., B.C., Can.	C4	69
Dean Channel, strt., B.C., Can.	C4	69
Deán Funes, Arg.	C4	56
Dearborn, Mi., U.S.	F7	99
Dearborn, co., In., U.S.	F7	91
Dearborn Heights, Mi., U.S.	p15	99
Dearg, Beinn, mtn., Scot., U.K.	D8	7
Dease Strait, strt., N.W. Ter., Can.	C11	66
Death Valley, val., Ca., U.S.	D5	82
Death Valley National Monument, U.S.	D5	82
Deauville, Fr.	C7	10
De Baca, co., N.M., U.S.	C5	108
De Bary, Fl., U.S.	D5	86
Debauch Mountain, mtn., Ak., U.S.	C8	79
Dębica, Pol.	E21	8
Debrecen, Hung.	H21	8
Debre Markos, Eth.	F2	46
Debre Tabor, Eth.	F2	46
De Cade, Lake, l., La., U.S.	E5	95
Decatur, Al., U.S.	A3	78
Decatur, Ar., U.S.	A1	81
Decatur, Ga., U.S.	C2	87
Decatur, Il., U.S.	D5	90
Decatur, In., U.S.	C8	91
Decatur, Mi., U.S.	F5	99
Decatur, Ms., U.S.	C4	101
Decatur, Ne., U.S.	B9	104
Decatur, Tn., U.S.	D9	119
Decatur, Tx., U.S.	C4	120
Decatur, co., Ga., U.S.	F2	87
Decatur, co., In., U.S.	F6	91
Decatur, co., Ia., U.S.	D4	92
Decatur, co., Ks., U.S.	C3	93
Decatur, co., Tn., U.S.	B3	119
Decaturville, Tn., U.S.	B3	119
Decazeville, Fr.	H9	10
Deccan, plat., India	E4	37
Deception, Mount, mtn., Wa., U.S.	B2	124
Decherd, Tn., U.S.	B5	119
Děčín, Czech.	E14	8
Decize, Fr.	F10	10
Deckerville, Mi., U.S.	E8	99
Decorah, Ia., U.S.	A6	92
Dedham, Ma., U.S.	B5	98
Dédougou, Burkina	F5	42
Dedovsk, Russia	F20	18
Deep, stm., N.C., U.S.	B3	110
Deep Creek, stm., Ut., U.S.	C2	121
Deep Creek, stm., Ut., U.S.	B3	121
Deep Creek, stm., Ut., U.S.	F3	121
Deep Creek, stm., Wa., U.S.	g13	124
Deep Creek Lake, res., Md., U.S.	K12	97
Deep Creek Mountains, mts., Id., U.S.	G6	89
Deep Fork, stm., Ok., U.S.	B5	113
Deep Inlet, b., Newf., Can.	g10	72
Deep Red Creek, stm., Ok., U.S.	C3	113
Deep River, Ont., Can.	A7	73
Deep River, Ct., U.S.	D6	84
Deer Creek Indian Reservation, Mn., U.S.	C5	100
Deerfield, Il., U.S.	h9	90
Deerfield, Ks., U.S.	E2	93
Deerfield, Ma., U.S.	A2	98
Deerfield, Mi., U.S.	G7	99
Deerfield, Wi., U.S.	E4	126
Deerfield, stm., U.S.	A2	98
Deerfield Beach, Fl., U.S.	F6	86
Deer Island, pen., Ma., U.S.	g12	98
Deer Island, i., Ms., U.S.	f8	101
Deer Isle, i., Me., U.S.	D4	96
Deer Lake, Newf., Can.	D3	72
Deer Lake, l., Newf., Can.	D3	72
Deer Lake, l., Mn., U.S.	C5	100
Deer Lodge, Mt., U.S.	D4	103
Deer Lodge, co., Mt., U.S.	E3	103
Deer Park, N.Y., U.S.	n15	109
Deer Park, Oh., U.S.	o13	112
Deer Park, Wa., U.S.	B8	124
Deer Peak, mtn., Co., U.S.	C5	83
Deer River, Mn., U.S.	C5	100
Deesa, India	H5	38
Defiance, Oh., U.S.	A1	112
Defiance, co., Oh., U.S.	A1	112
Defiance, Mount, mtn., Or., U.S.	B5	114
De Forest, Wi., U.S.	E4	126
De Funiak Springs, Fl., U.S.	u15	86
Degeh-Bur, Eth.	G3	46
Dégelis, Que., Can.	B9	74
Deggendorf, Ger.	G12	8
De Graff, Oh., U.S.	B2	112
De Gray Lake, res., Ar., U.S.	C2	81
Dehiwala-Mount Lavinia, Sri L.	I5	37
Dehra Dūn, India	E8	38
Dehri, India	H11	38
Dehu, India	C2	37
Dehui, China	C12	26
Dej, Rom.	B7	16
Deje, Swe.	G9	6
De Kalb, Il., U.S.	B5	90
De Kalb, Ms., U.S.	C5	101
De Kalb, Tx., U.S.	C5	120
De Kalb, co., Al., U.S.	A4	78
De Kalb, co., Ga., U.S.	C2	87
De Kalb, co., Il., U.S.	B5	90
De Kalb, co., In., U.S.	B7	91
De Kalb, co., Mo., U.S.	B3	102
De Kalb, co., Tn., U.S.	D8	119
Dekese, Zaire	B4	44
Delafield, Wi., U.S.	m11	126
Delanco, N.J., U.S.	C3	107
De Land, Fl., U.S.	C5	86
Delano, Ca., U.S.	E4	82
Delano, Mn., U.S.	E5	100
Delano Peak, mtn., Ut., U.S.	E3	121
Delaronde Lake, l., Sask., Can.	C2	75
Delavan, Il., U.S.	C4	90
Delavan, Wi., U.S.	F5	126
Delaware, Oh., U.S.	B2	112
Delaware, co., In., U.S.	D7	91
Delaware, co., Ia., U.S.	B6	92
Delaware, co., N.Y., U.S.	C5	109
Delaware, co., Oh., U.S.	B2	112
Delaware, co., Ok., U.S.	A7	113
Delaware, co., Pa., U.S.	G11	115
Delaware, state, U.S.	D3	85
Delaware, stm., U.S.	G11	115
Delaware, stm., Ks., U.S.	C8	93
Delaware, East Branch, stm., N.Y., U.S.	C5	109
Delaware Bay, b., U.S.	D11	76
Delaware City, De., U.S.	B3	85
Delaware Lake, res., Oh., U.S.	B3	112
Delaware Water Gap, N.J., U.S.	B2	107
Delaware Water Gap National Recreation Area, U.S.	B2	107
Delbarton, W.V., U.S.	D2	125
Delcambre, La., U.S.	E4	95
Del City, Ok., U.S.	B4	113
Delémont, Switz.	E14	10
De Leon, Tx., U.S.	C3	120
De Leon Springs, Fl., U.S.	C5	86
Delft, Neth.	C4	8
Delfzijl, Neth.	B6	8
Delgado, Cabo, c., Moz.	D8	44
Delhi, India	F7	38
Delhi, La., U.S.	B4	95
Delhi, N.Y., U.S.	C6	109
Delicias, Mex.	C7	62
De Lisle, Ms., U.S.	E4	101
Delitzsch, Ger.	D12	8
Dellenbaugh, Mount, mtn., Az., U.S.	A2	80
Dell Rapids, S.D., U.S.	D9	118
Del Mar, Ca., U.S.	o15	82
Delmar, De., U.S.	G3	85
Delmar, Md., U.S.	D6	97
Delmar, N.Y., U.S.	C7	109
Delmenhorst, Ger.	B8	8
Delnice, Cro.	D9	14
Del Norte, Co., U.S.	D4	83
Del Norte, co., Ca., U.S.	B2	82
De-Longa, Ostrova, is., Russia	B23	24
Deloraine, Man., Can.	E1	70
Del Park Manor, De., U.S.	i7	85
Delphi, In., U.S.	C4	91
Delphos, Oh., U.S.	B1	112
Delran, N.J., U.S.	C3	107
Delray Beach, Fl., U.S.	F6	86
Del Rio, Tx., U.S.	E2	120
Delson, Que., Can.	q19	74
Delta, Co., U.S.	C2	83
Delta, Oh., U.S.	A2	112
Delta, Ut., U.S.	D3	121
Delta, co., Co., U.S.	C3	83
Delta, co., Mi., U.S.	C3	99
Delta, co., Tx., U.S.	C5	120
Delta, reg., Ms., U.S.	B3	101
Delta Junction, Ak., U.S.	C10	79
Delta Peak, mtn., B.C., Can.	A3	69
Delta Reservoir, res., N.Y., U.S.	B5	109
Deltaville, Va., U.S.	C6	123
Deltona, Fl., U.S.	D5	86
Demarest, N.J., U.S.	h9	107
Deming, N.M., U.S.	E2	108
Demirci, Tur.	J12	16
Demirköy, Tur.	H11	16
Demmin, Ger.	B13	8
Demopolis, Al., U.S.	C2	78
Demorest, Ga., U.S.	B3	87
Demotte, In., U.S.	B3	91
Denain, Fr.	B10	10
Denali National Park, Ak., U.S.	C9	79
Denare Beach, Sask., Can.	C4	75
Denham Springs, La., U.S.	D5	95
Den Helder, Neth.	C4	8
Denia, Spain	G12	12
Denison, Ia., U.S.	B2	92
Denison, Tx., U.S.	C4	120
Denison Dam, U.S.	D5	113
Denizli, Tur.	H13	4
Denmark, S.C., U.S.	E5	117
Denmark, Wi., U.S.	D6	126
Denmark, ctry., Eur.	D9	4
Denmark Strait, strt.	C15	128
Dennehotso, Az., U.S.	A6	80
Dennis, Ma., U.S.	C7	98
Dennison, Oh., U.S.	B4	112
Dennis Port, Ma., U.S.	C7	98
Denny Terrace, S.C., U.S.	C5	117
Denpasar, Indon.	G6	32
Dent, co., Mo., U.S.	D6	102
Denton, Md., U.S.	C6	97
Denton, N.C., U.S.	B2	110
Denton, Tx., U.S.	C4	120
Denton, co., Tx., U.S.	C4	120
Denver, Co., U.S.	B6	83
Denver, Ia., U.S.	B5	92
Denver, Pa., U.S.	F9	115
Denver, co., Co., U.S.	B6	83
Denver City, Tx., U.S.	C1	120
Denville, N.J., U.S.	B4	107
Deoghar, India	H12	38
Deolāli, India	C2	37
Deoria, India	G10	38
De Pere, Wi., U.S.	D5	126
Depew, N.Y., U.S.	C2	109
Depoe Bay, Or., U.S.	C2	114
Deposit, N.Y., U.S.	C5	109
Depue, Il., U.S.	B4	90
Depok, Indon.	m13	33a
De Queen, Ar., U.S.	C1	81
De Queen Reservoir, res., Ar., U.S.	C1	81
De Quincy, La., U.S.	D2	95
Dera Ghāzi Khān, Pak.	E4	38
Dera Ismāïl Khān, Pak.	E4	38
Derby, Austl.	C4	50
Derby, Eng., U.K.	I11	7
Derby, Ct., U.S.	D3	84
Derby, Ks., U.S.	E6	93
Derby, Vt., U.S.	B4	122
Derby Line, Vt., U.S.	A4	122
Derg, Lough, l., Ire.	I4	7
De Ridder, La., U.S.	D2	95
Derma, Ms., U.S.	B4	101
Dermott, Ar., U.S.	D4	81
Dernieres, Isles, is., La., U.S.	E5	95
Derry, N.H., U.S.	E4	106
Derry, Pa., U.S.	F3	115
Derval, Fr.	E5	10
Derventa, Bos.	E12	14
Derwood, Md., U.S.	B3	97
Desaguadero, stm., Arg.	C3	56
Des Allemands, La., U.S.	E5	95
Des Arc, Ar., U.S.	C4	81
Desbiens, Que., Can.	A6	74
Descartes, Fr.	F7	10
Deschaillons [-sur-Saint-Laurent], Que., Can.	C5	74
Deschambault, Que., Can.	C6	74
Deschambault Lake, l., Sask., Can.	C4	75
Deschutes, co., Or., U.S.	D5	114
Deschutes, stm., Or., U.S.	B6	114
Dese, Eth.	F2	46
Deseado, stm., Arg.	F3	56
Deseret Peak, mtn., Ut., U.S.	C3	121
Deseronto, Ont., Can.	C7	73
Desert Creek Peak, mtn., Nv., U.S.	E2	105
Desert Hot Springs, Ca., U.S.	F5	82
Desert Peak, mtn., Ut., U.S.	B2	121
Desert Valley, val., Nv., U.S.	B3	105
Desha, Ar., U.S.	B5	81
Desha, co., Ar., U.S.	D4	81
Deshler, Ne., U.S.	D8	104
Deshler, Oh., U.S.	A2	112
Des Lacs, stm., N.D., U.S.	A4	111
Desloge, Mo., U.S.	D7	102
De Smet, S.D., U.S.	C8	118
Des Moines, Ia., U.S.	C4	92
Des Moines, Wa., U.S.	B3	124
Des Moines, co., Ia., U.S.	D6	92
Des Moines, stm., U.S.	D5	92
Desolación, Isla, i., Chile	G2	56
De Soto, Il., U.S.	F4	90
De Soto, Ia., U.S.	C3	92
De Soto, Ks., U.S.	D9	93
De Soto, Mo., U.S.	C7	102
De Soto, co., Fl., U.S.	E5	86
De Soto, co., La., U.S.	B2	95
De Soto, co., Ms., U.S.	A3	101
Despard, W.V., U.S.	k10	125
Des Peres, Mo., U.S.	f13	102
Des Plaines, Il., U.S.	A6	90
Des Plaines, stm., U.S.	k8	90
Desroches, Île, i., Sey.	C10	44
Dessau, Ger.	D12	8
Destin, Fl., U.S.	u15	86
Destrehan, La., U.S.	E5	95
Desvres, Fr.	B8	10
Detmold, Ger.	D8	8
Detour, Point, c., Mi., U.S.	C4	99
Detroit, Mi., U.S.	F7	99
Detroit Lake, res., Or., U.S.	C4	114
Detroit Lakes, Mn., U.S.	D3	100
Deuel, co., Ne., U.S.	C3	104
Deuel, co., S.D., U.S.	C9	118
Deutsche Bucht, b., Ger.	A7	8
Deutschlandsberg, Aus.	I15	8
Deux-Montagnes, Que., Can.	p19	74
Deux Montagnes, Lac des, l., Que., Can.	q19	74
Deva, Rom.	D6	16
Devakottai, India	H5	37
De Valls Bluff, Ar., U.S.	C4	81
Deventer, Neth.	C6	8
DeView, Bayou, stm., Ar., U.S.	B4	81
Devil's Island see Diable, Île du, i., Fr. Gu.	B8	54
Devils Lake, N.D., U.S.	A7	111
Devils Lake, l., N.D., U.S.	A6	111
Devils Paw, mtn., Ak., U.S.	k23	79
Devils Postpile National Monument, Ca., U.S.	D4	82
Devils Tower National Monument, Wy., U.S.	B8	127
Devil Track Lake, l., Mn., U.S.	k9	100
Devine, Tx., U.S.	E3	120
DeVola, Oh., U.S.	C4	112
Devon, Alta., Can.	C4	68
Devon Island, i., N.W. Ter., Can.	A15	66
Devonport, Austl.	H9	50
Devonport, N.Z.	B5	52
Devonshire, De., U.S.	h7	85
Dewa-kyūryō, hills, Japan	C13	30
Dewar, Ok., U.S.	B6	113
Dewās, India	I7	38
Dewees Inlet, b., S.C., U.S.	k12	117
Dewees Island, i., S.C., U.S.	F8	117
Dewey, Az., U.S.	C3	80
Dewey, Ok., U.S.	A6	113
Dewey, co., Ok., U.S.	B2	113
Dewey, co., S.D., U.S.	B4	118
Dewey Beach, De., U.S.	F5	85
Dewey Lake, res., Ky., U.S.	C7	94
Deweyville, Tx., U.S.	D6	120
De Witt, Ar., U.S.	C4	81
De Witt, Ia., U.S.	C7	92
De Witt, Mi., U.S.	F6	99
De Witt, N.Y., U.S.	B4	109
De Witt, co., Il., U.S.	C4	90
De Witt, co., Tx., U.S.	E4	120
Dexter, Ia., U.S.	C3	92
Dexter, Me., U.S.	C3	96
Dexter, Mi., U.S.	F7	99
Dexter, Mo., U.S.	E8	102
Dexter, N.M., U.S.	D5	108
Dexter, Lake, l., Fl., U.S.	C5	86
Dezfūl, Iran	B4	46
Dezhou, China	D10	26
Dhaka, Bngl.	I14	38
Dhamār, Yemen	F3	46
Dhamtari, India	B6	37
Dhānbād, India	I12	38
Dhār, India	I6	38
Dharmapuri, India	F5	37
Dharmavaram, India	E4	37
Dhārwār, India	E3	37
Dhawlāgiri, mtn., Nepal	F10	38
Dhodhekánisos (Dodecanese), is., Grc.	M10	16
Dholpur, India	G7	38
Dhorāji, India	J4	38
Dhrol, India	I4	38
Dhubri, India	G13	38
Dhule, India	B3	37
Diable, Île du, i., Fr. Gu.	B8	54
Diablo, Canyon, val., Az., U.S.	C4	80
Diablo, Mount, mtn., Ca., U.S.	h9	82
Diablo Dam, Wa., U.S.	A4	124
Diablo Lake, res., Wa., U.S.	A4	124
Diablo Range, mts., Ca., U.S.	D3	82
Diamante, Arg.	C4	56
Diamantina, Braz.	E7	57
Diamantino, Braz.	F7	54
Diamond Head, crat., Hi., U.S.	B4	88
Diamond Hill, R.I., U.S.	B4	116
Diamond Hill Reservoir, res., R.I., U.S.	A4	116
Diamond Lake, Il., U.S.	h9	90
Diamond Lake, l., Or., U.S.	D4	114
Diamond Mountains, mts., Nv., U.S.	D6	105
Diamond Peak, mtn., Co., U.S.	A2	83
Diamond Peak, mtn., Id., U.S.	E5	89
Diamond Peak, mtn., Or., U.S.	D4	114
Diamond Peak, mtn., Wa., U.S.	C8	124
Diamondville, Wy., U.S.	E2	127
Diaz, Ar., U.S.	B4	81
Dibaya, Zaire	C4	44
D'Iberville, Ms., U.S.	E5	101
Diboll, Tx., U.S.	D5	120
Dibrugarh, India	G16	38
Dickens, Tx., U.S.	C2	120
Dickens, co., Tx., U.S.	C2	120
Dickenson, co., Va., U.S.	e9	123
Dickerson, Md., U.S.	B3	97
Dickey, co., N.D., U.S.	C7	111
Dickeyville, Wi., U.S.	F3	126
Dickinson, N.D., U.S.	C3	111
Dickinson, co., Ia., U.S.	A2	92
Dickinson, co., Ks., U.S.	D6	93
Dickinson, co., Mi., U.S.	B3	99
Dickinson Dam, N.D., U.S.	C3	111
Dickson, Ok., U.S.	C5	113
Dickson, Tn., U.S.	A4	119
Dickson, co., Tn., U.S.	A4	119
Dickson City, Pa., U.S.	D10	115
Didsbury, Alta., Can.	D3	68
Die, Fr.	H12	10
Dieburg, Ger.	F8	8
Dieciocho de Marzo, Mex.	E11	62
Diefenbaker, Lake, res., Sask., Can.	F2	75
Diégo-Suarez see Antsiranana, Madag.	D9	44
Diepholz, Ger.	C8	8
Dieppe, N.B., Can.	C5	71
Dieppe, Fr.	C8	10
Dierks, Ar., U.S.	C1	81
Dieuze, Fr.	C13	10
Digboi, India	G16	38
Dighton, Ks., U.S.	D3	93
Digne, Fr.	H13	10
Digoin, Fr.	F10	10
Dijon, Fr.	E12	10
Dike, Ia., U.S.	B5	92
Dikson, Russia	C10	24
Dili, Indon.	G8	32
Dillard, Or., U.S.	D3	114
Dill City, Ok., U.S.	B2	113
Dilley, Tx., U.S.	E3	120
Dillingen [an der Donau], Ger.	G10	8
Dillingham, Ak., U.S.	D8	79
Dillon, Mt., U.S.	E4	103
Dillon, S.C., U.S.	C9	117
Dillon, co., S.C., U.S.	C9	117
Dillon Lake, res., Oh., U.S.	B3	112
Dillon Reservoir, res., Co., U.S.	B4	83
Dillonvale, Oh., U.S.	B5	112
Dillsboro, In., U.S.	F7	91
Dillsburg, Pa., U.S.	F7	115
Dilolo, Zaire	D4	44
Dilworth, Mn., U.S.	D2	100
Dimāpur, India	H15	38
Dimashq (Damascus), Syria	C5	40
Dimitrovgrad, Bul.	G9	16
Dimitrovgrad, Russia	G7	22
Dimmit, co., Tx., U.S.	E3	120
Dimmitt, Tx., U.S.	B1	120
Dimona, Isr.	D4	40
Dimondale, Mi., U.S.	F6	99
Dinagat Island, i., Phil.	C8	32
Dinājpur, Bngl.	H13	38
Dinan, Fr.	D4	10
Dinant, Bel.	E4	8
Dinara, mts., Eur.	F11	14
Dinard, Fr.	D4	10
Dinaric Alps see Dinara, mts., Eur.	F11	14
Dindigul, India	G4	37
Dinghai, China	E11	28
Dingle, Ire.	I2	7
Dingmans Ferry, Pa., U.S.	D12	115
Dingolfing, Ger.	G12	8
Dingqing, China	E16	38
Dingri, China	F12	38
Dingshan, China	D8	28
Dingwall, Scot., U.K.	D8	7
Dinh Lap, Viet.	D9	34
Dinner Point, c., Fl., U.S.	D4	86
Dinosaur National Monument, U.S.	C6	121
Dinuba, Ca., U.S.	D4	82
Dinwiddie, co., Va., U.S.	C5	123
Diourbel, Sen.	F2	42
Dipkarpaz, N. Cyp.	B4	40
Dipolog, Phil.	D7	32
Dire Dawa, Eth.	G3	46
Diriamba, Nic.	I4	64
Dirico, Ang.	E4	44
Dirk Hartog Island, i., Austl.	E2	50
Dirty Devil, stm., Ut., U.S.	E5	121
Disappointment, Cape, c., Falk. Is.	—	124
Disappointment, Lake, l., Austl.	D4	50
Disentis, Switz.	F15	10
Dishman, Wa., U.S.	g14	124
Disko, i., Grnld.	C22	66
Disko Bugt, b., Grnld.	C22	66
Dismal, stm., Ne., U.S.	C5	104
Disraëli, Que., Can.	D6	74
District of Columbia, dept., U.S.	f8	97
Diu, India	J4	38
Diu, ter., India	J4	38
Divernon, Il., U.S.	D4	90
Divide, co., N.D., U.S.	A2	111
Divide Peak, mtn., Wy., U.S.	E5	127
Divinópolis, Braz.	F6	57
Divisor, Serra do, plat., S.A.	E4	54
Dix, stm., Ky., U.S.	C5	94
Dixfield, Me., U.S.	D2	96
Dixie, co., Fl., U.S.	C3	86
Dixie Valley, val., Nv., U.S.	D3	105
Dixon, Il., U.S.	B4	90
Dixon, Ky., U.S.	C2	94
Dixon, Mo., U.S.	D5	102
Dixon, N.M., U.S.	A4	108
Dixon, co., Ne., U.S.	B9	104
Dixon Entrance, strt., N.A.	F6	66
Dixonville, Pa., U.S.	E3	115
Diyarbakır, Tur.	H16	4
Dja, stm., Afr.	H8	42
Djakarta see Jakarta, Indon.	m13	33a
Djambala, Congo	B2	44
Djanet, Alg.	D7	42
Djebel Abiod, Tun.	M4	14
Djebibina, Tun.	N5	14
Djerba, Île de, i., Tun.	B8	42
Djerid, Chott, sw., Tun.	B7	42
Djibouti, Dji.	F3	46
Djibouti, ctry., Afr.	F3	46
Dmitrija Lapteva, Proliv, strt., Russia	C22	24

Name	Map Ref	Page
...mitrov, Russia	E20	18
...nepr, stm., Eur.	H4	22
...neprodzeržinsk, Ukr.	H4	22
...nepropetrovsk, Ukr.	H4	22
...nestr, stm., Eur.	H3	22
...nieper see Dnepr, stm., Eur.	H4	22
...niester see Dnestr, stm., Eur.	H3	22
...no, Russia	D12	18
o Āb-e Mīkh-e Zarrīn, Afg.	C2	38
...oaktown, N.B., Can.	C3	71
...oany, Madag.	D9	44
...oba, Chad	E9	42
...obbiaco, Italy	C7	14
...obbs Ferry, N.Y., U.S.	g13	109
...öbeln, Ger.	D13	8
...oberai, Jazirah, pen., Indon.	F9	32
...obo, Indon.	G9	32
...oboj, Bos.	E2	16
...obrič, Bul.	F11	16
...obruš, Bela.	I14	18
...obson, N.C., U.S.	A2	110
...oce, stm., Braz.	E8	57
...ocena, Al., U.S.	f7	78
...ock Junction, Ga., U.S.	*E5	87
...octors Lake, l., Fl., U.S.	m8	86
...oddridge, co., W.V., U.S.	B4	125
...odecanese see Dhodhekánisos, is., Grc.	M10	16
...odge, Ne., U.S.	C9	104
...odge, co., Ga., U.S.	D3	87
...odge, co., Mn., U.S.	G6	100
...odge, co., Ne., U.S.	C9	104
...odge, co., Wi., U.S.	E5	126
...odge Center, Mn., U.S.	F6	100
...odge City, Ks., U.S.	E3	93
...odgeville, Wi., U.S.	F3	126
...odoma, Tan.	C7	44
...oerun, Ga., U.S.	E3	87
...oe Run, Mo., U.S.	D7	102
...oetinchem, Neth.	D6	8
...og, stm., Vt., U.S.	C3	122
...ogai Coring, l., China	C13	38
...og Island, l., China	C2	86
...og Keys Pass, strt., Ms., U.S.	g8	101
...og Lake, l., Man., Can.	D2	70
...ogondoutchi, Niger	F6	42
...oha see Ad-Dawḩah, Qatar	C5	46
...ohad, India	I6	38
...oiran, Lake, l., Eur.	H6	16
...okka, Nor.	F8	6
...okkum, Neth.	B5	8
...olak, Pulau, i., Indon.	G10	32
...olbeau, Que., Can.	k12	74
...ol-de-Bretagne, Fr.	D5	10
...olgeville, N.Y., U.S.	B6	109
...olianova, Italy	J4	14
...olisie, Congo	B2	44
...ollar Bay, Mi., U.S.	A2	99
...olomite, Al., U.S.	B3	78
...olomites see Dolomiti, mts., Italy	C6	14
...olomiti, mts., Italy	C6	14
...olores, Arg.	D5	56
...olores, Col.	F5	58
...olores, Co., U.S.	D2	83
...olores, co., Co., U.S.	D2	83
...olores, stm., U.S.	E7	121
...olores Hidalgo, Mex.	G9	62
...olphin and Union Strait, strt., N.W. Ter., Can.	C9	66
...olphin Island, i., Ut., U.S.	B3	121
...olton, Il., U.S.	k9	90
...ombás, Nor.	E7	6
...ome Mountain, mtn., Az., U.S.	k9	80
...ome Peak, mtn., Co., U.S.	B3	83
...omeyko, Chile	B2	56
...omeyko, Cordillera, mts., Chile	A3	56
...omfront, Fr.	D6	10
...ominica, ctry., N.A.	G17	64
...ominica Channel, strt., N.A.	G17	64
...ominican Republic, ctry., N.A.	E12	64
...ominion, Cape, c., N.W. Ter., Can.	C18	66
...omodedovo, Russia	F20	18
...omodossola, Italy	C3	14
...omžale, Slo.	C9	14
...on, stm., Russia	H6	22
...ona Ana, N.M., U.S.	E3	108
...ona Ana, co., N.M., U.S.	E2	108
...onaldsonville, La., U.S.	D4	95
...onalsonville, Ga., U.S.	E2	87
...onaueschingen, Ger.	H8	8
...onauwörth, Ger.	G10	8
...on Benito, Spain	G6	12
...oncaster, Eng., U.K.	H11	7
...ondo, Ang.	C2	44
...ondra Head, c., Ire.	J6	37
...oneck, Ukr.	H5	22
...onegal Bay, b., Ire.	G4	7
...oneraile, S.C., U.S.	C8	117
...onetsk see Doneck, Ukr.	H5	22
...onga, stm., Nig.	G8	42
...ongara, Austl.	E2	50
...ongchuan, China	A7	34
...ongfang, China	H8	26
...ongfang (Basuo), China	E10	34
...ongguan, China	L2	28
...onghai Dao, i., China	D11	34
...ong Hoi, Viet.	F9	34
...ongshan, China	L6	28
...ongtai, China	C9	28
...ongting Hu, l., China	F1	28
...oniphan, Mo., U.S.	E7	102
...oniphan, Ne., U.S.	D7	104
...oniphan, co., Ks., U.S.	C8	93
...onkey Creek, stm., Wy., U.S.	B7	127
...onkin, N.S., Can.	C10	71
...onley, co., Tx., U.S.	B2	120
...onna, Tx., U.S.	F3	120
...onnacona, Que., Can.	C6	74
...onner Pass, U.S.	C3	82
...onnellson, Ia., U.S.	D6	92
...onora, Pa., U.S.	F2	115
...onskoj, Russia	H21	18
...ooly, co., Ga., U.S.	D3	87
...oonerak, Mount, mtn., Ak., U.S.	B9	79

Name	Map Ref	Page
Door, co., Wi., U.S.	D6	126
Dora, Al., U.S.	B2	78
Doraville, Ga., U.S.	h8	87
Dorcheat, Bayou, stm., U.S.	B2	95
Dorchester, N.B., Can.	D5	71
Dorchester, Eng., U.K.	K10	7
Dorchester, Ne., U.S.	D8	104
Dorchester, co., Md., U.S.	D5	97
Dorchester, co., S.C., U.S.	E7	117
Dorchester, Cape, c., N.W. Ter., Can.	C17	66
Dordogne, stm., Fr.	H8	10
Dordrecht, Neth.	D4	8
Doré Lake, l., Sask., Can.	C2	75
Dorena Lake, res., Or., U.S.	D3	114
Dores do Indaiá, Braz.	E6	57
Dorgali, Italy	I4	14
Dori, Burkina	F5	42
Dorion-Vaudreuil, Que., Can.	q18	74
Dormont, Pa., U.S.	k13	115
Dornbirn, Aus.	H9	8
Dorothy Pond, Ma., U.S.	B4	98
Dorr, Mi., U.S.	F5	99
Dorset, Vt., U.S.	E2	122
Dorsey, Md., U.S.	B4	97
Dortmund, Ger.	D7	8
Dorton, Ky., U.S.	C7	94
Dorval, Que., Can.	q19	74
Dos Bahías, Cabo, c., Arg.	E3	56
Dothan, Al., U.S.	D4	78
Douai, Fr.	B10	10
Douala, Cam.	H7	42
Douarnenez, Fr.	D2	10
Double Beach, Ct., U.S.	D4	84
Doublespring Pass, Id., U.S.	E5	89
Double Springs, Al., U.S.	A2	78
Doubletop Peak, mtn., Wy., U.S.	C2	127
Doubs, stm., Eur.	E12	10
Dougherty, co., Ga., U.S.	E2	87
Douglas, I. of Man	G8	7
Douglas, Az., U.S.	F6	80
Douglas, Ga., U.S.	E4	87
Douglas, Mi., U.S.	F4	99
Douglas, Wy., U.S.	D7	127
Douglas, co., Co., U.S.	B6	83
Douglas, co., Ga., U.S.	C2	87
Douglas, co., Il., U.S.	D5	90
Douglas, co., Ks., U.S.	D8	93
Douglas, co., Mn., U.S.	E3	100
Douglas, co., Mo., U.S.	E5	102
Douglas, co., Ne., U.S.	C9	104
Douglas, co., Nv., U.S.	E2	105
Douglas, co., Or., U.S.	D3	114
Douglas, co., S.D., U.S.	D7	118
Douglas, co., Wa., U.S.	B6	124
Douglas, co., Wi., U.S.	B2	126
Douglas, Mount, mtn., Ak., U.S.	D9	79
Douglas Channel, strt., B.C., Can.	C3	69
Douglas Lake, l., Mi., U.S.	C6	99
Douglas Lake, res., Tn., U.S.	D10	119
Douglass, Ks., U.S.	E7	93
Douglastown, N.B., Can.	B4	71
Douglasville, Ga., U.S.	C2	87
Dourada, Serra, plat., Braz.	B4	57
Dourados, Braz.	G1	57
Douro (Duero), stm., Eur.	D4	12
Dousman, Wi., U.S.	E5	126
Dove Creek, Co., U.S.	D2	83
Dover, Eng., U.K.	J14	7
Dover, Ar., U.S.	B2	81
Dover, De., U.S.	D3	85
Dover, Fl., U.S.	D4	86
Dover, Ma., U.S.	h10	98
Dover, N.H., U.S.	D5	106
Dover, N.J., U.S.	B3	107
Dover, Oh., U.S.	B4	112
Dover, Pa., U.S.	F8	115
Dover, Tn., U.S.	A4	119
Dover, Strait of (Pas de Calais), strt., Eur.	J14	7
Dover Air Force Base, mil., De., U.S.	D4	85
Dover-Foxcroft, Me., U.S.	C3	96
Dover Plains, N.Y., U.S.	D7	109
Dowagiac, Mi., U.S.	G4	99
Dowlat Yār, Afg.	C1	38
Downers Grove, Il., U.S.	B5	90
Downey, Ca., U.S.	n12	82
Downey, Id., U.S.	G6	89
Downingtown, Pa., U.S.	F10	115
Downpatrick, N. Ire., U.K.	G7	7
Downpatrick Head, c., Ire.	G3	7
Downs, Ks., U.S.	C5	93
Downs Mountain, mtn., Wy., U.S.	C3	127
Downton, Mount, mtn., B.C., Can.	C5	69
Dows, Ia., U.S.	B4	92
Dowshī, Afg.	C3	38
Doylestown, Oh., U.S.	B4	112
Doylestown, Pa., U.S.	F11	115
Doyline, La., U.S.	B2	95
Draa, Oued, val., Afr.	C4	42
Dracena, Braz.	F3	57
Drachten, Neth.	B6	8
Dracut, Ma., U.S.	A5	98
Draguignan, Fr.	I13	10
Drain, Or., U.S.	D3	114
Drake Passage, strt.	D6	47
Drake Peak, mtn., Or., U.S.	E6	114
Dráma, Grc.	H8	16
Drammen, Nor.	G8	6
Draper, Ut., U.S.	C4	121
Drau (Drava), stm., Eur.	C8	14
Drava (Drau), stm., Eur.	D13	14
Drayton, Ont., Can.	D4	73
Drayton, N.D., U.S.	A8	111
Drayton, S.C., U.S.	B4	117
Drayton Plains, Mi., U.S.	F7	99
Drayton Valley, Alta., Can.	C3	68
Dresden, Ont., Can.	E2	73
Dresden, Ger.	D13	8
Dresden, Oh., U.S.	B3	112
Dresden, Tn., U.S.	A3	119
Dresslerville, Nv., U.S.	E2	105
Dreux, Fr.	D8	10
Drew, Ms., U.S.	B3	101
Drew, co., Ar., U.S.	D4	81
Drews Reservoir, res., Or., U.S.	E6	114
Drexel, Mo., U.S.	C3	102
Drexel, N.C., U.S.	B1	110

Name	Map Ref	Page
Drexel, Oh., U.S.	C1	112
Drift, Ky., U.S.	C7	94
Driggs, Id., U.S.	F7	89
Driskill Mountain, hill, La., U.S.	B3	95
Drogheda, Ire.	H6	7
Drumheller, Alta., Can.	D4	68
Drum Island, i., S.C., U.S.	k12	117
Drummond, Lake, l., Va., U.S.	D6	123
Drummond Island, i., Mi., U.S.	C7	99
Drummondville, Que., Can.	D5	74
Drumright, Ok., U.S.	B5	113
Družina, Russia	D23	24
Drybranch, W.V., U.S.	m13	125
Dry Cimarron, stm., U.S.	A6	108
Dry Creek Mountain, mtn., Nv., U.S.	B5	105
Dryden, Ont., Can.	o16	73
Dryden, N.Y., U.S.	C4	109
Dry Fork, stm., Mo., U.S.	D6	102
Dry Fork, stm., W.V., U.S.	D5	125
Dry Fork, stm., W.V., U.S.	D3	125
Dry Ridge, Ky., U.S.	B5	94
Dry Tortugas, is., Fl., U.S.	H5	86
Duarte, Pico, mtn., Dom. Rep.	E12	64
Dubach, La., U.S.	B3	95
Dubai see Dubayy, U.A.E.	C6	46
Dubawnt, stm., N.W. Ter., Can.	D12	66
Dubawnt Lake, l., N.W. Ter., Can.	D12	66
Du Bay, Lake, res., Wi., U.S.	D4	126
Dubbo, Austl.	F9	50
Dublin (Baile Átha Cliath), Ire.	H6	7
Dublin, Ga., U.S.	D4	87
Dublin, In., U.S.	E7	91
Dublin, N.H., U.S.	E2	106
Dublin, Oh., U.S.	k10	112
Dublin, Pa., U.S.	F11	115
Dublin, Tx., U.S.	C3	120
Dublin, Va., U.S.	C2	123
Dubna, Russia	E20	18
Dubois, In., U.S.	H4	91
Du Bois, Pa., U.S.	D4	115
Dubois, Wy., U.S.	C3	127
Dubois, co., In., U.S.	H4	91
Duboistown, Pa., U.S.	D7	115
Dubrovnik, Cro.	G13	14
Dubuque, Ia., U.S.	B7	92
Dubuque, co., Ia., U.S.	B7	92
Duchesne, Ut., U.S.	C5	121
Duchesne, co., Ut., U.S.	C5	121
Duchesne, stm., Ut., U.S.	C5	121
Duchess, Austl.	D7	50
Duck, stm., Tn., U.S.	B4	119
Duck Bay, Man., Can.	C1	70
Duck Creek, stm., Oh., U.S.	C4	112
Duck Creek, stm., Wi., U.S.	h9	126
Duck Lake, Sask., Can.	E2	75
Duck Lake, l., Me., U.S.	C4	96
Duck Mountain Provincial Park, Sask., Can.	F5	75
Duck Valley Indian Reservation, U.S.	B5	105
Duckwater Indian Reservation, Nv., U.S.	E6	105
Duckwater Peak, mtn., Nv., U.S.	E6	105
Dudelange, Lux.	F6	8
Dudinka, Russia	D11	24
Dudley, Ma., U.S.	B4	98
Duenweg, Mo., U.S.	D3	102
Duero (Douro), stm., Eur.	D5	12
Due West, S.C., U.S.	C3	117
Duffer Peak, mtn., Nv., U.S.	B3	105
Dufour Spitze, mtn., Eur.	G14	10
Duga Resa, Cro.	D10	14
Dugdemona, stm., La., U.S.	B3	95
Dugger, In., U.S.	F3	91
Duida, Cerro, mtn., Ven.	F10	58
Duifken Point, c., Austl.	B8	50
Duisburg, Ger.	D6	8
Duke Island, i., Ak., U.S.	n24	79
Dukes, co., Ma., U.S.	D6	98
Duk Fadiat, Sudan	G12	42
Dulce, N.M., U.S.	A2	108
Dulgalach, stm., Russia	D20	24
Duluth, Ga., U.S.	B2	87
Duluth, Mn., U.S.	D6	100
Dūmā, Syria	C5	40
Dumaguete, Phil.	D7	32
Dumaran Island, i., Phil.	C6	32
Dumaring, Indon.	E6	32
Dumas, Ar., U.S.	D4	81
Dumas, Tx., U.S.	B2	120
Dumbarton, Scot., U.K.	F8	7
Dumfries, Scot., U.K.	F9	7
Dumfries, Va., U.S.	B5	123
Dumont, Ia., U.S.	B5	92
Dumont, N.J., U.S.	B5	107
Dumyāṭ, Egypt	B12	42
Dunaújváros, Hung.	I18	8
Dunbar, Pa., U.S.	G2	115
Dunbar, W.V., U.S.	C3	125
Dunbar, B.C., Can.	E6	69
Duncan, Az., U.S.	E6	80
Duncan, Ok., U.S.	C4	113
Duncan, S.C., U.S.	B3	117
Duncan Falls, Oh., U.S.	C4	112
Duncan Lake, res., B.C., Can.	D9	69
Duncannon, Pa., U.S.	F7	115
Duncansville, Pa., U.S.	F5	115
Duncanville, Tx., U.S.	n10	120
Dundalk, Ont., Can.	C4	73
Dundalk, Ire.	G6	7
Dundalk, Md., U.S.	B4	97
Dundas, Ont., Can.	D5	73
Dundas Peninsula, pen., N.W. Ter., Can.	B10	66
Dundee, S. Afr.	G6	44
Dundee, Scot., U.K.	E9	7
Dundee, Fl., U.S.	D5	86
Dundee, Il., U.S.	A5	90
Dundee, Mi., U.S.	G7	99
Dundee, N.Y., U.S.	C3	109
Dundee, Or., U.S.	h11	114
Dundy, co., Ne., U.S.	D4	104
Dunedin, N.Z.	F3	52
Dunedin, Fl., U.S.	D4	86
Dunellen, N.J., U.S.	B4	107
Dunfermline, Scot., U.K.	E9	7
Dungarvan, Ire.	I5	7

Name	Map Ref	Page
Dungeness, stm., Wa., U.S.	A2	124
Dungun, Malay.	L7	34
Dunham, Que., Can.	D5	74
Dunhua, China	C12	26
Dunhuang, China	C5	26
Dunkard Creek, stm., U.S.	B4	125
Dunkerque, Fr.	A9	10
Dunkerton, Ia., U.S.	B5	92
Dunkirk, In., U.S.	D7	91
Dunkirk, N.Y., U.S.	C1	109
Dunkirk, Oh., U.S.	B2	112
Dunklin, co., Mo., U.S.	E7	102
Dunkwa, Ghana	G5	42
Dún Laoghaire, Ire.	H6	7
Dunlap, Il., U.S.	C4	90
Dunlap, In., U.S.	A6	91
Dunlap, Ia., U.S.	C2	92
Dunlap, Tn., U.S.	D8	119
Dunleith, De., U.S.	i7	85
Dunloup Creek, stm., W.V., U.S.	n13	125
Dunmore, Pa., U.S.	D10	115
Dunmore, Lake, l., Vt., U.S.	D2	122
Dunn, N.C., U.S.	B4	110
Dunn, co., N.D., U.S.	B3	111
Dunn, co., Wi., U.S.	D2	126
Dunnellon, Fl., U.S.	C4	86
Dunnville, Ont., Can.	E5	73
Dunqulah, Sudan	E12	42
Duns, Scot., U.K.	F10	7
Dunseith, N.D., U.S.	A5	111
Dunsmuir, Ca., U.S.	B2	82
Duntou, China	F8	28
Dunville, Newf., Can.	E5	72
Dunwoody, Ga., U.S.	h8	87
Duomaer, China	E2	26
Du Page, co., Il., U.S.	B5	90
Du Page, stm., Il., U.S.	k8	90
Duplin, co., N.C., U.S.	C5	110
Dupont, Co., U.S.	B6	83
Dupont, Pa., U.S.	n18	115
Dupont City, W.V., U.S.	m12	125
Dupont Manor, De., U.S.	B1	41
Dupont Manor, De., U.S.	D3	85
Duque de Caxias, Braz.	G7	57
Duque de York, Isla, i., Chile	G1	56
Duquesne, Pa., U.S.	F2	115
Du Quoin, Il., U.S.	E4	90
Durand, Il., U.S.	A4	90
Durand, Mi., U.S.	F6	99
Durand, Wi., U.S.	D2	126
Durango, Mex.	E7	62
Durango, Spain	B9	12
Durango, Co., U.S.	D3	83
Durant, Ia., U.S.	C7	92
Durant, Ms., U.S.	B4	101
Durant, Ok., U.S.	D5	113
Durazno, Ur.	C5	56
Durban, S. Afr.	G6	44
Ðurđevac, Cro.	C12	14
Düren, Ger.	E6	8
Durg, India	B6	37
Durgāpur, India	I12	38
Durham, Ont., Can.	C4	73
Durham, Eng., U.K.	G11	7
Durham, Ca., U.S.	C3	82
Durham, Ct., U.S.	D5	84
Durham, N.H., U.S.	D5	106
Durham, N.C., U.S.	B4	110
Durham, co., N.C., U.S.	A4	110
Durness, Scot., U.K.	C8	7
Durrell, Newf., Can.	D4	72
Durrës, Alb.	H3	16
Dursunbey, Tur.	J12	16
D'Urville, Tanjung, c., Indon.	F10	32
Duryea, Pa., U.S.	D10	115
Dušanbe, Taj.	J11	22
Dušekan, Russia	E15	24
Dushan, China	B9	34
Dushanbe see Dušanbe, Taj.	J11	22
Duson, La., U.S.	D3	95
Düsseldorf, Ger.	D6	8
Dutchess, co., N.Y., U.S.	D7	109
Dutch Island, i., R.I., U.S.	F4	116
Dutton, Ont., Can.	E3	73
Dutton, Mount, mtn., Ut., U.S.	E3	121
Duval, co., Fl., U.S.	B5	86
Duval, co., Tx., U.S.	F3	120
Duxbury, Ma., U.S.	B6	98
Duyun, China	A9	34
Dwight, Il., U.S.	B5	90
Dwight D. Eisenhower Lock, N.Y., U.S.	f9	109
Dworshak Reservoir, res., Id., U.S.	C3	89
Dyer, In., U.S.	A2	91
Dyer, Tn., U.S.	A3	119
Dyer, co., Tn., U.S.	A2	119
Dyer, Cape, c., N.W. Ter., Can.	C20	66
Dyer Island, i., R.I., U.S.	E5	116
Dyersburg, Tn., U.S.	A2	119
Dyersville, Ia., U.S.	B6	92
Dyess Air Force Base, mil., Tx., U.S.	C3	120
Dysart, Ia., U.S.	B5	92
Džalinda, Russia	G18	24
Džambul, Kaz.	I12	22
Dzaoudzi, May.	D9	44
Džardžan, Russia	D18	24
Dzavchan, stm., Mong.	B5	26
Dzeržinsk, Russia	E26	18
Dzeržinskoje, Kaz.	H10	24
Džezkazgan, Kaz.	H11	22
Dzhambul see Džambul, Kaz.	I12	22
Dzierżoniów (Reichenbach), Pol.	E16	8
Džugdžur, Chrebet, mts., Russia	F21	24

E

Name	Map Ref	Page
Eads, Co., U.S.	C8	83
Eagan, Mn., U.S.	n12	100
Eagar, Az., U.S.	C6	80
Eagle, Co., U.S.	B4	83
Eagle, Id., U.S.	F2	89
Eagle, Ne., U.S.	h12	104
Eagle, Wi., U.S.	F5	126
Eagle, co., Co., U.S.	B4	83
Eagle, stm., Newf., Can.	B2	72

Name	Map Ref	Page
Eagle Creek Reservoir, res., In., U.S.	E5	91
Eagle Grove, Ia., U.S.	B4	92
Eagle Key, i., Fl., U.S.	G6	86
Eagle Lake, Me., U.S.	A4	96
Eagle Lake, Mn., U.S.	F5	100
Eagle Lake, Tx., U.S.	E4	120
Eagle Lake, l., Ca., U.S.	B3	82
Eagle Lake, l., Me., U.S.	B3	96
Eagle Lake, l., Me., U.S.	A4	96
Eagle Lake, l., Ms., U.S.	C3	101
Eagle Lake, l., Wi., U.S.	C4	126
Eagle Mountain, mtn., Mn., U.S.	k9	100
Eagle Mountain Lake, res., Tx., U.S.	m9	120
Eagle Nest Lake, l., N.M., U.S.	A4	108
Eagle Pass, Tx., U.S.	E2	120
Eagle Peak, mtn., Ca., U.S.	B3	82
Eagle Point, Or., U.S.	E4	114
Eagle River, Wi., U.S.	C4	126
Eagletail Mountains, mts., Az., U.S.	D2	80
Eagletail Peak, mtn., Az., U.S.	D2	80
Eagletown, Ok., U.S.	C7	113
Earle, Ar., U.S.	B5	81
Earlham, Ia., U.S.	C3	92
Earlimart, Ca., U.S.	E4	82
Earlington, Ky., U.S.	C2	94
Earlville, Il., U.S.	B5	90
Earlville, Ia., U.S.	B6	92
Early, Ia., U.S.	B2	92
Early, co., Ga., U.S.	E2	87
Earth, Tx., U.S.	B1	120
Easley, S.C., U.S.	B3	117
East, stm., Ct., U.S.	D5	84
East, stm., N.Y., U.S.	k13	109
East, stm., Wi., U.S.	h9	126
East Alton, Il., U.S.	E3	90
East Angus, Que., Can.	D6	74
East Arlington, Vt., U.S.	E2	122
East Aurora, N.Y., U.S.	C2	109
East Bangor, Pa., U.S.	E11	115
East Bank, W.V., U.S.	m13	125
East Barre, Vt., U.S.	C4	122
East Baton Rouge, co., La., U.S.	D4	95
East Bay, b., Fl., U.S.	u16	86
East Bay, b., Tx., U.S.	R15	120
East Beckwith Mountain, mtn., Co., U.S.	C3	83
East Berlin, Ct., U.S.	C5	84
East Berlin, Pa., U.S.	G8	115
East Bernard, Tx., U.S.	E4	120
East Bernstadt, Ky., U.S.	C5	94
East Bethel, Mn., U.S.	E5	100
East Billerica, Ma., U.S.	f11	98
Eastborough, Ks., U.S.	g12	93
Eastbourne, Eng., U.K.	K13	7
East Brady, Pa., U.S.	E2	115
East Branch Clarion River Lake, res., Pa., U.S.	C4	115
East Brewton, Al., U.S.	D2	78
East Bridgewater, Ma., U.S.	B6	98
East Brimfield Lake, res., Ma., U.S.	B3	98
East Brooklyn, Ct., U.S.	B8	84
East Broughton, Que., Can.	C6	74
East Brunswick, N.J., U.S.	C4	107
East Butte, mtn., Mt., U.S.	B5	103
East Cache Creek, stm., Ok., U.S.	C3	113
East Cape, c., Fl., U.S.	G5	86
East Carbon, Ut., U.S.	D5	121
East Carroll, co., La., U.S.	B4	95
East Chicago, In., U.S.	A3	91
East China Sea, Asia	E12	26
East Chop, c., Ma., U.S.	D6	98
East Cleveland, Oh., U.S.	g9	112
East Cote Blanche Bay, b., La., U.S.	E4	95
East Dennis, Ma., U.S.	C7	98
East Derry, N.H., U.S.	E4	106
East Detroit, Mi., U.S.	p16	99
East Douglas, Ma., U.S.	B4	98
East Dubuque, Il., U.S.	A3	90
Eastend, Sask., Can.	H1	75
Easter Island see Pascua, Isla de, i., Chile		
Eastern Bay, b., Md., U.S.	C5	97
Eastern Channel see Tsushima-kaikyō, strt., Japan	I2	30
Eastern Ghāts, mts., India	F5	37
Eastern Neck Island, i., Md., U.S.	B5	97
Eastern Point, c., Ma., U.S.	f13	98
Easterville, Man., Can.	C2	70
East Falkland, i., Falk. Is.	G5	56
East Falmouth, Ma., U.S.	C6	98
East Feliciana, co., La., U.S.	D4	95
East Flat Rock, N.C., U.S.	f10	110
East Fork, stm., Wy., U.S.	D3	127
East Fork Lake, res., Oh., U.S.	C1	112
East Gaffney, S.C., U.S.	A4	117
East Galesburg, Il., U.S.	C3	90
East Granby, Ct., U.S.	B5	84
East Grand Forks, Mn., U.S.	C2	100
East Grand Rapids, Mi., U.S.	F5	99
East Greenville, Pa., U.S.	F10	115
East Greenwich, R.I., U.S.	D4	116
East Gwillimbury, Ont., Can.	C5	73
East Hampton, Ct., U.S.	C5	84
East Hampton, N.H., U.S.	E4	106
East Hampton, Ct., U.S.	C5	84
Easthampton, Ma., U.S.	B2	98
East Hanover, N.J., U.S.	*B4	107
East Hartford, Ct., U.S.	B5	84
East Hartland, Ct., U.S.	A4	84
East Haven, Ct., U.S.	D4	84
East Helena, Mt., U.S.	D5	103
East Jordan, Mi., U.S.	C5	99
Eastlake, Oh., U.S.	A4	112
East Lake Tohopekaliga, l., Fl., U.S.	D5	86
Eastland, Tx., U.S.	C3	120
Eastland, co., Tx., U.S.	C3	120
East Lansing, Mi., U.S.	F6	99
East Las Vegas, Nv., U.S.	G6	105
East Liverpool, Oh., U.S.	B5	112
East London (Oos-Londen), S. Afr.	H5	44
East Longmeadow, Ma., U.S.	B2	98
East Los Angeles, Ca., U.S.	m12	82
East Lyme, Ct., U.S.	D7	84

Name	Map Ref	Page
East Lynn Lake, res., W.V., U.S.	C2	125
Eastmain, stm., Que., Can.	F17	66
Eastmain-Opinaca, Réservoir, res., Que., Can.	h11	74
Eastman, Que., Can.	D5	74
Eastman, Ga., U.S.	D3	87
East Matunuck, R.I., U.S.	F3	116
East Middlebury, Vt., U.S.	D2	122
East Millinocket, Me., U.S.	C4	96
East Moline, Il., U.S.	B3	90
East Montpelier, Vt., U.S.	C4	122
East Naples, Fl., U.S.	F5	86
East Newnan, Ga., U.S.	C2	87
East Nishnabotna, stm., Ia., U.S.	C2	92
East Norriton, Pa., U.S.	o20	115
East Olympia, Wa., U.S.	C3	124
Easton, Md., U.S.	C5	97
Easton, Pa., U.S.	E11	115
Easton Reservoir, res., Ct., U.S.	E2	84
East Orange, N.J., U.S.	B4	107
East Orleans, Ma., U.S.	C8	98
Eastover, S.C., U.S.	D6	117
East Palatka, Fl., U.S.	C5	86
East Palestine, Oh., U.S.	B5	112
East Pass, strt., Fl., U.S.	C2	86
East Pea Ridge, W.V., U.S.	C2	125
East Peoria, Il., U.S.	C4	90
East Pepperell, Ma., U.S.	A4	98
East Petersburg, Pa., U.S.	F9	115
East Pittsburgh, Pa., U.S.	k14	115
Eastpoint, Fl., U.S.	C2	86
East Point, Ga., U.S.	C2	87
East Point, c., P.E.I., Can.	C8	71
East Point, c., Ma., U.S.	B6	98
East Point, c., N.J., U.S.	E2	107
Eastport, Newf., Can.	D5	72
Eastport, Me., U.S.	D6	96
East Prairie, Mo., U.S.	E8	102
East Providence, R.I., U.S.	C4	116
East Pryor Mountain, mtn., Mt., U.S.	E8	103
East Quogue, N.Y., U.S.	n16	109
East Range, mts., Nv., U.S.	C4	105
East Ridge, Tn., U.S.	h11	119
East River, Ct., U.S.	D5	84
East Rochester, N.Y., U.S.	B3	109
East Rockingham, N.C., U.S.	C3	110
East Rutherford, N.J., U.S.	h8	107
East Saint Louis, Il., U.S.	E3	90
East Selkirk, Man., Can.	D3	70
Eastsound, Wa., U.S.	A3	124
East Spencer, N.C., U.S.	B2	110
East Stroudsburg, Pa., U.S.	D11	115
East Tawas, Mi., U.S.	D7	99
East Troy, Wi., U.S.	F5	126
East Vestal, N.Y., U.S.	C4	109
East View, W.V., U.S.	k10	125
East Walker, stm., U.S.	E2	105
East Walpole, Ma., U.S.	h11	98
East Wareham, Ma., U.S.	C6	98
East Washington, Pa., U.S.	F1	115
East Wenatchee, Wa., U.S.	B5	124
East Windsor, N.J., U.S.	C3	107
East York, Ont., Can.	D5	73
Eaton, Co., U.S.	A6	83
Eaton, In., U.S.	D7	91
Eaton, Oh., U.S.	C1	112
Eaton, co., Mi., U.S.	F6	99
Eaton Rapids, Mi., U.S.	F6	99
Eatonton, Ga., U.S.	C3	87
Eatontown, N.J., U.S.	C4	107
Eatonville, Wa., U.S.	C3	124
Eau Claire, Wi., U.S.	D2	126
Eau Claire, co., Wi., U.S.	D2	126
Eau Claire, stm., Wi., U.S.	D2	126
Eau Claire, Lac à l', l., Que., Can.	g11	74
Eauze, Fr.	I7	10
Ebano, Mex.	F10	62
Ebba Ksour, Tun.	N3	14
Ebbw Vale, Wales, U.K.	J9	7
Ebensburg, Pa., U.S.	F4	115
Eberndorf, Aus.	I14	8
Eberswalde, Ger.	C13	8
Ebetsu, Japan	p19	30a
Ebingen, Ger.	G9	8
Ebinur Hu, l., China	B3	26
Eboli, Italy	I10	14
Ebolowa, Cam.	H8	42
Ebro, stm., Spain	E12	12
Ebro, Delta del, Spain	E12	12
Eccles, W.V., U.S.	n13	125
Echo Bay, Nv., U.S.	G7	105
Echo Lake, l., Me., U.S.	D3	96
Echo Lake, l., Vt., U.S.	B5	122
Echols, co., Ga., U.S.	F4	87
Écija, Spain	H6	12
Eckernförde, Ger.	A9	8
Eckhart Mines, Md., U.S.	k13	97
Eckville, Alta., Can.	C3	68
Eclectic, Al., U.S.	C3	78
Eclipse Sound, strt., N.W. Ter., Can.	B17	66
Écommoy, Fr.	E7	10
Econfina, stm., Fl., U.S.	B3	86
Economy, Pa., U.S.	*h13	115
Écorces, Rivière aux, stm., Que., Can.	A6	74
Écorse, Mi., U.S.	p15	99
Ecru, Ms., U.S.	A4	101
Ector, co., Tx., U.S.	D1	120
Ecuador, ctry., S.A.	D3	54
Ed, Swe.	G8	6
Edcouch, Tx., U.S.	F4	120
Eddy, co., N.M., U.S.	E5	108
Eddy, co., N.D., U.S.	B7	111
Eddystone, Pa., U.S.	p20	115
Eddyville, Ia., U.S.	C5	92
Eddyville, Ky., U.S.	e9	94
Ede, Neth.	C5	8
Edéa, Cam.	H8	42
Eden, Ga., U.S.	D5	87
Eden, Md., U.S.	D6	97
Eden, N.Y., U.S.	C2	109
Eden, N.C., U.S.	A3	110
Eden, Tx., U.S.	D3	120
Edenderry, Ire.	H5	7
Eden Prairie, Mn., U.S.	n12	100
Eden Valley, Mn., U.S.	E4	100
Edgar, Ne., U.S.	D8	104
Edgar, Wi., U.S.	D4	126
Edgar, co., Il., U.S.	D6	90
Edgard, La., U.S.	D5	95
Edgartown, Ma., U.S.	D6	98
Edgecombe, co., N.C., U.S.	B5	110
Edgecumbe, Cape, c., Ak., U.S.	m21	79
Edgefield, S.C., U.S.	D4	117
Edgefield, co., S.C., U.S.	D4	117
Edgeley, N.D., U.S.	C7	111
Edgemere, Md., U.S.	B5	97
Edgemont, S.D., U.S.	D2	118
Edgemoor, De., U.S.	A3	85
Edgerton, Ks., U.S.	D8	93
Edgerton, Mn., U.S.	G2	100
Edgerton, Oh., U.S.	A1	112
Edgerton, Wi., U.S.	F4	126
Edgerton, Wy., U.S.	C6	127
Edgewater, Al., U.S.	f7	78
Edgewater, Fl., U.S.	D6	86
Edgewater, Md., U.S.	C4	97
Edgewater, N.J., U.S.	h9	107
Edgewater Park, N.J., U.S.	C3	107
Edgewood, In., U.S.	D6	91
Edgewood, Ia., U.S.	B6	92
Edgewood, Ky., U.S.	h13	94
Edgewood, Md., U.S.	B5	97
Edgewood, N.M., U.S.	B3	108
Edgewood, Oh., U.S.	A5	112
Edgewood, Pa., U.S.	k14	115
Edgewood, Wa., U.S.	f11	124
Edgeworth, Pa., U.S.	h13	115
Edina, Mn., U.S.	F5	100
Edina, Mo., U.S.	A5	102
Edinboro, Pa., U.S.	C1	115
Edinburg, Il., U.S.	D4	90
Edinburg, Tx., U.S.	F3	120
Edinburg, Va., U.S.	B4	123
Edinburgh, Scot., U.K.	F9	7
Edinburgh, In., U.S.	F6	91
Edirne, Tur.	G13	4
Edison, Ga., U.S.	E2	87
Edison, N.J., U.S.	B4	107
Edisto, stm., S.C., U.S.	E6	117
Edisto Island, i., S.C., U.S.	F7	117
Edith, Mount, mtn., Mt., U.S.	D5	103
Edjeleh, Alg.	C7	42
Edmond, Ok., U.S.	B4	113
Edmonds, Wa., U.S.	B3	124
Edmondson Heights, Md., U.S.	*g10	97
Edmonson, co., Ky., U.S.	C3	94
Edmonton, Alta., Can.	C4	68
Edmonton, Ky., U.S.	D4	94
Edmore, Mi., U.S.	E5	99
Edmunds, co., S.D., U.S.	B6	118
Edmundston, N.B., Can.	B1	71
Edna, Tx., U.S.	E4	120
Edon, Oh., U.S.	A1	112
Édouard, Lac, l., Que., Can.	B5	74
Edremit, Tur.	J11	16
Edrengijn Nuruu, mts., Mong.	C6	26
Edsbyn, Swe.	F10	6
Edson, Alta., Can.	C2	68
Edson Butte, mtn., Or., U.S.	E2	114
Eduardo Castex, Arg.	D4	56
Edward, Lake, l., Afr.	B5	44
Edwards, Ms., U.S.	C3	101
Edwards, co., Il., U.S.	E5	90
Edwards, co., Ks., U.S.	E4	93
Edwards, co., Tx., U.S.	E2	120
Edwards Air Force Base, mil., Ca., U.S.	E5	82
Edwardsburg, Mi., U.S.	G4	99
Edwards Butte, mtn., Or., U.S.	B3	114
Edwardsville, Il., U.S.	E4	90
Edwardsville, Ks., U.S.	k16	93
Edwardsville, Pa., U.S.	n17	115
Eel, stm., Ca., U.S.	B2	82
Eel, stm., In., U.S.	F3	91
Eel, stm., In., U.S.	C6	91
Effigy Mounds National Monument, Ia., U.S.	A6	92
Effingham, Il., U.S.	D5	90
Effingham, co., Ga., U.S.	D5	87
Effingham, co., Il., U.S.	D5	90
Efland, N.C., U.S.	A3	110
Egan Range, mts., Nv., U.S.	E7	105
Eganville, Ont., Can.	B7	73
Egede og Rothes Fjord, Grnld.	C25	66
Egedesminde, Grnld.	C22	66
Eger, Hung.	H20	8
Egersund, Nor.	G5	6
Eggenfelden, Ger.	G12	8
Egg Harbor City, N.J., U.S.	D3	107
Egg Island Point, c., N.J., U.S.	E2	107
Egletons, Fr.	G9	10
Eglin Air Force Base, mil., Fl., U.S.	u15	86
Egmont, Mount, mtn., N.Z.	C5	52
Egmont Bay, b., P.E.I., Can.	C5	71
Egmont Channel, strt., Fl., U.S.	p10	86
Egmont Key, i., Fl., U.S.	p10	86
Egvekinot, Russia	D29	24
Egypt, ctry., Afr.	C11	42
Egypt, Lake of, res., Il., U.S.	F5	90
Ehingen, Ger.	G9	8
Ehrenberg, Az., U.S.	D1	80
Eibar, Spain	B9	12
Eichstätt, Ger.	G11	8
Eidsvoll, Nor.	F8	6
Eielson Air Force Base, mil., Ak., U.S.	C10	79
Eifel, mts., Ger.	E6	8
Eighty Mile Beach, Austl.	C4	50
Eil, Som.	G4	46
Eilenburg, Ger.	D12	8
Eindhoven, Neth.	D5	8
Einsiedeln, Switz.	E15	10
Eirunepé, Braz.	E5	54
Eisenach, Ger.	E10	8
Eisenberg, Ger.	E11	8
Eisenerz, Aus.	H14	8
Eisenhower, Mount, mtn., N.H., U.S.	B4	106
Eisenhüttenstadt, Ger.	C14	8
Eisenstadt, Aus.	H16	8
Eisleben, Ger.	D11	8
Ejea de los Caballeros, Spain	C10	12
Ekiatapskij Chrebet, mts., Russia	D29	24
Ekimčan, Russia	G20	24
Ekwan, stm., Ont., Can.	F16	66
El Aaiún, W. Sah.	C3	42
Elaine, Ar., U.S.	C5	81
El Asnam, Alg.	A6	42
Elat, Isr.	E4	40
El Avión, Mex.	E6	62
Elâzığ, Tur.	H15	4
Elba, Al., U.S.	D3	78
Elba, Isola d', i., Italy	G5	14
El Banco, Col.	C6	58
El Barco de Valdeorras, Spain	C5	12
Elbasan, Alb.	H4	16
El Baúl, Ven.	C8	58
Elbe (Labe), stm., Eur.	B9	8
Elberfeld, In., U.S.	H3	91
Elbert, co., Co., U.S.	B6	83
Elbert, co., Ga., U.S.	B4	87
Elbert, Mount, mtn., Co., U.S.	B4	83
Elberta, Ga., U.S.	D3	87
Elberton, Ga., U.S.	B4	87
Elbeuf, Fr.	C8	10
Elbing see Elbląg, Pol.	A19	8
El Bonillo, Spain	G9	12
El Bordo, Col.	F4	58
Elbow, stm., Alta., Can.	D3	68
Elbow Lake, Mn., U.S.	E3	100
El'brus, Gora (Mount Elbrus), mtn., Russia	I6	22
El Burgo de Osma, Spain	D8	12
Elburn, Il., U.S.	B5	90
Elburz Mountains see Alborz, Reshteh-ye Kūhhā-ye, mts., Iran	J8	22
El Cajon, Ca., U.S.	F5	82
El Callao, Ven.	D12	58
El Campo, Tx., U.S.	E4	120
El Capitan, mtn., Mt., U.S.	D2	103
El Capitan Reservoir, res., Ca., U.S.	o16	82
El Carmen, Arg.	A3	56
El Carmen de Bolívar, Col.	C5	58
El Centro, Ca., U.S.	F6	82
El Cerrito, Col.	F4	58
El Cerrito, Ca., U.S.	h8	82
Elche, Spain	G11	12
Elche de la Sierra, Spain	G9	12
El Cozón, Mex.	B3	62
El Cuervo Butte, mtn., N.M., U.S.	k9	108
Elda, Spain	G11	12
El Desemboque, Mex.	C3	62
El Diviso, Col.	G3	58
El Djouf, des., Afr.	D4	42
Eldon, Ia., U.S.	D5	92
Eldon, Mo., U.S.	C5	102
Eldora, Ia., U.S.	B4	92
Eldorado, Mex.	E6	62
Eldorado, Ar., U.S.	D3	81
Eldorado, Il., U.S.	F5	90
El Dorado, Ks., U.S.	E7	93
Eldorado, Tx., U.S.	D2	120
El Dorado, co., Ca., U.S.	C3	82
Eldorado Peak, mtn., Wa., U.S.	A4	124
Eldorado Springs, Co., U.S.	B5	83
El Dorado Springs, Mo., U.S.	D3	102
Eldoret, Kenya	A7	44
Eldridge, Ia., U.S.	C7	92
Eleanor, W.V., U.S.	C3	125
Electra, Tx., U.S.	C3	120
Electra Lake, res., Co., U.S.	D3	83
Electric Peak, mtn., Co., U.S.	B3	83
Electric Peak, mtn., Mt., U.S.	E6	103
Elektrostal', Russia	F21	18
El Encanto, Col.	H6	58
Elephant Butte Reservoir, res., N.M., U.S.	D2	108
El Estor, Guat.	G3	64
Eleuthera, i., Bah.	B9	64
Eleven Mile Canyon Reservoir, res., Co., U.S.	C5	83
Eleven Point, stm., U.S.	A4	81
Elevsís, Grc.	K7	16
El Fahs, Tun.	M4	14
El Ferrol del Caudillo, Spain	B3	12
El Galpón, Arg.	B4	56
Elgin, Scot., U.K.	D9	7
Elgin, Il., U.S.	A5	90
Elgin, Ia., U.S.	B6	92
Elgin, Mn., U.S.	F6	100
Elgin, Ne., U.S.	C7	104
Elgin, N.D., U.S.	C4	111
Elgin, Ok., U.S.	C3	113
Elgin, Or., U.S.	B9	114
Elgin, S.C., U.S.	B6	117
Elgin, Tx., U.S.	D4	120
El Goléa, Alg.	B6	42
El Golfo de Santa Clara, Mex.	B2	62
Elgon, Mount, mtn., Afr.	A6	44
El Hank, clf., Afr.	D4	42
El Haouaria, Tun.	L6	14
Elida, Oh., U.S.	B1	112
Élisabethville see Lubumbashi, Zaire	D5	44
Elizabeth, Austl.	F7	50
Elizabeth, Co., U.S.	B6	83
Elizabeth, N.J., U.S.	B4	107
Elizabeth, W.V., U.S.	B3	125
Elizabeth, Cape, c., Wa., U.S.	B1	124
Elizabeth City, N.C., U.S.	A6	110
Elizabeth Islands, is., Ma., U.S.	D6	98
Elizabeth Reef, atoll, Austl.	E11	50
Elizabethton, Tn., U.S.	C11	119
Elizabethtown, Ky., U.S.	C4	94
Elizabethtown, N.C., U.S.	C4	110
Elizabethtown, Pa., U.S.	F8	115
Elizabethville, Pa., U.S.	E8	115
El-Jadida, Mor.	B4	42
El Jebel, Ven.	B3	83
Etk, Pol.	B22	8
Elk, co., Ks., U.S.	E7	93
Elk, co., Pa., U.S.	D4	115
Elk, stm., U.S.	A2	78
Elk, stm., Co., U.S.	A4	83
Elk, stm., Ks., U.S.	E7	93
Elk, stm., W.V., U.S.	C3	125
Elk, stm., Wi., U.S.	C2	126
El Kairouan, Tun.	N5	14
Elk City, Id., U.S.	D3	89
Elk City, Ok., U.S.	B2	113
Elk City Lake, res., Ks., U.S.	E7	93
Elk Creek, stm., Ok., U.S.	B2	113
Elk Creek, stm., S.D., U.S.	C3	118
El Kef, Tun.	M3	14
Elkford, B.C., Can.	D10	69
Elk Grove, Ca., U.S.	C3	82
Elk Grove Village, Il., U.S.	h9	90
Elkhart, In., U.S.	A6	91
Elkhart, Ks., U.S.	E2	93
Elkhart, Tx., U.S.	D5	120
Elkhart, co., In., U.S.	A6	91
Elkhart, stm., In., U.S.	B6	91
Elkhart Lake, Wi., U.S.	E5	126
Elkhead Mountains, mts., Co., U.S.	A3	83
Elkhorn, Man., Can.	E1	70
Elk Horn, Ia., U.S.	C2	92
Elkhorn, Ne., U.S.	g12	104
Elkhorn, Wi., U.S.	F5	126
Elkhorn, stm., Ne., U.S.	B7	104
Elkhorn City, Ky., U.S.	C7	94
Elkhorn Peaks, mts., Id., U.S.	F7	89
Elkin, N.C., U.S.	A2	110
Elkins, Ar., U.S.	A1	81
Elkins, W.V., U.S.	C5	125
Elkland, Pa., U.S.	C7	115
Elk Mills, Md., U.S.	A6	97
Elk Mound, Wi., U.S.	D2	126
Elk Mountain, Wy., U.S.	E6	127
Elk Mountain, mtn., N.M., U.S.	D1	108
Elk Mountain, mtn., Wy., U.S.	E6	127
Elk Mountains, mts., U.S.	D1	118
Elk Mountains, mts., Co., U.S.	B3	83
Elko, Nv., U.S.	C6	105
Elko, co., Nv., U.S.	B6	105
Elk Peak, mtn., Mt., U.S.	D6	103
Elk Point, Alta., Can.	C5	68
Elk Point, S.D., U.S.	E9	118
Elk Rapids, Mi., U.S.	D5	99
El Krib, Tun.	M4	14
Elkridge, Md., U.S.	B4	97
Elk River, Mn., U.S.	E5	100
Elkton, Ky., U.S.	D2	94
Elkton, Md., U.S.	A6	97
Elkton, Mi., U.S.	E7	99
Elkton, S.D., U.S.	C9	118
Elkton, Va., U.S.	B4	123
Elkview, W.V., U.S.	m13	125
Elkville, Il., U.S.	F4	90
Ellaville, Ga., U.S.	D2	87
Ellen, Mount, mtn., Ut., U.S.	E5	121
Ellendale, De., U.S.	E4	85
Ellendale, N.D., U.S.	C7	111
Ellensburg, Wa., U.S.	C5	124
Ellenton, Fl., U.S.	E4	86
Ellenville, N.Y., U.S.	D6	109
Ellerbe, N.C., U.S.	B3	110
Ellerslie, Md., U.S.	k13	97
Ellesmere Island, i., N.W. Ter., Can.	A21	128
Ellettsville, In., U.S.	F4	91
Ellice Islands see Tuvalu, ctry., Oc.	G24	2
Ellicott City, Md., U.S.	B4	97
Ellijay, Ga., U.S.	B2	87
Ellington, Ct., U.S.	B6	84
Ellington, Mo., U.S.	D7	102
Ellinwood, Ks., U.S.	D5	93
Elliot Lake, Ont., Can.	A2	73
Elliott, Ms., U.S.	B4	101
Elliott, co., Ky., U.S.	B6	94
Elliott Bay, b., Wa., U.S.	e11	124
Elliott Key, i., Fl., U.S.	G6	86
Ellis, co., Ks., U.S.	D4	93
Ellis, co., Ok., U.S.	A2	113
Ellis, co., Tx., U.S.	C4	120
Ellis, stm., N.H., U.S.	B4	106
Elliston, Va., U.S.	C2	123
Ellisville, Ms., U.S.	D4	101
Ellisville, Mo., U.S.	f12	102
Ellon, Scot., U.K.	D10	7
Elloree, S.C., U.S.	D6	117
Ellport, Pa., U.S.	E1	115
Ellsworth, Ks., U.S.	D5	93
Ellsworth, Me., U.S.	D4	96
Ellsworth, Pa., U.S.	F1	115
Ellsworth, Wi., U.S.	D1	126
Ellsworth, co., Ks., U.S.	D5	93
Ellsworth Air Force Base, mil., S.D., U.S.	C2	118
Ellwangen, Ger.	G10	8
Ellwood City, Pa., U.S.	E1	115
Elm, stm., N.D., U.S.	B8	111
Elma, Wa., U.S.	C2	124
El Mahdia, Tun.	N6	14
Elm City, N.C., U.S.	B5	110
Elm Creek, Ne., U.S.	D6	104
El Manteco, Ven.	D11	58
El Médano, Mex.	E4	62
Elmendorf Air Force Base, mil., Ak., U.S.	C10	79
Elm Grove, Wi., U.S.	m11	126
Elmhurst, Il., U.S.	B6	90
Elmhurst, Pa., U.S.	D10	115
Elmira, N.Y., U.S.	C4	109
El Mirage, Az., U.S.	k8	80
Elmira Heights, N.Y., U.S.	C4	109
Elmont, N.Y., U.S.	k13	109
Elmora, Pa., U.S.	E4	115
Elmore, Mn., U.S.	G4	100
Elmore, Oh., U.S.	A2	112
Elmore, co., Al., U.S.	C3	78
Elmore, co., Id., U.S.	F3	89
El Morro National Monument, N.M., U.S.	B1	108
Elmsdale, N.S., Can.	E6	71
Elmshorn, Ger.	B9	8
Elm Springs, Ar., U.S.	A1	81
Elmvale, Ont., Can.	C5	73
Elmwood, Il., U.S.	C3	90
Elmwood, Wi., U.S.	D1	126
Elmwood Park, Il., U.S.	k9	90
Elmwood Park, N.J., U.S.	h8	107
Elmwood Place, Oh., U.S.	o13	112
Elne, Fr.	J9	10
Elnora, In., U.S.	G3	91
Eloise, Fl., U.S.	E5	86
Elon College, N.C., U.S.	A3	110
Elora, Ont., Can.	D4	73
Elorza, Ven.	D8	58
El Oued, Alg.	B7	42
Eloy, Az., U.S.	E4	80
El Palmar, Ven.	D12	58
El Paso, Il., U.S.	C4	90
El Paso, Tx., U.S.	o11	120
El Paso, co., Co., U.S.	C6	83
El Paso, co., Tx., U.S.	o11	120
El Pilar, Ven.	B11	58
El Pital, Cerro, mtn., N.A.	G3	64
El Portal, Fl., U.S.	s13	86
El Prado, N.M., U.S.	A4	108
El Progreso, Hond.	G4	64
El Puente del Arzobispo, Spain	F6	12
El Puerto de Santa María, Spain	I5	12
El Quelite, Mex.	F6	62
El Reno, Ok., U.S.	B4	113
Elrose, Sask., Can.	F1	75
Elroy, Wi., U.S.	E3	126
Elsa, Yukon, Can.	D5	66
Elsa, Tx., U.S.	F3	120
Elsah, Il., U.S.	E3	90
El Salto, Mex.	F7	62
El Salvador, ctry., N.A.	H3	64
El Sauce, Nic.	H4	64
El Sauzal, Mex.	B1	62
Elsberry, Mo., U.S.	B7	102
Elsie, Mi., U.S.	E6	99
Elsinore, Ut., U.S.	E3	121
Elsmere, De., U.S.	B3	85
Elsmere, Ky., U.S.	B5	94
El Socorro, Ven.	C10	58
El Sombrero, Ven.	C9	58
Elspe, Ger.	D8	8
Elsterwerda, Ger.	D13	8
El Tigre, Col.	F8	58
El Tigre, Ven.	C10	58
El Tocuyo, Ven.	C8	58
Elton, La., U.S.	D3	95
El Toro Marine Corps Air Station, mil., Ca., U.S.	n13	82
El Trapiche, Col.	F4	58
El Triunfo, Mex.	F4	62
El Turbio, Arg.	G2	56
Elūru, India	D6	37
El Vado Reservoir, res., N.M., U.S.	A3	108
Elvas, Port.	G4	12
Elverum, Nor.	F8	6
El Vigía, Ven.	C7	58
Elvins, Mo., U.S.	D7	102
Elwell, Lake, res., Mt., U.S.	B5	103
Elwha, stm., Wa., U.S.	A2	124
Elwood, In., U.S.	D6	91
Elwood, Ks., U.S.	C9	93
Elwood, Ne., U.S.	D6	104
Ely, Eng., U.K.	I13	7
Ely, Mn., U.S.	C7	100
Ely, Nv., U.S.	D7	105
Elyria, Oh., U.S.	A3	112
Elysburg, Pa., U.S.	E8	115
Emanuel, co., Ga., U.S.	D4	87
Embarcación, Arg.	A4	56
Embarras, stm., Il., U.S.	E6	90
Embarrass, stm., Wi., U.S.	D5	126
Embro, Ont., Can.	D4	73
Embrun, Fr.	H13	10
Emden, Ger.	B7	8
Emerald, Austl.	D9	50
Emerson, Man., Can.	E3	70
Emerson, Ga., U.S.	B2	87
Emerson, Ne., U.S.	B9	104
Emerson, N.J., U.S.	h8	107
Emery, co., Ut., U.S.	E5	121
Emily, Mn., U.S.	D5	100
Emily, Lake, l., Mn., U.S.	E3	100
Eminence, Ky., U.S.	B4	94
Emmaus, Pa., U.S.	E11	115
Emmen, Neth.	C6	8
Emmendingen, Ger.	G7	8
Emmet, co., Ia., U.S.	A3	92
Emmet, co., Mi., U.S.	C6	99
Emmetsburg, Ia., U.S.	A3	92
Emmett, Id., U.S.	F2	89
Emmiganūru, India	E4	37
Emmitsburg, Md., U.S.	A3	97
Emmonak, Ak., U.S.	C7	79
Emmons, co., N.D., U.S.	C5	111
Emory Peak, mtn., Tx., U.S.	E1	120
Empalme, Mex.	D4	62
Empangeni, S. Afr.	G6	44
Empedrado, Arg.	B5	56
Empire, La., U.S.	E6	95
Empire, Nv., U.S.	C2	105
Empoli, Italy	F5	14
Emporia, Ks., U.S.	D7	93
Emporia, Va., U.S.	D5	123
Emporium, Pa., U.S.	D5	115
Empty Quarter see Ar-Rab' al-Khālī, des., Asia	D5	46
Emsdetten, Ger.	C7	8
Emsworth, Pa., U.S.	h13	115
Encampment, Wy., U.S.	E6	127
Encarnación, Para.	B5	56
Encinitas, Ca., U.S.	F5	82
Encontrados, Ven.	C6	58
Ende, Indon.	G7	32
Enderby, B.C., Can.	D8	69
Enderby Land, reg., Ant.	C18	47
Enderlin, N.D., U.S.	C8	111
Enders Reservoir, res., Ne., U.S.	D4	104
Endicott, N.Y., U.S.	C4	109
Endicott Mountains, mts., Ak., U.S.	B9	79
Endless Lake, l., Me., U.S.	C4	96
Endwell, N.Y., U.S.	C4	109
Enfida, Tun.	M5	14
Enfield (Thompsonville), Ct., U.S.	B5	84
Enfield, N.H., U.S.	C2	106
Enfield, N.C., U.S.	A5	110
Engel's, Russia	G7	22
Enggano, Pulau, i., Indon.	G3	32

Name	Map Ref	Page
England, Ar., U.S.	C4	81
England, ter., U.K.	I11	7
England Air Force Base, mil., La., U.S.	C3	95
Englee, Newf., Can.	C3	72
Ingleside, Va., U.S.	g12	123
Inglewood, Co., U.S.	B6	83
Inglewood, Fl., U.S.	F4	86
Inglewood, N.J., U.S.	B5	107
Inglewood, Oh., U.S.	C1	112
Inglewood, Tn., U.S.	D9	119
Inglewood Cliffs, N.J., U.S.	h9	107
English, In., U.S.	H5	91
English Bāzār, India	H13	38
English Channel (La Manche), strt., Eur.	B5	10
Inguera, Spain	G11	12
Enid, Ok., U.S.	A4	113
Enid Lake, res., Ms., U.S.	A4	101
Enigma, Ga., U.S.	E3	87
Enka, N.C., U.S.	f10	110
Enkhuizen, Neth.	C5	8
Enköping, Swe.	G11	6
Enmelen, Russia	D30	24
Enna, Italy	L9	14
Ennadai Lake, l., N.W. Ter., Can.	D12	66
Ennedi, plat., Chad	E10	42
Ennis, Ire.	I4	7
Ennis, Mt., U.S.	E5	103
Ennis, Tx., U.S.	C4	120
Enniskillen, N. Ire., U.K.	G5	7
Enoch, Ut., U.S.	F2	121
Enola, Pa., U.S.	F8	115
Enon, Oh., U.S.	*C2	112
Enoree, S.C., U.S.	B4	117
Enoree, stm., S.C., U.S.	B3	117
Enosburg Falls, Vt., U.S.	B3	122
Enriquillo, Dom. Rep.	F12	64
Enschede, Neth.	C6	8
Ensenada, Mex.	B1	62
Enshi, China	E8	26
Enshū-nada, Japan	H10	30
Ensley, Fl., U.S.	u14	86
Entebbe, Ug.	A6	44
Enterprise, Al., U.S.	D4	78
Enterprise, Ks., U.S.	D6	93
Enterprise, Or., U.S.	B9	114
Enterprise, Ut., U.S.	F2	121
Enterprise, W.V., U.S.	B4	125
Entiat, stm., Wa., U.S.	B5	124
Entiat, Lake, l., Wa., U.S.	B5	124
Entiat Mountains, mts., Wa., U.S.	B5	124
Entraygues, Fr.	H9	10
Entre-Rios, Moz.	D7	44
Enugu, Nig.	G7	42
Enumclaw, Wa., U.S.	B4	124
Envigado, Col.	D5	58
Eola Hills, hills, Or., U.S.	h11	114
Epernay, Fr.	C10	10
Ephraim, Ut., U.S.	D4	121
Ephrata, Pa., U.S.	F9	115
Ephrata, Wa., U.S.	B6	124
Epila, Spain	D10	12
Epinal, Fr.	D13	10
Epping, N.H., U.S.	D4	106
Epworth, Ia., U.S.	B7	92
Equatorial Guinea, ctry., Afr.	H7	42
Eraclea, Italy	D7	14
Erath, La., U.S.	E3	95
Erath, co., Tx., U.S.	C3	120
Erdek, Tur.	I11	16
Erdemli, Tur.	A4	40
Erebus, Mount, mtn., Ant.	B29	47
Erechim, Braz.	B6	56
Erfurt, Ger.	E11	8
Erichsen Lake, l., N.W. Ter., Can.	B16	66
Erick, Ok., U.S.	B2	113
Erickson, Man., Can.	D2	70
Erie, Co., U.S.	A5	83
Erie, Il., U.S.	B3	90
Erie, Ks., U.S.	E8	93
Erie, Mi., U.S.	G7	99
Erie, Pa., U.S.	B1	115
Erie, co., N.Y., U.S.	C2	109
Erie, co., Oh., U.S.	A3	112
Erie, co., Pa., U.S.	C1	115
Erie, Lake, l., N.A.	C10	76
Erie Canal, N.Y., U.S.	B5	109
Erimo-misaki, c., Japan	r21	30a
Erin, Ont., Can.	D4	73
Erin, Tn., U.S.	A4	119
Eritrea, hist. reg., Eth.	E2	46
Erlangen, Ger.	F11	8
Erlanger, Ky., U.S.	A5	94
Erlian, China	C9	26
Erling, Lake, res., Ar., U.S.	D2	81
Ermelo, S. Afr.	G5	44
Ermenak, Tur.	A3	40
Ernakulam, India	H4	37
Erne, Lower Lough, l., N. Ire., U.K.	G5	7
Ernée, Fr.	D6	10
Erode, India	G4	37
Errigal, mtn., Ire.	F4	7
Ertai, China	B5	26
Erwin, N.C., U.S.	B4	110
Erwin, Tn., U.S.	C11	119
Erzgebirge (Krušné hory), mts., Eur.	E12	8
Erzincan, Tur.	H15	4
Erzurum, Tur.	H16	4
Esashi, Japan	A13	30
Esbjerg, Den.	I7	6
Escalante, Ut., U.S.	F4	121
Escalante, stm., Ut., U.S.	F4	121
Escalón, Mex.	D7	62
Escalon, Ca., U.S.	D3	82
Escambia, co., Al., U.S.	D2	78
Escambia, co., Fl., U.S.	u14	86
Escambia, stm., Fl., U.S.	u14	86
Escanaba, Mi., U.S.	C3	99
Escanaba, stm., Mi., U.S.	B3	99
Escarpada Point, c., Phil.	B7	32
Escatawpa, Ms., U.S.	E5	101
Escatawpa, stm., U.S.	D5	101
Esch-sur-Alzette, Lux.	F5	8
Eschwege, Ger.	D10	8
Escondido, Ca., U.S.	F5	82
Escoumins, Rivière des, stm., Que., Can.	A8	74
Escuinapa [de Hidalgo], Mex.	F7	62
Escuintla, Guat.	G2	64
Escuintla, Mex.	J13	62
Escuminac, Point, c., N.B., Can.	B5	71
Esfahān, Iran	B5	46
Eshkāshem, Afg.	B4	38
Eskilstuna, Swe.	G11	6
Eskimo Lakes, l., N.W. Ter., Can.	C6	66
Eskimo Point, N.W. Ter., Can.	D14	66
Eskişehir, Tur.	H14	4
Eşme, Tur.	K12	16
Esmeralda, co., Nv., U.S.	F4	105
Esmeraldas, Ec.	G3	58
Esmond, R.I., U.S.	B4	116
Espalion, Fr.	H9	10
Espanola, Ont., Can.	A3	73
Espanola, N.M., U.S.	B3	108
Esparto, Ca., U.S.	C2	82
Espelkamp, Ger.	C8	8
Esperance, Austl.	F4	50
Espinal, Col.	E5	58
Espinhaço, Serra do, mts., Braz.	C7	57
Espinho, Port.	D3	12
Espíritu Santo, Bahía del, b., Mex.	H16	62
Espíritu Santo, Isla del, i., Mex.	E4	62
Espoo (Esbo), Fin.	F15	6
Espy, Pa., U.S.	D9	115
Esquel, Arg.	E2	56
Esquimalt, B.C., Can.	E6	69
Esquina, Arg.	B5	56
Essaouira, Mor.	B4	42
Essen, Ger.	D7	8
Essendon, Mount, mtn., Austl.	D4	50
Essequibo, stm., Guy.	E13	58
Es Sers, Tun.	M4	14
Essex, Ont., Can.	E2	73
Essex, Ct., U.S.	D6	84
Essex, Ia., U.S.	D2	92
Essex, Md., U.S.	B5	97
Essex, Ma., U.S.	A6	98
Essex, Vt., U.S.	B2	122
Essex, co., Ma., U.S.	A5	98
Essex, co., N.J., U.S.	B4	107
Essex, co., N.Y., U.S.	B7	109
Essex, co., Vt., U.S.	B5	122
Essex, co., Va., U.S.	C6	123
Essex Junction, Vt., U.S.	C2	122
Essexville, Mi., U.S.	E7	99
Esslingen, Ger.	G9	8
Es Smala es Souassi, Tun.	N5	14
Est, Cap, c., Madag.	E10	44
Est, Pointe de l', c., Que., Can.	G20	71
Estacada, Or., U.S.	B4	114
Estaca de Bares, Punta de la, c., Spain	B4	12
Estacado, Llano, pl., U.S.	C1	120
Estados, Isla de los, i., Arg.	G4	56
Estancia, N.M., U.S.	C3	108
Estcourt, S. Afr.	G5	44
Este, Italy	D6	14
Estelí, Nic.	H4	64
Estella, Spain	C9	12
Estelline, S.D., U.S.	C9	118
Estepona, Spain	I6	12
Esternay, Fr.	D10	10
Estero Bay, b., Ca., U.S.	E3	82
Estero Bay, b., Fl., U.S.	F5	86
Estero Island, i., Fl., U.S.	F5	86
Estes Park, Co., U.S.	A5	83
Estherville, Ia., U.S.	A3	92
Estherwood, La., U.S.	D3	95
Estill, S.C., U.S.	F5	117
Estill, co., Ky., U.S.	C6	94
Estill Springs, Tn., U.S.	B5	119
Estonia, ctry., Eur.	C9	18
Estremoz, Port.	G4	12
Esztergom, Hung.	H18	8
Etah, Grnld.	B20	128
Etah, India	G8	38
Étampes, Fr.	D9	10
Étang-du-Nord, Que., Can.	B8	71
Étaples, Fr.	B8	10
Etāwah, India	G8	38
Ethel, W.V., U.S.	n12	125
Ethiopia, ctry., Afr.	G2	46
Etna, Pa., U.S.	k14	115
Etna, Monte, vol., Italy	L9	14
Etobicoke, Ont., Can.	D5	73
Etolin Island, i., Ak., U.S.	m23	79
Etolin Strait, strt., Ak., U.S.	C6	79
Etosha pan, pl., Nmb.	E3	44
Etowah, Tn., U.S.	D9	119
Etowah, co., Al., U.S.	A3	78
Etowah, stm., Ga., U.S.	B2	87
Ettelbruck, Lux.	F6	8
Ettlingen, Ger.	G8	8
Ettrick, Va., U.S.	C5	123
Eu, Fr.	B8	10
Eucla, Austl.	F5	50
Euclid, Oh., U.S.	A4	112
Eudora, Ar., U.S.	D4	81
Eudora, Ks., U.S.	D8	93
Eufaula, Al., U.S.	D4	78
Eufaula, Ok., U.S.	B6	113
Eufaula Lake, res., Ok., U.S.	B6	113
Eugene, Or., U.S.	C3	114
Eugenia, Punta, c., Mex.	D2	62
Eunice, La., U.S.	D3	95
Eunice, N.M., U.S.	E6	108
Eupora, Ms., U.S.	B4	101
Eureka, Ca., U.S.	B1	82
Eureka, Il., U.S.	C4	90
Eureka, Ks., U.S.	E7	93
Eureka, Mo., U.S.	f12	102
Eureka, Mt., U.S.	B1	103
Eureka, Nv., U.S.	D6	105
Eureka, S.C., U.S.	B5	117
Eureka, S.D., U.S.	B6	118
Eureka, co., Nv., U.S.	D5	105
Eureka Springs, Ar., U.S.	A2	81
Europa, Île, i., Reu.	F8	44
Europa Point, c., Gib.	I6	12
Europe	E11	4
Euskirchen, Ger.	E6	8
Eustis, Fl., U.S.	D5	86
Eutaw, Al., U.S.	C2	78
Eutin, Ger.	A10	8
Eutsuk Lake, l., B.C., Can.	C4	69
Evangeline, co., La., U.S.	D3	95
Evans, Co., U.S.	A6	83
Evans, Ga., U.S.	C4	87
Evans, co., Ga., U.S.	D5	87
Evans, W.V., U.S.	C3	125
Evans, Lac, l., Que., Can.	F17	66
Evans, Mount, mtn., Co., U.S.	B5	83
Evans City, Pa., U.S.	E1	115
Evansdale, Ia., U.S.	B5	92
Evans Strait, strt., N.W. Ter., Can.	D16	66
Evanston, Il., U.S.	A6	90
Evanston, Wy., U.S.	E2	127
Evansville, Il., U.S.	E4	90
Evansville, In., U.S.	I2	91
Evansville, Wi., U.S.	F4	126
Evart, Mi., U.S.	E5	99
Evarts, Ky., U.S.	D6	94
Eveleth, Mn., U.S.	C6	100
Everard, Lake, l., Austl.	F7	50
Everest, Mount, mtn., Asia	G12	38
Everett, Ma., U.S.	g11	98
Everett, Pa., U.S.	F5	115
Everett, Wa., U.S.	B3	124
Everett Lake, res., N.H., U.S.	D3	106
Everglades National Park, Fl., U.S.	G5	86
Evergreen, Al., U.S.	D3	78
Evergreen, Co., U.S.	B5	83
Evergreen Park, Il., U.S.	k9	90
Everly, Ia., U.S.	A2	92
Everson, Wa., U.S.	A3	124
Evesham, Eng., U.K.	I11	7
Evje, Nor.	G6	6
Évora, Port.	G4	12
Évreux, Fr.	C8	10
Évros (Marica) (Meriç), stm., Eur.	H10	16
E.V. Spence Reservoir, res., Tx., U.S.	D2	120
Évvoia, i., Grc.	K7	16
Ewa, Hi., U.S.	B3	88
Ewa Beach, Hi., U.S.	B3	88
Ewa Beach, Hi., U.S.	g9	88
Ewing Township, N.J., U.S.	C3	107
Ewo, Congo	B2	44
Excelsior Mountain, mtn., Ca., U.S.	C4	82
Excelsior Mountains, mts., Nv., U.S.	E3	105
Excelsior Springs, Mo., U.S.	B3	102
Executive Committee Range, mts., Ant.	B36	47
Exeter, Ont., Can.	D3	73
Exeter, Eng., U.K.	K9	7
Exeter, Ca., U.S.	D4	82
Exeter, Ne., U.S.	D8	104
Exeter, N.H., U.S.	E5	106
Exeter, Pa., U.S.	D10	115
Exeter, stm., N.H., U.S.	E5	106
Exeter Sound, strt., N.W. Ter., Can.	C20	66
Exira, Ia., U.S.	C3	92
Exmore, Va., U.S.	C7	123
Exmouth, Eng., U.K.	K9	7
Exmouth Gulf, b., Austl.	D2	50
Experiment, Ga., U.S.	C2	87
Exploits, stm., Newf., Can.	D3	72
Exploits, Bay of, b., Newf., Can.	D4	72
Export, Pa., U.S.	F2	115
Exuma Sound, strt., Bah.	B9	64
Eyasi, Lake, l., Tan.	B6	44
Eylar Mountain, mtn., Ca., U.S.	D12	103
Eymoutiers, Fr.	G8	10
Eyota, Mn., U.S.	G6	100
Eyre (North), Lake, l., Austl.	E7	50
Eyre (South), Lake, l., Austl.	E7	50
Eyre Peninsula, pen., Austl.	F7	50

F

Name	Map Ref	Page
Fabens, Tx., U.S.	o11	120
Fabius, stm., Mo., U.S.	A6	102
Fabriano, Italy	F7	14
Facatativá, Col.	E5	58
Factoryville, Pa., U.S.	C10	115
Fada, Chad	E10	42
Fada Ngourma, Burkina	F6	42
Faddejevskij, Ostrov, i., Russia	B22	24
Faenza, Italy	E6	14
Faeroe Islands, dep., Eur.	F7	6
Fagernes, Nor.	F10	6
Fagersta, Swe.	F10	6
Fairacres, N.M., U.S.	E3	108
Fairbank, Ia., U.S.	B5	92
Fairbanks, Ak., U.S.	C10	79
Fair Bluff, N.C., U.S.	C3	110
Fairborn, Oh., U.S.	C1	112
Fairburn, Ga., U.S.	C2	87
Fairbury, Il., U.S.	C5	90
Fairbury, Ne., U.S.	D8	104
Fairchance, Pa., U.S.	G2	115
Fairchild Air Force Base, mil., Wa., U.S.	g13	124
Fairdale, Ky., U.S.	B4	94
Fairfax, Ca., U.S.	C2	82
Fairfax, De., U.S.	A3	85
Fairfax, Mn., U.S.	F4	100
Fairfax, Mo., U.S.	A2	102
Fairfax, S.C., U.S.	F5	117
Fairfax, Va., U.S.	B5	123
Fairfax, co., Va., U.S.	B5	123
Fairfield, Al., U.S.	B3	78
Fairfield, Ca., U.S.	C2	82
Fairfield, Ct., U.S.	E2	84
Fairfield, Il., U.S.	E5	90
Fairfield, Ia., U.S.	C6	92
Fairfield, Me., U.S.	D3	96
Fairfield, Mt., U.S.	C5	103
Fairfield, Oh., U.S.	n12	112
Fairfield, Tx., U.S.	D4	120
Fairfield, co., Ct., U.S.	D2	84
Fairfield, co., Oh., U.S.	C3	112
Fairfield, co., S.C., U.S.	C5	117
Fairfield Bay, Ar., U.S.	B3	81
Fairfield Pond, l., Vt., U.S.	B3	122
Fair Grove, Mo., U.S.	D4	102
Fair Grove, N.C., U.S.	B2	110
Fairhaven, Ma., U.S.	C6	98
Fair Haven, Mi., U.S.	F8	99
Fair Haven, N.J., U.S.	C4	107
Fair Haven, Vt., U.S.	D2	122
Fairhope, Al., U.S.	E2	78
Fair Isle, i., Scot., U.K.	B11	7
Fairland, In., U.S.	E6	91
Fairland, Ok., U.S.	A7	113
Fair Lawn, N.J., U.S.	h8	107
Fairlawn, Va., U.S.	C2	123
Fairlea, W.V., U.S.	D4	125
Fairmont, Il., U.S.	C6	90
Fairmont, Mn., U.S.	G4	100
Fairmont, Ne., U.S.	D8	104
Fairmont, N.C., U.S.	C3	110
Fairmont, W.V., U.S.	B4	125
Fairmount, Ga., U.S.	B2	87
Fairmount, In., U.S.	D6	91
Fairmount Heights, Md., U.S.	f9	97
Fair Oaks, Ga., U.S.	h7	87
Fairoaks, Pa., U.S.	h13	115
Fair Plain, Mi., U.S.	F4	99
Fairport, N.Y., U.S.	B3	109
Fairport Harbor, Oh., U.S.	A4	112
Fairvale, N.B., Can.	D4	71
Fairview, Alta., Can.	A1	68
Fairview, Mt., U.S.	C12	103
Fairview, N.J., U.S.	h8	107
Fairview, Ok., U.S.	A3	113
Fairview, Pa., U.S.	B1	115
Fairview, Tn., U.S.	B4	119
Fairview, Ut., U.S.	D4	121
Fairview Heights, Il., U.S.	E3	90
Fairview Park, In., U.S.	E3	91
Fairview Park, Oh., U.S.	g9	112
Fairview Peak, mtn., Nv., U.S.	D3	105
Fairview Peak, mtn., Or., U.S.	D4	114
Fairway, Ks., U.S.	k16	93
Fairweather, Mount, mtn., N.A.	E5	66
Faisalabad, Pak.	E5	38
Faison, N.C., U.S.	B4	110
Faizābād, India	G10	38
Fakenham, Eng., U.K.	I13	7
Fakfak, Indon.	F9	32
Falaise, Fr.	D6	10
Falam, Burma	C2	34
Falconer, N.Y., U.S.	C1	109
Falcon Heights, Mn., U.S.	n12	100
Falcon Heights, Or., U.S.	E5	114
Falcon Reservoir, res., N.A.	D10	62
Falfurrias, Tx., U.S.	F3	120
Falher, Alta., Can.	B2	68
Falkenberg, Swe.	H9	6
Falkensee, Ger.	C13	8
Falkenstein, Ger.	E12	8
Falkland Islands (Islas Malvinas), dep., S.A.	G5	56
Falköping, Swe.	G9	6
Falkville, Al., U.S.	A3	78
Fall, stm., Ks., U.S.	E7	93
Fall Branch, Tn., U.S.	C11	119
Fallbrook, Ca., U.S.	F5	82
Fall City, Wa., U.S.	B4	124
Fall Creek, Wi., U.S.	D2	126
Falling Creek, stm., Va., U.S.	n17	123
Falling Rock Creek, stm., W.V., U.S.	m13	125
Fall Mountain Lake, Ct., U.S.	C4	84
Fallon, Nv., U.S.	D3	105
Fallon, co., Mt., U.S.	D12	103
Fallon Indian Reservation, Nv., U.S.	D3	105
Fallon Naval Air Station, mil., Nv., U.S.	D3	105
Fall River, Ma., U.S.	C5	98
Fall River, Wi., U.S.	E4	126
Fall River, co., S.D., U.S.	D2	118
Fall River Lake, res., Ks., U.S.	E7	93
Falls, co., Tx., U.S.	D4	120
Falls Church, Va., U.S.	g12	123
Falls City, Ne., U.S.	D10	104
Falls City, Or., U.S.	C3	114
Falls Creek, Pa., U.S.	D4	115
Fallston, Md., U.S.	A5	97
Falmouth, N.S., Can.	E5	71
Falmouth, Eng., U.K.	K7	7
Falmouth, Ky., U.S.	B5	94
Falmouth, Me., U.S.	E2	96
Falmouth, Ma., U.S.	C6	98
Falmouth, Va., U.S.	B5	123
False Cape, c., Fl., U.S.	D6	86
False Cape, c., Va., U.S.	D7	123
False Divi Point, c., India	E6	37
Falset, Spain	D12	12
Falun, Swe.	F10	6
Famagusta see Gazimağusa, N. Cyp.	B3	40
Famatina, Nevado de, mts., Arg.	B3	56
Fancy Farm, Ky., U.S.	f9	94
Fangcheng, China	B1	28
Fannin, co., Ga., U.S.	B2	87
Fannin, co., Tx., U.S.	C4	120
Fanny, Mount, mtn., Or., U.S.	B9	114
Fano, Italy	F8	14
Faradje, Zaire	H11	42
Faradofay, Madag.	G9	44
Farafangana, Madag.	F9	44
Farāh, Afg.	C1	36
Faranah, Gui.	F3	42
Farasān, Jazā'ir, is., Sau. Ar.	E3	46
Farewell, Cape, c., N.Z.	D4	52
Fargo, N.D., U.S.	C9	111
Faribault, Mn., U.S.	F5	100
Faribault, co., Mn., U.S.	G4	100
Farīdpur, Bngl.	I13	38
Färjestaden, Swe.	H11	6
Farley, Ia., U.S.	B6	92
Farmer City, Il., U.S.	C5	90
Farmers Branch, Tx., U.S.	n10	120
Farmersburg, In., U.S.	F3	91
Farmersville, La., U.S.	B3	95
Farmingdale, Me., U.S.	D3	96
Farmington, Ar., U.S.	A1	81
Farmington, Ct., U.S.	C4	84
Farmington, Il., U.S.	C3	90
Farmington, Ia., U.S.	D6	92
Farmington, Me., U.S.	D2	96
Farmington, Mn., U.S.	F5	100
Farmington, Mo., U.S.	D7	102
Farmington, N.H., U.S.	D4	106
Farmington, N.M., U.S.	A1	108
Farmington, Ut., U.S.	C4	121
Farmington, stm., Ct., U.S.	B4	84
Farmington Hills, Mi., U.S.	o15	99
Farmland, In., U.S.	D7	91
Farnham, Que., Can.	D5	74
Faro, Braz.	D7	54
Faro, Port.	H4	12
Faro, Punta del, c., Italy	K10	14
Fårösund, Swe.	H12	6
Farquhar Group, is., Sey.	D10	44
Farrell, Pa., U.S.	D1	115
Farrukhābād, India	G8	38
Fartak, Ra's, c., Yemen	E5	46
Farvel, Kap, c., Grnld.	E24	66
Farwell, Mi., U.S.	E5	99
Farwell, Tx., U.S.	B1	120
Fasano, Italy	I12	14
Fatehpur, India	H9	38
Fatehpur, India	G6	38
Faulk, co., S.D., U.S.	B6	118
Faulkland Heights, De., U.S.	i7	85
Faulkner, co., Ar., U.S.	B3	81
Faulkton, S.D., U.S.	B6	118
Fauquier, co., Va., U.S.	B5	123
Fauske, Nor.	C10	6
Favara, Italy	L8	14
Faverges, Fr.	G13	10
Fawnie Nose, mtn., B.C., Can.	C5	69
Fayette, Al., U.S.	B2	78
Fayette, Ia., U.S.	B6	92
Fayette, Mo., U.S.	B5	102
Fayette, Oh., U.S.	A1	112
Fayette, co., Al., U.S.	B2	78
Fayette, co., Ga., U.S.	C2	87
Fayette, co., Il., U.S.	D5	90
Fayette, co., In., U.S.	E7	91
Fayette, co., Ia., U.S.	B6	92
Fayette, co., Ky., U.S.	B5	94
Fayette, co., Oh., U.S.	C2	112
Fayette, co., Pa., U.S.	G2	115
Fayette, co., Tn., U.S.	B2	119
Fayette, co., Tx., U.S.	E4	120
Fayette, co., W.V., U.S.	C3	125
Fayetteville, Ar., U.S.	A1	81
Fayetteville, Ga., U.S.	C2	87
Fayetteville, N.C., U.S.	B4	110
Fayetteville, Pa., U.S.	G6	115
Fayetteville, Tn., U.S.	B5	119
Fayetteville, W.V., U.S.	C3	125
Fāzilka, India	E6	38
Fazzān (Fezzan), reg., Libya	C8	42
Fdérik, Maur.	D3	42
Fear, Cape, c., N.C., U.S.	D5	110
Feather, stm., Ca., U.S.	C3	82
Fécamp, Fr.	C7	10
Federalsburg, Md., U.S.	C6	97
Feeding Hills, Ma., U.S.	B2	98
Fehmarn Belt, strt., Eur.	A11	8
Feijó, Braz.	E4	54
Feira de Santana, Braz.	B9	57
Felanitx, Spain	F15	12
Feldbach, Aus.	I15	4
Feldkirch, Aus.	H9	8
Feldkirchen in Kärnten, Aus.	I14	4
Félix Gómez, Mex.	C4	62
Felletin, Fr.	G9	10
Fellsmere, Fl., U.S.	E6	86
Felton, Ca., U.S.	D2	82
Felton, De., U.S.	D3	85
Feltre, Italy	C6	14
Femundsenden, Nor.	F8	6
Fence, stm., Mi., U.S.	B2	99
Fence Lake, l., Wi., U.S.	C4	126
Fenelon Falls, Ont., Can.	C6	73
Fengcheng, China	G4	28
Fengzhen, China	C9	26
Fenimore Pass, strt., Ak., U.S.	E4	79
Fennimore, Wi., U.S.	F3	126
Fennville, Mi., U.S.	F4	99
Fenton, Mi., U.S.	F7	99
Fentress, co., Tn., U.S.	C9	119
Fenwick Island, i., S.C., U.S.	k11	117
Fenyang, China	D9	26
Feodosija, Ukr.	H5	22
Fer, Point au, c., La., U.S.	E4	95
Ferdinand, In., U.S.	H4	91
Fergana, Uzb.	I12	22
Fergus, Ont., Can.	D4	73
Fergus, co., Mt., U.S.	C7	103
Fergus Falls, Mn., U.S.	D2	100
Ferguson, Ky., U.S.	C5	94
Ferguson, Mo., U.S.	C7	102
Ferme-Neuve, Que., Can.	C2	74
Fermo, Italy	F8	14
Fermont, Que., Can.	h13	74
Fermoy, Ire.	I4	7
Fernandina Beach, Fl., U.S.	B5	86
Fernando de Noronha, Ilha, i., Braz.	D12	54
Fernandópolis, Braz.	F3	57
Fernando Póo see Bioko, i., Eq. Gui.	H7	42
Fernán-Núñez, Spain	H7	12
Fern Creek, Ky., U.S.	g11	94
Ferndale, Ca., U.S.	B1	82
Ferndale, Md., U.S.	B4	97
Ferndale, Mi., U.S.	p15	99
Ferndale, Pa., U.S.	F4	115
Ferndale, Wa., U.S.	A3	124
Fernie, B.C., Can.	E10	69
Fernley, Nv., U.S.	D2	105
Fern Ridge Lake, res., Or., U.S.	C3	114
Fernwood, Id., U.S.	B2	89
Fernwood, Ms., U.S.	D3	101
Ferrara, Italy	E6	14

Name	Map Ref	Page
Ferreira do Alentejo, Port.	G3	12
Ferrelo, Cape, c., Or., U.S.	E2	114
Ferriday, La., U.S.	C4	95
Ferris, Tx., U.S.	C4	120
Ferris Mountains, mts., Wy., U.S.	D5	127
Ferron, Ut., U.S.	D4	121
Ferrum, Va., U.S.	D2	123
Ferry, co., Wa., U.S.	A7	124
Ferry Farms, Va., U.S.	B5	123
Ferryland, Newf., Can.	E5	72
Ferry Point, c., N.J., U.S.	k7	107
Fertile, Mn., U.S.	C2	100
Fès, Mor.	B5	42
Feshi, Zaire	C3	44
Fessenden, N.D., U.S.	B6	111
Festus, Mo., U.S.	C7	102
Fethiye, Tur.	M13	16
Feuilles, Rivière aux, stm., Que., Can.	g12	74
Feurs, Fr.	G11	10
Feyzābād, Afg.	B4	38
Fez see Fès, Mor.	B5	42
Fianarantsoa, Madag.	F9	44
Ficksburg, S. Afr.	G5	44
Fidalgo Island, i., Wa., U.S.	A3	124
Fidenza, Italy	E5	14
Fieldale, Va., U.S.	D3	123
Fields, Lake, l., Fl., U.S.	B3	86
Fields, Lake, l., La., U.S.	k10	95
Fier, Alb.	I3	16
Fifteenmile Creek, stm., Wy., U.S.	B4	127
Fifteen Mile Falls Reservoir, res., U.S.	C5	122
Figeac, Fr.	H9	10
Figueira da Foz, Port.	E3	12
Figueras, Spain	C14	12
Figuig, Mor.	B5	42
Fiji, ctry., Oc.	H1	2
Filchner Ice Shelf, Ant.	B9	47
Filer, Id., U.S.	G4	89
Fillmore, Ca., U.S.	E4	82
Fillmore, Ut., U.S.	E3	121
Fillmore, co., Mn., U.S.	G6	100
Fillmore, co., Ne., U.S.	D8	104
Finale Ligure, Italy	E3	14
Findlay, Il., U.S.	D5	90
Findlay, Oh., U.S.	A2	112
Finisterre, Cabo de, c., Spain	C2	12
Finland, ctry., Eur.	C13	4
Finland, Gulf of, b., Eur.	G16	6
Finlay, stm., B.C., Can.	E7	66
Finley, Tn., U.S.	A2	119
Finney, co., Ks., U.S.	D3	93
Finn Mountain, mtn., Ak., U.S.	C8	79
Finse, Nor.	F6	6
Finspång, Swe.	G10	6
Finsterwalde, Ger.	D13	8
Fiorenzuola d'Arda, Italy	E4	14
Fircrest, Wa., U.S.	f10	124
Firebaugh, Ca., U.S.	D3	82
Firenze (Florence), Italy	F6	14
Firenzuola, Italy	E6	14
Firestone, Co., U.S.	A6	83
Firminy, Fr.	G11	10
Firozābād, India	G8	38
Firozpur, India	E6	38
First Connecticut Lake, l., N.H., U.S.	f7	106
Fish, stm., Al., U.S.	E2	78
Fish, stm., Me., U.S.	A4	96
Fish Creek, stm., W.V., U.S.	g8	125
Fisher, stm., N.C., U.S.	C5	90
Fisher, co., Tx., U.S.	C2	120
Fisher Bay, b., Man., Can.	D3	70
Fishermans Island, i., Va., U.S.	h15	123
Fishers, In., U.S.	C5	91
Fishers Island, i., N.Y., U.S.	m16	109
Fishers Peak, mtn., Co., U.S.	D6	83
Fisher Strait, strt., N.W. Ter., Can.	D16	66
Fishersville, Va., U.S.	B4	123
Fishing Bay, b., Md., U.S.	D5	97
Fishing Creek, Md., U.S.	D5	97
Fishing Creek, stm., N.C., U.S.	A5	110
Fishing Creek, stm., S.C., U.S.	B5	117
Fishing Creek, stm., W.V., U.S.	B4	125
Fishing Creek Reservoir, res., S.C., U.S.	B6	117
Fishkill, N.Y., U.S.	D7	109
Fish Lake, l., Ut., U.S.	E4	121
Fish River Lake, l., Me., U.S.	B4	96
Fishtrap Lake, res., Ky., U.S.	C7	94
Fiskdale, Ma., U.S.	B3	98
Fitchburg, Ma., U.S.	A4	98
Fitzgerald, Ga., U.S.	E3	87
Fitz Roy, Arg.	F3	56
Fitzroy, stm., Austl.	C4	50
Fitzroy, Monte (Cerro Chaltel), mtn., S.A.	F2	56
Fitzroy Crossing, Austl.	C5	50
Fitzwilliam, N.H., U.S.	E2	106
Fitzwilliam Island, i., Ont., Can.	B3	73
Five Island Lake, l., Ia., U.S.	A3	92
Fivemile Creek, stm., Wy., U.S.	C4	127
Five Points, N.M., U.S.	B3	108
Flagler, co., Fl., U.S.	C5	86
Flagler Beach, Fl., U.S.	C5	86
Flagstaff, Az., U.S.	B4	80
Flagstaff Lake, l., Or., U.S.	E7	114
Flambeau, stm., Wi., U.S.	C3	126
Flamborough Head, c., Eng., U.K.	G12	7
Flaming Gorge Dam, Ut., U.S.	C6	121
Flaming Gorge National Recreation Area, U.S.	E3	127
Flaming Gorge Reservoir, res., U.S.	E3	127
Flanagan, Il., U.S.	C5	90
Flandreau, S.D., U.S.	C9	118
Flandreau Indian Reservation, S.D., U.S.	C9	118
Flat, stm., Mi., U.S.	E5	99
Flat, stm., N.C., U.S.	A4	110
Flat, stm., R.I., U.S.	E2	116
Flat Brook, stm., N.J., U.S.	A3	107
Flathead, co., Mt., U.S.	B2	103
Flathead, South Fork, stm., Mt., U.S.	C3	103
Flathead Indian Reservation, Mt., U.S.	C2	103
Flathead Lake, l., Mt., U.S.	C2	103
Flathead Valley, val., Mt., U.S.	C2	103
Flat Lick, Ky., U.S.	D6	94
Flatonia, Tx., U.S.	E4	120
Flat River, Mo., U.S.	D7	102
Flat River Reservoir, res., R.I., U.S.	D3	116
Flat Rock, Il., U.S.	F7	99
Flat Rock, N.C., U.S.	f10	110
Flatrock, stm., In., U.S.	F6	91
Flattery, Cape, c., Wa., U.S.	A1	124
Flatwoods, Ky., U.S.	B7	94
Fleetwood, Eng., U.K.	H9	7
Fleetwood, Pa., U.S.	F10	115
Flekkefjord, Nor.	G6	6
Fleming, co., Ky., U.S.	B6	94
Fleming-Neon, Ky., U.S.	C7	94
Flemingsburg, Ky., U.S.	B6	94
Flemington, N.J., U.S.	B3	107
Flemington, Pa., U.S.	D7	115
Flensburg, Ger.	A9	8
Flers, Fr.	D6	10
Fletcher, N.C., U.S.	f10	110
Fletcher, Ok., U.S.	C3	113
Fleurance, Fr.	I7	10
Flin Flon, Man., Can.	B1	70
Flinders, stm., Austl.	C8	50
Flinders Island, i., Austl.	G9	50
Flint, Wales, U.K.	H9	7
Flint, Mi., U.S.	E7	99
Flint, stm., Ga., U.S.	E2	87
Flint City, Al., U.S.	A3	78
Flint Creek Range, mts., Mt., U.S.	D3	103
Flippin, Ar., U.S.	A3	81
Flomaton, Al., U.S.	D2	78
Flora, Il., U.S.	E5	90
Flora, In., U.S.	C4	91
Flora, Ms., U.S.	C3	101
Florala, Al., U.S.	D3	78
Floral City, Fl., U.S.	D4	86
Floral Park, N.Y., U.S.	*E7	109
Florence, Al., U.S.	A2	78
Florence, Az., U.S.	D4	80
Florence, Co., U.S.	C5	83
Florence, Ks., U.S.	D7	93
Florence, Ky., U.S.	A5	94
Florence, Ms., U.S.	C3	101
Florence, N.J., U.S.	C3	107
Florence, Or., U.S.	D2	114
Florence, S.C., U.S.	C8	117
Florence, co., S.C., U.S.	C8	117
Florence, co., Wi., U.S.	C5	126
Florence see Firenze, Italy	F6	14
Florenceville, N.B., Can.	C2	71
Florencia, Col.	G5	58
Flores, i., Indon.	G7	32
Flores, Laut (Flores Sea), Indon.	G6	32
Floresville, Tx., U.S.	E3	120
Florham Park, N.J., U.S.	B4	107
Floriano, Braz.	E10	54
Florianópolis, Braz.	B7	56
Florida, Col.	F4	58
Florida, Cuba	D8	64
Florida, N.Y., U.S.	D6	109
Florida, state, U.S.		86
Florida, Cape, c., Fl., U.S.	G6	86
Florida, Straits of, strt., N.A.	B7	64
Florida Bay, b., Fl., U.S.	H6	86
Floridablanca, Col.	D6	58
Florida City, Fl., U.S.	G6	86
Florida Keys, is., Fl., U.S.	H6	86
Florida Mountains, mts., N.M., U.S.	E2	108
Florida State Indian Reservation, Fl., U.S.	F5	86
Florien, La., U.S.	C2	95
Florissant, Mo., U.S.	f13	102
Florissant Fossil Beds National Monument, Co., U.S.	C5	83
Florø, Nor.	F5	6
Flossmoor, Il., U.S.	k9	90
Flovilla, Ga., U.S.	C3	87
Flower Brook, stm., Vt., U.S.	E2	122
Flowery Branch, Ga., U.S.	B3	87
Flowood, Ms., U.S.	C3	101
Floyd, co., Ga., U.S.	B1	87
Floyd, co., In., U.S.	H6	91
Floyd, co., Ia., U.S.	A5	92
Floyd, co., Ky., U.S.	C7	94
Floyd, co., Tx., U.S.	B2	120
Floyd, co., Va., U.S.	D2	123
Floyd, stm., Ia., U.S.	B1	92
Floydada, Tx., U.S.	C2	120
Floyds Fork, stm., Ky., U.S.	B4	94
Floyds Knobs, In., U.S.	H6	91
Flushing, Mi., U.S.	E7	99
Flushing, Oh., U.S.	B4	112
Flushing see Vlissingen, Neth.	D3	8
Fluvanna, co., Va., U.S.	C4	123
Fly, stm.	m15	50a
Foard, co., Tx., U.S.	B3	120
Foça, Tur.	K10	16
Focşani, Rom.	D11	16
Fogang (Shijiao), China	L2	28
Foggia, Italy	H10	14
Fogland Point, c., R.I., U.S.	E6	116
Fogo, Newf., Can.	D4	72
Fogo, Cape, c., Newf., Can.	D5	72
Fogo Island, i., Newf., Can.	D4	72
Fohnsdorf, Aus.	H14	8
Foix, Fr.	J8	10
Foley, Al., U.S.	E2	78
Foley, Mn., U.S.	E5	100
Foley Island, i., N.W. Ter., Can.	C17	66
Folkston, Ga., U.S.	F4	87
Follansbee, W.V., U.S.	A4	125
Follonica, Italy	G5	14
Folly Beach, S.C., U.S.	F8	117
Folly Island, i., S.C., U.S.	F8	117
Folsom, Ca., U.S.	C3	82
Fonda, Ia., U.S.	B3	92
Fond du Lac, Wi., U.S.	E5	126
Fond du Lac, co., Wi., U.S.	E5	126
Fond du Lac Indian Reservation, Mn., U.S.	D6	100
Fondi, Italy	H8	14
Fondouk el Aouareb, Tun.	N4	14
Fonni, Italy	I4	14
Fonseca, Col.	B6	58
Fonseca, Golfo de, b., N.A.	H4	64
Fontainebleau, Fr.	D9	10
Fontana, Ca., U.S.	m14	82
Fontana, Wi., U.S.	F5	126
Fontana Lake, res., N.C., U.S.	f9	110
Fontanelle, Ia., U.S.	C3	92
Fonte Boa, Braz.	D5	54
Fontenay-le-Comte, Fr.	F6	10
Fontenelle Reservoir, res., Wy., U.S.	D2	127
Fontur, c., Ice.	B5	4
Foochow see Fuzhou, China	I8	28
Footville, Wi., U.S.	F4	126
Foraker, Mount, mtn., Ak., U.S.	f16	79
Forbach, Fr.	C13	10
Forbach, Ger.	G8	8
Forbes, Mount, mtn., Alta., Can.	D2	68
Forcalquier, Fr.	I12	10
Forchheim, Ger.	F11	8
Ford, co., Il., U.S.	C5	90
Ford, co., Ks., U.S.	E4	93
Ford, stm., Mi., U.S.	C3	99
Ford City, Ca., U.S.	E4	82
Ford City, Pa., U.S.	E2	115
Førde, Nor.	F5	6
Fordoche, La., U.S.	D4	95
Fords Prairie, Wa., U.S.	C2	124
Fordyce, Ar., U.S.	D3	81
Forel, Mont, mtn., Grnld.	C25	66
Foreman, Ar., U.S.	D1	81
Forest, Ont., Can.	D2	73
Forest, Ms., U.S.	C4	101
Forest, Oh., U.S.	B2	112
Forest, co., Pa., U.S.	C3	115
Forest, co., Wi., U.S.	C5	126
Forest, stm., N.D., U.S.	A8	111
Forest Acres, S.C., U.S.	C6	117
Forest City, Ia., U.S.	A4	92
Forest City, N.C., U.S.	B1	110
Forest City, Pa., U.S.	C11	115
Forestdale, R.I., U.S.	B3	116
Forest Dale, Vt., U.S.	D2	122
Forest Glen, La., U.S.	h12	95
Forest Grove, Or., U.S.	B3	114
Forest Hill, Md., U.S.	A5	97
Forest Hills, Pa., U.S.	k14	115
Forest Knolls, Ca., U.S.	g7	82
Forest Lake, Mn., U.S.	E6	100
Forest Park, Ga., U.S.	h8	87
Forest Park, Il., U.S.	k9	90
Forest Park, La., U.S.	*B3	95
Forest Park, Oh., U.S.	*n12	112
Forfar, Scot., U.K.	E10	7
Forillon, Parc National de, Que., Can.	k14	74
Fork Creek, stm., W.V., U.S.	m12	125
Forked Deer, stm., Tn., U.S.	B2	119
Forkland, Al., U.S.	C2	78
Forks, Wa., U.S.	B1	124
Forlì, Italy	E7	14
Formia, Italy	H8	14
Formiga, Braz.	F6	57
Formosa, Arg.	B5	56
Formosa, Braz.	C5	57
Formosa, Serra, plat., Braz.	F8	54
Formosa see Taiwan, i., Asia	L9	28
Forney, Tx., U.S.	C4	120
Fornovo di Taro, Italy	E5	14
Forrest, Austl.	F5	50
Forrest, Il., U.S.	C5	90
Forrest, co., Ms., U.S.	D4	101
Forrest City, Ar., U.S.	B5	81
Forrester Island, i., Ak., U.S.	n23	79
Forreston, Il., U.S.	A4	90
Forsayth, Austl.	C8	50
Forst, Ger.	D14	8
Forsyth, Ga., U.S.	C3	87
Forsyth, Il., U.S.	D5	90
Forsyth, Mo., U.S.	E4	102
Forsyth, Mt., U.S.	D10	103
Forsyth, co., Ga., U.S.	B2	87
Forsyth, co., N.C., U.S.	A2	110
Fortaleza, Braz.	D11	54
Fort Apache Indian Reservation, Az., U.S.	D5	80
Fort-Archambault see Sarh, Chad	G9	42
Fort Ashby, W.V., U.S.	B6	125
Fort Atkinson, Wi., U.S.	F5	126
Fort Augustus, Scot., U.K.	D8	7
Fort Beaufort, S. Afr.	H5	44
Fort Belknap Indian Reservation, Mt., U.S.	B8	103
Fort Belvoir, mil., Va., U.S.	g12	123
Fort Bend, co., Tx., U.S.	E5	120
Fort Benjamin Harrison, mil., In., U.S.	k10	91
Fort Benning, mil., Ga., U.S.	D2	87
Fort Benton, Mt., U.S.	C6	103
Fort Berthold Indian Reservation, N.D., U.S.	B3	111
Fort Bidwell Indian Reservation, Ca., U.S.	B3	82
Fort Bliss, mil., Tx., U.S.	o11	120
Fort Bragg, Ca., U.S.	C2	82
Fort Bragg, mil., N.C., U.S.	B3	110
Fort Branch, In., U.S.	H2	91
Fort Calhoun, Ne., U.S.	C9	104
Fort Campbell, mil., U.S.	A4	119
Fort Carson, mil., Co., U.S.	C6	83
Fort Chipewyan, Alta., Can.	f8	68
Fort Clatsop National Memorial, hist., Or., U.S.	A3	114
Fort Cobb, Ok., U.S.	B3	113
Fort Cobb Reservoir, res., Ok., U.S.	B3	113
Fort Collins, Co., U.S.	A5	83
Fort Coulonge, Que., Can.	B8	73
Fort Davis, Tx., U.S.	o13	120
Fort Davis National Historic Site, hist., Tx., U.S.	o13	120
Fort Defiance, Az., U.S.	B6	80
Fort-de-France, Mart.	G17	64
Fort Deposit, Al., U.S.	D3	78
Fort Detrick, mil., Md., U.S.	B3	97
Fort Devens, mil., Ma., U.S.	f9	98
Fort Dix, mil., N.J., U.S.	C3	107
Fort Dodge, Ia., U.S.	B3	92
Fort Donelson National Battlefield, Tn., U.S.	A4	119
Fort Edward, N.Y., U.S.	B7	109
Fort Erie, Ont., Can.	E6	73
Fortescue, stm., Austl.	D3	50
Fort Eustis, mil., Va., U.S.	h14	123
Fort Fairfield, Me., U.S.	B5	96
Fort Frances, Ont., Can.	o16	73
Fort Franklin, N.W. Ter., Can.	C8	66
Fort Gaines, Ga., U.S.	E1	87
Fort Gay, W.V., U.S.	C2	125
Fort Gibson, Ok., U.S.	B6	113
Fort Gibson Lake, res., Ok., U.S.	A6	113
Fort Good Hope, N.W. Ter., Can.	C7	66
Fort Gordon, mil., Ga., U.S.	C4	87
Fort Greely, mil., Ak., U.S.	C10	79
Fort Hall, Id., U.S.	F6	89
Fort Hall Indian Reservation, Id., U.S.	F6	89
Fort Hood, mil., Tx., U.S.	D4	120
Fort Howard, Md., U.S.	B5	97
Fort Huachuca, mil., Az., U.S.	F5	80
Fortín Coronel Eugenio Garay, Para.	H6	54
Fort Jackson, mil., S.C., U.S.	C6	117
Fort Jefferson National Monument, Fl., U.S.	H4	86
Fort Kent, Me., U.S.	A4	96
Fort Knox, mil., Ky., U.S.	B4	94
Fort-Lamy see N'Djamena, Chad	F9	42
Fort Laramie, Wy., U.S.	D8	127
Fort Laramie National Historic Site, hist., Wy., U.S.	D8	127
Fort Lauderdale, Fl., U.S.	F6	86
Fort Lawn, S.C., U.S.	B6	117
Fort Leavenworth, mil., Ks., U.S.	C9	93
Fort Lee, N.J., U.S.	B5	107
Fort Lee, mil., Va., U.S.	C5	123
Fort Leonard Wood, mil., Mo., U.S.	D5	102
Fort Lewis, mil., Wa., U.S.	B3	124
Fort Liard, N.W. Ter., Can.	D8	66
Fort Loramie, Oh., U.S.	B1	112
Fort Loudon, Pa., U.S.	G6	115
Fort Loudoun Lake, res., Tn., U.S.	D9	119
Fort Lupton, Co., U.S.	A6	83
Fort MacArthur, mil., Ca., U.S.	n12	82
Fort Macleod, Alta., Can.	E4	68
Fort Madison, Ia., U.S.	D6	92
Fort Matanzas National Monument, Fl., U.S.	C5	86
Fort McClellan, mil., Al., U.S.	B4	78
Fort McDermitt Indian Reservation, U.S.	B4	105
Fort McDowell Indian Reservation, Az., U.S.	D4	80
Fort McHenry National Monument And Historic Shrine, Md., U.S.	g11	97
Fort McMurray, Alta., Can.	A5	68
Fort Meade, Fl., U.S.	E5	86
Fort Meade, mil., Md., U.S.	B4	97
Fort Meadow Reservoir, res., Ma., U.S.	g9	98
Fort Mill, S.C., U.S.	A6	117
Fort Mitchell, Al., U.S.	C4	78
Fort Mitchell, Ky., U.S.	h13	94
Fort Mojave Indian Reservation, U.S.	C1	80
Fort Monmouth, mil., N.J., U.S.	C4	107
Fort Monroe, mil., Va., U.S.	h15	123
Fort Morgan, Co., U.S.	A7	83
Fort Myer, mil., Va., U.S.	g12	123
Fort Myers, Fl., U.S.	F5	86
Fort Myers Beach, Fl., U.S.	F5	86
Fort Nelson, B.C., Can.	m18	69
Fort Norman, N.W. Ter., Can.	D7	66
Fort Oglethorpe, Ga., U.S.	B1	87
Fort Ord, mil., Ca., U.S.	D3	82
Fort Payne, Al., U.S.	A4	78
Fort Peck Indian Reservation, Mt., U.S.	B11	103
Fort Peck Lake, res., Mt., U.S.	C9	103
Fort Pierce, Fl., U.S.	E6	86
Fort Pierce Inlet, b., Fl., U.S.	E6	86
Fort Pierre, S.D., U.S.	C5	118
Fort Plain, N.Y., U.S.	C6	109
Fort Polk, mil., La., U.S.	C2	95
Fort Portal, Ug.	A6	44
Fort Providence, N.W. Ter., Can.	D9	66
Fort Randall Dam, S.D., U.S.	D7	118
Fort Recovery, Oh., U.S.	B1	112
Fort Reliance, N.W. Ter., Can.	D11	66
Fort Resolution, N.W. Ter., Can.	D10	66
Fort Richardson, mil., Ak., U.S.	C10	79
Fort Riley, mil., Ks., U.S.	C7	93
Fort Ritchie, mil., Md., U.S.	A3	97
Fort Rucker, mil., Al., U.S.	D4	78
Fort Saint James, B.C., Can.	B5	69
Fort Saint John, B.C., Can.	A7	69
Fort Sam Houston, mil., Tx., U.S.	k7	120
Fort Sandeman, Pak.	E3	38
Fort Saskatchewan, Alta., Can.	C4	68
Fort Scott, Ks., U.S.	E9	93
Fort Shafter, mil., Hi., U.S.	g10	88
Fort Shawnee, Oh., U.S.	B1	112
Fort Sheridan, mil., Il., U.S.	h9	90
Fort Sill, mil., Ok., U.S.	C3	113
Fort Simpson, N.W. Ter., Can.	D8	66
Fort Smith, N.W. Ter., Can.	D10	66
Fort Smith, Ar., U.S.	B1	81
Fort Stewart, mil., Ga., U.S.	D5	87
Fort Stockton, Tx., U.S.	D1	120
Fort Sumner, N.M., U.S.	C5	108
Fort Sumter National Monument, S.C., U.S.	k12	117
Fort Supply Lake, res., Ok., U.S.	A2	113
Fort Thomas, Ky., U.S.	h14	94
Fort Totten, N.D., U.S.	B7	111
Fort Totten Indian Reservation, N.D., U.S.	B7	111
Fortuna, Ca., U.S.	B1	82
Fortune, Newf., Can.	E4	72
Fortune Bay, b., Newf., Can.	E4	72
Fort Union National Monument, N.M., U.S.	B5	108
Fort Valley, Ga., U.S.	D3	87
Fort Vermilion, Alta., Can.	f7	68
Fortville, In., U.S.	E6	91
Fort Wainwright, mil., Ak., U.S.	C10	79
Fort Walton Beach, Fl., U.S.	u15	86
Fort Wayne, In., U.S.	B7	91
Fort Washington Forest, Md., U.S.	C4	97
Fort William, Scot., U.K.	E7	7
Fort Wingate, N.M., U.S.	B1	108
Fort Worth, Tx., U.S.	C4	120
Fort Wright, Ky., U.S.	h13	94
Forty Fort, Pa., U.S.	D10	115
Fort Yukon, Ak., U.S.	B10	79
Fort Yuma Indian Reservation, Ca., U.S.	F6	82
Foshan, China	L2	28
Fossano, Italy	E2	14
Fossil Butte National Monument, Wy., U.S.	E2	127
Fossil Lake, l., Or., U.S.	D6	114
Fossombrone, Italy	F7	14
Foss Reservoir, res., Ok., U.S.	B2	113
Fosston, Mn., U.S.	C3	100
Foster, Or., U.S.	C4	114
Foster, co., N.D., U.S.	B6	111
Foster Village, Hi., U.S.	g10	88
Fostoria, Oh., U.S.	A2	112
Fougamou, Gabon	B2	44
Fougères, Fr.	D5	10
Fouke, Ar., U.S.	D2	81
Foula, i., Scot., U.K.	A10	7
Foumban, Cam.	G8	42
Fountain, Co., U.S.	C6	83
Fountain, co., In., U.S.	D3	91
Fountain City, In., U.S.	E8	91
Fountain City, Wi., U.S.	D2	126
Fountain Hill, Pa., U.S.	E11	115
Fountain Inn, S.C., U.S.	B3	117
Fountain Peak, mtn., Ca., U.S.	E6	82
Fountain Place, La., U.S.	*D4	95
Fourche LaFave, stm., Ar., U.S.	C2	81
Fourche Maline, stm., Ok., U.S.	C6	113
Fourmies, Fr.	B11	10
Four Mountains, Islands of, is., Ak., U.S.	E6	79
Four Oaks, N.C., U.S.	B4	110
Fowler, Ca., U.S.	D4	82
Fowler, Co., U.S.	C6	83
Fowler, In., U.S.	C3	91
Fowlerville, Mi., U.S.	F6	99
Fox, stm., Man., Can.	B4	70
Fox, stm., U.S.	B5	90
Fox, stm., Mo., U.S.	A6	102
Fox, stm., Mi., U.S.	B4	99
Fox, stm., Wi., U.S.	D5	126
Foxboro, Ont., Can.	C7	73
Foxboro, Ma., U.S.	B5	98
Fox Creek, Alta., Can.	B2	68
Foxe Basin, b., N.W. Ter., Can.	C17	66
Foxe Channel, strt., N.W. Ter., Can.	D16	66
Foxe Peninsula, pen., N.W. Ter., Can.	D17	66
Fox Island, i., R.I., U.S.	E4	116
Fox Island, i., Wa., U.S.	f10	124
Fox Islands, is., Ak., U.S.	E6	79
Fox Lake, Il., U.S.	A5	90
Fox Lake, Wi., U.S.	E5	126
Fox Lake, l., Il., U.S.	h8	90
Fox Mountain, mtn., Nv., U.S.	B2	105
Fox Point, Wi., U.S.	E6	126
Fox River Grove, Il., U.S.	h8	90
Foxworth, Ms., U.S.	D4	101
Foz do Cunene, Ang.	E2	44
Foz do Iguaçu, Braz.	B6	56
Frackville, Pa., U.S.	E9	115
Fraga, Spain	D12	12
Framingham, Ma., U.S.	B5	98
Franca, Braz.	F5	57
Francavilla Fontana, Italy	I12	14
France, ctry., Eur.	F8	4
Francesville, In., U.S.	C4	91
Franceville, Gabon	B2	44
Francis, Lake, l., N.H., U.S.	f7	106
Francis Case, Lake, res., S.D., U.S.	D6	118
Francistown, Bots.	F5	44
Francofonte, Italy	L9	14
Franconia, N.H., U.S.	B3	106
Franconia Notch, N.H., U.S.	B3	106
Francs Peak, mtn., Wy., U.S.	C3	127
Frankenberg, Ger.	E13	8
Frankenberg-Eder, Ger.	D8	8
Frankenmuth, Mi., U.S.	E7	99
Frankford, Ont., Can.	C7	73
Frankford, De., U.S.	F5	85
Frankford, Il., U.S.	m9	90
Frankfort, In., U.S.	D4	91
Frankfort, Ks., U.S.	C7	93
Frankfort, Ky., U.S.	B5	94
Frankfort, Mi., U.S.	D4	99
Frankfort, N.Y., U.S.	B5	109
Frankfort, Oh., U.S.	C2	112
Frankfurt am Main, Ger.	E8	8
Frankfurt an der Oder, Ger.	C14	8
Franklin, Ga., U.S.	C1	87
Franklin, In., U.S.	F5	91
Franklin, Ky., U.S.	D3	94
Franklin, La., U.S.	E4	95
Franklin, Ma., U.S.	B5	98
Franklin, Ne., U.S.	D7	104
Franklin, N.H., U.S.	D3	106
Franklin, N.J., U.S.	A3	107
Franklin, N.C., U.S.	f9	110
Franklin, Oh., U.S.	C1	112
Franklin, Pa., U.S.	D2	115
Franklin, Tn., U.S.	B5	119
Franklin, Tx., U.S.	D4	120
Franklin, Va., U.S.	D6	123
Franklin, W.V., U.S.	C5	125
Franklin, Wi., U.S.	n11	126
Franklin, co., Ar., U.S.	B2	81
Franklin, co., Fl., U.S.	C2	86

Name	Map Ref	Page
Franklin, co., Ga., U.S.	B3	87
Franklin, co., Id., U.S.	G7	89
Franklin, co., Il., U.S.	E4	90
Franklin, co., In., U.S.	F7	91
Franklin, co., Ia., U.S.	B4	92
Franklin, co., Ks., U.S.	D8	93
Franklin, co., Ky., U.S.	B5	94
Franklin, co., La., U.S.	B4	95
Franklin, co., Me., U.S.	C2	96
Franklin, co., Ma., U.S.	A2	98
Franklin, co., Ms., U.S.	D3	101
Franklin, co., Mo., U.S.	C6	102
Franklin, co., Ne., U.S.	D7	104
Franklin, co., N.Y., U.S.	f10	109
Franklin, co., N.C., U.S.	A4	110
Franklin, co., Oh., U.S.	B2	112
Franklin, co., Pa., U.S.	G6	115
Franklin, co., Tn., U.S.	B5	119
Franklin, co., Tx., U.S.	C5	120
Franklin, co., Vt., U.S.	B2	122
Franklin, co., Va., U.S.	D3	123
Franklin, co., Wa., U.S.	C6	124
Franklin, Point, c., Ak., U.S.	A8	79
Franklin Bay, b., N.W. Ter., Can.	C7	66
Franklin D. Roosevelt Lake, res., Wa., U.S.	B7	124
Franklin Falls Reservoir, res., N.H., U.S.	C3	106
Franklin Grove, Il., U.S.	B4	90
Franklin Lake, l., Nv., U.S.	C6	105
Franklin Mountains, mts., N.W. Ter., Can.	D8	66
Franklin Park, Il., U.S.	k9	90
Franklin Park, Pa., U.S.	*h13	115
Franklin Strait, strt., N.W. Ter., Can.	B13	66
Franklinton, La., U.S.	D5	95
Franklinton, N.C., U.S.	A4	110
Franklinville, N.Y., U.S.	C2	109
Frankston, Tx., U.S.	C5	120
Frankton, In., U.S.	D6	91
Frascati, Italy	H7	14
Fraser, B.C., Can.	E7	69
Fraser, stm., Newf., Can.	g9	72
Fraser, Mount, mtn., Can.	C8	69
Fraserburgh, Scot., U.K.	D10	7
Fraser Lake, B.C., Can.	B5	69
Fraser Plateau, plat., B.C., Can.	D6	69
Frauenfeld, Switz.	E15	10
Frazee, Mn., U.S.	D3	100
Frazeysburg, Oh., U.S.	B3	112
Frazier Park, Ca., U.S.	E4	82
Fr'azino, Russia	F21	18
Frederic, Wi., U.S.	C1	126
Frederica, De., U.S.	D3	85
Fredericia, Den.	I7	6
Frederick, Co., U.S.	A6	83
Frederick, Md., U.S.	B3	97
Frederick, Ok., U.S.	C2	113
Frederick, co., Md., U.S.	B3	97
Frederick, co., Va., U.S.	A4	123
Fredericksburg, Ia., U.S.	B5	92
Fredericksburg, Tx., U.S.	D3	120
Fredericksburg, Va., U.S.	B5	123
Frederick Sound, strt., Ak., U.S.	m23	79
Fredericktown, Mo., U.S.	D7	102
Fredericktown, Oh., U.S.	B3	112
Fredericktown, Pa., U.S.	F1	115
Fredericton, N.B., Can.	D3	71
Fredericton Junction, N.B., Can.	D3	71
Frederikshåb, Grnld.	D23	66
Frederikshavn, Den.	H8	6
Fredonia, Az., U.S.	A3	80
Fredonia, Ks., U.S.	E8	93
Fredonia, N.Y., U.S.	C1	109
Fredonia, Wi., U.S.	E6	126
Fredrikstad, Nor.	G8	6
Freeborn, co., Mn., U.S.	G5	100
Freeburg, Il., U.S.	E4	90
Freedom, Pa., U.S.	E1	115
Freedom, Wy., U.S.	D2	127
Freehold, N.J., U.S.	C4	107
Freeland, Mi., U.S.	E6	99
Freeland, Pa., U.S.	D10	115
Freelandville, In., U.S.	G3	91
Freel Peak, mtn., Ca., U.S.	C4	82
Freels, Cape, c., Newf., Can.	D5	72
Freels, Cape, c., Newf., Can.	D5	72
Freeman, S.D., U.S.	D8	118
Freeman, Lake, l., In., U.S.	C4	91
Freemansburg, Pa., U.S.	E11	115
Freemason Island, i., La., U.S.	E7	95
Freeport, Bah.	A8	64
Freeport, Il., U.S.	A4	90
Freeport, Me., U.S.	E2	96
Freeport, N.Y., U.S.	n15	109
Freeport, Pa., U.S.	E2	115
Freeport, Tx., U.S.	E5	120
Freer, Tx., U.S.	F3	120
Freestone, co., Tx., U.S.	D4	120
Freetown, S.L.	G3	42
Freetown, In., U.S.	G5	91
Freezeout Mountains, mts., Wy., U.S.	D6	127
Fregenal de la Sierra, Spain	G5	12
Freiberg, Ger.	E13	8
Freiburg [im Breisgau], Ger.	H7	8
Freising, Ger.	G11	8
Freistadt, Aus.	G14	8
Freital, Ger.	D13	8
Fréjus, Fr.	I13	10
Fremont, Ca., U.S.	D2	82
Fremont, In., U.S.	A8	91
Fremont, Ia., U.S.	C5	92
Fremont, Mi., U.S.	E5	99
Fremont, Ne., U.S.	C9	104
Fremont, N.C., U.S.	B5	110
Fremont, Oh., U.S.	A2	112
Fremont, co., Co., U.S.	C5	83
Fremont, co., Id., U.S.	E7	89
Fremont, co., Ia., U.S.	C4	127
Fremont, co., Wy., U.S.	C4	127
Fremont, stm., Ut., U.S.	E4	121
Fremont Lake, l., Wy., U.S.	D3	127
Fremont Peak, mtn., Wy., U.S.	C3	127
French Broad, stm., U.S.	D10	119
French Creek, stm., Pa., U.S.	C2	115
French Frigate Shoals, rf., Hi., U.S.	m14	88
French Guiana, dep., S.A.	C8	54
French Lick, In., U.S.	G4	91
Frenchman Bay, b., Me., U.S.	D4	96
Frenchman Creek, stm., U.S.	D4	104
Frenchman Hills, hills, Wa., U.S.	C6	124
Frenchman Lake, l., Nv., U.S.	G6	105
French Polynesia, dep., Oc.	G3	2
French Settlement, La., U.S.	D5	95
Freshfield, Mount, mtn., Can.	D2	68
Fresnillo, Mex.	F8	62
Fresno, Ca., U.S.	D4	82
Fresno, co., Ca., U.S.	D4	82
Fresno Reservoir, res., Mt., U.S.	B6	103
Freudenstadt, Ger.	G8	8
Frewsburg, N.Y., U.S.	C1	109
Fria, Cape, c., Nmb.	E2	44
Friars Point, Ms., U.S.	A3	101
Frías, Arg.	B3	56
Fribourg (Freiburg), Switz.	F14	10
Friday Harbor, Wa., U.S.	A2	124
Fridley, Mn., U.S.	m12	100
Friedberg, Aus.	H16	8
Friedrichshafen, Ger.	H9	8
Friend, Ne., U.S.	D8	104
Friendship, Tn., U.S.	D9	119
Friendsville, Tn., U.S.	D2	123
Friesland, hist. reg., Neth.	B5	8
Frio, co., Tx., U.S.	E3	120
Frio, stm., Tx., U.S.	E3	120
Frio, Cabo, c., Braz.	G7	57
Friona, Tx., U.S.	B1	120
Fripps Island, i., S.C., U.S.	G7	117
Frisco, Co., U.S.	B4	83
Frisco City, Al., U.S.	D2	78
Frisco Peak, mtn., Ut., U.S.	E2	121
Frissell, Mount, mtn., U.S.	A2	84
Fritch, Tx., U.S.	B2	120
Fritzlar, Ger.	D9	8
Friza, Proliv, strt., Russia	H23	24
Frobisher Bay, b., N.W. Ter., Can.	D19	66
Frobisher Lake, l., Sask., Can.	m7	75
Frohnleiten, Aus.	H15	8
Frontenac, Ks., U.S.	E9	93
Frontier, co., Ne., U.S.	D5	104
Front Range, mts., Co., U.S.	A5	83
Front Royal, Va., U.S.	B4	123
Frosinone, Italy	H8	14
Frostburg, Md., U.S.	k13	97
Frostproof, Fl., U.S.	E5	86
Fruita, Co., U.S.	B2	83
Fruit Heights, Ut., U.S.	B4	121
Fruitland, Id., U.S.	F2	89
Fruitland, Md., U.S.	D6	97
Fruitland, N.M., U.S.	A1	108
Fruitland Park, Fl., U.S.	D5	86
Fruitport, Mi., U.S.	E4	99
Fruitvale, B.C., Can.	E9	69
Fruitvale, Co., U.S.	B2	83
Fruitvale, Wa., U.S.	C5	124
Fruitville, Fl., U.S.	E4	86
Frunze see Biškek, Kyrg.	I12	22
Frutigen, Switz.	F14	10
Fryeburg, Me., U.S.	D2	96
Fuchū, Japan	G7	12
Fuencaliente, Spain	G7	12
Fuente de Cantos, Spain	G5	12
Fuente-obejuna, Spain	G6	12
Fuerteventura, i., Spain	C3	42
Fuji, Japan	G11	30
Fuji, Mount see Fuji-san, vol., Japan	G11	30
Fujian, prov., China	F10	26
Fujin, China	B13	26
Fujinomiya, Japan	G11	30
Fujisawa, Japan	G12	30
Fuji-san (Fujiyama), vol., Japan	G11	30
Fujiyama see Fuji-san, vol., Japan	G11	30
Fuji-yoshida, Japan	G11	30
Fukagawa, Japan	p20	30a
Fukaya, Japan	F12	30
Fukuchiyama, Japan	G8	30
Fukue, Japan	J1	30
Fukui, Japan	F9	30
Fukuoka, Japan	I3	30
Fukushima, Japan	E13	30
Fukushima, Japan	r18	30a
Fukuyama, Japan	H6	30
Fülädï, Küh-e, mtn., Afg.	C2	38
Fulda, Ger.	E9	8
Fulda, Mn., U.S.	G3	100
Fullerton, Ca., U.S.	n13	82
Fullerton, Ne., U.S.	C8	104
Fulton, Il., U.S.	B3	90
Fulton, Ky., U.S.	f9	94
Fulton, Md., U.S.	B4	97
Fulton, Ms., U.S.	A5	101
Fulton, Mo., U.S.	C6	102
Fulton, N.Y., U.S.	B4	109
Fulton, co., Ar., U.S.	A4	81
Fulton, co., Ga., U.S.	C2	87
Fulton, co., Il., U.S.	C3	90
Fulton, co., In., U.S.	B5	91
Fulton, co., Ky., U.S.	f8	94
Fulton, co., N.Y., U.S.	B6	109
Fulton, co., Oh., U.S.	A1	112
Fulton, co., Pa., U.S.	G5	115
Fultondale, Al., U.S.	f7	78
Funabashi, Japan	G13	30
Funchal, Port.	B2	42
Fundación, Col.	B5	58
Fundy, Bay of, b., Can.	D4	71
Fundy National Park, N.B., Can.	D4	71
Funkstown, Md., U.S.	A2	97
Fuquay-Varina, N.C., U.S.	B4	110
Furano, Japan	p20	30a
Furmanov, Russia	D24	18
Furnace Brook, stm., Vt., U.S.	D3	122
Furnas, co., Ne., U.S.	D6	104
Furnas, Reprêsa de, res., Braz.	F5	57
Furneaux Group, is., Austl.	H9	50
Furqlus, Syria	B5	40
Fürstenfeld, Aus.	H16	8
Fürstenfeldbruck, Ger.	G11	8
Fürstenwalde, Ger.	C14	8
Fürth, Ger.	F10	8
Furth im Wald, Ger.	F12	8
Furudal, Swe.	C11	26
Fushun, China	C11	26
Füssen, Ger.	H10	8
Fuxian, China	D11	26
Fuxian, China	D8	26
Fuxinshi, China	C11	26
Fuyang, China	C4	28
Fuyang, China	G5	28
Fuzhou, China	I8	28
Fuzhou (Foochow), China	I8	28
Fyffe, Al., U.S.	A4	78

G

Name	Map Ref	Page
Gabbs, Nv., U.S.	E4	105
Gabès, Tun.	B8	42
Gabès, Golfe de, b., Tun.	B8	42
Gabon, ctry., Afr.	B2	44
Gaborone, Bots.	F5	44
Gabriel Strait, strt., N.W. Ter., Can.	D19	66
Gabriola, B.C., Can.	f12	69
Gabrovo, Bul.	G9	16
Gadag, India	E3	37
Gäddede, Swe.	D10	6
Gadsden, Al., U.S.	A3	78
Gadsden, co., Fl., U.S.	B2	86
Gaeta, Italy	H8	14
Gaffney, S.C., U.S.	A4	117
Gafsa, Tun.	B7	42
Gage, co., Ne., U.S.	D9	104
Gagetown, N.B., Can.	J13	14
Gagliano del Capo, Italy	J13	14
Gagnoa, I.C.	G4	42
Gahanna, Oh., U.S.	k11	112
Gaillac, Fr.	I8	10
Gaillard, Lake, l., Ct., U.S.	D5	84
Gaines, co., Tx., U.S.	C1	120
Gainesboro, Tn., U.S.	C8	119
Gaines Creek, stm., Ok., U.S.	C6	113
Gainesville, Fl., U.S.	C4	86
Gainesville, Ga., U.S.	B3	87
Gainesville, Mo., U.S.	E5	102
Gainesville, Tx., U.S.	C4	120
Gainesville, Va., U.S.	g11	123
Gairdner, Lake, l., Austl.	F7	50
Gaithersburg, Md., U.S.	B3	97
Galán, Cerro, mtn., Arg.	B3	56
Galapagos Islands see Colóon, Archipiélago de, is., Ec.	m15	58a
Galashiels, Scot., U.K.	F10	7
Galati, Rom.	D12	16
Galatia, Il., U.S.	F5	90
Galatina, Italy	I13	14
Galax, Va., U.S.	D2	123
Galena, Ak., U.S.	C8	79
Galena, Il., U.S.	A3	90
Galena, Ks., U.S.	E9	93
Galeota Point, c., Trin.	I17	64
Galera, Punta, c., Chile	D2	56
Galera, Punta, c., Ec.	G2	58
Galesburg, Il., U.S.	C3	90
Galesburg, Mi., U.S.	F5	99
Gales Ferry, Ct., U.S.	D7	84
Galesville, Md., U.S.	C4	97
Galesville, Wi., U.S.	D2	126
Galeton, Pa., U.S.	C6	115
Galič, Russia	C25	18
Galicia, hist. reg., Eur.	B3	12
Galicia, hist. reg., Spain	B3	12
Galilee, Sea of see Kinneret, Yam, l., Isr.	C4	40
Galion, Oh., U.S.	B3	112
Galisteo Creek, stm., N.M., U.S.	k8	108
Galiuro Mountains, mts., Az., U.S.	E5	80
Galka'yo, Som.	G4	46
Gallant, Al., U.S.	A3	78
Gallarate, Italy	D3	14
Gallatin, Mo., U.S.	B4	102
Gallatin, Tn., U.S.	A5	119
Gallatin, co., Il., U.S.	F5	90
Gallatin, co., Ky., U.S.	B5	94
Gallatin, co., Mt., U.S.	E5	103
Gallatin, stm., Mt., U.S.	E5	103
Gallatin Range, mts., Mt., U.S.	E5	103
Gallaway, Tn., U.S.	B2	119
Galle, Sri L.	I6	37
Gallia, co., Oh., U.S.	D3	112
Galliano, La., U.S.	E5	95
Gallinas, Punta, c., Col.	A7	58
Gallinas Mountains, mts., N.M., U.S.	C1	108
Gallipoli, Italy	I12	14
Gallipoli see Gelibolu, Tur.	I10	16
Gallipolis, Oh., U.S.	D3	112
Gallitzin, Pa., U.S.	F4	115
Gällivare, Swe.	C13	6
Gallo Mountains, mts., N.M., U.S.	C1	108
Galloo Island, i., N.Y., U.S.	B4	109
Galloway, Mull of, c., Scot., U.K.	G8	7
Gallup, N.M., U.S.	B1	108
Galt, Ca., U.S.	C3	82
Galtür, Aus.	I10	8
Galty Mountains, mts., Ire.	I4	7
Galva, Il., U.S.	B3	90
Galva, Ks., U.S.	D6	93
Galveston, In., U.S.	C5	91
Galveston, Tx., U.S.	E5	120
Galveston, co., Tx., U.S.	E5	120
Galveston Bay, b., Tx., U.S.	E5	120
Galveston Island, i., Tx., U.S.	E5	120
Gálvez, Arg.	C4	56
Galway, Ire.	H3	7
Gambela, Eth.	G1	46
Gambell, Ak., U.S.	C5	79
Gambia, ctry., Afr.	F2	42
Gambia (Gambie), stm., Afr.	F2	42
Gambier, Oh., U.S.	B3	112
Gambo, Newf., Can.	D4	72
Gambrills, Md., U.S.	B4	97
Gamleby, Swe.	H11	6
Ganado, Az., U.S.	B6	80
Ganado, Tx., U.S.	E4	120
Gananoque, Ont., Can.	C8	73
Ganda, Ang.	D2	44
Gandak, stm., Asia	G11	38
Gander, Newf., Can.	D4	72
Gander, stm., Newf., Can.	D4	72
Ganderkesee, Ger.	B8	8
Gander Lake, l., Newf., Can.	D4	72
Gandesa, Spain	D12	12
Gändhidhagar, India	I5	38
Gändhi Sägar, res., India	H6	38
Gandía, Spain	G11	12
Gangápur, India	G7	38
Gangäwati, India	E4	37
Gangdisê Shan, mts., China	E10	38
Ganges, B.C., Can.	g12	69
Ganges (Ganga) (Padma), stm., Asia	I13	38
Ganges, Mouths of the, mth., Asia	J13	38
Gang Mills, N.Y., U.S.	C3	109
Gangtok, India	G13	38
Gangu, China	E8	26
Gannat, Fr.	F10	10
Gannett Peak, mtn., Wy., U.S.	C3	127
Gansu, prov., China	D7	26
Gantt, S.C., U.S.	B3	117
Gantt Lake, res., Al., U.S.	D3	78
Ganzhou, China	J3	28
Ganzi, China	E7	26
Gao, Mali	E5	42
Gaokeng, China	H2	28
Gaoyou, China	C8	28
Gaozhou, China	D11	34
Gap, Fr.	H13	10
Gap, Pa., U.S.	G9	115
Gar, China	E9	38
Garanhuns, Braz.	E11	54
Garber, Ok., U.S.	A4	113
Garberville, Ca., U.S.	B2	82
Garça, Braz.	G4	57
Garda, Lago di, l., Italy	D5	14
Gardelegen, Ger.	C11	8
Garden, co., Ne., U.S.	C3	104
Gardena, Ca., U.S.	n12	82
Garden City, Ga., U.S.	D5	87
Garden City, Id., U.S.	F2	89
Garden City, Ks., U.S.	E3	93
Garden City, Mi., U.S.	p15	99
Garden City, Mo., U.S.	C3	102
Gardendale, Al., U.S.	B3	78
Garden Grove, Ca., U.S.	n13	82
Garden Island, i., Mi., U.S.	C5	99
Garden Plain, Ks., U.S.	E6	93
Garden Reach, India	I13	38
Gardiner, Me., U.S.	D3	96
Gardiner, Mt., U.S.	E6	103
Gardiner, Or., U.S.	D2	114
Gardiners Island, i., N.Y., U.S.	m16	109
Gardner, Il., U.S.	B5	90
Gardner, Ks., U.S.	D9	93
Gardner, Ma., U.S.	A4	98
Gardner Canal, strt., B.C., Can.	C3	69
Gardner Lake, l., Ct., U.S.	C6	84
Gardner Lake, l., Me., U.S.	D5	96
Gardner Pinnacles, Hi., U.S.	k14	88
Gardnerville, Nv., U.S.	E2	105
Gardone Val Trompia, Italy	D5	14
Garfield, N.J., U.S.	h8	107
Garfield, co., Co., U.S.	B2	83
Garfield, co., Mt., U.S.	C9	103
Garfield, co., Ne., U.S.	C6	104
Garfield, co., Ok., U.S.	A4	113
Garfield, co., Ut., U.S.	F4	121
Garfield, co., Wa., U.S.	C8	124
Garfield Heights, Oh., U.S.	h9	112
Garfield Mountain, mtn., Mt., U.S.	F4	103
Garfield Peak, mtn., Wy., U.S.	D5	127
Garibaldi, Or., U.S.	B3	114
Garibaldi, Mount, mtn., B.C., Can.	E6	69
Garies, S. Afr.	H3	44
Garissa, Kenya	B7	44
Garland, N.C., U.S.	n10	120
Garland, Tx., U.S.	B3	121
Garland, Ut., U.S.	C2	81
Garland, co., Ar., U.S.	I6	10
Garlin, Fr.	I6	10
Garm, ab, Afg.	D1	38
Garmisch-Partenkirchen, Ger.	H11	8
Garnavillo, Ia., U.S.	B6	92
Garner, Ia., U.S.	A4	92
Garner, N.C., U.S.	B4	110
Garnet Range, mts., Mt., U.S.	D3	103
Garnett, Ks., U.S.	D8	93
Garnish, Newf., Can.	E4	72
Garonne, stm., Eur.	H6	10
Garoua, Cam.	G8	42
Garrard, co., Ky., U.S.	C5	94
Garretson, S.D., U.S.	D9	118
Garrett, In., U.S.	B7	91
Garrett, co., Md., U.S.	k12	97
Garrett Park, Md., U.S.	B3	97
Garrettsville, Oh., U.S.	A4	112
Garrison, Ky., U.S.	B6	94
Garrison, Md., U.S.	B4	97
Garrison, N.D., U.S.	B4	111
Garrison Dam, N.D., U.S.	B4	111
Garrovillas, Spain	F5	12
Garry Lake, l., N.W. Ter., Can.	C12	66
Garsen, Kenya	B8	44
Garut, Indon.	m13	33a
Garvin, co., Ok., U.S.	C4	113
Gary, In., U.S.	A3	91
Gary, W.V., U.S.	D3	125
Garysburg, N.C., U.S.	A5	110
Garyville, La., U.S.	D5	95
Garza, co., Tx., U.S.	C2	120
Garza-Little Elm Reservoir, res., Tx., U.S.	C4	120
Garzón, Col.	F5	58
Gas City, In., U.S.	D6	91
Gasconade, co., Mo., U.S.	C6	102
Gasconade, stm., Mo., U.S.	C6	102
Gascoyne, stm., Austl.	E3	50
Gasparilla Island, i., Fl., U.S.	F4	86
Gaspé, Que., Can.	k14	74
Gaspésie, Péninsule de la, pen., Que., Can.	k13	74
Gassaway, W.V., U.S.	C4	125
Gassville, Ar., U.S.	A3	81
Gaston, In., U.S.	D7	91
Gaston, N.C., U.S.	A5	110
Gaston, S.C., U.S.	D5	117
Gaston, co., N.C., U.S.	B1	110
Gaston, Lake, res., U.S.	A5	110
Gaston Dam, N.C., U.S.	A5	110
Gastonia, N.C., U.S.	B1	110
Gátas, Akrotírion, c., Cyp.	B3	40
Gatčina, Russia	B13	18
Gate City, Va., U.S.	f9	123
Gates, N.Y., U.S.	*B3	109
Gates, Tn., U.S.	B2	119
Gates, co., N.C., U.S.	A6	110
Gateshead, Eng., U.K.	G11	7
Gateshead Island, i., N.W. Ter., Can.	B12	66
Gates of the Arctic National Park, Ak., U.S.	B9	79
Gatesville, Tx., U.S.	D4	120
Gatineau, Que., Can.	D2	74
Gatineau, stm., Que., Can.	D2	74
Gatineau, Parc de la, Que., Can.	D2	74
Gatlinburg, Tn., U.S.	D10	119
Gaucín, Spain	I6	12
Gauhäti, India	G14	38
Gauley, stm., W.V., U.S.	C3	125
Gauley Bridge, W.V., U.S.	C3	125
Gautier, Ms., U.S.	f8	101
Gauting, Ger.	G11	8
Gavá, Spain	D14	12
Gavins Point Dam, U.S.	B8	104
Gävle, Swe.	F11	6
Gavrilov-Jam, Russia	D22	18
Gawler Ranges, mts., Austl.	F7	50
Gaya, India	H11	38
Gay Head, c., Ma., U.S.	D6	98
Gaylord, Mi., U.S.	C6	99
Gaylord, Mn., U.S.	F4	100
Gayndah, Austl.	E10	50
Gaza see Ghazzah, Isr. Occ.	D4	40
Gaziantep, Tur.	H15	4
Gazimağusa, N. Cyp.	B3	40
Gazimağusa Körfezi, b., N. Cyp.	B4	40
Gbarnga, Lib.	G4	42
Gdańsk (Danzig), Pol.	A18	8
Gdynia, Pol.	A18	8
Gearhart, Or., U.S.	A3	114
Gearhart Mountain, mtn., Or., U.S.	E6	114
Geary, N.B., Can.	D3	71
Geary, Ok., U.S.	B3	113
Geary, co., Ks., U.S.	D7	93
Geauga, co., Oh., U.S.	A4	112
Gebze, Tur.	I13	16
Gediz, stm., Tur.	K11	16
Geel, Bel.	D4	8
Geelong, Austl.	G8	50
Ge'ermu, China	B16	38
Geesthacht, Ger.	B10	8
Geilo, Nor.	F7	6
Geislingen, Ger.	G9	8
Geistown, Pa., U.S.	F4	115
Geist Reservoir, res., In., U.S.	E6	91
Gejiu (Kokiu), China	C7	34
Gela, Italy	L9	14
Gelibolu, Tur.	I10	16
Gelibolu Yarimadasi (Gallipoli Peninsula), pen., Tur.	I10	16
Gelsenkirchen, Ger.	D7	8
Gem, co., Id., U.S.	E2	89
Gembloux, Bel.	E4	8
Gemena, Zaire	H9	42
Gemlik, Tur.	I13	16
Gemona del Friuli, Italy	C8	14
Genale (Juba), stm., Afr.	G3	46
General Alvear, Arg.	C3	56
General Bravo, Mex.	E10	62
General Carneiro, Braz.	C2	57
General Levalle, Arg.	C4	56
General Pico, Arg.	D4	56
General Pinedo, Arg.	B4	56
General Roca, Arg.	D3	56
General Villegas, Arg.	D4	56
Genesee, Mi., U.S.	E7	99
Genesee, co., Mi., U.S.	E7	99
Genesee, co., N.Y., U.S.	B2	109
Genesee, stm., N.Y., U.S.	B3	90
Geneseo, Il., U.S.	B3	90
Geneseo, N.Y., U.S.	C3	109
Geneva, Al., U.S.	D4	78
Geneva, Il., U.S.	B5	90
Geneva, In., U.S.	C8	91
Geneva, Ne., U.S.	D8	104
Geneva, N.Y., U.S.	C4	109
Geneva, Oh., U.S.	A5	112
Geneva, co., Al., U.S.	D4	78
Geneva, Lake, l., Eur.	F13	10
Geneva, Lake, l., Wi., U.S.	F5	126
Geneva see Genève, Switz.	F13	10
Geneva-on-the-Lake, Oh., U.S.	A5	112
Genève, Switz.	F13	10
Genk, Bel.	E5	8
Genkai-nada, Japan	I3	30
Genoa, Il., U.S.	A5	90
Genoa, Ne., U.S.	C8	104
Genoa, Nv., U.S.	D2	105
Genoa, Oh., U.S.	A2	112
Genoa City, Wi., U.S.	F5	126
Genoa see Genova, Italy	E3	14
Genola, Ut., U.S.	D4	121
Genova (Genoa), Italy	E3	14
Genova, Golfo di, b., Italy	E3	14
Gent (Gand), Bel.	D3	8
Genteng, Indon.	n17	33a
Genthin, Ger.	C12	8
Gentry, Ar., U.S.	A1	81
Gentry, co., Mo., U.S.	A3	102
Geographe Bay, b., Austl.	F3	50
George, S. Afr.	H4	44
George, Ia., U.S.	A2	92
George, co., Ms., U.S.	E5	101
George, stm., Que., Can.	g13	74
George, Cape, c., N.S., Can.	D8	71
George, Lake, l., Austl.	B6	44
George, Lake, l., Fl., U.S.	C5	86
George, Lake, l., N.Y., U.S.	B7	109
George Air Force Base, mil., Ca., U.S.	E5	82

Name	Map Ref	Page
George B. Stevenson Reservoir, res., Pa., U.S.	D6	115
George Peak, mtn., Ut., U.S.	B2	121
Georgetown, P.E.I., Can.	C7	71
Georgetown, Cay. Is.	E7	64
Georgetown, Gam.	F3	42
Georgetown, Guy.	D13	58
George Town (Pinang), Malay.	L6	34
Georgetown, Ca., U.S.	C3	82
Georgetown, Co., U.S.	B5	83
Georgetown, Ct., U.S.	D2	84
Georgetown, De., U.S.	F4	85
Georgetown, Ga., U.S.	E1	87
Georgetown, Il., U.S.	D6	90
Georgetown, In., U.S.	H6	91
Georgetown, Ky., U.S.	B5	94
Georgetown, Ma., U.S.	A6	98
Georgetown, Oh., U.S.	D2	112
Georgetown, S.C., U.S.	E9	117
Georgetown, Tx., U.S.	D4	120
Georgetown, co., S.C., U.S.	E9	117
George Washington Birthplace National Monument, Va., U.S.	B6	123
George Washington Carver National Monument, Mo., U.S.	E3	102
George West, Tx., U.S.	E3	120
Georgia, ctry., Asia	I6	22
Georgia, state, U.S.	D3	87
Georgia, Strait of, strt., N.A.	B2	76
Georgian Bay, b., Ont., Can.	B3	73
Georgina, stm., Austl.	D7	50
Gera, Ger.	E12	8
Gerald, Mo., U.S.	C6	102
Geraldine, Al., U.S.	A4	78
Geral do Paraná, Serra, hills, Braz.	C5	57
Geraldton, Austl.	E2	50
Geraldton, Ont., Can.	o18	73
Gérardmer, Fr.	D13	10
Gerber Reservoir, res., Or., U.S.	E5	114
Gerdine, Mount, mtn., Ak., U.S.	C9	79
Gereshk, Afg.	E1	38
Gérgal, Spain	H9	12
Gering, Ne., U.S.	C2	104
Gerlach, Nv., U.S.	C2	105
Germantown, Il., U.S.	E4	90
Germantown, Md., U.S.	B3	97
Germantown, Oh., U.S.	C1	112
Germantown, Tn., U.S.	B2	119
Germantown, Wi., U.S.	E5	126
Germany, ctry., Eur.	E10	4
Germiston, S. Afr.	G5	44
Gerona, Spain	D14	12
Geronimo, Ok., U.S.	C3	113
Gervais, Or., U.S.	B4	114
Geseke, Ger.	D8	8
Getafe, Spain	E8	12
Gettysburg, Pa., U.S.	G7	115
Gettysburg, S.D., U.S.	C6	118
Ghāghra, stm., Asia	G10	38
Ghana, ctry., Afr.	G5	42
Ghanzi, Bots.	F4	44
Gharbīyah, Aş-Şaḥrā' al- (Western Desert), des., Egypt	C11	42
Ghardaïa, Alg.	B6	42
Gharyān, Libya	B8	42
Ghāt, Libya	D8	42
Ghawdex, i., Malta	M9	14
Ghazāl, Bahr al-, stm., Sudan	G12	42
Ghāziābād, India	F7	38
Ghāzīpur, India	H10	38
Ghaznī, Afg.	D3	38
Ghazzah (Gaza), Isr. Occ.	D4	40
Ghedi, Italy	D5	14
Gheen, Mn., U.S.	C6	100
Ghent see Gent, Bel.	D3	8
Gheorghe Gheorghiu-Dej, Rom.	C10	16
Ghīn, Tall, mtn., Syria	C5	40
Ghudāmis, Libya	B7	42
Giants Neck, Ct., U.S.	D7	84
Gibbon, Mn., U.S.	F4	100
Gibbon, Ne., U.S.	D7	104
Gibbons, Alta., Can.	C4	68
Gibbstown, N.J., U.S.	D2	107
Gibeon, Nmb.	G3	44
Gibraltar, Gib.	I6	12
Gibraltar, dep., Eur.	H6	4
Gibraltar, Strait of (Estrecho de Gibraltar), strt.	J6	12
Gibraltar Point, c., Eng., U.K.	H13	7
Gibsland, La., U.S.	B2	95
Gibson, Ga., U.S.	C4	87
Gibson, co., In., U.S.	H2	91
Gibson, co., Tn., U.S.	A3	119
Gibsonburg, Oh., U.S.	A2	112
Gibson City, Il., U.S.	C5	90
Gibsonia, Pa., U.S.	h14	115
Gibson Desert, des., Austl.	D4	50
Gibson Island, i., Md., U.S.	B5	97
Gibsons, B.C., Can.	E6	69
Gibsonton, Fl., U.S.	p11	86
Gibsonville, N.C., U.S.	A3	110
Giddings, Tx., U.S.	D4	120
Gideon, Mo., U.S.	E8	102
Gien, Fr.	E9	10
Giessen, Ger.	E8	8
Gifford, Fl., U.S.	E6	86
Gifford, Il., U.S.	C5	90
Gifu, Japan	G9	30
Gig Harbor, Wa., U.S.	B3	124
Gihon, stm., Vt., U.S.	B3	122
Gijón, Spain	B6	12
Gila, co., Az., U.S.	D5	80
Gila, stm., U.S.	E4	76
Gila Bend, Az., U.S.	E3	80
Gila Bend Indian Reservation, Az., U.S.	D3	80
Gila Bend Mountains, mts., Az., U.S.	D2	80
Gila Cliff Dwellings National Monument, N.M., U.S.	D1	108
Gila Mountains, mts., Az., U.S.	D6	80
Gila Peak, mtn., Az., U.S.	D6	80
Gila River Indian Reservation, Az., U.S.	D4	80
Gilbert, Az., U.S.	D4	80
Gilbert, Ia., U.S.	B4	92
Gilbert, La., U.S.	B4	95
Gilbert, Mn., U.S.	C6	100
Gilbert Islands see Kiribati, ctry., Oc.	G24	2
Gilbert Peak, mtn., Wa., U.S.	C4	124
Gilbert Plains, Man., Can.	D1	70
Gilbertsville, Ky., U.S.	f9	94
Gilbertsville, Pa., U.S.	F10	115
Gilbertville, Ia., U.S.	B5	92
Gilbués, Braz.	E9	54
Gilchrist, Or., U.S.	D5	114
Gilchrist, co., Fl., U.S.	C4	86
Gilcrest, Co., U.S.	A6	83
Giles, co., Tn., U.S.	B4	119
Giles, co., Va., U.S.	C2	123
Gilford Island, i., B.C., Can.	C6	69
Gilgit, Pak.	C6	38
Gillam, Man., Can.	A4	70
Gillespie, Il., U.S.	D4	90
Gillespie, co., Tx., U.S.	D3	120
Gillespie Dam, Az., U.S.	D3	80
Gillett, Ar., U.S.	C4	81
Gillett, Wi., U.S.	D5	126
Gillette, Wy., U.S.	B7	127
Gilliam, co., Or., U.S.	B6	114
Gilman, Il., U.S.	C5	90
Gilman, Vt., U.S.	C5	122
Gilmanton, N.H., U.S.	D4	106
Gilmer, Tx., U.S.	C5	120
Gilmer, co., Ga., U.S.	B2	87
Gilmer, co., W.V., U.S.	C4	125
Gilo, stm., Eth.	G1	46
Gilpin, co., Co., U.S.	B5	83
Gilroy, Ca., U.S.	D3	82
Gil'uj, stm., Russia	G19	24
Giluwe, Mount, mtn., Pap. N. Gui.	m15	50a
Gimli, Man., Can.	D3	70
Ginosa, Italy	I11	14
Ginowan, Japan	y27	31b
Gioia del Colle, Italy	I11	14
Gioia Tauro, Italy	K10	14
Girard, Il., U.S.	D4	90
Girard, Ks., U.S.	E9	93
Girard, Oh., U.S.	A5	112
Girard, Pa., U.S.	B1	115
Girardot, Col.	E5	58
Girardville, Pa., U.S.	E9	115
Giridih, India	H12	38
Girifalco, Italy	K11	14
Girne, N. Cyp.	B3	40
Girwa, stm., Asia	F9	38
Gisborne, N.Z.	C7	52
Gisenyi, Rw.	B5	44
Gisors, Fr.	C8	10
Giugliano [in Campania], Italy	I9	14
Giulianova, Italy	G8	14
Giurgiu, Rom.	F9	16
Givet, Fr.	B11	10
Givors, Fr.	G11	10
Giyon, Eth.	G2	46
Giza see Al-Jīzah, Egypt	B12	42
Gižiga, Russia	E26	24
Gižiginskaja Guba, b., Russia	E25	24
Gjandžā, Azer.	I7	22
Gjirokastër, Alb.	I4	16
Gjoa Haven, N.W. Ter., Can.	C13	66
Glacier, co., Mt., U.S.	B3	103
Glacier Bay, b., Ak., U.S.	k21	79
Glacier Bay National Park, Ak., U.S.	D12	79
Glacier National Park, B.C., Can.	D9	69
Glacier National Park, Mt., U.S.	B2	103
Glacier Peak, mtn., Wa., U.S.	A4	124
Gladbrook, Ia., U.S.	B5	92
Glade Creek, stm., Wa., U.S.	C6	124
Glade Creek, stm., W.V., U.S.	n14	125
Glade Creek, stm., W.V., U.S.	n13	125
Glades, co., Fl., U.S.	F5	86
Glade Spring, Va., U.S.	f10	123
Gladewater, Tx., U.S.	C5	120
Gladstone, Austl.	D10	50
Gladstone, Man., Can.	D2	70
Gladstone, Mi., U.S.	C4	99
Gladstone, Mo., U.S.	h10	102
Gladstone, Or., U.S.	B4	114
Gladwin, Mi., U.S.	E6	99
Gladwin, co., Mi., U.S.	D6	99
Glåma, stm., Nor.	F8	6
Glarner Alpen, mts., Switz.	F15	10
Glarus, Switz.	E16	10
Glascock, co., Ga., U.S.	C4	87
Glasford, Il., U.S.	C4	90
Glasgow, Scot., U.K.	F8	7
Glasgow, Ky., U.S.	C4	94
Glasgow, Mo., U.S.	B5	102
Glasgow, Mt., U.S.	B10	103
Glasgow, Va., U.S.	C3	123
Glasgow, W.V., U.S.	m13	125
Glassboro, N.J., U.S.	D2	107
Glasscock, co., Tx., U.S.	D2	120
Glassport, Pa., U.S.	F2	115
Glastonbury, Ct., U.S.	C5	84
Glauchau, Ger.	E12	8
Glazier Lake, l., Me., U.S.	A3	96
Glazov, Russia	F8	22
Gleason, Tn., U.S.	A3	119
Gleisdorf, Aus.	H15	8
Glen Allan, Ms., U.S.	B2	101
Glen Allen, Va., U.S.	C5	123
Glenboro, Man., Can.	E2	70
Glenbrook, Nv., U.S.	D2	105
Glen Burnie, Md., U.S.	B4	97
Glen Canyon Dam, Az., U.S.	A4	80
Glen Canyon National Recreation Area, U.S.	F5	121
Glencoe, Ont., Can.	E3	73
Glencoe, Al., U.S.	B4	78
Glencoe, Il., U.S.	A6	90
Glencoe, Mn., U.S.	F4	100
Glen Cove, N.Y., U.S.	h13	109
Glendale, Az., U.S.	D3	80
Glendale, Ca., U.S.	m12	82
Glendale, Ms., U.S.	D4	101
Glendale, Oh., U.S.	C1	112
Glendale, Or., U.S.	E3	114
Glendale, R.I., U.S.	B2	116
Glendale, S.C., U.S.	B4	117
Glen Dale, W.V., U.S.	B4	125
Glendale, Wi., U.S.	m12	126
Glendale Heights, W.V., U.S.	g8	125
Glendive, Mt., U.S.	C12	103
Glendo, Wy., U.S.	D7	127
Glendo Reservoir, res., Wy., U.S.	D8	127
Glendora, Ca., U.S.	m13	82
Glenelg, Md., U.S.	B4	97
Glen Ellis Falls, wtfl, N.H., U.S.	B4	106
Glen Ellyn, Il., U.S.	k8	90
Glenham, N.Y., U.S.	D7	109
Glen Innes, Austl.	E10	50
Glen Jean, W.V., U.S.	D3	125
Glen Lake, l., Mi., U.S.	D5	99
Glen Lyon, Pa., U.S.	D9	115
Glenmora, La., U.S.	D3	95
Glenn, co., Ca., U.S.	C2	82
Glennallen, Ak., U.S.	f19	79
Glenns Ferry, Id., U.S.	G3	89
Glennville, Ga., U.S.	E5	87
Glenolden, Pa., U.S.	p20	115
Glenpool, Ok., U.S.	B5	113
Glen Raven, N.C., U.S.	A3	110
Glen Ridge, N.J., U.S.	h8	107
Glen Rock, N.J., U.S.	h8	107
Glen Rock, Pa., U.S.	G8	115
Glenrock, Wy., U.S.	D7	127
Glen Rose, Tx., U.S.	C4	120
Glens Falls, N.Y., U.S.	B7	109
Glen Ullin, N.D., U.S.	C4	111
Glenview, Il., U.S.	h9	90
Glenview Naval Air Station, mil., Il., U.S.	h9	90
Glenville, Mn., U.S.	G5	100
Glenville, W.V., U.S.	C4	125
Glenwood, Newf., Can.	D4	72
Glenwood, Ar., U.S.	C2	81
Glenwood, Ga., U.S.	D4	87
Glenwood, Ia., U.S.	C2	92
Glenwood, Mn., U.S.	E3	100
Glenwood, Va., U.S.	D3	123
Glenwood City, Wi., U.S.	C1	126
Glenwood Springs, Co., U.S.	B3	83
Glidden, Ia., U.S.	B3	92
Glide, Or., U.S.	D3	114
Glina, Cro.	D11	14
Glittertinden, mtn., Nor.	F7	6
Gliwice (Gleiwitz), Pol.	E18	8
Globe, Az., U.S.	D5	80
Gloggnitz, Aus.	H15	8
Gloster, Ms., U.S.	D2	101
Gloucester, Ont., Can.	h12	73
Gloucester, Eng., U.K.	J10	7
Gloucester, Ma., U.S.	A6	98
Gloucester, Va., U.S.	C6	123
Gloucester, co., N.J., U.S.	D2	107
Gloucester, co., Va., U.S.	C6	123
Gloucester City, N.J., U.S.	D2	107
Gloucester Point, Va., U.S.	C6	123
Glouster, Oh., U.S.	C3	112
Glover Island, i., Newf., Can.	D3	72
Gloversville, N.Y., U.S.	B6	109
Glovertown, Newf., Can.	D4	72
Gloverville, S.C., U.S.	E4	117
Gluck, S.C., U.S.	C2	117
Glücksburg, Ger.	A9	8
Glückstadt, Ger.	B9	8
Glyndon, Md., U.S.	B4	97
Glyndon, Mn., U.S.	D2	100
Glynn, co., Ga., U.S.	E5	87
Gmünd, Aus.	G14	8
Gmunden, Aus.	H13	8
Gnadenhutten, Oh., U.S.	B4	112
Gnarp, Swe.	E11	6
Gniezno, Pol.	C17	8
Gnjilane, Yugo.	G5	16
Gō, stm., Japan	H5	30
Goa, ter., India	E2	37
Goat Island, i., R.I., U.S.	F5	116
Goat Mountain, mtn., Mt., U.S.	C3	103
Goat Rock Dam, U.S.	C4	78
Goba, Eth.	G3	46
Gobabis, Nmb.	F3	44
Gobi, des., Asia	C7	26
Gobles, Mi., U.S.	F5	99
Godāvari, stm., India	D6	37
Goddard, Ks., U.S.	E6	93
Goderich, Ont., Can.	D3	73
Godfrey, Il., U.S.	E3	90
Godhavn, Grnld.	C22	66
Godhra, India	I5	38
Godoy Cruz, Arg.	C3	56
Gods, stm., Man., Can.	A5	70
Gods Lake, l., Man., Can.	B4	70
Godthåb, Grnld.	D22	66
Godwin Austen see K2, mtn., Asia	C7	38
Goéland, Lac au, l., Que., Can.	G17	66
Goélands, Lac aux, l., Que., Can.	E20	66
Goff Creek, stm., Ok., U.S.	e9	113
Goffstown, N.H., U.S.	D3	106
Gogebic, co., Mi., U.S.	n12	99
Gogebic, Lake, l., Mi., U.S.	m12	99
Goiana, Braz.	E12	54
Goiânia, Braz.	D4	57
Goiás, Braz.	C3	57
Goiás, estado, Braz.	C4	57
Gojra, Pak.	E5	38
Gokāk, India	D3	37
Gökçeada, i., Tur.	I9	16
Gol'čicha, Russia	C10	24
Golconda, Il., U.S.	F5	90
Golconda, Nv., U.S.	C4	105
Gold Bar, Wa., U.S.	B4	124
Gold Beach, Or., U.S.	E2	114
Golden, B.C., Can.	D9	69
Golden, Co., U.S.	B5	83
Golden City, Mo., U.S.	D3	102
Goldendale, Wa., U.S.	D5	124
Golden Gate Bridge, Ca., U.S.	h7	82
Golden Gate National Recreation Area, Ca., U.S.	h7	82
Golden Hinde, mtn., B.C., Can.	E5	69
Golden Meadow, La., U.S.	E5	95
Golden Spike National Historic Site, hist., Ut., U.S.	B3	121
Golden Valley, Mn., U.S.	n12	100
Golden Valley, co., Mt., U.S.	D7	103
Golden Valley, co., N.D., U.S.	B2	111
Goldfield, Ia., U.S.	B4	92
Goldfield, Nv., U.S.	F4	105
Gold Hill, Or., U.S.	E3	114
Goldsboro, N.C., U.S.	B5	110
Goldsby, Ok., U.S.	B4	113
Goldthwaite, Tx., U.S.	D3	120
Goleta, Ca., U.S.	E4	82
Golf Manor, Oh., U.S.	o13	112
Goliad, Tx., U.S.	E4	120
Goliad, co., Tx., U.S.	E4	120
Golspie, Scot., U.K.	D9	7
Gomati, stm., India	G9	38
Gombe, stm., Tan.	B6	44
Gomel', Bela.	I14	18
Gomera, i., Spain	C2	42
Gómez Palacio, Mex.	E8	62
Gonābād, Iran	K9	22
Gonaïves, Haiti	E11	64
Gonam, Russia	F20	24
Gonam, stm., Russia	F28	24
Gonâve, Golfe de la, b., Haiti	E11	64
Gonâve, Île de la, i., Haiti	E11	64
Gonda, India	G9	38
Gondal, India	J4	38
Gonder, Eth.	F2	46
Gondia, India	B6	37
Gondomar, Port.	D3	12
Gondrecourt-le-Château, Fr.	D12	10
Gönen, Tur.	I11	16
Gônoura, Japan	I2	30
Gonzales, Ca., U.S.	D3	82
Gonzales, La., U.S.	D5	95
Gonzales, Tx., U.S.	E4	120
Gonzales, co., Tx., U.S.	E4	120
Gonzalez, Fl., U.S.	u14	86
Goochland, co., Va., U.S.	C5	123
Goode, Mount, mtn., Ak., U.S.	g18	79
Goodfellow Air Force Base, mil., Tx., U.S.	D2	120
Good Hope, Cape of, c., S. Afr.	H3	44
Good Hope Mountain, mtn., B.C., Can.	D5	69
Goodhue, co., Mn., U.S.	F6	100
Gooding, Id., U.S.	G4	89
Gooding, co., Id., U.S.	F4	89
Goodland, In., U.S.	C3	91
Goodland, Ks., U.S.	C2	93
Goodlettsville, Tn., U.S.	g10	119
Goodman, Ms., U.S.	C4	101
Goodman, Mo., U.S.	E3	102
Good Pine, La., U.S.	C3	95
Goodsprings, Nv., U.S.	H6	105
Goodview, Mn., U.S.	F7	100
Goodwater, Al., U.S.	B3	78
Goodwell, Ok., U.S.	e9	113
Goodyear, Az., U.S.	D3	80
Goole, Eng., U.K.	H12	7
Goondiwindi, Austl.	E10	50
Goose, stm., N.D., U.S.	B8	111
Goose Bay, b., Newf., Can.	B1	72
Gooseberry Creek, stm., Wy., U.S.	B4	127
Goose Creek, S.C., U.S.	F7	117
Goose Creek, stm., U.S.	G5	89
Goose Creek, stm., Va., U.S.	C3	123
Goose Creek Reservoir, res., S.C., U.S.	k11	117
Goose Lake, l., U.S.	B3	82
Goose Pond, l., N.H., U.S.	C2	106
Göppingen, Ger.	G9	8
Gorakhpur, India	G10	38
Gorda, Punta, c., Cuba	C6	64
Gordil, Cen. Afr. Rep.	G10	42
Gordo, Al., U.S.	B2	78
Gordon, Ga., U.S.	D3	87
Gordon, Ne., U.S.	B3	104
Gordon, co., Ga., U.S.	B2	87
Gordonsville, Tn., U.S.	C8	119
Gordonsville, Va., U.S.	B4	123
Gore, Eth.	G2	46
Gore, N.Z.	G2	52
Gore, Ok., U.S.	B6	113
Gore Bay, Ont., Can.	B2	73
Gore Point, c., Ak., U.S.	h16	79
Gore Range, mts., Co., U.S.	B4	83
Goreville, Il., U.S.	F5	90
Gorey, Ire.	I6	7
Gorgān, Iran	J8	22
Gorge High Dam, Wa., U.S.	A4	124
Gorham, Me., U.S.	E2	96
Gorham, N.H., U.S.	B4	106
Gorinchem, Neth.	D4	8
Gorizia, Italy	D8	14
Gorki, Bela.	G13	18
Gorki see Nižnij Novgorod, Russia	E27	18
Gorkovskoje Vodochranilišče, res., Russia	D26	18
Görlitz, Ger.	B13	8
Gorlovka, Ukr.	H5	22
Gorman, Tx., U.S.	C3	120
Gornja Radgona, Slo.	C10	14
Gorno-Altajsk, Russia	G11	24
Gorodec, Russia	E26	18
Gorontalo, Indon.	E7	32
Gort, Ire.	H4	7
Gorzów Wielkopolski (Landsberg an der Warthe), Pol.	C15	8
Goshen, In., U.S.	A6	91
Goshen, N.Y., U.S.	D6	109
Goshen, Oh., U.S.	C1	112
Goshen, co., Wy., U.S.	D8	127
Goshute Indian Reservation, U.S.	D7	105
Goshute Lake, l., Nv., U.S.	C7	105
Goshute Mountains, mts., Nv., U.S.	C7	105
Goslar, Ger.	D10	8
Gosper, co., Ne., U.S.	D6	104
Gosport, In., U.S.	F4	91
Gotemba, Japan	G11	30
Gotha, Ger.	E10	8
Gothenburg, Ne., U.S.	D5	104
Gothenburg see Göteborg, Swe.	H8	6
Gotland, i., Swe.	H12	6
Gotō-rettō, is., Japan	J1	30
Göttingen, Ger.	D9	8
Gouda, Neth.	C4	8
Gouin, Réservoir, res., Que., Can.	k12	74
Goulburn, Austl.	F9	50
Goulburn Islands, is., Austl.	B6	50
Gould, Ar., U.S.	D4	81
Goulding, Fl., U.S.	u14	86
Gould Island, i., R.I., U.S.	E5	116
Goulds, Fl., U.S.	s13	86
Gourdon, Fr.	H8	10
Gouré, Niger	F8	42
Gourin, Fr.	D3	10
Gournay-en-Bray, Fr.	C8	10
Gouverneur, N.Y., U.S.	f9	109
Gove, co., Ks., U.S.	D3	93
Governador Valadares, Braz.	E8	57
Governors Harbour, Bah.	B9	64
Govind Balabh Pant Sāgar, res., India	H10	38
Govind Sāgar, res., India	E7	38
Gowanda, N.Y., U.S.	C2	109
Gower, Mo., U.S.	B3	102
Gowmal (Gumal), stm., Asia	D3	38
Gowmal Kalay, Afg.	D3	38
Gowrie, Ia., U.S.	B3	92
Goya, Arg.	B5	56
Gozo see Ghawdex, i., Malta	M9	14
Graaff-Reinet, S. Afr.	H4	44
Grabill, In., U.S.	B8	91
Grace, Id., U.S.	G7	89
Graceville, Fl., U.S.	u16	86
Graceville, Mn., U.S.	E2	100
Gracewood, Ga., U.S.	C4	87
Gracias a Dios, Cabo, c., N.A.	G6	64
Gradaús, Braz.	E8	54
Gradaús, Serra dos, plat., Braz.	E8	54
Grado, Italy	D8	14
Grady, co., Ga., U.S.	F2	87
Grady, co., Ok., U.S.	C4	113
Graettinger, Ia., U.S.	A3	92
Grafton, Austl.	E10	50
Grafton, Il., U.S.	E3	90
Grafton, Ma., U.S.	B4	98
Grafton, N.D., U.S.	A8	111
Grafton, Oh., U.S.	A3	112
Grafton, W.V., U.S.	B4	125
Grafton, Wi., U.S.	E6	126
Grafton, co., N.H., U.S.	C3	106
Grafton, Cape, c., Austl.	C9	50
Graham, N.C., U.S.	A3	110
Graham, Tx., U.S.	C3	120
Graham, co., Az., U.S.	E5	80
Graham, co., Ks., U.S.	C4	93
Graham, co., N.C., U.S.	f9	110
Graham, Lake, res., Tx., U.S.	C3	120
Graham, Mount, mtn., Az., U.S.	E6	80
Graham Island, i., B.C., Can.	C1	69
Graham Lake, l., Me., U.S.	D4	96
Graham Moore, Cape, c., N.W. Ter., Can.	B17	66
Grahamstown, S. Afr.	H5	44
Grahn, Ky., U.S.	B6	94
Grainger, co., Tn., U.S.	C10	119
Grain Valley, Mo., U.S.	B3	102
Grajaú, Braz.	E9	54
Gramat, Fr.	H8	10
Grambling, La., U.S.	B3	95
Gramercy, La., U.S.	h10	95
Grammichele, Italy	L9	14
Grampian Mountains, mts., Scot., U.K.	E8	7
Granada, Col.	F6	58
Granada, Nic.	I5	64
Granada, Spain	H8	12
Granard, Ire.	H5	7
Granbury, Tx., U.S.	C4	120
Granby, Que., Can.	D5	74
Granby, Ct., U.S.	A5	84
Granby, Mo., U.S.	E3	102
Granby, Lake, res., Co., U.S.	A5	83
Gran Canaria, i., Spain	C2	42
Gran Chaco, pl., S.A.	A4	56
Grand, co., Co., U.S.	A4	83
Grand, co., Ut., U.S.	E6	121
Grand, stm., Ont., Can.	D4	73
Grand, stm., Mi., U.S.	E5	99
Grand, stm., Mo., U.S.	A3	102
Grand, stm., Oh., U.S.	A4	112
Grand, stm., S.D., U.S.	B4	118
Grandas, Spain	B5	12
Grand Bahama, i., Bah.	A8	64
Grand Bank, Newf., Can.	E4	72
Grand-Bassam, I.C.	G5	42
Grand Bay, N.B., Can.	D3	71
Grand Bay, Al., U.S.	E1	78
Grand Bend, Ont., Can.	D3	73
Grand Blanc, Mi., U.S.	F7	99
Grand Caillou, La., U.S.	E5	95
Grand Canal, Ire.	H5	7
Grand Canal see Da Yunhe, China	E10	26
Grand Canyon, Az., U.S.	A3	80
Grand Canyon, val., Az., U.S.	A3	80
Grand Canyon National Park, Az., U.S.	B3	80
Grand Cayman, i., Cay. Is.	E7	64
Grand Centre, Alta., Can.	B5	68
Grand Coteau, La., U.S.	D3	95
Grand Coulee, Wa., U.S.	B6	124
Grand Coulee Dam, Wa., U.S.	B6	124
Grande, stm., Bol.	G6	53
Grande, stm., Braz.	E3	57
Grande, Bahía, b., Arg.	G3	53
Grande, Boca, mth., Ven.	C12	58
Grande, Ilha, i., Braz.	G6	57
Grande, Ilha, i., Braz.	G1	57
Grande, Rio (Bravo del Norte), stm., N.A.	F7	76
Grande-Anse, N.B., Can.	B4	71
Grande Cache, Alta., Can.	C1	68
Grande Comore, i., Com.	D8	44
Grande de Matagalpa, stm., Nic.	H5	64
Grande de Santiago, Río, stm., Mex.	G7	62
Grande do Gurupá, Ilha, i., Braz.	D8	54
Grande-Entrée, Que., Can.	B8	71
Grande Prairie, Alta., Can.	B1	68
Grand Erg de Bilma, des., Niger	E8	42
Grand Erg Occidental, des., Alg.	B6	42
Grand Erg Oriental, des., Alg.	B7	42
Grande rivière de la Baleine, stm., Que., Can.	g11	74

Name	Map Ref	Page
Grande Ronde, stm., U.S.	C8	124
Grandes, Salinas, pl., Arg.	B4	56
Grandes-Bergeronnes, Que., Can.	A8	74
Grande-Terre, i., Guad.	F17	64
Grand Falls (Grand-Sault), N.B., Can.	B2	71
Grand Falls, Newf., Can.	D4	72
Grand Falls, wtfl, Me., U.S.	C5	96
Grandfather Mountain, mtn., N.C., U.S.	A1	110
Grandfield, Ok., U.S.	C3	113
Grand Forks, B.C., Can.	E8	69
Grand Forks, N.D., U.S.	B8	111
Grand Forks, co., N.D., U.S.	B8	111
Grand Forks Air Force Base, mil., N.D., U.S.	B8	111
Grand-Fougeray, Fr.	E5	10
Grand Harbour, N.B., Can.	E3	71
Grand Haven, Mi., U.S.	E4	99
Grand Island, Ne., U.S.	D7	104
Grand Island, i., La., U.S.	D6	95
Grand Island, i., Mi., U.S.	B4	99
Grand Isle, La., U.S.	E6	95
Grand Isle, co., Vt., U.S.	B2	122
Grand Isle, i., La., U.S.	E6	95
Grand Junction, Co., U.S.	B2	83
Grand Junction, Ia., U.S.	B3	92
Grand Lake, i., N.B., Can.	D3	71
Grand Lake, i., Newf., Can.	D3	72
Grand Lake, i., La., U.S.	E3	95
Grand Lake, i., La., U.S.	E6	95
Grand Lake, i., Mi., U.S.	C7	99
Grand Lake, i., Oh., U.S.	B1	112
Grand Lake Matagamon, l., Me., U.S.	B4	96
Grand Lake Seboeis, l., Me., U.S.	B4	96
Grand Ledge, Mi., U.S.	F6	99
Grand Manan Island, i., N.B., Can.	E3	71
Grand Marais, Mn., U.S.	k9	100
Grand Meadow, Mn., U.S.	G6	100
Grand-Mère, Que., Can.	C5	74
Grand Mound, Ia., U.S.	C7	92
Grand Portage Indian Reservation, Mn., U.S.	k10	100
Grand Portage National Monument, Mn., U.S.	h10	100
Grand Prairie, Tx., U.S.	n10	120
Grand Rapids, Mi., U.S.	F5	99
Grand Rapids, Mn., U.S.	C5	100
Grand Rapids, Mi., U.S.	f6	112
Grand Rivière de la Baleine, stm., Que., Can.	E17	66
Grand-Saint-Bernard, Tunnel du, Eur.	G14	10
Grand Saline, Tx., U.S.	C5	120
Grand Terre Islands, is., La., U.S.	E6	95
Grand Teton, mtn., Wy., U.S.	C2	127
Grand Teton National Park, Wy., U.S.	C2	127
Grand Tower, Il., U.S.	F4	90
Grand Traverse, co., Mi., U.S.	D5	99
Grand Traverse Bay, b., Mi., U.S.	D5	99
Grand Turk, T./C. Is.	D12	64
Grand Valley, Ont., Can.	D4	73
Grandview, Man., Can.	D1	70
Grandview, In., U.S.	I4	91
Grandview, Mo., U.S.	C3	102
Grandview, Wa., U.S.	C6	124
Grandview Heights, Oh., U.S.	m10	112
Grandville, Mi., U.S.	F5	99
Grandy, N.C., U.S.	A7	110
Granger, In., U.S.	A5	91
Granger, Ia., U.S.	C4	92
Granger, Tx., U.S.	D4	120
Granger, Wa., U.S.	C5	124
Grangeville, Id., U.S.	D2	89
Granisle, B.C., Can.	B4	69
Granite, Ok., U.S.	C2	113
Granite, co., Mt., U.S.	D3	103
Granite City, Il., U.S.	E3	90
Granite Falls, Mn., U.S.	F3	100
Granite Falls, N.C., U.S.	B1	110
Granite Falls, Wa., U.S.	A4	124
Granite Lake, res., Newf., Can.	D3	72
Granite Mountain, mtn., Ak., U.S.	B7	79
Granite Mountains, mts., Az., U.S.	E2	80
Granite Mountains, mts., Wy., U.S.	D5	127
Granite Pass, Wy., U.S.	B5	127
Granite Peak, mtn., Mt., U.S.	E7	103
Granite Peak, mtn., Nv., U.S.	A4	105
Granite Peak, mtn., Nv., U.S.	C2	105
Granite Peak, mtn., Ut., U.S.	C2	121
Granite Peak, mtn., Ut., U.S.	E3	121
Granite Peak, mtn., Wy., U.S.	C4	127
Granite Quarry, N.C., U.S.	B2	110
Granite Range, mts., Nv., U.S.	C2	105
Graniteville, S.C., U.S.	D4	117
Graniteville, Vt., U.S.	C4	122
Granollers, Spain	D14	12
Grant, Al., U.S.	A3	78
Grant, Mi., U.S.	E5	99
Grant, Ne., U.S.	D4	104
Grant, co., Ar., U.S.	C3	81
Grant, co., In., U.S.	D6	91
Grant, co., Ks., U.S.	E2	93
Grant, co., Ky., U.S.	B5	94
Grant, co., La., U.S.	C3	95
Grant, co., Mn., U.S.	E2	100
Grant, co., Ne., U.S.	C4	104
Grant, co., N.M., U.S.	E1	108
Grant, co., N.D., U.S.	C4	111
Grant, co., Ok., U.S.	A4	113
Grant, co., Or., U.S.	C7	114
Grant, co., S.D., U.S.	B8	118
Grant, co., Wa., U.S.	B6	124
Grant, co., W.V., U.S.	B5	125
Grant, co., Wi., U.S.	F3	126
Grant, Mount, mtn., Nv., U.S.	E3	105
Grant City, Mo., U.S.	A3	102
Grantham, Eng., U.K.	I12	7
Grant Park, Il., U.S.	B6	90
Grant Range, mts., Nv., U.S.	E6	105
Grants, N.M., U.S.	B2	108
Grantsburg, Wi., U.S.	C1	126
Grants Pass, Or., U.S.	E3	114
Grantsville, Ut., U.S.	C3	121
Grantsville, W.V., U.S.	C3	125
Grant Town, W.V., U.S.	B4	125
Grantville, Ga., U.S.	C2	87
Granville, Fr.	D5	10
Granville, Il., U.S.	B4	90
Granville, N.Y., U.S.	B7	109
Granville, Oh., U.S.	B3	112
Granville, W.V., U.S.	h11	125
Granville, co., N.C., U.S.	A4	110
Granville Lake, l., Man., Can.	A1	70
Granvin, Nor.	F6	6
Grapeland, Tx., U.S.	D5	120
Grapeview, Wa., U.S.	B3	124
Grapevine, Tx., U.S.	C4	120
Grapevine Lake, res., Tx., U.S.	n9	120
Grapevine Peak, mtn., Nv., U.S.	G4	105
Gras, Lac de, l., N.W. Ter., Can.	D10	66
Grasonville, Md., U.S.	C5	97
Grass, stm., Man., Can.	B2	70
Grass, stm., N.Y., U.S.	f9	109
Grasse, Fr.	I13	10
Grass Lake, Il., U.S.	h8	90
Grass Lake, Mi., U.S.	F6	99
Grass Lake, l., Il., U.S.	h8	90
Grass Valley, Ca., U.S.	C3	82
Grassy Brook, stm., Vt., U.S.	E3	122
Grassy Lake, l., La., U.S.	k9	95
Grates Point, c., Newf., Can.	D5	72
Gratiot, co., Mi., U.S.	E6	99
Gratis, Oh., U.S.	C1	112
Grave Creek, stm., W.V., U.S.	g8	125
Gravelly Branch, stm., De., U.S.	F4	85
Gravelly Range, mts., Mt., U.S.	E4	103
Gravenhurst, Ont., Can.	C5	73
Grave Peak, mtn., Id., U.S.	C4	89
Graves, co., Ky., U.S.	f9	94
Gravette, Ar., U.S.	A1	81
Gravina in Puglia, Italy	I11	14
Gray, Fr.	E12	10
Gray, Ga., U.S.	C3	87
Gray, Ky., U.S.	D5	94
Gray, La., U.S.	k10	95
Gray, Me., U.S.	g7	96
Gray, co., Ks., U.S.	E3	93
Gray, co., Tx., U.S.	B2	120
Grayback Mountain, mtn., Or., U.S.	E3	114
Gray Court, S.C., U.S.	B3	117
Grayland, Wa., U.S.	C1	124
Grayling, Mi., U.S.	D6	99
Graylyn Crest, De., U.S.	A3	85
Grays Harbor, co., Wa., U.S.	B2	124
Grays Harbor, b., Wa., U.S.	C1	124
Grayslake, Il., U.S.	A5	90
Grays Lake, sw., Id., U.S.	F7	89
Grayson, Ky., U.S.	B7	94
Grayson, co., Ky., U.S.	C3	94
Grayson, co., Tx., U.S.	C4	120
Grayson, co., Va., U.S.	D1	123
Grayson Lake, res., Ky., U.S.	B7	94
Grays Peak, mtn., Co., U.S.	B5	83
Graysville, Al., U.S.	f7	78
Graysville, Tn., U.S.	D8	119
Grayville, Il., U.S.	E5	90
Graz, Aus.	H15	8
Gr'azi, Russia	I22	18
Great Abaco, i., Bah.	A9	64
Great Artesian Basin, Austl.	D8	50
Great Australian Bight, Austl.	F5	50
Great Averill Pond, l., Vt., U.S.	B5	122
Great Barrier Reef, rf., Austl.	C9	50
Great Barrington, Ma., U.S.	B1	98
Great Basin National Park, Nv., U.S.	E7	105
Great Bay, b., N.H., U.S.	D5	106
Great Bay, b., N.J., U.S.	D4	107
Great Bear Lake, l., N.W. Ter., Can.	C9	66
Great Bend, Ks., U.S.	D5	93
Great Captain Island, i., Ct., U.S.	F1	84
Great Channel, strt., Asia	K3	34
Great Dismal Swamp, sw., U.S.	D6	123
Great Divide Basin, Wy., U.S.	E4	127
Great Dividing Range, mts., Austl.	D9	50
Great East Lake, l., U.S.	C5	106
Great Egg Harbor, stm., N.J., U.S.	D3	107
Greater Antilles, is., N.A.	D10	64
Greater Sunda Islands, is., Asia	F4	32
Great Exuma, i., Bah.	C10	64
Great Falls, Mt., U.S.	C5	103
Great Falls, S.C., U.S.	B6	117
Great Falls, wtfl, Md., U.S.	B3	97
Great Falls Dam, Tn., U.S.	D6	119
Great Guana Cay, i., Bah.	B9	64
Great Himalaya Range, mts., Asia	F10	38
Great Inagua, i., Bah.	D11	64
Great Indian Desert (Thar Desert), des., Asia	G4	38
Great Island, spit, Ma., U.S.	C7	98
Great Island, i., N.C., U.S.	B6	110
Great Karroo, plat., S. Afr.	H4	44
Great Lakes Naval Training Center, mil., Il., U.S.	h9	90
Great Miami, stm., U.S.	C1	112
Great Misery Island, i., Ma., U.S.	f12	98
Great Moose Lake, l., Me., U.S.	D3	96
Great Neck, N.Y., U.S.	h13	109
Great Nicobar, i., India	K2	34
Great Pee Dee, stm., U.S.	D9	117
Great Plain of the Koukdjuak, pl., N.W. Ter., Can.	C18	66
Great Plains, pl., N.A.	E10	61
Great Point, c., Ma., U.S.	D7	98
Great Ruaha, stm., Tan.	C7	44
Great Sacandaga Lake, l., N.Y., U.S.	C6	109
Great Salt Lake, l., Ut., U.S.	B3	121
Great Salt Lake Desert, des., Ut., U.S.	C2	121
Great Salt Plains Lake, res., Ok., U.S.	A3	113
Great Salt Pond, b., R.I., U.S.	h7	116
Great Sand Dunes National Monument, Co., U.S.	D5	83
Great Sandy Desert, des., Austl.	D4	50
Great Slave Lake, l., N.W. Ter., Can.	D10	66
Great Smoky Mountains, mts., U.S.	B8	119
Great Smoky Mountains National Park, U.S.	B8	119
Great Swamp, sw., R.I., U.S.	F3	116
Great Victoria Desert, des., Austl.	E5	50
Great Village, N.S., Can.	D6	71
Great Wass Island, i., Me., U.S.	D5	96
Great Yarmouth, Eng., U.K.	I14	7
Greece, N.Y., U.S.	B3	109
Greece, ctry., Eur.	H12	4
Greeley, Co., U.S.	A6	83
Greeley, Pa., U.S.	D12	115
Greeley, co., Ks., U.S.	D2	93
Greeley, co., Ne., U.S.	C7	104
Green, Or., U.S.	D3	114
Green, co., Ky., U.S.	C4	94
Green, co., Wi., U.S.	F4	126
Green, stm., U.S.	D5	76
Green, stm., U.S.	A1	83
Green, stm., U.S.	F3	122
Green, stm., Il., U.S.	B4	90
Green, stm., Ky., U.S.	C2	94
Green, stm., Wa., U.S.	B3	124
Green Acres, De., U.S.	h8	85
Greenacres, Wa., U.S.	B8	124
Greenacres City, Fl., U.S.	F6	86
Greenback, Tn., U.S.	D9	119
Green Bay, Wi., U.S.	D6	126
Green Bay, b., U.S.	D3	99
Greenbelt, Md., U.S.	C4	97
Greenbriar, Va., U.S.	g12	123
Greenbrier, Ar., U.S.	B3	81
Green Brier, Tn., U.S.	A5	119
Greenbrier, co., W.V., U.S.	D4	125
Greenbrier, stm., W.V., U.S.	D4	125
Greenbush, Mn., U.S.	B2	100
Greencastle, In., U.S.	E4	91
Greencastle, Pa., U.S.	G6	115
Green City, Mo., U.S.	A5	102
Green Cove Springs, Fl., U.S.	C5	86
Greendale, In., U.S.	F8	91
Greendale, Wi., U.S.	F6	126
Greene, Ia., U.S.	B5	92
Greene, N.Y., U.S.	C5	109
Greene, co., Al., U.S.	C1	78
Greene, co., Ar., U.S.	A5	81
Greene, co., Ga., U.S.	C3	87
Greene, co., Il., U.S.	D3	90
Greene, co., In., U.S.	F4	91
Greene, co., Ia., U.S.	B3	92
Greene, co., Ms., U.S.	D5	101
Greene, co., Mo., U.S.	D4	102
Greene, co., N.Y., U.S.	C6	109
Greene, co., N.C., U.S.	B5	110
Greene, co., Oh., U.S.	C2	112
Greene, co., Pa., U.S.	G1	115
Greene, co., Tn., U.S.	C11	119
Greene, co., Va., U.S.	B4	123
Greeneville, Tn., U.S.	C11	119
Green Fall, stm., U.S.	F1	116
Greenfield, Ca., U.S.	D3	82
Greenfield, Il., U.S.	D3	90
Greenfield, In., U.S.	E6	91
Greenfield, Ia., U.S.	C3	92
Greenfield, Ma., U.S.	A2	98
Greenfield, Mo., U.S.	D4	102
Greenfield, N.H., U.S.	E3	106
Greenfield, Oh., U.S.	C2	112
Greenfield, Tn., U.S.	A3	119
Greenfield, Wi., U.S.	n12	126
Greenfield Plaza, Ia., U.S.	e8	92
Green Forest, Ar., U.S.	A2	81
Green Harbor, Ma., U.S.	B6	98
Green Hill Pond, l., R.I., U.S.	h7	116
Greenhills, Oh., U.S.	n12	112
Green Lake, Wi., U.S.	E5	126
Green Lake, co., Wi., U.S.	E4	126
Green Lake, l., Me., U.S.	D4	96
Green Lake, l., Wi., U.S.	E5	126
Greenland, Ar., U.S.	B1	81
Greenland, N.H., U.S.	D5	106
Greenland, dep., N.A.	B16	61
Greenland Sea	B13	128
Greenlee, co., Az., U.S.	D6	80
Green Lookout Mountain, mtn., Wa., U.S.	D3	124
Green Mountain, mtn., Wy., U.S.	D5	127
Green Mountain Reservoir, res., Co., U.S.	B4	83
Green Mountains, mts., Vt., U.S.	F2	122
Greenock, Scot., U.K.	F8	7
Greenock, Pa., U.S.	F2	115
Green Peter Lake, res., Or., U.S.	C4	114
Green Pond, Al., U.S.	B2	78
Green Pond, l., N.J., U.S.	A4	107
Greenport, N.Y., U.S.	m16	109
Green River, Ut., U.S.	E5	121
Green River, Wy., U.S.	E3	127
Green River Lake, res., Ky., U.S.	C4	94
Green River Lock and Dam, U.S.	I2	91
Green River Reservoir, res., Vt., U.S.	B3	122
Green Rock, Il., U.S.	B3	90
Greensboro, Al., U.S.	C2	78
Greensboro, Ga., U.S.	C3	87
Greensboro, Md., U.S.	C6	97
Greensboro, N.C., U.S.	A3	110
Greensburg, In., U.S.	F7	91
Greensburg, Ks., U.S.	E4	93
Greensburg, Ky., U.S.	C4	94
Greensburg, Pa., U.S.	F2	115
Greens Peak, mtn., Az., U.S.	C6	80
Green Springs, Oh., U.S.	A2	112
Greenville, Al., U.S.	D3	78
Greenville, Ca., U.S.	B3	82
Greenville, De., U.S.	A3	85
Greenville, Ga., U.S.	C2	87
Greenville, Il., U.S.	E4	90
Greenville, Ky., U.S.	C2	94
Greenville, Me., U.S.	C3	96
Greenville, Mi., U.S.	E5	99
Greenville, Ms., U.S.	B2	101
Greenville, N.H., U.S.	E3	106
Greenville, N.C., U.S.	B5	110
Greenville, Oh., U.S.	B1	112
Greenville, Pa., U.S.	D1	115
Greenville, R.I., U.S.	C3	116
Greenville, S.C., U.S.	B3	117
Greenville, Tx., U.S.	C4	120
Greenville, co., S.C., U.S.	B3	117
Greenville Creek, stm., Oh., U.S.	B1	112
Greenville Junction, Me., U.S.	C3	96
Greenwich, Ct., U.S.	E1	84
Greenwich, N.Y., U.S.	B7	109
Greenwich, Oh., U.S.	A3	112
Greenwich Bay, b., R.I., U.S.	D4	116
Greenwich Point, c., Ct., U.S.	E1	84
Greenwood, B.C., Can.	E8	69
Greenwood, Ar., U.S.	B1	81
Greenwood, De., U.S.	E3	85
Greenwood, In., U.S.	E5	91
Greenwood, La., U.S.	B2	95
Greenwood, Ms., U.S.	B3	101
Greenwood, Mo., U.S.	k11	102
Greenwood, Pa., U.S.	E5	115
Greenwood, S.C., U.S.	C3	117
Greenwood, Wi., U.S.	D3	126
Greenwood, co., Ks., U.S.	E7	93
Greenwood, co., S.C., U.S.	C3	117
Greenwood, Lake, res., In., U.S.	G4	91
Greenwood, Lake, res., S.C., U.S.	C4	117
Greenwood Lake, N.Y., U.S.	D6	109
Greenwood Lake, l., U.S.	A4	107
Greenwood Lake, l., Mn., U.S.	C7	100
Greer, S.C., U.S.	B3	117
Greer, co., Ok., U.S.	C2	113
Greers Ferry Lake, res., Ar., U.S.	B3	81
Greeson, Lake, res., Ar., U.S.	C2	81
Gregg, co., Tx., U.S.	C5	120
Gregory, S.D., U.S.	D6	118
Gregory, co., S.D., U.S.	D6	118
Greifswald, Ger.	A13	8
Greilickville, Mi., U.S.	D5	99
Greiz, Ger.	E12	8
Grenada, Ms., U.S.	B4	101
Grenada, co., Ms., U.S.	B4	101
Grenada, ctry., N.A.	H17	64
Grenada Lake, res., Ms., U.S.	B4	101
Grenadine Islands, is., N.A.	H17	64
Grenchen, Switz.	E14	10
Grenoble, Fr.	G12	10
Grenville, Que., Can.	D3	74
Grenville, Cape, c., Austl.	B8	50
Grenville, Point, c., Wa., U.S.	B1	124
Gresham, Or., U.S.	B4	114
Gresik, Indon.	m16	33a
Gretna, Man., Can.	E3	70
Gretna, Fl., U.S.	B2	86
Gretna, La., U.S.	E5	95
Gretna, Ne., U.S.	C9	104
Gretna, Va., U.S.	D3	123
Greven, Ger.	C7	8
Grevená, Grc.	I5	16
Grevenmühlen, Ger.	B11	8
Grey, stm., Newf., Can.	E3	72
Greybull, Wy., U.S.	B4	127
Greybull, stm., Wy., U.S.	B4	127
Greylock, Mount, mtn., Ma., U.S.	A1	98
Greymouth, N.Z.	E3	52
Greys, stm., Wy., U.S.	C2	127
Gridley, Ca., U.S.	C3	82
Gridley, Il., U.S.	C5	90
Griffin, Ga., U.S.	C2	87
Griffiss Air Force Base, mil., N.Y., U.S.	B5	109
Griffith, Austl.	F9	50
Griffith, In., U.S.	A3	91
Grifton, N.C., U.S.	B5	110
Griggs, co., N.D., U.S.	B7	111
Griggsville, Il., U.S.	D3	90
Grik, Malay.	L6	34
Grimes, Ia., U.S.	C4	92
Grimes, co., Tx., U.S.	D4	120
Grimmen, Ger.	A13	8
Grimsby, Ont., Can.	D5	73
Grimsby, Eng., U.K.	H12	7
Grimselpass, Switz.	F15	10
Grimshaw, Alta., Can.	A2	68
Grimsley, Tn., U.S.	C9	119
Grimstad, Nor.	G7	6
Grindall Creek, Va., U.S.	n18	123
Grinnell, Ia., U.S.	C5	92
Grinnell Peninsula, pen., N.W. Ter., Can.	A14	66
Gris-Nez, Cap, c., Fr.	B8	10
Grissom Air Force Base, mil., In., U.S.	C5	91
Griswold, Ia., U.S.	C2	92
Grizzly Mountain, mtn., Id., U.S.	B2	89
Grizzly Mountain, mtn., Or., U.S.	C6	114
Grizzly Mountain, mtn., Wa., U.S.	A7	124
Groais Island, i., Newf., Can.	C4	72
Grodno, Bela.	H6	18
Groesbeck, Tx., U.S.	D4	120
Grombalia, Tun.	M5	14
Gronau, Ger.	C6	8
Grong, Nor.	D9	6
Groningen, Neth.	B6	8
Groom Lake, l., Nv., U.S.	F6	105
Groom Range, mts., Nv., U.S.	F6	105
Groote Eylandt, i., Austl.	B7	50
Grootfontein, Nmb.	E3	44
Gros Morne National Park, Newf., Can.	D3	72
Grosse Isle Naval Air Station, mil., Mi., U.S.	p15	99
Grossenhain, Ger.	D13	8
Grosse Pointe, Mi., U.S.	*p16	99
Grosse Pointe Park, Mi., U.S.	p16	99
Grosse Pointe Woods, Mi., U.S.	p16	99
Grosseto, Italy	G6	14
Grossglockner, mtn., Aus.	H12	8
Grossmont, Ca., U.S.	o16	82
Gros Ventre, stm., Wy., U.S.	C2	127
Gros Ventre Range, mts., Wy., U.S.	C2	127
Groswater Bay, b., Newf., Can.	F21	66
Groton, Ct., U.S.	D7	84
Groton, N.Y., U.S.	C4	109
Groton, S.D., U.S.	B7	118
Groton Long Point, Ct., U.S.	D7	84
Grottaglie, Italy	I12	14
Grottaminarda, Italy	H10	14
Grottoes, Va., U.S.	B4	123
Grouse Creek, stm., U.S.	B2	121
Grouse Creek Mountain, mtn., Id., U.S.		89
Grove, Ok., U.S.	A7	113
Grove City, Fl., U.S.	F4	86
Grove City, Oh., U.S.	C2	112
Grove City, Pa., U.S.	D1	115
Grove Hill, Al., U.S.	D2	78
Groveland, Fl., U.S.	D5	86
Groveland, Ma., U.S.	A5	98
Grove Point, c., Md., U.S.	B5	97
Groveport, Oh., U.S.	C3	112
Grover City, Ca., U.S.	E3	82
Groves, Tx., U.S.	E6	120
Groveton, N.H., U.S.	A3	106
Groveton, Tx., U.S.	D5	120
Groveton, Va., U.S.	g12	123
Groveton Gardens, Va., U.S.	*B5	123
Grovetown, Ga., U.S.	C4	87
Groveville, N.J., U.S.	C3	107
Growler Peak, mtn., Az., U.S.	E2	80
Groznyj, Russia	I7	22
Grudziądz, Pol.	B18	8
Gruetli-Laager, Tn., U.S.	D8	119
Grulla, Tx., U.S.	F3	120
Grundy, Va., U.S.	e9	123
Grundy, co., Il., U.S.	B5	90
Grundy, co., Ia., U.S.	B5	92
Grundy, co., Mo., U.S.	A4	102
Grundy, co., Tn., U.S.	D8	119
Grundy Center, Ia., U.S.	B5	92
Grunthal, Man., Can.	E3	70
Gruver, Tx., U.S.	A2	120
Guacanayabo, Golfo de, b., Cuba	D9	64
Guachochic, Mex.	D6	62
Guadalajara, Mex.	G8	62
Guadalajara, Spain	E8	12
Guadalcanal, i., Sol.Is.	A11	50
Guadalquivir, stm., Spain	H6	12
Guadalupe, Mex.	E9	62
Guadalupe, Az., U.S.	m9	80
Guadalupe, Ca., U.S.	E3	82
Guadalupe, co., N.M., U.S.	C5	108
Guadalupe, co., Tx., U.S.	E4	120
Guadalupe Garzarón, Mex.	E9	62
Guadalupe Mountains, mts., U.S.	E5	108
Guadalupe Mountains National Park, Tx., U.S.	o12	120
Guadalupe Peak, mtn., Tx., U.S.	o12	120
Guadeloupe, dep., N.A.	F17	64
Guadeloupe Passage, strt., N.A.	F17	64
Guadiana, stm., Eur.	H4	12
Guadix, Spain	H8	12
Guafo, Isla, i., Chile	E2	56
Guajará Mirim, Braz.	F5	54
Gualeguay, Arg.	C5	56
Gualeguaychú, Arg.	C5	56
Gualicho, Salina, pl., Arg.	E3	56
Guam, dep., Oc.	F22	2
Guaminí, Arg.	D4	56
Guamo, Col.	E5	58
Guampí, Sierra de, mts., Ven.	B5	54
Guanaja, Isla de, i., Hond.	F5	64
Guanajuato, Mex.	G9	62
Guanambi, Braz.	C7	57
Guanare, Ven.	C8	58
Guanarito, Ven.	C8	58
Guandi Shan, China	E8	26
Guane, Cuba	C5	64
Guang'an, China	E8	26
Guangdong, prov., China	G9	26
Guanghua, China	E9	26
Guangxi Zhuang Zizhiqu, prov., China	G8	26
Guangyuan, China	E8	26
Guangzhou (Canton), China	L2	28
Guano Lake, l., Or., U.S.	E7	114
Guantánamo, Cuba	D10	64
Guanxian, China	E7	26
Guápiles, C.R.	I6	64
Guaporé (Iténez), stm., S.A.	F6	54
Guaqui, Bol.	G5	54
Guarabira, Braz.	E11	54
Guaranda, Ec.	H3	58
Guarapuava, Braz.	B6	56
Guaratinguetá, Braz.	G6	57
Guarda, Port.	E4	12
Guardo, Spain	C7	12
Guárico, Embalse del, res., Ven.	C9	58
Guarulhos, Braz.	G5	57
Guarus, Braz.	F8	57
Guasave, Mex.	E5	62
Guasdualito, Ven.	D7	58
Guatemala, Guat.	G2	64
Guatemala, ctry., N.A.	G2	64
Guaviare, stm., Col.	F8	58
Guaxupé, Braz.	F5	57
Guayama, P.R.	F14	64
Guayaquil, Ec.	I3	58
Guayaquil, Golfo de, b., S.A.	I2	58
Guaymallén, Arg.	C3	56
Guaymas, Mex.	D4	62
Gubbio, Italy	F7	14
Guben, Ger.	D14	8
Guchengzi, China	D7	26
Gudalür, India	G4	37
Gudiyāttam, India	F5	37
Gūdūr, India	E5	37
Guebwiller, Fr.	E14	10
Guelma, Alg.	A7	42
Guelph, Ont., Can.	D4	73
Guérande, Fr.	E4	10
Guéret, Fr.	F8	10
Guernsey, Wy., U.S.	D8	127
Guernsey, co., Oh., U.S.	B4	112
Guernsey, dep., Eur.	C4	10
Gueydan, La., U.S.	D3	95
Guga, Russia	G21	18
Guibes, Nmb.	G3	44
Güicán, Col.	D6	58
Guichen, Fr.	E5	10
Guiding, China	A9	34

Name	Map Ref	Page
Guijuelo, Spain	E6	12
Guilford, Ct., U.S.	D5	84
Guilford, Me., U.S.	C3	96
Guilford, co., N.C., U.S.	A3	110
Guilin (Kweilin), China	B11	34
Guillaumes, Fr.	H13	10
Guimarães, Port.	D3	12
Guin, Al., U.S.	B2	78
Guinea, ctry., Afr.	F3	42
Guinea, Gulf of, b., Afr.	H6	42
Guinea-Bissau, ctry., Afr.	F2	42
Güines, Cuba	C6	64
Guingamp, Fr.	D3	10
Güira de Melena, Cuba	C6	64
Guiratinga, Braz.	G8	54
Güiria, Ven.	B11	58
Guixian, China	C10	34
Guiyang (Kweiyang), China	A9	34
Guizhou, prov., China	F8	26
Gujarat, state, India	I4	37
Gūjar Khān, Pak.	D5	38
Gujrānwāla, Pak.	D6	38
Gujrāt, Pak.	D6	38
Gulbarga, India	D4	37
Guledagudda, India	D3	37
Gulf, co., Fl., U.S.	C1	86
Gulf Gate Estates, Fl., U.S.	E4	86
Gulf Islands National Seashore, U.S.	E5	101
Gulfport, Fl., U.S.	E4	86
Gulfport, Ms., U.S.	E4	101
Gulf Shores, Al., U.S.	E2	78
Gull Island, i., N.C., U.S.	B7	110
Gullivan Bay, b., Fl., U.S.	G5	86
Gull Lake, l., Alta., Can.	C4	68
Gull Lake, l., Mn., U.S.	D4	100
Güllük, Tur.	L11	16
Gülpınar, Tur.	J10	16
Gulu, Ug.	H12	42
Gumal (Gowmal), stm., Asia	D3	38
Gumboro, De., U.S.	G4	85
Gummersbach, Ger.	D7	8
Guna, India	H7	38
Gunisao, stm., Man., Can.	C3	70
Gunnarn, Swe.	D11	6
Gunnison, Co., U.S.	C4	83
Gunnison, Ms., U.S.	B3	101
Gunnison, Ut., U.S.	D4	121
Gunnison, co., Co., U.S.	C3	83
Gunnison, stm., Co., U.S.	C2	83
Gunnison, Mount, mtn., Co., U.S.	C3	83
Gunpowder Neck, c., Md., U.S.	B5	97
Gunpowder River, b., Md., U.S.	B5	97
Guntakal, India	E4	37
Gunter Air Force Base, mil., Al., U.S.	C3	78
Guntersville, Al., U.S.	A3	78
Guntersville Lake, res., Al., U.S.	A3	78
Guntown, Ms., U.S.	A5	101
Guntūr, India	D6	37
Gunungsitoli, Indon.	N4	34
Günzburg, Ger.	G10	8
Gunzenhausen, Ger.	F10	8
Gurdāspur, India	D6	38
Gurdon, Ar., U.S.	D2	81
Guri, Embalse, res., Ven.	D11	58
Gurjev, Kaz.	H8	22
Gurley, Al., U.S.	A3	78
Gurnee, Il., U.S.	h9	90
Gurnet Point, c., Ma., U.S.	B6	98
Gurupá, Braz.	F9	54
Gurupi, stm., Braz.	D9	54
Gusau, Nig.	F7	42
Gus'-Chrustal'nyj, Russia	F23	18
Gusev, Russia	G5	18
Gushi, China	C4	28
Gushikawa, Japan	y27	31b
Gusinoozersk, Russia	J3	18
Guspini, Italy	J3	14
Gustav Holm, Kap, c., Grnld.	C26	66
Gustine, Ca., U.S.	D3	82
Güstrow, Ger.	B12	8
Gütersloh, Ger.	D8	8
Guthrie, Ky., U.S.	D2	94
Guthrie, Ok., U.S.	B4	113
Guthrie, W.V., U.S.	m12	125
Guthrie, co., Ia., U.S.	C3	92
Guthrie Center, Ia., U.S.	C3	92
Guttenberg, Ia., U.S.	B6	92
Guttenberg, N.J., U.S.	h8	107
Guyana, ctry., S.A.	B7	54
Guyandotte, stm., W.V., U.S.	C2	125
Guymon, Ok., U.S.	e9	113
Guysborough, N.S., Can.	D8	71
Guyton, Ga., U.S.	D5	87
Güzelyurt Körfezi, b., N. Cyp.	B3	40
Gwādar, Pak.	D1	36
Gwai, Zimb.	E5	44
Gwalior, India	E5	44
Gwanda, Zimb.	F5	44
Gweru, Zimb.	E5	44
Gwinhurst, De., U.S.	h8	85
Gwinn, Mi., U.S.	B3	99
Gwinner, N.D., U.S.	C8	111
Gwinnett, co., Ga., U.S.	C2	87
Gwydyr Bay, b., Ak., U.S.	A10	79
Gwynns Falls, stm., Md., U.S.	g10	97
Gympie, Austl.	E10	50
Gyöngyös, Hung.	H19	8
Győr, Hung.	H17	8
Gypsum, Co., U.S.	B4	83

H

Name	Map Ref	Page
Haakon, co., S.D., U.S.	C4	118
Haapajärvi, Fin.	E15	6
Haapamäki, Fin.	E15	6
Haar, Ger.	G11	8
Haarlem, Neth.	C4	8
Haast, N.Z.	E2	52
Habersham, co., Ga., U.S.	B3	87
Habiganj, Bngl.	H14	38
Hachijō-jima, i., Japan	E14	26
Hachinohe, Japan	B14	30
Hachiōji, Japan	G12	30
Hackberry, La., U.S.	E2	95
Hackensack, N.J., U.S.	B4	107
Hackensack, stm., N.J., U.S.	h8	107
Hackettstown, N.J., U.S.	B3	107
Hackleburg, Al., U.S.	A2	78
Hadd, Ra's al-, c., Oman	D6	46
Haddam, Ct., U.S.	D5	84
Haddock, Ga., U.S.	C3	87
Haddonfield, N.J., U.S.	D2	107
Haddon Heights, N.J., U.S.	D2	107
Hadejia, stm., Nig.	F8	42
Hadera, Isr.	C4	40
Haderslev, Den.	I7	6
Hadīyah, Sau. Ar.	C2	46
Hadjeb el Aïoun, Tun.	N4	14
Hadley Bay, b., N.W. Ter., Can.	B11	66
Hadley Lake, l., Me., U.S.	D5	96
Hadlock, Wa., U.S.	A3	124
Ha Dong, Viet.	D8	34
Hadramawt, reg., Yemen	E4	46
Haeju, N. Kor.	D12	26
Hāfizābād, Pak.	D5	38
Hafun, Ras, c., Som.	F5	46
Hagan, Ga., U.S.	D5	87
Hagemeister Island, i., Ak., U.S.	D7	79
Hagen, Ger.	D7	8
Hagerman, Id., U.S.	G4	89
Hagerman, N.M., U.S.	D5	108
Hagerstown, In., U.S.	E7	91
Hagerstown, Md., U.S.	A2	97
Hagfors, Swe.	F9	6
Haggin, Mount, mtn., Mt., U.S.	D3	103
Hagi, Japan	H4	30
Ha Giang, Viet.	C8	34
Hague, Sask., Can.	E2	75
Hague, Cap de la, c., Fr.	C5	10
Haguenau, Fr.	D14	10
Hagues Peak, mtn., Co., U.S.	A5	83
Ha! Ha!, Baie des, b., Que., Can.	C2	72
Hahira, Ga., U.S.	F3	87
Hahnville, La., U.S.	E5	95
Haian, China	C9	28
Haicheng, China	C11	28
Hai Duong, Viet.	D9	34
Haifa see Hefa, Isr.	C4	40
Haikou, China	D11	34
Haiku, Hi., U.S.	C5	88
Hā'il, Sau. Ar.	C3	46
Hailaer, China	B10	26
Hailey, Id., U.S.	F4	89
Haileybury, Ont., Can.	p20	73
Haileyville, Ok., U.S.	C6	113
Haimen, China	G10	28
Haimen, China	L5	28
Hainan, China	H8	26
Hainan Dao, i., China	E10	34
Haines, Ak., U.S.	D12	79
Haines City, Fl., U.S.	D5	86
Haines Junction, Yukon, Can.	D5	66
Hainfeld, Aus.	G15	8
Haining, China	E9	28
Hai Phong, Viet.	D9	34
Haiti (Haïti), ctry., N.A.	E11	64
Haizhou, China	A8	28
Hakodate, Japan	r18	30a
Hāla, Pak.	H3	38
Halab (Aleppo), Syria	A5	40
Halā'ib, Sudan	D13	42
Halawa, Cape, c., Hi., U.S.	B5	88
Halawa Heights, Hi., U.S.	g10	88
Halbā, Leb.	B5	40
Halberstadt, Ger.	D11	8
Halden, Nor.	G8	6
Haldensleben, Ger.	C11	8
Haldimand, Ont., Can.	E5	73
Haldwāni, India	F8	38
Hale, Al., U.S.	C2	78
Hale, co., Tx., U.S.	B2	120
Haleakala Crater, crat., Hi., U.S.	C5	88
Haleakala National Park, Hi., U.S.	C6	88
Hale Center, Tx., U.S.	B2	120
Haleiwa, Hi., U.S.	B3	88
Hales Corners, Wi., U.S.	n11	126
Halethorpe, Md., U.S.	B4	97
Haleyville, Al., U.S.	A2	78
Half Moon Bay, Ca., U.S.	k8	82
Halfway, Md., U.S.	A2	97
Haliburton, Ont., Can.	B6	73
Halibut Point, c., Ma., U.S.	A6	98
Halifax, N.S., Can.	E6	71
Halifax, Va., U.S.	D4	123
Halifax, co., N.C., U.S.	A5	110
Halifax, co., Va., U.S.	D4	123
Halifax Bay, b., Austl.	C9	50
Halimaile, Hi., U.S.	C5	88
Halkirk, Scot., U.K.	C9	7
Hall, co., Ga., U.S.	B3	87
Hall, co., Ne., U.S.	D7	104
Hall, co., Tx., U.S.	B2	120
Hallam Peak, mtn., B.C., Can.	C8	69
Hallandale, Fl., U.S.	G6	86
Halla-san, mtn., S. Kor.	E12	26
Halle, Ger.	D11	8
Hällefors, Swe.	G10	6
Hallein, Aus.	H13	8
Hallettsville, Tx., U.S.	E4	120
Hallie, Wi., U.S.	D2	126
Hall Island, i., Ak., U.S.	C5	79
Hall Meadow Brook Reservoir, res., Ct., U.S.	B3	84
Hall Mountain, mtn., Wa., U.S.	A8	124
Hällnäs, Swe.	D12	6
Hallock, Mn., U.S.	B2	100
Hallowell, Me., U.S.	D3	96
Hall Peninsula, pen., N.W. Ter., Can.	D19	66
Halls, Tn., U.S.	B2	119
Hallsberg, Swe.	G10	6
Halls Creek, Austl.	C5	50
Halls Creek, stm., Ut., U.S.	F5	121
Halls Crossroads, Tn., U.S.	m14	119
Halls Stream, stm., N.H., U.S.	f7	106
Hallstavik, Swe.	F12	6
Hallstead, Pa., U.S.	C10	115
Hallsville, Mo., U.S.	B5	102
Hallsville, Tx., U.S.	C5	120
Halmahera, i., Indon.	E8	32
Halmahera, Laut, Indon.	F8	32
Halmstad, Swe.	H9	6
Halsey, Or., U.S.	C3	114
Hälsingborg see Helsingborg, Swe.	H9	6
Halstad, Mn., U.S.	C2	100
Halstead, Ks., U.S.	E6	93
Haltern, Ger.	D7	8
Hanford, Ca., U.S.	D4	82
Haltiatunturi, mtn., Eur.	B13	6
Halton Hills, Ont., Can.	D5	73
Hamada, Japan	H5	30
Hamadān, Iran	B4	46
Hamāh, Syria	B5	40
Hamamatsu, Japan	H10	30
Hamar, Nor.	F8	6
Hamblen, co., Tn., U.S.	C10	119
Hamburg, Ger.	B9	8
Hamburg, Ar., U.S.	D4	81
Hamburg, Ia., U.S.	D2	92
Hamburg, N.Y., U.S.	C2	109
Hamburg, Pa., U.S.	E10	115
Hamden, Ct., U.S.	D4	84
Hamden, Oh., U.S.	C3	112
Hämeenlinna, Fin.	F15	6
Hamel, Mn., U.S.	m11	100
Hamelin, Ger.	C9	8
Hamersley Range, mts., Austl.	D3	50
Hamhŭng, N. Kor.	D12	26
Hami, China	C5	26
Hamilton, Ber.	E14	76
Hamilton, Ont., Can.	D5	73
Hamilton, N.Z.	B5	52
Hamilton, Scot., U.K.	F8	7
Hamilton, Al., U.S.	A2	78
Hamilton, Il., U.S.	C2	90
Hamilton, In., U.S.	A8	91
Hamilton, Mi., U.S.	F4	99
Hamilton, Ms., U.S.	B5	101
Hamilton, Mo., U.S.	B3	102
Hamilton, Mt., U.S.	D2	103
Hamilton, N.Y., U.S.	C5	109
Hamilton, Oh., U.S.	C1	112
Hamilton, Tn., U.S.	D8	119
Hamilton, Tx., U.S.	D3	120
Hamilton, Va., U.S.	A5	123
Hamilton, co., Fl., U.S.	B3	86
Hamilton, co., Il., U.S.	E5	90
Hamilton, co., In., U.S.	D5	91
Hamilton, co., Ia., U.S.	B4	92
Hamilton, co., Ks., U.S.	E2	93
Hamilton, co., Ne., U.S.	D7	104
Hamilton, co., N.Y., U.S.	B6	109
Hamilton, co., Oh., U.S.	C1	112
Hamilton, co., Tn., U.S.	D8	119
Hamilton, co., Tx., U.S.	D3	120
Hamilton, Lake, res., Ar., U.S.	C2	81
Hamilton, Mount, mtn., Ak., U.S.	C8	79
Hamilton, Mount, mtn., Ca., U.S.	k9	82
Hamilton, Mount, mtn., Nv., U.S.	D6	105
Hamilton Inlet, b., Newf., Can.	A2	72
Hamilton Reservoir, res., Ma., U.S.	B3	98
Hamilton Sound, strt., Newf., Can.	D4	72
Hamilton Square, N.J., U.S.	C3	107
Hamiota, Man., Can.	D1	70
Hamlet, In., U.S.	B4	91
Hamlet, N.C., U.S.	C3	110
Hamlet, Mount, mtn., Ak., U.S.	B6	79
Hamlin, Pa., U.S.	D11	115
Hamlin, Tx., U.S.	C2	120
Hamlin, W.V., U.S.	C2	125
Hamlin, co., S.D., U.S.	C8	118
Hamlin Lake, l., Mi., U.S.	D4	99
Hamm, Ger.	D7	8
Hammamet, Tun.	M5	14
Hammam Lif, Tun.	M5	14
Hammerdal, Swe.	E10	6
Hammon, Ok., U.S.	B2	113
Hammonasset, stm., Ct., U.S.	D5	84
Hammonasset Point, c., Ct., U.S.	E5	84
Hammond, In., U.S.	A2	91
Hammond, La., U.S.	D5	95
Hammond, Wi., U.S.	D1	126
Hammond Bay, b., Mi., U.S.	C6	99
Hammonton, N.J., U.S.	D3	107
Hampden, Newf., Can.	D3	72
Hampden, Me., U.S.	D4	96
Hampden, co., Ma., U.S.	B2	98
Hampden Highlands, Me., U.S.	D4	96
Hampshire, Il., U.S.	A5	90
Hampshire, co., Ma., U.S.	B2	98
Hampshire, co., W.V., U.S.	B6	125
Hampstead, Md., U.S.	A4	97
Hampstead, N.C., U.S.	C5	110
Hampton, N.B., Can.	D4	71
Hampton, Ar., U.S.	D3	81
Hampton, Ga., U.S.	C2	87
Hampton, Ia., U.S.	B4	92
Hampton, N.H., U.S.	E5	106
Hampton, S.C., U.S.	F5	117
Hampton, Tn., U.S.	C11	119
Hampton, Va., U.S.	C6	123
Hampton, co., S.C., U.S.	F5	117
Hampton Bays, N.Y., U.S.	n16	109
Hampton Beach, N.H., U.S.	E5	106
Hampton Butte, mtn., Or., U.S.	D6	114
Hampton Roads, Va., U.S.	k15	123
Hampton Roads Bridge-Tunnel, Va., U.S.	k15	123
Hams Fork, stm., Wy., U.S.	E2	127
Hamtramck, Mi., U.S.	p15	99
Hana, Hi., U.S.	C6	88
Hanahan, S.C., U.S.	F7	117
Hanalei Bay, b., Hi., U.S.	A2	88
Hanamaki, Japan	C14	30
Hanamanulu, Hi., U.S.	B2	88
Hanapepe, Hi., U.S.	B2	88
Hanau, Ger.	E8	8
Hanceville, Al., U.S.	A3	78
Hancock, Md., U.S.	A1	97
Hancock, Mi., U.S.	A2	99
Hancock, Mn., U.S.	E3	100
Hancock, co., Ga., U.S.	C3	87
Hancock, co., Il., U.S.	C2	90
Hancock, co., Ia., U.S.	A4	92
Hancock, co., Ky., U.S.	C3	94
Hancock, co., Me., U.S.	D4	96
Hancock, co., Ms., U.S.	E4	101
Hancock, co., Oh., U.S.	A2	112
Hancock, co., Tn., U.S.	C10	119
Hancock, co., W.V., U.S.	A4	125
Hand, co., S.D., U.S.	C6	118
Handa, Japan	H9	30
Handan, China	D9	26
Hando, Som.	F5	46
HaNegev, reg., Isr.	D4	40
Hangchow see Hangzhou, China	E9	28
Hangman Creek, stm., Wa., U.S.	B8	124
Hangö (Hanko), Fin.	G14	6
Hangzhou (Hangchow), China	E9	28
Hangzhou Wan, b., China	E9	28
Hanīsh, Jazā'ir, is., Yemen	F3	46
Hanjiang, China	J8	29
Hankinson, N.D., U.S.	C9	111
Hanna, Alta., Can.	D5	68
Hanna, Wy., U.S.	E6	127
Hanna City, Il., U.S.	C4	90
Hannahville Indian Reservation, Mi., U.S.	C3	99
Hannibal, Mo., U.S.	B6	102
Hannover, Ger.	C9	8
Hanover, Ont., Can.	C3	73
Hanover, Il., U.S.	A3	90
Hanover, In., U.S.	G7	91
Hanover, Ks., U.S.	C7	93
Hanover, Ma., U.S.	B6	98
Hanover, N.H., U.S.	C2	106
Hanover, Pa., U.S.	G8	115
Hanover, co., Va., U.S.	C5	123
Hanover Park, Il., U.S.	k8	90
Hansen, Id., U.S.	G4	89
Hansford, co., Tx., U.S.	A2	120
Hanson, Ma., U.S.	B6	98
Hanson, co., S.D., U.S.	D8	118
Hantsport, N.S., Can.	D5	71
Hanzhong, China	E8	26
Haparanda, Swe.	D15	6
Hapeville, Ga., U.S.	C2	87
Happy Valley, N.M., U.S.	E5	108
Happy Valley-Goose Bay, Newf., Can.	B1	72
Harahan, La., U.S.	k11	95
Haralson, co., Ga., U.S.	C1	87
Harare, Zimb.	E6	44
Harash, Bi'r al-, well, Libya	C10	42
Harbeson, De., U.S.	F4	85
Harbin, China	B12	26
Harbor, Or., U.S.	E2	114
Harbor Beach, Mi., U.S.	E8	99
Harborcreek, Pa., U.S.	B2	115
Harbor Springs, Mi., U.S.	C6	99
Harbour Breton, Newf., Can.	E4	72
Harbour Grace, Newf., Can.	E5	72
Harcuvar Mountains, mts., Az., U.S.	D2	80
Harda, India	I7	38
Hardangerfjorden, Nor.	F5	6
Hardee, co., Fl., U.S.	E5	86
Hardeeville, S.C., U.S.	G5	117
Hardeman, co., Tn., U.S.	B2	119
Hardeman, co., Tx., U.S.	B3	120
Hardin, Il., U.S.	D3	90
Hardin, Mt., U.S.	E9	103
Hardin, co., Il., U.S.	F5	90
Hardin, co., Ia., U.S.	B4	92
Hardin, co., Ky., U.S.	C4	94
Hardin, co., Oh., U.S.	B2	112
Hardin, co., Tn., U.S.	B3	119
Hardin, co., Tx., U.S.	D5	120
Harding, co., N.M., U.S.	B5	108
Harding, co., S.D., U.S.	B2	118
Harding, Lake, res., U.S.	C4	78
Hardinsburg, Ky., U.S.	C3	94
Hardisty, Alta., Can.	C5	68
Hardwār, India	F8	38
Hardwick, Ga., U.S.	C3	87
Hardwick, Vt., U.S.	B4	122
Hardwood Ridge, mtn., Pa., U.S.	D11	115
Hardy, co., W.V., U.S.	B6	125
Hardy Lake, res., In., U.S.	G6	91
Hare Bay, Newf., Can.	D4	72
Hare Bay, b., Newf., Can.	C4	72
Harer, Eth.	G3	46
Harford, co., Md., U.S.	A5	97
Hargeysa, Som.	G3	46
Harihar, India	E3	37
Harīrūd (Tedžen), stm., Asia	J10	22
Harkers Island, N.C., U.S.	C6	110
Harlan, Ia., U.S.	C2	92
Harlan, Ky., U.S.	D6	94
Harlan, co., Ky., U.S.	D6	94
Harlan, co., Ne., U.S.	D6	104
Harlan County Lake, res., Ne., U.S.	E6	104
Harlem, Fl., U.S.	F6	86
Harlem, Ga., U.S.	C4	87
Harlem, Mt., U.S.	B8	103
Harleysville, Pa., U.S.	F11	115
Harlingen, Neth.	B5	8
Harlingen, Tx., U.S.	F4	120
Harlow, Eng., U.K.	J13	7
Harlowton, Mt., U.S.	D7	103
Harmon, co., Ok., U.S.	C2	113
Harmon Creek, stm., W.V., U.S.	f8	125
Harmony, In., U.S.	E3	91
Harmony, Mn., U.S.	G6	100
Harmony, Pa., U.S.	E1	115
Harmony, R.I., U.S.	B3	116
Harnett, co., N.C., U.S.	B4	110
Harney, co., Or., U.S.	D7	114
Harney Lake, l., Or., U.S.	D7	114
Harney Peak, mtn., S.D., U.S.	D2	118
Härnösand, Swe.	E11	6
Haro, Spain	C9	12
Haro Strait, strt., Wa., U.S.	A2	124
Harper, Lib.	H4	42
Harper, Ks., U.S.	E5	93
Harper, co., Ks., U.S.	E5	93
Harper, co., Ok., U.S.	A2	113
Harper, Mount, mtn., Ak., U.S.	C11	79
Harpers Ferry, W.V., U.S.	B7	125
Harpers Ferry National Historical Park, W.V., U.S.	B7	125
Harpersville, Al., U.S.	B3	78
Harpeth, stm., Tn., U.S.	A5	119
Harquahala Mountain, mtn., Az., U.S.	D2	80
Harquahala Mountains, mts., Az., U.S.	D2	80
Harrah, Ok., U.S.	B4	113
Harricana, stm., Can.	F17	66
Harriman, Tn., U.S.	D9	119
Harriman Reservoir, res., Vt., U.S.	F3	122
Harrington, De., U.S.	E3	85
Harrington Park, N.J., U.S.	h9	107
Harris, Mn., U.S.	E6	100
Harris, R.I., U.S.	D3	116
Harris, co., Ga., U.S.	D2	87
Harris, co., Tx., U.S.	E5	120
Harris, Lake, l., Fl., U.S.	D5	86
Harrisburg, Ar., U.S.	B5	81
Harrisburg, Il., U.S.	F5	90
Harrisburg, Or., U.S.	C3	114
Harrisburg, Pa., U.S.	F8	115
Harrisburg, S.D., U.S.	D9	118
Harrison, Ar., U.S.	A2	81
Harrison, Mi., U.S.	D6	99
Harrison, N.J., U.S.	k8	107
Harrison, N.Y., U.S.	h13	109
Harrison, Oh., U.S.	C1	112
Harrison, Tn., U.S.	h11	119
Harrison, co., In., U.S.	H5	91
Harrison, co., Ia., U.S.	C2	92
Harrison, co., Ky., U.S.	B5	94
Harrison, co., Ms., U.S.	E4	101
Harrison, co., Mo., U.S.	A3	102
Harrison, co., Oh., U.S.	B4	112
Harrison, co., Tx., U.S.	C5	120
Harrison, co., W.V., U.S.	B4	125
Harrison Bay, b., Ak., U.S.	A9	79
Harrisonburg, Va., U.S.	B4	123
Harrison Hot Springs, B.C., Can.	f14	69
Harrisonville, L., B.C., Can.	E7	69
Harrisonville, Mo., U.S.	C3	102
Harriston, Ont., Can.	D4	73
Harristown, Il., U.S.	D4	90
Harrisville, R.I., U.S.	B2	116
Harrisville, Ut., U.S.	B4	121
Harrisville, W.V., U.S.	B3	125
Harrodsburg, Ky., U.S.	C5	94
Harrogate, Eng., U.K.	G11	7
Harrow, Ont., Can.	E2	73
Harry S. Truman Reservoir, res., Mo., U.S.	C4	102
Harry Strunk Lake, res., Ne., U.S.	D5	104
Harstad, Nor.	B11	6
Hart, Mi., U.S.	E4	99
Hart, Tx., U.S.	B1	120
Hart, co., Ga., U.S.	B4	87
Hart, co., Ky., U.S.	C4	94
Hart, Lake, l., Fl., U.S.	D5	86
Hartford, Al., U.S.	D4	78
Hartford, Ar., U.S.	B1	81
Hartford, Ct., U.S.	B5	84
Hartford, Il., U.S.	E3	90
Hartford, Ia., U.S.	C4	92
Hartford, Ky., U.S.	C3	94
Hartford, Mi., U.S.	F4	99
Hartford, S.D., U.S.	D9	118
Hartford, Vt., U.S.	D4	122
Hartford, Wi., U.S.	E5	126
Hartford, co., Ct., U.S.	B4	84
Hartford City, In., U.S.	D7	91
Hartington, Ne., U.S.	B8	104
Hart Lake, l., Or., U.S.	E7	114
Hartland, N.B., Can.	C2	71
Hartland, Me., U.S.	D3	96
Hartland Point, c., Eng., U.K.	J8	7
Hartlepool, Eng., U.K.	G11	7
Hartley, Ia., U.S.	A2	92
Hartley, co., Tx., U.S.	B1	120
Hartney, Man., Can.	E1	70
Hartselle, Al., U.S.	A3	78
Hartshorne, Ok., U.S.	C6	113
Hartsville, S.C., U.S.	C7	117
Hartsville, Tn., U.S.	A5	119
Hartville, Oh., U.S.	B4	112
Hartwell, Ga., U.S.	B4	87
Hartwell Lake, res., U.S.	B1	117
Hārūnābād, Pak.	F5	38
Hārūt, stm., Afg.	C1	36
Harvard, Il., U.S.	A5	90
Harvard, Ne., U.S.	D7	104
Harvard, Mount, mtn., Co., U.S.	C4	83
Harvey, Il., U.S.	B6	90
Harvey, La., U.S.	E5	95
Harvey, Mi., U.S.	B3	99
Harvey, N.D., U.S.	B6	111
Harvey, co., Ks., U.S.	D6	93
Harvey Lake, res., Me., U.S.	m16	115
Harveys Creek, stm., Pa., U.S.	n16	115
Harwich, Eng., U.K.	J14	7
Harwich Port, Ma., U.S.	C7	98
Harwinton, Ct., U.S.	B3	84
Haryana, state, India	F7	38
Harz, mts., Ger.	D10	8
Hasbrouck Heights, N.J., U.S.	h8	107
Haskell, Ar., U.S.	C3	81
Haskell, Ok., U.S.	B6	113
Haskell, Tx., U.S.	C3	120
Haskell, co., Ks., U.S.	E3	93
Haskell, co., Ok., U.S.	B6	113
Haskell, co., Tx., U.S.	C3	120
Haskovo, Bul.	H9	16
Hassan, India	F4	37
Hassayampa, stm., Az., U.S.	D3	80
Hasselt, Bel.	E5	8
Hassfurt, Ger.	E10	8
Hässleholm, Swe.	H9	6
Hastings, Ont., Can.	C7	73
Hastings, N.Z.	C6	52
Hastings, Eng., U.K.	K13	7
Hastings, Mi., U.S.	F5	99
Hastings, Mn., U.S.	F6	100
Hastings, Ne., U.S.	D7	104
Hastings, Pa., U.S.	E4	115
Hastings-on-Hudson, N.Y., U.S.	h13	109
Hatch, N.M., U.S.	E2	108
Hatchet Lake, l., Sask., Can.	E6	71
Hatchie, stm., Tn., U.S.	B2	119
Hatchineha, Lake, l., Fl., U.S.	D5	86

Name	Map Ref	Page
Hat Creek, stm., S.D., U.S.	E2	118
Hatfield, In., U.S.	I3	91
Hatfield, Pa., U.S.	F11	115
Hathras, India	G8	38
Ha Tinh, Viet.	E8	34
Hat Mountain, mtn., Az., U.S.	E3	80
Hatteras, N.C., U.S.	B7	110
Hatteras, Cape, c., N.C., U.S.	B7	110
Hatteras Inlet, b., N.C., U.S.	B7	110
Hattiesburg, Ms., U.S.	D4	101
Hatton, N.D., U.S.	B8	111
Hat Yai, Thai.	K6	34
Haubstadt, In., U.S.	H2	91
Haugesund, Nor.	G5	6
Haughton, La., U.S.	B2	95
Haukivuori, Fin.	E16	6
Hauser, Or., U.S.	D2	114
Haut, Isle au, i., Me., U.S.	D4	96
Haut Atlas, mts., Mor.	B4	42
Hauula, Hi., U.S.	B4	88
Havana, Cuba	B2	86
Havana, Il., U.S.	C3	90
Havana see La Habana, Cuba	C6	64
Havant, Eng., U.K.	K12	7
Havasu, Lake, res., U.S.	C1	80
Havasupai Indian Reservation, Az., U.S.	A3	80
Havelberg, Ger.	C12	8
Havelock, Ont., Can.	C7	73
Havelock, N.C., U.S.	C6	110
Haven, Ks., U.S.	E6	93
Haverford [Township], Pa., U.S.	o20	115
Haverhill, Ma., U.S.	A5	98
Hāveri, India	E3	37
Haverstraw, N.Y., U.S.	D7	109
Haviland, Ks., U.S.	E4	93
Havirov, Czech.	F18	8
Havre, Mt., U.S.	B7	103
Havre de Grace, Md., U.S.	A5	97
Havre North, Mt., U.S.	B7	103
Haw, stm., N.C., U.S.	B3	110
Hawaii, co., Hi., U.S.	D6	88
Hawaii, state, U.S.	C5	88
Hawaii, i., Hi., U.S.	D6	88
Hawaiian Islands, is., Hi., U.S.	m14	88
Hawaii Volcanoes National Park, Hi., U.S.	D6	88
Hawarden, Ia., U.S.	A1	92
Hawesville, Ky., U.S.	C3	94
Hawi, Hi., U.S.	C6	88
Hawick, Scot., U.K.	F10	7
Hawke Bay, b., N.Z.	C6	52
Hawkesbury, Ont., Can.	B10	73
Hawkesbury Island, i., B.C., Can.	C3	69
Hawkins, co., Tn., U.S.	C11	119
Hawkinsville, Ga., U.S.	D3	87
Hawley, Mn., U.S.	D2	100
Hawley, Pa., U.S.	D11	115
Haworth, N.J., U.S.	h9	107
Haw River, N.C., U.S.	A3	110
Hawthorne, Ca., U.S.	n12	82
Hawthorne, Fl., U.S.	C4	86
Hawthorne, Nv., U.S.	E3	105
Hawthorne, N.J., U.S.	B4	107
Hawthorne, N.Y., U.S.	g13	109
Haxtun, Co., U.S.	A8	83
Hay, Austl.	F8	50
Hay, stm., Austl.	D7	50
Hay, stm., Can.	E9	66
Hay, Cape, c., N.W. Ter., Can.	B10	66
Hayange, Fr.	C13	10
Hayden, Az., U.S.	E5	80
Hayden, Co., U.S.	A3	83
Hayden Lake, l., Id., U.S.	B2	89
Hayes, co., Ne., U.S.	D3	95
Hayes, stm., Man., Can.	D4	104
Hayes, Mount, mtn., Ak., U.S.	B5	70
Hayfield, Mn., U.S.	C10	79
Hayford Peak, mtn., Nv., U.S.	G6	100
Haymock Lake, l., Me., U.S.	G6	105
Haynesville, La., U.S.	B3	96
Hayneville, Al., U.S.	B2	95
Hayrabolu, Tur.	C3	78
Hay River, N.W. Ter., Can.	H11	16
Hays, Ks., U.S.	D9	66
Hays, N.C., U.S.	D4	93
Hays, co., Tx., U.S.	A1	110
Hays Canyon Peak, mtn., Nv., U.S.	D3	120
Hay Springs, Ne., U.S.	B2	105
Haystack Mountain, mtn., Nv., U.S.	B3	104
Haysville, Ks., U.S.	B6	105
Hayti, Mo., U.S.	g12	93
Hayti Heights, Mo., U.S.	E8	102
Hayward, Ca., U.S.	E8	102
Hayward, Wi., U.S.	h8	82
Haywood, co., N.C., U.S.	B2	126
Haywood, co., Tn., U.S.	f9	110
Hazard, Ky., U.S.	B2	119
Hazardville, Ct., U.S.	C6	94
Hazārībāgh, India	B5	84
Hazel Crest, Il., U.S.	I11	38
Hazel Dell, Wa., U.S.	k9	90
Hazel Green, Al., U.S.	D3	124
Hazel Green, Wi., U.S.	A3	78
Hazel Park, Mi., U.S.	F3	126
Hazelton, N.D., U.S.	p15	99
Hazelton, Pa., U.S.	f10	110
Hazen, Ar., U.S.	B6	92
Hazen, N.D., U.S.	C4	81
Hazen Bay, b., Ak., U.S.	B4	111
Hazlehurst, Ga., U.S.	C6	79
Hazlehurst, Ms., U.S.	E4	87
Hazlet, N.J., U.S.	D3	101
Hazleton, Ia., U.S.	C4	107
Hazleton, Pa., U.S.	B6	92
Head Harbor Island, i., Me., U.S.	E9	115
Headland, Al., U.S.	D5	96
Headley, Mount, mtn., Mt., U.S.	C1	78
Healdsburg, Ca., U.S.	C1	103
Healdton, Ok., U.S.	C2	82
Healy, co., Ga., U.S.	C10	113
Heard, co., Ga., U.S.	C1	87
Hearne, Tx., U.S.	D4	120
Hearst, Ont., Can.	o19	73
Heart, stm., N.D., U.S.	C3	111
Heart Butte Dam, N.D., U.S.	C4	111
Heart Lake, l., Wy., U.S.	B2	127
Heart's Content, Newf., Can.	E5	72
Heath, Oh., U.S.	B3	112
Heath Springs, S.C., U.S.	B6	117
Heavener, Ok., U.S.	C7	113
Hebbronville, Tx., U.S.	F3	120
Hebei, prov., China	D10	26
Heber, Az., U.S.	C5	80
Heber City, Ut., U.S.	C4	121
Heber Springs, Ar., U.S.	B3	81
Hébertville, Que., Can.	A6	74
Hebgen Lake, res., Mt., U.S.	F5	103
Hebrides, is., Scot., U.K.	D6	4
Hebron, N.S., Can.	F3	71
Hebron, Il., U.S.	A5	90
Hebron, In., U.S.	B3	91
Hebron, Ky., U.S.	h13	94
Hebron, Md., U.S.	D6	97
Hebron, Ne., U.S.	D8	104
Hebron, N.D., U.S.	C3	111
Hebron, Oh., U.S.	C3	112
Hebron see Al-Khalīl, Jord.	D4	40
Hecate Strait, strt., B.C., Can.	C2	69
Hechi, China	B9	34
Hechingen, Ger.	G8	8
Hechuan, China	E8	26
Hecla Island, i., Man., Can.	D3	70
Hector, Mn., U.S.	F4	100
Hedemora, Swe.	F10	6
He Devil, mtn., Id., U.S.	D2	89
Hedrick, Ia., U.S.	C5	92
Heerenveen, Neth.	C5	8
Heerlen, Neth.	E5	8
Hefa (Haifa), Isr.	C4	40
Hefei, China	D6	28
Heflin, Al., U.S.	B4	78
Hefner, Lake, res., Ok., U.S.	B4	113
Hegang, China	B13	26
Hegins, Pa., U.S.	E9	115
Heide, Ger.	A9	8
Heidelberg, Ger.	F8	8
Heidelberg, Ms., U.S.	D5	101
Heidenheim, Ger.	F10	8
Heidenreichstein, Aus.	G15	8
Heidrick, Ky., U.S.	D6	94
Heihe (Naqung), China	E14	38
Heilbron, S. Afr.	G5	44
Heilbronn, Ger.	F9	8
Heiligenstadt, Ger.	D10	8
Heilongjiang, prov., China	B12	26
Heilongjiang (Amur), stm., Asia	G19	24
Heinola, Fin.	F16	6
Hejaz see Al-Hijāz, reg., Sau. Ar.	C2	46
Hekla, vol., Ice.	C4	4
Hekou, China	C7	34
Helena, Al., U.S.	B3	78
Helena, Ar., U.S.	C5	81
Helena, Ga., U.S.	D4	87
Helena, Mt., U.S.	D4	103
Helena, Ok., U.S.	A3	113
Helensburgh, Scot., U.K.	E8	7
Helgoland, i., Ger.	A7	8
Helgoländer Bucht, b., Ger.	A8	8
Hellam, Pa., U.S.	G8	115
Hellertown, Pa., U.S.	E11	115
Hellesylt, Nor.	E6	6
Hellín, Spain	G10	12
Hells Canyon, val., U.S.	B10	114
Hells Canyon National Recreation Area, U.S.	B10	114
Hell-Ville, Madag.	D9	44
Helmand, stm., Asia	C2	36
Helmond, Neth.	D5	8
Helmsdale, Scot., U.K.	C9	7
Helmstedt, Ger.	C10	8
Helotes, Tx., U.S.	h7	120
Helper, Ut., U.S.	D5	121
Helsingborg, Swe.	H9	6
Helsingfors see Helsinki, Fin.	F15	6
Helsingør (Elsinore), Den.	H9	6
Helsinki (Helsingfors), Fin.	F15	6
Hematite, Mo., U.S.	C7	102
Hemet, Ca., U.S.	F5	82
Hemingford, Ne., U.S.	B2	104
Hemingway, S.C., U.S.	D9	117
Hemlock, Mi., U.S.	E6	99
Hemlock Reservoir, res., Ct., U.S.	E2	84
Hemmingford, Que., Can.	D4	74
Hemphill, Tx., U.S.	D6	120
Hemphill, co., Tx., U.S.	B2	120
Hempstead, N.Y., U.S.	n15	109
Hempstead, Tx., U.S.	D4	120
Hempstead, co., Ar., U.S.	D2	81
Hemse, Swe.	H12	6
Henagar, Al., U.S.	A4	78
Henan, prov., China	E9	26
Henderson, Ky., U.S.	C2	94
Henderson, La., U.S.	D4	95
Henderson, Mn., U.S.	F5	100
Henderson, Ne., U.S.	D8	104
Henderson, Nv., U.S.	G7	105
Henderson, N.C., U.S.	A4	110
Henderson, Tn., U.S.	B3	119
Henderson, Tx., U.S.	C5	120
Henderson, co., Il., U.S.	C3	90
Henderson, co., Ky., U.S.	C2	94
Henderson, co., N.C., U.S.	f10	110
Henderson, co., Tn., U.S.	B3	119
Henderson, co., Tx., U.S.	C5	120
Henderson's Point, Ms., U.S.	g7	101
Hendersonville, N.C., U.S.	f10	110
Hendersonville, Tn., U.S.	A5	119
Hendricks, Mn., U.S.	F2	100
Hendricks, co., In., U.S.	E4	91
Hendry, co., Fl., U.S.	F5	86
Hengelo, Neth.	C6	8
Hengshan, China	H1	28
Hengyang, China	F9	26
Henlawson, W.V., U.S.	n12	125
Henlopen, Cape, c., De., U.S.	E5	85
Hennef, Ger.	E7	8
Hennepin, co., Mn., U.S.	E5	100
Hennessey, Ok., U.S.	A4	113
Henniker, N.H., U.S.	D3	106
Henning, Mn., U.S.	D3	100
Henning, Tn., U.S.	B2	119
Henrico, co., Va., U.S.	C5	123
Henrietta, N.C., U.S.	B1	110
Henrietta, Tx., U.S.	C3	120
Henrietta Maria, Cape, c., Ont., Can.	n19	73
Henry, Il., U.S.	B4	90
Henry, co., Al., U.S.	D4	78
Henry, co., Ga., U.S.	C2	87
Henry, co., Il., U.S.	B3	90
Henry, co., In., U.S.	E7	91
Henry, co., Ia., U.S.	C6	92
Henry, co., Ky., U.S.	B4	94
Henry, co., Mo., U.S.	C4	102
Henry, co., Oh., U.S.	A1	119
Henry, co., Tn., U.S.	A3	119
Henry, co., Va., U.S.	D3	123
Henry, Mount, mtn., Mt., U.S.	B1	103
Henryetta, Ok., U.S.	B6	113
Henry Kater, Cape, c., N.W. Ter., Can.	C19	66
Henrys Fork, stm., U.S.	E2	127
Henryville, Que., Can.	D4	74
Henryville, In., U.S.	G6	91
Hensall, Ont., Can.	D3	73
Henzada, Burma	F3	34
Hephzibah, Ga., U.S.	C4	87
Heppner, Or., U.S.	B7	114
Hepu (Lianzhou), China	D10	34
Herät, Afg.	C1	36
Herbes, Isle aux, i., Al., U.S.	E1	78
Herbignac, Fr.	E4	10
Herculaneum, Mo., U.S.	C7	102
Hereford, Eng., U.K.	I10	7
Hereford, Md., U.S.	A4	97
Hereford, Tx., U.S.	B1	120
Hereford Inlet, b., N.J., U.S.	E3	107
Herford, Ger.	C8	8
Herington, Ks., U.S.	D7	93
Herkimer, N.Y., U.S.	B6	109
Herkimer, co., N.Y., U.S.	B5	109
Hermann, Mo., U.S.	C6	102
Hermantown, Mn., U.S.	D6	100
Hermanus, S. Afr.	H3	44
Herminie, Pa., U.S.	F2	115
Hermiston, Or., U.S.	B7	114
Hermitage, Newf., Can.	E4	72
Hermitage, Ar., U.S.	D3	81
Hermitage Bay, b., Newf., Can.	E3	72
Hermosillo, Mex.	C4	62
Hernando, Fl., U.S.	D4	86
Hernando, Ms., U.S.	A4	101
Hernando, co., Fl., U.S.	D4	86
Herndon, Va., U.S.	B5	123
Herne, Ger.	D7	8
Heron Lake, Mn., U.S.	G3	100
Herrera del Duque, Spain	F6	12
Herrera de Pisuerga, Spain	C7	12
Herrin, Il., U.S.	F4	90
Herring Bay, b., Md., U.S.	C4	97
Herring Cove, N.S., Can.	E6	71
Herrington Lake, res., Ky., U.S.	C5	94
Herscher, Il., U.S.	B5	90
Hershey, Pa., U.S.	F8	115
Hertford, N.C., U.S.	A6	110
Hertford, co., N.C., U.S.	A5	110
Hervás, Spain	E6	12
Hesdin, Fr.	B9	10
Hesperia, Ca., U.S.	E5	82
Hesperia, Mi., U.S.	E4	99
Hesperus Mountain, mtn., Co., U.S.	D2	83
Hesston, Ks., U.S.	D6	93
Hetian, China	B8	38
Hettinger, N.D., U.S.	D3	111
Hettinger, co., N.D., U.S.	C3	111
Heyburn, Id., U.S.	G5	89
Heyworth, Il., U.S.	C5	90
Hialeah, Fl., U.S.	G6	86
Hiawatha, Ia., U.S.	B6	92
Hiawatha, Ks., U.S.	C8	93
Hibbing, Mn., U.S.	C6	100
Hickam Air Force Base, mil., Hi., U.S.	g10	88
Hickman, Ky., U.S.	f8	94
Hickman, Ne., U.S.	D9	104
Hickman, co., Ky., U.S.	f8	94
Hickman, co., Tn., U.S.	B4	119
Hickory, N.C., U.S.	B1	110
Hickory, co., Mo., U.S.	D4	102
Hicksville, N.Y., U.S.	E7	109
Hicksville, Oh., U.S.	A1	112
Hico, Tx., U.S.	D3	120
Hico, W.V., U.S.	C3	125
Hidaka-sammyaku, mts., Japan	q20	30a
Hidalgo, Mex.	E10	62
Hidalgo, Tx., U.S.	F3	120
Hidalgo, co., N.M., U.S.	F1	108
Hidalgo, co., Tx., U.S.	F3	120
Hidalgo del Parral, Mex.	D7	62
Hieroglyphic Mountains, mts., Az., U.S.	k8	80
Hierro, i., Spain	C2	42
Higashiōsaka, Japan	H8	30
Higbee, Mo., U.S.	B5	102
Higganum, Ct., U.S.	D5	84
Higgins Lake, l., Mi., U.S.	D6	99
Higgins Millpond, res., Md., U.S.	C6	97
Higginsville, Mo., U.S.	B4	102
High Bridge, N.J., U.S.	B3	107
High Falls Reservoir, res., Wi., U.S.	C5	126
High Island, i., Mi., U.S.	C5	99
Highland, Il., U.S.	E4	90
Highland, In., U.S.	A3	91
Highland, Ks., U.S.	C8	93
Highland, Mi., U.S.	o14	99
Highland, N.Y., U.S.	D7	109
Highland, Wi., U.S.	E3	126
Highland, co., Oh., U.S.	C2	112
Highland, co., Va., U.S.	B3	123
Highland Lake, l., Me., U.S.	g7	96
Highland Lakes, N.J., U.S.	A4	107
Highland Park, Il., U.S.	A6	90
Highland Park, Mi., U.S.	p15	99
Highland Park, Tx., U.S.	n10	120
Highland Peak, mtn., Ca., U.S.	C4	82
Highland Point, c., Fl., U.S.	G5	86
Highlands, N.J., U.S.	C5	107
Highlands, N.C., U.S.	f9	110
Highlands, Tx., U.S.	r14	120
Highlands, co., Fl., U.S.	E5	86
Highland Springs, Va., U.S.	C5	123
High Level, Alta., Can.	F7	68
Highmore, S.D., U.S.	C6	118
High Point, N.C., U.S.	B2	110
High Prairie, Alta., Can.	B2	68
High Ridge, Mo., U.S.	g12	102
High River, Alta., Can.	D4	68
Highrock Lake, l., Man., Can.	B1	70
High Rock Lake, res., N.C., U.S.	B2	110
High Spire, Pa., U.S.	F8	115
High Springs, Fl., U.S.	C4	86
Hightstown, N.J., U.S.	C3	107
Highwood, Il., U.S.	A6	90
Highwood Baldy, mtn., Mt., U.S.	C6	103
Highwood Mountains, mts., Mt., U.S.	C6	103
Higuerote, Ven.	B9	58
Higüey, Dom. Rep.	E13	64
Híjar, Spain	D11	12
Hikari, Japan	I4	30
Hikone, Japan	G9	30
Hiko Range, mts., Nv., U.S.	F6	105
Hilbert, Wi., U.S.	D5	126
Hildale, Ut., U.S.	F3	121
Hilden, N.S., Can.	D6	71
Hildesheim, Ger.	C9	8
Hill, co., Mt., U.S.	B6	103
Hill, co., Tx., U.S.	D4	120
Hill City, Ks., U.S.	C4	93
Hill City, S.D., U.S.	D2	118
Hillcrest, Il., U.S.	B4	90
Hillcrest Heights, Md., U.S.	C4	97
Hilliard, Fl., U.S.	B5	86
Hilliard, Oh., U.S.	k10	112
Hill Island Lake, l., N.W. Ter., Can.	D11	66
Hills, Ia., U.S.	C6	92
Hills, Mn., U.S.	G2	100
Hillsboro, Il., U.S.	D4	90
Hillsboro, Ks., U.S.	D6	93
Hillsboro, Mo., U.S.	C7	102
Hillsboro, N.H., U.S.	D3	106
Hillsboro, N.D., U.S.	B8	111
Hillsboro, Oh., U.S.	C2	112
Hillsboro, Or., U.S.	B4	114
Hillsboro, Tx., U.S.	C4	120
Hillsboro, Wi., U.S.	E3	126
Hillsboro Canal, Fl., U.S.	F6	86
Hillsborough, N.B., Can.	D5	71
Hillsborough, N.C., U.S.	A3	110
Hillsborough, co., Fl., U.S.	E4	86
Hillsborough, co., N.H., U.S.	E3	106
Hillsborough Bay, b., P.E.I., Can.	C6	71
Hillsburgh, Ont., Can.	D4	73
Hills Creek Lake, res., Or., U.S.	D4	114
Hillsdale, Mi., U.S.	G6	99
Hillsdale, N.J., U.S.	g8	107
Hillsdale, co., Mi., U.S.	G6	99
Hillside, N.J., U.S.	k8	107
Hillsville, Pa., U.S.	D1	115
Hillsville, Va., U.S.	D2	123
Hilo, Hi., U.S.	D6	88
Hilo Bay, b., Hi., U.S.	D6	88
Hilton, N.Y., U.S.	B3	109
Hilton Head Island, S.C., U.S.	G6	117
Hilton Head Island, i., S.C., U.S.	G6	117
Hilversum, Neth.	C5	8
Himachal Pradesh, ter., India	E7	38
Himalayas, mts., Asia	F10	38
Himeji, Japan	H7	30
Himi, Japan	F9	30
Hims (Homs), Syria	B5	40
Hinchinbrook Island, i., Austl.	C9	50
Hinchinbrook Island, i., Ak., U.S.	g18	79
Hinckley, Il., U.S.	B5	90
Hinckley, Mn., U.S.	D6	100
Hinckley, Ut., U.S.	D3	121
Hinckley Reservoir, res., N.Y., U.S.	B5	109
Hindaun, India	G7	38
Hindman, Ky., U.S.	C7	94
Hinds, co., Ms., U.S.	C3	101
Hindu Kush, mts., Asia	B4	38
Hindupur, India	F4	37
Hines, Or., U.S.	D7	114
Hinesville, Ga., U.S.	E5	87
Hinganghät, India	B5	37
Hingham, Ma., U.S.	B6	98
Hingham Bay, b., Ma., U.S.	g12	98
Hingoli, India	C4	37
Hinojosa del Duque, Spain	G6	12
Hinsdale, Il., U.S.	k9	90
Hinsdale, N.H., U.S.	E2	106
Hinsdale, co., Co., U.S.	D3	83
Hinton, Alta., Can.	C2	68
Hinton, Ia., U.S.	B1	92
Hinton, Ok., U.S.	B3	113
Hinton, W.V., U.S.	D4	125
Hirado, Japan	I2	30
Hīrākud, res., India	J10	38
Hiram, Ga., U.S.	C2	87
Hiram, Oh., U.S.	A4	112
Hirara, Japan	G12	26
Hiratsuka, Japan	G12	30
Hirosaki, Japan	B13	30
Hiroshima, Japan	H5	30
Hirson, Fr.	C11	10
Hīsār, India	F6	38
Hispaniola, i., N.A.	E12	64
Hita, Japan	I3	30
Hitachi, Japan	F13	30
Hitchcock, Tx., U.S.	r14	120
Hitchcock, co., Ne., U.S.	D4	104
Hitchcock Lake, Ct., U.S.	C4	84
Hitoyoshi, Japan	J3	30
Hitra, i., Nor.	E7	6
Hiwassee, stm., Tn., U.S.	D9	119
Hiwassee Lake, res., N.C., U.S.	f8	110
Hjørring, Den.	G6	42
Ho, Ghana	G6	42
Hoa Binh, Viet.	D8	34
Hoagland, In., U.S.	C8	91
Hoback, stm., Wy., U.S.	C2	127
Hobart, Austl.	H9	50
Hobart, In., U.S.	A3	91
Hobart, Ok., U.S.	B2	113
Hobbs, N.M., U.S.	E6	108
Hobe Sound, Fl., U.S.	E6	86
Hoboken, N.J., U.S.	k8	107
Höchstadt an der Aisch, Ger.	F10	8
Hockessin, De., U.S.	A3	85
Hocking, co., Oh., U.S.	C3	112
Hocking, stm., Oh., U.S.	C3	112
Hockley, co., Tx., U.S.	C1	120
Hodgeman, co., Ks., U.S.	D4	93
Hodgenville, Ky., U.S.	C4	94
Hodges Village Reservoir, res., Ma., U.S.	B4	98
Hódmezővásárhely, Hung.	I20	8
Hodna, Chott el, l., Alg.	J16	12
Hodonín, Czech.	G17	8
Hof, Ger.	E11	8
Hoffman Estates, Il., U.S.	h8	90
Hofgeismar, Ger.	D9	8
Hofheim in Unterfranken, Ger.	E10	8
Hofors, Swe.	F11	6
Hōfu, Japan	H4	30
Hogansville, Ga., U.S.	C2	87
Hogback Mountain, mtn., Mt., U.S.	F4	103
Hog Island, i., Fl., U.S.	C3	86
Hog Island, i., Mi., U.S.	C5	99
Hog Island, i., N.C., U.S.	B6	110
Hog Island, i., R.I., U.S.	D5	116
Hog Island, i., Va., U.S.	C7	123
Hoh, stm., Wa., U.S.	B1	124
Hohenau an der March, Aus.	G16	8
Hohenwald, Tn., U.S.	B4	119
Hohe Tauern, mts., Aus.	H12	8
Hoh Head, c., Wa., U.S.	B1	124
Hohhot, China	C9	26
Hohoe, Ghana	G5	42
Hōhoku, Japan	H3	30
Ho-Ho-Kus, N.J., U.S.	h8	107
Hoh Xil Shan, mts., China	C13	38
Hoi An, Viet.	G10	34
Hoisington, Ks., U.S.	D5	93
Hokah, Mn., U.S.	G7	100
Hoke, co., N.C., U.S.	B3	110
Hokes Bluff, Al., U.S.	B4	78
Hokitika, N.Z.	E3	52
Hokkaidō, i., Japan	p20	30a
Holbrook, Az., U.S.	C5	80
Holbrook, Ma., U.S.	B5	98
Holcomb, Ks., U.S.	E3	93
Holden, Ma., U.S.	B4	98
Holden, Mo., U.S.	C4	102
Holden, W.V., U.S.	D2	125
Holdenville, Ok., U.S.	B5	113
Holdrege, Ne., U.S.	D6	104
Hole in the Mountain Peak, mtn., Nv., U.S.	C6	105
Holgate, Oh., U.S.	A1	112
Holguín, Cuba	D9	64
Höljes, Swe.	F9	6
Hollabrunn, Aus.	G16	8
Holladay, Ut., U.S.	C4	121
Holland, Mi., U.S.	H3	91
Holland, Mi., U.S.	F4	99
Holland, Oh., U.S.	A2	112
Holland, Tx., U.S.	D4	120
Hollandale, Ms., U.S.	B3	101
Holland Island, i., Md., U.S.	D5	97
Holland see Netherlands, ctry., Eur.	E9	4
Holland Point, c., Md., U.S.	C4	97
Holland Straits, strt., Md., U.S.	D5	97
Holley, N.Y., U.S.	B2	109
Holliday, Tx., U.S.	C3	120
Hollidaysburg, Pa., U.S.	F5	115
Hollins, Va., U.S.	C3	123
Hollis, Ok., U.S.	C2	113
Hollister, Ca., U.S.	D3	82
Hollister, Mo., U.S.	E4	102
Holliston, Ma., U.S.	B5	98
Holloman Air Force Base, mil., N.M., U.S.	E3	108
Hollow Rock, Tn., U.S.	A3	119
Hollowtop Mountain, mtn., Mt., U.S.	E4	103
Holly, Co., U.S.	C8	83
Holly, Mi., U.S.	F7	99
Holly Grove, Ar., U.S.	C4	81
Holly Hill, Fl., U.S.	C5	86
Holly Hill, S.C., U.S.	E7	117
Holly Pond, Al., U.S.	A3	78
Holly Ridge, N.C., U.S.	C5	110
Holly Shelter Swamp, sw., N.C., U.S.	C5	110
Holly Springs, Ga., U.S.	B2	87
Holly Springs, Ms., U.S.	A4	101
Holly Springs, N.C., U.S.	B4	110
Hollywood, Al., U.S.	A4	78
Hollywood, Fl., U.S.	F6	86
Hollywood, Md., U.S.	D4	97
Hollywood, S.C., U.S.	k11	117
Hollywood Indian Reservation, Fl., U.S.	r3	86
Holman Island, N.W. Ter., Can.	B9	66
Holmen, Wi., U.S.	E2	126
Holmes, co., Fl., U.S.	u16	86
Holmes, co., Ms., U.S.	B3	101
Holmes, co., Oh., U.S.	B4	112
Holmes, Mount, mtn., Wy., U.S.	B2	127
Holmes Reefs, rf., Austl.	C9	50
Holstebro, Den.	H7	6
Holstein, Ia., U.S.	B2	92
Holsteinsborg, Grnld.	C22	66
Holston, stm., Tn., U.S.	C11	119
Holston, Middle Fork, stm., Va., U.S.	f10	123
Holston High Knob, mtn., Tn., U.S.	C11	119
Holsworthy, Eng., U.K.	K8	7
Holt, Al., U.S.	B2	78
Holt, Mi., U.S.	F6	99
Holt, co., Mo., U.S.	A2	102
Holt, co., Ne., U.S.	B7	104
Holt Lake, res., Al., U.S.	B2	78
Holton, Ks., U.S.	C8	93
Holtville, Ca., U.S.	F6	82

Name	Map Ref	Page
Holualoa, Hi., U.S.	D6	88
Holy Cross, Mountain of the, mtn., Co., U.S.	B4	83
Holyhead, Wales, U.K.	H8	7
Holyoke, Co., U.S.	A8	83
Holyoke, Ma., U.S.	B2	98
Holyoke Range, hills, Ma., U.S.	B2	98
Holzminden, Ger.	D9	8
Hombori Tondo, mtn., Mali	E5	42
Homburg, Ger.	F7	8
Home Bay, b., N.W. Ter., Can.	C19	66
Homecroft, In., U.S.	m10	91
Homedale, Id., U.S.	F2	89
Home Hill, Austl.	C9	50
Homeland, Ga., U.S.	F4	87
Home Place, In., U.S.	E5	91
Homer, Ak., U.S.	D9	79
Homer, Ga., U.S.	B3	87
Homer, Il., U.S.	C6	90
Homer, La., U.S.	B2	95
Homer, Mi., U.S.	F6	99
Homer, N.Y., U.S.	C4	109
Homer City, Pa., U.S.	E3	115
Homerville, Ga., U.S.	E4	87
Homer Youngs Peak, mtn., Mt., U.S.	E3	103
Homestead, Fl., U.S.	G6	86
Homestead, Pa., U.S.	k14	115
Homestead Air Force Base, mil., Fl., U.S.	G6	86
Homestead National Monument of America, Ne., U.S.	D9	104
Homewood, Al., U.S.	g7	78
Homewood, Il., U.S.	B6	90
Homewood, Oh., U.S.	C1	112
Hominy, Ok., U.S.	A5	113
Hominy Creek, stm., Ok., U.S.	A5	113
Homme Dam, N.D., U.S.	A8	111
Homochitto, stm., Ms., U.S.	D2	101
Homosassa, Fl., U.S.	D4	86
Homs see Hims, Syria		
Honaker, Va., U.S.	e10	123
Honanunu, Hi., U.S.	D6	88
Honda, Col.	E5	58
Honda, Japan	J3	30
Hondo, Tx., U.S.	E3	120
Hondo, stm., N.A.	H15	62
Hondo, Rio, stm., N.M., U.S.	D4	108
Honduras, ctry., N.A.	G4	64
Honduras, Gulf of, b., N.A.	F4	64
Honea Path, S.C., U.S.	C3	117
Hønefoss, Nor.	F8	6
Honeoye Falls, N.Y., U.S.	C3	109
Honesdale, Pa., U.S.	C11	115
Honey Brook, Pa., U.S.	F10	115
Honey Grove, Tx., U.S.	C5	120
Honey Lake, l., Ca., U.S.	B3	82
Honeypot Glen, Ct., U.S.	C4	84
Honeyville, Ut., U.S.	B3	121
Hon Gai, Viet.	D9	34
Honga River, b., Md., U.S.	D5	97
Hongdong, China	D9	26
Honghu, China	F2	28
Hong Kong, dep., Asia	M3	28
Hongliuyuan, China	C6	26
Honguedo, Détroit d', strt., Que., Can.	G20	66
Hongze Hu, l., China	B7	28
Honiara, Sol.Is.	A11	50
Honjō, Japan	F12	30
Honningsvåg, Nor.	A15	6
Honokaa, Hi., U.S.	C6	88
Honolulu, Hi., U.S.	B4	88
Honolulu, co., Hi., U.S.	B3	88
Honolulu International Airport, Hi., U.S.	g10	88
Honomu, Hi., U.S.	D6	88
Honouliuli, Hi., U.S.	g9	88
Honshū, i., Japan	F10	30
Honuapo Bay, b., Hi., U.S.	D6	88
Hood, co., Tx., U.S.	C4	120
Hood, Mount, mtn., Or., U.S.	B5	114
Hood Canal, b., Wa., U.S.	B2	124
Hoodoo Peak, mtn., Wa., U.S.	A5	124
Hood River, Or., U.S.	B5	114
Hood River, co., Or., U.S.	B5	114
Hoodsport, Wa., U.S.	B2	124
Hoogeveen, Neth.	C5	8
Hooker, Ok., U.S.	e9	113
Hooker, co., Ne., U.S.	C4	104
Hook Head, c., Ire.	I6	7
Hooksett, N.H., U.S.	D4	106
Hoonah, Ak., U.S.	D12	79
Hoopa Valley Indian Reservation, Ca., U.S.	B2	82
Hooper, Ne., U.S.	C9	104
Hooper Bay, Ak., U.S.	C6	79
Hooper Islands, is., Md., U.S.	D5	97
Hooper Strait, strt., Md., U.S.	D5	97
Hoopes Reservoir, res., De., U.S.	A3	85
Hoopeston, Il., U.S.	C6	90
Hoorn, Neth.	C5	8
Hoosac Range, mts., U.S.	A1	98
Hoosic, stm., U.S.	C7	109
Hoosick Falls, N.Y., U.S.	C7	109
Hoover Dam, U.S.	G7	105
Hoover Reservoir, res., Oh., U.S.	B3	112
Hooverson Heights, W.V., U.S.	f8	125
Hopatcong, N.J., U.S.	B3	107
Hopatcong, Lake, l., N.J., U.S.	A3	107
Hope, B.C., Can.	E7	69
Hope, Ar., U.S.	D2	81
Hope, In., U.S.	F6	91
Hope, R.I., U.S.	D3	116
Hope, Ben, mtn., Scot., U.K.	C8	7
Hope, Point, c., Ak., U.S.	B6	79
Hopedale, Il., U.S.	C4	90
Hopedale, Ma., U.S.	B4	98
Hopedale, l., R.I., U.S.	B5	116
Hope Mills, N.C., U.S.	C4	110
Hopes Advance, Cap, c., Que., Can.	f13	74
Hopetown, S. Afr.	G4	44
Hope Valley, R.I., U.S.	E2	116
Hopewell, Va., U.S.	C5	123
Hopewell Junction, N.Y., U.S.	D7	109

Name	Map Ref	Page
Hopi Indian Reservation, Az., U.S.	A5	80
Hopkins, Mn., U.S.	n12	100
Hopkins, S.C., U.S.	D6	117
Hopkins, co., Ky., U.S.	C2	94
Hopkins, co., Tx., U.S.	C5	120
Hopkinsville, Ky., U.S.	D2	94
Hopkinton, Ia., U.S.	B6	92
Hopkinton, Ma., U.S.	B4	98
Hopkinton, R.I., U.S.	F1	116
Hopkinton Lake, res., N.H., U.S.	D3	106
Hopwood, Pa., U.S.	G2	115
Hoquiam, Wa., U.S.	C2	124
Horace, N.D., U.S.	C9	111
Horace Mountain, mtn., Ak., U.S.	B10	79
Horatio, Ar., U.S.	D1	81
Horgen, Switz.	E15	10
Horicon, Wi., U.S.	E5	126
Horine, Mo., U.S.	C7	102
Hormuz, Strait of, strt., Asia	C6	46
Horn, Aus.	G15	8
Horn, Cape see Hornos, Cabo de, c., Chile	H3	56
Hornell, N.Y., U.S.	C3	109
Hornersville, Mo., U.S.	E7	102
Horn Island, i., Ms., U.S.	E5	101
Horn Island Pass, strt., Ms., U.S.	g8	101
Horn Lake, Ms., U.S.	A3	101
Hornos, Cabo de (Cape Horn), c., Chile	H3	56
Horn Plateau, plat., N.W. Ter., Can.	D9	66
Horqin Youyi Qianqi, China	B11	26
Horry, co., S.C., U.S.	D10	117
Horse, stm., Ct., U.S.	C6	84
Horse Cave, Ky., U.S.	C4	94
Horse Creek, stm., U.S.	E8	127
Horse Creek Reservoir, res., Co., U.S.	C7	83
Horsehead Lake, l., N.D., U.S.	B6	111
Horseheads, N.Y., U.S.	C4	109
Horse Heaven Hills, hills, Wa., U.S.	C6	124
Horsens, Den.	I7	6
Horse Peak, mtn., N.M., U.S.	D1	108
Horseshoe Bend National Military Park, Al., U.S.	C4	78
Horseshoe Cove, b., Fl., U.S.	C3	86
Horseshoe Point, c., Fl., U.S.	C3	86
Horseshoe Reservoir, res., Az., U.S.	C4	80
Horsham, Austl.	G8	50
Horten, Nor.	G8	6
Horton, Ks., U.S.	C8	93
Hortonia, Lake, l., Vt., U.S.	D2	122
Hortonville, Wi., U.S.	D5	126
Hoschton, Ga., U.S.	B3	87
Hoshangābād, India	I7	38
Hoshiārpur, India	E6	38
Hospers, Ia., U.S.	A2	92
Hospet, India	E4	37
Hospitalet, Spain	D14	12
Hosta Butte, mtn., N.M., U.S.	B1	108
Hoste, Isla, i., Chile	H3	56
Hotchkiss, Co., U.S.	C3	83
Hot Creek Range, mts., Nv., U.S.	E5	105
Hot Creek Valley, val., Nv., U.S.	E5	105
Hoting, Swe.	D11	6
Hot Spring, co., Ar., U.S.	C2	81
Hot Springs, S.D., U.S.	D2	118
Hot Springs, co., Wy., U.S.	C4	127
Hot Springs National Park, Ar., U.S.	C2	81
Hot Springs National Park, Ar., U.S.	C2	81
Hot Springs Peak, mtn., Ca., U.S.	B3	82
Hot Springs Peak, mtn., Ca., U.S.	B4	105
Hottah Lake, l., N.W. Ter., Can.	C9	66
Houghton, Mi., U.S.	A2	99
Houghton, N.Y., U.S.	C2	109
Houghton, co., Mi., U.S.	B2	99
Houghton Lake, Mi., U.S.	D6	99
Houghton Lake, l., Mi., U.S.	D6	99
Houghton Lake Heights, Mi., U.S.	D6	99
Houlton, Me., U.S.	B5	96
Houma, China	D9	26
Houma, La., U.S.	E5	95
Housatonic, stm., U.S.	D3	84
House Springs, Mo., U.S.	g12	102
Houston, De., U.S.	E3	85
Houston, Mn., U.S.	G7	100
Houston, Ms., U.S.	B4	101
Houston, Mo., U.S.	D6	102
Houston, Pa., U.S.	F1	115
Houston, Tx., U.S.	E5	120
Houston, co., Al., U.S.	D4	78
Houston, co., Ga., U.S.	D3	87
Houston, co., Mn., U.S.	G7	100
Houston, co., Tn., U.S.	A4	119
Houston, co., Tx., U.S.	D5	120
Houston, stm., La., U.S.	D2	95
Houston Intercontinental Airport, Tx., U.S.	r14	120
Houtman Rocks, Austl.	E2	50
Houtzdale, Pa., U.S.	E5	115
Hovenweep National Monument, Ut., U.S.	F6	121
Hovmantorp, Swe.	H10	6
Howard, Ks., U.S.	E7	93
Howard, S.D., U.S.	C8	118
Howard, Wi., U.S.	D5	126
Howard, co., Ar., U.S.	C2	81
Howard, co., In., U.S.	C5	91
Howard, co., Ia., U.S.	A5	92
Howard, co., Md., U.S.	B4	97
Howard, co., Mo., U.S.	B5	102
Howard, co., Ne., U.S.	C7	104
Howard, co., Tx., U.S.	C2	120
Howard City, Mi., U.S.	E5	99
Howard Hanson Reservoir, res., Wa., U.S.	B4	124
Howard Lake, Mn., U.S.	E4	100
Howard Prairie Lake, res., Or., U.S.	E4	114
Howards Grove-Millersville, Wi., U.S.	E6	126
Howell, Mi., U.S.	F7	99
Howell, co., Mo., U.S.	E6	102

Name	Map Ref	Page
Howells, Ne., U.S.	C8	104
Howe Sound, strt., B.C., Can.	E6	69
Howick, Que., Can.	D4	74
Howland, Me., U.S.	C4	96
Howrah, India	I13	38
Hoxie, Ar., U.S.	A5	81
Hoxie, Ks., U.S.	C3	93
Höxter, Ger.	D9	8
Hoy, i., Scot., U.K.	C9	7
Høyanger, Nor.	F6	6
Hoyerswerda, Ger.	D14	8
Hoyos, Spain	E5	12
Hoyt Lakes, Mn., U.S.	C6	100
Hradec Králové, Czech.	E15	8
Hsilo, Tai.	L9	28
Hsinchu, Tai.	K9	28
Hsüehchia, Tai.	L9	28
Huacho, Peru	F3	54
Huachuca City, Az., U.S.	F5	80
Hua Hin, Thai.	H5	34
Huahua, stm., Nic.	G6	64
Huaian, China	B8	28
Huainan, China	C6	28
Huaiyang, China	B3	28
Huaiyin, China	B8	28
Huaiyuan, China	C6	28
Hualalai, vol., Hi., U.S.	D6	88
Hualapai Indian Reservation, Az., U.S.	B2	80
Hualapai Mountains, mts., Az., U.S.	C2	80
Hualapai Peak, mtn., Az., U.S.	B2	80
Hualien, Tai.	L10	28
Huallaga, stm., Peru	E3	54
Huallanca, Peru	E3	54
Huamachuco, Peru	E3	54
Huambo, Ang.	D3	44
Huancayo, Peru	F3	54
Huang (Yellow), stm., China	D10	26
Huangchuan, China	C4	28
Huanggang, China	D8	28
Huangshi, China	E4	28
Huangyan, China	G10	28
Huánuco, Peru	E3	54
Huaraz, Peru	E3	54
Huascarán, Nevado, mtn., Peru	E3	54
Huasco, Chile	B2	56
Huatabampo, Mex.	D5	62
Huauchinango, Mex.	G10	62
Hubbard, Ia., U.S.	B4	92
Hubbard, Oh., U.S.	A5	112
Hubbard, Or., U.S.	B4	114
Hubbard, Tx., U.S.	D4	120
Hubbard, co., Mn., U.S.	C4	100
Hubbard Creek Lake, res., Tx., U.S.	C3	120
Hubbard Lake, l., Mi., U.S.	D7	99
Hubbardton, stm., Vt., U.S.	D2	122
Hubbell, Mi., U.S.	A2	99
Hubei, prov., China	E9	26
Hubli, India	E3	37
Huckleberry Mountain, mtn., Or., U.S.	D4	114
Huddersfield, Eng., U.K.	H11	7
Huddinge, Swe.	G11	6
Hudiksvall, Swe.	F11	6
Hudson, Que., Can.	D3	74
Hudson, Co., U.S.	A6	83
Hudson, Fl., U.S.	D4	86
Hudson, Il., U.S.	C5	90
Hudson, Ia., U.S.	B5	92
Hudson, Ma., U.S.	B4	98
Hudson, Mi., U.S.	G6	99
Hudson, N.H., U.S.	E4	106
Hudson, N.Y., U.S.	C7	109
Hudson, N.C., U.S.	B1	110
Hudson, Oh., U.S.	A4	112
Hudson, Wi., U.S.	D1	126
Hudson, Wy., U.S.	D4	127
Hudson, co., N.J., U.S.	B4	107
Hudson, stm., U.S.	E7	109
Hudson, Lake, res., Ok., U.S.	A6	113
Hudson Bay, b., Can.	D15	66
Hudson Falls, N.Y., U.S.	B7	109
Hudson Hope, B.C., Can.	A6	69
Hudson Lake, In., U.S.	A4	91
Hudson Strait, strt., Can.	D18	66
Hudsonville, Mi., U.S.	F5	99
Hudspeth, co., Tx., U.S.	o12	120
Hue, Viet.	F9	34
Huehuetenango, Guat.	G2	64
Huelma, Spain	H8	12
Huelva, Spain	H5	12
Huércal-Overa, Spain	H10	12
Huerfano, co., Co., U.S.	D5	83
Huerfano, stm., Co., U.S.	D6	83
Huerfano Mountain, mtn., N.M., U.S.	A2	108
Huesca, Spain	C11	12
Hueytown, Al., U.S.	g6	78
Huffakers, Nv., U.S.	D2	105
Hugh Butler Lake, res., Ne., U.S.	D5	104
Hughenden, Austl.	D8	50
Hughes, Ar., U.S.	C5	81
Hughes, co., Ok., U.S.	B5	113
Hughes, co., S.D., U.S.	C5	118
Hughes, North Fork, stm., W.V., U.S.	B3	125
Hughes, South Fork, stm., W.V., U.S.	B3	125
Hughesville, Md., U.S.	C4	97
Hughesville, Pa., U.S.	D8	115
Hugo, Co., U.S.	B7	83
Hugo, Mn., U.S.	m13	100
Hugo, Ok., U.S.	C6	113
Hugo Lake, res., Ok., U.S.	C6	113
Hugoton, Ks., U.S.	E2	93
Huidong, China	A7	34
Huila, Nevado del, mtn., Col.	A7	34
Huili, China	A7	34
Huinan, China	C12	26
Huittinen (Lauttakylä), Fin.	F14	6
Huitzuco [de los Figueroa], Mex.	H10	62
Huixtla, Mex.	J13	62
Huiyang (Huizhou), China	L3	28
Hulah Lake, res., Ok., U.S.	A5	113
Hulan, China	B12	26
Hulett, Wy., U.S.	B8	127
Hull, Que., Can.	D2	74

Name	Map Ref	Page
Hull, Ia., U.S.	A1	92
Hull, Ma., U.S.	B6	98
Hultsfred, Swe.	H10	6
Hulun Nur, l., China	B10	26
Humaitá, Braz.	E6	54
Humansville, Mo., U.S.	D4	102
Humber, stm., Eng., U.K.	H12	7
Humble, Tx., U.S.	E5	120
Humboldt, Az., U.S.	C3	80
Humboldt, Ia., U.S.	B3	92
Humboldt, Ks., U.S.	E8	93
Humboldt, Ne., U.S.	D10	104
Humboldt, Tn., U.S.	B3	119
Humboldt, co., Ca., U.S.	B2	82
Humboldt, co., Ia., U.S.	B3	92
Humboldt, co., Nv., U.S.	B3	105
Humboldt, stm., Nv., U.S.	C3	105
Humboldt Range, mts., Nv., U.S.	C3	105
Hummels Wharf, Pa., U.S.	E8	115
Humphrey, Ar., U.S.	C4	81
Humphrey, Ne., U.S.	C8	104
Humphreys, co., Ms., U.S.	B3	101
Humphreys, co., Tn., U.S.	A4	119
Humphreys, Mount, mtn., Ca., U.S.	D4	82
Humphreys Peak, mtn., Az., U.S.	B4	80
Hunedoara, Rom.	D6	16
Hünfeld, Ger.	E9	8
Hungary, ctry., Eur.	F11	4
Hungt'ou Hsü, i., Tai.	M10	28
Hungry Horse, Mt., U.S.	B2	103
Hungry Horse Reservoir, res., Mt., U.S.	B3	103
Hunt, co., Tx., U.S.	C4	120
Hunt, stm., R.I., U.S.	D4	116
Hunterdon, co., N.J., U.S.	B3	107
Hunter Island, i., Austl.	H8	50
Hunter Island, i., B.C., Can.	D3	69
Huntertown, In., U.S.	B7	91
Huntingburg, In., U.S.	H4	91
Huntingdon, Que., Can.	D3	74
Huntingdon, Pa., U.S.	F6	115
Huntingdon, co., Pa., U.S.	F5	115
Huntington, Ar., U.S.	B1	81
Huntington, In., U.S.	C7	91
Huntington, N.Y., U.S.	E7	109
Huntington, Tx., U.S.	D5	120
Huntington, Ut., U.S.	D5	121
Huntington, W.V., U.S.	C2	125
Huntington, co., In., U.S.	C6	91
Huntington Beach, Ca., U.S.	F4	82
Huntington Lake, res., In., U.S.	C7	91
Huntington Woods, Mi., U.S.	p15	99
Huntingtown, Md., U.S.	C4	97
Huntland, Tn., U.S.	B5	119
Huntley, Il., U.S.	A5	90
Huntley, Mt., U.S.	E8	103
Huntsville, Ont., Can.	B5	73
Huntsville, Al., U.S.	A3	78
Huntsville, Ar., U.S.	A2	81
Huntsville, Mo., U.S.	B5	102
Huntsville, Tn., U.S.	C9	119
Huntsville, Tx., U.S.	D5	120
Huon Gulf, b., Pap. N. Gui.	m16	50a
Hurao, China	B13	26
Hurd, Cape, c., Ont., Can.	B3	73
Hurley, Ms., U.S.	E5	101
Hurley, N.M., U.S.	E1	108
Hurley, N.Y., U.S.	D6	109
Hurley, Wi., U.S.	B3	126
Hurlock, Md., U.S.	C6	97
Huron, Oh., U.S.	A3	112
Huron, S.D., U.S.	C7	118
Huron, co., Mi., U.S.	E7	99
Huron, co., Oh., U.S.	A3	112
Huron, stm., Mi., U.S.	p14	99
Huron, Lake, l., N.A.	C10	76
Huron Mountains, hills, Mi., U.S.	B3	99
Hurricane, Ut., U.S.	F2	121
Hurricane, W.V., U.S.	C2	125
Hurst, Il., U.S.	F4	90
Hurt, Va., U.S.	C3	123
Hurtsboro, Al., U.S.	C4	78
Húsavík, Ice.	B4	4
Huskvarna, Swe.	H10	6
Hustisford, Wi., U.S.	E5	126
Husum, Ger.	A9	8
Hutchins, Tx., U.S.	n10	120
Hutchinson, Ks., U.S.	D6	93
Hutchinson, Mn., U.S.	F4	100
Hutchinson, co., S.D., U.S.	D8	118
Hutchinson, co., Tx., U.S.	B2	120
Hutchinson Island, i., Fl., U.S.	E6	86
Hutchinson Island, i., S.C., U.S.	k11	117
Hutch Mountain, mtn., Az., U.S.	C4	80
Hüttental, Ger.	E8	8
Huttig, Ar., U.S.	D3	81
Huwei, Tai.	L9	28
Huxley, Ia., U.S.	C4	92
Huy, Bel.	E5	8
Huzhou, China	E9	28
Hvannadalshnúkur, mtn., Ice.	C4	4
Hvar, Cro.	F11	14
Hwange, Zimb.	E5	44
Hwang Ho see Huang, stm., China	D10	26
Hyannis, Ma., U.S.	C7	98
Hyannis Port, Ma., U.S.	C7	98
Hyattsville, Md., U.S.	C4	97
Hybla Valley, Va., U.S.	g12	123
Hyco, stm., U.S.	D3	123
Hyco Lake, res., N.C., U.S.	A3	110
Hyde, Pa., U.S.	D5	115
Hyde, co., N.C., U.S.	B6	110
Hyde, co., S.D., U.S.	C6	118
Hyde Park, Guy.	D13	58
Hyde Park, N.Y., U.S.	D7	109
Hyde Park, Ut., U.S.	B4	121
Hyder, Ak., U.S.	D13	79
Hyderābād, India	D5	37
Hyderābād, Pak.	H3	38
Hydeville, Vt., U.S.	D2	122

Name	Map Ref	Page
Hydro, Ok., U.S.	B3	113
Hyères, Fr.	I13	10
Hyesan, N. Kor.	C12	26
Hymera, In., U.S.	F3	91
Hyndman, Pa., U.S.	G4	115
Hyndman Peak, mtn., Id., U.S.	F4	89
Hyrum, Ut., U.S.	B4	121
Hythe, Alta., Can.	B1	68
Hyūga, Japan	J4	30
Hyūga-nada, Japan	J4	30
Hyvinkää, Fin.	F15	6

I

Name	Map Ref	Page
Iamonia, Lake, l., Fl., U.S.	B2	86
Iaşi, Rom.	B11	16
Iatt, Lake, res., La., U.S.	C3	95
Ibadan, Nig.	G6	42
Ibagué, Col.	E5	58
Ibapah Peak, mtn., Ut., U.S.	D2	121
Ibarra, Ec.	G3	58
Ibb, Yemen	F3	46
Iberia, Mo., U.S.	C5	102
Iberia, co., La., U.S.	E4	95
Iberville, Que., Can.	D4	74
Iberville, co., La., U.S.	D4	95
Iberville, Mont d' (Mount Caubvick), mtn., Can.	g14	72
Ibiá, Braz.	E5	57
Ibicaraí, Braz.	C9	57
Ibiza, Spain	G13	12
Ibiza, i., Spain	G13	12
Ibo, Moz.	D8	44
Ica, Peru	F3	54
Içá (Putumayo), stm., S.A.	I8	58
Içana, Braz.	C5	54
Içana, stm., S.A.	C5	54
Ice Harbor Dam, Wa., U.S.	C7	124
İçel, Tur.	H14	4
Iceland, ctry., Eur.	B4	4
Ichalkaranji, India	D3	37
Ich Bogd Uul, mts., Mong.	C7	26
Ichinomiya, Japan	G9	30
Ichinoseki, Japan	D14	30
Icicle Creek, stm., Wa., U.S.	B5	124
Icó, Braz.	E11	54
Icy Cape, c., Ak., U.S.	A7	79
Icy Strait, strt., Ak., U.S.	k22	79
Ida, Mi., U.S.	G7	99
Ida, co., Ia., U.S.	B2	92
Ida, Lake, l., Mn., U.S.	D3	100
Idabel, Ok., U.S.	D7	113
Ida Grove, Ia., U.S.	B2	92
Idaho, co., Id., U.S.	D3	89
Idaho, state, U.S.	E3	89
Idaho City, Id., U.S.	F3	89
Idaho Falls, Id., U.S.	F6	89
Idaho Springs, Co., U.S.	B5	83
Idalou, Tx., U.S.	C2	120
Idamay, W.V., U.S.	k10	125
Idanha-a-Nova, Port.	F4	12
Idappādi, India	G4	37
Idar-Oberstein, Ger.	F7	8
Idaville, In., U.S.	C4	91
Ider, Al., U.S.	A4	78
Idfū, Egypt	D12	42
Idlib, Syria	B5	40
Ídolo, Isla del, i., Mex.	G11	62
Ieper, Bel.	E2	8
Ierápetra, Grc.	N9	16
Iesi, Italy	F8	14
Ife, Nig.	G6	42
Iferouâne, Niger	E7	42
Iforas, Adrar des, mts., Afr.	D6	42
Iglesias, Italy	J3	14
Igloolik, N.W. Ter., Can.	C16	66
Ignacio, Co., U.S.	D3	83
Iguaçu, Saltos do (Iguassu Falls), wtfl, S.A.	B6	56
Iguala, Mex.	H10	62
Igualada, Spain	D13	12
Iguape, Braz.	A7	56
Iguatu, Braz.	E11	54
Iguéla, Gabon	B1	44
Iguidi, Erg, dunes, Afr.	C4	42
Ihosy, Madag.	F9	44
Iida, Japan	G10	30
Iisalmi, Fin.	E16	6
Iizuka, Japan	I3	30
IJmuiden, Neth.	C4	8
IJsselmeer (Zuiderzee), Neth.	C5	8
Ika, Russia	F15	24
Ikela, Zaire	B4	44
Ikerre, Nig.	G7	42
Ila, Nig.	G6	42
Ilagan, Phil.	B7	32
Ilan, Tai.	K10	28
Ilbenge, Russia	E18	24
Île-à-la-Crosse, Lac, l., Sask., Can.	B2	75
Ilebo, Zaire	B4	44
Île-de-France, hist. reg., Fr.	C9	10
Île-Perrot, Que., Can.	q19	74
Ilhéus, Braz.	C9	57
Ili, stm., Asia	I13	22
Iliamna Lake, l., Ak., U.S.	D8	79
Iliamna Volcano, vol., Ak., U.S.	C9	79
Ilio Point, c., Hi., U.S.	B4	88
Ilirska Bistrica, Slo.	D9	14
Iljinskij, Russia	H22	24
Ilkal, India	E4	37
Illampu, Nevado, mtn., Bol.	G5	54
Illapel, Chile	C2	56
Illescas, Mex.	F8	62
Illiers, Fr.	D8	10
Illimani, Nevado, mtn., Bol.	G5	54
Illinois, state, U.S.	C4	90
Illinois, stm., U.S.	A7	113
Illinois, stm., Il., U.S.	B5	90
Illinois, stm., Or., U.S.	E3	114
Illinois Peak, mtn., Id., U.S.	B3	89
Illiopolis, Il., U.S.	D4	90
Illizi, Alg.	C7	42
Illmo, Mo., U.S.	D8	102
Il'men', Ozero, l., Russia	C14	18
Ilo, Peru	G4	54
Iloilo, Phil.	C7	32

Name	Map Ref	Page
omantsi, Fin.	E18	6
orin, Nig.	G6	42
pyrskij, Russia	F26	24
waco, Wa., U.S.	C1	124
nabari, Japan	H6	30
man, Russia	H20	24
nari, Japan	I2	30
natra, Fin.	F17	6
nboden, Ar., U.S.	A4	81
nlay, Nv., U.S.	C3	105
nlay City, Mi., U.S.	E7	99
nmenstadt, Ger.	H10	8
nmokalee, Fl., U.S.	F5	86
nnaha, stm., Or., U.S.	B10	114
nola, Ind.	E6	14
nperatriz, Braz.	E9	54
nperia, Italy	F3	14
nperia, Ca., U.S.	F6	82
nperial, Mo., U.S.	C7	102
nperial, Ne., U.S.	D4	104
nperial, Pa., U.S.	k13	115
nperial Beach, Ca., U.S.	o15	82
nperial Dam, U.S.	E1	80
nperial Reservoir, res., U.S.	E1	80
nperial Valley, val., Ca., U.S.	F6	82
npfondo, Congo	A3	44
nphāl, India	H15	38
nst, Aus.	H10	8
nuris, Mex.	B4	62
na, Japan	G10	30
nari, Fin.	B16	6
nca, Spain	F14	12
ncekum Burnu, c., Tur.	A3	40
nch'ŏn, S. Kor.	D12	26
ncline Village, Nv., U.S.	D2	105
ndependence, Ia., U.S.	B6	92
ndependence, Ks., U.S.	E8	93
ndependence, Ky., U.S.	B5	94
ndependence, La., U.S.	D5	95
ndependence, Mo., U.S.	B3	102
ndependence, Or., U.S.	C3	114
ndependence, Or., U.S.	D1	123
ndependence, Wi., U.S.	D2	126
ndependence, co., Ar., U.S.	B4	81
ndependence, stm., N.Y., U.S.	B5	109
ndependence Mountains, mts., Nv., U.S.	C5	105
ndependence National Historical Park, Pa., U.S.	p21	115
ndependence Rock, mtn., Wy., U.S.	D5	127
ndia, ctry., Asia	E4	36
ndian, stm., Ont., Can.	B7	73
ndian, stm., On., U.S.	F4	85
ndian, stm., Mi., U.S.	B4	99
ndian, stm., N.Y., U.S.	A5	109
ndiana, Pa., U.S.	E3	115
ndiana, co., Pa., U.S.	E3	115
ndiana, state, U.S.	E5	91
ndiana Dunes National Lakeshore, In., U.S.	A3	91
ndianapolis, In., U.S.	E5	91
ndian Bay, b., Fl., U.S.	D4	86
ndian Cedar Swamp, sw., R.I., U.S.	F2	116
ndian Creek, stm., Oh., U.S.	C1	112
ndian Creek, stm., S.D., U.S.	B2	118
ndian Creek, stm., Tn., U.S.	B3	119
ndian Creek, stm., W.V., U.S.	D4	125
ndian Creek, stm., W.V., U.S.	k9	125
ndian Head, Md., U.S.	C3	97
ndian Lake, l., Mi., U.S.	C4	99
ndian Lake, l., N.Y., U.S.	B6	109
ndian Lake, l., Oh., U.S.	B2	112
ndian Lake, l., R.I., U.S.	F4	116
ndian Neck, Ct., U.S.	D4	84
ndian Ocean	G17	2
ndianola, Ia., U.S.	C4	92
ndianola, Ms., U.S.	B3	101
ndianola, Ne., U.S.	D5	104
ndian Peak, mtn., Ut., U.S.	E2	121
ndian Peak, mtn., Wy., U.S.	B3	127
ndian Prairie Canal, Fl., U.S.	E5	86
ndian River, co., Fl., U.S.	E6	86
ndian River, b., De., U.S.	D6	86
ndian River Bay, b., De., U.S.	F5	85
ndian Rock, mtn., Wa., U.S.	D5	124
ndian Rocks Beach, Fl., U.S.	p10	86
ndian Springs, Nv., U.S.	G6	105
ndian Stream, stm., N.H., U.S.	f7	106
ndiantown, Fl., U.S.	E6	86
ndian Trail, N.C., U.S.	B2	110
ndigirka, stm., Russia	C23	24
ndio, Ca., U.S.	F5	82
ndispensable Reefs, rf., Sol.Is.	B8	50
ndonesia, ctry., Asia	F6	32
ndore, India	I6	38
ndoukâl-n-Taghès, mtn., Niger	E7	42
ndramayu, Indon.	m14	32
ndrāvati, stm., India	C6	37
ndus, stm., Asia	H2	38
negöl, Tur.	I13	16
nfiernillo, Presa del, res., Mex.	H9	62
-n-Gall, Niger	E7	42
ngalls, In., U.S.	E6	91
ngalls Park, Il., U.S.	B5	90
ngersoll, Ont., Can.	D4	73
ngham, co., Mi., U.S.	F6	99
ngleside, Tx., U.S.	F4	120
nglewood, Ca., U.S.	n12	82
ngolstadt, Ger.	G11	8
ngraham, Lake, l., Fl., U.S.	G5	86
n Guezzam, Alg.	E7	42
nhambane, Moz.	F7	44
nhambupe, Braz.	F11	54
nhaminga, Moz.	E6	44
nharrime, Moz.	F7	44
nírida, stm., Col.	F8	58
nkerman, N.B., Can.	B5	71
nkom, Al., U.S.	G6	89
nkster, Mi., U.S.	p15	99
nland Sea see Seto-naikai, Japan	H6	30
Inle Lake, l., Burma	D4	34
Inman, Ks., U.S.	D6	93
Inman, S.C., U.S.	A3	117
Inn (En), stm., Eur.	G13	8
Innamincka, Austl.	E8	50
Innisfail, Alta., Can.	C4	68
Innsbruck, Aus.	H11	8
Inola, Ok., U.S.	A6	113
Inongo, Zaire	B3	44
Inowrocław, Pol.	C18	8
In Salah, Alg.	C6	42
Inscription House Ruin, hist., Az., U.S.	A5	80
Insein, Burma	F4	34
Institute, W.V., U.S.	m12	125
Interlachen, Fl., U.S.	C5	86
Interlaken, Switz.	F14	10
International Falls, Mn., U.S.	B5	100
Inthanon, Doi, mtn., Thai.	E5	34
Intiyaco, Arg.	B4	56
Intracoastal Waterway, U.S.	E4	95
Inukjuak, Que., Can.	g11	74
Inver Grove Heights, Mn., U.S.	n12	100
Invermere, B.C., Can.	D9	69
Inverness, Scot., U.K.	D8	7
Inverness, Ca., U.S.	C2	82
Inverness, Fl., U.S.	D4	86
Inverness, Ms., U.S.	B3	101
Inverurie, Scot., U.K.	D10	7
Investigator Group, is., Austl.	F6	50
Investigator Strait, strt., Austl.	G7	50
Invisible Mountain, mtn., Id., U.S.	F5	89
Inwood, Ia., U.S.	A1	92
Inwood, N.Y., U.S.	k13	109
Inwood, W.V., U.S.	B6	125
Inyangani, mtn., Zimb.	E6	44
Inyan Kara Creek, stm., Wy., U.S.	B8	127
Inyan Kara Mountain, mtn., Wy., U.S.	B8	127
Inyo, co., Ca., U.S.	D5	82
Inyo, Mount, mtn., Ca., U.S.	D5	82
Inyo Mountains, mts., Ca., U.S.	D4	82
Ioánnina, Grc.	J4	16
Iola, Ks., U.S.	E8	93
Iola, Wi., U.S.	D4	126
Ione, Ca., U.S.	C3	82
Ionia, Mi., U.S.	F5	99
Ionia, co., Mi., U.S.	F5	99
Ionian Islands see Iónioi Nísoi, is., Grc.		
Ionian Sea, Eur.	H11	4
Iónioi Nísoi, is., Grc.	K4	16
Iosco, co., Mi., U.S.	D7	99
Iota, La., U.S.	D3	95
Iowa, La., U.S.	D2	95
Iowa, co., Ia., U.S.	C5	92
Iowa, co., Wi., U.S.	E3	126
Iowa, stm., Ia., U.S.	C4	92
Iowa, state, U.S.	C6	92
Iowa, West Branch, stm., Ia., U.S.	B4	92
Iowa City, Ia., U.S.	C6	92
Iowa Falls, Ia., U.S.	B4	92
Iowa Indian Reservation, U.S.	C8	93
Iowa Lake, l., U.S.	A3	92
Iowa Park, Tx., U.S.	C3	120
Ipameri, Braz.	D5	57
Iphigenia Bay, b., Ak., U.S.	n22	79
Ipiales, Col.	G4	58
Ipiaú, Braz.	C9	57
Ipoh, Malay.	L6	34
Ipswich, Austl.	E10	50
Ipswich, Eng., U.K.	I14	7
Ipswich, Ma., U.S.	A6	98
Ipswich, S.D., U.S.	B6	118
Ipswich, stm., Ma., U.S.	A5	98
Ipu, Braz.	D10	54
Iqaluit, N.W. Ter., Can.	D19	66
Iquique, Chile	H4	54
Iquitos, Peru	D4	54
Iraan, Tx., U.S.	D2	120
Iráklion, Grc.	N9	16
Iran, ctry., Asia	B5	46
Iran Mountains, mts., Asia	E5	32
Iränshahr, Iran	C7	46
Irapa, Ven.	B11	58
Irapuato, Mex.	G9	62
Iraq, ctry., Asia	B3	46
Irazú, Volcán, vol., C.R.	J6	64
Irbid, Jord.	C4	40
Irbil, Iraq	A3	46
Iredell, co., N.C., U.S.	B2	110
Ireland, ctry., Eur.	E6	4
Iriga, Phil.	r20	32
Iringa, Tan.	C7	44
Irion, co., Tx., U.S.	D2	120
Iriri, stm., Braz.	D8	54
Irish, Mount, mtn., Nv., U.S.	F6	105
Irish Sea, Eur.	H8	7
Irkutsk, Russia	G14	24
Irmo, S.C., U.S.	C5	117
Iron, co., Mi., U.S.	B2	99
Iron, co., Mo., U.S.	D7	102
Iron, co., Ut., U.S.	F2	121
Iron, co., Wi., U.S.	B3	126
Irondale, Al., U.S.	f7	78
Irondequoit, N.Y., U.S.	B3	109
Iron Gate, val., Eur.	E6	16
Iron Gate Reservoir, res., Eur.	E5	16
Iron Gate Reservoir, res., Ca., U.S.	B2	82
Iron Mountain, Mi., U.S.	C2	99
Iron Mountain, mtn., Az., U.S.	D4	80
Iron Mountains, mts., U.S.	D1	123
Iron Ridge, Wi., U.S.	E5	126
Iron River, Mi., U.S.	B2	99
Iron River, Wi., U.S.	B2	126
Ironton, Mo., U.S.	D7	102
Ironton, Oh., U.S.	D3	112
Ironwood, Mi., U.S.	n11	99
Iroquois, Ont., Can.	C9	73
Iroquois, co., Il., U.S.	C6	90
Iroquois, stm., U.S.	C6	90
Iroquois, Lake, l., Vt., U.S.	B2	122
Iroquois Falls, Ont., Can.	o19	73
Irrawaddy see Ayeyarwady, stm., Burma	G3	34
Irricana, Alta., Can.	D4	68
Irrigon, Or., U.S.	B7	114
Irtyš (Ertix), stm., Asia	F11	22
Irumu, Zaire	A5	44
Irún, Spain	B10	12
Irurzun, Spain	C10	12
Irú Tepuy, mtn., Ven.	E12	58
Irvine, Scot., U.K.	F8	7
Irvine, Ca., U.S.	n13	82
Irvine, Ky., U.S.	C6	94
Irving, Tx., U.S.	n10	120
Irvington, Al., U.S.	E1	78
Irvington, Il., U.S.	E4	90
Irvington, Ky., U.S.	C3	94
Irvington, N.J., U.S.	k8	107
Irvington, N.Y., U.S.	g13	109
Irwin, Pa., U.S.	F2	115
Irwin, co., Ga., U.S.	E3	87
Irwinton, Ga., U.S.	D3	87
Isabel, Mount, mtn., Wy., U.S.	D2	127
Isabella, co., Mi., U.S.	E6	99
Isabella, Cordillera, mts., Nic.	G5	64
Isabella Indian Reservation, Mi., U.S.	E6	99
Isabella Lake, l., Mn., U.S.	C7	100
Isafjördur, Ice.	B3	4
Isahaya, Japan	J3	30
Isanti, Mn., U.S.	E5	100
Isanti, co., Mn., U.S.	E5	100
Isar, stm., Eur.	G11	8
Ischia, Italy	I8	14
Ise, Japan	H9	30
Isernia, Italy	H9	14
Isesaki, Japan	F12	30
Ise-wan, b., Japan	H9	30
Isherton, Guy.	F13	58
Ishikari-wan, b., Japan	p18	30a
Ishinomaki, Japan	D14	30
Ishpeming, Mi., U.S.	B3	99
Isinglass, stm., N.H., U.S.	D4	106
Isiolo, Kenya	A7	44
Isiro, Zaire	H11	42
Iskele, N. Cyp.	B3	40
İskenderun, Tur.	A4	40
İskenderun Körfezi, b., Tur.	A4	40
Iskitim, Russia	G10	24
Islâhiye, Tur.	A5	40
Islāmābād, Pak.	D5	38
Islamorada, Fl., U.S.	H6	86
Isla Mujeres, Mex.	G16	62
Island, co., Wa., U.S.	A3	124
Island Beach, N.J., U.S.	D4	107
Island City, Or., U.S.	B8	114
Island Falls, Me., U.S.	B4	96
Island Lake, l., Man., Can.	C4	70
Island Park, R.I., U.S.	E6	116
Island Park Reservoir, res., Id., U.S.	E7	89
Island Pond, Vt., U.S.	B5	122
Island Pond, l., N.H., U.S.	E4	106
Islands, Bay of, b., Newf., Can.	D2	72
Isla Vista, Ca., U.S.	E4	82
Islay, I., Scot., U.K.	F6	7
Isle-aux-Morts, Newf., Can.	E2	72
Isle of Man, dep., Eur.	E7	4
Isle of Palms, S.C., U.S.	k12	117
Isle of Wight, co., Va., U.S.	D6	123
Isle of Wight Bay, b., Md., U.S.	D7	97
Isle Royale National Park, Mi., U.S.	h9	99
Islesboro Island, i., Me., U.S.	D4	96
Isleta, N.M., U.S.	C3	108
Isleta Indian Reservation, N.M., U.S.	C3	108
Islington, Ma., U.S.	h11	98
Isola, Ms., U.S.	B3	101
Isola della Scala, Italy	D5	14
Ispica, Italy	M9	14
Israel (Yisra'el), ctry., Asia	D4	40
Israel, stm., N.H., U.S.	B3	106
Issano, Guy.	E13	58
Issaquah, Wa., U.S.	B3	124
Issaquena, co., Ms., U.S.	C2	101
Issoire, Fr.	G10	10
Issoudun, Fr.	F8	10
Is-sur-Tille, Fr.	E12	10
İstanbul, Tur.	G13	4
Issyk-Kul', Kyrg.	I9	24
İstanbul Boğazı (Bosporus), strt., Tur.	H13	16
Isto, Mount, mtn., Ak., U.S.	B11	79
Istokpoga, Lake, l., Fl., U.S.	E5	86
Itabaiana, Braz.	F11	54
Itaberaí, Braz.	G9	54
Itabira, Braz.	E7	57
Itabuna, Braz.	C9	57
Itacoatiara, Braz.	D7	54
Itagüí, Col.	D5	58
Itaituba, Braz.	D7	54
Itajaí, Braz.	B7	56
Itajubá, Braz.	G6	57
Itapira, Braz.	G5	57
Itapetinga, Braz.	C8	57
Itapetininga, Braz.	G4	57
Itapeva, Braz.	G4	57
Itapicuru, stm., Braz.	D10	54
Itaquari, Braz.	F8	57
Itararé, Braz.	H4	57
Itārsi, India	I7	38
Itasca, Il., U.S.	k8	90
Itasca, Tx., U.S.	C4	120
Itasca, co., Mn., U.S.	C5	100
Itasca, Lake, l., Mn., U.S.	C3	100
Itawamba, co., Ms., U.S.	A5	101
Ithaca, Mi., U.S.	E6	99
Ithaca, N.Y., U.S.	C4	109
Itō, Japan	H12	30
Itta Bena, Ms., U.S.	B3	101
Ittiri, Italy	I3	14
Ituberá, Braz.	B9	57
Ituiutaba, Braz.	E4	57
Itumbiara, Braz.	E4	57
Ituni, Guy.	E13	58
Ituri, stm., Zaire	A5	44
Iturup, Ostrov (Etorofu-tō), i., Russia	I23	24
Ituverava, Braz.	F5	57
Ituxi, stm., Braz.	E5	54
Itzehoe, Ger.	B9	8
Iuka, Ms., U.S.	A5	101
Iva, S.C., U.S.	C2	117
Ivalo, Fin.	B16	6
Ivanhoe, Mn., U.S.	F2	100
Ivanić Grad, Cro.	D11	14
Ivano-Frankovsk, Ukr.	H2	22
Ivanovo, Russia	D23	18
Ivigtut, Grnld.	D23	66
Ivinheima, stm., Braz.	G2	57
Ivins, Ut., U.S.	F2	121
Ivory Coast, ctry., Afr.	G4	42
Ivoryton, Ct., U.S.	D6	84
Ivrea, Italy	D2	14
Iwaki (Taira), Japan	E13	30
Iwakuni, Japan	H5	30
Iwanai, Japan	q18	30a
Iwanuma, Japan	D13	30
Iwo, Nig.	G6	42
Ixtacihuatl, vol., Mex.	H10	62
Iyo-nada, Japan	I5	30
Izabal, Lago de, l., Guat.	G3	64
Izard, co., Ar., U.S.	A4	81
Izegem, Bel.	E3	8
Iževsk, Russia	F8	22
İzmir, Tur.	H13	4
İzmit, Tur.	G13	4
Iznalloz, Spain	H8	12
Iznik Gölü, l., Tur.	I13	16
Izozog, Bañados de, sw., Bol.	G6	54
Izúcar de Matamoros, Mex.	H10	62
Izuhara, Japan	H2	30
Izumo, Japan	G5	30
Izu-shotō, is., Japan	H12	30
Izvestij CIK, Ostrova, is., Russia	B10	24

J

Name	Map Ref	Page
Jabalpur, India	I8	38
Jabbūl, Sabkhat al-, l., Syria	A5	40
Jablah, Syria	B4	40
Jablonec nad Nisou, Czech.	E15	8
Jaboatão, Braz.	E11	54
Jabrīn, well, Sau. Ar.	D4	46
Jaca, Spain	C11	12
Jacarèzinho, Braz.	G4	57
Jáchal, Arg.	C3	56
Jacinto City, Tx., U.S.	r14	120
Jack, co., Tx., U.S.	C3	120
Jackfish Lake, l., Sask., Can.	D1	75
Jackman, Me., U.S.	C2	96
Jackman Station, Me., U.S.	C2	96
Jack Mountain, mtn., Mt., U.S.	D4	103
Jack Mountain, mtn., Wa., U.S.	A5	124
Jackpot, Nv., U.S.	B7	105
Jacksboro, Tn., U.S.	C9	119
Jacksboro, Tx., U.S.	C3	120
Jacks Mountain, mtn., Pa., U.S.	E6	115
Jackson, Al., U.S.	D2	78
Jackson, Ca., U.S.	C3	82
Jackson, Ky., U.S.	C6	94
Jackson, La., U.S.	D4	95
Jackson, Mi., U.S.	F6	99
Jackson, Mn., U.S.	G4	100
Jackson, Ms., U.S.	C3	101
Jackson, Mo., U.S.	D8	102
Jackson, Oh., U.S.	C3	112
Jackson, S.C., U.S.	E4	117
Jackson, Tn., U.S.	B3	119
Jackson, Wi., U.S.	E5	126
Jackson, Wy., U.S.	C2	127
Jackson, co., Al., U.S.	A3	78
Jackson, co., Ar., U.S.	B4	81
Jackson, co., Co., U.S.	A4	83
Jackson, co., Fl., U.S.	B1	86
Jackson, co., Ga., U.S.	B3	87
Jackson, co., Il., U.S.	F4	90
Jackson, co., In., U.S.	G5	91
Jackson, co., Ia., U.S.	B7	92
Jackson, co., Ks., U.S.	C8	93
Jackson, co., Ky., U.S.	C5	94
Jackson, co., La., U.S.	B3	95
Jackson, co., Mi., U.S.	F6	99
Jackson, co., Mn., U.S.	G3	100
Jackson, co., Ms., U.S.	E5	101
Jackson, co., Mo., U.S.	B3	102
Jackson, co., N.C., U.S.	f9	110
Jackson, co., Oh., U.S.	C3	112
Jackson, co., Ok., U.S.	C2	113
Jackson, co., Or., U.S.	E4	114
Jackson, co., S.D., U.S.	D4	118
Jackson, co., Tn., U.S.	C8	119
Jackson, co., Tx., U.S.	E4	120
Jackson, co., W.V., U.S.	C3	125
Jackson, co., Wi., U.S.	D3	126
Jackson, Lake, l., Fl., U.S.	E5	86
Jackson, Lake, l., Fl., U.S.	B2	86
Jackson, Mount, mtn., N.H., U.S.	B4	106
Jackson Center, Oh., U.S.	B1	112
Jackson Lake, res., Wy., U.S.	C2	127
Jackson Mountains, mts., Nv., U.S.	B3	105
Jackson's Arm, Newf., Can.	D3	72
Jacksons Gap, Al., U.S.	C4	78
Jacksonville, Al., U.S.	B4	78
Jacksonville, Ar., U.S.	C3	81
Jacksonville, Fl., U.S.	B5	86
Jacksonville, Il., U.S.	D3	90
Jacksonville, N.C., U.S.	C5	110
Jacksonville, Tx., U.S.	D5	120
Jacksonville Beach, Fl., U.S.	B5	86
Jacksonville Naval Air Station, mil., Fl., U.S.	B5	86
Jacks Peak, mtn., Ut., U.S.	E3	121
Jacmel, Haiti	E11	64
Jacobābād, Pak.	F3	38
Jacques-Cartier, Mount, mtn., Que., Can.	B6	74
Jacques-Cartier, Détroit de, strt., Que., Can.	h8	72
Jacquet River, N.B., Can.	B4	71
Jadraque, Spain	E9	12
Jaén, Peru	E3	54
Jaén, Spain	H8	12
Jaffna, Sri L.	H6	37
Jaffrey, N.H., U.S.	E2	106
Jafr, Qā' al-, depr., Jord.	D5	40
Jagādhri, India	E7	38
Jagdalpur, India	C7	37
Jagersfontein, S. Afr.	G5	44
Jagodnoje, Russia	E23	24
Jagtiāl, India	C5	37
Jaguarão, Braz.	C6	56
Jahrom, Iran	C5	46
Jaidak, Afg.	E2	38
Jaipur, India	G6	38
Jajce, Bos.	E12	14
Jakarta, Indon.	m13	32
Jakobshavn, Grnld.	C22	66
Jakobstad (Pietarsaari), Fin.	E14	6
Jakutsk, Russia	E19	24
Jal, N.M., U.S.	E6	108
Jalālābād, Afg.	C4	38
Jalapa, Guat.	G3	64
Jalapa Enríquez, Mex.	H11	62
Jālgaon, India	B3	37
Jālna, India	C3	37
Jalostotitlán, Mex.	G8	62
Jalpaiguri, India	G13	38
Jalta, Ukr.	I4	22
Jaltepec, stm., Mex.	I12	62
Jamaica, ctry., N.A.	E9	64
Jamaica Bay, b., N.Y., U.S.	k13	109
Jamaica Channel, strt., N.A.	E10	64
Jamālpur, Bngl.	H13	38
Jamālpur, India	H12	38
Jamame, Som.	A8	44
Jambi, Indon.	F3	32
Jambol, Bul.	G10	16
James, stm., Mo., U.S.	C7	76
James, stm., Mo., U.S.	E4	102
James, stm., Va., U.S.	C5	123
James, Lake, l., In., U.S.	A7	91
James, Lake, res., N.C., U.S.	B1	110
James Bay, b., Can.	F16	66
James Branch, stm., De., U.S.	F3	85
Jamesburg, N.J., U.S.	C4	107
James City, N.C., U.S.	B5	110
James City, co., Va., U.S.	C6	123
James Island, S.C., U.S.	k12	117
James Island, i., Md., U.S.	C5	97
James Island, i., S.C., U.S.	F8	117
James River Bridge, Va., U.S.	k15	123
Jamestown, In., U.S.	E4	91
Jamestown, Ky., U.S.	D4	94
Jamestown, N.Y., U.S.	C1	109
Jamestown, N.C., U.S.	B3	110
Jamestown, N.D., U.S.	C7	111
Jamestown, Oh., U.S.	C2	112
Jamestown, R.I., U.S.	F5	116
Jamestown, Tn., U.S.	C9	119
James Town, Wy., U.S.	E3	127
Jamestown Dam, N.D., U.S.	C7	111
Jamestown Reservoir, res., N.D., U.S.	C7	111
Jamiltepec, Mex.	I11	62
Jamkhandi, India	D3	37
Jammu, India	D6	38
Jammu and Kashmir, dep., Asia	C6	38
Jāmnagar, India	I4	38
Jāmpur, Pak.	F4	38
Jämsä, Fin.	F15	6
Jamshedpur, India	I12	38
Jamsk, Russia	F24	24
Jamūi, India	H12	38
Jamuna, stm., Bngl.	H13	38
Jana, stm., Russia	C21	24
Janaucu, Ilha, i., Braz.	C8	54
Janesville, Ca., U.S.	B3	82
Janesville, Ia., U.S.	B5	92
Janesville, Mn., U.S.	F5	100
Janesville, Wi., U.S.	F4	126
Jangipur, India	H13	38
Janīn, Jord.	C4	40
Janskij, Russia	D20	24
Janskij Zaliv, b., Russia	C21	24
Januária, Braz.	C6	57
Jaora, India	I6	38
Japan, ctry., Asia	D14	26
Japan, Sea of, Asia	D13	26
Japurá (Caquetá), stm., S.A.	D5	54
Jaqué, Pan.	K8	64
Jarābulus, Syria	A6	40
Jaraiz de la Vera, Spain	E6	12
Jarash, Jord.	C4	40
Jarceovo, Russia	F15	18
Jardines de la Reina, is., Cuba	D8	64
Jari, stm., Braz.	D8	54
Jaridih, India	I12	38
Jaroslavl', Russia	D22	18
Jarosław, Pol.	E22	8
Jarrettsville, Md., U.S.	A5	97
Järvenpää, Fin.	F15	6
Järvsö, Swe.	F11	6
Jask, Iran	C6	46
Jasmine Estates, Fl., U.S.	D4	86
Jasnyj, Russia	G19	24
Jasonville, In., U.S.	F3	91
Jasper, Al., U.S.	B2	78
Jasper, Fl., U.S.	B4	86
Jasper, Ga., U.S.	B2	87
Jasper, In., U.S.	H4	91
Jasper, Mo., U.S.	D3	102
Jasper, Tn., U.S.	D8	119
Jasper, Tx., U.S.	D6	120
Jasper, co., Ga., U.S.	C3	87
Jasper, co., Il., U.S.	D5	90
Jasper, co., In., U.S.	B3	91
Jasper, co., Ia., U.S.	C4	92
Jasper, co., Ms., U.S.	C4	101
Jasper, co., Mo., U.S.	D3	102
Jasper, co., S.C., U.S.	G5	117
Jasper, co., Tx., U.S.	C1	120
Jasper National Park, Alta., Can.	C1	68
Jataí, Braz.	D3	57
Játiva, Spain	G11	12

Name	Map Ref	Page
Jatni, India	J11	38
Jaú, Braz.	G4	57
Jauaperi, stm., Braz.	C6	54
Jauja, Peru	F3	54
Jaunpur, India	H10	38
Java see Jawa, i., Indon.	G4	32
Javari (Yavari), stm., S.A.	D4	54
Java Sea see Jawa, Laut, Indon.	G4	32
Jävre, Swe.	D13	6
Jawa, i., Indon.	G4	32
Jawa, Laut (Java Sea), Indon.	G4	32
Jaworzno, Pol.	E19	8
Jay, Ok., U.S.	A7	113
Jay, co., In., U.S.	D7	91
Jaya, Puncak, mtn., Indon.	F10	32
Jayapura, Indon.	F11	32
Jayb, Wādī al-, val., Asia	D4	40
J. B. Thomas, Lake, res., Tx., U.S.	C2	120
Jean, Nv., U.S.	H6	105
Jeanerette, La., U.S.	E4	95
Jean Lafitte National Historical Park, La., U.S.	k12	95
Jeannette, Pa., U.S.	F2	115
Jebba, Nig.	G6	42
Jeddore Lake, res., Newf., Can.	D3	72
Jeff Davis, co., Ga., U.S.	E4	87
Jeff Davis, co., Tx., U.S.	o12	120
Jefferson, Ga., U.S.	B3	87
Jefferson, Ia., U.S.	B3	92
Jefferson, La., U.S.	k11	95
Jefferson, N.C., U.S.	A1	110
Jefferson, Oh., U.S.	A5	112
Jefferson, Or., U.S.	C3	114
Jefferson, S.C., U.S.	B7	117
Jefferson, Tx., U.S.	C5	120
Jefferson, Wi., U.S.	E5	126
Jefferson, co., Al., U.S.	B3	78
Jefferson, co., Ar., U.S.	C3	81
Jefferson, co., Co., U.S.	B5	83
Jefferson, co., Fl., U.S.	B3	86
Jefferson, co., Ga., U.S.	C4	87
Jefferson, co., Id., U.S.	F6	89
Jefferson, co., Il., U.S.	E5	90
Jefferson, co., In., U.S.	G6	91
Jefferson, co., Ia., U.S.	C5	92
Jefferson, co., Ks., U.S.	C8	93
Jefferson, co., Ky., U.S.	B4	94
Jefferson, co., La., U.S.	E5	95
Jefferson, co., Ms., U.S.	D2	101
Jefferson, co., Mo., U.S.	C7	102
Jefferson, co., Mt., U.S.	D4	103
Jefferson, co., Ne., U.S.	D8	104
Jefferson, co., N.Y., U.S.	A5	109
Jefferson, co., Oh., U.S.	B5	112
Jefferson, co., Ok., U.S.	C4	113
Jefferson, co., Or., U.S.	C5	114
Jefferson, co., Pa., U.S.	D3	115
Jefferson, co., Tn., U.S.	C10	119
Jefferson, co., Tx., U.S.	E5	120
Jefferson, co., Wa., U.S.	B1	124
Jefferson, co., W.V., U.S.	B7	125
Jefferson, co., Wi., U.S.	E5	126
Jefferson, stm., Mt., U.S.	E5	103
Jefferson, Mount, mtn., Id., U.S.	E7	89
Jefferson, Mount, mtn., Nv., U.S.	E5	105
Jefferson, Mount, mtn., Or., U.S.	C5	114
Jefferson City, Mo., U.S.	C5	102
Jefferson City, Tn., U.S.	C10	119
Jefferson Davis, co., La., U.S.	D3	95
Jefferson Davis, co., Ms., U.S.	D4	101
Jefferson Farms, De., U.S.	i7	85
Jefferson Proving Ground, mil., In., U.S.	G7	91
Jeffersontown, Ky., U.S.	B4	94
Jeffersonville, Ga., U.S.	D3	87
Jeffersonville, In., U.S.	H6	91
Jeffersonville, Ky., U.S.	C6	94
Jeffersonville, Oh., U.S.	C2	112
Jeffrey, W.V., U.S.	D3	125
Jeffrey City, Wy., U.S.	D5	127
Jeffries Creek, stm., S.C., U.S.	C8	117
Jefremov, Russia	H21	18
Jegorjevsk, Russia	F22	18
Jehossee Island, i., S.C., U.S.	k11	117
Jejsk, Russia	H5	22
Jekaterinburg, Russia	F10	22
Jekyll Island, i., Ga., U.S.	E5	87
Jelec, Russia	I21	18
Jelenia Góra (Hirschberg), Pol.	E15	8
Jelgava, Lat.	E6	18
Jellico, Tn., U.S.	C9	119
Jelm Mountain, mtn., Wy., U.S.	E7	127
Jeloguj, stm., Russia	E11	24
Jember, Indon.	n16	32
Jemez, stm., N.M., U.S.	k7	108
Jemez Canyon Dam, N.M., U.S.	k7	108
Jemez Indian Reservation, N.M., U.S.	h7	108
Jemez Pueblo, N.M., U.S.	B3	108
Jemison, Al., U.S.	C3	78
Jena, Ger.	E11	8
Jena, La., U.S.	C3	95
Jenašimskij Polkan, Gora, mtn., Russia	F12	24
Jendouba (Souk el Arba), Tun.	M3	14
Jenisej, stm., Russia	D11	24
Jenisejsk, Russia	F12	24
Jenisejskij Zaliv, b., Russia	C10	24
Jenkins, Ky., U.S.	C7	94
Jenkins, co., Ga., U.S.	D5	87
Jenkintown, Pa., U.S.	o21	115
Jenks, Ok., U.S.	A6	113
Jennings, La., U.S.	D3	95
Jennings, Mo., U.S.	f13	102
Jennings, co., In., U.S.	G6	91
Jensen Beach, Fl., U.S.	E6	86
Jepara, Indon.	m15	33a
Jequié, Braz.	B8	57
Jequitinhonha, stm., Braz.	D9	57
Jerada, Mor.	B6	42
Jerauld, co., S.D., U.S.	C7	118
Jérémie, Haiti	E10	64
Jeremoabo, Braz.	F11	54
Jerevan, Arm.	I6	22
Jerez de García Salinas, Mex.	F8	62
Jerez de la Frontera, Spain	I5	12
Jerez de los Caballeros, Spain	G5	12
Jericho, Vt., U.S.	B3	122
Jericho see Arīḥā, Jord.	D4	40
Jerimoth Hill, hill, R.I., U.S.	C1	116
Jermyn, Pa., U.S.	C10	115
Jerofej Pavlovič, Russia	G18	24
Jerome, Az., U.S.	C4	80
Jerome, Id., U.S.	G4	89
Jerome, Pa., U.S.	F4	115
Jerome, co., Id., U.S.	G4	89
Jeropol, Russia	D27	24
Jersey, co., Il., U.S.	D3	90
Jersey, dep., Eur.	C4	10
Jersey City, N.J., U.S.	B4	107
Jersey Mountain, mtn., Id., U.S.	E3	89
Jersey Shore, Pa., U.S.	D7	115
Jerseyville, Il., U.S.	D3	90
Jerusalem see Yerushalayim, Isr.	D4	40
Jervis Inlet, b., B.C., Can.	D6	69
Jesenice, Slo.	C9	14
Jessore, Bngl.	I13	38
Jessup, Md., U.S.	B4	97
Jessup, Pa., U.S.	m18	115
Jesup, Ga., U.S.	E5	87
Jesup, Ia., U.S.	B5	92
Jesup, Lake, l., Fl., U.S.	D5	86
Jésus, Île, i., Que., Can.	p19	74
Jesús Carranza, Mex.	I12	62
Jetmore, Ks., U.S.	D4	93
Jeumont, Fr.	B11	10
Jever, Ger.	B7	8
Jevpatorija, Ukr.	H4	22
Jewel Cave National Monument, S.D., U.S.	D2	118
Jewell, Ia., U.S.	B4	92
Jewell, co., Ks., U.S.	C5	93
Jewett City, Ct., U.S.	C8	84
Jeypore, India	C7	37
Jhang Maghiāna, Pak.	E5	38
Jhānsi, India	H8	38
Jharia, India	I12	38
Jhelum, Pak.	D5	38
Jhelum, stm., Asia	E5	38
Jiading, China	D10	28
Jiaganj, India	H13	38
Jiamusi, China	B13	26
Jian, China	H3	28
Jianchuan, China	A5	34
Jiangmen, China	M2	28
Jiangsu, prov., China	E10	26
Jiangxi, prov., China	F10	26
Jiangyin, China	D9	28
Jiangzi, China	F13	38
Jianou, China	H7	28
Jianshui, China	C7	34
Jiaoxian, China	D10	26
Jiaozuo, China	D9	26
Jiashan, China	C6	28
Jiawang, China	A4	28
Jiaxian, China	A2	28
Jiaxing, China	E9	28
Jiazi, China	M5	28
Jicarilla Apache Indian Reservation, N.M., U.S.	A2	108
Jiddah, Sau. Ar.	D2	46
Jieshou, China	B4	28
Jieyang, China	L5	28
Jihlava, Czech.	F15	8
Jijiga, Eth.	G3	46
Jijona, Spain	G11	12
Jilemutu, China	A11	26
Jilin, China	C12	26
Jilin, prov., China	C12	26
Jill, Kediet ej, mtn., Maur.	D3	42
Jima, Eth.	G2	46
Jimena de la Frontera, Spain	I6	12
Jim Hogg, co., Tx., U.S.	F3	120
Jim Lake, res., N.D., U.S.	B7	111
Jim Thorpe, Pa., U.S.	E10	115
Jim Wells, co., Tx., U.S.	F3	120
Jinan (Tsinan), China	D10	26
Jind, India	F7	38
Jingdezhen (Kingtechen), China	F6	28
Jingjiang, China	C9	28
Jingxi, China	C9	34
Jinhua, China	F7	28
Jining, China	D10	26
Jining, China	C9	26
Jinja, Ug.	A6	44
Jinning (Jiukunyang), China	B7	34
Jinotega, Nic.	H4	64
Jinotepe, Nic.	H4	64
Jinshi, China	F9	26
Jinxian, China	D11	26
Jinzhou, China	C11	26
Jiparaná, stm., Braz.	E6	54
Jipijapa, Ec.	H2	58
Jirjā, Egypt	C12	42
Jirjā, India	G16	38
Jisr ash-Shughūr, Syria	B5	40
Jiujiang, China	F4	28
Jiuling Shan, mts., China	G3	28
Jiumangya, China	B14	38
Jiuquan, China	D6	26
Jixi, China	B13	26
Joaçaba, Braz.	B6	56
Joanna, S.C., U.S.	C4	117
João Pessoa, Braz.	E12	54
Joaquín V. González, Arg.	B4	56
Job Peak, mtn., Nv., U.S.	D3	105
Jobson (Vera), Arg.	B5	56
Jocassee, Lake, res., U.S.	B1	117
Jódar, Spain	H8	12
Jo Daviess, co., Il., U.S.	A3	90
Jodhpur, India	G5	38
Joe Batt's Arm [-Barr'd Islands-Shoal Bay], Newf., Can.	D4	72
Joensuu, Fin.	E17	6
Joes Brook, stm., Vt., U.S.	C4	122
Joes Creek, stm., W.V., U.S.	m12	125
Joffre, Mount, mtn., Can.	D3	68
Jogjakarta see Yogyakarta, Indon.	G5	32
Johannesburg, S. Afr.	G5	44
Johar, Som.	H4	46
John, Cape, c., N.S., Can.	D6	71
John Day, Or., U.S.	C8	114
John Day, stm., Or., U.S.	B6	114
John Day Dam, U.S.	D5	124
John Day Fossil Beds National Monument, Or., U.S.	C6	114
John F. Kennedy Space Center, sci., Fl., U.S.	D6	86
John H. Kerr Dam, Va., U.S.	D4	123
John H. Kerr Reservoir, res., U.S.	D4	123
John Martin Reservoir, res., Co., U.S.	C7	83
John Muir National Historical Site, hist., Ca., U.S.	h8	82
John o' Groats, Scot., U.K.	C9	7
John Redmond Reservoir, res., Ks., U.S.	D8	93
John Sevier, Tn., U.S.	m14	119
Johns Island, i., S.C., U.S.	F7	117
Johnson, Ks., U.S.	E2	93
Johnson, Vt., U.S.	B3	122
Johnson, co., Ar., U.S.	B2	81
Johnson, co., Ga., U.S.	D4	87
Johnson, co., Il., U.S.	F5	90
Johnson, co., In., U.S.	F5	91
Johnson, co., Ia., U.S.	C6	92
Johnson, co., Ks., U.S.	D9	93
Johnson, co., Ky., U.S.	C7	94
Johnson, co., Mo., U.S.	C4	102
Johnson, co., Ne., U.S.	D9	104
Johnson, co., Tn., U.S.	C12	119
Johnson, co., Tx., U.S.	C4	120
Johnson, co., Wy., U.S.	B6	127
Johnsonburg, Pa., U.S.	D4	115
Johnson City, N.Y., U.S.	C5	109
Johnson City, Tn., U.S.	C11	119
Johnson City, Tx., U.S.	D3	120
Johnson Creek, Wi., U.S.	E5	126
Johnsonville, S.C., U.S.	D9	117
Johns Pass, strt., Fl., U.S.	p10	86
Johnston, Ia., U.S.	e8	92
Johnston, R.I., U.S.	C4	116
Johnston, S.C., U.S.	D4	117
Johnston, co., N.C., U.S.	B4	110
Johnston, co., Ok., U.S.	C5	113
Johnston City, Il., U.S.	F5	90
Johnston Key, i., Fl., U.S.	H5	86
Johnstown, Co., U.S.	A6	83
Johnstown, N.Y., U.S.	B6	109
Johnstown, Oh., U.S.	B3	112
Johnstown, Pa., U.S.	F4	115
John W. Flannagan Reservoir, res., Va., U.S.	e9	123
Johor Baharu, Malay.	N7	34
Joigny, Fr.	E10	10
Joiner, Ar., U.S.	B5	81
Joinville, Braz.	B7	56
Joinville, Fr.	D12	10
Jokkmokk, Swe.	C12	6
Joliet, Il., U.S.	B5	90
Joliette, Que., Can.	C4	74
Jolo Island, i., Phil.	D7	32
Jombang, Indon.	m16	33a
Jones, Ok., U.S.	B4	113
Jones, co., Ga., U.S.	C3	87
Jones, co., Ia., U.S.	B6	92
Jones, co., Ms., U.S.	D4	101
Jones, co., N.C., U.S.	B5	110
Jones, co., S.D., U.S.	D5	118
Jones, co., Tx., U.S.	C3	120
Jonesboro, Ar., U.S.	B5	81
Jonesboro, Ga., U.S.	C2	87
Jonesboro, Il., U.S.	F4	90
Jonesboro, In., U.S.	D6	91
Jonesboro, La., U.S.	B3	95
Jonesborough, Tn., U.S.	C11	119
Jonesburg, Mo., U.S.	C6	102
Jones Creek, Tx., U.S.	s14	120
Jones Mill, Ar., U.S.	C3	81
Jonesport, Me., U.S.	D5	96
Jones Sound, strt., N.W. Ter., Can.	A15	66
Jonestown, Ms., U.S.	A3	101
Jonesville, La., U.S.	C4	95
Jonesville, Mi., U.S.	G6	99
Jonesville, N.C., U.S.	A2	110
Jonesville, S.C., U.S.	B4	117
Jonesville, Va., U.S.	f8	123
Jongkha, China	F11	38
Jönköping, Swe.	H10	6
Jonquière, Que., Can.	A6	74
Jonzac, Fr.	G6	10
Joplin, Mo., U.S.	D3	102
Joppatowne, Md., U.S.	B5	97
Jordan, Mn., U.S.	F5	100
Jordan, ctry., Asia	D5	40
Jordan, stm., Asia	C4	40
Jordan, stm., Ut., U.S.	C4	121
Jordan Creek, stm., U.S.	E9	114
Jordan Lake, res., Al., U.S.	C3	78
Jorhāt, India	G16	38
Jörn, Swe.	D13	6
Jornado del Muerto, des., N.M., U.S.	D3	108
Jos, Nig.	G7	42
José Battle y Ordóñez, Ur.	C5	56
Joseph, Or., U.S.	B9	114
Joseph, Lac, l., Newf., Can.	h8	72
Joseph Bonaparte Gulf, b., Austl.	B5	50
Joseph City, Az., U.S.	C5	80
Josephine, co., Or., U.S.	E3	114
Joshua, Tx., U.S.	n9	120
Joshua Tree, co., U.S.	E5	82
Joshua Tree National Monument, Ca., U.S.	F6	82
Joškar-Ola, Russia	F7	22
Jourdanton, Tx., U.S.	E3	120
Joutsijärvi, Fin.	C16	6
Jovellanos, Cuba	C7	64
J. Percy Priest Lake, res., Tn., U.S.	A5	119
Juab, co., Ut., U.S.	D2	121
Juan Aldama, Mex.	E8	62
Juan de Fuca, Strait of, strt., N.A.	G8	66
Juan de Nova, Île, i., Reu.	E8	44
Juárez, Arg.	D5	56
Juàzeiro, Braz.	E10	54
Juàzeiro do Norte, Braz.	E11	54
Jūbā, Sudan	H12	42
Juba (Genale), stm., Afr.	H3	46
Juchitán [de Zaragoza], Mex.	I12	62
Judenburg, Aus.	H14	8
Judith, stm., Mt., U.S.	C7	103
Judith, Point, c., R.I., U.S.	G4	85
Judith Basin, co., Mt., U.S.	C6	103
Judith Gap, l., N.C., U.S.	B6	110
Judith Mountains, mts., Mt., U.S.	C7	103
Judith Peak, mtn., Mt., U.S.	C7	103
Judoma, stm., Russia	F21	24
Judsonia, Ar., U.S.	B4	81
Juigalpa, Nic.	H5	64
Juiz de Fora, Braz.	F7	57
Jukagirskoje Ploskogorje, plat., Russia	D24	24
Jukte, Russia	E15	24
Julesburg, Co., U.S.	A8	83
Juliaca, Peru	G4	54
Julian, Ca., U.S.	F5	82
Julian, W.V., U.S.	C3	125
Julian Alps, mts., Eur.	C8	14
Juliana Top, mtn., Sur.	C7	54
Julianehåb, Grnld.	D23	66
Jülich, Ger.	E6	8
Jullundur, India	E6	38
Jumbo Peak, mtn., Nv., U.S.	G7	105
Jumentos Cays, is., Bah.	C10	64
Jumet, Bel.	E4	8
Jumilla, Spain	G10	12
Jump, stm., Wi., U.S.	C3	126
Junàgadh, India	J4	38
Junction, Tx., U.S.	D3	120
Junction City, Ar., U.S.	D3	81
Junction City, Ks., U.S.	C7	93
Junction City, Ky., U.S.	C5	94
Junction City, La., U.S.	A3	95
Junction City, Or., U.S.	C3	114
Jundiaí, Braz.	G5	57
Juneau, Ak., U.S.	D13	79
Juneau, Wi., U.S.	E5	126
Juneau, co., Wi., U.S.	E3	126
June in Winter, Lake, l., Fl., U.S.	E5	86
Jungfrau, mtn., Switz.	F14	10
Junggar Pendi, China	B4	26
Juniata, Ne., U.S.	D7	104
Juniata, co., Pa., U.S.	F7	115
Juniata, stm., Pa., U.S.	F7	115
Junín, Arg.	C4	56
Junín, Lago de, l., Peru	F3	54
Junín de los Andes, Arg.	D2	56
Junior, Lake, l., Me., U.S.	C5	96
Juniper Mountains, mts., Az., U.S.	B2	80
Junípero Serra Peak, mtn., Ca., U.S.	D3	82
Junsele, Swe.	E11	6
Jupiter, Fl., U.S.	F6	86
Jupiter Inlet, b., Fl., U.S.	F6	86
Jupiter Island, i., Fl., U.S.	E6	86
Jura, mts., Eur.	F13	10
Jura, i., Scot., U.K.	F7	7
Jurga, Russia	F10	24
Jūrmala, Lat.	E6	18
Juruá, stm., S.A.	D5	54
Juruena, stm., Braz.	E7	54
Justin, Tx., U.S.	C4	120
Justo Daract, Arg.	C3	56
Jutaí, stm., Braz.	D5	54
Jüterbog, Ger.	D13	8
Jutiapa, Guat.	G3	64
Juticalpa, Hond.	G4	64
Jutland see Jylland, pen., Den.	H7	6
Juventud, Isla de la (Isle of Pines), i., Cuba	D6	64
Juwara, Oman		
Juža, Russia	E25	18
Južno-Sachalinsk, Russia	H22	24
Južnyj, Mys, c., Russia	F25	24
Južnyj Bug, stm., Ukr.	H3	22
Jwayyā, Leb.	C4	40
Jylland, pen., Den.	H7	6
Jyväskylä, Fin.	E15	6

K

K2 (Qogir Feng), mtn., Asia	C7	38
Kaaawa, Hi., U.S.	f10	88
Kaala, mtn., Hi., U.S.	f9	88
Kaala Djerda, Tun.	N3	14
Kaalualu Bay, b., Hi., U.S.	E6	88
Kaaumakua, Puu, mtn., Hi., U.S.	f10	88
Kabale, Ug.	B5	44
Kabalo, Zaire	C5	44
Kabambare, Zaire	B5	44
Kâdbalis, Swe.	C12	6
Kabetogama Lake, l., Mn., U.S.	B5	100
Kabīr Kūh, mts., Iran	B4	46
Kābol, Afg.	C3	38
Kabompo, stm., Zam.	C4	44
Kabongo, Zaire	C5	44
Kābul, stm., Asia	C4	38
Kabwe (Broken Hill), Zam.	D5	44
K'achta, Russia	G15	24
Kačug, Russia	G15	24
Kadan Kyun, i., Burma	H5	34
Kadiri, India	E5	37
Kadoka, S.D., U.S.	D4	118
Kaduna, Nig.	F7	42
Kāduqlī, Sudan	F11	42
Kadykčan, Russia	E23	24
Kaédi, Maur.	E3	42
Kaena Point, c., Hi., U.S.	B3	88
Kaesŏng, N. Kor.	D12	26
Kafia Kingi, Sudan	G10	42
Kafue, stm., Zam.	D5	44
Kaga, Japan	F9	30
Kagamigahara, Japan	G9	30
Kagaznagar, India	C5	37
Kagoshima, Japan	K3	30
Kahaluu, Hi., U.S.	g10	88
Kahana Bay, b., Hi., U.S.	f10	88
Kahemba, Zaire	C3	44
Kahoka, Mo., U.S.	A6	102
Kahoolawe, i., Hi., U.S.	C5	88
Kahuku, Hi., U.S.	B4	88
Kahuku Point, c., Hi., U.S.	B4	88
Kahului, Hi., U.S.	C5	88
Kahului Bay, b., Hi., U.S.	C5	88
Kai, Kepulauan, is., Indon.	G9	32
Kaibab Indian Reservation, Az., U.S.	A3	80
Kaieteur Fall, wtfl, Guy.	E13	58
Kaifeng, China	E9	26
Kaikoura, N.Z.	E4	52
Kaili, China	A10	34
Kailua, Hi., U.S.	B4	88
Kailua Bay, b., Hi., U.S.	g11	88
Kailua Kona, Hi., U.S.	D6	88
Kaimana, Indon.	F9	32
Kaimanawa Mountains, mts., N.Z.	C5	52
Kainan, Japan	H8	30
Kaiserslautern, Ger.	F7	8
Kaitangata, N.Z.	G2	52
Kaiwi Channel, strt., Hi., U.S.	B4	88
Kajaani, Fin.	D16	6
Kajakī, Band-e, res., Afg.	D1	38
Kajan, stm., Indon.	E6	32
Kajang, Malay.	M6	34
Kakamas, S. Afr.	G4	44
Kaka Point, c., Hi., U.S.	C5	88
Kake, Ak., U.S.	D13	79
Kakegawa, Japan	H11	30
Kakie, Bots.	F4	44
Kākināda, India	D7	37
Kakogawa, Japan	H7	30
Kaladan, stm., Asia	D2	34
Ka Lae, c., Hi., U.S.	E6	88
Kalahari Desert, des., Afr.	F4	44
Kālahasti, India	F5	37
Kalaheo, Hi., U.S.	B2	88
Kalajoki, Fin.	D14	6
Kalakan, Russia	F17	24
Kalām, Pak.	C5	38
Kalama, Wa., U.S.	C3	124
Kalámai, Grc.	L6	16
Kalamazoo, Mi., U.S.	F5	99
Kalamazoo, co., Mi., U.S.	F5	99
Kalamazoo, stm., Mi., U.S.	F5	99
Kalasin, Thai.	F7	34
Kalāt, Pak.	F2	38
Kalaupapa Peninsula, pen., Hi., U.S.	B5	88
Kalawao, co., Hi., U.S.	B5	88
Kalb, Ra's al-, c., Yemen	F4	46
Kale, Tur.	L12	16
Kaleden, B.C., Can.	E8	69
Kalemie (Albertville), Zaire	C5	44
Kalena, Puu, mtn., Hi., U.S.	g9	88
Kalgin Island, i., Ak., U.S.	g16	79
Kalgoorlie, Austl.	F4	50
Kalima, Zaire	B5	44
Kálimnos, Grc.	M10	16
Kaliningrad (Königsberg), Russia	G3	18
Kalinkoviči, Bela.	I12	18
Kalispel Indian Reservation, Wa., U.S.	A8	124
Kalispell, Mt., U.S.	B2	103
Kalkaska, Mi., U.S.	D5	99
Kalkaska, co., Mi., U.S.	D5	99
Kalmar, Swe.	H11	6
Kalohi Channel, strt., Hi., U.S.	C4	88
Kālol, India	I5	38
Kaloli Point, c., Hi., U.S.	D7	88
Kalona, Ia., U.S.	C6	92
Kalone Peak, mtn., B.C., Can.	C4	121
Kaluga, Russia	G19	18
Kalutara, Sri L.	I5	37
Kamaishi, Japan	C14	30
Kamakou, mtn., Hi., U.S.	B5	88
Kamakura, Japan	G12	31
Kamālia, Pak.	E5	38
Kamarān, i., Yemen	E3	46
Kamas, Ut., U.S.	C4	121
Kamba, China	F13	38
Kambam, India	H4	37
Kambar, Pak.	G2	38
Kamčatka, stm., Russia	F25	24
Kamčatka, Poluostrov, pen., Russia	F25	24
Kamčatskij Zaliv, b., Russia	F26	24
Kamen', Gora, mtn., Russia	D12	24
Kamen'-na-Obi, Russia	G10	24
Kamenz, Ger.	D14	8
Kamiah, Id., U.S.	C2	89
Kamiak Butte, mtn., Wa., U.S.	C8	124
Kamienna Góra, Pol.	E16	8
Kamilukuak Lake, l., N.W. Ter., Can.	D12	66
Kamina, Zaire	C5	44
Kaminak Lake, l., N.W. Ter., Can.	D13	66
Kaminuriak Lake, l., N.W. Ter., Can.	D13	66
Kamitsushima, Japan	H2	30
Kamloops, B.C., Can.	D7	69
Kamo, Japan	E12	30
Kāmoke, Pak.	E6	38
Kampala, Ug.	A6	44
Kampar, Malay.	L6	34
Kampen, Neth.	C5	8
Kampeska, Lake, l., S.D., U.S.	C8	118
Kâmpóng Cham, Camb.	H8	34
Kâmpóng Chhnăng, Camb.	H8	34
Kâmpôt, Camb.	I8	34
Kâmpóng Saôm, Chhâk, b., Camb.	I7	34
Kâmpóng Thum, Camb.	H8	34
Kâmpôt, Camb.	I8	34
Kāmthi, India	B5	37
Kamuela (Waimea), Hi., U.S.	C6	88
Kamui-misaki, c., Japan	p18	30a
Kan, stm., Asia	H9	34
Kanab, Ut., U.S.	F3	121
Kanab Creek, stm., U.S.	A3	80
Kanabec, co., Mn., U.S.	E5	100
Kanaga Island, i., Ak., U.S.	E4	79

Name	Map Ref	Page
'anairiktok, stm., Newf., Can.	g9	72
'ananga (Luluabourg), Zaire	C4	44
'anapou Bay, b., Hi., U.S.	C5	88
'anata, Ont., Can.	B9	73
'anawha, Ia., U.S.	B4	92
'anawha, co., W.V., U.S.	C3	125
'anawha, stm., W.V., U.S.	C3	125
'anazawa, Japan	F9	30
'anchanaburi, Thai.	G5	34
'änchenjunga, mtn., Asia	G13	38
'änchipuram, India	F5	37
'andhkot, Pak.	F3	38
'ändi, India	I13	38
'andiyohi, co., Mn., U.S.	E3	100
'andy, Sri L.	I6	37
'ane, Pa., U.S.	C4	115
'ane, co., Il., U.S.	B5	90
'ane, co., Ut., U.S.	F3	121
'aneohe, Hi., U.S.	B4	88
'aneohe Bay, b., Hi., U.S.	g10	88
'aneohe Bay Marine Corps Air Station, mil., Hi., U.S.	g10	88
'angar, Malay.	K6	34
'angaroo Island, i., Austl.	G7	50
'angean, Kepulauan, is., Indon.	G6	32
'angnüng, S. Kor.	D12	26
'ango, Gabon	A2	44
'angto, mtn., Asia	G15	38
'aniama, Zaire	C4	44
'ankakee, Il., U.S.	B6	90
'ankakee, co., Il., U.S.	B6	90
'ankakee, stm., U.S.	B5	90
'ankan, Gui.	F4	42
'anmaw Kyun, i., Burma	I5	34
'annapolis, N.C., U.S.	B2	110
'annauj, India	G8	38
'annonkoski, Fin.	E15	6
'annus, Fin.	E14	6
'ano, Fin.	F7	42
'anonji, Japan	H6	30
'anopolis, Il., U.S.	D5	93
'anopolis Lake, res., Ks., U.S.	D5	93
'anoya, Japan	K3	30
'änpur, India	G9	38
'ansas, Il., U.S.	D6	90
'ansas, state, U.S.	D5	93
'ansas, stm., Ks., U.S.	C7	93
'ansas City, Ks., U.S.	C9	93
'ansas City, Mo., U.S.	B3	102
'ansk, Russia	F13	24
'antō-sammyaku, mts., Japan	F11	30
'anuma, Japan	F12	30
'anye, Bots.	F5	44
'aohsiung, Tai.	M9	28
'aohsiunghsien, Tai.	M9	28
'aolack, Sen.	E2	44
'aokoveld, plat., Nmb.	E2	44
'apaa, Hi., U.S.	A2	88
'apaau, Hi., U.S.	C6	88
'apadvanj, India	I5	38
'apanga, Zaire	C4	44
'apapa Island, i., Hi., U.S.	g10	88
'apfenberg, Aus.	H15	8
'aplan, La., U.S.	D3	95
'aposvár, Hung.	I17	8
'aptai, Bngl.	I15	38
'apuas, stm., Indon.	F4	32
'apūrthala, India	E6	38
'apuskasing, Ont., Can.	o19	73
'arabük, Tur.	G14	4
'aracabey, Tur.	I12	16
'aracaköy, Tur.	H12	16
'arāchi, Pak.	H2	38
'arād, India	D3	37
'araganda, Kaz.	H8	24
'araginskij, Ostrov, i., Russia	F26	24
'araginskij Zaliv, b., Russia	F26	24
'aragoš, Gora, mtn., Russia	G11	24
'araikkudi, India	G5	37
'arakelong, Pulau, i., Indon.	E8	32
'arakoram Range, mts., Asia	C7	38
'arakumskij kanal, Turk.	J10	22
'araman, Tur.	H14	4
'araman, Tur.	L13	16
'aramay, China	B3	26
'aramürsel, Tur.	I13	16
'āranja, India	B4	37
'arasburg, Nmb.	G3	44
'arasjok, Nor.	B15	6
'aratsu, Japan	I2	30
'araul, Russia	C10	24
'arauli, India	G7	38
'arawang, Indon.	m13	33a
'arawanken, mts., Eur.	C9	14
'arbalā', Iraq	B3	46
'ärböle, Swe.	F10	6
'arcag, Hung.	H20	8
'ardhitsa, Grc.	J5	16
'ârdžali, Bul.	H9	16
'argasok, Russia	F10	24
'arhula, Fin.	F16	6
'ariba, Zimb.	E5	44
'ariba, Lake, res., Afr.	E5	44
'aribib, Nmb.	F3	44
'arigasniemi, Fin.	B15	6
'arimata, Kepulauan, is., Indon.	F4	32
'arimata, Selat (Karimata Strait), strt., Indon.	F4	32
'arīmganj, India	H15	38
'arimnagar, India	C5	37
'arin, Som.	F4	46
'ariya, Japan	H9	30
'aris (Karjaa), Fin.	F14	6
'arjaa, Japan	H9	30
'arkabet, Eth.	E2	46
'arlobac, Cro.	D10	14
'arlovo, Bul.	G8	16
'arlovy Vary, Czech.	E12	8
'arlshamn, Swe.	H10	6
'arlskoga, Swe.	G10	6
'arlskrona, Swe.	H10	6
'arlsruhe, Ger.	F8	8
'arlstad, Swe.	G9	6
'arlstad, Mn., U.S.	B2	100

Name	Map Ref	Page
Karnāl, India	F7	38
Karnaphuli Reservoir, res., Bngl.	I15	38
Karnataka, state, India	E3	37
Karnes, co., Tx., U.S.	E4	120
Karnes City, Tx., U.S.	E4	120
Karns, Tn., U.S.	n13	119
Karonga, Mwi.	C6	44
Kárpathos, i., Grc.	N11	16
Karpenísion, Grc.	K5	16
Kars, Tur.	G16	4
Kärsämäki, Fin.	E15	6
Karši, Uzb.	J11	22
Kartal, Tur.	I13	16
Karufa, Indon.	F9	32
Karungi, Swe.	C14	6
Karūr, India	G5	37
Karviná, Czech.	F18	8
Kārwār, India	E3	37
Kasai (Cassai), stm., Afr.	B3	44
Kasaji, Zaire	D4	44
Kasama, Zam.	D6	44
Kasanga, Tan.	C6	44
Kasaoka, Japan	H6	30
Kāsaragod, India	F3	37
Kasba Lake, l., N.W. Ter., Can.	D12	66
Kaseda, Japan	K3	30
Kasempa, Zam.	D5	44
Kasenga, Zaire	D5	44
Kasese, Zaire	B5	46
Kāsganj, India	G8	38
Kāshān, Iran	B5	46
Kashi, China	D2	26
Kashima-nada, Japan	F13	30
Kashīpur, India	F8	38
Kashiwa, Japan	G12	30
Kashiwazaki, Japan	E11	30
Kashmir see Jammu and Kashmir, dep., Asia	C6	38
Kasimov, Russia	G24	18
Kašin, Russia	D20	18
Kašira, Russia	G21	18
Kaskaskia, stm., Il., U.S.	D5	90
Kaskö (Kaskinen), Fin.	E13	6
Kaslo, B.C., Can.	E9	69
Kasongo, Zaire	B5	44
Kasota, Mn., U.S.	F5	100
Kasr, Ra's, c., Sudan	E13	42
Kassalā, Sudan	E13	42
Kassel, Ger.	D9	8
Kasson, Mn., U.S.	F6	100
Kastoría, Grc.	I5	16
Kasugai, Japan	G9	30
Kasūr, Pak.	E6	38
Katahdin, Mount, mtn., Me., U.S.	C4	96
Katanga Plateau, plat., Zaire	D5	44
Katchall Island, i., India	K2	34
Kateríni, Grc.	I6	16
Kates Needle, mtn., Ak., U.S.	m24	79
Katherine, Austl.	B6	50
Kāthiāwār, pen., India	I4	38
Kathleen, Fl., U.S.	k7	120
Kaṭhmāndau, Nepal	G11	38
Katihār, India	H12	38
Katiola, I.C.	G4	42
Katmai, Mount, mtn., Ak., U.S.	D9	79
Katmai National Park, Ak., U.S.	D9	79
Katmandu see Kāthmāndau, Nepal	G11	38
Katowice, Pol.	E19	8
Kātrīnā, Jabal, mtn., Egypt	C12	42
Katríneholm, Swe.	G11	6
Katsina, Nig.	F7	42
Katsuta, Japan	F13	30
Kattegat, strt., Eur.	H8	6
Katy, Tx., U.S.	r14	120
Kauai, co., Hi., U.S.	B1	88
Kauai, i., Hi., U.S.	A2	88
Kauai Channel, strt., Hi., U.S.	B3	88
Kau Desert, des., Hi., U.S.	D6	88
Kaufbeuren, Ger.	H10	8
Kaufman, Tx., U.S.	C4	120
Kaufman, co., Tx., U.S.	C4	120
Kauhajoki, Fin.	E14	6
Kaukauna, Wi., U.S.	D5	126
Kaukauveld, mts., Afr.	F3	44
Kaula Island, i., Hi., U.S.	m15	88
Kaulakahi Channel, strt., Hi., U.S.	A2	88
Kaumakani, Hi., U.S.	B2	88
Kaunakakai, Hi., U.S.	B4	88
Kauna Point, c., Hi., U.S.	D6	88
Kaunas, Lith.	G6	18
Kaura Namoda, Nig.	F7	42
Kaustinen, Fin.	E14	6
Kavača, Russia	E27	24
Kavacik, Tur.	J12	16
Kavalerovo, Russia	I21	24
Kavála, Grc.	I8	16
Kavaratti, India	G2	37
Kavieng, Pap. N. Gui.	k17	50a
Kawagoe, Japan	G12	30
Kawaguchi, Japan	G12	30
Kawaihoa Point, c., Hi., U.S.	B1	88
Kawaikini, mtn., Hi., U.S.	A2	88
Kawambwa, Zam.	C5	44
Kawanoe, Japan	H6	30
Kawasaki, Japan	G12	30
Kawich Peak, mtn., Nv., U.S.	F5	105
Kawich Range, mts., Nv., U.S.	F5	105
Kaw Lake, res., Ok., U.S.	A5	113
Kawm Umbū, Egypt	D12	42
Kay, co., Ok., U.S.	A4	113
Kayankulam, India	H4	37
Kaycee, Wy., U.S.	C6	127
Kayenta, Az., U.S.	A5	80
Kayes, Mali	F3	42
Kayseri, Tur.	H15	4
Kaysville, Ut., U.S.	B4	121
Kažačinskoje, Russia	F12	24
Kazačje, Russia	C21	24
Kazakhstan, ctry., Asia	H11	22
Kazan', Russia	F7	22
Kazanlâk, Bul.	G9	16
Kāzerūn, Iran	C5	46
Kazincbarcika, Russia	D6	18
Keahiakahoe, Puu, mtn., Hi., U.S.	g10	88
Keahole Point, c., Hi., U.S.	D5	88

Name	Map Ref	Page
Kealaikahiki Channel, strt., Hi., U.S.	C5	88
Kealaikahiki Point, c., Hi., U.S.	C5	88
Kealakekua, Hi., U.S.	D6	88
Kealia, Hi., U.S.	A2	88
Keams Canyon, Az., U.S.	B5	80
Keanapapa Point, c., Hi., U.S.	C4	88
Keansburg, N.J., U.S.	C4	107
Kearney, Mo., U.S.	B3	102
Kearney, co., Ne., U.S.	D7	104
Kearny, Az., U.S.	D5	80
Kearny, N.J., U.S.	h8	107
Kearny, co., Ks., U.S.	D2	93
Kebri Dehar, Eth.	G3	46
Kecskemét, Hung.	I19	8
Kedges Straits, strt., Md., U.S.	D5	97
Kedgwick, N.B., Can.	B2	71
Kediri, Indon.	m16	32
Kedon, Russia	E25	24
Kédougou, Sen.	F3	42
Keego Harbor, Mi., U.S.	o15	99
Keele Peak, mtn., Yukon, Can.	D6	66
Keelung see Chilung, Tai.	J10	28
Keene, N.H., U.S.	E2	106
Keene, Tx., U.S.	n9	120
Keeper Hill, hill, Ire.	I4	7
Keeseville, N.Y., U.S.	f11	109
Keesler Air Force Base, mil., Ms., U.S.	E5	101
Keetmanshoop, Nmb.	G3	44
Keet Seel Ruin, hist., Az., U.S.	A5	80
Keewatin, Ont., Can.	E4	70
Keewatin, Mn., U.S.	C5	100
Kefallinía, i., Grc.	K4	16
Keffi, Nig.	G7	42
Keflavík, Ice.	C3	4
Ke Ga, Mui, c., Viet.	H10	34
Kegonsa, Lake, l., Wi., U.S.	F4	126
Keiser, Ar., U.S.	B5	81
Keith, Scot., U.K.	D10	7
Keith, co., Ne., U.S.	C4	104
Keizer, Or., U.S.	C3	114
Kejimkujik National Park, N.S., Can.	E4	71
Kekaha, Hi., U.S.	B2	88
Kelafo, Eth.	G3	46
Kelang, Malay.	M6	34
Kelheim, Ger.	G11	8
Kelibia, Tun.	M6	14
Keller, Tx., U.S.	n9	120
Kellett, Cape, c., N.W. Ter., Can.	B7	66
Kelleys Island, i., Oh., U.S.	A3	112
Kellogg, Id., U.S.	B2	89
Kellogg, Ia., U.S.	C5	92
Kelloselkä, Fin.	C17	6
Kelly Air Force Base, mil., Tx., U.S.	k7	120
Kelly Island, i., De., U.S.	D4	85
Kellyville, Ok., U.S.	B5	113
Kélo, Chad	G9	42
Kelottijärvi, Fin.	B14	6
Kelowna, B.C., Can.	E8	69
Kelso, Wa., U.S.	C3	124
Keluang, Malay.	M7	34
Kemerovo, Russia	F11	24
Kemi, Fin.	D15	6
Kemijärvi, Fin.	C16	6
Kemijoki, stm., Fin.	C15	6
Kemmerer, Wy., U.S.	E2	127
Kemp, Lake, res., Tx., U.S.	C3	120
Kemper, co., Ms., U.S.	C5	101
Kemps Bay, Bah.	B9	64
Kempt, Lac, l., Que., Can.	G18	66
Kempten [Allgäu], Ger.	H10	8
Kemptville, Ont., Can.	B9	73
Kemul, Kong, mtn., Indon.	E6	32
Kenai, Ak., U.S.	C9	79
Kenai Fjords National Park, Ak., U.S.	D10	79
Kenai Mountains, mts., Ak., U.S.	h16	79
Kenai Peninsula, pen., Ak., U.S.	h16	79
Kenansville, N.C., U.S.	C5	110
Kenbridge, Va., U.S.	D4	123
Kendall, Fl., U.S.	s13	86
Kendall, co., Il., U.S.	B5	90
Kendall, co., Tx., U.S.	E3	120
Kendall, Cape, c., N.W. Ter., Can.	D15	66
Kendall Park, N.J., U.S.	C3	107
Kendallville, In., U.S.	A7	91
Kendari, Indon.	F7	32
Kenedy, Tx., U.S.	E4	120
Kenedy, co., Tx., U.S.	F4	120
Kenema, S.L.	G3	42
Kenesaw, Ne., U.S.	D7	104
Kenhardt, S. Afr.	G4	44
Kenilworth, Il., U.S.	h9	90
Kenitra, Mor.	B4	42
Kenly, N.C., U.S.	B4	110
Kenmare, N.D., U.S.	A3	111
Kenmore, N.Y., U.S.	C2	109
Kennaday Peak, mtn., Wy., U.S.	E6	127
Kennebago Lake, l., Me., U.S.	C2	96
Kennebec, co., Me., U.S.	D3	96
Kennebec, stm., Me., U.S.	D3	96
Kennebunk, Me., U.S.	E2	96
Kennebunkport, Me., U.S.	E2	96
Kennedy Entrance, strt., Ak., U.S.	D9	79
Kennedy Peak, mtn., Burma	C2	34
Kenner, La., U.S.	E5	95
Kennesaw, Ga., U.S.	B2	87
Kennesaw Mountain, mtn., Ga., U.S.	C2	87
Kennett, Mo., U.S.	E7	102
Kennett Square, Pa., U.S.	G10	115
Kennewick, Wa., U.S.	C6	124
Kenn Reefs, rf., Austl.	D11	50
Keno, Or., U.S.	E5	114
Kénogami, Lac, l., Que., Can.	A6	74
Kenora, Ont., Can.	o16	73

Name	Map Ref	Page
Kenosha, Wi., U.S.	F6	126
Kenosha, co., Wi., U.S.	F5	126
Kenova, W.V., U.S.	C2	125
Kensett, Ar., U.S.	B4	81
Kensico Reservoir, res., N.Y., U.S.	g13	109
Kensington, P.E.I., Can.	C6	71
Kensington, Ct., U.S.	C4	84
Kensington, Md., U.S.	B3	97
Kent, Oh., U.S.	A4	112
Kent, Wa., U.S.	B3	124
Kent, co., Ne., U.S.	D7	104
Kent, co., Md., U.S.	B5	97
Kent, co., Mi., U.S.	E5	99
Kent, co., R.I., U.S.	D2	116
Kent, co., Tx., U.S.	C2	120
Kent City, Mi., U.S.	E5	99
Kent Island, i., De., U.S.	D4	85
Kent Island, i., Md., U.S.	C5	97
Kentland, In., U.S.	C3	91
Kenton, De., U.S.	D3	85
Kenton, Oh., U.S.	B2	112
Kenton, Tn., U.S.	A2	119
Kenton, co., Ky., U.S.	B5	94
Kent Peninsula, pen., N.W. Ter., Can.	C11	66
Kent Point, c., Md., U.S.	C5	97
Kentucky, state, U.S.	C4	94
Kentucky, stm., Ky., U.S.	B5	94
Kentwood, La., U.S.	D5	95
Kentwood, Mi., U.S.	F5	99
Kenvil, N.J., U.S.	B3	107
Kenvir, Ky., U.S.	D6	94
Kenya, ctry., Afr.	B7	44
Kenya, Mount see Kirinyaga, mtn., Kenya	B7	44
Kenyon, Mn., U.S.	F6	100
Kenyon, R.I., U.S.	F2	116
Keokea, Hi., U.S.	C5	88
Keokuk, Ia., U.S.	D6	92
Keokuk, co., Ia., U.S.	C5	92
Keokuk Lock and Dam, U.S.	D6	92
Keosauqua, Ia., U.S.	D6	92
Keota, Ia., U.S.	C6	92
Keota, Ok., U.S.	B7	113
Keowee, Lake, res., S.C., U.S.	B2	117
Kepi, Indon.	G10	32
Kerala, state, India	G4	37
Kerč', Ukr.	H5	22
Keremeos, B.C., Can.	E8	69
Keren, Eth.	E2	46
Kerens, Tx., U.S.	C4	120
Kerguélen, Îles, is., F.S.A.T.	J17	2
Kerhonkson, N.Y., U.S.	D6	109
Kericho, Kenya	B7	44
Kerinci, Gunung, mtn., Indon.	F3	32
Kerkhoven, Mn., U.S.	E3	100
Kérkira (Corfu), Grc.	J3	16
Kérkira, i., Grc.	J3	16
Kermān, Iran	B6	46
Kerme Körfezi, b., Tur.	M11	16
Kermit, Tx., U.S.	D1	120
Kermode, Mount, mtn., B.C., Can.	C2	69
Kern, co., Ca., U.S.	E4	82
Kern, stm., Ca., U.S.	E4	82
Kernersville, N.C., U.S.	A2	110
Kernville, Ca., U.S.	E4	82
Kerr, co., Tx., U.S.	D3	120
Kerrville, Tx., U.S.	D3	120
Kerry Head, c., Ire.	I3	7
Kersey, Co., U.S.	A6	83
Kershaw, S.C., U.S.	B6	117
Kershaw, co., S.C., U.S.	C6	117
Kerulen (Cherlen), stm., Asia	B9	26
Kesagami Lake, l., Ont., Can.	F16	66
Keşan, Tur.	I10	16
Kesennuma, Japan	D14	30
Keshena, Wi., U.S.	D5	126
Ket', stm., Russia	F11	24
Keta, Ozero, l., Russia	D11	24
Ketchikan, Ak., U.S.	D13	79
Ketchum, Id., U.S.	F4	89
Kettering, Eng., U.K.	I12	7
Kettering, Oh., U.S.	C1	112
Kettle, stm., Mn., U.S.	D6	100
Kettle Creek, stm., Pa., U.S.	D6	115
Kettle Creek Lake, res., Pa., U.S.	D6	115
Kettle Falls, Wa., U.S.	A7	124
Keuka Lake, l., N.Y., U.S.	C3	109
Kew, T./C. Is.	D11	64
Kewanee, Il., U.S.	B4	90
Kewaskum, Wi., U.S.	E5	126
Kewaunee, Wi., U.S.	D6	126
Kewaunee, co., Wi., U.S.	D6	126
Keweenaw, co., Mi., U.S.	A2	99
Keweenaw Bay, b., Mi., U.S.	B2	99
Keweenaw Peninsula, pen., Mi., U.S.	A3	99
Keweenaw Point, c., Mi., U.S.	A3	99
Keya Paha, co., Ne., U.S.	B6	104
Keya Paha, stm., U.S.	A5	104
Keyhole Reservoir, res., Wy., U.S.	B8	127
Key Largo, Fl., U.S.	G6	86
Keyport, N.J., U.S.	C4	107
Keyser, W.V., U.S.	B6	125
Keystone, W.V., U.S.	D3	125
Keystone Heights, Fl., U.S.	C4	86
Keystone Lake, res., Ok., U.S.	A5	113
Keystone Peak, mtn., Az., U.S.	F4	80
Keysville, Va., U.S.	C4	123
Key West, Fl., U.S.	H5	86
Key West Naval Air Station, mil., Fl., U.S.	H5	86
Kezar Falls, Me., U.S.	E2	96
Kezar Lake, l., Me., U.S.	D2	96
Kežma, Russia	F14	24
Khadki (Kirkee), India	C2	37
Khairpur, Pak.	G3	38
Khalkis, Grc.	K7	16
Khambhāliya, India	I3	38
Khambhāt, Gulf of, b., India	B2	37
Khāmgaon, India	B4	37
Khammam, India	D6	37
Khānābād, Afg.	B3	38
Khānaqīn, Iraq	B4	46
Khandwa, India	B4	37

Name	Map Ref	Page
Khānewāl, Pak.	E4	38
Khaniá, Grc.	N8	16
Khanna, India	E7	38
Khānpur, Pak.	F4	38
Khān Yūnus, Isr. Occ.	D4	40
Kharagpur, India	I12	38
Khargon, India	J6	38
Kharkov see Char'kov, Ukr.	G5	22
Khartoum see Al-Kharṭūm, Sudan	E12	42
Kherson see Cherson, Ukr.	H4	22
Khíos, Grc.	K10	16
Kholm, Afg.	B2	38
Khong, Laos	G8	34
Khong Sédone, Laos	G8	34
Khon Kaen, Thai.	F7	34
Khóra Sfakíon, Grc.	N8	16
Khorramābād, Iran	B4	46
Khorramshahr, Iran	B4	46
Khouribga, Mor.	B4	42
Khowst, Afg.	D3	38
Khulna, Bngl.	I13	38
Khunjerab Pass, Asia	B6	38
Khurja, India	F7	38
Khūryān Mūryān (Kuria Muria Isla, is., Oman	E6	46
Khushāb, Pak.	D5	38
Khvājeh Moḥammad, Kūh-e, mts., Afg.	B4	38
Khvoy, Iran	J6	22
Khyber Pass, Asia	C4	38
Kiamichi, stm., Ok., U.S.	C6	113
Kiamika, stm., Que., Can.	C2	74
Kiana, Ak., U.S.	B7	79
Kiawah Island, i., S.C., U.S.	F7	117
Kibangou, Congo	B2	44
Kibombo, Zaire	B5	44
Kibre Mengist, Eth.	G2	46
Kičevo, Mac.	H4	16
Kichčik, Russia	G25	24
Kickamuit, stm., R.I., U.S.	D5	116
Kickapoo, stm., Wi., U.S.	E3	126
Kickapoo, Lake, res., Tx., U.S.	C3	120
Kickapoo Indian Reservation, Ks., U.S.	C8	93
Kicking Horse Pass, Can.	D2	68
Kidal, Mali	E6	42
Kidder, co., N.D., U.S.	C6	111
Kidira, Sen.	F3	42
Kiefer, Ok., U.S.	B5	113
Kiel, Wi., U.S.	E5	126
Kieler Bucht, b., Ger.	A10	8
Kielce, Pol.	E20	8
Kiel, Wi., U.S.	E5	126
Kiester, Mn., U.S.	G5	100
Kiev see Kijev, Ukr.	G4	22
Kiffa, Maur.	E3	42
Kigali, Rw.	B6	44
Kigoma, Tan.	B5	44
Kihei, Hi., U.S.	C5	88
Kihniö, Fin.	E14	6
Kiholo Bay, b., Hi., U.S.	D5	88
Kii-suidō, strt., Japan	I7	30
Kijev (Kiev), Ukr.	G4	22
Kikinda, Yugo.	D4	16
Kikládhes, is., Grc.	L8	16
Kikwit, Zaire	C3	44
Kilauea, Hi., U.S.	A2	88
Kilauea Crater, crat., Hi., U.S.	D6	88
Kilauea Point, c., Hi., U.S.	A2	88
Kilgore, Tx., U.S.	C5	120
Kilimanjaro, mtn., Tan.	B7	44
Kilis, Tur.	A5	40
Kilkee, Ire.	I5	7
Kilkenny, Ire.	I5	7
Kilkís, Grc.	H6	16
Killala, Ire.	G3	7
Killaloe Station, Ont., Can.	B7	73
Killam, Alta., Can.	C5	68
Killarney, Man., Can.	E2	70
Killarney, Ire.	I3	7
Killarney Provincial Park, Ont., Can.	A3	73
Killdeer, N.D., U.S.	B3	111
Killeen, Tx., U.S.	D4	120
Killen, Al., U.S.	A2	78
Killian, La., U.S.	h10	95
Killik, stm., Ak., U.S.	B9	79
Killona, La., U.S.	h11	95
Killorglin, Ire.	I3	7
Kilmarnock, Scot., U.K.	F8	7
Kilmarnock, Va., U.S.	C6	123
Kilmichael, Ms., U.S.	B4	101
Kiln, Ms., U.S.	E4	101
Kilombero, stm., Tan.	C7	44
Kilosa, Tan.	C7	44
Kilpisjärvi, Fin.	B13	6
Kilwa, Zaire	C5	44
Kilwa Kivinje, Tan.	C7	44
Kimball, Mn., U.S.	E4	100
Kimball, Ne., U.S.	C2	104
Kimball, S.D., U.S.	D7	118
Kimball, co., Ne., U.S.	C2	104
Kimball, Mount, mtn., Ak., U.S.	C11	79
Kimberley, B.C., Can.	E9	69
Kimberley, S. Afr.	G4	44
Kimberley Plateau, plat., Austl.	C5	50
Kimberlin Heights, Tn., U.S.	n14	119
Kimberly, Id., U.S.	B3	78
Kimberly, Id., U.S.	G5	89
Kimberly, W.V., U.S.	m13	125
Kimberly, Wi., U.S.	h9	126
Kimble, co., Tx., U.S.	D3	120
Kimch'aek, N. Kor.	C12	26
Kimovsk, Russia	H21	18
Kimry, Russia	E20	18
Kinabalu, Gunong, mtn., Malay.	D6	32
Kinbasket Lake, res., B.C., Can.	D8	69
Kincaid, Il., U.S.	D4	90
Kincaid, W.V., U.S.	m13	125
Kincaid, Lake, res., Il., U.S.	D4	90
Kincardine, Ont., Can.	C3	73
Kincheloe Air Force Base, mil., Mi., U.S.	B6	99
Kinder, La., U.S.	D3	95
Kindia, Gui.	F3	42
Kindu, Zaire	B5	44

157

Name	Map Ref	Page
Kinešma, Russia	D25	18
King, N.C., U.S.	A2	110
King, Wi., U.S.	D4	126
King, co., Tx., U.S.	C2	120
King, co., Wa., U.S.	B3	124
King and Queen, co., Va., U.S.	C6	123
Kingaroy, Austl.	E10	50
King City, Ca., U.S.	D3	82
King City, Mo., U.S.	A3	102
King Cove, Ak., U.S.	E7	79
Kingfield, Me., U.S.	D2	96
Kingfisher, Ok., U.S.	B4	113
Kingfisher, co., Ok., U.S.	B3	113
King George, co., Va., U.S.	B5	123
King Island, i., Austl.	G8	50
King Island, i., B.C., Can.	C4	69
King Lear Peak, mtn., Nv., U.S.	B3	105
Kirwin Reservoir, res., Ks., U.S.	C4	93
King Leopold Ranges, mts., Austl.	C5	50
Kingman, Az., U.S.	B1	80
Kingman, Ks., U.S.	E5	93
Kingman, co., Ks., U.S.	E5	93
King Mountain, mtn., Or., U.S.	E3	114
King Mountain, mtn., Or., U.S.	D8	114
King Peak, mtn., Ca., U.S.	B1	82
Kings, Ms., U.S.	C3	101
Kings, co., Ca., U.S.	D4	82
Kings, co., N.Y., U.S.	E7	109
Kings, stm., Ar., U.S.	A2	81
Kings, stm., Ca., U.S.	D4	82
Kings, stm., Nv., U.S.	B3	105
King Salmon, Ak., U.S.	D8	79
Kingsburg, Ca., U.S.	D4	82
Kingsbury, co., S.D., U.S.	C8	118
Kings Canyon National Park, Ca., U.S.	D4	82
Kingsey-Falls, Que., Can.	D5	74
Kingsford, Mi., U.S.	C2	99
Kingsland, Ga., U.S.	F5	87
Kingsland, Tx., U.S.	D3	120
Kingsley, Ia., U.S.	B2	92
Kingsley, Mi., U.S.	D5	99
King's Lynn, Eng., U.K.	I13	7
Kings Mountain, N.C., U.S.	B1	110
King Sound, strt., Austl.	C4	50
Kings Park West, Va., U.S.	*B5	123
Kings Peak, mtn., Ut., U.S.	C5	121
King's Point, Newf., Can.	D3	72
Kingsport, Tn., U.S.	C11	119
Kingston, Ont., Can.	C8	73
Kingston, Jam.	E9	64
Kingston, Ga., U.S.	B2	87
Kingston, Id., U.S.	B2	89
Kingston, Ma., U.S.	C6	98
Kingston, N.H., U.S.	E4	106
Kingston, N.Y., U.S.	D6	109
Kingston, Oh., U.S.	C3	112
Kingston, Ok., U.S.	D5	113
Kingston, Pa., U.S.	D10	115
Kingston, R.I., U.S.	F3	116
Kingston, Tn., U.S.	D9	119
Kingston Springs, Tn., U.S.	A4	119
Kingston upon Hull, Eng., U.K.	H12	7
Kingstown, St. Vin.	H17	64
Kingstown, Md., U.S.	B5	97
Kingstree, S.C., U.S.	D8	117
Kingsville, Ont., Can.	E2	73
Kingsville, Md., U.S.	B5	97
Kingsville (North Kingsville), Oh., U.S.	A5	112
Kingsville, Tx., U.S.	F4	120
Kingsville Naval Air Station, mil., Tx., U.S.	F4	120
King William, co., Va., U.S.	C5	123
King William Island, i., N.W. Ter., Can.	C13	66
King William's Town, S. Afr.	H5	44
Kingwood, W.V., U.S.	B5	125
Kinistino, Sask., Can.	E3	75
Kinkaid Lake, res., Il., U.S.	F4	90
Kinloch, Mo., U.S.	f13	102
Kinmundy, Il., U.S.	E5	90
Kinna, Swe.	H9	6
Kinnairds Head, c., Scot., U.K.	D10	7
Kinnelon, N.J., U.S.	B4	107
Kinneret, Yam, l., Isr.	C4	40
Kinney, co., Tx., U.S.	E2	120
Kinross, Scot., U.K.	E9	7
Kinsale, Ire.	J4	7
Kinsarvik, Nor.	F6	6
Kinsey, Al., U.S.	D4	78
Kinshasa (Léopoldville), Zaire	B3	44
Kinsley, Ks., U.S.	E4	93
Kinston, N.C., U.S.	B5	110
Kintyre, pen., Scot., U.K.	F7	7
Kintyre, Mull of, c., Scot., U.K.	F7	7
Kinyeti, mtn., Sudan	H12	42
Kiowa, Ks., U.S.	E5	93
Kiowa, Ok., U.S.	C6	113
Kiowa, co., Co., U.S.	C8	83
Kiowa, co., Ks., U.S.	E4	93
Kiowa, co., Ok., U.S.	C2	113
Kiowa Creek, stm., Ok., U.S.	A1	113
Kipembawe, Tan.	C6	44
Kipili, Tan.	C6	44
Kipnuk, Ak., U.S.	C7	79
Kipushi, Zaire	D5	44
Kirbyville, Tx., U.S.	D6	120
Kirchdorf an der Krems, Aus.	H14	8
Kirenga, stm., Russia	F15	24
Kirensk, Russia	F15	24
Kirghizia see Kyrgyzstan, ctry., Asia	I12	22
Kiribati, ctry., Oc.	G24	2
Kırıkhan, Tur.	A5	40
Kırıkkale, Tur.	H14	4
Kirin see Jilin, China	C12	26
Kirinyaga (Mount Kenya), mtn., Kenya	B7	44
Kırkağaç, Tur.	J11	16
Kirkcaldy, Scot., U.K.	E9	7
Kirkcudbright, Scot., U.K.	G8	7
Kirkenes, Nor.	B18	6
Kirkland, Il., U.S.	A5	90

Kirkland, Wa., U.S.	B3	124
Kirkland Lake, Ont., Can.	o19	73
Kirklin, In., U.S.	D5	91
Kirksville, Mo., U.S.	A5	102
Kirkūk, Iraq	A3	46
Kirkwall, Scot., U.K.	C10	7
Kirkwood, De., U.S.	B3	85
Kirkwood, Il., U.S.	C3	90
Kirkwood, Mo., U.S.	f13	102
Kirov, Russia	F7	22
Kirov, Russia	G17	18
Kirovograd, Ukr.	H4	22
Kirovski, Russia	G25	24
Kırşehir, Tur.	H14	4
Kirthar Range, mts., Pak.	G2	38
Kirtland, N.M., U.S.	A1	108
Kirtland Air Force Base, mil., N.M., U.S.	k7	108
Kiruna, Swe.	C13	6
Kiryū, Japan	F12	30
Kisa, Swe.	H10	6
Kisangani (Stanleyville), Zaire	A5	44
Kisarazu, Japan	G12	30
K.I. Sawyer Air Force Base, mil., Mi., U.S.	B3	99
Kisel'ovsk, Russia	G11	24
Kishanganj, India	G12	38
Kishangarh, India	G6	38
Kishinev see Kišin'ov, Mol.	H3	22
Kishiwada, Japan	H8	30
Kishorganj, Bngl.	H14	38
Kishwaukee, stm., Il., U.S.	A5	90
Kišin'ov, Mol.	H3	22
Kiska Island, i., Ak., U.S.	E3	79
Kiskunfélegyháza, Hung.	I19	8
Kiskunhalas, Hung.	I19	8
Kislovodsk, Russia	I6	22
Kismayu, Som.	B8	44
Kissidougou, Gui.	G3	42
Kissimmee, Fl., U.S.	D5	86
Kissimmee, stm., Fl., U.S.	E5	86
Kissimmee, Lake, l., Fl., U.S.	E5	86
Kississing Lake, l., Man., Can.	B1	70
Kistanje, Cro.	F10	14
Kistler, W.V., U.S.	D3	125
Kisumu, Kenya	B6	44
Kitaibaraki, Japan	F13	30
Kitakami, Japan	C14	30
Kitakami-sanchi, mts., Japan	C14	30
Kitakyūshū, Japan	I3	30
Kitale, Kenya	A6	44
Kitami, Japan	p21	30a
Kitami-sanchi, mts., Japan	o20	30a
Kit Carson, co., Co., U.S.	B8	83
Kitchener, Ont., Can.	D4	73
Kíthira, i., Grc.	M6	16
Kitimat, B.C., Can.	B3	69
Kitsap, co., Wa., U.S.	B3	124
Kitscoty, Alta., Can.	C5	68
Kittanning, Pa., U.S.	E2	115
Kittatinny Mountain, mtn., U.S.	B2	107
Kittery, Me., U.S.	E2	96
Kittery Point, Me., U.S.	E2	96
Kittilä, Fin.	C15	6
Kittitas, Wa., U.S.	C5	124
Kittitas, co., Wa., U.S.	B4	124
Kitts, Ky., U.S.	D6	94
Kittson, co., Mn., U.S.	B2	100
Kitty Hawk, N.C., U.S.	A7	110
Kitty Hawk Bay, b., N.C., U.S.	A7	110
Kitwe, Zam.	D5	44
Kitzbühel, Aus.	H12	8
Kitzingen, Ger.	F10	8
Kivu, Lac, l., Afr.	B5	44
Kızıl, stm., Tur.	G14	4
Kjustendil, Bul.	G6	16
Kladno, Czech.	E14	8
Klagenfurt, Aus.	I14	8
Klaipėda (Memel), Lith.	F4	18
Klamath, co., Or., U.S.	E5	114
Klamath, stm., U.S.	B2	82
Klamath Falls, Or., U.S.	E5	114
Klamath Mountains, mts., U.S.	E2	114
Klangenan, Indon.	m14	33a
Klarälven, stm., Eur.	F9	6
Klawock, Ak., U.S.	D13	79
Kleberg, co., Tx., U.S.	F4	120
Klerksdorp, S. Afr.	G5	44
Kleve, Ger.	D6	8
Klickitat, Wa., U.S.	D4	124
Klickitat, co., Wa., U.S.	C4	124
Klickitat, stm., Wa., U.S.	C4	124
Klimovsk, Russia	F20	18
Klin, Russia	E19	18
Klincy, Russia	I15	18
Kłodzko, Pol.	E16	8
Klondike, hist. reg., Yukon, Can.	D5	66
Klondike Gold Rush National Historical Park, Ak., U.S.	k22	79
Klosterneuburg, Aus.	G16	8
Kluane Lake, l., Yukon, Can.	D5	66
Klutina Lake, l., Ak., U.S.	g19	79
Knapp Creek, stm., W.V., U.S.	C5	125
Knee Lake, l., Man., Can.	B4	70
Kneža, Bul.	F8	16
Knife, stm., N.D., U.S.	B3	111
Knightdale, N.C., U.S.	B4	110
Knight Inlet, b., B.C., Can.	D5	69
Knight Island, i., Ak., U.S.	g18	79
Knightstown, In., U.S.	E6	91
Knightsville, In., U.S.	E3	91
Knightville Reservoir, res., Ma., U.S.	B2	98
Knin, Cro.	E11	14
Knittelfeld, Aus.	H14	8
Knob Noster, Mo., U.S.	C4	102
Knokke, Bel.	D3	8
Knollwood, W.V., U.S.	m12	125
Knott, co., Ky., U.S.	C6	94
Knox, In., U.S.	B4	91
Knox, Pa., U.S.	D2	115
Knox, co., Il., U.S.	B3	90
Knox, co., In., U.S.	G3	91
Knox, co., Ky., U.S.	D6	94

Knox, co., Me., U.S.	D4	96
Knox, co., Mo., U.S.	A5	102
Knox, co., Ne., U.S.	B8	104
Knox, co., Oh., U.S.	B3	112
Knox, co., Tn., U.S.	C10	119
Knox, co., Tx., U.S.	C3	120
Knox, Cape, c., B.C., Can.	B1	69
Knox City, Tx., U.S.	C3	120
Knoxville, Il., U.S.	C3	90
Knoxville, Ia., U.S.	C4	92
Knoxville, Tn., U.S.	D10	119
Knysna, S. Afr.	H4	44
Kōbe, Japan	H8	30
København (Copenhagen), Den.	I9	6
Koblenz, Ger.	E7	8
Kobrin, Bela.	I7	18
Kobuk, stm., Ak., U.S.	B8	79
Kobuk Valley National Park, Ak., U.S.	B8	79
Kočani, Mac.	H6	16
Kočevje, Slo.	D9	14
Kōchi, Japan	I6	30
Koch Peak, mtn., Mt., U.S.	E5	103
Kodiak, Ak., U.S.	D9	79
Kodiak Island, i., Ak., U.S.	D9	79
Koes, Nmb.	G3	44
Kofa Mountains, mts., Az., U.S.	D2	80
Köflach, Aus.	H15	8
Kōfu, Japan	G11	30
Koga, Japan	F12	30
Kogaluc, Baie, b., Que., Can.	E17	66
Kogaluk, stm., Newf., Can.	g9	72
Køge Bugt, b., Grnld.	D24	66
Kohala Mountains, mts., Hi., U.S.	C6	88
Kohāt, Pak.	D4	38
Kohīma, India	H16	38
Kohler, Wi., U.S.	E6	126
Kohtla-Järve, Est.	B10	18
Kokand, Uzb.	I12	22
Kokanee Glacier Provincial Park, B.C., Can.	E9	69
Kokemäki, Fin.	F14	6
Kokkola (Gamlakarleby), Fin.	E14	6
Koko Head, c., Hi., U.S.	B4	88
Kokolik, stm., Ak., U.S.	B7	79
Kokomo, In., U.S.	D5	91
Kokonau, Indon.	F10	32
Kokopo, Pap. N. Gui.	k17	50a
Kokosing, stm., Oh., U.S.	B3	112
Koksoak, stm., Que., Can.	E19	66
Kokstad, S. Afr.	H5	44
Kolaka, Indon.	F7	32
Kola Peninsula see Kol'skij poluostrov, pen., Russia	D5	22
Kolār, India	F5	37
Kolār Gold Fields, India	F5	37
Kol'čugino, Russia	E22	18
Kolda, Sen.	F3	42
Kolding, Den.	I7	6
Kolhāpur, India	D3	37
Kolín, Czech.	E15	8
Kollegāl, India	F4	37
Köln (Cologne), Ger.	E6	8
Koloa, Hi., U.S.	B2	88
Kołobrzeg, Pol.	A15	8
Kolomna, Russia	F21	18
Kolpaševo, Russia	F10	24
Kolpino, Russia	B13	18
Kol'skij poluostrov (Kola Peninsula), pen., Russia	D5	22
Kolwezi, Zaire	D5	44
Kolyma, stm., Russia	D25	24
Kolymskaja Nizmennost', pl., Russia	D24	24
Komárno, Czech.	H18	8
Komatsu, Japan	F9	30
Komló, Hung.	I18	8
Kommunizma, pik, mtn., Taj.	J12	22
Komoé, stm., Afr.	G5	42
Komomolec, Ostrov, i., Russia	A12	24
Komomol'sk-na-Amure, Russia	G21	24
Komsomol'skoj Pravdy, Ostrova, is., Russia	B15	24
Konahuanui, Puu, mtn., Hi., U.S.	g10	88
Konakovo, Russia	E19	18
Konawa, Ok., U.S.	C5	113
Konch, India	H8	38
Kondrovo, Russia	G18	18
Kong, Kaôh, i., Camb.	I7	34
Kongolo, Zaire	C5	44
Kongsberg, Nor.	G7	6
Kongsvinger, Nor.	F8	6
Kongsvoll, Nor.	E7	6
Kongur Shan, mtn., China	A6	38
Königs Wusterhausen, Ger.	C13	8
Konin, Pol.	C18	8
Konjic, Bos.	F12	14
Konomoc, Lake, res., Ct., U.S.	D7	84
Konqi, stm., China	C4	26
Konstanz, Ger.	H9	8
Kontagora, Nig.	F7	42
Kontiomäki, Fin.	D17	6
Kon Tum, Viet.	G10	34
Konya, Tur.	H14	4
Konza, Kenya	B7	44
Koochiching, co., Mn., U.S.	B4	100
Koolau Range, mts., Hi., U.S.	f10	88
Koontz Lake, In., U.S.	B5	91
Kooskia, Id., U.S.	C3	89
Kootenai, co., Id., U.S.	B2	89
Kootenay Lake, l., B.C., Can.	E9	69
Kootenay National Park, B.C., Can.	D9	69
Kopargaon, India	C3	37
Koper, Slo.	D8	14
Kopetdag, chrebet, mts., Asia	J9	22
Köping, Swe.	G10	6
Koppal, India	E4	37
Koppang, Nor.	F8	6
Koppel, Pa., U.S.	E1	115
Koprivnica, Cro.	C11	14
Kor'akskoje Nagorje, mts., Russia	E27	24
Korba, India	I10	38
Korbach, Ger.	D8	8
Korçë, Alb.	I4	16

Korčula, Cro.	G12	14
Korea, North, ctry., Asia	C12	26
Korea, South, ctry., Asia	D12	26
Korea Bay, b., Asia	D11	26
Korea Strait, strt., Asia	E12	26
Korf, Russia	E27	24
Korhogo, I.C.	G4	42
Korinthiakós Kólpos, b., Grc.	K6	16
Kórinthos (Corinth), Grc.	L6	16
Kōriyama, Japan	E13	30
Korliki, Russia	E10	24
Korogwe, Tan.	C7	44
Koronis, Lake, l., Mn., U.S.	E4	100
Koro Toro, Chad	E9	42
Korovin Volcano, vol., Ak., U.S.	E5	79
Korsakov, Russia	H22	24
Korsnäs, Fin.	E13	6
Korso, Fin.	F15	6
Kortrijk (Courtrai), Bel.	E3	8
Koruçam Burnu, c., N. Cyp.	B3	40
Koš-Ãgač, Russia	G11	24
Kosciusko, Ms., U.S.	B4	101
Kosciusko, co., In., U.S.	B6	91
Kosciusko, Mount, mtn., Austl.	G9	50
Koshkonong, Lake, l., Wi., U.S.	F5	126
Košice, Czech.	G21	8
Koso, Hi., U.S.	C5	88
Kosovska Mitrovica, Yugo.	G4	16
Kossuth, co., Ia., U.S.	A3	92
Kostroma, Russia	D23	18
Koszalin (Köslin), Pol.	A16	8
Kota, India	H6	38
Kota Baharu, Malay.	K7	34
Kotabumi, Indon.	F3	32
Kot Addu, Pak.	E4	38
Kota Kinabalu (Jesselton), Malay.	D6	32
Kotel'nyj, Ostrov, i., Russia	B21	24
Köthen, Ger.	D11	8
Kotka, Fin.	F16	6
Kot Kapūra, India	E6	38
Kotlas, Russia	E7	22
Kotlik, Ak., U.S.	C7	79
Kotor Varoš, Bos.	E12	14
Kotovsk, Russia	I24	18
Kotri, Pak.	H3	38
Kötschach [-Mauthen], Aus.	I12	8
Kottagüdem, India	D6	37
Kottayam, India	H4	37
Kotte, Sri L.	I5	37
Kotto, stm., Cen. Afr. Rep.	G10	42
Kotuj, stm., Russia	C14	24
Kotzebue, Ak., U.S.	B7	79
Kotzebue Sound, strt., Ak., U.S.	B7	79
Kouchibouguac National Park, N.B., Can.	C5	71
Koudougou, Burkina	F5	42
Koula-Moutou, Gabon	B2	44
Koumra, Chad	G9	42
Kountze, Tx., U.S.	D5	120
Koussi, Emi, mtn., Chad	E9	42
Koutiala, Mali	F4	42
Kouts, In., U.S.	B3	91
Kouvola, Fin.	F16	6
Kovrov, Russia	E24	18
Kowkcheh, stm., Afg.	B4	38
Kowloon (Jiulong), H.K.	M3	28
Kowt-e 'Ashrow, Afg.	C3	38
Koyukuk, stm., Ak., U.S.	B8	79
Koza, Japan	y27	31b
Kozáni, Grc.	I5	16
Kra, Isthmus of, Asia	I5	34
Krāchéh, Camb.	H9	34
Kragerø, Nor.	G7	6
Kragujevac, Yugo.	E4	16
Kraków, Pol.	E19	8
Kraljevica, Cro.	D9	14
Kraljevo, Yugo.	F4	16
Kramfors, Swe.	E11	6
Krångede, Swe.	E11	6
Krasneno, Russia	E28	24
Krasnodar, Russia	H5	22
Krasnogorsk, Russia	F20	18
Krasnojarsk, Russia	F12	24
Krasnoje, Ozero, l., Russia	E28	24
Krasnosel'kup, Russia	D10	24
Krasnozavodsk, Russia	E21	18
Krebs, Ok., U.S.	C6	113
Kremenčug, Ukr.	H4	22
Kremmling, Co., U.S.	A4	83
Krems an der Donau, Aus.	G15	8
Kresta, Zaliv, b., Russia	D30	24
Kribi, Cam.	H7	42
Krichev, Bela.	H14	18
Krishna, stm., India	D5	37
Krishnanagar, India	I13	38
Kristiansand, Nor.	G7	6
Kristianstad, Swe.	H10	6
Kristiansund, Nor.	E6	6
Kristinehamn, Swe.	G10	6
Kríti, i., Grc.	N8	16
Kritikón Pélagos, Grc.	N8	16
Krivoj Rog, Ukr.	H4	22
Krivoy Rog see Krivoj Rog, Ukr.	H4	22
Krnov, Czech.	E17	8
Kroken, Nor.	D10	6
Kroměříž, Czech.	F17	8
Kronach, Ger.	E11	8
Krŏng Khémôréah Phumint, Camb.	I7	34
Kronockij Zaliv, b., Russia	G26	24
Kronoki, Russia	G26	24
Kronštadt, Russia	B12	18
Kroonstad, S. Afr.	G5	44
Kropotkin, Russia	F17	24
Krosno, Pol.	F21	8
Krotz Springs, La., U.S.	D4	95
Krško, Slo.	D10	14
Kr'ukovo, Russia	D25	24
Krung Thep (Bangkok), Thai.	H6	34
Kruševac, Yugo.	F5	16
Krušné hory (Erzgebirge), mts., Eur.	E12	8
Kruzenšterna, Proliv, strt., Russia	H24	24
Kruzof Island, i., Ak., U.S.	m21	79
Krymskij poluostrov (Crimea), pen., Ukr.	H4	22

Ksar-es-Souk, Mor.	B5	42
Ksenjevka, Russia	G17	24
Ksour Essaf, Tun.	N5	14
Kuala Kangsar, Malay.	L6	34
Kualakapuas, Indon.	F5	32
Kuala Krai, Malay.	L7	34
Kuala Kubu Baharu, Malay.	M6	34
Kuala Lumpur, Malay.	M6	34
Kuala Nerang, Malay.	K6	34
Kuala Pilah, Malay.	M7	34
Kuala Terengganu, Malay.	L7	34
Kuantan, Malay.	M7	34
Kubokawa, Japan	I6	30
Kuche, China	C3	26
Kuching, Malay.	E5	32
Kudat, Malay.	D6	32
Kudus, Indon.	m15	32
Kuee Ruins, hist., Hi., U.S.	D6	88
Kufstein, Aus.	H12	8
Kuhmo, Fin.	D17	6
Kuito, Ang.	D3	44
Kuiu Island, i., Ak., U.S.	m23	79
Kuivaniemi, Fin.	D15	6
Kukawa, Nig.	F8	42
Kula, Tur.	K12	16
Kula, Hi., U.S.	C5	88
Kul'ab, Taj.	B3	38
Kula Kangri, mtn., Bhu.	F14	38
Kulebaki, Russia	F25	18
Kulen Vakuf, Bos.	E11	14
Kulim, Malay.	L6	34
Kulmbach, Ger.	E11	8
Kulpmont, Pa., U.S.	E9	115
Kulunqi, China	C11	26
Kumagaya, Japan	F12	30
Kumajri, Arm.	I6	22
Kumamoto, Japan	J3	30
Kumano, Japan	I9	30
Kumano-nada, Japan	I9	30
Kumanovo, Mac.	G5	16
Kumasi, Ghana	G5	42
Kumbakonam, India	G5	37
Kume-shima, i., Japan	y26	31
Kumo, Nig.	F8	42
Kumon Range, mts., Burma	B4	34
Kumukahi, Cape, c., Hi., U.S.	D7	88
Kuna, Id., U.S.	F2	89
Kunašir, Ostrov (Kunashir-tō), i., Russia	I23	24
Kundian, Pak.	D4	38
Kundla, India	J4	38
Kunes, Nor.	A16	6
Kunghit Island, i., B.C., Can.	C2	69
Kuningan, Indon.	m14	33a
Kunlun Shan, mts., China	B12	38
Kunming, China	B7	34
Kunsan, S. Kor.	D12	26
Kunshan, China	D9	28
Kuopio, Fin.	E16	6
Kupang, Indon.	H7	32
Kupreanof Island, i., Ak., U.S.	m23	79
Kupres, Bos.	E12	14
Kura, stm., Asia	I7	22
Kurashiki, Japan	H6	30
Kurayoshi, Japan	G6	30
Kure, Japan	H5	30
Kure Island, i., Hi., U.S.	k12	88
Kurejka, stm., Russia	D11	24
Kurenalus, Fin.	D16	6
Kurgan-T'ube, Taj.	B3	38
Kurikka, Fin.	E14	6
Kuril'sk, Russia	H23	24
Kuril'skije Ostrova (Kuril Islands), is., Russia	H23	24
Kurmuk, Sudan	F12	42
Kurnool, India	E5	37
Kurow, N.Z.	F3	52
Kursk, Russia	G5	22
Kurtistown, Hi., U.S.	D6	88
Kuruman, S. Afr.	G4	44
Kurume, Japan	I3	30
Kurumkan, Russia	G16	24
Kurunegala, Sri L.	I6	37
Kuşadasi Körfezi, b., Tur.	L11	16
Kuş Gölü, l., Tur.	K4	30
Kushima, Japan	K4	30
Kushiro, Japan	q22	30a
Kushui, China	C5	26
Kuskokwim, stm., Ak., U.S.	C8	79
Kuskokwim Bay, b., Ak., U.S.	D7	79
Kuskokwim Mountains, mts., Ak., U.S.	C8	79
Küstī, Sudan	F12	42
K'us'ur, Russia	C19	24
Kut, Ko, i., Thai.	I7	34
Kutaisi, Geor.	I6	22
Küt al-Imāra, Iraq	B4	46
Kutch, Gulf of, b., India	I3	38
Kutina, Cro.	D11	14
Kutno, Pol.	C19	8
Kutu, Zaire	B3	44
Kutztown, Pa., U.S.	E10	115
Kuujjuaq, Que., Can.	g13	74
Kuusamo, Fin.	D17	6
Kuusankoski, Fin.	F16	6
Kuvango, Ang.	D3	44
Kuwait, ctry., Asia	C4	46
Kuwait see Al-Kuwayt, Kuw.	C4	46
Kuwana, Japan	G9	30
Kuybyshev see Samara, Russia	G8	22
Kuzneck, Russia	G7	22
Kvikkjokk, Swe.	C11	6
Kwando (Cuando), stm., Afr.	D4	44
Kwangchow see Guangzhou, China	L2	28
Kwangju, S. Kor.	D12	26
Kwango (Cuango), stm., Afr.	C3	44
Kwekwe, Zimb.	E5	44
Kwethluk, Ak., U.S.	C7	79
Kwidzyn, Pol.	B18	8
Kwigillingok, Ak., U.S.	D7	79
Kwilu (Cuilo), stm., Afr.	B3	44
Kyaikkami, Burma	F4	34
Kyaikto, Burma	F4	34
Kyle, Tx., U.S.	E4	120

Name	Map Ref	Page
Kyle of Lochalsh, Scot., U.K.	D7	7
Kyoga, Lake, l., Ug.	A6	44
Kyōto, Japan	G8	30
Kyuquot Sound, strt., B.C., Can.	E4	69
Kyūshū, i., Japan	I3	30
Kyūshū-sanchi, mts., Japan	J4	30
Kyyjärvi, Fin.	E15	6
Kyrgyzstan, ctry., Asia	I12	22
Kyzyl, Russia	G12	24
Kyzyl-Orda, Kaz.	I11	22
Laa an der Thaya, Aus.	G16	8
La Almunia de Doña Godina, Spain	D10	12
La Asunción, Ven.	B11	58
Laau Point, c., Hi., U.S.	B4	88
L'Abacou, Pointe, c., Haiti	E11	64
Labadieville, La., U.S.	E5	95
La Bañeza, Spain	C6	12
La Barca, Mex.	G8	62
La Barge, Wy., U.S.	D2	127
La Barge Creek, stm., Wy., U.S.	D2	127
La Baule, Fr.	E4	10
Labé, Gui.	F3	42
Labe (Elbe), stm., Eur.	E14	8
Laghouat, Alg.	B6	42
Labouheyre, Fr.	H6	10
Labrador, reg., Newf., Can.	g9	72
Labrador City, Newf., Can.	h8	72
Labrador Sea, N.A.	E6	54
Lábrea, Braz.	E6	54
Labutta, Burma	F3	34
La Canada Flintridge, Ca., U.S.	m12	82
Lacanau, Fr.	H5	10
La Cañiza, Spain	C3	12
La Canourgue, Fr.	H10	10
La Carolina, Spain	G8	12
Lacaune, Fr.	I9	10
Lac-Bouchette, Que., Can.	A5	74
Lac-Brome, Que., Can.	D5	74
Laccadive Sea, Asia	H3	37
Lac-Carré, Que., Can.	C3	74
Lac Courte Oreilles Indian Reservation, Wi., U.S.	C2	126
Lac du Bonnet, Man., Can.	D3	70
Lac du Flambeau, Wi., U.S.	B4	126
Lac du Flambeau Indian Reservation, Wi., U.S.	C3	126
La Ceiba, Hond.	G4	64
La Ceiba, Ven.	C7	58
La Center, Ky., U.S.	e9	94
Lac-Etchemin, Que., Can.	C7	74
Lacey, Wa., U.S.	B3	124
La Charité [-sur-Loire], Fr.	E10	10
La Châtre, Fr.	F8	10
La Chaux-de-Fonds, Switz.	E13	10
Lachine, Que., Can.	D4	74
La Chorrera, Col.	H6	58
La Chorrera, Pan.	J8	64
Lachute, Que., Can.	D3	74
La Ciotat, Fr.	I12	10
Lackawanna, N.Y., U.S.	C2	109
Lackawanna, co., Pa., U.S.	D10	115
Lackland Air Force Base, mil., Tx., U.S.	k7	120
Lac La Biche, Alta., Can.	B5	68
Lac la Hache, B.C., Can.	D7	69
Lac-Mégantic, Que., Can.	D7	74
Lacolle, Que., Can.	D4	74
Lacombe, Alta., Can.	C4	68
Lacombe, La., U.S.	D6	95
Lacon, Il., U.S.	B4	90
Laconia, N.H., U.S.	C4	106
La Conner, Wa., U.S.	A3	124
Lacoochee, Fl., U.S.	D4	86
La Coruña, Spain	B3	12
Lac qui Parle, co., Mn., U.S.	F2	100
Lac qui Parle, stm., Mn., U.S.	F2	100
La Creek Lake, S.D., U.S.	D4	118
La Crete, Alta., Can.	f7	68
La Crosse, In., U.S.	B4	91
La Crosse, Ks., U.S.	D4	93
La Crosse, Wi., U.S.	E2	126
La Crosse, co., Wi., U.S.	E2	126
La Crosse, stm., Wi., U.S.	E3	126
La Cruz, Nic.	H5	64
La Cygne, Ks., U.S.	D9	93
Ladd, Il., U.S.	B4	90
Ladies Island, i., S.C., U.S.	G6	117
Ladiz, Iran	C7	46
Lādnun, India	G6	38
Ladoga, In., U.S.	E4	91
Ladoga, Lake see Ladožskoje Ozero, l., Russia	F18	6
La Dorada, Col.	E5	58
Ladožskoje Ozero (Lake Ladoga), l., Russia	F18	6
Ladson, S.C., U.S.	F7	117
Lady Lake, Fl., U.S.	D5	86
Lady Laurier, Mount, mtn., B.C., Can.	A6	69
Ladysmith, B.C., Can.	E6	69
Ladysmith, S. Afr.	G5	44
Ladysmith, Wi., U.S.	C2	126
Lae, Pap. N. Gui.	m16	50a
La Encantada, Cerro de, mtn., Mex.	B2	62
La Esmeralda, Ven.	F10	58
La Esperanza, Hond.	G3	64
La Estrada, Spain	C3	12
La Farge, Wi., U.S.	E3	126
Lafayette, Al., U.S.	C4	78
Lafayette, Co., U.S.	B5	83
Lafayette, Ga., U.S.	B1	87
Lafayette, In., U.S.	D4	91
Lafayette, La., U.S.	D3	95
Lafayette, N.C., U.S.	B3	110
La Fayette, R.I., U.S.	E4	116
La Fayette, Tn., U.S.	A5	119
Lafayette, Or., U.S.	B3	114
Lafayette, co., Fl., U.S.	C3	86
Lafayette, co., La., U.S.	D3	95
Lafayette, co., Ms., U.S.	A4	101
Lafayette, co., Mo., U.S.	B4	102
Lafayette, co., Wi., U.S.	F3	126
Lafayette, Mount, mtn., N.H., U.S.	B3	106
La Feria, Tx., U.S.	F4	120
La Ferté-Bernard, Fr.	D7	10
La Ferté-Macé, Fr.	D6	10
La Ferté-Saint-Aubin, Fr.	E8	10
Lafia, Nig.	G7	42
Lafitte, La., U.S.	k11	95
La Flèche, Fr.	E6	10
La Follette, Tn., U.S.	C9	119
La Fontaine, In., U.S.	C6	91
La Fortuna, C.R.	I5	64
Lafourche, co., La., U.S.	E5	95
Lafourche, stm., La., U.S.	E5	95
La France, S.C., U.S.	B2	117
La Fregeneda, Spain	E5	12
La Fría, Ven.	C6	58
La Fuente de San Esteban, Spain	E5	12
Lågen, stm., Nor.	F8	6
Lago, Mount, mtn., Wa., U.S.	A5	124
Lagonegro, Italy	I10	14
Lagos, Nig.	G6	42
Lagos de Moreno, Mex.	G9	62
La Goulette, Tun.	M5	14
La Grand'Combe, Fr.	H11	10
La Grande, Or., U.S.	B8	114
La Grande, stm., Que., Can.	h11	74
La Grande Deux, Réservoir, res., Que., Can.	h11	74
La Grange, Austl.	C4	50
La Grange, Ga., U.S.	C1	87
La Grange, Il., U.S.	B6	90
Lagrange, In., U.S.	A7	91
La Grange, Ky., U.S.	B4	94
Lagrange, Mo., U.S.	A6	102
La Grange, N.C., U.S.	B5	110
Lagrange, Oh., U.S.	A3	112
La Grange, Tx., U.S.	E4	120
Lagrange, co., In., U.S.	A7	91
La Grange Park, Il., U.S.	k9	90
La Gran Sabana, pl., Ven.	E12	58
La Grita, Ven.	C7	58
La Guadeloupe (Saint-Evariste), Que., Can.	D7	74
La Guaira, Ven.	B9	58
La Guajira, Península de, pen., S.A.	A7	58
Laguardia, Spain	C9	12
La Guardia, Spain	D3	12
La Guerche-de-Bretagne, Fr.	E5	10
La Guerche-sur-l'aubois, Fr.	F9	10
Laguiole, Fr.	H9	10
Laguna, N.M., U.S.	B2	108
Laguna Beach, Ca., U.S.	F5	82
Laguna Dam, U.S.	E1	80
Laguna Indian Reservation, N.M., U.S.	C2	108
Lagunillas, Bol.	G6	54
La Habana (Havana), Cuba	C6	64
La Habra, Ca., U.S.	n13	82
Lahaina, Hi., U.S.	C5	88
La Harpe, Il., U.S.	C3	90
La Harpe, Ks., U.S.	E8	93
Lahat, Indon.	F3	32
La Have, stm., N.S., Can.	E5	71
La Haye-du-Puits, Fr.	C5	10
Lahij, Yemen	F3	46
Laholm, Swe.	H9	6
Lahontan Reservoir, res., Nv., U.S.	D2	105
Lahore, Pak.	E6	38
Lahr, Ger.	G7	8
Lahti, Fin.	F15	6
Laie, Hi., U.S.	B4	88
L'Aigle, Fr.	D7	10
Laignes, Fr.	E11	10
Laihia, Fin.	E14	6
Laingsburg, S. Afr.	H4	44
Laingsburg, Mi., U.S.	F6	99
Lairg, Scot., U.K.	C8	7
Laissac, Fr.	H9	10
Laiyang, China	D11	26
La Jara, Co., U.S.	D5	83
Lajes, Braz.	E11	54
La Jolla, Point, c., Ca., U.S.	o15	82
La Joya, Mex.	A2	62
La Junta, Mex.	C6	62
La Junta, Co., U.S.	D7	83
Lake, co., Ca., U.S.	C2	82
Lake, co., Co., U.S.	B4	83
Lake, co., Fl., U.S.	D5	86
Lake, co., Il., U.S.	A6	90
Lake, co., In., U.S.	B3	91
Lake, co., Mi., U.S.	E5	99
Lake, co., Mn., U.S.	C7	100
Lake, co., Mt., U.S.	C2	103
Lake, co., Oh., U.S.	A4	112
Lake, co., Or., U.S.	E6	114
Lake, co., S.D., U.S.	C8	118
Lake, co., Tn., U.S.	A2	119
Lake Alfred, Fl., U.S.	D5	86
Lake Andes, S.D., U.S.	D7	118
Lake Ariel, Pa., U.S.	D11	115
Lake Arrowhead, Ca., U.S.	E5	82
Lake Arthur, La., U.S.	D3	95
Lake Barcroft, Va., U.S.	*B5	123
Lake Benton, Mn., U.S.	F2	100
Lake Bluff, Il., U.S.	A6	90
Lake Butler, Fl., U.S.	B4	86
Lake Charles, La., U.S.	D2	95
Lake Chelan National Recreation Area, Wa., U.S.	A5	124
Lake City, Ar., U.S.	B5	81
Lake City, Fl., U.S.	B4	86
Lake City, Ia., U.S.	B3	92
Lake City, Mi., U.S.	D5	99
Lake City, Mn., U.S.	F6	100
Lake City, Pa., U.S.	B1	115
Lake City, S.C., U.S.	D8	117
Lake City, Tn., U.S.	C9	119
Lake Clark National Park, Ak., U.S.	C9	79
Lake Cowichan, B.C., Can.	g11	69
Lake Creek, stm., Wa., U.S.	B7	124
Lake Crystal, Mn., U.S.	F4	100
Lake Delta, N.Y., U.S.	B5	109
Lake Delton, Wi., U.S.	E4	126
Lake District National Park, Eng., U.K.	G9	7
Lake Elsinore, Ca., U.S.	F5	82
Lake Erie Beach, N.Y., U.S.	C1	109
Lakefield, Ont., Can.	C6	73
Lakefield, Mn., U.S.	G3	100
Lake Forest, Il., U.S.	A6	90
Lake Fork, stm., Ut., U.S.	C5	121
Lake Geneva, Wi., U.S.	F5	126
Lake Hamilton, Ar., U.S.	g7	81
Lake Harbour, N.W. Ter., Can.	D19	66
Lake Havasu City, Az., U.S.	C1	80
Lake Helen, Fl., U.S.	D5	86
Lakehurst, N.J., U.S.	C4	107
Lakehurst Naval Air Station, mil., N.J., U.S.	C4	107
Lake in the Hills, Il., U.S.	h8	90
Lake Jackson, Tx., U.S.	r14	120
Lake Katrine, N.Y., U.S.	D7	109
Lakeland, Fl., U.S.	D5	86
Lakeland, Ga., U.S.	E3	87
Lake Linden, Mi., U.S.	A2	99
Lake Louise, Alta., Can.	D2	68
Lake Magdalene, Fl., U.S.	o11	86
Lake Mary, Fl., U.S.	D5	86
Lake Mead National Recreation Area, U.S.	H7	105
Lake Meredith National Recreation Area, Tx., U.S.	B2	120
Lake Mills, Ia., U.S.	A4	92
Lake Mills, Wi., U.S.	E5	126
Lakemore, Oh., U.S.	A4	112
Lake Mountain, mtn., Wy., U.S.	E6	127
Lake Nebagamon, Wi., U.S.	B2	126
Lake Odessa, Mi., U.S.	F5	99
Lake of the Woods, co., Mn., U.S.	B4	100
Lake Orion, Mi., U.S.	F7	99
Lake Oswego, Or., U.S.	B4	114
Lake Ozark, Mo., U.S.	C5	102
Lake Park, Fl., U.S.	F6	86
Lake Park, Ia., U.S.	A2	92
Lake Park, Mn., U.S.	D2	100
Lake Placid, Fl., U.S.	E5	86
Lake Placid, N.Y., U.S.	A7	109
Lake Pontchartrain Causeway, La., U.S.	h11	95
Lakeport, Ca., U.S.	C2	82
Lake Preston, S.D., U.S.	C8	118
Lake Providence, La., U.S.	B4	95
Lake Range, mts., Nv., U.S.	C2	105
Lake Ridge, Va., U.S.	*B5	123
Lake Shore, Md., U.S.	B5	97
Lakeshore, Ms., U.S.	E4	101
Lakeside, Az., U.S.	C6	80
Lakeside, Ca., U.S.	F5	82
Lakeside, Ct., U.S.	D3	84
Lakeside, Mt., U.S.	B2	103
Lakeside, Oh., U.S.	A3	112
Lakeside, Or., U.S.	D2	114
Lakeside Park, Ky., U.S.	h13	94
Lake Station, In., U.S.	A3	91
Lake Station, Ok., U.S.	A5	113
Lake Stevens, Wa., U.S.	A3	124
Lake Superior Provincial Park, Ont., Can.	p18	73
Lake Swamp, stm., S.C., U.S.	D8	117
Lake Tansi Village, Tn., U.S.	D8	119
Lake Valley, val., Nv., U.S.	E7	105
Lake View, Ia., U.S.	B2	92
Lakeview, Mi., U.S.	E5	99
Lakeview, Oh., U.S.	B2	112
Lakeview, Or., U.S.	E6	114
Lake View, S.C., U.S.	C9	117
Lake Villa, Il., U.S.	h8	90
Lake Village, Ar., U.S.	D4	81
Lake Village, In., U.S.	B3	91
Lakeville, Ct., U.S.	B2	84
Lakeville, In., U.S.	A5	91
Lakeville, Ma., U.S.	C6	98
Lakeville, Mn., U.S.	F5	100
Lake Waccamaw, N.C., U.S.	C4	110
Lake Wales, Fl., U.S.	E5	86
Lakewood, Ca., U.S.	n12	82
Lakewood, Co., U.S.	B5	83
Lakewood, Il., U.S.	D5	90
Lakewood, Ia., U.S.	f8	92
Lakewood, N.J., U.S.	C4	107
Lakewood, N.Y., U.S.	C1	109
Lakewood, Oh., U.S.	A4	112
Lakewood Center, Wa., U.S.	f11	124
Lake Worth, Fl., U.S.	F6	86
Lake Worth Inlet, b., Fl., U.S.	F7	86
Lake Zurich, Il., U.S.	h8	90
Lakhimpur, India	G9	38
Lakin, Ks., U.S.	E2	93
Lakota, N.D., U.S.	A7	111
Lakselv, Nor.	A15	6
Lakshadweep, state, India	H3	37
Lakshadweep, is., India	H2	37
Lalbenque, Fr.	H8	10
La Libertad, Guat.	F2	64
La Libertad, Mex.	C3	62
Lalinde, Fr.	H8	10
La Línea, Spain	I6	12
Lalitpur, India	I8	38
Lalitpur, Nepal	G11	38
La Loupe, Fr.	D8	10
La Luz, N.M., U.S.	E4	108
Lama, Ozero, l., Russia	D12	24
La Maddalena, Italy	H4	14
La Madrid, Arg.	B3	56
La Malbaie, Que., Can.	B7	74
La Mancha, Mex.	E8	62
La Mancha, reg., Spain	G8	12
Lamar, Ar., U.S.	B2	81
Lamar, Co., U.S.	C8	83
Lamar, Mo., U.S.	D3	102
Lamar, Pa., U.S.	D7	115
Lamar, S.C., U.S.	C7	117
Lamar, co., Al., U.S.	B1	78
Lamar, co., Ga., U.S.	C2	87
Lamar, co., Ms., U.S.	D4	101
Lamar, co., Tx., U.S.	C5	120
Lamar, stm., Wy., U.S.	B2	127
Lamarche, Fr.	D12	10
La Mauricie, Parc National de, Que., Can.	C5	74
Lamb, co., Tx., U.S.	B1	120
Lamballe, Fr.	D4	10
Lambaréné, Gabon	B2	44
Lambert Glacier, Ant.	B19	47
Lambert, Ms., U.S.	A3	101
Lamberton, Mn., U.S.	F3	100
Lambert's Bay, S. Afr.	H3	44
Lambertville, Mi., U.S.	G7	99
Lambertville, N.J., U.S.	C3	107
Lambton, Cape, c., N.W. Ter., Can.	B8	66
Lame Deer, Mt., U.S.	E10	103
Lamego, Port.	D4	12
Lamèque, N.B., Can.	B5	71
Lamèque, Île, i., N.B., Can.	B5	71
La Mesa, Ca., U.S.	F5	82
La Mesa, N.M., U.S.	E3	108
Lamesa, Tx., U.S.	C2	120
Lamia, Grc.	K6	16
Lamoille, Nv., U.S.	C6	105
Lamoille, co., Vt., U.S.	B3	122
Lamoille, stm., Vt., U.S.	B3	122
La Moine, stm., Il., U.S.	C3	90
Lamoni, Ia., U.S.	D4	92
Lamont, Alta., Can.	C4	68
Lamont, Ca., U.S.	E4	82
La Monte, Mo., U.S.	C4	102
La Motte, Isle, i., Vt., U.S.	B2	122
Lamotte-Beuvron, Fr.	E9	10
La Moure, N.D., U.S.	C7	111
La Moure, co., N.D., U.S.	C7	111
Lampang, Thai.	E5	34
Lampasas, Tx., U.S.	D3	120
Lampasas, co., Tx., U.S.	D3	120
Lampedusa, Isola di, i., Italy	N7	14
Lampertheim, Ger.	F8	8
Lampman, Sask., Can.	H4	75
Lamprey, stm., N.H., U.S.	D4	106
Lamu, Kenya	B8	44
La Mure, Fr.	H12	10
Lanai, i., Hi., U.S.	C4	88
Lanai City, Hi., U.S.	C5	88
Lanaihale, mtn., Hi., U.S.	C5	88
Lanark, Ont., Can.	C8	73
Lanark, Il., U.S.	A4	90
Lanark, W.V., U.S.	D3	125
Lanbi Kyun, i., Burma	I5	34
Lancaster, Ont., Can.	B10	73
Lancaster, Eng., U.K.	G10	7
Lancaster, Ca., U.S.	E4	82
Lancaster, Ky., U.S.	C5	94
Lancaster, Mo., U.S.	A5	102
Lancaster, N.H., U.S.	B3	106
Lancaster, N.Y., U.S.	C2	109
Lancaster, Oh., U.S.	C3	112
Lancaster, Pa., U.S.	F9	115
Lancaster, S.C., U.S.	B6	117
Lancaster, Tx., U.S.	n10	120
Lancaster, Wi., U.S.	F3	126
Lancaster, co., Ne., U.S.	D9	104
Lancaster, co., Pa., U.S.	G9	115
Lancaster, co., S.C., U.S.	B6	117
Lancaster, co., Va., U.S.	C6	123
Lancaster Sound, strt., N.W. Ter., Can.	B16	66
Lance Creek, stm., Wy., U.S.	C8	127
Lanciano, Italy	G9	14
Landau, Ger.	F8	8
Landau an der Isar, Ger.	G12	8
Land Between the Lakes, park, U.S.	f9	94
Lander, Wy., U.S.	D4	127
Lander, co., Nv., U.S.	C4	105
Landerneau, Fr.	D2	10
Landess, In., U.S.	C6	91
Landete, Spain	F10	12
Landis, N.C., U.S.	B2	110
Lando, S.C., U.S.	B5	117
Landquart, Switz.	F16	10
Landrum, S.C., U.S.	A3	117
Land's End, c., Eng., U.K.	K7	7
Lands End, c., R.I., U.S.	F5	116
Landshut, Ger.	G12	8
Landskrona, Swe.	I9	6
Lane, co., Ks., U.S.	D3	93
Lane, co., Or., U.S.	C4	114
Lanesboro, Mn., U.S.	G7	100
Lanett, Al., U.S.	C4	78
Langar, Afg.	B5	38
Langdon, N.D., U.S.	A7	111
Langeac, Fr.	G10	10
Langeais, Fr.	E7	10
Langeloth, Pa., U.S.	F1	115
Langenhagen, Ger.	C9	8
Langenthal, Switz.	E14	10
Langhorne, Pa., U.S.	F12	115
Langlade, co., Wi., U.S.	C4	126
Langley, B.C., Can.	f13	69
Langley, S.C., U.S.	E4	117
Langley, Wa., U.S.	A3	124
Langley Air Force Base, mil., Va., U.S.	h15	123
Langley Park, Md., U.S.	f9	97
Langnau, Switz.	F14	10
Langogne, Fr.	H10	10
Langon, Fr.	H6	10
Langres, Fr.	E1	10
Langsa, Indon.	E2	32
Lang Son, Viet.	D9	34
Langston, Ok., U.S.	B4	113
Languedoc, hist. reg., Fr.	I9	10
L'Anguille, stm., Ar., U.S.	B5	81
Langzhong, China	E8	26
Lanham, Md., U.S.	C4	97
Lanier, co., Ga., U.S.	E3	87
Lannemezan, Fr.	I7	10
Lannilis, Fr.	D2	10
Lannion, Fr.	D2	10
Lannon, Wi., U.S.	m11	126
L'Annonciation, Que., Can.	C3	74
Lansdale, Pa., U.S.	F11	115
Lansdowne, Md., U.S.	B4	97
L'Anse, Mi., U.S.	B2	99
L'Anse-au-Loup, Newf., Can.	C3	72
L'Anse Indian Reservation, Mi., U.S.	B2	99
Lansford, Pa., U.S.	E10	115
Lansing, Il., U.S.	B6	90
Lansing, Ia., U.S.	A6	92
Lansing, Ks., U.S.	C9	93
Lansing, Mi., U.S.	F6	99
Lantana, Fl., U.S.	F6	86
Lantau Island, i., H.K.	M2	28
Lanusei, Italy	J4	14
Lanxi, China	F8	28
Lanzarote, i., Spain	C3	42
Lanzhou, China	D7	26
Laoag, Phil.	B7	32
Lao Cai, Viet.	C7	34
Laon, Fr.	C10	10
La Oroya, Peru	F3	54
Laos, ctry., Asia	B3	32
Lapalisse, Fr.	F10	10
La Palma, Col.	E5	58
La Palma, Pan.	J8	64
La Palma, i., Spain	C2	42
La Paragua, Ven.	D11	58
La Paz, Arg.	C3	56
La Paz, Bol.	G5	54
La Paz, Mex.	E4	62
La Paz, co., Az., U.S.	D2	80
La Paz, Bahía de, b., Mex.	E4	62
Lapeer, Mi., U.S.	E7	99
Lapeer, co., Mi., U.S.	E7	99
Lapel, In., U.S.	D6	91
La Perouse Strait, strt., Asia	B15	26
La Piedad [Cavadas], Mex.	G8	62
La Pine, Or., U.S.	D5	114
Lapinlahti, Fin.	E16	6
La Place, La., U.S.	h11	95
Lapland, reg., Eur.	C14	6
La Plata, Arg.	C5	56
La Plata, Md., U.S.	C4	97
La Plata, Mo., U.S.	A5	102
La Plata, co., Co., U.S.	D3	83
La Plata Mountains, mts., Co., U.S.	D3	83
La Plata Peak, mtn., Co., U.S.	B4	83
La Platte, stm., Vt., U.S.	C2	122
La Pocatière, Que., Can.	B7	74
Laporte, Co., U.S.	A5	83
La Porte, In., U.S.	A4	91
La Porte, Tx., U.S.	r14	120
La Porte, co., In., U.S.	A4	91
La Porte City, Ia., U.S.	B5	92
Lappeenranta, Fin.	F17	6
La Prairie, Que., Can.	D4	74
La Pryor, Tx., U.S.	E3	120
Laptevych, More (Laptev Sea), Russia	B19	24
Lapua, Fin.	E14	6
La Puebla, Spain	F15	12
La Puebla de Montalbán, Spain	F7	12
La Push, Wa., U.S.	B1	124
Lapwai, Id., U.S.	C2	89
La Quiaca, Arg.	A3	56
L'Aquila, Italy	G8	14
Lār, Iran	C5	46
Larache, Mor.	A4	42
Laramie, Wy., U.S.	E7	127
Laramie, co., Wy., U.S.	E8	127
Laramie, stm., Wy., U.S.	E7	127
Laramie Mountains, mts., Wy., U.S.	D7	127
Laramie Peak, mtn., Wy., U.S.	D7	127
Larantuka, Indon.	G7	32
L'Arbresle, Fr.	G11	10
Lärbro, Swe.	H12	6
Larche, Col de, Eur.	H13	10
Larchmont, N.Y., U.S.	h13	109
Larchwood, Ia., U.S.	A1	92
Laredo, Tx., U.S.	F3	120
La Réole, Fr.	H6	10
Largeau, Chad	E9	42
L'argentière-la-Bessée, Fr.	H13	10
Lar Gerd, Afg.	C2	38
Largo, Fl., U.S.	E4	86
Largo, Cañon, val., N.M., U.S.	A2	108
Largo, Key, i., Fl., U.S.	G6	86
Largs, Scot., U.K.	F8	7
Larimer, co., Co., U.S.	A5	83
Larimore, N.D., U.S.	B8	111
La Rioja, Arg.	B3	56
Lárisa, Grc.	J6	16
Larjak, Russia	E10	24
Lärkäna, Pak.	G3	38
Lark Harbour, Newf., Can.	D2	72
Larkspur, Ca., U.S.	h7	82
Lárnax (Larnaca), Cyp.	B3	40
Larne, N. Ire., U.K.	G7	7
Larned, Ks., U.S.	D4	93
La Robla, Spain	C6	12
La Roca de la Sierra, Spain	F5	12
La Rochefoucauld, Fr.	G7	10
La Rochelle, Fr.	F5	10
La Roche-sur-Yon, Fr.	F5	10
La Roda, Spain	F9	12
La Romana, Dom. Rep.	E13	64
Laroquebrou, Fr.	H9	10
Larose, La., U.S.	E5	95
La Rubia, Arg.	C4	56
Larue, co., Ky., U.S.	C4	94
Laruns, Fr.	J6	10

Name	Map Ref	Page
Larvik, Nor.	G7	6
LaSalle, Que., Can.	q19	74
La Salle, Co., U.S.	A6	83
La Salle, Il., U.S.	B4	90
La Salle, co., Il., U.S.	B4	90
La Salle, co., La., U.S.	C3	95
La Salle, co., Tx., U.S.	E3	120
Las Animas, Co., U.S.	C7	83
Las Animas, co., Co., U.S.	D6	83
Las Anod, Som.	G4	46
La Sarre, Que., Can.	k11	74
Las Casitas, Cerro, mtn., Mex.	F5	62
Las Choapas, Mex.	I12	62
La Scie, Newf., Can.	D4	72
Las Colimas, Mex.	E10	62
Las Cruces, N.M., U.S.	E3	108
Las Delicias, Mex.	J14	62
La Selle, Pic, mtn., Haiti	E11	64
La Serena, Chile	B2	56
Las Escobas, Mex.	B2	62
La Seyne, Fr.	I12	10
Las Flores, Arg.	D5	56
Lashio, Burma	C4	34
Laško, Slo.	C10	14
Las Lomitas, Arg.	A4	56
Las Minas, Cerro, mtn., Hond.	G3	64
La Solana, Spain	G8	12
Las Palmas de Gran Canaria, Spain	C2	42
La Spezia, Italy	E4	14
Las Piedras, Ur.	C5	56
La Plumas, Arg.	E3	56
Lassen, co., Ca., U.S.	B3	82
Lassen Peak, vol., Ca., U.S.	B3	82
Lassen Volcanic National Park, Ca., U.S.	B3	82
L'Assomption, Que., Can.	D4	74
Las Termas, Arg.	B4	56
Last Mountain Lake, l., Sask., Can.	F3	75
Las Tórtolas, Cerro, mtn., S.A.	B3	56
Las Varas, Mex.	C5	62
Las Vegas, Nv., U.S.	G6	105
Las Vegas, N.M., U.S.	B4	108
Latacunga, Ec.	H3	58
Latah, co., Id., U.S.	C2	89
Latakia see Al-Lādhiqīyah, Syria	A4	40
Lathrop, Mo., U.S.	B3	102
Lathrop Wells, Nv., U.S.	G5	105
Latimer, co., Ok., U.S.	C6	113
Latina, Italy	H7	14
Laton, Ca., U.S.	D4	82
La Tortuga, Isla, i., Ven.	B10	58
Latour Peak, mtn., Id., U.S.	B2	89
Latrobe, Pa., U.S.	F3	115
Latta, S.C., U.S.	C9	117
La Tuque, Que., Can.	B5	74
Lātūr, India	C4	37
Latvia, ctry., Eur.	E7	18
Lauchhammer, Ger.	D13	8
Lauderdale, Ms., U.S.	C5	101
Lauderdale, co., Al., U.S.	A2	78
Lauderdale, co., Ms., U.S.	C5	101
Lauderdale, co., Tn., U.S.	B2	119
Lauderdale Lakes, Fl., U.S.	r13	86
Lauenburg, Ger.	B10	8
Laughlin, Nv., U.S.	H7	105
Laughlin Air Force Base, mil., Tx., U.S.	E2	120
Laughlin Peak, mtn., N.M., U.S.	A5	108
Laughlintown, Pa., U.S.	F3	115
Launceston, Austl.	H9	50
Launceston, Eng., U.K.	K8	7
Launching Point, c., P.E.I., Can.	C7	71
La Unión, El Sal.	H4	64
La Unión, Spain	H11	12
La Unión, Ven.	C9	58
La Urbana, Ven.	D9	58
Laurel, De., U.S.	F3	85
Laurel, Fl., U.S.	E4	86
Laurel, Md., U.S.	B4	97
Laurel, Ms., U.S.	D4	101
Laurel, Mt., U.S.	E8	103
Laurel, Ne., U.S.	B8	104
Laurel, Va., U.S.	C5	123
Laurel, co., Ky., U.S.	C5	94
Laurel, stm., Ky., U.S.	D5	94
Laurel Bay, S.C., U.S.	G6	117
Laurel Creek, stm., W.V., U.S.	n14	125
Laurel Creek, stm., W.V., U.S.	m12	125
Laureldale, Pa., U.S.	F10	115
Laurel Fork, stm., W.V., U.S.	C5	125
Laurel Hill, N.C., U.S.	C3	110
Laurel River Lake, res., Ky., U.S.	D5	94
Laurence G. Hanscom Air Force Base, mil., Ma., U.S.	g10	98
Laurence Harbor, N.J., U.S.	C4	107
Laurens, Ia., U.S.	B3	92
Laurens, S.C., U.S.	B3	117
Laurens, co., Ga., U.S.	D4	87
Laurens, co., S.C., U.S.	C4	117
Laurentides, Que., Can.	D4	74
Laurentides, Parc Provincial des, Que., Can.	B6	74
Laurier, Que., Can.	C6	74
Laurière, Fr.	F8	10
Laurinville, Que., Can.	C6	74
Laurinburg, N.C., U.S.	C3	110
Laurium, Mi., U.S.	A2	99
Lausanne, Switz.	F13	10
Laut, Pulau, i., Indon.	F6	32
Laut, Pulau, i., Indon.	L9	34
Lautaro, Chile	D2	56
Lauterbach, Ger.	E9	8
Laut Kecil, Kepulauan, is., Indon.	F6	32
Lauzon, Que., Can.	C6	74
Lava Beds National Monument, Ca., U.S.	B3	82
Lavaca, Ar., U.S.	B1	81
Lavaca, co., Tx., U.S.	E4	120
Lavagh More, mtn., Ire.	G4	7
Laval, Que., Can.	D4	74
Laval, Fr.	D6	10
La Vale, Md., U.S.	k13	97
Lavaltrie, Que., Can.	D4	74
Lavapié, Punta, c., Chile	D2	56
Laveen, Az., U.S.	m8	80
La Vega, Dom. Rep.	E12	64
La Vela, Cabo de, c., Col.	A6	58
Lavello, Italy	H10	14
L'Avenir, Que., Can.	D5	74
La Vergne, Tn., U.S.	A5	119
La Verkin, Ut., U.S.	F2	121
La Verne, Ca., U.S.	m13	82
La Veta, Co., U.S.	D5	83
Lavia, Fin.	F14	6
La Vista, Ga., U.S.	*h8	87
La Vista, Ne., U.S.	g12	104
Lavonia, Ga., U.S.	B3	87
Lavon Lake, res., Tx., U.S.	m10	120
La Voulte-sur-Rhône, Fr.	H11	10
Lavras, Braz.	F6	57
Lawai, Hi., U.S.	B2	88
Lawang, Indon.	m16	33a
Lawers, Ben, mtn., Scot., U.K.	E8	7
Lawn, Newf., Can.	E4	72
Lawrence, In., U.S.	E5	91
Lawrence, Ks., U.S.	D8	93
Lawrence, Ma., U.S.	A5	98
Lawrence, Mi., U.S.	F4	99
Lawrence, N.Y., U.S.	k13	109
Lawrence, co., Al., U.S.	A2	78
Lawrence, co., Ar., U.S.	A4	81
Lawrence, co., Il., U.S.	E6	90
Lawrence, co., In., U.S.	G4	91
Lawrence, co., Ky., U.S.	B7	94
Lawrence, co., Ms., U.S.	D3	101
Lawrence, co., Mo., U.S.	D4	102
Lawrence, co., Oh., U.S.	D3	112
Lawrence, co., Pa., U.S.	E1	115
Lawrence, co., Tn., U.S.	B4	119
Lawrenceburg, In., U.S.	F8	91
Lawrenceburg, Ky., U.S.	B5	94
Lawrenceburg, Tn., U.S.	B4	119
Lawrence Park, Pa., U.S.	B1	115
Lawrenceville, Ga., U.S.	C3	87
Lawrenceville, Il., U.S.	E6	90
Lawrenceville, Va., U.S.	D5	123
Lawson, Mo., U.S.	B3	102
Lawsonia, Md., U.S.	E6	97
Lawtell, La., U.S.	D3	95
Lawton, Mi., U.S.	F5	99
Lawton, Ok., U.S.	C3	113
Lawz, Jabal al-, mtn., Sau. Ar.	C2	46
Lay Lake, res., Al., U.S.	B3	78
Laysan Island, i., Hi., U.S.	k13	88
Layton, Ut., U.S.	B4	121
La Zarca, Mex.	E7	62
Lazarev, Russia	G22	24
Lazi, China	F12	38
Lea, co., N.M., U.S.	D6	108
Leachville, Ar., U.S.	B5	81
Lead, S.D., U.S.	C2	118
Leadbetter Point, c., Wa., U.S.	C1	124
Leadville, Co., U.S.	B4	83
Leadwood, Mo., U.S.	D7	102
Leaf, stm., Ms., U.S.	D5	101
Leaf Rapids, Man., Can.	A1	70
Leake, co., Ms., U.S.	C4	101
Leakesville, Ms., U.S.	D5	101
Lealman, Fl., U.S.	p10	86
Leamington, Ont., Can.	E2	73
Leary, Ga., U.S.	E2	87
Leatherman Peak, mtn., Id., U.S.	E5	89
Leavenworth, Ks., U.S.	C9	93
Leavenworth, Wa., U.S.	B5	124
Leavenworth, co., Ks., U.S.	C8	93
Leavittsburg, Oh., U.S.	A5	112
Leawood, Ks., U.S.	D9	93
Lebanon, De., U.S.	D4	85
Lebanon, Il., U.S.	E4	90
Lebanon, In., U.S.	D5	91
Lebanon, Ky., U.S.	C4	94
Lebanon, Mo., U.S.	D5	102
Lebanon, N.H., U.S.	C2	106
Lebanon, Oh., U.S.	C1	112
Lebanon, Or., U.S.	C4	114
Lebanon, Pa., U.S.	F9	115
Lebanon, Tn., U.S.	A5	119
Lebanon, Va., U.S.	f9	123
Lebanon, co., Pa., U.S.	F8	115
Lebanon, ctry., Asia	C4	40
Lebanon Junction, Ky., U.S.	C4	94
Le Blanc, Fr.	F8	10
Lebo, Ks., U.S.	D8	93
Lębork, Pol.	A17	8
Lebrija, Spain	I5	12
Lecce, Italy	I13	14
Lecco, Italy	D4	14
Le Center, Mn., U.S.	F5	100
Le Cheylard, Fr.	H11	10
Le Claire, Ia., U.S.	C7	92
Lecompte, La., U.S.	C3	95
Lecompton, Ks., U.S.	C8	93
Le Creusot, Fr.	F11	10
Le Dorat, Fr.	F8	10
Leduc, Alta., Can.	C4	68
Lee, Ma., U.S.	B1	98
Lee, co., Al., U.S.	C4	78
Lee, co., Ar., U.S.	C5	81
Lee, co., Fl., U.S.	F5	86
Lee, co., Ga., U.S.	E2	87
Lee, co., Il., U.S.	B4	90
Lee, co., Ia., U.S.	D6	92
Lee, co., Ky., U.S.	C6	94
Lee, co., Ms., U.S.	A5	101
Lee, co., N.C., U.S.	B3	110
Lee, co., S.C., U.S.	C7	117
Lee, co., Tx., U.S.	D4	120
Lee, Lake, l., Ms., U.S.	B3	101
Leechburg, Pa., U.S.	E2	115
Leech Lake, l., Mn., U.S.	C4	100
Leech Lake Indian Reservation, Mn., U.S.	C4	100
Lee Creek, stm., U.S.	B1	81
Leeds, Eng., U.K.	H11	7
Leeds, Al., U.S.	B3	78
Leelanau, co., Mi., U.S.	D5	99
Leelanau, Lake, l., Mi., U.S.	C5	99
Lee Park, Pa., U.S.	n17	115
Leer, Ger.	B7	8
Leesburg, Fl., U.S.	D5	86
Leesburg, Ga., U.S.	E2	87
Leesburg, Oh., U.S.	C2	112
Leesburg, Va., U.S.	A5	123
Lees Summit, Mo., U.S.	C3	102
Leesville, La., U.S.	C2	95
Leesville, S.C., U.S.	D4	117
Leesville Lake, res., Va., U.S.	C3	123
Leeton, Mo., U.S.	C4	102
Leetonia, Oh., U.S.	B5	112
Leetsdale, Pa., U.S.	h13	115
Leeuwarden, Neth.	B5	8
Leeuwin, Cape, c., Austl.	F3	50
Leeward Islands, is., N.A.	F17	64
Leflore, co., Ms., U.S.	B3	101
Le Flore, co., Ok., U.S.	C7	113
Legal, Alta., Can.	C4	68
Leghorn see Livorno, Italy	F5	14
Legnago, Italy	D6	14
Legnano, Italy	D3	14
Legnica (Liegnitz), Pol.	D16	8
Le Grand, Ca., U.S.	D3	82
Le Grand, Ia., U.S.	B5	92
Le Havre, Fr.	C7	10
Lehi, Ut., U.S.	C4	121
Lehigh, co., Pa., U.S.	E10	115
Lehigh, stm., Pa., U.S.	E10	115
Lehigh Acres, Fl., U.S.	F5	86
Lehighton, Pa., U.S.	E10	115
Lehua Island, i., Hi., U.S.	A1	88
Lehututu, Bots.	F4	44
Leiah, Pak.	E4	38
Leibnitz, Aus.	I15	8
Leicester, Eng., U.K.	I11	7
Leicester, Ma., U.S.	B4	98
Leichhardt, stm., Austl.	C7	50
Leiden, Neth.	C4	8
Leighton, Al., U.S.	A2	78
Leikanger, Nor.	F6	6
Leinster, hist. reg., Ire.	H5	7
Leinster, Mount, mtn., Ire.	I6	7
Leipsic, De., U.S.	D3	85
Leipsic, Oh., U.S.	A2	112
Leipsic, stm., De., U.S.	C3	85
Leipzig, Ger.	D12	8
Leiria, Port.	F3	12
Leisler, Mount, mtn., Austl.	D5	50
Leisure City, Fl., U.S.	s13	86
Leitchfield, Ky., U.S.	C3	94
Leitrim, Ire.	G4	7
Leiyang, China	I1	28
Leizhou Bandao, pen., China	D11	34
Leland, Il., U.S.	B5	90
Leland, Ms., U.S.	B3	101
Lelewi Point, c., Hi., U.S.	D7	88
Leleque, Arg.	E2	56
Le Lion-d'Angers, Fr.	E6	10
Leli Shan, mtn., China	D9	38
Le Locle, Switz.	E13	10
Le Lude, Fr.	E7	10
Le Maire, Estrecho de, strt., Arg.	G4	56
Le Mans, Fr.	D7	10
Le Mars, Ia., U.S.	B1	92
Leme, Braz.	G5	57
Lemesós (Limassol), Cyp.	B3	40
Lemgo, Ger.	C8	8
Lemhi, co., Id., U.S.	E4	89
Lemhi, stm., Id., U.S.	E5	89
Lemhi Pass, Id., U.S.	E5	89
Lemhi Range, mts., Id., U.S.	E5	89
Lemmon, S.D., U.S.	B3	118
Lemmon, Mount, mtn., Az., U.S.	E5	80
Lemmon Valley, Nv., U.S.	D2	105
Lemon, Lake, l., In., U.S.	F5	91
Lemon Fair, stm., Vt., U.S.	C2	122
Lemon Grove, Ca., U.S.	o15	82
Lemon Island, i., S.C., U.S.	G6	117
Lemont, Il., U.S.	B5	90
Lemont, Pa., U.S.	E6	115
Lemonweir, stm., Wi., U.S.	D3	126
Lemoore, Ca., U.S.	D4	82
Lemoore Naval Air Station, mil., Ca., U.S.	D4	82
Lempa, stm., N.A.	H3	64
Lem Peak, mtn., Id., U.S.	E5	89
Lena, Il., U.S.	A4	90
Lena, stm., Russia	C19	24
Lenawee, co., Mi., U.S.	G6	99
Lenclître, Fr.	F7	10
Lenghu, China	D5	26
Leninabad, Taj.	I11	22
Leningrad see Sankt-Peterburg, Russia	B13	18
Leninogorsk, Kaz.	G10	24
Leninsk-Kuzneckij, Russia	G11	24
Leninskoje, Russia	H20	24
Lennox, S.D., U.S.	D9	118
Lennoxville, Que., Can.	D6	74
Lenoir, N.C., U.S.	B1	110
Lenoir, co., N.C., U.S.	B5	110
Lenoir City, Tn., U.S.	D9	119
Lenore Lake, l., Sask., Can.	E3	75
Lenore Lake, l., Wa., U.S.	B6	124
Lenox, Ga., U.S.	E3	87
Lenox, Ia., U.S.	D3	92
Lenox, Ma., U.S.	B1	98
Lens, Fr.	B9	10
Lensk, Russia	E16	24
Lentini, Italy	L10	14
Leo, In., U.S.	B7	91
Leoben, Aus.	H15	8
Leominster, hist. reg., U.K.	I10	7
Leominster, Ma., U.S.	A4	98
León, Nic.	H4	64
León, Spain	C6	12
Leon, Ia., U.S.	D4	92
Leon, Ks., U.S.	E7	93
Leon, co., Fl., U.S.	B2	86
Leon, co., Tx., U.S.	D4	120
Leonard, Tx., U.S.	C4	120
Leonardo, N.J., U.S.	C4	107
Leonardtown, Md., U.S.	D4	97
Leonberg, Ger.	G9	8
León [de los Aldamas], Mex.	G9	62
Leonia, N.J., U.S.	h9	107
Leonora, Austl.	E4	50
Leonville, La., U.S.	D4	95
Léopold II, Lac see Mai-Ndombe, Lac, l., Zaire	B3	44
Leopoldina, Braz.	F7	57
Léopoldville see Kinshasa, Zaire	B3	44
Leoti, Ks., U.S.	D2	93
Le Palais, Fr.	E3	10
Lepanto, Ar., U.S.	B5	81
Lepe, Spain	H4	12
Leping, China	G6	28
L'Épiphanie, Que., Can.	D4	74
Le Puy, Fr.	G10	10
Lercara Friddi, Italy	L8	14
Lerici, Italy	E4	14
Lérida, Col.	G7	58
Lérida, Spain	D12	12
Lerma, Spain	C8	12
Le Roy, Il., U.S.	C5	90
Le Roy, Mn., U.S.	G6	100
Le Roy, N.Y., U.S.	C3	109
Lerwick, Scot., U.K.	A11	7
Léry, Que., Can.	q19	74
Léry, Lake, l., La., U.S.	k12	95
Les Andelys, Fr.	C8	10
Lesbos see Lésvos, i., Grc.	J10	16
Les Cayes, Haiti	E11	64
Les Échelles, Fr.	G12	10
Les Herbiers, Fr.	F5	10
Leskovac, Yugo.	G5	16
Leslie, Mi., U.S.	F6	99
Leslie, S.C., U.S.	B6	117
Leslie, co., Ky., U.S.	C6	94
Lesotho, ctry., Afr.	G5	44
Lesozavodsk, Russia	H20	24
Les Sables-d'Olonne, Fr.	F5	10
Lesser Antilles, is.	G17	64
Lesser Slave Lake, l., Alta., Can.	B3	68
Lesser Sunda Islands, is., Indon.	G6	32
Lester Prairie, Mn., U.S.	F4	100
Le Sueur, Mn., U.S.	F5	100
Le Sueur, co., Mn., U.S.	F5	100
Lésvos (Lesbos), i., Grc.	J10	16
Leszno, Pol.	D16	8
Letcher, co., Ky., U.S.	C7	94
Lethbridge, Alta., Can.	E4	68
Lethbridge, Newf., Can.	D5	72
Lethem, Guy.	F13	58
Leti, Kepulauan, is., Indon.	G8	32
Leticia, Col.	J8	58
Le Tréport, Fr.	B8	10
Letsôk-Aw Kyun, i., Burma	I5	34
Letterkenny, Ire.	G5	7
Leuven (Louvain), Bel.	E4	8
Levádhia, Grc.	K6	16
Levante, Riviera di, Italy	E4	14
Levelland, Tx., U.S.	C1	120
Leveque, Cape, c., Austl.	C4	50
Leverkusen, Ger.	D6	8
Lévis, Que., Can.	C6	74
Levisa Fork, stm., U.S.	C7	94
Levittown, N.Y., U.S.	E7	109
Levittown, Pa., U.S.	F12	115
Levy, co., Fl., U.S.	C4	86
Levy Lake, l., Fl., U.S.	C4	86
Lewes, Eng., U.K.	K13	7
Lewes, De., U.S.	E5	85
Lewes and Rehoboth Canal, De., U.S.	F5	85
Lewis, co., Id., U.S.	C2	89
Lewis, co., Ky., U.S.	B6	94
Lewis, co., Mo., U.S.	A6	102
Lewis, co., N.Y., U.S.	B5	109
Lewis, co., Tn., U.S.	B4	119
Lewis, co., Wa., U.S.	C3	124
Lewis, co., W.V., U.S.	C4	125
Lewis, stm., Wa., U.S.	C4	124
Lewis, Mount, mtn., Nv., U.S.	C5	105
Lewis, Isle of, i., Scot., U.K.	C6	7
Lewis and Clark, co., Mt., U.S.	C4	103
Lewis and Clark Lake, res., U.S.	E8	118
Lewisburg, Ky., U.S.	D3	94
Lewisburg, Oh., U.S.	C1	112
Lewisburg, Pa., U.S.	E8	115
Lewisburg, Tn., U.S.	B5	119
Lewisburg, W.V., U.S.	D4	125
Lewis Creek, stm., Vt., U.S.	C2	122
Lewis Lake, l., Wy., U.S.	B2	127
Lewisport, Ky., U.S.	C3	94
Lewisporte, Newf., Can.	D4	72
Lewis Smith Lake, res., Al., U.S.	B2	78
Lewiston, Id., U.S.	C1	89
Lewiston, Me., U.S.	D2	96
Lewiston, Mn., U.S.	G7	100
Lewiston, N.Y., U.S.	B1	109
Lewiston, Ut., U.S.	B4	121
Lewiston Peak, mtn., Ut., U.S.	C3	121
Lewiston Woodville, N.C., U.S.	A5	110
Lewistown, Il., U.S.	C3	90
Lewistown, Mt., U.S.	C7	103
Lewistown, Pa., U.S.	E6	115
Lewisville, Ar., U.S.	D2	81
Lewisville, Tx., U.S.	C4	120
Lewisville Lake, res., Tx., U.S.	C4	120
Lexington, Al., U.S.	A2	78
Lexington, Il., U.S.	C5	90
Lexington, Ky., U.S.	B5	94
Lexington, Ma., U.S.	B5	98
Lexington, Ms., U.S.	B3	101
Lexington, Mo., U.S.	B4	102
Lexington, N.C., U.S.	B2	110
Lexington, Oh., U.S.	B3	112
Lexington, Ok., U.S.	B4	113
Lexington, S.C., U.S.	D5	117
Lexington, Tn., U.S.	B3	119
Lexington, Va., U.S.	C3	123
Lexington, co., S.C., U.S.	D5	117
Lexington Park, Md., U.S.	D5	97
Leyte, i., Phil.	C7	32
Leyte Gulf, b., Phil.	C8	32
Lhasa, China	F14	38
Lhokseumawe, Indon.	D2	32
Lianhua Shan, mts., China	L4	28
Lianxian, China	G9	26
Lianyungang, China	E10	26
Liao, stm., China	C11	26
Liaocheng, China	D10	26
Liaodong Wan, b., China	C11	26
Liaoning, prov., China	C11	26
Liaotung, Gulf of see Liaodong Wan, b., China	C11	26
Liaoyang, China	C11	26
Liaoyuan, China	C12	26
Liard, stm., Can.	E8	66
Libby, Mt., U.S.	B1	103
Libenge, Zaire	H9	42
Liberal, Ks., U.S.	E3	93
Liberal, Mo., U.S.	D3	102
Liberec, Czech.	E15	8
Liberia, C.R.	I5	64
Liberia, ctry., Afr.	G4	42
Libertad, Ven.	C8	58
Liberty, In., U.S.	E8	91
Liberty, Ky., U.S.	C5	94
Liberty, Ms., U.S.	D3	101
Liberty, Mo., U.S.	B3	102
Liberty, N.Y., U.S.	D6	109
Liberty, N.C., U.S.	B3	110
Liberty, S.C., U.S.	B2	117
Liberty, Tx., U.S.	D5	120
Liberty, co., Fl., U.S.	B2	86
Liberty, co., Ga., U.S.	E5	87
Liberty, co., Mt., U.S.	B5	103
Liberty, co., Tx., U.S.	D5	120
Liberty Center, Oh., U.S.	A1	112
Liberty Lake, Wa., U.S.	g14	124
Liberty Lake, res., Md., U.S.	B4	97
Libertyville, Il., U.S.	A6	90
Libīyah, Aş-Şaḥrā' al- (Libyan Desert), des., Afr.	D11	42
Libourne, Fr.	H6	10
Libreville, Gabon	A1	44
Libuse, La., U.S.	C3	95
Libya, ctry., Afr.	C9	42
Libyan Desert see Libīyah, Aş-Şaḥrā' al-, des., Afr.	D11	42
Licata, Italy	L8	14
Lichinga, Moz.	D7	44
Lichtenfels, Ger.	E11	8
Lick Creek, stm., Tn., U.S.	C11	119
Licking, Mo., U.S.	D6	102
Licking, co., Oh., U.S.	B3	112
Licking, stm., Ky., U.S.	B6	94
Lida, Bela.	H8	18
Lida, Lake, l., Mn., U.S.	D3	100
Lidgerwood, N.D., U.S.	C8	111
Lidköping, Swe.	G9	6
Lido di Ostia, Italy	H7	14
Liechtenstein, ctry., Eur.	F9	4
Liège, Bel.	E5	8
Lieksa, Fin.	E18	6
Lienz, Aus.	I12	8
Liepāja, Lat.	E4	18
Lier, Bel.	D4	8
Liestal, Switz.	E14	10
Liévin, Fr.	B9	10
Lièvre, Rivière du, stm., Que., Can.	D2	74
Liezen, Aus.	H14	8
Lifford, Ire.	G5	7
Ligao, Phil.	r20	33b
Lighthouse Inlet, b., S.C., U.S.	k12	117
Lighthouse Point, c., Fl., U.S.	C2	86
Lighthouse Point, c., Mi., U.S.	C5	99
Lightning Creek, stm., Wy., U.S.	C8	127
Ligny-en-Barrois, Fr.	D12	10
Ligonier, In., U.S.	B6	91
Ligonier, Pa., U.S.	F3	115
Ligurian Sea, Eur.	E3	14
Lihou Reefs, rf., Austl.	C10	50
Lihue, Hi., U.S.	B2	88
Lijiang, China	F7	26
Likasi (Jadotville), Zaire	D5	44
Likino-Dulevo, Russia	F22	18
Liknes, Nor.	G6	6
Likouala, stm., Congo	B3	44
Lilbourn, Mo., U.S.	E8	102
Lilburn, Ga., U.S.	h8	87
Liling, China	H2	28
Lille, Fr.	B10	10
Lillehammer, Nor.	F8	6
Lillestrøm, Nor.	G8	6
Lillian, Al., U.S.	E2	78
Lillington, N.C., U.S.	B4	110
Lillinonah, Lake, l., Ct., U.S.	C2	84
Lillo, Spain	F8	12
Lillooet, B.C., Can.	D7	69
Lillooet, stm., B.C., Can.	D6	69
Lilly, Pa., U.S.	F4	115
Lilly Fork, stm., W.V., U.S.	m13	125
Lilly Grove, W.V., U.S.	D3	125
Lilongwe, Mwi.	D6	44
Lily, Ky., U.S.	C5	94
Lima, Peru	F3	54
Lima, N.Y., U.S.	C3	109
Lima, Oh., U.S.	B1	112
Lima Reservoir, res., Mt., U.S.	F4	103
Limassol see Lemesós, Cyp.	B3	40
Limbdi, India	I4	38
Limburg an der Lahn, Ger.	E8	8
Limeira, Braz.	G5	57
Limerick, Ire.	I4	7
Limestone, Me., U.S.	A5	96
Limestone, co., Al., U.S.	A2	78
Limestone, co., Tx., U.S.	D4	120
Limestone Point, pen., Man., Can.	C2	10
Liminka, Fin.	D15	6

Name	Map Ref	Page
ímmen Bight, Austl.	B7	50
ímnos, i., Grc.	J9	16
ímoges, Ont., Can.	B9	73
ímoges, Fr.	G8	10
ímón, C.R.	I6	64
ímón, Hond.	G5	64
ímon, Co., U.S.	B7	83
ímousins, Plateau du, plat., Fr.	G8	10
ímoux, Fr.	I9	10
ímpopo, stm., Afr.	F6	44
ínares, Chile	D2	56
ínares, Col.	G4	58
ínares, Mex.	E10	62
ínares, Spain	G8	12
íncoln, Arg.	C4	56
íncoln, Ont., Can.	D5	73
íncoln, Eng., U.K.	H12	7
íncoln, Al., U.S.	B3	78
íncoln, Ar., U.S.	B1	81
íncoln, Ca., U.S.	C3	82
íncoln, De., U.S.	E4	85
íncoln, Id., U.S.	F6	89
íncoln, Il., U.S.	C4	90
íncoln, Ks., U.S.	C5	93
íncoln, Me., U.S.	C4	96
íncoln, Ma., U.S.	g10	98
íncoln, Mo., U.S.	C4	102
íncoln, Ne., U.S.	D9	104
íncoln, N.H., U.S.	B3	106
íncoln, co., Ar., U.S.	D4	81
íncoln, co., Co., U.S.	C7	83
íncoln, co., Ga., U.S.	C4	87
íncoln, co., Id., U.S.	G4	89
íncoln, co., Ks., U.S.	C5	93
íncoln, co., Ky., U.S.	C5	94
íncoln, co., La., U.S.	B3	95
íncoln, co., Me., U.S.	D3	96
íncoln, co., Mn., U.S.	F2	100
íncoln, co., Ms., U.S.	D3	101
íncoln, co., Mo., U.S.	B7	102
íncoln, co., Mt., U.S.	B1	103
íncoln, co., Ne., U.S.	D5	104
íncoln, co., Nv., U.S.	F6	105
íncoln, co., N.M., U.S.	D4	108
íncoln, co., N.C., U.S.	B1	110
íncoln, co., Ok., U.S.	B5	113
íncoln, co., Or., U.S.	C3	114
íncoln, co., S.D., U.S.	D9	118
íncoln, co., Tn., U.S.	B5	119
íncoln, co., Wa., U.S.	B7	124
íncoln, co., W.V., U.S.	C2	125
íncoln, co., Wi., U.S.	C4	126
íncoln, co., Wy., U.S.	D2	127
íncoln, Mount, mtn., Co., U.S.	B4	83
íncoln Acres, Ca., U.S.	o15	82
íncoln City, Or., U.S.	C3	114
íncoln Heights, Oh., U.S.	o13	112
íncoln Park, Co., U.S.	C5	83
íncoln Park, Ga., U.S.	D2	87
íncoln Park, Mi., U.S.	p15	99
íncoln Park, N.J., U.S.	B4	107
íncolnshire, Il., U.S.	h9	90
íncoln Tomb State Memorial, hist., Il., U.S.	D4	90
íncolnton, Ga., U.S.	C4	87
íncolnton, N.C., U.S.	B1	110
íncolnville, S.C., U.S.	h11	117
íncolnwood, Il., U.S.	h9	90
íncroft, N.J., U.S.	C4	107
índale, Ga., U.S.	B1	87
índale, Tx., U.S.	C5	120
índau, Ger.	H9	8
índen, Al., U.S.	C2	78
índen, In., U.S.	D4	91
índen, Mi., U.S.	F7	99
índen, N.J., U.S.	k8	107
índen, Tn., U.S.	B4	119
índen, Tx., U.S.	C5	120
índenhurst, Il., U.S.	h8	90
índenhurst, N.Y., U.S.	n15	109
índenwold, N.J., U.S.	D3	107
índesnes, c., Nor.	G6	6
índi, Tan.	C7	44
índon, Ut., U.S.	C4	121
índsay, Ont., Can.	C6	73
índsay, Ca., U.S.	D4	82
índsay, Ok., U.S.	C4	113
índsborg, Ks., U.S.	D6	93
índstrom, Mn., U.S.	E6	100
ínesville, Pa., U.S.	E1	115
íneville, Al., U.S.	B4	78
íngao, China	D10	34
íngayen, Phil.	B7	32
ínge, Ger.	C7	8
íngga, Kepulauan, is., Indon.	F3	32
íngle, U.S.	D8	127
ínglestown, Pa., U.S.	F8	115
íngling, China	A11	34
ính, Ngoc, mtn., Viet.	G9	34
ínhai, China	G10	28
ínière, Que., Can.	C7	74
ínjiang, China	C12	26
ínköping, Swe.	G10	6
ínkou, China	B13	26
ínn, Mo., U.S.	C6	102
ínn, co., Ia., U.S.	B6	92
ínn, co., Ks., U.S.	D9	93
ínn, co., Mo., U.S.	B4	102
ínn, co., Or., U.S.	C4	114
íno Lakes, Mn., U.S.	m12	100
ínqing, China	D10	26
ínru, China	A1	28
íns, Braz.	F4	57
íntao, China	D7	26
ínthicum Heights, Md., U.S.	B4	97
ínton, In., U.S.	F3	91
ínton, N.D., U.S.	C5	111
ínwood, N.J., U.S.	E3	107
ínxi, China	C10	26
ínxia, China	D7	26
ínyi, China	D10	26
ínz, Aus.	G14	8
íon, Golfe du, b., Fr.	I11	10
Lipa, Phil.	r19	33b
Lipeck, Russia	I22	18
Lippstadt, Ger.	D8	8
Lipscomb, Al., U.S.	B3	78
Lipscomb, co., Tx., U.S.	A2	120
Lira, Ug.	H12	42
Liria, Spain	F11	12
Lisala, Zaire	A4	44
Lisboa (Lisbon), Port.	G2	12
Lisbon, Ia., U.S.	C6	92
Lisbon, Me., U.S.	D2	96
Lisbon, Md., U.S.	B3	97
Lisbon, N.H., U.S.	B3	106
Lisbon, N.D., U.S.	C8	111
Lisbon, Oh., U.S.	B5	112
Lisbon Center, Me., U.S.	f7	96
Lisbon Falls, Me., U.S.	E2	96
Lisbon see Lisboa, Port.	G2	12
Lisburne, Cape, c., Ak., U.S.	B6	79
Lishui, China	G8	28
Lisianski Island, i., Hi., U.S.	k13	88
Lisičansk, Ukr.	H5	22
Lisieux, Fr.	C7	10
L'Isle Jourdain, Fr.	F7	10
L'Isle-Jourdain, Fr.	I8	10
L'Islet-sur-Mer, Que., Can.	B7	74
L'Isle-Verte, Que., Can.	A8	74
Lismore, Austl.	E10	50
Listowel, Ont., Can.	D4	73
Listowel, Ire.	I3	7
Lit, Swe.	E10	6
Litang, China	G8	26
Litchfield, Ct., U.S.	C3	84
Litchfield, Il., U.S.	D4	90
Litchfield, Mi., U.S.	F6	99
Litchfield, Mn., U.S.	E4	100
Litchfield, co., Ct., U.S.	B2	84
Litchfield Park, Az., U.S.	m8	80
Lithia Springs, Ga., U.S.	h7	87
Lithonia, Ga., U.S.	C2	87
Lithuania, ctry., Eur.	F6	18
Litija, Slo.	C9	14
Lititz, Pa., U.S.	F9	115
Litovko, Russia	H21	24
Little, stm., U.S.	B5	81
Little, stm., U.S.	D7	113
Little, stm., Ct., U.S.	C7	84
Little, stm., Ky., U.S.	D2	94
Little, stm., La., U.S.	C3	95
Little, stm., N.C., U.S.	B3	110
Little, stm., Ok., U.S.	B5	113
Little, stm., S.C., U.S.	C2	117
Little, stm., Tn., U.S.	n14	119
Little, stm., Vt., U.S.	C3	122
Little, stm., Va., U.S.	D2	123
Little Abaco Island, i., Bah.	A9	64
Little Acres, Az., U.S.	D5	80
Little Andaman, i., India	I2	34
Little Arkansas, stm., Ks., U.S.	D6	93
Little Belt Mountains, mts., Mt., U.S.	D6	103
Little Bighorn, stm., U.S.	E9	103
Little Black, stm., Me., U.S.	A3	96
Little Blue, stm., U.S.	C6	93
Little Blue, stm., In., U.S.	H5	91
Little Bow, stm., Alta., Can.	D4	68
Little Cacapon, stm., W.V., U.S.	B6	125
Little Catalina, Newf., Can.	D5	72
Little Cayman, i., Cay. Is.	E7	64
Little Cedar, stm., Ia., U.S.	A5	92
Little Churchill, stm., Man., Can.	A4	70
Little Chute, Wi., U.S.	D5	126
Little Coal, stm., W.V., U.S.	C3	125
Little Colorado, stm., Az., U.S.	B4	80
Little Compton, R.I., U.S.	E6	116
Little Creek, De., U.S.	D4	85
Little Creek Naval Amphibious Base, mil., Va., U.S.	k15	123
Little Creek Peak, mtn., Ut., U.S.	F3	121
Little Current, Ont., Can.	B3	73
Little Diomede Island, i., Ak., U.S.	B6	79
Little Egg Harbor, b., N.J., U.S.	D4	107
Little Egg Inlet, b., N.J., U.S.	E4	107
Little Falls, Mn., U.S.	E4	100
Little Falls, N.J., U.S.	B4	107
Little Falls, N.Y., U.S.	B6	109
Little Ferry, N.J., U.S.	h8	107
Littlefield, Tx., U.S.	C1	120
Little Fishing Creek, stm., W.V., U.S.	h9	125
Littlefork, Mn., U.S.	B5	100
Little Fork, stm., Mn., U.S.	B5	100
Little Goose Creek, stm., Wy., U.S.	B6	127
Little Gunpowder Falls, stm., Md., U.S.	A4	97
Little Humboldt, stm., Nv., U.S.	B4	105
Little Inagua, i., Bah.	D11	64
Little Kanawha, stm., W.V., U.S.	C4	125
Little Lake, Mi., U.S.	B3	99
Little Lake, i., La., U.S.	E5	95
Little Lynches, stm., S.C., U.S.	C7	117
Little Manatee, stm., Fl., U.S.	p11	86
Little Mecatina, stm., Can.	h9	72
Little Miami, stm., Oh., U.S.	C1	112
Little Minch, strt., Scot., U.K.	D6	7
Little Missouri, stm., U.S.	B6	76
Little Missouri, stm., Ar., U.S.	D2	81
Little Muddy, stm., Il., U.S.	E4	90
Little Muddy, stm., N.D., U.S.	A2	111
Little Nicobar, i., India	K2	34
Little Osage, stm., U.S.	E9	93
Little Otter Creek, stm., Vt., U.S.	C2	122
Little Owyhee, stm., U.S.	B5	105
Little Pee Dee, stm., S.C., U.S.	C9	117
Little Powder, stm., U.S.	F11	103
Little Red, stm., Ar., U.S.	B4	81
Little River, co., Ar., U.S.	D1	81
Little River Inlet, b., S.C., U.S.	D10	117
Little Rock, Ar., U.S.	C3	81
Little Rock, stm., U.S.	A1	92
Little Rock Air Force Base, mil., Ar., U.S.	C3	81
Little Sable Point, c., Mi., U.S.	E4	99
Little Salt Lake, l., Ut., U.S.	F3	121
Little Sandy, stm., Ky., U.S.	B6	94
Little Sandy Creek, stm., Wy., U.S.	D3	127
Little Sebago Lake, l., Me., U.S.	g7	96
Little Silver, N.J., U.S.	C4	107
Little Sioux, stm., U.S.	B2	92
Little Sioux, West Fork, stm., Ia., U.S.	B2	92
Little Smoky, stm., Alta., Can.	B2	68
Little Snake, stm., U.S.	A2	83
Little Spokane, stm., Wa., U.S.	B8	124
Littlestown, Pa., U.S.	G7	115
Little Tallapoosa, stm., U.S.	B4	78
Little Tenmile Creek, stm., W.V., U.S.	k10	125
Little Tennessee, stm., U.S.	D7	119
Littleton, Co., U.S.	B6	83
Littleton, Il., U.S.	C3	90
Littleton, Ma., U.S.	f10	98
Littleton, N.H., U.S.	B3	106
Littleton, N.C., U.S.	A5	110
Littleville, Al., U.S.	A2	78
Little Wabash, stm., Il., U.S.	E5	90
Little Walnut, stm., Ks., U.S.	g13	93
Little White, stm., S.D., U.S.	D5	118
Little Wolf, stm., Wi., U.S.	D4	126
Little Wood, stm., Id., U.S.	F4	89
Liuan, China	D5	28
Liuhe, China	C7	28
Liuzhou, China	B10	34
Live Oak, Ca., U.S.	C3	82
Live Oak, Fl., U.S.	B4	86
Live Oak, co., Tx., U.S.	E3	120
Livermore, Ca., U.S.	h9	82
Livermore, Ky., U.S.	C2	94
Livermore, Mount, mtn., Tx., U.S.	o12	120
Livermore Falls, Me., U.S.	D2	96
Liverpool, Eng., U.K.	H10	7
Liverpool, Cape, c., N.W. Ter., Can.	B17	66
Livingston, Al., U.S.	C1	78
Livingston, Ca., U.S.	D3	82
Livingston, Il., U.S.	E4	90
Livingston, La., U.S.	D5	95
Livingston, Mt., U.S.	E6	103
Livingston, N.J., U.S.	B4	107
Livingston, Tn., U.S.	C8	119
Livingston, Tx., U.S.	D5	120
Livingston, co., Il., U.S.	C5	90
Livingston, co., Ky., U.S.	e9	94
Livingston, co., La., U.S.	D5	95
Livingston, co., Mi., U.S.	F7	99
Livingston, co., Mo., U.S.	B4	102
Livingston, co., N.Y., U.S.	C3	109
Livingston, Lake, res., Tx., U.S.	D5	120
Livingstone, Zam.	E5	44
Livingstonia, Mwi.	D6	44
Livno, Bos.	F12	14
Livny, Russia	I20	18
Livonia, La., U.S.	D4	95
Livonia, Mi., U.S.	F7	99
Livorno (Leghorn), Italy	F5	14
Liyang, China	D8	28
Lizard Head Pass, Co., U.S.	D3	83
Lizard Head Peak, mtn., Wy., U.S.	D3	127
Lizard Point, c., Eng., U.K.	L7	7
Lizella, Ga., U.S.	D3	87
Ljubljana, Slo.	C9	14
Ljungby, Swe.	H9	6
Ljusdal, Swe.	F11	6
Llandudno, Wales, U.K.	H9	7
Llanelli, Wales, U.K.	J8	7
Llanes, Spain	B7	12
Llanidloes, Wales, U.K.	I9	7
Llano, Tx., U.S.	D3	120
Llano, co., Tx., U.S.	D3	120
Llano, stm., Tx., U.S.	D3	120
Llanos, pl., S.A.	E7	58
Llanwrtyd Wells, Wales, U.K.	I9	7
Llera, Mex.	F10	62
Llerena, Spain	G5	12
Lloyd, Ky., U.S.	B7	94
Lloydminster, Alta., Can.	C5	68
Lloyds, stm., Newf., Can.	D3	72
Lluchmayor, Spain	F14	12
Llullaillaco, Volcán, vol., S.A.	A3	56
Lo, stm., Viet.	C8	34
Loami, Il., U.S.	D4	90
Loange, stm., Afr.	C3	44
Löbau, Ger.	D14	8
Lobaye, stm., Cen. Afr. Rep.	G9	42
Lobelville, Tn., U.S.	B4	119
Lobito, Ang.	D2	44
Lobos de Afuera, Islas, is., Peru	E2	54
Lobos de Tierra, Isla, i., Peru	E2	54
Lobster Lake, l., Me., U.S.	C3	96
Locarno, Switz.	F15	10
Lochaline, Scot., U.K.	E7	7
Lochboisdale, Scot., U.K.	D5	7
Loches, Fr.	E7	10
Lochgilphead, Scot., U.K.	E7	7
Lochsa, stm., Id., U.S.	C3	89
Lockeport, N.S., Can.	F4	71
Lockesburg, Ar., U.S.	D1	81
Lockhart, Tx., U.S.	E4	120
Lock Haven, Pa., U.S.	D7	115
Lockland, Oh., U.S.	o13	112
Lockney, Tx., U.S.	B2	120
Lockport, Il., U.S.	B5	90
Lockport, La., U.S.	E5	95
Lockport, N.Y., U.S.	B2	109
Lockwood, Mo., U.S.	D4	102
Lockwood, Mt., U.S.	E8	103
Loc Ninh, Viet.	I9	34
Locust, N.C., U.S.	B2	110
Locust Fork, stm., Al., U.S.	B3	78
Locust Grove, Ga., U.S.	C2	87
Locust Grove, Ok., U.S.	A6	113
Lod, Isr.		
Lodejnoje Polje, Russia	A16	18
Lodeve, Fr.	I10	10
Lodgepole Creek, stm., U.S.	C3	104
Lodi, Italy	D4	14
Lodi, Ca., U.S.	C3	82
Lodi, N.J., U.S.	h8	107
Lodi, Oh., U.S.	A3	112
Lodi, Wi., U.S.	E4	126
Lodja, Zaire	B4	44
Lodwar, Kenya	H2	46
Łódź, Pol.	D19	8
Loffa, stm., Afr.	G3	42
Logan, Ia., U.S.	C2	92
Logan, Ks., U.S.	C4	93
Logan, N.M., U.S.	B6	108
Logan, Oh., U.S.	C3	112
Logan, Ut., U.S.	B4	121
Logan, W.V., U.S.	D3	125
Logan, co., Ar., U.S.	B2	81
Logan, co., Co., U.S.	A7	83
Logan, co., Il., U.S.	C4	90
Logan, co., Ks., U.S.	D2	93
Logan, co., Ky., U.S.	D3	94
Logan, co., Ne., U.S.	C5	104
Logan, co., N.D., U.S.	C6	111
Logan, co., Oh., U.S.	B2	112
Logan, co., Ok., U.S.	B4	113
Logan, co., W.V., U.S.	D3	125
Logan, Mount, mtn., Yukon, Can.	D4	66
Logan, Mount, mtn., Wa., U.S.	A5	124
Logandale, Nv., U.S.	G7	105
Logan Lake, B.C., Can.	D7	69
Logan Martin Lake, res., Al., U.S.	B3	78
Logan Pass, Mt., U.S.	B2	103
Logansport, In., U.S.	C5	91
Logansport, La., U.S.	C2	95
Loganville, Ga., U.S.	C3	87
Loganville, Pa., U.S.	G8	115
Loggieville, N.B., Can.	B4	71
Logone, stm., Afr.	F9	42
Logroño, Spain	C9	12
Logrosán, Spain	F6	12
Lohr, Ger.	E9	8
Loi-Kaw, Burma	E4	34
Loimaa, Fin.	F14	6
Loire, stm., Fr.	E5	10
Loja, Ec.	J3	58
Loja, Spain	H7	12
Lokolama, Zaire	B3	44
Lol, stm., Sudan	G11	42
Lola, Mount, mtn., Ca., U.S.	C3	82
Lolo, Mt., U.S.	D2	103
Lolo Pass, U.S.	C4	89
Lomami, stm., Zaire	B4	44
Lombard, Il., U.S.	k8	90
Lomblen, Pulau, i., Indon.	G7	32
Lombok, i., Indon.	G6	32
Lomé, Togo	G6	42
Lomela, Zaire	B4	44
Lomela, stm., Zaire	B4	44
Lomira, Wi., U.S.	E5	126
Lomond, Loch, l., Scot., U.K.	E8	7
Lomonosov, Russia	B12	18
Lompoc, Ca., U.S.	E3	82
Łomża, Pol.	B22	8
Lonaconing, Md., U.S.	k13	97
Lonāvale, India	C2	37
Loncoche, Chile	D2	56
London, Ont., Can.	E3	73
London, Eng., U.K.	J12	7
London, Ar., U.S.	B2	81
London, Ky., U.S.	C5	94
London, Oh., U.S.	C2	112
Londonderry, N. Ire., U.K.	G5	7
Londonderry, N.H., U.S.	E4	106
Londonderry, Cape, c., Austl.	B5	50
Londonderry, Isla, i., Chile	H2	56
Londontown, Md., U.S.	C4	97
Londrina, Braz.	G3	57
Lone Grove, Ok., U.S.	C4	113
Lone Mountain, mtn., Nv., U.S.	E4	105
Lone Pine, Ca., U.S.	D4	82
Lone Tree, Ia., U.S.	C6	92
Long, co., Ga., U.S.	E5	87
Longa, Proliv, strt., Russia	C29	24
Longarone, Italy	C7	14
Long Bar Harbor, Md., U.S.	B5	97
Long Beach, Ca., U.S.	F4	82
Long Beach, In., U.S.	A4	91
Long Beach, Md., U.S.	D5	97
Long Beach, Ms., U.S.	g7	101
Long Beach, N.Y., U.S.	E7	109
Long Beach, Wa., U.S.	C1	124
Long Beach Naval Shipyard, mil., Ca., U.S.	n12	82
Longboat Key, i., Fl., U.S.	q10	86
Longboat Key, i., Fl., U.S.	E4	86
Longboat Pass, strt., Fl., U.S.	q10	86
Long Branch, N.J., U.S.	C5	107
Longbranch, Wa., U.S.	B3	124
Long Creek Mountain, mtn., Wy., U.S.	D5	127
Longeau, Fr.	E12	10
Long Grove, Ia., U.S.	C7	92
Long Harbour [-Mount Arlington Heights], Newf., Can.	E5	72
Long Island, i., Bah.	C10	64
Long Island, i., N.S., Can.	E3	71
Long Island, i., Me., U.S.	g7	96
Long Island, i., Ma., U.S.	g12	98
Long Island, i., N.Y., U.S.	E7	109
Long Island Sound, strt., U.S.	E7	109
Longjiang, China	B11	26
Long Key, i., Fl., U.S.	H6	86
Long Lake, Il., U.S.	h8	90
Long Lake, l., Me., U.S.	D2	96
Long Lake, l., Me., U.S.	A4	96
Long Lake, l., Mi., U.S.	C7	99
Long Lake, l., Mi., U.S.	D5	99
Long Lake, l., Mn., U.S.	D4	100
Long Lake, l., N.Y., U.S.	B6	109
Long Lake, l., N.D., U.S.	C6	111
Long Lake, l., Wa., U.S.	f10	124
Long Lake, l., Wi., U.S.	C2	126
Longli, China	A9	34
Longmeadow, Ma., U.S.	B2	98
Longmont, Co., U.S.	A5	83
Long Point, c., Man., Can.	C2	70
Long Point, pen., Ont., Can.	E4	73
Long Pond, res., Fl., U.S.	C4	86
Long Prairie, Mn., U.S.	E4	100
Long Range Mountains, mts., Newf., Can.	D3	72
Longreach, Austl.	D8	50
Longsheng, China	B11	34
Longs Peak, mtn., Co., U.S.	A5	83
Longué, Fr.	E6	10
Longueuil, Que., Can.	D4	74
Longuyon, Fr.	C12	10
Long View, N.C., U.S.	B1	110
Longview, Tx., U.S.	C5	120
Longview, Wa., U.S.	C3	124
Longwy, Fr.	C12	10
Long Xuyen, Viet.	I8	34
Lonigo, Italy	D6	14
Löningen, Ger.	C7	8
Lonoke, Ar., U.S.	C4	81
Lonoke, co., Ar., U.S.	C4	81
Lønsdal, Nor.	C10	6
Lonsdale, Mn., U.S.	F5	100
Lonsdale, R.I., U.S.	B4	116
Lons-le-Saunier, Fr.	F12	10
Loogootee, In., U.S.	G4	91
Lookout, Ky., U.S.	C7	94
Lookout, Cape, c., N.C., U.S.	C6	110
Lookout, Point, c., Mi., U.S.	d7	99
Lookout Mountain, Tn., U.S.	h11	119
Lookout Mountain, mtn., U.S.	D8	119
Lookout Mountain, mtn., Or., U.S.	C6	114
Lookout Pass, U.S.	B3	89
Lookout Point Lake, res., Or., U.S.	D4	114
Loon Lake, Wa., U.S.	A8	124
Loon Lake, l., Me., U.S.	B3	96
Loop Creek, stm., W.V., U.S.	m13	125
Loop Head, c., Ire.	I3	7
Loosahatchie, stm., Tn., U.S.	B2	119
Lopatina, Gora, mtn., Russia	G22	24
Lopatka, Mys, c., Russia	G25	24
Lop Buri, Thai.	G6	34
Lopez, Cap, c., Gabon	B1	44
López Collada, Mex.	B3	62
Lopez Island, i., Wa., U.S.	A3	124
Lop Nur, l., China	C5	26
Lora del Río, Spain	H6	12
Lorain, Oh., U.S.	A3	112
Lorain, co., Oh., U.S.	A3	112
Loramie, Lake, res., Oh., U.S.	B1	112
Lorca, Spain	H10	12
Lord Howe Island, i., Austl.	F11	50
Lordsburg, N.M., U.S.	E1	108
Loreauville, La., U.S.	D4	95
Lorena, Braz.	G6	57
Lorenzo, Tx., U.S.	C2	120
Loreto, Braz.	E9	54
Loreto, Col.	I7	58
Loreto, Mex.	F9	62
Lorette, Man., Can.	E3	70
Loretteville, Que., Can.	C6	74
Loretto, Ky., U.S.	C4	94
Loretto, Pa., U.S.	F4	115
Loretto, Tn., U.S.	B4	119
L'Orignal, Ont., Can.	B10	73
Loring Air Force Base, mil., Me., U.S.	B5	96
Loriol [-du-Comtat], Fr.	H11	10
Loris, S.C., U.S.	C10	117
Lorne, N.B., Can.	B3	71
Lörrach, Ger.	H7	8
Lorraine, hist. reg., Fr.	D13	10
Los Alamos, N.M., U.S.	B3	108
Los Alamos, co., N.M., U.S.	B3	108
Los Aldamas, Mex.	D10	62
Los Altos, Ca., U.S.	k8	82
Los Ángeles, Chile	D2	56
Los Angeles, Ca., U.S.	E4	82
Los Angeles, co., Ca., U.S.	E4	82
Los Angeles Aqueduct, Ca., U.S.	E4	82
Los Banos, Ca., U.S.	D3	82
Los Blancos, Arg.	A4	56
Los Fresnos, Tx., U.S.	F4	120
Los Gatos, Ca., U.S.	D2	82
Los Lagos, Chile	D2	56
Los Lunas, N.M., U.S.	C3	108
Los Mochis, Mex.	E5	62
Los Palacios y Villafranca, Spain	H6	12
Los Pinos, stm., Co., U.S.	D3	83
Los Ranchos de Albuquerque, N.M., U.S.	B3	108
Los Roques, Islas, is., Ven.	B9	58
Lost, stm., In., U.S.	G4	91
Lost, stm., Wa., U.S.	A5	124
Lost, stm., W.V., U.S.	B6	125
Lost Creek, stm., Wy., U.S.	D4	127
Los Teques, Ven.	B9	58
Los Testigos, Islas, is., Ven.	B11	58
Lost Peak, mtn., U.S.	F2	121
Lost Ranger Peak, mtn., Co., U.S.	A4	83
Lost River Glacial Caverns, N.H., U.S.	B3	106
Lost River Range, mts., Id., U.S.	E5	89
Lost Trail Pass, U.S.	D5	89
Los Vilos, Chile	C2	56
Los Yébenes, Spain	F8	12
Lota, Chile	D2	56
Lotawana, Lake, res., Mo., U.S.	k11	102
Lotbinière, Que., Can.	C6	74
Louang Namtha, Laos	D6	34
Louangphrabang, Laos	E7	34
Loudéac, Fr.	D4	10
Loudon, Tn., U.S.	D9	119
Loudon, co., Tn., U.S.	D9	119
Loudonville, Oh., U.S.	B3	112
Loudoun, co., Va., U.S.	A5	123
Loudun, Fr.	E7	10
Louga, Sen.	E2	42
Loughrea, Ire.	H4	7
Louhans, Fr.	F12	10
Louisa, Ky., U.S.	B7	94
Louisa, co., Ia., U.S.	C6	92
Louisa, co., Va., U.S.	C5	123

161

Name	Map Ref	Page
Louisa, Lake, l., Fl., U.S.	D5	86
Louisbourg, N.S., Can.	D10	71
Louisburg, Ks., U.S.	D9	93
Louisburg, N.C., U.S.	A4	110
Louisdale, N.S., Can.	D8	71
Louise, Lake, l., Ak., U.S.	f18	79
Louise Island, i., B.C., Can.	C2	69
Louiseville, Que., Can.	C5	74
Louisiade Archipelago, is., Pap. N. Gui.	B10	50
Louisiana, Mo., U.S.	B6	102
Louisiana, state, U.S.	C3	95
Louisiana Point, c., La., U.S.	E2	95
Louis Trichardt, S. Afr.	F5	44
Louisville, Al., U.S.	D4	78
Louisville, Co., U.S.	B5	83
Louisville, Ga., U.S.	C4	87
Louisville, Il., U.S.	E5	90
Louisville, Ky., U.S.	B4	94
Louisville, Ms., U.S.	B4	101
Louisville, Ne., U.S.	D9	104
Louisville, Oh., U.S.	B4	112
Louis-XIV, Pointe, c., Que., Can.	h11	74
Loulé, Port.	H3	12
Loup, co., Ne., U.S.	C6	104
Loup, stm., Ne., U.S.	C8	104
Loup City, Ne., U.S.	C7	104
Lourdes, Newf., Can.	D2	72
Lourdes, Fr.	I6	10
Lourenço Marques see Maputo, Moz.	G6	44
Louth, Eng., U.K.	H12	7
Louviers, Fr.	C8	10
Louviers, Co., U.S.	B6	83
Love, co., Ok., U.S.	D4	113
Loveč, Bul.	F8	16
Loveland, Co., U.S.	A5	83
Loveland, Oh., U.S.	n13	112
Loveland Park, Oh., U.S.	C1	112
Loveland Pass, Co., U.S.	B5	83
Lovell, Wy., U.S.	B4	127
Lovelock, Nv., U.S.	C3	105
Lovely, Ky., U.S.	C7	94
Lovenia, Mount, mtn., Ut., U.S.	C5	121
Love Point, c., Md., U.S.	B5	97
Lovere, Italy	D5	14
Loves Park, Il., U.S.	A4	90
Lovettsville, Va., U.S.	A5	123
Loving, N.M., U.S.	E5	108
Loving, co., Tx., U.S.	D1	120
Lovington, Il., U.S.	D5	90
Lovington, Ia., U.S.	e8	92
Lovington, N.M., U.S.	E6	108
Lövstabruk, Swe.	F11	6
Low, Cape, c., N.W. Ter., Can.	D15	66
Lowden, Ia., U.S.	C7	92
Lowell, Ar., U.S.	A1	81
Lowell, In., U.S.	B3	91
Lowell, Ma., U.S.	A5	98
Lowell, Mi., U.S.	F5	99
Lowell, N.C., U.S.	B1	110
Lowell, Or., U.S.	D4	114
Lowell, Lake, res., Id., U.S.	F2	89
Lowellville, Oh., U.S.	B5	112
Lower Arrow Lake, res., B.C., Can.	E8	69
Lower Brule Indian Reservation, S.D., U.S.	C6	118
Lower California see Baja California, pen., Mex.	D3	62
Lower Hutt, N.Z.	D5	52
Lower Klamath Lake, l., Ca., U.S.	B3	82
Lower Matecumbe Key, i., Fl., U.S.	H6	86
Lower Monumental Lake, res., Wa., U.S.	C7	124
Lower New York Bay, b., N.J., U.S.	B4	107
Lower Otay Lake, res., Ca., U.S.	o16	82
Lower Paia, Hi., U.S.	C5	88
Lower Red Lake, l., Mn., U.S.	C3	100
Lower Rice Lake, l., Mn., U.S.	C3	100
Lower Salmon Dam, Id., U.S.	G4	89
Lower West Pubnico, N.S., Can.	F4	71
Lowestoft, Eng., U.K.	I14	7
Lowndes, co., Al., U.S.	C3	78
Lowndes, co., Ga., U.S.	F3	87
Lowndes, co., Ms., U.S.	B5	101
Lowry Air Force Base, mil., Co., U.S.	B6	83
Lowry City, Mo., U.S.	C4	102
Lowville, N.Y., U.S.	B5	109
Loxley, Al., U.S.	E2	78
Loyal, Wi., U.S.	D3	126
Loyall, Ky., U.S.	D6	94
Loyalsock Creek, stm., Pa., U.S.	D8	115
Loznica, Yugo.	E3	16
Lozoyuela, Spain	E8	12
Lua, stm., Zaire	H9	42
Lualaba, stm., Zaire	B5	44
Lua Makika, crat., Hi., U.S.	C5	88
Luanda, Ang.	C2	44
Luang Praban Range, mts., Asia	E6	34
Luanguinga, stm., Afr.	D4	44
Luangwa, stm., Afr.	D6	44
Luanshya, Zam.	D5	44
Luarca, Spain	B5	12
Luau, Ang.	D4	44
Lubang Island, i., Phil.	C7	32
Lubango, Ang.	D2	44
Lübben, Ger.	D13	8
Lübbenau, Ger.	D13	8
Lubbock, Tx., U.S.	C2	120
Lubbock, co., Tx., U.S.	C2	120
Lubec, Me., U.S.	D6	96
Lübeck, Ger.	B10	8
Lübecker Bucht, b., Ger.	A11	8
L'ubercy, Russia	F20	18
Lubilash, stm., Zaire	C4	44
Lubin, Pol.	D16	8
Lublin, Pol.	D22	8
Lubudi, Zaire	C4	44
Lubuksikaping, Indon.	N6	34
Lubumbashi (Élisabethville), Zaire	D5	44
Lubutu, Zaire	B5	44
Lucama, N.C., U.S.	B4	110
Lucan, Ont., Can.	D3	73
Lucania, Mount, mtn., Yukon, Can.	D4	66
Lucas, co., Ia., U.S.	C4	92
Lucas, co., Oh., U.S.	A2	112
Lucasville, Oh., U.S.	D3	112
Lucca, Italy	F5	14
Luce, co., Mi., U.S.	B5	99
Luce Bay, b., Scot., U.K.	G8	7
Lucedale, Ms., U.S.	E5	101
Lucena, Phil.	r19	33b
Lucena, Spain	H7	12
Lucena del Cid, Spain	E11	12
Luc-en-Diois, Fr.	H12	10
Lucera, Italy	H10	14
Lucerne, Ca., U.S.	C2	82
Lucerne see Luzern, Switz.	E15	10
Lucernemines, Pa., U.S.	E3	115
Lucerne Valley, Ca., U.S.	E5	82
Luceville, Que., Can.	A9	74
Luchiang, Tai.	K9	28
Lüchow, Ger.	C11	8
Lucira, Ang.	D2	44
Luck, Ukr.	G3	22
Luck, Wi., U.S.	C1	126
Luckeesarai, India	H12	38
Luckenwalde, Ger.	C13	8
Lucknow, Ont., Can.	D3	73
Lucknow, India	G9	38
Lucky Peak Lake, res., Id., U.S.	F3	89
Luçon, Fr.	F5	10
Lüderitz, Nmb.	G3	44
Ludhiāna, India	E6	38
Ludington, Mi., U.S.	E4	99
L'udinovo, Russia	H17	18
Ludlow, Ky., U.S.	h13	94
Ludlow, Ma., U.S.	B3	98
Ludlow, Vt., U.S.	E3	122
Ludowici, Ga., U.S.	E5	87
Ludvika, Swe.	F10	6
Ludwigsburg, Ger.	G9	8
Ludwigsfelde, Ger.	C13	8
Ludwigshafen, Ger.	F8	8
Luena, stm., Ang.	D4	44
Luene, Ang.	D3	44
Lufeng, China	M4	28
Lufkin, Tx., U.S.	D5	120
Luga, Russia	C12	18
Lugano, Switz.	F15	10
Lugansk, Ukr.	H5	22
Lugenda, stm., Moz.	D7	44
Lugh Ganane, Som.	H3	46
Lugnaquillia Mountain, mtn., Ire.	I6	7
Lugo, Italy	E6	14
Lugo, Spain	B4	12
Lugoff, S.C., U.S.	C6	117
Lugoj, Rom.	D5	16
Luhit, stm., Asia	G16	38
Luilaka, stm., Zaire	B4	44
Luino, Italy	C3	14
Lukachukai, Az., U.S.	A6	80
Luke Air Force Base, mil., Az., U.S.	D3	80
Lukulu, Zam.	D4	44
Lula, Ga., U.S.	B3	87
Luleå, Swe.	D14	6
Lüleburgaz, Tur.	H11	16
Luling, La., U.S.	k11	95
Luling, Tx., U.S.	E4	120
Lulonga, stm., Zaire	A3	44
Lumajang, Indon.	n16	33a
Lumber, stm., U.S.	C9	117
Lumber City, Ga., U.S.	E4	87
Lumberport, W.V., U.S.	B4	125
Lumberton, Ms., U.S.	D4	101
Lumberton, N.C., U.S.	C3	110
Lumbrales, Spain	E5	12
Lumby, B.C., Can.	D8	69
Lumding, India	H15	38
Lummi Indian Reservation, Wa., U.S.	A3	124
Lumpkin, Ga., U.S.	D2	87
Lumpkin, co., Ga., U.S.	B2	87
Lumsden, Newf., Can.	D5	72
Luna, co., N.M., U.S.	E2	108
Luna Pier, Mi., U.S.	G7	99
Lund, Swe.	I9	6
Lund, Nv., U.S.	E6	105
Lundar, Man., Can.	D2	70
Lundazi, Zam.	D6	44
Lüneburg, Ger.	B10	8
Lüneburger Heide, reg., Ger.	B10	8
Lunel, Fr.	I11	10
Lunenburg, Ma., U.S.	A4	98
Lunenburg, co., Va., U.S.	D4	123
Lunéville, Fr.	D13	10
Lunga, stm., Zam.	D5	44
Luohe, China	B3	28
Luolong, China	E17	38
Luopu, China	B9	38
Luoyang, China	E9	26
Lürah, stm., Afg.	D2	38
Luray, Va., U.S.	B4	123
Lure, Fr.	E13	10
Lure, Lake, res., N.C., U.S.	f10	110
Lurgan, N. Ire., U.K.	G6	7
Lúrio, stm., Moz.	D7	44
Lusaka, Zam.	E5	44
Lusambo, Zaire	B4	44
Lusby, Md., U.S.	C4	97
Luseland, Sask., Can.	E1	75
Lushan, China	B1	28
Lushnje, Alb.	I3	16
Lushoto, Tan.	B7	44
Lüshun (Port Arthur), China	D11	26
Lusk, Wy., U.S.	D8	127
Lussac-les-Châteaux, Fr.	F7	10
Lüt, Dasht-e, des., Iran	B6	46
Luther, Ok., U.S.	B4	113
Luthersville, Ga., U.S.	C2	87
Lutherville-Timonium, Md., U.S.	B4	97
Luton, Eng., U.K.	J12	7
Lutsk see Luck, Ukr.	G3	22
Luttrell, Tn., U.S.	C10	119
Lutz, Fl., U.S.	D4	86
Luverne, Al., U.S.	D3	78
Luverne, Mn., U.S.	G2	100
Luwegu, stm., Tan.	C7	44
Luxapallila Creek, stm., U.S.	B5	101
Luxembourg, Lux.	F6	8
Luxembourg, ctry., Eur.	F9	4
Luxemburg, Wi., U.S.	D6	126
Luxomni, Ga., U.S.	h8	87
Luxora, Ar., U.S.	B6	81
Luzern, Switz.	E15	10
Luzerne, co., Pa., U.S.	D9	115
Luzhou, China	F8	26
Luzon, i., Phil.	B7	32
Luzon Strait, strt., Asia	G11	26
Luzy, Fr.	F10	10
L'vov, Ukr.	H2	22
Lyckele, Swe.	D12	6
Lycoming, co., Pa., U.S.	D7	115
Lycoming Creek, stm., Pa., U.S.	D7	115
Lydenburg, S. Afr.	G6	44
Lyell, Mount, mtn., Can.	D2	68
Lyford, Tx., U.S.	F4	120
Lykens, Pa., U.S.	E8	115
Lyle, Wa., U.S.	D4	124
Lyman, S.C., U.S.	B3	117
Lyman, Wy., U.S.	E2	127
Lyman, co., S.D., U.S.	D6	118
Lyman Lake, res., Az., U.S.	C6	80
Lynch, Ky., U.S.	D7	94
Lynchburg, Oh., U.S.	C2	112
Lynchburg, Tn., U.S.	B5	119
Lynchburg, Va., U.S.	C3	123
Lynches, stm., S.C., U.S.	D8	117
Lynden, Wa., U.S.	A3	124
Lynde Point, c., Ct., U.S.	D6	84
Lyndhurst, N.J., U.S.	h8	107
Lyndhurst, Oh., U.S.	g9	112
Lyndon, Ks., U.S.	D8	93
Lyndon, Ky., U.S.	g11	94
Lyndon B. Johnson National Historical Site, hist., Tx., U.S.	D3	120
Lyndon B. Johnson Space Center, sci., Tx., U.S.	r14	120
Lyndonville, Vt., U.S.	B4	122
Lyndora, Pa., U.S.	E2	115
Lynher Reef, rf., Austl.	C4	50
Lynn, Al., U.S.	A2	78
Lynn, In., U.S.	D8	91
Lynn, Ma., U.S.	B6	98
Lynn, co., Tx., U.S.	C2	120
Lynn, Lake, res., W.V., U.S.	B5	125
Lynn Canal, b., Ak., U.S.	k22	79
Lynne Acres, Md., U.S.	*B4	97
Lynnfield, Ma., U.S.	f11	98
Lynn Garden, Tn., U.S.	C11	119
Lynn Garden, Tn., U.S.	A9	119
Lynn Haven, Fl., U.S.	u16	86
Lynnhaven Roads, b., Va., U.S.	k15	123
Lynnville, In., U.S.	H3	91
Lynnwood, Wa., U.S.	B3	124
Lynton, Eng., U.K.	J9	7
Lynwood, Ca., U.S.	n12	82
Lyon, co., Ia., U.S.	A1	92
Lyon, co., Ks., U.S.	D7	93
Lyon, co., Ky., U.S.	C1	94
Lyon, co., Mn., U.S.	F3	100
Lyon, co., Nv., U.S.	D2	105
Lyons, Co., U.S.	A5	83
Lyons, Ga., U.S.	D4	87
Lyons, Il., U.S.	k9	90
Lyons, In., U.S.	G3	91
Lyons, Ks., U.S.	D5	93
Lyons, Mi., U.S.	F6	99
Lyons, Ne., U.S.	C9	104
Lyons, N.Y., U.S.	B3	109
Lyons, Or., U.S.	C4	114
Lyster Station, Que., Can.	C6	74
Lytle, Tx., U.S.	E3	120

M

Name	Map Ref	Page
Ma, stm., Asia	D8	34
Maalaea Bay, b., Hi., U.S.	C5	88
Ma'ān, Jord.	D4	40
Maanshan, China	D7	28
Ma'arrat an-Nu'mān, Syria	B5	40
Maas (Meuse), stm., Eur.	D5	8
Maastricht, Neth.	E5	8
Mabank, Tx., U.S.	C4	120
Mabaruma, Guy.	C13	58
Mabel, Mn., U.S.	G7	100
Maben, Ms., U.S.	B4	101
Mableton, Ga., U.S.	h7	87
Mabscott, W.V., U.S.	D3	125
Mabton, Wa., U.S.	C5	124
Mača, Russia	F17	24
Macaé, Braz.	G8	57
Macão, Port.	F3	12
Macao see Macau, dep., Asia	M2	28
Macapá, Braz.	C8	54
Macará, Ec.	J3	58
Macarani, Braz.	C8	57
Macas, Ec.	I3	58
Macau, Braz.	E11	54
Macau (Aomen), Macao	M2	28
Macau (Aomen), dep., Asia	M2	28
MacClenny, Fl., U.S.	B4	86
MacDill Air Force Base, mil., Fl., U.S.	E4	86
Macdonnell Ranges, mts., Austl.	D6	50
MacDowell Reservoir, res., N.H., U.S.	E2	106
Macduff, Scot., U.K.	D10	7
Macedo de Cavaleiros, Port.	D5	12
Macedonia, Oh., U.S.	A4	112
Macedonia, ctry., Eur.	H5	16
Macedonia, hist. reg., Eur.	H6	16
Maceió, Braz.	E11	54
Macerata, Italy	F8	14
Maces Bay, b., N.B., Can.	D3	71
MacGregor, Man., Can.	E2	70
Machačkala, Russia	I7	22
Machagai, Arg.	B4	56
Machala, Ec.	I3	58
Machecoul, Fr.	E5	10
Machias, Me., U.S.	D5	96
Machias, stm., Me., U.S.	B4	96
Machias, stm., Me., U.S.	D5	96
Machias Bay, b., Me., U.S.	D5	96
Machias Lakes, l., Me., U.S.	C5	96
Machilipatnam (Bandar), India	D6	37
Machiques, Ven.	B6	58
Macho, Arroyo del, val., N.M., U.S.	C4	108
Machupicchu, Peru	F4	54
Macina, reg., Mali	F4	42
Mackay, Austl.	D9	50
Mackay, Lake, l., Austl.	D5	50
MacKenzie, B.C., Can.	B6	69
Mackenzie, stm., N.W. Ter., Can.	C6	66
Mackenzie Bay, b., Can.	C5	66
Mackenzie Mountains, mts., Can.	D7	66
Mackinac, co., Mi., U.S.	B5	99
Mackinac, Straits of, strt., Mi., U.S.	C6	99
Mackinac Bridge, Mi., U.S.	C6	99
Mackinac Island, i., Mi., U.S.	C6	99
Mackinaw, Il., U.S.	C4	90
Mackinaw, stm., Il., U.S.	C4	90
Mackinaw City, Mi., U.S.	C6	99
Maclear, S. Afr.	H5	44
Macmillan, stm., Yukon, Can.	D6	66
Macomb, Il., U.S.	C3	90
Macomb, co., Mi., U.S.	F8	99
Macomer, Italy	I3	14
Mâcon, Fr.	F11	10
Macon, Ga., U.S.	D3	87
Macon, Il., U.S.	D5	90
Macon, Ms., U.S.	B5	101
Macon, Mo., U.S.	B5	102
Macon, co., Al., U.S.	C4	78
Macon, co., Ga., U.S.	D2	87
Macon, co., Il., U.S.	D4	90
Macon, co., Mo., U.S.	B5	102
Macon, co., N.C., U.S.	f9	110
Macon, co., Tn., U.S.	A5	119
Macon, Bayou, stm., U.S.	B4	95
Macoupin, co., Il., U.S.	D4	90
MacTier, Ont., Can.	C4	50
Macungie, Pa., U.S.	E10	115
Mad, stm., Ca., U.S.	B2	82
Mad, stm., Ct., U.S.	B3	84
Mad, stm., N.H., U.S.	C3	106
Mad, stm., Oh., U.S.	C2	112
Mad, stm., Vt., U.S.	C3	122
Ma'dabā, Jord.	D4	40
Madagascar, ctry., Afr.	E9	44
Madame, Isle, i., N.S., Can.	D9	71
Madanapalle, India	F5	37
Madang, Pap. N. Gui.	m16	50a
Mādārīpur, Bngl.	I14	38
Madawaska, Me., U.S.	A4	96
Madawaska, stm., Ont., Can.	B7	73
Madawaska Lake, l., Me., U.S.	A4	96
Maddaloni, Italy	H9	14
Madeira, Oh., U.S.	o13	112
Madeira, i., Port.	B2	42
Madeira, stm., S.A.	E6	54
Madeira, Arquipélago da (Madeira Islands), is., Port.	B2	42
Mädelegabel, mtn., Eur.	E17	10
Madeleine, Îles de la, is., Que., Can.	B8	71
Madelia, Mn., U.S.	F4	100
Madeline Island, i., Wi., U.S.	B3	126
Madera, Ca., U.S.	D3	82
Madera, co., Ca., U.S.	D4	82
Madhubani, India	G12	38
Madhya Pradesh, state, India	I8	38
Madill, Ok., U.S.	C5	113
Madīnat ash-Sha'b, Yemen	F3	46
Madingou, Congo	B2	44
Madison, Al., U.S.	A3	78
Madison, Ar., U.S.	B5	81
Madison, Ct., U.S.	D5	84
Madison, Fl., U.S.	B3	86
Madison, Ga., U.S.	C3	87
Madison, Il., U.S.	E3	90
Madison, In., U.S.	G7	91
Madison, Ks., U.S.	D7	93
Madison, Me., U.S.	D3	96
Madison, Mn., U.S.	E2	100
Madison, Ms., U.S.	C3	101
Madison, Ne., U.S.	C8	104
Madison, N.J., U.S.	B4	107
Madison, N.C., U.S.	A3	110
Madison, S.D., U.S.	D8	118
Madison, W.V., U.S.	C3	125
Madison, Wi., U.S.	E4	126
Madison, co., Al., U.S.	A3	78
Madison, co., Ar., U.S.	B2	81
Madison, co., Fl., U.S.	B3	86
Madison, co., Ga., U.S.	B3	87
Madison, co., Id., U.S.	F7	89
Madison, co., Il., U.S.	E4	90
Madison, co., In., U.S.	D6	91
Madison, co., Ia., U.S.	C3	92
Madison, co., Ky., U.S.	C5	94
Madison, co., La., U.S.	B4	95
Madison, co., Ms., U.S.	C3	101
Madison, co., Mo., U.S.	D7	102
Madison, co., Mt., U.S.	E5	103
Madison, co., Ne., U.S.	C8	104
Madison, co., N.Y., U.S.	C5	109
Madison, co., N.C., U.S.	f10	110
Madison, co., Oh., U.S.	C2	112
Madison, co., Tn., U.S.	B3	119
Madison, co., Tx., U.S.	D5	120
Madison, co., Va., U.S.	B4	123
Madison, stm., Mt., U.S.	E5	103
Madison Heights, Mi., U.S.	o15	99
Madison Heights, Va., U.S.	C3	123
Madison Lake, Mn., U.S.	F5	100
Madison Range, mts., Mt., U.S.	E5	103
Madisonville, Ky., U.S.	C2	94
Madisonville, La., U.S.	D5	95
Madisonville, Tn., U.S.	D9	119
Madisonville, Tx., U.S.	D5	120
Madiun, Indon.	m15	33a
Madoc, Ont., Can.	C7	73
Mado Gashi, Kenya	B7	44
Madras, India	F6	37
Madras, Or., U.S.	C5	114
Madre, Laguna, b., Mex.	E11	62
Madre, Laguna, b., Tx., U.S.	F4	120
Madre, Sierra, mts., N.A.	J14	62
Madre, Sierra, mts., Phil.	B7	32
Madre de Dios, stm., S.A.	F5	54
Madre de Dios, Isla, i., Chile	G2	56
Madre del Sur, Sierra, mts., Mex.	I10	62
Madre Occidental, Sierra, mts., Mex.	E6	62
Madre Oriental, Sierra, mts., Mex.	F9	62
Madrid, Spain	E8	12
Madrid, Ia., U.S.	C4	92
Madridejos, Spain	F8	12
Maduo, China	E6	26
Madura, i., Indon.	G5	32
Madurai, India	H5	37
Maebashi, Japan	F12	30
Mae Hong Son, Thai.	E4	34
Maeser, Ut., U.S.	C6	121
Mae Sot, Thai.	F5	34
Maestra, Sierra, mts., Cuba	D9	64
Maevatanana, Madag.	E9	44
Mafia Island, i., Tan.	C7	44
Mafikeng, S. Afr.	G5	44
Mafra, Braz.	B7	56
Magadan, Russia	F24	24
Magadi, Kenya	B7	44
Magallanes, Estrecho de (Strait of Magellan), strt., S.A.	G2	56
Magangué, Col.	C5	58
Magazine, Ar., U.S.	B2	81
Magazine Mountain, mtn., Ar., U.S.	B2	81
Magdagači, Russia	G19	24
Magdalena, Bol.	F6	54
Magdalena, Mex.	B4	62
Magdalena, N.M., U.S.	C2	108
Magdalena, stm., Col.	B5	58
Magdalena, Bahía, b., Mex.	E3	62
Magdalena, Isla, i., Chile	E2	56
Magdalena Mountains, mts., N.M., U.S.	D2	108
Magdeburg, Ger.	C11	8
Magee, Ms., U.S.	D4	101
Magelang, Indon.	m15	33a
Magellan, Strait of see Magallanes, Estrecho de, strt., S.A.	G2	56
Magenta, Italy	D3	14
Maggie Creek, stm., Nv., U.S.	C5	105
Maggiore, Lago, l., Eur.	C3	14
Magic Reservoir, res., Id., U.S.	F4	89
Magione, Italy	F7	14
Magna, Ut., U.S.	C3	121
Magnetawan, stm., Ont., Can.	B4	73
Magnitogorsk, Russia	G9	22
Magnolia, Ar., U.S.	D2	81
Magnolia, Ky., U.S.	C4	94
Magnolia, Ms., U.S.	D3	101
Magnolia, N.C., U.S.	B4	110
Magnolia, Oh., U.S.	B4	112
Magoffin, co., Ky., U.S.	C6	94
Magog, Que., Can.	D5	74
Magothy River, b., Md., U.S.	B4	97
Magpie, Lac, l., Que., Can.	F20	66
Magrath, Alta., Can.	E4	68
Magruder Mountain, mtn., Nv., U.S.	F4	105
Maguarinho, Cabo, c., Braz.	D9	54
Magway, Burma	D3	34
Magwe, Burma	G11	38
Mahābād, Iran	J7	22
Mahābhārat Range, mts., Nepal	F10	38
Mahaicony Village, Guy.	D14	58
Mahajamba, Baie de la, b., Madag.	E9	44
Mahajanga, Madag.	E9	44
Mahakam, stm., Indon.	E6	32
Mahānadi, stm., India	J11	38
Mahanoro, Madag.	E9	44
Mahanoy City, Pa., U.S.	E9	115
Mahārāshtra, state, India	C3	37
Maha Sarakham, Thai.	F7	34
Mahaska, co., Ia., U.S.	C5	92
Mahattat al-Qaṭrānah, Jord.	D5	40
Mahattat Harad, Sau. Ar.	D4	46
Mahbūbnagar, India	D4	37
Mahé Island, i., Sey.	B11	44
Mahenge, Tan.	C7	44
Mahi, stm., India	I5	38
Mahmūd-e 'Erāqī, Afg.	C3	38
Mahnomen, Mn., U.S.	C3	100
Mahnomen, co., Mn., U.S.	C3	100
Mahoba, India	H8	38
Mahogany Mountain, mtn., Or., U.S.	D9	114
Mahomet, Il., U.S.	C5	90
Mahón, Spain	F16	12
Mahone Bay, N.S., Can.	E5	71
Mahoning, co., Oh., U.S.	B5	112
Mahoning, stm., U.S.	A5	112
Mahopac, N.Y., U.S.	D7	109
Mahuva, India	J4	38
Mahwah, N.J., U.S.	A4	107
Maiden, N.C., U.S.	B1	110
Maidstone, Eng., U.K.	J13	7
Maidstone Lake, l., Vt., U.S.	B5	122
Maiduguri, Nig.	F8	42
Maili, Hi., U.S.	g9	88
Maili Point, c., Hi., U.S.	g9	88
Maillezais, Fr.	F6	10
Main, stm., Ger.	F9	8
Mainburg, Ger.	G11	8
Main Channel, strt., Ont., Can.	B3	73
Mai-Ndombe, Lac, l., Zaire	B3	44
Maine, state, U.S.	C3	96
Mainland, i., Scot., U.K.	B9	7

Name	Map Ref	Page
Mainland, i., Scot., U.K.	A11	7
Main Pass, strt., La., U.S.	E6	95
Mainz, Ger.	E8	8
Maipo, Volcán, vol., S.A.	C3	56
Maipú, Arg.	D5	56
Maiquetía, Ven.	B9	58
Maisonnette, N.B., Can.	B4	71
Maitland, Austl.	F10	50
Maitland, Ont., Can.	C9	73
Maize, Ks., U.S.	g12	93
Maizuru, Japan	G8	30
Maja, stm., Russia	F20	24
Majene, Indon.	F6	32
Maji, Eth.	G2	46
Majkop, Russia	I6	22
Majno-Pyl'gino, Russia	E29	24
Major, co., Ok., U.S.	A3	113
Majorca see Mallorca, i., Spain	F15	12
Makaha, Hi., U.S.	g9	88
Makaha Point, c., Hi., U.S.	A2	88
Makakilo City, Hi., U.S.	g9	88
Makakilo, Indon.	F6	32
Makale, Indon.	F6	32
Makapuu Head, c., Hi., U.S.	B4	88
Makarska, Cro.	F12	14
Makasar, Selat (Makassar Strait), strt., Indon.	F6	32
Makasar see Ujungpandang, Indon.	G6	32
Makawao, Hi., U.S.	C5	88
Makaweli, Hi., U.S.	B2	88
Makeni, S.L.	G3	42
Makgadikgadi Pans, pl., Bots.	F5	44
Makhachkala see Machačkala, Russia	I7	22
Makindu, Kenya	B7	44
M'akit, Russia	E24	24
Makkah (Mecca), Sau. Ar.	D2	46
Maklakovo, Russia	F12	24
Makó, Hung.	I20	8
Makokou, Gabon	A2	44
Makthar, Tun.	N4	14
Makumbi, Zaire	C4	44
Makurazaki, Japan	K3	30
Makurdi, Nig.	G7	42
Makushin Volcano, vol., Ak., U.S.	E6	79
Malabar, Fl., U.S.	D6	86
Malabo, Eq. Gui.	H7	42
Malacca, Strait of, strt., Asia	M6	34
Malad City, Id., U.S.	G6	89
Málaga, Col.	D6	58
Málaga, Spain	I7	12
Malagón, Spain	F8	12
Malaimbandy, Madag.	F9	44
Malaja Kuril'skaja Gr'ada (Habomai-shotō), is., Russia	p24	30a
Malakál, Sudan	G12	42
Malakoff, Tx., U.S.	C4	120
Malang, Indon.	m16	32
Malanje, Ang.	C3	44
Malanville, Benin	F6	42
Mälaren, l., Swe.	G11	6
Malargüe, Arg.	D3	56
Malartic, Que., Can.	k11	74
Malaspina Glacier, Ak., U.S.	D11	79
Malatya, Tur.	H15	4
Malawi, ctry., Afr.	D6	44
Malaya, reg., Malay.	M7	34
Malay Peninsula, pen., Asia	K6	34
Malaysia, ctry., Asia	E3	32
Malbaie, stm., Que., Can.	B7	74
Malbork, Pol.	A19	8
Malcolm, Austl.	E4	50
Malden, Ma., U.S.	B5	98
Malden, Mo., U.S.	E8	102
Malden, W.V., U.S.	m12	125
Maldives, ctry., Asia	I2	37
Maldonado, Ur.	C6	56
Mālegaon, India	B3	37
Malek Dīn, Afg.	D3	38
Malha Wells, Sudan	E11	42
Malheur, co., Or., U.S.	D9	114
Malheur, stm., Or., U.S.	D9	114
Malheur Lake, l., Or., U.S.	D8	114
Mali, ctry., Afr.	E5	42
Malibu, Ca., U.S.	m11	82
Malik, Wādī al-, val., Sudan	E11	42
Malin, Or., U.S.	E5	114
Malindi, Kenya	B8	44
Malino, Bukit, mtn., Indon.	E7	32
Malka, Russia	G25	24
Malkāpur, India	B4	37
Malkara, Tur.	I10	16
Mallaig, Scot., U.K.	D7	7
Mallawī, Egypt	C12	42
Malletts Bay, b., Vt., U.S.	B2	122
Mallnitz, Aus.	I13	8
Mallorca, i., Spain	F14	12
Mallow, Ire.	I4	7
Malmberget, Swe.	C13	6
Malmédy, Bel.	E6	8
Malmesbury, S. Afr.	H3	44
Malmö, Swe.	I9	6
Malmstrom Air Force Base, mil., Mt., U.S.	C5	103
Malolos, Phil.	q19	33b
Malone, N.Y., U.S.	f10	109
Maloney Reservoir, res., Ne., U.S.	C5	104
Måløy, Nor.	F5	6
Malpaso, Presa de, res., Mex.	I13	62
Malpelo, Isla de, i., Col.	C2	54
Malpeque Bay, b., P.E.I., Can.	C6	71
Malta, Il., U.S.	B5	90
Malta, Mt., U.S.	B9	103
Malta, ctry., Eur.	H10	4
Malta Channel, strt., Eur.	M9	14
Maltahöhe, Nmb.	F3	44
Maluku (Moluccas), is., Indon.	F8	32
Maluku, Laut (Molucca Sea), Indon.	F7	32
Malung, Swe.	F9	6
Malvern, Ar., U.S.	C3	81
Malvern, Ia., U.S.	D2	92
Malvern, Oh., U.S.	B4	112
Malvern, Pa., U.S.	o19	115
Malverne, N.Y., U.S.	k13	109
Malyj An'uj, stm., Russia	D26	24
Malyj Tajmyr, Ostrov, i., Russia	B15	24
Mama, Russia	F16	24
Mamala Bay, b., Hi., U.S.	g10	88
Mamaroneck, N.Y., U.S.	h13	109
Mamberamo, stm., Indon.	F10	32
Mamers, Fr.	D7	10
Mamfe, Cam.	G7	42
Mammoth, Az., U.S.	E5	80
Mammoth Cave National Park, Ky., U.S.	C4	94
Mammoth Lakes, Ca., U.S.	D4	82
Mammoth Spring, Ar., U.S.	A4	81
Mamoré, stm., S.A.	F5	54
Mamou, Gui.	F3	42
Mamou, La., U.S.	D3	95
Man, I.C.	G4	42
Man, W.V., U.S.	D3	125
Manacapuru, Braz.	D6	54
Manacor, Spain	F15	12
Manado, Indon.	E7	32
Managua, Nic.	H4	64
Managua, Lago de, l., Nic.	H4	64
Manakara, Madag.	F9	44
Manama see Al-Manāmah, Bahr.	C5	46
Manana Island, i., Hi., U.S.	g11	88
Mananara, Madag.	E9	44
Mananjary, Madag.	F9	44
Manantico Creek, stm., N.J., U.S.	E3	107
Manas, China	C4	26
Manasquan, N.J., U.S.	C4	107
Manasquan, stm., N.J., U.S.	C4	107
Manassa, Co., U.S.	D5	83
Manassas, Va., U.S.	B5	123
Manassas National Battlefield Park, Va., U.S.	g11	123
Manassas Park, Va., U.S.	B5	123
Manatee, co., Fl., U.S.	E4	86
Manatee, stm., Fl., U.S.	E4	86
Manaus, Braz.	D6	54
Manawa, Wi., U.S.	D5	126
Manbij, Syria	A5	40
Mancelona, Mi., U.S.	D5	99
Mancha Real, Spain	H8	12
Manchester, Eng., U.K.	H10	7
Manchester, Ct., U.S.	B5	84
Manchester, Ga., U.S.	D2	87
Manchester, Ia., U.S.	B6	92
Manchester, Ky., U.S.	C6	94
Manchester, Me., U.S.	D3	96
Manchester, Md., U.S.	A4	97
Manchester, Ma., U.S.	A6	98
Manchester, Mi., U.S.	F6	99
Manchester, Mo., U.S.	f12	102
Manchester, N.H., U.S.	E4	106
Manchester, N.Y., U.S.	C3	109
Manchester, Oh., U.S.	D2	112
Manchester, Pa., U.S.	F8	115
Manchester, Tn., U.S.	B5	119
Manchester, Vt., U.S.	E2	122
Manchester Center, Vt., U.S.	E2	122
Manchuria, reg., China	B12	26
Manciano, Italy	G6	14
Mancos, Co., U.S.	D2	83
Mancos, stm., U.S.	D2	83
Mand, stm., Iran	C5	46
Manda, Tan.	D6	44
Mandal, Nor.	G6	6
Mandalay, Burma	C4	34
Mandalgov', Mong.	B8	26
Mandan, N.D., U.S.	C5	111
Mandas, Italy	J4	14
Mandasor, India	H6	38
Mandeb, Bāb el-, strt.	F3	46
Mandeville, Ar., U.S.	D2	81
Mandeville, La., U.S.	D5	95
Mandi Bahāuddīn, Pak.	D5	38
Mandimba, Moz.	D7	44
Mandla, India	I9	38
Manduria, Italy	I12	14
Māndvi, India	I3	38
Mandya, India	F4	37
Manerbio, Italy	D5	14
Manfredonia, Italy	H10	14
Mangabeiras, Chapada das, hills, Braz.	F9	54
Mangalore, India	F3	37
Mangkalihat, Tanjung, c., Indon.	E6	32
Manglares, Cabo, c., Col.	G3	58
Mangoche, Mwi.	D7	44
Mangoky, stm., Madag.	F8	44
Mangole, Pulau, i., Indon.	F8	32
Mangrove Cay, i., Bah.	B9	64
Mangualde, Port.	E4	12
Mangum, Ok., U.S.	C2	113
Mangya, China	D5	26
Manhattan, Ks., U.S.	C7	93
Manhattan, Mt., U.S.	E5	103
Manhattan Beach, Ca., U.S.	n12	82
Manhattan Island, i., N.Y., U.S.	h13	109
Manheim, Pa., U.S.	F9	115
Manhuaçu, Braz.	F7	57
Manicoré, Braz.	E6	54
Manicouagan, stm., Que., Can.	F19	66
Manicouagan, Réservoir, res., Que., Can.	h13	74
Manila, Phil.	q19	32
Manila, Ar., U.S.	B5	81
Manila Bay, b., Phil.	C7	32
Manilla, Ia., U.S.	C2	92
Manipur, ter., India	H15	38
Manisa, Tur.	K11	16
Manistee, Mi., U.S.	D4	99
Manistee, co., Mi., U.S.	D4	99
Manistee, stm., Mi., U.S.	D5	99
Manistique, Mi., U.S.	C4	99
Manistique, stm., Mi., U.S.	B4	99
Manistique Lake, l., Mi., U.S.	B5	99
Manito, Il., U.S.	C4	90
Manitoba, prov., Can.	C3	70
Manitoba, Lake, l., Man., Can.	D2	70
Manitou, Man., Can.	E2	70
Manitou, Lake, l., Ont., Can.	B3	73
Manitou Island, i., Mi., U.S.	A3	99
Manitou Lake, l., Sask., Can.	E1	75
Manitoulin Island, i., Ont., Can.	B3	73
Manitou Springs, Co., U.S.	C6	83
Manitowoc, Wi., U.S.	D6	126
Manitowoc, co., Wi., U.S.	D6	126
Manitowoc, stm., Wi., U.S.	h10	126
Maniwaki, Que., Can.	C2	74
Manizales, Col.	E5	58
Manjacaze, Moz.	F6	44
Mānjra, stm., India	C4	37
Mankato, Ks., U.S.	C5	93
Mankato, Mn., U.S.	F5	100
Mankoya, Zam.	D4	44
Manlius, N.Y., U.S.	C5	109
Manlléu, Spain	C14	12
Manly, Ia., U.S.	A4	92
Manmād, India	B3	37
Mannar, Gulf of, b., Asia	H5	37
Mannārgudi, India	G5	37
Mannar Island, i., Sri L.	H5	37
Mannford, Ok., U.S.	A5	113
Mannheim, Ger.	F8	8
Manning, Alta., Can.	A2	68
Manning, Ia., U.S.	C2	92
Manning, S.C., U.S.	D7	117
Mannington, W.V., U.S.	B4	125
Mannville, Alta., Can.	C5	68
Manns Creek, stm., W.V., U.S.	n14	125
Manokin, stm., Md., U.S.	D6	97
Manokotak, Ak., U.S.	D8	79
Manokwari, Indon.	F9	32
Manomet, Ma., U.S.	C6	98
Manomet Point, c., Ma., U.S.	C6	98
Manono, Zaire	C5	44
Manor, Tx., U.S.	D4	120
Manosque, Fr.	I12	10
Manouane, Lac, l., Que., Can.	h12	74
Manresa, Spain	D13	12
Mānsa, India	F6	38
Mansa, Zam.	D5	44
Manseau, Que., Can.	C5	74
Mansel Island, i., N.W. Ter., Can.	D17	66
Mansfield, Eng., U.K.	H11	7
Mansfield, Il., U.S.	C5	90
Mansfield, La., U.S.	B2	95
Mansfield, Ma., U.S.	B5	98
Mansfield, Mo., U.S.	D5	102
Mansfield, Oh., U.S.	B3	112
Mansfield, Pa., U.S.	C7	115
Mansfield, Tx., U.S.	n9	120
Mansfield, Mount, mtn., Vt., U.S.	B3	122
Mansfield Center, Ct., U.S.	B7	84
Mansfield Hollow Lake, res., Ct., U.S.	B7	84
Manson, Ia., U.S.	B3	92
Manson, Wa., U.S.	B5	124
Mansonville, Que., Can.	D5	74
Mansura, La., U.S.	C3	95
Manta, Ec.	H2	58
Mantachie, Ms., U.S.	A5	101
Manteca, Ca., U.S.	D3	82
Manteno, Il., U.S.	B6	90
Manteo, N.C., U.S.	B7	110
Mantes-la-Jolie, Fr.	D8	10
Manti, Ut., U.S.	D4	121
Mantiqueira, Serra da, mts., Braz.	F6	57
Manton, Mi., U.S.	D5	99
Mantorville, Mn., U.S.	F6	100
Mantova, Italy	D5	14
Mantua, Oh., U.S.	A4	112
Mantua, Ut., U.S.	B4	121
Manturovo, Russia	C27	18
Manukau Harbour, b., N.Z.	B5	52
Manumuskin, stm., N.J., U.S.	E3	107
Manus Island, i., Pap. N. Gui.	k16	50a
Manvel, Tx., U.S.	r14	120
Manville, N.J., U.S.	B4	107
Manville, R.I., U.S.	B4	116
Many, La., U.S.	C2	95
Many Farms, Az., U.S.	A6	80
Manzanares, Spain	F8	12
Manzanillo, Cuba	D9	64
Manzanillo, Mex.	H7	62
Manzano Mountains, mts., N.M., U.S.	C3	108
Manzano Peak, mtn., N.M., U.S.	C3	108
Manzhouli, China	B10	26
Mao, Chad	F9	42
Maoke, Pegunungan, mts., Indon.	F10	32
Mapastepec, Mex.	J13	62
Mapi, Indon.	G10	32
Mapia, Kepulauan, is., Indon.	E9	32
Mapimí, Mex.	E8	62
Mapimí, Bolsón de, des., Mex.	D8	62
Mapire, Ven.	D10	58
Maple, stm., Ia., U.S.	B2	92
Maple, stm., N.D., U.S.	C8	111
Maple Bluff, Wi., U.S.	E4	126
Maple Grove, Mn., U.S.	m12	100
Maple Heights, Oh., U.S.	h9	112
Maple Lake, Mn., U.S.	E5	100
Maple Plain, Mn., U.S.	m11	100
Maple Shade, N.J., U.S.	D2	107
Maplesville, Al., U.S.	C3	78
Mapleton, Ia., U.S.	B2	92
Mapleton, Mn., U.S.	G5	100
Mapleton, N.D., U.S.	C8	111
Mapleton, Or., U.S.	C3	114
Mapleton, Ut., U.S.	C4	121
Maple Valley, Wa., U.S.	f11	124
Mapleville, R.I., U.S.	B2	116
Maplewood, Mn., U.S.	n12	100
Maplewood, Mo., U.S.	f13	102
Mapuera, stm., Braz.	D7	54
Maputo (Lourenço Marques), Moz.	G6	44
Maqueda, Spain	E7	12
Maquela do Zombo, Ang.	C3	44
Maquinchao, Arg.	E3	56
Maquoketa, Ia., U.S.	B7	92
Maquoketa, stm., Ia., U.S.	B6	92
Maquoketa, North Fork, stm., Ia., U.S.	B7	92
Mar, Serra do, clf, Braz.	A7	56
Marabá, Braz.	E9	54
Maracá, Ilha de, i., Braz.	C8	54
Maracaibo, Ven.	B7	58
Maracaibo, Lago de, l., Ven.	C7	58
Maracay, Ven.	B9	58
Marādah, Libya	C9	42
Maradi, Niger	F7	42
Marāgheh, Iran	J7	22
Maragogipe, Braz.	B9	57
Marahuaca, Cerro, mtn., Ven.	F10	58
Marais des Cygnes, stm., U.S.	D8	93
Marajó, Baía de, b., Braz.	D9	54
Marajó, Ilha de, i., Braz.	D9	54
Maralal, Kenya	A7	44
Marana, Az., U.S.	E4	80
Marand, Iran	J7	22
Marang, Malay.	L7	34
Marañón, stm., Peru	D3	54
Marans, Fr.	F5	10
Marapanim, Braz.	D9	54
Marathon, Fl., U.S.	H5	86
Marathon, Tx., U.S.	o12	120
Marathon, co., Wi., U.S.	D4	126
Marawī, Sudan	E1	46
Marble, Mn., U.S.	C5	100
Marble, N.C., U.S.	f9	110
Marble Bar, Austl.	D3	50
Marble Canyon, val., Az., U.S.	A4	80
Marble Falls, Tx., U.S.	D3	120
Marblehead, Ma., U.S.	B6	98
Marble Hill, Mo., U.S.	D8	102
Marbleton, Wy., U.S.	D2	127
Marburg an der Lahn, Ger.	E8	8
Marbury, Md., U.S.	C3	97
Marcaria, Italy	D5	14
Marceline, Mo., U.S.	B5	102
Marcellus, Mi., U.S.	F5	99
March (Morava), stm., Eur.	G16	8
Marche-en-Famenne, Bel.	E5	8
Marchena, Spain	H6	12
Mar Chiquita, Laguna, l., Arg.	C4	56
Marco, Fl., U.S.	G5	86
Marcus, Ia., U.S.	B2	92
Marcus Baker, Mount, mtn., Ak., U.S.	g18	79
Marcus Hook, Pa., U.S.	G11	115
Marcy, Mount, mtn., N.Y., U.S.	A7	109
Mardān, Pak.	C5	38
Mar del Plata, Arg.	D5	56
Mardin, Tur.	H16	4
Mareeba, Austl.	C9	50
Marengo, Il., U.S.	A5	90
Marengo, Ia., U.S.	C5	92
Marengo, co., Al., U.S.	C2	78
Marennes, Fr.	G5	10
Marfa, Tx., U.S.	o12	120
Margaret, Al., U.S.	B3	78
Margarita, Isla de, i., Ven.	B10	58
Margate, Fl., U.S.	F6	86
Margate City, N.J., U.S.	E3	107
Margherita Peak, mtn., Afr.	A5	44
Marghī, Afg.	C2	38
Margrethe, Lac, l., Mi., U.S.	D6	99
Marianao, Cuba	C6	64
Mariana, Ar., U.S.	C5	81
Marianna, Fl., U.S.	B1	86
Marias, stm., Mt., U.S.	B4	103
Marias, Islas, is., Mex.	G6	62
Marias Pass, Mt., U.S.	B3	103
Mariato, Punta, c., Pan.	K7	64
Mariazell, Aus.	H15	8
Maribor, Slo.	C10	14
Marica (Évros/Meriç), stm., Eur.	G9	16
Maricopa, Ca., U.S.	E4	82
Maricopa, Az., U.S.	E3	80
Maricopa, co., Az., U.S.	D3	80
Maricopa Mountains, mts., Az., U.S.	m7	80
Marie-Galante, i., Guad.	G17	64
Mariehamn, Fin.	F12	6
Mariemont, Oh., U.S.	o13	112
Mariental, Nmb.	F3	44
Marienville, Pa., U.S.	D3	115
Maries, co., Mo., U.S.	C6	102
Mariestad, Swe.	G9	6
Marietta, Ga., U.S.	C2	87
Marietta, Oh., U.S.	C4	112
Marietta, Ok., U.S.	D4	113
Marietta, S.C., U.S.	A2	117
Marieville, Que., Can.	D4	74
Marília, Braz.	G4	57
Marimba, Ang.	C3	44
Marín, Spain	C3	12
Marin, co., Ca., U.S.	C2	82
Marinduque Island, i., Phil.	C7	32
Marine, Il., U.S.	E4	90
Marine City, Mi., U.S.	F8	99
Marine On St. Croix, Mn., U.S.	E6	100
Marinette, Wi., U.S.	C6	126
Marinette, co., Wi., U.S.	C5	126
Maringá, Braz.	G3	57
Marinha Grande, Port.	F3	12
Marion, Ar., U.S.	B5	81
Marion, Al., U.S.	C2	78
Marion, Il., U.S.	F5	90
Marion, In., U.S.	C6	91
Marion, Ia., U.S.	B6	92
Marion, Ks., U.S.	D6	93
Marion, Ky., U.S.	e9	94
Marion, La., U.S.	B3	95
Marion, Mi., U.S.	D5	99
Marion, Ms., U.S.	C5	101
Marion, N.C., U.S.	B1	110
Marion, Oh., U.S.	B2	112
Marion, Pa., U.S.	G6	115
Marion, S.C., U.S.	C9	117
Marion, S.D., U.S.	D8	118
Marion, Va., U.S.	f10	123
Marion, Wi., U.S.	D5	126
Marion, co., Al., U.S.	A2	78
Marion, co., Ar., U.S.	A3	81
Marion, co., Fl., U.S.	C4	86
Marion, co., Ga., U.S.	D2	87
Marion, co., Il., U.S.	E4	90
Marion, co., In., U.S.	E5	91
Marion, co., Ia., U.S.	C4	92
Marion, co., Ks., U.S.	D6	93
Marion, co., Ky., U.S.	C4	94
Marion, co., Ms., U.S.	D4	101
Marion, co., Mo., U.S.	B6	102
Marion, co., Oh., U.S.	B2	112
Marion, co., Or., U.S.	C4	114
Marion, co., S.C., U.S.	C9	117
Marion, co., Tn., U.S.	D8	119
Marion, co., Tx., U.S.	C5	120
Marion, co., W.V., U.S.	B4	125
Marion, Lake, res., S.C., U.S.	E7	117
Marion Station, Md., U.S.	D6	97
Marionville, Mo., U.S.	D4	102
Maripa, Ven.	D10	58
Mariposa, co., Ca., U.S.	D3	82
Mariscal Estigarribia, Para.	A4	56
Marissa, Il., U.S.	E4	90
Maritime Alps, mts., Eur.	H14	10
Mariupol' (Zdanov), Ukr.	H5	22
Marka, Som.	H3	46
Markaryd, Swe.	H9	6
Markdale, Ont., Can.	C4	73
Marked Tree, Ar., U.S.	B5	81
Markesan, Wi., U.S.	E5	126
Markham, Ont., Can.	D5	73
Markham, Il., U.S.	k9	90
Markham, Tx., U.S.	E4	120
Markham, Mount, mtn., Ant.	A29	47
Markland Lock and Dam, U.S.	B5	94
Markle, In., U.S.	C7	91
Markovo, Russia	E28	24
Marks, Ms., U.S.	A3	101
Marksville, La., U.S.	C3	95
Marktredwitz, Ger.	E12	8
Mark Twain Lake, res., Mo., U.S.	B6	102
Marlboro, N.Y., U.S.	D6	109
Marlboro, Va., U.S.	n17	123
Marlboro, co., S.C., U.S.	B8	117
Marlborough, Ct., U.S.	C6	84
Marlborough, Ma., U.S.	B4	98
Marlborough, N.H., U.S.	E2	106
Marle, Fr.	C10	10
Marlette, Mi., U.S.	E7	99
Marley, Md., U.S.	B4	97
Marlin, Tx., U.S.	D4	120
Marlinton, W.V., U.S.	C4	125
Marlow, Ok., U.S.	C4	113
Marlowe, W.V., U.S.	B7	125
Marlton, N.J., U.S.	D3	107
Marmaduke, Ar., U.S.	A5	81
Marmande, Fr.	H7	10
Marmara Adasi, i., Tur.	I11	16
Marmara Denizi (Sea of Marmara), Tur.	I12	16
Marmaris, Tur.	M12	16
Marmet, W.V., U.S.	C3	125
Marmora, Ont., Can.	C7	73
Marne, Fr.	C10	10
Maroa, Il., U.S.	C5	90
Maroa, Ven.	F9	58
Maroantsetra, Madag.	E9	44
Maromokotro, mtn., Madag.	D9	44
Marondera, Zimb.	E6	44
Maros (Mureş), stm., Eur.	C4	16
Maroua, Cam.	F8	42
Marovoay, Madag.	E9	44
Marquesas Keys, is., Fl., U.S.	H4	86
Marquette, Mi., U.S.	B3	99
Marquette, co., Mi., U.S.	B3	99
Marquette, co., Wi., U.S.	E4	126
Marquette Heights, Il., U.S.	C4	90
Marquise, Fr.	B8	10
Marrah, Jabal, mtn., Sudan	F10	42
Marrakech, Mor.	B4	42
Marrero, La., U.S.	E5	95
Mars, Pa., U.S.	E1	115
Marsabit, Kenya	H2	46
Marsala, Italy	L7	14
Marsā Matrūh, Egypt	B11	42
Marseille, Fr.	I12	10
Marseille-en-Beauvaisis, Fr.	C8	10
Marseilles, Il., U.S.	B5	90
Marshall, Sask., Can.	D1	75
Marshall, Ar., U.S.	B3	81
Marshall, Il., U.S.	D6	90
Marshall, Mi., U.S.	F6	99
Marshall, Mn., U.S.	F3	100
Marshall, Mo., U.S.	B4	102
Marshall, N.C., U.S.	f10	110
Marshall, Tx., U.S.	C5	120
Marshall, Va., U.S.	B5	123
Marshall, Wi., U.S.	E4	126
Marshall, co., Al., U.S.	A3	78
Marshall, co., Il., U.S.	B4	90
Marshall, co., In., U.S.	B5	91
Marshall, co., Ia., U.S.	B4	92
Marshall, co., Ks., U.S.	C7	93
Marshall, co., Ky., U.S.	f9	94
Marshall, co., Mn., U.S.	B2	100
Marshall, co., Ms., U.S.	A4	101
Marshall, co., Ok., U.S.	C5	113
Marshall, co., S.D., U.S.	B8	118
Marshall, co., Tn., U.S.	B5	119
Marshall, co., W.V., U.S.	B4	125
Marshallton, De., U.S.	i7	85
Marshalltown, Ia., U.S.	B5	92
Marshallville, Ga., U.S.	D3	87
Marshes Siding, Ky., U.S.	D5	94
Marshfield, Ma., U.S.	B6	98

Name	Map Ref	Page
Marshfield, Mo., U.S.	D5	102
Marshfield, Wi., U.S.	D3	126
Marshfield Hills, Ma., U.S.	B6	98
Marsh Fork, stm., W.V., U.S.	n13	125
Marsh Harbour, Bah.	A9	64
Mars Hill, Me., U.S.	B5	96
Mars Hill, N.C., U.S.	f10	110
Marsh Island, i., La., U.S.	E4	95
Marsh Lake, res., Mn., U.S.	E2	100
Marshville, N.C., U.S.	C2	110
Marsing, Id., U.S.	F2	89
Märsta, Swe.	G11	6
Marston, Mo., U.S.	E8	102
Mart, Tx., U.S.	D4	120
Martaban, Gulf of, b., Burma	F4	34
Marthasville, Mo., U.S.	C6	102
Martha's Vineyard, i., Ma., U.S.	D6	98
Martigny, Switz.	F14	10
Martigues, Fr.	I12	10
Martin, Czech.	F18	8
Martin, Ky., U.S.	C7	94
Martin, S.D., U.S.	D4	118
Martin, Tn., U.S.	A3	119
Martin, co., Fl., U.S.	E6	86
Martin, co., In., U.S.	G4	91
Martin, co., Ky., U.S.	C7	94
Martin, co., Mn., U.S.	G4	100
Martin, co., N.C., U.S.	B5	110
Martin, co., Tx., U.S.	C2	120
Martina Franca, Italy	I12	14
Martinez, Ca., U.S.	C2	82
Martinez, Ga., U.S.	C4	87
Martínez de la Torre, Mex.	G11	62
Martinique, dep., N.A.	G17	64
Martin Lake, res., Al., U.S.	C4	78
Martin Point, c., Ak., U.S.	A11	79
Martinsberg, Aus.	G15	8
Martinsburg, Pa., U.S.	F5	115
Martinsburg, W.V., U.S.	B7	125
Martins Ferry, Oh., U.S.	B5	112
Martinsville, Il., U.S.	D6	90
Martinsville, In., U.S.	F5	91
Martinsville, Va., U.S.	D3	123
Martos, Spain	H8	12
Martre, Lac la, l., N.W. Ter., Can.	D9	66
Martti, Fin.	C17	6
Marugame, Japan	H6	30
Ma'rūt, Afg.	E2	38
Marvejols, Fr.	H10	10
Marvell, Ar., U.S.	C5	81
Marvine, Mount, mtn., Ut., U.S.	E4	121
Mary, Turk.	J10	22
Mary, Lake, l., Mn., U.S.	E3	100
Mary, Lake, l., Ms., U.S.	D2	101
Maryborough, Austl.	E10	50
Maryland, state, U.S.	B4	97
Maryland City, Md., U.S.	B4	97
Maryland Heights, Mo., U.S.	f13	102
Maryland Point, c., Md., U.S.	D3	97
Maryport, Eng., U.K.	G9	7
Marys, stm., Nv., U.S.	B6	105
Marys Peak, mtn., Or., U.S.	C3	114
Marystown, Newf., Can.	E4	72
Marysville, Ca., U.S.	C3	82
Marysville, Ks., U.S.	C7	93
Marysville, Mi., U.S.	F8	99
Marysville, Oh., U.S.	B2	112
Marysville, Pa., U.S.	F8	115
Marysville, Wa., U.S.	A3	124
Maryville, Mo., U.S.	A3	102
Maryville, Tn., U.S.	D10	119
Marzūq, Libya	C8	42
Marzūq, Idehan, reg., Libya	C8	42
Masai Steppe, plat., Tan.	B7	44
Masaka, Ug.	B6	44
Masan, S. Kor.	D12	26
Masasi, Tan.	D7	44
Masaya, Nic.	I4	64
Masbate Island, i., Phil.	C7	32
Mascarene Islands, is., Afr.	F11	44
Mascoma, stm., N.H., U.S.	C2	106
Mascoma Lake, l., N.H., U.S.	C2	106
Mascot, Tn., U.S.	C10	119
Mascota, Mex.	G7	62
Mascouche, Que., Can.	D4	74
Mascoutah, Il., U.S.	E4	90
Maseru, Leso.	G5	44
Mashābih, i., Sau. Ar.	C2	46
Mashapaug Pond, l., Ct., U.S.	A7	84
Masherbrum, mtn., Pak.	C7	38
Mashhad, Iran	J9	22
Masi Manimba, Zaire	B3	44
Masindi, Ug.	H12	42
Mask, Lough, l., Ire.	H3	7
Maskanah, Syria	A6	40
Maskinongé, Que., Can.	C4	74
Mason, Mi., U.S.	F6	99
Mason, Nv., U.S.	E2	105
Mason, Oh., U.S.	C1	112
Mason, Tx., U.S.	D3	120
Mason, W.V., U.S.	B2	125
Mason, co., Il., U.S.	C4	90
Mason, co., Ky., U.S.	B6	94
Mason, co., Mi., U.S.	D4	99
Mason, co., Tx., U.S.	D3	120
Mason, co., Wa., U.S.	B2	124
Mason, co., W.V., U.S.	C3	125
Mason City, Il., U.S.	C4	90
Mason City, Ia., U.S.	A4	92
Masontown, Pa., U.S.	G2	115
Masontown, W.V., U.S.	B5	125
Massa, Italy	E5	14
Massac, co., Il., U.S.	F5	90
Massachusetts, state, U.S.	B4	98
Massachusetts Bay, b., Ma., U.S.	B6	98
Massacre Lake, l., Nv., U.S.	B2	105
Massafra, Italy	I12	14
Massa Marittima, Italy	F5	14
Massangena, Moz.	F6	44
Massapoag Lake, l., Ma., U.S.	h11	98
Massarosa, Italy	F5	14
Massasecum, Lake, l., N.H., U.S.	D3	106
Massena, N.Y., U.S.	f10	109
Massenya, Chad	F9	42
Masset, B.C., Can.	C1	69
Massey, Ont., Can.	A2	73
Massif Central see Central, Massif, mts., Fr.	G10	10
Massillon, Oh., U.S.	B4	112
Massive, Mount, mtn., Co., U.S.	B4	83
Masterton, N.Z.	D5	52
Mastic Beach, N.Y., U.S.	n16	109
Mastung, Pak.	F2	38
Masuda, Japan	H4	30
Masury, Oh., U.S.	A5	112
Matadi, Zaire	C2	44
Matagalpa, Nic.	H5	64
Matagorda, co., Tx., U.S.	E5	120
Matagorda Bay, b., Tx., U.S.	E4	120
Matagorda Island, i., Tx., U.S.	E4	120
Matagorda Peninsula, pen., Tx., U.S.	E5	120
Matale, Sri L.	I6	37
Matamoras, Pa., U.S.	D12	115
Matamoros, Mex.	E11	62
Matamoros de la Laguna, Mex.	E8	62
Matandu, stm., Tan.	C7	44
Matane, Que., Can.	k13	74
Matanuska, stm., Ak., U.S.	g18	79
Matanzas, Cuba	C7	64
Matanzas Inlet, b., Fl., U.S.	C5	86
Matara, Sri L.	J6	37
Mataró, Spain	D14	12
Matatiele, S. Afr.	H5	44
Matawan, N.J., U.S.	C4	107
Matawin, stm., Que., Can.	C4	74
Matehuala, Mex.	F9	62
Mateira, Braz.	E3	57
Matelica, Italy	F7	14
Matera, Italy	I11	14
Mateur, Tun.	L4	14
Matewan, W.V., U.S.	D2	125
Mather, Pa., U.S.	G1	115
Mather Air Force Base, mil., Ca., U.S.	C3	82
Mather Peaks, mts., Wy., U.S.	B5	127
Mathews, La., U.S.	E5	95
Mathews, Va., U.S.	C6	123
Mathews, co., Va., U.S.	C6	123
Mathews, Lake, l., Ca., U.S.	n14	82
Mathis, Tx., U.S.	E4	120
Mathiston, Ms., U.S.	B4	101
Mathura, India	G7	38
Matías Romero, Mex.	I12	62
Matinicus Island, i., Me., U.S.	E3	96
Mātli, Pak.	H3	38
Mato, Cerro, mtn., Ven.	D10	58
Matoaca, Va., U.S.	n18	123
Mato Grosso, Braz.	F7	54
Mato Grosso, Planalto do, plat., Braz.	G7	54
Matosinhos, Port.	D3	12
Matou, Tai.	L9	28
Matraḥ, Oman	D6	46
Matsqui, B.C., Can.	f13	69
Matsudo, Japan	G12	30
Matsue, Japan	G6	30
Matsumae, Japan	r18	30a
Matsumoto, Japan	F10	30
Matsusaka, Japan	H9	30
Matsu Tao, i., Tai.	I8	28
Matsuyama, Japan	I5	30
Mattagami, stm., Ont., Can.	F16	66
Mattamiscontis Lake, l., Me., U.S.	C4	96
Mattamuskeet, Lake, l., N.C., U.S.	B6	110
Mattāncheri, India	H4	37
Mattapoisett, Ma., U.S.	C6	98
Mattaponi, stm., Va., U.S.	C5	123
Mattawa, Ont., Can.	A6	73
Mattawamkeag, Me., U.S.	C4	96
Mattawamkeag, stm., Me., U.S.	C4	96
Mattawamkeag Lake, l., Me., U.S.	C4	96
Matterhorn, mtn., Eur.	G14	10
Matterhorn, mtn., Nv., U.S.	B6	105
Matteson, Il., U.S.	k9	90
Matthews, Mo., U.S.	E8	102
Matthews, N.C., U.S.	B2	110
Matthews Ridge, Guy.	D12	58
Matthew Town, Bah.	D11	64
Mattighofen, Aus.	G13	8
Mattituck, N.Y., U.S.	n16	109
Mattoon, Il., U.S.	D5	90
Mattoon, Lake, res., Il., U.S.	D5	90
Mattydale, N.Y., U.S.	B4	109
Matunuck, R.I., U.S.	G3	116
Maturín, Ven.	C11	58
Maúa, Moz.	D7	44
Maubeuge, Fr.	B10	10
Maud, Ok., U.S.	B5	113
Maugansville, Md., U.S.	A2	97
Maui, co., Hi., U.S.	B5	88
Maui, i., Hi., U.S.	C6	88
Mauldin, S.C., U.S.	B3	117
Mauléon-Licharre, Fr.	I6	10
Maulvi Bāzār, Bngl.	H14	38
Maumee, Oh., U.S.	A2	112
Maumee, stm., U.S.	A2	112
Maumee Bay, b., U.S.	G7	99
Maumelle, Lake, res., Ar., U.S.	C3	81
Maun, Bots.	E4	44
Mauna Kea, vol., Hi., U.S.	D6	88
Maunaloa, Hi., U.S.	B4	88
Mauna Loa, vol., Hi., U.S.	D6	88
Maunalua Bay, b., Hi., U.S.	g10	88
Maunath Bhanjan, India	H10	38
Maunawili, Hi., U.S.	g10	88
Mau Rānipur, India	H8	38
Maurepas, Lake, l., La., U.S.	D5	95
Mauriac, Fr.	G9	10
Maurice, Ia., U.S.	B1	92
Maurice, stm., N.J., U.S.	E2	107
Mauritania, ctry., Afr.	D3	42
Mauritius, ctry., Afr.	F11	44
Maurs, Fr.	H9	10
Maury, co., Tn., U.S.	B4	119
Maury City, Tn., U.S.	B2	119
Maury Island, i., Wa., U.S.	f11	124
Mauston, Wi., U.S.	E3	126
Mauterndorf, Aus.	H13	8
Mauthausen, Aus.	G14	8
Maverick, co., Tx., U.S.	E2	120
Maw-Daung Pass, Asia	I5	34
Mawlaik, Burma	C3	34
Mawlamyine (Moulmein), Burma	F4	34
Maw Taung, mtn., Asia	I5	34
Maxinkuckee, Lake, l., In., U.S.	B5	91
Max Meadows, Va., U.S.	D2	123
Maxton, N.C., U.S.	C3	110
Maxville, Ont., Can.	B10	73
Maxwell, Ia., U.S.	C4	92
Maxwell Acres, W.V., U.S.	g8	125
Maxwell Air Force Base, mil., Al., U.S.	C3	78
Mayaguana, i., Bah.	C11	64
Mayaguana Passage, strt., Bah.	C11	64
Mayagüez, P.R.	E14	64
Maya Mountains, mts., N.A.	F3	64
Maybole, Scot., U.K.	F8	7
Mayen, Ger.	E7	8
Mayenne, Fr.	D6	10
Mayer, Az., U.S.	C3	80
Mayerthorpe, Alta., Can.	C3	68
Mayes, co., Ok., U.S.	A6	113
Mayesville, S.C., U.S.	D7	117
Mayfield, Ky., U.S.	f9	94
Mayfield, Pa., U.S.	C10	115
Mayfield Heights, Oh., U.S.	A4	112
Mayfield Lake, res., Wa., U.S.	C3	124
Mayflower, Ar., U.S.	C3	81
Mayking, Ky., U.S.	C7	94
Maykop see Majkop, Russia	I6	22
Maymyo, Burma	C4	34
Maynard, Ma., U.S.	B5	98
Maynardville, Tn., U.S.	C10	119
Mayne, B.C., Can.	g12	69
Mayo, Yukon, Can.	D5	66
Mayo, Md., U.S.	C4	97
Mayo, S.C., U.S.	A4	117
Mayodan, N.C., U.S.	A3	110
Mayotte, ter., Afr.	D9	44
Mayotte, i., May.	D9	44
May Park, Or., U.S.	B8	114
Mayport Naval Station, mil., Fl., U.S.	B5	86
Maysville, Ga., U.S.	B3	87
Maysville, Ky., U.S.	B6	94
Maysville, Mo., U.S.	B3	102
Maysville, N.C., U.S.	C5	110
Maysville, Ok., U.S.	C4	113
Mayumba, Gabon	B2	44
Mayūram, India	G5	37
Mayville, Mi., U.S.	E7	99
Mayville, N.Y., U.S.	C1	109
Mayville, N.D., U.S.	B8	111
Mayville, Wi., U.S.	E5	126
Maywood, Il., U.S.	k9	90
Maywood, N.J., U.S.	h8	107
Maywood Park, Or., U.S.	*B4	114
Mazabuka, Zam.	E5	44
Mazamet, Fr.	I9	10
Mazara del Vallo, Italy	L7	14
Mazār-e Sharīf, Afg.	B2	38
Mazaruni, stm., Guy.	E13	58
Mazatenango, Guat.	G2	64
Mazatlán, Mex.	F6	62
Mazatzal Mountains, mts., Az., U.S.	C4	80
Mazatzal Peak, mtn., Az., U.S.	C4	80
Mazeppa, Mn., U.S.	F6	100
Mazoe, stm., Afr.	E6	44
Mazomanie, Wi., U.S.	E4	126
Mazon, Il., U.S.	B5	90
Mbabane, Swaz.	G6	44
Mbaïki, Cen. Afr. Rep.	H9	42
Mbala, Zam.	C6	44
Mbale, Ug.	A6	44
Mbandaka (Coquilhatville), Zaire	A3	44
Mbanza-Ngungu, Zaire	C2	44
Mbeya, Tan.	C6	44
Mbomou (Bomu), stm., Afr.	H10	42
Mbout, Maur.	E3	42
Mbuji-Mayi (Bakwanga), Zaire	C4	44
McAdam, N.B., Can.	D2	71
McAdoo, Pa., U.S.	E9	115
McAfee Peak, mtn., Nv., U.S.	B6	105
McAlester, Ok., U.S.	C6	113
McAlester, Lake, res., Ok., U.S.	B6	113
McAllen, Tx., U.S.	F3	120
McAlmont, Ar., U.S.	h10	81
McAlpine, Md., U.S.	B4	97
McAlpine Lock and Dam, U.S.	H6	91
McArthur, Oh., U.S.	C3	112
McBee, S.C., U.S.	C7	117
McCall, Id., U.S.	E2	89
McCalla, Al., U.S.	g6	78
McCamey, Tx., U.S.	D1	120
McCammon, Id., U.S.	G6	89
McCandless, Pa., U.S.	h13	115
McCartney Mountain, mtn., Mt., U.S.	E4	103
McCaysville, Ga., U.S.	B2	87
McChord Air Force Base, mil., Wa., U.S.	f11	124
McClain, co., Ok., U.S.	C4	113
McCleary, Wa., U.S.	B2	124
McClellan Air Force Base, mil., Ca., U.S.	C3	82
McClintock, Mount, mtn., Ant.	A28	47
McCloud, Ca., U.S.	B2	82
McClure, Pa., U.S.	E7	115
McColl, S.C., U.S.	B8	117
McComas, W.V., U.S.	D3	125
McComb, Ms., U.S.	D3	101
McComb, Oh., U.S.	A2	112
McCone, co., Mt., U.S.	C11	103
McConnell Air Force Base, mil., Ks., U.S.	g12	93
McConnellsburg, Pa., U.S.	G6	115
McConnellsville, Oh., U.S.	C4	112
McCook, Ne., U.S.	D5	104
McCook, co., S.D., U.S.	D8	118
McCordsville, In., U.S.	E6	91
McCormick, S.C., U.S.	D3	117
McCormick, co., S.C., U.S.	D3	117
McCracken, co., Ky., U.S.	e9	94
McCreary, Man., Can.	D2	70
McCreary, co., Ky., U.S.	D5	94
McCrory, Ar., U.S.	B4	81
McCulloch, co., Tx., U.S.	D3	120
McCullough Mountain, mtn., Nv., U.S.	H6	105
McCurtain, co., Ok., U.S.	C7	113
McDermitt, Nv., U.S.	B4	105
McDonald, co., Mo., U.S.	E3	102
McDonough, Ga., U.S.	C2	87
McDonough, co., Il., U.S.	C3	90
McDougall, Mount, mtn., Wy., U.S.	D2	127
McDowell, Ky., U.S.	C7	94
McDowell, co., N.C., U.S.	f10	110
McDowell, co., W.V., U.S.	D3	125
McDowell Mountains, mts., Az., U.S.	k9	80
McDowell Peak, mtn., Az., U.S.	k9	80
McDuffie, co., Ga., U.S.	C4	87
McElroy Creek, stm., W.V., U.S.	k9	125
McEwen, Tn., U.S.	A4	119
McFarland, Ca., U.S.	E4	82
McFarland, Wi., U.S.	E4	126
McGehee, Ar., U.S.	D4	81
McGill, Nv., U.S.	D7	105
McGrath, Ak., U.S.	C8	79
McGregor, Ia., U.S.	A6	92
McGregor, Tx., U.S.	D4	120
McGregor, stm., B.C., Can.	B7	69
McGregor Lake, l., Alta., Can.	D4	68
McGuire, Mount, mtn., Id., U.S.	D4	89
McGuire Air Force Base, mil., N.J., U.S.	C3	107
McHenry, Il., U.S.	A5	90
McHenry, Md., U.S.	k12	97
McHenry, co., Il., U.S.	A5	90
McHenry, co., N.D., U.S.	A5	111
McIntosh, Mn., U.S.	C2	100
McIntosh, co., Ga., U.S.	E5	87
McIntosh, co., N.D., U.S.	C6	111
McIntosh, co., Ok., U.S.	B6	113
McKean, co., Pa., U.S.	C4	115
McKee, Ky., U.S.	C6	94
McKeesport, Pa., U.S.	F2	115
McKees Rocks, Pa., U.S.	F1	115
McKenzie, Tn., U.S.	A3	119
McKenzie, co., N.D., U.S.	B2	111
McKenzie, stm., Or., U.S.	C4	114
McKinley, co., N.M., U.S.	B1	108
McKinley, Mount, mtn., Ak., U.S.	C9	79
McKinleyville, Ca., U.S.	B1	82
McKinney, Tx., U.S.	C4	120
McKinney, Lake, l., Ks., U.S.	E2	93
McKittrick Summit, mtn., Ca., U.S.	E4	82
McLaughlin, S.D., U.S.	B5	118
McLean, Il., U.S.	C4	90
McLean, Va., U.S.	g12	123
McLean, co., Il., U.S.	C4	90
McLean, co., Ky., U.S.	C2	94
McLean, co., N.D., U.S.	B4	111
McLeansboro, Il., U.S.	E5	90
McLennan, Alta., Can.	B2	68
McLennan, co., Tx., U.S.	D4	120
McLeod, co., Mn., U.S.	F4	100
McLeod, Lake, l., Austl.	D2	50
M'Clintock Channel, strt., N.W. Ter., Can.	B12	66
McLoud, Ok., U.S.	B4	113
McLoughlin, Mount, mtn., Or., U.S.	E4	114
McLouth, Ks., U.S.	C8	93
McMechen, W.V., U.S.	B4	125
McMillan, Lake, res., N.M., U.S.	E5	108
McMinn, co., Tn., U.S.	D9	119
McMinnville, Or., U.S.	B3	114
McMinnville, Tn., U.S.	D8	119
McMullen, co., Tx., U.S.	E3	120
McNairy, co., Tn., U.S.	B3	119
McNary, Az., U.S.	C6	80
McNary Dam, U.S.	B7	114
McNeil, Ar., U.S.	D2	81
McNeil, Mount, mtn., B.C., Can.	B2	69
McNeil Island, i., Wa., U.S.	f10	124
McNeill, Ms., U.S.	E4	101
McPherson, Ks., U.S.	D6	93
McPherson, co., Ks., U.S.	D6	93
McPherson, co., Ne., U.S.	C4	104
McPherson, co., S.D., U.S.	B6	118
McQueeney, Tx., U.S.	h7	120
McRae, Ar., U.S.	B4	81
McRae, Ga., U.S.	D4	87
McRoberts, Ky., U.S.	C7	94
McSherrystown, Pa., U.S.	G7	115
Mead, Wa., U.S.	B8	124
Mead, Lake, res., U.S.	A1	80
Meade, Ks., U.S.	E3	93
Meade, co., Ks., U.S.	E3	93
Meade, co., Ky., U.S.	C3	94
Meade, co., S.D., U.S.	C3	118
Meade, stm., Ak., U.S.	B8	79
Meade Peak, mtn., Id., U.S.	G7	89
Meadow, stm., W.V., U.S.	C4	125
Meadow Creek, stm., W.V., U.S.	n14	125
Meadow Lands, Pa., U.S.	F1	115
Meadow Valley Wash, val., Nv., U.S.	F7	105
Meadowview, Va., U.S.	f10	123
Meadville, Pa., U.S.	C1	115
Meaford, Ont., Can.	C4	73
Meagher, co., Mt., U.S.	D6	103
Mealhada, Port.	E3	12
Meander Creek Reservoir, res., Oh., U.S.	A5	112
Meath, hist. reg., Ire.	H5	7
Meaux, Fr.	C10	10
Mebane, N.C., U.S.	A3	110
Mecca, Ca., U.S.	F5	82
Mecca see Makkah, Sau. Ar.	D2	46
Mechanic Falls, Me., U.S.	D2	96
Mechanicsburg, Oh., U.S.	B2	112
Mechanicsburg, Pa., U.S.	F7	115
Mechanicsville, Ia., U.S.	C6	92
Mechanicsville, Md., U.S.	D4	97
Mechanicsville, Va., U.S.	C5	123
Mechanicville, N.Y., U.S.	C7	109
Mechant, Lake, l., La., U.S.	E4	95
Mechelen, Bel.	D4	8
Mecklenburg, co., N.C., U.S.	B2	110
Mecklenburg, co., Va., U.S.	D4	123
Mecklenburg, hist. reg., Ger.	B12	8
Mecklenburger Bucht, b., Ger.	A11	8
Mecosta, co., Mi., U.S.	E5	99
Medan, Indon.	E2	32
Medanosa, Punta, c., Arg.	F3	56
Medaryville, In., U.S.	B4	91
Meddybumps Lake, l., Me., U.S.	C5	96
Medeiros Neto, Braz.	D8	57
Medellín, Col.	D5	58
Médenine, Tun.	B8	42
Medfield, Ma., U.S.	h10	98
Medford, Ma., U.S.	B5	98
Medford, Mn., U.S.	F5	100
Medford, Ok., U.S.	A4	113
Medford, Or., U.S.	E4	114
Medford, Wi., U.S.	C3	126
Medford Lakes, N.J., U.S.	D3	107
Medgidia, Rom.	E12	16
Media, Pa., U.S.	G11	115
Mediapolis, Ia., U.S.	C6	92
Mediaş, Rom.	C8	16
Medical Lake, Wa., U.S.	B8	124
Medicine Bow, Wy., U.S.	E6	127
Medicine Bow, stm., Wy., U.S.	E6	127
Medicine Bow Mountains, mts., U.S.	E6	127
Medicine Bow Peak, mtn., Wy., U.S.	E6	127
Medicine Hat, Alta., Can.	D5	68
Medicine Lodge, Ks., U.S.	E5	93
Medicine Lodge, stm., U.S.	E4	93
Medina, N.Y., U.S.	B2	109
Medina, Oh., U.S.	A4	112
Medina, Tn., U.S.	B3	119
Medina, Wa., U.S.	e11	124
Medina, co., Oh., U.S.	A4	112
Medina, co., Tx., U.S.	E3	120
Medina, stm., Tx., U.S.	k7	120
Medina see Al-Madīnah, Sau. Ar.	D2	46
Medinaceli, Spain	D9	12
Medina del Campo, Spain	D7	12
Medina de Ríoseco, Spain	D6	12
Mediterranean Sea	D14	2
Médoc, reg., Fr.	G5	10
Medora, In., U.S.	G5	91
Médouneu, Gabon	A2	44
Medway, Me., U.S.	C4	96
Medway, stm., N.S., Can.	E5	71
Meekatharra, Austl.	E3	50
Meeker, Co., U.S.	A3	83
Meeker, Ok., U.S.	B5	113
Meeker, co., Mn., U.S.	E4	100
Meelpaeg Lake, res., Newf., Can.	D3	72
Meerut, India	F7	38
Meeteetse, Wy., U.S.	B4	127
Mega, Eth.	H2	46
Mégantic, Lac, l., Que., Can.	D7	74
Mégantic, Mont, mtn., Que., Can.	D6	74
Mégara, Grc.	K7	16
Meggett, S.C., U.S.	F7	117
Meghalaya, state, India	H14	38
Meherrin, stm., U.S.	A4	110
Mehlville, Mo., U.S.	f13	102
Mehsāna, India	I5	38
Mehtar Lām, Afg.	C4	38
Mehun-sur-Yèvre, Fr.	E9	10
Meigs, Ga., U.S.	E2	87
Meigs, co., Oh., U.S.	C3	112
Meigs, co., Tn., U.S.	D9	119
Meiktila, Burma	D3	34
Meiningen, Ger.	E10	8
Meissen, Ger.	D13	8
Meixian, China	K5	28
Mekambo, Gabon	A2	44
Mekele, Eth.	F2	46
Meknès, Mor.	B4	42
Mekong, stm., Asia	H8	34
Melaka, Malay.	M7	34
Melanesia, is., Oc.	G23	50
Melbourne, Austl.	G9	50
Melbourne, Ar., U.S.	A4	81
Melbourne, Fl., U.S.	D6	86
Melbourne, Ia., U.S.	C4	92
Melbourne, Ky., U.S.	h14	94
Melbourne Beach, Fl., U.S.	D6	86
Melcher, Ia., U.S.	C4	92
Meldorf, Ger.	A9	8
Mélèzes, Rivière aux, stm., Que., Can.	g12	74
Melfi, Chad	F9	42
Melfi, Italy	I10	14
Melgaço, Port.	C3	12
Melhus, Nor.	E8	6
Melilla, Sp. N. Afr.	A5	42
Melita, Man., Can.	E1	70
Melito di Porto Salvo, Italy	L10	14
Melitopol', Ukr.	H5	22
Melk, Aus.	G15	8
Mellansel, Swe.	E12	6
Melle, Fr.	F6	10
Mellen, Wi., U.S.	B3	126
Mellerud, Swe.	G9	6
Mellette, co., S.D., U.S.	D5	118
Mellish Reef, atoll, Austl.	C11	50
Melo, Ur.	C6	56
Melocheville, Que., Can.	q19	74
Melrose, Fl., U.S.	C4	86
Melrose, Ma., U.S.	B5	98
Melrose, Mn., U.S.	E4	100
Melrose, N.M., U.S.	C6	108
Meltaus, Fin.	C15	6
Melton Hill Lake, res., Tn., U.S.	D9	119
Melton Mowbray, Eng., U.K.	I12	7

Name	Map Ref	Page
Melun, Fr.	D9	10
Melvern Lake, res., Ks., U.S.	D8	93
Melville, La., U.S.	D4	95
Melville, Lake, l., Newf., Can.	B2	72
Melville Hills, hills, N.W. Ter., Can.	C8	66
Melville Island, i., Austl.	B6	50
Melville Island, i., N.W. Ter., Can.	A10	66
Melville Peninsula, pen., N.W. Ter., Can.	C16	66
Melvin, Ky., U.S.	C7	94
Memmingen, Ger.	H10	8
Memphis, Fl., U.S.	p10	86
Memphis, Mi., U.S.	F8	99
Memphis, Mo., U.S.	A5	102
Memphis, Tn., U.S.	B1	119
Memphis, Tx., U.S.	B2	120
Memphis Naval Air Station, mil., Tn., U.S.	B2	119
Mena, Ar., U.S.	C1	81
Menahga, Mn., U.S.	D3	100
Ménaka, Mali	E6	42
Menan, Id., U.S.	F7	89
Menands, N.Y., U.S.	C7	109
Menard, Tx., U.S.	D3	120
Menard, co., Il., U.S.	C4	90
Menard, co., Tx., U.S.	D3	120
Menasha, Wi., U.S.	D5	126
Mendawai, stm., Indon.	F5	32
Mende, Fr.	H10	10
Mendenhall, Ms., U.S.	D4	101
Méndez, Ec.	I3	58
Mendham, N.J., U.S.	B3	107
Mendi, Eth.	G2	46
Mendip Hills, hills, Eng., U.K.	J10	7
Mendocino, co., Ca., U.S.	C2	82
Mendon, Il., U.S.	C2	90
Mendon, Mi., U.S.	F5	99
Mendon, Ut., U.S.	B4	121
Mendota, Ca., U.S.	D3	82
Mendota, Il., U.S.	B4	90
Mendota, Lake, l., Wi., U.S.	E4	126
Mendoza, Arg.	C3	56
Mene de Mauroa, Ven.	B7	58
Mene Grande, Ven.	C7	58
Menemen, Tur.	K11	16
Menfi, Italy	L7	14
Mengzhi, China	C7	34
Mengzi, China	B5	34
Menifee, co., Ky., U.S.	C6	94
Menlo Park, Ca., U.S.	k8	82
Menno, S.D., U.S.	D8	118
Menominee, Mi., U.S.	C3	99
Menominee, co., Mi., U.S.	C3	99
Menominee, co., Wi., U.S.	C5	126
Menominee, stm., U.S.	C6	126
Menominee Indian Reservation, Wi., U.S.	C5	126
Menomonee, stm., Wi., U.S.	m11	126
Menomonee Falls, Wi., U.S.	E5	126
Menomonie, Wi., U.S.	D2	126
Menongue, Ang.	D3	44
Menorca, i., Spain	F16	12
Mentawai, Kepulauan, is., Indon.	F2	32
Menton, Fr.	I14	10
Mentone, In., U.S.	B5	91
Mentor, Oh., U.S.	A4	112
Mentor-on-the-Lake, Oh., U.S.	A4	112
Menzel Bourguiba, Tun.	L4	14
Meoqui, Mex.	C7	62
Meppel, Neth.	C6	8
Meppen, Ger.	C7	8
Mequon, Wi., U.S.	E6	126
Mer, Fr.	E8	10
Meramec, stm., Mo., U.S.	C7	102
Merano (Meran), Italy	C6	14
Merasheen Island, i., Newf., Can.	E4	72
Merauke, Indon.	G11	32
Meraux, La., U.S.	k12	95
Mercaderes, Col.	G4	58
Merced, Ca., U.S.	D3	82
Merced, co., Ca., U.S.	D3	82
Merced, stm., Ca., U.S.	D3	82
Mercedes, Arg.	B5	56
Mercedes, Arg.	C3	56
Mercedes, Tx., U.S.	F4	120
Mercedes, Ur.	C5	56
Mercer, Pa., U.S.	D1	115
Mercer, Wi., U.S.	B3	126
Mercer, co., Il., U.S.	B3	90
Mercer, co., Ky., U.S.	C5	94
Mercer, co., Mo., U.S.	A4	102
Mercer, co., N.J., U.S.	C3	107
Mercer, co., N.D., U.S.	B4	111
Mercer, co., Oh., U.S.	B1	112
Mercer, co., Pa., U.S.	D1	115
Mercer, co., W.V., U.S.	D3	125
Mercer Island, Wa., U.S.	B3	124
Mercer Island, i., Wa., U.S.	e11	124
Mercersburg, Pa., U.S.	G6	115
Mercerville, N.J., U.S.	C3	107
Mercier, Que., Can.	D4	74
Meredith, N.H., U.S.	C3	106
Meredith, Lake, l., Co., U.S.	C7	83
Meredith, Lake, res., Tx., U.S.	B2	120
Meredosia, Il., U.S.	D3	90
Meredosia Lake, l., Il., U.S.	D3	90
Mergui (Myeik), Burma	H5	34
Mergui Archipelago, is., Burma	H4	34
Meriç (Marica) (évros), stm., Eur.	H10	16
Mérida, Mex.	G15	62
Mérida, Spain	G5	12
Mérida, Ven.	C4	84
Meriden, Ct., U.S.	C5	84
Meriden, Ks., U.S.	C8	93
Meridian, Id., U.S.	F2	89
Meridian, Ms., U.S.	C5	101
Meridian, Pa., U.S.	E2	115
Meridian, Tx., U.S.	D4	120
Meridian Hills, In., U.S.	k10	91
Meridian Naval Air Station, mil., Ms., U.S.	C5	101
Meridianville, Al., U.S.	A3	78
Mérignac, Fr.	H6	10
Merikarvia, Fin.	F13	6
Meriwether, co., Ga., U.S.	C2	87
Merkel, Tx., U.S.	C2	120
Merlin, Ont., Can.	E2	73
Mermentau, La., U.S.	D3	95
Mermentau, stm., La., U.S.	E3	95
Meron, Hare, mtn., Isr.	C4	40
Merriam, Ks., U.S.	k16	93
Merrick, co., Ne., U.S.	C7	104
Merrickville, Ont., Can.	C9	73
Merrill, Ia., U.S.	B1	92
Merrill, Mi., U.S.	E6	99
Merrill, Or., U.S.	E5	114
Merrill, Wi., U.S.	C4	126
Merrillville, In., U.S.	B3	91
Merrimac, Ma., U.S.	A5	98
Merrimack, N.H., U.S.	E4	106
Merrimack, co., N.H., U.S.	D3	106
Merrimack, stm., U.S.	A5	98
Merritt, B.C., Can.	D7	69
Merritt Island, Fl., U.S.	D6	86
Merritt Reservoir, res., Ne., U.S.	B5	104
Merrymeeting Lake, l., N.H., U.S.	D4	106
Merryville, La., U.S.	D2	95
Merseburg, Ger.	D11	8
Merthyr Tydfil, Wales, U.K.	J9	7
Mértola, Port.	H4	12
Merton, Wi., U.S.	m11	126
Méru, Fr.	C9	10
Merwin Lake, res., Wa., U.S.	C3	124
Merzig, Ger.	F6	8
Mesa, Az., U.S.	D4	80
Mesa, co., Co., U.S.	C2	83
Mesabi Range, hills, Mn., U.S.	C6	100
Mesagne, Italy	I12	14
Mesa Mountain, mtn., Co., U.S.	D4	83
Mesa Verde National Park, Co., U.S.	D2	83
Mescalero, N.M., U.S.	D4	108
Mescalero Indian Reservation, N.M., U.S.	D4	108
Mesilla, N.M., U.S.	E3	108
Mesolóngion, Grc.	K5	16
Mesopotamia, reg., Asia	B3	46
Mesquite, Nv., U.S.	G7	105
Mesquite, N.M., U.S.	E3	108
Mesquite, Tx., U.S.	n10	120
Messalo, stm., Moz.	D7	44
Messalonskee Lake, l., Me., U.S.	D3	96
Messina, Italy	K10	14
Messina, S. Afr.	F5	44
Messina, Stretto di, strt., Italy	K10	14
Mesta (Néstos), stm., Eur.	H7	16
Mestre, Italy	D7	14
Meta, stm., S.A.	D9	58
Métabetchouan, Que., Can.	A6	74
Métabetchouane, stm., Que., Can.	A5	74
Metairie, La., U.S.	k11	95
Metamora, Il., U.S.	C4	90
Metán, Arg.	B3	56
Metcalfe, Ont., Can.	B9	73
Metcalfe, Ms., U.S.	B2	101
Metcalfe, co., Ky., U.S.	C4	94
Metedeconk, North Branch, stm., N.J., U.S.	C4	107
Metedeconk, South Branch, stm., N.J., U.S.	C3	107
Meteghan, N.S., Can.	E3	71
Meteghan River, N.S., Can.	E3	71
Meteor Crater, crat., Az., U.S.	C4	80
Methow, stm., Wa., U.S.	A5	124
Methuen, Ma., U.S.	A5	98
Metković, Cro.	F12	14
Metlakatla, Ak., U.S.	D13	79
Metlatonoc, Mex.	I10	62
Metlika, Slo.	D10	14
Metonga, Lake, l., Wi., U.S.	C5	126
Metro, Indon.	k12	33a
Metropolis, Il., U.S.	F5	90
Mettawee, stm., U.S.	E2	122
Metter, Ga., U.S.	D4	87
Mettür, India	G4	37
Metuchen, N.J., U.S.	B4	107
Metz, Fr.	C13	10
Metzger, Or., U.S.	h12	114
Meuse (Maas), stm., Eur.	E5	8
Mexia, Tx., U.S.	D4	120
Mexia, Lake, res., Tx., U.S.	D4	120
Mexiana, Ilha, i., Braz.	D9	54
Mexicali, Mex.	A2	62
Mexico, In., U.S.	C5	91
Mexico, Mo., U.S.	B6	102
Mexico (México), ctry., N.A.	F8	62
Mexico, Gulf of, b., N.A.	F9	76
Mexico City see Ciudad de México, Mex.	H10	62
Meximieux, Fr.	G12	10
Meycauayan, Phil.	q19	33b
Meyersdale, Pa., U.S.	G3	115
Meymaneh, Afg.	C1	38
Meyrueis, Fr.	H10	10
Mèze, Fr.	I10	10
Mezőtúr, Hung.	H20	8
Mezquital, Mex.	F7	62
Mezzolombardo, Italy	C6	14
Mhow, India	I6	38
Miami, Az., U.S.	D5	80
Miami, Fl., U.S.	G6	86
Miami, Ok., U.S.	A7	113
Miami, co., In., U.S.	C5	91
Miami, co., Ks., U.S.	D9	93
Miami, co., Oh., U.S.	B1	112
Miami Beach, Fl., U.S.	G6	86
Miami Canal, Fl., U.S.	F6	86
Miami International Airport, Fl., U.S.	G6	86
Miamisburg, Oh., U.S.	C1	112
Miami Shores, Fl., U.S.	G6	86
Miami Springs, Fl., U.S.	s13	86
Miandrivazo, Madag.	E9	44
Miāneh, Iran	J7	22
Mianus Reservoir, res., U.S.	E1	84
Miānwāli, Pak.	D4	38
Mica Mountain, mtn., Az., U.S.	E5	80
Micco, Fl., U.S.	E6	86
Miccosukee, Lake, res., Fl., U.S.	B2	86
Michelson, Mount, mtn., Ak., U.S.	B11	79
Michie, Tn., U.S.	B3	119
Michigamme, Lake, l., Mi., U.S.	B2	99
Michigamme Reservoir, res., Mi., U.S.	B2	99
Michigan, state, U.S.	E6	99
Michigan, stm., Co., U.S.	A4	83
Michigan, Lake, l., U.S.	C9	76
Michigan Center, Mi., U.S.	F6	99
Michigan City, In., U.S.	A4	91
Michigan Island, i., Wi., U.S.	B3	126
Michikamau Lake, l., Newf., Can.	F20	66
Michipicoten Island, i., Ont., Can.	G15	66
Micronesia, is., Oc.	F23	2
Mičurinsk, Russia	I23	18
Middelburg, Neth.	D3	8
Middelburg, S. Afr.	H4	44
Middelharnis, Neth.	D4	8
Middle, stm., Ia., U.S.	C3	92
Middle Andaman, i., India	H2	34
Middleboro (Middleborough Center), Ma., U.S.	C6	98
Middlebourne, W.V., U.S.	B4	125
Middleburg, Fl., U.S.	B5	86
Middleburg, Pa., U.S.	E7	115
Middleburg Heights, Oh., U.S.	h9	112
Middlebury, Ct., U.S.	C3	84
Middlebury, In., U.S.	A6	91
Middlebury, Vt., U.S.	C2	122
Middlefield, Ct., U.S.	C5	84
Middlefield, Oh., U.S.	A4	112
Middle Island Creek, stm., W.V., U.S.	B3	125
Middle Nodaway, stm., Ia., U.S.	C3	92
Middle Park, val., Co., U.S.	A4	83
Middle Patuxent, stm., Md., U.S.	B4	97
Middleport, N.Y., U.S.	B2	109
Middleport, Oh., U.S.	C3	112
Middle Raccoon, stm., Ia., U.S.	C3	92
Middle River, Md., U.S.	B5	97
Middlesboro, Ky., U.S.	D6	94
Middlesex, N.J., U.S.	B4	107
Middlesex, N.C., U.S.	B4	110
Middlesex, co., Ct., U.S.	D5	84
Middlesex, co., Ma., U.S.	A5	98
Middlesex, co., N.J., U.S.	C4	107
Middlesex, co., Va., U.S.	C6	123
Middlesex Fells Reservation, Ma., U.S.	g11	98
Middleton, N.S., Can.	E4	71
Middleton, Id., U.S.	F2	89
Middleton, Ma., U.S.	A5	98
Middleton, Wi., U.S.	E4	126
Middleton Reef, atoll, Austl.	E11	50
Middletown, Ca., U.S.	C2	82
Middletown, Ct., U.S.	C5	84
Middletown, De., U.S.	C3	85
Middletown, In., U.S.	D6	91
Middletown, Ky., U.S.	g11	94
Middletown, Md., U.S.	B2	97
Middletown, N.J., U.S.	C4	107
Middletown, N.Y., U.S.	D6	109
Middletown, Oh., U.S.	C1	112
Middletown, Pa., U.S.	F8	115
Middletown, R.I., U.S.	E5	116
Middletown, Va., U.S.	A4	123
Middleville, Mi., U.S.	F5	99
Midfield, Al., U.S.	g7	78
Midland, Ont., Can.	C5	73
Midland, Mi., U.S.	E6	99
Midland, N.C., U.S.	B2	110
Midland, Pa., U.S.	E1	115
Midland, Tx., U.S.	D1	120
Midland, co., Mi., U.S.	E6	99
Midland, co., Tx., U.S.	D1	120
Midland City, Al., U.S.	D4	78
Midland Park, Ks., U.S.	g12	93
Midland Park, N.J., U.S.	B4	107
Midland Park, S.C., U.S.	k11	117
Midleton, Ire.	J4	7
Midlothian, Il., U.S.	k9	90
Midlothian, Tx., U.S.	C4	120
Midnapore, India	I12	38
Midongy Sud, Madag.	F9	44
Midvale, Ut., U.S.	C4	121
Midville, Ga., U.S.	D4	87
Midway, B.C., Can.	E8	69
Midway, De., U.S.	F5	85
Midway, Ky., U.S.	B5	94
Midway, Pa., U.S.	G7	115
Midway, Ut., U.S.	C4	121
Midway Islands, dep., Oc.	E1	2
Midwest, Wy., U.S.	C6	127
Midwest City, Ok., U.S.	B4	113
Mielec, Pol.	E21	8
Mieres, Spain	B6	12
Miesbach, Ger.	H11	8
Mifflin, co., Pa., U.S.	E6	115
Mifflinburg, Pa., U.S.	E7	115
Mifflinville, Pa., U.S.	D9	115
Miguel Alemán, Presa, res., Mex.	H11	62
Miguel Auza, Mex.	E8	62
Mihailovgrad, Bul.	F7	16
Mihara, Japan	H6	30
Mikasa, Japan	p19	30a
Mikkeli, Fin.	F16	6
Mikumi, Tan.	C7	44
Milaca, Mn., U.S.	E5	100
Milagro, Arg.	C3	56
Milagro, Ec.	I3	58
Milam, co., Tx., U.S.	D4	120
Milan, Ga., U.S.	D3	87
Milan, Il., U.S.	B3	90
Milan, In., U.S.	F7	91
Milan, Mi., U.S.	F7	99
Milan, Mo., U.S.	A4	102
Milan, N.M., U.S.	B2	108
Milan, Oh., U.S.	A3	112
Milan, Tn., U.S.	B3	119
Milan see Milano, Italy	D4	14
Milano (Milan), Italy	D4	14
Milâs, Tur.	L11	16
Milazzo, Italy	K10	14
Milbank, S.D., U.S.	B9	118
Mildmay, Ont., Can.	C3	73
Mildura, Austl.	F8	50
Milesburg, Pa., U.S.	E6	115
Miles City, Mt., U.S.	D11	103
Milestone, Sask., Can.	G3	75
Milford, Ct., U.S.	E3	84
Milford, De., U.S.	E4	85
Milford, Il., U.S.	C6	90
Milford, In., U.S.	B6	91
Milford, Ia., U.S.	A2	92
Milford, Me., U.S.	D4	96
Milford, Ma., U.S.	B4	98
Milford, Mi., U.S.	F7	99
Milford, Ne., U.S.	D8	104
Milford, N.H., U.S.	E3	106
Milford, Oh., U.S.	C1	112
Milford, Pa., U.S.	D12	115
Milford, Ut., U.S.	E2	121
Milford Haven, Wales, U.K.	J7	7
Milford Lake, res., Ks., U.S.	C6	93
Milford Station, N.S., Can.	D6	71
Mililani Town, Hi., U.S.	g9	88
Milk, stm., Mt., U.S.	h9	98
Milk River, Alta., Can.	E4	68
Mill, stm., Ma., U.S.	h9	98
Millard, co., Ut., U.S.	D2	121
Millau, Fr.	H10	10
Millbrae, Ca., U.S.	h8	82
Millbrook, Ont., Can.	C6	73
Millbrook, Al., U.S.	C3	78
Mill Brook, stm., Vt., U.S.	B5	122
Millburn, N.J., U.S.	B4	107
Millbury, Ma., U.S.	B4	98
Millbury, Oh., U.S.	e7	112
Mill City, Or., U.S.	C4	114
Millcreek, Ut., U.S.	C4	121
Mill Creek, W.V., U.S.	C5	125
Mill Creek, stm., N.J., U.S.	C4	107
Mill Creek, stm., Oh., U.S.	B2	112
Mill Creek, stm., Tn., U.S.	g10	119
Mill Creek, stm., W.V., U.S.	C3	125
Mill Creek, stm., W.V., U.S.	m13	125
Millcreek Township, Pa., U.S.	B1	115
Milledgeville, Ga., U.S.	C3	87
Milledgeville, Il., U.S.	B4	90
Mille Îles, Rivière des, stm., Que., Can.	p19	74
Mille Lacs, co., Mn., U.S.	E5	100
Mille Lacs, Lac des, l., Ont., Can.	G14	66
Mille Lacs Indian Reservation, Mn., U.S.	D5	100
Mille Lacs Lake, l., Mn., U.S.	D5	100
Millen, Ga., U.S.	D5	87
Miller, S.D., U.S.	C7	118
Miller, co., Ar., U.S.	D2	81
Miller, co., Ga., U.S.	E2	87
Miller, co., Mo., U.S.	C5	102
Miller, Mount, mtn., Ak., U.S.	C11	79
Miller Peak, mtn., Az., U.S.	F5	80
Miller Run, stm., Vt., U.S.	B4	122
Millers, stm., Ma., U.S.	A3	98
Millersburg, In., U.S.	A6	91
Millersburg, Ky., U.S.	B5	94
Millersburg, Oh., U.S.	B4	112
Millersburg, Pa., U.S.	E8	115
Millersport, Oh., U.S.	C3	112
Millersville, Pa., U.S.	F9	115
Millet, Alta., Can.	C4	68
Mill Hall, Pa., U.S.	D7	115
Milliken, Co., U.S.	A6	83
Millington, Mi., U.S.	E7	99
Millington, Tn., U.S.	B2	119
Millinocket, Me., U.S.	C4	96
Millinocket Lake, l., Me., U.S.	C4	96
Millis, Ma., U.S.	B5	98
Millport, Al., U.S.	B1	78
Millry, Al., U.S.	D1	78
Mills, Wy., U.S.	D6	127
Mills, co., Ia., U.S.	C2	92
Mills, co., Tx., U.S.	D3	120
Millsboro, De., U.S.	F4	85
Millsboro, Pa., U.S.	G1	115
Millstadt, Il., U.S.	E3	90
Millstone, stm., N.J., U.S.	C4	107
Milltown, In., U.S.	H5	91
Milltown, N.J., U.S.	C4	107
Milltown, Wi., U.S.	C1	126
Milltown [-Head of Bay d'Espoir], Newf., Can.	E4	72
Milltown Malbay, Ire.	I3	7
Millvale, Pa., U.S.	k14	115
Mill Valley, Ca., U.S.	D2	82
Millville, Ma., U.S.	B4	98
Millville, N.J., U.S.	E2	107
Millville, Pa., U.S.	D9	115
Millville, Ut., U.S.	B4	121
Millville Lake, N.H., U.S.	E4	106
Millwood, Wa., U.S.	g14	124
Millwood Lake, res., Ar., U.S.	D1	81
Milner Dam, Id., U.S.	G5	89
Milnor, N.D., U.S.	C8	111
Milo, Ia., U.S.	C4	92
Milo, Me., U.S.	C4	96
Milparinka, Austl.	F7	91
Milroy, In., U.S.	E6	91
Milroy, Pa., U.S.	E6	115
Milstead, Ga., U.S.	C3	87
Milton, Ont., Can.	D5	73
Milton, N.S., Can.	E5	71
Milton, De., U.S.	F4	85
Milton, Fl., U.S.	u14	86
Milton, Ky., U.S.	B4	94
Milton, Ma., U.S.	B5	98
Milton, N.H., U.S.	D5	106
Milton, Pa., U.S.	D8	115
Milton, Vt., U.S.	B2	122
Milton, Wa., U.S.	f11	124
Milton, W.V., U.S.	C2	125
Milton, Wi., U.S.	F5	126
Milton, Lake, l., Oh., U.S.	A4	112
Milton-Freewater, Or., U.S.	B8	114
Miltona, Lake, l., Mn., U.S.	D3	100
Milton Reservoir, res., Co., U.S.	A6	83
Milverton, Ont., Can.	D4	73
Milwaukee, Wi., U.S.	E6	126
Milwaukee, co., Wi., U.S.	E6	126
Milwaukee, stm., Wi., U.S.	m12	126
Milwaukie, Or., U.S.	B4	114
Mimizan, Fr.	H5	10
Mims, Fl., U.S.	D6	86
Min, stm., China	I7	28
Mina, Nv., U.S.	E3	105
Minahasa, pen., Indon.	E7	32
Minamata, Japan	J3	30
Minas, Ur.	C5	56
Minas, Sierra de las, mts., Guat.	G3	64
Minas Basin, b., N.S., Can.	D5	71
Minas Channel, strt., N.S., Can.	D5	71
Minas de Barroterán, Mex.	D9	62
Minas Novas, Braz.	D7	57
Minatare, Ne., U.S.	C2	104
Minatitlán, Mex.	I12	62
Minco, Ok., U.S.	B4	113
Mindanao, i., Phil.	D7	32
Mindanao, stm., Phil.	D7	32
Mindanao Sea, Phil.	D7	32
Mindelheim, Ger.	G10	8
Minden, Ger.	C8	8
Minden, La., U.S.	B2	95
Minden, Ne., U.S.	D7	104
Minden, Nv., U.S.	E2	105
Minden, W.V., U.S.	D3	125
Mindoro, i., Phil.	C7	32
Mindoro Strait, strt., Phil.	C7	32
Mine Hill, N.J., U.S.	B3	107
Mineiros, Braz.	D2	57
Mineola, N.Y., U.S.	E7	109
Mineola, Tx., U.S.	C5	120
Miner, Mo., U.S.	E8	102
Miner, co., S.D., U.S.	D8	118
Mineral, Ca., U.S.	B3	82
Mineral, co., Co., U.S.	D4	83
Mineral, co., Mt., U.S.	C1	103
Mineral, co., Nv., U.S.	E3	105
Mineral, co., W.V., U.S.	B6	125
Mineral Point, Wi., U.S.	F3	126
Mineral Springs, Ar., U.S.	D2	81
Mineral Wells, Tx., U.S.	C3	120
Minersville, Pa., U.S.	E9	115
Minersville, Ut., U.S.	E3	121
Minerva, Oh., U.S.	B4	112
Minervino Murge, Italy	H11	14
Minetto, N.Y., U.S.	B4	109
Mingo, co., W.V., U.S.	D2	125
Mingo Junction, Oh., U.S.	B5	112
Minho (Miño), stm., Eur.	D3	12
Minidoka, co., Id., U.S.	G5	89
Minidoka Dam, Id., U.S.	G5	89
Minier, Il., U.S.	C4	90
Minisink Island, i., N.J., U.S.	A3	107
Minitonas, Man., Can.	C1	70
Minna, Nig.	G7	42
Minneapolis, Ks., U.S.	C6	93
Minneapolis, Mn., U.S.	F5	100
Minnedosa, Man., Can.	D2	70
Minnedosa, stm., Man., Can.	D1	70
Minnehaha, co., S.D., U.S.	D9	118
Minneola, Ks., U.S.	E3	93
Minneota, Mn., U.S.	F3	100
Minnesota, state, U.S.	F2	100
Minnesota, stm., Mn., U.S.	G5	100
Minnetonka, Mn., U.S.	n12	100
Minnetonka, Lake, l., Mn., U.S.	n11	100
Minnewaska, Lake, l., Mn., U.S.	E3	100
Miño (Minho), stm., Eur.	D3	12
Minocqua, Wi., U.S.	C4	126
Minonk, Il., U.S.	C4	90
Minooka, Il., U.S.	B5	90
Minot, N.D., U.S.	A4	111
Minot Air Force Base, mil., N.D., U.S.	A4	111
Minquadale, De., U.S.	i7	85
Minsk, Bela.	H10	18
Mińsk Mazowiecki, Pol.	C21	8
Minster, Oh., U.S.	B1	112
Mint Hill, N.C., U.S.	B2	110
Minto, N.B., Can.	C3	71
Minto Inlet, b., N.W. Ter., Can.	B9	66
Minturn, Co., U.S.	B4	83
Minturno, Italy	H8	14
Minusinsk, Russia	G12	24
Minute Man National Historical Park, Ma., U.S.	g10	98
Minxian, China	E7	26
Mio, Mi., U.S.	D6	99
Mira, Italy	D7	14
Mirabel, Que., Can.	D3	74
Mirabeau, Col.	E6	58
Miraflores, Col.	G6	58
Miraj, India	D3	37
Miramar, Fl., U.S.	s13	86
Miramar Naval Air Station, mil., Ca., U.S.	F5	82
Miramas, Fr.	I11	10
Mirambeau, Fr.	G6	10
Miramichi Bay, b., N.B., Can.	B5	71
Miranda de Ebro, Spain	C9	12
Miranda do Douro, Port.	D5	12
Mirande, Fr.	I7	10
Mirandela, Port.	D4	12
Mirandola, Italy	E6	14
Mirbāt, Oman	E5	46
Mirebeau-sur-Bèze, Fr.	E12	10
Miri, Malay.	E5	32
Mirnyj, Russia	E16	24
Mírpur Khās, Pak.	H3	38
Mirror Lake, l., N.H., U.S.	C4	106
Mirzāpur, India	H10	38
Misawa, Japan	B14	30
Miscouche, P.E.I., Can.	C6	71
Miscou Island, i., N.B., Can.	B5	71
Miscou Point, c., N.B., Can.	A5	71
Misenheimer, N.C., U.S.	B2	110
Mishawaka, In., U.S.	A5	91
Misheguk Mountain, mtn., Ak., U.S.	B7	79
Mishicot, Wi., U.S.	D6	126
Mishmi Hills, hills, Asia	F16	38
Misima Island, i., Pap. N. Gui.	B10	50
Miskitos, Cayos, is., Nic.	G6	64
Miskolc, Hung.	G20	8

Name	Map Ref	Page
Misool, Pulau, i., Indon.	F9	32
Mispillion, stm., De., U.S.	E4	85
Misrātah, Libya	B9	42
Missaukee, co., Mi., U.S.	D5	99
Missaukee, Lake, l., Mi., U.S.	D5	99
Mission, Ks., U.S.	m16	93
Mission, S.D., U.S.	D5	118
Mission, Tx., U.S.	F3	120
Mission Range, mts., Mt., U.S.	C3	103
Mission Viejo, Ca., U.S.	n13	82
Missisquoi, stm., Vt., U.S.	B3	122
Missisquoi Bay, b., Vt., U.S.	A2	122
Mississauga, Ont., Can.	D5	73
Mississinewa, stm., U.S.	D7	91
Mississinewa Lake, res., In., U.S.	C6	91
Mississippi, co., Ar., U.S.	B5	81
Mississippi, co., Mo., U.S.	E8	102
Mississippi, state, U.S.	C4	101
Mississippi, stm., U.S.	E8	76
Mississippi Delta, La., U.S.	E6	95
Mississippi Sound, strt., U.S.	E5	101
Mississippi State, Ms., U.S.	B5	101
Missoula, Mt., U.S.	D2	103
Missoula, co., Mt., U.S.	D2	103
Missouri, state, U.S.	C5	102
Missouri, stm., U.S.	C7	76
Missouri City, Tx., U.S.	r14	120
Missouri Valley, Ia., U.S.	C2	92
Mistassini, Que., Can.	h12	74
Mistassini, Lac, l., Que., Can.	h12	74
Misti, Volcán, vol., Peru	G4	54
Mistretta, Italy	L9	14
Mita, Punta de, c., Mex.	G7	62
Mitchell, Austl.	E9	50
Mitchell, Ont., Can.	D3	73
Mitchell, Il., U.S.	E3	90
Mitchell, In., U.S.	G5	91
Mitchell, Ne., U.S.	C2	104
Mitchell, S.D., U.S.	D7	118
Mitchell, co., Ga., U.S.	E2	87
Mitchell, co., Ia., U.S.	A5	92
Mitchell, co., Ks., U.S.	C5	93
Mitchell, co., N.C., U.S.	e10	110
Mitchell, co., Tx., U.S.	C2	120
Mitchell, stm., Austl.	C8	50
Mitchell, Lake, l., Mi., U.S.	D5	99
Mitchell, Lake, res., Al., U.S.	C3	78
Mitchell, Mount, mtn., N.C., U.S.	f10	110
Mitchell Island, i., La., U.S.	E6	95
Mitchellville, Ia., U.S.	C4	92
Mitilíni, Grc.	J10	16
Mitkof Island, i., Ak., U.S.	m23	79
Mito, Japan	F13	30
Mitsiwa, Eth.	E2	46
Mitsuke, Japan	E11	30
Mittenwald, Ger.	H11	8
Mittweida, Ger.	E12	8
Mitú, Col.	G7	58
Mitumba, Monts, mts., Zaire	C5	44
Mitwaba, Zaire	C5	44
Mitzic, Gabon	A2	44
Miura, Japan	G12	30
Mixian, China	A2	28
Miyako, Japan	C14	30
Miyako-jima, i., Japan	G12	26
Miyakonojō, Japan	K4	30
Miyazaki, Japan	K4	30
Miyoshi, Japan	H5	30
Miyun, China	C10	26
Mizdah, Libya	B8	42
Mizen Head, c., Ire.	J3	7
Mizoram, ter., India	I15	38
Mizpe Ramon, Isr.	D4	40
Mizque, Bol.	G5	54
Mjölby, Swe.	G10	6
Mjøsa, l., Nor.	F8	6
Mkalama, Tan.	B6	44
Mladá Boleslav, Czech.	E14	8
Mława, Pol.	B20	8
Mo, Nor.	C10	6
Moab, Ut., U.S.	E6	121
Moapa River Indian Reservation, Nv., U.S.	G7	105
Moate, Ire.	H5	7
Mobara, Japan	G13	30
Mobaye, Cen. Afr. Rep.	H10	42
Moberly, Mo., U.S.	B5	102
Mobile, Al., U.S.	E1	78
Mobile, co., Al., U.S.	E1	78
Mobile, stm., Al., U.S.	E1	78
Mobile Bay, b., Al., U.S.	E1	83
Mobridge, S.D., U.S.	B5	118
Moçambique, Moz.	E8	44
Moçanaqua, Pa., U.S.	D9	115
Mocha, Isla, i., Chile	D2	56
Mochudi, Bots.	F5	44
Mocksville, N.C., U.S.	B2	110
Moclips, Wa., U.S.	B1	124
Môco, Serra do, mtn., Ang.	D3	44
Mocoa, Col.	G4	58
Mococa, Braz.	F5	57
Moctezuma, Mex.	C5	62
Mocuba, Moz.	E7	44
Modane, Fr.	G13	10
Model Reservoir, res., Co., U.S.	D6	83
Modena, Italy	E5	14
Modesto, Ca., U.S.	D3	82
Modica, Italy	M9	14
Mödling, Aus.	G16	8
Modoc, co., Ca., U.S.	B3	82
Modowi, Indon.	F9	32
Moengo, Sur.	B8	54
Moenkopi, Az., U.S.	A4	80
Moffat, Scot., U.K.	F9	7
Moffat, co., Co., U.S.	A2	83
Moffat Tunnel, Co., U.S.	B5	83
Moffett Field Naval Air Station, mil., Ca., U.S.	k8	82
Moga, India	E6	38
Mogadishu see Muqdisho, Som.	H4	46
Mogadore, Oh., U.S.	A4	112
Mogadouro, Port.	D5	12
Mogaung, Burma	B4	34
Mogi das Cruzes, Braz.	G5	57
Mogil'ov, Bela.	H13	18
Mogi-Mirim, Braz.	G5	57
Mogincual, Moz.	E8	44
Mogočа, Russia	G17	24
Mogočin, Russia	F10	24
Mogok, Burma	C4	34
Mogollon Mountains, mts., N.M., U.S.	D1	108
Mogollon Rim, clf, Az., U.S.	C5	80
Mogotón, Pico, mtn., N.A.	H4	64
Mohall, N.D., U.S.	A4	111
Mohave, co., Az., U.S.	B1	80
Mohave, Lake, res., U.S.	H7	105
Mohave Mountains, mts., Az., U.S.	C1	80
Mohave Valley, Az., U.S.	C1	80
Mohawk, N.Y., U.S.	C5	109
Mohawk, stm., N.H., U.S.	g7	106
Mohawk, stm., N.Y., U.S.	C6	109
Mohawk Lake, l., N.J., U.S.	A3	107
Mohawk Mountains, mts., Az., U.S.	E2	80
Moheli, i., Com.	D8	44
Mohican, stm., Oh., U.S.	B3	112
Mohinora, Cerro, mtn., Mex.	D6	62
Mohnton, Pa., U.S.	F10	115
Moi, Nor.	G6	6
Moisie, Que., Can.	h8	72
Moisie, stm., Que., Can.	F19	66
Moissac, Fr.	H8	10
Mojave, Ca., U.S.	E4	82
Mojave, stm., Ca., U.S.	E5	82
Mojave Desert, des., Ca., U.S.	E5	82
Mojjero, stm., Russia	D14	24
Mojo, Eth.	G2	46
Mokapu Peninsula, pen., Hi., U.S.	g10	88
Mokapu Point, c., Hi., U.S.	g11	88
Mokelumne, stm., Ca., U.S.	C3	82
Mokena, Il., U.S.	k9	90
Mokp'o, S. Kor.	E12	26
Moku Manu, i., Hi., U.S.	g11	88
Mol, Bel.	D5	8
Molalla, Or., U.S.	B4	114
Moldau see Vltava, stm., Czech.	F14	8
Molde, Nor.	E6	6
Moldova, ctry., Eur.	H3	22
Molepolole, Bots.	F5	44
Molfetta, Italy	H11	14
Molina de Aragón, Spain	E10	12
Molina de Segura, Spain	G10	12
Moline, Il., U.S.	B3	90
Moline, Mi., U.S.	F5	99
Molino, Fl., U.S.	u14	86
Molins de Rey, Spain	D14	12
Mollendo, Peru	G4	54
Mölln, Ger.	B10	8
Mölndal, Swe.	H9	6
Molodečno, Bela.	G9	18
Molokai, i., Hi., U.S.	B5	88
Molokini, i., Hi., U.S.	C5	88
Molson Lake, l., Man., Can.	B3	70
Molucca Sea see Maluku, Laut, Indon.	F7	32
Moluccas see Maluku, is., Indon.	F8	32
Moma, Moz.	E7	44
Moma, stm., Russia	D22	24
Mombasa, Kenya	B7	44
Mombetsu, Japan	o21	30a
Momence, Il., U.S.	B6	90
Momotombo, Volcán, vol., Nic.	H4	64
Mon, stm., Burma	D3	34
Mona, Canal de la, strt., N.A.	E14	64
Mona, Isla, i., P.R.	E14	64
Monaca, Pa., U.S.	E1	115
Monaco, ctry., Eur.	G9	4
Monadhliath Mountains, mts., Scot., U.K.	D8	7
Monadnock, Mount, mtn., N.H., U.S.	E2	106
Monadnock Mountain, mtn., Vt., U.S.	B5	122
Monahans, Tx., U.S.	D1	120
Monarch Mills, S.C., U.S.	B4	117
Monarch Pass, Co., U.S.	C4	83
Monashee Mountains, mts., B.C., Can.	D8	69
Monastir, Tun.	N5	14
Moncalieri, Italy	D2	14
Monção, Braz.	D9	54
Mönchengladbach, Ger.	D6	8
Monchique, Port.	H3	12
Moncks Corner, S.C., U.S.	E7	117
Monclova, Mex.	D9	62
Moncton, N.B., Can.	C5	71
Mondoñedo, Spain	B4	12
Mondovì, Italy	E2	14
Mondovi, Wi., U.S.	D2	126
Mondragone, Italy	H8	14
Monee, Il., U.S.	B6	90
Monessen, Pa., U.S.	F2	115
Monett, Mo., U.S.	E4	102
Monette, Ar., U.S.	B5	81
Monfalcone, Italy	D8	14
Monforte de Lemos, Spain	C4	12
Monfort Heights, Oh., U.S.	*o12	112
Mong Cai, Viet.	D9	34
Mông Hsat, Burma	D5	34
Monghyr, India	H12	38
Mongo, Chad	F9	42
Mongol Altajn Nuruu, mts., Asia	B5	26
Mongolia, ctry., Asia	B7	26
Mongu, Zam.	E4	44
Monhegan Island, i., Me., U.S.	E3	96
Monida Pass, U.S.	E6	89
Moniteau, co., Mo., U.S.	C5	102
Monitor Range, mts., Nv., U.S.	E5	105
Monitor Valley, val., Nv., U.S.	D5	105
Monmouth, Il., U.S.	C3	90
Monmouth, Or., U.S.	C3	114
Monmouth, co., N.J., U.S.	C4	107
Monmouth Beach, N.J., U.S.	C5	107
Monmouth Mountain, mtn., B.C., Can.	D6	69
Mono, co., Ca., U.S.	D4	82
Monocacy, stm., Md., U.S.	B3	97
Mono Lake, l., Ca., U.S.	D4	82
Monomonac, Lake, l., U.S.	E3	106
Monomoy Island, i., Ma., U.S.	C7	98
Monomoy Point, c., Ma., U.S.	C7	98
Monon, In., U.S.	C4	91
Monona, Ia., U.S.	A6	92
Monona, Wi., U.S.	E4	126
Monona, co., Ia., U.S.	B1	92
Monona, Lake, l., Wi., U.S.	E4	126
Monongah, W.V., U.S.	B4	125
Monongahela, Pa., U.S.	F2	115
Monongahela, stm., U.S.	G2	115
Monongalia, co., W.V., U.S.	B4	125
Monopoli, Italy	I12	14
Monóvar, Spain	G11	12
Monreal del Campo, Spain	E10	12
Monroe, Ga., U.S.	C3	87
Monroe, In., U.S.	C8	91
Monroe, Ia., U.S.	C4	92
Monroe, La., U.S.	B3	95
Monroe, Mi., U.S.	G7	99
Monroe, N.Y., U.S.	D6	109
Monroe, N.C., U.S.	C2	110
Monroe, Oh., U.S.	C1	112
Monroe, Ut., U.S.	E3	121
Monroe, Wa., U.S.	B4	124
Monroe, Wi., U.S.	F4	126
Monroe, co., Al., U.S.	D2	78
Monroe, co., Ar., U.S.	C4	81
Monroe, co., Fl., U.S.	G5	86
Monroe, co., Ga., U.S.	D3	87
Monroe, co., Il., U.S.	E3	90
Monroe, co., In., U.S.	F4	91
Monroe, co., Ia., U.S.	D5	92
Monroe, co., Ky., U.S.	D4	94
Monroe, co., Mi., U.S.	G7	99
Monroe, co., Ms., U.S.	B5	101
Monroe, co., Mo., U.S.	B6	102
Monroe, co., N.Y., U.S.	B3	109
Monroe, co., Oh., U.S.	C4	112
Monroe, co., Pa., U.S.	D11	115
Monroe, co., Tn., U.S.	D9	119
Monroe, co., W.V., U.S.	D4	125
Monroe, co., Wi., U.S.	E3	126
Monroe Center, Ct., U.S.	D3	84
Monroe Lake, res., In., U.S.	F5	91
Monroe Park, De., U.S.	h7	85
Monroeville, Al., U.S.	D2	78
Monroeville, In., U.S.	C8	91
Monroeville, Oh., U.S.	A3	112
Monroeville, Pa., U.S.	k14	115
Monrovia, Lib.	G3	42
Monrovia, Ca., U.S.	m13	82
Monrovia, In., U.S.	E5	91
Mons, Bel.	E3	8
Monson, Ma., U.S.	B3	98
Montague, P.E.I., Can.	C7	71
Montague, Ca., U.S.	B2	82
Montague, Mi., U.S.	E4	99
Montague, co., Tx., U.S.	C4	120
Montague, Isla, i., Mex.	B2	62
Montague Island, i., Ak., U.S.	D10	79
Montague Peak, mtn., Ak., U.S.	g18	79
Montague Strait, strt., Ak., U.S.	h18	79
Montaigu, Fr.	F5	10
Montalbán, Spain	E11	12
Montalcino, Italy	F6	14
Montalegre, Port.	D4	12
Mont Alto, Pa., U.S.	G6	115
Montana, state, U.S.	D7	103
Montánchez, Spain	F5	12
Montargis, Fr.	D9	10
Montauban, Fr.	H8	10
Montauk, N.Y., U.S.	m17	109
Montbard, Fr.	E11	10
Montbéliard, Fr.	E13	10
Mont Belvieu, Tx., U.S.	E5	120
Montblanch, Spain	D13	12
Montbrison, Fr.	G11	10
Montcalm, co., Mi., U.S.	E5	99
Montchanin, De., U.S.	h7	85
Montclair, Ca., U.S.	m13	82
Montclair, N.J., U.S.	B4	107
Mont Clare, Pa., U.S.	o19	115
Mont-de-Marsan, Fr.	I6	10
Montdidier, Fr.	C9	10
Monteagle, Tn., U.S.	D8	119
Monteagudo, Bol.	G6	54
Monte Azul, Braz.	C7	57
Montebello, Que., Can.	D3	74
Montebello, Ca., U.S.	m12	82
Monte Caseros, Arg.	B5	56
Montecatini Terme, Italy	F5	14
Monte Comán, Arg.	C3	56
Montecristi, Dom. Rep.	E12	64
Montecristi, Ec.	H2	58
Montefiascone, Italy	G7	14
Montego Bay, Jam.	E9	64
Montegut, La., U.S.	E5	95
Montélimar, Fr.	H11	10
Montello, Nv., U.S.	B7	105
Montello, Wi., U.S.	E4	126
Montemorelos, Mex.	E10	62
Montemor-o-Novo, Port.	G3	12
Montendre, Fr.	G6	10
Montenegro, state, Yugo.	G3	16
Montenero di Bisaccia, Italy	H9	14
Montepuez, Moz.	D8	44
Monte Quemado, Arg.	B4	56
Montereau-faut-Yonne, Fr.	D9	10
Monterey, Ca., U.S.	D3	82
Monterey, Tn., U.S.	C8	119
Monterey, co., Ca., U.S.	D3	82
Monterey Bay, b., Ca., U.S.	D2	82
Monterey Park, Ca., U.S.	m12	82
Montería, Col.	C5	58
Monterotondo, Italy	G7	14
Monterrey, Mex.	E9	62
Montesano, Wa., U.S.	C2	124
Monte Sant'Angelo, Italy	H10	14
Montes Claros, Braz.	D7	57
Montevallo, Al., U.S.	B3	78
Montevarchi, Italy	F6	14
Montevideo, Mn., U.S.	F3	100
Montevideo, Ur.	C5	56
Monte Vista, Co., U.S.	D4	83
Montezuma, Ga., U.S.	D2	87
Montezuma, Ia., U.S.	C5	92
Montezuma, Ks., U.S.	E3	93
Montezuma, co., Co., U.S.	D2	83
Montezuma Castle National Monument, Az., U.S.	C4	80
Montezuma Peak, mtn., Az., U.S.	D3	80
Montgomery, Al., U.S.	C3	78
Montgomery, Il., U.S.	B5	90
Montgomery, La., U.S.	C3	95
Montgomery, Mn., U.S.	F5	100
Montgomery, N.Y., U.S.	D6	109
Montgomery, Oh., U.S.	o13	112
Montgomery, Pa., U.S.	D8	115
Montgomery, W.V., U.S.	C3	125
Montgomery, co., Al., U.S.	C3	78
Montgomery, co., Ar., U.S.	C2	81
Montgomery, co., Ga., U.S.	D4	87
Montgomery, co., Il., U.S.	D4	90
Montgomery, co., In., U.S.	D4	91
Montgomery, co., Ia., U.S.	C2	92
Montgomery, co., Ks., U.S.	E8	93
Montgomery, co., Ky., U.S.	B6	94
Montgomery, co., Md., U.S.	B3	97
Montgomery, co., Ms., U.S.	B4	101
Montgomery, co., Mo., U.S.	C6	102
Montgomery, co., N.Y., U.S.	C6	109
Montgomery, co., N.C., U.S.	B3	110
Montgomery, co., Oh., U.S.	C1	112
Montgomery, co., Pa., U.S.	F11	115
Montgomery, co., Tn., U.S.	A4	119
Montgomery, co., Tx., U.S.	D5	120
Montgomery, co., Va., U.S.	C2	123
Montgomery City, Mo., U.S.	C6	102
Monthey, Switz.	F13	10
Monticello, Fl., U.S.	B3	86
Monticello, Ga., U.S.	C3	87
Monticello, Il., U.S.	C5	90
Monticello, In., U.S.	C4	91
Monticello, Ia., U.S.	B6	92
Monticello, Ky., U.S.	D5	94
Monticello, Mn., U.S.	E5	100
Monticello, Ms., U.S.	D3	101
Monticello, N.Y., U.S.	D6	109
Monticello, Ut., U.S.	F6	121
Monticello, Wi., U.S.	F4	126
Montichiari, Italy	D5	14
Montignac, Fr.	G8	10
Montijo, Port.	G3	12
Montijo, Spain	G5	12
Montilla, Spain	H7	12
Montivilliers, Fr.	C7	10
Mont-Joli, Que., Can.	A9	74
Mont-Laurier, Que., Can.	C2	74
Mont-Louis, Fr.	J9	10
Montluçon, Fr.	F9	10
Montmagny, Que., Can.	C7	74
Montmorenci, S.C., U.S.	D4	117
Montmorency, co., Mi., U.S.	C6	99
Montmorillon, Fr.	F7	10
Montmort, Fr.	D10	10
Montoro, Spain	G7	12
Montour, co., Pa., U.S.	D8	115
Montour Falls, N.Y., U.S.	C4	109
Montoursville, Pa., U.S.	D8	115
Montpelier, Id., U.S.	G7	89
Montpelier, In., U.S.	C7	91
Montpelier, Vt., U.S.	C3	122
Montpellier, Fr.	I10	10
Montréal, Que., Can.	D4	74
Montreal, Wi., U.S.	B3	126
Montréal, Île de, i., Que., Can.	q19	74
Montréal-Est, l., Sask., Can.	C3	75
Montréal-Nord, Que., Can.	p19	74
Montreat, N.C., U.S.	f10	110
Montreuil-Bellay, Fr.	E6	10
Montreux, Switz.	F13	10
Mont-Rolland, Que., Can.	D3	74
Montrose, B.C., Can.	E9	69
Montrose, Scot., U.K.	E10	7
Montrose, Al., U.S.	E2	78
Montrose, Co., U.S.	C3	83
Montrose, Ia., U.S.	D6	92
Montrose, Mi., U.S.	E7	99
Montrose, Pa., U.S.	C10	115
Montrose, Va., U.S.	m18	123
Montrose, co., Co., U.S.	C2	83
Mont-Royal, Que., Can.	p19	74
Montserrat, dep., N.A.	F16	64
Mont-Tremblant, Parc Provincial du, Que., Can.	C3	74
Montvale, N.J., U.S.	A4	107
Montville, Ct., U.S.	D7	84
Monument, Co., U.S.	B6	83
Monument Beach, Ma., U.S.	C6	98
Monument Peak, mtn., Co., U.S.	B3	83
Monument Peak, mtn., Id., U.S.	G4	89
Monument Valley, val., Az., U.S.	A5	80
Monywa, Burma	C3	34
Monza, Italy	D4	14
Monzón, Spain	D12	12
Moodus, Ct., U.S.	D6	84
Moodus Reservoir, res., Ct., U.S.	C6	84
Moody, Tx., U.S.	D4	120
Moody, co., S.D., U.S.	C9	118
Moon Lake, l., Ms., U.S.	A3	101
Moora, Austl.	F3	50
Moorcroft, Wy., U.S.	B8	127
Moore, Ok., U.S.	B4	113
Moore, co., N.C., U.S.	B3	110
Moore, co., Tn., U.S.	B5	119
Moore, co., Tx., U.S.	B2	120
Moore Dam, U.S.	B3	106
Moore Haven, Fl., U.S.	F5	86
Mooreland, Ok., U.S.	A2	113
Moore Reservoir, res., U.S.	B3	106
Moores Creek National Military Park, N.C., U.S.	C4	110
Moores Hill, In., U.S.	F7	91
Moorestown, N.J., U.S.	D3	107
Mooresville, In., U.S.	E5	91
Mooresville, N.C., U.S.	B2	110
Moorhead, Mn., U.S.	D2	100
Moorhead, Ms., U.S.	B3	101
Mooringsport, La., U.S.	B2	95
Moose, stm., N.H., U.S.	B4	106
Moose, stm., N.Y., U.S.	B5	109
Moose, stm., Wi., U.S.	B5	122
Moosehead Lake, l., Me., U.S.	C3	96
Moose Jaw, stm., Sask., Can.	G3	75
Moose Lake, Man., Can.	C1	70
Moose Lake, Mn., U.S.	D6	100
Moose Lake, l., Wi., U.S.	B2	126
Mooseleuk Stream, stm., Me., U.S.	B4	96
Mooselookmeguntic Lake, l., Me., U.S.	D2	96
Moose Mountain Creek, stm., Sask., Can.	H4	75
Moose Mountain Provincial Park, Sask., Can.	H4	75
Moosic, Pa., U.S.	m18	115
Moosup, Ct., U.S.	C8	84
Moosup, stm., U.S.	C1	116
Mopang Lake, l., Me., U.S.	D5	96
Mopti, Mali	F5	42
Moquegua, Peru	G4	54
Mora, Port.	G3	12
Mora, Spain	F8	12
Mora, Swe.	F10	6
Mora, Mn., U.S.	E5	100
Mora, N.M., U.S.	B4	108
Mora, co., N.M., U.S.	A5	108
Mora, stm., N.M., U.S.	B5	108
Morādābād, India	F8	38
Morada Nova de Minas, Braz.	E6	57
Morafenobe, Madag.	E8	44
Moraleda, Canal, strt., Chile	E2	56
Morant Cays, is., Jam.	F9	64
Mor'arovskij Zaton, Russia	F10	24
Moratuwa, Sri L.	I5	37
Morava, hist. reg., Czech.	F17	8
Morava (March), stm., Eur.	G16	8
Moravia, Ia., U.S.	D5	92
Moravia see Morava, hist. reg., Czech.	F17	8
Morawhanna, Guy.	C13	58
Moray Firth, est., Scot., U.K.	D9	7
Morden, Man., Can.	E2	70
More, Ben, mtn., Scot., U.K.	E8	7
More Assynt, Ben, mtn., Scot., U.K.	C8	7
Moreau, stm., S.D., U.S.	B3	118
Moreauville, La., U.S.	C4	95
Morecambe, Eng., U.K.	G10	7
Moree, Austl.	E9	50
Morehead, Ky., U.S.	B6	94
Morehead City, N.C., U.S.	C6	110
Morehouse, Mo., U.S.	E8	102
Morehouse, co., La., U.S.	B4	95
Morelia, Mex.	H9	62
Morella, Spain	E11	12
Morena, India	G8	38
Morenci, Az., U.S.	D6	80
Morenci, Mi., U.S.	G6	99
Moresby Island, i., B.C., Can.	C2	69
Moreuil, Fr.	C9	10
Morey, Lake, l., Vt., U.S.	D4	122
Morey Peak, mtn., Nv., U.S.	E5	105
Morgan, Mn., U.S.	F4	100
Morgan, Ut., U.S.	B4	121
Morgan, co., Al., U.S.	A3	78
Morgan, co., Co., U.S.	A7	83
Morgan, co., Ga., U.S.	C3	87
Morgan, co., Il., U.S.	D3	90
Morgan, co., In., U.S.	F5	91
Morgan, co., Ky., U.S.	C6	94
Morgan, co., Mo., U.S.	C5	102
Morgan, co., Oh., U.S.	C4	112
Morgan, co., Tn., U.S.	C9	119
Morgan, co., Ut., U.S.	B4	121
Morgan, co., W.V., U.S.	B6	125
Morgan City, La., U.S.	E4	95
Morganfield, Ky., U.S.	C2	94
Morgan Hill, Ca., U.S.	D3	82
Morgan Island, i., S.C., U.S.	G6	117
Morgan Point, c., Ct., U.S.	E4	84
Morganton, N.C., U.S.	B1	110
Morgantown, Ky., U.S.	C3	94
Morgantown, Ms., U.S.	D2	101
Morgantown, W.V., U.S.	B5	125
Morganza, La., U.S.	D4	95
Mori, Japan	q18	30a
Moriah, Mount, mtn., Nv., U.S.	D7	105
Moriarty, N.M., U.S.	C3	108
Morinville, Alta., Can.	C4	68
Morioka, Japan	C14	30
Morkoka, stm., Russia	D16	24
Morlaix, Fr.	D3	10
Morley, Mo., U.S.	D8	102
Mormon Peak, mtn., Nv., U.S.	G7	105
Morning Sun, Ia., U.S.	C6	92
Mornington Island, i., Austl.	C7	50
Morobe, Pap. N. Gui.	m16	50a
Morocco, In., U.S.	C3	91
Morocco, ctry., Afr.	B4	42
Morogoro, Tan.	C7	44
Moro Gulf, b., Phil.	D7	32
Morombe, Madag.	F8	44
Morón, Cuba	C8	64
Morondava, Madag.	F8	44
Morón de la Frontera, Spain	H6	12
Moroni, Com.	D8	44
Moroni, Ut., U.S.	D4	121
Morošečnoje, Russia	F25	25
Morotai, i., Indon.	E8	32
Morrill, co., Ne., U.S.	C2	104
Morrilton, Ar., U.S.	B3	81
Morrinhos, Braz.	D4	57
Morris, Man., Can.	E3	70
Morris, Al., U.S.	B3	78
Morris, Il., U.S.	B5	90

Name	Map Ref	Page
Morris, Mn., U.S.	E3	100
Morris, Ok., U.S.	B6	113
Morris, co., Ks., U.S.	D7	93
Morris, co., N.J., U.S.	B3	107
Morris, co., Tx., U.S.	C5	120
Morrisburg, Ont., Can.	C9	73
Morris Island, i., S.C., U.S.	F8	117
Morrison, Il., U.S.	B4	90
Morrison, Ok., U.S.	A4	113
Morrison, co., Mn., U.S.	D4	100
Morrison City, Tn., U.S.	C11	119
Morrisonville, Il., U.S.	D4	90
Morrisonville, N.Y., U.S.	f11	109
Morris Plains, N.J., U.S.	B4	107
Morristown, In., U.S.	E6	91
Morristown, Mn., U.S.	F5	100
Morristown, N.J., U.S.	B4	107
Morristown, Tn., U.S.	C10	119
Morristown National Historical Park, N.J., U.S.	B3	107
Morrisville, N.Y., U.S.	C5	109
Morrisville, Pa., U.S.	F12	115
Morrisville, Vt., U.S.	B3	122
Morro, Ec.	I2	58
Morro, Punta c., Chile	B2	56
Morro Bay, Ca., U.S.	E3	82
Morro do Chapéu, Braz.	F10	54
Morrow, Ga., U.S.	C2	87
Morrow, Oh., U.S.	C1	112
Morrow, co., Oh., U.S.	B3	112
Morrow, co., Or., U.S.	B7	114
Moršansk, Russia	H24	18
Morse, La., U.S.	D3	95
Morse Reservoir, res., In., U.S.	D5	91
Morses Creek, stm., N.J., U.S.	k8	107
Mortagne, Fr.	D7	10
Mortagne-sur-Sèvre, Fr.	E6	10
Mortara, Italy	D3	14
Mortes, Rio das, stm., Braz.	G8	54
Morton, Il., U.S.	C4	90
Morton, Ms., U.S.	C4	101
Morton, Tx., U.S.	C1	120
Morton, Wa., U.S.	C3	124
Morton, co., Ks., U.S.	E2	93
Morton, co., N.D., U.S.	C4	111
Morton Grove, Il., U.S.	h9	90
Morton Pass, Wy., U.S.	E7	127
Mortons Gap, Ky., U.S.	C2	94
Morven, mtn., Scot., U.K.	C9	7
Morvi, India	I4	38
Morwell, Austl.	G9	50
Mosbach, Ger.	F9	8
Moscos Islands, is., Burma	G4	34
Moscow, Id., U.S.	C2	89
Moscow, Pa., U.S.	m18	115
Moscow see Moskva, Russia	F20	18
Moscow Mills, Mo., U.S.	C7	102
Mosel (Moselle), stm., Eur.	F6	8
Moselle, Ms., U.S.	D4	101
Moselle (Mosel), stm., Eur.	F6	8
Moses Coulee, val., Wa., U.S.	B6	124
Moses Lake, Wa., U.S.	B6	124
Moses Lake, l., Wa., U.S.	B6	124
Mosheim, Tn., U.S.	C11	119
Moshi, Tan.	B7	44
Mosinee, Wi., U.S.	D4	126
Mosjøen, Nor.	D9	6
Moskva (Moscow), Russia	F20	18
Mosquera, Col.	F3	58
Mosquito Creek Lake, res., Oh., U.S.	A5	112
Mosquito Lagoon, b., Fl., U.S.	D6	86
Mosquitos, Golfo de los, b., Pan.	J7	64
Moss, Nor.	G8	6
Mossaka, Congo	B3	44
Moss Bluff, La., U.S.	D2	95
Mosselbaai, S. Afr.	H4	44
Mossendjo, Congo	B2	44
Mossoró, Braz.	E11	54
Moss Point, Ms., U.S.	E5	101
Most, Czech.	A6	42
Mostaganem, Alg.	A6	42
Mostar, Bos.	F12	14
Mostardas, Braz.	C6	56
Møsting, Kap, c., Grnld.	D24	66
Moswansicut Pond, l., R.I., U.S.	C3	116
Mota del Marqués, Spain	D6	12
Motala, Swe.	G10	6
Motherwell, Scot., U.K.	F8	7
Motīhāri, India	G11	38
Motilla del Palancar, Spain	F10	12
Motley, co., Tx., U.S.	B2	120
Motril, Spain	I8	12
Mott, N.D., U.S.	C3	111
Motueka, N.Z.	D4	52
Motul de Felipe Carrillo Puerto, Mex.	G15	62
Motygino, Russia	F12	24
Mouchoir Passage, strt., N.A.	D12	64
Moudjéria, Maur.	B2	44
Mouila, Gabon	G8	50
Moulamein Creek, stm., Austl.	F10	10
Moulins, Fr.	F10	10
Moulmeingyun, Burma	F3	34
Moulouya, Oued, stm., Mor.	B5	42
Moulton, Al., U.S.	A2	78
Moulton, Ia., U.S.	D5	92
Moultrie, Ga., U.S.	E3	87
Moultrie, co., Il., U.S.	D5	90
Moultrie, Lake, res., S.C., U.S.	E7	117
Mound, Mn., U.S.	n11	100
Mound Bayou, Ms., U.S.	B3	101
Mound City, Il., U.S.	F4	90
Mound City, Ks., U.S.	D9	93
Mound City, Mo., U.S.	A2	102
Mound City Group National Monument, Oh., U.S.	C2	112
Moundcu, Chad	G9	42
Moundridge, Ks., U.S.	D6	93
Mounds, Il., U.S.	F4	90
Mounds, Ok., U.S.	B5	113
Mounds View, Mn., U.S.	m12	100
Moundsville, W.V., U.S.	B4	125
Moundville, Al., U.S.	C2	78
Mountainair, N.M., U.S.	C3	108
Mountainaire, Az., U.S.	B4	80
Mountain Brook, Al., U.S.	g7	78
Mountain City, Ga., U.S.	B3	87
Mountain City, Nv., U.S.	B6	105
Mountain City, Tn., U.S.	C12	119
Mountain Fork, stm., U.S.	C7	113
Mountain Grove, Mo., U.S.	D5	102
Mountain Home, Ar., U.S.	A3	81
Mountain Home, Id., U.S.	F3	89
Mountain Home Air Force Base, mil., Id., U.S.	F3	89
Mountain Iron, Mn., U.S.	C6	100
Mountain Lake, Mn., U.S.	G4	100
Mountain Lake Park, Md., U.S.	m12	97
Mountain Nile (Baḥr al-Jabal), stm., Sudan	G12	42
Mountain Pine, Ar., U.S.	C2	81
Mountainside, N.J., U.S.	B4	107
Mountain View, Ar., U.S.	B3	81
Mountain View, Ca., U.S.	k8	82
Mountain View, Mo., U.S.	D6	102
Mountain View, N.M., U.S.	C3	108
Mountain View, Ok., U.S.	B3	113
Mountain View, Wy., U.S.	E2	127
Mountain Village, Ak., U.S.	C7	79
Mount Airy, Md., U.S.	B3	97
Mount Airy, N.C., U.S.	A2	110
Mount Albert, Ont., Can.	C5	73
Mount Angel, Or., U.S.	B4	114
Mount Arlington, N.J., U.S.	B3	107
Mount Ayr, Ia., U.S.	D3	92
Mount Carmel, Il., U.S.	E6	90
Mount Carmel, Oh., U.S.	o13	112
Mount Carmel, Pa., U.S.	E9	115
Mount Carmel [-Mitchell's Brook-Saint Catherine's], Newf., Can.	E5	72
Mount Carroll, Il., U.S.	A4	90
Mount Clare, W.V., U.S.	B4	125
Mount Clemens, Mi., U.S.	F8	99
Mount Desert Island, i., Me., U.S.	D4	96
Mount Dora, Fl., U.S.	D5	86
Mount Forest, Ont., Can.	D4	73
Mount Gambier, Austl.	G8	50
Mount Gay, W.V., U.S.	D2	125
Mount Gilead, N.C., U.S.	B3	110
Mount Gilead, Oh., U.S.	B3	112
Mount Healthy, Oh., U.S.	o12	112
Mount Holly, N.J., U.S.	D3	107
Mount Holly, N.C., U.S.	B1	110
Mount Holly Springs, Pa., U.S.	F7	115
Mount Hope, Austl.	F7	50
Mount Hope, Ks., U.S.	E6	93
Mount Hope, W.V., U.S.	D3	125
Mount Hope, stm., Ct., U.S.	B7	84
Mount Hope Bay, b., U.S.	D6	116
Mount Horeb, Wi., U.S.	E4	126
Mount Ida, Ar., U.S.	C2	81
Mount Isa, Austl.	D7	50
Mount Jackson, Va., U.S.	B4	123
Mount Jewett, Pa., U.S.	C4	115
Mount Joy, Pa., U.S.	F9	115
Mount Juliet, Tn., U.S.	A5	119
Mount Kisco, N.Y., U.S.	D7	109
Mount Lebanon, Pa., U.S.	F1	115
Mount Magnet, Austl.	E3	50
Mount Morris, Il., U.S.	A4	90
Mount Morris, Mi., U.S.	E7	99
Mount Morris, N.Y., U.S.	C3	109
Mount Olive, Al., U.S.	B3	78
Mount Olive, Il., U.S.	D4	90
Mount Olive, Ms., U.S.	D4	101
Mount Olive, N.C., U.S.	B4	110
Mount Olive, Tn., U.S.	n14	119
Mount Orab, Oh., U.S.	C2	112
Mount Pearl, Newf., Can.	E5	72
Mount Penn, Pa., U.S.	F10	115
Mount Pleasant, Ia., U.S.	D6	92
Mount Pleasant, Mi., U.S.	E6	99
Mount Pleasant, N.C., U.S.	B2	110
Mount Pleasant, S.C., U.S.	F8	117
Mount Pleasant, Tn., U.S.	B4	119
Mount Pleasant, Tx., U.S.	C5	120
Mount Pleasant, Ut., U.S.	D4	121
Mount Pocono, Pa., U.S.	D11	115
Mount Prospect, Il., U.S.	A6	90
Mount Pulaski, Il., U.S.	C4	90
Mount Rainier, Md., U.S.	f9	97
Mount Rainier National Park, Wa., U.S.	C4	124
Mount Revelstoke National Park, B.C., Can.	D8	69
Mount Rogers National Recreation Area, Va., U.S.	D1	123
Mount Rushmore National Memorial, hist., S.D., U.S.	D2	118
Mount Savage, Md., U.S.	k13	97
Mount Shasta, Ca., U.S.	B2	82
Mount Sterling, Il., U.S.	D3	90
Mount Sterling, Ky., U.S.	B6	94
Mount Sterling, Oh., U.S.	C2	112
Mount Uniacke, N.S., Can.	E6	71
Mount Union, Pa., U.S.	F6	115
Mount Vernon, Al., U.S.	D1	78
Mount Vernon, Ga., U.S.	D4	87
Mount Vernon, Il., U.S.	E5	90
Mount Vernon, In., U.S.	I2	91
Mount Vernon, Ia., U.S.	C6	92
Mount Vernon, Ky., U.S.	C5	94
Mount Vernon, Mo., U.S.	D4	102
Mount Vernon, N.Y., U.S.	h13	109
Mount Vernon, Oh., U.S.	B3	112
Mount Vernon, Tx., U.S.	C5	120
Mount Vernon, Wa., U.S.	A3	124
Mount View, R.I., U.S.	D4	116
Mount Washington, Ky., U.S.	B4	94
Mount Wolf, Pa., U.S.	F8	115
Mount Zion, Il., U.S.	D5	90
Moura, Braz.	D6	54
Moura, Port.	G4	12
Mourne Mountains, mts., N. Ire., U.K.	G6	7
Moussoro, Chad	F9	42
Moutong, Indon.	E7	32
Moville, Ia., U.S.	B1	92
Moweaqua, Il., U.S.	D4	90
Mower, co., Mn., U.S.	G6	100
Moxee City, Wa., U.S.	C5	124
Moxos, Llanos de, pl., Bol.	G6	54
Moyahua, Mex.	G8	62
Moyale, Kenya	H2	46
Moyen Atlas, mts., Mor.	B5	42
Moyeuvre-Grande, Fr.	C13	10
Moyock, N.C., U.S.	A6	110
Moyu, China	B8	38
Možajsk, Russia	F19	18
Mozambique, ctry., Afr.	E6	44
Mozambique Channel, strt., Afr.	E8	44
Mozyr', Bela.	G3	22
Mpanda, Tan.	C6	44
Mpika, Tan.	D6	44
Mrkonjić Grad, Bos.	E12	14
Msaken, Tun.	N5	14
Mtwara, Tan.	D8	44
Muang Khammouan, Laos	F8	34
Muang Pakxan, Laos	E7	34
Muar, Malay.	M7	34
Muaratewe, Indon.	F5	32
Muāri, Rās, c., Pak.	H2	38
Mücheln, Ger.	D11	8
Muchinga Mountains, mts., Zam.	D6	44
Muckleshoot Indian Reservation, Wa., U.S.	f11	124
Mud, stm., Ky., U.S.	C3	94
Mud, stm., Mn., U.S.	B3	100
Mud, stm., W.V., U.S.	C2	125
Mudanjiang, China	C12	26
Mud Creek, stm., Ok., U.S.	C4	113
Muddy Boggy Creek, stm., Ok., U.S.	C6	113
Muddy Creek, stm., Ut., U.S.	E4	121
Muddy Creek, stm., Wy., U.S.	D6	127
Muddy Creek, stm., Wy., U.S.	E5	127
Muddy Creek, stm., Wy., U.S.	C4	127
Muddy Creek, stm., Wy., U.S.	E2	127
Muddy Mountains, mts., Nv., U.S.	G7	105
Muddy Peak, mtn., Nv., U.S.	G7	105
Mud Lake, l., Me., U.S.	A4	96
Mud Lake, l., Nv., U.S.	F4	105
Mudon, Burma	F4	34
Muenster, Tx., U.S.	C4	120
Mufulira, Zam.	D5	44
Mu Gia, Deo (Mu Gia Pass), Asia	E7	34
Muğla, Tur.	H13	4
Mühldorf, Ger.	G12	8
Muhlenberg, co., Ky., U.S.	C2	94
Mühlhausen, Ger.	D10	8
Mühlviertel, reg., Aus.	G14	8
Muhola, Fin.	E15	6
Muirkirk, Md., U.S.	B4	97
Muiron Islands, is., Austl.	D2	50
Muir Woods National Monument, Ca., U.S.	h7	82
Mukden see Shenyang, China	C11	26
Mukilteo, Wa., U.S.	B3	124
Mukwonago, Wi., U.S.	F5	126
Mula, Spain	G10	12
Mulanje, Mwi.	E7	44
Mulberry, Ar., U.S.	B1	81
Mulberry, Fl., U.S.	E4	86
Mulberry, In., U.S.	D4	91
Mulberry, N.C., U.S.	A1	110
Mulberry, stm., Ar., U.S.	B1	81
Mulberry Fork, stm., Al., U.S.	B3	78
Muldraugh, Ky., U.S.	C4	94
Muldrow, Ok., U.S.	B7	113
Muleshoe, Tx., U.S.	B1	120
Mulgrave, N.S., Can.	D8	71
Mulhacén, mtn., Spain	H8	12
Mulhouse, Fr.	E14	10
Mull, Island of, i., Scot., U.K.	E6	7
Mullan, Id., U.S.	B3	89
Mullan Pass, Mt., U.S.	D4	103
Mullens, W.V., U.S.	D3	125
Muller, Pegunungan, mts., Indon.	E5	32
Mullet Key, i., Fl., U.S.	p10	86
Mullett Lake, l., Mi., U.S.	C6	99
Mullewa, Austl.	E3	50
Mullica, stm., N.J., U.S.	D3	107
Mullins, S.C., U.S.	C9	117
Multān, Pak.	E4	38
Multnomah, co., Or., U.S.	B4	114
Mulvane, Ks., U.S.	E6	93
Mumbwa, Zam.	D5	44
Mummy Range, mts., Co., U.S.	A5	83
Muna, Pulau, i., Indon.	F7	32
Muncar, Indon.	n17	33a
München (Munich), Ger.	G11	9
Muncie, In., U.S.	D7	91
Muncy, Pa., U.S.	D8	115
Munday, Tx., U.S.	C3	120
Mundelein, Il., U.S.	A5	90
Münden, Ger.	D9	8
Munford, Al., U.S.	B4	78
Munford, Tn., U.S.	B2	119
Munfordville, Ky., U.S.	C4	94
Mungbere, Zaire	H11	42
Munhall, Pa., U.S.	k14	115
Munhango, Ang.	D3	44
Munich see München, Ger.	G11	9
Munising, Mi., U.S.	B4	99
Munster, Ger.	C10	8
Münster, Ger.	D7	8
Munster, In., U.S.	A2	91
Munster, hist. reg., Ire.	I4	7
Munsungan Lake, l., Me., U.S.	B3	96
Munuscong Lake, l., Mi., U.S.	B6	99
Muong Sing, Laos	D6	34
Muqayshiţ, i., U.A.E.	D5	46
Muqdisho, Som.	H4	46
Mur (Mura), stm., Eur.	I15	8
Mura (Mur), stm., Eur.	I16	8
Murat, Fr.	G9	10
Murat, stm., Tur.	H16	4
Murau, Aus.	H14	8
Muravera, Italy	J4	14
Murča, Port.	D4	12
Murchison, stm., Austl.	E3	50
Murcia, Spain	H10	12
Murderkill, stm., De., U.S.	D4	85
Murdo, S.D., U.S.	D5	118
Mureş (Maros), stm., Eur.	C5	16
Muret, Fr.	I8	10
Murfreesboro, Ar., U.S.	C2	81
Murfreesboro, N.C., U.S.	A5	110
Murfreesboro, Tn., U.S.	B5	119
Mūriān, Hāmūn-e, l., Iran	C6	46
Murmansk, Russia	D4	22
Murom, Russia	F25	18
Muroran, Japan	q18	30a
Muros, Spain	C2	12
Muroto, Japan	I7	30
Muroto-zaki, c., Japan	I7	30
Murphy, Mo., U.S.	g13	102
Murphy, N.C., U.S.	f8	110
Murphy Island, i., S.C., U.S.	E9	117
Murphysboro, Il., U.S.	F4	90
Murray, Ia., U.S.	C4	92
Murray, Ky., U.S.	f9	94
Murray, Ut., U.S.	C4	121
Murray, co., Ga., U.S.	B2	87
Murray, co., Mn., U.S.	F3	100
Murray, co., Ok., U.S.	C4	113
Murray, stm., Austl.	F7	50
Murray, Lake, res., Ok., U.S.	C4	113
Murray, Lake, res., S.C., U.S.	C5	117
Murray Head, c., P.E.I., Can.	C7	71
Murraysburg, S. Afr.	H4	44
Murrayville, Ga., U.S.	B3	87
Murrells Inlet, S.C., U.S.	D9	117
Murrells Inlet, b., S.C., U.S.	D10	117
Murten, Switz.	F14	10
Murukta, Russia	D14	24
Murwāra, India	I9	38
Murwillumbah, Austl.	E10	50
Mürzzuschlag, Aus.	H15	8
Muş, Tur.	H16	4
Musayʿīd, Qatar	D5	46
Muscat and Oman see Oman, ctry., Asia	D6	46
Muscatatuck, stm., In., U.S.	G5	91
Muscatine, Ia., U.S.	C6	92
Muscatine, co., Ia., U.S.	C6	92
Muscat see Masqaţ, Oman	D6	46
Mus-Chaja, Gora, mtn., Russia	E22	24
Muscle Shoals, Al., U.S.	A2	78
Musclow, Mount, mtn., B.C., Can.	C4	69
Muscoda, Wi., U.S.	E3	126
Muscogee, co., Ga., U.S.	D2	87
Musconetcong, stm., N.J., U.S.	B4	107
Muscooten Bay, l., Il., U.S.	C3	90
Muse, Fi., U.S.	F1	115
Musgrave, Austl.	B8	50
Musgrave Harbour, Newf., Can.	D5	72
Musgrave Ranges, mts., Austl.	E6	50
Musgravetown, Newf., Can.	D5	72
Muskeg Bay, b., Mn., U.S.	B3	100
Muskeget Island, i., Ma., U.S.	D7	98
Muskego, Wi., U.S.	F5	126
Muskego Lake, l., Wi., U.S.	n11	126
Muskegon, Mi., U.S.	E4	99
Muskegon, co., Mi., U.S.	E4	99
Muskegon, stm., Mi., U.S.	E4	99
Muskegon Heights, Mi., U.S.	E4	99
Muskegon Lake, l., Mi., U.S.	E4	99
Muskingum, co., Oh., U.S.	B4	112
Muskingum, stm., Oh., U.S.	C4	112
Muskogee, Ok., U.S.	B6	113
Muskogee, co., Ok., U.S.	B6	113
Musoma, Tan.	B6	44
Musquacook Lakes, l., Me., U.S.	B3	96
Musquodoboit Harbour, N.S., Can.	E6	71
Musselshell, co., Mt., U.S.	D8	103
Musselshell, stm., Mt., U.S.	D9	103
Mussidan, Fr.	G7	10
Mussuma, Ang.	D4	44
Mustafakemalpaşa, Tur.	I12	16
Mustang, Ok., U.S.	B4	113
Mustinka, stm., Mn., U.S.	E2	100
Mut, Tur.	A3	40
Mutare, Zimb.	E6	44
Mutoraj, Russia	E14	24
Mutsu, Japan	A14	30
Mutsu-wan, b., Japan	A13	30
Mutton Mountains, mts., Or., U.S.	C5	114
Muzaffarābād, Pak.	C5	38
Muzaffarnagar, India	F7	38
Muzaffarpur, India	G11	38
Muzon, Cape, c., Ak., U.S.	n23	79
Muztag, mtn., China	B9	38
Muztag, mtn., China	B12	38
Mvuma, Zimb.	E6	44
Mwanza, Tan.	B6	44
Mweelrea, mtn., Ire.	H3	7
Mweka, Zaire	B4	44
Mwenezi, Zimb.	F6	44
Mweru, Lake, l., Afr.	C5	44
Mwinilunga, Zam.	D4	44
Myakka, stm., Fl., U.S.	E4	86
Myanaung, Burma	E3	34
Myaungmya, Burma	F3	34
Myerstown, Pa., U.S.	F9	115
Myingyan, Burma	D3	34
Myitkyinā, Burma	B4	34
Myllymäki, Fin.	E15	6
Mymensingh, Bngl.	H14	38
Mynämäki, Fin.	F13	6
Myrskylä (Mörskom), Fin.	F15	6
Myrtle Beach, S.C., U.S.	D10	117
Myrtle Beach Air Force Base, mil., S.C., U.S.	D10	117
Myrtle Grove, Fl., U.S.	u14	86
Myrtle Point, Or., U.S.	D2	114
Mysen, Nor.	G8	6
Mysore, India	F4	37
Mys Šmidta, Russia	D30	24
Mystic, Ct., U.S.	D8	84
Mystic Lakes, l., Ma., U.S.	g11	98
My Tho, Viet.	I9	34
Mytišči, Russia	F20	18
Mzimba, Mwi.	D6	44
Mzuzu, Mwi.	D6	44

N

Name	Map Ref	Page
Naalehu, Hi., U.S.	D6	88
Naas, Ire.	H6	7
Nabadwīp, India	I13	38
Naberežnyje Čelny, Russia	F8	22
Nabeul, Tun.	M5	14
Nabī Shuʿayb, Jabal an-, mtn., Yemen	E3	46
Nabnasset, Ma., U.S.	A5	98
Nābulus, Isr. Occ.	C4	40
Nacala-Velha, Moz.	D8	44
Naches, stm., Wa., U.S.	C5	124
Nachingwea, Tan.	D7	44
Nachodka, Russia	I20	24
Nacimiento, Lake, res., Ca., U.S.	E3	82
Naco, Mex.	B5	62
Naco, Az., U.S.	F6	80
Nacogdoches, Tx., U.S.	D5	120
Nacogdoches, co., Tx., U.S.	D5	120
Nadiād, India	I5	38
Nadym, stm., Russia	E8	24
Næstved, Den.	I8	6
Naga, Phil.	r20	32
Nagahama, Japan	G9	30
Nagaland, state, India	H16	38
Nagano, Japan	F11	30
Nagaoka, Japan	E11	30
Nāgappattinam, India	G5	37
Nagasaki, Japan	J2	30
Nāgaur, India	G5	38
Nāgda, India	I6	38
Nāgercoil, India	H4	37
Nago, Japan	y27	31b
Nagornyj, Russia	F18	24
Nagoya, Japan	G9	30
Nāgpur, India	B5	37
Nags Head, N.C., U.S.	B7	110
Nagykanizsa, Hung.	I16	8
Nagykőrös, Hung.	H19	8
Naha, Japan	y27	31b
Nahant, Ma., U.S.	g12	98
Nahariyya, Isr.	C4	40
Nahmakanta Lake, l., Me., U.S.	C3	96
Nahunta, Ga., U.S.	E5	87
Naidong, China	F14	38
Naʿīn, Iran	g9	72
Naʿīn, Iran	B5	46
Nairn, Scot., U.K.	D9	7
Nairobi, Kenya	B7	44
Najafābād, Iran	B5	46
Nájera, Spain	C9	12
Najin, N. Kor.	C13	26
Nakaminato, Japan	F13	30
Nakatsu, Japan	I4	30
Nakatsugawa, Japan	G10	30
Nakhon Pathom, Thai.	H6	34
Nakhon Phanom, Thai.	F8	34
Nakhon Ratchasima, Thai.	G7	34
Nakhon Sawan, Thai.	G6	34
Nakhon Si Thammarat, Thai.	J5	34
Nakina, Ont., Can.	o18	73
Naknek, Ak., U.S.	D8	79
Naknek Lake, l., Ak., U.S.	D8	79
Nakskov, Den.	I8	6
Nakuru, Kenya	B7	44
Nakusp, B.C., Can.	D9	69
Nalchik see Nal'čik, Russia	I6	22
Nal'čik, Russia	I6	22
Nalgonda, India	D5	37
Nālūt, Libya	B8	42
Namak, Daryācheh-ye, l., Iran	K8	22
Namangan, Uzb.	I12	22
Namanock Island, i., N.J., U.S.	A3	107
Namapa, Moz.	D7	44
Namatanai, Pap. N. Gui.	k17	50a
Nambour, Austl.	E10	50
Namcha Barwa see Namjagbarwa Feng, mtn., China	F16	38
Nam Co, l., China	E14	38
Nam Dinh, Viet.	D9	34
Namekagon, stm., Wi., U.S.	B2	126
Namekagon Lake, l., Wi., U.S.	B2	126
Namhkam, Burma	C4	34
Namib Desert, des., Nmb.	F2	44
Namibe, Ang.	E2	44
Namibia, ctry., Afr.	F3	44
Namjagbarwa Feng, mtn., China	F16	38
Namlea, Indon.	F8	32
Nampa, Id., U.S.	F2	89
Namp'o, N. Kor.	D12	26
Nampula, Moz.	E7	44
Namsos, Nor.	D8	6
Namur, Bel.	E4	8
Nanaimo, B.C., Can.	E5	69
Nanakuli, Hi., U.S.	B3	88
Nanao, Japan	E9	30
Nance, co., Ne., U.S.	C7	104
Nanchang, China	G4	28
Nanchong, China	E8	28
Nancy, Fr.	D13	10
Nanda Devi, mtn., India	E8	38
Nānded, India	C4	37
Nandurbār, India	B3	37
Nandyāl, India	E5	37
Nānga Parbat, mtn., Pak.	C6	38
Nangqian (Xiangda), China	D17	38
Nanjing (Nanking), China	C7	28
Nanking see Nanjing, China	C7	28
Nankoku, Japan	I6	30
Nankou, China	C10	26
Nan Ling, mts., China	F9	28
Nanning, China	C10	34
Nanping, China	I7	28
Nansei-shotō (Ryukyu Islands), is., Japan	k12	31b
Nansemond, stm., Va., U.S.	k14	123
Nantes, Fr.	E5	10
Nanticoke, Ont., Can.	E4	73
Nanticoke, Pa., U.S.	D10	115
Nanticoke, stm., U.S.	D6	97
Nanton, Alta., Can.	D4	68
Nantong, China	C9	28

Name	Map Ref	Page
Nant'ou, Tai.	L9	28
Nantua, Fr.	F12	10
Nantucket, Ma., U.S.	D7	98
Nantucket, co., Ma., U.S.	D7	98
Nantucket Island, i., Ma., U.S.	D7	98
Nantucket Sound, strt., Ma., U.S.	C7	98
Nantuxent Point, c., N.J., U.S.	E2	107
Nanty Glo, Pa., U.S.	F4	115
Nanuet, N.Y., U.S.	g12	109
Nanuque, Braz.	D8	57
Nanxiang, China	D10	28
Nanxiong, China	J3	28
Nanyang, China	B1	28
Naoetsu, Japan	E11	30
Naoma, W.V., U.S.	n13	125
Naomi Peak, mtn., Ut., U.S.	B4	121
Náousa, Grc.	I6	16
Napa, Ca., U.S.	C2	82
Napa, co., Ca., U.S.	C2	82
Napanee, Ont., Can.	C8	73
Napatree Point, c., R.I., U.S.	G1	116
Napavine, Wa., U.S.	C3	124
Naperville, Il., U.S.	B5	90
Napier, N.Z.	C6	52
Napierville, Que., Can.	D4	74
Naples, Fl., U.S.	F5	86
Naples, Tx., U.S.	C5	120
Naples, Ut., U.S.	C6	121
Naples see Napoli, Italy	I9	14
Napo, stm., S.A.	I6	58
Napoleon, N.D., U.S.	C6	111
Napoleon, Oh., U.S.	A1	112
Napoleonville, La., U.S.	E4	95
Napoli (Naples), Italy	I9	14
Nappanee, In., U.S.	B5	91
Nara, Japan	H8	30
Nara, Mali	E4	42
Naracoorte, Austl.	G8	50
Naramata, B.C., Can.	E8	69
Naranja, Fl., U.S.	G6	86
Narasapur, India	D6	37
Narasaraopet, India	D6	37
Narathiwat, Thai.	K6	34
Nārāyanganj, Bngl.	I14	38
Narberth, Pa., U.S.	p20	115
Narbonne, Fr.	I9	10
Nardò, Italy	I13	14
Narew, stm., Eur.	C21	8
Nārīn Ghar, Afg.	B3	38
Narita, Japan	G13	30
Narmada, stm., India	J5	38
Nārnaul, India	F7	38
Narni, Italy	G7	14
Naro-Fominsk, Russia	F19	18
Narragansett, R.I., U.S.	F4	116
Narragansett Bay, b., R.I., U.S.	E5	116
Narraguagus, stm., Me., U.S.	D5	96
Narrows, Va., U.S.	C2	123
Narsimhapur, India	I8	38
Narssaq, Grnld.	D23	66
Naruto, Japan	H7	30
Narva, Est.	B11	18
Narvik, Nor.	B11	6
Naselle, Wa., U.S.	C2	124
Nash, Tx., U.S.	C5	120
Nash, co., N.C., U.S.	A4	110
Nashawena Island, i., Ma., U.S.	D6	98
Nashua, Ia., U.S.	B5	92
Nashua, N.H., U.S.	E4	106
Nashua, stm., U.S.	E3	106
Nashville, Ar., U.S.	D2	81
Nashville, Ga., U.S.	E3	87
Nashville, Il., U.S.	E4	90
Nashville, In., U.S.	F5	91
Nashville, Mi., U.S.	F5	99
Nashville, N.C., U.S.	B5	110
Nashville, Tn., U.S.	A5	119
Nashwauk, Mn., U.S.	C5	100
Nāsik, India	C2	37
Nāsir, Sudan	G12	42
Naskaupi, stm., Newf., Can.	g9	72
Nassau, Bah.	B9	64
Nassau, co., Fl., U.S.	B5	86
Nassau, co., N.Y., U.S.	E7	109
Nassau, stm., Fl., U.S.	k8	86
Nassau Sound, b., Fl., U.S.	B5	86
Nasser, Lake, res., Afr.	D12	42
Nässjö, Swe.	H10	6
Nasukoin Mountain, mtn., Mt., U.S.	B2	103
Natal, Braz.	E11	54
Natalbany, La., U.S.	D5	95
Natalia, Tx., U.S.	E3	120
Natashquan, stm., Can.	h9	72
Natchaug, stm., Ct., U.S.	B7	84
Natchez, Ms., U.S.	D2	101
Natchitoches, La., U.S.	C2	95
Natchitoches, co., La., U.S.	C2	95
Nāthdwāra, India	H5	38
Natick, Ma., U.S.	B5	98
National City, Ca., U.S.	F5	82
Natron, Lake, l., Afr.	B7	44
Natrona, co., Wy., U.S.	D5	127
Natrona Heights, Pa., U.S.	E2	115
Nattaung, mtn., Burma	E4	34
Natuna Besar, i., Indon.	M10	34
Natuna Besar, Kepulauan, is., Indon.	M10	34
Natuna Selatan, Kepulauan, is., Indon.	M10	34
Natural Bridge, Ut., U.S.	F3	121
Natural Bridge, Va., U.S.	C3	123
Natural Bridges National Monument, Ut., U.S.	F6	121
Naturaliste, Cape, c., Austl.	F3	50
Nauen, Ger.	C12	8
Naugatuck, Ct., U.S.	D3	84
Naugatuck, stm., Ct., U.S.	D3	84
Naumburg, Ger.	D11	8
Naushon Island, i., Ma., U.S.	D6	98
Nautilus Park, Ct., U.S.	D7	84
Nauvoo, Il., U.S.	C2	90
Nava del Rey, Spain	D6	12
Navahermosa, Spain	F7	12
Navajo, co., Az., U.S.	B5	80
Navajo Dam, N.M., U.S.	A2	108
Navajo Indian Reservation, U.S.	A4	80
Navajo Mountain, mtn., Ut., U.S.	F5	121
Navajo National Monument, Az., U.S.	A5	80
Navajo Reservoir, res., U.S.	A2	108
Navalcarnero, Spain	E7	12
Navalmoral de la Mata, Spain	F6	12
Navalvillar de Pela, Spain	F6	12
Navan, Ont., Can.	B9	73
Navan, Ire.	H6	7
Navarin, Mys, c., Russia	E29	24
Navarino, Isla, i., Chile	H3	56
Navarre, Oh., U.S.	B4	112
Navarro, co., Tx., U.S.	D4	120
Navasota, Tx., U.S.	D4	120
Navassa Island, i., N.A.	E10	64
Navoi, Uzb.	I11	22
Navojoa, Mex.	D5	62
Navolato, Mex.	E6	62
Navsāri, India	B2	37
Nawābganj, Bngl.	H13	38
Nawābganj, India	G9	38
Nawābshāh, Pak.	G3	38
Nāwah, Afg.	D2	38
Nawalgarh, India	G6	38
Nawiliwili Bay, b., Hi., U.S.	B2	88
Nayak, Afg.	C2	38
Naylor, Mo., U.S.	E7	102
Nayoro, Japan	o20	30a
Nazaré, Braz.	B9	57
Nazaré, Port.	F2	12
Nazareth, Pa., U.S.	E11	115
Nazca, Peru	F4	54
Naze, Japan	w29	31b
Nazilli, Tur.	L12	16
Nazko, stm., B.C., Can.	C6	69
Ndélé, Cen. Afr. Rep.	G10	42
N'Djamena (Fort-Lamy), Chad	F9	42
Ndola, Zam.	D5	44
Neagh, Lough, l., N. Ire., U.K.	G6	7
Neah Bay, Wa., U.S.	A1	124
Néa Páfos (Paphos), Cyp.	B3	40
Neápolis, Grc.	M7	16
Near Islands, is., Ak., U.S.	E2	79
Nebo, Mount, mtn., Ut., U.S.	D4	121
Nebraska, state, U.S.	C6	104
Nebraska City, Ne., U.S.	D10	104
Nechako, stm., B.C., Can.	C5	69
Neches, stm., Tx., U.S.	D5	120
Nechí, Col.	C5	58
Neckar, stm., Ger.	F9	8
Necker Island, i., Hi., U.S.	m15	88
Necochea, Arg.	D5	56
Nederland, Co., U.S.	B5	83
Nederland, Tx., U.S.	E6	120
Nedrow, N.Y., U.S.	C4	109
Needham, Ma., U.S.	g11	98
Needle Mountain, mtn., Wy., U.S.	B3	127
Needles, Ca., U.S.	E6	82
Needville, Tx., U.S.	r14	120
Neenah, Wi., U.S.	D5	126
Neepawa, Man., Can.	D2	70
Neffs, Oh., U.S.	B5	112
Neffsville, Pa., U.S.	F9	115
Negage, Ang.	C3	44
Negaunee, Mi., U.S.	B3	99
Negele, Eth.	G2	46
Negev Desert see Hanegev, reg., Isr.	D4	40
Negley, Oh., U.S.	B5	112
Negombo, Sri L.	I5	37
Negra, Punta, c., Peru	E2	54
Negro, stm., Arg.	E4	56
Negro, stm., S.A.	H12	58
Negros, i., Phil.	C7	32
Neguac, N.B., Can.	B4	71
Nehalem, stm., Or., U.S.	A3	114
Nehbandān, Iran	B7	46
Neiba, Bahía de, b., Dom. Rep.	E12	64
Neijiang, China	F8	26
Neill Point, c., Wa., U.S.	f11	124
Neillsville, Wi., U.S.	D3	126
Nei Monggol Zizhiqu (Inner Mongolia), prov., China	C10	26
Neisse (Nysa Łużycka), stm., Eur.	D14	8
Neiva, Col.	F5	58
Neja, Russia	C26	18
Nekemte, Eth.	G2	46
Nekoosa, Wi., U.S.	D4	126
Nelidovo, Russia	E15	18
Neligh, Ne., U.S.	B7	104
Nel'kan, Russia	F21	24
Nellikuppam, India	G5	37
Nellis Air Force Base, mil., Nv., U.S.	G6	105
Nellore, India	E5	37
Nelson, B.C., Can.	E9	69
Nelson, N.Z.	D4	52
Nelson, Ne., U.S.	D7	104
Nelson, co., Ky., U.S.	C4	94
Nelson, co., N.D., U.S.	B7	111
Nelson, co., Va., U.S.	C4	123
Nelson, stm., Man., Can.	A4	70
Nelsonville, Oh., U.S.	C3	112
Néma, Maur.	E4	42
Nemacolin, Pa., U.S.	G2	115
Nemadji, stm., U.S.	B1	126
Nemaha, co., Ks., U.S.	C7	93
Nemaha, co., Ne., U.S.	D10	104
Nemours, Fr.	D9	10
Nemuro, Japan	p23	30a
Nemuro Strait, strt., Asia	o23	30a
Nenagh, Ire.	I4	7
Nenana, Ak., U.S.	C10	79
Neodesha, Ks., U.S.	E8	93
Neoga, Il., U.S.	D5	90
Neola, Ia., U.S.	C2	92
Neola, Ut., U.S.	C5	121
Neopit, Wi., U.S.	D5	126
Neosho, Mo., U.S.	E3	102
Neosho, co., Ks., U.S.	E8	93
Neosho, stm., Ok., U.S.	A6	113
Nepal (Nepāl), ctry., Asia	D5	36
Nepālganj, Nepal	F9	38
Nepaug Reservoir, res., Ct., U.S.	B3	84
Nepean, Ont., Can.	h12	73
Nepewassi Lake, l., Ont., Can.	A4	73
Nephi, Ut., U.S.	D4	121
Nepisiguit, stm., N.B., Can.	B3	71
Nepisiguit Bay, b., N.B., Can.	B4	71
Neponset, stm., Ma., U.S.	h11	98
Neptune, N.J., U.S.	C4	107
Neptune Beach, Fl., U.S.	B5	86
Neptune City, N.J., U.S.	C4	107
Nérac, Fr.	H7	10
Nerastro, Sarīr, des., Libya	D10	42
Nerčinskij Zavod, Russia	G17	24
Nerehta, Russia	D23	18
Neriquinha, Ang.	E4	44
Nerva, Spain	H5	12
Nesbyen, Nor.	F7	6
Nescopeck, Pa., U.S.	D9	115
Neshanic, stm., N.J., U.S.	C3	107
Neshoba, co., Ms., U.S.	C4	101
Neskaupstaður, Ice.	B5	4
Nesna, Nor.	C9	6
Nesowadnehunk, l., Me., U.S.	B3	96
Nesquehoning, Pa., U.S.	E10	115
Ness, co., Ks., U.S.	D4	93
Ness, Loch, l., Scot., U.K.	D8	7
Ness City, Ks., U.S.	D4	93
Néstos (Mesta), stm., Eur.	H8	16
Netanya, Isr.	C4	40
Netcong, N.J., U.S.	B3	107
Netherlands, ctry., Eur.	E9	4
Netherlands Antilles (Nederlandse Antillen), dep., N.A.	H13	64
Netrakona, Bngl.	H14	38
Nett Lake, l., Mn., U.S.	B5	100
Nettilling Lake, l., N.W. Ter., Can.	C18	66
Nett Lake Indian Reservation, Mn., U.S.	B6	100
Nettleton, Ms., U.S.	A5	101
Nettuno, Italy	H7	14
Neubrandenburg, Ger.	B13	8
Neuburg an der Donau, Ger.	G11	8
Neuchâtel, Switz.	F13	10
Neuchâtel, Lac de, l., Switz.	F13	10
Neufchâteau, Bel.	F5	8
Neufchâteau, Fr.	D12	10
Neufchâtel-en-Bray, Fr.	C8	10
Neuillé-Pont-Pierre, Fr.	E7	10
Neumarkt in der Oberpfalz, Ger.	F11	8
Neumünster, Ger.	A9	8
Neunkirchen, Aus.	H16	8
Neunkirchen/Saar, Ger.	F7	8
Neuquén, Arg.	D3	56
Neuruppin, Ger.	C12	8
Neuse, stm., N.C., U.S.	B6	110
Neusiedler See, l., Eur.	H16	8
Neuss, Ger.	D6	8
Neustadt an der Aisch—, Ger.	F10	8
Neustadt an der Weinstrasse, Ger.	F8	8
Neustadt in Holstein, Ger.	A10	8
Neustrelitz, Ger.	B13	8
Neu-Ulm, Ger.	G10	8
Neuville, Que., Can.	C6	74
Neuville-de-Poitou, Fr.	F7	10
Neuwied, Ger.	E7	8
Nevada, Ia., U.S.	B4	92
Nevada, Mo., U.S.	D3	102
Nevada, co., Ar., U.S.	D2	81
Nevada, co., Ca., U.S.	C3	82
Nevada, state, U.S.	D5	105
Nevada, Sierra, mts., Spain	H8	12
Nevada, Sierra, mts., Ca., U.S.	D4	82
Nevada City, Ca., U.S.	C3	82
Nevado, Cerro, mtn., Arg.	D3	56
Nevado, Cerro, mtn., Col.	F5	58
Nevel', Russia	E11	18
Nevers, Fr.	E10	10
Neversink, stm., N.Y., U.S.	D6	109
Nevis, i., St. K./N.	F16	64
Nevis, Ben, mtn., Scot., U.K.	E7	7
New, stm., Az., U.S.	k8	80
New, stm., N.C., U.S.	C5	110
New Albany, In., U.S.	H6	91
New Albany, Ms., U.S.	A4	101
New Albany, Oh., U.S.	k11	112
New Amsterdam, Guy.	D14	58
Newark, Ar., U.S.	B4	81
Newark, Ca., U.S.	h8	82
Newark, De., U.S.	B3	85
Newark, Il., U.S.	B5	90
Newark, N.J., U.S.	B4	107
Newark, N.Y., U.S.	B3	109
Newark, Oh., U.S.	B3	112
Newark Bay, b., N.J., U.S.	k8	107
Newark Lake, l., Nv., U.S.	D6	105
New Athens, Il., U.S.	E4	90
New Augusta, Ms., U.S.	D4	101
Newaygo, Mi., U.S.	E5	99
Newaygo, co., Mi., U.S.	E5	99
New Baden, Il., U.S.	E4	90
New Baltimore, Mi., U.S.	F8	99
New Bedford, Ma., U.S.	C6	98
New Bedford, Pa., U.S.	D1	115
New Berlin, Il., U.S.	D4	90
New Berlin, Wi., U.S.	n11	126
New Bern, N.C., U.S.	B5	110
Newbern, Tn., U.S.	A2	119
Newberry, Fl., U.S.	C4	86
Newberry, Mi., U.S.	B5	99
Newberry, S.C., U.S.	C4	117
Newberry, co., S.C., U.S.	C4	117
New Bethlehem, Pa., U.S.	D3	115
New Bloomfield, Pa., U.S.	F7	115
New Boston, Mi., U.S.	p15	99
New Boston, Oh., U.S.	D3	112
New Boston, Tx., U.S.	C5	120
New Braunfels, Tx., U.S.	E3	120
New Bremen, Oh., U.S.	B1	112
New Brighton, Mn., U.S.	m12	100
New Brighton, Pa., U.S.	E1	115
New Britain, Ct., U.S.	C4	84
New Britain, i., Pap. N. Gui.	m16	50a
New Brockton, Al., U.S.	D4	78
New Brunswick, N.J., U.S.	C4	107
New Brunswick, prov., Can.	C3	71
New Buffalo, Mi., U.S.	G4	99
Newburg, Wi., U.S.	E5	126
Newburgh, Ont., Can.	C8	73
Newburgh, In., U.S.	I3	91
Newburgh, N.Y., U.S.	D6	109
Newburgh Heights, Oh., U.S.	h9	112
Newburyport, Ma., U.S.	A6	98
New Caledonia, dep., Oc.	H24	2
New Canaan, Ct., U.S.	E2	84
New Carlisle, In., U.S.	A4	91
New Carlisle, Oh., U.S.	C1	112
Newcastle, Austl.	F10	50
Newcastle, N.B., Can.	C4	71
Newcastle, Ont., Can.	D6	73
Newcastle, S. Afr.	G5	44
New Castle, Al., U.S.	B3	78
New Castle, Co., U.S.	B3	83
New Castle, De., U.S.	B3	85
New Castle, In., U.S.	E7	91
New Castle, Ky., U.S.	B4	94
Newcastle, Ok., U.S.	B4	113
New Castle, Pa., U.S.	D1	115
Newcastle, Wy., U.S.	C8	127
New Castle, co., De., U.S.	B3	85
Newcastle upon Tyne, Eng., U.K.	G11	7
Newcastle Waters, Austl.	C6	50
Newcomerstown, Oh., U.S.	B4	112
New Concord, Oh., U.S.	C4	112
New Cumberland, Pa., U.S.	F8	115
New Cumberland, W.V., U.S.	A4	125
Newdegate, Austl.	F3	50
New Delhi, India	F7	38
New Ellenton, S.C., U.S.	E4	117
New England, N.D., U.S.	C3	111
Newenham, Cape, c., Ak., U.S.	D7	79
New Fairfield, Ct., U.S.	D2	84
Newfane, N.Y., U.S.	B2	109
Newfields, N.H., U.S.	D5	106
New Florence, Mo., U.S.	C6	102
Newfound Gap, U.S.	f9	110
Newfound Lake, l., N.H., U.S.	C3	106
Newfoundland, prov., Can.	D4	72
Newfoundland, i., Newf., Can.	D3	72
New Franklin, Mo., U.S.	B5	102
New Freedom, Pa., U.S.	G8	115
New Georgia, i., Sol.Is.	A11	50
New Glarus, Wi., U.S.	F4	126
New Guinea, i.	m14	50a
New Hampshire, state, U.S.	C3	106
New Hampton, Ia., U.S.	A5	92
New Hanover, co., N.C., U.S.	C5	110
New Hanover, i., Pap. N. Gui.	k17	50a
New Harbour, Newf., Can.	E5	72
New Harmony, In., U.S.	H2	91
New Hartford, Ct., U.S.	B4	84
New Hartford, Ia., U.S.	B5	92
New Haven, Ct., U.S.	D4	84
New Haven, In., U.S.	B7	91
New Haven, Ky., U.S.	C4	94
New Haven, Mi., U.S.	F8	99
New Haven, Mo., U.S.	C6	102
New Haven, W.V., U.S.	C3	125
New Haven, co., Ct., U.S.	D4	84
New Haven Harbor, b., Ct., U.S.	E4	84
New Hazelton, B.C., Can.	B4	69
New Hebrides see Vanuatu, ctry., Oc.	H24	2
New Holland, Ga., U.S.	B3	87
New Holland, Pa., U.S.	F9	115
New Holstein, Wi., U.S.	E5	126
New Hope, Al., U.S.	A3	78
New Hope, Ky., U.S.	C4	94
New Hope, Pa., U.S.	F12	115
New Hudson, Mi., U.S.	o14	99
New Iberia, La., U.S.	D4	95
Newington, Ct., U.S.	C5	84
New Inlet, b., N.C., U.S.	D5	110
New Ireland, i., Pap. N. Gui.	k17	50a
New Jersey, state, U.S.	C4	107
New Johnsonville, Tn., U.S.	A4	119
New Kensington, Pa., U.S.	E2	115
New Kent, co., Va., U.S.	C5	123
Newkirk, Ok., U.S.	A4	113
New Laguna, N.M., U.S.	B2	108
New Lake, l., N.C., U.S.	B6	110
New Lenox, Il., U.S.	B6	90
New Lexington, Oh., U.S.	C3	112
New Lisbon, Wi., U.S.	E3	126
New Liskeard, Ont., Can.	p20	73
Newllano, La., U.S.	C2	95
New London, Ct., U.S.	D7	84
New London, Ia., U.S.	D6	92
New London, Mn., U.S.	E4	100
New London, Mo., U.S.	B6	102
New London, N.H., U.S.	D3	106
New London, Oh., U.S.	A3	112
New London, Wi., U.S.	D5	126
New London, co., Ct., U.S.	C7	84
New London Submarine Base, mil., Ct., U.S.	D7	84
New Madison, Oh., U.S.	C1	112
New Madrid, Mo., U.S.	E8	102
New Madrid, co., Mo., U.S.	E8	102
Newman, Ca., U.S.	D3	82
Newman, Il., U.S.	D6	90
Newman Grove, Ne., U.S.	C8	104
Newman Lake, l., Wa., U.S.	B8	124
Newmanstown, Pa., U.S.	F9	115
Newmarket, Ont., Can.	C5	73
New Market, Al., U.S.	A3	78
New Market, In., U.S.	E4	91
New Market, Tn., U.S.	C10	119
New Market, Va., U.S.	B4	123
New Martinsville, W.V., U.S.	B4	125
New Matamoras, Oh., U.S.	C4	112
New Mexico, state, U.S.	C3	108
New Miami, Oh., U.S.	C1	112
New Milford, Ct., U.S.	C2	84
New Milford, N.J., U.S.	h8	107
New Milford, Pa., U.S.	C10	115
Newnan, Ga., U.S.	C2	87
Newnans Lake, l., Fl., U.S.	C4	86
New Norfolk, Austl.	H9	50
New Orleans, La., U.S.	E5	95
New Orleans Naval Air Station, mil., La., U.S.	k11	95
New Oxford, Pa., U.S.	G7	115
New Palestine, In., U.S.	E6	91
New Paltz, N.Y., U.S.	D6	109
New Paris, In., U.S.	B6	91
New Paris, Oh., U.S.	C1	112
New Philadelphia, Oh., U.S.	B4	112
New Philadelphia, Pa., U.S.	E9	115
New Plymouth, N.Z.	C5	52
New Plymouth, Id., U.S.	F2	89
New Point Comfort, c., Va., U.S.	C6	123
Newport, Eng., U.K.	K11	7
Newport, Wales, U.K.	J9	7
Newport, Ar., U.S.	B4	81
Newport, De., U.S.	B3	85
Newport, In., U.S.	E3	91
Newport, Ky., U.S.	A5	94
Newport, Me., U.S.	D3	96
Newport, Mi., U.S.	G7	99
Newport, Mn., U.S.	n13	100
Newport, N.H., U.S.	D2	106
Newport, N.C., U.S.	C6	110
Newport, Oh., U.S.	C4	112
Newport, Or., U.S.	C2	114
Newport, Pa., U.S.	F7	115
Newport, R.I., U.S.	F5	116
Newport, Tn., U.S.	D10	119
Newport, Vt., U.S.	B4	122
Newport, Wa., U.S.	A8	124
Newport, co., R.I., U.S.	E5	116
Newport Beach, Ca., U.S.	n13	82
Newport News, Va., U.S.	D6	123
New Port Richey, Fl., U.S.	D4	86
New Prague, Mn., U.S.	F5	100
New Preston, Ct., U.S.	C2	84
New Providence, N.J., U.S.	B4	107
New Providence, i., Bah.	B9	64
Newquay, Eng., U.K.	K7	7
New Richland, Mn., U.S.	G5	100
New Richmond, Que., Can.	A4	71
New Richmond, Oh., U.S.	D1	112
New Richmond, Wi., U.S.	C1	126
New River Inlet, b., N.C., U.S.	C5	110
New Roads, La., U.S.	D4	95
New Rochelle, N.Y., U.S.	E7	109
New Rockford, N.D., U.S.	B6	111
New Ross, Ire.	I6	7
Newry, N. Ire., U.K.	G6	7
New Salem, N.D., U.S.	C4	111
New Sarpy, La., U.S.	k11	95
New Sharon, Ia., U.S.	C5	92
New Site, Al., U.S.	B4	78
New Smyrna Beach, Fl., U.S.	C6	86
New South Wales, state, Austl.	F9	50
New Straitsville, Oh., U.S.	C3	112
New Tazewell, Tn., U.S.	C10	119
Newton, Al., U.S.	D4	78
Newton, Ga., U.S.	E2	87
Newton, Il., U.S.	E5	90
Newton, Ia., U.S.	C4	92
Newton, Ks., U.S.	D6	93
Newton, Ma., U.S.	B5	98
Newton, Ms., U.S.	C4	101
Newton, N.J., U.S.	A3	107
Newton, N.C., U.S.	B1	110
Newton, Tx., U.S.	D6	120
Newton, Ut., U.S.	B4	121
Newton, co., Ar., U.S.	B2	81
Newton, co., Ga., U.S.	C3	87
Newton, co., In., U.S.	B3	91
Newton, co., Ms., U.S.	C4	101
Newton, co., Mo., U.S.	E3	102
Newton, co., Tx., U.S.	D6	120
Newton Falls, Oh., U.S.	A5	112
Newton Lake, res., Il., U.S.	E5	90
Newton Stewart, Scot., U.K.	G8	7
Newtown, Ct., U.S.	D2	84
Newtown, N.D., U.S.	B3	111
Newtown, Oh., U.S.	C1	112
Newtownabbey, N. Ire., U.K.	G7	7
Newtown Square, Pa., U.S.	p20	115
New Ulm, Mn., U.S.	F4	100
New Vienna, Oh., U.S.	C2	112
Newville, Pa., U.S.	F7	115
New Washington, In., U.S.	G6	91
New Washington, Oh., U.S.	B3	112
New Waterford, Oh., U.S.	B5	112
New Westminster, B.C., Can.	E6	69
New Whiteland, In., U.S.	E5	91
New Wilmington, Pa., U.S.	D1	115
New Windsor, Il., U.S.	B3	90
New Windsor, Md., U.S.	A3	97
New Windsor, N.Y., U.S.	D6	109
New World Island, i., Newf., Can.	D4	72
New York, N.Y., U.S.	E7	109
New York, co., N.Y., U.S.	k13	109
New York, state, U.S.	C6	109
New York Mills, Mn., U.S.	D3	100
New Zealand, ctry., Oc.	D4	52
Nežin, Ukr.	G4	22
Nez Perce, co., Id., U.S.	C2	89
Nez Perce Indian Reservation, Id., U.S.	C2	89
Ngami, Lake, l., Bots.	F4	44
Nganglong Kangri, mts., China	D10	38
Nganjuk, Indon.	m15	33a
Ngaoundéré, Cam.	G8	42

Name	Map Ref	Page
Nguigmi, Niger	F8	42
Nguru, Nig.	F8	42
Nha Trang, Viet.	H10	34
Niafounké, Mali	E5	42
Niagara, Wi., U.S.	C6	126
Niagara, N.Y., U.S.	B2	109
Niagara Falls, Ont., Can.	D5	73
Niagara Falls, N.Y., U.S.	B1	109
Niagara-on-the-Lake, Ont., Can.	D5	73
Niamey, Niger	F6	42
Niangara, Zaire	H11	42
Niangua, stm., Mo., U.S.	D5	102
Niantic, Ct., U.S.	D7	84
Nias, Pulau, i., Indon.	N4	34
Nibley, Ut., U.S.	B4	121
Nicaragua, ctry., N.A.	H5	64
Nicaragua, Lago de, l., Nic.	I5	64
Nicatous Lake, l., Me., U.S.	C4	96
Nice, Fr.	I14	10
Niceville, Fl., U.S.	u15	86
Nichinan, Japan	K4	30
Nicholas, co., Ky., U.S.	B6	94
Nicholas, co., W.V., U.S.	C4	125
Nicholas Channel, strt., N.A.	C7	64
Nicholasville, Ky., U.S.	C5	94
Nicholls, Ga., U.S.	E4	87
Nichols Hills, Ok., U.S.	B4	113
Nicholson, Ms., U.S.	E4	101
Nickajack Lake, res., Tn., U.S.	D8	119
Nickel Centre, Ont., Can.	p19	73
Nickerson, Ks., U.S.	D5	93
Nicobar Islands, is., India	J2	34
Nicolet, Que., Can.	C5	74
Nicolet, stm., Que., Can.	C5	74
Nicolet, Lake, l., Mi., U.S.	B6	99
Nicollet, Mn., U.S.	F4	100
Nicollet, co., Mn., U.S.	F4	100
Nicolls Town, Bah.	B8	64
Nicoma Park, Ok., U.S.	B4	113
Nicosia, Cyp.	B3	40
Nicosia, N. Cyp.	B3	40
Nicosia, Italy	L9	14
Nicoya, Golfo de, b., C.R.	J5	64
Nicoya, Península de, pen., C.R.	I5	64
Niebüll, Ger.	A8	8
Nienburg, Ger.	C9	8
Nieuw Nickerie, Sur.	B7	54
Nieves, Mex.	E8	62
Nigadoo, N.B., Can.	B4	71
Niger, ctry., Afr.	E7	42
Niger, stm., Afr.	G7	42
Nigeria, ctry., Afr.	G7	42
Nigrita, Grc.	I7	16
Nihoa, i., Hi., U.S.	m15	88
Niigata, Japan	E12	30
Niihama, Japan	I6	30
Niihau, i., Hi., U.S.	B1	88
Niinisalo, Fin.	F14	6
Niitsu, Japan	E12	30
Nijar, Spain	I9	12
Nijmegen, Neth.	D5	8
Nikishka, Ak., U.S.	g16	79
Nikkō, Japan	F12	30
Nikolajev, Ukr.	H4	22
Nikolajevsk-na-Amure, Russia	G22	24
Nikolayev see Nikolajev, Ukr.	H4	22
Nikšić, Yugo.	G2	16
Niland, Ca., U.S.	F6	82
Nile (Nahr an-Nīl), stm., Afr.	C12	42
Niles, Il., U.S.	h9	90
Niles, Mi., U.S.	G4	99
Niles, Oh., U.S.	A5	112
Nileshwar, India	F3	37
Nīmach, India	H6	38
Nimba, Mont, mtn., Afr.	G4	42
Nîmes, Fr.	I11	10
Nimrod Lake, res., Ar., U.S.	C2	81
Nine Degree Channel, strt., India	H2	37
Nine Mile Creek, stm., Ut., U.S.	D5	121
Ninemile Point, c., Mi., U.S.	C6	99
Ninety Six, S.C., U.S.	C3	117
Ningbo, China	F10	28
Ningming, China	C9	34
Ningxia Huizu Zizhiqu, prov., China	D8	26
Ninh Binh, Viet.	D8	34
Ninilchik, Ak., U.S.	C9	79
Ninnescah, stm., Ks., U.S.	E6	93
Niobrara, co., Wy., U.S.	C8	127
Niobrara, stm., U.S.	B7	104
Niono, Mali	F4	42
Nioro du Sahel, Mali	E4	42
Niort, Fr.	F6	10
Niota, Tn., U.S.	D9	119
Nipāni, India	D3	37
Nipigon, Lake, l., Ont., Can.	o17	73
Nipissing, Lake, l., Ont., Can.	A5	73
Nipomo, Ca., U.S.	E3	82
Nipple Mountain, mtn., Co., U.S.	D2	83
Nirmal, India	C5	37
Niš, Yugo.	F5	16
Nisa, Port.	F4	12
Nishinoomote, Japan	u30	31b
Nishiwaki, Japan	H7	30
Niskayuna, N.Y., U.S.	C7	109
Nisqually, stm., Wa., U.S.	C3	124
Nisswa, Mn., U.S.	D4	100
Niterói, Braz.	G7	57
Nitra, Czech.	G18	8
Nitro, W.V., U.S.	C3	125
Niue, dep., Oc.	H1	2
Nivelles, Bel.	E4	8
Niverville, Man., Can.	E3	70
Niwot, Co., U.S.	A5	83
Nixa, Mo., U.S.	D4	102
Nixon, Nv., U.S.	D2	105
Nixon, Tx., U.S.	E4	120
Nizāmābād, India	C5	37
Nizip, Tur.	A5	40
Nižn'aja Pojma, Russia	F13	24
Nižn'aja Tunguska, stm., Russia	E12	24
Nižneangarsk, Russia	F15	24
Nižneilimsk, Russia	F14	24
Nižneudinsk, Russia	G13	24
Nižnij Novgorod (Gorki), Russia	E27	18
Nizza Monferrato, Italy	E3	14
Njombe, Tan.	C6	44
Nkhota Kota, Mwi.	D6	44
Nkongsamba, Cam.	H7	42
Noākhāli, Bngl.	I14	38
Noank, Ct., U.S.	D8	84
Noatak, Ak., U.S.	B7	79
Noatak, stm., Ak., U.S.	B7	79
Nobel, Ont., Can.	B4	73
Nobeoka, Japan	J4	30
Noble, Ok., U.S.	B4	113
Noble, co., In., U.S.	B7	91
Noble, co., Oh., U.S.	C4	112
Noble, co., Ok., U.S.	A4	113
Nobles, co., Mn., U.S.	G3	100
Noblesville, In., U.S.	D6	91
Noboribetsu, Japan	q19	30a
Nocatee, Fl., U.S.	E5	86
Nocera [Inferiore], Italy	I9	14
Nochixtlán, Mex.	I11	62
Nocona, Tx., U.S.	C4	120
Nodaway, co., Mo., U.S.	A3	102
Nodaway, stm., U.S.	A2	102
Noel, Mo., U.S.	E3	102
Nogales, Mex.	B4	62
Nogales, Az., U.S.	F5	80
Nogent-le-Rotrou, Fr.	D7	10
Noginsk, Russia	F21	18
Nogoyá, Arg.	C5	56
Noirmoutier, Fr.	E4	10
Nojima-zaki, c., Japan	H12	30
Nokia, Fin.	F14	6
Nokomis, Fl., U.S.	E4	86
Nokomis, Il., U.S.	D4	90
Nokomis, Lake, res., Wi., U.S.	C4	126
Nolan, co., Tx., U.S.	C2	120
Nolichucky, stm., Tn., U.S.	C10	119
Nolin, stm., Ky., U.S.	C3	94
Nolin Lake, res., Ky., U.S.	C3	94
Nomans Land, i., Ma., U.S.	D6	98
Nombre de Dios, Mex.	F7	62
Nome, Ak., U.S.	C6	79
Nominingue, Que., Can.	C2	74
Nonacho Lake, l., N.W. Ter., Can.	D11	66
Nonesuch, stm., Me., U.S.	g7	96
Nong'an, China	C12	26
Nong Khai, Thai.	F7	34
Nonquit Pond, l., R.I., U.S.	E6	116
Nontron, Fr.	G7	10
Nooksack, North Fork, stm., Wa., U.S.	A4	124
Nooksack, South Fork, stm., Wa., U.S.	A3	124
Noordoost Polder, reg., Neth.	C5	8
Noorvik, Ak., U.S.	B7	79
Nootka Island, i., B.C., Can.	G7	66
Nootka Sound, strt., B.C., Can.	E4	69
No Point, Point, c., Md., U.S.	D5	97
Noquebay, Lake, l., Wi., U.S.	C6	126
Noranda, Que., Can.	k11	74
Nora Springs, Ia., U.S.	A5	92
Norborne, Mo., U.S.	B4	102
Norco, La., U.S.	E5	95
Norcross, Ga., U.S.	C2	87
Norden, Ger.	B7	8
Nordenham, Ger.	B8	8
Nordenšeľda, Archipelag, is., Russia	B13	24
Norderney, i., Ger.	B7	8
Nordfjordeid, Nor.	F5	6
Nordfold, Nor.	C10	6
Nordhausen, Ger.	D10	8
Nordhorn, Ger.	C7	8
Nordkapp, c., Nor.	A15	6
Nordkjosbotn, Nor.	B12	6
Nördlingen, Ger.	G10	8
Nordmaling, Swe.	E12	6
Nordreisa, Nor.	B13	6
Nordre Strømfjord, Grnld.	C22	66
Nordvik, Russia	C16	24
Norfolk, Ct., U.S.	B3	84
Norfolk, Ne., U.S.	B8	104
Norfolk, N.Y., U.S.	f9	109
Norfolk, Va., U.S.	D6	123
Norfolk, co., Ma., U.S.	B5	98
Norfolk Naval Base, mil., Va., U.S.	k15	123
Norfolk Naval Shipyard, mil., Va., U.S.	k15	123
Norfork Dam, Ar., U.S.	A3	81
Norfork Lake, res., Ar., U.S.	A3	81
Noril'sk, Russia	D11	24
Norland, Fl., U.S.	s13	86
Norlina, N.C., U.S.	A4	110
Normal, Il., U.S.	C5	90
Norman, Ok., U.S.	B4	113
Norman, co., Mn., U.S.	C2	100
Norman, Lake, res., N.C., U.S.	B2	110
Normandie, hist. reg., Fr.	D6	10
Normandy, Mo., U.S.	f13	102
Normandy see Normandie, hist. reg., Fr.	D6	10
Normanton, Austl.	C8	50
Norman Wells, N.W. Ter., Can.	C7	66
Norphlet, Ar., U.S.	D3	81
Norquinco, Arg.	E2	56
Norridge, Il., U.S.	k9	90
Norridgewock, Me., U.S.	D3	96
Norris, S.C., U.S.	B2	117
Norris, Tn., U.S.	C9	119
Norris Arm, Newf., Can.	D4	72
Norris City, Il., U.S.	F5	90
Norris Dam, Tn., U.S.	C9	119
Norris Lake, res., Tn., U.S.	C10	119
Norris Point, Newf., Can.	D3	72
Norristown, Pa., U.S.	F11	115
Norrköping, Swe.	G11	6
Norrtälje, Swe.	G12	6
Norseman, Austl.	F4	50
Norsk, Russia	G19	24
Norte, Serra do, plat., Braz.	F7	54
North, S.C., U.S.	D5	117
North, stm., Al., U.S.	B2	78
North, stm., Ia., U.S.	f8	92
North, stm., Ma., U.S.	h12	98
North, stm., W.V., U.S.	B6	125
North, Cape, c., N.S., Can.	B9	71
North America	E10	61
North Amherst, Ma., U.S.	B2	98
Northampton, Eng., U.K.	I12	7
Northampton, Ma., U.S.	B2	98
Northampton, Pa., U.S.	E11	115
Northampton, co., N.C., U.S.	A5	110
Northampton, co., Pa., U.S.	E11	115
Northampton, co., Va., U.S.	C7	123
North Andaman, i., India	H2	34
North Andover, Ma., U.S.	A5	98
North Andrews Gardens, Fl., U.S.	*r13	86
North Anna, stm., Va., U.S.	B5	123
North Anson, Me., U.S.	D3	96
North Apollo, Pa., U.S.	E2	115
North Arapaho Peak, mtn., Co., U.S.	A5	83
North Arlington, N.J., U.S.	h8	107
North Atlanta, Ga., U.S.	h8	87
North Attleboro, Ma., U.S.	C5	98
North Aurora, Il., U.S.	k8	90
North Baltimore, Oh., U.S.	A2	112
North Bay, Ont., Can.	A5	73
North Beach, Md., U.S.	C4	97
North Belmont, N.C., U.S.	B1	110
North Bend, Ne., U.S.	C9	104
North Bend, Or., U.S.	D2	114
North Bend, Wa., U.S.	B4	124
North Bennington, Vt., U.S.	F2	122
North Bergen, N.J., U.S.	h8	107
North Berwick, Me., U.S.	E2	96
North Billerica, Ma., U.S.	A5	98
Northborough, Ma., U.S.	B4	98
North Branch, Mi., U.S.	E7	99
North Branch, Mn., U.S.	E6	100
North Branch, N.H., U.S.	D3	106
North Branch, N.J., U.S.	B3	107
North Branford, Ct., U.S.	D4	84
Northbridge, Ma., U.S.	B4	98
Northbrook, Il., U.S.	h9	90
North Brookfield, Ma., U.S.	B3	98
North Brunswick, N.J., U.S.	C4	107
North Caldwell, N.J., U.S.	B4	107
North Canadian, stm., Ok., U.S.	A5	113
North Canton, Ga., U.S.	B2	87
North Canton, Oh., U.S.	B4	112
North Cape, c., P.E.I., Can.	B5	71
North Cape May, N.J., U.S.	F3	107
North Cape see Nordkapp, c., Nor.	A15	6
North Caribou Lake, l., Ont., Can.	F14	66
North Carolina, state, U.S.	B3	110
North Cascades National Park, Wa., U.S.	A4	124
North Channel, strt., Ont., Can.	A2	73
North Channel, strt., U.K.	F7	7
North Charleston, S.C., U.S.	F8	117
North Chicago, Il., U.S.	A6	90
North Clarendon, Vt., U.S.	D3	122
North College Hill, Oh., U.S.	o12	112
North Conway, N.H., U.S.	B4	106
North Corbin, Ky., U.S.	D5	94
North Crossett, Ar., U.S.	D4	81
North Cyprus, ctry., Asia	B3	40
North Dakota, state, U.S.	B5	111
North Dartmouth, Ma., U.S.	C5	98
North Druid Hills, Ga., U.S.	*h8	87
North Eagle Butte, S.D., U.S.	B4	118
North East, Md., U.S.	A6	97
North East, Pa., U.S.	B2	115
Northeast, stm., Md., U.S.	A6	97
Northeast Cape, c., Ak., U.S.	C6	79
Northeast Cape Fear, stm., N.C., U.S.	C5	110
Northeast Harbor, Me., U.S.	D4	96
Northeast Henrietta, N.Y., U.S.	*B3	109
North East Pond, l., N.H., U.S.	D5	106
Northeast Providence Channel, strt., Bah.	B9	64
North Edisto, stm., S.C., U.S.	k11	117
Northeim, Ger.	D9	8
North English, Ia., U.S.	C5	92
North English, stm., Ia., U.S.	C5	92
North Enid, Ok., U.S.	A4	113
Northern Cheyenne Indian Reservation, Mt., U.S.	E10	103
Northern Indian Lake, l., Man., Can.	A3	70
Northern Ireland, ter., U.K.	G6	7
Northern Territory, ter., Austl.	C6	50
North Falmouth, Ma., U.S.	C6	98
Northfield, Mn., U.S.	F5	100
Northfield, N.H., U.S.	D3	106
Northfield, N.J., U.S.	E3	107
Northfield, Oh., U.S.	h9	112
Northfield, Vt., U.S.	C3	122
Northfield Falls, Vt., U.S.	C3	122
North Flinders Ranges, mts., Austl.	F7	50
North Fond du Lac, Wi., U.S.	E5	126
Northford, Ct., U.S.	D4	84
North Fork Reservoir, res., Or., U.S.	B4	114
North Fort Myers, Fl., U.S.	F5	86
North Fox Island, i., Mi., U.S.	C5	99
North Frisian Islands, is., Eur.	A8	8
North Gower, Ont., Can.	B9	73
North Grafton, Ma., U.S.	B4	98
North Grosvenordale, Ct., U.S.	B8	84
North Gulfport, Ms., U.S.	E4	101
North Haledon, N.J., U.S.	B4	107
North Hampton, N.H., U.S.	E5	106
North Hartland Reservoir, res., Vt., U.S.	D4	122
North Hatley, Que., Can.	D6	74
North Haven, Ct., U.S.	D4	84
North Head, N.B., Can.	E3	71
North Hero Island, i., Vt., U.S.	B2	122
North Horn Lake, l., Tn., U.S.	e8	119
North Industry, Oh., U.S.	B4	112
North Inlet, b., S.C., U.S.	E9	117
North Island, i., N.Z.	C5	52
North Island, i., S.C., U.S.	E9	117
North Island Naval Air Station, mil., Ca., U.S.	o15	82
North Islands, is., La., U.S.	E7	95
North Judson, In., U.S.	B4	91
North Kansas City, Mo., U.S.	h10	102
North Kingstown, R.I., U.S.	E4	116
North Kingsville, Oh., U.S.	A5	112
North La Junta, Co., U.S.	C7	83
North La Veta Pass, Co., U.S.	D5	83
North Lake Park, Fl., U.S.	—	—
North Laramie, stm., Wy., U.S.	D7	127
North Las Vegas, Nv., U.S.	G6	105
North Lewisburg, Oh., U.S.	B2	112
North Liberty, In., U.S.	A5	91
North Liberty, Ia., U.S.	C6	92
North Lima, Oh., U.S.	B5	112
North Little Rock, Ar., U.S.	C3	81
North Logan, Ut., U.S.	B4	121
North Loon Mountain, mtn., Id., U.S.	D3	89
North Magnetic Pole	B22	128
North Mamm Peak, mtn., Co., U.S.	B3	83
North Manchester, In., U.S.	C6	91
North Manitou Island, i., Mi., U.S.	C4	99
North Mankato, Mn., U.S.	F4	100
North Miami, Fl., U.S.	G6	86
North Miami Beach, Fl., U.S.	s13	86
North Middletown, Ky., U.S.	B5	94
North Moose Lake, l., Man., Can.	B1	70
North Mountain, mtn., Pa., U.S.	D9	115
North Muskegon, Mi., U.S.	E4	99
North Myrtle Beach, S.C., U.S.	D10	117
North Naples, Fl., U.S.	F5	86
North New River Canal, Fl., U.S.	F6	86
North Ogden, Ut., U.S.	B4	121
North Olmsted, Oh., U.S.	h9	112
North Palisade, mtn., Ca., U.S.	D4	82
North Park, Il., U.S.	A4	90
North Park, val., Co., U.S.	A4	83
North Pass, strt., La., U.S.	E7	95
North Pembroke, Ma., U.S.	B6	98
North Plainfield, N.J., U.S.	B4	107
North Plains, Or., U.S.	B4	114
North Plains, pl., N.M., U.S.	C1	108
North Platte, Ne., U.S.	C5	104
North Platte, stm., U.S.	C6	76
North Point, c., Md., U.S.	B5	97
North Point, c., Mi., U.S.	C7	99
North Pole	A12	128
Northport, Al., U.S.	B2	78
North Prairie, Wi., U.S.	F5	126
North Providence, R.I., U.S.	C4	116
North Raccoon, stm., Ia., U.S.	C3	92
North Reading, Ma., U.S.	f11	98
North Richland Hills, Tx., U.S.	n9	120
Northridge, Oh., U.S.	C2	112
North Ridgeville, Oh., U.S.	A3	112
North Royalton, Oh., U.S.	h9	112
North Rustico, P.E.I., Can.	C6	71
North Salem, N.H., U.S.	E4	106
North Salt Lake, Ut., U.S.	C4	121
North Santee, stm., S.C., U.S.	E9	117
North Saskatchewan, stm., Can.	F10	66
North Schell Peak, mtn., Nv., U.S.	D7	105
North Scituate, Ma., U.S.	h12	98
North Sea, Eur.	D8	4
North Shoshone Peak, mtn., Nv., U.S.	D4	105
North Sioux City, S.D., U.S.	E9	118
North Skunk, stm., Ia., U.S.	C5	92
North Springfield, Vt., U.S.	E3	122
North Springfield Reservoir, res., Vt., U.S.	E4	122
North Star, De., U.S.	A3	85
North St. Paul, Mn., U.S.	m13	100
North Stratford, N.H., U.S.	A3	106
North Sudbury, Ma., U.S.	g10	98
North Swanzey, N.H., U.S.	E2	106
North Syracuse, N.Y., U.S.	B4	109
North Tarrytown, N.Y., U.S.	D7	109
North Terre Haute, In., U.S.	E3	91
North Thompson, stm., B.C., Can.	D8	69
North Tonawanda, N.Y., U.S.	B2	109
North Troy, Vt., U.S.	B4	122
North Tunica, Ms., U.S.	A3	101
North Twin Lake, l., Wi., U.S.	C4	126
Northumberland, Pa., U.S.	E8	115
Northumberland, co., Pa., U.S.	D8	115
Northumberland, co., Va., U.S.	C6	123
Northumberland National Park, Eng., U.K.	F10	7
Northumberland Strait, strt., Can.	C6	71
North Umpqua, stm., Or., U.S.	D3	114
North Uxbridge, Ma., U.S.	B4	98
Northvale, N.J., U.S.	g9	107
North Vancouver, B.C., Can.	E6	69
North Vassalboro, Me., U.S.	D3	96
North Vernon, In., U.S.	F6	91
Northville, Mi., U.S.	p15	99
North Wales, Pa., U.S.	F11	115
North Walpole, N.H., U.S.	D2	106
North Warren, Pa., U.S.	C3	115
North Webster, In., U.S.	B6	91
North West Cape, c., Austl.	D2	50
Northwest Miramichi, stm., N.B., Can.	B3	71
Northwest Providence Channel, strt., Bah.	A8	64
Northwest Territories, prov., Can.	C13	66
North Wildwood, N.J., U.S.	E3	107
North Wilkesboro, N.C., U.S.	A1	110
North Windham, Ct., U.S.	C7	84
North Windham, Me., U.S.	E2	96
Northwood, Ia., U.S.	A4	92
Northwood, N.D., U.S.	B8	111
Northwoods, Mo., U.S.	—	—
North Woodstock, N.H., U.S.	B3	106
North Haven, Ct., U.S.	—	—
North York, Ont., Can.	D5	73
North York, Pa., U.S.	G8	115
North York Moors National Park, Eng., U.K.	G12	7
Norton, N.B., Can.	D4	71
Norton, Ks., U.S.	C4	93
Norton, Ma., U.S.	C5	98
Norton, Oh., U.S.	A4	112
Norton, Va., U.S.	f9	123
Norton, co., Ks., U.S.	C4	93
Norton Air Force Base, mil., Ca., U.S.	E5	82
Norton Bay, b., Ak., U.S.	C7	79
Norton Pond, l., Vt., U.S.	B5	122
Norton Reservoir, res., Ks., U.S.	C3	93
Norton Shores, Mi., U.S.	E4	99
Norton Sound, strt., Ak., U.S.	C6	79
Nortonville, Ks., U.S.	C8	93
Nortonville, Ky., U.S.	C2	94
Norwalk, Ca., U.S.	n12	82
Norwalk, Ct., U.S.	E2	84
Norwalk, Ia., U.S.	C4	92
Norwalk, Oh., U.S.	A3	112
Norwalk, stm., Ct., U.S.	E2	84
Norwalk Islands, is., Ct., U.S.	E2	84
Norway, Me., U.S.	D2	96
Norway, Mi., U.S.	C3	99
Norway, ctry., Eur.	C9	4
Norway Bay, b., N.W. Ter., Can.	B12	66
Norway House, Man., Can.	C3	70
Norway Lake, l., Mn., U.S.	E3	100
Norwegian Sea, Eur.	C12	128
Norwich, Eng., U.K.	I14	7
Norwich, Ct., U.S.	C7	84
Norwich, N.Y., U.S.	C5	109
Norwich, Vt., U.S.	D4	122
Norwood, Ont., Can.	C7	73
Norwood, Ma., U.S.	B5	98
Norwood, Mn., U.S.	F5	100
Norwood, N.J., U.S.	h9	107
Norwood, N.Y., U.S.	f10	109
Norwood, N.C., U.S.	B2	110
Norwood, Oh., U.S.	o13	112
Norwood, Pa., U.S.	p20	115
Norwoodville, Ia., U.S.	e8	92
Noshiro, Japan	B13	30
Notasulga, Al., U.S.	C4	78
Notch Peak, mtn., Ut., U.S.	D2	121
Noto, Italy	M10	14
Notodden, Nor.	G7	6
Notre Dame, Monts, mts., Que., Can.	k13	74
Notre Dame Bay, b., Newf., Can.	D4	72
Notre Dame de Lourdes, Man., Can.	E2	70
Notre-Dame-du-Lac, Que., Can.	B9	74
Nottawasaga Bay, b., Ont., Can.	C4	73
Nottaway, stm., Que., Can.	h11	74
Nottingham, Eng., U.K.	I11	7
Nottingham Island, i., N.W. Ter., Can.	D17	66
Nottoway, co., Va., U.S.	C4	123
Nottoway, stm., Va., U.S.	D5	123
Nouadhibou, Maur.	D2	42
Nouakchott, Maur.	E2	42
Nouamrhar, Maur.	E2	42
Noupoort, S. Afr.	H4	44
Nouveau-Québec, Cratère du, crat., Que., Can.	D18	66
Nova América, Braz.	C4	57
Nova Cruz, Braz.	E11	54
Nova Freixo, Moz.	D7	44
Nova Friburgo, Braz.	G7	57
Nova Gaia, Ang.	D3	44
Nova Gradiška, Cro.	D12	14
Nova Iguaçu, Braz.	G7	57
Novaja Sibir', Ostrov, i., Russia	B23	24
Novaja Zeml'a, is., Russia	C5	24
Nova Lima, Braz.	E7	57
Nova Lisboa see Huambo, Ang.	D3	44
Nova Mambone, Moz.	F7	44
Novara, Italy	D3	14
Nova Scotia, prov., Can.	D6	71
Nova Sofala, Moz.	F6	44
Novato, Ca., U.S.	C2	82
Novelda, Spain	G11	12
Nové Zámky, Czech.	H18	8
Novgorod, Russia	C14	18
Novi, Mi., U.S.	p15	99
Novi Ligure, Italy	E3	14
Novi Pazar, Bul.	F11	16
Novi Pazar, Yugo.	F4	16
Novi Sad, Yugo.	D3	16
Novoaltajsk, Russia	G10	24
Novo Aripuanã, Braz.	E6	54
Novogrudok, Bela.	H8	18
Novokuzneck, Russia	G11	24
Novo Mesto, Slo.	D10	14
Novo Redondo, Ang.	D2	44
Novorossijsk, Russia	I5	22
Novosibirsk, Russia	C15	24
Novosibirskoje Vodochranilišče, res., Russia	G10	24
Novotroick, Russia	G9	22
Novozybkov, Russia	I14	18
Novska, Cro.	D11	14
Nowa Sól (Neusalz), Pol.	D15	8
Nowata, Ok., U.S.	A6	113
Nowata, co., Ok., U.S.	A6	113
Nowgong, India	G15	38
Nowood, stm., Wy., U.S.	B5	127
Nowshāk, mtn., Asia	B4	38
Nowshera, Pak.	C4	38
Nowy Sącz, Pol.	F20	8
Nowy Targ, Pol.	F20	8
Noxon Reservoir, res., Mt., U.S.	C1	103
Noxontown Lake, res., De., U.S.	C3	85
Noxubee, co., Ms., U.S.	B5	101
Noxubee, stm., U.S.	B5	101
Noyes Island, i., Ak., U.S.	n22	79
Noyon, Fr.	C9	10
Nozay, Fr.	E5	10
Nsanje, Mwi.	E7	44
Nsawam, Ghana	G5	42

169

Name	Map Ref	Page
Nubanusit Lake, l., N.H., U.S.	E2	106
Nubian Desert, des., Sudan	D12	42
Nuckolls, co., Ne., U.S.	D7	104
Nucla, Co., U.S.	C2	83
Nueces, co., Tx., U.S.	F4	120
Nueces, stm., Tx., U.S.	E3	120
Nueltin Lake, l., Can.	E13	66
Nueva Casas Grandes, Mex.	B6	62
Nueva Rosita, Mex.	D9	62
Nueva San Salvador, El Sal.	H3	64
Nueve de Julio, Arg.	D4	56
Nuevitas, Cuba	D9	64
Nuevo, Golfo, b., Arg.	E4	56
Nuevo Laredo, Mex.	D10	62
Nuevo Rocafuerte, Ec.	H5	58
Nuits-Saint-Georges, Fr.	E11	10
Nukus, Uzb.	I9	22
Nulato, Ak., U.S.	C8	79
Nulhegan, stm., Vt., U.S.	B5	122
Nullagine, Austl.	D4	50
Nullarbor Plain, pl., Austl.	F5	50
Numata, Japan	F12	30
Numazu, Japan	G11	30
Numfoor, Pulau, i., Indon.	F9	32
Nun, stm., China	A12	26
Nunivak Island, i., Ak., U.S.	D6	79
Nunjiang, China	B12	26
Nuoro, Italy	I4	14
N'urba, Russia	E17	24
Nuremberg, Pa., U.S.	E9	115
Nuremberg see Nürnberg, Ger.	F11	8
Nürnberg, Ger.	F11	8
Nurri, Italy	J4	14
Nutley, N.J., U.S.	B4	107
Nutter Fort, W.V., U.S.	k10	125
Nutting Lake, Ma., U.S.	f10	98
Nuuanu Pali, Hi., U.S.	g10	88
Nyack, N.Y., U.S.	D7	109
Nyainqêntanglha Shan, mts., China	E13	38
Nyala, Sudan	F10	42
Nyanda, Zimb.	F6	44
Nyasa, Lake, l., Afr.	D6	44
Nyaunglebin, Burma	F4	34
Nybro, Swe.	H10	6
Nye, co., Nv., U.S.	E5	105
Nyenyam, China	F11	38
Nyeri, Kenya	B7	44
Nyíregyháza, Hung.	H21	8
Nykøbing, Den.	I8	6
Nyköping, Swe.	G11	6
Nylstroom, S. Afr.	F5	44
Nynäshamn, Swe.	G11	6
Nyngan, Austl.	F9	50
Nyon, Switz.	F13	10
Nyons, Fr.	H12	10
Nysa, Pol.	F11	8
Nysa Łużycka (Neisse) (Nisa), stm., Eur.	D14	8
Nyssa, Or., U.S.	D9	114
Nzérékoré, Gui.	G4	42
N'zeto, Ang.	C2	44

O

Name	Map Ref	Page
Oahe, Lake, res., U.S.	B6	76
Oahe Dam, S.D., U.S.	C5	118
Oahu, i., Hi., U.S.	B4	88
Oak Bay, B.C., Can.	h12	69
Oak Bluffs, Ma., U.S.	D6	98
Oak Creek, Co., U.S.	A4	83
Oak Creek, Wi., U.S.	n12	126
Oakdale, Ca., U.S.	D3	82
Oakdale, Ga., U.S.	h8	87
Oakdale, La., U.S.	D3	95
Oakdale, Pa., U.S.	k13	115
Oakes, N.D., U.S.	C7	111
Oakfield, N.Y., U.S.	B2	109
Oakfield, Wi., U.S.	E5	126
Oak Forest, Il., U.S.	k9	90
Oak Grove, Ky., U.S.	D2	94
Oak Grove, La., U.S.	B4	95
Oak Grove, Or., U.S.	B4	114
Oak Harbor, Oh., U.S.	A2	112
Oak Harbor, Wa., U.S.	A3	124
Oak Hill, Mi., U.S.	D4	99
Oak Hill, Oh., U.S.	D3	112
Oak Hill, W.V., U.S.	D3	125
Oak Hill, mtn., Ma., U.S.	f9	98
Oakhurst, Ok., U.S.	A5	113
Oak Island, i., Wi., U.S.	B3	126
Oak Lake, l., Man., Can.	E1	70
Oakland, Ca., U.S.	D2	82
Oakland, Il., U.S.	D5	90
Oakland, Ia., U.S.	C2	92
Oakland, Me., U.S.	D3	96
Oakland, Md., U.S.	m12	97
Oakland, Ne., U.S.	C9	104
Oakland, N.J., U.S.	A4	107
Oakland, Ok., U.S.	C5	113
Oakland, Or., U.S.	D3	114
Oakland, R.I., U.S.	B2	116
Oakland, co., Mi., U.S.	F7	99
Oakland City, In., U.S.	H3	91
Oakland Park, Fl., U.S.	r13	86
Oak Lawn, Il., U.S.	B6	90
Oaklawn, Ks., U.S.	g12	93
Oakley, Id., U.S.	G5	89
Oakley, Ks., U.S.	C3	93
Oakman, Al., U.S.	B2	78
Oakmont, Pa., U.S.	E2	115
Oak Mountain, mtn., Ga., U.S.	D2	87
Oak Orchard, De., U.S.	F5	85
Oak Park, Il., U.S.	B6	90
Oak Park, Mi., U.S.	p15	99
Oak Ridge, N.C., U.S.	A3	110
Oak Ridge, Tn., U.S.	C9	119
Oak Ridge Reservoir, res., N.J., U.S.	A3	107
Oakton, Va., U.S.	g12	123
Oaktown, In., U.S.	G3	91
Oak Valley, N.J., U.S.	D2	107
Oakville, Ont., Can.	D5	73
Oakville, Ct., U.S.	C3	84
Oakville, Mo., U.S.	g13	102
Oakwood, Ga., U.S.	B3	87
Oakwood, Il., U.S.	C6	90
Oakwood, Oh., U.S.	C1	112
Oamaru, N.Z.	F3	52
Oaxaca [de Juárez], Mex.	I11	62
Ob', stm., Russia	D7	24
Oban, Scot., U.K.	E7	7
Obbia, Som.	G4	46
Obed, stm., Tn., U.S.	C9	119
Oberlin, Ks., U.S.	C3	93
Oberlin, La., U.S.	D3	95
Oberlin, Oh., U.S.	A3	112
Oberwart, Aus.	H16	8
Obetz, Oh., U.S.	C3	112
Obi, Kepulauan, is., Indon.	F8	32
Obi, Pulau, i., Indon.	F8	32
Óbidos, Braz.	D7	54
Obihiro, Japan	q21	30a
Obion, Tn., U.S.	A2	119
Obion, co., Tn., U.S.	A2	119
Obion, stm., Tn., U.S.	A2	119
Oblong, Il., U.S.	D6	90
Obluče, Russia	H20	24
Obninsk, Russia	F19	18
Obock, Dji.	F3	46
O'Brien, co., Ia., U.S.	A2	92
Obrovac, Cro.	E10	14
Observation Peak, mtn., Ca., U.S.	B3	82
Observatoire, Caye de l', i., N. Cal.	D11	50
Obuasi, Ghana	G5	42
Ocala, Fl., U.S.	C4	86
Ocaña, Col.	C6	58
Ocaña, Spain	F8	12
Occidental, Cordillera, mts., Col.	E4	58
Occidental, Cordillera, mts., Peru	F4	54
Ocean, co., N.J., U.S.	D4	107
Oceana, W.V., U.S.	D3	125
Oceana, co., Mi., U.S.	E4	99
Oceana Naval Air Station, mil., Va., U.S.	k15	123
Ocean Bluff, Ma., U.S.	B6	98
Ocean City, Fl., U.S.	u15	86
Ocean City, Md., U.S.	D7	97
Ocean City, N.J., U.S.	E3	107
Ocean Grove, Ma., U.S.	C5	98
Ocean Park, Wa., U.S.	C1	124
Oceanport, N.J., U.S.	C4	107
Oceanside, Ca., U.S.	F5	82
Ocean Springs, Ms., U.S.	E5	101
Ocean [Township], N.J., U.S.	C4	107
Ocean View, De., U.S.	F5	85
Ocha, Russia	G22	24
Ocheda Lake, l., Mn., U.S.	G3	100
Ocheyedan, stm., Ia., U.S.	A2	92
Ochiltree, co., Tx., U.S.	A2	120
Ochlockonee, stm., Fl., U.S.	B2	86
Ochoco Lake, res., Or., U.S.	C6	114
Ocho Rios, Jam.	E9	64
Ochota, stm., Russia	F22	24
Ochotsk, Russia	F22	24
Ochsenfurt, Ger.	F10	8
Ocilla, Ga., U.S.	E3	87
Ockelbo, Swe.	F11	6
Ocmulgee, stm., Ga., U.S.	D3	87
Ocoee, Fl., U.S.	D5	86
Ocoee, Lake, res., Tn., U.S.	D9	119
Oconee, co., Ga., U.S.	C3	87
Oconee, co., S.C., U.S.	B1	117
Oconee, stm., Ga., U.S.	C3	87
Oconee, Lake, res., Ga., U.S.	C3	87
Oconomowoc, Wi., U.S.	E5	126
Oconto, Wi., U.S.	D6	126
Oconto, co., Wi., U.S.	D5	126
Oconto, stm., Wi., U.S.	D5	126
Oconto Falls, Wi., U.S.	D5	126
Ocotal, Nic.	H4	64
Ocotlán, Mex.	G8	62
Ocracoke Inlet, b., N.C., U.S.	B6	110
Ocracoke Island, i., N.C., U.S.	B7	110
Octoraro Creek, stm., U.S.	A5	97
Ocumare del Tuy, Ven.	B9	58
Ocussi, Indon.	G7	32
Oda, Ghana	G5	42
Oda, Jabal, mtn., Sudan	D13	42
Ōdate, Japan	B13	30
Odawara, Japan	G12	30
Odda, Nor.	F6	6
Odebolt, Ia., U.S.	B2	92
Odell, Il., U.S.	B5	90
Odell, Or., U.S.	B5	114
Odell Lake, l., Or., U.S.	E5	114
Odem, Tx., U.S.	F4	120
Odemira, Port.	H3	12
Ödemiş, Tur.	K11	16
Odense, Den.	I8	6
Odenton, Md., U.S.	B4	97
Odenville, Al., U.S.	B3	78
Oder (Odra), stm., Eur.	C14	8
Oderberg, Ger.	C14	8
Odessa, Ont., Can.	C8	73
Odessa, Ukr.	H4	22
Odessa, De., U.S.	C3	85
Odessa, Mo., U.S.	C4	102
Odessa, Tx., U.S.	D1	120
Odessa, Wa., U.S.	B7	124
Odienné, I.C.	G4	42
Odin, Il., U.S.	E4	90
Odincovo, Russia	F20	18
Odon, In., U.S.	G4	91
O'Donnell, Tx., U.S.	C2	120
Odra (Oder), stm., Eur.	C14	8
Oelsnitz, Ger.	E12	8
Oelwein, Ia., U.S.	B6	92
O'Fallon, Il., U.S.	E4	90
O'Fallon, Mo., U.S.	f12	102
Offenbach, Ger.	E8	8
Offenburg, Ger.	G7	8
Offutt Air Force Base, mil., Ne., U.S.	g3	104
Ōfunato, Japan	C14	30
Ōgaki, Japan	G9	30
Ogallala, Ne., U.S.	C4	104
Ogbomosho, Nig.	G6	42
Ogden, Ia., U.S.	B3	92
Ogden, Ks., U.S.	C7	93
Ogden, Ut., U.S.	B4	121
Ogden, Mount, mtn., N.A.	k23	79
Ogdensburg, N.J., U.S.	A3	107
Ogdensburg, N.Y., U.S.	f9	109
Ogeechee, stm., Ga., U.S.	D5	87
Ogemaw, co., Mi., U.S.	D6	99
Ogilvie Mountains, mts., Yukon, Can.	D5	66
Ogle, co., Il., U.S.	A4	90
Oglesby, Il., U.S.	B4	90
Oglethorpe, Ga., U.S.	D2	87
Oglethorpe, co., Ga., U.S.	C3	87
Oglethorpe, Mount, mtn., Ga., U.S.	B2	87
Ogooué, stm., Afr.	B2	44
Ogulin, Cro.	D10	14
Ogunquit, Me., U.S.	E2	96
Oğuzeli, Tur.	A5	40
Ohanet, Alg.	C7	42
Ōhata, Japan	A14	30
Ohatchee, Al., U.S.	B3	78
O'Higgins, Lago (Lago San Martín), l., S.A.	F2	56
Ohio, co., In., U.S.	G7	91
Ohio, co., Ky., U.S.	C3	94
Ohio, co., W.V., U.S.	A4	125
Ohio, state, U.S.	B3	112
Ohio, stm., U.S.	D9	76
Ohio Brush Creek, stm., Oh., U.S.	D2	112
Ohio City, Oh., U.S.	B1	112
Ohio Peak, mtn., Co., U.S.	C3	83
Ohioville, Pa., U.S.	E1	115
Ohoopee, stm., Ga., U.S.	D4	87
Ohrid, Lake, l., Eur.	H4	16
Öhringen, Ger.	F9	8
Oiapoque, Braz.	C8	54
Oil City, La., U.S.	B2	95
Oil City, Pa., U.S.	D2	115
Oil Creek, stm., Pa., U.S.	C2	115
Oildale, Ca., U.S.	E4	82
Oil Springs, Ont., Can.	E2	73
Oilton, Ok., U.S.	A5	113
Ōita, Japan	I4	30
Ojai, Ca., U.S.	E4	82
Ojinaga, Mex.	C7	62
Ojm'akon, Russia	E22	24
Ojo de Liebre, Laguna, b., Mex.	D2	62
Ojos del Salado, Cerro, mtn., S.A.	B3	56
Oka, stm., Russia	G14	24
Oka, stm., Russia	F25	16
Okaba, Indon.	G10	32
Okahandja, Nmb.	F3	44
Okaloosa, co., Fl., U.S.	u15	86
Okamanpeedan Lake, l., U.S.	A3	92
Okanagan Falls, B.C., Can.	E8	69
Okanagan Lake, l., B.C., Can.	D8	69
Okanagan Landing, B.C., Can.	D8	69
Okanogan, Wa., U.S.	A6	124
Okanogan, co., Wa., U.S.	A5	124
Okara, Pak.	E5	38
Okatibee Reservoir, res., Ms., U.S.	C5	101
Okauchee Lake, Wi., U.S.	*E5	126
Okavango (Cubango), stm., Afr.	E3	44
Okavango Swamp, sw., Bots.	E4	44
Ōkawa, Japan	I3	30
Okawville, Il., U.S.	E4	90
Okaya, Japan	F11	30
Okayama, Japan	H6	30
Okazaki, Japan	H10	30
Okeechobee, Fl., U.S.	E6	86
Okeechobee, co., Fl., U.S.	E6	86
Okeechobee, Lake, l., Fl., U.S.	F6	86
Okeene, Ok., U.S.	A3	113
Okefenokee Swamp, sw., U.S.	F4	87
Okemah, Ok., U.S.	B5	113
Okfuskee, co., Ok., U.S.	B5	113
Okhotsk, Sea of (Ochotskoje More), Asia	G23	24
Oki-guntō, is., Japan	F6	30
Okinawa-jima, i., Japan	y27	31b
Okinoerabu-shima, i., Japan	x28	31b
Okino-Tori-shima, i., Japan	G14	26
Oklahoma, co., Ok., U.S.	B4	113
Oklahoma, state, U.S.	B4	113
Oklahoma City, Ok., U.S.	B4	113
Oklawaha, Fl., U.S.	C5	86
Oklawaha, stm., Fl., U.S.	C5	86
Oklawaha, Lake, res., Fl., U.S.	C5	86
Okmulgee, Ok., U.S.	B6	113
Okmulgee, co., Ok., U.S.	B5	113
Okoboji, Ia., U.S.	A2	92
Okobojo Creek, stm., S.D., U.S.	C5	118
Okolona, Ky., U.S.	g11	94
Okolona, Ms., U.S.	B5	101
Okotoks, Alta., Can.	D4	68
Okt'abr'skoj Revol'ucii, Ostrov, i., Russia	B13	24
Oktibbeha, co., Ms., U.S.	B5	101
Ola, Ar., U.S.	B2	81
Olancha Peak, mtn., Ca., U.S.	D4	82
Olanchito, Hond.	G4	64
Öland, i., Swe.	H11	6
Olanta, S.C., U.S.	D8	117
Olathe, Co., U.S.	C3	83
Olathe, Ks., U.S.	D9	93
Olavarría, Arg.	D4	56
Olcott, N.Y., U.S.	B2	109
Old Bahama Channel, strt., N.A.	C8	64
Old Bridge, N.J., U.S.	C4	107
Oldenburg, Ger.	B8	8
Oldenburg, In., U.S.	F7	91
Oldenburg [in Holstein], Ger.	A10	8
Old Faithful Geyser, Wy., U.S.	B2	127
Old Forge, Pa., U.S.	D10	115
Old Fort, N.C., U.S.	f10	110
Oldham, Ky., U.S.	B4	94
Oldham, co., Tx., U.S.	B1	120
Old Harbor, Ak., U.S.	D9	79
Old Head of Kinsale, c., Ire.	J4	7
Old Hickory Lake, res., Tn., U.S.	A5	119
Oldman, stm., Alta., Can.	E4	68
Old Man of the Mountain, N.H., U.S.	B3	106
Oldmans Creek, stm., N.J., U.S.	D2	107
Old Orchard Beach, Me., U.S.	E2	96
Old Perlican, Newf., Can.	D5	72
Old Point Comfort, c., Va., U.S.	h15	123
Old Rhodes Key, i., Fl., U.S.	G6	86
Old River Lake, l., Ar., U.S.	k10	81
Olds, Alta., Can.	D3	68
Old Saybrook, Ct., U.S.	D6	84
Oldsmar, Fl., U.S.	o10	86
Old Tampa Bay, b., Fl., U.S.	p10	86
Old Tappan, N.J., U.S.	g9	107
Old Topsail Inlet, b., N.C., U.S.	C5	110
Old Town, Me., U.S.	D4	96
Old Wives Lake, l., Sask., Can.	G2	75
Olean, N.Y., U.S.	C2	109
O'Leary, P.E.I., Can.	C5	71
Ølen, Nor.	G5	6
Olenij, Ostrov, i., Russia	C9	24
Olen'ok, Russia	D16	24
Olen'ok, stm., Russia	C18	24
Olen'okskij Zaliv, b., Russia	C18	24
Olentangy, stm., Oh., U.S.	B3	112
Oleśnica, Pol.	D17	8
Ol'ga, Russia	I21	24
Olga, Mount, mtn., Austl.	E6	50
Olhão, Port.	H4	12
Ólimbos, mtn., Cyp.	B3	40
Ólimbos, Óros, mtn., Grc.	I6	16
Olímpia, Braz.	F4	57
Olin, Ia., U.S.	B6	92
Olinda, Braz.	E12	54
Olite, Spain	C10	12
Oliva, Arg.	C4	56
Oliva, Spain	G11	12
Oliva de la Frontera, Spain	G5	12
Olive Branch, Ms., U.S.	A4	101
Olive Hill, Ky., U.S.	B6	94
Olivehurst, Ca., U.S.	C3	82
Oliveira, Braz.	F6	57
Olivenza, Spain	G4	12
Oliver, B.C., Can.	E8	69
Oliver, Pa., U.S.	G2	115
Oliver, co., N.D., U.S.	B4	111
Oliver Dam, U.S.	C5	78
Oliver Springs, Tn., U.S.	C9	119
Olivet, Mi., U.S.	F6	99
Olivia, Mn., U.S.	F4	100
Olla, La., U.S.	C3	95
Ollagüe, Chile	A3	56
Olmedo, Spain	D7	12
Olmito, Tx., U.S.	F4	120
Olmos, Peru	E3	54
Olmos Park, Tx., U.S.	k7	120
Olmsted, co., Mn., U.S.	G6	100
Olmsted Falls, Oh., U.S.	h9	112
Olney, Il., U.S.	E5	90
Olney, Md., U.S.	B3	97
Olney, Tx., U.S.	C3	120
Oloj, stm., Russia	D26	24
Ol'okma, stm., Russia	F18	24
Ol'okminsk, Russia	E18	24
Olomouc, Czech.	F17	8
Olongapo, Phil.	q19	33b
Oloron-Sainte-Marie, Fr.	I6	10
Olot, Spain	C14	12
Olov'annaja, Russia	G17	24
Olsztyn (Allenstein), Pol.	B20	8
Olten, Switz.	E14	10
Olton, Tx., U.S.	B1	120
Oluan Pi, c., Tai.	N9	28
Olustee, Ok., U.S.	C2	113
Olympia, Wa., U.S.	B3	124
Olympic Mountains, mts., Wa., U.S.	B2	124
Olympic National Park, Wa., U.S.	B2	124
Olympus, Mount, mtn., Wa., U.S.	B2	124
Olympus, Mount see Ólimbos, Óros, mtn., Grc.	I6	16
Olyphant, Pa., U.S.	D10	115
Omae-zaki, c., Japan	H11	30
Omagh, N. Ire., U.K.	G5	7
Omaha, Ne., U.S.	C10	104
Omaha Indian Reservation, Ne., U.S.	B9	104
Omak, Wa., U.S.	A6	124
Omak Lake, l., Wa., U.S.	A6	124
Oman, ctry., Asia	D6	46
Oman, Gulf of, b., Asia	D6	46
Omar, W.V., U.S.	D3	125
Ōma-zaki, c., Japan	A13	30
Omčak, Russia	E23	24
Omega, Ga., U.S.	E3	87
Omegna, Italy	D3	14
Omemee, Ont., Can.	C6	73
Omerville, Que., Can.	D5	74
Ometepe, Isla de i., Nic.	I5	64
Ometepec, Mex.	I10	62
Omineca, stm., B.C., Can.	B5	69
Omineca Mountains, mts., B.C., Can.	A4	69
Ōmiya, Japan	G12	30
Ommaney, Cape, c., Ak., U.S.	D12	79
Ommanney Bay, b., N.W. Ter., Can.	B12	66
Ommen, Neth.	C6	8
Omo, stm., Eth.	G2	46
Omolon, stm., Russia	D25	24
Ompompanoosuc, stm., Vt., U.S.	D4	122
Omro, Wi., U.S.	D5	126
Omsk, Russia	F8	24
Omsukčan, Russia	E25	24
Ōmura, Japan	J2	30
Ōmuta, Japan	I3	30
Onaga, Ks., U.S.	C7	93
Onalaska, Wi., U.S.	E2	126
Onamia, Mn., U.S.	D5	100
Onancock, Va., U.S.	C7	123
Onarga, Il., U.S.	C6	90
Onawa, Ia., U.S.	B1	92
Onawa, Lake, l., Me., U.S.	C3	96
Onaway, Mi., U.S.	C6	99
Onda, Spain	F11	12
Ondangua, Nmb.	E3	44
Ondjiva, Ang.	E3	44
Öndörchaan, Mong.	B9	28
Oneco, Fl., U.S.	E4	86
Onega, Lake see Onežskoje ozero, l., Russia	E5	22
One Hundred Fifty Mile House, B.C., Can.	C7	69
One Hundred Mile House, B.C., Can.	D7	69
Oneida, Ky., U.S.	C6	94
Oneida, N.Y., U.S.	B5	109
Oneida, Oh., U.S.	C1	112
Oneida, Tn., U.S.	C9	119
Oneida, co., Id., U.S.	G6	89
Oneida, co., N.Y., U.S.	B5	109
Oneida, co., Wi., U.S.	C4	126
Oneida Lake, l., N.Y., U.S.	B5	109
O'Neill, Ne., U.S.	B7	104
Onekotan, Ostrov, i., Russia	H24	24
Oneonta, Al., U.S.	B3	78
Oneonta, N.Y., U.S.	C5	109
Onežskoje ozero, l., Russia	E5	22
Ongole, India	E6	37
Onida, S.D., U.S.	C5	118
Onitsha, Nig.	G7	42
Onoda, Japan	I4	30
Onomichi, Japan	H6	30
Onondaga, co., N.Y., U.S.	C4	109
Onondaga Indian Reservation, N.Y., U.S.	C4	109
Onota Lake, l., Ma., U.S.	B1	98
Onoway, Alta., Can.	C3	68
Onset, Ma., U.S.	C6	98
Onslow, Austl.	D3	50
Onslow, co., N.C., U.S.	C5	110
Onslow Bay, b., N.C., U.S.	C5	110
Onsted, Mi., U.S.	F6	99
Ontario, Ca., U.S.	E5	82
Ontario, Oh., U.S.	B3	112
Ontario, Or., U.S.	C10	114
Ontario, co., N.Y., U.S.	C3	109
Ontario, prov., Can.	C6	73
Ontario, Lake, l., N.A.	C11	76
Onteniente, Spain	G11	12
Ontonagon, Mi., U.S.	m12	99
Ontonagon, co., Mi., U.S.	m12	99
Ontonagon Indian Reservation, Mi., U.S.	B1	99
Onverwacht, Sur.	B7	54
Oodnadatta, Austl.	E7	50
Ooldea, Austl.	F6	50
Oolitic, In., U.S.	G4	91
Oologah, Ok., U.S.	A6	113
Oologah Lake, res., Ok., U.S.	A6	113
Ooltewah, Tn., U.S.	D8	119
Oostburg, Wi., U.S.	E6	126
Oostende (Ostende), Bel.	D2	8
Oosterhout, Neth.	D4	8
Ootacamund, India	G4	37
Ootsa Lake, l., B.C., Can.	C4	69
Opala, Zaire	B4	44
Opa-Locka, Fl., U.S.	s13	86
Opatija, Cro.	D9	14
Opava, Czech.	F17	8
Opelika, Al., U.S.	C4	78
Opelousas, La., U.S.	D3	95
Opequon Creek, stm., W.V., U.S.	B6	125
Opiscotéo, Lac, l., Que., Can.	F19	72
Opole (Oppeln), Pol.	E17	8
Opotiki, N.Z.	C6	52
Opp, Al., U.S.	D3	78
Oppdal, Nor.	E7	6
Oppelo, Ar., U.S.	B3	81
Opportunity, Wa., U.S.	B8	124
Optima Reservoir, res., Ok., U.S.	e9	113
Oquawka, Il., U.S.	C3	90
Ora, Italy	C6	14
Oracle, Az., U.S.	E5	80
Oradea, Rom.	B5	16
Oradell, N.J., U.S.	h8	107
Oradell Reservoir, res., N.J., U.S.	h9	107
Orai, India	H8	38
Oraibi, Az., U.S.	B5	80
Oran (Wahran), Alg.	A5	42
Oran, Mo., U.S.	D8	102
Orange, Austl.	F9	50
Orange, Fr.	H11	10
Orange, Ca., U.S.	n13	82
Orange, Ct., U.S.	D3	84
Orange, Ma., U.S.	A3	98
Orange, N.J., U.S.	B4	107
Orange, Tx., U.S.	D6	120
Orange, Va., U.S.	B4	123
Orange, co., Ca., U.S.	F5	82
Orange, co., Fl., U.S.	D5	86
Orange, co., In., U.S.	G4	91
Orange, co., N.Y., U.S.	D6	109
Orange, co., N.C., U.S.	A3	110
Orange, co., Tx., U.S.	D6	120
Orange, co., Vt., U.S.	D3	122
Orange, co., Va., U.S.	B4	123
Orange (Oranje), stm., Afr.	G3	44
Orange, Cabo, c., Braz.	C8	54
Orange Beach, Al., U.S.	E2	78
Orangeburg, S.C., U.S.	E6	117
Orangeburg, co., S.C., U.S.	E6	117
Orange City, Fl., U.S.	D5	86
Orange City, Ia., U.S.	B1	92
Orange Grove, Ms., U.S.	E5	101
Orange Grove, Tx., U.S.	F4	120
Orange Lake, l., Fl., U.S.	C4	86
Orange Park, Fl., U.S.	B5	86
Orangeville, Ont., Can.	D4	73
Orangeville, Ut., U.S.	D4	121
Orange Walk, Belize	E3	64
Orani, Phil.	q19	33b
Oranienburg, Ger.	C13	8
Oranjestad, Aruba	H12	64
Orbetello, Italy	G6	14
Orbost, Austl.	G9	50
Örbyhus, Swe.	F11	6
Orcas Island, i., Wa., U.S.	A3	124

Name	Map Ref	Page
Orcera, Spain	G9	12
Orchard City, Co., U.S.	C3	83
Orchard Homes, Mt., U.S.	D2	103
Orchard Park, N.Y., U.S.	C2	109
Orchards, Wa., U.S.	D3	124
Orchard Valley, Wy., U.S.	E8	127
Orchila, Isla, i., Ven.	B9	58
Orchon, stm., Mong.	B7	26
Orcutt, Ca., U.S.	E3	82
Ord, Ne., U.S.	C7	104
Ord, Mount, mtn., Austl.	C5	50
Ordenes, Spain	B3	12
Ordway, Co., U.S.	C7	83
Ordzhonikidze see Vladikavkaz, Russia	I6	22
Oreana, Il., U.S.	D5	90
Örebro, Swe.	G10	6
Orechovo-Zujevo, Russia	F21	18
Oregon, Il., U.S.	A4	90
Oregon, Mo., U.S.	B2	102
Oregon, Oh., U.S.	A2	112
Oregon, Wi., U.S.	F4	126
Oregon, co., Mo., U.S.	E6	102
Oregon, state, U.S.	C6	114
Oregon Caves National Monument, Or., U.S.	E2	114
Oregon City, Or., U.S.	B4	114
Oregon Inlet, b., N.C., U.S.	B7	110
Orem, Ut., U.S.	C4	121
Orenburg, Russia	G9	22
Orense, Spain	C4	12
Orestiás, Grc.	H10	16
Orfordville, Wi., U.S.	F4	126
Organ Mountains, mts., N.M., U.S.	E3	108
Organ Pipe Cactus National Monument, Az., U.S.	E3	80
Orgün, Afg.	D3	38
Oriental, N.C., U.S.	B6	110
Oriental, Cordillera, mts., Col.	E6	58
Oriental, Cordillera, mts., Peru	F4	54
Orihuela, Spain	G11	12
Orillia, Ont., Can.	C5	73
Orinoco, stm., S.A.	C11	58
Orinoco, Delta del, Ven.	C12	58
Orion, Il., U.S.	B3	90
Oripää, Fin.	F14	6
Orissa, state, India	J11	38
Oristano, Italy	I3	14
Orivesi, Fin.	F15	6
Orizaba, Mex.	H11	62
Orizaba, Pico de (Volcán Citlaltépetl), vol., Mex.	H11	62
Orkney Islands, is., Scot., U.K.	B9	7
Orland, Ca., U.S.	C2	82
Orlando, Fl., U.S.	D5	86
Orland Park, Il., U.S.	k9	90
Orléans, Fr.	E8	10
Orleans, Ma., U.S.	C7	98
Orleans, Vt., U.S.	B4	122
Orleans, co., La., U.S.	E6	95
Orleans, co., N.Y., U.S.	B2	109
Orleans, co., Vt., U.S.	B4	122
Orléans, Île d', i., Que., Can.	C7	74
Orman Dam, S.D., U.S.	C2	118
Ormond Beach, Fl., U.S.	C5	86
Ormož, Slo.	C11	14
Ormstown, Que., Can.	D3	74
Ornans, Fr.	E13	10
Örnsköldsvik, Swe.	E12	6
Orocué, Col.	E7	58
Orofino, Id., U.S.	C2	89
Or'ol, Russia	I19	18
Oromocto, N.B., Can.	D3	71
Oromocto Lake, l., N.B., Can.	D2	71
Orono, Me., U.S.	D4	96
Oronoco, Mn., U.S.	F6	100
Oroville, Ca., U.S.	C3	82
Oroville, Wa., U.S.	A6	124
Oroville, Lake, res., Ca., U.S.	C3	82
Orrick, Mo., U.S.	B3	102
Orrville, Oh., U.S.	B4	112
Orsk, Russia	G9	22
Orta Nova, Italy	H10	14
Ortegal, Cabo, c., Spain	B4	12
Orting, Wa., U.S.	B3	124
Ortiz, Ven.	C9	58
Ortona, Italy	G9	14
Ortonville, Mn., U.S.	F7	99
Ortonville, Mn., U.S.	E2	100
Orümiyeh (Rezā'īyeh), Iran	J7	22
Orümiyeh, Daryächeh-ye, l., Iran	J7	22
Oruro, Bol.	G5	54
Orüzgän (Qala-I-Hazär Qadam), Afg.	D2	38
Orvieto, Italy	G7	14
Orwell, Oh., U.S.	A5	112
Orwigsburg, Pa., U.S.	E9	115
Oš, Kyrg.	I12	22
Osa, Península de, pen., C.R.	J6	64
Osage, Ia., U.S.	A5	92
Osage, Wy., U.S.	C8	127
Osage, co., Ks., U.S.	D8	93
Osage, co., Mo., U.S.	C6	102
Osage, co., Ok., U.S.	A5	113
Osage, co., Mo., U.S.	C5	102
Osage Beach, Mo., U.S.	C5	102
Osage City, Ks., U.S.	D8	93
Ōsaka, Japan	H8	30
Ōsaka-wan, b., Japan	H8	30
Osakis, Mn., U.S.	E3	100
Osakis, Lake, l., Mn., U.S.	E3	100
Osawatomie, Ks., U.S.	D9	93
Osborne, Ks., U.S.	C5	93
Osborne, co., Ks., U.S.	C5	93
Osburn, Id., U.S.	B3	89
Osceola, Ar., U.S.	B6	81
Osceola, In., U.S.	A5	91
Osceola, Mo., U.S.	C4	102
Osceola, Ne., U.S.	C8	104
Osceola, Wi., U.S.	C1	126
Osceola, co., Fl., U.S.	E5	86
Osceola, co., Ia., U.S.	A2	92
Osceola, co., Mi., U.S.	E5	99
Osceola Mills, Pa., U.S.	E5	115
Oscoda, Mi., U.S.	D7	99
Oscoda, co., Mi., U.S.	D6	99
Oscura Mountains, mts., N.M., U.S.	D3	108
Osen, Nor.	D8	6
Osgood, In., U.S.	F7	91
Oshawa, Ont., Can.	D6	73
Oshima-hantō, pen., Japan	q18	30a
Oshkosh, Ne., U.S.	C3	104
Oshkosh, Wi., U.S.	D5	126
Oshogbo, Nig.	G6	42
Osh see Oš, Kyrg.	I12	22
Oshwe, Zaire	B3	44
Osijek, Cro.	D2	16
Osimo, Italy	F8	14
Osinniki, Russia	G11	24
Osipoviči, Bela.	H11	18
Oskaloosa, Ia., U.S.	C5	92
Oskaloosa, Ks., U.S.	C8	93
Oskarshamn, Swe.	H11	6
Oslo, Nor.	G8	6
Osmānābād, India	C4	37
Osmaniye, Tur.	A5	40
Osmond, Ne., U.S.	B8	104
Osnabrück, Ger.	C8	8
Osorno, Chile	E2	56
Osorno, Spain	C7	12
Osoyoos, B.C., Can.	E8	69
Osoyoos Lake, l., Wa., U.S.	A6	124
Ospino, Ven.	C8	58
Osprey, Fl., U.S.	E4	86
Osprey Reef, rf., Austl.	B9	50
Ossa, Mount, mtn., Austl.	H9	50
Ossabaw Island, i., Ga., U.S.	E5	87
Osseo, Mn., U.S.	m12	100
Osseo, Wi., U.S.	D2	126
Ossian, In., U.S.	C7	91
Ossian, Ia., U.S.	A6	92
Ossining, N.Y., U.S.	D7	109
Ossipee, Ma., U.S.	C5	106
Ossipee Lake, l., N.H., U.S.	C4	106
Ostaškov, Russia	D16	18
Osterholz-Scharmbeck, Ger.	B8	8
Osterode, Ger.	D10	8
Östersund, Swe.	E10	6
Osterville, Ma., U.S.	C7	98
Ostrava, Czech.	F18	8
Ostrołęka, Pol.	B21	8
Ostrov, Russia	D11	18
Ostrowiec Świętokrzyski, Pol.	E21	8
Ostrów Wielkopolski, Pol.	D17	8
Ostuni, Italy	I12	14
Ōsumi-kaikyō, strt., Japan	L3	30
Ōsumi-shotō, is., Japan	u30	31b
Osuna, Spain	H6	12
Osvaldo Cruz, Braz.	F3	57
Oswegatchie, stm., N.Y., U.S.	f9	109
Oswego, Il., U.S.	B5	90
Oswego, Ks., U.S.	E8	93
Oswego, N.Y., U.S.	B4	109
Oswego, co., N.Y., U.S.	B4	109
Oswego, stm., N.J., U.S.	D4	107
Oswego, stm., N.Y., U.S.	B4	109
Oswestry, Eng., U.K.	I9	7
Oświęcim, Pol.	E19	8
Ōta, Japan	F12	30
Otaki, N.Z.	D5	52
Otaru, Japan	p18	30a
Otavi, Nmb.	E3	44
Oteen, N.C., U.S.	f10	110
Otero, co., Co., U.S.	D7	83
Otero, co., N.M., U.S.	E3	108
Othello, Wa., U.S.	C6	124
Oti, stm., Afr.	G6	42
Otis, Orchards, Wa., U.S.	g14	124
Otis Reservoir, res., Ma., U.S.	B1	98
Otisville, Mi., U.S.	E7	99
Otjiwarongo, Nmb.	F3	44
Otočac, Cro.	E10	14
Otoe, co., Ne., U.S.	D9	104
Otranto, Italy	I13	14
Otranto, Strait of, mth., Eur.	I2	16
Otsego, Mi., U.S.	F5	99
Otsego, co., Mi., U.S.	C6	99
Otsego, co., N.Y., U.S.	C5	109
Otsego Lake, l., N.Y., U.S.	C6	109
Ōtsu, Japan	G8	30
Otta, Nor.	F7	6
Ottauquechee, stm., Vt., U.S.	D4	122
Ottawa, Ont., Can.	B9	73
Ottawa, Il., U.S.	B5	90
Ottawa, Ks., U.S.	D8	93
Ottawa, Oh., U.S.	A1	112
Ottawa, co., Ks., U.S.	C6	93
Ottawa, co., Mi., U.S.	F4	99
Ottawa, co., Oh., U.S.	A2	112
Ottawa, co., Ok., U.S.	A7	113
Ottawa, stm., Can.	G17	66
Ottawa, stm., Oh., U.S.	e6	112
Ottawa Hills, Oh., U.S.	e6	112
Ottawa Islands, is., N.W. Ter., Can.	E16	66
Ottenby, Swe.	H11	6
Otterbein, In., U.S.	D3	91
Otter Brook, stm., N.H., U.S.	E2	106
Otter Brook Lake, res., N.H., U.S.	E2	106
Otter Creek, stm., Ut., U.S.	E4	121
Otter Creek, stm., Vt., U.S.	C2	122
Otter Creek Reservoir, res., Ut., U.S.	E4	121
Otter Islands, is., S.C., U.S.	m11	117
Otter Tail, co., Mn., U.S.	D3	100
Otter Tail, stm., Mn., U.S.	D2	100
Otter Tail Lake, l., Mn., U.S.	D3	100
Otterville, Ont., Can.	E4	73
Oyama, Japan	F12	30
Oyem, Gabon	A2	44
Oyen, Alta., Can.	D5	68
Oyonnax, Fr.	F12	10
Oyster Bay, N.Y., U.S.	E7	109
Oyster Keys, is., Fl., U.S.	G6	86
Ottumwa, Ia., U.S.	C5	92
Otwock, Pol.	C21	8
Ötztaler Alpen, mts., Eur.	C5	14
Ouachita, co., Ar., U.S.	D3	81
Ouachita, co., La., U.S.	B3	95
Ouachita, Lake, res., Ar., U.S.	C2	81
Ouachita Mountains, mts., U.S.	E8	76
Ouadda, Cen. Afr. Rep.	G10	42
Ouagadougou, Burkina	F5	42
Ouahigouya, Burkina	F5	42
Oualâta, Maur.	E4	42
Ouallene, Alg.	D6	42
Ouanda Djallé, Cen. Afr. Rep.	G10	42
Ouarane, reg., Maur.	D3	42
Ouargla, Alg.	B7	42
Ouarzazate, Mor.	B4	42
Oubangui, stm., Afr.	A3	44
Oudtshoorn, S. Afr.	H4	44
Oued Meliz, Tun.	M3	14
Oued Zarga, Tun.	M4	14
Ouémé, stm., Benin	G6	42
Ouesso, Congo	A3	44
Ouezzane, Mor.	B4	42
Oujda, Mor.	B5	42
Oulu, Fin.	D15	6
Oulujärvi, l., Fin.	D16	6
Oum Chalouba, Chad	E10	42
Ounianga Kébir, Chad	E10	42
Ouray, Co., U.S.	C3	83
Ouray, co., Co., U.S.	C3	83
Ouray, Mount, mtn., Co., U.S.	C4	83
Ourinhos, Braz.	G4	57
Ourique, Port.	H3	12
Ouro Prêto, Braz.	F7	57
Ōu-sammyaku, mts., Japan	D13	30
Outagamie, co., Wi., U.S.	D5	126
Outardes Quatre, Réservoir, res., Que., Can.	h13	74
Outer Hebrides, is., Scot., U.K.	D5	7
Outer Island, i., Wi., U.S.	A3	126
Outer Santa Barbara Passage, strt., Ca., U.S.	F4	82
Outpost Mountain, mtn., Ak., U.S.	B9	79
Outremont, Que., Can.	p19	74
Ovalle, Chile	C2	56
Ovamboland, hist. reg., Nmb.	E3	44
Ovana, Cerro, mtn., Ven.	E9	58
Ovar, Port.	E3	12
Overbrook, Ks., U.S.	D8	93
Overgaard, Az., U.S.	C5	80
Overland, Mo., U.S.	f13	102
Overland Park, Ks., U.S.	m16	93
Overlea, Md., U.S.	B4	97
Overton, Nv., U.S.	G7	105
Overton, Tx., U.S.	C5	120
Overton, co., Tn., U.S.	C8	119
Övertorneå, Swe.	C14	6
Ovett, Ms., U.S.	D4	101
Ovid, Mi., U.S.	E6	99
Oviedo, Spain	B6	12
Owando, Congo	B3	44
Owasco Lake, l., N.Y., U.S.	C4	109
Owase, Japan	H9	30
Owasso, Ok., U.S.	A6	113
Owatonna, Mn., U.S.	F5	100
Owego, N.Y., U.S.	C4	109
Owen, Wi., U.S.	D3	126
Owen, co., In., U.S.	F4	91
Owen, co., Ky., U.S.	B5	94
Owen, Lake, l., Wi., U.S.	B2	126
Owen, Mount, mtn., Co., U.S.	C3	83
Owens, stm., Ca., U.S.	D4	82
Owensboro, Ky., U.S.	C2	94
Owens Cross Roads, Al., U.S.	A3	78
Owens Lake, l., Ca., U.S.	D5	82
Owensville, In., U.S.	H2	91
Owensville, Mo., U.S.	C6	102
Owensville, Oh., U.S.	C1	112
Owenton, Ky., U.S.	B5	94
Owings Mills, Md., U.S.	B4	97
Owingsville, Ky., U.S.	B6	94
Owl Creek, stm., Wy., U.S.	C4	127
Owl Creek Mountains, mts., Wy., U.S.	C4	127
Owo, Nig.	G7	42
Owosso, Mi., U.S.	E6	99
Owsley, co., Ky., U.S.	C6	94
Owyhee, Nv., U.S.	B5	105
Owyhee, co., Id., U.S.	G2	89
Owyhee, stm., U.S.	E9	114
Owyhee, Lake, res., Or., U.S.	D9	114
Owyhee Dam, Or., U.S.	D9	114
Owyhee Mountains, mts., U.S.	G2	89
Oxbow Dam, U.S.	E2	89
Oxelösund, Swe.	G11	6
Oxford, N.S., Can.	D6	71
Oxford, N.Z.	E4	52
Oxford, Eng., U.K.	J11	7
Oxford, Al., U.S.	B4	78
Oxford, Ct., U.S.	D3	84
Oxford, Ga., U.S.	C3	87
Oxford, In., U.S.	C3	91
Oxford, Ia., U.S.	C6	92
Oxford, Md., U.S.	C5	97
Oxford, Ma., U.S.	B4	98
Oxford, Mi., U.S.	F7	99
Oxford, Ms., U.S.	A4	101
Oxford, Ne., U.S.	D6	104
Oxford, N.Y., U.S.	C5	109
Oxford, N.C., U.S.	A4	110
Oxford, Oh., U.S.	C1	112
Oxford, Pa., U.S.	G10	115
Oxford, co., Me., U.S.	D2	96
Oxford Lake, l., Man., Can.	B4	70
Oxford Peak, mtn., Id., U.S.	G6	89
Oxnard, Ca., U.S.	E4	82
Oxon Hill, Md., U.S.	f9	97
Oxus see Amu Darya, stm., Asia	I10	22
Oyama, B.C., Can.	D8	69
Ozark, Al., U.S.	D4	78
Ozark, Ar., U.S.	B2	81
Ozark, Mo., U.S.	D4	102
Ozark, co., Mo., U.S.	E5	102
Ozark Plateau, plat., U.S.	D8	76
Ozark Reservoir, res., Ar., U.S.	B1	81
Ozarks, Lake of the, res., Mo., U.S.	C5	102
Ozaukee, co., Wi., U.S.	E6	126
Ózd, Hung.	G20	8
Ozernovskij, Russia	G25	24
Ozette Lake, l., Wa., U.S.	A1	124
Ozieri, Italy	I3	14
Ožogino, Ozero, l., Russia	D23	24
Ozona, Fl., U.S.	o10	86
Ozona, Tx., U.S.	D2	120
Ōzu, Japan	I5	30

P

Name	Map Ref	Page
Paarl, S. Afr.	H3	44
Paauilo, Hi., U.S.	C6	88
Pabianice, Pol.	D19	8
Pābna, Bngl.	H13	38
Pacasmayo, Peru	E3	54
Pace, Fl., U.S.	u14	86
Pachaug Pond, l., Ct., U.S.	C8	84
Pachino, Italy	M10	14
Pachuca [de Soto], Mex.	G10	62
Pacific, Mo., U.S.	C7	102
Pacific, Wa., U.S.	f11	124
Pacific, co., Wa., U.S.	C2	124
Pacifica, Ca., U.S.	h8	82
Pacific Beach, Wa., U.S.	B1	124
Pacific City, Or., U.S.	B3	114
Pacific Creek, stm., Wy., U.S.	D3	127
Pacific Grove, Ca., U.S.	D3	82
Pacific Ocean	F2	2
Pacific Palisades, Hi., U.S.	g10	88
Pacific Ranges, mts., B.C., Can.	D4	69
Pacific Rim National Park, B.C., Can.	E5	69
Pack Monadnock Mountain, mtn., N.H., U.S.	E3	106
Packwood, Wa., U.S.	C4	124
Pacolet, S.C., U.S.	B4	117
Pacolet, stm., S.C., U.S.	A4	117
Pacolet Mills, S.C., U.S.	B4	117
Pactola Reservoir, res., S.D., U.S.	C2	118
Padang, Indon.	F3	32
Padangpanjang, Indon.	O6	34
Padangsidempuan, Indon.	N5	34
Paddock Lake, Wi., U.S.	n11	126
Paden City, W.V., U.S.	B4	125
Paderborn, Ger.	D8	8
Padova, Italy	D6	14
Padre Island, i., Tx., U.S.	F4	120
Padre Island National Seashore, Tx., U.S.	F4	120
Padrón, Spain	C3	12
Padstow, Eng., U.K.	K8	7
Padua see Padova, Italy	D6	14
Paducah, Ky., U.S.	e9	94
Paducah, Tx., U.S.	B2	120
Paektu-san, mtn., Asia	C12	26
Pafúri, Moz.	F6	44
Pag, Cro.	E10	14
Pagai Selatan, Pulau, i., Indon.	F3	32
Pagai Utara, Pulau, i., Indon.	F3	32
Page, Az., U.S.	A4	80
Page, W.V., U.S.	C3	125
Page, co., Ia., U.S.	D2	92
Page, co., Va., U.S.	B4	123
Pageland, S.C., U.S.	B7	117
Pagoda Peak, mtn., Co., U.S.	A3	83
Pagoda Point, c., Burma	G3	34
Pagosa Springs, Co., U.S.	D3	83
Paguate, N.M., U.S.	B2	108
Pahala, Hi., U.S.	D6	88
Pahang, stm., Malay.	M7	34
Pahoa, Hi., U.S.	D7	88
Pahokee, Fl., U.S.	F6	86
Pahrump, Nv., U.S.	G6	105
Pahute Mesa, mtn., Nv., U.S.	F5	105
Paia, Hi., U.S.	C5	88
Päijänne, l., Fin.	F15	6
Pailolo Channel, strt., Hi., U.S.	B5	88
Paimpol, Fr.	D3	10
Paincourtville, La., U.S.	k9	95
Painesville, Oh., U.S.	A4	112
Paint, stm., Mi., U.S.	B2	99
Paint Creek, stm., Oh., U.S.	C2	112
Paint Creek, stm., Oh., U.S.	m13	125
Paint Creek, North Fork, stm., Oh., U.S.	C2	112
Paint Creek Lake, res., Oh., U.S.	C2	112
Painted Desert, des., Az., U.S.	B4	80
Painted Post, N.Y., U.S.	C3	109
Painted Rock Reservoir, res., Az., U.S.	D3	80
Paintsville, Ky., U.S.	C7	94
Paisley, Ont., Can.	C3	73
Paisley, Scot., U.K.	F8	7
Paita, Peru	E2	54
Pajala, Swe.	C14	6
Pají, Ec.	H2	58
Pakanbaru, Indon.	E3	32
Pakaraima Mountains, mts., S.A.	E12	58
Pakistan (Pākistān), ctry., Asia	D2	36
Pakistan, East see Bangladesh, ctry., Asia	E6	36
Pakokku, Burma	D3	34
Pakowki Lake, l., Alta., Can.	E5	68
P'akupur, stm., Russia	D15	24
Pakxé, Laos	G8	34
Pala, Chad	G8	42
Palacios, Tx., U.S.	E4	120
Palamós, Spain	D15	12
Palana, Russia	F25	24
Pālanpur, India	H5	38
Palaoa Point, c., Hi., U.S.	C4	88
Palapye, Bots.	F5	44
Palatine, Il., U.S.	A5	90
Palatka, Russia	E24	24
Palatka, Fl., U.S.	C5	86
Palawan, i., Phil.	D6	32
Pälayankottai, India	H4	37
Palembang, Indon.	F3	32
Palencia, Spain	C7	12
Palermo, Italy	K8	14
Palestine, Ar., U.S.	C5	81
Palestine, Il., U.S.	D6	90
Palestine, Tx., U.S.	D5	120
Palestine, ctry., Asia	C4	40
Palestine, Lake, res., Tx., U.S.	C5	120
Paletwa, Burma	D2	34
Pālghāt, India	G4	37
Pāli, India	H5	38
Palikea, mtn., Hi., U.S.	g9	88
Palisade, Co., U.S.	B2	83
Palisades Park, N.J., U.S.	h8	107
Palisades Reservoir, res., U.S.	F7	89
Pälitäna, India	J4	38
Palk Strait, strt., Asia	H5	37
Pallastunturi, mtn., Fin.	B14	6
Palma, Moz.	D8	44
Palma del Río, Spain	H6	12
Palma [de Mallorca], Spain	F14	12
Palma di Montechiaro, Italy	L8	14
Palmanova, Italy	D8	14
Palmarito, Ven.	D7	58
Palmas, Cape, c., Lib.	H4	42
Palma Soriano, Cuba	D9	64
Palm Bay, Fl., U.S.	D6	86
Palm Beach, Fl., U.S.	F6	86
Palm Beach, co., Fl., U.S.	F6	86
Palm Beach Gardens, Fl., U.S.	*F6	86
Palmdale, Ca., U.S.	E4	82
Palmeira, Braz.	D4	57
Palmer, Ak., U.S.	C10	79
Palmer, Ma., U.S.	B3	98
Palmer, Mi., U.S.	B3	99
Palmer, Ms., U.S.	D4	101
Palmer, Ne., U.S.	C7	104
Palmer, Tn., U.S.	D8	119
Palmer, Tx., U.S.	n10	120
Palmer Lake, Co., U.S.	B6	83
Palmerston, Ont., Can.	D4	73
Palmerston, Cape, c., Austl.	D9	50
Palmerston North, N.Z.	D5	52
Palmerton, Pa., U.S.	E10	115
Palmetto, Fl., U.S.	E4	86
Palmetto, Ga., U.S.	C2	87
Palm Harbor, Fl., U.S.	o10	86
Palmi, Italy	K10	14
Palmira, Col.	F4	58
Palmira, Ec.	I3	58
Palms, Isle of, i., S.C., U.S.	F8	117
Palm Springs, Ca., U.S.	F5	82
Palm Springs, Fl., U.S.	*F6	86
Palmyra, In., U.S.	H5	91
Palmyra, Mo., U.S.	B6	102
Palmyra, N.J., U.S.	C2	107
Palmyra, N.Y., U.S.	B3	109
Palmyra, Pa., U.S.	F8	115
Palmyra, Wi., U.S.	F5	126
Palni, India	G4	37
Palo Alto, Ca., U.S.	D2	82
Palo Alto, co., Ia., U.S.	A3	92
Paloich, Sudan	F12	42
Palomar Mountain, mtn., Ca., U.S.	F5	82
Palomas Mountains, mts., Az., U.S.	D2	80
Palo Pinto, co., Tx., U.S.	C3	120
Palos Park, Il., U.S.	k9	90
Palos Verdes Estates, Ca., U.S.	n12	82
Palourde, Lake, l., La., U.S.	k9	95
Palouse, Wa., U.S.	C8	124
Palouse, stm., Wa., U.S.	C7	124
Palu, Indon.	F6	32
Palwal, India	F7	38
Pamekasan, Indon.	m16	33a
Pamiers, Fr.	I8	10
Pamir, mts., Asia	B3	36
Pamlico, co., N.C., U.S.	B6	110
Pamlico, stm., N.C., U.S.	B6	110
Pamlico Sound, strt., N.C., U.S.	B6	110
Pampa, Tx., U.S.	B2	120
Pampas, reg., Arg.	C4	56
Pamplico, S.C., U.S.	D8	117
Pamplona, Col.	D6	58
Pamplona, Spain	C10	12
Pamunkey, stm., Va., U.S.	C5	123
Pana, Il., U.S.	D4	90
Panaca, Nv., U.S.	F7	105
Panache, Lake, l., Ont., Can.	A3	73
Panaji (Panjim), India	E2	37
Panamá, Pan.	J8	64
Panama, Ok., U.S.	B7	113
Panama, ctry., N.A.	J7	64
Panama, Gulf of, b., Pan.	J8	64
Panama, Isthmus of, Pan.	J8	64
Panama Canal, Pan.	J8	64
Panama City, Fl., U.S.	u16	86
Panama City Beach, Fl., U.S.	u16	86
Panamint Range, mts., Ca., U.S.	D5	82
Panay, i., Phil.	C7	32
Pancake Range, mts., Nv., U.S.	E6	105
Pandharpur, India	D3	37
Pandora, Oh., U.S.	B2	112
P'andž (Panj), stm., Asia	A4	38
Panevėžys, Lith.	F7	18
Pangala, Congo	B2	44
Pangburn, Ar., U.S.	*F5	81
Pangkalanbuun, Indon.	F5	32
Pangkalpinang, Indon.	F4	32
Pangnirtung, N.W. Ter., Can.	C19	66
Panguitch, Ut., U.S.	F3	121
Pangutaran Group, is., Phil.	D7	32
Panhandle, Tx., U.S.	B2	120
Paniau, mtn., Hi., U.S.	B1	88
Pānīpat, India	F7	38
Panj (P'andž), stm., Asia	B4	38
Panjāb, Afg.	C2	38
Panjgür, Pak.	D1	36
Panola, co., Ms., U.S.	A3	101
Panola, co., Tx., U.S.	C5	120
Panora, Ia., U.S.	C3	92
Pantelleria, Italy	M6	14
Panvel, India	C2	37
Panxian, China	B8	34

Name	Map Ref	Page
Panyam, Nig.	G7	42
Panyu, China	M2	28
Paola, Italy	J11	14
Paola, Ks., U.S.	D9	93
Paoli, In., U.S.	G5	91
Paoli, Pa., U.S.	o20	115
Paonia, Co., U.S.	C3	83
Pápa, Hung.	H17	8
Papago Indian Reservation, Az., U.S.	E3	80
Papaikou, Hi., U.S.	D6	88
Papantla [de Olarte], Mex.	G11	62
Papawai Point, c., Hi., U.S.	C5	88
Papenburg, Ger.	B7	8
Papillion, Ne., U.S.	C9	104
Papineauville, Que., Can.	D2	74
Papua, Gulf of, b., Pap. N. Gui.	m15	50a
Papua New Guinea, ctry., Oc.	m15	50a
Pará, stm., Braz.	D9	54
Paracatu, Braz.	D5	57
Paracatu, stm., Braz.	D6	57
Paracel Islands, is., Asia	B5	32
Parachute, Co., U.S.	B2	83
Paradis, La., U.S.	k11	95
Paradise, Ca., U.S.	C3	82
Paradise, Nv., U.S.	G6	105
Paradise, stm., Newf., Can.	B3	72
Paradise Hills, N.M., U.S.	B3	108
Paradise Valley, Az., U.S.	k9	80
Paradise Valley, Nv., U.S.	B4	105
Paragould, Ar., U.S.	A5	81
Paraguaçu Paulista, Braz.	G3	57
Paraguaipoa, Ven.	B7	58
Paraguaná, Península de, pen., Ven.	B7	58
Paraguarí, Para.	B5	56
Paraguay, ctry., S.A.	A5	56
Paraguay, stm., S.A.	A5	56
Paraíba do Sul, stm., Braz.	F7	57
Parakou, Benin	G6	42
Paramagudi, India	H5	37
Paramaribo, Sur.	B7	54
Paramirim, Braz.	B7	57
Paramount, Md., U.S.	A2	97
Paramus, N.J., U.S.	h8	107
Paramušir, Ostrov, i., Russia	G25	24
Paraná, Arg.	C4	56
Paraná, Braz.	B5	57
Paraná, stm., Braz.	B5	57
Paraná, stm., S.A.	C5	56
Paranaguá, Braz.	B7	56
Paranaíba, Braz.	E3	57
Paranaíba, stm., Braz.	E3	57
Paranapanema, stm., Braz.	G3	57
Paranavaí, Braz.	G3	57
Parangaba, Braz.	D11	54
Paratinga, Braz.	B7	57
Paraúna, Braz.	D3	57
Pārbati, stm., India	H7	38
Parbhani, India	C4	37
Parchim, Ger.	B11	8
Parchment, Mi., U.S.	F5	99
Pardeeville, Wi., U.S.	E4	126
Pardo, stm., Braz.	F5	57
Pardubice, Czech.	E15	8
Parece Vela see Okino-Tori-shima, i., Japan	G14	26
Parecis, Serra dos, mts., Braz.	F7	54
Paredes de Nava, Spain	C7	12
Paren', Russia	E26	24
Parepare, Indon.	F6	32
Pargas (Parainen), Fin.	F14	6
Paria, stm., U.S.	A4	80
Paria, Gulf of, b.	I16	64
Pariaguán, Ven.	C10	58
Pariaman, Indon.	O6	34
Parícutin, vol., Mex.	H8	62
Parima, Sierra, mts., S.A.	F10	58
Pariñas, Punta, c., Peru	D2	54
Parintins, Braz.	D7	54
Paris, Ont., Can.	D4	73
Paris, Fr.	D9	10
Paris, Ar., U.S.	B2	81
Paris, Il., U.S.	D6	90
Paris, Ky., U.S.	B5	94
Paris, Mo., U.S.	B5	102
Paris, Tn., U.S.	A3	119
Paris, Tx., U.S.	C5	120
Paris Peak, mtn., Id., U.S.	G7	89
Parit Buntar, Malay.	L6	34
Park, co., Co., U.S.	B5	83
Park, co., Mt., U.S.	E6	103
Park, co., Wy., U.S.	B3	127
Park, stm., N.D., U.S.	A8	111
Parkano, Fin.	E14	6
Park City, Ks., U.S.	g12	93
Park City, Ut., U.S.	C4	121
Parkdale, P.E.I., Can.	C6	71
Parke, co., In., U.S.	E3	91
Parker, Az., U.S.	C1	80
Parker, Co., U.S.	B6	83
Parker, Fl., U.S.	u16	86
Parker, S.D., U.S.	D8	118
Parker, co., Tx., U.S.	C4	120
Parker, Cape, c., N.W. Ter., Can.	A17	66
Parker City, In., U.S.	D7	91
Parker Dam, U.S.	C1	80
Parkersburg, Ia., U.S.	B5	92
Parkersburg, W.V., U.S.	B3	125
Parkers Prairie, Mn., U.S.	D3	100
Parkesburg, Pa., U.S.	G10	115
Park Falls, Wi., U.S.	C3	126
Park Forest, Il., U.S.	B6	90
Park Hall, Md., U.S.	D5	97
Park Hills, Ky., U.S.	h13	94
Parkin, Ar., U.S.	B5	81
Parkland, Wa., U.S.	f11	124
Park Layne, Oh., U.S.	C1	112
Park Range, mts., Co., U.S.	A4	83
Park Rapids, Mn., U.S.	D3	100
Park Ridge, Il., U.S.	B6	90
Park Ridge, N.J., U.S.	g8	107
Park River, N.D., U.S.	A8	111
Parkrose, Or., U.S.	B4	114
Parksley, Va., U.S.	C7	123
Parkston, S.D., U.S.	D8	118
Parksville, B.C., Can.	E5	69
Parkville, Md., U.S.	B4	97
Parkville, Mo., U.S.	B3	102
Parkwater, Wa., U.S.	g14	124
Parkwood, N.C., U.S.	B4	110
Pārlākimidi, India	C8	37
Parle, Lac qui, l., Mn., U.S.	E3	100
Parlier, Ca., U.S.	D4	82
Parma, Italy	E5	14
Parma, Id., U.S.	F2	89
Parma, Mi., U.S.	F6	99
Parma, Mo., U.S.	E8	102
Parma, Oh., U.S.	A4	112
Parmachenee Lake, l., Me., U.S.	C2	96
Parma Heights, Oh., U.S.	h9	112
Parmer, co., Tx., U.S.	B1	120
Parnaíba, Braz.	D10	54
Parnaíba, stm., Braz.	D10	54
Pärnu, Est.	C7	18
Paro, Bhu.	G13	38
Parowan, Ut., U.S.	F3	121
Par Pond, res., S.C., U.S.	D5	117
Parral, Chile	D2	56
Parramore Island, i., Va., U.S.	C7	123
Parras de la Fuente, Mex.	E8	62
Parrish, Al., U.S.	B2	78
Parrsboro, N.S., Can.	D5	71
Parry, Cape, c., N.W. Ter., Can.	B8	66
Parry, Mount, mtn., B.C., Can.	C3	69
Parry Bay, b., N.W. Ter., Can.	C16	66
Parry Sound, Ont., Can.	B4	73
Parshall, N.D., U.S.	B3	111
Parsons, Ks., U.S.	E8	93
Parsons, Tn., U.S.	B3	119
Parsons, W.V., U.S.	B5	125
Parsonsburg, Md., U.S.	D7	97
Parthenay, Fr.	F6	10
Partinico, Italy	K8	14
Partridge Point, c., Newf., Can.	C3	72
Paru, stm., Braz.	D8	54
Pārvatīpuram, India	C7	37
Parys, S. Afr.	G5	44
Pasadena, Newf., Can.	D3	72
Pasadena, Ca., U.S.	E4	82
Pasadena, Md., U.S.	B4	97
Pasadena, Tx., U.S.	r14	120
Pascagoula, Ms., U.S.	E5	101
Pascagoula, stm., Ms., U.S.	E5	101
Pascagoula Bay, b., Ms., U.S.	f8	101
Pasco, Wa., U.S.	C6	124
Pasco, co., Fl., U.S.	D4	86
Pascoag, R.I., U.S.	B2	116
Pascoag Reservoir, res., R.I., U.S.	B2	116
Pascua, Isla de (Easter Island), i., Chile	H5	2
Pasewalk, Ger.	B13	8
Pasig, Phil.	q19	33b
P'asina, stm., Russia	C11	24
P'asino, Ozero, l., Russia	D11	24
P'asinskij Zaliv, b., Russia	C10	24
Pasirpengarajan, Indon.	N6	34
Pasir Puteh, Malay.	L7	34
Pasni, Pak.	D1	36
Paso de Indios, Arg.	E3	56
Paso de los Libres, Arg.	B5	56
Paso Robles, Ca., U.S.	E3	82
Pasque Island, i., Ma., U.S.	D6	98
Pasquotank, co., N.C., U.S.	A6	110
Passage, Braz.	B7	57
Passaic, N.J., U.S.	B4	107
Passaic, co., N.J., U.S.	A4	107
Passaic, stm., N.J., U.S.	h8	107
Passamaquoddy Bay, b., Me., U.S.	C6	96
Passau, Ger.	G13	8
Pass Christian, Ms., U.S.	E4	101
Passo Fundo, Braz.	B6	56
Passos, Braz.	F5	57
Passumpsic, stm., Vt., U.S.	C4	122
Pasto, Col.	G4	58
Pastora Peak, mtn., Az., U.S.	A6	80
Pastrana, Spain	E9	12
Pasuruan, Indon.	m16	33a
Patagonia, Az., U.S.	F5	80
Patagonia, reg., Arg.	E3	56
Pātan, India	I5	38
Patapsco, stm., Md., U.S.	B4	97
Pataskala, Oh., U.S.	C3	112
Patchet Brook Reservoir, res., R.I., U.S.	E6	116
Patchogue, N.Y., U.S.	n15	109
Pate Island, i., Kenya	B8	44
Paternò, Italy	L9	14
Paterson, N.J., U.S.	B4	107
Pathānkot, India	D6	38
Pathein, Burma	F3	34
Pathfinder Reservoir, res., Wy., U.S.	D6	127
Pati, Indon.	m15	33a
Patiāla, India	E7	38
Patience Island, i., R.I., U.S.	D5	116
P'atigorsk, Russia	I6	22
Pātkai Range, mts., Asia	G16	38
Patman, Lake, res., Tx., U.S.	C5	120
Patna, India	H11	38
Patoka, In., U.S.	H2	91
Patoka, stm., In., U.S.	H2	91
Patoka Lake, res., In., U.S.	H4	91
Patos, Braz.	E11	54
Patos, Lagoa dos, b., Braz.	C6	56
Patos de Minas, Braz.	E5	57
Patquía, Arg.	C3	56
Pátrai, Grc.	K5	16
Patricio Lynch, Isla, i., Chile	F1	56
Patrick, co., Va., U.S.	D2	123
Patrick Air Force Base, mil., Fl., U.S.	D6	86
Patrocínio, Braz.	E5	57
Pattani, Thai.	K6	34
Patten, Me., U.S.	C4	96
Patterson, Ga., U.S.	E4	87
Patterson, La., U.S.	E4	95
Patterson Creek, stm., W.V., U.S.	B5	125
Pattoki, Pak.	E5	38
Patton, Pa., U.S.	E4	115
Patuākhāli, Bngl.	I14	38
Patuca, stm., Hond.	G5	64
Patuxent, stm., Md., U.S.	D4	97
Patuxent Naval Air Test Center, mil., Md., U.S.	D5	97
Pátzcuaro, Mex.	H9	62
Pau, Fr.	I6	10
Paul, Id., U.S.	G5	89
Paulding, Oh., U.S.	A1	112
Paulding, co., Ga., U.S.	C2	87
Paulding, co., Oh., U.S.	A1	112
Paulina, La., U.S.	h10	95
Paulina Mountains, mts., Or., U.S.	D5	114
Paulina Peak, mtn., Or., U.S.	E5	114
Paulins Kill, stm., N.J., U.S.	A3	107
Paulistana, Braz.	E10	54
Paulo Afonso, Braz.	E11	54
Paulsboro, N.J., U.S.	D2	107
Paungde, Burma	E3	34
Pavia, Italy	D4	14
Pavilion Key, i., Fl., U.S.	G5	86
Pavlodar, Kaz.	G9	24
Pavlof Volcano, vol., Ak., U.S.	D7	79
Pavlovo, Russia	F26	18
Pavlovsk, Russia	G7	22
Pavlovskij Posad, Russia	F21	18
Pavo, Ga., U.S.	F3	87
Pavón, Col.	F6	58
Pavullo nel Frignano, Italy	E5	14
Pawcatuck, Ct., U.S.	D8	84
Pawcatuck, stm., R.I., U.S.	G1	116
Paw Creek, N.C., U.S.	B2	110
Pawhuska, Ok., U.S.	A5	113
Pawling, N.Y., U.S.	D7	109
Pawnee, Il., U.S.	D4	90
Pawnee, Ok., U.S.	A5	113
Pawnee, co., Ks., U.S.	D4	93
Pawnee, co., Ne., U.S.	D9	104
Pawnee, co., Ok., U.S.	A5	113
Pawnee, stm., Ks., U.S.	D3	93
Pawnee City, Ne., U.S.	D9	104
Pawpaw, Il., U.S.	B5	90
Paw Paw, Mi., U.S.	F5	99
Paw Paw, stm., Mi., U.S.	F4	99
Pawpaw Creek, stm., W.V., U.S.	h10	125
Pawtuckaway Pond, l., N.H., U.S.	D4	106
Pawtucket, R.I., U.S.	C4	116
Pawtuxet, stm., R.I., U.S.	C4	116
Paxton, Il., U.S.	C5	90
Paxton, Ma., U.S.	B4	98
Payakumbuh, Indon.	O6	34
Payette, Id., U.S.	E2	89
Payette, co., Id., U.S.	E2	89
Payette, North Fork, stm., Id., U.S.	E2	89
Payette, South Fork, stm., Id., U.S.	E3	89
Payette Lake, res., Id., U.S.	E3	89
Payne, Oh., U.S.	A1	112
Payne, co., Ok., U.S.	A4	113
Paynesville, Mn., U.S.	E4	100
Paysandú, Ur.	C5	56
Payson, Az., U.S.	C4	80
Payson, Il., U.S.	D2	90
Payson, Ut., U.S.	C4	121
Pazardžik, Bul.	G8	16
Paz de Río, Col.	E6	58
Pazin, Cro.	D8	14
Pea, stm., Al., U.S.	D3	78
Peabody, Ks., U.S.	D6	93
Peabody, Ma., U.S.	A6	98
Peabody, stm., N.H., U.S.	B4	106
Peace, stm., Can.	E9	66
Peace, stm., Fl., U.S.	E5	86
Peace Dale, R.I., U.S.	F3	116
Peace River, Alta., Can.	A2	68
Peach, co., Ga., U.S.	D3	87
Peacham Pond, res., Vt., U.S.	C4	122
Peach Point, c., Ma., U.S.	f12	98
Peach Springs, Az., U.S.	B2	80
Peak District National Park, Eng., U.K.	H11	7
Peaks Island, i., Me., U.S.	g7	96
Peale, Mount, mtn., Ut., U.S.	E6	121
Pea Patch Island, i., De., U.S.	B3	85
Pea Ridge, Ar., U.S.	A1	81
Pea Ridge National Military Park, Ar., U.S.	A1	81
Pearisburg, Va., U.S.	C2	123
Pearl, Ms., U.S.	C3	101
Pearl, stm., U.S.	D3	101
Pearland, Tx., U.S.	r14	120
Pearl and Hermes Reef, rf., Hi., U.S.	k12	88
Pearl City, Hi., U.S.	B4	88
Pearl Harbor, b., Hi., U.S.	B3	88
Pearl Harbor Naval Station, mil., Hi., U.S.	g10	88
Pearlington, Ms., U.S.	E4	101
Pearl River, La., U.S.	D6	95
Pearl River, N.Y., U.S.	g12	109
Pearl River, co., Ms., U.S.	E4	101
Pearsall, Tx., U.S.	E3	120
Pearson, Ga., U.S.	E4	87
Pearsoll Peak, mtn., Or., U.S.	E3	114
Peary Land, reg., Grnld.	A16	128
Pease, stm., Tx., U.S.	B3	120
Pease Air Force Base, mil., N.H., U.S.	D5	106
Pebane, Moz.	E7	44
Peć, Yugo.	G4	16
Pecatonica, Il., U.S.	A4	90
Pecatonica, stm., U.S.	A4	90
Pecatonica, East Branch, stm., Wi., U.S.	F4	126
Peckerwood Lake, res., Ar., U.S.	C4	81
Pečora, stm., Russia	D5	24
Pecos, N.M., U.S.	B4	108
Pecos, Tx., U.S.	D1	120
Pecos, co., Tx., U.S.	D1	120
Pecos, stm., U.S.	E6	76
Pecos National Monument, N.M., U.S.	B4	108
Pécs, Hung.	I18	8
Peculiar, Mo., U.S.	C3	102
Peddocks Island, i., Ma., U.S.	g12	98
Pedernales, Ven.	C11	58
Pedregal, Ven.	B7	58
Pedro, Point, c., Sri L.	H6	37
Pedro de Valdivia, Chile	A3	56
Pedro Juan Caballero, Para.	G1	57
Pedro Point, c., N.W. Ter., Can.	B10	66
Peebles, Oh., U.S.	D2	112
Peekskill, N.Y., U.S.	D7	109
Peel, I. of Man	G8	7
Peel, stm., Can.	C5	66
Peel Point, c., N.W. Ter., Can.	B10	66
Peel Sound, strt., N.W. Ter., Can.	B13	66
Pegram, Tn., U.S.	A4	119
Pehuajó, Arg.	D4	56
Peikang, Tai.	L9	28
Peine, Ger.	C10	8
Pekalongan, Indon.	m14	32
Pekan, Malay.	M7	34
Pekin, Il., U.S.	C4	90
Pekin, In., U.S.	G5	91
Peking see Beijing, China	D10	26
Pelagie, Isole, is., Italy	N7	14
Pelahatchie, Ms., U.S.	C4	101
Pelée, Montagne, mtn., Mart.	G17	64
Pelee Island, i., Ont., Can.	F2	73
Peleng, Pulau, i., Indon.	F7	32
Pelham, Ont., Can.	D5	73
Pelham, Al., U.S.	B3	78
Pelham, Ga., U.S.	E2	87
Pelham, N.H., U.S.	E4	106
Pelham Manor, N.Y., U.S.	h13	109
Pelican Bay, b., Man., Can.	C1	70
Pelican Lake, l., Man., Can.	C1	70
Pelican Lake, l., Mn., U.S.	C1	100
Pelican Lake, l., Mn., U.S.	D3	100
Pelican Lake, l., Mn., U.S.	B6	100
Pelican Lake, l., Mn., U.S.	E5	100
Pelican Lake, l., Wi., U.S.	C4	126
Pelican Mountain, mtn., Alta., Can.	B4	68
Pelican Rapids, Mn., U.S.	D2	100
Pella, Ia., U.S.	C5	92
Pell City, Al., U.S.	B3	78
Pell Lake, Wi., U.S.	n11	126
Pello, Fin.	C14	6
Pelly Mountains, mts., Yukon, Can.	D6	66
Pelopónnisos, reg., Grc.	L5	16
Pelotas, Braz.	C6	56
Pelton, Lake, l., La., U.S.	E5	95
Pemadumcook Lake, l., Me., U.S.	C3	96
Pemalang, Indon.	m14	33a
Pematangsiantar, Indon.	E2	32
Pemba, Moz.	D8	44
Pemba Island, i., Tan.	C7	44
Pemberton, Austl.	F3	50
Pemberville, Oh., U.S.	A2	112
Pembina, N.D., U.S.	A8	111
Pembina, co., N.D., U.S.	A8	111
Pembina, stm., Alta., Can.	C3	68
Pembroke, Wales, U.K.	J8	7
Pembroke, Ont., Can.	B7	73
Pembroke, Ga., U.S.	D5	87
Pembroke, Ky., U.S.	D2	94
Pembroke, Ma., U.S.	B6	98
Pembroke, N.C., U.S.	C3	110
Pembroke, Va., U.S.	C2	123
Pembroke Pines, Fl., U.S.	r13	86
Pemigewasset, stm., N.H., U.S.	C3	106
Pemiscot, co., Mo., U.S.	E8	102
Peñafiel, Spain	D7	12
Peñalsordo, Spain	G6	12
Penápolis, Braz.	F3	57
Peñaranda de Bracamonte, Spain	E6	12
Pen Argyl, Pa., U.S.	E11	115
Peñarroya-Pueblonuevo, Spain	G6	12
Penas, Golfo de, b., Chile	F1	56
Penasco, N.M., U.S.	A4	108
Peñasco, Rio, stm., N.M., U.S.	E4	108
Penbrook, Pa., U.S.	F8	115
Pender, Ne., U.S.	B9	104
Pender, co., N.C., U.S.	C4	110
Pendleton, In., U.S.	E6	91
Pendleton, Or., U.S.	B8	114
Pendleton, S.C., U.S.	B2	117
Pendleton, co., Ky., U.S.	B5	94
Pendleton, co., W.V., U.S.	C5	125
Pendley Hills, Ga., U.S.	*h8	87
Pend Oreille, co., Wa., U.S.	A8	124
Pend Oreille, Lake, l., Id., U.S.	A2	89
Pend Oreille, Mount, mtn., Id., U.S.	A2	89
Penetanguishene, Ont., Can.	C5	73
P'enghu Liehtao, is., Tai.	L8	28
Penglai, China	D11	26
Penhold, Alta., Can.	C4	68
Peniche, Port.	F2	12
Penjamo, Mex.	G9	62
Pennant Point, c., N.S., Can.	E6	71
Pennask Mountain, mtn., B.C., Can.	E7	69
Penne, Italy	G8	14
Pennell, Mount, mtn., Ut., U.S.	F5	121
Penner, stm., India	C5	37
Penn Hills, Pa., U.S.	k14	115
Pennines, mts., Eng., U.K.	G10	7
Pennines, Alpes, mts., Eur.	F14	10
Pennington, co., Mn., U.S.	B2	100
Pennington, co., S.D., U.S.	D2	118
Pennington Gap, Va., U.S.	f8	123
Pennsauken, N.J., U.S.	D2	107
Pennsboro, W.V., U.S.	B4	125
Pennsburg, Pa., U.S.	F11	115
Penns Grove, N.J., U.S.	D2	107
Pennsville, N.J., U.S.	D1	107
Pennsylvania, state, U.S.	E7	115
Pennville, In., U.S.	D7	91
Penn Yan, N.Y., U.S.	C3	109
Penobscot, co., Me., U.S.	C4	96
Penobscot, stm., Me., U.S.	C4	96
Penobscot Bay, b., Me., U.S.	D3	96
Penobscot Lake, l., Me., U.S.	C2	96
Penonomé, Pan.	J7	64
Penrith, Eng., U.K.	G10	7
Pensacola, Fl., U.S.	u14	86
Pensacola Bay, b., Fl., U.S.	u14	86
Pensacola Dam, Ok., U.S.	A6	113
Pensacola Naval Air Station, mil., Fl., U.S.	u14	86
Pentagon Mountain, mtn., Mt., U.S.	C3	103
Penticton, B.C., Can.	E8	69
Pentland Firth, strt., Scot., U.K.	C9	7
Pentwater, Mi., U.S.	E4	99
Penyu, Kepulauan, is., Indon.	G8	32
Penza, Russia	G7	22
Penzance, Eng., U.K.	K7	7
Penžina, stm., Russia	E27	24
Penžinskaja Guba, b., Russia	E26	24
Penžinskij Chrebet, mts., Russia	E27	24
Peonan Point, c., Man., Can.	D2	70
Peoria, Az., U.S.	D3	80
Peoria, Il., U.S.	C4	90
Peoria, co., Il., U.S.	C4	90
Peoria Heights, Il., U.S.	C4	90
Peotone, Il., U.S.	B6	90
Pepacton Reservoir, res., N.Y., U.S.	C6	109
Pepeekeo, Hi., U.S.	D6	88
Pepin, Wi., U.S.	D1	126
Pepin, co., Wi., U.S.	D2	126
Pepin, Lake, l., U.S.	D1	126
Pepperell, Ma., U.S.	A4	98
Pequannock, N.J., U.S.	B4	107
Pequest, stm., N.J., U.S.	B2	107
Pequop Mountains, mts., Nv., U.S.	C7	105
Pequot Lakes, Mn., U.S.	D4	100
Perabumulih, Indon.	F3	32
Percy, Il., U.S.	E4	90
Perdido, Al., U.S.	D2	78
Perdido, stm., U.S.	E2	78
Perdido Bay, b., Al., U.S.	E2	78
Pereira, Col.	E5	58
Pere Marquette, stm., Mi., U.S.	E4	99
Pereslavl'-Zalesskij, Russia	E21	18
Pergamino, Arg.	C4	56
Pergine Valsugana, Italy	C6	14
Perham, Mn., U.S.	D3	100
Péribonca, stm., Que., Can.	G18	74
Péridot, Az., U.S.	D5	80
Périgueux, Fr.	G7	10
Perijá, Sierra de, mts., S.A.	C6	58
Perkasie, Pa., U.S.	F11	115
Perkins, Ok., U.S.	B4	113
Perkins, co., Ne., U.S.	D4	104
Perkins, co., S.D., U.S.	B3	118
Perkinston, Ms., U.S.	E4	101
Perlas, Archipiélago de las, is., Pan.	J8	64
Perlas, Laguna de b., Nic.	H6	64
Perleberg, Ger.	B11	8
Perm', Russia	F9	22
Pernik, Bul.	G7	16
Péronne, Fr.	C9	10
Perpignan, Fr.	J9	10
Perquimans, co., N.C., U.S.	A6	110
Perrine, Fl., U.S.	G6	86
Perris, Ca., U.S.	F5	82
Perro, Laguna del, l., N.M., U.S.	C4	108
Perros-Guirec, Fr.	D3	10
Perrot, Île, i., Que., Can.	q19	74
Perry, Fl., U.S.	B3	86
Perry, Ga., U.S.	D3	87
Perry, Ia., U.S.	C3	92
Perry, Ks., U.S.	C8	93
Perry, Mi., U.S.	F6	99
Perry, Mo., U.S.	B6	102
Perry, N.Y., U.S.	C2	109
Perry, Oh., U.S.	A4	112
Perry, Ok., U.S.	A4	113
Perry, Ut., U.S.	B3	121
Perry, co., Al., U.S.	C2	78
Perry, co., Ar., U.S.	C3	81
Perry, co., Il., U.S.	E4	90
Perry, co., In., U.S.	H4	91
Perry, co., Ky., U.S.	C6	94
Perry, co., Ms., U.S.	D4	101
Perry, co., Mo., U.S.	D8	102
Perry, co., Oh., U.S.	C3	112
Perry, co., Pa., U.S.	F7	115
Perry, co., Tn., U.S.	B4	119
Perry Hall, Md., U.S.	B5	97
Perry Lake, res., Ks., U.S.	C8	93
Perryman, Md., U.S.	B5	97
Perrysburg, Oh., U.S.	A2	112
Perry Stream, stm., N.H., U.S.	f7	106
Perry's Victory and International Peace Memorial, hist., Oh., U.S.	A2	112
Perryton, Tx., U.S.	A2	120
Perryville, Ar., U.S.	B3	81
Perryville, Ky., U.S.	C5	94
Perryville, Md., U.S.	A5	97
Perryville, Mo., U.S.	D8	102
Pershing, co., Nv., U.S.	C3	105
Persia see Iran, ctry., Asia	B5	46
Person, co., N.C., U.S.	A3	110
Perth, Austl.	F3	50
Perth, Ont., Can.	C8	73
Perth, Scot., U.K.	E9	7
Perth Amboy, N.J., U.S.	B4	107
Perth-Andover, N.B., Can.	D10	71
Pertuis, Fr.	I12	10
Peru, Il., U.S.	B4	90
Peru, In., U.S.	C5	91
Peru, Ne., U.S.	D10	104
Peru, N.Y., U.S.	f11	109
Peru (Perú), ctry., S.A.	E3	54
Perugia, Italy	F7	14
Perušić, Cro.	E10	14
Pesaro, Italy	F7	14
Pescadores see P'enghu Liehtao, is., Tai.	L8	28
Pescara, Italy	G9	14

Name	Map Ref	Page
escia, Italy	F5	14
eshastin, Wa., U.S.	B5	124
eshāwar, Pak.	C4	38
eshtigo, Wi., U.S.	C6	126
eshtigo, stm., Wi., U.S.	C5	126
esqueira, Braz.	E11	54
essac, Fr.	H6	10
etaḥ Tiqwa, Isr.	C4	40
etal, Ms., U.S.	D4	101
etaluma, Ca., U.S.	C2	82
etatlán, Mex.	I9	62
etawawa, Ont., Can.	B7	73
etawawa, stm., Ont., Can.	A6	73
etenwell Lake, res., Wi., U.S.	D4	126
eterborough, Austl.	F7	50
eterborough, Ont., Can.	C6	73
eterborough, Eng., U.K.	I12	7
eterborough, N.H., U.S.	E3	106
eterhead, Scot., U.K.	D11	7
eter Pond Lake, l., Sask., Can.	m7	75
etersburg, Ak., U.S.	D13	79
etersburg, Il., U.S.	C4	90
etersburg, In., U.S.	H3	91
etersburg, Mi., U.S.	G7	99
etersburg, Oh., U.S.	B5	112
etersburg, Tx., U.S.	C2	120
etersburg, Va., U.S.	C5	123
etersburg, W.V., U.S.	B5	125
eters Creek, stm., W.V., U.S.	m14	125
eterson, Al., U.S.	B2	78
eterson Field, mil., Co., U.S.	C6	83
etersville, Al., U.S.	A2	78
etit Bois Island, i., Ms., U.S.	E5	101
etitcodiac, N.B., Can.	D4	71
etitcodiac, stm., N.B., Can.	C5	71
etite Amite, stm., La., U.S.	h10	95
etit Jean, stm., Ar., U.S.	B2	81
etit Lac Des Allemands, l., La., U.S.	k11	95
etit Lake, l., La., U.S.	k12	95
etitot, stm., Can.	E8	66
etit-Rocher, N.B., Can.	B4	71
etitsikapau Lake, l., Newf., Can.	g8	72
etlād, India	I5	38
etone, N.Z.	D5	52
etoskey, Mi., U.S.	C6	99
etrified Forest National Park, Az., U.S.	B6	80
etrila, Rom.	D7	16
etrinja, Cro.	D11	14
etroleum, co., Mt., U.S.	C8	103
etrolia, Ont., Can.	E2	73
etrolina, Braz.	E10	54
etropavlovsk-Kamčatskij, Russia	G25	24
etrópolis, Braz.	G7	57
etros, Tn., U.S.	C9	119
etroşani, Rom.	D7	16
etrovsk-Zabajkal'skij, Russia	G15	24
etrozavodsk, Russia	E4	22
ettaquamscutt Lake Shores, R.I., U.S.	F4	116
ettingell Peak, mtn., Co., U.S.	B5	83
ettis, co., Mo., U.S.	C4	102
evek, Russia	D28	24
evely, Mo., U.S.	g13	102
ewaukee, Wi., U.S.	E5	126
ewaukee Lake, l., Wi., U.S.	m11	126
ewee Valley, Ky., U.S.	B4	94
ézenas, Fr.	I10	10
forzheim, Ger.	G8	8
fungstadt, Ger.	F8	8
ha-an, Burma	F4	34
hagwāra, India	E6	38
haltan, India	D3	37
halsbourg, Fr.	D14	10
hangan, Ko., i., Thai.	J6	34
hangnga, Thai.	J5	34
hanom Dongrak, Thiu Khao, mts., Asia	G7	34
han Rang, Viet.	I10	34
han Si Pan, mtn., Viet.	C7	34
han Thiet, Viet.	I10	34
harr, Tx., U.S.	F3	120
hatthalung, Thai.	K6	34
hayao, Thai.	E5	34
helps, Ky., U.S.	C7	94
helps, N.Y., U.S.	C3	109
helps, Wi., U.S.	B4	126
helps, co., Mo., U.S.	D6	102
helps, co., Ne., U.S.	D6	104
helps Lake, l., N.C., U.S.	B6	110
henix City, Al., U.S.	C4	78
hetchaburi, Thai.	H5	34
hiladelphia, Ms., U.S.	C4	101
hiladelphia, Pa., U.S.	G11	115
hiladelphia, co., Pa., U.S.	G12	115
hiladelphia Naval Shipyard, mil., Pa., U.S.	P21	115
hil Campbell, Al., U.S.	A2	78
hilip, S.D., U.S.	C4	118
hilippeville, Bel.	E4	8
hilippi, W.V., U.S.	B4	125
hilippines, ctry., Asia	C7	32
hilippine Sea	E21	2
hilipsburg, Mt., U.S.	D3	103
hilipsburg, Pa., U.S.	E5	115
hilleo Lake, l., Wa., U.S.	h14	124
hillips, Me., U.S.	D2	96
hillips, Tx., U.S.	B2	120
hillips, Wi., U.S.	C3	126
hillips, co., Co., U.S.	A8	83
hillips, co., Ks., U.S.	C4	93
hillips, co., Mt., U.S.	B8	103
hillips Brook, stm., N.H., U.S.	A4	106
hillipsburg, Ks., U.S.	C4	93
hillipsburg, N.J., U.S.	B2	107
hilmont, N.Y., U.S.	C7	109
hilo, Il., U.S.	C5	90
hilomath, Or., U.S.	C3	114
hilpots Island, i., N.W. Ter., Can.	B17	66
hilpott Reservoir, res., Va., U.S.	D2	123
hitsanulok, Thai.	F6	34
Phnom Penh see Phnum Pénh, Camb.	I8	34
Phnum Pénh (Phnom Penh), Camb.	I8	34
Phoenix, Az., U.S.	D3	80
Phoenix, Il., U.S.	k9	90
Phoenix, N.Y., U.S.	B4	109
Phoenix, Or., U.S.	E4	114
Phoenixville, Pa., U.S.	F10	115
Phôngsali, Laos	D7	34
Phrae, Thai.	E6	34
Phra Nakhon Si Ayutthaya, Thai.	G6	34
Phuket, Thai.	K5	34
Phuket, Ko, i., Thai.	K5	34
Phumi Béng, Camb.	H8	34
Phumi Kâmpóng Trâbêk, Camb.	H8	34
Phu Quoc, Dao, i., Viet.	I7	34
Phu Tho, Viet.	D8	34
Piacenza, Italy	D4	14
Piatra-Neamţ, Rom.	C10	16
Piatt, co., Il., U.S.	D5	90
Piazza Armerina, Italy	L9	14
Pibor Post, Sudan	G12	42
Picardie, hist. reg., Fr.	C9	10
Picayune, Ms., U.S.	E4	101
Piccadilly, Newf., Can.	D2	72
Pichanal, Arg.	A4	56
Picher, Ok., U.S.	A7	113
Pickaway, co., Oh., U.S.	C2	112
Pickens, Ms., U.S.	C4	101
Pickens, S.C., U.S.	B2	117
Pickens, co., Al., U.S.	B1	78
Pickens, co., Ga., U.S.	B2	87
Pickens, co., S.C., U.S.	B2	117
Pickerel Lake, l., Wi., U.S.	C5	126
Pickering, Ont., Can.	D5	73
Pickerington, Oh., U.S.	C3	112
Pickett, co., Tn., U.S.	C8	119
Pickwick Lake, res., U.S.	A6	101
Pickworth Point, c., Ma., U.S.	f12	98
Pico Rivera, Ca., U.S.	n12	82
Picos, Braz.	E10	54
Picquigny, Fr.	C9	10
Picton, Ont., Can.	D7	73
Pictou Island, i., N.S., Can.	D7	71
Picture Butte, Alta., Can.	E4	68
Pictured Rocks National Lakeshore, Mi., U.S.	B4	99
Pidálion, Akrotírion, c., Cyp.	B4	40
Pidurutalagala, mtn., Sri L.	I6	37
Piedmont, Al., U.S.	B4	78
Piedmont, Ca., U.S.	h8	82
Piedmont, Mo., U.S.	D7	102
Piedmont, Ok., U.S.	B4	113
Piedmont, S.C., U.S.	B3	117
Piedmont, W.V., U.S.	B5	125
Piedmont Lake, l., Oh., U.S.	B4	112
Piedra, stm., Co., U.S.	D3	83
Piedrabuena, Spain	F7	12
Piedrahita, Spain	E6	12
Piedras Blancas, Point, c., Ca., U.S.	E3	82
Piedras Negras, Guat.	F2	64
Piedras Negras, Mex.	C9	62
Pieksämäki, Fin.	E16	6
Pierce, Co., U.S.	A6	83
Pierce, Id., U.S.	C3	89
Pierce, Ne., U.S.	B8	104
Pierce, co., Ga., U.S.	E4	87
Pierce, co., Ne., U.S.	B8	104
Pierce, co., N.D., U.S.	A5	111
Pierce, co., Wa., U.S.	C3	124
Pierce, co., Wi., U.S.	D1	126
Pierce, Lake, l., Fl., U.S.	E5	86
Pierce City, Mo., U.S.	E3	102
Pierceton, In., U.S.	B6	91
Pierre, S.D., U.S.	C5	118
Pierre-Buffière, Fr.	G8	10
Pierrefonds, Que., Can.	q19	74
Pierre Part, La., U.S.	k9	95
Pierreville, Que., Can.	C5	74
Pierson, Fl., U.S.	C5	86
Pierz, Mn., U.S.	E4	100
Pietermaritzburg, S. Afr.	G6	44
Pietersburg, S. Afr.	F5	44
Pietrasanta, Italy	F5	14
Piet Retief, S. Afr.	G6	44
Pigeon, Mi., U.S.	E7	99
Pigeon, stm., U.S.	f9	110
Pigeon, stm., In., U.S.	A6	91
Pigeon, stm., Mn., U.S.	h10	100
Pigeon, stm., Wi., U.S.	k10	126
Pigeon Cove, Ma., U.S.	A6	98
Pigeon Forge, Tn., U.S.	D10	119
Pigeon Point, c., Mn., U.S.	h10	100
Pigg, stm., Va., U.S.	D3	123
Piggott, Ar., U.S.	A5	81
Pijijiapan, Mex.	J13	62
Pikal'ovo, Russia	B17	18
Pike, co., Al., U.S.	D4	78
Pike, co., Ar., U.S.	C2	81
Pike, co., Ga., U.S.	C2	87
Pike, co., Il., U.S.	D3	90
Pike, co., In., U.S.	H3	91
Pike, co., Ky., U.S.	C7	94
Pike, co., Ms., U.S.	D3	101
Pike, co., Mo., U.S.	B6	102
Pike, co., Oh., U.S.	C2	112
Pike, co., Pa., U.S.	D11	115
Pike, stm., Wi., U.S.	C6	126
Pike Island Dam, U.S.	f8	125
Pike Lake, Mn., U.S.	D6	100
Pikes Peak, mtn., Co., U.S.	C5	83
Pikesville, Md., U.S.	B4	97
Piketberg, S. Afr.	H3	44
Pikeville, Oh., U.S.	C2	112
Pikeville, Ky., U.S.	C7	94
Pikeville, Tn., U.S.	D8	119
Piła (Schneidemühl), Pol.	B16	8
Pilar do Sul, Braz.	G5	57
Pilcomayo, stm., S.A.	A4	56
Pilibhīt, India	F8	38
Pillar Point, c., Ca., U.S.	k7	82
Pilot Grove, Mo., U.S.	C5	102
Pilot Knob, Mo., U.S.	D7	102
Pilot Knob, mtn., Id., U.S.	D3	89
Pilot Mound, Man., Can.	E2	70
Pilot Mountain, N.C., U.S.	A2	110
Pilot Peak, mtn., Nv., U.S.	B7	105
Pilot Peak, mtn., Nv., U.S.	E4	105
Pilot Peak, mtn., Wy., U.S.	B3	127
Pilot Point, Tx., U.S.	C4	120
Pilot Range, mts., Nv., U.S.	B7	105
Pilot Rock, Or., U.S.	B8	114
Pilot Station, Ak., U.S.	C7	79
Pima, Az., U.S.	E6	80
Pima, co., Az., U.S.	E3	80
Pimental, Peru	E3	54
Pimmit Hills, Va., U.S.	g12	123
Pina, Spain	D11	12
Pinal, co., Az., U.S.	E4	80
Pinaleno Mountains, mts., Az., U.S.	E5	80
Pinal Mountains, mts., Az., U.S.	D5	80
Pinang see George Town, Malay.	L6	34
Pinar del Río, Cuba	C6	64
Pinardville, N.H., U.S.	E3	106
Pincher Creek, Alta., Can.	E4	68
Pinckard, Al., U.S.	D4	78
Pinckney, Mi., U.S.	F7	99
Pinckney Island, i., S.C., U.S.	G6	117
Pinckneyville, Il., U.S.	E4	90
Pinconning, Mi., U.S.	E7	99
Píndhos Óros, mts., Grc.	J5	16
Pindi Gheb, Pak.	D5	38
Pindus Mountains see Píndhos Óros, mts., Grc.	J5	16
Pine, Az., U.S.	C4	80
Pine, co., Mn., U.S.	D6	100
Pine, stm., Mi., U.S.	D5	99
Pine, stm., Mi., U.S.	D7	99
Pine, stm., N.H., U.S.	C4	106
Pine, stm., Wi., U.S.	C5	126
Pine, stm., Wi., U.S.	C4	126
Pine Barrens, reg., N.J., U.S.	D3	107
Pine Bluff, Ar., U.S.	C3	81
Pinebluff, N.C., U.S.	B3	110
Pine Bluffs, Wy., U.S.	E8	127
Pine Bridge, Ct., U.S.	D3	84
Pine Castle, Fl., U.S.	D5	86
Pine City, Mn., U.S.	E6	100
Pine Creek, stm., Nv., U.S.	C5	105
Pine Creek, stm., Pa., U.S.	C6	115
Pine Creek, stm., Wa., U.S.	B8	124
Pine Creek Lake, res., Ok., U.S.	C6	113
Pinedale, Wy., U.S.	D3	127
Pine Falls, Man., Can.	D3	70
Pine Forest Range, mts., Nv., U.S.	B3	105
Pine Grove, Pa., U.S.	E9	115
Pine Grove Mills, Pa., U.S.	E6	115
Pine Hill, N.J., U.S.	D3	107
Pine Hills, Fl., U.S.	D5	86
Pinehouse Lake, Sask., Can.	B2	75
Pinehouse Lake, l., Sask., Can.	B2	75
Pinehurst, Ma., U.S.	f11	98
Pinehurst, N.C., U.S.	B3	110
Pine Island, Mn., U.S.	F6	100
Pine Island, i., Fl., U.S.	F4	86
Pine Island Sound, strt., Fl., U.S.	F4	86
Pine Key, i., Fl., U.S.	p10	86
Pine Knot, Ky., U.S.	D5	94
Pine Lake, Ga., U.S.	h8	87
Pine Lake, l., In., U.S.	A4	91
Pine Lake, l., Wi., U.S.	C5	126
Pine Lawn, Mo., U.S.	f13	102
Pine Level, N.C., U.S.	B4	110
Pinellas, co., Fl., U.S.	D4	86
Pinellas, Point, c., Fl., U.S.	p10	86
Pinellas Park, Fl., U.S.	E4	86
Pine Mountain, Ga., U.S.	D2	87
Pine Mountain, mtn., Or., U.S.	D6	114
Pine Mountain, mtn., Wy., U.S.	E3	127
Pine Point, N.W. Ter., Can.	D10	66
Pine Point, Me., U.S.	E2	96
Pine Prairie, La., U.S.	D3	95
Pine Ridge, S.D., U.S.	D3	118
Pine Ridge Indian Reservation, S.D., U.S.	D3	118
Pine River, Mn., U.S.	D4	100
Pinerolo, Italy	E2	14
Pines, Lake O' the, res., Tx., U.S.	C5	120
Pinesdale, Mt., U.S.	D2	103
Pinetops, N.C., U.S.	B5	110
Pine Valley, val., Ut., U.S.	E2	121
Pineville, Ky., U.S.	D6	94
Pineville, La., U.S.	C3	95
Pineville, N.C., U.S.	B2	110
Pineville, W.V., U.S.	D3	125
Pinewood, S.C., U.S.	D7	117
Piney Creek, stm., W.V., U.S.	n13	125
Piney Fork, stm., W.V., U.S.	h9	125
Piney Point, Md., U.S.	D4	97
Piney View, W.V., U.S.	n13	125
Ping, stm., Thai.	F5	34
Pingdingshan, China	E9	26
Pinghu, China	E10	28
Pingliang, China	D8	26
Pingtan Dao, i., China	J8	28
P'ingtung, Tai.	M9	28
Pingxiang, China	H2	28
Pingyao, China	D9	26
Pinhel, Port.	E4	12
Pinnacles National Monument, Ca., U.S.	D3	82
Pinneberg, Ger.	B9	8
Pinole, Ca., U.S.	h8	82
Pinopolis Dam, S.C., U.S.	E8	117
Pinos, Mount, mtn., Ca., U.S.	E4	82
Pins, Pointe aux, c., Ont., Can.	E3	73
Pinsk, Bela.	I9	18
Pinson, Al., U.S.	f7	78
Pinta, Sierra, mts., Az., U.S.	E2	80
Pintwater Range, mts., Nv., U.S.	F7	105
Pioche, Nv., U.S.	F7	105
Piombino, Italy	G5	14
Pioneer, Oh., U.S.	A1	112
Pioneer Mountains, mts., Id., U.S.	F5	89
Pioneer Mountains, mts., Mt., U.S.	E3	103
Pioner, Ostrov, i., Russia	B12	24
Piotrków Trybunalski, Pol.	D19	8
Pipe Spring National Monument, Az., U.S.	A3	80
Pipestem Creek, stm., N.D., U.S.	B6	111
Pipestone, Mn., U.S.	G2	100
Pipestone, co., Mn., U.S.	F2	100
Pipestone, stm., Ont., Can.	F14	66
Pipestone National Monument, Mn., U.S.	G2	100
Pipestone Pass, Mt., U.S.	E4	103
Pipmuacan, Réservoir, res., Que., Can.	k12	74
Piqua, Oh., U.S.	B1	112
Piracicaba, Braz.	G5	57
Piraeus see Piraiévs, Grc.	L7	16
Piraí do Sul, Braz.	A7	56
Piraiévs (Piraeus), Grc.	L7	16
Piraju, Braz.	G4	57
Piran, Slo.	D8	14
Pirané, Arg.	B5	56
Pirapora, Braz.	D6	57
Pires do Rio, Braz.	D4	57
Pírgos, Grc.	L5	16
Pirmasens, Ger.	F7	8
Pirna, Ger.	E13	8
Pirtleville, Az., U.S.	F6	80
Piru, Indon.	F8	32
Pisa, Italy	F5	14
Pisagua, Chile	G4	54
Piscataqua, stm., N.H., U.S.	D5	106
Piscataquis, co., Me., U.S.	C3	96
Piscataquis, stm., Me., U.S.	C3	96
Piscataquog, stm., N.H., U.S.	D3	106
Piscataway, N.J., U.S.	B4	107
Pisco, Peru	F3	54
Piseco Lake, l., N.Y., U.S.	B6	109
Písek, Czech.	F14	8
Pisgah, Al., U.S.	A4	78
Pisgah, Oh., U.S.	n13	112
Pisgah, Mount, mtn., Wy., U.S.	B8	127
Pisgah Forest, N.C., U.S.	f10	110
Pishan, China	B8	38
Pismo Beach, Ca., U.S.	E3	82
Pisticci, Italy	I11	14
Pistoia, Italy	F5	14
Pistolet Bay, b., Newf., Can.	C4	72
Pit, stm., Ca., U.S.	B3	82
Pitalito, Col.	G4	58
Pitcairn, Pa., U.S.	k14	115
Pitcairn, dep., Oc.	H4	2
Piteå, Swe.	D13	6
Piteşti, Rom.	E8	16
Pithāpuram, India	D7	37
Pithiviers, Fr.	D9	10
Pitiquito, Mex.	B3	62
Pitkin, co., Co., U.S.	B4	83
Pitlochry, Scot., U.K.	E9	7
Pitman, N.J., U.S.	D2	107
Pitt, co., N.C., U.S.	B5	110
Pitt Island, i., B.C., Can.	C3	69
Pittsboro, In., U.S.	E5	91
Pittsboro, N.C., U.S.	B3	110
Pittsburg, Ca., U.S.	g9	82
Pittsburg, Ks., U.S.	E9	93
Pittsburg, Ky., U.S.	C5	94
Pittsburg, Tx., U.S.	C5	120
Pittsburg, co., Ok., U.S.	C6	113
Pittsburgh, Pa., U.S.	F1	115
Pittsfield, Il., U.S.	D3	90
Pittsfield, Ma., U.S.	B1	98
Pittsfield, N.H., U.S.	D4	106
Pittsford, Vt., U.S.	D2	122
Pittston, Pa., U.S.	D10	115
Pittsville, Md., U.S.	D7	97
Pittsville, Wi., U.S.	D3	126
Pittsylvania, co., Va., U.S.	D3	123
Piu, Cerro, mtn., Nic.	H5	64
Piura, Peru	E2	54
Piute, co., Ut., U.S.	E3	121
Piute Peak, mtn., Ca., U.S.	E4	82
Piute Reservoir, res., Ut., U.S.	E3	121
Pixley, Ca., U.S.	E4	82
Pizzo, Italy	K11	14
Placentia, Newf., Can.	E5	72
Placentia Bay, b., Newf., Can.	E4	72
Placer, co., Ca., U.S.	C3	82
PLacer Mountain, mtn., N.M., U.S.	k8	108
Placerville, Ca., U.S.	C3	82
Placetas, Cuba	C8	64
Placid, Lake, l., Fl., U.S.	E5	86
Placid, Lake, l., N.Y., U.S.	f11	109
Placitas, N.M., U.S.	B3	108
Plain City, Oh., U.S.	B2	112
Plain City, Ut., U.S.	B3	121
Plain Dealing, La., U.S.	B2	95
Plainfield, Ct., U.S.	C8	84
Plainfield, Il., U.S.	B5	90
Plainfield, In., U.S.	E5	91
Plainfield, N.J., U.S.	B4	107
Plainfield, Vt., U.S.	C4	122
Plainfield, Wi., U.S.	D4	126
Plainfield Heights, Mi., U.S.	*E5	99
Plains, Ga., U.S.	D2	87
Plains, Ks., U.S.	E3	93
Plains, Mt., U.S.	C1	103
Plains, Pa., U.S.	n17	115
Plains, Tx., U.S.	C1	120
Plainview, Ar., U.S.	C2	81
Plainview, Mn., U.S.	F6	100
Plainview, Ne., U.S.	B8	104
Plainview, Tx., U.S.	B2	120
Plainville, Ct., U.S.	C4	84
Plainville, Ks., U.S.	C4	93
Plainville, Ma., U.S.	B5	98
Plainwell, Mi., U.S.	F5	99
Plaistow, N.H., U.S.	E4	106
Plankinton, S.D., U.S.	D7	118
Plano, Il., U.S.	B5	90
Plano, Tx., U.S.	C4	120
Plantagenet, Ont., Can.	B9	73
Plantation, Fl., U.S.	r13	86
Plant City, Fl., U.S.	D4	86
Plantersville, Al., U.S.	C3	78
Plantersville, Ms., U.S.	A5	101
Plantsite, Az., U.S.	D6	80
Plantsville, Ct., U.S.	C4	84
Plaquemine, La., U.S.	D4	95
Plaquemines, co., La., U.S.	E6	95
Plasencia, Spain	E5	12
Plaški, Cro.	D10	14
Plaster Rock, N.B., Can.	C2	71
Plata, Río de la, est., S.A.	D5	56
Platte, S.D., U.S.	D7	118
Platte, co., Mo., U.S.	B3	102
Platte, co., Ne., U.S.	C8	104
Platte, co., Wy., U.S.	D7	127
Platte, stm., U.S.	B3	102
Platte, stm., Mo., U.S.	E4	102
Platte, stm., Ne., U.S.	D6	104
Platte City, Mo., U.S.	B3	102
Platte Island, i., Sey.	C11	44
Platteville, Co., U.S.	A6	83
Platteville, Wi., U.S.	F3	126
Plattling, Ger.	G12	8
Plattsburg, Mo., U.S.	B3	102
Plattsburgh, N.Y., U.S.	f11	109
Plattsburgh Air Force Base, mil., N.Y., U.S.	f11	109
Plattsmouth, Ne., U.S.	D10	104
Plau, Ger.	B12	8
Plauen, Ger.	E12	8
Playas Lake, l., N.M., U.S.	F2	108
Play Cu, Viet.	H9	34
Playgreen Lake, l., Man., Can.	B2	70
Pleasant, stm., Me., U.S.	C3	96
Pleasant, Lake, res., Az., U.S.	D3	80
Pleasant Gap, Pa., U.S.	E6	115
Pleasant Garden, N.C., U.S.	B3	110
Pleasant Grove, Al., U.S.	g7	78
Pleasant Grove, Ut., U.S.	C4	121
Pleasant Hill, Ca., U.S.	h8	82
Pleasant Hill, Il., U.S.	D3	90
Pleasant Hill, Ia., U.S.	e8	92
Pleasant Hill, La., U.S.	C2	95
Pleasant Hill, Mo., U.S.	C3	102
Pleasant Hill, Oh., U.S.	B1	112
Pleasant Lake, In., U.S.	A7	91
Pleasant Lake, l., N.H., U.S.	D4	106
Pleasanton, Ca., U.S.	h9	82
Pleasanton, Ks., U.S.	D9	93
Pleasanton, Tx., U.S.	E3	120
Pleasant Prairie, Wi., U.S.	n12	126
Pleasants, co., W.V., U.S.	B3	125
Pleasant Valley, Ia., U.S.	g11	92
Pleasant Valley, Mo., U.S.	h11	102
Pleasant View, Ut., U.S.	B3	121
Pleasantville, Ia., U.S.	C4	92
Pleasantville, N.J., U.S.	E3	107
Pleasantville, N.Y., U.S.	D7	109
Pleasantville, Oh., U.S.	C3	112
Pleasure Beach, Ct., U.S.	D7	84
Pleasure Ridge Park, Ky., U.S.	g11	94
Pleasureville, Ky., U.S.	B4	94
Pleiku see Play Cu, Viet.	H9	34
Pléneuf, Fr.	D4	10
Plenty, Bay of, b., N.Z.	B6	52
Plentywood, Mt., U.S.	B12	103
Plessisville, Que., Can.	C6	74
Pleternica, Cro.	D12	14
Plétipi, Lac, l., Que., Can.	F18	66
Pleven, Bul.	F8	16
Pljevlja, Yugo.	F3	16
Ploče, Cro.	F12	14
Płock, Pol.	C19	8
Ploërmel, Fr.	E4	10
Ploieşti, Rom.	E10	16
Plomosa Mountains, mts., Az., U.S.	D1	80
Plonge, Lac la, l., Sask., Can.	B2	75
Plouguenast, Fr.	D4	10
Plovdiv, Bul.	G8	16
Plover, Wi., U.S.	D4	126
Plover, stm., Wi., U.S.	D4	126
Plum, Pa., U.S.	k14	115
Plumas, co., Ca., U.S.	B3	82
Plum Coulee, Man., Can.	E3	70
Plumerville, Ar., U.S.	B3	81
Plum Island, i., Ma., U.S.	A6	98
Plummer, Id., U.S.	B2	89
Plumsteadville, Pa., U.S.	F11	115
Plumtree, Zimb.	F5	44
Plymouth, Monts.	F16	64
Plymouth, Eng., U.K.	K8	7
Plymouth, Ct., U.S.	C3	84
Plymouth, Fl., U.S.	D5	86
Plymouth, In., U.S.	B5	91
Plymouth, Ma., U.S.	C6	98
Plymouth, Mi., U.S.	p15	99
Plymouth, Mn., U.S.	m12	100
Plymouth, N.H., U.S.	C3	106
Plymouth, N.C., U.S.	B6	110
Plymouth, Oh., U.S.	A3	112
Plymouth, Pa., U.S.	D10	115
Plymouth, Wi., U.S.	E6	126
Plymouth, co., Ia., U.S.	B1	92
Plymouth, co., Ma., U.S.	C6	98
Plymouth Bay, b., Ma., U.S.	C6	98
Plzeň, Czech.	F13	8
Po, stm., Italy	E7	14
Po, stm., Va., U.S.	B5	123
Pobeda, Gora, mtn., Russia	D23	24
Pocahontas, Ar., U.S.	A5	81
Pocahontas, Il., U.S.	E4	90
Pocahontas, Ia., U.S.	B3	92
Pocahontas, co., Ia., U.S.	B3	92
Pocahontas, co., W.V., U.S.	C4	125
Pocasset, Ma., U.S.	C6	98
Pocatalico, W.V., U.S.	C3	125
Pocatalico, stm., W.V., U.S.	C3	125
Pocatello, Id., U.S.	G6	89
Počep, Russia	I16	18
Pochutla, Mex.	J11	62
Poções, Braz.	C8	57
Pocola, Ok., U.S.	B7	113
Pocomoke, stm., Md., U.S.	D7	97
Pocomoke City, Md., U.S.	D6	97
Pocomoke Sound, strt., Md., U.S.	E6	97

Name	Map Ref	Page
Pocono Mountains, hills, Pa., U.S.	E11	115
Pocono Pines, Pa., U.S.	D11	115
Poços de Caldas, Braz.	F5	57
Pocotopaug Lake, res., Ct., U.S.	C6	84
Podensac, Fr.	H6	10
Podkamennaja Tunguska, Russia	E12	24
Podkamennaja Tunguska, stm., Russia	E13	24
Podol'sk, Russia	F20	22
Podor, Sen.	E3	42
Podravska Slatina, Cro.	D12	14
Pofadder, S. Afr.	G3	44
Poge, Cape, c., Ma., U.S.	D7	98
Poggibonsi, Italy	F6	14
P'ohang, S. Kor.	D12	26
Pohénégamook, Que., Can.	B8	74
Pohue Bay, b., Hi., U.S.	E6	88
Poinsett, co., Ar., U.S.	B5	81
Poinsett, Lake, l., Fl., U.S.	D6	86
Poinsett, Lake, l., S.D., U.S.	C8	118
Point Clear, Al., U.S.	E2	78
Pointe a la Hache, La., U.S.	E6	95
Pointe-à-Pitre, Guad.	F17	64
Pointe-au-Pic, Que., Can.	B7	74
Pointe-Calumet, Que., Can.	p19	74
Pointe-Claire, Que., Can.	D4	74
Pointe Coupee, co., La., U.S.	D4	95
Pointe-des-Cascades, Que., Can.	q19	74
Point Edward, Ont., Can.	D2	73
Pointe-Noire, Congo	B2	44
Pointe-Verte, N.B., Can.	B4	71
Point Fortin, Trin.	I17	64
Point Hope, Ak., U.S.	B6	79
Point Imperial, mtn., Az., U.S.	A4	80
Point Judith Pond, l., R.I., U.S.	F4	116
Point Lake, l., N.W. Ter., Can.	C10	66
Point Leamington, Newf., Can.	D4	72
Point Marion, Pa., U.S.	G2	115
Point Mugu Naval Air Station, mil., Ca., U.S.	E4	82
Point of Rocks, Md., U.S.	B2	97
Point Pelee National Park, Ont., Can.	F2	73
Point Pleasant, N.J., U.S.	C4	107
Point Pleasant, W.V., U.S.	C2	125
Point Pleasant Beach, N.J., U.S.	C4	107
Point Reyes National Seashore, Ca., U.S.	C2	82
Point Roberts, Wa., U.S.	A2	124
Poipu, Hi., U.S.	B2	88
Poison Creek, stm., Wy., U.S.	C5	127
Poisson Blanc, Lac du, res., Que., Can.	C2	74
Poitiers, Fr.	F7	10
Poitou, reg., Fr.	F6	10
Poix, Fr.	C8	10
Pokegama Lake, l., Mn., U.S.	C5	100
Pokegama Lake, l., Wi., U.S.	C2	126
Polacca, Az., U.S.	B5	80
Poland, ctry., Eur.	E11	4
Polar Bear Provincial Park, Ont., Can.	n18	73
Polecat Creek, stm., Ok., U.S.	B5	113
Pol-e Khomrī, Afg.	C3	38
Polesje, reg., Eur.	I10	18
Pólis, Cyp.	B3	40
Polistena, Italy	K11	14
Polk, Pa., U.S.	D2	115
Polk, co., Ar., U.S.	C1	81
Polk, co., Fl., U.S.	E5	86
Polk, co., Ga., U.S.	C1	87
Polk, co., Ia., U.S.	C4	92
Polk, co., Mn., U.S.	C2	100
Polk, co., Mo., U.S.	D4	102
Polk, co., Ne., U.S.	C8	104
Polk, co., N.C., U.S.	f10	110
Polk, co., Or., U.S.	C3	114
Polk, co., Tn., U.S.	D9	119
Polk, co., Tx., U.S.	D5	120
Polk, co., Wi., U.S.	C1	126
Polk City, Fl., U.S.	D5	86
Polk City, Ia., U.S.	C4	92
Pol'kino, Russia	C13	24
Polo, Il., U.S.	B4	90
Polock, Bela.	F11	18
Polson, Mt., U.S.	C2	103
Poltava, Ukr.	H4	22
Polynesia, is., Oc.	G2	2
Pomabamba, Peru	E3	54
Pomaro, Mex.	H8	62
Pombal, Port.	F3	12
Pomerania, hist. reg., Pol.	A16	8
Pomeranian Bay, b., Eur.	A14	8
Pomeroy, Ia., U.S.	B3	92
Pomeroy, Oh., U.S.	C3	112
Pomeroy, Wa., U.S.	C8	124
Pomme de Terre, stm., Mn., U.S.	E3	100
Pomme de Terre, stm., Mo., U.S.	D4	102
Pomme de Terre Lake, res., Mo., U.S.	D4	102
Pomona, Ca., U.S.	E5	82
Pomona, Ks., U.S.	D8	93
Pomona Lake, res., Ks., U.S.	D7	93
Pompano Beach, Fl., U.S.	F6	86
Pompton Lakes, N.J., U.S.	A4	107
Ponaganset, stm., R.I., U.S.	C2	116
Ponaganset Reservoir, res., R.I., U.S.	B2	116
Ponca, Ne., U.S.	B9	104
Ponca City, Ok., U.S.	A4	113
Ponca Creek, stm., U.S.	A6	104
Ponca Indian Reservation, Ne., U.S.	B7	104
Ponce, P.R.	E14	64
Ponce de Leon Bay, b., Fl., U.S.	G5	86
Ponce de Leon Inlet, b., Fl., U.S.	C6	86
Poncha Pass, Co., U.S.	C4	83
Ponchatoula, La., U.S.	D5	95
Pond, stm., Ky., U.S.	C2	94
Pond Creek, Ok., U.S.	A4	113
Pondera, co., Mt., U.S.	B4	103
Pond Fork, stm., W.V., U.S.	D3	125

Name	Map Ref	Page
Pondicherry, India	G5	37
Pondicherry, ter., India	G5	37
Pond Inlet, N.W. Ter., Can.	B17	66
Pone Island, i., Md., U.S.	D5	97
Ponferrada, Spain	C5	12
Ponoka, Alta., Can.	C4	68
Ponorogo, Indon.	m15	33a
Pons, Fr.	G6	10
Ponta Grossa, Braz.	B6	56
Pont-à-Mousson, Fr.	D13	10
Ponta Porã, Braz.	G1	57
Pontarlier, Fr.	F13	10
Pontassieve, Italy	F6	14
Pont-Audemer, Fr.	C7	10
Pontchartrain, Lake, l., La., U.S.	D5	95
Pontchâteau, Fr.	E4	10
Pont de Suert, Spain	C12	12
Ponte Branca, Braz.	D2	57
Ponte da Barca, Port.	D3	12
Pontedera, Italy	F5	14
Ponte de Sor, Port.	F3	12
Ponteix, Sask., Can.	H2	75
Ponte Nova, Braz.	F7	57
Ponte Vedra Beach, Fl., U.S.	B5	86
Pontevedra, Spain	C3	12
Pontgibaud, Fr.	F9	10
Pontiac, Il., U.S.	C5	90
Pontiac, Mi., U.S.	F7	99
Pontianak, Indon.	F4	32
Pontivy, Fr.	D4	10
Pont-l'Abbé, Fr.	E2	10
Pontoise, Fr.	C9	10
Pontoosuc Lake, l., Ma., U.S.	B1	98
Pontorson, Fr.	D5	10
Pontotoc, Ms., U.S.	A4	101
Pontotoc, co., Ms., U.S.	A4	101
Pontotoc, co., Ok., U.S.	C5	113
Pont-Rouge, Que., Can.	C6	74
Pontypool, Ont., Can.	C6	73
Pontypool, Wales, U.K.	J9	7
Poole, Eng., U.K.	K11	7
Pooler, Ga., U.S.	D5	87
Pooles Island, i., Md., U.S.	B5	97
Poolesville, Md., U.S.	B3	97
Poopó, Lago de, l., Bol.	G5	54
Popayán, Col.	F4	58
Pope, co., Ar., U.S.	B2	81
Pope, co., Il., U.S.	F5	90
Pope, co., Mn., U.S.	E3	100
Pope Air Force Base, mil., N.C., U.S.	B3	110
Poplar, Mt., U.S.	B11	103
Poplar, stm., Mn., U.S.	C2	100
Poplar Bluff, Mo., U.S.	E7	102
Poplar Island, i., Md., U.S.	C5	97
Poplarville, Ms., U.S.	E4	101
Popocatépetl, Volcán, vol., Mex.	H10	62
Popokabaka, Zaire	C3	44
Popomanasiu, Mount, mtn., Sol.Is.	A11	50
Popondetta, Pap. N. Gui.	m16	50a
Popple, stm., Wi., U.S.	C5	126
Poquonock, Ct., U.S.	B5	84
Poquonock Bridge, Ct., U.S.	D7	84
Poquoson, Va., U.S.	C6	123
Porangatu, Braz.	F9	54
Porbandar, India	J3	38
Porcher Island, i., B.C., Can.	C2	69
Porcupine Mountains, mts., Mi., U.S.	m12	99
Pordenone, Italy	D7	14
Poreč, Cro.	D8	14
Pori, Fin.	F13	6
Porkkala, Fin.	G15	6
Porlamar, Ven.	B11	58
Porlezza, Port.	F4	12
Poronajsk, Russia	H22	24
Porsgrunn, Nor.	G7	6
Portadown, N. Ire., U.K.	G6	7
Portage, In., U.S.	A3	91
Portage, Mi., U.S.	F5	99
Portage, Pa., U.S.	F4	115
Portage, Wi., U.S.	E4	126
Portage, co., Oh., U.S.	A4	112
Portage, co., Wi., U.S.	D4	126
Portage, stm., Oh., U.S.	B2	112
Portage Bay, b., Man., Can.	D2	70
Portage Head, c., Wa., U.S.	A1	124
Portage Lake, l., Me., U.S.	B4	96
Portage Lakes, Oh., U.S.	B4	112
Portage la Prairie, Man., Can.	D2	70
Portageville, Mo., U.S.	E8	102
Portalegre, Port.	F4	12
Portales, N.M., U.S.	C6	108
Port Alice, B.C., Can.	D4	69
Port Allegany, Pa., U.S.	C5	115
Port Allen, La., U.S.	D4	95
Port Angeles, Wa., U.S.	A2	124
Port Antonio, Jam.	E9	64
Port Aransas, Tx., U.S.	F4	120
Port Arthur, Tx., U.S.	E6	120
Port Arthur see Lüshun, China	D11	26
Port Augusta, Austl.	F7	50
Port au Port Bay, b., Newf., Can.	D2	72
Port au Port [West-Aguathuna-Felix Cove], Newf., Can.	D2	72
Port-au-Prince, Haiti	E11	64
Port au Prince Peninsula, pen., Newf., Can.	D2	72
Port Austin, Mi., U.S.	D7	99
Port Barre, La., U.S.	D4	95
Port-Bergé, Madag.	D9	44
Port Blair, India	I2	34
Port Blandford, Newf., Can.	D4	72
Port Bolivar, Tx., U.S.	E5	120
Port Burwell, Ont., Can.	E4	73
Port Byron, Il., U.S.	B3	90
Port Carbon, Pa., U.S.	E9	115
Port Carling, Ont., Can.	B5	73
Port-Cartier-Ouest, Que., Can.	k13	74
Port Chalmers, N.Z.	F3	52
Port Charlotte, Fl., U.S.	F4	86
Port Chester, N.Y., U.S.	E7	109
Port Clinton, Oh., U.S.	A3	112
Port Colborne, Ont., Can.	E5	73
Port Coquitlam, B.C., Can.	E6	69

Name	Map Ref	Page
Port Deposit, Md., U.S.	A5	97
Port Dickinson, N.Y., U.S.	C5	109
Port Dickson, Malay.	M6	34
Port Edward, B.C., Can.	B2	69
Port Edwards, Wi., U.S.	D4	126
Portel, Braz.	D8	54
Portel, Port.	G4	12
Port Elgin, Ont., Can.	C3	73
Port Elizabeth, S. Afr.	H5	44
Port Ellen, Scot., U.K.	F6	7
Porter, In., U.S.	A3	91
Porter, Tx., U.S.	D5	120
Porter, co., In., U.S.	B3	91
Porter Creek, stm., W.V., U.S.	m13	125
Porterdale, Ga., U.S.	C3	87
Porterville, Ca., U.S.	D4	82
Port Ewen, N.Y., U.S.	D7	109
Port Gamble Indian Reservation, Wa., U.S.	B3	124
Port-Gentil, Gabon	B1	44
Port Gibson, Ms., U.S.	D3	101
Port Harcourt, Nig.	H7	42
Port Hedland, Austl.	D3	50
Port Hood, N.S., Can.	C8	71
Port Hope, Ont., Can.	D6	73
Port Hope Simpson, Newf., Can.	B3	72
Port Hueneme, Ca., U.S.	E4	82
Port Huron, Mi., U.S.	F8	99
Portimão, Port.	H3	12
Port Isabel, Tx., U.S.	F4	120
Port Jefferson, N.Y., U.S.	n15	109
Port Jervis, N.Y., U.S.	D6	109
Portland, Austl.	G8	50
Portland, Ct., U.S.	C5	84
Portland, In., U.S.	D8	91
Portland, Me., U.S.	E2	96
Portland, Mi., U.S.	F6	99
Portland, N.D., U.S.	B8	111
Portland, Or., U.S.	B4	114
Portland, Tn., U.S.	A5	119
Portland, Tx., U.S.	F4	120
Portland, Bill of, c., Eng., U.K.	K10	7
Portland Inlet, b., B.C., Can.	B2	69
Portland Point, c., Jam.	F9	64
Port Lavaca, Tx., U.S.	E4	120
Port Lincoln, Austl.	F7	50
Port Loko, S.L.	G3	42
Port Louis, Mrts.	F11	44
Port Ludlow, Wa., U.S.	B3	124
Port-Lyautey see Kenitra, Mor.	B4	42
Port Macquarie, Austl.	F10	50
Port Madison Indian Reservation, Wa., U.S.	B3	124
Port McNeil, B.C., Can.	D4	69
Port McNicoll, Ont., Can.	C5	73
Port Monmouth, N.J., U.S.	C4	107
Port Moresby, Pap. N. Gui.	m16	50a
Port Morien, N.S., Can.	C10	71
Port Neches, Tx., U.S.	E6	120
Portneuf, Que., Can.	C6	74
Port Nolloth, S. Afr.	G3	44
Porto, Port.	D3	12
Porto Alegre, Braz.	C6	56
Porto Amboim, Ang.	D2	44
Portobelo, Pan.	J8	64
Porto de Moz, Braz.	D8	54
Porto Esperança, Braz.	G7	54
Porto Esperidião, Braz.	G7	54
Pôrto Feliz, Braz.	G5	57
Portoferraio, Italy	G5	14
Pôrto Ferreira, Braz.	F5	57
Port of Spain, Trin.	I17	64
Portogruaro, Italy	D7	14
Portola, Ca., U.S.	C3	82
Porto Murtinho, Braz.	H7	54
Porto Nacional, Braz.	F9	54
Porto-Novo, Benin	G6	42
Port Orange, Fl., U.S.	C6	86
Port Orchard, Wa., U.S.	B3	124
Port Orford, Or., U.S.	E2	114
Porto San Giorgio, Italy	F8	14
Porto Santo Stefano, Italy	G6	14
Pôrto São José, Braz.	G2	57
Pôrto Seguro, Braz.	D9	57
Porto Torres, Italy	I3	14
Porto União, Braz.	B6	56
Porto Velho, Braz.	E6	54
Portoviejo, Ec.	H2	58
Port Penn, De., U.S.	B3	85
Port Pirie, Austl.	F7	50
Port Richey, Fl., U.S.	D4	86
Port Rowan, Ont., Can.	E4	73
Port Royal, S.C., U.S.	G6	117
Port Royal Island, i., S.C., U.S.	G6	117
Port Royal Sound, strt., S.C., U.S.	G6	117
Port Said see Būr Sa'īd, Egypt	B12	42
Port-Sainte-Marie, Fr.	H7	10
Port Saint Joe, Fl., U.S.	C1	86
Port Saint Johns, S. Afr.	H5	44
Port Saint Lucie, Fl., U.S.	E6	86
Port Salerno, Fl., U.S.	E6	86
Port Saunders, Newf., Can.	C3	72
Port Shepstone, S. Afr.	H6	44
Portsmouth, Eng., U.K.	K11	7
Portsmouth, N.H., U.S.	D5	106
Portsmouth, Oh., U.S.	D3	112
Portsmouth, R.I., U.S.	E6	116
Portsmouth, Va., U.S.	D6	123
Portsmouth Naval Shipyard, mil., Me., U.S.	D5	106
Port Stanley, Ont., Can.	E3	73
Port Sulphur, La., U.S.	E6	95
Port Talbot, Wales, U.K.	J9	7
Port Townsend, Wa., U.S.	A3	124
Portugal, ctry., Eur.	H6	4
Portugalete, Spain	B8	12
Portuguese Guinea see Guinea-Bissau, ctry., Afr.	F2	42
Portumna, Ire.	H4	7
Port Union, Newf., Can.	D5	72
Port-Vendres, Fr.	J10	10
Porum, Ok., U.S.	B6	113
Porz, Ger.	E7	8

Name	Map Ref	Page
Porzuna, Spain	F7	12
Posadas, Arg.	B5	56
Poschiavo, Switz.	F17	10
Posen, i., P.I., U.S.	k9	90
Posen, Il., U.S.	k9	90
Posey, co., In., U.S.	H2	91
Poseyville, In., U.S.	H2	91
Poso, Indon.	F7	32
Posse, Braz.	F4	54
Possession, Braz.	p19	74
Pössneck, Ger.	E11	8
Post, Tx., U.S.	C2	120
Post Falls, Id., U.S.	B2	89
Post Maurice Cortier (Bidon Cinq), Alg.	D6	42
Potchefstroom, S. Afr.	G5	44
Poté, Braz.	D8	57
Poteau, Ok., U.S.	B7	113
Poteau, stm., U.S.	B7	113
Poteet, Tx., U.S.	E3	120
Potenza, Italy	I10	14
Potes, Spain	B7	12
Potgietersrus, S. Afr.	F5	44
Poth, Tx., U.S.	E3	120
Potholes Reservoir, res., Wa., U.S.	B6	124
Potiraguá, Braz.	C9	57
Potiskum, Nig.	F8	42
Potlatch, Id., U.S.	C2	89
Potomac, Md., U.S.	B3	97
Potomac, stm., U.S.	D4	97
Potomac Heights, Md., U.S.	C3	97
Potomac Park, Md., U.S.	k13	97
Potosí, Bol.	G5	54
Potosi, Mo., U.S.	D7	102
Potosí, Cerro, mtn., Mex.	E9	62
Potsdam, Ger.	C13	8
Potsdam, N.Y., U.S.	f10	109
Pottawatomie, co., Ks., U.S.	C7	93
Pottawatomie, co., Ok., U.S.	B4	113
Pottawattamie, co., Ia., U.S.	C2	92
Potter, Ne., U.S.	C6	115
Potter, co., Pa., U.S.	C6	115
Potter, co., S.D., U.S.	B6	118
Potter, co., Tx., U.S.	B2	120
Potter Valley, Ca., U.S.	C2	82
Potts Creek, stm., U.S.	C2	123
Pottstown, Pa., U.S.	F10	115
Pottsville, Ar., U.S.	B2	81
Pottsville, Pa., U.S.	E9	115
Potwin, Ks., U.S.	E6	93
Pouce Coupe, B.C., Can.	B7	69
Pouch Cove, Newf., Can.	E5	72
Poughkeepsie, N.Y., U.S.	D7	109
Poulan, Ga., U.S.	E3	87
Poulsbo, Wa., U.S.	B3	124
Poultney, Vt., U.S.	D2	122
Poultney, stm., Vt., U.S.	D2	122
Pound, Va., U.S.	e9	123
Pound Gap, U.S.	C7	94
Pouso Alegre, Braz.	G6	57
Pouzauges, Fr.	F6	10
Póvoa de Varzim, Port.	D3	12
Povungnituk, Que., Can.	f11	74
Powassan, Ont., Can.	A5	73
Poway, Ca., U.S.	F5	82
Powder, stm., Or., U.S.	C9	114
Powder, Middle Fork, stm., Wy., U.S.	C6	127
Powder, North Fork, stm., Wy., U.S.	C6	127
Powder, South Fork, stm., Wy., U.S.	C6	127
Powder River, co., Mt., U.S.	E11	103
Powder River Pass, Wy., U.S.	B5	127
Powder Springs, Ga., U.S.	h8	87
Powell, Oh., U.S.	B2	112
Powell, Tn., U.S.	m13	119
Powell, Wy., U.S.	B4	127
Powell, co., Ky., U.S.	C6	94
Powell, co., Mt., U.S.	D4	103
Powell, stm., U.S.	C10	119
Powell, Lake, res., U.S.	F5	121
Powell, Mount, mtn., Co., U.S.	B4	83
Powell, Mount, mtn., N.M., U.S.	B1	108
Powell Butte, Or., U.S.	C5	114
Powell Park, reg., Co., U.S.	A2	83
Powell River, B.C., Can.	E5	69
Powellton, W.V., U.S.	C3	125
Power, co., Id., U.S.	G5	89
Powers, Or., U.S.	E2	114
Powerview, Man., Can.	D3	70
Poweshiek, co., Ia., U.S.	C5	92
Powhatan, co., Va., U.S.	C5	123
Powhatan Point, Oh., U.S.	C5	112
Poxoreu, Braz.	C1	57
Poyang, China	F5	28
Poyang Hu, l., China	F5	28
Poygan, Lake, l., Wi., U.S.	D5	126
Poynette, Wi., U.S.	E4	126
Poza Rica de Hidalgo, Mex.	G11	62
Poznań, Pol.	C16	8
Pozo Alcón, Spain	H9	12
Pozoblanco, Spain	G7	12
Pozo Redondo Mountains, mts., Az., U.S.	E3	80
Pozuelo de Alarcón, Spain	E8	12
Pozzuoli, Italy	I9	14
Prachin Buri, Thai.	G6	34
Prachuap Khiri Khan, Thai.	I5	34
Prague, Ok., U.S.	B5	113
Prague see Praha, Czech.	E14	8
Praha (Prague), Czech.	E14	8
Prainha, Braz.	E6	54
Prairie, co., Ar., U.S.	C4	81
Prairie, co., Mt., U.S.	D11	103
Prairie, stm., Mn., U.S.	C5	100
Prairie City, Ia., U.S.	C4	92
Prairie City, Or., U.S.	C8	114

Name	Map Ref	Page
Prairie Creek Reservoir, res., In., U.S.	D7	91
Prairie Dog Creek, stm., U.S.	C3	93
Prairie du Chien, Wi., U.S.	E2	126
Prairie du Sac, Wi., U.S.	E4	126
Prairie Grove, Ar., U.S.	B1	81
Prairies, Rivière des, stm., Que., Can.	p19	74
Prairie View, Tx., U.S.	D5	120
Prairie Village, Ks., U.S.	m16	93
Praslin Island, i., Sey.	B11	44
Pratas Islands see Tungsha Tao, is., Tai.	G10	26
Prat de Llobregat, Spain	D14	12
Prater Mountain, mtn., Wy., U.S.	C2	127
Prato, Italy	F6	14
Pratt, Ks., U.S.	E5	93
Pratt, co., Ks., U.S.	E5	93
Prattville, S. Afr.	C3	78
Prattville, Al., U.S.	C3	78
Pravia, Spain	B5	12
Preble, co., Oh., U.S.	C1	112
Predazzo, Italy	C6	14
Predlitz [-Turrach], Aus.	H13	8
Pré-en-Pail, Fr.	D6	10
Preetz, Ger.	A10	8
Premont, Tx., U.S.	F3	120
Prentiss, Ms., U.S.	D4	101
Prentiss, co., Ms., U.S.	A5	101
Prenzlau, Ger.	B13	8
Preparis Island, i., Burma	G2	34
Preparis North Channel, strt., Burma	G2	34
Preparis South Channel, strt., Burma	G2	34
Přerov, Czech.	F17	8
Prescott, Ont., Can.	C9	73
Prescott, Az., U.S.	C3	80
Prescott, Ar., U.S.	D2	81
Prescott, Wi., U.S.	D1	126
Presho, S.D., U.S.	D5	118
Presidencia Roca, Arg.	B5	56
Presidente Epitácio, Braz.	F2	57
Presidente Prudente, Braz.	G3	57
Presidential Range, mts., N.H., U.S.	B4	106
Presidio, Tx., U.S.	p12	120
Presidio, co., Tx., U.S.	o12	120
Presidio of San Francisco, mil., Ca., U.S.	h8	82
Prešov, Czech.	F21	8
Prespa, Lake, l., Eur.	I4	16
Presque Isle, Me., U.S.	B5	96
Presque Isle, co., Mi., U.S.	C6	99
Preston, Eng., U.K.	H10	7
Preston, Id., U.S.	G7	89
Preston, Ia., U.S.	B7	92
Preston, Mn., U.S.	G6	100
Preston, co., W.V., U.S.	B5	125
Preston Peak, mtn., Ca., U.S.	B2	82
Prestonsburg, Ky., U.S.	C7	94
Presumpscot, stm., Me., U.S.	g7	96
Pretoria, S. Afr.	G5	44
Prettyboy Reservoir, res., Md., U.S.	A4	97
Pretty Prairie, Ks., U.S.	E5	93
Préveza, Grc.	K4	16
Prewitt Reservoir, res., Co., U.S.	A7	83
Prey Vêng, Camb.	I8	34
Pribilof Islands, is., Ak., U.S.	D5	79
Příbram, Czech.	F14	8
Price, Ut., U.S.	D5	121
Price, co., Wi., U.S.	C3	126
Price, stm., Ut., U.S.	D5	121
Price Inlet, b., S.C., U.S.	k12	117
Prichard, Al., U.S.	E1	78
Priego, Spain	E9	12
Priego de Córdoba, Spain	H7	12
Prien, Ger.	H12	8
Prieska, S. Afr.	G4	44
Priest Lake, l., Id., U.S.	A2	89
Priest Rapids Dam, Wa., U.S.	C6	124
Priest Rapids Lake, res., Wa., U.S.	C6	124
Priest River, Id., U.S.	A2	89
Prievidza, Czech.	G18	8
Prijedor, Bos.	E11	14
Prilep, Mac.	H5	16
Prim, Point, c., P.E.I., Can.	C6	71
Primghar, Ia., U.S.	A2	92
Primrose, R.I., U.S.	B3	116
Primrose Lake, l., Can.	F11	75
Prince, Lake, res., Va., U.S.	k14	123
Prince Albert National Park, Sask., Can.	C2	75
Prince Albert Sound, strt., N.W. Ter., Can.	B9	66
Prince Charles Island, i., N.W. Ter., Can.	C17	66
Prince-de-Galles, Cap du, c., Que., Can.	D18	74
Prince Edward, co., Va., U.S.	C4	123
Prince Edward Island, prov., Can.	C6	71
Prince Edward Island National Park, P.E.I., Can.	C6	71
Prince Frederick, Md., U.S.	C4	97
Prince George, B.C., Can.	C6	69
Prince George, co., Va., U.S.	C5	123
Prince Georges, co., Md., U.S.	C4	97
Prince of Wales, Cape, c., Ak., U.S.	B6	79
Prince of Wales Island, i., Austl.	B8	50
Prince of Wales Island, i., N.W. Ter., Can.	B13	66
Prince of Wales Island, i., Ak., U.S.	n23	79
Prince of Wales Strait, strt., N.W. Ter., Can.	B9	66
Prince Regent Inlet, b., N.W. Ter., Can.	B14	66
Prince Rupert, B.C., Can.	B2	69
Princes Lakes, In., U.S.	F5	91
Princess Anne, Md., U.S.	D6	97
Princess Royal Channel, strt., B.C., Can.	C3	69
Princess Royal Island, i., B.C., Can.	C3	69

Name	Map Ref	Page
rinceton, B.C., Can.	E7	69
rinceton, Fl., U.S.	G6	86
rinceton, Il., U.S.	B4	90
rinceton, In., U.S.	H2	91
rinceton, Ia., U.S.	C7	92
rinceton, Ky., U.S.	C2	94
rinceton, Me., U.S.	C5	96
rinceton, Mn., U.S.	E5	100
rinceton, Mo., U.S.	A4	102
rinceton, N.J., U.S.	C3	107
rinceton, N.C., U.S.	B4	110
rinceton, W.V., U.S.	D3	125
rinceton, Wi., U.S.	E4	126
rinceton, Mount, mtn., Co., U.S.	C4	83
rinceville, Que., Can.	C6	74
rinceville, Il., U.S.	C4	90
rinceville, N.C., U.S.	B5	110
rineville, Or., U.S.	C6	114
rineville Reservoir, res., Or., U.S.	C6	114
ringsewu, Indon.	k12	33a
rior Lake, Mn., U.S.	F5	100
riština, Yugo.	G5	16
ritchards Island, i., S.C., U.S.	G6	117
ritzwalk, Ger.	B12	8
rivas, Fr.	H11	10
rivolžsk, Russia	D24	18
robolinggo, Indon.	m16	33a
roctor, Mn., U.S.	D6	100
roctor, Vt., U.S.	D2	122
roctor Lake, res., Tx., U.S.	C3	120
roctorsville, Vt., U.S.	E3	122
roddatür, India	E5	37
rofessor Dr. Ir. W.J. van Blommestein Meer, res., Sur.	C7	54
rogreso, Mex.	G15	62
rokopjevsk, Russia	G11	24
rokuplje, Yugo.	F5	16
romontory Mountains, mts., Ut., U.S.	B3	121
rophetstown, Il., U.S.	B4	90
rospect, Ct., U.S.	C4	84
rospect, Ky., U.S.	g11	94
rospect, Oh., U.S.	B2	112
rospect, Pa., U.S.	E4	114
rospect, Pa., U.S.	E1	115
rospect Hill, mtn., Or., U.S.	k11	114
rospect Park, N.J., U.S.	B4	107
rospect Park, Pa., U.S.	p20	115
rosperity, S.C., U.S.	C4	117
rosperity, W.V., U.S.	n13	125
rosser, Wa., U.S.	C6	124
rostějov, Czech.	F17	8
rotection, Ks., U.S.	E4	93
rotville, Tun.	M5	14
rovence, hist. reg., Fr.	I13	10
rovidence, Ky., U.S.	C2	94
rovidence, R.I., U.S.	C4	116
rovidence, Ut., U.S.	B4	121
rovidence, co., R.I., U.S.	C2	116
rovidence, co., R.I., U.S.	C5	116
rovidence Island, i., Sey.	C10	44
rovidence Point, c., R.I., U.S.	D5	116
rovidencia, Isla de i., Col.	H7	64
rovidenija, Russia	E31	24
rovince Lake, l., N.H., U.S.	C5	106
rovincetown, Ma., U.S.	B7	98
rovins, Fr.	D10	10
rovo, Ut., U.S.	C4	121
rovo, stm., Ut., U.S.	C4	121
rovost, Alta., Can.	C5	68
rowers, co., Co., U.S.	D8	83
rozor, Bos.	F12	14
rudenville, Mi., U.S.	D6	99
rudhoe Bay, Ak., U.S.	A10	79
rudhoe Bay, b., Ak., U.S.	A10	79
rüm, Ger.	E6	8
ruszków, Pol.	C20	8
rut, stm., Eur.	D12	16
ryor, Mt., U.S.	E8	103
ryor, Ok., U.S.	A6	113
ryor Mountains, mts., Mt., U.S.	E8	103
rzemyśl, Pol.	F22	8
skov, Russia	D11	18
tolemais, Grc.	I5	16
tolemais, Grc.	C10	14
ucallpa, Peru	E4	54
ucheng, China	H7	28
uckaway Lake, l., Wi., U.S.	E4	126
udukkottai, India	G5	37
uebla de Sanabria, Spain	C5	12
uebla de Trives, Spain	C4	12
uebla [de Zaragoza], Mex.	H10	62
ueblo, Co., U.S.	C6	83
ueblo, co., Co., U.S.	C6	83
ueblo Hundido, Chile	B2	56
ueblo Mountain, mtn., Or., U.S.	E8	114
ueblo Mountains, mts., Or., U.S.	E8	114
ueblo Reservoir, res., Co., U.S.	C6	83
uentedeume, Spain	B3	12
uente-Genil, Spain	H7	12
ueo Point, c., Hi., U.S.	B1	88
uerco, stm., U.S.	C6	80
uerco, Rio, stm., N.M., U.S.	B2	108
uerto Aisén, Chile	F2	56
uerto Alfonso, Col.	I7	58
uerto Ángel, Mex.	J11	62
uerto Armuelles, Pan.	J6	64
uerto Asís, Col.	G4	58
uerto Ayacucho, Ven.	E9	58
uerto Barrios, Guat.	G3	64
uerto Berrío, Col.	D5	58
uerto Boyacá, Col.	E5	58
uerto Cabello, Ven.	B8	58
uerto Cabezas, Nic.	G6	64
Puerto Carreño, Col.	D9	58
Puerto Casado, Para.	A5	56
Puerto Chicama, Peru	E3	54
Puerto Cortés, C.R.	J6	64
Puerto Cortés, Hond.	G4	64
Puerto Cumarebo, Ven.	B8	58
Puerto de Pollensa, Spain	F15	12
Puerto de San José, Guat.	H2	64
Puerto Deseado, Arg.	F3	56
Puerto Escondido, Mex.	J11	62
Puerto Francisco de Orellana, Ec.	H4	58
Puerto Inírida, Col.	F9	58
Puerto Juárez, Mex.	G16	62
Puerto la Cruz, Ven.	B10	58
Puerto Leguízamo, Col.	H5	58
Puerto Limón, Col.	F6	58
Puertollano, Spain	G7	12
Puerto Lobos, Arg.	E3	56
Puerto Madryn, Arg.	E3	56
Puerto Maldonado, Peru	F5	54
Puerto Montt, Chile	E2	56
Puerto Morelos, Mex.	G16	62
Puerto Nariño, Col.	E9	58
Puerto Natales, Chile	G2	56
Puerto Padre, Cuba	D9	64
Puerto Peñasco, Mex.	B3	62
Puerto Plata, Dom. Rep.	E12	64
Puerto Princesa, Phil.	D6	32
Puerto Real, Spain	I5	12
Puerto Rico, dep., N.A.	E14	64
Puerto Rondón, Col.	D7	58
Puerto Suárez, Bol.	G7	54
Puerto Tejada, Col.	F4	58
Puerto Vallarta, Mex.	G7	62
Puerto Wilches, Col.	D6	58
Puget Sound, strt., Wa., U.S.	B3	124
Puget Sound Naval Shipyard, mil., Wa., U.S.	e10	124
Pugwash, N.S., Can.	D6	71
Puhi, Hi., U.S.	B2	88
Puigcerdá, Spain	C13	12
Pukalani, Hi., U.S.	C5	88
Pukaskwa National Park, Ont., Can.	o18	73
Pukch'ŏng, N. Kor.	C12	26
Pukë, Alb.	G3	16
Pukeashun Mountain, mtn., B.C., Can.	D8	69
Pukekohe, N.Z.	B5	52
Pukou, China	C7	28
Pula, Cro.	E8	14
Pulacayo, Bol.	H5	54
Pulaski, N.Y., U.S.	B4	109
Pulaski, Tn., U.S.	B4	119
Pulaski, Va., U.S.	C2	123
Pulaski, Wi., U.S.	D5	126
Pulaski, co., Ar., U.S.	C3	81
Pulaski, co., Ga., U.S.	D3	87
Pulaski, co., Il., U.S.	F4	90
Pulaski, co., In., U.S.	B4	91
Pulaski, co., Ky., U.S.	C5	94
Pulaski, co., Mo., U.S.	D5	102
Pulaski, co., Va., U.S.	C2	123
Puli, Tai.	L9	28
Puliyangudi, India	H4	37
Pulkkila, Fin.	D15	6
Pullman, Wa., U.S.	C8	124
Pulog, Mount, mtn., Phil.	B7	32
Pumphrey, Md., U.S.	h11	97
Puná, Isla, i., Ec.	I2	58
Punakha, Bhu.	G13	38
Pünch, India	D6	38
Pungo Lake, l., N.C., U.S.	B6	110
Punjab, state, India	E6	38
Puno, Peru	G4	54
Punta, Cerro de, mtn., P.R.	E14	64
Punta Alta, Arg.	D4	56
Punta Arenas, Chile	G2	56
Punta Delgada, Arg.	E4	56
Punta de Mata, Ven.	C11	58
Punta Gorda, Belize	F3	64
Punta Gorda, Nic.	I6	64
Punta Gorda, Fl., U.S.	F4	86
Puntarenas, C.R.	I5	64
Punto Fijo, Ven.	B7	58
Punxsutawney, Pa., U.S.	E4	115
Puolanka, Fin.	D16	6
Purcell, Ok., U.S.	B4	113
Purcellville, Va., U.S.	A5	123
Purdy, Mo., U.S.	E4	102
Purgatoire, stm., Co., U.S.	D7	83
Purgatoire Peak, mtn., Co., U.S.	D5	83
Puri, India	K11	38
Purli, India	C4	37
Purnea, India	H12	38
Purūlia, India	I12	38
Purus (Purús), stm., S.A.	D6	54
Purvis, Ms., U.S.	D4	101
Purwakarta, Indon.	m13	33a
Purwokerto, Indon.	m14	32
Purworejo, Indon.	m15	33a
Pusan, S. Kor.	D12	26
Pushaw Lake, l., Me., U.S.	D4	96
Pushmataha, co., Ok., U.S.	C6	113
Puškin, Russia	B13	18
Puškino, Russia	E20	18
Putao, Burma	F6	26
Puting, Tanjung, c., Indon.	F5	32
Putnam, Ct., U.S.	B8	84
Putnam, co., Fl., U.S.	C5	86
Putnam, co., Ga., U.S.	C3	87
Putnam, co., Il., U.S.	B4	90
Putnam, co., In., U.S.	E4	91
Putnam, co., Mo., U.S.	A4	102
Putnam, co., N.Y., U.S.	D7	109
Putnam, co., Oh., U.S.	B1	112
Putnam, co., Tn., U.S.	C8	119
Putnam, co., W.V., U.S.	C3	125
Putney, Ga., U.S.	E2	87
Putney, Vt., U.S.	F3	122
Putorana, Plato, plat., Russia	D12	24
Puttalam, Sri L.	H5	37
Puttgarden, Ger.	A11	8
Putumayo (Içá), stm., S.A.	I7	58
Putuo, China	F11	28
Puukohola Heiau National Historic Site, hist., Hi., U.S.	D6	88
Puxico, Mo., U.S.	E7	102
Puyallup, Wa., U.S.	B3	124
Puyallup, stm., Wa., U.S.	C3	124
Puy de Dôme, mtn., Fr.	G9	10
Puy de Sancy, mtn., Fr.	G9	10
Puylaurens, Fr.	I9	10
Puyo, Ec.	H4	58
Pweto, Zaire	C5	44
Pwllheli, Wales, U.K.	I8	7
Pyapon, Burma	F3	34
Pyatigorsk see P'atigorsk, Russia	I6	22
Pyè (Prome), Burma	E3	34
Pyhäjoki, Fin.	D15	6
Pyhäselkä, Fin.	E17	6
Pyinmana, Burma	E4	34
Pyles Fork, stm., W.V., U.S.	h10	125
Pymatuning Reservoir, res., U.S.	C1	115
P'yŏngyang, N. Kor.	D12	26
Pyramid Lake, l., Nv., U.S.	C2	105
Pyramid Lake Indian Reservation, Nv., U.S.	D2	105
Pyramid Mountains, mts., N.M., U.S.	E1	108
Pyramid Peak, mtn., N.M., U.S.	E1	108
Pyramid Peak, mtn., Wy., U.S.	C2	127
Pyrenees, mts., Eur.	C12	12
Pyskowice, Pol.	E18	8
Pyu, Burma	E4	34

Q

Name	Map Ref	Page
Qaidam Pendi, China	B16	38
Qalāt, Afg.	D2	38
Qal'at Bīshah, Sau. Ar.	E3	46
Qal'eh-ye Kānsī, Afg.	C2	36
Qal'eh-ye Sarkārī, Afg.	C2	38
Qallābāt, Sudan	F13	42
Qamar, Ghubbat al-, b., Yemen	E5	46
Qamdo, China	E6	26
Qandahār, Afg.	E1	38
Qandala, Som.	F4	46
Qarqan, stm., China	B11	38
Qarqīn, Afg.	B2	38
Qasr al-Burayqah, Libya	B9	42
Qasr al-Farāfirah, Egypt	C11	42
Qatanā, Syria	C5	40
Qatar, ctry., Asia	C5	46
Qazvīn, Iran	J8	22
Qeshm, i., Iran	C6	46
Qeyşār, Afg.	C1	38
Qezī'ot, Isr.	D4	40
Qiemo, China	A11	38
Qijiang, China	F8	26
Qinā, Egypt	C12	42
Qingdao (Tsingtao), China	D11	26
Qinghai, prov., China	D6	26
Qinghai Hu, l., China	D7	26
Qingjiang, China	G4	28
Qinglong, China	B8	34
Qingyang, China	D8	26
Qingyuan, China	G8	26
Qingyuan, China	L2	28
Qinhuangdao, China	D10	26
Qin Ling, mts., China	E8	26
Qinzhou, China	D10	34
Qiongzhou Haixia, strt., China	D11	34
Qiqihar, China	B11	26
Qiryat Shemona, Isr.	C4	40
Qitai, China	C4	26
Qīzān, Sau. Ar.	E3	46
Qom, Iran	B5	46
Qomsheh, Iran	B5	46
Qondūz, Afg.	B3	38
Qondūz, stm., Afg.	C3	38
Quabbin Reservoir, res., Ma., U.S.	B3	98
Quaddick Reservoir, res., Ct., U.S.	B8	84
Quail Oaks, Va., U.S.	n18	123
Quaker Hill, Ct., U.S.	D7	84
Quakertown, Pa., U.S.	F11	115
Qualicum Beach, B.C., Can.	E5	69
Quanah, Tx., U.S.	B3	120
Quang Ngai, Viet.	G10	34
Quannapowitt, Lake, l., Ma., U.S.	f11	98
Quantico, Va., U.S.	B5	123
Quantico Marine Corps Air Station, mil., Va., U.S.	B5	123
Quanzhou, China	K7	28
Quapaw, Ok., U.S.	A7	113
Qu'Appelle, Sask., Can.	G4	75
Qu'Appelle, stm., Can.	G4	75
Quarryville, Pa., U.S.	G9	115
Quartu Sant'Elena, Italy	J4	14
Quartz Lake, l., N.W. Ter., Can.	B16	66
Quartz Mountain, mtn., Or., U.S.	D4	114
Quartzsite, Az., U.S.	D1	80
Quassapaug, Lake, l., Ct., U.S.	C3	84
Quatsino Sound, strt., B.C., Can.	D3	69
Quay, co., N.M., U.S.	C6	108
Québec, Que., Can.	C6	74
Quebec, prov., Can.	C5	74
Quechee, Vt., U.S.	D4	122
Quedlinburg, Ger.	D11	8
Queen, stm., R.I., U.S.	E3	116
Queen Annes, co., Md., U.S.	B5	97
Queen Bess, Mount, mtn., B.C., Can.	D5	69
Queen Charlotte, B.C., Can.	C1	69
Queen Charlotte Islands, is., B.C., Can.	C1	69
Queen Charlotte Mountains, mts., B.C., Can.	C1	69
Queen Charlotte Sound, strt., B.C., Can.	n17	69
Queen Charlotte Strait, strt., B.C., Can.	D4	69
Queen City, Mo., U.S.	A5	102
Queen City, Tx., U.S.	C5	120
Queen Creek, Az., U.S.	m9	80
Queen Maud Gulf, b., N.W. Ter., Can.	C12	66
Queen Maud Land, reg., Ant.	B14	47
Queens, co., N.Y., U.S.	E7	109
Queens Channel, strt., N.W. Ter., Can.	A13	66
Queensland, state, Austl.	D8	50
Queenstown, N.Z.	F2	52
Queenstown, S. Afr.	H5	44
Quelimane, Moz.	E7	44
Quemoy see Chinmen Tao, i., Tai.	K7	28
Querétaro, Mex.	G9	62
Querobabi, Mex.	B4	62
Quesnel, B.C., Can.	C6	69
Quesnel, stm., B.C., Can.	C6	69
Quesnel Lake, l., B.C., Can.	C7	69
Questa, N.M., U.S.	A4	108
Questembert, Fr.	E4	10
Quetico Provincial Park, Ont., Can.	o17	73
Quetta, Pak.	E2	38
Quevedo, Ec.	H3	58
Quevedo, stm., Ec.	H3	58
Quezaltenango, Guat.	G2	64
Quezon City, Phil.	q19	32
Qufu, China	D10	26
Quibdó, Col.	E4	58
Quiberon, Fr.	E3	10
Quicksand Pond, l., R.I., U.S.	E6	116
Quidnessett, R.I., U.S.	E4	116
Quidnick, R.I., U.S.	D3	116
Quidnick Reservoir, res., R.I., U.S.	D2	116
Quilá, Mex.	E6	62
Quilcene, Wa., U.S.	B3	124
Quileute Indian Reservation, Wa., U.S.	B1	124
Quillan, Fr.	J9	10
Quilon, India	H4	37
Quilpie, Austl.	E8	50
Quimper, Fr.	D2	10
Quimperlé, Fr.	E3	10
Quinault, stm., Wa., U.S.	B1	124
Quinault, Lake, l., Wa., U.S.	B2	124
Quinault Indian Reservation, Wa., U.S.	B1	124
Quincemil, Peru	F4	54
Quincy, Ca., U.S.	C3	82
Quincy, Fl., U.S.	B2	86
Quincy, Il., U.S.	D2	90
Quincy, Ma., U.S.	B5	98
Quincy, Mi., U.S.	G6	99
Quincy, Wa., U.S.	B6	124
Quincy Bay, b., Ma., U.S.	g12	98
Quinebaug, Ct., U.S.	A8	84
Quinebaug, stm., Ct., U.S.	C8	84
Quinhagak, Ak., U.S.	D7	79
Qui Nhon, Viet.	H10	34
Quinlan, Tx., U.S.	C4	120
Quinn, stm., Nv., U.S.	B3	105
Quinn Canyon Range, mts., Nv., U.S.	F6	105
Quinnesec, Mi., U.S.	C3	99
Quinnipiac, stm., Ct., U.S.	D4	84
Quintanar de la Orden, Spain	F8	12
Quinter, Ks., U.S.	C3	93
Quinton, Ok., U.S.	B6	113
Quiroga, Spain	C4	12
Quitman, Ar., U.S.	B3	81
Quitman, Ga., U.S.	F3	87
Quitman, Ms., U.S.	C5	101
Quitman, Tx., U.S.	C5	120
Quitman, co., Ga., U.S.	E1	87
Quitman, co., Ms., U.S.	A3	101
Quito, Ec.	H3	58
Quixadá, Braz.	D11	54
Qujing, China	B7	34
Qumalai (Sewugou), China	C16	38
Quoich, stm., N.W. Ter., Can.	D14	66
Quonnipaug Lake, l., Ct., U.S.	D5	84
Quonochontaug, R.I., U.S.	G2	116
Quonochontaug Pond, l., R.I., U.S.	G2	116
Quonset Point, c., R.I., U.S.	E4	116
Qutdligssat, Grnld.	B22	66
Quthing, Leso.	H5	44
Quxian, China	G7	28

R

Name	Map Ref	Page
Raalte, Neth.	C6	8
Rab, Cro.	E9	14
Raba, Indon.	G6	32
Rába (Raab), stm., Eur.	H17	8
Rábade, Spain	B4	12
Rabat (Victoria), Malta	M9	14
Rabat, Mor.	B4	42
Rabaul, Pap. N. Gui.	k17	50a
Rabbit Creek, stm., S.D., U.S.	B3	118
Rabbit Ears Pass, Co., U.S.	A4	83
Rābigh, Sau. Ar.	D2	46
Rabun, co., Ga., U.S.	B3	87
Rabun Bald, mtn., Ga., U.S.	B3	87
Raccoon Creek, stm., Oh., U.S.	D3	112
Raccourci Island, i., La., U.S.	D4	95
Race, Cape, c., Newf., Can.	E5	72
Raceland, Ky., U.S.	B7	94
Raceland, La., U.S.	E5	95
Race Point, c., Ma., U.S.	B7	98
Rach Gia, Viet.	I8	34
Racibórz (Ratibor), Pol.	E18	8
Racine, W.V., U.S.	C3	125
Racine, Wi., U.S.	F6	126
Racine, co., Wi., U.S.	F5	126
Racine Dam, Wi., U.S.	C3	125
Radcliff, Ky., U.S.	C4	94
Radeberg, Ger.	D13	8
Radebeul, Ger.	D13	8
Radeče, Slo.	C10	14
Radford, Va., U.S.	C2	123
Radolfzell, Ger.	H8	8
Radom, Pol.	D21	8
Radomsko, Pol.	D19	8
Rae, N.W. Ter., Can.	D9	66
Rae Bareli, India	G9	38
Rae Isthmus, N.W. Ter., Can.	C15	66
Rae Strait, strt., N.W. Ter., Can.	C13	66
Raetihi, N.Z.	C5	52
Rafaela, Arg.	C4	56
Rafah, Isr. Occ.	D4	40
Rafhā', Sau. Ar.	C3	46
Rafsanjān, Iran	K9	22
Rafsanjān, Iran	B6	46
Raft, stm., Id., U.S.	G5	89
Raft River Mountains, mts., Ut., U.S.	B2	121
Raga, Sudan	G11	42
Ragged Island, i., Me., U.S.	E4	96
Ragged Lake, l., Me., U.S.	C3	96
Ragged Top Mountain, mtn., Wy., U.S.	E7	127
Ragland, Al., U.S.	B3	78
Ragusa, Italy	M9	14
Ragusa see Dubrovnik, Cro.	G13	14
Rahway, N.J., U.S.	B4	107
Rahway, stm., N.J., U.S.	k7	107
Rāichūr, India	D4	37
Raigarh, India	B7	37
Railroad Valley, val., Nv., U.S.	E6	105
Rainbow Bridge National Monument, Ut., U.S.	F5	121
Rainbow Falls, wtfl, Tn., U.S.	D10	119
Rainbow Flowage, res., Wi., U.S.	C4	126
Rainbow Lake, l., Me., U.S.	C3	96
Rainelle, W.V., U.S.	D4	125
Rainier, Or., U.S.	A4	114
Rainier, Wa., U.S.	C3	124
Rainier, Mount, mtn., Wa., U.S.	C5	124
Rains, co., Tx., U.S.	C5	120
Rainsville, Al., U.S.	A4	78
Rainy Lake, l., N.A.	G14	66
Rainy Lake, l., Mn., U.S.	B5	100
Rainy River, Ont., Can.	o16	73
Raipur, India	B6	37
Rājahmundry, India	H4	37
Rājapālaiyam, India	H4	37
Rājasthān, prov., India	G5	38
Rājasthān Canal, India	D5	38
Raj-Nāndgaon, India	B6	37
Rājpīpla, India	J5	38
Rajshahi, India	H13	38
Rākaposhi, mtn., Pak.	B6	38
Rakata, Pulau, i., Indon.	m12	33a
Råkvåg, Nor.	E8	6
Raleigh, Ms., U.S.	C4	101
Raleigh, N.C., U.S.	B4	110
Raleigh, co., W.V., U.S.	D3	125
Raleigh Bay, b., N.C., U.S.	C6	110
Ralls, Tx., U.S.	C2	120
Ralls, co., Mo., U.S.	B6	102
Ralston, Ne., U.S.	g12	104
Ralston Valley, val., Nv., U.S.	E5	105
Rama, Nic.	H5	64
Ramah, N.M., U.S.	B1	108
Ramah Indian Reservation, N.M., U.S.	C1	108
Rām Allāh, Jord.	D4	40
Ramapo, stm., N.J., U.S.	A4	107
Ramblewood, N.J., U.S.	D3	107
Rambouillet, Fr.	D8	10
Ramea, Newf., Can.	E3	72
Ramenskoje, Russia	F21	18
Rāmeswaram, India	H5	37
Rāmgarh, Bngl.	I14	38
Ramla, Isr.	D4	40
Ramlo, mtn., Eth.	F3	46
Ramona, Ca., U.S.	F5	82
Rampart Range, mts., Co., U.S.	B5	83
Rāmpur, India	F8	38
Ramree Island, i., Burma	E2	34
Ramsay, Mi., U.S.	n12	99
Ramsey, I. of Man	J14	7
Ramsey, Il., U.S.	D4	90
Ramsey, Mn., U.S.	*E5	100
Ramsey, N.J., U.S.	A4	107
Ramsey, co., Mn., U.S.	E5	100
Ramsey, co., N.D., U.S.	A7	111
Ramsgate, Eng., U.K.	J14	7
Ramshorn Peak, mtn., Mt., U.S.	E5	103
Ramshorn Peak, mtn., Wy., U.S.	C3	127
Rāmu, Bngl.	J15	38
Ramu, stm., Pap. N. Gui.	m16	50a
Rancagua, Chile	C2	56
Rancharia, Braz.	G3	57
Rancheria Rock, Or., U.S.	C6	114
Ranchester, Wy., U.S.	B5	127
Ranchi, India	I11	38
Rancho Palos Verdes, Ca., U.S.	*n12	82
Ranchos de Taos, N.M., U.S.	A4	108
Rancocas Creek, stm., N.J., U.S.	C3	107
Rand, W.V., U.S.	C3	125
Randall, co., Tx., U.S.	B2	120
Randallstown, Md., U.S.	B4	97
Randazzo, Italy	L9	14
Randers, Den.	H8	6
Randle, Wa., U.S.	C4	124
Randleman, N.C., U.S.	B3	110
Randolph, Me., U.S.	D3	96
Randolph, Ma., U.S.	B5	98
Randolph, Ne., U.S.	B8	104
Randolph, Vt., U.S.	D3	122
Randolph, Wi., U.S.	E5	126
Randolph, co., Al., U.S.	B4	78
Randolph, co., Ar., U.S.	A4	81
Randolph, co., Ga., U.S.	E2	87
Randolph, co., Il., U.S.	E4	90
Randolph, co., In., U.S.	D7	91
Randolph, co., Mo., U.S.	B5	102
Randolph, co., N.C., U.S.	B3	110
Randolph, co., W.V., U.S.	C5	125
Randolph Air Force Base, mil., Tx., U.S.	h7	120
Randolph Hills, Md., U.S.	B3	97
Random Island, i., Newf., Can.	D5	72
Random Lake, Wi., U.S.	E6	126
Rangeley, Me., U.S.	D2	96

Name	Map Ref	Page
Rangeley Lake, l., Me., U.S.	D2	96
Rangely, Co., U.S.	A2	83
Ranger, Tx., U.S.	C3	120
Ranger Lake, l., N.M., U.S.	D6	108
Rangoon see Yangon, Burma	B2	32
Rangpur, Bngl.	H13	38
Rankin, Pa., U.S.	k14	115
Rankin, co., Ms., U.S.	C4	101
Rankin Inlet, N.W. Ter., Can.	D14	66
Rann of Kutch, pl., Asia	H3	38
Ransom, co., N.D., U.S.	C8	111
Ranson, W.V., U.S.	B7	125
Rantauprapat, Indon.	E2	32
Rantekombola, Bulu, mtn., Irdon.	F7	32
Rantoul, Il., U.S.	C5	90
Raoping, China	L6	28
Raoul, Ga., U.S.	B3	87
Rapallo, Italy	E4	14
Rapid, stm., Mn., U.S.	B4	100
Rapid City, S.D., U.S.	C2	118
Rapides, co., La., U.S.	C3	95
Rapid River, Mi., U.S.	C4	99
Rapids City, Il., U.S.	B3	90
Rappahannock, co., Va., U.S.	B4	123
Rappahannock, stm., Va., U.S.	B5	123
Raquette, stm., N.Y., U.S.	f10	109
Raquette Lake, l., N.Y., U.S.	B6	109
Raritan, N.J., U.S.	B3	107
Raritan, stm., N.J., U.S.	C4	107
Raritan Bay, b., N.J., U.S.	C4	107
Ra's al-'Ayn, Syria	A7	40
Ra's an-Naqb, Jord.	D4	40
Ras Dashen, mtn., Eth.	F2	46
Ras Djebel, Tun.	L5	14
Rasht, Iran	J7	22
Rāsipuram, India	G5	37
Rasskazovo, Russia	I24	18
Rastatt, Ger.	G8	8
Ratangarh, India	F6	38
Rätansbyn, Swe.	E10	6
Rathbun Lake, res., Ia., U.S.	D5	92
Rathdrum, Id., U.S.	B2	89
Rathenow, Ger.	C12	8
Rathkeale, Ire.	I4	7
Rathlin Island, i., N. Ire., U.K.	F6	7
Rat Islands, is., Ak., U.S.	E3	79
Ratlām, India	I6	38
Ratnāgiri, India	D2	37
Ratnapura, Sri L.	I6	37
Raton, N.M., U.S.	A5	108
Raton Pass, N.M., U.S.	A5	108
Rattlesnake Creek, stm., Oh., U.S.	C2	112
Rattlesnake Creek, stm., Wa., U.S.	C6	124
Rättvik, Swe.	F10	6
Ratz, Mount, mtn., B.C., Can.	E6	66
Ratzeburg, Ger.	B10	8
Raub, Malay.	M6	34
Rauch, Arg.	D5	56
Rauma, Fin.	F13	6
Raurkela, India	I11	38
Ravalli, co., Mt., U.S.	D2	103
Raven, Va., U.S.	e10	123
Ravena, N.Y., U.S.	C7	109
Ravenel, S.C., U.S.	k11	117
Ravenna, Italy	E7	14
Ravenna, Ky., U.S.	C6	94
Ravenna, Mi., U.S.	E5	99
Ravenna, Ne., U.S.	C7	104
Ravenna, Oh., U.S.	A4	112
Raven Park, reg., Co., U.S.	A2	83
Ravensburg, Ger.	H9	8
Ravenshoe, Austl.	C9	50
Ravensthorpe, Austl.	F3	50
Ravenswood, W.V., U.S.	C3	125
Rāwalpindi, Pak.	D5	38
Rawdon, Que., Can.	C4	74
Rawhide Creek, stm., Wy., U.S.	D8	127
Rawlings, Md., U.S.	k13	97
Rawlinna, Austl.	F5	50
Rawlins, Wy., U.S.	E5	127
Rawlins, co., Ks., U.S.	C2	93
Rawson, Arg.	E3	56
Ray, N.D., U.S.	A2	111
Ray, co., Mo., U.S.	B3	102
Ray, Cape, c., Newf., Can.	E2	72
Raya, Bukit, mtn., Indon.	F5	32
Rāyadrug, India	E4	37
Ray City, Ga., U.S.	E3	87
Raymond, Alta., Can.	E4	68
Raymond, Il., U.S.	D4	90
Raymond, Mn., U.S.	E3	100
Raymond, Ms., U.S.	C3	101
Raymond, N.H., U.S.	D4	106
Raymond, Wa., U.S.	C2	124
Raymondville, Tx., U.S.	F4	120
Raymore, Sask., Can.	F3	75
Raymore, Mo., U.S.	C3	102
Rayne, La., U.S.	D3	95
Raynham, Ma., U.S.	C5	98
Raynham Center, Ma., U.S.	C5	98
Raytown, Mo., U.S.	h11	102
Rayville, La., U.S.	B4	95
R'azan', Russia	G22	18
Razgrad, Bul.	F10	16
R'ažsk, Russia	H23	18
Reader, W.V., U.S.	B4	125
Reading, Eng., U.K.	J12	7
Reading, Ma., U.S.	A5	98
Reading, Mi., U.S.	G6	99
Reading, Oh., U.S.	C1	112
Reading, Pa., U.S.	F10	115
Readlyn, Ia., U.S.	B5	92
Reagan, co., Tx., U.S.	D2	120
Real, co., Tx., U.S.	E3	120
Realicó, Arg.	C4	56
Réalmont, Fr.	I9	10
Reamstown, Pa., U.S.	F9	115
Recanati, Italy	F8	14
Recherche, Archipelago of the, is., Austl.	F4	50
Rečica, Bela.	I13	18
Recife, Braz.	E12	54
Recklinghausen, Ger.	D7	8
Recreo, Arg.	B3	56
Rector, Ar., U.S.	A5	81
Red (Hong) (Yuan), stm., Asia	C8	34
Red, stm., N.A.	B7	76
Red, stm., U.S.	E8	76
Red, stm., Ky., U.S.	C6	94
Red, stm., Tn., U.S.	A4	119
Red Bank, N.J., U.S.	C4	107
Red Bank, Tn., U.S.	D8	119
Red Bay, Al., U.S.	A1	78
Redberry Lake, l., Sask., Can.	E2	75
Redbird, Oh., U.S.	A4	112
Red Bird, stm., Ky., U.S.	C6	94
Red Bluff, Ca., U.S.	B2	82
Red Bluff Lake, res., U.S.	o12	120
Red Boiling Springs, Tn., U.S.	C8	119
Red Bud, Il., U.S.	E4	90
Red Butte, mtn., Ut., U.S.	B2	121
Red Cedar, stm., Mi., U.S.	C2	126
Red Cedar Lake, l., Wi., U.S.	C2	126
Redcliff, Alta., Can.	D5	68
Redcliffe, Mount, mtn., Austl.	E4	50
Red Cliff Indian Reservation, Wi., U.S.	B2	126
Red Cloud, Ne., U.S.	D7	104
Redcloud Peak, mtn., Co., U.S.	D3	83
Red Deer, Alta., Can.	C4	68
Red Deer, stm., Can.	D4	68
Red Deer, stm., Can.	E4	75
Redding, Ca., U.S.	B2	82
Redding, Ct., U.S.	D2	84
Redeye, stm., Mn., U.S.	D3	100
Redfield, Ar., U.S.	C3	81
Redfield, Ia., U.S.	C3	92
Redfield, S.D., U.S.	C7	118
Redford, Mi., U.S.	F7	99
Redgranite, Wi., U.S.	D4	126
Red Hook, N.Y., U.S.	C7	109
Red Indian Lake, l., Newf., Can.	D3	72
Red Jacket, W.V., U.S.	D2	125
Redkey, In., U.S.	D7	91
Red Lake, co., Mn., U.S.	C2	100
Red Lake, l., Az., U.S.	B1	80
Red Lake, l., Mn., U.S.	C2	100
Red Lake Falls, Mn., U.S.	C2	100
Red Lake Indian Reservation, Mn., U.S.	B3	100
Redlands, Ca., U.S.	E5	82
Red Lion, Pa., U.S.	G8	115
Red Lodge, Mt., U.S.	E7	103
Red Mill Pond, l., De., U.S.	E5	85
Redmond, Or., U.S.	C5	114
Redmond, Ut., U.S.	E4	121
Redmond, Wa., U.S.	e11	124
Red Mountain, mtn., Ca., U.S.	B2	82
Red Mountain, mtn., Mt., U.S.	C4	103
Red Mountain Pass, Co., U.S.	D3	83
Red Oak, Ga., U.S.	h7	87
Red Oak, Ia., U.S.	D2	92
Red Oak, Ok., U.S.	C6	113
Red Oak, Tx., U.S.	n10	120
Red Oaks, La., U.S.	h9	95
Redon, Fr.	E4	10
Redondela, Spain	C3	12
Redondo, Port.	G4	12
Redondo, Wa., U.S.	f11	124
Redondo Beach, Ca., U.S.	n12	82
Redoubt Volcano, vol., Ak., U.S.	g15	79
Red Peak, mtn., Co., U.S.	B4	83
Red River, co., La., U.S.	B2	95
Red River, co., Tx., U.S.	C5	120
Red Rock, stm., Mt., U.S.	F4	103
Red Rock, Lake, res., Ia., U.S.	C4	92
Red Sea	D2	46
Red Springs, N.C., U.S.	C3	110
Red Table Mountain, mts., Co., U.S.	B4	83
Redwater, Alta., Can.	C4	68
Redwater, stm., Mt., U.S.	C11	103
Red Willow, co., Ne., U.S.	D5	104
Redwillow, stm., Can.	B7	69
Red Wing, Mn., U.S.	F6	100
Redwood, co., Mn., U.S.	F3	100
Redwood, stm., Mn., U.S.	F3	100
Redwood City, Ca., U.S.	D2	82
Redwood Falls, Mn., U.S.	F3	100
Redwood National Park, Ca., U.S.	B2	82
Redwood Valley, Ca., U.S.	C2	82
Ree, Lough, l., Ire.	H4	7
Reed City, Mi., U.S.	E5	99
Reedley, Ca., U.S.	D4	82
Reedsburg, Wi., U.S.	E3	126
Reeds Peak, mtn., N.M., U.S.	D2	108
Reedsport, Or., U.S.	D2	114
Reedsville, Pa., U.S.	E6	115
Reedsville, Wi., U.S.	D6	126
Reedy, stm., S.C., U.S.	C3	117
Reedy Lake, l., Fl., U.S.	E5	86
Reelfoot Lake, l., Tn., U.S.	A2	119
Reese, Mi., U.S.	E7	99
Reese, stm., Nv., U.S.	C4	105
Reese Air Force Base, mil., Tx., U.S.	C1	120
Reeves, co., Tx., U.S.	o13	120
Reform, Al., U.S.	B1	78
Refugio, Tx., U.S.	E4	120
Refugio, co., Tx., U.S.	E4	120
Regen, Ger.	G13	8
Regencia, Braz.	E9	57
Regensburg, Ger.	F12	8
Reggane, Alg.	C6	42
Reggio di Calabria, Italy	K10	14
Reggio nell'Emilia, Italy	E5	14
Regina, Sask., Can.	G3	75
Regina Beach, Sask., Can.	G3	75
Rehoboth, Nmb.	F3	44
Rehoboth, Nmb.	F3	44
Rehoboth Bay, b., De., U.S.	F5	85
Rehoboth Beach, De., U.S.	F5	85
Rehovot, Isr.	D4	40
Reichenbach, Ger.	E12	8
Reid, Mount, mtn., Ak., U.S.	n24	79
Reidland, Ky., U.S.	e9	94
Reidsville, Ga., U.S.	D4	87
Reidsville, N.C., U.S.	A3	110
Reims, Fr.	C11	10
Reina Adelaida, Archipiélago, is., Chile	G2	56
Reinbeck, Ia., U.S.	B5	92
Reindeer Island, i., Man., Can.	C3	70
Reindeer Lake, l., Can.	m8	75
Reinosa, Spain	B7	12
Reisterstown, Md., U.S.	B4	97
Reliance, Wy., U.S.	E3	127
Remada, Tun.	B8	42
Remanso, Braz.	E10	54
Rembang, Indon.	m15	33a
Remington, In., U.S.	C3	91
Remiremont, Fr.	D13	10
Remmel Dam, Ar., U.S.	g8	81
Remscheid, Ger.	D7	8
Remsen, Ia., U.S.	B2	92
Rend Lake, res., Il., U.S.	E5	90
Rendova, i., Sol.Is.	A11	50
Rendsburg, Ger.	A9	8
Renforth, N.B., Can.	D4	71
Renfrew, Ont., Can.	B8	73
Rengat, Indon.	O7	34
Rennell Island, i., Sol.Is.	B12	50
Rennes, Fr.	D5	10
Reno, Nv., U.S.	D2	105
Reno, co., Ks., U.S.	E5	93
Reno, Lake, l., Mn., U.S.	E3	100
Reno Hill, mtn., Wy., U.S.	D6	127
Renovo, Pa., U.S.	D6	115
Rensselaer, In., U.S.	C3	91
Rensselaer, N.Y., U.S.	C7	109
Rensselaer, co., N.Y., U.S.	C7	109
Renton, Wa., U.S.	B3	124
Renville, Mn., U.S.	F3	100
Renville, co., Mn., U.S.	F4	100
Renville, co., N.D., U.S.	A4	111
Reo, Indon.	G7	32
Repentigny, Que., Can.	D4	74
Republic, Mi., U.S.	B3	99
Republic, Mo., U.S.	D4	102
Republic, Pa., U.S.	G2	115
Republic, Wa., U.S.	A7	124
Republic, co., Ks., U.S.	C6	93
Republican, stm., U.S.	C6	93
Repulse Bay, N.W. Ter., Can.	C15	66
Repvåg, Nor.	A15	6
Réquista, Fr.	H9	10
Reschenpass, Eur.	C5	14
Reserve, La., U.S.	h10	95
Resistencia, Arg.	B5	56
Reşiţa, Rom.	D5	16
Resolute, N.W. Ter., Can.	B14	66
Resolution Island, i., N.W. Ter., Can.	D20	66
Reston, Man., Can.	E1	70
Reston, Va., U.S.	B5	123
Resülhınzır, c., Tur.	A4	40
Retalhuleu, Guat.	G2	64
Rethel, Fr.	C11	10
Réthimnon, Grc.	N8	16
Reunion (Réunion), dep., Afr.	F11	44
Reus, Spain	D13	12
Reutlingen, Ger.	G9	8
Revelo, Ky., U.S.	D5	94
Revelstoke, B.C., Can.	D8	69
Revelstoke, Lake, res., B.C., Can.	D8	69
Revere, Ma., U.S.	g11	98
Revillagigedo, Islas de, is., Mex.	H4	62
Revillagigedo Island, i., Ak., U.S.	n24	79
Revin, Fr.	C11	10
Rewa, India	H9	38
Rewāri, India	F7	38
Rex, Ga., U.S.	h8	87
Rexburg, Id., U.S.	F7	89
Rexton, N.B., Can.	C5	71
Rey, Iran	J8	22
Rey, Isla del, i., Pan.	J8	64
Reyes, Bol.	F5	54
Reyes, Point, c., Ca., U.S.	C2	82
Reyhanlı, Tur.	A5	40
Reykjavík, Ice.	C3	4
Reynolds, Ga., U.S.	D2	87
Reynolds, co., Mo., U.S.	D6	102
Reynoldsburg, Oh., U.S.	C3	112
Reynoldsville, Pa., U.S.	D4	115
Reynosa, Mex.	D10	62
Rēzekne, Lat.	E10	18
Rhaetian Alps, mts., Eur.	F16	10
Rhea, co., Tn., U.S.	D9	119
Rheine, Ger.	C7	8
Rheydt, Ger.	D6	8
Rhine (Rhein) (Rhin), stm., Eur.	D6	8
Rhinebeck, N.Y., U.S.	D7	109
Rhinelander, Wi., U.S.	C4	126
Rho, Italy	D4	14
Rhode Island, state, U.S.	D3	116
Rhode Island, i., R.I., U.S.	E5	116
Rhode Island Sound, strt., U.S.	F5	116
Rhodesia see Zimbabwe, ctry., Afr.	E5	44
Rhodes Peak, mtn., Id., U.S.	C4	89
Rhodes see Ródhos, Grc.	M12	16
Rhodope Mountains, mts., Eur.	H8	16
Rhondda, Wales, U.K.	J9	7
Rhône, stm., Eur.	H11	10
Rialto, Ca., U.S.	m14	82
Riaza, Spain	D8	12
Riau, Kepulauan, is., Indon.	N8	34
Ribadeo, Spain	B4	12
Ribadesella, Spain	B6	12
Ribeirão Prêto, Braz.	F5	57
Ribera, Italy	L8	14
Riberalta, Bol.	F5	54
Rib Lake, Wi., U.S.	C3	126
Ribnitz-Damgarten, Ger.	A12	8
Riccione, Italy	F7	14
Rice, Mn., U.S.	E4	100
Rice, co., Ks., U.S.	D5	93
Rice, co., Mn., U.S.	F5	100
Riceboro, Ga., U.S.	E5	87
Rice Lake, Wi., U.S.	C2	126
Rice Lake, l., Ont., Can.	C6	73
Rice Lake, l., Mn., U.S.	D5	100
Riceville, Ia., U.S.	A5	92
Rich, co., Ut., U.S.	B4	121
Rich, Cape, c., Ont., Can.	C4	73
Richards-Gebaur Air Force Base, mil., Mo., U.S.	C3	102
Richards Island, i., N.W. Ter., Can.	C6	66
Richardson, Tx., U.S.	n10	120
Richardson, co., Ne., U.S.	D10	104
Richardson Lakes, l., Me., U.S.	D2	96
Richardson Mountains, mts., Can.	C5	66
Richardson, N.D., U.S.	C3	111
Rich Creek, Va., U.S.	C2	123
Richfield, Mn., U.S.	F5	100
Richfield, Ut., U.S.	E3	121
Richford, Vt., U.S.	B3	122
Rich Hill, Mo., U.S.	C3	102
Richibucto, N.B., Can.	C5	71
Richland, Ga., U.S.	D2	87
Richland, Mo., U.S.	D5	102
Richland, Wa., U.S.	C6	124
Richland, co., Il., U.S.	E5	90
Richland, co., La., U.S.	B4	95
Richland, co., Mt., U.S.	C12	103
Richland, co., N.D., U.S.	C8	111
Richland, co., Oh., U.S.	B3	112
Richland, co., S.C., U.S.	D6	117
Richland, co., Wi., U.S.	E3	126
Richland Balsam, mtn., N.C., U.S.	f10	110
Richland Center, Wi., U.S.	E3	126
Richland Creek, stm., Tn., U.S.	B5	119
Richlands, N.C., U.S.	C5	110
Richlands, Va., U.S.	e10	123
Richlandtown, Pa., U.S.	F11	115
Richmond, Austl.	D8	50
Richmond, B.C., Can.	E6	69
Richmond, Que., Can.	D5	74
Richmond, Ca., U.S.	D2	82
Richmond, Il., U.S.	A5	90
Richmond, In., U.S.	E8	91
Richmond, Ky., U.S.	C5	94
Richmond, Me., U.S.	D3	96
Richmond, Mi., U.S.	F8	99
Richmond, Mo., U.S.	B4	102
Richmond, Tx., U.S.	E5	120
Richmond, Ut., U.S.	B4	121
Richmond, Vt., U.S.	C3	122
Richmond, Va., U.S.	C5	123
Richmond, co., Ga., U.S.	C4	87
Richmond, co., N.Y., U.S.	E6	109
Richmond, co., N.C., U.S.	B3	110
Richmond, co., Va., U.S.	C6	123
Richmond Beach, Wa., U.S.	B3	124
Richmond Heights, Fl., U.S.	s13	86
Richmond Heights, Mo., U.S.	f13	102
Richmond Highlands, Wa., U.S.	B3	124
Richmond Hill, Ont., Can.	D5	73
Richmond Hill, Ga., U.S.	E5	87
Richmond National Battlefield Park, Va., U.S.	n18	123
Rich Square, N.C., U.S.	A5	110
Richthofen, Mount, mtn., Co., U.S.	A5	83
Richton, Ms., U.S.	D5	101
Richwood, Oh., U.S.	B2	112
Richwood, W.V., U.S.	C4	125
Rickenbacker Air Force Base, mil., Oh., U.S.	m11	112
Rickman, Tn., U.S.	C8	119
Riddle, Or., U.S.	E3	114
Riddle Mountain, mtn., Or., U.S.	D8	114
Rideau, stm., Ont., Can.	B9	73
Ridgecrest, Ca., U.S.	E5	82
Ridge Farm, Il., U.S.	D6	90
Ridgefield, Ct., U.S.	D2	84
Ridgefield, N.J., U.S.	h8	107
Ridgefield, Wa., U.S.	D3	124
Ridgefield Park, N.J., U.S.	h8	107
Ridgeland, Ms., U.S.	C3	101
Ridgeland, S.C., U.S.	G6	117
Ridgeley, W.V., U.S.	B6	125
Ridgely, Md., U.S.	C6	97
Ridgely, Tn., U.S.	A2	119
Ridge Spring, S.C., U.S.	D4	117
Ridgetop, Tn., U.S.	A5	119
Ridgetown, Ont., Can.	E3	73
Ridgeview, W.V., U.S.	C3	125
Ridgeville, In., U.S.	D7	91
Ridgeville, S.C., U.S.	E7	117
Ridgeway, Va., U.S.	D3	123
Ridgewood, N.J., U.S.	B4	107
Ridgway, Il., U.S.	F5	90
Ridgway, Pa., U.S.	D4	115
Riding Mountain National Park, Man., Can.	D1	70
Ridley Park, Pa., U.S.	p20	115
Ried im Innkreis, Aus.	G13	8
Riesa, Ger.	D13	8
Riesi, Italy	L9	14
Rieti, Italy	G7	14
Riffe Lake, res., Wa., U.S.	C3	124
Rifle, Co., U.S.	B3	83
Rifle, stm., Mi., U.S.	D6	99
Rift Valley, val., Afr.	B5	44
Riga, Lat.	E7	18
Riga, Gulf of, b., Eur.	D6	18
Rigaud, Que., Can.	D3	74
Rigby, Id., U.S.	F7	89
Rīgestān, reg., Afg.	C1	36
Riihimäki, Fin.	F15	6
Rijeka, Cro.	D9	14
Riley, Ks., U.S.	C7	93
Riley, co., Ks., U.S.	C7	93
Riley, Mount, mtn., N.M., U.S.	F2	108
Rimbey, Alta., Can.	C3	68
Rimersburg, Pa., U.S.	D2	115
Rimini, Italy	F7	14
Rimouski, Que., Can.	A9	74
Rimouski-Est, Que., Can.	A9	74
Rimrock Lake, res., Wa., U.S.	C5	124
Rincon, Ga., U.S.	D5	87
Rincon Mountains, mts., Az., U.S.	E5	80
Rindal, Nor.	E7	6
Ringebu, Nor.	F8	6
Ringgold, Ga., U.S.	B1	87
Ringgold, La., U.S.	B2	95
Ringgold, co., Ia., U.S.	D3	92
Ringling, Ok., U.S.	C4	113
Ringwood, N.J., U.S.	A4	107
Rio, Fl., U.S.	E6	86
Rio, Wi., U.S.	E4	126
Rio Arriba, co., N.M., U.S.	A2	108
Riobamba, Ec.	H3	58
Río Benito, Eq. Gui.	H7	42
Rio Branco, Braz.	E5	54
Río Blanco, co., Co., U.S.	B2	83
Río Claro, Braz.	G5	57
Río Colorado, Arg.	D4	56
Río Cuarto, Arg.	C4	56
Rio de Janeiro, Braz.	G7	57
Rio Dell, Ca., U.S.	B1	82
Rio do Sul, Braz.	B7	56
Ríos Gallegos, Arg.	G3	56
Rio Grande, Arg.	G3	56
Rio Grande, Braz.	C6	56
Río Grande, Mex.	F8	62
Rio Grande, Nic.	H6	64
Rio Grande, Oh., U.S.	D3	112
Rio Grande, co., Co., U.S.	D4	83
Rio Grande City, Tx., U.S.	F3	120
Rio Grande Reservoir, res., Co., U.S.	D3	83
Ríohacha, Col.	B6	58
Rio Hondo, Tx., U.S.	F4	120
Rioja, Peru	E3	54
Riom, Fr.	G10	10
Río Mayo, Arg.	F2	56
Río Negro, Embalse del, res., Ur.	C5	56
Río Negro, Pantanal do, sw., Braz.	G7	54
Rionero in Vulture, Italy	I10	14
Río Pardo, Braz.	B6	56
Rio Pardo de Minas, Braz.	G10	57
Río Rancho, N.M., U.S.	B3	108
Río Sucio, Col.	E5	58
Río Verde, Braz.	D3	57
Ríoverde, Mex.	G10	62
Rio Vista, Ca., U.S.	C3	82
Rioz, Fr.	E13	10
Ripley, Ms., U.S.	A5	101
Ripley, Oh., U.S.	D2	112
Ripley, Tn., U.S.	B2	119
Ripley, W.V., U.S.	C3	125
Ripley, co., In., U.S.	F7	91
Ripley, co., Mo., U.S.	E7	102
Ripoll, Spain	C14	12
Ripon, Eng., U.K.	G11	7
Ripon, Wi., U.S.	E5	126
Rippowam, stm., Ct., U.S.	E1	84
Ririe Lake, res., Id., U.S.	F7	89
Rishon leZiyyon, Isr.	D4	40
Rising Sun, De., U.S.	D3	85
Rising Sun, In., U.S.	G8	91
Rising Sun, Md., U.S.	A5	97
Rison, Ar., U.S.	D3	81
Ritchie, co., W.V., U.S.	B3	125
Ritter, Mount, mtn., Ca., U.S.	D4	82
Rittman, Oh., U.S.	B4	112
Ritzville, Wa., U.S.	B7	124
Riva, Italy	D5	14
Rivanna, stm., Va., U.S.	C4	123
Rivas, Nic.	I5	64
Rivera, Ur.	C5	56
Riverbank, Ca., U.S.	D3	82
River Bourgeois, N.S., Can.	D9	71
Riverdale, Ca., U.S.	D4	82
Riverdale, Il., U.S.	k9	90
River Edge, N.J., U.S.	h8	107
River Falls, Al., U.S.	D3	78
River Falls, Wi., U.S.	D1	126
River Forest, Il., U.S.	k9	90
River Grove, Il., U.S.	k9	90
Riverhead, N.Y., U.S.	n16	109
River Hebert, N.S., Can.	D5	71
River Heights, Ut., U.S.	B4	121
River Hills, Wi., U.S.	m12	126
River Pines, Ma., U.S.	f10	98
River Ridge, La., U.S.	k11	95
River Road, Or., U.S.	C3	114
River Rouge, Mi., U.S.	p15	99
Rivers, Man., Can.	D1	70
Riverside, Al., U.S.	B3	78
Riverside, Ca., U.S.	F5	82
Riverside, Il., U.S.	k9	90
Riverside, Ia., U.S.	C6	92
Riverside, N.J., U.S.	C3	107
Riverside, Pa., U.S.	E8	115
Riverside, co., Ca., U.S.	F5	82
Riverside Reservoir, res., Co., U.S.	A6	83
Riverton, Man., Can.	D3	70
Riverton, Il., U.S.	D4	90
Riverton, Ks., U.S.	E9	93
Riverton, N.J., U.S.	C3	107
Riverton, Ut., U.S.	C4	121
Riverton, Vt., U.S.	C3	122
Riverton, Wy., U.S.	C4	127
Riverton Heights, Wa., U.S.	f11	124
River Vale, N.J., U.S.	h8	107
Riverview, Fl., U.S.	p11	86
Riverview, Mi., U.S.	p15	99
Rivesaltes, Fr.	J9	10
Riviera Beach, Fl., U.S.	F6	86
Riviera Beach, Md., U.S.	B4	97
Rivière-du-Loup, Que., Can.	B8	74
Rivière-Verte, N.B., Can.	B1	71
Rivoli, Italy	D2	14
Riyadh see Ar-Riyāḍ, Sau. Ar.	D4	46
Rize, Tur.	G16	22
Roa, Spain	C8	12
Roachdale, In., U.S.	E4	91
Roane, co., Tn., U.S.	D9	119
Roane, co., W.V., U.S.	C3	125
Roan Mountain, Tn., U.S.	C11	119
Roanne, Fr.	F11	10
Roanoke, Al., U.S.	B4	78

Name	Map Ref	Page
oanoke, Il., U.S.	C4	90
oanoke, In., U.S.	C7	91
oanoke, La., U.S.	D3	95
oanoke, Tx., U.S.	m9	120
oanoke, Va., U.S.	C3	123
oanoke, co., Va., U.S.	C2	123
oanoke, stm., U.S.	A5	110
oanoke Island, i., N.C., U.S.	B7	110
oanoke Rapids, N.C., U.S.	A5	110
oanoke Rapids Lake, res., U.S.	A5	110
oaring Fork, stm., Co., U.S.	C4	83
oaring Spring, Pa., U.S.	F5	115
oatán, Isla de, i., Hond.	F4	64
obbins, Il., U.S.	k9	90
obbins, N.C., U.S.	B3	110
obbinsdale, Mn., U.S.	m12	100
obbinsville, N.C., U.S.	f9	110
öbel, Ger.	B12	8
obersonville, N.C., U.S.	B5	110
oberta, Ga., U.S.	D2	87
obert Lee, Tx., U.S.	D2	120
oberts, Wi., U.S.	C1	126
oberts, co., S.D., U.S.	B8	118
oberts, co., Tx., U.S.	B2	120
oberts, Point, c., Wa., U.S.	A2	124
obert's Arm, Newf., Can.	D4	72
oberts Creek Mountain, mtn., Nv., U.S.	D5	105
obertsdale, Al., U.S.	E2	78
obertsfors, Swe.	D13	6
obert S. Kerr Reservoir, res., Ok., U.S.	B6	113
oberts Mountain, mtn., Ak., U.S.	C6	79
oberts Mountain, mtn., Wy., U.S.	D3	127
obertson, co., Ky., U.S.	B5	94
obertson, co., Tn., U.S.	A5	119
obertson, co., Tx., U.S.	D4	120
obertsonville, Que., Can.	C6	74
oberts Peak, mtn., B.C., Can.	F8	66
obertsport, Lib.	G3	42
obertville, N.B., Can.	B4	71
oberval, Que., Can.	A5	74
obeson, co., N.C., U.S.	C3	110
obins, Ia., U.S.	B6	92
obinson, Il., U.S.	D6	90
obinson Fork, stm., W.V., U.S.	m14	125
obinson Fork, stm., W.V., U.S.	k9	125
oblin, Man., Can.	D1	70
oboré, Bol.	G7	54
obson, Mount, mtn., B.C., Can.	C8	69
obstown, Tx., U.S.	F4	120
oca Partida, Isla, i., Mex.	H3	62
oca Partida, Punta, c., Mex.	H12	62
ocas, Atol das, atoll, Braz.	D12	54
occastrada, Italy	F6	14
ochefort, Fr.	G6	10
ochelle, Ga., U.S.	E3	87
ochelle, Il., U.S.	B4	90
ochelle Park, N.J., U.S.	h8	107
ochester, Il., U.S.	D4	90
ochester, In., U.S.	B5	91
ochester, Mi., U.S.	F7	99
ochester, Mn., U.S.	F6	100
ochester, N.H., U.S.	D5	106
ochester, N.Y., U.S.	B3	109
ochester, Pa., U.S.	E1	115
ochester, Vt., U.S.	D3	122
ochester, Wa., U.S.	C2	124
ochester, Wi., U.S.	n11	126
ock, co., Mn., U.S.	G2	100
ock, co., Ne., U.S.	B6	104
ock, co., Wi., U.S.	F4	126
ock, stm., U.S.	B3	90
ock, stm., U.S.	A1	92
ockall, i., Scot., U.K.	D5	4
ockaway, N.J., U.S.	B3	107
ockaway, Or., U.S.	B3	114
ockbridge, co., Va., U.S.	C3	123
ockcastle, co., Ky., U.S.	C5	94
ockcastle, stm., Ky., U.S.	C5	94
ockcliffe Park, Ont., Can.	h12	73
ock Creek, Mn., U.S.	E6	100
ock Creek, stm., U.S.	B3	97
ock Creek, stm., U.S.	h14	124
ock Creek, stm., Nv., U.S.	C5	105
ock Creek, stm., Wa., U.S.	B6	114
ock Creek, stm., Wa., U.S.	B8	124
ock Creek, stm., Wa., U.S.	D5	124
ock Creek, stm., Wy., U.S.	E6	127
ock Creek Butte, mtn., Or., U.S.	C8	114
ockdale, Il., U.S.	B5	90
ockdale, Md., U.S.	B4	97
ockdale, Tx., U.S.	D4	120
ockdale, co., Ga., U.S.	C3	87
ockfall, Ct., U.S.	C5	84
ock Falls, Il., U.S.	B4	90
ockford, Il., U.S.	A4	90
ockford, Ia., U.S.	A5	92
ockford, Mi., U.S.	E5	99
ockford, Mn., U.S.	E5	100
ockford, Oh., U.S.	B1	112
ockford, Tn., U.S.	D10	119
ock Hall, Md., U.S.	B5	97
ock Hill, S.C., U.S.	B5	117
ockhampton, Austl.	D10	50
ock Hill, S.C., U.S.	B5	117
ockingham, co., N.H., U.S.	D4	106
ockingham, co., N.C., U.S.	A3	110
ockingham, co., Va., U.S.	B4	123
ock Island, Que., Can.	D5	74
ock Island, Il., U.S.	B3	90
ock Island, co., Il., U.S.	B3	90
ock Island, i., Fl., U.S.	C3	86
ock Island, i., Wi., U.S.	C7	126
ock Lake, l., Wa., U.S.	B8	124
ockland, Ont., Can.	B9	73
ockland, Me., U.S.	D3	96
ockland, Ma., U.S.	B6	98
ockland, co., N.Y., U.S.	D6	109
ockledge, Fl., U.S.	D6	86
ockledge, Pa., U.S.	o20	115
Rocklin, Ca., U.S.	C3	82
Rockmart, Ga., U.S.	B1	87
Rock Mountain, mtn., Co., U.S.	D3	83
Rockport, In., U.S.	I3	91
Rockport, Ma., U.S.	A6	98
Rockport, Mo., U.S.	A2	103
Rock Port, Mo., U.S.	A2	102
Rockport, Tx., U.S.	F4	120
Rock Rapids, Ia., U.S.	A1	92
Rock River, Wy., U.S.	E7	127
Rock Sound, Bah.	B9	64
Rocksprings, Tx., U.S.	D2	120
Rock Springs, Wy., U.S.	E3	127
Rockstone, Guy.	E13	58
Rock Valley, Ia., U.S.	A1	92
Rockville, In., U.S.	E3	91
Rockville, Md., U.S.	B3	97
Rockville Centre, N.Y., U.S.	n15	109
Rockwall, Tx., U.S.	C4	120
Rockwall, co., Tx., U.S.	C4	120
Rockwell, Ia., U.S.	B4	92
Rockwell, N.C., U.S.	B2	110
Rockwell City, Ia., U.S.	B3	92
Rockwell Park, N.C., U.S.	B2	110
Rockwood, Mi., U.S.	F7	99
Rockwood, Pa., U.S.	G3	115
Rockwood, Tn., U.S.	D9	119
Rocky, stm., N.C., U.S.	B2	110
Rocky, stm., S.C., U.S.	C2	117
Rocky, East Branch, stm., Oh., U.S.	h9	112
Rocky, West Branch, stm., Oh., U.S.	h9	112
Rocky Boys Indian Reservation, Mt., U.S.	B7	103
Rocky Ford, Co., U.S.	C7	83
Rocky Fork Lake, l., Oh., U.S.	C2	112
Rocky Harbour, Newf., Can.	D3	72
Rocky Hill, Ct., U.S.	C5	84
Rocky Lake, l., Me., U.S.	D5	96
Rocky Mount, N.C., U.S.	B5	110
Rocky Mount, Va., U.S.	D3	123
Rocky Mountain, mtn., Mt., U.S.	C4	103
Rocky Mountain House, Alta., Can.	C3	68
Rocky Mountain National Park, Co., U.S.	A5	83
Rocky Mountains, mts., N.A.	E9	61
Rocky Ripple, In., U.S.	k10	91
Rocky River, Oh., U.S.	A4	112
Rocky Top, mtn., Or., U.S.	C4	114
Roddickton, Newf., Can.	C3	72
Roderfield, W.V., U.S.	D3	125
Rodez, Fr.	H9	10
Ródhos (Rhodes), Grc.	M12	16
Ródhos, i., Grc.	M11	16
Rodney, Ont., Can.	E3	73
Rodney, Cape, c., Ak., U.S.	C6	79
Rodney Village, De., U.S.	D3	85
Rodniki, Russia	D24	18
Roebourne, Austl.	D3	50
Roebuck, S.C., U.S.	B4	117
Roeland Park, Ks., U.S.	k16	93
Roeselare, Bel.	E3	8
Roes Welcome Sound, strt., N.W. Ter., Can.	D15	66
Roff, Ok., U.S.	C5	113
Rogagua, Lago, l., Bol.	F5	54
Roger Mills, co., Ok., U.S.	B2	113
Rogers, Ar., U.S.	A1	81
Rogers, Mn., U.S.	E5	100
Rogers, Tx., U.S.	D4	120
Rogers, co., Ok., U.S.	A6	113
Rogers, Mount, mtn., Va., U.S.	f10	123
Rogers City, Mi., U.S.	C7	99
Rogers Lake, res., Ct., U.S.	D6	84
Rogers Pass, Mt., U.S.	C4	103
Rogersville, N.B., Can.	C4	71
Rogersville, Al., U.S.	A2	78
Rogersville, Mo., U.S.	D4	102
Rogersville, Tn., U.S.	C10	119
Roggiano Gravina, Italy	J11	14
Rogue, stm., Or., U.S.	E2	114
Rogue River, Or., U.S.	E3	114
Rohtak, India	F7	38
Roi Et, Thai.	F7	34
Rojo, Cabo, c., Mex.	G11	62
Roiand, Ia., U.S.	B4	92
Roland, Ok., U.S.	B7	113
Roland, Lake, res., Md., U.S.	g11	97
Rolândia, Braz.	G3	57
Rolette, N.D., U.S.	A6	111
Rolette, co., N.D., U.S.	A6	111
Rolfe, Ia., U.S.	B3	92
Rolla, Mo., U.S.	D6	102
Rolla, N.D., U.S.	A6	111
Rollingbay, Wa., U.S.	e10	124
Rolling Fork, Ms., U.S.	C3	101
Rolling Fork, stm., Ky., U.S.	C1	94
Rolling Fork, stm., Ky., U.S.	C4	94
Rolling Meadows, Il., U.S.	h8	90
Rollingstone, Mn., U.S.	F7	100
Rollinsford, N.H., U.S.	D5	106
Roma (Rome), Italy	H7	14
Roma, Tx., U.S.	F3	120
Roman, Rom.	C10	16
Romania, ctry., Eur.	F13	4
Roman Nose Mountain, mtn., Or., U.S.	D3	114
Romano, Cape, c., Fl., U.S.	G5	86
Romano, Cayo, i., Cuba	C8	64
Romans [-sur-Isère], Fr.	G12	10
Romanzof, Cape, c., Ak., U.S.	C6	79
Romanzof Mountains, mts., Ak., U.S.	B11	79
Rome, Ga., U.S.	B1	87
Rome, Il., U.S.	C4	90
Rome, N.Y., U.S.	B5	109
Rome City, In., U.S.	B7	91
Romeo, Mi., U.S.	F7	99
Romeoville, Il., U.S.	k8	90
Rome see Roma, Italy	H7	14
Romilly-sur-Seine, Fr.	D10	10
Romney, W.V., U.S.	B6	125
Romorantin-Lanthenay, Fr.	E8	10
Romulus, Mi., U.S.	p15	99
Ron, Mui, c., Viet.	E9	34
Ronan, Mt., U.S.	C2	103
Roncador, Serra do, plat., Braz.	F8	54
Roncesvalles, Spain	B10	12
Ronceverte, W.V., U.S.	D4	125
Ronda, Spain	I6	12
Rondônia, Braz.	F6	54
Rondonópolis, Braz.	D1	57
Ronge, Lac la, l., Sask., Can.	B3	75
Rønne, Den.	I10	6
Ronneby, Swe.	H10	6
Ronne Ice Shelf, Ant.	B6	47
Ronse, Bel.	E3	8
Roodhouse, Il., U.S.	D3	90
Rooks, co., Ks., U.S.	C4	93
Roorkee, India	F7	38
Roosendaal, Neth.	D4	8
Roosevelt, Ut., U.S.	C5	121
Roosevelt, co., Mt., U.S.	B11	103
Roosevelt, co., N.M., U.S.	C6	108
Roosevelt, stm., Braz.	E6	54
Roosevelt Park, Mi., U.S.	E4	99
Root, stm., Mn., U.S.	G7	100
Root, stm., Wi., U.S.	n12	126
Roper, N.C., U.S.	B6	110
Roquefort, Fr.	H6	10
Roraima, Mount, mtn., S.A.	E12	58
Røros, Nor.	E8	6
Rorschach, Switz.	E16	10
Rørvik, Nor.	D8	6
Roŝal', Russia	F22	18
Rosamond, Ca., U.S.	E4	82
Rosamorada, Mex.	F7	62
Rosario, Arg.	C4	56
Rosário, Braz.	D10	54
Rosario, Mex.	F7	62
Rosario, Mex.	D4	14
Rosario, Ven.	B6	58
Rosário Oeste, Braz.	F7	54
Rosarno, Italy	K10	14
Rosas, Golfo de, b., Spain	C15	12
Roscoe, Il., U.S.	A5	90
Roscoe, Tx., U.S.	C2	120
Roscommon, Ire.	H4	7
Roscommon, Mi., U.S.	D6	99
Roscommon, co., Mi., U.S.	D6	99
Roscrea, Ire.	I5	7
Rose, Mount, mtn., Nv., U.S.	D2	105
Roseau, Dom.	G17	64
Roseau, Mn., U.S.	B3	100
Roseau, co., Mn., U.S.	B3	100
Roseau, South Fork, stm., Mn., U.S.	B3	100
Rose-Blanche [-Harbour le Cou], Newf., Can.	E2	72
Roseboro, N.C., U.S.	C4	110
Rosebud, S.D., U.S.	D5	118
Rosebud, Tx., U.S.	D4	120
Rosebud, co., Mt., U.S.	D10	103
Rosebud Indian Reservation, S.D., U.S.	D5	118
Roseburg, Or., U.S.	D3	114
Rosedale, In., U.S.	E3	91
Rosedale, Md., U.S.	g11	97
Rosedale, Ms., U.S.	B2	101
Rose Hill, Ks., U.S.	E6	93
Rose Hill, N.C., U.S.	C4	110
Rose Hill, Va., U.S.	f8	123
Roseland, Fl., U.S.	E6	86
Roseland, La., U.S.	D5	95
Roseland, Oh., U.S.	B3	112
Roselle, Il., U.S.	k8	90
Roselle, N.J., U.S.	k7	107
Roselle Park, N.J., U.S.	k7	107
Rosemère, Que., Can.	p19	74
Rosemount, Mn., U.S.	F5	100
Rosenberg, Tx., U.S.	E5	120
Rosendale, Wi., U.S.	E5	126
Rosenheim, Ger.	H12	8
Rose Peak, mtn., Az., U.S.	D6	80
Rosepine, La., U.S.	D2	95
Rose Point, c., B.C., Can.	B2	69
Roseto, Pa., U.S.	E11	115
Roseville, Ca., U.S.	C3	82
Roseville, Il., U.S.	C3	90
Roseville, Mi., U.S.	o16	99
Roseville, Mn., U.S.	m12	100
Roseville, Oh., U.S.	C3	112
Rosewood Heights, Il., U.S.	E3	90
Rosiclare, Il., U.S.	F5	90
Rosignano Marittimo, Italy	F5	14
Roskilde, Den.	I9	6
Roslags-Näsby, Swe.	G12	6
Roslavl', Russia	H15	18
Roslyn, Wa., U.S.	B4	124
Roslyn Heights, N.Y., U.S.	h13	109
Ross, Oh., U.S.	C1	112
Ross, co., Oh., U.S.	C2	112
Rossano, Italy	J11	14
Rossan Point, c., Ire.	G4	7
Ross Barnett Reservoir, res., Ms., U.S.	C3	101
Rossburn, Man., Can.	D1	70
Ross Dam, Wa., U.S.	A4	124
Rossel Island, i., Pap. N. Gui.	B10	50
Rossford, Oh., U.S.	A2	112
Ross Ice Shelf, Ant.	A31	47
Rossignol, Lake, l., N.S., Can.	E4	71
Ross Island, i., Man., Can.	B3	70
Ross Lake National Recreation Area, Wa., U.S.	A5	124
Rossland, B.C., Can.	E9	69
Rosslare, Ire.	I6	7
Rosso, Maur.	E2	42
Ross River, Yukon, Can.	D6	66
Ross Sea, Ant.	B31	47
Rossville, Ga., U.S.	B1	87
Rossville, Il., U.S.	C6	90
Rossville, In., U.S.	D4	91
Rossville, Ks., U.S.	C8	93
Rostock, Ger.	A12	8
Rostov, Russia	D22	18
Rostov-na-Donu, Russia	H5	22
Roswell, Ga., U.S.	B2	87
Roswell, N.M., U.S.	D5	108
Rotan, Tx., U.S.	C2	120
Rotenburg, Ger.	B9	8
Rothaargebirge, mts., Ger.	D8	8
Rothenburg ob der Tauber, Ger.	F10	8
Rothesay, N.B., Can.	D4	71
Rothschild, Wi., U.S.	D4	126
Rothsay, Mn., U.S.	D2	100
Rothville, Pa., U.S.	F9	115
Roti, Pulau, i., Indon.	H7	32
Rotondella, Italy	I11	14
Rotorua, N.Z.	C6	52
Rotterdam, Neth.	D4	8
Rotterdam, N.Y., U.S.	C6	109
Rottweil, Ger.	G8	8
Roubaix, Fr.	B10	10
Rouen, Fr.	C8	10
Rouge, stm., Que., Can.	D3	74
Rough, stm., Ky., U.S.	C3	94
Rough River Lake, res., Ky., U.S.	C3	94
Roulette, Pa., U.S.	C5	115
Round Island, i., Ms., U.S.	g8	101
Round Lake, Il., U.S.	h8	90
Round Lake Beach, Il., U.S.	h8	90
Round Mountain, Nv., U.S.	E4	105
Round Rock, Tx., U.S.	D4	120
Roundup, Mt., U.S.	D8	103
Round Valley Indian Reservation, Ca., U.S.	C2	82
Round Valley Reservoir, res., N.J., U.S.	B3	107
Rouses Point, N.Y., U.S.	f11	109
Roussillon, hist. reg., Fr.	J9	10
Routt, co., Co., U.S.	A3	83
Rouyn, Que., Can.	k11	74
Rouzerville, Pa., U.S.	G6	115
Rovaniemi, Fin.	C15	6
Rovato, Italy	D4	14
Rovereto, Italy	D6	14
Rovigo, Italy	D6	14
Rovinj, Cro.	D8	14
Rovno, Ukr.	G3	22
Rowan, co., Ky., U.S.	B6	94
Rowan, co., N.C., U.S.	B2	110
Rowland, N.C., U.S.	C3	110
Rowlesburg, W.V., U.S.	B5	125
Rowley Island, i., N.W. Ter., Can.	C17	66
Rowley Shoals, rf., Austl.	C3	50
Roxboro, N.C., U.S.	A4	110
Roxton Falls, Que., Can.	D5	74
Roxton Pond, Que., Can.	D5	74
Roy, Ut., U.S.	B3	121
Royal, stm., Me., U.S.	g7	96
Royal Canal, Ire.	H5	7
Royal Center, In., U.S.	C4	91
Royale, Isle, i., Mi., U.S.	h9	99
Royal Gorge, val., Co., U.S.	C5	83
Royal Oak, Mi., U.S.	F7	99
Royal Pines, N.C., U.S.	f10	110
Royalton, Il., U.S.	F4	90
Royalton, Mn., U.S.	E4	100
Royan, Fr.	G5	10
Royersford, Pa., U.S.	F10	115
Royerton, In., U.S.	D7	91
Royse City, Tx., U.S.	C4	120
Royston, B.C., Can.	E5	69
Royston, Ga., U.S.	B3	87
Rubbestadneset, Nor.	G5	6
Rubcovsk, Russia	G10	24
Rubidoux, Ca., U.S.	n14	82
Rubio, Ven.	D6	58
Ruby Dome, mtn., Nv., U.S.	C6	105
Ruby Lake, l., Nv., U.S.	C6	105
Ruby Mountains, mts., Nv., U.S.	C6	105
Ruby Range, mts., Co., U.S.	C3	83
Ruby Range, mts., Mt., U.S.	E4	103
Rudolf, Lake, l., Afr.	H2	46
Rudolstadt, Ger.	E11	8
Rudyard, Mi., U.S.	B6	99
Rue, Fr.	B8	10
Rufā'ah, Sudan	F12	42
Ruffec, Fr.	F7	10
Rufino, Arg.	C4	56
Rufus Woods Lake, res., Wa., U.S.	A6	124
Rugao, China	C9	28
Rugby, Eng., U.K.	I11	7
Rugby, N.D., U.S.	A6	111
Ruian, China	H9	28
Ruidoso, N.M., U.S.	D4	108
Ruidoso Downs, N.M., U.S.	D4	108
Ruijin, China	F10	26
Ruijin, China	J4	28
Rukwa, Lake, l., Tan.	C6	44
Ruleville, Ms., U.S.	B3	101
Rum, stm., Mn., U.S.	D5	100
Ruma, Yugo.	D3	16
Rumbek, Sudan	G11	42
Rum Cay, i., Bah.	C10	64
Rum Creek, stm., W.V., U.S.	n12	125
Rumford, Me., U.S.	D2	96
Rumia, Pol.	A18	8
Rum Jungle, Austl.	B6	50
Rumoi, Japan	p19	30a
Rumson, N.J., U.S.	C4	107
Rumstick Point, c., R.I., U.S.	D5	116
Ru'nan, China	B3	28
Runanga, N.Z.	E3	52
Runge, Tx., U.S.	E4	120
Rungwa, Tan.	C6	44
Runnels, co., Tx., U.S.	D3	120
Runnemede, N.J., U.S.	D2	107
Ruoqiang, China	D4	26
Rupert, Id., U.S.	G5	89
Rupert, W.V., U.S.	D4	125
Rupert, Rivière de, stm., Que., Can.	h11	74
Rural Hall, N.C., U.S.	A2	110
Rural Retreat, Va., U.S.	D1	123
Rusagonis, N.B., Can.	D3	71
Ruse, Bul.	F9	16
Rush, co., In., U.S.	E6	91
Rush, co., Ks., U.S.	D4	93
Rush, stm., Wi., U.S.	D1	126
Rush City, Mn., U.S.	E6	100
Rush Creek, stm., Oh., U.S.	B2	112
Rush Creek, stm., Ok., U.S.	C4	113
Rushford, Mn., U.S.	G7	100
Rush Lake, l., Mn., U.S.	E5	100
Rush Lake, l., Mn., U.S.	D3	100
Rush Lake, l., Wi., U.S.	E5	126
Rushmere, Va., U.S.	h14	123
Rush Springs, Ok., U.S.	C4	113
Rushville, Il., U.S.	C3	90
Rushville, In., U.S.	E7	91
Rushville, Ne., U.S.	B3	104
Rusk, Tx., U.S.	D5	120
Rusk, co., Tx., U.S.	C5	120
Rusk, co., Wi., U.S.	C2	126
Ruskin, Fl., U.S.	E4	86
Russas, Braz.	D11	54
Russell, Man., Can.	D1	70
Russell, Ont., Can.	B9	73
Russell, Ks., U.S.	D5	93
Russell, Ky., U.S.	B7	94
Russell, Pa., U.S.	C3	115
Russell, co., Al., U.S.	C4	78
Russell, co., Ks., U.S.	D5	93
Russell, co., Ky., U.S.	D4	94
Russell, co., Va., U.S.	f9	123
Russell, Mount, mtn., Ak., U.S.	f16	79
Russell Cave National Monument, Al., U.S.	A4	78
Russell Fork, stm., U.S.	C7	94
Russell Island, i., N.W. Ter., Can.	B13	66
Russell Springs, Ky., U.S.	C4	94
Russellville, Al., U.S.	A2	78
Russellville, Ar., U.S.	B2	81
Russellville, Ky., U.S.	D3	94
Russellville, Mo., U.S.	C5	102
Russellville, Tn., U.S.	C10	119
Rüsselsheim, Ger.	E8	8
Russia, ctry., Eur.	E15	22
Russian, stm., Ca., U.S.	C2	82
Russiaville, In., U.S.	D5	91
Rustavi, Geor.	I7	22
Rustburg, Va., U.S.	C3	123
Rustenburg, S. Afr.	G5	44
Ruston, La., U.S.	B3	95
Ruston, Wa., U.S.	B3	124
Ruth, Nv., U.S.	D6	105
Rutherford, N.J., U.S.	B4	107
Rutherford, Tn., U.S.	A3	119
Rutherford, co., N.C., U.S.	B1	110
Rutherford, co., Tn., U.S.	B5	119
Rutherfordton, N.C., U.S.	B1	110
Ruthven, Ia., U.S.	A3	92
Rutland, Ma., U.S.	B4	98
Rutland, Vt., U.S.	D3	122
Rutland, co., Vt., U.S.	D2	122
Rutledge, Ga., U.S.	C3	87
Rutledge, Tn., U.S.	C10	119
Ruukki, Fin.	D15	6
Ruvuma (Rovuma), stm., Afr.	D7	44
Ružomberok, Czech.	F19	8
Rwanda, ctry., Afr.	B5	44
Ryan, Ok., U.S.	C4	113
Ryan Peak, mtn., Id., U.S.	F4	89
Rybinsk, Russia	C21	18
Rybinskoje Vodochranilišče, res., Russia	C21	18
Rybnik, Pol.	E18	8
Rycroft, Alta., Can.	B1	68
Rye, Eng., U.K.	K11	7
Rye, N.H., U.S.	D5	106
Rye, N.Y., U.S.	h13	109
Rye Beach, N.H., U.S.	E5	106
Rye Patch Dam, Nv., U.S.	C3	105
Rye Patch Reservoir, res., Nv., U.S.	C3	105
Ryfoss, Nor.	F7	6
Ryōtsu, Japan	D11	30
Rysy, mtn., Eur.	F20	8
Ryukyu Islands see Nansei-shotō, is., Japan	F12	26
Rzeszów, Pol.	E21	8
Ržev, Russia	E17	18

S

Name	Map Ref	Page
Saalfeld, Ger.	E11	8
Saarbrücken, Ger.	F6	8
Saaremaa, i., Est.	C5	18
Saarijärvi, Fin.	E15	6
Saarlouis, Ger.	F6	8
Sab, Tônlé, l., Camb.	H7	34
Saba, i., Neth. Ant.	F16	64
Sabadell, Spain	D14	12
Sabae, Japan	G9	30
Sabana, Archipiélago de, is., Cuba	C8	64
Sabanagrande, Hond.	H4	64
Sabanalarga, Col.	B5	58
Sabang, Indon.	E6	32
Sabanilla, Mex.	E9	62
Sabará, Braz.	E7	57
Sabattus, Me., U.S.	D2	96
Sabetha, Ks., U.S.	C8	93
Sabhah, Libya	C8	42
Sabi (Save), stm., Afr.	F6	44
Sabillasville, Md., U.S.	A3	97
Sabina, Oh., U.S.	C2	112
Sabinal, Tx., U.S.	E3	120
Sabiñánigo, Spain	C11	12
Sabinas, Mex.	D9	62
Sabinas Hidalgo, Mex.	D9	62
Sabine, co., La., U.S.	D2	95
Sabine, co., Tx., U.S.	D6	120
Sabine, stm., U.S.	E2	95
Sabine Lake, l., U.S.	E2	95
Sabine Pass, strt., U.S.	E2	95
Sable, Cape, c., N.S., Can.	H19	66
Sable, Cape, c., Fl., U.S.	G5	86
Sable, Îles de, i., N. Cal.	C11	50
Sable Island, i., N.S., Can.	F10	71
Sabula, Ia., U.S.	B7	92
Sabzevār, Iran	J9	22
Sac, co., Ia., U.S.	B2	92
Sac, stm., Mo., U.S.	D4	102
Sacajawea, Lake, res., Wa., U.S.	C7	124

Index

Name	Map Ref	Page
Sacajawea Peak, mtn., Or., U.S.	B9	114
Sacandaga Lake, l., N.Y., U.S.	B6	109
Sac and Fox Indian Reservation, Ia., U.S.	C5	92
Sacaton, Az., U.S.	D4	80
Sac City, Ia., U.S.	B2	92
Sacedón, Spain	E9	12
Sachalin, Ostrov (Sakhalin), i., Russia	G22	24
Sachalinskij Zaliv, b., Russia	G22	24
Sachigo, stm., Ont., Can.	F14	66
Sachse, Tx., U.S.	n10	120
Sachs Harbour, N.W. Ter., Can.	B8	66
Šachty, Russia	H6	22
Sachuest Point, c., R.I., U.S.	F6	116
Sackville, N.B., Can.	D5	71
Saco, Me., U.S.	E2	96
Saco, stm., U.S.	E2	96
Saco, East Branch, stm., N.H., U.S.	B4	106
Sacramento, Ca., U.S.	C3	82
Sacramento, co., Ca., U.S.	C3	82
Sacramento, stm., Ca., U.S.	C3	82
Sacramento, stm., N.M., U.S.	E4	108
Sacramento Mountains, mts., N.M., U.S.	E4	108
Sacramento Valley, val., Ca., U.S.	C2	82
Sacré-Coeur-Saguenay, Que., Can.	A8	74
Sacred Heart, Mn., U.S.	F3	100
Sádaba, Spain	C10	12
Şa'dah, Yemen	E3	46
Saddle, stm., N.J., U.S.	h8	107
Saddleback Mountain, mtn., Az., U.S.	k8	80
Saddle Brook, N.J., U.S.	h8	107
Saddlebunch Keys, is., Fl., U.S.	H5	86
Saddle Mountain, mtn., Or., U.S.	B3	114
Saddle Mountains, mts., Wa., U.S.	C5	124
Saddle River, N.J., U.S.	A4	107
Sa Dec, Viet.	I8	34
Sādiqābad, Pak.	F4	38
Sado, i., Japan	D11	30
Sado-kaikyō, strt., Japan	E11	30
Saegertown, Pa., U.S.	C1	115
Safety Harbor, Fl., U.S.	o11	86
Säffle, Swe.	G9	6
Safford, Az., U.S.	E6	80
Safi, Mor.	B4	42
Safid, stm., Afg.	B1	38
Säfid Küh, Selseleh-ye, mts., Afg.	C1	36
Safonovo, Russia	F16	18
Saga, Japan	I3	30
Sagadahoc, co., Me., U.S.	E3	96
Sagaing, Burma	D3	34
Sagamihara, Japan	G12	30
Sagami-nada, b., Japan	G12	30
Sagamore Hills, Oh., U.S.	h9	112
Saganaga Lake, l., Mn., U.S.	B7	100
Sāgar, India	E3	37
Sāgar, India	I8	38
Sag Harbor, N.Y., U.S.	m16	109
Saginaw, Mi., U.S.	E7	99
Saginaw, Tx., U.S.	n9	120
Saginaw, co., Mi., U.S.	E6	99
Saginaw Bay, b., Mi., U.S.	E7	99
Saglek Bay, b., Newf., Can.	f9	72
Sagres, Port.	H3	12
Saguache, Co., U.S.	C4	83
Sagua de Tánamo, Cuba	D10	64
Sagua la Grande, Cuba	C7	64
Saguaro Lake, res., Az., U.S.	k10	80
Saguaro National Monument (Tucson Mountain Section), Az., U.S.	E4	80
Saguaro National Monument, Az., U.S.	E5	80
Saguenay, stm., Que., Can.	A7	74
Sagunto, Spain	F11	12
Sahagún, Col.	C5	58
Sahagún, Spain	C6	12
Sahara, des., Afr.	D6	42
Sahāranpur, India	F7	38
Sāhiwāl (Montgomery), Pak.	E5	38
Sahuaripa, Mex.	C5	62
Sahuarita, Az., U.S.	F5	80
Sahuayo, Mex.	G8	62
Saibai, i., Austl.	A8	50
Saïda, Alg.	B6	42
Saidpur, Bngl.	H13	38
Saidu, Pak.	C5	38
Saigō, Japan	F9	30
Saigon see Thanh Pho Ho Chi Minh, Viet.	I9	34
Saijō, Japan	I6	30
Saimaa, l., Fin.	F16	6
Saint Abb's Head, c., Scot., U.K.	F10	7
Saint Adolphe, Man., Can.	E3	70
Saint-Affrique, Fr.	I9	10
Sainte-Agathe, Que., Can.	C6	74
Sainte-Agathe-des-Monts, Que., Can.	C3	74
Saint-Aimé (Massueville), Que., Can.	D5	74
Saint-Alban, Que., Can.	C5	74
Saint Alban's, Newf., Can.	E4	72
Saint Albans, Eng., U.K.	J12	7
Saint Albans, Vt., U.S.	B2	122
Saint Albans, W.V., U.S.	C3	125
Saint Albans Bay, b., Vt., U.S.	B2	122
Saint Albert, Alta., Can.	C4	68
Saint-Amand-Mont-Rond, Fr.	F9	10
Saint-Ambroise, Que., Can.	A6	74
Saint-Ambroix, Fr.	H11	10
Saint-André, Cap, c., Madag.	E8	44
Saint-André-Avellin, Que., Can.	D2	74
Saint-André-Est, Que., Can.	D3	74
Saint-André-les-Alpes, Fr.	I13	10
Saint Andrew Bay, b., Fl., U.S.	u16	86
Saint Andrews, N.B., Can.	D2	71
Saint Andrews, Scot., U.K.	E10	7
Saint Andrews, S.C., U.S.	F7	117
Saint Andrews, S.C., U.S.	C5	117
Saint Anne, Il., U.S.	B6	90
Sainte-Anne-de-Beaupré, Que., Can.	B7	74
Sainte-Anne [-de-Bellevue], Que., Can.	q19	74
Sainte-Anne-de-Madawaska, N.B., Can.	B1	71
Sainte-Anne-des-Chênes, Man., Can.	E3	70
Sainte-Anselme, Que., Can.	C7	74
Saint Ansgar, Ia., U.S.	A5	92
Saint Anthony, Newf., Can.	C4	72
Saint Anthony, Id., U.S.	F7	89
Saint Antoine, N.B., Can.	C5	71
Saint-Apollinaire, Que., Can.	C6	74
Saint Arthur, N.B., Can.	B3	71
Saint-Astier, Fr.	G7	10
Saint-Aubert, Que., Can.	B7	74
Saint Augustin, Que., Can.	C2	72
Saint Augustine, Fl., U.S.	C5	86
Saint-Austell, Eng., U.K.	K8	7
Saint-Avold, Fr.	C13	10
Saint-Barthélemy, i., Guad.	F16	64
Saint Basile, N.B., Can.	B1	71
Saint-Basile [-Sud], Que., Can.	C6	74
Saint-Benoît-du-Sault, Fr.	F8	10
Saint-Bernard, Que., Can.	C6	74
Saint Bernard, Al., U.S.	A3	78
Saint Bernard, La., U.S.	E6	95
Saint Bernard, Oh., U.S.	o13	112
Saint Bernard, co., La., U.S.	E6	95
Saint Bernice, In., U.S.	E2	91
Saint Bride, Mount, mtn., Alta., Can.	D3	68
Saint Bride's, Newf., Can.	E4	72
Saint-Brieuc, Fr.	D4	10
Saint-Bruno, Que., Can.	A6	74
Saint-Calais, Fr.	E7	10
Saint-Casimir, Que., Can.	C5	74
Saint Catharines, Ont., Can.	D5	73
Saint Catherine, Lake, l., Vt., U.S.	E2	122
Saint Catherines Island, i., Ga., U.S.	E5	87
Saint-Célestin (Annaville), Que., Can.	C5	74
Saint-Céré, Fr.	H8	10
Saint-Césaire, Que., Can.	D4	74
Saint-Chamond, Fr.	G11	10
Saint-Charles, Que., Can.	C7	74
Saint Charles, Il., U.S.	B5	90
Saint Charles, Mi., U.S.	E6	99
Saint Charles, Mn., U.S.	G6	100
Saint Charles, Mo., U.S.	C7	102
Saint Charles, co., La., U.S.	E5	95
Saint Charles, co., Il., U.S.	E3	90
Saint Charles, co., Mi., U.S.	F8	99
Saint Charles, co., Mo., U.S.	C4	102
Saint Charles, co., Mo., U.S.	C3	102
Saint-Chély-d'Apcher, Fr.	H10	10
Saint Christopher (Saint Kitts), i., St. K./N.	F16	64
Saint Christopher-Nevis see Saint Kitts and Nevis, ctry., N.A.	F16	64
Saint-Chrysostome, Que., Can.	D4	74
Saint Clair, Mi., U.S.	F8	99
Saint Clair, Mn., U.S.	F5	100
Saint Clair, Mo., U.S.	C6	102
Saint Clair, Pa., U.S.	E9	115
Saint Clair, co., Al., U.S.	B3	78
Saint Clair, co., Il., U.S.	E3	90
Saint Clair, co., Mi., U.S.	F8	99
Saint Clair, co., Mo., U.S.	C4	102
Saint Clair Shores, Mi., U.S.	p16	99
Saint Clairsville, Oh., U.S.	B5	112
Saint Claude, Man., Can.	E2	70
Saint-Claude, Fr.	F12	10
Saint Cloud, Fl., U.S.	D5	86
Saint Cloud, Mn., U.S.	E4	100
Saint-Coeur-de-Marie, Que., Can.	A6	74
Saint-Constant, Que., Can.	q19	74
Sainte-Croix, Que., Can.	C6	74
Saint Croix, co., Wi., U.S.	C1	126
Saint Croix, i., V.I.U.S.	F15	64
Saint Croix, stm., U.S.	C1	126
Saint Croix, Lake, l., U.S.	D1	126
Saint Croix Falls, Wi., U.S.	C1	126
Saint Croix Stream, stm., Me., U.S.	B4	96
Saint-Damase, Que., Can.	D4	74
Saint David, Az., U.S.	F5	80
Saint-David-de-l'Auberivière, Que., Can.	n17	74
Saint David's, Wales, U.K.	J7	7
Saint-Denis, Fr.	D9	10
Saint-Denis, Reu.	F11	44
Saint-Dié, Fr.	D13	10
Saint-Dizier, Fr.	D11	10
Saint-Dominique, Que., Can.	D5	74
Saint Edward, Ne., U.S.	C8	104
Saint Eleanor's, P.E.I., Can.	C6	71
Saint Elias, Cape, c., Ak., U.S.	D11	79
Saint Elmo, Al., U.S.	E1	78
Saint Elmo, Il., U.S.	D5	90
Saint-Éphrem [-de-Tring], Que., Can.	C7	74
Saint Étienne, Fr.	G11	10
Saint-Eustache, Que., Can.	D4	74
Saint-Félicien, Que., Can.	A5	74
Saint-Félix-de-Valois, Que., Can.	C4	74
Saint-Ferdinand (Bernierville), Que., Can.	C6	74
Saint-Ferréol [-les-Neiges], Que., Can.	B7	74
Saint-Flavien, Que., Can.	C6	74
Saint-Florentin, Fr.	D10	10
Saint-Florent-sur-Cher, Fr.	F9	10
Saint-Flour, Fr.	G10	10
Sainte-Foy, Que., Can.	n17	74
Sainte-Foy-la-Grande, Fr.	H7	10
Saint Francis, Ks., U.S.	C2	93
Saint Francis, Mn., U.S.	E5	100
Saint Francis, S.D., U.S.	D5	118
Saint Francis, Wi., U.S.	n12	126
Saint Francis, co., Ar., U.S.	B5	81
Saint Francis, stm., U.S.	A5	81
Saint Francis, Cape, c., Newf., Can.	E5	72
Saint Francisville, Il., U.S.	E6	90
Saint Francisville, La., U.S.	D4	95
Saint Francois, co., Mo., U.S.	D7	102
Saint-François, stm., Que., Can.	D5	74
Saint-François, Lac, l., Que., Can.	D6	74
Saint Francois Mountains, hills, Mo., U.S.	D7	102
Saint Froid Lake, l., Me., U.S.	B4	96
Saint-Fulgence, Que., Can.	A7	74
Saint-Gabriel, Que., Can.	C4	74
Saint-Gaudens, Fr.	I7	10
Saint-Gédéon, Que., Can.	D7	74
Sainte Genevieve, Mo., U.S.	D7	102
Sainte Genevieve, co., Mo., U.S.	D7	102
Saint George, Austl.	E9	50
Saint George, N.B., Can.	D3	71
Saint George, Ont., Can.	D4	73
Saint George, S.C., U.S.	E6	117
Saint George, Ut., U.S.	F2	121
Saint George, Cape, c., Newf., Can.	D2	72
Saint George, Cape, c., Fl., U.S.	C1	86
Saint George Island, i., Ak., U.S.	D6	79
Saint George Island, i., Fl., U.S.	C2	86
Saint-Georges, Que., Can.	C5	74
Saint-Georges, Fr. Gu.	C8	54
Saint George's, Gren.	H17	64
Saint George's, De., U.S.	B3	85
Saint George's Bay, b., Newf., Can.	D2	72
Saint George's Bay, b., N.S., Can.	D8	71
Saint George's Channel, strt., Eur.	J6	7
Saint-Georges-Ouest, Que., Can.	C7	74
Saint-Germain, Fr.	D9	10
Saint-Gervais, Que., Can.	C7	74
Saint-Gilles, Que., Can.	C6	74
Saint-Gilles-Croix-de-Vie, Fr.	F5	10
Saint-Girons, Fr.	J8	10
Saint-Grégoire (Larochelle), Que., Can.	C5	74
Saint-Guénolé, Fr.	E2	10
Saint-Guillaume-d'Upton, Que., Can.	D5	74
Saint Helen, Lake, l., Mi., U.S.	D6	99
Saint Helena, Ca., U.S.	C2	82
Saint Helena, co., La., U.S.	D5	95
Saint Helena Bay, b., S. Afr.	H3	44
Saint Helena Island, i., S.C.	G6	117
Saint Helena Sound, strt., S.C., U.S.	G7	117
Saint Helens, Or., U.S.	B4	114
Saint Helens, Mount, vol., Wa., U.S.	C3	124
Saint Helier, Jersey	C4	10
Saint Henry, Oh., U.S.	B1	112
Saint-Hippolyte, Fr.	E13	10
Saint-Honoré, Que., Can.	D7	74
Saint-Hubert, Que., Can.	q20	74
Saint-Hubert-de-Témiscouata, Que., Can.	B8	74
Saint-Hyacinthe, Que., Can.	D5	74
Saint Ignace, Mi., U.S.	C6	99
Saint Ignatius, Mt., U.S.	C2	103
Saint Ignace Island, i., Ont., Can.	G15	66
Saint Isidore de Prescott, Ont., Can.	B10	73
Saint Jacobs, Ont., Can.	D4	73
Saint Jacques, N.B., Can.	B1	71
Saint-Jacques, Que., Can.	D4	74
Saint James, Mn., U.S.	G4	100
Saint James, Mo., U.S.	D6	102
Saint James, co., La., U.S.	D5	95
Saint James, Cape, c., B.C., Can.	D2	69
Saint James City, Fl., U.S.	F4	86
Saint-Jean, stm., Que., Can.	A7	74
Saint-Jean, Lac, l., Que., Can.	A5	74
Saint Jean Baptiste, Man., Can.	E3	70
Saint-Jean-Chrysostome, Que., Can.	o17	74
Saint-Jean-d'Angély, Fr.	G6	10
Saint-Jean-de-Luz, Fr.	I5	10
Saint-Jean-de-Maurienne, Fr.	G13	10
Saint-Jean-de-Monts, Fr.	F4	10
Saint-Jean-Pied-de-Port, Fr.	I5	10
Saint-Jean-sur-Richelieu, Que., Can.	D4	74
Saint-Jérôme, Que., Can.	D3	74
Saint Jo, Tx., U.S.	C4	120
Saint-Joachim, Que., Can.	B7	74
Saint Joe, stm., Id., U.S.	B3	89
Saint John, In., U.S.	B3	91
Saint John, Ks., U.S.	E5	93
Saint John, i., V.I.U.S.	E15	64
Saint John, stm., U.S.	G19	66
Saint John, Cape, c., Newf., Can.	D4	72
Saint John Bay, b., Newf., Can.	C3	72
Saint Johns, Antig.	F17	64
Saint John's, Newf., Can.	E5	72
Saint Johns, Az., U.S.	C6	80
Saint Johns, Mi., U.S.	F6	99
Saint Johns, co., Fl., U.S.	C5	86
Saint Johns, stm., Fl., U.S.	B5	86
Saint Johnsbury, Vt., U.S.	C4	122
Saint Johnsville, N.Y., U.S.	B6	109
Saint John the Baptist, co., La., U.S.	D5	95
Saint Jones, stm., De., U.S.	D4	85
Saint Joseph, N.B., Can.	D5	71
Saint Joseph, Il., U.S.	C5	90
Saint Joseph, La., U.S.	C4	95
Saint Joseph, Mi., U.S.	F4	99
Saint Joseph, Mn., U.S.	E4	100
Saint Joseph, Mo., U.S.	B3	102
Saint Joseph, Tn., U.S.	B4	119
Saint Joseph, co., In., U.S.	A5	91
Saint Joseph, co., Mi., U.S.	G5	99
Saint-Joseph, stm., U.S.	F5	99
Saint-Joseph, Lac, l., Que., Can.	n16	74
Saint Joseph, Lake, l., Ont., Can.	o17	73
Saint Joseph Bay, b., Fl., U.S.	C1	86
Saint-Joseph-de-Beauce, Que., Can.	C7	74
Saint Joseph Point, c., Fl., U.S.	v16	86
Saint Joseph Sound, strt., Fl., U.S.	o10	86
Saint-Jovite, Que., Can.	C3	74
Saint-Julien-en-Born, Fr.	H5	10
Saint-Junien, Fr.	G7	10
Saint-Just-en-Chaussée, Fr.	C9	10
Saint Kilda, i., Scot., U.K.	D4	7
Saint Kitts-Nevis, ctry., N.A.	F16	64
Saint-Lambert, Que., Can.	p19	74
Saint Landry, co., La., U.S.	D3	95
Saint-Laurent, Que., Can.	p19	74
Saint Lawrence, Newf., Can.	E4	72
Saint Lawrence, co., N.Y., U.S.	A5	109
Saint Lawrence, stm., N.A.	G19	66
Saint Lawrence, Cape, c., N.S., Can.	B9	71
Saint Lawrence, Gulf of, b., Can.	G20	66
Saint Lawrence Island, i., Ak., U.S.	C5	79
Saint Lawrence Islands National Park, Ont., Can.	C9	73
Saint Léonard, N.B., Can.	B2	71
Saint-Léonard [-d'Aston], Que., Can.	C5	74
Saint-Liboire, Que., Can.	D5	74
Saint-Lô, Fr.	C6	10
Saint Louis, Sen.	E2	42
Saint Louis, Mi., U.S.	E6	99
Saint Louis, Mo., U.S.	C7	102
Saint Louis, co., Mn., U.S.	C6	100
Saint Louis, co., Mo., U.S.	C7	102
Saint Louis, stm., U.S.	D6	100
Saint-Louis, Lac, l., Que., Can.	q19	74
Saint Louis Bay, b., Ms., U.S.	f7	101
Saint-Louis-de-Gonzague, Que., Can.	D3	74
Saint Louis-du-Ha! Ha!, Que., Can.	B8	74
Saint Louis Park, Mn., U.S.	n12	100
Saint-Luc, Que., Can.	D4	74
Saint Lucia, ctry., N.A.	H17	64
Saint Lucia Channel, strt., N.A.	G17	64
Saint Lucie, co., Fl., U.S.	E6	86
Saint Lucie Canal, Fl., U.S.	F6	86
Saint Lucie Inlet, b., Fl., U.S.	E6	86
Sainte-Madeleine, Que., Can.	D4	74
Saint-Malo, Man., Can.	E3	70
Saint-Malo, Fr.	D4	10
Saint-Malo, Golfe de, b., Fr.	C4	10
Saint-Marc, Haiti	E11	64
Saint-Marc [-des-Carrières], Que., Can.	C5	74
Saint-Marcellin, Fr.	G12	10
Saint Margaret Bay, b., Newf.	C3	72
Sainte-Marguerite, stm., Que., Can.	A7	74
Sainte-Marie, Que., Can.	C6	74
Sainte-Marie, Cap, c., Madag.	G9	44
Saint Maries, Id., U.S.	B2	89
Sainte-Marthe, Que., Can.	D3	74
Saint Martin, co., La., U.S.	D4	95
Saint-Martin (Sint Maarten), i., N.A.	E16	64
Saint Martin, Lake, l., Man., Can.	D2	70
Saint Martin Island, i., Mi., U.S.	C4	99
Saint Martinville, La., U.S.	D4	95
Saint Mary, co., La., U.S.	E4	95
Saint Mary-of-the-Woods, In., U.S.	E3	91
Saint Mary Peak, mtn., Austl.	F7	50
Saint Marys, Austl.	H9	50
Saint Mary's, Newf., Can.	E5	72
Saint Marys, Ak., U.S.	C7	79
Saint Marys, Ga., U.S.	F5	87
Saint Marys, In., U.S.	A5	91
Saint Marys, Ks., U.S.	C7	93
Saint Marys, Oh., U.S.	B1	112
Saint Marys, Pa., U.S.	D4	115
Saint Marys, W.V., U.S.	B3	125
Saint Marys, co., Md., U.S.	D4	97
Saint Marys, stm., N.S., Can.	D8	71
Saint Marys, stm., U.S.	F5	87
Saint Marys, stm., U.S.	C8	91
Saint Marys, stm., Md., U.S.	D5	97
Saint Mary's, Cape, c., Newf., Can.	E4	72
Saint Mary's Bay, b., Newf., Can.	E5	72
Saint Marys Bay, b., N.S., Can.	E3	71
Saint Marys City, Md., U.S.	D5	97
Saint-Mathieu, Pointe de, c., Fr.	D2	10
Saint Matthew Island, i., Ak., U.S.	C5	79
Saint Matthews, Ky., U.S.	B4	94
Saint Matthews, S.C., U.S.	D6	117
Sainte-Maure-du-Touraine, Fr.	E7	10
Sainte-Maxime, Fr.	I13	10
Sainte-Maurice, stm., Que., Can.	C5	74
Saint-Méen-le-Grand, Fr.	D4	10
Sainte-Menehould, Fr.	C11	10
Sainte-Mère-Église, Fr.	C5	10
Saint Michael, Mn., U.S.	E5	100
Saint Michaels, Md., U.S.	C5	97
Saint-Michel [-de-Bellechasse], Que., Can.	C7	74
Saint-Mihiel, Fr.	D12	10
Saint-Moritz see Sankt Moritz, Switz.	F16	10
Saint-Nazaire, Fr.	E4	10
Saint-Nicolas, Que., Can.	o17	74
Saint-Odilon, Que., Can.	C7	74
Saint-Omer, Fr.	B9	10
Saint-Ours, Que., Can.	D4	74
Saint-Pacôme, Que., Can.	B8	74
Saint-Pamphile, Que., Can.	C8	74
Saint Paris, Oh., U.S.	B2	112
Saint-Pascal, Que., Can.	B8	74
Saint Paul, Alta., Can.	B5	68
Saint Paul, Ak., U.S.	D5	79
Saint Paul, In., U.S.	F6	91
Saint Paul, Ks., U.S.	E8	93
Saint Paul, Mn., U.S.	F5	100
Saint Paul, Ne., U.S.	C7	104
Saint Paul, Va., U.S.	f9	123
Saint Paul Island, i., Ak., U.S.	D5	79
Saint Paul Park, Mn., U.S.	n12	100
Saint Pauls, N.C., U.S.	C4	110
Sainte-Perpétue-de-L'Islet, Que., Can.	B8	74
Saint Peter, Mn., U.S.	F5	100
Saint Peter Port, Guernsey	C4	10
Saint Peters, N.S., Can.	D9	71
Saint Peters, Mo., U.S.	C7	102
Saint Petersburg, Fl., U.S.	E4	86
Saint Petersburg Beach, Fl., U.S.	p10	86
Saint Petersburg see Sankt-Peterburg, Russia	B13	18
Saint Phillips Island, i., S.C., U.S.	G6	117
Saint-Pie, Que., Can.	D5	74
Saint-Pierre, Reu.	F11	44
Saint-Pierre, St. P./M.	E3	72
Saint-Pierre, Lac, l., Que., Can.	C5	74
Saint Pierre and Miquelon, dep., N.A.	G21	66
Saint Pierre Island, i., Sey.	C10	44
Saint-Pierre-Jolys, Man., Can.	E3	70
Saint-Pierre-le-Moûtier, Fr.	F10	10
Saint-Pol-de-Léon, Fr.	D3	10
Saint-Pons, Fr.	I9	10
Saint-Pourçain-sur-Sioule, Fr.	F10	10
Saint-Prime, Que., Can.	A5	74
Saint Quentin, N.B., Can.	B2	71
Saint-Quentin, Fr.	C10	10
Saint-Raphaël, Que., Can.	C7	74
Saint-Raphaël, Fr.	I13	10
Saint-Raymond, Que., Can.	C6	74
Saint-Rédempteur, Que., Can.	o17	74
Saint Regis, West Branch, stm., N.Y., U.S.	f10	109
Saint-Rémi, Que., Can.	D4	74
Saint-Romuald, Que., Can.	C6	74
Saint Rose, La., U.S.	k11	95
Sainte Rose du Lac, Man., Can.	D2	70
Saintes, Fr.	G6	10
Saint Sauveur, N.B., Can.	B4	71
Saint-Sauveur-des-Monts, Que., Can.	D3	74
Saint-Sébastien, Cap, c., Madag.	D9	44
Saint-Siméon, Que., Can.	B8	74
Saint Simons Island, Ga., U.S.	E5	87
Saint Simons Island, i., Ga., U.S.	E5	87
Saint Stephen, N.B., Can.	D2	71
Saint Stephen, S.C., U.S.	E8	117
Saint Tammany, co., La., U.S.	C5	95
Sainte-Thècle, Que., Can.	C4	74
Sainte-Thérèse, Que., Can.	D4	74
Saint Thomas, Ont., Can.	E3	73
Saint Thomas, i., V.I.U.S.	E15	64
Saint Timothée, Que., Can.	q18	74
Saint-Tite, Que., Can.	C5	74
Saint-Tropez, Fr.	I13	10
Saint-Valéry-en-Caux, Fr.	C7	10
Saint-Varent, Fr.	F6	10
Saint-Véronique, Que., Can.	C3	74
Saint-Victor, Que., Can.	C7	74
Saint-Vincent, Cap, c., Madag.	F8	44
Saint Vincent, Gulf, b., Austl.	F7	50
Saint Vincent and the Grenadines, ctry., N.A.	H17	64
Saint Vincent Island, i., Fl., U.S.	C1	86
Saint Vincent Passage, strt., N.A.	H17	64
Saint Vincent's [-Saint Stephens-Peter's River], Newf., Can.	E5	72
Saint-Vith, Bel.	E6	8
Saint Walburg, Sask., Can.	D1	75
Saint-Zacharie, Que., Can.	C7	74
Sairecábur, Cerro, mtn., S.A.	A3	56
Saito, Japan	J4	30
Saitula, China	B8	38
Sajama, Nevado, mtn., Bol.	G5	54
Sajia, China	F13	38
Sajnśand, Mong.	C9	26
Sakai, Japan	H8	30
Sakaide, Japan	H6	30
Sakai-minato, Japan	G6	30
Sakakawea, Lake, res., N.D., U.S.	B3	111
Sakami, Lac, l., Que., Can.	F17	66
Sakata, Japan	D12	30
Sakhalin see Sachalin, Ostrov, i., Russia	G22	24
Säkhar, Afg.	D1	38
Sakishima-shotō, is., Japan	G11	26
Sakon Nakhon, Thai.	F8	34
Sakonnet, stm., R.I., U.S.	E6	116
Sakonnet Point, c., R.I., U.S.	F6	116
Saku, Japan	F12	30
Sakurai, Japan	H8	30
Sal, Point, c., Ca., U.S.	E3	82
Sala, Swe.	G11	6
Salaberry-de-Valleyfield, Que., Can.	D3	74
Sala Consilina, Italy	I10	14
Salado, stm., Arg.	C4	56
Salado, Rio, stm., N.M., U.S.	E2	108
Salālah, Oman	E5	46
Salamanca, Mex.	G9	62
Salamanca, Spain	E6	12
Salamanca, N.Y., U.S.	C2	109
Salamina, Col.	E5	58
Salamonie, stm., In., U.S.	C6	91
Salamonie, Lake, res., In., U.S.	C6	91
Salatiga, Indon.	m15	33
Salavat, Russia	G9	22
Salawati, i., Indon.	F9	32
Saldanha, S. Afr.	H3	44
Sale, Austl.	G9	50
Sale Creek, Tn., U.S.	D8	119
Salem, India	G5	37
Salem, Ar., U.S.	A4	81
Salem, Il., U.S.	E5	90
Salem, In., U.S.	G5	91
Salem, Ky., U.S.	e9	94
Salem, Ma., U.S.	A6	98
Salem, Mo., U.S.	D6	102
Salem, N.H., U.S.	E4	106
Salem, N.J., U.S.	D2	107
Salem, Oh., U.S.	B5	112
Salem, Or., U.S.	C4	114
Salem, S.D., U.S.	D8	118
Salem, Ut., U.S.	C4	121

Name	Map Ref	Page
Salem, Va., U.S.	C2	123
Salem, W.V., U.S.	B4	125
Salem, Wi., U.S.	n11	126
Salem, co., N.J., U.S.	D2	107
Salem, stm., N.J., U.S.	D2	107
Salem Lake, l., Vt., U.S.	B4	122
Salemi, Italy	L7	14
Sälen, Swe.	F9	6
Salerno, Italy	I9	14
Salford, Eng., U.K.	H10	7
Salgótarján, Hung.	G19	8
Sali, Cro.	F10	14
Salida, Co., U.S.	C5	83
Salies-de-Béarn, Fr.	I6	10
Salihli, Tur.	K12	16
Salina, Ks., U.S.	D6	93
Salina, Ok., U.S.	A6	113
Salina, Ut., U.S.	E4	121
Salina Cruz, Mex.	I12	62
Salinas, Braz.	D7	57
Salinas, Ca., U.S.	D3	82
Salinas, stm., Ca., U.S.	D3	82
Salinas de Hidalgo, Mex.	F9	62
Salinas Peak, mtn., N.M., U.S.	D3	108
Salinas Pueblo Missions National Monument, N.M., U.S.	C3	108
Saline, Mi., U.S.	F7	99
Saline, co., Ar., U.S.	C3	81
Saline, co., Il., U.S.	F5	90
Saline, co., Ks., U.S.	D6	93
Saline, co., Mo., U.S.	B4	102
Saline, co., Ne., U.S.	D8	104
Saline, stm., Ar., U.S.	D4	81
Saline, stm., Ar., U.S.	C1	81
Saline, stm., Ks., U.S.	C3	93
Saline, North Fork, stm., Il., U.S.	F5	90
Saline Lake, res., La., U.S.	C3	95
Salineville, Oh., U.S.	B5	112
Salisbury, N.B., Can.	C4	71
Salisbury, Eng., U.K.	J11	7
Salisbury, Ct., U.S.	B2	84
Salisbury, Md., U.S.	D6	97
Salisbury, Ma., U.S.	A6	98
Salisbury, Mo., U.S.	B5	102
Salisbury, N.C., U.S.	B2	110
Salisbury see Harare, Zimb.	E6	44
Salisbury Island, i., N.W. Ter., Can.	D17	66
Salisbury Plain, pl., Eng., U.K.	J11	7
Salish Mountains, mts., Mt., U.S.	B2	103
Salkehatchie, stm., S.C., U.S.	E5	117
Salkhad, Syria	C5	40
Salles-Curan, Fr.	H9	10
Sallisaw, Ok., U.S.	B7	113
Salluit, Que., Can.	f11	74
Salmo, B.C., Can.	E9	69
Salmon, Id., U.S.	D5	89
Salmon, stm., N.B., Can.	C4	71
Salmon, stm., Id., U.S.	D3	89
Salmon Creek, Wa., U.S.	D3	124
Salmon Creek Reservoir, res., Id., U.S.	G4	89
Salmon Falls, stm., U.S.	D5	106
Salmon Falls Creek, stm., U.S.	G4	89
Salmon Mountains, mts., Ca., U.S.	B2	82
Salmon Point, c., Ont., Can.	D7	73
Salmon River Mountains, mts., Id., U.S.	E3	89
Salmon River Reservoir, res., N.Y., U.S.	B5	109
Salo, Fin.	F14	6
Salome, Az., U.S.	D2	80
Salon-De-Provence, Fr.	I12	10
Saloniki see Thessaloníki, Grc.	I6	16
Salsomaggiore Terme, Italy	E4	14
Salt, stm., Az., U.S.	D4	80
Salt, stm., Ky., U.S.	C4	94
Salt, stm., Mo., U.S.	B6	102
Salta, Arg.	A3	56
Salt Creek, stm., N.M., U.S.	D5	108
Salt Creek, stm., Oh., U.S.	C3	112
Salt Creek, stm., Wy., U.S.	C6	127
Salter Path, N.C., U.S.	C6	110
Salt Fork Lake, res., Oh., U.S.	B4	112
Saltillo, Mex.	E9	62
Saltillo, Ms., U.S.	A5	101
Salt Lake, co., Ut., U.S.	C3	121
Salt Lake, l., Hi., U.S.	g10	88
Salt Lake, l., N.M., U.S.	E6	108
Salt Lake City, Ut., U.S.	C4	121
Salto, Ur.	C5	56
Salton Sea, l., Ca., U.S.	F5	82
Saltpond, Gh.	H5	42
Saltville, Va., U.S.	f10	123
Salt Wells Creek, stm., Wy., U.S.	E4	127
Saluda, S.C., U.S.	C4	117
Saluda, co., S.C., U.S.	C4	117
Saluda, stm., S.C., U.S.	C4	117
Saluda Dam, S.C., U.S.	C5	117
Salūr, India	C7	37
Saluzzo, Italy	E2	14
Salvador, Braz.	B9	57
Salvador, Lake, l., La., U.S.	E5	95
Salvatierra, Mex.	G9	62
Salween (Nu) (Thanlwin), stm., Asia	D5	34
Salyersville, Ky., U.S.	C6	94
Salzburg, Aus.	H13	8
Salzgitter, Ger.	C10	8
Salzwedel, Ger.	C11	8
Sama [de Langreo], Spain	B6	12
Samaná, Bahía de, b., Dom. Rep.	E13	64
Samana Cay, i., Bah.	C11	64
Samandağı, Tur.	A4	40
Samar, i., Phil.	C8	32
Samara, Russia	G8	22
Samarai, Pap. N. Gui.	n17	50a
Samariapo, Ven.	E9	58
Samarinda, Indon.	F6	32
Samarkand, Uzb.	J11	22
Sāmarrā', Iraq	B3	46
Samāstipur, India	H11	38
Sambalpur, India	J10	38
Sambas, Indon.	E4	32
Sambava, Madag.	D10	44
Sambhal, India	F8	38
Sāmbhar, India	G6	38
Samborondón, Ec.	H3	58
Sammamish Lake, l., Wa., U.S.	e11	124
Samneua, Laos	D8	34
Samobor, Cro.	D10	14
Sámos, i., Grc.	L10	16
Samoset, Fl., U.S.	q10	86
Sampit, Indon.	F5	32
Sampit, stm., S.C., U.S.	E9	117
Sampson, co., N.C., U.S.	B4	110
Sam Rayburn Reservoir, res., Tx., U.S.	D5	120
Samson, Al., U.S.	D3	78
Samsun, Tur.	G15	4
Samuels, Id., U.S.	A2	89
Samui, Ko, i., Thai.	J6	34
Samut Prakan, Thai.	H6	34
Samut Sakhon, Thai.	H6	34
San, Mali	F5	42
San, stm., Eur.	E22	8
Şan'ā', Yemen	E3	46
Sanaga, stm., Cam.	H7	42
San Agustín, Col.	G4	58
San Agustin, Cape, c., Phil.	D8	32
San Agustin, Plains of, pl., N.M., U.S.	C2	108
Sanak Islands, is., Ak., U.S.	E7	79
Sanana, Pulau, i., Indon.	F8	32
Sanandaj, Iran	A4	40
San Andreas, Ca., U.S.	C3	82
San Andrés, Isla de, i., Col.	H7	64
San Andres Mountains, mts., N.M., U.S.	E3	108
San Andres Peak, mtn., N.M., U.S.	E3	108
San Andrés Tuxtla, Mex.	H12	62
San Angelo, Tx., U.S.	D2	120
San Anselmo, Ca., U.S.	h7	82
San Antonio, Tx., U.S.	E3	120
San Antonio, Cabo, c., Arg.	D5	56
San Antonio, Cabo, c., Cuba	D5	64
San Antonio Abad, Spain	G13	12
San Antonio Bay, b., Tx., U.S.	E4	120
San Antonio de Bravo, Mex.	B7	62
San Antonio de los Cobres, Arg.	A3	56
San Antonio del Táchira, Ven.	D6	58
San Antonio Mountain, mtn., N.M., U.S.	A3	108
San Antonio Oeste, Arg.	E4	56
San Augustine, Tx., U.S.	D5	120
San Augustine, co., Tx., U.S.	D5	120
San Benedetto del Tronto, Italy	G8	14
San Benedicto, Isla, i., Mex.	H4	62
San Benito, Guat.	F3	64
San Benito, Tx., U.S.	F4	120
San Benito, co., Ca., U.S.	D3	82
San Benito Mountain, mtn., Ca., U.S.	D3	82
San Bernardino, Ca., U.S.	E5	82
San Bernardino, co., Ca., U.S.	E5	82
San Bernardo, Chile	C2	56
San Blas, Mex.	G7	62
San Blas, Mex.	D5	62
San Blas, Cape, c., Fl., U.S.	v16	86
San Borja, Bol.	F5	54
Sanborn, Ia., U.S.	A2	92
Sanborn, co., S.D., U.S.	D7	118
Sanbornville, N.H., U.S.	C4	106
San Bruno, Ca., U.S.	D2	82
San Carlos, Nic.	I5	64
San Carlos, Az., U.S.	D5	80
San Carlos, Ca., U.S.	k8	82
San Carlos, Ven.	C8	58
San Carlos de Bariloche, Arg.	E2	56
San Carlos de Guaroa, Col.	F6	58
San Carlos de la Rápita, Spain	E12	12
San Carlos del Zulia, Ven.	C7	58
San Carlos de Río Negro, Ven.	G9	58
San Carlos Indian Reservation, Az., U.S.	D5	80
San Carlos Lake, res., Az., U.S.	D5	80
San Cataldo, Italy	L9	14
Sancerre, Fr.	E9	10
Sánchez, Mex.	D10	62
San Clemente, Ca., U.S.	F5	82
San Clemente Island, i., Ca., U.S.	F4	82
Sancoins, Fr.	F9	10
San Cristóbal, Arg.	C4	56
San Cristóbal, Col.	D6	58
San Cristóbal, Volcán, vol., Nic.	H4	64
San Cristóbal las Casas, Mex.	I13	62
Sancti-Spíritus, Cuba	D8	64
Sand, Nor.	G6	6
Sandakan, Malay.	D6	32
Sanday, i., Scot., U.K.	B10	7
Sand Creek, stm., Wy., U.S.	C7	127
Sanders, Az., U.S.	B6	80
Sanders, co., Mt., U.S.	C1	103
Sanderson, Tx., U.S.	D1	120
Sandersville, Ga., U.S.	D4	87
Sandersville, Ms., U.S.	D4	101
Sand Hill, Ma., U.S.	h13	98
Sand Hill, stm., Mn., U.S.	C2	100
Sandia, Peru	F5	54
Sandia Crest, mtn., N.M., U.S.	k8	108
Sandia Indian Reservation, N.M., U.S.	k7	108
Sandia Mountains, mts., N.M., U.S.	k8	108
San Diego, Ca., U.S.	F5	82
San Diego, Tx., U.S.	F3	120
San Diego, co., Ca., U.S.	F5	82
San Diego, stm., Ca., U.S.	o15	82
San Diego Naval Station, mil., Ca., U.S.	o15	82
San Diego Naval Training Center, mil., Ca., U.S.	o15	82
Sand Island, i., Hi., U.S.	g10	88
Sand Island, i., Wi., U.S.	B3	126
Sand Key, i., Fl., U.S.	E4	86
Sandlick Creek, stm., W.V., U.S.	n13	125
Sandnes, Nor.	G5	6
Sandoa, Zaire	C4	44
San Donà di Piave, Italy	D7	14
Sandoval, Il., U.S.	E4	90
Sandoval, co., N.M., U.S.	B2	108
Sandoway, Burma	E3	34
Sand Point, Ak., U.S.	D7	79
Sandpoint, Id., U.S.	A2	89
Sands Key, i., Fl., U.S.	s3	86
Sand Springs, Ok., U.S.	A5	113
Sandston, Va., U.S.	m18	123
Sandstone, Mn., U.S.	D6	100
Sandusky, Oh., U.S.	A3	112
Sandusky, co., Oh., U.S.	A2	112
Sandusky, stm., Oh., U.S.	B2	112
Sandviken, Swe.	F11	6
Sandwich, Il., U.S.	B5	90
Sandwich, Ma., U.S.	C7	98
Sandwich Bay, b., Newf., Can.	B3	72
Sandy, Or., U.S.	B4	114
Sandy, Ut., U.S.	C4	121
Sandy, stm., Me., U.S.	D2	96
Sandy Creek, stm., Oh., U.S.	B4	112
Sandy Creek, stm., Ok., U.S.	C2	113
Sandy Hook, Ct., U.S.	D2	84
Sandy Hook, spit, N.J., U.S.	C5	107
Sandy Island, i., S.C., U.S.	D9	117
Sandy Lake, l., Newf., Can.	D3	72
Sandy Lake, l., Ont., Can.	n16	73
Sandy Neck, pen., Ma., U.S.	C7	98
Sandy Point, c., R.I., U.S.	h7	116
Sandy Springs, Ga., U.S.	h8	87
Sandy Springs, S.C., U.S.	B2	117
Sandyville, Md., U.S.	A4	97
San Felipe, Ven.	B8	58
San Felipe Indian Reservation, N.M., U.S.	k8	108
San Felipe Pueblo, N.M., U.S.	B3	108
San Feliu de Guixols, Spain	D15	12
San Fernando, Chile	C2	56
San Fernando, Mex.	E10	62
San Fernando, Phil.	q19	32
San Fernando, Phil.	B7	32
San Fernando, Spain	I5	12
San Fernando, Trin.	I17	64
San Fernando, Ca., U.S.	m12	82
San Fernando de Apure, Ven.	D9	58
San Fernando de Atabapo, Ven.	E9	58
Sanford, Co., U.S.	D5	83
Sanford, Fl., U.S.	D5	86
Sanford, Me., U.S.	E2	96
Sanford, Mi., U.S.	E6	99
Sanford, N.C., U.S.	B3	110
Sanford, Mount, mtn., Ak., U.S.	C11	79
San Francisco, Arg.	C4	56
San Francisco, Ca., U.S.	D2	82
San Francisco, co., Ca., U.S.	D2	82
San Francisco, stm., U.S.	D6	80
San Francisco Bay, b., Ca., U.S.	h8	82
San Francisco de Borja, Mex.	D6	62
San Francisco del Oro, Mex.	D7	62
San Francisco del Rincón, Mex.	G9	62
San Francisco de Macorís, Dom. Rep.	E12	64
San Fratello, Italy	K9	14
San Gabriel, Ec.	G4	58
San Gabriel, Ca., U.S.	*m12	82
San Gabriel Mountains, mts., Ca., U.S.	m12	82
Sangamner, India	C3	37
Sangamon, co., Il., U.S.	D4	90
Sangamon, stm., Il., U.S.	C3	90
San Gavino Monreale, Italy	J3	14
Sangay, Volcán, vol., Ec.	H3	58
Sang-e Māsheh, Afg.	D2	38
Sanger, Ca., U.S.	D4	82
Sanger, Tx., U.S.	C4	120
Sangerhausen, Ger.	D11	8
Sangha, stm., Afr.	B3	44
Sanghar, Pak.	G3	38
Sangihe, Kepulauan, is., Indon.	E8	32
Sangihe, Pulau, i., Indon.	E8	32
San Gil, Col.	D6	58
San Giovanni in Fiore, Italy	J11	14
San Giovanni in Persiceto, Italy	E6	14
San Giovanni Valdarno, Italy	F6	14
Sāngli, India	D3	37
Sangolquí, Ec.	H3	58
San Gorgonio Mountain, mtn., Ca., U.S.	E5	82
San Gregorio, Ur.	C5	56
Sangrūr, India	E6	38
Sangüesa, Spain	C10	12
Sanibel, Fl., U.S.	F4	86
Sanibel Island, i., Fl., U.S.	F4	86
San Ignacio, Arg.	B5	56
San Ignacio, Hond.	G4	64
Sanilac, co., Mi., U.S.	E8	99
San Isidro, Arg.	C5	56
San Isidro, C.R.	J6	64
San Jacinto, Col.	C5	58
San Jacinto, Ca., U.S.	F5	82
San Jacinto, stm., Ca., U.S.	F5	82
San Jacinto, stm., Tx., U.S.	r14	120
Sanjō, Japan	E11	30
San Joaquin, co., Ca., U.S.	D3	82
San Joaquin, stm., Ca., U.S.	D3	82
San Joaquin Valley, val., Ca., U.S.	D3	82
San Jorge, Golfo b., Arg.	F3	56
San Jorge, Golfo de b., Spain	E12	12
San José, C.R.	J5	64
San Jose, Ca., U.S.	D3	82
San Jose, Isla, i., Mex.	E5	62
San José de Chiquitos, Bol.	G6	54
San José de Guanipa, Ven.	C10	58
San José del Cabo, Mex.	F5	62
San José del Guaviare, Col.	F6	58
San José de Mayo, Ur.	C5	56
San José de Ocuné, Col.	E7	58
San José de Raíces, Mex.	E9	62
San Jose Island, i., Tx., U.S.	E4	120
San Juan, Arg.	C3	56
San Juan, Mex.	D8	62
San Juan, P.R.	E14	64
San Juan, co., Co., U.S.	D3	83
San Juan, co., N.M., U.S.	A1	108
San Juan, co., Ut., U.S.	F5	121
San Juan, co., Wa., U.S.	A2	124
San Juan, stm., N.A.	I6	64
San Juan Capistrano, Ca., U.S.	F5	82
San Juan de Colón, Ven.	C6	58
San Juan [de la Maguana], Dom. Rep.	E12	64
San Juan del Norte, Nic.	I6	64
San Juan de los Cayos, Ven.	B8	58
San Juan de los Morros, Ven.	C9	58
San Juan del Río, Mex.	G9	62
San Juan del Sur, Nic.	I5	64
San Juan Island, i., Wa., U.S.	A2	124
San Juan Mountains, mts., Co., U.S.	D3	83
San Julián, Arg.	F3	56
San Justo, Arg.	C4	56
Sankt Gallen, Aus.	H14	8
Sankt Gallen, Switz.	E16	10
Sankt Johann im Pongau, Aus.	H13	8
Sankt Moritz, Switz.	F16	10
Sankt Peter, Ger.	A8	8
Sankt-Peterburg (Saint Petersburg), Russia	B13	18
Sankt Pölten, Aus.	G15	8
Sankt Veit an der Glan, Aus.	I14	8
Sankt Wendel, Ger.	F7	8
Sankuru, stm., Zaire	B4	44
San Lázaro, Cabo, c., Mex.	E3	62
San Leandro, Ca., U.S.	h8	82
San Lope, Col.	D7	58
San Lorenzo, Arg.	C4	56
San Lorenzo, Ec.	G3	58
San Lorenzo, Isla, i., Peru	F3	54
San Lorenzo de El Escorial, Spain	E7	12
San Lorenzo de la Parrilla, Spain	F9	12
Sanlúcar de Barrameda, Spain	I5	12
San Lucas, Ec.	I3	58
San Lucas, Cabo, c., Mex.	F5	62
San Luis, Arg.	C3	56
San Luis, Guat.	F3	64
San Luis, Az., U.S.	E1	80
San Luis, Co., U.S.	D5	83
San Luis, Ven.	B8	58
San Luis, Lago de, l., Bol.	F6	54
San Luis, Point, c., Ca., U.S.	E3	82
San Luis de la Paz, Mex.	G9	62
San Luis Obispo, Ca., U.S.	E3	82
San Luis Obispo, co., Ca., U.S.	E3	82
San Luis Pass, strt., Tx., U.S.	r14	120
San Luis Peak, mtn., Co., U.S.	D4	83
San Luis Potosí, Mex.	F9	62
San Luis Río Colorado, Mex.	A2	62
San Luis Valley, val., Co., U.S.	D4	83
San Manuel, Az., U.S.	E5	80
San Marcos, Col.	C5	58
San Marcos, Mex.	D8	62
San Marcos, Tx., U.S.	E4	120
San Marcos, stm., Tx., U.S.	h8	120
San Marino, Ca., U.S.	m12	82
San Marino, ctry., Eur.	G10	4
San Martín de Valdeiglesias, Spain	E7	12
San Mateo, Spain	E12	12
San Mateo, Ca., U.S.	D2	82
San Mateo, co., Ca., U.S.	D2	82
San Mateo Mountains, mts., N.M., U.S.	D2	108
San Mateo Mountains, mts., N.M., U.S.	B2	108
San Matías, Golfo, b., Arg.	E4	56
San Miguel, El Sal.	H3	64
San Miguel, Ca., U.S.	D2	83
San Miguel, co., Co., U.S.	D2	83
San Miguel, co., N.M., U.S.	B5	108
San Miguel, stm., Bol.	F6	54
San Miguel, stm., Co., U.S.	C2	83
San Miguel de Allende, Mex.	G9	62
San Miguel del Monte, Arg.	D5	56
San Miguel de Tucumán, Arg.	B3	56
San Miguel el Alto, Mex.	G8	62
San Miguel Island, i., Ca., U.S.	E3	82
San Miguel Mountains, mts., Co., U.S.	D2	83
Sannār, Sudan	F12	42
Sannicandro Garganico, Italy	H10	14
San Nicolás, Phil.	o19	33b
San Nicolás de los Arroyos, Arg.	C4	56
San Nicolas Island, i., Ca., U.S.	F4	82
Sannikova, Proliv, strt., Russia	C21	24
Sanniquellie, Lib.	G4	42
Sano, Japan	F12	30
Sanok, Pol.	F22	8
San Onofre, Col.	C5	58
San Pablo, Col.	C5	58
San Pablo, Phil.	q19	32
San Pablo Balleza, Mex.	D6	62
San Pablo Bay, b., Ca., U.S.	g8	82
San Patricio, co., Tx., U.S.	E4	120
San Pedro, Punta, c., Chile	B2	56
San Pedro, stm., Az., U.S.	E5	80
San Pedro, Volcán, vol., Chile	A3	56
San Pedro Bay, b., Ca., U.S.	n12	82
San Pedro Carchá, Guat.	G2	64
San Pedro de las Colonias, Mex.	E8	62
San Pedro de Macorís, Dom. Rep.	E13	64
San Pedro Mártir, Sierra, mts., Mex.	B2	62
San Pedro Peaks, mts., N.M., U.S.	A3	108
San Pedro Sula, Hond.	G4	64
Sanpete, co., Ut., U.S.	D4	121
Sanpoil, stm., Wa., U.S.	A7	124
San Quintín, Cabo, c., Mex.	B1	62
San Rafael, Arg.	C3	56
San Rafael, Mex.	E9	62
San Rafael, Ca., U.S.	D2	82
San Rafael, N.M., U.S.	B2	108
San Rafael, stm., Ut., U.S.	D5	121
San Rafael Knob, mtn., Ut., U.S.	E5	121
San Rafael Mountains, mts., Ca., U.S.	E4	82
San Ramón, Nic.	G5	64
San Ramon, Ca., U.S.	h9	82
San Remo, Italy	F2	14
San Saba, Tx., U.S.	D3	120
San Saba, co., Tx., U.S.	D3	120
San Salvador, El Sal.	H3	64
San Salvador (Watling Island), i., Bah.	B10	64
San Salvador de Jujuy, Arg.	A3	56
Sansanné-Mango, Togo	F6	42
San Sebastián, Spain	B10	12
Sansepolcro, Italy	F7	14
San Severo, Italy	H10	14
San Simon, stm., Az., U.S.	E6	80
Sanski Most, Bos.	E11	14
Santa Ana, Bol.	F5	54
Santa Ana, Bol.	G5	54
Santa Ana, El Sal.	H3	64
Santa Ana, Mex.	E9	62
Santa Ana, Mex.	B4	62
Santa Ana, Ca., U.S.	F5	82
Santa Ana, stm., Ca., U.S.	n13	82
Santa Ana Indian Reservation, N.M., U.S.	h7	108
Santa Ana Mountains, mts., Ca., U.S.	n13	82
Santa Anna, Tx., U.S.	D3	120
Santa Bárbara, Mex.	D7	62
Santa Barbara, Ca., U.S.	E4	82
Santa Barbara, co., Ca., U.S.	E3	82
Santa Barbara Channel, strt., Ca., U.S.	E3	82
Santa Barbara Island, i., Ca., U.S.	F4	82
Santa Catalina, Gulf of, b., Ca., U.S.	F5	82
Santa Catalina Island, i., Ca., U.S.	F4	82
Santa Catalina Mountains, mts., Az., U.S.	E5	80
Santa Catarina, Ilha de, i., Braz.	B7	56
Santa Catarina, Cuba	C8	64
Santa Clara, Ca., U.S.	D2	82
Santa Clara, Ut., U.S.	F2	121
Santa Clara, co., Ca., U.S.	D3	82
Santa Clara, stm., Ca., U.S.	E4	82
Santa Claus, In., U.S.	H4	91
Santa Coloma de Farnés, Spain	D14	12
Santa Comba Dão, Port.	E3	12
Santa Cruz, Arg.	F3	56
Santa Cruz, Bol.	G6	54
Santa Cruz, C.R.	I5	64
Santa Cruz, Phil.	q19	33b
Santa Cruz, Ca., U.S.	D2	82
Santa Cruz, N.M., U.S.	B3	108
Santa Cruz, co., Az., U.S.	F5	80
Santa Cruz, co., Ca., U.S.	D2	82
Santa Cruz, stm., Az., U.S.	E4	80
Santa Cruz del Quiché, Guat.	G2	64
Santa Cruz de Tenerife, Spain	C2	42
Santa Cruz do Rio Pardo, Braz.	G4	57
Santa Cruz Island, i., Ca., U.S.	F4	82
Santa Elena, Punta, c., Ec.	I2	58
Santa Elena, Punta, c., Ec.	I2	58
Santa Eugenia, Spain	C2	12
Santa Eulalia, Spain	E10	12
Santa Eulalia del Río, Spain	G13	12
Santa Fe, Arg.	C4	56
Santa Fé, Braz.	C3	57
Santa Fé, Cuba	D6	64
Santa Fe, Spain	H8	12
Santa Fe, N.M., U.S.	B4	108
Santa Fe, Tx., U.S.	r14	120
Santa Fe, co., N.M., U.S.	B3	108
Santa Fe, stm., N.M., U.S.	h8	108
Santa Fe Baldy, mtn., N.M., U.S.	B4	108
Santa Fe de Bogotá, Col.	E5	58
Santa Inés, Isla, i., Chile	G2	56
Santa Isabel, Ec.	I3	58
Santa Isabel, i., Sol.Is.	A11	50
Santa Isabel see Malabo, Eq. Gui.	H7	42
Santa Lucia Range, mts., Ca., U.S.	E3	82
Santa Magdalena, Isla, i., Mex.	E3	62
Santa Margarita, Ca., U.S.	E3	82
Santa Margarita, Isla de, i., Mex.	E4	62
Santa Maria, Braz.	B6	56
Santa Maria, stm., Az., U.S.	C2	80
Santa Maria, Cabo de, c., Ang.	D2	44
Santa Maria do Suaçuí, Braz.	E7	57
Santa Maria Mountains, mts., Az., U.S.	C3	80
Santa Marta, Col.	B5	58
Santa Monica, Ca., U.S.	m12	82
Santana do Livramento, Braz.	C5	56
Santander, Col.	F4	58
Santander, Spain	B8	12
Sant' Antioco, Italy	J3	14
Santa Paula, Ca., U.S.	E4	82
Santaquín, Ut., U.S.	D4	121
Sant'Arcangelo, Italy	I11	14
Santarém, Braz.	D8	54
Santarém, Port.	F3	12
Santa Rita, Hond.	G6	58
Santa Rita, Hond.	G4	64
Santa Rosa, Arg.	D4	56
Santa Rosa, Arg.	C3	56
Santa Rosa, Ec.	I3	58
Santa Rosa, Ca., U.S.	C2	82
Santa Rosa, co., Fl., U.S.	u14	86
Santa Rosa Island, i., Ca., U.S.	E5	58
Santa Rosa [de Copán], Hond.	G3	64
Santa Rosa Island, i., Ca., U.S.	F3	82
Santa Rosa Island, i., Fl., U.S.	u14	86
Santa Rosa Range, mts., Nv., U.S.	B4	105
Šantarskije Ostrova, is., Russia	F21	24
Santa Teresa Gallura, Italy	H4	14
Santa Vitória do Palmar, Braz.	C6	56
Santa Ynez, Ca., U.S.	E3	82

Name	Map Ref	Page
Santee, Ca., U.S.	o16	82
Santee, stm., S.C., U.S.	E8	117
Santee Dam, S.C., U.S.	E7	117
Santee Indian Reservation, Ne., U.S.	B8	104
Santhià, Italy	D3	14
Santiago, Chile	C2	56
Santiago, Dom. Rep.	E12	64
Santiago, Pan.	J7	64
Santiago de Compostela, Spain	C3	12
Santiago de Cuba, Cuba	D10	64
Santiago del Estero, Arg.	B4	56
Santiago do Cacém, Port.	G3	12
Santiago Ixcuintla, Mex.	G7	62
Santiago Papasquiaro, Mex.	E7	62
Santiago Peak, mtn., Ca., U.S.	n13	82
Santiago Reservoir, res., Ca., U.S.	n13	82
Santiaguillo, Laguna de, l., Mex.	E7	62
Santiam Pass, Or., U.S.	C4	114
Sãntipur, India	I13	38
Santisteban del Puerto, Spain	G8	12
Santo Amaro, Braz.	B9	57
Santo Anastácio, Braz.	F3	57
Santo André, Braz.	G5	57
Santo Ângelo, Braz.	B6	56
Santo Antônio de Jesus, Braz.	B9	57
Santo Antônio do Içá, Braz.	D5	54
Santo Domingo, Dom. Rep.	E12	64
Santo Domingo, Nic.	H5	64
Santo Domingo de la Calzada, Spain	C9	12
Santo Domingo de los Colorados, Ec.	H3	58
Santo Domingo Indian Reservation, N.M., U.S.	h8	108
Santo Domingo Pueblo, N.M., U.S.	B3	108
Santoña, Spain	B8	12
Santos, Braz.	G5	57
Santos Dumont, Braz.	F7	57
Santo Tomás, Mex.	B1	62
Santo Tomé, Arg.	B5	56
San Valentín, Monte, mtn., Chile	F2	56
San Vicente, El Sal.	H3	64
San Vicente, Mex.	B1	62
San Vicente de Baracaldo, Spain	B9	12
San Vicente de la Barquera, Spain	B7	12
San Vicente del Caguán, Col.	F5	58
San Vicente Reservoir, res., Ca., U.S.	o16	82
San Xavier Indian Reservation, Az., U.S.	E4	80
Sanzao Dao, i., China	M2	28
Sanza Pombo, Ang.	C3	44
São Bento, Braz.	D10	54
São Borja, Braz.	B5	56
São Caetano do Sul, Braz.	G5	57
São Carlos, Braz.	G5	57
São Domingos, Braz.	B5	57
São Francisco, stm., Braz.	E11	54
São Francisco do Sul, Braz.	B7	56
São Gabriel, Braz.	E8	57
São João da Boa Vista, Braz.	F5	57
São João da Madeira, Port.	E3	12
São João del Rei, Braz.	F6	57
São Joaquim da Barra, Braz.	F5	57
São José do Rio Prêto, Braz.	F4	57
São José dos Campos, Braz.	G6	57
São Leopoldo, Braz.	B6	56
São Lourenço, Braz.	G6	57
São Lourenço, Pantanal de, sw., Braz.	G7	54
São Luís, Braz.	D10	54
São Manuel, Braz.	G4	57
São Mateus, Braz.	E9	57
Saona, Isla, i., Dom. Rep.	E13	64
Saône, stm., Fr.	F11	10
São Paulo, Braz.	G5	57
São Pedro do Ivaí, Braz.	G3	57
São Pedro do Sul, Port.	E3	12
São Romão, Braz.	D6	57
São Roque, Cabo de, c., Braz.	E11	54
São Sebastião, Ponta, c., Moz.	F7	44
São Sebastião do Paraíso, Braz.	F5	57
São Tomé, S. Tom./P.	A1	44
São Tomé, i., S. Tom./P.	A1	44
Sao Tome and Principe, ctry., Afr.	A1	44
São Vicente, Braz.	G5	57
São Vicente, Cabo de, c., Port.	H2	12
Sapé, Braz.	E11	54
Sapele, Nig.	G7	42
Sapelo Island, i., Ga., U.S.	E5	87
Sapitwa, mtn., Mwi.	E7	44
Sappa Creek, stm., U.S.	E5	104
Sapphire Mountains, mts., Mt., U.S.	D3	103
Sappington, Mo., U.S.	f13	102
Sapporo, Japan	p19	30a
Sapri, Italy	I10	14
Sapulpa, Ok., U.S.	B5	113
Sara Buri, Thai.	G6	34
Sarajevo, Bos.	F2	16
Saraland, Al., U.S.	E1	78
Saranac, Mi., U.S.	F5	99
Saranac, stm., N.Y., U.S.	F11	109
Saranac Lake, N.Y., U.S.	f10	109
Saranac Lakes, l., N.Y., U.S.	f10	109
Sarangani Islands, is., Phil.	D8	32
Saransk, Russia	G7	22
Sarapul, Russia	F8	22
Sarasota, Fl., U.S.	E4	86
Sarasota, co., Fl., U.S.	E4	86
Sarasota Bay, b., Fl., U.S.	E4	86
Saratoga, Ca., U.S.	k8	82
Saratoga, Tx., U.S.	D5	120
Saratoga, Wy., U.S.	E6	127
Saratoga, co., N.Y., U.S.	B7	109
Saratoga Lake, l., N.Y., U.S.	C7	109
Saratoga National Historical Park, N.Y., U.S.	B7	109
Saratoga Springs, N.Y., U.S.	B7	109
Saratov, Russia	G7	22
Saravane, Laos	G9	34
Sarcoxie, Mo., U.S.	D3	102
Sardalas, Libya	C8	42
Sardārshahr, India	F6	38
Sardegna, i., Italy	I3	14
Sardinia see Sardegna, i., Italy	I3	14
Sardis, Ga., U.S.	D5	87
Sardis, Ms., U.S.	A4	101
Sardis Lake, res., Ms., U.S.	A4	101
Sar-e Pol, Afg.	B1	38
Sarepta, La., U.S.	B2	95
Sarera, Teluk, b., Indon.	F10	32
Sargent, Ga., U.S.	C2	87
Sargent, Ne., U.S.	C6	104
Sargent, co., N.D., U.S.	C8	111
Sargodha, Pak.	D5	38
Sarh, Chad	G9	42
Sariñena, Spain	D11	12
Şarköy, Tur.	I11	16
Sarlat-la-Canéda, Fr.	H8	10
Sarmi, Indon.	F10	32
Sarmiento, Arg.	F3	56
Sãrna, Swe.	F9	6
Sarnia, Ont., Can.	E2	73
Sarpy, co., Ne., U.S.	C9	104
Sarralbe, Fr.	C14	10
Sarrebourg, Fr.	D14	10
Sarreguemines, Fr.	C14	10
Sarria, Spain	C4	12
Sartang, stm., Russia	D20	24
Sartell, Mn., U.S.	E4	100
Sarthe, stm., Fr.	E6	10
Sarufutsu, Japan	n20	30a
Sarzeau, Fr.	E4	10
Sasarām, India	H11	38
Sasebo, Japan	I2	30
Saskatchewan, prov., Can.	E3	75
Saskatchewan, stm., Can.	F12	66
Saskylach, Russia	C16	24
Sasovo, Russia	G24	18
Sassafras, stm., Md., U.S.	B5	97
Sassafras Mountain, mtn., U.S.	A2	117
Sassandra, I.C.	H4	42
Sassandra, stm., I.C.	G4	42
Sassari, Italy	I3	14
Sassnitz, Ger.	A13	8
Sassuolo, Italy	E5	14
Sastown, Lib.	H4	42
Satah Mountain, mtn., B.C., Can.	C5	69
Sata-misaki, c., Japan	L3	30
Satanta, Ks., U.S.	E3	93
Sãtāra, India	D2	37
Satilla, stm., Ga., U.S.	E5	87
Satka, Russia	F21	18
Satkānia, Bngl.	I15	38
Satna, India	H9	38
Sātpura Range, mts., India	J7	38
Satsuma, Al., U.S.	E1	78
Satsunan-shotō, is., Japan	v29	31b
Satu Mare, Rom.	B6	16
Satura, Russia	F22	18
Satus Creek, stm., Wa., U.S.	C5	124
Sauceda Mountains, mts., Az., U.S.	E3	80
Sauda, Nor.	G6	6
Saudi Arabia, ctry., Asia	D4	46
Saufley Field Naval Air Station, mil., Fl., U.S.	u14	86
Saugatuck, Mi., U.S.	F4	99
Saugatuck, Ct., U.S.	D2	84
Saugatucket, stm., R.I., U.S.	F4	116
Saugatuck Reservoir, res., Ct., U.S.	D2	84
Saugerties, N.Y., U.S.	C7	109
Saugus, Ma., U.S.	B5	98
Saugus, stm., Ma., U.S.	g11	98
Sauk, co., Wi., U.S.	E4	126
Sauk, stm., Mn., U.S.	E4	100
Sauk, stm., Wa., U.S.	A4	124
Sauk Centre, Mn., U.S.	E4	100
Sauk City, Wi., U.S.	E4	126
Sauk Rapids, Mn., U.S.	E4	100
Saukville, Wi., U.S.	E6	126
Saulgau, Ger.	G9	8
Saulnierville, N.S., Can.	E3	71
Sault-au-Mouton, Que., Can.	A8	74
Sault Sainte Marie, Ont., Can.	p18	73
Sault Sainte Marie, Mi., U.S.	B6	99
Saumarez Reef, rf., Austl.	D10	50
Saumur, Fr.	E6	10
Saunders, co., Ne., U.S.	C9	104
Saunderstown, R.I., U.S.	E4	116
Saurimo, Ang.	C4	44
Sausalito, Ca., U.S.	D2	82
Sava, Italy	I12	14
Sava, stm., Eur.	E3	16
Savage, Md., U.S.	B4	97
Savage, stm., Md., U.S.	k12	97
Savage River Reservoir, res., Md., U.S.	k12	97
Savanna, Il., U.S.	A3	90
Savanna, Ok., U.S.	C6	113
Savannah, Ga., U.S.	D5	87
Savannah, Mo., U.S.	B3	102
Savannah, Tn., U.S.	B3	119
Savannah, stm., U.S.	F5	117
Savannah River Plant, sci., S.C., U.S.	E4	117
Savannakhet, Laos	F8	34
Savanna Lake, l., Md., U.S.	D6	97
Savanna-la-Mar, Jam.	E8	64
Savaştepe, Tur.	J11	16
Save (Sabi), stm., Afr.	F6	44
Savenay, Fr.	E5	10
Saverdun, Fr.	I8	10
Saverne, Fr.	D14	10
Savigliano, Italy	E2	14
Saville Dam, Ct., U.S.	B4	84
Savona, Italy	E3	14
Savonlinna, Fin.	F17	6
Savonranta, Fin.	E17	6
Savoonga, Ak., U.S.	C5	79
Savoy, Il., U.S.	C5	90
Savu Sea see Sawu, Laut, Indon.	G7	32
Sawai Mādhopur, India	G7	38
Sawākin, Sudan	E13	42
Sawang, Indon.	N7	34
Sawatch Range, mts., Co., U.S.	B4	83
Sawdā', Qurnat as-, mtn., Leb.	B5	40
Sawel Mountain, mtn., N. Ire., U.K.	G5	7
Sawhāj, Egypt	C12	42
Sawknah, Libya	C9	42
Sawnee Mountain, mtn., Ga., U.S.	B2	87
Sawtooth Mountains, mts., Id., U.S.	F4	89
Sawtooth National Recreation Area, Id., U.S.	E3	89
Sawu, Laut (Savu Sea), Indon.	G7	32
Sawu, Pulau, i., Indon.	H7	32
Sawwān, Ard as-, pl., Jord.	D5	40
Sawyer, co., Wi., U.S.	C2	126
Sawyerville, Que., Can.	D6	74
Saxmundham, Eng., U.K.	I14	7
Saxonburg, Pa., U.S.	E2	115
Saxtons, stm., Vt., U.S.	E3	122
Saxtons River, Vt., U.S.	E3	122
Sayaboury, Laos	E6	34
Sayan Mountains (Sajany), mts., Asia	G12	24
Sayaxché, Guat.	F2	64
Saybrook, Il., U.S.	C5	90
Saybrook, Mo., U.S.	D8	102
Saybrook Manor, Ct., U.S.	D6	84
Saydā (Sidon), Leb.	C4	40
Saydel, U.S.	e8	92
Sayhūt, Yemen	E5	46
Saylesville, R.I., U.S.	B4	116
Saylorsburg, Pa., U.S.	E11	115
Saylorville, Ia., U.S.	e8	92
Saylorville Lake, res., Ia., U.S.	C4	92
Sayre, Al., U.S.	B3	78
Sayre, Ok., U.S.	B2	113
Sayre, Pa., U.S.	C8	115
Sayreville, N.J., U.S.	C4	107
Sayula, Mex.	H8	62
Say'ūn, Yemen	E4	46
Sayville, N.Y., U.S.	n15	109
Scafell Pikes, mtn., Eng., U.K.	G9	7
Scalp Level, Pa., U.S.	F4	115
Scanlon, Mn., U.S.	D6	100
Scapegoat Mountain, mtn., Mt., U.S.	C3	103
Ščapino, Russia	F25	24
Scappoose, Or., U.S.	B4	114
Scarborough, Ont., Can.	m15	73
Scarborough, Trin.	I17	64
Scarborough, Me., U.S.	E2	96
Scarbro, W.V., U.S.	n13	125
Scarsdale, N.Y., U.S.	h13	109
Ščelkovo, Russia	F21	18
Ščerbakovo, Russia	D26	24
Schaefferstown, Pa., U.S.	F9	115
Schaffhausen, Switz.	E15	10
Schaller, Ia., U.S.	B2	92
Schaumburg, Il., U.S.	h8	90
Schell Creek Range, mts., Nv., U.S.	D7	105
Schenectady, N.Y., U.S.	C7	109
Schenectady, co., N.Y., U.S.	C6	109
Schererville, In., U.S.	B3	91
Schertz, Tx., U.S.	h7	120
Schiller Park, Il., U.S.	k9	90
Schio, Italy	D6	14
Schladming, Aus.	H13	8
Schleicher, co., Tx., U.S.	D2	120
Schleiden, Ger.	E6	8
Schleswig, Ger.	A9	8
Schleswig, Ia., U.S.	B2	92
Schley, co., Ga., U.S.	D2	87
Schneverdingen, Ger.	B9	8
Schofield, Wi., U.S.	D4	126
Schofield Barracks, mil., Hi., U.S.	g9	88
Schoharie, N.Y., U.S.	C6	109
Schoharie, co., N.Y., U.S.	C6	109
Schoharie Creek, stm., N.Y., U.S.	C6	109
Schönebeck, Ger.	B13	8
Schongau, Ger.	H10	8
Schoodic Lake, l., Me., U.S.	C4	96
Schoolcraft, Mi., U.S.	F5	99
Schoolcraft, co., Mi., U.S.	B4	99
Schramberg, Ger.	G8	8
Schroon Lake, l., N.Y., U.S.	B7	109
Schulenburg, Tx., U.S.	E4	120
Schulter, Ok., U.S.	B6	113
Schurz, Nv., U.S.	E3	105
Schuyler, Ne., U.S.	C8	104
Schuyler, co., Il., U.S.	C3	90
Schuyler, co., Mo., U.S.	A5	102
Schuyler, co., N.Y., U.S.	C4	109
Schuylkill, co., Pa., U.S.	E9	115
Schuylkill, stm., Pa., U.S.	F10	115
Schuylkill Haven, Pa., U.S.	E9	115
Schwabach, Ger.	F11	8
Schwaben, hist. reg., Ger.	G10	8
Schwäbische Alb, mts., Ger.	G9	8
Schwäbisch Gmünd, Ger.	G9	8
Schwäbisch Hall, Ger.	F9	8
Schwandorf in Bayern, Ger.	F12	8
Schwaner, Pegunungan, mts., Indon.	F5	32
Schwarzwald, mts., Ger.	G8	8
Schwaz, Aus.	H11	8
Schwechat, Aus.	G16	8
Schwedt, Ger.	B14	8
Schweinfurt, Ger.	E10	8
Schwerin, Ger.	B11	8
Schwyz, Switz.	E15	10
Sciacca, Italy	L8	14
Scicli, Italy	M9	14
Science Hill, Ky., U.S.	C5	94
Scilly, Isles of, is., Eng., U.K.	L6	7
Scio, Or., U.S.	C4	114
Scioto, co., Oh., U.S.	D3	112
Scioto, stm., Oh., U.S.	B2	112
Scituate, Ma., U.S.	B6	98
Scituate, co., R.I., U.S.	C3	116
Scituate Reservoir, res., R.I., U.S.	C3	116
Scobey, Mt., U.S.	B11	103
Scofield Reservoir, res., Ut., U.S.	D4	121
Ščokino, Russia	G20	18
Scotch Plains, N.J., U.S.	B4	107
Scotia, Ca., U.S.	B1	82
Scotia, N.Y., U.S.	C7	109
Scotland, Ont., Can.	D4	73
Scotland, S.D., U.S.	D8	118
Scotland, co., Mo., U.S.	A5	102
Scotland, co., N.C., U.S.	C3	110
Scotland, ter., U.K.	D8	7
Scotland Neck, N.C., U.S.	A5	110
Scotlandville, La., U.S.	D4	95
Scotrun, Pa., U.S.	D11	115
Scott, co., Ar., U.S.	C1	81
Scott, co., Il., U.S.	D3	90
Scott, co., In., U.S.	G6	91
Scott, co., Ia., U.S.	C7	92
Scott, co., Ks., U.S.	D3	93
Scott, co., Ky., U.S.	B5	94
Scott, co., Mn., U.S.	F5	100
Scott, co., Mo., U.S.	D8	102
Scott, co., Tn., U.S.	C9	119
Scott, co., Va., U.S.	f9	123
Scott, Cape, c., B.C., Can.	D3	69
Scott, Mount, mtn., Or., U.S.	E4	114
Scott Air Force Base, mil., Il., U.S.	E4	90
Scott City, Ks., U.S.	D3	93
Scott City, Mo., U.S.	D8	102
Scottdale, Ga., U.S.	h8	87
Scottdale, Pa., U.S.	F2	115
Scott Islands, is., B.C., Can.	F7	66
Scott Mountain, mtn., Id., U.S.	E3	89
Scott Peak, mtn., Id., U.S.	E6	89
Scott Reef, rf., Austl.	B4	50
Scott Reservoir, res., N.C., U.S.	A1	110
Scottsbluff, Ne., U.S.	C2	104
Scotts Bluff, co., Ne., U.S.	C2	104
Scotts Bluff National Monument, Ne., U.S.	C2	104
Scottsboro, Al., U.S.	A3	78
Scottsburg, In., U.S.	G6	91
Scottsdale, Austl.	H9	50
Scottsdale, Az., U.S.	D4	80
Scottsville, Ky., U.S.	D3	94
Scottsville, N.Y., U.S.	B3	109
Scottville, Mi., U.S.	E4	99
Scourie, Scot., U.K.	C7	7
Scranton, Ks., U.S.	D8	93
Scranton, Pa., U.S.	D10	115
Scranton, S.C., U.S.	D8	117
Screven, Ga., U.S.	E4	87
Screven, co., Ga., U.S.	D5	87
Scribner, Ne., U.S.	C9	104
Scugog, Lake, l., Ont., Can.	C6	73
Scurry, co., Tx., U.S.	C2	120
Scutari, Lake, l., Eur.	G3	16
Seaboard, N.C., U.S.	A5	110
Seabreeze, De., U.S.	F5	85
Seabrook, N.H., U.S.	E5	106
Seabrook, Tx., U.S.	r14	120
Seabrook Island, i., S.C., U.S.	F7	117
Seadrift, Tx., U.S.	E4	120
Seaford, De., U.S.	F3	85
Seaford, Va., U.S.	h15	123
Seaforth, Ont., Can.	D3	73
Seagoville, Tx., U.S.	n10	120
Seagraves, Tx., U.S.	C1	120
Seaham, Eng., U.K.	G11	7
Sea Isle City, N.J., U.S.	E3	107
Seal, stm., Man., Can.	E13	66
Seal Cove, Newf., Can.	D3	72
Seal Point, c., P.E.I., Can.	C5	71
Seal Rock, Or., U.S.	C2	114
Sealy, Tx., U.S.	E4	120
Seaman, Oh., U.S.	D2	112
Seaman Range, mts., Nv., U.S.	F6	105
Searchlight, Nv., U.S.	H7	105
Searcy, Ar., U.S.	B4	81
Searcy, co., Ar., U.S.	B3	81
Searles Lake, l., Ca., U.S.	E5	82
Searsport, Me., U.S.	D4	96
Seaside, Or., U.S.	B3	114
Seat Pleasant, Md., U.S.	C4	97
Seattle, Wa., U.S.	B3	124
Seattle-Tacoma International Airport, Wa., U.S.	f11	124
Seaview, Wa., U.S.	C1	124
Sebago Lake, Me., U.S.	E2	96
Šebalino, Russia	G11	24
Sebastian, Fl., U.S.	E6	86
Sebastian, co., Ar., U.S.	B1	81
Sebastian, Cape, c., Or., U.S.	E2	114
Sebastian Inlet, b., Fl., U.S.	E6	86
Sebastián Vizcaíno, Bahía, b., Mex.	C2	62
Sebastícook Lake, l., Me., U.S.	D3	96
Sebec Lake, l., Me., U.S.	C3	96
Sebeka, Mn., U.S.	D3	100
Sebewaing, Mi., U.S.	E7	99
Seboeis, stm., Me., U.S.	B4	96
Seboeis Lake, l., Me., U.S.	C4	96
Seboomook Lake, l., Me., U.S.	C3	96
Sebree, Ky., U.S.	C2	94
Sebring, Fl., U.S.	E5	86
Sebring, Oh., U.S.	B4	112
Secaucus, N.J., U.S.	h8	107
Sechelt, B.C., Can.	E6	69
Second Lake, l., N.H., U.S.	f7	106
Second Mesa, Az., U.S.	B5	80
Secret Lake, l., R.I., U.S.	E4	116
Section, Al., U.S.	A4	78
Security, Co., U.S.	C6	83
Sedalia, Mo., U.S.	C4	102
Sedan, Fr.	C11	10
Sedan, Ks., U.S.	E7	93
Sedano, Spain	C8	12
Sedgewick, Alta., Can.	C5	68
Sedgwick, Mount, mtn., N.M., U.S.	B1	108
Sedgwick, Ks., U.S.	E6	93
Sedgwick, co., Co., U.S.	A8	83
Sedgwick, co., Ks., U.S.	E6	93
Sedley, Va., U.S.	D6	123
Sedona, Az., U.S.	C4	80
Sedro Woolley, Wa., U.S.	A3	124
Seeheim, Nmb.	G3	44
Seekonk, Ma., U.S.	C5	98
Seekonk, stm., R.I., U.S.	C4	116
Seeley, Ca., U.S.	F6	82
Seeley Lake, Mt., U.S.	C3	103
Seelyville, In., U.S.	F3	91
Sées, Fr.	D7	10
Segamat, Malay.	M7	34
Ségou, Mali	F4	42
Segovia, Col.	D5	58
Segovia, Spain	E7	12
Segré, Fr.	E6	10
Seguam Island, i., Ak., U.S.	E5	79
Seguam Pass, strt., Ak., U.S.	E5	79
Séguédine, Niger	D8	42
Seguin, Tx., U.S.	E4	120
Sehore, India	I7	38
Seia, Port.	E4	12
Seiling, Ok., U.S.	A3	113
Seinäjoki, Fin.	E14	6
Seine, stm., Fr.	C7	10
Seki, Tur.	M13	16
Sekiu, Wa., U.S.	A1	124
Sekondi-Takoradi, Ghana	H5	42
Selah, Wa., U.S.	C5	124
Selaru, stm., Indon.	G9	32
Selatan, Tanjung, c., Indon.	F5	32
Selawik, Ak., U.S.	B7	79
Selawik Lake, l., Ak., U.S.	B7	79
Selayar, Pulau, i., Indon.	G7	32
Selb, Ger.	E12	8
Selby, S.D., U.S.	B5	118
Selbyville, De., U.S.	G5	85
Selçuk, Tur.	L11	16
Seldovia, Ak., U.S.	D9	79
Selemdža, stm., Russia	G20	24
Selenn'ach, stm., Russia	D21	24
Sélestat, Fr.	D14	10
Sélibaby, Maur.	E3	42
Selichova, Zaliv, b., Russia	E25	24
Seligman, Az., U.S.	B3	80
Selinsgrove, Pa., U.S.	E8	115
Selkirk, Man., Can.	D3	70
Selkirk, Scot., U.K.	F10	7
Selkirk Mountains, mts., N.A.	F9	66
Sellersburg, In., U.S.	H6	91
Sellersville, Pa., U.S.	F11	115
Selles-sur-Cher, Fr.	E8	10
Sells, Az., U.S.	F4	80
Selma, Al., U.S.	C2	78
Selma, Ca., U.S.	D4	82
Selma, In., U.S.	D7	91
Selma, N.C., U.S.	B4	110
Selmer, Tn., U.S.	B3	119
Selva, Arg.	B4	56
Selvas, pr., Braz.	E6	54
Selway, stm., Id., U.S.	C3	89
Selwyn Mountains, mts., Can.	D6	66
Semara, W. Sah.	C3	42
Semarang, Indon.	m15	32
Semeru, Gunung, vol., Indon.	n16	33a
Seminoe Mountains, mts., Wy., U.S.	D6	127
Seminoe Reservoir, res., Wy., U.S.	D6	127
Seminole, Ok., U.S.	B5	113
Seminole, Tx., U.S.	C1	120
Seminole, co., Fl., U.S.	D5	86
Seminole, co., Ga., U.S.	F2	87
Seminole, co., Ok., U.S.	B5	113
Seminole, Lake, res., U.S.	F2	87
Semipalatinsk, Kaz.	G10	24
Semisopochnoi Island, i., Ak., U.S.	E3	79
Semmes, Al., U.S.	E1	78
Semonaicha, Kaz.	G10	24
Semur-en-Auxois, Fr.	E11	10
Sên, stm., Camb.	H8	34
Sena, Moz.	E6	44
Senachwine Lake, l., Il., U.S.	B4	90
Senador Pompeu, Braz.	E11	54
Sena Madureira, Braz.	E5	54
Senanga, Zam.	E4	44
Senath, Mo., U.S.	E7	102
Senatobia, Ms., U.S.	A4	101
Sendai, Japan	K3	30
Sendai, Japan	D13	30
Seneca, Il., U.S.	B5	90
Seneca, Ks., U.S.	C7	93
Seneca, Mo., U.S.	E3	102
Seneca, Pa., U.S.	D2	115
Seneca, S.C., U.S.	B2	117
Seneca, co., N.Y., U.S.	C4	109
Seneca, co., Oh., U.S.	A2	112
Seneca Falls, N.Y., U.S.	C4	109
Seneca Lake, l., N.Y., U.S.	C4	109
Senecaville Lake, res., Oh., U.S.	C4	112
Senegal (Sénégal), ctry., Afr.	F3	42
Sénégal, stm., Afr.	E3	42
Senekal, S. Afr.	G5	44
Senftenberg, Ger.	D13	8
Senigallia, Italy	F8	14
Senise, Italy	I11	14
Senmonorom, Camb.	H9	34
Senneterre, Que., Can.	k11	74
Sennori, Italy	I3	14
Senoia, Ga., U.S.	C2	87
Sens, Fr.	D10	10
Senta, Yugo.	D4	16
Sentinel, Ok., U.S.	B2	113
Seo de Urgel, Spain	C13	12
Seoni, India	I8	38
Seoul see Sŏul, S. Kor.	D12	30
Sept-Îles (Seven Islands), Que., Can.	h13	74
Sepulga, stm., Al., U.S.	D3	78
Sepúlveda, Spain	D8	12
Sequatchie, co., Tn., U.S.	D8	119
Sequatchie, stm., Tn., U.S.	D8	119
Sequim, Wa., U.S.	A2	124
Sequoia National Park, Ca., U.S.	D4	82
Sequoyah, co., Ok., U.S.	B7	113
Seraing, Bel.	E5	8
Seram, i., Indon.	F8	32
Seram, Laut (Ceram Sea), Indon.	F8	32
Serang, Indon.	m13	33a
Serbia, state, Yugo.	F5	16
Seremban, Malay.	M6	34
Serengeti Plain, pl., Tan.	B6	44

Name	Map Ref	Page
erenje, Zam.	D6	44
ergeant Bluff, Ia., U.S.	B1	92
ergeja Kirova, Ostrova, is., Russia	B11	24
ergijev Podad, Russia	E21	18
erowe, Bots.	F5	44
erpa, Port.	H4	12
erpuchov, Russia	G20	18
errai, Grc.	H7	16
erra San Bruno, Italy	K11	14
erra Talhada, Braz.	E11	54
erres, Fr.	H12	10
errezuela, Arg.	C3	56
erri, Italy	J4	14
errinha, Braz.	F11	54
ertã, Port.	F3	12
esfontein, Nmb.	E2	44
esheke, Zam.	E4	44
essa Aurunca, Italy	H8	14
esser, Il., U.S.	E4	90
estri Levante, Italy	E4	14
ete Lagoas, Braz.	E6	57
eth, W.V., U.S.	C3	125
étif, Alg.	A7	42
eto, Japan	G10	30
eto-naikai, Japan	H6	30
etúbal, Port.	G3	12
eul, Lac, l., Ont., Can.	o16	73
eul Choix Point, c., Mi., U.S.	C5	99
evan, ozero, l., Arm.	I7	22
evastopol', Ukr.	I4	22
evčenko, Kaz.	I8	22
even Devils Lake, res., Ar., U.S.	D4	81
even Devils Mountains, mts., Id., U.S.	D2	89
even Hills, Oh., U.S.	h9	112
even Mile Beach, N.J., U.S.	E3	107
évérac-le-Château, Fr.	H10	10
evern, Md., U.S.	B4	97
evern, stm., Ont., Can.	n17	73
evern, stm., Eng., U.K.	J10	7
evernaja Dvina, stm., Russia	E6	22
evernaja Zeml'a, is., Russia	B13	24
everna Park, Md., U.S.	B4	97
ever River, b., Md., U.S.	B4	97
everodvinsk, Russia	E5	22
evero-Kuril'sk, Russia	G25	24
Severo-Sibirskaja Nizmennost', pl., Russia	C13	24
Severo-Zadonsk, Russia	G21	18
evettijärvi, Fin.	B17	6
Sevier, co., Ar., U.S.	D1	81
Sevier, co., Tn., U.S.	D10	119
Sevier, co., Ut., U.S.	E4	121
Sevier, stm., Ut., U.S.	D3	121
Sevier Bridge Reservoir, res., Ut., U.S.	D4	121
Sevier Lake, l., Ut., U.S.	E2	121
evierville, Tn., U.S.	D10	119
evilla, Col.	E5	58
evilla, Spain	H6	12
eville, Oh., U.S.	A4	112
eville see Sevilla, Spain	H6	12
ewanee, Tn., U.S.	D8	119
eward, Ak., U.S.	C10	79
eward, Ne., U.S.	D8	104
eward, co., Ks., U.S.	E3	93
eward, co., Ne., U.S.	D8	104
eward Peninsula, pen., Ak., U.S.	B7	79
ewickley, Pa., U.S.	E1	115
exsmith, Alta., Can.	B1	68
eychelles, ctry., Afr.	B11	44
eydisfjörður, Ice.	B5	4
eymour, Ct., U.S.	D3	84
eymour, In., U.S.	G6	91
eymour, Ia., U.S.	D4	92
eymour, Mo., U.S.	D5	102
eymour, Tx., U.S.	C3	120
eymour, Wi., U.S.	D5	126
eymour Inlet, b., B.C., Can.	D4	69
Seymour Johnson Air Force Base, mil., N.C., U.S.	B5	110
eymour Lake, l., Vt., U.S.	B4	122
eymourville, La., U.S.	h9	95
eyne, Fr.	H13	10
eyssel, Fr.	G12	10
ézanne, Fr.	D10	10
ezze, Italy	H8	14
fax, Tun.	B8	42
's-Gravenhage (The Hague), Neth.	C4	8
Shabbona, Il., U.S.	B5	90
Shache, China	A7	38
Shackelford, co., Tx., U.S.	C3	120
Shackleton Ice Shelf, Ant.	C22	47
Shaddādī, Syria	A7	40
Shadehill Dam, S.D., U.S.	B3	118
Shadehill Reservoir, res., S.D., U.S.	B3	118
Shadow Mountain National Recreation Area, Co., U.S.	A4	83
Shady Cove, Or., U.S.	E4	114
Shady Side, Md., U.S.	C4	97
Shadyside, Oh., U.S.	C5	112
Shady Spring, W.V., U.S.	D3	125
Shafer, Lake, l., In., U.S.	C4	91
Shafer Butte, mtn., Id., U.S.	F2	89
Shafter, Ca., U.S.	E4	82
Shaftsbury, Vt., U.S.	E2	122
Shāhdādkot, Pak.	G2	38
Shahdol, India	I9	38
Shāhjahānpur, India	G8	38
Shāh Jūy, Afg.	D2	38
Shahrak, Afg.	C1	38
Shājāpur, India	I7	38
Shakawe, Bots.	E4	44
Shaker Heights, Oh., U.S.	A4	112
Shakhty see Sachty, Russia	G6	22
Shaki, Nig.	G6	42
Shakopee, Mn., U.S.	F5	100
Shaler Mountains, mts., N.W. Ter., Can.	B10	66
Shallotte, N.C., U.S.	D4	110
Shallotte Inlet, b., N.C., U.S.	D4	110
Shallowater, Tx., U.S.	C2	120
Shām, Bādiyat ash-, des., Asia	C6	40
Shām, Jabal ash-, mtn., Oman	C6	46
Shamokin, Pa., U.S.	E8	115
Shamokin Dam, Pa., U.S.	E8	115
Shamrock, Tx., U.S.	B2	120
Shandī, Sudan	E12	42
Shandong, prov., China	D10	26
Shandong Bandao, pen., China	D11	26
Shanghai, China	D10	28
Shanghai Shih, China	E11	26
Shangqiu, China	A4	28
Shangrao, China	G6	28
Shangshui, China	B3	28
Shangzhi, China	B12	28
Shannock, R.I., U.S.	B1	87
Shannon, Il., U.S.	A4	90
Shannon, Ms., U.S.	A5	101
Shannon, co., Mo., U.S.	D6	102
Shannon, co., S.D., U.S.	D3	118
Shannon, stm., Ire.	I3	7
Shannon, Lake, l., Wa., U.S.	A4	124
Shannontown, S.C., U.S.	D7	117
Shantou (Swatow), China	L5	28
Shantung Peninsula see Shandong Bandao, pen., China	D11	26
Shānxī, prov., China	D8	26
Shānxī, prov., China	D9	26
Shanyin, China	D9	26
Shaoguan, China	K2	28
Shaowu, China	H6	28
Shaoxing, China	E9	28
Shaoyang, China	F9	26
Shark Bay, b., Austl.	E2	50
Sharkey, co., Ms., U.S.	C3	101
Shark Point, c., Fl., U.S.	H5	86
Sharktooth Mountain, mtn., B.C., Can.		
Sharon, Ct., U.S.	B2	84
Sharon, Ma., U.S.	B5	98
Sharon, Pa., U.S.	D1	115
Sharon, Tn., U.S.	A3	119
Sharon, Wi., U.S.	F5	126
Sharon Hill, Pa., U.S.	p20	115
Sharon Park, Oh., U.S.	n12	112
Sharon Springs, Ks., U.S.	D2	93
Sharonville, Oh., U.S.	n13	112
Sharp, co., Ar., U.S.	A4	81
Sharpe, Lake, l., res., S.D., U.S.	C6	118
Sharpes, Fl., U.S.	D6	86
Sharpley, De., U.S.	h7	85
Sharpsburg, Md., U.S.	B2	97
Sharpsburg, N.C., U.S.	B5	110
Sharpsburg, Pa., U.S.	k14	115
Sharpsville, In., U.S.	D5	91
Sharpsville, Pa., U.S.	D1	115
Sharptown, Md., U.S.	C6	97
Sharqīyah, Aṣ-Ṣaḥrā' ash- (Arabian Desert), des., Egypt	C12	42
Shashi, China	E9	26
Shashi, stm., Afr.	F5	44
Shasta, co., Ca., U.S.	B3	82
Shasta, Mount, vol., Ca., U.S.	B2	82
Shasta, Lake, res., Ca., U.S.	B2	82
Shattuck, Ok., U.S.	A2	113
Shaw, Ms., U.S.	B3	101
Shaw Air Force Base, mil., S.C., U.S.	D7	117
Shawano, Wi., U.S.	D5	126
Shawano, co., Wi., U.S.	D5	126
Shawano Lake, l., Wi., U.S.	D5	126
Shawinigan, Que., Can.	C5	74
Shawinigan-Sud, Que., Can.	C5	74
Shawnee, Ks., U.S.	k16	93
Shawnee, Ok., U.S.	B5	113
Shawnee, co., Ks., U.S.	D8	93
Shawneetown, Il., U.S.	F5	90
Shawsheen, stm., Ma., U.S.	f11	98
Shaybārā, i., Sau. Ar.	C2	46
Shaykh, Jabal ash-, mtn., Asia	C4	40
Shebele (Shebelle), stm., Afr.	G3	46
Sheberghān, Afg.	B1	38
Sheboygan, Wi., U.S.	E6	126
Sheboygan, co., Wi., U.S.	E6	126
Sheboygan, stm., Wi., U.S.	k10	126
Sheboygan Falls, Wi., U.S.	E6	126
Shediac, N.B., Can.	C5	71
Sheenjek, stm., Ak., U.S.	B11	79
Sheep Mountain, mtn., Az., U.S.	E1	80
Sheep Mountain, mtn., Wy., U.S.	B5	127
Sheep Mountain, mtn., Wy., U.S.	C2	127
Sheep Peak, mtn., Nv., U.S.	G6	105
Sheep Range, mts., Nv., U.S.	G6	105
Sheet Harbour, N.S., Can.	E7	71
Sheffield, Eng., U.K.	H11	7
Sheffield, Al., U.S.	A2	78
Sheffield, Il., U.S.	B4	90
Sheffield, Ia., U.S.	B4	92
Sheffield, Pa., U.S.	C3	115
Sheffield Lake, Oh., U.S.	A3	112
Sheila, N.B., Can.	B5	71
Shēkhābād, Afg.	C3	38
Shekhūpura, India	E5	38
Shelagyote Peak, mtn., B.C., Can.	B4	69
Shelbiana, Ky., U.S.	C7	94
Shelbina, Mo., U.S.	B5	102
Shelburn, In., U.S.	F3	91
Shelburne, Ont., Can.	C4	73
Shelburne Falls, Ma., U.S.	A2	98
Shelburne Pond, l., Vt., U.S.	C2	122
Shelby, Al., U.S.	B3	78
Shelby, In., U.S.	B3	91
Shelby, Ia., U.S.	C2	92
Shelby, Mi., U.S.	E4	99
Shelby, Ms., U.S.	B3	101
Shelby, Mt., U.S.	B5	103
Shelby, Ne., U.S.	C8	104
Shelby, N.C., U.S.	B1	110
Shelby, Oh., U.S.	B3	112
Shelby, co., Al., U.S.	B3	78
Shelby, co., Il., U.S.	D5	90
Shelby, co., Ia., U.S.	C2	92
Shelby, co., Ky., U.S.	B4	94
Shelby, co., Mo., U.S.	B5	102
Shelby, co., Oh., U.S.	B1	112
Shelby, co., Tn., U.S.	B2	119
Shelby, co., Tx., U.S.	D5	120
Shelbyville, Il., U.S.	D5	90
Shelbyville, In., U.S.	F6	91
Shelbyville, Ky., U.S.	B4	94
Shelbyville, Tn., U.S.	B5	119
Shelbyville, Lake, res., Il., U.S.	D5	90
Sheldon, Ia., U.S.	A2	92
Sheldon, Tx., U.S.	r14	120
Shelikof Strait, strt., Ak., U.S.	D9	79
Shell Creek, stm., Wy., U.S.	A2	83
Shell Creek, stm., Wy., U.S.	B5	127
Shelley, Id., U.S.	F6	89
Shell Lake, Wi., U.S.	C2	126
Shell Lake, l., Mn., U.S.	D3	100
Shell Lake, l., Wi., U.S.	C2	126
Shellman, Ga., U.S.	E2	87
Shell Rock, Ia., U.S.	B5	92
Shell Rock, stm., Ia., U.S.	B5	92
Shellsburg, Ia., U.S.	B6	92
Shelly Mountain, mtn., Id., U.S.	F5	89
Shelter Island, N.Y., U.S.	m16	109
Shelton, Ct., U.S.	D3	84
Shelton, Ne., U.S.	D7	104
Shelton, Wa., U.S.	B2	124
Shemya Air Force Base, mil., Ak., U.S.	E2	79
Shenandoah, Ia., U.S.	D2	92
Shenandoah, Pa., U.S.	E9	115
Shenandoah, Va., U.S.	B4	123
Shenandoah, co., Va., U.S.	B4	123
Shenandoah, stm., U.S.	A5	123
Shenandoah, North Fork, stm., Va., U.S.	B4	123
Shenandoah, South Fork, stm., Va., U.S.	B4	123
Shenandoah Mountain, mtn., U.S.	B3	123
Shenandoah National Park, Va., U.S.	B4	123
Shenango River Lake, res., U.S.	D1	115
Shengfang, China	D10	26
Shengze, China	E9	28
Shenipsit Lake, l., Ct., U.S.	B6	84
Shenyang (Mukden), China	C11	26
Shenzha, China	E13	38
Shepaug, stm., Ct., U.S.	C2	84
Shepaug Dam, Ct., U.S.	D2	84
Shepaug Reservoir, res., Ct., U.S.	C2	84
Shepherd, Mi., U.S.	E6	99
Shepherd, Tx., U.S.	D5	120
Shepherdstown, W.V., U.S.	B7	125
Shepherdsville, Ky., U.S.	C4	94
Sheppard Air Force Base, mil., Tx., U.S.	C3	120
Shepparton, Austl.	G9	50
Sherborn, Ma., U.S.	h10	98
Sherbro Island, i., S.L.	G3	42
Sherbrooke, Que., Can.	D6	74
Sherburn, Mn., U.S.	G4	100
Sherburne, co., Mn., U.S.	E5	100
Sheridan, Ar., U.S.	C3	81
Sheridan, Il., U.S.	B5	90
Sheridan, In., U.S.	D5	91
Sheridan, Mi., U.S.	E5	99
Sheridan, Mt., U.S.	E4	103
Sheridan, Or., U.S.	B3	114
Sheridan, Wy., U.S.	B6	127
Sheridan, co., Ks., U.S.	C3	93
Sheridan, co., Mt., U.S.	B12	103
Sheridan, co., Ne., U.S.	B3	104
Sheridan, co., N.D., U.S.	B5	111
Sheridan, co., Wy., U.S.	B5	127
Sheridan, Mount, mtn., Wy., U.S.	B2	127
Sheringham Cromer, Eng., U.K.	I14	7
Sherman, Tx., U.S.	C4	120
Sherman, co., Ks., U.S.	C2	93
Sherman, co., Ne., U.S.	C6	104
Sherman, co., Or., U.S.	B6	114
Sherman, co., Tx., U.S.	A2	120
Sherman Reservoir, res., Ne., U.S.	C7	104
Sherrelwood, Co., U.S.	*B6	83
Sherrill, N.Y., U.S.	B5	109
's-Hertogenbosch, Neth.	D5	8
Sherwood, Ar., U.S.	C3	81
Sherwood, Or., U.S.	h12	114
Sherwood, Wi., U.S.	h9	126
Sherwood Manor, Ct., U.S.	B5	84
Sherwood Park, De., U.S.	i7	85
Shetek, Lake, l., Mn., U.S.	G3	100
Shetland Islands, is., Scot., U.K.	A11	7
Shetucket, stm., Ct., U.S.	C8	84
Sheyenne, stm., N.D., U.S.	B7	111
Sheyenne Lake, res., N.D., U.S.	B5	111
Shiawassee, co., Mi., U.S.	F6	99
Shibata, Japan	E12	30
Shibetsu, Japan	p23	30
Shibukawa, Japan	F11	30
Shickshinny, Pa., U.S.	D9	115
Shijiazhuang, China	D9	26
Shijushan, China	D8	26
Shikārpur, Pak.	G3	38
Shikohābād, India	G8	38
Shikoku, i., Japan	I6	30
Shikoku-sanchi, mts., Japan	I6	30
Shikotsu-ko, l., Japan	q19	30a
Shillington, Pa., U.S.	F10	115
Shillong, India	H14	38
Shiloh National Military Park, Tn., U.S.	B3	119
Shilong, China	L2	28
Shimabara, Japan	J3	30
Shimada, Japan	H11	30
Shimbiris, mtn., Som.	F4	46
Shimizu, Japan	G11	30
Shimminato, Japan	F12	30
Shimoga, India	I3	37
Shimonoseki, Japan	I3	30
Shinano, stm., Japan	E11	30
Shīndand, Afg.	C1	36
Shiner, Tx., U.S.	E4	120
Shinglehouse, Pa., U.S.	C5	115
Shingū, Japan	I8	30
Shinjō, Japan	D13	30
Shinnston, W.V., U.S.	B4	125
Shinshār, Syria	B5	40
Shinyanga, Tan.	B6	44
Shiocton, Wi., U.S.	D5	126
Shiogama, Japan	D14	30
Shiojiri, Japan	F10	30
Shiping, China	C7	34
Ship Island, i., Ms., U.S.	E5	101
Ship Island Pass, strt., Ms., U.S.	g7	101
Shippagan, N.B., Can.	B5	71
Shippensburg, Pa., U.S.	F6	115
Shiprock, N.M., U.S.	A1	108
Ship Rock, mtn., N.M., U.S.	A1	108
Shirakawa, Japan	E13	30
Shīrāz, Iran	C5	46
Shire, stm., Afr.	E6	44
Shiretoko-misaki, c., Japan	o23	30a
Shirley, In., U.S.	E6	91
Shirley, Ma., U.S.	A4	98
Shirley Mountains, mts., Wy., U.S.	D6	127
Shirpur, India	B3	37
Shishaldin Volcano, vol., Ak., U.S.	E7	79
Shishmaref, Ak., U.S.	B6	79
Shively, Ky., U.S.	B4	94
Shivpuri, India	H7	38
Shizuoka, Japan	H11	30
Shkodër, Alb.	G3	16
Shoal Creek, stm., U.S.	B4	119
Shoal Harbour, Newf., Can.	D4	72
Shoal Lake, Man., Can.	D1	70
Shoals, In., U.S.	G4	91
Shoals, Isles of, is., Me., U.S.	E2	96
Shoalwater, Cape, c., Wa., U.S.	C1	124
Shōdo-shima, i., Japan	H7	30
Shoemakersville, Pa., U.S.	F10	115
Sholāpur, India	D3	37
Shongopovi, Az., U.S.	A5	80
Shonto, Az., U.S.	A5	80
Shores Acres, R.I., U.S.	E4	116
Shoreview, Mn., U.S.	m12	100
Shorewood, Il., U.S.	k8	90
Shorewood, Mn., U.S.	n11	100
Shorewood, Wi., U.S.	E6	126
Short Beach, Ct., U.S.	D4	84
Shoshone, Id., U.S.	G4	89
Shoshone, co., Id., U.S.	B2	89
Shoshone, co., Wy., U.S.	B4	127
Shoshone Falls, wtfl, Id., U.S.	G4	89
Shoshone Lake, l., Wy., U.S.	B2	127
Shoshone Mountains, mts., Nv., U.S.	E4	105
Shoshone Peak, mtn., Nv., U.S.	G5	105
Shoshone Range, mts., Nv., U.S.	C5	105
Shoshong, Bots.	F5	44
Shoshoni, Wy., U.S.	C5	127
Shoup, Id., U.S.	D4	89
Shouxian, China	C5	28
Show Low, Az., U.S.	C5	80
Shreve, Oh., U.S.	B3	112
Shreveport, La., U.S.	B2	95
Shrewsbury, Eng., U.K.	I10	7
Shrewsbury, Ma., U.S.	B4	98
Shrewsbury, N.J., U.S.	C4	107
Shrewsbury, Pa., U.S.	G8	115
Shuajingsi, China	E7	26
Shuangcheng, China	B12	26
Shuangyashan, China	B13	26
Shubenacadie, N.S., Can.	D6	71
Shuksan, Mount, mtn., Wa., U.S.	A4	124
Shullsburg, Wi., U.S.	F3	126
Shumagin Islands, is., Ak., U.S.	E7	79
Shunde, China	M2	28
Shungnak, Ak., U.S.	B8	79
Shuqrā', Yemen	F4	46
Shūshtar, Iran	B4	46
Shuswap Lake, l., B.C., Can.	D8	69
Shwebo, Burma	C3	34
Shymkent see Čimkent, Kaz.	N7	34
Siaksriinderapura, Indon.	D6	38
Siālkot, Pak.		
Siam, Gulf of see Thailand, Gulf of, b., Asia	J6	34
Sian see Xi'an, China	E8	26
Siargao Island, i., Phil.	D8	32
Šiaškotan, Ostrov, i., Russia	H24	24
Šiauliai, Lith.	F6	18
Šibenik, Cro.	F10	14
Siberia see Sibir', reg., Russia	D16	24
Siberut, Pulau, i., Indon.	F2	32
Sibi, Pak.	F2	38
Sibir' (Siberia), reg., Russia	D16	24
Sibir'akova, Ostrov, i., Russia	C9	24
Sibiti, Congo	B2	44
Sibiu, Rom.	D8	16
Sibley, Ia., U.S.	A2	92
Sibley, La., U.S.	B2	95
Sibley, co., Mn., U.S.	F4	100
Sibolga, Indon.	E2	32
Sibsāgar, India	G16	38
Sibu, Malay.	E5	32
Sibutu Island, i., Phil.	E6	32
Sibuyan Island, i., Phil.	C7	32
Sibuyan Sea, Phil.	C7	32
Sicamous, B.C., Can.	D8	69
Sichote-Alin', mts., Russia	H21	24
Sichuan, prov., China	E7	26
Sicié, Cap, c., Fr.	I12	10
Sicilia, i., Italy	L9	14
Sicily, Strait of, strt.	L7	14
Sicily see Sicilia, i., Italy	L9	14
Sico, stm., Hond.	G5	64
Sicuani, Peru	F4	54
Siddipet, India	C5	37
Siderno, Italy	K11	14
Sidhpur, India	I5	38
Sidi bel Abbès, Alg.	A5	42
Sidi Ifni, Mor.	C2	42
Sidmouth, Eng., U.K.	K9	7
Sidney, B.C., Can.	g11	69
Sidney, Ia., U.S.	D2	92
Sidney, Il., U.S.	C5	90
Sidney, Mt., U.S.	C12	103
Sidney, Ne., U.S.	C3	104
Sidney, N.Y., U.S.	C5	109
Sidney, Oh., U.S.	B1	112
Sidney Lanier, Lake, res., Ga., U.S.	B2	87
Sidon see Ṣaydā, Leb.	C4	40
Sidra, Gulf of see Surt, Khalīj, b., Libya	B9	42
Siedlce, Pol.	C22	8
Siegburg, Ger.	E7	8
Siegen, Ger.	E8	8
Siĕmréab, Camb.	H7	34
Siena, Italy	F6	14
Sierra, co., Ca., U.S.	C3	82
Sierra, co., N.M., U.S.	D2	108
Sierra Blanca Peak, mtn., N.M., U.S.	D4	108
Sierra Colorada, Arg.	E3	56
Sierra Estrella, mts., Az., U.S.	m8	80
Sierra Leone, ctry., Afr.	G3	42
Sierra Madre, Ca., U.S.	m12	82
Sierra Vista, Az., U.S.	F5	80
Sierre, Switz.	F14	10
Siesta Key, i., Fl., U.S.	E4	86
Sighetul Marmației, Rom.	B7	16
Sighișoara, Rom.	C8	16
Siglufjörður, Ice.	B4	4
Signal Mountain, Tn., U.S.	D8	119
Signal Peak, mtn., Az., U.S.	D1	80
Signal Peak, mtn., Ut., U.S.	F2	121
Signy-l'Abbaye, Fr.	C11	10
Sigourney, Ia., U.S.	C5	92
Sigüenza, Spain	D9	12
Sigües, Spain	C10	12
Siguiri, Gui.	F4	42
Siilinjärvi, Fin.	E16	6
Si-Kacha, Thai.	H6	34
Šikar, India	G6	38
Sikeston, Mo., U.S.	E8	102
Sikiá, Grc.	I7	16
Síkinos, Grc.	M9	16
Sikkim, state, India	G13	38
Sikotan, Ostrov (Shikotan-tō), i., Russia	I23	24
Sikt'ach, Russia	D19	24
Silandro, Italy	C5	14
Silao, Mex.	G9	62
Silay, Phil.	C7	32
Silba, Cro.	E9	14
Silchar, India	H15	38
Siler City, N.C., U.S.	B3	110
Silesia, hist. reg., Pol.	E16	8
Siletz, Or., U.S.	C3	114
Silifke, Tur.	A3	40
Siliguri, India	G13	38
Siling Co, l., China	E13	38
Silistra, Bul.	E11	16
Šilka, Russia	G18	24
Šilka, stm., Russia	G17	24
Silkeborg, Den.	H7	6
Sillamäe, Est.	B10	18
Sillé-le-Guillaume, Fr.	D6	10
Sillery, Que., Can.	n17	74
Sillon de Talbert, pen., Fr.	D3	10
Siloam Springs, Ar., U.S.	A1	81
Silsbee, Tx., U.S.	D5	120
Silt, Co., U.S.	B3	83
Silvânia, Braz.	G9	54
Silvassa, India	B3	37
Silver Bay, Mn., U.S.	C7	100
Silver Bow, co., Mt., U.S.	E4	103
Silver City, Nv., U.S.	D2	105
Silver City, N.M., U.S.	E1	108
Silver Creek, Ne., U.S.	C8	104
Silver Creek, N.Y., U.S.	C1	109
Silver Creek, stm., Or., U.S.	D7	114
Silverdale, Wa., U.S.	B3	124
Silver Grove, Ky., U.S.	h14	94
Silver Hill, Md., U.S.	f9	97
Silver Lake, Ks., U.S.	C8	93
Silver Lake, Ma., U.S.	f11	98
Silver Lake, Mn., U.S.	F4	100
Silver Lake, Wi., U.S.	F5	126
Silver Lake, l., De., U.S.	D3	85
Silver Lake, l., Ia., U.S.	A3	92
Silver Lake, l., Me., U.S.	C3	96
Silver Lake, l., N.H., U.S.	E2	106
Silver Lake, l., N.H., U.S.	C4	106
Silver Lake, l., Or., U.S.	D7	114
Silver Lake, l., Wa., U.S.	g13	124
Silverpeak, Nv., U.S.	F4	105
Silver Peak Range, mts., Nv., U.S.	F4	105
Silver Spring, Md., U.S.	C3	97
Silver Springs, Nv., U.S.	D2	105
Silver Star Mountain, mtn., Wa., U.S.	A5	124
Silverthrone Mountain, mtn., B.C., Can.	D4	69
Silvertip Mountain, mtn., Mt., U.S.	C3	103
Silverton, Co., U.S.	D3	83
Silverton, Id., U.S.	B3	89
Silverton, N.J., U.S.	C4	107
Silverton, Or., U.S.	C4	114
Silvi, Italy	G9	14
Silvies, stm., Or., U.S.	D7	114
Silview, De., U.S.	B3	85
Silvis, Il., U.S.	B3	90
Simanggang, Malay.	E5	32
Simanovsk, Russia	G19	24
Simav, Tur.	J12	16
Simcoe, Ont., Can.	E4	73
Simcoe, Lake, l., Ont., Can.	C5	73
Simeulue, Pulau, i., Indon.	M3	34
Simferopol', Ukr.	I4	22
Simi Valley, Ca., U.S.	E4	82
Simla, India	E7	38
Simla, Co., U.S.	B6	83
Simmesport, La., U.S.	D4	95
Simms Stream, stm., N.H., U.S.	g7	106
Simojovel [de Allende], Mex.	I13	62
Simonette, stm., Alta., Can.	B1	68
Simplon Pass, Switz.	F15	10
Simpson, co., Ky., U.S.	D3	94
Simpson, co., Ms., U.S.	D4	101
Simpson Creek, stm., W.V., U.S.	k10	125

Name	Map Ref	Page
Simpson Desert, des., Austl.	D7	50
Simpson Peninsula, pen., N.W. Ter., Can.	C15	66
Simpsonville, Ky., U.S.	B4	94
Simpsonville, S.C., U.S.	B3	117
Simsboro, La., U.S.	B3	95
Simsbury, Ct., U.S.	B4	84
Simušir, Ostrov, i., Russia	H24	24
Sīnā', Shibh Jazīrat (Sinai Peninsula), pen., Egypt	C12	42
Sinabang, Indon.	M4	34
Sinai Peninsula see Sīnā', Shibh Jazīrat, pen., Egypt	C12	42
Sin'aja, stm., Russia	E18	24
Sinaloa, stm., Mex.	E5	62
Sināwan, Libya	B8	42
Sincé, Col.	C5	58
Sincé, Col.	J10	64
Sincelejo, Col.	C5	58
Sinclair, Wy., U.S.	E5	127
Sindri, India	I12	38
Sines, Port.	H3	12
Sinfães, Port.	D3	12
Singānallūr, India	G4	37
Singapore, Sing.	N7	34
Singapore, ctry., Asia	E3	32
Singapore Strait, strt., Asia	N7	34
Singen [Hohentwiel], Ger.	H8	8
Singida, Tan.	B6	44
Singkang, Indon.	F7	32
Singkawang, Indon.	E4	32
Siniscola, Italy	I4	14
Sinj, Cro.	F11	14
Sinjah, Sudan	F12	42
Sinkāt, Sudan	E13	42
Sinnamary, Fr. Gu.	B8	54
Sinnemahoning Creek, stm., Pa., U.S.	D5	115
Sinop, Tur.	G15	4
Sinskoje, Russia	E19	24
Sintang, Indon.	E5	32
Sint Eustatius, i., Neth. Ant.	F16	64
Sint Marten (Saint-Martin), i., N.A.	E16	64
Sint-Niklaas, Bel.	D4	8
Sinton, Tx., U.S.	E4	120
Sintra, Port.	G2	12
Sinŭiju, N. Kor.	C11	26
Sion, Switz.	F14	10
Sioux, co., Ia., U.S.	A1	92
Sioux, co., Ne., U.S.	B2	104
Sioux, co., N.D., U.S.	C4	111
Sioux Center, Ia., U.S.	A1	92
Sioux City, Ia., U.S.	B1	92
Sioux Falls, S.D., U.S.	D9	118
Sioux Lookout, Ont., Can.	o17	73
Sioux Rapids, Ia., U.S.	B2	92
Siping, China	C11	26
Sipiwesk Lake, l., Man., Can.	B3	70
Sipsey, stm., Al., U.S.	B2	78
Sipsey Fork, stm., Al., U.S.	A2	78
Siracusa, Italy	L10	14
Sirājganj, Bngl.	H13	38
Sir Douglas, Mount, mtn., Can.	D3	68
Sir Edward Pellew Group, is., Austl.	C7	50
Siren, Wi., U.S.	C1	126
Siret, stm., Eur.	C11	16
Sirevåg, Nor.	G5	6
Sir James MacBrien, Mount, mtn., N.W. Ter., Can.	D5	66
Sirohi, India	H5	38
Sirsa, India	F6	38
Sir Sandford, Mount, mtn., B.C., Can.	D9	69
Sirsi, India	E3	37
Sir Wilfrid Laurier, Mount, mtn., B.C., Can.	C8	69
Sisak, Cro.	D11	14
Siskiyou, co., Ca., U.S.	B2	82
Siskiyou Mountains, mts., U.S.	F3	114
Siskiyou Pass, Or., U.S.	E4	114
Sisseton, S.D., U.S.	B8	118
Sisseton Indian Reservation, U.S.	B8	118
Sissiboo, stm., N.S., Can.	E4	71
Sisson Branch Reservoir, res., N.B., Can.	B2	71
Sissonville, W.V., U.S.	C3	125
Sisteron, Fr.	H12	10
Sisters, Or., U.S.	C5	114
Sistersville, W.V., U.S.	B4	125
Sītāpur, India	G9	38
Sitka, Ak., U.S.	D12	79
Sitka National Historical Park, Ak., U.S.	m22	79
Sitka Sound, strt., Ak., U.S.	m22	79
Sittard, Neth.	D5	8
Sittoung, stm., Burma	E4	34
Sittwe (Akyab), Burma	D2	34
Situbondo, Indon.	m16	33a
Sivas, Tur.	H15	4
Siwah, Egypt	C11	42
Siwān, India	G11	38
Sjælland, i., Den.	I8	6
Skagen, Den.	H8	6
Skagerrak, strt., Eur.	H7	6
Skagit, co., Wa., U.S.	A4	124
Skagway, Ak., U.S.	D12	79
Skaidi, Nor.	A15	6
Skamania, co., Wa., U.S.	D3	124
Skaneateles, N.Y., U.S.	C4	109
Skaneateles Lake, l., N.Y., U.S.	C4	109
Skārdu, Pak.	C6	38
Skarżysko-Kamienna, Pol.	D20	8
Skeena Mountains, mts., B.C., Can.	E7	66
Skegness, Eng., U.K.	H13	7
Skeleton Lake, l., Ont., Can.	B5	73
Skellefteå, Swe.	D13	6
Skelleftehamn, Swe.	D13	6
Skiatook, Ok., U.S.	A5	113
Skiatook Reservoir, res., Ok., U.S.	A5	113
Skibotn, Nor.	B13	6
Skiddaw, mtn., Eng., U.K.	G9	7
Skien, Nor.	G7	6
Skierniewice, Pol.	D20	8
Skihist Mountain, mtn., B.C., Can.	D7	69
Skikda, Alg.	A7	42
Skillet Fork, stm., Il., U.S.	E5	90
Skillingaryd, Swe.	H10	6
Sklad, Russia	C18	24
Škofja Loka, Slo.	C9	14
Skokie, Il., U.S.	A6	90
Skokomish Indian Reservation, Wa., U.S.	B2	124
Skopje, Mac.	H5	16
Skövde, Swe.	G9	6
Skovorodino, Russia	G18	24
Skowhegan, Me., U.S.	D3	96
Skull Valley, val., Ut., U.S.	C3	121
Skull Valley Indian Reservation, Ut., U.S.	C3	121
Skuna, stm., Ms., U.S.	B4	101
Skunk, stm., Ia., U.S.	D6	92
Skwentna, stm., Ak., U.S.	g15	79
Skykomish, stm., Wa., U.S.	B4	124
Skyland, Nv., U.S.	D2	105
Skyland, N.C., U.S.	f10	110
Skyline, Al., U.S.	A3	78
Slagnäs, Swe.	D12	6
Slamet, Gunung, vol., Indon.	m14	33a
Slancy, Russia	B11	18
Slano, Cro.	G12	14
Slater, Ia., U.S.	C4	92
Slater, Mo., U.S.	B4	102
Slater, S.C., U.S.	A3	117
Slatersville, R.I., U.S.	A3	116
Slatersville Reservoir, res., R.I., U.S.	B3	116
Slatington, Pa., U.S.	E10	115
Slaton, Tx., U.S.	C2	120
Slaughter, La., U.S.	D4	95
Slave, stm., Can.	D10	66
Slave Lake, Alta., Can.	B3	68
Slavonia see Slavonija, reg., Cro.	D12	14
Slavonija, reg., Cro.	D12	14
Slavonska Požega, Cro.	D12	14
Slavonski Brod, Cro.	D2	16
Slayton, Mn., U.S.	G3	100
Sleeping Bear Dunes National Lakeshore, Mi., U.S.	D4	99
Sleeping Bear Point, c., Mi., U.S.	D4	99
Sleepy Eye, Mn., U.S.	F4	100
Slickville, Pa., U.S.	F2	115
Slidell, La., U.S.	D6	95
Sliderock Mountain, mtn., Mt., U.S.	D3	103
Sligo, Ire.	G4	7
Slinger, Wi., U.S.	E5	126
Slippery Rock, Pa., U.S.	D1	115
Sliven, Bul.	G10	16
Sloan, Ia., U.S.	B1	92
Sloan, N.Y., U.S.	C2	109
Slocomb, Al., U.S.	D4	78
Slonim, Bela.	H8	18
Slope, co., N.D., U.S.	C2	111
Slovakia see Slovensko, hist. reg., Czech.	G19	8
Slovenia, ctry., Eur.	C9	14
Slovenjgradec, Slo.	C10	14
Slovenska Bistrica, Slo.	C10	14
Slovensko, hist. reg., Czech.	G19	8
Sluck, Bela.	H10	18
Słupsk (Stolp), Pol.	A17	8
Sl'ud'anka, Russia	G14	24
Smackover, Ar., U.S.	D3	81
Small Point, c., Me., U.S.	g8	96
Smallwood Reservoir, res., Newf., Can.	g8	72
Smederevo, Yugo.	E4	16
Smethport, Pa., U.S.	C5	115
Šmidovič, Russia	H20	24
Šmidta, Ostrov, i., Russia	A12	24
Smith, co., Ks., U.S.	C5	93
Smith, co., Ms., U.S.	C4	101
Smith, co., Tn., U.S.	A5	119
Smith, co., Tx., U.S.	C5	120
Smith, stm., De., U.S.	D3	123
Smith, stm., Mt., U.S.	D5	103
Smith and Sayles Reservoir, res., R.I., U.S.	B2	116
Smith Bay, b., Ak., U.S.	A9	79
Smith Canyon, val., Co., U.S.	D7	83
Smith Center, Ks., U.S.	C5	93
Smithers, B.C., Can.	B4	69
Smithers, W.V., U.S.	C3	125
Smithfield, N.C., U.S.	B4	110
Smithfield, Pa., U.S.	G2	115
Smithfield, Ut., U.S.	B4	121
Smithfield, Va., U.S.	D6	123
Smith Island, i., U.S.	D5	97
Smith Island, i., Va., U.S.	C7	123
Smith Mountain Lake, res., Va., U.S.	C3	123
Smith Peak, mtn., U.S.	A2	89
Smith Point, c., Ma., U.S.	D7	98
Smith Point, c., Va., U.S.	C6	123
Smiths, Al., U.S.	C4	78
Smithsburg, Md., U.S.	A2	97
Smiths Falls, Ont., Can.	C8	73
Smiths Grove, Ky., U.S.	C3	94
Smithton, Austl.	H9	50
Smithton, Il., U.S.	E4	90
Smithtown, N.Y., U.S.	n15	109
Smithville, Ga., U.S.	E2	87
Smithville, Ms., U.S.	A5	101
Smithville, Mo., U.S.	B3	102
Smithville, Oh., U.S.	B4	112
Smithville, Tn., U.S.	D8	119
Smithville, Tx., U.S.	D4	120
Smithville Lake, res., Mo., U.S.	B3	102
Smoke Creek Desert, des., Nv., U.S.	C2	105
Smokey, Cape, c., N.S., Can.	C9	71
Smokey Dome, mtn., Id., U.S.	F4	89
Smoky, stm., Alta., Can.	B1	68
Smoky Hill, stm., U.S.	D5	93
Smoky Lake, Alta., Can.	B4	68
Smoky Mountains, mts., Id., U.S.	F4	89
Smolensk, Russia	G15	18
Smoothstone Lake, l., Sask., Can.	C2	75
Smooth Rock Falls, Ont., Can.	o19	73
Smyrna, De., U.S.	C3	85
Smyrna, Ga., U.S.	C2	87
Smyrna, Tn., U.S.	B5	119
Smyrna, stm., De., U.S.	C3	85
Smyth, co., Va., U.S.	f10	123
Smythe, Mount, mtn., B.C., Can.	E8	66
Snake, stm., U.S.	D5	100
Snake, stm., Mn., U.S.	B1	100
Snake, stm., Ne., U.S.	B4	104
Snake Range, mts., Nv., U.S.	E7	105
Snake River Plain, pl., Id., U.S.	F2	89
Snake River Range, mts., U.S.	C2	127
Sneads, Fl., U.S.	B2	86
Sneedville, Tn., U.S.	C10	119
Sneek, Neth.	B5	8
Snipe Keys, is., Fl., U.S.	H5	86
Snohomish, Wa., U.S.	B3	124
Snohomish, co., Wa., U.S.	A4	124
Snoqualmie, Wa., U.S.	B4	124
Snoqualmie, stm., Wa., U.S.	B4	124
Snoqualmie Pass, Wa., U.S.	B4	124
Snowbank Lake, l., Mn., U.S.	B7	100
Snowdon, mtn., Wales, U.K.	H8	7
Snowdonia National Park, Wales, U.K.	I9	7
Snowdrift, N.W. Ter., Can.	D10	66
Snowflake, Az., U.S.	C5	80
Snow Hill, Md., U.S.	D7	97
Snow Hill, N.C., U.S.	B5	110
Snowking Mountain, mtn., Wa., U.S.	A4	124
Snow Lake, Man., Can.	B1	70
Snowmass Mountain, mtn., Co., U.S.	B3	83
Snow Peak, mtn., Wa., U.S.	A7	124
Snowshoe Lake, l., Me., U.S.	B4	96
Snowshoe Peak, mtn., Mt., U.S.	B1	103
Snow Water Lake, l., Nv., U.S.	C7	105
Snowyside Peak, mtn., Id., U.S.	F4	89
Snyder, Ok., U.S.	C3	113
Snyder, Tx., U.S.	C2	120
Snyder, co., Pa., U.S.	E7	115
Soacha, Col.	E5	58
Soalala, Madag.	E9	44
Soap Lake, Wa., U.S.	B6	124
Sobat, stm., Sudan	G12	42
Sobinka, Russia	F23	18
Sobral, Braz.	D10	54
Socastee, S.C., U.S.	D9	117
Sochi see Soči, Russia	I5	22
Soči, Russia	I5	22
Social Circle, Ga., U.S.	C3	87
Social Hill, S.C., U.S.	B8	117
Society Hill, S.C., U.S.	C8	117
Socorro, Col.	D6	58
Socorro, N.M., U.S.	C3	108
Socorro, co., N.M., U.S.	D2	108
Socorro, Isla, i., Mex.	H4	62
Socotra see Suquţrā, i., Yemen	F5	46
Soc Trang, Viet.	J8	34
Socuéllamos, Spain	F9	12
Sodankylä, Fin.	C16	6
Soda Springs, Id., U.S.	G7	89
Soddy-Daisy, Tn., U.S.	D8	119
Söderhamn, Swe.	F11	6
Södertälje, Swe.	G11	6
Sodo, Eth.	G2	46
Sodus, N.Y., U.S.	B3	109
Soest, Ger.	D8	8
Sofia, stm., Madag.	E9	44
Sofia see Sofija, Bul.	G7	16
Sofija (Sofia), Bul.	G7	16
Sogamoso, Col.	E6	58
Sognafjorden, Nor.	F5	6
Søgne, Nor.	G6	6
Soignies, Bel.	E4	8
Sointula, B.C., Can.	D4	69
Soissons, Fr.	C10	10
Sokodé, Togo	G6	42
Sokol, Russia	C19	24
Sokol, Russia	B23	18
Sokoto, Nig.	F7	42
Sol, Costa del, Spain	I7	12
Solana, Fl., U.S.	F5	86
Solano, Phil.	p19	33b
Solano, co., Ca., U.S.	C3	82
Solbad Hall in Tirol, Aus.	H11	8
Soldier, stm., Ia., U.S.	C2	92
Soldier Key, i., Fl., U.S.	s3	86
Soldotna, Ak., U.S.	g16	79
Soledad, Col.	B5	58
Soledad, Ca., U.S.	D3	82
Soledad, Ven.	C11	58
Soleduck, stm., Wa., U.S.	B1	124
Solingen, Ger.	D7	8
Soileftea, Swe.	E11	6
Sollentuna, Swe.	G11	6
Sóller, Spain	F14	12
Solnečnogorsk, Russia	E19	18
Sologoncy, Russia	D16	24
Solok, Indon.	O6	34
Solomon, Ks., U.S.	D6	93
Solomon, stm., Ks., U.S.	C6	93
Solomon Islands, ctry., Oc.	G23	2
Solomons, Md., U.S.	D5	97
Solomon Sea, Oc.	A10	50
Solon, Ia., U.S.	C6	92
Solon, Oh., U.S.	A4	112
Solon Springs, Wi., U.S.	B2	126
Solothurn, Switz.	E14	10
Solsona, Spain	D13	12
Soltau, Ger.	C9	8
Solvay, N.Y., U.S.	B4	109
Solwezi, Zam.	D5	44
Soma, Tur.	J11	16
Somalia, ctry., Afr.	G4	46
Sombor, Yugo.	D3	16
Sombrerete, Mex.	F8	62
Somerdale, N.J., U.S.	D2	107
Somers, Ct., U.S.	B6	84
Somers, Mt., U.S.	B2	103
Somerset, Man., Can.	E2	70
Somerset, Ky., U.S.	C5	94
Somerset, Ma., U.S.	C5	98
Somerset, N.J., U.S.	B3	107
Somerset, Oh., U.S.	C3	112
Somerset, Pa., U.S.	F3	115
Somerset, Tx., U.S.	k7	120
Somerset, Wi., U.S.	C1	126
Somerset, co., De., U.S.	C3	85
Somerset, co., Md., U.S.	D6	97
Somerset, co., N.J., U.S.	B3	107
Somerset, co., Pa., U.S.	G3	115
Somerset Island, i., N.W. Ter., Can.	B14	66
Somers Point, N.J., U.S.	E3	107
Somersville, Ct., U.S.	B6	84
Somersworth, N.H., U.S.	D5	106
Somerton, Az., U.S.	E1	80
Somervell, co., Tx., U.S.	C4	120
Somerville, Ma., U.S.	B5	98
Somerville, N.J., U.S.	B3	107
Somerville, Tn., U.S.	B2	119
Somerville, Tx., U.S.	D4	120
Somerville Lake, res., Tx., U.S.	D4	120
Someş (Szamos), stm., Eur.	B6	16
Sömmerda, Ger.	D11	8
Somonauk, Il., U.S.	B5	90
Somoto, Nic.	H4	64
Son, stm., India	H10	38
Sønderborg, Den.	I7	6
Sondershausen, Ger.	D10	8
Søndre Strømfjord, Grnld.	C22	66
Sondrio, Italy	C4	14
Song Cau, Viet.	H10	34
Songea, Tan.	D7	44
Songhua, stm., China	B12	26
Songjiang, China	D10	28
Songnim, N. Kor.	D12	26
Sonipat, India	F7	38
Sonneberg, Ger.	E11	8
Sonoita, Mex.	B3	62
Sonoma, Ca., U.S.	C2	82
Sonoma, co., Ca., U.S.	C2	82
Sonoma Peak, mtn., Nv., U.S.	C4	105
Sonoma Range, mts., Nv., U.S.	C4	105
Sonora, Ca., U.S.	D3	82
Sonora, Tx., U.S.	D2	120
Sonora, stm., Mex.	C4	62
Sonsonate, El Sal.	H3	64
Sonsón, Col.	E5	58
Sonsorol Islands, is., T.T.P.I.	D9	32
Soochow see Suzhou, China	D9	28
Soperton, Ga., U.S.	D4	87
Sophia, W.V., U.S.	D3	125
Sopot, Pol.	A18	8
Sopron, Hung.	H16	8
Sopur, India	C6	38
Sora, Italy	H8	14
Sore, Fr.	H6	10
Sorel, Que., Can.	C4	74
Sorgono, Italy	I4	14
Sorgues, Fr.	H11	10
Soria, Spain	D9	12
Sorocaba, Braz.	G5	57
Sorong, Indon.	F9	32
Soroti, Ug.	H12	42
Sorrento, Italy	I9	14
Sorrento, La., U.S.	D5	95
Sorsele, Swe.	D11	6
Sorsogon, Phil.	C7	32
Sort, Spain	C13	12
Sorūbī, Afg.	C3	38
Sos del Rey Católico, Spain	C10	12
Sosnovo-Oz'orskoje, Russia	G16	24
Sosnowiec, Pol.	E19	8
Šoštanj, Slo.	C10	14
Sotkamo, Fin.	D17	6
Soto la Marina, Mex.	F10	62
Sotteville, Fr.	C8	10
Soucook, stm., N.H., U.S.	D4	106
Soudan, Mn., U.S.	C6	100
Souderton, Pa., U.S.	F11	115
Souhegan, stm., N.H., U.S.	E3	106
Souillac, Fr.	H8	10
Soûl (Seoul), S. Kor.	D12	26
Soulac-sur-Mer, Fr.	G5	10
Souris, Man., Can.	E1	70
Souris, P.E.I., Can.	C7	71
Sousa, Braz.	E11	54
Sousse, Tun.	N5	14
South, stm., Ia., U.S.	C4	92
South, stm., N.C., U.S.	C4	110
South Acton, Ma., U.S.	g10	98
South Africa, ctry., Afr.	G5	44
South Amboy, N.J., U.S.	C4	107
South America	E4	53
South Amherst, Ma., U.S.	B2	98
South Amherst, Oh., U.S.	A3	112
Southampton, Ont., Can.	C3	73
Southampton, Eng., U.K.	K11	7
Southampton, N.Y., U.S.	n16	109
Southampton, co., Va., U.S.	D5	123
Southampton Island, i., N.W. Ter., Can.	D16	66
South Andaman, i., India	I2	34
South Anna, stm., Va., U.S.	C5	123
South Aulatsivik Island, i., Newf., Can.	E20	66
South Australia, state, Austl.	F7	50
South Bald Mountain, mtn., Co., U.S.	A5	83
South Baldy, mtn., N.M., U.S.	D2	108
South Bay, Fl., U.S.	F6	86
South Beloit, Il., U.S.	A4	90
South Bend, Wa., U.S.	C2	124
South Berwick, Me., U.S.	E2	96
South Bloomfield, Oh., U.S.	C3	112
South Boston, Va., U.S.	D4	123
South Bound Brook, N.J., U.S.	B3	107
South Branch Lake, l., Me., U.S.	C4	96
Southbridge, Ma., U.S.	B3	98
South Bristol, Me., U.S.	E3	96
South Britain, Ct., U.S.	D3	84
South Broadway, Wa., U.S.	C5	124
South Bruny, i., Austl.	H9	50
South Burlington, Vt., U.S.	C2	122
Southbury, Ct., U.S.	D3	84
South Carolina, state, U.S.	D6	117
South Charleston, Oh., U.S.	C2	112
South Charleston, W.V., U.S.	C3	125
South Chicago Heights, Il., U.S.	m9	90
South China Sea, Asia	C5	32
South Coffeyville, Ok., U.S.	A6	113
South Congaree, S.C., U.S.	D5	117
South Connellsville, Pa., U.S.	G2	115
South Dakota, state, U.S.	C5	118
South Dartmouth, Ma., U.S.	C6	98
South Daytona, Fl., U.S.	C5	86
South Deerfield, Ma., U.S.	B2	98
South Dennis, Ma., U.S.	C7	98
South Duxbury, Ma., U.S.	B6	98
South East Cape, c., Austl.	H9	50
Southeast Cape, c., Ak., U.S.	C6	79
Southeast Pass, strt., La., U.S.	E7	95
Southeast Point, c., R.I., U.S.	h7	116
South Elgin, Il., U.S.	B5	90
Southend-on-Sea, Eng., U.K.	J13	7
Southern Alps, mts., N.Z.	E3	52
Southern Cross, Austl.	F3	50
Southern Indian Lake, l., Man., Can.	f8	70
Southern Pines, N.C., U.S.	B3	110
Southern Ute Indian Reservation, Co., U.S.	D2	83
South Euclid, Oh., U.S.	g9	112
South Fabius, stm., Mo., U.S.	A5	102
South Fallsburg, N.Y., U.S.	D6	109
Southfield, Mi., U.S.	o15	99
South Fork, Pa., U.S.	F4	115
South Fox Island, i., Mi., U.S.	C5	99
South Fulton, Tn., U.S.	A3	119
South Gastonia, N.C., U.S.	B1	110
South Gate, Ca., U.S.	n12	82
Southgate, Ky., U.S.	h14	94
Southgate, Mi., U.S.	p15	99
South Georgia, i., Falk. Is.	G9	65
South Glastonbury, Ct., U.S.	C5	84
South Glens Falls, N.Y., U.S.	B7	109
South Grafton, Ma., U.S.	B4	98
South Grand, stm., Mo., U.S.	C3	102
South Hadley, Ma., U.S.	B2	98
South Hadley Falls, Ma., U.S.	B2	98
South Hamilton, Ma., U.S.	A6	98
South Haven, In., U.S.	A3	91
South Haven, Mi., U.S.	F4	99
South Henik Lake, l., N.W. Ter., Can.	D13	66
South Hero Island, i., Vt., U.S.	B2	122
South Hill, Va., U.S.	D4	123
South Hingham, Ma., U.S.	h12	98
South Holland, Il., U.S.	k9	90
South Holston Lake, res., U.S.	A9	119
South Hooksett, N.H., U.S.	D4	106
South Hopkinton, R.I., U.S.	F1	116
South Houston, Tx., U.S.	r14	120
South Hutchinson, Ks., U.S.	f11	93
South Indian Lake, Man., Can.	A2	70
Southington, Ct., U.S.	C4	84
South International Falls, Mn., U.S.	B5	100
South Island, i., N.Z.	E3	52
South Jacksonville, Il., U.S.	D3	90
South Jordan, Ut., U.S.	C3	121
South Kenosha, Wi., U.S.	F6	126
South Lake Tahoe, Ca., U.S.	C4	82
South Lancaster, Ma., U.S.	B4	98
South Laurel, Md., U.S.	*B4	97
South Lebanon, Oh., U.S.	C1	112
South Lyon, Mi., U.S.	F7	99
South Magnetic Pole	C26	97
South Manitou Island, i., Mi., U.S.	C4	99
South Marsh Island, i., Md., U.S.	D5	97
South Miami, Fl., U.S.	G6	86
South Miami Heights, Fl., U.S.	s13	86
South Mills, N.C., U.S.	A6	110
South Milwaukee, Wi., U.S.	F6	126
Southmont, N.C., U.S.	B2	110
South Moose Lake, l., Man., Can.	C1	70
South Mountain, mtn., Id., U.S.	G2	89
South Mountain, mtn., N.M., U.S.	k8	108
South Mountains, mts., Az., U.S.	m8	80
South Mountains, mts., N.C., U.S.	B1	110
South Nahanni, stm., N.W. Ter., Can.	D7	66
South New River Canal, Fl., U.S.	r3	86
South Ogden, Ut., U.S.	B4	121
South Orange, N.J., U.S.	B4	107
South Orkney Islands, is., B.A.T.	C8	47
South Paris, Me., U.S.	D2	96
South Park, val., Co., U.S.	B5	83
South Pass, Wy., U.S.	D4	127
South Pass, strt., La., U.S.	F6	95
South Patrick Shores, Fl., U.S.	D6	86
South Pekin, Il., U.S.	C4	90
South Pittsburg, Tn., U.S.	D8	119
South Plainfield, N.J., U.S.	B4	107
South Platte, stm., U.S.	C6	76
South Point, c., Mi., U.S.	D7	99
South Pole, Ant.	A12	47
Southport, Eng., U.K.	H9	7
Southport, Fl., U.S.	u16	86
Southport, In., U.S.	E5	91
Southport, N.Y., U.S.	C4	109
Southport, N.C., U.S.	D4	110
South Portland, Me., U.S.	E2	96
South Portsmouth, Ky., U.S.	B6	94
South Range, Mi., U.S.	A2	99
South River, Ont., Can.	B5	73

Name	Map Ref	Page
South River, N.J., U.S.	C4	107
South River, b., Md., U.S.	C4	97
South Ronaldsay, i., Scot., U.K.	C10	7
South Royalton, Vt., U.S.	D3	122
South Saint Paul, Mn., U.S.	n12	100
South Sandwich Islands, is., Falk. Is.	D10	47
South San Francisco, Ca., U.S.	h8	82
South Saskatchewan, stm., Can.	F11	66
South Shetland Islands, is., B.A.T.	C7	47
South Shields, Eng., U.K.	F11	7
Southside, Al., U.S.	B3	78
Southside Place, Tx., U.S.	r14	120
South Sioux City, Ne., U.S.	B9	104
South Skunk, stm., Ia., U.S.	C4	92
South Stony Brook, N.Y., U.S.	*n15	109
South Streator, Il., U.S.	B5	90
South Toms River, N.J., U.S.	D4	107
South Torrington, Wy., U.S.	D8	127
South Tucson, Az., U.S.	E5	80
South Valley Stream, N.Y., U.S.	*n15	109
South Venice, Fl., U.S.	E4	86
South Ventana Cone, vol., Ca., U.S.	D3	82
South Waverly, Pa., U.S.	C8	115
South Wellfleet, Ma., U.S.	C8	98
South Wellington, B.C., Can.	f12	69
South West Africa see Namibia, ctry., Afr.	F3	44
South Westbury, N.Y., U.S.	*n15	109
South West Cape, c., Austl.	H9	50
Southwest Channel, strt., Fl., U.S.	E4	86
Southwest Harbor, Me., U.S.	D4	96
Southwest Head, c., N.B., Can.	E3	71
Southwest Miramichi, stm., N.B., Can.	C3	71
Southwest Pass, strt., La., U.S.	E3	95
Southwest Pass, strt., La., U.S.	F6	95
Southwest Point, c., R.I., U.S.	h7	116
South Weymouth Naval Air Station, mil., Ma., U.S.	h12	98
South Whitley, In., U.S.	B6	91
South Williamson, Ky., U.S.	C7	94
South Williamsport, Pa., U.S.	D7	115
South Windham, Ct., U.S.	C7	84
South Windham, Me., U.S.	E2	96
South Windsor, Ct., U.S.	B5	84
Southwood, Co., U.S.	*B6	83
Southwood Acres, Ct., U.S.	A5	84
South Woodstock, Ct., U.S.	B8	84
South Yarmouth, Ma., U.S.	C7	98
South Zanesville, Oh., U.S.	C3	112
Sovetsk (Tilsit), Russia	F4	18
Sovetskaja Gavan', Russia	H22	24
Spa, Bel.	E5	8
Spain, ctry., Eur.	G7	4
Spalding, co., Ga., U.S.	C2	87
Spanaway, Wa., U.S.	B3	124
Spangler, Pa., U.S.	E4	115
Spaniard's Bay, Newf., Can.	E5	72
Spanish Fork, Ut., U.S.	C4	121
Spanish Fort, Al., U.S.	E2	78
Spanish Lake, Mo., U.S.	f13	102
Spanish North Africa, dep., Afr.	A4	42
Spanish Peak, mtn., Or., U.S.	C7	114
Spanish Sahara see Western Sahara, dep., Afr.	D3	42
Spanish Town, Jam.	E9	64
Sparks, Ga., U.S.	E3	87
Sparks, Nv., U.S.	D2	105
Sparta, Ga., U.S.	C4	87
Sparta, Il., U.S.	E4	90
Sparta, Mi., U.S.	E5	99
Sparta, Mo., U.S.	D4	102
Sparta (Lake Mohawk), N.J., U.S.	A3	107
Sparta, N.C., U.S.	A1	110
Sparta, Tn., U.S.	D8	119
Sparta, Wi., U.S.	E3	126
Spartanburg, S.C., U.S.	B4	117
Spartanburg, co., S.C., U.S.	B3	117
Sparta see Spárti, Grc.	L6	16
Spartel, Cap, c., Mor.	J6	12
Spárti (Sparta), Grc.	L6	16
Spartivento, Capo, c., Italy	E10	69
Sparwood, B.C., Can.	I20	12
Spassk-Dal'nij, Russia		
Spavinaw Creek, stm., Ok., U.S.	A7	113
Spear, Cape, c., Newf., Can.	E5	72
Spearfish, S.D., U.S.	C2	118
Spearman, Tx., U.S.	A2	120
Spearville, Ks., U.S.	E4	93
Speed, In., U.S.	H6	91
Speedway, In., U.S.	E5	91
Spence Bay, N.W. Ter., Can.	C14	66
Spencer, In., U.S.	F4	91
Spencer, Ia., U.S.	A2	92
Spencer, Ma., U.S.	B4	98
Spencer, N.C., U.S.	B2	110
Spencer, Tn., U.S.	D8	119
Spencer, W.V., U.S.	C3	125
Spencer, Wi., U.S.	D3	126
Spencer, co., In., U.S.	H4	91
Spencer, co., Ky., U.S.	B4	94
Spencer, Cape, c., Ak., U.S.	k21	79
Spencer Gulf, b., Austl.	F7	50
Spencer Lake, l., Me., U.S.	C2	96
Spencerport, N.Y., U.S.	B3	109
Spencerville, Md., U.S.	B4	97
Spencerville, Oh., U.S.	B1	112
Sperry, Ok., U.S.	A6	113
Spesutie Island, i., Md., U.S.	B5	97
Spey, stm., Scot., U.K.	D9	7
Speyer, Ger.	F8	8
Spiceland, In., U.S.	E7	91
Spicer, Mn., U.S.	E4	100
Spider Lake, l., Wi., U.S.	B3	126
Spindale, N.C., U.S.	B1	110
Spink, co., S.D., U.S.	C7	118
Spirit Lake, Id., U.S.	B2	89
Spirit Lake, Ia., U.S.	A2	92
Spirit Lake, l., Ia., U.S.	A2	92
Spirit Lake, l., Wa., U.S.	C3	124

Spirit River, Alta., Can.	B1	68
Spirit River Flowage, res., Wi., U.S.	C4	126
Spiro, Ok., U.S.	B7	113
Spittal an der Drau, Aus.	I13	8
Spitz, Aus.	G15	8
Split, Cro.	F11	14
Split, Cape, c., N.S., Can.	D5	71
Split Lake, l., Man., Can.	A4	70
Split Rock Creek, stm., U.S.	G2	100
Splügen, Switz.	F16	10
Spofford Lake, l., N.H., U.S.	E2	106
Spokane, Wa., U.S.	B8	124
Spokane, co., Wa., U.S.	B8	124
Spokane, stm., U.S.	B8	124
Spokane, Mount, mtn., Wa., U.S.	B8	124
Spokane Indian Reservation, Wa., U.S.	B8	124
Spoleto, Italy	G7	14
Spoon, stm., Il., U.S.	C3	90
Spooner, Wi., U.S.	C2	126
Spooner Lake, l., Wi., U.S.	C2	126
Spornoje, Russia	E24	24
Spotswood, N.J., U.S.	C4	107
Spotsylvania, co., Va., U.S.	B5	123
Sprague, W.V., U.S.	n13	125
Sprague, stm., Or., U.S.	E5	114
Sprague Lake, l., Wa., U.S.	B7	124
Spremberg, Ger.	D14	8
Spring, stm., Ar., U.S.	A4	81
Spring Arbor, Mi., U.S.	F6	99
Spring Bay, b., Ut., U.S.	B3	121
Springbok, S. Afr.	G3	44
Springboro, Oh., U.S.	C1	112
Spring Brook, stm., Pa., U.S.	n18	115
Spring City, Pa., U.S.	F10	115
Spring City, Tn., U.S.	D9	119
Spring City, Ut., U.S.	D4	121
Spring Creek, stm., Nv., U.S.	D4	104
Spring Creek, stm., Nv., U.S.	C4	105
Spring Creek, stm., N.D., U.S.	B3	111
Springdale, Newf., Can.	D3	72
Springdale, Ar., U.S.	A1	81
Springdale, Oh., U.S.	n13	112
Springdale, Pa., U.S.	E2	115
Springdale, S.C., U.S.	D5	117
Springer, N.M., U.S.	A5	108
Springerville, Az., U.S.	C6	80
Springfield, Co., U.S.	D8	83
Springfield, Fl., U.S.	u16	86
Springfield, Ga., U.S.	D5	87
Springfield, Il., U.S.	D4	90
Springfield, Ky., U.S.	C4	94
Springfield, Ma., U.S.	B2	98
Springfield, Mn., U.S.	F4	100
Springfield, Mo., U.S.	D4	102
Springfield, Ne., U.S.	C9	104
Springfield, N.J., U.S.	B4	107
Springfield, Oh., U.S.	C2	112
Springfield, Or., U.S.	C4	114
Springfield, Pa., U.S.	p20	115
Springfield, S.D., U.S.	E8	118
Springfield, Tn., U.S.	A5	119
Springfield, Vt., U.S.	E4	122
Springfield, Va., U.S.	g12	123
Springfield, Lake, res., Il., U.S.	D4	90
Springfontein, S. Afr.	H5	44
Spring Garden, Guy.	D13	58
Spring Glen, Ut., U.S.	D5	121
Spring Green, Wi., U.S.	E3	126
Spring Grove, Il., U.S.	h8	90
Spring Grove, Mn., U.S.	G7	100
Spring Grove, Pa., U.S.	G8	115
Spring Hill, Fl., U.S.	D4	86
Spring Hill, Ks., U.S.	D9	93
Springhill, La., U.S.	A2	95
Spring Hill, Tn., U.S.	B5	119
Spring Hope, N.C., U.S.	B4	110
Spring Island, i., S.C., U.S.	G6	117
Spring Lake, Mi., U.S.	E4	99
Spring Lake, N.J., U.S.	C4	107
Spring Lake, N.C., U.S.	B4	110
Spring Lake, l., Me., U.S.	C2	96
Spring Lake, res., N.J., U.S.	B3	107
Spring Lake Heights, N.J., U.S.	C4	107
Spring Mountains, mts., Nv., U.S.	G6	105
Springport, Mi., U.S.	F6	99
Springs, S. Afr.	G5	44
Springside, Sask., Can.	F4	75
Springvale, Me., U.S.	E2	96
Spring Valley, Ca., U.S.	o16	82
Spring Valley, Il., U.S.	B4	90
Spring Valley, Mn., U.S.	G6	100
Spring Valley, N.Y., U.S.	g12	109
Spring Valley, Wi., U.S.	D1	126
Springville, Al., U.S.	B3	78
Springville, Ia., U.S.	B6	92
Springville, N.Y., U.S.	C2	109
Springville, Ut., U.S.	C4	121
Spruce Fork, stm., W.V., U.S.	m12	125
Spruce Grove, Alta., Can.	C4	68
Spruce Knob, mtn., W.V., U.S.	C6	125
Spruce Knob-Seneca Rocks National Recreation Area, W.V., U.S.	C5	125
Spruce Mountain, mtn., Az., U.S.	C3	80
Spruce Mountain, mtn., Nv., U.S.	C7	105
Spruce Pine, N.C., U.S.	f10	110
Spruce Run Reservoir, res., N.J., U.S.	B3	107
Spur, Tx., U.S.	C2	120
Spurr, Mount, mtn., Ak., U.S.	g15	79
Squam Lake, l., N.H., U.S.	C4	106
Squapan Lake, l., Me., U.S.	B4	96
Square Lake, l., Me., U.S.	A4	96
Squatec, Que., Can.	B9	74
Squaw Cap Mountain, mtn., N.B., Can.	B3	71
Squaw Hill, mtn., Wy., U.S.	E7	127
Squaw Peak, mtn., Mt., U.S.	C2	103
Squibnocket Point, c., Ma., U.S.	D6	98
Squinzano, Italy	I13	14
Squire, W.V., U.S.	D3	125
Sragen, Indon.	m15	33a
Sredinnyj Chrebet, mts., Russia	F26	24

Srednekolymsk, Russia	D24	24
Srednerusskaja Vozvyšennost', plat., Russia	H20	18
Srednesibirskoje Ploskogorje, plat., Russia	D14	24
Sremska Mitrovica, Yugo.	E3	16
Sri Gangānagar, India	F5	38
Srīkākulam, India	C7	37
Sri Lanka, ctry., Asia	H5	36
Srīnagar, India	C6	38
Srīrampur, India	C3	37
Stack Reservoir, res., R.I., U.S.	C3	116
Stade, Ger.	B9	8
Stadthagen, Ger.	C9	8
Stafford, Eng., U.K.	I10	7
Stafford, Ks., U.S.	D5	93
Stafford, Va., U.S.	B5	123
Stafford, co., Ks., U.S.	D5	93
Stafford, co., Va., U.S.	B5	123
Stafford Pond, l., R.I., U.S.	D6	116
Stafford Springs, Ct., U.S.	B6	84
Staked Plain see Estacado, Llano, pl., U.S.	E6	76
Stalheim, Nor.	F6	6
Stalingrad see Volgograd, Russia	H6	22
Stalowa Wola, Pol.	E22	8
Stambaugh, Mi., U.S.	B2	99
Stamford, Ct., U.S.	E1	84
Stamford, Tx., U.S.	C3	120
Stamford, Vt., U.S.	F2	122
Stamford, Lake, res., Tx., U.S.	C3	120
Stamping Ground, Ky., U.S.	B5	94
Stamps, Ar., U.S.	D2	81
Stanaford, W.V., U.S.	D3	125
Stanberry, Mo., U.S.	A3	102
Standerton, S. Afr.	G5	44
Standing Rock Indian Reservation, U.S.	B4	118
Standish, Mi., U.S.	E7	99
Stanfield, Az., U.S.	E3	80
Stanfield, Or., U.S.	B7	114
Stanford, Ky., U.S.	C5	94
Stanhope, N.J., U.S.	B3	107
Stanislaus, co., Ca., U.S.	D3	82
Stanke Dimitrov, Bul.	G7	16
Stanley, Falk. Is.	G5	56
Stanley, N.C., U.S.	B1	110
Stanley, N.D., U.S.	A3	111
Stanley, Va., U.S.	B4	123
Stanley, Wi., U.S.	D3	126
Stanley, co., S.D., U.S.	C5	118
Stanley Falls, wtfl, Zaire	A5	44
Stanleytown, Va., U.S.	D3	123
Stanleyville, N.C., U.S.	A2	110
Stanleyville see Kisangani, Zaire	A5	44
Stanly, co., N.C., U.S.	B2	110
Stann Creek, Belize	F3	64
Stanovoj Chrebet, mts., Russia	F19	24
Stanovoje Nagorje (Stanovoy Mountains), mts., Russia	F16	24
Stanstead, Que., Can.	D5	74
Stanton, Ia., U.S.	D2	92
Stanton, Ky., U.S.	C6	94
Stanton, Mi., U.S.	E5	99
Stanton, Ne., U.S.	C8	104
Stanton, Tx., U.S.	C2	120
Stanton, co., Ks., U.S.	E2	93
Stanton, co., Ne., U.S.	C8	104
Stantonsburg, N.C., U.S.	B5	110
Stanwood, Ia., U.S.	C6	92
Stanwood, Wa., U.S.	A3	124
Staples, Mn., U.S.	D4	100
Stapleton, Al., U.S.	E2	78
Star, Id., U.S.	F2	89
Star, N.C., U.S.	B3	110
Starachowice, Pol.	D21	8
Staraja Russa, Russia	C14	18
Stara Planina (Balkan Mountains), mts., Eur.	G8	16
Stara Zagora, Bul.	G9	16
Starbuck, Mn., U.S.	E3	100
Star City, Ar., U.S.	D4	81
Star City, W.V., U.S.	B5	125
Stargard Szczeciński (Stargard in Pommern), Pol.	B15	8
Stargo, Az., U.S.	D6	80
Stark, co., Il., U.S.	B4	90
Stark, co., N.D., U.S.	C3	111
Stark, co., Oh., U.S.	B4	112
Starke, Fl., U.S.	C4	86
Starke, co., In., U.S.	B4	91
Starks, La., U.S.	D2	95
Starkville, Ms., U.S.	B5	101
Star Lake, l., Mn., U.S.	D3	100
Starnberg, Ger.	G11	8
Starogard Gdański, Pol.	B18	8
Star Peak, mtn., Nv., U.S.	C3	105
Starr, co., Tx., U.S.	F3	120
Startex, S.C., U.S.	B3	117
Start Point, c., Eng., U.K.	K9	7
Startup, Wa., U.S.	B4	124
State Center, Ia., U.S.	B4	92
State College, Pa., U.S.	E6	115
Stateline, Nv., U.S.	E2	105
State Line, Pa., U.S.	G6	115
Staten Island, i., N.Y., U.S.	k12	109
Statenville, Ga., U.S.	F4	87
Statesboro, Ga., U.S.	D5	87
Statesville, N.C., U.S.	B2	110
Statham, Ga., U.S.	C3	87
Statue of Liberty National Monument, N.J., U.S.	k8	107
Staunton, Il., U.S.	D4	90
Staunton, Va., U.S.	B3	123
Stavanger, Nor.	G5	6
Stavropol', Russia	H6	22
Stayner, Ont., Can.	C4	73
Stayton, Or., U.S.	C4	114
Steamboat, Nv., U.S.	D2	105
Steamboat Mountain, mtn., Mt., U.S.	C4	103
Steamboat Mountain, mtn., Wy., U.S.	E4	127
Steamboat Springs, Co., U.S.	A4	83
Stearns, Ky., U.S.	D5	94
Stearns, co., Mn., U.S.	E4	100

Stearns Brook, stm., N.H., U.S.	A4	106
Stebbins, Ak., U.S.	C7	79
Steele, Al., U.S.	B3	78
Steele, Mo., U.S.	E8	102
Steele, N.D., U.S.	C6	111
Steele, co., Mn., U.S.	F5	100
Steele, co., N.D., U.S.	B8	111
Steele, Mount, mtn., Wy., U.S.	E6	127
Steeleville, Il., U.S.	E4	90
Steelton, Pa., U.S.	F8	115
Steelville, Mo., U.S.	D6	102
Steenkool, Indon.	F9	32
Steens Mountain, mts., Or., U.S.	E8	114
Stefansson Island, i., N.W. Ter., Can.	B11	66
Steger, Il., U.S.	B6	90
Steilacoom, Wa., U.S.	f10	124
Steinbach, Man., Can.	E3	70
Steinhatchee, stm., Fl., U.S.	C3	86
Steinkjer, Nor.	D8	6
Stellenbosch, S. Afr.	H3	44
Stenay, Fr.	C12	10
Stendal, Ger.	C11	8
Stephen, Mn., U.S.	B2	100
Stephens, Ar., U.S.	D2	81
Stephens, co., Ga., U.S.	B3	87
Stephens, co., Ok., U.S.	C4	113
Stephens, co., Tx., U.S.	C3	120
Stephens City, Va., U.S.	A4	123
Stephens Lake, res., Man., Can.	A4	70
Stephenson, Mi., U.S.	C3	99
Stephenson, co., Il., U.S.	A4	90
Stephens Passage, strt., Ak., U.S.	m23	79
Stephenville, Newf., Can.	D2	72
Stephenville, Tx., U.S.	C3	120
Stephenville Crossing, Newf., Can.	D2	72
Sterling, Ak., U.S.	g16	79
Sterling, Co., U.S.	A7	83
Sterling, Il., U.S.	B4	90
Sterling, Ks., U.S.	D5	93
Sterling, Va., U.S.	A5	123
Sterling, co., Tx., U.S.	D2	120
Sterling City, Tx., U.S.	D2	120
Sterling Heights, Mi., U.S.	o15	99
Sterling Reservoir, res., Co., U.S.	A7	83
Sterlington, La., U.S.	B3	95
Sterlitamak, Russia	G9	22
Stettin see Szczecin, Pol.	B14	8
Stettler, Alta., Can.	C4	68
Steuben, co., In., U.S.	A7	91
Steuben, co., N.Y., U.S.	C3	109
Steubenville, Oh., U.S.	B5	112
Stevenage, Eng., U.K.	J12	7
Stevens, co., Mn., U.S.	E2	100
Stevens, co., Wa., U.S.	A7	124
Stevens Creek Dam, U.S.	C4	87
Stevenson, Al., U.S.	A4	78
Stevenson, Ct., U.S.	D3	84
Stevenson, Wa., U.S.	D4	124
Stevenson Lake, l., Man., Can.	C4	70
Stevens Pass, Wa., U.S.	B4	124
Stevens Peak, mtn., Id., U.S.	B3	89
Stevens Point, Wi., U.S.	D4	126
Stevensville, Md., U.S.	C5	97
Stevensville, Mi., U.S.	F4	99
Stevensville, Mt., U.S.	D2	103
Stewart, co., Ga., U.S.	D2	87
Stewart, co., Tn., U.S.	A4	119
Stewart Island, i., N.Z.	G1	52
Stewart Mountain, mtn., Az., U.S.	k9	80
Stewartstown, Pa., U.S.	G8	115
Stewartsville, Mo., U.S.	B3	102
Stewartville, Mn., U.S.	G6	100
Stewiacke, N.S., Can.	D6	71
Steyr, Aus.	G14	8
Stigler, Ok., U.S.	I11	14
Stigliano, Italy	I11	14
Stikine, stm., B.C., Can.	D13	79
Stikine, stm., Ak., U.S.	D13	79
Stikine Ranges, mts., B.C., Can.	E6	66
Still, stm., Ct., U.S.	B3	84
Stillaguamish, North Fork, stm., Wa., U.S.	A4	124
Stillaguamish, South Fork, stm., Wa., U.S.	A4	124
Stillhouse Hollow Lake, res., Tx., U.S.	D4	120
Stillman Valley, Il., U.S.	A4	90
Stillmore, Ga., U.S.	D4	87
Stillwater, Mn., U.S.	E6	100
Stillwater, Ok., U.S.	A4	113
Stillwater, co., Mt., U.S.	E7	103
Stillwater Range, mts., Nv., U.S.	D3	105
Stillwater Reservoir, res., N.Y., U.S.	B5	109
Stillwater Reservoir, res., R.I., U.S.	B3	116
Stilwell, Ok., U.S.	B7	113
Stimson, Mount, mtn., Mt., U.S.	B3	103
Stine Mountain, mtn., Mt., U.S.	E4	103
Stinking Lake, l., N.M., U.S.	A3	108
Stinnett, Tx., U.S.	B2	120
Štip, Mac.	H6	16
Stirling, Alta., Can.	E4	68
Stirling, Ont., Can.	C7	73
Stirling, Scot., U.K.	E9	7
Stjørdalshalsen, Nor.	E8	6
Stockbridge, Ga., U.S.	C2	87
Stockbridge, Mi., U.S.	F6	99
Stockbridge-Munsee Indian Reservation, Wi., U.S.	D5	126
Stockdale, Tx., U.S.	E4	120
Stockerau, Aus.	G16	8
Stockholm, Swe.	G12	6
Stockton, Ca., U.S.	D3	82
Stockton, Il., U.S.	A3	90
Stockton, Ks., U.S.	C4	93
Stockton, Md., U.S.	D7	97
Stockton, Mo., U.S.	D4	102
Stockton Island, i., Wi., U.S.	B3	126
Stockton Lake, res., Mo., U.S.	D4	102
Stoddard, Wi., U.S.	E2	126
Stoddard, co., Mo., U.S.	E8	102

Stoke-on-Trent, Eng., U.K.	H10	7
Stokes, co., N.C., U.S.	A2	110
Stokesdale, N.C., U.S.	A3	110
Stolbovoj, Ostrov, i., Russia	C21	24
Stollings, W.V., U.S.	n12	125
Ston, Cro.	G12	14
Stone, co., Ar., U.S.	B3	81
Stone, co., Ms., U.S.	E4	101
Stone, co., Mo., U.S.	E4	102
Stoneboro, Pa., U.S.	D1	115
Stone Corral Lake, l., Or., U.S.	E7	114
Stoneham, Ma., U.S.	g11	98
Stonehaven, Scot., U.K.	E10	7
Stone Mountain, Ga., U.S.	C2	87
Stone Mountain, mtn., Ga., U.S.	C2	87
Stones River National Battlefield, hist., Tn., U.S.	B4	119
Stoneville, N.C., U.S.	A3	110
Stonewall, Man., Can.	D3	70
Stonewall, La., U.S.	B2	95
Stonewall, Ms., U.S.	C5	101
Stonewall, co., Tx., U.S.	C2	120
Stonewood, W.V., U.S.	k10	125
Stoney Creek, Ont., Can.	D5	73
Stonington, Ct., U.S.	D8	84
Stonington, Il., U.S.	D4	90
Stonington, Me., U.S.	D4	96
Stono, stm., S.C., U.S.	k11	117
Stono Inlet, b., S.C., U.S.	F8	117
Stony Brook, N.Y., U.S.	n15	109
Stony Brook, stm., N.J., U.S.	C3	107
Stony Creek, stm., Va., U.S.	C5	123
Stony Island, i., N.Y., U.S.	B4	109
Stony Plain, Alta., Can.	C3	68
Stony Point, N.C., U.S.	B1	110
Storby, Fin.	F12	6
Støren, Nor.	E8	6
Storey, co., Nv., U.S.	D2	105
Storfors, Swe.	G10	6
Storkerson Peninsula, pen., N.W. Ter., Can.	B11	66
Storlien, Swe.	E9	6
Storm Lake, Ia., U.S.	B2	92
Storm Lake, l., Ia., U.S.	B2	92
Storm Mountain, mtn., Ak., U.S.	h16	79
Stornoway, Scot., U.K.	C6	7
Storrs, Ct., U.S.	B7	84
Storuman, Swe.	D11	6
Storvreta, Swe.	G11	6
Story, Wy., U.S.	B6	127
Story, co., Ia., U.S.	B4	92
Story City, Ia., U.S.	B4	92
Stoughton, Sask., Can.	H4	75
Stoughton, Ma., U.S.	B5	98
Stoughton, Wi., U.S.	F4	126
Stover, Mo., U.S.	C5	102
Stow, Oh., U.S.	A4	112
Stow Creek, stm., N.J., U.S.	E2	107
Stowe, Pa., U.S.	F10	115
Stowe, Vt., U.S.	C3	122
Stoyoma Mountain, mtn., B.C., Can.	E7	69
Strabane, Pa., U.S.	F1	115
Strafford, Mo., U.S.	D4	102
Strafford, co., N.H., U.S.	D4	106
Straffordville, Ont., Can.	E4	73
Strahan, Austl.	H9	50
Strakonice, Czech.	F13	8
Stralsund, Ger.	A13	8
Stranraer, Scot., U.K.	G7	7
Strasbourg, Fr.	D14	10
Strasburg, Co., U.S.	B6	83
Strasburg, Oh., U.S.	B4	112
Strasburg, Pa., U.S.	G9	115
Strasburg, Va., U.S.	A4	123
Stratford, Ont., Can.	D3	73
Stratford, Ct., U.S.	E3	84
Stratford, Ia., U.S.	B4	92
Stratford, N.J., U.S.	D2	107
Stratford, Ok., U.S.	C5	113
Stratford, Tx., U.S.	A1	120
Stratford, Wi., U.S.	D3	126
Stratford, co., U.S.	E3	84
Stratford Point, c., Ct., U.S.	E3	84
Stratford-upon-Avon, Eng., U.K.	I11	7
Stratham, N.H., U.S.	D5	106
Strathmore, Alta., Can.	D4	68
Strathmore, Ca., U.S.	D4	82
Strathroy, Ont., Can.	E3	73
Stratton, Co., U.S.	B8	83
Straubing, Ger.	G12	8
Strausberg, Ger.	C13	8
Strawberry, stm., Ar., U.S.	A4	81
Strawberry, stm., Ut., U.S.	C5	121
Strawberry Mountain, mtn., Or., U.S.	C8	114
Strawberry Point, Ia., U.S.	B6	92
Strawberry Point, c., Ma., U.S.	B6	98
Strawberry Range, mts., Or., U.S.	C8	114
Strawberry Reservoir, res., Ut., U.S.	C4	121
Streator, Il., U.S.	B5	90
Stretensk, Russia	G17	24
Strickland, stm., Pap. N. Gui.	m15	50a
Strimón (Struma), stm., Eur.	I7	16
Stromness, Scot., U.K.	C9	7
Stromsburg, Ne., U.S.	C8	104
Strömstad, Swe.	G8	6
Strömsund, Swe.	E10	6
Strong, Ar., U.S.	D3	81
Strong, Me., U.S.	D2	96
Strong, stm., Ms., U.S.	C4	101
Strong City, Ks., U.S.	D7	93
Stronghurst, Il., U.S.	C3	90
Strongsville, Oh., U.S.	A4	112
Stronsay, i., Scot., U.K.	B10	7
Stroud, Ok., U.S.	B5	113
Stroudsburg, Pa., U.S.	E11	115
Stroudwater, stm., Me., U.S.	g7	96
Strum, Wi., U.S.	D2	126
Struma (Strimón), stm., Eur.	H7	16
Strumble Head, c., Wales, U.K.	I7	7
Strumica, Mac.	E21	18
Strunino, Russia	A5	18
Struthers, Oh., U.S.	A5	112
Stryker, Oh., U.S.	A1	112
Stuart, Fl., U.S.	E6	86

183

Name	Map Ref	Page
Stuart, Ia., U.S.	C3	92
Stuart, Ne., U.S.	B6	104
Stuart, Va., U.S.	D2	123
Stuart, Mount, mtn., Wa., U.S.	B5	124
Stuart Lake, l., B.C., Can.	B5	69
Stuarts Draft, Va., U.S.	B5	123
Stull, stm., Can.	B5	70
Stump Lake, l., N.D., U.S.	B7	111
Stump Pond, res., R.I., U.S.	D2	116
Stung Treng, Camb.	H8	34
Stupino, Russia	G21	18
Sturbridge, Ma., U.S.	B3	98
Sturgeon, Mo., U.S.	B5	102
Sturgeon, stm., Mi., U.S.	B4	99
Sturgeon Bay, Wi., U.S.	D6	126
Sturgeon Bay, b., Man., Can.	C3	70
Sturgeon Falls, Ont., Can.	A5	73
Sturgeon Lake, l., Ont., Can.	C6	73
Sturgis, Sask., Can.	F4	75
Sturgis, Ky., U.S.	e10	94
Sturgis, Mi., U.S.	G5	99
Sturgis, S.D., U.S.	C2	118
Sturtevant, Wi., U.S.	F6	126
Stutsman, co., N.D., U.S.	B6	111
Stuttgart, Ger.	G9	8
Stuttgart, Ar., U.S.	C4	81
Suaita, Col.	D6	58
Subang, Indon.	m13	33a
Subansiri, stm., Asia	G16	38
Subiaco, Italy	H8	14
Sublette, Ks., U.S.	E3	93
Sublette, co., Wy., U.S.	D2	127
Sublett Range, mts., Id., U.S.	G6	89
Sublimity, Or., U.S.	C4	114
Subotica, Yugo.	C3	16
Sučan, Russia	I20	24
Sucarnoochee, stm., Al., U.S.	C1	78
Succasunna, N.J., U.S.	B3	107
Suceava, Rom.	B10	16
Süchbaatar, Mong.	A8	26
Suchumi, Geor.	I6	22
Sucre, Bol.	G5	54
Sucuaro, Col.	E8	58
Sudan, ctry., Afr.	F12	42
Sudan, reg., Afr.	F7	42
Sudbury, Ont., Can.	A4	73
Sudbury, Ma., U.S.	B5	98
Sudbury, stm., Ma., U.S.	B5	98
Sudbury Center, Ma., U.S.	g10	98
Sudbury Reservoir, res., Ma., U.S.	g10	98
Sudeten see Sudety, mts., Eur.	E15	8
Sudety, mts., Eur.	E15	8
Sue, stm., Sudan	G11	42
Sueca, Spain	F11	12
Suez see As-Suways, Egypt	C12	42
Suez Canal see Suways, Qanāt as-, Egypt	D3	40
Suffern, N.Y., U.S.	D6	109
Suffield, Ct., U.S.	B5	84
Suffolk, Va., U.S.	D6	123
Suffolk, co., Ma., U.S.	B5	98
Suffolk, co., N.Y., U.S.	n15	109
Sugar, stm., U.S.	F4	126
Sugar, stm., N.H., U.S.	D2	106
Sugar City, Id., U.S.	F7	89
Sugar Creek, Mo., U.S.	h11	102
Sugarcreek, Pa., U.S.	D2	115
Sugar Creek, stm., Oh., U.S.	C2	112
Sugar Creek, stm., Pa., U.S.	C8	115
Sugar Grove, Va., U.S.	D1	123
Sugar Hill, Ga., U.S.	B2	87
Sugar Island, i., Mi., U.S.	B6	99
Sugar Land, Tx., U.S.	E5	120
Sugarland Run, Va., U.S.	*A5	123
Sugar Loaf, l., U.S.	C3	123
Sugarloaf Mountain, mtn., Mt., U.S.	C4	103
Sugar Notch, Pa., U.S.	n17	115
Suggi Lake, l., Sask., Can.	C4	75
Sugoj, stm., Russia	E25	24
Şuḥār, Oman	D6	46
Suhl, Ger.	E10	8
Suiattle, stm., Wa., U.S.	A4	124
Suide, China	D9	26
Suihua, China	B12	26
Suining, China	E8	26
Suiping, China	B2	28
Suitland, Md., U.S.	C4	97
Şuizhong, China	C11	26
Šuja, Russia	E24	18
Sukabumi, Indon.	m13	33a
Sukagawa, Japan	E13	30
Sukhumi see Suchumi, Geor.	I6	22
Sukkertoppen, Grnld.	C22	66
Sukkur, Pak.	G3	38
Sukumo, Japan	J5	30
Sula, Kepulauan, is., Indon.	F8	32
Sulaimān Range, mts., Pak.	F3	38
Sulawesi (Celebes), i., Indon.	F7	32
Sullana, Peru	D2	54
Sulligent, Al., U.S.	B1	78
Sullivan, Il., U.S.	D5	90
Sullivan, In., U.S.	F3	91
Sullivan, Mo., U.S.	C6	102
Sullivan, co., In., U.S.	F3	91
Sullivan, co., Mo., U.S.	A4	102
Sullivan, co., N.H., U.S.	D2	106
Sullivan, co., N.Y., U.S.	D6	109
Sullivan, co., Pa., U.S.	D9	115
Sullivan, co., Tn., U.S.	C11	119
Sullivan Lake, l., Alta., Can.	D5	68
Sullivans Island, S.C., U.S.	k12	117
Sully, Fr.	E9	10
Sully, Ia., U.S.	C5	92
Sully, co., S.D., U.S.	C5	118
Sulmona, Italy	G8	14
Sulphur, La., U.S.	D2	95
Sulphur, Ok., U.S.	C5	113
Sulphur, stm., U.S.	D2	81
Sulphur Spring Range, mts., Nv., U.S.	C5	105
Sulphur Springs, Tx., U.S.	C5	120
Sultan, Wa., U.S.	B4	124
Sultānpur, India	G10	38
Sulu Archipelago, is., Phil.	D7	32
Sulu Sea, Asia	D6	32
Sulzbach-Rosenberg, Ger.	F11	8
Sumas, Wa., U.S.	A3	124
Sumatera (Sumatra), i., Indon.	F3	32
Sumatra see Sumatera, i., Indon.	F3	32
Sumba, i., Indon.	G7	32
Sumbawa, i., Indon.	G6	32
Sumbawanga, Tan.	C6	44
Sumedang, Indon.	m13	33a
Sumen, Bul.	F10	16
Sumenep, Indon.	m16	33a
Sumgait, Azer.	I7	22
Sumiton, Al., U.S.	B2	78
Summerfield, N.C., U.S.	A3	110
Summerford, Newf., Can.	D4	72
Summer Island, i., Mi., U.S.	C4	99
Summer Lake, l., Or., U.S.	E6	114
Summerland, B.C., Can.	E8	69
Summers, co., W.V., U.S.	D4	125
Summerside, P.E.I., Can.	C6	71
Summersville, W.V., U.S.	C4	125
Summersville Lake, res., W.V., U.S.	C4	125
Summerton, S.C., U.S.	D7	117
Summertown, Tn., U.S.	B4	119
Summerville, Ga., U.S.	B1	87
Summerville, S.C., U.S.	E7	117
Summit, Il., U.S.	k9	90
Summit, Ms., U.S.	D3	101
Summit, N.J., U.S.	B4	107
Summit, Tn., U.S.	h11	119
Summit, co., Co., U.S.	B4	83
Summit, co., Oh., U.S.	A4	112
Summit, co., Ut., U.S.	C5	121
Summit Hill, Pa., U.S.	E10	115
Summit Lake, l., Ia., U.S.	C3	92
Summit Lake Indian Reservation, Nv., U.S.	B2	105
Summit Mountain, mtn., Nv., U.S.	D5	105
Summit Peak, mtn., Co., U.S.	D4	83
Summitville, In., U.S.	D6	91
Sumner, Il., U.S.	E6	90
Sumner, Ia., U.S.	B5	92
Sumner, Wa., U.S.	B3	124
Sumner, co., Ks., U.S.	E6	93
Sumner, co., Tn., U.S.	A5	119
Sumner, Lake, res., N.M., U.S.	C5	108
Sumner Dam, N.M., U.S.	C5	108
Sumner Strait, strt., Ak., U.S.	m23	79
Sumoto, Japan	H7	30
Šumperk, Czech.	F16	8
Şumrall, Ms., U.S.	D4	101
Šumšu, Ostrov, i., Russia	G25	24
Sumter, S.C., U.S.	D7	117
Sumter, co., Al., U.S.	C1	78
Sumter, co., Fl., U.S.	D4	86
Sumter, co., Ga., U.S.	D2	87
Sumter, co., S.C., U.S.	D7	117
Sumy, Ukr.	G4	22
Sun, stm., Mt., U.S.	C4	103
Sunagawa, Japan	p19	30a
Sunapee, N.H., U.S.	D2	106
Sunapee Lake, l., N.H., U.S.	D2	106
Sunbright, Tn., U.S.	C9	119
Sunbury, Oh., U.S.	B3	112
Sunbury, Pa., U.S.	E8	115
Sunchales, Arg.	C4	56
Sun City, Az., U.S.	k8	80
Suncook, N.H., U.S.	D4	106
Suncook, stm., N.H., U.S.	D4	106
Suncook Lakes, l., N.H., U.S.	D4	106
Sunda, Selat, strt., Indon.	G4	32
Sundance, Wy., U.S.	B8	127
Sundance Mountain, mtn., Wy., U.S.	B8	127
Sundarbans, reg., Asia	J13	38
Sunderland, Ont., Can.	C5	73
Sunderland, Eng., U.K.	G11	7
Sundown, Tx., U.S.	C1	120
Sundre, Alta., Can.	D3	68
Sundridge, Ont., Can.	B5	73
Sundsvall, Swe.	E11	6
Sunflower, Ms., U.S.	B3	101
Sunflower, co., Ms., U.S.	B3	101
Sunflower, Mount, mtn., Ks., U.S.	C2	93
Sungaidareh, Indon.	O6	34
Sungei Patani, Malay.	L6	34
Suniteyouqi, China	C9	26
Sunland Park, N.M., U.S.	F3	108
Sunlight Creek, stm., Wy., U.S.	B3	127
Sunman, In., U.S.	F7	91
Sunndalsøra, Nor.	E7	6
Sunnyside, Newf., Can.	E5	72
Sunnyside, Wa., U.S.	C5	124
Sunnyvale, Ca., U.S.	k8	82
Sun Prairie, Wi., U.S.	E4	126
Sunray, Tx., U.S.	A2	120
Sunrise Manor, Nv., U.S.	*G6	105
Sunset, La., U.S.	D3	95
Sunset, Ut., U.S.	B4	121
Sunset Beach, Hi., U.S.	f9	88
Sunset Crater National Monument, Az., U.S.	B4	80
Sunset Lake, l., Vt., U.S.	D2	122
Suntar, Russia	E17	24
Suntar-Chajata, Chrebet, mts., Russia	E22	24
Suntaug Lake, l., Ma., U.S.	f11	98
Sun Valley, Id., U.S.	F4	89
Sun Valley, Nv., U.S.	D2	105
Sunyani, Ghana	G5	42
Suō-nada, Japan	I4	30
Suonenjoki, Fin.	E16	6
Suordach, Russia	D20	24
Superior, Az., U.S.	D4	80
Superior, Mt., U.S.	C2	103
Superior, Ne., U.S.	D7	104
Superior, Wi., U.S.	B1	126
Superior, Wy., U.S.	E4	127
Superior, Lake, l., N.A.	B9	76
Superstition Mountains, mts., Az., U.S.	m10	80
Supetar, Cro.	F11	14
Suphan Buri, Thai.	G6	34
Suqian, China	B7	28
Suquamish, Wa., U.S.	B3	124
Suquţrā (Socotra), i., Yemen	F5	46
Şūr (Tyre), Leb.	C4	40
Şūr, Oman	D6	46
Sur, Point, c., Ca., U.S.	D3	82
Surabaya, Indon.	m16	32
Surakarta, Indon.	m15	32
Şūrān, Syria	B5	40
Surat, India	B2	37
Surat Thani (Ban Don), Thai.	J5	34
Surendranagar, India	I4	38
Surfside, Fl., U.S.	s13	86
Surfside Beach, S.C., U.S.	D10	117
Surgoinsville, Tn., U.S.	C11	119
Sūri, India	I12	38
Surigao, Phil.	D8	32
Surin, Thai.	G7	34
Suriname, ctry., S.A.	C7	54
Surprise, Az., U.S.	k8	80
Surrey, N.D., U.S.	A4	111
Surry, co., N.C., U.S.	A2	110
Surry, co., Va., U.S.	C6	123
Surry Mountain Lake, res., N.H., U.S.	D2	106
Surt, Libya	B9	42
Surt, Khalīj, b., Libya	B9	42
Sürüç, Tur.	A6	40
Suruga-wan, b., Japan	H11	30
Susa, Italy	D2	14
Susanville, Ca., U.S.	B3	82
Susitna, stm., Ak., U.S.	C10	79
Susquehanna, Pa., U.S.	C10	115
Susquehanna, co., Pa., U.S.	C10	115
Susquehanna, stm., U.S.	A5	97
Susquehanna, West Branch, stm., Pa., U.S.	D5	115
Sussex, N.B., Can.	D4	71
Sussex, N.J., U.S.	A3	107
Sussex, Wi., U.S.	m11	126
Sussex, co., De., U.S.	F4	85
Sussex, co., N.J., U.S.	A3	107
Sussex, co., Va., U.S.	D5	123
Susurluk, Tur.	J12	16
Sutherland, S. Afr.	H4	44
Sutherland, Ia., U.S.	B2	92
Sutherland, Ne., U.S.	C4	104
Sutherlin, Or., U.S.	D3	114
Sutlej (Satluj) (Langqên), stm., Asia	F4	38
Sutter, co., Ca., U.S.	C3	82
Sutter Creek, Ca., U.S.	C3	82
Sutton, Que., Can.	D5	74
Sutton, Ne., U.S.	D8	104
Sutton, W.V., U.S.	C4	125
Sutton, co., Tx., U.S.	D2	120
Sutton Lake, res., W.V., U.S.	C4	125
Sutwik Island, i., Ak., U.S.	D8	79
Suur Munamägi, hill, Est.	D10	18
Suwa, Japan	F11	30
Suwałki, Pol.	A22	8
Suwannee, co., Fl., U.S.	B3	86
Suwannee, stm., U.S.	C4	86
Suwannee Sound, strt., Fl., U.S.	C3	86
Suways, Qanāt as- (Suez Canal), Egypt	D3	40
Suwŏn, S. Kor.	D12	26
Suxian, China	B5	28
Suzaka, Japan	F11	30
Suzhou (Soochow), China	D9	28
Suzuka, Japan	H9	30
Suzu-misaki, c., Japan	E10	30
Suzzara, Italy	D5	14
Svappavaara, Swe.	C13	6
Svartenhuk, pen., Grnld.	B22	66
Sv'atoj Nos, Mys, c., Russia	C22	24
Sveg, Swe.	E10	6
Svenljunga, Swe.	H9	6
Svensen, Or., U.S.	A3	114
Sverdlovsk see Jekaterinburg, Russia	F10	22
Svetlaja, Russia	H21	24
Svetlyj, Russia	F17	24
Svištov, Bul.	F9	16
Svobodnyj, Russia	G19	24
Svolvær, Nor.	B11	6
Swain, co., N.C., U.S.	f9	110
Swainsboro, Ga., U.S.	D4	87
Swakopmund, Nmb.	F2	44
Swampscott, Ma., U.S.	B6	98
Swan, stm., Can.	C1	70
Swan Creek, stm., Oh., U.S.	e6	112
Swan Falls, wtfl, Id., U.S.	F2	89
Swan Hill, Austl.	G8	50
Swan Hills, Alta., Can.	B3	68
Swan Islands, is., Hond.	F6	64
Swan Lake, l., Man., Can.	C1	70
Swan Lake, l., Me., U.S.	D4	96
Swan Lake, l., Ne., U.S.	C3	104
Swannanoa, N.C., U.S.	f10	110
Swan Peak, mtn., Mt., U.S.	C3	103
Swan Range, mts., Mt., U.S.	C3	103
Swan River, Man., Can.	C1	70
Swansboro, N.C., U.S.	C5	110
Swansea, Wales, U.K.	J9	7
Swansea, Il., U.S.	E4	90
Swanson Lake, res., Ne., U.S.	D4	104
Swanton, Oh., U.S.	A2	112
Swanton, Vt., U.S.	B2	122
Swanzey Center, N.H., U.S.	E2	106
Swarthmore, Pa., U.S.	p20	115
Swartswood Lake, l., N.J., U.S.	A3	107
Swartz Creek, Mi., U.S.	F7	99
Swayzee, In., U.S.	C6	91
Swaziland, ctry., Afr.	G6	44
Swea City, Ia., U.S.	A3	92
Sweden, ctry., Eur.	C10	4
Sweeny, Tx., U.S.	r14	120
Sweet Grass, co., Mt., U.S.	E7	103
Sweet Home, Or., U.S.	C4	114
Sweetser, In., U.S.	C6	91
Sweet Springs, Mo., U.S.	C4	102
Sweetwater, Tn., U.S.	D9	119
Sweetwater, Tx., U.S.	C2	120
Sweetwater, co., Wy., U.S.	E3	127
Sweetwater, stm., Wy., U.S.	D4	127
Sweetwater Creek, Fl., U.S.	p10	86
Sweetwater Creek, stm., Ok., U.S.		
Swellendam, S. Afr.	H4	44
Swepsonville, N.C., U.S.	A3	110
Swift, co., Mn., U.S.	E3	100
Swift, co., N.H., U.S.	B4	106
Swift Creek, stm., N.C., U.S.	B5	110
Swift Creek Reservoir, res., Wa., U.S.	C3	124
Swift Diamond, stm., N.H., U.S.	g7	106
Swifton, Ar., U.S.	B4	81
Swinburne, Cape, c., N.W. Ter., Can.	B13	66
Swindon, Eng., U.K.	J11	7
Swinomish Indian Reservation, Wa., U.S.	A3	124
Świnoujście (Swinemünde), Pol.	B14	8
Swisher, Ia., U.S.	C6	92
Swisher, co., Tx., U.S.	B2	120
Swissvale, Pa., U.S.	k14	115
Switzer, W.V., U.S.	D3	125
Switzerland, Fl., U.S.	m8	86
Switzerland, co., In., U.S.	G7	91
Switzerland, ctry., Eur.	F9	4
Swoyerville, Pa., U.S.	D10	115
Syalach, Russia	D18	24
Sycamore, Al., U.S.	B3	78
Sycamore, Il., U.S.	B5	90
Sycamore, Oh., U.S.	B2	112
Sycamore Creek, stm., W.V., U.S.	m13	125
Sydenham, Ont., Can.	C8	73
Sydney, Austl.	F10	50
Syke, Ger.	C8	8
Sykesville, Md., U.S.	B4	97
Sykesville, Pa., U.S.	D4	115
Sykkylven, Nor.	E6	6
Syktyvkar, Russia	E8	22
Sylacauga, Al., U.S.	B3	78
Sylhet, Bngl.	H14	38
Sylva, N.C., U.S.	f9	110
Sylvania, Al., U.S.	A4	78
Sylvania, Ga., U.S.	D5	87
Sylvania, Oh., U.S.	A2	112
Sylvan Lake, Alta., Can.	C3	68
Sylvan Lake, Mi., U.S.	o15	99
Sylvan Lake, l., In., U.S.	B7	91
Sylvan Pass, Wy., U.S.	B2	127
Sylvester, Ga., U.S.	E3	87
Sym, Russia	E11	24
Symmes Creek, stm., Oh., U.S.	D3	112
Symsonia, Ky., U.S.	f9	94
Syracuse, In., U.S.	B6	91
Syracuse, Ks., U.S.	E2	93
Syracuse, Ne., U.S.	D9	104
Syracuse, N.Y., U.S.	B4	109
Syracuse, Ut., U.S.	B3	121
Syrdarja (Syr Darya), stm., Asia	I11	22
Syria, ctry., Asia	B5	40
Syriam, Burma	F4	34
Syrian Desert see Shām, Bādiyat ash-, des., Asia	C6	40
Sysladobsis Lake, l., Me., U.S.	C4	96
Syzran', Russia	G7	22
Szamos (Someş), stm., Eur.	B6	16
Szczecin (Stettin), Pol.	B14	8
Szczecinek (Neustettin), Pol.	B16	8
Szeged, Hung.	I20	8
Székesfehérvár, Hung.	H18	8
Szentes, Hung.	I20	8
Szolnok, Hung.	H20	8
Szombathely, Hung.	H16	8

T

Name	Map Ref	Page
Taal, Lake, l., Phil.	r19	33b
Tabaco, Phil.	r20	33b
Tabarka, Tun.	M3	14
Tabatinga, Serra da, hills, Braz.	F10	54
Tabbys Peak, mtn., Ut., U.S.	C3	121
Tabelbala, Alg.	C5	42
Taber, Alta., Can.	E4	68
Tabernes de Valldigna, Spain	F11	12
Tablas Island, i., Phil.	C7	32
Table Head, c., Newf., Can.	B4	72
Table Mountain, mtn., Az., U.S.	E5	80
Table Rock Lake, res., U.S.	E4	102
Table Top, mtn., Az., U.S.	E3	80
Tabor, Russia	C24	24
Tabor, Ia., U.S.	D2	92
Tabora, Tan.	C6	44
Tabor City, N.C., U.S.	C4	110
Tabou, I.C.	H4	42
Tabrīz, Iran	J7	22
Tabūk, Sau. Ar.	C2	46
Tacámbaro de Codallos, Mex.	H9	62
Tachikawa, Japan	G12	30
Tacna, Peru	G4	54
Tacoma, Wa., U.S.	B3	124
Taconic Range, mts., U.S.	A1	98
Tacuarembó, Ur.	C5	56
Tacubaya, Mex.	C7	62
Tadjerouine, Tun.	N3	14
Tadoule Lake, l., Man., Can.	E13	66
Tadoussac, Que., Can.	A8	74
Tādpatri, India	E5	37
Taegu, S. Kor.	D12	26
Taejŏn, S. Kor.	D12	26
Tafalla, Spain	C10	12
Taft, Ca., U.S.	E4	82
Taft, Tx., U.S.	F4	120
Tagajō, Japan	D13	30
Taganrog, Russia	H5	22
Taglio di Po, Italy	D7	14
Taguatinga, Braz.	B5	57
Taguke, China	D11	38
Tagula Island, i., Pap. N. Gui.	B10	50
Tagus (Tejo) (Tajo), stm., Eur.	F3	12
Tahan, Gunong, mtn., Malay.	L7	34
Tahat, mtn., Alg.	D7	42
Tahlequah, Ok., U.S.	B7	113
Tahoe, Lake, l., U.S.	E1	105
Tahoka, Tx., U.S.	C2	120
Taholah, Wa., U.S.	B1	124
Tahoua, Niger	F7	42
Tahquamenon, stm., Mi., U.S.	B5	99
Tahsis, B.C., Can.	E4	69
Tahtsa Peak, mtn., B.C., Can.	C4	69
T'aichung, Tai.	K9	28
T'aichunghsien, Tai.	K9	28
Taihape, N.Z.	C5	52
Tai Hu, l., China	D9	28
Tailai, China	B11	26
Tain, Scot., U.K.	D8	7
T'ainan, Tai.	L9	28
T'aipei, Tai.	J10	28
T'aipeihsien, Tai.	J10	28
Taiping, Malay.	L6	34
Taishun, China	H8	28
Taitao, Península de, pen., Chile	F2	56
T'aitung, Tai.	M10	28
Taivalkoski, Fin.	D17	6
Taiwan (T'aiwan), ctry., Asia	G11	26
Taiwan Strait, strt., Asia	K8	28
Taixian, China	C9	28
Taixing, China	C9	28
Taizhou, China	C8	28
Ta'izz, Yemen	F3	46
Tajikistan, ctry., Asia	J12	22
Tajitos, Mex.	B3	62
Tajmyr, Ozero, l., Russia	C14	24
Tajmyr, Poluostrov, pen., Russia	B14	24
Tajšet, Russia	F13	24
Tajumulco, Volcán, vol., Guat.	G2	64
Tak, Thai.	F5	34
Takada, Japan	E11	30
Takalar, Indon.	G6	32
Takamatsu, Japan	H7	30
Takaoka, Japan	F10	30
Takapuna, N.Z.	B5	52
Takasaki, Japan	F12	30
Takatsuki, Japan	H8	30
Takawa, Japan	I3	30
Takayama, Japan	F10	30
Takefu, Japan	G9	30
Takêv, Camb.	I8	34
Takijuq Lake, l., N.W. Ter., Can.	C10	66
Takikawa, Japan	p19	30a
Takla Lake, l., B.C., Can.	B5	69
Taklimakan Shamo, des., China	D3	26
Takoma Park, Md., U.S.	f8	97
Taku Glacier, Ak., U.S.	k22	79
Tala, Mex.	G8	62
Talagang, Pak.	D5	38
Talaimannar, Sri L.	H5	37
Talara, Peru	D2	54
Talarrubias, Spain	F6	12
Talasea, Pap. N. Gui.	m17	50a
Talaud, Kepulauan, is., Indon.	E8	32
Talavera de la Reina, Spain	F7	12
Talawdī, Sudan	F12	42
Talbot, co., Ga., U.S.	D2	87
Talbot, co., Md., U.S.	C5	97
Talbot Island, i., Fl., U.S.	B5	86
Talbot Lake, l., Man., Can.	B2	70
Talbotton, Ga., U.S.	D2	87
Talca, Chile	D2	56
Talcahuano, Chile	D2	56
Talent, Or., U.S.	E4	114
Taliabu, Pulau, i., Indon.	F7	32
Taliaferro, co., Ga., U.S.	C4	87
Talihina, Ok., U.S.	C6	113
Talkeetna, Ak., U.S.	C10	79
Talkeetna Mountains, mts., Ak., U.S.	f17	79
Talladega, Al., U.S.	B3	78
Talladega, co., Al., U.S.	B3	78
Tallahassee, Fl., U.S.	B2	86
Tallahatchie, co., Ms., U.S.	B3	101
Tallahatchie, stm., Ms., U.S.	B3	101
Tallapoosa, Ga., U.S.	C1	87
Tallapoosa, co., Al., U.S.	C4	78
Tallapoosa, stm., Al., U.S.	C3	78
Tallassee, Al., U.S.	C4	78
Talleyville, De., U.S.	A3	85
Tallinn, Est.	B7	18
Tall Kalakh, Syria	B5	40
Tallmadge, Oh., U.S.	A4	112
Tall Tamir, Syria	A7	40
Tallulah, La., U.S.	B4	95
Tal'menka, Russia	G10	24
Talo, mtn., Eth.	F2	46
Tāloqān, Afg.	B3	38
Talquin, Lake, res., Fl., U.S.	B2	86
Talu, Indon.	N5	34
Taluk, Indon.	O6	34
Tama, Ia., U.S.	C5	92
Tama, co., Ia., U.S.	B5	92
Tamale, Ghana	G5	42
Tamalpais, Mount, mtn., Ca., U.S.	h7	82
Tamana, Japan	J3	30
Tamanrasset, Alg.	D7	42
Tamaqua, Pa., U.S.	E10	115
Tamaroa, Il., U.S.	E4	90
Tamazula de Gordiano, Mex.	H8	62
Tamazunchale, Mex.	G10	62
Tambacounda, Sen.	F3	42
Tambohorano, Madag.	E8	44
Tambov, Russia	I24	18
Tambura, Sudan	G11	42
Tamchaket, Maur.	E3	42
Tamel Aike, Arg.	F2	56
Tamiahua, Laguna de, b., Mex.	G11	62
Tamiami Canal, Fl., U.S.	G6	86
Tamil Nadu, state, India	G5	37
Tam Ky, Viet.	G10	34
Tampa, Fl., U.S.	E4	86
Tampa Bay, b., Fl., U.S.	E4	86
Tampere, Fin.	F14	6
Tampico, Mex.	F11	62
Tampico, Il., U.S.	B4	90
Tamrida, Yemen	F5	46
Tamsagbulag, Mong.	B10	26
Tamworth, Austl.	F10	50

Name	Map Ref	Page
ana, Nor.	A17	6
ana, stm., Eur.	A16	6
ana, stm., Kenya	B7	44
ana, Lake, l., Eth.	F2	46
anabe, Japan	I8	30
anaga Island, i., Ak., U.S.	E4	79
anahjampea, Pulau, i., Indon.	G7	32
anami Desert, des., Austl.	C5	50
anana, Ak., U.S.	B9	79
anana, stm., Ak., U.S.	C10	79
ananarive see Antananarivo, Madag.	E9	44
ānda, India	G10	38
andil, Arg.	D5	56
ando Ādam, Pak.	H3	38
ando Muhammad Khān, Pak.	H3	38
anega-shima, i., Japan	u30	31b
aney, co., Mo., U.S.	E4	102
aneycomo, Lake, res., Mo., U.S.	E4	102
aneytown, Md., U.S.	A3	97
anezrouft, des., Afr.	D5	42
anga, Tan.	C7	44
angail, Bngl.	H13	38
anganyika, Lake, l., Afr.	C5	44
anger (Tangier), Mor.	A4	42
angerang, Indon.	m13	33a
angermünde, Ger.	C11	8
anggula Shan, mts., China	D13	38
angier, Va., U.S.	C7	123
angier Island, i., Va., U.S.	C6	123
angier Sound, strt., Md., U.S.	D6	97
angier see Tanger, Mor.	A4	42
angipahoa, co., La., U.S.	D5	95
angipahoa, stm., La., U.S.	D5	95
angra Yumco, l., China	E12	38
angshan, China	D10	26
anguan, is., Indon.	G9	32
animber, Kepulauan, is., Indon.	M5	34
anjungbalai, Indon.	M5	34
anjungkarang-Telukbetung, Indon.	k12	32
anjungpinang, Indon.	N8	34
anjungselor, Indon.	E6	32
ānk, Pak.	D4	38
ännäs, Swe.	E9	6
anner, Al., U.S.	A3	78
ânout, Niger	F7	42
anshui, Tai.	J10	28
anṭā, Egypt	B12	42
anuku, India	D6	37
anzania, ctry., Afr.	C6	44
aos, Mo., U.S.	C5	102
aos, N.M., U.S.	A4	108
aos, co., N.M., U.S.	A4	108
aos Pueblo, N.M., U.S.	A4	108
aoudenni, Mali	D5	42
apachula, Mex.	J13	62
apah, Malay.	L6	34
apajós, stm., Braz.	E7	54
aphan Hin, Thai.	F6	34
āpi, stm., India	B2	37
appahannock, Va., U.S.	C6	123
appan, N.Y., U.S.	g13	109
appan, Lake, res., N.J., U.S.	g9	107
appan Lake, res., Oh., U.S.	B4	112
aqaṭu' Hayyā, Sudan	E13	42
aquaritinga, Braz.	F4	57
ar, stm., N.C., U.S.	B5	110
ara, Ont., Can.	C3	73
arābulus (Tripoli), Leb.	B4	40
arābulus (Tripoli), Libya	B4	42
arābulus (Tripolitania), reg., Libya	B8	42
arakan, Indon.	E6	32
arancón, Spain	E8	12
aranto, Italy	I12	14
aranto, Golfo di b., Italy	I12	14
arapacá, Col.	I8	58
arare, Fr.	G11	10
arascon, Fr.	J8	10
arata, Bol.	G5	54
arazona, Spain	D10	12
arazona de la Mancha, Spain	F10	12
arbert, Scot., U.K.	F7	7
arbert, Scot., U.K.	D6	7
arbes, Fr.	I7	10
arboro, N.C., U.S.	B5	110
arcento, Italy	C8	14
aree, Austl.	F10	50
areja, Russia	C12	24
arentum, Pa., U.S.	E2	115
arfaya, Mor.	C3	42
arghee Pass, U.S.	E7	89
arifa, Punta de, c., Spain	I6	12
ariffville, Ct., U.S.	B4	84
arija, Bol.	H6	54
arim, stm., China	C3	26
arīn Kowt, Afg.	D1	38
arkio, Mo., U.S.	A2	102
arkwa, Ghana	G5	42
arlac, Phil.	q19	32
arn, stm., Fr.	I8	10
arnaby, Swe.	D10	6
arnak, stm., Afg.	D2	38
arnów, Pol.	E20	8
arnowskie Góry, Pol.	E18	8
arpey, Ca., U.S.	D4	82
arpon, Lake, l., Fl., U.S.	o10	86
arpon Springs, Fl., U.S.	D4	86
arquinia, Italy	G6	14
arragona, Spain	D13	12
arrant, Al., U.S.	B3	78
arrant, co., Tx., U.S.	C4	120
arrasa, Spain	D14	12
arrayall Mountains, mts., Co., U.S.	B5	83
arrytown, N.Y., U.S.	D7	109
arsus, Tur.	A4	40
artas, Arg.	A4	56
artas, Fr.	I6	10
artu, Est.	C9	18
arṭūs, Syria	B4	40
arutung, Indon.	M5	34
aşauz, Turk.	I9	22
asejeva, stm., Russia	F12	24
Tasejevo, Russia	F12	24
Taseko Mountain, mtn., B.C., Can.	D6	69
Tashi Gang Dzong, Bhu.	G14	38
Tashkent see Taškent, Uzb.	I11	22
Tasikmalaya, Indon.	m14	32
Taškent, Uzb.	I11	22
Tasmania, state, Austl.	H9	50
Tasman Sea, Oc.	G11	50
Tasso, Tn., U.S.	D9	119
Taštagol, Russia	G11	24
Tatabánya, Hung.	H18	8
Tatarskij Proliv, strt., Russia	H22	24
Tate, Ga., U.S.	B2	87
Tate, co., Ms., U.S.	A4	101
Tateville, Ky., U.S.	D5	94
Tateyama, Japan	H12	30
Tathlina Lake, l., N.W. Ter., Can.	D9	66
Tatnam, Cape, c., Man., Can.	f9	70
Tatta, Pak.	H2	38
Tattnall, co., Ga., U.S.	D4	87
Tatum, N.M., U.S.	D6	108
Tatvan, Tur.	H16	4
Tau, Nor.	G5	6
Taubaté, Braz.	G6	57
Tauberbischofsheim, Ger.	F9	8
Taujskaja Guba, b., Russia	F24	24
Taumarunui, N.Z.	C5	52
Taum Sauk Mountain, mtn., Mo., U.S.	D6	102
Taungdwingyi, Burma	D3	34
Taunggyi, Burma	D4	34
Taungup Pass, Burma	E3	34
Taunton, Eng., U.K.	J9	7
Taunton, Ma., U.S.	C5	98
Taunton, stm., Ma., U.S.	C5	98
Taupo, Lake, l., N.Z.	C5	52
Tauranga, N.Z.	B6	52
Taureau, Réservoir, res., Que., Can.	C4	74
Taurus Mountains see Toros Dağları, mts., Tur.	H14	4
Tauste, Spain	D10	12
Tavares, Fl., U.S.	D5	86
Tavernier, Fl., U.S.	G6	86
Tavira, Port.	H4	12
Tavoy Point, c., Burma	H5	34
Tavşanlı, Tur.	J13	16
Tawakoni, Lake, res., Tx., U.S.	C4	120
Tawas City, Mi., U.S.	D7	99
Tawas Lake, l., Mi., U.S.	D7	99
Tawau, Malay.	E6	32
Tawitawi Island, i., Phil.	D6	32
Tawkar, Sudan	E13	42
Taxco de Alarcón, Mex.	H10	62
Tay, Loch, l., Scot., U.K.	E8	7
Taylor, B.C., Can.	A7	69
Taylor, Az., U.S.	C5	80
Taylor, Ar., U.S.	D2	81
Taylor, Mi., U.S.	p15	99
Taylor, Pa., U.S.	D10	115
Taylor, Tx., U.S.	D4	120
Taylor, co., Fl., U.S.	B3	86
Taylor, co., Ga., U.S.	D2	87
Taylor, co., Ia., U.S.	D3	92
Taylor, co., Ky., U.S.	C4	94
Taylor, co., Tx., U.S.	C3	120
Taylor, co., W.V., U.S.	B4	125
Taylor, co., Wi., U.S.	C3	126
Taylor, stm., Co., U.S.	C4	83
Taylor, Mount, mtn., N.M., U.S.	B2	108
Taylor Mill, Ky., U.S.	k14	94
Taylor Park Reservoir, res., Co., U.S.	C4	83
Taylors, S.C., U.S.	B3	117
Taylors Falls, Mn., U.S.	E6	100
Taylors Island, i., Md., U.S.	D5	97
Taylorsville, In., U.S.	F6	91
Taylorsville, Ky., U.S.	B4	94
Taylorsville, Ms., U.S.	D4	101
Taylorsville, N.C., U.S.	B1	110
Taylorville, Il., U.S.	D4	90
Taymá', Sau. Ar.	C2	46
Tay Ninh, Viet.	I9	34
Tayoltita, Mex.	E7	62
Taytay, Phil.	C6	32
Taz, stm., Russia	D10	24
Taza, Mor.	B5	42
Tazewell, Tn., U.S.	C10	119
Tazewell, Va., U.S.	e10	123
Tazewell, co., Il., U.S.	C4	90
Tazewell, co., Va., U.S.	e10	123
Tazin Lake, l., Sask., Can.	E11	66
Tbessa, Alg.	A7	42
Tbilisi, Geor.	I6	22
Tbong, Camb.	H8	34
Tchefuncta, stm., La., U.S.	D5	95
Tchibanga, Gabon	B2	44
Tchien, Lib.	G4	42
Tchula, Ms., U.S.	B3	101
Tczew, Pol.	A18	8
Tea, S.D., U.S.	D9	118
Teacapán, Mex.	F7	62
Teague, Tx., U.S.	D4	120
Teakean Butte, mtn., Id., U.S.	C2	89
Te Anau, Lake, l., N.Z.	F1	52
Teaneck, N.J., U.S.	h8	107
Teano, Italy	H9	14
Teaticket, Ma., U.S.	C6	98
Tebingtinggi, Indon.	M5	34
Téboursouk, Tun.	M4	14
Tecate, Mex.	A1	62
Tecolotlán, Mex.	G7	62
Tecomán, Mex.	H8	62
Tecpan de Galeana, Mex.	I9	62
Tecuala, Mex.	F7	62
Tecuci, Rom.	D11	16
Tecumseh, Ont., Can.	E2	73
Tecumseh, Ks., U.S.	k14	93
Tecumseh, Mi., U.S.	G7	99
Tecumseh, Ne., U.S.	D9	104
Tecumseh, Ok., U.S.	B5	113
Tedžen (Harīrūd), stm., Asia	J10	22
Teeswater, Ont., Can.	C3	73
Tefé, Braz.	D6	54
Tegal, Indon.	m14	32
Tegucigalpa, Hond.	G4	64
Tehachapi, Ca., U.S.	E4	82
Tehachapi Mountains, mts., Ca., U.S.	E4	82
Tehama, co., Ca., U.S.	B2	82
Tehrān, Iran	J8	22
Tehuacán, Mex.	H11	62
Tehuantepec, Mex.	I12	62
Tehuantepec, Golfo de, b., Mex.	J12	62
Tehuantepec, Istmo de, Mex.	I12	62
Teide, Pico de, mtn., Spain	C2	42
Tejamén, Mex.	E7	62
Tejkovo, Russia	E23	18
Tejupan, Punta, c., Mex.	H8	62
Tekamah, Ne., U.S.	C9	104
Tekirdağ, Tur.	I11	16
Tekoa, Wa., U.S.	B8	124
Tekonsha, Mi., U.S.	F5	99
Tela, Hond.	G4	64
Telavåg, Nor.	F5	6
Tel Aviv-Yafo, Isr.	C4	40
Teleckoje, Ozero, l., Russia	G11	24
Telén, Arg.	D3	56
Telescope Peak, mtn., Ca., U.S.	D5	82
Teles Pires, stm., Braz.	E7	54
Telfair, co., Ga., U.S.	E4	87
Telford, Pa., U.S.	F11	115
Telfs, Aus.	H11	8
Teli, Russia	G12	24
Telkwa, B.C., Can.	B4	69
Tell City, In., U.S.	I4	91
Teller, co., Co., U.S.	C5	83
Tellicherry, India	G3	37
Tellico Plains, Tn., U.S.	D9	119
Telluride, Co., U.S.	D3	83
Telok Anson, Malay.	L6	34
Telos Lake, l., Me., U.S.	B3	96
Temagami, Lake, l., Ont., Can.	G16	66
Tembeling, stm., Malay.	L7	34
Tembenčí, stm., Russia	D13	24
Temecula, Ca., U.S.	F5	82
Temerloh, Malay.	M7	34
Teminabuan, Indon.	F9	32
Témiscouata, Lac, l., Que., Can.	B9	74
Te-Moak Indian Reservation, Nv., U.S.	C6	105
Temósachic, Mex.	C6	62
Tempe, Az., U.S.	D4	80
Temperance, Mi., U.S.	G7	99
Temperance, stm., Mn., U.S.	C8	100
Tempio Pausania, Italy	I4	14
Temple, Ok., U.S.	C3	113
Temple, Pa., U.S.	F10	115
Temple, Tx., U.S.	D4	120
Temple Terrace, Fl., U.S.	o11	86
Templin, Ger.	B13	8
Temuco, Chile	D2	56
Tena, Ec.	H4	58
Tenafly, N.J., U.S.	B5	107
Tenaha, Tx., U.S.	D5	120
Tenāli, India	D6	37
Tende, Col de, Eur.	H14	10
Ten Degree Channel, strt., India	J2	34
Ténéré, des., Niger	E8	42
Tenerife, i., Spain	C2	42
Tengchong, China	B5	34
Tenino, Wa., U.S.	C3	124
Tenkāsi, India	H4	37
Tenkiller Ferry Lake, res., Ok., U.S.	B6	113
Tenkodogo, Burkina	F5	42
Tenmile, stm., U.S.	B5	119
Tenmile Creek, stm., W.V., U.S.	k10	125
Tenmile Lake, l., Mn., U.S.	D4	100
Tennant Creek, Austl.	C6	50
Tennessee, state, U.S.	B5	119
Tennessee, stm., U.S.	D9	76
Tennessee Pass, Co., U.S.	B4	83
Tennessee Ridge, Tn., U.S.	A4	119
Tennille, Ga., U.S.	D4	87
Tenom, Malay.	E6	32
Tenryū, stm., Japan	G10	30
Tensas, co., La., U.S.	B4	95
Tensas, stm., La., U.S.	B4	95
Tensaw, stm., Al., U.S.	E2	78
Ten Sleep, Wy., U.S.	B5	127
Tenterfield, Austl.	E10	50
Ten Thousand Islands, is., Fl., U.S.	G5	86
Teocaltiche, Mex.	G8	62
Teófilo Otoni, Braz.	G8	57
Tepa, Indon.	G8	32
Tepatitlán [de Morelos], Mex.	G8	62
Tepic, Mex.	G7	62
Teplice, Czech.	E13	8
Teramo, Italy	G8	14
Teresina, Braz.	E10	54
Teresópolis, Braz.	G7	57
Termez, Uzb.	B3	38
Termini Imerese, Italy	L8	14
Términos, Laguna de, b., Mex.	H14	62
Termoli, Italy	G9	14
Ternej, Russia	H21	24
Terni, Italy	G7	14
Ternopol', Ukr.	H3	22
Terpenija, stm., Russia	H22	24
Terpenija, Zaliv, b., Russia	H22	24
Terra Alta, W.V., U.S.	B5	125
Terrace, B.C., Can.	B3	69
Terracina, Italy	H8	14
Terralba, Italy	J3	14
Terra Nova National Park, Newf., Can.	D4	72
Terrebonne, Que., Can.	D4	74
Terrebonne, Or., U.S.	C5	114
Terrebonne, co., La., U.S.	E5	95
Terrebonne Bay, b., La., U.S.	E5	95
Terre Haute, In., U.S.	F3	91
Terre Hill, Pa., U.S.	F9	115
Terrell, Tx., U.S.	C4	120
Terrell, co., Ga., U.S.	E2	87
Terrell, co., Tx., U.S.	D1	120
Terrell Hills, Tx., U.S.	k7	120
Terrenceville, Newf., Can.	E4	72
Terry, Ms., U.S.	C3	101
Terry, Mt., U.S.	D11	103
Terry, co., Tx., U.S.	C1	120
Terrytown, Ne., U.S.	C2	104
Terryville, Ct., U.S.	C3	84
Teruel, Spain	E10	12
Tervola, Fin.	C15	6
Teseney, Eth.	E2	46
Teshekpuk Lake, l., Ak., U.S.	A9	79
Teshio, Japan	o19	30a
Teslin, Yukon, Can.	D6	66
Teslin, stm., Can.	D6	66
Tesouro, Braz.	D2	57
Tessalit, Mali	D6	42
Tesuque, N.M., U.S.	B4	108
Tete, Moz.	E6	44
Teterow, Ger.	B12	8
Teton, co., Id., U.S.	F7	89
Teton, co., Mt., U.S.	C4	103
Teton, co., Wy., U.S.	C2	127
Teton, stm., Mt., U.S.	C5	103
Teton Range, mts., Wy., U.S.	C2	127
Teton Village, Wy., U.S.	C2	127
Tétouan, Mor.	A4	42
Tetovo, Mac.	G4	16
Tet'uche, Russia	I21	24
Teulada, Italy	K3	14
Teulon, Man., Can.	D3	70
Teutopolis, Il., U.S.	D5	90
Teuva, Fin.	E13	6
Tevere (Tiber), stm., Italy	G7	14
Teverya, Isr.	C4	40
Tewksbury, Ma., U.S.	A5	98
Texada Island, i., B.C., Can.	E5	69
Texarkana, Ar., U.S.	D1	81
Texarkana, Tx., U.S.	C5	120
Texas, co., Mo., U.S.	D5	102
Texas, co., Ok., U.S.	e9	113
Texas, state, U.S.	D3	120
Texas City, Tx., U.S.	E5	120
Texhoma, Ok., U.S.	e9	113
Texico, N.M., U.S.	C6	108
Texoma, Lake, res., U.S.	D5	113
Teyvareh, Afg.	D1	38
Teziutlán, Mex.	H11	62
Tezpur, India	G15	38
Thabazimbi, S. Afr.	F5	44
Thai Binh, Viet.	D9	34
Thailand, ctry., Asia	B3	32
Thailand, Gulf of, b., Asia	J6	34
Thai Nguyen, Viet.	D8	34
Thal, Pak.	D4	38
Thames, stm., Ont., Can.	E3	73
Thames, stm., Eng., U.K.	J14	7
Thames, stm., Ct., U.S.	D7	84
Thamesville, Ont., Can.	E3	73
Thāna, India	C2	37
Thanh Hoa, Viet.	E8	34
Thanh Pho Ho Chi Minh (Saigon), Viet.	I9	34
Thanjāvūr, India	G5	37
Thar Desert (Great Indian Desert), des., Asia	G3	38
Thargomindah, Austl.	E8	50
Thatcher, Az., U.S.	E6	80
Thaton, Burma	F4	34
Thayer, Mo., U.S.	E6	102
Thayer, co., Ne., U.S.	D8	104
Thayetmyo, Burma	E3	34
Thayne, Wy., U.S.	D1	127
Thealka, Ky., U.S.	C7	94
The Barrens, plat., Tn., U.S.	B5	119
The Bight, Bah.	B10	64
The Cheviot, mtn., Eng., U.K.	F10	7
The Colony, Tx., U.S.	*C4	120
The Dalles, Or., U.S.	B5	114
The Dells, val., Wi., U.S.	E4	126
Thedford, Ont., Can.	D3	73
The English Company's Islands, is., Austl.	B7	50
The Everglades, sw., Fl., U.S.	G6	86
The Fens, sw., Eng., U.K.	I12	7
The Flat Tops, mts., Co., U.S.	B3	83
The Flume, wtfl, N.H., U.S.	B3	106
The Graves, is., Ma., U.S.	g12	98
The Hague see 's-Gravenhage, Neth.	C4	8
The Heads, c., Or., U.S.	E2	114
Thelon, stm., N.W. Ter., Can.	D12	66
The Narrows, strt., Wa., U.S.	f10	124
Theodore, Austl.	D10	50
Theodore, Al., U.S.	E1	78
Theodore Roosevelt Lake, res., Az., U.S.	D4	80
Theodore Roosevelt National Park (South Unit), N.D., U.S.	C2	111
Theodore Roosevelt National Park (North Unit), N.D., U.S.	B2	111
The Pas, Man., Can.	C1	70
The Plains, Oh., U.S.	C3	112
Theresa, Wi., U.S.	E5	126
Thermopolis, Wy., U.S.	C4	127
The Rockies, mts., Wa., U.S.	C3	124
Thessalon, Ont., Can.	p19	73
Thessaloníki (Salonika), Grc.	I6	16
Thetford Mines, Que., Can.	C6	74
The Thimbles, is., Ct., U.S.	E5	84
The Village, Ok., U.S.	B4	113
The Warburton, stm., Austl.	E7	50
The Wash, b., Eng., U.K.	I13	7
The Weald, reg., Eng., U.K.	J13	7
Thibodaux, La., U.S.	E5	95
Thief, stm., Mn., U.S.	B2	100
Thief Lake, l., Mn., U.S.	B3	100
Thief River Falls, Mn., U.S.	B2	100
Thielsen, Mount, mtn., Or., U.S.	D4	114
Thiene, Italy	D6	14
Thiensville, Wi., U.S.	E6	126
Thiers, Fr.	G10	10
Thiès, Sen.	F2	42
Thika, Kenya	B7	44
Thimphu, Bhu.	G13	38
Thingangyun, Burma	F4	34
Thionville, Fr.	C13	10
Thíra, i., Grc.	M9	16
Third Lake, l., N.H., U.S.	f7	106
Thirsk, Eng., U.K.	G11	7
Thisted, Den.	H7	6
Thívai (Thebes), Grc.	K7	16
Thiviers, Fr.	G7	10
Thomas, Ok., U.S.	B3	113
Thomas, co., Ga., U.S.	F3	87
Thomas, co., Ks., U.S.	C2	93
Thomas, co., Ne., U.S.	C5	104
Thomasboro, Il., U.S.	C5	90
Thomaston, Ct., U.S.	C3	84
Thomaston, Ga., U.S.	D2	87
Thomaston, Me., U.S.	D3	96
Thomaston Reservoir, res., Ct., U.S.	C3	84
Thomastown, Ire.	I5	7
Thomasville, Al., U.S.	D2	78
Thomasville, Ga., U.S.	F3	87
Thomasville, N.C., U.S.	B2	110
Thompson, Man., Can.	B3	70
Thompson, Ct., U.S.	B8	84
Thompson, N.D., U.S.	B8	111
Thompson, stm., U.S.	A4	102
Thompson Falls, Mt., U.S.	C1	103
Thompson Island, i., Ma., U.S.	g11	98
Thompson Lake, l., U.S.	D2	96
Thompson Peak, mtn., Ca., U.S.	B2	82
Thompson Peak, mtn., N.M., U.S.	h9	108
Thompson Reservoir, res., Or., U.S.	E5	114
Thomsen, stm., N.W. Ter., Can.	B9	66
Thomson, Ga., U.S.	C4	87
Thon Buri, Thai.	H6	34
Thongwa, Burma	F4	34
Thonon-les-Bains, Fr.	F13	10
Thonotosassa, Fl., U.S.	D4	86
Thonze, Burma	F3	34
Thorburn, N.S., Can.	D7	71
Thoreau, N.M., U.S.	B1	108
Thornbury, Ont., Can.	C4	73
Thorndale, Tx., U.S.	D4	120
Thornton, Ont., Can.	C5	73
Thorntown, In., U.S.	D4	91
Thorold, Ont., Can.	D5	73
Thorp, Wi., U.S.	D3	126
Thorsby, Al., U.S.	C3	78
Thouars, Fr.	F6	10
Thousand Islands, is., N.Y., U.S.	A4	109
Thousand Lake Mountain, mtn., Ut., U.S.	E4	121
Thousand Springs Creek, stm., U.S.	B7	105
Thrace, hist. reg., Eur.	G13	4
Thrakikón Pélagos, Grc.	I8	16
Three Fingered Jack, mtn., Or., U.S.	C5	114
Three Forks, Mt., U.S.	E5	103
Three Hills, Alta., Can.	D4	68
Three Lakes, Wi., U.S.	C4	126
Three Mile Plains, N.S., Can.	E5	71
Three Oaks, Mi., U.S.	G4	99
Three Pagodas Pass, Asia	G5	34
Three Points, Cape, c., Ghana	H5	42
Three Rivers, Ma., U.S.	B3	98
Three Rivers, Mi., U.S.	G5	99
Three Rivers, Tx., U.S.	E3	120
Three Sisters, mtn., Or., U.S.	C5	114
Three Springs, Austl.	E3	50
Throckmorton, co., Tx., U.S.	C3	120
Throop, Pa., U.S.	m18	115
Throssell Range, mts., Austl.	D4	50
Thule, Grnld.	B19	128
Thun, Switz.	F14	10
Thunder Bay, Ont., Can.	o17	73
Thunder Bay, b., Mi., U.S.	D7	99
Thunder Bay, stm., Mi., U.S.	D6	99
Thunderbird, Lake, res., Ok., U.S.	B4	113
Thunderbolt, Ga., U.S.	D5	87
Thunder Butte Creek, stm., S.D., U.S.	B3	118
Thunersee, l., Switz.	F14	10
Thüringen, hist. reg., Ger.	D11	8
Thurles, Ire.	I5	7
Thurmont, Md., U.S.	A3	97
Thurso, Que., Can.	D2	74
Thurso, Scot., U.K.	C9	7
Thurston, co., Ne., U.S.	B9	104
Thurston, co., Wa., U.S.	C2	124
Tiancang, China	C7	26
Tiandong, China	C9	28
Tianjin (Tientsin), China	D10	26
Tianjun, China	D6	26
Tianmen, China	E2	28
Tianshui, China	E8	26
Tiaret, Alg.	A6	42
Tibagi, Braz.	A6	56
Tibasti, Sarīr, des., Libya	D9	42
Tiber see Tevere, stm., Italy	G7	14
Tibesti, mts., Chad	D9	42
Tibet, hist. reg., China	E12	38
Tiburón, Isla, i., Mex.	C3	62
Tice, Fl., U.S.	F5	86
Tichît, Maur.	E4	42
Tichvin, Russia	C16	18
Tickfaw, stm., La., U.S.	C5	95
Ticonderoga, N.Y., U.S.	B7	109
Ticul, Mex.	G15	62
Tide Head, N.B., Can.	B3	71
Tidjikdja, Maur.	E3	42
Tieling, China	C11	26
Tien Shan, mts., Asia	C2	26
Tientsin see Tianjin, China	D10	26
Tierra Amarilla, N.M., U.S.	A3	108
Tierra Blanca, Mex.	H11	62
Tierra del Fuego, Isla Grande de, i., S.A.	G3	56
Tierralta, Col.	C4	58
Tietê, stm., Braz.	F3	57
Tieton, Wa., U.S.	C5	124
Tieton, stm., Wa., U.S.	C4	124
Tieton Dam, Wa., U.S.	C4	124
Tiffany Mountain, mtn., Wa., U.S.	A6	124
Tiffin, Oh., U.S.	A2	112

185

Name	Map Ref	Page
Tiffin, stm., Oh., U.S.	A1	112
Tift, co., Ga., U.S.	E3	87
Tifton, Ga., U.S.	E3	87
Tigard, Or., U.S.	h12	114
Tigerton, Wi., U.S.	D4	126
Tigil', Russia	F25	24
Tignall, Ga., U.S.	C4	87
Tignish, P.E.I., Can.	C5	71
Tigre, stm., Peru	D3	54
Tigris (Dijlah), stm., Asia	A3	46
Tiguentourine, Alg.	C7	42
Tijesno, Cro.	F10	14
Tijuana, Mex.	A1	62
Tikamgarh, India	H8	38
Tikrīt, Iraq	B3	46
Tilburg, Neth.	D5	8
Tilbury, Ont., Can.	E2	73
Tilden, Il., U.S.	E4	90
Tilden, Ne., U.S.	B8	104
Tilghman, Md., U.S.	C5	97
Tilghman Island, i., Md., U.S.	C5	97
Tilhar, India	G8	38
Tillabéry, Niger	F6	42
Tillamook, Or., U.S.	B3	114
Tillamook, co., Or., U.S.	B3	114
Tillanchong Island, i., India	J2	34
Tillery, Lake, res., N.C., U.S.	B2	110
Tillman, co., Ok., U.S.	C2	113
Tillmans Corner, Al., U.S.	E1	78
Tillsonburg, Ont., Can.	E4	73
Tilton, Il., U.S.	C6	90
Tilton, N.H., U.S.	D3	106
Tiltonsville, Oh., U.S.	B5	112
Timaru, N.Z.	F3	52
Timbalier Island, i., La., U.S.	E5	95
Timberlake, Va., U.S.	C3	123
Timberville, Va., U.S.	B4	123
Timbuktu see Tombouctou, Mali	E5	42
Timimoun, Alg.	C6	42
Timiris, Cap, c., Maur.	E2	42
Timişoara, Rom.	D5	16
Timmins, Ont., Can.	o19	73
Timmonsville, S.C., U.S.	C8	117
Timms Hill, hill, Wi., U.S.	C3	126
Timor, i., Indon.	G8	32
Timor Sea	B5	50
Timotes, Ven.	C7	58
Timpanogos Cave National Monument, Ut., U.S.	C4	121
Timpton, stm., Russia	F19	24
Tims Ford Lake, res., Tn., U.S.	B5	119
Tinaquillo, Ven.	C8	58
Tindivanam, India	F5	37
Tindouf, Alg.	C4	42
Tingmerkpuk Mountain, mtn., Ak., U.S.	B7	79
Tingo María, Peru	E3	54
Tingvoll, Nor.	E7	6
Tinharé, Ilha de, i., Braz.	F11	54
Tinker Air Force Base, mil., Ok., U.S.	B4	113
Tinley Park, Il., U.S.	k9	90
Tinniswood, Mount, mtn., B.C., Can.	D6	69
Tinogasta, Arg.	B3	56
Tinsukia, India	G16	38
Tinton Falls, N.J., U.S.	C4	107
Tioga, La., U.S.	C3	95
Tioga, N.D., U.S.	A3	111
Tioga, co., N.Y., U.S.	C4	109
Tioga, co., Pa., U.S.	C7	115
Tioga, stm., Pa., U.S.	B7	115
Tiogue Lake, res., R.I., U.S.	D3	116
Tioman, Pulau, i., Malay.	M8	34
Tionesta Creek, stm., Pa., U.S.	C3	115
Tionesta Lake, res., Pa., U.S.	D3	115
Tioughnioga, stm., N.Y., U.S.	C4	109
Tippah, co., Ms., U.S.	A5	101
Tippah, stm., Ms., U.S.	A4	101
Tipp City, Oh., U.S.	C1	112
Tippecanoe, co., In., U.S.	D4	91
Tippecanoe, stm., In., U.S.	C4	91
Tipperary, Ire.	I4	7
Tipton, Ca., U.S.	D4	82
Tipton, In., U.S.	D5	91
Tipton, Ia., U.S.	C6	92
Tipton, Mo., U.S.	C5	102
Tipton, Ok., U.S.	C2	113
Tipton, co., In., U.S.	D5	91
Tipton, co., Tn., U.S.	B2	119
Tipton, Mount, mtn., Az., U.S.	B1	80
Tiptonville, Tn., U.S.	A2	119
Tiquisate, Guat.	G2	64
Tiracambu, Serra do, plat., Braz.	D9	54
Tīrān, Maḍīq, strt.	F4	40
Tiran, Strait of see Tīrān, Maḍīq, strt.	F4	40
Tiranë, Alb.	H3	16
Tirano, Italy	C6	14
Tiraspol', Mol.	H3	22
Tirat Karmel, Isr.	C4	40
Tire, Tur.	K11	16
Tiree, i., Scot., U.K.	E6	7
Tîrgovişte, Rom.	E9	16
Tîrgu-Jiu, Rom.	D7	16
Tîrgu Mureş, Rom.	C8	16
Tîrgu-Ocna, Rom.	C10	16
Tîrnavos, Grc.	J6	16
Tirschenreuth, Ger.	F12	8
Tiruchchīrāppalli, India	G5	37
Tirunelveli, India	H4	37
Tirupati, India	F5	37
Tiruppattūr, India	F5	37
Tiruppur, India	G4	37
Tiruvannāmalai, India	F5	37
Tishomingo, Ok., U.S.	C5	113
Tishomingo, co., Ms., U.S.	A5	101
Tiskilwa, Il., U.S.	B4	90
Tisza (Tisa), stm., Eur.	C4	16
Tit-Ary, Russia	C19	24
Titicaca, Lago, l., S.A.	G5	54
Titograd, Yugo.	G3	16
Titonka, Ia., U.S.	A3	92
Titovo Užice, Yugo.	F3	16
Titov Veles, Mac.	H5	16
Titule, Zaire	H11	42
Titus, co., Tx., U.S.	C5	120
Titusville, Fl., U.S.	D6	86
Titusville, Pa., U.S.	C2	115
Tiverton, Ont., Can.	C3	73
Tiverton, Eng., U.K.	K9	7
Tiverton, R.I., U.S.	D6	116
Tivoli, Italy	H7	14
Tizimín, Mex.	G15	62
Tizi-Ouzou, Alg.	A6	42
Tlahualilo de Zaragoza, Mex.	D8	62
Tlaltenango de Sánchez Román, Mex.	G8	62
Tlaxiaco, Mex.	I11	62
Tlemcen, Alg.	B5	42
Tlētē Ouâte Gharbī, Jabal, mtn., Syria	B6	40
Toamasina, Madag.	E9	44
Toano, Va., U.S.	C6	123
Toano Range, mts., Nv., U.S.	C7	105
Toast, N.C., U.S.	A2	110
Toba, Japan	H9	30
Toba, Danau, l., Indon.	M5	34
Tobacco Root Mountains, mts., Mt., U.S.	E5	103
Tobago, i., Trin.	I17	64
Toba Inlet, b., B.C., Can.	D5	69
Toba Kākar Range, mts., Pak.	E2	38
Tobarra, Spain	G10	12
Tobermory, Scot., U.K.	E6	7
Tobin, Mount, mtn., Nv., U.S.	C4	105
Tobin Lake, l., Sask., Can.	D4	75
Tobin Range, mts., Nv., U.S.	C4	105
Tobique, stm., N.B., Can.	B2	71
Tobruk see Ţubruq, Libya	B10	42
Tobyhanna, Pa., U.S.	D11	115
Tocantínia, Braz.	E9	54
Tocantinópolis, Braz.	E9	54
Tocantins, stm., Braz.	D9	54
Toccoa, Ga., U.S.	B3	87
Toccoa, stm., Ga., U.S.	B2	87
Toccoa Falls, Ga., U.S.	B3	87
Tochigi, Japan	F12	30
Töcksfors, Swe.	G8	6
Toco, Chile	A3	56
Tocopilla, Chile	A2	56
Todd, co., Ky., U.S.	D2	94
Todd, co., Mn., U.S.	D4	100
Todd, co., S.D., U.S.	D5	118
Todi, Italy	G7	14
Todos Santos, Mex.	F4	62
Todtnau, Ger.	H7	8
Tofield, Alta., Can.	C4	68
Tofino, B.C., Can.	E5	69
Togiak, Ak., U.S.	D7	79
Togian, Kepulauan, is., Indon.	F7	32
Togo, ctry., Afr.	G6	42
Togwotee Pass, Wy., U.S.	C2	127
Tohakum Peak, mtn., Nv., U.S.	C2	105
Tohatchi, N.M., U.S.	B1	108
Tohopekaliga, Lake, l., Fl., U.S.	D5	86
Toiyabe Range, mts., Nv., U.S.	D4	105
Tok, Ak., U.S.	C11	79
Tōkamachi, Japan	E11	30
Tokara-kaikyō, strt., Japan	u30	31b
Tokara-rettō, is., Japan	v29	31b
Tokat, Tur.	G15	4
Tokelau Islands, dep., Oc.	G1	2
Toki, Japan	G10	30
Tokuno-shima, i., Japan	x28	31b
Tokushima, Japan	H7	30
Tokuyama, Japan	H4	30
Tōkyō, Japan	G12	30
Tokzār, Afg.	C2	38
Toleak Point, c., Wa., U.S.	B1	124
Toledo, Spain	F7	12
Toledo, Il., U.S.	D5	90
Toledo, Ia., U.S.	B5	92
Toledo, Oh., U.S.	A2	112
Toledo, Or., U.S.	C3	114
Toledo Bend Reservoir, res., U.S.	C2	95
Tolentino, Italy	F8	14
Toler, Ky., U.S.	C7	94
Toliara, Madag.	F8	44
Toljatti, Russia	G7	22
Tol'ka, Russia	E10	24
Tolland, Ct., U.S.	B6	84
Tolland, co., Ct., U.S.	B6	84
Tollesboro, Ky., U.S.	B6	94
Tolleson, Az., U.S.	m8	80
Tolmezzo, Italy	C8	14
Tolmin, Slo.	C8	14
Tolo, Teluk, b., Indon.	F7	32
Tolono, Il., U.S.	D5	90
Tolosa, Spain	B9	12
Tolstoj, Mys, c., Russia	F25	24
Tolt Reservoir, res., Wa., U.S.	B4	124
Toluca, Il., U.S.	C4	90
Toluca, Nevado de, vol., Mex.	H10	62
Toluca [de Lerdo], Mex.	H10	62
Tom', stm., Russia	F11	24
Tomah, Wi., U.S.	E3	126
Tomahawk, Wi., U.S.	C4	126
Tomahawk Lake, l., Wi., U.S.	C4	126
Tomakomai, Japan	q19	30a
Tomar, Port.	F3	12
Tomaszów Mazowiecki, Pol.	D20	8
Tomatlán, Mex.	H7	62
Tombador, Serra do, plat., Braz.	F7	54
Tomball, Tx., U.S.	D5	120
Tombigbee, stm., U.S.	D1	78
Tombouctou (Timbuktu), Mali	E5	42
Tombstone, Az., U.S.	F5	80
Tombua, Ang.	E2	44
Tomelloso, Spain	F9	12
Tom Green, co., Tx., U.S.	D2	120
Tomini, Teluk, b., Indon.	F7	32
Tommot, Russia	F19	24
Tom Nevers Head, c., Ma., U.S.	D8	98
Tomo, stm., Col.	E8	58
Tompkins, co., N.Y., U.S.	C4	109
Tompkinsville, Ky., U.S.	D4	94
Tomptokan, Russia	F20	24
Tomra, Nor.	E6	6
Toms, stm., N.J., U.S.	C4	107
Tomsk, Russia	F10	24
Toms River, N.J., U.S.	D4	107
Tonalá, Mex.	I13	62
Tonasket, Wa., U.S.	A6	124
Tonawanda Indian Reservation, N.Y., U.S.	B2	109
Tondabayashi, Japan	H8	30
Tone, stm., Japan	F12	30
Tonga, ctry., Oc.	H1	2
Tonganoxie, Ks., U.S.	C8	93
Tongbai, China	C2	28
Tongchuan, China	D8	26
Tongeren, Bel.	E5	8
Tongguan, China	E9	26
Tonghai, China	B7	34
Tonghua, China	C12	26
Tongliao, China	C11	26
Tongling, China	E6	28
Tongsa Dzong, Bhu.	G14	38
Tongtianheyan, China	D15	38
Tongue, Scot., U.K.	C8	7
Tongue, stm., Mt., U.S.	E10	103
Tongue, stm., Tx., U.S.	p13	120
Tongzi, China	F8	26
Tonk, India	G6	38
Tonkawa, Ok., U.S.	A4	113
Tonkin, Gulf of, b., Asia	E9	34
Tonle Sap see Sab, Tônlé, l., Camb.	H7	34
Tonneins, Fr.	H7	10
Tonnerre, Fr.	E10	10
Tonopah, Nv., U.S.	E4	105
Tønsberg, Nor.	G8	6
Tonstad, Nor.	G6	6
Tonto National Monument, Az., U.S.	D4	80
Tonto Natural Bridge, Az., U.S.	C4	80
Tooele, Ut., U.S.	C3	121
Tooele, co., Ut., U.S.	C2	121
Toole, co., Mt., U.S.	B5	103
Toombs, co., Ga., U.S.	D4	87
Toomsboro, Ga., U.S.	D3	87
Toowoomba, Austl.	E10	50
Topeka, In., U.S.	A6	91
Topeka, Ks., U.S.	C8	93
Topia, Mex.	E6	62
Topock, Az., U.S.	C1	80
Toppenish, Wa., U.S.	C5	124
Topsfield, Ma., U.S.	A6	98
Topsham, Me., U.S.	E3	96
Topton, Pa., U.S.	F10	115
Toquima Range, mts., Nv., U.S.	E5	105
Torbay, Newf., Can.	E5	72
Torbert, Mount, mtn., Ak., U.S.	g15	79
Torch Lake, l., Mi., U.S.	D5	99
Tordesillas, Spain	D6	12
Töre, Swe.	D14	6
Torgau, Ger.	D12	8
Torhout, Bel.	D3	8
Torino (Turin), Italy	D2	14
Torit, Sudan	H12	42
Torkestān, Band-e, mts., Afg.	C2	38
Tornäälven, stm., Eur.	B12	4
Torngat Mountains, mts., Can.	f8	72
Toro, Spain	D6	12
Toronto, Ont., Can.	D5	73
Toronto, Oh., U.S.	B5	112
Toronto Lake, l., Ks., U.S.	E7	93
Toro Peak, mtn., Ca., U.S.	F5	82
Tororo, Ug.	A6	44
Torquay (Torbay), Eng., U.K.	K9	7
Torquemada, Spain	C7	12
Torrance, Ca., U.S.	n12	82
Torrance, co., N.M., U.S.	C3	108
Torrão, Port.	G3	12
Torre Annunziata, Italy	I9	14
Torre Baja, Spain	E10	12
Torreblanca, Spain	E12	12
Torrecilla en Cameros, Spain	C9	12
Torre de Moncorvo, Port.	D4	12
Torredonjimeno, Spain	H8	12
Torrelaguna, Spain	E8	12
Torrelavega, Spain	B7	12
Torremaggiore, Italy	H10	14
Torremolinos, Spain	I7	12
Torrens, Lake, l., Austl.	F7	50
Torrente, Spain	F11	12
Torreón, Mex.	E8	62
Torres Novas, Port.	F3	12
Torres Strait, strt., Oc.	B8	50
Torres Vedras, Port.	F2	12
Torrevieja, Spain	H11	12
Torridon, Scot., U.K.	D7	7
Torriglia, Italy	E4	14
Torrijos, Spain	F7	12
Torrington, Ct., U.S.	B3	84
Torrington, Wy., U.S.	D8	127
Torrox, Spain	I8	12
Torsby, Swe.	F9	6
Tórshavn, Faer. Is.	C6	4
Tortola, i., Br. Vir. Is.	E15	64
Tortoli, Italy	J4	14
Tortona, Italy	E3	14
Tortosa, Spain	E12	12
Tortue, Île de la, i., Haiti	D11	64
Toruń, Pol.	B18	8
Toržok, Russia	D17	18
Tosa-shimizu, Japan	J5	30
Tosa-wan, b., Japan	I6	30
Tostado, Arg.	B4	56
Totagatic, stm., Wi., U.S.	B2	126
Totana, Spain	H10	12
Toteng, Bots.	F4	44
Tôtes, Fr.	C8	10
Totness, N.C., U.S.	B5	110
Totowa, N.J., U.S.	B4	107
Totson Mountain, mtn., Ak., U.S.	C8	79
Tottenham, Ont., Can.	C5	73
Tottori, Japan	G7	30
Toubkal, Jbel, mtn., Mor.	B4	42
Touchet, stm., Wa., U.S.	C7	124
Touggourt, Alg.	B7	42
Touisset, Ma., U.S.	C5	98
Toul, Fr.	D12	10
Toulon, Fr.	I12	10
Toulon, Il., U.S.	B4	90
Toulouse, Fr.	I8	10
Tounan, Tai.	L9	28
Toungoo, Burma	E4	34
Tourcoing, Fr.	B10	10
Tournai, Bel.	E3	8
Tournon, Fr.	G11	10
Tournus, Fr.	F11	10
Tours, Fr.	E7	10
Touside, Pic, mtn., Chad	D9	42
Toussaint Creek, stm., Oh., U.S.	f7	112
Toutle, North Fork, stm., Wa., U.S.	C3	124
Tovar, Ven.	C7	58
Towanda, Il., U.S.	C5	90
Towanda, Ks., U.S.	E7	93
Towanda, Pa., U.S.	C9	115
Towanda Creek, stm., Pa., U.S.	C8	115
Tower City, Pa., U.S.	E8	115
Tower Peak, mtn., Ca., U.S.	D3	82
Town Creek, Al., U.S.	A2	78
Towner, N.D., U.S.	A5	111
Towner, co., N.D., U.S.	A6	111
Towns, co., Ga., U.S.	B3	87
Townsend, De., U.S.	C3	85
Townsend, Mt., U.S.	D5	103
Townshend Reservoir, res., Vt., U.S.	E3	122
Townsville, Austl.	C9	50
Towson, Md., U.S.	B4	97
Toyama, Japan	F10	30
Toyohashi, Japan	H10	30
Toyokawa, Japan	H10	30
Toyonaka, Japan	H8	30
Toyooka, Japan	G7	30
Toyota, Japan	G10	30
Tozeur, Tun.	B7	42
Trabzon, Tur.	G15	4
Tracadie, N.B., Can.	B5	71
Tracy, N.B., Can.	D3	71
Tracy, Que., Can.	C4	74
Tracy, Mn., U.S.	F3	100
Tracy City, Tn., U.S.	D8	119
Tracyton, Wa., U.S.	e10	124
Tradewater, stm., Ky., U.S.	C2	94
Traer, Ia., U.S.	B5	92
Trafford, Al., U.S.	k14	115
Trafford, Lake, l., Fl., U.S.	F5	86
Trail, B.C., Can.	E9	69
Trail Creek, In., U.S.	A4	91
Traill, co., N.D., U.S.	B8	111
Trail Ridge, mtn., U.S.	F4	87
Tralee, Ire.	I3	7
Tranås, Swe.	G10	6
Trancas, Arg.	B3	56
Trang, Thai.	K5	34
Trangan, Pulau, i., Indon.	G9	32
Trani, Italy	H11	14
Transylvania, co., N.C., U.S.	f10	110
Transylvania, hist. reg., Rom.	C7	16
Transylvanian Alps see Carpaţii Meridionali, mts., Rom.	D8	16
Trapani, Italy	K7	14
Trappe, Md., U.S.	C5	97
Trapper Peak, mtn., Mt., U.S.	E2	103
Traun, Aus.	G14	8
Traunstein, Ger.	H12	8
Travelers Rest, S.C., U.S.	B3	117
Traverse, co., Mn., U.S.	E2	100
Traverse, Lake, l., U.S.	B9	118
Traverse City, Mi., U.S.	D5	99
Travis, co., Tx., U.S.	D4	120
Travis Air Force Base, mil., Ca., U.S.	C2	82
Travnik, Bos.	E12	14
Tray Mountain, mtn., Ga., U.S.	B3	87
Treasure, co., Mt., U.S.	D9	103
Treasure Island Naval Station, mil., Ca., U.S.	h8	82
Trecate, Italy	D3	14
Trego, co., Ks., U.S.	D4	93
Tregosse Islets, is., Austl.	C10	50
Tréguier, Fr.	D3	10
Treherne, Man., U.S.	E2	70
Treinta y Tres, Ur.	C6	56
Trélazé, Fr.	E6	10
Trelew, Arg.	E3	56
Trelleborg, Swe.	I9	6
Tremblant, Mont, mtn., Que., Can.	C3	74
Tremont, Il., U.S.	C4	90
Tremont, Pa., U.S.	E9	115
Tremonton, Ut., U.S.	B3	121
Tremp, Spain	C12	12
Trempealeau, Wi., U.S.	D2	126
Trempealeau, co., Wi., U.S.	D2	126
Trempealeau, stm., Wi., U.S.	D2	126
Trenche, stm., Que., Can.	B5	74
Trenčín, Czech.	G18	8
Trenque Lauquen, Arg.	D4	56
Trent, stm., N.C., U.S.	B5	110
Trente et un Milles, Lac des, l., Que., Can.	C2	74
Trentino, Italy	C6	14
Trenton, Ont., Can.	C7	73
Trenton, Fl., U.S.	C4	86
Trenton, Ga., U.S.	B1	87
Trenton, Il., U.S.	E4	90
Trenton, Mi., U.S.	F7	99
Trenton, Mo., U.S.	A4	102
Trenton, Ne., U.S.	D4	104
Trenton, N.J., U.S.	C3	107
Trenton, Oh., U.S.	C1	112
Trepassey, Newf., Can.	E5	72
Trepassey Bay, b., Newf., Can.	E5	72
Tres Arroyos, Arg.	D4	56
Tresckow, Pa., U.S.	E10	115
Três Corações, Braz.	F6	57
Tres Esquinas, Col.	G5	58
Três Lagoas, Braz.	F3	57
Três Marias, Reprêsa, res., Braz.	E6	57
Tres Picos, Cerro, mtn., Arg.	D4	56
Três Pontas, Braz.	F6	57
Tres Puntas, Cabo, c., Arg.	F3	56
Três Rios, Braz.	G7	57
Treutlen, co., Ga., U.S.	D4	87
Treviglio, Italy	D4	14
Treviso, Italy	D7	14
Trevor, Wi., U.S.	n11	126
Trevorton, Pa., U.S.	E8	115
Treynor, Ia., U.S.	C2	92
Trezevant, Tn., U.S.	A3	119
Triadelphia, W.V., U.S.	A4	125
Triadelphia Reservoir, res., Md., U.S.	B3	97
Triangle, Va., U.S.	B5	123
Tribune, Ks., U.S.	D2	93
Trichūr, India	G4	37
Tri City, Or., U.S.	E3	114
Trident Peak, mtn., Nv., U.S.	B3	105
Trieben, Aus.	H14	8
Trier, Ger.	F6	8
Trieste, Italy	D8	14
Trigg, co., Ky., U.S.	D2	94
Triglav, mtn., Slo.	C8	14
Trigo Mountains, mts., Az., U.S.	D1	80
Trikala, Grc.	J5	16
Trikora, Puncak, mtn., Indon.	F10	32
Tri Lakes, In., U.S.	B7	91
Trim, Ire.	H6	7
Trimble, Tn., U.S.	A2	119
Trimble, co., Ky., U.S.	B4	94
Trimont, Mn., U.S.	G4	100
Trincheras, Mex.	B4	62
Trincomalee, Sri L.	H6	37
Třinec, Czech.	F18	8
Tring Jonction, Que., Can.	C6	74
Trinidad, Bol.	F6	54
Trinidad, Col.	E7	58
Trinidad, Cuba	D8	64
Trinidad, Co., U.S.	D6	83
Trinidad, Tx., U.S.	C4	120
Trinidad, i., Trin.	I17	64
Trinidad and Tobago, ctry., N.A.	I17	64
Trinidad Head, c., Ca., U.S.	B1	82
Trinity, Al., U.S.	A2	78
Trinity, Tx., U.S.	D5	120
Trinity, co., Ca., U.S.	B2	82
Trinity, co., Tx., U.S.	D5	120
Trinity, stm., Ca., U.S.	B2	82
Trinity, stm., Tx., U.S.	D5	120
Trinity Bay, b., Newf., Can.	D5	72
Trinity Islands, is., Ak., U.S.	D9	79
Trinity Mountain, mtn., Id., U.S.	F3	89
Trinity Mountains, mts., Ca., U.S.	B2	82
Trinity Peak, mtn., Nv., U.S.	C3	105
Trinity Range, mts., Nv., U.S.	C3	105
Trion, Ga., U.S.	B1	87
Tripoli, Ia., U.S.	B5	92
Tripolis, Grc.	L6	16
Tripoli see Ţarābulus, Leb.	B4	40
Tripoli see Ţarābulus, Libya	B8	42
Tripp, S.D., U.S.	D8	118
Tripp, co., S.D., U.S.	D6	118
Triumph, La., U.S.	E6	95
Trivandrum, India	H4	37
Trnava, Czech.	G17	8
Troarn, Fr.	C6	10
Trobriand Islands, is., Pap. N. Gui.	A10	50
Trochu, Alta., Can.	D4	68
Trogir, Cro.	F11	14
Trois-Pistoles, Que., Can.	A8	74
Trois-Rivières, Que., Can.	C5	74
Trois-Rivières-Ouest, Que., Can.	C5	74
Trojan, Bul.	G8	16
Trollhättan, Swe.	G9	6
Trombetas, stm., Braz.	C7	54
Tromelin, i., Afr.	E10	44
Tromsø, Nor.	B12	6
Trona, Ca., U.S.	E5	82
Tronador, Monte, mtn., S.A.	E2	56
Trondheim, Nor.	E8	6
Trondheimsfjorden, Nor.	E8	6
Tropea, Italy	K10	14
Trophy Mountain, mtn., B.C., Can.	D8	69
Trotwood, Oh., U.S.	C1	112
Troup, co., Ga., U.S.	C1	87
Trousdale, co., Tn., U.S.	A5	119
Trout, stm., Fl., U.S.	m8	86
Trout, stm., Vt., U.S.	B3	122
Trout Creek, Ont., Can.	B5	73
Trout Creek Pass, Co., U.S.	C5	83
Trout Lake, Wa., U.S.	D4	124
Trout Lake, l., N.W. Ter., Can.	D8	66
Trout Lake, l., Ont., Can.	o16	73
Trout Lake, l., Mn., U.S.	B6	100
Trout Lake, l., Wi., U.S.	B4	126
Troutman, N.C., U.S.	B2	110
Trout Peak, mtn., Wy., U.S.	B3	127
Trout River, Newf., Can.	D2	72
Trouville [-sur-Mer], Fr.	C7	10
Troy, Al., U.S.	D4	78
Troy, Id., U.S.	C2	89
Troy, Il., U.S.	E4	90
Troy, Ks., U.S.	C8	93
Troy, Mi., U.S.	o15	99
Troy, Mo., U.S.	C7	102
Troy, Mt., U.S.	B1	103
Troy, N.H., U.S.	E2	106
Troy, N.Y., U.S.	C7	109
Troy, N.C., U.S.	B3	110
Troy, Oh., U.S.	B1	112
Troy, Pa., U.S.	C8	115
Troy, Tn., U.S.	A2	119
Troyes, Fr.	D11	10
Troy Peak, mtn., Nv., U.S.	E6	105
Truchas Peak, mtn., N.M., U.S.	B4	108
Trucial States see United Arab Emirates, ctry., Asia	D5	46
Truckee, Ca., U.S.	C3	82
Truckee, stm., U.S.	D2	105
Trujillo, Hond.	G4	64
Trujillo, Peru	E3	54
Trujillo, Spain	F6	12
Trujillo, Ven.	C7	58
Truman, Mn., U.S.	G4	100
Trumann, Ar., U.S.	B5	81
Trumansburg, N.Y., U.S.	C4	109
Trumbull, Ct., U.S.	E3	84
Trumbull, co., Oh., U.S.	A5	112

Name	Map Ref	Page
rumbull, Mount, mtn., Az., U.S.	A2	80
uro, Eng., U.K.	K7	7
russville, Al., U.S.	B3	78
rustom Pond, l., R.I., U.S.	G3	116
ruth or Consequences (Hot Springs), N.M., U.S.	D2	108
utnov, Czech.	E15	8
ryon, N.C., U.S.	f10	110
žič, Slo.	C9	14
sala Apopka Lake, l., Fl., U.S.	D4	86
saratanana, Madag.	E9	44
saratanana, Massif du, mts., Madag.	D9	44
shabong, Bots.	G4	44
shangalele, Lac, l., Zaire	D5	44
shikapa, Zaire	C4	44
shofa, Zaire	C5	44
shuapa, stm., Zaire	B4	44
soying, Tai.	M9	28
su, Japan	H9	30
subame, Japan	E11	30
suchiura, Japan	F13	30
sugaru-kaikyō, strt., Japan	A13	30
sukumi, Japan	I4	30
sukushi-sanchi, mts., Japan	I3	30
sumeb, Nmb.	E3	44
suruga, Japan	G9	30
suruoka, Japan	D12	30
sushima, is., Japan	H2	30
sushima-kaikyō, strt., Japan	I2	30
suyama, Japan	G7	30
ual, Indon.	G9	32
ualatin, stm., Or., U.S.	h11	114
uba City, Az., U.S.	A4	80
uban, Indon.	m16	33a
ubarão, Braz.	B7	56
ubruq, Libya	B10	42
ucannon, stm., Wa., U.S.	C8	124
ucano, Braz.	F11	54
uckahoe, N.Y., U.S.	h13	109
uckahoe, stm., N.J., U.S.	E3	107
ucker, Ga., U.S.	h8	87
ucker, co., W.V., U.S.	B5	125
ucker Island, i., N.J., U.S.	E4	107
uckerman, Ar., U.S.	B4	81
uckernuck Island, i., Ma., U.S.	D7	98
uckerton, N.J., U.S.	D4	107
ucson, Az., U.S.	E5	80
ucumcari, N.M., U.S.	B6	108
ucumcari Mountain, mtn., N.M., U.S.	B6	108
ucupita, Ven.	C11	58
ucuruí, Braz.	D9	54
udela, Spain	C10	12
udmur (Palmyra), Syria	B6	40
ugaloo Lake, res., U.S.	B1	117
ug Fork, stm., U.S.	C2	125
uguegarao, Phil.	p19	32
ugur, Russia	G21	24
ukangbesi, Kepulauan, is., Indon.	G7	32
uktoyaktuk, N.W. Ter., Can.	C6	66
ukwila, Wa., U.S.	f11	124
ula, Mex.	F10	62
ula, Russia	G20	18
ulalip Indian Reservation, Wa., U.S.	A3	124
ulancingo, Mex.	G10	62
ulare, Ca., U.S.	D4	82
ulare, co., Ca., U.S.	D4	82
ulare Lake, l., Ca., U.S.	D4	82
ularosa, N.M., U.S.	D3	108
ularosa Mountains, mts., N.M., U.S.	D1	108
ularosa Valley, val., N.M., U.S.	E3	108
ulcán, Ec.	G4	58
ulcea, Rom.	D12	16
ule Lake, sw., Ca., U.S.	B3	82
ule River Indian Reservation, Ca., U.S.	E4	82
ule Valley, val., Ut., U.S.	D2	121
ulia, Tx., U.S.	B2	120
ulkarm, Jord.	C4	40
ullahoma, Tn., U.S.	B5	119
ullamore, Ire.	H5	7
ulle, Fr.	G8	10
ullins, Fr.	G12	10
ulsa, Ok., U.S.	A6	113
ulsa, co., Ok., U.S.	B6	113
uluá, Col.	E4	58
ulum, Mex.	G16	62
ulun, Russia	G14	24
ulungagung, Indon.	n15	33a
uma, lm., Nic.	H5	64
umacacori National Monument, Az., U.S.	F4	80
umaco, Col.	G3	58
uman-gang, stm., Asia	C12	26
umany, Russia	E25	24
umatumari, Guy.	E13	58
umba, Lac, l., Zaire	B3	44
umbes, Peru	D2	54
umble Mountain, mtn., Mt., U.S.	E7	103
umbler Ridge, B.C., Can.	B7	69
umen, China	C12	26
umiritinga, Braz.	E8	57
umkūr, India	F4	37
ummo, Libya	D8	42
umsar, India	B5	37
umuc-Humac Mountains, mts., S.A.	C8	54
umwater, Wa., U.S.	B3	124
unbridge Wells, Eng., U.K.	J13	7
unduru, Tan.	D7	44
undža, stm., Eur.	G10	16
'ung, stm., Russia	D17	24
ungabhadra, India	E4	37
ungabhadra Reservoir, res., India	E4	37
ungchiang, Tai.	M9	28
ungsha Tao (Pratas Islands), is., Tai.	G10	26
ungshih, Tai.	K9	28
unica, Ms., U.S.	A3	101
Tunica, co., Ms., U.S.	A3	101
Tunis, Tun.	M5	14
Tunisia, ctry., Afr.	B7	42
Tunja, Col.	E6	58
Tunkhannock, Pa., U.S.	C10	115
Tunk Lake, l., Me., U.S.	D4	96
Tunnel Hill, Ga., U.S.	B1	87
Tunp Range, mts., Wy., U.S.	D2	127
Tununak, Ak., U.S.	C6	79
Tunxi, China	F7	28
Tuobuja, Russia	E18	24
Tuolumne, Ca., U.S.	D3	82
Tuolumne, co., Ca., U.S.	C4	82
Tuolumne, stm., Ca., U.S.	D3	82
Tupã, Braz.	F3	57
Tupaciguara, Braz.	E4	57
Tupanciretã, Braz.	B6	56
Tupelo, Ms., U.S.	A5	101
Tupiza, Bol.	H5	54
Tupper Lake, N.Y., U.S.	A6	109
Tupper Lake, l., N.Y., U.S.	A6	109
Túquerres, Col.	G4	58
Tura, India	H14	38
Tura, Russia	E14	24
Turan, Russia	G12	24
Turbat, Pak.	D1	36
Turbeville, S.C., U.S.	D7	117
Turbo, Col.	C4	58
Turda, Rom.	C7	16
Turgutlu, Tur.	K11	16
Turimiquire, Cerro, mtn., Ven.	B11	58
Turin see Torino, Italy	D2	14
Turkey, ctry., Asia	H14	4
Turkey, stm., Ia., U.S.	B6	92
Turkey Creek, stm., Ok., U.S.	A3	113
Turkey Point, c., Md., U.S.	B5	97
Turkmenistan, ctry., Asia	I9	22
Turks and Caicos Islands, dep., N.A.	D12	64
Turks Islands, is., T./C. Is.	D12	64
Turku (Åbo), Fin.	F14	6
Turley, Ok., U.S.	A6	113
Turlock, Ca., U.S.	D3	82
Turnbull, Mount, mtn., Az., U.S.	D5	80
Turneffe Islands, is., Belize	F4	64
Turner, Or., U.S.	C4	114
Turner, co., Ga., U.S.	E3	87
Turner, co., S.D., U.S.	D8	118
Turners Falls, Ma., U.S.	A2	98
Turner Valley, Alta., Can.	D3	68
Turnhout, Bel.	D4	8
Turnor Lake, l., Sask., Can.	m7	75
Turnu-Măgurele, Rom.	F8	16
Turpan, China	C4	26
Turquino, Pico, mtn., Cuba	E9	64
Turrell, Ar., U.S.	B5	81
Turret Peak, mtn., Az., U.S.	C4	80
Turtle Creek, Pa., U.S.	k14	115
Turtle Flambeau Flowage, res., Wi., U.S.	B3	126
Turtle Lake, N.D., U.S.	B5	111
Turtle Lake, Wi., U.S.	C1	126
Turtle Lake, l., Sask., Can.	D1	75
Turtle Mountain Indian Reservation, N.D., U.S.	A6	111
Turu, stm., Russia	D14	24
Turuchan, stm., Russia	D11	24
Turuchansk, Russia	D11	24
Tuscaloosa, Al., U.S.	B2	78
Tuscaloosa, co., Al., U.S.	B2	78
Tuscarawas, co., Oh., U.S.	B4	112
Tuscarawas, stm., Oh., U.S.	B4	112
Tuscarora Indian Reservation, N.Y., U.S.	B2	109
Tuscarora Mountain, mtn., Pa., U.S.	F6	115
Tuscarora Mountains, mts., Nv., U.S.	B5	105
Tuscola, Il., U.S.	D5	90
Tuscola, co., Mi., U.S.	E7	99
Tuscumbia, Al., U.S.	A2	78
Tuskegee, Al., U.S.	C4	78
Tusket, stm., N.S., Can.	E4	71
Tustumena Lake, l., Ak., U.S.	g16	79
Tuticorin, India	H5	37
Tutóia, Braz.	D10	54
Tuttle, Ok., U.S.	B4	113
Tuttle Creek Lake, res., Ks., U.S.	C7	93
Tututalak Mountain, mtn., Ak., U.S.	B7	79
Tutwiler, Ms., U.S.	A3	101
Tuvalu, ctry., Oc.	G24	2
Tuwayq, Jabal, mts., Sau. Ar.	D4	46
Tuxedo, N.C., U.S.	f10	110
Tuxedo Park, De., U.S.	i7	85
Tuxpan, Mex.	G7	62
Tuxpan de Rodríguez Cano, Mex.	G11	62
Tuxtla Gutiérrez, Mex.	I13	62
Túy, Spain	C3	12
Tuy Hoa, Viet.	H10	34
Tuz Gölü, l., Tur.	H14	4
Tuzigoot National Monument, Az., U.S.	C3	80
Tuzla, Bos.	E2	16
Tveitsund, Nor.	G7	6
Tver', Russia	E18	18
Tweed, Ont., U.S.	C7	73
Tweedsmuir Provincial Park, B.C., Can.	C4	69
Tweedy Mountain, mtn., Mt., U.S.	E4	103
Twelvepole Creek, stm., W.V., U.S.	C2	125
Twentymile Creek, stm., W.V., U.S.	C3	125
Twentynine Palms, Ca., U.S.	E5	82
Twentynine Palms Marine Corps Base, mil., Ca., U.S.	E5	82
Twiggs, co., Ga., U.S.	D3	87
Twillingate, Newf., Can.	D4	72
Twin Buttes, mtn., Or., U.S.	C4	114
Twin Buttes Reservoir, res., Tx., U.S.	D2	120
Twin City, Ga., U.S.	D4	87
Twin Creek, stm., Oh., U.S.	C1	112
Twin Falls, Id., U.S.	G4	89
Twin Falls, co., Id., U.S.	G4	89
Twin Knolls, Az., U.S.	m9	80
Twin Lakes, Ga., U.S.	F3	87
Twin Lakes, Wi., U.S.	F5	126
Twin Lakes, l., Ct., U.S.	A2	84
Twin Lakes, l., Ia., U.S.	B3	92
Twin Lakes, l., Me., U.S.	C4	96
Twin Mountains, mtn., Wy., U.S.	E7	127
Twin Peaks, mts., Id., U.S.	E4	89
Twin Rivers, N.J., U.S.	C4	107
Twinsburg, Oh., U.S.	A4	112
Twin Valley, Mn., U.S.	C2	100
Twisp, Wa., U.S.	A5	124
Two Harbors, Mn., U.S.	C7	100
Two Hills, Alta., Can.	C5	68
Two Mile Beach, N.J., U.S.	F3	107
Two Rivers, Wi., U.S.	D6	126
Two Rivers, North Branch, stm., Mn., U.S.	B2	100
Two Rivers, South Branch, stm., Mn., U.S.	B2	100
Tybee Island, Ga., U.S.	D6	87
Tychy, Pol.	E18	8
Tygart Lake, res., W.V., U.S.	B5	125
Tygart River, Falls of the, wtfl, W.V., U.S.	k10	125
Tygart Valley, stm., W.V., U.S.	B4	125
Tyger, stm., S.C., U.S.	B4	117
Tyler, Mn., U.S.	F2	100
Tyler, Tx., U.S.	C5	120
Tyler, co., Tx., U.S.	D5	120
Tyler, co., W.V., U.S.	B4	125
Tyler, Lake, res., Tx., U.S.	C5	120
Tyler Branch, stm., Vt., U.S.	B3	122
Tyler Heights, W.V., U.S.	C3	125
Tylertown, Ms., U.S.	D3	101
Tymochtee Creek, stm., Oh., U.S.	B2	112
Tyndall, S.D., U.S.	E8	118
Tyndall Air Force Base, mil., Fl., U.S.	u16	86
Tyonek, Ak., U.S.	C9	79
Tyre see Şūr, Leb.	C4	40
Tyrma, Russia	G20	24
Tyrone, N.M., U.S.	E1	108
Tyrone, Ok., U.S.	e9	113
Tyrone, Pa., U.S.	E5	115
Tyronza, Ar., U.S.	B5	81
Tyrrell, co., N.C., U.S.	B6	110
Tyrrhenian Sea (Mare Tirreno), Eur.	I6	14
Tysse, Nor.	F5	6
Tzaneen, S. Afr.	F6	44

U

Name	Map Ref	Page
Uaturnã, stm., Braz.	D7	54
Uaupés, Braz.	D5	54
Ubá, Braz.	F7	57
Ubangi (Oubangui), stm., Afr.	H9	42
Ube, Japan	I4	30
Úbeda, Spain	G8	12
Uberaba, Braz.	E5	57
Uberlândia, Braz.	E4	57
Ubly, Mi., U.S.	E8	99
Ubon Ratchathani, Thai.	G8	34
Ubundi, Zaire	B5	44
Učami, Russia	E13	24
Ucayali, stm., Peru	E4	54
Uchiura-wan, b., Japan	q18	30a
Ucluelet, B.C., Can.	E5	69
Ucon, Id., U.S.	F7	89
Uda, stm., Russia	G13	24
Uda, stm., Russia	G20	24
Udaipur, India	H5	38
Udall, Ks., U.S.	E6	93
Uddevalla, Swe.	G8	6
Udgīr, India	C4	37
Udine, Italy	C8	14
Udipi, India	F3	37
Udon Thani, Thai.	F7	34
Udskaja Guba, b., Russia	G21	24
Udža, Russia	C17	24
Ueckermünde, Ger.	B14	8
Ueda, Japan	F11	30
Uele, stm., Zaire	H10	42
Uelen, Russia	D31	24
Uelzen, Ger.	C10	8
Ueno, Japan	H9	30
Uere, stm., Zaire	H11	42
Ufa, Russia	G9	22
Uganda, ctry., Afr.	A6	44
Ugashik Lakes, l., Ak., U.S.	D8	79
Ugine, Fr.	G13	10
Uglegorsk, Russia	H22	24
Uglič, Russia	D21	18
Uhrichsville, Oh., U.S.	B4	112
Uíge, Ang.	C3	44
Uijõngbu, S. Kor.	D12	26
Uinta, co., Wy., U.S.	E2	127
Uinta, stm., Ut., U.S.	C5	121
Uintah, co., Ut., U.S.	D6	121
Uintah and Ouray Indian Reservation, Ut., U.S.	C5	121
Uinta Mountains, mts., Ut., U.S.	C5	121
Uitenhage, S. Afr.	H5	44
Uivak, Cape, c., Newf., Can.	f9	72
Ujandina, stm., Russia	D22	24
Uji, Japan	H8	30
Ujiji, Tan.	B5	44
Ujjain, India	I6	38
Ujungpandang, Indon.	G6	32
Uka, Russia	F26	24
Ukiah, Ca., U.S.	C2	82
Ukiah, Or., U.S.	B7	114
Ukraine, ctry., Eur.	H4	22
Ulaanbaatar (Ulan Bator), Mong.	B8	26
Ulaangom, Mong.	B5	26
Ulak Island, i., Ak., U.S.	E4	79
Ulan Bator see Ulaanbaatar, Mong.	B8	26
Ulan-Ude, Russia	G15	24
Ulhāsnagar, India	C2	37
Uliastaj, Mong.	B6	26
Ulindi, stm., Zaire	B5	44
Ulja, Russia	F22	24
Uljanovsk, Russia	G7	22
Ullapool, Scot., U.K.	D7	7
Ullŭng-do, i., S. Kor.	D13	26
Ulm, Ger.	G10	8
Ulsan, S. Kor.	D12	26
Ulster, co., N.Y., U.S.	D6	109
Ulster, hist. reg., Eur.	G5	7
Ulu, Russia	E19	24
Ulubat Gölü, l., Tur.	I12	16
Ulungur Hu, l., China	B4	26
Ulysses, Ks., U.S.	E2	93
Umag, Cro.	D8	14
Uman', Ukr.	H4	22
Umanak, Grnld.	B22	66
Umanak Fjord, Grnld.	B22	66
Umatilla, Fl., U.S.	D5	86
Umatilla, Or., U.S.	B7	114
Umatilla, co., Or., U.S.	B8	114
Umatilla, stm., Or., U.S.	B7	114
Umatilla Indian Reservation, Or., U.S.	B8	114
Umbagog Lake, l., U.S.	A4	106
Umcolcus Lake, l., Me., U.S.	B4	96
Umeå, Swe.	E13	6
Umm Durmān (Omdurman), Sudan	E12	42
Umnak Island, i., Ak., U.S.	E6	79
Umnäs, Swe.	D11	6
Umpqua, stm., Or., U.S.	D3	114
Umsaskis Lake, l., Me., U.S.	B3	96
Umtata, S. Afr.	H5	44
Umzinto, S. Afr.	H6	44
Unadilla, Ga., U.S.	D3	87
Unadilla, stm., N.Y., U.S.	C5	109
Unalakleet, Ak., U.S.	C7	79
Unalaska Island, i., Ak., U.S.	E6	79
'Unayzah, Sau. Ar.	C3	46
Uncasville, Ct., U.S.	D7	84
Uncompahgre, stm., Co., U.S.	C3	83
Uncompahgre Mountains, mts., Co., U.S.	C3	83
Uncompahgre Peak, mtn., Co., U.S.	C3	83
Underwood, Al., U.S.	B3	78
Underwood, N.D., U.S.	B4	111
Ungava, Péninsule d', pen., Que., Can.	g12	74
Ungava Bay, b., Can.	E19	66
União dos Palmares, Braz.	E11	54
Unicoi, Tn., U.S.	C11	119
Unicoi, co., Tn., U.S.	C11	119
Unicoi Mountains, mts., U.S.	D9	119
Unimak Island, i., Ak., U.S.	D7	79
Unimak Pass, strt., Ak., U.S.	E6	79
Union, Ky., U.S.	k13	94
Union, Ms., U.S.	C4	101
Union, Mo., U.S.	C6	102
Union, Or., U.S.	B9	114
Union, S.C., U.S.	B4	117
Union, Wa., U.S.	B2	124
Union, co., Ar., U.S.	D3	81
Union, co., Fl., U.S.	B4	86
Union, co., Ga., U.S.	B2	87
Union, co., Il., U.S.	F4	90
Union, co., Ia., U.S.	C3	92
Union, co., Ky., U.S.	C2	94
Union, co., La., U.S.	B3	95
Union, co., Ms., U.S.	A4	101
Union, co., N.J., U.S.	B4	107
Union, co., N.M., U.S.	A6	108
Union, co., N.C., U.S.	B2	110
Union, co., Oh., U.S.	B2	112
Union, co., Or., U.S.	B8	114
Union, co., Pa., U.S.	E7	115
Union, co., S.C., U.S.	B4	117
Union, co., S.D., U.S.	E9	118
Union, co., Tn., U.S.	C10	119
Union, West Branch, stm., Me., U.S.	D4	96
Union Beach, N.J., U.S.	C4	107
Union Bridge, Md., U.S.	A3	97
Union City, Ga., U.S.	C2	87
Union City, In., U.S.	D8	91
Union City, Mi., U.S.	F5	99
Union City, N.J., U.S.	h8	107
Union City, Oh., U.S.	B1	112
Union City, Ok., U.S.	B4	113
Union City, Pa., U.S.	C2	115
Union City, Tn., U.S.	A2	119
Union Flat, stm., Wa., U.S.	C8	124
Union Gap, Wa., U.S.	C5	124
Union Grove, Wi., U.S.	F5	126
Union Lake, l., N.J., U.S.	E2	107
Union Pier, Mi., U.S.	G4	99
Union Point, Ga., U.S.	C3	87
Union Springs, Al., U.S.	C4	78
Uniontown, Al., U.S.	C2	78
Uniontown, Ky., U.S.	C2	94
Uniontown, Oh., U.S.	B4	112
Uniontown, Pa., U.S.	G2	115
Union Village, R.I., U.S.	B3	116
Union Village Reservoir, res., Vt., U.S.	D4	122
Unionville, Ct., U.S.	B4	84
Unionville, Mo., U.S.	A4	102
United Arab Emirates, ctry., Asia	D5	46
United Kingdom, ctry., Eur.	E7	4
United Nations Headquarters, N.Y., U.S.	h12	109
United States, ctry., N.A.	D7	76
United States Air Force Academy, mil., Co., U.S.	B6	83
United States Military Academy, mil., N.Y., U.S.	C6	109
United States Naval Academy, mil., Md., U.S.	C4	97
Unity Reservoir, res., Or., U.S.	C8	114
University City, Mo., U.S.	C7	102
University Heights, Ia., U.S.	C6	92
University Heights, Oh., U.S.	h9	112
University Park, Ia., U.S.	C5	92
University Park, N.M., U.S.	E3	108
University Park, Tx., U.S.	n10	120
University Place, Wa., U.S.	f10	124
Unnão, India	G9	38
Uozu, Japan	F10	30
Upata, Ven.	C11	58
Upemba, Lac, l., Zaire	C5	44
Upernavik, Grnld.	B21	66
Upington, S. Afr.	G4	44
Upland, Ca., U.S.	E5	82
Upland, In., U.S.	D7	91
Upleta, India	J4	38
Upolu Point, c., Hi., U.S.	C6	88
Upper Ammonoosuc, stm., N.H., U.S.	A4	106
Upper Arlington, Oh., U.S.	B2	112
Upper Arrow Lake, l., B.C., Can.	F9	66
Upper Arrow Lake, res., B.C., Can.	D9	69
Upperco, Md., U.S.	A4	97
Upper Darby, Pa., U.S.	G11	115
Upper Greenwood Lake, N.J., U.S.	A4	107
Upper Humber, stm., Newf., Can.	D3	72
Upper Iowa, stm., Ia., U.S.	A5	92
Upper Island Cove, Newf., Can.	E5	72
Upper Kapuas Mountains, mts., Asia	E5	32
Upper Klamath Lake, l., Or., U.S.	E4	114
Upper Marlboro, Md., U.S.	C4	97
Upper New York Bay, b., U.S.	k8	107
Upper Red Lake, l., Mn., U.S.	B4	100
Upper Saddle River, N.J., U.S.	A4	107
Upper Sandusky, Oh., U.S.	B2	112
Upper Sheila, N.B., Can.	B5	71
Upper Volta see Burkina Faso, ctry., Afr.	F5	42
Uppsala, Swe.	G11	6
Upright, Cape, c., Ak., U.S.	C5	79
Upshur, co., Tx., U.S.	C5	120
Upshur, co., W.V., U.S.	C4	125
Upson, co., Ga., U.S.	D2	87
Upton, Ky., U.S.	C4	94
Upton, Ma., U.S.	B4	98
Upton, Wy., U.S.	B8	127
Upton, co., Tx., U.S.	D2	120
Uquía, Cerro, mtn., Ven.	E11	58
Urabá, Golfo de, b., Col.	C4	58
Ural, stm., Asia	H8	22
Ural Mountains see Ural'skije gory, mts., Russia	F9	22
Ural'sk, Kaz.	G8	22
Urania, La., U.S.	C3	95
Urbana, Il., U.S.	C5	90
Urbana, Oh., U.S.	B2	112
Urbancrest, Oh., U.S.	m10	112
Urbandale, Ia., U.S.	C4	92
Urbino, Italy	F7	14
Urfa, Tur.	H15	4
Urgenč, Uzb.	I10	22
Uribe, Col.	F5	58
Uribia, Col.	B6	58
Urla, Tur.	K10	16
Uruaçu, Braz.	C4	57
Uruapan [del Progreso], Mex.	H8	62
Urubamba, stm., Peru	F4	54
Urucuia, stm., Braz.	D6	57
Uruguaiana, Braz.	B5	56
Uruguay, ctry., S.A.	C5	56
Uruguay (Uruguai), stm., S.A.	C5	56
Ürümqi, China	C4	26
Ur'ung-Chaja, Russia	C16	24
Urun-Islāmpur, India	D3	37
Urup, Ostrov, i., Russia	H23	24
Usa, Japan	I4	30
Uşak, Tur.	K13	16
Usedom, i., Eur.	B14	8
Ushibuka, Japan	J3	30
Ushuaia, Arg.	G3	56
Usolje-Sibirskoje, Russia	G14	24
Usquepaug, R.I., U.S.	F3	116
Ussel, Fr.	G9	10
Ussuri (Wusuli), stm., Asia	B14	26
Ussurijsk, Russia	I20	24
Ust'-Barguzin, Russia	G15	24
Ust'-Belaja, Russia	D28	24
Ust'-Čaun, Russia	D28	24
Ústí nad Labem, Czech.	E14	8
Ust'-Kamčatsk, Russia	F26	24
Ust'-Kamenogorsk, Kaz.	H10	24
Ust'-Kut, Russia	F15	24
Ust'-Maja, Russia	E20	24
Ust'-Nera, Russia	E22	24
Usu, China	C3	26
Usuki, Japan	I4	30
Usulután, El Sal.	H3	64
Usumacinta, stm., N.A.	I14	62
Utah, co., Ut., U.S.	C4	121
Utah, state, U.S.	D4	121
Utah Lake, l., Ut., U.S.	C4	121
Utashinai, Japan	p20	30a
Ute Creek, stm., N.M., U.S.	A6	108
Ute Mountain Indian Reservation, U.S.	D2	83
Ute Reservoir, res., N.M., U.S.	B6	108
Utete, Tan.	C7	44
Uthai Thani, Thai.	G6	34
Utiariti, Braz.	F7	54
Utica, Il., U.S.	B5	90
Utica, Mi., U.S.	F7	99
Utica, Ms., U.S.	C3	101
Utica, Ne., U.S.	D8	104
Utica, N.Y., U.S.	B5	109
Utica, Oh., U.S.	B3	112
Utiel, Spain	F10	12
Utikuma Lake, l., Alta., Can.	B3	68
Utrecht, Neth.	C5	8
Utrera, Spain	H6	12
Utsunomiya, Japan	F12	30
Uttar Pradesh, state, India	G8	38
Uusikaupunki (Nystad), Fin.	F13	6
Uvá, stm., Col.	F7	58
Uvalde, Tx., U.S.	E3	120
Uvalde, co., Tx., U.S.	E3	120
Uvdal, Nor.	F7	6
Uvinza, Tan.	C6	44
Uvs Nuur, l., Asia	A5	26
Uwajima, Japan	I5	30
'Uwaynāt, Jabal al-, mtn., Afr.	D10	42
Uwharrie, stm., N.C., U.S.	B3	110

Name	Map Ref	Page
Uxbridge, Ma., U.S.	B4	98
Uyuni, Bol.	H5	54
Uyuni, Salar de, pl., Bol.	H5	54
Uzbekistan, state, Asia	I10	22
Uzerche, Fr.	G8	10
Uzès, Fr.	H11	10
Uzlovaja, Russia	H21	18
Uzunköprü, Tur.	H10	16
Užur, Russia	F11	24

V

Name	Map Ref	Page
Vaala, Fin.	D16	6
Vaasa (Vasa), Fin.	E13	6
Vác, Hung.	H19	8
Vaca Key, i., Fl., U.S.	H5	86
Vacaville, Ca., U.S.	C3	82
Vaccarès, Étang de, b., Fr.	I11	10
Vach, stm., Russia	E9	24
Vacherie, La., U.S.	h10	95
Vadsø, Nor.	A17	6
Vaduz, Liech.	H9	8
Váh, stm., Czech.	G18	8
Vaiden, Ms., U.S.	B4	101
Vail, Co., U.S.	B4	83
Vākhān, stm., Afg.	B5	38
Vākhān, reg., Afg.	B5	38
Vålådalen, Swe.	E9	6
Val-Bélair, Que., Can.	n17	74
Valcheta, Arg.	E3	56
Valcourt, Que., Can.	D5	74
Valdagno, Italy	D6	14
Val-David, Que., Can.	C3	74
Valdecañas, Embalse de, res., Spain	F6	12
Valdemarsvik, Swe.	G11	6
Valdepeñas, Spain	G8	12
Valderrobres, Spain	E12	12
Valders, Wi., U.S.	D6	126
Valdés, Península, pen., Arg.	E4	56
Valdese, N.C., U.S.	B1	110
Valdez, Ak., U.S.	C10	79
Val-d'Isère, Fr.	G13	10
Valdivia, Col.	D2	56
Valdivia, Col.	D5	58
Val-d'Or, Que., Can.	k11	74
Valdosta, Ga., U.S.	F3	87
Vale, Or., U.S.	D9	114
Valemount, B.C., Can.	C8	69
Valença, Braz.	B9	57
Valença, Port.	D3	12
Valençay, Fr.	E8	10
Valence, Fr.	H11	10
Valencia, Spain	F11	12
Valencia, Az., U.S.	m7	80
Valencia, Ven.	C8	58
Valencia, co., N.M., U.S.	C3	108
Valencia, Golfo de, b., Spain	F12	12
Valencia de Alcántara, Spain	F4	12
Valencia de Don Juan, Spain	C6	12
Valencia Heights, S.C., U.S.	D6	117
Valentine, Ne., U.S.	B5	104
Valenza, Italy	D3	14
Valera, Ven.	C7	58
Valga, Est.	D9	18
Valhalla, N.Y., U.S.	D7	109
Valhermoso Springs, Al., U.S.	A3	78
Valjevo, Yugo.	E3	16
Valkeakoski, Fin.	F15	6
Valkenswaard, Neth.	D5	8
Valladolid, Mex.	G15	62
Valladolid, Spain	D7	12
Valle de Uxó, Spain	F11	12
Vallecito Reservoir, res., Co., U.S.	D3	83
Valle de Guanape, Ven.	C10	58
Valle de la Pascua, Ven.	C9	58
Valle de Santiago, Mex.	G9	62
Valle de Zaragoza, Mex.	D7	62
Valledupar, Col.	B6	58
Vallée-Jonction, Que., Can.	C7	74
Valle Hermoso, Mex.	E11	62
Vallejo, Ca., U.S.	C2	82
Vallelunga Pratameno, Italy	L8	14
Vallenar, Chile	B2	56
Valletta, Malta	N9	14
Valley, Ne., U.S.	C9	104
Valley, co., Id., U.S.	E3	89
Valley, co., Mt., U.S.	B10	103
Valley, co., Ne., U.S.	C6	104
Valley, stm., Man., Can.	D1	70
Valley Center, Ks., U.S.	E6	93
Valley City, N.D., U.S.	C8	111
Valley Cottage, N.Y., U.S.	g13	109
Valley East, Ont., Can.	p19	73
Valley Falls, Ks., U.S.	C8	93
Valley Falls, R.I., U.S.	B4	116
Valley Forge, Pa., U.S.	o20	115
Valley Mills, Tx., U.S.	D4	120
Valley Park, Mo., U.S.	f12	102
Valley Springs, S.D., U.S.	D9	118
Valley Station, Ky., U.S.	g11	94
Valley Stream, N.Y., U.S.	n15	109
Valleyview, Alta., Can.	B2	68
Valley View, Pa., U.S.	E8	115
Valliant, Ok., U.S.	D6	113
Vallo della Lucania, Italy	I10	14
Valls, Spain	D13	12
Vallscreek, W.V., U.S.	D3	125
Valmeyer, Il., U.S.	E3	90
Valognes, Fr.	C5	10
Valparaíso, Chile	C2	56
Valparaíso, Mex.	F8	62
Valparaiso, Fl., U.S.	u15	86
Valparaiso, In., U.S.	B3	91
Valréas, Fr.	H11	10
Val Verda, Ut., U.S.	C4	121
Valverde, Dom. Rep.	E12	64
Val Verde, co., Tx., U.S.	E2	120

Name	Map Ref	Page
Valverde del Camino, Spain	H5	12
Van, Tur.	H16	4
Van, Tx., U.S.	C5	120
Van, W.V., U.S.	n12	125
Van Alstyne, Tx., U.S.	C4	120
Vanavara, Russia	E14	24
Van Buren, Ar., U.S.	B1	81
Van Buren, Me., U.S.	A5	96
Van Buren, In., U.S.	C6	91
Van Buren, co., Ar., U.S.	B3	81
Van Buren, co., Ia., U.S.	D6	92
Van Buren, co., Mi., U.S.	F4	99
Van Buren, co., Tn., U.S.	D8	119
Vance, co., N.C., U.S.	A4	110
Vance Air Force Base, mil., Ok., U.S.	A3	113
Vanceboro, N.C., U.S.	B5	110
Vanceburg, Ky., U.S.	B6	94
Vancleave, Ms., U.S.	E5	101
Vancouver, B.C., Can.	E6	69
Vancouver, Wa., U.S.	D3	124
Vancouver, Cape, c., Austl.	G3	50
Vancouver Island, i., B.C., Can.	E4	69
Vancouver Island Ranges, mts., B.C., Can.	D4	69
Vandalia, Il., U.S.	E4	90
Vandalia, Mo., U.S.	B6	102
Vandenberg Air Force Base, mil., Ca., U.S.	E3	82
Vander, N.C., U.S.	B4	110
Vanderbilt Peak, mtn., N.M., U.S.	E1	108
Vanderburgh, co., In., U.S.	H2	91
Vandergrift, Pa., U.S.	E2	115
Vanderhoof, B.C., Can.	C5	69
Van Diemen Gulf, b., Austl.	B6	50
Vänern, l., Swe.	G9	6
Vänersborg, Swe.	G9	6
Vangaindrano, Madag.	F9	44
Van Gölü, l., Tur.	H16	4
Vangunu, i., Sol.Is.	A11	50
Van Horn, Tx., U.S.	o12	120
Van Horne, Ia., U.S.	B5	92
Vanier, Ont., Can.	h12	73
Vāniyambādi, India	F5	37
Vankarem, Russia	D30	24
Vankleek Hill, Ont., Can.	B10	73
Van Kull, Kill, stm., N.J., U.S.	k8	107
Van Lear, Ky., U.S.	C7	94
Van Meter, Ia., U.S.	C4	92
Vännäs, Swe.	E12	6
Vannes, Fr.	E4	10
Van Rees, Pegunungan, mts., Indon.	F10	32
Vanrhynsdorp, S. Afr.	H3	44
Vansant, Va., U.S.	e9	123
Vansbro, Swe.	F10	6
Vansittart Island, i., N.W. Ter., Can.	C16	66
Vanuatu, ctry., Oc.	H24	2
Van Vleck, Tx., U.S.	r14	120
Van Wert, Oh., U.S.	B1	112
Van Wert, co., Oh., U.S.	B1	112
Van Zandt, co., Tx., U.S.	C5	120
Varades, Fr.	E5	10
Vārānasi (Benares), India	H10	38
Varaždin, Cro.	C11	14
Varazze, Italy	E3	14
Varberg, Swe.	H9	6
Vardaman, Ms., U.S.	B4	101
Vardar (Axiós), stm., Eur.	H6	16
Vardø, Nor.	A18	6
Varennes, Que., Can.	D4	74
Varennes-sur-Allier, Fr.	F10	10
Varese, Italy	D3	14
Varginha, Braz.	F6	57
Varina, Va., U.S.	C5	123
Varkaus, Fin.	E16	6
Varkhān, stm., Afg.	D1	38
Varna, Bul.	F11	16
Värnamo, Swe.	H10	6
Varnville, S.C., U.S.	F5	117
Varzy, Fr.	E10	10
Vasai (Bassein), India	C2	37
Vashon, Point, c., Wa., U.S.	e11	124
Vashon Island, i., Wa., U.S.	f11	124
Vass, N.C., U.S.	B3	110
Vassar, Mi., U.S.	E7	99
Västerås, Swe.	G11	6
Västervik, Swe.	H11	6
Vasto, Italy	G9	14
Vas'ugan, stm., Russia	F9	24
Vatican City (Città del Vaticano), ctry., Eur.	H7	14
Vatnajökull, Ice.	C4	4
Vättern, l., Swe.	G10	6
Vaucouleurs, Fr.	D12	10
Vaudreuil, Que., Can.	D3	74
Vaughan, Ont., Can.	D5	73
Vaughn, Mt., U.S.	C5	103
Vaughn, N.M., U.S.	C4	108
Vaupés (Uaupés), stm., S.A.	G7	58
Vauxhall, Alta., Can.	D4	68
Vazante, Braz.	D5	57
V'azemskij, Russia	H20	24
V'az'ma, Russia	F17	18
V'azniki, Russia	E25	18
Veazie, Me., U.S.	D4	96
Vechta, Ger.	C8	8
Veedersburg, In., U.S.	D3	91
Veendam, Neth.	B6	8
Vegreville, Alta., Can.	C4	68
Vejer de la Frontera, Spain	I6	12
Vejle, Den.	I7	6
Vela Luka, Cro.	G11	14
Velda Rose Estates, Az., U.S.	*D4	80
Velenje, Slo.	C10	14
Vélez-Málaga, Spain	I7	12
Vélez Rubio, Spain	H9	12
Velhas, Rio das, stm., Braz.	D6	57
Velike Lašče, Slo.	D9	14
Velikije Luki, Russia	E13	18
Veliko Tŭrnovo, Bul.	F9	16
Vella Lavella, i., Sol.Is.	A11	50
Velletri, Italy	H7	14

Name	Map Ref	Page
Vellore, India	F5	37
Velma, Ok., U.S.	C4	113
Velva, N.D., U.S.	A5	111
Venado Tuerto, Arg.	C4	56
Venango, co., Pa., U.S.	D2	115
Venda Nova, Braz.	E7	57
Vendeuvre-sur-Barse, Fr.	D11	10
Vendôme, Fr.	E8	10
Veneta, Or., U.S.	C3	114
Venezia (Venice), Italy	D7	14
Venezuela, ctry., S.A.	B5	54
Venezuela, Golfo de, b., S.A.	B7	58
Veniaminof, Mount, mtn., Ak., U.S.	D8	79
Venice, Fl., U.S.	E4	86
Venice, Il., U.S.	E3	90
Venice, Gulf of, b., Eur.	D7	14
Venice see Venezia, Italy	D7	14
Vénissieux, Fr.	G11	10
Venlo, Neth.	D6	8
Venosa, Italy	I10	14
Ventnor City, N.J., U.S.	E4	107
Ventspils, Lat.	D4	18
Ventuari, stm., Ven.	E9	58
Ventura (San Buenaventura), Ca., U.S.	E4	82
Ventura, co., Ca., U.S.	E4	82
Venustiano Carranza, Mex.	I13	62
Vera, Spain	H10	12
Veracruz [Llave], Mex.	H11	62
Verāval, India	J4	38
Verbania, Italy	D3	14
Vercelli, Italy	D3	14
Verchères, Que., Can.	D4	74
Verchn'aja Amga, Russia	F19	24
Verchneimbatskoje, Russia	E11	24
Verchojansk, Russia	D20	24
Verchojanskij Chrebet, mts., Russia	D19	24
Verda, Ky., U.S.	D6	94
Verde, stm., Az., U.S.	C4	80
Verden, Ger.	C9	8
Verdi, Nv., U.S.	D2	105
Verdigre, Ne., U.S.	B7	104
Verdigris, Ok., U.S.	A6	113
Verdigris, stm., U.S.	A6	113
Verdi Peak, mtn., Nv., U.S.	C6	105
Verdun, Que., Can.	q19	74
Verdun, Fr.	C12	10
Vereeniging, S. Afr.	G5	44
Vergara, Spain	B9	12
Vergennes, Vt., U.S.	C2	122
Verissimo, Braz.	E4	57
Vermilion, Alta., Can.	C5	68
Vermilion, Oh., U.S.	A3	112
Vermilion, co., Il., U.S.	C6	90
Vermilion, co., La., U.S.	E3	95
Vermilion, stm., Alta., Can.	C5	68
Vermilion, stm., Il., U.S.	C5	90
Vermilion, stm., La., U.S.	E3	95
Vermilion, stm., Mn., U.S.	B6	100
Vermilion, stm., Oh., U.S.	A3	112
Vermilion Bay, b., La., U.S.	E3	95
Vermilion Lake, l., Mn., U.S.	C6	100
Vermilion Pass, Can.	D2	68
Vermillion, S.D., U.S.	E9	118
Vermillion, co., In., U.S.	E2	91
Vermilion, East Fork, stm., S.D., U.S.	D8	118
Vermillon, stm., Que., Can.	B4	74
Vermont, Il., U.S.	C3	90
Vermont, state, U.S.	D3	122
Vermontville, Mi., U.S.	F5	99
Vernal, Ut., U.S.	C6	121
Verneuil-sur-Avre, Fr.	D7	10
Vernon, B.C., Can.	D8	69
Vernon, Fr.	C8	10
Vernon, Al., U.S.	B1	78
Vernon, Tx., U.S.	B3	120
Vernon, co., La., U.S.	C2	95
Vernon, co., Mo., U.S.	D3	102
Vernon, co., Wi., U.S.	E3	126
Vernon Hills, Il., U.S.	h9	90
Vernonia, Or., U.S.	B3	114
Vero Beach, Fl., U.S.	E6	86
Véroia, Grc.	I6	16
Verona, Ont., Can.	C8	73
Verona, Italy	D6	14
Verona, Ms., U.S.	A5	101
Verona, N.J., U.S.	B4	107
Verona, Pa., U.S.	k14	115
Verona, Wi., U.S.	E4	126
Verret, Lake, l., La., U.S.	E4	95
Versailles, Fr.	D9	10
Versailles, In., U.S.	F7	91
Versailles, Ky., U.S.	B5	94
Versailles, Mo., U.S.	C5	102
Versailles, Oh., U.S.	B1	112
Vert, Cap, c., Sen.	F2	42
Vertientes, Cuba	D8	64
Vertou, Fr.	E5	10
Verviers, Bel.	E5	8
Vesoul, Fr.	E13	10
Vestal, N.Y., U.S.	C4	109
Vestavia Hills, Al., U.S.	g7	78
Vestmannaeyjar, Ice.	C3	4
Vesuvio, vol., Italy	I9	14
Vesuvius see Vesuvio, vol., Italy	I9	14
Veszprém, Hung.	H17	8
Vetlanda, Swe.	H10	6
Vevay, In., U.S.	G7	91
Vevey, Switz.	F13	10
Veynes, Fr.	H12	10
Viadana, Italy	E5	14
Vian, Ok., U.S.	B7	113
Viana do Bollo, Spain	C4	12
Viana do Alentejo, Port.	G3	12
Viana do Castelo, Port.	D3	12
Viangchan, Laos	F7	34
Viareggio, Italy	F5	14
Viborg, Den.	H7	6
Viborg, S.D., U.S.	D8	118
Vibo Valentia, Italy	K11	14
Viburnum, Mo., U.S.	D6	102
Vic-en-Bigorre, Fr.	I7	10

Name	Map Ref	Page
Vicente, Point, c., Ca., U.S.	n12	82
Vicenza, Italy	D6	14
Vich, Spain	D14	12
Vichada, stm., Col.	E8	58
Vichy, Fr.	F10	10
Vici, Ok., U.S.	A2	113
Vicksburg, Mi., U.S.	F5	99
Vicksburg, Ms., U.S.	C3	101
Vicksburg National Military Park, Ms., U.S.	C3	101
Viçosa, Braz.	F7	57
Victor, Ia., U.S.	C5	92
Victor, N.Y., U.S.	C3	109
Victoria, B.C., Can.	E6	69
Victoria, Newf., Can.	E5	72
Victoria (Xianggang), H.K.	M3	28
Victoria, Sey.	B11	44
Victoria, Ks., U.S.	D4	93
Victoria, Tx., U.S.	E4	120
Victoria, Va., U.S.	*C4	123
Victoria, state, Austl.	G9	50
Victoria, co., Tx., U.S.	E4	120
Victoria, Lake, l., Afr.	B6	44
Victoria, Mount, mtn., Burma	D2	34
Victoria de las Tunas, Cuba	D9	64
Victoria Falls, wtfl, Afr.	E5	44
Victoria Harbour, Ont., Can.	C5	73
Victoria Island, i., N.W. Ter., Can.	B10	66
Victoria Lake, res., Newf., Can.	D3	72
Victoria Land, reg., Ant.	B28	47
Victoria Nile, stm., Ug.	H12	42
Victoria Peak, mtn., Belize	F3	64
Victoria Strait, strt., N.W. Ter., Can.	C12	66
Victoriaville, Que., Can.	C6	74
Victoria West, S. Afr.	H4	44
Victorville, Ca., U.S.	E5	82
Vičuga, Russia	D24	18
Vidalia, Ga., U.S.	D4	87
Vidalia, La., U.S.	C3	95
Vidisha, India	I7	38
Vidor, Tx., U.S.	D5	120
Viechtach, Ger.	F12	8
Viedma, Arg.	E4	56
Viedma, Lago, l., Arg.	F2	56
Viella, Spain	C12	12
Vienna, Ga., U.S.	D3	87
Vienna, Il., U.S.	F5	90
Vienna, Mo., U.S.	C6	102
Vienna, Va., U.S.	B5	123
Vienna, W.V., U.S.	B3	125
Vienna see Wien, Aus.	G16	8
Vienne, Fr.	G11	10
Vientiane see Viangchan, Laos	F7	34
Vieques, Isla de, i., P.R.	E15	64
Vieremä, Fin.	E16	6
Vierwaldstätter See, l., Switz.	F15	10
Vierzon, Fr.	E9	10
Vieste, Italy	H11	14
Vietnam, ctry., Asia	B4	32
Vieux Desert, Lac, l., Wi., U.S.	B4	126
Vigan, Phil.	p19	33b
Vigevano, Italy	D3	14
Vignola, Italy	E5	14
Vigo, Spain	C3	12
Vigo, co., In., U.S.	F3	91
Vijayawāda, India	D6	37
Vijosë (Aóös), stm., Eur.	I3	16
Vikajärvi, Fin.	C16	6
Viking, Alta., Can.	C5	68
Vila Coutinho, Moz.	D6	44
Vila do Conde, Port.	D3	12
Vila Fontes, Moz.	E7	44
Vilafranca de Xira, Port.	G3	12
Vilanculos, Moz.	F7	44
Vila Nova de Famalicão, Port.	D3	12
Vila Nova de Foz Côa, Port.	D4	12
Vila Nova de Gaia, Port.	D3	12
Vila Pery, Moz.	E6	44
Vila Real, Port.	D4	12
Vila Velha de Ródão, Port.	F4	12
Vilar Formoso, Port.	E4	12
Vila Velha, Braz.	F8	57
Vilas, co., Wi., U.S.	B4	126
Vil'kickogo, Proliv, strt., Russia	B14	24
Villa Ahumada, Mex.	B6	62
Villa Bella, Bol.	F5	54
Villablino, Spain	C5	12
Villa Bruzual, Ven.	C8	58
Villacañas, Spain	F8	12
Villacarriedo, Spain	B8	12
Villacarrillo, Spain	G8	12
Villach, Aus.	I13	8
Villacidro, Italy	J3	14
Villa Colón (Caucete), Arg.	C3	56
Villa del Rosario, Ven.	I11	64
Villa de Méndez, Mex.	E10	62
Villadiego, Spain	C7	12
Villafranca del Bierzo, Spain	C5	12
Villafranca de los Barros, Spain	G5	12
Villafranca di Verona, Italy	D5	14
Villa Frontera, Mex.	D9	62
Villagarcía, Spain	C3	12
Villa Grove, Il., U.S.	D5	90
Villaguay, Arg.	C5	56
Villa Hayes, Para.	B5	56
Villahermosa, Mex.	I13	62
Villajoyosa, Spain	G11	12
Villalón de Campos, Spain	C6	12
Villalonga, Arg.	D4	56
Villalpando, Spain	D6	12
Villa María, Arg.	C4	56
Villamartín, Spain	I6	12
Villa Montes, Bol.	H6	54
Villanova Monteleone, Italy	I3	14
Villanueva, Col.	B6	58
Villanueva de Córdoba, Spain	G7	12
Villanueva de la Serana, Spain	G6	12
Villanueva de los Infantes, Spain	G8	12
Villanueva del Río y Minas, Spain	H6	12
Villanueva y Geltrú, Spain	D13	12
Villa Park, Il., U.S.	k8	90
Villa Pedro Montoya, Mex.	G10	62

Name	Map Ref	Page
Villarcayo, Spain	C8	12
Villa Rica, Ga., U.S.	C2	87
Villarreal, Spain	F11	12
Villarrica, Chile	D2	56
Villarrobledo, Spain	F9	12
Villas, N.J., U.S.	E3	107
Villa San Giovanni, Italy	K10	14
Villasayas, Spain	D9	12
Villa Unión, Arg.	B4	56
Villavicencio, Col.	E6	58
Villaviciosa de Córdoba, Spain	G6	12
Villedieu, Fr.	D5	10
Villefort, Fr.	H10	10
Villefranche, Fr.	G11	10
Villefranche-de-Rouergue, Fr.	H9	10
Villena, Spain	G11	12
Villeneuve-de-Berg, Fr.	H11	10
Villeneuve-Saint-Georges, Fr.	D9	10
Villeneuve-sur-Lot, Fr.	H7	10
Ville Platte, La., U.S.	D3	95
Villers-Bocage, Fr.	C6	10
Villers-Cotterêts, Fr.	C10	10
Ville Saint-Georges, Que., Can.	C7	74
Villeurbanne, Fr.	G11	10
Villingen-Schwenningen, Ger.	G8	8
Villisca, Ia., U.S.	D3	92
Villupuram, India	F5	37
Vilnius, Lith.	G8	18
Vilonia, Ar., U.S.	B3	81
Vilsbiburg, Ger.	G12	8
Vil'uj, stm., Russia	E18	24
Vil'ujsk, Russia	E18	24
Vimianzo, Spain	B2	12
Vimoutiers, Fr.	D7	10
Vina, stm., Cam.	G8	42
Viña del Mar, Chile	C2	56
Vinalhaven, Me., U.S.	D4	96
Vinalhaven Island, i., Me., U.S.	D4	96
Vinaroz, Spain	E12	12
Vincennes, In., U.S.	G2	91
Vincent, Al., U.S.	B3	78
Vinces, Ec.	H3	58
Vindeln, Swe.	D12	6
Vindhya Range, mts., India	I7	38
Vine Brook, stm., Ma., U.S.	g11	98
Vinegar Hill, mtn., Or., U.S.	C8	114
Vine Grove, Ky., U.S.	C4	94
Vineland, N.J., U.S.	E2	107
Vineyard Haven, Ma., U.S.	D6	98
Vineyard Sound, strt., Ma., U.S.	D6	98
Vinh, Viet.	E8	34
Vinhais, Port.	D4	12
Vinh Long, Viet.	I8	34
Vinita, Ok., U.S.	A6	113
Vinkovci, Cro.	D2	16
Vinnica, Ukr.	H3	22
Vinnitsa see Vinnica, Ukr.	H3	22
Vinson Massif, mtn., Ant.	B4	47
Vinton, Ia., U.S.	B5	92
Vinton, La., U.S.	D2	95
Vinton, Va., U.S.	C3	123
Vinton, co., Oh., U.S.	C3	112
Viola, Il., U.S.	B3	90
Violet, La., U.S.	k12	95
Vipava, Slo.	D8	14
Vipiteno, Italy	C6	14
Virac, Phil.	C7	32
Viramgām, India	I5	38
Viranşehir, Tur.	A6	40
Virden, Man., Can.	E1	70
Virden, Il., U.S.	D4	90
Vire, Fr.	D6	10
Virgin, stm., U.S.	G8	105
Virginia, S. Afr.	G5	44
Virginia, Al., U.S.	g6	78
Virginia, Il., U.S.	D3	90
Virginia, Mn., U.S.	C6	100
Virginia, state, U.S.	C4	123
Virginia Beach, Va., U.S.	D7	123
Virginia City, Nv., U.S.	D2	105
Virginia Peak, mtn., Nv., U.S.	D2	105
Virgin Islands, dep., N.A.	E15	64
Virje, Cro.	C11	14
Virkie, Scot., U.K.	B11	7
Viroqua, Wi., U.S.	E3	126
Virovitica, Cro.	D12	14
Virtaniemi, Fin.	B17	6
Virudunagar, India	H4	37
Vis, Cro.	F11	14
Visalia, Ca., U.S.	D4	82
Visby, Swe.	H12	6
Viscount Melville Sound, strt., N.W. Ter., Can.	B10	66
Viseu, Port.	E4	12
Vishākhapatnam, India	D7	37
Vislinskij Zaliv, b., Eur.	A19	8
Visnagar, India	I5	38
Vista, Ca., U.S.	F5	82
Vistula see Wisła, stm., Pol.	A18	8
Vitarte, Peru	F3	54
Vitebsk, Bela.	F13	18
Viterbo, Italy	G7	14
Vitigudino, Spain	D5	12
Vitim, Russia	F16	24
Vitim, stm., Russia	F16	24
Vitória, Braz.	F8	57
Vitoria, Spain	C9	12
Vitória da Conquista, Braz.	C8	57
Vitré, Fr.	D5	10
Vitry-le-François, Fr.	D11	10
Vitteaux, Fr.	E11	10
Vittel, Fr.	D12	10
Vittoria, Italy	M9	14
Vittorio Veneto, Italy	D7	14
Viver, Spain	F11	12
Vivero, Spain	B4	12
Vivian, La., U.S.	B2	95
Viviers, Fr.	H11	10
Vivonne, Fr.	F7	10
Vizcachas, Meseta de las, plat., Arg.	G2	56
Vizcaíno, Desierto de, des., Mex.	D3	62
Vizianagaram, India	C7	37
Vizille, Fr.	G12	10
Vladikavkaz, Russia	I6	22

Name	Map Ref	Page
adimir, Russia	E23	18
adivostok, Russia	E35	128
issingen (Flushing), Neth.	D3	8
orë, Alb.	I3	16
tava, stm., Czech.	F14	8
öcklabruck, Aus.	G13	8
odnjan, Cro.	E8	14
ogelsberg, mts., Ger.	E9	8
oghera, Italy	E4	14
ohenstrauss, Ger.	F12	8
ohibinany, Madag.	E9	44
ohimarina, Madag.	D10	44
oi, Kenya	B7	46
oinjama, Lib.	G4	42
oiron, Fr.	G12	10
oitsberg, Aus.	H15	8
olcano, Hi., U.S.	D6	88
olchov, Russia	B15	18
olda, Nor.	E6	6
olga, S.D., U.S.	C9	118
olga, stm.	H7	22
olgograd (Stalingrad), Russia	H6	22
olkovysk, Bela.	H7	18
oločanka, Russia	C12	24
ologda, Russia	B22	18
olokolamsk, Russia	E18	18
olos, Grc.	J6	16
olta, Lake, res., Ghana	G5	42
olta Blanche (White Volta), stm., Afr.	F5	42
olta Noire (Black Volta), stm., Afr.	F6	42
olta Redonda, Braz.	G6	57
olterra, Italy	F5	14
olusia, co., Fl., U.S.	C5	86
olžskij, Russia	H6	22
on Frank Mountain, mtn., Ak., U.S.	C9	79
onore, Tn., U.S.	D9	119
oriai Sporádhes, is., Grc.	J7	16
oronež, Russia	G5	22
oronež, stm., Voronež, Russia	G5	22
osges, mts., Fr.	D14	10
oskresensk, Russia	F21	18
oss, Nor.	F6	6
ostočno-Sibirskoje More (East Siberian Sea), Russia	C25	24
ostočnyj Sajan, mts., Russia	G13	24
otkinsk, Russia	F8	22
otuporanga, Braz.	F4	57
ouziers, Fr.	C11	10
oyageurs National Park, Mn., U.S.	B5	100
aca, Bul.	F7	16
angel'a, Ostrov, i., Russia	C29	24
anje, Yugo.	G5	16
annika, Slo.	D9	14
yburg, S. Afr.	G4	44
yheid, S. Afr.	G6	44
evidof, Mount, mtn., Ak., U.S.	E6	79
evoložsk, Russia	A13	18
okovar, Cro.	D2	16
olcan, Alta., Can.	D4	68
ng Tau (Cap-St.-Jacques), Viet.	I9	34
oggatjålme, Swe.	C11	6
oksenniska, Fin.	F17	6
borg, Russia	A11	18
ška, Russia	D18	18
šnij Voločok, Russia	D17	18
sokogornyj, Russia	G21	24
a, Ghana	F5	42
aawaa, Puu, mtn., Hi., U.S.	D6	88
abana (Bell Island), Newf., Can.	E5	72
abasca, Alta., Can.	B4	68
abasca, stm., Alta., Can.	f1	68
abash, In., U.S.	C6	91
abash, co., Il., U.S.	E6	90
abash, co., In., U.S.	C6	91
abash, stm., U.S.	H2	91
abasha, Mn., U.S.	F6	100
abasha, co., Mn., U.S.	F6	100
abasso, Fl., U.S.	E6	86
abasso, stm.	F3	100
abaunsee, co., Ks., U.S.	D7	93
abeno, Wi., U.S.	C5	126
abowden, Man., Can.	B2	70
abush, Newf., Can.	h8	72
accamaw, stm., U.S.	D9	117
accamaw, Lake, res., U.S.	C4	110
accasassa Bay, b., Fl., U.S.	C4	86
achusett Mountain, mtn., Ma., U.S.	B4	98
achusett Reservoir, res., Ma., U.S.	B4	98
aco, Tx., U.S.	D4	120
aco Lake, res., Tx., U.S.	D4	120
aconda Lake, res., Ks., U.S.	C5	93
aconia, Mn., U.S.	F5	100
addeneilanden, is., Neth.	B5	8
addenzee, Neth.	B5	8
addi, Chappal, mtn., Nig.	G8	42
addington, Mount, mtn., B.C., Can.	D5	69
adena, Mn., U.S.	D3	100
adena, co., Mn., U.S.	D4	100
adenswil, Switz.	E15	10
adesboro, N.C., U.S.	C2	110
ading, stm., N.J., U.S.	D3	107
adley, Ga., U.S.	D4	87
ad Madanī, Sudan	F12	42
admalaw Island, i., S.C., U.S.	F7	117
adsworth, Il., U.S.	h9	90
adsworth, Nv., U.S.	D2	105
adsworth, Oh., U.S.	A4	112
agener, S.C., U.S.	D5	117
ageningen, Neth.	D5	8
ager Bay, b., N.W. Ter., Can.	C15	66
agga Wagga, Austl.	G9	50
Wagin, Austl.	F3	50
Wagner, S.D., U.S.	D7	118
Wagoner, Ok., U.S.	B6	113
Wagoner, co., Ok., U.S.	B6	113
Wagontire Mountain, mtn., Or., U.S.	D7	114
Wagrowiec, Pol.	C17	8
Wah, Pak.	D5	38
Waha, Libya	C9	42
Wahiawa, Hi., U.S.	B3	88
Wahiawa Reservoir, res., Hi., U.S.	g9	88
Wahkiakum, co., Wa., U.S.	C2	124
Wahoo, Ne., U.S.	C9	104
Wahpeton, N.D., U.S.	C9	111
Wahweap Creek, stm., Ut., U.S.	F4	121
Waialua, Hi., U.S.	B3	88
Waialua Bay, b., Hi., U.S.	B3	88
Waianae, Hi., U.S.	B3	88
Waianae Range, mts., Hi., U.S.	f9	88
Waidhofen an der Ybbs, Aus.	H14	8
Waigeo, Pulau, i., Indon.	F9	32
Waihi, N.Z.	B5	52
Waikapu, Hi., U.S.	C5	88
Waikiki Beach, Hi., U.S.	g10	88
Wailua, Hi., U.S.	A2	88
Wailuku, Hi., U.S.	C5	88
Waimanalo, Hi., U.S.	B4	88
Waimanalo Bay, b., Hi., U.S.	g11	88
Waimea, Hi., U.S.	B2	88
Waimea, Hi., U.S.	f9	88
Wainwright, Alta., Can.	C5	68
Wainwright, Ak., U.S.	A8	79
Waipahu, Hi., U.S.	B3	88
Waipio Acres, Hi., U.S.	g9	88
Waipio Peninsula, pen., Hi., U.S.	g10	88
Waipukurau, N.Z.	D6	52
Waite Park, Mn., U.S.	E4	100
Waits, stm., Vt., U.S.	C4	122
Waitsburg, Wa., U.S.	C7	124
Wajir, Kenya	H3	46
Wakarusa, In., U.S.	A5	91
Wakarusa, stm., Ks., U.S.	D8	93
Wakasa-wan, b., Japan	G8	30
Wakatomika Creek, stm., Oh., U.S.	B3	112
Wakayama, Japan	H8	30
Wake, co., N.C., U.S.	B4	110
WaKeeney, Ks., U.S.	C4	93
Wakefield, Que., Can.	D2	74
Wakefield, Ks., U.S.	C6	93
Wakefield, Ma., U.S.	B5	98
Wakefield, Mi., U.S.	n12	99
Wakefield, Ne., U.S.	B9	104
Wakefield, R.I., U.S.	F3	116
Wakefield, Va., U.S.	D6	123
Wake Forest, N.C., U.S.	B4	110
Wake Island, dep., Oc.	E24	2
Wakema, Burma	F3	34
Wakeman, Oh., U.S.	A3	112
Wakkanai, Japan	n19	30a
Wakulla, co., Fl., U.S.	B2	86
Walbridge, Oh., U.S.	e6	112
Wałbrzych (Waldenburg), Pol.	E16	8
Walcott, Ia., U.S.	C7	92
Walcott, Lake, res., Id., U.S.	G5	89
Walden, Ont., Can.	A3	73
Walden, Co., U.S.	A4	83
Walden, N.Y., U.S.	D6	109
Walden Ridge, mtn., Tn., U.S.	D8	119
Waldheim, Sask., Can.	E2	75
Waldo, Ar., U.S.	D2	81
Waldo, co., Me., U.S.	D3	96
Waldoboro, Me., U.S.	D3	96
Waldo Lake, l., Ma., U.S.	h11	98
Waldo Lake, l., Or., U.S.	D4	114
Waldport, Or., U.S.	C2	114
Waldron, Ar., U.S.	C1	81
Waldshut, Ger.	H8	8
Waldwick, N.J., U.S.	A4	107
Wales, ter., U.K.	I9	7
Wales Island, i., N.W. Ter., Can.	C15	66
Waleska, Ga., U.S.	B2	87
Walgett, Austl.	E9	50
Walhalla, N.D., U.S.	A8	111
Walhalla, S.C., U.S.	B1	117
Walhonding, stm., Oh., U.S.	B3	112
Walker, La., U.S.	D5	95
Walker, Mi., U.S.	E5	99
Walker, Mn., U.S.	C4	100
Walker, co., Al., U.S.	B2	78
Walker, co., Ga., U.S.	B1	87
Walker, co., Tx., U.S.	D5	120
Walker, stm., Nv., U.S.	D3	105
Walker Lake, l., Nv., U.S.	E3	105
Walker River Indian Reservation, Nv., U.S.	D3	105
Walkersville, Md., U.S.	B3	97
Walkerton, Ont., Can.	C3	73
Walkerton, In., U.S.	B5	91
Walkertown, N.C., U.S.	A2	110
Walkerville, Mt., U.S.	D4	103
Wall, S.D., U.S.	D3	118
Wallace, Id., U.S.	B3	89
Wallace, N.C., U.S.	B4	110
Wallace, co., Ks., U.S.	D2	93
Wallaceburg, Ont., Can.	E2	73
Wallace Lake, res., La., U.S.	B2	95
Walla Walla, Wa., U.S.	C7	124
Walla Walla, co., Wa., U.S.	C7	124
Walla Walla, stm., U.S.	C7	124
Walled Lake, Mi., U.S.	o15	99
Wallen, In., U.S.	B7	91
Wallenpaupack, Lake, l., Pa., U.S.	D11	115
Waller, Tx., U.S.	q14	120
Waller, co., Tx., U.S.	E4	120
Wallingford, Ct., U.S.	D4	84
Wallingford, Vt., U.S.	E3	122
Wallington, N.J., U.S.	h8	107
Wallis and Futuna, dep., Oc.	G1	2
Wallkill, N.Y., U.S.	D6	109
Wallkill, stm., N.Y., U.S.	D6	109
Wall Lake, Ia., U.S.	B2	92
Wall Lake, l., Ia., U.S.	B4	92
Walloomsac, stm., U.S.	F2	122
Walloon Lake, l., Mi., U.S.	C6	99
Wallowa, Or., U.S.	B9	114
Wallowa, co., Or., U.S.	B9	114
Wallowa Mountains, mts., Or., U.S.	B9	114
Wallula, Lake, res., U.S.	C7	124
Wallum Lake, l., U.S.	A1	116
Walnut, Il., U.S.	B4	90
Walnut, Ia., U.S.	C2	92
Walnut, stm., Ks., U.S.	E6	93
Walnut Canyon National Monument, Az., U.S.	B4	80
Walnut Cove, N.C., U.S.	A2	110
Walnut Creek, Ca., U.S.	h8	82
Walnut Creek, stm., Ks., U.S.	D4	93
Walnut Grove, Al., U.S.	A3	78
Walnut Grove, Mn., U.S.	F3	100
Walnut Ridge, Ar., U.S.	A5	81
Walnutport, Pa., U.S.	E10	115
Walpole, Ma., U.S.	B5	98
Walpole, N.H., U.S.	D2	106
Walsall, Eng., U.K.	I11	7
Walsenburg, Co., U.S.	D6	83
Walsh, Co., U.S.	D8	83
Walsh, co., N.D., U.S.	A8	111
Walsrode, Ger.	C9	8
Walterboro, S.C., U.S.	F6	117
Walter F. George Dam, U.S.	D4	78
Walter F. George Lake, res., U.S.	D4	78
Walters, Ok., U.S.	C3	113
Walthall, co., Ms., U.S.	D3	101
Waltham, Ma., U.S.	B5	98
Walthill, Ne., U.S.	B9	104
Walthourville, Ga., U.S.	E5	87
Walton, In., U.S.	C5	91
Walton, Ky., U.S.	B5	94
Walton, N.Y., U.S.	C5	109
Walton, co., Fl., U.S.	u15	86
Walton, co., Ga., U.S.	C3	87
Walvisbaai (Walvis Bay), S. Afr.	F2	44
Walworth, Wi., U.S.	F5	126
Walworth, co., S.D., U.S.	B5	118
Walworth, co., Wi., U.S.	F5	126
Wamac, Il., U.S.	E4	90
Wamba, stm., Afr.	C3	44
Wamego, Ks., U.S.	C7	93
Wamesit, Ma., U.S.	A5	98
Wamsutter, Wy., U.S.	E5	127
Wanaka, N.Z.	F2	52
Wanamingo, Mn., U.S.	F6	100
Wanapum Dam, Wa., U.S.	C6	124
Wanapum Lake, res., Wa., U.S.	B6	124
Wanaque, N.J., U.S.	A4	107
Wanaque Reservoir, res., N.J., U.S.	A4	107
Wanatah, In., U.S.	B4	91
Wanchese, N.C., U.S.	B7	110
Wando, stm., S.C., U.S.	F8	117
Wando Woods, S.C., U.S.	k11	117
Wanganui, N.Z.	C5	52
Wanganui, stm., N.Z.	C5	52
Wangaratta, Austl.	G9	50
Wangen [im Allgäu], Ger.	H9	8
Wangpan Yang, b., China	E10	28
Wänkäner, India	I4	38
Wanxian, China	E8	26
Wapakoneta, Oh., U.S.	B1	112
Wapato, Wa., U.S.	C5	124
Wapawekka Lake, l., Sask., Can.	C3	75
Wapello, Ia., U.S.	C6	92
Wapello, co., Ia., U.S.	C5	92
Wapiti, stm., Can.	B1	68
Wappapello Lake, res., Mo., U.S.	D7	102
Wappingers Falls, N.Y., U.S.	D7	109
Wapsipinicon, stm., Ia., U.S.	B6	92
War, W.V., U.S.	D3	125
Waramaug, Lake, l., Ct., U.S.	C2	84
Warangal, India	C5	37
Ward, Ar., U.S.	B4	81
Ward, co., N.D., U.S.	A4	111
Ward, co., Tx., U.S.	D1	120
Warden, Wa., U.S.	C6	124
Wardha, India	B5	37
Ward Mountain, mtn., Mt., U.S.	D2	103
Ware, Ma., U.S.	B3	98
Ware, co., Ga., U.S.	E4	87
Ware, stm., Ma., U.S.	B3	98
War Eagle Mountain, mtn., Id., U.S.	G2	89
Wareham, Ma., U.S.	C6	98
Warehouse Point, Ct., U.S.	B5	84
Waren, Ger.	B12	8
Warendorf, Ger.	D7	8
Ware Shoals, S.C., U.S.	C3	117
Warfield, B.C., Can.	E9	69
Warminster, Eng., U.K.	J10	7
Warminster, Pa., U.S.	F11	115
Warm Springs Indian Reservation, Or., U.S.	C5	114
Warm Springs Reservoir, res., Or., U.S.	D8	114
Warnemünde, Ger.	A12	8
Warner, N.H., U.S.	D3	106
Warner, Ok., U.S.	B6	113
Warner, stm., N.H., U.S.	D3	106
Warner Mountains, mts., Ca., U.S.	B3	82
Warner Peak, mtn., Or., U.S.	E7	114
Warner Robins, Ga., U.S.	D3	87
Warr Acres, Ok., U.S.	B4	113
Warren, Ar., U.S.	D3	81
Warren, Il., U.S.	A4	90
Warren, In., U.S.	C7	91
Warren, Ma., U.S.	B3	98
Warren, Mi., U.S.	F7	99
Warren, Mn., U.S.	B2	100
Warren, Oh., U.S.	A5	112
Warren, Pa., U.S.	C3	115
Warren, R.I., U.S.	D5	116
Warren, Vt., U.S.	C3	122
Warren, co., Ga., U.S.	C4	87
Warren, co., Il., U.S.	C3	90
Warren, co., In., U.S.	D3	91
Warren, co., Ia., U.S.	C4	92
Warren, co., Ky., U.S.	C3	94
Warren, co., Ms., U.S.	C3	101
Warren, co., Mo., U.S.	C6	102
Warren, co., N.J., U.S.	B3	107
Warren, co., N.Y., U.S.	B7	109
Warren, co., N.C., U.S.	A4	110
Warren, co., Oh., U.S.	C1	112
Warren, co., Pa., U.S.	C3	115
Warren, co., Tn., U.S.	D8	119
Warren, co., Va., U.S.	B4	123
Warren, co., U.S.	D5	116
Warren Park, In., U.S.	k10	91
Warren Peaks, mts., Wy., U.S.	B8	127
Warrensburg, Il., U.S.	D4	90
Warrensburg, Mo., U.S.	C4	102
Warrensburg, N.Y., U.S.	B7	109
Warrensville Heights, Oh., U.S.	h9	112
Warrenton, S. Afr.	G4	44
Warrenton, Ga., U.S.	C4	87
Warrenton, Mo., U.S.	C6	102
Warrenton, N.C., U.S.	A4	110
Warrenton, Or., U.S.	A3	114
Warrenton, Va., U.S.	B5	123
Warrenville, Il., U.S.	k8	90
Warrenville, S.C., U.S.	D4	117
Warri, Nig.	G7	42
Warrick, co., In., U.S.	H3	91
Warrina, Austl.	E7	50
Warrington, Eng., U.K.	H10	7
Warrington, Fl., U.S.	u14	86
Warrior, Al., U.S.	B3	78
Warrior Lake, res., Al., U.S.	C2	78
Warrnambool, Austl.	G8	50
Warroad, Mn., U.S.	B3	100
Warsaw, Il., U.S.	C2	90
Warsaw, In., U.S.	B6	91
Warsaw, Ky., U.S.	B5	94
Warsaw, Mo., U.S.	C4	102
Warsaw, N.Y., U.S.	C2	109
Warsaw, N.C., U.S.	B4	110
Warsaw, Va., U.S.	C6	123
Warsaw see Warszawa, Pol.	C21	8
Warszawa (Warsaw), Pol.	C21	8
Warta, stm., Pol.	C15	8
Wartburg, Tn., U.S.	C9	119
Warthe see Warta, stm., Pol.	C15	8
Warwick, Austl.	E10	50
Warwick, Que., Can.	D6	74
Warwick, Eng., U.K.	I11	7
Warwick, Md., U.S.	B6	97
Warwick, N.Y., U.S.	D6	109
Warwick, R.I., U.S.	D4	116
Wasaga Beach, Ont., Can.	C4	73
Wasatch, co., Ut., U.S.	C5	121
Wasco, Ca., U.S.	E4	82
Wasco, co., Or., U.S.	B5	114
Waseca, Mn., U.S.	F5	100
Waseca, co., Mn., U.S.	F5	100
Washakie, co., Wy., U.S.	C5	127
Washakie Needles, mts., Wy., U.S.	C3	127
Washburn, Il., U.S.	C4	90
Washburn, Me., U.S.	B5	96
Washburn, N.D., U.S.	B5	111
Washburn, Wi., U.S.	B3	126
Washburn, co., Wi., U.S.	C2	126
Washburn, Mount, mtn., Wy., U.S.	B2	127
Washington, D.C., U.S.	C3	97
Washington, Ga., U.S.	C4	87
Washington, Il., U.S.	C4	90
Washington, In., U.S.	G3	91
Washington, Ia., U.S.	C6	92
Washington, Ks., U.S.	C6	93
Washington, Ky., U.S.	B6	94
Washington, La., U.S.	D3	95
Washington, Mo., U.S.	C6	102
Washington, N.J., U.S.	B3	107
Washington, N.C., U.S.	B5	110
Washington, Pa., U.S.	F1	115
Washington, Ut., U.S.	F2	121
Washington, co., Al., U.S.	D1	78
Washington, co., Ar., U.S.	A1	81
Washington, co., Co., U.S.	B7	83
Washington, co., Fl., U.S.	u16	86
Washington, co., Ga., U.S.	C4	87
Washington, co., Id., U.S.	E2	89
Washington, co., Il., U.S.	E4	90
Washington, co., In., U.S.	G5	91
Washington, co., Ia., U.S.	C6	92
Washington, co., Ks., U.S.	C6	93
Washington, co., Ky., U.S.	C4	94
Washington, co., Me., U.S.	D5	96
Washington, co., Md., U.S.	A2	97
Washington, co., Mn., U.S.	E6	100
Washington, co., Ms., U.S.	B3	101
Washington, co., Mo., U.S.	D7	102
Washington, co., Ne., U.S.	C9	104
Washington, co., N.Y., U.S.	B7	109
Washington, co., N.C., U.S.	B6	110
Washington, co., Oh., U.S.	C4	112
Washington, co., Ok., U.S.	A6	113
Washington, co., Or., U.S.	B3	114
Washington, co., Pa., U.S.	F1	115
Washington, co., R.I., U.S.	E2	116
Washington, co., Tn., U.S.	C11	119
Washington, co., Tx., U.S.	D4	120
Washington, co., Ut., U.S.	F2	121
Washington, co., Vt., U.S.	C3	122
Washington, co., Va., U.S.	f9	123
Washington, co., Wi., U.S.	E5	126
Washington, state, U.S.	B5	124
Washington, Lake, l., Fl., U.S.	D6	86
Washington, Lake, l., Mn., U.S.	E4	100
Washington, Lake, l., Wa., U.S.	e11	124
Washington, Mount, mtn., N.H., U.S.	B4	106
Washington Court House, Oh., U.S.	C2	112
Washington Island, i., Wi., U.S.	C7	126
Washington Park, Il., U.S.	E3	90
Washington Terrace, Ut., U.S.	B4	121
Washita, co., Ok., U.S.	B2	113
Washita, stm., Ok., U.S.	C4	113
Washoe, co., Nv., U.S.	C2	105
Washoe City, Nv., U.S.	D2	105
Washougal, Wa., U.S.	D3	124
Washow Bay, b., Man., Can.	D3	70
Washtenaw, co., Mi., U.S.	F7	99
Wasilla, Ak., U.S.	C10	79
Wasior, Indon.	F9	32
Waskom, Tx., U.S.	C5	120
Waspán, Nic.	G5	64
Wasque Point, c., Ma., U.S.	D7	98
Wassen, Switz.	F15	10
Wassookeag, Lake, l., Me., U.S.	C3	96
Wassuk Range, mts., Nv., U.S.	E3	105
Wataga, Il., U.S.	B3	90
Watauga, co., N.C., U.S.	A1	110
Watauga, stm., Tn., U.S.	C12	119
Watauga Lake, res., Tn., U.S.	C12	119
Watchaug Pond, l., R.I., U.S.	F2	116
Watch Hill Point, c., R.I., U.S.	G1	116
Watchung, N.J., U.S.	B4	107
Waterbury, Ct., U.S.	C3	84
Waterbury, Vt., U.S.	C3	122
Waterbury Center, Vt., U.S.	C3	122
Waterbury Reservoir, res., Vt., U.S.	C3	122
Wateree, stm., S.C., U.S.	D6	117
Wateree Lake, res., S.C., U.S.	C6	117
Waterford, Ire.	I5	7
Waterford, Ct., U.S.	D7	84
Waterford, N.Y., U.S.	C7	109
Waterford, Pa., U.S.	C2	115
Waterford, Wi., U.S.	F5	126
Waterhen Lake, l., Man., Can.	C2	70
Waterloo, Bel.	E4	8
Waterloo, Ont., Can.	D4	73
Waterloo, Que., Can.	D5	74
Waterloo, Il., U.S.	E3	90
Waterloo, In., U.S.	B7	91
Waterloo, Ia., U.S.	B5	92
Waterloo, N.Y., U.S.	C4	109
Waterloo, Wi., U.S.	E5	126
Waterman, Il., U.S.	B5	90
Waterman Reservoir, res., R.I., U.S.	B3	116
Waterproof, La., U.S.	C4	95
Watersmeet, Mi., U.S.	n12	99
Waterton Lakes National Park, Alta., Can.	E3	68
Watertown, Ct., U.S.	C3	84
Watertown, Ma., U.S.	g11	98
Watertown, N.Y., U.S.	B5	109
Watertown, S.D., U.S.	C8	118
Watertown, Tn., U.S.	A5	119
Watertown, Wi., U.S.	E5	126
Water Valley, Ms., U.S.	A4	101
Waterville, Ks., U.S.	C7	93
Waterville, Me., U.S.	D3	96
Waterville, Mn., U.S.	F5	100
Waterville, N.Y., U.S.	C5	109
Waterville, Oh., U.S.	A2	112
Waterville, Wa., U.S.	B5	124
Watervliet, Mi., U.S.	F4	99
Watervliet, N.Y., U.S.	C7	109
Watford, Ont., Can.	E3	73
Watford City, N.D., U.S.	B2	111
Wathena, Ks., U.S.	C9	93
Watkins, Mn., U.S.	E4	100
Watkins Glen, N.Y., U.S.	C4	109
Watkinsville, Ga., U.S.	C3	87
Watonga, Ok., U.S.	B3	113
Watonwan, co., Mn., U.S.	F4	100
Watonwan, stm., Mn., U.S.	G4	100
Watseka, Il., U.S.	C6	90
Watson Lake, Yukon, Can.	D7	66
Watsontown, Pa., U.S.	D8	115
Watsonville, Ca., U.S.	D3	82
Watts Bar Dam, Tn., U.S.	D9	119
Watts Bar Lake, res., Tn., U.S.	D9	119
Wattsville, S.C., U.S.	B4	117
Wattwil, Switz.	E16	10
Watubela, Kepulauan, is., Indon.	F9	32
Waubaushene, Ont., Can.	C5	73
Waubay, S.D., U.S.	B8	118
Waubay Lake, l., S.D., U.S.	B8	118
Wauchula, Fl., U.S.	E5	86
Wauconda, Il., U.S.	h8	90
Waugh Mountain, mtn., Id., U.S.	D4	89
Waukee, Ia., U.S.	C4	92
Waukegan, Il., U.S.	A6	90
Waukesha, Wi., U.S.	F5	126
Waukesha, co., Wi., U.S.	E5	126
Waukewan, Lake, l., N.H., U.S.	C3	106
Waukomis, Ok., U.S.	A4	113
Waukon, Ia., U.S.	A6	92
Waunakee, Wi., U.S.	E4	126
Wauneta, Ne., U.S.	D4	104
Waungumbaug Lake, l., Ct., U.S.	B6	84
Waupaca, Wi., U.S.	D5	126
Waupaca, co., Wi., U.S.	D5	126
Waupun, Wi., U.S.	E5	126
Wauregan, Ct., U.S.	C8	84
Waurika, Ok., U.S.	C4	113
Wausau, Wi., U.S.	D4	126
Wausau, Lake, res., Wi., U.S.	D4	126
Wauseon, Oh., U.S.	A1	112
Waushara, co., Wi., U.S.	D4	126
Wautoma, Wi., U.S.	D4	126
Wauwatosa, Wi., U.S.	m12	126
Wave Hill, Austl.	C6	50
Waveland, Ms., U.S.	E4	101
Waverley, N.S., Can.	E6	71
Waverly, Il., U.S.	D4	90
Waverly, Ia., U.S.	B5	92
Waverly, Ks., U.S.	D8	93
Waverly, Mn., U.S.	E5	100
Waverly, Mo., U.S.	B4	102
Waverly, Ne., U.S.	D9	104
Waverly, N.Y., U.S.	C4	109
Waverly, Oh., U.S.	C3	112
Waverly, Tn., U.S.	A4	119
Waverly, Va., U.S.	C5	123
Waverly, W.V., U.S.	B3	125
Waverly Hall, Ga., U.S.	D2	87
Wāw, Sudan	G11	42
Wawanesa, Man., Can.	E2	70
Wawasee, Lake, l., In., U.S.	B6	91

Name	Map Ref	Page
Wawayanda Lake, l., N.J., U.S.	A4	107
Wawota, Sask., Can.	H4	75
Waxahachie, Tx., U.S.	C4	120
Waxhaw, N.C., U.S.	C2	110
Waycross, Ga., U.S.	E4	87
Wayland, Ia., U.S.	C6	92
Wayland, Ma., U.S.	g10	98
Wayland, Mi., U.S.	F5	99
Wayland, N.Y., U.S.	C3	109
Waylyn, S.C., U.S.	k12	117
Waymart, Pa., U.S.	C11	115
Wayne, Mi., U.S.	p15	99
Wayne, Ne., U.S.	B8	104
Wayne, N.J., U.S.	B4	107
Wayne, W.V., U.S.	C2	125
Wayne, co., Ga., U.S.	E5	87
Wayne, co., Il., U.S.	E5	90
Wayne, co., In., U.S.	E7	91
Wayne, co., Ia., U.S.	D4	92
Wayne, co., Ky., U.S.	D5	94
Wayne, co., Mi., U.S.	F7	99
Wayne, co., Ms., U.S.	D5	101
Wayne, co., Mo., U.S.	D7	102
Wayne, co., Ne., U.S.	B8	104
Wayne, co., N.Y., U.S.	B3	109
Wayne, co., N.C., U.S.	B4	110
Wayne, co., Oh., U.S.	B4	112
Wayne, co., Pa., U.S.	C11	115
Wayne, co., Tn., U.S.	B4	119
Wayne, co., Ut., U.S.	E4	121
Wayne, co., W.V., U.S.	C2	125
Wayne City, Il., U.S.	E5	90
Waynesboro, Ga., U.S.	C4	87
Waynesboro, Ms., U.S.	D5	101
Waynesboro, Pa., U.S.	G6	115
Waynesboro, Tn., U.S.	B4	119
Waynesboro, Va., U.S.	B4	123
Waynesburg, Oh., U.S.	B4	112
Waynesburg, Pa., U.S.	G1	115
Waynesville, Mo., U.S.	D5	102
Waynesville, N.C., U.S.	f10	110
Waynesville, Oh., U.S.	C1	112
Waynetown, In., U.S.	D3	91
Waynewood, Va., U.S.	g12	123
Waynoka, Ok., U.S.	A3	113
Wayzata, Mn., U.S.	n11	100
Wazīrābād, Pak.	D6	38
Weakley, co., Tn., U.S.	A3	119
Weatherford, Ok., U.S.	B3	113
Weatherford, Tx., U.S.	C4	120
Weatherly, Pa., U.S.	E10	115
Weatogue, Ct., U.S.	B4	84
Weaver, Al., U.S.	B4	78
Weaver Mountains, mts., Az., U.S.	C3	80
Weaverville, Ca., U.S.	B2	82
Weaverville, N.C., U.S.	f10	110
Webb, Al., U.S.	D4	78
Webb, Ms., U.S.	B3	101
Webb, co., Tx., U.S.	F3	120
Webb City, Mo., U.S.	D3	102
Webbers Falls, Ok., U.S.	B6	113
Webberville, Mi., U.S.	F6	99
Webb Lake, l., Me., U.S.	D2	96
Weber, co., Ut., U.S.	B4	121
Weber City, Va., U.S.	f9	123
Webster, Ma., U.S.	B4	98
Webster, N.Y., U.S.	B3	109
Webster, Pa., U.S.	F2	115
Webster, S.D., U.S.	B8	118
Webster, co., Ga., U.S.	D2	87
Webster, co., Ia., U.S.	B3	92
Webster, co., Ky., U.S.	C2	94
Webster, co., La., U.S.	B2	95
Webster, co., Ms., U.S.	B4	101
Webster, co., Mo., U.S.	D5	102
Webster, co., Ne., U.S.	D7	104
Webster, co., W.V., U.S.	C4	125
Webster City, Ia., U.S.	B4	92
Webster Groves, Mo., U.S.	f13	102
Webster Reservoir, res., Ks., U.S.	C4	93
Websterville, Vt., U.S.	C4	122
Weddell Sea, Ant.	B8	47
Wedgeport, N.S., Can.	F4	71
Wedgewood, Mo., U.S.	f13	102
Wedowee, Al., U.S.	B4	78
Weed, Ca., U.S.	B2	82
Weed Heights, Nv., U.S.	E2	105
Weedon, Que., Can.	D6	74
Weedsport, N.Y., U.S.	B4	109
Weedville, Pa., U.S.	D5	115
Weehawken, N.J., U.S.	h8	107
Weeksbury, Ky., U.S.	C7	94
Weeping Water, Ne., U.S.	D9	104
Wegscheid, Ger.	G13	8
Weiden in der Oberpfalz, Ger.	F12	8
Weifang, China	D10	26
Weihai, China	D11	26
Weilburg, Ger.	E8	8
Weilheim, Ger.	H11	8
Weimar, Ger.	E11	8
Weimar, Tx., U.S.	E4	120
Weiner, Ar., U.S.	B5	81
Weinheim, Ger.	F8	8
Weipa, Austl.	B8	50
Weippe, Id., U.S.	C3	89
Weir, Ks., U.S.	E9	93
Weir, Lake, l., Fl., U.S.	C5	86
Weirsdale, Fl., U.S.	D5	86
Weirton, W.V., U.S.	A4	125
Weiser, Id., U.S.	E2	89
Weiser, stm., Id., U.S.	E2	89
Weishi, China	A3	28
Weissenburg in Bayern, Ger.	F10	8
Weissenfels, Ger.	D11	8
Weiss Lake, res., U.S.	A4	78
Weisswasser, Ger.	D14	8
Weiz, Aus.	H15	8
Wejherowo, Pol.	A18	8
Welch, W.V., U.S.	D3	125
Welcome, Mn., U.S.	G4	100
Welcome, S.C., U.S.	B3	117

Name	Map Ref	Page
Weld, co., Co., U.S.	A6	83
Weldon, N.C., U.S.	A5	110
Weldon Spring, Mo., U.S.	f12	102
Weleetka, Ok., U.S.	B5	113
Welkom, S. Afr.	G5	44
Welland, Ont., Can.	E5	73
Wellesley, Ont., Can.	D4	73
Wellesley, Ma., U.S.	B5	98
Wellesley Islands, is., Austl.	C7	50
Wellford, S.C., U.S.	B3	117
Wellington, Ont., Can.	D7	73
Wellington, N.Z.	D5	52
Wellington, Co., U.S.	A5	83
Wellington, Ks., U.S.	E6	93
Wellington, Mo., U.S.	B4	102
Wellington, Nv., U.S.	E2	105
Wellington, Oh., U.S.	A3	112
Wellington, Tx., U.S.	B2	120
Wellington, Ut., U.S.	D5	121
Wellington, Isla, i., Chile	F2	56
Wellington Channel, strt., N.W. Ter., Can.	A14	66
Wellman, Ia., U.S.	C6	92
Wells, Me., U.S.	E2	96
Wells, Mi., U.S.	C3	99
Wells, Mn., U.S.	G5	100
Wells, Nv., U.S.	B7	105
Wells, co., In., U.S.	C7	91
Wells, co., N.D., U.S.	B6	111
Wells, stm., Vt., U.S.	C4	122
Wellsboro, Pa., U.S.	C7	115
Wellsburg, Ia., U.S.	B5	92
Wellsburg, W.V., U.S.	A4	125
Wellston, Oh., U.S.	C3	112
Wellston, Ok., U.S.	B4	113
Wellsville, Ks., U.S.	D8	93
Wellsville, Mo., U.S.	B6	102
Wellsville, N.Y., U.S.	C3	109
Wellsville, Oh., U.S.	B5	112
Wellsville, Ut., U.S.	B4	121
Wellton, Az., U.S.	E1	80
Wels, Aus.	G14	8
Welsh, La., U.S.	D3	95
Welshpool, Wales, U.K.	I9	7
Wembley, Alta., Can.	B1	68
Wenatchee, Wa., U.S.	B5	124
Wenatchee, stm., Wa., U.S.	B5	124
Wenatchee Lake, l., Wa., U.S.	B5	124
Wenatchee Mountains, mts., Wa., U.S.	B5	124
Wendell, Id., U.S.	G4	89
Wendell, N.C., U.S.	B4	110
Wendover, Ut., U.S.	C1	121
Wenham, Ma., U.S.	A6	98
Wenham Lake, l., Ma., U.S.	f12	98
Wenona, Il., U.S.	B4	90
Wenshan, China	C8	34
Wentworth, Lake, l., N.H., U.S.	C4	106
Wentzville, Mo., U.S.	C7	102
Wenzhou, China	G9	28
Weohyakapka, Lake, l., Fl., U.S.	E5	86
Wernigerode, Ger.	D10	8
Wertheim, Ger.	F9	8
Wesel, Ger.	D6	8
Weser, stm., Ger.	B8	8
Weslaco, Tx., U.S.	F4	120
Wesley, Newf., Can.	D5	72
Wesleyville, Pa., U.S.	B2	115
Wessel Islands, is., Austl.	B7	50
Wesserunsett Lake, l., Me., U.S.	D3	96
Wessington Springs, S.D., U.S.	C7	118
Wesson, Ms., U.S.	D3	101
West, Tx., U.S.	D4	120
West, stm., Ct., U.S.	D5	84
West, stm., Ma., U.S.	h9	98
West, stm., Vt., U.S.	E3	122
West Acton, Ma., U.S.	g10	98
West Alexandria, Oh., U.S.	C1	112
West Allis, Wi., U.S.	m11	126
West Alton, Mo., U.S.	f13	102
West Andover, Ma., U.S.	A5	98
West Baden Springs, In., U.S.	G4	91
West Baton Rouge, co., La., U.S.	D4	95
West Bay, b., Fl., U.S.	u16	86
West Bay, b., N.C., U.S.	B6	110
West Bay, b., Tx., U.S.	r15	120
West Bend, Ia., U.S.	B3	92
West Bend, Wi., U.S.	E5	126
West Bengal, state, India	I12	38
West Berlin, N.J., U.S.	D3	107
West Blocton, Al., U.S.	B2	78
Westborough, Ma., U.S.	B4	98
West Bountiful, Ut., U.S.	C4	121
West Boylston, Ma., U.S.	B4	98
West Branch, Ia., U.S.	C6	92
West Branch, Mi., U.S.	D6	99
West Branch Reservoir, res., Ct., U.S.	B3	84
West Bridgewater, Ma., U.S.	B5	98
Westbrook, Ct., U.S.	D6	84
Westbrook, Me., U.S.	E2	96
Westbrook, Mn., U.S.	F3	100
West Burlington, Ia., U.S.	D6	92
West Butte, mtn., Mt., U.S.	B5	103
Westby, Wi., U.S.	E3	126
West Cache Creek, stm., Ok., U.S.	C3	113
West Caldwell, N.J., U.S.	B4	107
West Canada Creek, stm., N.Y., U.S.	B6	109
West Carroll, co., La., U.S.	B4	95
West Carrollton, Oh., U.S.	C1	112
West Carthage, N.Y., U.S.	B5	109
Westchester, Il., U.S.	k9	90
West Chester, Pa., U.S.	G10	115
Westchester, co., N.Y., U.S.	D7	109
West Chicago, Il., U.S.	k8	90
West Chop, c., Ma., U.S.	D6	98
West College Corner, In., U.S.	E8	91
West Columbia, S.C., U.S.	D5	117
West Columbia, Tx., U.S.	E5	120
West Concord, Ma., U.S.	g10	98
West Concord, Mn., U.S.	F6	100
West Concord, N.C., U.S.	B2	110

Name	Map Ref	Page
Westconnaug Reservoir, res., R.I., U.S.	C2	116
West Cote Blanche Bay, b., La., U.S.	E4	95
West Covina, Ca., U.S.	m13	82
West Crossett, Ar., U.S.	D4	81
West Cumberland, Me., U.S.	E2	96
West Dennis, Ma., U.S.	C7	98
West Des Moines, Ia., U.S.	C4	92
West Elk Mountains, mts., Co., U.S.	C3	83
West Elk Peak, mtn., Co., U.S.	C3	83
Westerly, R.I., U.S.	F1	116
Western Australia, state, Austl.	D4	50
Western Desert see Gharbīyah, Aş-Şaḥrāʾ al-, des., Egypt	C11	42
Western Ghāts, mts., India	E3	37
Westernport, Md., U.S.	m12	97
Western Sahara, dep., Afr.	D3	42
Western Samoa, ctry., Oc.	G1	2
Western Springs, Il., U.S.	k9	90
Westerstede, Ger.	B7	8
Westerville, Oh., U.S.	B3	112
West Falkland, i., Falk. Is.	G4	56
West Falmouth, Ma., U.S.	C6	98
West Fargo, N.D., U.S.	C9	111
West Feliciana, co., La., U.S.	D4	95
Westfield, In., U.S.	D5	91
Westfield, Ma., U.S.	B2	98
Westfield, N.J., U.S.	B4	107
Westfield, N.Y., U.S.	C1	109
Westfield, Pa., U.S.	C6	115
Westfield, Wi., U.S.	E4	126
Westfield, stm., Ma., U.S.	B2	98
West Fork, Ar., U.S.	B1	81
West Fork, stm., W.V., U.S.	B4	125
West Frankfort, Il., U.S.	F5	90
West Freehold, N.J., U.S.	C4	107
West Friendship, Md., U.S.	B4	97
Westgate, Fl., U.S.	F6	86
West Grand Lake, l., Me., U.S.	C5	96
West Grove, Pa., U.S.	G10	115
West Hanover, Ma., U.S.	h12	98
West Hartford, Ct., U.S.	B4	84
West Haven, Ct., U.S.	D4	84
West Hazleton, Pa., U.S.	E9	115
West Helena, Ar., U.S.	C5	81
West Hill Reservoir, res., Ma., U.S.	B4	98
Westhope, N.D., U.S.	A4	111
West Indies, is.	E12	64
West Island, i., Ma., U.S.	C6	98
West Jefferson, N.C., U.S.	A1	110
West Jefferson, Oh., U.S.	C2	112
West Jordan, Ut., U.S.	C3	121
West Kingston, R.I., U.S.	F3	116
West Lafayette, In., U.S.	D4	91
West Lafayette, Oh., U.S.	B4	112
Westlake, La., U.S.	D2	95
Westlake, Oh., U.S.	h9	112
West Lake, l., Me., U.S.	C4	96
Westland, Mi., U.S.	F7	99
West Laramie, Wy., U.S.	E7	127
West Lawn, Pa., U.S.	F10	115
West Lebanon, In., U.S.	D3	91
West Liberty, Ia., U.S.	C6	92
West Liberty, Ky., U.S.	C6	94
West Liberty, Oh., U.S.	B2	112
West Liberty, W.V., U.S.	f8	125
West Linn, Or., U.S.	B4	114
Westlock, Alta., Can.	B4	68
West Long Branch, N.J., U.S.	C4	107
West Lorne, Ont., Can.	E3	73
West Marion, N.C., U.S.	f10	110
West Medway, Ma., U.S.	B5	98
West Memphis, Ar., U.S.	B5	81
West Miami, Fl., U.S.	s13	86
West Middlesex, Pa., U.S.	D1	115
West Mifflin, Pa., U.S.	F2	115
West Milton, Oh., U.S.	C1	112
West Milwaukee, Wi., U.S.	m12	126
Westminster, Ca., U.S.	n12	82
Westminster, Co., U.S.	B5	83
Westminster, Md., U.S.	A4	97
Westminster, S.C., U.S.	B1	117
West Monroe, La., U.S.	B3	95
Westmont, Ca., U.S.	*n12	82
Westmont, Il., U.S.	k9	90
Westmont, N.J., U.S.	D2	107
Westmont, Pa., U.S.	F4	115
Westmoreland, Tn., U.S.	A5	119
Westmoreland, co., Pa., U.S.	F2	115
Westmoreland, co., Va., U.S.	B6	123
Westmorland, Ca., U.S.	F6	82
West Musquash Lake, l., Me., U.S.	C5	96
West Mystic, Ct., U.S.	D8	84
West Newton, Pa., U.S.	F2	115
West New York, N.J., U.S.	h8	107
West Nishnabotna, stm., Ia., U.S.	C2	92
West Norriton, Pa., U.S.	o20	115
Weston, Ct., U.S.	E2	84
Weston, Ma., U.S.	g10	98
Weston, Mo., U.S.	B3	102
Weston, Oh., U.S.	A2	112
Weston, Or., U.S.	B8	114
Weston, W.V., U.S.	B4	125
Weston, co., Wy., U.S.	C8	127
Weston-super-Mare, Eng., U.K.	J10	7
West Orange, N.J., U.S.	B4	107
Westover, Md., U.S.	D6	97
Westover, W.V., U.S.	B5	125
Westover Air Force Base, mil., Ma., U.S.	B2	98
West Palm Beach, Fl., U.S.	F6	86
West Pawlet, Vt., U.S.	E2	122
West Pearl, stm., La., U.S.	D6	95
West Pelzer, S.C., U.S.	B3	117
West Pensacola, Fl., U.S.	u14	86
West Peoria, Il., U.S.	C4	90
Westphalia, Mi., U.S.	F6	99
West Pittsburg, Pa., U.S.	E1	115
West Pittston, Pa., U.S.	m17	115
West Plains, Mo., U.S.	E6	102

Name	Map Ref	Page
West Point, Ca., U.S.	C3	82
West Point, Ga., U.S.	D1	87
West Point, Ky., U.S.	C4	94
West Point, Ms., U.S.	B5	101
West Point, Ne., U.S.	C9	104
West Point, N.Y., U.S.	D7	109
West Point, Va., U.S.	C6	123
West Point, mtn., Ak., U.S.	C11	79
West Point Lake, res., U.S.	C1	87
Westport, Ont., Can.	C8	73
Westport, N.Z.	D3	52
Westport, Ct., U.S.	E2	84
Westport, In., U.S.	F6	91
Westport, Wa., U.S.	C1	124
West Portsmouth, Oh., U.S.	D2	112
West Quoddy Head, c., Me., U.S.	D6	96
West Reading, Pa., U.S.	F10	115
West Rutland, Vt., U.S.	D2	122
West Saint Paul, Mn., U.S.	n12	100
West Salem, Il., U.S.	E5	90
West Salem, Oh., U.S.	B3	112
West Salem, Wi., U.S.	E2	126
West Scarborough, Me., U.S.	E2	96
West Seneca, N.Y., U.S.	C2	109
West Simsbury, Ct., U.S.	B4	84
West Slope, Or., U.S.	g12	114
West Spanish Peak, mtn., Co., U.S.	D6	83
West Springfield, Ma., U.S.	B2	98
West Springfield, Va., U.S.	g12	123
West Swanzey, N.H., U.S.	E2	106
West Terre Haute, In., U.S.	F3	91
West Thompson Lake, res., Ct., U.S.	B8	84
West Union, Ia., U.S.	B6	92
West Union, Oh., U.S.	D2	112
West Union, W.V., U.S.	B4	125
West Unity, Oh., U.S.	A1	112
West University Place, Tx., U.S.	r14	120
West Valley City, Ut., U.S.	C4	121
West Vancouver, B.C., Can.	f12	69
West Van Lear, Ky., U.S.	C7	94
West View, Pa., U.S.	h13	115
Westville, Il., U.S.	C6	90
Westville, In., U.S.	A4	91
Westville, N.H., U.S.	E4	106
Westville, N.J., U.S.	D2	107
Westville, Ok., U.S.	A7	113
Westville Lake, res., Ma., U.S.	B3	98
West Virginia, state, U.S.	C4	125
West Walker, stm., U.S.	E2	105
West Wareham, Ma., U.S.	C6	98
West Warwick, R.I., U.S.	D3	116
Westwego, La., U.S.	k11	95
Westwood, Ca., U.S.	B3	82
Westwood, Ks., U.S.	k16	93
Westwood, Ky., U.S.	B7	94
Westwood, Ma., U.S.	B5	98
Westwood, N.J., U.S.	B4	107
Westwood Lakes, Fl., U.S.	s13	86
West Wyoming, Pa., U.S.	n17	115
West Yarmouth, Ma., U.S.	C7	98
West Yellowstone, Mt., U.S.	F5	103
West York, Pa., U.S.	G8	115
Wetar, Pulau, i., Indon.	G8	32
Wetaskiwin, Alta., Can.	C4	68
Wethersfield, Ct., U.S.	C5	84
Wet Mountains, mts., Co., U.S.	C5	83
Wetumka, Ok., U.S.	B5	113
Wetumpka, Al., U.S.	C3	78
Wetzel, co., W.V., U.S.	B4	125
Wetzlar, Ger.	E8	8
Wewak, Pap. N. Gui.	k15	50a
Wewahitchka, Fl., U.S.	B1	86
Wewoka, Ok., U.S.	B5	113
Wexford, Ire.	I6	7
Wexford, co., Mi., U.S.	D5	99
Weyauwega, Wi., U.S.	D5	126
Weymouth, Eng., U.K.	K10	7
Weymouth, Ma., U.S.	B6	98
Whaleysville, Md., U.S.	D7	97
Whalsay, i., Scot., U.K.	A12	7
Whangarei, N.Z.	A5	52
Wharton, N.J., U.S.	B3	107
Wharton, Tx., U.S.	E4	120
Wharton, co., Tx., U.S.	E4	120
What Cheer, Ia., U.S.	C5	92
Whatcom, co., Wa., U.S.	A4	124
Whatcom, Lake, l., Wa., U.S.	A3	124
Wheatfield, In., U.S.	B3	91
Wheatland, Ca., U.S.	C3	82
Wheatland, Ia., U.S.	C7	92
Wheatland, Wy., U.S.	D8	127
Wheatland, co., Mt., U.S.	D7	103
Wheatland Reservoir, res., Wy., U.S.	E7	127
Wheatley, Ont., Can.	E2	73
Wheaton, Il., U.S.	B5	90
Wheaton, Md., U.S.	B3	97
Wheaton, Mn., U.S.	E2	100
Wheaton, Mo., U.S.	E3	102
Wheat Ridge, Co., U.S.	B5	83
Wheelbarrow Peak, mtn., Nv., U.S.	F5	105
Wheeler, Ms., U.S.	A5	101
Wheeler, Tx., U.S.	B2	120
Wheeler, co., Ga., U.S.	D4	87
Wheeler, co., Ne., U.S.	C7	104
Wheeler, co., Or., U.S.	C6	114
Wheeler, co., Tx., U.S.	B2	120
Wheeler Air Force Base, mil., Hi., U.S.	g9	88
Wheeler Lake, res., Al., U.S.	A2	78
Wheeler Peak, mtn., Ca., U.S.	C4	82
Wheeler Peak, mtn., Nv., U.S.	E7	105
Wheeler Peak, mtn., N.M., U.S.	A4	108
Wheelersburg, Oh., U.S.	D3	112
Wheeling, Il., U.S.	h9	90
Wheeling, W.V., U.S.	A4	125
Wheeling Creek, stm., W.V., U.S.	f8	125
Wheelwright, Ky., U.S.	C7	94
Whetstone, stm., U.S.	E2	100
Whidbey Island, i., Wa., U.S.	A3	124

Name	Map Ref	Page
Whidbey Island Naval Air Station, mil., Wa., U.S.	A3	124
Whigham, Ga., U.S.	F2	87
Whiskey Peak, mtn., Wy., U.S.	D5	127
Whiskeytown-Shasta-Trinity National Recreation Area, Ca., U.S.	B2	82
Whistler, B.C., Can.	D6	69
Whitacres, Ct., U.S.	A5	84
Whitakers, N.C., U.S.	A5	110
Whitbourne, Newf., Can.	E5	72
Whitby, Ont., Can.	D6	73
Whitchurch-Stouffville, Ont., Can.	D5	73
White, co., Ar., U.S.	B4	81
White, co., Ga., U.S.	B3	87
White, co., Il., U.S.	E5	90
White, co., In., U.S.	C4	91
White, co., Tn., U.S.	D8	119
White, stm., N.A.	D4	66
White, stm., U.S.	C4	81
White, stm., U.S.	D5	118
White, stm., U.S.	C7	121
White, stm., Az., U.S.	D5	80
White, stm., In., U.S.	H2	91
White, stm., Mi., U.S.	E4	99
White, stm., Ne., U.S.	E6	105
White, stm., Tx., U.S.	C2	120
White, stm., Vt., U.S.	D4	122
White, stm., Wa., U.S.	B5	124
White, stm., U.S.	B4	124
White Lake, l., Austl.	D5	50
White Bay, b., Newf., Can.	D3	72
White Bear, stm., Newf., Can.	E3	72
White Bear Lake, Mn., U.S.	E5	100
White Bluff, Tn., U.S.	A4	119
White Butte, mtn., N.D., U.S.	C2	111
White Castle, La., U.S.	D4	95
White Center, Wa., U.S.	e11	124
White City, Or., U.S.	E4	114
White Clay Creek, stm., U.S.	A3	104
White Cloud, Mi., U.S.	E5	99
Whitecourt, Alta., Can.	B3	68
White Creek, stm., U.S.	E2	122
Whiteday, stm., W.V., U.S.	h10	125
White Deer, Tx., U.S.	B2	120
White Earth Indian Reservation, Mn., U.S.	C3	100
White Lake, l., Mn., U.S.	C3	100
Whiteface, stm., Mn., U.S.	C6	100
Whiteface Mountain, mtn., N.Y., U.S.	f11	109
Whitefield, N.H., U.S.	B3	106
Whitefish, Mt., U.S.	B2	103
Whitefish Bay, Wi., U.S.	m12	126
Whitefish Bay, b., Mi., U.S.	B6	99
Whitefish Lake, l., Mn., U.S.	D4	100
Whitefish Range, mts., Mt., U.S.	B2	103
Whiteford, Md., U.S.	A5	97
White Hall, Al., U.S.	C3	78
White Hall, Ar., U.S.	C3	81
White Hall, Il., U.S.	D3	90
Whitehall, Mi., U.S.	E4	99
Whitehall, Mt., U.S.	E4	103
Whitehall, N.Y., U.S.	B7	109
Whitehall, Oh., U.S.	m11	112
Whitehall, Wi., U.S.	D2	126
Whitehall Reservoir, res., Ma., U.S.	h9	98
Whitehaven, Eng., U.K.	G9	7
White Haven, Pa., U.S.	D10	115
Whitehorn, Point, c., Wa., U.S.	A3	124
Whitehorse, Yukon, Can.	D5	66
White Horse, N.J., U.S.	C3	107
Whitehouse, Oh., U.S.	A2	112
White House, Tn., U.S.	A5	119
White Island Shores, Ma., U.S.	C6	98
White Knob Mountains, mts., Id., U.S.	F5	89
White Lake, l., La., U.S.	E3	95
Whiteman Air Force Base, mil., Mo., U.S.	C4	102
White Meadow Lake, N.J., U.S.	*B3	107
White Mesa Natural Bridge, Az., U.S.	A4	80
White Mountain Peak, mtn., Ca., U.S.	D4	82
White Mountains, mts., U.S.	D4	82
White Mountains, mts., N.H., U.S.	B3	106
Whitemouth, stm., Man., Can.	E4	70
Whitemouth Lake, l., Man., Can.	E4	70
White Nile (Al-Baḥr al-Abyaḍ), stm., Sudan	F12	42
White Oak, Oh., U.S.	o12	112
White Oak Creek, stm., Oh., U.S.	D2	112
Whiteoak Creek, stm., Tn., U.S.	A4	119
White Oak Lake, res., Ar., U.S.	D2	81
White Pigeon, Mi., U.S.	G5	99
White Pine, Mi., U.S.	m12	99
White Pine, Tn., U.S.	C10	119
White Pine, co., Nv., U.S.	D6	105
White Plains, Md., U.S.	C4	97
White Plains, N.Y., U.S.	D7	109
Whiteriver, Az., U.S.	D6	80
White River Junction, Vt., U.S.	D4	122
White Rock, B.C., Can.	E6	69
White Russia see Belarus, ctry., Eur.	G3	18
White Salmon, Wa., U.S.	D4	124
White Salmon, stm., Wa., U.S.	D4	124
White Sands Missile Range, mil., N.M., U.S.	E3	108
White Sands National Monument, N.M., U.S.	E3	108
Whitesboro, N.Y., U.S.	B5	109
Whitesboro, Tx., U.S.	C4	120
Whitesburg, Ga., U.S.	C2	87
Whitesburg, Ky., U.S.	C7	94
Whites Creek, stm., Tn., U.S.	g10	119
White Sea see Beloje more, Russia	D5	22
Whiteside, co., Il., U.S.	B3	90
Whiteside, co., Il., U.S.	B3	90
White Sulphur Springs, Mt., U.S.	D6	103
White Sulphur Springs, W.V., U.S.	D4	125
Whitesville, Ky., U.S.	C3	94
White Swan, Wa., U.S.	C5	124

Name	Map Ref	Page

Name	Map Ref	Page
/hite Tank Mountains, mts., Az., U.S.	k7	80
hiteville, N.C., U.S.	C4	110
hiteville, Tn., U.S.	B2	119
hite Volta (Volta Blanche), stm., Afr.	F5	42
hitewater, Ks., U.S.	E6	93
hitewater, Wi., U.S.	F5	126
hitewater, stm., U.S.	F7	91
hitewater, stm., U.S.	E6	93
hitewater Baldy, mtn., N.M., U.S.	D1	108
hitewater Bay, b., Fl., U.S.	G6	86
hitewood, S.D., U.S.	C2	118
hitewright, Tx., U.S.	C4	120
hitfield, co., Ga., U.S.	B2	87
hitfield Estates, Fl., U.S.	q10	86
hiting, In., U.S.	A3	91
hiting, Ia., U.S.	B1	92
hiting, Wi., U.S.	D4	126
hiting Field Naval Air Station, mil., Fl., U.S.	u14	86
hitinsville, Ma., U.S.	B4	98
hitley, co., In., U.S.	B6	91
hitley, co., Ky., U.S.	D5	94
hitley City, Ky., U.S.	D5	94
hitman, Ma., U.S.	B6	98
hitman, W.V., U.S.	D2	125
hitman, co., Wa., U.S.	B8	124
hitman Square, N.J., U.S.	D2	107
hitmire, S.C., U.S.	B4	117
hitmore Lake, Mi., U.S.	p14	99
hitmore Village, Hi., U.S.	f9	88
hitney, S.C., U.S.	B4	117
hitney, Tx., U.S.	D4	120
hitney, Lake, res., Tx., U.S.	D4	120
hitney, Mount, mtn., Ca., U.S.	D4	82
hitney Point Lake, res., N.Y., U.S.	C5	109
hittier, Ak., U.S.	C10	79
hittier, Ca., U.S.	F4	82
hitwell, Tn., U.S.	D8	119
holdaia Lake, l., N.W. Ter., Can.	D12	66
hyalla, Austl.	F7	50
iarton, Ont., Can.	C3	73
ibaux, Mt., U.S.	D12	103
ibaux, co., Mt., U.S.	D12	103
ichita, Ks., U.S.	E6	93
ichita, co., Ks., U.S.	D2	93
ichita, co., Tx., U.S.	B3	120
ichita Falls, Tx., U.S.	C3	120
ichita Mountains, mts., Ok., U.S.	C3	113
ick, Scot., U.K.	C9	7
ickenburg, Az., U.S.	D3	80
ickiup Reservoir, res., Or., U.S.	E5	114
ickliffe, Ky., U.S.	f8	94
ickliffe, Oh., U.S.	A4	112
icklow, Ire.	I6	7
icklow Head, c., Ire.	I6	7
icklow Mountains, mts., Ire.	H6	7
icomico, co., Md., U.S.	D6	97
icomico, stm., Md., U.S.	D6	97
iconisco, Pa., U.S.	E8	115
idefield, Co., U.S.	C6	83
ielkopolska, reg., Pol.	D17	8
ien (Vienna), Aus.	G16	8
iener Neustadt, Aus.	H16	8
iesbaden, Ger.	E8	8
iesloch, Ger.	F8	8
iggins, Ms., U.S.	E4	101
iggins Peak, mtn., Wy., U.S.	C3	127
kwemikong, Ont., Can.	B3	73
ilbarger, co., Tx., U.S.	B3	120
ilber, Ne., U.S.	D9	104
ilberforce, Oh., U.S.	C2	112
ilbraham, Ma., U.S.	B3	98
ilbur, Wa., U.S.	B7	124
ilburton, Ok., U.S.	C6	113
ilcannia, Austl.	F8	50
ilcox, Pa., U.S.	C4	115
ilcox, co., Al., U.S.	D2	78
ilcox, co., Ga., U.S.	E3	87
ild, stm., U.S.	B4	106
ild Ammonoosuc, stm., N.H., U.S.	B3	106
ild Branch, stm., Vt., U.S.	B4	122
ilder, Id., U.S.	F2	89
ilder, Vt., U.S.	D4	122
ilder Dam, U.S.	C2	106
ildhorse Creek, stm., Ok., U.S.	C3	113
ild Horse Reservoir, res., Nv., U.S.	B6	105
ildorado, Tx., U.S.	B1	120
ild Rice, stm., Mn., U.S.	C2	100
ild Rice, stm., N.D., U.S.	C8	111
ildwood, Fl., U.S.	D4	86
ildwood, N.J., U.S.	F3	107
ildwood Crest, N.J., U.S.	F3	107
ilhelm, Mount, mtn., Pap. N. Gui.	m16	50a
ilhelmina Gebergte, mts., Sur.	C7	54
ilhelmina Peak see Trikora, Puntjak, mtn., Indon.	F10	32
ilhelmshaven, Ger.	B8	8
ilkes, co., Ga., U.S.	C4	87
ilkes, co., N.C., U.S.	A1	110
ilkes-Barre, Pa., U.S.	D10	115
ilkesboro, N.C., U.S.	A1	110
ilkes Land, reg., Ant.	C24	47
ilkin, co., Mn., U.S.	D2	100
ilkinsburg, Pa., U.S.	F2	115
ilkinson, W.V., U.S.	D3	125
ilkinson, co., Ga., U.S.	D3	87
ilkinson, co., Ms., U.S.	D2	101
ill, co., Il., U.S.	B5	90
illacoochee, Ga., U.S.	E3	87
illacy, co., Tx., U.S.	F4	120
illamette, stm., Or., U.S.	C3	114
illamette Pass, Or., U.S.	D4	114
illamina, Or., U.S.	B3	114
illapa Bay, b., Wa., U.S.	C1	124
illard, Mo., U.S.	D4	102
Willard, Oh., U.S.	A3	112
Willard, Ut., U.S.	B3	121
Willard Bay, b., Ut., U.S.	B3	121
Willards, Md., U.S.	D7	97
Willard Stream, stm., Vt., U.S.	B5	122
Willcox, Az., U.S.	E6	80
Willcox Playa, l., Az., U.S.	E6	80
Willemstad, Neth. Ant.	H13	64
William "Bill" Dannelly Reservoir, res., Al., U.S.	C2	78
Williams, Az., U.S.	B3	80
Williams, Ca., U.S.	C2	82
Williams, co., N.D., U.S.	A2	111
Williams, co., Oh., U.S.	A1	112
Williams, stm., Vt., U.S.	E3	122
Williams, stm., W.V., U.S.	C4	125
Williams Air Force Base, mil., Az., U.S.	D4	80
Williams Bay, Wi., U.S.	F5	126
Williamsburg, In., U.S.	E8	91
Williamsburg, Ia., U.S.	C5	92
Williamsburg, Ky., U.S.	D5	94
Williamsburg, Oh., U.S.	C1	112
Williamsburg, Pa., U.S.	F5	115
Williamsburg, Va., U.S.	C6	123
Williamsburg, co., S.C., U.S.	D8	117
Williams Fork, stm., Co., U.S.	A3	83
Williams Lake, B.C., Can.	C6	69
Williamson, N.Y., U.S.	B3	109
Williamson, W.V., U.S.	D2	125
Williamson, co., Il., U.S.	F4	90
Williamson, co., Tn., U.S.	B5	119
Williamson, co., Tx., U.S.	D4	120
Williamsport, In., U.S.	D3	91
Williamsport, Md., U.S.	A2	97
Williamsport, Pa., U.S.	D7	115
Williamston, Mi., U.S.	F6	99
Williamston, N.C., U.S.	B5	110
Williamston, S.C., U.S.	B3	117
Williamstown, Ky., U.S.	B5	94
Williamstown, Ma., U.S.	A1	98
Williamstown, N.J., U.S.	D3	107
Williamstown, Pa., U.S.	E8	115
Williamstown, Vt., U.S.	C4	122
Williamstown, W.V., U.S.	B3	125
Williamsville, Il., U.S.	D4	90
Williamsville, N.Y., U.S.	C2	109
Willimantic, Ct., U.S.	C7	84
Willimantic, stm., Ct., U.S.	B6	84
Willimantic Reservoir, res., Ct., U.S.	C7	84
Willingboro, N.J., U.S.	C3	107
Willis, Tx., U.S.	D5	120
Willis Islets, is., Austl.	C9	50
Williston, Fl., U.S.	C4	86
Williston, N.D., U.S.	A2	111
Williston, S.C., U.S.	E5	117
Williston Lake, res., B.C., Can.	B6	69
Willits, Ca., U.S.	C2	82
Willmar, Mn., U.S.	E3	100
Willoughby, Oh., U.S.	A4	112
Willoughby, Lake, l., Vt., U.S.	B4	122
Willoughby Hills, Oh., U.S.	A4	112
Willow, Ak., U.S.	g17	79
Willow Creek, stm., U.S.	C19	16
Willow Creek, stm., Ut., U.S.	D6	121
Willow Creek, stm., Wy., U.S.	C6	127
Willow Grove Naval Air Station, mil., Pa., U.S.	F11	115
Willowick, Oh., U.S.	A4	112
Willowmore, S. Afr.	H4	44
Willow Reservoir, res., Wi., U.S.	C3	126
Willow Run, De., U.S.	i7	85
Willow Run, Mi., U.S.	p14	99
Willows, Ca., U.S.	C2	82
Willow Springs, Il., U.S.	k9	90
Willow Springs, Mo., U.S.	E6	102
Willston, Va., U.S.	*B5	123
Wilmar, Ar., U.S.	D4	81
Wilmerding, Pa., U.S.	k14	115
Wilmette, Il., U.S.	A6	90
Wilmington, De., U.S.	B3	85
Wilmington, Il., U.S.	B5	90
Wilmington, Ma., U.S.	A5	98
Wilmington, N.C., U.S.	C5	110
Wilmington, Oh., U.S.	C2	112
Wilmington, Vt., U.S.	F3	122
Wilmington Manor, De., U.S.	i7	85
Wilmore, Ky., U.S.	C5	94
Wilmot, Ar., U.S.	D4	81
Wilson, Ar., U.S.	B5	81
Wilson, Ks., U.S.	D5	93
Wilson, La., U.S.	D4	95
Wilson, N.C., U.S.	B5	110
Wilson, Ok., U.S.	C4	113
Wilson, Pa., U.S.	E11	115
Wilson, Wy., U.S.	C2	127
Wilson, co., Ks., U.S.	E8	93
Wilson, co., N.C., U.S.	B5	110
Wilson, co., Tn., U.S.	A5	119
Wilson, co., Tx., U.S.	E3	120
Wilson, Cape, c., N.W. Ter., Can.	C16	66
Wilson, Mount, mtn., Az., U.S.	B5	80
Wilson, Mount, mtn., Ca., U.S.	m12	82
Wilson, Mount, mtn., Co., U.S.	D2	83
Wilson, Mount, mtn., Nv., U.S.	E7	105
Wilson, Mount, mtn., Wa., U.S.	B5	124
Wilson Creek, stm., Wa., U.S.	B5	124
Wilson Creek, stm., Wa., U.S.	C5	120
Wilson Lake, res., Al., U.S.	A2	78
Wilson Lake, res., Ks., U.S.	D4	93
Wilsons Beach, N.B., Can.	E3	71
Wilsonville, Al., U.S.	B3	78
Wilsonville, Or., U.S.	h12	114
Wilton, Ct., U.S.	E2	84
Wilton, Ia., U.S.	C6	92
Wilton, Me., U.S.	D2	96
Wilton, N.H., U.S.	E3	106
Wilton, N.D., U.S.	B5	111
Wiluna, Austl.	E4	50
Wimauma, Fl., U.S.	E4	86
Wimico, Lake, l., Fl., U.S.	C1	86
Wincheck Pond, l., R.I., U.S.	E1	116
Winchendon, Ma., U.S.	A3	98
Winchester, Ont., Can.	B9	73
Winchester, Eng., U.K.	J11	7
Winchester, Il., U.S.	D3	90
Winchester, In., U.S.	D8	91
Winchester, Ks., U.S.	k15	93
Winchester, Ky., U.S.	C5	94
Winchester, Ma., U.S.	g11	98
Winchester, Nv., U.S.	G6	105
Winchester, N.H., U.S.	E2	106
Winchester, Oh., U.S.	D2	112
Winchester, Tn., U.S.	B5	119
Winchester, Va., U.S.	A4	123
Winchester Bay, Or., U.S.	D2	114
Wind, stm., U.S.	D4	124
Wind, stm., Wy., U.S.	C4	127
Windber, Pa., U.S.	F4	115
Wind Cave National Park, S.D., U.S.	D2	118
Winder, Ga., U.S.	C3	87
Windermere, Eng., U.K.	G10	7
Windfall, In., U.S.	D6	91
Windgap, Pa., U.S.	E11	115
Windham, Ct., U.S.	C7	84
Windham, Oh., U.S.	A4	112
Windham, co., Ct., U.S.	B7	84
Windham, co., Vt., U.S.	F3	122
Windhoek, Nmb.	F3	44
Wind Lake, Wi., U.S.	F5	126
Wind Lake, l., Wi., U.S.	n11	126
Windmill Point, c., Va., U.S.	C6	123
Windom, Mn., U.S.	G3	100
Windom Peak, mtn., Co., U.S.	D3	83
Windorah, Austl.	E8	50
Window Rock, Az., U.S.	B6	80
Wind Point, Wi., U.S.	n12	126
Wind River Indian Reservation, Wy., U.S.	C4	127
Wind River Peak, mtn., Wy., U.S.	D3	127
Wind River Range, mts., Wy., U.S.	C3	127
Windsor, Newf., Can.	D4	72
Windsor, Ont., Can.	E1	73
Windsor, Que., Can.	D5	74
Windsor, Eng., U.K.	J12	7
Windsor, Co., U.S.	A6	83
Windsor, Ct., U.S.	B5	84
Windsor, Il., U.S.	D5	90
Windsor, Mo., U.S.	C4	102
Windsor, N.C., U.S.	A6	110
Windsor, Pa., U.S.	G8	115
Windsor, Vt., U.S.	E4	122
Windsor, Va., U.S.	D6	123
Windsor, co., Vt., U.S.	D3	122
Windsor Heights, Ia., U.S.	e8	92
Windsor Locks, Ct., U.S.	B5	84
Windward Islands, is., N.A.	H17	64
Windward Passage, strt., N.A.	E10	64
Windy Hill, S.C., U.S.	C8	117
Windy Peak, mtn., Wa., U.S.	A6	124
Winefred Lake, l., Alta., Can.	B5	68
Winfield, Al., U.S.	B2	78
Winfield, Ia., U.S.	C6	92
Winfield, Ks., U.S.	E7	93
Winfield, Mo., U.S.	C7	102
Winfield, W.V., U.S.	C3	125
Wing, stm., Mn., U.S.	D3	100
Wingate, N.C., U.S.	C2	110
Wingham, Ont., Can.	D3	73
Winifrede, W.V., U.S.	m12	125
Winisk, stm., Ont., Can.	n18	73
Winisk Lake, l., Ont., Can.	F15	66
Wink, Tx., U.S.	D1	120
Winkelman, Az., U.S.	E5	80
Winkler, Man., Can.	E3	70
Winkler, co., Tx., U.S.	D1	120
Winlock, Wa., U.S.	C3	124
Winn, co., La., U.S.	C3	95
Winnebago, Il., U.S.	A4	90
Winnebago, Mn., U.S.	G4	100
Winnebago, Ne., U.S.	B9	104
Winnebago, Wi., U.S.	h8	126
Winnebago, co., Il., U.S.	A4	90
Winnebago, co., Ia., U.S.	A4	92
Winnebago, co., Wi., U.S.	D5	126
Winnebago, stm., Ia., U.S.	A4	92
Winnebago, Lake, l., Wi., U.S.	E5	126
Winnebago Indian Reservation, Ne., U.S.	B9	104
Winneconne, Wi., U.S.	D5	126
Winnemucca, Nv., U.S.	C4	105
Winnemucca Lake, l., Nv., U.S.	C2	105
Winner, S.D., U.S.	D6	118
Winneshiek, co., Ia., U.S.	A6	92
Winnetka, Il., U.S.	A6	90
Winnfield, La., U.S.	C3	95
Winnibigoshish, Lake, l., Mn., U.S.	C4	100
Winnipeg, Man., Can.	E3	70
Winnipeg, stm., Can.	D4	70
Winnipeg, Lake, l., Man., Can.	C3	70
Winnipeg Beach, Man., Can.	D3	70
Winnipegosis, Lake, l., Man., Can.	C2	70
Winnipesaukee, Lake, l., N.H., U.S.	C4	106
Winnsboro, La., U.S.	B4	95
Winnsboro, S.C., U.S.	C5	117
Winnsboro, Tx., U.S.	C5	120
Winnsboro Mills, S.C., U.S.	C5	117
Winona, Mn., U.S.	F7	100
Winona, Ms., U.S.	B4	101
Winona, Mo., U.S.	D6	102
Winona, co., Mn., U.S.	F7	100
Winona Lake, In., U.S.	B6	91
Winona Lake, l., Vt., U.S.	C2	122
Winooski, Vt., U.S.	C2	122
Winooski, stm., Vt., U.S.	C3	122
Winslow, Az., U.S.	C5	80
Winslow, In., U.S.	H3	91
Winslow, Me., U.S.	D3	96
Winsted, Mn., U.S.	F4	100
Winsted, Ct., U.S.	B3	84
Winston, Fl., U.S.	D4	86
Winston, Or., U.S.	D3	114
Winston, co., Al., U.S.	A2	78
Winston, co., Ms., U.S.	B4	101
Winston-Salem, N.C., U.S.	A2	110
Winter Garden, Fl., U.S.	D5	86
Winter Harbor, Me., U.S.	D4	96
Winter Haven, Fl., U.S.	D5	86
Winter Park, Fl., U.S.	D5	86
Winter Park, N.C., U.S.	C5	110
Winterport, Me., U.S.	D4	96
Winter Ridge, mtn., Or., U.S.	E6	114
Winters, Ca., U.S.	C2	82
Winters, Tx., U.S.	D3	120
Winterset, Ia., U.S.	C4	92
Wintersville, Oh., U.S.	B5	112
Winterswijk, Neth.	D6	9
Winterthur, Switz.	E15	10
Winterville, Ga., U.S.	C3	87
Winterville, N.C., U.S.	B5	110
Winthrop, Ia., U.S.	B6	92
Winthrop, Me., U.S.	D3	96
Winthrop, Ma., U.S.	B6	98
Winthrop, Mn., U.S.	F4	100
Winthrop, Lake, l., Ma., U.S.	h10	98
Winthrop Harbor, Il., U.S.	A6	90
Winton, Austl.	D8	50
Winton, N.C., U.S.	A6	110
Winton Lake, res., Oh., U.S.	o12	113
Winyah Bay, b., S.C., U.S.	E9	117
Wirt, co., W.V., U.S.	B3	125
Wiscasset, Me., U.S.	D3	96
Wisconsin, state, U.S.	D4	126
Wisconsin, stm., Wi., U.S.	E3	126
Wisconsin, Lake, res., Wi., U.S.	E4	126
Wisconsin Dells, Wi., U.S.	E4	126
Wisconsin Rapids, Wi., U.S.	D4	126
Wise, Va., U.S.	f9	123
Wise, co., Tx., U.S.	C4	120
Wise, co., Va., U.S.	e9	123
Wishek, N.D., U.S.	C6	111
Wishram, Wa., U.S.	D4	124
Wisła, stm., Pol.	A18	8
Wismar, Ger.	B11	8
Wisner, La., U.S.	C4	95
Wisner, Ne., U.S.	C9	104
Wissota, Lake, res., Wi., U.S.	D2	126
Wister, Ok., U.S.	C7	113
Wister Lake, res., Ok., U.S.	C7	113
Witbank, S. Afr.	G5	44
Withamsville, Oh., U.S.	C1	112
Witherspoon, Mount, mtn., Ak., U.S.	g18	79
Withlacoochee, stm., U.S.	B3	86
Withlacoochee, stm., Fl., U.S.	C4	86
Witless Bay, Newf., Can.	E5	72
Witt, Il., U.S.	D4	90
Wittenberg, Ger.	D12	8
Wittenberg, Wi., U.S.	D4	126
Wittenberge, Ger.	B11	8
Wittlich, Ger.	F6	8
Wittman, Md., U.S.	C5	97
Wittmann, Az., U.S.	D3	80
Wittstock, Ger.	B12	8
Wixom, Mi., U.S.	o14	99
Wixom Lake, res., Mi., U.S.	E6	99
Włocławek, Pol.	C19	8
Woburn, Ma., U.S.	B5	98
Wokam, Pulau, i., Indon.	G9	32
Woking, Eng., U.K.	J12	7
Wolcott, Ct., U.S.	C4	84
Wolcott, In., U.S.	C3	91
Wolcottville, In., U.S.	A7	91
Wolf, stm., Ms., U.S.	E4	101
Wolf, stm., Tn., U.S.	e9	119
Wolf, stm., Wi., U.S.	C5	126
Wolf Creek, Or., U.S.	E3	114
Wolf Creek, stm., U.S.	A2	113
Wolf Creek, stm., W.V., U.S.	m13	125
Wolf Creek Pass, Co., U.S.	D3	83
Wolfe, co., Ky., U.S.	C6	94
Wolfeboro, N.H., U.S.	C4	106
Wolfeboro Falls, N.H., U.S.	C4	106
Wolfe City, Tx., U.S.	C4	120
Wolfen, Ger.	D12	8
Wolfenbüttel, Ger.	C10	8
Wolf Lake, Mi., U.S.	E4	99
Wolf Lake, l., Il., U.S.	k9	90
Wolf Mountain, mtn., Ak., U.S.	B9	79
Wolf Point, Mt., U.S.	B11	103
Wolfsberg, Aus.	I14	8
Wolfsburg, Ger.	C10	8
Wolf Swamp, sw., N.C., U.S.	C5	110
Wolgast, Ger.	A13	8
Wollaston, Cape, c., N.W. Ter., Can.	C10	66
Wollaston, Islas, is., Chile	H3	56
Wollaston Lake, l., Sask., Can.	m8	75
Wollaston Peninsula, pen., N.W. Ter., Can.	C10	66
Wollongong, Austl.	F10	50
Wolverhampton, Eng., U.K.	I10	7
Woman Lake, l., Mn., U.S.	D4	100
Womelsdorf, Pa., U.S.	F9	115
Wonder Lake, Il., U.S.	A5	90
Wonewoc, Wi., U.S.	E3	126
Wŏnsan, N. Kor.	D12	26
Wood, co., Oh., U.S.	A2	112
Wood, co., Tx., U.S.	C5	120
Wood, co., W.V., U.S.	B3	125
Wood, co., Wi., U.S.	D3	126
Wood, stm., Sask., Can.	H2	75
Wood, stm., R.I., U.S.	F2	116
Wood, stm., Wy., U.S.	C3	127
Wood, Mount, mtn., Mt., U.S.	E7	103
Woodall Mountain, mtn., Ms., U.S.	A5	101
Woodbine, Ga., U.S.	F5	87
Woodbine, Ia., U.S.	C2	92
Woodbine, Ky., U.S.	D5	94
Woodbine, N.J., U.S.	E3	107
Woodbridge, Ct., U.S.	D3	84
Woodbridge, Va., U.S.	B5	123
Woodbridge [Township], N.J., U.S.	B4	107
Woodburn, In., U.S.	B8	91
Woodburn, Or., U.S.	B4	114
Woodbury, Ct., U.S.	C3	84
Woodbury, Ga., U.S.	D2	87
Woodbury, Mn., U.S.	F6	100
Woodbury, N.J., U.S.	D2	107
Woodbury, Tn., U.S.	B5	119
Woodbury, co., Ia., U.S.	B1	92
Woodcliff Lake, N.J., U.S.	g8	107
Woodcliff Lake, l., N.J., U.S.	g8	107
Wood Dale, Il., U.S.	k9	90
Wood End, spit, Ma., U.S.	B7	98
Woodfield, S.C., U.S.	C6	117
Woodford, co., Il., U.S.	C4	90
Woodford, co., Ky., U.S.	B5	94
Woodhull, Il., U.S.	B3	90
Woodlake, Ca., U.S.	D4	82
Woodland, Ca., U.S.	C3	82
Woodland, Me., U.S.	C5	96
Woodland, N.C., U.S.	A5	110
Woodland, Wa., U.S.	D3	124
Woodland Acres, Co., U.S.	D6	83
Woodland Park, Co., U.S.	C5	83
Woodlark Island, i., Pap. N. Gui.	A10	50
Woodlawn, Ky., U.S.	e9	94
Woodlawn, Md., U.S.	g10	97
Woodlawn, Oh., U.S.	n13	112
Woodlawn, Va., U.S.	D2	123
Woodmont, Ct., U.S.	E4	84
Woodmoor, Md., U.S.	B4	97
Woodridge, Il., U.S.	k8	90
Wood-Ridge, N.J., U.S.	h8	107
Wood River, Il., U.S.	E3	90
Wood River, Ne., U.S.	D7	104
Woodroffe, Mount, mtn., Austl.	E6	50
Woodruff, S.C., U.S.	B3	117
Woodruff, Wi., U.S.	C4	126
Woodruff, co., Ar., U.S.	B4	81
Woods, co., Ok., U.S.	A3	113
Woods, Lake, res., Tn., U.S.	B5	119
Woods, Lake of the, l., N.A.	G14	66
Woodsboro, Tx., U.S.	E4	120
Woods Cross, Ut., U.S.	C4	121
Woodsfield, Oh., U.S.	C4	112
Woods Hole, Ma., U.S.	C6	98
Woodson, Ar., U.S.	C3	81
Woodson, co., Ks., U.S.	E8	93
Woodstock, N.B., Can.	C2	71
Woodstock, Ont., Can.	D4	73
Woodstock, Ga., U.S.	B2	87
Woodstock, Il., U.S.	A5	90
Woodstock, Md., U.S.	B4	97
Woodstock, N.Y., U.S.	C6	109
Woodstock, Vt., U.S.	D3	122
Woodstock, Va., U.S.	B4	123
Woodstown, N.J., U.S.	D2	107
Woodsville, N.H., U.S.	B2	106
Woodville, N.Z.	D5	52
Woodville, Fl., U.S.	B2	86
Woodville, Ms., U.S.	D2	101
Woodville, Oh., U.S.	A2	112
Woodville, Tx., U.S.	D5	120
Woodville, Wi., U.S.	D1	126
Woodward, Ia., U.S.	C4	92
Woodward, Ok., U.S.	A2	113
Woodward, co., Ok., U.S.	A2	113
Woodworth, La., U.S.	C3	95
Woolmarket, Ms., U.S.	E5	101
Woolrich, Pa., U.S.	D7	115
Woolsey Peak, mtn., Az., U.S.	D3	80
Woomera, Austl.	F7	50
Woonsocket, R.I., U.S.	A3	116
Woonsocket, S.D., U.S.	C7	118
Woonsocket Reservoir Number Three, res., R.I., U.S.	B3	116
Wooramel, Austl.	E2	50
Wooster, Oh., U.S.	B4	112
Worcester, S. Afr.	H3	44
Worcester, Eng., U.K.	I10	7
Worcester, Ma., U.S.	B4	98
Worcester, co., Md., U.S.	D7	97
Worcester, co., Ma., U.S.	A3	98
Worden, Il., U.S.	E4	90
Worden Pond, l., R.I., U.S.	F3	116
Workington, Eng., U.K.	G9	7
Worland, Wy., U.S.	B5	127
Worms, Ger.	F8	8
Worth, Il., U.S.	k9	90
Worth, co., Ga., U.S.	E3	87
Worth, co., Ia., U.S.	A4	92
Worth, co., Mo., U.S.	A3	102
Worthing, Eng., U.K.	K12	7
Worthington, In., U.S.	F4	91
Worthington, Ky., U.S.	B7	94
Worthington, Mn., U.S.	G3	100
Worthington, Oh., U.S.	B2	112
Worthington Peak, mtn., Nv., U.S.	F6	105
Wowoni, Pulau, i., Indon.	F7	32
Wrangell, Ak., U.S.	D13	79
Wrangell, Cape, Ak., U.S.	E2	79
Wrangell, Mount, mtn., Ak., U.S.	I19	79
Wrangell Island, i., Ak., U.S.	m24	79
Wrangell Mountains, mts., Ak., U.S.	C11	79
Wrangell-Saint Elias National Park, Ak., U.S.	C11	79
Wrath, Cape, c., Scot., U.K.	C7	7
Wray, Co., U.S.	A8	83
Wreck Reefs, rf., Austl.	D11	50
Wrens, Ga., U.S.	C4	87
Wrentham, Ma., U.S.	B5	98
Wrexham, Wales, U.K.	H9	7
Wright, co., Ia., U.S.	B4	92
Wright, co., Mn., U.S.	E4	100
Wright, co., Mo., U.S.	D5	102
Wright, Mount, mtn., Mt., U.S.	C4	103
Wright Brothers National Memorial, hist., N.C., U.S.	A7	110
Wright City, Mo., U.S.	C8	102
Wright City, Ok., U.S.	C6	113
Wright-Patterson Air Force Base, mil., Oh., U.S.	C1	112
Wrightson, Mount, mtn., Az., U.S.	F5	80
Wrightstown, N.J., U.S.	C3	107
Wrightstown, Wi., U.S.	D5	126
Wrightsville, Ar., U.S.	C3	81
Wrightsville, Ga., U.S.	D4	87
Wrightsville, Pa., U.S.	F8	115
Wrightsville Beach, N.C., U.S.	C5	110

Name	Map Ref	Page
Wrightsville Reservoir, res., Vt., U.S.	C3	122
Wrigley, N.W. Ter., Can.	D8	66
Wrocław (Breslau), Pol.	D17	8
Wuchuan, China	D11	34
Wudu, China	E7	26
Wugang, China	F9	26
Wuhan, China	E3	28
Wuhu, China	D7	28
Wunstorf, Ger.	C9	8
Wupatki National Monument, Az., U.S.	B4	80
Wuppertal, Ger.	D7	8
Würzburg, Ger.	F9	8
Wurzen, Ger.	D12	8
Wushan, China	E8	26
Wushenqi, China	D8	26
Wusong, China	D10	28
Wutongqiao, China	F7	26
Wuwei, China	D7	26
Wuwei, China	D6	28
Wuxi (Wuhsi), China	D9	28
Wuyi Shan, mts., China	I5	28
Wuyuan, China	C8	26
Wuzhong, China	D8	26
Wuzhou (Wuchow), China	C11	34
Wyaconda, stm., Mo., U.S.	A6	102
Wyandot, co., Oh., U.S.	B2	112
Wyandotte, Mi., U.S.	F7	99
Wyandotte, co., Ks., U.S.	C9	93
Wyanet, Il., U.S.	B4	90
Wyk, Ger.	A8	8
Wylie, Lake, res., U.S.	A5	117
Wyman Lake, res., Me., U.S.	C3	96
Wymore, Ne., U.S.	D9	104
Wyndham, Austl.	C5	50
Wynndel, B.C., Can.	E9	69
Wynne, Ar., U.S.	B5	81
Wynnewood, Ok., U.S.	C4	113
Wynoochee, stm., Wa., U.S.	B2	124
Wyoming, Ont., Can.	E2	73
Wyoming, De., U.S.	D3	85
Wyoming, Il., U.S.	B4	90
Wyoming, Ia., U.S.	B6	92
Wyoming, Mi., U.S.	F5	99
Wyoming, Mn., U.S.	E6	100
Wyoming, Oh., U.S.	o13	112
Wyoming, Pa., U.S.	n17	115
Wyoming, R.I., U.S.	E2	116
Wyoming, co., N.Y., U.S.	C2	109
Wyoming, co., Pa., U.S.	D9	115
Wyoming, co., W.V., U.S.	D3	125
Wyoming, state, U.S.	C5	127
Wyoming Peak, mtn., Wy., U.S.	D2	127
Wyoming Range, mts., Wy., U.S.	D2	127
Wyomissing, Pa., U.S.	F10	115
Wysocking Bay, b., N.C., U.S.	B7	110
Wythe, co., Va., U.S.	D1	123
Wytheville, Va., U.S.	D1	123

X

Xai-Xai, Moz.	G6	44
Xangongo, Ang.	E3	44
Xánthi, Grc.	H8	16
Xapuri, Braz.	F5	54
Xenia, Oh., U.S.	C2	112
Xertigny, Fr.	D13	10
Xi, stm., China	G9	26
Xiaguan, China	E9	26
Xiahe, China	D7	26
Xiamen (Amoy), China	K7	28
Xi'an (Sian), China	E8	26
Xiangcheng, China	B2	28
Xiangfan, China	E9	26
Xiangkhoang, Laos	E7	34
Xiangride, China	D6	26
Xiangtan, China	H1	28
Xianyou, China	J7	28
Xiaogan, China	E2	28
Xiaolan, China	M2	28
Xiashi, China	E9	28
Xichang, China	F7	26
Xiegeer, China	F12	38
Xigazê, China	F13	38
Xihua, China	B3	28
Xilinhaote, China	C10	26
Xinavane, Moz.	G6	44
Xingtai, China	D9	26
Xingu, stm., Braz.	D8	54
Xingyi, China	B8	34
Xinhui, China	M2	28
Xining, China	D7	26
Xinjiang Uygur Zizhiqu, prov., China	B9	38
Xinxiang, China	D9	26
Xinyang, China	C3	28
Xiping, China	B3	28
Xique-Xique, Braz.	F10	54
Xizang Zizhiqu, prov., China	D12	38
Xuancheng, China	E7	28
Xuanhua, China	C10	26
Xuchang, China	A2	28
Xuwen, China	D11	34
Xuyong, China	F8	26
Xuzhou (Süchow), China	A6	28

Y

Yaan, China	E7	26

Yacolt, Wa., U.S.	D3	124
Yacuiba, Bol.	H6	54
Yādgīr, India	D4	37
Yadkin, co., N.C., U.S.	A2	110
Yadkin, stm., N.C., U.S.	B2	110
Yadkinville, N.C., U.S.	A2	110
Yainax Butte, mtn., Or., U.S.	E5	114
Yaizu, Japan	H11	30
Yakima, Wa., U.S.	C5	124
Yakima, co., Wa., U.S.	C4	124
Yakima, stm., Wa., U.S.	C6	124
Yakima Indian Reservation, Wa., U.S.	C5	124
Yakobi Island, i., Ak., U.S.	m21	79
Yakumo, Japan	q18	30a
Yaku-shima, i., Japan	u30	31b
Yakutat, Ak., U.S.	D12	79
Yakutat Bay, b., Ak., U.S.	D11	79
Yala, Thai.	K6	34
Yale, Mi., U.S.	E8	99
Yale, Ok., U.S.	A5	113
Yale Lake, res., Wa., U.S.	D3	124
Yale, Mount, mtn., Co., U.S.	C5	83
Yalobusha, co., Ms., U.S.	A4	101
Yalobusha, stm., Ms., U.S.	B4	101
Yalu (Amnok-kang), stm., Asia	C12	26
Yamachiche, Que., Can.	C5	74
Yamagata, Japan	D13	30
Yamaguchi, Japan	H4	30
Yamato-takada, Japan	H8	30
Yambio, Sudan	H11	42
Yamdena, Pulau, i., Indon.	G9	32
Yamethin, Burma	D4	34
Yamhill, Or., U.S.	h11	114
Yamhill, co., Or., U.S.	B3	114
Yamoussoukro, I.C.	G4	42
Yampa, stm., Co., U.S.	A2	83
Yamsay Mountain, mtn., Or., U.S.	E5	114
Yamuna, stm., India	H9	38
Yanbu', Sau. Ar.	D2	46
Yancey, co., N.C., U.S.	f10	110
Yanceyville, N.C., U.S.	A3	110
Yanchang, China	D9	26
Yancheng, China	B9	28
Yandoon, Burma	F3	34
Yangjiang, China	G9	26
Yangon (Rangoon), Burma	B2	32
Yangquan, China	D9	26
Yangtze see Chang, stm., China	E10	26
Yangzhou, China	C8	28
Yanji, China	C12	26
Yankton, S.D., U.S.	E8	118
Yankton, co., S.D., U.S.	D8	118
Yanqi, China	C4	26
Yantai (Chefoo), China	D11	26
Yantic, stm., Ct., U.S.	C7	84
Yaoundé, Cam.	H8	42
Yapen, Pulau, i., Indon.	F10	32
Yaqui, stm., Mex.	C5	62
Yaraka, Austl.	D8	50
Yardley, Pa., U.S.	F12	115
Yardville, N.J., U.S.	C3	107
Yaritagua, Ven.	B8	58
Yarmouth, Me., U.S.	E2	96
Yarnell, Az., U.S.	C3	80
Yarumal, Col.	D5	58
Yashiro-jima, i., Japan	I5	30
Yates, co., N.Y., U.S.	C3	109
Yates Center, Ks., U.S.	E8	93
Yates City, Il., U.S.	C3	90
Yathkyed Lake, I., N.W. Ter., Can.	D13	66
Yatsushiro, Japan	J3	30
Yatta Plateau, plat., Kenya	B7	44
Yaupi, Ec.	I4	58
Yavapai, co., Az., U.S.	C3	80
Yavarí (Javari), stm., S.A.	D4	54
Yavatmāl, India	B5	37
Yaví, Cerro, mtn., Ven.	E10	58
Yaviza, Pan.	J9	64
Yawatahama, Japan	I5	30
Yawgoog Pond, I., R.I., U.S.	E1	116
Yaxian, China	E10	34
Yazd, Iran	B5	46
Yazoo, co., Ms., U.S.	C3	101
Yazoo, stm., Ms., U.S.	C3	101
Yazoo City, Ms., U.S.	C3	101
Ye, Burma	G4	34
Yeadon, Pa., U.S.	p21	115
Yeagertown, Pa., U.S.	E6	115
Yecheng, China	B7	38
Yecla, Spain	G10	12
Yei, stm., Sudan	G12	42
Yell, co., Ar., U.S.	B2	81
Yell, i., Scot., U.K.	A11	7
Yellow, stm., In., U.S.	u15	86
Yellow, stm., In., U.S.	B4	91
Yellow, stm., Wi., U.S.	D3	126
Yellow, stm., Wi., U.S.	C3	126
Yellow Creek, stm., Tn., U.S.	A4	119
Yellow see Huang, stm., China	D10	26
Yellow Lake, I., Wi., U.S.	C1	126
Yellow Medicine, co., Mn., U.S.	F2	100
Yellow Sea, Asia	D11	26
Yellow Springs, Oh., U.S.	C2	112
Yellowhead Pass, Can.	C1	68
Yellowknife, N.W. Ter., Can.	D10	66
Yellowjacket Mountains, mts., Id., U.S.	D4	89
Yellowstone, co., Mt., U.S.	D8	103
Yellowstone, stm., U.S.	D10	103
Yellowstone Lake, I., Wy., U.S.	B2	127
Yellowstone National Park, co., Mt., U.S.	E6	103
Yellowstone National Park, U.S.	B2	127

Yellville, Ar., U.S.	A3	81
Yelm, Wa., U.S.	C3	124
Yemassee, S.C., U.S.	F6	117
Yemen, ctry., Asia	E4	46
Yenangyaung, Burma	D3	34
Yen Bai, Viet.	D8	34
Yendéré, Burkina	F5	42
Yendi, Ghana	G5	42
Yenisey see Jenisej, stm., Russia	D11	24
Yenshui, Tai.	L9	28
Yentna, stm., Ak., U.S.	f16	79
Yeovil, Eng., U.K.	K10	7
Yerevan see Jerevan, Arm.	I6	22
Yerington, Nv., U.S.	E2	105
Yerington Indian Reservation, Nv., U.S.	D2	105
Yermasóyia, Cyp.	B3	40
Yermo, Ca., U.S.	E5	82
Yerupajá, Nevado, mtn., Peru	F3	54
Yerushalayim (Jerusalem), Isr.	D4	40
Yeste, Spain	G9	12
Yexian, China	B2	28
Yiannitsá, Grc.	I6	16
Yibin, China	F7	26
Yichang, China	E9	26
Yichun, China	B12	26
Yichun, China	H3	28
Yilan, China	B12	26
Yiliang, China	B7	34
Yinchuan, China	D8	26
Yingde, China	K2	28
Yingkou, China	C11	26
Yining, China	C3	26
Yirga Alem, Eth.	G2	46
Yishan, China	B10	34
Yíthion, Grc.	M6	16
Yitulihe, China	A11	26
Yiyang, China	F9	26
Ylivieska, Fin.	D15	6
Ynykčanskij, Russia	E21	24
Yoakum, Tx., U.S.	E4	120
Yoakum, co., Tx., U.S.	C1	120
Yockanookany, stm., Ms., U.S.	C4	101
Yocona, stm., Ms., U.S.	A4	101
Yogyakarta, Indon.	m15	32
Yoho National Park, B.C., Can.	D9	69
Yokkaichi, Japan	H9	30
Yokohama, Japan	G12	30
Yokosuka, Japan	G12	30
Yokote, Japan	C13	30
Yola, Nig.	G8	42
Yolo, co., Ca., U.S.	C2	82
Yolombó, Col.	D5	58
Yomba Indian Reservation, Nv., U.S.	D4	105
Yonago, Japan	G6	30
Yoncalla, Or., U.S.	D3	114
Yonezawa, Japan	E13	30
Yongdeng, China	D7	26
Yongdingzhen, China	A6	34
Yongfeng, China	H4	28
Yonkers, N.Y., U.S.	E7	109
Yopal, Col.	E6	58
York, Ont., Can.	D5	73
York, Al., U.S.	C1	78
York, Me., U.S.	E2	96
York, Ne., U.S.	D8	104
York, Pa., U.S.	G8	115
York, S.C., U.S.	B5	117
York, co., Me., U.S.	E2	96
York, co., Ne., U.S.	D8	104
York, co., Pa., U.S.	G8	115
York, co., S.C., U.S.	A5	117
York, co., Va., U.S.	C6	123
York, stm., Ont., Can.	B7	73
York, stm., Va., U.S.	C6	123
York, Cape, c., Austl.	B8	50
York Beach, Me., U.S.	E2	96
York Harbor, Me., U.S.	E2	96
Yorklyn, De., U.S.	A3	85
Yorktown, In., U.S.	D7	91
Yorktown, Tx., U.S.	E4	120
Yorktown, Va., U.S.	C6	123
Yorktown Manor, R.I., U.S.	E4	116
Yorkville, Il., U.S.	B5	90
Yorkville, N.Y., U.S.	B5	109
Yorkville, Oh., U.S.	B5	112
Yoro, Hond.	G4	64
Yoron-jima, i., Japan	x28	31b
Yosemite National Park, Ca., U.S.	D4	82
Yŏsu, S. Kor.	E12	26
Youbou, B.C., Can.	g11	69
Youghal, Ire.	J5	7
Youghiogheny, stm., U.S.	F2	115
Youghiogheny River Lake, res., U.S.	G3	115
Young, Az., U.S.	C5	80
Young, co., Tx., U.S.	C3	120
Young Harris, Ga., U.S.	B3	87
Youngs, Lake, I., Wa., U.S.	f11	124
Youngstown, N.Y., U.S.	B1	109
Youngstown, Oh., U.S.	A5	112
Youngsville, La., U.S.	D3	95
Youngsville, Pa., U.S.	C3	115
Youngtown, Az., U.S.	k8	80
Youngwood, Pa., U.S.	F2	115
Youyang, China	F8	26
Ypres see Ieper, Bel.	E2	8
Ypsilanti, Mi., U.S.	F7	99
Yreka, Ca., U.S.	B2	82
Yssingeaux, Fr.	G11	10
Ystad, Swe.	I9	6
Yu, stm., China	C10	34

Yuanling, China	F9	26
Yuba, co., Ca., U.S.	C3	82
Yuba, stm., Ca., U.S.	C3	82
Yuba City, Ca., U.S.	C3	82
Yūbari, Japan	p19	30a
Yucatan Channel, strt., N.A.	C4	64
Yucatan Peninsula, pen., N.A.	H15	62
Yucca Lake, I., Nv., U.S.	F5	105
Yucca Mountain, mtn., Nv., U.S.	G5	105
Yuci, China	D9	26
Yueyang, China	F2	28
Yugoslavia, ctry., Eur.	G11	4
Yukon, Ok., U.S.	B4	113
Yukon, prov., Can.	D6	66
Yukon, stm., N.A.	m19	76a
Yukuhashi, Japan	I3	30
Yulee, Fl., U.S.	B5	86
Yulin, China	D8	26
Yulin, China	C11	34
Yuma, Az., U.S.	E1	80
Yuma, Co., U.S.	A8	83
Yuma, co., Az., U.S.	E1	80
Yuma, co., Co., U.S.	A8	83
Yuma Marine Corps Air Station, mil., Az., U.S.	E1	80
Yumen, China	D6	26
Yuncheng, China	D9	26
Yunnan, prov., China	F7	26
Yurimaguas, Peru	E3	54
Yuriria, Mex.	G9	62
Yü Shan, mtn., Tai.	L9	28
Yushu, China	E6	26
Yutan, Ne., U.S.	C9	104
Yutian, China	B9	38
Yuty, Para.	B5	56
Yuxian, China	A2	28
Yuyao, China	E10	28
Yverdon, Switz.	F13	10
Yvetot, Fr.	C7	10

Z

Zaandam, Neth.	C4	8
Zabīd, Yemen	F3	46
Zabrze, Pol.	E18	8
Zacapa, Guat.	G3	64
Zacapu, Mex.	H9	62
Zacatecas, Mex.	F8	62
Zachary, La., U.S.	D4	95
Zacualtipán, Mex.	G10	62
Zadar, Cro.	E10	14
Zadetkyi Kyun, i., Burma	J5	34
Zafer Burnu, c., N. Cyp.	B4	40
Zafra, Spain	G5	12
Zagreb, Cro.	D10	14
Zāgros, Kūhhā-ye, mts., Iran	B5	46
Zāhedān, Iran	C7	46
Zahlah, Leb.	C4	40
Zaire, ctry., Afr.	B4	44
Zajsan, Kaz.	H10	24
Zajsan, Ozero, I., Kaz.	H10	24
Zákinthos, i., Grc.	L4	16
Zakopane, Pol.	F19	8
Zalaegerszeg, Hung.	I16	8
Zambezi (Zambeze), stm., Afr.	E6	44
Zambia, ctry., Afr.	D5	44
Zamboanga, Phil.	D7	32
Zamfara, stm., Nig.	F7	42
Zamora, Ec.	J3	58
Zamora, Spain	D6	12
Zamora de Hidalgo, Mex.	H8	62
Zanesville, Oh., U.S.	C4	112
Zanjān, Iran	J7	22
Zanzibar, Tan.	C7	44
Zanzibar, i., Tan.	C7	44
Zaouia el Mgaïz, Tun.	M5	14
Zaouiet el Kahla, Alg.	C7	42
Zaoz'ornyj, Russia	F12	24
Zapadnyj Sajan, mts., Russia	G12	24
Zapala, Arg.	D2	56
Zapata, Tx., U.S.	F3	120
Zapata, co., Tx., U.S.	F3	120
Zapata, Península de, pen., Cuba	C7	64
Zaporozh'ye see Zaporožje, Ukr.	H5	22
Zaporožje, Ukr.	H5	22
Zaragoza, Spain	D11	12
Zarajsk, Russia	G21	18
Zárate, Arg.	C5	56
Zaraza, Ven.	C10	58
Zard Kūh, mtn., Iran	B5	46
Zarembo Island, i., Ak., U.S.	m23	79
Zaria, Nig.	F7	42
Zarzal, Col.	E4	58
Zāskār, stm., India	D7	38
Zāskār Mountains, mts., Asia	C4	36
Zavala, co., Tx., U.S.	E3	120
Zavolžje, Russia	E26	18
Zavol'zsk, Russia	D25	18
Zawiercie, Pol.	E19	8
Zduńska Wola, Pol.	D18	8
Zearing, Ia., U.S.	B4	92
Zebulon, Ga., U.S.	C2	87
Zebulon, N.C., U.S.	B4	110
Zeehan, Austl.	H9	50
Zeeland, Mi., U.S.	F5	99
Zeerust, S. Afr.	G5	44
Zehdenick, Ger.	C13	8
Zeigler, Il., U.S.	F4	90

Zeila, Som.	F3	46
Zeitz, Ger.	D12	8
Zeja, Russia	G19	24
Zeja, stm., Russia	G19	24
Železnogorsk-Ilimskij, Russia	F14	24
Zelienople, Pa., U.S.	E1	115
Zelina, Cro.	D11	14
Zell, Ger.	E7	8
Zell am See, Aus.	H12	8
Zemio, Cen. Afr. Rep.	G11	42
Zenica, Bos.	E12	14
Zenith, Wa., U.S.	f11	124
Zenobia Peak, mtn., Co., U.S.	A2	83
Zephyr Cove, Nv., U.S.	E2	105
Zephyrhills, Fl., U.S.	D4	86
Zerbst, Ger.	D12	8
Zereh, Gowd-e, I., Afg.	D1	36
Zermatt, Switz.	F14	10
Zeytindağ, Tur.	K11	16
Zgierz, Pol.	D19	8
Zhalutegi, China	C11	26
Zhangjiakou (Kalgan), China	C9	26
Zhangzhou (Longxi), China	K6	28
Zhanjiang, China	D11	34
Zhaoan, China	L6	28
Zhaotong, China	D8	26
Zhaxigang, China	D8	26
Zhejiang, prov., China	F10	26
Zhengzhou, China	E9	26
Zhenjiang, China	C8	28
Zhenyuan, China	F8	26
Zhitomir see Žitomir, Ukr.	G3	22
Zhob, stm., Pak.	E3	38
Zhongba, China	E3	38
Zhongshan, China	M2	28
Zhoushan Dao, i., China	E11	28
Zhoushan Qundao, is., China	E11	28
Zhujiangkou, stm., Asia	M2	28
Zhumadian, China	C3	28
Zhungeerqi, China	D9	26
Zhuoxian, China	D10	26
Zhuzhou, China	H2	28
Zia Indian Reservation, N.M., U.S.	h7	108
Zibo, China	D10	26
Ziebach, co., S.D., U.S.	C4	118
Ziel, Mount, mtn., Austl.	D6	50
Zielona Góra (Grünberg), Pol.	D15	8
Žigalovo, Russia	G15	24
Žigansk, Russia	D18	24
Zigong, China	F8	26
Ziguinchor, Sen.	F2	42
Zihuatanejo, Mex.	I9	62
Žilina, Czech.	F18	8
Zillah, Wa., U.S.	C5	124
Zillertaler Alpen, mts., Eur.	B6	14
Zilwaukee, Mi., U.S.	E7	99
Zima, Russia	G14	24
Zimbabwe, ctry., Afr.	E5	44
Zimmerman, Mn., U.S.	E5	100
Zinder, Niger	F7	42
Zion, Il., U.S.	A6	90
Zion National Park, Ut., U.S.	F3	121
Zion Reservoir, res., Az., U.S.	C6	80
Zionsville, In., U.S.	E5	91
Zipaquirá, Col.	E5	58
Zirkel, Mount, mtn., Co., U.S.	A5	83
Ziro, India	G15	38
Zitácuaro, Mex.	H9	62
Žitomir, Ukr.	G3	22
Zittau, Ger.	E14	8
Ziway, Lake, I., Eth.	G2	46
Žižickoje, Ozero, I., Russia	E14	18
Zlarin, Cro.	F10	14
Zlín, Czech.	F17	8
Žlobin, Bela.	I13	18
Zmeinogorsk, Russia	G10	24
Znojmo, Czech.	G16	8
Zolfo Springs, Fl., U.S.	E5	86
Zomba, Mwi.	E7	44
Zonguldak, Tur.	G14	4
Zorita, Spain	F6	12
Zouar, Chad	D9	42
Zrenjanin, Yugo.	D4	14
Zuckerhütl, mtn., Aus.	I11	8
Zudáñez, Bol.	G6	54
Zuera, Spain	D11	12
Zug, Switz.	E15	10
Zugspitze, mtn., Eur.	H10	8
Zuiderzee see IJsselmeer, Neth.	C4	8
Zumba, Ec.	J3	58
Zumbo, Moz.	E6	44
Zumbro, stm., Mn., U.S.	F6	100
Zumbrota, Mn., U.S.	F6	100
Zuni (Zuni Pueblo), N.M., U.S.	B1	108
Zuni, stm., U.S.	C6	80
Zuni Indian Reservation, N.M., U.S.	B1	108
Zuni Mountains, mts., N.M., U.S.	B1	108
Zunyi, China	F8	26
Zuqar, Jazīrat, i., Yemen	F3	46
Zurich, Ont., Can.	D3	73
Zürich, Switz.	E15	10
Zürichsee, I., Switz.	E15	10
Zutphen, Neth.	C6	8
Zvishavane, Zimb.	F6	44
Zvolen, Czech.	G19	8
Zwettl, Aus.	G15	8
Zwickau, Ger.	E12	8
Zwolle, La., U.S.	C2	95
Zwolle, Neth.	C6	8
Zyr'anka, Russia	D24	24
Żyrardów, Pol.	C20	8

World Political Information

This table lists the area, population, population density, form of government, political status, and capital for every country in the world.

The populations are estimates for January 1, 1992 made by Rand McNally on the basis of official data, United Nations estimates, and other available information. Area figures include inland water.

The political units listed in the table are categorized by political status, as follows:

A–independent countries; B–internally independent political entities which are under the protection of other countries in matters of defense and foreign affairs; C–colonies and other dependent political units; D–the major administrative subdivisions of Australia, Canada, China, the Soviet Union, the United Kingdom, the United States, and Yugoslavia. For comparison, the table also includes the continents and the world.

All footnotes to this table appear on page 196.

Country, Division or Region English (Conventional)	Area in sq. mi.	Area in sq. km.	Estimated Population 1/1/92	Pop. per sq. mi.	Pop. per sq. km.	Form of Government and Political Status		Capital
† Afghanistan	251,826	652,225	16,880,000	67	26	Republic	A	Kābol (Kabul)
Africa	11,700,000	30,300,000	694,000,000	59	23			
Alabama	52,423	135,775	4,099,000	78	30	State (U.S.)	D	Montgomery
Alaska	656,424	1,700,139	560,000	0.9	0.3	State (U.S.)	D	Juneau
† Albania	11,100	28,748	3,352,000	302	117	Socialist republic	A	Tiranë
Alberta	255,287	661,190	2,499,000	9.8	3.8	Province (Canada)	D	Edmonton
† Algeria	919,595	2,381,741	26,360,000	29	11	Socialist republic	A	Alger (Algiers)
American Samoa	77	199	49,000	636	246	Unincorporated territory (U.S.)	C	Pago Pago
Andorra	175	453	54,000	309	119	Coprincipality (Spanish and French protection)	B	Andorra
† Angola	481,354	1,246,700	10,425,000	22	8.4	Socialist republic	A	Luanda
Anguilla	35	91	7,000	200	77	Dependent territory (U.K. protection)	B	The Valley
Anhui	53,668	139,000	58,250,000	1,085	419	Province (China)	D	Hefei
Antarctica	5,400,000	14,000,000	(1)	—	—			
† Antigua and Barbuda	171	443	64,000	374	144	Parliamentary state	A	St. Johns
† Argentina	1,073,400	2,780,092	32,860,000	31	12	Republic	A	Buenos Aires and Viedma [6]
Arizona	114,006	295,276	3,780,000	33	13	State (U.S.)	D	Phoenix
Arkansas	53,182	137,742	2,383,000	45	17	State (U.S.)	D	Little Rock
Armenia	11,506	29,800	3,360,000	292	113	Republic	A	Jerevan
Aruba	75	193	64,000	853	332	Self-governing terr. (Netherlands protection)	B	Oranjestad
Asia	17,300,000	44,900,000	3,331,500,000	193	74			
† Australia	2,966,155	7,682,300	17,420,000	5.9	2.3	Federal parliamentary state	A	Canberra
Australian Capital Territory	927	2,400	294,000	317	123	Territory (Australia)	D	Canberra
† Austria	32,377	83,855	7,681,000	237	92	Federal republic	A	Wien (Vienna)
Azerbaijan	33,436	86,600	7,170,000	214	83	Republic	A	Baku
† Bahamas	5,382	13,939	260,000	48	19	Parliamentary state	A	Nassau
† Bahrain	267	691	546,000	2,045	790	Monarchy	A	Al-Manāmah
† Bangladesh	55,598	143,998	118,000,000	2,122	819	Islamic republic	A	Dhaka (Dacca)
† Barbados	166	430	257,000	1,548	598	Parliamentary state	A	Bridgetown
Beijing Shi	6,487	16,800	11,700,000	1,804	696	Autonomous city (China)	D	Beijing (Peking)
† Belarus	80,155	207,600	10,390,000	130	50	Republic	A	Minsk
† Belgium	11,783	30,518	9,932,000	843	325	Constitutional monarchy	A	Bruxelles (Brussels)
† Belize	8,866	22,963	232,000	26	10	Parliamentary state	A	Belmopan
† Benin	43,475	112,600	4,914,000	113	44	Republic	A	Porto-Novo and Cotonou
Bermuda	21	54	60,000	2,857	1,111	Dependent territory (U.K.)	C	Hamilton
† Bhutan	17,954	46,500	1,614,000	90	35	Monarchy (Indian protection)	B	Thimphu
† Bolivia	424,165	1,098,581	7,243,000	17	6.6	Republic	A	La Paz and Sucre
Bosnia and Hercegovina	19,741	51,129	4,519,000	229	88	Republic	A	Sarajevo
† Botswana	224,711	582,000	1,345,000	6.0	2.3	Republic	A	Gaborone
† Brazil	3,286,488	8,511,965	156,750,000	48	18	Federal republic	A	Brasília
British Columbia	365,948	947,800	3,106,000	8.5	3.3	Province (Canada)	D	Victoria
British Indian Ocean Territory	23	60	(1)	—	—	Dependent territory (U.K.)	C	
† Brunei	2,226	5,765	411,000	185	71	Monarchy	A	Bandar Seri Begawan
† Bulgaria	42,823	110,912	8,902,000	208	80	Republic	A	Sofija (Sofia)
† Burkina Faso	105,869	274,200	9,510,000	90	35	Provisional military government	A	Ouagadougou
† Burma (Myanmar)	261,228	676,577	42,615,000	163	63	Provisional military government	A	Yangon (Rangoon)
† Burundi	10,745	27,830	5,924,000	551	213	Provisional military government	A	Bujumbura
California	163,707	424,002	30,680,000	187	72	State (U.S.)	D	Sacramento
† Cambodia	69,898	181,035	8,543,000	122	47	Socialist republic	A	Phnum Pénh (Phnom Penh)
† Cameroon	183,569	475,442	11,550,000	63	24	Republic	A	Yaoundé
† Canada	3,849,674	9,970,610	26,985,000	7.0	2.7	Federal parliamentary state	A	Ottawa
† Cape Verde	1,557	4,033	393,000	252	97	Republic	A	Praia
Cayman Islands	100	259	28,000	280	108	Dependent territory (U.K.)	C	Georgetown
† Central African Republic	240,535	622,984	2,990,000	12	4.8	Republic	A	Bangui
† Chad	495,755	1,284,000	5,178,000	10	4.0	Republic	A	N'Djamena
† Chile	292,135	756,626	13,395,000	46	18	Republic	A	Santiago
† China (excl. Taiwan)	3,689,631	9,556,100	1,181,580,000	320	124	Socialist republic	A	Beijing (Peking)
Christmas Island	52	135	2,300	44	17	External territory (Australia)	C	
Cocos (Keeling) Islands	5.4	14	700	130	50	Part of Australia	C	
† Colombia	440,831	1,141,748	33,170,000	75	29	Republic	A	Santa Fe de Bogotá
Colorado	104,100	269,620	3,356,000	32	12	State (U.S.)	D	Denver
† Comoros (excl. Mayotte)	863	2,235	484,000	561	217	Federal Islamic republic	A	Moroni
† Congo	132,047	342,000	2,344,000	18	6.9	Socialist republic	A	Brazzaville
Connecticut	5,544	14,358	3,336,000	602	232	State (U.S.)	D	Hartford
Cook Islands	91	236	18,000	198	76	Self-governing territory (New Zealand protection)	B	Avarua
† Costa Rica	19,730	51,100	3,151,000	160	62	Republic	A	San José
Cote d'Ivoire, see Ivory Coast	—	—	—	—	—			
Croatia	21,829	56,538	4,800,000	220	85	Republic	A	Zagreb
† Cuba	42,804	110,861	10,785,000	252	97	Socialist republic	A	
† Cyprus (excl. North Cyprus)	2,276	5,896	713,000	313	121	Republic	A	Nicosia (Levkosía)
Cyprus, North [2]	1,295	3,355	192,000	148	57	Republic	A	Nicosia (Lefkoşa)
† Czechoslovakia	49,382	127,899	15,755,000	319	123	Federal republic	A	Praha (Prague)
Delaware	2,489	6,447	679,000	273	105	State (U.S.)	D	Dover
† Denmark	16,638	43,093	5,154,000	310	120	Constitutional monarchy	A	København (Copenhagen)
District of Columbia	68	177	611,000	8,985	3,452	Federal district (U.S.)	D	Washington
† Djibouti	8,958	23,200	351,000	39	15	Republic	A	Djibouti
† Dominica	305	790	87,000	285	110	Republic	A	Roseau
† Dominican Republic	18,704	48,442	8,124,000	434	168	Republic	A	Santo Domingo
† Ecuador	109,484	283,561	10,880,000	99	38	Republic	A	Quito
† Egypt	386,662	1,001,449	55,105,000	143	55	Socialist republic	A	Al-Qāhirah (Cairo)
† El Salvador	8,124	21,041	5,473,000	674	260	Republic	A	San Salvador
England	50,363	130,439	48,015,000	953	368	Administrative division (U.K.)	D	London
† Equatorial Guinea	10,831	28,051	384,000	35	14	Republic	A	Malabo
† Estonia	17,413	45,100	1,606,000	92	36	Republic	A	Tallinn
† Ethiopia	483,123	1,251,282	54,040,000	112	43	Socialist republic	A	Adis Abeba
Europe	3,800,000	9,900,000	695,200,000	183	70			
Faeroe Islands	540	1,399	48,000	89	34	Self-governing territory (Danish protection)	B	Tórshavn
Falkland Islands [3]	4,700	12,173	2,000	0.4	0.2	Dependent territory (U.K.)	C	Stanley
† Fiji	7,078	18,333	747,000	106	41	Republic	A	Suva
† Finland	130,559	338,145	5,001,000	38	15	Republic	A	Helsinki (Helsingfors)
Florida	65,758	170,313	13,360,000	203	78	State (U.S.)	D	Tallahassee

193

World Political Information

Country, Division or Region English (Conventional)	Area in sq. mi.	Area in sq. km.	Estimated Population 1/1/92	Pop. per sq. mi.	Pop. per sq. km.	Form of Government and Political Status	Capital
† France (excl. Overseas Departments)	211,208	*547,026*	57,010,000	270	*104*	Republic A	Paris
French Guiana	35,135	*91,000*	104,000	3.0	*1.1*	Overseas department (France) C	Cayenne
French Polynesia	1,544	*4,000*	198,000	128	*50*	Overseas territory (France) C	Papeete
Fujian	46,332	*120,000*	30,840,000	666	*257*	Province (China) D	Fuzhou
† Gabon	103,347	*267,667*	1,088,000	11	*4.1*	Republic A	Libreville
† Gambia	4,127	*10,689*	889,000	215	*83*	Republic A	Banjul
Gansu	173,746	*450,000*	23,275,000	134	*52*	Province (China) D	Lanzhou
Georgia	59,441	*153,953*	6,657,000	112	*43*	State (U.S.) D	Atlanta
Georgia	26,911	*69,700*	5,550,000	206	*80*	Republic A	Tbilisi
† Germany	137,822	*356,955*	79,710,000	578	*223*	Federal republic A	Berlin and Bonn
† Ghana	92,098	*238,533*	15,865,000	172	*67*	Provisional military government A	Accra
Gibraltar	2.3	*6.0*	31,000	13,478	*5,167*	Dependent territory (U.K.) C	Gibraltar
† Greece	50,962	*131,990*	10,285,000	202	*78*	Republic A	Athínai (Athens)
Greenland	840,004	*2,175,600*	57,000	0.1	—	Self-governing territory (Danish protection) B	Godthåb (Nuuk)
† Grenada	133	*344*	98,000	737	*285*	Parliamentary state A	St. George's
Guadeloupe (incl. Dependencies)	687	*1,780*	346,000	504	*194*	Overseas department (France) C	Basse-Terre
Guam	209	*541*	147,000	703	*272*	Unincorporated territory (U.S.) C	Agana
Guangdong	68,726	*178,000*	63,800,000	928	*358*	Province (China) D	Guangzhou (Canton)
† Guatemala	42,042	*108,889*	9,386,000	223	*86*	Republic A	Guatemala
Guernsey (incl. Dependencies)	30	*78*	58,000	1,933	*744*	Bailiwick (Channel Islands) C	St. Peter Port
† Guinea	94,926	*245,857*	7,553,000	80	*31*	Provisional military government A	Conakry
† Guinea-Bissau	13,948	*36,125*	1,036,000	74	*29*	Republic A	Bissau
Guizhou	65,637	*170,000*	33,795,000	515	*199*	Province (China) D	Guiyang
† Guyana	83,000	*214,969*	748,000	9.0	*3.5*	Republic A	Georgetown
Hainan	13,127	*34,000*	7,090,000	540	*209*	Province (China) D	Haikou
† Haiti	10,714	*27,750*	6,361,000	594	*229*	Republic A	Port-au-Prince
Hawaii	10,932	*28,313*	1,133,000	104	*40*	State (U.S.) D	Honolulu
Hebei	73,359	*190,000*	62,860,000	857	*331*	Province (China) D	Shijiazhuang
Heilongjiang	181,082	*469,000*	37,690,000	208	*80*	Province (China) D	Harbin
Henan	64,479	*167,000*	87,670,000	1,360	*525*	Province (China) D	Zhengzhou
† Honduras	43,277	*112,088*	5,342,000	123	*48*	Republic A	Tegucigalpa
Hong Kong	414	*1,072*	5,874,000	14,188	*5,479*	Chinese territory under British administration C	Victoria (Xianggang)
Hubei	72,356	*187,400*	56,360,000	779	*301*	Province (China) D	Wuhan
Hunan	81,081	*210,000*	63,810,000	787	*304*	Province (China) D	Changsha
† Hungary	35,920	*93,033*	10,555,000	294	*113*	Republic A	Budapest
† Iceland	39,769	*103,000*	261,000	6.6	*2.5*	Republic A	Reykjavík
Idaho	83,574	*216,456*	1,065,000	13	*4.9*	State (U.S.) D	Boise
Illinois	57,918	*150,007*	11,575,000	200	*77*	State (U.S.) D	Springfield
† India (incl. part of Jammu and Kashmir)	1,237,062	*3,203,975*	874,150,000	707	*273*	Federal republic A	New Delhi
Indiana	36,420	*94,328*	5,615,000	154	*60*	State (U.S.) D	Indianapolis
† Indonesia	752,410	*1,948,732*	195,300,000	260	*100*	Republic A	Jakarta
Inner Mongolia (Nei Mongol Zizhiqu)	456,759	*1,183,000*	22,685,000	50	*19*	Autonomous region (China) D	Hohhot
Iowa	56,276	*145,754*	2,801,000	50	*19*	State (U.S.) D	Des Moines
† Iran	632,457	*1,638,057*	60,000,000	95	*37*	Islamic republic A	Tehrān
† Iraq	169,235	*438,317*	19,915,000	118	*45*	Republic A	Baghdād
† Ireland	27,137	*70,285*	3,484,000	128	*50*	Republic A	Dublin (Baile Átha Cliath)
Isle of Man	221	*572*	64,000	290	*112*	Self-governing territory (U.K. protection) B	Douglas
† Israel (excl. Occupied Areas)	8,019	*20,770*	4,393,000	548	*212*	Republic A	Yerushalayim (Jerusalem)
Israeli Occupied Areas (4)	2,947	*7,632*	1,789,000	607	*234*		
† Italy	116,324	*301,277*	57,830,000	497	*192*	Republic A	Roma (Rome)
† Ivory Coast (Côte d'Ivoire)	124,518	*322,500*	13,240,000	106	*41*	Republic A	Abidjan and Yamoussoukro (5)
† Jamaica	4,244	*10,991*	2,501,000	589	*228*	Parliamentary state A	Kingston
† Japan	145,870	*377,801*	124,270,000	852	*329*	Constitutional monarchy A	Tōkyō
Jersey	45	*116*	85,000	1,889	*733*	Bailiwick (Channel Islands) C	St. Helier
Jiangsu	39,614	*102,600*	69,830,000	1,763	*681*	Province (China) D	Nanjing
Jiangxi	64,325	*166,600*	39,110,000	608	*235*	Province (China) D	Nanchang
Jilin	72,201	*187,000*	25,760,000	357	*138*	Province (China) D	Changchun
† Jordan	35,135	*91,000*	3,485,000	99	*38*	Constitutional monarchy A	'Ammān
Kansas	82,282	*213,110*	2,517,000	31	*12*	State (U.S.) D	Topeka
Kazakhstan	1,049,156	*2,717,300*	16,880,000	16	*6.2*	Republic A	Alma-Ata
Kentucky	40,411	*104,665*	3,727,000	92	*36*	State (U.S.) D	Frankfort
† Kenya	224,961	*582,646*	25,695,000	114	*44*	Republic A	Nairobi
Kiribati	313	*811*	72,000	230	*89*	Republic A	Bairiki
† Korea, North	46,540	*120,538*	22,250,000	478	*185*	Socialist republic A	P'yŏngyang
† Korea, South	38,230	*99,016*	43,305,000	1,133	*437*	Republic A	Sŏul (Seoul)
† Kuwait	6,880	*17,818*	2,244,000	326	*126*	Constitutional monarchy A	Al-Kuwayt (Kuwait)
Kwangsi Chuang (Guangxi Zhuang Zizhiqu)	91,236	*236,300*	44,310,000	486	*188*	Autonomous region (China) D	Nanning
Kyrgyzstan	76,641	*198,500*	4,385,000	57	*22*	Republic A	Biškek
† Laos	91,429	*236,800*	4,158,000	45	*18*	Socialist republic A	Viangchan (Vientiane)
† Latvia	24,595	*63,700*	2,737,000	111	*43*	Republic A	Rīga
† Lebanon	4,015	*10,400*	3,409,000	849	*328*	Republic A	Bayrūt (Beirut)
† Lesotho	11,720	*30,355*	1,824,000	156	*60*	Constitutional monarchy A	Maseru
Liaoning	56,255	*145,700*	41,590,000	739	*285*	Province (China) D	Shenyang (Mukden)
† Liberia	38,250	*99,067*	2,776,000	73	*28*	Republic A	Monrovia
† Libya	679,362	*1,759,540*	4,416,000	6.5	*2.5*	Socialist republic A	Ṭarābulus (Tripoli)
† Liechtenstein	62	*160*	28,000	452	*175*	Constitutional monarchy A	Vaduz
† Lithuania	25,174	*65,200*	3,767,000	150	*58*	Republic A	Vilnius
Louisiana	51,843	*134,275*	4,251,000	82	*32*	State (U.S.) D	Baton Rouge
† Luxembourg	998	*2,586*	390,000	391	*151*	Constitutional monarchy A	Luxembourg
Macau	6.6	*17*	448,000	67,879	*26,353*	Chinese terr. under Portuguese administration C	Macau
Macedonia	9,928	*25,713*	2,120,000	214	*82*	Republic A	Skopje
† Madagascar	226,658	*587,041*	12,380,000	55	*21*	Republic A	Antananarivo
Maine	35,387	*91,653*	1,252,000	35	*14*	State (U.S.) D	Augusta
† Malawi	45,747	*118,484*	9,523,000	208	*80*	Republic A	Lilongwe
† Malaysia	129,251	*334,758*	18,200,000	141	*54*	Federal constitutional monarchy A	Kuala Lumpur
† Maldives	115	*298*	230,000	2,000	*772*	Republic A	Male
† Mali	478,767	*1,240,000*	8,438,000	18	*6.8*	Republic A	Bamako
† Malta	122	*316*	357,000	2,926	*1,130*	Republic A	Valletta
Manitoba	250,947	*649,950*	1,129,000	4.5	*1.7*	Province (Canada) D	Winnipeg
† Marshall Islands	70	*181*	49,000	700	*271*	Republic A	Majuro (island)
Martinique	425	*1,100*	347,000	816	*315*	Overseas department (France) C	Fort-de-France
Maryland	12,407	*32,135*	4,895,000	395	*152*	State (U.S.) D	Annapolis
Massachusetts	10,555	*27,337*	6,107,000	579	*223*	State (U.S.) D	Boston
† Mauritania	395,956	*1,025,520*	2,028,000	5.1	*2.0*	Provisional military government A	Nouakchott

Country, Division or Region English (Conventional)	Area in sq. mi.	Area in sq. km.	Estimated Population 1/1/92	Pop. per sq. mi.	Pop. per sq. km.	Form of Government and Political Status		Capital
† Mauritius (incl. Dependencies)	788	2,040	1,085,000	1,377	532	Parliamentary state	A	Port Louis
Mayotte (6)	144	374	77,000	535	206	Territorial collectivity (France)	C	Dzaoudzi and Mamoudzou (5)
† Mexico	756,066	1,958,201	91,000,000	120	46	Federal republic	A	Ciudad de México (Mexico City)
Michigan	96,810	250,738	9,423,000	97	38	State (U.S.)	D	Lansing
† Micronesia, Federated States of	271	702	109,000	402	155	Republic	A	Kolonia and Paliker (5)
Midway Islands	2.0	5.2	500	250	96	Unincorporated territory (U.S.)	C	....
Minnesota	86,943	225,182	4,459,000	51	20	State (U.S.)	D	St. Paul
Mississippi	48,434	125,443	2,604,000	54	21	State (U.S.)	D	Jackson
Missouri	69,709	180,546	5,200,000	75	29	State (U.S.)	D	Jefferson City
Moldova	13,012	33,700	4,440,000	341	132	Republic	A	Kišin'ov (Chişinău)
Monaco	0.7	1.9	30,000	42,857	15,789	Constitutional monarchy	A	Monaco
† Mongolia	604,829	1,566,500	2,278,000	3.8	1.5	Socialist republic	A	Ulaanbaatar (Ulan Bator)
Montana	147,046	380,850	806,000	5.5	2.1	State (U.S.)	D	Helena
Montenegro	5,333	13,812	647,000	121	47	Republic (Yugoslavia)	D	Titograd
Montserrat	39	102	13,000	333	127	Dependent territory (U.K.)	C	Plymouth
† Morocco (excl. Western Sahara)	172,414	446,550	26,470,000	154	59	Constitutional monarchy	A	Rabat
† Mozambique	308,642	799,380	15,460,000	50	19	Republic	A	Maputo
Myanmar, see Burma	—	—	—	—	—			
† Namibia (excl. Walvis Bay)	317,818	823,144	1,548,000	4.9	1.9	Republic	A	Windhoek
Nauru	8.1	21	9,000	1,111	429	Republic	A	Yaren District
Nebraska	77,358	200,358	1,615,000	21	8.1	State (U.S.)	D	Lincoln
† Nepal	56,827	147,181	19,845,000	349	135	Constitutional monarchy	A	Kāthmāndāu (Kathmandu)
† Netherlands	16,133	41,785	15,065,000	934	361	Constitutional monarchy	A	Amsterdam and 's-Gravenhage (The Hague)
Netherlands Antilles	309	800	190,000	615	238	Self-governing terr. (Netherlands protection)	B	Willemstad
Nevada	110,567	286,368	1,257,000	11	4.4	State (U.S.)	D	Carson City
New Brunswick	28,355	73,440	743,000	26	10	Province (Canada)	D	Fredericton
New Caledonia	7,358	19,058	174,000	24	9.1	Overseas territory (France)	C	Nouméa
Newfoundland	156,649	405,720	591,000	3.8	1.5	Province (Canada)	D	St. John's
New Hampshire	9,351	24,219	1,138,000	122	47	State (U.S.)	D	Concord
New Jersey	8,722	22,590	7,850,000	900	347	State (U.S.)	D	Trenton
New Mexico	121,598	314,939	1,550,000	13	4.9	State (U.S.)	D	Santa Fe
New South Wales	309,500	801,600	5,930,000	19	7.4	State (Australia)	D	Sydney
New York	54,475	141,089	18,260,000	335	129	State (U.S.)	D	Albany
† New Zealand	103,519	268,112	3,463,000	33	13	Parliamentary state	A	Wellington
† Nicaragua	50,054	129,640	3,805,000	76	29	Republic	A	Managua
† Niger	489,191	1,267,000	8,113,000	17	6.4	Provisional military government	A	Niamey
† Nigeria	356,669	923,768	124,300,000	349	135	Provisional military government	A	Lagos and Abuja (5)
Ningsia Hui (Ningxia Huizu Zizhiqu)	25,637	66,400	4,845,000	189	73	Autonomous region (China)	D	Yinchuan
Niue	100	258	1,800	18	7.0	Self-governing terr. (New Zealand protection)	B	Alofi
Norfolk Island	14	36	2,600	186	72	External territory (Australia)	C	Kingston
North America	9,500,000	24,700,000	436,300,000	46	18			....
North Carolina	53,821	139,397	6,770,000	126	49	State (U.S.)	D	Raleigh
North Dakota	70,704	183,123	644,000	9.1	3.5	State (U.S.)	D	Bismarck
Northern Ireland	5,452	14,121	1,596,000	293	113	Administrative division (U.K.)	D	Belfast
Northern Mariana Islands	184	477	46,000	250	96	Commonwealth (U.S. protection)	B	Saipan (island)
Northern Territory	519,771	1,346,200	160,000	0.3	0.1	Territory (Australia)	D	Darwin
Northwest Territories	1,322,910	3,426,320	54,000	—	—	Territory (Canada)	D	Yellowknife
† Norway (incl. Svalbard and Jan Mayen)	149,412	386,975	4,286,000	29	11	Constitutional monarchy	A	Oslo
Nova Scotia	21,425	55,490	920,000	43	17	Province (Canada)	D	Halifax
Oceania (incl. Australia)	3,300,000	8,500,000	27,300,000	8.3	3.2			....
Ohio	44,828	116,103	10,980,000	245	95	State (U.S.)	D	Columbus
Oklahoma	69,903	181,049	3,169,000	45	18	State (U.S.)	D	Oklahoma City
† Oman	82,030	212,457	1,562,000	19	7.4	Monarchy	A	Masqaţ (Muscat)
Ontario	412,581	1,068,580	9,820,000	24	9.2	Province (Canada)	D	Toronto
Oregon	98,386	254,819	2,895,000	29	11	State (U.S.)	D	Salem
† Pakistan (incl. part of Jammu and Kashmir)	339,732	879,902	119,000,000	350	135	Federal Islamic republic	A	Islāmābād
Palau (Belau)	196	508	15,000	77	30	Part of Trust Territory of the Pacific Islands	B	Koror and Melekeok (5)
† Panama	29,157	75,517	2,503,000	86	33	Republic	A	Panamá
† Papua New Guinea	178,704	462,840	3,960,000	22	8.6	Parliamentary state	A	Port Moresby
† Paraguay	157,048	406,752	4,871,000	31	12	Republic	A	Asunción
Pennsylvania	46,058	119,291	12,042,000	261	101	State (U.S.)	D	Harrisburg
† Peru	496,225	1,285,216	22,585,000	46	18	Republic	A	Lima
† Philippines	115,831	300,000	62,380,000	539	208	Republic	A	Manila
Pitcairn (incl. Dependencies)	19	49	40	2.1	0.8	Dependent territory (U.K.)	C	Adamstown
† Poland	120,728	312,683	37,840,000	313	121	Republic	A	Warszawa (Warsaw)
† Portugal	35,516	91,985	10,410,000	293	113	Republic	A	Lisboa (Lisbon)
Prince Edward Island	2,185	5,660	134,000	61	24	Province (Canada)	D	Charlottetown
Puerto Rico	3,515	9,104	3,528,000	1,004	388	Commonwealth (U.S. protection)	B	San Juan
† Qatar	4,416	11,437	532,000	120	47	Monarchy	A	Ad-Dawḥah (Doha)
Qinghai	277,994	720,000	4,725,000	17	6.6	Province (China)	D	Xining
Quebec	594,860	1,540,680	6,911,000	12	4.5	Province (Canada)	D	Québec
Queensland	666,876	1,727,200	2,981,000	4.5	1.7	State (Australia)	D	Brisbane
Reunion	969	2,510	613,000	633	244	Overseas department (France)	C	Saint-Denis
Rhode Island	1,545	4,002	1,019,000	660	255	State (U.S.)	D	Providence
† Romania	91,699	237,500	23,465,000	256	99	Republic	A	Bucureşti (Bucharest)
† Russia	6,592,849	17,075,400	150,505,000	23	8.8	Republic	A	Moskva (Moscow)
† Rwanda (incl. Dependencies)	10,169	26,338	8,053,000	792	306	Provisional military government	A	Kigali
St. Helena (incl. Dependencies)	121	314	7,000	58	22	Dependent territory (U.K.)	C	Jamestown
† St. Kitts and Nevis	104	269	42,000	404	156	Parliamentary state	A	Basseterre
† St. Lucia	238	616	155,000	651	252	Parliamentary state	A	Castries
St. Pierre and Miquelon	93	242	6,000	65	25	Territorial collectivity (France)	C	Saint-Pierre
† St. Vincent and the Grenadines	150	388	115,000	767	296	Parliamentary state	A	Kingstown
San Marino	24	61	23,000	958	377	Republic	A	San Marino
† Sao Tome and Principe	372	964	130,000	349	135	Republic	A	São Tomé
Saskatchewan	251,866	652,330	1,052,000	4.2	1.6	Province (Canada)	D	Regina
† Saudi Arabia	830,000	2,149,690	16,690,000	20	7.8	Monarchy	A	Ar-Riyāḍ (Riyadh)
Scotland	30,414	78,772	5,125,000	169	65	Administrative division (U.K.)	D	Edinburgh
† Senegal	75,951	196,712	7,569,000	100	38	Republic	A	Dakar
Serbia	34,116	88,361	9,975,000	292	113	Republic (Yugoslavia)	D	Beograd (Belgrade)
† Seychelles	175	453	69,000	394	152	Republic	A	Victoria
Shandong	59,074	153,000	87,550,000	1,482	572	Province (China)	D	Jinan
Shanghai Shi	2,394	6,200	13,705,000	5,725	2,210	Autonomous city (China)	D	Shanghai
Shansi (Shānxī)	60,232	156,000	29,895,000	496	192	Province (China)	D	Taiyuan
Shensi (Shǎnxī)	79,151	205,000	34,030,000	430	166	Province (China)	D	Xi'an (Sian)
Sichuan	220,078	570,000	114,970,000	522	202	Province (China)	D	Chengdu

World Political Information

Country, Division or Region English (Conventional)	Area in sq. mi.	Area in sq. km.	Estimated Population 1/1/92	Pop. per sq. mi.	Pop. per sq. km.	Form of Government and Political Status		Capital
† Sierra Leone	27,925	72,325	4,330,000	155	60	Republic	A	Freetown
† Singapore	246	636	3,062,000	12,447	4,814	Republic	A	Singapore
Sinkiang (Xinjiang Uygur Zizhiqu)...	617,764	1,600,000	15,715,000	25	9.8	Autonomous region (China)	D	Ürümqi
Slovenia	7,819	20,251	1,989,000	254	98	Republic	A	Ljubljana
† Solomon Islands	10,954	28,370	353,000	32	12	Parliamentary state	A	Honiara
† Somalia	246,201	637,657	6,823,000	28	11	Provisional military government	A	Muqdisho (Mogadishu)
† South Africa (incl. Walvis Bay)	433,680	1,123,226	36,765,000	85	33	Republic	A	Pretoria, Cape Town, and Bloemfontein
South America	6,900,000	17,800,000	306,700,000	44	17			
South Australia	379,925	984,000	1,465,000	3.9	1.5	State (Australia)	D	Adelaide
South Carolina	32,007	82,898	3,559,000	111	43	State (U.S.)	D	Columbia
South Dakota	77,121	199,745	673,000	8.7	3.4	State (U.S.)	D	Pierre
South Georgia (incl. Dependencies)	1,450	3,755	(1)	—	—	Dependent territory (U.K.)	C	
† Spain	194,885	504,750	39,465,000	203	78	Constitutional monarchy	A	Madrid
Spanish North Africa [7]	12	32	137,000	11,417	4,281	Five possessions (Spain)	C	
† Sri Lanka	24,962	64,652	17,530,000	702	271	Socialist republic	A	Colombo and Kotte
† Sudan	967,500	2,505,813	27,630,000	29	11	Islamic Republic	A	Al-Khartūm (Khartoum)
† Suriname	63,251	163,820	405,000	6.4	2.5	Republic	A	Paramaribo
† Swaziland	6,704	17,364	875,000	131	50	Monarchy	A	Mbabane and Lobamba
† Sweden	173,732	449,964	8,581,000	49	19	Constitutional monarchy	A	Stockholm
Switzerland	15,943	41,293	6,804,000	427	165	Federal republic	A	Bern (Berne)
† Syria	71,498	185,180	13,210,000	185	71	Socialist republic	A	Dimashq (Damascus)
Taiwan	13,900	36,002	20,785,000	1,495	577	Republic	A	T'aipei
Tajikistan	55,251	143,100	5,210,000	94	36	Republic	A	Dušanbe
† Tanzania	364,900	945,087	27,325,000	75	29	Republic	A	Dar es Salaam and Dodoma [5]
Tasmania	26,178	67,800	463,000	18	6.8	State (Australia)	D	Hobart
Tennessee	42,146	109,158	4,959,000	118	45	State (U.S.)	D	Nashville
Texas	268,601	695,676	17,355,000	65	25	State (U.S.)	D	Austin
† Thailand	198,115	513,115	57,200,000	289	111	Constitutional monarchy	A	Krung Thep (Bangkok)
Tianjin Shi	4,363	11,300	9,100,000	2,086	805	Autonomous city (China)	D	Tianjin (Tientsin)
Tibet (Xizang Zizhiqu)	471,045	1,220,000	2,245,000	4.8	1.8	Autonomous region (China)	D	Lhasa
† Togo	21,925	56,785	3,880,000	177	68	Republic	A	Lomé
Tokelau Islands	4.6	12	1,700	370	142	Island territory (New Zealand)	C	
Tonga	290	750	103,000	355	137	Constitutional monarchy	A	Nuku'alofa
† Trinidad and Tobago	1,980	5,128	1,293,000	653	252	Republic	A	Port of Spain
† Tunisia	63,170	163,610	8,367,000	132	51	Republic	A	Tunis
† Turkey	300,948	779,452	58,850,000	196	76	Republic	A	Ankara
Turkmenistan	188,456	488,100	3,615,000	19	7.4	Republic	A	Ašchabad
Turks and Caicos Islands	193	500	12,000	62	24	Dependent territory (U.K.)	C	Grand Turk
Tuvalu	10	26	9,000	900	346	Parliamentary state	A	Funafuti
† Uganda	93,104	241,139	18,485,000	199	77	Republic	A	Kampala
† Ukraine	233,090	603,700	52,800,000	227	87	Republic	A	Kijev (Kiev)
† United Arab Emirates	32,278	83,600	2,459,000	76	29	Federation of monarchs	A	Abū Zaby (Abu Dhabi)
† United Kingdom	94,248	244,100	57,630,000	611	236	Constitutional monarchy	A	London
† United States	3,787,425	9,809,431	253,510,000	67	26	Federal republic	A	Washington
† Uruguay	68,500	177,414	3,130,000	46	18	Republic	A	Montevideo
Utah	84,904	219,900	1,757,000	21	8.0	State (U.S.)	D	Salt Lake City
Uzbekistan	172,742	447,400	20,325,000	118	45	Republic	A	Taškent
† Vanuatu	4,707	12,190	153,000	33	13	Republic	A	Port Vila
Vatican City	0.2	0.4	800	4,000	2,000	Ecclesiastical city-state	A	Città del Vaticano (Vatican City)
† Venezuela	352,145	912,050	20,430,000	58	22	Federal republic	A	Caracas
Vermont	9,615	24,903	583,000	61	23	State (U.S.)	D	Montpelier
Victoria	87,877	227,600	4,455,000	51	20	State (Australia)	D	Melbourne
† Vietnam	128,066	331,689	68,310,000	533	206	Socialist republic	A	Ha Noi
Virginia	42,769	110,771	6,333,000	148	57	State (U.S.)	D	Richmond
Virgin Islands (U.S.)	133	344	103,000	774	299	Unincorporated territory (U.S.)	C	Charlotte Amalie
Virgin Islands, British	59	153	14,000	237	92	Dependent territory (U.K.)	C	Road Town
Wake Island	3.0	7.8	200	67	26	Unincorporated territory (U.S.)	C	
Wales	8,019	20,768	2,894,000	361	139	Administrative division (U.K.)	D	Cardiff
Wallis and Futuna	98	255	17,000	173	67	Overseas territory (France)	C	Mata-Utu
Washington	71,303	184,674	4,984,000	70	27	State (U.S.)	D	Olympia
Western Australia	975,101	2,525,500	1,672,000	1.7	0.7	State (Australia)	D	Perth
Western Sahara	102,703	266,000	200,000	1.9	0.8	Occupied by Morocco		
† Western Samoa	1,093	2,831	192,000	176	68	Constitutional monarchy	A	Apia
West Virginia	24,231	62,759	1,775,000	73	28	State (U.S.)	D	Charleston
Wisconsin	65,503	169,653	4,964,000	76	29	State (U.S.)	D	Madison
Wyoming	97,818	253,349	448,000	4.6	1.8	State (U.S.)	D	Cheyenne
† Yemen	205,356	531,869	11,825,000	58	22	Republic	A	San'ā'
† Yugoslavia	39,449	102,173	10,622,000	269	104	Federal socialist republic	A	Beograd (Belgrade)
Yukon Territory	186,661	483,450	26,000	0.1	0.1	Territory (Canada)	D	Whitehorse
Yunnan	152,124	394,000	38,875,000	256	99	Province (China)	D	Kunming
† Zaire	905,446	2,345,095	38,475,000	42	16	Republic	A	Kinshasa
† Zambia	290,586	752,614	8,201,000	28	11	Republic	A	Lusaka
Zhejiang	39,305	101,800	45,255,000	1,151	445	Province (China)	D	Hangzhou
† Zimbabwe	150,873	390,759	9,748,000	65	25	Republic	A	Harare
WORLD	57,900,000	150,100,000	5,491,000,000	95	37			

† Member of the United Nations (1991).
(1) No permanent population.
(2) North Cyprus unilaterally declared its independence from Cyprus in 1983.
(3) Claimed by Argentina.
(4) Includes West Bank, Golan Heights, and Gaza Strip.
(5) Future capital.
(6) Claimed by Comoros.
(7) Comprises Ceuta, Melilla, and several small islands.

World Geographical Information

General

MOVEMENTS OF THE EARTH

The earth makes one complete revolution around the sun every 365 days, 5 hours, 48 minutes, and 46 seconds.

The earth makes one complete rotation on its axis in 23 hours, 56 minutes and 4 seconds.

The earth revolves in its orbit around the sun at a speed of 66,700 miles per hour (107,343 kilometers per hour).

The earth rotates on its axis at an equatorial speed of more than 1,000 miles per hour (1,600 kilometers per hour).

MEASUREMENTS OF THE EARTH

Estimated age of the earth, at least 4.6 billion years.

Equatorial diameter of the earth, 7,926.38 miles (12,756.27 kilometers).

Polar diameter of the earth, 7,899.80 miles (12,713.50 kilometers).

Mean diameter of the earth, 7,917.52 miles (12,742.01 kilometers).

Equatorial circumference of the earth, 24,901.46 miles (40,075.02 kilometers).

Polar circumference of the earth, 24,855.34 miles (40,000.79 kilometers).

Difference between equatorial and polar circumferences of the earth, 46.12 miles (74.23 kilometers).

Weight of the earth, 6,600,000,000,000,000,000,000 tons, or 6,600 billion billion tons (6,000 billion billion metric tons).

THE EARTH'S SURFACE

Total area of the earth, 197,000,000 square miles (510,000,000 square kilometers).

Total land area of the earth (including inland water and Antarctica), 57,900,000 square miles (150,100,000 square kilometers).

Highest point on the earth's surface, Mt. Everest, Asia, 29,028 feet (8,848 meters).

Lowest point on the earth's land surface, shores of the Dead Sea, Asia, 1,299 feet (396 meters) below sea level.

Greatest known depth of the ocean, the Mariana Trench, southwest of Guam, Pacific Ocean, 35,810 feet (10,915 meters).

THE EARTH'S INHABITANTS

Population of the earth is estimated to be 5,491,000,000 (January 1, 1992).

Estimated population density of the earth, 93 per square mile (36 per square kilometer).

EXTREMES OF TEMPERATURE AND RAINFALL OF THE EARTH

Highest temperature ever recorded, 136° F. (58° C.) at Al-'Azīzīyah, Libya, Africa, on September 13, 1922.

Lowest temperature ever recorded, -129° F. (-89° C.) at Vostok, Antarctica on July 21, 1983.

Highest mean annual temperature, 94° F. (34° C.) at Dallol, Ethiopia.

Lowest mean annual temperature, -70° F. (-50° C.) at Plateau Station, Antarctica.

The greatest local average annual rainfall is at Mt. Waialeale, Kauai, Hawaii, 460 inches (11,680 millimeters).

The greatest 24-hour rainfall, 74 inches (1,880 millimeters), is at Cilaos, Reunion Island, March 15-16, 1952.

The lowest local average annual rainfall is at Arica, Chile, .03 inches (8 millimeters).

The longest dry period, over 14 years, is at Arica, Chile, October 1903 to January 1918.

The Continents

CONTINENT	Area (sq. mi.) (sq. km.)	Estimated Population Jan. 1, 1992	Population per sq. mi. (sq. km.)	Mean Elevation (feet) (M.)	Highest Elevation (feet) (m.)	Lowest Elevation (feet) (m.)	Highest Recorded Temperature	Lowest Recorded Temperature
North America	9,500,000 (24,700,000)	436,300,000	46 (18)	2,000 (610)	Mt. McKinley, Alaska, United States 20,320 (6,194)	Death Valley, California, United States 282 (84) below sea level	Death Valley, California 134° F (57° C)	Northice, Greenland -87° F (-66° C)
South America	6,900,000 (17,800,000)	306,700,000	44 (17)	1,800 (550)	Cerro Aconcagua, Argentina 22,831 (6,959)	Salinas Chicas, Argentina 138 (42) below sea level	Rivadavia, Argentina 120° F (49° C)	Sarmiento, Argentina -27° F (-33° C)
Europe	3,800,000 (9,900,000)	695,200,000	183 (70)	980 (300)	Gora El'brus, Russia 18,510 (5,642)	Caspian Sea, Asia-Europe 92 (28) below sea level	Sevilla, Spain 122° F (50° C)	Ust' Ščugor, Russia -67° F (-55° C)
Asia	17,300,000 (44,900,000)	3,331,500,000	193 (74)	3,000 (910)	Mt. Everest, China-Nepal 29,028 (8,848)	Dead Sea, Israel-Jordan 1,299 (396) below sea level	Tirat Zevi, Israel 129° F (54° C)	Ojm'akon and Verchojansk, Russia -90° F (-68° C)
Africa	11,700,000 (30,300,000)	694,000,000	59 (23)	1,900 (580)	Kilimanjaro, Tanzania 19,340 (5,895)	Lac Assal, Djibouti 502 (153) below sea level	Al-'Azīzīyah, Libya 136° F (58° C)	Ifrane, Morocco -11° F (-24° C)
Oceania, incl. Australia	3,300,000 (8,500,000)	27,300,000	8.3 (3.2)	....	Mt. Wilhelm, Papua New Guinea 14,793 (4,509)	Lake Eyre, South Australia, Australia 52 (16) below sea level	Cloncurry, Queensland, Australia 128° F (53° C)	Charlotte Pass, New South Wales, Australia -8° F (-22° C)
Australia	2,966,155 (7,682,300)	17,420,000	5.9 (2.3)	1,000 (300)	Mt. Kosciusko, New South Wales 7,316 (2,230)	Lake Eyre, South Australia, Australia 52 (16) below sea level	Cloncurry, Queensland 128° F (53° C)	Charlotte Pass, New South Wales -8° F (-22° C)
Antarctica	5,400,000 (14,000,000)	....	....	6,000 (1830)	Vinson Massif 16,066 (4,897)	sea level	Vanda Station 59° F (15° C)	Vostok -129° F (-89° C)
World	57,900,000 (150,100,000)	5,491,000,000	95 (37)	....	Mt. Everest, China-Nepal 29,028 (8,848)	Dead Sea, Israel-Jordan 1,299 (396) below sea level	Al-'Azīzīyah, Libya 136° F (58° C)	Vostok, Antarctica -129° F (-89° C)

Historical Populations *

AREA	1650	1750	1800	1850	1900	1920	1950	1970	1980	1990
North America	5,000,000	5,000,000	13,000,000	39,000,000	106,000,000	147,000,000	219,000,000	316,600,000	365,000,000	423,600,000
South America	8,000,000	7,000,000	12,000,000	20,000,000	38,000,000	61,000,000	111,000,000	187,400,000	239,000,000	293,700,000
Europe	100,000,000	140,000,000	190,000,000	265,000,000	400,000,000	453,000,000	530,000,000	623,700,000	660,300,000	688,000,000
Asia	335,000,000	476,000,000	593,000,000	754,000,000	932,000,000	1,000,000,000	1,418,000,000	2,086,200,000	2,581,000,000	3,156,100,000
Africa	100,000,000	95,000,000	90,000,000	95,000,000	118,000,000	140,000,000	199,000,000	346,900,000	463,800,000	648,300,000
Oceania, incl. Australia	2,000,000	2,000,000	2,000,000	2,000,000	6,000,000	9,000,000	13,000,000	19,200,000	22,700,000	26,300,000
Australia	*	*	*	*	4,000,000	6,000,000	8,000,000	12,460,000	14,510,000	16,950,000
World	550,000,000	725,000,000	900,000,000	1,175,000,000	1,600,000,000	1,810,000,000	2,490,000,000	3,580,000,000	4,332,000,000	5,236,000,000

* Figures prior to 1970 are rounded to the nearest million.   Figures in italics represent very rough estimates.

Largest Countries : Population

		Population 1/1/92				Population 1/1/92
1	China	1,181,580,000	16	Turkey		58,850,000
2	India	874,150,000	17	Italy		57,830,000
3	United States	253,510,000	18	United Kingdom		57,630,000
4	Indonesia	195,300,000	19	Thailand		57,200,000
5	Brazil	156,750,000	20	France		57,010,000
6	Russia	150,505,000	21	Egypt		55,105,000
7	Nigeria	124,300,000	22	Ethiopia		54,040,000
8	Japan	124,270,000	23	Ukraine		52,800,000
9	Pakistan	119,000,000	24	South Korea		43,305,000
10	Bangladesh	118,000,000	25	Burma (Myanmar)		42,615,000
11	Mexico	91,000,000	26	Spain		39,465,000
12	Germany	79,710,000	27	Zaire		38,475,000
13	Vietnam	68,310,000	28	Poland		37,840,000
14	Philippines	62,380,000	29	South Africa		36,765,000
15	Iran	60,000,000	30	Colombia		33,170,000

Largest Countries : Area

		Area (sq. mi.)	Area (sq. km.)			Area (sq. mi.)	Area (sq. km.)
1	Russia	6,592,849	17,075,400	16	Indonesia	752,410	1,948,732
2	Canada	3,849,674	9,970,610	17	Libya	679,362	1,759,540
3	United States	3,787,425	9,809,431	18	Iran	632,457	1,638,057
4	China	3,689,631	9,556,100	19	Mongolia	604,829	1,566,500
5	Brazil	3,286,488	8,511,965	20	Peru	496,225	1,285,216
6	Australia	2,966,155	7,682,300	21	Chad	495,755	1,284,000
7	India	1,237,062	3,203,975	22	Niger	489,191	1,267,000
8	Argentina	1,073,400	2,780,092	23	Ethiopia	483,123	1,251,282
9	Kazakhstan	1,049,156	2,717,300	24	Angola	481,354	1,246,700
10	Sudan	967,500	2,505,813	25	Mali	478,767	1,240,000
11	Algeria	919,595	2,381,741	26	Colombia	440,831	1,141,748
12	Zaire	905,446	2,345,095	27	South Africa	433,680	1,123,226
13	Greenland	840,004	2,175,600	28	Bolivia	424,165	1,098,581
14	Saudi Arabia	830,000	2,149,690	29	Mauritania	395,956	1,025,520
15	Mexico	756,066	1,958,201	30	Egypt	386,662	1,001,449

World Geographical Information

Principal Mountains

NORTH AMERICA

	Height (feet)	Height (meters)
McKinley, Mt., Δ Alaska (Δ United States; Δ North America)	20,320	*6,194*
Logan, Mt., Δ Canada (Δ Yukon; Δ St. Elias Mts.)	19,524	*5,951*
Orizaba, Pico de, Δ Mexico	18,406	*5,610*
St. Elias, Mt., Alaska-Canada	18,008	*5,489*
Popocatépetl, Volcán, Mexico	17,930	*5,465*
Foraker, Mt., Alaska	17,400	*5,304*
Ixtacihuatl, Mexico	17,159	*5,230*
Lucania, Mt., Canada	17,147	*5,226*
Fairweather, Mt., Alaska-Canada (Δ British Columbia)	15,300	*4,663*
Whitney, Mt., Δ California,	14,494	*4,418*
Elbert, Mt., Δ Colorado (Δ Rocky Mts.)	14,433	*4,399*
Massive, Mt., Colorado	14,421	*4,396*
Harvard, Mt., Colorado	14,420	*4,395*
Rainier, Mt., Δ Washington (Δ Cascade Range)	14,410	*4,392*
Williamson, Mt., California	14,375	*4,382*
Blanca Pk., Colorado (Δ Sangre de Cristo Mts.)	14,345	*4,372*
La Plata Pk., Colorado	14,336	*4,370*
Uncompahgre Pk., Colorado (Δ San Juan Mts.)	14,309	*4,361*
Grays Pk., Colorado (Δ Front Range)	14,270	*4,349*
Evans, Mt., Colorado	14,264	*4,348*
Longs Pk., Colorado	14,255	*4,345*
Wrangell, Mt., Alaska	14,163	*4,317*
Shasta, Mt., California	14,162	*4,317*
Pikes Pk., Colorado	14,110	*4,301*
Colima, Nevado de, Mexico	13,993	*4,265*
Tajumulco, Volcán, Δ Guatemala (Δ Central America)	13,845	*4,220*
Gannett Pk., Δ Wyoming	13,804	*4,207*
Mauna Kea, Δ Hawaii	13,796	*4,205*
Grand Teton, Wyoming	13,770	*4,197*
Mauna Loa, Hawaii	13,679	*4,169*
Kings Pk., Δ Utah	13,528	*4,123*
Cloud Pk., Wyoming (Δ Bighorn Mts.)	13,167	*4,013*
Wheeler Pk., Δ New Mexico	13,161	*4,011*
Boundary Pk., Δ Nevada	13,143	*4,006*
Waddington, Mt., Canada (Δ Coast Mts.)	13,104	*3,994*
Robson, Mt., Canada (Δ Canadian Rockies)	12,972	*3,954*
Granite Pk., Δ Montana	12,799	*3,901*
Borah Pk., Δ Idaho	12,662	*3,859*
Humphreys Pk., Δ Arizona	12,633	*3,851*
Chirripó, Cerro, Δ Costa Rica	12,530	*3,819*
Columbia, Mt., Canada (Δ Alberta)	12,294	*3,747*
Adams, Mt., Washington	12,276	*3,742*
Gunnbjørn Mtn., Δ Greenland	12,139	*3,700*
San Gorgonio Mtn., California	11,499	*3,505*
Barú, Volcán, Δ Panama	11,411	*3,475*
Hood, Mt., Δ Oregon	11,239	*3,426*
Lassen Pk., California	10,457	*3,187*
Duarte, Pico, Δ Dominican Rep. (Δ West Indies)	10,417	*3,175*
Haleakala Crater, Hawaii (Δ Maui)	10,023	*3,055*
Paricutín, Mexico	9,213	*2,808*
El Pital, Cerro, Δ El Salvador-Honduras	8,957	*2,730*
La Selle, Pic, Δ Haiti	8,773	*2,674*
Guadalupe Pk., Δ Texas	8,749	*2,667*
Olympus, Mt., Washington (Δ Olympic Mts.)	7,965	*2,428*
Blue Mountain Pk., Δ Jamaica	7,402	*2,256*
Harney Pk., Δ South Dakota (Δ Black Hills)	7,242	*2,207*
Mitchell, Mt., Δ North Carolina (Δ Appalachian Mts.)	6,684	*2,037*
Clingmans Dome, North Carolina-Δ Tennessee (Δ Great Smoky Mts.)	6,643	*2,025*
Turquino, Pico, Δ Cuba	6,470	*1,972*
Washington, Mt., Δ New Hampshire (Δ White Mts.)	6,288	*1,917*
Rogers, Mt., Δ Virginia	5,729	*1,746*
Marcy, Mt., Δ New York (Δ Adirondack Mts.)	5,344	*1,629*
Katahdin, Mt., Δ Maine	5,268	*1,606*
Kawaikini, Hawaii (Δ Kauai)	5,243	*1,598*
Spruce Knob, Δ West Virginia	4,862	*1,482*
Pelée, Montagne, Δ Martinique	4,583	*1,397*
Mansfield, Mt., Δ Vermont (Δ Green Mts.)	4,393	*1,339*
Punta, Cerro de, Δ Puerto Rico	4,389	*1,338*
Black Mtn., Δ Kentucky-Virginia	4,145	*1,263*
Kaala, Hawaii (Δ Oahu)	4,040	*1,231*

SOUTH AMERICA

Aconcagua, Cerro, Δ Argentina; Δ Andes; (Δ South America)	22,831	*6,959*
Ojos del Salado, Nevado, Argentina-Δ Chile	22,615	*6,893*
Illimani, Nevado, Δ Bolivia	22,579	*6,882*
Bonete, Cerro, Argentina	22,546	*6,872*
Huascarán, Nevado, Δ Peru	22,133	*6,746*
Llullaillaco, Volcán, Argentina-Chile	22,057	*6,723*
Yerupaja, Nevado, Peru	21,765	*6,634*
Tupungato, Cerro, Argentina-Chile	21,555	*6,570*
Sajama, Nevado, Bolivia	21,463	*6,542*
Illampu, Nevado, Bolivia	20,873	*6,362*
Chimborazo, Δ Ecuador	20,702	*6,310*
Antofalla, Volcán, Argentina	20,013	*6,100*
Cotopaxi, Ecuador	19,347	*5,897*
Misti, Volcán, Peru	19,101	*5,822*
Huila, Nevado del, Colombia (Δ Cordillera Central)	16,896	*5,150*
Bolívar, Pico, Δ Venezuela	16,427	*5,007*
Fitzroy, Monte (Cerro Chaltel), Argentina-Chile	11,073	*3,375*
Neblina, Pico da, Δ Brazil-Venezuela	9,888	*3,014*

EUROPE

El'brus, gora, Δ Russia (Δ Caucasus; Δ Europe)	18,510	*5,642*
Dykh-Tau, Mt., Russia	17,073	*5,204*
Shkhara, Mt., Δ Georgia-Russia	16,627	*5,068*
Blanc, Mont (Monte Bianco), Δ France-Δ Italy (Δ Alps)	15,771	*4,807*
Dufourspitze, Italy-Δ Switzerland	15,203	*4,634*
Weisshorn, Switzerland	14,783	*4,506*
Matterhorn, Italy-Switzerland	14,692	*4,478*
Finsteraarhorn, Switzerland	14,022	*4,274*
Jungfrau, Switzerland	13,642	*4,158*
Écrins, Barre des, France	13,458	*4,102*
Viso, Monte, Italy (Δ Alpes Cottiennes)	12,602	*3,841*
Grossglockner, Δ Austria	12,457	*3,797*
Teide, Pico de, Δ Spain (Δ Canary Is.)	12,188	*3,715*
Mulhacén, Δ Spain (continental)	11,410	*3,478*
Aneto, Pico de, Spain (Δ Pyrenees)	11,168	*3,404*
Perdido, Monte, Spain	11,007	*3,355*
Etna, Monte, Italy (Δ Sicily)	10,902	*3,323*
Zugspitze, Austria-Δ Germany	9,721	*2,963*
Musala, Δ Bulgaria	9,596	*2,925*
Olympus, Mount (Óros Ólimbos), Δ Greece	9,570	*2,917*
Corno Grande, Italy (Δ Apennines)	9,554	*2,912*
Triglav, Δ Slovenia	9,393	*2,863*
Korabit, Maja e Δ Albania-Macedonia	9,035	*2,754*
Cinto, Monte, France (Δ Corsica)	8,878	*2,706*
Gerlachovský Štít, Δ Czechoslovakia (Δ Carpathian Mts.)	8,711	*2,655*
Moldoveanu, Δ Romania	8,346	*2,544*
Rysy, Czechoslovakia-Δ Poland	8,199	*2,499*
Glittertinden, Δ Norway (Δ Scandinavia)	8,110	*2,472*
Parnassos, Greece	8,061	*2,457*
Ídhi, Óros, Greece (Δ Crete)	8,057	*2,456*
Pico, Ponta do, Δ Portugal (Δ Azores Is.)	7,713	*2,351*
Hvannadalshnúkur, Δ Iceland	6,952	*2,119*
Kebnekaise, Δ Sweden	6,926	*2,111*
Estrela, Δ Portugal (continental)	6,539	*1,993*
Narodnaja, gora, Russia (Δ Ural Mts.)	6,217	*1,895*
Sancy, Puy de, France (Δ Massif Central)	6,184	*1,885*
Marmora, Punta la, Italy (Δ Sardinia)	6,017	*1,834*
Hekla, Iceland	4,892	*1,491*
Nevis, Ben, Δ United Kingdom (Δ Scotland)	4,406	*1,343*
Haltiatunturi, Δ Finland-Norway	4,357	*1,328*
Vesuvio, Italy	4,190	*1,277*
Snowdon, United Kingdom (Δ Wales)	3,560	*1,085*
Carrauntoohil, Δ Ireland	3,406	*1,038*
Kékes, Δ Hungary	3,330	*1,015*
Scafell Pikes, United Kingdom (Δ England)	3,210	*978*

ASIA

Everest, Mount, Δ China-Δ Nepal (Δ Tibet; Δ Himalayas; Δ Asia; Δ World)	29,028	*8,848*
K2 (Qogir Feng), China-Δ Pakistan (Δ Kashmir; Δ Karakoram Range)	28,250	*8,611*
Kānchenjunga, Δ India-Nepal	28,208	*8,598*
Makālu, China-Nepal	27,825	*8,481*
Dhawlagiri, Nepal	26,810	*8,172*
Nānga Parbat, Pakistan	26,660	*8,126*
Annapurna, Nepal	26,504	*8,078*
Gasherbrum, China-Pakistan	26,470	*8,068*
Xixabangma Feng, China	26,286	*8,012*
Nanda Devi, India	25,645	*7,817*
Kamet, China-India	25,447	*7,756*
Namjagbarwa Feng, China	25,442	*7,755*
Muztag, China (Δ Kunlun Shan)	25,338	*7,723*
Tirich Mir, Pakistan (Δ Hindu Kush)	25,230	*7,690*
Gongga Shan, China	24,790	*7,556*
Kula Kangri, Δ Bhutan	24,784	*7,554*
Kommunizma, pik, Δ Tajikistan (Δ Pamir)	24,590	*7,495*
Nowshāk, Δ Afghanistan-Pakistan	24,557	*7,485*
Pobedy, pik, China-Russia	24,406	*7,439*
Chomo Lhari, Bhutan-China	23,997	*7,314*
Muztag, China	23,891	*7,282*
Lenin, pik, Δ Kyrgyzstan-Tajikistan	23,406	*7,134*
Api, Nepal	23,399	*7,132*
Kangrinboqê Feng, China	22,028	*6,714*
Hkakabo Razi, Δ Burma	19,296	*5,881*
Damāvend, Qollah-ye, Δ Iran	18,386	*5,604*
Ağrı Dağı, Δ Turkey	16,804	*5,122*
Jaya, Puncak, Δ Indonesia (Δ New Guinea)	16,503	*5,030*
Fūlādī, Kūh-e, Afghanistan	16,243	*4,951*
Kl'učevskaja Sopka, vulkan, Russia (Δ Puluostrov Kamčatka)	15,584	*4,750*
Trikora, Puncak, Indonesia	15,584	*4,750*
Belucha, gora, Russia-Kazakhstan	14,783	*4,506*
Munch Chajrchan Ula, Mongolia	14,311	*4,362*
Kinabalu, Gunong, Δ Malaysia (Δ Borneo)	13,455	*4,101*
Yü Shan, Δ Taiwan	13,114	*3,997*
Erciyes Dağı, Turkey	12,851	*3,917*
Kerinci, Gunung, Indonesia (Δ Sumatra)	12,467	*3,800*
Fuji-san, Δ Japan (Δ Honshu)	12,388	*3,776*
Rinjani, Indonesia (Δ Lombok)	12,224	*3,726*
Semeru, Indonesia (Δ Java)	12,060	*3,676*
Nabī Shu'ayb, Jabal an-, Δ Yemen (Δ Arabian Peninsula)	12,008	*3,660*
Rantekombola, Bulu, Indonesia (Δ Celebes)	11,335	*3,455*
Slamet, Indonesia	11,247	*3,428*
Phan Si Pan, Δ Vietnam	10,312	*3,143*
Shām, Jabal ash-, Δ Oman	9,957	*3,035*
Apo, Mount, Δ Philippines (Δ Mindanao)	9,692	*2,954*
Pulog, Mount, Philippines (Δ Luzon)	9,626	*2,934*
Bia, Phou, Δ Laos	9,249	*2,819*
Shaykh, Jabal ash-, Lebanon-Δ Syria	9,232	*2,814*
Paektu-san, Δ North Korea-China	9,003	*2,744*
Inthanon, Doi, Δ Thailand	8,530	*2,600*
Pidurutalagala, Δ Sri Lanka	8,281	*2,524*
Mayon Volcano, Philippines	8,077	*2,462*
Asahi-dake, Japan (Δ Hokkaidō)	7,513	*2,290*
Tahan, Gunong, Malaysia (Δ Malaya)	7,174	*2,187*
Ólimbos, Δ Cyprus	6,401	*1,951*
Halla-san, Δ South Korea	6,398	*1,950*
Aôral, Phnum, Δ Cambodia	5,948	*1,813*
Kujū-san, Japan (Δ Kyūshū)	5,863	*1,787*
Ramm, Jabal, Δ Jordan	5,755	*1,754*
Meron, Hare, Δ Israel	3,963	*1,208*
Carmel, Mt., Israel	1,791	*546*

AFRICA

Kilimanjaro, Δ Tanzania (Δ Africa)	19,340	*5,895*
Kirinyaga (Mount Kenya), Δ Kenya	17,058	*5,199*
Margherita Peak, Δ Uganda-Δ Zaire	16,763	*5,109*
Ras Dashen Terara, Δ Ethiopia	15,158	*4,620*
Meru, Mount, Tanzania	14,978	*4,565*
Karisimbi, Volcan, Δ Rwanda-Zaire	14,787	*4,507*
Elgon, Mount, Kenya-Uganda	14,178	*4,321*
Toubkal, Jbel, Δ Morocco (Δ Atlas Mts.)	13,665	*4,165*
Cameroon Mountain, Δ Cameroon	13,451	*4,100*
Ntlenyana, Thabana, Δ Lesotho	11,425	*3,482*
eNjesuthi, Δ South Africa	11,306	*3,446*
Koussi, Emi, Δ Chad (Δ Tibesti)	11,204	*3,415*
Kinyeti, Δ Sudan	10,456	*3,187*
Santa Isabel, Pico de, Δ Equatorial Guinea (Δ Bioko)	9,869	*3,008*
Tahat, Δ Algeria (Δ Ahaggar)	9,541	*2,908*
Maromokotro, Δ Madagascar	9,436	*2,876*
Kātrīnā, Jabal, Δ Egypt	8,668	*2,642*
Sao Tome, Pico de, Δ Sao Tome	6,640	*2,024*

OCEANIA

Wilhelm, Mount, Δ Papua New Guinea	14,793	*4,509*
Giluwe, Mount, Papua New Guinea	14,330	*4,368*
Bangeta, Mt., Papua New Guinea	13,520	*4,121*
Victoria, Mount, Papua New Guinea (Δ Owen Stanley Range)	13,238	*4,035*
Cook, Mount, Δ New Zealand (Δ South Island)	12,349	*3,764*
Ruapehu, New Zealand (Δ North Island)	9,177	*2,797*
Balbi, Papua New Guinea (Δ Solomon Is.)	9,000	*2,743*
Egmont, Mount, New Zealand	8,260	*2,518*
Orohena, Mont, Δ French Polynesia (Δ Tahiti)	7,352	*2,241*
Kosciusko, Mount, Δ Australia (Δ New South Wales)	7,316	*2,230*
Silisili, Mount, Δ Western Samoa	6,096	*1,858*
Panié, Mont, Δ New Caledonia	5,341	*1,628*
Bartle Frere, Australia (Δ Queensland)	5,322	*1,622*
Ossa, Mount, Australia (Δ Tasmania)	5,305	*1,617*
Woodroffe, Mount, Australia (Δ South Australia)	4,724	*1,440*
Sinewit, Mt., Papua New Guinea (Δ Bismarck Archipelago)	4,462	*1,360*
Tomanivi, Δ Fiji (Δ Viti Levu)	4,341	*1,323*
Meharry, Mt., Australia (Δ Western Australia)	4,104	*1,251*
Ayers Rock, Australia	2,844	*867*

ANTARCTICA

Vinson Massif, Δ Antarctica	16,066	*4,897*
Kirkpatrick, Mount, Antarctica	14,856	*4,528*
Markham, Mount, Antarctica	14,049	*4,282*
Jackson, Mount, Antarctica	13,747	*4,190*
Sidley, Mount, Antarctica	13,717	*4,181*
Wade, Mount, Antarctica	13,399	*4,084*

Δ *Highest mountain in state, country, range, or region named.*

Oceans, Seas and Gulfs

	Area (sq. mi.)	Area (sq. km.)
Pacific Ocean	63,800,000	165,200,000
Atlantic Ocean	31,800,000	82,400,000
Indian Ocean	28,900,000	74,900,000
Arctic Ocean	5,400,000	14,000,000
Arabian Sea	1,492,000	3,864,000
South China Sea	1,331,000	3,447,000
Caribbean Sea	1,063,000	2,753,000
Mediterranean Sea	967,000	2,505,000
Bering Sea	876,000	2,269,000
Bengal, Bay of	839,000	2,173,000
Okhotsk, Sea of	619,000	1,603,000
Norwegian Sea	597,000	1,546,000
Mexico, Gulf of	596,000	1,544,000
Hudson Bay	475,000	1,230,000
Greenland Sea	465,000	1,204,000

Principal Lakes

	Area (sq. mi.)	Area (sq. km.)
Caspian Sea, Asia—Europe (Salt)	143,240	370,990
Superior, Lake, Canada—U.S.	31,700	82,100
Victoria, Lake, Kenya—Tanzania—Uganda	26,820	69,463
Aral Sea, Asia (Salt)	24,700	64,100
Huron, Lake, Canada—U.S.	23,000	60,000
Michigan, Lake, U.S.	22,300	57,800
Tanganyika, Lake, Africa	12,350	31,986
Bajkal, ozero, Russia	12,200	31,500
Great Bear Lake, Canada	12,095	31,326
Malawi, Lake (Lake Nyasa), Malawi—Mozambique—Tanzania	11,150	28,878
Great Slave Lake, Canada	11,030	28,568
Erie, Lake, Canada—U.S.	9,910	25,667
Winnipeg, Lake, Canada	9,416	24,387
Ontario, Lake, Canada—U.S.	7,540	19,529
Balchaš, ozero, Kazakhstan	Δ 7,100	18,300
Ladožskoje ozero, Russia	6,833	17,700
Chad, Lake (Lac Tchad), Cameroon—Chad—Nigeria	6,300	16,300
Onežskoje ozero, Russia	3,753	9,720
Eyre, Lake, Australia (Salt)	Δ 3,700	9,500
Titicaca, Lago, Bolivia—Peru	3,200	8,300
Nicaragua, Lago de, Nicaragua	3,150	8,158
Mai—Ndombe, Lac, Zaire	Δ 3,100	8,000
Athabasca, Lake, Canada	3,064	7,935
Reindeer Lake, Canada	2,568	6,650
Tônlé Sab, Cambodia	Δ 2,500	6,500
Rudolf, Lake, Ethiopia—Kenya (Salt)	2,473	6,405
Issyk-Kul', ozero, Kyrgyzstan (Salt)	2,425	6,280
Torrens, Lake, Australia (Salt)	2,300	5,900
Albert, Lake, Uganda—Zaire	2,160	5,594
Vänern, Sweden	2,156	5,584
Nettilling Lake, Canada	2,140	5,542
Winnipegosis, Lake, Canada	2,075	5,374
Bangweulu, Lake, Zambia	1,930	4,999
Nipigon, Lake, Canada	1,872	4,848
Orūmīyeh, Daryācheh-ye, Iran (Salt)	Δ 1,815	4,701
Manitoba, Lake, Canada	1,785	4,624
Woods, Lake of the, Canada—U.S.	1,727	4,472
Kyoga, Lake, Uganda	1,710	4,429
Gairdner, Lake, Australia (Salt)	Δ 1,700	4,300
Great Salt Lake, U.S. (Salt)	1,680	4,351

Δ Due to seasonal fluctuations in water level, areas of these lakes vary considerably.

Principal Rivers

	Length (miles)	Length (km.)
Nile, Africa	4,145	6,671
Amazon-Ucayali, South America	4,000	6,400
Yangtze (Chang), Asia	3,900	6,300
Mississippi-Missouri, North America	3,740	6,019
Huang (Yellow), Asia	3,395	5,464
Ob'-Irtyš, Asia	3,362	5,410
Río de la Plata-Paraná, South America	3,030	4,876
Congo (Zaïre), Africa	2,900	4,700
Paraná, South America	2,800	4,500
Amur-Argun', Asia	2,761	4,444
Amur (Heilong), Asia	2,744	4,416
Lena, Asia	2,700	4,400
Mackenzie, North America	2,635	4,241
Mekong, Asia	2,600	4,200
Niger, Africa	2,600	4,200
Jenisej, Asia	2,543	4,092
Missouri-Red Rock, North America	2,533	4,076
Mississippi, North America	2,348	3,779
Murray-Darling, Australia	2,330	3,750
Missouri, North America	2,315	3,726
Volga, Europe	2,194	3,531
Madeira, South America	2,013	3,240
São Francisco, South America	1,988	3,199
Grande, Rio (Río Bravo), North America	1,885	3,034
Purús, South America	1,860	2,993
Indus, Asia	1,800	2,900
Danube, Europe	1,776	2,858
Brahmaputra, Asia	1,770	2,849
Yukon, North America	1,770	2,849
Salween (Nu), Asia	1,750	2,816
Zambezi, Africa	1,700	2,700
Vil'uj, Asia	1,647	2,650
Tocantins, South America	1,640	2,639
Orinoco South America	1,600	2,600
Paraguay, South America	1,610	2,591
Amu Darya, Asia	1,578	2,540
Murray, Australia	1,566	2,520
Ganges, Asia	1,560	2,511
Pilcomayo, South America	1,550	2,494
Euphrates, Asia	1,510	2,430
Ural, Asia	1,509	2,428
Arkansas, North America	1,459	2,348
Colorado, North America (U.S.-Mexico)	1,450	2,334
Aldan, Asia	1,412	2,273
Syrdarja, Asia	1,370	2,205
Dnepr, Europe	1,400	2,200
Araguaia, South America	1,400	2,200
Kasai (Cassai), Africa	1,338	2,153
Tarim, Asia	1,328	2,137
Kolyma, Asia	1,323	2,129
Orange, Africa	1,300	2,100
Negro, South America	1,300	2,100
Ayeyarwady, Asia	1,300	2,100
Red, North America	1,270	2,044
Juruá, South America	1,250	2,012
Columbia, North America	1,200	2,000
Xingu, South America	1,230	1,979
Ucayali, South America	1,220	1,963
Saskatchewan-Bow, North America	1,205	1,939
Peace North America,	1,195	1,923
Tigris, Asia	1,180	1,899
Don, Europe	1,162	1,870
Songhua, Asia	1,140	1,835
Pečora, Europe	1,124	1,809
Kama, Europe	1,122	1,805
Limpopo, Africa	1,100	1,800
Angara, Asia	1,105	1,779
Snake, North America	1,038	1,670
Uruguay, South America	1,025	1,650
Churchill, North America	1,000	1,600
Marañón, South America	1,000	1,600
Tobol, Asia	989	1,591
Ohio, North America	981	1,579
Magdalena, South America	950	1,529
Roosevelt, South America	950	1,529
Oka, Europe	900	1,500
Xiang, Asia	930	1,497
Godāvari, Asia	930	1,497
Canadian, North America	906	1,458
Brazos, North America	900	1,400
Salado, South America	900	1,400
Darling, Australia	864	1,390
Fraser, North America	851	1,370
Parnaíba, South America	850	1,368
Colorado, North America (Texas)	840	1,352
Dnestr, Europe	840	1,352
Rhine, Europe	820	1,320
Narmada, Asia	800	1,300
St. Lawrence, North America	800	1,300
Ottawa, North America	790	1,271
Athabasca, North America	765	1,231
Pecos, North America	735	1,183
Severskij Donec, Europe	735	1,183
Green, North America	730	1,175
White, North America (Ar.-Mo.)	720	1,159
Cumberland, North America	720	1,159
Elbe (Labe), Europe	720	1,159
James, North America (N./S. Dakota)	710	1,143
Gambia, Africa	680	1,094
Yellowstone, North America	671	1,080
Tennessee, North America	652	1,049
Gila, North America	630	1,014
Wisła (Vistula), Europe	630	1,014
Tagus (Tejo) (Tajo), Europe	625	1,006
Loire, Europe	625	1,006
Cimarron, North America	600	1,000
North Platte, North America	618	995
Albany, North America	610	982
Tisza (Tisa), Europe	607	977
Back, North America	605	974
Ouachita, North America	605	974
Sava, Europe	585	941
Nemunas (Neman), Europe	582	937
Branco, South America	580	933
Meuse (Maas), Europe	575	925
Oder (Odra), Europe	565	909
Rhône, Europe	500	800

Principal Islands

	Area (sq. mi.)	Area (sq. km.)
Grønland (Greenland), North America	840,000	2,175,600
New Guinea, Asia—Oceania	309,000	800,000
Borneo (Kalimantan), Asia	287,300	744,100
Madagascar, Africa	226,500	587,000
Baffin Island, Canada	195,928	507,451
Sumatera (Sumatra), Indonesia	182,860	473,606
Honshū, Japan	89,176	230,966
Great Britain, United Kingdom	88,795	229,978
Victoria Island, Canada	83,897	217,291
Ellesmere Island, Canada	75,767	196,236
Sulawesi (Celebes), Indonesia	73,057	189,216
South Island, New Zealand	57,708	149,463
Jawa (Java), Indonesia	51,038	132,187
North Island, New Zealand	44,332	114,821
Cuba, North America	42,800	110,800
Newfoundland, Canada	42,031	108,860
Luzon, Philippines	40,420	104,688
Ísland (Iceland), Europe	39,800	103,000
Mindanao, Philippines	36,537	94,630
Ireland, Europe	32,600	84,400
Hokkaidō, Japan	32,245	83,515
Novaja Zeml'a (Novaya Zemlya), Russia	31,900	82,600
Sachalin, ostrov (Sakhalin), Russia	29,500	76,400
Hispaniola, North America	29,400	76,200
Banks Island, Canada	27,038	70,028
Tasmania, Australia	26,200	67,800
Sri Lanka, Asia	24,900	64,600
Devon Island, Canada	21,331	55,247
Tierra del Fuego, Isla Grande de, South America	18,600	48,200
Kyūshū, Japan	17,129	44,363
Melville Island, Canada	16,274	42,149
Southampton Island, Canada	15,913	41,214
Spitsbergen, Norway	15,260	39,523
New Britain, Papua New Guinea	14,093	36,500
T'aiwan, Asia	13,900	36,000
Hainan Dao, Asia	13,100	34,000
Prince of Wales Island, Canada	12,872	33,339
Vancouver Island, Canada	12,079	31,285
Sicilia (Sicily), Italy	9,926	25,709
Somerset Island, Canada	9,570	24,786
Sardegna (Sardinia), Italy	9,301	24,090
Shikoku, Japan	7,258	18,799
Seram (Ceram)	7,191	18,625
Nordaustlandet (North East Land), Norway	6,350	16,446
New Caledonia, Oceania	6,252	16,192
Timor, Indonesia	5,743	14,874
Flores, Indonesia	5,502	14,250
Samar, Philippines	5,100	13,080
Negros, Philippines	4,907	12,710
Palawan, Philippines	4,550	11,785
Panay, Philippines	4,446	11,515
Jamaica, North America	4,200	11,000
Hawaii, United States	4,034	10,448
Cape Breton Island, Canada	3,981	10,311
Mindoro, Philippines	3,759	9,735
Kodiak Island, United States	3,670	9,505
Bougainville, Papua New Guinea	3,600	9,300
Cyprus, Asia	3,572	9,251
Puerto Rico, North America	3,500	9,100
New Ireland, Papua New Guinea	3,500	9,000
Corse (Corsica), France	3,367	8,720
Kríti (Crete), Greece	3,189	8,259
Vrangel'a, ostrov (Wrangel Island), Russia	2,800	7,300
Leyte, Philippines	2,785	7,214
Guadalcanal, Solomon Islands	2,060	5,336
Long Island, United States	1,377	3,566

World Populations

This table includes every urban center of 50,000 or more population in the world, as well as many other important or well-known cities and towns.

The population figures are all from recent censuses (designated C) or official estimates (designated E), except for a few cities for which only unofficial estimates are available (designated U). The date of the census or estimate is specified for each country. Individual exceptions are dated in parentheses.

For many cities, a second population figure is given accompanied by a star (★). The starred population refers to the city's entire metropolitan area, including suburbs. These metropolitan areas have been defined by Rand McNally, following consistent rules to facilitate comparisons among the urban centers of various countries. Where a place is part of the metropolitan area of another city, that city's name is specified in parentheses preceded by a (★). Some important places that are considered to be secondary central cities of their areas are designated by (★ ★) preceding the name of the metropolitan area's main city. A population preceded by a triangle (▲) refers to an entire municipality, commune, or other district, which includes rural areas in addition to the urban center itself. The names of capital cities appear in CAPITALS; the largest city in each country is designated by the symbol (•).

For more recent population totals for countries, see the Rand McNally population estimates in the World Political Information table.

AFGHANISTAN / Afghānestān

1988 E 15,513,000

Cities and Towns

Herāt 177,300
Jalālābād (1982 E) 58,000
• KĀBOL 1,424,400
Mazār-e Sharīf 130,600
Qandahār 225,500
Qondūz (1982 E) 57,000

ALBANIA / Shqipëri

1987 E 3,084,000

Cities and Towns

Durrës 78,700
Elbasan 78,300
Korçë 61,500
Shkodër 76,300
• TIRANË 255,700
Vlorë 67,700

ALGERIA / Algérie / Djazaïr

1987 C 23,038,942

Cities and Towns

Aïn el Beïda 61,997
Aïn Oussera 44,270
Aïn Témouchent 47,479
• ALGER (ALGIERS) (★ 2,547,983) 1,507,241
Annaba (Bône) 305,526
Bab Ezzouar (★ Alger) 55,211
Barika 56,488
Batna 181,601
Béchar 107,311
Bejaïa (Bougie) 114,534
Biskra 128,281
Blida 170,935
Bordj Bou Arreridj 84,264
Bordj el Kiffan (★ Alger) 61,035
Bou Saada 66,688
Constantine 440,842
El Asnam 129,976
El Djelfa 84,207
El Eulma 67,933
El Wad 70,073
Ghardaïa 89,415
Ghilizane 80,091
Guelma 77,821
Jijel 62,793
Khemis 55,335
Khenchla 69,743
Laghouat 67,214
Lemdiyya 85,195
Maghniyya 52,275
Mostaganem 114,037
Mouaskar 64,691
M'Sila 65,805
Oran 628,558
Saïda 80,825
Sidi bel Abbès 152,778
Skikda 128,747
Souq Ahras 83,015
Stif 170,182
Tébessa 107,559
Tihert 95,821
Tizi-Ouzou 61,163
Tlemcen 126,882
Touggourt 70,645
Wargla 81,721

AMERICAN SAMOA / Amerika Samoa

1980 C 32,279

Cities and Towns

• PAGO PAGO 3,075

ANDORRA

1986 C 46,976

Cities and Towns

• ANDORRA 18,463

ANGOLA

1989 E 9,739,100

Cities and Towns

Benguela (1983 E) 155,000
Huambo (Nova Lisboa) (1983 E) 203,000
Lobito (1983 E) 150,000
• LUANDA 1,459,900
Lubango (1984 E) 95,915
Namibe (1981 E) 100,000

ANGUILLA

1984 C 6,680

Cities and Towns

• THE VALLEY 1,042

ANTIGUA AND BARBUDA

1977 E 72,000

Cities and Towns

• SAINT JOHNS 24,359

ARGENTINA

1980 C 27,947,446

Cities and Towns

Almirante Brown (★ Buenos Aires) 331,919
Avellaneda (★ Buenos Aires) 334,145
Bahía Blanca 223,818
Berazategui (★ Buenos Aires) 201,862
Berisso (★ Buenos Aires) 66,152
• BUENOS AIRES (★ 10,750,000) 2,922,829
Campana (★ Buenos Aires) 54,832
Caseros (Tres de Febrero) (★ Buenos Aires) 345,424
Catamarca (★ 90,000) 78,799
Comodoro Rivadavia 96,817
Concordia 94,222
Córdoba (★ 1,070,000) 993,055
Corrientes 180,612
Esteban Echeverría (★ Buenos Aires) 188,923
Florencio Varela (★ Buenos Aires) 173,452
Formosa 93,603
General San Martín (★ Buenos Aires) 385,625
General Sarmiento (San Miguel) (★ Buenos Aires) 502,926
Godoy Cruz (★ Mendoza) 142,408
Gualeguaychú 51,400
Junín 62,458
Lanús (★ Buenos Aires) 466,980
La Plata (★★ Buenos Aires) 477,175
La Rioja 67,043
Las Heras (★ Mendoza) 101,579
Lomas de Zamora (★ Buenos Aires) 510,130
Mar del Plata 414,696
Mendoza (★ 650,000) 119,088
Mercedes 50,992
Merlo (★ Buenos Aires) 292,587
Moreno (★ Buenos Aires) 194,440
Morón (★ Buenos Aires) 598,420
Necochea 51,069
Neuquén 90,089
Olavarría 64,097
Paraná 161,638
Pergamino 68,612
Pilar (★ Buenos Aires) 84,429
Posadas 143,889
Presidencia Roque Sáenz Peña 49,341
Punta Alta 56,620
Quilmes (★ Buenos Aires) 446,587
Rafaela 53,273
Resistencia 220,104
Río Cuarto 110,254
Rosario (★ 1,045,000) 938,120
Salta 260,744
San Carlos de Bariloche 48,980
San Fernando (★ Buenos Aires) 133,624
San Francisco (★ 58,536) 51,932
San Isidro (★ Buenos Aires) 289,170
San Juan (★ 300,000) 118,046
San Justo (★ Buenos Aires) 949,566
San Lorenzo (★ Rosario) 96,891
San Luis 70,999
San Miguel de Tucumán (★ 525,000) 392,888
San Nicolás de los Arroyos 98,495
San Rafael 70,959
San Salvador de Jujuy 124,950
Santa Fe 292,165
Santiago del Estero (★ 200,000) 148,758
San Vicente (★ Buenos Aires) 55,803
Tandil 79,429
Tigre (★ Buenos Aires) 206,349
Trelew 52,372
Vicente López (★ Buenos Aires) 291,072
Villa Krause (★ San Juan) 66,693
Villa María 67,560
Villa Nueva (★ Mendoza) 164,670
Zárate 67,143

ARMENIA / Hayastan

1989 C 3,283,000

Cities and Towns

Abovjan (1987 E) 53,000
Čardžou 161,000
Ečmiadzin (★ Jerevan) (1987 E) 53,000
• JEREVAN (★ 1,315,000) 1,199,000
Kirovakan (1987 E) 169,000
Kumajri 120,000
Razdan (1987 E) 56,000

ARUBA

1987 E 64,763

Cities and Towns

• ORANJESTAD 19,800

AUSTRALIA

1989 E 16,833,100

Cities and Towns

Adelaide (★ 1,036,747) 12,340
Albury (★ 66,530) 40,730
Auburn (★ Sydney) 49,950
Ballarat (★ 80,090) 36,680
Bankstown (★ Sydney) 158,750
Bendigo (★ 67,920) 32,050
Berwick (★ Melbourne) 64,100
Blacktown (★ Sydney) 210,900
Blue Mountains (★ Sydney) 70,800
Brisbane (★ 1,273,511) 744,828
Broadmeadows (★ Melbourne) 105,500
Cairns (★ 80,875) 42,839
Camberwell (★ Melbourne) 87,700
Campbelltown (★ Sydney) 139,500
CANBERRA (★ 271,362) (1986 C) 247,194
Canning (★ Perth) 69,104
Canterbury (★ Sydney) 135,200
Caulfield (★ Melbourne) 70,100
Coburg (★ Melbourne) 54,500
Cockburn (★ Perth) 49,802
Dandenong (★ Melbourne) 59,400
Darwin (★ 72,937) 63,900
Doncaster (★ Melbourne) 107,300
Enfield (★ Adelaide) 64,058
Essendon (★ Melbourne) 55,300
Fairfield (★ Sydney) 176,350
Footscray (★ Melbourne) 48,700
Frankston (★ Melbourne) 90,500
Geelong (★ 148,980) 13,190
Gosford 126,600
Gosnells (★ Perth) 71,862
Heidelberg (★ Melbourne) 63,500
Hobart (★ 181,210) 47,280
Holroyd (★ Sydney) 82,500
Hurstville (★ Sydney) 66,350
Ipswich (★ Brisbane) 75,283
Keilor (★ Melbourne) 103,700
Knox (★ Melbourne) 121,300
Lake Macquarie (★ Newcastle) 161,700
Launceston (★ 92,350) 32,150
Leichhardt (★ Sydney) 58,950
Liverpool (★ Sydney) 99,750
Logan (★ Brisbane) 142,222
Mackay (★ 50,885) 22,583
Marion (★ Adelaide) 74,631
Marrickville (★ Sydney) 84,650
Melbourne (★ 3,039,100) 55,300
Melville (★ Perth) 85,590
Mitcham (★ Adelaide) 63,301
Moorabbin (★ Melbourne) 98,900
Newcastle (★ 425,610) 130,940
Noarlunga (★ Adelaide) 77,352
Northcote (★ Melbourne) 49,100
North Sydney (★ Sydney) 53,400
Nunawading (★ Melbourne) 96,400
Oakleigh (★ Melbourne) 57,600
Parramatta (★ Sydney) 134,600
Penrith (★ Sydney) 152,650
Perth (★ 1,158,387) 82,413
Preston (★ Melbourne) 82,000
Randwick (★ Sydney) 119,200
Redcliffe (★ Brisbane) 48,123
Rockdale (★ Sydney) 88,200
Rockhampton (★ 61,694) 58,890
Ryde (★ Sydney) 94,400
Salisbury (★ Adelaide) 106,129
Shoalhaven 64,070
Southport (★ 254,861) 135,408
South Sydney (★ Sydney) 74,100
Springvale (★ Melbourne) 88,700
Stirling (★ Perth) 181,556
Sunshine (★ Melbourne) 97,700
• Sydney (★ 3,623,550) 9,800
Tea Tree Gully (★ Adelaide) 82,324
Toowoomba 81,071
Townsville (★ 111,972) 83,339
Wagga Wagga 52,180
Wanneroo (★ Perth) 163,324
Waverley (★ Melbourne) 126,300
Waverley (★ Sydney) 61,850
Willoughby (★ Sydney) 53,950
Wollongong (★ 236,690) 174,770
Woodville (★ Adelaide) 82,590
Woollahra (★ Sydney) 53,850

AUSTRIA / Österreich

1981 C 7,555,338

Cities and Towns

Graz (★ 325,000) 243,166
Innsbruck (★ 185,000) 117,287
Klagenfurt (★ 115,000) 87,321
Linz (★ 335,000) 199,910
Salzburg (★ 220,000) 139,426
Sankt Pölten (★ 67,000) 50,419
Villach (★ 65,000) 52,692
Wels (★ 76,000) 51,060
• WIEN (VIENNA) (★ 1,875,000) (1988 E) 1,482,800

AZERBAIJAN / Azerbajdžan

1989 C 7,029,000

Cities and Towns

Ali-Bajramly (1987 E) 51,000
• BAKU (★ 2,020,000) 1,150,000
Chudžand 160,000
Gjandža 278,000
Kurgan-T'ube (1987 E) 55,000
Mingečaur (1987 E) 78,000
Nachičevan' (1987 E) 51,000
Šeki (Nucha) (1987 E) 54,000
Sumgait (★ Baku) 231,000

BAHAMAS

1982 E 218,000

Cities and Towns

• NASSAU 135,000

BAHRAIN / Al-Baḥrayn

1981 C 350,798

Cities and Towns

• AL-MANĀMAH (★ 224,643) 115,054
Al-Muharraq (★ Al-Manāmah) 57,688

BANGLADESH

1981 C 87,119,965

Cities and Towns

Barisāl 172,905
Begamganj 69,623
Bhairab Bāzār 63,563
Bogra 68,749
Brāhmanbāria 87,570
Chāndpur 85,656
Chittagong (★ 1,391,877) 980,000
Chuādanga 76,000
Comilla 184,132
• DHAKA (DACCA) (★ 3,430,312) 2,365,695
Dinājpur 96,718
Farīdpur 66,579
Gulshan (★ Dhaka) 215,444
Jamālpur 91,815
Jessore 148,927
Khulna 648,359
Kishorganj 52,302
Kushtia 74,892
Mādārīpur 63,917
Mīrpur (★ Dhaka) 349,031
Mymensingh 190,991
Naogaon 52,975
Nārāyanganj (★★ Dhaka) 405,562
Narsinghdi 76,841
Nawābganj 87,724
Noākhāli 59,065
Pābna 109,065
Patuākhāli 48,121
Rājshāhi 253,740
Rangpur 153,174
Saidpur 126,608
Sātkhira 52,156
Sherpur 48,214
Sirājganj 106,774
Sītākunda (★ Chittagong) 237,520
Sylhet 168,371
Tangail 77,518
Tongi (★ Dhaka) 94,580

BARBADOS

1980 C 244,228

Cities and Towns

• BRIDGETOWN (★ 115,000) 7,466

BELARUS / Byelarus'

1989 C 10,200,000

Cities and Towns

Baranoviči 159,000
Bobrujsk 223,000
Borisov 144,000
Brest 258,000
Gomel' 500,000
Grodno 270,000
Lida (1987 E) 81,000
• MINSK (★ 1,650,000) 1,589,000
Mogil'ov 356,000
Molodečno (1987 E) 87,000
Mozyr' 101,000
Novopolock (1987 E) 90,000
Orša 123,000
Pinsk 119,000
Polock (1987 E) 80,000
Rečica (1987 E) 71,000
Sluck (1987 E) 55,000
Soligorsk (1987 E) 92,000
Svetlogorsk (1987 E) 68,000
Vitebsk 350,000
Žlobin (1987 E) 52,000
Žodino (1987 E) 51,000

BELGIUM / België / Belgique

1987 E 9,864,751

Cities and Towns

Aalst (Alost) (★ Bruxelles) 77,113
Anderlecht (★ Bruxelles) 88,849
Antwerpen (★ 1,100,000) 479,748
Brugge (Bruges) (★ 223,000) 117,755
• BRUXELLES (BRUSSEL) (★ 2,385,000) 136,920
Charleroi (★ 480,000) 209,395
Forest (★ Bruxelles) 48,266
Genk (★★ Hasselt) 61,391
Gent (Gand) (★ 465,000) 233,856
Hasselt (★ 290,000) 65,563
Ixelles (★ Bruxelles) 76,241
Kortrijk (Courtrai) (★ 202,000) 76,216
La Louvière (★ 147,000) 76,340
Leuven (Louvain) (★ 173,000) 84,583
Liège (Luik) (★ 750,000) 200,891
Mechelen (Malines) (★ 121,000) 75,808
Molenbeek-St.-Jean (★ Bruxelles) 69,764
Mons (Bergen) (★ 242,000) 89,697
Mouscron (★ Lille, France) 53,713
Namur (★ 147,000) 102,670
Oostende (Ostende) (★ 122,000) 68,318

C Census. E Official estimate. U Unofficial estimate.
• Largest city in country.

★ Population or designation of metropolitan area, including suburbs (see headnote).
▲ Population of an entire municipality, commune, or district, including rural area.

Roeselare (Roulers) ... 51,963
Schaerbeek (★ Bruxelles) ... 104,919
Seraing (★ Liège) ... 61,731
Sint-Niklaas (Saint-Nicolas) ... 68,082
Tournai (Doornik) (▲ 66,998) ... 44,900
Uccle (★ Bruxelles) ... 75,876
Verviers (★ 101,000) ... 53,498

BELIZE

1985 E ... 166,400

Cities and Towns

• Belize City ... 47,000
BELMOPAN ... 4,500

BENIN / Bénin

1984 E ... 3,825,000

Cities and Towns

Abomey ... 53,000
• COTONOU ... 478,000
Natitingou (1975 E) ... 51,000
Ouidah (1979 E) ... 53,000
Parakou ... 92,000
PORTO-NOVO ... 164,000

BERMUDA

1985 E ... 56,000

Cities and Towns

• HAMILTON (★ 15,000) ... 1,676

BHUTAN / Druk-Yul

1982 E ... 1,333,000

Cities and Towns

• THIMPHU ... 12,000

BOLIVIA

1985 E ... 6,429,226

Cities and Towns

Cochabamba ... 317,251
• LA PAZ ... 992,592
Oruro ... 178,393
Potosí ... 113,380
Santa Cruz ... 441,717
SUCRE ... 86,609
Tarija ... 60,621

BOSNIA AND HERCEGOVINA / Bosna i Hercegovina

1987 E ... 4,400,464

Cities and Towns

Banja Luka (▲ 193,890) ... 130,900
• SARAJEVO (▲ 479,688) ... 341,200
Tuzla (▲ 129,967) ... 67,300
Zenica (▲ 144,869) ... 67,500

BOTSWANA

1987 E ... 1,169,000

Cities and Towns

Francistown (1986 E) ... 43,837
• GABORONE ... 107,677
Selebi Phikwe (1986 E) ... 41,382

BRAZIL / Brasil

1985 E ... 135,564,395

Cities and Towns

Alagoinhas (▲ 116,959) ... 87,500
Alegrete (▲ 71,898) ... 56,700
Alvorada ... 105,730
Americana ... 156,030
Anápolis ... 225,840
Apucarana (▲ 92,812) ... 73,700
Aracaju ... 360,013
Araçatuba ... 129,304
Araguari (▲ 96,035) ... 84,300
Arapiraca (▲ 147,879) ... 91,400
Araraquara (▲ 145,042) ... 87,500
Araras (▲ 71,652) ... 59,900
Araxá ... 61,418
Assis (▲ 74,238) ... 63,100
Bagé (▲ 106,155) ... 70,800
Barbacena (▲ 99,337) ... 80,200
Barra do Piraí (▲ 78,189) ... 55,700
Barra Mansa (★ Volta Redonda) ... 149,200
Barretos ... 80,202
Bauru ... 220,105
Bayeux (★ João Pessoa) ... 67,182
Belém (★ 1,200,000) ... 1,116,578
Belford Roxo (★ Rio de Janeiro) ... 340,700
Belo Horizonte (★ 2,950,000) ... 2,114,429
Betim (★ Belo Horizonte) ... 96,810
Blumenau ... 192,074
Boa Vista ... 66,028
Botucatu (▲ 71,139) ... 62,600
Bragança Paulista (▲ 105,099) ... 76,300
BRASÍLIA ... 1,567,709
Caçapava (▲ 64,213) ... 56,600
Cachoeira do Sul (▲ 91,492) ... 58,900
Cachoeirinha (★ Porto Alegre) ... 73,117
Cachoeiro de Itapemirim (▲ 138,156) ... 95,000
Campina Grande ... 279,929
Campinas (★ 1,125,000) ... 841,016
Campo Grande ... 384,398
Campos (▲ 366,716) ... 187,900
Campos Elyseos (★ Rio de Janeiro) ... 188,200
Canoas (★ Porto Alegre) ... 261,222
Carapicuíba (★ São Paulo) ... 265,856
Carazinho (▲ 62,108) ... 48,500
Cariacica (★ Vitória) ... 74,300
Caruaru (▲ 190,794) ... 152,100
Cascavel (▲ 200,485) ... 123,100
Castanhal (▲ 89,703) ... 71,200
Catanduva (▲ 80,309) ... 71,400
Caucaia (★ Fortaleza) ... 78,500
Cavaleiro (★ Recife) ... 106,600
Caxias (▲ 148,230) ... 66,300
Caxias do Sul ... 266,809
Chapecó (▲ 100,997) ... 64,200
Coelho da Rocha (★ Rio de Janeiro) ... 164,400
Colatina (▲ 106,260) ... 58,600
Colombo (★ Curitiba) ... 65,900
Conselheiro Lafaiete ... 77,958
Contagem (★ Belo Horizonte) ... 152,700
Corumbá (▲ 80,666) ... 65,800
Crato (▲ 86,371) ... 52,700
Criciúma (▲ 128,410) ... 85,900
Cruz Alta (▲ 71,817) ... 58,300
Cruzeiro ... 63,918
Cubatão (★ Santos) ... 98,322
Cuiabá (▲ 279,651) ... 220,400
Curitiba (★ 1,700,000) ... 1,279,205
Diadema (★ São Paulo) ... 320,187
Divinópolis ... 139,940
Dourados (▲ 123,757) ... 89,200
Duque de Caxias (★ Rio de Janeiro) ... 353,200
Embu (★ São Paulo) ... 119,791
Erechim (▲ 70,709) ... 54,300
Esteio (★ Porto Alegre) ... 58,964
Feira de Santana (▲ 355,201) ... 278,600
Ferraz de Vasconcelos (★ São Paulo) ... 68,831
Florianópolis (★ 365,000) ... 178,400
Fortaleza (★ 1,825,000) ... 1,582,414
Foz do Iguaçu (▲ 182,101) ... 124,900
Franca ... 182,820
Garanhuns ... 73,100
Goiânia (★ 990,000) ... 923,333
Governador Valadares (▲ 216,957) ... 192,300
Guaratinguetá (▲ 93,534) ... 80,400
Guarujá (★ Santos) ... 83,500
Guarulhos (★ São Paulo) ... 571,700
Ijuí (▲ 82,064) ... 64,400
Ilhéus (▲ 145,810) ... 79,400
Imperatriz (▲ 235,453) ... 119,500
Ipatinga (★ 270,000) ... 149,100
Ipiíba (★ Rio de Janeiro) ... 116,200
Itabira (▲ 81,771) ... 66,300
Itabuna (▲ 167,543) ... 142,200
Itajaí ... 104,232
Itajubá (▲ 69,675) ... 61,500
Itapecerica da Serra (★ São Paulo) ... 65,500
Itapetininga (▲ 105,512) ... 76,700
Itapevi (★ São Paulo) ... 66,825
Itaquaquecetuba (★ São Paulo) ... 91,366
Itaguari (★ Vitória) ... 163,900
Itaúna ... 61,446
Itu (▲ 92,786) ... 77,900
Ituiutaba (▲ 85,365) ... 74,900
Itumbiara (▲ 78,844) ... 57,200
Jaboatão (★ Recife) ... 82,900
Jacareí ... 149,061
Jaú (▲ 92,547) ... 74,500
Jequié (▲ 127,070) ... 92,100
João Pessoa (★ 550,000) ... 348,500
Joinvile ... 302,877
Juàzeiro (★ Petrolina) ... 78,600
Juàzeiro do Norte ... 159,806
Juiz de Fora ... 349,720
Jundiaí (▲ 313,652) ... 268,900
Lajes (▲ 143,246) ... 103,600
Lavras ... 52,100
Limeira ... 186,986
Linhares (▲ 122,453) ... 53,400
Londrina (▲ 346,676) ... 296,400
Lorena ... 63,230
Luziânia (▲ 98,408) ... 71,400
Macapá (▲ 168,839) ... 109,400
Maceió ... 482,195
Manaus ... 809,914
Marabá (▲ 133,559) ... 92,700
Marília (▲ 136,187) ... 116,100
Maringá ... 196,871
Mauá (★ São Paulo) ... 269,321
Mesquita (★ Rio de Janeiro) ... 161,300
Mogi das Cruzes (★ São Paulo) ... 144,800
Mogi-Guaçu (▲ 91,994) ... 81,800
Mogi-Mirim (▲ 63,313) ... 52,300
Monjolo (★ Rio de Janeiro) ... 113,900
Montes Claros (▲ 214,472) ... 183,500
Mossoró (▲ 158,723) ... 128,300
Muriaé (▲ 80,466) ... 57,600
Muribeca dos Guararapes (★ Recife) ... 171,200
Natal ... 510,106
Neves (★ Rio de Janeiro) ... 163,600
Nilópolis (★ Rio de Janeiro) ... 112,800
Niterói (★ Rio de Janeiro) ... 441,684
Nova Friburgo (▲ 143,529) ... 103,500
Nova Iguaçu (★ Rio de Janeiro) ... 592,800
Novo Hamburgo (★ Porto Alegre) ... 167,744
Olinda (★ Recife) ... 316,600
Osasco (★ São Paulo) ... 591,568
Ourinhos (▲ 65,841) ... 58,100
Paranaguá (▲ 94,809) ... 82,300
Paranavaí (▲ 75,511) ... 60,900
Parnaíba (▲ 116,206) ... 90,200
Parque Industrial (★ Belo Horizonte) ... 228,400
Passo Fundo (▲ 137,843) ... 117,500
Passos (▲ 79,393) ... 65,500
Patos ... 74,298
Patos de Minas (▲ 99,027) ... 69,000
Paulo Afonso (▲ 86,182) ... 75,300
Pelotas (▲ 277,730) ... 210,300
Petrolina (★ 225,000) ... 92,100
Petrópolis (★ Rio de Janeiro) ... 170,300
Pindamonhangaba (▲ 86,990) ... 64,100
Pinheirinho (★ Curitiba) ... 51,600
Piracicaba (▲ 252,079) ... 211,000
Poá (★ São Paulo) ... 66,006
Poços de Caldas ... 100,004
Ponta Grossa ... 223,154
Porto Alegre (★ 2,600,000) ... 1,272,121
Porto Velho (▲ 202,011) ... 152,700
Pouso Alegre (▲ 65,958) ... 58,300
Praia Grande (★ Santos) ... 67,800
Presidente Prudente ... 155,883
Queimados (★ Rio de Janeiro) ... 113,700
Recife (★ 2,625,000) ... 1,287,623
Ribeirão Prêto ... 383,125
Rio Branco (▲ 145,486) ... 109,800
Rio Claro ... 129,859
Rio de Janeiro (★ 10,150,000) ... 5,603,388
Rio Grande ... 164,221
Rio Verde (▲ 92,954) ... 59,400
Rondonópolis (▲ 101,642) ... 65,500
Salvador (★ 2,050,000) ... 1,804,438
Santa Bárbara d'Oeste ... 95,818
Santa Cruz do Sul (▲ 115,288) ... 60,300
Santa Maria (▲ 196,827) ... 163,900
Santana do Livramento (▲ 70,489) ... 60,100
Santarém (▲ 226,618) ... 120,800
Santa Rita (★ João Pessoa) ... 60,100
Santo André (★ São Paulo) ... 635,129
Santo Angelo (▲ 107,559) ... 57,700
Santos (★ 1,065,000) ... 460,100
São Bernardo do Campo (★ São Paulo) ... 562,485
São Caetano do Sul (★ São Paulo) ... 171,005
São Carlos ... 140,383
São Gonçalo (★ Rio de Janeiro) ... 262,400
São João da Boa Vista (▲ 61,653) ... 50,400
São João del Rei (▲ 74,385) ... 61,400
São João de Meriti (★ Rio de Janeiro) ... 241,700
São José do Rio Prêto ... 229,221
São José dos Campos ... 372,578
São José dos Pinhais (★ Curitiba) ... 64,100
São Leopoldo (★ Porto Alegre) ... 114,065
São Lourenço da Mata (★ Recife) ... 65,936
São Luís (★ 600,000) ... 227,900
• São Paulo (★ 15,175,000) ... 10,063,110
São Vicente (★ Santos) ... 239,778
Sapucaia do Sul (★ Porto Alegre) ... 91,820
Sete Lagoas ... 121,418
Sete Pontes (★ Rio de Janeiro) ... 72,300
Sobral (▲ 112,275) ... 69,400
Sorocaba ... 327,468
Suzano (★ São Paulo) ... 128,924
Taboão da Serra (★ São Paulo) ... 122,112
Tatuí (▲ 69,358) ... 56,000
Taubaté ... 205,120
Teófilo Otoni (▲ 126,265) ... 82,700
Teresina (★ 525,000) ... 425,300
Teresópolis (▲ 115,859) ... 92,600
Timon (★ Teresina) ... 68,300
Tubarão (▲ 82,082) ... 70,400
Uberaba ... 244,875
Uberlândia ... 312,024
Uruguaiana (▲ 105,862) ... 91,500
Varginha ... 74,630
Vicente de Carvalho (★ Santos) ... 102,700
Vila Velha (★ Vitória) ... 91,900
Vitória (★ 735,000) ... 201,500
Vitória da Conquista (▲ 198,150) ... 145,800
Vitória de Santo Antão (▲ 100,450) ... 67,800
Volta Redonda (★ 375,000) ... 219,267

BRITISH VIRGIN ISLANDS

1980 C ... 12,034

Cities and Towns

• ROAD TOWN ... 2,479

BRUNEI

1981 C ... 192,832

Cities and Towns

• BANDAR SERI BEGAWAN (★ 64,000) ... 22,777

BULGARIA / Bâlgarija

1986 E ... 9,913,000

Cities and Towns

Blagoevgrad ... 67,766
Burgas ... 186,369
Dimitrovgrad ... 54,898
Dobrič ... 110,471
Gabrovo ... 81,688
Haskovo ... 89,273
Jambol ... 92,321
Kârdžali ... 56,906
Kazanlâk ... 61,780
Kjustendil ... 54,773
Loveč (1985 E) ... 48,862
Mihajlovgrad ... 53,529
Pazardžik ... 79,198
Pernik ... 96,277
Pleven ... 132,206
Plovdiv ... 349,148
Razgrad ... 51,277
Ruse ... 186,428
Silistra ... 54,627
Sliven ... 104,345
• SOFIJA (SOFIA) (★ 1,205,000) ... 1,119,152
Stara Zagora ... 153,538
Šumen ... 102,886
Varna ... 303,071
Veliko Târnovo ... 70,610
Vidin ... 63,813
Vraca ... 77,934

BURKINA FASO

1985 C ... 7,964,705

Cities and Towns

Bobo Dioulasso ... 228,668
Koudougou ... 51,926
• OUAGADOUGOU ... 441,514

BURMA / Myanmar

1983 C ... 34,124,908

Cities and Towns

Bago (Pegu) ... 150,528
Chauk ... 51,437
Dawei (Tavoy) ... 69,882
Henzada ... 82,005
Kale ... 52,628
Lashio ... 88,590
Magway ... 54,881
Mandalay ... 532,949
Mawlamyine (Moulmein) ... 219,961
Maymyo ... 63,782
Meiktila ... 96,496
Mergui (Myeik) ... 88,600
Mogok ... 49,392
Monywa ... 106,843
Myingyan ... 77,060
Myitkyinā ... 56,427
Pakokku ... 71,860
Pathein (Bassein) ... 144,096
Pyè (Prome) ... 83,332
Pyinmana ... 52,962
Shwebo ... 52,185
Sittwe (Akyab) ... 107,621
Taunggyi ... 108,231
Thaton ... 61,790
Toungoo ... 65,861
• YANGON (RANGOON) (★ 2,800,000) ... 2,705,039
Yenangyaung ... 62,582

BURUNDI

1986 E ... 4,782,000

Cities and Towns

• BUJUMBURA ... 273,000
Gitega ... 95,000

CAMBODIA / Kâmpŭchéa

1986 E ... 7,492,000

Cities and Towns

Kâmpóng Saôm (1981 E) ... 53,000
• PHNUM PENH ... 700,000

CAMEROON / Cameroun

1986 E ... 10,446,409

Cities and Towns

Bafoussam (1985 E) ... 89,000
Bamenda (1985 E) ... 72,000
• Douala ... 1,029,731
Foumban (1985 E) ... 50,000
Garoua (1985 E) ... 96,000
Kumba (1985 E) ... 67,000
Maroua ... 103,653
Ngaoundéré (1985 E) ... 61,000
Nkongsamba ... 123,149
YAOUNDÉ ... 653,670

CANADA

1986 C ... 25,354,064

CANADA: ALBERTA

1986 C ... 2,375,278

Cities and Towns

Calgary (★ 671,326) ... 636,104
Edmonton (★ 785,465) ... 573,982
Fort McMurray (★ 48,497) ... 34,949
Lethbridge ... 58,841
Medicine Hat (★ 50,734) ... 41,804
Red Deer ... 54,425

CANADA: BRITISH COLUMBIA

1986 C ... 2,889,207

Cities and Towns

Burnaby (★ Vancouver) ... 145,161
Chilliwack (★ 50,288) ... 41,337
Kamloops ... 61,773
Kelowna (★ 89,730) ... 61,213
Matsqui (★ 88,420) ... 51,449
Nanaimo (★ 60,420) ... 49,029
Prince George ... 67,621
Richmond (★ Vancouver) ... 108,492
Vancouver (★ 1,380,729) ... 431,147
Victoria (★ 255,547) ... 66,303

CANADA: MANITOBA

1986 C ... 1,071,232

Cities and Towns

Brandon ... 38,708
Portage la Prairie ... 13,198
Winnipeg (★ 625,304) ... 594,551

CANADA: NEW BRUNSWICK

1986 C ... 710,422

Cities and Towns

Fredericton (★ 65,768) ... 44,352
Moncton (★ 102,084) ... 55,468
Saint John (★ 121,265) ... 76,381

CANADA: NEWFOUNDLAND

1986 C ... 568,349

Cities and Towns

Corner Brook (★ 33,730) ... 22,719
Gander ... 10,207
Saint John's (★ 161,901) ... 96,216

CANADA: NORTHWEST TERRITORIES

1986 C ... 52,238

Cities and Towns

Inuvik ... 3,389
Yellowknife ... 11,753

CANADA: NOVA SCOTIA

1986 C ... 873,199

Cities and Towns

Dartmouth (★ Halifax) ... 65,243
Halifax (★ 295,990) ... 113,577
Sydney (★ 119,470) ... 27,754

CANADA: ONTARIO

1986 C ... 9,113,515

Cities and Towns

Barrie (★ 67,703) ... 48,287

C Census. E Official estimate. U Unofficial estimate.
• Largest city in country.
★ Population or designation of metropolitan area, including suburbs (see headnote).
▲ Population of an entire municipality, commune, or district, including rural area.

Brampton (★ Toronto) 188,498
Brantford (★ 90,521) 76,146
Burlington (★ Hamilton) 116,675
Cambridge (Galt)
(★★ Kitchener) 79,920
East York (★ Toronto) 101,085
Etobicoke (★ Toronto) 302,973
Gloucester (★ Ottawa) 89,810
Guelph (★ 85,962)............78,235
Hamilton (★ 557,029).......306,728
Kingston (★ 122,350)........55,050
Kitchener (★ 311,195) 150,604
London (★ 342,302) 269,140
Markham (★ Toronto) 114,597
Mississauga
(★ Toronto) 374,005
Nepean (★ Ottawa)...........95,490
Niagara Falls (★★ Saint
Catharines)................72,107
North Bay (★ 57,422)........50,623
North York (★ Toronto) 556,297
Oakville (★ Toronto) 87,107
Oshawa (★ 203,543) 123,651
OTTAWA (★ 819,263) 300,763
Peterborough
(★ 87,083) 61,049
Saint Catharines
(★ 343,258) 123,455
Sarnia (★ 85,700) 49,033
Sault Sainte Marie
(★ 84,617) 80,905
Scarborough
(★ Toronto) 484,676
Sudbury (★ 148,877) 88,717
Thunder Bay
(★ 122,217) 112,272
• Toronto (★ 3,427,168) 612,289
Vaughan (★ Toronto) 65,058
Waterloo (★ Kitchener) 58,718
Windsor (★ 253,988) 193,111
York (★ Toronto) 135,401

CANADA: PRINCE EDWARD ISLAND

1986 C.......................126,646

Cities and Towns

Charlottetown
(★ 53,868) 15,776
Summerside (★ 15,614) 8,020

CANADA: QUÉBEC

1986 C....................6,540,276

Cities and Towns

Beauport (★ Québec)........62,869
Brossard (★ Montréal) 57,441
Charlesbourg
(★ Québec) 68,996
Chicoutimi (★ 158,468) 61,083
Gatineau (★ Ottawa)..........81,244
Hull (★ Ottawa)................58,722
Jonquière
(★★ Chicoutimi) 58,467
LaSalle (★ Montréal)..........75,621
Laval (★ Montréal)...........284,164
Longueuil (★ Montréal) 125,441
Montréal (★ 2,921,357) ..1,015,420
Montréal-Nord
(★ Montréal) 90,303
Québec (★ 603,267).........164,580
Sainte-Foy (★ Québec) 69,615
Saint-Hubert
(★ Montréal) 66,218
Saint-Laurent
(★ Montréal) 67,002
Saint-Léonard
(★ Montréal) 75,947
Sherbrooke
(★ 129,960) 74,438
Trois-Rivières
(★ 128,888) 50,122
Verdun (★ Montréal)..........60,246

CANADA: SASKATCHEWAN

1986 C....................1,010,198

Cities and Towns

Moose Jaw (★ 37,219) 35,073
Prince Albert
(★ 40,841) 33,686
Regina (★ 186,521).........175,064
Saskatoon (★ 200,665) 177,641

CANADA: YUKON

1986 C.........................23,504

Cities and Towns

Dawson 896
Whitehorse 15,199

CAPE VERDE / Cabo Verde

1990 C.......................336,798

Cities and Towns

• PRAIA 61,797

CAYMAN ISLANDS

1988 E.........................25,900

Cities and Towns

• GEORGETOWN 13,700

CENTRAL AFRICAN REPUBLIC / République centrafricaine

1984 E.....................2,517,000

Cities and Towns

• BANGUI 473,817
Bouar (1982 E) 48,000

CHAD / Tchad

1979 E.....................4,405,000

Cities and Towns

Abéché 54,000
Moundou 66,000
• N'DJAMENA 303,000
Sarh 65,000

CHILE

1982 C...................11,329,736

Cities and Towns

Antofagasta 185,486
Apoquindo (★ Santiago) 175,735
Arica 139,320
Calama 81,684
Cerrillos (★ Santiago) 67,013
Cerro Navia
(★ Santiago) 137,777
Chillán 118,163
Concepción
(★ 675,000) 267,891
Conchalí (★ Santiago) 157,884
Copiapó 69,045
Coquimbo 62,186
Coronel (★ Concepción) 65,918
Curicó 60,550
El Bosque (★ Santiago) 143,717
Huechuraba
(★ Santiago) 56,313
Independencia
(★ Santiago) 86,724
Iquique 110,153
La Cisterna
(★ Santiago) 95,863
La Florida (★ Santiago) 191,883
La Granja (★ Santiago) 109,168
La Pintana (★ Santiago) 73,932
La Reina (★ Santiago) 80,452
La Serena 83,283
Las Rejas (★ Santiago) 147,918
Lo Espejo (★ Santiago) 124,462
Lo Prado (★ Santiago) 103,575
Los Ángeles 70,529
Macul (★ Santiago) 113,100
Maipú (★ Santiago) 114,117
Ñuñoa (★ Santiago) 168,919
Osorno 95,286
Pedro Aguirre Cerda
(★ Santiago) 145,207
Peñalolén (★ Santiago) 137,298
Providencia
(★ Santiago) 115,449
Pudahuel (★ Santiago) 97,578
Puente Alto
(★ Santiago) 109,239
Puerto Montt 84,410
Punta Arenas 95,332
Quilpué (★ Valparaíso) 84,136
Quinta Normal
(★ Santiago) 128,989
Rancagua 139,925
Recoleta (★ Santiago) 164,292
Renca (★ Santiago)...........93,928
San Antonio 61,486
San Bernardo
(★ Santiago) 117,132
San Joaquín
(★ Santiago) 123,904
San Miguel
(★ Santiago) 88,764
San Ramón
(★ Santiago) 99,410
• SANTIAGO
(★ 4,100,000) 232,667
Talca 128,544
Talcahuano
(★★ Concepción)...........202,368
Temuco 157,297
Valdivia 100,046
Valparaíso (★ 675,000) 265,355
Villa Alemana
(★ Valparaíso) 55,766
Viña del Mar
(★ Valparaíso)...............244,899
Vitacura (★ Santiago).........72,038

CHINA / Zhongguo

1988 E................1,103,983,000

Cities and Towns

Abagnar Qi (▲ 100,700)
(1986 E) 71,700
Acheng (1985 E) 100,304
Aihui (▲ 135,000)
(1986 E) 76,700
Akesu (▲ 345,900)
(1986 E) 143,100
Altay (▲ 141,700)
(1986 E) 62,800
Anci (Langfang)
(▲ 522,800) (1986 E) 122,100
Anda (▲ 425,500)
(1986 E) 130,200
Andong (1986 E) 579,800
Ankang (1985 E) 89,188
Anqing (▲ 433,900)
(1986 E) 213,200
Anshan 1,330,000
Anshun (▲ 214,700)
(1986 E) 128,800
Anyang (▲ 541,900)
(1986 E) 361,200
Baicheng (▲ 282,000)
(1986 E) 198,600
Baiquan (1985 E) 50,996
Baiyin (▲ 301,900)
(1986 E) 157,100
Baoding (▲ 535,100)
(1986 E) 423,200
Baoji (▲ 359,500)
(1986 E) 286,200
Baoshan (▲ 688,400)
(1986 E) 52,300
Baotou (Paotow) 1,130,000
Baoying (1985 E) 50,479
Bei'an (▲ 440,500)
(1986 E) 199,500
Beihai (▲ 175,900)
(1986 E) 119,000
BEIJING (PEKING)
(★ 6,450,000) 6,710,000
Beipiao (▲ 603,700)
(1986 E) 180,900
Bengbu (▲ 612,600)
(1986 E) 403,900
Benxi (Penhsi) 860,000
Bijie (1985 E) 54,871
Binxian (▲ 177,900)
(1986 E) 86,700
Binxian (1982 C) 127,326
Boli (1985 E) 61,990
Bose (▲ 271,400)
(1986 E) 82,000
Boshan (1975 U) 100,000
Boxian (1985 E) 63,222
Boxing (1982 C) 57,554
Boyang (1985 E) 60,688
Butha Qi (Zalantun)
(▲ 389,500) (1986 E) 111,300
Cangshan (Bianzhuang)
(1982 C) 79,334
Cangzhou (▲ 293,600)
(1986 E) 196,700
Changchun
(▲ 2,000,000) 1,822,000
Changde (▲ 220,800)
(1986 E) 178,200
Changge (1982 C)..............67,002
Changji (▲ 233,400)
(1986 E) 110,500
Changqing (1982 C) 65,094
Changsha 1,230,000
Changshou (1985 E)...........51,923
Changshu (▲ 998,000)
(1986 E) 281,300
Changtu (1985 E) 49,937
Changyi (1982 C)................64,513
Changzhi (▲ 463,400)
(1986 E) 273,000
Changzhou
(Changchow)
(1986 E) 522,700
Chaoan (▲ 1,214,500)
(1986 E) 265,400
Chaoxian (▲ 739,500)
(1986 E) 116,800
Chaoyang, Guangdong
prov. (1985 E)..................85,968
Chaoyang, Liaoning
prov. (▲ 318,900)
(1986 E) 180,300
Chengde (▲ 330,400)
(1986 E) 226,600
Chengdu (Chengtu)
(▲ 2,960,000) 1,884,000
Chenghai (1985 E)..............50,631
Chenxian (▲ 191,900)
(1986 E) 143,500
Chifeng (Ulanhad)
(▲ 882,900) (1986 E) 299,000
Chongqing (Chungking)
(▲ 2,890,000) 2,502,000
Chuxian (▲ 365,000)
(1986 E) 113,300
Chuxiong (▲ 379,400)
(1986 E) 67,700
Da'an (1985 E) 70,552
Dachangzhen (1975 U) 50,000
Dalian (Dairen)...............2,280,000
Danyang (1985 E) 48,449
Daqing (▲ 880,000) 640,000
Dashiqiao (1985 E) 68,898
Datong (1985 E)..................55,529
Datong (▲ 1,040,000) 810,000
Dawa (1985 E) 142,581
Daxian (▲ 209,400)
(1986 E) 142,000
Dehui (1985 E) 60,247
Dengfeng (1982 C) 49,746
Deqing (1982 C)..................48,726
Deyang (▲ 753,400)
(1986 E) 184,800
Dezhou (▲ 276,200)
(1986 E) 161,300
Didao (1975 U) 50,000
Dinghai (1985 E) 50,161
Dongchuan (Xincun)
(▲ 275,100) (1986 E) 67,400
Dongguan
(▲ 1,208,500)
(1986 E) 254,900
Dongsheng (▲ 121,300)
(1986 E) 57,500
Dongtai (1985 E) 65,788
Dongying (▲ 514,400)
(1986 E) 178,100
Dukou (▲ 551,200)
(1986 E) 380,200
Dunhua (▲ 448,000)
(1986 E) 217,100
Duyun (▲ 386,600)
(1986 E) 123,800
Echeng (▲ 938,000)
(1986 E) 217,400
Enshi (▲ 679,000)
(1986 E) 84,300
Ergun Zuoqi (1985 E)..........55,970
Feixian (1982 C).................73,246
Fengcheng (1985 E) 66,745
Foshan (▲ 312,700)
(1986 E) 243,500
Fujin (1985 E) 60,948
Fuling (▲ 973,500)
(1986 E) 166,300
Fushun (Funan)..............1,290,000
Fuxian (Wafangdian)
(▲ 960,700) (1986 E) 246,200
Fuxinshi 700,000
Fuyang (▲ 195,200)
(1986 E) 143,400
Fuyu, Heilongjiang
prov. (1985 E)..................48,670
Fuyu, Jilin prov.
(1985 E) 98,373
Fuzhou, Fujian prov.
(▲ 1,240,000) 910,000
Fuzhou, Jiangxi prov.
(▲ 171,800) (1986 E) 106,700
Gaixian (1985 E) 67,587
Ganhe (1985 E) 48,128
Ganzhou (▲ 346,000)
(1986 E) 191,600
Gaoqing (Tianzhen)
(1982 C) 70,411
Gaoyou (1985 E) 57,844
Gejiu (Kokiu)
(▲ 341,700) (1986 E) 193,600
Golmud (1986 E) 60,300
Gongchangling
(1982 C) 49,281
Guanghua (▲ 420,000)
(1986 E) 104,400
Guangyuan (▲ 805,500)
(1986 E) 162,200
Guangzhou (Canton)
(▲ 3,420,000) 3,100,000
Guanxian, Shandong
prov. (1982 C) 49,782
Guanxian, Sichuan
prov. (1985 E)..................65,039
Guilin (Kweilin)
(▲ 457,500) (1986 E) 324,200
Guixian (1985 E) 61,970
Guiyang (Kweiyang)
(▲ 1,430,000) 1,030,000
Haicheng (▲ 984,800)
(1986 E) 210,700
Haifeng (1985 E) 50,401
Haikou (▲ 289,600)
(1986 E) 209,200
Hailaer (1986 E) 180,000
Hailin (1985 E)...................58,909
Hailong (Meihekou)
(▲ 534,200) (1986 E) 117,500
Hailun (1985 E) 83,448
Haiyang (Dongcun)
(1982 C) 77,098
Hami (Kumul)
(▲ 270,300) (1986 E) 146,400
Hancheng (▲ 304,200)
(1986 E) 66,600
Handan (▲ 1,030,000) 870,000
Hangu (1975 U) 100,000
Hangzhou (Hangchow) ..1,290,000
Hanzhong (▲ 415,000)
(1986 E) 151,700
Harbin 2,710,000
Hebi (▲ 321,600)
(1986 E) 158,500
Hechi (▲ 266,800)
(1986 E) 74,400
Hechuan (1985 E) 65,237
Hefei (▲ 930,000) 740,000
Hegang (1986 E) 588,300
Helong (1985 E) 62,665
Hengshui (▲ 286,500)
(1986 E) 83,100
Hengyang (▲ 601,300)
(1986 E) 419,200
Heze (Caozhou)
(▲ 1,001,500)
(1986 E) 115,400
Hohhot (▲ 830,000) 670,000
Hongjiang (▲ 67,000)
(1986 E) 54,300
Horqin Youyi Qianqi
(Ulan Hot)
(▲ 192,100) (1986 E) 129,100
Hotan (▲ 122,800)
(1986 E) 71,700
Houma (▲ 158,500)
(1986 E) 67,000
Huadian (1985 E)................75,183
Huaian (1985 E)..................65,673
Huaibei (▲ 447,200)
(1986 E) 252,100
Huaide (▲ 899,400)
(1986 E) 187,600
Huaihua (▲ 427,100)
(1986 E) 102,000
Huainan (▲ 1,110,000) 700,000
Huaiyin (Wangying)
(▲ 382,500) (1986 E) 201,700
Huanan (1985 E) 66,596
Huanggang (1982 C) 65,961
Huangshi (1986 E)............451,900
Huayun (Huarong)
(▲ 313,500) (1986 E) 81,000
Huinan (Chaoyang)
(1985 E) 52,429
Huizhou (▲ 182,100)
(1986 E) 117,000
Hulan (1985 E) 74,989
Hunjiang (Badaojiang)
(▲ 687,700) (1986 E) 442,600
Huzhou (▲ 964,400)
(1986 E) 208,500
Jiading (1985 E) 60,718
Jiamusi (Kiamusze)
(▲ 557,700) (1986 E) 429,800
Jian (▲ 184,300)
(1986 E) 132,200
Jiangling (1985 E) 77,887
Jiangmen (▲ 231,700)
(1986 E) 168,800
Jiangyin (1985 E)................66,476
Jiangyou (1985 E) 72,663
Jianou (1985 E) 55,180
Jiaohe (1985 E) 51,504
Jiaojiang (▲ 385,200)
(1986 E) 82,300
Jiaoxian (1985 E).................51,869
Jiaozuo (▲ 509,900)
(1986 E) 335,400
Jiawang (1975 U).................50,000
Jiaxing (▲ 686,500)
(1986 E) 210,200
Jiayuguan (▲ 102,100)
(1986 E) 73,800
Jiexiu (1985 E) 51,300
Jieyang (1985 E) 98,531
Jilin (Kirin) 1,200,000
Jinan (Tsinan)
(▲ 2,140,000) 1,546,000
Jinchang (Baijiazui)
(▲ 136,000) (1986 E) 90,500
Jincheng (▲ 612,700)
(1986 E) 99,900
Jingdezhen
(Kingtechen)
(▲ 569,700) (1986 E) 304,000
Jingmen (▲ 946,500)
(1986 E) 227,000
Jinhua (▲ 799,900)
(1986 E) 147,800
Jining, Nei Monggol
prov. (1986 E)................163,300
Jining, Shandong prov.
(▲ 765,700) (1986 E) 222,600
Jinshi (▲ 219,700)
(1986 E) 73,700
Jinxi (▲ 634,300)
(1986 E) 223,100
Jinxian (1985 E) 95,761
Jinzhou (Chinchou)
(▲ 810,000)...................710,000
Jishou (▲ 194,500)
(1986 E) 59,500
Jishu (1985 E).....................75,587
Jiujiang (▲ 382,300)
(1986 E) 248,500
Jiuquan (Suzhou)
(▲ 269,900) (1986 E) 56,300
Jiutai (1985 E) 63,021
Jixi (▲ 820,000) 700,000
Jixian (1985 E) 59,725
Juancheng (1982 C)............54,110
Junan (Shizilu) (1982 C) 90,222
Junxian (▲ 423,400)
(1986 E) 97,000
Juxian (1982 C) 51,666
Kaifeng (▲ 629,100)
(1986 E) 458,800
Kaili (▲ 342,100)
(1986 E) 96,600
Kaiping (1985 E).................54,145
Kaiyuan (▲ 342,100)
(1986 E) 96,600
Kaiyuan (1985 E) 85,762
Karamay (1986 E) 185,300
Kashi (▲ 194,500)
(1986 E) 146,300
Keshan (1985 E) 65,088
Korla (▲ 219,000)
(1986 E) 129,400
Kunming (▲ 1,550,000) ..1,310,000
Kuqa (1985 E).....................63,847
Kuytun (1986 E)...................60,200
Laiwu (▲ 1,041,800)
(1986 E) 143,500
Langxiang (1985 E).............64,658
Lanxi (1985 E) 53,236
Lanxi (▲ 606,800)
(1986 E) 70,500
Lanzhou (Lanchow)
(▲ 1,420,000) 1,297,000
Lechang (1986 E) 56,913
Lengshuijiang
(▲ 277,600) (1986 E) 101,700
Lengshuitan
(▲ 362,000) (1986 E) 60,900
Leshan (▲ 972,300)
(1986 E) 307,300
Lhasa (▲ 107,700)
(1986 E) 84,400
Lianyungang (Xinpu)
(▲ 459,400) (1986 E) 288,000
Liaocheng (▲ 724,300)
(1986 E) 119,000
Liaoyang (▲ 576,900)
(1986 E) 442,600
Liaoyuan (1986 E) 370,400
Liling (▲ 856,300)
(1986 E) 107,100
Linfen (▲ 530,100)
(1986 E) 157,600

C Census. E Official estimate. U Unofficial estimate.
• Largest city in country.

★ Population or designation of metropolitan area, including suburbs (see headnote).
▲ Population of an entire municipality, commune, or district, including rural area.

- Lingling (▲ 515,300) (1986 E) ... 72,700
- Lingyuan (1985 E) ... 66,825
- Linhai (1985 E) ... 52,653
- Linhe (▲ 365,900) (1986 E) ... 99,800
- Linkou (1985 E) ... 52,936
- Linqing (▲ 603,000) (1986 E) ... 87,000
- Linqu (1982 C) ... 84,196
- Linxia (▲ 150,200) (1986 E) ... 72,900
- Linyi (▲ 1,365,000) (1986 E) ... 190,000
- Liuzhou ... 680,000
- Longjiang (1985 E) ... 51,156
- Longyan (▲ 378,500) (1986 E) ... 114,500
- Loudi (▲ 254,300) (1986 E) ... 84,200
- Lu'an (▲ 163,400) (1986 E) ... 122,600
- Lufeng (1985 E) ... 53,015
- Luohe (▲ 159,100) (1986 E) ... 102,300
- Luoyang (Loyang) (▲ 1,090,000) ... 760,000
- Luzhou (▲ 360,300) (1986 E) ... 237,800
- Maanshan (▲ 367,000) (1986 E) ... 258,900
- Manzhouli (1986 E) ... 116,600
- Maoming (▲ 434,900) (1986 E) ... 118,600
- Meixian (▲ 740,600) (1986 E) ... 169,100
- Mengxian ... 55,000
- Mengyin (1982 C) ... 70,602
- Mianyang, Sichuan prov. (▲ 848,500) (1986 E) ... 233,900
- Minhang (1975 U) ... 60,000
- Mishan (1985 E) ... 54,919
- Mixian (1982 C) ... 64,776
- Mudanjiang ... 650,000
- Nahe (1985 E) ... 49,725
- N'aizishen (1985 E) ... 51,982
- Nancha (1975 U) ... 50,000
- Nanchang (▲ 1,260,000) ... 1,090,000
- Nanchong (▲ 238,100) (1986 E) ... 158,000
- Nanjing (Nanking) ... 2,390,000
- Nanning (▲ 1,000,000) ... 720,000
- Nanpiao (1982 C) ... 67,274
- Nanping (▲ 420,800) (1986 E) ... 157,100
- Nantong (▲ 411,000) (1986 E) ... 308,800
- Nanyang (▲ 294,800) (1986 E) ... 199,400
- Neihuang (1982 C) ... 56,039
- Neijiang (▲ 298,500) (1986 E) ... 191,100
- Ning'an (1985 E) ... 49,334
- Ningbo (▲ 1,050,000) ... 570,000
- Ningyang (1982 C) ... 55,424
- Nong'an (1985 E) ... 55,966
- Nunjiang (1985 E) ... 59,276
- Orogen Zizhiqi (1985 E) ... 48,042
- Panshan (▲ 343,100) (1986 E) ... 248,100
- Panshi (1985 E) ... 59,270
- Pingdingshan (▲ 819,900) (1986 E) ... 363,200
- Pingliang (▲ 362,500) (1986 E) ... 85,400
- Pingxiang (▲ 1,286,700) (1986 E) ... 368,700
- Pingyi (1982 C) ... 89,373
- Pingyin (1982 C) ... 62,827
- Potou (▲ 456,100) (1986 E) ... 59,000
- Puqi (1985 E) ... 65,239
- Putian (▲ 265,400) (1986 E) ... 64,600
- Putuo (1985 E) ... 50,962
- Puyang (▲ 1,086,100) (1986 E) ... 131,000
- Qian Gorlos (1985 E) ... 79,494
- Qingdao (Tsingtao) ... 1,300,000
- Qingjiang (▲ 246,617) (1982 C) ... 150,000
- Qingyuan (1985 E) ... 51,756
- Qinhuangdao (Chinwangtao) (★ 436,000) (1986 E) ... 307,500
- Qinzhou (▲ 923,400) (1986 E) ... 97,100
- Qiqihar (Tsitsihar) (▲ 1,330,000) ... 1,180,000
- Qitaihe (▲ 309,900) (1986 E) ... 166,400
- Qixia (1982 C) ... 54,158
- Qixian (1982 C) ... 53,041
- Quanzhou (Chuanchou) (▲ 436,000) (1986 E) ... 157,000
- Qujing (▲ 758,000) (1986 E) ... 135,000
- Quxian (▲ 704,800) (1986 E) ... 124,000
- Raoping (1985 E) ... 54,831
- Rizhao (▲ 970,300) (1986 E) ... 93,300
- Rongcheng (1982 C) ... 52,878
- Rugao (1985 E) ... 50,643
- Ruian (1985 E) ... 57,993
- Sanmenxia (Shanxian) (▲ 150,000) (1986 E) ... 79,000
- Sanming (▲ 214,300) (1986 E) ... 144,900
- • Shanghai (★ 9,300,000) ... 7,220,000
- Shangqiu (Zhuji) (▲ 199,400) (1986 E) ... 135,400
- Shangrao (▲ 142,500) (1986 E) ... 113,000
- Shangshui (1982 C) ... 50,191
- Shantou (Swatow) (▲ 790,000) ... 560,000
- Shanwei (1985 E) ... 61,234
- Shaoguan (1986 E) ... 363,100
- Shaowu (▲ 266,700) (1986 E) ... 81,400
- Shaoxing (▲ 250,900) (1986 E) ... 167,100
- Shaoyang (▲ 465,900) (1986 E) ... 218,600
- Shashi (1986 E) ... 253,700
- Shenxian (1982 C) ... 50,208
- Shenyang (Mukden) (▲ 4,370,000) ... 3,910,000
- Shenzhen (▲ 231,900) (1986 E) ... 189,600
- Shiguaigou (1975 U) ... 50,000
- Shihezi (▲ 549,300) (1987 E) ... 304,700
- Shijiazhuang ... 1,220,000
- Shiyan (▲ 332,600) (1986 E) ... 227,300
- Shizuishan (▲ 317,400) (1986 E) ... 225,500
- Shouguang (1982 C) ... 83,400
- Shuangcheng (1985 E) ... 91,163
- Shuangliao (1985 E) ... 67,326
- Shuangyashan (1986 E) ... 427,300
- Shuicheng (▲ 2,216,500) (1986 E) ... 363,500
- Shulan (1986 E) ... 50,582
- Shunde (1985 E) ... 50,262
- Siping (▲ 357,800) (1986 E) ... 280,100
- Sishui (1982 C) ... 82,990
- Songjiang (1985 E) ... 71,864
- Songjianghe (1985 E) ... 53,023
- Suihua (▲ 732,100) (1986 E) ... 200,400
- Suileng (1985 E) ... 68,399
- Suining (▲ 1,174,900) (1986 E) ... 118,500
- Suixian (▲ 1,281,600) (1986 E) ... 187,700
- Suqian (1985 E) ... 50,742
- Suxian (▲ 218,600) (1986 E) ... 123,300
- Suzhou (Soochow) ... 740,000
- Tai'an (▲ 1,325,400) (1986 E) ... 215,900
- Taiyuan (▲ 1,980,000) ... 1,700,000
- Taizhou (▲ 210,800) (1987 E) ... 143,200
- Tancheng (1982 C) ... 61,857
- Tangshan (▲ 1,440,000) ... 1,080,000
- Tao'an (1985 E) ... 76,269
- Tengxian (1985 E) ... 53,254
- Tianjin (Tientsin) (▲ 5,540,000) ... 4,950,000
- Tianshui (▲ 953,200) (1986 E) ... 209,500
- Tiefa (▲ 146,367) (1982 C) ... 60,000
- Tieli (1985 E) ... 102,527
- Tieling (▲ 454,100) (1986 E) ... 326,100
- Tongchuan (▲ 393,200) (1986 E) ... 268,900
- Tonghua (▲ 367,400) (1986 E) ... 290,200
- Tongliao (▲ 253,100) (1986 E) ... 190,100
- Tongling (▲ 216,400) (1986 E) ... 182,900
- Tongren (1985 E) ... 50,307
- Tongxian (1985 E) ... 97,168
- Tumen (▲ 99,700) (1986 E) ... 77,600
- Tunxi (▲ 104,500) (1986 E) ... 61,800
- Turpan (▲ 196,800) (1986 E) ... 52,300
- Ürümqi ... 1,060,000
- Wangkui (1985 E) ... 52,021
- Wangqing (1985 E) ... 61,237
- Wanxian (▲ 280,800) (1986 E) ... 138,700
- Weifang (▲ 1,042,200) (1986 E) ... 312,500
- Weihai (▲ 220,800) (1986 E) ... 83,000
- Weinan (▲ 699,400) (1986 E) ... 111,300
- Weishan (Xiazhen) (1982 C) ... 57,932
- Weixian (Hanting) (1982 C) ... 50,180
- Wenzhou (▲ 530,600) (1986 E) ... 372,200
- Wuchang (1985 E) ... 64,403
- Wuhai (1986 E) ... 266,000
- Wuhan ... 3,570,000
- Wuhu (▲ 502,200) (1986 E) ... 396,000
- Wulian (Hongning) (1982 C) ... 51,718
- Wusong (1982 C) ... 64,017
- Wuwei (Liangzhou) (▲ 804,000) (1986 E) ... 115,500
- Wuxi (Wuhsi) ... 880,000
- Wuzhong (▲ 402,400) (1986 E) ... 48,600
- Wuzhou (Wuchow) (▲ 261,500) (1986 E) ... 194,800
- Xiaguan (▲ 395,800) (1986 E) ... 112,100
- Xiamen (Amoy) (▲ 546,400) (1986 E) ... 343,700
- Xi'an (Sian) (▲ 2,580,000) ... 2,210,000
- Xiangfan (▲ 421,200) (1986 E) ... 314,900
- Xiangtan (▲ 511,100) (1986 E) ... 389,500
- Xianning (▲ 402,200) (1986 E) ... 122,200
- Xianyang (▲ 641,800) (1986 E) ... 285,900
- Xiaogan (▲ 1,204,400) (1986 E) ... 125,500
- Xiaoshan (1985 E) ... 63,074
- Xichang (▲ 161,000) (1986 E) ... 105,000
- Xinghua (1985 E) ... 75,573
- Xinglongzhen (1982 C) ... 52,961
- Xingtai (▲ 350,800) (1986 E) ... 265,600
- Xinhui (1985 E) ... 77,381
- Xining (Sining) ... 620,000
- Xinmin (1985 E) ... 47,900
- Xintai (▲ 1,157,300) (1986 E) ... 171,400
- Xinwen (Suncun) (1975 U) ... 50,000
- Xinxian (▲ 398,600) (1986 E) ... 74,200
- Xinxiang (▲ 540,500) (1986 E) ... 411,000
- Xinyang (▲ 234,200) (1986 E) ... 169,100
- Xinyu (▲ 610,600) (1986 E) ... 140,200
- Xuancheng (1985 E) ... 52,387
- Xuanhua (1975 U) ... 140,000
- Xuanwei (1982 C) ... 70,081
- Xuchang (▲ 247,200) (1986 E) ... 167,800
- Xuguit Qi (Yakeshi) (1986 E) ... 390,000
- Xuzhou (Süchow) ... 860,000
- Yaan (▲ 277,600) (1986 E) ... 89,200
- Yan'an (▲ 259,800) (1986 E) ... 86,700
- Yancheng (▲ 1,251,400) (1986 E) ... 258,400
- Yangcheng (1982 C) ... 57,255
- Yangjiang (1986 E) ... 91,433
- Yangquan (▲ 478,900) (1986 E) ... 295,100
- Yangzhou (▲ 417,300) (1986 E) ... 321,500
- Yanji (▲ 216,900) (1986 E) ... 175,000
- Yanji (Longjing) (1985 E) ... 55,035
- Yanling (1982 C) ... 52,679
- Yantai (Chefoo) (▲ 717,300) (1986 E) ... 327,000
- Yanzhou (1985 E) ... 48,972
- Yaxian (Sanya) (▲ 321,700) (1986 E) ... 70,500
- Yi'an (1986 E) ... 54,253
- Yibin (Ipin) (▲ 636,500) (1986 E) ... 218,800
- Yichang (Ichang) (1986 E) ... 410,500
- Yichuan (1982 C) ... 58,914
- Yichun, Heilongjiang prov. ... 840,000
- Yichun, Jiangxi prov. (▲ 770,200) (1986 E) ... 132,600
- Yidu (1985 E) ... 54,838
- Yilan (1985 E) ... 50,436
- Yima (▲ 84,800) (1986 E) ... 53,700
- Yinan (Jiehu) (1982 C) ... 67,803
- Yinchuan (▲ 396,900) (1986 E) ... 268,200
- Yingchengzi (1985 E) ... 59,072
- Yingkou (▲ 480,000) (1986 E) ... 366,900
- Yingtan (▲ 116,200) (1986 E) ... 64,500
- Yining (Kuldja) (▲ 232,000) (1986 E) ... 153,200
- Yiyang (▲ 365,000) (1986 E) ... 155,300
- Yiyuan (Nanma) (1982 C) ... 53,800
- Yongan (▲ 269,000) (1986 E) ... 105,100
- Yongchuan (1985 E) ... 70,444
- Yuci (▲ 420,700) (1986 E) ... 171,000
- Yueyang (▲ 411,300) (1986 E) ... 239,500
- Yulin, Guangxi Zhuangzu prov. (▲ 1,228,800) (1986 E) ... 115,600
- Yulin, Shaanxi prov. (1985 E) ... 51,610
- Yumen (Laojunmiao) (▲ 160,100) (1986 E) ... 84,300
- Yuncheng, Shandong prov. (1982 C) ... 54,262
- Yuncheng, Shansi prov. (▲ 434,900) (1986 E) ... 87,000
- Yunyang (1982 C) ... 54,903
- Yushu (1985 E) ... 57,222
- Yuyao (▲ 772,700) (1986 E) ... 169,700
- Zaozhuang (▲ 1,592,000) (1986 E) ... 292,200
- Zhangjiakou (Kalgan) (▲ 640,000) ... 500,000
- Zhangye (▲ 394,200) (1986 E) ... 73,000
- Zhangzhou (Longxi) (▲ 310,400) (1986 E) ... 159,400
- Zhanhua (Fuguo) (1982 C) ... 48,193
- Zhanjiang (▲ 920,900) (1986 E) ... 335,500
- Zhaodong (1985 E) ... 99,836
- Zhaoqing (Gaoyao) (▲ 187,600) (1986 E) ... 145,700
- Zhaotong (▲ 546,600) (1986 E) ... 77,500
- Zhaoyuan (1982 C) ... 56,389
- Zhengzhou (Chengchow) (▲ 1,580,000) ... 1,150,000
- Zhenjiang (1986 E) ... 412,400
- Zhongshan (Shiqizhen) (▲ 1,059,700) (1986 E) ... 238,700
- Zhoucun (1975 U) ... 50,000
- Zhoukouzhen (▲ 220,400) (1986 E) ... 110,500
- Zhuhai (▲ 155,000) (1986 E) ... 88,800
- Zhumadian (▲ 149,500) (1986 E) ... 99,400
- Zhuoxian (1985 E) ... 54,523
- Zhuzhou (Chuchow) (▲ 499,600) (1986 E) ... 344,800
- Zibo (Zhangdian) (▲ 2,370,000) ... 840,000
- Zigong (Tzukung) (▲ 909,300) (1986 E) ... 361,700
- Zixing (▲ 334,300) (1986 E) ... 97,100
- Ziyang (1985 E) ... 57,349
- Zouping (1982 C) ... 49,274
- Zouxian (1985 E) ... 61,578
- Zunyi (▲ 347,600) (1986 E) ... 236,600

COLOMBIA

1985 C ... 27,867,326

Cities and Towns

- Armenia ... 187,130
- Barrancabermeja ... 137,406
- Barranquilla (★ 1,140,000) ... 899,781
- Bello (★ Medellín) ... 212,861
- Bucaramanga (★ 550,000) ... 352,326
- Buenaventura ... 160,342
- Buga ... 82,992
- Cali (★ 1,400,000) ... 1,350,565
- Cartagena ... 531,426
- Cartago ... 97,791
- Ciénaga ... 56,860
- Cúcuta (★ 445,000) ... 379,478
- Dos Quebradas (★ Pereira) ... 101,480
- Duitama ... 56,390
- Envigado (★ Medellín) ... 91,391
- Florencia ... 66,430
- Floridablanca (★ Bucaramanga) ... 143,824
- Girardot ... 70,078
- Ibagué ... 292,965
- Itagüí (★ Medellín) ... 137,623
- Magangué ... 49,160
- Malambo (★ Barranquilla) ... 52,584
- Manizales (★ 330,000) ... 299,352
- Medellín (★ 2,095,000) ... 1,468,089
- Montería ... 157,466
- Neiva ... 194,556
- Ocaña ... 51,443
- Palmira ... 175,186
- Pasto ... 197,407
- Pereira (★ 390,000) ... 233,271
- Popayán ... 141,964
- • SANTA FE DE BOGOTÁ (★ 4,260,000) ... 3,982,941
- Santa Marta ... 177,922
- Sincelejo ... 120,537
- Soacha (★ Santa Fe de Bogotá) ... 109,051
- Sogamoso ... 64,437
- Soledad (★ Barranquilla) ... 165,791
- Tuluá ... 99,721
- Tunja ... 93,792
- Valledupar ... 142,771
- Villa Rosario (★ Cúcuta) ... 63,615
- Villavicencio ... 178,685

COMOROS / Al-Qumur / Comores

1990 E ... 452,742

Cities and Towns

- • MORONI ... 23,432

CONGO

1984 C ... 1,912,429

Cities and Towns

- • BRAZZAVILLE ... 585,812
- Dolisie ... 49,134
- Pointe-Noire ... 294,203

COOK ISLANDS

1986 C ... 18,155

Cities and Towns

- • AVARUA ... 9,678

COSTA RICA

1988 E ... 2,851,000

Cities and Towns

- Limón (▲ 62,600) ... 40,400
- • SAN JOSÉ (★ 670,000) ... 278,600

CROATIA / Hrvatska

1987 E ... 4,673,517

Cities and Towns

- Osijek (▲ 162,490) ... 106,800
- Rijeka (▲ 199,282) ... 166,400
- Split ... 197,074
- • ZAGREB ... 697,925

CUBA

1987 E ... 10,288,000

Cities and Towns

- Bayamo ... 108,716
- Camagüey ... 265,588
- Cárdenas (1981 C) ... 59,352
- Cienfuegos ... 112,225
- Guantánamo ... 179,091
- Holguín ... 199,861
- • LA HABANA (HAVANA) (★ 2,125,000) ... 2,036,800
- Manzanillo (1981 C) ... 87,830
- Matanzas ... 106,954
- Palma Soriano (1981 C) ... 55,851
- Pinar del Río ... 108,109
- Santa Clara ... 182,349
- Santiago de Cuba ... 364,554
- Victoria de las Tunas (1985 E) ... 91,400

CYPRUS / Kıbrıs / Kípros

1982 C ... 512,097

Cities and Towns

- Lemesós (Limassol) (★ 107,161) ... 74,782
- • NICOSIA (LEVKOSÍA) (★ 185,000) ... 48,221

CYPRUS, NORTH / Kuzey Kıbrıs

1985 E ... 160,287

Cities and Towns

- • NICOSIA (LEFKOŞA) ... 37,400

CZECHOSLOVAKIA / Československo

1990 E ... 15,661,734

Cities and Towns

- Banská Bystrica ... 87,834
- Bratislava ... 442,999
- Brno (★ 450,000) ... 392,285
- České Budějovice (★ 114,000) ... 99,428
- Chomutov (★ 80,000) ... 55,735
- Děčín (★ 72,000) ... 56,034
- Frýdek-Místek (★ Ostrava) ... 66,791
- Havířov (★ Ostrava) ... 92,037
- Hradec Králové (★ 113,000) ... 101,302
- Jihlava ... 54,855
- Karlovy Vary (Carlsbad) ... 58,039
- Karviná (★★ Ostrava) ... 69,521
- Kladno (★ 88,500) ... 73,347
- Košice ... 237,099
- Liberec (★ 175,000) ... 104,256
- Martin ... 66,678
- Mladá Boleslav ... 49,195
- Most (★ 135,000) ... 71,360
- Nitra ... 91,297
- Olomouc (★ 126,000) ... 107,044
- Opava (★ 77,500) ... 63,440
- Ostrava (★ 760,000) ... 331,557
- Pardubice ... 95,909
- Plzeň (★ 210,000) ... 175,038
- Poprad ... 53,039
- • PRAHA (PRAGUE) (★ 1,325,000) ... 1,215,656
- Přerov ... 51,996
- Prešov ... 90,121
- Prievidza ... 52,624
- Prostějov ... 52,074
- Teplice (★ 94,000) ... 55,287
- Trenčín ... 57,813
- Trnava ... 72,866
- Ústí nad Labem (★ 115,000) ... 106,499
- Žilina ... 97,508
- Zlín (★ 124,000) ... 87,189

C Census. E Official estimate. U Unofficial estimate.
• Largest city in country.

★ Population or designation of metropolitan area, including suburbs (see headnote).
▲ Population of an entire municipality, commune, or district, including rural area.

DENMARK / Danmark
1990 E 5,135,409
Cities and Towns
Ålborg (▲ 155,019) 114,000
Århus (▲ 261,437) 202,300
Esbjerg (▲ 81,504) 71,900
Frederiksberg (★ København) 85,611
Gentofte (★ København) 65,303
Gladsakse (★ København) 60,882
Helsingør (Elsinore) (★ København) 56,701
• KØBENHAVN (★ 1,685,000) 466,723
Kongens Lyngby (★ København) 49,317
Odense (▲ 176,133) 140,100
Randers 61,020

DJIBOUTI
1976 E 226,000
Cities and Towns
• DJIBOUTI 120,000

DOMINICA
1984 E 77,000
Cities and Towns
• ROSEAU 9,348

DOMINICAN REPUBLIC / República Dominicana
1981 C 5,647,977
Cities and Towns
Barahona 49,334
La Romana 91,571
San Cristóbal 58,520
San Francisco de Macorís 64,906
San Juan [de la Maguana] 49,764
San Pedro de Macorís 78,562
Santiago [de los Caballeros] 278,638
• SANTO DOMINGO 1,313,172

ECUADOR
1987 E 9,923,000
Cities and Towns
Alfaro (★ Guayaquil) (1982 C) 51,023
Ambato 126,067
Cuenca 201,490
Esmeraldas 120,387
• Guayaquil (★ 1,580,000) 1,572,615
Ibarra (1982 C) 53,428
Loja (1982 C) 71,652
Machala 144,396
Manta 135,990
Milagro 102,884
Portoviejo 141,568
Quevedo (1982 C) 67,023
QUITO (★ 1,300,000) 1,137,705
Riobamba (1982 C) 75,455
Santo Domingo de los Colorados 104,059

EGYPT / Mișr
1986 C 48,205,049
Cities and Towns
Abū Kabīr 69,509
Akhmīm 70,602
Al-'Arīsh 67,638
Al-Fayyūm 212,523
Al-Ḥawāmidīyah (★ Al-Qāhirah) 73,060
Al-Iskandarīyah (Alexandria) (★ 3,350,000) 2,917,327
Al-Ismā53 īlīyah (★ 235,000) 212,567
Al-Jīzah (Giza) (★ Al-Qāhirah) 1,870,508
Al-Maḥallah al-Kubrā 358,844
Al-Manṣūrah (★ 375,000) 316,870
Al-Manzilah 55,090
Al-Maṭarīyah 74,554
Al-Minyā 179,136
• AL-QĀHIRAH (CAIRO) (★ 9,300,000) 6,052,836
Al-Uqṣur (Luxor) 125,404
Armant 54,650
Ashmūn 54,450
As-Sinbillāwayn 60,285
As-Suways (Suez) 326,820
Aswān 191,461
Asyūṭ 273,191
Az-Zaqāzīq 245,496
Bahtīm (★ Al-Qāhirah) 275,807
Banhā 115,571
Banī Suwayf 151,813
Bilbays 96,540
Bilqās Qism Awwal 73,162
Būlāq ad-Dakrūr (★ Al-Qāhirah) 148,787
Būr Sa'īd (Port Said) 399,793
Būsh 54,482
Damanhūr 190,840
Disūq 78,119
Dumyāṭ (Damietta) 89,498
Hawsh 'Īsā (1980 C) 53,619
Idkū 70,729
Jirjā 70,899
Kafr ad-Dawwār (★ Al-Iskandarīyah) 195,102
Kafr ash-Shaykh 102,910
Kafr az-Zayyāt 58,061
Kawm Umbū 52,131
Maghāghah 50,807
Mallawī 99,062
Manfalūṭ 52,644
Minūf 69,883
Mīt Ghamr (★ 100,000) 92,253
Qalyūb 86,684
Qinā 119,794
Rashīd (Rosetta) 52,014
Rummānah 50,014
Samālūṭ 62,404
Sāqiyat Makkī 51,062
Sawhāj 132,965
Shibīn al-Kawm 132,751
Shubrā al-Khaymah (★ Al-Qāhirah) 710,794
Sinnūris 55,323
Ṭahṭā 58,516
Ṭalkhā (★ Al-Manṣūrah) 55,757
Ṭanṭā 334,505
Warrāq al-'Arab (★ Al-Qāhirah) 127,108
Ziftā (★★ Mīt Ghamr) 69,050

EL SALVADOR
1985 E 5,337,896
Cities and Towns
Delgado (★ San Salvador) 67,684
Mejicanos (★ San Salvador) 91,465
Nueva San Salvador (★ San Salvador) 53,688
San Miguel 88,520
• SAN SALVADOR (★ 920,000) 462,652
Santa Ana 137,879
Soyapango (★ San Salvador) 60,000

EQUATORIAL GUINEA / Guinea Ecuatorial
1983 C 300,000
Cities and Towns
• MALABO 31,630

ESTONIA / Eesti
1989 C 1,573,000
Cities and Towns
Kohtla-Järve (1987 E) 78,000
Narva (1987 E) 81,000
Pärnu (1987 E) 53,000
• TALLINN 482,000
Tartu 114,000

ETHIOPIA / Ityopiya
1984 C 42,019,418
Cities and Towns
• ADIS ABEBA (★ 1,500,000) (1988 E) 1,686,300
Akaki Beseka (★ Adis Abeba) 54,146
Asmera (1988 E) 319,353
Bahir Dar 54,800
Debre Zeyit 51,143
Dese 68,848
Dire Dawa (1988 E) 117,042
Gonder 68,958
Harer 62,160
Jima 60,992
Mekele 61,583
Nazret 76,284

FAEROE ISLANDS / Føroyar
1990 E 47,946
Cities and Towns
• TÓRSHAVN 14,767

FALKLAND ISLANDS
1986 C 1,916
Cities and Towns
• STANLEY 1,200

FIJI
1986 C 715,375
Cities and Towns
Lautoka (★ 39,057) 28,728
• SUVA (★ 141,273) 69,665

FINLAND / Suomi
1988 E 4,938,602
Cities and Towns
Espoo (Esbo) (★ Helsinki) 164,569
Hämeenlinna 42,486
• HELSINKI (HELSINGFORS) (★ 1,040,000) 490,034
Joensuu 47,099
Jyväskylä (★ 93,000) 65,719
Kotka 57,745
Kouvola (★ 53,821) 31,933
Kuopio 78,916
Lahti (★ 108,000) 74,300
Lappeenranta (▲ 53,780) 47,400
Oulu (★ 121,000) 98,582
Pori 77,395
Tampere (★ 241,000) 170,533
Turku (Åbo) (★ 228,000) 160,456
Vaasa (Vasa) 53,737
Vantaa (Vanda) (★ Helsinki) 149,063

FRANCE
1982 C 54,334,871
Cities and Towns
Aix-en-Provence (★ 126,552) 121,327
Ajaccio 54,089
Albi (★ 60,181) 45,947
Alès (★ 70,180) 43,268
Amiens (★ 154,498) 131,332
Angers (★ 195,859) 136,038
Angoulême (★ 103,552) 46,197
Annecy (★ 112,632) 49,965
Antibes (★★ Cannes) 62,859
Antony (★ Paris) 54,610
Argenteuil (★ Paris) 95,347
Arras (★ 80,477) 41,736
Asnières [-sur-Seine] (★ Paris) 71,077
Aubervilliers (★ Paris) 67,719
Aulnay-sous-Bois (★ Paris) 75,996
Avignon (★ 174,264) 89,132
Bayonne (★ 127,477) 41,381
Beauvais (★ 55,817) 52,365
Belfort (★ 76,221) 51,206
Besançon (★ 120,772) 113,283
Béthune (★ 258,383) 25,508
Béziers (★ 81,347) 76,647
Bordeaux (★ 640,012) 208,159
Boulogne-Billancourt (★ Paris) 102,582
Boulogne-sur-Mer (★ 98,566) 47,653
Bourges (★ 92,202) 76,432
Brest (★ 201,145) 156,060
Brive-la-Gaillarde (★ 64,301) 51,511
Caen (★ 183,526) 114,068
Calais (★ 100,823) 76,527
Cannes (★ 295,525) 72,259
Châlons-sur-Marne (★ 63,061) 51,137
Chalon-sur-Saône (★ 78,064) 56,194
Chambéry (★ 96,163) 53,427
Champigny-sur-Marne (★ Paris) 76,176
Charleville-Mézières (★ 67,694) 58,667
Châteauroux (★ 66,851) 51,942
Cherbourg (★ 85,485) 28,442
Cholet 55,524
Clermont-Ferrand (★ 256,189) 147,361
Colmar (★ 82,468) 62,483
Colombes (★ Paris) 78,777
Courbevoie (★ Paris) 59,830
Créteil (★ Paris) 71,693
Dieppe (★ 41,812) 35,957
Dijon (★ 215,865) 140,942
Douai (★ 202,366) 42,576
Drancy (★ Paris) 60,183
Dunkerque (★ 195,705) 73,120
Épinay-sur-Seine (★ Paris) 50,314
Fontenay-sous-Bois (★ Paris) 52,627
Forbach (★ 99,606) 27,187
Grenoble (★ 392,021) 156,637
Hagondange (★ 119,669) 9,091
Ivry-sur-Seine (★ Paris) 55,699
La Rochelle (★ 102,143) 75,840
La Seyne [-sur-Mer] (★ Toulon) 57,659
Laval (★ 55,984) 50,360
Le Havre (★ 254,595) 199,388
Le Mans (★ 191,080) 147,697
Levallois-Perret (★ Paris) 53,500
Lille (★ 1,020,000) 168,424
Limoges (★ 171,689) 140,400
Lorient (★ 104,025) 62,554
Lyon (★ 1,275,000) 413,095
Maisons-Alfort (★ Paris) 51,065
Mantes-la-Jolie (★ 170,265) 43,564
Marseille (★ 1,225,000) 874,436
Maubeuge (★ 105,714) 36,061
Melun (★ 82,479) 35,005
Mérignac (★ Bordeaux) 51,306
Metz (★ 186,437) 114,232
Montbéliard (★ 128,194) 31,836
Montluçon (★ 67,963) 49,912
Montpellier (★ 221,307) 197,231
Montreuil-sous-Bois (★ Paris) 93,368
Mulhouse (Mülhausen) (★ 220,613) 112,157
Nancy (★ 306,982) 96,317
Nanterre (★ Paris) 88,578
Nantes (★ 464,857) 240,539
Neuilly-sur-Seine (★ Paris) 64,170
Nice (★ 449,496) 337,085
Nîmes (★ 132,343) 124,220
Niort (★ 61,959) 58,203
Orléans (★ 220,478) 102,710
• PARIS (★ 9,775,000) (1987 E) 2,078,900
Pau (★ 131,265) 83,790
Perpignan (★ 137,915) 111,669
Pessac (★ Bordeaux) 50,267
Poitiers (★ 103,204) 79,350
Quimper 56,907
Reims (★ 199,388) 194,656
Rennes (★ 234,418) 117,234
Roanne (★ 81,786) 48,705
Roubaix (★★ Lille) 101,602
Rouen (★ 379,879) 101,945
Rueil-Malmaison (★ Paris) 63,412
Saint-Brieuc (★ 83,900) 48,563
Saint-Chamond (★ 82,059) 40,267
Saint-Denis (★ Paris) 90,829
Saint-Étienne (★ 317,228) 204,955
Saint-Maur-des-Fossés (★ Paris) 80,811
Saint-Nazaire (★ 130,271) 68,348
Saint-Quentin (★ 71,887) 63,567
Sarcelles (★ Paris) 53,630
Strasbourg (★ 400,000) 248,712
Tarbes (★ 78,056) 51,422
Thionville (★ 138,034) 40,573
Toulon (★ 410,393) 179,423
Toulouse (★ 541,271) 347,995
Tourcoing (★★ Lille) 96,908
Tours (★ 262,786) 132,209
Troyes (★ 125,240) 63,581
Valence (★ 106,041) 66,356
Valenciennes (★ 349,505) 40,275
Vénissieux (★ Lyon) 64,804
Versailles (★ Paris) 91,494
Villejuif (★ Paris) 52,448
Villeneuve-d'Ascq (★ Lille) 59,527
Villeurbanne (★ Lyon) 115,960
Vitry-sur-Seine (★ Paris) 85,263

FRENCH GUIANA / Guyane française
1982 C 73,022
Cities and Towns
• CAYENNE 38,091

FRENCH POLYNESIA / Polynésie française
1988 C 188,814
Cities and Towns
• PAPEETE (★ 80,000) 23,555

GABON
1985 E 1,312,000
Cities and Towns
Franceville 58,800
Lambaréné 49,500
• LIBREVILLE 235,700
Port Gentil 124,400

GAMBIA
1983 C 696,000
Cities and Towns
• BANJUL (★ 95,000) 44,536

GEORGIA / Sakartvelo
1989 C 5,449,000
Cities and Towns
Batumi 136,000
Gori (1987 E) 62,000
Kutaisi 235,000
Poti (1977 E) 54,000
Rustavi (★ Tbilisi) 159,000
Suchumi 121,000
• TBILISI (★ 1,460,000) 1,260,000

GERMANY / Deutschland
1989 E 78,389,735
Cities and Towns
Aachen (★ 535,000) 233,255
Aalen (★ 80,000) 62,812
Ahlen 52,836
Altenburg 53,288
Arnsberg 73,912
Aschaffenburg (★ 145,000) 62,048
Augsburg (★ 405,000) 247,731
Baden-Baden 50,761
Bad Homburg (★ Frankfurt am Main) 51,035
Bad Salzuflen (★★ Herford) 50,875
Bamberg (★ 120,000) 69,809
Bautzen 52,394
Bayreuth (★ 90,000) 70,933
Bergheim (★ Köln) 55,997
Bergisch Gladbach (★ Köln) 101,983
Bergkamen (★ Essen) 48,489
BERLIN (★ 3,825,000) 3,352,848
Bielefeld (★ 515,000) 311,946
Bitterfeld (★ 105,000) 20,513
Bocholt 67,565
Bochum (★★ Essen) 389,087
BONN (★ 570,000) 282,190
Bottrop (★ Essen) 116,363
Brandenburg 94,872
Braunschweig (★ 330,000) 253,794
Bremen (★ 800,000) 535,058
Bremerhaven (★ 190,000) 126,934
Castrop-Rauxel (★ Essen) 77,660
Celle 71,050
Chemnitz (★ 450,000) 311,765
Cottbus 128,639
Cuxhaven 55,249
Darmstadt (★ 305,000) 136,067
Delmenhorst (★★ Bremen) 72,901
Dessau (★ 140,000) 103,867
Detmold 66,809
Dinslaken (★ Essen) 63,246
Dormagen (★ Köln) 55,935
Dorsten (★ Essen) 75,518
Dortmund (★★ Essen) 587,328
Dresden (★ 670,000) 518,057
Duisburg (★★ Essen) 527,447
Düren (★ 110,000) 83,120
Düsseldorf (★ 1,190,000) 569,641
Eberswalde 54,822
Eisenhüttenstadt 53,048
Emden 49,803
Erfurt 220,016
Erlangen (★★ Nürnberg) 100,583
Eschweiler (★★ Aachen) 53,516
• Essen (★ 4,950,000) 620,594
Esslingen (★ Stuttgart) 90,537
Flensburg (★ 103,000) 85,830
Frankfurt am Main (★ 1,855,000) 625,258
Frankfurt an der Oder 87,863
Freiberg 51,341
Freiburg [im Breisgau] (★ 225,000) 183,979
Friedrichshafen 52,295
Fulda (★ 79,000) 54,320
Fürth (★★ Nürnberg) 98,832
Garbsen (★ Hannover) 59,225
Garmisch-Partenkirchen 25,908
Gelsenkirchen (★★ Essen) 287,255
Gera 134,834
Giessen (★ 160,000) 71,751
Gladbeck (★ Essen) 79,187
Göppingen (★ 155,000) 52,873
Görlitz 77,609
Goslar (★ 84,000) 45,614
Gotha 57,365
Göttingen 118,073
Greifswald 68,597
Grevenbroich (★ Düsseldorf) 59,204
Gummersbach 49,017
Gütersloh (★★ Bielefeld) 83,407
Hagen (★★ Essen) 210,640
Halle (★ 475,000) 236,044
Halle-Neustadt (★ Halle) 93,446
Hamburg (★ 2,225,000) 1,603,070
Hameln (★ 72,000) 57,642
Hamm 173,611
Hanau (★★ Frankfurt am Main) 84,300
Hannover (★ 1,000,000) 498,495
Hattingen (★ Essen) 56,242
Heidelberg (★★ Mannheim) 131,429
Heidenheim (★ 89,000) 48,497
Heilbronn (★ 230,000) 112,278
Herford (★ 120,000) 61,700
Herne (★ Essen) 174,664
Herten (★ Essen) 68,111
Hilden (★ Düsseldorf) 53,725
Hildesheim (★ 140,000) 103,512
Hof 50,938
Hoyerswerda 69,361
Hürth (★ Köln) 49,094
Ingolstadt (★ 138,000) 97,702
Iserlohn 93,337
Jena 108,010
Kaiserslautern (★ 138,000) 96,990
Karlsruhe (★ 485,000) 265,100
Kassel (★ 360,000) 189,156
Kempten (Allgäu) 60,052
Kerpen (★ Köln) 54,699
Kiel (★ 335,000) 240,675
Kleve 44,416
Koblenz (★ 180,000) 107,286
Köln (Cologne) (★ 1,760,000) 937,482

C Census. E Official estimate. U Unofficial estimate.
• Largest city in country.
★ Population or designation of metropolitan area, including suburbs (see headnote).
▲ Population of an entire municipality, commune, or district, including rural area.

Konstanz 72,862
Krefeld (★★ Essen) 235,423
Landshut 57,194
Langenfeld (★ Düsseldorf) 50,777
Leipzig (★ 700,000) 545,307
Leverkusen (★ Köln) 157,358
Lippstadt 60,396
Lübeck (★ 260,000) 210,681
Lüdenscheid 76,118
Ludwigsburg (★ Stuttgart) 79,342
Ludwigshafen (★★ Mannheim) 158,478
Lüneburg 60,053
Lünen (★ Essen) 85,584
Magdeburg (★ 400,000) 290,579
Mainz (★★ Wiesbaden) 174,828
Mannheim (★ 1,400,000) 300,468
Marburg an der Lahn 70,905
Marl (★ Essen) 89,651
Meerbusch (★ Düsseldorf) 50,452
Menden 54,899
Minden (★ 125,000) 75,169
Moers (★ Essen) 101,809
Mönchengladbach (★ 410,000) 252,910
Mülheim an der Ruhr (★ Essen) 175,454
München (Munich) (★ 1,955,000) 1,211,617
Münster 248,919
Neubrandenburg 90,471
Neumünster 79,574
Neunkirchen (★ 135,000) 50,784
Neuss (★ Düsseldorf) 143,976
Neustadt an der Weinstrasse 50,453
Neuwied (★ 150,000) 60,665
Norderstedt (★ Hamburg) 66,747
Nürnberg (★ 1,030,000) 480,078
Oberhausen (★★ Essen) 221,017
Offenbach (★ Frankfurt am Main) 112,450
Offenburg 51,730
Oldenburg 140,785
Osnabrück (★ 270,000) 154,594
Paderborn 114,148
Passau 49,137
Pforzheim (★ 220,000) 108,887
Plauen 77,593
Potsdam (★ Berlin) 142,862
Ratingen (★ Düsseldorf) 89,880
Ravensburg (★ 75,000) 44,146
Recklinghausen (★ Essen) 121,666
Regensburg (★ 205,000) 119,078
Remscheid (★★ Wuppertal) 120,979
Reutlingen (★ 160,000) 100,400
Rheine 69,324
Rosenheim 54,304
Rostock 253,990
Rüsselsheim (★★ Wiesbaden) 58,426
Saarbrücken (★ 385,000) 188,467
Saarlouis (★ 115,000) 37,662
Salzgitter 111,674
Sankt Augustin (★ Bonn) 50,230
Schwäbisch Gmünd 57,861
Schwedt 52,419
Schweinfurt (★ 110,000) 52,818
Schwerin 130,685
Schwerte (★ Essen) 49,017
Siegburg (★ 170,000) 34,402
Siegen (★ 200,000) 106,160
Sindelfingen (★ Stuttgart) 57,524
Solingen (★★ Wuppertal) 160,824
Stendal 49,906
Stolberg (★★ Aachen) 56,182
Stralsund 75,498
Stuttgart (★ 1,925,000) 562,658
Suhl 56,345
Trier (★ 125,000) 95,692
Troisdorf (★★ Siegburg) 62,011
Tübingen 76,046
Ulm (★ 210,000) 106,508
Unna (★ Essen) 61,989
Velbert (★ Essen) 88,058
Viersen (★★ Mönchengladbach) 76,163
Villingen-Schwenningen 76,258
Weimar 63,412
Wesel 57,986
Wetzlar (★ 105,000) 50,299
Wiesbaden (★ 795,000) 254,209
Wilhelmshaven (★ 135,000) 89,892
Wismar 58,058
Witten (★ Essen) 109,637
Wittenberg 53,358
Wolfenbüttel (★★ Braunschweig) 50,960
Wolfsburg 125,831
Worms (★★ Mannheim) 74,809
Wuppertal (★ 830,000) 371,283
Würzburg (★ 210,000) 125,589
Zweibrücken (★ 105,000) 33,377
Zwickau (★ 165,000) 121,749

GHANA
1984 C 12,205,574
Cities and Towns
• ACCRA (★ 1,250,000) 859,640
Ashiaman (★ Accra) 49,427
Cape Coast 86,620
Koforidua 54,400
Kumasi (★ 600,000) 348,880
Obuasi 60,146
Sekondi-Takoradi (★ 175,352) 93,882
Tafo (★ Kumasi) 50,432
Tamale (★ 168,091) 136,828
Tema (★★ Accra) 99,608
Teshie (★ Accra) 62,954

GIBRALTAR
1988 E 30,077
Cities and Towns
• GIBRALTAR 30,077

GREECE / Ellás
1981 C 9,740,417
Cities and Towns
Aiyáleo (★ Athínai) 81,906
• ATHÍNAI (ATHENS) (★ 3,027,331) 885,737
Áyios Dhimítrios (★ Athínai) 51,421
Galátsion (★ Athínai) 50,096
Ilioúpolis (★ Athínai) 69,560
Iráklion (★ 110,958) 102,398
Kalamariá (★ Thessaloníki) 51,676
Kallithéa (★ Athínai) 117,319
Kavála 56,375
Keratsínion (★ Athínai) 74,179
Khalándrion (★ Athínai) 54,320
Khaniá (★ 61,976) 47,451
Khíos (★ 29,742) 24,070
Koridhallós (★ Athínai) 61,313
Lárisa 102,048
Néa Ionía (★ Athínai) 59,202
Néa Liósia (★ Athínai) 72,427
Néa Smírni (★ Athínai) 67,408
Níkaia (★ Athínai) 90,368
Palaión Fáliron (★ Athínai) 53,273
Pátrai (★ 154,596) 142,163
Peristérion (★ Athínai) 140,858
Piraiévs (Piraeus) (★★ Athínai) 196,389
Spárti (Sparta) (★ 14,388) 12,975
Thessaloníki (Salonika) (★ 706,180) 406,413
Víron (★ Athínai) 57,880
Vólos (★ 107,407) 71,378
Zográfos (★ Athínai) 84,548

GREENLAND / Grønland / Kalaallit Nunaat
1990 E 55,558
Cities and Towns
• GODTHÅB (NUUK) 12,217

GRENADA
1981 C 89,088
Cities and Towns
• SAINT GEORGE'S (★ 25,000) 4,788

GUADELOUPE
1982 C 328,400
Cities and Towns
BASSE-TERRE (★ 26,600) 13,656
Les Abymes (★ Pointe-à-Pitre) 56,165
• Pointe-à-Pitre (★ 83,000) 25,310

GUAM
1980 C 105,979
Cities and Towns
• AGANA (★ 44,000) 896

GUATEMALA
1989 E 8,935,395
Cities and Towns
Escuintla 60,673
• GUATEMALA (★ 1,400,000) 1,057,210
Quetzaltenango 88,769

GUERNSEY
1986 C 55,482
Cities and Towns
• SAINT PETER PORT (★ 36,000) 16,085

GUINEA / Guinée
1986 E 6,225,000
Cities and Towns
• CONAKRY 800,000
Kankan 100,000
Kindia 80,000
Labé 110,000
Nzérékoré (1983 C) 55,356

GUINEA-BISSAU / Guiné-Bissau
1988 E 945,000
Cities and Towns
• BISSAU 125,000

GUYANA
1983 E 918,000
Cities and Towns
• GEORGETOWN (★ 188,000) 78,500

HAITI / Haïti
1987 E 5,531,802
Cities and Towns
Cap-Haïtien 72,161
• PORT-AU-PRINCE (★ 880,000) 797,000

HONDURAS
1988 C 4,376,839
Cities and Towns
Choluteca 53,799
El Progreso 55,523
La Ceiba 68,289
San Pedro Sula 279,356
• TEGUCIGALPA 551,606

HONG KONG
1986 C 5,395,997
Cities and Towns
Kowloon (Jiulong) (★★ Victoria) 774,781
Kwai Chung (★ Victoria) 131,362
New Kowloon (Xinjiulong) (★★ Victoria) 1,526,910
Sha Tin (★ Victoria) 355,810
Sheung Shui 87,206
Tai Po 119,679
Tsuen Wan (Quanwan) (★ Victoria) 514,241
Tuen Mun (★ Victoria) 262,458
• VICTORIA (★ 4,770,000) 1,175,860
Yuen Long 75,740

HUNGARY / Magyarország
1990 C 10,375,000
Cities and Towns
Békéscsaba (▲ 67,621) 58,800
• BUDAPEST (★ 2,565,000) 2,016,132
Debrecen 212,247
Dunaújváros 59,049
Eger 61,908
Győr 129,356
Kaposvár 71,793
Kecskemét (▲ 102,528) 81,200
Miskolc 196,449
Nagykanizsa 54,059
Nyíregyháza (▲ 114,166) 88,500
Pécs 170,119
Sopron 55,088
Szeged 175,338
Székesfehérvár 108,990
Szolnok 78,333
Szombathely 85,418
Tatabánya 74,271
Veszprém 63,902
Zalaegerszeg 62,221

ICELAND / Ísland
1987 E 247,357
Cities and Towns
• REYKJAVÍK (★ 137,941) 93,425

INDIA / Bharat
1981 C 685,184,692
Cities and Towns
Abohar 86,334
Achalpur 81,186
Ādilābād 53,482
Ādityapur (★ Jamshedpur) 53,421
Ādoni 108,939
Agartala 132,186
Āgra (★ 747,318) 694,191
Ahmadābād (★ 2,400,000) 2,059,725
Ahmadnagar (★ 181,210) 143,937
Ajmer 375,593
Akola 225,412
Akot 51,936
Alandur (★ Madras) 97,449
Alīgarh 320,861
Alījal 74,493
Allahābād (★ 650,070) 616,051
Alleppey 169,940
Alwar 145,795
Amalner 67,516
Amarnāth (★ Bombay) 96,347
Ambāla (★ 233,110) 104,565
Ambāla Sadar (★ Ambāla) 80,741
Ambattur (★ Madras) 115,901
Āmbūr 66,042
Amrāvati 261,404
Amreli (★ 58,241) 56,598
Amritsar 594,844
Amroha 112,682
Anakāpalle 73,179
Ānand 83,936
Anantapur 119,531
Arcot (★ 94,363) 38,836
Arkonam 59,405
Arni 49,365
Arrah 125,111
Aruppukkottai 72,245
Asansol (★ 1,050,000) 183,375
Ashoknagar-Kalyangarh (★ Hābra) 55,176
Āttūr 50,517
Aurangābād (★ 316,421) 284,607
Avadi (★ Madras) 124,701
Azamgarh 66,523
Badagara 64,174
Bāgalkot 67,858
Baharampur (★ 102,311) 92,889
Bahraich 99,889
Baidyabāti (★ Calcutta) 70,573
Bālāghāt (★ 53,183) 49,564
Balāngīr 54,943
Balasore 65,779
Ballālpur 61,398
Ballia 61,704
Bālly (★ Calcutta) 147,735
Bālly (★ Calcutta) 54,859
Bālurghāt (★ 112,621) 104,646
Bānda 72,379
Bangalore (★ 2,950,000) 2,476,355
Bangaon 69,885
Bānkura 94,954
Bansberia (★ Calcutta) 77,020
Bāpatla 55,347
Bārākpur (★ Calcutta) 115,253
Baranagar (★ Calcutta) 170,343
Bārāsat (★ Calcutta) 66,504
Bareilly (★ 449,425) 386,734
Barmer 55,554
Baroda (★ 744,881) 734,473
Bārsi 72,537
Bāruni 56,366
Basīrhāt 81,040
Basti 69,357
Batala (★ 101,966) 87,135
Beāwar 89,998
Begusarai (★ 68,305) 56,633
Behāla (South Suburban) (★ Calcutta) 378,765
Bela 49,932
Belgaum (★ 300,372) 274,430
Bellary 201,579
Berhampur 162,550
Bettiah 72,167
Bhadrakh 60,600
Bhadrāvati (★ 130,606) 53,551
Bhadrāvati New Town (★★ Bhadrāvati) 77,055
Bhadreswar (★ Calcutta) 58,858
Bhāgalpur 225,062
Bhandāra 56,025
Bharatpur 105,274
Bhathinda 124,453
Bhātpāra (★ Calcutta) 260,761
Bhaunagar (★ 308,642) 307,121
Bhilai (★ 490,214) 290,090
Bhīlwāra 122,625
Bhīmavaram 101,894
Bhind 74,515
Bhiwandi (★ Bombay) 115,298
Bhiwāni 101,277
Bhopāl 671,018
Bhubaneswar 219,211
Bhuj (★ 70,211) 69,693
Bhusāwal (★ 132,142) 123,133
Bīdar 78,856
Bihār 151,343
Bijāpur 147,313
Bijnor 56,713
Bīkaner (★ 287,712) 253,174
Bilāspur (★ 187,104) 147,218
Bīr 80,287
Bodhan 50,807
Bodināyakkanūr 59,168
Bokāro Steel City (★ 264,480) 224,099
Bombay (★ 9,950,000) 8,243,405
Botād 50,274
Brajrajnagar 54,033
Broach (★ 120,524) 110,070
Budaun 93,004
Budge Budge (★ Calcutta) 66,424
Bulandshahr 103,436
Bulsār (★ Bombay) 54,017
Burdwān 167,364
Burhānpur 140,896
• Calcutta (★ 11,100,000) 3,305,006
Calicut (★ 546,058) 394,447
Cambay 68,791
Cannanore (★ 157,797) 60,904
Chākdaha 59,308
Chakradharpur (★ 44,532) 29,272
Chālisgaon 59,342
Champdāni (★ Calcutta) 76,138
Chandannagar (★ Calcutta) 101,925
Chandausi 66,970
Chandīgarh (★ 422,841) 373,789
Chandrapur 115,777
Changanācheri 51,955
Channapatna 50,725
Chāpra 111,564
Chhatarpur 51,959
Chhindwāra 75,178
Chidambaram (★ 62,543) 55,920
Chikmagalūr 60,582
Chilakalurupet 61,645
Chīrāla 72,040
Chitradurga 74,580
Chittaranjan (★ 61,045) 50,748
Chittoor 86,230
Churu (★ 62,070) 61,811
Cochin (★ 685,836) 513,249
Coimbatore (★ 965,000) 704,514
Cooch Behār (★ 80,101) 62,127
Coonoor (★ 92,242) 44,750
Cuddalore 127,625
Cuddapah 103,125
Cuttack (★ 327,412) 269,950
Dabgram 76,402
Dāhod (★ 82,256) 55,256
Dāltonganj 51,952
Damoh (★ 76,758) 75,573
Dānāpur (★ Patna) 58,684
Darbhanga 176,301
Darjiling 57,603
Datia 49,386
Dāvangere 196,621
Dehra Dūn (★ 293,010) 211,416
Dehri 90,409
Delhi (★ 7,200,000) 4,884,234
Delhi Cantonment (★ Delhi) 85,166
Deoband 51,270
Deoghar (★ 59,120) 52,904
Deolāli (★★ Nāsik) 77,666
Deolāli Cantonment (★ Nāsik) 57,745
Deoria 55,720
Dewās 83,465
Dhamtari 55,797
Dhānbād (★ 825,000) 120,221
Dharmapuri 51,223
Dharmavaram 50,969
Dhorāji (★ 77,716) 76,556
Dhrāngadhra 51,280
Dhule 210,759
Dibrugarh (1971 C) 80,348
Dindigul 164,103
Dombivli (★ Bombay) 103,222
Durg (★★ Bhilai) 114,637
Durgāpur 311,798
Elūru 168,154
English Bāzār 79,010
Erode (★ 275,999) 142,252
Etah 53,784
Etāwah 112,174
Faizābād (★ 143,167) 101,873
Farīdābad New Township (★ Delhi) 330,864
Farrukhābād (★ 160,796) 145,793
Fatehpur, Rājasthān state 51,084
Fatehpur, Uttar Pradesh state 84,831
Fīrozābād 202,338
Fīrozpur (★ 105,840) 61,162
Gadag 117,368
Gandhidham (★ 61,489) 61,415
Gandhinagar 62,443
Gangāwati 58,735
Garden Reach (★ Calcutta) 191,107
Gārulia (★ Calcutta) 57,061
Gauhāti (★ 200,377) (1971 C) 123,783
Gaya 247,075
Ghāziābād (★ 287,170) 271,730
Ghāzīpur 60,725
Giridih 65,444
Godhra (★ 86,228) 85,784
Gonda 70,847
Gondal (★ 66,818) 66,096
Gondia 100,423
Gorakhpur (★ 307,501) 290,814
Gudivāda 80,198
Gudiyāttam (★ 80,674) 75,044
Gulbarga 221,325
Guna (★ 64,659) 60,255
Guntakal 84,599
Guntūr 367,699
Gurgaon (★ 100,877) 89,115
Gwalior (★ 555,862) 539,015
Hābra (★ 129,610) 74,434
Hājīpur 62,520
Haldwāni 77,300
Hālisahar (★ Calcutta) 95,579
Hānsi 50,365
Hanumāngarh 60,071
Hāpur 102,837

C Census. E Official estimate. U Unofficial estimate.
• Largest city in country.
★ Population or designation of metropolitan area, including suburbs (see headnote).
▲ Population of an entire municipality, commune, or district, including rural area.

Hardoi 67,259
Hardwār (★ 145,946) 114,180
Harihar 52,334
Hassan 71,534
Hāthras 92,962
Hazārībāgh 80,155
Hindupur 55,901
Hinganghāt 59,075
Hisār (★ 137,369) 131,309
Hoshiārpur 85,648
Hospet (★ 115,351) 90,572
Howrah (★ Calcutta) 744,429
Hubli-Dhārwār 527,108
Hugli-Chinsurah (★ Calcutta) 125,193
Hyderābād (★ 2,750,000) 2,187,262
Ichalkaranji 133,751
Imphāl 156,622
Indore (★ 850,000) 829,327
Itārsi (★ 69,619) 62,499
Jabalpur (★ 757,303) 614,162
Jabalpur Cantonment (★ Jabalpur) 61,026
Jādabpur (★ Calcutta) 251,968
Jagdalpur (★ 63,632) 51,286
Jagtiāl 53,213
Jaipur (★ 1,025,000) 977,165
Jālgaon 145,335
Jālna 122,276
Jalpaiguri 61,743
Jamālpur 78,356
Jammu (★ 223,361) 206,135
Jāmnagar (★ 317,362) 277,615
Jamshedpur (★ 669,580) 438,385
Jangoon 70,727
Jaridih (★ 101,946) 46,477
Jaunpur 105,140
Jetpur (★ 63,074) 62,806
Jeypore 53,981
Jhānsi (★ 284,141) 246,172
Jharia (★★ Dhanbād) 57,496
Jhārsuguda 54,859
Jīnd 56,748
Jodhpur 506,345
Jotacamund 78,277
Jullundur (★ 441,552) 408,186
Junāgadh (★ 120,416) 118,646
Kadaiyanallūr 60,306
Kadiri 52,774
Kaithal 58,385
Kākināda 226,409
Kālahasti 51,306
Kālol (★ Ahmadābād) 69,946
Kalyān (★ Bombay) 136,052
Kāmārhāti (★ Calcutta) 234,951
Kambam 50,340
Kāmthi (★ Nāgpur) 67,364
Kānchipuram (★ 145,254) 130,926
Kānchrāpāra (★ Calcutta) 88,798
Kānpur (★ 1,875,000) 1,481,789
Kānpur Cantonment (★ Kānpur) 90,311
Kapūrthala 50,300
Karād 54,364
Kāraikkudi (★ 100,141) 66,993
Karīmnagar 86,125
Karnāl 132,107
Karūr (★ 93,810) 72,692
Kāsganj 61,402
Kashīpur 51,773
Katihār (★ 122,005) 104,781
Kayankulam 61,327
Kerkend (★ Dhanbād) 75,186
Khadki Cantonment (★ Pune) 80,835
Khāmgaon 61,992
Khammam 98,757
Khandwa 114,725
Khanna 53,761
Kharagpur (★ 232,575) 150,475
Kharagpur Railway Settlement (★ Kharagpur) 82,100
Khargon 52,749
Khurja 67,119
Kishanganj 51,790
Kishangarh 62,032
Kolār 65,834
Kolār Gold Fields (★ 144,385) 77,679
Kolhāpur (★ 351,392) 340,625
Konnagar (★ Calcutta) 51,211
Korba 83,387
Kota 358,241
Kottagūdem 94,894
Kottayam 64,431
Kovilpatti 63,964
Krishnanagar 98,141
Kumbakonam (★ 141,794) 132,832
Kundla (★ 51,431) 49,740
Kurnool 206,362
Lakhīmpur 61,003
Lalitpur 55,756
Lātūr 111,986
Lucknow (★ 1,060,000) 895,721
Lucknow Cantonment (★ Lucknow) 59,614
Ludhiāna 607,052
Machilīpatnam (Bandar) 138,530
Madanapalle 54,938
Madgaon (Margao) (★ 64,858) 53,076
Madras (★ 4,475,000) 3,276,622
Madurai (★ 960,000) 820,891
Mahbūbnagar 87,503
Mahuva (★ 56,072) 53,625
Mainpuri 58,928
Mālegaon 245,883
Māler Kotla 65,756
Malkajgiri (★ Hyderābād) 65,776
Mandasor 77,603
Mandya 100,285
Mangalore (★ 306,078) 172,252
Mango (★ Jamshedpur) 67,284
Manjeri 53,959
Manmād 51,439
Mannārgudi 51,738
Mathura (★ 160,995) 147,493
Maunath Bhanjan 86,326
Māyūram 67,675
Meerut (★ 536,615) 417,395
Meerut Cantonment (★ Meerut) 94,210
Mehsāna (★ 73,024) 72,872
Melappālaiyam (★ Tirunelveli) 57,683
Mettuppālaiyam 59,537
Mhow (★ 76,037) 70,130
Midnapore 86,118
Miraj (★★ Sāngli) 105,455
Mirzāpur 127,787
Modinagar (★ 87,665) 78,243
Moga 80,272
Mokāma 51,047
Monghyr 129,260
Morādābād (★ 345,350) 330,051
Morena 69,864
Mormugao 69,684
Morvi 73,327
Motihāri (★ 63,212) 57,911
Muktsar 50,941
Murwāra (★ 123,017) 77,862
Muzaffarnagar 171,816
Muzaffarpur 190,416
Mysore (★ 479,081) 441,754
Nabadwip (★ 129,800) 109,108
Nadiād 142,689
Nāgappattinam (★ 90,650) 82,828
Nāgda 56,602
Nāgercoil 171,648
Nagīna 50,405
Nāgpur (★ 1,302,066) 1,219,461
Naihāti (★ Calcutta) 114,607
Najībābād 55,109
Nalgonda 62,458
Nānded 191,269
Nandurbār 65,394
Nandyāl 88,185
Nangi (★ Calcutta) 54,035
Narasaraopet 67,032
Nāsik (★ 429,034) 262,428
Navsāri (★ 129,266) 106,793
Nawābganj (★ 62,216) 51,518
Neemuch (★ 68,853) 65,860
Nellore 237,065
NEW DELHI (★★ Delhi) 273,036
Neyveli (★ 98,866) 88,000
Nizāmābād 183,061
North Bārākpur (★ Calcutta) 81,758
North Dum Dum (★ Calcutta) 96,418
Nowgong (1971 C) 56,537
Ongole 85,302
Orai 66,397
Outer Burnpur (★ Asansol) 86,803
Pālanpur 61,262
Pālayankottai (★★ Tirunelveli) 87,302
Pālghāt (★ 117,986) 111,245
Pāli 91,568
Pallavaram (★ Madras) 83,901
Palni (★ 68,389) 64,444
Pānchur (★ Calcutta) 51,223
Pandharpur 64,380
Pānihāti (★ Calcutta) 205,718
Pānīpat 137,927
Paramagudi 61,149
Parbhani 109,364
Pātan 79,196
Pathānkot 110,039
Patiāla (★ 206,254) 205,141
Patna (★ 1,025,000) 776,371
Pattukkottai 49,484
Phagwāra (★ 75,961) 72,499
Pīlibhīt 88,548
Pimpri-Chinchwad (★ Pune) 220,966
Pollāchi (★ 114,971) 82,354
Pondicherry (★ 251,420) 162,636
Ponmalai (★ Tiruchchirāppalli) 55,995
Ponnūru Nidubrolu 50,206
Porbandar (★ 133,307) 115,182
Port Blair 49,634
Proddatūr 107,070
Pudukkottai 87,952
Pune (Poona) (★ 1,775,000) 1,203,351
Pune Cantonment (★ Pune) 85,986
Puri 100,942
Purnea (★ 109,875) 91,144
Purūlia 73,904
Quilon (★ 167,598) 137,943
Rabkavi Banhatti 51,693
Rāe Bareli 89,697
Rāichūr 124,762
Raiganj (★ 66,705) 60,343
Raigarh (★ 69,791) 68,060
Raipur 338,245
Rājahmundry (★ 268,370) 203,358
Rājapālaiyam 101,640
Rajhara-Jharandalli 55,307
Rājkot 445,076
Rāj-Nāndgaon 86,367
Rājpura 58,645
Rāmpur 204,610
Rānāghāt (★ 83,744) 58,356
Rānchī (★ 502,771) 489,626
Rānībennur 58,118
Rānīganj (★ 119,101) 48,702
Ratlām (★ 155,578) 142,319
Raurkela (★ 322,610) 206,821
Raurkela Civil Township (★ Raurkela) 96,000
Rewa 100,641
Rewāri 51,562
Rishra (★ Calcutta) 81,001
Robertson Pet (★ Kolār Gold Fields) 61,099
Rohtak 166,767
Roorkee (★ 79,076) 61,851
Sāgar (★ 207,479) 160,392
Sahāranpur 295,355
Saharsa 57,580
Sahijpur Bogha (★ Ahmadābād) 65,327
Salem (★ 518,615) 361,394
Sambalpur (★ 162,214) 110,282
Sambhal 108,232
Sāngli (★ 268,988) 152,339
Sāntipur 82,980
Sardarnagar (★ Ahmadābād) 50,128
Sardārshahr (★ 56,388) 55,473
Sasarām 73,457
Sātāra 83,336
Satna (★ 96,667) 90,476
Saunda (★ 99,990) 70,780
Secunderābād Cantonment (★ Hyderābād) 135,994
Sehore 52,190
Seoni 54,017
Serampore (★ Calcutta) 127,304
Shāhjahānpur (★ 205,095) 185,396
Shāmli 51,850
Shillong (★ 174,703) 109,244
Shimoga 151,783
Shivpuri 75,738
Sholāpur (★ 514,860) 511,103
Shrirampur 55,491
Sidhpur (★ 52,706) 51,953
Sīkar 102,970
Silchar (1971 C) 52,596
Silīguri 154,378
Simla 70,604
Sindri (★★ Dhanbād) 70,645
Sirsa 89,068
Sītāpur 101,210
Sivakāsi (★ 83,072) 59,827
Siwān 51,284
Sonīpat 109,369
South Dum Dum (★ Calcutta) 230,266
Sri Gangānagar 123,692
Srīkākulam 68,145
Srīnagar (★ 606,002) 594,775
Srīrangam (★ Tiruchchirāppalli) 64,241
Srīvilliputtūr 61,458
Sujāngarh 55,546
Surat (★ 913,806) 776,583
Surendranagar (★ 130,602) 89,619
Tādepallegūdem 62,574
Tādpatri 53,920
Tāmbaram (★ Madras) 86,923
Tānda 54,474
Tanuku 53,618
Tellicherry (★ 98,704) 75,561
Tenāli 119,257
Tenkāsi 49,214
Thāna (★ Bombay) 309,897
Thānesar 49,052
Thanjāvūr 184,015
Theni-Allinagaram 53,018
Tindivanam 56,520
Tinsukia (1971 C) 54,911
Tiruchchirāppalli (★ 609,548) 362,045
Tiruchengodu 53,941
Tirunelveli (★ 323,344) 128,850
Tirupati 115,292
Tiruppattūr 52,422
Tiruppur (★ 215,859) 165,223
Tiruvannāmalai 89,462
Tiruvottiyūr (★ Madras) 134,014
Titāgarh (★ Calcutta) 104,534
Tonk 77,653
Trichūr (★ 170,122) 77,923
Trivandrum (★ 520,125) 483,086
Tumkūr 108,670
Tuticorin (★ 250,677) 192,949
Udaipur 232,588
Udamalpet 54,852
Udgīr 50,564
Ujjain (★ 282,203) 278,454
Ulhāsnagar (★ Bombay) 273,668
Unnāo 75,983
Upleta 54,907
Uttarpara-Kotrung (★ Calcutta) 79,598
Valparai 115,452
Vāniyambādi (★ 75,042) 59,107
Vārānasi (Benares) (★ 925,000) 708,647
Vellore (★ 274,041) 174,247
Verāval (★ 105,307) 85,048
Vidisha 65,521
Vijayawāda (★ 543,008) 454,577
Vikramasingapuram 49,319
Villupuram 77,091
Virudunagar 68,047
Vishākhapatnam (★ 603,630) 565,321
Vizianagaram 114,806
Warangal 335,150
Wardha 88,495
Yamunānagar (★ 160,424) 109,304
Yavatmāl 89,071
Yemmiganur 50,701

INDONESIA

1980 C 147,490,298

Cities and Towns

Ambon (▲ 207,702) 111,914
Balikpapan (▲ 279,852) 208,040
Banda Aceh (Kuturaja) 71,868
Bandung (★ 1,800,000) (1985 C) 1,633,000
Banjarmasin (1983 E) 424,000
Banyuwangi 90,378
Batang 49,328
Bekasi (★ Jakarta) 144,290
Binjai 71,444
Blitar (★ 100,000) 78,503
Bogor (★ 560,000) 246,946
Bojonegoro 57,483
Bukittinggi (▲ 70,691) 55,577
Cianjur 105,655
Cibinong 87,580
Cilacap 127,017
Cimahi (★ Bandung) (1971 C) 72,367
Ciparay 66,854
Cirebon (★ 275,000) 223,504
Denpasar 159,233
Depok (★ Jakarta) 126,693
Garut 145,624
Genteng 59,481
Gorontalo (▲ 97,610) 63,554
Gresik 86,418
• JAKARTA (★ 1,000,000) (1989 E) 9,200,000
Jambi (▲ 230,046) 155,761
Jayapura (Sukarnapura) 60,641
Jember 171,284
Jombang 58,800
Karawang 72,195
Kediri (▲ 221,830) 176,261
Kisaran 58,129
Klangenang 64,013
Klaten 117,560
Kudus 154,478
Kupang 84,587
Lumajang 58,495
Madiun (★ 180,000) 150,562
Magelang (★ 160,000) 123,358
Majalaya 87,474
Malang (1983 E) 547,000
Manado 217,091
Mataram 210,485
Medan (1985 E) 2,110,000
Mojokerto 68,849
Padang (▲ 657,000) (1983 E) 405,600
Padangsidempuan 56,984
Palangkaraya (▲ 60,447) 51,686
Palembang (1983 E) 874,000
Pangkalpinang 90,078
Parepare (▲ 86,360) 62,865
Pasuruan (★ 125,000) 95,864
Pati 50,159
Pekalongan (★ 260,000) 132,413
Pekanbaru 186,199
Pemalang 72,663
Pematangsiantar (★ 175,000) 150,296
Ponorogo 55,523
Pontianak (1983 E) 343,000
Pringsewu 56,115
Probolinggo 100,296
Purwakarta 61,995
Purwokerto 143,787
Salatiga 85,740
Samarinda (▲ 264,012) 182,473
Semarang (1983 E) 1,206,000
Serang 78,209
Sibolga 59,466
Sidoarjo 56,090
Singaraja 53,368
Singkawang 58,693
Situbondo 58,299
Sorong 52,041
Subang 52,041
Sukabumi (★ 225,000) 109,898
Surabaya (1985 E) 2,345,000
Surakarta (★ 575,000) (1983 E) 491,000
Taman 64,358
Tangerang 97,091
Tanjungkarang-Telukbetung (★ 375,000) 284,167
Tasikmalaya 192,267
Tebingtinggi (▲ 92,068) 69,569
Tegal (★ 340,000) 131,440
Tembilahan 52,140
Tulungagung 91,585
Ujungpandang (Makasar) (1983 E) 841,000
Yogyakarta (★ 510,000) (1983 E) 421,000

IRAN / Īrān

1986 C 49,445,010

Cities and Towns

Ābādān (1976 C) 296,081
Āghā Jārī (1982 E) 64,000
Ahar (1982 E) 52,000
Ahvāz 579,826
Āmol 118,242
Andīmeshk (1982 E) 53,000
Arāk 265,349
Ardabīl 281,973
Bābol 115,320
Bakhtarān (Kermānshāh) 560,514
Bandar-e 'Abbās 201,642
Bandar-e Anzalī (Bandar-e Pahlavī) (1982 E) 83,000
Bandar-e Būshehr 120,787
Bandar-e Māh Shahr (1982 E) 88,000
Behbahān (1982 E) 84,000
Bīrjand (1982 E) 68,000
Bojnūrd (1982 E) 82,000
Borāzjān (1982 E) 53,000
Borūjerd 183,879
Dezfūl 151,420
Do Rūd (1982 E) 52,000
Emāmshahr (Shāhrūd) (1982 E) 68,000
Eşfahān (★ 1,175,000) 986,753
Eslāmābād (1982 E) 71,000
Eslāmshahr (★ Tehrān) 215,129
Fasā (1982 E) 67,000
Gonbad-e Qābūs (1982 E) 75,000
Gorgān 139,430
Hamadān 272,499
Īlām (1982 E) 75,000
Jahrom (1982 E) 68,000
Karaj (★ Tehrān) 275,100
Kāshān 138,599
Kāzerūn (1982 E) 63,000
Kermān 257,284
Khomeynīshahr (★ Eşfahān) 104,647
Khorramābād 208,592
Khorramshahr (1976 C) 146,709
Khvoy 115,343
Mahābād (1982 E) 63,000
Malāyer 103,640
Marāgheh 100,679
Marand (1982 E) 59,000
Marv Dasht (1982 E) 72,000
Mashhad 1,463,508
Masjed Soleymān 104,787
Mīāndoāb (1982 E) 52,000
Mīāneh (1982 E) 57,000
Najafābād 129,058
Neyshābūr 109,258
Orūmīyeh (Reẕā'īyeh) 300,746
Qā'emshahr 109,288
Qazvīn 248,591
Qom 543,139
Qomsheh (1982 E) 67,000
Qūchān (1982 E) 61,000
Rafsanjān (1982 E) 61,000
Rāmhormoz (1982 E) 53,000
Rasht 290,897
Sabzevār 129,103
Sanandaj 204,537
Saqqez (1982 E) 76,000
Sārī 141,020
Semnān (1982 E) 54,000
Shahr-e Kord (1982 E) 63,000
Shīrāz 848,289
Sīrjān (1982 E) 67,000
Tabrīz 971,482
• TEHRĀN (★ 7,500,000) 6,042,584
Torbat-e Heydarīyeh (1982 E) 62,000
Varāmīn (1982 E) 51,000
Yazd 230,483
Zābol (1982 E) 58,000
Zāhedān 281,923
Zanjān 215,261
Zarrīn Shahr (1982 E) 69,000

IRAQ / Al 'Irāq

1985 E 15,584,987

Cities and Towns

Ad-Dīwānīyah (1970 E) 62,300
Al-'Amārah 131,758
Al-Başrah 616,700
Al-Hillah 215,249
Al-Kūt 73,022
Al-Mawşil 570,926
An-Najaf 242,603
An-Nāşirīyah 138,842
Ar-Ramādī 137,388
As-Samāwah 75,293
As-Sulaymānīyah 279,424
• BAGHDĀD (1987 C) 3,841,268
Ba'qūbah 114,516
Irbīl 333,903
Karbalā' 184,574
Kirkūk (1970 E) 207,900

IRELAND / Éire

1986 C 3,540,643

C Census. E Official estimate. U Unofficial estimate.
• Largest city in country.
★ Population or designation of metropolitan area, including suburbs (see headnote).
▲ Population of an entire municipality, commune, or district, including rural area.

Cities and Towns

Cork (★ 173,694) 133,271
• DUBLIN (BAILE ÁTHA CLIATH) (★ 1,140,000) 502,749
Dún Laoghaire (★ Dublin) 54,715
Galway 47,104
Limerick (★ 76,557) 56,279
Waterford (★ 41,054) 39,529

ISLE OF MAN

1986 C 64,282

Cities and Towns

• DOUGLAS (★ 28,500) 20,368

ISRAEL / Isrā'īl / Yisra'el

1989 E 4,386,000

Cities and Towns

Ashdod 74,700
Ashqelon 56,300
Bat Yam (★ Tel Aviv-Yafo) 133,100
Be'ér Sheva (Beersheba) 113,200
Bene Beraq (★ Tel Aviv-Yafo) 109,400
Elat 24,700
Giv'atayim (★ Tel Aviv-Yafo) 45,600
Ḥefa (★ 435,000) 222,600
Herzliyya (★ Tel Aviv-Yafo) 71,600
Holon (★ Tel Aviv-Yafo) 146,100
Kefar Sava (★ Tel Aviv-Yafo) 54,800
Lod (Lydda) (★ Tel Aviv-Yafo) 41,300
Nazerat (Nazareth) (★ 77,000) 50,600
Netanya (★ Tel Aviv-Yafo) 117,800
Petaḥ Tiqwa (★ Tel Aviv-Yafo) 133,600
Ra'anana (★ Tel Aviv-Yafo) 49,400
Ramat Gan (★ Tel Aviv-Yafo) 115,700
Reḥovot (★ Tel Aviv-Yafo) 72,500
Rishon leẔiyyon (★ Tel Aviv-Yafo) 123,800
• Tel Aviv-Yafo (★ 1,735,000) 317,800
YERUSHALAYIM (AL-QUDS) (JERUSALEM) (★ 530,000) 493,500

ISRAELI OCCUPIED TERRITORIES

1989 E 1,574,700

Cities and Towns

Al-Khalīl (Hebron) (1971 E) 43,000
Al-Quds (Jerusalem) (★ Yerushalayim) (1976 E) 90,000
Arīḥā (Jericho) (1967 C) 6,829
Bayt Laḥm (Bethlehem) (1971 E) 25,000
• Ghazzah (1967 C) 118,272
Khān Yūnis (1967 C) 52,997
Nābulus (1971 E) 64,000
Rafaḥ (1967 C) 49,812

ITALY / Italia

1987 E 57,290,519

Cities and Towns

Afragola (★ Napoli) 59,397
Alessandria (▲ 96,014) 76,100
Altamura 54,784
Ancona 104,409
Andria 88,348
Arezzo (▲ 91,681) 74,200
Asti (▲ 75,459) 63,600
Avellino 56,407
Aversa (★ Napoli) 57,827
Bari (★ 475,000) 362,524
Barletta 86,954
Benevento (▲ 65,661) 54,400
Bergamo (★ 345,000) 118,959
Biella 51,788
Bitonto 51,962
Bologna (★ 525,000) 432,406
Bolzano 101,515
Brescia 199,286
Brindisi 92,280
Busto Arsizio (★ Milano) 78,056
Cagliari (★ 305,000) 220,574
Caltanissetta 62,352
Carpi (▲ 60,614) 49,500
Carrara (★★ Massa) 69,229
Caserta 65,974
Casoria (★ Napoli) 54,100
Castellammare [di Stabia] (★ Napoli) 68,491
Catania (★ 550,000) 372,486
Catanzaro 102,558
Cava de'Tirreni (★ Salerno) 52,028
Cerignola 53,463
Cesena (▲ 90,012) 72,600
Chieti 55,827
Cinisello Balsamo (★ Milano) 78,917
Civitavecchia 50,806
Collegno (★ Torino) 49,334
Cologno Monzese (★ Milano) 52,554
Como (★ 165,000) 91,738
Cosenza (★ 150,000) 106,026
Cremona 76,979
Crotone (▲ 61,005) 53,600
Ercolano (★ Napoli) 62,783
Ferrara (▲ 143,950) 113,300
Firenze (★ 640,000) 425,835
Foggia 155,051
Forlì (▲ 110,482) 91,200
Gela 79,378
Genova (Genoa) (★ 805,000) 727,427
Giugliano in Campania (★ Napoli) 51,187
Grosseto (▲ 70,592) 56,400
La Spezia (★ 185,000) 108,937
Latina (▲ 98,479) 67,800
Lecce 100,981
Livorno 174,065
Lucca 88,024
Manfredonia 57,707
Mantova (▲ 56,817) 49,000
Marsala 80,468
Massa (★ 145,000) 66,872
Matera 52,819
Messina 268,896
Mestre (★ Venezia) 189,700
• Milano (Milan) (★ 3,750,000) 1,495,260
Modena 176,880
Molfetta 64,519
Moncalieri (★ Torino) 62,306
Monza (★ Milano) 122,064
Napoli (Naples) (★ 2,875,000) 1,204,211
Nicastro (▲ 67,562) 52,100
Novara 102,742
Padova (★ 270,000) 225,769
Palermo 723,732
Parma 175,842
Pavia 82,065
Perugia (▲ 146,713) 106,700
Pesaro (▲ 90,336) 78,700
Pescara 131,027
Piacenza 105,626
Pisa 104,384
Pistoia (▲ 90,689) 76,800
Pordenone 50,825
Portici (★ Napoli) 76,302
Potenza (▲ 67,114) 57,600
Pozzuoli (★ Napoli) 65,000
Prato (★ 215,000) 164,595
Quartu Sant'Elena 52,838
Ragusa 67,748
Ravenna (▲ 136,016) 86,500
Reggio di Calabria 178,821
Reggio nell'Emilia (▲ 130,086) 107,300
Rho (★ Milano) 50,876
Rimini (▲ 130,698) 114,600
Rivoli (★ Torino) 50,786
ROMA (ROME) (★ 3,175,000) 2,815,457
Salerno (★ 250,000) 154,848
San Giorgio a Cremano (★ Napoli) 63,656
San Remo 60,797
San Severo 55,239
Sassari 120,152
Savona (★ 112,000) 62,300
Scandicci (★ Firenze) 54,367
Sesto San Giovanni (★ Milano) 91,624
Siena 59,712
Siracusa 122,857
Taranto 244,997
Terni (▲ 111,157) 94,500
Torino (★ 1,550,000) 1,035,565
Torre Annunziata (★ Napoli) 57,508
Torre del Greco (★ Napoli) 105,066
Trapani (▲ 73,083) 63,000
Trento (▲ 100,202) 81,500
Treviso 85,083
Trieste (Triest) 239,031
Udine (★ 126,000) 100,211
Varese 88,353
Venezia (Venice) (★ 420,000) 88,700
Vercelli 51,008
Verona 259,151
Viareggio (▲ 59,146) 50,300
Vicenza 110,449
Vigevano 62,671
Vittoria 54,795

IVORY COAST / Côte d'Ivoire

1983 E 9,300,000

Cities and Towns

• ABIDJAN 1,950,000
Bouaké 275,000
Daloa 70,000
Korhogo 125,000
Man 55,000
YAMOUSSOUKRO 80,000

JAMAICA

1982 C 2,190,357

Cities and Towns

• KINGSTON (★ 770,000) (1987 E) 646,400
Montego Bay 70,265
Portmore (★ Kingston) 73,426
Spanish Town (★ Kingston) 89,097

JAPAN / Nihon

1985 C 121,048,923

Cities and Towns

Abiko (★ Tōkyō) 111,659
Ageo (★ Tōkyō) 178,587
Aizu-wakamatsu 118,140
Akashi (★ Ōsaka) 263,363
Akishima (★ Tōkyō) 97,543
Akita 296,400
Akō 52,374
Amagasaki (★ Ōsaka) 509,115
Anjō 133,059
Aomori 294,045
Arao (★ Ōmuta) 62,570
Asahikawa 363,631
Asaka (★ Tōkyō) 94,431
Ashikaga 167,656
Ashiya (★ Ōsaka) 87,127
Atami 49,374
Atsugi (★ Tōkyō) 175,600
Ayase (★ Tōkyō) 71,152
Beppu 134,775
Bisai (★ Nagoya) 56,234
Chiba (★ Tōkyō) 788,930
Chichibu 61,013
Chigasaki (★ Tōkyō) 185,030
Chikushino (★ Fukuoka) 63,242
Chiryū (★ Nagoya) 50,506
Chita (★ Nagoya) 70,013
Chitose 73,610
Chōfu (★ Tōkyō) 191,071
Chōshi 87,883
Daitō (★ Ōsaka) 122,441
Dazaifu (★ Fukuoka) 57,737
Ebetsu (★ Sapporo) 90,328
Ebina (★ Tōkyō) 93,159
Fuchū (★ Tōkyō) 201,972
Fuji (★ 370,000) 214,448
Fujieda (★ Shizuoka) 111,985
Fujiidera (★ Ōsaka) 65,252
Fujimi (★ Tōkyō) 85,697
Fujinomiya (★★ Fuji) 112,642
Fujisawa (★ Tōkyō) 328,387
Fuji-yoshida 54,796
Fukaya (▲ 89,121) 71,600
Fukuchiyama (▲ 65,995) 56,200
Fukui 250,261
Fukuoka (★ 1,750,000) 1,160,440
Fukushima 270,762
Fukuyama 360,261
Funabashi (★ Tōkyō) 506,966
Fussa (★ Tōkyō) 51,478
Gamagōri 85,580
Gifu 411,743
Ginowan 69,206
Gotemba 74,882
Gushikawa 51,351
Gyōda 79,359
Habikino (★ Ōsaka) 111,394
Hachinohe 241,430
Hachiōji (★ Tōkyō) 426,654
Hadano (★ Tōkyō) 141,803
Hagi 52,740
Hakodate 319,194
Hamada 51,071
Hamakita 77,228
Hamamatsu 514,118
Hanamaki (▲ 69,886) 54,500
Handa (★ Nagoya) 92,883
Hannō (★ Tōkyō) 66,550
Hashima 59,760
Hasuda (★ Tōkyō) 53,991
Hatogaya (★ Tōkyō) 55,424
Hatsukaichi (★ Hiroshima) 52,020
Hekinan 63,778
Higashihiroshima (★ Hiroshima) 84,717
Higashikurume (★ Tōkyō) 110,079
Higashimatsuyama 70,426
Higashimurayama (★ Tōkyō) 123,798
Higashiōsaka (★ Ōsaka) 522,805
Higashiyamato (★ Tōkyō) 69,881
Hikari (★ Tokuyama) 49,246
Hikone 94,204
Himeji (★ 660,000) 452,917
Himi (▲ 62,112) 52,300
Hino (★ Tōkyō) 156,031
Hirakata (★ Ōsaka) 382,257
Hiratsuka (★ Tōkyō) 229,990
Hirosaki (▲ 176,082) 134,800
Hiroshima (★ 1,575,000) 1,044,118
Hita (▲ 65,730) 57,900
Hitachi 206,074
Hōfu 118,067
Honjō 56,495
Hōya (★ Tōkyō) 91,568
Hyūga 59,163
Ibaraki (★ Ōsaka) 250,463
Ichihara (★ Tōkyō) 237,617
Ichikawa (★ Tōkyō) 397,822
Ichinomiya (★★ Nagoya) 257,388
Ichinoseki (▲ 60,941) 49,200
Iida (▲ 92,401) 65,000
Iizuka (★ 110,000) 81,868
Ikeda (★ Ōsaka) 101,683
Ikoma (★ Ōsaka) 86,293
Imabari 125,115
Imari (▲ 62,044) 50,700
Inagi (★ Tōkyō) 50,766
Inazawa (★ Nagoya) 94,479
Inuyama (★ Nagoya) 68,723
Iruma (★ Tōkyō) 118,603
Isahaya 88,376
Ise (Uji-yamada) 105,455
Isesaki 112,459
Ishinomaki 122,674
Itami (★ Ōsaka) 182,731
Itō 70,197
Iwaki (Taira) 350,569
Iwakuni 111,833
Iwamizawa 81,664
Iwata 80,810
Iwatsuki (★ Tōkyō) 100,903
Izumi (★ Ōsaka) 137,641
Izumi (★ Sendai) 124,216
Izumi-ōtsu (★ Ōsaka) 67,755
Izumi-sano (★ Ōsaka) 91,563
Izumo (▲ 80,749) 68,000
Jōyō (★ Ōsaka) 81,850
Kadoma (★ Ōsaka) 140,590
Kaga 68,630
Kagoshima 530,502
Kainan (★ Wakayama) 50,779
Kaizuka (★ Ōsaka) 79,591
Kakamigahara 124,464
Kakegawa (▲ 68,724) 55,600
Kakogawa (★ Ōsaka) 227,311
Kamagaya (★ Tōkyō) 85,705
Kamaishi 60,007
Kamakura (★ Tōkyō) 175,495
Kameoka 76,207
Kamifukuoka (★ Tōkyō) 57,638
Kanazawa 430,481
Kani (★ Nagoya) 69,630
Kanoya (▲ 76,029) 60,200
Kanuma (▲ 88,078) 73,200
Karatsu (▲ 78,744) 70,100
Kariya (★ Nagoya) 112,403
Kasai 52,107
Kasaoka (▲ 60,598) 53,500
Kashihara (★ Ōsaka) 112,888
Kashiwa (★ Tōkyō) 273,128
Kashiwara (★ Ōsaka) 73,252
Kashiwazaki (▲ 86,020) 73,350
Kasuga (★ Fukuoka) 75,555
Kasugai (★ Nagoya) 256,990
Kasukabe (★ Tōkyō) 171,890
Katano (★ Ōsaka) 64,205
Katsuta 102,763
Kawachi-nagano (★ Ōsaka) 91,313
Kawagoe (★ Tōkyō) 285,437
Kawaguchi (★ Tōkyō) 403,015
Kawanishi (★ Ōsaka) 136,376
Kawasaki (★ Tōkyō) 1,088,624
Kesennuma 68,137
Kimitsu (▲ 84,310) 71,900
Kiryū 131,267
Kisarazu 120,201
Kishiwada (★ Ōsaka) 185,731
Kitaibaraki 51,035
Kitakyūshū (★ 1,525,000) 1,056,402
Kitami 107,281
Kitamoto (★ Tōkyō) 58,114
Kiyose (★ Tōkyō) 65,066
Kōbe (★★ Ōsaka) 1,410,834
Kōchi 312,241
Kodaira (★ Tōkyō) 158,673
Kōfu 202,405
Koga (★ Tōkyō) 57,541
Koganei (★ Tōkyō) 104,642
Kokubunji (★ Tōkyō) 95,467
Komae (★ Tōkyō) 73,784
Komaki (★ Nagoya) 113,284
Komatsu 106,041
Kōnan (★ Nagoya) 92,049
Kōnosu (★ Tōkyō) 60,565
Kōriyama 301,673
Koshigaya (★ Tōkyō) 253,479
Kudamatsu (★★ Tokuyama) 54,445
Kuki (★ Tōkyō) 58,636
Kumagaya 143,496
Kumamoto 555,719
Kunitachi (★ Tōkyō) 64,881
Kurashiki 413,632
Kure (★★ Hiroshima) 226,488
Kurume 222,847
Kusatsu (★ Ōsaka) 87,542
Kushiro 214,541
Kuwana (★ Nagoya) 94,731
Kyōto (★★ Ōsaka) 1,479,218
Machida (★ Tōkyō) 321,188
Maebashi 277,319
Maizuru 98,775
Marugame 74,272
Matsubara (★ Ōsaka) 136,455
Matsudo (★ Tōkyō) 427,473
Matsue 140,005
Matsumoto 197,340
Matsusaka 116,886
Matsuyama 426,658
Mihara 85,975
Miki (★ Ōsaka) 74,527
Minō (★ Ōsaka) 114,770
Misato (★ Tōkyō) 107,964
Mishima (★★ Numazu) 99,600
Mitaka (★ Tōkyō) 166,252
Mito 228,985
Miura (★ Tōkyō) 50,471
Miyako 61,654
Miyakonojō (▲ 132,098) 107,600
Miyazaki 279,114
Mobara 76,929
Moriguchi (★ Ōsaka) 159,400
Morioka 235,469
Moriyama 53,052
Mukō (★ Ōsaka) 52,216
Munakata 60,971
Muroran (★ 195,000) 136,208
Musashimurayama (★ Tōkyō) 60,930
Musashino (★ Tōkyō) 138,783
Mutsu 49,292
Nabari 56,474
Nagahama 55,531
Nagano 336,973
Nagaoka 183,756
Nagaokakyō (★ Ōsaka) 75,242
Nagareyama (★ Tōkyō) 124,682
Nagasaki 449,382
Nagoya (★ 4,800,000) 2,116,381
Naha 303,674
Nakama (★ Kitakyūshū) 50,294
Nakatsu 66,260
Nakatsugawa 53,277
Nanao 50,582
Nara (★ Ōsaka) 327,702
Narashino (★ Tōkyō) 136,365
Narita 77,181
Naruto 64,329
Naze 49,765
Neyagawa (★ Ōsaka) 258,228
Niigata 475,630
Niihama 132,184
Niitsu (▲ 63,846) 55,600
Niiza (★ Tōkyō) 129,287
Nishinomiya (★ Ōsaka) 421,267
Nishio 91,930
Nobeoka 136,381
Noboribetsu (★ Muroran) 58,370
Noda (★ Tōkyō) 105,937
Nōgata 64,479
Noshiro (▲ 59,170) 50,400
Numazu (★ 495,000) 210,490
Obihiro 162,932
Ōbu (★ Nagoya) 66,696
Ōdate (▲ 71,794) 60,900
Odawara 185,941
Ōgaki 145,910
Ōita 390,096
Okaya 61,747
Okayama 572,479
Okazaki 284,996
Okegawa (★ Tōkyō) 61,499
Okinawa 101,210
Ōme (★ Tōkyō) 110,828
Ōmi-hachiman (★ Ōsaka) 63,791
Ōmiya (★ Tōkyō) 373,022
Ōmura 69,472
Ōmuta (★ 225,000) 159,424
Ōnojō (★ Fukuoka) 69,435
Onomichi 100,640
Ōsaka (★ 16,450,000) 2,636,249
Ōta 133,670
Otaru (★★ Sapporo) 172,486
Ōtsu (★ Ōsaka) 234,551
Owariashi (★ Nagoya) 57,415
Oyama (▲ 134,242) 113,100
Sabae 61,452
Saeki 54,706
Saga 168,252
Sagamihara (★ Tōkyō) 482,778
Saijō 56,516
Sakado (★ Tōkyō) 87,586
Sakai (★ Ōsaka) 818,271
Sakaide 66,087
Sakata 101,392
Sakura (★ Tōkyō) 121,213
Sakurai 58,894
Sanjō 86,325
Sano 80,753
Sapporo (★ 1,900,000) 1,542,979
Sasebo 250,633
Satte 51,462
Sayama (★ Tōkyō) 144,366
Sayama (★ Ōsaka) 50,246
Seki 64,149
Sendai, Kagoshima pref. (▲ 71,444) 57,800
Sendai, Miyagi pref. (★ 1,175,000) 700,254
Sennan (★ Ōsaka) 60,059
Seto 124,623
Settsu (★ Ōsaka) 86,332
Shibata (▲ 77,219) 62,800
Shijōnawate (★ Ōsaka) 50,352
Shiki (★ Tōkyō) 58,935
Shimada (▲ 72,388) 63,200
Shimizu (★★ Shizuoka) 242,166
Shimodate (▲ 63,958) 52,400
Shimonoseki (★★ Kitakyūshū) 269,169
Shiogama (★ Sendai) 61,825
Shizuoka (★ 975,000) 468,362
Sōka (★ Tōkyō) 194,205
Suita (★ Ōsaka) 348,948
Suwa 52,329
Suzuka 164,936
Tachikawa (★ Tōkyō) 146,523
Tagajō (★ Sendai) 54,436
Tagawa 59,727
Tajimi (★ Nagoya) 84,829
Takada 130,659
Takaishi (★ Ōsaka) 66,974
Takamatsu 326,999

C Census. E Official estimate. U Unofficial estimate.
• Largest city in country.
★ Population or designation of metropolitan area, including suburbs (see headnote).
▲ Population of an entire municipality, commune, or district, including rural area.

Takaoka (★ 220,000) 175,780
Takarazuka (★ Ōsaka) 194,273
Takasago (★ Ōsaka) 91,434
Takasaki 231,766
Takatsuki (★ Ōsaka) 348,784
Takayama 65,033
Takefu 69,148
Takikawa 52,004
Tama (★ Tōkyō) 122,135
Tamano 76,954
Tanabe (▲ 70,835) 59,800
Tanashi (★ Tōkyō) 71,331
Tatebayashi 75,141
Tenri 69,129
Tochigi 86,290
Toda (★ Tōkyō) 76,960
Tōkai (★ Nagoya) 95,278
Toki 65,308
Tokoname (★ Nagoya) 53,077
Tokorozawa (★ Tōkyō) 275,168
Tokushima 257,884
Tokuyama (★ 250,000) 112,638
• TŌKYŌ (★ 27,700,000) 8,354,615
Tomakomai 158,061
Tondabayashi (★ Ōsaka) 102,619
Toride (★ Tōkyō) 78,608
Tosu 55,791
Tottori 137,060
Toyama 314,111
Toyoake (★ Nagoya) 57,969
Toyohashi 322,142
Toyokawa 107,430
Toyonaka (★ Ōsaka) 413,213
Toyota 308,111
Tsu 150,690
Tsuchiura 120,175
Tsuruga 65,670
Tsuruoka 100,200
Tsushima (★ Nagoya) 58,735
Tsuyama 86,837
Ube (★ 230,000) 174,855
Ueda 116,178
Ueno (▲ 60,812) 51,800
Uji (★ Ōsaka) 165,411
Uozu 49,825
Urasoe 81,611
Urawa (★ Tōkyō) 377,235
Urayasu (★ Tōkyō) 93,756
Ushiku 51,926
Utsunomiya 405,375
Uwajima 71,381
Wakayama (★ 495,000) 401,352
Wakkanai 51,854
Wakō (★ Tōkyō) 55,212
Warabi (★ Tōkyō) 70,408
Yachiyo (★ Tōkyō) 142,184
Yaizu (★ Shizuoka) 108,558
Yamagata 245,158
Yamaguchi 124,213
Yamato (★ Tōkyō) 177,669
Yamato-kōriyama (★ Ōsaka) 89,624
Yamato-takada (★ Ōsaka) 65,223
Yao (★ Ōsaka) 276,394
Yashio (★ Tōkyō) 67,635
Yatsushiro (▲ 108,790) 88,700
Yawata (★ Ōsaka) 72,356
Yokkaichi 263,001
Yokohama (★★ Tōkyō) 2,992,926
Yokosuka (★ Tōkyō) 427,116
Yonago 131,792
Yonezawa 93,721
Yono (★ Tōkyō) 71,597
Yotsukaidō (★ Tōkyō) 67,008
Yukuhashi 65,527
Zama (★ Tōkyō) 100,000
Zushi (★ Tōkyō) 57,656

JERSEY
1986 C 80,212

Cities and Towns

• SAINT HELIER (★ 46,500) 27,083

JORDAN / Al-Urdun
1989 E 3,111,000

Cities and Towns

Al-Baq'ah (★ 'Ammān) 63,985
• 'AMMĀN (★ 1,450,000) 936,300
Ar-Ruṣayfah (★ 'Ammān) 72,580
Az-Zarqā' (★★ 'Ammān) 318,055
Irbid 167,785

KAZAKHSTAN
1989 C 16,538,000

Cities and Towns

Akt'ubinsk 253,000
• ALMA-ATA (★ 1,190,000) 1,128,000
Arkalyk (1987 E) 71,000
Balchaš (1987 E) 84,000
Čelinograd 277,000
Čimkent 393,000
Džambul 307,000
Džezkazgan 109,000
Ekibastuz 135,000
Gurjev 149,000
Karaganda 614,000
Kentau (1987 E) 60,000
Kokčetav 137,000
Kustanaj 224,000
Kzyl-Orda 153,000
Leninogorsk (1987 E) 69,000
Pavlodar 331,000
Petropavlovsk 241,000
Rudnyj 124,000
Šachtinsk (1987 E) 62,000
Saptajev (1987 E) 64,000
Šaran' (1987 E) 64,000
Ščučinsk (1987 E) 53,000
Semipalatinsk 334,000
Ševčenko 159,000
Taldy-Kurgan 119,000
Temirtau 212,000
Turkestan (1987 E) 77,000
Ural'sk 200,000
Ust'-Kamenogorsk 324,000
Zanatas (1987 E) 53,000
Zyr'anovsk (1987 E) 55,000

KENYA
1990 E 24,870,000

Cities and Towns

Eldoret (1979 C) 50,503
Kisumu (1984 E) 167,100
Machakos (1983 E) 92,300
Meru (1979 C) 72,049
Mombasa 537,000
• NAIROBI 1,505,000
Nakuru (1984 E) 101,700

KIRIBATI
1988 E 68,207

Cities and Towns

BAIRIKI 2,230
• Bikenibeu 4,580

KOREA, NORTH / Chosŏn-minjujuŭi-inmīn-konghwaguk
1981 E 18,317,000

Cities and Towns

Ch'ŏngjin 490,000
Haeju (1983 E) 213,000
Hamhŭng (1970 E) 150,000
Hŭngnam (1976 E) 260,000
Kaesŏng 259,000
Kanggye (1967 E) 130,000
Kimch'aek (Sŏngjin) (1967 E) 265,000
Namp'o 241,000
• P'YŎNGYANG (★ 1,600,000) 1,283,000
Sinŭiju 305,000
Songnim (1944 C) 53,035
Wŏnsan (1981 E) 398,000

KOREA, SOUTH / Taehan-min'guk
1985 C 40,448,486

Cities and Towns

Andong 114,216
Anyang (★ Sŏul) 361,577
Bucheon (★ Sŏul) 456,292
Changwŏn (★ Masan) 173,508
Chech'on 102,274
Cheju 202,911
Chinhae 121,341
Chinju 227,309
Ch'ŏnan 170,196
Ch'ŏngju 350,256
Chŏnju 79,323
Chŏnju, Chŏlla Pukdo prov. 426,473
Ch'unch'ŏn 162,988
Ch'ungju 113,331
Ch'ungmu 87,459
Inch'ŏn (★★ Sŏul) (1989 E) 1,628,000
Iri 192,269
Kangnŭng 132,897
Kimch'ŏn 77,254
Kimhae 77,903
Kumi 142,094
Kŭmsŏng 58,897
Kunsan 185,649
Kwangju (1989 E) 1,165,000
Kwangmyŏng (★ Sŏul) 219,611
Kyŏngju 127,544
Masan (★ 625,000) 448,746
Mokp'o 236,085
Namwŏn 61,447
P'ohang 260,691
Pusan (★ 3,800,000) (1989 E) 3,773,000
P'yŏngt'aek (▲ 180,513) 63,400
Samch'ŏnp'o 62,466
Sŏgwipo 82,311
Sŏkch'o 69,501
Sŏngnam (★ Sŏul) 447,692
Sŏngtan 66,357
• SŎUL (★ 15,850,000) (1989 E) 10,522,000
Sunch'ŏn (▲ 116,323) 121,958
Suwŏn (★ Sŏul) 430,752
T'aebaek 113,997
Taegu (1989 C) 2,207,000
Taejŏn (1989 E) 1,041,000
Tongduch'ŏn 68,633
Tonghae 91,691
Ŭijŏngbu (★ Sŏul) 162,700
Ulsan 551,014
Wŏnju 151,165
Yŏngch'ŏn 52,811
Yŏngju 84,742
Yŏsu 171,933

KUWAIT / Al-Kuwayt
1985 C 1,697,301

Cities and Towns

Al-Aḥmadī (★ 285,000) 26,899
Al-Farwānīyah (★ Al-Kuwayt) 68,701
Al-Fuḥayḥīl (★ Al-Aḥmadī) 50,081
Al-Jahrah (★ Al-Kuwayt) 111,222
• AL-KUWAYT (★ 1,375,000) 44,335
As-Sālimīyah (★ Al-Kuwayt) 153,359
Aṣ-Ṣulaybīyah (★ Al-Kuwayt) 51,314
Hawallī (★ Al-Kuwayt) 145,126
Qalīb ash-Shuyūkh (★ Al-Kuwayt) 114,771
South Khīṭān (★ Al-Kuwayt) 69,256
Subahiya (★ Al-Aḥmadī) 60,787

KYRGYZSTAN
1989 C 4,291,000

Cities and Towns

• BIŠKEK 616,000
Džalal-Abad (1987 E) 74,000
Kara-Balta (1987 E) 55,000
Oš 213,000
Prževal'sk (1987 E) 64,000
Tokmak (1987 E) 71,000

LAOS / Lao
1985 C 3,584,803

Cities and Towns

Savannakhet (1975 E) 53,000
Viangchan (Vientiane) 377,409

LATVIA / Latvija
1989 C 2,681,000

Cities and Towns

Daugavpils 127,000
Jelgava (1987 E) 72,000
Jūrmala (★ Rīga) (1987 E) 65,000
Liepāja 114,000
• RĪGA (★ 1,005,000) 915,000
Ventspils (1987 E) 52,000

LEBANON / Lubnān
1982 U 2,637,000

Cities and Towns

• BAYRŪT (★ 1,675,000) 509,000
Ṣaydā 105,000
Ṭarābulus (Tripoli) 198,000

LESOTHO
1986 C 1,577,536

Cities and Towns

• MASERU 109,382

LIBERIA
1986 E 2,221,000

Cities and Towns

• MONROVIA 465,000

LIBYA / Lībiyā
1984 C 3,637,488

Cities and Towns

Banghāzī 435,886
Darnah 62,179
Misrātah 131,031
• ṬARĀBULUS (TRIPOLI) 990,697
Ṭubruq (Tobruk) 75,282
Zāwiyat al-Bayḍā' 67,120

LIECHTENSTEIN
1990 E 28,452

Cities and Towns

• VADUZ 4,874

LITHUANIA / Lietuva
1989 C 3,690,000

Cities and Towns

Alytus (1987 E) 71,000
Kaunas 423,000
Klaipėda (Memel) 204,000
Panevėžys 126,000
Šiauliai 145,000
• VILNIUS 582,000

LUXEMBOURG
1985 E 366,000

Cities and Towns

• LUXEMBOURG (★ 136,000) 76,130

MACAU
1987 E 429,000

Cities and Towns

• MACAU 429,000

MACEDONIA / Makedonija
1987 E 2,064,581

Cities and Towns

Bitola (▲ 143,090) 76,000
• SKOPJE (▲ 547,214) 444,900

MADAGASCAR / Madagasikara
1984 E 9,731,000

Cities and Towns

• ANTANANARIVO (1985 E) 663,000
Antsirabe (▲ 95,000) 50,100
Antsiranana 100,000
Fianarantsoa 130,000
Mahajanga 85,000
Toamasina 100,000
Toliara 55,000

MALAWI / Malaŵi
1987 C 7,982,607

Cities and Towns

• Blantyre 331,588
LILONGWE 233,973

MALAYSIA
1980 C 13,136,109

Cities and Towns

Alor Setar 69,435
Batu Pahat 64,727
Butterworth (★★ George Town) 77,982
George Town (Pinang) (★ 495,000) 248,241
Ipoh 293,849
Johor Baharu (★ Singapore, Sing.) 246,395
Kelang 192,080
Keluang 50,315
Kota Baharu 167,872
Kota Kinabalu (Jesselton) 55,997
• KUALA LUMPUR (★ 1,475,000) 919,610
Kuala Terengganu 180,296
Kuantan 131,547
Kuching 72,555
Melaka 87,494
Miri 52,125
Muar (Bandar Maharani) 65,151
Petaling Jaya (★ Kuala Lumpur) 207,805
Sandakan 70,420
Seremban 132,911
Sibu 85,231
Taiping 146,000
Telok Anson 49,148

MALDIVES
1985 C 181,453

Cities and Towns

• MALE 46,334

MALI
1987 C 7,620,225

Cities and Towns

• BAMAKO 646,163
Gao 54,874
Mopti 73,979
Ségou 88,877
Sikasso 73,050
Tombouctou (Timbuktu) 31,925

MALTA
1989 E 349,014

Cities and Towns

• VALLETTA (★ 215,000) 9,210

MARSHALL ISLANDS
1980 C 30,873

Cities and Towns

• Jarej-Uliga-Delap 8,583

MARTINIQUE
1982 C 328,566

Cities and Towns

• FORT-DE-FRANCE (★ 116,017) 99,844

MAURITANIA / Mauritanie / Mūrītāniyā
1987 E 2,007,000

Cities and Towns

• NOUAKCHOTT 285,000

MAURITIUS
1987 E 1,008,864

Cities and Towns

Beau Bassin-Rose Hill (★ Port Louis) 93,125
Curepipe (★ Port Louis) 64,243
• PORT LOUIS (★ 420,000) 139,730
Quatre Bornes (★ Port Louis) 65,480
Vacoas-Phoenix (★ Port Louis) 55,667

MAYOTTE
1985 E 67,205

Cities and Towns

• DZAOUDZI (★ 6,979) 5,865

MEXICO / México
1980 C 67,395,826

Cities and Towns

Acapulco [de Juárez] 301,902
Aguascalientes 293,152
Atlixco 53,207
Campeche 128,434
Cancún 33,273
Celaya 141,675
Chihuahua 385,603
Chilpancingo [de los Bravo] 67,498
Ciudad Chetumal 56,709
Ciudad del Carmen 72,489
• CIUDAD DE MÉXICO (MEXICO CITY) (★ 14,100,000) 8,831,079
Ciudad de Valles 65,609
Ciudad Guzmán 60,938
Ciudad Juárez 544,496
Ciudad Madero (★ Tampico) 132,444
Ciudad Mante 70,647
Ciudad Obregón 165,572
Ciudad Victoria 140,161
Coatzacoalcos 127,170
Colima 86,044
Córdoba 99,972
Cuernavaca 192,770
Culiacán 304,826
Delicias 65,504
Durango 257,915
Ecatepec (★ Ciudad de México) 741,821
Ensenada 120,483
Fresnillo 56,066
Garza García (★ Monterrey) 81,974
Gómez Palacio (★★ Torreón) 116,967
Guadalajara (★ 2,325,000) 1,626,152
Guadalupe (★ Monterrey) 370,524
Guaymas 54,826
Hermosillo 297,175
Hidalgo del Parral 75,590
Iguala 66,005
Irapuato 170,138
Jalapa Enríquez 204,594
La Paz 91,453
León [de los Aldamas] 593,002
Los Mochis 122,531
Matamoros 188,745
Mazatlán 199,830
Mérida 400,142
Mexicali (★ 365,000) 341,559
Minatitlán 106,765
Monclova 115,786
Monterrey (★ 2,015,000) 1,090,009
Morelia 297,544
Naucalpan de Juárez (★ Ciudad de México) 723,723
Navojoa 62,901
Nezahualcóyotl (★ Ciudad de México) 1,341,230
Nogales 65,603
Nuevo Laredo 201,731
Oaxaca [de Juárez] 154,223
Orizaba (★ 215,000) 114,848
Pachuca [de Soto] 110,351
Piedras Negras 67,455
Poza Rica de Hidalgo 166,799
Puebla [de Zaragoza] (★ 1,055,000) 835,759
Puerto Vallarta 38,645
Querétaro 215,976
Reynosa 194,693
Río Bravo 55,236
Salamanca 96,703
Saltillo 284,937
San Luis Potosí (★ 470,000) 362,371
San Luis Río Colorado 76,684
San Nicolás de los Garza (★ Monterrey) 280,696
Santa Catarina (★ Monterrey) 87,673

C Census. E Official estimate. U Unofficial estimate.
• Largest city in country.
★ Population or designation of metropolitan area, including suburbs (see headnote).
▲ Population of an entire municipality, commune, or district, including rural area.

Soledad Díez Gutiérrez
(★ San Luis Potosí) ...49,173
Tampico (★ 435,000) ...267,957
Tapachula ...85,766
Tehuacán ...79,547
Tepic ...145,741
Tijuana ...429,500
Tlalnepantla (★ Ciudad de México) ...778,173
Tlaquepaque (★ Guadalajara) ...133,500
Toluca [de Lerdo] ...199,778
Torreón (★ 575,000) ...328,086
Tulancingo ...53,400
Tuxpan de Rodríguez Cano ...56,037
Tuxtla Gutiérrez ...131,096
Uruapan [del Progreso] ...122,828
Veracruz [Llave] (★ 385,000) ...284,822
Villahermosa ...158,216
Zacatecas ...80,088
Zamora de Hidalgo ...86,998
Zapopan (★ Guadalajara) ...345,390

MICRONESIA, FEDERATED STATES OF
1985 E ...94,534
Cities and Towns
• KOLONIA ...6,306

MOLDOVA
1989 C ...4,341,000
Cities and Towns
Bel'c' ...159,000
Bendery ...130,000
• KISIN'OV ...665,000
Rybnica (1987 E) ...58,000
Tiraspol' ...182,000

MONACO
1982 C ...27,063
Cities and Towns
• MONACO (★ 87,000) ...27,063

MONGOLIA / Mongol Ard Uls
1989 E ...2,040,000
Cities and Towns
Darchan (1985 E) ...69,800
• ULAANBAATAR ...548,400

MONTSERRAT
1980 C ...11,606
Cities and Towns
• PLYMOUTH ...1,568

MOROCCO / Al-Magreb
1982 C ...20,419,555
Cities and Towns
Agadir ...110,479
Beni-Mellal ...95,003
Berkane ...60,490
• Casablanca (Dar-el-Beida) (★ 2,475,000) ...2,139,204
El-Jadida (Mazagan) ...81,455
Fès (★ 535,000) ...448,823
Kenitra ...188,194
Khemisset ...58,925
Khouribga ...127,181
Ksar-el-Kebir ...73,541
Larache ...63,893
Marrakech (★ 535,000) ...439,728
Meknès (★ 375,000) ...319,783
Mohammedia (Fedala) (★ Casablanca) ...105,120
Nador ...62,040
Oued-Zem ...58,744
Oujda ...260,082
RABAT (★ 980,000) ...518,616
Safi ...197,309
Salé (★★ Rabat) ...289,391
Settat ...65,203
Sidi Kacem ...55,833
Sidi Slimane ...50,457
Tanger (Tangier) (★ 370,000) ...266,346
Taza ...77,216
Tétouan ...199,615

MOZAMBIQUE / Moçambique
1989 E ...15,326,476
Cities and Towns
Beira ...291,604
Chimoio (1986 E) ...86,928
Inhambane (1986 E) ...64,274
• MAPUTO ...1,069,727
Nacala-Velha ...101,615
Nampula ...197,379
Pemba (1986 E) ...50,215
Quelimane ...78,520
Tete (1986 E) ...56,178
Xai-Xai (1986 E) ...51,620

NAMIBIA
1988 E ...1,760,000

Cities and Towns
• WINDHOEK ...114,500

NAURU / Naoero
1987 E ...8,000

NEPAL / Nepāl
1981 C ...15,022,839
Cities and Towns
Birātnagar ...93,544
• KĀTHMĀNDAU (★ 320,000) ...235,160

NETHERLANDS / Nederland
1989 E ...14,880,000
Cities and Towns
Alkmaar (★ 121,000) (1987 E) ...87,034
Almelo (1986 E) ...62,421
Alphen aan den Rijn (1986 E) ...55,812
Amersfoort (★ 130,158) (1986 E) ...89,596
Amstelveen (★ Amsterdam) (1986 E) ...68,090
• AMSTERDAM (★ 1,860,000) ...696,500
Apeldoorn ...147,300
Arnhem (★ 296,362) ...129,000
Breda (★ 155,613) ...121,400
Delft (★★ 's-Gravenhage) (1986 E) ...87,440
Den Helder (1986 E) ...63,231
Deventer (1986 E) ...64,806
Dordrecht (★ 202,126) ...108,300
Eindhoven (★ 379,377) ...190,700
Enschede (★ 288,000) ...145,200
Gouda (1986 E) ...60,927
Groningen (★ 206,781) ...167,800
Haarlem (★ Amsterdam) ...149,200
Heerlen (★ 266,617) (1986 E) ...93,871
Helmond (1987 E) ...63,909
Hengelo (★★ Enschede) (1986 E) ...76,694
Hilversum (★ Amsterdam) (1986 E) ...86,125
Hoorn (1987 E) ...53,788
IJmuiden (★ Amsterdam) (1986 E) ...57,157
Kerkrade (★ Heerlen) (1986 E) ...52,885
Leeuwarden (1986 E) ...84,966
Leiden (★ 182,244) ...109,200
Maastricht (★ 160,026) ...116,400
Nieuwegein (★ Utrecht) (1987 E) ...56,719
Nijmegen (★ 240,085) ...145,400
Oss (1986 E) ...50,343
Purmerend (★ Amsterdam) (1987 E) ...52,257
Roosendaal (1986 E) ...57,385
Rotterdam (★ 1,110,000) ...576,300
Schiedam (★ Rotterdam) (1986 E) ...69,078
'S-GRAVENHAGE (THE HAGUE) (★ 770,000) ...443,900
's-Hertogenbosch (★ 189,067) (1986 E) ...89,039
Spijkenisse (★ Rotterdam) (1987 E) ...62,394
Tilburg (★ 224,934) ...155,100
Utrecht (★ 518,779) ...230,700
Venlo (★ 87,000) (1986 E) ...63,475
Vlaardingen (★ Rotterdam) (1986 E) ...75,536
Zaandam (★ Amsterdam) ...129,600
Zeist (★ Utrecht) (1986 E) ...59,743
Zoetermeer (★ 's-Gravenhage) (1987 E) ...85,349
Zwolle (1986 E) ...88,438

NETHERLANDS ANTILLES / Nederlandse Antillen
1990 E ...189,687
Cities and Towns
• WILLEMSTAD (★ 130,000) (1981 C) ...31,883

NEW CALEDONIA / Nouvelle-Calédonie
1989 C ...164,173
Cities and Towns
• NOUMÉA (★ 88,000) ...65,110

NEW ZEALAND
1986 C ...3,307,084

Cities and Towns
• Auckland (★ 850,000) ...149,046
Christchurch (★ 320,000) ...168,200
Dunedin (★ 109,000) ...76,964
Hamilton (★ 101,814) ...94,511
Lower Hutt (★ Wellington) ...63,862
Manukau (★ Auckland) ...177,248
Napier (★ 107,060) ...49,428
Palmerston North (★ 67,405) ...60,503
Takapuna (★ Auckland) ...69,419
Waitemata (★ Auckland) ...96,365
WELLINGTON (★ 350,000) ...137,495

NICARAGUA
1985 E ...3,272,100
Cities and Towns
Chinandega ...75,000
Granada (1981 E) ...64,642
León ...101,000
• MANAGUA ...682,000
Masaya ...75,000
Matagalpa ...68,000

NIGER
1988 C ...7,250,383
Cities and Towns
Agadez ...50,164
Maradi ...112,965
• NIAMEY ...398,265
Tahoua ...51,607
Zinder ...120,892

NIGERIA
1987 E ...101,907,000
Cities and Towns
Aba ...239,800
Abakaliki ...56,800
Abeokuta ...341,300
Ado-Ekiti ...287,000
Afikpo ...65,790
Agege ...83,810
Akure ...129,600
Amaigbo ...53,690
Apomu ...49,570
Awka ...88,800
Azare ...50,020
Bauchi ...68,840
Benin City ...183,200
Bida ...100,200
Calabar ...139,800
Deba ...110,600
Duku ...52,880
Ede ...245,200
Effon-Alaiye ...122,300
Ejigbo ...84,570
Emure-Ekiti ...58,750
Enugu ...252,500
Epe ...80,560
Erin-Oshogbo ...59,940
Eruwa ...49,140
Fiditi ...49,440
Gboko ...49,390
Gbongan ...53,990
Gombe ...86,120
Gusau ...126,200
Ibadan ...1,144,000
Idah ...50,550
Idanre ...56,080
Ife ...237,000
Ifon-Oshogbo ...65,980
Igbo-Ora ...68,060
Igede-Ekiti ...56,570
Ihiala ...73,240
Ijebu-Igbo ...78,680
Ijebu-Ode ...124,900
Ijero-Ekiti ...76,420
Ikare ...112,500
Ikerre ...195,400
Ikire ...94,450
Ikirun ...144,900
Ikole ...71,860
Ikorodu ...147,700
Ikot Ekpene ...69,440
Ila ...210,800
Ilawe-Ekiti ...147,300
Ilesha ...302,100
Ilobu ...159,000
Ilorin ...380,000
Inisa ...95,630
Ipoti-Ekiti ...53,220
Ise-Ekiti ...82,580
Iseyin ...173,500
Iwo ...289,100
Jimeta ...66,130
Jos ...164,700
Kaduna ...273,200
Kano ...538,300
Katsina ...165,000
Kaura Namoda ...52,910
Keffi ...57,790
Kishi ...77,210
Kumo ...118,200
Lafia ...97,810
Lafiagi ...57,580
• LAGOS (★ 3,800,000) ...1,213,000
Lalupon ...56,130
Lere ...49,670
Maiduguri ...255,100

Makurdi ...98,350
Minna ...109,300
Mubi ...51,190
Mushin (★ Lagos) ...266,100
Nguru ...78,770
Offa ...157,500
Ogbomosho ...582,900
Oka ...114,400
Oke-Mesi ...55,040
Okwe ...52,550
Olupona ...65,720
Ondo ...135,300
Onitsha ...298,200
Opobo ...64,620
Oron ...62,260
Oshogbo ...380,800
Owo ...146,600
Oyan ...50,930
Oyo ...204,700
Pindiga ...64,130
Port Harcourt ...327,300
Potiskum ...56,490
Sapele ...111,200
Shagamu ...93,610
Shaki ...139,000
Shomolu (★ Lagos) ...120,700
Sokoto ...163,700
Ugep ...81,910
Umuahia ...52,550
Uyo ...60,500
Warri ...100,700
Zaria ...302,800

NIUE
1986 C ...2,531
Cities and Towns
• ALOFI ...811

NORTHERN MARIANA ISLANDS
1980 C ...16,780
Cities and Towns
• Chalan Kanoa ...2,678

NORWAY / Norge
1987 E ...4,190,000
Cities and Towns
Bærum (★ Oslo) (1985 E) ...83,000
Bergen (★ 239,000) ...209,320
Drammen (★ 73,000) (1985 E) ...50,700
Fredrikstad (★ 52,000) (1983 E) ...27,618
Hammerfest (1983 E) ...7,208
Kristiansand (1985 E) ...62,200
• OSLO (★ 720,000) ...452,415
Stavanger (★ 132,000) (1985 E) ...94,200
Tromsø (1985 E) ...47,800
Trondheim ...135,010

OMAN / 'Umān
1981 C ...919,000
Cities and Towns
• MASQAT (MUSCAT) ...50,000
Sūr (1980 E) ...30,000

PAKISTAN / Pākistān
1981 C ...84,253,644
Cities and Towns
Ahmadpur East ...56,979
Bahāwalnagar ...74,533
Bahāwalpur (★ 180,263) ...152,009
Chārsadda ...62,530
Chīchāwatni ...50,241
Chiniot ...105,559
Chishtiān Mandi ...61,959
Daska ...55,555
Dera Ghāzi Khān ...102,007
Dera Ismāil Khān (★ 68,145) ...64,358
Drigh Road Cantonment (★ Karāchi) ...56,742
Faisalabad (Lyallpur) ...1,104,209
Gojra ...68,000
Gujrānwāla (★ 658,753) ...600,993
Gujrānwāla Cantonment (★ Gujrānwāla) ...57,760
Gujrāt ...155,058
Hāfizābād ...83,464
Hyderābād (★ 800,000) ...702,539
ISLAMABAD (★★ Rāwalpindi) ...204,364
Jacobābād ...79,365
Jarānwāla ...69,459
Jhang Maghiāna ...195,558
Jhelum (★ 106,462) ...92,646
Kāmālia ...61,107
Kāmoke ...71,097
• Karāchi (★ 5,300,000) ...4,901,627
Karāchi Cantonment (★ Karāchi) ...181,981
Kasūr ...155,523
Khairpur ...61,447
Khānewāl ...89,090
Khānpur ...70,589
Khushāb ...56,274
Kohāt (★ 77,604) ...55,832
Lahore (★ 3,025,000) ...2,707,215

Lahore Cantonment (★ Lahore) ...245,474
Lārkāna ...123,890
Leiah ...51,482
Mandi Būrewāla ...86,311
Mardān (★ 147,977) ...141,842
Miānwāli ...59,159
Mingāora ...88,078
Mīrpur Khās ...124,371
Multān (★ 732,070) ...696,316
Muzaffargarh ...53,000
Nawābshāh ...102,139
Okāra (★ 153,483) ...127,455
Pākpattan ...69,820
Peshāwar (★ 566,248) ...506,896
Peshāwar Cantonment (★ Peshāwar) ...59,352
Quetta (★ 285,719) ...244,842
Rahīmyār Khān (★ 132,635) ...119,036
Rāwalpindi (★ 1,040,000) ...457,091
Rāwalpindi Cantonment (★ Rāwalpindi) ...337,752
Sādiqābād ...63,935
Sāhīwal ...150,954
Sargodha (★ 291,362) ...231,895
Sargodha Cantonment (★ Sargodha) ...59,467
Shekhūpura ...141,168
Shikārpur ...88,138
Siālkot (★ 302,009) ...258,147
Sukkur ...190,551
Tando Ādam ...62,744
Turbat ...52,337
Vihāri ...53,799
Wāh ...122,335
Wazīrābād ...62,725

PALAU / Belau
1986 C ...13,873
Cities and Towns
• KOROR ...8,629

PANAMA / Panamá
1990 C ...2,315,047
Cities and Towns
Colón (★ 96,000) ...54,469
David ...65,635
• PANAMÁ (★ 770,000) ...411,549
San Miguelito (★ Panamá) ...242,529

PAPUA NEW GUINEA
1987 E ...3,479,400
Cities and Towns
Lae ...79,600
• PORT MORESBY ...152,100
Rabaul (1980 C) ...14,954

PARAGUAY
1985 E ...3,279,000
Cities and Towns
• ASUNCIÓN (★ 700,000) ...477,100
Fernando de la Mora (★ Asunción) ...80,000
Lambaré (★ Asunción) ...84,000
Puerto Presidente Stroessner ...64,000
San Lorenzo (★ Asunción) (1982 C) ...74,632

PERU / Perú
1981 C ...17,031,221
Cities and Towns
Arequipa (★ 446,942) ...108,023
Ayacucho (★ 69,533) ...57,432
Breña (★ Lima) ...112,398
Cajamarca ...62,259
Callao (★★ Lima) ...264,133
Cerro de Pasco (★ 66,373) ...55,597
Chiclayo (★ 279,527) ...213,095
Chimbote ...223,341
Chorrillos (★ Lima) ...141,881
Chosica (★ Lima) ...65,139
Cuzco (★ 184,550) ...89,563
Huancayo (★ 164,954) ...84,845
Huánuco ...61,812
Ica ...114,786
Iquitos ...178,738
Jesús María (★ Lima) ...83,179
Juliaca ...87,651
La Victoria (★ Lima) ...270,778
• LIMA (★ 4,608,010) ...371,122
Lince (★ Lima) ...80,456
Magdalena (★ Lima) ...55,535
Miraflores (★ Lima) ...103,453
Pisco ...55,604
Piura (★ 207,934) ...144,609
Pucallpa ...112,263
Pueblo Libre (★ Lima) ...83,985
Puno ...67,397
Rímac (★ Lima) ...184,484
San Isidro (★ Lima) ...71,203
San Martin de Porras (★ Lima) ...404,856
Santiago de Surco (★ Lima) ...146,636

C Census. E Official estimate. U Unofficial estimate.
• Largest city in country.

★ Population or designation of metropolitan area, including suburbs (see headnote).
▲ Population of an entire municipality, commune, or district, including rural area.

Sullana 89,037
Surquillo (★ Lima) 134,158
Tacna 97,173
Talara 57,351
Trujillo (★ 354,301) 202,469
Vitarte (★ Lima) 145,504

PHILIPPINES / Pilipinas

1990 C 60,477,000

Cities and Towns

Angeles 236,000
Antipolo (▲ 68,912) (1980 C) 54,117
Bacolod 364,000
Bacoor (★ Manila) (1980 C) 90,364
Baguio 183,000
Baliuag (1980 C) 70,555
Biñan (★ Manila) (1980 C) 83,684
Binangonan (1980 C) 80,980
Bocaue (1980 C) 49,693
Butuan (▲ 228,000) 99,000
Cabanatuan (▲ 173,000) 75,700
Cagayan de Oro (▲ 340,000) 255,000
Cainta (★ Manila) (1980 C) 59,025
Calamba (▲ 121,175) (1980 C) 72,359
Caloocan (★ Manila) 746,000
Carmona (★ Manila) (1980 C) 65,014
Cavite (★ 175,000) 92,000
Cebu (★ 720,000) 610,000
Cotabato 127,000
Dagupan 122,000
Davao (▲ 850,000) 569,300
Dumaguete 80,000
General Santos (Dadiangas) (▲ 250,000) 157,600
Guagua (1980 C) 72,609
Iloilo 311,000
Isabela (Basilan) (▲ 49,891) (1980 C) 11,491
Jolo (1980 C) 52,429
Lapu-Lapu (Opon) 146,000
Las Piñas (★ Manila) (1984 E) 190,364
Legaspi (▲ 121,000) 63,000
Lucena 151,000
Mabalacat (▲ 80,966) (1980 C) 54,988
Makati (★ Manila) (1984 E) 408,991
Malabon (★ Manila) (1984 E) 212,930
Malolos (1980 C) 95,699
Mandaluyong (★ Manila) (1984 E) 226,670
Mandaue (★ Cebu) 180,000
Mangaldan (1980 C) 50,434
• MANILA (★ 6,800,000) 1,587,000
Marawi 92,000
Marikina (★ Manila) (1984 E) 248,183
Meycauayan (★ Manila) (1980 C) 83,579
Muntinglupa (★ Manila) (1984 E) 172,421
Naga 115,000
Navotas (★ Manila) (1984 E) 146,899
Olongapo 192,000
Pagadian (▲ 107,000) 52,400
Parañaque (★ Manila) (1984 E) 252,791
Pasay (★ Manila) 354,000
Pasig (★ Manila) (1984 E) 318,853
Puerto Princesa (▲ 92,000) 52,000
Quezon City (★ Manila) 1,632,000
San Fernando (1980 C) 110,891
San Juan del Monte (★ Manila) (1984 E) 139,126
San Pablo (▲ 161,000) 83,900
San Pedro (1980 C) 74,556
Santa Cruz (1980 C) 60,620
Santa Rosa (★ Manila) (1980 C) 64,325
Tacloban 138,000
Tagbilaran 56,000
Tagig (★ Manila) (1984 E) 130,719
Taytay (★ Manila) (1980 C) 75,328
Valenzuela (★ Manila) (1984 E) 275,725
Zamboanga (▲ 444,000) 107,000

PITCAIRN

1988 C 59

Cities and Towns

• ADAMSTOWN 59

POLAND / Polska

1989 E 37,775,100

Cities and Towns

Będzin (★ Katowice) 77,300
Bełchatów 53,600
Biała Podlaska 50,900
Białystok 263,900
Bielsko-Biała 179,600
Bydgoszcz 377,900
Bytom (Beuthen) (★★ Katowice) 228,000
Chełm 63,300
Chorzów (★★ Katowice) 133,300
Częstochowa 254,600
Dąbrowa Górnicza (★ Katowice) 133,200
Elbląg (Elbing) 124,600
Ełk 49,600
Gdańsk (Danzig) (★ 909,000) 461,500
Gdynia (★★ Gdańsk) 250,200
Gliwice (Gleiwitz) (★★ Katowice) 222,500
Głogów 70,100
Gniezno 68,900
Gorzów Wielkopolski (Landsberg an der Warthe) 121,500
Grudziądz 99,900
Inowrocław 75,100
Jastrzębie-Zdrój 102,200
Jaworzno (★ Katowice) 97,400
Jelenia Góra (Hirschberg) 92,700
Kalisz 105,600
• Katowice (★ 2,778,000) 365,800
Kędzierzyn Kozle 71,600
Kielce 211,100
Konin 78,500
Koszalin (Köslin) 105,600
Kraków (★ 828,000) 743,700
Legionowo (★ Warszawa) 50,000
Legnica (Liegnitz) 102,800
Leszno 56,700
Łódź (★ 1,061,000) 851,500
Łomża 56,300
Lubin 78,800
Lublin (★ 389,000) 339,500
Mielec 58,600
Mysłowice (★ Katowice) 91,200
Nowy Sącz 75,100
Olsztyn (Allenstein) 158,800
Opole (Oppeln) 125,800
Ostrowiec Świętokrzyski 76,300
Ostrów Wielkopolski 71,200
Pabianice (★ Łódź) 74,400
Piekary Śląskie (★ Katowice) 68,200
Piła (Schneidemühl) (1988 E) 70,000
Piotrków Trybunalski 80,100
Płock 119,300
Poznań (★ 672,000) 586,500
Pruszków (★ Warszawa) 52,700
Przemyśl 67,300
Puławy 52,200
Racibórz (Ratibor) 61,700
Radom 223,600
Radomsko 49,700
Ruda Śląska (★ Katowice) 167,700
Rybnik 140,000
Rzeszów 148,600
Siedlce 69,200
Siemianowice Śląskie (★ Katowice) 79,200
Skarżysko-Kamienna 50,200
Słupsk (Stolp) 98,500
Sosnowiec (★★ Katowice) 258,700
Stalowa Wola 67,600
Starachowice 55,400
Stargard Szczeciński (Stargard in Pommern) 68,400
Suwałki 57,900
Świdnica (Schweidnitz) 61,800
Świętochłowice (★ Katowice) 58,700
Szczecin (Stettin) (★ 449,000) 409,500
Tarnów 119,100
Tarnowskie Góry (★ Katowice) 72,700
Tczew 58,400
Tomaszów Mazowiecki 69,200
Toruń 199,600
Tychy (★ Katowice) 187,600
Wałbrzych (Waldenburg) (★ 207,000) 141,400
• WARSZAWA (★ 2,323,000) 1,651,200
Włocławek 119,500
Wodzisław Śląski 109,800
Wrocław (Breslau) 637,400
Zabrze (Hindenburg) (★★ Katowice) 201,400
Zamość 59,000
Zawiercie 55,700
Zgierz (★ Łódź) 58,500
Zielona Góra (Grünberg) 111,800
Żory 65,300

PORTUGAL

1981 C 9,833,014

Cities and Towns

Amadora (★ Lisboa) 95,518
Barreiro (★ Lisboa) 50,863
Braga 63,033
Coimbra 74,616
• LISBOA (LISBON) (★ 2,250,000) 807,167
Porto (★ 1,225,000) 327,368
Setúbal 77,885
Vila Nova de Gaia (★ Porto) 62,469

PUERTO RICO

1980 C 3,196,520

Cities and Towns

Aguadilla (★ 152,793) 22,039
Arecibo (★ 160,336) 48,779
Bayamón (★ San Juan) 185,087
Caguas (★ San Juan) 87,214
Carolina (★ San Juan) 147,835
Guaynabo (★ San Juan) 65,075
Mayagüez (★ 200,464) 82,968
Ponce (★ 232,551) 161,739
• SAN JUAN (★ 1,775,260) 424,600

QATAR / Qaṭar

1986 C 369,079

Cities and Towns

• AD-DAWHAH (DOHA) (★ 310,000) 217,294
Ar-Rayyān (★ Ad-Dawḥah) 91,996

REUNION / Réunion

1982 C 515,814

Cities and Towns

• SAINT-DENIS (▲ 109,072) 84,400

ROMANIA / România

1986 E 22,823,479

Cities and Towns

Alba-Iulia 66,100
Alexandria 52,802
Arad 187,744
Bacău 179,877
Baia-Mare 139,704
Bîrlad 70,365
Bistriţa 77,267
Botoşani 108,775
Brăila 235,620
Braşov 351,493
• BUCUREŞTI (BUCHAREST) (★ 2,275,000) 1,989,823
Buzău 136,080
Călăraşi 69,350
Cluj-Napoca 310,017
Constanţa 327,676
Craiova 281,044
Deva 77,976
Drobeta-Turnu-Severin 99,366
Focşani 86,411
Galaţi 295,372
Gheorghe Gheorghiu-Dej 52,329
Giurgiu 68,002
Hunedoara 88,514
Iaşi 313,060
Lugoj 53,665
Medgidia 48,409
Mediaş 72,816
Oradea 213,846
Petroşani (★ 76,000) 49,131
Piatra-Neamţ 109,393
Piteşti 157,190
Ploieşti (★ 310,000) 234,886
Reşiţa 105,914
Rîmnicu-Vîlcea 96,051
Roman 72,415
Satu Mare 130,082
Sfîntu-Gheorghe 67,587
Sibiu 177,511
Slatina 76,714
Suceava 96,317
Timişoara 325,272
Tîrgovişte 91,990
Tîrgu-Jiu 87,693
Tîrgu-Mureş 158,998
Tulcea 86,336
Turda 61,594
Vaslui 65,070
Zalău 57,283

RUSSIA / Rossija

1989 C 147,386,000

Cities and Towns

Abakan 154,000
Achtubinsk (1987 E) 53,000
Ačinsk 122,000
Alapajevsk (1987 E) 51,000
Aleksandrov (1987 E) 66,000
Aleksin (1987 E) 72,000
Al'metjevsk 129,000
Amursk (1987 E) 54,000
Angarsk 266,000
Anžero-Sudžensk 108,000
Apatity (1987 E) 80,000
Archangel'sk 416,000
Armavir 161,000
Arsenjev (1987 E) 67,000
Art'om (1987 E) 73,000
Arzamas 109,000
Asbest (1987 E) 83,000
Astrachan' 509,000
Azov (1987 E) 81,000
Balakovo 198,000
Balašicha (★ Moskva) 136,000
Balašov (1987 E) 99,000
Barnaul (★ 665,000) 602,000
Batajsk (★ Rostov-na-Donu) (1987 E) 98,000
Belebej (1987 E) 51,000
Belgorod 300,000
Belogorsk (1987 E) 71,000
Beloreck (1987 E) 75,000
Belovo (1987 E) 118,000
Berdsk (★ Novosibirsk) (1987 E) 77,000
Berezniki 201,000
Ber'ozovskij (1987 E) 51,000
Bijsk 233,000
Birobidžan (1987 E) 82,000
Blagoveščensk 206,000
Bor (★ Nižnij Novgorod) (1987 E) 65,000
Borisoglebsk (1987 E) 69,000
Boroviči (1987 E) 64,000
Br'ansk 452,000
Bratsk 255,000
Bud'onnovsk (1987 E) 54,000
Bugul'ma (1987 E) 88,000
Buguruslan (1987 E) 53,000
Bujnaksk (1987 E) 53,000
Buzuluk (1987 E) 82,000
Čajkovskij (1987 E) 83,000
Čapajevsk (1987 E) 87,000
Čeboksary 420,000
Čechov (1987 E) 57,000
Čel'abinsk (★ 1,325,000) 1,143,000
Čeremchovo (1987 E) 73,000
Čerepovec 310,000
Čerkessk 113,000
Černogorsk (1987 E) 80,000
Chabarovsk 601,000
Chasav'urt (1987 E) 74,000
Chimki (★ Moskva) 133,000
Cholmsk (1987 E) 50,000
Čistopol' (1987 E) 65,000
Čita 366,000
Čusovoj (1987 E) 59,000
Derbent (1987 E) 83,000
Dimitrovgrad 124,000
Dmitrov (1987 E) 64,000
Dolgoprudnyj (★ Moskva) (1987 E) 71,000
Domodedovo (★ Moskva) (1987 E) 51,000
Dubna (1987 E) 64,000
Dzeržinsk (★ Nižnij Novgorod) 285,000
Elektrostal' 153,000
Elista (1987 E) 85,000
Engel's (★★ Saratov) 182,000
Fr'azino (★ Moskva) (1987 E) 52,000
Gatčina (★ Sankt-Peterburg) (1987 E) 81,000
Georgijevsk (1987 E) 62,000
Glazov 104,000
Groznyj 401,000
Gubkin (1987 E) 75,000
Gukovo (1987 E) 72,000
Gus'-Chrustal'nyj (1987 E) 75,000
Inta (1987 E) 58,000
Irbit (1987 E) 53,000
Irkutsk 626,000
Išim (1987 E) 65,000
Išimbaj (1987 E) 67,000
Iskitim (1987 E) 69,000
Ivanovo 481,000
Ivantejevka (★ Moskva) (1987 E) 53,000
Iževsk 635,000
Jakutsk 187,000
Jaroslavl' 633,000
Jefremov (1987 E) 58,000
Jegorjevsk (1987 E) 73,000
Jejsk (1987 E) 77,000
Jekaterinburg (Sverdlovsk) (★ 1,620,000) 1,367,000
Jelec 120,000
Jermolajevo (1987 E) 62,000
Jessentuki (1987 E) 84,000
Joškar-Ola 242,000
Jurga (1987 E) 92,000
Južno-Sachalinsk 157,000
Kaliningrad (Königsberg) 401,000
Kaliningrad (★ Moskva) 160,000
Kaluga 312,000
Kamensk-Šachtinskij (1987 E) 75,000
Kamensk-Ural'skij 209,000
Kamyšin 122,000
Kanaš (1987 E) 53,000
Kansk 110,000
Kaspijsk (1987 E) 61,000
Kazan' (★ 1,140,000) 1,094,000
Kemerovo 520,000
Kimry (1987 E) 61,000
Kinel' (1979 C) 40,873
Kinešma 105,000
Kiriši (1987 E) 51,000
Kirov 441,000
Kirovo-Čepeck (1987 E) 89,000
Kisel'ovsk (★★ Prokopjevsk) 128,000
Kislovodsk 114,000
Kizel (1979 C) 40,157
Klimovsk (★ Moskva) (1987 E) 57,000
Klin (1987 E) 95,000
Klincy (1987 E) 72,000
Kol'čugino (1979 C) 43,686
Kolomna 162,000
Kolpino (★ Sankt-Peterburg) 142,000
Komsomol'sk-na-Amure 315,000
Kopejsk (★ Čel'abinsk) (1987 E) 99,000
Korkino (1981 E) 63,000
Korsakov (1979 C) 43,348
Kostroma 278,000
Kotlas (1987 E) 69,000
Kovrov 160,000
Krasnodar 620,000
Krasnogorsk (★ Moskva) (1987 E) 89,000
Krasnojarsk 912,000
Krasnokamensk (1987 E) 70,000
Krasnokamsk (1987 E) 58,000
Krasnoturjinsk (1987 E) 66,000
Krasnoufimsk (1979 C) 40,027
Krasnoural'sk (1979 C) 38,212
Krasnyj Sulin (1979 C) 42,281
Kropotkin (1987 E) 73,000
Krymsk (1983 E) 50,000
Kstovo (★ Nižnij Novgorod) (1987 E) 64,000
Kujbyšev (1987 E) 51,000
Kulebaki (1979 C) 48,302
Kungur (1987 E) 83,000
Kurgan 356,000
Kursk 424,000
Kušva (1979 C) 43,089
Kuzneck (1987 E) 98,000
Kyzyl (1987 E) 80,000
Labinsk (1987 E) 58,000
Leninogorsk (1987 E) 61,000
Leninsk-Kuzneckij 165,000
Lipeck 450,000
Liski (1987 E) 54,000
Livny (1987 E) 51,000
Lobn'a (★ Moskva) (1987 E) 59,000
L'ubercy (★ Moskva) 165,000
Lys'va (1987 E) 77,000
Lytkarino (★ Moskva) (1987 E) 51,000
Machačkala 315,000
Magadan 152,000
Magnitogorsk 440,000
Majkop 149,000
Meždurečensk 107,000
Miass 168,000
Michajlovka (1987 E) 58,000
Mičurinsk 109,000
Mineral'nyje Vody (1987 E) 75,000
Minusinsk (1987 E) 72,000
Mončegorsk (1987 E) 65,000
Moršansk (1987 E) 51,000
• MOSKVA (MOSCOW) (★ 13,100,000) 8,769,000
Murmansk 468,000
Murom 124,000
Mytišči (★ Moskva) 154,000
Naberežnyje Čelny 501,000
Nachodka 165,000
Nal'čik 235,000
Naro-Fominsk (1987 E) 60,000
Nazarovo (1987 E) 63,000
Neftejugansk (1987 E) 86,000
Ner'ungri (1987 E) 68,000
Nevinnomyssk 121,000
Nikolo-Berjozovka 107,000
Nižnekamsk 191,000
Nižnevartovsk 242,000
Nižnij Novgorod (★ 2,025,000) 1,438,000
Nižnij Tagil 440,000
Noginsk 123,000
Nojabr'sk (1987 E) 77,000
Noril'sk 174,000
Novgorod 229,000
Novoaltajsk (★ Barnaul) (1987 E) 51,000
Novočeboksarsk 115,000
Novočerkassk 187,000
Novodvinsk (1987 E) 50,000
Novokujbyševsk (★ Kujbyšev) 113,000
Novokuzneck 600,000
Novomoskovsk (★ 365,000) 146,000
Novorossijsk 186,000
Novošachtinsk 106,000
Novosibirsk (★ 1,600,000) 1,436,000
Novotroick 106,000
Novyj Urengoj (1987 E) 79,000
Obninsk 100,000
Odincovo (★ Moskva) 125,000
Okt'abr'skij 105,000
Omsk (★ 1,175,000) 1,148,000
Orechovo-Zujevo (★ 205,000) 137,000
Orenburg 547,000
Or'ol 337,000
Orsk 271,000
Osinniki (1987 E) 63,000
Partizansk (1979 C) 45,628
P'atigorsk 129,000
Pavlovo (1987 E) 72,000

C Census. E Official estimate. U Unofficial estimate.
• Largest city in country.
★ Population or designation of metropolitan area, including suburbs (see headnote).
▲ Population of an entire municipality, commune, or district, including rural area.

Pavlovskij Posad (1987 E) 71,000
Pečora (1987 E) 64,000
Penza 543,000
Perm' (★ 1,160,000) 1,091,000
Pervoural'sk 142,000
Petrodvorec (★ Sankt-Peterburg) (1987 E) 77,000
Petropavlovsk-Kamčatskij 269,000
Petrozavodsk 270,000
Podol'sk (★ Moskva) 210,000
Polevskoj (1987 E) 71,000
Prochladnyj (1987 E) 53,000
Prokopjevsk (★ 410,000) 274,000
Pskov 204,000
Puškin (★ Sankt-Peterburg) (1987 E) 97,000
Puškino (1987 E) 74,000
Ramenskoje (1987 E) 86,000
R'azan' 515,000
Reutov (★ Moskva) (1987 E) 68,000
Revda (1987 E) 66,000
Roslavl' (1987 E) 61,000
Rossoš' (1987 E) 55,000
Rostov-na-Donu (★ 1,165,000) 1,020,000
Rubcovsk 172,000
Ruzajevka (1987 E) 53,000
Rybinsk 252,000
Ržev (1987 E) 70,000
Šachty 224,000
Šadrinsk (1987 E) 87,000
Safonovo (1987 E) 56,000
Salavat 150,000
Sal'sk (1987 E) 62,000
Samara (★ 1,505,000) 1,257,000
Sankt-Peterburg (Saint Petersburg) (★ 5,825,000) 4,456,000
Saransk 312,000
Sarapul 111,000
Saratov (★ 1,155,000) 905,000
Ščelkovo (★ Moskva) 109,000
Ščokino (1987 E) 70,000
Sergijev Posad 115,000
Serov 104,000
Serpuchov 144,000
Severodvinsk 249,000
Severomorsk (1987 E) 55,000
Slav'ansk-Na-Kubani (1987 E) 57,000
Smolensk 341,000
Soči 337,000
Sokol (1979 C) 45,424
Solikamsk 110,000
Solncevo (★ Moskva) (1984 E) 62,000
Solnečnogorsk (★ Moskva) (1987 E) 53,000
Sosnovyj Bor (1987 E) 56,000
Spassk-Dal'nij (1987 E) 60,000
Staryj Oskol 174,000
Stavropol' 318,000
Sterlitamak 248,000
Stupino (1987 E) 73,000
Suja (1987 E) 72,000
Surgut 248,000
Svobodnyj (1987 E) 78,000
Syktyvkar 233,000
Syzran' 174,000
Taganrog 291,000
Talnach (1987 E) 54,000
Tambov 305,000
Tichoreck (1987 E) 67,000
Tichvin (1987 E) 70,000
Tobol'sk (1987 E) 82,000
Toljatti 630,000
Tomsk 502,000
Toržok (1987 E) 51,000
Troick (1987 E) 91,000
Tuapse (1987 E) 64,000
Tujmazy (1987 E) 54,000
Tula (★ 640,000) 540,000
Tulun (1987 E) 56,000
T'umen' 477,000
Tver' 451,000
Tyndinskij (1987 E) 61,000
Uchta 111,000
Ufa (★ 1,100,000) 1,083,000
Uglič (1979 C) 39,872
Ulan-Ude 353,000
Uljanovsk 625,000
Usolje-Sibirskoje 107,000
Ussurijsk 162,000
Ust'-Ilimsk 109,000
Ust'-Kut (1987 E) 58,000
Uzlovaja (★ Novomoskovsk) (1987 E) 63,000
V'az'ma (1987 E) 57,000
Velikije Luki 114,000
Verchn'aja Salda (1987 E) 56,000
Vičuga (1987 E) 51,000
Vladikavkaz 300,000
Vladimir 350,000
Vladivostok 648,000
Volchov (1987 E) 51,000
Volgodonsk 176,000
Volgograd (Stalingrad) (★ 1,360,000) 999,000
Vologda 283,000
Vol'sk (1987 E) 66,000
Volžsk (1987 E) 60,000
Volžskij (★ Volgograd) 269,000
Vorkuta 116,000
Voronež 887,000
Voskresensk (1987 E) 80,000
Votkinsk 103,000
Vyborg (1987 E) 81,000
Vyksa (1987 E) 60,000
Vyšnij Voloček (1987 E) 70,000
Zelenograd (★ Moskva) 158,000
Železnodorožnyj (★ Moskva) (1987 E) 90,000
Železnogorsk (1987 E) 81,000
Zel'onodol'sk (1987 E) 93,000
Žigulevsk (1977 E) 50,000
Zima (1987 E) 51,000
Zlatoust 208,000
Žukovskij 101,000

RWANDA

1983 E 5,762,000

Cities and Towns

Butare 30,000
• KIGALI 181,600

SAINT HELENA

1987 C 5,644

Cities and Towns

• JAMESTOWN 1,413

SAINT KITTS AND NEVIS

1980 C 44,404

Cities and Towns

• BASSETERRE 14,725
Charlestown 1,771

SAINT LUCIA

1987 E 142,342

Cities and Towns

• CASTRIES 53,933

SAINT PIERRE AND MIQUELON / Saint-Pierre-et-Miquelon

1982 C 6,041

Cities and Towns

• SAINT-PIERRE 5,371

SAINT VINCENT AND THE GRENADINES

1987 E 112,589

Cities and Towns

• KINGSTOWN (★ 28,936) 19,028

SAN MARINO

1988 E 22,304

Cities and Towns

• SAN MARINO 2,777

SAO TOME AND PRINCIPE / São Tomé e Príncipe

1970 C 73,631

Cities and Towns

• SÃO TOMÉ 17,380

SAUDI ARABIA / Al-'Arabīyah as-Su'ūdīyah

1980 E 9,229,000

Cities and Towns

Abhā (1974 C) 30,150
Ad-Dammām 200,000
Al-Hufūf (1974 C) 101,271
Al-Khubar (1974 C) 48,817
Al-Madīnah (Medina) 290,000
Al-Mubarraz (1974 C) 54,325
AR-RIYĀD (RIYADH) 1,250,000
At-Tā'if 300,000
Buraydah (1974 C) 69,940
Hā'il (1974 C) 40,502
• Jiddah 1,300,000
Makkah (Mecca) 550,000
Najran (1974 C) 47,501
Tabūk (1974 C) 74,825

SENEGAL / Sénégal

1988 C 6,881,919

Cities and Towns

• DAKAR 1,447,642
Diourbel 77,548
Kaolack 152,007
Louga 52,763
Saint-Louis 160,689
Thiès 184,902
Ziguinchor 124,283

SEYCHELLES

1984 E 64,718

Cities and Towns

• VICTORIA 23,000

SIERRA LEONE

1985 C 3,515,812

Cities and Towns

Bo 59,768
• FREETOWN (★ 525,000) 469,776
Kenema 52,473
Koidu 82,474
Makeni 49,038

SINGAPORE

1989 E 2,685,400

Cities and Towns

• SINGAPORE (★ 3,025,000) 2,685,400

SLOVENIA / Slovenija

1987 E 1,936,606

Cities and Towns

• LJUBLJANA (▲ 316,607) 233,200
Maribor (▲ 187,651) 107,400

SOLOMON ISLANDS

1986 C 285,176

Cities and Towns

• HONIARA 30,413

SOMALIA / Somaliya

1984 E 5,423,000

Cities and Towns

Berbera 65,000
Hargeysa 70,000
Kismayu 70,000
Marka 60,000
• MUQDISHO 600,000

SOUTH AFRICA / Suid-Afrika

1985 C 23,385,645

Cities and Towns

Alberton (★ Johannesburg) 66,155
Alexandra (★ Johannesburg) 67,276
Atteridgeville (★ Pretoria) 73,439
Bellville (★ Cape Town) 68,915
Benoni (★ Johannesburg) 94,926
Bloemfontein (★ 235,000) 104,381
Boksburg (★ Johannesburg) 110,832
Botshabelo (★ Bloemfontein) 95,625
CAPE TOWN (KAAPSTAD) (★ 1,790,000) 776,617
Carletonville (★ 120,499) 97,874
Daveyton (★ Johannesburg) 99,056
Diepmeadow (★ Johannesburg) 192,682
Durban (★ 1,550,000) 634,301
East London (Oos-Londen) (★ 320,000) 85,699
Elsies River (★ Cape Town) 70,067
Evaton (★ Vereeniging) 52,559
Galeshewe (★ Kimberley) 63,238
Germiston (★★ Johannesburg) 116,718
Grassy Park (★ Cape Town) 50,193
Guguleto (★ Cape Town) 63,893
• Johannesburg (★ 3,650,000) 632,369
Kagiso (★ Johannesburg) 50,647
Katlehong (★ Johannesburg) 137,745
Kayamnandi (★ Port Elizabeth) 220,548
Kempton Park (★ Johannesburg) 87,721
Kimberley (★ 145,000) 74,061
Klerksdorp (★ 205,000) 48,947
Kroonstad (★ 65,165) 22,886
Krugersdorp (★ Johannesburg) 73,767
Kwa Makuta (★ Durban) 71,378
Kwa Mashu (★ Durban) 111,593
Kwanobuhle (★ Port Elizabeth) 52,376
Kwa-Thema (★ Johannesburg) 78,640
Ladysmith (★ 31,670) 25,102
Lekoa (Shapeville) (★ Vereeniging) 218,392
Madadeni (★ Newcastle) 65,832
Mamelodi (★ Pretoria) 127,033
Mangaung (★ Bloemfontein) 79,851
Newcastle (★ 155,000) 34,931
Ntuzuma (★ Durban) 61,834
Nyanga (★ Cape Town) 148,882
Ozisweni (★ Newcastle) 51,934
Paarl (★★ Cape Town) 63,671
Parow (★ Cape Town) 60,294
Pietermaritzburg (★ 230,000) 133,809
Pinetown (★ Durban) 55,770
Port Elizabeth (★ 690,000) 272,844
PRETORIA (★ 960,000) 443,059
Randburg (★ Johannesburg) 74,347
Roodepoort-Maraisburg (★ Johannesburg) 141,764
Sandton (★ Johannesburg) 86,089
Soshanguve (★ Pretoria) 68,598
Soweto (★ Johannesburg) 521,948
Springs (★ Johannesburg) 68,235
Tembisa (★ Johannesburg) 149,282
Uitenhage (★★ Port Elizabeth) 54,987
Umlazi (★ Durban) 194,933
Vanderbijlpark (★★ Vereeniging) 59,865
Vereeniging (★ 525,000) 60,584
Verwoerdburg (★ Pretoria) 49,891
Vosloosrus (★ Johannesburg) 52,061
Walvisbaai (Walvis Bay) (★ 16,607) 9,687
Welkom (★ 215,000) 54,488
Witbank (★ 77,171) 41,784

SPAIN / España

1988 E 39,217,804

Cities and Towns

Albacete 125,997
Alcalá de Guadaira 50,935
Alcalá de Henares (★ Madrid) 150,021
Alcobendas (★ Madrid) 73,455
Alcorcón (★ Madrid) 139,796
Alcoy 66,074
Algeciras 99,528
Alicante 261,051
Almería 157,644
Avilés (★ 131,000) 87,811
Badajoz (▲ 122,407) 106,400
Badalona (★ Barcelona) 225,229
Baracaldo (★ Bilbao) 113,502
Barcelona (★ 4,040,000) 1,714,355
Bilbao (★ 985,000) 384,733
Burgos 160,561
Cáceres 71,598
Cádiz (★ 240,000) 156,591
Cartagena (▲ 172,710) 70,000
Castelló de la Plana 131,809
Ciudad Real 56,300
Córdoba 302,301
Cornella (★ Barcelona) 86,866
Coslada (★ Madrid) 68,765
Dos Hermanas (▲ 68,456) 60,600
Elche (▲ 180,256) 158,300
Elda 56,756
El Ferrol del Caudillo (★ 129,000) 86,503
El Puerto de Santa María (▲ 62,285) 49,900
Fuenlabrada (★ Madrid) 128,872
Getafe (★ Madrid) 135,367
Gijón 262,156
Granada 263,334
Granollers (★ Barcelona) 49,045
Guadalajara 61,309
Hospitalet (★ Barcelona) 278,449
Huelva 137,826
Irún 54,886
Jaén 106,435
Jerez de la Frontera (▲ 183,007) 156,200
La Coruña 248,862
La Línea 60,956
Las Palmas de Gran Canaria (▲ 366,347) 319,000
Leganés (★ Madrid) 168,403
León (★ 159,000) 136,558
Lérida (▲ 109,795) 91,500
Linares 58,622
Logroño 119,038
Lugo (▲ 78,795) 68,700
• MADRID (★ 4,650,000) 3,102,846
Málaga 574,456
Manresa 65,607
Mataró 100,817
Mérida 52,368
Móstoles (★ Madrid) 181,648
Murcia (▲ 314,124) 149,800
Orense 106,042
Oviedo (▲ 190,073) 168,900
Palencia 76,692
Palma [de Mallorca] (▲ 314,608) 249,000
Parla (★ Madrid) 66,253
Portugalete (★ Bilbao) 57,813
Prat del Llobregat (★ Barcelona) 64,193
Puertollano 52,284
Reus 83,800
Sabadell (★ Barcelona) 189,489
Salamanca 159,342
San Baudilio de Llobregat (★ Barcelona) 77,502
San Fernando (★★ Cádiz) 81,975
San Sebastián (★ 285,000) 177,622
San Sebastián de los Reyes (★ Madrid) 51,653
Santa Coloma de Gramanet (★ Barcelona) 136,042
Santa Cruz de Tenerife 215,228
Santander (▲ 190,795) 166,800
Santiago de Compostela (▲ 88,110) 68,800
Santurce-Antiguo (★ Bilbao) 52,334
Segovia 54,402
Sevilla (★ 945,000) 663,132
Talavera de la Reina 68,158
Tarragona (▲ 109,586) 63,500
Tarrasa (★ Barcelona) 161,410
Toledo 59,551
Torrejón de Ardoz (★ Madrid) 83,267
Torrente (★ València) 55,751
Valencia (★ 1,270,000) 743,933
Valladolid 331,461
Vigo (▲ 271,128) 179,500
Vitoria (Gasteiz) 204,264
Zamora 62,047
Zaragoza 582,239

SPANISH NORTH AFRICA / Plazas de Soberanía en el Norte de África

1988 E 122,905

Cities and Towns

• Ceuta 67,188
Melilla 55,717

SRI LANKA

1986 E 16,117,000

Cities and Towns

Battaramulla (★ Colombo) (1981 C) 56,535
• COLOMBO (★ 2,050,000) 683,000
Dehiwala-Mount Lavinia (★ Colombo) 191,000
Galle 109,000
Jaffna 143,000
Kandy 130,000
KOTTE (★ Colombo) 104,000
Maharagama (★ Colombo) (1981 C) 49,765
Matale (1985 E) 57,000
Matara (1985 E) 57,000
Moratuwa (★ Colombo) 138,000
Negombo (1985 E) 76,000
Ratnapura (1985 E) 51,000
Trincomalee (1985 E) 51,000

SUDAN / As-Sūdān

1983 C 20,564,364

Cities and Towns

Al-Fāshir (1973 C) 51,932
• AL-KHARṬŪM (★ 1,450,000) 476,218
Al-Kharṭūm Bahrī (★ Al-Kharṭūm) 341,146
Al-Qaḍārif (1973 C) 66,465
Al-Ubayyiḍ 140,000
Atbarah 73,000
Būr Sūdān (Port Sudan) 206,727
Jūbā (1980 E) 116,000
Kassalā 143,000
Kūstī (1973 C) 65,257
Nyala (1973 C) 59,852
Umm Durmān (Omdurman) (★★ Al-Kharṭūm) 526,287
Wad Madanī 141,000
Wāw (1980 E) 116,000

SURINAME

1988 E 392,000

Cities and Towns

• PARAMARIBO (★ 296,000) 241,000

SWAZILAND

1986 C 712,131

Cities and Towns

LOBAMBA 0
Manzini (★ 30,000) 18,084
• MBABANE 38,290

SWEDEN / Sverige

1990 E 8,527,036

Cities and Towns

Borås 101,231
Borlänge 46,424
Eskilstuna 89,460

C Census. E Official estimate. U Unofficial estimate.
• Largest city in country.
★ Population or designation of metropolitan area, including suburbs (see headnote).
▲ Population of an entire municipality, commune, or district, including rural area.

Gävle (▲ 88,081) ... 67,500
Göteborg (★ 710,894) ... 431,840
Halmstad (▲ 79,362) ... 50,900
Helsingborg ... 108,359
Huddinge (★ Stockholm) ... 73,107
Järfälla (★ Stockholm) ... 56,386
Jönköping ... 110,860
Karlstad ... 76,120
Linköping ... 120,562
Luleå ... 67,903
Lund (★★ Malmö) ... 86,412
Malmö (★ 445,000) ... 232,908
Mölndal (★ Göteborg) ... 51,767
Nacka (★ Stockholm) ... 63,114
Norrköping ... 119,921
Örebro ... 120,353
Södertälje (★ Stockholm) ... 81,460
Sollentuna (★ Stockholm) ... 50,606
Solna (★ Stockholm) ... 51,427
• STOCKHOLM (★ 1,449,972) ... 672,187
Sundsvall (▲ 93,404) ... 50,600
Täby (★ Stockholm) ... 56,553
Trollhättan ... 50,602
Tumba (★ Stockholm) ... 68,255
Umeå (▲ 90,004) ... 58,700
Uppsala ... 164,754
Västerås ... 118,386
Växjö (▲ 68,849) ... 45,500

SWITZERLAND / Schweiz / Suisse / Svizzera

1990 E ... 6,673,850

Cities and Towns

Arbon (★ 41,100) ... 12,284
Baden (★ 70,700) ... 14,545
Basel (Bâle) (★ 575,000) ... 169,587
BERN (BERNE) (★ 298,800) ... 134,393
Biel (Bienne) (★ 81,900) ... 52,023
Fribourg (Freiburg) (★ 56,800) ... 33,962
Genève (Geneva) (★ 460,000) ... 165,404
Lausanne (★ 259,900) ... 122,600
Locarno (★ 42,350) ... 14,149
Lugano (★ 94,800) ... 26,055
Luzern (★ 159,500) ... 59,115
Sankt Gallen (★ 125,000) ... 73,191
Sankt Moritz (1987 E) ... 5,335
Solothurn (★ 56,800) ... 15,429
Thun (★ 77,200) ... 37,707
Winterthur (★ 107,400) ... 85,174
• Zürich (★ 860,000) ... 342,861

SYRIA / Sūrīyah

1988 E ... 11,338,000

Cities and Towns

Al-Hasakah (1981 C) ... 73,426
Al-Lādhiqīyah (Latakia) ... 249,000
Al-Qāmishlī ... 126,236
As-Suwaydā' ... 46,844
Dar'ā (1981 C) ... 49,534
Dārayyā ... 53,204
Dayr az-Zawr ... 112,000
• DIMASHQ (DAMASCUS) (★ 1,950,000) ... 1,326,000
Dūmā (★ Dimashq) ... 66,130
Halab (Aleppo) (★ 1,275,000) ... 1,261,000
Hamāh ... 222,000
Hims ... 447,000
Idlib (1981 C) ... 51,682
Jaramānah (★ Dimashq) ... 96,681
Madīnat ath Thawrah ... 58,151
Tartūs (1981 C) ... 52,589

TAIWAN / T'aiwan

1988 E ... 19,672,612

Cities and Towns

Changhua (▲ 206,603) ... 158,400
Chiai ... 254,875
Chilung ... 348,541
Chungho (★ T'aipei) ... 343,389
Chungli ... 247,639
Chutung ... 104,797
Fangshan (★ Kaohsiung) ... 276,259
Fengyüan (▲ 144,434) ... 115,300
Hsichih (★ T'aipei) (1980 C) ... 70,031
Hsinchu ... 309,899
Hsinchuang (★ T'aipei) ... 259,001
Hsintien (★ T'aipei) ... 205,094
Hualien ... 106,658
Ilan (▲ 81,751) (1980 C) ... 70,900
Kangshan (1980 C) ... 78,049
Kaohsiung (★ 1,845,000) ... 1,342,797
Lotung (1980 C) ... 57,925
Lukang (1980 C) ... 72,019
Miaoli (1980 C) ... 81,500
Nant'ou (1980 C) ... 84,038
P'ingchen (★ T'aipei) ... 134,925
P'ingtung (▲ 204,990) ... 167,600
Sanchung (★ T'aipei) ... 362,171
Shulin (★ T'aipei) (1980 C) ... 75,700
Tach'i (1980 C) ... 67,209
T'aichung ... 715,107
T'ainan ... 656,927
• T'AIPEI (★ 6,130,000) ... 2,637,100
T'aipeihsien (★ T'aipei) ... 506,220
T'aitung (▲ 109,358) ... 79,800
Taoyüan ... 220,255
T'oufen (1980 C) ... 66,536
T'uch'eng (★ T'aipei) ... 70,500
Yangmei (1980 C) ... 84,353
Yüanlin (▲ 116,936) ... 51,300
Yungho (★ T'aipei) ... 242,252
Yungkang (▲ 114,904) ... 59,600

TAJIKISTAN

1989 C ... 5,112,000

Cities and Towns

Chudžand ... 160,000
• DUŠANBE ... 595,000
Kul'ab (1987 E) ... 71,000

TANZANIA

1984 E ... 21,062,000

Cities and Towns

Arusha ... 69,000
• DAR ES SALAAM ... 1,300,000
Dodoma ... 54,000
Iringa ... 67,000
Kigoma (1978 C) ... 50,044
Mbeya ... 93,000
Morogoro ... 72,000
Moshi ... 62,000
Mtwara (1978 C) ... 48,510
Mwanza (1978 C) ... 110,611
Tabora ... 87,000
Tanga ... 121,000
Zanzibar (1985 E) ... 133,000

THAILAND / Prathet Thai

1988 E ... 54,960,917

Cities and Towns

Chiang Mai ... 164,030
Hat Yai ... 138,046
Khon Kaen ... 131,340
• KRUNG THEP (BANGKOK) (★ 6,450,000) ... 5,716,779
Nakhon Ratchasima ... 204,982
Nakhon Sawan ... 105,220
Nakhon Si Thammarat ... 72,407
Nonthaburi (★ Krung Thep) ... 218,354
Pattaya ... 56,402
Phitsanulok ... 77,675
Phra Nakhon Si Ayutthaya ... 60,847
Samut Prakan (★ Krung Thep) ... 73,327
Samut Sakhon ... 53,984
Saraburi ... 61,206
Songkhla ... 84,433
Ubon Ratchathani ... 100,374
Udon Thani ... 81,202
Yala ... 67,383

TOGO

1981 C ... 2,702,945

Cities and Towns

• LOMÉ (1984 E) ... 400,000
Sokodé ... 48,098

TOKELAU

1986 C ... 1,690

TONGA

1986 C ... 94,535

Cities and Towns

• NUKU'ALOFA ... 21,265

TRINIDAD AND TOBAGO

1990 C ... 1,234,388

Cities and Towns

• PORT OF SPAIN (★ 370,000) ... 50,878
San Fernando (★ 75,000) ... 30,092

TUNISIA / Tunis / Tunisie

1984 C ... 6,975,450

Cities and Towns

Ariana (★ Tunis) ... 98,655
Bardo (★ Tunis) ... 65,669
Béja ... 46,708
Ben Arous (★ Tunis) ... 52,105
Binzert ... 94,509
Gabès ... 92,258
Gafsa ... 60,970
Hammam Lif (★ Tunis) ... 47,009
Houmt Essouk ... 92,269
Kairouan ... 72,254
Kasserine ... 47,606
La Goulette (★ Tunis) ... 61,609
Menzel Bourguiba ... 51,399
Nabeul (★ 75,000) ... 39,531
Sfax (★ 310,000) ... 231,911
Sousse (★ 160,000) ... 83,509
• TUNIS (★ 1,225,000) ... 596,654
Zarzis ... 49,063

TURKEY / Türkiye

1990 C ... 56,969,109

Cities and Towns

Adana ... 931,555
Adapazarı ... 174,353
Adıyaman ... 101,306
Afyon ... 98,618
Ağrı ... 57,837
Akhisar ... 74,002
Aksaray ... 92,038
Akşehir ... 51,669
Amasya ... 55,602
ANKARA (★ 2,650,000) ... 2,553,209
Antakya (Antioch) ... 124,443
Antalya ... 378,726
Aydın ... 106,603
Bafra ... 66,209
Balıkesir ... 171,967
Bandırma ... 77,211
Batman ... 148,121
Bolu ... 60,600
Burdur ... 56,095
Bursa ... 838,323
Çanakkale ... 53,887
Ceyhan ... 85,000
Çorlu ... 77,025
Çorum ... 116,260
Denizli ... 203,130
Diyarbakır ... 375,767
Dörtyol ... 48,030
Düzce ... 62,606
Edirne ... 102,325
Elazığ ... 211,720
Elbistan ... 55,114
Ereğli, Konya prov. ... 74,332
Ereğli, Zonguldak prov. ... 63,776
Erzincan ... 90,799
Erzurum ... 241,344
Eskişehir ... 413,305
Gaziantep ... 627,584
Gebze (★ İstanbul) ... 156,594
Gemlik ... 50,212
Giresun ... 67,536
Gölcük ... 65,000
İçel (Mersin) ... 420,750
İnegöl ... 71,095
İskenderun ... 156,198
Isparta ... 111,706
• İstanbul (★ 7,550,000) ... 6,748,435
İzmir (★ 1,900,000) ... 1,762,849
İzmit ... 254,768
Kadirli ... 55,193
Kahramanmaraş ... 229,066
Karabük ... 104,869
Karaman ... 76,682
Kars ... 79,496
Kastamonu ... 52,363
Kayseri ... 416,276
Kilis ... 81,469
Kırıkhan ... 69,323
Kırıkkale ... 203,666
Kırşehir ... 74,546
Kızıltepe ... 60,445
Konya ... 509,208
Kozan ... 54,934
Kütahya ... 131,286
Lüleburgaz ... 51,978
Malatya ... 276,666
Manisa ... 158,283
Mardin ... 52,994
Nazilli ... 80,209
Nevşehir ... 52,514
Niğde ... 54,822
Nizip ... 58,259
Nusaybin ... 50,605
Ödemiş ... 511,110
Ordu ... 101,306
Osmaniye ... 122,315
Polatlı ... 61,026
Rize ... 51,586
Salihli ... 71,035
Samsun ... 301,412
Siirt ... 66,607
Silvan (Miyafarkin) ... 59,959
Sincan (★ Ankara) ... 92,262
Sivas ... 219,122
Siverek ... 63,366
Söke ... 50,598
Soma ... 50,165
Tarsus ... 191,333
Tatvan ... 52,404
Tekirdağ ... 80,207
Tokat ... 83,174
Trabzon ... 144,805
Turgutlu ... 73,734
Turhal ... 71,406
Urfa ... 278,516
Uşak ... 104,980
Van ... 153,525
Viranşehir ... 58,394
Yalova ... 72,874
Yarımca (1985 C) ... 48,420
Yozgat ... 51,360
Zonguldak (★ 220,000) ... 120,300

TURKMENISTAN

1989 C ... 3,534,000

Cities and Towns

• AŠCHABAD ... 398,000
Mary (1987 E) ... 89,000
Nebit-Dag (Krasnovodsk) (1987 E) ... 59,000
Nebit-Dag (1987 E) ... 85,000
Tašauz ... 112,000

TURKS AND CAICOS ISLANDS

1990 C ... 12,350

Cities and Towns

• GRAND TURK ... 3,761

TUVALU

1979 C ... 7,349

Cities and Towns

• FUNAFUTI ... 2,191

UGANDA

1990 E ... 17,213,407

Cities and Towns

Jinja (1982 E) ... 55,000
• KAMPALA ... 1,008,707

UKRAINE / Ukrayina

1989 C ... 51,704,000

Cities and Towns

Aleksandrija ... 103,000
Antracit (★★ Krasnyj Luč) (1987 E) ... 70,000
Art'omovsk (1987 E) ... 91,000
Belaja Cerkov' ... 197,000
Belgorod-Dnestrovskij (1987 E) ... 54,000
Berd'ansk ... 132,000
Berdičev (1987 E) ... 89,000
Br'anka (★ Stachanov) (1987 E) ... 65,000
Brovary (★ Kijev) (1987 E) ... 73,000
Čerkassy ... 290,000
Černigov ... 296,000
Černovcy ... 257,000
Červonograd (1987 E) ... 71,000
Charcyzsk (★ Doneck) (1987 E) ... 69,000
Char'kov (★ 1,940,000) ... 1,611,000
Cherson ... 355,000
Chmel'nickij ... 237,000
Dimitrov (★★ Krasnoarmejsk) (1987 E) ... 62,000
Dneprodzeržinsk (★★ Dnepropetrovsk) ... 282,000
Dnepropetrovsk (★ 1,600,000) ... 1,179,000
Doneck (★ 2,200,000) ... 1,110,000
Drogobyč (1987 E) ... 76,000
Družkovka (★ Kramatorsk) (1987 E) ... 70,000
Džankoj (1987 E) ... 51,000
Fastov (1987 E) ... 55,000
Feodosija (1987 E) ... 83,000
Gorlovka (★ 710,000) ... 337,000
Iljičovsk (★ Odessa) (1987 E) ... 52,000
Ivano-Frankovsk ... 214,000
Izmail (1987 E) ... 90,000
Iz'um (1987 E) ... 63,000
Jalta (1987 E) ... 89,000
Jenakijevo (★★ Gorlovka) ... 121,000
Jevpatorija ... 108,000
Kaluš (1987 E) ... 67,000
Kamenec-Podol'skij ... 102,000
Kerč' ... 174,000
• KIJEV (★ 2,900,000) ... 2,587,000
Kirovograd ... 269,000
Kolomyja (1987 E) ... 63,000
Kommunarsk (★ Stachanov) ... 126,000
Konotop (1987 E) ... 93,000
Konstantinovka ... 108,000
Korosten' (1987 E) ... 72,000
Kovel' (1987 E) ... 66,000
Kramatorsk (★ 465,000) ... 198,000
Krasnoarmejsk (★ 175,000) (1987 E) ... 70,000
Krasnodon (1987 E) ... 52,000
Krasnyj Luč (★ 250,000) ... 113,000
Kremenčug ... 236,000
Krivoj Rog ... 713,000
Lisičansk (★ 410,000) ... 127,000
Lozovaja (1987 E) ... 68,000
Lubny (1987 E) ... 58,000
Luck ... 198,000
Lugansk ... 497,000
L'vov ... 790,000
Makejevka (★★ Doneck) ... 430,000
Marganec (1987 E) ... 55,000
Mariupol' (Ždanov) ... 517,000
Melitopol' ... 174,000
Mukačevo (1987 E) ... 88,000
Nežin (1987 E) ... 81,000
Nikolajev ... 503,000
Nikopol' ... 158,000
Novaja Kachovka (1987 E) ... 53,000
Novograd-Volynskij (1987 E) ... 52,000
Novomoskovsk (1987 E) ... 76,000
Novovolynsk (1987 E) ... 54,000
Odessa (★ 1,185,000) ... 1,115,000
Pavlograd ... 131,000
Pervomajsk (1987 E) ... 79,000
Poltava ... 315,000
Priluki (1987 E) ... 73,000
Romny (1987 E) ... 53,000
Roven'ki (1987 E) ... 68,000
Rovno ... 228,000
Rubežnoje (★★ Lisičansk) (1987 E) ... 72,000
Šacht'orsk (★★ Torez) (1987 E) ... 73,000
Sevastopol' ... 356,000
Severodoneck (★★ Lisičansk) ... 131,000
Simferopol' ... 344,000
Slav'ansk (★★ Kramatorsk) ... 135,000
Smela (1987 E) ... 76,000
Snežnoje (★ Torez) (1987 E) ... 68,000
Šostka (1987 E) ... 87,000
Stachanov (★ 610,000) ... 112,000
Stryj (1987 E) ... 63,000
Sumy ... 291,000
Sverdlovsk (1987 E) ... 84,000
Svetlovodsk (1987 E) ... 55,000
Ternopol' ... 205,000
Torez (★ 290,000) (1987 E) ... 88,000
Uman' (1987 E) ... 89,000
Užgorod ... 117,000
Vinnica ... 374,000
Zaporožje ... 884,000
Žitomir ... 292,000
Žoltyje Vody (1987 E) ... 61,000

UNITED ARAB EMIRATES / Al-Imārāt al-'Arabīyah al-Muttaḥidah

1980 C ... 980,000

Cities and Towns

ABŪ ZABY (ABU DHABI) ... 242,975
Al-'Ayn ... 101,663
Ash-Shāriqah ... 125,149
• Dubayy ... 265,702

UNITED KINGDOM

1981 C ... 55,678,079

UNITED KINGDOM: ENGLAND

1981 C ... 46,220,955

Cities and Towns

Aldershot (★ London) ... 53,665
Aylesbury ... 51,999
Barnsley ... 76,783
Barrow-in-Furness ... 50,174
Basildon (★ London) ... 94,800
Basingstoke ... 73,027
Bath ... 84,283
Bebington (★ Liverpool) ... 62,618
Bedford ... 75,632
Beeston and Stapleford (★ Nottingham) ... 64,785
Benfleet (★ London) ... 50,783
Birkenhead (★ Liverpool) ... 99,075
Birmingham (★ 2,675,000) ... 1,013,995
Blackburn (★ 221,900) ... 109,564
Blackpool (★ 280,000) ... 146,297
Bognor Regis ... 50,323
Bolton (★★ Manchester) ... 143,960
Bootle ... 70,860
Bournemouth (★ 315,000) ... 142,829
Bracknell (★ London) ... 52,257
Bradford (★★ Leeds) ... 293,336
Brentwood (★ London) ... 51,212
Brighton (★ 420,000) ... 134,581
Bristol (★ 630,000) ... 413,861
Burnley (★ 160,000) ... 76,365
Burton [upon Trent] ... 59,040
Bury (★ Manchester) ... 61,785
Cambridge ... 87,111
Cannock (★ Birmingham) ... 54,503
Canterbury ... 34,546
Carlisle ... 72,206
Chatham (★ London) ... 65,835
Cheadle and Gatley (★ Manchester) ... 59,478
Chelmsford (★ London) ... 91,109
Cheltenham ... 87,188
Cheshunt (★ London) ... 49,616
Chester ... 80,154
Chesterfield (★ 127,000) ... 73,352
Colchester ... 87,476
Corby ... 48,704
Coventry (★ 645,000) ... 318,718
Crawley (★ London) ... 80,113
Crewe ... 59,097
Crosby (★ Liverpool) ... 54,103
Darlington ... 85,519
Dartford (★ London) ... 62,032
Derby (★ 275,000) ... 218,026
Dewsbury (★★ Leeds) ... 49,612
Doncaster ... 74,727

C Census. E Official estimate. U Unofficial estimate.
• Largest city in country.

★ Population or designation of metropolitan area, including suburbs (see headnote).
▲ Population of an entire municipality, commune, or district, including rural area.

Dover 33,461
Dudley (★★ Birmingham) 186,513
Eastbourne 86,715
Eastleigh (★ Southampton) 58,585
Ellesmere Port (★ Liverpool) 65,829
Epsom and Ewell (★ London) 65,830
Exeter 88,235
Fareham / Portchester (★ Portsmouth) 55,563
Farnborough (★ London) 48,063
Gateshead (★ Newcastle upon Tyne) 91,429
Gillingham (★ London) 92,531
Gloucester (★ 115,000) 106,526
Gosport (★ Portsmouth) 69,664
Gravesend (★ London) 53,450
Greasby / Moreton (★ Liverpool) 56,410
Great Yarmouth 54,777
Grimsby (★ 145,000) 91,532
Guildford (★ London) 61,509
Halesowen (★ Birmingham) 57,533
Halifax 76,675
Harlow (★ London) 79,150
Harrogate 63,637
Hartlepool (★★ Teesside) 91,749
Hastings 74,979
Havant (★ Portsmouth) 50,098
Hemel Hempstead (★ London) 80,110
Hereford 48,277
High Wycombe (▲ 156,800) 69,575
Hove (★ Brighton) 65,587
Huddersfield (▲ 377,400) 147,825
Huyton-with-Roby (★ Liverpool) 62,011
Ipswich 129,661
Keighley (★ Leeds) 49,188
Kidderminster 50,385
Kingston upon Hull (★ 350,000) 322,144
Kingswood (★ Bristol) 54,736
Kirkby (★ Liverpool) 52,825
Leeds (★ 1,540,000) 445,242
Leicester (★ 495,000) 324,394
Lincoln 79,980
Littlehampton 46,028
Liverpool (★ 1,525,000) 538,809
• LONDON (★ 11,100,000) 6,574,009
Lowestoft 59,430
Luton (★ 220,000) 163,209
Macclesfield 47,525
Maidenhead (★ London) 59,809
Maidstone 86,067
Manchester (★ 2,775,000) 437,612
Mansfield (★ 198,000) 71,325
Margate 53,137
Middleton (★ Manchester) 51,373
Milton Keynes 36,886
Newcastle-under-Lyme (★★ Stoke-on-Trent) 73,208
Newcastle upon Tyne (★ 1,300,000) 199,064
Northampton 154,172
Norwich (★ 230,000) 169,814
Nottingham (★ 655,000) 273,300
Nuneaton (★★ Coventry) 60,337
Oldbury / Smethwick (★ Birmingham) 153,268
Oldham (★★ Manchester) 107,095
Oxford (★ 230,000) 113,847
Penzance 18,501
Peterborough 113,404
Plymouth (★ 290,000) 238,583
Poole (★★ Bournemouth) 122,815
Portsmouth (★ 485,000) 174,218
Preston (★ 250,000) 166,675
Ramsgate 36,678
Reading (★ 200,000) 194,727
Redditch (★ Birmingham) 61,639
Rochdale (★★ Manchester) 97,292
Rotherham (★★ Sheffield) 122,374
Royal Leamington Spa (★★ Coventry) 56,552
Rugby 59,039
Runcorn (★ Liverpool) 63,995
Saint Albans (★ London) 76,709
Saint Helens 114,397
Sale (★ Manchester) 57,872
Salford (★ Manchester) 96,525
Scunthorpe 79,043
Sheffield (★ 710,000) 470,685
Shrewsbury 57,731
Slough (★ London) 106,341
Solihull (★ Birmingham) 93,940
Southampton (★ 415,000) 211,321
Southend-on-Sea (★ London) 155,720
Southport (★★ Liverpool) 88,596
South Shields (★★ Newcastle upon Tyne) 86,488
Stafford 60,915
Staines (★ London) 51,949
Stevenage 74,757
Stockport (★ Manchester) 135,489
Stoke-on-Trent (★ 440,000) 272,446
Stourbridge (★ Birmingham) 55,136
Stratford-upon-Avon 20,941
Stretford (★ Manchester) 47,522
Sunderland (★★ Newcastle upon Tyne) 195,064
Sutton Coldfield (★ Birmingham) 102,572
Swindon 127,348
Tanworth 63,260
Taunton 47,793
Teesside (★ 580,000) 245,215
Torquay (★ 112,400) 54,430
Tunbridge Wells 57,699
Wakefield (★★ Leeds) 74,764
Wallasey (★ Liverpool) 62,465
Walsall (★★ Birmingham) 177,923
Walton and Weybridge (★ London) 50,031
Warrington 81,366
Waterlooville (★ Portsmouth) 57,296
Watford (★ London) 109,503
West Bromwich (★ Birmingham) 153,725
Weston-super-Mare 60,821
Widnes 55,973
Wigan (★★ Manchester) 88,725
Winchester 34,127
Windsor (★ London) 30,832
Woking (★ London) 92,667
Wolverhampton (★★ Birmingham) 263,501
Worcester 75,466
Worthing (★★ Brighton) 90,687
York (★ 145,000) 123,126

UNITED KINGDOM: NORTHERN IRELAND

1987 E 1,575,200

Cities and Towns

Antrim (1981 C) 22,342
Ballymena (1981 C) 28,166
Bangor (★ Belfast) 70,700
Belfast (★ 685,000) 303,800
Castlereagh (★ Belfast) 57,900
Londonderry (★ 97,200) 97,500
Lurgan (★ 63,000) (1981 C) 20,991
Newtownabbey (★ Belfast) 72,300

UNITED KINGDOM: SCOTLAND

1989 E 5,090,700

Cities and Towns

Aberdeen 210,700
Ayr (★ 100,000) (1981 C) 48,493
Clydebank (★ Glasgow) (1981 C) 51,832
Coatbridge (1981 C) 50,831
Cumbernauld (★ Glasgow) 50,300
Dundee 172,540
Dunfermline (★ 125,817) (1981 C) 52,105
East Kilbride (★ Glasgow) 69,500
Edinburgh (★ 630,000) 433,200
Glasgow (★ 1,800,000) 695,630
Greenock (★ 101,000) (1981 C) 58,436
Hamilton (★ Glasgow) (1981 C) 51,666
Irvine (★ 94,000) 55,900
Kilmarnock (★ 84,000) (1981 C) 51,799
Kirkcaldy (★ 148,171) (1981 C) 46,356
Paisley (★ Glasgow) (1981 C) 84,330
Stirling (★ 61,000) (1981 C) 36,640

UNITED KINGDOM: WALES

1981 C 2,790,462

Cities and Towns

Barry (★ Cardiff) 44,443
Cardiff (★ 625,000) 262,313
Cwmbran (★ Newport) 44,592
Llanelli 45,336
Neath (★★ Swansea) 48,687
Newport (★ 310,000) 115,896
Port Talbot (★ 130,000) 40,078
Rhondda (★★ Cardiff) 70,980
Swansea (★ 275,000) 172,433

UNITED STATES

1990 C 248,709,873

UNITED STATES: ALABAMA

1990 C 4,040,587

Cities and Towns

Birmingham 265,968
Decatur 48,761
Dothan 53,589
Florence 36,426
Gadsden 42,523
Huntsville 159,789
Mobile 196,278
Montgomery 187,106
Tuscaloosa 77,759

UNITED STATES: ALASKA

1990 C 550,043

Cities and Towns

Anchorage 226,338
Fairbanks 30,843
Juneau 26,751

UNITED STATES: ARIZONA

1990 C 3,665,228

Cities and Towns

Chandler 90,533
Flagstaff 45,857
Glendale 148,134
Mesa 288,091
Peoria 50,618
Phoenix 900,013
Scottsdale 130,069
Sun City 57,000
Tempe 141,865
Tucson 405,390
Yuma 54,923

UNITED STATES: ARKANSAS

1990 C 2,350,725

Cities and Towns

Fort Smith 72,798
Little Rock 175,795
North Little Rock 61,741
Pine Bluff 57,140

UNITED STATES: CALIFORNIA

1990 C 29,760,021

Cities and Towns

Alameda 76,459
Alhambra 82,106
Anaheim 266,406
Antioch 62,195
Bakersfield 174,820
Baldwin Park 69,330
Bellflower 61,815
Berkeley 102,724
Beverly Hills 31,971
Buena Park 68,784
Burbank 93,643
Camarillo 52,303
Carlsbad 63,126
Carson 83,995
Cerritos 53,240
Chino 59,682
Chula Vista 135,163
Citrus Heights 107,439
Clovis 50,323
Compton 90,454
Concord 111,348
Corona 76,095
Costa Mesa 96,357
Cucamonga 101,409
Daly City 92,311
Diamond Bar 53,672
Downey 91,444
East Los Angeles 126,379
El Cajon 88,693
El Monte 106,209
Encinitas 55,386
Escondido 108,635
Fairfield 77,211
Fontana 87,535
Fountain Valley 53,691
Fremont 173,339
Fresno 354,202
Fullerton 114,144
Gardena 49,847
Garden Grove 143,050
Glendale 180,038
Hacienda Heights 52,354
Hawthorne 71,349
Hayward 111,498
Hesperia 50,418
Huntington Beach 181,519
Huntington Park 56,065
Inglewood 109,602
Irvine 110,330
La Habra 51,266
Lakewood 73,557
La Mesa 52,931
Lancaster 97,291
Livermore 56,741
Lodi 51,874
Long Beach 429,433
Los Angeles 3,485,398
Lynwood 61,945
Merced 56,216
Milpitas 50,686
Mission Viejo 72,820
Modesto 164,730
Montebello 59,564
Monterey Park 60,738
Moreno Valley 118,779
Mountain View 67,460
Napa 61,842
National City 54,249
Newport Beach 66,643
Norwalk 94,279
Oakland 372,242
Oceanside 128,398
Ontario 133,179
Orange 110,658
Oxnard 142,216
Palmdale 68,842
Palm Springs 40,181
Palo Alto 55,900
Pasadena 131,591
Pico Rivera 59,177
Pleasanton 50,553
Pomona 131,723
Redding 66,462
Redlands 60,394
Redondo Beach 60,167
Redwood City 66,072
Rialto 72,388
Richmond 87,425
Riverside 226,505
Rosemead 51,638
Sacramento 369,365
Salinas 108,777
San Bernardino 164,164
San Diego 1,110,549
San Francisco 723,959
San Jose 782,248
San Leandro 68,223
San Mateo 85,486
Santa Ana 293,742
Santa Barbara 85,571
Santa Clara 93,613
Santa Clarita 110,642
Santa Cruz 49,040
Santa Maria 61,284
Santa Monica 86,905
Santa Rosa 113,313
Santee 52,902
Simi Valley 100,217
South Gate 86,284
South San Francisco 54,312
Stockton 210,943
Sunnyvale 117,229
Thousand Oaks 104,352
Torrance 133,107
Tustin 50,689
Union City 53,762
Upland 63,374
Vacaville 71,479
Vallejo 109,199
Ventura (San Buenaventura) 92,575
Visalia 75,636
Vista 71,872
Walnut Creek 60,569
West Covina 96,086
Westminster 78,118
Whittier 77,671
Yorba Linda 52,422

UNITED STATES: COLORADO

1990 C 3,294,394

Cities and Towns

Arvada 89,235
Aurora 222,103
Boulder 83,312
Colorado Springs 281,140
Denver 467,610
Fort Collins 87,758
Greeley 60,536
Lakewood 126,481
Longmont 51,555
Pueblo 98,640
Thornton 55,031
Westminster 74,625

UNITED STATES: CONNECTICUT

1990 C 3,287,116

Cities and Towns

Bridgeport 141,686
Bristol 60,640
Danbury 65,585
East Hartford 50,452
Fairfield 52,400
Greenwich 58,000
Hamden 53,100
Hartford 139,739
Manchester 51,000
Meriden 59,479
Milford 48,168
New Britain 75,491
New Haven 130,474
Norwalk 78,331
Stamford 108,056
Stratford 50,400
Waterbury 108,961
West Hartford 59,100
West Haven 54,021

UNITED STATES: DELAWARE

1990 C 666,168

Cities and Towns

Dover 27,630
Newark 25,098
Wilmington 71,529

UNITED STATES: DISTRICT OF COLUMBIA

1990 C 606,900

Cities and Towns

WASHINGTON 606,900

UNITED STATES: FLORIDA

1990 C 12,937,926

Cities and Towns

Boca Raton 61,492
Cape Coral 74,991
Carol City 52,800
City of Sunrise 64,407
Clearwater 98,784
Corol Springs 79,443
Daytona Beach 61,921
Delray Beach 47,181
Fort Lauderdale 149,377
Gainesville 84,770
Hialeah 188,004
Hollywood 121,697
Jacksonville 635,230
Kendall 53,100
Lakeland 70,576
Largo 65,674
Lauderhill 49,708
Melbourne 59,646
Miami 358,548
Miami Beach 92,639
North Miami 49,998
Orlando 164,693
Palm Bay 62,632
Pembroke Pines 65,452
Pensacola 58,165
Plantation 66,692
Pompano Beach 72,411
Port Saint Lucie 55,866
Saint Petersburg 238,629
Sarasota 50,961
Tallahassee 124,773
Tampa 280,015
West Palm Beach 67,643

UNITED STATES: GEORGIA

1990 C 6,478,216

Cities and Towns

Albany 78,122
Athens 45,734
Atlanta 394,017
Columbus 178,681
Macon 106,612
Savannah 137,560

UNITED STATES: HAWAII

1990 C 1,108,229

Cities and Towns

Hilo 37,808
Honolulu 365,272
Pearl City 30,993

UNITED STATES: IDAHO

1990 C 1,006,749

Cities and Towns

Boise 125,738
Idaho Falls 43,929
Pocatello 46,080

UNITED STATES: ILLINOIS

1990 C 11,430,602

Cities and Towns

Arlington Heights 75,460
Aurora 99,581
Bloomington 51,972
Champaign 63,502
Chicago 2,783,726
Cicero 67,436
Decatur 83,885
Des Plaines 53,223
Elgin 77,010
Evanston 73,233
Joliet 76,836
Mount Prospect 53,170
Naperville 85,351
Oak Lawn 56,182
Oak Park 53,648
Peoria 113,504
Rockford 139,426
Schaumburg 68,586
Skokie 59,432
Springfield 105,227
Waukegan 69,392
Wheaton 51,464

UNITED STATES: INDIANA

1990 C 5,544,159

Cities and Towns

Anderson 59,459
Bloomington 60,633
Evansville 126,272
Fort Wayne 173,072
Gary 116,646
Hammond 84,236
Indianapolis 731,327
Kokomo 44,962
Lafayette 43,764
Michigan City 33,822
Muncie 71,035

C Census. E Official estimate. U Unofficial estimate.
• Largest city in country.

★ Population or designation of metropolitan area, including suburbs (see headnote).
▲ Population of an entire municipality, commune, or district, including rural area.

South Bend 105,511
Terre Haute 57,483

UNITED STATES: IOWA
1990 C 2,776,755

Cities and Towns

Ames 47,198
Cedar Rapids 108,751
Council Bluffs 54,315
Davenport 95,333
Des Moines 193,187
Dubuque 57,546
Iowa City 59,738
Sioux City 80,505
Waterloo 66,467

UNITED STATES: KANSAS
1990 C 2,477,574

Cities and Towns

Kansas City 149,767
Lawrence 65,608
Olathe 63,352
Overland Park 111,790
Topeka 119,883
Wichita 304,011

UNITED STATES: KENTUCKY
1990 C 3,685,296

Cities and Towns

Frankfort 25,968
Lexington 225,366
Louisville 269,063
Owensboro 53,549

UNITED STATES: LOUISIANA
1990 C 4,219,973

Cities and Towns

Alexandria 49,188
Baton Rouge 219,531
Bossier City 52,721
Houma 96,982
Kenner 72,033
Lafayette 94,440
Lake Charles 70,580
Metairie 149,428
Monroe 54,909
New Orleans 496,938
Shreveport 198,525

UNITED STATES: MAINE
1990 C 1,227,928

Cities and Towns

Augusta 21,325
Bangor 33,181
Lewiston 39,757
Portland 64,358

UNITED STATES: MARYLAND
1990 C 4,781,468

Cities and Towns

Annapolis 33,187
Baltimore 736,014
Bethesda 62,936
Columbia 75,883
Dundalk 65,800
Rockville 44,835
Silver Spring 76,200
Towson 49,445
Wheaton 58,300

UNITED STATES: MASSACHUSETTS
1990 C 6,016,425

Cities and Towns

Boston 574,283
Brockton 92,788
Brookline 54,718
Cambridge 95,802
Chicopee 56,632
Fall River 92,703
Framingham 64,989
Haverhill 51,418
Holyoke 43,704
Lawrence 70,207
Lowell 103,439
Lynn 81,245
Malden 53,884
Medford 57,407
New Bedford 99,922
Newton 82,585
Peabody 47,039
Pittsfield 48,622
Quincy 84,985
Salem 38,091
Somerville 76,210
Springfield 156,983
Taunton 49,832
Waltham 57,878
Weymouth 54,063
Worcester 169,759

UNITED STATES: MICHIGAN
1990 C 9,295,297

Cities and Towns

Ann Arbor 109,592
Battle Creek 53,540
Clinton 85,866
Dearborn 89,286
Dearborn Heights 60,838
Detroit 1,027,974
East Lansing 50,677
Farmington Hills 74,652
Flint 140,761
Grand Rapids 189,126
Kalamazoo 80,277
Lansing 127,321
Livonia 100,850
Pontiac 71,166
Redford 54,387
Rochester Hills 61,766
Roseville 51,412
Royal Oak 65,410
Saginaw 69,512
Saint Clair Shores 68,107
Southfield 75,728
Sterling Heights 117,810
Taylor 70,811
Troy 72,884
Warren 144,864
Westland 84,724
Wyoming 63,891

UNITED STATES: MINNESOTA
1990 C 4,375,099

Cities and Towns

Bloomington 86,335
Brooklyn Park 56,381
Burnsville 51,288
Coon Rapids 52,978
Duluth 85,493
Minneapolis 368,383
Minnetonka 48,370
Plymouth 50,889
Rochester 70,745
Saint Cloud 48,812
Saint Paul 272,235

UNITED STATES: MISSISSIPPI
1990 C 2,573,216

Cities and Towns

Biloxi 46,319
Hattiesburg 41,882
Jackson 196,637

UNITED STATES: MISSOURI
1990 C 5,117,073

Cities and Towns

Columbia 69,101
Florissant 51,206
Independence 112,301
Jefferson City 35,481
Kansas City 435,146
Saint Charles 54,555
Saint Joseph 71,852
Saint Louis 396,685
Springfield 140,494

UNITED STATES: MONTANA
1990 C 799,065

Cities and Towns

Billings 81,151
Great Falls 55,097
Helena 24,569

UNITED STATES: NEBRASKA
1990 C 1,578,385

Cities and Towns

Grand Island 39,386
Lincoln 191,972
Omaha 335,795

UNITED STATES: NEVADA
1990 C 1,201,833

Cities and Towns

Carson City 40,443
Henderson 64,942
Las Vegas 258,295
Paradise 124,682
Reno 133,850
Sparks 53,367
Sunrise Manor 95,362

UNITED STATES: NEW HAMPSHIRE
1990 C 1,109,252

Cities and Towns

Concord 36,006
Manchester 99,567
Nashua 79,662

UNITED STATES: NEW JERSEY
1990 C 7,730,188

Cities and Towns

Atlantic City 37,986
Bayonne 61,444
Brick [Township] 64,800
Camden 87,492
Cherry Hill 69,319
Clifton 71,742
East Orange 73,552
Edison 88,680
Elizabeth 110,002
Irvington 59,774
Jersey City 228,537
Newark 275,221
Passaic 58,041
Paterson 140,891
Trenton 88,675
Union 50,024
Union City 58,012
Vineland 54,780
Woodbridge [Township] (1986 U) 95,100

UNITED STATES: NEW MEXICO
1990 C 1,515,069

Cities and Towns

Albuquerque 384,736
Las Cruces 62,126
Roswell 44,654
Santa Fe 55,859

UNITED STATES: NEW YORK
1990 C 17,990,455

Cities and Towns

Albany 101,082
Binghamton 53,008
Buffalo 328,123
Cheektowaga 84,387
Greece 64,600
Irondequoit 52,322
Levittown 53,286
Mount Vernon 67,153
New Rochelle 67,265
• New York 7,322,564
Niagara Falls 61,840
Rochester 231,636
Schenectady 65,566
Syracuse 163,860
Tonawanda 65,284
Troy 54,269
Utica 68,637
Yonkers 188,082

UNITED STATES: NORTH CAROLINA
1990 C 6,628,637

Cities and Towns

Asheville 61,607
Charlotte 395,934
Durham 136,611
Fayetteville 75,695
Gastonia 54,732
Greensboro 183,521
High Point 69,496
Raleigh 207,951
Rocky Mount 48,997
Wilmington 55,530
Winston-Salem 143,485

UNITED STATES: NORTH DAKOTA
1990 C 638,800

Cities and Towns

Bismarck 49,256
Fargo 74,111
Grand Forks 49,425

UNITED STATES: OHIO
1990 C 10,847,115

Cities and Towns

Akron 223,019
Canton 84,161
Cincinnati 364,040
Cleveland 505,616
Cleveland Heights 54,052
Columbus 632,910
Dayton 182,044
Elyria 56,746
Euclid 54,875
Hamilton 61,368
Kettering 60,569
Lakewood 59,718
Lorain 71,245
Mansfield 50,627
Parma 87,876
Springfield 70,487
Toledo 332,943
Warren 50,793
Youngstown 95,732

UNITED STATES: OKLAHOMA
1990 C 3,145,585

Cities and Towns

Broken Arrow 58,043
Edmond 52,315
Lawton 80,561
Midwest City 52,267
Norman 80,071
Oklahoma City 444,719
Tulsa 367,302

UNITED STATES: OREGON
1990 C 2,842,321

Cities and Towns

Beaverton 53,310
Eugene 112,669
Gresham 68,235
Portland 437,319
Salem 107,786

UNITED STATES: PENNSYLVANIA
1990 C 11,881,643

Cities and Towns

Abington Township 59,300
Allentown 105,090
Altoona 51,881
Bensalem 56,788
Bethlehem 71,428
Bristol 57,129
Erie 108,718
Harrisburg 52,376
Haverford Township 51,800
Lancaster 55,551
Lower Merion 58,003
Penn Hills 51,430
Philadelphia 1,585,577
Pittsburgh 369,879
Reading 78,380
Scranton 81,805
Upper Darby 86,100

UNITED STATES: RHODE ISLAND
1990 C 1,003,464

Cities and Towns

Cranston 76,060
East Providence 50,380
Pawtucket 72,644
Providence 160,728
Warwick 85,427

UNITED STATES: SOUTH CAROLINA
1990 C 3,486,703

Cities and Towns

Charleston 80,414
Columbia 98,052
Greenville 58,282
North Charleston 70,218

UNITED STATES: SOUTH DAKOTA
1990 C 696,004

Cities and Towns

Pierre 12,906
Rapid City 54,523
Sioux Falls 100,814

UNITED STATES: TENNESSEE
1990 C 4,877,185

Cities and Towns

Chattanooga 152,466
Clarksville 75,494
Jackson 48,949
Knoxville 165,121
Memphis 610,337
Nashville 487,969

UNITED STATES: TEXAS
1990 C 16,986,510

Cities and Towns

Abilene 106,654
Amarillo 157,615
Arlington 261,721
Austin 465,622
Baytown 63,850
Beaumont 114,323
Brownsville 98,962
Bryan 55,002
Carrollton 82,169
College Station 52,456
Corpus Christi 257,453
Dallas 1,006,877
Denton 66,270
El Paso 515,342
Fort Worth 447,619
Galveston 59,070
Garland 180,650
Grand Prairie 99,616
Houston 1,630,553
Irving 155,037
Killeen 63,535
Laredo 122,899
Longview 70,311
Lubbock 186,206
McAllen 84,021
Mesquite 101,484
Midland 89,443
Odessa 89,699
Pasadena 119,363
Plano 128,713
Port Arthur 58,724
Richardson 74,840
San Angelo 84,474
San Antonio 935,933
Tyler 75,450
Victoria 55,076
Waco 103,590
Wichita Falls 96,259

UNITED STATES: UTAH
1990 C 1,722,850

Cities and Towns

Ogden 63,909
Orem 67,561
Provo 86,835
Salt Lake City 159,936
Sandy 75,058
West Valley City 86,976

UNITED STATES: VERMONT
1990 C 562,758

Cities and Towns

Burlington 39,127
Montpelier 8,247
Rutland 18,230

UNITED STATES: VIRGINIA
1990 C 6,187,358

Cities and Towns

Alexandria 111,183
Arlington 170,936
Chesapeake 151,976
Danville 53,056
Hampton 133,793
Lynchburg 66,049
Newport News 170,045
Norfolk 261,229
Petersburg 38,386
Portsmouth 103,907
Richmond 203,056
Roanoke 96,397
Suffolk 52,141
Virginia Beach 393,069

UNITED STATES: WASHINGTON
1990 C 4,866,692

Cities and Towns

Bellevue 86,874
Bellingham 52,179
Everett 69,961
Lakewood Center 62,000
Olympia 33,840
Seattle 516,259
Spokane 177,196
Tacoma 176,664
Yakima 54,827

UNITED STATES: WEST VIRGINIA
1990 C 1,793,477

Cities and Towns

Charleston 57,287
Huntington 54,844
Parkersburg 33,862
Wheeling 34,882

UNITED STATES: WISCONSIN
1990 C 4,891,769

Cities and Towns

Appleton 65,695
Eau Claire 56,856
Fond du Lac 37,757
Green Bay 96,466
Janesville 52,133
Kenosha 80,352
La Crosse 51,003
Madison 191,262
Milwaukee 628,088
Oshkosh 55,006
Racine 84,298
Sheboygan 49,676
Waukesha 56,958
Wausau 37,060
Wauwatosa 49,366
West Allis 63,221

UNITED STATES: WYOMING
1990 C 453,588

Cities and Towns

Casper 46,742
Cheyenne 50,008
Laramie 26,687

URUGUAY
1985 C 2,955,241

Cities and Towns

Las Piedras (★ Montevideo) 58,288
• MONTEVIDEO (★ 1,550,000) 1,251,647
Paysandú 76,191
Rivera 57,316
Salto 80,823

UZBEKISTAN / Üzbekiston
1989 C 19,906,000

Cities and Towns

Almalyk 114,000
Andižan 293,000
Angren 131,000
Bekabad (1987 E) 80,000
Buchara 224,000
Chodžejli (1987 E) 55,000
Čirčik (★ Taškent) 156,000
Denau (1987 E) 53,000
Džizak 102,000

C Census. E Official estimate. U Unofficial estimate.
• Largest city in country.
★ Population or designation of metropolitan area, including suburbs (see headnote).
▲ Population of an entire municipality, commune, or district, including rural area.

Fergana	.200,000
Gulistan (1987 E)	.51,000
Jangijul' (1987 E)	.71,000
Karši	.156,000
Kattakurgan (1987 E)	.63,000
Kokand	.182,000
Margilan	.125,000
Namangan	.308,000
Navoi	.107,000
Nukus	.169,000
Samarkand	.366,000
• TAŠKENT (★ 2,325,000)	.2,073,000
Termez (1987 E)	.72,000
Urgenč	.128,000

VANUATU

1989 C 142,419

Cities and Towns

• PORT VILA (★ 23,000) 18,905

VATICAN CITY / Città del Vaticano

1988 E 766

VENEZUELA

1981 C 14,516,735

Cities and Towns

Acarigua	.91,662
Barcelona	.156,461
Barinas	.110,462
Barquisimeto	.497,635
Baruta (★ Caracas)	.200,063
Cabimas	.140,435
Cagua	.53,704
Calabozo	.61,995
• CARACAS (★ 3,600,000)	.1,816,901
Carora	.58,694
Carúpano	.64,579
Catia La Mar (★ Caracas)	.87,916
Chacao (★ Caracas)	.72,703
Ciudad Bolívar	.182,941
Ciudad Guayana	.314,497
Ciudad Ojeda (Lagunillas)	.83,565
Coro	.96,339

Cumaná	.179,814
El Limón	.65,122
El Tigre	.73,595
Guacara	.72,727
Guanare	.64,025
Guarenas (★ Caracas)	.101,742
La Victoria	.70,828
Los Dos Caminos (★ Caracas)	.63,346
Los Teques (★ Caracas)	.112,857
Maiquetía (★ Caracas)	.66,056
Maracaibo	.890,643
Maracay	.322,560
Maturín	.154,976
Mérida	.143,209
Petare (★ Caracas)	.395,715
Porlamar	.51,079
Pozuelos	.80,342
Puerto Cabello	.71,759
Puerto La Cruz	.53,881
Punto Fijo	.71,114
San Cristóbal	.198,793
San Felipe	.57,526
San Fernando de Apure	.57,308
San Juan de los Morros	.57,219
Turmero	.111,186
Valencia	.616,224
Valera	.102,068
Valle de la Pascua	.55,761

VIETNAM / Viet Nam

1979 C 52,741,766

Cities and Towns

Bac Giang	.54,506
Bien Hoa	.187,254
Buon Me Thuot	.71,815
Ca Mau	.67,484
Cam Pha	.76,697
Cam Ranh (1973 E)	.118,111
Can Tho	.182,856
Da Lat	.87,136
Da Nang	.318,653
Hai Duong	.54,579
Hai Phong (▲ 1,279,067) (1989 C)	.456,000
HA NOI (★ 1,500,000) (1989 C)	.1,089,000

Hoa Binh	.51,187
Hon Gai	.114,573
Hue	.165,710
Long Xuyen	.112,485
Minh Hai	.72,517
My Tho	.101,493
Nam Dinh	.160,179
Nha Trang	.172,663
Phan Thiet	.75,241
Play Cu	.58,088
Qui Nhon	.127,211
Rach Gia	.81,075
Sa Dec	.73,104
Soc Trang	.74,967
Thai Binh	.79,566
Thai Nguyen	.138,023
Thanh Hoa	.72,646
• Thanh Pho Ho Chi Minh (Saigon) (★ 3,100,000) (1989 C)	.3,169,000
Tra Vinh	.44,020
Tuy Hoa	.46,617
Viet Tri	.72,108
Vinh	.159,753
Vinh Long	.71,505
Vung Tau	.81,694

VIRGIN ISLANDS OF THE UNITED STATES

1980 C 96,569

Cities and Towns

• CHARLOTTE AMALIE (★ 32,000) 11,842

WALLIS AND FUTUNA / Wallis et Futuna

1983 E 12,408

Cities and Towns

• MATA-UTU 815

WESTERN SAHARA

1982 E 142,000

Cities and Towns

• EL AAIÚN 93,875

WESTERN SAMOA / Samoa i Sisifo

1981 C 156,349

Cities and Towns

• APIA 33,170

YEMEN / Al-Yaman

1990 E 11,282,000

Cities and Towns

'Adan (★ 318,000) (1984 E)	.176,100
Al-Hudaydah (1986 C)	.155,110
Al-Mukallā (1984 E)	.58,000
• SAN'Ā' (1986 C)	.427,150
Ta'izz (1986 C)	.178,043

YUGOSLAVIA / Jugoslavija

1987 E 10,342,020

Cities and Towns

• BEOGRAD (★ 1,400,000)	.1,130,000
Kragujevac (▲ 171,609)	.94,800
Niš (▲ 240,219)	.168,400
Novi Sad (▲ 266,772)	.176,000
Pančevo (★ Beograd)	.62,700
Priština (▲ 244,830)	.125,400
Subotica (▲ 153,306)	.100,500
Titograd (▲ 145,163)	.82,500
Zrenjanin (▲ 140,009)	.65,400

ZAIRE / Zaïre

1984 C 29,671,407

Cities and Towns

Bandundu	.63,189
Beni	.73,319
Boma	.88,556
Bukavu	.171,064
Butembo	.78,633
Gandajika	.60,263
Gemena	.62,641
Goma	.76,745
Ilebo (Port-Francqui)	.48,831
Isiro	.78,871

Kabinda	.81,752
Kalemie (Albertville)	.70,694
Kananga (Luluabourg)	.290,898
Kikwit	.146,784
Kindu	.68,044
• KINSHASA (LÉOPOLDVILLE) (1986 E)	.3,000,000
Kisangani (Stanleyville)	.282,650
Kolwezi	.201,382
Likasi (Jadotville)	.194,465
Lubumbashi (Élisabethville)	.543,268
Manono	.51,755
Matadi	.144,742
Mbandaka (Coquilhatville)	.125,263
Mbuji-Mayi (Bakwanga)	.423,363
Mwene-Ditu	.72,567
Tshikapa	.105,484
Yangambi	.53,726

ZAMBIA

1980 C 5,661,801

Cities and Towns

Chililabombwe (Bancroft) (★ 56,582)	.25,900
Chingola	.130,872
Kabwe (Broken Hill)	.127,420
Kalulushi	.53,383
Kitwe (★ 283,962)	.207,500
Livingstone	.61,296
Luanshya (★ 113,422)	.61,600
• LUSAKA	.535,830
Mufulira (★ 138,824)	.77,100
Ndola	.250,490

ZIMBABWE

1983 E 7,740,000

Cities and Towns

Bulawayo	.429,000
Chitungwiza (★ Harare)	.202,000
Gweru (1982 C)	.78,940
• HARARE (★ 890,000)	.681,000
Kwekwe (1982 C)	.47,976
Mutare (1982 C)	.75,358

United States General Information

Geographical Facts

ELEVATION

The highest elevation in the United States is Mount McKinley, Alaska, 20,320 feet.

The lowest elevation in the United States is in Death Valley, California, 282 feet below sea level.

The average elevation of the United States is 2,500 feet.

EXTREMITIES

Direction	Location	Latitude Longitude
North	Point Barrow, Ak.	71° 23'N. 156° 29'W.
South	Ka Lae (point) Hi.	18° 56'N. 155° 41'W.
East	West Quoddy Head, Me.	44° 49'N. 66° 57'W.
West	Cape Wrangell, Ak.	52° 55'N. 172° 27'E.

LENGTH OF BOUNDARIES

The total length of the Canadian boundary of the United States is 5,525 miles.

The total length of the Mexican boundary of the United States is 1,933 miles.

The total length of the Atlantic coastline of the United States is 2,069 miles.

The total length of the Pacific and Arctic coastline of the United States is 8,683 miles.

The total length of the Gulf of Mexico coastline of the United States is 1,631 miles.

The total length of all coastlines and land boundaries of the United States is 19,841 miles.

The total length of the tidal shoreline and land boundaries of the United States is 96,091 miles.

GEOGRAPHIC CENTERS

The geographic center of the United States (including Alaska and Hawaii) is in Butte County, South Dakota at 44° 58'N., 103° 46'W.

The geographic center of North America is in North Dakota, a few miles west of Devils Lake, at 48° 10'N., 100° 10'W.

EXTREMES OF TEMPERATURE

The highest temperature ever recorded in the United States was 134° F., at Greenland Ranch, Death Valley, California, on July 10, 1913.

The lowest temperature ever recorded in the United States was -80° F., at Prospect Creek, Alaska, on January 23, 1971.

Historical Facts

TERRITORIAL ACQUISITIONS

Accession	Date	Area (sq. mi.)	Cost in Dollars
Original territory of the Thirteen States	1790	888,685	
Purchase of Louisiana Territory, from France	1803	827,192	$11,250,000
By treaty with Spain: Florida	1819	58,560	5,000,000
Other areas	1819	13,443	
Annexation of Texas	1845	390,144	
Oregon Territory, by treaty with Great Britain	1846	285,580	
Mexican Cession	1848	529,017	$15,000,000
Gadsden Purchase, from Mexico	1853	29,640	$10,000,000
Purchase of Alaska, from Russia	1867	586,412	7,200,000
Annexation of Hawaiian Islands	1898	6,450	
Puerto Rico, by treaty with Spain	1899	3,435	
Guam, by treaty with Spain	1899	212	
American Samoa, by treaty with Great Britain and Germany	1900	76	
Virgin Islands, by purchase from Denmark	1917	133	$25,000,000

Note: The Philippines, ceded by Spain in 1898 for $20,000,000 were a territorial possession of the United States from 1898 to 1946. On July 4, 1946 they became the independent Republic of the Philippines.

Note: The Canal Zone, ceded by Panama in 1903 for $10,000,000 was a territory of the United States from 1903 to 1979. As a result of treaties signed in 1977, sovereignty over the Canal Zone reverted to Panama in 1979.

WESTWARD MOVEMENT OF CENTER OF POPULATION

Year	U.S.Population Total at Census	Approximate Location
1790	3,929,214	23 miles east of Baltimore, Md.
1800	5,308,483	18 miles west of Baltimore, Md.
1810	7,239,881	40 miles northwest of Washington, D.C.
1820	9,638,453	16 miles east of Moorefield, W. Va.
1830	12,866,020	19 miles southwest of Moorefield, W. Va.
1840	17,069,453	16 miles south of Clarksburg, W. Va.
1850	23,191,876	23 miles southeast of Parkersburg, W. Va.
1860	31,443,321	20 miles southwest of Chillicothe, Ohio
1870	39,818,449	48 miles northeast of Cincinnati, Ohio
1880	50,155,783	8 miles southwest of Cincinnati, Ohio
1890	62,947,714	20 miles east of Columbus, Ind.
1900	75,994,575	6 miles southeast of Columbus, Ind.
1910	91,972,266	Bloomington, Ind.
1920	105,710,620	8 miles southwest of Spencer, Ind.
1930	122,775,046	3 miles northeast of Linton, Ind.
1940	131,669,275	2 miles southeast of Carlisle, Ind.
1950	150,697,361	8 miles northwest of Olney, Ill.
1960	179,323,175	6 miles northwest of Centralia, Ill.
1970	204,816,296	5 miles southeast of Mascoutah, Ill.
1980	226,549,010	1/4 mile west of DeSoto, Mo.
1990	248,709,873	10 miles southeast of Steelville, Mo.

State Areas and Populations

STATE	Land Area* square miles	Water Area* square miles	Total Area* square miles	Area Rank land area	1990 Population	1990 Population per square mile	1980 Population	1970 Population	1960 Population	Population Rank 1990	1980	1970
Alabama	50,750	1,673	52,423	28	4,040,587	80	3,894,046	3,444,354	3,266,740	22	22	21
Alaska	570,374	86,051	656,424	1	550,043	1.0	401,851	302,583	226,167	49	50	50
Arizona	113,642	364	114,006	6	3,665,228	32	2,716,756	1,775,399	1,302,161	24	29	33
Arkansas	52,075	1,107	53,182	27	2,350,725	45	2,286,357	1,923,322	1,786,272	33	33	32
California	155,973	7,734	163,707	3	29,760,021	191	23,667,372	19,971,069	15,717,204	1	1	1
Colorado	103,730	371	104,100	8	3,294,394	32	2,889,735	2,209,596	1,753,947	26	28	30
Connecticut	4,845	698	5,544	48	3,287,116	678	3,107,576	3,032,217	2,535,234	27	25	24
Delaware	1,955	535	2,489	49	666,168	341	594,317	548,104	446,292	46	47	41
District of Columbia	61	7	68	.....	606,900	9,949	638,432	756,668	763,956	.....	.....	.....
Florida	53,997	11,761	65,758	26	12,937,926	240	9,747,015	6,791,418	4,951,560	4	7	9
Georgia	57,919	1,522	59,441	21	6,478,216	112	5,462,982	4,587,930	3,943,116	11	13	15
Hawaii	6,423	4,508	10,932	47	1,108,229	173	964,691	769,913	632,772	41	39	40
Idaho	82,751	823	83,574	11	1,006,749	12	944,127	713,015	667,191	42	41	43
Illinois	55,593	2,325	57,918	24	11,430,602	206	11,427,414	11,110,285	10,081,158	6	5	5
Indiana	35,870	550	36,420	38	5,544,159	155	5,490,212	5,195,392	4,662,498	14	12	11
Iowa	55,875	401	56,276	23	2,776,755	50	2,913,808	2,825,368	2,757,537	30	27	25
Kansas	81,823	459	82,282	13	2,477,574	30	2,364,236	2,249,071	2,178,611	32	32	28
Kentucky	39,732	679	40,411	36	3,685,296	93	3,660,324	3,220,711	3,038,156	23	23	23
Louisiana	43,566	8,277	51,843	33	4,219,973	97	4,206,098	3,644,637	3,257,022	21	19	20
Maine	30,865	4,523	35,387	39	1,227,928	40	1,125,043	993,722	969,265	38	38	38
Maryland	9,775	2,633	12,407	42	4,781,468	489	4,216,933	3,923,897	3,100,689	19	18	18
Massachusetts	7,838	2,717	10,555	45	6,016,425	768	5,737,093	5,689,170	5,148,578	13	11	10
Michigan	56,809	40,001	96,810	22	9,295,297	164	9,262,044	8,881,826	7,823,194	8	8	7
Minnesota	79,617	7,326	86,943	14	4,375,099	55	4,075,970	3,806,103	3,413,864	20	21	19
Mississippi	46,914	1,520	48,434	31	2,573,216	55	2,520,698	2,216,994	2,178,141	31	31	29
Missouri	68,898	811	69,709	18	5,117,073	74	4,916,759	4,677,623	4,319,813	15	15	13
Montana	145,556	1,490	147,046	4	799,065	5.5	786,690	694,409	674,767	44	44	44
Nebraska	76,878	481	77,358	15	1,578,385	21	1,569,825	1,485,333	1,411,330	36	35	35
Nevada	109,806	761	110,567	7	1,201,833	11	800,508	488,738	285,278	39	43	47
New Hampshire	8,969	382	9,351	44	1,109,252	124	920,610	737,681	606,921	40	42	42
New Jersey	7,419	1,303	8,722	46	7,730,188	1,042	7,365,011	7,171,112	6,066,782	9	9	8
New Mexico	121,365	234	121,598	5	1,515,069	12	1,303,542	1,017,055	951,023	37	37	37
New York	47,224	7,251	54,475	30	17,990,455	381	17,558,165	18,241,391	16,782,304	2	2	2
North Carolina	48,718	5,103	53,821	29	6,628,637	136	5,880,415	5,084,411	4,556,155	10	10	12
North Dakota	68,994	1,710	70,704	17	638,800	9.3	652,717	617,792	632,446	47	46	46
Ohio	40,953	3,875	44,828	35	10,847,115	265	10,797,603	10,657,423	9,706,397	7	6	6
Oklahoma	68,679	1,224	69,903	19	3,145,585	46	3,025,487	2,559,463	2,328,284	28	26	27
Oregon	96,003	2,383	98,386	10	2,842,321	30	2,633,156	2,091,533	1,768,687	29	30	31
Pennsylvania	44,820	1,239	46,058	32	11,881,643	265	11,864,751	11,800,766	11,319,366	5	4	3
Rhode Island	1,045	500	1,545	50	1,003,464	960	947,154	949,723	859,488	43	40	39
South Carolina	30,111	1,896	32,007	40	3,486,703	116	3,120,730	2,590,713	2,382,594	25	24	26
South Dakota	75,898	1,224	77,121	16	696,004	9.2	690,768	666,257	680,514	45	45	45
Tennessee	41,220	926	42,146	34	4,877,185	118	4,591,023	3,926,018	3,567,089	17	17	17
Texas	261,914	6,687	268,601	2	16,986,510	65	14,225,288	11,198,655	9,579,677	3	3	4
Utah	82,168	2,736	84,904	12	1,722,850	21	1,461,037	1,059,273	890,627	35	36	36
Vermont	9,249	366	9,615	43	562,758	61	511,456	444,732	389,881	48	48	48
Virginia	39,598	3,171	42,769	37	6,187,358	156	5,346,797	4,651,448	3,966,949	12	14	14
Washington	66,582	4,721	71,303	20	4,866,692	73	4,132,353	3,413,244	2,853,214	18	20	22
West Virginia	24,087	145	24,231	41	1,793,477	74	1,950,186	1,744,237	1,860,421	34	34	34
Wisconsin	54,314	11,190	65,503	25	4,891,769	90	4,705,642	4,417,831	3,951,777	16	16	16
Wyoming	97,105	714	97,818	9	453,588	4.7	469,557	332,416	330,066	50	49	49
United States	3,536,342	251,083	3,787,425	.....	248,709,873	70	226,542,360	203,302,031	179,323,175	.....	.....	.....

*Area figures for all states does not equal U.S. total due to rounding.

United States Populations and Zip Codes

The following alphabetical list shows populations for all counties and over 15,000 selected cities and towns in the United States. ZIP codes are shown for all of the cities listed in the table. The state abbreviation following each name is that used by the United States Postal Service.

ZIP codes are listed for cities and towns after the state abbreviations. For each city with more than one ZIP code, the range of numbers assigned to the city is shown: For example, the ZIP code range for Chicago is 60601–99, and this indicates that the numbers between 60601 and 60699 are valid Chicago ZIP codes. ZIP codes are not listed for counties.

Populations for cities and towns appear as *italics* after the ZIP codes, and populations for counties appear after the state abbreviations. These populations are either 1990 census figures or, where census data are not available, estimates created by Rand McNally. City populations are for central cities, not metropolitan areas. For New England, 1990 census populations are given for incorporated cities. Estimates are used for unincorporated places that are not treated separately by the census. 'Town' (or 'township') populations are not included unless the town is considered to be primarily urban and contains only one commonly used placename.

Counties are identified by a square symbol (□).

Abbreviations for State Names

AK	Alaska	**IA**	Iowa	**MS**	Mississippi	**PA**	Pennsylvania
AL	Alabama	**ID**	Idaho	**MT**	Montana	**RI**	Rhode Island
AR	Arkansas	**IL**	Illinois	**NC**	North Carolina	**SC**	South Carolina
AZ	Arizona	**IN**	Indiana	**ND**	North Dakota	**SD**	South Dakota
CA	California	**KS**	Kansas	**NE**	Nebraska	**TN**	Tennessee
CO	Colorado	**KY**	Kentucky	**NH**	New Hampshire	**TX**	Texas
CT	Connecticut	**LA**	Louisiana	**NJ**	New Jersey	**UT**	Utah
DC	District of Columbia	**MA**	Massachusetts	**NM**	New Mexico	**VA**	Virginia
		MD	Maryland	**NV**	Nevada	**VT**	Vermont
DE	Delaware	**ME**	Maine	**NY**	New York	**WA**	Washington
FL	Florida	**MI**	Michigan	**OH**	Ohio	**WI**	Wisconsin
GA	Georgia	**MN**	Minnesota	**OK**	Oklahoma	**WV**	West Virginia
HI	Hawaii	**MO**	Missouri	**OR**	Oregon	**WY**	Wyoming

A

Abbeville, AL 36310 • *3,173*
Abbeville, LA 70510–11 • *11,187*
Abbeville, SC 29620 • *5,778*
Abbeville □, SC • *23,862*
Abbotsford, WI 54405 • *1,916*
Abbott Run Valley, RI 02864 • *1,050*
Aberdeen, ID 83210 • *1,406*
Aberdeen, MD 21001 • *13,087*
Aberdeen, MS 39730 • *6,837*
Aberdeen, NC 28315 • *2,700*
Aberdeen, OH 45101 • *1,329*
Aberdeen, SD 57401–02 • *24,927*
Aberdeen, WA 98520 • *16,565*
Abernathy, TX 79311 • *2,720*
Abilene, KS 67410 • *6,242*
Abilene, TX 79601–08 • *106,654*
Abingdon, IL 61410 • *3,597*
Abingdon, VA 24210 • *7,003*
Abington, MA 02351 • *13,817*
Abington [Township], PA 19001 • *59,084*
Abita Springs, LA 70420 • *1,296*
Absarokee, MT 59001 • *1,067*
Absecon, NJ 08201 • *7,298*
Academia, OH 43050 • *1,447*
Acadia □, LA • *55,882*
Accomack □, VA • *31,703*
Ackerman, MS 39735 • *1,573*
Ackley, IA 50601 • *1,696*
Acton, CA 93510 • *1,471*
Acton, MA 01720 • *2,300*
Acushnet, MA 02743 • *6,030*
Acworth, GA 30101 • *4,519*
Ada, MN 56510 • *1,708*
Ada, OH 45810 • *5,413*
Ada, OK 74820–21 • *15,820*
Ada □, ID • *205,775*
Adair □, IA • *8,409*
Adair □, KY • *15,360*
Adair □, MO • *24,577*
Adair □, OK • *18,421*
Adairsville, GA 30103 • *2,131*
Adams, CO 80022 • *2,200*
Adams, MA 01220 • *6,356*
Adams, NY 13605 • *1,753*
Adams, WI 53910 • *1,715*
Adams □, CO • *265,038*
Adams □, ID • *3,254*
Adams □, IL • *66,090*
Adams □, IN • *31,095*
Adams □, IA • *4,866*
Adams □, MS • *35,356*
Adams □, NE • *29,625*
Adams □, ND • *3,174*
Adams □, OH • *25,371*
Adams □, PA • *78,274*
Adams □, WA • *13,603*
Adams □, WI • *15,682*
Adams Center, NY 13606 • *1,675*
Adamstown, PA 19501 • *1,108*
Adamsville, AL 35005 • *4,161*
Adamsville, RI 02801 • *600*
Adamsville, TN 38310 • *1,745*
Addis, LA 70710 • *1,222*
Addison, CT 06033 • *2,460*
Addison, IL 60101 • *32,058*
Addison, NY 14801 • *1,842*
Addison, TX 75001 • *8,783*
Addison □, VT • *32,953*
Addyston, OH 45001 • *1,198*
Adel, GA 31620 • *5,093*
Adel, IA 50003 • *3,304*
Adelanto, CA 92301 • *8,517*
Adelphi, MD 20783 • *13,524*
Adobe Acres, NM 87105 • *2,400*
Adrian, MI 49221 • *22,097*
Adrian, MN 56110 • *1,141*
Adrian, MO 64720 • *1,582*
Advance, MO 63730 • *1,139*
Affton, MO 63123 • *21,106*
Afton, DE 19810 • *1,200*
Afton, MN 55001 • *2,645*
Afton, WY 83110 • *1,394*
Agawam, MA 01001 • *10,190*
Agoura Hills, CA 91301 • *20,390*
Ahoskie, NC 27910 • *4,391*
Aiea, HI 96701 • *8,906*
Aiken, SC 29801–03 • *19,872*
Aiken □, SC • *120,940*
Ainsworth, NE 69210 • *1,870*
Air Park West, NE 68524 • *3,100*
Aitkin, MN 56431 • *1,698*
Aitkin □, MN • *12,425*
Ajo, AZ 85321 • *2,919*
Akiachak, AK 99551 • *400*
Akron, CO 80720 • *1,599*
Akron, IA 51001 • *1,450*
Akron, NY 14001 • *2,906*
Akron, OH 44301–98 • *223,019*
Akron, PA 17501 • *3,869*
Alabaster, AL 35007 • *14,732*
Alachua, FL 32615 • *4,529*
Alachua □, FL • *181,596*
Alakanuk, AK 99554 • *544*
Alamance □, NC • *108,213*
Alameda, CA 94501 • *76,459*
Alameda, NM 87114 • *5,900*
Alameda □, CA • *1,279,182*
Alamo, CA 94507 • *12,277*
Alamo, NV 89001 • *400*
Alamo, TN 38001 • *2,426*
Alamo, TX 78516 • *8,210*
Alamogordo, NM 88310–11 • *27,596*
Alamo Heights, TX 78208 • *6,502*
Alamosa, CO 81101–02 • *7,579*
Alamosa □, CO • *13,617*
Alamosa East, CO 81101 • *1,389*
Albany, CA 94706 • *16,327*
Albany, GA 31701–07 • *78,122*
Albany, IN 47320 • *2,357*
Albany, KY 42602 • *2,062*
Albany, MN 56307 • *1,548*
Albany, MO 64402 • *1,958*
Albany, NY 12201–60 • *101,082*
Albany, OR 97321 • *29,462*
Albany, TX 76430 • *1,962*
Albany, WI 53502 • *1,140*
Albany □, NY • *292,594*
Albany □, WY • *30,797*
Albemarle, NC 28001–02 • *14,939*
Albemarle □, VA • *68,040*
Albert Lea, MN 56007 • *18,310*
Albertson, NY 11507 • *5,166*
Albertville, AL 35950 • *14,507*
Albertville, MN 55301 • *1,251*
Albia, IA 52531 • *3,870*
Albion, IL 62806 • *2,116*
Albion, IN 46701 • *1,823*
Albion, MI 49224 • *10,066*
Albion, NE 68620 • *1,916*
Albion, NY 14411 • *5,863*
Albion, PA 16401 • *1,575*
Albion, RI 02802 • *1,600*
Albuquerque, NM 87101–99 • *384,736*
Alburtis, PA 18011 • *1,415*
Alcester, SD 57001 • *843*
Alcoa, TN 37701 • *6,400*
Alcona □, MI • *10,145*
Alcorn □, MS • *31,722*
Alden, NY 14004 • *2,457*
Alderson, WV 24910 • *1,152*
Alderwood Manor, WA 98011 • *16,524*
Aledo, IL 61231 • *3,681*
Alexander □, IL • *10,626*
Alexander □, NC • *27,544*
Alexander City, AL 35010 • *14,917*
Alexandria, IN 46001 • *5,709*
Alexandria, KY 41001 • *5,592*
Alexandria, LA 71301–15 • *49,188*
Alexandria, MN 56308 • *7,838*
Alexandria, VA 22301–20 • *111,183*
Alexandria Bay, NY 13607 • *1,194*
Alfalfa □, OK • *6,416*
Alfred, NY 14802 • *4,559*
Alger □, MI • *8,972*
Algoma, WI 54201 • *3,353*
Algona, IA 50511 • *6,015*
Algona, WA 98001 • *1,694*
Algonac, MI 48001 • *4,551*
Algonquin, IL 60102 • *11,663*
Algood, TN 38501 • *2,399*
Alhambra, CA 91801–99 • *82,106*
Alice, TX 78332–33 • *19,788*
Aliceville, AL 35442 • *3,009*
Aliquippa, PA 15001 • *13,374*
Allamakee □, IA • *13,855*
Allegan, MI 49010 • *4,547*
Allegan □, MI • *90,509*
Allegany, NY 14706 • *1,980*
Allegany □, MD • *74,946*
Allegany □, NY • *50,470*
Alleghany □, NC • *9,590*
Alleghany □, VA • *13,176*
Allegheny □, PA • *1,336,449*
Allen, TX 75002 • *18,309*
Allen, TX 75002 • *18,309*
Allen □, IN • *300,836*
Allen □, KS • *14,638*
Allen □, KY • *14,628*
Allen □, LA • *21,226*
Allen □, OH • *109,755*
Allendale, NJ 07401 • *5,900*
Allendale, SC 29810 • *4,410*
Allendale □, SC • *11,722*
Allen Park, MI 48101 • *31,092*
Allenton, RI 02852 • *600*
Allentown, NJ 08501 • *1,828*
Allentown, PA 18101–95 • *105,090*
Alliance, NE 69301 • *9,765*
Alliance, OH 44601 • *23,376*
Allison, IA 50602 • *1,000*
Allison Park, PA 15101 • *5,600*
Allouez, WI 54301 • *14,431*
Alloway, NJ 08001 • *1,371*
Allyn, WA 98524 • *1,100*
Alma, AR 72921 • *2,959*
Alma, GA 31510 • *3,663*
Alma, MI 48801 • *9,034*
Alma, NE 68920 • *1,226*
Almont, MI 48003 • *2,354*
Aloha, OR 97006 • *34,284*
Alondra Park, CA 90249 • *12,215*
Alpena, MI 49707 • *11,354*
Alpena □, MI • *30,605*
Alpha, NJ 08865 • *2,530*
Alpharetta, GA 30201–02 • *13,002*
Alpine, CA 91901 • *9,695*
Alpine, NJ 07620 • *1,716*
Alpine, TX 79830–31 • *5,637*
Alpine, UT 84003 • *3,492*
Alpine □, CA • *1,113*
Alsip, IL 60658 • *18,227*
Alta, IA 51002 • *1,820*
Altadena, CA 91001–02 • *42,658*
Altamont, IL 62411 • *2,296*
Altamont, KS 67330 • *1,048*
Altamont, NY 12009 • *1,519*
Altamont, OR 97601 • *18,591*
Altamonte Springs, FL 32701 • *34,879*
Alta Sierra, CA 95949 • *5,709*
Altavista, VA 24517 • *3,686*
Alto, TX 75925 • *1,027*
Alton, IL 62002 • *32,905*
Alton, IA 51003 • *1,063*
Alton, NH 03809 • *975*
Alton Bay, NH 03810 • *1,000*
Altoona, FL 32702 • *1,300*
Altoona, IA 50009 • *7,191*
Altoona, PA 16601–03 • *51,881*
Altoona, WI 54720 • *5,889*
Alturas, CA 96101 • *3,231*
Altus, OK 73521–23 • *21,910*
Alva, FL 33920 • *1,200*
Alva, OK 73717 • *5,495*
Alvarado, TX 76009 • *2,918*
Alvin, TX 77511–12 • *19,220*
Amador □, CA • *30,039*
Amagansett, NY 11930 • *2,188*
Amana, IA 52203 • *540*
Amarillo, TX 79101–76 • *157,615*
Ambler, PA 19002 • *6,609*
Amboy, IL 61310 • *2,377*
Ambridge, PA 15003 • *8,133*
Amelia, LA 70340 • *2,447*
Amelia, OH 45102 • *1,837*
Amelia □, VA • *8,787*
Amenia, NY 12501 • *1,057*
American Canyon, CA 94589 • *7,706*
American Falls, ID 83211 • *3,757*
American Fork, UT 84003–04 • *15,696*
Americus, GA 31709 • *16,512*
Amery, WI 54001 • *2,657*
Ames, IA 50010 • *47,198*
Amesbury, MA 01913 • *12,109*
Amherst, MA 01002–04 • *17,824*
Amherst, NH 03031 • *850*
Amherst, NY 14226 • *45,600*
Amherst, OH 44001 • *10,332*
Amherst, VA 24521 • *1,060*
Amherst □, VA • *28,578*
Amherstdale, WV 25607 • *1,200*
Amite, LA 70422 • *4,236*
Amite □, MS • *13,328*
Amity, OR 97101 • *1,175*
Amityville, NY 11701 • *9,286*
Ammon, ID 83401 • *5,002*
Amory, MS 38821 • *7,093*
Amsterdam, NY 12010 • *20,714*
Anaconda, MT 59711 • *10,278*
Anacortes, WA 98221 • *11,451*
Anadarko, OK 73005 • *6,586*
Anaheim, CA 92801–25 • *266,406*
Anahola, HI 96703 • *1,181*
Anahuac, TX 77514 • *1,993*
Anamosa, IA 52205 • *5,100*
Anandale, LA 71301 • *2,000*
Anchorage, AK 99501–40 • *226,338*
Anchorage, KY 40223 • *2,082*
Andalusia, AL 36420 • *9,269*
Anderson, AK 99744 • *628*
Anderson, CA 96007 • *8,299*
Anderson, IN 46011–18 • *59,459*
Anderson, MO 64831 • *1,432*
Anderson, SC 29621–25 • *26,184*
Anderson □, KS • *7,803*
Anderson □, KY • *14,571*
Anderson □, SC • *145,196*
Anderson □, TN • *68,250*
Anderson □, TX • *48,024*
Andover, KS 67002 • *4,047*
Andover, MA 01810 • *8,242*
Andover, MN 55304 • *15,216*
Andover, NY 14806 • *1,125*
Andover, OH 44003 • *1,216*
Andrew □, MO • *14,632*
Andrews, IN 46702 • *1,118*
Andrews, NC 28901 • *2,551*
Andrews, SC 29510 • *3,050*
Andrews, TX 79714 • *10,678*
Andrews □, TX • *14,338*
Androscoggin □, ME • *105,259*
Angelina □, TX • *69,884*
Angels Camp, CA 95222 • *2,409*
Angier, NC 27501 • *2,235*
Angle Lake, WA 98188 • *5,000*
Angleton, TX 77515–16 • *17,140*
Angola, IN 46703 • *5,824*
Angola, NY 14006 • *2,231*
Angoon, AK 99820 • *638*
Aniak, AK 99557 • *540*
Anita, IA 50020 • *1,068*
Ankeny, IA 50021 • *18,482*
Anna, IL 62906 • *4,805*
Anna, OH 45302 • *1,164*
Annalee Heights, VA 22042 • *1,750*
Anna Maria, FL 34216 • *1,744*
Annandale, MN 55302 • *2,054*
Annandale, VA 22003 • *50,975*
Annapolis, MD 21401–05 • *33,187*
Ann Arbor, MI 48103–08 • *109,592*
Anne Arundel □, MD • *427,239*
Anniston, AL 36201–06 • *26,623*
Annville, PA 17003 • *4,294*
Anoka, MN 55303–04 • *17,192*
Anoka □, MN • *243,641*
Anson, TX 79501 • *2,644*
Anson □, NC • *23,474*
Ansonia, CT 06401 • *18,403*
Ansonia, OH 45303 • *1,279*
Ansted, WV 25812 • *1,643*
Antelope □, NE • *7,965*
Anthony, FL 32617 • *1,200*
Anthony, KS 67003 • *2,516*
Anthony, NM 88021 • *5,160*
Anthony, RI 02816 • *2,980*
Anthony, TX 88021 • *3,328*
Antigo, WI 54409 • *8,276*
Antioch, CA 94509 • *62,195*
Antioch, IL 60002 • *6,105*
Antlers, OK 74523 • *2,524*
Anton, TX 79313 • *1,212*
Antrim, NH 03440 • *1,325*
Antrim □, MI • *18,185*
Antwerp, OH 45813 • *1,677*
Apache, OK 73006 • *1,591*
Apache □, AZ • *61,591*
Apache Junction, AZ 85217–20 • *18,100*
Apalachicola, FL 32320 • *2,602*
Apalachin, NY 13732 • *1,208*
Apex, NC 27502 • *4,968*
Aplington, IA 50604 • *1,034*
Apollo, PA 15613 • *1,895*
Apollo Beach, FL 33572 • *6,025*
Apopka, FL 32703–04 • *13,512*
Appalachia, VA 24216 • *1,994*
Appanoose □, IA • *13,743*
Appleton, MN 56208 • *1,552*
Appleton, WI 54911–15 • *65,695*
Appleton City, MO 64724 • *1,280*
Apple Valley, CA 92307–08 • *46,079*
Apple Valley, MN 55124 • *34,598*
Applewood, CO 80401 • *11,069*
Appleyard, WA 98801 • *1,207*
Appling □, GA • *15,744*
Appomattox, VA 24522 • *1,707*
Appomattox □, VA • *12,298*
Aptos, CA 95003 • *9,061*
Aquia Harbour, VA 22554 • *6,308*
Arab, AL 35016 • *6,321*
Arabi, LA 70032 • *8,787*
Aransas □, TX • *17,892*
Aransas Pass, TX 78336 • *7,180*
Arapahoe, NE 68922 • *1,001*
Arapahoe □, CO • *391,511*
Arbuckle, CA 95912 • *1,912*
Arcade, CA 95821 • *47,900*
Arcade, NY 14009 • *2,081*
Arcadia, CA 91006–07 • *48,290*
Arcadia, FL 33821 • *6,488*
Arcadia, IN 46030 • *1,468*
Arcadia, LA 71001 • *3,079*
Arcadia, SC 29320 • *2,088*
Arcadia, WI 54612 • *2,166*
Arcanum, OH 45304 • *1,953*
Arcata, CA 95521 • *15,197*
Archbald, PA 18403 • *6,291*
Archbold, OH 43502 • *3,440*
Archdale, NC 27263 • *6,913*
Archer, FL 32618 • *1,372*
Archer □, TX • *7,973*
Archer City, TX 76351 • *1,748*
Archuleta □, CO • *5,345*
Arco, ID 83213 • *1,016*
Arcola, IL 61910 • *2,678*
Arden, CA 95825 • *62,900*
Arden Hills, MN 55112 • *9,199*
Ardmore, AL 35739 • *1,090*
Ardmore, IN 46628 • *2,250*
Ardmore, OK 73401–03 • *23,079*
Ardsley, NY 10502 • *4,272*
Arenac □, MI • *14,931*
Argos, IN 46501 • *1,642*
Arizona Sunsites, AZ 85625 • *1,100*
Arkadelphia, AR 71923 • *10,014*
Arkansas □, AR • *21,653*
Arkansas City, KS 67005 • *12,762*
Arkoma, OK 74901 • *2,393*
Arlington, GA 31713 • *1,513*
Arlington, MA 02174 • *44,630*
Arlington, MN 55307 • *1,886*
Arlington, NE 68002 • *1,178*
Arlington, NY 12603 • *11,948*
Arlington, OH 45814 • *1,267*
Arlington, SD 57212 • *908*
Arlington, TN 38002 • *1,541*
Arlington, TX 76010–18 • *261,721*
Arlington, VT 05250 • *1,311*
Arlington, VA 22201–19 • *170,936*
Arlington, WA 98223 • *4,037*
Arlington □, VA • *170,936*
Arlington Heights, IL 60004–07 • *75,460*
Arma, KS 66712 • *1,542*
Armada, MI 48005 • *1,548*
Armijo, NM 87105 • *14,600*
Armonk, NY 10504 • *2,745*
Armour, SD 57313 • *854*
Armstrong, IA 50514 • *1,025*
Armstrong □, PA • *73,478*
Armstrong □, TX • *2,021*
Arnaudville, LA 70512 • *1,444*
Arnold, MD 21012 • *20,261*
Arnold, MN 55803 • *1,500*
Arnold, MO 63010 • *18,828*
Arnold, PA 15068 • *6,113*
Arnold Mills, RI 02864 • *600*
Aroostook □, ME • *86,936*
Arroyo Grande, CA 93420–21 • *14,378*
Artesia, CA 90701–03 • *15,464*
Artesia, NM 88210–11 • *10,610*
Arthur, IL 61911 • *2,112*
Arthur □, NE • *462*
Arundel Village, MD 21225 • *3,370*
Arvada, CO 80001–06 • *89,235*
Arvin, CA 93203 • *9,286*
Asbury Park, NJ 07712 • *16,799*
Ascension □, LA • *58,214*
Ashaway, RI 02804 • *1,584*
Ashburn, GA 31714 • *4,827*
Ashburnham, MA 01430 • *1,300*
Ashdown, AR 71822 • *5,150*
Ashe □, NC • *22,209*
Asheboro, NC 27203 • *16,362*
Asherton, TX 78827 • *1,608*
Asheville, NC 28801–16 • *61,607*
Ashford, AL 36312 • *1,926*
Ash Grove, MO 65604 • *1,128*
Ashland, AL 36251 • *2,034*
Ashland, CA 94541 • *16,590*
Ashland, IL 62612 • *1,257*
Ashland, KS 67831 • *1,032*
Ashland, KY 41101–05 • *23,622*
Ashland, MA 01721 • *9,165*
Ashland, MO 65010 • *1,252*
Ashland, NE 68003 • *2,136*
Ashland, NH 03217 • *1,915*
Ashland, OH 44805 • *20,079*
Ashland, OR 97520 • *16,234*
Ashland, PA 17921 • *3,859*
Ashland, VA 23005 • *5,864*
Ashland, WI 54806 • *8,695*
Ashland □, OH • *47,507*
Ashland □, WI • *16,307*
Ashland City, TN 37015 • *2,552*
Ashley, ND 58413 • *1,052*
Ashley, OH 43003 • *1,059*
Ashley, PA 18706 • *3,291*
Ashley □, AR • *24,319*
Ashtabula, OH 44004 • *21,633*
Ashtabula □, OH • *99,821*
Ashton, ID 83420 • *1,114*
Ashton, IL 61006 • *1,042*
Ashton, MD 20861 • *1,800*
Ashton, RI 02864 • *820*
Ashville, AL 35953 • *1,494*
Ashville, OH 43103 • *2,254*
Ashwaubenon, WI 54304 • *16,376*
Asotin □, WA • *17,605*
Aspen, CO 81611–15 • *5,049*
Aspen Hill, MD 20906 • *45,494*
Aspermont, TX 79502 • *1,214*
Aspinwall, PA 15215 • *2,880*
Assinippi, MA 02339 • *1,400*
Assonet, MA 02702 • *1,200*
Assumption, IL 62510 • *1,244*
Assumption □, LA • *22,753*
Astoria, IL 61501 • *1,205*
Astoria, OR 97103 • *10,069*
Atascadero, CA 93422–23 • *23,138*
Atascosa □, TX • *30,533*
Atchison, KS 66002 • *10,656*
Atchison □, KS • *16,932*
Atchison □, MO • *7,457*
Atco, NJ 08004 • *2,020*
Athens, AL 35611 • *16,901*
Athens, GA 30601–13 • *45,734*
Athens, IL 62613 • *1,404*
Athens, NY 12015 • *1,708*
Athens, OH 45701 • *21,265*
Athens, PA 18810 • *3,468*
Athens, TN 37303 • *12,054*
Athens, TX 75751 • *10,967*
Athens □, OH • *59,549*
Atherton, CA 94027 • *7,163*
Athol, MA 01331 • *8,732*
Atkins, AR 72823 • *2,834*
Atkins, VA 24311 • *1,130*
Atkinson, NE 68713 • *1,380*
Atkinson □, GA • *613*
Atlanta, GA 30301–83 • *394,017*
Atlanta, IL 61723 • *1,616*
Atlanta, TX 75551 • *6,118*
Atlantic, IA 50022 • *7,432*
Atlantic □, NJ • *224,327*
Atlantic Beach, FL 32233 • *11,636*
Atlantic City, NJ 08401–06 • *37,986*
Atlantic Highlands, NJ 07716 • *4,629*
Atmore, AL 36502 • *8,046*
Atoka, OK 74525 • *3,298*
Atoka □, OK • *12,778*
Attala □, MS • *18,481*
Attalla, AL 35954 • *6,859*
Attica, IN 47918 • *3,457*
Attica, NY 14011 • *2,630*
Attleboro, MA 02703 • *38,383*
Atwater, CA 95301 • *22,282*
Atwater, MN 56209 • *1,053*
Atwood, IL 61913 • *1,253*
Atwood, KS 67730 • *1,388*
Atwood, TN 38220 • *1,066*
Auberry, CA 93602 • *1,866*
Auburn, AL 36830–49 • *33,830*
Auburn, CA 95603–04 • *10,592*

United States Populations and ZIP Codes

Auburn, GA 30203 • 3,139
Auburn, IL 62615 • 3,724
Auburn, IN 46706 • 9,379
Auburn, KY 42206 • 1,273
Auburn, ME 04210–12 • 24,309
Auburn, MA 01501 • 14,845
Auburn, MI 48611 • 1,855
Auburn, NE 68305 • 3,443
Auburn, NY 13021–24 • 31,258
Auburn, WA 98001–02 • 33,102
Auburndale, FL 33823 • 8,858
Auburn Heights, MI 48321 • 17,076
Audrain □, MO • 23,599
Audubon, IA 50025 • 2,524
Audubon, NJ 08106 • 9,205
Audubon, PA 19407 • 6,328
Audubon □, IA • 7,334
Auglaize □, OH • 44,585
August, CA 95201 • 6,376
Augusta, AR 72006 • 2,759
Augusta, GA 30901–19 • 44,639
Augusta, KS 67010 • 7,876
Augusta, KY 41002 • 1,336
Augusta, ME 04330–38 • 21,325
Augusta, WI 54722 • 1,510
Augusta □, VA • 54,677
Aulander, NC 27805 • 1,209
Ault, CO 80610 • 1,107
Aumsville, OR 97325 • 1,650
Aurora, CO 80010–19 • 222,103
Aurora, IL 60504–07 • 99,581
Aurora, IN 47001 • 3,825
Aurora, MN 55705 • 1,965
Aurora, MO 65605 • 6,459
Aurora, NE 68818 • 3,810
Aurora, OH 44202 • 9,192
Aurora □, SD • 3,135
Au Sable, MI 48750 • 1,542
Au Sable Forks, NY 12912 • 2,100
Austell, GA 30001 • 4,173
Austin, IN 47102 • 4,310
Austin, MN 55912 • 21,907
Austin, NV 89310 • 370
Austin, TX 78701–89 • 465,622
Austin □, TX • 19,832
Austintown, OH 44512 • 32,371
Autauga □, AL • 34,222
Ava, MO 65608 • 2,938
Avalon, CA 90704 • 2,918
Avalon, NJ 08202 • 1,809
Avalon, PA 15202 • 5,784
Avella, PA 15312 • 1,200
Avenal, CA 93204 • 9,770
Avenel, MD • 5,600
Avenel, NJ 07001 • 15,504
Aventura, FL 33180 • 14,914
Averill Park, NY 12018 • 1,656
Avery □, NC • 14,867
Avilla, IN 46710 • 1,366
Avis, PA 17721 • 1,506
Avoca, IA 51521 • 1,497
Avoca, NY 14809 • 1,033
Avoca, PA 18641 • 2,897
Avocado Heights, CA 91746 • 14,232
Avon, CT 06001 • 13,937
Avon, MA 02322 • 5,026
Avon, NY 14414 • 2,995
Avon, OH 44011 • 7,337
Avon by the Sea, NJ 07717 • 2,165
Avondale, AZ 85323 • 16,169
Avondale, LA 70094 • 5,813
Avondale, OH 45404 • 5,000
Avondale Estates, GA 30002 • 2,209
Avon Lake, OH 44012 • 15,066
Avonmore, PA 15618 • 1,089
Avon Park, FL 33825 • 8,042
Avoyelles □, LA • 39,159
Ayden, NC 28513 • 4,740
Ayer, MA 01432 • 2,889
Azalea Park, FL 32807 • 8,926
Azle, TX 76020 • 8,868
Aztec, NM 87410 • 5,479
Azusa, CA 91702 • 41,333

B

Babbitt, MN 55706 • 1,562
Babbitt, NV • 1,800
Babylon, NY 11702–04 • 12,249
Baca □, CO • 4,556
Bacliff, TX 77518 • 5,549
Bacon □, GA • 9,566
Bad Axe, MI 48413 • 3,484
Baden, PA 15005 • 5,074
Badin, NC 28009 • 1,481
Bagdad, AZ 86321 • 1,858
Bagdad, FL 32530 • 1,457
Baggs, WY 82321 • 272
Bagley, MN 56621 • 1,388
Bailey □, TX • 7,064
Baileys Crossroads, VA 22041 • 19,507
Bainbridge, GA 31717 • 10,712
Bainbridge, NY 13733 • 1,550
Baird, TX 79504 • 1,658
Bairdford, PA 15006 • 1,200
Baker, LA 70714 • 13,233
Baker, MT 59313 • 1,818
Baker, OR 97814 • 9,140
Baker □, FL • 18,486
Baker □, GA • 3,615
Baker □, OR • 15,317
Bakersfield, CA 93301–89 • 174,820
Balch Springs, TX 75180 • 17,406
Bald Knob, AR 72010 • 2,653
Baldwin, FL 32234 • 1,450
Baldwin, GA 30511 • 1,439
Baldwin, LA 70514 • 2,379
Baldwin, NY 11510 • 22,719
Baldwin, PA 15234 • 21,923
Baldwin, WI 54002 • 2,022
Baldwin □, AL • 98,280
Baldwin □, GA • 39,530
Baldwin City, KS 66006 • 2,961
Baldwin Park, CA 91706 • 69,330
Baldwinsville, NY 13027 • 6,591
Baldwinville, MA 01436 • 1,795
Baldwyn, MS 38824 • 3,204
Balfour, NC 28706 • 1,118
Ball, LA 71405 • 3,305
Ballard □, KY • 7,902
Ballardvale, MA 01810 • 1,270
Ballinger, TX 76821 • 3,975
Ballston Spa, NY 12020 • 4,937
Ballwin, MO 63011 • 21,816
Balmville, NY 12550 • 2,963
Baltic, CT 06330 • 2,000
Baltimore, MD 21201–99 • 736,014
Baltimore, OH 43105 • 2,971
Baltimore □, MD • 692,134
Baltimore Highlands, MD 21227 • 7,300
Bamberg, SC 29003 • 3,843
Bamberg □, SC • 16,902
Bandera □, TX • 10,562
Bandon, OR 97411 • 2,215
Bangor, ME 04401–02 • 33,181
Bangor, MI 49013 • 1,922
Bangor, PA 18013 • 5,383
Bangor, WI 54614 • 1,076
Bangor Township, MI 48706 • 17,494
Bangs, TX 76823 • 1,555
Banks □, GA • 10,308
Banner □, NE • 852
Banning, CA 92220 • 20,570
Bannock □, ID • 66,026
Baraboo, WI 53913 • 9,203
Baraga, MI 49908 • 1,231
Baraga □, MI • 7,954
Barataria, LA 70036 • 1,160
Barber □, KS • 5,874
Barberton, OH 44203 • 27,623
Barbour □, AL • 25,417
Barbour □, WV • 15,699
Barboursville, WV 25504 • 2,774
Barbourville, KY 40906 • 3,658
Bardstown, KY 40004 • 6,801
Bargersville, IN 46106 • 1,681
Bar Harbor, ME 04609 • 2,768
Barker Heights, NC 28739 • 1,137
Barling, AR 72923 • 4,078
Barnegat, NJ 08005 • 1,160
Barnes □, ND • 12,545
Barnesboro, PA 15714 • 2,530
Barnesville, GA 30204 • 4,747
Barnesville, MN 56514 • 2,066
Barnesville, OH 43713 • 4,326
Barnsdall, OK 74002 • 1,316
Barnstable, MA 02630 • 2,790
Barnstable □, MA • 186,605
Barnwell, SC 29812 • 5,255
Barnwell □, SC • 20,293
Barrackville, WV 26559 • 1,443
Barre, MA 01005 • 1,094
Barre, VT 05641 • 9,482
Barren □, KY • 34,001
Barrington, IL 60010–11 • 9,504
Barrington, NJ 08007 • 6,774
Barrington, RI 02806 • 15,849
Barron, WI 54812 • 2,986
Barron □, WI • 40,750
Barron Lake, MI 49120 • 1,600
Barrow, AK 99723 • 3,469
Barrow □, GA • 29,721
Barry, IL 62312 • 1,391
Barry □, MI • 50,057
Barry □, MO • 27,547
Barstow, CA 92310–12 • 21,472
Bartholomew □, IN • 63,657
Bartlesville, OK 74003–06 • 34,256
Bartlett, IL 60103 • 19,373
Bartlett, TN 38134 • 26,989
Bartlett, TX 76511 • 1,439
Barton, OH 43905 • 1,039
Barton, VT 05822 • 908
Barton □, KS • 29,382
Barton □, MO • 11,312
Bartonville, IL 61607 • 5,643
Bartow, FL 33830 • 14,716
Bartow □, GA • 55,911
Barview, OR 97420 • 1,402
Basalt, CO 81621 • 1,128
Basehor, KS 66007 • 1,591
Basile, LA 70515 • 1,808
Basin, WY 82410 • 1,180
Basking Ridge, NJ 07920 • 3,060
Bassett, VA 24055 • 1,579
Bass Lake, IN 46534 • 1,500
Bastrop, LA 71220–21 • 13,916
Bastrop, TX 78602 • 4,044
Bastrop □, TX • 38,263
Batavia, IL 60510 • 17,076
Batavia, NY 14020–21 • 16,310
Batavia, OH 45103 • 1,700
Bates □, MO • 15,025
Batesburg, SC 29006 • 4,082
Batesville, AR 72501–03 • 9,187
Batesville, IN 47006 • 4,720
Batesville, MS 38606 • 6,403
Bath, ME 04530 • 9,799
Bath, NY 14810 • 5,801
Bath, PA 18014 • 2,358
Bath, SC 29816 • 2,242
Bath □, KY • 9,692
Bath □, VA • 4,799
Baton Rouge, LA 70801–98 • 219,531
Battle Creek, MI 49015–17 • 53,540
Battle Ground, WA 98604 • 3,758
Battle Mountain, NV 89820 • 3,542
Baudette, MN 56623 • 1,146
Bawcomville, LA 71291 • 2,250
Baxley, GA 31513 • 3,841
Baxter, MN 56425 • 3,695
Baxter, TN 38544 • 1,289
Baxter □, AR • 31,186
Baxter Springs, KS 66713 • 4,351
Bay, AR 72411 • 1,660
Bay □, FL • 126,994
Bay □, MI • 111,723
Bayard, NE 69334 • 1,196
Bayard, NM 88023 • 2,598
Bayberry, NY 13088 • 6,710
Bay City, MI 48706–08 • 38,936
Bay City, OR 97107 • 1,027
Bay City, TX 77414 • 18,170
Bayfield, CO 81122 • 1,090
Bayfield □, WI • 14,008
Bay Head, NJ 08742 • 1,226
Baylor □, TX • 4,385
Bay Minette, AL 36507 • 7,168
Bayonet Point, FL 34667 • 21,860
Bayonne, NJ 07002 • 61,444
Bayou Cane, LA 70359 • 15,876
Bayou George, FL 32401 • 1,500
Bayou La Batre, AL 36509 • 2,456
Bay Pines, FL 33504 • 4,171
Bayport, MN 55003 • 3,200
Bayport, NY 11705 • 7,702
Bay Ridge, MD 21403 • 1,989
Bay Saint Louis, MS 39520–21 • 8,063
Bay Shore, NY 11706 • 21,279
Bayshore Gardens, FL 34207 • 17,062
Bayside, WI 53217 • 4,789
Bay Springs, MS 39422 • 1,729
Baytown, TX 77520–22 • 63,850
Bay Village, OH 44140 • 17,000
Bayville, NY 11709 • 7,193
Beach, IL 60085 • 9,513
Beach, ND 58621 • 1,205
Beach Haven, NJ 08008 • 1,475
Beachwood, NJ 08722 • 9,324
Beachwood, OH 44122 • 10,677
Beacon, NY 12508 • 13,243
Beacon Falls, CT 06403 • 1,285
Beacon Square, FL 34652 • 6,265
Beadle □, SD • 18,253
Bear, DE 19701 • 1,200
Bearden, AR 71720 • 1,021
Beardstown, IL 62618 • 5,270
Bear Lake □, ID • 6,084
Bear Town, MS 39648 • 1,277
Beatrice, NE 68310 • 12,354
Beatty, NV 89003 • 1,623
Beattyville, KY 41311 • 1,131
Beaufort, NC 28516 • 3,808
Beaufort, SC 29901–03 • 9,576
Beaufort □, NC • 42,283
Beaufort □, SC • 86,425
Beaumont, CA 92223 • 9,685
Beaumont, MS 39423 • 1,054
Beaumont, TX 77701–26 • 114,323
Beauregard □, LA • 30,083
Beaver, OK 73932 • 1,584
Beaver, PA 15009 • 5,028
Beaver, UT 84713 • 1,998
Beaver, WV 25813 • 1,244
Beaver □, OK • 6,023
Beaver □, PA • 186,093
Beaver □, UT • 4,765
Beavercreek, OH 45385 • 33,626
Beaverdale, PA 15921 • 1,000
Beaver Dam, KY 42320 • 2,904
Beaver Dam, WI 53916 • 14,196
Beaver Falls, PA 15010 • 10,687
Beaverhead □, MT • 8,424
Beaverton, MI 48612 • 1,150
Beaverton, OR 97005–07 • 53,310
Beckemeyer, IL 62219 • 1,070
Becker □, MN • 27,881
Beckham □, OK • 18,812
Beckley, WV 25801–02 • 18,296
Bedford, IN 47421 • 13,817
Bedford, IA 50833 • 1,528
Bedford, MA 01730 • 13,067
Bedford, NH 03102 • 1,400
Bedford, OH 44146 • 14,822
Bedford, PA 15522 • 3,137
Bedford, TX 76021–22 • 43,762
Bedford, VA 24523 • 6,073
Bedford □, PA • 47,919
Bedford □, TN • 30,411
Bedford □, VA • 45,656
Bedford Heights, OH 44146 • 12,131
Bedford Hills, NY 10507 • 3,140
Bee □, TX • 25,135
Beebe, AR 72012 • 4,455
Beecher, IL 60401 • 2,032
Beecher, MI 48458 • 14,465
Beech Grove, IN 46107 • 13,383
Beech Island, SC 29842 • 1,500
Bee Ridge, FL 34233 • 6,406
Beeville, TX 78102–04 • 13,547
Beggs, OK 74421 • 1,150
Bel Air, MD 21014 • 8,860
Bel Aire, KS 67220 • 3,695
Belchertown, MA 01007 • 2,339
Belcourt, ND 58316 • 2,458
Belding, MI 48809 • 5,969
Belen, NM 87002 • 6,547
Belfast, ME 04915 • 6,355
Belfast, NY 14711 • 1,100
Belfield, ND 58622 • 887
Belford, NJ 07718 • 6,300
Belgrade, MT 59714 • 3,411
Belhaven, NC 27810 • 2,269
Belington, WV 26250 • 1,850
Belknap □, NH • 49,216
Bell, CA 90201 • 34,365
Bell □, KY • 31,506
Bell □, TX • 191,088
Bellair, FL 32073 • 5,200
Bellaire, MI 49615 • 1,104
Bellaire, OH 43906 • 6,028
Bellaire, TX 77401–02 • 13,842
Bella Vista, AR 72712 • 9,083
Bellbrook, OH 45305 • 6,511
Belle, MO 65013 • 1,218
Belle, WV 25015 • 1,421
Belleair, FL 34616 • 3,968
Belle Chasse, LA 70037 • 8,512
Bellefontaine, OH 43311 • 12,142
Bellefontaine Neighbors, MO 63137 • 10,922
Bellefonte, DE 19809 • 1,243
Bellefonte, PA 16823 • 6,358
Belle Fourche, SD 57717 • 4,335
Belle Glade, FL 33430 • 16,177
Belle Isle, FL 32809 • 5,272
Belle Meade, TN 37205 • 2,839
Bellemoor, DE 19802 • 1,040
Belle Plaine, IA 52208 • 2,834
Belle Plaine, KS 67013 • 1,649
Belle Plaine, MN 56011 • 3,149
Belle Vernon, PA 15012 • 1,213
Belleview, FL 32506 • 8,000
Belleview, FL 32620 • 2,666
Belle View, VA 22307 • 3,500
Belleville, IL 62220–25 • 42,785
Belleville, KS 66935 • 2,517
Belleville, MI 48111–12 • 3,270
Belleville, NJ 07109 • 34,213
Belleville, PA 17004 • 1,589
Belleville, WI 53508 • 1,456
Bellevue, ID 83313 • 1,275
Bellevue, IA 52031 • 2,239
Bellevue, KY 41073 • 6,997
Bellevue, MI 49021 • 1,401
Bellevue, NE 68005 • 30,982
Bellevue, OH 44811 • 8,146
Bellevue, PA 15202 • 9,126
Bellevue, WA 98004–09 • 86,874
Bellflower, CA 90706–07 • 61,815
Bell Gardens, CA 90201 • 42,355
Bellingham, MA 02019 • 4,535
Bellingham, WA 98225–27 • 52,179
Bellmawr, NJ 08031 • 12,603
Bellmead, TX 76705 • 8,336
Bellmore, NY 11710 • 16,438
Bellows Falls, VT 05101 • 3,313
Bellport, NY 11713 • 2,572
Bells, TN 38006 • 1,643
Bellville, OH 44813 • 1,568
Bellville, TX 77418 • 3,378
Bellwood, IL 60104 • 20,241
Bellwood, PA 16617 • 1,976
Bellwood, VA 23234 • 6,178
Belmar, NJ 07719 • 5,877
Belmond, IA 50421 • 2,500
Belmont, CA 94002 • 24,127
Belmont, MA 02178 • 24,720
Belmont, MS 38827 • 1,554
Belmont, NY 14813 • 1,006
Belmont, NC 28012 • 8,434
Belmont □, OH • 71,074
Bel-Nor, MO 63133 • 2,935
Beloit, KS 67420 • 4,066
Beloit, OH 44609 • 1,037
Beloit, WI 53511–12 • 35,573
Beloit North, WI 53511 • 5,457
Belpre, OH 45714 • 6,796
Belt, MT 59412 • 571
Belton, MO 64012 • 18,150
Belton, SC 29627 • 4,646
Belton, TX 76513 • 12,476
Beltrami □, MN • 34,384
Beltsville, MD 20705 • 14,476
Belvedere, GA 30032 • 6,100
Belvedere, SC 29841 • 6,133
Belvedere Park, GA 30032 • 18,089
Belvidere, IL 61008 • 15,958
Belvidere, NJ 07823 • 2,669
Belzoni, MS 39038 • 2,536
Bement, IL 61813 • 1,668
Bemidji, MN 56601–19 • 11,245
Benavides, TX 78341 • 1,788
Benbrook, TX 76126 • 19,564
Bend, OR 97701–09 • 20,469
Benewah □, ID • 7,937
Ben Hill □, GA • 16,245
Benicia, CA 94510 • 24,437
Benkelman, NE 69021 • 1,193
Benld, IL 62009 • 1,604
Ben Lomond, CA 95005 • 7,884
Bennett, CO 80102 • 1,757
Bennett □, SD • 3,206
Bennettsville, SC 29512 • 9,345
Bennington, VT 05201 • 9,532
Bennington □, VT • 35,845
Bennion, UT 84118 • 9,575
Bensalem, PA 19020–21 • 52,368
Bensenville, IL 60106 • 17,767
Bensley, VA 23234 • 5,093
Benson, AZ 85602 • 3,824
Benson, MN 56215 • 3,235
Benson, NC 27504 • 2,810
Benson □, ND • 7,198
Bent □, CO • 5,048
Bentleyville, PA 15314 • 2,673
Benton, AR 72015 • 18,177
Benton, IL 62812 • 7,216
Benton, KY 42025 • 3,899
Benton, LA 71006 • 2,047
Benton □, AR • 97,499
Benton □, IN • 9,441
Benton □, IA • 22,429
Benton □, MN • 30,185
Benton □, MS • 8,046
Benton □, MO • 13,859
Benton □, OR • 70,811
Benton □, TN • 14,524
Benton □, WA • 112,560
Benton City, WA 99320 • 1,806
Benton Harbor, MI 49022–23 • 12,818
Benton Heights, MI 49022 • 5,465
Bentonville, AR 72712–14 • 11,257
Benwood, WV 26031 • 1,669
Benzie □, MI • 12,200
Beowawe, NV 89821 • 250
Berea, KY 40403 • 9,126
Berea, OH 44017 • 19,051
Berea, SC 29611 • 13,535
Beresford, SD 57004 • 1,849
Bergen, NY 14416 • 1,103
Bergen □, NJ • 825,380
Bergenfield, NJ 07621 • 24,458
Berkeley, CA 94701–10 • 102,724
Berkeley, IL 60163 • 5,137
Berkeley, MO 63134 • 12,450
Berkeley, RI 02864 • 830
Berkeley □, SC • 128,776
Berkeley □, WV • 59,253
Berkeley Heights, NJ 07922 • 11,980
Berkley, MI 48072 • 16,960
Berks □, PA • 336,523
Berkshire □, MA • 139,352
Berlin, CT 06037 • 1,040
Berlin, MD 21811 • 2,616
Berlin, NH 03570 • 11,824
Berlin, NJ 08009 • 5,672
Berlin, NY 12022 • 1,200
Berlin, PA 15530 • 2,064
Berlin, WI 54923 • 5,371
Bernalillo, NM 87004 • 5,960
Bernalillo □, NM • 480,577
Bernardsville, NJ 07924 • 6,597
Berne, IN 46711 • 3,559
Bernice, LA 71222 • 1,543
Bernie, MO 63822 • 1,847
Berrien □, GA • 14,153
Berrien □, MI • 161,378
Berrien Springs, MI 49103 • 1,927
Berry, AL 35546 • 1,218
Berryville, AR 72616 • 3,212
Berryville, VA 22611 • 3,097
Berthoud, CO 80513 • 2,990
Bertie □, NC • 20,388
Bertrand, MI 49120 • 5,500
Berwick, LA 70342 • 4,375
Berwick, ME 03901 • 2,378
Berwick, PA 18603 • 10,976
Berwyn, IL 60402 • 45,426
Berwyn, PA 19312 • 8,150
Bessemer, AL 35020–23 • 33,497
Bessemer, MI 49911 • 2,272
Bessemer, PA 16112 • 1,196
Bessemer City, NC 28016 • 4,698
Bethalto, IL 62010 • 9,507
Bethany, CT 06525 • 1,170
Bethany, IL 61914 • 1,369
Bethany, MO 64424 • 3,005
Bethany, OK 73008 • 20,075
Bethany, WV 26032 • 1,139
Bethany Beach, DE 19930 • 326
Bethel, AK 99559 • 4,674
Bethel, CT 06801 • 8,835
Bethel, ME 04217 • 1,225
Bethel, NC 27812 • 1,842
Bethel, OH 45106 • 2,407
Bethel, VT 05032 • 1,866
Bethel Acres, OK 74801 • 2,505
Bethel Park, PA 15102 • 33,823
Bethesda, MD 20813–17 • 62,936
Bethesda, OH 43719 • 1,161
Bethlehem, CT 06751 • 1,976
Bethlehem, PA 18015–18 • 71,428
Bethpage, NY 11714 • 15,761
Bettendorf, IA 52722 • 28,132
Beulah, ND 58523 • 3,363
Beverly, MA 01915 • 38,195
Beverly, NJ 08010 • 2,973
Beverly, OH 45715 • 1,444
Beverly Hills, CA 90209–13 • 31,971
Beverly Hills, FL 32665 • 6,163
Beverly Hills, MI 48009 • 10,610
Bexar □, TX • 1,185,394
Bexley, OH 43209 • 13,088
Bibb □, AL • 16,576
Bibb □, GA • 149,967
Bicknell, IN 47512 • 3,357
Biddeford, ME 04005 • 20,710
Bienville □, LA • 15,979
Big Bear City, CA 92314 • 3,500
Big Bend, WI 53103 • 1,299
Big Delta, AK 99737 • 400
Big Flats, NY 14814 • 2,658
Bigfork, MT 59911 • 1,080
Biggs, CA 95917 • 1,581
Big Horn □, MT • 11,337
Big Horn □, WY • 10,525
Big Lake, MN 55309 • 3,113
Big Lake, TX 76932 • 3,672
Big Pine, CA 93513 • 1,158
Big Piney, WY 83113 • 454
Big Rapids, MI 49307 • 12,603
Big Sandy, MT 59520 • 740
Big Sandy, TX 75755 • 1,185
Big Spring, TX 79720–21 • 23,093
Big Stone □, MN • 6,285
Big Stone Gap, VA 24219 • 4,748
Big Timber, MT 59011 • 1,557
Billerica, MA 01821–22 • 6,840
Billings, MT 59101–08 • 81,151
Billings □, ND • 1,108
Billings Heights, MT 59105 • 8,480
Biloxi, MS 39530–35 • 46,319
Biltmore Forest, NC 28803 • 1,327
Bingham, ME 04920 • 1,071
Bingham □, ID • 37,583
Binghamton, NY 13901–05 • 53,008
Birchwood City, MD 20745 • 4,870
Birchwood Park, DE 19711 • 2,250
Bird Island, MN 55310 • 1,326
Birdsboro, PA 19508 • 4,222
Birmingham, AL 35201–61 • 265,968
Birmingham, MI 48009–12 • 19,997
Bisbee, AZ 85603 • 6,288
Biscayne Gardens, FL 33168 • 13,000
Biscayne Park, FL 33161 • 3,068
Biscoe, NC 27209 • 1,484
Bishop, CA 93514–15 • 3,475
Bishop, TX 78343 • 3,337
Bishopville, SC 29010 • 3,560
Bismarck, MO 63624 • 1,579
Bismarck, ND 58501–07 • 49,256
Biwabik, MN 55708 • 1,097
Bixby, OK 74008 • 9,502
Black Canyon City, AZ 85324 • 1,811
Black Creek, WI 54106 • 1,152
Black Diamond, WA 98010 • 1,422
Black Earth, WI 53515 • 1,248
Blackfoot, ID 83221 • 9,646
Blackford □, IN • 14,067
Black Forest, CO 80908 • 8,143
Black Hawk, SD 57718 • 1,955
Black Hawk □, IA • 123,798
Black Jack, MO 63031 • 6,128
Black Lick, PA 15716 • 1,100
Blacklick Estates, OH 43227 • 10,080
Black Mountain, NC 28711 • 5,418
Black Point Beach Club, CT 06357 • 1,200
Black River, NY 13612 • 1,349
Black River Falls, WI 54615 • 3,490
Blacksburg, SC 29702 • 1,907
Blacksburg, VA 24060–63 • 34,590
Blackshear, GA 31516 • 3,263
Blackstone, MA 01504 • 4,460
Blackstone, VA 23824 • 3,497
Blackville, SC 29817 • 2,688
Blackwell, OK 74631 • 7,538
Blackwood, NJ 08012 • 5,120
Bladen □, NC • 28,663
Bladenboro, NC 28320 • 1,821
Bladensburg, MD 20710 • 8,064
Blades, DE 19973 • 834
Blaine, MN 55433 • 38,975
Blaine, TN 37709 • 1,326
Blaine, WA 98230 • 2,489
Blaine □, ID • 13,552
Blaine □, MT • 6,728
Blaine □, NE • 675
Blaine □, OK • 11,470
Blair, NE 68008 • 6,860
Blair, WI 54616 • 1,126
Blair □, PA • 130,542
Blairsville, PA 15717 • 3,595
Blakely, GA 31723 • 5,595
Blakely, PA 18447 • 7,222
Blanchard, LA 71009 • 1,175
Blanchard, OK 73010 • 1,922
Blanchester, OH 45107 • 4,206
Blanco, TX 78606 • 1,238
Blanco □, TX • 5,972
Bland □, VA • 6,514
Blanding, UT 84511 • 3,162
Blasdell, NY 14219 • 2,900

Blauvelt, NY 10913 • 4,470
Blawnox, PA 15238 • 1,626
Bleckley □, GA • 10,430
Bledsoe □, TN • 9,669
Blende, CO 81006 • 1,330
Blennerhassett, WV 26101 • 2,924
Blissfield, MI 49228 • 3,172
Block Island, RI 02807 • 620
Bloomer, WI 54724 • 3,085
Bloomfield, CT 06002 • 7,120
Bloomfield, IN 47424 • 2,592
Bloomfield, IA 52537 • 2,580
Bloomfield, MO 63825 • 1,800
Bloomfield, NE 68718 • 1,181
Bloomfield, NJ 07003 • 45,061
Bloomfield, NM 87413 • 5,214
Bloomfield Hills, MI 48302–04 • 4,288
Bloomfield Township, MI 48302 • 42,137
Bloomingdale, GA 31302 • 2,271
Bloomingdale, IL 60108 • 16,614
Bloomingdale, NJ 07403 • 7,530
Bloomingdale, TN 37660 • 10,953
Blooming Prairie, MN 55917 • 2,043
Bloomington, CA 92316 • 15,116
Bloomington, IL 61701–04 • 51,972
Bloomington, IN 47401–08 • 60,633
Bloomington, MN 55420 • 86,335
Bloomington, TX 77951 • 1,888
Bloomsburg, PA 17815 • 12,439
Blossburg, PA 16912 • 1,571
Blossom, TX 75416 • 1,440
Blount □, AL • 39,248
Blount □, TN • 85,969
Blountstown, FL 32424 • 2,404
Blountsville, AL 35031 • 1,527
Blountville, TN 37617 • 2,605
Blowing Rock, NC 28605 • 1,257
Blue Ash, OH 45242 • 11,860
Blue Diamond, NV 89004 • 420
Blue Earth, MN 56013 • 3,745
Blue Earth □, MN • 54,044
Bluefield, VA 24605 • 5,363
Bluefield, WV 24701 • 12,756
Blue Grass, IA 52726 • 1,214
Blue Hills, CT 06002 • 3,206
Blue Island, IL 60406 • 21,203
Blue Lake, CA 95525 • 1,235
Blue Mound, IL 62513 • 1,161
Blue Rapids, KS 66411 • 1,131
Blue Ridge, GA 30513 • 1,336
Blue Ridge, VA 24064 • 2,840
Blue Ridge Summit, PA 17214 • 1,800
Blue Springs, MO 64014–15 • 40,153
Bluewell, WV 24701 • 2,752
Bluff City, TN 37618 • 1,390
Bluffdale, UT 84065 • 2,152
Bluff Park, AL 35226 • 8,000
Bluffton, IN 46714 • 9,020
Bluffton, OH 45817 • 3,367
Blythe, CA 92225–26 • 8,428
Blytheville, AR 72315–19 • 22,906
Boalsburg, PA 16827 • 2,206
Boardman, OH 44512 • 38,596
Boardman, OR 97818 • 1,387
Boaz, AL 35957 • 6,928
Boca Grande, FL 33921 • 1,200
Boca Raton, FL 33431–34 • 61,492
Boerne, TX 78006 • 4,274
Bogalusa, LA 70427–29 • 14,280
Bogart, GA 30622 • 1,018
Bogata, TX 75417 • 1,421
Boger City, NC 28092 • 1,373
Bogota, NJ 07603 • 7,824
Bohemia, NY 11716 • 9,556
Boiling Springs, NC 28017 • 2,445
Boiling Springs, PA 17007 • 1,978
Boise, ID 83701–15 • 125,738
Boise □, ID • 3,509
Boise City, OK 73933 • 1,509
Bolingbrook, IL 60440 • 40,843
Bolivar, MO 65613 • 6,845
Bolivar, NY 14715 • 1,261
Bolivar, TN 38008 • 5,969
Bolivar □, MS • 41,875
Bollinger □, MO • 10,619
Bolton Landing, NY 12814 • 1,600
Bon Air, VA 23235 • 16,413
Bonaventure, FL 33317 • 6,000
Bond □, IL • 14,991
Bondsville, MA 01009 • 1,992
Bonduel, WI 54107 • 1,210
Bondurant, IA 50035 • 1,584
Bonham, TX 75418 • 6,686
Bon Homme □, SD • 7,089
Bonifay, FL 32425 • 2,612
Bonita, CA 91903 • 12,542
Bonita Springs, FL 33923 • 13,600
Bonneauville, PA 17325 • 1,282
Bonner □, ID • 26,622
Bonners Ferry, ID 83805 • 2,193
Bonner Springs, KS 66012 • 6,413
Bonne Terre, MO 63628 • 3,871
Bonneville □, ID • 72,207
Bonney Lake, WA 98390 • 7,494
Bonnie Doone, NC 28303 • 3,893
Bono, AR 72416 • 1,220
Booker, TX 79005 • 1,236
Boomer, WV 25031 • 1,051
Boone, IA 50036 • 12,392
Boone, NC 28607 • 12,915
Boone □, AR • 28,297
Boone □, IL • 30,806
Boone □, IN • 38,147
Boone □, IA • 25,186
Boone □, KY • 57,589
Boone □, MO • 112,379
Boone □, NE • 6,667
Boone □, WV • 25,870
Booneville, AR 72927 • 3,804
Booneville, MS 38829 • 7,955
Boonsboro, MD 21713 • 2,445
Boonton, NJ 07005 • 8,343
Boonville, CA 95415 • 1,000
Boonville, IN 47601 • 6,724
Boonville, MO 65233 • 7,095
Boonville, NY 13309 • 2,220
Boonville, NC 27011 • 1,009
Boothbay Harbor, ME 04538 • 1,267
Borden □, TX • 799
Bordentown, NJ 08505 • 4,341
Borger, TX 79007–08 • 15,675
Boron, CA 93516 • 2,101
Borrego Springs, CA 92004 • 2,244
Boscobel, WI 53805 • 2,706
Bosque □, TX • 15,125
Bossert Estates, NJ 08505 • 1,830
Bossier □, LA • 86,088
Bossier City, LA 71111–13 • 52,721
Boston, GA 31626 • 1,395
Boston, MA 02101–99 • 574,283
Boswell, PA 15531 • 1,485
Botetourt □, VA • 24,992
Bothell, WA 98011–12 • 12,345
Botkins, OH 45306 • 1,340
Bottineau, ND 58318 • 2,598
Bottineau □, ND • 8,011
Boulder, CO 80301–08 • 83,312
Boulder, MT 59632 • 1,316
Boulder □, CO • 225,339
Boulder City, NV 89005–06 • 12,567
Boulder Creek, CA 95006 • 6,725
Boulder Hill, IL 60538 • 8,894
Boulevard Heights, MD 20743 • 1,820
Boundary □, ID • 8,332
Bound Brook, NJ 08805 • 9,487
Bountiful, UT 84010–11 • 36,659
Bourbon, IN 46504 • 1,672
Bourbon, MO 65441 • 1,188
Bourbon □, KS • 14,966
Bourbon □, KY • 19,236
Bourbonnais, IL 60914 • 13,934
Bourg, LA 70343 • 2,073
Bourne, MA 02532 • 1,284
Boutte, LA 70039 • 1,200
Bovina, TX 79009 • 1,549
Bowdon, GA 30108 • 1,981
Bowie, MD 20715–21 • 37,589
Bowie, TX 76230 • 4,990
Bowie □, TX • 81,665
Bowling Green, FL 33834 • 1,836
Bowling Green, KY 42101–04 • 40,641
Bowling Green, MO 63334 • 2,976
Bowling Green, OH 43402 • 28,176
Bowman, ND 58623 • 1,741
Bowman, SC 29018 • 1,063
Bowman □, ND • 3,596
Box Butte □, NE • 13,130
Box Elder, SD 57719 • 2,680
Box Elder □, UT • 36,485
Boxford, MA 01921 • 2,072
Boyce, LA 71409 • 1,361
Boyd □, KY • 51,150
Boyd □, NE • 2,835
Boyertown, PA 19512 • 3,759
Boyes Hot Springs, CA 95416 • 5,973
Boyle □, KY • 25,641
Boyne City, MI 49712 • 3,478
Boynton Beach, FL 33435–37 • 46,194
Bozeman, MT 59715 • 22,660
Bracken □, KY • 7,766
Brackenridge, PA 15014 • 3,784
Brackettville, TX 78832 • 1,740
Braddock, PA 15104 • 4,682
Braddock Heights, MD 21714 • 4,778
Bradenton, FL 34201–10 • 43,779
Bradenville, PA 15620 • 1,100
Bradford, OH 45308 • 2,005
Bradford, PA 16701 • 9,625
Bradford, RI 02808 • 1,604
Bradford, TN 38316 • 1,154
Bradford, VT 05033 • 672
Bradford □, FL • 22,515
Bradford □, PA • 60,967
Bradfordwoods, PA 15015 • 1,329
Bradley, FL 33835 • 1,108
Bradley, IL 60915 • 10,792
Bradley, WV 25818 • 2,144
Bradley □, AR • 11,793
Bradley □, TN • 73,712
Bradley Beach, NJ 07720 • 4,475
Bradner, OH 43406 • 1,093
Brady, TX 76825 • 5,946
Braham, MN 55006 • 1,139
Braidwood, IL 60408 • 3,584
Brainerd, MN 56401 • 12,353
Braintree, MA 02184 • 33,836
Branch □, MI • 41,502
Branch Village, RI 02895 • 400
Branchville, SC 29432 • 1,107
Brandenburg, KY 40108 • 1,857
Brandon, FL 33510 • 57,985
Brandon, MS 39042–43 • 11,077
Brandon, SC 29611 • 2,170
Brandon, SD 57005 • 3,543
Brandon, VT 05733 • 1,902
Brandywine, MD 20613 • 1,406
Branford, CT 06405 • 27,603
Branford Hills, CT 06405 • 3,460
Branson, MO 65616 • 3,706
Brantley, AL 36009 • 1,015
Brantley □, GA • 11,077
Brant Rock, MA 02020 • 1,850
Bratenahl, OH 44108 • 1,356
Brattleboro, VT 05301–04 • 8,612
Brawley, CA 92227 • 18,923
Braxton □, WV • 12,998
Brazil, IN 47834 • 7,640
Brazoria, TX 77422 • 2,717
Brazoria □, TX • 191,707
Brazos □, TX • 121,862
Brea, CA 92621–22 • 32,873
Breathitt □, KY • 15,703
Breaux Bridge, LA 70517 • 6,515
Breckenridge, CO 80424 • 1,285
Breckenridge, MI 48615 • 1,301
Breckenridge, MN 56520 • 3,708
Breckenridge, TX 76024 • 5,665
Breckenridge Hills, MO 63114 • 5,404
Breckinridge □, KY • 16,312
Brecksville, OH 44141 • 11,818
Breese, IL 62230 • 3,567
Bremen, GA 30110 • 4,356
Bremen, IN 46506 • 4,725
Bremen, OH 43107 • 1,386
Bremer □, IA • 22,813
Bremerton, WA 98310–15 • 38,142
Bremond, TX 76629 • 1,110
Brenham, TX 77833–34 • 11,952
Brent, AL 35034 • 2,776
Brent, FL 32503 • 21,624
Brentwood, CA 94513 • 7,563
Brentwood, MD 20722 • 3,005
Brentwood, MO 63144 • 8,150
Brentwood, NY 11717 • 45,218
Brentwood, NY • 45,218
Brentwood, OH 45231 • 3,568
Brentwood, PA 15227 • 10,823
Brentwood, SC 29405 • 2,000
Brentwood, TN 37027 • 16,392
Brevard, NC 28712 • 5,388
Brevard □, FL • 398,978
Brewer, ME 04412 • 9,021
Brewster, MA 02631 • 1,818
Brewster, NY 10509 • 1,566
Brewster, OH 44613 • 2,307
Brewster, WA 98812 • 1,633
Brewster □, TX • 8,681
Brewton, AL 36426–27 • 5,885
Briarcliff Manor, NY 10510 • 7,070
Brick [Township], NJ 08723 • 55,473
Bridge City, LA 70094 • 8,327
Bridge City, TX 77611 • 8,034
Bridgehampton, NY 11932 • 1,997
Bridgeport, AL 35740 • 2,936
Bridgeport, CT 06601–50 • 141,686
Bridgeport, IL 62417 • 2,118
Bridgeport, MI 48722 • 8,569
Bridgeport, NE 69336 • 1,581
Bridgeport, OH 43912 • 2,318
Bridgeport, PA 19405 • 4,292
Bridgeport, TX 76026 • 3,581
Bridgeport, WA 98813 • 1,498
Bridgeport, WV 26330 • 6,739
Bridger, MT 59014 • 692
Bridgeton, MO 63044 • 17,779
Bridgeton, NJ 08302 • 18,942
Bridgetown, OH 45211 • 11,460
Bridgeview, IL 60455 • 14,402
Bridgeville, DE 19933 • 1,210
Bridgeville, PA 15017 • 5,445
Bridgewater, MA 02324 • 7,242
Bridgewater, NJ 08807 • 5,630
Bridgewater, VA 22812 • 3,918
Bridgman, MI 49106 • 2,140
Bridgton, ME 04009 • 2,195
Brielle, NJ 08730 • 4,406
Brigantine, NJ 08203 • 11,354
Brigham City, UT 84302 • 15,644
Brighton, AL 35020 • 4,518
Brighton, CO 80601 • 14,203
Brighton, IL 62012 • 2,270
Brighton, MI 48116 • 5,686
Brighton, NY 14610 • 34,455
Brilliant, OH 43913 • 1,672
Brillion, WI 54110 • 2,840
Brinkley, AR 72021 • 4,234
Briscoe □, TX • 1,971
Bristol, CT 06010–11 • 60,640
Bristol, IN 46507 • 1,133
Bristol, NH 03222 • 1,483
Bristol, RI 02809 • 21,625
Bristol, TN 37620–25 • 23,421
Bristol, VT 05443 • 1,801
Bristol, VA 24201–03 • 18,426
Bristol □, MA • 506,325
Bristol □, RI • 48,859
Bristol [Township], PA 19007 • 58,773
Bristow, OK 74010 • 4,062
Britt, IA 50423 • 2,133
Britton, SD 57430 • 1,394
Broadalbin, NY 12025 • 1,397
Broad Brook, CT 06016 • 1,280
Broadkill Beach, DE 19968 • 390
Broadus, MT 59317 • 572
Broadview, IL 60153 • 8,713
Broadview Heights, OH 44141 • 12,219
Broadview Park, FL 33314 • 6,109
Broadwater □, MT • 3,318
Broadway, VA 22815 • 1,209
Brockport, NY 14420 • 8,749
Brockton, MA 02401–05 • 92,788
Brockway, PA 15824 • 2,207
Brocton, NY 14716 • 1,387
Brodhead, KY 40409 • 1,140
Brodhead, WI 53520 • 3,165
Brodheadsville, PA 18322 • 1,500
Broken Arrow, OK 74011–14 • 58,043
Broken Bow, NE 68822 • 3,778
Broken Bow, OK 74728 • 3,961
Bronson, MI 49028 • 2,342
Bronx □, NY • 1,203,789
Bronxville, NY 10708 • 6,028
Brooke □, WV • 26,992
Brookfield, CT 06804 • 1,500
Brookfield, IL 60513 • 18,876
Brookfield, MA 01506 • 2,968
Brookfield, MO 64628 • 4,888
Brookfield, VA 22021 • 2,100
Brookfield, WI 53005 • 35,184
Brookfield Center, CT 06804 • 1,400
Brookhaven, MS 39601 • 10,243
Brookhaven, PA 19015 • 8,567
Brookhaven, WV 26505 • 3,836
Brookings, OR 97415 • 4,400
Brookings, SD 57006 • 16,270
Brookings □, SD • 25,207
Brooklawn, NJ 08030 • 1,805
Brookline, MA 02146 • 54,718
Brooklyn, CT 06234 • 1,400
Brooklyn, IN 46111 • 1,162
Brooklyn, IA 52211 • 1,439
Brooklyn, OH 44144 • 11,706
Brooklyn, SC 29720 • 1,850
Brooklyn Center, MN 55429 • 28,887
Brooklyn Park, MD 21225 • 10,987
Brooklyn Park, MN 55443 • 56,381
Brookneal, VA 24528 • 1,344
Brook Park, OH 44142 • 22,865
Brookport, IL 62910 • 1,070
Brooks, KY 40109 • 2,464
Brooks □, GA • 15,398
Brooks □, TX • 8,204
Brookshire, TX 77423 • 2,922
Brookside, AL 35036 • 1,365
Brookside, DE 19713 • 15,307
Brookston, IN 47923 • 1,804
Brooksville, FL 34601–14 • 7,440
Brooksville, MS 39739 • 1,098
Brookville, IN 47012 • 2,529
Brookville, NY 11545 • 3,716
Brookville, OH 45309 • 4,621
Brookville, PA 15825 • 4,184
Brookwood, NJ 08527 • 5,500
Broomall, PA 19008 • 10,930
Broome □, NY • 212,160
Broomfield, CO 80020–21 • 24,638
Broussard, LA 70518 • 3,213
Broward □, FL • 1,255,488
Browardale, FL 33311 • 6,257
Brown □, IL • 5,836
Brown □, IN • 14,080
Brown □, KS • 11,128
Brown □, MN • 26,984
Brown □, NE • 3,657
Brown □, OH • 34,966
Brown □, SD • 35,580
Brown □, TX • 34,371
Brown □, WI • 194,594
Brown City, MI 48416 • 1,244
Brown Deer, WI 53209 • 12,236
Brownfield, TX 79316 • 9,560
Brownfields, LA 70811 • 5,229
Browning, MT 59417 • 1,170
Brownsburg, IN 46112 • 7,628
Browns Mills, NJ 08015 • 11,429
Brownstown, IN 47220 • 2,872
Brownsville, FL 33142 • 15,607
Brownsville, OR 97327 • 1,281
Brownsville, PA 15417 • 3,164
Brownsville, TN 38012 • 10,019
Brownsville, TX 78520–26 • 98,962
Brownville, LA 71291 • 1,700
Brownville, NY 13615 • 1,138
Brownwood, TX 76803–04 • 18,387
Broxton, GA 31519 • 1,211
Broyhill Park, VA 22042 • 3,600
Bruce, MS 38915 • 2,127
Bruceton, TN 38317 • 1,586
Brule □, SD • 5,485
Brundidge, AL 36010 • 2,472
Brunswick, GA 31520–22 • 16,433
Brunswick, ME 04011 • 14,683
Brunswick, MD 21716 • 5,117
Brunswick, MO 65236 • 1,074
Brunswick, OH 44212 • 28,230
Brunswick □, NC • 50,985
Brunswick □, VA • 15,987
Brush, CO 80723 • 4,165
Brusly, LA 70719 • 1,824
Bryan, OH 43506 • 8,348
Bryan, TX 77801–06 • 55,002
Bryan □, GA • 15,438
Bryan □, OK • 32,089
Bryans Road, MD 20616 • 3,809
Bryant, AR 72022 • 5,269
Bryantville, MA 02327 • 1,800
Bryn Mawr, WA 98178 • 1,500
Bryson City, NC 28713 • 1,145
Buchanan, GA 30113 • 1,009
Buchanan, MI 49107 • 4,992
Buchanan, VA 24066 • 1,222
Buchanan □, IA • 20,844
Buchanan □, MO • 83,083
Buchanan □, VA • 31,333
Buckeye, AZ 85326 • 5,038
Buckeye Lake, OH 43008 • 2,986
Buckhannon, WV 26201 • 5,909
Buckingham □, VA • 12,873
Buckley, WA 98321 • 3,516
Bucknell Manor, VA 22307 • 2,300
Buckner, MO 64016 • 2,873
Bucks □, PA • 541,174
Bucksport, ME 04416 • 2,989
Bucksport, SC 29527 • 1,022
Bucyrus, OH 44820 • 13,496
Buda, TX 78610 • 1,795
Budd Lake 0L, NJ • 7,272
Buechel, KY 40218 • 7,081
Buena, NJ 08310 • 4,441
Buena Park, CA 90620–24 • 68,784
Buena Vista, CO 81211 • 1,752
Buena Vista, FL 34691 • 3,000
Buena Vista, GA 31803 • 1,472
Buena Vista, VA 24416 • 6,406
Buena Vista □, IA • 19,965
Buffalo, IA 52728 • 1,260
Buffalo, MN 55313 • 6,856
Buffalo, MO 65622 • 2,414
Buffalo, NY 14201–40 • 328,123
Buffalo, OK 73834 • 1,312
Buffalo, SC 29321 • 1,569
Buffalo, TX 75831 • 1,555
Buffalo, WY 82834 • 3,302
Buffalo □, NE • 37,447
Buffalo □, SD • 1,759
Buffalo □, WI • 13,584
Buffalo Center, IA 50424 • 1,081
Buffalo Grove, IL 60089 • 36,427
Buford, GA 30518 • 8,771
Buhl, ID 83316 • 3,516
Buhler, KS 67522 • 1,277
Buies Creek, NC 27506 • 2,085
Bullhead City, AZ 86430 • 21,951
Bullitt □, KY • 47,567
Bulloch □, GA • 43,125
Bullock □, AL • 11,042
Bull Shoals, AR 72619 • 1,534
Buna, TX 77612 • 1,900
Bunche Park, FL 33054 • 4,000
Buncombe □, NC • 174,821
Bunker Hill, IL 62014 • 1,722
Bunker Hill, OR 97420 • 1,242
Bunkerville, NV 89007 • 300
Bunkie, LA 71322 • 5,044
Bunnell, FL 32110 • 1,873
Buras, LA 70041 • 1,600
Burbank, CA 91501–10 • 93,643
Burbank, IL 60459 • 27,600
Burdickville, RI 02808 • 500
Bureau □, IL • 35,688
Burgaw, NC 28425 • 1,807
Burgettstown, PA 15021 • 1,634
Burgin, KY 40310 • 1,009
Burien, WA 98062 • 25,089
Burkburnett, TX 76354 • 10,145
Burke, SD 57523 • 756
Burke, VA 22015 • 57,734
Burke □, GA • 20,579
Burke □, NC • 75,744
Burke □, ND • 3,002
Burkesville, KY 42717 • 1,815
Burleigh □, ND • 60,131
Burleson, TX 76028 • 16,113
Burleson □, TX • 13,625
Burley, ID 83318 • 8,702
Burlingame, CA 94010–11 • 26,801
Burlingame, KS 66413 • 1,074
Burlington, CO 80807 • 2,941
Burlington, IA 52601 • 27,208
Burlington, KS 66839 • 2,735
Burlington, KY 41005 • 6,070
Burlington, MA 01803 • 23,302
Burlington, NJ 08016 • 9,835
Burlington, NC 27215–17 • 39,498
Burlington, ND 58722 • 995
Burlington, VT 05401–04 • 39,127
Burlington, WA 98233 • 4,349
Burlington, WI 53105 • 8,855
Burlington □, NJ • 395,066
Burnet, TX 78611 • 3,423
Burnet □, TX • 22,677
Burnett □, WI • 13,084
Burney, CA 96013 • 3,423
Burnham, PA 17009 • 2,197
Burns, OR 97720 • 2,913
Burns, TN 37029 • 1,127
Burns, WY 82053 • 254
Burns Flat, OK 73624 • 1,027
Burnsville, MN 55337 • 51,288
Burnsville, NC 28714 • 1,482
Burnt Hills, NY 12027 • 1,550
Burr Ridge, IL 60521 • 7,669
Burt □, NE • 7,868
Burton, MI 48509 • 27,617
Burton, OH 44021 • 1,349
Burton, SC 29902 • 6,917
Burtonsville, MD 20866 • 5,853
Burwell, NE 68823 • 1,278
Bushnell, FL 33513 • 1,998
Bushnell, IL 61422 • 3,288
Butler, AL 36904 • 1,872
Butler, GA 31006 • 1,673
Butler, IN 46721 • 2,601
Butler, MO 64730 • 4,099
Butler, NJ 07405 • 7,392
Butler, PA 16001–03 • 15,714
Butler, WI 53007 • 2,079
Butler □, AL • 21,892
Butler □, IA • 15,731
Butler □, KS • 50,580
Butler □, KY • 11,245
Butler □, MO • 38,765
Butler □, NE • 8,601
Butler □, OH • 291,479
Butler □, PA • 152,013
Butner, NC 27509 • 4,679
Butte, MT 59701–03 • 33,336
Butte □, CA • 182,120
Butte □, ID • 2,918
Butte □, SD • 7,914
Buttonwillow, CA 93206 • 1,301
Butts □, GA • 15,326
Buxton, NC 27920 • 1,300
Buzzards Bay, MA 02532 • 3,250
Byers, CO 80103 • 1,065
Byesville, OH 43723 • 2,435
Byfield, MA 01922 • 1,200
Bylas, AZ 85530 • 1,219
Byron, GA 31008 • 2,276
Byron, IL 61010 • 2,284
Byron, MN 55920 • 2,441
Byron, WY 82412 • 470

C

Cabarrus □, NC • 98,935
Cabell □, WV • 96,827
Cabin Creek, WV 25035 • 1,300
Cabin John, MD 20818 • 1,690
Cabool, MO 65689 • 2,006
Cabot, AR 72023 • 8,319
Cache, OK 73527 • 2,251
Cache □, UT • 70,183
Caddo □, LA • 248,253
Caddo □, OK • 29,550
Cadillac, MI 49601 • 10,104
Cadiz, KY 42211 • 2,148
Cadiz, OH 43907 • 3,439
Cadott, WI 54727 • 1,328
Cahaba Heights, AL 35243 • 4,778
Cahokia, IL 62206 • 17,550
Cairnbrook, PA 15924 • 1,081
Cairo, GA 31728 • 9,035
Cairo, IL 62914 • 4,846
Cairo, NY 12413 • 1,273
Calais, ME 04619 • 3,963
Calaveras □, CA • 31,998
Calavo Gardens, CA 91941 • 6,100
Calcasieu □, LA • 168,134
Calcutta, OH 43920 • 1,212
Caldwell, ID 83605–06 • 18,400
Caldwell, KS 67022 • 1,351
Caldwell, NJ 07006 • 7,549
Caldwell, OH 43724 • 1,786
Caldwell, TX 77836 • 3,181
Caldwell □, KY • 13,232
Caldwell □, LA • 9,810
Caldwell □, MO • 8,380
Caldwell □, NC • 70,709
Caldwell □, TX • 26,392
Caledonia, MN 55921 • 2,846
Caledonia, NY 14423 • 2,262
Caledonia □, VT • 27,846
Calera, AL 35040 • 2,136
Calera, OK 74730 • 1,536
Calexico, CA 92231–32 • 18,633
Calhoun, GA 30701 • 7,135
Calhoun □, AL • 116,034
Calhoun □, AR • 5,826
Calhoun □, FL • 11,011
Calhoun □, GA • 5,013
Calhoun □, IL • 5,322
Calhoun □, IA • 11,508
Calhoun □, MI • 135,982
Calhoun □, MS • 14,908
Calhoun □, SC • 12,753
Calhoun □, TX • 19,053
Calhoun □, WV • 7,885
Calhoun City, MS 38916 • 1,838
Calhoun Falls, SC 29628 • 2,328
Caliente, NV 89008 • 1,111
Califon, NJ 07830 • 1,073
California, MD 20619 • 7,626
California, MO 65018 • 3,465
California, PA 15419 • 5,748
Calipatria, CA 92233 • 2,690
Calistoga, CA 94515 • 4,468
Callahan □, TX • 11,859
Callaway, FL 32401 • 12,253
Callaway □, MO • 32,809
Calloway □, KY • 30,735
Calmar, IA 52132 • 1,026
Calumet □, WI • 34,291

Calumet City, IL 60409 • 37,840
Calumet Park, IL 60643 • 8,418
Calvert, TX 77837 • 1,536
Calvert □, MD • 51,372
Calvert City, KY 42029 • 2,531
Calverton, MD 20705 • 12,046
Calverton Park, MO 63136 • 1,404
Camanche, IA 52730 • 4,436
Camarillo, CA 93010–11 • 52,303
Camas, WA 98607 • 6,442
Camas □, ID • 727
Cambria, CA 93428 • 5,382
Cambria □, PA • 163,029
Cambrian Park, CA 95124 • 2,998
Cambridge, IL 61238 • 2,124
Cambridge, MD 21613 • 11,514
Cambridge, MA 02138 • 95,802
Cambridge, MN 55008 • 5,094
Cambridge, NE 69022 • 1,107
Cambridge, NY 12816 • 1,906
Cambridge, OH 43725 • 11,748
Cambridge City, IN 47327 • 2,091
Cambridge Springs, PA 16403 • 1,837
Camden, AL 36726 • 2,414
Camden, AR 71701 • 14,380
Camden, DE 19934 • 1,899
Camden, ME 04843 • 4,022
Camden, NJ 08101–10 • 87,492
Camden, NY 13316 • 2,552
Camden, OH 45311 • 2,210
Camden, SC 29020 • 6,696
Camden, TN 38320 • 3,643
Camden □, GA • 30,167
Camden □, MO • 27,495
Camden □, NJ • 502,824
Camden □, NC • 5,904
Camdenton, MO 65020 • 2,561
Camelot, WA 98002 • 4,900
Cameron, LA 70631 • 2,041
Cameron, MO 64429 • 4,831
Cameron, TX 76520 • 5,580
Cameron, WV 26033 • 1,177
Cameron, WI 54822 • 1,273
Cameron □, LA • 9,260
Cameron □, PA • 5,913
Cameron □, TX • 260,120
Cameron Park, CA 95682 • 11,897
Camilla, GA 31730 • 5,008
Camino, CA 95709 • 1,500
Camp □, TX • 9,904
Campbell, CA 95008–09 • 36,048
Campbell, FL 34746 • 3,884
Campbell, MO 63933 • 2,165
Campbell, OH 44405 • 10,038
Campbell □, KY • 83,866
Campbell □, SD • 1,965
Campbell □, TN • 35,079
Campbell □, VA • 47,572
Campbell □, WY • 29,370
Campbellsport, WI 53010 • 1,732
Campbellsville, KY 42718–19 • 9,577
Camp Hill, AL 36850 • 1,415
Camp Hill, PA 17011 • 7,831
Camp Point, IL 62320 • 1,230
Camp Springs, MD 20748 • 16,392
Camp Verde, AZ 86322 • 6,243
Canaan, CT 06018 • 1,194
Canadensis, PA 18325 • 1,200
Canadian, TX 79014 • 2,417
Canadian □, OK • 74,409
Canajoharie, NY 13317 • 2,278
Canal Fulton, OH 44614 • 4,157
Canal Winchester, OH 43110 • 2,617
Canandaigua, NY 14424–25 • 10,725
Canastota, NY 13032 • 4,673
Canby, MN 56220 • 1,826
Canby, OR 97013 • 8,983
Candler □, GA • 7,744
Candlewood Isle, CT 06812 • 1,100
Candlewood Shores, CT 06804 • 1,620
Cando, ND 58324 • 1,564
Caney, KS 67333 • 2,062
Canfield, OH 44406 • 5,409
Canisteo, NY 14823 • 2,421
Cannelton, IN 47520 • 1,786
Cannon □, TN • 10,467
Cannon Beach, OR 97110 • 1,221
Cannondale, CT 06897 • 1,500
Cannon Falls, MN 55009 • 3,232
Canon City, CO 81212 • 12,687
Canonsburg, PA 15317 • 9,200
Canterbury, DE 19943 • 500
Canton, CT 06019 • 1,563
Canton, GA 30114 • 4,817
Canton, IL 61520 • 13,922
Canton, MA 02021 • 18,182
Canton, MI 48187 • 57,047
Canton, MS 39046 • 10,062
Canton, MO 63435 • 2,623
Canton, NY 13617 • 6,379
Canton, NC 28716 • 3,790
Canton, OH 44701–99 • 84,161
Canton, PA 17724 • 1,966
Canton, SD 57013 • 2,787
Canton, TX 75103 • 2,949
Cantonment, FL 32533 • 3,200
Canutillo, TX 79835 • 4,500
Canyon, TX 79015 • 11,365
Canyon □, ID • 90,076
Canyon Lake, CA 92380 • 7,938
Canyon Lake, TX 78130 • 9,975
Canyonville, OR 97417 • 1,219
Capac, MI 48014 • 1,583
Cape Canaveral, FL 32920 • 8,014
Cape Charles, VA 23310 • 1,398
Cape Coral, FL 33904 • 74,991
Cape Elizabeth, ME 04107 • 8,854
Cape Girardeau, MO 63701–02 • 34,438
Cape Girardeau □, MO • 61,633
Cape May, NJ 08204 • 4,668
Cape May □, NJ • 95,089
Cape May Court House, NJ 08210 • 4,426
Cape Saint Claire, MD 21401 • 7,878
Capitola, CA 95010 • 10,171
Capitol Heights, MD 20743 • 3,633
Capitol View, SC 29209 • 10,456
Captain Cook, HI 96704 • 2,595
Captiva, FL 33924 • 1,200
Caraway, AR 72419 • 1,178
Carbon □, MT • 8,080
Carbon □, PA • 56,846
Carbon □, UT • 20,228
Carbon □, WY • 16,659
Carbondale, CO 81623 • 3,004
Carbondale, IL 62901–03 • 27,033
Carbondale, KS 66414 • 1,526
Carbondale, PA 18407 • 10,664
Carbon Hill, AL 35549 • 2,115
Cardington, OH 43315 • 1,770
Carencro, LA 70520 • 5,429
Carey, OH 43316 • 3,684
Caribou, ME 04736 • 9,415
Caribou □, ID • 6,963
Carle Place, NY 11514 • 5,107
Carleton, MI 48117 • 2,770
Carlin, NV 89822 • 2,220
Carlinville, IL 62626 • 5,416
Carlisle, AR 72024 • 2,253
Carlisle, IA 50047 • 3,241
Carlisle, KY 40311 • 1,639
Carlisle, OH 45005 • 4,872
Carlisle, PA 17013 • 18,419
Carlisle □, KY • 5,238
Carl Junction, MO 64834 • 4,123
Carlsbad, CA 92008–09 • 63,126
Carlsbad, NM 88220–21 • 24,952
Carlstadt, NJ 07072 • 5,510
Carlton, OR 97111 • 1,289
Carlton □, MN • 29,259
Carlyle, IL 62231 • 3,474
Carmel, CA 93921–23 • 4,239
Carmel, IN 46032 • 25,380
Carmel, NY 10512 • 3,395
Carmi, IL 62821 • 5,564
Carmichael, CA 95608–09 • 48,702
Carnation, WA 98014 • 1,243
Carnegie, OK 73015 • 1,593
Carnegie, PA 15106 • 9,278
Carney, MD 21234 • 25,578
Carneys Point, NJ 08069 • 7,686
Carnot, PA 15108 • 4,750
Caro, MI 48723 • 4,054
Carol City, FL 33055 • 53,331
Caroleen, NC 28019 • 1,100
Carolina Beach, NC 28428 • 3,630
Caroline □, MD • 27,035
Caroline □, VA • 19,217
Carol Stream, IL 60188 • 31,716
Carpentersville, IL 60110 • 23,049
Carpinteria, CA 93013–14 • 13,747
Carrabelle, FL 32322 • 1,200
Carrboro, NC 27510 • 11,553
Carrier Mills, IL 62917 • 1,991
Carrington, ND 58421 • 2,267
Carrizo Springs, TX 78834 • 5,745
Carrizozo, NM 88301 • 1,075
Carroll, IA 51401 • 9,579
Carroll □, AR • 18,654
Carroll □, GA • 71,422
Carroll □, IL • 16,805
Carroll □, IN • 18,809
Carroll □, IA • 21,423
Carroll □, KY • 9,292
Carroll □, MD • 123,372
Carroll □, MS • 9,237
Carroll □, MO • 10,748
Carroll □, NH • 35,410
Carroll □, OH • 26,521
Carroll □, TN • 27,514
Carroll □, VA • 26,594
Carrollton, AL 35447 • 1,170
Carrollton, GA 30117 • 16,029
Carrollton, IL 62016 • 2,507
Carrollton, KY 41008 • 3,715
Carrollton, MI 48724 • 6,521
Carrollton, MO 64633 • 4,406
Carrollton, OH 44615 • 3,042
Carrollton, TX 75006–08 • 82,169
Carrolltown, PA 15722 • 1,286
Carrollwood, FL 33618 • 11,400
Carson, CA 90749 • 83,995
Carson □, TX • 6,576
Carson City, MI 48811 • 1,158
Carson City, NV 89701–21 • 40,443
Carter □, KY • 24,340
Carter □, MO • 5,515
Carter □, MT • 1,503
Carter □, OK • 42,919
Carter □, TN • 51,505
Carteret, NJ 07008 • 19,025
Carteret □, NC • 52,556
Carter Lake, IA 51510 • 3,200
Cartersville, GA 30120 • 12,035
Carterville, IL 62918 • 3,630
Carterville, MO 64835 • 2,013
Carthage, IL 62321 • 2,657
Carthage, MS 39051 • 3,819
Carthage, MO 64836 • 10,747
Carthage, NY 13619 • 4,344
Carthage, TN 37030 • 2,386
Carthage, TX 75633 • 6,496
Caruthersville, MO 63830 • 7,389
Carver, MA 02330 • 1,500
Carver □, MN • 47,915
Carver Ranch Estates, FL 33023 • 5,600
Carville, LA 70721 • 1,108
Cary, IL 60013 • 10,043
Cary, NC 27511 • 43,858
Caryville, TN 37714 • 1,751
Casa de Oro, CA 92077 • 9,500
Casa Grande, AZ 85222 • 19,082
Casas Adobes, AZ 85704 • 12,155
Cascade, CO 80809 • 1,000
Cascade, ID 83611 • 877
Cascade, IA 52033 • 1,812
Cascade, MT 59421 • 729
Cascade □, MT • 77,691
Cascade Vista, WA 98058 • 7,800
Casey, IL 62420 • 2,914
Casey □, KY • 14,211
Cashion, AZ 85329 • 3,014
Cashmere, WA 98815 • 2,544
Casper, WY 82601–15 • 46,742
Caspian, MI 49915 • 1,031
Cass □, IL • 13,437
Cass □, IN • 38,413
Cass □, IA • 15,128
Cass □, MI • 49,477
Cass □, MN • 21,791
Cass □, MO • 63,808
Cass □, NE • 21,318
Cass □, ND • 102,874
Cass □, TX • 29,982
Cass City, MI 48726 • 2,276
Casselberry, FL 32707–08 • 18,911
Casselton, ND 58012 • 1,601
Cassia □, ID • 19,532
Cassopolis, MI 49031 • 1,822
Cassville, MO 65625 • 2,371
Cassville, WI 53806 • 1,144
Castanea, PA 17726 • 1,123
Castile, NY 14427 • 1,078
Castle Dale, UT 84513 • 1,704
Castle Hayne, NC 28429 • 1,182
Castle Hills, DE 19720 • 1,475
Castle Park, CA 92011 • 6,300
Castle Point, MO 63136 • 7,800
Castle Rock, CO 80104 • 8,708
Castle Rock, WA 98611 • 2,067
Castle Shannon, PA 15234 • 9,135
Castleton, VT 05735 • 600
Castleton on Hudson, NY 12033 • 1,491
Castlewood, VA 24224 • 2,110
Castro □, TX • 9,070
Castro Valley, CA 94546 • 48,619
Castroville, TX 78009 • 2,159
Caswell □, NC • 20,693
Catahoula □, LA • 11,065
Catalina Foothills, AZ 85718 • 1,470
Catasauqua, PA 18032 • 6,662
Cataumet, MA 02534 • 1,500
Catawba □, NC • 118,412
Catawissa, PA 17820 • 1,683
Cathedral City, CA 92234–35 • 30,085
Catlettsburg, KY 41129 • 2,231
Catlin, IL 61817 • 2,173
Catonsville, MD 21228 • 35,233
Catoosa, OK 74015 • 2,954
Catoosa □, GA • 42,464
Catron □, NM • 2,563
Catskill, NY 12414 • 4,690
Cattaraugus, NY 14719 • 1,100
Cattaraugus □, NY • 84,234
Cavalier, ND 58220 • 1,508
Cavalier □, ND • 6,064
Cave City, AR 72521 • 1,503
Cave City, KY 42127 • 1,953
Cave Creek, AZ 85331 • 2,925
Cave Junction, OR 97523 • 1,126
Cave Spring, VA 24018 • 24,053
Cavetown, MD 21720 • 1,533
Cayce, SC 29033 • 11,163
Cayuga, IN 47928 • 1,083
Cayuga □, NY • 82,313
Cayuga Heights, NY 14850 • 3,457
Cazenovia, NY 13035 • 3,007
Cecil □, MD • 71,347
Cedar □, IA • 17,381
Cedar □, MO • 12,093
Cedar □, NE • 10,131
Cedar Bluff, AL 35959 • 1,174
Cedar Bluff Two, TN 37722 • 2,000
Cedarburg, WI 53012 • 9,895
Cedar City, UT 84720–22 • 13,443
Cedar Crest, NM 87008 • 1,200
Cedaredge, CO 81413 • 1,380
Cedar Falls, IA 50613 • 34,298
Cedar Grove, NJ 07009 • 12,053
Cedar Grove, WV 25039 • 1,213
Cedar Grove, WI 53013 • 1,521
Cedar Hill, MO 63016 • 1,966
Cedar Hill, TX 75104 • 19,976
Cedar Hills, OR 97005 • 9,294
Cedarhurst, NY 11516 • 5,716
Cedar Lake, IN 46303 • 8,885
Cedar Rapids, IA 52401–10 • 108,751
Cedar Springs, MI 49319 • 2,600
Cedartown, GA 30125 • 7,978
Cedarville, NJ 08311 • 1,100
Cedarville, OH 45314 • 3,210
Celina, OH 45822 • 9,650
Celina, TN 38551 • 1,493
Celina, TX 75009 • 1,737
Celoron, NY 14720 • 1,232
Cementon, PA 18052 • 1,050
Center, CO 81125 • 1,963
Center, ND 58530 • 826
Center, TX 75935 • 4,950
Centerburg, OH 43011 • 1,323
Centereach, NY 11720 • 26,720
Center Line, MI 48015 • 9,026
Center Moriches, NY 11934 • 5,987
Center Point, AL 35215 • 22,657
Center Point, IA 52213 • 1,693
Centerville, IN 47330 • 2,398
Centerville, IA 52544 • 5,936
Centerville, MA 02632 • 9,190
Centerville, OH 45459 • 21,082
Centerville, PA 15417 • 3,842
Centerville, SD 57014 • 887
Centerville, TN 37033 • 3,616
Centerville, UT 84014 • 11,500
Central, NM 88026 • 1,835
Central, SC 29630 • 2,438
Central City, CO 80427 • 335
Central City, IL 62801 • 1,390
Central City, IA 52214 • 1,063
Central City, KY 42330 • 4,979
Central City, NE 68826 • 2,868
Central City, PA 15926 • 1,246
Central Falls, RI 02863 • 17,637
Central Heights, AZ 85501 • 1,500
Centralia, IL 62801 • 14,274
Centralia, MO 65240 • 3,414
Centralia, WA 98531 • 12,101
Central Islip, NY 11722 • 26,028
Central Park, WA 98520 • 2,669
Central Point, OR 97502 • 7,509
Central Square, NY 13036 • 1,671
Central Valley, CA 96019 • 4,340
Central Valley, NY 10917 • 1,929
Central Village, CT 06332 • 1,600
Centre, AL 35960 • 2,893
Centre □, PA • 123,786
Centre City, NJ 08051 • 2,070
Centre Hall, PA 16828 • 1,203
Centreville, AL 35042 • 2,508
Centreville, IL 62207 • 7,489
Centreville, MD 21617 • 2,097
Centreville, MI 49032 • 1,516
Centreville, MS 39631 • 1,771
Centreville, VA 22020 • 26,585
Century, FL 32535 • 1,989
Century Village, FL 33409 • 8,363
Ceredo, WV 25507 • 1,916
Ceres, CA 95307 • 26,314
Cerritos, CA 90703 • 53,240
Cerro Gordo, IL 61818 • 1,436
Cerro Gordo □, IA • 46,733
Chadbourn, NC 28431 • 2,005
Chadds Ford, PA 19317 • 1,200
Chadron, NE 69337 • 5,588
Chadwicks, NY 13319 • 2,000
Chaffee, MO 63740 • 3,059
Chaffee □, CO • 12,684
Chaffin, MA 01520 • 3,980
Chagrin Falls, OH 44022 • 4,146
Chalfonte, DE 19810 • 1,740
Challis, ID 83226 • 1,073
Chalmette, LA 70043–44 • 31,860
Chama, NM 87520 • 1,048
Chamberlain, SD 57325 • 2,347
Chambers □, AL • 36,876
Chambers □, TX • 20,088
Chambersburg, PA 17201 • 16,647
Chamblee, GA 30341 • 7,668
Champaign, IL 61820–21 • 63,502
Champaign □, IL • 173,025
Champaign □, OH • 36,019
Champion, OH 44481 • 5,270
Champlain, NY 12919 • 1,273
Champlin, MN 55316 • 16,849
Chandler, AZ 85224–27 • 90,533
Chandler, IN 47610 • 3,099
Chandler, OK 74834 • 2,596
Chandler, TX 75758 • 1,630
Chandler Heights, AZ 85227 • 1,000
Chanhassen, MN 55317 • 11,732
Channahon, IL 60410 • 4,266
Channel Lake, IL 60002 • 1,660
Channelview, TX 77530 • 25,564
Chantilly, VA 22021–22 • 29,337
Chanute, KS 66720 • 9,488
Chapel Hill, NC 27514–16 • 38,719
Chapel Square, VA 22003 • 2,400
Chapman, KS 67431 • 1,264
Chapmanville, WV 25508 • 1,110
Chappaqua, NY 10514 • 6,380
Chardon, OH 44024 • 4,446
Chariton, IA 50049 • 4,616
Chariton □, MO • 9,202
Charleroi, PA 15022 • 5,014
Charles □, MD • 101,154
Charles City, IA 50616 • 7,878
Charles City □, VA • 6,282
Charles Mix □, SD • 9,131
Charleston, AR 72933 • 2,128
Charleston, IL 61920 • 20,398
Charleston, MS 38921 • 2,328
Charleston, MO 63834 • 5,085
Charleston, SC 29401–22 • 80,414
Charleston, WV 25301–75 • 57,287
Charleston □, SC • 295,039
Charlestown, IN 47111 • 5,889
Charlestown, NH 03603 • 1,173
Charlestown, RI 02813 • 1,500
Charles Town, WV 25414 • 3,122
Charlevoix, MI 49720 • 3,116
Charlevoix □, MI • 21,468
Charlotte, MI 48813 • 8,083
Charlotte, NC 28201–41 • 395,934
Charlotte, TX 78011 • 1,475
Charlotte □, FL • 110,975
Charlotte □, VA • 11,688
Charlotte Hall, MD 20622 • 1,992
Charlotte Harbor, FL 33980 • 3,327
Charlottesville, VA 22901–08 • 40,341
Charlton □, GA • 8,496
Charlton City, MA 01508 • 1,400
Charter Oak, CA 91724 • 8,858
Chase □, KS • 3,021
Chase □, NE • 4,381
Chase City, VA 23924 • 2,442
Chaska, MN 55318 • 11,339
Chatfield, MN 55923 • 2,226
Chatham, IL 62629 • 6,074
Chatham, MA 02633 • 1,916
Chatham, NJ 07928 • 8,007
Chatham, NY 12037 • 1,920
Chatham, VA 24531 • 1,354
Chatham □, GA • 216,935
Chatham □, NC • 38,759
Chatom, AL 36518 • 1,094
Chatsworth, GA 30705 • 2,865
Chatsworth, IL 60921 • 1,186
Chattahoochee, FL 32324 • 4,382
Chattahoochee □, GA • 16,934
Chattanooga, TN 37401–22 • 152,466
Chattaroy, WV 25667 • 1,182
Chattooga □, GA • 22,242
Chautauqua □, KS • 4,407
Chautauqua □, NY • 141,895
Chauvin, LA 70344 • 3,375
Chaves □, NM • 57,849
Chazy, NY 12921 • 1,000
Cheatham □, TN • 27,140
Cheboygan, MI 49721 • 4,999
Cheboygan □, MI • 21,398
Checotah, OK 74426 • 3,290
Cheektowaga, NY 14225 • 84,387
Chehalis, WA 98532 • 6,527
Chelan, WA 98816 • 2,969
Chelan □, WA • 52,250
Chelmsford, MA 01824 • 32,388
Chelsea, MA 02150 • 28,710
Chelsea, MI 48118 • 3,772
Chelsea, OK 74016 • 1,620
Chelsea Estates, DE 19720 • 1,320
Cheltenham Township, PA 19012 • 35,509
Chemung □, NY • 95,195
Chenango □, NY • 51,768
Chenango Bridge, NY 13745 • 2,890
Cheney, KS 67025 • 1,560
Cheney, WA 99004 • 7,723
Cheneyville, LA 71325 • 1,005
Chenoa, IL 61726 • 1,732
Chenoweth, OR 97058 • 3,246
Chepachet, RI 02814 • 900
Cheraw, SC 29520 • 5,505
Cherokee, AL 35616 • 1,479
Cherokee, IA 51012 • 6,026
Cherokee, OK 73728 • 1,787
Cherokee □, AL • 19,543
Cherokee □, GA • 90,204
Cherokee □, IA • 14,098
Cherokee □, KS • 21,374
Cherokee □, NC • 20,170
Cherokee □, OK • 34,049
Cherokee □, SC • 44,506
Cherokee □, TX • 41,049
Cherokee Village, AR 72525 • 3,200
Cherry □, NE • 6,307
Cherry Hill, NJ 08002–03 • 69,319
Cherry Hills Village, CO 80110 • 5,245
Cherryland, CA 94541 • 11,088
Cherryvale, KS 67335 • 2,464
Cherry Valley, CA 92223 • 5,945
Cherry Valley, IL 61016 • 1,615
Cherry Valley, MA 01611 • 1,120
Cherryville, NC 28021 • 4,756
Chesaning, MI 48616 • 2,567
Chesapeake, OH 45619 • 1,073
Chesapeake, VA 23320–28 • 151,976
Chesapeake, WV 25315 • 1,896
Chesapeake Beach, MD 20732 • 2,403
Cheshire, CT 06410 • 25,684
Cheshire, MA 01225 • 1,100
Cheshire □, NH • 70,121
Chesilhurst, NJ 08089 • 1,526
Chesnee, SC 29323 • 1,280
Chester, CA 96020 • 2,082
Chester, CT 06412 • 1,563
Chester, IL 62233 • 8,194
Chester, MT 59522 • 942
Chester, NJ 07930 • 1,214
Chester, NY 10918 • 3,270
Chester, PA 19013–16 • 41,856
Chester, SC 29706 • 7,158
Chester, VT 05143 • 550
Chester, VA 23831 • 14,896
Chester, WV 26034 • 2,905
Chester □, PA • 376,396
Chester □, SC • 32,170
Chester □, TN • 12,819
Chester Depot, VT 05144 • 500
Chesterfield, IN 46017 • 2,730
Chesterfield, SC 29709 • 1,373
Chesterfield □, SC • 38,577
Chesterfield □, VA • 209,274
Chesterton, IN 46304 • 9,124
Chestertown, MD 21620 • 4,005
Chester Township, PA 19013 • 5,399
Chestnut Hill Estates, DE 19713 • 1,730
Chestnut Ridge, NY 10952 • 7,517
Cheswick, PA 15024 • 1,971
Cheswold, DE 19936 • 321
Chetek, WI 54728 • 1,953
Chetopa, KS 67336 • 1,357
Chevak, AK 99563 • 598
Cheverly, MD 20785 • 6,023
Cheviot, OH 45211 • 9,616
Chevy Chase, MD 20815 • 8,559
Chewelah, WA 99109 • 1,945
Cheyenne, WY 82001–09 • 50,008
Cheyenne □, CO • 2,397
Cheyenne □, KS • 3,243
Cheyenne □, NE • 9,494
Cheyenne Wells, CO 80810 • 1,128
Chicago, IL 60601–66 • 2,783,726
Chicago Heights, IL 60411 • 33,072
Chicago Ridge, IL 60415 • 13,643
Chickamauga, GA 30707 • 2,149
Chickasaw, AL 36611 • 6,649
Chickasaw □, IA • 13,295
Chickasaw □, MS • 18,085
Chickasha, OK 73018 • 14,988
Chico, CA 95926–28 • 40,079
Chicopee, MA 01013–22 • 56,632
Chicora, PA 16025 • 1,058
Chiefland, FL 32626 • 1,917
Childersburg, AL 35044 • 4,579
Childress, TX 79201 • 5,055
Childress □, TX • 5,953
Chilhowie, VA 24319 • 1,971
Chili Center, NY 14624 • 4,360
Chillicothe, IL 61523 • 5,959
Chillicothe, MO 64601 • 8,804
Chillicothe, OH 45601 • 21,923
Chillum, MD 20783 • 31,309
Chilton, WI 53014 • 3,240
Chilton □, AL • 32,458
Chimayo, NM 87522 • 2,789
China Grove, NC 28023 • 2,732
Chincoteague, VA 23336 • 3,572
Chinle, AZ 86503 • 5,059
Chino, CA 91708–10 • 59,682
Chinook, MT 59523 • 1,512
Chino Valley, AZ 86323 • 4,837
Chipley, FL 32428 • 3,866
Chippewa □, MI • 34,604
Chippewa □, MN • 13,228
Chippewa □, WI • 52,360
Chippewa Falls, WI 54729 • 12,727
Chisago □, MN • 30,521
Chisago City, MN 55013 • 2,009
Chisholm, ME 04239 • 1,653
Chisholm, MN 55719 • 5,290
Chittenango, NY 13037 • 4,734
Chittenden □, VT • 131,761
Choctaw, OK 73020 • 8,545
Choctaw □, AL • 16,018
Choctaw □, MS • 9,071
Choctaw □, OK • 15,302
Choteau, MT 59422 • 1,741
Chouteau, OK 74337 • 1,771
Chouteau □, MT • 5,452
Chowan □, NC • 13,506
Chowchilla, CA 93610 • 5,930
Chrisman, IL 61924 • 1,136
Christian □, IL • 34,418
Christian □, KY • 68,941
Christian □, MO • 32,644
Christiana, DE 19702 • 500
Christiana, PA 17509 • 1,045
Christiansburg, VA 24073 • 15,004
Christmas, FL 32709 • 1,200
Christopher, IL 62822 • 2,774
Chubbuck, ID 83202 • 7,791
Chugwater, WY 82210 • 192
Chula Vista, CA 91909–15 • 135,163
Church Hill, TN 37642 • 4,834
Churchill, OH 44505 • 7,700
Churchill □, NV • 17,938
Church Point, LA 70525 • 4,677
Churchville, NY 14428 • 1,731
Churubusco, IN 46723 • 1,781
Cibola □, NM • 23,794
Cicero, IL 60650 • 67,436
Cicero, IN 46034 • 3,268
Cimarron, KS 67835 • 1,626
Cimarron □, OK • 3,301
Cimarron Hills, CO 80906 • 11,160
Cincinnati, OH 45201–75 • 364,040
Cinnaminson, NJ 08077 • 14,583
Circle, MT 59215 • 805

Circle Pines, MN 55014 • 4,704
Circleville, OH 43113 • 11,666
Cisco, TX 76437 • 3,813
Citra, FL 32113 • 1,500
Citronelle, AL 36522 • 3,671
Citrus, CA 91702 • 9,481
Citrus □, FL • 93,515
Citrus Heights, CA 95610–11 • 107,439
City Of Sunrise, FL 33313 • 64,407
City View, SC 29611 • 1,490
Clackamas, OR 97015 • 2,578
Clackamas □, OR • 278,850
Claiborne, LA 71291 • 8,300
Claiborne □, LA • 17,405
Claiborne □, MS • 11,370
Claiborne □, TN • 26,137
Clair-Mel City, FL 33619 • 7,000
Clairton, PA 15025 • 9,656
Clallam □, WA • 56,464
Clanton, AL 35045 • 7,669
Clara City, MN 56222 • 1,307
Clare, MI 48617 • 3,021
Clare □, MI • 24,952
Claremont, CA 91711 • 32,503
Claremont, NH 03743 • 13,902
Claremore, OK 74017–18 • 13,280
Clarence, MO 63437 • 1,026
Clarendon, AR 72029 • 2,072
Clarendon, TX 79226 • 2,067
Clarendon □, SC • 28,450
Clarendon Hills, IL 60514 • 6,994
Claridge, PA 15623 • 1,200
Clarinda, IA 51632 • 5,104
Clarion, IA 50525 • 2,703
Clarion, PA 16214 • 6,457
Clarion □, PA • 41,699
Clark, NJ 07066 • 14,629
Clark, SD 57225 • 1,292
Clark □, AR • 21,437
Clark □, ID • 762
Clark □, IL • 15,921
Clark □, IN • 87,777
Clark □, KS • 2,418
Clark □, KY • 29,496
Clark □, MO • 7,547
Clark □, NV • 741,459
Clark □, OH • 147,548
Clark □, SD • 4,403
Clark □, WA • 238,053
Clark □, WI • 31,647
Clarkdale, AZ 86324 • 2,144
Clarke □, AL • 27,240
Clarke □, GA • 87,594
Clarke □, IA • 8,287
Clarke □, MS • 17,313
Clarke □, VA • 12,101
Clarkesville, GA 30523 • 1,151
Clarksburg, WV 26301–02 • 18,059
Clarksdale, MS 38614 • 19,717
Clarks Summit, PA 18411 • 5,433
Clarkston, GA 30021 • 5,385
Clarkston, MI 48346–48 • 1,005
Clarkston, WA 99403 • 6,753
Clarksville, AR 72830 • 5,833
Clarksville, DE 19970 • 500
Clarksville, IN 47129 • 19,833
Clarksville, IA 50619 • 1,382
Clarksville, TN 37040–43 • 75,494
Clarksville, TX 75426 • 4,311
Clarksville, VA 23927 • 1,243
Clarkton, MO 63837 • 1,113
Clatskanie, OR 97016 • 1,629
Clatsop □, OR • 33,301
Claude, TX 79019 • 1,199
Clawson, MI 48017 • 13,874
Claxton, GA 30417 • 2,464
Clay, KY 42404 • 1,173
Clay □, AL • 13,252
Clay □, AR • 18,107
Clay □, FL • 105,986
Clay □, GA • 3,364
Clay □, IL • 14,460
Clay □, IN • 24,705
Clay □, IA • 17,585
Clay □, KS • 9,158
Clay □, KY • 21,746
Clay □, MN • 50,422
Clay □, MS • 21,120
Clay □, MO • 153,411
Clay □, NE • 7,123
Clay □, NC • 7,155
Clay □, SD • 13,186
Clay □, TN • 7,238
Clay □, TX • 10,024
Clay □, WV • 9,983
Clay Center, KS 67432 • 4,613
Clay City, KY 40312 • 1,258
Claymont, DE 19702 • 9,800
Claypool, AZ 85532 • 1,942
Claysburg, PA 16625 • 1,399
Clayton, AL 36016 • 1,564
Clayton, DE 19938 • 1,163
Clayton, GA 30525 • 1,613
Clayton, MO 63105 • 13,874
Clayton, NJ 08312 • 6,155
Clayton, NM 88415 • 2,484
Clayton, NY 13624 • 2,160
Clayton, NC 27520 • 4,756
Clayton □, GA • 182,052
Clayton □, IA • 19,054
Clear Creek □, CO • 7,619
Clearfield, KY 40313 • 1,250
Clearfield, PA 16830 • 6,633
Clearfield, UT 84015 • 21,435
Clearfield □, PA • 78,097
Clearlake, CA 95422 • 11,804
Clear Lake, IA 50428 • 8,183
Clear Lake, SD 57226 • 1,247
Clearlake, WA 98235 • 1,100
Clear Lake Shores, TX 77565 • 1,096
Clearwater, FL 34615–30 • 98,784
Clearwater, KS 67026 • 1,875
Clearwater, SC 29822 • 4,731
Clearwater □, ID • 8,505
Clearwater □, MN • 8,309
Cleburne, TX 76031–33 • 22,205
Cleburne □, AL • 12,730
Cleburne □, AR • 19,411
Cle Elum, WA 98922 • 1,778
Cleland Heights, DE 19805 • 1,120
Clementon, NJ 08021 • 5,601
Clemmons, NC 27012 • 6,020
Clemson, SC 29631–33 • 11,096
Clendenin, WV 25045 • 1,203
Cleona, PA 17042 • 2,322
Clermont, FL 34711–12 • 6,910
Clermont □, OH • 150,187
Cleveland, GA 30528 • 1,653
Cleveland, MS 38732–33 • 15,384
Cleveland, OH 44101–99 • 505,616
Cleveland, OK 74020 • 3,156
Cleveland, TN 37311–12 • 30,354
Cleveland, TX 77327–28 • 7,124
Cleveland, WI 53015 • 1,398
Cleveland □, AR • 7,781
Cleveland □, NC • 84,714
Cleveland □, OK • 174,253
Cleveland Heights, OH 44118 • 54,052
Cleves, OH 45002 • 2,208
Clewiston, FL 33440 • 6,085
Cliffside Park, NJ 07010 • 20,393
Clifton, AZ 85533 • 2,840
Clifton, CO 81520 • 12,671
Clifton, IL 60927 • 1,347
Clifton, NJ 07011–15 • 71,742
Clifton, TX 76634 • 3,195
Clifton Forge, VA 24422 • 4,679
Clifton Heights, PA 19018 • 7,111
Clifton Knolls, NY 12065 • 5,636
Clifton Springs, NY 14432 • 2,175
Clinch □, GA • 6,160
Clint, TX 79836 • 1,035
Clinton, AR 72031 • 2,213
Clinton, CT 06413 • 3,439
Clinton, IL 61727 • 7,437
Clinton, IN 47842 • 5,040
Clinton, IA 52732–33 • 29,201
Clinton, KY 42031 • 1,547
Clinton, LA 70722 • 1,904
Clinton, ME 04927 • 1,485
Clinton, MD 20735 • 19,987
Clinton, MA 01510 • 7,943
Clinton, MI 49236 • 2,475
Clinton, MS 39056 • 21,847
Clinton, MO 64735 • 8,703
Clinton, NJ 08809 • 2,054
Clinton, NY 13323 • 2,238
Clinton, NC 28328 • 8,204
Clinton, OK 73601 • 9,298
Clinton, SC 29325 • 7,987
Clinton, TN 37716 • 8,972
Clinton, UT 84015 • 7,945
Clinton, WA 98236 • 2,000
Clinton, WI 53525 • 1,849
Clinton □, IL • 33,944
Clinton □, IN • 30,974
Clinton □, IA • 51,040
Clinton □, KY • 9,135
Clinton □, MI • 57,883
Clinton □, MO • 16,595
Clinton □, NY • 85,969
Clinton □, OH • 35,415
Clinton □, PA • 37,182
Clinton Township, MI 48043 • 85,866
Clintonville, WI 54929 • 4,351
Clintwood, VA 24228 • 1,542
Clio, AL 36017 • 1,365
Clio, MI 48420 • 2,629
Clive, IA 50322 • 7,462
Cloquet, MN 55720 • 10,885
Closter, NJ 07624 • 8,094
Cloud □, KS • 11,023
Clover, SC 29710 • 3,422
Cloverdale, CA 95425 • 4,924
Cloverdale, IN 46120 • 1,681
Cloverleaf, TX 77015 • 18,230
Cloverport, KY 40111 • 1,207
Clovis, CA 93612–13 • 50,323
Clovis, NM 88101–03 • 30,954
Clute, TX 77531 • 8,910
Clyde, NY 14433 • 2,409
Clyde, NC 28721 • 1,041
Clyde, OH 43410 • 5,776
Clyde, TX 79510 • 3,002
Clymer, PA 15728 • 1,499
Coachella, CA 92236 • 16,896
Coahoma, TX 79511 • 1,133
Coahoma □, MS • 31,665
Coal □, OK • 5,780
Coal City, IL 60416 • 3,907
Coal Fork, WV 25306 • 2,100
Coalgate, OK 74538 • 1,895
Coal Grove, OH 45638 • 2,251
Coalinga, CA 93210 • 8,212
Coalville, UT 84017 • 1,065
Coatesville, PA 19320 • 11,038
Coats, NC 27521 • 1,493
Cobb □, GA • 447,745
Cobden, IL 62920 • 1,090
Cobleskill, NY 12043 • 5,268
Cochise □, AZ • 97,624
Cochituate, MA 01778 • 6,046
Cochran, GA 31014 • 4,390
Cochran □, TX • 4,377
Cochranton, PA 16314 • 1,174
Cocke □, TN • 29,141
Cockeysville, MD 21030 • 18,668
Cockrell Hill, TX 75211 • 3,746
Cocoa, FL 32922–27 • 17,722
Cocoa Beach, FL 32931–32 • 12,123
Coconino □, AZ • 96,591
Coconut Creek, FL 33060 • 27,485
Codington □, SD • 22,698
Cody, WY 82414 • 7,897
Coeburn, VA 24230 • 2,165
Coeur d'Alene, ID 83814 • 24,563
Coffee □, AL • 40,240
Coffee □, GA • 29,592
Coffee □, TN • 40,339
Coffey □, KS • 8,404
Coffeyville, KS 67337 • 12,917
Cohasset, MA 02025 • 6,800
Cohoes, NY 12047 • 16,825
Cokato, MN 55321 • 2,180
Coke □, TX • 3,424
Cokeville, WY 83114 • 493
Colbert, OK 74733 • 1,043
Colbert □, AL • 51,666
Colby, KS 67701 • 5,396
Colby, WI 54421 • 1,532
Colchester, CT 06415 • 3,212
Colchester, IL 62326 • 1,645
Cold Bay, AK 99571 • 148
Cold Spring, KY 41076 • 2,880
Cold Spring, MN 56320 • 2,459
Cold Spring Harbor, NY 11724 • 4,789
Coldwater, MI 49036 • 9,607
Coldwater, MS 38618 • 1,502
Coldwater, OH 45828 • 4,335
Cole □, MO • 63,579
Colebrook, NH 03576 • 2,444
Cole Camp, MO 65325 • 1,054
Coleman, MI 48618 • 1,237
Coleman, TX 76834 • 5,410
Coleman □, TX • 9,710
Coleraine, MN 55722 • 1,041
Coles □, IL • 51,644
Colfax, CA 95713 • 1,306
Colfax, IA 50054 • 2,462
Colfax, LA 71417 • 1,696
Colfax, WA 99111 • 2,713
Colfax, WI 54730 • 1,110
Colfax □, NE • 9,139
Colfax □, NM • 12,925
College, AK 99701 • 11,249
Collegedale, TN 37315 • 5,048
College Park, GA 30337 • 20,457
College Park, MD 20740–41 • 21,927
College Place, WA 99324 • 6,308
College Station, AR 72053 • 3,800
College Station, TX 77840–45 • 52,456
Collegeville, PA 19426 • 4,227
Colleton □, SC • 34,377
Colleyville, TX 76034 • 12,724
Collier □, FL • 152,099
Collierville, TN 38017 • 14,427
Collin □, TX • 264,036
Collingdale, PA 19023 • 9,175
Collingswood, NJ 08108 • 15,289
Collingsworth □, TX • 3,573
Collins, MS 39428 • 2,541
Collins Park, DE 19720 • 2,100
Collinsville, AL 35961 • 1,429
Collinsville, CT 06022 • 2,591
Collinsville, IL 62234 • 22,446
Collinsville, OK 74021 • 3,612
Collinsville, VA 24078 • 7,280
Collinwood, TN 38450 • 1,014
Colmar Manor, MD 20722 • 1,249
Coloma, MI 49038 • 1,679
Colon, MI 49040 • 1,224
Colonia, NJ 07067 • 18,238
Colonial Beach, VA 22443 • 3,132
Colonial Heights, TN 37663 • 6,716
Colonial Heights, VA 23834 • 16,064
Colonial Park, PA 17109 • 13,777
Colonie, NY 12212 • 8,019
Colorado □, TX • 18,383
Colorado City, AZ 86021 • 2,426
Colorado City, CO 81019 • 1,149
Colorado City, TX 79512 • 4,749
Colorado Springs, CO 80901–99 • 281,140
Colquitt, GA 31737 • 1,991
Colquitt □, GA • 36,645
Colstrip, MT 59323 • 3,035
Colton, CA 92324 • 40,213
Columbia, CA 95310 • 1,799
Columbia, IL 62236 • 5,524
Columbia, KY 42728 • 3,845
Columbia, MD 21044–46 • 75,883
Columbia, MS 39429 • 6,815
Columbia, MO 65201–05 • 69,101
Columbia, PA 17512 • 10,701
Columbia, SC 29201–92 • 98,052
Columbia, TN 38401–02 • 28,583
Columbia □, AR • 25,691
Columbia □, FL • 42,613
Columbia □, GA • 66,031
Columbia □, NY • 62,982
Columbia □, OR • 37,557
Columbia □, PA • 63,202
Columbia □, WA • 4,024
Columbia □, WI • 45,088
Columbia City, IN 46725 • 5,706
Columbia City, OR 97018 • 1,003
Columbia Falls, MT 59912 • 2,942
Columbia Heights, MN 55421 • 18,910
Columbiana, AL 35051 • 2,968
Columbiana, OH 44408 • 4,961
Columbiana □, OH • 108,276
Columbine, CO 80123 • 23,969
Columbus, GA 31901–09 • 178,681
Columbus, IN 47201–03 • 31,802
Columbus, KS 66725 • 3,268
Columbus, MS 39701–05 • 23,799
Columbus, MT 59019 • 1,573
Columbus, NE 68601 • 19,480
Columbus, OH 43201–91 • 632,910
Columbus, TX 78934 • 3,367
Columbus, WI 53925 • 4,093
Columbus □, NC • 49,587
Columbus Grove, OH 45830 • 2,231
Columbus Junction, IA 52738 • 1,616
Colusa, CA 95932 • 4,934
Colusa □, CA • 16,275
Colver, PA 15927 • 1,024
Colville, WA 99114 • 4,360
Colwich, KS 67030 • 1,091
Comal □, TX • 51,832
Comanche, OK 73529 • 1,695
Comanche, TX 76442 • 4,087
Comanche □, KS • 2,313
Comanche □, OK • 111,486
Comanche □, TX • 13,381
Combee Settlement, FL 33801 • 5,463
Combined Locks, WI 54113 • 2,190
Comfort, TX 78013 • 1,477
Commack, NY 11725 • 36,124
Commerce, CA 90040 • 12,135
Commerce, GA 30529 • 4,108
Commerce, OK 74339 • 2,426
Commerce, TX 75428 • 6,825
Commerce City, CO 80022 • 16,466
Common Fence Point, RI 02871 • 860
Como, MS 38619 • 1,387
Compton, CA 90220–24 • 90,454
Comstock, MI 49041 • 5,600
Comstock Park, MI 49321 • 6,530
Concho □, TX • 3,044
Concord, CA 94518–24 • 111,348
Concord, MA 01742 • 4,680
Concord, MO 63128 • 19,859
Concord, NH 03301–03 • 36,006
Concord, NC 28025–27 • 27,347
Concord, TN 37901 • 3,420
Concordia, KS 66901 • 6,167
Concordia, MO 64020 • 2,160
Concordia □, LA • 20,828
Conecuh □, AL • 14,054
Conejos □, CO • 7,453
Conemaugh, PA 15909 • 1,470
Congers, NY 10920 • 8,003
Conklin, NY 13748 • 1,800
Conley, GA 30027 • 5,528
Conneaut, OH 44030 • 13,241
Connell, WA 99326 • 2,005
Connellsville, PA 15425 • 9,229
Connersville, IN 47331 • 15,550
Conover, NC 28613 • 5,465
Conrad, MT 59425 • 2,891
Conroe, TX 77301–05 • 27,610
Conshohocken, PA 19428 • 8,064
Constantia, NY 13044 • 1,140
Constantine, MI 49042 • 2,032
Continental, OH 45831 • 1,214
Contoocook, NH 03229 • 1,334
Contra Costa □, CA • 803,732
Converse, IN 46919 • 1,144
Converse, SC 29329 • 1,173
Converse, TX 78109 • 8,887
Converse □, WY • 11,128
Convoy, OH 45832 • 1,200
Conway, AR 72032 • 26,481
Conway, FL 32809 • 13,159
Conway, NH 03818 • 1,604
Conway, PA 15027 • 2,424
Conway, SC 29526–27 • 9,819
Conway □, AR • 19,151
Conway Springs, KS 67031 • 1,384
Conyers, GA 30207–08 • 7,380
Cook □, GA • 13,456
Cook □, IL • 5,105,067
Cook □, MN • 3,868
Cooke □, TX • 30,777
Cookeville, TN 38501–02 • 21,744
Coolidge, AZ 85228 • 6,927
Coon Rapids, IA 50058 • 1,266
Coon Rapids, MN 55433 • 52,978
Cooper, TX 75432 • 2,153
Cooper □, MO • 14,835
Cooper City, FL 33328 • 20,791
Cooper Road, LA 71107 • 11,050
Coopersburg, PA 18036 • 2,599
Cooperstown, NY 13326 • 2,180
Cooperstown, ND 58425 • 1,247
Coopersville, MI 49404 • 3,421
Coos □, NH • 34,828
Coos □, OR • 60,273
Coosa □, AL • 11,063
Coos Bay, OR 97420 • 15,076
Copake, NY 12516 • 1,200
Copiague, NY 11726 • 20,769
Copiah □, MS • 27,592
Coplay, PA 18037 • 3,267
Copperas Cove, TX 76522 • 24,079
Coquille, OR 97423 • 4,121
Coral Gables, FL 33134 • 40,091
Coral Hills, MD 20743 • 11,032
Coral Springs, FL 33065 • 79,443
Coral Terrace, FL 33157 • 23,255
Coralville, IA 52241 • 10,347
Coral Way Village, FL 33155 • 9,000
Coram, NY 11727 • 30,111
Coraopolis, PA 15108 • 6,747
Corbin, KY 40701–02 • 7,419
Corcoran, CA 93212 • 13,364
Corcoran, MN 55340 • 5,199
Cordaville, MA 01772 • 1,530
Cordele, GA 31015 • 10,321
Cordell, OK 73632 • 2,903
Cordova, AL 35550 • 2,623
Cordova, AK 99574 • 2,110
Cordova, NC 28330 • 1,200
Corinth, MS 38834 • 11,820
Corinth, NY 12822 • 2,760
Cornelia, GA 30531 • 3,219
Cornelius, NC 28031 • 2,581
Cornelius, OR 97113 • 6,148
Cornell, WI 54732 • 1,541
Corning, AR 72422 • 3,323
Corning, CA 96021 • 5,870
Corning, IA 50841 • 1,806
Corning, NY 14830 • 11,938
Cornville, AZ 86325 • 1,200
Cornwall, PA 17016 • 3,231
Cornwall on Hudson, NY 12520 • 3,093
Corona, CA 91718–20 • 76,095
Coronado, CA 92118 • 26,540
Coronado, CO 80229 • 6,890
Corpus Christi, TX 78401–82 • 257,453
Corrigan, TX 75939 • 1,764
Corriganville, MD 21524 • 1,020
Corry, PA 16407 • 7,216
Corsicana, TX 75110 • 22,911
Corson □, SD • 4,195
Corte Madera, CA 94925 • 8,272
Cortez, CO 81321 • 7,284
Cortez, FL 34215 • 4,509
Cortland, NY 13045 • 19,801
Cortland, OH 44410 • 5,666
Cortland □, NY • 48,963
Corunna, MI 48817 • 3,091
Corvallis, OR 97330–33 • 44,757
Corydon, IN 47112 • 2,661
Corydon, IA 50060 • 1,675
Coryell □, TX • 64,213
Coshocton, OH 43812 • 12,193
Coshocton □, OH • 35,427
Cosmopolis, WA 98537 • 1,372
Costa Mesa, CA 92626–28 • 96,357
Costilla □, CO • 3,190
Cottage Grove, MN 55016 • 22,935
Cottage Grove, OR 97424 • 7,402
Cottle □, TX • 2,247
Cottleville, MO 63338 • 2,936
Cotton □, OK • 6,651
Cottondale, AL 35453 • 1,960
Cotton Plant, AR 72036 • 1,150
Cottonport, LA 71327 • 2,600
Cotton Valley, LA 71018 • 1,130
Cottonwood, AL 36320 • 1,385
Cottonwood, AZ 86326 • 5,918
Cottonwood, CA 96022 • 1,747
Cottonwood, ID 83522 • 822
Cottonwood, UT 84121 • 11,554
Cottonwood □, MN • 12,694
Cottonwood Heights, UT 84121 • 28,766
Cotuit, MA 02635 • 1,750
Cotulla, TX 78014 • 3,694
Coudersport, PA 16915 • 2,854
Coulee Dam, WA 99116 • 1,087
Council, ID 83612 • 831
Council Bluffs, IA 51501–03 • 54,315
Council Grove, KS 66846 • 2,228
Country Club Hills, IL 60478 • 15,431
Country Homes, WA 99218 • 5,126
Countryside, IL 60525 • 5,716
Coupeville, WA 98239 • 1,377
Coushatta, LA 71019 • 1,845
Covedale, OH 45238 • 6,669
Covelo, CA 95428 • 1,057
Coventry, CT 06238 • 10,063
Coventry, DE 19720 • 1,165
Coventry, RI 02816 • 6,980
Covina, CA 91722–24 • 43,207
Covington, GA 30209 • 10,026
Covington, IN 47932 • 2,747
Covington, KY 41011–18 • 43,264
Covington, LA 70433–34 • 7,691
Covington, OH 45318 • 2,603
Covington, TN 38019 • 7,487
Covington, VA 24426 • 6,991
Covington □, AL • 36,478
Covington □, MS • 16,527
Cowan, TN 37318 • 1,738
Cowarts, AL 36321 • 1,400
Coweta, OK 74429 • 6,159
Coweta □, GA • 53,853
Cowley, WY 82420 • 477
Cowley □, KS • 36,915
Cowlitz □, WA • 82,119
Cowpens, SC 29330 • 2,176
Coxsackie, NY 12051 • 2,789
Cozad, NE 69130 • 3,823
Crab Orchard, WV 25827 • 2,919
Crabtree, PA 15624 • 1,000
Crafton, PA 15205 • 7,188
Craig, AK 99921 • 1,260
Craig, CO 81625–26 • 8,091
Craig □, OK • 14,104
Craig □, VA • 4,372
Craighead □, AR • 68,956
Craigsville, WV 26205 • 1,955
Cramerton, NC 28032 • 2,371
Cranbury, NJ 08512 • 1,255
Crandall, TX 75114 • 1,652
Crandon, WI 54520 • 1,958
Crane, AZ 85365 • 2,650
Crane, MO 65633 • 1,218
Crane, TX 79731 • 3,533
Crane □, TX • 4,652
Cranford, NJ 07016 • 22,624
Cranston, RI 02910 • 76,060
Craven □, NC • 81,613
Crawford, NE 69339 • 1,115
Crawford □, AR • 42,493
Crawford □, GA • 8,991
Crawford □, IL • 19,464
Crawford □, IN • 9,914
Crawford □, IA • 16,775
Crawford □, KS • 35,568
Crawford □, MI • 12,260
Crawford □, MO • 19,173
Crawford □, OH • 47,870
Crawford □, PA • 86,169
Crawford □, WI • 15,940
Crawfordsville, IN 47933 • 13,584
Crawfordville, FL 32327 • 1,110
Creedmoor, NC 27522 • 1,504
Creek □, OK • 60,915
Creighton, NE 68729 • 1,223
Creighton, PA 15030 • 1,658
Crenshaw □, AL • 13,635
Creola, AL 36525 • 1,896
Cresaptown, MD 21502 • 4,645
Crescent, OK 73028 • 1,236
Crescent City, CA 95531 • 4,380
Crescent City, FL 32112 • 1,859
Crescent Springs, KY 41016 • 2,179
Cresco, IA 52136 • 3,669
Cresskill, NJ 07626 • 7,558
Cresson, PA 16630 • 1,784
Cressona, PA 17929 • 1,694
Cresthaven, FL 33064 • 2,400
Crest Hill, IL 60435 • 10,643
Crestline, CA 92325 • 8,594
Crestline, OH 44827 • 4,934
Creston, IA 50801 • 7,911
Creston, OH 44217 • 1,848
Crestview, FL 32536 • 9,886
Crestview, HI 96797 • 1,000
Crestwood, IL 60445 • 10,823
Crestwood, KY 40014 • 1,435
Crestwood, MO 63126 • 11,234
Crestwood Village, NJ 08759 • 8,030
Creswell, OR 97426 • 2,431
Crete, IL 60417 • 6,773
Crete, NE 68333 • 4,841
Creve Coeur, IL 61611 • 5,938
Creve Coeur, MO 63141 • 12,304
Crewe, VA 23930 • 2,276
Cricket, NC 28659 • 2,015
Cridersville, OH 45806 • 1,885
Crisfield, MD 21817 • 2,880
Crisp □, GA • 20,011
Crittenden □, AR • 49,939
Crittenden □, KY • 9,196
Crocker, MO 65452 • 1,077
Crockett, CA 94525 • 3,228
Crockett, TX 75835 • 7,024
Crockett □, TN • 13,378
Crockett □, TX • 4,078
Crofton, MD 21114 • 12,781
Cromwell, CT 06416 • 1,100
Crook □, OR • 14,111
Crook □, WY • 5,294
Crookston, MN 56716 • 8,119
Crooksville, OH 43731 • 2,601
Crosby, MN 56441 • 2,073
Crosby, ND 58730 • 1,312
Crosby, TX 77532 • 1,811
Crosby □, TX • 7,304
Crosbyton, TX 79322 • 2,026
Cross □, AR • 19,225
Cross City, FL 32628 • 2,041
Crossett, AR 71635 • 6,282
Crosslake, MN 56442 • 1,132
Cross Lanes, WV 25313 • 10,878
Cross Plains, TN 37049 • 1,025
Cross Plains, TX 76443 • 1,063
Cross Plains, WI 53528 • 2,098
Crossville, AL 35962 • 1,350
Crossville, TN 38555 • 6,930
Croswell, MI 48422 • 2,174

Crothersville, IN 47229 • *1,687*
Croton-on-Hudson, NY 10520 • *7,018*
Crow Agency, MT 59022 • *1,446*
Crowell, TX 79227 • *1,230*
Crowley, LA 70526-27 • *13,983*
Crowley, TX 76036 • *6,974*
Crowley □, CO • *3,946*
Crown Point, IN 46307 • *17,728*
Crownpoint, NM 87313 • *2,108*
Crow Wing □, MN • *44,249*
Crozet, VA 22932 • *2,256*
Crystal, MN 55428 • *23,788*
Crystal Bay, NV 89402 • *1,200*
Crystal Beach, FL 34681 • *1,450*
Crystal City, MO 63019 • *4,088*
Crystal City, TX 78839 • *8,263*
Crystal Falls, MI 49920 • *1,922*
Crystal Lake, CT 06029 • *1,200*
Crystal Lake, FL 33803 • *5,300*
Crystal Lake, IL 60014 • *24,512*
Crystal Lawns, IL 60435 • *1,660*
Crystal River, FL 32629 • *4,044*
Crystal Springs, MS 39059 • *5,643*
Cuba, IL 61427 • *1,440*
Cuba, MO 65453 • *2,537*
Cuba, NY 14727 • *1,690*
Cuba City, WI 53807 • *2,024*
Cucamonga, CA 91730 • *101,409*
Cudahy, CA 90201 • *22,817*
Cudahy, WI 53110 • *18,659*
Cuero, TX 77954 • *6,700*
Culberson □, TX • *3,407*
Culbertson, MT 59218 • *796*
Cullen, LA 71021 • *1,642*
Cullman, AL 35055-56 • *13,367*
Cullman □, AL • *67,613*
Culloden, WV 25510 • *2,907*
Cullowhee, NC 28723 • *1,200*
Culpeper, VA 22701 • *8,581*
Culpeper □, VA • *27,791*
Culver, IN 46511 • *1,404*
Culver City, CA 90230-33 • *38,793*
Cumberland, KY 40823 • *3,112*
Cumberland, MD 21501-05 • *23,706*
Cumberland, WI 54829 • *2,163*
Cumberland □, IL • *10,670*
Cumberland □, KY • *6,784*
Cumberland □, ME • *243,135*
Cumberland □, NJ • *138,053*
Cumberland □, NC • *274,566*
Cumberland □, PA • *195,257*
Cumberland □, TN • *34,736*
Cumberland □, VA • *7,825*
Cumberland Center, ME 04021 • *1,890*
Cumberland Foreside, ME 04110 • *1,000*
Cumberland Hill, RI 02864 • *6,379*
Cuming □, NE • *10,117*
Cumming, GA 30130 • *2,828*
Cupertino, CA 95014-16 • *40,263*
Currituck □, NC • *13,736*
Curry □, NM • *42,207*
Curry □, OR • *19,327*
Curtisville, PA 15032 • *1,285*
Curwensville, PA 16833 • *2,924*
Cushing, OK 74023 • *7,218*
Cusseta, GA 31805 • *1,107*
Custer, SD 57730 • *1,741*
Custer □, CO • *1,926*
Custer □, ID • *4,133*
Custer □, MT • *11,697*
Custer □, NE • *12,270*
Custer □, OK • *26,897*
Custer □, SD • *6,179*
Cut Bank, MT 59427 • *3,329*
Cutchogue, NY 11935 • *1,730*
Cuthbert, GA 31740 • *3,730*
Cutler, FL 33157 • *16,201*
Cutler Ridge, FL 33157 • *21,268*
Cutlerville, MI 49508 • *11,228*
Cut Off, LA 70345 • *5,325*
Cuyahoga □, OH • *1,412,140*
Cuyahoga Falls, OH 44221-24 • *48,950*
Cynthiana, KY 41031 • *6,497*
Cypress, CA 90630 • *42,655*
Cypress Lake, FL 33919 • *10,491*
Cypress Quarters, FL 34972 • *1,343*
Cyril, OK 73029 • *1,072*

D

Dacono, CO 80514 • *2,228*
Dacula, GA 30211 • *2,217*
Dade □, FL • *1,937,094*
Dade □, GA • *13,147*
Dade □, MO • *7,449*
Dade City, FL 33525-26 • *5,633*
Dadeville, AL 36853 • *3,276*
Daggett □, UT • *690*
Dagsboro, DE 19939 • *398*
Dahlonega, GA 30533 • *3,086*
Daingerfield, TX 75638 • *2,572*
Dakota □, MN • *275,227*
Dakota □, NE • *16,742*
Dakota City, IA 50529 • *1,024*
Dakota City, NE 68731 • *1,470*
Dale, IN 47523 • *1,553*
Dale □, AL • *49,633*
Dale City, VA 22193 • *47,170*
Daleville, AL 36322 • *5,117*
Daleville, IN 47334 • *1,681*
Dalhart, TX 79022 • *6,246*
Dallam □, TX • *5,461*
Dallas, GA 30132 • *2,810*
Dallas, NC 28034 • *3,012*
Dallas, OR 97338 • *9,422*
Dallas, PA 18612 • *2,567*
Dallas, TX 75201-99 • *1,006,877*
Dallas □, AL • *48,130*
Dallas □, AR • *9,614*
Dallas □, IA • *29,755*
Dallas □, MO • *12,646*
Dallas □, TX • *1,852,810*
Dallas Center, IA 50063 • *1,454*
Dallas City, IL 62330 • *1,037*
Dallastown, PA 17313 • *3,974*
Dalton, GA 30720-22 • *21,761*
Dalton, MA 01226-27 • *6,797*
Dalton, OH 44618 • *1,377*
Dalton, PA 18414 • *1,369*
Dalton Gardens, ID 83814 • *1,951*
Daly City, CA 94014-17 • *92,311*
Damascus, MD 20872 • *9,817*
Dana Point, CA 92629 • *31,896*
Danbury, CT 06810-13 • *65,585*
Danbury, TX 77534 • *1,447*
Dandridge, TN 37725 • *1,540*
Dane □, WI • *367,085*
Dania, FL 33004 • *13,024*
Daniels □, MT • *2,266*
Danielson, CT 06239 • *4,441*
Dannemora, NY 12929 • *4,005*
Dansville, NY 14437 • *5,002*
Dante, VA 24237 • *1,083*
Danvers, MA 01923 • *24,174*
Danville, AR 72833 • *1,585*
Danville, CA 94526 • *31,306*
Danville, IL 61832-34 • *33,828*
Danville, IN 46122 • *4,345*
Danville, KY 40422-23 • *12,420*
Danville, OH 43014 • *1,001*
Danville, PA 17821 • *5,165*
Danville, VA 24540-43 • *53,056*
Daphne, AL 36526 • *11,290*
Darby, PA 19023 • *11,140*
Darby Township, PA 19036 • *10,955*
Dardanelle, AR 72834 • *3,722*
Dare □, NC • *22,746*
Darien, CT 06820 • *18,130*
Darien, GA 31305 • *1,783*
Darien, IL 60559 • *18,341*
Darien, WI 53114 • *1,158*
Darke □, OH • *53,619*
Darley Woods, DE 19810 • *1,220*
Darlington, SC 29532 • *7,311*
Darlington, WI 53530 • *2,235*
Darlington □, SC • *61,851*
Darrington, WA 98241 • *1,042*
Dartmouth Woods, DE 19810 • *1,970*
Dassel, MN 55325 • *1,082*
Dauphin □, PA • *237,813*
Davenport, FL 33837 • *1,529*
Davenport, IA 52801-09 • *95,333*
Davenport, WA 99122 • *1,502*
David City, NE 68632 • *2,522*
Davidson, NC 28036 • *4,046*
Davidson □, NC • *126,677*
Davidson □, TN • *510,784*
Davidsville, PA 15928 • *1,167*
Davie, FL 33328 • *47,217*
Davie □, NC • *27,859*
Daviess □, IN • *27,533*
Daviess □, KY • *87,189*
Daviess □, MO • *7,865*
Davis, CA 95616-17 • *46,209*
Davis, OK 73030 • *2,543*
Davis □, IA • *8,312*
Davis □, UT • *187,941*
Davison, MI 48423 • *5,693*
Davison □, SD • *17,503*
Davisville, RI 02852 • *500*
Dawes □, NE • *9,021*
Dawson, GA 31742 • *5,295*
Dawson, MN 56232 • *1,626*
Dawson □, GA • *9,429*
Dawson □, MT • *9,505*
Dawson □, NE • *19,940*
Dawson □, TX • *14,349*
Dawson Springs, KY 42408 • *3,129*
Day □, SD • *6,978*
Dayton, KY 41074 • *6,576*
Dayton, MN 55327 • *4,443*
Dayton, NV 89403 • *2,217*
Dayton, NJ 08810 • *1,200*
Dayton, OH 45401-90 • *182,044*
Dayton, OR 97114 • *1,526*
Dayton, TN 37321 • *5,671*
Dayton, TX 77535 • *5,151*
Dayton, WA 99328 • *2,468*
Dayton, WY 82836 • *565*
Daytona Beach, FL 32114-25 • *61,921*
Dayville, CT 06241 • *1,500*
Deadwood, SD 57732 • *1,830*
Deaf Smith □, TX • *19,153*
Deal, NJ 07723 • *1,179*
Deale, MD 20751 • *4,151*
Dearborn, MI 48120-26 • *89,286*
Dearborn □, IN • *38,835*
Dearborn Heights, MI 48127 • *60,838*
De Baca □, NM • *2,252*
De Bary, FL 32713 • *7,176*
Decatur, AL 35601-03 • *48,761*
Decatur, GA 30030-37 • *17,336*
Decatur, IL 62521-26 • *83,885*
Decatur, IN 46733 • *8,644*
Decatur, MI 49045 • *1,760*
Decatur, MS 39327 • *1,248*
Decatur, TN 37322 • *1,361*
Decatur, TX 76234 • *4,252*
Decatur □, GA • *25,511*
Decatur □, IN • *23,645*
Decatur □, IA • *8,338*
Decatur □, KS • *4,021*
Decatur □, TN • *10,472*
Decherd, TN 37324 • *2,196*
Deckerville, MI 48427 • *1,015*
Decorah, IA 52101 • *8,063*
Dedham, MA 02026 • *23,782*
Deep River, CT 06417 • *2,520*
Deerfield, IL 60015 • *17,327*
Deerfield, WI 53531 • *1,617*
Deerfield Beach, FL 33441-43 • *46,325*
Deer Lodge, MT 59722 • *3,378*
Deer Lodge □, MT • *10,278*
Deer Park, NY 11729 • *28,840*
Deer Park, OH 45236 • *6,181*
Deer Park, TX 77536 • *27,652*
Deer Park, WA 99006 • *2,278*
Defiance, OH 43512 • *16,768*
Defiance □, OH • *39,350*
De Forest, WI 53532 • *4,882*
De Funiak Springs, FL 32433 • *5,120*
De Graff, OH 43318 • *1,331*
De Kalb, IL 60115 • *34,925*
De Kalb, MS 39328 • *1,073*
De Kalb, TX 75559 • *1,976*
De Kalb □, AL • *54,651*
De Kalb □, GA • *545,837*
De Kalb □, IL • *77,932*
De Kalb □, IN • *35,324*
De Kalb □, MO • *9,967*
De Kalb □, TN • *14,360*
Delafield, WI 53018 • *5,347*
Del Aire, CA 90250 • *8,040*
Delanco, NJ 08075 • *3,316*
De Land, FL 32720-24 • *16,491*
Delano, CA 93215-16 • *22,762*
Delano, MN 55328 • *2,709*
Delavan, IL 61734 • *1,642*
Delavan, WI 53115 • *6,073*
Delavan Lake, WI 53115 • *2,177*
Delaware, OH 43015 • *20,030*
Delaware □, IN • *119,659*
Delaware □, IA • *18,035*
Delaware □, NY • *47,225*
Delaware □, OH • *66,929*
Delaware □, OK • *28,070*
Delaware □, PA • *547,651*
Delaware City, DE 19706 • *1,682*
Delcambre, LA 70528 • *1,978*
Del City, OK 73115 • *23,928*
De Leon, TX 76444 • *2,190*
De Leon Springs, FL 32130 • *1,481*
Delevan, NY 14042 • *1,214*
Delhi, LA 71232 • *3,169*
Delhi, NY 13753 • *3,064*
Delhi Hills, OH 45238 • *27,647*
Dell Rapids, SD 57022 • *2,484*
Dellwood, MO 63136 • *5,245*
Del Mar, CA 92014 • *4,860*
Delmar, DE 19940 • *962*
Delmar, MD 21875 • *1,430*
Delmar, NY 12054 • *8,360*
Del Norte, CO 81132 • *1,674*
Del Norte □, CA • *23,460*
Del Park Manor, DE 19808 • *1,550*
Delphi, IN 46923 • *2,531*
Delphos, OH 45833 • *7,093*
Delran, NJ 08075 • *14,811*
Delray Beach, FL 33444-47 • *47,181*
Del Rio, FL 33617 • *8,248*
Del Rio, TX 78840-42 • *30,705*
Delta, CO 81416 • *3,789*
Delta, OH 43515 • *2,849*
Delta, UT 84624 • *2,998*
Delta □, CO • *20,980*
Delta □, MI • *37,780*
Delta □, TX • *4,857*
Delta Junction, AK 99737 • *652*
Deltaville, VA 23043 • *1,082*
Deltona, FL 32725 • *50,828*
Demarest, NJ 07627 • *4,800*
Deming, NM 88030-31 • *10,970*
Demopolis, AL 36732 • *7,512*
Demorest, GA 30535 • *1,088*
Demotte, IN 46310 • *2,482*
Denham Springs, LA 70726-27 • *8,381*
Denison, IA 51442 • *6,604*
Denison, TX 75020-21 • *21,505*
Denmark, SC 29042 • *3,762*
Denmark, WI 54208 • *1,612*
Dennis, MA 02638 • *2,500*
Dennison, OH 44621 • *3,282*
Dennis Port, MA 02639 • *2,775*
Denny Terrace, SC 29203 • *1,885*
Dent □, MO • *13,702*
Denton, MD 21629 • *2,977*
Denton, NC 27239 • *1,292*
Denton, TX 76201-06 • *66,270*
Denton □, TX • *273,525*
Dentsville, SC 29204 • *11,839*
Denver, CO 80201-95 • *467,610*
Denver, IA 50622 • *1,600*
Denver, PA 17517 • *2,861*
Denver □, CO • *467,610*
Denver City, TX 79323 • *5,145*
Denville, NJ 07834 • *14,380*
De Pere, WI 54115 • *16,569*
Depew, NY 14043 • *17,673*
Deposit, NY 13754 • *1,936*
Depue, IL 61322 • *1,729*
De Queen, AR 71832 • *4,633*
De Quincy, LA 70633 • *3,474*
Derby, CT 06418 • *12,199*
Derby, KS 67037 • *14,699*
Derby, NY 14047 • *1,200*
Derby Line, VT 05830 • *855*
De Ridder, LA 70634 • *9,868*
Dermott, AR 71638 • *4,715*
Derry, NH 03038 • *20,446*
Derry, PA 15627 • *2,950*
Derwood, MD 20855 • *1,500*
Des Allemands, LA 70030 • *2,504*
Des Arc, AR 72040 • *2,001*
Deschutes □, OR • *74,958*
Desert Hot Springs, CA 92240 • *11,668*
Desha □, AR • *16,798*
Deshler, OH 43516 • *1,876*
Desloge, MO 63601 • *4,150*
De Smet, SD 57231 • *1,172*
Des Moines, IA 50301-95 • *193,187*
Des Moines, WA 98188 • *17,283*
Des Moines □, IA • *42,614*
De Soto, IL 62924 • *1,500*
De Soto, IA 50069 • *1,033*
De Soto, KS 66018 • *2,291*
De Soto, MO 63020 • *5,993*
De Soto, TX 75115 • *30,544*
De Soto □, FL • *23,865*
De Soto □, LA • *25,346*
De Soto □, MS • *67,910*
Despard, WV 26301 • *1,018*
Des Peres, MO 63131 • *8,395*
Des Plaines, IL 60016-19 • *53,223*
Destin, FL 32540-41 • *8,080*
Destrehan, LA 70047 • *8,031*
Detroit, MI 48201-44 • *1,027,974*
Detroit Lakes, MN 56501-02 • *6,635*
Deuel □, NE • *2,237*
Deuel □, SD • *4,522*
Devils Lake, ND 58301 • *7,782*
Devine, TX 78016 • *3,928*
Devola, OH 45750 • *2,736*
Devon, PA 19333 • *6,620*
Devonshire, DE 19810 • *2,120*
Dewey, OK 74029 • *3,326*
Dewey □, OK • *5,551*
Dewey □, SD • *5,523*
Dewey Beach, DE 19971 • *204*
Deweyville, TX 77614 • *1,218*
De Witt, AR 72042 • *3,553*
De Witt, IA 52742 • *4,514*
De Witt, MI 48820 • *3,964*
De Witt, NY 13214 • *8,244*
De Witt □, IL • *16,516*
De Witt □, TX • *18,840*
Dexter, ME 04930 • *2,650*
Dexter, MI 48130 • *1,497*
Dexter, MO 63841 • *7,559*
Dexter, NY 13634 • *1,030*
Diamond Bar, CA 91765 • *53,672*
Diamond Hill, RI 02864 • *810*
Diamond Lake, IL 60060 • *1,500*
Diamond Springs, CA 95619 • *2,872*
Diamondville, WY 83116 • *864*
Diaz, AR 72043 • *1,363*
D'Iberville, MS 39532 • *6,566*
Diboll, TX 75941 • *4,341*
Dickens □, TX • *2,571*
Dickenson □, VA • *17,620*
Dickey □, ND • *6,107*
Dickinson, ND 58601-02 • *16,097*
Dickinson, TX 77539 • *9,497*
Dickinson □, IA • *14,909*
Dickinson □, KS • *18,958*
Dickinson □, MI • *26,831*
Dickson, TN 37055 • *8,791*
Dickson □, TN • *35,061*
Dickson City, PA 18519 • *6,276*
Dierks, AR 71833 • *1,263*
Dighton, KS 67839 • *1,361*
Dighton, MA 02715 • *1,100*
Dillard, OR 97432 • *1,000*
Dilley, TX 78017 • *2,632*
Dillingham, AK 99576 • *2,017*
Dillon, MT 59725 • *3,991*
Dillon, SC 29536 • *6,829*
Dillon □, SC • *29,114*
Dillsboro, IN 47018 • *1,200*
Dillsburg, PA 17019 • *1,925*
Dilworth, MN 56529 • *2,562*
Dimmit □, TX • *10,433*
Dimmitt, TX 79027 • *4,408*
Dimondale, MI 48821 • *1,247*
Dingmans Ferry, PA 18328 • *1,200*
Dinuba, CA 93618 • *12,743*
Dinwiddie □, VA • *20,960*
Dishman, WA 99213 • *9,671*
District Heights-Forestville, MD 20747 • *6,704*
District of Columbia 0T15, DC •
Divernon, IL 62530 • *1,178*
Divide □, ND • *2,899*
Dixfield, ME 04224 • *1,300*
Dix Hills, NY 11746 • *25,849*
Dixie □, FL • *10,585*
Dixon, CA 95620 • *10,401*
Dixon, IL 61021 • *15,144*
Dixon, MO 65459 • *1,585*
Dixon □, NE • *6,143*
Dixonville, PA 15734 • *1,000*
Dobbs Ferry, NY 10522 • *9,940*
Dobson, NC 27017 • *1,195*
Docena, AL 35060 • *1,000*
Dock Junction, GA 31520 • *7,094*
Doddridge □, WV • *6,994*
Dodge □, GA • *17,607*
Dodge □, MN • *15,731*
Dodge □, NE • *34,500*
Dodge □, WI • *76,559*
Dodge Center, MN 55927 • *1,954*
Dodge City, KS 67801 • *21,129*
Dodge Park, MD 20785 • *4,842*
Dodgeville, WI 53533 • *3,882*
Dolgeville, NY 13329 • *2,452*
Dolomite, AL 35061 • *2,590*
Dolores □, CO • *1,504*
Dolton, IL 60419 • *23,930*
Dona Ana, NM 88032 • *950*
Dona Ana □, NM • *135,510*
Donaldsonville, LA 70346 • *7,949*
Donalsonville, GA 31745 • *2,761*
Doneraile, SC 29532 • *1,276*
Doniphan, MO 63935 • *1,713*
Doniphan □, KS • *8,134*
Donley □, TX • *3,696*
Donna, TX 78537 • *12,652*
Donora, PA 15033 • *5,928*
Dooly □, GA • *9,901*
Door □, WI • *25,690*
Dora, AL 35062 • *2,214*
Doraville, GA 30340 • *7,626*
Dorchester □, MD • *30,236*
Dorchester □, SC • *83,060*
Dormont, PA 15216 • *9,772*
Dorothy Pond, MA 01527 • *1,670*
Dorr, MI 49323 • *1,450*
Dorset, VT 05251 • *550*
Dorsey, MD 21227 • *1,186*
Dothan, AL 36301-04 • *53,589*
Double Springs, AL 35553 • *1,138*
Dougherty □, GA • *96,311*
Douglas, AZ 85607-08 • *12,822*
Douglas, GA 31533 • *10,464*
Douglas, MI 49406 • *1,040*
Douglas, WY 82633 • *5,076*
Douglas □, CO • *60,391*
Douglas □, GA • *71,120*
Douglas □, IL • *19,464*
Douglas □, KS • *81,798*
Douglas □, MN • *28,674*
Douglas □, MO • *11,876*
Douglas □, NE • *416,444*
Douglas □, NV • *27,637*
Douglas □, OR • *94,649*
Douglas □, SD • *3,746*
Douglas □, WA • *26,205*
Douglas □, WI • *41,758*
Douglass, KS 67039 • *1,722*
Douglasville, GA 30133-35 • *11,635*
Dousman, WI 53118 • *1,277*
Dover, AR 72837 • *1,055*
Dover, DE 19901-03 • *27,630*
Dover, FL 33527 • *2,606*
Dover, MA 02030 • *2,163*
Dover, NH 03820 • *25,042*
Dover, NJ 07801 • *15,115*
Dover, OH 44622 • *11,329*
Dover, PA 17315 • *1,884*
Dover, TN 37058 • *1,341*
Dover-Foxcroft, ME 04426 • *3,077*
Dover Plains, NY 12522 • *1,847*
Dowagiac, MI 49047 • *6,409*
Downers Grove, IL 60515-17 • *46,858*
Downey, CA 90239-42 • *91,444*
Downingtown, PA 19335 • *7,749*
Downs, KS 67437 • *1,119*
Downsville, NY 13755 • *1,100*
Doylestown, OH 44230 • *2,668*
Doylestown, PA 18901 • *8,575*
Dracut, MA 01826 • *25,594*
Drain, OR 97435 • *1,011*
Draper, UT 84020 • *7,257*
Drayton, ND 58225 • *961*
Drayton, SC 29333 • *1,443*
Drayton Plains, MI 48330 • *18,000*
Dreamland Villa, AZ 85205 • *3,400*
Dresden, OH 43821 • *1,581*
Dresden, TN 38225 • *2,488*
Dresslerville, NV 89410 • *180*
Drew, MS 38737 • *2,349*
Drew □, AR • *17,369*
Drexel, NC 28619 • *1,746*
Drexel, OH 45427 • *5,143*
Drexel Hill, PA 19026 • *29,744*
Dripping Springs, TX 78620 • *1,033*
Druid Hills, GA 30333 • *12,174*
Drumright, OK 74030 • *2,799*
Dryden, NY 13053 • *1,908*
Dry Ridge, KY 41035 • *1,601*
Duarte, CA 91010 • *20,688*
Dublin, CA 94568 • *23,229*
Dublin, GA 31021 • *16,312*
Dublin, OH 43017 • *16,366*
Dublin, PA 18917 • *1,985*
Dublin, TX 76446 • *3,190*
Dublin, VA 24084 • *2,012*
Du Bois, PA 15801 • *8,286*
Dubois, WY 82513 • *895*
Dubois □, IN • *36,616*
Duboistown, PA 17701 • *1,201*
Dubuque, IA 52001-04 • *57,546*
Dubuque □, IA • *86,403*
Duchesne, UT 84021 • *1,308*
Duchesne □, UT • *12,645*
Dudley, MA 01570-71 • *3,700*
Due West, SC 29639 • *1,220*
Dukes □, MA • *11,639*
Dulce, NM 87528 • *2,438*
Duluth, GA 30136 • *9,029*
Duluth, MN 55801-16 • *85,493*
Dumas, AR 71639 • *5,520*
Dumas, TX 79029 • *12,871*
Dumfries, VA 22026 • *4,282*
Dumont, NJ 07628 • *17,187*
Dunaire, GA 30032 • *7,170*
Dunbar, PA 15431 • *1,213*
Dunbar, WV 25064 • *8,697*
Duncan, OK 73533-34 • *21,732*
Duncan, SC 29334 • *2,152*
Duncan Falls, OH 43734 • *1,200*
Duncannon, PA 17020 • *1,450*
Duncansville, PA 16635 • *1,309*
Duncanville, TX 75116 • *35,748*
Dundalk, MD 21222 • *65,800*
Dundee, FL 33838 • *2,335*
Dundee, IL 60118 • *3,728*
Dundee, MI 48131 • *2,664*
Dundee, NY 14837 • *1,588*
Dundee, OR 97115 • *1,663*
Dundy □, NE • *2,582*
Dunedin, FL 34697-98 • *34,012*
Dunellen, NJ 08812 • *6,528*
Dunkirk, IN 47336 • *2,739*
Dunkirk, NY 14048 • *13,989*
Dunklin □, MO • *33,112*
Dunlap, IN 46514 • *5,705*
Dunlap, IA 51529 • *1,251*
Dunlap, TN 37327 • *3,731*
Dunleith, DE 19801 • *2,600*
Dunmore, PA 18512 • *15,403*
Dunn, NC 28334-35 • *8,336*
Dunn □, ND • *4,005*
Dunn □, WI • *35,909*
Dunnellon, FL 32630 • *1,624*
Dunn Loring Woods, VA 22180 • *2,800*
Dunseith, ND 58329 • *723*
Dunsmuir, CA 96025 • *2,129*
Dunwoody, GA 30338 • *26,302*
Du Page □, IL • *781,666*
Duplin □, NC • *39,995*
Dupont, CO 80024 • *5,200*
Dupont, PA 18641 • *2,984*
Dupont Manor, DE 19901 • *1,059*
Duquesne, PA 15110 • *8,525*
Du Quoin, IL 62832 • *6,697*
Durand, IL 61024 • *1,100*
Durand, MI 48429 • *4,283*
Durand, WI 54736 • *2,003*
Durango, CO 81301-02 • *12,430*
Durant, IA 52747 • *1,549*
Durant, MS 39063 • *2,838*
Durant, OK 74701-02 • *12,823*
Durham, CA 95938 • *1,500*
Durham, CT 06422 • *2,650*
Durham, NH 03824 • *9,236*
Durham, NC 27701-22 • *136,611*
Durham □, NC • *181,835*
Duryea, PA 18642 • *4,869*
Duson, LA 70529 • *1,465*
Dutchess □, NY • *259,462*
Duval □, FL • *672,971*
Duval □, TX • *12,918*
Duxbury, MA 02331-32 • *1,637*
Dwight, IL 60420 • *4,230*
Dyer, IN 46311 • *10,923*
Dyer, TN 38330 • *2,204*
Dyer □, TN • *34,854*
Dyersburg, TN 38024-25 • *16,317*
Dyersville, IA 52040 • *3,703*
Dysart, IA 52224 • *1,230*

E

Eagan, MN 55121 • *47,409*
Eagar, AZ 85925 • *4,025*
Eagle, CO 81631 • *1,580*
Eagle, ID 83616 • *3,327*
Eagle, NE 68347 • *1,047*
Eagle, WI 53119 • *1,182*
Eagle □, CO • *21,928*
Eagle Grove, IA 50533 • *3,671*
Eagle Lake, MN 56024 • *1,703*
Eagle Lake, TX 77434 • *3,551*
Eagle Lake, WI 53139 • *1,000*
Eagle Pass, TX 78852-53 • *20,651*
Eagle Point, OR 97524 • *3,008*
Eagle River, WI 54521 • *1,374*
Eagleton Village, TN 37801 • *5,331*
Earle, AR 72331 • *3,393*
Earlham, IA 50072 • *1,157*
Earlimart, CA 93219 • *5,881*

Earlington, KY 42410 • 1,833
Earlville, IL 60518 • 1,435
Early ☐, GA • 11,854
Earth, TX 79031 • 1,228
Easley, SC 29640–42 • 15,195
East Alton, IL 62024 • 7,063
East Arlington, VT 05252 • 600
East Aurora, NY 14052 • 6,647
East Bangor, PA 18013 • 1,006
East Barre, VT 05649 • 700
East Baton Rouge ☐, LA • 380,105
East Berlin, PA 17316 • 1,175
East Bernard, TX 77435 • 1,544
East Bethel, MN 55005 • 8,050
East Billerica, MA 01821 • 3,830
East Brady, PA 16028 • 1,047
East Brewton, AL 36426 • 2,579
East Bridgewater, MA 02333 • 3,270
East Brookfield, MA 01515 • 1,396
East Brooklyn, CT 06239 • 1,481
East Brunswick, NJ 08816 • 43,548
East Carbon, UT 84520 • 1,270
East Carroll ☐, LA • 9,709
Eastchester, NY 10709 • 18,537
East Chicago, IN 46312 • 33,892
East Cleveland, OH 44112 • 33,096
East Compton, CA 90221 • 7,967
East Dennis, MA 02641 • 1,500
East Detroit, MI 48021 • 35,283
East Douglas, MA 01516 • 1,945
East Dubuque, IL 61025 • 1,914
East Falmouth, MA 02536 • 5,577
East Farmingdale, NY 11735 • 4,510
East Feliciana ☐, LA • 19,211
East Flat Rock, NC 28726 • 3,218
East Gaffney, SC 29340 • 3,278
Eastgate, WA 98007 • 4,434
East Glenville, NY 12302 • 6,518
East Granby, CT 06026 • 1,200
East Grand Forks, MN 56721 • 8,658
East Grand Rapids, MI 49506 • 10,807
East Greenville, PA 18041 • 3,117
East Greenwich, RI 02818 • 11,865
East Half Hollow Hills, NY 11746 • 7,010
Eastham, MA 02642 • 1,150
East Hampton, CT 06424 • 2,167
Easthampton, MA 01027 • 15,580
East Hampton, NY 11937 • 1,402
East Hanover, NJ • 9,926
East Hartford, CT 06128 • 50,452
East Haven, CT 06512 • 26,144
East Helena, MT 59635 • 1,538
East Hemet, CA 92343 • 17,611
East Hills, NY 11576 • 6,746
East Islip, NY 11730 • 14,325
East Jordan, MI 49727 • 2,240
Eastlake, OH 44094 • 21,161
East La Mirada, CA 90638 • 9,367
Eastland, TX 76448 • 3,690
Eastland ☐, TX • 18,488
East Lansing, MI 48823–26 • 50,677
East Las Vegas, NM 89112 • 11,087
East Liverpool, OH 43920 • 13,654
East Longmeadow, MA 01028 • 12,905
East Los Angeles, CA 90022 • 126,379
East Lyme, CT 06333 • 1,200
Eastman, GA 31023 • 5,153
East Marietta, NJ 30062 • 11,900
East Marion, NY 11939 • 1,500
East Matunuck, RI 02879 • 500
East Meadow, NY 11554 • 36,609
East Middlebury, VT 05740 • 500
East Midvale, UT 84047 • 3,800
East Millinocket, ME 04430 • 2,075
East Moline, IL 61244 • 20,147
East Montpelier, VT 05651 • 600
East Naples, FL 33962 • 22,951
East Newark, NJ 07029 • 2,157
East Newnan, GA 30263 • 1,173
East Norriton, PA 19401 • 13,324
East Northport, NY 11731 • 20,411
Easton, MD 21601 • 9,372
Easton, PA 18042–44 • 26,276
East Orange, NJ 07017–19 • 73,552
East Orleans, MA 02643 • 1,850
Eastover, SC 29044 • 1,044
East Palatka, FL 32131 • 1,989
East Palestine, OH 44413 • 5,168
East Palo Alto, CA 94303 • 23,451
East Patchogue, NY 11772 • 20,195
East Pea Ridge, WV 25705 • 4,980
East Peoria, IL 61611 • 21,378
East Pepperell, MA 01463 • 2,296
East Petersburg, PA 17520 • 4,197
East Pittsburgh, PA 15112 • 2,160
Eastpoint, FL 32328 • 1,577
East Point, GA 30344 • 34,402
Eastport, ME 04631 • 1,965
Eastport, NY 11941 • 1,500
East Porterville, CA 93257 • 5,790
East Port Orchard, WA 98366 • 5,409
East Prairie, MO 63845 • 3,416
East Providence, RI 02914 • 50,380
East Quogue, NY 11942 • 4,372
East Richmond, CA 94805 • 5,100
East Ridge, TN 37412 • 21,101
East River, CT 06423 • 3,440
East Rochester, NY 14445 • 6,932
East Rockaway, NY 11518 • 10,152
East Rockingham, NC 28379 • 4,158
East Rutherford, NJ 07073 • 7,902
East Saint Louis, IL 62201–08 • 40,944
Eastsound, WA 98245 • 1,100
East Spencer, NC 28039 • 2,055
East Stroudsburg, PA 18301 • 8,781
East Tawas, MI 48730 • 2,887
East Templeton, MA 01438 • 1,300
East Troy, WI 53120 • 2,664
East Tustin, CA 92705 • 10,000
East Vestal, NY 13902 • 6,310
East View, WV 26301 • 1,222
East Walpole, MA 02032 • 3,760
East Wareham, MA 02538 • 1,500
East Washington, PA 15301 • 2,126
East Wenatchee, WA 98802 • 2,701
East Windsor, NJ 08520 • 15,000
Eastwood, MI 49001 • 6,340
Eastwood Hills, UT 84106 • 1,200
Eaton, CO 80615 • 1,959
Eaton, IN 47338 • 1,614
Eaton, OH 45320 • 7,396
Eaton ☐, MI • 92,879
Eaton Rapids, MI 48827 • 4,695

Eatonton, GA 31024 • 4,737
Eatontown, NJ 07724 • 13,800
Eatonville, WA 98328 • 1,374
Eau Claire, WI 54701–03 • 56,856
Eau Claire ☐, WI • 85,183
Ebensburg, PA 15931 • 3,872
Eccles, WV 25836 • 1,162
Echo Bay, NV 89040 • 120
Echols ☐, GA • 2,334
Eckhart Mines, MD 21528 • 1,333
Eclectic, AL 36024 • 1,087
Economy, PA 15005 • 9,519
Ecorse, MI 48229 • 12,180
Ector ☐, TX • 118,934
Edcouch, TX 78538 • 2,878
Eddy, NM • 48,605
Eddy ☐, ND • 2,951
Eddystone, PA 19013 • 2,446
Eddyville, IA 52553 • 1,010
Eddyville, KY 42038 • 1,889
Eden, NY 14057 • 3,088
Eden, NC 27288 • 15,238
Edenton, NC 27932 • 5,268
Edgar, WI 54426 • 1,318
Edgar ☐, IL • 19,595
Edgartown, MA 02539 • 3,062
Edgecombe ☐, NC • 56,558
Edgefield, SC 29824 • 2,563
Edgefield ☐, SC • 18,375
Edgeley, ND 58433 • 1,567
Edgemere, MD 21221 • 9,226
Edgemont, SD 57735 • 906
Edgemoor, DE 19802 • 5,853
Edgerton, KS 66021 • 1,244
Edgerton, MN 56128 • 1,106
Edgerton, OH 43517 • 1,896
Edgerton, WI 53534 • 4,254
Edgerton, WY 82635 • 247
Edgewater, AL 35224 • 1,120
Edgewater, CO 80214 • 4,613
Edgewater, FL 32132 • 6,337
Edgewater, MD 21037 • 1,600
Edgewater, NJ 07020 • 5,001
Edgewater Park, NJ 08010 • 8,388
Edgewood, IN 46011 • 2,057
Edgewood, KY 41017 • 8,143
Edgewood, MD • 3,470
Edgewood, MD 21040 • 23,903
Edgewood, OH 44004 • 5,189
Edgewood, PA 15218 • 3,581
Edgewood, WA 98372 • 2,650
Edgeworth, PA 15143 • 1,670
Edina, MN 55410 • 46,070
Edina, MO 63537 • 1,283
Edinboro, PA 16412 • 7,736
Edinburg, TX 78539–40 • 29,885
Edinburgh, IN 46124 • 4,536
Edison, GA 31746 • 1,182
Edison, NJ 08817–20 • 88,680
Edmond, OK 73034 • 52,315
Edmonds, WA 98020 • 30,744
Edmondson Heights, MD 21207 • 4,750
Edmonson ☐, KY • 10,357
Edmonton, KY 42129 • 1,477
Edmore, MI 48829 • 1,126
Edmunds ☐, SD • 4,356
Edna, TX 77957 • 5,343
Edwards, MS 39066 • 1,279
Edwards ☐, IL • 7,440
Edwards ☐, KS • 3,787
Edwards ☐, TX • 2,266
Edwardsburg, MI 49112 • 1,142
Edwardsville, IL 62025 • 14,579
Edwardsville, KS 66113 • 3,979
Edwardsville, PA 18704 • 5,399
Effingham, IL 62401 • 11,851
Effingham ☐, GA • 25,687
Effingham ☐, IL • 31,704
Egg Harbor City, NJ 08215 • 4,583
Egypt, MA 02066 • 1,100
Egypt Lake, FL 33614 • 14,580
Ehrenberg, AZ 85334 • 1,500
Elba, AL 36323 • 4,011
Elbert ☐, CO • 9,646
Elbert ☐, GA • 18,949
Elberta, GA 31093 • 1,559
Elberton, GA 30635 • 5,682
Elbow Lake, MN 56531 • 1,186
Elburn, IL 60119 • 1,275
El Cajon, CA 92019–22 • 88,693
El Campo, TX 77437 • 10,511
El Centro, CA 92243–44 • 31,384
El Cerrito, CA 94530 • 22,869
Eldersburg, MD 21784 • 9,720
Eldon, IA 52554 • 1,070
Eldon, MO 65026 • 4,419
Eldora, IA 50627 • 3,038
El Dorado, AR 71730–31 • 23,146
Eldorado, IL 62930 • 4,601
El Dorado, KS 67042 • 11,504
Eldorado, TX 76936 • 2,019
El Dorado ☐, CA • 125,995
El Dorado Hills, CA 95630 • 6,395
El Dorado Springs, MO 64744 • 3,830
Eldridge, IA 52748 • 3,378
Eleanor, WV 25070 • 1,256
Electra, TX 76360 • 3,113
Eleele, HI 96705 • 1,489
El Encanto Heights, CA 93117 • 7,700
Elfers, FL 34680 • 12,356
Elgin, IL 60120–23 • 77,010
Elgin, ND 58533 • 765
Elgin, OR 97827 • 1,586
Elgin, TX 78621 • 4,846
Elida, OH 45807 • 1,486
Elizabeth, NJ 07201–08 • 110,002
Elizabeth, PA 15037 • 1,486
Elizabeth City, NC 27909 • 14,292
Elizabethton, TN 37643–44 • 11,931
Elizabethtown, KY 42701–02 • 18,167
Elizabethtown, NC 28337 • 3,704
Elizabethtown, PA 17022 • 9,952
Elizabethville, PA 17023 • 1,467
Elk ☐, KS • 3,327
Elk ☐, PA • 34,878
Elkader, IA 52043 • 1,510
Elk City, OK 73644 • 10,118
Elk Grove, CA 95624 • 17,483
Elk Grove Village, IL 60009 • 33,429
Elkhart, IN 46514–17 • 43,627
Elkhart, KS 67950 • 2,318
Elkhart, TX 75839 • 1,076

Elkhart ☐, IN • 156,198
Elkhart Lake, WI 53020 • 1,019
Elkhorn, NE 68022 • 1,398
Elkhorn, WI 53121 • 5,337
Elkin, NC 28621 • 3,790
Elkins, WV 26241 • 7,420
Elkland, PA 16920 • 1,849
Elk Mountain, WY 82324 • 174
Elko, NV 89801–02 • 14,736
Elko ☐, NV • 33,530
Elk Point, SD 57025 • 1,423
Elk Rapids, MI 49629 • 1,626
Elkridge, MD 21227 • 12,953
Elk River, MN 55330 • 11,143
Elkton, KY 42220 • 1,789
Elkton, MD 21921–22 • 9,073
Elkton, VA 22827 • 1,935
Elkview, WV 25071 • 1,047
Ellaville, GA 31806 • 1,724
Ellendale, DE 19941 • 313
Ellendale, ND 58436 • 1,798
Ellensburg, WA 98926 • 12,361
Ellenton, FL 34222 • 2,573
Ellenville, NY 12428 • 4,243
Ellerbe, NC 28338 • 1,132
Ellerslie, MD 21529 • 1,500
Ellettsville, IN 47429 • 3,275
Ellicott City, MD 21043 • 41,396
Ellijay, GA 30540 • 1,178
Ellington, CT 06029 • 1,500
Ellinwood, KS 67526 • 2,329
Elliott ☐, KY • 6,455
Ellis, KS 67637 • 1,814
Ellis ☐, KS • 26,004
Ellis ☐, OK • 4,497
Ellis ☐, TX • 85,167
Ellisville, MS 39437 • 3,634
Ellisville, MO 63011 • 7,545
Ellport, PA 16117 • 1,243
Ellsworth, KS 67439 • 2,294
Ellsworth, ME 04605 • 5,975
Ellsworth, PA 15331 • 1,048
Ellsworth, WI 54011 • 2,706
Ellsworth ☐, KS • 6,586
Ellwood City, PA 16117 • 8,894
Elma, WA 98541 • 3,011
Elm City, NC 27822 • 1,624
Elmer, NJ 08318 • 1,571
Elm Grove, WI 53122 • 6,261
Elmhurst, IL 60126 • 42,029
Elmira, NY 14901–05 • 33,724
El Mirage, AZ 85335 • 5,001
Elmira Heights, NY 14903 • 4,359
Elmont, NY 11003 • 28,612
El Monte, CA 91731–34 • 106,209
Elmora, PA 15737 • 1,500
Elmore, OH 43416 • 1,334
Elmore ☐, AL • 49,210
Elmore ☐, ID • 21,205
Elmwood, IL 61529 • 1,841
Elmwood Park, IL 60635 • 23,206
Elmwood Park, NJ 07407 • 17,623
Elmwood Place, OH 45216 • 2,937
Eloise, FL 33880 • 1,408
Elon College, NC 27244 • 4,394
Eloy, AZ 85231 • 7,211
El Paso, IL 61738 • 2,499
El Paso, TX 79901–99 • 515,342
El Paso ☐, CO • 397,014
El Paso ☐, TX • 591,610
El Portal, FL 33138 • 2,457
El Reno, OK 73036 • 15,414
Elroy, WI 53929 • 1,533
Elsa, TX 78543 • 5,242
Elsberry, MO 63343 • 1,898
El Segundo, CA 90245 • 15,223
Elsmere, DE 19805 • 5,935
Elsmere, KY 41018 • 6,847
Elsmere, NY 12054 • 4,180
El Sobrante, CA 94803 • 9,852
Elton, LA 70532 • 1,277
El Toro, CA 92630 • 62,685
Elvins, MO 63601 • 1,391
Elwood, IN 46036 • 9,494
Elwood, KS 66024 • 1,079
Elwood, NJ 08217 • 1,400
Elwood, NY 11731 • 10,916
Ely, MN 55731 • 3,968
Ely, NV 89301 • 4,756
Elyria, OH 44035–39 • 56,746
Elysburg, PA 17824 • 1,890
Emanuel ☐, GA • 20,546
Emerson, GA 30137 • 1,201
Emerson, NJ 07630 • 6,930
Emery ☐, UT • 10,332
Eminence, KY 40019 • 2,055
Emmaus, PA 18049 • 11,157
Emmet ☐, IA • 11,569
Emmet ☐, MI • 25,040
Emmetsburg, IA 50536 • 3,940
Emmett, ID 83617 • 4,601
Emmitsburg, MD 21727 • 1,688
Emmonak, AK 99581 • 642
Emmons ☐, ND • 4,830
Empire, NV 89405 • 300
Emporia, KS 66801 • 25,512
Emporia, VA 23847 • 5,306
Emporium, PA 15834 • 2,513
Emsworth, PA 15202 • 2,892
Encampment, WY 82325 • 490
Encinitas, CA 92023–24 • 55,386
Enderlin, ND 58027 • 997
Endicott, NY 13760 • 13,531
Endwell, NY 13760 • 12,602
Enfield (Thompsonville), CT 06082–83 • 8,458
Enfield, NH 03748 • 1,560
Enfield, NC 27823 • 3,082
England, AR 72046 • 3,351
Engleside, VA 22309 • 24,058
Englewood, CO 80110–12 • 29,387
Englewood, FL 34223–24 • 15,025
Englewood, NJ 07631–32 • 24,850
Englewood, OH 45322 • 11,432
Englewood, TN 37329 • 1,611
Englewood Cliffs, NJ 07632 • 5,634
Englishtown, NJ 07726 • 1,268
Enid, OK 73701–06 • 45,309
Enka, NC 28728 • 5,567
Ennis, MT 59729 • 773
Ennis, TX 75119–20 • 13,883
Enoch, UT 84720 • 1,947
Enola, PA 17025 • 5,961

Enon, OH 45323 • 2,605
Enoree, SC 29335 • 1,107
Enosburg Falls, VT 05450 • 1,350
Ensley, FL 32504 • 16,362
Enterprise, AL 36330–31 • 20,123
Enterprise, OR 97828 • 1,905
Enterprise, WV 26568 • 1,058
Enumclaw, WA 98022 • 7,227
Ephraim, UT 84627 • 3,363
Ephrata, PA 17522 • 12,133
Ephrata, WA 98823 • 5,349
Epping, NH 03042 • 1,384
Epworth, IA 52045 • 1,297
Erath, LA 70533 • 2,428
Erath ☐, TX • 27,991
Erial, NJ 08081 • 2,500
Erick, OK 73645 • 1,083
Erie, CO 80516 • 1,258
Erie, IL 61250 • 1,572
Erie, KS 66733 • 1,276
Erie, PA 16501–65 • 108,718
Erie ☐, NY • 968,532
Erie ☐, OH • 76,779
Erie ☐, PA • 275,572
Erin, TN 37061 • 1,586
Erlanger, KY 41018 • 15,979
Erma, NJ 08204 • 2,045
Errol Heights, OR 97266 • 10,487
Erwin, NC 28339 • 4,061
Erwin, TN 37650 • 5,015
Escalon, CA 95320 • 4,437
Escambia ☐, AL • 35,518
Escambia ☐, FL • 262,798
Escanaba, MI 49829 • 13,659
Escatawpa, MS 39552 • 3,902
Escondido, CA 92025–27 • 108,635
Esmeralda ☐, NV • 1,344
Esmond, RI 02917 • 4,320
Espanola, NM 87532 • 8,389
Esparto, CA 95627 • 1,487
Esperance, NM 98043 • 11,236
Espy, PA 17815 • 1,430
Essex, CT 06426 • 2,500
Essex, MD 21221 • 40,872
Essex, MA 01929 • 1,507
Essex, VT 05451 • 800
Essex ☐, MA • 670,080
Essex ☐, NJ • 778,206
Essex ☐, NY • 37,152
Essex ☐, VT • 6,405
Essex ☐, VA • 8,689
Essex Fells, NJ 07021 • 2,363
Essex Junction, VT 05452–53 • 8,396
Essexville, MI 48732 • 4,088
Estacada, OR 97023 • 2,016
Estelle, LA 70072 • 14,091
Estell Manor, NJ 08319 • 1,404
Estes Park, CO 80517 • 3,184
Estherville, IA 51334 • 6,720
Estill, SC 29918 • 2,387
Estill ☐, KY • 14,614
Estill Springs, TN 37330 • 1,408
Etna, PA 15223 • 4,200
Etowah, TN 37331 • 3,815
Etowah ☐, AL • 99,840
Ettrick, VA 23803 • 5,290
Euclid, OH 44117 • 54,875
Eudora, AR 71640 • 3,155
Eudora, KS 66025 • 3,006
Eufaula, AL 36027 • 13,220
Eufaula, OK 74432 • 2,652
Eugene, OR 97401–05 • 112,669
Euless, TX 76039–40 • 38,149
Eunice, LA 70535 • 11,162
Eunice, NM 88231 • 2,676
Eupora, MS 39744 • 2,145
Eureka, CA 95501–02 • 27,025
Eureka, IL 61530 • 4,435
Eureka, KS 67045 • 2,974
Eureka, MO 63025 • 4,683
Eureka, MT 59917 • 1,043
Eureka, NV 89316 • 650
Eureka, SC 29706 • 1,738
Eureka, SD 57437 • 1,197
Eureka ☐, NV • 1,547
Eureka Springs, AR 72632 • 1,900
Eustis, FL 32726–27 • 12,967
Eutaw, AL 35462 • 2,281
Evangeline ☐, LA • 33,274
Evans, CO 80620 • 5,877
Evans, GA 30809 • 2,000
Evans ☐, GA • 8,724
Evans City, PA 16033 • 2,054
Evansdale, IA 50707 • 4,638
Evanston, IL 60201–04 • 73,233
Evanston, WY 82930–31 • 10,903
Evansville, IN 47701–37 • 126,272
Evansville, WI 53536 • 3,174
Evansville, WY 82636 • 1,403
Evart, MI 49631 • 1,744
Evarts, KY 40828 • 1,063
Eveleth, MN 55734 • 4,064
Everett, MA 02149 • 35,701
Everett, PA 15537 • 1,777
Everett, WA 98201–08 • 69,961
Evergreen, AL 36401 • 3,911
Evergreen, CO 80439 • 7,582
Evergreen Park, IL 60642 • 20,874
Everman, TX 76140 • 5,672
Everson, WA 98247 • 1,490
Ewa, HI 96706 • 3,780
Ewa Beach, HI 96706–07 • 14,315
Ewing Township, NJ 08618 • 34,185
Excelsior Springs, MO 64024 • 10,354
Exeter, CA 93221 • 7,276
Exeter, NH 03833 • 9,556
Exeter, PA 18643 • 5,691
Exmore, VA 23350 • 1,115
Experiment, GA 30223 • 3,762
Eyota, MN 55934 • 1,448

F

Fabens, TX 79838 • 5,599
Factoryville, PA 18419 • 1,310
Fairbank, IA 50629 • 1,018
Fairbanks, AK 99701 • 30,843
Fair Bluff, NC 28439 • 1,068
Fairborn, OH 45324 • 31,300
Fairburn, GA 30213 • 4,013
Fairbury, IL 61739 • 3,643

Fairbury, NE 68352 • 4,335
Fairchance, PA 15436 • 1,918
Fairdale, KY 40118 • 6,563
Fairfax, DE 19803 • 2,075
Fairfax, MN 55332 • 1,276
Fairfax, OK 74637 • 1,749
Fairfax, SC 29827 • 2,317
Fairfax, VA 22030–39 • 19,622
Fairfax ☐, VA • 818,584
Fairfield, AL 35064 • 12,200
Fairfield, CA 94533 • 77,211
Fairfield, CT 06430–32 • 53,418
Fairfield, IL 62837 • 5,439
Fairfield, IA 52556 • 9,768
Fairfield, ME 04937 • 2,794
Fairfield, NJ 07004 • 7,615
Fairfield, OH 45014 • 39,729
Fairfield, TX 75840 • 3,234
Fairfield ☐, CT • 827,645
Fairfield ☐, OH • 103,461
Fairfield ☐, SC • 22,295
Fairfield Bay, AR 72088 • 2,332
Fair Grove, NC 27360 • 1,500
Fairhaven, MA 02719 • 15,759
Fair Haven, NJ 07704 • 5,270
Fair Haven, VT 05743 • 2,432
Fairhope, AL 36532–33 • 8,485
Fair Lawn, NJ 07410 • 30,548
Fairlawn, OH 44313 • 5,779
Fairlawn, VA 24141 • 2,399
Fairlea, WV 24902 • 1,743
Fairless Hills, PA 19030 • 9,026
Fairmont, IL 60441 • 2,260
Fairmont, MN 56031 • 11,265
Fairmont, NC 28340 • 2,489
Fairmont, WV 26554–55 • 20,210
Fairmount, IN 46928 • 3,130
Fairmount, NY 13031 • 12,266
Fairmount Heights, MD 20743 • 1,238
Fair Oaks, CA 95628 • 26,867
Fair Oaks, GA 30060 • 6,996
Fairoaks, PA 15003 • 1,854
Fair Plain, MI 49022 • 8,051
Fairport, NY 14450 • 5,943
Fairport Harbor, OH 44077 • 2,978
Fairton, NJ 08320 • 1,359
Fairview, MT 59221 • 869
Fairview, NJ 07022 • 10,733
Fairview, OK 73737 • 2,936
Fairview, OR 97024 • 2,391
Fairview, PA 16415 • 1,988
Fairview, TN 37062 • 4,210
Fairview Heights, IL 62208 • 14,351
Fairview Park, IN 47842 • 1,446
Fairview Park, OH 44126 • 18,028
Fairview Shores, FL 32804 • 13,192
Fairway, KS 66205 • 4,173
Falcon Heights, MN 55113 • 5,380
Falfurrias, TX 78355 • 5,788
Falkville, AL 35622 • 1,337
Fall Branch, TN 37656 • 1,203
Fallbrook, CA 92028 • 22,095
Fall City, WA 98024 • 1,582
Fall Creek, WI 54742 • 1,034
Fallon, NV 89406 • 6,438
Fallon ☐, MT • 3,103
Fall River, MA 02720–26 • 92,703
Fall River ☐, SD • 7,353
Falls ☐, TX • 17,712
Falls Church, VA 22040–46 • 9,578
Falls City, NE 68355 • 4,769
Falls Creek, PA 15840 • 1,087
Fallston, MD 21047 • 5,700
Falls Township, PA 19054 • 36,083
Falmouth, KY 41040 • 2,378
Falmouth, MA 02540 • 7,610
Falmouth, ME 04105 • 7,610
Falmouth, MA 02540 • 4,047
Falmouth, VA 22405 • 3,541
Fannin ☐, GA • 15,992
Fannin ☐, TX • 24,804
Fanwood, NJ 07023 • 7,115
Fargo, ND 58102–09 • 74,111
Faribault, MN 55021 • 17,085
Faribault ☐, MN • 16,937
Farley, IA 52046 • 1,354
Farmer City, IL 61842 • 2,114
Farmers Branch, TX 75234 • 24,250
Farmersburg, IN 47850 • 1,159
Farmersville, CA 93223 • 6,235
Farmerville, LA 71241 • 3,334
Farmingdale, ME 04345 • 2,070
Farmingdale, NJ 07727 • 1,462
Farmingdale, NY 11735 • 8,022
Farmington, AR 72730 • 1,322
Farmington, CT 06032 • 2,500
Farmington, IL 61531 • 2,535
Farmington, ME 04938 • 4,197
Farmington, MI 48335–36 • 10,132
Farmington, MN 55024 • 5,940
Farmington, MO 63640 • 11,598
Farmington, NH 03835 • 3,567
Farmington, NM 87401–02 • 33,997
Farmington, UT 84025 • 9,028
Farmington Hills, MI 48331–34 • 74,652
Farmingville, NY 11738 • 14,842
Farmland, IN 47340 • 1,412
Farmville, NC 27828 • 4,392
Farmville, VA 23901 • 6,046
Farragut, TN 37922 • 12,793
Farrell, PA 16121 • 6,841
Farwell, TX 79325 • 1,373
Faulk ☐, SD • 2,744
Faulkland Heights, DE 19808 • 1,300
Faulkner ☐, AR • 60,006
Faulkton, SD 57438 • 809
Fauquier ☐, VA • 48,741
Fayette, AL 35555 • 4,909
Fayette, IA 52142 • 1,317
Fayette, MS 39069 • 1,853
Fayette, MO 65248 • 2,888
Fayette, OH 43521 • 1,248
Fayette ☐, AL • 17,962
Fayette ☐, GA • 62,415
Fayette ☐, IL • 20,893
Fayette ☐, IN • 26,015
Fayette ☐, IA • 21,843
Fayette ☐, KY • 225,366
Fayette ☐, OH • 27,466
Fayette ☐, PA • 145,351

Fayette □, TN • 25,559
Fayette □, TX • 20,095
Fayette □, WV • 47,952
Fayetteville, AR 72701-03 • 42,099
Fayetteville, GA 30214 • 5,827
Fayetteville, NC 28301-14 • 75,695
Fayetteville, PA 17222 • 3,033
Fayetteville, TN 37334 • 6,921
Fayetteville, WV 25840 • 2,182
Fayville, MA 01745 • 1,000
Federal Heights, CO 80221 • 9,342
Federalsburg, MD 21632 • 2,365
Federal Way, WA 98003 • 67,554
Feeding Hills, MA 01030 • 5,470
Fellowship, NJ 08057 • 4,250
Fellsmere, FL 32948 • 2,179
Felton, CA 95041 • 5,350
Felton, DE 19943 • 683
Fennimore, WI 53809 • 2,378
Fennville, MI 49408 • 1,023
Fenton, MI 48430 • 8,444
Fentress □, TN • 14,669
Ferdinand, IN 47532 • 2,318
Fergus □, MT • 12,083
Fergus Falls, MN 56537-38 • 12,362
Ferguson, MO 63135 • 22,286
Fernandina Beach, FL 32034 • 8,765
Fern Creek, KY 40291 • 16,406
Ferndale, CA 95536 • 1,331
Ferndale, MD 21061 • 16,355
Ferndale, MI 48220 • 25,084
Ferndale, PA 15905 • 2,020
Ferndale, WA 98248 • 5,398
Fernley, NV 89408 • 5,164
Fern Park, FL 32730 • 8,294
Fernway, PA 16063 • 9,072
Ferriday, LA 71334 • 4,111
Ferris, TX 75125 • 2,212
Ferron, UT 84523 • 1,606
Ferry □, WA • 6,295
Ferry Farms, VA 22405 • 1,600
Fessenden, ND 58438 • 655
Festus, MO 63028 • 8,105
Fieldale, VA 24089 • 1,018
Fig Garden, CA 93704 • 9,000
Filer, ID 83328 • 1,511
Fillmore, CA 93015-16 • 11,992
Fillmore, UT 84631 • 1,956
Fillmore □, MN • 20,777
Fillmore □, NE • 7,103
Findlay, OH 45839-40 • 35,703
Finley, ND 58030 • 1,014
Finney □, KS • 33,070
Fircrest, WA 98466 • 5,258
Firebaugh, CA 93622 • 4,429
Firestone, CO 80520 • 1,358
Fisher, IL 61843 • 1,526
Fisher □, TX • 4,842
Fishers, IN 46038 • 7,508
Fishkill, NY 12524 • 1,957
Fiskdale, MA 01518 • 2,189
Fitchburg, MA 01420 • 41,194
Fitzgerald, GA 31750 • 8,612
Five Points, NM 87105 • 4,200
Flagler □, FL • 28,701
Flagler Beach, FL 32136 • 3,820
Flagstaff, AZ 86001-16 • 45,857
Flanders, NJ 07836 • 3,040
Flandreau, SD 57028 • 2,311
Flathead □, MT • 59,218
Flatonia, TX 78941 • 1,295
Flat River, MO 63601 • 4,823
Flat Rock, MI 48134 • 7,290
Flat Rock, NC 28731 • 1,200
Flatwoods, KY 41139 • 7,799
Fleetwood, PA 19522 • 3,478
Fleming □, KY • 12,292
Flemingsburg, KY 41041 • 3,071
Flemington, NJ 08822 • 4,047
Flemington, PA 17745 • 1,321
Fletcher, NC 28732 • 2,787
Fletcher, OK 73541 • 1,002
Flint, MI 48501-32 • 140,761
Flint City, AL 35601 • 1,033
Flippin, AR 72634 • 1,006
Flomaton, AL 36441 • 1,811
Flora, IL 62839 • 5,054
Flora, IN 46929 • 2,179
Flora, MS 39071 • 1,482
Florala, AL 36442 • 2,075
Floral City, FL 32636 • 2,609
Floral Park, NY 11001-05 • 15,947
Florence, AZ 85232 • 7,510
Florence, AL 35630-33 • 36,426
Florence, AL 90001 • 43,900
Florence, CO 81226 • 2,990
Florence, KY 41042 • 18,624
Florence, MS 39073 • 1,831
Florence, NJ 08518 • 4,203
Florence, OR 97439 • 5,162
Florence, SC 29501-06 • 29,813
Florence □, SC • 114,344
Florence □, WI • 4,590
Floresville, TX 78114 • 5,247
Florham Park, NJ 07932 • 8,521
Florida, NY 10921 • 2,497
Florida City, FL 33034 • 5,806
Florida Ridge, FL 32960 • 12,218
Florin, CA 95828 • 24,330
Florissant, MO 63031-34 • 51,206
Floissant, IL 60422 • 8,651
Flower Hill, NY 11050 • 4,490
Flowery Branch, GA 30542 • 1,251
Flowood, MS 39208 • 2,860
Floyd □, GA • 81,251
Floyd □, IN • 64,404
Floyd □, IA • 17,058
Floyd □, KY • 43,586
Floyd □, TX • 8,497
Floyd □, VA • 12,005
Floydada, TX 79235 • 3,896
Flushing, MI 48433 • 8,542
Flushing, OH 43977 • 1,042
Fluvanna □, VA • 12,429
Foard □, TX • 1,794
Folcroft, PA 19032 • 7,506
Foley, AL 36535-36 • 4,937
Foley, MN 56329 • 1,854
Folkston, GA 31537 • 2,285
Follansbee, WV 26037 • 3,339
Folly Beach, SC 29439 • 1,398
Folsom, CA 95630 • 29,802
Folsom, NJ 08037 • 2,181

Fonda, NY 12068 • 1,007
Fond du Lac, WI 54935-36 • 37,757
Fond du Lac □, WI • 90,083
Fontana, CA 92334-36 • 87,535
Fontana, WI 53125 • 1,635
Foothill Farms, CA 95841 • 17,135
Ford □, IL • 14,275
Ford □, KS • 27,463
Ford City, CA 93268 • 3,781
Ford City, PA 16226 • 3,413
Ford Heights, IL 60411 • 4,259
Fords, NJ 08863 • 14,392
Fords Prairie, WA 98531 • 2,480
Fordyce, AR 71742 • 4,729
Foreman, AR 71836 • 1,267
Forest, MS 39074 • 5,060
Forest, OH 45843 • 1,594
Forest □, PA • 4,802
Forest □, WI • 8,776
Forest Acres, SC 29206 • 7,197
Forest City, IA 50436 • 4,430
Forest City, NC 28043 • 7,475
Forest City, PA 18421 • 1,846
Forestdale, AL 35214 • 10,395
Forestdale, RI 02824 • 530
Forest Dale, VT 05745 • 350
Forest Grove, OR 97116 • 13,559
Forest Hill, TX 76119 • 11,482
Forest Hills, PA 15221 • 7,335
Forest Knolls, CA 94933 • 2,000
Forest Lake, MN 55025 • 5,833
Forest Park, GA 30050-51 • 16,925
Forest Park, IL 60130 • 14,918
Forest Park, LA 71291 • 1,400
Forest Park, OH 45240 • 18,609
Forked River, NJ 08731 • 1,950
Forks, WA 98331 • 2,862
Forney, TX 75126 • 4,070
Forrest, IL 61741 • 1,124
Forrest □, MS • 68,314
Forrest City, AR 72335 • 13,364
Forreston, IL 61030 • 1,361
Forsyth, GA 31029 • 4,268
Forsyth □, GA 62535 • 1,275
Forsyth, MO 65653 • 1,175
Forsyth, MT 59327 • 2,178
Forsyth □, GA • 44,083
Forsyth □, NC • 265,878
Fort Ashby, WV 26719 • 1,288
Fort Atkinson, WI 53538 • 10,227
Fort Bend □, TX • 225,421
Fort Benton, MT 59442 • 1,660
Fort Bragg, CA 95437 • 6,078
Fort Branch, IN 47648 • 2,447
Fort Collins, CO 80521-26 • 87,758
Fort Covington, NY 12937 • 1,200
Fort Davis, TX 79734 • 1,100
Fort Defiance, AZ 86504 • 4,489
Fort Deposit, AL 36032 • 1,240
Fort Dodge, IA 50501 • 25,894
Fort Edward, NY 12828 • 3,561
Fort Fairfield, ME 04742 • 1,729
Fort Gaines, GA 31751 • 1,248
Fort Gibson, OK 74434 • 3,359
Fort Hall, ID 83203 • 2,681
Fort Kent, ME 04743 • 2,123
Fort Laramie, WY 82212 • 243
Fort Lauderdale, FL 33301-51 • 149,377
Fort Lee, NJ 07024 • 31,997
Fort Loramie, OH 45845 • 1,042
Fort Loudon, PA 17224 • 1,200
Fort Lupton, CO 80621 • 5,159
Fort Madison, IA 52627 • 11,618
Fort McKinley, OH 45426 • 9,740
Fort Meade, FL 33841 • 4,976
Fort Mill, SC 29715 • 4,930
Fort Mitchell, KY 41017 • 7,438
Fort Morgan, CO 80701 • 9,068
Fort Myers, FL 33901-19 • 45,206
Fort Myers Beach, FL 33931-32 • 9,284
Fort Myers Shores, FL 33905 • 5,460
Fort Oglethorpe, GA 30742 • 5,880
Fort Payne, AL 35967 • 11,838
Fort Pierce, FL 34945-54 • 36,830
Fort Pierre, SD 57532 • 1,854
Fort Plain, NY 13339 • 2,416
Fort Recovery, OH 45846 • 1,313
Fort Scott, KS 66701 • 8,362
Fort Shawnee, OH 45804 • 4,128
Fort Smith, AR 72901-17 • 72,798
Fort Stockton, TX 79735 • 8,524
Fort Sumner, NM 88119 • 1,269
Fort Thomas, KY 41075 • 16,032
Fortuna, CA 95540 • 8,788
Fort Valley, GA 31030 • 8,198
Fortville, IN 46040 • 2,690
Fort Walton Beach, FL 32547-48 • 21,471
Fort Washington Forest, MD 20744 • 1,010
Fort Wayne, IN 46801-99 • 173,072
Fort Wingate, NM 87316 • 950
Fort Worth, TX 76101-85 • 447,619
Fort Wright, KY 41011 • 6,570
Forty Fort, PA 18704 • 5,049
Fort Yukon, AK 99740 • 580
Fosston, MN 56542 • 1,529
Foster □, ND • 3,983
Foster City, CA 94404 • 28,176
Foster Village, HI 96818 • 3,700
Fostoria, OH 44830 • 14,983
Fountain, CO 80817 • 9,984
Fountain □, IN • 17,808
Fountain Hill, PA 18015 • 4,637
Fountain Inn, SC 29644 • 4,388
Fountain Place, LA • 9,200
Fountain Valley, CA 92708 • 53,691
Four Corners, OR 97301 • 12,156
Four Oaks, NC 27524 • 1,308
Fowler, CA 93625 • 3,208
Fowler, CO 81039 • 1,154
Fowler, IN 47944 • 2,333
Fowlerville, MI 48836 • 2,648
Foxboro, MA 02035 • 5,706
Fox Chapel, PA 15238 • 5,319
Fox Lake, IL 60020 • 7,478
Fox Lake, WI 53933 • 1,269
Fox Point, WI 53217 • 7,238
Fox River Grove, IL 60021 • 3,551
Frackville, PA 17931 • 4,700
Framingham, MA 01701 • 64,994
Franconia, VA 22310 • 19,882
Frankenmuth, MI 48734 • 4,408
Frankford, DE 19945 • 591
Frankfort, IL 60423 • 7,180

Frankfort, IN 46041 • 14,754
Frankfort, KY 40601-22 • 25,968
Frankfort, MI 49635 • 1,546
Frankfort, NY 13340 • 2,693
Frankfort, OH 45628 • 1,065
Franklin, KY 42134-35 • 7,607
Franklin, LA 70538 • 9,004
Franklin, MA 02038 • 9,965
Franklin, NH 03235 • 8,304
Franklin, NJ 07416 • 4,977
Franklin, NC 28734 • 2,873
Franklin, OH 45005 • 11,026
Franklin, PA 16323 • 7,329
Franklin, TN 37064-65 • 20,098
Franklin, TX 77856 • 1,336
Franklin, VA 23851 • 7,864
Franklin, WI 53132 • 21,855
Franklin □, AL • 27,814
Franklin □, AR • 14,897
Franklin □, FL • 8,967
Franklin □, GA • 16,650
Franklin □, ID • 9,232
Franklin □, IL • 40,319
Franklin □, IN • 19,580
Franklin □, IA • 11,364
Franklin □, KS • 21,994
Franklin □, KY • 43,781
Franklin □, LA • 22,387
Franklin □, ME • 29,008
Franklin □, MA • 70,092
Franklin □, MS • 8,377
Franklin □, MO • 80,603
Franklin □, NE • 3,938
Franklin □, NY • 46,540
Franklin □, NC • 36,414
Franklin □, OH • 961,437
Franklin □, PA • 121,082
Franklin □, TN • 34,725
Franklin □, TX • 7,802
Franklin □, VT • 39,980
Franklin □, VA • 39,549
Franklin □, WA • 37,473
Franklin Lakes, NJ 07417 • 9,873
Franklin Park, IL 60131 • 18,485
Franklin Park, PA 15143 • 10,109
Franklin Square, NY 11010 • 28,205
Franklinton, LA 70438 • 4,007
Franklinton, NC 27525 • 1,615
Franklinville, NJ 08322 • 1,020
Franklinville, NY 14737 • 1,739
Frankston, TX 75763 • 1,127
Frankton, IN 46044 • 1,736
Fraser, MI 48026 • 13,899
Frazee, MN 56544 • 1,176
Frazeysburg, OH 43822 • 1,165
Frazier Park, CA 93225 • 2,201
Frederic, WI 54837 • 1,124
Frederica, DE 19946 • 761
Frederick, MD 21701-02 • 40,148
Frederick, OK 73542 • 5,221
Frederick □, MD • 150,208
Frederick □, VA • 45,723
Fredericksburg, IA 50630 • 1,011
Fredericksburg, TX 78624 • 6,934
Fredericksburg, VA 22401-08 • 19,027
Fredericktown, MO 63645 • 3,950
Fredericktown, OH 43019 • 2,443
Fredericktown, PA 15333 • 1,052
Fredonia, AZ 86022 • 1,207
Fredonia, KS 66736 • 2,599
Fredonia, NY 14063 • 10,436
Fredonia, WI 53021 • 1,558
Freeborn □, MN • 33,060
Freeburg, IL 62243 • 3,115
Freedom, CA 95019 • 8,361
Freedom, PA 15042 • 1,897
Freedom, WY 83120 • 450
Freehold, NJ 07728 • 10,742
Freeland, MI 48623 • 1,421
Freeland, PA 18224 • 3,909
Freeman, SD 57029 • 1,293
Freeport, IL 61032 • 25,840
Freeport, ME 04032 • 1,829
Freeport, NY 11520 • 39,894
Freeport, PA 16229 • 1,983
Freeport, TX 77541 • 11,389
Freer, TX 78357 • 3,271
Freestone □, TX • 15,818
Fremont, CA 94536-39 • 173,339
Fremont, IN 46737 • 1,407
Fremont, MI 49412 • 3,875
Fremont, NE 68025 • 23,680
Fremont, NC 27830 • 1,710
Fremont, OH 43420 • 17,648
Fremont □, CO • 32,273
Fremont □, ID • 10,937
Fremont □, IA • 8,226
Fremont □, WY • 33,662
French Island, WI 54601 • 4,478
French Lick, IN 47432 • 2,087
Frenchtown, NJ 08825 • 1,528
Fresno, CA 93701-94 • 354,202
Fresno □, CA • 667,490
Frewsburg, NY 14738 • 1,317
Friars Point, MS 38631 • 1,334
Friday Harbor, WA 98250 • 1,492
Fridley, MN 55432 • 28,335
Friend, NE 68359 • 1,111
Friendship, NY 14739 • 1,423
Friendswood, TX 77546 • 22,814
Frio □, TX • 13,472
Friona, TX 79035 • 3,688
Frisco, CO 80443 • 1,601
Frisco City, AL 36445 • 1,581
Fritch, TX 79036 • 2,335
Frontenac, KS 66762 • 2,588
Frontier □, NE • 3,101
Front Royal, VA 22630 • 11,880
Frostburg, MD 21532 • 8,075
Frostproof, FL 33843 • 2,808
Fruita, CO 81521 • 4,045
Fruit Heights, UT 84037 • 3,900
Fruitland, ID 83619 • 2,400
Fruitland, MD 21826 • 3,511
Fruitland Park, FL 34731 • 2,754
Fruitport, MI 49415 • 1,090
Fruitvale, CO 81504 • 1,570
Fruitvale, WA 98902 • 4,125
Fruitville, FL 34232 • 9,808
Fryeburg, ME 04037 • 1,580

Fulda, MN 56131 • 1,212
Fullerton, CA 92631-35 • 114,144
Fullerton, NE 68638 • 1,452
Fulton, IL 61252 • 3,698
Fulton, KY 42041 • 3,078
Fulton, MS 38843 • 3,387
Fulton, MO 65251 • 10,033
Fulton, NY 13069 • 12,929
Fulton □, AR • 10,037
Fulton □, GA • 648,951
Fulton □, IL • 38,080
Fulton □, IN • 18,840
Fulton □, KY • 8,271
Fulton □, NY • 54,191
Fulton □, OH • 38,498
Fulton □, PA • 13,837
Fultondale, AL 35068 • 6,400
Funkstown, MD 21734 • 1,136
Fuquay-Varina, NC 27526 • 4,562
Furnas □, NE • 5,553
Fyffe, AL 35971 • 1,094

G

Gabbs, NV 89409 • 667
Gadsden, AL 35901-05 • 42,523
Gadsden □, FL • 41,105
Gaffney, SC 29340-42 • 13,145
Gage □, NE • 22,794
Gages Lake, IL 60030 • 8,349
Gahanna, OH 43230 • 27,791
Gaines □, TX • 14,123
Gainesboro, TN 38562 • 1,002
Gainesville, FL 32601-14 • 84,770
Gainesville, GA 30501-07 • 17,885
Gainesville, TX 76240 • 14,256
Gaithersburg, MD 20877-79 • 39,542
Galax, VA 24333 • 6,670
Galena, AK 99741 • 833
Galena, IL 61036 • 3,647
Galena, KS 66739 • 3,308
Galesburg, IL 61401-02 • 33,530
Galesburg, MI 49053 • 1,863
Gales Ferry, CT 06335 • 1,191
Galesville, WI 54630 • 1,278
Galeton, PA 16922 • 1,370
Galeville, NY 13088 • 4,695
Galion, OH 44833 • 11,859
Gallatin, MO 64640 • 1,864
Gallatin, TN 37066 • 18,794
Gallatin □, IL • 6,909
Gallatin □, KY • 5,393
Gallatin □, MT • 50,463
Gallia □, OH • 30,954
Galliano, LA 70354 • 4,294
Gallipolis, OH 45631 • 4,831
Gallitzin, PA 16641 • 2,003
Gallup, NM 87301-05 • 19,154
Galt, CA 95632 • 8,889
Galva, IL 61434 • 2,742
Galveston, IN 46932 • 1,609
Galveston, TX 77550-54 • 59,070
Galveston □, TX • 217,399
Gambell, AK 99742 • 525
Gambier, OH 43022 • 2,073
Gambrills, MD 21054 • 1,200
Ganado, AZ 86505 • 3,400
Ganado, TX 77962 • 1,701
Gang Mills, NY 14870 • 2,738
Gantt, SC 29605 • 13,891
Gap, PA 17527 • 1,200
Garberville, CA 95440 • 1,200
Garden □, NE • 2,460
Gardena, CA 90247-49 • 49,847
Garden City, GA 31408 • 7,410
Garden City, ID 83704 • 6,369
Garden City, KS 67846 • 24,097
Garden City, MI 48135-36 • 31,846
Garden City, NY 11530 • 21,686
Garden City Park, NY 11040 • 7,437
Garden Grove, CA 92640-45 • 143,050
Garden Home, OR 97223 • 5,500
Gardiner, ME 04345 • 6,746
Gardner, IL 60424 • 1,237
Gardner, KS 66030 • 3,191
Gardner, MA 01440 • 20,125
Gardnerville, NV 89410 • 2,177
Gardnerville Ranchos, NV 89410 • 7,455
Garfield, NJ 07026 • 26,727
Garfield □, CO • 29,974
Garfield □, MT • 1,589
Garfield □, NE • 2,141
Garfield □, OK • 56,735
Garfield □, UT • 3,980
Garfield □, WA • 2,248
Garfield Heights, OH 44125 • 31,739
Garfield Park, DE 19720 • 1,415
Garland, TX 75040-48 • 180,650
Garland, UT 84312 • 1,637
Garland □, AR • 73,397
Garner, IA 50438 • 2,916
Garner, NC 27529 • 14,967
Garnett, KS 66032 • 3,210
Garrard □, KY • 11,579
Garretson, SD 57030 • 924
Garrett, IN 46738 • 5,349
Garrett □, MD • 28,138
Garrettsville, OH 44231 • 2,014
Garrison, ND 21055 • 5,045
Garrison, ND 58540 • 1,530
Garvin □, OK • 26,605
Garwood, NJ 07027 • 4,227
Gary, IN 46401-11 • 116,646
Gary, WV 24836 • 1,355
Garysburg, NC 27831 • 1,057
Garyville, LA 70051 • 3,181
Garza □, TX • 5,143
Gas City, IN 46933 • 6,296
Gasconade □, MO • 14,006
Gasport, NY 14067 • 1,336
Gassville, AR 72635 • 1,167
Gaston, NC 27832 • 1,068
Gaston □, NC • 175,093
Gastonia, NC 28051-56 • 54,732
Gate City, VA 24251 • 2,214
Gates, NY 14624 • 30,000
Gates □, NC • 9,305
Gatesville, TX 76528 • 11,492
Gatlinburg, TN 37738 • 3,417

Gautier, MS 39553 • 10,088
Gaylord, MI 49735 • 3,256
Gaylord, MN 55334 • 1,935
Gearhart, OR 97138 • 1,027
Geary, OK 73040 • 1,347
Geary □, KS • 30,453
Geauga □, OH • 81,129
Gem □, ID • 11,844
Genesee, ID 83832 • 725
Genesee, MI 48437 • 1,400
Genesee □, MI • 430,459
Genesee □, NY • 60,060
Geneseo, IL 61254 • 5,990
Geneseo, NY 14454 • 7,187
Geneva, AL 36340 • 4,681
Geneva, IL 60134 • 12,617
Geneva, IN 46740 • 1,280
Geneva, NE 68361 • 2,310
Geneva, NY 14456 • 14,143
Geneva, OH 44041 • 6,597
Geneva □, AL • 23,647
Geneva-on-the-Lake, OH 44041 • 1,626
Genoa, IL 60135 • 3,083
Genoa, NE 68640 • 1,082
Genoa, NV 89411 • 190
Genoa □, OH 43430 • 2,262
Genoa City, WI 53128 • 1,277
Gentry, AR 72734 • 1,726
Gentry □, MO • 6,848
George, IA 51237 • 1,066
George □, MS • 16,673
Georgetown, CA 95634 • 2,000
Georgetown, CT 06829 • 1,694
Georgetown, DE 19947 • 3,732
Georgetown, IL 61846 • 3,678
Georgetown, IN 47122 • 2,092
Georgetown, KY 40324 • 11,414
Georgetown, MA 01833 • 2,100
Georgetown, OH 45121 • 3,627
Georgetown, SC 29440-42 • 9,517
Georgetown, TX 78626-28 • 14,842
Georgetown □, SC • 46,302
George West, TX 78022 • 2,586
Georgiana, AL 36033 • 1,933
Gering, NE 69341 • 7,946
Gerlach, NV 89412 • 200
Germantown, IL 62245 • 1,167
Germantown, MD 20874 • 41,145
Germantown, OH 45327 • 4,916
Germantown, TN 38138 • 32,893
Germantown, WI 53022 • 13,658
Gettysburg, PA 17325 • 7,025
Gettysburg, SD 57442 • 1,510
Giants Neck, CT 06357 • 1,200
Gibbon, NE 68840 • 1,525
Gibbstown, NJ 08027 • 5,404
Gibsland, LA 71028 • 1,224
Gibson □, IN • 31,913
Gibson □, TN • 46,315
Gibsonburg, OH 43431 • 2,579
Gibson City, IL 60936 • 3,396
Gibsonia, FL 33805 • 5,168
Gibsonia, PA 15044 • 3,500
Gibsonton, FL 33534 • 7,706
Gibsonville, NC 27249 • 3,441
Giddings, TX 78942 • 4,093
Gideon, MO 63848 • 1,112
Gifford, FL 32960 • 6,278
Gig Harbor, WA 98335 • 3,236
Gila □, AZ • 40,216
Gila Bend, AZ 85337 • 1,747
Gilbert, AZ 85234 • 29,188
Gilbert, MN 55741 • 1,934
Gilbert, OR 97266 • 4,000
Gilbertsville, PA 19525 • 3,994
Gilbertville, MA 01031 • 1,029
Gilchrist □, FL • 9,667
Gilcrest, CO 80623 • 1,084
Giles □, TN • 25,741
Giles □, VA • 16,366
Gilford Park, NJ 08753 • 8,668
Gillespie, IL 62033 • 3,645
Gillespie □, TX • 17,204
Gillett, WI 54124 • 1,303
Gillette, WY 82716-17 • 17,635
Gilliam □, OR • 1,717
Gilman, IL 60938 • 1,816
Gilman, VT 05904 • 500
Gilmer, TX 75644 • 4,822
Gilmer □, GA • 13,368
Gilmer □, WV • 7,669
Gilpin □, CO • 3,070
Gilroy, CA 95020-21 • 31,487
Girard, IL 62640 • 2,164
Girard, KS 66743 • 2,794
Girard, OH 44420 • 11,304
Girard, PA 16417 • 2,879
Girardville, PA 17935 • 1,889
Glacier □, MT • 12,121
Glades □, FL • 7,591
Glade Spring, VA 24340 • 1,435
Gladeview, FL 33138 • 15,637
Gladewater, TX 75647 • 6,027
Gladstone, MI 49837 • 4,565
Gladstone, MO 64118 • 26,243
Gladstone, NY 12432 • 1,538
Gladstone, OR 97027 • 10,152
Gladwin, MI 48624 • 2,682
Gladwin □, MI • 21,896
Glasco, NY 12432 • 1,538
Glascock □, GA • 2,357
Glasford, IL 61533 • 1,115
Glasgow, KY 42141-42 • 12,351
Glasgow, MO 65254 • 1,295
Glasgow, MT 59230 • 3,572
Glasgow, VA 24555 • 1,140
Glasgow Village, MO 63137 • 5,199
Glassboro, NJ 08028 • 15,614
Glascock □, TX • 1,447
Glassport, PA 15045 • 5,582
Glastonbury, CT 06033 • 7,082
Gleason, TN 38229 • 1,402
Glen Allen, VA 23060 • 9,010
Glen Avon, CA • 12,663
Glenbrook, NV 89413 • 400
Glen Burnie, MD 21061 • 37,305
Glen Burnie Park, MD 21061 • 3,260
Glen Carbon, IL 62034 • 7,731
Glencoe, AL 35905 • 4,670
Glencoe, IL 60022 • 8,499
Glencoe, MN 55336 • 4,648
Glen Cove, NY 11542 • 24,149

Glendale, AZ 85301-12 • 148,134
Glendale, CA 91201-14 • 180,038
Glendale, CO 80222 • 2,453
Glendale, MS 39401 • 1,329
Glendale, MO 63122 • 5,945
Glendale, OH 45246 • 2,445
Glendale, RI 02826 • 700
Glendale, SC 29346 • 1,049
Glen Dale, WV 26038 • 1,612
Glendale, WI 53209 • 14,088
Glendale Heights, IL 60139 • 27,973
Glendive, MT 59330 • 4,802
Glendo, WY 82213 • 195
Glendola, NJ 07719 • 2,340
Glendora, CA 91740 • 47,828
Glendora, NJ 08029 • 5,201
Glen Ellyn, IL 60137-38 • 24,944
Glen Gardner, NJ 08826 • 1,665
Glenham, NY 12527 • 2,832
Glen Head, NY 11545 • 6,870
Glen Lyon, PA 18617 • 2,082
Glenmora, LA 71433 • 1,686
Glenn □, CA • 24,798
Glennallen, AK 99588 • 451
Glenn Dale, MD 20769 • 9,689
Glenns Ferry, ID 83623 • 1,304
Glennville, GA 30427 • 3,676
Glenolden, PA 19036 • 7,260
Glenpool, OK 74033 • 6,688
Glen Raven, NC 27215 • 2,616
Glen Ridge, NJ 07028 • 7,076
Glen Rock, NJ 07452 • 10,883
Glen Rock, PA 17327 • 1,688
Glenrock, WY 82637 • 2,153
Glen Rose, TX 76043 • 1,949
Glens Falls, NY 12801 • 15,023
Glenside, PA 19038 • 8,704
Glen Ullin, ND 58631 • 927
Glenview, IL 60025 • 37,093
Glenville, WV 26351 • 1,923
Glenwood, AR 71943 • 1,354
Glenwood, IL 60425 • 9,289
Glenwood, IA 51534 • 4,571
Glenwood, MN 56334 • 2,573
Glenwood, VA 24541 • 2,276
Glenwood City, WI 54013 • 1,026
Glenwood Farms, VA 23223 • 3,200
Glenwood Hills, GA 30032 • 5,240
Glenwood Springs, CO 81601-02 • 6,561
Glidden, IA 51443 • 1,099
Globe, AZ 85501-02 • 6,062
Gloster, MS 39638 • 1,323
Gloucester, MA 01930-31 • 28,716
Gloucester, VA 23061 • 1,200
Gloucester □, NJ • 230,082
Gloucester □, VA • 30,131
Gloucester City, NJ 08030 • 12,649
Gloucester Point, VA 23062 • 8,509
Glouster, OH 45732 • 2,001
Gloversville, NY 12078 • 16,656
Gloverville, SC 29828 • 2,753
Glynn □, GA • 62,496
Gnadenhutten, OH 44629 • 1,226
Goddard, KS 67052 • 1,804
Godfrey, IL 62035 • 5,436
Goffstown, NH 03045 • 2,700
Gogebic □, MI • 18,052
Golconda, NV 89414 • 200
Gold Bar, WA 98251 • 1,078
Gold Beach, OR 97444 • 1,546
Golden, CO 80401-03 • 13,116
Goldendale, WA 98620 • 3,319
Golden Gate, FL 33999 • 14,148
Golden Glades, FL 33055 • 25,474
Golden Meadow, LA 70357 • 2,049
Golden Valley, MN 55427 • 20,971
Golden Valley □, MT • 912
Golden Valley □, ND • 2,108
Goldfield, NV 89013 • 600
Goldsboro, NC 27530-34 • 40,709
Goldthwaite, TX 76844 • 1,658
Goleta, CA 93117 • 28,600
Golf Manor, OH 45237 • 4,154
Goliad, TX 77963 • 1,946
Goliad □, TX • 5,980
Gonzales, CA 93926 • 4,660
Gonzales, LA 70737 • 7,003
Gonzales, TX 78629 • 6,527
Gonzales □, TX • 17,205
Gonzalez, FL 32560 • 7,669
Goochland □, VA • 14,163
Goodhue □, MN • 40,690
Gooding, ID 83330 • 2,820
Gooding □, ID • 11,633
Goodland, FL 33933 • 1,000
Goodland, IN 47948 • 1,033
Goodland, KS 67735 • 4,983
Goodlettsville, TN 37072 • 11,219
Goodman, MS 39079 • 1,256
Goodman, MO 64843 • 1,094
Goodsprings, NV 89019 • 150
Goodview, MN 55987 • 2,878
Goodwater, AL 35072 • 1,840
Goodwell, OK 73939 • 1,065
Goodyear, AZ 85338 • 6,258
Goose Creek, SC 29445 • 24,692
Gordo, AL 35466 • 1,918
Gordon, GA 31031 • 2,468
Gordon, NE 69343 • 1,803
Gordon □, GA • 35,072
Gordonsville, VA 22942 • 1,351
Gorham, ME 04038 • 3,618
Gorham, NH 03581 • 1,910
Gorman, TX 76454 • 1,290
Goshen, IN 46526 • 23,797
Goshen, NY 10924 • 5,255
Goshen, OH 45122 • 1,400
Goshen □, WY • 12,373
Gosnell, AR 72319 • 3,783
Gosper □, NE • 1,928
Gothenburg, NE 69138 • 3,232
Gould, AR 71643 • 1,470
Goulding, FL 32503 • 4,159
Goulds, FL 33170 • 7,284
Gouverneur, NY 13642 • 4,604
Gove □, KS • 3,231
Gowanda, NY 14070 • 2,901
Gower, MO 64454 • 1,249
Gowrie, IA 50543 • 1,028
Grace, ID 83241 • 973
Graceville, FL 32440 • 2,675
Gracewood, GA 30812 • 1,000
Grady □, GA • 20,279
Grady □, OK • 41,747
Grafton, MA 01519 • 1,520
Grafton, ND 58237 • 4,840
Grafton, OH 44044 • 3,344
Grafton, WV 26354 • 5,524
Grafton, WI 53024 • 9,340
Grafton □, NH • 74,929
Graham, CA 90002 • 10,600
Graham, NC 27253 • 10,426
Graham, TX 76046 • 8,986
Graham □, AZ • 26,554
Graham □, KS • 3,543
Graham □, NC • 7,196
Grainger □, TN • 17,095
Grain Valley, MO 64029 • 1,898
Grambling, LA 71245 • 5,484
Gramercy, LA 70052 • 2,412
Granbury, TX 76048-49 • 4,045
Granby, CT 06035 • 9,369
Granby, MA 01033 • 1,327
Granby, MO 64844 • 1,945
Grand □, CO • 7,966
Grand □, UT • 6,620
Grand Bay, AL 36541 • 3,383
Grand Blanc, MI 48439 • 7,760
Grand Caillou, LA 70360 • 1,400
Grand Canyon, AZ 86023 • 1,499
Grand Coteau, LA 70541 • 1,118
Grandfield, OK 73546 • 1,224
Grand Forks, ND 58201-06 • 49,425
Grand Forks □, ND • 70,683
Grand Haven, MI 49417 • 11,951
Grand Island, NE 68801-03 • 39,386
Grand Isle, LA 70358 • 1,455
Grand Isle □, VT • 5,318
Grand Junction, CO 81501-06 • 29,034
Grand Ledge, MI 48837 • 7,579
Grand Marais, MN 55604 • 1,171
Grand Prairie, TX 75050-54 • 99,616
Grand Rapids, MI 49501-99 • 189,126
Grand Rapids, MN 55744 • 7,976
Grand Saline, TX 75140 • 2,630
Grand Terrace, CA 92324 • 10,946
Grand Traverse □, MI • 64,273
Grandview, MO 64030 • 24,967
Grandview, WA 98930 • 7,169
Grandview Heights, OH 43212 • 7,010
Grandville, MI 49418 • 15,624
Granger, IN 46530 • 20,241
Granger, TX 76530 • 1,190
Granger, WA 98932 • 2,053
Grangeville, ID 83530 • 3,226
Granite, OK 73547 • 1,844
Granite □, MT • 2,548
Granite City, IL 62040 • 32,862
Granite Falls, MN 56241 • 3,083
Granite Falls, NC 28630 • 3,253
Granite Falls, WA 98252 • 1,060
Granite Quarry, NC 28072 • 1,646
Graniteville, MA 01886 • 1,010
Graniteville, SC 29829 • 1,158
Graniteville, VT 05654 • 500
Grant, NE 69140 • 1,239
Grant □, AR • 13,948
Grant □, IN • 74,169
Grant □, KS • 7,159
Grant □, KY • 15,737
Grant □, LA • 17,526
Grant □, MN • 6,246
Grant □, NE • 769
Grant □, NM • 27,676
Grant □, ND • 3,549
Grant □, OK • 5,689
Grant □, OR • 7,853
Grant □, SD • 8,372
Grant □, WA • 54,758
Grant □, WV • 10,428
Grant □, WI • 49,264
Grant Park, IL 60940 • 1,024
Grants, NM 87020 • 8,626
Grantsburg, WI 54840 • 1,144
Grants Pass, OR 97526-27 • 17,488
Grantsville, UT 84029 • 4,500
Grantville, GA 30220 • 1,180
Granville, IL 61326 • 1,407
Granville, NY 12832 • 2,646
Granville, OH 43023 • 4,353
Granville □, NC • 38,345
Grapeland, TX 75844 • 1,450
Grapevine, TX 76051 • 29,202
Grasonville, MD 21638 • 2,439
Grass Lake, IL 60002 • 2,191
Grass Valley, CA 95945 • 9,048
Gratiot □, MI • 38,982
Graves □, KY • 33,550
Gravette, AR 72736 • 1,412
Gray, GA 31032 • 2,189
Gray, LA 70359 • 1,500
Gray □, KS • 5,396
Gray □, TX • 23,967
Grayling, MI 49738 • 1,944
Graylyn Crest, DE 19810 • 4,380
Grays Harbor □, WA • 64,175
Grayslake, IL 60030 • 7,388
Grayson, KY 41143 • 3,510
Grayson □, KY • 21,050
Grayson □, TX • 95,021
Grayson □, VA • 16,278
Graysville, AL 35073 • 2,241
Graysville, TN 37338 • 1,301
Grayville, IL 62844 • 2,043
Great Barrington, MA 01230 • 2,810
Great Bend, KS 67530 • 15,427
Great Falls, MT 59401-06 • 55,097
Great Falls, SC 29055 • 2,307
Great Falls, VA 22066 • 6,945
Great Neck, NY 11020-27 • 8,745
Great Neck Estates, NY 11021 • 2,790
Greece, NY 14626 • 15,632
Greece, NY • 15,632
Greeley, CO 80631-34 • 60,536
Greeley □, KS • 1,774
Greeley □, NE • 3,006
Green, OR 97470 • 5,076
Green □, KY • 10,371
Green □, WI • 30,339
Greenacres, CA 93308 • 7,379
Green Acres, DE 19803 • 1,140
Greenacres, WA 99016 • 4,250
Greenacres City, FL 33463 • 18,683
Green Bay, WI 54301-24 • 96,466
Greenbelt, MD 20770 • 21,096
Greenbriar, VA 22033 • 6,200
Greenbrier, AR 72058 • 2,130
Green Brier, TN 37073 • 2,873
Greenbrier □, WV • 34,693
Green Brook, NJ 08812 • 2,380
Greencastle, IN 46135 • 8,984
Greencastle, PA 17225 • 3,600
Green Cove Springs, FL 32043 • 4,497
Greendale, IN 47025 • 3,881
Greendale, WI 53129 • 15,128
Greene, IA 50636 • 1,142
Greene, NY 13778 • 1,812
Greene □, AL • 10,153
Greene □, AR • 31,804
Greene □, GA • 11,793
Greene □, IL • 15,317
Greene □, IN • 30,410
Greene □, IA • 10,045
Greene □, MS • 10,220
Greene □, MO • 207,949
Greene □, NY • 44,739
Greene □, NC • 15,384
Greene □, OH • 136,731
Greene □, PA • 39,550
Greene □, TN • 55,853
Greene □, VA • 10,297
Greeneville, TN 37743-44 • 13,532
Greenfield, CA 93927 • 7,464
Greenfield, IL 62044 • 1,162
Greenfield, IN 46140 • 11,657
Greenfield, IA 50849 • 2,074
Greenfield, MA 01301-02 • 14,016
Greenfield, MO 65661 • 1,416
Greenfield, OH 45123 • 5,172
Greenfield, TN 38230 • 2,105
Greenfield, WI 53220 • 33,403
Greenfield Plaza, IA 50315 • 2,200
Green Forest, AR 72638 • 2,050
Green Harbor, MA 02041 • 1,900
Greenhills, OH 45218 • 4,393
Green Island, NY 12183 • 2,490
Green Lake, WI 54941 • 1,064
Green Lake □, WI • 18,651
Greenlawn, NY 11740 • 13,208
Greenlee □, AZ • 8,008
Greenock, PA 15047 • 2,500
Greenport, NY 11944 • 2,070
Green River, WY 82935 • 12,711
Green Rock, IL 61241 • 2,615
Greensboro, AL 36744 • 3,047
Greensboro, GA 30642 • 2,860
Greensboro, MD 21639 • 1,441
Greensboro, NC 27401-95 • 183,521
Greensburg, IN 47240 • 9,286
Greensburg, KS 67054 • 1,792
Greensburg, KY 42743 • 1,990
Greensburg, PA 15601 • 16,318
Green Springs, OH 44836 • 1,446
Greensville □, VA • 8,853
Greentown, IN 46936 • 2,172
Green Tree, PA 15220 • 4,905
Greenup, IL 62428 • 1,616
Greenup, KY 41144 • 1,158
Greenup □, KY • 36,742
Green Valley, AZ 85614 • 13,231
Green Valley, MD 21771 • 9,424
Greenview, SC 29203 • 5,515
Greenville, AL 36037 • 7,492
Greenville, CA 95947 • 1,396
Greenville, DE 19807 • 800
Greenville, GA 30222 • 1,167
Greenville, IL 62246 • 4,806
Greenville, KY 42345 • 4,689
Greenville, ME 04441 • 1,601
Greenville, MI 48838 • 8,101
Greenville, MS 38701-04 • 45,226
Greenville, NH 03048 • 1,135
Greenville, NY 10583 • 9,528
Greenville, NC 27834-36 • 44,972
Greenville, OH 45331 • 12,863
Greenville, PA 16125 • 6,734
Greenville, RI 02828 • 8,303
Greenville, SC 29601-16 • 58,282
Greenville, TX 75401-03 • 23,071
Greenville □, SC • 320,167
Greenwich, CT 06830-36 • 58,441
Greenwich, NY 12834 • 1,961
Greenwich, OH 44837 • 1,442
Greenwood, AR 72936 • 3,984
Greenwood, DE 19950 • 578
Greenwood, IN 46142 • 26,265
Greenwood, LA 71033 • 2,092
Greenwood, MS 38930 • 18,906
Greenwood, MO 64034 • 1,505
Greenwood, PA 16601 • 1,650
Greenwood, SC 29646-49 • 20,807
Greenwood □, KS • 7,847
Greenwood □, SC • 59,567
Greenwood Lake, NY 10925 • 3,208
Greenwood Village, CO 80111 • 7,589
Greer, SC 29650-52 • 10,322
Greer □, OK • 6,559
Gregg □, TX • 104,948
Gregory, SD 57533 • 1,384
Gregory □, SD • 5,359
Greilickville, MI 49684 • 1,060
Grenada, MS 38901 • 10,864
Grenada □, MS • 21,555
Gresham, OR 97030 • 68,235
Gresham Park, GA 30316 • 9,000
Gretna, FL 32332 • 1,981
Gretna, LA 70053-54 • 17,208
Gretna, NE 68028 • 2,249
Gretna, VA 24557 • 1,339
Greybull, WY 82426 • 1,789
Gridley, CA 95948 • 4,631
Gridley, IL 61744 • 1,304
Griffin, GA 30223-24 • 21,347
Griffith, IN 46319 • 17,916
Grifton, NC 28530 • 2,393
Griggs □, ND • 3,303
Griggsville, IL 62340 • 1,218
Grimes, IA 50111 • 2,653
Grimes □, TX • 18,828
Grindall Creek, VA 23234 • 1,710
Grinnell, IA 50112 • 8,902
Griswold, IA 51535 • 1,049
Groesbeck, OH 45239 • 6,684
Groesbeck, TX 76642 • 3,185
Grosse Ile, MI 48138 • 9,781
Grosse Pointe, MI 48236 • 5,681
Grosse Pointe Farms, MI 48236 • 10,092
Grosse Pointe Park, MI 48230 • 12,857
Grosse Pointe Woods, MI 48225 • 17,715
Grossmont, CA 91941 • 2,600
Groton, CT 06340 • 9,837
Groton, MA 01450 • 1,044
Groton, NY 13073 • 2,398
Groton, SD 57445 • 1,196
Grottoes, VA 24441 • 1,455
Grove, OK 74344 • 4,020
Grove City, FL 34224 • 2,374
Grove City, OH 43123 • 19,661
Grove City, PA 16127 • 8,240
Grove Hill, AL 36451 • 1,551
Groveland, FL 34736 • 2,300
Groveland, MA 01834 • 3,780
Groveport, OH 43125 • 2,948
Grover City, CA 93433 • 11,656
Groves, TX 77619 • 16,513
Groveton, NH 03582 • 1,255
Groveton, TX 75845 • 1,071
Groveton, VA 22303 • 19,997
Groveton Gardens, VA 22303 • 2,600
Grovetown, GA 30813 • 3,596
Groveville, NJ 08620 • 2,900
Gruetli-Laager, TN 37339 • 1,810
Grulla, TX 78548 • 1,335
Grundy, VA 24614 • 1,305
Grundy □, IL • 32,337
Grundy □, IA • 12,029
Grundy □, MO • 10,536
Grundy □, TN • 13,362
Grundy Center, IA 50638 • 2,491
Gruver, TX 79040 • 1,172
Guadalupe, AZ 85283 • 5,458
Guadalupe, CA 93434 • 5,479
Guadalupe □, NM • 4,156
Guadalupe □, TX • 64,873
Guernsey, WY 82214 • 1,155
Guernsey □, OH • 39,024
Gueydan, LA 70542 • 1,611
Guilford, CT 06437 • 2,588
Guilford, ME 04443 • 1,082
Guilford □, NC • 347,420
Guin, AL 35563 • 2,464
Gulf □, FL • 11,504
Gulf Breeze, FL 32561 • 5,530
Gulf Gate Estates, FL 34231 • 11,622
Gulfport, FL 33707 • 11,727
Gulfport, MS 39501-07 • 40,775
Gulf Shores, AL 36542 • 3,261
Gumboro, DE 19945 • 200
Gunnison, CO 81230 • 4,636
Gunnison, UT 84634 • 1,298
Gunnison □, CO • 10,273
Guntersville, AL 35976 • 7,038
Gurdon, AR 71743 • 2,199
Gurley, AL 35748 • 1,007
Gurnee, IL 60031 • 13,701
Gustine, CA 95322 • 3,931
Guthrie, KY 42234 • 1,504
Guthrie, OK 73044 • 10,518
Guthrie □, IA • 10,935
Guthrie Center, IA 50115 • 1,614
Guttenberg, IA 52052 • 2,257
Guttenberg, NJ 07093 • 8,268
Guymon, OK 73942 • 7,803
Gwinhurst, DE 19809 • 1,340
Gwinn, MI 49841 • 2,370
Gwinner, ND 58040 • 585
Gwinnett □, GA • 352,910
Gypsum, CO 81637 • 1,750

H

Haakon □, SD • 2,624
Habersham □, GA • 27,621
Hacienda Heights, CA 91745 • 52,354
Hackensack, NJ 07601-08 • 37,049
Hackettstown, NJ 07840 • 8,120
Hackleburg, AL 35564 • 1,161
Haddam, CT 06438 • 1,200
Haddonfield, NJ 08033 • 11,628
Haddon Heights, NJ 08035 • 7,860
Hadlock, WA 98339 • 1,752
Hagerman, NM 88232 • 961
Hagerstown, IN 47346 • 1,835
Hagerstown, MD 21740 • 35,445
Hahira, GA 31632 • 1,353
Hahnville, LA 70057 • 2,599
Hailey, ID 83333 • 3,687
Haines, AK 99827 • 1,238
Haines City, FL 33844 • 11,683
Hainesport, NJ 08036 • 1,250
Halawa Heights, HI 96701 • 7,000
Hale □, AL • 15,498
Hale □, TX • 34,671
Hale Center, TX 79041 • 2,067
Haledon, NJ 07508 • 6,951
Haleiwa, HI 96712 • 2,442
Hales Corners, WI 53130 • 7,623
Halethorpe, MD 21227 • 19,750
Haleyville, AL 35565 • 4,452
Half Hollow Hills, NY 11746 • 5,110
Half Moon, NC 28540 • 6,306
Half Moon Bay, CA 94019 • 8,886
Halfway, MD 21740 • 8,873
Halifax □, NC • 55,516
Halifax □, VA • 29,033
Haliimaile, HI 96768 • 841
Hall □, GA • 95,428
Hall □, NE • 48,925
Hall □, TX • 3,905
Hallandale, FL 33009 • 30,996
Hallettsville, TX 77964 • 2,718
Hallie, WI 54729 • 1,300
Hallock, MN 56728 • 1,304
Hallowell, ME 04347 • 2,534
Halls, TN 37918 • 6,450
Halls, TN 38040 • 2,431
Halls Crossroads, TN 37918 • 1,900
Hallstead, PA 18822 • 1,274
Hallsville, TX 75650 • 2,288
Halstead, KS 67056 • 2,015
Haltom City, TX 76117 • 32,856
Hamblen □, TN • 50,480
Hamburg, AR 71646 • 3,098
Hamburg, IA 51640 • 1,248
Hamburg, NJ 07419 • 2,566
Hamburg, NY 14075 • 10,442
Hamburg, PA 19526 • 3,987
Hamden, CT 06514 • 52,434
Hamel, MN 55340 • 3,096
Hamilton, AL 35570 • 5,787
Hamilton, IL 62341 • 3,281
Hamilton, MA 01936 • 1,000
Hamilton, MI 49419 • 1,000
Hamilton, MO 64644 • 1,737
Hamilton, MT 59840 • 2,737
Hamilton, NY 13346 • 3,790
Hamilton, OH 45011-18 • 61,368
Hamilton, TX 76531 • 2,937
Hamilton □, FL • 10,930
Hamilton □, IL • 8,499
Hamilton □, IN • 108,936
Hamilton □, IA • 16,071
Hamilton □, KS • 2,388
Hamilton □, NE • 8,862
Hamilton □, NY • 5,279
Hamilton □, OH • 866,228
Hamilton □, TN • 285,536
Hamilton □, TX • 7,733
Hamilton City, CA 95951 • 1,811
Hamilton Square, NJ 08690 • 10,970
Ham Lake, MN 55304 • 8,924
Hamlet, NC 28345 • 6,196
Hamlin, TX 79520 • 2,791
Hamlin, WV 25523 • 1,030
Hamlin □, SD • 4,974
Hammond, IN 46320-27 • 84,236
Hammond, LA 70401-04 • 15,871
Hammond, WI 54015 • 1,097
Hammonton, NJ 08037 • 12,208
Hampden, ME 04444 • 3,895
Hampden □, MA • 456,310
Hampden Highlands, ME 04444 • 1,540
Hampshire, IL 60140 • 1,843
Hampshire □, MA • 146,568
Hampshire □, WV • 16,498
Hampstead, MD 21074 • 2,608
Hampton, AR 71744 • 1,562
Hampton, GA 30228 • 2,694
Hampton, IA 50441 • 4,133
Hampton, NH 03842 • 7,989
Hampton, NJ 08827 • 1,515
Hampton, SC 29924 • 2,997
Hampton, TN 37658 • 2,236
Hampton, VA 23651-70 • 133,793
Hampton □, SC • 18,191
Hampton Bays, NY 11946 • 7,893
Hamtramck, MI 48212 • 18,372
Hana, HI 96713 • 683
Hanahan, SC 29406 • 13,176
Hanamaulu, HI 96715 • 3,611
Hanapepe, HI 96716 • 1,395
Hanceville, AL 35077 • 2,246
Hancock, MD 21750 • 1,926
Hancock, MI 49930 • 4,547
Hancock, NY 13783 • 1,330
Hancock □, GA • 8,908
Hancock □, IL • 21,373
Hancock □, IN • 45,527
Hancock □, IA • 12,638
Hancock □, KY • 7,864
Hancock □, ME • 46,948
Hancock □, MS • 31,760
Hancock □, OH • 65,536
Hancock □, TN • 6,739
Hancock □, WV • 35,233
Hand □, SD • 4,272
Hanford, CA 93230-32 • 30,897
Hankinson, ND 58041 • 1,038
Hanna, WY 82327 • 1,076
Hanna City, IL 61536 • 1,205
Hannibal, MO 63401 • 18,004
Hanover, IN 47243 • 3,610
Hanover, MA 02339 • 2,500
Hanover, NH 03755 • 6,538
Hanover, PA 17331 • 14,399
Hanover □, VA • 63,306
Hanover Center, MA 02339 • 1,000
Hanover Park, IL 60103 • 32,895
Hanover Township, NJ 07981 • 11,538
Hansen, ID 83334 • 848
Hansford □, TX • 5,848
Hanson, MA 02341 • 2,188
Hanson □, SD • 2,994
Hapeville, GA 30354 • 5,483
Happy Valley, OR 97236 • 1,519
Harahan, LA 70123 • 9,927
Haralson □, GA • 21,966
Harbeson, DE 19951 • 500
Harbor, OR 97415 • 2,143
Harbor Beach, MI 48441 • 2,089
Harborcreek, PA 16421 • 1,500
Harbor Springs, MI 49740 • 1,540
Hardee □, FL • 19,499
Hardeeville, SC 29927 • 1,583
Hardeman □, TN • 23,377
Hardeman □, TX • 5,283
Hardin, IL 62047 • 1,071
Hardin, MT 59034 • 2,940
Hardin □, IL • 5,189
Hardin □, IA • 19,094
Hardin □, KY • 89,240
Hardin □, OH • 31,111
Hardin □, TN • 22,633
Hardin □, TX • 41,320
Harding □, NM • 987
Harding □, SD • 1,669
Hardinsburg, KY 40143 • 1,906
Hardwick, GA 31034 • 8,800
Hardwick, VT 05843 • 1,400
Hardy □, WV • 10,977
Harford □, MD • 182,132
Hargill, TX 78549 • 1,030
Harker Heights, TX 76543 • 12,841
Harkers Island, NC 28531 • 1,759
Harlan, IN 46743 • 1,200
Harlan, IA 51537 • 5,148
Harlan, KY 40831 • 2,686
Harlan □, KY • 36,574
Harlan □, NE • 3,810
Harlem, FL 33440 • 2,826
Harlem, GA 30814 • 2,199
Harlem, MT 59526 • 882
Harleysville, PA 19438 • 7,405
Harlingen, TX 78550-52 • 48,735
Harlowton, MT 59036 • 1,049
Harmon □, OK • 3,793
Harmony, MN 55939 • 1,081
Harmony, PA 16037 • 1,054
Harmony, RI 02829 • 820
Harnett □, NC • 67,822
Harney □, OR • 7,060
Harper, KS 67058 • 1,735
Harper □, KS • 7,124

Harper □, OK • 4,063
Harpers Ferry, WV 25425 • 308
Harper Woods, MI 48225 • 14,903
Harrah, OK 73045 • 4,206
Harriman, TN 37748 • 7,119
Harrington, DE 19952 • 2,311
Harrington Park, NJ 07640 • 4,623
Harris, RI 02816 • 1,050
Harris □, GA • 17,788
Harris □, TX • 2,818,199
Harrisburg, AR 72432 • 1,943
Harrisburg, IL 62946 • 9,289
Harrisburg, OR 97446 • 1,939
Harrisburg, PA 17101–13 • 52,376
Harris Hill, NY 14221 • 4,577
Harrison, AR 72601–02 • 9,922
Harrison, MI 48625 • 1,835
Harrison, NJ 07029 • 13,425
Harrison, NY 10528 • 23,308
Harrison, OH 45030 • 7,518
Harrison, TN 37341 • 7,191
Harrison □, IN • 29,890
Harrison □, IA • 14,730
Harrison □, KY • 16,248
Harrison □, MS • 165,365
Harrison □, MO • 8,469
Harrison □, OH • 16,085
Harrison □, TX • 57,483
Harrison □, WV • 69,371
Harrisonburg, VA 22801 • 30,707
Harrison Township, MI 48045 • 24,685
Harrisonville, MO 64701 • 7,683
Harristown, IL 62537 • 1,319
Harrisville, RI 02830 • 1,654
Harrisville, UT 84404 • 3,004
Harrisville, WV 26362 • 1,839
Harrodsburg, KY 40330 • 7,335
Hart, MI 49420 • 1,942
Hart, TX 79043 • 1,221
Hart □, GA • 19,712
Hart □, KY • 14,890
Hartford, AL 36344 • 2,448
Hartford, CT 06101–99 • 139,739
Hartford, IL 62048 • 1,676
Hartford, KY 42347 • 2,532
Hartford, MI 49057 • 2,341
Hartford, SD 57033 • 1,262
Hartford, VT 05047 • 500
Hartford, WI 53027 • 8,188
Hartford □, CT • 851,783
Hartford City, IN 47348 • 6,960
Hartington, NE 68739 • 1,583
Hartland, ME 04943 • 1,038
Hartland, WI 53029 • 6,906
Hartley, IA 51346 • 1,632
Hartley □, TX • 3,634
Hartsdale, NY 10530 • 9,587
Hartselle, AL 35640 • 10,795
Hartshorne, OK 74547 • 2,120
Hartsville, SC 29550 • 8,372
Hartsville, TN 37074 • 2,188
Hartville, OH 44632 • 2,031
Hartwell, GA 30643 • 4,555
Harvard, IL 60033 • 5,975
Harvard, MA 01451 • 1,200
Harvey, IL 60426 • 29,771
Harvey, LA 70058 • 21,222
Harvey, MI 49855 • 1,377
Harvey, ND 58341 • 2,263
Harvey □, KS • 31,028
Harwich, MA 02645 • 4,399
Harwich Port, MA 02646 • 2,300
Harwinton, CT 06791 • 5,228
Harwood Heights, IL 60656 • 7,680
Hasbrouck Heights, NJ 07604 • 11,488
Haskell, AR 72015 • 1,342
Haskell, OK 74436 • 2,143
Haskell, TX 79521 • 3,362
Haskell □, KS • 3,886
Haskell □, OK • 10,940
Haskell □, TX • 6,820
Haslett, MI 48840 • 10,230
Hastings, MI 49058 • 6,549
Hastings, MN 55033 • 15,445
Hastings, NE 68901–02 • 22,837
Hastings, PA 16646 • 1,431
Hastings-on-Hudson, NY 10706 • 8,000
Hatboro, PA 19040 • 7,382
Hatch, NM 87937 • 1,136
Hatfield, MA 01038 • 1,234
Hatfield, PA 19440 • 2,650
Hatteras, NC 27943 • 1,000
Hattiesburg, MS 39401–07 • 41,882
Hatton, ND 58240 • 800
Haubstadt, IN 47639 • 1,455
Haughton, LA 71037 • 1,664
Hauppauge, NY 11788 • 19,750
Hauula, HI 96717 • 3,479
Havana, FL 32333 • 1,654
Havana, IL 62644 • 3,610
Havelock, NC 28532 • 20,268
Haven, KS 67543 • 1,198
Haverford [Township], PA 19083 • 52,371
Haverhill, MA 01830–35 • 51,418
Haverstraw, NY 10927 • 9,438
Havre, MT 59501 • 10,201
Havre de Grace, MD 21078 • 8,952
Havre North, MT 59501 • 1,110
Hawaii □, HI • 120,317
Hawaiian Gardens, CA 90716 • 13,639
Hawarden, IA 51023 • 2,439
Hawi, HI 96719 • 924
Hawkins □, TN • 44,565
Hawkinsville, GA 31036 • 3,527
Hawley, MN 56549 • 1,655
Hawley, PA 18428 • 1,244
Haworth, NJ 07641 • 3,384
Haw River, NC 27258 • 1,855
Hawthorne, CA 90250–51 • 71,349
Hawthorne, FL 32640 • 1,305
Hawthorne, NV 89415–16 • 4,162
Hawthorne, NJ 07506 • 17,084
Hawthorne, NY 10532 • 4,764
Hayden, CO 81639 • 1,444
Hayden, ID 83835 • 3,744
Hayes □, NE • 1,222
Hayesville, OR 97303 • 14,318
Hayfield, MN 55940 • 1,283
Hayfield, VA 22310 • 2,300
Hayfork, CA 96041 • 2,605
Haynesville, LA 71038 • 2,854
Hays, KS 67601 • 17,767
Hays □, TX • 65,614
Haysville, KS 67060 • 8,364
Hayti, MO 63851 • 3,280
Hayward, CA 94540–46 • 111,498
Hayward, WI 54843 • 1,897
Hayward Addition, SD 57106 • 1,000
Haywood □, NC • 46,942
Haywood □, TN • 19,437
Hazard, KY 41701 • 5,416
Hazardville, CT 06082 • 5,179
Hazel Crest, IL 60429 • 13,334
Hazel Dell, WA 98660 • 15,386
Hazel Green, AL 35750 • 2,208
Hazel Green, WI 53811 • 1,171
Hazel Park, MI 48030 • 20,051
Hazelwood, MO 63042–45 • 15,324
Hazelwood, NC 28738 • 1,678
Hazen, AR 72064 • 1,668
Hazen, ND 58545 • 2,818
Hazlehurst, GA 31539 • 4,202
Hazlehurst, MS 39083 • 4,221
Hazlet, NJ 07730 • 23,013
Hazleton, PA 18201 • 24,730
Headland, AL 36345 • 3,266
Healdsburg, CA 95448 • 9,469
Healdton, OK 73438 • 2,872
Healy, AK 99743 • 487
Heard □, GA • 8,628
Hearne, TX 77859 • 5,132
Heath, OH 43056 • 7,231
Heavener, OK 74937 • 2,601
Hebbronville, TX 78361 • 4,465
Heber City, UT 84032 • 4,782
Heber Springs, AR 72543 • 5,628
Hebron, IN 46341 • 3,183
Hebron, KY 41048 • 1,200
Hebron, NE 68370 • 1,765
Hebron, ND 58638 • 888
Hebron, OH 43025 • 2,076
Hector, MN 55342 • 1,145
Heeia, HI 96744 • 5,010
Heflin, AL 36264 • 2,906
Hegins, PA 17938 • 1,200
Helena, AL 35080 • 3,918
Helena, AR 72342 • 7,491
Helena, GA 31037 • 1,256
Helena, MT 59601–26 • 24,569
Helena, OK 73741 • 1,043
Hellam, PA 17406 • 1,375
Hellertown, PA 18055 • 5,662
Helmetta, NJ 08828 • 1,211
Helotes, TX 78023 • 1,535
Helper, UT 84526 • 2,148
Hemet, CA 92343–44 • 36,094
Hemlock, MI 48626 • 1,601
Hemphill, TX 75948 • 1,182
Hemphill □, TX • 3,720
Hempstead, NY 11550–54 • 49,453
Hempstead, TX 77445 • 3,551
Hempstead □, AR • 21,621
Henagar, AL 35978 • 1,934
Henderson, KY 42420 • 25,945
Henderson, LA 70517 • 1,543
Henderson, NV 89015–16 • 64,942
Henderson, NC 27536 • 15,655
Henderson, TN 38340 • 4,760
Henderson, TX 75652–53 • 11,139
Henderson □, IL • 8,096
Henderson □, KY • 43,044
Henderson □, NC • 69,285
Henderson □, TN • 21,844
Henderson □, TX • 58,543
Henderson's Point, MS 39571 • 1,114
Hendersonville, NC 28739 • 7,284
Hendersonville, TN 37075 • 32,188
Hendricks □, IN • 75,717
Hendry □, FL • 25,773
Hennepin □, MN • 1,032,431
Hennessey, OK 73742 • 1,902
Henniker, NH 03242 • 1,693
Henrico □, VA • 217,881
Henrietta, NY 14467 • 1,200
Henrietta, NC 28076 • 1,412
Henrietta, TX 76365 • 2,896
Henry, IL 61537 • 2,591
Henry □, AL • 15,374
Henry □, GA • 58,741
Henry □, IL • 51,159
Henry □, IN • 48,139
Henry □, IA • 19,226
Henry □, KY • 12,823
Henry □, MO • 20,044
Henry □, OH • 29,108
Henry □, TN • 27,888
Henry □, VA • 56,942
Henryetta, OK 74437 • 5,872
Henryville, IN 47126 • 1,132
Hephzibah, GA 30815 • 2,466
Heppner, OR 97836 • 1,412
Herculaneum, MO 63048 • 2,263
Hercules, CA 94547 • 16,829
Hereford, TX 79045 • 14,745
Herington, KS 67449 • 2,685
Heritage Village, CT 06488 • 9,700
Herkimer, NY 13350 • 7,945
Herkimer □, NY • 65,797
Hermann, MO 65041 • 2,754
Hermantown, MN 55811 • 6,761
Herminie, PA 15637 • 2,000
Hermiston, OR 97838 • 10,040
Hermitage, PA 16148 • 15,300
Hermosa Beach, CA 90254 • 18,219
Hernando, FL 32642 • 2,103
Hernando, MS 38632 • 3,125
Hernando □, FL • 101,115
Herndon, VA 22070–71 • 16,139
Herrin, IL 62948 • 10,857
Herscher, IL 60941 • 1,278
Hershey, PA 17033 • 11,860
Hertford, NC 27944 • 2,105
Hertford □, NC • 22,523
Hesperia, CA 92345 • 50,418
Hesston, KS 67062 • 3,012
Hettinger, ND 58639 • 1,574
Hettinger □, ND • 3,445
Hewitt, TX 76643 • 8,983
Hewlett, NY 11557 • 6,620
Heyburn, ID 83336 • 2,714
Heyworth, IL 61745 • 1,627
Hialeah, FL 33010–16 • 188,004
Hiawatha, IA 52233 • 4,986
Hiawatha, KS 66434 • 3,603
Hibbing, MN 55746–47 • 18,046
Hickman, KY 42050 • 2,689
Hickman, NE 68372 • 1,081
Hickman □, KY • 5,566
Hickman □, TN • 16,754
Hickory, NC 28601–03 • 28,301
Hickory □, MO • 7,335
Hickory Hills, IL 60457 • 13,021
Hicksville, NY 11801–05 • 40,174
Hicksville, OH 43526 • 3,664
Hico, TX 76457 • 1,342
Hidalgo, TX 78557 • 3,292
Hidalgo □, NM • 5,958
Hidalgo □, TX • 383,545
Higganum, CT 06441 • 1,692
Higginsville, MO 64037 • 4,693
High Bridge, NJ 08829 • 3,886
Highland, CA 92346 • 34,439
Highland, IL 62249 • 7,525
Highland, IN 46322 • 23,696
Highland, MI 48356–57 • 750
Highland, NY 12528 • 4,492
Highland □, OH • 35,728
Highland □, VA • 2,635
Highland Falls, NY 10928 • 3,937
Highland Heights, OH 44124 • 6,249
Highland Lakes, NJ 07422 • 4,550
Highland Park, IL 60035 • 30,575
Highland Park, MI 48203 • 20,121
Highland Park, NJ 08904 • 13,279
Highland Park, TX 75205 • 8,739
Highlands, NJ 07732 • 4,849
Highlands, TX 77562 • 6,632
Highlands □, FL • 68,432
Highland Springs, VA 23075 • 13,823
Highmore, SD 57345 • 835
High Point, NC 27260–65 • 69,496
High Ridge, MO 63049 • 2,380
High Spire, PA 17034 • 2,668
High Springs, FL 32643 • 3,144
Hightstown, NJ 08520 • 5,126
Highview, KY 40228 • 14,814
Highwood, IL 60040 • 5,331
Hilbert, WI 54129 • 1,211
Hildale, UT 84784 • 1,325
Hill □, MT • 17,654
Hill □, TX • 27,146
Hill City, KS 67642 • 1,835
Hillcrest, NY 10977 • 6,447
Hillcrest Center, CA 93306 • 26,900
Hillcrest Heights, MD 20748 • 17,136
Hilliard, FL 32046 • 1,751
Hilliard, OH 43026 • 11,796
Hillsboro, IL 62049 • 4,400
Hillsboro, KS 67063 • 2,704
Hillsboro, MO 63050 • 1,625
Hillsboro, NH 03244 • 1,826
Hillsboro, ND 58045 • 1,488
Hillsboro, OH 45133 • 6,235
Hillsboro, OR 97123–24 • 37,520
Hillsboro, TX 76645 • 7,072
Hillsboro, WI 54634 • 1,288
Hillsborough, CA 94010 • 10,667
Hillsborough, NC 27278 • 4,263
Hillsborough □, FL • 834,054
Hillsborough □, NH • 336,073
Hillsdale, MI 49242 • 8,170
Hillsdale, NJ 07642 • 9,750
Hillsdale □, MI • 43,431
Hillside, IL 60162 • 7,672
Hillside, NJ 07205 • 21,044
Hillside Heights, DE 19711 • 1,500
Hillsville, VA 24343 • 2,008
Hillview, KY 40229 • 6,119
Hilo, HI 96720–21 • 37,808
Hilton, NY 14468 • 5,216
Hilton Head Island, SC 29928 • 23,694
Hinckley, IL 60520 • 1,682
Hinds □, MS • 254,441
Hines, OR 97738 • 1,452
Hinesville, GA 31313 • 21,603
Hingham, MA 02043 • 5,454
Hinsdale, IL 60521–22 • 16,029
Hinsdale, NH 03451 • 1,718
Hinsdale □, CO • 467
Hinton, OK 73047 • 1,233
Hinton, WV 25951 • 3,433
Hiram, GA 30141 • 1,389
Hiram, OH 44234 • 1,330
Hitchcock, TX 77563 • 5,868
Hitchcock □, NE • 3,750
Hitchcock Lake, CT 06716 • 1,640
Hobart, IN 46342 • 21,822
Hobart, OK 73651 • 4,305
Hobbs, NM 88240–41 • 29,115
Hobe Sound, FL 33455 • 11,507
Hoboken, NJ 07030 • 33,397
Hockessin, DE 19707 • 2,430
Hocking □, OH • 25,533
Hockley □, TX • 24,199
Hodgeman □, KS • 2,177
Hodgenville, KY 42748 • 2,721
Hoffman Estates, IL 60194–95 • 46,561
Hogansville, GA 30230 • 2,976
Hohenwald, TN 38462 • 3,760
Ho-Ho-Kus, NJ 07423 • 3,935
Hoisington, KS 67544 • 3,182
Hoke □, NC • 22,856
Hokes Bluff, AL 35903 • 3,739
Holbrook, AZ 86025–29 • 4,686
Holbrook, MA 02343 • 11,041
Holbrook, NY 11741 • 25,273
Holcomb, KS 67851 • 1,400
Holden, MA 01520 • 4,040
Holden, MO 64040 • 2,389
Holden, WV 25625 • 1,246
Holden Heights, FL 32805 • 4,387
Holdenville, OK 74848 • 4,792
Holdrege, NE 68949 • 5,671
Holgate, OH 43527 • 1,290
Holiday, FL 34690 • 19,360
Holiday City at Berkeley, NJ 08757 • 5,750
Holladay, UT 84117 • 22,189
Holland, MI 49422–24 • 30,745
Holland, NY 14080 • 1,288
Holland, OH 43528 • 1,210
Holland, PA 18966 • 5,250
Holland, TX 76534 • 1,118
Hollandale, MS 38748 • 3,576
Holley, NY 14470 • 1,890
Holliday, TX 76366 • 1,475
Hollidaysburg, PA 16648 • 5,624
Hollins, VA 24019 • 13,305
Hollis, OK 73550 • 2,584
Hollister, CA 95023–24 • 19,212
Hollister, MO 65672 • 2,628
Holliston, MA 01746 • 12,622
Holly, MI 48442 • 5,595
Holly Hill, FL 32117 • 11,141
Holly Hill, SC 29059 • 1,478
Holly Springs, GA 30142 • 2,406
Holly Springs, MS 38634–35 • 7,261
Hollywood, FL 33019–29 • 121,697
Hollywood, SC 29449 • 2,094
Holmen, WI 54636 • 3,220
Holmes □, FL • 15,778
Holmes □, MS • 21,604
Holmes □, OH • 32,849
Holstein, IA 51025 • 1,449
Holt, AL 35404 • 4,125
Holt, MI 48842 • 11,744
Holt □, MO • 6,034
Holt □, NE • 12,599
Holton, KS 66436 • 3,196
Holtsville, NY 11742 • 14,972
Holtville, CA 92250 • 4,820
Holualoa, HI 96725 • 3,834
Holyoke, CO 80734 • 1,931
Holyoke, MA 01040–41 • 43,704
Homedale, ID 83628 • 1,963
Home Gardens, CA 91720 • 7,780
Homeland Park, SC 29621 • 6,569
Home Place, IN 46240 • 1,300
Homer, AK 99603 • 3,660
Homer, IL 61849 • 1,264
Homer, LA 71040 • 4,152
Homer, MI 49245 • 1,758
Homer, NY 13077 • 3,476
Homer City, PA 15748 • 1,809
Homerville, GA 31634 • 2,560
Homestead, FL 33030–35 • 26,866
Homestead, PA 15120 • 4,179
Hometown, IL 60456 • 4,769
Homewood, AL 35209 • 22,922
Homewood, IL 60430 • 19,278
Homewood, OH 45015 • 2,550
Hominy, OK 74035 • 2,342
Homosassa, FL 32646 • 2,113
Hondo, TX 78861 • 6,018
Honea Path, SC 29654 • 3,841
Honeoye Falls, NY 14472 • 2,340
Honesdale, PA 18431 • 4,972
Honey Brook, PA 19344 • 1,184
Honey Grove, TX 75446 • 1,681
Honeypot Glen, CT 06410 • 1,200
Honeyville, UT 84314 • 1,112
Honokaa, HI 96727 • 2,186
Honolulu, HI 96801–50 • 365,272
Honolulu □, HI • 836,231
Honomu, HI 96728 • 532
Hood □, TX • 28,981
Hood River, OR 97031 • 4,632
Hood River □, OR • 16,903
Hoodsport, WA 98548 • 1,100
Hooker, OK 73945 • 1,551
Hooker □, NE • 793
Hooksett, NH 03106 • 2,573
Hoonah, AK 99829 • 795
Hooper Bay, AK 99604 • 845
Hoopeston, IL 60942 • 5,871
Hoosick Falls, NY 12090 • 3,490
Hoover, AL 35216 • 39,788
Hooverson Heights, WV 26037 • 3,056
Hopatcong, NJ 07843 • 15,586
Hope, AR 71801 • 9,643
Hope, IN 47246 • 2,171
Hope, RI 02831 • 270
Hopedale, MA 01747 • 3,961
Hope Mills, NC 28348 • 8,184
Hope Valley, RI 02832 • 1,446
Hopewell, NJ 08525 • 1,968
Hopewell, VA 23860 • 23,101
Hopewell Junction, NY 12533 • 1,786
Hopkins, MN 55343–47 • 16,534
Hopkins, SC 29061 • 1,600
Hopkins □, KY • 46,126
Hopkins □, TX • 28,833
Hopkinsville, KY 42240–41 • 29,809
Hopkinton, MA 01748 • 2,305
Hopkinton, RI 02833 • 550
Hopwood, PA 15445 • 2,021
Hoquiam, WA 98550 • 8,972
Horicon, WI 53032 • 3,873
Hornell, NY 14843 • 9,877
Horn Lake, MS 38637 • 9,069
Horry □, SC • 144,053
Horse Cave, KY 42749 • 2,284
Horseheads, NY 14844–45 • 6,802
Horsham, PA 19044 • 15,051
Horton, KS 66439 • 1,885
Hortonville, WI 54944 • 2,029
Hot Spring □, AR • 26,115
Hot Springs, SD 57747 • 4,325
Hot Springs □, WY • 4,809
Hot Springs National Park, AR 71901–14 • 32,462
Hot Springs Village, AR 71901 • 6,361
Houghton, MI 49931 • 7,498
Houghton, NY 14744 • 1,740
Houghton □, MI • 35,446
Houghton Lake, MI 48629 • 3,353
Houghton Lake Heights, MI 48630 • 2,449
Houlton, ME 04730 • 5,627
Houma, LA 70360–64 • 96,982
Housatonic, MA 01236 • 1,184
Houston, DE 19954 • 487
Houston, MN 55943 • 1,013
Houston, MS 38851 • 3,903
Houston, MO 65483 • 2,118
Houston, PA 15342 • 1,445
Houston, TX 77001–99 • 1,630,553
Houston □, AL • 81,331
Houston □, GA • 89,208
Houston □, MN • 18,497
Houston □, TN • 7,018
Houston □, TX • 21,375
Houtzdale, PA 16651 • 1,204
Howard, SD 57349 • 1,156
Howard, WI 54303 • 9,874
Howard □, AR • 13,569
Howard □, IN • 80,827
Howard □, IA • 9,809
Howard □, MD • 187,328
Howard □, MO • 9,631
Howard □, NE • 6,055
Howard □, TX • 32,343
Howard City, MI 49329 • 1,351
Howard Lake, MN 55349 • 1,343
Howards Grove-Millersville, WI 53083 • 2,329
Howell, MI 48843–44 • 8,184
Howell □, MO • 31,447
Howland, ME 04448 • 1,304
Howland, OH 44484 • 6,732
Hoxie, AR 72433 • 2,676
Hoxie, KS 67740 • 1,342
Hoyt Lakes, MN 55750 • 2,348
Huachuca City, AZ 85616 • 1,782
Hubbard, OH 44425 • 8,248
Hubbard, OR 97032 • 1,881
Hubbard, TX 76648 • 1,589
Hubbard □, MN • 14,939
Hubbell, MI 49934 • 1,174
Huber Heights, OH 45424 • 38,696
Huber Ridge, OH 43081 • 5,255
Huber South, OH 45439 • 4,800
Hudson, FL 34667 • 7,344
Hudson, IL 61748 • 1,006
Hudson, IA 50643 • 2,037
Hudson, MA 01749 • 14,267
Hudson, MI 49247 • 2,580
Hudson, NH 03051 • 7,626
Hudson, NY 12534 • 8,034
Hudson, NC 28638 • 2,819
Hudson, OH 44236 • 5,159
Hudson, WI 54016 • 6,378
Hudson, WY 82515 • 392
Hudson □, NJ • 553,099
Hudson Falls, NY 12839 • 7,651
Hudson Lake, IN 46552 • 1,347
Hudsonville, MI 49426 • 6,170
Hudspeth □, TX • 2,915
Huerfano □, CO • 6,009
Hueytown, AL 35023 • 15,280
Huffakers, NV 89501 • 150
Hughes, AR 72348 • 1,810
Hughes □, OK • 13,023
Hughes □, SD • 14,817
Hughesville, MD 20637 • 1,319
Hughesville, PA 17737 • 2,049
Hugo, MN 55038 • 4,417
Hugo, OK 74743 • 5,978
Hugoton, KS 67951 • 3,179
Hulett, WY 82720 • 429
Hull, IA 51239 • 1,724
Hull, MA 02045 • 10,466
Humansville, MO 65674 • 1,084
Humble, TX 77338–39 • 12,060
Humboldt, IA 50548 • 4,438
Humboldt, KS 66748 • 2,178
Humboldt, NE 68376 • 1,003
Humboldt, TN 38343 • 9,651
Humboldt □, CA • 119,118
Humboldt □, IA • 10,756
Humboldt □, NV • 12,844
Hummels Wharf, PA 17831 • 1,069
Humphreys □, MS • 12,134
Humphreys □, TN • 15,795
Hunt □, TX • 64,343
Hunterdon □, NJ • 107,776
Huntertown, IN 46748 • 1,330
Huntingburg, IN 47542 • 5,242
Huntingdon, PA 16652 • 6,843
Huntingdon, TN 38344 • 4,180
Huntingdon □, PA • 44,164
Huntington, IN 46750 • 16,389
Huntington, MA 01050 • 1,200
Huntington, NY 11743 • 18,243
Huntington, TX 75949 • 1,794
Huntington, UT 84528 • 1,875
Huntington, VA 22303 • 7,489
Huntington, WV 25701–79 • 54,844
Huntington □, IN • 35,427
Huntington Bay, NY 11743 • 1,521
Huntington Beach, CA 92646–49 • 181,519
Huntington Park, CA 90255 • 56,065
Huntington Station, NY 11746 • 28,247
Huntington Woods, MI 48070 • 6,419
Huntley, IL 60142 • 2,453
Huntsville, AL 35801–24 • 159,789
Huntsville, AR 72740 • 1,605
Huntsville, MO 65259 • 1,567
Huntsville, TX 77340–44 • 27,925
Hurley, NM 88043 • 1,534
Hurley, NY 12443 • 4,644
Hurley, WI 54534 • 1,782
Hurlock, MD 21643 • 1,706
Huron, OH 44839 • 7,030
Huron, SD 57350 • 12,448
Huron □, MI • 34,951
Huron □, OH • 56,240
Hurricane, UT 84737 • 3,915
Hurricane, WV 25526 • 4,461
Hurst, TX 76053–54 • 33,574
Hurt, VA 24563 • 1,294
Hutchins, TX 75141 • 2,719
Hutchinson, KS 67501–05 • 39,308
Hutchinson, MN 55350 • 11,523
Hutchinson □, SD • 8,262
Hutchinson □, TX • 25,689
Huxley, IA 50124 • 2,047
Hyannis, MA 02601 • 14,120
Hyannis Port, MA 02647 • 1,100
Hyattsville, MD 20780–89 • 13,864
Hybla Valley, VA 22306 • 15,491
Hydaburg, AK 99922 • 384
Hyde, PA 16843 • 1,643
Hyde □, NC • 5,411
Hyde □, SD • 1,696
Hyde Park, NY 12538 • 2,550
Hyde Park, UT 84318 • 2,190
Hydeville, VT 05750 • 450
Hyndman, PA 15545 • 1,019
Hyrum, UT 84319 • 4,829

I

Iberia □, LA • 68,297
Iberville □, LA • 31,049
Ida, MI 48140 • 1,000
Ida □, IA • 8,365
Idabel, OK 74745 • 6,957
Ida Grove, IA 51445 • 2,357
Idaho □, ID • 13,783
Idaho Falls, ID 83401–15 • 43,929
Idaho Springs, CO 80452 • 1,834
Idalou, TX 79329 • 2,074
Ilion, NY 13357 • 8,888

Illmo, MO 63780 • 1,368
Imlay, NV 89418 • 250
Imlay City, MI 48444 • 2,921
Immokalee, FL 33934 • 14,120
Imperial, CA 92251 • 4,113
Imperial, NE 69033 • 2,007
Imperial, PA 15126 • 3,200
Imperial □, CA • 109,303
Imperial Beach, CA 91932–33 • 26,512
Incline Village, NV 89450 • 4,500
Independence, CA 93526 • 1,000
Independence, IA 50644 • 5,972
Independence, KS 67301 • 9,942
Independence, KY 41051 • 10,444
Independence, LA 70443 • 1,632
Independence, MO 64050–58 • 112,301
Independence, OH 44131 • 6,500
Independence, OR 97351 • 4,425
Independence, WI 54747 • 1,041
Independence □, AR • 31,192
Indiana, PA 15701 • 15,174
Indiana □, PA • 89,994
Indianapolis, IN 46201–90 • 731,327
Indian Harbour Beach, FL 32937 • 6,933
Indian Head, MD 20640 • 3,531
Indian Heights, IN 46902 • 3,669
Indian Hills, CO 80454 • 2,000
Indian Neck, CT 06405 • 2,430
Indianola, IA 50125 • 11,340
Indianola, MS 38751 • 11,809
Indian Ridge Estates, AZ 85715 • 1,260
Indian River □, FL • 90,208
Indian Rocks Beach, FL 34635 • 3,963
Indian Springs, NV 89018 • 1,164
Indiantown, FL 34956 • 4,794
Indian Trail, NC 28079 • 1,942
Indio, CA 92201–02 • 36,793
Ingalls Park, IL 60431 • 2,730
Ingham □, MI • 281,912
Ingleside, TX 78362 • 5,696
Inglewood, CA 90301–12 • 109,602
Inglewood, TX 98011 • 6,500
Ingram, PA 15205 • 3,901
Inkom, ID 83245 • 769
Inkster, MI 48141 • 30,772
Inman, KS 67546 • 1,035
Inman, SC 29349 • 1,742
Inniswold, LA 70809 • 1,100
Inola, OK 74036 • 1,444
Institute, WV 25112 • 1,400
Interlachen, FL 32148 • 1,160
International Falls, MN 56649 • 8,325
Inver Grove Heights, MN 55076–77 • 22,477
Inverness, CA 94937 • 1,422
Inverness, FL 32650–52 • 5,797
Inverness, IL 60067 • 6,503
Inverness, MS 38753 • 1,174
Inwood, FL 33880 • 6,824
Inwood, NY 11696 • 7,767
Inwood, WV 25428 • 1,360
Inyo □, CA • 18,281
Iola, KS 66749 • 6,351
Iola, WI 54945 • 1,125
Iona, ID 83427 • 1,049
Ione, CA 95640 • 6,516
Ionia, MI 48846 • 5,935
Ionia □, MI • 57,024
Iosco □, MI • 30,209
Iota, LA 70543 • 1,256
Iowa, LA 70647 • 2,588
Iowa □, IA • 14,630
Iowa □, WI • 20,150
Iowa City, IA 52240–46 • 59,738
Iowa Falls, IA 50126 • 5,424
Iowa Park, TX 76367 • 6,072
Ipswich, MA 01938 • 4,132
Ipswich, SD 57451 • 965
Iraan, TX 79744 • 1,322
Iredell □, NC • 92,931
Irion □, TX • 1,629
Irmo, SC 29063 • 11,280
Iron □, MI • 13,175
Iron □, MO • 10,726
Iron □, UT • 20,789
Iron □, WI • 6,153
Irondale, AL 35210 • 9,454
Irondequoit, NY 14617 • 52,322
Ironia, NJ 07845 • 1,110
Iron Mountain, MI 49801 • 8,525
Iron River, MI 49935 • 2,095
Ironton, MO 63650 • 1,539
Ironton, OH 45638 • 12,751
Ironwood, MI 49938 • 6,849
Iroquois □, IL • 30,787
Irvine, CA 92713–20 • 110,330
Irvine, KY 40336 • 2,836
Irving, TX 75060–63 • 155,037
Irvington, KY 40146 • 1,180
Irvington, NJ 07111 • 59,774
Irvington, NY 10533 • 6,348
Irwin, PA 15642 • 4,604
Irwin □, GA • 8,649
Isabella □, MI • 54,624
Isanti, MN 55040 • 1,228
Isanti □, MN • 25,921
Iselin, NJ 08830 • 16,141
Ishpeming, MI 49849 • 7,200
Islamorada, FL 33036 • 1,220
Island □, WA • 60,195
Island Heights, NJ 08732 • 1,470
Island Park, NY 11558 • 4,860
Island Park, RI 02871 • 1,240
Island Pond, VT 05846 • 1,222
Isla Vista, CA 93117 • 20,395
Isle of Palms, SC 29451 • 3,680
Isle of Wight □, VA • 25,053
Isleta, NM 87022 • 1,703
Islington, MA 02090 • 4,920
Islip, NY 11751 • 18,924
Islip Terrace, NY 11752 • 5,530
Issaquah, WA 98027 • 7,786
Issaquena □, MS • 1,909
Italy, TX 76651 • 1,699
Itasca, IL 60143 • 6,947
Itasca, TX 76055 • 1,523
Itasca □, MN • 40,863
Itawamba □, MS • 20,017
Ithaca, MI 48847 • 3,009
Ithaca, NY 14850–52 • 29,541
Itta Bena, MS 38941 • 2,377
Iuka, MS 38852 • 3,122
Iva, SC 29655 • 1,174
Ives Estates, FL 33162 • 13,531
Ivins, UT 84738 • 1,630
Ivoryton, CT 06442 • 2,200
Izard □, AR • 11,364

J

Jacinto City, TX 77029 • 9,343
Jack □, TX • 6,981
Jackpot, NV 89825 • 570
Jacksboro, TN 37757 • 1,568
Jacksboro, TX 76056 • 3,350
Jackson, AL 36545 • 5,819
Jackson, CA 95642 • 3,545
Jackson, GA 30233 • 4,076
Jackson, KY 41339 • 2,466
Jackson, LA 70748 • 3,891
Jackson, MI 49201–04 • 37,446
Jackson, MN 56143 • 3,559
Jackson, MS 39201–98 • 196,637
Jackson, MO 63755 • 9,256
Jackson, OH 45640 • 6,144
Jackson, SC 29831 • 1,681
Jackson, TN 38301–08 • 48,949
Jackson, WI 53037 • 2,486
Jackson, WY 83001–02 • 4,472
Jackson □, AL • 47,796
Jackson □, AR • 18,944
Jackson □, CO • 1,605
Jackson □, FL • 41,375
Jackson □, GA • 30,005
Jackson □, IL • 61,067
Jackson □, IN • 37,730
Jackson □, IA • 19,950
Jackson □, KS • 11,525
Jackson □, KY • 11,955
Jackson □, LA • 15,705
Jackson □, MI • 149,756
Jackson □, MN • 11,677
Jackson □, MS • 115,243
Jackson □, MO • 633,232
Jackson □, NC • 26,846
Jackson □, OH • 30,230
Jackson □, OK • 28,764
Jackson □, OR • 146,389
Jackson □, SD • 2,811
Jackson □, TN • 9,297
Jackson □, TX • 13,039
Jackson □, WV • 25,938
Jackson □, WI • 16,588
Jackson Center, OH 45334 • 1,398
Jacksonville, AL 36265 • 10,283
Jacksonville, AR 72076 • 29,101
Jacksonville, FL 32201–98 • 635,230
Jacksonville, IL 62650–51 • 19,324
Jacksonville, NC 28540–46 • 30,013
Jacksonville, OR 97530 • 1,896
Jacksonville, TX 75766 • 12,765
Jacksonville Beach, FL 32250 • 17,839
Jaffrey, NH 03452 • 2,558
Jal, NM 88252 • 2,156
Jamesburg, NJ 08831 • 5,294
James City, NC 28560 • 4,279
James City □, VA • 34,859
James Island, SC 29412 • 24,124
Jamestown, CA 95327 • 2,178
Jamestown, KY 42629 • 1,641
Jamestown, NY 14701–02 • 34,681
Jamestown, NC 27282 • 2,600
Jamestown, ND 58401–02 • 15,571
Jamestown, OH 45335 • 1,794
Jamestown, RI 02835 • 2,156
Jamestown, TN 38556 • 1,862
James Town, WY 82935 • 280
Janesville, CA 96114 • 1,200
Janesville, MN 56048 • 1,969
Janesville, WI 53545–47 • 52,133
Jarrettsville, MD 21084 • 2,148
Jasmine Estates, FL 34668 • 17,136
Jasonville, IN 47438 • 2,200
Jasper, AL 35501–02 • 13,553
Jasper, FL 32052 • 2,099
Jasper, GA 30143 • 1,772
Jasper, IN 47546–47 • 10,030
Jasper, TN 37347 • 2,780
Jasper, TX 75951 • 6,959
Jasper □, GA • 8,453
Jasper □, IL • 10,609
Jasper □, IN • 24,960
Jasper □, IA • 34,795
Jasper □, MS • 17,114
Jasper □, MO • 90,465
Jasper □, SC • 15,487
Jasper □, TX • 31,102
Jay, OK 74346 • 2,220
Jay □, IN • 21,512
Jean, NV 89019 • 150
Jeanerette, LA 70544 • 6,205
Jeannette, PA 15644 • 11,221
Jeff Davis □, GA • 12,032
Jeff Davis □, TX • 1,946
Jefferson, GA 30549 • 2,763
Jefferson, IA 50129 • 4,292
Jefferson, LA 70121 • 14,521
Jefferson, NC 28640 • 1,300
Jefferson, OH 44047 • 3,331
Jefferson, OR 97352 • 1,805
Jefferson, PA 15025 • 9,533
Jefferson, TX 75657 • 2,199
Jefferson, WI 53549 • 6,078
Jefferson □, AL • 651,525
Jefferson □, AR • 85,487
Jefferson □, CO • 438,430
Jefferson □, FL • 11,296
Jefferson □, GA • 17,408
Jefferson □, ID • 16,543
Jefferson □, IL • 37,020
Jefferson □, IN • 29,797
Jefferson □, IA • 16,310
Jefferson □, KS • 15,905
Jefferson □, KY • 664,937
Jefferson □, LA • 448,306
Jefferson □, MS • 8,653
Jefferson □, MO • 171,380
Jefferson □, MT • 7,939
Jefferson □, NE • 8,759
Jefferson □, NY • 110,943
Jefferson □, OH • 80,298
Jefferson □, OK • 7,010
Jefferson □, OR • 13,676
Jefferson □, PA • 46,083
Jefferson □, TN • 33,016
Jefferson □, TX • 239,397
Jefferson □, WA • 20,146
Jefferson □, WV • 35,926
Jefferson □, WI • 67,783
Jefferson City, MO 65101–10 • 35,481
Jefferson City, TN 37760 • 5,494
Jefferson Davis □, LA • 30,722
Jefferson Davis □, MS • 14,051
Jefferson Farms, DE 19720 • 3,130
Jefferson Manor, VA 22303 • 2,300
Jeffersontown, KY 40299 • 23,221
Jefferson Valley, NY 10535 • 6,420
Jefferson Village, VA 22042 • 2,500
Jeffersonville, GA 31044 • 1,545
Jeffersonville, IN 47129–31 • 21,841
Jeffersonville, KY 40337 • 1,854
Jeffersonville, OH 43128 • 1,281
Jeffrey City, WY 82310 • 1,882
Jellico, TN 37762 • 2,447
Jemez Pueblo, NM 87024 • 1,301
Jemison, AL 35085 • 1,898
Jena, LA 71342 • 2,626
Jenison, MI 49428–29 • 17,882
Jenkins, KY 41537 • 2,751
Jenkins □, GA • 8,247
Jenkintown, PA 19046 • 4,574
Jenks, OK 74037 • 7,493
Jennings, LA 70546 • 11,305
Jennings, MO 63136 • 15,905
Jennings □, IN • 23,661
Jennings Lodge, OR 97222 • 11,480
Jensen Beach, FL 34957–58 • 9,884
Jerauld □, SD • 2,425
Jericho, NY 11753 • 13,141
Jericho, VT 05465 • 1,300
Jermyn, PA 18433 • 2,263
Jerome, ID 83338 • 6,529
Jerome, PA 15937 • 1,074
Jerome □, ID • 15,138
Jersey □, IL • 20,539
Jersey City, NJ 07301–11 • 228,537
Jersey Shore, PA 17740 • 4,353
Jerseyville, IL 62052 • 7,382
Jessamine □, KY • 30,508
Jessup, MD 20794 • 6,537
Jessup, PA 18434 • 4,605
Jesup, GA 31545 • 8,958
Jesup, IA 50648 • 2,121
Jewell, IA 50130 • 1,106
Jewell □, KS • 4,251
Jewett City, CT 06351 • 3,349
Jim Hogg □, TX • 5,109
Jim Thorpe, PA 18229 • 5,048
Jim Wells □, TX • 37,679
Joanna, SC 29351 • 1,735
Jo Daviess □, IL • 21,821
John Day, OR 97845 • 1,836
Johnson, KS 67855 • 1,348
Johnson, VT 05656 • 1,470
Johnson □, AR • 18,221
Johnson □, GA • 8,329
Johnson □, IL • 11,347
Johnson □, IN • 88,109
Johnson □, IA • 96,119
Johnson □, KS • 355,054
Johnson □, KY • 23,248
Johnson □, MO • 42,514
Johnson □, NE • 4,673
Johnson □, TN • 13,766
Johnson □, TX • 97,165
Johnson □, WY • 6,145
Johnsonburg, PA 15845 • 3,350
Johnson City, NY 13790 • 16,890
Johnson City, TN 37601–15 • 49,381
Johnson Creek, WI 53038 • 1,259
Johnsonville, SC 29555 • 1,415
Johnston, IA 50131 • 4,702
Johnston, RI 02919 • 26,542
Johnston, SC 29832 • 2,688
Johnston □, NC • 81,306
Johnston □, OK • 10,032
Johnston City, IL 62951 • 3,706
Johnstown, CO 80534 • 1,579
Johnstown, NY 12095 • 9,058
Johnstown, OH 43031 • 3,237
Johnstown, PA 15901–09 • 28,134
Joliet, IL 60431–36 • 76,836
Jones, OK 73049 • 2,424
Jones □, GA • 20,739
Jones □, IA • 19,444
Jones □, MS • 62,031
Jones □, NC • 9,414
Jones □, SD • 1,324
Jones □, TX • 16,490
Jonesboro, AR 72401–03 • 46,535
Jonesboro, GA 30236–37 • 3,635
Jonesboro, IL 62952 • 1,728
Jonesboro, IN 46938 • 2,073
Jonesboro, LA 71251 • 4,305
Jonesborough, TN 37659 • 3,091
Jones Creek, TX 77541 • 2,160
Jonesport, ME 04649 • 1,525
Jonestown, MS 38639 • 1,467
Jonesville, LA 71343 • 2,720
Jonesville, MI 49250 • 2,283
Jonesville, NC 28642 • 1,549
Jonesville, SC 29353 • 1,205
Joplin, MO 64801–04 • 40,961
Joppatowne, MD 21085 • 11,084
Jordan, MN 55352 • 2,909
Jordan, NY 13080 • 1,325
Joseph, OR 97846 • 1,073
Josephine □, OR • 62,649
Joshua, TX 76058 • 3,828
Joshua Tree, CA 92252 • 3,898
Jourdanton, TX 78026 • 3,220
Juab □, UT • 5,817
Juanita, WA 98033 • 10,500
Judith Basin □, MT • 2,282
Judsonia, AR 72081 • 1,915
Julesburg, CO 80737 • 1,295
Julian, CA 92036 • 1,284
Junction, TX 76849 • 2,654
Junction City, KS 66441 • 20,604
Junction City, KY 40440 • 1,983
Junction City, OR 97448 • 3,670
Juneau, AK 99801–03 • 26,751
Juneau, WI 53039 • 2,157
Juneau □, WI • 21,650
Juniata □, PA • 20,625
Jupiter, FL 33458 • 24,986
Justice, IL 60458 • 11,137
Justin, TX 76247 • 1,234

K

Kaaawa, HI 96730 • 1,138
Kadoka, SD 57543 • 736
Kahaluu, HI 96725 • 380
Kahaluu, HI 96744 • 3,068
Kahoka, MO 63445 • 2,195
Kahuku, HI 96731 • 2,063
Kahului, HI 96732–33 • 16,889
Kailua, HI 96734 • 36,818
Kailua Kona, HI 96739–40 • 9,126
Kake, AK 99830 • 700
Kalaheo, HI 96741 • 3,592
Kalama, WA 98625 • 1,210
Kalamazoo, MI 49001–09 • 80,277
Kalamazoo □, MI • 223,411
Kalawao □, HI • 130
Kalispell, MT 59901 • 11,917
Kalkaska, MI 49646 • 1,952
Kalkaska □, MI • 13,497
Kalona, IA 52247 • 1,942
Kamas, UT 84036 • 1,061
Kamiah, ID 83536 • 1,157
Kamuela (Waimea), HI 96743 • 5,972
Kanab, UT 84741 • 3,289
Kanabec □, MN • 12,802
Kanawha □, WV • 207,619
Kandiyohi □, MN • 38,761
Kane, PA 16735 • 4,590
Kane □, IL • 317,471
Kane □, UT • 5,169
Kaneohe, HI 96744 • 35,448
Kankakee, IL 60901 • 27,575
Kankakee □, IL • 96,255
Kannapolis, NC 28081–83 • 29,696
Kansas City, KS 66101–19 • 149,767
Kansas City, MO 64101–99 • 435,146
Kapaa, HI 96746 • 8,149
Kapaau, HI 96755 • 1,083
Kaplan, LA 70548 • 4,535
Karnes □, TX • 12,455
Karnes City, TX 78118 • 2,916
Karns, TN 37921 • 1,458
Kasson, MN 55944 • 3,514
Kathleen, FL 33849 • 2,743
Katy, TX 77449–50 • 8,005
Kauai □, HI • 51,177
Kaufman, TX 75142 • 5,238
Kaufman □, TX • 52,220
Kaukauna, WI 54130 • 11,982
Kaumakani, HI 96747 • 803
Kaunakakai, HI 96748 • 2,658
Kay □, OK • 48,056
Kaycee, WY 82639 • 256
Kayenta, AZ 86033 • 4,372
Kaysville, UT 84037 • 13,961
Keaau, HI 96749 • 1,584
Kealakekua, HI 96750 • 1,453
Kealia, HI 96751 • 700
Keansburg, NJ 07734 • 11,069
Kearney, MO 64060 • 1,790
Kearney, NE 68847–48 • 24,396
Kearney □, NE • 6,629
Kearns, UT 84118 • 28,374
Kearny, AZ 85237 • 2,262
Kearny, NJ 07031–32 • 34,874
Kearny □, KS • 4,027
Keego Harbor, MI 48320 • 2,932
Keene, NH 03431 • 22,430
Keene, TX 76059 • 3,944
Keeseville, NY 12944 • 1,854
Keewatin, MN 55753 • 1,118
Keith □, NE • 8,584
Keizer, OR 97303 • 21,884
Kekaha, HI 96752 • 3,506
Keller, TX 76248 • 13,683
Kellogg, ID 83837 • 2,591
Kelseyville, CA 95451 • 2,861
Kelso, WA 98626 • 11,820
Kemmerer, WY 83101 • 3,020
Kemp, TX 75143 • 1,184
Kemper □, MS • 10,356
Kenai, AK 99611 • 6,327
Kenbridge, VA 23944 • 1,264
Ken Caryl, CO 80123 • 24,391
Kendall, FL 33156 • 87,271
Kendall □, IL • 39,413
Kendall □, TX • 14,589
Kendall Park, NJ 08824 • 7,127
Kendallville, IN 46755 • 7,773
Kenedy, TX 78119 • 3,763
Kenedy □, TX • 460
Kenilworth, IL 60043 • 2,402
Kenilworth, NJ 07033 • 7,574
Kenly, NC 27542 • 1,549
Kenmare, ND 58746 • 1,214
Kenmore, NY 14217 • 17,180
Kenmore, WA 98028 • 8,917
Kennebec □, ME • 115,904
Kennebunk, ME 04043 • 4,206
Kennebunkport, ME 04046 • 1,100
Kennedy Heights, LA 70094 • 2,000
Kennedy Township, PA 15108 • 7,152
Kenner, LA 70062–65 • 72,033
Kennesaw, GA 30144 • 8,936
Kennett, MO 63857 • 10,941
Kennett Square, PA 19348 • 5,218
Kennewick, WA 99336–37 • 42,155
Kennydale, WA 98056 • 2,000
Kenosha, WI 53140–44 • 80,352
Kenosha □, WI • 128,181
Kenova, WV 25530 • 3,748
Ken Rock, IL 61109 • 3,300
Kensett, AR 72082 • 1,741
Kensington, CA 94707 • 4,974
Kensington, CT 06037 • 8,306
Kensington, MD 20895 • 1,713
Kent, OH 44240 • 28,835
Kent, WA 98031–32 • 37,960
Kent □, DE • 110,993
Kent □, MD • 17,842
Kent □, MI • 500,631
Kent □, RI • 161,135
Kent □, TX • 1,010
Kentfield, CA 94904 • 6,030
Kentland, IN 47951 • 1,798
Kenton, DE 19955 • 232
Kenton, OH 43326 • 8,356
Kenton, TN 38233 • 1,366
Kenton □, KY • 142,031
Kentwood, LA 70444 • 2,468
Kentwood, MI 49508 • 37,826
Kenvil, NJ 07847 • 3,050
Kenwood, OH 45236 • 7,469
Kenyon, MN 55946 • 1,552
Kenyon, RI 02836 • 400
Keokea, HI 96790 • 900
Keokuk, IA 52632 • 12,451
Keokuk □, IA • 11,624
Keosauqua, IA 52565 • 1,020
Keota, IA 52248 • 1,000
Kerens, TX 75144 • 1,702
Kerhonkson, NY 12446 • 1,629
Kermit, TX 79745 • 6,875
Kern □, CA • 543,477
Kernersville, NC 27284–85 • 10,836
Kernville, CA 93238 • 1,656
Kerr □, TX • 36,304
Kerrville, TX 78028–29 • 17,384
Kershaw, SC 29067 • 1,814
Kershaw □, SC • 43,599
Ketchikan, AK 99901 • 8,263
Ketchum, ID 83340 • 2,523
Kettering, MD 20772 • 9,901
Kettering, OH 45429 • 60,569
Kettle Falls, WA 99141 • 1,272
Kewanee, IL 61443 • 12,969
Kewaskum, WI 53040 • 2,515
Kewaunee, WI 54216 • 2,750
Kewaunee □, WI • 18,878
Keweenaw □, MI • 1,701
Keya Paha □, NE • 1,029
Key Biscayne, FL 33149 • 8,854
Key Largo, FL 33037 • 11,336
Keyport, NJ 07735 • 7,586
Keyser, WV 26726 • 5,870
Keystone Heights, FL 32656 • 1,315
Key West, FL 33040–41 • 24,832
Kiana, AK 99749 • 385
Kidder □, ND • 3,332
Kiel, WI 53042 • 2,910
Kihei, HI 96753 • 11,107
Kilauea, HI 96754 • 1,685
Kilgore, TX 75662–63 • 11,066
Killdeer, ND 58640 • 722
Killeen, TX 76540–47 • 63,535
Killen, AL 35645 • 1,047
Kilmarnock, VA 22482 • 1,109
Kimball, NE 69145 • 2,574
Kimball □, NE • 4,108
Kimberly, AL 35091 • 1,096
Kimberly, ID 83341 • 2,367
Kimberly, WI 54136 • 5,406
Kimble □, TX • 4,122
Kincaid, IL 62540 • 1,353
Kinder, LA 70648 • 2,246
Kinderhook, NY 12106 • 1,293
King, NC 27021 • 4,059
King □, TX • 354
King □, WA • 1,507,319
King and Queen □, VA • 6,289
King City, CA 93930 • 7,634
King Cove, AK 99612 • 451
Kingfisher, OK 73750 • 4,095
Kingfisher □, OK • 13,212
King George □, VA • 13,527
Kingman, AZ 86401–02 • 12,722
Kingman, KS 67068 • 3,196
Kingman □, KS • 8,292
King of Prussia, PA 19406 • 18,406
Kings, MS 39180 • 1,165
Kings □, CA • 101,469
Kings □, NY • 2,300,664
King Salmon, AK 99613 • 696
Kingsburg, CA 93631 • 7,205
Kingsbury □, SD • 5,925
Kingsford, MI 49801 • 5,480
Kingsgate, WA 98011 • 14,259
Kingsland, GA 31548 • 4,699
Kingsland, TX 78639 • 2,725
Kingsley, IA 51028 • 1,129
Kings Mountain, NC 28086 • 8,763
Kings Park, NY 11754 • 17,773
Kings Park, VA 22151 • 6,000
Kings Park West, VA 22032 • 6,000
Kings Point, FL 33484 • 12,422
Kings Point, NY 11024 • 4,843
Kingsport, TN 37660–65 • 36,365
Kingston, ID 83839 • 1,000
Kingston, MA 02364 • 4,774
Kingston, NJ 08528 • 1,200
Kingston, NY 12401 • 23,095
Kingston, OH 45644 • 1,153
Kingston, OK 73439 • 1,237
Kingston, PA 18704 • 14,507
Kingston, RI 02881 • 6,504
Kingston, TN 37763 • 4,552
Kingston Springs, TN 37082 • 1,529
Kingstown, MD 21620 • 1,660
Kingstree, SC 29556 • 3,858
Kingsville, MD 21087 • 3,550
Kingsville (North Kingsville), OH 44048 • 1,243
Kingsville, TX 78363–64 • 25,276
King William □, VA • 10,913
Kingwood, TX 77339 • 37,397
Kingwood, WV 26537 • 3,243
Kinloch, MO 63140 • 2,702
Kinnelon, NJ 07405 • 8,470
Kinney □, TX • 3,119
Kinsey, AL 36301 • 1,679
Kinsley, KS 67547 • 1,875
Kinston, NC 28501–03 • 25,295
Kiowa, KS 67070 • 1,160
Kiowa □, CO • 1,688
Kiowa □, KS • 3,660
Kiowa □, OK • 11,347
Kipnuk, AK 99614 • 470
Kirby, TX 78219 • 8,326
Kirbyville, TX 75956 • 1,871
Kirkland, IL 60146 • 1,011
Kirkland, WA 98033–34 • 40,052
Kirksville, MO 63501 • 17,152
Kirkwood, DE 19708 • 350
Kirkwood, MO 63122 • 27,291
Kirtland, NM 87417 • 3,552
Kirtland, OH 44094 • 5,881
Kissimmee, FL 34741–46 • 30,050
Kit Carson □, CO • 7,140
Kitsap □, WA • 189,731
Kittanning, PA 16201 • 5,120
Kittery, ME 03904 • 5,151

Kittery Point, ME 03905 • 1,093
Kittitas □, WA • 26,725
Kittson □, MN • 5,767
Kitty Hawk, NC 27949 • 1,937
Klamath □, OR • 57,702
Klamath Falls, OR 97601–03 • 17,737
Klawock, AK 99925 • 722
Kleberg □, TX • 30,274
Klein, TX 77379 • 12,000
Klickitat □, WA • 16,616
Knightdale, NC 27545 • 1,884
Knights Landing, CA 95645 • 1,000
Knightstown, IN 46148 • 2,048
Knob Noster, MO 65336 • 2,261
Knott □, KY • 17,906
Knox, IN 46534 • 3,705
Knox, PA 16232 • 1,182
Knox □, IL • 56,393
Knox □, IN • 39,884
Knox □, KY • 29,676
Knox □, ME • 36,310
Knox □, MO • 4,482
Knox □, NE • 9,534
Knox □, OH • 47,473
Knox □, TN • 335,749
Knox □, TX • 4,837
Knox City, TX 79529 • 1,440
Knoxville, IL 61448 • 3,243
Knoxville, IA 50138 • 8,232
Knoxville, TN 37901–50 • 165,121
Kodiak, AK 99615 • 6,365
Kohler, WI 53044 • 1,817
Kokomo, IN 46901–04 • 44,962
Koloa, HI 96756 • 1,791
Konawa, OK 74849 • 1,508
Koochiching □, MN • 16,299
Koontz Lake, IN 46574 • 1,615
Kootenai □, ID • 69,795
Koppel, PA 16136 • 1,024
Kosciusko, MS 39090 • 6,986
Kosciusko □, IN • 65,294
Kossuth □, IA • 18,591
Kotlik, AK 99620 • 461
Kotzebue, AK 99752 • 2,751
Kountze, TX 77625 • 2,056
Kouts, IN 46347 • 1,603
Krebs, OK 74554 • 1,955
Kremmling, CO 80459 • 1,166
Krotz Springs, LA 70750 • 1,285
Kula, HI 96790 • 1,300
Kulpmont, PA 17834 • 3,233
Kuna, ID 83634 • 1,955
Kurtistown, HI 96760 • 910
Kutztown, PA 19530 • 4,704
Kwethluk, AK 99621 • 558
Kwigillingok, AK 99622 • 278
Kyle, TX 78640 • 2,225

L

Labadieville, LA 70372 • 1,821
La Barge, WY 83123 • 493
La Belle, FL 33935 • 2,703
Labette □, KS • 23,693
La Canada Flintridge, CA 91011 • 19,378
Lac du Flambeau, WI 54538 • 1,180
La Center, KY 42056 • 1,040
Lacey, WA 98503 • 19,279
Lackawanna, NY 14218 • 20,585
Lackawanna □, PA • 219,039
Laclede □, MO • 27,158
Lacombe, LA 70445 • 6,523
Lacon, IL 61540 • 1,986
Laconia, NH 03246–47 • 15,743
Lacoochee, FL 33537 • 2,072
Lac qui Parle □, MN • 8,924
La Crescent, MN 55947 • 4,311
La Crescenta, CA 91214 • 12,500
La Crosse, KS 67548 • 1,427
La Crosse, WI 54601–03 • 51,003
La Crosse □, WI • 97,904
La Cygne, KS 66040 • 1,066
Ladd, IL 61329 • 1,283
Ladera Heights, CA 90045 • 6,316
Ladoga, IN 47954 • 1,124
Ladson, SC 29456 • 13,540
Ladue, MO 63124 • 8,847
Lady Lake, FL 32159 • 8,071
Ladysmith, WI 54848 • 3,938
Lafayette, AL 36862 • 3,151
Lafayette, CA 94549 • 23,501
Lafayette, CO 80026 • 14,548
Lafayette, GA 30728 • 6,313
Lafayette, IN 47901–06 • 43,764
Lafayette, LA 70501–09 • 94,440
Lafayette, NC 28304 • 3,200
Lafayette, OR 97127 • 1,292
La Fayette, RI 02852 • 640
Lafayette, TN 37083 • 3,641
Lafayette □, AR • 9,643
Lafayette □, FL • 5,578
Lafayette □, LA • 164,762
Lafayette □, MS • 31,826
Lafayette □, MO • 31,107
Lafayette □, WI • 16,076
Lafayette Southwest, LA • 5,500
La Feria, TX 78559 • 4,360
Lafitte, LA 70067 • 1,507
La Follette, TN 37766 • 7,192
Lafourche □, LA • 85,860
La Grande, OR 97850 • 11,766
La Grange, GA 30240–41 • 25,597
La Grange, IL 60525 • 15,362
Lagrange, IN 46761 • 2,382
La Grange, KY 40031 • 3,853
La Grange, MO 63448 • 1,102
La Grange, NC 28551 • 2,805
Lagrange, OH 44050 • 1,199
La Grange, TX 78945 • 3,951
Lagrange □, IN • 29,477
La Grange Highlands, IL 60525 • 3,660
La Grange Park, IL 60525 • 12,861
Laguna Beach, CA 92651–54 • 23,170
Laguna Hills, CA 92653 • 46,731
Laguna Niguel, CA 92677 • 44,400
La Habra, CA 90631–33 • 51,266
Lahaina, HI 96761 • 9,073
La Harpe, IL 61450 • 1,407
Laie, HI 96762 • 5,577
Laingsburg, MI 48848 • 1,148
La Junta, CO 81050 • 7,637

Lake □, CA • 50,631
Lake □, CO • 6,007
Lake □, FL • 152,104
Lake □, IL • 516,418
Lake □, IN • 475,594
Lake □, MI • 8,583
Lake □, MN • 10,415
Lake □, MT • 21,041
Lake □, OH • 215,499
Lake □, OR • 7,186
Lake □, SD • 10,550
Lake □, TN • 7,129
Lake Alfred, FL 33850 • 3,622
Lake Andes, SD 57356 • 846
Lake Arrowhead, CA 92317 • 6,539
Lake Arthur, LA 70549 • 3,194
Lake Barcroft, VA 22041 • 8,686
Lake Bluff, IL 60044 • 5,513
Lake Butler, FL 32054 • 2,116
Lake Carmel, NY 10512 • 8,489
Lake Charles, LA 70601–29 • 70,580
Lake City, AR 72437 • 1,833
Lake City, FL 32055–56 • 10,005
Lake City, IA 51449 • 1,841
Lake City, MN 55041 • 4,391
Lake City, PA 16423 • 2,519
Lake City, SC 29560 • 7,153
Lake City, TN 37769 • 2,166
Lake Crystal, MN 56055 • 2,084
Lake Delta, NY 13440 • 1,980
Lake Delton, WI 53940 • 1,470
Lake Elmo, MN 55042 • 5,903
Lake Elsinore, CA 92330–31 • 18,285
Lake Erie Beach, NY 14006 • 4,509
Lakefield, MN 56150 • 1,679
Lake Forest, FL 33023 • 5,400
Lake Forest, IL 60045 • 17,836
Lake Geneva, WI 53147 • 5,979
Lake Grove, NY 11755 • 9,612
Lake Hamilton, AR 71913 • 1,331
Lake Havasu City, AZ 86403–05 • 24,363
Lake Helen, FL 32744 • 2,344
Lakehurst, NJ 08733 • 3,078
Lake in the Hills, IL 60102 • 5,866
Lake Jackson, TX 77566 • 22,776
Lake Katrine, NY 12449 • 1,998
Lakeland, FL 33801–13 • 70,576
Lakeland, GA 31635 • 2,467
Lakeland Highlands, FL 33801 • 9,972
Lakeland Village, CA 92330 • 5,159
Lake Linden, MI 49945 • 1,203
Lake Lorraine, FL 32569 • 6,779
Lake Luzerne, NY 12846 • 1,160
Lake Magdalene, FL 33612 • 15,973
Lake Mary, FL 32746 • 5,929
Lake Mills, IA 50450 • 2,143
Lake Mills, WI 53551 • 4,143
Lakemore, OH 44250 • 2,684
Lake Odessa, MI 48849 • 2,256
Lake Of The Woods □, MN • 4,076
Lake Orion, MI 48360–62 • 3,057
Lake Oswego, OR 97034–35 • 30,576
Lake Park, FL 33403 • 6,704
Lake Placid, FL 33852 • 1,158
Lake Placid, NY 12946 • 2,485
Lakeport, CA 95453 • 4,390
Lake Preston, SD 57249 • 663
Lake Providence, LA 71254 • 5,380
Lake Ridge, VA 22192 • 23,862
Lake Ronkonkoma, NY 11779 • 18,997
Lake Shore, MD 21122 • 13,269
Lakeside, CA 92040 • 39,412
Lakeside, CT 06488 • 1,200
Lakeside, FL 32073 • 29,137
Lakeside, OR 97449 • 1,437
Lakeside, VA 23228 • 12,081
Lakeside Park, KY 41017 • 3,131
Lakeside-Pinetop, AZ 85935 • 2,422
Lake Station, IN 46405 • 13,899
Lake Stevens, WA 98258 • 3,380
Lake Telemark, NJ 07866 • 1,121
Lakeview, GA 30741 • 5,237
Lake View, IA 51450 • 1,303
Lakeview, MI 48850 • 1,108
Lake View, NY 14085 • 1,460
Lakeview, NY 11552 • 5,476
Lakeview, OH 43331 • 1,056
Lakeview, OR 97630 • 2,526
Lake Villa, IL 60046 • 2,857
Lake Village, AR 71653 • 2,791
Lakeville, CT 06039 • 1,800
Lakeville, MA 02346 • 1,948
Lakeville, MN 55044 • 24,854
Lakeville, NY 14480 • 1,000
Lake Wales, FL 33853 • 9,670
Lake Wissota, WI 54729 • 2,175
Lakewood, CA 90711–16 • 73,557
Lakewood, CO 80215 • 126,481
Lakewood, IL 60014 • 1,609
Lakewood, IA 50211 • 1,950
Lakewood, NJ 08701 • 26,095
Lakewood, NY 14750 • 3,564
Lakewood, OH 44107 • 59,718
Lakewood, WA 98259 • 58,412
Lakewood Center, WA 98499 • 58,412
Lakewood Park, FL 34951 • 7,211
Lake Worth, FL 33460–67 • 28,564
Lake Zurich, IL 60047 • 14,947
Lakin, KS 67860 • 2,060
Lakota, ND 58344 • 898
La Luz, NM 88337 • 1,625
Lamar, CO 81052 • 8,343
Lamar, MO 64759 • 4,168
Lamar, PA 16848 • 1,200
Lamar, SC 29069 • 1,125
Lamar □, AL • 15,715
Lamar □, GA • 13,038
Lamar □, MS • 30,424
Lamar □, TX • 43,949
La Marque, TX 77568 • 14,120
Lamb □, TX • 15,072
Lambert, MS 38643 • 1,131
Lambertville, MI 48144 • 7,860
Lambertville, NJ 08530 • 3,927
La Mesa, CA 91941–44 • 52,931
La Mesa, NM 88044 • 900
Lamesa, TX 79331 • 10,809
La Mirada, CA 90637–38 • 40,452
Lamoille, NV 89828 • 110
Lamoille □, VT • 19,735
Lamoni, IA 50140 • 2,319
Lamont, CA 93241 • 11,517
La Moure, ND 58458 • 970

La Moure □, ND • 5,383
Lampasas, TX 76550 • 6,382
Lampasas □, TX • 13,521
Lanai City, HI 96763 • 2,400
Lanark, IL 61046 • 1,382
Lancashire, DE 19810 • 1,175
Lancaster, CA 93534–39 • 97,291
Lancaster, KY 40444 • 3,421
Lancaster, NH 03584 • 1,859
Lancaster, NY 14086 • 11,940
Lancaster, OH 43130 • 34,507
Lancaster, PA 17601–05 • 55,551
Lancaster, SC 29720–21 • 8,914
Lancaster, TX 75146 • 22,117
Lancaster, WI 53813 • 4,192
Lancaster □, NE • 213,641
Lancaster □, PA • 422,822
Lancaster □, SC • 54,516
Lancaster □, VA • 10,896
Lancaster Village, DE 19805 • 1,100
Landen, OH 45040 • 9,263
Lander, WY 82520 • 7,023
Lander □, NV • 6,266
Landess, IN 46944 • 1,500
Landis, NC 28088 • 2,333
Land O' Lakes, FL 34639 • 7,892
Landover, MD 20784 • 5,052
Landrum, SC 29356 • 2,347
Lane □, KS • 2,375
Lane □, OR • 282,912
Lanesboro, MA 01237 • 1,000
Lanett, AL 36863 • 8,985
Langdon, ND 58249 • 2,241
Langeloth, PA 15054 • 1,112
Langhorne, PA 19047 • 1,361
Langlade □, WI • 19,505
Langley, SC 29834 • 1,714
Langley Park, MD 20783 • 17,474
Langston, OK 73050 • 1,471
Lanham, MD 20706 • 5,000
Lanier □, GA • 5,531
Lansdale, PA 19446 • 16,362
Lansdowne, MD 21227 • 9,430
Lansdowne, PA 19050 • 11,712
L'Anse, MI 49946 • 2,151
Lansford, PA 18232 • 4,583
Lansing, IL 60438 • 28,086
Lansing, IA 52151 • 1,007
Lansing, KS 66043 • 7,120
Lansing, MI 48901–33 • 127,321
Lantana, FL 33462 • 8,392
La Palma, CA 90623 • 15,392
La Paz □, AZ • 13,844
Lapeer, MI 48446 • 7,759
Lapeer □, MI • 74,768
Lapel, IN 46051 • 1,742
La Place, LA 70068–69 • 24,194
La Plata, MD 20646 • 5,841
La Plata, MO 63549 • 1,401
La Plata □, CO • 32,284
Laporte, CO 80535 • 1,300
La Porte, IN 46350 • 21,507
La Porte, TX 77571–72 • 27,910
La Porte □, IN • 107,066
La Porte City, IA 50651 • 2,128
La Pryor, TX 78872 • 1,343
La Puente, CA 91744–49 • 36,955
Lapwai, ID 83540 • 932
Laramie, WY 82063–71 • 26,687
Laramie □, WY • 73,142
Larchmont, NY 10538 • 6,181
Larchmont North, NY 10538 • 11,240
Laredo, TX 78040–44 • 122,899
Largo, FL 34640–49 • 65,674
Larimer □, CO • 186,136
Larimore, ND 58251 • 1,464
La Riviera, CA 95826 • 10,986
Larkspur, CA 94939 • 11,070
Larksville, PA 18704 • 4,700
Larned, KS 67550 • 4,490
Larose, LA 70373 • 5,772
Larue □, KY • 11,679
La Salle, CO 80645 • 1,783
La Salle, IL 61301 • 9,717
La Salle □, IL • 106,913
La Salle □, LA • 13,662
La Salle □, TX • 5,254
Las Animas, CO 81054 • 2,481
Las Animas □, CO • 13,765
Las Cruces, NM 88001–08 • 62,126
Lassen □, CA • 27,598
Las Vegas, NV 89101–99 • 258,295
Las Vegas, NM 87701 • 14,753
Latah □, ID • 30,617
Lathrop, MO 64465 • 1,794
Lathrop Wells, NV 89020 • 350
Latimer □, OK • 10,333
Laton, CA 93242 • 1,415
Latrobe, PA 15650 • 9,265
Latta, SC 29565 • 1,565
Lauderdale □, AL • 79,661
Lauderdale □, MS • 75,555
Lauderdale □, TN • 23,491
Lauderdale Lakes, FL 33313 • 27,341
Lauderhill, FL 33313 • 49,708
Laughlin, NV 89028–29 • 140
Laughlintown, PA 15655 • 1,000
Laurel, DE 19956 • 3,226
Laurel, FL 34272 • 8,245
Laurel, MD 20707–09 • 19,438
Laurel, MS 39440–42 • 18,827
Laurel, MT 59044 • 5,686
Laurel, VA 23060 • 13,011
Laurel □, KY • 43,438
Laurel Bay, SC 29902 • 4,972
Laureldale, PA 19605 • 3,726
Laurel Hill, NC 28351 • 2,314
Laurence Harbor, NJ 08879 • 6,361
Laurens, IA 50554 • 1,550
Laurens, SC 29360 • 9,694
Laurens □, GA • 39,988
Laurens □, SC • 58,092
Laurinburg, NC 28352–53 • 11,643
Laurium, MI 49913 • 2,268
Lavaca, AR 72941 • 1,253
Lavaca □, TX • 18,690
La Vale, MD 21502 • 5,000
Lavallette, NJ 08735 • 2,299
La Vergne, TN 37086 • 7,499
La Verkin, UT 84745 • 1,771
La Verne, CA 91750 • 30,897
Laverne, OK 73848 • 1,269
La Vista, GA 30329 • 4,900

La Vista, NE 68128 • 9,840
Lavonia, GA 30553 • 1,840
Lawai, HI 96765 • 1,787
Lawndale, CA 90260–61 • 27,331
Lawnside, NJ 08045 • 2,841
Lawrence, IN 46226 • 26,763
Lawrence, KS 66044–46 • 65,608
Lawrence, MA 01840–45 • 70,207
Lawrence, NY 11559 • 6,513
Lawrence □, AL • 31,513
Lawrence □, AR • 17,457
Lawrence □, IL • 15,972
Lawrence □, IN • 42,836
Lawrence □, KY • 13,998
Lawrence □, MS • 12,458
Lawrence □, MO • 30,236
Lawrence □, OH • 61,834
Lawrence □, PA • 96,246
Lawrence □, TN • 35,303
Lawrenceburg, IN 47025 • 4,375
Lawrenceburg, KY 40342 • 5,911
Lawrenceburg, TN 38464 • 10,412
Lawrence Park, PA 16511 • 4,310
Lawrenceville, GA 30243–46 • 16,848
Lawrenceville, IL 62439 • 4,897
Lawrenceville, NJ 08648 • 6,446
Lawrenceville, VA 23868 • 1,486
Lawson, MO 64062 • 1,876
Lawsonia, MD 21817 • 1,326
Lawtell, LA 70550 • 1,014
Lawton, MI 49065 • 1,685
Lawton, OK 73501–07 • 80,561
Layton, UT 84040–41 • 41,784
Laytonville, CA 95454 • 1,133
Lea □, NM • 55,765
Leachville, AR 72438 • 1,743
Lead, SD 57754 • 3,632
Leadville, CO 80461 • 2,629
Leadwood, MO 63653 • 1,247
League City, TX 77573–74 • 30,159
Leake □, MS • 18,436
Leakesville, MS 39451 • 1,129
Lealman, FL 33714 • 21,748
Leavenworth, KS 66048 • 38,495
Leavenworth, WA 98826 • 1,692
Leavenworth □, KS • 64,371
Leavittsburg, OH 44430 • 2,220
Leawood, KS 66206 • 19,693
Lebanon, DE 19901 • 130
Lebanon, IL 62254 • 3,688
Lebanon, IN 46052 • 12,059
Lebanon, KY 40033 • 5,695
Lebanon, MO 65536 • 9,983
Lebanon, NH 03766 • 12,183
Lebanon, NJ 08833 • 1,036
Lebanon, OH 45036 • 10,453
Lebanon, OR 97355 • 10,950
Lebanon, PA 17042 • 24,800
Lebanon, TN 37087–88 • 15,208
Lebanon, VA 24266 • 3,386
Lebanon □, PA • 113,744
Lebanon Junction, KY 40150 • 1,741
Le Center, MN 56057 • 2,006
Le Claire, IA 52753 • 2,734
Lecompte, LA 71346 • 1,592
Lee, MA 01238 • 2,020
Lee □, AL • 87,146
Lee □, AR • 13,053
Lee □, FL • 335,113
Lee □, GA • 16,250
Lee □, IL • 34,392
Lee □, IA • 38,687
Lee □, KY • 7,422
Lee □, MS • 65,581
Lee □, NC • 41,374
Lee □, SC • 18,437
Lee □, TX • 12,854
Lee □, VA • 24,496
Leechburg, PA 15656 • 2,504
Leedom Estates, DE 19720 • 1,100
Leeds, AL 35094 • 9,946
Leelanau □, MI • 16,527
Lee Park, PA 18702 • 3,800
Leesburg, FL 34748–49 • 14,903
Leesburg, GA 31763 • 1,452
Leesburg, OH 45135 • 1,063
Leesburg, VA 22075 • 16,202
Lees Summit, MO 64063–64 • 46,418
Leesville, LA 71446 • 7,638
Leesville, SC 29070 • 2,025
Leetonia, OH 44431 • 2,070
Leetsdale, PA 15056 • 1,387
Leflore □, MS • 37,341
Le Flore □, OK • 43,270
Le Grand, CA 95333 • 1,205
Lehi, UT 84043 • 8,475
Lehigh □, PA • 291,130
Lehigh Acres, FL 33936 • 13,611
Lehighton, PA 18235 • 5,914
Leicester, MA 01524 • 3,200
Leipsic, DE 19901 • 236
Leipsic, OH 45856 • 2,203
Leisure City, FL 33033 • 19,379
Leitchfield, KY 42754–55 • 4,965
Leland, MS 38756 • 6,366
Le Mars, IA 51031 • 8,454
Lemay, MO 63125 • 18,005
Lemhi □, ID • 6,899
Lemmon, SD 57638 • 1,614
Lemmon Valley, NV 89501 • 4,100
Lemon Grove, CA 91945–46 • 23,984
Lemont, IL 60439 • 7,348
Lemont, PA 16851 • 2,613
Lemoore, CA 93245 • 13,622
Lena, IL 61048 • 2,605
Lenawee □, MI • 91,476
Lenexa, KS 66215 • 34,034
Lennox, CA 90304 • 22,757
Lennox, SD 57039 • 1,767
Lenoir, NC 28645 • 14,192
Lenoir □, NC • 57,274
Lenoir City, TN 37771 • 6,147
Lenox, IA 50851 • 1,303
Lenox, MA 01240 • 1,687
Leo, IN 46765 • 1,200
Leominster, MA 01453 • 38,145
Leon, IA 50144 • 2,047
Leon □, FL • 192,493
Leon □, TX • 12,665
Leonard, TX 75452 • 1,744
Leonardo, NJ 07737 • 3,720
Leonardtown, MD 20650 • 1,475
Leonia, NJ 07605 • 8,365

Leon Valley, TX 78238 • 9,581
Leoti, KS 67861 • 1,738
Lepanto, AR 72354 • 2,033
Le Roy, IL 61752 • 2,777
Le Roy, NY 14482 • 4,974
Leslie, MI 49251 • 1,872
Leslie, SC 29730 • 1,102
Leslie □, KY • 13,642
Lester Prairie, MN 55354 • 1,180
Le Sueur, MN 56058 • 3,714
Le Sueur □, MN • 23,239
Letcher □, KY • 27,000
Levelland, TX 79336–38 • 13,986
Levittown, NY 11756 • 53,286
Levittown, PA 19058 • 55,362
Levy □, FL • 25,923
Lewes, DE 19958 • 2,295
Lewis □, ID • 3,516
Lewis □, KY • 13,029
Lewis □, MO • 10,233
Lewis □, NY • 26,796
Lewis □, TN • 9,247
Lewis □, WA • 59,358
Lewis □, WV • 17,223
Lewis and Clark □, MT • 47,495
Lewisburg, OH 45338 • 1,584
Lewisburg, PA 17837 • 5,785
Lewisburg, TN 37091 • 9,879
Lewisburg, WV 24901 • 3,598
Lewisport, KY 42351 • 1,778
Lewiston, ID 83501 • 28,082
Lewiston, ME 04240–43 • 39,757
Lewiston, MN 55952 • 1,298
Lewiston, NY 14092 • 3,048
Lewiston, UT 84320 • 1,532
Lewistown, IL 61542 • 2,572
Lewistown, MT 59457 • 6,051
Lewistown, PA 17044 • 9,341
Lewisville, AR 71845 • 1,424
Lewisville, TX 75067 • 46,521
Lexington, IL 61753 • 1,809
Lexington, KY 40501–96 • 225,366
Lexington, MA 02173 • 28,974
Lexington, MS 39095 • 2,227
Lexington, MO 64067 • 4,860
Lexington, NE 68850 • 6,601
Lexington, NC 27292–93 • 16,581
Lexington, OH 44904 • 4,124
Lexington, OK 73051 • 1,776
Lexington, SC 29071–73 • 3,289
Lexington, TN 38351 • 5,810
Lexington, VA 24450 • 6,959
Lexington □, SC • 167,611
Lexington Park, MD 20653 • 9,943
Libby, MT 59923 • 2,532
Liberal, KS 67901–05 • 16,573
Liberty, IN 47353 • 2,051
Liberty, KY 42539 • 1,937
Liberty, MO 64068 • 20,459
Liberty, NY 12754 • 4,128
Liberty, NC 27298 • 2,047
Liberty, SC 29657 • 3,228
Liberty, TX 77575 • 7,733
Liberty □, FL • 5,569
Liberty □, GA • 52,745
Liberty □, MT • 2,295
Liberty □, TX • 52,726
Liberty Acres, CA 90250 • 4,700
Liberty Center, OH 43532 • 1,084
Liberty Lake, WA 99019 • 2,015
Libertyville, IL 60048 • 19,174
Licking, MO 65542 • 1,328
Licking □, OH • 128,300
Lidgerwood, ND 58053 • 799
Lighthouse Point, FL 33064 • 10,378
Ligonier, IN 46767 • 3,443
Ligonier, PA 15658 • 1,638
Lihue, HI 96766 • 5,536
Lilbourn, MO 63862 • 1,378
Lilburn, GA 30247 • 9,301
Lillington, NC 27546 • 2,048
Lilly, PA 15938 • 1,162
Lima, NY 14485 • 2,165
Lima, OH 45801–09 • 45,549
Limestone, ME 04750–51 • 1,245
Limestone □, AL • 54,135
Limestone □, TX • 20,946
Limon, CO 80828 • 1,831
Lincoln, AL 35096 • 2,941
Lincoln, AR 72744 • 1,460
Lincoln, CA 95648 • 7,248
Lincoln, DE 19960 • 500
Lincoln, IL 62656 • 15,418
Lincoln, KS 67455 • 1,381
Lincoln, ME 04457 • 3,399
Lincoln, MA 01773 • 2,860
Lincoln, NE 68501–72 • 191,972
Lincoln □, AR • 13,690
Lincoln □, CO • 4,529
Lincoln □, GA • 7,442
Lincoln □, ID • 3,308
Lincoln □, KS • 3,653
Lincoln □, KY • 20,045
Lincoln □, LA • 41,745
Lincoln □, ME • 30,357
Lincoln □, MN • 6,890
Lincoln □, MS • 30,278
Lincoln □, MO • 28,892
Lincoln □, MT • 17,481
Lincoln □, NE • 32,508
Lincoln □, NV • 3,775
Lincoln □, NM • 12,219
Lincoln □, NC • 50,319
Lincoln □, OK • 29,216
Lincoln □, OR • 38,889
Lincoln □, SD • 15,427
Lincoln □, TN • 28,157
Lincoln □, WA • 8,864
Lincoln □, WV • 21,382
Lincoln □, WI • 26,993
Lincoln □, WY • 12,625
Lincoln Acres, CA 91947 • 1,800
Lincoln City, OR 97367 • 5,892
Lincoln Heights, OH 45215 • 4,805
Lincoln Park, CO 81212 • 3,728
Lincoln Park, GA 30286 • 1,755
Lincoln Park, MI 48146 • 41,832
Lincoln Park, NJ 07035 • 10,978
Lincolnshire, IL 60069 • 4,931
Lincolnton, GA 30817 • 1,476
Lincolnton, NC 28092 • 6,847
Lincoln Village, CA 95207 • 4,236
Lincoln Village, OH 43228 • 9,958

Lincolnwood, IL 60645 • 11,365
Lincroft, NJ 07738 • 4,740
Linda, CA 95901 • 13,033
Lindale, GA 30147 • 4,187
Lindale, TX 75771 • 2,428
Linden, AL 36748 • 2,548
Linden, MI 48451 • 2,415
Linden, NJ 07036 • 36,701
Linden, TN 37096 • 1,099
Linden, TX 75563 • 2,375
Lindenhurst, IL 60046 • 8,038
Lindenhurst, NY 11757 • 26,879
Lindenwold, NJ 08021 • 18,734
Lindgren Acres, FL 33177 • 22,290
Lindon, UT 84042 • 3,818
Lindsay, CA 93247 • 8,338
Lindsay, OK 73052 • 2,947
Lindsborg, KS 67456 • 3,076
Lindstrom, MN 55045 • 2,461
Linesville, PA 16424 • 1,166
Lineville, AL 36266 • 2,394
Lingle, WY 82223 • 473
Linglestown, PA 17112 • 3,700
Linn, MO 65051 • 1,148
Linn □, IA • 168,767
Linn □, KS • 8,254
Linn □, MO • 13,885
Linn □, OR • 91,227
Lino Lakes, MN 55014 • 8,807
Linthicum Heights, MD • 2,950
Linthicum Heights, MD 21090 • 7,547
Linton, IN 47441 • 5,814
Linton, ND 58552 • 1,410
Linwood, NJ 08221 • 6,866
Lipscomb, AL 35020 • 2,892
Lipscomb □, TX • 3,143
Lisbon, IA 52253 • 1,452
Lisbon, ME 04250 • 1,240
Lisbon, NH 03585 • 1,246
Lisbon, ND 58054 • 2,177
Lisbon, OH 44432 • 3,037
Lisbon Falls, ME 04252 • 4,674
Lisle, IL 60532 • 19,512
Litchfield, CT 06759 • 1,378
Litchfield, IL 62056 • 6,883
Litchfield, MI 49252 • 1,317
Litchfield, MN 55355 • 6,041
Litchfield □, CT • 174,092
Litchfield Park, AZ 85340 • 3,303
Lithia Springs, GA 30057 • 11,403
Lithonia, GA 30058 • 2,448
Lititz, PA 17543 • 8,280
Little Canada, MN 55110 • 8,971
Little Chute, WI 54140 • 9,207
Little Compton, RI 02837 • 500
Little Creek, DE 19961 • 167
Little Falls, MN 56345 • 7,232
Little Falls, NJ 07424 • 11,294
Little Falls, NY 13365 • 5,829
Little Ferry, NJ 07643 • 9,989
Littlefield, TX 79339 • 6,489
Little River □, AR • 13,966
Little Rock, AR 72201–31 • 175,795
Little Silver, NJ 07739 • 5,721
Littlestown, PA 17340 • 2,974
Littleton, CO 80120–27 • 33,685
Littleton, MA 01460 • 2,867
Littleton, NH 03561 • 4,633
Little Valley, NY 14755 • 1,188
Live Oak, CA 95062 • 15,212
Live Oak, CA 95953 • 4,320
Live Oak, FL 32060 • 6,332
Live Oak, TX 78233 • 10,023
Live Oak □, TX • 9,556
Live Oak Manor, LA 70094 • 2,150
Livermore, CA 94550 • 56,741
Livermore, KY 42352 • 1,534
Livermore Falls, ME 04254 • 1,935
Livingston, AL 35470 • 3,530
Livingston, CA 95334 • 7,317
Livingston, MT 59047 • 6,701
Livingston, NJ 07039 • 26,609
Livingston, TN 38570 • 3,809
Livingston, TX 77351 • 5,019
Livingston □, IL • 39,301
Livingston □, KY • 9,062
Livingston □, LA • 70,526
Livingston □, MI • 115,645
Livingston □, MO • 14,592
Livingston □, NY • 62,372
Livingston Manor, NY 12758 • 1,482
Livonia, MI 48150–54 • 100,850
Livonia, NY 14487 • 1,434
Llangollen Estates, DE 19720 • 1,070
Llano, TX 78643 • 2,962
Llano □, TX • 11,631
Lloyd Harbor, NY 11743 • 3,343
Lochearn, MD 21207 • 25,240
Loch Lomond, VA 22110 • 3,292
Lockhart, FL 32810 • 11,636
Lockhart, TX 78644 • 9,205
Lock Haven, PA 17745 • 9,230
Lockland, OH 45215 • 4,357
Lockney, TX 79241 • 2,207
Lockport, IL 60441 • 9,401
Lockport, LA 70374 • 2,503
Lockport, NY 14094 • 24,426
Lockwood, MO 65682 • 1,041
Lockwood, MT 59101 • 3,967
Locust, NC 28097 • 1,940
Locust Grove, GA 30248 • 1,681
Locust Grove, OK 74352 • 1,326
Lodi, CA 95240–42 • 51,874
Lodi, NJ 07644 • 22,355
Lodi, OH 44254 • 3,042
Lodi, WI 53555 • 2,093
Logan, IA 51546 • 1,401
Logan, OH 43138 • 6,725
Logan, UT 84321 • 32,762
Logan, WV 25601 • 2,206
Logan □, AR • 20,557
Logan □, CO • 17,567
Logan □, IL • 30,798
Logan □, KS • 3,081
Logan □, KY • 24,416
Logan □, NE • 878
Logan □, ND • 2,847
Logan □, OH • 42,310
Logan □, OK • 29,011
Logan □, WV • 43,032
Logandale, NV 89021 • 500
Logansport, IN 46947 • 16,812
Logansport, LA 71049 • 1,390
Loganville, GA 30249 • 3,180
Lolo, MT 59847 • 2,746
Loma Linda, CA 92354 • 17,400
Lombard, IL 60148 • 39,408
Lomira, WI 53048 • 1,542
Lomita, CA 90717 • 19,382
Lompoc, CA 93436 • 37,649
Lonaconing, MD 21539 • 1,122
London, KY 40741 • 5,757
London, OH 43140 • 7,807
Londonderry, NH 03053 • 10,114
Londontown, MD 21037 • 6,992
Lone Grove, OK 73443 • 4,114
Lone Pine, CA 93545 • 1,818
Long □, GA • 6,202
Long Beach, CA 90801–88 • 429,433
Long Beach, IN 46360 • 2,044
Long Beach, MS 39560 • 15,804
Long Beach, NY 11561 • 33,510
Long Beach, WA 98631 • 1,236
Longboat Key, FL 34228 • 5,937
Long Branch, NJ 07740 • 28,658
Long Lake, IL 60041 • 2,888
Longmeadow, MA 01106 • 15,467
Longmont, CO 80501–02 • 51,555
Longport, NJ 08403 • 1,224
Long Prairie, MN 56347 • 2,786
Long Valley, NJ 07853 • 1,744
Long View, NC 28601 • 3,229
Longview, TX 75601–15 • 70,311
Longview, WA 98632 • 31,499
Longwood, FL 32750 • 13,316
Lonoke, AR 72086 • 4,022
Lonoke □, AR • 39,268
Lonsdale, MN 55046 • 1,252
Lonsdale, RI 02865 • 3,850
Loogootee, IN 47553 • 2,884
Lookout Mountain, TN 37350 • 1,901
Lorain, OH 44052–55 • 71,245
Lorain □, OH • 271,126
Lordsburg, NM 88045 • 2,951
Lorenzo, TX 79343 • 1,208
Loretto, PA 15940 • 1,072
Loretto, TN 38469 • 1,515
Loris, SC 29569 • 2,067
Lorton, VA 22079 • 15,385
Los Alamitos, CA 90720–21 • 11,676
Los Alamos, NM 87544 • 11,455
Los Alamos □, NM • 18,115
Los Altos, CA 94022–24 • 26,303
Los Altos Hills, CA 94022 • 7,514
Los Angeles, CA 90001–99 • 3,485,398
Los Angeles □, CA • 8,863,164
Los Banos, CA 93635 • 14,519
Los Fresnos, TX 78566 • 2,473
Los Gatos, CA 95030–32 • 27,357
Los Lunas, NM 87031 • 6,013
Los Molinos, CA 96055 • 1,709
Los Nietos, CA 90606 • 7,100
Los Osos, CA 93402 • 8,000
Los Padillas, NM 87105 • 2,400
Los Ranchos de Albuquerque, NM 87107 • 3,955
Los Serranos, CA 91709 • 7,099
Lost Hills, CA 93249 • 1,212
Loudon, TN 37774 • 4,026
Loudon □, TN • 31,255
Loudonville, NY 12211 • 10,822
Loudonville, OH 44842 • 2,915
Loudoun □, VA • 86,129
Louisa, KY 41230 • 1,990
Louisa, VA 23093 • 1,088
Louisa □, IA • 11,592
Louisa □, VA • 20,325
Louisburg, KS 66053 • 1,964
Louisburg, NC 27549 • 3,037
Louisiana, MO 63353 • 3,967
Louisville, CO 80027 • 12,361
Louisville, GA 30434 • 2,429
Louisville, IL 62858 • 1,098
Louisville, KY 40201–99 • 269,063
Louisville, MS 39339 • 7,169
Louisville, OH 44641 • 8,087
Loup □, NE • 683
Loup City, NE 68853 • 1,104
Love □, OK • 8,157
Loveland, CO 80537–39 • 37,352
Loveland, OH 45140 • 9,990
Loveland Park, OH 45140 • 1,357
Lovell, WY 82431 • 2,131
Lovelock, NV 89419 • 2,069
Loves Park, IL 61111 • 15,462
Loving, NM 88256 • 1,243
Loving □, TX • 107
Lovington, IL 61937 • 1,143
Lovington, NM 88260 • 9,322
Lowell, AR 72745 • 1,224
Lowell, IN 46356 • 6,430
Lowell, MA 01850–54 • 103,439
Lowell, MI 49331 • 3,983
Lowell, NC 28098 • 2,704
Lowellville, OH 44436 • 1,349
Lower Burrell, PA 15068 • 12,251
Lower Merion Township, PA 19003 • 59,629
Lower Paia, HI 96779 • 1,500
Lowndes □, AL • 12,658
Lowndes □, GA • 75,981
Lowndes □, MS • 59,308
Lowville, NY 13367 • 3,632
Loxley, AL 36551 • 1,161
Loyal, WI 54446 • 1,244
Loyall, KY 40854 • 1,100
Lubbock, TX 79401–99 • 186,206
Lubbock □, TX • 222,636
Lucas □, IA • 9,070
Lucas □, OH • 462,361
Lucasville, OH 45648 • 1,575
Luce □, MI • 5,763
Lucedale, MS 39452 • 2,592
Lucerne, CA 95458 • 2,011
Lucernemines, PA 15754 • 1,074
Lucerne Valley, CA 92356 • 1,300
Luck, WI 54853 • 1,022
Ludington, MI 49431 • 8,507
Ludlow, KY 41016 • 4,736
Ludlow, MA 01056 • 18,150
Ludlow, VT 05149 • 1,123
Ludowici, GA 31316 • 1,291
Lufkin, TX 75901–03 • 30,206
Lugoff, SC 29078 • 3,211
Lula, GA 30554 • 1,018
Luling, LA 70070 • 2,803
Luling, TX 78648 • 4,661
Lumber City, GA 31549 • 1,429
Lumberport, WV 26386 • 1,014
Lumberton, MS 39455 • 2,121
Lumberton, NC 28358–59 • 18,601
Lumpkin, GA 31815 • 1,250
Lumpkin □, GA • 14,573
Luna □, NM • 18,110
Luna Pier, MI 48157 • 1,507
Lund, NV 89317 • 330
Lunenburg, MA 01462 • 1,694
Lunenburg □, VA • 11,419
Luray, VA 22835 • 4,587
Lusk, WY 82225 • 1,504
Lutcher, LA 70071 • 3,907
Luther, OK 73054 • 1,560
Lutherville-Timonium, MD 21093 • 16,442
Lutz, FL 33549 • 10,552
Luverne, AL 36049 • 2,555
Luverne, MN 56156 • 4,382
Luxemburg, WI 54217 • 1,151
Luxora, AR 72358 • 1,338
Luzerne, PA 18709 • 3,206
Luzerne □, PA • 328,149
Lycoming □, PA • 118,710
Lyford, TX 78569 • 1,674
Lykens, PA 17048 • 1,986
Lyman, SC 29365 • 2,271
Lyman, WY 82937 • 1,896
Lyman □, SD • 3,638
Lynbrook, NY 11563 • 19,208
Lynch, KY 40855 • 1,166
Lynchburg, OH 45142 • 1,212
Lynchburg, TN 37352 • 4,721
Lynchburg, VA 24501–06 • 66,049
Lyncourt, NY 13208 • 4,516
Lynden, WA 98264 • 5,709
Lyndhurst, NJ 07071 • 18,262
Lyndhurst, OH 44124 • 15,982
Lyndon, KY 40222 • 8,037
Lyndonville, VT 05851 • 1,255
Lyndora, PA 16045 • 3,000
Lynn, IN 47355 • 1,183
Lynn, MA 01901–08 • 81,245
Lynn □, TX • 6,758
Lynne Acres, MD 21207 • 5,910
Lynnfield, MA 01940 • 11,274
Lynn Garden, TN 37665 • 7,213
Lynn Garden, TN 37665 • 3,950
Lynn Haven, FL 32444 • 9,298
Lynnwood, WA 98036–37 • 28,695
Lynwood, CA 90262 • 61,945
Lyon □, IA • 11,952
Lyon □, KS • 34,732
Lyon □, KY • 6,624
Lyon □, MN • 24,789
Lyon □, NV • 20,001
Lyon Mountain, NY 12952 • 1,000
Lyons, CO 80540 • 1,227
Lyons, GA 30436 • 4,502
Lyons, IL 60534 • 9,828
Lyons, KS 67554 • 3,688
Lyons, NE 68038 • 1,144
Lyons, NY 14489 • 4,280
Lytle, TX 78052 • 2,255

M

Mabank, TX 75147 • 1,739
Mableton, GA 30059 • 25,725
Mabscott, WV 25871 • 1,543
Mabton, WA 98935 • 1,482
MacClenny, FL 32063 • 3,966
Macedon, NY 14502 • 1,400
Macedonia, OH 44056 • 7,509
Machesney Park, IL 61111 • 19,033
Machias, ME 04654 • 1,773
Mackinac □, MI • 10,674
Mackinaw, IL 61755 • 1,331
Mackinaw City, MI 49701 • 875
Macomb, IL 61455 • 19,952
Macomb □, MI • 717,400
Macon, GA 31201–95 • 106,612
Macon, IL 62544 • 1,282
Macon, MS 39341 • 2,256
Macon, MO 63552 • 5,571
Macon □, AL • 24,928
Macon □, GA • 13,114
Macon □, IL • 117,206
Macon □, MO • 15,345
Macon □, NC • 23,499
Macon □, TN • 15,906
Macoupin □, IL • 47,679
Macungie, PA 18062 • 2,597
Madawaska, ME 04756 • 3,653
Madeira, OH 45243 • 9,141
Madelia, MN 56062 • 2,237
Madera, CA 93637–39 • 29,281
Madera □, CA • 88,090
Madill, OK 73446 • 3,069
Madison, AL 35758 • 14,904
Madison, AR 72359 • 1,263
Madison, CT 06443 • 2,139
Madison, FL 32340 • 3,345
Madison, GA 30650 • 3,483
Madison, IL 62060 • 4,629
Madison, IN 47250 • 12,006
Madison, ME 04950 • 2,956
Madison, MN 56256 • 1,951
Madison, MS 39110 • 7,471
Madison, NE 68748 • 2,135
Madison, NJ 07940 • 15,850
Madison, NC 27025 • 2,371
Madison, OH 44057 • 2,477
Madison, SD 57042 • 6,257
Madison, WV 25130 • 3,051
Madison, WI 53701–19 • 191,262
Madison □, AL • 238,912
Madison □, AR • 11,618
Madison □, FL • 16,569
Madison □, GA • 21,050
Madison □, ID • 23,674
Madison □, IL • 249,238
Madison □, IN • 130,669
Madison □, IA • 12,483
Madison □, KY • 57,508
Madison □, LA • 12,463
Madison □, MS • 53,794
Madison □, MO • 11,127
Madison □, MT • 5,989
Madison □, NE • 32,655
Madison □, NY • 69,120
Madison □, NC • 16,953
Madison □, OH • 37,068
Madison □, TN • 77,982
Madison □, TX • 10,931
Madison □, VA • 11,949
Madison Heights, MI 48071 • 32,196
Madison Heights, VA 24572 • 11,700
Madisonville, KY 42431 • 16,200
Madisonville, TN 37354 • 3,033
Madisonville, TX 77864 • 3,569
Madras, OR 97741 • 3,443
Madrid, IA 50156 • 2,395
Maeser, UT 84078 • 2,598
Magalia, CA 95954 • 8,987
Magdalena, NM 87825 • 861
Magee, MS 39111 • 3,607
Magna, UT 84044 • 17,829
Magnolia, AR 71753 • 11,151
Magnolia, MS 39652 • 2,245
Magnolia, NJ 08049 • 4,861
Magoffin □, KY • 13,077
Mahanoy City, PA 17948 • 5,209
Mahaska □, IA • 21,522
Mahnomen, MN 56557 • 1,154
Mahnomen □, MN • 5,044
Mahomet, IL 61853 • 3,103
Mahoning □, OH • 264,806
Mahopac, NY 10541 • 7,755
Mahwah, NJ 07430 • 7,500
Maiden, NC 28650 • 2,574
Maili, HI 96792 • 6,059
Maine, NY 13802 • 1,110
Maitland, FL 32751 • 9,110
Maize, KS 67101 • 1,520
Major □, OK • 8,055
Makaha, HI 96792 • 7,990
Makakilo City, HI 96706 • 9,828
Makawao, HI 96768 • 5,405
Makaweli, HI 96769 • 700
Malabar, FL 32950 • 1,977
Malad City, ID 83252 • 1,946
Malaga, NJ 08328 • 2,140
Malakoff, TX 75148 • 2,038
Malden, MA 02148 • 53,884
Malden, MO 63863 • 5,123
Malheur □, OR • 26,038
Malibu, CA 90264–65 • 10,000
Malone, NY 12953 • 6,777
Malta, MT 59538 • 2,340
Malvern, AR 72104 • 9,256
Malvern, IA 51551 • 1,210
Malvern, OH 44644 • 1,112
Malvern, PA 19355 • 2,944
Malverne, NY 11565 • 9,054
Mamaroneck, NY 10543 • 17,325
Mammoth, AZ 85618 • 1,845
Mammoth Lakes, CA 93546 • 4,785
Mammoth Spring, AR 72554 • 1,097
Mamou, LA 70554 • 3,483
Manahawkin, NJ 08050 • 1,594
Manasquan, NJ 08736 • 5,369
Manassas, VA 22110–11 • 27,957
Manassas Park, VA 22111 • 6,734
Manatee □, FL • 211,707
Manawa, WI 54949 • 1,169
Mancelona, MI 49659 • 1,370
Manchaug, MA 01526 • 1,000
Manchester, CT 06040 • 51,618
Manchester, GA 31816 • 4,104
Manchester, IA 52057 • 5,137
Manchester, KY 40962 • 1,634
Manchester, MD 21102 • 2,810
Manchester, MA 01944 • 5,424
Manchester, MI 48158 • 1,753
Manchester, MO 63011 • 6,542
Manchester, NH 03101–10 • 99,567
Manchester, NY 14504 • 1,598
Manchester, OH 45144 • 2,223
Manchester, PA 17345 • 1,830
Manchester, TN 37355 • 7,709
Manchester, VT 05254 • 561
Manchester Center, VT 05255 • 1,574
Mandan, ND 58554 • 15,177
Mandeville, LA 70448 • 7,083
Mangum, OK 73554 • 3,344
Manhasset, NY 11030 • 7,718
Manhattan, KS 66502 • 37,712
Manhattan, MT 59741 • 1,034
Manhattan Beach, CA 90266 • 32,063
Manheim, PA 17545 • 5,011
Manila, AR 72442 • 2,635
Manistee, MI 49660 • 6,734
Manistee □, MI • 21,265
Manistique, MI 49854 • 3,456
Manito, IL 61546 • 1,711
Manitou Springs, CO 80829 • 4,535
Manitowoc, WI 54220–21 • 32,520
Manitowoc □, WI • 80,421
Mankato, KS 66956 • 1,037
Mankato, MN 56001–03 • 31,477
Manlius, NY 13104 • 4,764
Manly, IA 50456 • 1,349
Mannford, OK 74044 • 1,826
Manning, IA 51455 • 1,484
Manning, SC 29102 • 4,428
Mannington, WV 26582 • 2,184
Manokotak, AK 99628 • 385
Manomet, MA 02345 • 1,500
Manor, TX 78653 • 1,041
Manorhaven, NY 11050 • 5,672
Mansfield, AR 72944 • 1,018
Mansfield, LA 71052 • 5,389
Mansfield, MA 02048 • 7,170
Mansfield, MO 65704 • 1,429
Mansfield, OH 44901–07 • 50,627
Mansfield, PA 16933 • 3,538
Mansfield, TX 76063 • 15,607
Mansfield Center, CT 06250 • 1,043
Manson, IA 50563 • 1,844
Mansura, LA 71350 • 1,601
Manteca, CA 95336 • 40,773
Manteno, IL 60950 • 3,488
Manti, UT 84642 • 2,268
Manton, MI 49663 • 1,161
Mantua, NJ 08051 • 1,350
Mantua, OH 44255 • 1,178
Mantua Hills, VA 22031 • 1,600
Manvel, TX 77578 • 3,733
Manville, NJ 08835 • 10,567
Manville, RI 02838 • 3,030
Many, LA 71449 • 3,112
Many Farms, AZ 86538 • 1,294
Maple Bluff, WI 53704 • 1,352
Maple Grove, MN 55369 • 38,736
Maple Heights, OH 44137 • 27,089
Maple Lake, MN 55358 • 1,394
Maple Plain, MN 55359 • 2,005
Maple Shade, NJ 08052 • 19,211
Mapleton, IA 51034 • 1,294
Mapleton, MN 56065 • 1,526
Mapleton, UT 84663 • 3,572
Maple Valley, WA 98038 • 1,211
Mapleville, RI 02839 • 1,300
Maplewood, MN 55109 • 30,954
Maplewood, MO 63143 • 9,962
Maplewood, NJ 07040 • 21,756
Maquoketa, IA 52060 • 6,111
Marana, AZ 85653 • 2,187
Marathon, FL 33050 • 8,857
Marathon, NY 13803 • 1,107
Marathon, WI 54448 • 1,606
Marathon □, WI • 115,400
Marble Falls, TX 78654 • 4,007
Marblehead, MA 01945 • 19,971
Marble Hill, MO 63764 • 1,447
Marbleton, WY 83113 • 634
Marbury, MD 20658 • 1,244
Marceline, MO 64658 • 2,645
Marcellus, MI 49067 • 1,193
Marco, FL 33937 • 9,493
Marcus, IA 51035 • 1,171
Marcus Hook, PA 19061 • 2,546
Marengo, IL 60152 • 4,768
Marengo, IA 52301 • 2,270
Marengo □, AL • 23,084
Marfa, TX 79843 • 2,424
Margate, FL 33063 • 42,985
Margate, MD 21060 • 1,900
Margate City, NJ 08402 • 8,431
Marianna, AR 72360 • 5,910
Marianna, FL 32446 • 6,292
Maricopa, AZ 85239 • 1,600
Maricopa, CA 93252 • 1,193
Maricopa □, AZ • 2,122,101
Mariemont, OH 45227 • 3,118
Marienville, PA 16239 • 1,400
Maries □, MO • 7,976
Marietta, GA 30060–68 • 44,129
Marietta, OH 45750 • 15,026
Marietta, OK 73448 • 2,306
Marin □, CA • 230,096
Marina, CA 93933 • 26,436
Marina del Rey, CA 90292 • 7,431
Marine City, MI 48039 • 4,556
Marinette, WI 54143 • 11,843
Marinette □, WI • 40,548
Maringouin, LA 70757 • 1,149
Marion, AL 36756 • 4,211
Marion, AR 72364 • 4,391
Marion, IL 62959 • 14,545
Marion, IN 46952–53 • 32,618
Marion, IA 52302 • 20,403
Marion, KS 66861 • 1,906
Marion, KY 42064 • 3,320
Marion, MA 02738 • 1,426
Marion, MS 39342 • 1,359
Marion, NY 14505 • 1,080
Marion, NC 28752 • 4,765
Marion, OH 43301–02 • 34,075
Marion, PA 17235 • 1,000
Marion, SC 29571 • 7,658
Marion, SD 57043 • 831
Marion, VA 24354 • 6,630
Marion, WI 54950 • 1,242
Marion □, AL • 29,830
Marion □, AR • 12,001
Marion □, FL • 194,833
Marion □, GA • 5,590
Marion □, IL • 41,561
Marion □, IN • 797,159
Marion □, IA • 30,001
Marion □, KS • 12,888
Marion □, KY • 16,499
Marion □, MS • 25,544
Marion □, MO • 27,682
Marion □, OH • 64,274
Marion □, OR • 228,483
Marion □, SC • 33,899
Marion □, TN • 24,860
Marion □, TX • 9,984
Marion □, WV • 57,249
Marionville, MO 65705 • 1,920
Mariposa, CA 95338 • 1,152
Mariposa □, CA • 14,302
Marissa, IL 62257 • 2,375
Marked Tree, AR 72365 • 3,100
Markesan, WI 53946 • 1,496
Markham, IL 60426 • 13,136
Markham, TX 77456 • 1,206
Markle, IN 46770 • 1,208
Marks, MS 38646 • 1,758
Marksville, LA 71351 • 5,526
Marlboro, NY 12542 • 2,200
Marlboro □, SC • 29,361
Marlborough, CT 06447 • 5,535
Marlborough, MA 01752 • 31,813
Marlborough, NH 03455 • 1,211
Marlene Village, OR 97005 • 1,500
Marlette, MI 48453 • 1,924
Marley, MD 21060 • 7,100
Marlin, TX 76661 • 6,386
Marlinton, WV 24954 • 1,148
Marlow, OK 73055 • 4,416
Marlow Heights, MD 20748 • 5,885
Marlton, NJ 08053 • 10,228
Marmaduke, AR 72443 • 1,164
Marmet, WV 25315 • 1,879
Maroa, IL 61756 • 1,602
Marquette, MI 49855 • 21,977
Marquette □, MI • 70,887
Marquette □, WI • 12,321
Marquette Heights, IL 61554 • 3,077
Marrero, LA 70072–73 • 36,671
Mars, PA 16046 • 1,713
Marseilles, IL 61341 • 4,811
Marshall, AR 72650 • 1,318
Marshall, IL 62441 • 3,555
Marshall, MI 49068 • 6,891
Marshall, MN 56258 • 12,023
Marshall, MO 65340 • 12,711
Marshall, TX 75670–71 • 23,682
Marshall, WI 53559 • 2,329
Marshall □, AL • 70,832
Marshall □, IL • 12,846
Marshall □, IN • 42,182

United States Populations and ZIP Codes

Marshall □, IA • *38,276*
Marshall □, KS • *11,705*
Marshall □, KY • *27,205*
Marshall □, MN • *10,993*
Marshall □, MS • *30,361*
Marshall □, OK • *10,829*
Marshall □, SD • *4,844*
Marshall □, TN • *21,539*
Marshall □, WV • *37,356*
Marshallton, DE 19808 • *1,765*
Marshalltown, IA 50158 • *25,178*
Marshallville, GA 31057 • *1,457*
Marshfield, MA 02050 • *4,002*
Marshfield, MO 65706 • *4,374*
Marshfield, WI 54449 • *19,291*
Marshfield Hills, MA 02051 • *2,201*
Mars Hill, ME 04758 • *1,500*
Mars Hill, NC 28754 • *1,611*
Marshville, NC 28103 • *2,020*
Marsing, ID 83639 • *798*
Marstons Mills, MA 02648 • *8,017*
Mart, TX 76664 • *2,004*
Martha Lake, WA 98012 • *10,155*
Martin, SD 57551 • *1,151*
Martin, TN 38237 • *8,600*
Martin □, FL • *100,900*
Martin □, IN • *10,369*
Martin □, KY • *12,526*
Martin □, MN • *22,914*
Martin □, NC • *25,078*
Martin □, TX • *4,956*
Martinez, CA 94553 • *31,808*
Martinez, GA 30907 • *33,731*
Martinsburg, PA 16662 • *2,119*
Martinsburg, WV 25401 • *14,073*
Martins Ferry, OH 43935 • *7,990*
Martinsville, IL 62442 • *1,161*
Martinsville, IN 46151 • *11,677*
Martinsville, VA 24112–15 • *16,162*
Marvell, AR 72366 • *1,545*
Maryland City, MD 20724 • *6,813*
Maryland Heights, MO 63043 • *25,407*
Marysville, CA 95901 • *12,324*
Marysville, KS 66508 • *3,359*
Marysville, MI 48040 • *8,515*
Marysville, OH 43040 • *9,656*
Marysville, PA 17053 • *2,425*
Marysville, WA 98270 • *10,328*
Maryville, MO 64468 • *10,663*
Maryville, TN 37801–04 • *19,208*
Mascot, TN 37806 • *2,138*
Mascoutah, IL 62258 • *5,511*
Mason, MI 48854 • *6,768*
Mason, NV 89447 • *400*
Mason, OH 45040 • *11,452*
Mason, TX 76856 • *2,041*
Mason, WV 25260 • *1,053*
Mason □, IL • *16,269*
Mason □, KY • *16,666*
Mason □, MI • *25,537*
Mason □, TX • *3,423*
Mason □, WA • *38,341*
Mason □, WV • *25,178*
Masonboro, NC 28403 • *7,010*
Mason City, IL 62664 • *2,323*
Mason City, IA 50401 • *29,040*
Masontown, PA 15461 • *3,759*
Massac □, IL • *14,752*
Massapequa, NY 11758 • *22,018*
Massapequa Park, NY 11762 • *18,044*
Massena, NY 13662 • *11,719*
Massillon, OH 44646–48 • *31,007*
Mastic, NY 11950 • *13,778*
Mastic Beach, NY 11951 • *10,293*
Masury, OH 44438 • *1,836*
Matagorda □, TX • *36,928*
Matamoras, PA 18336 • *1,934*
Matawan, NJ 07747 • *9,270*
Mather, PA 15346 • *1,300*
Mathews □, VA • *8,348*
Mathis, TX 78368 • *5,423*
Matoaca, VA 23803 • *1,967*
Mattapoisett, MA 02739 • *2,949*
Matteson, IL 60443 • *11,378*
Matthews, NC 28105–06 • *13,651*
Mattituck, NY 11952 • *3,902*
Mattoon, IL 61938 • *18,441*
Mattydale, NY 13211 • *6,418*
Matunuck, RI 02879 • *550*
Maud, OK 74854 • *1,204*
Maugansville, MD 21767 • *1,707*
Maui □, HI • *100,374*
Mauldin, SC 29662 • *11,587*
Maumee, OH 43537 • *15,561*
Maunaloa, HI 96770 • *405*
Maunawili, HI 96734 • *4,847*
Maury □, TN • *54,812*
Mauston, WI 53948 • *3,439*
Maverick □, TX • *36,378*
Maxton, NC 28364 • *2,373*
Maxwell Acres, WV 26041 • *1,000*
Mayer, AZ 86333 • *1,800*
Mayes □, OK • *33,366*
Mayfield, KY 42066 • *9,935*
Mayfield, PA 18433 • *1,890*
Mayfield Heights, OH 44124 • *19,847*
Mayflower, AR 72106 • *1,415*
Mayflower Village, CA 91016 • *4,978*
Maynard, MA 01754 • *10,325*
Maynardville, TN 37807 • *1,298*
Mayo, MD 21106 • *2,537*
Mayodan, NC 27027 • *2,471*
Mays Landing, NJ 08330 • *2,090*
Maysville, KY 41056 • *7,169*
Maysville, MO 64469 • *1,176*
Maysville, OK 73057 • *1,203*
Mayville, MI 48744 • *1,010*
Mayville, NY 14757 • *1,636*
Mayville, ND 58257 • *2,092*
Mayville, WI 53050 • *4,374*
Maywood, CA 90270 • *27,850*
Maywood, IL 60153–54 • *27,139*
Maywood, NJ 07607 • *9,473*
Mazomanie, WI 53560 • *1,377*
McAdoo, PA 18237 • *2,459*
McAlester, OK 74501–02 • *16,370*
McAllen, TX 78501–04 • *84,021*
McAlmont, AR 72117 • *1,800*
McAlpine, MD 21043 • *2,230*
McArthur, OH 45651 • *1,541*
McCall, ID 83638 • *2,005*
McCamey, TX 79752 • *2,493*
McCandless, PA 15237 • *28,781*
McCaysville, GA 30555 • *1,065*
McClain □, OK • *22,795*
McCleary, WA 98557 • *1,235*
McCloud, CA 96057 • *1,555*
McClure, PA 17841 • *1,070*
McColl, SC 29570 • *2,685*
McComb, MS 39648 • *11,591*
McComb, OH 45858 • *1,544*
McCone □, MT • *2,276*
McConnellsburg, PA 17233 • *1,106*
McConnelsville, OH 43756 • *1,804*
McCook, NE 69001 • *8,112*
McCook □, SD • *5,688*
McCormick, SC 29835 • *1,659*
McCormick □, SC • *8,868*
McCracken □, KY • *62,879*
McCreary □, KY • *15,603*
McCrory, AR 72101 • *1,971*
McCulloch □, TX • *8,778*
McCurtain □, OK • *33,433*
McDermitt, NV 89421 • *373*
McDonald □, MO • *16,938*
McDonough, GA 30253 • *2,929*
McDonough □, IL • *35,244*
McDowell □, NC • *35,681*
McDowell □, WV • *35,233*
McDuffie □, GA • *20,119*
McEwen, TN 37101 • *1,442*
McFarland, CA 93250 • *7,005*
McFarland, WI 53558 • *5,232*
McGehee, AR 71654 • *4,997*
McGill, NV 89318 • *1,258*
McGrath, AK 99627 • *528*
McGraw, NY 13101 • *1,074*
McGregor, TX 76657 • *4,683*
McHenry, IL 60050–51 • *16,177*
McHenry □, IL • *183,241*
McHenry □, ND • *6,528*
McIntosh □, GA • *8,634*
McIntosh □, ND • *4,021*
McIntosh □, OK • *16,779*
McKean □, PA • *47,131*
McKee City, NJ 08232 • *1,200*
McKeesport, PA 15130–35 • *26,016*
McKees Rocks, PA 15136 • *7,691*
McKenzie, TN 38201 • *5,168*
McKenzie □, ND • *6,383*
McKinley □, NM • *60,686*
McKinleyville, CA 95521 • *10,749*
McKinney, TX 75069–70 • *21,283*
McLaughlin, SD 57642 • *780*
McLean, VA 22101 • *38,168*
McLean □, IL • *129,180*
McLean □, KY • *9,628*
McLean □, ND • *10,457*
McLeansboro, IL 62859 • *2,677*
McLennan □, TX • *189,123*
McLeod □, MN • *32,030*
McLoud, OK 74851 • *2,493*
McMechen, WV 26040 • *2,130*
McMinn □, TN • *42,383*
McMinnville, OR 97128 • *17,894*
McMinnville, TN 37110 • *11,194*
McMullen □, TX • *817*
McNairy □, TN • *22,422*
McPherson, KS 67460 • *12,422*
McPherson □, KS • *27,268*
McPherson □, NE • *546*
McPherson □, SD • *3,228*
McQueeney, TX 78123 • *2,063*
McRae, GA 31055 • *3,007*
McRoberts, KY 41835 • *1,101*
McSherrystown, PA 17344 • *2,769*
Mead, WA 99021 • *2,150*
Meade, KS 67864 • *1,526*
Meade □, KS • *4,247*
Meade □, KY • *24,170*
Meade □, SD • *21,878*
Meadowbrook, FL 32808 • *5,200*
Meadowood, DE 19711 • *2,100*
Meadville, PA 16335 • *14,318*
Meagher □, MT • *1,819*
Mebane, NC 27302 • *4,754*
Mecca, CA 92254 • *1,966*
Mechanic Falls, ME 04256 • *2,388*
Mechanicsburg, OH 43044 • *1,803*
Mechanicsburg, PA 17055 • *9,452*
Mechanicsville, IA 52306 • *1,012*
Mechanicsville, VA 23111 • *22,027*
Mechanicville, NY 12118 • *5,249*
Mecklenburg □, NC • *511,433*
Mecklenburg □, VA • *29,241*
Mecosta □, MI • *37,308*
Medfield, MA 02052 • *5,985*
Medford, MA 02155 • *57,407*
Medford, NJ 08055 • *1,800*
Medford, NY 11763 • *21,274*
Medford, OK 73759 • *1,172*
Medford, OR 97501–04 • *46,951*
Medford, WI 54451 • *4,283*
Medford Lakes, NJ 08055 • *4,462*
Media, PA 19063–65 • *5,957*
Mediapolis, IA 52637 • *1,637*
Medical Lake, WA 99022 • *3,664*
Medicine Bow, WY 82329 • *389*
Medicine Lodge, KS 67104 • *2,453*
Medina, NY 14103 • *6,686*
Medina, OH 44256 • *19,231*
Medina, WA 98039 • *2,981*
Medina □, OH • *122,354*
Medina □, TX • *27,312*
Medway, MA 02053 • *3,890*
Meeker, CO 81641 • *2,098*
Meeker, OK 74855 • *1,003*
Meeker □, MN • *20,846*
Meeteetse, WY 82433 • *368*
Mehlville, MO 63129 • *27,557*
Meigs, GA 31765 • *1,120*
Meigs □, OH • *22,987*
Meigs □, TN • *8,033*
Meiners Oaks, CA 93023 • *3,329*
Melbourne, AR 72556 • *1,562*
Melbourne, FL 32901–10 • *59,646*
Melbourne Beach, FL 32951 • *3,021*
Melcher, IA 50163 • *1,302*
Mellette □, SD • *2,137*
Melrose, FL 32666 • *1,700*
Melrose, MA 02176 • *28,150*
Melrose, MN 56352 • *2,561*
Melrose Park, FL 33312 • *6,477*
Melrose Park, IL 60160–63 • *20,859*
Melville, LA 71353 • *1,562*
Melville, NY 11747 • *12,586*
Melvindale, MI 48122 • *11,216*
Memphis, FL 34221 • *6,760*
Memphis, MI 48041 • *1,221*
Memphis, MO 63555 • *2,094*
Memphis, TN 38101–87 • *610,337*
Memphis, TX 79245 • *2,465*
Mena, AR 71953 • *5,475*
Menahga, MN 56464 • *1,076*
Menands, NY 12204 • *4,333*
Menard, TX 76859 • *1,606*
Menard □, IL • *11,164*
Menard □, TX • *2,252*
Menasha, WI 54952 • *14,711*
Mendenhall, MS 39114 • *2,463*
Mendham, NJ 07945 • *4,890*
Mendocino, CA 95460 • *1,008*
Mendocino □, CA • *80,345*
Mendota, CA 93640 • *6,821*
Mendota, IL 61342 • *7,018*
Mendota Heights, MN 55118 • *9,431*
Menifee □, KY • *5,092*
Menlo Park, CA 94025–28 • *28,040*
Menno, SD 57045 • *768*
Menominee, MI 49858 • *9,398*
Menominee □, MI • *24,920*
Menominee □, WI • *3,890*
Menomonee Falls, WI 53051–52 • *26,840*
Menomonie, WI 54751 • *13,547*
Mentor, OH 44060–61 • *47,358*
Mentor-on-the-Lake, OH 44060 • *8,271*
Mequon, WI 53092 • *18,885*
Meraux, LA 70075 • *8,000*
Merced, CA 95339–44 • *56,216*
Merced □, CA • *178,403*
Mercedes, TX 78570 • *12,694*
Mercer, PA 16137 • *2,444*
Mercer, WI 54547 • *1,300*
Mercer □, IL • *17,290*
Mercer □, KY • *19,148*
Mercer □, MO • *3,723*
Mercer □, NJ • *325,824*
Mercer □, ND • *9,808*
Mercer □, OH • *39,443*
Mercer □, PA • *121,003*
Mercer □, WV • *64,980*
Mercer Island, WA 98040 • *20,816*
Mercersburg, PA 17236 • *1,640*
Mercerville, NJ 08619 • *15,600*
Merchantville, NJ 08109 • *4,095*
Meredith, NH 03253 • *1,654*
Meredosia, IL 62665 • *1,134*
Meriden, CT 06450 • *59,479*
Meridian, ID 83642 • *9,596*
Meridian, MS 39301–09 • *41,036*
Meridian, PA 16001 • *3,473*
Meridian, TX 76665 • *1,390*
Meridian Hills, IN 46260 • *1,728*
Meridianville, AL 35759 • *2,852*
Meriwether □, GA • *22,411*
Merkel, TX 79536 • *2,469*
Merriam, KS 66203 • *11,821*
Merrick, NY 11566 • *23,042*
Merrick □, NE • *8,042*
Merrifield, VA 22031 • *8,399*
Merrill, WI 54452 • *9,860*
Merrillville, IN 46410 • *27,257*
Merrimac, MA 01860 • *2,050*
Merrimack, NH 03054 • *1,300*
Merrimack □, NH • *120,005*
Merritt Island, FL 32952–54 • *32,886*
Merryville, LA 70653 • *1,235*
Merton, WI 53056 • *1,199*
Mesa, AZ 85201–16 • *288,091*
Mesa □, CO • *93,145*
Mescalero, NM 88340 • *1,159*
Mesilla, NM 88046 • *1,975*
Mesquite, NV 89024 • *1,871*
Mesquite, TX 75149–50 • *101,484*
Metairie, LA 70001–11 • *149,428*
Metamora, IL 61548 • *2,520*
Metcalfe, MS 38760 • *1,092*
Metcalfe □, KY • *8,963*
Methuen, MA 01844 • *39,990*
Metlakatla, AK 99926 • *1,407*
Metropolis, IL 62960 • *6,734*
Metter, GA 30439 • *3,707*
Metuchen, NJ 08840 • *12,804*
Metzger, OR 97223 • *3,149*
Mexia, TX 76667 • *6,933*
Mexico, ME 04257 • *2,302*
Mexico, MO 65265 • *11,290*
Mexico, NY 13114 • *1,555*
Meyersdale, PA 15552 • *2,518*
Miami, AZ 85539 • *2,018*
Miami, FL 33101–99 • *358,548*
Miami, OK 74354–55 • *13,142*
Miami □, IN • *36,897*
Miami □, KS • *23,466*
Miami □, OH • *93,182*
Miami Beach, FL 33139 • *92,639*
Miami Lakes, FL 33014 • *12,750*
Miamisburg, OH 45342–43 • *17,834*
Miami Shores, FL 33138 • *10,084*
Miami Springs, FL 33166 • *13,268*
Micco, FL 32958 • *8,757*
Michigan Center, MI 49254 • *4,863*
Michigan City, IN 46360 • *33,822*
Middleboro (Middleborough Center), MA 02346 • *6,837*
Middleburg, FL 32068 • *6,223*
Middleburg, PA 17842 • *1,422*
Middleburgh, NY 12122 • *1,436*
Middleburg Heights, OH 44130 • *14,702*
Middlebury, CT 06762 • *4,140*
Middlebury, IN 46540 • *2,004*
Middlebury, VT 05753 • *6,007*
Middlefield, CT 06455 • *1,200*
Middlefield, OH 44062 • *1,898*
Middle Island, NY 11953 • *7,848*
Middleport, NY 14105 • *1,876*
Middleport, OH 45760 • *2,725*
Middle River, MD 21220 • *24,616*
Middlesboro, KY 40965 • *11,328*
Middlesex, NJ 08846 • *13,055*
Middlesex □, CT • *143,196*
Middlesex □, MA • *1,398,468*
Middlesex □, NJ • *671,780*
Middlesex □, VA • *8,653*
Middleton, ID 83644 • *1,851*
Middleton, MA 01949 • *4,135*
Middleton, WI 53562 • *13,289*
Middletown, CA 95461 • *2,000*
Middletown, CT 06457 • *42,762*
Middletown, DE 19709 • *3,834*
Middletown, IN 47356 • *2,333*
Middletown, KY 40243 • *5,016*
Middletown, MD 21769 • *1,834*
Middletown, NJ 07718 • *62,298*
Middletown, NY 10940 • *24,160*
Middletown, OH 45042–44 • *46,022*
Middletown, PA 17057 • *9,254*
Middletown, RI 02840 • *3,350*
Middletown, VA 22645 • *1,061*
Middletown Township, PA 19037 • *6,866*
Middleville, MI 49333 • *1,966*
Midfield, AL 35228 • *5,559*
Midland, MI 48640–42 • *38,053*
Midland, PA 15059 • *3,321*
Midland, TX 79701–12 • *89,443*
Midland □, MI • *75,651*
Midland □, TX • *106,611*
Midland City, AL 36350 • *1,819*
Midland Park, KS 67216 • *1,200*
Midland Park, NJ 07432 • *7,047*
Midland Park, SC 29405 • *1,300*
Midlothian, IL 60445 • *14,372*
Midlothian, TX 76065 • *5,141*
Midvale, UT 84047 • *11,886*
Midway, DE 19971 • *500*
Midway, KY 40347 • *1,290*
Midway, OR 97233 • *19,000*
Midway, PA 15060 • *1,043*
Midway, UT 84049 • *1,554*
Midwest, WY 82643 • *495*
Midwest City, OK 73110 • *52,267*
Mifflin □, PA • *46,197*
Mifflinburg, PA 17844 • *3,480*
Mifflinville, PA 18631 • *1,329*
Milaca, MN 56353 • *2,182*
Milam □, TX • *22,946*
Milan, GA 31060 • *1,056*
Milan, IL 61264 • *5,831*
Milan, IN 47031 • *1,529*
Milan, MI 48160 • *4,040*
Milan, MO 63556 • *1,767*
Milan, NM 87021 • *1,911*
Milan, OH 44846 • *1,464*
Milan, TN 38358 • *7,512*
Milbank, SD 57252 • *3,879*
Milesburg, PA 16853 • *1,144*
Miles City, MT 59301 • *8,461*
Milford, CT 06460 • *48,168*
Milford, DE 19963 • *6,040*
Milford, IL 60953 • *1,512*
Milford, IN 46542 • *1,388*
Milford, IA 51351 • *2,170*
Milford, ME 04461 • *2,228*
Milford, MA 01757 • *23,339*
Milford, MI 48380–82 • *5,511*
Milford, NE 68405 • *1,886*
Milford, NH 03055 • *8,015*
Milford, NJ 08848 • *1,273*
Milford, OH 45150 • *5,660*
Milford, PA 18337 • *1,064*
Milford, UT 84751 • *1,107*
Mililani Town, HI 96789 • *29,359*
Millard □, UT • *11,333*
Millbrae, CA 94030 • *20,412*
Millbrook, AL 36054 • *6,050*
Millbrook, NY 12545 • *1,339*
Millburn, NJ 07041 • *18,630*
Millbury, MA 01527 • *4,940*
Millbury, OH 43447 • *1,081*
Mill City, OR 97360 • *1,555*
Millcreek, UT 84109 • *32,230*
Millcreek Township, PA 16505 • *46,100*
Milledgeville, GA 31061 • *17,727*
Milledgeville, IL 61051 • *1,076*
Mille Lacs □, MN • *18,670*
Millen, GA 30442 • *3,808*
Miller, SD 57362 • *1,678*
Miller □, AR • *38,467*
Miller □, GA • *6,280*
Miller □, MO • *20,700*
Miller Place, NY 11764 • *9,315*
Millersburg, OH 44654 • *3,051*
Millersburg, PA 17061 • *2,729*
Millers Falls, MA 01349 • *1,084*
Millersport, OH 43046 • *1,010*
Millersville, PA 17551 • *8,099*
Mill Hall, PA 17751 • *1,702*
Milliken, CO 80543 • *1,605*
Millington, MI 48746 • *1,114*
Millington, TN 38053 • *17,866*
Millinocket, ME 04462 • *6,922*
Millis, MA 02054 • *3,777*
Millport, AL 35576 • *1,203*
Mills, WY 82644 • *1,574*
Mills □, IA • *13,202*
Mills □, TX • *4,531*
Millsboro, DE 19966 • *1,643*
Millstadt, IL 62260 • *2,566*
Milltown, NJ 08850 • *6,968*
Millvale, PA 15209 • *4,341*
Mill Valley, CA 94941–42 • *13,038*
Millville, MA 01529 • *1,693*
Millville, NJ 08332 • *25,992*
Millville, UT 84326 • *1,202*
Millwood, WA 99212 • *1,559*
Milnor, ND 58060 • *651*
Milo, ME 04463 • *2,129*
Milpitas, CA 95035–36 • *50,686*
Milroy, PA 17063 • *1,456*
Milstead, GA 30207 • *1,500*
Milton, DE 19968 • *1,417*
Milton, FL 32570–71 • *7,216*
Milton, MA 02186 • *25,725*
Milton, NH 03851 • *1,000*
Milton, NY 12547 • *1,140*
Milton, PA 17847 • *6,746*
Milton, VT 05468 • *1,578*
Milton, WA 98354 • *4,995*
Milton, WV 25541 • *2,242*
Milton, WI 53563 • *4,434*
Milton-Freewater, OR 97862 • *5,533*
Milwaukee, WI 53201–95 • *628,088*
Milwaukee □, WI • *959,275*
Milwaukie, OR 97222 • *18,692*
Mimosa Park, LA 70070 • *4,516*
Mims, FL 32754 • *9,412*
Mina, NV 89422 • *400*
Minco, OK 73059 • *1,411*
Minden, LA 71055 • *13,661*
Minden, NE 68959 • *2,749*
Minden, NV 89423 • *1,441*
Mine Hill, NJ 07801 • *3,250*
Mineola, NY 11501 • *18,994*
Mineola, TX 75773 • *4,321*
Miner, MO 63801 • *1,218*
Miner □, SD • *3,272*
Mineral □, CO • *558*
Mineral □, MT • *3,315*
Mineral □, NV • *6,475*
Mineral □, WV • *26,697*
Mineral Point, WI 53565 • *2,428*
Mineral Springs, AR 71851 • *1,004*
Mineral Wells, TX 76067 • *14,870*
Minersville, PA 17954 • *4,877*
Minerva, OH 44657 • *4,318*
Minetto, NY 13115 • *1,252*
Mineville, NY 12956 • *1,000*
Mingo □, WV • *33,739*
Mingo Junction, OH 43938 • *4,297*
Minidoka □, ID • *19,361*
Minier, IL 61759 • *1,155*
Minneapolis, KS 67467 • *1,983*
Minneapolis, MN 55401–80 • *368,383*
Minnehaha □, SD • *123,809*
Minneota, MN 56264 • *1,417*
Minnetonka, MN 55345 • *48,370*
Minocqua, WI 54548 • *1,280*
Minonk, IL 61760 • *1,982*
Minooka, IL 60447 • *2,561*
Minot, ND 58701–02 • *34,544*
Minquadale, DE 19720 • *790*
Minster, OH 45865 • *2,650*
Mint Hill, NC 28212 • *11,567*
Minturn, CO 81645 • *1,066*
Mio, MI 48647 • *1,500*
Mira Loma, CA 91752 • *15,786*
Miramar, FL 33023 • *40,663*
Misenheimer, NC 28109 • *1,000*
Mishawaka, IN 46544–46 • *42,608*
Mishicot, WI 54228 • *1,296*
Missaukee □, MI • *12,147*
Mission, KS 66205 • *9,504*
Mission, TX 78572 • *28,653*
Mission Hills, KS 66205 • *3,446*
Mission Viejo, CA 92691 • *72,820*
Mississippi □, AR • *57,525*
Mississippi □, MO • *14,442*
Mississippi State, MS 39762 • *12,400*
Missoula, MT 59801–07 • *42,918*
Missoula □, MT • *78,687*
Missouri City, TX 77459 • *36,176*
Missouri Valley, IA 51555 • *2,888*
Mitchell, IL 62040 • *1,320*
Mitchell, IN 47446 • *4,669*
Mitchell, NE 69357 • *1,743*
Mitchell, SD 57301 • *13,798*
Mitchell □, GA • *20,275*
Mitchell □, IA • *10,928*
Mitchell □, KS • *7,203*
Mitchell □, NC • *14,433*
Mitchell □, TX • *8,016*
Mitchellville, IA 50169 • *1,670*
Mizpah, NJ 08342 • *1,000*
Moab, UT 84532 • *3,971*
Moberly, MO 65270 • *12,839*
Mobile, AL 36601–95 • *196,278*
Mobile □, AL • *378,643*
Mobridge, SD 57601 • *3,768*
Mocanaqua, PA 18655 • *1,100*
Mocksville, NC 27028 • *3,399*
Modesto, CA 95350–56 • *164,730*
Modoc □, CA • *9,678*
Moenkopi, AZ 86045 • *1,200*
Moffat □, CO • *11,357*
Mogadore, OH 44260 • *4,008*
Mohall, ND 58761 • *931*
Mohave □, AZ • *93,497*
Mohawk, NY 13407 • *2,986*
Mohnton, PA 19540 • *2,484*
Mojave, CA 93501–02 • *3,763*
Mokena, IL 60448 • *6,128*
Molalla, OR 97038 • *3,651*
Moline, IL 61265 • *43,202*
Molino, FL 32577 • *1,207*
Momence, IL 60954 • *2,968*
Monaca, PA 15061 • *6,739*
Monahans, TX 79756 • *8,101*
Monarch Mills, SC 29379 • *2,214*
Moncks Corner, SC 29461 • *5,607*
Mondovi, WI 54755 • *2,491*
Monee, IL 60449 • *1,044*
Monessen, PA 15062 • *9,901*
Monett, MO 65708 • *6,529*
Monette, AR 72447 • *1,115*
Monfort Heights, OH 45239 • *9,745*
Moniteau □, MO • *12,298*
Monmouth, IL 61462 • *9,489*
Monmouth, OR 97361 • *6,288*
Monmouth □, NJ • *553,124*
Monmouth Beach, NJ 07750 • *3,303*
Monmouth Junction, NJ 08852 • *1,570*
Mono □, CA • *9,956*
Monon, IN 47959 • *1,585*
Monona, IA 52159 • *1,520*
Monona, WI 53716 • *8,637*
Monona □, IA • *10,034*
Monongah, WV 26554 • *1,018*
Monongahela, PA 15063 • *4,928*
Monongalia □, WV • *75,509*
Monroe, GA 30655 • *9,759*
Monroe, IA 50170 • *1,739*
Monroe, LA 71201–13 • *54,909*
Monroe, MI 48161 • *22,902*
Monroe, NY 10950 • *6,672*
Monroe, NC 28110–12 • *16,127*
Monroe, OH 45050 • *4,490*
Monroe, UT 84754 • *1,472*
Monroe, WA 98272 • *4,278*
Monroe, WI 53566 • *10,241*
Monroe □, AL • *23,968*
Monroe □, AR • *11,333*
Monroe □, FL • *78,024*
Monroe □, GA • *17,113*
Monroe □, IL • *22,422*
Monroe □, IN • *108,978*
Monroe □, IA • *8,114*
Monroe □, KY • *11,401*
Monroe □, MI • *133,600*
Monroe □, MS • *36,582*
Monroe □, MO • *9,104*
Monroe □, NY • *713,968*
Monroe □, OH • *15,497*
Monroe □, PA • *95,709*
Monroe □, TN • *30,541*
Monroe □, WV • *12,406*

Monroe □, WI • 36,633
Monroe Center, CT 06468 • 7,900
Monroe City, MO 63456 • 2,701
Monroe Park, DE 19807 • 1,000
Monroeville, AL 36460–61 • 6,993
Monroeville, IN 46773 • 1,232
Monroeville, OH 44847 • 1,381
Monroeville, PA 15146 • 29,169
Monrovia, CA 91016 • 35,761
Monsey, NY 10952 • 13,986
Monson, MA 01057 • 2,101
Montague, CA 96064 • 1,415
Montague, MI 49437 • 2,276
Montague □, TX • 17,274
Mont Alto, PA 17237 • 1,395
Montauk, NY 11954 • 3,001
Mont Belvieu, TX 77580 • 1,323
Montcalm □, MI • 53,059
Montchanin, DE 19710 • 500
Montclair, CA 91763 • 28,434
Montclair, NJ 07042–44 • 37,729
Mont Clare, PA 19453 • 1,800
Monteagle, TN 37356 • 1,138
Montebello, CA 90640 • 59,564
Montecito, CA 93108 • 9,300
Montello, NV 89830 • 200
Montello, WI 53949 • 1,329
Monterey, CA 93940 • 31,954
Monterey, TN 38574 • 2,559
Monterey □, CA • 355,660
Monterey Park, CA 91754 • 60,738
Montesano, WA 98563 • 3,064
Montevallo, AL 35115 • 4,239
Montevideo, MN 56265 • 5,499
Monte Vista, CO 81144 • 4,324
Montezuma, GA 31063 • 4,506
Montezuma, IN 47862 • 1,134
Montezuma, IA 50171 • 1,651
Montezuma □, CO • 18,672
Montgomery, AL 36101–99 • 187,106
Montgomery, IL 60538 • 4,267
Montgomery, MN 56069 • 2,399
Montgomery, NY 12549 • 2,696
Montgomery, OH 45242 • 9,753
Montgomery, PA 17752 • 1,631
Montgomery, WV 25136 • 2,449
Montgomery □, AL • 209,085
Montgomery □, AR • 7,841
Montgomery □, GA • 7,163
Montgomery □, IL • 30,728
Montgomery □, IN • 34,436
Montgomery □, IA • 12,076
Montgomery □, KS • 38,816
Montgomery □, KY • 19,561
Montgomery □, MD • 757,027
Montgomery □, MS • 12,388
Montgomery □, MO • 11,355
Montgomery □, NY • 51,981
Montgomery □, NC • 23,346
Montgomery □, OH • 573,809
Montgomery □, PA • 678,111
Montgomery □, TN • 100,498
Montgomery □, TX • 182,201
Montgomery □, VA • 73,913
Montgomery City, MO 63361 • 2,281
Montgomery Village, MD 20879 • 32,315
Monticello, AR 71655 • 8,116
Monticello, FL 32344 • 2,573
Monticello, GA 31064 • 2,289
Monticello, IL 61856 • 4,549
Monticello, IN 47960 • 5,237
Monticello, IA 52310 • 3,522
Monticello, KY 42633 • 5,357
Monticello, MN 55362 • 4,941
Monticello, MS 39654 • 1,755
Monticello, NY 12701 • 6,597
Monticello, UT 84535 • 1,806
Monticello, WI 53570 • 1,140
Montmorency □, MI • 8,936
Montour □, PA • 17,735
Montour Falls, NY 14865 • 1,845
Montoursville, PA 17754 • 4,983
Montpelier, ID 83254 • 2,656
Montpelier, IN 47359 • 1,880
Montpelier, OH 43543 • 4,299
Montpelier, VT 05601–02 • 8,247
Montrose, AL 36559 • 1,400
Montrose, CO 81401–02 • 8,854
Montrose, MI 48457 • 1,811
Montrose, PA 18801 • 1,982
Montrose, VA 23231 • 6,405
Montrose □, CO • 24,423
Montvale, NJ 07645 • 6,946
Montville, CT 06353 • 16,673
Montville, NJ 07045 • 2,600
Monument, CO 80132 • 1,020
Monument Beach, MA 02553 • 1,800
Monument Heights, VA 23226 • 2,500
Moodus, CT 06469 • 1,170
Moody, TX 76557 • 1,329
Moody □, SD • 6,507
Moonachie, NJ 07074 • 2,817
Moorcroft, WY 82721 • 768
Moore, OK 73160 • 40,318
Moore □, NC • 59,013
Moore □, TN • 4,721
Moore □, TX • 17,865
Moorefield, WV 26836 • 2,148
Moore Haven, FL 33471 • 1,432
Mooreland, OK 73852 • 1,157
Moorestown, NJ 08057 • 16,500
Mooresville, IN 46158 • 5,541
Mooresville, NC 28115 • 9,317
Moorhead, MN 56560–61 • 32,295
Moorhead, MS 38761 • 2,417
Moorpark, CA 93020–21 • 25,494
Moose Lake, MN 55767 • 1,206
Moosic, PA 18507 • 5,339
Moosup, CT 06354 • 3,289
Mora, MN 55051 • 2,905
Mora, NM 87732 • 1,200
Mora □, NM • 4,264
Moraga, CA 94556 • 15,852
Moraine, OH 45439 • 5,989
Moravia, NY 13118 • 1,559
Morehead, KY 40351 • 8,357
Morehead City, NC 28557 • 6,046
Morehouse, MO 63868 • 1,068
Morehouse □, LA • 31,938
Morenci, AZ 85540 • 1,799
Morenci, MI 49256 • 2,342
Moreno Valley, CA 92387–88 • 118,779
Morgan, UT 84050 • 2,023

Morgan □, AL • 100,043
Morgan □, CO • 21,939
Morgan □, GA • 12,883
Morgan □, IL • 36,397
Morgan □, IN • 55,920
Morgan □, KY • 11,648
Morgan □, MO • 15,574
Morgan □, OH • 14,194
Morgan □, TN • 17,300
Morgan □, UT • 5,528
Morgan □, WV • 12,128
Morgan City, LA 70380–81 • 14,531
Morganfield, KY 42437 • 3,776
Morgan Hill, CA 95037–38 • 23,928
Morganton, NC 28655 • 15,085
Morgantown, KY 42261 • 2,284
Morgantown, MS 39120 • 3,288
Morgantown, WV 26502–07 • 25,879
Moriarty, NM 87035 • 1,399
Morningdale, MA 01505 • 1,130
Morocco, IN 47963 • 1,044
Moroni, UT 84646 • 1,115
Morrill □, NE • 5,423
Morrilton, AR 72110 • 6,551
Morris, AL 35116 • 1,136
Morris, IL 60450 • 10,270
Morris, MN 56267 • 5,613
Morris, OK 74445 • 1,216
Morris □, KS • 6,198
Morris □, NJ • 421,353
Morris □, TX • 13,200
Morrison, IL 61270 • 4,363
Morrison □, MN • 29,604
Morrison City, TN 37660 • 2,032
Morrisonville, IL 62546 • 1,113
Morrisonville, NY 12962 • 1,742
Morris Plains, NJ 07950 • 5,219
Morristown, NJ 07960–63 • 16,189
Morristown, TN 37813–16 • 21,385
Morrisville, NY 13408 • 2,732
Morrisville, PA 19067 • 9,765
Morrisville, VT 05661 • 1,984
Morro Bay, CA 93442–43 • 9,664
Morrow, GA 30260 • 5,168
Morrow, OH 45152 • 1,206
Morrow □, OH • 27,749
Morrow □, OR • 7,625
Morton, IL 61550 • 13,799
Morton, MS 39117 • 3,212
Morton, TX 79346 • 2,597
Morton, WA 98356 • 1,130
Morton □, KS • 3,480
Morton □, ND • 23,700
Morton Grove, IL 60053 • 22,408
Moscow, ID 83843 • 18,519
Moscow, PA 18444 • 1,527
Moses Lake, WA 98837 • 11,235
Mosheim, TN 37818 • 1,451
Mosinee, WI 54455 • 3,820
Moss Bluff, LA 70611 • 8,039
Moss Point, MS 39563 • 17,837
Motley □, TX • 1,532
Mott, ND 58646 • 1,019
Moulton, AL 35650 • 3,248
Moultrie, GA 31768 • 14,865
Moultrie □, IL • 13,930
Mound, MN 55364 • 9,634
Mound Bayou, MS 38762 • 2,222
Mound City, MO 64470 • 1,273
Moundridge, KS 67107 • 1,531
Mounds, IL 62964 • 1,407
Mounds View, MN 55432 • 12,541
Moundsville, WV 26041 • 10,753
Moundville, AL 35474 • 1,348
Mountainair, NM 87036 • 926
Mountain Brook, AL 35223 • 19,810
Mountain City, NV 89831 • 110
Mountain City, TN 37683 • 2,169
Mountain Grove, MO 65711 • 4,182
Mountain Home, AR 72653 • 9,027
Mountain Home, ID 83647 • 7,913
Mountain Iron, MN 55768 • 3,362
Mountain Lake, MN 56159 • 1,906
Mountain Lake Park, MD 21550 • 1,938
Mountain Lakes, NJ 07046 • 3,847
Mountain Park, GA 30087 • 11,025
Mountainside, NJ 07092 • 6,657
Mountain View, AR 72560 • 2,439
Mountain View, CA 94039–43 • 67,460
Mountain View, CO 80521 • 2,100
Mountain View, MO 65548 • 2,036
Mountain View, NM 87105 • 2,300
Mountain View, OK 73062 • 1,086
Mountain View, WY 82604 • 1,200
Mountain View, WY 82939 • 1,189
Mountain Village, AK 99632 • 674
Mount Airy, MD 21771 • 3,730
Mount Airy, NC 27030 • 7,156
Mount Angel, OR 97362 • 2,778
Mount Arlington, NJ 07856 • 3,630
Mount Ayr, IA 50854 • 1,796
Mount Carmel, IL 62863 • 8,287
Mount Carmel, PA 17851 • 7,196
Mount Carroll, IL 61053 • 1,726
Mount Clemens, MI 48043–46 • 18,405
Mount Dora, FL 32757 • 7,196
Mount Ephraim, NJ 08059 • 4,517
Mount Freedom, NJ 07970 • 1,920
Mount Gay, WV 25637 • 1,200
Mount Gilead, NC 27306 • 1,336
Mount Gilead, OH 43338 • 2,846
Mount Healthy, OH 45231 • 7,580
Mount Holly, NJ 08060 • 10,639
Mount Holly, NC 28120 • 7,710
Mount Holly Springs, PA 17065 • 1,925
Mount Hope, WV 25880 • 1,573
Mount Horeb, WI 53572 • 4,182
Mount Jackson, VA 22842 • 1,583
Mount Jewett, PA 16740 • 1,029
Mount Joy, PA 17552 • 6,398
Mount Juliet, TN 37122 • 5,389
Mount Kisco, NY 10549 • 9,108
Mountlake Terrace, WA 98043 • 19,320
Mount Lebanon, PA 15228 • 33,362
Mount Morris, IL 61054 • 2,919
Mount Morris, MI 48458 • 3,292
Mount Morris, NY 14510 • 3,102
Mount Olive, AL 35117 • 2,270
Mount Olive, IL 62069 • 2,126
Mount Olive, NC 28365 • 4,582
Mount Olympus, UT 84117 • 7,413
Mount Orab, OH 45154 • 1,929
Mount Penn, PA 19606 • 2,883

Mount Pleasant, IA 52641 • 8,027
Mount Pleasant, MI 48858–59 • 23,285
Mount Pleasant, NC 28124 • 1,027
Mount Pleasant, PA 15666 • 4,787
Mount Pleasant, SC 29464–65 • 30,108
Mount Pleasant, TN 38474 • 4,278
Mount Pleasant, TX 75455 • 12,291
Mount Pleasant, UT 84647 • 2,092
Mount Pocono, PA 18344 • 1,795
Mount Prospect, IL 60056 • 53,170
Mount Pulaski, IL 62548 • 1,610
Mountrail □, ND • 7,021
Mount Rainier, MD 20712 • 7,954
Mount Savage, MD 21545 • 1,640
Mount Shasta, CA 96067 • 3,460
Mount Sinai, NY 11766 • 8,023
Mount Sterling, IL 62353 • 1,922
Mount Sterling, KY 40353 • 5,362
Mount Sterling, OH 43143 • 1,647
Mount Union, PA 17066 • 2,878
Mount Vernon, GA 30445 • 1,914
Mount Vernon, IL 62864 • 16,988
Mount Vernon, IN 47620 • 7,217
Mount Vernon, IA 52314 • 3,657
Mount Vernon, KY 40456 • 2,654
Mount Vernon, MO 65712 • 3,726
Mount Vernon, NY 10550–53 • 67,153
Mount Vernon, OH 43050 • 14,550
Mount Vernon, TX 75457 • 2,219
Mount Vernon, WA 98273 • 17,647
Mount View, RI 02852 • 610
Mount Washington, KY 40047 • 5,226
Mount Wolf, PA 17347 • 1,365
Mount Zion, IL 62549 • 4,522
Moville, IA 51039 • 1,306
Moweaqua, IL 62550 • 1,785
Mower □, MN • 37,385
Moyock, NC 27958 • 1,400
Muenster, TX 76252 • 1,387
Muhlenberg □, KY • 31,318
Mukilteo, WA 98275 • 7,007
Mukwonago, WI 53149 • 4,457
Mulberry, AR 72947 • 1,448
Mulberry, FL 33860 • 2,988
Mulberry, IN 46058 • 1,262
Mulberry, NC 28659 • 2,339
Muldraugh, KY 40155 • 1,376
Muldrow, OK 74948 • 2,889
Muleshoe, TX 79347 • 4,571
Mullan, ID 83846 • 821
Mullens, WV 25882 • 2,006
Mullica Hill, NJ 08062 • 1,117
Mullins, SC 29574 • 5,910
Multnomah □, OR • 583,887
Mulvane, KS 67110 • 4,674
Muncie, IN 47302–08 • 71,035
Muncy, PA 17756 • 2,702
Munday, TX 76371 • 1,600
Mundelein, IL 60060 • 21,215
Munford, TN 38058 • 2,326
Munfordville, KY 42765 • 1,556
Munhall, PA 15120 • 13,158
Munising, MI 49862 • 2,783
Munster, IN 46321 • 19,949
Murfreesboro, AR 71958 • 1,542
Murfreesboro, NC 27855 • 2,580
Murfreesboro, TN 37129–33 • 44,922
Murphy, MO 63026 • 9,342
Murphy, NC 28906 • 1,575
Murphys, CA 95247 • 1,517
Murphysboro, IL 62966 • 9,176
Murray, KY 42071 • 14,439
Murray, UT 84107 • 31,282
Murray □, GA • 26,147
Murray □, MN • 9,660
Murray □, OK • 12,042
Murrells Inlet, SC 29576 • 3,334
Murrysville, PA 15668 • 17,240
Muscatine, IA 52761 • 22,881
Muscatine □, IA • 39,907
Muscle Shoals, AL 35661 • 9,611
Muscoda, WI 53573 • 1,287
Muscogee □, GA • 179,278
Muscoy, CA 92405 • 7,541
Muse, PA 15350 • 1,250
Muskego, WI 53150 • 16,813
Muskegon, MI 49440–45 • 40,283
Muskegon □, MI • 158,983
Muskegon Heights, MI 49444 • 13,176
Muskingum □, OH • 82,068
Muskogee, OK 74401–03 • 37,708
Muskogee □, OK • 68,078
Musselshell □, MT • 4,106
Mustang, OK 73064 • 10,434
Myerstown, PA 17067 • 3,236
Myrtle Beach, SC 29577–78 • 24,848
Myrtle Grove, FL 32506 • 17,402
Myrtle Point, OR 97458 • 2,712
Mystic, CT 06355 • 2,618
Mystic Island, NJ 08087 • 7,400

N

Naalehu, HI 96772 • 1,027
Naamans Gardens, DE 19810 • 1,500
Nabnasset, MA 01886 • 3,600
Nacogdoches, TX 75961–63 • 30,872
Nacogdoches □, TX • 54,753
Nags Head, NC 27959 • 1,838
Nahant, MA 01908 • 3,828
Nahunta, GA 31553 • 1,049
Nampa, ID 83651–53 • 28,365
Nanakuli, HI 96792 • 9,575
Nance □, NE • 4,275
Nanticoke, PA 18634 • 12,267
Nantucket, MA 02554 • 3,069
Nantucket □, MA • 6,012
Nanty Glo, PA 15943 • 3,190
Nanuet, NY 10954 • 14,065
Napa, CA 94558–59 • 61,842
Napa □, CA • 110,765
Napanoch, NY 12458 • 1,068
Naperville, IL 60540 • 85,351
Naples, FL 33939–42 • 19,505
Naples, NY 14512 • 1,237
Naples, TX 75568 • 1,508
Naples, UT 84078 • 1,334
Naples Park, FL 33963 • 8,002
Napoleon, ND 58561 • 930
Napoleon, OH 43545 • 8,884
Nappanee, IN 46550 • 5,510

Naranja, FL 33032 • 5,790
Narberth, PA 19072 • 4,278
Narragansett, RI 02882 • 3,721
Narrows, VA 24124 • 2,082
Naselle, WA 98638 • 1,000
Nash, TX 75569 • 2,162
Nash □, NC • 76,677
Nashua, IA 50658 • 1,476
Nashua, NH 03060–63 • 79,662
Nashville, AR 71852 • 4,639
Nashville, GA 31639 • 4,782
Nashville, IL 62263 • 3,202
Nashville, MI 49073 • 1,654
Nashville, NC 27856 • 3,617
Nashville, TN 37201–35 • 487,969
Nashwauk, MN 55769 • 1,026
Nassau, NY 12123 • 1,254
Nassau □, FL • 43,941
Nassau □, NY • 1,287,348
Nassau Shores, NY 11758 • 5,110
Natalia, TX 78059 • 1,216
Natchez, MS 39120–22 • 19,460
Natchitoches, LA 71457–58 • 16,609
Natchitoches □, LA • 36,689
Natick, MA 01760 • 30,100
National City, CA 91950–51 • 54,249
National Park, NJ 08063 • 3,413
Natrona □, WY • 61,226
Natrona Heights, PA 15065 • 12,200
Naugatuck, CT 06770 • 30,625
Nautilus Park, CT 06340 • 6,500
Nauvoo, IL 62354 • 1,108
Navajo □, AZ • 77,658
Navarre, OH 44662 • 1,635
Navarro □, TX • 39,926
Navasota, TX 77868–69 • 6,296
Navesink, NJ 07752 • 1,420
Nazareth, PA 18064 • 5,713
Neah Bay, WA 98357 • 1,300
Nebraska City, NE 68410 • 6,547
Nederland, CO 80466 • 1,099
Nederland, TX 77627 • 16,192
Nedrow, NY 13120 • 2,980
Needham, MA 02192 • 27,557
Needles, CA 92363 • 5,191
Needville, TX 77461 • 2,199
Neenah, WI 54956–57 • 23,219
Neffs, OH 43940 • 1,213
Negaunee, MI 49866 • 4,741
Neillsville, WI 54456 • 2,680
Nekoosa, WI 54457 • 2,557
Neligh, NE 68756 • 1,742
Nelson □, KY • 29,710
Nelson □, ND • 4,410
Nelson □, VA • 12,778
Nelsonville, OH 45764 • 4,563
Nemacolin, PA 15351 • 1,097
Nemaha □, KS • 10,446
Nemaha □, NE • 7,980
Nenana, AK 99760 • 393
Neodesha, KS 66757 • 2,837
Neoga, IL 62447 • 1,678
Neosho, MO 64850 • 9,254
Neosho □, KS • 17,035
Nephi, UT 84648 • 3,515
Neptune, NJ 07753 • 28,366
Neptune Beach, FL 32233 • 6,816
Neptune City, NJ 07753 • 4,997
Nesconset, NY 11767 • 10,712
Nescopeck, PA 18635 • 1,651
Neshoba □, MS • 24,800
Nesquehoning, PA 18240 • 3,364
Ness □, KS • 4,033
Ness City, KS 67560 • 1,724
Netcong, NJ 07857 • 3,311
Nether Providence Township, PA 19013 • 13,229
Nettleton, MS 38858 • 2,462
Nevada, IA 50201 • 6,009
Nevada, MO 64772 • 8,597
Nevada □, AR • 10,101
Nevada □, CA • 78,510
Nevada City, CA 95959 • 2,855
New Albany, IN 47150–51 • 36,322
New Albany, MS 38652 • 6,775
New Albany, OH 43054 • 1,621
Newark, AR 72562 • 1,159
Newark, CA 94560 • 37,861
Newark, DE 19711–15 • 25,098
Newark, NJ 07101–75 • 275,221
Newark, NY 14513 • 9,849
Newark, OH 43055–58 • 44,389
Newark Valley, NY 13811 • 1,082
New Athens, IL 62264 • 2,010
Newaygo, MI 49337 • 1,336
Newaygo □, MI • 38,202
New Baden, IL 62265 • 2,602
New Baltimore, MI 48047 • 5,798
New Bedford, MA 02740–48 • 99,922
Newberg, OR 97132 • 13,086
New Berlin, NY 13411 • 1,220
New Berlin, WI 53151 • 33,592
New Bern, NC 28560–64 • 17,363
Newbern, TN 38059 • 2,515
Newberry, FL 32669 • 1,644
Newberry, MI 49868 • 1,873
Newberry, SC 29108 • 10,542
Newberry □, SC • 33,172
New Bethlehem, PA 16242 • 1,151
New Bloomfield, PA 17068 • 1,092
New Boston, MI 48164 • 1,200
New Boston, OH 45662 • 2,717
New Boston, TX 75570 • 5,057
New Braunfels, TX 78130–33 • 27,334
New Bremen, OH 45869 • 2,558
New Brighton, MN 55112 • 22,207
New Brighton, PA 15066 • 6,854
New Britain, CT 06050–53 • 75,491
New Brockton, AL 36351 • 1,184
New Brunswick, NJ 08901–06 • 41,711
New Buffalo, MI 49117 • 2,317
Newburg, KY 40218 • 21,647
Newburgh, IN 47629–30 • 2,880
Newburgh, NY 12550–53 • 26,454
Newburgh Heights, OH 44105 • 2,310
Newburyport, MA 01950–52 • 16,317
New Canaan, CT 06840 • 17,864
New Carlisle, IN 46552 • 1,446
New Carlisle, OH 45344 • 6,049
New Carrollton, MD 20784 • 12,002
New Cassel, NY 11590 • 10,257
New Castle, AL 35119 • 1,100
New Castle, DE 19720 • 4,837

New Castle, IN 47362 • 17,753
Newcastle, OK 73065 • 4,214
New Castle, PA 16101–08 • 28,334
Newcastle, WY 82701 • 3,003
New Castle □, DE • 441,946
New City, NY 10956 • 33,673
Newcomerstown, OH 43832 • 4,012
New Concord, OH 43762 • 2,086
New Cumberland, PA 17070 • 7,665
New Cumberland, WV 26047 • 1,363
New Egypt, NJ 08533 • 2,327
Newell, IA 50568 • 1,089
Newell, WV 26050 • 1,724
New Ellenton, SC 29809 • 2,515
Newellton, LA 71357 • 1,576
New England, ND 58647 • 663
New Fairfield, CT 06812 • 4,600
Newfane, NY 14108 • 3,001
Newfield, NJ 08344 • 1,592
New Franklin, MO 65274 • 1,107
New Freedom, PA 17349 • 2,920
New Glarus, WI 53574 • 1,899
New Hampton, IA 50659 • 3,660
New Hanover □, NC • 120,284
New Hartford, CT 06057 • 1,269
New Haven, CT 06501–36 • 130,474
New Haven, IN 46774 • 9,320
New Haven, MI 48048 • 2,331
New Haven, MO 63068 • 1,757
New Haven, WV 25265 • 1,632
New Haven □, CT • 804,219
New Holland, GA 30501 • 1,200
New Holland, PA 17557 • 4,484
New Holstein, WI 53061 • 3,342
New Hope, AL 35760 • 2,248
New Hope, MN 55428 • 21,853
New Hope, NC 27604 • 5,694
New Hope, PA 18938 • 1,400
New Hyde Park, NY 11040 • 9,728
New Iberia, LA 70560–62 • 31,828
Newington, CT 06131 • 29,208
Newington, VA 22122 • 17,965
New Johnsonville, TN 37134 • 1,643
New Kensington, PA 15068 • 15,894
New Kent □, VA • 10,445
Newkirk, OK 74647 • 2,168
New Lenox, IL 60451 • 9,627
New Lexington, OH 43764 • 5,117
New Lisbon, WI 53950 • 1,491
Newllano, LA 71461 • 2,660
New London, CT 06320 • 28,540
New London, IA 52645 • 1,922
New London, NH 03257 • 3,180
New London, OH 44851 • 2,642
New London, WI 54961 • 6,658
New London □, CT • 254,957
New Madrid, MO 63869 • 3,350
New Madrid □, MO • 20,928
Newman, CA 95360 • 4,151
Newmanstown, PA 17073 • 1,410
Newmarket, NH 03857 • 4,917
New Market, TN 37820 • 1,086
New Market, VA 22844 • 1,435
New Martinsville, WV 26155 • 6,705
New Matamoras, OH 45767 • 1,002
New Miami, OH 45011 • 2,555
New Milford, CT 06776 • 5,775
New Milford, NJ 07646 • 15,990
Newnan, GA 30263–65 • 12,497
New Orleans, LA 70101–95 • 496,938
New Oxford, PA 17350 • 1,617
New Paltz, NY 12561 • 5,463
New Paris, IN 46553 • 1,007
New Paris, OH 45347 • 1,801
New Philadelphia, OH 44663 • 15,698
New Philadelphia, PA 17959 • 1,283
New Plymouth, ID 83655 • 1,313
Newport, AR 72112 • 7,459
Newport, DE 19804 • 1,240
Newport, KY 41071–76 • 18,871
Newport, ME 04953 • 1,843
Newport, MI 48166 • 1,100
Newport, MN 55055 • 3,720
Newport, NH 03773 • 3,772
Newport, NC 28570 • 2,516
Newport, OR 97365 • 8,437
Newport, PA 17074 • 1,568
Newport, RI 02840 • 28,227
Newport, TN 37821 • 7,123
Newport, VT 05855 • 4,434
Newport, WA 99156 • 1,691
Newport □, RI • 87,194
Newport Beach, CA 92657–63 • 66,643
Newport East, RI 02840 • 11,080
Newport Hills, WA 98002 • 14,736
Newport News, VA 23601–09 • 170,045
New Port Richey, FL 34652–56 • 14,044
New Prague, MN 56071 • 3,569
New Preston, CT 06777 • 1,217
New Providence, NJ 07974 • 11,439
New Richland, MN 56072 • 1,237
New Richmond, OH 45157 • 2,408
New Richmond, WI 54017 • 5,106
New River Station, NC 28542 • 9,732
New Roads, LA 70760 • 5,303
New Rochelle, NY 10801–05 • 67,265
New Rockford, ND 58356 • 1,604
New Salem, ND 58563 • 909
New Sarpy, LA 70078 • 2,946
New Sharon, IA 50207 • 1,136
New Smyrna Beach, FL 32168–70 • 16,543
New Tazewell, TN 37825 • 1,864
Newton, AL 36352 • 1,580
Newton, IL 62448 • 3,154
Newton, IA 50208 • 14,789
Newton, KS 67114 • 16,700
Newton, MA 02158 • 82,585
Newton, MS 39345 • 3,701
Newton, NJ 07860 • 7,521
Newton, NC 28658 • 9,304
Newton, TX 75966 • 1,885
Newton □, AR • 7,666
Newton □, GA • 41,808
Newton □, IN • 13,551
Newton □, MS • 20,291
Newton □, MO • 44,445
Newton □, TX • 13,569
Newton Falls, OH 44444 • 4,866
Newtown, CT 06470 • 1,800
New Town, ND 58763 • 1,388
Newtown, OH 45244 • 1,589
Newtown Square, PA 19073 • 11,366

United States Populations and ZIP Codes

New Ulm, MN 56073 • 13,132
Newville, PA 17241 • 1,349
New Washington, OH 44854 • 1,057
New Washoe City, NV 89701 • 2,875
New Waterford, OH 44445 • 1,278
New Whiteland, IN 46184 • 4,097
New Wilmington, PA 16142 • 2,706
New Windsor, NY 12553 • 8,898
New York, NY 10001–99 • 7,322,564
New York □, NY • 1,487,536
Nez Perce □, ID • 33,754
Niagara, WI 54151 • 1,999
Niagara □, NY • 220,756
Niagara Falls, NY 14301–05 • 61,840
Niantic, CT 06357 • 3,048
Nibley, UT 84321 • 1,167
Niceville, FL 32578 • 10,507
Nicholas □, KY • 6,725
Nicholas □, WV • 26,775
Nicholasville, KY 40356 • 13,603
Nicholls, GA 31554 • 1,003
Nichols Hills, OK 73116 • 4,020
Nickerson, KS 67561 • 1,137
Nicollet □, MN • 28,076
Nicoma Park, OK 73066 • 2,353
Nikishka, AK 99635 • 1,109
Niland, CA 92257 • 1,183
Niles, IL 60648 • 28,284
Niles, MI 49120 • 12,458
Niles, OH 44446 • 21,128
Ninety Six, SC 29666 • 2,099
Ninilchik, AK 99639 • 456
Niobrara □, WY • 2,499
Nipomo, CA 93444 • 7,109
Niskayuna, NY 12309 • 4,942
Nisswa, MN 56468 • 1,391
Nitro, WV 25143 • 6,851
Niwot, CO 80544 • 2,666
Nixa, MO 65714 • 4,707
Nixon, NV 89424 • 150
Nixon, TX 78140 • 1,995
Noank, CT 06340 • 1,406
Noble, OK 73068 • 4,710
Noble □, IN • 37,877
Noble □, OH • 11,336
Noble □, OK • 11,045
Nobles □, MN • 20,098
Noblesville, IN 46060 • 17,655
Nocatee, FL 33864 • 1,300
Nocona, TX 76255 • 2,870
Nodaway □, MO • 21,709
Noel, MO 64854 • 1,169
Nogales, AZ 85621 • 19,489
Nokomis, FL 34274–75 • 3,448
Nokomis, IL 62075 • 2,534
Nolan □, TX • 16,594
Nome, AK 99762 • 3,500
Noorvik, AK 99763 • 531
Nora Springs, IA 50458 • 1,505
Norco, CA 91760 • 23,302
Norco, LA 70079 • 3,385
Norcross, GA 30071 • 5,947
Norfolk, CT 06058 • 1,500
Norfolk, NE 68701 • 21,476
Norfolk, NY 13667 • 1,412
Norfolk, VA 23501–93 • 261,229
Norfolk □, MA • 616,087
Norland, FL 33169 • 22,109
Normal, IL 61761 • 40,023
Norman, OK 73069–72 • 80,071
Norman □, MN • 7,975
Normandy, MO 63121 • 4,480
Norridge, IL 60656 • 14,459
Norridgewock, ME 04957 • 1,496
Norris, TN 37828 • 1,303
Norris City, IL 62869 • 1,341
Norristown, PA 19401–09 • 30,749
North Adams, MA 01247 • 16,797
North Albany, OR 97321 • 4,325
North Amherst, MA 01059 • 6,239
North Amityville, NY 11701 • 13,849
Northampton, MA 01060–61 • 29,289
Northampton, PA 18067 • 8,717
Northampton □, NC • 20,798
Northampton □, PA • 247,105
Northampton □, VA • 13,061
North Andover, MA 01845 • 20,129
North Andrews Gardens, FL 33308 • 9,002
North Apollo, PA 15673 • 1,391
North Arlington, NJ 07032 • 13,790
North Atlanta, GA 30319 • 27,812
North Attleboro, MA 02760–63 • 16,178
North Auburn, CA 95603 • 10,301
North Augusta, SC 29841 • 15,351
North Aurora, IL 60542 • 5,940
North Babylon, NY 11703 • 18,081
North Baltimore, OH 45872 • 3,139
North Bay Shore, NY 11706 • 12,799
North Beach, MD 20714 • 1,173
North Bellmore, NY 11710 • 19,707
North Bellport, NY 11713 • 8,182
North Belmont, NC 28012 • 10,762
North Bend, NE 68649 • 1,249
North Bend, OR 97459 • 9,614
North Bend, WA 98045 • 2,578
North Bennington, VT 05257 • 1,520
North Bergen, NJ 07047 • 48,414
North Berwick, ME 03906 • 1,568
North Billerica, MA 01862 • 5,400
Northborough, MA 01532 • 5,761
North Braddock, PA 15104 • 7,036
North Branch, MI 48461 • 1,023
North Branch, MN 55056 • 1,867
North Branch, NJ 08876 • 2,620
North Branford, CT 06471 • 6,600
Northbridge, MA 01534 • 3,570
Northbrook, IL 60062 • 32,308
Northbrook, OH 45231 • 11,471
North Brookfield, MA 01535 • 2,635
North Brunswick, NJ 08902 • 31,287
North Brunswick Township, NJ 08902 • 31,287
North Caldwell, NJ 07006 • 5,832
North Canton, OH 44720 • 14,748
North Cape May, NJ 08204 • 3,574
North Charleston, SC 29406 • 70,218
North Chicago, IL 60064 • 34,978
North City, WA 98155 • 8,200
North Cohasset, MA 02025 • 1,045
North College Hill, OH 45239 • 11,002
North Collins, NY 14111 • 1,335
North Conway, NH 03860 • 2,032
North Corbin, KY 40701 • 1,601
North Crossett, AR 71635 • 3,358
North Dartmouth, MA 02747 • 8,080
North Decatur, GA 30033 • 13,936
North Dighton, MA 02764 • 1,174
North Druid Hills, GA 30033 • 14,170
North Eagle Butte, SD 57625 • 1,423
North East, MD 21901 • 1,913
North East, PA 16428 • 4,617
North Eastham, MA 02651 • 1,570
Northeast Henrietta, NY 14534 • 10,650
North Easton, MA 02356 • 4,420
North Fair Oaks, CA 94025 • 13,912
North Falmouth, MA 02556 • 3,150
Northfield, IL 60093 • 4,635
Northfield, MA 01360 • 1,322
Northfield, MN 55057 • 14,684
Northfield, NH 03276 • 1,375
Northfield, NJ 08225 • 7,305
Northfield, OH 44067 • 3,624
Northfield, VT 05663 • 1,889
Northfield Falls, VT 05664 • 600
North Fond du Lac, WI 54935 • 4,292
Northford, CT 06472 • 3,180
North Fort Myers, FL 33903 • 30,027
Northglenn, CO 80233 • 27,195
North Grafton, MA 01536 • 3,050
North Great River, NY 11722 • 3,964
North Grosvenordale, CT 06255 • 1,705
North Gulfport, MS 39501 • 4,966
North Haledon, NJ 07508 • 7,987
North Hampton, NH 03862 • 1,000
North Haven, CT 06473 • 22,249
North Highlands, CA 95660 • 42,105
North Hill, WA 98166 • 5,706
North Houston, TX 77086 • 12,800
North Hudson, WI 54016 • 3,101
North Industry, OH 44707 • 3,250
North Judson, IN 46366 • 1,582
North Kansas City, MO 64116 • 4,130
North Kingstown, RI 02852–54 • 2,750
North Kingsville, OH 44068 • 2,672
North La Junta, CO 81050 • 1,076
Northlake, IL 60164 • 12,505
North Las Vegas, NV 89030–31 • 47,707
North Lauderdale, FL 33068 • 26,506
North Lewisburg, OH 43060 • 1,160
North Liberty, IN 46554 • 1,366
North Liberty, IA 52317 • 2,926
North Lindenhurst, NY 11757 • 10,563
North Little Rock, AR 72114–20 • 61,741
North Logan, UT 84321 • 3,768
North Madison, OH 44057 • 8,699
North Manchester, IN 46962 • 6,383
North Mankato, MN 56001 • 10,164
North Massapequa, NY 11758 • 19,365
North Merrick, NY 11566 • 12,113
North Merrydale, LA 70812 • 4,000
North Miami, FL 33161 • 49,998
North Miami Beach, FL 33162 • 35,359
North Muskegon, MI 49445 • 3,919
North Myrtle Beach, SC 29582 • 8,636
North Naples, FL 33963 • 13,422
North New Hyde Park, NY 11040 • 14,359
North Ogden, UT 84404 • 11,668
North Olmsted, OH 44070 • 34,204
North Oxford, MA 01537 • 1,250
North Palm Beach, FL 33408 • 11,343
North Park, IL 61111 • 15,806
North Patchogue, NY 11772 • 7,374
North Pembroke, MA 02358 • 2,485
North Plainfield, NJ 07060 • 18,820
North Platte, NE 69101–03 • 22,605
Northport, AL 35476 • 17,366
North Port, FL 34287 • 11,973
Northport, NY 11768 • 7,572
North Prairie, WI 53153 • 1,322
North Providence, RI 02911 • 32,090
North Reading, MA 01864 • 11,455
North Richland Hills, TX 76118 • 45,895
Northridge, OH 45502 • 5,939
Northridge, OH 45414 • 9,448
North Ridgeville, OH 44039 • 21,564
North Riverside, IL 60546 • 6,005
North Royalton, OH 44133 • 23,197
North Salt Lake, UT 84054 • 6,474
North Sarasota, FL 34234 • 6,702
North Scituate, MA 02060 • 4,891
North Sioux City, SD 57049 • 2,019
North Springfield, OR 97477 • 5,451
North Springfield, VT 05150 • 750
North Springfield, VA 22151 • 8,996
North Star, DE 19711 • 1,030
North St. Paul, MN 55109 • 12,376
North Sudbury, MA 01776 • 2,630
North Syracuse, NY 13212 • 7,363
North Tarrytown, NY 10591 • 8,152
North Terre Haute, IN 47805 • 2,000
North Tewksbury, MA 01876 • 1,030
North Tonawanda, NY 14120 • 34,989
North Troy, VT 05859 • 723
North Tunica, MS 38676 • 1,314
Northumberland, PA 17857 • 3,860
Northumberland □, PA • 96,771
Northumberland □, VA • 10,524
North Uxbridge, MA 01538 • 1,500
Northvale, NJ 07647 • 4,563
North Valley Stream, NY 11580 • 14,574
North Vernon, IN 47265 • 5,311
North Versailles, PA 15137 • 12,302
Northview, MI 49505 • 13,712
Northview, OH 45322 • 10,337
Northville, MI 48167 • 6,226
Northville, NY 12134 • 1,180
North Wales, PA 19454 • 3,802
North Wantagh, NY 11793 • 12,276
North Warren, PA 16365 • 1,232
North Wildwood, NJ 08260 • 5,017
North Wilkesboro, NC 28659 • 3,384
North Windham, ME 04062 • 4,077
Northwood, IA 50459 • 1,940
Northwood, ND 58267 • 1,166
Northwood, OH 43619 • 5,506
Northwoods, MO 63121 • 5,106
North York, PA 17404 • 1,689
Norton, KS 67654 • 3,017
Norton, MA 02766 • 1,899
Norton, OH 44203 • 11,477
Norton, VA 24273 • 4,247
Norton □, KS • 5,947
Norton Shores, MI 49441 • 21,755
Nortonville, KY 42442 • 1,209
Norwalk, CA 90650–52 • 94,279
Norwalk, CT 06850–56 • 78,331
Norwalk, IA 50211 • 5,726
Norwalk, OH 44857 • 14,731
Norway, ME 04268 • 3,023
Norway, MI 49870 • 2,910
Norwell, MA 02061 • 1,200
Norwich, CT 06360 • 37,391
Norwich, NY 13815 • 7,613
Norwich, VT 05055 • 1,000
Norwood, MA 02062 • 28,700
Norwood, MN 55368 • 1,351
Norwood, NJ 07648 • 4,858
Norwood, NY 13668 • 1,841
Norwood, NC 28128 • 1,617
Norwood, OH 45212 • 23,674
Norwood, PA 19074 • 6,162
Norwoodville, IA 50317 • 1,200
Nottoway □, VA • 14,993
Novato, CA 94947–49 • 47,585
Novi, MI 48374–77 • 32,998
Nowata, OK 74048 • 3,896
Nowata □, OK • 9,992
Noxubee □, MS • 12,604
Nuckolls □, NE • 5,786
Nueces □, TX • 291,145
Nulato, AK 99765 • 359
Nunda, NY 14517 • 1,347
Nutley, NJ 07110 • 27,099
Nutter Fort, WV 26301 • 1,819
Nutting Lake, MA 01865 • 3,180
Nyack, NY 10960 • 6,558
Nye □, NV • 17,781
Nyssa, OR 97913 • 2,629

O

Oak Bluffs, MA 02557 • 1,124
Oak Brook, IL 60521 • 9,178
Oak Creek, WI 53154 • 19,513
Oakdale, CA 95361 • 11,961
Oakdale, GA 30080 • 1,080
Oakdale, LA 71463 • 6,832
Oakdale, MN 55128 • 18,374
Oakdale, NY 11769 • 7,875
Oakdale, PA 15071 • 1,752
Oakes, ND 58474 • 1,775
Oakfield, NY 14125 • 1,818
Oakfield, WI 53065 • 1,003
Oak Forest, IL 60452 • 26,203
Oak Grove, KY 42262 • 2,863
Oak Grove, LA 71263 • 2,126
Oak Grove, OR 97267 • 12,576
Oak Grove, SC 29073 • 7,173
Oak Harbor, OH 43449 • 2,637
Oak Harbor, WA 98277 • 17,176
Oak Hill, MI 49660 • 1,000
Oak Hill, OH 45656 • 1,831
Oak Hill, WV 25901 • 6,812
Oakhurst, OK 74050 • 2,200
Oakland, CA 94601–62 • 372,242
Oakland, IA 51560 • 1,496
Oakland, ME 04963 • 3,510
Oakland, MD 21550 • 2,078
Oakland, NE 68045 • 1,279
Oakland, NJ 07436 • 11,997
Oakland, RI 02830 • 600
Oakland □, MI • 1,083,592
Oakland City, IN 47660 • 2,810
Oakland Park, FL 33334 • 26,326
Oak Lawn, IL 60453–59 • 56,182
Oaklawn, KS 67216 • 4,200
Oakley, CA 94561 • 18,374
Oakley, KS 67748 • 2,045
Oaklyn, NJ 08107 • 4,430
Oakmont, PA 15139 • 6,961
Oak Orchard, DE 19966 • 350
Oak Park, CA 91301 • 5,000
Oak Park, IL 60301–05 • 53,648
Oak Park, MI 48237 • 30,462
Oak Ridge, FL 32809 • 15,388
Oakridge, OR 97463 • 3,063
Oak Ridge, TN 37830 • 27,310
Oakton, VA 22124 • 24,610
Oak Valley, NJ 08090 • 5,400
Oakville, CT 06779 • 8,741
Oakville, MO 63129 • 31,750
Oakwood, GA 30566 • 1,464
Oakwood, IL 61858 • 1,533
Oakwood, OH 45419 • 3,392
Oberlin, KS 67749 • 2,197
Oberlin, LA 70655 • 1,808
Oberlin, OH 44074 • 8,191
Obetz, OH 43207 • 3,167
Obion, TN 38240 • 1,241
Obion □, TN • 31,717
Oblong, IL 62449 • 1,616
O'Brien □, IA • 15,444
Ocala, FL 32670–78 • 42,045
Ocean □, NJ • 433,203
Oceana, WV 24870 • 1,791
Oceana □, MI • 22,454
Ocean Bluff, MA 02065 • 2,500
Ocean City, FL 32548 • 5,422
Ocean City, MD 21842 • 5,146
Ocean City, NJ 08226 • 15,512
Ocean Gate, NJ 08740 • 2,078
Ocean Grove, MA 02777 • 4,560
Oceano, CA 93445 • 6,169
Ocean Park, WA 98640 • 1,650
Ocean Port, NJ 07757 • 6,146
Oceanside, CA 92054–56 • 128,398
Oceanside, NY 11572 • 32,423
Ocean Springs, MS 39564–65 • 14,658
Ocean [Township], NJ 07712 • 23,570
Ocean View, DE 19970 • 606
Oceanville, NJ 08231 • 1,000
Ochiltree □, TX • 9,128
Ocilla, GA 31774 • 3,182
Ocoee, FL 34761 • 12,778
Oconee □, GA • 17,618
Oconee □, SC • 57,494
Oconomowoc, WI 53066 • 10,993
Oconto, WI 54153 • 4,474
Oconto □, WI • 30,226
Oconto Falls, WI 54154 • 2,584
Odebolt, IA 51458 • 1,158
Odell, IL 60460 • 1,030
Odem, TX 78370 • 2,366
Odenton, MD 21113 • 12,833
Odessa, DE 19730 • 303
Odessa, MO 64076 • 3,695
Odessa, TX 79760–68 • 89,699
Odin, IL 62870 • 1,150
Odon, IN 47562 • 1,475
O'Donnell, TX 79351 • 1,102
Oelwein, IA 50662 • 6,493
O'Fallon, IL 62269 • 16,073
O'Fallon, MO 63366 • 18,698
Ogallala, NE 69153 • 5,095
Ogden, IA 50212 • 1,909
Ogden, KS 66517 • 1,494
Ogden, UT 84401–14 • 63,909
Ogdensburg, NJ 07439 • 2,722
Ogdensburg, NY 13669 • 13,521
Ogemaw □, MI • 18,681
Ogle □, IL • 45,957
Oglesby, IL 61348 • 3,619
Oglethorpe, GA 31068 • 1,302
Oglethorpe □, GA • 9,763
Ogunquit, ME 03907 • 1,492
Ohatchee, AL 36271 • 1,042
Ohio □, IN • 5,315
Ohio □, KY • 21,105
Ohio □, WV • 50,871
Ohioville, PA 15059 • 3,865
Oil City, LA 71061 • 1,282
Oil City, PA 16301 • 11,949
Oildale, CA 93308 • 26,553
Oilton, OK 74052 • 1,060
Ojai, CA 93023–24 • 7,613
Okaloosa □, FL • 143,776
Okanogan, WA 98840 • 2,370
Okanogan □, WA • 33,350
Okarche, OK 73762 • 1,160
Okauchee, WI 53069 • 2,300
Okauchee Lake, WI 53058 • 3,819
Okawville, IL 62271 • 1,274
Okeechobee, FL 34972–74 • 4,943
Okeechobee □, FL • 29,627
Okeene, OK 73763 • 1,343
Okemah, OK 74859 • 3,085
Okemos, MI 48864 • 20,216
Okfuskee □, OK • 11,551
Oklahoma □, OK • 599,611
Oklahoma City, OK 73101–80 • 444,719
Oklawaha, FL 32179 • 1,200
Okmulgee, OK 74447 • 13,441
Okmulgee □, OK • 36,490
Okolona, KY 40219 • 18,902
Okolona, MS 38860 • 3,267
Oktibbeha □, MS • 38,375
Ola, AR 72853 • 1,090
Olathe, CO 81425 • 1,263
Olathe, KS 66061–62 • 63,352
Olcott, NY 14126 • 1,432
Old Bethpage, NY 11804 • 5,610
Old Bridge, NJ 08857 • 22,151
Old Forge, NY 13420 • 1,061
Old Forge, PA 18518 • 8,834
Oldham □, KY • 33,263
Oldham □, TX • 2,278
Old Harbor, AK 99643 • 284
Old Orchard Beach, ME 04064 • 7,789
Old Saybrook, CT 06475 • 1,820
Oldsmar, FL 34677 • 8,361
Old Tappan, NJ 07675 • 4,254
Old Town, ME 04468 • 8,317
Olean, NY 14760 • 16,946
Olive Branch, MS 38654 • 3,567
Olive Hill, KY 41164 • 1,809
Olivehurst, CA 95961 • 9,738
Oliver, PA 15472 • 3,271
Oliver □, ND • 2,381
Oliver Springs, TN 37840 • 3,433
Olivet, MI 49076 • 1,604
Olivette, MO 63132 • 7,573
Olivia, MN 56277 • 2,623
Olla, LA 71465 • 1,410
Olmito, TX 78575 • 1,400
Olmos Park, TX 78212 • 2,161
Olmsted □, MN • 106,470
Olmsted Falls, OH 44138 • 6,741
Olney, IL 62450 • 8,664
Olney, MD 20832 • 23,019
Olney, TX 76374 • 3,519
Olton, TX 79064 • 2,116
Olympia, WA 98501–07 • 33,840
Olympia Heights, FL 33175 • 36,900
Olyphant, PA 18447 • 5,222
Omaha, NE 68101–72 • 335,795
Omak, WA 98841 • 4,117
Omro, WI 54963 • 2,836
Onalaska, WI 54650 • 11,284
Onancock, VA 23417 • 1,434
Onarga, IL 60955 • 1,281
Onawa, IA 51040 • 2,936
Onaway, MI 49765 • 1,039
Oneco, FL 34264 • 6,417
Oneida, NY 13421 • 10,850
Oneida, OH 45042 • 1,650
Oneida, TN 37841 • 3,502
Oneida □, ID • 3,492
Oneida □, NY • 250,836
Oneida □, WI • 31,679
O'Neill, NE 68763 • 3,852
Oneonta, AL 35121 • 4,844
Oneonta, NY 13820 • 13,954
Onida, SD 57564 • 761
Onondaga □, NY • 468,973
Onset, MA 02558 • 1,461
Onslow □, NC • 149,838
Ontario, CA 91761–62 • 133,179
Ontario, OH 44862 • 4,026
Ontario, OR 97914 • 9,392
Ontario □, NY • 95,101
Ontonagon, MI 49953 • 2,040
Ontonagon □, MI • 8,854
Oolitic, IN 47451 • 1,424
Ooltewah, TN 37363 • 1,200
Oostburg, WI 53070 • 1,931
Opal Cliffs, CA 95062 • 5,940
Opa-Locka, FL 33054–56 • 15,283
Opelika, AL 36801–03 • 22,122
Opelousas, LA 70570–71 • 18,151
Opp, AL 36467 • 6,985
Opportunity, WA 99206 • 22,326
Oquawka, IL 61469 • 1,442
Oracle, AZ 85623 • 3,043
Oradell, NJ 07649 • 8,024
Oran, MO 63771 • 1,164
Orange, CA 92664–69 • 110,658
Orange, CT 06477 • 12,830
Orange, MA 01364 • 3,791
Orange, NJ 07050–52 • 29,925
Orange, TX 77630–31 • 19,381
Orange, VA 22960 • 2,582
Orange □, CA • 2,410,556
Orange □, FL • 677,491
Orange □, IN • 18,409
Orange □, NY • 307,647
Orange □, NC • 93,851
Orange □, TX • 80,509
Orange □, VT • 26,149
Orange □, VA • 21,421
Orange Beach, AL 36561 • 2,253
Orangeburg, SC 29115–16 • 13,739
Orangeburg □, SC • 84,803
Orange City, FL 32763 • 5,347
Orange City, IA 51041 • 4,940
Orange Grove, MS 39503 • 15,676
Orange Grove, TX 78372 • 1,175
Orange Lake, FL 32681 • 1,000
Orange Park, FL 32073 • 9,488
Orangevale, CA 95662 • 26,266
Orangeville, UT 84537 • 1,459
Orchard City, CO 81410 • 2,218
Orchard Homes, MT 59801 • 10,317
Orchard Mesa, CO 81501 • 5,977
Orchard Park, NY 14127 • 3,280
Orchards, WA 98662 • 8,828
Orchard Valley, WY 82007 • 3,321
Orcutt, CA 93455 • 1,500
Ord, NE 68862 • 2,481
Ordway, CO 81063 • 1,025
Oregon, IL 61061 • 3,891
Oregon, OH 43616 • 18,334
Oregon, WI 53575 • 4,519
Oregon □, MO • 9,470
Oregon City, OR 97045 • 14,698
Orem, UT 84057–59 • 67,561
Orfordville, WI 53576 • 1,219
Orient, NY 11957 • 1,000
Orinda, CA 94563 • 16,642
Orion, IL 61273 • 1,821
Oriskany, NY 13424 • 1,450
Orland, CA 95963 • 5,052
Orlando, FL 32801–72 • 164,693
Orland Park, IL 60462 • 35,720
Orleans, IN 47452 • 2,083
Orleans, IN 47452 • 2,161
Orleans, MA 02653 • 1,699
Orleans, VT 05860 • 806
Orleans □, LA • 496,938
Orleans □, NY • 41,846
Orleans □, VT • 24,053
Orlovista, FL 32811 • 5,990
Ormond Beach, FL 32174–76 • 29,721
Ormond By The Sea, FL 32174 • 8,157
Orofino, ID 83544 • 2,868
Orono, ME 04473 • 9,789
Orono, MN 55323 • 7,285
Orosi, CA 93647 • 5,486
Oroville, CA 95965–66 • 11,960
Oroville, WA 98844 • 1,505
Orrville, OH 44667 • 7,712
Orting, WA 98360 • 2,106
Ortonville, MI 48462 • 1,252
Ortonville, MN 56278 • 2,205
Orwell, OH 44076 • 1,258
Orwigsburg, PA 17961 • 2,780
Osage, IA 50461 • 3,439
Osage, WY 82723 • 350
Osage □, KS • 15,248
Osage □, MO • 12,018
Osage □, OK • 41,645
Osage Beach, MO 65065 • 2,599
Osage City, KS 66523 • 2,689
Osakis, MN 56360 • 1,256
Osawatomie, KS 66064 • 4,590
Osborne, KS 67473 • 1,778
Osborne □, KS • 4,867
Osburn, ID 83849 • 1,579
Osceola, AR 72370 • 8,930
Osceola, IN 46561 • 1,999
Osceola, IA 50213 • 4,164
Osceola, WI 54020 • 2,075
Osceola □, FL • 107,728
Osceola □, IA • 7,267
Osceola □, MI • 20,146
Osceola Mills, PA 16666 • 1,310
Oscoda, MI 48750 • 1,061
Oscoda □, MI • 7,842
Osgood, IN 47037 • 1,688
Oshkosh, WI 54901–04 • 55,006
Oskaloosa, IA 52577 • 10,632
Oskaloosa, KS 66066 • 1,074
Osprey, FL 34229 • 2,597
Osseo, MN 55369 • 2,704
Osseo, WI 54758 • 1,551
Ossian, IN 46777 • 2,428
Ossining, NY 10562 • 22,582
Osterville, MA 02655 • 2,911
Oswego, IL 60543 • 3,876
Oswego, KS 67356 • 1,870
Oswego, NY 13126 • 19,195
Oswego □, NY • 121,771
Otay, CA 92010 • 6,400
Oteen, NC 28805 • 1,400
Otego, NY 13825 • 1,068
Otero □, CO • 20,185
Otero □, NM • 51,928
Othello, WA 99327 • 4,638
Otis Orchards, WA 99027 • 3,200
Otoe □, NE • 14,252
Otsego, MI 49078 • 3,937
Otsego □, MI • 17,957
Otsego □, NY • 60,517
Ottawa, IL 61350 • 17,451
Ottawa, KS 66067 • 10,667
Ottawa, OH 45875 • 3,999
Ottawa □, KS • 5,634
Ottawa □, MI • 187,768
Ottawa □, OH • 40,029
Ottawa □, OK • 30,561
Ottawa Hills, OH 43606 • 4,543
Otterbein, IN 47970 • 1,291
Otter Tail □, MN • 50,714
Ottumwa, IA 52501 • 24,488
Ouachita □, AR • 30,574
Ouachita □, LA • 142,191
Ouray, CO 81427 • 644
Ouray □, CO • 2,295
Outagamie □, WI • 140,510
Overland, MO 63114 • 17,987
Overland Park, KS 66204 • 111,790
Overlea, MD 21206 • 12,137
Overlook, OH 45431 • 6,000
Overton, NV 89040 • 1,111

Overton, TX 75684 • 2,105
Overton □, TN • 17,636
Ovid, MI 48866 • 1,442
Owasso, OK 74055 • 11,151
Owatonna, MN 55060 • 19,386
Owego, NY 13827 • 4,442
Owen □, IN • 17,281
Owen □, KY • 9,035
Owensboro, KY 42301-03 • 53,549
Owensville, IN 47665 • 1,053
Owensville, MO 65066 • 2,325
Owensville, OH 45160 • 1,019
Owenton, KY 40359 • 1,306
Owings Mills, MD 21117 • 9,474
Owingsville, KY 40360 • 1,491
Owosso, MI 48867 • 16,322
Owsley □, KY • 5,036
Owyhee, NV 89832 • 908
Owyhee □, ID • 8,392
Oxford, AL 36203 • 9,362
Oxford, CT 06483 • 1,600
Oxford, GA 30267 • 1,945
Oxford, IN 47971 • 1,273
Oxford, KS 67119 • 1,143
Oxford, MA 01540 • 5,969
Oxford, MI 48370-71 • 2,929
Oxford, MS 38655 • 9,984
Oxford, NJ 07863 • 1,767
Oxford, NY 13830 • 1,738
Oxford, NC 27565 • 7,913
Oxford, OH 45056 • 18,937
Oxford, PA 19363 • 3,769
Oxford □, ME • 52,602
Oxnard, CA 93030-35 • 142,216
Oxon Hill, MD 20745 • 36,267
Oyster Bay, NY 11771 • 6,687
Ozark, AL 36360-61 • 12,922
Ozark, AR 72949 • 3,330
Ozark, MO 65721 • 4,243
Ozark □, MO • 8,598
Ozaukee □, WI • 72,831
Ozona, FL 34660 • 1,500
Ozona, TX 76943 • 3,181

P

Paauilo, HI 96776 • 620
Pace, FL 32571 • 6,277
Pacific, MO 63069 • 4,350
Pacific, WA 98047 • 4,622
Pacific □, WA • 18,882
Pacifica, CA 94044 • 37,670
Pacific Beach, WA 98571 • 1,200
Pacific City, OR 97135 • 1,500
Pacific Grove, CA 93950 • 16,117
Pacific Palisades, HI 96782 • 10,000
Packwood, WA 98361 • 1,010
Pacolet, SC 29372 • 1,736
Paddock Lake, WI 53168 • 2,662
Paden City, WV 26159 • 2,862
Paducah, KY 42001-03 • 27,256
Paducah, TX 79248 • 1,788
Page, AZ 86040 • 6,598
Page □, IA • 16,870
Page □, VA • 21,690
Pageland, SC 29728 • 2,666
Page Manor, OH 45431 • 9,300
Pagosa Springs, CO 81147 • 1,207
Pahala, HI 96777 • 1,520
Pahoa, HI 96778 • 1,027
Pahokee, FL 33476 • 6,822
Pahrump, NV 89041 • 7,424
Paia, HI 96779 • 2,091
Paincourtville, LA 70391 • 1,550
Painesville, OH 44077 • 15,699
Painted Post, NY 14870 • 1,950
Paintsville, KY 41240 • 4,354
Pajarito, NM 87105 • 1,400
Palacios, TX 77465 • 4,418
Palatine, IL 60067 • 39,253
Palatka, FL 32177 • 10,201
Palestine, IL 62451 • 1,619
Palestine, TX 75801-02 • 18,042
Palisade, CO 81526 • 1,871
Palisades Park, NJ 07650 • 14,536
Palm Bay, FL 32905 • 62,632
Palm Beach, FL 33480 • 9,814
Palm Beach □, FL • 863,518
Palm Beach Gardens, FL 33410 • 22,965
Palm Coast, FL 32135 • 14,287
Palmdale, CA 93550-51 • 68,842
Palm Desert, CA 92260-61 • 23,252
Palmer, AK 99645 • 2,866
Palmer, MA 01069 • 4,069
Palmer, MS 39401 • 2,765
Palmer, TX 75152 • 1,659
Palmer Lake, CO 80133 • 1,480
Palmer Park, MD 20785 • 7,019
Palmerton, PA 18071 • 5,394
Palmetto, FL 34220-21 • 9,268
Palmetto, GA 30268 • 2,612
Palmetto Estates, FL 33157 • 12,293
Palm Harbor, FL 34682-85 • 50,256
Palm Springs, CA 92262-64 • 40,181
Palm Springs, FL 33460 • 9,763
Palm Springs North, FL 33015 • 5,300
Palm Valley, FL 32082 • 9,960
Palmyra, MO 63461 • 3,371
Palmyra, NJ 08065 • 7,056
Palmyra, NY 14522 • 3,566
Palmyra, PA 17078 • 6,910
Palmyra, WI 53156 • 1,539
Palo Alto, CA 94301-09 • 55,900
Palo Alto □, IA • 10,669
Palo Pinto □, TX • 25,055
Palos Heights, IL 60463 • 11,478
Palos Hills, IL 60465 • 17,803
Palos Park, IL 60464 • 4,199
Palos Verdes Estates, CA 90274 • 13,512
Pamlico □, NC • 11,372
Pampa, TX 79065-66 • 19,959
Pamplico, SC 29583 • 1,314
Pana, IL 62557 • 5,796
Panaca, NV 89042 • 700
Panama, OK 74951 • 1,528
Panama City, FL 32401-13 • 34,378
Panama City Beach, FL 32407-08 • 4,051
Pandora, OH 45877 • 1,009
Panguitch, UT 84759 • 1,444
Panhandle, TX 79068 • 2,353
Panola □, MS • 29,996
Panola □, TX • 22,035
Panora, IA 50216 • 1,100
Panthersville, GA 30032 • 9,874
Paola, KS 66071 • 4,698
Paoli, IN 47454 • 3,542
Paoli, PA 19301 • 5,603
Paonia, CO 81428 • 1,403
Papaikou, HI 96781 • 1,634
Papillion, NE 68046 • 10,372
Paradise, CA 95969 • 25,408
Paradise, NV 89109 • 124,682
Paradise Hills, NM 87114 • 5,513
Paradise Valley, AZ 85253 • 11,671
Paradise Valley, NV 89426 • 150
Paragould, AR 72450-51 • 18,540
Paramount, CA 90723 • 47,669
Paramount, MD 21740 • 1,878
Paramus, NJ 07652-53 • 25,067
Parchment, MI 49004 • 1,958
Pardeeville, WI 53954 • 1,630
Paris, AR 72855 • 3,674
Paris, IL 61944 • 8,987
Paris, KY 40361-62 • 8,730
Paris, MO 65275 • 1,486
Paris, TN 38242 • 9,332
Paris, TX 75460-61 • 24,699
Park □, CO • 7,174
Park □, MT • 14,562
Park □, WY • 23,178
Park City, KS 67219 • 5,050
Park City, UT 84060 • 4,468
Parke □, IN • 15,410
Parker, AZ 85344 • 2,897
Parker, CO 80134 • 5,450
Parker, FL 32401 • 4,598
Parker, SD 57053 • 984
Parker □, TX • 64,785
Parker City, IN 47368 • 1,323
Parkersburg, IA 50665 • 1,804
Parkersburg, WV 26101-06 • 33,862
Parkesburg, PA 19365 • 2,981
Park Falls, WI 54552 • 3,104
Park Forest, IL 60466 • 24,656
Park Hills, KY 41015 • 3,321
Parkin, AR 72373 • 1,847
Parkland, WA 98444 • 20,882
Park Layne, OH 45344 • 4,895
Park Rapids, MN 56470 • 2,863
Park Ridge, IL 60068 • 36,175
Park Ridge, NJ 07656 • 8,102
Park River, ND 58270 • 1,725
Parkrose, OR 97230 • 21,108
Parkston, SD 57366 • 1,572
Parkville, MD 21234 • 31,617
Parkville, MO 64152 • 2,402
Parkwater, WA 99211 • 4,300
Parkway, CA 95823 • 12,000
Parkwood, NC 27713 • 4,123
Parkwood, WA 98366 • 6,853
Parlier, CA 93648 • 7,938
Parma, ID 83660 • 1,597
Parma, OH 44129 • 87,876
Parma Heights, OH 44130 • 21,448
Parmer □, TX • 9,863
Parole, MD 21401 • 10,054
Parowan, UT 84761 • 1,873
Parrish, AL 35580 • 1,433
Parshall, ND 58770 • 943
Parsons, KS 67357 • 11,924
Parsons, TN 38363 • 2,033
Parsons, WV 26287 • 1,453
Pasadena, CA 91101-09 • 131,591
Pasadena, MD 21122 • 10,012
Pasadena, TX 77501-08 • 119,363
Pascagoula, MS 39567-68 • 25,899
Pasco, WA 99301-02 • 20,337
Pasco □, FL • 281,131
Pascoag, RI 02859 • 5,011
Paso Robles, CA 93446-47 • 18,583
Pasquotank □, NC • 31,298
Passaic, NJ 07055 • 58,041
Passaic □, NJ • 453,060
Pass Christian, MS 39571 • 5,557
Pataskala, OH 43062 • 3,046
Patchogue, NY 11772 • 11,060
Paterson, NJ 07501-44 • 140,891
Patrick □, VA • 17,473
Patten, ME 04765 • 1,256
Patterson, LA 70392 • 4,736
Patterson, NY 12563 • 1,200
Patton, PA 16668 • 2,206
Paul, ID 83347 • 901
Paulding, OH 45879 • 2,605
Paulding □, GA • 41,611
Paulding □, OH • 20,488
Paullina, IA 51046 • 1,134
Paulsboro, NJ 08066 • 6,577
Pauls Valley, OK 73075 • 6,150
Pawcatuck, CT 06379 • 5,289
Paw Creek, NC 28130 • 1,700
Pawhuska, OK 74056 • 3,825
Pawling, NY 12564 • 1,974
Pawnee, IL 62558 • 2,384
Pawnee, OK 74058 • 2,197
Pawnee □, KS • 7,555
Pawnee □, NE • 3,317
Pawnee □, OK • 15,575
Pawnee City, NE 68420 • 1,008
Paw Paw, MI 49079 • 3,169
Pawtucket, RI 02860-65 • 72,644
Paxton, IL 60957 • 4,289
Paxton, MA 01612 • 1,550
Payette, ID 83661 • 5,592
Payette □, ID • 16,434
Payne, OH 45880 • 1,244
Payne □, OK • 61,507
Paynesville, MN 56362 • 2,275
Payson, AZ 85541 • 8,377
Payson, IL 62360 • 1,114
Payson, UT 84651 • 9,510
Peabody, KS 66866 • 1,349
Peabody, MA 01960-61 • 47,039
Peace Dale, RI 02883 • 3,100
Peach □, GA • 21,189
Peach Orchard, GA 30906 • 13,800
Peachtree City, GA 30269 • 19,027
Pea Ridge, AR 72751 • 1,620
Pearisburg, VA 24134 • 2,064
Pearl, MS 39208 • 19,588
Pearland, TX 77581 • 18,697
Pearl City, HI 96782 • 30,993
Pearl River, LA 70452 • 1,507
Pearl River, NY 10965 • 15,314
Pearl River □, MS • 38,714
Pearsall, TX 78061 • 6,924
Pearson, GA 31642 • 1,714
Pecatonica, IL 61063 • 1,760
Pecos, NM 87552 • 1,012
Pecos, TX 79772 • 12,069
Pecos □, TX • 14,675
Peculiar, MO 64078 • 1,777
Pedricktown, NJ 08067 • 1,500
Peebles, OH 45660 • 1,782
Peekskill, NY 10566 • 19,536
Pegram, TN 37143 • 1,371
Pekin, IL 61554-55 • 32,254
Pekin, IN 47165 • 1,095
Pelahatchie, MS 39145 • 1,553
Pelham, AL 35124 • 9,765
Pelham, GA 31779 • 3,869
Pelham, NY 10803 • 6,413
Pelham Manor, NY 10803 • 5,443
Pelican Rapids, MN 56572 • 1,886
Pella, IA 50219 • 9,270
Pell City, AL 35125 • 8,118
Pell Lake, WI 53157 • 2,018
Pemberton, NJ 08068 • 1,367
Pemberville, OH 43450 • 1,279
Pembina □, ND • 9,238
Pembroke, GA 31321 • 1,503
Pembroke, MA 02359 • 2,000
Pembroke, NC 28372 • 2,241
Pembroke, VA 24136 • 1,064
Pembroke Park, FL 33009 • 4,933
Pembroke Pines, FL 33024 • 65,452
Pemiscot □, MO • 21,921
Pen Argyl, PA 18072 • 3,492
Penbrook, PA 17103 • 2,791
Pender, NE 68047 • 1,208
Pender □, NC • 28,855
Pendleton, IN 46064 • 2,309
Pendleton, OR 97801 • 15,126
Pendleton, SC 29670 • 3,314
Pendleton □, KY • 12,036
Pendleton □, WV • 8,054
Pendley Hills, GA 30032 • 5,400
Pend Oreille □, WA • 8,915
Penfield, NY 14526 • 6,260
Penn Acres, DE 19720 • 2,430
Penn Hills, PA 15235 • 51,430
Pennington, NJ 08534 • 2,537
Pennington □, MN • 13,306
Pennington □, SD • 81,343
Pennington Gap, VA 24277 • 1,922
Pennsauken, NJ 08110 • 34,733
Pennsboro, WV 26415 • 1,282
Pennsburg, PA 18073 • 2,460
Penns Grove, NJ 08069 • 5,228
Pennsville, NJ 08070 • 12,218
Penn Yan, NY 14527 • 5,248
Penobscot □, ME • 146,601
Pensacola, FL 32501-26 • 58,165
Pentwater, MI 49449 • 1,050
Peoria, AZ 85345 • 50,618
Peoria, IL 61601-56 • 113,504
Peoria □, IL • 182,827
Peoria Heights, IL 61614 • 6,930
Peotone, IL 60468 • 2,947
Pepeekeo, HI 96783 • 1,813
Pepin □, WI • 7,107
Pepperell, MA 01463 • 2,350
Pepper Pike, OH 44124 • 6,185
Pequannock, NJ 07440 • 12,844
Perdido, AL 36562 • 1,200
Perham, MN 56573 • 2,075
Perkasie, PA 18944 • 7,878
Perkins, OK 74059 • 1,925
Perkins □, NE • 3,367
Perkins □, SD • 3,932
Perquimans □, NC • 10,447
Perrine, FL 33157 • 15,576
Perris, CA 92370 • 21,460
Perry, FL 32347 • 7,151
Perry, GA 31069 • 9,452
Perry, IA 50220 • 6,652
Perry, MI 48872 • 2,163
Perry, NY 14530 • 4,219
Perry, OH 44081 • 1,012
Perry, OK 73077 • 4,978
Perry, UT 84302 • 1,211
Perry □, AL • 12,759
Perry □, AR • 7,969
Perry □, IL • 21,412
Perry □, IN • 19,107
Perry □, KY • 30,283
Perry □, MS • 10,865
Perry □, MO • 16,648
Perry □, OH • 31,557
Perry □, PA • 41,172
Perry □, TN • 6,612
Perry Hall, MD 21128 • 22,723
Perry Heights, OH 44646 • 9,055
Perryman, MD 21130 • 2,160
Perrysburg, OH 43551-52 • 12,551
Perryton, TX 79070 • 7,607
Perryville, AR 72126 • 1,141
Perryville, MD 21903 • 2,456
Perryville, MO 63775 • 6,933
Pershing □, NV • 4,336
Person □, NC • 30,180
Perth Amboy, NJ 08861-63 • 41,967
Peru, IL 61354 • 9,302
Peru, IN 46970 • 12,843
Peru, NE 68421 • 1,110
Peru, NY 12972 • 1,565
Peshtigo, WI 54157 • 3,154
Petal, MS 39465 • 7,883
Petaluma, CA 94952-55 • 43,184
Peterborough, NH 03458 • 2,685
Petersburg, AK 99833 • 3,207
Petersburg, IL 62675 • 2,261
Petersburg, IN 47567 • 2,449
Petersburg, MI 49270 • 1,201
Petersburg, TX 79250 • 1,292
Petersburg, VA 23801-05 • 38,386
Petersburg, WV 26847 • 2,360
Petersville, AL 35633 • 1,730
Petoskey, MI 49770 • 6,056
Petroleum □, MT • 519
Petros, TN 37845 • 1,286
Pettis □, MO • 35,437
Pevely, MO 63070 • 2,831
Pewaukee, WI 53072 • 4,941
Pewee Valley, KY 40056 • 1,283
Pharr, TX 78577 • 32,921
Phelps, KY 41553 • 1,120
Phelps, NY 14532 • 1,978
Phelps □, MO • 35,248
Phelps □, NE • 9,715
Phenix City, AL 36867-69 • 25,312
Philadelphia, MS 39350 • 6,758
Philadelphia, NY 13673 • 1,478
Philadelphia, PA 19101-96 • 1,585,577
Philadelphia □, PA • 1,585,577
Phil Campbell, AL 35581 • 1,317
Philip, SD 57567 • 1,077
Philippi, WV 26416 • 3,132
Philipsburg, MT 59858 • 925
Philipsburg, PA 16866 • 3,048
Phillips, TX 79007 • 1,729
Phillips, WI 54555 • 1,592
Phillips □, AR • 28,838
Phillips □, CO • 4,189
Phillips □, KS • 6,590
Phillips □, MT • 5,163
Phillipsburg, KS 67661 • 2,828
Phillipsburg, NJ 08865 • 15,757
Philmont, NY 12565 • 1,623
Philo, IL 61864 • 1,028
Philomath, OR 97370 • 2,983
Phoenix, AZ 85001-82 • 983,403
Phoenix, IL 60426 • 2,217
Phoenix, NY 13135 • 2,435
Phoenix, OR 97535 • 3,239
Phoenixville, PA 19460 • 15,066
Piatt □, IL • 15,548
Picayune, MS 39466 • 10,633
Picher, OK 74360 • 1,714
Pickaway □, OH • 48,255
Pickens, MS 39146 • 1,285
Pickens, SC 29671 • 3,042
Pickens □, AL • 20,699
Pickens □, GA • 14,432
Pickens □, SC • 93,894
Pickerington, OH 43147 • 5,668
Pickett □, TN • 4,548
Pico Rivera, CA 90660-61 • 59,177
Piedmont, AL 36272 • 5,288
Piedmont, CA 94611 • 10,602
Piedmont, MO 63957 • 2,166
Piedmont, OK 73078 • 2,522
Piedmont, SC 29673 • 4,143
Piedmont, WV 26750 • 1,094
Pierce, ID 83546 • 746
Pierce, NE 68767 • 1,615
Pierce □, GA • 13,328
Pierce □, NE • 7,827
Pierce □, ND • 5,052
Pierce □, WA • 586,203
Pierce □, WI • 32,765
Pierce City, MO 65723 • 1,382
Pierceton, IN 46562 • 1,030
Pierre, SD 57501 • 12,906
Pierre Part, LA 70339 • 3,053
Pierson, FL 32180 • 2,988
Pierz, MN 56364 • 1,014
Pigeon, MI 48755 • 1,207
Pigeon Cove, MA 01966 • 1,660
Pigeon Forge, TN 37863 • 3,027
Piggott, AR 72454 • 3,777
Pike □, AL • 27,595
Pike □, AR • 10,086
Pike □, GA • 10,224
Pike □, IL • 17,577
Pike □, IN • 12,509
Pike □, KY • 72,583
Pike □, MS • 36,882
Pike □, MO • 15,969
Pike □, OH • 24,249
Pike □, PA • 27,966
Pike Lake, MN 55811 • 1,004
Pikesville, MD 21208 • 24,815
Piketon, OH 45661 • 1,717
Pikeville, KY 41501-02 • 6,324
Pikeville, TN 37367 • 1,771
Pilot Mountain, NC 27041 • 1,181
Pilot Point, TX 76258 • 2,538
Pilot Rock, OR 97868 • 1,478
Pilot Station, AK 99650 • 463
Pima, AZ 85543 • 1,725
Pima □, AZ • 666,880
Pimmit Hills, VA 22043 • 6,019
Pinal □, AZ • 116,379
Pinardville, NH 03045 • 4,654
Pinckney, MI 48169 • 1,603
Pinckneyville, IL 62274 • 3,372
Pinconning, MI 48650 • 1,291
Pine □, MN • 21,264
Pine Bluff, AR 71601-13 • 57,140
Pine Bluffs, WY 82082 • 1,054
Pine Bridge, CT 06403 • 1,160
Pine Bush, NY 12566 • 1,445
Pine Castle, FL 32809 • 8,276
Pine City, MN 55063 • 2,613
Pinedale, WY 82941 • 1,181
Pine Grove, PA 17963 • 2,118
Pine Grove Mills, PA 16868 • 1,129
Pine Hill, NJ 08021 • 9,854
Pine Hills, FL 32808 • 35,322
Pinehurst, MA 01866 • 6,614
Pinehurst, NJ 08201 • 1,850
Pinehurst, NC 28374 • 5,103
Pine Island, MN 55963 • 2,125
Pine Island, NY 10969 • 1,200
Pine Knot, KY 42635 • 1,549
Pine Lawn, MO 63120 • 5,092
Pine Level, NC 27568 • 1,217
Pinellas □, FL • 851,659
Pinellas Park, FL 34664-66 • 43,426
Pine Plains, NY 12567 • 1,312
Pine Ridge, SD 57770 • 2,596
Pinetops, NC 27864 • 1,514
Pine Valley, CA 91962 • 1,297
Pineville, KY 40977 • 2,198
Pineville, LA 71360-61 • 12,251
Pineville, NC 28134 • 2,970
Pinewald, NJ 08721 • 1,700
Pinewood, FL 33168 • 15,518
Pinewood Park, FL 33168 • 8,300
Piney Point, MD 20674 • 1,200
Piney View, WV 25906 • 1,085
Pinole, CA 94564 • 17,460
Pinson, AL 35126 • 1,430
Pioche, NV 89043 • 830
Pioneer, OH 43554 • 1,287
Pipestone, MN 56164 • 4,554
Pipestone □, MN • 10,491
Piqua, OH 45356 • 20,612
Pirtleville, AZ 85626 • 1,364
Piscataquis □, ME • 18,653
Piscataway, NJ 08854-55 • 42,223
Pisgah, OH 45069 • 15,660
Pisgah Forest, NC 28768 • 1,899
Pismo Beach, CA 93448-49 • 7,669
Pitcairn, PA 15140 • 4,087
Pitkin □, CO • 12,661
Pitman, NJ 08071 • 9,365
Pitt □, NC • 107,924
Pittsboro, NC 27312 • 1,436
Pittsburg, CA 94565 • 47,564
Pittsburg, KS 66762 • 17,775
Pittsburg, TX 75686 • 4,007
Pittsburg □, OK • 40,581
Pittsburgh, PA 15201-90 • 369,879
Pittsfield, IL 62363 • 4,231
Pittsfield, ME 04967 • 3,222
Pittsfield, MA 01201-03 • 48,622
Pittsfield, NH 03263 • 1,717
Pittsford, VT 05763 • 650
Pittston, PA 18640-44 • 9,389
Pittsylvania □, VA • 55,655
Piute □, UT • 1,277
Pixley, CA 93256 • 2,457
Placentia, CA 92670 • 41,259
Placer □, CA • 172,796
Placerville, CA 95667 • 8,355
Plain City, OH 43064 • 2,278
Plain City, UT 84404 • 2,722
Plain Dealing, LA 71064 • 1,074
Plainedge, NY 11714 • 8,739
Plainfield, CT 06374 • 2,856
Plainfield, IL 60544 • 4,557
Plainfield, IN 46168 • 10,433
Plainfield, NJ 07059-63 • 46,567
Plainfield, VT 05667 • 600
Plainfield Heights, MI 49505 • 5,000
Plains, MT 59859 • 992
Plains, PA 18705 • 4,694
Plains, TX 79355 • 1,422
Plainsboro, NJ 08536 • 1,560
Plainview, MN 55964 • 2,768
Plainview, NE 68769 • 1,333
Plainview, NY 11803 • 26,207
Plainview, TX 79072-73 • 21,700
Plainville, CT 06062 • 17,392
Plainville, KS 67663 • 2,173
Plainville, MA 02762 • 5,857
Plainwell, MI 49080 • 4,057
Plaistow, NH 03865 • 1,850
Plano, IL 60545 • 5,104
Plano, TX 75074-75 • 128,713
Plantation, FL 33317 • 66,692
Plant City, FL 33564-67 • 22,754
Plantersville, MS 38862 • 1,046
Plantsite, AZ 85540 • 1,500
Plantsville, CT 06479 • 7,050
Plaquemine, LA 70764-65 • 7,186
Plaquemines □, LA • 25,575
Platte, SD 57369 • 1,311
Platte □, MO • 57,867
Platte □, NE • 29,820
Platte □, WY • 8,145
Platte City, MO 64079 • 2,947
Platteville, CO 80651 • 1,515
Platteville, WI 53818 • 9,708
Plattsburg, MO 64477 • 2,248
Plattsburgh, NY 12901 • 21,255
Plattsmouth, NE 68048 • 6,412
Pleasant Gap, PA 16823 • 1,699
Pleasant Garden, NC 27313 • 2,228
Pleasant Grove, AL 35127 • 8,458
Pleasant Grove, UT 84062 • 13,476
Pleasant Hill, CA 94523 • 31,585
Pleasant Hill, IL 62366 • 1,030
Pleasant Hill, IA 50301 • 3,671
Pleasant Hill, MO 64080 • 3,827
Pleasant Hill, OH 45359 • 1,066
Pleasant Hills, PA 15236 • 8,884
Pleasanton, CA 94566 • 50,553
Pleasanton, KS 66075 • 1,231
Pleasanton, TX 78064 • 7,678
Pleasant Prairie, WI 53158 • 11,961
Pleasants □, WV • 7,546
Pleasant Valley, MO 64068 • 2,731
Pleasant Valley, NY 12569 • 1,688
Pleasant View, CO 80401 • 3,460
Pleasant View, UT 84404 • 3,603
Pleasantville, IA 50225 • 1,536
Pleasantville, NJ 08232 • 16,027
Pleasantville, NY 10570-72 • 6,592
Pleasure Beach, CT 06385 • 1,356
Pleasure Ridge Park, KY 40258 • 25,131
Plentywood, MT 59254 • 2,136
Plover, WI 54467 • 8,176
Plum, PA 15239 • 25,609
Plumas □, CA • 19,739
Plumsteadville, PA 18949 • 1,200
Plymouth, CT 06782 • 1,070
Plymouth, FL 32768 • 2,700
Plymouth, IN 46563 • 8,303
Plymouth, MA 02360-61 • 7,258
Plymouth, MI 48170 • 9,560
Plymouth, MN 55441 • 50,889
Plymouth, NH 03264 • 3,967
Plymouth, NC 27962 • 4,328
Plymouth, OH 44865 • 1,942
Plymouth, PA 18651 • 7,134
Plymouth, WI 53073 • 6,769
Plymouth □, IA • 23,388
Plymouth □, MA • 435,276
Plymouth Township, PA 19401 • 17,168
Poca, WV 25159 • 1,124
Pocahontas, AR 72455 • 6,151
Pocahontas, IA 50574 • 2,085
Pocahontas □, IA • 9,525
Pocahontas □, WV • 9,008
Pocasset, MA 02559 • 2,200
Pocatalico, WV 25320 • 2,450
Pocatello, ID 83201-06 • 46,080
Pocola, OK 74902 • 3,664
Pocomoke City, MD 21851 • 3,922
Poinsett □, AR • 24,664
Point Clear, AL 36564 • 2,125
Pointe Coupee □, LA • 22,540
Point Hope, AK 99766 • 639
Point Marion, PA 15474 • 1,344
Point Pleasant, NJ 08742 • 18,177
Point Pleasant, WV 25550 • 4,996
Point Pleasant Beach, NJ 08742 • 5,112
Poipu, HI 96756 • 975
Polk, PA 16342 • 1,267
Polk □, AR • 17,347

Polk □, FL • 405,382
Polk □, GA • 33,815
Polk □, IA • 327,140
Polk □, MN • 32,498
Polk □, MO • 21,826
Polk □, NE • 5,675
Polk □, NC • 14,416
Polk □, OR • 49,541
Polk □, TN • 13,643
Polk □, TX • 30,687
Polk □, WI • 34,773
Polk City, FL 33868 • 1,439
Polk City, IA 50226 • 1,908
Polo, IL 61064 • 2,514
Polson, MT 59860 • 3,283
Pomeroy, OH 45769 • 2,259
Pomeroy, WA 99347 • 1,393
Pomona, CA 91765–69 • 131,723
Pomona, NJ 08240 • 2,624
Pompano Beach, FL 33060–69 • 72,411
Pompano Beach Highlands, FL 33060 • 17,915
Pompton Lakes, NJ 07442 • 10,539
Ponca City, OK 74601–04 • 26,359
Ponchatoula, LA 70454 • 5,425
Pondera □, MT • 6,433
Ponte Vedra Beach, FL 32082 • 1,700
Pontiac, IL 61764 • 11,428
Pontiac, MI 48340–43 • 71,166
Pontotoc, MS 38863 • 4,570
Pontotoc □, MS • 22,237
Pontotoc □, OK • 34,119
Pooler, GA 31322 • 4,453
Poolesville, MD 20837 • 3,796
Pope □, AR • 45,883
Pope □, IL • 4,373
Pope □, MN • 10,745
Poplar, MT 59255 • 881
Poplar Bluff, MO 63901 • 16,996
Poplarville, MS 39470 • 2,561
Poquonock Bridge, CT 06340 • 2,770
Poquoson, VA 23662 • 11,005
Portage, IN 46368 • 29,060
Portage, MI 49081 • 41,042
Portage, PA 15946 • 3,105
Portage, WI 53901 • 8,640
Portage □, OH • 142,585
Portage □, WI • 61,405
Portage Lakes, OH 44319 • 13,373
Portageville, MO 63873 • 3,401
Portales, NM 88130 • 10,690
Port Allegany, PA 16743 • 2,391
Port Allen, LA 70767 • 6,277
Port Angeles, WA 98362 • 17,710
Port Aransas, TX 78373 • 2,233
Port Arthur, TX 77640–43 • 58,724
Port Barre, LA 70577 • 2,144
Port Bolivar, TX 77650 • 1,600
Port Byron, IL 61275 • 1,002
Port Byron, NY 13140 • 1,359
Port Carbon, PA 17965 • 2,134
Port Charlotte, FL 33952 • 41,535
Port Chester, NY 10573 • 24,728
Port Clinton, OH 43452 • 7,106
Port Dickinson, NY 13901 • 1,785
Port Edwards, WI 54469 • 1,848
Porter, IN 46304 • 3,118
Porter, TX 77365 • 7,000
Porter □, IN • 128,932
Porterdale, GA 30270 • 1,278
Porterville, CA 93257–58 • 29,563
Port Ewen, NY 12466 • 3,444
Port Gibson, MS 39150 • 1,810
Port Henry, NY 12974 • 1,263
Port Hueneme, CA 93041–44 • 20,319
Port Huron, MI 48060–61 • 33,694
Port Isabel, TX 78578 • 4,467
Port Jefferson, NY 11777 • 7,455
Port Jefferson Station, NY 11776 • 7,232
Port Jervis, NY 12771 • 9,060
Portland, CT 06480 • 5,645
Portland, IN 47371 • 6,483
Portland, ME 04101–12 • 64,358
Portland, MI 48875 • 3,889
Portland, OR 97201–99 • 437,319
Portland, TN 37148 • 5,165
Portland, TX 78374 • 12,224
Port Lavaca, TX 77979 • 10,886
Port Monmouth, NJ 07758 • 3,800
Port Neches, TX 77651 • 12,974
Port Norris, NJ 08349 • 1,701
Port O'Connor, TX 77982 • 1,031
Portola, CA 96122 • 2,193
Port Orange, FL 32127 • 35,317
Port Orchard, WA 98366 • 4,984
Port Orford, OR 97465 • 1,025
Port Penn, DE 19731 • 300
Port Richey, FL 34667–74 • 2,523
Port Royal, SC 29935 • 2,985
Port Saint Joe, FL 32456 • 4,044
Port Saint Lucie, FL 34952 • 55,866
Port Salerno, FL 34992 • 7,786
Portsmouth, NH 03801–02 • 25,925
Portsmouth, OH 45662 • 22,676
Portsmouth, RI 02871 • 3,540
Portsmouth, VA 23701–09 • 103,907
Port St. John, FL 32922 • 8,933
Port Sulphur, LA 70083 • 3,523
Port Townsend, WA 98368 • 7,001
Portville, NY 14770 • 1,000
Port Vue, PA 15133 • 4,641
Port Washington, NY 11050 • 15,387
Port Washington, WI 53074 • 9,338
Port Wentworth, GA 31407 • 4,012
Posen, IL 60469 • 4,226
Posey □, IN • 25,968
Poseyville, IN 47633 • 1,089
Post, TX 79356 • 3,768
Post Falls, ID 83854 • 7,349
Postville, IA 52162 • 1,472
Poteau, OK 74953 • 7,210
Poteet, TX 78065 • 3,206
Poth, TX 78147 • 1,642
Potlatch, ID 83855 • 790
Potomac, MD 20851 • 45,634
Potomac Heights, MD 20640 • 1,524
Potomac Park, MD 21502 • 1,800
Potosi, MO 63664 • 2,683
Potsdam, NY 13676 • 10,251
Pottawatomie □, KS • 16,128
Pottawattamie □, OK • 58,760
Pottawattamie □, IA • 82,628
Potter □, PA • 16,717

Potter □, SD • 3,190
Potter □, TX • 97,874
Potter Valley, CA 95469 • 1,500
Pottstown, PA 19464 • 21,831
Pottsville, PA 17901 • 16,603
Poughkeepsie, NY 12601–03 • 28,844
Poulsbo, WA 98370 • 4,848
Poultney, VT 05764 • 1,731
Poway, CA 92064 • 43,516
Powder River □, MT • 2,090
Powder Springs, GA 30073 • 6,893
Powell, OH 43065 • 2,154
Powell, TN 37849 • 7,534
Powell, WY 82435 • 5,292
Powell □, KY • 11,686
Powell □, MT • 6,620
Powellhurst, OR 97236 • 28,756
Powellton, WV 25161 • 1,905
Power □, ID • 7,086
Poweshiek, IA • 19,033
Powhatan □, VA • 15,328
Powhatan Point, OH 43942 • 1,807
Poydras, LA 70085 • 4,029
Poynette, WI 53955 • 1,662
Prague, OK 74864 • 2,308
Prairie □, AR • 9,518
Prairie □, MT • 1,383
Prairie City, IA 50228 • 1,360
Prairie City, OR 97869 • 1,117
Prairie du Chien, WI 53821 • 5,659
Prairie du Sac, WI 53578 • 2,380
Prairie Grove, AR 72753 • 1,761
Prairie View, TX 77446 • 4,004
Prairie Village, KS 66208 • 23,186
Pratt, KS 67124 • 6,687
Pratt □, KS • 9,702
Prattville, AL 36066–67 • 19,587
Preble □, OH • 40,113
Premont, TX 78375 • 2,914
Prentiss, MS 39474 • 1,487
Prentiss □, MS • 23,278
Prescott, AZ 86301–14 • 26,455
Prescott, AR 71857 • 3,673
Prescott, WI 54021 • 3,243
Presho, SD 57568 • 654
Presidio, TX 79845 • 3,072
Presidio □, TX • 6,637
Presque Isle, ME 04769 • 10,550
Presque Isle □, MI • 13,743
Preston, ID 83263 • 3,710
Preston, IA 52069 • 1,025
Preston, MN 55965 • 1,530
Preston □, WV • 29,037
Prestonsburg, KY 41653 • 3,558
Price, UT 84501 • 8,712
Price □, WI • 15,600
Prichard, AL 36610 • 34,311
Priest River, ID 83856 • 1,560
Primrose, IN 02895 • 500
Prince Edward □, VA • 17,320
Prince Frederick, MD 20678 • 1,885
Prince George □, MD • 729,268
Prince George □, VA • 27,394
Princes Lakes, IN 46164 • 1,055
Princess Anne, MD 21853 • 1,666
Princeton, FL 33032 • 7,073
Princeton, IL 61356 • 7,197
Princeton, IN 47670 • 8,127
Princeton, KY 42445 • 6,940
Princeton, MN 55371 • 3,719
Princeton, MO 64673 • 1,021
Princeton, NJ 08540–43 • 12,016
Princeton, NC 27569 • 1,181
Princeton, WV 24740 • 7,043
Princeton, WI 54968 • 1,458
Princeton Junction, NJ 08550 • 2,362
Princeville, IL 61559 • 1,421
Princeville, NC 27886 • 1,652
Prince William □, VA • 215,686
Prineville, OR 97754 • 5,355
Prior Lake, MN 55372 • 11,482
Proctor, MN 55810 • 2,974
Proctor, VT 05765 • 1,979
Proctorsville, VT 05153 • 480
Prophetstown, IL 61277 • 1,749
Prospect, CT 06712 • 6,807
Prospect, KY 40059 • 2,788
Prospect, OH 43342 • 1,148
Prospect, OR 97536 • 1,200
Prospect, PA 16052 • 1,122
Prospect Heights, IL 60070 • 15,239
Prospect Park, NJ 07508 • 5,053
Prospect Park, PA 19076 • 6,764
Prosperity, SC 29127 • 1,116
Prosperity, WV 25909 • 1,322
Prosser, WA 99350 • 4,476
Providence, KY 42450 • 4,123
Providence, RI 02901–40 • 160,728
Providence, UT 84332 • 3,344
Providence □, RI • 596,270
Provincetown, MA 02657 • 3,374
Provo, UT 84601–06 • 86,835
Prowers □, CO • 13,347
Prudenville, MI 48651 • 1,100
Prudhoe Bay, AK 99734 • 47
Pryor, OK 74361–62 • 8,327
Pueblo, CO 81001–19 • 98,640
Pueblo □, CO • 123,051
Puhi, HI 96766 • 1,210
Pukalani, HI 96788 • 5,879
Pulaski, NY 13142 • 2,525
Pulaski, TN 38478 • 7,895
Pulaski, VA 24301 • 9,985
Pulaski, WI 54162 • 2,200
Pulaski □, AR • 349,660
Pulaski □, GA • 8,108
Pulaski □, IL • 7,523
Pulaski □, IN • 12,643
Pulaski □, KY • 49,489
Pulaski □, MO • 41,307
Pulaski □, VA • 34,496
Pullman, WA 99163–65 • 23,478
Pumphrey, MD 21227 • 5,483
Punta Gorda, FL 33948–55 • 10,747
Punxsutawney, PA 15767 • 6,782
Purcell, OK 73080 • 4,784
Purcellville, VA 22132 • 1,744
Purvis, MS 39475 • 2,140
Pushmataha □, OK • 10,997
Putnam, CT 06260 • 6,835
Putnam □, FL • 65,070
Putnam □, GA • 14,137
Putnam □, IL • 5,730

Putnam □, IN • 30,315
Putnam □, MO • 5,079
Putnam □, NY • 83,941
Putnam □, OH • 33,819
Putnam □, TN • 51,373
Putnam □, WV • 42,835
Putney, VT 05346 • 1,100
Puyallup, WA 98371–74 • 23,875

Q

Quail Oaks, VA 23234 • 1,500
Quaker Hill, CT 06375 • 2,052
Quakertown, PA 18951 • 8,982
Quanah, TX 79252 • 3,413
Quarryville, PA 17566 • 1,642
Quartz Hill, CA 93536 • 9,626
Quartzsite, AZ 85346 • 1,876
Quay □, NM • 10,823
Quechee, VT 05059 • 550
Queen Annes □, MD • 33,953
Queen City, TX 75572 • 1,748
Queen Creek, AZ 85242 • 2,667
Queens □, NY • 1,951,598
Queensborough, WA 98021 • 4,850
Questa, NM 87556 • 1,707
Quidnessett, RI 02852 • 3,300
Quidnick, RI 02816 • 2,300
Quilcene, WA 98376 • 1,200
Quincy, CA 95971 • 2,700
Quincy, FL 32351 • 7,444
Quincy, IL 62301–06 • 39,681
Quincy, MA 02169 • 84,985
Quincy, MI 49082 • 1,680
Quincy, WA 98848 • 3,738
Quinebaug, CT 06262 • 1,031
Quinhagak, AK 99655 • 501
Quinlan, TX 75474 • 1,360
Quinton, OK 74561 • 1,133
Quitman, GA 31643 • 5,292
Quitman, MS 39355 • 2,736
Quitman, TX 75783 • 1,684
Quitman □, GA • 2,209
Quitman □, MS • 10,490
Quonochontaug, RI 02813 • 1,500

R

Rabun □, GA • 11,648
Raceland, KY 41169 • 2,256
Raceland, LA 70394 • 5,564
Racine, WI 53401–08 • 84,298
Racine □, WI • 175,034
Radcliff, KY 40159–60 • 19,772
Radford, VA 24141–43 • 15,940
Radnor Township, PA 19087 • 28,705
Raeford, NC 28376 • 3,469
Ragland, AL 35131 • 1,807
Rahway, NJ 07065–67 • 25,325
Rainbow City, AL 35901 • 7,673
Rainelle, WV 25962 • 1,681
Rainier, OR 97048 • 1,674
Rains □, TX • 6,715
Rainsville, AL 35986 • 3,875
Raleigh, MS 39153 • 1,291
Raleigh, NC 27601–61 • 207,951
Raleigh □, WV • 76,819
Raleigh Hills, OR 97225 • 6,066
Ralls, TX 79357 • 2,172
Ralls □, MO • 8,476
Ralston, NE 68127 • 6,236
Rambleton Acres, DE 19720 • 1,700
Ramblewood, NJ 08054 • 6,181
Ramona, CA 92065 • 13,040
Ramsay, MI 49959 • 1,075
Ramseur, NC 27316 • 1,168
Ramsey, MN 55303 • 12,408
Ramsey, NJ 07446 • 13,228
Ramsey □, MN • 485,765
Ramsey □, ND • 12,681
Ranchester, WY 82839 • 676
Rancho Cordova, CA 95670 • 48,731
Rancho Mirage, CA 92270 • 9,778
Rancho Palos Verdes, CA 90274 • 41,659
Rancho Rinconado, CA 95014 • 4,206
Ranchos de Taos, NM 87557 • 1,779
Rancocas Woods, NJ 08060 • 1,250
Rand, WV 25306 • 2,400
Randall □, TX • 89,673
Randallstown, MD 21133 • 26,277
Randleman, NC 27317 • 2,612
Randolph, ME 04345 • 1,949
Randolph, MA 02368 • 30,093
Randolph, NY 14772 • 1,298
Randolph, VT 22090 • 4,556
Randolph, WI 53956 • 1,729
Randolph □, AL • 19,881
Randolph □, AR • 16,558
Randolph □, GA • 8,023
Randolph □, IL • 34,583
Randolph □, IN • 27,148
Randolph □, MO • 24,370
Randolph □, NC • 106,546
Randolph □, WV • 27,803
Randolph Hills, MD 20852 • 4,180
Random Lake, WI 53075 • 1,439
Rangely, CO 81648 • 2,278
Ranger, TX 76470 • 2,803
Rankin, PA 15104 • 2,503
Rankin, TX 79778 • 1,011
Rankin □, MS • 87,161
Ransom □, ND • 5,921
Ransomville, NY 14131 • 1,542
Ranson, WV 25438 • 2,890
Rantoul, IL 61866 • 17,212
Raoul, GA 30510 • 1,400
Rapid City, SD 57701–09 • 54,523
Rapides □, LA • 131,556
Rapid Valley, SD 57701 • 5,968
Rappahannock □, VA • 6,622
Raritan, NJ 08869 • 5,798
Raton, NM 87740 • 7,372
Ravalli □, MT • 25,010
Raven, VA 24639 • 2,640
Ravena, NY 12143 • 3,547
Ravenel, SC 29470 • 2,165
Ravenna, NE 68869 • 1,317
Ravenna, OH 44266 • 12,069
Ravenswood, WV 26164 • 4,189

Rawlins, WY 82301 • 9,380
Rawlins □, KS • 3,404
Ray, ND 58849 • 603
Ray □, MO • 21,971
Raymond, CA 93654 • 2,275
Raymond, NH 03077 • 2,516
Raymond, WA 98577 • 2,901
Raymondville, TX 78580 • 8,880
Raymore, MO 64083 • 5,592
Rayne, LA 70578 • 8,502
Raynham, MA 02767 • 3,709
Raynham Center, MA 02768 • 3,709
Raytown, MO 64133 • 30,601
Rayville, LA 71269 • 4,411
Reading, PA 18951 • 22,539
Reading, MI 49274 • 1,127
Reading, OH 45215 • 12,038
Reading, PA 19601–12 • 78,380
Reagan □, TX • 4,514
Real □, TX • 2,412
Reamstown, PA 17567 • 2,649
Rector, AR 72461 • 2,268
Red Bank, NJ 07701–04 • 10,636
Red Bank, SC 29073 • 6,112
Red Bank, TN 37415 • 12,322
Red Bay, AL 35582 • 3,451
Redbird, OH 44057 • 1,600
Red Bluff, CA 96080 • 12,363
Red Bud, IL 62278 • 2,918
Red Cloud, NE 68970 • 1,204
Redding, CA 96001–03 • 66,462
Redding, CT 06875 • 1,000
Redfield, AR 72132 • 1,082
Redfield, SD 57469 • 2,770
Redford, MI 48239 • 54,387
Redgranite, WI 54970 • 1,009
Red Hook, NY 12571 • 1,794
Redkey, IN 47373 • 1,383
Red Lake □, MN • 4,525
Red Lake Falls, MN 56750 • 1,481
Redlands, CA 92373–75 • 60,394
Red Lion, PA 17356 • 6,130
Red Lodge, MT 59068 • 1,958
Redmond, OR 97756 • 7,163
Redmond, WA 98052–53 • 35,800
Red Oak, GA 30272 • 2,800
Red Oak, IA 51566 • 6,264
Red Oak, TX 75154 • 3,124
Red Oaks, LA 70815 • 1,600
Red Oaks Mill, NY 12603 • 4,906
Redondo Beach, CA 90277–78 • 60,167
Red River □, LA • 9,387
Red River □, TX • 14,317
Red Springs, NC 28377 • 3,799
Red Willow □, NE • 11,705
Red Wing, MN 55066 • 15,134
Redwood, UT 84119 • 1,850
Redwood □, MN • 17,254
Redwood City, CA 94061–65 • 66,072
Redwood Falls, MN 56283 • 4,859
Redwood Valley, CA 95470 • 1,300
Reed City, MI 49677 • 2,379
Reedley, CA 93654 • 15,791
Reedsburg, WI 53959 • 5,834
Reedsport, OR 97467 • 4,796
Reedsville, PA 17084 • 1,030
Reedsville, WI 54230 • 1,182
Reedurban, OH 44710 • 6,650
Reese, MI 48757 • 1,414
Reeves □, TX • 15,852
Reform, AL 35481 • 2,105
Refugio, TX 78377 • 3,158
Refugio □, TX • 7,976
Rehoboth Beach, DE 19971 • 1,234
Reidland, KY 42001 • 4,054
Reidsville, GA 30453 • 2,469
Reidsville, NC 27320–23 • 12,183
Reinbeck, IA 50669 • 1,605
Reisterstown, MD 21136 • 19,314
Reliance, WY 82943 • 500
Remington, IN 47977 • 1,247
Remsen, IA 51050 • 1,513
Reno, NV 89501–70 • 133,850
Reno □, KS • 62,389
Renovo, PA 17764 • 1,526
Rensselaer, IN 47978 • 5,045
Rensselaer, NY 12144 • 8,255
Rensselaer □, NY • 154,429
Renton, WA 98055–59 • 41,688
Renville, MN 56284 • 1,315
Renville □, MN • 17,673
Renville □, ND • 3,160
River Edge, NJ 07661 • 10,603
Republic, MI 49879 • 1,100
Republic, MO 65738 • 6,292
Republic, PA 15475 • 1,400
Republic □, KS • 6,482
Reserve, LA 70084 • 8,847
Reston, VA 22090 • 48,556
Revere, MA 02151 • 42,786
Rexburg, ID 83440 • 14,302
Reynolds, GA 31076 • 1,166
Reynolds □, MO • 6,661
Reynoldsburg, OH 43068 • 25,748
Reynoldsville, PA 15851 • 2,818
Rhea □, TN • 24,344
Rhinebeck, NY 12572 • 2,725
Rhinelander, WI 54501 • 7,427
Rialto, CA 92376–77 • 72,388
Rice □, KS • 10,610
Rice □, MN • 49,183
Rice Lake, WI 54868 • 7,998
Rich □, UT • 1,725
Richardson, TX 75080–83 • 74,840
Richardson □, NE • 9,937
Richardson Park, DE 19804 • 1,100
Richardton, ND 58652 • 625
Richboro, PA 18954 • 5,332
Richfield, MN 55423 • 35,710
Richfield, UT 84701 • 5,593
Richfield Springs, NY 13439 • 1,565
Richford, VT 05476 • 1,425
Rich Hill, MO 64779 • 1,317
Richland, GA 31825 • 1,668
Richland, MO 65556 • 2,029
Richland, WA 99352 • 32,315
Richland □, IL • 16,545
Richland □, LA • 20,629
Richland □, MT • 10,716
Richland □, ND • 18,148
Richland □, OH • 126,137
Richland □, SC • 285,720
Richland □, WI • 17,521
Richland Center, WI 53581 • 5,018

Richland Hills, TX 76118 • 7,978
Richlands, VA 24641 • 4,456
Richlandtown, PA 18955 • 1,195
Richmond, CA 94801–08 • 87,425
Richmond, IL 60071 • 1,070
Richmond, IN 47374–75 • 38,705
Richmond, KY 40475–76 • 21,155
Richmond, ME 04357 • 1,775
Richmond, MI 48062 • 4,141
Richmond, MO 64085 • 5,738
Richmond, TX 77469 • 9,801
Richmond, UT 84333 • 1,955
Richmond, VT 05477 • 650
Richmond, VA 23201–94 • 203,056
Richmond □, GA • 189,719
Richmond □, NY • 378,977
Richmond □, NC • 44,518
Richmond □, VA • 7,273
Richmond Beach, WA 98160 • 5,000
Richmond Heights, FL 33156 • 8,583
Richmond Heights, MO 63117 • 10,448
Richmond Heights, OH 44143 • 9,611
Richmond Highlands, WA 98133 • 26,037
Richmond Hill, GA 31324 • 2,934
Rich Square, NC 27869 • 1,058
Richton, MS 39476 • 1,034
Richton Park, IL 60471 • 10,523
Richwood, OH 43344 • 2,186
Richwood, WV 26261 • 2,808
Riddle, OR 97469 • 1,143
Ridge, NY 11961 • 11,734
Ridgecrest, CA 93555 • 27,725
Ridgecrest, WA 98155 • 5,500
Ridgefield, CT 06877 • 6,363
Ridgefield, NJ 07657 • 9,996
Ridgefield, WA 98642 • 1,297
Ridgefield Park, NJ 07660 • 12,454
Ridgeland, MS 39157–58 • 11,714
Ridgeland, SC 29936 • 1,071
Ridgely, MD 21660 • 1,034
Ridgely, TN 38080 • 1,775
Ridgetop, TN 37152 • 1,132
Ridgeville, SC 29472 • 1,625
Ridgewood, NJ 07450–52 • 24,152
Ridgway, IL 62979 • 1,103
Ridgway, PA 15853 • 4,793
Ridley Park, PA 19078 • 7,592
Ridley Township, PA 19018 • 33,771
Rifle, CO 81650 • 4,636
Rigby, ID 83442 • 2,681
Riley □, KS • 67,139
Rimersburg, PA 16248 • 1,053
Rincon, GA 31326 • 2,697
Ringgold, GA 30736 • 1,675
Ringgold, LA 71068 • 1,856
Ringgold □, IA • 5,420
Ringling, OK 73456 • 1,250
Ringwood, NJ 07456 • 6,478
Rio, FL 34957 • 1,054
Rio Arriba □, NM • 34,365
Rio Blanco □, CO • 5,972
Rio Dell, CA 95562 • 3,012
Rio Del Mar, CA 95003 • 8,919
Rio Grande, NJ 08242 • 2,505
Rio Grande □, CO • 10,770
Rio Grande City, TX 78582 • 9,891
Rio Hondo, TX 78583 • 1,793
Rio Linda, CA 95673 • 9,481
Rio Rancho, NM 87124 • 32,505
Rio Vista, CA 94571 • 3,316
Ripley, MS 38663 • 5,371
Ripley, NY 14775 • 1,189
Ripley, OH 45167 • 1,816
Ripley, TN 38063 • 6,188
Ripley, WV 25271 • 3,023
Ripley □, IN • 24,616
Ripley □, MO • 12,303
Ripon, WI 54971 • 7,241
Rising Sun, IN 47040 • 2,311
Rising Sun, MD 21911 • 1,263
Rison, AR 71665 • 1,258
Ritchie □, WV • 15,034
Rittman, OH 44270 • 6,147
Ritzville, WA 99169 • 1,725
Riverbank, CA 95367 • 8,547
Riverdale, CA 93656 • 1,980
Riverdale, GA 30274 • 9,359
Riverdale, IL 60627 • 13,671
Riverdale, MD 20737–38 • 5,185
Riverdale, NJ 07457 • 2,370
Riverdale, UT 84405 • 6,419
River Edge, NJ 07661 • 10,603
River Falls, WI 54022 • 10,610
River Forest, IL 60305 • 11,669
River Grove, IL 60171 • 9,961
Riverhead, NY 11901 • 8,814
River Heights, UT 84321 • 1,274
River Hills, WI 53217 • 1,612
River Oaks, TX 76114 • 6,580
River Pines, MA 01821 • 3,620
River Ridge, LA 70123 • 14,800
River Road, OR 97404 • 9,443
River Rouge, MI 48218 • 11,314
Riverside, AL 35135 • 1,004
Riverside, CA 92501–19 • 226,505
Riverside, IL 60546 • 8,774
Riverside, NJ 08075 • 7,974
Riverside, PA 17868 • 1,991
Riverside □, CA • 1,170,413
Riverton, IL 62561 • 2,638
Riverton, NJ 08077 • 2,775
Riverton, UT 84065 • 11,261
Riverton, VT 05663 • 150
Riverton, WY 82501 • 9,202
Riverton Heights, WA 98188 • 14,182
River Vale, NJ 07675 • 9,410
Riverview, FL 33569 • 6,478
Riverview, MI 48192 • 13,894
Rivesville, WV 26588 • 1,064
Riviera Beach, FL 33404 • 27,639
Riviera Beach, MD 21122 • 11,376
Roane □, TN • 47,227
Roane □, WV • 15,120
Roan Mountain, TN 37687 • 1,220
Roanoke, AL 36274 • 6,362
Roanoke, IL 61561 • 1,910
Roanoke, VA 46783 • 1,018
Roanoke, TX 76262 • 1,616
Roanoke, VA 24001–38 • 96,397
Roanoke □, VA • 79,332
Roanoke Rapids, NC 27870 • 15,722
Roaring Spring, PA 16673 • 2,615

Robbins, IL 60472 • *7,498*
Robbinsdale, MN 55422 • *14,396*
Robersonville, NC 27871 • *1,940*
Robert Lee, TX 76945 • *1,276*
Roberts, WI 54023 • *1,043*
Roberts □, SD • *9,914*
Roberts □, TX • *1,025*
Robertsdale, AL 36567 • *2,401*
Robertson □, KY • *2,124*
Robertson □, TN • *41,494*
Robertson □, TX • *15,511*
Robertsville, NJ 07746 • *9,841*
Robeson □, NC • *105,179*
Robinson, IL 62454 • *6,740*
Robinson, TX 76706 • *7,111*
Robstown, TX 78380 • *12,849*
Rochdale, MA 01542 • *1,105*
Rochelle, GA 31079 • *1,510*
Rochelle, IL 61068 • *8,769*
Rochelle Park, NJ 07662 • *5,587*
Rochester, IL 62563 • *2,676*
Rochester, IN 46975 • *5,969*
Rochester, MI 48306–09 • *7,130*
Rochester, MN 55901–06 • *70,745*
Rochester, NH 03867–68 • *26,630*
Rochester, NY 14601–92 • *231,636*
Rochester, PA 15074 • *4,156*
Rochester, VT 05767 • *500*
Rochester, WA 98579 • *1,150*
Rochester Hills, MI 48309 • *61,766*
Rock □, MN • *9,806*
Rock □, NE • *2,019*
Rock □, WI • *139,510*
Rockaway, NJ 07866 • *6,243*
Rockbridge □, VA • *18,350*
Rockcastle □, KY • *14,803*
Rock Creek, MN 55067 • *1,040*
Rock Creek 0M, OR • *8,282*
Rockdale, IL 60436 • *1,709*
Rockdale, MD 21207 • *5,885*
Rockdale, TX 76567 • *5,235*
Rockdale □, GA • *54,091*
Rock Falls, IL 61071 • *9,654*
Rockford, IL 61101–32 • *139,426*
Rockford, MI 49341 • *3,750*
Rockford, MN 55373 • *2,665*
Rockford, OH 45882 • *1,119*
Rock Hall, MD 21661 • *1,584*
Rock Hill, MO 63124 • *5,217*
Rock Hill, SC 29730–32 • *41,643*
Rockingham, NC 28379 • *9,399*
Rockingham □, NH • *245,845*
Rockingham □, NC • *86,064*
Rockingham □, VA • *57,482*
Rock Island, IL 61201–04 • *40,552*
Rock Island □, IL • *148,723*
Rockland, ME 04841 • *7,972*
Rockland, MA 02370 • *15,695*
Rockland □, NY • *265,475*
Rockledge, FL 32955–56 • *16,023*
Rockledge, PA 19111 • *2,679*
Rocklin, CA 95677 • *19,033*
Rockmart, GA 30153 • *3,356*
Rockport, IN 47635 • *2,315*
Rockport, ME 04856 • *1,100*
Rockport, MA 01966 • *4,690*
Rock Port, MO 64482 • *1,438*
Rockport, TX 78382 • *4,753*
Rock Rapids, IA 51246 • *2,601*
Rock River, WY 82083 • *190*
Rocksprings, TX 78880 • *1,339*
Rock Springs, WY 82901–02 • *19,050*
Rockton, IL 61072 • *2,928*
Rock Valley, IA 51247 • *2,540*
Rockville, IN 47872 • *2,706*
Rockville, MD 20847–59 • *44,835*
Rockville Centre, NY 11570–71 • *24,727*
Rockwall, TX 75087 • *10,486*
Rockwall □, TX • *25,604*
Rockwell, IA 50469 • *1,008*
Rockwell, NC 28138 • *1,598*
Rockwell City, IA 50579 • *1,981*
Rockwell Park, NC 28213 • *2,600*
Rockwood, MI 48173 • *3,141*
Rockwood, OR 97233 • *11,000*
Rockwood, PA 15557 • *1,014*
Rockwood, TN 37854 • *5,348*
Rocky Creek, FL 33615 • *7,800*
Rocky Ford, CO 81067 • *4,162*
Rocky Hill, CT 06067 • *14,559*
Rocky Mount, NC 27801–04 • *48,997*
Rocky Mount, VA 24151 • *4,098*
Rocky Point, NY 11778 • *8,596*
Rocky River, OH 44116 • *20,410*
Rodeo, CA 94572 • *7,589*
Roderfield, WV 24881 • *1,200*
Rodney Village, DE 19901 • *1,745*
Roebling, NJ 08554 • *2,415*
Roebuck, SC 29376 • *1,966*
Roeland Park, KS 66203 • *7,706*
Roessleville, NY 12205 • *10,753*
Roger Mills □, OK • *4,147*
Rogers, AR 72756–57 • *24,692*
Rogers, TX 76569 • *1,131*
Rogers □, OK • *55,170*
Rogers City, MI 49779 • *3,642*
Rogersville, AL 35652 • *1,125*
Rogersville, TN 37857 • *4,149*
Rogue River, OR 97537 • *1,759*
Rohnert Park, CA 94927–28 • *36,326*
Roland, IA 50236 • *1,035*
Roland, OK 74954 • *2,481*
Rolette □, ND • *12,772*
Rolla, MO 65401 • *14,090*
Rolla, ND 58367 • *1,286*
Rolling Fork, MS 39159 • *2,444*
Rolling Hills Estates, CA 90274 • *7,789*
Rolling Meadows, IL 60008 • *22,591*
Rollinsford, NH 03869 • *2,645*
Roma, TX 78584 • *8,059*
Rome, GA 30161–65 • *30,326*
Rome, IL 61562 • *1,902*
Rome, NY 13440 • *44,350*
Rome City, IN 46784 • *1,138*
Romeo, MI 48065 • *3,520*
Romeoville, IL 60441 • *14,074*
Romney, WV 26757 • *1,966*
Romulus, MI 48174 • *22,897*
Ronan, MT 59864 • *1,547*
Ronceverte, WV 24970 • *1,754*
Ronkonkoma, NY 11779 • *20,391*
Roodhouse, IL 62082 • *2,139*
Rooks □, KS • *6,039*
Roosevelt, NY 11575 • *15,030*
Roosevelt, UT 84066 • *3,915*
Roosevelt □, MT • *10,999*
Roosevelt □, NM • *16,702*
Roosevelt Park, MI 49441 • *3,885*
Rosamond, CA 93560 • *7,430*
Roscoe, IL 61073 • *2,079*
Roscoe, TX 79545 • *1,446*
Roscommon □, MI • *19,776*
Roseau, MN 56751 • *2,396*
Roseau □, MN • *15,026*
Roseboro, NC 28382 • *1,441*
Rosebud, TX 76570 • *1,638*
Rosebud □, MT • *10,505*
Roseburg, OR 97470 • *17,032*
Rosedale, MD 21237 • *18,703*
Rosedale, MS 38769 • *2,595*
Rose Hill, KS 67133 • *2,399*
Rose Hill, NC 28458 • *1,287*
Rose Hill, VA 22310 • *12,675*
Roseland, CA 95407 • *8,779*
Roseland, FL 32957 • *1,379*
Roseland, LA 70456 • *1,093*
Roseland, NJ 07068 • *4,847*
Roseland, OH 44906 • *3,000*
Roselle, IL 60172 • *20,819*
Roselle, NJ 07203 • *20,314*
Roselle Park, NJ 07204 • *12,805*
Rosemead, CA 91770 • *51,638*
Rosemont, CA 95826 • *22,851*
Rosemount, MN 55068 • *8,622*
Rosenberg, TX 77471 • *20,183*
Rosepine, LA 70659 • *1,135*
Roseto, PA 18013 • *1,555*
Roseville, CA 95678 • *44,685*
Roseville, IL 61473 • *1,151*
Roseville, MI 48066 • *51,412*
Roseville, MN 55113 • *33,485*
Roseville, OH 43777 • *1,847*
Rosewood Heights, IL 62024 • *4,821*
Rosiclare, IL 62982 • *1,378*
Roslyn Heights, NY 11577 • *6,405*
Ross, OH 45061 • *2,124*
Ross □, OH • *69,330*
Rossford, OH 43460 • *5,861*
Rossmoor, CA 90720 • *9,893*
Ross Township, PA 15237 • *33,482*
Rossville, GA 30741–42 • *3,601*
Rossville, IL 60963 • *1,334*
Rossville, IN 46065 • *1,175*
Rossville, KS 66533 • *1,052*
Roswell, GA 30075–77 • *47,923*
Roswell, NM 88201–02 • *44,654*
Rotan, TX 79546 • *1,913*
Rothschild, WI 54474 • *3,310*
Rothsville, PA 17543 • *2,097*
Rotterdam, NY 12303 • *21,228*
Roulette, PA 16746 • *1,500*
Round Lake, IL 60073 • *3,550*
Round Lake Beach, IL 60073 • *16,434*
Round Mountain, NV 89045 • *210*
Round Rock, TX 78664 • *30,923*
Roundup, MT 59072 • *1,808*
Rouses Point, NY 12979 • *2,377*
Routt □, CO • *14,088*
Rouzerville, PA 17250 • *1,188*
Rowan □, KY • *20,353*
Rowan □, NC • *110,605*
Rowland, NC 28383 • *1,139*
Rowland Heights, CA 91748 • *32,700*
Rowlett, TX 75088 • *23,260*
Rowley, MA 01969 • *1,144*
Roxboro, NC 27573 • *7,332*
Roy, UT 84067 • *24,603*
Royal Oak, MI 48067–73 • *65,410*
Royal Pines, NC 28704 • *1,600*
Royalton, IL 62983 • *1,191*
Royersford, PA 19468 • *4,458*
Royse City, TX 75089 • *2,206*
Royston, GA 30662 • *2,758*
Rubidoux, CA 92509 • *24,367*
Rugby, ND 58368 • *2,909*
Ruidoso, NM 88345 • *4,600*
Ruidoso Downs, NM 88346 • *920*
Ruleville, MS 38771 • *3,245*
Rumford, ME 04276 • *5,419*
Rumson, NJ 07760 • *6,701*
Runge, TX 78151 • *1,139*
Runnels □, TX • *11,294*
Runnemede, NJ 08078 • *9,042*
Rupert, ID 83350 • *5,455*
Rupert, WV 25984 • *1,104*
Rural Hall, NC 27045 • *1,652*
Rush □, IN • *18,129*
Rush □, KS • *3,842*
Rush City, MN 55069 • *1,497*
Rushford, MN 55971 • *1,485*
Rushmere, VA 23430 • *1,064*
Rush Springs, OK 73082 • *1,229*
Rushville, IL 62681 • *3,229*
Rushville, IN 46173 • *5,533*
Rushville, NE 69360 • *1,127*
Rusk, TX 75785 • *4,366*
Rusk □, TX • *43,735*
Rusk □, WI • *15,079*
Ruskin, FL 33570–73 • *6,046*
Russell, KS 67665 • *4,781*
Russell, KY 41169 • *4,014*
Russell, PA 16345 • *1,000*
Russell □, AL • *46,860*
Russell □, KS • *7,835*
Russell □, KY • *14,716*
Russell □, VA • *28,667*
Russell Springs, KY 42642 • *2,363*
Russellville, AL 35653 • *7,812*
Russellville, AR 72801 • *21,260*
Russellville, KY 42276 • *7,454*
Russellville, OR 97216 • *6,500*
Russellville, TN 37860 • *1,069*
Ruston, LA 71270–73 • *20,027*
Ruth, NV 89319 • *550*
Rutherford, NJ 07070–75 • *17,790*
Rutherford, TN 38369 • *1,303*
Rutherford □, NC • *56,918*
Rutherford □, TN • *118,570*
Rutherfordton, NC 28139 • *3,617*
Rutland, MA 01543 • *2,145*
Rutland, VT 05701–02 • *18,230*
Rutland □, VT • *62,142*
Rye, NH 03870 • *835*
Rye, NY 10580 • *14,936*
Rye Brook, NY 10573 • *7,765*

S

Sabattus, ME 04280 • *3,696*
Sabetha, KS 66534 • *2,341*
Sabina, OH 45169 • *2,662*
Sabinal, TX 78881 • *1,584*
Sabine □, LA • *22,646*
Sabine □, TX • *9,586*
Sac □, IA • *12,324*
Sacaton, AZ 85221 • *1,452*
Sac City, IA 50583 • *2,492*
Sachse, TX 75040 • *5,346*
Sackets Harbor, NY 13685 • *1,313*
Saco, ME 04072 • *15,181*
Sacramento, CA 95801–66 • *369,365*
Sacramento □, CA • *1,041,219*
Saddle Brook, NJ 07662 • *13,296*
Saddle River, NJ 07458 • *2,950*
Saegertown, PA 16433 • *1,066*
Safety Harbor, FL 34695 • *15,124*
Safford, AZ 85546 • *7,359*
Sagadahoc □, ME • *33,535*
Sagamore, MA 02561 • *2,589*
Sagamore Hills, OH 44067 • *4,700*
Sag Harbor, NY 11963 • *2,134*
Saginaw, MI 48601–08 • *69,512*
Saginaw, TX 76179 • *8,551*
Saginaw □, MI • *211,946*
Saguache □, CO • *4,619*
Saint Albans, VT 05478 • *7,339*
Saint Albans, WV 25177 • *11,194*
Saint Andrews, SC 29407 • *9,908*
Saint Andrews, SC 29210 • *25,692*
Saint Ann, MO 63074 • *14,489*
Saint Anne, IL 60964 • *1,153*
Saint Ansgar, IA 50472 • *1,063*
Saint Anthony, ID 83445 • *3,010*
Saint Anthony, MN 55418 • *7,727*
Saint Augustine, FL 32084–86 • *11,692*
Saint Bernard, OH 45217 • *5,344*
Saint Bernard □, LA • *66,631*
Saint Charles, IL 60174–75 • *22,501*
Saint Charles, MD 20601 • *28,717*
Saint Charles, MI 48655 • *2,144*
Saint Charles, MN 55972 • *2,642*
Saint Charles, MO 63301–03 • *54,555*
Saint Charles □, LA • *42,437*
Saint Charles □, MO • *212,907*
Saint Charles Mesa, CO 81006 • *7,050*
Saint Clair, MI 48079 • *5,116*
Saint Clair, MO 63077 • *3,917*
Saint Clair, PA 17970 • *3,524*
Saint Clair □, AL • *50,009*
Saint Clair □, IL • *262,852*
Saint Clair □, MI • *145,607*
Saint Clair □, MO • *8,457*
Saint Clair Shores, MI 48080–82 • *68,107*
Saint Clairsville, OH 43950 • *5,162*
Saint Cloud, FL 34769–73 • *12,453*
Saint Cloud, MN 56301–04 • *48,812*
Saint Croix □, WI • *50,251*
Saint Croix Falls, WI 54024 • *1,640*
Saint David, AZ 85630 • *1,500*
Saint Elmo, IL 62458 • *1,473*
Saint Francis, KS 67756 • *1,495*
Saint Francis, MN 55070 • *2,538*
Saint Francis, SD 57572 • *815*
Saint Francis, WI 53207 • *9,245*
Saint Francis □, AR • *28,497*
Saint Francisville, LA 70775 • *1,700*
Saint Francois □, MO • *48,904*
Sainte Genevieve, MO 63670 • *4,411*
Sainte Genevieve □, MO • *16,037*
Saint George, SC 29477 • *2,077*
Saint George, UT 84770–71 • *28,502*
Saint Georges, DE 19733 • *500*
Saint Helena, CA 94574 • *4,990*
Saint Helena □, LA • *9,874*
Saint Helens, OR 97051 • *7,535*
Saint Henry, OH 45883 • *1,907*
Saint Ignace, MI 49781 • *2,568*
Saint Ignatius, MT 59865 • *778*
Saint James, MN 56081 • *4,364*
Saint James, MO 65559 • *3,256*
Saint James, NY 11780 • *12,703*
Saint James □, LA • *20,879*
Saint James City, FL 33956 • *1,094*
Saint Jo, TX 76265 • *1,048*
Saint John, IN 46373 • *4,921*
Saint John, KS 67576 • *1,357*
Saint Johns, AZ 85936 • *3,294*
Saint Johns, MI 48879 • *7,284*
Saint Johns, MO 63114 • *7,466*
Saint Johns □, FL • *83,829*
Saint Johnsbury, VT 05819 • *6,424*
Saint Johnsville, NY 13452 • *1,825*
Saint John the Baptist □, LA • *39,996*
Saint Joseph, IL 61873 • *2,052*
Saint Joseph, LA 71366 • *1,517*
Saint Joseph, MI 49085 • *9,214*
Saint Joseph, MN 56374 • *3,294*
Saint Joseph, MO 64501–08 • *71,852*
Saint Joseph □, IN • *247,052*
Saint Joseph □, MI • *58,913*
Saint Landry □, LA • *80,331*
Saint Lawrence □, NY • *111,974*
Saint Leo, FL 33574 • *1,009*
Saint Louis, MI 48880 • *3,828*
Saint Louis, MO 63101–88 • *396,685*
Saint Louis □, MN • *198,213*
Saint Louis □, MO • *993,529*
Saint Louis Park, MN 55426 • *43,787*
Saint Lucie □, FL • *150,171*
Saint Maries, ID 83861 • *2,442*
Saint Martin □, LA • *43,978*
Saint Martinville, LA 70582 • *7,137*
Saint Mary □, LA • *58,086*
Saint Marys, AK 99658 • *441*
Saint Marys, GA 31558 • *8,187*
Saint Marys, IN 46556 • *1,800*
Saint Marys, KS 66536 • *1,791*
Saint Marys, OH 45885 • *8,441*
Saint Marys, PA 15857 • *5,511*
Saint Marys, WV 26170 • *2,148*
Saint Marys □, MD • *75,974*
Saint Marys City, MD 20686 • *3,200*
Saint Matthews, KY 40207 • *15,800*
Saint Matthews, SC 29135 • *2,345*
Saint Michael, MN 55376 • *2,506*
Saint Michaels, MD 21663 • *1,301*
Saint Paris, OH 43072 • *1,842*
Saint Paul, AK 99660 • *763*
Saint Paul, IN 47272 • *1,032*
Saint Paul, MN 55101–89 • *272,235*
Saint Paul, MO 63366 • *1,192*
Saint Paul, NE 68873 • *2,009*
Saint Paul, VA 24283 • *1,007*
Saint Paul Park, MN 55071 • *4,965*
Saint Pauls, NC 28384 • *1,992*
Saint Peter, MN 56082 • *9,421*
Saint Peters, MO 63376 • *45,779*
Saint Petersburg, FL 33701–84 • *238,629*
Saint Petersburg Beach, FL 33706 • *9,200*
Saint Rose, LA 70087 • *2,800*
Saint Simons Island, GA 31522 • *12,026*
Saint Stephen, SC 29479 • *1,697*
Saint Stephens, NC 28601 • *8,734*
Saint Tammany □, LA • *144,508*
Salamanca, NY 14779 • *6,566*
Sale Creek, TN 37373 • *1,050*
Salem, AR 72576 • *1,474*
Salem, IL 62881 • *7,470*
Salem, IN 47167 • *5,619*
Salem, MA 01970–71 • *38,091*
Salem, MO 65560 • *4,486*
Salem, NH 03079 • *12,000*
Salem, NJ 08079 • *6,883*
Salem, OH 44460 • *12,233*
Salem, OR 97301–14 • *107,786*
Salem, SD 57058 • *1,289*
Salem, UT 84653 • *2,284*
Salem, VA 24153 • *23,756*
Salem, WV 26426 • *2,063*
Salem, WI 53168 • *1,020*
Salem □, NJ • *65,294*
Salida, CO 81201 • *4,737*
Salina, KS 67401–02 • *42,303*
Salina, OK 74365 • *1,153*
Salina, UT 84654 • *1,943*
Salinas, CA 93901–15 • *108,777*
Saline, MI 48176 • *6,660*
Saline □, AR • *64,183*
Saline □, IL • *26,551*
Saline □, KS • *49,301*
Saline □, MO • *23,523*
Saline □, NE • *12,715*
Salineville, OH 43945 • *1,474*
Salisbury, CT 06068 • *1,600*
Salisbury, MD 21801–03 • *20,592*
Salisbury, MA 01952 • *3,729*
Salisbury, MO 65281 • *1,881*
Salisbury, NC 28144–46 • *23,087*
Sallisaw, OK 74955 • *7,122*
Salmon, ID 83467 • *2,941*
Salmon Creek, WA 98665 • *11,989*
Saltillo, MS 38866 • *1,782*
Salt Lake □, UT • *725,956*
Salt Lake City, UT 84101–90 • *159,936*
Salt Springs, FL 32113 • *1,500*
Saltville, VA 24370 • *2,300*
Saltwater, WA 98188 • *2,200*
Saluda, SC 29138 • *2,798*
Saluda □, SC • *16,357*
Salyersville, KY 41465 • *1,917*
Samoset, FL 34208 • *3,119*
Sampson □, NC • *47,297*
Samson, AL 36477 • *2,190*
Samtown, LA 71301 • *3,500*
San Andreas, CA 95249 • *2,115*
San Angelo, TX 76901–06 • *84,474*
San Anselmo, CA 94960 • *11,743*
San Antonio, TX 78201–99 • *935,933*
Sanatoga, PA 19464 • *5,534*
San Augustine, TX 75972 • *2,337*
San Augustine □, TX • *7,999*
San Benito, TX 78586 • *20,125*
San Benito □, CA • *36,697*
San Bernardino, CA 92401–27 • *164,164*
San Bernardino □, CA • *1,418,380*
Sanborn, IA 51248 • *1,345*
Sanborn □, SD • *2,833*
San Bruno, CA 94066 • *38,961*
San Carlos, AZ 85550 • *2,918*
San Carlos, CA 94070 • *26,167*
San Carlos Park, FL 33912 • *11,785*
San Clemente, CA 92672–74 • *41,100*
Sandalfoot Cove, FL 33433 • *14,214*
Sanders □, MT • *8,669*
Sanderson, TX 79848 • *1,128*
Sandersville, GA 31082 • *6,290*
Sand Hill, MA 02066 • *1,800*
Sandia, NM 87047 • *6,742*
San Diego, CA 92101–99 • *1,110,549*
San Diego, TX 78384 • *4,983*
San Diego □, CA • *2,498,016*
San Dimas, CA 91773 • *32,397*
Sandoval, IL 62882 • *1,535*
Sandoval □, NM • *63,319*
Sand Point, AK 99661 • *878*
Sandpoint, ID 83862–65 • *5,203*
Sand Springs, OK 74063 • *15,346*
Sandston, VA 23150 • *3,630*
Sandstone, MN 55072 • *2,057*
Sandusky, MI 48471 • *2,403*
Sandusky, OH 44870–71 • *29,764*
Sandusky □, OH • *61,963*
Sandwich, IL 60548 • *5,567*
Sandwich, MA 02563 • *2,998*
Sandy, OR 97055 • *4,152*
Sandy, UT 84070 • *75,058*
Sandy Hook, CT 06482 • *1,100*
Sandy Springs, GA 30328 • *67,842*
Sandy Springs, SC 29677 • *1,200*
San Felipe Pueblo, NM 87001 • *1,557*
San Fernando, CA 91340–46 • *22,580*
Sanford, FL 32771–73 • *32,387*
Sanford, ME 04073 • *10,296*
Sanford, NC 27330–31 • *14,475*
San Francisco, CA 94101–88 • *723,959*
San Francisco □, CA • *723,959*
Sangamon □, IL • *178,386*
Sanger, CA 93657 • *16,839*
Sanger, TX 76266 • *3,508*
Sanibel, FL 33957 • *5,468*
Sanilac □, MI • *39,928*
San Jacinto, CA 92383 • *16,210*
San Jacinto □, TX • *16,372*
San Joaquín □, CA • *480,628*
San Jose, CA 95101–96 • *782,248*
San Juan, TX 78589 • *10,815*
San Juan □, CO • *745*
San Juan □, NM • *91,605*
San Juan □, UT • *12,621*
San Juan □, WA • *10,035*
San Juan Capistrano, CA 92690–93 • *26,183*
San Leandro, CA 94577–79 • *68,223*
San Lorenzo, CA 94580 • *19,987*
San Luis, AZ 85634 • *4,212*
San Luis Obispo, CA 93401–12 • *41,958*
San Luis Obispo □, CA • *217,162*
San Manuel, AZ 85631 • *4,009*
San Marcos, CA 92069 • *38,974*
San Marcos, TX 78666–67 • *28,743*
San Marino, CA 91108 • *12,959*
San Mateo, CA 94401–04 • *85,486*
San Mateo □, CA • *649,623*
San Miguel □, CO • *3,653*
San Miguel □, NM • *25,743*
San Pablo, CA 94806 • *25,158*
San Patricio □, TX • *58,749*
Sanpete □, UT • *16,259*
San Rafael, CA 94901–15 • *48,404*
San Ramon, CA 94583 • *35,303*
San Remo, NY 11754 • *7,770*
San Saba, TX 76877 • *2,626*
San Saba □, TX • *5,401*
Sans Souci, SC 29609 • *7,612*
Santa Ana, CA 92701–08 • *293,742*
Santa Anna, TX 76878 • *1,249*
Santa Barbara, CA 93101–90 • *85,571*
Santa Barbara □, CA • *369,608*
Santa Clara, CA 95050–56 • *93,613*
Santa Clara, OR 97404 • *12,834*
Santa Clara, UT 84765 • *2,322*
Santa Clara □, CA • *1,497,577*
Santa Cruz, CA 95060–67 • *49,040*
Santa Cruz, NM 87567 • *975*
Santa Cruz □, AZ • *29,676*
Santa Cruz □, CA • *229,734*
Santa Fe, NM 87501–06 • *55,859*
Santa Fe, TX 77510 • *8,429*
Santa Fe □, NM • *98,928*
Santa Fe Springs, CA 90670–71 • *15,520*
Santa Margarita, CA 93453 • *1,200*
Santa Maria, CA 93454–56 • *61,284*
Santa Monica, CA 90401–11 • *86,905*
Santa Paula, CA 93060–61 • *25,062*
Santaquin, UT 84655 • *2,386*
Santa Rosa, CA 95401–09 • *113,313*
Santa Rosa, NM 88435 • *2,263*
Santa Rosa □, FL • *81,608*
Santa Venetia, CA 94901 • *6,000*
Santa Ynez, CA 93460 • *4,200*
Santee, CA 92071 • *52,902*
Santo Domingo Pueblo, NM 87052 • *2,866*
San Ygnacio, TX 78067 • *1,000*
Sappington, MO 63126 • *10,917*
Sapulpa, OK 74066–67 • *18,074*
Saraland, AL 36571 • *11,751*
Saranac, MI 48881 • *1,461*
Saranac Lake, NY 12983 • *5,377*
Sarasota, FL 34230–43 • *50,961*
Sarasota □, FL • *277,776*
Sarasota Springs, FL 34232 • *16,088*
Saratoga, CA 95070–71 • *28,061*
Saratoga, TX 77585 • *1,200*
Saratoga, WY 82331 • *1,969*
Saratoga □, NY • *181,276*
Saratoga Springs, NY 12866 • *25,001*
Sarcoxie, MO 64862 • *1,330*
Sardis, GA 30456 • *1,116*
Sardis, MS 38666 • *2,128*
Sargent □, ND • *4,549*
Sarpy □, NE • *102,583*
Sartell, MN 56377 • *5,393*
Satanta, KS 67870 • *1,073*
Satellite Beach, FL 32937 • *9,889*
Satsuma, AL 36572 • *5,194*
Saugerties, NY 12477 • *3,915*
Saugus, MA 01906 • *25,549*
Sauk □, WI • *46,975*
Sauk Centre, MN 56378 • *3,581*
Sauk City, WI 53583 • *3,019*
Sauk Rapids, MN 56379 • *7,825*
Sauk Village, IL 60411 • *9,926*
Saukville, WI 53080 • *3,695*
Sault Sainte Marie, MI 49783 • *14,689*
Saunders □, NE • *18,285*
Saunderstown, RI 02874 • *400*
Sausalito, CA 94965–66 • *7,152*
Savage, MD 20763 • *2,850*
Savage, MN 55378 • *9,906*
Savanna, IL 61074 • *3,819*
Savannah, GA 31401–20 • *137,560*
Savannah, MO 64485 • *4,352*
Savannah, TN 38372 • *6,547*
Savoonga, AK 99769 • *519*
Savoy, IL 61874 • *2,674*
Sawyer □, WI • *14,181*
Saxonburg, PA 16056 • *1,345*
Saxtons River, VT 05154 • *541*
Saybrook Manor, CT 06475 • *1,073*
Saydel, IA 50313 • *3,500*
Saylesville, RI 02865 • *3,510*
Saylorsburg, PA 18353 • *1,500*
Sayre, OK 73662 • *2,881*
Sayre, PA 18840 • *5,791*
Sayreville, NJ 08872 • *34,986*
Sayville, NY 11782 • *16,550*
Scalp Level, PA 15963 • *1,158*
Scappoose, OR 97056 • *3,529*
Scarborough, ME 04074 • *2,586*
Scarsdale, NY 10583 • *16,987*
Schaumburg, IL 60192–94 • *68,586*
Schenectady, NY 12301–09 • *65,566*
Schenectady □, NY • *149,285*
Schererville, IN 46375 • *19,926*
Schertz, TX 78154 • *10,555*
Schiller Park, IL 60176 • *11,189*
Schleicher □, TX • *2,990*
Schley □, GA • *3,588*
Schofield, WI 54476 • *2,415*
Schoharie, NY 12157 • *1,045*
Schoharie □, NY • *31,859*
Schoolcraft, MI 49087 • *1,517*
Schoolcraft □, MI • *8,302*
Schroon Lake, NY 12870 • *1,100*
Schulenburg, TX 78956 • *2,455*
Schurz, NV 89427 • *617*
Schuyler, NE 68661 • *4,052*
Schuyler □, IL • *7,498*
Schuyler □, MO • *4,236*
Schuyler □, NY • *18,662*
Schuylerville, NY 12871 • *1,364*
Schuylkill □, PA • *152,585*

United States Populations and ZIP Codes

Schuylkill Haven, PA 17972 • *5,610*
Scioto □, OH • *80,327*
Scituate, MA 02066 • *5,180*
Scobey, MT 59263 • *1,154*
Scotch Plains, NJ 07076 • *21,160*
Scotchtown, NY 10940 • *8,765*
Scotia, CA 95565 • *1,200*
Scotia, NY 12302 • *7,359*
Scotland, SD 57059 • *968*
Scotland □, MO • *4,822*
Scotland □, NC • *33,754*
Scotland Neck, NC 27874 • *2,575*
Scotlandville, LA 70807 • *15,113*
Scott, LA 70583 • *4,912*
Scott □, AR • *10,205*
Scott □, IL • *5,644*
Scott □, IN • *20,991*
Scott □, IA • *150,979*
Scott □, KS • *5,289*
Scott □, KY • *23,867*
Scott □, MN • *57,846*
Scott □, MS • *24,137*
Scott □, MO • *39,376*
Scott □, TN • *18,358*
Scott □, VA • *23,204*
Scott City, KS 67871 • *3,785*
Scott City, MO 63780 • *4,292*
Scottdale, GA 30079 • *8,636*
Scottdale, PA 15683 • *5,184*
Scott Lake, FL 33055 • *14,588*
Scottsbluff, NE 69361–63 • *13,711*
Scotts Bluff □, NE • *36,025*
Scottsboro, AL 35768 • *13,786*
Scottsburg, IN 47170 • *5,334*
Scottsdale, AZ 85250–71 • *130,069*
Scotts Valley, CA 95066–67 • *8,615*
Scottsville, KY 42164 • *4,278*
Scottsville, NY 14546 • *1,912*
Scott Township, PA 15106 • *17,118*
Scottville, MI 49454 • *1,287*
Scranton, PA 18501–19 • *81,805*
Screven □, GA • *13,842*
Scurry □, TX • *18,634*
Seabreeze, DE 19971 • *350*
Sea Bright, NJ 07760 • *1,693*
Seabrook, MD 20706 • *7,660*
Seabrook, NJ 08302 • *1,457*
Seabrook, TX 77586 • *6,685*
Sea Cliff, NY 11579 • *5,054*
Seadrift, TX 77983 • *1,277*
Seaford, DE 19973 • *5,689*
Seaford, NY 11783 • *15,597*
Seaford, VA 23696 • *2,340*
Seagate, NC 28403 • *5,444*
Sea Girt, NJ 08750 • *2,099*
Seagoville, TX 75159 • *8,969*
Seagraves, TX 79359 • *2,398*
Sea Isle City, NJ 08243 • *2,692*
Seal Beach, CA 90740 • *25,098*
Sealy, TX 77474 • *4,541*
Seaman, OH 45679 • *1,013*
Searchlight, NV 89029 • *430*
Searcy, AR 72143 • *15,180*
Searcy □, AR • *7,841*
Searsport, ME 04974 • *1,151*
Seaside, CA 93955 • *38,901*
Seaside, OR 97138 • *5,359*
Seaside Heights, NJ 08751 • *2,366*
Seaside Park, NJ 08752 • *1,871*
Seat Pleasant, MD 20743 • *5,359*
Seattle, WA 98101–99 • *516,259*
Sebastian, FL 32958 • *10,205*
Sebastian □, AR • *99,590*
Sebewaing, MI 48759 • *1,923*
Sebree, KY 42455 • *1,510*
Sebring, FL 33870–72 • *8,900*
Sebring, OH 44672 • *4,848*
Secaucus, NJ 07094 • *14,061*
Security, CO 80911 • *6,660*
Sedalia, MO 65301–02 • *19,800*
Sedan, KS 67361 • *1,306*
Sedgwick, KS 67135 • *1,438*
Sedgwick □, CO • *2,690*
Sedgwick □, KS • *403,662*
Sedona, AZ 86336 • *7,720*
Sedro Woolley, WA 98284 • *6,031*
Seekonk, MA 02771 • *12,269*
Seeley, CA 92273 • *1,228*
Seelyville, IN 47878 • *1,090*
Seguin, TX 78155–56 • *18,853*
Seiling, OK 73663 • *1,031*
Selah, WA 98942 • *5,113*
Selawik, AK 99770 • *596*
Selby, SD 57472 • *707*
Selbyville, DE 19975 • *1,335*
Selden, NY 11784 • *20,608*
Seldovia, AK 99663 • *316*
Selinsgrove, PA 17870 • *5,384*
Sellersburg, IN 47172 • *5,745*
Sellersville, PA 18960 • *4,479*
Sells, AZ 85634 • *2,750*
Selma, AL 36701–02 • *23,755*
Selma, CA 93662 • *14,757*
Selma, NC 27576 • *4,600*
Selmer, TN 38375 • *3,838*
Seminole, OK 74868 • *7,071*
Seminole, TX 79360 • *6,342*
Seminole □, FL • *287,529*
Seminole □, GA • *9,010*
Seminole □, OK • *25,412*
Seminole Park, FL 34647 • *8,000*
Semmes, AL 36575 • *2,250*
Senath, MO 63876 • *1,622*
Senatobia, MS 38668 • *4,772*
Seneca, IL 61360 • *1,878*
Seneca, KS 66538 • *2,027*
Seneca, MO 64865 • *1,885*
Seneca, PA 16346 • *1,300*
Seneca, SC 29678–79 • *7,726*
Seneca □, NY • *33,683*
Seneca □, OH • *59,733*
Seneca Falls, NY 13148 • *7,370*
Sequatchie □, TN • *8,863*
Sequim, WA 98382 • *3,616*
Sequoyah □, OK • *33,828*
Sergeant Bluff, IA 51054 • *2,772*
Sesser, IL 62884 • *2,087*
Seven Hills, OH 44131 • *12,339*
Seven Oaks, SC 29210 • *15,722*
Severn, MD 21144 • *24,499*
Severna Park, MD 21146 • *25,879*
Sevier □, AR • *13,637*
Sevier □, TN • *51,043*
Sevier □, UT • *15,431*
Sevierville, TN 37862 • *7,178*
Seville, OH 44273 • *1,810*
Sewanee, TN 37375 • *2,128*
Seward, AK 99664 • *2,699*
Seward, NE 68434 • *5,634*
Seward □, KS • *18,743*
Seward □, NE • *15,450*
Sewell, NJ 08080 • *1,870*
Sewickley, PA 15143 • *4,134*
Seymour, CT 06483 • *14,288*
Seymour, IN 47274 • *15,576*
Seymour, MO 65746 • *1,636*
Seymour, TN 37865 • *7,026*
Seymour, TX 76380 • *3,185*
Seymour, WI 54165 • *2,782*
Seymourville, LA 70764 • *2,891*
Shackelford □, TX • *3,316*
Shady Cove, OR 97539 • *1,351*
Shady Side, MD 20764 • *4,107*
Shadyside, OH 43947 • *3,934*
Shady Spring, WV 25918 • *1,929*
Shafter, CA 93263 • *8,409*
Shaftsbury, VT 05262 • *700*
Shaker Heights, OH 44120 • *30,831*
Shakopee, MN 55379 • *11,739*
Shaler Township, PA 15116 • *30,533*
Shallowater, TX 79363 • *1,708*
Shamokin, PA 17872 • *9,184*
Shamokin Dam, PA 17876 • *1,690*
Shamrock, TX 79079 • *2,286*
Shannock, RI 02875 • *950*
Shannon, GA 30172 • *1,703*
Shannon, MS 38868 • *1,419*
Shannon □, MO • *7,613*
Shannon □, SD • *9,902*
Shannontown, SC 29150 • *7,900*
Sharkey □, MS • *7,066*
Sharon, MA 02067 • *5,893*
Sharon, PA 16146 • *17,493*
Sharon, TN 38255 • *1,047*
Sharon, WI 53585 • *1,250*
Sharon Hill, PA 19079 • *5,771*
Sharonville, OH 45241 • *13,153*
Sharp □, AR • *14,109*
Sharpes, FL 32922 • *3,348*
Sharpley, DE 19803 • *1,250*
Sharpsburg, MD 21782 • *659*
Sharpsburg, NC 27878 • *1,536*
Sharpsburg, PA 15215 • *3,781*
Sharpsville, PA 16150 • *4,729*
Shasta □, CA • *147,036*
Shattuck, OK 73858 • *1,454*
Shaw, MS 38773 • *2,349*
Shawano, WI 54166 • *7,598*
Shawano □, WI • *37,157*
Shawnee, KS 66203 • *37,993*
Shawnee, OK 74801–02 • *26,017*
Shawnee □, KS • *160,976*
Shawneetown, IL 62984 • *1,575*
Sheboygan, WI 53081–83 • *49,676*
Sheboygan □, WI • *103,877*
Sheboygan Falls, WI 53085 • *5,823*
Sheffield, AL 35660–62 • *10,380*
Sheffield, IA 50475 • *1,174*
Sheffield, MA 01257 • *1,100*
Sheffield, PA 16347 • *1,294*
Sheffield Lake, OH 44054 • *9,825*
Shelbina, MO 63468 • *2,172*
Shelburn, IN 47879 • *1,147*
Shelburne Falls, MA 01370 • *1,996*
Shelby, MI 49455 • *48,655*
Shelby, MS 38774 • *2,806*
Shelby, MT 59474 • *2,763*
Shelby, NC 28150–51 • *14,669*
Shelby, OH 44875 • *9,564*
Shelby □, AL • *99,358*
Shelby □, IL • *22,261*
Shelby □, IN • *40,307*
Shelby □, IA • *13,230*
Shelby □, KY • *24,824*
Shelby □, MO • *6,942*
Shelby □, OH • *44,915*
Shelby □, TN • *826,330*
Shelby □, TX • *22,034*
Shelbyville, IL 62565 • *4,943*
Shelbyville, IN 46176 • *15,336*
Shelbyville, KY 40065 • *6,238*
Shelbyville, TN 37160 • *14,049*
Sheldon, IL 60966 • *1,109*
Sheldon, IA 51201 • *4,937*
Sheldon, TX 77028 • *1,653*
Shelley, ID 83274 • *3,536*
Shell Lake, WI 54871 • *1,161*
Shellman, GA 31786 • *1,162*
Shell Rock, IA 50670 • *1,385*
Shelter Island, NY 11964 • *1,193*
Shelton, CT 06484 • *35,418*
Shelton, WA 98584 • *7,241*
Shenandoah, IA 51601 • *5,572*
Shenandoah, PA 17976 • *6,221*
Shenandoah, VA 22849 • *2,213*
Shenandoah □, VA • *31,636*
Shepherd, MI 48883 • *1,413*
Shepherd, TX 77371 • *1,812*
Shepherdstown, WV 25443 • *1,287*
Shepherdsville, KY 40165 • *4,805*
Sherborn, MA 01770 • *1,490*
Sherburn, MN 56171 • *1,105*
Sherburne, NY 13460 • *1,531*
Sherburne □, MN • *41,945*
Sheridan, AR 72150 • *3,098*
Sheridan, CO 80110 • *4,976*
Sheridan, IL 60551 • *1,288*
Sheridan, IN 46069 • *2,046*
Sheridan, OR 97378 • *3,979*
Sheridan, WY 82801 • *13,900*
Sheridan □, KS • *3,043*
Sheridan □, MT • *4,732*
Sheridan □, NE • *6,750*
Sheridan □, ND • *2,148*
Sheridan □, WY • *23,562*
Sheridan Beach, WA 98155 • *6,518*
Sherman, TX 75090–91 • *31,601*
Sherman □, KS • *6,926*
Sherman □, NE • *3,718*
Sherman □, OR • *1,918*
Sherman □, TX • *2,858*
Sherrelwood, CO 80221 • *16,636*
Sherrill, NY 13461 • *2,864*
Sherwood, AR 72116 • *18,893*
Sherwood, OR 97140 • *3,093*
Sherwood Manor, CT 06082 • *6,357*
Sherwood Park, DE 19808 • *2,000*
Shiawassee □, MI • *69,770*
Shickshinny, PA 18655 • *1,108*
Shillington, PA 19607 • *5,062*
Shiloh, OH 44878 • *11,607*
Shiloh, PA 17404 • *8,245*
Shiner, TX 77984 • *2,074*
Shinglehouse, PA 16748 • *1,243*
Shinnston, WV 26431 • *2,543*
Ship Bottom, NJ 08008 • *1,352*
Shippensburg, PA 17257 • *5,331*
Shiprock, NM 87420 • *7,687*
Shirley, MA 01464 • *1,559*
Shirley, NY 11967 • *22,936*
Shishmaref, AK 99772 • *456*
Shively, KY 40216 • *15,535*
Shoemakersville, PA 19555 • *1,443*
Shore Acres, MA 02066 • *1,200*
Shores Acres, RI 02852 • *410*
Shoreview, MN 55112 • *24,587*
Shorewood, IL 60435 • *6,264*
Shorewood, MN 55331 • *5,917*
Shorewood, WI 53211 • *14,116*
Shorewood Hills, WI 53705 • *1,680*
Short Beach, CT 06405 • *2,500*
Shortsville, NY 14548 • *1,485*
Shoshone, ID 83352 • *1,249*
Shoshone □, ID • *13,931*
Shoshoni, WY 82649 • *497*
Show Low, AZ 85901 • *5,019*
Shreve, OH 44676 • *1,584*
Shreveport, LA 71101–10 • *198,525*
Shrewsbury, MA 01545 • *23,400*
Shrewsbury, MO 63119 • *6,416*
Shrewsbury, NJ 07702 • *3,096*
Shrewsbury, PA 17361 • *2,672*
Shullsburg, WI 53586 • *1,236*
Shungnak, AK 99773 • *223*
Sibley, IA 51249 • *2,815*
Sibley □, MN • *14,366*
Sicklerville, NJ 08081 • *1,750*
Sidney, IL 61877 • *1,027*
Sidney, IA 51652 • *1,253*
Sidney, MT 59270 • *5,217*
Sidney, NE 69162 • *5,959*
Sidney, NY 13838 • *4,720*
Sidney, OH 45365 • *18,710*
Siegle, LA 71291 • *1,600*
Sierra □, CA • *3,318*
Sierra □, NM • *9,912*
Sierra Madre, CA 91024 • *10,762*
Sierra Vista, AZ 85635–36 • *32,983*
Siesta Key, FL 34242 • *7,772*
Signal Hill, CA 90806 • *8,371*
Signal Mountain, TN 37377 • *7,034*
Sigourney, IA 52591 • *2,111*
Sikeston, MO 63801 • *17,641*
Siler City, NC 27344 • *4,808*
Siloam Springs, AR 72761 • *8,151*
Silsbee, TX 77656 • *6,368*
Silt, CO 81652 • *1,095*
Silver Bay, MN 55614 • *1,894*
Silver Bow □, MT • *33,941*
Silver City, NV 89428 • *100*
Silver City, NM 88061–62 • *10,683*
Silver Creek, NY 14136 • *2,927*
Silverdale, WA 98383 • *7,660*
Silver Grove, KY 41085 • *1,102*
Silver Hill, MD 20746 • *1,580*
Silver Lake, KS 66539 • *1,390*
Silver Lake, MA 01887 • *2,900*
Silver Lake, WI 53170 • *1,801*
Silverpeak, NV 89047 • *190*
Silver Spring, MD 20901–12 • *76,046*
Silver Springs, FL 32688 • *1,082*
Silver Springs, NV 89429 • *2,253*
Silver Springs Shores, FL 32672 • *6,421*
Silverton, NJ 08753 • *9,175*
Silverton, OH 45236 • *5,859*
Silverton, OR 97381 • *5,635*
Silview, DE 19804 • *1,500*
Silvis, IL 61282 • *6,926*
Simi Valley, CA 93062–65 • *100,217*
Simmesport, LA 71369 • *2,092*
Simpson, PA 18407 • *1,670*
Simpson □, KY • *15,145*
Simpson □, MS • *23,953*
Simpsonville, SC 29681 • *11,708*
Simsbury, CT 06070 • *5,577*
Sinclair, WY 82334 • *500*
Sinton, TX 78387 • *5,549*
Sioux □, IA • *29,903*
Sioux □, NE • *1,549*
Sioux □, ND • *3,761*
Sioux Center, IA 51250 • *5,074*
Sioux City, IA 51101–11 • *80,505*
Sioux Falls, SD 57101–18 • *100,814*
Siskiyou □, CA • *43,531*
Sisseton, SD 57262 • *2,181*
Sistersville, WV 26175 • *1,797*
Sitka, AK 99835 • *8,588*
Skagit □, WA • *79,555*
Skagway, AK 99840 • *692*
Skamania □, WA • *8,289*
Skaneateles, NY 13152 • *2,724*
Skiatook, OK 74070 • *4,910*
Skokie, IL 60076–77 • *59,432*
Skowhegan, ME 04976 • *6,990*
Sky Lake, FL 32809 • *6,202*
Skyland, NV 89448 • *660*
Skyland, NC 28776 • *1,100*
Skyway, WA 98178 • *8,500*
Slackwoods, NJ 08638 • *8,100*
Slater, IA 50244 • *1,268*
Slater, MO 65349 • *2,186*
Slater, SC 29683 • *1,000*
Slatersville, RI 02876 • *2,330*
Slatington, PA 18080 • *4,678*
Slaton, TX 79364 • *6,078*
Slayton, MN 56172 • *2,147*
Sleepy Eye, MN 56085 • *3,694*
Slickville, PA 15684 • *1,178*
Slidell, LA 70458–61 • *24,124*
Slinger, WI 53086 • *2,340*
Slippery Rock, PA 16057 • *3,008*
Sloan, NY 14225 • *3,830*
Sloatsburg, NY 10974 • *3,035*
Slocomb, AL 36375 • *1,906*
Slope □, ND • *907*
Smackover, AR 71762 • *2,232*
Smethport, PA 16749 • *1,734*
Smith □, KS • *5,078*
Smith □, MS • *14,798*
Smith □, TN • *14,143*
Smith □, TX • *151,309*
Smith Center, KS 66967 • *2,016*
Smithers, WV 25186 • *1,162*
Smithfield, NC 27577 • *7,540*
Smithfield, PA 15478 • *1,000*
Smithfield, UT 84335 • *5,566*
Smithfield, VA 23430 • *4,686*
Smith River, CA 95567 • *1,000*
Smiths, AL 36877 • *1,700*
Smithsburg, MD 21783 • *1,221*
Smithton, IL 62285 • *1,587*
Smithtown, NY 11787 • *25,638*
Smithville, MO 64089 • *2,525*
Smithville, OH 44677 • *1,354*
Smithville, TN 37166 • *3,791*
Smithville, TX 78957 • *3,196*
Smyrna, DE 19977 • *5,231*
Smyrna, GA 30080–82 • *30,981*
Smyrna, TN 37167 • *13,647*
Smyth □, VA • *32,370*
Sneads, FL 32460 • *1,746*
Sneedville, TN 37869 • *1,446*
Snellville, GA 30278 • *12,084*
Snohomish, WA 98290 • *6,499*
Snohomish □, WA • *465,642*
Snoqualmie, WA 98065 • *1,546*
Snowflake, AZ 85937 • *3,679*
Snow Hill, MD 21863 • *2,217*
Snow Hill, NC 28580 • *1,378*
Snyder, OK 73566 • *1,619*
Snyder, TX 79549 • *12,195*
Snyder □, PA • *36,680*
Soap Lake, WA 98851 • *1,149*
Socastee, SC 29577 • *10,426*
Social Circle, GA 30279 • *2,755*
Socorro, NM 87801 • *8,159*
Socorro □, NM • *14,764*
Soda Springs, ID 83276 • *3,111*
Soddy-Daisy, TN 37379 • *8,240*
Sodus, NY 14551 • *1,904*
Sodus Point, NY 14555 • *1,190*
Solana, FL 33950 • *1,128*
Solana Beach, CA 92075 • *12,962*
Solano □, CA • *340,421*
Soldotna, AK 99669 • *3,482*
Soledad, CA 93960 • *7,146*
Solomons, MD 20688 • *1,500*
Solon, IA 52333 • *1,050*
Solon, OH 44139 • *18,548*
Solvay, NY 13209 • *6,717*
Somerdale, NJ 08083 • *5,440*
Somers, CT 06071 • *9,108*
Somerset, KY 42501–02 • *10,733*
Somerset, MA 02725 • *17,655*
Somerset, NJ 08873–75 • *22,070*
Somerset, OH 43783 • *1,390*
Somerset, PA 15501 • *6,454*
Somerset, TX 78069 • *1,144*
Somerset, WI 54025 • *1,065*
Somerset □, ME • *49,767*
Somerset □, MD • *23,440*
Somerset □, NJ • *240,279*
Somerset □, PA • *78,218*
Somers Point, NJ 08244 • *11,216*
Somersville, CT 06072 • *1,200*
Somersworth, NH 03878 • *11,249*
Somerton, AZ 85350 • *5,282*
Somervell □, TX • *5,360*
Somerville, MA 02143 • *76,210*
Somerville, NJ 08876–77 • *11,632*
Somerville, TN 38068 • *2,047*
Somerville, TX 77879 • *1,542*
Somonauk, IL 60552 • *1,263*
Sonoma, CA 95476 • *8,121*
Sonoma □, CA • *388,222*
Sonora, CA 95370 • *4,153*
Sonora, TX 76950 • *2,751*
Soperton, GA 30457 • *2,797*
Sophia, WV 25921 • *1,182*
Soquel, CA 95073 • *9,188*
Sorrento, LA 70778 • *1,119*
Souderton, PA 18964 • *5,957*
Sound Beach, NY 11789 • *9,102*
South Acton, MA 01720 • *3,220*
South Amboy, NJ 08879 • *7,863*
South Amherst, MA 01002 • *5,053*
South Amherst, OH 44001 • *1,765*
Southampton, NY 11968–69 • *3,980*
Southampton □, VA • *17,550*
South Ashburnham, MA 01466 • *1,110*
Southaven, MS 38671 • *17,949*
South Barre, VT 05670 • *1,314*
South Bay, FL 33493 • *3,558*
South Belmar, NJ 07719 • *1,482*
South Beloit, IL 61080 • *4,072*
South Bend, IN 46601–80 • *105,511*
South Bend, WA 98586 • *1,551*
South Berwick, ME 03908 • *5,877*
Southborough, MA 01772 • *1,450*
South Boston, VA 24592 • *6,997*
South Bound Brook, NJ 08880 • *4,185*
South Bradenton, FL 34205 • *20,398*
Southbridge, MA 01550 • *13,631*
South Broadway, WA 98902 • *2,735*
South Burlington, VT 05403 • *12,809*
Southbury, CT 06488 • *3,000*
South Charleston, OH 45368 • *1,626*
South Charleston, WV 25303 • *13,645*
South Chicago Heights, IL 60411 • *3,597*
South Congaree, SC 29169 • *2,406*
South Connellsville, PA 15425 • *2,204*
South Dartmouth, MA 02748 • *9,850*
South Daytona, FL 32121 • *12,482*
South Decatur, GA 30034 • *19,350*
South Deerfield, MA 01373 • *1,906*
South Dennis, MA 02660 • *2,500*
South Duxbury, MA 02332 • *3,017*
South Easton, MA 02375 • *1,530*
South Elgin, IL 60177 • *7,474*
South El Monte, CA 91733 • *20,850*
Southern Pines, NC 28387–88 • *9,129*
South Euclid, OH 44121 • *23,866*
South Fallsburg, NY 12779 • *2,115*
South Farmingdale, NY 11735 • *15,377*
Southfield, MI 48034 • *75,728*
South Fork, PA 15956 • *1,197*
South Fulton, TN 38257 • *2,688*
South Gastonia, NC 28052 • *5,487*
South Gate, CA 90280 • *86,284*
Southgate, FL 34239 • *7,324*
Southgate, KY 41071 • *3,266*
South Gate, MD 21061 • *27,564*
Southgate, MI 48195 • *30,771*
South Glastonbury, CT 06073 • *1,570*
Southglenn, CO 80122 • *43,087*
South Glens Falls, NY 12801 • *3,506*
South Grafton, MA 01560 • *2,610*
South Hackensack, NJ 07606 • *2,229*
South Hadley, MA 01075 • *5,340*
South Hadley Falls, MA 01075 • *5,100*
South Hamilton, MA 01982 • *2,720*
South Haven, IN 46383 • *6,112*
South Haven, MI 49090 • *5,563*
South Hill, NY 14850 • *5,423*
South Hill, VA 23970 • *4,217*
South Hingham, MA 02043 • *4,080*
South Holland, IL 60473 • *22,105*
South Hooksett, NH 03106 • *3,638*
South Hopkinton, RI 02813 • *900*
South Houston, TX 77587 • *14,207*
South Huntington, NY 11746 • *9,624*
South Hutchinson, KS 67505 • *2,444*
Southington, CT 06489 • *38,518*
South International Falls, MN 56679 • *2,806*
South Jacksonville, IL 62650 • *3,187*
South Jordan, UT 84065 • *12,220*
South Lake Tahoe, CA 95702 • *21,586*
South Lancaster, MA 01561 • *1,772*
South Laramie, WY 82070 • *1,500*
South Laurel, MD 20708 • *18,591*
South Lebanon, OH 45065 • *2,696*
South Lockport, NY 14094 • *7,112*
South Lyon, MI 48178 • *5,857*
South Miami, FL 33143 • *10,404*
South Miami Heights, FL 33157 • *30,030*
South Milwaukee, WI 53172 • *20,958*
South Nyack, NY 10960 • *3,352*
South Ogden, UT 84403 • *12,105*
Southold, NY 11971 • *5,192*
South Orange, NJ 07079 • *16,390*
South Paris, ME 04281 • *2,320*
South Pasadena, CA 91030 • *23,936*
South Patrick Shores, FL 32937 • *10,249*
South Pekin, IL 61564 • *1,184*
South Pittsburg, TN 37380 • *3,295*
South Plainfield, NJ 07080 • *20,489*
Southport, FL 32409 • *1,992*
Southport, IN 46227 • *1,969*
Southport, NY 14904 • *7,753*
Southport, NC 28461 • *2,369*
South Portland, ME 04106 • *23,163*
South River, NJ 08882 • *13,692*
South Royalton, VT 05068 • *700*
South Saint Paul, MN 55075–77 • *20,197*
South Salt Lake, UT 84115 • *10,129*
South San Francisco, CA 94080–83 • *54,312*
South San Gabriel, CA 91770 • *7,700*
South San Jose Hills, CA 91744 • *17,814*
South Sarasota, FL 34239 • *5,298*
South Setauket, NY 11733 • *5,990*
Southside, AL 35901 • *5,580*
Southside Place, TX 77005 • *1,392*
South Sioux City, NE 68776 • *9,677*
South Stony Brook, NY 11790 • *6,120*
South Streator, IL 61364 • *2,334*
South Sumter, SC 29150 • *4,371*
South Toms River, NJ 08757 • *3,869*
South Torrington, WY 82240 • *300*
South Tucson, AZ 85713 • *5,093*
South Valley Stream, NY 11581 • *5,328*
South Venice, FL 34293 • *11,951*
South Walpole, MA 02071 • *1,300*
South Waverly, PA 14892 • *1,049*
South Wellfleet, MA 02663 • *2,300*
South Westbury, NY 11590 • *9,732*
Southwest Harbor, ME 04679 • *1,952*
South Whitley, IN 46787 • *1,482*
South Whittier, CA 90605 • *51,100*
Southwick, MA 01077 • *1,170*
South Williamsport, PA 17701 • *6,496*
South Windham, CT 06266 • *1,644*
South Windham, ME 04082 • *1,350*
South Windsor, CT 06074 • *10,800*
Southwood, CO 80120 • *2,050*
Southwood Acres, CT 06082 • *8,963*
South Woodstock, CT 06267 • *1,112*
South Yarmouth, MA 02664 • *10,358*
South Yuba City, CA 95991 • *8,816*
South Zanesville, OH 43701 • *1,969*
Spalding □, GA • *54,457*
Spanaway, WA 98387 • *15,001*
Spangler, PA 15775 • *2,068*
Spanish Fork, UT 84660 • *11,272*
Spanish Fort, AL 36527 • *3,732*
Spanish Lake, MO 63138 • *20,322*
Sparks, GA 31647 • *1,205*
Sparks, NV 89431–36 • *53,367*
Sparr, FL 32192 • *1,100*
Sparta, GA 31087 • *1,710*
Sparta, IL 62286 • *4,853*
Sparta, MI 49345 • *3,968*
Sparta (Lake Mohawk), NJ 07871 • *8,930*
Sparta, NC 28675 • *1,957*
Sparta, TN 38583 • *4,681*
Sparta, WI 54656 • *7,788*
Spartanburg, SC 29301–18 • *43,467*
Spartanburg □, SC • *226,800*
Spearfish, SD 57783 • *6,966*
Spearman, TX 79081 • *3,197*
Speedway, IN 46224 • *13,092*
Spencer, IN 47460 • *2,609*
Spencer, IA 51301 • *11,066*
Spencer, MA 01562 • *6,306*
Spencer, NC 28159 • *3,219*
Spencer, TN 38585 • *1,125*
Spencer, WV 25276 • *2,279*
Spencer, WI 54479 • *1,757*
Spencer □, IN • *19,490*
Spencer □, KY • *6,801*
Spencerport, NY 14559 • *3,606*
Spencerville, MD 20868 • *1,780*
Spencerville, OH 45887 • *2,288*
Spicer, MN 56288 • *1,020*
Spindale, NC 28160 • *4,040*
Spink □, SD • *7,981*
Spirit Lake, ID 83869 • *790*
Spirit Lake, IA 51360 • *3,871*
Spiro, OK 74959 • *2,146*
Spokane, WA 99201–28 • *177,196*
Spokane □, WA • *361,364*
Spooner, WI 54801 • *2,464*
Spotswood, NJ 08884 • *7,983*
Spotsylvania □, VA • *57,403*
Sprague, WV 25926 • *2,090*

Spring, TX 77373 • *33,111*
Spring Arbor, MI 49283 • *2,010*
Springboro, OH 45066 • *6,590*
Spring City, PA 19475 • *3,433*
Spring City, TN 37381 • *2,199*
Spring Creek 0M, NV • *5,866*
Springdale, AR 72764–66 • *29,941*
Springdale, OH 45246 • *10,621*
Springdale, PA 15144 • *3,992*
Springdale, SC 29169 • *3,226*
Springer, NM 87747 • *1,262*
Springerville, AZ 85938 • *1,802*
Springfield, CO 81073 • *1,475*
Springfield, FL 32401 • *8,715*
Springfield, GA 31329 • *1,415*
Springfield, IL 62701–94 • *105,227*
Springfield, KY 40069 • *2,875*
Springfield, MA 01101–05 • *156,983*
Springfield, MI 49015 • *5,582*
Springfield, MN 56087 • *2,173*
Springfield, MO 65801–99 • *140,494*
Springfield, NE 68059 • *1,426*
Springfield, NJ 07081 • *13,240*
Springfield, OH 45501–06 • *70,487*
Springfield, OR 97477–78 • *44,683*
Springfield, PA 19064 • *24,160*
Springfield, SD 57062 • *834*
Springfield, TN 37172 • *11,227*
Springfield, VT 05156 • *4,207*
Springfield, VA 22150 • *23,706*
Spring Garden, PA 17403 • *11,127*
Spring Green, WI 53588 • *1,283*
Spring Grove, IL 60081 • *1,066*
Spring Grove, MN 55974 • *1,153*
Spring Grove, PA 17362 • *1,863*
Spring Hill, FL 34606 • *31,117*
Spring Hill, KS 66083 • *2,191*
Springhill, LA 71075 • *5,668*
Spring Hill, TN 37174 • *1,464*
Spring Hope, NC 27882 • *1,221*
Spring Lake, MI 49456 • *2,537*
Spring Lake, NJ 07762 • *3,499*
Spring Lake, NC 28390 • *7,524*
Spring Lake Heights, NJ 07762 • *5,341*
Spring Lake Park, MN 55432 • *6,532*
Springvale, ME 04083 • *3,542*
Spring Valley, IL 61362 • *5,246*
Spring Valley, MN 55975 • *2,461*
Spring Valley, NY 10977 • *21,802*
Spring Valley, WI 54767 • *1,051*
Springville, AL 35146 • *1,910*
Springville, IA 52336 • *1,068*
Springville, NY 14141 • *4,310*
Springville, UT 84663–64 • *13,950*
Spruce Pine, NC 28777 • *2,010*
Spur, TX 79370 • *1,300*
Staatsburg, NY 12580 • *1,100*
Stafford, KS 67578 • *1,344*
Stafford □, KS • *5,365*
Stafford □, VA • *61,236*
Stafford Springs, CT 06076 • *4,100*
Stambaugh, MI 49964 • *1,281*
Stamford, CT 06901–12 • *108,056*
Stamford, NY 12167 • *1,211*
Stamford, TX 79553 • *3,817*
Stamford, VT 05352 • *400*
Stamps, AR 71860 • *2,478*
Stanaford, WV 25927 • *1,706*
Stanberry, MO 64489 • *1,310*
Standish, MI 48658 • *1,377*
Stanfield, AZ 85272 • *1,700*
Stanfield, OR 97875 • *1,568*
Stanford, CA 94305 • *18,097*
Stanford, KY 40484 • *2,686*
Stanhope, NJ 07874 • *3,393*
Stanislaus □, CA • *370,522*
Stanley, NC 28164 • *2,823*
Stanley, ND 58784 • *1,371*
Stanley, VA 22851 • *1,186*
Stanley, WI 54768 • *2,011*
Stanley □, SD • *2,453*
Stanleytown, VA 24168 • *1,563*
Stanleyville, NC 27045 • *4,779*
Stanly □, NC • *51,765*
Stanton, CA 90680 • *30,491*
Stanton, KY 40380 • *2,795*
Stanton, MI 48888 • *1,504*
Stanton, NE 68779 • *1,549*
Stanton, TX 79782 • *2,576*
Stanton □, KS • *2,333*
Stanton □, NE • *6,244*
Stanwood, WA 98292 • *1,961*
Staples, MN 56479 • *2,754*
Stapleton, AL 36578 • *1,300*
Starbuck, MN 56381 • *1,143*
Star City, AR 71667 • *2,138*
Star City, WV 26505 • *1,251*
Stargo, AZ 85540 • *1,038*
Stark □, IL • *6,534*
Stark □, ND • *22,832*
Stark □, OH • *367,585*
Starke, FL 32091 • *5,226*
Starke □, IN • *22,747*
Starkville, MS 39759 • *18,458*
Starr □, TX • *40,518*
Startex, SC 29377 • *1,162*
State Center, IA 50247 • *1,248*
State College, PA 16801–05 • *38,923*
Stateline, NV 89449 • *1,379*
State Line, PA 17263 • *1,253*
Statesboro, GA 30458 • *15,854*
Statesville, NC 28677 • *17,567*
Statham, GA 30666 • *1,360*
Staunton, IL 62088 • *4,806*
Staunton, VA 24401 • *24,461*
Stayton, OR 97383 • *5,011*
Steamboat, NV 89511 • *450*
Steamboat Springs, CO 80487 • *6,695*
Stearns, KY 42647 • *1,550*
Stearns □, MN • *118,791*
Stebbins, AK 99671 • *400*
Steele, AL 35987 • *1,046*
Steele, MO 63877 • *2,395*
Steele, ND 58482 • *762*
Steele □, MN • *30,729*
Steele □, ND • *2,420*
Steeleville, IL 62288 • *2,059*
Steelton, PA 17113 • *5,152*
Steelville, MO 65565 • *1,465*
Steger, IL 60475 • *8,584*
Steilacoom, WA 98388 • *5,728*
Stephens, AR 71764 • *1,137*
Stephens □, GA • *23,257*
Stephens □, OK • *42,299*
Stephens □, TX • *9,010*
Stephens City, VA 22655 • *1,186*
Stephenson □, IL • *48,052*
Stephenville, TX 76401 • *13,502*
Sterling, AK 99672 • *3,802*
Sterling, CO 80751 • *10,362*
Sterling, IL 61081 • *15,132*
Sterling, KS 67579 • *2,115*
Sterling, MA 01564 • *1,250*
Sterling, VA 22170 • *20,512*
Sterling □, TX • *1,438*
Sterling City, TX 76951 • *1,096*
Sterling Heights, MI 48310–14 • *117,810*
Sterlington, LA 71280 • *1,140*
Steuben □, IN • *27,446*
Steuben □, NY • *99,088*
Steubenville, OH 43952 • *22,125*
Stevens □, KS • *5,048*
Stevens □, MN • *10,634*
Stevens □, WA • *30,948*
Stevenson, AL 35772 • *2,046*
Stevenson, WA 98648 • *1,147*
Stevens Point, WI 54481 • *23,006*
Stevensville, MI 49127 • *1,230*
Stevensville, MT 59870 • *1,221*
Stewart □, GA • *5,654*
Stewart □, TN • *9,479*
Stewartstown, PA 17363 • *1,308*
Stewartville, MN 55976 • *4,520*
Stickney, IL 60402 • *5,678*
Stigler, OK 74462 • *2,574*
Stillwater, MN 55082–83 • *13,882*
Stillwater, NY 12170 • *1,531*
Stillwater, OK 74074–76 • *36,676*
Stillwater □, MT • *6,536*
Stilwell, OK 74960 • *2,663*
Stinnett, TX 79083 • *2,166*
Stirling, NJ 07980 • *1,800*
Stockbridge, GA 30281 • *3,359*
Stockbridge, MA 01262 • *2,408*
Stockbridge, MI 49285 • *1,202*
Stockdale, TX 78160 • *1,268*
Stockholm, NJ 07460 • *1,200*
Stockton, CA 95201–19 • *210,943*
Stockton, IL 61085 • *1,871*
Stockton, KS 67669 • *1,507*
Stockton, MO 65785 • *1,579*
Stoddard □, MO • *28,895*
Stokes □, NC • *37,223*
Stokesdale, NC 27357 • *2,134*
Stollings, WV 25646 • *1,200*
Stone □, AR • *9,775*
Stone □, MS • *10,750*
Stone □, MO • *19,078*
Stoneboro, PA 16153 • *1,091*
Stoneham, MA 02180 • *22,203*
Stone Harbor, NJ 08247 • *1,025*
Stone Mountain, GA 30083 • *6,494*
Stoneville, NC 27048 • *1,109*
Stonewall, LA 71078 • *1,266*
Stonewall, MS 39363 • *1,148*
Stonewall □, TX • *2,013*
Stonewood, WV 26301 • *1,996*
Stonington, CT 06378 • *1,100*
Stonington, IL 62567 • *1,006*
Stony Brook, NY 11790 • *13,726*
Stony Point, NY 10980 • *10,587*
Stony Point, NC 28678 • *1,286*
Storey □, NV • *2,526*
Storm Lake, IA 50588 • *8,769*
Storrs, CT 06268 • *12,198*
Story, WY 82842 • *700*
Story □, IA • *74,252*
Story City, IA 50248 • *2,959*
Stottville, NY 12172 • *1,369*
Stoughton, MA 02072 • *26,777*
Stoughton, WI 53589 • *8,786*
Stow, MA 01775 • *1,200*
Stow, OH 44224 • *27,702*
Stowe, PA 19464 • *3,598*
Stowe, VT 05672 • *450*
Stowe Township, PA 15136 • *7,681*
Strabane, PA 15363 • *1,200*
Strafford, MO 65757 • *1,166*
Strafford □, NH • *104,233*
Strasburg, CO 80136 • *1,005*
Strasburg, OH 44680 • *1,995*
Strasburg, PA 17579 • *2,568*
Strasburg, VA 22657 • *3,762*
Stratford, CT 06497 • *49,389*
Stratford, DE 19720 • *1,950*
Stratford, NJ 08084 • *7,614*
Stratford, OK 74872 • *1,404*
Stratford, TX 79084 • *1,781*
Stratford, WI 54484 • *1,515*
Stratford Landing, VA 22308 • *2,800*
Strathmore, CA 93267 • *2,353*
Strathmore, NJ 07747 • *7,060*
Strawberry Point, IA 52076 • *1,357*
Streamwood, IL 60103 • *30,987*
Streator, IL 61364 • *14,121*
Streetsboro, OH 44241 • *9,932*
Stromsburg, NE 68666 • *1,241*
Strongsville, OH 44136 • *35,308*
Stroud, OK 74079 • *2,666*
Stroudsburg, PA 18360 • *5,312*
Struthers, OH 44471 • *12,284*
Stryker, OH 43557 • *1,468*
Stuart, FL 34994–97 • *11,936*
Stuart, IA 50250 • *1,522*
Stuarts Draft, VA 24477 • *5,087*
Sturbridge, MA 01566 • *2,093*
Sturgeon Bay, WI 54235 • *9,176*
Sturgis, KY 42459 • *2,184*
Sturgis, MI 49091 • *10,130*
Sturgis, SD 57785 • *5,330*
Sturtevant, WI 53177 • *3,803*
Stutsman □, ND • *22,241*
Stuttgart, AR 72160 • *10,420*
Sublette, KS 67877 • *1,378*
Sublette □, WY • *4,843*
Sublimity, OR 97385 • *1,491*
Succasunna, NJ 07876 • *7,750*
Sudbury, MA 01776 • *1,860*
Sudbury Center, MA 01776 • *2,590*
Sudley, VA 22110 • *7,321*
Suffern, NY 10901 • *11,055*
Suffield, CT 06078 • *1,353*
Suffolk, VA 23432–38 • *52,141*
Suffolk □, MA • *663,906*
Suffolk □, NY • *1,321,864*
Sugar City, ID 83448 • *1,275*
Sugar Creek, MO 64054 • *3,982*
Sugarcreek, PA 16323 • *5,532*
Sugar Grove, VA 24375 • *1,027*
Sugar Hill, GA 30518 • *4,557*
Sugar Land, TX 77478–79 • *24,529*
Sugarland Run, VA 22170 • *9,357*
Sugar Loaf, VA 24018 • *2,000*
Sugar Notch, PA 18706 • *1,044*
Suisun City, CA 94585 • *22,686*
Suitland, MD 20746 • *35,400*
Sulligent, AL 35586 • *1,886*
Sullivan, IL 61951 • *4,354*
Sullivan, IN 47882 • *4,663*
Sullivan, MO 63080 • *5,661*
Sullivan □, IN • *18,993*
Sullivan □, MO • *6,326*
Sullivan □, NH • *38,592*
Sullivan □, NY • *69,277*
Sullivan □, PA • *6,104*
Sullivan □, TN • *143,596*
Sullivans Island, SC 29482 • *1,623*
Sully □, SD • *1,589*
Sulphur, LA 70663–64 • *20,125*
Sulphur, OK 73086 • *4,824*
Sulphur Springs, TX 75482 • *14,062*
Sultan, WA 98294 • *2,236*
Sumiton, AL 35148 • *2,604*
Summerfield, NC 27358 • *2,051*
Summers □, WV • *14,204*
Summersville, WV 26651 • *2,906*
Summerville, GA 30747 • *5,025*
Summerville, SC 29483–85 • *22,519*
Summit, IL 60501 • *9,971*
Summit, MS 39666 • *1,566*
Summit, NJ 07901 • *19,757*
Summit, TN 37363 • *8,307*
Summit □, CO • *12,881*
Summit □, OH • *514,990*
Summit □, UT • *15,518*
Summit Hill, PA 18250 • *3,332*
Sumner, IL 62466 • *1,083*
Sumner, IA 50674 • *2,078*
Sumner, WA 98390 • *6,281*
Sumner □, KS • *25,841*
Sumner □, TN • *103,281*
Sumter, SC 29150–54 • *41,943*
Sumter □, AL • *16,174*
Sumter □, FL • *31,577*
Sumter □, GA • *30,228*
Sumter □, SC • *102,637*
Sunbury, OH 43074 • *2,046*
Sunbury, PA 17801 • *11,591*
Sun City, AZ 85351 • *38,126*
Sun City, CA 92381 • *14,930*
Sun City Center, FL 33573 • *8,326*
Suncook, NH 03275 • *5,214*
Sundance, WY 82729 • *1,139*
Sundown, TX 79372 • *1,759*
Sunflower □, MS • *32,867*
Sunland Park, NM 88063 • *8,179*
Sunny Isles, FL 33160 • *11,772*
Sunnyside, CA 93727 • *5,000*
Sunnyside, WA 98944 • *11,238*
Sunnyvale, CA 94086–89 • *117,229*
Sun Prairie, WI 53590 • *15,333*
Sunray, TX 79086 • *1,729*
Sunrise Manor, NV 89110 • *95,362*
Sunset, FL 33143 • *15,810*
Sunset, LA 70584 • *2,201*
Sunset, UT 84015 • *5,128*
Sunset Beach, HI 96712 • *800*
Sun Valley, ID 83353–54 • *938*
Sun Valley, NV 89433 • *11,391*
Superior, AZ 85273 • *3,468*
Superior, MT 59872 • *881*
Superior, NE 68978 • *2,397*
Superior, WI 54880 • *27,134*
Superior, WY 82945 • *273*
Suquamish, WA 98392 • *3,105*
Surf City, NJ 08008 • *1,375*
Surfside, FL 33154 • *4,108*
Surfside Beach, SC 29575 • *3,845*
Surgoinsville, TN 37873 • *1,499*
Surprise, AZ 85374 • *7,122*
Surrey, ND 58785 • *856*
Surry □, NC • *61,704*
Surry □, VA • *6,145*
Susanville, CA 96130 • *7,279*
Susquehanna, PA 18847 • *1,760*
Susquehanna □, PA • *40,380*
Sussex, NJ 07461 • *2,201*
Sussex, WI 53089 • *5,039*
Sussex □, DE • *113,229*
Sussex □, NJ • *130,943*
Sussex □, VA • *10,248*
Sutherland, NE 69165 • *1,032*
Sutherlin, OR 97479 • *5,020*
Sutter □, CA • *64,415*
Sutter Creek, CA 95685 • *1,835*
Sutton, NE 68979 • *1,353*
Sutton □, TX • *4,135*
Suwanee, GA 30174 • *2,412*
Suwannee □, FL • *26,780*
Swain □, NC • *11,268*
Swainsboro, GA 30401 • *7,361*
Swampscott, MA 01907 • *13,650*
Swannanoa, NC 28778 • *3,538*
Swansboro, NC 28584 • *1,165*
Swansea, IL 62221 • *8,201*
Swanton, OH 43558 • *3,557*
Swanton, VT 05488 • *2,360*
Swanwyck Estates, DE 19720 • *1,320*
Swarthmore, PA 19081 • *6,157*
Swartz Creek, MI 48473 • *4,851*
Swatara Township, PA 17111 • *19,700*
Swayzee, IN 46986 • *1,059*
Swedesboro, NJ 08085 • *2,024*
Sweeny, TX 77480 • *3,297*
Sweet Grass □, MT • *3,154*
Sweet Home, OR 97386 • *6,850*
Sweet Springs, MO 65351 • *1,595*
Sweetwater, FL 33152 • *13,909*
Sweetwater, TN 37874 • *5,066*
Sweetwater, TX 79556 • *11,967*
Sweetwater □, WY • *38,823*
Sweetwater Creek, FL 33614 • *18,000*
Swift □, MN • *10,724*
Swisher □, TX • *8,133*
Swissvale, PA 15218 • *10,637*
Switzer, WV 25647 • *1,004*
Switzerland, FL 32043 • *2,400*
Switzerland □, IN • *7,738*
Swoyerville, PA • *5,630*
Sycamore, AL 35149 • *1,250*
Sycamore, IL 60178 • *9,708*
Sykesville, MD 21784 • *2,303*
Sykesville, PA 15865 • *1,387*
Sylacauga, AL 35150 • *12,520*
Sylva, NC 28779 • *1,809*
Sylvan Beach, NY 13157 • *1,119*
Sylvania, GA 30467 • *2,871*
Sylvania, OH 43560 • *17,301*
Sylvan Lake, MI 48320 • *1,884*
Sylvester, GA 31791 • *5,702*
Syosset, NY 11791 • *18,967*
Syracuse, IN 46567 • *2,729*
Syracuse, KS 67878 • *1,606*
Syracuse, NE 68446 • *1,646*
Syracuse, NY 13201–90 • *163,860*
Syracuse, UT 84075 • *4,658*

T

Tabor City, NC 28463 • *2,330*
Tacoma, WA 98401–99 • *176,664*
Taft, CA 93268 • *5,902*
Taft, TX 78390 • *3,222*
Tahlequah, OK 74464–65 • *10,398*
Tahoe City, CA 95730 • *1,300*
Tahoka, TX 79373 • *2,868*
Takoma Park, MD 20912 • *16,700*
Talbot □, GA • *6,524*
Talbot □, MD • *30,549*
Talbotton, GA 31827 • *1,046*
Talent, OR 97540 • *3,274*
Taliaferro □, GA • *1,915*
Talihina, OK 74571 • *1,297*
Talladega, AL 35160 • *18,175*
Talladega □, AL • *74,107*
Tallahassee, FL 32301–17 • *124,773*
Tallahatchie □, MS • *15,210*
Tallapoosa, GA 30176 • *2,805*
Tallapoosa □, AL • *38,826*
Tallassee, AL 36078 • *5,112*
Talleyville, DE 19803 • *6,346*
Tallmadge, OH 44278 • *14,870*
Tallulah, LA 71282–84 • *8,526*
Tama, IA 52339 • *2,697*
Tama □, IA • *17,419*
Tamalpais Valley, CA 94941 • *5,000*
Tamaqua, PA 18252 • *7,943*
Tamarac, FL 33321 • *44,822*
Tamiami, FL 33165 • *33,845*
Tampa, FL 33601–97 • *280,015*
Tanana, AK 99777 • *345*
Taney □, MO • *25,561*
Taneytown, MD 21787 • *3,695*
Tangipahoa □, LA • *85,709*
Taos, NM 87571 • *4,065*
Taos □, NM • *23,118*
Taos Pueblo, NM 87571 • *1,030*
Tappahannock, VA 22560 • *1,550*
Tappan, NY 10983 • *6,867*
Tara Hills, CA 94564 • *6,000*
Tarboro, NC 27886 • *11,037*
Tarentum, PA 15084 • *5,674*
Tariffville, CT 06081 • *1,477*
Tarkio, MO 64491 • *2,243*
Tarpey, CA 93727 • *4,000*
Tarpon Springs, FL 34688–91 • *17,906*
Tarrant, AL 35217 • *8,046*
Tarrant □, TX • *1,170,103*
Tarrytown, NY 10591 • *10,739*
Tate, GA 30177 • *1,000*
Tate □, MS • *21,432*
Tattnall □, GA • *17,722*
Taunton, MA 02780 • *49,832*
Tavares, FL 32778 • *7,383*
Tavernier, FL 33070 • *2,433*
Tawas City, MI 48763–64 • *2,009*
Taylor, AZ 85939 • *2,418*
Taylor, MI 48180 • *70,811*
Taylor, PA 18517 • *6,941*
Taylor, TX 76574 • *11,472*
Taylor □, FL • *17,111*
Taylor □, GA • *7,642*
Taylor □, IA • *7,114*
Taylor □, KY • *21,146*
Taylor □, TX • *119,655*
Taylor □, WV • *15,144*
Taylor □, WI • *18,901*
Taylor Mill, KY 41015 • *5,530*
Taylors, SC 29687 • *19,619*
Taylorsville, IN 47280 • *1,044*
Taylorsville, MS 39168 • *1,412*
Taylorsville, NC 28681 • *1,566*
Taylorville, IL 62568 • *11,133*
Tazewell, TN 37879 • *2,150*
Tazewell, VA 24651 • *4,176*
Tazewell □, IL • *123,692*
Tazewell □, VA • *45,960*
Tchula, MS 39169 • *2,186*
Teague, TX 75860 • *3,268*
Teaneck, NJ 07666 • *37,825*
Teaticket, MA 02536 • *2,600*
Tecumseh, MI 49286 • *7,462*
Tecumseh, NE 68450 • *1,702*
Tecumseh, OK 74873 • *5,750*
Tehachapi, CA 93561 • *5,791*
Tehama □, CA • *49,625*
Tekamah, NE 68061 • *1,852*
Telfair □, GA • *11,000*
Telford, PA 18969 • *4,238*
Tell City, IN 47586 • *8,088*
Teller □, CO • *12,468*
Telluride, CO 81435 • *1,309*
Temecula, CA 92390 • *27,099*
Tempe, AZ 85280–85 • *141,865*
Temperance, MI 48182 • *6,542*
Temple, GA 30179 • *1,870*
Temple, OK 73568 • *1,223*
Temple, PA 19560 • *1,491*
Temple, TX 76501–05 • *46,109*
Temple City, CA 91780 • *31,100*
Temple Terrace, FL 33617 • *16,444*
Templeton, MA 01468 • *1,000*
Tenafly, NJ 07670 • *13,326*
Tenaha, TX 75974 • *1,072*
Tenino, WA 98589 • *1,292*
Tennessee Ridge, TN 37178 • *1,271*
Tennille, GA 31089 • *1,552*
Tensas □, LA • *7,103*
Ten Sleep, WY 82442 • *311*
Terra Alta, WV 26764 • *1,713*
Terrebonne □, LA • *96,982*
Terre Haute, IN 47801–08 • *57,483*
Terre Hill, PA 17581 • *1,282*
Terrell, TX 75160 • *12,490*
Terrell □, GA • *10,653*
Terrell □, TX • *1,410*
Terrell Hills, TX 78209 • *4,592*
Terry, MT 59349 • *659*
Terry □, TX • *13,218*
Terrytown, LA 70053 • *23,787*
Terryville, CT 06786 • *5,426*
Terryville, NY 11776 • *7,380*
Tesuque, NM 87574 • *1,490*
Teton □, ID • *3,439*
Teton □, MT • *6,271*
Teton □, WY • *11,172*
Teton Village, WY 83025 • *250*
Teutopolis, IL 62467 • *1,417*
Tewksbury, MA 01876 • *10,540*
Texarkana, AR 75502 • *22,631*
Texarkana, TX 75501–05 • *31,656*
Texas □, MO • *21,476*
Texas □, OK • *16,419*
Texas City, TX 77590–92 • *40,822*
Texico, NM 88135 • *966*
Thatcher, AZ 85552 • *3,763*
Thayer, MO 65791 • *1,996*
Thayer □, NE • *6,635*
Thayne, WY 83127 • *267*
The Colony, TX 75056 • *22,113*
The Dalles, OR 97058 • *11,060*
Theodore, AL 36582 • *6,509*
The Plains, OH 45780 • *2,644*
Thermalito, CA 95965 • *5,646*
Thermopolis, WY 82443 • *3,247*
The Village, OK 73120 • *10,353*
The Village of Indian Hill, OH 45243 • *5,383*
The Woodlands, TX 77380 • *29,205*
Thibodaux, LA 70301–02 • *14,035*
Thief River Falls, MN 56701 • *8,010*
Thiensville, WI 53092 • *3,301*
Thomas, OK 73669 • *1,246*
Thomas □, GA • *38,986*
Thomas □, KS • *8,258*
Thomas □, NE • *851*
Thomasboro, IL 61878 • *1,250*
Thomaston, CT 06787 • *3,590*
Thomaston, GA 30286 • *9,127*
Thomaston, ME 04861 • *2,445*
Thomasville, AL 36784 • *4,301*
Thomasville, GA 31792 • *17,457*
Thomasville, NC 27360–61 • *15,915*
Thompson, ND 58278 • *930*
Thompson Falls, MT 59873 • *1,319*
Thomson, GA 30824 • *6,862*
Thonotosassa, FL 33592 • *1,500*
Thoreau, NM 87323 • *1,099*
Thorndale, TX 76577 • *1,092*
Thorndike, MA 01079 • *1,100*
Thornton, CO 80229 • *55,031*
Thorntown, IN 46071 • *1,506*
Thornwood, NY 10594 • *7,025*
Thorofare, NJ 08086 • *1,800*
Thorp, WI 54771 • *1,657*
Thorsby, AL 35171 • *1,465*
Thousand Oaks, CA 91359–62 • *104,352*
Three Forks, MT 59752 • *1,203*
Three Oaks, MI 49128 • *1,786*
Three Rivers, MA 01080 • *3,006*
Three Rivers, MI 49093 • *7,413*
Three Rivers, TX 78071 • *1,889*
Throckmorton, TX 76083 • *1,036*
Throckmorton □, TX • *1,880*
Throop, PA 18512 • *4,070*
Thunderbolt, GA 31404 • *2,786*
Thurmont, MD 21788 • *3,398*
Thurston □, NE • *6,936*
Thurston □, WA • *161,238*
Tiburon, CA 94920 • *7,532*
Tice, FL 33905 • *3,971*
Ticonderoga, NY 12883 • *2,770*
Tierra Amarilla, NM 87575 • *900*
Tiffin, OH 44883 • *18,604*
Tift □, GA • *34,998*
Tifton, GA 31793–94 • *14,215*
Tigard, OR 97223 • *29,344*
Tillamook, OR 97141 • *4,001*
Tillamook □, OR • *21,570*
Tillman □, OK • *10,384*
Tillmans Corner, AL 36619 • *17,988*
Tillson, NY 12486 • *1,688*
Tilton, IL 61833 • *2,729*
Tilton, NH 03276 • *1,380*
Tiltonsville, OH 43963 • *1,517*
Timberlake, VA 24502 • *10,314*
Timberville, VA 22853 • *1,596*
Timmonsville, SC 29161 • *2,182*
Timpson, TX 75975 • *1,029*
Tinley Park, IL 60477 • *37,121*
Tinton Falls, NJ 07724 • *12,361*
Tioga, LA 71477 • *1,200*
Tioga, ND 58852 • *1,278*
Tioga □, NY • *52,337*
Tioga □, PA • *41,126*
Tippah □, MS • *19,523*
Tipp City, OH 45371 • *6,027*
Tippecanoe □, IN • *130,598*
Tipton, CA 93272 • *1,383*
Tipton, IN 46072 • *4,751*
Tipton, IA 52772 • *2,998*
Tipton, MO 65081 • *2,026*
Tipton, OK 73570 • *1,043*
Tipton □, IN • *16,119*
Tipton □, TN • *37,568*
Tiptonville, TN 38079 • *2,149*
Tishomingo, OK 73460 • *3,116*
Tishomingo □, MS • *17,683*
Titus □, TX • *24,009*
Titusville, FL 32780–83 • *39,394*
Titusville, PA 16354 • *6,434*
Tiverton, RI 02878 • *7,259*
Tivoli, NY 12583 • *1,035*
Toast, NC 27049 • *2,125*
Tobyhanna, PA 18466 • *1,200*
Toccoa, GA 30577 • *8,266*
Todd □, KY • *10,940*
Todd □, MN • *23,363*
Todd □, SD • *8,352*
Todd Estates, DE 19713 • *2,000*
Togiak, AK 99678 • *613*
Tohatchi, NM 87325 • *661*
Tok, AK 99780 • *935*
Toledo, IL 62468 • *1,199*

Toledo, IA 52342 • 2,380
Toledo, OH 43601–99 • 332,943
Toledo, OR 97391 • 3,174
Tolland, CT 06084 • 1,200
Tolland □, CT • 128,699
Tolleson, AZ 85353 • 4,434
Tolono, IL 61880 • 2,605
Toluca, IL 61369 • 1,315
Tomah, WI 54660 • 7,570
Tomahawk, WI 54487 • 3,328
Tomball, TX 77375 • 6,370
Tombstone, AZ 85638 • 1,220
Tom Green □, TX • 98,458
Tompkins □, NY • 94,097
Tompkinsville, KY 42167 • 2,861
Toms River, NJ 08753–57 • 7,524
Tonawanda, NY 14150–51 • 17,284
Tonawanda, NY 14223 • 65,284
Tonganoxie, KS 66086 • 2,347
Tonkawa, OK 74653 • 3,127
Tonopah, NV 89049 • 3,616
Tooele, UT 84074 • 13,887
Tooele □, UT • 26,601
Toole □, MT • 5,046
Toombs □, GA • 24,072
Topeka, KS 66601–99 • 119,883
Toppenish, WA 98948 • 7,419
Topsfield, MA 01983 • 2,711
Topsham, ME 04086 • 6,147
Topton, PA 19562 • 1,987
Toronto, OH 43964 • 6,127
Torrance, CA 90501–10 • 133,107
Torrance □, NM • 10,285
Torrington, CT 06790 • 33,687
Torrington, WY 82240 • 5,651
Totowa, NJ 07512 • 10,177
Touisset, MA 02777 • 1,520
Toulon, IL 61483 • 1,328
Towaco, NJ 07082 • 1,020
Towanda, KS 67144 • 1,289
Towanda, PA 18848 • 3,242
Tower City, PA 17980 • 1,518
Town and Country, WA 99210 • 4,921
Town Creek, AL 35672 • 1,379
Towner, ND 58788 • 669
Towner □, ND • 3,627
Town 'n Country, FL 33615 • 60,946
Towns □, GA • 6,754
Townsend, DE 19734 • 322
Townsend, MA 01469 • 1,164
Townsend, MT 59644 • 1,635
Towson, MD 21204 • 49,445
Tracy, CA 95376–78 • 33,558
Tracy, MN 56175 • 2,059
Tracy City, TN 37387 • 1,556
Tracyton, WA 98393 • 2,621
Traer, IA 50675 • 1,552
Trafford, PA 15085 • 3,345
Trail Creek, IN 46360 • 2,463
Traill □, ND • 8,752
Transylvania □, NC • 25,520
Travelers Rest, SC 29690 • 3,069
Traverse □, MN • 4,463
Traverse City, MI 49684 • 15,155
Travis □, TX • 576,407
Treasure □, MT • 874
Treasure Island, FL 33706 • 7,266
Trego □, KS • 3,694
Tremont, IL 61568 • 2,088
Tremont, PA 17981 • 1,814
Tremonton, UT 84337 • 4,264
Trempealeau, WI 54661 • 1,039
Trempealeau □, WI • 25,263
Trenton, FL 32693 • 1,287
Trenton, GA 30752 • 1,994
Trenton, IL 62293 • 2,481
Trenton, MI 48183 • 20,586
Trenton, MO 64683 • 6,129
Trenton, NJ 08601–91 • 88,675
Trenton, OH 45067 • 6,189
Trenton, TN 38382 • 4,836
Tresckow, PA 18254 • 1,033
Treutlen □, GA • 5,994
Trevorton, PA 17881 • 2,058
Triangle, VA 22172 • 4,740
Tri City, OR 97457 • 3,585
Trigg □, KY • 10,361
Tri Lakes, IN 46725 • 3,299
Trimble □, KY • 6,090
Trinidad, CO 81082 • 8,580
Trinidad, TX 75163 • 1,056
Trinity, AL 35673 • 1,380
Trinity, NC 27370 • 5,469
Trinity, TX 75862 • 2,648
Trinity □, CA • 13,063
Trinity □, TX • 11,445
Trion, GA 30753 • 1,661
Tripoli, IA 50676 • 1,188
Tripp □, SD • 6,924
Triumph, LA 70041 • 1,200
Trona, CA 93562 • 1,400
Trooper, PA 19401 • 5,137
Trotwood, OH 45426 • 8,816
Troup □, GA • 55,536
Trousdale □, TN • 5,920
Troutdale, OR 97060 • 7,852
Troutman, NC 28166 • 1,493
Troy, AL 36081 • 13,051
Troy, ID 83871 • 699
Troy, IL 62294 • 6,046
Troy, KS 66087 • 1,073
Troy, MI 48083–84 • 72,884
Troy, MO 63379 • 3,811
Troy, MT 59935 • 953
Troy, NH 03465 • 2,097
Troy, NY 12180–83 • 54,269
Troy, NC 27371 • 3,404
Troy, OH 45373 • 19,478
Troy, PA 16947 • 1,262
Troy, TN 38260 • 1,047
Truckee, CA 95734 • 3,484
Truman, MN 56088 • 1,292
Trumann, AR 72472 • 6,304
Trumansburg, NY 14886 • 1,611
Trumbull, CT 06611 • 32,000
Trumbull □, OH • 227,813
Trussville, AL 35173 • 8,266
Truth or Consequences (Hot Springs), NM 87901 • 6,221
Tryon, NC 28782 • 1,680
Tualatin, OR 97062 • 15,013
Tuba City, AZ 86045 • 7,323
Tuckahoe, NY 10707 • 6,302
Tucker, GA 30084 • 25,781
Tucker □, WV • 7,728
Tuckerman, AR 72473 • 2,020
Tuckerton, NJ 08087 • 3,048
Tucson, AZ 85701–51 • 405,390
Tucumcari, NM 88401 • 6,831
Tukwila, WA 98188 • 11,874
Tulare, CA 93274–75 • 33,249
Tulare □, CA • 311,921
Tularosa, NM 88352 • 2,615
Tulelake, CA 96134 • 1,010
Tulia, TX 79088 • 4,699
Tullahoma, TN 37388 • 16,761
Tulsa, OK 74101–94 • 367,302
Tulsa □, OK • 503,341
Tumwater, WA 98502 • 9,976
Tunica, MS 38676 • 1,175
Tunica □, MS • 8,164
Tunkhannock, PA 18657 • 2,251
Tununak, AK 99681 • 316
Tuolumne, CA 95379 • 1,686
Tuolumne □, CA • 48,456
Tupelo, MS 38801–03 • 30,685
Tupper Lake, NY 12986 • 4,087
Turley, OK 74156 • 2,930
Turlock, CA 95380–81 • 42,198
Turner, OR 97392 • 1,281
Turner □, GA • 8,703
Turner □, SD • 8,576
Turners Falls, MA 01376 • 4,731
Turtle Creek, PA 15145 • 6,556
Turtle Lake, ND 58575 • 681
Tuscaloosa, AL 35401–06 • 77,759
Tuscaloosa □, AL • 150,522
Tuscarawas □, OH • 84,090
Tuscola, IL 61953 • 4,155
Tuscola □, MI • 55,498
Tuscumbia, AL 35674 • 8,413
Tuskegee, AL 36083 • 12,257
Tustin, CA 92680–81 • 50,689
Tuttle, OK 73089 • 2,807
Tutwiler, MS 38963 • 1,391
Tuxedo Park, DE 19804 • 1,300
Twentynine Palms, CA 92277–78 • 11,821
Twiggs □, GA • 9,806
Twin City, GA 30471 • 1,466
Twin Falls, ID 83301–03 • 27,591
Twin Falls □, ID • 53,580
Twin Knolls, AZ 85207 • 5,210
Twin Lakes, CA 95060 • 5,379
Twin Lakes, WI 53181 • 3,989
Twin Rivers, NJ 08520 • 7,715
Twinsburg, OH 44087 • 9,606
Two Harbors, MN 55616 • 3,651
Two Rivers, WI 54241 • 13,030
Tybee Island, GA 31328 • 2,842
Tyler, MN 56178 • 1,257
Tyler, TX 75701–13 • 75,450
Tyler □, TX • 16,646
Tyler □, WV • 9,796
Tyler Heights, WV 25312 • 4,070
Tylertown, MS 39667 • 1,938
Tyndall, SD 57066 • 1,201
Tyrone, NM 88065 • 950
Tyrone, PA 16686 • 5,743
Tyrrell □, NC • 3,856
Tysons Corner, VA 22102 • 13,124

U

Ucon, ID 83454 • 895
Uhrichsville, OH 44683 • 5,604
Uinta □, WY • 18,705
Uintah □, UT • 22,211
Ukiah, CA 95482 • 14,599
Uleta, FL 33162 • 10,000
Ulster □, NY • 165,304
Ulysses, KS 67880 • 5,474
Umatilla, FL 32784 • 2,350
Umatilla, OR 97882 • 3,046
Umatilla □, OR • 59,249
Unadilla, GA 31091 • 1,620
Unadilla, NY 13849 • 1,265
Unalakleet, AK 99684 • 714
Unalaska, AK 99685 • 3,089
Uncasville, CT 06382 • 1,597
Underwood, AL 35630 • 1,950
Underwood, ND 58576 • 976
Unicoi □, TN • 16,549
Union, KY 41091 • 1,001
Union, MS 39365 • 1,875
Union, MO 63084 • 5,909
Union, NJ 07083 • 50,024
Union, OH 45322 • 5,501
Union, OR 97883 • 1,847
Union, SC 29379 • 9,836
Union, UT 84047 • 13,684
Union □, AR • 46,719
Union □, FL • 10,252
Union □, GA • 11,993
Union □, IL • 17,619
Union □, IN • 6,976
Union □, IA • 12,750
Union □, KY • 16,557
Union □, LA • 20,690
Union □, MS • 22,085
Union □, NJ • 493,819
Union □, NM • 4,124
Union □, NC • 84,211
Union □, OH • 31,969
Union □, OR • 23,598
Union □, PA • 36,176
Union □, SC • 30,337
Union □, SD • 10,189
Union □, TN • 13,694
Union Beach, NJ 07735 • 6,156
Union City, CA 94587 • 53,762
Union City, GA 30291 • 8,375
Union City, IN 47390 • 3,612
Union City, MI 49094 • 1,767
Union City, NJ 07087 • 58,012
Union City, OH 45390 • 1,984
Union City, OK 73090 • 1,000
Union City, PA 16438 • 3,537
Union City, TN 38261 • 10,513
Uniondale, NY 11553 • 20,328
Union Gap, WA 98903 • 3,120
Union Grove, WI 53182 • 3,669
Union Lake, MI 48386–87 • 8,500
Union Park, FL 32817 • 6,890
Union Pier, MI 49129 • 1,039
Union Point, GA 30669 • 1,753
Union Springs, AL 36089 • 3,975
Union Springs, NY 13160 • 1,142
Uniontown, AL 36786 • 1,730
Uniontown, KY 42461 • 1,008
Uniontown, OH 44685 • 1,500
Uniontown, PA 15401 • 12,034
Union Village, RI 02895 • 2,150
Unionville, CT 06085 • 3,500
Unionville, MO 63565 • 1,989
Universal City, TX 78148 • 13,057
University City, MO 63130 • 40,087
University Gardens, NY 11020 • 4,600
University Heights, IA 52240 • 1,042
University Heights, OH 44118 • 14,790
University Park, IL 60466 • 6,204
University Park, NM 88003 • 4,520
University Park, TX 75205 • 22,259
University Place, WA 98465 • 27,701
Upland, CA 91785–86 • 63,374
Upland, IN 46989 • 3,295
Upper Arlington, OH 43221 • 34,128
Upper Darby, PA 19082–83 • 84,054
Upper Dublin Township, PA 19002 • 22,348
Upper Greenwood Lake, NJ 07421 • 2,734
Upper Merion Township, PA 19406 • 26,138
Upper Moreland Township, PA 19090 • 25,874
Upper Providence Township, PA 19063 • 9,727
Upper Saddle River, NJ 07458 • 7,198
Upper Saint Clair, PA 15241 • 19,692
Upper Sandusky, OH 43351 • 5,906
Upshur □, TX • 31,370
Upshur □, WV • 22,867
Upson □, GA • 26,300
Upton, MA 01568 • 1,500
Upton, WY 82730 • 980
Upton □, TX • 4,447
Urbana, IL 61801 • 36,344
Urbana, OH 43078 • 11,353
Urbandale, IA 50322 • 23,500
Usquepaug, RI 02892 • 400
Utah □, UT • 263,590
Utica, MI 48315–18 • 5,081
Utica, MS 39175 • 1,033
Utica, NY 13501–05 • 68,637
Utica, OH 43080 • 1,997
Uvalde, TX 78801–02 • 14,729
Uvalde □, TX • 23,340
Uxbridge, MA 01569 • 3,340

V

Vacaville, CA 95687–88 • 71,479
Vacherie, LA 70090 • 2,169
Vadnais Heights, MN 55110 • 11,041
Vail, CO 81657–58 • 3,659
Valatie, NY 12184 • 1,487
Valdese, NC 28690 • 3,914
Valdez, AK 99686 • 4,068
Valdosta, GA 31601–04 • 39,806
Vale, OR 97918 • 1,491
Valencia, AZ 85326 • 1,200
Valencia □, NM • 45,235
Valencia Heights, SC 29205 • 4,122
Valentine, NE 69201 • 2,826
Valhalla, NY 10595 • 6,200
Valinda, CA 91744 • 18,735
Vallejo, CA 94589–92 • 109,199
Valle Vista, CA 92343 • 8,751
Valley, AL 36854 • 8,173
Valley, NE 68064 • 1,775
Valley □, ID • 6,109
Valley □, MT • 8,239
Valley □, NE • 5,169
Valley Center, KS 67147 • 3,624
Valley City, ND 58072 • 7,163
Valley Cottage, NY 10989 • 9,007
Valley Falls, KS 66088 • 1,253
Valley Falls, RI 02864 • 11,175
Valley Forge, PA 19481–82 • 1,500
Valley Mills, TX 76689 • 1,085
Valley Park, MO 63088 • 4,165
Valley Ridge, WA 98188 • 6,500
Valley Springs, SD 57068 • 739
Valley Station, KY 40272 • 22,840
Valley Stream, NY 11580–82 • 33,946
Valley View, PA 17983 • 1,749
Valparaiso, FL 32580 • 4,672
Valparaiso, IN 46383–84 • 24,414
Val Verda, UT 84010 • 3,712
Val Verde □, TX • 38,721
Van, TX 75790 • 1,854
Van Alstyne, TX 75095 • 2,090
Van Buren, AR 72956 • 14,979
Van Buren, ME 04785 • 2,759
Van Buren □, AR • 14,008
Van Buren □, IA • 7,676
Van Buren □, MI • 70,060
Van Buren □, TN • 4,846
Vance □, NC • 38,892
Vanceburg, KY 41179 • 1,713
Vancleave, MS 39564 • 3,214
Vancouver, WA 98660–68 • 46,380
Vandalia, IL 62471 • 6,114
Vandalia, MO 63382 • 2,683
Vandalia, OH 45377 • 13,882
Vandenberg Village, CA 93436 • 5,871
Vander, NC 28301 • 1,179
Vanderburgh □, IN • 165,058
Vandergrift, PA 15690 • 5,904
Van Horn, TX 79855 • 2,930
Van Lear, KY 41265 • 1,050
Vansant, VA 24656 • 1,187
Van Vleck, TX 77482 • 1,534
Van Wert, OH 45891 • 10,891
Van Wert □, OH • 30,464
Van Zandt □, TX • 37,944
Varina, VA 23231 • 2,500
Varnville, SC 29944 • 1,970
Vassar, MI 48768 • 2,559
Vaughn, MT 59487 • 2,270
Veazie, ME 04401 • 1,610
Veedersburg, IN 47987 • 2,192
Velda Rose Estates, AZ 85205 • 2,330
Velva, ND 58790 • 968
Venango □, PA • 59,381
Veneta, OR 97487 • 2,519
Venice, FL 34292–93 • 16,922
Venice, IL 62090 • 3,571
Venice Gardens, FL 34293 • 7,701
Ventnor City, NJ 08406 • 11,005
Ventura (San Buenaventura), CA 93001–07 • 92,575
Ventura □, CA • 669,016
Veradale, WA 99037 • 7,836
Verda, KY 40828 • 1,133
Verdi, NV 89439 • 1,140
Vergennes, VT 05491 • 2,578
Vermilion, OH 44089 • 11,127
Vermilion □, IL • 88,257
Vermilion □, LA • 50,055
Vermillion, SD 57069 • 10,034
Vermillion □, IN • 16,773
Vernal, UT 84078–79 • 6,644
Vernon, AL 35592 • 2,247
Vernon, CT 06066 • 30,200
Vernon, TX 76384 • 12,001
Vernon □, LA • 61,961
Vernon □, MO • 19,041
Vernon □, WI • 25,617
Vernon Hills, IL 60061 • 15,319
Vernonia, OR 97064 • 1,808
Vero Beach, FL 32960–68 • 17,350
Verona, MS 38879 • 2,893
Verona, NJ 07044 • 13,597
Verona, PA 15147 • 3,260
Verona, WI 53593 • 5,374
Versailles, IN 47042 • 1,791
Versailles, KY 40383 • 7,269
Versailles, MO 65084 • 2,365
Versailles, OH 45380 • 2,351
Vestal, NY 13850–51 • 5,530
Vestavia Hills, AL 35216 • 19,749
Vevay, IN 47043 • 1,393
Vian, OK 74962 • 1,414
Vicksburg, MI 49097 • 2,216
Vicksburg, MS 39180–82 • 20,908
Victor, NY 14564 • 2,308
Victoria, KS 67671 • 1,157
Victoria, TX 77901–05 • 55,076
Victoria, VA 23974 • 1,830
Victoria □, TX • 74,361
Victorville, CA 92392–93 • 40,674
Vidalia, GA 30474 • 11,078
Vidalia, LA 71373 • 4,953
Vidor, TX 77662 • 10,935
Vienna, GA 31092 • 2,708
Vienna, IL 62995 • 1,446
Vienna, VA 22180–83 • 14,852
Vienna, WV 26105 • 10,862
View Park, CA 90043 • 5,900
Vigo □, IN • 106,107
Vilas □, WI • 17,707
Villa Grove, IL 61956 • 2,734
Villa Hills, KY 41016 • 7,739
Villa Park, CA 92667 • 6,299
Villa Park, IL 60181 • 22,253
Villa Rica, GA 30180 • 6,542
Villas, NJ 08251 • 8,136
Ville Platte, LA 70586 • 9,037
Villisca, IA 50864 • 1,332
Vilonia, AR 72173 • 1,133
Vincennes, IN 47591 • 19,859
Vincent, AL 35178 • 1,767
Vine Grove, KY 40175 • 3,586
Vineland, NJ 08360 • 54,780
Vineyard Haven, MA 02568 • 1,762
Vinita, OK 74301 • 5,804
Vinton, IA 52349 • 5,103
Vinton, LA 70668 • 3,154
Vinton, VA 24179 • 7,665
Vinton □, OH • 11,098
Viola, NY 10952 • 4,504
Violet, LA 70092 • 8,574
Virden, IL 62690 • 3,635
Virginia, IL 62691 • 1,767
Virginia, MN 55792 • 9,410
Virginia Beach, VA 23450–67 • 393,069
Virginia City, NV 89440 • 920
Viroqua, WI 54665 • 3,922
Visalia, CA 93277–79 • 75,636
Vista, CA 92083–84 • 71,872
Vivian, LA 71082 • 4,156
Volcano, HI 96785 • 1,516
Volga, SD 57071 • 1,263
Volusia □, FL • 370,712

W

Wabash, IN 46992 • 12,127
Wabash □, IL • 13,111
Wabash □, IN • 35,069
Wabasha, MN 55981 • 2,384
Wabasha □, MN • 19,744
Wabasso, FL 32970 • 1,145
Wabaunsee □, KS • 6,603
Waco, TX 76701–16 • 103,590
Waconia, MN 55387 • 3,498
Wade Hampton, SC 29607 • 20,014
Wadena, MN 56482 • 4,131
Wadena □, MN • 13,154
Wadesboro, NC 28170 • 3,645
Wading River, NY 11792 • 5,317
Wadley, GA 30477 • 2,473
Wadsworth, IL 60083 • 1,826
Wadsworth, NV 89442 • 640
Wadsworth, OH 44281 • 15,718
Wagner, SD 57380 • 1,462
Wagoner, OK 74467 • 6,894
Wagoner □, OK • 47,883
Wahiawa, HI 96786 • 17,386
Wahkiakum □, WA • 3,327
Wahoo, NE 68066 • 3,681
Wahpeton, ND 58074–75 • 8,751
Waialua, HI 96791 • 3,943
Waianae, HI 96792 • 8,758
Waikapu, HI 96793 • 729
Wailua, HI 96746 • 2,018
Wailuku, HI 96793 • 10,688
Waimanalo, HI 96795 • 3,508
Waimea, HI 96712 • 600
Waimea, HI 96796 • 5,972
Wainwright, AK 99782 • 492
Waipahu, HI 96797 • 31,435
Waipio Acres, HI 96786 • 5,304
Waite Park, MN 56387 • 5,020
Wakarusa, IN 46573 • 1,667
Wake □, NC • 423,380
Wa Keeney, KS 67672 • 2,161
Wakefield, MA 01880 • 24,825
Wakefield, MI 49968 • 2,318
Wakefield, NE 68784 • 1,082
Wakefield, RI 02879–83 • 3,450
Wakefield, VA 23888 • 1,070
Wake Forest, NC 27587–88 • 5,769
Wakulla □, FL • 14,202
Walbridge, OH 43465 • 2,736
Walcott, IA 52773 • 1,356
Walden, NY 12586 • 5,836
Waldo, AR 71770 • 1,495
Waldo, FL 32694 • 1,017
Waldo □, ME • 33,018
Waldoboro, ME 04572 • 1,420
Waldport, OR 97394 • 1,595
Waldron, AR 72958 • 3,024
Waldwick, NJ 07463 • 9,757
Walhalla, ND 58282 • 1,131
Walhalla, SC 29691 • 3,755
Walker, LA 70785 • 3,727
Walker, MI 49504 • 17,279
Walker □, AL • 67,670
Walker □, GA • 58,340
Walker □, TX • 50,917
Walkersville, MD 21793 • 4,145
Walkerton, IN 46574 • 2,061
Walkertown, NC 27051 • 1,200
Walkerville, MT 59701 • 605
Wall, SD 57790 • 834
Wallace, ID 83873 • 1,010
Wallace, NC 28466 • 2,939
Wallace □, KS • 1,821
Walla Walla, WA 99362 • 26,478
Walla Walla □, WA • 48,439
Walled Lake, MI 48390 • 6,278
Wallen, IN 46806 • 1,000
Waller, TX 77484 • 1,493
Waller □, TX • 23,390
Wallingford, CT 06492 • 17,827
Wallingford, VT 05773 • 1,148
Wallington, NJ 07057 • 10,828
Wallis, TX 77485 • 1,001
Wallkill, NY 12589 • 2,125
Wallowa □, OR • 6,911
Walnut, CA 91789 • 29,105
Walnut, IL 61376 • 1,463
Walnut Cove, NC 27052 • 1,088
Walnut Creek, CA 94593–98 • 60,569
Walnut Park, CA 90255 • 14,722
Walnutport, PA 18088 • 2,055
Walnut Ridge, AR 72476 • 4,388
Walpole, MA 02081 • 5,495
Walsenburg, CO 81089 • 3,300
Walsh □, ND • 13,840
Walterboro, SC 29488 • 5,492
Walters, OK 73572 • 2,519
Walthall □, MS • 14,352
Waltham, MA 02154 • 57,878
Walthourville, GA 31333 • 2,024
Walton, IN 46994 • 1,053
Walton, KY 41094 • 2,034
Walton, NY 13856 • 3,326
Walton □, FL • 27,760
Walton □, GA • 38,586
Walworth, WI 53184 • 1,614
Walworth □, SD • 6,087
Walworth □, WI • 75,000
Wamac, IL 62801 • 1,501
Wamego, KS 66547 • 3,706
Wamesit, MA 01876 • 2,700
Wamsutter, WY 82336 • 240
Wanaque, NJ 07465 • 9,711
Wanchese, NC 27981 • 1,380
Wando Woods, SC 29405 • 5,253
Wantagh, NY 11793 • 18,567
Wapakoneta, OH 45895 • 9,214
Wapato, WA 98951 • 3,795
Wapello, IA 52653 • 2,013
Wapello □, IA • 35,687
Wappingers Falls, NY 12590 • 4,605
War, WV 24892 • 1,081
Ward, AR 72176 • 1,269
Ward □, ND • 57,921
Ward □, TX • 13,115
Warden, WA 98857 • 1,639
Ware, MA 01082 • 6,533
Ware □, GA • 35,471
Wareham, MA 02571 • 2,607
Warehouse Point, CT 06088 • 1,880
Ware Shoals, SC 29692 • 2,497
Waretown, NJ 08758 • 1,283
Warminster, PA 18974 • 35,463
Warner, OK 74469 • 1,479
Warner Robins, GA 31088 • 43,726
Warr Acres, OK 73132 • 9,288
Warren, AR 71671 • 6,455
Warren, IL 61087 • 1,550
Warren, IN 46792 • 1,185
Warren, MA 01083 • 1,516
Warren, MI 48089–93 • 144,864
Warren, MN 56762 • 1,813
Warren, OH 44481–85 • 50,793
Warren, PA 16365 • 11,122
Warren, RI 02885 • 11,385
Warren, VT 05674 • 350
Warren □, GA • 6,078
Warren □, IL • 19,181
Warren □, IN • 8,176
Warren □, IA • 36,033
Warren □, KY • 76,673
Warren □, MS • 47,880
Warren □, MO • 19,534
Warren □, NJ • 91,607
Warren □, NY • 59,209
Warren □, NC • 17,265
Warren □, OH • 113,909
Warren □, PA • 45,050
Warren □, TN • 32,992
Warren □, VA • 26,142
Warren Park, IN 46219 • 1,763
Warrensburg, IL 62573 • 1,274
Warrensburg, MO 64093 • 15,244
Warrensburg, NY 12885 • 3,204
Warrensville Heights, OH 44122 • 15,745
Warrenton, GA 30828 • 2,056
Warrenton, MO 63383 • 3,564
Warrenton, OR 97146 • 2,681
Warrenton, VA 22186 • 4,830
Warrenville, IL 60555 • 11,333
Warrenville, SC 29851 • 1,029
Warrick □, IN • 44,920
Warrington, FL 32507 • 16,040
Warrington, PA 18976 • 6,980

Warrior, AL 35180 • *3,280*
Warroad, MN 56763 • *1,679*
Warsaw, IL 62379 • *1,882*
Warsaw, IN 46580–81 • *10,968*
Warsaw, KY 41095 • *1,202*
Warsaw, MO 65355 • *1,696*
Warsaw, NY 14569 • *3,830*
Warsaw, NC 28398 • *2,859*
Warwick, NY 10990 • *5,984*
Warwick, RI 02886–89 • *85,427*
Wasatch □, UT • *10,089*
Wasco, CA 93280 • *12,412*
Wasco □, OR • *21,683*
Waseca, MN 56093 • *8,385*
Waseca □, MN • *18,079*
Washakie □, WY • *8,388*
Washburn, IL 61570 • *1,075*
Washburn, IA 50706 • *1,400*
Washburn, ME 04786 • *1,880*
Washburn, ND 58577 • *1,506*
Washburn, WI 54891 • *2,285*
Washburn □, WI • *13,772*
Washington, DC 20001–99 • *606,900*
Washington, GA 30673 • *4,279*
Washington, IL 61571 • *10,099*
Washington, IN 47501 • *10,838*
Washington, IA 52353 • *7,074*
Washington, KS 66968 • *1,304*
Washington, LA 70589 • *1,253*
Washington, MO 63090 • *10,704*
Washington, NJ 07882 • *6,474*
Washington, NC 27889 • *9,075*
Washington, PA 15301 • *15,864*
Washington, UT 84780 • *4,198*
Washington □, AL • *16,694*
Washington □, AR • *113,409*
Washington □, CO • *4,812*
Washington □, FL • *16,919*
Washington □, GA • *19,112*
Washington □, ID • *8,550*
Washington □, IL • *14,965*
Washington □, IN • *23,717*
Washington □, IA • *19,612*
Washington □, KS • *7,073*
Washington □, KY • *10,441*
Washington □, LA • *43,185*
Washington □, ME • *35,308*
Washington □, MD • *121,393*
Washington □, MN • *145,896*
Washington □, MS • *67,935*
Washington □, MO • *20,380*
Washington □, NE • *16,607*
Washington □, NY • *59,330*
Washington □, NC • *13,997*
Washington □, OH • *62,254*
Washington □, OK • *48,066*
Washington □, OR • *311,554*
Washington □, PA • *204,584*
Washington □, RI • *110,006*
Washington □, TN • *92,315*
Washington □, TX • *26,154*
Washington □, UT • *48,560*
Washington □, VT • *54,928*
Washington □, VA • *45,887*
Washington □, WI • *95,328*
Washington Court House, OH 43160 • *12,983*
Washington Park, FL 33314 • *6,930*
Washington Park, IL 62204 • *7,431*
Washington Terrace, UT 84403 • *8,189*
Washington Township, NJ 07675 • *9,245*
Washita □, OK • *11,441*
Washoe □, NV • *254,667*
Washoe City, NV 89701 • *400*
Washougal, WA 98671 • *4,764*
Washtenaw □, MI • *282,937*
Wasilla, AK 99687 • *4,028*
Waskom, TX 75692 • *1,812*
Watauga, TX 76148 • *20,009*
Watauga □, NC • *36,952*
Watchung, NJ 07060 • *5,110*
Waterbury, CT 06701–26 • *108,961*
Waterbury, VT 05676 • *1,702*
Waterbury Center, VT 05677 • *500*
Waterford, CT 06385 • *17,930*
Waterford, MI 48327–29 • *66,692*
Waterford, NY 12188 • *2,370*
Waterford, PA 16441 • *1,492*
Waterford, WI 53185 • *2,431*
Waterford Works, NJ 08089 • *1,200*
Waterloo, IL 62298 • *5,072*
Waterloo, IN 46793 • *2,040*
Waterloo, IA 50701–07 • *66,467*
Waterloo, NY 13165 • *5,116*
Waterloo, WI 53594 • *2,712*
Waterman, IL 60556 • *1,074*
Waterproof, LA 71375 • *1,080*
Watertown, CT 06795 • *20,456*
Watertown, FL 32055 • *3,340*
Watertown, MA 02172 • *33,284*
Watertown, NY 13601–03 • *29,429*
Watertown, SD 57201 • *17,592*
Watertown, TN 37184 • *1,250*
Watertown, WI 53094 • *19,142*
Water Valley, MS 38965 • *3,610*
Waterville, ME 04901–03 • *17,173*
Waterville, MN 56096 • *1,771*
Waterville, NY 13480 • *1,664*
Waterville, OH 43566 • *4,517*
Watervliet, MI 49098 • *1,867*
Watervliet, NY 12189 • *11,061*
Watford City, ND 58854 • *1,784*
Wathena, KS 66090 • *1,160*
Watkins Glen, NY 14891 • *2,207*
Watkinsville, GA 30677 • *1,600*
Watonga, OK 73772 • *3,408*
Watonwan □, MN • *11,682*
Watseka, IL 60970 • *5,424*
Watsontown, PA 17777 • *2,310*
Watsonville, CA 95076–77 • *31,099*
Wattsville, SC 29360 • *1,324*
Wauchula, FL 33873 • *3,253*
Wauconda, IL 60084 • *6,294*
Waukee, IA 50263 • *2,512*
Waukegan, IL 60085–87 • *69,392*
Waukesha, WI 53186–88 • *56,958*
Waukesha □, WI • *304,715*
Waukomis, OK 73773 • *1,322*
Waukon, IA 52172 • *4,019*
Waunakee, WI 53597 • *5,897*
Waupaca, WI 54981 • *4,957*
Waupaca □, WI • *46,104*
Waupun, WI 53963 • *8,207*

Wauregan, CT 06387 • *1,200*
Waurika, OK 73573 • *2,088*
Wausau, WI 54401–02 • *37,060*
Wauseon, OH 43567 • *6,322*
Waushara □, WI • *19,385*
Wautoma, WI 54982 • *1,784*
Wauwatosa, WI 53213 • *49,366*
Waveland, MS 39576 • *5,369*
Waverly, IL 62692 • *1,402*
Waverly, IA 50677 • *8,539*
Waverly, MI 48917 • *15,614*
Waverly, NE 68462 • *1,869*
Waverly, NY 14892 • *4,787*
Waverly, OH 45690 • *4,477*
Waverly, TN 37185 • *3,925*
Waverly, VA 23890 • *2,223*
Waxahachie, TX 75165 • *18,168*
Waxhaw, NC 28173 • *1,294*
Waycross, GA 31501 • *16,410*
Wayland, MA 01778 • *2,550*
Wayland, MI 49348 • *2,751*
Wayland, NY 14572 • *1,976*
Waylyn, SC 29405 • *2,400*
Waymart, PA 18472 • *1,337*
Wayne, MI 48184–88 • *19,899*
Wayne, NE 68787 • *5,142*
Wayne, NJ 07470–74 • *47,025*
Wayne, WV 25570 • *1,128*
Wayne □, GA • *22,356*
Wayne □, IL • *17,241*
Wayne □, IN • *71,951*
Wayne □, IA • *7,067*
Wayne □, KY • *17,468*
Wayne □, MI • *2,111,687*
Wayne □, MS • *19,517*
Wayne □, MO • *11,543*
Wayne □, NE • *9,364*
Wayne □, NY • *89,123*
Wayne □, NC • *104,666*
Wayne □, OH • *101,461*
Wayne □, PA • *39,944*
Wayne □, TN • *13,935*
Wayne □, UT • *2,177*
Wayne □, WV • *41,636*
Wayne City, IL 62895 • *1,099*
Waynesboro, GA 30830 • *5,701*
Waynesboro, MS 39367 • *5,143*
Waynesboro, PA 17268 • *9,578*
Waynesboro, TN 38485 • *1,824*
Waynesboro, VA 22980 • *18,549*
Waynesburg, OH 44688 • *1,068*
Waynesburg, PA 15370 • *4,270*
Waynesville, MO 65583 • *3,207*
Waynesville, NC 28786 • *6,758*
Waynesville, OH 45068 • *1,949*
Waynewood, VA 22308 • *5,000*
Wayzata, MN 55391 • *3,806*
Weakley □, TN • *31,972*
Weatherford, OK 73096 • *10,124*
Weatherford, TX 76086–87 • *14,804*
Weatherly, PA 18255 • *2,640*
Weatogue, CT 06089 • *2,521*
Weaver, AL 36277 • *2,715*
Weaverville, CA 96093 • *3,370*
Weaverville, NC 28787 • *2,107*
Webb, AL 36376 • *1,039*
Webb □, TX • *133,239*
Webb City, MO 64870 • *7,449*
Webberville, MI 48892 • *1,698*
Weber □, UT • *158,330*
Weber City, VA 24251 • *1,377*
Webster, MA 01570 • *11,849*
Webster, NY 14580 • *5,464*
Webster, PA 15087 • *1,000*
Webster, SD 57274 • *2,017*
Webster □, GA • *2,263*
Webster □, IA • *40,342*
Webster □, KY • *13,955*
Webster □, LA • *41,989*
Webster □, MS • *10,222*
Webster □, MO • *23,753*
Webster □, NE • *4,279*
Webster □, WV • *10,729*
Webster City, IA 50595 • *7,894*
Webster Groves, MO 63119 • *22,987*
Websterville, VT 05678 • *600*
Wedgewood, MO 63031 • *6,700*
Weed, CA 96094 • *3,062*
Weed Heights, NV 89447 • *230*
Weedsport, NY 13166 • *1,996*
Weehawken, NJ 07087 • *12,385*
Weeping Water, NE 68463 • *1,008*
Weigelstown, PA 17315 • *8,665*
Weimar, TX 78962 • *2,052*
Weippe, ID 83553 • *532*
Weirsdale, FL 32195 • *1,500*
Weirton, WV 26062 • *22,124*
Weiser, ID 83672 • *4,571*
Wekiva Springs, FL 32750 • *23,026*
Welch, WV 24801 • *3,028*
Welcome, SC 29611 • *6,560*
Weld □, CO • *131,821*
Weldon, NC 27890 • *1,392*
Weleetka, OK 74880 • *1,112*
Wellesley, MA 02181 • *26,615*
Wellfleet, MA 02667 • *1,200*
Wellford, SC 29385 • *2,511*
Wellington, CO 80549 • *1,340*
Wellington, FL 33414 • *20,670*
Wellington, KS 67152 • *8,411*
Wellington, NV 89444 • *280*
Wellington, OH 44090 • *4,140*
Wellington, TX 79095 • *2,456*
Wellington, UT 84542 • *1,632*
Wellman, IA 52356 • *1,085*
Wells, ME 04090 • *1,200*
Wells, MI 49894 • *1,150*
Wells, MN 56097 • *2,465*
Wells, NV 89835 • *1,256*
Wells □, IN • *25,948*
Wells □, ND • *5,864*
Wellsboro, PA 16901 • *3,430*
Wellsburg, WV 26070 • *3,385*
Wellston, OH 45692 • *6,049*
Wellsville, KS 66092 • *1,563*
Wellsville, MO 63384 • *1,430*
Wellsville, NY 14895 • *5,241*
Wellsville, OH 43968 • *4,532*
Wellsville, UT 84339 • *2,206*
Wellton, AZ 85356 • *1,066*
Welsh, LA 70591 • *3,299*
Wenatchee, WA 98801–07 • *21,756*
Wendell, ID 83355 • *1,963*

Wendell, NC 27591 • *2,822*
Wendover, UT 84083 • *1,127*
Wenham, MA 01984 • *3,897*
Wenonah, NJ 08090 • *2,331*
Wentzville, MO 63385 • *5,088*
Weslaco, TX 78596 • *21,877*
Wesleyville, PA 16510 • *3,655*
Wessington Springs, SD 57382 • *1,083*
Wesson, MS 39191 • *1,510*
West, TX 76691 • *2,515*
West Acton, MA 01720 • *5,230*
West Alexandria, OH 45381 • *1,460*
West Allis, WI 53214 • *63,221*
West Andover, MA 01810 • *1,970*
West Athens, CA 90247 • *8,859*
West Babylon, NY 11704 • *42,410*
West Barnstable, MA 02668 • *1,000*
West Baton Rouge □, LA • *19,419*
West Bay Shore, NY 11706 • *4,907*
West Bend, WI 53095 • *23,916*
West Berlin, NJ 08091 • *2,970*
West Billerica, MA 01862 • *1,920*
West Blocton, AL 35184 • *1,468*
Westborough, MA 01581 • *3,917*
West Bountiful, UT 84087 • *4,477*
West Boylston, MA 01583 • *3,130*
West Bradenton, FL 34205 • *4,528*
West Branch, IA 52358 • *1,908*
West Branch, MI 48661 • *1,914*
West Bridgewater, MA 02379 • *2,140*
Westbrook, CT 06498 • *2,060*
Westbrook, ME 04092 • *16,121*
West Brookfield, MA 01585 • *1,419*
West Burlington, IA 52655 • *3,083*
Westbury, NY 11590 • *13,060*
Westby, WI 54667 • *1,866*
West Caldwell, NJ 07004 • *10,422*
West Cape May, NJ 08204 • *1,026*
West Carroll □, LA • *12,093*
West Carrollton, OH 45449 • *14,403*
West Carson, CA 90502 • *20,143*
West Carthage, NY 13619 • *2,166*
West Chatham, MA 02669 • *1,504*
Westchester, FL 33136 • *29,883*
Westchester, IL 60153 • *17,301*
West Chester, PA 19380–82 • *18,041*
Westchester □, NY • *874,866*
West Chicago, IL 60185–86 • *14,796*
West Columbia, SC 29169–72 • *10,588*
West Columbia, TX 77486 • *4,372*
West Compton, CA 90220 • *5,451*
West Concord, MA 01742 • *5,761*
West Concord, NC 28027 • *5,859*
West Covina, CA 91790–93 • *96,086*
West Crossett, AR 71635 • *2,019*
West Dennis, MA 02670 • *2,307*
West Des Moines, IA 50265 • *31,702*
West Elmira, NY 14905 • *5,218*
Westerly, RI 02891 • *16,477*
Westernport, MD 21562 • *2,454*
Western Springs, IL 60558 • *11,984*
Westerville, OH 43081–82 • *30,269*
West Fairview, PA 17025 • *1,403*
West Falmouth, MA 02574 • *1,600*
West Fargo, ND 58078 • *12,287*
West Feliciana □, LA • *12,915*
Westfield, IN 46074 • *3,304*
Westfield, MA 01085–86 • *38,372*
Westfield, NJ 07090–92 • *28,870*
Westfield, NY 14787 • *3,451*
Westfield, PA 16950 • *1,119*
Westfield, WI 53964 • *1,125*
Westford, MA 01886 • *1,200*
West Fork, AR 72774 • *1,607*
West Frankfort, IL 62896 • *8,526*
West Freehold, NJ 07728 • *11,166*
Westgate, FL 33401 • *2,100*
West Gate, VA 22110 • *6,565*
West Gate of Lomond, VA 22110 • *5,400*
West Glens Falls, NY 12801 • *5,964*
West Goshen, PA 19380 • *8,948*
West Grove, PA 19390 • *2,128*
Westham, VA 23229 • *3,200*
West Hanover, MA 02339 • *1,700*
West Hartford, CT 06127 • *60,110*
West Haven, CT 06516 • *54,021*
West Haven, OR 97225 • *3,400*
West Haverstraw, NY 10993 • *9,183*
West Hazleton, PA 18201 • *4,136*
West Helena, AR 72390 • *9,695*
West Hempstead, NY 11552 • *17,689*
West Hollywood, CA 90069 • *36,118*
Westhope, ND 58793 • *578*
West Hyannisport, MA 02672 • *1,200*
West Islip, NY 11795 • *28,419*
West Jefferson, NC 28694 • *1,002*
West Jefferson, OH 43162 • *4,504*
West Jordan, UT 84084 • *42,892*
West Kingston, RI 02892 • *1,150*
West Lafayette, IN 47906–07 • *25,907*
West Lafayette, OH 43845 • *2,129*
Westlake, LA 70669 • *5,007*
Westlake, OH 44145 • *27,018*
Westlake Village, CA 91361 • *7,455*
Westland, MI 48185 • *84,724*
West Lawn, PA 19609 • *1,606*
West Liberty, IA 52776 • *2,935*
West Liberty, KY 41472 • *1,887*
West Liberty, OH 43357 • *1,613*
West Liberty, WV 26074 • *1,434*
West Linn, OR 97068 • *16,367*
West Long Branch, NJ 07764 • *7,690*
West Marion, NC 28752 • *1,291*
West Medway, MA 02053 • *1,940*
West Melbourne, FL 32901 • *8,399*
West Memphis, AR 72301 • *28,259*
Westmere, NY 12203 • *6,750*
West Miami, FL 33174 • *5,727*
West Mifflin, PA 15122–23 • *23,644*
West Milford, NJ 07480 • *25,430*
West Milton, OH 45383 • *4,348*
West Milwaukee, WI 53214 • *3,973*
Westminster, CA 92683–84 • *78,118*
Westminster, CO 80030–31 • *74,625*
Westminster, MD 21157 • *13,068*
Westminster, SC 29693 • *3,120*
West Modesto, CA 95351 • *6,135*
West Monroe, LA 71291–94 • *14,096*
Westmont, CA 90044 • *31,100*
Westmont, IL 60559 • *21,228*
Westmont, NJ 08108 • *5,630*
Westmont, PA 15905 • *5,789*
Westmoreland, TN 37186 • *1,726*

Westmoreland □, PA • *370,321*
Westmoreland □, VA • *15,480*
Westmorland, CA 92281 • *1,380*
West Mystic, CT 06388 • *3,595*
West Newton, PA 15089 • *3,152*
West New York, NJ 07093 • *38,125*
West Norriton, PA 19401 • *15,209*
West Nyack, NY 10960 • *3,437*
Weston, CT 06883 • *1,370*
Weston, MA 02193 • *11,169*
Weston, MO 64098 • *1,528*
Weston, OH 43569 • *1,716*
Weston, WV 26452 • *4,994*
Weston, WI 54476 • *9,714*
Weston □, WY • *6,518*
West Orange, NJ 07052 • *39,103*
Westover, WV 26505 • *4,201*
West Palm Beach, FL 33401–20 • *67,643*
West Pasco, WA 99301 • *7,312*
West Paterson, NJ 07424 • *10,982*
West Pawlet, VT 05775 • *350*
West Pensacola, FL 32505 • *22,107*
West Peoria, IL 61604 • *5,314*
West Pittsburg, CA 94565 • *17,453*
West Pittsburg, PA 16160 • *1,133*
West Pittston, PA 18643 • *5,590*
West Plains, MO 65775 • *8,913*
West Point, CA 95255 • *1,500*
West Point, GA 31833 • *3,571*
West Point, IA 52656 • *1,079*
West Point, KY 40177 • *1,216*
West Point, MS 39773 • *8,489*
West Point, NE 68788 • *3,250*
West Point, NY 10996–97 • *8,024*
West Point, UT 84015 • *4,258*
West Point, VA 23181 • *2,938*
Westport, CT 06880–83 • *24,407*
Westport, IN 47283 • *1,478*
Westport, WA 98595 • *1,892*
West Portsmouth, OH 45662 • *3,551*
West Puente Valley, CA 91744 • *20,254*
West Reading, PA 19611 • *4,142*
West Rutland, VT 05777 • *2,246*
West Sacramento, CA 95691 • *28,898*
West Saint Paul, MN 55118 • *19,248*
West Salem, IL 62476 • *1,042*
West Salem, OH 44287 • *1,534*
West Salem, WI 54669 • *3,611*
West Sayville, NY 11796 • *4,680*
West Seneca, NY 14224 • *47,866*
West Simsbury, CT 06092 • *2,149*
West Slope, OR 97225 • *7,959*
West Springfield, MA 01089–90 • *27,537*
West Springfield, VA 22152 • *28,126*
West Swanzey, NH 03469 • *1,055*
West Terre Haute, IN 47885 • *2,495*
West Union, IA 52175 • *2,490*
West Union, OH 45693 • *3,096*
West Unity, OH 43570 • *1,677*
West University Place, TX 77005 • *12,920*
West Upton, MA 01587 • *1,300*
Westvale, NY 13219 • *5,952*
West Valley City, UT 84120 • *86,976*
Westview, FL 33168 • *9,668*
West View, PA 15229 • *7,734*
Westville, IL 61883 • *3,387*
Westville, IN 46391 • *5,255*
Westville, NJ 08093 • *4,573*
Westville, OK 74965 • *1,374*
West Wareham, MA 02576 • *2,059*
West Warren, MA 01092 • *1,200*
West Warwick, RI 02893 • *29,268*
West Webster, NY 14580 • *8,690*
Westwego, LA 70094–96 • *11,218*
West Whittier, CA 90606 • *13,800*
West Willow, MI 48198 • *4,300*
Westwood, CA 96137 • *2,017*
Westwood, KS 66205 • *1,772*
Westwood, KY 41101 • *5,300*
Westwood, MA 02090 • *6,500*
Westwood, MI 49007 • *8,957*
Westwood, NJ 07675 • *10,446*
Westwood Lakes, FL 33165 • *11,522*
West Wyoming, PA 18644 • *3,117*
West Yarmouth, MA 02673 • *5,409*
West Yellowstone, MT 59758 • *913*
West York, PA 17404 • *4,283*
Wethersfield, CT 06129 • *25,651*
Wetumka, OK 74883 • *1,427*
Wetumpka, AL 36092 • *4,670*
Wetzel □, WV • *19,258*
Wewahitchka, FL 32465 • *1,779*
Wewoka, OK 74884 • *4,050*
Wexford □, MI • *26,360*
Weyauwega, WI 54983 • *1,665*
Weymouth, MA 02188 • *54,063*
Whalom, MA 01420 • *1,340*
Wharton, NJ 07885 • *5,405*
Wharton, TX 77488 • *9,011*
Wharton □, TX • *39,955*
Whatcom □, WA • *127,780*
Wheatland, CA 95692 • *1,631*
Wheatland, WY 82201 • *3,271*
Wheatland □, MT • *2,246*
Wheaton, IL 60187–89 • *51,464*
Wheaton, MD 20902 • *58,300*
Wheaton, MN 56296 • *1,615*
Wheat Ridge, CO 80033–34 • *29,419*
Wheeler, TX 79096 • *1,393*
Wheeler □, GA • *4,903*
Wheeler □, NE • *948*
Wheeler □, OR • *1,396*
Wheeler □, TX • *5,879*
Wheelersburg, OH 45694 • *5,113*
Wheeling, IL 60090 • *29,911*
Wheeling, WV 26003 • *34,882*
Whitacres, CT 06082 • *2,410*
White □, AR • *54,676*
White □, GA • *13,006*
White □, IL • *16,522*
White □, IN • *23,265*
White □, TN • *20,090*
White Bear Lake, MN 55110 • *24,704*
White Bluff, TN 37187 • *1,988*
White Castle, LA 70788 • *2,102*
White Center, WA 98126 • *15,700*
White City, OR 97503 • *5,891*
White City, UT 84070 • *6,506*
White Cloud, MI 49349 • *1,147*
White Deer, TX 79097 • *1,125*
Whitefield, NH 03598 • *1,041*
Whitefish, MT 59937 • *4,368*
Whitefish Bay, WI 53217 • *14,272*

White Hall, AR 71602 • *3,849*
White Hall, IL 62092 • *2,814*
Whitehall, MI 49461 • *3,027*
Whitehall, MT 59759 • *1,067*
Whitehall, NY 12887 • *3,071*
Whitehall, OH 43213 • *20,572*
Whitehall, PA 15227 • *14,451*
Whitehall, WI 54773 • *1,494*
White Haven, PA 18661 • *1,132*
White Horse, NJ 08610 • *9,397*
White Horse Beach, MA 02381 • *1,200*
Whitehouse, OH 43571 • *2,528*
White House, TN 37188 • *2,987*
White House Station, NJ 08889 • *1,400*
White Island Shores, MA 02538 • *2,000*
White Meadow Lake, NJ 07866 • *8,002*
White Oak, MD 20901 • *18,671*
White Oak, OH 45239 • *12,430*
White Oak, PA 15131 • *8,761*
White Pigeon, MI 49099 • *1,458*
White Pine, MI 49971 • *1,142*
White Pine, TN 37890 • *1,771*
White Pine □, NV • *9,264*
White Plains, MD 20695 • *3,560*
White Plains, NY 10601–07 • *48,718*
Whiteriver, AZ 85941 • *3,775*
White River Junction, VT 05001 • *2,521*
White Rock, NM 87544 • *6,192*
White Salmon, WA 98672 • *1,861*
Whitesboro, NY 13492 • *4,195*
Whitesboro, TX 76273 • *3,209*
Whitesburg, KY 41858 • *1,636*
White Settlement, TX 76108 • *15,472*
Whiteside □, IL • *60,186*
White Sulphur Springs, MT 59645 • *963*
White Sulphur Springs, WV 24986 • *2,779*
Whiteville, NC 28472 • *5,078*
Whiteville, TN 38075 • *1,050*
Whitewater, WI 53190 • *12,636*
Whitewood, SD 57793 • *891*
Whitewright, TX 75491 • *1,713*
Whitfield □, GA • *72,462*
Whitfield Estates, FL 34243 • *3,152*
Whiting, IN 46394 • *5,155*
Whiting, WI 54481 • *1,838*
Whitinsville, MA 01588 • *5,639*
Whitley □, IN • *27,651*
Whitley □, KY • *33,326*
Whitley City, KY 42653 • *1,133*
Whitman, MA 02382 • *13,534*
Whitman, WV 25652 • *1,651*
Whitman □, WA • *38,775*
Whitman Square, NJ 08012 • *3,490*
Whitmire, SC 29178 • *1,702*
Whitmore Lake, MI 48189 • *3,251*
Whitmore Village, HI 96786 • *3,373*
Whitney, SC 29303 • *4,052*
Whitney, TX 76692 • *1,626*
Whitney Point, NY 13862 • *1,054*
Whittier, AK 99693 • *243*
Whittier, CA 90601–12 • *77,671*
Whitwell, TN 37397 • *1,622*
Wibaux, MT 59353 • *628*
Wibaux □, MT • *1,191*
Wichita, KS 67201–78 • *304,011*
Wichita □, KS • *2,758*
Wichita □, TX • *122,378*
Wichita Falls, TX 76301–11 • *96,259*
Wickenburg, AZ 85358 • *4,515*
Wickliffe, OH 44092 • *14,558*
Wickliffe, OH 44515 • *7,240*
Wicomico □, MD • *74,339*
Wiconisco, PA 17097 • *1,321*
Widefield, CO 80911 • *12,112*
Wiggins, MS 39577 • *3,185*
Wilbarger □, TX • *15,121*
Wilber, NE 68465 • *1,527*
Wilberforce, OH 45384 • *2,639*
Wilbraham, MA 01095 • *3,352*
Wilburton, OK 74578 • *3,092*
Wilcox, PA 15870 • *1,000*
Wilcox □, AL • *13,568*
Wilcox □, GA • *7,008*
Wilder, ID 83676 • *1,232*
Wilder, VT 05088 • *1,576*
Wildorado, TX 79098 • *2,000*
Wildwood, FL 34785 • *3,421*
Wildwood, IL 60030 • *2,034*
Wildwood, NJ 08260 • *4,484*
Wildwood Crest, NJ 08260 • *3,631*
Wilkes □, GA • *10,597*
Wilkes □, NC • *59,393*
Wilkes-Barre, PA 18701–73 • *47,523*
Wilkesboro, NC 28697 • *2,573*
Wilkin □, MN • *7,516*
Wilkinsburg, PA 15221 • *21,080*
Wilkinson □, GA • *10,228*
Wilkinson □, MS • *9,678*
Wilkins Township, PA 15145 • *7,487*
Will □, IL • *357,313*
Willacoochee, GA 31650 • *1,205*
Willacy □, TX • *17,705*
Willamina, OR 97396 • *1,717*
Willard, MO 65781 • *2,177*
Willard, NY 14588 • *1,339*
Willard, OH 44890 • *6,210*
Willard, UT 84340 • *1,298*
Willcox, AZ 85643 • *3,122*
Williams, AZ 86046 • *2,532*
Williams, CA 95987 • *2,297*
Williams □, ND • *21,129*
Williams □, OH • *36,956*
Williams Bay, WI 53191 • *2,108*
Williamsburg, IA 52361 • *2,174*
Williamsburg, KY 40769 • *5,493*
Williamsburg, MA 01096 • *1,200*
Williamsburg, OH 45176 • *2,322*
Williamsburg, PA 16693 • *1,456*
Williamsburg, VA 23185–88 • *11,530*
Williamsburg □, SC • *36,815*
Williamson, NY 14589 • *1,768*
Williamson, WV 25661 • *4,154*
Williamson □, IL • *57,733*
Williamson □, TN • *81,021*
Williamson □, TX • *139,551*
Williamsport, IN 47993 • *1,798*
Williamsport, MD 21795 • *2,103*
Williamsport, PA 17701–03 • *31,933*
Williamston, MI 48895 • *2,922*
Williamston, NC 27892 • *5,503*
Williamston, SC 29697 • *3,876*
Williamstown, KY 41097 • *3,023*
Williamstown, MA 01267 • *4,791*

United States Populations and ZIP Codes

Williamstown, NJ 08094 • 10,891
Williamstown, PA 17098 • 1,509
Williamstown, WV 26187 • 2,774
Williamsville, IL 62693 • 1,140
Williamsville, NY 14221 • 5,583
Willimantic, CT 06226 • 14,746
Willingboro, NJ 08046 • 36,291
Willis, TX 77378 • 2,764
Williston, FL 32696 • 2,179
Williston, ND 58801–02 • 13,131
Williston, SC 29853 • 3,099
Williston Park, NY 11596 • 7,516
Willits, CA 95490 • 5,027
Wilmar, MN 56201 • 17,531
Willoughby, OH 44094–95 • 20,510
Willoughby Hills, OH 44092 • 8,427
Willow Brook, CA 90222 • 32,772
Willowbrook, IL 60521 • 8,598
Willow Grove, PA 19090 • 16,325
Willowick, OH 44094 • 15,269
Willow Run, DE 19805 • 1,600
Willow Run, MI 48198 • 7,200
Willows, CA 95988 • 5,988
Willow Springs, IL 60480 • 4,509
Willow Springs, MO 65793 • 2,038
Willston, VA 22044 • 2,000
Wilmette, IL 60091 • 26,690
Wilmington, DE 19801–99 • 71,529
Wilmington, IL 60481 • 4,743
Wilmington, MA 01887 • 17,654
Wilmington, NC 28401–12 • 55,530
Wilmington, OH 45177 • 11,199
Wilmington, VT 05363 • 550
Wilmington Island, GA 31410 • 11,230
Wilmington Manor, DE 19720 • 8,568
Wilmington Manor Gardens, DE 19720 • 1,500
Wilmore, KY 40390 • 4,215
Wilmot, AR 71676 • 1,047
Wilson, AR 72395 • 1,068
Wilson, NY 14172 • 1,307
Wilson, NC 27893–95 • 36,930
Wilson, OK 73463 • 1,639
Wilson, PA 18042 • 7,830
Wilson, WY 83014 • 500
Wilson □, KS • 10,289
Wilson □, NC • 66,061
Wilson □, TN • 67,675
Wilson □, TX • 22,650
Wilsonville, AL 35186 • 1,185
Wilsonville, OR 97070 • 7,106
Wilton, CT 06897 • 7,200
Wilton, IA 52778 • 2,577
Wilton, ME 04294 • 2,453
Wilton, NH 03086 • 1,165
Wilton, ND 58579 • 728
Wilton Manors, FL 33334 • 11,804
Wimauma, FL 33598 • 2,932
Winamac, IN 46996 • 2,262
Winchendon, MA 01475 • 4,316
Winchester, IL 62694 • 1,769
Winchester, IN 47394 • 5,095
Winchester, KY 40391–92 • 15,799
Winchester, MA 01890 • 20,267
Winchester, NH 03470 • 1,735
Winchester, NV 89101 • 23,365
Winchester, TN 37398 • 6,305
Winchester, VA 22601 • 21,947
Windber, PA 15963 • 4,756
Windcrest, TX 78239 • 5,331
Winder, GA 30680 • 7,373
Windgap, PA 18091 • 2,741
Windham, CT 06280 • 1,100
Windham, OH 44288 • 2,943
Windham □, CT • 102,525
Windham □, VT • 41,588
Wind Lake, WI 53185 • 3,000
Windom, MN 56101 • 4,283
Window Rock, AZ 86515 • 3,306
Wind Point, WI 53402 • 1,941
Windsor, CO 80550 • 5,062
Windsor, CT 06095 • 27,817
Windsor, IL 61957 • 1,143
Windsor, MO 65360 • 3,044

Windsor, NC 27983 • 2,056
Windsor, PA 17366 • 1,355
Windsor, VT 05089 • 3,478
Windsor, VA 23487 • 1,025
Windsor □, VT • 54,055
Windsor Heights, IA 50311 • 5,190
Windsor Hills, CA 90052 • 6,200
Windsor Locks, CT 06096 • 12,358
Windy Hill, SC 29506 • 1,622
Windy Hills, DE 19711 • 1,130
Winfield, AL 35594 • 3,689
Winfield, IA 52659 • 1,051
Winfield, KS 67156 • 11,931
Winfield, NJ 07036 • 1,785
Winfield, WV 25213 • 1,164
Wingate, NC 28174 • 2,821
Wink, TX 79789 • 1,189
Winkler □, TX • 8,626
Winlock, WA 98596 • 1,027
Winn □, LA • 16,269
Winnebago, IL 61088 • 1,840
Winnebago, MN 56098 • 1,565
Winnebago, WI 54985 • 1,433
Winnebago □, IL • 252,913
Winnebago □, IA • 12,122
Winnebago □, WI • 140,320
Winneconne, WI 54986 • 2,059
Winner, SD 57580 • 3,354
Winneshiek □, IA • 20,847
Winnetka, IL 60093 • 12,174
Winnfield, LA 71483 • 6,138
Winnsboro, LA 71295 • 5,755
Winnsboro, SC 29180 • 3,475
Winnsboro, TX 75494 • 2,904
Winnsboro Mills, SC 29180 • 2,275
Winona, MN 55987 • 25,399
Winona, MS 38967 • 5,705
Winona, MO 65588 • 1,081
Winona □, MN • 47,828
Winona Lake, IN 46590 • 4,053
Winooski, VT 05404 • 6,649
Winslow, AZ 86047 • 8,190
Winslow, ME 04901 • 5,436
Winsted, CT 06098 • 8,254
Winsted, MN 55395 • 1,581
Winston, FL 33801 • 9,118
Winston, OR 97496 • 3,773
Winston □, AL • 22,053
Winston □, MS • 19,433
Winston-Salem, NC 27101–27 • 143,485
Winter Garden, FL 34787 • 5,351
Winter Haven, FL 33880–84 • 24,725
Winter Park, FL 32789–90 • 22,242
Winter Park, NC 28403 • 4,504
Winterport, ME 04496 • 1,274
Winters, CA 95694 • 4,639
Winters, TX 79567 • 2,905
Winterset, IA 50273 • 4,196
Winter Springs, FL 32708 • 22,151
Wintersville, OH 43952 • 4,102
Winterville, NC 28590 • 2,816
Winthrop, ME 04364 • 2,819
Winthrop, MA 02152 • 18,127
Winthrop, MN 55396 • 1,279
Winthrop Harbor, IL 60096 • 6,240
Winton, CA 95388 • 7,559
Wirt □, WV • 5,192
Wiscasset, ME 04578 • 1,350
Wisconsin Dells, WI 53965 • 2,393
Wisconsin Rapids, WI 54494–95 • 18,245
Wise, VA 24293 • 3,193
Wise □, TX • 34,679
Wise □, VA • 39,573
Wishek, ND 58495 • 1,171
Wisner, LA 71378 • 1,153
Wisner, NE 68791 • 1,253
Withamsville, OH 45245 • 5,000
Witherbee, NY 12998 • 1,000
Wittenberg, WI 54499 • 1,145
Wixom, MI 48393 • 8,550
Woburn, MA 01801 • 35,943
Wolcott, CT 06716 • 6,070
Wolcott, NY 14590 • 1,544
Wolfe □, KY • 6,503
Wolfeboro, NH 03894 • 2,783

Wolfe City, TX 75496 • 1,505
Wolf Lake, MI 49442 • 4,110
Wolf Point, MT 59201 • 2,880
Wolf Trap, VA 22182 • 13,133
Womelsdorf, PA 19567 • 2,270
Wonder Lake, IL 60097 • 6,664
Wood □, OH • 113,269
Wood □, TX • 29,380
Wood □, WV • 86,915
Wood □, WI • 73,605
Woodbine, GA 31569 • 1,212
Woodbine, IA 51579 • 1,500
Woodbine, NJ 08270 • 2,678
Woodbourne, NY 12788 • 1,155
Woodbourne, OH 45459 • 6,000
Woodbridge, CT 06525 • 7,924
Woodbridge, NJ 07095 • 17,434
Woodbridge, VA 22191–94 • 26,401
Woodbridge [Township], NJ 07095 • 17,434
Woodburn, IN 46797 • 1,321
Woodburn, OR 97071 • 13,404
Woodbury, CT 06798 • 1,212
Woodbury, GA 30293 • 1,429
Woodbury, MN 55125 • 20,075
Woodbury, NJ 08096 • 10,904
Woodbury, NY 11797 • 8,008
Woodbury, TN 37190 • 2,287
Woodbury □, IA • 98,276
Woodcliff Lake, NJ 07675 • 5,303
Wood Dale, IL 60191 • 12,425
Woodfield, SC 29206 • 8,862
Woodford □, IL • 32,653
Woodford □, KY • 19,955
Woodhaven, MI 48183 • 11,631
Woodlake, CA 93286 • 5,678
Woodland, CA 95695 • 39,802
Woodland, ME 04694 • 1,287
Woodland, WA 98674 • 2,500
Woodland Park, CO 80863 • 4,610
Woodlawn, KY 42001 • 1,600
Woodlawn, MD 21207 • 5,329
Woodlawn, MD 20784 • 5,329
Woodlawn, OH 45215 • 2,674
Woodlawn, VA 24381 • 1,689
Woodlynne, NJ 08107 • 2,547
Woodmere, NY 11598 • 15,578
Woodmont, CT 06460 • 1,770
Woodmoor, MD 21207 • 8,630
Woodridge, IL 60517 • 26,256
Wood-Ridge, NJ 07075 • 7,506
Wood River, IL 62095 • 11,490
Wood River, NE 68883 • 1,156
Woodruff, SC 29388 • 4,365
Woodruff, WI 54568 • 1,500
Woodruff □, AR • 9,520
Woods □, OK • 9,103
Woodsboro, TX 78393 • 1,731
Woods Cross, UT 84087 • 5,384
Woodsfield, OH 43793 • 2,832
Woods Hole, MA 02543 • 1,080
Woodside, CA 94062 • 5,035
Woodson □, KS • 4,116
Woodstock, GA 30188 • 4,361
Woodstock, IL 60098 • 14,353
Woodstock, NY 12498 • 1,870
Woodstock, VT 05091 • 1,037
Woodstock, VA 22664 • 3,182
Woodstown, NJ 08098 • 3,154
Woodsville, NH 03785 • 1,122
Woodville, FL 32362 • 2,760
Woodville, MS 39669 • 1,393
Woodville, OH 43469 • 1,953
Woodville, TX 75979 • 2,636
Woodward, IA 50276 • 1,197
Woodward, OK 73801–02 • 12,340
Woodward □, OK • 18,976
Woodway, TX 76710 • 8,695
Woonsocket, RI 02895 • 43,877
Woonsocket, SD 57385 • 766
Wooster, OH 44691 • 22,191
Worcester, MA 01601–15 • 169,759
Worcester □, MD • 35,028
Worcester □, MA • 709,705
Worland, WY 82401 • 5,742

Worth, IL 60482 • 11,208
Worth □, GA • 19,745
Worth □, IA • 7,991
Worth □, MO • 2,440
Wortham, TX 76693 • 1,020
Worthington, IN 47471 • 1,473
Worthington, KY 41183 • 1,751
Worthington, MN 56187 • 9,977
Worthington, OH 43085 • 14,869
Wrangell, AK 99929 • 2,479
Wray, CO 80758 • 1,998
Wrens, GA 30833 • 2,414
Wrentham, MA 02093 • 2,110
Wright, FL 32548 • 18,945
Wright □, IA • 14,269
Wright □, MN • 68,710
Wright □, MO • 16,758
Wright City, MO 63390 • 1,250
Wrightstown, NJ 08562 • 3,843
Wrightsville, AR 72183 • 1,062
Wrightsville, GA 31096 • 2,331
Wrightsville, PA 17368 • 2,396
Wrightsville Beach, NC 28480 • 2,937
Wrightwood, CA 92397 • 3,308
Wurtsboro, NY 12790 • 1,048
Wyandanch, NY 11798 • 8,950
Wyandot □, OH • 22,254
Wyandotte, MI 48192 • 30,938
Wyandotte □, KS • 161,993
Wyanet, IL 61379 • 1,017
Wyckoff, NJ 07481 • 15,372
Wymore, NE 68466 • 1,611
Wynne, AR 72396–97 • 8,187
Wynnewood, OK 73098 • 2,451
Wyoming, DE 19934 • 977
Wyoming, IL 61491 • 1,462
Wyoming, MI 49509 • 63,891
Wyoming, MN 55092 • 2,142
Wyoming, OH 45215 • 8,128
Wyoming, PA 18644 • 3,255
Wyoming □, NY • 42,507
Wyoming □, PA • 28,076
Wyoming □, WV • 28,990
Wyomissing, PA 19610 • 7,332
Wythe □, VA • 25,466
Wytheville, VA 24382 • 8,038

X

Xenia, OH 45385 • 24,664

Y

Yadkin □, NC • 30,488
Yadkinville, NC 27055 • 2,525
Yakima, WA 98901–09 • 54,827
Yakima □, WA • 188,823
Yakutat, AK 99689 • 534
Yale, MI 48097 • 1,977
Yale, OK 74085 • 1,392
Yalobusha □, MS • 12,033
Yamhill □, OR • 65,551
Yancey □, NC • 15,419
Yanceyville, NC 27379 • 1,973
Yankton, SD 57078 • 12,703
Yankton □, SD • 19,252
Yaphank, NY 11980 • 5,000
Yardley, PA 19067 • 2,288
Yardville, NJ 08620 • 6,190
Yarmouth, ME 04096 • 3,338
Yarmouth, MA 02675 • 1,200
Yarnell, AZ 85362 • 1,500
Yates □, NY • 22,810
Yates Center, KS 66783 • 1,815
Yavapai □, AZ • 107,714
Yazoo □, MS • 25,506
Yazoo City, MS 39194 • 12,427
Yeadon, PA 19050 • 11,980
Yeagertown, PA 17099 • 1,150
Yell □, AR • 17,759
Yellow Medicine □, MN • 11,684

Yellow Springs, OH 45387 • 3,973
Yellowstone □, MT • 113,419
Yellowstone National Park, WY 82190 • 400
Yellowstone National Park □, MT • 52
Yellville, AR 72687 • 1,181
Yelm, WA 98597 • 1,337
Yerington, NV 89447 • 2,367
Yermo, CA 92398 • 1,092
Yoakum, TX 77995 • 5,611
Yoakum □, TX • 8,786
Yolo □, CA • 141,092
Yonkers, NY 10701–10 • 188,082
Yorba Linda, CA 92686 • 52,422
York, AL 36925 • 3,160
York, ME 03909 • 3,130
York, NE 68467 • 7,884
York, PA 17401–07 • 42,192
York, SC 29745 • 6,709
York □, ME • 164,587
York □, NE • 14,428
York □, PA • 339,574
York □, SC • 131,497
York □, VA • 42,422
Yorketown, NJ 07726 • 6,313
York Harbor, ME 03911 • 2,555
Yorklyn, DE 19736 • 600
Yorkshire, NY 14173 • 1,340
Yorktown, IN 47396 • 4,106
Yorktown, NY 10598 • 5,270
Yorktown, TX 78164 • 2,207
Yorktown, VA 23690–93 • 270
Yorktown Heights, NY 10598 • 7,690
Yorktown Manor, RI 02852 • 2,520
Yorkville, IL 60560 • 3,925
Yorkville, NY 13495 • 2,972
Yorkville, OH 43971 • 1,246
Yosemite National Park, CA 95389 • 1,073
Young □, TX • 18,126
Youngstown, NY 14174 • 2,075
Youngstown, OH 44501–15 • 95,732
Youngsville, LA 70592 • 1,195
Youngsville, PA 16371 • 1,775
Youngtown, AZ 85363 • 2,542
Youngwood, PA 15697 • 3,372
Ypsilanti, MI 48197–98 • 24,846
Yreka, CA 96097 • 6,948
Yuba □, CA • 58,228
Yuba City, CA 95991–92 • 27,437
Yucaipa, CA 92399 • 20,000
Yucca Valley, CA 92284–86 • 13,701
Yukon, OK 73099 • 20,935
Yulee, FL 32097 • 6,915
Yuma, AZ 85364–69 • 54,923
Yuma, CO 80759 • 2,719
Yuma □, AZ • 106,895
Yuma □, CO • 8,954

Z

Zachary, LA 70791 • 9,036
Zanesville, OH 43701–02 • 26,778
Zapata, TX 78076 • 7,119
Zapata □, TX • 9,279
Zavala □, TX • 12,162
Zebulon, GA 30295 • 1,035
Zebulon, NC 27597 • 3,173
Zeeland, MI 49464 • 5,417
Zeigler, IL 62999 • 1,746
Zelienople, PA 16063 • 4,158
Zenith, WA 98188 • 1,100
Zephyr Cove, NV 89448 • 1,700
Zephyrhills, FL 33539–44 • 8,220
Ziebach □, SD • 2,220
Zillah, WA 98953 • 1,911
Zilwaukee, MI 48604 • 1,850
Zimmerman, MN 55398 • 1,350
Zion, IL 60099 • 19,775
Zionsville, IN 46077 • 5,281
Zolfo Springs, FL 33890 • 1,219
Zumbrota, MN 55992 • 2,312
Zuni (Zuni Pueblo), NM 87327 • 5,857
Zwolle, LA 71486 • 1,779